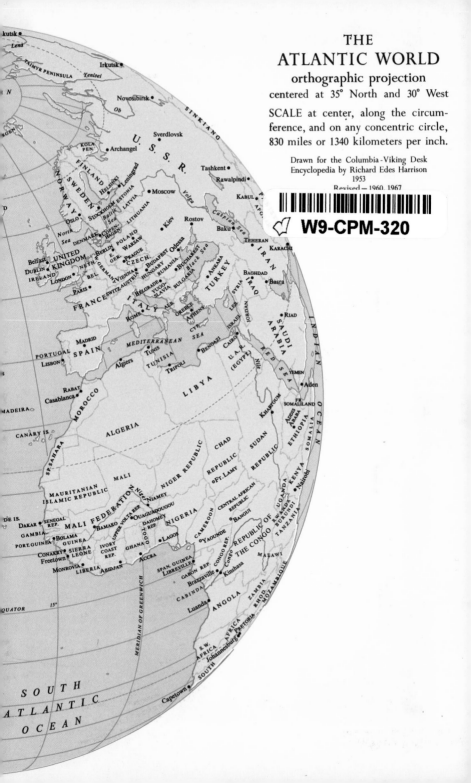

PRONUNCIATION KEY

ā fate (fāt), fail (fāl), vacation (vākā′shùn)
â care (kâr), Mary (mâ′rē)
ă bat (băt), add (ăd), marry (mă′rē)
ä father (fä′dhùr), marble (mär′bul)
ã French tant (tã), Rouen (rōōä′), and similar sounds in some other languages
b back (băk), cab (kăb)
ch chap (chăp)
d dock (dŏk), cod (kŏd)
dh father (fä′dhùr), then (dhĕn). Compare with th.
ē even (ē′vùn), clearing (klēr′ĭng), obvious (ŏb′vēùs)
ĕ end (ĕnd), met (mĕt), merry (mĕ′rē)
ē French vin (vē), bien (byē), and similar sounds in some other languages
f fat (făt), Philip (fĭ′lĭp)
g get (gĕt), tag (tăg)
h hat (hăt). See also ch, dh, kh, sh, th, zh, and hw
hw where (hwâr), what (hwŏt)
ī fine (fīn), buyer (bī′ùr)
ĭ pin (pĭn), pit (pĭt), spirit (spĭ′rĭt), fated (fā′tĭd)
j jam (jăm), edge (ĕj), ginger (jĭn′jùr)
k cook (kŏŏk), tackle (tă′kùl)
kh loch (lŏkh), German Aachen (ä′khùn), Licht (lĭkht), and similar sounds in some other languages
l peal (pēl), pull (pŏŏl)
m hammer (hă′mùr)
n dinner (dĭ′nùr)
ng singing (sĭng′ĭng), finger (fĭng′gùr), sang (săng), sank (săngk)
ō hope (hōp), potato (pùtā′tō)
ô orbit (ôr′bĭt), fall (fôl)
ŏ hot (hŏt), toddy (tŏ′dē), borrow (bŏ′rō)
õ French dont (dõ), chanson (shăsõ′), and similar sounds in some other languages
oi boil (boil), royal (roi′ùl)
ōō boot (bōōt), lose (lōōz)
ŏŏ foot (fŏŏt), purely (pyŏŏr′lē), manipulate (mùnĭ′pyŏŏlāt)
ou scout (skout), crowd (kroud)

p pipe (pīp), happy (hă′pē)
r road (rōd), appeared (ùpērd′), carpenter (kär′pùntùr)
s saw (sô), case (kās)
sh shall (shăl), nation (nā′shùn)
t tight (tīt), rating (rā′tĭng)
th thin (thĭn), myth (mĭth). Compare with dh.
ū fume (fūm), euphemism (ū′fùmĭzm)
û curl (kûrl), Hamburg (hăm′bûrg), French œuvre (û′vrù), peu (pû), German schön (shûn), Goethe (gû′tù), and similar sounds in some other languages
ŭ butter (bŭ′tùr), suds (sŭdz), hurry (hŭ′rē)
ù affair (ùfâr′), sofa (sō′fù), contravene (kŏntrùvēn′), monopoly (mùnŏ′pùlē), suburban (sùbûr′bùn), callous (kă′lùs), rather (ră′dhùr)
ü French Cluny (klünē′), German Lübeck (lü′bĕk), and similar sounds in some other languages
ũ French Melun (mùlũ′), Chambrun (shăbrũ′), and similar sounds in some other languages
v vest (vĕst), trivial (trĭ′vēùl)
w wax (wăks)
y you (yōō), bunion (bŭ′nyùn)
z zipper (zĭ′pùr), ease (ēz), treads (trĕdz)
zh pleasure (plĕ′zhùr), rouge (rōōzh)

′ main accent, written after accented vowel or syllable: Nebraska (nùbră′skù), James Buchanan (jāmz′ būkă′nùn)

″ secondary accent: Mississippi (mĭ″sùsĭ′pē)

— dash, replacing obvious portion of pronunciation: hegemony (hĭjĕ′mùnē, hē—, hĕ′jùmō″nē, hĕ′gù—)

- hyphen, to prevent ambiguity: Erlanger (ûr′lăng-ùr), dishearten dĭs-här′tùn)

NOTES

The purpose of the pronunciation symbols is to give at least one serviceable way in which the word in question may be pronounced when used by careful speakers of English.

In this work a pronunciation is ordinarily indicated for words printed in boldface when this pronunciation is not obvious to the English-speaking reader. Of two or more words or names in succession spelled and pronounced alike, a pronunciation is frequently indicated for the first occurrence only.

For names of localities in English-speaking areas the local pronunciation is preferred, provided it is acceptable to careful speakers.

For foreign words and names the speaker of English desires to use a pronunciation that will be acceptable to other speakers of English (unless he is speaking in a foreign language). In many cases (e.g., Paris) there is a traditional pronunciation that resembles little the current native pronunciation, and attempts to introduce into English conversation an approximation of the native form (something like pärē′) are regarded as an affectation. It is customary with foreign names that have no conventional English form to pronounce them with English sounds approximating the foreign ones. Such an approximation is indicated in this work, whenever there is no established usage to follow.

Actual good foreign-language pronunciations can be acquired only through imitation and study. Nevertheless, Englishmen and Americans have for many years made a practice of imitating roughly five French sounds: ã, ē, õ, ũ, and ü. A speaker of English can attain ã by saying äng without the closure at the back of the mouth necessary to make ng, breathing through nose and mouth as well; ē is similarly like the beginning of äng, õ like that of õng, and ũ like that of ûng. To approximate ü say ōō with vigor, then, keeping the lips rounded, change the sound quickly to ē.

For Latin words the venerable English tradition is followed [e.g., Caesar (sē′zùr)], except where some other pronunciation is well established, as in ecclesiastical names [e.g., Salve Regina (säl′vä räjē′nù)]. The so-called classical pronunciation, which approximates the pronunciation Caesar used [e.g., Caesar (kī′sär)], is not given, as being not usual in English conversation.

THE COLUMBIA-
VIKING DESK
ENCYCLOPEDIA

VOLUME ONE
Aa-Lavaca Bay

THE COLUMBIA-VIKING DESK ENCYCLOPEDIA

Compiled and edited at Columbia University

by the staff of The Columbia Encyclopedia

WILLIAM BRIDGWATER, Editor-in-chief

Third Edition

PUBLISHED BY THE VIKING PRESS

NEW YORK

PREFACE

Herewith we present the Third Edition of *The Columbia-Viking Desk Encyclopedia*. It is a complete revision of the Second Edition. All the articles have been reviewed, and well over half of them have been changed. We have tried to bring the articles up to date by adding to the entries for countries and living people accounts not only of events in the recent past but also of recent discoveries about older events. We have set out to include all the new headings that are significant for our coverage. The current maps, the illustrations, charts, and tables, and the page on the cabinet of U.S. Presidents all enhance the value of the text, supplementing it with graphic materials that are frequently clearer than words of description.

The original *Columbia-Viking Desk Encyclopedia* was prepared in order to present information in a brief and portable form—what might properly be called finger-tip information. It was derived from *The Columbia Encyclopedia,* Second Edition. The purpose was to provide a small volume, suitable for ordinary desk use. The articles were for the most part reduced from the large encyclopedia, though some new ones were supplied. Similarly, the present edition is derived from *The Columbia Encyclopedia,* Third Edition, and many new articles have been included.

This work is an encyclopedia and makes no attempt to be a dictionary. Entries that would give no more than dictionary information have been rigorously excluded. Space for each entry is limited. Preference has been given to specific headings and to those which would be of interest to the ordinary reader. We have therefore been compelled to omit articles on general topics such as American literature and Italian art. Yet you will find articles on particular authors of American literature and important artists and political figures of the Italian Renaissance that will give information on the more general subject. The book makes no pretense of being what is called an encyclopedic dictionary. It is, instead, a parallel to what is known in Europe as a hand encyclopedia, a small work usually derived from a larger one.

The encyclopedia is American, and therefore stress has been laid on persons and places important in United States history, past and present. There is also some stress upon Canada, upon Mexico, and upon the rest of Latin America. Yet the European tradition has been considered in all the articles on Western civilization, whether in Europe or in America, and interest in Asia and continuing change in Africa have required close attention to recent developments and older traditions in those areas. All material is dated as of August 1, 1967.

In order to give as much information as possible in a very short form, we have had to use many abbreviations. They are all clear to the ordinary reader. Similarly, when the subject of a sentence is clear it has been omitted. So have other words when the statement is clear without them. When, however, the needs of the reader cannot be fulfilled without complete statements, sentences have been made complete. The seeming inconsistency between clipped and full sentences was adopted in order to save as much space as possible with full benefit to the reader. In shorter articles abbreviations are used more than in the longer, but we hope that even the shortest is comprehensible. Abridged forms are used only when they will not hinder the flow of the short articles.

In this book the cross references are of the utmost importance. Information cannot be repeated, and the reader must find it at the primary appearance. Writers have avoided repeating information under two or more headings to use space to its utmost possibility. These cross references within articles are indicated by small capitals. The references are not used recklessly; they appear only when the reader will find under the other heading information that would be useful. It is easy to learn the method of following cross references and gaining extra knowledge.

The illustrations in the book are intended to broaden information. They tell things that are not contained in the text itself. Each is a unit of information, and the reader can use it, sometimes with reference to the text, sometimes without it. The charts and tables, too, contain extra information that embellishes the text. They are articles presented in graphic form.

Figures for population are derived from the latest reliable census information. In general, the 1960 United States census figures are given, and note has been made in the few instances where later special census reports were used. Figures for areas of countries, for altitudes of mountains, and for depths of the sea have also been adjusted to fit the latest information available.

All the articles in the book were written for American readers. English-language forms are used throughout. The pronunciations offered are those that are current among educated Americans. Whenever a foreign spelling, differing from the English form, would seem to be an absolute necessity for the reader, that spelling is given in italics after the ordinary spelling in English. In general, the material is kept to the usage that would be requisite for the reader who knows little of foreign languages.

Because the articles are capsules of information, too small for extended discussion, the editors have found it impossible to include all the variant views of a situation. Yet every effort has been made to examine our statements with an eye to avoiding possible bias. In some cases it has been necessary to elaborate articles to give several views of a controversy. As a consequence, the articles cannot be judged for their importance by length alone. One person is important for a single unchallenged achievement, another is known for many small contributions to civilization; a third is the subject of controversy. The space allotted to them must vary: there is no escape from the difficulty. We must in some cases give more space to a less important figure, less space to a more prominent one.

The staff of The Viking Press learned through two previous editions the hardships of publishing a reference book. It met the many problems of this edition with patience and understanding. Marshall A. Best, as always, offered constructive editorial criticism and guided the book to completion, while Teresa Egan provided indispensable day-to-day liaison between editors and publisher. Typography and design, retained from the earlier editions, were the work of Milton B. Glick, who was primarily responsible for the original project at Viking.

The editing of the book depended upon the editors whose names appear in the editorial staff list. The fields for which they were responsible have not been delineated; in certain cases their activities crossed several fields. Each made an essential contribution to the work as a whole. One must be singled out: Edith P. Hazen as senior assistant

editor coordinated the work of editors, contributors, and proofreaders, keeping always in mind the aims and standards to which the book is heir.

The book is ultimately derived from *The Columbia Encyclopedia*. In the creation of that work, the guiding spirit was Clarke Fisher Ansley, who was determined that there should be in English a one-volume encyclopedia worthy to be compared with European small encyclopedias. He succeeded far beyond his expectations. To assist him he had Elizabeth J. Sherwood, dedicated to the same ideals which have also dominated *The Columbia-Viking Desk Encyclopedia*. To provide him with understanding and encouragement, he had Charles G. Proffitt, now President and Director of Columbia University Press.

The tradition that Dr. Ansley began in the first edition of *The Columbia Encyclopedia* was carried on by William Bridgwater, who edited the second edition (with Elizabeth Sherwood) and the third (with Seymour Kurtz), as well as the first two editions of *The Columbia-Viking Desk Encyclopedia*. This third edition was begun under the supervision of the late Dr. Bridgwater, who died in December, 1966. His policies have been continued by the staff, under Mrs. Hazen's guidance, so far as possible; the words of this Preface describing policies are his. His death is a loss to Columbia University Press and the world of scholarly editing.

HENRY H. WIGGINS
ASSISTANT DIRECTOR
COLUMBIA UNIVERSITY PRESS

November, 1967

ARTISTS

Illustrations for the first edition were by
I. N. STEINBERG and Associates;
with NATALIE RAYMOND as Research Editor

Illustrations for the second and third editions by

Allen Beechel
Nancy Dixon
R. L. Gates
Charles Lichtenstein
Frank Pulliam

Marjorie Rudolph
Howard W. Vreeland
Vance Weaver
Marilyn Weber

CARTOGRAPHERS

Continental maps for the first edition were by:
JACK LUBOFF (*New York Herald Tribune*)

Consultant: GERARD L. ALEXANDER
(*Map Division, New York Public Library*)

Maps of Africa, Polar Regions, and United States by:
DANIEL BROWNSTEIN (*New York Times*)

World maps by RICHARD EDES HARRISON

ILLUSTRATIONS, CHARTS, AND TABLES

Grouped under subject headings for convenient comparison of related material. A number of subjects have been included in the illustrations, though not in the text, when it was felt that graphic or tabular material served the purpose better than words.

MAPS AND LISTS

MAPS

As a rule the articles on places do not give cross references to maps; but countries, principal cities, large rivers, and many other geographic features may be located on the maps of their respective continents.

WORLD MAPS

CONTINENT MAPS

LISTS

Some of the ready-reference material in the text is located as follows

ACKNOWLEDGMENTS

Grateful acknowledgment is made to the following publishers for permission to use their material as a basis for certain of our drawings: Duell, Sloan & Pearce, Inc., for two illustrations from Giovanna Calastri Lawford, *The Human Frame* (1952); Henry Holt and Company, Inc., for the sectional view of a gasoline engine and the gas turbine from Charles E. Dull, H. Clark Metcalfe, and William O. Brooks, *Modern Physics* (1955); W. W. Norton & Company, Inc., for drawings of various Asiatic musical instruments in Curt Sachs, *History of Musical Instruments* (1940); John Wiley & Sons, Inc., for the drawing of the prehistoric lakes Agassiz and Nipissing of North America from R. F. Flint, *Glacial Geology and the Pleistocene Epoch* (1947) and for the drawings of a typical river cycle, the Ice Age in North America, and the formation of the Appalachians from C. R. Longwell, Adolph Knopf, and R. F. Flint, *Physical Geology* (3d ed., 1948). All these are reproduced with permission. The representation of the turbojet engine is based on the "Schematic Flow Diagram of General Electric's TG-180 Engine" by permission of General Electric Company. The drawings of the Japanese samisen and the Javanese saron are based on illustrations in Curt Sachs, *Geist und Werden der Musikinstrumente* (Berlin, 1929) and the Chinese sona on one in his *Real-Lexikon der Musikinstrumente* (Berlin, 1913).

THE COLUMBIA-VIKING DESK ENCYCLOPEDIA

VOLUME ONE
Aa-Lavaca Bay

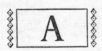

A

Aa (ä), name of many small streams of N Europe and Switzerland. The word is derived from an Indo-European root meaning "water."

Aachen (ä′khůn) or Aix-la-Chapelle (äks′-lä-shůpĕl′), city (1964 est. pop. 175,964), West Germany, in North Rhine–Westphalia, near Dutch and Belgian borders, in a hard-coal dist. Machinery, rubber, textile mfg. Hot mineral baths in use since Roman times. Charlemagne built splendid palace and founded cathedral (rebuilt 10th cent.; partly Byzantine, partly Gothic), which contains his tomb. German kings were crowned at Aachen until 1531. Free imperial city until annexed by France (1801); awarded to Prussia 1814. For treaties signed here 1668 and 1748, see AIX-LA-CHAPELLE, TREATY OF.

Aakjaer, Jeppe (yĕp′ů ôk′yâr), 1866–1930, Danish poet, author of *Songs of the Rye* (1906) and *Heimdal's Wanderings* (1924). Also wrote novels.

Aaland Islands, Finland: see ALAND ISLANDS.

Aalborg, Dan. *Ålborg* or *Aalborg* (all: ôl′bôrg), city (pop. 85,800), Denmark, in N Jutland; a port on S shore of Lim Fjord.

Aalesund, Norway: see ALESUND.

Aalst, Belgium: see ALOST.

Aalto, Alvar (öl′vär äl′tō), 1899–, Finnish architect and furniture designer. Adapted Finnish building traditions to modern European techniques. Pioneered in evolving functional plywood furniture.

Aanrud, Hans (ôn′rōŏd), 1863–1953, Norwegian writer of stories, plays, and books for children. Portrayed life in his home valley, Gudbrandsdal.

Aar (är) or Aare (är′ů), river, c.183 mi. long, Switzerland, rising in Bernese Alps and flowing through L. Brienz and L. Thun, past Bern, Solothurn, and Aarau, into the Rhine.

Aarau (ä′rou), town (pop. 17,045), cap. of Aargau canton, N Switzerland, on the Aar. Mfg. shoes, scientific instruments.

aardvark (ärd′värk), nocturnal mammal, order Tubulidentata. Two species (genus *Orycteropus*), one in central, one in S Africa. Long snout, erect ears; naked or sparse hair on body; c.6 ft. long; long tail; an ant-eating burrower. Also called ant bear.

Aargau (är′gou), canton (542 sq. mi.; pop. 360,940), N Switzerland; cap. Aarau. Traversed by fertile Aar valley. Swiss possession since 1415; canton since 1803. Pop. is Protestant, German-speaking.

Aarhus, Dan. *Århus* or *Aarhus* (all: ôr′hŏŏs), city (pop. 119,568), Denmark, in E Jutland, on Aarhus Bay, which opens on the Kattegat. Second largest Danish city; commercial and industrial center. An episcopal see since 13th cent., it has a medieval cathedral and many fine Renaissance houses.

Aaron (â′run), in Bible, first high priest, brother of Moses and his spokesman in Egypt. Descendants served as temple priests. Jehovah performed miracles through him (e.g., blossoming of Aaron's rod). Aaron rebuked for making golden calf and allowing its worship.

Aasen, Ivar Andreas (ē′vär ändrā′äs ô′sůn), 1813–96, Norwegian lexicographer. By standardizing the dia-

lects of his people he created a speech (i.e., Landsmaal) which became the second national language.

abacá: see MANILA HEMP.

abacus, in mathematics, simple calculating device. One type is frame with movable counters on parallel rods or in grooves.

Abadan (äbädän′), city (pop. c.172,000), E Iran, on Abadan isl., in delta of the Shatt-el-Arab at head of Persian Gulf. Site of huge oil refinery.

Abaddon (ůbăd′ůn) [Heb.,= destruction], Hebrew name of the destroying angel. See SATAN.

Abakan (ůbúkän′), city (1965 est. pop. 71,000), cap. of Khakass Autonomous Oblast, Krasnoyarsk Territory, RSFSR, in S central Siberia. A commercial center on the South Siberian RR; founded 1707. Called Ust-Abakanskoye until 1931.

abalone (ăbůlō′nē), spiral-shelled gastropod univalve mollusk, genus *Haliotis*, also called ear shell or sea ear. Common food on California coast.

Abana (ůbā′nů), river of Damascus. 2 Kings 5.12. It is probably the Barada, flowing near Damascus.

Abarbanel, Isaac: see ABRAVANEL, ISAAC.

A battery: see BATTERY, ELECTRIC.

Abbadides (ă′bůdĭdz), Arabian dynasty in Spain; ruled emirate of SEVILLE 1023–91. Succeeding the caliphs of Córdoba as chief Moorish power in Spain, they were replaced in turn by the ALMORAVIDES.

Abbas (ă′bůs, äbäs′), d. 652, uncle of Mohammed; ancestor of Abbasid caliphs.

Abbas I (Abbas the Great), 1557–1628, shah of Persia (1587–1628), of Safavid dynasty. Took large area from the Turks 1603–23; estab. order.

Abbas II (Abbas Hilmi), 1874–1944, khedive of Egypt (1892–1914), deposed by the British.

Abbasid (ůbä′sĭd, ă′bůsĭd) or Abbaside (–sĭd, –sĭd), Arabic family, descended from Abbas (uncle of Mohammed), which held caliphate 749–1258. First caliph was ABU-L-ABBAS AS-SAFFAH; second was MANSUR. Early years of Abbasid rule were brilliant, especially under HARUN-AL-RASHID and MAMUN. Rival caliphs (see CALIPHATE) helped to weaken power of the Abbasid, who were finally overthrown 1258 by Hulagu Khan (grandson of Jenghiz Khan).

Abbe, Cleveland (ăb′ē), 1838–1916, American meteorologist. As Cincinnati Observatory director, he inaugurated daily weather forecasting based on telegraph reports. Influenced establishment of, and served in, government weather service.

Abbe, Ernst (ĕrnst ä′bů), 1840–1905, German physicist; owner of Zeiss optical works. Invented Abbe refractometer.

Abbeville (äbvēl′), town (est. pop. 19,502), Somme dept., N France, on Somme R. Textile mfg., especially linen. Chartered 1184, was prosperous town until revocation of Edict of NANTES (1685).

Abbeville (ăb′ēvĭl), town (pop. 10,414), S La., N of Vermilion Bay, in rice-growing area. Town grew around Roman Catholic chapel built 1845 by the French.

Abbey, Edwin Austin, 1852–1911, American artist, noted for book illustrations. Official painter of coronation of Edward VII.

SMALL CAPITALS = cross references. Pronunciation key on inside end pages. Abbreviations: p. 2.

1

Abbey Theatre, Irish theatrical company. Experiments resulted in forming (1902) of Irish Natl. Theatre Society, whose playwright-directors included Yeats, A. E., Lady Gregory, Synge. The Abbey Theatre in Dublin (donated for free use by Miss A. E. F. Horniman 1904) was purchased 1910. First to present plays of such writers as Sean O'Casey and Paul Vincent Carroll. Often toured the U.S.

Abbot, Charles Greeley, 1872–, American astrophysicist, authority on solar radiation. Associated with Smithsonian Institution from 1896.

Abbotsford, estate (1812–32) of Sir Walter Scott, Roxburghshire, Scotland. Contains relics of Scott.

Abbott, Edith: see ABBOTT, GRACE.

Abbott, George, 1889–, American theatrical producer, playwright, and director. Recognized as a master of crackling farce since the success of his *Three Men on a Horse* (1935).

Abbott, Grace, 1878–1939, American social worker, director of Child Labor Division of U.S. Children's Bureau (1921–34). Her sister, **Edith Abbott,** 1876–1957,

became (1924) dean of School of Social Service Administration, Univ. of Chicago.

Abbott, Jacob, 1803–79, American teacher, author of more than 180 books for boys (*Rollo* series). His son **Lyman Abbott,** 1835–1922, American clergyman, edited *Christian Union* (later *Outlook*) with Henry Ward Beecher. Succeeded him at Plymouth Church, Brooklyn, 1888; resigned 1899 for editorial duties. Leader in "social gospel" movement.

abbreviation, in writing, arbitrary shortening of a word, usually by cutting off letters from the end, e.g., U.S.A., Geo. (George). Contraction serves the same purpose but is understood strictly to be the shortening of a word by cutting out letters in the middle, the omission sometimes being indicated by an apostrophe. Many writers hold that a contraction (in which last letter of the word appears) should not be followed by a period, though an abbreviation should. Recent usage, however, differs widely (NATO vs. U.S.). A period is never used when apostrophes appear. A select list of widely used abbreviations, including those that are used in this volume, follows:

LIST OF ABBREVIATIONS

a = are [100 sq. meters]
a.= acre, acres
A.A.= Alcoholics Anonymous
AAA = Agricultural Adjustment Agency
A.A.A.= American Automobile Association
A.B.= Able-bodied Seaman; *Artium Baccalaureus* [Bachelor of Arts]
abbr. (*or* abbrev.) = abbreviation
Abp.= Archbishop
abr.= abridged
AC = alternating current
Acad.= Academy
acct.= account
A.D.= *anno Domini* [in the year of the Lord] (often small capitals)
ad fin.= *ad finem* [to the end, at the end]
adj.= adjective
Adjt.= Adjutant
ad lib.= *ad libitum* [at pleasure]
Adm.= Admiral, Admiralty
adv.= adverb
ad val. (*or* adv.) = *ad valorem* [on the value]
advt. (*or* adv.) = advertisement
AEC = Atomic Energy Commission
A.E.F.= American Expeditionary Force
aet. (*or* aetat.) = *aetatis* [of age]
AFL (*or* A.F. of L.) = American Federation of Labor
AFL–CIO = American Federation of Labor–Congress of Industrial Organizations
Afr.= Africa
agr.= agriculture, agricultural
agt.= agent
A.H.= *anno Hegirae* [in the year of the Hegira] (often small capitals)
A.I.A.= American Institute of Architects

AID = Agency for International Development
A.L.A.=American Library Association
Ala.= Alabama
alt.= altitude
Alta.= Alberta
A.M.= *ante meridiem* [before noon] (often small capitals); *anno mundi* [in the year of the world] (often small capitals); *Artium Magister* [Master of Arts]
AM = amplitude modulation
A.M.A.= American Medical Association
A.M.D.G.= *ad majorem Dei gloriam* [to the greater glory of God]
Amer. (*or* Am.) = America, American
amp.= ampere, amperes
amt.= amount
anc.= ancient
ann.= annual, annals
anon.= anonymous
AP = Associated Press
APO = Army Post Office
app.= appendix, appointed
apt.= apartment
APRA = *Alianza Popular Revolucionaria Americana*
Arch.= Archipelago
Ariz.= Arizona
Ark.= Arkansas
art.= article
A.S. (*or* AS) = Anglo-Saxon
ASCAP = American Society of Composers, Authors, and Publishers
A.S.P.C.A.= American Society for the Prevention of Cruelty to Animals
assn.= association
ASSR=Autonomous Soviet Socialist Republic
asst.= assistant
ATP = adenosine triphosphate
atty.= attorney
at. wt.= atomic weight

A.U.C.=*ab urbe condita* [from the founding of the city] or *anno urbis conditae* [in the year of the founding of the city] (often small capitals)
Aug.= August
AV = Authorized Version
Av. (*or* Ave.) =Avenue
av.= average, avoirdupois
AVC= American Veterans Committee
avdp. (*or* av.) = avoirdupois
Ave. (*or* Av.) =Avenue
AWOL= absent without leave
b.= born, born in
B.A.= Bachelor of Arts
bal.= balance
Bapt.= Baptist
B.Arch.= Bachelor of Architecture
Bart.= Baronet
B.B.C.= British Broadcasting Corporation
bbl.= barrel
B.C.=before Christ (often small capitals); British Columbia
B.D.= Bachelor of Divinity
bd.= board
Bev = billion electron volt
bf = boldface
Bl.= Blessed
Bldg.= Building
B.Lit.= Bachelor of Literature
Blvd.= Boulevard
B.Mus.= Bachelor of Music
bor.= borough
Bp.= Bishop
B.P.O.E.= Benevolent Protective Order of Elks
Br. (*or* Brit.)=British
Brig. Gen.= Brigadier General
Brit. (*or* Br.)=British
bro.= brother
B.S.= Bachelor of Science
B.Sc.= Bachelor of Science
B.T.U.= British thermal unit
bu.= bushel, bushels
bul.= bulletin

Bulg.= Bulgarian
bur.= bureau
B.V.M.= Blessed Virgin Mary
B.W.I.= British West Indies
C.= centigrade, Caius
c.= copyright
c. (*or* ca.) = *circa* [about]
ca = centare
CACM = Central American Common Market
cal.= calorie
Calif.= California
Can.= Canadian
can.= canon, canto
Cant.= Canticles (Song of Solomon)
Cantab.= *Cantabrigiensis* [of Cambridge]
cap.= capital, capital letter, capitulum [chapter]
Capt.= Captain
car. (*or* k.)=carat
CARE=Cooperative for American Remittances to Everywhere, Inc.
Cath.= Catholic
C.B.= Companion of the Order of the Bath
C.C.= Chamber of Commerce
c.c. (*or* cc.)= cubic centimeter, carbon copy
CCC = Civilian Conservation Corps, Commodity Credit Corporation
C.E.= Civil Engineer
cen.= central
cent.= century, centuries
CENTO = Central Treaty Organization
CERN = European Organization for Nuclear Research
cf.= *confer* [compare]
cgs = centimeter-gram-second
chap.= chapter
Chem.E.= Chemical Engineer
Chron.= Chronicles
CIA = Central Intelligence Agency
Cia = *Compañía* [Company]
C.I.D.= Criminal Investigation Department

Cie=*Compagnie* [Company]
CINC=Commander in Chief
CIO = Congress of Industrial Organizations
C.J.= Chief Justice
cm = centimeter, centimeters
Cn.= Cneius
Co.= Company
co.= county
c/o = care of
C.O.D.= cash (also collect) on delivery
coed.= coeducational
Col.= College, Colonel, Colossians
col.= collector, column
Coll.= Collection
Colo.= Colorado
Comdr.= Commander
COMECON = Council for Mutual Economic Assistance
comp.= compiled, compiler
Comsat = Communications Satellite Corporation
Cong.= Congregational, Congressional
conj.= conjunction
Conn.= Connecticut
cont.= continued
COPE = Committee on Political Education
Cor.= Corinthians
cor.= corrected
CORE = Congress of Racial Equality
corp.= corporation
CP = Communist party
c.p.= candle power
C.P.A.= Certified Public Accountant
Cpl.= Corporal
CPO = Chief Petty Officer
Cr.= credit, creditor
C.S.= Christian Science
C.S.A.= Confederate States of America
cu.= cubic
CVA = Columbia Valley Authority
cwt.= hundredweight
C.Z.= Canal Zone
D.= Don or Doña (Span. address), Dom or Dona (Port. address); Decimus
d.= daughter; *denarius* [penny], *denarii* [pence]; died, died in
D.A.= District Attorney
Dan.= Daniel, Danish
D.A.R.= Daughters of the American Revolution
DC = direct current
D.C.= District of Columbia
D.C.L.= Doctor of Civil Law
D.D.= Doctor of Divinity
D.D.S.= Doctor of Dental Surgery
DDT = Dichloro-diphenyl-trichloro-ethane
Dec.= December
deg.= degree, degrees
Del.= Delaware
Dem.= Democrat, Democratic
dept.= department
Deut.= Deuteronomy
dial.= dialect, dialectical

diam.= diameter
dict.= dictionary
dist.= district
div.= division
DM = Deutschemark
DNA = deoxyribonucleic acid
do.= ditto [the same]
doz.= dozen, dozens
DP = displaced person
Dr.= debtor, Doctor
dr.= dram, drams
D.S.C.= Distinguished Service Cross
D.Sc.= Doctor of Science
D.S.M.= Distinguished Service Medal
D.S.O.=Companion of the Distinguished Service Order
Du.= Dutch
D.V.= *Deo volente* [God willing]
dwt.= pennyweight
E = east
ECA = Economic Cooperation Administration
Eccles.= Ecclesiastes
Ecclus.= Ecclesiasticus
ECSC = European Coal and Steel Community
ed.= edited, edition, editor, educated
EDC = European Defense Community
E.E.= Electrical Engineer
EEC = European Economic Community
EFTA = European Free Trade Association
e.g.= *exempli gratia* [for example]
E.M.= Engineer of Mines
EMA = European Monetary Agreement
emf = electromotive force
ency. (*or* encyc.) = encyclopedia
ENE = east-northeast
Eng.= English
engr.= engraved
enl.= enlarged
Eph.= Ephesians
Epis. (*or* Episc.) = Episcopal
EPU = European Payments Union
ERP=European Recovery Program
ESE = east-southeast
esp.= especially
Esq.= Esquire
est.= estimated
estab.= establish, established
et al.= *et alibi* [and elsewhere]; *et alii* [and others]
etc.= *et cetera* [and others, and so forth]
et seq.= *et sequens* [and the following]
et sqq.= *et sequentes, et sequentia* [and those following]
Eur.= Europe
Ex.= Exodus
ex.= example, except
Ezek.= Ezekiel
F.= Fahrenheit, Fellow
F. (*or* Fri.) = Friday
f.= and the following page

f. (*or* fem.) = feminine
fac.= facsimile
F.A.G.S.= Fellow of the American Geographical Society
F. and A.M.=Free and Accepted Masons
FAO = Food and Agriculture Organization of the United Nations
FBI = Federal Bureau of Investigation
FCA = Farm Credit Administration
FCC = Federal Communications Commission
Feb.= February
fed.= federated, federation
fem. (*or* f.)=feminine
FEPC=Fair Employment Practices Committee
ff.= and the following pages
fig.= figure
fl.= *floruit* [flourished]
Fla.= Florida
FLN = *Front de Libération nationale* [National Liberation Front]
fl. oz.= fluid ounce
FM = frequency modulation
fn.= footnote
fo.= folio
f.o.b.= free on board
FPO = Fleet Post Office
Fr.= French, Father, Friar
fr.= franc
F.R.A.S.= Fellow of the Royal Astronomical Society
F.R.C.P.= Fellow of the Royal College of Physicians
F.R.C.S.= Fellow of the Royal College of Surgeons
F.R.G.S.= Fellow of the Royal Geographical Society
Fri. (*or* F.) = Friday
front.= frontispiece
F.R.S.= Fellow of the Royal Society
ft.= foot, feet, fort
FTC = Federal Trade Commission
g = gram, grams
Ga.= Georgia
Gal.= Galatians
gal.= galley, gallon, gallons
Gall.= Gallery
G.A.R.= Grand Army of the Republic
G.C.= Knight Grand Cross; Knight Grand Commander (of various British orders, when followed by abbreviation designating the order)
G.C.B.= Knight Grand Cross of the Order of the Bath
Gen.= General, Genesis
Ger.= German
GHQ = General Headquarters
G.I.= general issue (term for common soldier); gastrointestinal
gloss.= glossary
G.M.T.= Greenwich mean time
g.n.p.= gross national product
G.O.P.=Grand Old Party (Republican Party)
Gov.= Governor
govt.= government

GPU (*or* OGPU *or* Ogpu) = *Otdelenie Gosudarstvenni Politcheskoi Upravi* [Unified State Political Administration]
Gr.= Greek
gr.= grain, grains
grad.= graduate, graduated, graduated at
ha = hectare
Hab.= Habakkuk
Hag.= Haggai
Heb.= Hebrew, Hebrews (NT)
hhd.= hogshead
H.M.S.= His (Her) Majesty's Ship; His (Her) Majesty's Service
HOLC = Home Owners' Loan Corporation
Hon.= the Honorable
hp = horsepower
hq.= headquarters
H.R.= House of Representatives
hr.= hour, hours
H.R.H.= His (Her) Royal Highness
ht.= height
HUD = Housing and Urban Development
Hung.= Hungarian
ib. (*or* ibid.) = *ibidem* [in the same place]
ICA = International Cooperation Administration
ICAO = International Civil Aviation Organization
ICBM = intercontinental ballistic missile
ICC=Interstate Commerce Commission
I.E. (*or* I-E *or* IE) = Indo-European
i.e.= *id est* [that is]
IGY = International Geophysical Year
IHS = *Iesus Hominum Salvator* [Jesus, the Savior of Men]; *in hoc signo* [in this sign] (originally three letters of the Greek for Jesus)
Ill.= Illinois
ill. (*or* illus.) = illustrated, illustration
ILO = International Labor Organization
ILS = instrument-landing system
in.= inch, inches
inc.= incorporated
incl.= including, inclusive
incog.= incognito [unknown, unrecognized]
Ind.= Indiana
ind.= index
inf.= infinitive, *infra* [below]
I.N.R.I.= *Iesus Nazarenus, Rex Iudaeorum* [Jesus of Nazareth, King of the Jews]
Inst.= Institute, Institution
inst.= instant [the present month]
int.= interest
internatl.= international
introd.= introduction
I.O.O.F.= Independent Order of Odd Fellows

SMALL CAPITALS = cross references. Pronunciation key on inside end pages. Abbreviations: p. 2.

I O U = I owe you

I.Q. (or IQ) = intelligence quotient

IQSY = International Quiet Sun Year

Ir.= Irish

IRA = Irish Republican Army

IRBM = intermediate-range ballistic missile

IRO = International Refugee Organization

Isa.= Isaiah

isl.= island

Ital. (or It.) = Italian

ital = italic type

ITO = International Trade Organization

ITU = International Telecommunications Union

IWW = Industrial Workers of the World

JAG = Judge Advocate General

Jan.= January

Jap.= Japanese

J.D.= *Juris Doctor* [Doctor of Laws]

Jer.= Jeremiah

jg = junior grade (in U.S. Navy)

jour.= journal

J.P.= Justice of the Peace

Jr.= Junior

J.U.D.= *Juris Utriusque Doctor* [Doctor of Both Civil and Canon Laws]

K.= Kelvin

k. (or car.) = carat

K.C.= King's Counsel; Knight Commander (of various British orders, when followed by abbreviation designating the order)

K.C. (or K. of C.) = Knights of Columbus

kc = kilocycle, kilocycles

K.G.= Knight of the Order of the Garter

kg = kilogram, kilograms

KJV = King James Version

K.K.K.= Ku Klux Klan

kl = kiloliter, kiloliters

km=kilometer, kilometers

K. of C. (or K.C.) = Knights of Columbus

K.P.= Knights of Pythias

K.T.= Knight Templar

Kt.= Knight

kw = kilowatt, kilowatts

kwh = kilowatt hour, kilowatt hours

Ky.= Kentucky

L.= Lake; Left (in stage directions); Lucius

£.= *libra* [pound]

l.= liter, liters

l.= line

La.= Louisiana

Lab.= Labrador

LAFTA = Latin American Free Trade Association

Lam.= Lamentations

Lat.= Latin

lat.= latitude

lb.= *libra* [pound], *librae* [pounds]

l.c.= lower case [not capitalized]

Lev.= Leviticus

L.H.D.= *Litterarum Humaniorum Doctor* [Doctor of Humane Letters]

L.I.= Long Island

Lieut.= Lieutenant

Litt.B.= *Litterarum Baccalaureus* [Bachelor of Literature]

Litt.D.= *Litterarum Doctor* [Doctor of Literature]

ll.= lines

LL.B.= *Legum Baccalaureus* [Bachelor of Laws]

LL.D.= *Legum Doctor* [Doctor of Laws]

loc. cit.= *loco citato* [in the place cited]

log.= logarithm

long.= longitude

Lt.= Lieutenant

Ltd.= Limited

Luth.= Lutheran

M.= mark [German coin]; *meridies* [noon] (often small capitals); Monsieur [Mr., Sir]; Marcus

m = meter, meters

m.= married

m. (or masc.) = masculine

M.A.= Master of Arts

Mac.= Maccabees

Maj.= Major

Mal.= Malachi

Man.= Manitoba

masc. (or m.) = masculine

Mass.= Massachusetts

Mat.= Matthew

max.= maximum

M.D.= *Medicinae Doctor* [Doctor of Medicine]

Md.= Maryland

mdse.= merchandise

M.E.= Mechanical Engineer, Methodist Episcopal

M.E. (or ME or Mid. Eng.)= Middle English

memo.= memorandum

Messrs.= Messieurs [Gentlemen] (plural of Mr.)

Met. E.= Metallurgical Engineer

Meth.= Methodist

Mex.= Mexican

mfg.= manufacturing

M.F.H.= Master of Foxhounds

mg = milligram, milligrams

Mgr = Monsignor

mgr.= manager

M.H.G. (or MHG) = Middle High German

mi.= mile, miles

Mich.= Michigan

Mid. Eng. (or M.E. or ME)= Middle English

min.=minimum, minute, minutes

Minn.= Minnesota

misc.= miscellaneous

Miss.= Mississippi

ml = milliliter, milliliters

Mlle = Mademoiselle [Miss]

MM.= Messieurs [Gentlemen] (plural of M.)

mm = millimeter, millimeters

Mme = Madame

Mo.= Missouri

mo.= month

Mon.= Monday

Mont.= Montana

M.P.= Member of Parliament

mph = miles per hour

Mr.= Mister (always abbreviated)

MRA = Moral Re-Armament

Mrs.= Mistress (always abbreviated)

MS = manuscript

M.S. (or M.Sc.) = Master of Science

Msgr = Monsignor

MSS = manuscripts

mt.= mount, mountain

mus.= museum, music

Mus.B.= *Musicae Baccalaureus* [Bachelor of Music]

Mus.D.=*Musicae Doctor* [Doctor of Music]

MVA = Missouri Valley Authority

MVD = *Ministerstvo Vnutrennikh Del* [Soviet Ministry of Internal Affairs]

N = noun

n.= *natus* [born], neuter, noun

n. (or nom.)=nominative

N.A.=National Academy, North America

NAACP = National Association for the Advancement of Colored People

N.A.M.= National Association of Manufacturers

NASA = National Aeronautics and Space Administration

natl.= national

NATO=North Atlantic Treaty Organization

N.B.= New Brunswick; *nota bene* [note well]

N.C.= North Carolina

NCO = Noncommissioned Officer

n.d.= no date

N.Dak.= North Dakota

NE = northeast

N.E.A.= National Education Association

Nebr.= Nebraska

Neh.= Nehemiah

NEP = New Economic Policy

neut. (or n.)=neuter

Nev.= Nevada

N.F.= Newfoundland

N.H.= New Hampshire

N.J.= New Jersey

NKVD = *Narodnyi Komissariat Vnutrennikh Del* [People's Commissariat of Internal Affairs]

NLRB = National Labor Relations Board

N.Mex.= New Mexico

NNE = north-northeast

NNW = north-northwest

No., no.= *numero* [number]

Nor.= Norwegian

Nov.= November

N.P.= Notary Public

NRA = National Recovery Administration

NROTC = Naval Reserve Officers' Training Corps

N.S.= New Style; Nova Scotia; new series (of a periodical)

NT = New Testament

Num.= Numbers

NW = northwest

N.Y.= New York

NYA = National Youth Administration

OAS = *Organisation de l'Armée secrète* [Secret Army Organization]: Organization of American States

OAU = Organization of African Unity

ob.= *obiit* [died]

Obad.= Obadiah

obs.= obsolete

Oct.= October

O.E. (or OE) = Old English

OECD = Organization for Economic Cooperation and Development

OEEC = Organization for European Economic Cooperation

O.F.M.=*Ordo Fratrum Minorum* [Order of Friars Minor] (Franciscan)

O.Fr. (or O.F. or OF)= Old French

OGPU (or Ogpu or GPU)= *Otdelenie Gosudarstvennoi Politcheskoi Upravi* [Unified State Political Administration]

O.H.G. (or OHG)= Old High German

O.Ir.= Old Irish

O.K. (or OK) = correct

Okla.= Oklahoma

O.M.= Order of Merit

O.N. (or ON) = Old Norse

Ont.= Ontario

O.P.=Order of Preachers (Dominicans)

op.= *opus* [work]

OPA = Office of Price Administration

op. cit.= *opere citato* [in the work cited]

opp.= opposite

O.S.= Old Style

O.S.B.= *Ordo Sancti Benedicti* [Order of St. Benedict] (Benedictines)

OSS = Office of Strategic Services

OT = Old Testament

Oxon.= *Oxoniensis* [of Oxford]

oz.= ounce, ounces

P.= Publius

p.= page

Pa.= Pennsylvania

PAC = Political Action Committee

Pat. Off.= Patent Office

p.c.= per cent

pd.= paid

Pd. D.= *Pedagogiae Doctor* [Doctor of Pedagogy]

P.E.= Protestant Episcopal

P.E.I.= Prince Edward Island

PFC (or Pfc) = Private First Class

Pg. (or Port.) = Portuguese

Ph.B.= *Philosophiae Baccalaureus* [Bachelor of Philosophy]

Ph.D.= *Philosophiae Doctor* [Doctor of Philosophy]
Philip.= Philippians
P.I.= Philippine Islands
pinx.= *pinxit* [he painted]
pk.= peck
PKU = phenylketonuria
pl.= plate
pl. (*or* plur.) = plural
plur. (*or* pl.) = plural
P.M.= Postmaster; *post meridiem* [afternoon] (often small capitals)
PO = Petty Officer
P.O.= post office
Pol.= Polish
pop.= population
Port. (*or* Pg.) = Portuguese
POW = prisoner of war
pp.= pages
P.R.= Puerto Rico
pref.= preface
prep.= preparatory, preposition
Pres.= President
Presb.= Presbyterian
pron.= pronoun, pronounced
Prot.= Protestant
pro tem.= *pro tempore* [temporarily]
Prov.= Proverbs
prov.= province
prox.= *proximo* [of the next month]
P.S.= *post scriptum* [postscript]
Ps.= Psalm
pseud.= pseudonym
Pss.= Psalms
pt.= part, pint, pints, point
pub.= published, publisher
Pvt.= Private
PWA = Public Works Administration
Q.= Quintus, question
Q.C.= Queen's Counsel
Q.E.D.= *quod erat demonstrandum* [which was to be demonstrated]
Q.E.F.= *quod erat faciendum* [which was to be done]
QM = Quartermaster
qq.v.= *quae vide* [which see] (plural)
qt.= quart, quarts
Que.= Quebec
q.v.= *quod vide* [which see]
R.= River; Réaumur; *Rex* [King]; *Regina* [Queen]; Right (stage direction)
R.A.= Royal Academician
RAF = Royal Air Force
R.C.=Red Cross, Roman Catholic
Rd.= Road
RDF = radio direction finder
REA = Rural Electrification Administration
recd.= received
rect. (*or* rept.) = receipt
reestab.= reestablish, reestablished
Regt.= Regiment
Rep.= Republican, Representative
rept.= report
rept. (*or* rect.) = receipt

Ret.= Retired
Rev.= Revelations, the Reverend
rev.= revised
RFC = Reconstruction Finance Corporation
R.F.D.= rural free delivery
R.I.= Rhode Island
R.I.P.=*requiescat in pace* [may he rest in peace]
RM.= Reichsmark
R.N.= Registered Nurse, Royal Navy
RNA = ribonucleic acid
Rom.= Romans
rom = roman type
ROTC = Reserve Officers' Training Corps
rpm.= revolutions per minute
RR = railroad
RSFSR = Russian Soviet Federated Socialist Republic
RSV = Revised Standard Version
R.S.V.P.= *Répondez, s'il vous plaît* [An answer is requested]
Rt. Rev.= The Right Reverend
Rus.= Russian
RV = Revised Version
Ry.= railway
S = south
S.= *San, Santa, Santo,* or *São* [Saint]
S. (*or* Sun.)=Sunday
s.= *solidus* [shilling], *solidi* [shillings]
S.A.= Salvation Army; South America; *Sociedad Anónima, Société Anonyme* [Limited]
SACLANT = Supreme Allied Commander Atlantic
Sam.= Samuel
S.A.R.= Sons of the American Revolution
Sask.= Saskatchewan
Sat.= Saturday
S.C.= South Carolina
s.c.= small capitals
sc.= *scilicet* [namely]
Sc.D.= *Scientiae Doctor* [Doctor of Science]
S.Dak.= South Dakota
SE = southeast
SEATO = Southeast Asia Treaty Organization
SEC = Securities and Exchange Commission
sec.= second, seconds, section, sections
secy.= secretary
Sen.= Senator
Sept.= September
ser.= series
Sex.= Sextus
Sgt.= Sergeant
SHAEF = Supreme Headquarters, Allied Expeditionary Force
SHAPE=Supreme Headquarters, Allied Powers in Europe
sing.= singular
S.J.= *Societas Jesu* [Society of Jesus]
Skt.= Sanskrit
Soc.= society

SOS = distress signal (not a true abbreviation)
Span. (*or* Sp.) = Spanish
S.P.C.C.= Society for the Prevention of Cruelty to Children
sp. gr.= specific gravity
S.P.Q.R.= *Senatus Populusque Romanus* [the Senate and People of Rome]
sq.= *sequens* [the following]; square
sqq.= *sequentes, sequentia* [those following]
Sr.= Senior
SS.= Saints
S.S.=Steamship, Sunday School
SSE = south-southeast
SSR = Soviet Socialist Republic
SSW = south-southwest
St.= Saint, Street
S.T.D.= *Sacrae Theologiae Doctor* [Doctor of Sacred Theology]
Ste = *Sainte* [Saint, feminine]
Sun. (*or* S.) = Sunday
sup.= supplement, *supra* [above]
Supt.= Superintendent
s.v.= *sub verbo* (under the entry)
SW = southwest
Swed. (*or* Sw.) = Swedish
T.= Titus
Tenn.= Tennessee
Th. (*or* Thurs.) = Thursday
Thess.= Thessalonians
Thurs. (*or* Th.) = Thursday
Ti.= Tiberius
Tim.= Timothy
TNEC = Temporary National Economic Committee
T.N.T. (*or* TNT)=trinitrotoluene, trinitrotoluol
tp.= township
t.p. (*or* t.-p.) = title page
tr.=transitive, translated, translation, translator, transpose
treas.= treasurer
Tu. (*or* Tues.) = Tuesday
TVA = Tennessee Valley Authority
UAR = United Arab Republic
U.C.V.= United Confederate Veterans
U.D.C.= United Daughters of the Confederacy
UHF = ultra high frequency
UK = United Kingdom of Great Britain and Northern Ireland
ult.= *ultimo* [of the preceding month]
UN = United Nations
UNCTAD = United Nations Conference on Trade and Development
UNESCO = United Nations Educational, Scientific, and Cultural Organization
uninc.= unincorporated
Unit.= Unitarian
Univ.= Universalist, University
UNRRA = United Nations Relief and Rehabilitation Administration

UPI = United Press International
U.S.= United States
USA = United States Army
U.S.A.= United States of America
USAF = United States Air Force
USBGN = United States Board on Geographic Names
USCG = United States Coast Guard
USMC = United States Marine Corps
USN = United States Navy
USO = United Service Organizations
U.S.S.= United States Ship
USSR = Union of Soviet Socialist Republics
v.= *vide* [see]
v, (*or* vb.)= verb
v, (*or* vs.) = *versus* [against]
VA=Veterans' Administration
Va.= Virginia
V.C.= Victoria Cross
Ved.= Vedic
Ven.= the Venerable
VHF = very high frequency
V.I.= Virgin Islands
viz.= *videlicet* [namely]
vol.= volume, volunteer
vs.= verse, versus
Vt.= Vermont
W = west
W. (*or* Wed.) = Wednesday
WAC = Women's Army Corps
Wash.= Washington
WAVES = Women Accepted for Voluntary Emergency Service (United States Women's Naval Reserve)
W.C.T.U.= Woman's Christian Temperance Union
Wed. (*or* W.) = Wednesday
WEU = Western European Union
WHO = World Health Organization
W.I.= West Indies
Wis.= Wisconsin
wk.= week
WMO = World Meteorological Organization
WNW = west-northwest
WO = Warrant Officer
WPA=Work Projects Administration
WSW = west-southwest
wt.= weight
W.Va.= West Virginia
Wyo.= Wyoming
yd.= yard, yards
Y.M.C.A.=Young Men's Christian Association
Y.M.H.A.= Young Men's Hebrew Association
yr.= year
Y.W.C.A.= Young Women's Christian Association
Y.W.H.A.= Young Women's Hebrew Association
Zech.= Zechariah
Zeph.= Zephaniah

SMALL CAPITALS = cross references. Pronunciation key on inside end pages. Abbreviations: p. 2.

Abd al-Rahman. For Moslem rulers thus named, see ABDU-R-RAHMAN.

Abd-el-Krim (ăb″dĕl-krēm′), 1882?–1963, leader of Riffian tribes of Morocco. Defeated 1925 by a joint Franco-Spanish army and deported to Réunion isl. Escaped 1947 to Egypt, where he became a leader of the N African independence movement.

Abdera (ăbdēr′ŭ), Gr. *Avdera*, town (pop. 1,222), Greece, in SW Thrace. Agr. market. Founded c.650 B.C. Protagoras and Democritus lived here.

Abderhalden, Emil (ä′mēl äp′dúrhäl″dŭn), 1877–1950, Swiss physiologist and biochemist. Worked on enzymes and food metabolism. Devised pregnancy test.

Abdias: see OBADIAH.

abdication, renunciation of high public office, usually by a monarch. Known from antiquity and in many lands, act may be voluntary (e.g., Emperor Charles V) or forced (many cases in China, including Hsüan t'ung emperor in 1912). Forbidden in Great Britain since 1688 unless with consent of Parliament, as in the case of Edward VIII (1936).

abdomen, portion of trunk below diaphragm. Cavity, lined by membrane (peritoneum), contains stomach, intestines, liver, pancreas, spleen, kidneys; in lower part (called pelvis) are bladder, rectum, some of reproductive organs. See *ill.*, p. 657.

Abdu-l-Aziz IV (äb″dōōl-äzēz′), 1881?–1943, sultan of Morocco (1894–1908). French influence in Morocco was strengthened during his weak and unpopular reign. Deposed by his brother Abdu-l-Hafid.

Abdu-l-Aziz, 1830–76, Ottoman sultan (1861–76). During his reign Turkey became financially dependent on the West; Rumania, Serbia, Egypt gained virtual independence. Overthrown by MIDHAT PASHA, he died a few days later (probably by suicide).

Abdu-l-Aziz ibn Saud: see IBN SAUD.

Abdu-l-Hamid (–hämēd′), Ottoman sultans. **Abdu-l-Hamid I,** 1725–89, reigned 1774–89. Made peace with Russia in Treaty of KUCHUK-KAINARJI (1774); renewed war 1787. **Abdu-l-Hamid II,** 1842–1918, reigned 1876–1909. He suspended the constitution; disposed of MIDHAT PASHA. After Congress of BERLIN (1878), he began a pro-German policy. Called Red Sultan for his part in Armenian massacres (1894–96). Deposed by Young Turks 1909.

Abdu-l-Kadir (–kädēr′), c.1807–83, Algerian leader, of Arab descent. As emir of Mascara, he extended his power over much of N Algeria (1832–39). In 1839 declared a holy war against the French. Driven by Gen. Bugeaud into Morocco, where he won the sultan's support. Defeated 1844 at Isly, surrendered 1847, imprisoned in France until 1852.

Abdullah (äbdŭ′lŭ, äbdōōlä′), d. c.570, father of Mohammed.

Abdullah, 1882–1951, first king of Jordan (1946–51), b. Mecca. Lost Hejaz to Ibn Saud. Led British-trained Arab Legion against Israel in 1948. Assassinated 1951.

Abdu-l-Malik (äb″dōōl-mùlīk′), c.646–705, the 5th OMAYYAD caliph (685–705). Overthrew rival caliphs and united Islam.

Abdu-l-Mejid (–mējēd′), 1823–61, Ottoman sultan (1839–61). Promoted reform. Revolt of MOHAMMED ALI was checked by Great Powers. CRIMEAN WAR and Congress of PARIS (1856) brought Turkey no gain. After his time decline of sultanate began.

Abdu-l-Mumin (–mōō′mĭn), 1094–1163, founder of the ALMOHADES. Conquered Morocco in the 1140s, became dominant in Spain in 1151, and extended his African domain as far east as Tripoli, 1158–59.

Abdu-r-Rahman (äb″dōōr-rä′män, –rämän′) or **Abd al-Rahman** (äb″dōōl-), OMAYYAD rulers of Córdoba. **Abdu-r-Rahman I,** d. 788, fled Damascus, seized power in Córdoba (756), ruled as emir till his death. **Abdu-r-Rahman III,** 891–961, ruled as emir from 912, as caliph from 929. Under him Moslem Spain reached height of glory. Also ruled Moslem part of N Africa 939–47.

Abdu-r-Rahman or **Abd al-Rahman,** d. 732, Moslem governor in Spain. Defeated and slain in battle near Tours by CHARLES MARTEL.

Abed-nego (ùbĕd′nēgō), one of THREE HOLY CHILDREN.

Abel, shepherd son of Adam and Eve, killed by Cain, his brother. Gen. 4.1–8.

Abel, Sir Frederick Augustus, 1826–1902, English chemist. Improved guncotton manufacture. Invented cordite (with Dewar) and Abel test for flash point of petroleum.

Abel, John Jacob, 1857–1938, American pharmacologist, associated with Johns Hopkins from 1893. He isolated epinephrine (adrenaline), crystalline form of insulin, and amino acids from blood.

Abel, Niels Henrik, 1802–29, Norwegian mathematician. Proved insolubility of general algebraic equation of fifth degree by elementary operations alone. Worked also on elliptic functions.

Abelard, Peter (ā′bùlärd), Fr. *Pierre Abélard,* 1079–1142, French scholastic. Regarded as founder of Univ. of Paris. His romance and secret marriage with his pupil Heloise, niece of Fulbert, a canon of Notre Dame, ended when Fulbert had him emasculated by hired ruffians. Abelard became monk at Saint-Denis; left in 1120 to teach. Hostility of St. Bernard of Clairvaux caused condemnation of certain of his doctrines at Council of Soissons (1121). Abelard built a hermitage near Troyes, adding a monastery, the Paraclete, to house students; later he gave it to Heloise, who became abbess of a sisterhood there. To avoid condemnation at Council of Sens (1140), he made submission and retired to Cluny. Abelard applied logical methods to truths of faith; considered universals as existing only in thought but with basis in particulars (see SCHOLASTICISM). Chief work: *Sic et non* (collection of contradictory statements of Church Fathers). *Historia calamitatum* is autobiographical. Letters of Abelard and Heloise belong to world literature.

Abell, Kjeld (kyĕl′ ä′bĕl), 1901–61, Danish dramatist, innovator in stage techniques. Among his plays on social problems are *Anna Sophie Hedvig* (1939) and *The Queen Walks Again* (1943).

Abeokuta (ä′bēō″kōōtù), city (pop. c.187,300), SW Nigeria. Founded c.1830 as one of Yoruba citystates. Modern industrial center.

Abercromby, Sir Ralph, 1734–1801, British general. Won major military reputation for campaigns against the French, especially in Flanders (1794–95) and W Indies. Killed in successful battle at Aboukir.

Aberdeen, George Hamilton-Gordon, 4th earl of (äbŭr-dēn′), 1784–1860, British statesman. By Treaty of Töplitz (1813) cemented Austria to anti-Napoleonic coalition. By Webster-Ashburton Treaty (1842) settled Northeast Boundary Dispute with U.S. Prime Minister (1852–55), he resigned after failure to stop British involvement in unpopular Crimean War.

Aberdeen, city (pop. 185,379), Aberdeenshire and Kincardine, Scotland, on North Sea at mouth of the Dee; chief port and largest city of NE Scotland. Called the Granite City. Univ. of Aberdeen includes King's Col. (1493) and Marischal Col. (1593).

Aberdeen. 1 Town (pop. 9,679), NE Md., NE of Baltimore, in farm region. U.S. army's Aberdeen Proving Ground is nearby. **2** City (pop. 23,073), NE S. Dak., NW of Watertown; settled 1880. Trade center for agr. region. **3** City (pop. 18,741), W Wash., on Grays Harbor ESE of Hoquiam; settled 1867. Owes growth mainly to lumber and fish-canning.

Aberdeenshire, county (1,971 sq. mi.; pop. 298,503), NE Scotland; county town Aberdeen. Chief occupations agr., fishing, and cattle breeding. At Braemar is British royal residence, Balmoral Castle.

Aberhart, William (ä′bùrhärt), 1878–1943, Canadian statesman. Organizer of Social Credit party of Alberta; premier of Alberta (1935–43).

aberration, optics, blurring or loss of clearness in images produced by lenses or mirrors. It is spherical when rays of light from a point are not brought to a single focus, chromatic when image is blurred and fringes of color appear at its edges.

Abertawe, Glamorganshire, Wales: see SWANSEA.

Aberystwyth (ăbŭrist'with), municipal borough (pop. 10,418), Cardiganshire, Wales; summer resort on Cardigan Bay. Has a constituent college of Univ. of Wales and Natl. Library of Wales.

Abgar, Epistles of: see PSEUDEPIGRAPHA.

Abiathar (ŭbī'–), priest, son of Ahimelech. After escaping massacre ordered by Saul, remained loyal to David. 1 Sam. 22.9–23; 2 Sam. 15.27,29; I Kings 1.7; 2.27; Mark 2.26. Name sometimes exchanged with his father's.

Abidjan (ăbĭjän'), industrial city (pop. c.225,000), cap. of Republic of the Ivory Coast, on the Ebrie Lagoon, off the Gulf of Guinea. Access to ocean is by Vridi Canal through lagoon bar. Exports coffee, cacao, rubber, and timber. Also rail terminus.

Abigail (ăb'ĭgăl) [Heb.,= my father is joy]. **1** Wife of Nabal. After his death, she married David. 1 Sam. 25; 2 Sam. 3.3; 1 Chron. 3.1. **2** David's stepsister. 2 Sam. 17.25; 1 Chron. 2.16,17.

Abihu (ŭbī'hū), son of Aaron, destroyed for offering "strange" fire. Ex. 6.23; 24.1,9; 28.1; Lev. 10.1; Num. 3.2,4; 26.60,61; 1 Chron. 6.3; 24.1,2.

Abijah (ŭbī'jù), died c.911 B.C., king of Judah (c.914–c.911 B.C.); successor of Rehoboam. Jeroboam warred against him. 2 Chron. 13. Abijam: 1 Kings 15.1–8.

Abilene. 1 City (pop. 6,746), central Kansas, on Smoky Hill R., W of Topeka. One of wildest cow towns of old West, it was railhead for CHISHOLM TRAIL. Now a shipping point for wheat and farm area. Eisenhower Center has old family homestead, museum, and library. **2** City (pop. 90,368), W central Texas, WSW of Fort Worth; founded 1881. Shipping point for cattle; financial, commercial, and educational center; hq. of regional petroleum industry. Seat of Hardin-Simmons Univ., Abilene Christian Col., and McMurry Col. Dyess Air Force Base is SW.

Abimelech (ŭbĭm'ŭlĕk). **1** See AHIMELECH. **2** Son of Gideon. Slew his 70 brothers, except Jotham, and became "king." Judges 9.1–57; 2 Sam. 11.21.

Abinadab (ŭbĭn'ŭdăb). **1** Son of King Saul, killed at battle of Mt. Gilboa. **1** Sam. 31.2; 1 Chron. 10.2. **2** Keeper of ark for 20 years. 1 Sam. 7.1,2; 2 Sam. 6.3,4; 1 Chron. 13.7.

Abington, town (pop. 10,607), E Mass., NE of Brockton; settled 1668.

Abiram (ŭbī'rŭm), rebel (with KORAH) against Moses.

Abishag (ăb'–), handmaid to David in his old age. Adonijah wanted to marry her after David's death, and thus incurred Solomon's wrath. 1 Kings 1; 2.

Abitibi, Fort (ăbŭtĭb'ē), important Canadian fur-trading post, on Abitibi L., NE Ont., built 1686.

Abkhaz Autonomous Soviet Socialist Republic (ăbkäz', Rus. ŭpkhäs') or **Abkhasia,** autonomous state (3,300 sq. mi.; 1965 est. pop. 456,000), NW Georgian SSR; cap. Sukhum. Abkhasians (15% of pop.), who call themselves Apsua, are Orthodox Christians and Mohammedans. Annexed by Russia from Turkey 1810. Became autonomous republic 1922.

ablative: see CASE.

ablaut (äp'lout), in inflection, the variation between vowels in related words (e.g., English, *ring, rang, rung*) indicating a corresponding modification of meaning. At an earlier unknown period the corresponding forms of the language had differences in accent, not differences in vowel.

Abner, head of Saul's army. Killed by Joab. 1 Sam. 14.50,51; 17.55; 2 Sam. 2;3.

Abo, Finland: see TURKU.

abolitionists, in U.S. history, especially 1830–60, advocates of compulsory freeing of Negro slaves, as distinguished from free-soilers, opposed only to extension of slavery. Active campaign had mainspring in religious revival in 1820s and reached crusading stage in 1830s led by T. D. Weld, Tappan brothers, and W.

L. GARRISON. American Anti-Slavery Society, estab. 1833, flooded slave states with literature and lobbied in Washington. Writers such as J. G. Whittier and orators such as Wendell Phillips lent strength to cause. Despite unanimity on goal, there was division over methods, Garrison advocating moral suasion, others direct political action. Stringent fugitive slave laws in 1850 increased activity on UNDERGROUND RAILROAD. Harriet B. Stowe's *Uncle Tom's Cabin* and the Kansas question aroused both North and South, culminating in John Brown's raid on Harpers Ferry. Uncompromising temper of movement helped bring on the Civil War. See also SLAVERY.

abominable snowman or **yeti,** manlike creature reported to live in Himalayan regions. Unknown except for tracks ascribed to him and alleged sightings; described as 6–7 ft. tall, walking upright, and covered with long, dark hair. Variously considered a form of unclassified ape, a remnant of Neanderthal man, or a myth.

abortion, expulsion of product of conception before fetus can survive. Spontaneous abortion in humans popularly called miscarriage. Induced abortion is criminal offense in most states of U.S. except to save mother's life; Colorado liberalized its statutes on abortion in April, 1967. Legal on various grounds in several other countries.

Aboukir or **Abukir** (both: ăʺbōōkēr'), village, Egypt, on Aboukir Bay, SW of Rosetta mouth of the Nile. Nelson's victory here over the French fleet in 1798 restored British prestige in the Mediterranean. The battle is sometimes called the battle of the Nile.

abracadabra (ăb'rŭkŭdăb'rù), magic formula used by Gnostics in 2d cent. to invoke aid of benevolent spirits to ward off affliction; usually engraved on amulets as protective charm. The word gradually lost occult significance; now means any hocus-pocus.

Abraham [according to Gen. 17.5 = father of many] or **Abram** [Heb.,= the father is high], forefather of the Hebrews through his son Isaac and of the Arabs through his son Ishmael. Chiefly important as the founder of Judaism. He instituted circumcision and received God's word that his people would gain the promised land of Canaan. Revered by many faiths as a symbol of devotion to, and trust in, God (as shown in willingness to sacrifice Isaac, kindliness to his wayward nephew Lot). Gen. 11–25.

Abraham, Plains of, field adjoining upper part of Quebec city. Here the English under Wolfe defeated French under Montcalm (1759), ending FRENCH AND INDIAN WARS and deciding fate of Canada.

Abram: see ABRAHAM.

Abramovich Sholem Yakob: see MENDELE MOCHER SFORIM.

Abramovitz, Max, 1908–, American architect. Designed Philharmonic Hall at Lincoln Center.

abrasive, material used in grinding, cutting, polishing. Natural forms include DIAMOND, CORUNDUM, emery, SAND, PUMICE, chalk. Alundum (see ALUMINA) and Carborundum (see SILICON CARBIDE) are artificial. For special purposes powdered abrasives are often mixed with oil or water, molded with cement into wheels or sticks, or glued on cloth or paper.

Abravanel or **Abarbanel, Isaac** (ùbrä'vùnĕl, ùbärbù–), 1437–1508, Jewish philosopher and Biblical commentator. Minister of finance to kings of Portugal and Spain. Attempted to prevent expulsion of Jews from Spain in 1492. His son, **Judah Leon Abravanel,** c.1460–1525, called Leone Ebreo, was also a philosopher. His Neoplatonic *Dialoghi di Amore* had strong impact on Renaissance poetry and Spinoza.

Abruzzi, Luigi Amedeo, duca degli (ăbrōōt'tsē), 1873–1933, Italian naval officer, mountain climber, and arctic explorer, b. Madrid. Duke of the Abruzzi was cousin of Victor Emmanuel III.

Abruzzi e Molise (–ā môlē'zĕ), region (5,881 sq. mi.; pop. 1,584,777), central Italy, along Adriatic and in most rugged part of Apennines (Gran Sasso d'Italia);

cap. Aquila. Vineyards, olives, sheep raising. Shared history of kingdom of NAPLES.

Absalom (ăb'sŭlŏm), beloved but treacherous son of David. He fled after murdering his brother Amnon. Forgiven by David but led abortive revolt and was slain. 2 Sam. 3.3; 13–19; 2 Chron. 11.20,21.

Absalon (ăp'sälôn) or **Axel** (äk'sŭl), c.1128–1201, Danish churchman, archbishop of Lund. Held great political influence, warred against Wends, defeated Duke Bogislav of Pomerania in naval battle (1184). Patron of Saxo Grammaticus. Outstanding intellectual figure.

Absaroka Indians: see CROW INDIANS.

Absaroka Range (ăbsŭrō'kŭ), part of Rocky Mts., c.150 mi. long, NW Wyo. and S Mont.. partly in Yellowstone Natl. Park. Francs (or Franks) Peak is 13,140 ft. high.

abscess, accumulation of pus in tissues as result of infection. Characterized by inflammation and painful swelling. Occurs in various parts of body such as skin, eyelids, middle ear (see MASTOID), and rectoanal area (see HEMORRHOIDS). In tuberculosis abscesses (tubercules) occur in lung. Surgical drainage may be required unless abscess discharges spontaneously.

absentee proprietorship, system under which a person controls, and derives income from, land or capital in a region in which he does not live. Notable abuse in Ireland in 18th and 19th cent. and in E Europe until 20th cent. Recently term applied to concentrated control of wealth through corporate devices, shutting investor from conduct of business.

Absolute, the, in Western metaphysics, the unconditional principle that underlies the universe. Considered in Christian religion as equivalent to God. In philosophy term is most familiar in the thought of HEGEL. In Buddhism it is used for the final stage of illumination (Suchness).

absolute zero: see TEMPERATURE.

absorption: see GAS; OSMOSIS; SPECTRUM.

abstract art, nonrepresentational art in general. May be more or less naturalistic, but generally distinguished by elements not photographically realistic. Term applied in wide sense to many earlier artists, but more especially to 20th-cent. schools such as fauvism, cubism, expressionism, and their successors. A form of abstract art is nonobjective art (an early leader was Kandinsky in 1910), in which lines, textures, shapes, and colors are without reference to recognizable objects. Later varieties were CONSTRUCTIVISM and DE STIJL.

abstract expressionism, movement of abstract painting that emerged in New York city during the mid-1940s and attained singular prominence in American art in the following decade. It was the first important school in American painting to declare its independence from European styles and to influence the development of art abroad. Important artists include Arshile Gorky, Jackson Pollock, Willem de Kooning, Hans Hofmann, Robert Motherwell, Philip Guston, and Franz Kline. Also called action painting and the New York school.

Abubacer: see IBN TUFAIL.

Abubakar Tafawa Balewa, Alhaji Sir: see BALEWA, ALHAJI SIR ABUBAKAR TAFAWA.

Abu Bakr (ä'boo bä'kŭr), 573–634, 1st caliph, father of AYESHA, Mohammed's wife; most zealous convert, first outside Prophet's family. Mohammed's only companion on the Hegira. During his critical two-year caliphate Arabian opposition was crushed; extension of Islam as world religion began.

Abu Hanifa (–hänē'fä), 699–767, Moslem jurist, founder of a system of Islamic jurisprudence.

Abu Khasim, Arabian physician: see ABULCASIS.

Abukir, Egypt: see ABOUKIR.

Abu-l-Abbas as-Saffah (ä'bool-äbäs'äs-säfä'), d. 754, 1st ABBASID caliph (749–54). Took caliphate from the Omayyad with help of Abu Muslim.

Abu-l-Ala al-Maarri (–äl-mä-är-rē'), 973–1057, blind Arabic poet. Known for youthful verses of radical originality, he reverted to classicism after 35.

Abulcasis (ä'boolkä'sĭs) or **Abu Khasim** (ä'boo kä'-sĭm), fl. 11th cent., Arabian physician, author of influential text, *Tasrif*, on medicine and surgery.

Abu-l-Faraj Ali of Isfahan (ä'boolfä'räj), 897–967, Arabic scholar. His *Book of Songs* is an annotated compilation of Arabic poems set to music.

Abu-l-Walid Merwan ibn Janah: see JONAH, RABBI.

Abu Muslim (ä'boo moo'slĭm), c.728–755, Persian revolutionist. Won the caliphate for the Abbasid, who later killed him.

Abu Nuwas (–noowäs'), d. c.810, Arabic poet. His poetry echoes extravagance of Baghdad court.

Abu Said ibn Abi-l-Khair (sä'ĭd ä'bĕl-khīr'), 967–1049, Persian poet, a Sufi. Adapted rubaiyat poetic form to express Sufi mysticism.

Abu-Simbel (ä'boo-sĭm'bŭl) or **Ipsambul** (ĭp"sämbool'), village, S Egypt, on Nile river. Site of two temples hewn out of rock cliffs (c.1250 B.C.) during reign of Ramses II. Through efforts of UNESCO to save them from flooding behind Aswan High Dam, the temples were cut into sections and raised above water level.

Abu Tammam Habib ibn Aus: see HAMASA.

abutilon (übū'tĭlŭn) or **flowering maple,** tropical shrubs (*Abutilon*), with yellow, white, or pink bell-shaped flowers, lobed leaves. House plant in North.

Abydos (übī'dŭs), city of anc. Egypt, NW of Thebes; center of worship of Osiris. Burial place of Seti I and Ramses II.

Abyssinia: see ETHIOPIA.

Ac, chemical symbol of the element ACTINIUM.

acacia (ükä'shŭ), leguminous, tropical or subtropical trees or shrubs of genus *Acacia*, with fluffy clusters of yellow or white flowers. Known as wattle in Australia. Yield GUM arabic, dyes, tanning aids, furniture wood, CATECHU, and SHITTIM WOOD mentioned in the Bible.

academic freedom, right of scholars to teach, pursue research, and publish unrestrained by employing institution. A civil right in democratic countries, it usually includes right of tenure. Academic freedom is based on beliefs that open investigation best reveals truth and that scholars ought to pursue research regardless of personal opinion. The idea of completely free inquiry, evolving in the period of Enlightenment, was first accepted in Prussia and other German states. In England, Jeremy Bentham, Herbert Spencer, Charles Darwin, and Thomas Huxley showed value of free investigation. In U.S. the Association of University Professors maintains standards of academic freedom and obligation.

Académie française: see FRENCH ACADEMY.

Academy, garden near Athens where PLATO taught (c.387 B.C.), and his followers met until banned by Justinian (A.D. 529).

Acadia (ükä'dèu), region and former French colony, E Canada, centered on Nova Scotia but including Prince Edward Isl. and mainland coast from Gulf of St. Lawrence S into Maine. First and chief town, Port Royal, was founded 1605. Attacked and taken by British 1710. In 1755 French settlers who refused to swear allegiance to Great Britain were deported. Exiles found refuge in many places. Longfellow's *Evangeline* tells of those in St. Martinville, La., where the Cajuns—as they are popularly called—maintain a separate folk culture. In 1762 a new mass deportation was thwarted, and gradually some exiles returned. Today in Canada, Acadian (French *Acadien*) means a French-speaking inhabitant of Maritime Provs.

Acadia National Park: see MOUNT DESERT ISLAND.

Acadia University: see WOLFVILLE, N.S.

acanthus (ükăn'–), perennial herbs (*Acanthus*), with deeply cut leaves often copied in architectural motif.

Acapulco (äkäpool'kō), city (pop. c.29,000), Guerrero, SW Mexico; Pacific port. Winter resort.

Acarya: see BHASCARA.

Accad: see AKKAD.

Aecault, Michel, French explorer: see ACO.

accent, in language, emphasis given a particular sound. In English each independently spoken form has an accented vowel. The English accent is phonemic (or significant), for there are words different from each other only in their accent, e.g., *contract,* verb and noun. In French the accent is entirely different, but the so-called accents in French, acute (´), grave (`), and circumflex (^), are borrowed from Greek writing and are mainly orthographic devices to indicate vowel quality.

accessory, in law, a person connected with a crime other than the principal perpetrator. The law usually distinguishes between one who in some way abets the committing of crime (before the fact) and who aids the criminal after the crime is committed (after the fact), but has nothing to do with the criminal act.

accordion, small portable musical instrument, consisting of rectangular bellows expanded and contracted between the hands. Buttons or keys operated by the player determine tones. Introduced in 1822; keyboard added in 1852. Similar to the concertina, which is smaller and has bellows attached to hexagonal blocks that have handles and buttons.

Accra (ŭkrä´), city (pop. c.491,000), cap. of the Republic of Ghana; mfg. and industrial port on Gulf of Guinea. Railway terminus. Univ. of Ghana is at nearby Legon.

accusative: see CASE.

Aceldama (ŭsĕl´dŭmŭ), "field of blood," apparently place where Judas died. Money given him for betraying Jesus was used to buy this place for burial of strangers. Earlier it had been called "potter's field," hence term for paupers' burying ground. Mat. 27.3–10; Acts 1.16–19.

acetaldehyde: see ALDEHYDE.

acetic acid (ŭsē´tĭk), weak organic acid (constituent of vinegar), a colorless liquid with pungent odor; boils at 118.5°C. Miscible with water; heat evolved. Pure (99.5%) acid called glacial acetic acid. Its compounds used in plastics, medicines, lacquers, and as mordants.

acetone (ăs´ĭtōn), colorless, inflammable liquid with minty taste and odor; boils at 56.1°C. Used as a solvent for organic substances and in making celluloid, smokeless powders, and chloroform. It is the simplest KETONE; two methyl radicals are joined to the carbonyl group.

acetylcholine (ăs´ŭtĭlkō´lēn), organic compound of carbon, hydrogen, oxygen, and nitrogen. Liberated at nerve endings, it is believed to be a factor in stimulation of muscles and organs.

acetylene (ŭsĕt´ĭlēn), colorless gas, boiling at −84°C., with ethereal odor when pure. Forms explosive mixture with air; explosive when liquefied. Used as illuminant and for cutting and welding metals (see OXYACETYLENE FLAME). The molecule is composed of two carbon atoms, triply bound to each other, and two hydrogen atoms, each attached to one of the carbons.

Achad Haam [Heb.,= one from among the people], pseud. of **Asher Ginzberg,** 1856–1927, Jewish philosopher and essayist, b. Ukraine, d. Tel Aviv. Founder of cultural Zionism. Interpreted core of Judaism as concern for justice.

Achaea (ŭkē´ŭ), region of anc. Greece, in N Peloponnesus, on Gulf of Corinth; the home of the **Achaeans,** powerful in Greece by c.1250 B.C. Their cities were formed before 5th cent. B.C. in the first **Achaean League,** which lasted until it opposed Philip II of Macedon (338 B.C.) and was then dissolved. The second Achaean League was formed in 3d cent. B.C. and tried to liberate Greece from Macedonian rule but ran into opposition of Sparta. In 198 B.C. the league got Roman help and gained power. Later suspected by Rome of sympathy for Macedon, many Achaeans were deported (168 B.C.) to Italy. In 146 B.C. Achaeans waged suicidal war against Rome.

Achaemenidae (ăkĭmĕ´nĭdē) or **Achaemenids** (ăkĭmĕ´nĭdz), dynasty of ancient Persia, c.550–330 B.C., founded by CYRUS THE GREAT.

Achard, Franz Karl (äkh´ärt), 1753–1821, German chemist. Pioneered in producing sugar from beets (1806); work based on discoveries by MARGGRAF. Also developed method for working platinum.

Achelous (ăkĭlō´ŭs), in Greek religion, river-god. The son of Oceanus and Tethys, he was father of the Sirens and other nymphs.

Achelous (ăkhĕlō´ôs), river, 137 mi. long, NW Greece, flowing from Pindus mts. S to the Ionian Sea. Also known as Aspropotamos.

Acheron (ă´kŭrŏn), in Greek religion, river of Hades.

Acheson, Dean (Gooderham) (ăch´ĭsŭn), 1893–, U.S. Secretary of State (1949–53). He was Asst. Secretary of State 1941–45, Undersecretary 1945–47.

Acheson, Edward Goodrich, 1856–1931, American inventor. Discovered carborundum; developed processes for producing silicon, aluminum, synthetic graphite.

Acheulian (ŭshōō´lēŭn), phase of Paleolithic period named for Saint-Acheul, France, where typical implements were found.

Achilles (ŭkĭl´lēz), in Greek legend, hero of the *Iliad,* prominent Greek warrior in TROJAN WAR; son of Peleus and Thetis. His mother, hearing prophecy of his death at Troy, dipped him in river Styx to make him invulnerable, but the water did not touch the heel she held. She disguised him as a girl and hid him at Skyros. Odysseus persuaded him to join expedition against Troy. He quarreled with AGAMEMNON and sulked in his tent, but to avenge the death of his friend PATROCLUS, he fought again and slew Hector. He was killed by Paris, who wounded his heel.

Achitophel, variant of AHITHOPHEL.

acid, according to ionization theory (see ION), compound yielding hydrogen ions when dissolved in water. Properties result from presence of hydrogen ion: in aqueous solution acids taste sour, turn blue litmus red, react with bases and basic oxides (see NEUTRALIZATION) to form salts and water. Can conduct electricity. Most acids are solids, few are liquids, and very few are gases. Strong acids (e.g., nitric) are largely ionized in solution; weak acids (e.g., acetic) are little ionized. Classified also by number of replaceable hydrogen ions in molecule as monobasic (e.g., nitric), dibasic (e.g., sulphuric), tribasic (e.g., phosphoric). Carboxyl group (−COOH) characteristic of organic acids.

acidosis, reduction of the body's alkali reserve resulting from starvation, diabetes, nephritis, infectious diseases. It does not imply real acidity of the blood. Alkalosis is abnormal increase in alkali reserve.

Acmeists (ăk´mēĭsts), school of Russian poets, started 1912 in reaction against symbolists. Strove after concreteness of image, clarity of expression. Leading Acmeists: Akhmatova, Gumilev, Mandelstam.

acne (ăk´nē), disease of sebaceous glands common during adolescence. Characterized by pink pimples (papules) surrounding blackheads, especially on face, back, and chest. Sometimes chronic. In most cases acne can be controlled by diet and strict cleanliness.

Aco or **Accault, Michel** (äkō´), fl. 1680–1702, French explorer of region of upper Mississippi R.; lieutenant of La Salle.

Acoma or **Ácoma** (both: ä´kŭmŭ), pueblo (pop. 1,414), W central N.Mex., WSW of Albuquerque. A "sky city," difficult of access, on mesa more than 350 ft. high. Visited by Coronado's men (1540), Juan de Oñate (1598), and Fray Juan Ramírez (1629). Revolted in 1599 and joined 1680 uprising of PUEBLO INDIANS. Western Keresan spoken. Farming and pottery-making. Holds festival to St. Stephen, Sept. 2.

Aconcagua (äkōnkä´gwä), peak, 22,835 ft. high, W Argentina, in ANDES. Long considered highest peak in W Hemisphere.

aconite (ăk´-), **monkshood,** or **wolfsbane** (*Aconitum*), hardy plant with blue, purple, yellow, or white hooded flowers. Drug aconite, a sedative, contains poisonous alkaloid aconitine. Winter aconite (*Eranthis*) has small, yellow flowers in spring.

Açores: see AZORES.

acorn: see OAK.

Acosta, Uriel or **Uriel da Costa,** 1585–1640, Jewish philosopher, b. Portugal; precursor of Spinoza. At one time a Catholic, he reverted to Judaism in Amsterdam. Criticized rabbinical Judaism; rejected belief in immortality, and for this was excommunicated. Later committed suicide. Gutzkow wrote drama about him.

acoustics (ŭkŏō′stĭks), science of sound, its production, transmission, and effects. Acoustical problems in buildings include reverberation (repeated reflection of sound waves from smooth surface in enclosed space) and interference (from reflection of sound waves of different frequencies). Some reverberation avoids sound deadening; interference either reinforces or destroys sound.

acquired characteristics, modifications produced in organisms by environmental influence, mutilation, or disease. Lamarck and Lysenko believed them inheritable; Darwin and Mendel did not.

Acre (ä′kŭr, ä′kŭr), Arabic *Acca*, Heb. *Acco*, city (pop. c.18,000), N Israel, port on Bay of Acre opposite Haifa. Biblical names are Accho and Ptolemais. Taken by Arabs 638, held by Crusaders 1104–87 and by Knights Hospitalers 1190–1291. Surrender to Saracens in 1291 marked decline of Latin Kingdom of Jerusalem and the Crusades. Held by Turkey 1517–1832, 1840–1918, by Egypt 1832–40, and by Great Britain 1918–48. Partition of Palestine in 1948 assigned Acre to Arabs, but Israeli forces captured it.

Acre (ä′krä), river rising at border of Peru and Brazil and flowing NE. Treaty of Petrópolis (1903) gave Brazil most of territory surrounding river, with large indemnity to Bolivia.

acre, land measure used by English-speaking peoples, now set at 160 sq. rods (4,840 sq. yd.; 43,560 sq. ft.; ¹⁄₆₄₀ sq. mi.). Local variations survive.

Acrocraunia: see CERAUNIAN MOUNTAINS.

Acrocorinthus (ă″krōkŭrĭn′thŭs), rock, 1,886 ft. high, site of the Acropolis of Old CORINTH, Greece. On its summit stood temple of Aphrodite; below was fountain of Pirene, from which Pegasus drank.

acropolis (ŭkrŏp′ŭlĭs), elevated, fortified section of ancient Greek cities. Athenian Acropolis, a hill c.260 ft. high, was adorned, chiefly during time of Cimon and Pericles, with some of world's greatest architectural works (PROPYLAEA, PARTHENON, ERECHTHEUM). See ELGIN MARBLES.

Actaeon (ăk-tē′ŭn), in Greek legend, a hunter. Because he saw Artemis bathing, she changed him into a stag, and his own dogs killed him.

ACTH (adrenocorticotropin), pituitary hormone that stimulates adrenal cortex to produce adrenocortical substance, chiefly CORTISONE. Used in treatment of arthritis and muscle diseases; may have undesirable side-effects.

actinide series or **actinides,** heavy radioactive metallic elements (see ELEMENT, table), atomic numbers 89–103, having chemical properties similar to actinium. They are ACTINIUM, THORIUM, PROTACTINIUM, URANIUM, NEPTUNIUM, PLUTONIUM, AMERICIUM, CURIUM, BERKELIUM, CALIFORNIUM, EINSTEINIUM, FERMIUM, MENDELEVIUM, NOBELIUM, and LAWRENCIUM.

actinium (ăktĭn′ēŭm), radioactive element (symbol = Ac; see also ELEMENT, table). Found in all uranium ores. Emits beta rays.

action painting: see ABSTRACT EXPRESSIONISM.

Actium (ăk′tēŭm, ăk′shēŭm), Gr. *Aktion*, promontory NW Greece. Here forces of Octavian (later AUGUSTUS) defeated Antony and Cleopatra (31 B.C.).

active: see VOICE.

act of God, accident caused by an extraordinary, unforeseeable, and unavoidable natural force. The injured party has in general no right to damages.

Acton, John Emerich Edward Dalberg Acton, 1st Baron, 1834–1902, English historian. Taught at Cambridge from 1895. Planned *Cambridge Modern History.* Notable as a liberal and a Roman Catholic. Wrote *History of Freedom* (1907), essays.

Acton, Sir John Francis Edward, 1736?–1811, Neapolitan statesman of British origin. Favorite of Marie Caroline. Chief minister 1779–1804.

Acton, London: see EALING.

Actors' Studio, American theater group founded 1947 by Elia Kazan and Cheryl Crawford as a workshop for professional actors. Formal training in Stanislavsky's method supervised by Lee STRASBERG; membership is free and highly competitive. Program later expanded to include directors and writers.

Acts of the Apostles, book of Bible between Gospels and Epistles, only contemporary historical account of early spread of Christianity. Written in Greek A.D. c.60–80. Traditional author is St. Luke. Three critical events are: descent of the Holy Ghost, martyrdom of St. Stephen, conversion of St. Paul, St. Paul's missions to Gentiles.

actuary, at first, registrar recording court acts or managing joint stock company. Now an INSURANCE statistician who calculates probability.

Acuña, Cristóbal de (krěstō′bäl dä äkōō′nyä), 1597–1676?, Spanish Jesuit missionary and explorer. Accompanied Teixeira on journey down Amazon (1638), wrote earliest major firsthand description of the river (1639).

Acushnet (ŭkōōsh′nĭt), town (pop. 5,755), SE Mass., NE of New Bedford; settled c.1660. Devastated in King Philip's War.

Ada. 1 Village (pop. 3,918), NW Ohio, E of Lima, in farm area; laid out 1853. Seat of Ohio Northern Univ. **2** City (pop. 14,347), S central Okla., near Canadian R., SE of Oklahoma City; settled 1889. Center for oil and agr. area.

Adak (ä′dăk, ä′däk), off W Alaska, one of ALEUTIAN ISLANDS. Was U.S. military base in Second World War.

Adalbert, d. 1072, archbishop of Hamburg-Bremen, a diocese which included Scandinavia. Favorite of Emperor Henry III; guardian of Henry IV. Relentlessly ambitious, he helped to consolidate imperial authority despite opposition of nobles and clergy.

Adalia, Turkey: see ANTALYA.

Adam [Heb.,= mankind], in Bible, the first man. His story from creation to expulsion from Garden of Eden (with his wife EVE) is told in Gen. 1.26–5.5. To St. Paul, Adam represented earthly side of man (1 Cor. 15.20–22,42–58). Higher criticism compares Adam's story with Babylonian myths of creation. For examples of Judaic and Islamic legends stemming from biblical account, see LILITH; PSEUDEPIGRAPHA.

Adam, Adolphe (ädôlf′ ädä′), 1803–56, French composer of comic opera and other stage works, known for his ballet *Giselle* and the popular *Cantique de Noël.*

Adam, Robert (ăd′ŭm), 1728–92, and **James Adam,** 1730–94, Scottish architects, brothers. Chiefly inspired by classic architecture, they created a style of great elegance. Principles also applied to furniture.

Adam de la Halle (ädä′ dù lä äl′), 1237?–c.1285, French dramatist. Author of *Le Jeu de Robin et de Marion,* a pastoral comedy with music.

Adams, family of distinguished Americans from Mass. **John Adams,** 1735–1826, was 2d President of the United States (1797–1801). A patriot leader who opposed British measures leading to American Revolution, he later served in both Continental Congresses and argued eloquently for the Declaration of Independence, which he signed. Served as Washington's Vice President (1789–97). His administration as President revealed his honest and stubborn integrity; though allied with the conservative Federalists, he was not dominated by them in their struggle against the Jeffersonians. By conciliation he prevented war with France; he had reservations about the ALIEN AND SEDITION

ACTS. His wife, **Abigail (Smith) Adams**, 1744–1818, was one of the most distinguished and influential first ladies in U.S. history. Their son, **John Quincy Adams**, 1767–1848, was 6th President of the United States (1825–29). As U.S. Senator from Mass. (1803–8), he outraged his fellow Federalists by supporting Jeffersonian policies. Served in several ministerial positions. Best-known achievement as U.S. Secretary of State (1817–25) was MONROE DOCTRINE. Elected President in House of Representatives through support of Henry Clay, Adams had an unhappy, ineffective administration. Won new renown as U.S. Representative from Mass. (1831–48); eloquently attacked all measures expanding slavery. Promoted Smithsonian Inst. His diary is a valuable historical document. His son, **Charles Francis Adams**, 1807–86, was minister to Great Britain (1861–68). He won British respect for wisdom in upholding Northern cause, especially in *Trent* and *Alabama* incidents. Later represented U.S. in settlement of Alabama claims. His son, **Charles Francis Adams**, 1835–1915, American historian and railroad expert, was president of the Union Pacific (1884–90). Author of *Three Episodes of Massachusetts History* (1892). His brother, **Brooks Adams**, 1848–1927, was also an historian. He developed theory that civilization rose and fell according to growth and decline of commerce in *The Law of Civilization and Decay* (1895). His ideas influenced another brother, **Henry (Brooks) Adams**, 1838–1918, also an historian. In developing a basic philosophy of history he found a unifying principle in force or energy. Applied this theory in two books, *Mont-Saint-Michel and Chartres* (privately printed 1904, pub. 1913), and *The Education of Henry Adams* (privately printed 1906, pub. 1918). Also wrote study of administrations of Jefferson and Madison. **Charles Francis Adams**, 1866–1954, grandson of Charles Francis Adams (1807–86), was U.S. Secretary of the Navy (1929–33). The first volume of the writings of the Adams family (ed. by Lyman H. Butterfield) appeared in 1961.

Adams, James Truslow, 1878–1949, American historian. His books on the American scene include *The Epic of America* (1931), *The Adams Family* (1930), and *Henry Adams* (1933). Editor in chief of *Dictionary of American History*, *Atlas of American History*, and *Album of American History*.

Adams, John: see ADAMS, family.

Adams, John Couch, 1819–92, English astronomer. Calculated position of then unknown planet NEPTUNE.

Adams, John Quincy: see ADAMS, family.

Adams, Maude, 1872–1953, American actress, real name Kiskadden. She gained fame in Barrie plays; starred in his *Little Minister* (1897), *Quality Street* (1901), *What Every Woman Knows* (1908), and *Peter Pan* (1905), role for which she is best known.

Adams, Roger, 1889–, American chemist. Developed methods of identification, preparation, and synthesis. Among first to synthesize the local anesthetics butyn and procaine.

Adams, Samuel, 1722–1803, American Revolutionary patriot, signer of Declaration of Independence; second cousin of John Adams. Leader of extremists in colonial resistance to British.

Adams, Will(iam), 1564?–1620, first Englishman to visit Japan. He became a favorite of IEYASU soon after his arrival (1600). Japan profited by his knowledge of shipbuilding, navigation, mathematics, and Western affairs. A successful trader, he acquired the Japanese name Anjin Sama, or Mr. Pilot.

Adams, town (pop. 12,391), NW Mass., in Berkshires, on Hoosic R. and S of North Adams; settled 1762. Has paper mills and limestone quarries. Birthplace of Susan B. Anthony.

Adams, Mount. 1 Peak, N.H.: see PRESIDENTIAL RANGE. **2** Peak, Wash.: see CASCADE RANGE.

Adam's Bridge: see PALK STRAIT.

Adam's Peak, Singhalese *Sri Padastanaya* and *Samanaliya*, c.7,360 ft. high, S central Ceylon. Goal of pilgrimage for Buddhists, Hindus, and Moslems.

Adana (ä'dänä), city (pop. 231,454), S Turkey, on Seyhan R. Once a Roman colony, it is now a commercial center.

adaptation, in biology, adjustment of an organism to its total environment, a basic difference between living and nonliving matter. See ECOLOGY; EVOLUTION; GENETICS; PROTECTIVE COLORATION; NATURAL SELECTION.

Adda (äd'dä), river, c.194 mi. long, N Italy. Flows from Alps, through L. Como, S into Po R. Furnishes electric power.

Addams, Jane, 1860–1935, American social worker. Founded (1899, with Ellen G. Starr) noted social settlement, Hull House, in Chicago. Leader in woman-suffrage and peace movements. Shared 1931 Nobel Peace Prize with Nicholas Murray Butler. Wrote *Twenty Years at Hull-House* (1910).

adder, poisonous snake of European viper family. Species also found in Asia, Africa, Australia. In U.S. name is applied to various harmless snakes.

Adder's tongue: see DOGTOOTH VIOLET.

adding machine: see CALCULATING MACHINE.

Addington, Henry: see SIDMOUTH, HENRY ADDINGTON, VISCOUNT.

Addis Ababa (ä'dïs ä'bŭbŭ), city (pop. c.500,000), cap. of Ethiopia. Founded 1887 by Menelik II to be his cap.; was cap. of Italian East Africa 1936–41. Hq. of Organization of African Unity, seat of imperial palace and of Haile Selassie Univ. Rail and communications center; exports coffee, tobacco, and hides.

Addison, Joseph, 1672–1719, English essayist. First achieved notice with epic poem *The Campaign* (1704) and later wrote poems, dramas (e.g., tragedy, *Cato*, 1713) and criticism (notably on *Paradise Lost*, praising Milton), but he is best remembered for witty, urbane essays, some of the finest in English. He began in 1710 to contribute to Richard Steele's *Tatler* and later continued his essays in the *Spectator* (1711–12). His most popular papers were on the imaginary squire, Sir Roger de Coverley (invented by Steele), and his coterie. Addison held a seat in Parliament and government posts.

Addison, Thomas: see ADDISON'S DISEASE.

Addison. 1 Village (pop. 16,977), NE Ill., WNW of Chicago. **2** Town, W.Va.: see WEBSTER SPRINGS.

Addison's disease is characterized by emaciation, anemia, brown skin pigmentation; caused by malfunction of cortex of adrenal glands. First described by Thomas Addison, 1793–1860, English pathologist.

address, forms of. Both spoken and written salutations differ widely even in English-speaking countries. Monarchical traditions and hereditary titles give rise to great complexity; England has a multiplicity of forms and a strict code of address. The U.S. has fewer and simpler forms, which have grown out of custom and convenience rather than inheritance and are indicative, not of a man's birth or family, but of his professional or political position. However, in all official and diplomatic correspondence and in formal social intercourse, modes of addressing letters and invitations, as well as the manner of personal address, are of great importance. The President of the U.S. is addressed in speech as *Mr. President*, in writing as *The President, The White House, Washington*. The formal opening of a letter may be *Sir*, the informal opening *My Dear Mr. President*. Ambassadors, in speech, are *Your Excellency*, in writing *His Excellency the Ambassador of Great Britain*. A governor of a state is spoken of formally as *His Excellency the Governor of Ohio*. An invitation would read *The Honorable the Governor of New York*. The Vice President, heads of executive departments (cabinet members), justices of the higher courts, mayors of cities, American ministers, Senators and Representatives, and ex-Presidents are addressed as

The Honorable, e.g., *The Honorable the Vice President of the United States, The Honorable the Secretary of State.* The secretary to the President, heads of independent boards and commissions, assistant secretaries of executive departments, are also addressed as *Honorable. Esquire* is used after the names of chief clerks and chiefs of the bureaus of executive departments, diplomatic officers below the rank of minister, consular officers, clerk of the Supreme Court, and officers of other courts. *Reverend* or *Honorable* should be preceded by the word *the* and should not be abbreviated; letters after the heading should begin (this is known as the salutation) *Dear Mr.* ——. Professional titles precede the name, and professional abbreviations follow. Church dignitaries are addressed in writing thus: the pope, *His Holiness Pope Paul VI,* in the salutation *Your Holiness* or *Most Holy Father;* cardinals, *His Eminence the Cardinal Archbishop of New York* or (when not an archbishop) *His Eminence Cardinal* ——, salutation *Your Eminence;* archbishops, *His Grace the Archbishop of* ——, salutation *My Lord Archbishop* or *Your Grace;* bishops, *The Right Reverend Bishop* —— or *The Right Reverend Bishop of* ——, salutation *Dear Sir* or *My Lord;* Methodist Episcopal bishops, *The Reverend Bishop* —— ——, salutation *Dear Sir;* deans, *The Very Reverend* —— ——, salutation *Very Reverend Sir.* English titles are numerous and complex. The king and the queen, in speech with intimates, are *Sir* and *Ma'am.* Addressed by letter, the king is *His Most Gracious Majesty the King;* the salutation of the letter is *Sire* or *Your Majesty.* The queen in writing is *Her Most Gracious Majesty the Queen,* salutation *Madame* or *Your Majesty.* A prince is in writing *His Royal Highness the Prince of* ——, a princess *Her Royal Highness the Princess Margaret Rose.* A duke is in writing *His Grace the Duke of* ——, salutation *My Lord Duke* or *Your Grace.* A countess is in writing *The Right Honourable the Countess of* ——, salutation *Madame* or *Your Ladyship.* An earl is in writing *The Right Honourable the Earl of* ——, salutation *My Lord* or *Your Lordship.* Members of Parliament add the letters M.P. to their address. A privy councilor is *The Right Honourable* —— ——. In addressing invitations the full title is used except in the case of barons. The title *Right Honourable* belongs to all peers and is the right of members of the privy council and of cabinet ministers. Professional titles precede titles of rank as *Captain the Honourable John Blank.* The use of *Esquire,* formerly limited to lawyers, country gentlemen, and eldest sons of knights, is now more general. The title *Honourable* is ignored in conversation and is never used on visiting cards.

Ade, George, 1866–1944, American journalist, humorist, dramatist, satirist of the Midwest. Notable book among a large number is *Fables in Slang* (1900).

Adelaide, empress: see OTTO I, Holy Roman emperor.

Adelaide, city (pop. of metropolitan area, 570,000), cap. of South Australia, on Torrens R., near Gulf St. Vincent. Founded 1836, it is the state's oldest city. Seat of Univ. of Adelaide. Has knitting mills.

Adelard of Bath (ä'dŭlärd), fl. 12th cent., English scholastic philosopher, noted for Arabic studies.

Adelheid, empress: see OTTO I, emperor.

Adélie Coast, region, Antarctica, in Australian quadrant, W of George V Coast and E of Wilkes Land. Heavily glaciated, has strongest winds in world. Discovered 1840.

Adelsberg, Yugoslavia: see POSTOJNA.

Aden (ä'dŭn, ä'–), British crown colony (80 sq. mi.; pop. c.140,000 including PERIM), SW Arabia, on Gulf of Aden. Captured by Moslems 636; occupied by Turks almost continuously 1538–1630; under British administration as part of India 1839–1937. Town of Aden is free port. British protectorate of Aden (c.112,000 sq. mi.; pop. c.700,000) is mountainous and dry. Inhabitants are Moslems. Protectorate is divided into eastern and western sections. In 1960 six of the small states in the western section formed the Aden Federation, which was given promise of future independence by Britain. In 1963 Aden colony and Aden Federation merged into the Federation of South Arabia. Nationalist, anti-British terrorism flared in mid-1967 as Britain scheduled independence for Jan., 1968.

Aden, Gulf of, W arm of Arabian Sea, between Aden protectorate and Somaliland. On trade route from Mediterranean Sea to Indian Ocean via Suez Canal.

Adenauer, Konrad (kôn'rät ä'dŭnou"ŭr), 1876–1967, German statesman. Founded Christian Democratic Union 1945; became chancellor of West GERMANY 1949 and was foreign minister 1951–55. Insisted on German reunification through free elections and championed W European cooperation and, with de GAULLE, a Europe independent of U.S. Resigned 1963.

adenoids, pharyngeal tonsils, masses of lymphoid tissue in upper part of throat. When enlarged they may interfere with normal breathing and speech.

adenosine triphosphate: see ATP.

adhesive, substance used for bonding surfaces. Animal glue, made from hides, hoofs, bones, probably was known to prehistoric man. In 19th cent. appeared many vegetable adhesives including gums, resins, mucilage, and starch. Other adhesives are made from casein, soybeans, rubber, cellulose, and synthetic substances.

Adige (ä'dējĕ) Ger. *Etsch,* river, 255 mi. long, N Italy. Flows from Alps, past Verona, to Adriatic.

Adighe: see ADYGE AUTONOMOUS OBLAST.

Adirondack Mountains (ădĭrôn'dăk), NE N.Y., sometimes mistakenly included in Appalachian system. Group bounded E by L. Champlain and L. George region and extends from foothills near St. Lawrence R. on N to Mohawk valley on S. Geologically region resembles LAURENTIAN PLATEAU. Its pre-Cambrian metamorphic rock with intruded igneous rock has been uplifted and eroded for countless years. E portion most rugged. Layers of sedimentary rock with marine fossils of Cambrian and Ordovician times tilted against mts. Rises to 5,344 ft. in Mt. Marcy, highest point in N.Y. Other peaks are Whiteface, MacIntyre, Haystack, Algonquin, and Skylight. Part of region—noted for wild scenery, beautiful forests, many lakes—is in Adirondack Forest Preserve (2,273,378 acres). Several lakes, including L. Placid, L. George, and Saranac Lake, have resorts. Hudson, Ausable, and Black rivers have sources here. Had yielded iron ore, titanium, vanadium, and talc.

Adlai (ăd'lī, ăd'lā), father of Shaphat, one of David's officers. 1 Chron. 27.29.

Adler, Alfred (ăd'lŭr), 1870–1937, Austrian psychiatrist, founder of school of individual psychology. He rejected Freudian emphasis on sex and maintained that all personality difficulties or behavior disorders are overcompensation for deficiencies, environmental repressions, or feelings of inferiority. Later Adler lectured and practiced in U.S.

Adler, Cyrus, 1863–1940, leader of conservative Judaism in the U.S. First president of Dropsie Col., president Jewish Theological Seminary; founder American Jewish Historical Society; an editor of *Jewish Encyclopedia* and *American-Jewish Year Book.*

Adler, Felix, 1851–1933, American educator and founder of ETHICAL CULTURE MOVEMENT, b. Germany. Was professor of ethics, Columbia Univ., after 1902 and leader in social welfare activities.

Adler, Viktor, 1852–1918, Austrian politician, founder of Austrian Social Democratic party. His son, **Friedrich Adler,** 1879–1960, Socialist leader, shot Count STÜRGKH (1916); amnestied 1918.

Adlum, John, 1759–1836, American horticulturist. Originated the Catawba grape used in wine making.

Admetus (ădmē'tŭs), in Greek legend, Thessalian king, whom Apollo served. On condition that his life be spared, his wife, ALCESTIS, gave her life, but Hercules saved her by grappling with Death.

administrative law, in U.S., governs jurisdiction of administrative agencies, their powers, and operating procedures as well as availability of judicial review of their activities. Administrative agencies existed as early as 1789 to administer small fields (e.g., customs laws), but their greatest development came after 1880s in response to need for regulation of economic and social problems such as railroads and labor. Agency procedures are regulated by the Administrative Procedure Act (1946) which provides safeguards against unfair agency action.

Admiralty Inlet, Wash.: see PUGET SOUND.

Admiralty Island, off SE Alaska, in ALEXANDER ARCHIPELAGO SW of Juneau. Large (1,664 sq. mi.), heavily forested, and mountainous. Abounds in wildlife. Separated from mainland by Stephens Passage.

Admiralty Islands, volcanic group (area c.800 sq. mi.; pop. c.16,752), SW Pacific, in Bismarck Archipelago, part of Territory of New Guinea. UN trust territory since 1947, it is administered by Australia from Manus, its chief island.

Admiralty Range, N part of great mountain range in Victoria Land, W of Ross Sea, Antarctica. Its peaks reach 10,000 ft.

adolescence (ă″dŭlĕ′sŭns), physical stage between puberty and maturity lasting generally from ages of 12 to 21. Adolescent physiological changes strengthen heterosexual drives and strivings for independence. Typical emotional difficulties arise from conflicting biological changes and inability to express new needs in socially acceptable form.

Adolf of Nassau, d. 1298, German king (1292–98). Deposed by diet; defeated and slain by army of Albert I.

Adonijah (ăd″nī′jŭ, ŭdŏn′ŭjŭ), son of David. He schemed for the throne, but David gave it to Solomon. 2 Sam. 3.4; 1 Kings 1; 2.1–25.

Adonis (ŭdō′nĭs), in Greek religion, young man loved by APHRODITE. When he was killed by a wild boar, Aphrodite persuaded the gods to let him live for six months of each year. Hence his death and resurrection were celebrated in midsummer festival Adonia, symbolizing yearly growth and decay.

adoptionism, heresy in Spain in late 8th cent., centered on belief that Christ in His divine nature was the true son of God but in His human nature the adoptive son (by baptism). Related to doctrine of ancient monarchianism and Nestorianism. Some theologians call heretical followers of Abelard neo-adoptionists. Also adoptianism.

Adoula, Cyrille (sērĭl′ ädōō′lŭ), 1922–, African statesman in Republic of the Congo. Elected to Senate upon country's independence (1960); was member of cabinet; in Aug., 1961, became prime minister. Replaced in July, 1964, by Moise Tshombe. Served as ambassador to Belgium and in Aug., 1966, was appointed ambassador to U.S.

Adour (ädōōr′), river, 210 mi. long, SW France. Rises in Pyrenees, enters Bay of Biscay near Bayonne. Forms N limit of Basque country.

Adowa, Ethiopia: see ADUWA.

Adrammelech (ŭdrăm′–), in Bible, one of two men named as murderers of their father, Sennacherib; Sharezer was the other. 2 Kings 19.37 (= Isa. 37.38).

adrenal gland (ădrē′nŭl) or **suprarenal gland** (sōōprŭrē′nŭl), one of two small, endocrine glands, one resting on upper part of each kidney. Inner portion (medulla) secretes hormone adrenaline. Outer layer (cortex) secretes a number of hormones influencing various functions including carbohydrate metabolism, kidney action, retention of sodium in the body, sexual characteristics. Hormone production of the adrenal cortex is regulated in part by ACTH, a hormone produced by the pituitary gland.

adrenaline (ŭdrĕn′ŭlĭn) or **epinephrine** (ĕpĭnĕf′rĭn), hormone secreted by medulla of adrenal gland. It contracts capillaries, stimulates sympathetic nervous system. Used in treating hemorrhage, shock, asthma, heart failure. Takamine extracted it (1901) in pure form; first synthesized (1904) by Frederick Stolz.

Adria (ā′drĕŭ), ancient name of the Adriatic, extended to mean central Mediterranean in Acts 27.27.

Adrian I, d. 795, pope (772–95). Called on CHARLEMAGNE to repulse Lombard king, Desiderius. Increased papal lands through Donation of Charlemagne. Supported Empress IRENE against ICONOCLASM.

Adrian IV, d. 1159, pope (1154–59), an Englishman named Nicholas Breakspear. Driven from Rome by ARNOLD OF BRESCIA, he returned by 1155 and put down rebels with help of FREDERICK I, whom he crowned. Adrian had difficulties with William I of Sicily and Frederick. His donation of Ireland as fief to Henry II of England much disputed.

Adrian, emperor: see HADRIAN.

Adrian, Edgar Douglas Adrian, Baron, 1889–, English physiologist, authority on nervous system. Shared 1932 Nobel Prize in Physiology and Medicine for work on function of neuron. Awarded barony (1955).

Adrian, city (pop. 20,347), S Mich., SW of Detroit; settled 1825. Farm trade center. Adrian Col. and Siena Heights Col. are here.

Adrianople (ā″drēŭnō′pŭl) or **Edirne** (ĕdēr′nĕ), town (pop. 31,865), European Turkey, in Thrace. Commercial center; silk and cotton mfg. Founded by Emperor Hadrian A.D. c.125, it was the scene of a fateful Visigothic victory over Emperor VALENS in 378. Passed to the Turks 1361; residence of the sultans 1361–1453. To Russians twice in Russo-Turkish Wars (19th cent.). Briefly held by Bulgaria in the Balkan Wars (1913), it was given to Greece in 1920 and restored to Turkey in 1923. Chief among landmarks is the Mosque of Selim I, built by Sinan.

Adrianople, Treaty of, 1829, ended Russo-Turkish War of 1828–29. Turkey gave Russia mouth of Danube and additional territory on Black Sea; Russia occupied Moldavia and Walachia; Dardanelles opened to all commercial vessels; autonomy given to Serbia and promised to Greece.

Adriatic Sea (ādrēā′tĭk), arm of the Mediterranean, between Italy and Balkan Peninsula; 500 mi. long, 60–140 mi. wide, max. depth 4,035 ft. Low W and N shores belong to Italy, rugged E shore to Yugoslavia and Albania. Chief ports: Trieste, Venice, Bari, Rijeke (Fiume), and Dubrovnik.

adsorption, attraction and adhesion of molecules of one substance to surface of another; no chemical change. Certain solids (e.g., charcoal) readily adsorb gases. Particles in colloidal solution may adsorb much of the solvent. Adsorption used in removing colors from solutions, in photography, in hydrogenation of oils, and in gas analysis.

Adullam (ŭdŭl′–), town of Judah, SW of Jerusalem. David hid in Cave of Adullam when fleeing from Saul. 1 Sam. 22; 2 Sam. 23.13–17; 1 Chron. 11.15–19.

adult education, training of adults beyond school age. Usual forms are lecture, reading, discussion groups. Formal attempts to organize adult education in 19th-cent. Europe gave rise to continuation schools in Switzerland and Germany, the FOLK SCHOOL in Denmark. In U.S. lectures of the LYCEUM and of the Lowell Institute of Boston long preceded the CHAUTAUQUA MOVEMENT. Lectures augmented by extension and correspondence courses offered by many colleges in 20th cent. Political and labor organs have promoted adult education, including vocational education. Libraries have also advanced adult education groups, as has the Federal government. A separate program is that of the "great books" groups, which began meeting in 1947. American Association for Adult Education was estab. (1926) to systematize philosophy and methods.

Aduwa or Adowa (both: ä′dŭwä), town (pop. c.10,-000), N Ethiopia. Scene in 1896 of decisive victory by Menelik II over Italian invaders.

Advent, four-week penitential season. In West, from Sunday nearest Nov. 30 (St. Andrew's) to Christmas. First season of church year.

Adventists, religious groups centering belief on second coming of Christ. William MILLER led Millerites or Second Adventists; Advent Christian Church (1861) was a branch. Seventh-day Adventists adopted (1846) observance of Saturday as Sabbath. Organized formally in 1863, this largest branch is fundamentally evangelical in its theology. Other Adventist groups are Church of God (1888), the Life and Advent Union (1863), and Primitive Advent Christian Church, a branch of Advent Christian Church organized only in W.Va.

advertising, offering of goods, services, or ideas through medium of public communication; evolved in 18th cent., now handled by specialized agencies. Played role in economic growth of U.S., which still supports bulk of world advertising. Usual media include television, radio, newspapers, periodicals, billboards, signs.

Ady, Andrew (ŏ'dē), Hung. *Ady Endre,* 1877–1919, Hungarian modernist poet.

Adyge Autonomous Oblast (ŭdĭgyĕ'), administrative division (1,700 sq. mi.; 1965 est. pop. 353,000), Krasnodar Territory, SE European RSFSR; cap. Maikop. Farming, livestock raising, and food processing. Population is largely Moslem Adyge, a people related to the Circassians (see CIRCASSIA). Conquered (1830–64) by Russia, it became an autonomous oblast 1922. Region is also called Adighe.

Adzhar Autonomous Soviet Socialist Republic (ùjär', ä'jär) or **Adzharistan** (ùjä'rīstän"), autonomous state (1,100 sq. mi.; 1965 est. pop. 288,000, largely Mohammedan), SW Georgian SSR; cap. BATUM. Annexed by Russia from Turkey 1829 and 1878.

A. E., poet: see RUSSELL, GEORGE WILLIAM.

Aeëtes, king of Colchis: see JASON; MEDEA.

Aegadian Isles (ēgā'dēùn), Latin *Aegates,* small archipelago, Italy, in Mediterranean off W Sicily. Here Roman naval victory (241 B.C.) ended First Punic War.

Aegean civilization (ējē'ùn), general term for cultures of early heroic Greece. MINOAN CIVILIZATION was a rich culture of Crete (early 3d millennium B.C.). MYCENAEAN CIVILIZATION occupied mainland of Greece later. Other centers at Troy and in Cyclades.

Aegean Sea, arm of Mediterranean, c.400 mi. long and c.200 mi. wide, between Greece and Asia Minor; connected by Dardanelles with the Sea of Marmara. Its ancient name, Archipelago, now applies to its numerous islands, which include EUBOEA, N and S SPORADES, CYCLADES, and DODECANESE.

Aegeus (ē'jēùs, ē'jōōs), legendary king of Athens. Believing his son, Theseus, killed by the Minotaur, drowned himself in the sea (hence called Aegean).

Aegina (ējī'nù), Gr. *Aigina,* island (32 sq. mi.; pop. 8,958), off SE Greece, in the Gulf of Aegina (Saronic Gulf), an arm of the Aegean, near Athens; chief town Aegina (pop. 4,989), on NW shore. Agr.; sulfur springs. Influenced by MINOAN CIVILIZATION, island was conquered c.1000 B.C. by Dorian Greeks. It struck first Greek coins and rose to great commercial importance. Was sacked by Athens against whom it sided in Peloponnesian War (431 B.C.). AEGINETAN MARBLES discovered near by (1811).

Aegina, Gulf of, Greece: see SARONIC GULF.

Aegineta, Paulus: see PAUL OF AEGINA.

Aeginetan marbles (ē"jīnē'tùn), Greek sculptures, probably of the 5th cent. B.C., discovered 1811 in Aegina. Depict story of Troy. Now in Munich.

Aegisthus (ējīs'thùs), in Greek legend, lover of Clytemnestra. The lovers killed her husband, Agamemnon. In revenge her son, ORESTES, killed both.

Aegospotamos (ē"gùspŏ'tùmùs), river of anc. Thrace. At its mouth occurred the final battle of the PELOPONNESIAN WAR (405 B.C.) when Lysander of Sparta destroyed the Athenian fleet.

Ælfric (ăl'frĭk), c.955–1020, English churchman, author of homilies, saints' lives, free version of first seven books of the Bible in Anglo-Saxon.

Aemilian Way: see ROMAN ROADS.

Aeneas (ĭnē'ùs), in classical legend, Trojan who escaped from Troy. He tarried at Carthage with Queen Dido and then went on to Italy where his descendants founded Rome. The **Aeneid** (ĭnē'ĭd), a 12-book Latin epic by VERGIL, tells of his adventures.

Aeolia, ancient Greek region: see AEOLIS.

Aeolian Islands: see LIPARI ISLANDS.

Aeolis (ē'ùlĭs) or **Aeolia** (ēō'lēù), collective term for cities on NW coast of Asia Minor planted by the Aeolians, Hellenic peoples from Boeotia and Thessaly.

Aeolus (ē'ùlùs), in Greek mythology. **1** Wind-god, who kept winds in cave on Aeolia. **2** Son of Hellen and ancestor of Aeolian branch of Hellenic race.

aerial: see ANTENNA.

aerodynamics: see FLIGHT.

aeroembolism, physiologic disorder caused by too rapid decrease in atmospheric pressure. This releases body nitrogen as gas bubbles which block small veins and arteries and collect in tissues. Oxygen supply is thus cut off, and nausea, pain in joints and abdomen, and paralysis occur. May be prevented by gradual return to normal atmospheric pressure, often through pressurized locks. Inhalation of pure oxygen helps to clear nitrogen from body. Also called caisson disease, bends, altitude sickness.

aeroplane: see AIRPLANE.

Aeschines (ē'skĭnēs), c.390–314? B.C., Athenian orator, rival of Demosthenes.

Aeschylus (ēs'kĭlùs, ēs–), 525–456 B.C., first of three great Greek poets of TRAGEDY. Added an actor and increased possibilities of the drama; won 13 first prizes. Author of perhaps 90 plays, seven in full extant: *The Suppliants, The Persians, The Seven against Thebes, Prometheus Bound,* and only extant ancient trilogy, the *Oresteia,* which contains the plays *Agamemnon, The Choëphoroe,* and *The Eumenides.*

Aesculapius: see ASCLEPIUS.

Aesir, Norse Olympian gods: see ASGARD.

Aesop (ē'sùp, –sŏp), 6th cent. B.C., legendary composer of Greek fables; supposedly a slave. See FABLE.

aesthetics, philosophy concerned with the basic principles underlying work in all the arts. From the time of Plato and Aristotle to the present a major branch of philosophic theory, on the nature of beauty. Notable later philosophers of aesthetics are Leo Tolstoy, Bernard Bosanquet, Paul Valéry, and Benedetto Croce.

aestivation: see HIBERNATION.

Æthelbald (ē'thùlbôld, ă'–), Anglo-Saxon kings. **Æthelbald,** d. 757, king of Mercia (716–57). A strong ruler, by 731 he controlled all England S of the Humber. Murdered by his bodyguard. **Æthelbald,** d. 860, king of Wessex, son of ÆTHELWULF and brother of ALFRED. Refused to allow his father to return to the kingdom after a pilgrimage to Rome. Married his father's widow, Judith of France, 858.

Æthelbert (–bùrt, –bûrt), Anglo-Saxon kings. **Æthelbert,** d. 616, king of Kent (560?–616), was strongest ruler S of the Humber. St. Augustine converted him to Christianity and made his cap., Canterbury, a great Christian center. His laws are earliest extant body of laws in any Germanic language. **Æthelbert,** d. 865, king of Wessex (860–65), was son of Æthelwulf and brother of Alfred.

Æthelflæd (–flēd) or **Ethelfleda** (ēthùlflē'dù), d. 918, daughter of ALFRED. Reigned over Mercia alone from 911; was known as Lady of the Mercians. Her wise government made her known as one of English history's outstanding women.

Æthelfrith (–frĭth), d. 616, king of Northumbria; first great leader of N Angles. He forced his brother-in-law EDWIN (who pretended to throne) into exile. Killed in battle by Edwin's supporters near Nottingham.

Æthelred (-rĕd), Anglo-Saxon kings. **Æthelred,** d. 871, king of Wessex (865–71), son of ÆTHELWULF and brother of ALFRED. **Æthelred,** 965?–1016, king of England (978–1016), called Æthelred the Unready [Old Eng., = without counsel]. Son of Edgar, brother of EDWARD THE MARTYR. A weak king, he reigned at height of Danish power. Frequent levies of DANEGELD begun 991. Danes returned in 997; stayed to plunder until 1000. He married (1002) Emma, sister of duke of Normandy, possibly to gain an ally. National navy built by 1009 was rendered useless by treason of its commanders. Danish king SWEYN was received by the DANELAW in 1013; London capitulated; Æthelred fled to Normandy. Restored on Sweyn's death (1014). Æthelred's son EDMUND IRONSIDE succeeded him (1016) and made treaty with CANUTE, son of Sweyn, who ruled England and married Æthelred's widow.

Æthelstan, English king: see ATHELSTAN.

Æthelwulf (-wŏŏlf), d. 858, king of Wessex (839–56), son of EGBERT and father of ÆTHELBALD, ÆTHELBERT, ÆTHELRED, and ALFRED. With Æthelbald won notable victory over Danes at Aclea (851). Married Judith of France in 856. A man of great piety, he learned while on pilgrimage in Rome that Æthelbald would resist his return; he left his son as king of Wessex and ruled in Kent and dependencies.

Aetius (āē'shēŭs), c.396–454, Roman general. Defeated the Germans in Gaul. Repulsed Attila and the Huns at Châlons (451). Murdered by Valentinian III.

Aetna: see ETNA.

Aetolia (ētōl'yu), region of anc. Greece, N of Gulf of Corinth and Gulf of Calydon. Its people, the Aetolians, were farmers and shepherds. Cities of Aetolia joined in **Aetolian League** in 4th cent. B.C. to oppose Achaean League and the Macedonians. With Roman help it defeated Philip V of Macedon in 197 B.C. but then joined Antiochus III and went down with his defeat (189 B.C.).

Afanasyev, Aleksandr Nikolayevich (ŭlyĭksän'dŭr nyĭkŭlī'ŭvĭch ŭfŭnä'syŭf), 1826–71, Russian folklorist. His collections of popular tales introduced Russian folklore to world literature.

Afghanistan (ăfgă'nĭstăn″), kingdom (253,000 sq. mi.; pop. c.13,000,000), S central Asia; cap. Kabul. Bounded on N by USSR, on W by Iran, on S and E by Pakistan. Mostly mountainous ranges fan out from the Hindu Kush. Wheat, barley, and fruits are grown in fertile valleys; chief export is karakul. Helmand is longest river, with Amu Darya R. marking part of boundary with USSR. To the N are Afghan Turkistan and highlands of Badakshan (noted for lapis lazuli). Communications are poor (there are no railroads), and industry is in stage of infancy. Diversified population comprises Afghans, Tadzhiks, Hazaras, Turkmen, and Uzbeks; unifying factor is religion, for almost all are Moslem. Chief languages are Afghan or Pushtu and Iranian. Area was annexed 516 B.C. by Darius I and conquered 326 B.C. by Alexander the Great on his way to India. Kingdom of BACTRIA (fl. 3d cent.–2d cent. B.C.) fell to Parthians and rebellious tribes. Buddhism spread from the E but had brief survival; stable religion was provided by Moslem conquest, begun in 7th cent. Greatest of many Moslem states was that of Mahmud of Ghazni, who in 11th cent. conquered parts of Persia and India. Area was later conquered by Jenghiz Khan and Tamerlane, and in 16th cent. Baber used Kabul as base for conquest of India. Unified state covering most of present Afghanistan was estab. in 18th cent. by AHMED SHAH. Reigns of DOST MOHAMMED and SHERE ALI saw Afghan Wars (1839–42, 1878–81), resulting from rivalry between Britain and Russia for Afghan buffer state. Anglo-Russian agreement (1907) guaranteeing country's independence under British influence roused anti-British feeling and led to short war in 1919. Emirate was changed to a kingdom in 1926 under Amanullah, who was deposed in 1929 by fanatical Moslem subjects who resented his radical reforms. His successor, Mo-

hammed Nadir Shah, was assassinated in 1933 for continuing the program of modernization. He was succeeded by his son, Mohammed Zahir Shah. Despite Afghan opposition, Pakistan in 1950 took over the vaguely defined lands of Pathan tribes within Durand line (boundary estab. 1893 by Sir Mortimer Durand between North-West Frontier Prov., India, and Afghanistan). Afghan support of an independent Pushtu state caused break with Pakistan. In 1957 relations were resumed. Afghanistan in 1955 renewed the 1931 treaty with the USSR. Taking a neutralist position in international politics, Afghanistan receives large amounts of aid from the U.S. and USSR. Afghanistan is a member of the UN.

Afghan language (ăf'găn, -gŭn), occasional name for the PASHTO language.

AFL–CIO: see AMERICAN FEDERATION OF LABOR-CONGRESS OF INDUSTRIAL ORGANIZATIONS.

Afonso. For rulers thus named, see ALFONSO.

Africa, continent (with adjacent islands incl. Madagascar c.11,684,000 sq. mi.; pop. c.263,000,000), separated from Europe by Strait of Gibraltar, from Asia by Suez Canal. Few natural harbors, varied climate. Mainly a plateau with its highest point at Mt. Kilimanjaro (19,565 ft.). In east is L. Victoria, its greatest lake. Vast river systems include the Nile, Niger, Congo, and Zambezi. The deserts, notably the Sahara, are edged by savannas. Jungles cover W equatorial Africa. In the civilization of Egypt (dating from before 3000 B.C.) Africa may claim one of the world's most ancient settled cultures. The N African coast was colonized by Rome after the defeat of Carthage (149 B.C.). Islam was brought by the Arab invasion, 7th–11th cent. Moslem peoples (chiefly Moors) from N Africa launched a series of European invasions which ended in 15th cent. European exploration of the coast began in 15th cent. with Diaz's voyage around the Cape of Good Hope in 1488. The Portuguese were followed by Dutch, British, and French traders, 16th–17th cent. Explorations of interior revealed Africa's great wealth and led to large-scale colonization. By 1912 the European powers had partitioned Africa, with only Egypt, Ethiopia, and Liberia retaining a measure of independence. After First World War Germany lost her colonies to France and England (see BRITISH EMPIRE; FRENCH COMMUNITY). Powers with lesser interests in Africa are Belgium, Portugal, and Spain. Italy after Second World War was shorn by the UN of virtually all her African holdings. In Second World War a series of major campaigns in NORTH AFRICA ended in 1943 with Axis defeat. After Second World War the movement for autonomy and independence by nationalists went on apace. In 1945 Ethiopia, Egypt, Liberia, and the Union of South Africa were the only free states in Africa. Nationalism emerged in the 1950s with Libya's independence 1951, formation of Federation of Rhodesia and Nyasaland 1953, independence for Sudan, Morocco, and Tunisia in 1956, Ghana in 1957, and Guinea in 1958. The high tide of African nationalism was reached in 1960. In that year the following republics were created from former French colonies: Cameroon, Central African Republic, Chad, Congo Republic, Dahomey, Gabon, Ivory Coast, Malagasy, Mali (formerly the Sudanese Republic), Mauretania, Niger, Senegal, and Upper Volta; 1960 saw also the formation of the Republic of the Congo, the Federation of Nigeria, Somali Republic, and Togo. In 1961 Sierra Leone and Tanganyika gained sovereignty. In 1962 Algeria, Burundi, Rwanda, and Uganda achieved independence. Kenya followed in 1963, Malawi and Zambia in 1964; Tanganyika and Zanzibar joined to become United Republic of Tanzania in 1964, and Gambia gained independence in 1965. Rhodesia unilaterally declared her independence in 1965. Botswana and Lesotho became separate free states in 1966. By late 1966 there were few European colonies left in Africa. Portugal still held Angola,

AFRICA

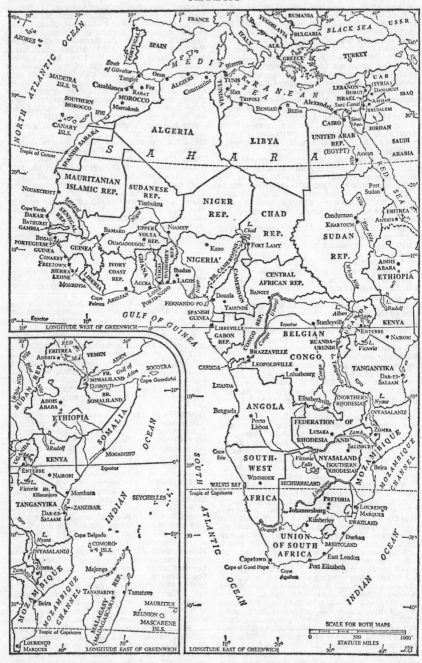

Cabinda, Mozambique, Portuguese Guinea, and São Tomé and Príncipe. Spain's possessions were Spanish Sahara, Ifni, the Canary Isls., and Spanish Guinea (Río Muni and Fernando Po). France retained French Somaliland, the Comoro Isls., and the island of Réunion. Britain held the colony of Mauritius, the high commission territory of Swaziland, and the Seychelles protectorate. The Republic of South Africa held South-West Africa. Pan-African and anti-European movements were rampant in many parts of the continent. See separate articles on the African countries.

African Methodist Episcopal Church, American Negro denomination, founded (1816) by Richard ALLEN.

African Methodist Episcopal Zion Church, Negro Protestant denomination. Founded 1796 by Negro members of Methodist Episcopal church in New York city; organized nationally 1821.

African Negro literature. Earliest examples of this literature are to be found in anc. Moslem religious books written by African Negroes in Swahili and Arabic. Modern writings have been in both native and European languages. One of the first modern writers was Thomas Mofolo (c.1875–1948), who wrote in Sesuto. Negro writers from Francophone Africa made Paris their center. There the periodical *Présence Africaine* provided them with direction. Outstanding among them were the novelist René Maran, poet and essayist Léopold Sedar Senghor of Senegal, and Paul Hazoumé of Dahomey. Other outstanding African writers in French are Camara Laye of Guinea, Malagasy poet Jean-Joseph Rabearivelo, Ferdinand Oyono and Mongo Beti of Cameroon, and David Diop, born in France of a Senegalese father and a Camerounian mother. Much of French African literature has been concerned with *negritude*. Among the many Africans writing in English are the Nigerians Chinua Achebe, Cyprian Ekwensi, Wole Soyinka, Amos Tutuola, George Awwonor Williams of Ghana, David Rubadiri of Malawi, William Conton from Gambia and Sierra Leone, and Peter Abrahams and Ezekiel Mphahlele from South Africa.

African Negro music is rhythmic and percussive with the distinctive use of two or more rhythms simultaneously. There are many variations, some primitive, of wind, string, and percussion instruments. The influence of this music on the American Negro spiritual and jazz is debated.

Afrikaans (ăˈfrĭkäns', -känz'), standard language of the South African Boers, a Germanic language of Indo-European family. See LANGUAGE (table).

Afro-Asian bloc, independent African and Asian nations consulting together or collaborating, especially in the UN. First formally constituted meeting was BANDUNG CONFERENCE (1955). Bloc's efforts achieved UN resolution in 1960 calling for immediate end of "colonialism" in Africa and Asia and subsequent establishment of UN Special Committee on Colonialism. The Casablanca group, formed 1961 by Ghana, Guinea, Mali, Morocco, and Egypt (UAR), opposed "imperialism" most strongly. More pro-Western in sympathy was Monrovia group, formed 1961 by Tunisia, Kenya, Liberia, Nigeria, Tanganyika, and most former French colonies of equatorial and W Africa (latter are known as the Brazzaville group). The Monrovia group favored loose alliance rather than centralized Union of African States favored by Casablanca group.

Afro-Asiatic languages, family including languages of the Near East and N Africa. The term Hamito-Semitic languages, formerly applied to this group is misleading since it falsely suggests for the non-Semitic languages an ethnic and linguistic unity like that of the Semitic group. See LANGUAGE (table).

Afton, river of Ayrshire, Scotland. It is the "sweet Afton" of Burns's poem.

Ag, chemical symbol of the element SILVER.

Agade, ancient Mesopotamian city: see AKKAD.

Agadir (ägädĕr'), town (pop. c.16,695), SW Morocco, a port on the Atlantic. Occupied and fortified by the Portuguese 1505–41. In 1911 when French troops were intervening in a Moroccan revolt, the German cruiser *Panther* appeared here, ostensibly to protect German property. The incident created a tense situation, later eased when the French ceded large part of French Congo. City devastated by earthquake in 1960. Seaside resort; has sardine canneries.

Aga Khan (äˈgä khän'), 1877–1957, Indian leader, the hereditary head of Mohammedan Ismaili sect. Founded All-India Moslem League in 1906. Represented India at League of Nations in 1930s. Famed for his wealth, he was succeeded by grandson Karim.

Agamemnon (ăˈgŭmĕmˈnŏn), in Greek legend, leader of Greek armies in TROJAN WAR; brother of Menelaus. Quarrel with Achilles is a main theme of the *Iliad*. He married CLYTEMNESTRA, who bore him ELECTRA, ORESTES, and IPHIGENIA. Murdered by his wife and Aegisthus, he was avenged by Orestes.

Aga Mohamad Khan or **Agha Mohammed Khan,** d. 1797, shah of Persia, founder of the Kajar (or Qajar) dynasty. His cruelty is proverbial.

Agana (ägäˈnyä), city (pop. 1,642), capital of Guam, on W coast ENE of Apra Harbor. Largest and most important city on island. Nearby is Anderson Air Force Base.

Aganippe (ăgˈŭnĭpˈē), in Greek legend, nymph whose fountain on HELICON gives poetic inspiration to all who drink from it. Muses are often called Aganippides [Gr.,= daughters of Aganippe].

agar (äˈgär), or **agar-agar,** gelatinous product from red algae or seaweed, used as a laxative, sizing, food thickening, and culture medium for bacteria.

Agassiz, (Jean) Louis (Rodolphe) (zhäˈ lwē rōdŏlfˈ ăgˈūsē), 1807–73), Swiss-American zoologist, geologist. His research on fossil fish, exposition of glacial movement and deposit, and his teaching made Univ. of Neuchâtel a center of scientific study. As professor of zoology and geology at Lawrence Scientific School at Harvard he stimulated scientific study of nature in U.S. Agassiz's first wife died in Germany in 1848. His second wife **Elizabeth Cary Agassiz,** 1822–1907, was an author and educator. She accompanied her husband on expeditions to Brazil (1865–66) and along the E and W coasts of the Americas (1871–72). Influential in the founding of Radcliffe College, she served to 1903 as its first president. With her husband she wrote *A Journey in Brazil* (1868) and with her stepson Alexander, *Seaside Studies in Natural History* (1865). **Alexander Agassiz,** 1835–1910, son of Louis Agassiz, was from 1862 connected with Harvard and its Museum of Comparative Zoology. Much of the wealth he acquired from copper mines was used for scientific expeditions and research publication. Noted also as oceanographer.

Agassiz, Lake, c.700 mi. long, 250 mi. wide, of Pleistocene epoch, formed by melting of continental ice sheet c.10,000 years ago over much of present NW Minn., NE N.Dak., S Manitoba, and SW Ont. Named 1879 for Louis Agassiz. As ice melted, water drained E into L. Superior and N into Hudson Bay, leaving many smaller lakes. Its bed is now rich wheat-growing Red R. valley.

agate, variety of QUARTZ banded in two or more colors. Used as semiprecious gem. Found in Brazil, India, Uruguay, and U.S.

Agatharchus (ăgˈūthärˈkŭs), 5th cent. B.C., Greek painter, credited with discoveries in perspective.

agave: see SISAL HEMP.

Agawam (ăˈgŭwäm). Town (pop. 15,718), SW Mass.; on Connecticut R. below W Springfield; settled 1635. 2 Former name of IPSWICH, Mass.

Agee, James (äˈgē), 1909–55, American writer. Film critic for *Time* and the *Nation*, his works include *Let Us Now Praise Famous Men* (1941); a novel, *A Death in the Family* (1957); and the collection *Agee on Film* (2 vols., 1958–60).

Agen (äzhĕ'), town (est. pop. 32,593), cap. of Lot-et-Garonne dept., SW France, on Garonne R. Vineyards and orchards. Romanesque cathedral.

Agenor (ùjĕ'–), Phoenician king; father of CADMUS and EUROPA.

ageratum (ăj"ùrā'tùm), popular annual (*Ageratum*), also called flossflower, with clustered lavender flowers. It is grown in borders and pots.

Agesander: see LAOCOÖN.

Agesilaus II (ùjĕ"sĭlā'ùs), c.444–360 B.C., king of Sparta; successor of Agis I. Though admired by Xenophon, he gave Greek cities to Persia by King's Peace (386) and, having excluded Thebes from a peace treaty, was defeated by Epaminondas at Leuctra (371 B.C.).

agglutination: see INFLECTION.

Agincourt (ă'jĭnkôrt), modern Fr. *Azincourt* (äzĕkoor'), village, Pas-de-Calais dept., N France. Here Henry V of England routed French Oct. 25, 1415.

Agis I (ā'jĭs), d. 398? B.C., king of Sparta, victor at Mantinea (418 B.C.). Sometimes called Agis II.

Aglaia, one of the GRACES.

Agnes, Saint, 4th cent., noble Roman virgin martyred at 13 for rejecting pagan suitor. Feast: Jan. 21.

Agnes Scott College, at Decatur, Ga.; for women; opened 1889; acquired present name 1906.

Agnon, Shmuel Yosef, 1888–, Hebrew writer, b. Galicia. Awarded 1966 Nobel Prize in Literature. His works concern Eastern European Jewish life. Originally named Czaczkes.

agnosticism, suspension of belief and disbelief in God or gods. The teaching, known from early times in the East and West, holds that metaphysics is untenable by reason and therefore to be rejected. It does not, however, shut out the possibility of the belief in metaphysical realities, merely maintaining that they are not subject to proof and therefore cannot be accepted. The agnostic belief stops short of ATHEISM.

Agnus Dei (än'yōōs dā'ē) [Latin,= Lamb of God, i.e., Jesus Christ], precommunion hymn in the Mass, so called from opening words; final number of sung Masses. The figure is of crucified Christ as sacrifice for mankind (sacrificial lamb).

Agoult, Marie (de Flavigny), comtesse d' (märĕ' dù flävēnyĕ' kōtĕs' dägōō'), pseud. Daniel Stern, 1805–76, French author of autobiographical romances and social and political writings. Mistress of Liszt; mother of Cosima WAGNER.

agouti (ùgōō'tē), rodents of genera *Dasyprocta* and *Myoprocta* of Central and South America, West Indies. Length c.1½ ft.; coat speckled reddish to black; legs long, slender.

Agra (ä'grù), city (pop. 333,530), W Uttar Pradesh, India, on Jumna R. Founded 1566 by Akbar as cap. of Mogul empire. Outstanding among many splendid buildings are the TAJ MAHAL, Pearl Mosque, and Great Mosque. Important rail junction. Cotton spinning and carpet mfg. Seat of Agra Univ.

Agra and Oudh, India: see UTTAR PRADESH.

Agram, Yugoslavia: see ZAGREB.

Agrapha of Jesus (ăg'rùfù) [Gr.,= not written], sayings attributed to Jesus not found in the four Gospels. There are quotations in the New Testament (e.g., Acts 20.35), and Agrapha from oral tradition appear in early Christian literature. Many are probably pseudepigrapha.

agrarian laws, in ancient Rome, regulated disposition of public lands. Patricians tended to gain (and hold) large areas, nominally as state tenants. Poorer classes' land hunger gave rise to laws, mostly ineffectual, beginning in 5th cent. B.C. Despite Licinian Rogations (367 B.C.), Sempronian Law (133 B.C.) and its revival (123 B.C.), and later large-scale reassignments, Domitian's edict (1st cent. A.D.) giving lands to their holders only confirmed long trend toward dependency of the poor upon the powerful, which foreshadowed the greater dependency of feudalism.

agrarian reform, in narrow sense, redistribution of land; in modern sense includes changes in institutions (e.g., credit, rents). Reform of land tenure conditions is a recurrent theme in history. Many peasant rebellions in Middle Ages were triggered by demand for land reform. Advent of socialist and communist ideologies added new aspect in advocacy of collective ownership of land (see COLLECTIVE FARM). Land reform is a particularly acute question in Latin America.

Agricola (Cneius Julius Agricola) (ùgrĭ'kùlù), A.D. c.37–A.D. 93, Roman general, governor and pacifier of Britain; father-in-law of Tacitus.

Agricola, Georg (gā'ôrk), 1490?–1555, German physician and scientist, pioneer in scientific classification of minerals, and author of *De re metallica* (1556; Eng. tr. 1912).

Agricola, Johann or Johannes (yō'hän, yōhän'ùs), c.1494–1566, German Protestant minister (family name Schnitter, originally Schneider). Early associated with Luther and active in founding of Protestantism. Broke with Luther (1536) by upholding antinomianism. Helped draw up Augsburg Interim (1548).

Agricultural Adjustment Administration (AAA), U.S. government agency estab. in Dept. of Agriculture (1933) as part of New Deal program. Designed to help farmers by cutting supplies of staple crops, thus raising farm prices and changing agr. pattern from overproduction of staple crops to more diversified farming. In 1936 Supreme Court declared important sections of act invalid for infringing on powers of the states. Soil Conservation and Domestic Allotment Act (1936) subsidized conservation. Agricultural Adjustment Act of 1938 estab. "ever-normal granary"; empowered AAA to store surplus crops and maintain balance of prices between years of low yield and years of high yield. In 1945 its functions were taken over by the Production and Marketing Administration.

Agricultural and Technical College, at Greensboro, N.C.; land grant, state supported; coed.; opened for first instruction 1890, estab. 1891. Formerly called Agr. and Technical Col. of North Carolina.

agricultural subsidies, financial assistance to farmers through government-sponsored price-support programs. Programs to reduce instability of farm prices and raise farm income are common in most industrialized countries since 1930s. After agr. collapse in 1920s due to overproduction, Federal government expanded credit for farmers (1923). Agricultural Marketing Act (1929) initiated program of direct aid to agr. Agricultural Adjustment Act (1933) attempted to reduce supply of basic crops. Goal was estab. of parity principle; parity prices were computed to give farm produce same buying power as in a previous selected period. By 1949 demand for U.S. farm products declined, leading to increased surpluses. Estimated value of government-held surpluses was over $9 billion in 1960. Subsidies once introduced proved difficult to end, and price support programs are still controversial.

agriculture, in its narrow sense, is tilling the soil; more broadly, it includes stock raising, forestry, some mfg. (e.g., buttermaking). In prehistory, the change from hunting economy to tillage and domestication of beasts marked beginning of settlement, hence beginning of civilization. European agr. has long been mixed farming, much of it on subsistence level; in U.S., because of conquest of vast frontiers, increased growth of cities, and mechanization, farming tends to be on larger scale. Agr. colleges and government bureaus seek to increase productivity by disseminating knowledge of improved agr. practices (e.g., ROTATION OF CROPS, soil chemistry). Modern large-scale agriculture subject to much government regulation.

Agriculture, United States Department of, division of U.S. government. Federal aid to agr. began modestly in 1839; Dept. of Agriculture, under a commissioner, was created 1862; Secretary of Agriculture became Cabinet member 1889. One of chief research, planning, service, and regulatory agencies of government; helps farmers with production, marketing, farm organization, land tenure, and land utilization problems, conducts huge research program, serves urban consumers, and issues many valuable publications.

Agrigento (ägrējĕn'tō), city (pop. 47,094), S Sicily, Italy, on a height 2 mi. from sea. Now an agr. market and sulfur-exporting center. Founded as Acragas c.580 B.C. by Greek colonists from Gela; one of most splendid cities of anc. Grecian world. Remains of Doric temples (6th–5th cent. B.C.). Birthplace of Greek philosopher, Empedocles, for whom nearby Porto Empedocle is named.

agrimony (ăg'rĭmō"nē), perennial plant of genus *Agrimonia*. Grows wild in N temperate zone and is cultivated in herb gardens. It has aromatic leaves and yellow flowers, followed by top-shaped burs.

Agrippa, in Palestinian history: see HEROD.

Agrippa, Marcus Vipsanius (mär'kŭs vĭpsā'nēŭs ŭgrĭ'pŭ), c.63 B.C.–c.12 B.C. Roman general, lieutenant and son-in-law of Augustus. Fought against Sextus Pompeius and in the victory over Antony at Actium.

Agrippina I (ă"grĭpī'nù), d. A.D. 33, Roman matron, daughter of Agrippa, granddaughter of Augustus, mother of Caligula. She accused Tiberius of having her husband Germanicus poisoned. Her daughter, **Agrippina II,** d. A.D. 59, was mother of NERO by her first marriage; after marriage to her uncle CLAUDIUS I she persuaded him to adopt Nero, then probably poisoned him to advance Nero, who had her murdered.

agronomy, branch of agr. dealing with crop production and field management. Aim is to increase yield and quality of food, seed, forage, and fiber crops by using land to fullest capacity and greatest efficiency.

Agua (ä'gwä), inactive volcano, 12,310 ft. high, S Guatemala. In 1541 a flood from the mountain destroyed Ciudad Vieja, then cap. of Guatemala.

Aguascalientes (ä"gwäskälyän'täs), state (2,499 sq. mi.; pop. 208,800), N central Mexico, on central plateau; cap. Aguascalientes (pop. c.130,000), founded 1575, a health resort with mineral springs. State is rich in agr. produce, cattle, and minerals.

Aguinaldo, Emilio (ägwĭnäl'dō; āmē'lyō ägēnäl'dō), 1869?–1964, Philippine leader. Led insurrection against Spain in 1896 and, after brief alliance with U.S. in Spanish-American War, against U.S. 1899–1901.

Aguirre, Lope de (lō'pä dä ägē'rä), c.1510–1561, Spanish rebel in colonial South America, noted for violence and cruelty. On expedition down Marañón and Amazon (1560), he killed Ursúa, the leader, laid waste Indian villages; held Margarita Isl. in terror (1561); and proclaimed rebellion against Spain. Surrounded at Barquisimeto, before he surrendered and was shot, he had his own daughter murdered.

Agulhas, Cape (ùgù'lùs), W Cape Prov., South Africa; most southerly point of Africa. On dividing line between Atlantic and Indian oceans.

Agustini, Delmira (dĕlmē'rä ägōōstē'nē), c.1886–1914, Uruguayan lyric poet.

Ahab (ā'hăb), d. c.853 B.C., king of Israel (c.874–c.853 B.C.), politically one of its greatest kings, religiously one of its wickedest; successor of Omri. He consolidated foreign relations by strategic marriages: his own to JEZEBEL of Tyre, his daughter Athaliah's to son of king of Judah. Bible account concerned chiefly with religious aspects of his reign. His foreign wife, who encouraged worship of Baal, led him into clashes with ELIJAH. He died in battle against Ben-hadad of Syria. Ruins of palace have been excavated at Samaria. 1 Kings 16.28–22.40.

Ahaggar: see SAHARA.

Ahasuerus (ăhăs"ūē'rùs), Hebrew form of Xerxes used in Bible. In Esther probably Xerxes I; in Tobit 14.15

may be Cyaxares I, destroyer of Nineveh. Father of DARIUS THE MEDE given as Ahasuerus.

Ahaz (ā'hăz), d. c.727 B.C., king of Judah (c.731–727 B.C.). His reign marks end of Judah's real independence. Coalition of Israel and Syria attacked him and nearly took Jerusalem. He appealed to Assyrians, who defeated his enemies but demanded tribute, which he paid with Temple gold. For this and other heathen practices (e.g., human sacrifice) he is denounced in the Bible. Isaiah opposed his alliance with Assyria. Succeeded by Hezekiah. 2 Kings 16.2; 2 Chron. 28; Isa. 7. Achaz: Mat. 1.9.

Ahaziah (āhùzī'ù). **1** Died c.852 B.C., king of Israel (c.853–852 B.C.), son of Ahab. 1 Kings 22.51–53; 2 Kings 1; 2 Chron. 20.35–37. **2** Died c.846 B.C., king of Judah (c.846 B.C.), son of Jehoram **2** and Athaliah. Killed in Jehu's coup d'état. His mother succeeded him. 2 Kings 8.25–29; 9; 2 Chron. 22.

Ahidjo, Ahmadou (ämä'dō ähhē'jō), 1922–, African statesman, president of Federal Republic of Cameroon (1960–). From the Moslem Northern Region, he succeeded André-Marie M'Bida as premier in 1958 and was elected first president when the republic gained full independence.

Ahijah, prophet from Shiloh in the time of Jeroboam. May be same as AHIMELECH. 1 Kings 11.29; 12.15; 14.1–18; 2 Chron. 10.15.

Ahimelech (ùhĭm'ulĕk), priest, brother of (or perhaps same as) Ahijah. Saul had him killed for helping David. 1 Sam. 22.9–19. Abimelech: 1 Chron. 18.16.

Ahithophel (ùhĭth'ùfĕl), David's counselor. Plotted with Absalom; his counsel ignored, he killed himself. 2 Sam. 15.12; 16:20–17.23; 23.34. Dryden's satire, *Absalom and Achitophel,* uses instead the Vulgate form of name.

Ahlin, Lars (lärsh älēn'), 1915–, Swedish novelist. Works marked by great creative vitality, psychological realism, and a concern with spiritual values. Wrote *If* (1946) and *The Cinnamon Stick* (1953).

Ahmadabad, India: see AHMEDABAD.

Ahmad Khan, Sir Sayyid (sä'yēd ä'mäd kän'), 1817–98, Indian Moslem educator and leader. Through his books he inspired numerous changes in the moribund life and society of 19th-cent. Moslem India.

Ahmed, Ottoman sultans. **Ahmed I,** 1589–1617, reigned 1603–17. Made peace with Austria (1606), recognizing Transylvanian independence. Lost Tabriz to ABBAS I. **Ahmed III,** 1673–1736, reigned 1703–30. Harbored CHARLES XII of Sweden. In war with Russia (1710–11) he recovered Azov. Defeated by the Austrians, he signed Treaty of PASSAROWITZ (1718). He was overthrown by the Janizaries.

Ahmed, 1898–1930, shah of Persia (1909–25), last of Kajar dynasty; deposed by Reza Shah Pahlevi.

Ahmedabad or **Ahmadabad** (both: ăm"ùdùbäd'), city, (pop. 1,400,000), Gujarat state, W India. Sacred to the Jains. Cotton mills.

Ahmed al-Mansur (ä'mĕd äl mänsōōr') [al-Mansur = the victorious], d.1603, emir of Morocco (1578–1603). Proclaimed ruler after his brother's death at the battle of Alcazarquivir. Extended Moroccan rule S of the Sahara by conquest of Gao and Timbuktu (1590–91).

Ahmed Shah (ä'mĕd shä'), c.1723–1773, Afghan ruler, founder of Durani dynasty. Won Afghan rule by supporting Nadir Shah of Iran.

Ahriman: see ZOROASTRIANISM.

Ahura Mazdah: see ZOROASTRIANISM.

Ahvenanmaa, Finland: see ALAND ISLANDS.

aids, in feudalism, type of feudal due paid by a vassal to his suzerain or lord. Their exact nature is subject to controversy. In English-speaking countries, as specified in MAGNA CARTA of 1215, aids were due on knighting of lord's eldest son, on marriage of his eldest daughter, for ransom when lord was in captivity. In France aids were converted into a form of royal tax and continued to 1789. See also SCUTAGE; TALLAGE.

Aiea (ä"ēä'ä), town (pop. 11,826), Hawaii, on S Oahu, near Pearl Harbor, in sugar-cane region.

Aigues-Mortes (ĕg-môrt'), town (est. pop. 3,746), Gard dept., S France, near Mediterranean. Louis IX built port (now silted up). Medieval towers, ramparts.

Aijalon (ā'jŭ-, ĭ'jŭ-, ā'jŭ-), valley over which Joshua commanded moon to stand still. Joshua 10.12.

Aiken, Conrad (ā'kĭn), 1889-, American poet. His work reflects preoccupation with music and with psychoanalytic theory. Volumes of poetry include *The Jig of Forslin* (1916), *Selected Poems* (1961), *Cats and Bats and Things with Wings* (1965). Has also written criticism, novels (*Blue Voyage*, 1927; *Collected Novels*, 1964), an autobiography (1952), and short stories (e.g., "Mr. Arcularis").

Aiken, city (pop. 11,243), W S.C., NE of Augusta, Ga. A resort and industrial center in area of sand hills and pine forests. Savannah R. plant of the Atomic Energy Commission is nearby.

ailanthus (ālăn'-) or **tree of heaven,** hardy deciduous tree (*Ailanthus*), with large compound leaves. Native to China, common in European and American cities. Is tolerant of smoke and other handicaps.

Ailly, Pierre d' (pyĕr'dāyē'), 1350-1420, French cardinal. Favored calling of general council to end Great Schism and was prominent in Council of Constance. His astronomical work, *Imago mundi,* studied by Columbus.

Ailsa Craig (āl'sŭ), conspicuous rocky island (1,114 ft. high) off SW Scotland, in Ayrshire.

Ain (ĕ), department (2,229 sq. mi.; pop. 327,146), E central France, in Burgundy; cap. Bourg-en-Bresse.

Aintab, Turkey: see GAZIANTEP.

Aintree, difficult and dangerous racecourse, Lancashire, England. The Grand National is run here.

Ainu (ī'nōō), aborigines of Japan. Forced to retreat to N islands, they now live as hunters and fishermen in Hokkaido and in the Soviet islands of Sakhalin and the Kuriles. They are short, stocky, hairy, resembling Europeans more than Mongoloids. Their language is unrelated to any known speech.

air: see ATMOSPHERE; LIQUID AIR; VENTILATION.

air-conditioning, mechanical control of humidity, temperature, cleanliness, and circulation of indoor air. Gas flowing in a closed circuit is heated by compression. After losing heat to air outdoors, it cools further by expansion and absorbs heat from air indoors. An intake fan draws fresh air through cooling coils and filters it into building. Some units use circulating cold water to extract and remove heat.

aircraft carrier, ship designed to store, launch, and land aircraft. Used experimentally in First World War; most important of capital ships in Second World War battles.

air-cushion vehicle or hovercraft, device supported above ground or water by downdraft of air produced by horizontal propeller or fan.

air lock, access chamber connecting work area under higher air pressure in caisson or tunnel with area of normal pressure. For entry to work area, men and materials are sealed in air lock, compressed air is admitted, and when pressure in air lock equals that of work area, door separating them is opened.

air mail. Demonstrated in U.S. and England in 1911. Army pilots and aircraft began regular U.S. civilian service with New York-to-Washington flight May 15, 1918; continued by Post Office Dept. 1920-21. Coast-to-coast service (all by air) operated by Post Office Dept. 1924 for first time. Commercial contracts authorized 1925. Service extends to most of world.

Aïr Mountains: see SAHARA.

airplane or aeroplane, heavier-than-air craft developing propulsive power and sustained by air action on external surfaces. First man-carrying, power-driven, heavier-than-air flight was that of Wright brothers' biplane (Kitty Hawk, N.C., Dec. 17, 1903). Airplanes are usually monoplane (one wing). Main structures: fuselage (main body); wing surface (for support); landing gear; movable control surfaces (ailerons for longitudinal control, rudder for horizontal control, elevator for vertical control); and one or more power plants (engines or motors). Airplanes are powered by piston internal-combustion engine or by JET PROPULSION. See *ill.,* p. 368.

air plant or **epiphyte,** plant, such as orchid and Spanish moss, not normally rooted in soil, but unlike PARASITE, able to make its food by PHOTOSYNTHESIS. Grows on another plant or other support and gets water from atmosphere.

air pollution may be natural or man-made. Smog, such as that in Los Angeles, is largely composed of automobile exhaust and smoke from factories; geography, climate, and local pattern of air movement also influence smog development. Smog may contain noxious elements; it irritates nose and throat, stunts plant growth, and may be a factor causing lung cancer. Large cities have set up commissions to control smog. Summer haze is a phenomenon of nature resulting from organic emanations of living plants.

airport, land area for landing and departure of aircraft. Provides taxiing and parking strips; hangars; repair and fueling facilities; traffic tower; radio and meteorological apparatus; passenger and cargo stations; beacons, floodlights, obstacle lights, other illumination; radar and other devices for guiding blind flight and blind landings. Introduction of jet aircraft into commercial air travel has made extension of runways necessary and has raised other problems. See also AIRWAY.

air power. Use of aircraft in First World War led some theorists (notably American William Mitchell and Italian Giulio Douhet) to develop idea of predominance of air power—victory by aircraft alone. Fascist Germany, Italy, and Japan were among first to develop air power, and planes were used extensively in Second World War. Loss of air supremacy in 1944-45 played large role in defeat of Axis. Aircraft carriers were prominent in Pacific warfare. Unsettled question of victory by air alone complicated by introduction of atomic bomb, jet propulsion, and guided missiles.

airship, self-propelled, steerable (dirigible) balloon. Internal gas pressure shapes nonrigid (e.g., blimp) and semirigid types. Rigid airships (largest type) are elongated, have rigid frame or latticework of aluminum or duraluminum compartmentation for gas cells and covered by fabric. Engines inside drive propellers outside. Lift is provided by hydrogen gas (most buoyant) or helium (noninflammable). Airships have been entirely superseded in commercial use by the airplane, but they are still widely used by the military, particularly in antisubmarine work.

airsickness: see MOTION SICKNESS.

airway, air route between air traffic centers over terrain most suitable for emergency landings, spaced with landing fields equipped with air navigation and radio facilities. Civil Aeronautics Authority supervises U.S. airway traffic and facilities and enforces flight rules.

Aisha: see AYESHA.

Aisne (ān, Fr. ĕn), department (2,868 sq. mi.; pop. 512,920), NE France; cap. Laon. Towns; Soissons, Château-Thierry, Saint-Quentin. Aisne R., tributary of Oise, was important battle line in First World War.

Aix-en-Provence (ĕks'-ā-prôvās', ĕk"sā-), city (pop. 67,943), Bouches-du-Rhône dept., SE France. Founded c.122 B.C. by Romans as Aquae Sextiae; scene of Marius' victory over Teutons (102 B.C.); cap. of Provence (1501-1789); center of medieval Provençal culture. University founded 1409, now partly in Marseilles.

Aix-la-Chapelle, Germany: see AACHEN.

Aix-la-Chapelle, Treaty of. 1 Compact of May 2, 1668, which ended War of DEVOLUTION. France kept most of its conquests in Flanders but returned Franche-Comté to Spain. Spanish possessions in Low Countries were guaranteed by TRIPLE ALLIANCE. 2 Treaty of 1748, ending War of the AUSTRIAN SUCCESSION. It generally restored the prewar map, but awarded Silesia to Prussia and conferred Parma, Piacenza, and Guastalla on the Spanish infante, Philip. PRAGMATIC SANCTION was confirmed.

Aix-les-Bains (ĕks'-lã-bē'), town (est. pop. 15,680), Savoie dept., E France, on L. Bourget; spa.

Ajaccio (Fr. äzhäksyō', Ital. äyät'chô), city (est. pop. 32,997), cap. of Corsica, France; seaport. Birthplace of Napoleon I.

Ajanta (ûjŭn'tû), village, NW Bombay, India. Here are cave dwellings and shrines decorated with Buddhist art (200 B.C.–A.D. 600).

Ajax (ā'jăks), Gr. *Aias,* in Greek legend. 1 Telamonian Ajax, hero of Trojan War, was a giant, courageous but slow of mind and speech. He and Odysseus rescued Achilles' body. When Odysseus received Achilles' armor, Ajax killed himself. 2 Locrian Ajax, leader of Locrian forces in Trojan War, violated Cassandra. Rescued from shipwreck by Poseidon, he was struck dead when defying lightning.

Aiivika (äjē'vĭkû), religious sect of medieval India. Founded by Gosala (d. c.484 B.C.) who believed transmigration was controlled wholly by *Niyati,* or destiny. Atheistic and anti-Brahmanical, its pessimistic doctrines are related to JAINISM. Flourished under Asoka and then saw rapid decline. Survived until 14th cent.

Ajmer (äjmēr', ŭj–), former state, NW India, now part of Rajasthan state. Ajmer city (pop. 196,633), former cap., was founded 12th cent. Trade center.

Ajo (ä'hō), town (pop. 7,049), SW Ariz., SW of Gila; settled 1854. Health resort and one of state's oldest active copper-mining towns. Organ Pipe Cactus Natl. Monument is nearby.

Ajodhya, India: see FYZABAD.

Akademgordok, RSFSR: see NOVOSIBIRSK.

Akbar (ăk'bär), 1542–1605, Mogul emperor of India (1556–1605), grandson of Baber. Enlarged his original domain in N central India to include Afghanistan and all of N India. Known for administrative reforms and religious tolerance.

Akeley, Carl Ethan (āk'lē), 1864–1926, American naturalist, sculptor. Noted for improved methods of mounting habitat groups, invention of cement gun and Akeley camera, and bronze works of sculpture of African wildlife and natives. Made numerous African expeditions for American museums. Author of *In Brightest Africa* (1923).

Akershus (ä'kûrs-hōōs"), province (1,895 sq. mi.; pop. 226,948), SE Norway, W and NW of Oslo Fjord; cap. OSLO. Has many farms and forests. Products include food, textiles, and iron.

Akhenaton: see IKHNATON.

Akhetaton: see TEL-EL AMARNA.

Akhmatova, Anna (ûkhmä'tûvŭ), pseud. of Anna Andreyevna Gorenko, 1888–1966, Russian poet (see ACMEISTS). Her poems of love and tragedy are sculptured in their simplicity yet rhythmic in the tradition of Pushkin. Long very popular in Soviet Russia, she was criticized in 1946 by the Communist party for "bourgeois aristocratic aestheticism," but her political poems published after 1950 met with favor.

Akiba ben Joseph, A.D. c.50–c.132, Jewish expositor of the legal tradition, supported BAR KOKHBA as Messiah. His life and martyr's death became a favorite subject of legend.

Akihito (äkē'hētō), 1933–, Japanese prince, son of Emperor Hirohito; heir apparent. First member Japanese royal family to wed commoner, 1959. His son, Naruhito (1960–), is next in succession to throne.

Akkad (ă'kăd, ä'käd), northern part of Babylonia, in Mesopotamia; the southern part was Sumer. From the 4th millennium B.C. a Semitic people flourished and under Sargon (c.2340) became an imperial power. Under Hammurabi Akkad and Sumer were united as Babylonia. Also spelled Accad.

Akkerman: see BELGOROD-DNESTROVSKY, Ukraine.

Aklavik (ăklä'vĭk), settlement on Mackenzie R., Mackenzie dist., Northwest Territories, Canada. Administrative center for Eskimos and Indians of region with airfield, radio station, schools, and hospital.

Akmolinsk: see TSELINOGRAD, Kazakh SSR.

Akron, city (pop. 290,351), NE Ohio, on Little Cuyahoga R., S of Cleveland; settled 1807. Growth spurred by opening of Ohio and Erie Canal. Important industrial center and hub of U.S. rubber industry; mfg. of automobile and aircraft parts, metal products, chemicals, and machinery. Also U.S. center for lighter-than-air-craft, with dirigible airdock (*Akron* and *Macon* dirigibles built here). First important application of sit-down strike technique occurred here 1936. Seat of the Univ. of Akron and its Inst. of Rubber Research.

Aksakov, Sergei Timofeyevich (syĭrgä' tyĭmûfyä'ûvĭch üksä'kûf), 1791–1859, Russian writer. Author of *The Family Chronicle* (1856; Eng. tr., 1916–24), a remarkable picture of life of landed gentry.

Aksum or **Axum** (both: äksōōm'), town (pop. c.10,000), N Ethiopia. Was cap. of dynasty (1st–6th cent.) which ruled over parts of modern Ethiopia and the Sudan. A major center of Coptic Christianity.

Akte, Greek peninsula: see ATHOS.

Aktyubinsk (ûktyōō'bĭnsk), city (1965 est. pop. 127,-000), NW Kazakh SSR. On the Trans-Caspian RR, it has metallurgical and machine-building plants.

Akureyri (ä'kürä"rē), port (pop. 9,532), N Iceland, on Evja Fjord. Fishing, commercial, and industrial center. Second largest city of Iceland.

Al, chemical symbol of the element ALUMINUM.

Alabama, state (51,609 sq. mi.; pop. 3,266,740), SE U.S.; admitted 1819 as 22d state (slaveholding); cap. MONTGOMERY. Largest city is BIRMINGHAM. Except for Cumberland Plateau in NE, state is rolling plain. Touches Gulf of Mexico in SW; seaport is MOBILE. Plains, drained by Alabama and Tombigbee rivers, given over to agr. Black Belt yields cotton, corn, and peanuts. Where Tennessee R. loops across N, TENNESSEE VALLEY AUTHORITY has developed industry. Mineral riches include coal, stone, petroleum. Birmingham is a leading U.S. iron and steel center. Lumbering and Gulf fishing also important. Area first explored by Spanish (esp. De Soto 1540); first settled 1702 in Mobile area by French under BIENVILLE. Ceded to Great Britain 1763 after French and Indian Wars, to U.S. 1783 after Revolution. Defeat of Creek Indians by Andrew Jackson (1814) spurred settlement. Alabama became territory 1817. The state seceded from Union Jan. 11, 1861; Confederate government was organized at Montgomery Feb. 4. In 1868 Alabama was readmitted to Union. Two world wars stimulated industrialization and crop diversification. Heightened racial tension after Supreme Court desegregation ruling (1954) continued into 1960s.

Alabama, navigable river formed in central Ala. by confluence of Coosa and Tallapoosa rivers above Montgomery. Flows c.315 mi. W, SW, then S to join Tombigbee R. and form Mobile R. N of Mobile.

Alabama, ship: see CONFEDERATE CRUISERS.

Alabama, University of, mainly at University, near Tuscaloosa; state supported; coed.; chartered 1820, opened 1831. Medical center at Birmingham. Extension centers at Birmingham, Dothan, Gadsden, Huntsville, Mobile, and Montgomery.

Alabama claims, damages sought by U.S. from Great Britain for losses to merchant marine caused by British-financed CONFEDERATE CRUISERS. Tribunal at Geneva (1871–72) awarded U.S. $15,500,000 for damage by *Florida, Alabama,* and *Shenandoah.*

alabaster, (ăl'ûbăs"tûr), fine-grained, translucent variety of GYPSUM, white or streaked with reddish brown. Used for statues, decorations. Very soft, hence easily worked but subject to breaking and other damage. Alabaster of the ancients is marble.

Alacoque, Margaret Mary: see MARGARET MARY, SAINT.

Alagez, Mount: see ARAGATS, MOUNT.

Alagoas (älägō'ús), state (c.10,700 sq. mi.; pop. c.1,271,100), NE Brazil on Atlantic Ocean; cap. Maceió. Chief products are cattle and cotton from semiarid interior, cacao and sugar from forested coastal belt where oil has been found.

Alain-Fournier (alã'-fŏornyã'), 1886–1914, French writer of mystical novel *Le Grand Meaulnes* (1913; Eng. tr., *The Wanderer*, 1928). Real name was Henri Alban Fournier.

Alais: see ALÈS.

Alameda (ălŭmē'dù). **1** City (pop. 63,855), W central Calif., on isl. off E shore of San Francisco Bay, S of Oakland; settled 1850. A mfg., shipbuilding, shipping center, with U.S. naval installations. Bridges and tunnels to mainland. **2** City (pop. 10,660), SE Idaho, suburb NNE of Pocatello.

Alamein (ălŭmān', ä–) or **El Alamein** (ĕl), town, N Egypt, on Mediterranean coast, 70 mi. W of Alexandria. Here in Second World War British under Montgomery defeated Germans under Rommel (Nov. 1–2, 1942).

Alamo, the (ăl'ŭmō) [Spanish,= cottonwood], building in San Antonio, Texas, "the cradle of Texas liberty." Heroic but hopeless defense of the fortified building in Feb., 1836, against Santa Anna's demands for surrender, roused fighting anger among Texans, who six weeks later defeated the Mexicans at San Jacinto, crying, "Remember the Alamo!"

Alamogordo (ăl'ŭmûgôr'dō, –dù), city (pop. 21,723), S N.Mex., near Sacramento Mts., NNE of El Paso, Texas; settled 1898. Holloman Air Force Base and a center for weapons research and testing are here. First atomic bomb exploded July 16, 1945, in desert nearby (see WHITE SANDS). Also a trade center of livestock, timber, resort area. White Sands Natl. Monument and Apache Indian Reservation are near.

Alamosa (ălŭmō'sù), city (pop. 6,205; alt. 7,500 ft.), S Colo., SW of Pueblo, on Rio Grande; founded 1878. In an irrigated farm region of San Luis Valley. Adams State Col. of Colorado is here. Great Sand Dunes Natl. Monument (see NATIONAL PARKS AND MONUMENTS, table) is near.

Åland Islands (ä'lùnd, ô'–), Finnish *Ahvenanmaa*, Swed. *Ålandsöerna*, archipelago (572 sq. mi.; pop. 29,-000), Finland, in Baltic Sea, strategically placed at entrance to Gulf of Bothnia; chief town Mariehamn. Pop. largely Swedish. Shipping, farming. Ceded by Sweden to Russia 1809; became part of independent Finland 1917. Finnish-Swedish dispute over islands was settled 1921 by League of Nations, which awarded islands to Finland (with autonomous status) and forbade remilitarization. Russo-Finnish demilitarization agreement (1940) was renewed after World War II. Also spelled Aaland.

Alarcón, Hernando de (ĕrnän'dō dã älärkōn'), fl. 1540, Spanish explorer in American Southwest, discovered Colorado R.

Alarcón, Pedro Antonio de (pād'rō äntō'nyō), 1833–91, Spanish writer and diplomat. His short novel *El sombrero de tres picos* (1874; Eng. tr. *Three-cornered Hat*) is basis of popular ballet by Manuel de Falla.

Alarcón y Mendoza, Juan Ruiz de (hwän' rŏoēth' dã älärkōn' ē mändō'thä), 1581?–1639, Spanish dramatic poet of the Golden Age, b. Mexico. His classical comedies are noted for characterization. Best known is *La verdad sospechosa* [the suspicious truth], adapted by Corneille in *Le Menteur*.

Alaric I (ă' lùrĭk), c.370–410, Visigothic king. Led his troops in rebellion after death of Theodosius I, devastated S Balkans until stopped by Stilicho. Invaded Italy (408); sacked Rome (410).

Alaric II, d. 507, Visigothic king of Spain and S Gaul (c.484–507). Issued BREVIARY OF ALARIC. Routed and slain by Clovis I at Vouillé.

Alaska, state (571,065 sq. mi.; with water surface 586,400 sq. mi.; pop. 226,167), NW North America; admitted 1959 as 49th state; cap. JUNEAU. Largest but least populous state in U.S. Bounded N by Arctic Ocean, S by Pacific, E by Canada. Seward Peninsula on W separated from Asiatic USSR by narrow BERING STRAIT, widening in N to Chukchi Sea, in S to BERING SEA (with PRIBILOF ISLANDS). Alaska Peninsula (with ALEUTIAN RANGE) extends SW toward ALEUTIAN ISLANDS. S shore indented by Gulf of Alaska inlets, Prince William Sound, and Cook Inlet. Kenai Peninsula extends SW toward KODIAK ISLAND. Narrow Panhandle in SE, with ALEXANDER ARCHIPELAGO, is most populous region. Coastal mountains and ALASKA RANGE, with Mt. McKINLEY, rim valleys in S (esp. the MATANUSKA VALLEY, with ANCHORAGE, the state's largest city). Arctic Alaska, N of BROOKS RANGE, is mostly barren grounds, permanently frozen. Vitus BERING and Aleksey CHIRIKOV first reached Alaska from Russia 1741, and Russian fur traders followed. Grigori SHELEKHOV founded first permanent settlement on Kodiak Isl. 1784. From 1799 to 1817 area was dominated by Aleksandr BARANOV, who extended fur trade S to Calif. British-American conflict ended in negotiated settlement of S boundary 1824. U.S. purchased Alaska 1867 through efforts of W. H. SEWARD. First government estab. in 1884 after gold discovery in Juneau area. Gold strikes (Nome 1899, Fairbanks 1902) followed 1896 Klondike strike, brought prospectors and adventurers. Boundaries set 1903. BERING SEA FUR-SEAL CONTROVERSY settled 1911. Alaska became U.S. territory 1912. Area was strategic in Second World War. Improved transportation, permanent defense bases, and successful arctic farming have contributed to its rapid development. Fishing, lumbering, mining (oil, iron ore, copper, coal, gold). Severe earthquake in 1964 devastated broad area.

Alaska, University of, at Fairbanks; land grant, state supported; coed.; chartered 1917. Opened 1922 as Alaska Agr. Col. and School of Mines; became university 1935. Has branches at Anchorage, Juneau-Douglas, Ketchikan, Palmer, and Sitka.

Alaska Highway, 1,523 mi. long, from Dawson Creek, B.C., Canada, to Fairbanks, Alaska, formerly called Alaska Military Highway, Alaska International Highway, and Alcan Highway. Noted engineering feat, built March–Sept., 1942, by U.S. troops to supply Alaskan forces. Haines Cutoff connects it with Alaska's Panhandle. Last stretch to Fairbanks uses previously built Richardson Highway. Canadian part of road transferred 1946 to Canadian control. Opened to unrestricted travel 1947.

Alaska Range, S central Alaska, rising to 20,320 ft. in Mt. McKinley, highest point in North America. Range divides S central Alaska from great interior plateau.

Alastor (ùlă'stùr), in Greek mythology, the spirit of vengeance.

Ala-Tau (ä'lä-tou'), six mountain ranges of the Tien Shan system, central Asia, near L. Issyk Kul. Four of them rise to more than 16,000 ft.

Álava, Spain: see BASQUE PROVINCES.

Alba or **Alva, Fernando Álvarez de Toledo, duque de** (fĕrnän'dō äl'väräth dã tōlā'dhō dŏo'kä dã äl'vä), 1508–1582, duke of Alba, Spanish general. Succeeded (1567) Margaret of Parma as regent in Netherlands for Philip II. To suppress rebellion set up "Court of Blood" (18,000 executed, including EGMONT). Resigned 1573. Conquered Portugal (1580); seized Lisbon, permitted massacre there.

Albacete (älbäthä'tä) city (pop. 75,187), cap. of Albacete prov., SE Spain, in Murcia; agr. center.

Alba-Iulia (äl'bä-yōo'lyä), Hung. *Gyulafehérvár*, Ger. *Karlsburg*, city (est. pop. 15,000), central Rumania. Wine-growing region. Former seat of Translyvanian princes. Fortress built by Emperor Charles VI.

Alba Longa (äl'bù lông'gù), city of anc. Latium. In legend founded by son of Aeneas; birthplace of Romulus and Remus; destroyed by Roman king, Tullus Hostilius (c.600 B.C.?).

Albania (älbä'nyù), Albanian *Shqipnija* or *Shqiperia*, republic (11,097 sq. mi.; est. pop. 1,814,000), SE Europe, on Adriatic coast of Balkan Peninsula, between Yugoslavia and Greece; cap. Tirana. A mountainous country (except for a fertile coastal strip, with ports of DURAZZO and Valona), it has oil, copper, and coal deposits but is economically underdeveloped. The people are mainly hill tribes of very ancient stock; c.60% are Moslem, 20% Greek Orthodox, 10% Roman Catholic. Large Albanian minorities live in Yugoslavia and Greece. Including parts of ancient ILLYRIA and EPIRUS, Albania has known many masters (notably Macedon, Rome, Byzantium, and Turkey), but their domination was never effective among the inland mountain clans. Italian penetration began with ROBERT GUISCARD (11th cent.). It was continued by Naples and Venice, which held Durazzo until 1501, when the Turkish conquest, long delayed by SCANDERBEG, became final. Independence from Turkey was proclaimed 1912 during the first Balkan War. An international commission assigned large areas claimed by Albania to Montenegro, Serbia, and Greece (1913). A battleground and the scene of political chaos during and after second Balkan War and First World War, Albania passed in turn under kingship of William, prince of Wied, the dictatorship of ESSAD PASHA, and the dictatorship (kingship after 1928) of ZOG. Occupied by Italy in 1939, Albania fought with the Axis powers in Second World War. After the Allied landing (1944), power passed to antifascist guerrilla leader Enver Hoxha, who set up a Communist dictatorship in 1946. A WARSAW TREATY nation, Albania was admitted to the United Nations in 1955. Became China's spokesman in dispute with USSR (1960); broke with Moscow (1961) and Warsaw nations.

Albano, Lake (älbä'nō), crater lake, central Italy, in Alban Hills, SE of Rome; circumference 6 mi. Underground tunnel, built 4th cent. B.C., is still its only outlet. Alba Longa was near by.

Albany, dukes of: see STUART, ALEXANDER and ROBERT.

Albany, Louisa, countess of, 1752–1824, wife of Charles Edward STUART. Married in 1772, she left her dissolute husband after eight years. Was mistress of poet Vittorio Alfieri until his death (1803) and then mistress of French artist François Fabre.

Albany, ancient and literary name of Scotland.

Albany. 1 Residential city (pop. 14,804), W Calif., on San Francisco Bay adjoining Berkeley. Has U.S. Dept. of Agr. research laboratory. **2** City (pop. 55,890), SW Ga., on Flint R.; founded 1836. Tourist center and industrial city in pecan and peanut area of coastal plain. Albany State Col. is here. Nearby are Radium Springs resort, Turner Air Force Base, and U.S. Marine Corps supply center. **3** City (pop. 129,726), E N.Y., state cap. (since 1797), on W bank of Hudson R. Site visited by Henry Hudson, 1609; Dutch estab. Fort Nassau nearby 1613; in 1624 Walloons began permanent settlement at Fort Orange (renamed Albany 1664 when English took control). Long important as fur-trade center. ALBANY CONGRESS met here 1754. Trade grew especially after Champlain and Erie canals opened in 1820s. Major transshipment point; has breweries and mfg. of chemicals, paper, textiles, woodwork. Seat of UNION UNIVERSITY and Albany Inst. of History and Art; a university center of the State Univ. of NEW YORK is here. Has many old buildings, including Schuyler mansion (1762; Elizabeth Schuyler married to Alexander Hamilton here). **4** City (pop. 12,926), NW Oregon, on Willamette R., S of Salem; founded 1848. Lumbering and processing center in farm area. Titanium and zirconium mines in area.

Albany, river rising in W central Ont., Canada, and flowing c.600 mi. E and NE to James Bay.

Albany, Fort, fur-trading post, at mouth of Albany R. on James Bay, Ont., Canada. One of earliest Hudson's Bay Co. forts (before 1682). From 1697 to 1713 was only post in region in possession of British company.

Albany Congress, 1754, meeting at Albany, N.Y., in which treaty was concluded between seven British colonies and the Iroquois. Benjamin Franklin's Plan of Union for the colonies, though accepted favorably, was later rejected by colonial legislatures and the crown.

Albany Regency, informal group of leaders of Democratic party in N.Y. after 1820. Enforced party regularity and controlled elections, partly through SPOILS SYSTEM. Martin Van Buren was member. Slavery issue and quarrel between BARNBURNERS and HUNKERS led to decay; prestige dwindled after 1848.

albatross (âl'bûtrôs), sea bird, order of tube-nosed swimmers (includes petrels, shearwaters, fulmars), found chiefly in S Pacific. Wandering albatross (of Coleridge's *Rime of the Ancient Mariner*) has wingspread 10–12 ft.

Albee, Edward, 1928–, American playwright. His clever, often satiric, plays include the one-act *The Zoo Story* (1960) and *The American Dream* (1961) and the full-length *Who's Afraid of Virginia Woolf?* (1962), *Tiny Alice* (1964), and *A Delicate Balance* (1966).

Albemarle, George Monck or **Monk, 1st duke of:** see MONCK OR MONK, GEORGE.

Albemarle, town (pop. 12,261), central N.C., ENE of Charlotte; estab. 1842. Marketing center in timber, dairy, and grain region.

Albemarle Sound, arm of Atlantic Ocean, NE N.C., extending inland c.60 mi. Chowan and Roanoke rivers empty into it. Bridged near Edenton.

Albéniz, Isaac (ēsäk' älbä'nēth), 1860–1909, Spanish pianist and composer; used Spanish folk themes in his music. Best known is his piano suite, *Iberia.*

Alberdi, Juan Bautista (hwän' boutē'stä älbēr'dē), 1810–84, Argentine publicist, diplomat. Suggestions in his *Bases y puntos de partida para la organización política de la república argentina* were incorporated into 1853 constitution.

Alberoni, Giulio (jōō'lyō älbärō'nē), 1664–1752, Italian cardinal, chief minister to Philip V of Spain. His efforts to nullify Peace of Utrecht were stopped by Quadruple Alliance. Dismissed 1719.

Albert, rulers of Holy Roman Empire. **Albert I,** c.1250–1308, son of Rudolf I, was elected German king after his victory over ADOLF OF NASSAU (1298). Put down revolt of Rhenish archbishops and elector palatine (1300–1302); secured crowns of Hungary and Bohemia for his son Rudolf (1306). Assassinated by conspirators. **Albert II,** 1397–1439, German king and king of Bohemia and Hungary (1438–39); son-in-law of Emperor Sigismund. Was unable to suppress revolt of Bohemia. With him began continuous HAPSBURG rule over empire.

Albert I, 1875–1934, king of the Belgians (1909–34). Led Belgian resistance to German invasion in First World War; improved social conditions in Belgium and Belgian Congo; won great popularity through his democratic ways. Died in rock-climbing accident. Married Queen ELIZABETH 1900.

Albert (Prince Albert), 1819–61, royal consort of VICTORIA of Great Britain; son of Ernest I of Saxe-Coburg-Gotha. Initial unpopularity was modified through his devotion to queen and responsible concern with public affairs. His insistence on moderate approach to Trent affair may have averted war with the U.S.

Albert, A. Adrian, 1905–, American mathematician. Began teaching at Univ. of Chicago 1931. Noted for work in algebra and on numbers theory.

Albert, Lake: see ALBERT NYANZA.

Alberta, province (c.248,800 sq. mi.; with water surface 255,285 sq. mi.; pop. 1,331,944), W Canada; cap. EDMONTON. Other cities are CALGARY, LETHBRIDGE, MEDICINE HAT, and RED DEER. Westernmost of the Prairie Provs., it has grass-covered plains to S and woodlands to N. W in the Rockies are Banff, Jasper, and WatertonLakes national parks. Drained by Peace, Athabaska, Red Deer, St. Mary, and Milk rivers, and north and south branches of the Saskatchewan. Largest lakes are ATHABASKA and LESSER SLAVE. Population is centered in S and in wheatlands of Peace R. valley. Farming, supplemented by ranching and dairying, is basic industry. Province produces much of Canada's domestic supply of crude oil, natural gas, and coal. After exploration by fur traders in mid-18th cent., North West and Hudson's Bay companies estab. trading posts. Area ceded to Canada by Hudson's Bay Co. 1870 and incorporated into Northwest Territories. Became a district 1882, a province 1905. Canadian Pacific RR arrived 1883.

Alberta, University of, at Edmonton; provincially supported, coed.; chartered 1906, opened 1908. Affiliated are two men's colleges, St. Joseph's (R.C.) and St. Stephen's (United Church). Banff School of Fine Arts is one of its extensions.

Albert Canal, waterway, 81 mi. long, Belgium, from Meuse R. at Liège to Scheldt R. at Antwerp. Inaugurated 1939. Connects vital industrial area of Liège with Antwerp, chief Belgian port.

Alberti, Domenico (älbĕr'tē), c.1710–c.1740, Venetian composer. Developed a type of broken-chord bass accompaniment, now called Alberti bass.

Alberti, Leone Battista (lāo'nä bät-tēs'tä), 1404–72, Italian architect. Wrote the first printed book on architecture; it helped spread appreciation for the classical Roman style.

Albert Lea (lē), city (1965 pop. 18,454), S Minn., near Iowa line S of Minneapolis; settled 1835. A trade and mfg. center in a farm area.

Albert Nile: see BAHR-EL-JEBEL.

Albert Nyanza (nĭän'zŭ), lake, area 2,064 sq. mi., E central Africa, on border of Republic of the Congo and Uganda; part of Great Rift Valley. Alt. 2,018 ft., average depth 2,200 ft. Drained by Albert Nile. Also called L. Albert.

Albert of Brandenburg, 1490–1568, grand master of TEUTONIC KNIGHTS (1511–25), first duke of PRUSSIA (1525–68). Turned to Protestantism 1525 and transformed dominions of his order into hereditary duchy, under Polish suzerainty.

Albert the Bear, c.1100–1170, first margrave of Brandenburg (1150–1170). A loyal follower of Lothair II and Conrad III, he temporarily held Austria and Saxony, but is most notable for obtaining, partly by peaceful methods, the Wendish territory of BRANDENBURG. He helped to Christianize NE Germany.

Albertus Magnus (Albert the Great), b. 1193 or 1206, d. 1280, scholastic philosopher, who attempted in his *Summa theologiae* to reconcile Aristotelianism and Christian doctrine. His pupil was Thomas Aquinas. Albertus was deeply interested in natural science.

Albertville (älbĕrvēl') town (pop. c.30,000), E Republic of the Congo, on L. Tanganyika. Rail-steamer transfer point and commercial center; mfg. of textiles and cement.

Albi (älbē'), city (est. pop. 34,693), cap. of Tarn dept., S France. Famous as former center of the ALBIGENSES and for well-preserved medieval architecture (mostly in red brick), including Gothic cathedral, episcopal palace, 11th-cent. bridge.

Albigenses (ălbĭjĕn'sēz), religious group of S France, strong in 12th and 13th cent. Officially called heretics, they were actually non-Christian Cathari who believed in absolute Manichaean dualism of good and evil and held that Jesus lived only in semblance. An ascetic, enthusiastic sect, the Albigenses had powerful preachers and gained protectors—notably RAYMOND VI of Toulouse (backed by the Catholic Peter II of Aragon). St. Bernard of Clairvaux tried to convert them, as did the Dominicans. Murder of a Cistercian set off the **Albigensian Crusade,** proclaimed by Pope Innocent III (1208). Troops led by Simon de Montfort in interests of France turned this into a political affair and victory at Muret (1213) paved the way for Louis IX of France to get Toulouse (1229) from Ray-

mond VII, son of Raymond VI. Use of the Inquisition and ardent preaching converted Albigensians slowly.

albino (ălbī'nō), animal or plant entirely lacking pigmentation. In animals the absence of pigment is observed in the body covering (skin, hair, and feathers) and in the iris of the eye. Blood vessels of the iris show through, giving it a pinkish color, and eyes are very sensitive to light. Albinism is inherited as a Mendelian recessive character.

Albion, ancient and literary name of Britain.

Albion (ăl'bĕŭn). **1** City (pop. 2,025), SE Ill., E. of Belleville; founded 1818 by Englishmen led by Morris Birkbeck and George Flower. **2** Industrial city (pop. 12,749), S Mich., on Kalamazoo R., S of Lansing; settled 1833. Seat of Albion Col.

Albo, Joseph, c.1380–1444, Jewish philosopher of religion, b. Spain. Based Judaism on principles of existence of God, revelation, divine retribution.

Alboin (ăl'boin), d. 572?, Lombard chieftain. Conquered most of N and central Italy (568–72); crowned first Lombard king 569. See also ROSAMOND.

Alborg, Denmark: see AALBORG.

Albornoz, Gil Álvarez Carrillo de (hēl' äl'väräth kärē'lyō dä älbôrnōth'), 1310?–1367, cardinal, Spanish and papal statesman and general. Sent (1353) by pope (then at Avignon) as legate to Papal States and entered Rome with RIENZI. Temporarily restored papal authority in Marches and Romagna.

Albrecht. For rulers thus named, see ALBERT.

Albret, Jeanne d': see JEANNE D'ALBRET.

Albret (älbrā'), former fief, SW France, in the Landes of Gascony. By his marriage (1494) with the heiress of Foix, Lord Jean d'Albret acquired Navarre, Foix, and Béarn. His son, Henri d'Albret, married (1527) Margaret of Navarre, who had inherited Armagnac from her first husband. In 1556 Albret was made a duchy. Henry IV of France, son of JEANNE D'ALBRET, added duchy to royal domain (1607).

albumin (ălbū'mĭn), member of class of PROTEINS that is water soluble and coagulated by heat. Varieties are found widely in plant and animal tissues, e.g., egg white, muscle, blood serum, wheat. In humans it helps to transport drugs and organic acids and to control water distribution throughout circulatory system. Used in treatment of shock as well as in textile printing, dye fixation, and sugar refining.

Albuquerque, Afonso de (äfō'zō dù äl″bùkĕr'kù), 1453–1515, Portuguese admiral, founder of Portuguese Empire in East. Succeeded Almeida in India; took Goa (1510), Malacca (1511), also Socotra Isl. and Hormuz. Died off Goa after his dismissal.

Albuquerque (ăl'bùkûr″kē), city (pop. 201,189), W central N.Mex., on upper Rio Grande R., SW of Santa Fe; old town founded 1706, new town platted 1880. State's largest city, it is important commercial, industrial, and transportation center of timber, livestock, and farm area. Has railroad shops. Indian jewelry and curios are made. In mountain region, it is also health resort with many sanatoriums and hospitals (incl. U.S. veterans' hospital and U.S. Indian hospital). Here are Univ. of NEW MEXICO, U.S. school for Indians, Church of San Felipe de Neri (1706), and old-town plaza. Kirtland Air Force Base and several Indian pueblos and reservations are nearby.

Alcaeus (ălsē'ùs), d. c.580 B.C., Greek lyric poet, associate of Sappho. His Alcaic strophe (ălkā'ĭk) was widely imitated by the Greeks and by Horace.

Alcalá de Henares (älkälä' dä änä'räs), town (pop. 25,123), Madrid prov., central Spain, in New Castile. Great university founded 1508; transferred to Madrid 1836. Birthplace of Cervantes.

Alcalá Zamora, Niceto (nēthä'tō älkälä' thämō'rä), 1877–1949, first president (1931–36) of Spanish republic, a middle-of-the-road liberal.

alcalde (älkäl'dē) [Span., from Arabic,= the judge], Spanish official title. In 11th cent. it designated a judge with certain administrative functions. Since

19th cent. it has stood for chief of municipal government and representative of central government.

Alcamenes (ăl"kŭmē'nēz), 5th cent. B.C., Athenian sculptor. His *Aphrodite of the Gardens* was one of the great masterpieces of antiquity.

Alcántara (älkän'tärä), town (pop. 3,564), Cáceres prov., W Spain, in Estremadura. Military religious Order of Alcántara founded here in 13th cent. Roman bridge and ruins of order's church and convent survive.

Alcatraz (ăl'kŭträz), rocky isl. in San Francisco Bay, W Calif. Fortified by Spanish. Used as U.S. military prison after 1859 and Federal prison after 1933. Was symbol of impregnable fortress prison, with maximum security. Closed 1963.

Alcazarquivir (älkä"thärkēvēr'), city (pop. c.34,035), W Morocco. At this place in 1578 Ahmed IV's Moroccan army decisively defeated the Portuguese forces led by King Sebastian, who was killed.

Alcestis (ălsĕ'stĭs), in Greek mythology, daughter of Pelias. She married ADMETUS, who met her father's demand that suitor come for her in chariot drawn by wild animals. Her wifely devotion led her to sacrifice herself to save her husband's life.

alchemy (ăl'kŭmē), learning, originating either in anc. Egypt or China, and dealing with attempts to change one substance into another (notably to turn base metals into gold). The alchemical belief in a miraculous philosopher's stone may have originated in Alexandria. Alchemy was influenced by Hellenistic philosophy, later (probably after 8th cent.) by Moslems. In 12th cent. it reached Europe through the Arabs. There the art, though symbolic and cryptic, gave rise gradually to modern chemistry. The TRANSMUTATION OF ELEMENTS has now been accomplished. Alchemy long a sister science of astrology.

Alcibiades (ălsĭbī'ŭdēz), c.450–404 B.C., Athenian statesman. Leader in the struggle against Sparta in the PELOPONNESIAN WAR, he was defeated at Mantinea (418 B.C.). Promoted Sicilian campaign (415), but was accused (probably falsely) of sacrilege and was called home for trial. Instead he fled to Sparta (where he counseled Agis I), then to Persian lands. Back in Athens after 411, he won a naval victory (410), but Athenian forces were defeated at Notium (406) by Lysander, who procured the murder of Alcibiades (then in exile).

Alcinoüs (ălsĭ'nōŭs), in Greek legend, father of Nausicaä, host to Odysseus and to Jason and Medea.

Alciphron (ăl'sĭfrŏn), fl. A.D. c.200?, Greek satirist. Wrote imaginary letters, supposedly by Athenians of 4th cent. B.C.

Alcmaeon (ălkmē'ŭn), in Greek legend, one of the EPIGONI. Having killed his mother, Eriphyle, for the murder of his father, he was pursued by the Furies. Later, for his wife Callirrhoë, he tried to get the robe and necklace of Harmonia from his former wife, Arsinoë, but was killed.

Alcmaeonidae (ălk"mēō'nĭdē), powerful Athenian family, 7th–5th cent. B.C. Members were CLEISTHENES, PERICLES, and ALCIBIADES.

Alcmene (ălkmē'nē), in Greek legend, wife of AMPHITRYON. She bore twins, Hercules by Zeus and Iphicles by Amphitryon.

Alcoa (ălkō'ů), industrial city (pop. 6,395), E Tenn., S of Knoxville. Founded 1913 by Aluminum Co. of America, which had large reduction plants here.

Alcobaça (älkōōbä'sů), town (pop. 5,174), Leiria dist., W central Portugal, in Estremadura. Cistercian abbey (begun 1152), greatest of medieval Portugal, is burial place of early kings.

alcohol, organic compound of carbon, hydrogen, and oxygen. Molecule has one or more hydroxyl radicals (see HYDROXIDE) linked to carbon atoms not involved in a benzene ring. In popular use, alcohol means ETHYL ALCOHOL. Classes (by number of hydroxyl groups in molecule): monohydric (one group), e.g.,

methyl; dihydric (two groups), e.g., glycol; trihydric (three groups), e.g., glycerin.

alcoholism, abnormal and persistent desire to drink excessive amounts of ethyl alcohol; also, the condition resulting from that drinking. Acute form connected with action of alcohol on central nervous system. Chronic alcoholism is generally considered a symptom of psychic instability. It may produce psychological and structural changes. Problem attacked through scientific studies, clinics for inebriates, organizations such as Alcoholics Anonymous (founded 1934), and Research Council on Problems of Alcohol (organized 1937).

Alcott, (Amos) Bronson (ôl'kŭt), 1799–1888, American educational reformer, transcendentalist philosopher; father of Louisa May Alcott. Founded Temple School (Boston, 1834), "Fruitlands" community (1843). Both failed, but ideas gained notice.

Alcott, Louisa May, 1832–88, American author. *Little Women* is her beloved classic of girls' literature. Among other works (many in series) are *Little Men* (1871), *Eight Cousins* (1875), and *Jo's Boys* (1886).

Alcuin (ăl'kwĭn), 735?–804, English churchman, scholar at court of Charlemagne, center of Carolingian renaissance. He estab. study of the seven liberal arts which became the curriculum for medieval Western Europe.

Aldan (ŭldän'), city (pop. 12,200), Yakut ASSR, RSFSR, in E Siberia. Gold mining.

Aldanov, Mark (ŭldä'nŭf), pseud. of Mark Aleksandrovich Landau, 1886–1957, Russian author. Went to France after 1917, to America in 1941; became U.S. citizen. Among his works are the tetralogy *The Thinker* (4 vols., 1921–27; on the Napoleonic era) and, on Bolshevism, *The Fifth Seal* (1939), *The Escape* (1950), and *To Live As We Wish* (1952).

aldehyde (ăl'dĭhĭd), organic compound with a carbon-hydrogen-oxygen (CHO) group. Used in synthetic resins and dyestuffs. The term aldehyde is often used to mean acetaldehyde, prepared from oxidation of ethyl alcohol; oxidizes to acetic acid. FORMALDEHYDE is simplest aldehyde. See also FURFURAL.

Alden, John, c.1599–1687, Puritan settler in Plymouth Colony. His marriage to Priscilla Mullens gave rise to the romantic legend made familiar by Longfellow's poem *The Courtship of Miles Standish*.

Alder, Kurt (äl'dŭr), 1902–58, German organic chemist. Shared 1950 Nobel Prize in Chemistry for discovering and developing Diels-Alder reaction, a method of synthesis of benzene ring hydrocarbons.

alder, deciduous tree and shrub of genus *Alnus*, with conelike fruits, widely found in N Hemisphere. Bark of black alder is used for dyes and tanning, wood of Western red alder for furniture.

Alderney: see CHANNEL ISLANDS.

Aldershot, municipal borough (pop. 31,260), Hampshire, England; site of largest and most complete military training center (estab. 1854) in United Kingdom.

Aldington, Richard (ôl–), 1892–, English poet. Once a leader of imagists, he later opposed them. Also a novelist, biographer, editor, and translator.

Aldrich, Nelson Wilmarth, 1841–1915, U.S. Senator from R.I. (1881–1911). Spokesman of big business in Republican party. Co-author of Payne-Aldrich Tariff Act (1909). Concerned with monetary problems.

Aldrich, Thomas Bailey, 1836–1907, American author, editor. His *Story of a Bad Boy* (1870) is based on his Portsmouth, N.H., boyhood. Edited (1881–90) *Atlantic Monthly*.

Aldus Manutius (mùnū'shùs), 1450–1515, Venetian printer, humanist. Through Aldine Press (with dolphin and anchor mark), made classical manuscripts available to scholars. Had *italic* type designed (1501).

ale: see BEER.

Aleandro, Girolamo (jĕrō'lämō älään'drō), 1480–1542, Italian scholar, cardinal of the Roman Church, called Hieronymus Aleander. He obtained the condemnation of Luther at Diet of Worms (1521).

Alecsandri, Vasile (väsē'lĕ älĕksän'drē), 1821–90, Rumanian poet and statesman.

Alegría, Ciro (sē'rō älägrē'ä), 1909–67, Peruvian novelist. Wrote novels of social protest, e.g., *El mundo es ancho y ajeno* (Latin American Novel Prize, 1941; Eng. tr., *Broad and Alien Is the World,* 1941).

Aleichem, Sholom (shō'lŭm älā'khŭm) [Heb.,= Peace be upon you! (a Yiddish greeting)], 1859–1916, author of tragicomic Yiddish tales about late 19th-cent. Russian Jewry. His *Tevye der Milchiger* was adapted for the stage as "Fiddler on the Roof." Real name Sholem Rabinowitz.

Aleijadinho (ûlā"zhŭdē'nyō), 1730–1814, Brazilian sculptor, b. Minas Gerais. Though crippled, he created fine Churrigueresque church sculpture.

Alekhine, Alexander (ûlyĕkh'ēn), 1892–1946, Russian-French chess player. He was world champion 1927–35, 1937–46.

Aleksandropol: see LENINAKAN, Armenia.

Aleksandrov (ûlyĭksän'drŭf), city (pop. c.36,600), W central European RSFSR. Residence of Ivan IV (1564–81). Site of first printing plant in Russia.

Aleksandrov-Grushevski: see SHAKHTY.

Aleksandrovsk, Ukraine: see ZAPOROZHE.

Aleksandrovsk-Sakhalinski (ûlyĭksän'drŭfsk-sŭkhŭlyēn'skē), city (pop. 21,900), SE Asiatic RSFSR, on N Sakhalin; port on Tatar Strait. Coal mining.

Alemán, Mateo (mätä'ō älämän'), 1547–1614?, Spanish novelist, author of picaresque *Guzmán de Alfarache* (two parts, 1599, 1604).

Alemán, Miguel (mēgĕl' älämän'), 1902–, president of Mexico (1946–52).

Alemanni (ălĭmä'nĭ), Germanic tribe which settled in upper Italy in 3d cent. and along Rhine (present Alsace, Baden, NE Switzerland) in 5th cent. Defeated by Franks under Clovis I (496), they retired to Rhaetia, and in 536 passed under Frankish rule. High German dialects of SW Germany and Switzerland are called Alemannic. See also GERMANS.

Alembert, Jean le Rond d' (zhä' lù rō däläbâr'), 1717–83, French mathematician and philosopher. As coeditor of Diderot's ENCYCLOPÉDIE he wrote its remarkable "Preliminary discourse." For his work in dynamics, see D'ALEMBERT'S PRINCIPLE.

Alemtejo, Portugal: see ALENTEJO.

Alençon, François, duc d': see FRANCIS, duke of Alençon and Anjou.

Alençon (äläsō'), town (est. pop. 21,893), cap. of Orne dept., N France, on Sarthe R.; famous for lace.

Alentejo (äläntä'zhō), historic province, SE Portugal, now divided into Upper Alentejo (4,888 sq. mi.; pop. c.219,895; cap. Évora) and Lower Alentejo (5,318 sq. mi.; pop. c.276,895; cap. Beja). "Granary of Portugal"; also livestock, wine, olives, fruit. Formerly spelled Alemtejo.

Alep (ûlĕp') or **Aleppo** (ûlĕ'pō), city (pop. 407,613), NW Syria. Was the Greek and biblical Beroea or Berea. Ancient city on main caravan route across Syria to Baghdad, center of a Hittite kingdom before 1000 B.C. Flourished as city of Byzantine Empire. Taken by Arabs in 7th cent. and by Seljuk Turks in 11th cent. Crusaders besieged it unsuccessfully 1124, Saladin took it 1183. Mongols seized Alep in 1260 and 1401. Held by the Turks (1517–1832, 1840–1920) and by Egypt (1832–40). Produces silk and cotton textiles; trades in wool, hides, and fruit.

Alès (älĕs'), formerly **Alais** (älä', älĕs'), city (est. pop. 36,893), Gard dept., S France. Industrial and coal-mining region.

Alesia (ûlē'zhû), town in anc. Gaul, held by Vercingetorix, besieged by Caesar (52 B.C.). Its surrender because of starvation marked the end of Gallic resistance.

Alessandria (älĕs-sän'drēä), city (pop. 92,291), cap. of Alessandria prov., in Piedmont, N Italy. Commerce and mfg. (felt hats). Founded 1168 as Lombard League stronghold.

Alesund or **Aalesund,** Nor. *Ålesund* (all: ô'lùsöōn), city (pop. 18,957), W Norway, on three small islands at mouth of Stor Fjord. Largest Norwegian fishing harbor; whaling base.

Aletsch (ä'lĕch), largest glacier (66 sq. mi.) of Swiss Alps, between Jungfrau and Aletschhorn (13,721 ft.), one of highest in Bernese Alps.

Aleutian Islands (ûlōō'shŭn), chain of volcanic islands SW from tip of Alaska Peninsula and approaching Russian Komandorski Isls. Partially submerged, they are a continuation of Aleutian Range dividing the Bering Sea from the Pacific. There are four main groups. Fox Isls. nearest Alaska include Unimak, Unalaska (with Dutch Harbor on small Amaknak Isl.) and Umnak. Andreanof Isls. are many, including Adak. Important in Rat Isls. are Amchitka and Kiska. Near Isls., farthest W and smallest group of all, include Attu. Islands are generally rugged, of volcanic action, and have few good harbors, owing to reefs. Temperature is relatively moderate, but fog is constant. They are almost completely treeless with dense vegetation. Vitus BERING discovered islands 1741. Russian fur traders exploited native Aleuts. Fishing and fur hunting are now state controlled. Dutch Harbor became transshipping point for Nome 1900, and U.S. naval base 1940. Japanese occupied Attu and Kiska 1942–43; withdrawal forced by bitter U.S. fighting.

Aleutian Range, mountain chain, SW Alaska, extending along entire Alaska Peninsula and continuing, partly submerged, in Aleutian Isls. Violent volcanic eruption was notable at Katmai, now in KATMAI NATIONAL MONUMENT.

Alexander III, d. 1181, pope (1159–81), a Sienese named Orlando Bandinelli. A learned canon lawyer, he issued many legal rules for governing church. Backed Lombard League in opposing Emperor Frederick I, who exiled him to France. His rule contested by antipopes until 1178. Convened Third LATERAN COUNCIL.

Alexander VI, 1431–1503, pope (1492–1503), a Spaniard named Rodrigo de Borja (of BORGIA family). Notorious in following centuries as corrupt and worldly Renaissance pope, he showered money and favors on his children by a Roman woman, Cesare and Lucrezia Borgia. Opposed Charles VIII of France, who invaded Italy. Proclaimed the line of demarcation between Spanish and Portuguese colonial spheres (1494).

Alexander, emperors of Russia. **Alexander I,** 1777–1825? (reigned 1801–25), succeeded his father, PAUL I, in whose murder he may have had indirect part. His early liberalism did not lead to internal reform. Alexander joined coalition against NAPOLEON I (1805); was defeated at Austerlitz, Friedland; made peace at TILSIT 1807. After repulsing French invasion (1812), led allies into Paris (1814) and attended Congress of VIENNA. Under influence of Metternich and Julie de KRÜDENER he turned to extreme reaction and promoted HOLY ALLIANCE. Officially, he died at Taganrog; according to popular belief–shared by some historians–he retired to live in penitence as a hermit. His tomb, opened 1926, was empty. His brother, Nicholas I, succeeded him. **Alexander II,** 1818–81, son of Nicholas I, reigned 1855–81. A liberal reformer, he abolished serfdom (1861; see EMANCIPATION, EDICT OF), introduced ZEMSTVO system of local government and new judicial system (1864). Reforms did not satisfy the radicals. Terrorism and NIHILISM increased; led to Alexander's assassination. Other events of reign: end of CRIMEAN WAR; Russian expansion in Asia; and Russo-Turkish War of 1877–78. Succeeded by his son, **Alexander III,** 1845–94 (reigned 1881–94), a fanatic reactionary. Fostered persecution of Jews and forcible Russification of minorities. Suppressed liberal thought, but promoted peace policy and industrial development. Nicholas II succeeded him.

Alexander, 1893–1920, king of the Hellenes (1917–20). Succeeded his deposed father, Constantine, with aid of Allies, who favored him over his elder brother (later King George II).

Alexander, kings of Scotland. Alexander I, 1078?–1124, ruled 1107–24. He opposed English efforts to rule church in Scotland. Estab. abbeys at Inchcolm and Scone. **Alexander II,** 1198–1249, ruled 1214–49. **Alexander III,** 1241–86, ruled 1249–86. Acquired for Scotland Western Isles and Isle of Man, already claimed from Norway. After his death struggle between ROBERT I and John de BALIOL (1249–1315) began.

Alexander, rulers of Serbia and Yugoslavia. **Alexander** (Alexander Karageorgevich), 1806–85, prince of Serbia (1842–58); son of KARAGEORGE. Deposed. **Alexander** (Alexander Obrenovich), 1876–1903, king of Serbia (1889–1903); son and successor of MILAN. Abolished liberal constitution 1894. His marriage in 1900 to Draga Mashin, a lady of scandalous past, aggravated the opposition. Royal couple was assassinated by an army clique, the Obrenovich dynasty deposed, and Peter I made king. **Alexander,** 1888–1934, king of Yugoslavia (1921–34); son and successor of Peter I. Became regent of kingdom of Serbs, Croats, and Slovenes 1918; ruled dictatorially 1929–31 to unify kingdom, which he renamed Yugoslavia. Antagonized Croatian and Macedonian separatists. In foreign policy he was loyal to French alliance and LITTLE ENTENTE. Assassinated, with Louis BARTHOU, by Yugoslav terrorist at Marseilles, France.

Alexander (Alexander of BATTENBERG), 1857–93, prince of Bulgaria (1879–86). He was elected with Russian support and ruled under Turkish overlordship. His annexation of E RUMELIA (1885) antagonized Russia and caused Serbia to declare war. Though victorious, he was deposed by a pro-Russian faction.

Alexander, in Greek legend, another name for PARIS.

Alexander, Grover Cleveland, 1887–1950, American baseball player. One of game's great right-hand pitchers; pitched 696 games, won 373.

Alexander, Harold Rupert Leofric George, Earl Alexander of Tunis, 1891–, British field marshal. In Second World War commanded retreats of Dunkirk and Burma and triumphs in N Africa and Sicily. Governor general of Canada 1946–52. Made defense minister in Churchill cabinet 1952.

Alexander, Samuel, 1859–1938, British naturalist philosopher. He held that space-time was ultimate principle of all existence.

Alexander, Sir William, d. 1640: see STIRLING, WILLIAM ALEXANDER, EARL OF.

Alexander Archipelago, just off SE Alaska. It and mountainous coast make up Alaska's Panhandle, the state's most populous area. A submerged mountain system, the islands rise steeply from sea. Deep channels separate them, cut them from the mainland, making part of the Inside Passage from Seattle to Alaska. Included are CHICHAGOF ISLAND, ADMIRALTY ISLAND, BARANOF ISLAND (with Sitka), WRANGELL ISLAND (with Wrangell), REVILLAGIGEDO ISLAND (with Ketchikan), and PRINCE OF WALES ISLAND.

Alexander Balas (bā′–), d. 145 B.C., ruler of Syria. Seized power from his uncle Demetrius I. Jonathan the Maccabee supported him. Eventually defeated by Ptolemy Philometor. 1 Mac. 10–11.

Alexander Bay, town (pop. c.900), NW Cape Prov., Republic of South Africa, at mouth of Orange R. Rich alluvial diamond deposits.

Alexander City, city (pop. 13,140), E central Ala., SE of Birmingham, in farm area; founded mid-19th cent. on site of Indian village.

Alexander Nevski, Saint (nĕv′skē), 1220–1263, grand duke of Vladimir-Suzdal; Russian national hero. Defeated Swedes on the Neva (1240) and Livonian Knights near Lake Peipus (1242).

Alexander of Hales (hālz), d. 1245, English scholastic philosopher, called the Unanswerable Doctor, a Franciscan who taught at Univ. of Paris. Introduced Aristotle as authority in systematic exposition of Christian doctrine.

Alexander Severus (Marcus Aurelius Alexander Severus) (sĭvēr′ŭs), d. 235, Roman emperor (222–35).

Alexanderson, Ernest Frederik Werner, 1878–, American electrical engineer and inventor, b. Uppsala, Sweden. Pioneered in use of electricity for ship and railroad propulsion; noted for work in television.

Alexander the Great (Alexander III), 356–323 B.C., king of Macedon (336–323); son of PHILIP II. He put down rebellion in Greece, and in 334 he undertook what was to be the widest conquest of ancient times. Victories at the Granicus (334), the Issus (333), and Gaugamela (or Arbela, 331) punctuated his seizure of Asia Minor, peaceful occupation of Egypt, and overthrow of the Persian Empire of Darius III. He pushed on through Bactria and into India. There his men refused to go farther. A fleet was sent back under Nearchus, but Alexander led his men back across deserts, reaching Susa in 324. Married Roxana, a Bactrian princess, and adopted Persian ways. Died of a fever at 33. One of the greatest generals of all time, he was also one of the most romantic figures of antiquity. His great empire was broken by wars of the DIADOCHI.

Alexandra, 1844–1925, queen consort of Edward VII of Great Britain; daughter of Christian IX of Denmark. Married Edward 1863.

Alexandra, Mount: see RUWENZORI.

Alexandra Feodorovna (fēŏ″dŭrŏv′nŭ), 1872–1918, Russian empress, consort of NICHOLAS II; a Hessian princess, granddaughter of Queen Vietoria. Under influence of RASPUTIN, she encouraged tsar's reactionary policies. Shot by Bolsheviks 1918.

Alexandretta, Turkey: see ISKENDERUN.

Alexandretta, sanjak of (sän″jäk′, ä″līgzän̄drĕ′tŭ), former name of Hatay prov. (2,141 sq. mi.; pop. 441,-209), S Turkey, comprising cities of Antioch (now Antakya) and its port Alexandretta (now Iskenderun). Awarded 1920 to Syria, given autonomous status 1937. Turkish-Arab riots resulted 1938 in joint military control by France and Turkey. To Turkey 1939.

Alexandria, Arabic *Al Iskandariya,* city (pop. 1,513,-000), N Egypt, major Mediterranean port. Estab. 332 B.C. by Alexander the Great. Cap. of the Ptolemies (304–30 B.C.), it received much Mediterranean trade and soon outgrew Carthage to become largest city in West. The great center of Hellenistic and Jewish culture. Became part of Roman Empire (30 B.C.) and was greatest provincial cap. with free population of 300,000. In 642 fell to the Arabs who moved the cap. to modern Cairo. Today handles most of Egypt's foreign trade.

Alexandria. 1 City (pop. 40,279), central La., on Red R., SW of Shreveport, in cotton, sugar-cane, and timber area; laid out 1810. England Air Force Base is NNW. **2** City (pop. 6,713), W Minn., SE of Fergus Falls, in farm and lake-resort area; settled 1857. Has KENSINGTON RUNE STONE. **3** City (pop. 91,023), N Va., S of Washington, D.C., on Potomac R. Primarily a residential suburb. Has railroad yards and repair shops. Permanently settled in early 18th cent., it was part of D.C., 1789–1847. Its historic buildings (many associated with George Washington) include Gadsby's Tavern (1752), Carlyle House (1752), Christ Church (1767–73), and Ramsay House (1749–51). George Washington Masonic Natl. Memorial Temple has Washington mementos. Woodlawn, Washington family estate, was made nat. shrine 1949. Mt. Vernon is nearby.

Alexandria Bay, resort village (pop. 1,583), N N.Y., on St. Lawrence, N of Watertown. Nearby Thousand Isls. Bridge spans St. Lawrence to Canada.

alexandrine, in prosody, a line of 12 syllables (or 13 if the last syllable is unstressed), deriving its name probably from a 12th-cent. French romance about Alexander. Rhyming alexandrine couplets of equal length are the classic French poetic form (in works of Ronsard, Corneille, Racine). In English an iambic hexameter line is often called an alexandrine; used notably by SPENSER in Spenserian stanza.

Alexandroupolis (ălĕksăndrōō'pōlēs), city (pop. 18,-712), W Thrace, Greece, near Turkish border, on Aegean Sea. Agr., trading, and commercial center with rail connections to Salonica and Adrianople. Originally called Dedeagach.

Alexis, 1629–76, tsar of Russia (1645–76), successor of Michael Romanov. He acquired part of Ukraine, began a schism by deposing Patriarch NIKON, suppressed Stenka RAZIN rebellion, and promulgated law code of 1648, which favored landowners but tied peasants to soil. His son Feodor III succeeded him. Peter the Great was his son by a second marriage.

Alexius (ŭlĕk'sēŭs), Byzantine emperors. **Alexius I** (Comnenus), 1048–1118; nephew of Isaac I. Gained throne by overthrowing Nicephorus III (1081). Withstood Norman invasions under ROBERT GUISCARD and BOHEMOND; defeated Petchenegs (1091) and Cumans (1095). In the First Crusade he persuaded leaders to pledge their conquests to him, later forced Bohemond to recognize his suzerainty over Antioch. His last years brought struggle with the Turks and intrigues of his daughter ANNA COMNENA against his son John II. Restored Byzantine prestige. **Alexius III** (Angelus), d. after 1210. Gained throne by deposing his brother ISAAC II (1195). This gave the leaders of the Fourth Crusade a pretext for attacking Constantinople (1203). Alexius III fled; Isaac was restored, with his son **Alexius IV** (d. 1204) as joint emperor. In 1204 **Alexius V** (Ducas Mourtzouphlos), son-in-law of Alexius III, led the Byzantine national party in the overthrow of Isaac and Alexius IV. This act brought the sack of Constantinople by the Crusaders, who had Alexius V executed (1204) and set up the Latin Empire of Constantinople.

alfalfa or **lucern**, perennial (*Medicago sativa*). North America's most important hay and pasture plant. High protein content and prolific growth. Valued in crop rotation and soil improvement because of nitrogen-fixing bacteria in roots.

Al-Farabi, d. 950, Arabian philosopher, who continued the tradition of Al-Kindi. He adapted Aristotelian thought to the Islamic tradition.

Alfieri, Vittorio, Conte (vĕt-tō'rēō kōn'tä älfyä'rē), 1749–1803, Italian tragic poet, b. Piedmont. After a dissipated youth, he became a poet and poured his hatred of tyranny into tragedies, intentionally harsh and unornamented—*Saul* (1782), *Antigone* (1783), *Maria Stuart* (1804). Also wrote comedies, satires, political tracts, autobiography. Allied with Louisa, countess of Albany.

Alfonsine tables, improved revision of Ptolemaic planetary tables, made at Toledo by astronomers assembled by Alfonso X of Spain. Completed c.1252; printed 1483 in Venice.

Alfonso, kings of Aragon. **Alfonso I**, d. 1134, king of Aragon and Navarre (1104–34), husband of URRACA of Castile. Took Saragossa and Calatayud from Moors. **Alfonso II**, 1152–96, king of Aragon (1164–96), count of Barcelona (1162–96). Inherited Provence (1166); Roussillon (1172). Wrote Provençal poetry. **Alfonso V** (the Magnanimous), 1396–1458, king of Aragon and Sicily (1416–58), became king of Naples (1443–58) after defeating René of Anjou. His splendid court at Naples was center of arts and letters.

Alfonso, kings of Portugal. **Alfonso I** (Port. *Afonso Henriques*), 1111?–1185, became first king of Portugal (1139), took Santarém and Lisbon (1147). **Alfonso II** (the Fat), 1185–1223, reigned 1211–23. **Alfonso III** (Port. *Afonso o Bolonhez*), 1210–79, reigned 1248–79. Completed reconquest of Portugal from Moors; quarreled with Alfonso X of Castile over Algarve, and with Church; and called Cortes of Leiria (1254; first to include commoners). Fostered commerce and cultural revival. **Alfonso IV**, 1291–1357, reigned 1325–57. Approved murder of Inés de CASTRO. **Alfonso V** (the African), 1432–81, reigned 1438–81. Took Tangier

(1471). His marriage with Juana la Beltraneja led to unsuccessful war with Ferdinand and Isabella. **Alfonso VI** (the Victorious), 1643–83, reigned 1656–67. Physically and mentally defective, he yet ousted his mother from regency with aid of count of Castelho Melhor, who took over the government and repulsed the Spanish in 1663. Alfonso's wife, Marie Françoise of Savoy, and his brother (later Peter II) forced him to abdicate. After having her marriage annulled, the queen married Peter, who ruled as regent.

Alfonso, Spanish kings. **Alfonso I** (the Catholic), 693?–757, king of Asturias (739–57), conquered parts of Galicia, Leon, and Santander from Moors. **Alfonso III** (the Great), 838?–911?, king of Asturias (866–910?), consolidated kingdom. **Alfonso V** (the Noble), 994?–1027, king of Asturias and Leon (999–1027), gave Leon its *fuero* [code of laws]. **Alfonso VI**, 1030–1109, king of Leon (1065–1109) and Castile (1072–1109), took Galicia from his brother García (1073), and Toledo from Moors (1085). His court at Toledo was meeting place of Christian and Moorish cultures. **Alfonso VII** (the Emperor), 1104–57, king of Castile and Leon (1126–57). Recovered places lost by his mother, URRACA, to her second husband; had himself crowned emperor in Leon (1135); and took Almería from Moors. **Alfonso VIII** (the Noble), 1155–1214, king of Castile (1158–1214), won great victory of Navas de Tolosa (1212) over Moors. **Alfonso X** (the Wise), 1221–84, king of Castile and Leon (1252–84), grandson of Emperor Philip of Swabia, was elected German king (1256) by faction of German princes, but renounced claim in 1275. Took Cádiz from Moors (1262). Patron of learning; largely responsible for great legal compilation, *Siete partidas*, and ALFONSINE TABLES. **Alfonso XI**, 1311–50, king of Castile and Leon (1312–50), defeated Moors at Tarifa (1340), took Algeciras (1344), died in siege of Gibraltar. **Alfonso XII**, 1857–85, king of Spain (1870–85), son of Isabella II, lived in exile (1868–75) during Carlist revolt. Proclaimed king 1874; returned to Madrid 1875 and restored order. **Alfonso XIII**, 1886–1941, king of Spain (1886–1931), supported dictatorship of Primo de Rivera (1923–30). Went into exile when republicans won election (1931).

Alfred [Old Eng. Ælfred], 849–99, king of Wessex (871–99), sometimes called Alfred the Great. Victory over Danes at Ashdown being followed by defeats, he decided, in face of their threat to overrun England, to pay DANEGELD. His flight to the fens of Somerset (878) gave basis for legend of Alfred and the cakes. Victory over Danes at Ethandun (Edington) led to program of reform and to code of laws combining Christian doctrine with strong centralized monarchy. His greatest achievements were creation of a navy, revival of learning among the clergy, education for youths and nobles at court, the establishment of old English literary prose, his own English translation of Latin works, and his influence on extant form of ANGLO-SAXON CHRONICLE. Many heroic legends later embroidered his career. See editions of his own works and contemporary biography by Bishop Asser, *Life of King Alfred* (1906).

Alfred, village (1965 pop. 3,383), SW N.Y., SW of Hornell. Alfred Univ. is here.

Alfred University, at Alfred, N.Y., near Hornell; state and private support; coed.; opened as school 1836, chartered 1857 as Alfred Univ. Its college of ceramics is affiliated with State Univ. of New York.

Alfsborg, county, Sweden: see ALVSBORG.

algae (ăl'jē), primitive plants lacking true roots, stems, leaves, and flowers, but having chlorophyll. Chief aquatic plants in fresh and salt water (including pond scum and SEAWEED) are algae, ranging from microscopic size to 100 ft. long (e.g., kelp). Most do not move, but certain microscopic forms have flagella. Different types of algae have various combinations of pigments; classes of algae include the blue-green, green, yellow-green, golden-brown, brown, and red algae. Algae serve as food for many small and large animals; they indirectly provide food for many carnivorous animals. See also DIATOM; GULFWEED; IRISH MOSS. See *ill.*, p. 859.

Algardi, Alessandro (älĕs-sän'drō älgär'dē), 1595–1654, Italian baroque classicist sculptor, b. Bologna. Second only to Bernini in 17th-cent. Rome.

Algarve (älgär'vù), southernmost province (1,958 sq. mi.; pop. c.314,841), Portugal; cap. Faro. Grows much fruit; has offshore tuna and sardine fisheries.

Al-Gazel: see AL-GHAZALI.

algebra, branch of mathematics which generalizes arithmetic operations. Elementary algebra achieves this by use of letters to represent numbers. Product of several numbers and letters, e.g., a term such as $6xy^3$, depends on values of unknowns x and y; number 6 is a coefficient; number ^{3} (written above, to right of y) is an exponent. There are rules for addition, subtraction, multiplication, and division of such expressions and for simplifying resulting expressions, often involving factoring, combining like terms, canceling, removing parentheses (grouping symbols). Algebra is used in most mathematics branches (geometry, trigonometry, calculus) and in other fields, e.g., physics, statistics; in these it is usually needed to solve equations expressing the relation of unknown to known quantities. Modern abstract algebra generalizes not only numbers but also operations.

Algeciras (äljúsēr'ùs, Span. älhäthē'räs), city (pop. 66,317), Cádiz prov., S Spain, in Andalusia; Mediterranean port on Bay of Algeciras opposite Gibraltar. British victory here in 1801 over French-Spanish fleet.

Algeciras Conference: see MOROCCO.

Alger, Horatio (äl'jùr), 1834–99, American writer of boys' stories. His more than 100 books show success gained by exemplary living, heroic deeds, struggle against odds.

Alger, Russell Alexander, 1836–1907, U.S. Secretary of War (1897–99) and U.S. Senator from Mich. (1902–7).

Algeria (äl'jērēù), republic (c.920,000 sq. mi.; pop. c.11,600,000), NW Africa; cap. ALGIERS. The Atlas Mts. are between the long Mediterranean coastal strip and the fertile well-populated Tell region. In the interior are semiarid plateaus and the great Sahara, with but a few date-bearing oases. Hoggar massif rises to SE. Agr., fishing, and livestock raising. Mineral resources in iron ore, zinc, phosphate, lead, and silver; production of oil and gas begun 1956. Good road and rail networks serve major ports of ORAN, Algiers, and BÔNE. Population is mainly of mixed Arab and Berber stock. Arabic is official language, with French as second language. Carthage was first to dominate area. The richness of the Tell attracted the Roman conquerors, who subjugated Numidia and Mauretania. In the Christian days of the empire, St. Augustine was bishop at Hippo Regius (now Bône). The declining civilization was conquered by Vandals (430–31) and by Byzantines (534). Arab invasion (7th cent.) brought Islam, which profoundly affected Algerian culture. In the 16th cent. the Turks estab. their control over the coast, which became a stronghold for pirates (see BARBARY STATES). In 1847 France won complete control over Algeria, except for the Saharan area (subdued 1900–1909). New crops (esp. grapes and tobacco) were introduced, and the exploitation of mineral resources was begun. Algeria played a vital part in Second World War. The postwar era gave birth to an Algerian independence movement and, late in 1954, open rebellion under leadership of the Natl. Liberation Front (FLN). France, unwilling to withdraw, boycotted a UN discussion in 1955 and waged a costly war. Army elements committed to de Gaulle seized control of Algeria in May, 1958. The Algerian Republic was then proclaimed, with provisional hq. in Tunis. In Sept., 1959, de Gaulle

recognized the right of Algerians to determine their own future. In Jan., 1961, a referendum gave Algerian self-determination; negotiations ended in ceasefire in March, 1962, but terrorist activity against Moslem civilians, unleased by the right-wing Secret Army Organization (OAS), resulted in vast numbers of killed, wounded, and homeless. Algeria became independent July, 1962. Threat of civil war was averted when army was aligned with Ahmed BEN BELLA. Ben Bella was elected premier 1962 and became president Aug., 1963, but was overthrown in coup d'état led by Houari Boumedienne in June, 1965. In June, 1967, Algeria joined the Arab nations in the war against Israel. American-owned oil interests were confiscated and diplomatic relations with Britain and the U.S. were broken off over their support of Israel.

Algerine War: see DECATUR, STEPHEN; TRIPOLITAN WAR.

Al-Ghazali, c.1058–1111, Arabian philosopher. He rejected the rationalism of Al-Kindi and Al-Farabi in favor of devotion to the faith of Islam. Also Al-Gazel.

Algiers (äljērz'), Fr. *Alger,* city (pop. c.883,880), N Algeria, cap. of Algeria; major port of N Africa. Founded in late 10th cent. by the Berbers on site of the Roman Icosium. Became important after establishment of Turkish rule by Barbarossa in 1518. A base for Barbary pirates, it was visited by several European punitive expeditions. Occupied in 1830 by the French, who later built modern city along the harbor. The 16th-cent. Casbah (fortress), surmounting a height, gives its name to whole of old quarter. In Second World War, after capture by Allies in Nov., 1942, it became hq. of Gen. de Gaulle's government. Revolt in Algeria in May, 1958, helped end French Fourth Republic and brought de Gaulle to power a second time. Prior to Algerian independence in 1962, frequent bombings by the Secret Army Organization (OAS), French terrorists, damaged many industrial and communications facilities.

Algonquian (älgŏng'kwēùn, –kēun), largest family of Algonquian-Mosan linguistic stock, a widespread stock among Canadian and U.S. Indians. See LANGUAGE (table).

Algonquin Indians (älgŏng'kwĭn, –kūn), North American Indian tribe in Canada, of Algonquian linguistic family. Friendly to the French, they were dispersed by Iroquois in 17th cent.

Algonquin Provincial Park, 2,741 sq. mi., S Ont., Canada; estab. 1893 as game preserve and recreation area.

algum: see ALMUG.

Alhambra (älhäm'brù), city (pop. 54,807), S Calif., ENE of Los Angeles; founded 1881.

Alhambra [Arabic,= the red], group of Moorish buildings on a hill overlooking Granada, Spain. Comprises citadel remains, palace of kings, and quarters of nobles and officials. Halls and chambers, with intricate geometric ornament and honeycomb vaulting, surround a series of open courts with fountains and gardens. Built 1238–1354, it was mutilated after expulsion of the Moors in 1492 and extensively restored after 1828.

Ali (ä'lē, älē'), 600?–661, 4th caliph (656–61); first cousin and faithful follower of Mohammed, husband of Fatima. Caliphate opposed by Ayesha and Muawiya. Shiite-Sunnite division in Islam stems from this period. Ali and his son HUSEIN major Shiite saints.

Alicante (älēkän'tä), city (pop. 127,967), cap. of Alicante prov., Valencia, SE Spain; Mediterranean port.

Alice, city (pop. 20,861), S Texas, W of Corpus Christi. Cattle-shipping rail junction with oil wells and farms nearby.

Alice Springs, town (pop. 4,000), Northern Territory, Australia, at terminus of Central Australian RR. Formerly called Stuart, it was cap. of Central Australia 1926–31. Opal mining.

SMALL CAPITALS = cross references. Pronunciation key on inside end pages. Abbreviations: p. 2.

alien, person foreign to political group with which he associates. Governments have right to exclude aliens or to estab. conditions for entry. Aliens are subject to laws of country of residence. They owe allegiance to home country and may ask it to intercede on their behalf with the country of residence. In wartime, laws governing aliens, particularly enemy aliens, are stricter.

Alien and Sedition Acts, 1798, passed by U.S. Congress when warfare with France threatened (see XYZ AF-FAIR). Empowered President to expel "dangerous" aliens; provided for indictment of those who should "unlawfully combine or conspire" against the administration or should write or speak "with intent to defame" the government, the Congress, or the President. Acts provoked KENTUCKY AND VIRGINIA RESOLUTIONS.

Aligarh (ülēgŭr'), city (pop. 141,618), W Uttar Pradesh, India; trade center. Moslem university.

alimentary canal, tubular passage (c.30 ft. long) from mouth to anus functioning in DIGESTION and absorption of food. Includes pharynx, esophagus, STOMACH, INTESTINE, and rectum.

alimony, allowance which by court order a husband pays to wife not living with him. Temporary alimony is allowed pending a suit for separation, divorce, or nullity of marriage; permanent alimony, only after a decree has been rendered.

Ali Pasha (ä'lē päshä'), 1744?–1822, Turkish governor of Yannina (1787–1820); called the Lion of Yannina. Originally an Albanian brigand chief, he ruled as quasi-independent despot over most of Albania and Epirus. Ordered deposed for his ambitious plans (1820), he rebelled and resisted Turkish troops (badly needed in fight against Greek insurrection) until his assassination by a Turkish agent. Byron described his rugged court in *Childe Harold*.

Aliquippa (ălĭkwĭp'ŭ), borough (pop. 26,369), W Pa., on Ohio R., in industrial region NW of Pittsburgh. Grew after expansion of steel mills 1909.

Alisal, town (pop. 16,473), W Calif., E of Salinas; settled 1933, principally by migratory farm workers. Also called The Alisal; formerly called East Salinas.

alizarin (ŭlĭz'ŭrĭn), MORDANT vegetable dye prepared originally from MADDER root. Now synthesized from coal-tar derivatives using method discovered by Karl LIEBERMANN. With a metallic salt (e.g., that of aluminum, tin, or iron) it forms a brilliant red, brown, or violet LAKE.

Aljubarrota (älzhōōbŭrô'tŭ), village, Leiria dist., Estremadura, W central Portugal. Here Portuguese, aided by English, defeated Spanish, kept independence (1385).

alkali (ăl'kŭlī), in chemistry, a strong BASE, e.g., sodium hydroxide (see LYE). Has properties of bases: soluble in water and neutralizes acids. Strongly CAUSTIC. Used to make soap, cotton goods, paper. **Alkali metals** are cesium, rubidium, potassium, sodium, and lithium. Oxides of barium, strontium, calcium, and sometimes magnesium called **alkaline earths** because they act like alkalis. **Alkali soils** contain excess of soluble salts natural to soils.

alkaloid, organic compound composed of carbon, hydrogen, nitrogen, and usually oxygen. Derived from plants; name indicates properties of a BASE. Examples: ATROPINE, CAFFEINE, COCAINE, MORPHINE, NICOTINE, QUININE, STRYCHNINE, codeine.

alkalosis: see ACIDOSIS.

Al-Khowarizmi (äl-khōwärēz'mē), fl. 820, Arabian mathematician, noted for treatises on Hindu arithmetic and algebra. He is said to have given algebra its name. Latin translations of his works were a major source of knowledge in medieval Europe.

Al-Kindi, 9th-cent. Arabian philosopher, who devoted himself to reconciling the views of Plato and Aristotle, in the light of Islamic thought. He was followed by Al-Farabi and Al-Ghazali.

Alkmaar (älk'mär), municipality (pop. 47,512) and town, North Holland prov., NW Netherlands. Market

center; iron foundries. Weekly cheese market in front of ancient weighhouse is famous.

alkyl: see RADICAL.

Allah (ä'lŭ, ä'lŭ), Arabic name for God, used in Islam and Arabic-speaking Christian countries.

Allahabad (äl'ŭhŭbäd'), city pop. c.431,000), S Uttar Pradesh, India. On site of Prayag, ancient Aryan holy city, at junction of the sacred Jumna and Ganges rivers. Trade center.

All-American Canal, SE Calif.; built 1934–40. A part of Federal irrigation system of Hoover Dam. Taps Colorado R. at Imperial Dam, N of Yuma, Ariz., and runs 80 mi. W, past Calexico, Calif. Serves IM-PERIAL VALLEY and Coachella Valley.

Allan, Sir Hugh, 1810–82, Canadian financier and shipowner, b. Scotland. Involved in PACIFIC SCANDAL over construction of Canadian Pacific Ry.

Allegany (ăl'ŭgā''nē), village (pop. 2,064), SW N.Y., on Allegheny R., W of Olean. St. Bonaventure Univ. and Allegany Indian Reservation are nearby.

Alleghany, variant spelling: see ALLEGHENY.

Allegheny (ä'lŭgā''nē), river rising in N Pa., and flowing NW to N.Y., then SW into Pa., joining the Monongahela at Pittsburgh to form the Ohio; 325 mi. long. Transports some freight. Dams on tributaries include Crooked Creek, Mahoning, and Allegheny River.

Allegheny Mountains, a W part of Appalachian Mts., extending SW from N Pa. through Md., W.Va., and Va. Heights vary from c.2,000 ft. in N to over 4,000 ft. in S. E portion has Allegheny Front, a steep escarpment; W portion is plateau reaching into E Ohio and Ky. Allegheny upland, extending into Cumberland upland on S, was largely formed by folding of sedimentary rock. Much subsequent erosion and leveling. Has yielded coal, iron, oil, and gas.

allegory (ăl'ĭgôr''ē), literary work expressing through elaborate symbols a commentary or account of social, political, or artistic ideas. Characters are types or personifications. Spenser's *Faerie Queene* and Bunyan's *Pilgrim's Progress* are famous examples.

Alleluia, Latin form of HALLELUJAH.

Allen, Ethan, 1738–89, hero of American Revolution, leader of GREEN MOUNTAIN BOYS. Helped capture Ticonderoga (1775). Captured by British on expedition against Canada (1775). Promoted independence and statehood of Vt. His brother, **Ira Allen,** 1751–1814, was a political leader in early Vt.

Allen, Hervey, 1889–1949, American author. Best known for historical novels, especially *Anthony Adverse* (1933), one of the longest and best-selling novels of the century.

Allen, Horatio, 1802–89, American civil and mechanical engineer. Operated first steam locomotive (English-built) to run on rails in U.S.; designed steamboats.

Allen, Ira: see ALLEN, ETHAN.

Allen, James Lane, 1849–1925, American novelist. Wrote stories, poems on Ky. Novels include *A Kentucky Cardinal* (1894), *The Choir Invisible* (1897).

Allen, Richard, 1760–1831, founder of the African Methodist Episcopal Church (1794). He was born a slave in Philadelphia.

Allen, Zachariah, 1795–1882, American inventor. Devised belt lines to replace cogwheels for transmitting power. Credited with developing (1821) first hot-air central heating system.

Allenby, Edmund Henry Hynman Allenby, 1st Viscount (ä'lŭnbē), 1861–1936, British field marshal. Invaded Palestine and ended Turkish resistance (1918). British high commissioner for Egypt 1919–25.

Allen Park, city (pop. 37,494), SE Mich., a suburb SW of Detroit; settled c.1819.

Allenstein (ä'lŭnstīn) or **Olsztyn,** city (est. pop. 73,-000), N Poland (since 1945), formerly in E Prussia. Trade, mfg., and rail center. Founded 1348 by Teutonic Knights, who built its great castle. Resettled by Poles after Second World War and made cap. of Olsztyn prov.

Allentown, industrial city (pop. 108,347), E Pa., on Lehigh R., N of Philadelphia; laid out 1762, settled by German religious groups. Trade center for farmers in Pennsylvania Dutch region. Machinery, clothing, truck and coach bodies, textiles, cement are produced. Liberty Bell brought here (1777) for safekeeping; munitions center for Continental army. Seat of Cedar Crest and Muhlenberg colleges.

allergy, excessive sensitivity to a usually harmless substance, typically a protein. Agents (known as allergens) include air-borne pollen and dust, hair and fur, bacteria, poison ivy, various foods. Allergen (a kind of antigen) causes body to produce antibodies. When allergen reacts with antibody in blood stream, allergen is neutralized; the organism is said to be immune. When allergen reaches cells and there reacts with antibodies, allergic disorders (anaphylaxis) result. The allergic symptoms are due in part to liberation of histamine in the cells. Allergic disorders include skin rashes (hives, dermatitis), asthma, hay fever, digestive disturbances, some migraine headaches.

Alleyn, Edward (ăl′ĭn), 1566–1626. English actor; rival of Richard Burbage. Famous for portrayals in Marlowe's *Tamburlaine, Jew of Malta,* and *Faustus.*

Allia (ă′lĕŭ), river, Latium, Italy, tributary of Tiber. Gauls defeated Romans on Allia 390 B.C.

Alliance, city, pop. 28,362), NE Ohio, SE of Akron, on Mahoning R.; laid out 1838. An industrial, distributing, and rail center. Seat of Mt. Union Col. with Clarke Observatory.

Alliance for Progress (*Alianza para Progreso*), economic assistance program announced 1961 by Pres. J. F. Kennedy to help solve economic and social problems of Latin America. Latin American countries (excluding Cuba) pledged $80,000,000,000 in capital investment over ten-year period and agreed to carry out tax and land reforms; U.S. and private investors were to provide 60% of $20,000,000,000 in outside financing.

Allier (älyä′), department (2,850 sq. mi; pop. 380,221), central France, in Bourbonnais; cap. Moulins. Traversed by Allier R. (tributary of Loire).

Allier, river, rising in central France, in the Cévennes. Flows c.255 mi. NW past Vichy and Moulins to join the Loire below Nevers.

alligator, large reptile (order Crocodilia) similar to CROCODILE. American alligator, c.12 to 14 ft. long, ranges N Carolina to Florida, Gulf states. Adults black, young dark brown or black with yellow bands. Snout short and broad. Eats water life.

alligator pear: see AVOCADO.

allotropy (ŭlŏt′rŭpē), occurrence of chemical element in two or more forms differing in atomic arrangement and physical properties but alike in chemical properties. Among elements showing allotropy: arsenic, carbon, oxygen, phosphorus, sulfur.

Allouez, Claude Jean (klōd′ zhä′ älwä′), 1622–89, French Jesuit missionary in Canada and Old Northwest. Founded missions in present Wis.

alloy (ăl′oi), combination of metal with metallic or nonmetallic elements to form mixture or compound having metallic properties suitable for special purposes. May be heterogeneous (composed of crystals embedded in a matrix or of interlocking crystals of several types) or homogeneous (solid solution with uniform physical properties). See also BRASS; BRONZE; GOLD; STEEL.

All Souls College: see OXFORD UNIVERSITY.

allspice: see PIMENTO.

Allston, Washington, 1779–1843, American painter, a pupil of Benjamin West. His work is usually biblical or classical in subject.

Alma, town (pop. 13,309), S Que., Canada, on Saguenay R. and NW of Chicoutimi. Wool carding, lumbering, mfg. of paper products and bricks. Named St. Joseph d'Alma until 1954.

Alma. 1 City (pop. 8,978), S Mich., N. of Lansing; settled 1853. Seat of Alma Col. **2** City (pop. 1,342),

S Nebr., SW of Grand Isl. on Republican R. near Kansas line, in farm area; founded 1871. Harlan Co. Dam is near.

Alma-Ata (ăl′mŭ-ä′tä, Rus. ŭlmä″-ŭtä′), city (1965 est. pop. 623,000), cap. of Kazakh SSR, on Turk-Sib. RR. Machine-building, electrical, and textile plants. University founded 1928. City called Verny until 1921.

Almadén (älmädhän′), town (pop. 14,125), central Spain, in New Castile. Center of rich mercury mines exploited since Roman times.

Almagest: see PTOLEMY (Claudius).

Almagro, Diego de (dyä′gō dä älmä′grō), c.1475–1538, Spanish conquistador, a leader with Pizarros in conquest of Peru. Led expedition into Chile 1535.

Al-Mamun: see MAMUN.

Al-Mansur: see MANSUR; AHMED AL-MANSUR.

Almeida, Francisco de (fränsēsh′kō dù älmä′dù), c.1450–1510, Portuguese admiral. Became (1505) viceroy of Portuguese India and fortified E coast of Africa. Routed Egyptians and their Indian allies off Diu (1509). Sought Portuguese supremacy on seas. Killed by Hottentots on way home.

Almeida Garrett, João Batista de (zhwāō′ bùtēsh′tù dù älmä′dù gùrĕt′), 1799–1854, Portuguese romantic dramatist and poet. Notable are plays *Alfageme de Santarém* and *Frei Luis de Sousa,* and long poems *Camões* and *Dona Branca.*

Almería (älmärē′ä), city (pop. 90,543), cap. of Almería prov., S Spain, in Andalusia; Mediterranean port. Ships fruits, esparto, minerals. Probably founded by Phoenicians. Flourished (13th–15th cent.) under Moors. Gothic cathedral.

Almohades (ăl′mŭhädz, –hädz) or **Almohads** (–hädz), Berber Moslem dynasty, 12th–13th cent. of Morocco and Spain. Puritanical anti-ALMORAVIDES sect founded by Mohammed ibn Tumart c.1120. His successors conquered Morocco, Moslem Spain, displacing Almoravides by 1174. Defeated by Spanish and Portuguese 1212; by Merenide dynasty in Morocco 1269.

almond, fruit kernel of an orchard tree (*Prunus amygdalus*), resembling the peach and bearing single or double spring blossoms, pink in sweet, white in bitter. Both yield almond oil, and the bitter yields also amygdalin, which on decomposing gives prussic acid. Sweet almond nut used in confections. Flowering almonds are ornamental shrubs of other *Prunus* species.

Almoravides (älmō′ rùvīdz, –vīdz) or **Almoravids** (–vīdz), Berber Moslem dynasty, 11th–12th cent., of Morocco and Spain; militant puritanical reform sect founded by Abdullah ibn Yasin (d. 1059). His successors founded Marrakesh (1062), helped Spanish Moors stem Christian reconquest (1086), then took over Moslem Spain. Overthrown by ALMOHADES by 1174.

Almquist, Carl Jonas Love (kärl′ yōō′näs lōō′vù älm′kvĭst), 1793–1866, Swedish writer. Novels, plays, poems, and short stories are in *The Book of the Thorn Rose* (14 vols., 1832–51).

almug or **algum,** precious wood, mentioned in Bible, used in the Temple and Solomon's palace. 2 Chron. 2.8; 9.10, 11. Perhaps a red sandalwood.

aloe (ăl′ō), perennial of genus *Aloe* (ăl′ōē), with stiff, fleshy leaf clusters, red or yellow flowers. Some are a few inches high, others tree size. Native to South Africa; tub plant elsewhere. Yields drugs and fibers (for cords and nets). The fragrant wood of an unrelated East Indian tree is also called aloe.

Alost (älōst′), Flemish *Aalst,* town (est. pop. 45,476), East Flanders, Belgium. Textile mfg.

alpaca (ălpăk′ù), partially domesticated South American hoofed mammal of camel family. Of same genus (*Lama*) as wild guanaco (probably descended from it) and vicuña. Bred chiefly for long, lustrous wool (black through shades of brown to white) by Indians in highlands of Peru, Chile, Bolivia.

Alp Arslan (älp ärslän′), 1029–72, Seljuk sultan of Persia (1063–72). Vigorous conqueror of Christians; victor of MANZIKERT.

Alpena, resort city (pop. 14,682), N Mich., on Thunder Bay of L. Huron and NNE of Bay City; laid out 1856. Has limestone quarries and busy commercial harbor.

Alpes, Basses- and Hautes-, France: see BASSES-ALPES and HAUTES-ALPES.

Alpes-Maritimes (älp'-märētēm'), department (1,644 sq. mi.; pop. 618,625—incl. BRIGUE AND TENDE), SE France, on French RIVIERA; cap. Nice.

alphabet, system of writing, theoretically having a one-to-one relation between character (or letter) and phoneme (see PHONETICS). Few alphabets have achieved the ideal exactness. An alphabet is called a syllabary when one character represents a syllable rather than a phoneme (e.g., kana of Japan). The modern Western European alphabet is that of Rome (developed from Greek), the base of most alphabets used for newly written languages of Africa and America. The Cyrillic alphabet, an augmented Greek alphabet, is used for Russian, Serbian, Bulgarian, and many languages of the USSR. Greek (developed from Phoenician), Hebrew, Arabic, and Devanagari of India (with syllabic features) all have their own alphabets, based ultimately on Egyptian HIEROGLYPHIC writing. This, though not alphabetic, bore the germ of phonemic writing in the phonogram. A similar development created Persian CUNEIFORM syllabary. See also RUNES and OGHAM. See *ill.*, p. 1187.

alpha particle and **alpha ray:** see RADIOACTIVITY; RADIUM; RAY.

Alpheus (älfē'ŭs), Gr. *Alpheios,* river, 69 mi. long, S Greece, flowing from Taygetus mts. NW through Peloponnesus to the Ionian Sea. In mythology its waters were said to pass under the sea and emerge as fountain of Arethusa at Syracuse. Hercules turned the river through Augeas' stables to clean them. It is the river Alph of Coleridge's *Kubla Khan.*

Alphonso. For rulers thus named, see ALFONSO.

Alphonsus Liguori, Saint (älfŏn'sŭs lĭgwô'rē), 1696–1787, Italian Catholic churchman, Doctor of the Church, founder of Redemptorist order. Wrote many hymns. Original name Alfonso Maria de' Liguori. Feast: Aug. 2.

Alpine, town (pop. 4,740), W Texas, in mtns. N of Big Bend of Rio Grande; founded 1882. A rail junction, it ships cattle and sheep. Sul Ross State Col. is here. Big Bend Natl. Park (see NATIONAL PARKS and MONUMENTS, table) is nearby.

alpine plants, high-altitude flowering plants of dwarfed form, many preferring shade. Cultivated for use in alpine and ROCK GARDENS.

Alps, mountain system, S central Europe, forming great arc from Mediterranean coast between France and Italy to Adriatic coast of Yugoslavia. Covering most of Switzerland and Austria, the Alps separate Po plain (N Italy) from France (W), Germany (N), and Danubian plain (E). Many rivers (Rhine, Rhone, Po) originate in the Alpine watershed. Cattle raising, dairying are common in high Alps; agr., orchards, vineyards in valleys. Hydroelectric plants. Beautiful, varied scenery attracts many tourists. Towering peaks, covered by glaciers and perpetual snow, rise above the relatively low base level (3,000–4,000 ft.) and the many fine lakes, e.g., Geneva, Lucerne, Como, Garda, Maggiore. Best-known peaks include Mont Blanc (15,-781 ft.; highest of chain), Monte Rosa, Matterhorn (all in W Alps); Jungfrau, Finsteraarhorn, Piz Bernina (Central Alps, in Bernese Oberland and Engadine); Ortles, Grossglockner, Zugspitze (E Alps, including Dolomites, Hohe Tauern, Bavarian Alps). Principal tunnels and highway passes: Mont CENIS, SIMPLON, SAINT GOTTHARD, ARLBERG, BRENNER PASS, Great and Little SAINT BERNARD, FURKA, MALOJA, STELVIO PASS.

Als (äls), Ger. *Alsen,* island (121 sq. mi.; pop. c.50,-000), Denmark, in the Little Belt, separated from S Jutland by narrow Als Sound; chief city Sonderborg. Agr., fruitgrowing. Held by Prussia 1864–1920.

Alsace (äl'säs, äl'säs, Fr. älzäs'), Ger. *Elsass* (ĕl'zäs), region and former province, E France, along Rhine border with Germany; crossed by Vosges mts. Comprises Bas-Rhin, Haut-Rhin, and Territory of Belfort depts. Chief cities: Strasbourg, Colmar, Mulhouse. Bilingual (French, German), 25% of pop. is Protestant. Agr., vineyards, cotton mfg., and potash mines. Included in East Frankish (later German) kingdom (870); Peace of Westphalia (1648) and annexations by Louis XIV (1680–97) gave most of Alsace to France; rest annexed in French Revolution. Ceded (except Belfort) to Germany with part of Lorraine (1871), but recovered by France (1918). Occupied by Germany (1940–44).

Alsen, Denmark: see ALS.

alsike: see CLOVER.

Alston, Walter, 1911–, American baseball player and manager. Led Brooklyn and Los Angeles Dodgers to five pennants and four world championships from 1955 to 1965.

Altadena (ältúdē'nů), residential city (pop. 40,568), S Calif., N of Pasadena, in orange and avocado area; founded 1887.

Altai or **Sharasume** (shäräsōōmä'), town (pop. c.30,-000), N Sinkiang, China, on slopes of Altai mts. Part of Mongolia until 1907. Administered by Ili Kazakh Autonomous Region since 1955. Trade center. Gold mined nearby. Chinese name is Chenghwa.

Altai or **Altay** (äl'tī, ältī'), mountain system of SW Siberia, RSFSR and Kazakh SSR, and of W Mongolia. Highest peak, Belukha (14,780 ft.), is in Katun range, RSFSR. Forests, meadows, rich mineral deposits (lead, zinc, silver, wolfram, copper, mercury, gold). Larger part of mountains is administratively included in **Altai Territory** (101,042 sq. mi.; 1965 est. pop. 2,772,000), RSFSR, with one of richest black-earth areas of Siberia; cap. Barnaul. Drained by Ob R. Population is largely Russian; in mountains Altai-speaking Oirats or Oirots predominate. Oirats were seminomadic until recent settlement on collective farms.

Altaic (ältā'īk), family of languages which includes Turkish, Mongolian, and Manchu. See LANGUAGE (table).

Altamira (äl''tämē'rä) site of the caverns in N Spain, near Santander, where famous examples of CAVE ART were discovered in 1879.

Altamirano, Ignacio Manuel (ēgnä'syō mänwĕl' ältämērä'nō), 1834–93, Mexican novelist, of pure Indian blood. Key figure in reconstruction of republic after collapse of Maximilian's empire. Wrote novels *Clemencia* and *La navidad en las montañas.*

Altamont (äl'tůmônt), town (pop. 10,811), S Oregon, suburb SE of Klamath Falls.

Altay: see ALTAI.

Altdorf (ält'dôrf), town (pop. 7,477), cap. of Uri, Switzerland. Scene of William Tell's exploits.

Altdorfer, Albrecht (äl'brĕkht ältdôr'fùr), 1480–1538, German painter and engraver, follower of Dürer. Landscape was among his major interests.

Altenburg, Germany: see SAXE-ALTENBURG.

alternating current: see ELECTRICITY; GENERATOR.

Altgeld, John Peter (ält'gĕlt), 1847–1902, governor of Ill. (1892–96), b. Germany. A Democrat and sturdy champion of human rights, he pardoned the men convicted for Haymarket riots and opposed sending of Federal troops when there was a strike at PULLMAN (1894).

althea, shrubby: see MALLOW.

Althing (äl'thing), parliament of Iceland. Oldest assembly in Europe, first convened 930. Dissolved 1800, revived as advisory body 1843, restored 1874.

Altichiero da Zevio (ältēkyä'rō dä tsäv'yō), c.1330–c.1395, Italian painter, follower of Giotto, founder of school of Verona.

altimeter (ältīm'ītùr, äl'tīmē''tùr), altitude-measuring device for aircraft, usually a BAROMETER indicating altitude above sea level only. Newer type uses radio waves and shows actual distance.

altitude sickness: see AEROEMBOLISM.

Alto Adige, Italy: see TRENTINO-ALTO ADIGE.

Alton (ôl'tŭn), city (pop. 43,047), SW Ill., on bluffs above Mississippi R. and N of St. Louis; laid out 1815. Shipping and industrial center. Has monument to E. P. LOVEJOY and tablet marking scene of Lincoln-Douglas debate (1858). PRINCIPIA COLLEGE is at nearby Elsah.

Altona, Germany: see HAMBURG.

Altoona, industrial city (pop. 69,407), central Pa., near source of Juniata R., E of Pittsburgh; settled c.1769. A rail center with shops, E of scenic Horseshoe Curve of Pennsylvania RR. Bituminous coal mines nearby.

Altus (ăl'tŭs), city (pop. 21,225), SW Okla., W of Lawton, in cotton and cattle area; founded c.1892. Altus Air Force Base is NE. L. Altus, chief unit of W. C. Austin reclamation project, is N.

alum (ăl'ŭm), double crystalline salt, a sulphate of a univalent and a trivalent cation (positively charged atom or radical). Alum in popular use means double sulphate of potassium and aluminum, i.e., potassium alum or potash alum.

alumina (ûlŏo'mĭnŭ) or **aluminum oxide,** occurs nearly pure as CORUNDUM and is combined with silica in clay. Corundum and emery (an impure form) are among the hardest of abrasives. Alundum is an artificial form used as an abrasive. Alumina from BAUXITE is important source of metallic aluminum.

aluminum, silvery-white metallic element (symbol = Al; see also ELEMENT, table). Ductile and malleable; resists corrosion; excellent conductor of heat and electricity; very light. Used in airplanes, autos, construction, window frames, kitchen utensils, wrapping foil, high-tension wires. It is produced commercially from BAUXITE by the electrolysis of alumina; process developed (1886) by Charles Martin HALL and Paul Héroult, working independently.

Alum Rock, town (pop. 18,942), W central Calif., a suburb NE of San Jose. Has mineral springs.

alundum: see ALUMINA.

Alva, Fernando de: see ALBA.

Alvarado, Juan Bautista (hwän' boutĕs'tä älvärä'dhō), 1809-82, governor of Alta California (present California) 1836-42. Local rivalries and immigration of U.S. citizens brought about recurrent disturbances.

Alvarado, Pedro de (pā'dhrō dä), 1486-1541, Spanish conquistador. Served under Hernán Cortés in conquest of Mexico. Sent out by Cortés, he conquered Guatemala and Salvador (1523). Governor of Guatemala until his death; his wife, Beatriz de la Cueva, succeeded him. Tried unsuccessfully (1534) to share Inca booty in Ecuador. Died in action against Indians of W Mexico.

Álvarez Quintero, Serafín (säräfĕn' äl'väräth kēntä'ro), 1871-1938, and **Joaquín Álvarez Quintero** (hwäkēn'), 1873-1944, Spanish dramatists; brothers. Collaborators on comedies about Andalusian middle-class life.

Alvord, Henry Elijah, 1844-1904, American agriculturist, educator, and dairy specialist; developed cooperative creamery system.

Alvsborg, Swed. *Älvsborgs län,* county (4,919 sq. mi.; pop. 375,037), SE Sweden; cap. Vanersborg. N section, W of Vanern lake, is agr. and lumbering district; important textile plants in S; large power works at TROLLHATTAN. Alfsborg and Elfsborg are former spellings.

alyssum (-lĭs'-), plant of genus *Alyssum,* low perennials with yellow flowers, used in borders and rock gardens. **Sweet alyssum** is an annual species of *Lobularia* with fragrant white or lavender flowers.

Am, chemical symbol of the element AMERICIUM.

Amadeus VIII (ămŭdē'ŭs), 1383-1451, duke of Savoy, antipope (1439-49), as Felix V. Had few supporters and yielded to Nicholas V.

Amadeus, 1845-90, king of Spain (1870-73), duke of Aosta, son of Victor Emmanuel II of Italy. Elected king after expulsion of Isabella II. His difficulties with his own government, and with the rebel CARLISTS, compelled him to abdicate.

Amadis of Gaul (ă'mŭdĭs), romance of chivalry, first composed in Spain or Portugal (13th or 14th cent.), probably based on French sources. Often rewritten and translated, it gives ideal of perfect knight.

Amado, Jorge (zhôr'zhŭ ŭmä'dō), 1912-, Brazilian novelist. Wrote with grim realism of Brazilian life, especially of the economically oppressed.

Amagansett (ă'mŭgăn'sĭt), fishing and resort village (pop. 1,095), SE N.Y., on S shore of Long Island, ENE of Southampton; settled 1650.

Amagasaki (ä'mägäsä'kē), industrial city (pop. 405,-955), S Honshu, Japan; a port on Osaka Bay.

Amager (ä'mägŭr), island (25 sq. mi.; pop. 178,184), Denmark, in the Oresund. N end is occupied by part of Copenhagen.

Amakusa Islands. (ämäkōō'sä), archipelago (341 sq. mi.), in East China Sea, W of Kyushu, Japan. A group of c.67 islands. Major 16th-cent. center of Christianity. Hondo is chief town.

Amalasuntha (ä'mŭlŭsŭn'thŭ), d. 535, Ostrogothic queen in Italy, daughter of Theodoric the Great. Regent for son Athalaric (526-34); ruled after his death till murdered by order of her husband.

Amalekites (ăm'ŭlŭkīts), people of Canaan, descendants of Esau, hereditary enemies of Hebrews until dispersed by Saul and David. Gen. 14.7; Ex. 17.8-16; Gen. 36.12,16; Num. 13.29; 14.25,45; 24.20; Judges 3.13; 6.3,33; 7.12; 1 Sam. 15.5-8; 30.1-20; 1 Chron. 1.36; 4.43.

Amalfi (ämäl'fē), town (est. pop. 6,663), Campania, S Italy, on Gulf of Salerno. Early Italian maritime republic (9th cent.); duchy from 953 until fall to Normans (1131). Cathedral in Sicilian-Arabic style was begun in 10th cent.

amalgam, ALLOY of mercury with any metal except platinum or iron. Most are made artificially. Amalgamation process extracts gold and silver, which are dissolved from ores.

Amalric (ŭmăl'rĭk) or **Amaury** (ŭmô'rē), Latin kings of Jerusalem. **Amalric I,** c.1137-74, reigned 1162-74. Lost suzerainty of Egypt to NUREDDIN. **Amalric II,** c.1155-1205. gained the title in 1197 through marriage to Isabella, eldest daughter of Amalric I. Succeeded his brother Guy of Lusignan as king of Cyprus 1194.

Amalthaea (ămŭlthē'ŭ), nurse of Zeus, often represented as a goat with wonderful horns; one horn became the CORNUCOPIA.

Amana Society (ŭmän'ŭ), corporate name of seven villages, E central Iowa, grouped around Iowa R. WNW of Iowa City; settled 1855 by members of Community of True Inspiration. Community originated in 17th-cent. German religious sect. Fled to U.S. 1843 under Christian Metz to escape persecution. Settled first near Buffalo, N.Y. One of most successful U.S. communal communities. Made cooperative corporation with separation of religious and economic administration, 1932. Wool and wood handicrafts prominent.

amaranth (ăm'-), coarse annual plant (*Amaranthus*), with colorful foliage and chaffy flower spikes. Garden kinds include love-lies-bleeding or tassel flower, Joseph's coat. Some species are weeds, e.g., pigweed, TUMBLEWEED.

Amarapura (ŭ'mŭräpōō'rä), town, Upper Burma, on Irrawaddy R. Was cap. of Burma 1783-1823, 1837-60.

Amarillo, city (pop. 137,969), N Texas. Area known to Indians, buffalo hunters, and cowboys before arrival of railroad 1887. A former cow town, it is now banking and commercial metropolis of Panhandle. It mushroomed into industrial city after discovery of oil and gas. U.S. helium plant nearby.

amaryllis (ăm'ŭrĭl'ĭs), South African bulbous plant (*Amaryllis belladonna*), the belladonna lily, often cultivated for its rose-red, fragrant flowers. Name used for related plants, especially for those of the genus *Hippeastrum*, whose heavy stalks bear clusters of vivid lilylike flowers.

Amasa (ăm'ùsù), cousin of Absalom with whom he revolted. 2 Sam. 17.25; 19.13; 20.4–13; 1 Kings 2.5.

Amasis I (ùmā'sĭs) (Ahmose), d. c.1557 B.C., king of Egypt. Founded XVIII dynasty and drove out HYKSOS.

Amati (ämä'tē), family of violinmakers of Cremona, beginning with Andrea Amati (c.1535–c.1578). Niccolò Amati (1596–1684) brought the Amati violin to its peak. Antonio Stradivari was his pupil.

Amaury. For persons thus named, see AMALRIC.

Amaziah (ăm''ŭzī'ù), died c.775 B.C., king of Judah c.802–c.775 B.C.), successor of Jehoash of Judah. Two events of reign were conquest of Edom and unprovoked attack on King Jehoash of Israel. Jehoash took Amaziah prisoner, entered Jerusalem, sacked the Temple. Amaziah was killed. 2 Kings 14; 2 Chron. 25.

Amazon (ă'mŭzŏn), in Greek legend, one of tribe of women who spent time in hunting and warfare. One of Hercules' 12 labors was to steal girdle of Queen Hippolyte. In Trojan War they fought against Greeks, and their leader, Penthesilea, was slain by Achilles.

Amazon, Port. *Amazonas* (ämùzŏ'nùsh), river rising in Peruvian Andes in two major headstreams, MARAÑÓN and Ucayali, and flowing across Brazil to Atlantic. Carries more water than any other river. Length is c.3,500 mi. with Marañón or c.3,700 with Ucayali. Extremely low gradient, enormous drainage basin. In lowlands E of Andes is world's largest rain forest. Principal tributaries from N are NEGRO, NAPO, PUTU-MAYO, Caquetá; from S are JURUÁ, PURUS, MADEIRA, XINGU, TAPAJÓS, TOCANTINS. Below Xingu, Amazon reaches delta and divides around MARAJÓ isl.; S stream called Pará. Basin sparsely peopled, mostly by Indians. Early explorers include Vicente Yañez Pinzón (lower part, 1500), ORELLANA (from Napo, 1540–41; his fanciful story of female warriors gave Amazon its name), Pedro de Ursúa (1559), TEIXEIRA (1637–38). Resources of basin are principally wild rubber (important in early 20th cent.), cacao, woods, jute. Brazilian government in recent years, aided by UNESCO, undertook intensive development of area and estab. health services.

Amazonas, state (c.602,000 sq. mi.; pop. c.721,215), NW Brazil; cap. Manaus. Covering major part of Amazon basin, it is largest but least populated Brazilian state.

Ambato (ämbä'tō), city (pop. c.39,000), central Ecuador, a resort town and commercial hub in high Andean valley.

amber, fossil resin exuded as gum by coniferous trees in past geologic time. It is either transparent or cloudy and is used in making beads, ornaments, and cigarette holders. Ancient Greeks knew that rubbing it with fur produced static electricity.

ambergris (ăm'bùrgrēs), waxlike substance produced by abnormal conditions in sperm whale's digestive tract. Floats in tropical seas as yellow, gray, black, or variegated mass. Perfume fixative.

Ambers, Lou, 1913–, American boxer, called Herkimer Kid. World lightweight champion 1936–38, 1939–40.

Ambiorix (ämbī'ùrĭks), fl. 54 B.C., Gallic chieftain. Though earlier in Roman favor, he joined in attacking Caesar's legates. When Caesar approached, he fled across the Rhine and disappeared from history.

Ambler, Eric, 1909–, English author of suspense novels. They include *A Coffin for Demetrios* (1939), *Journey into Fear* (1940), and *Passage of Arms* (1959).

Ambleside, village, Westmorland, England; Lake District tourist center. Church has stained glass window given by admirers of Wordsworth.

Amboina (ämboi'nù), Malay Ambon, island (c.314 sq. mi.; pop. 56,037), E Indonesia, one of the Moluccas.

Amboina, chief city and port, exports spices and copra.

Amboise, Georges d' (zhôrzh' däbwäz'), 1460–1510, cardinal, French statesman. Chief minister of Louis XII; patron of arts and letters.

Amboise (äbwäz'), town (est. pop. 6,736), Indre-et-Loire dept., N central France, on the Loire. Famous castle was royal residence 15th-16th cent.

Amboise, conspiracy of, 1560, unsuccessful plot of French Huguenots and others to abduct Francis II from Amboise and to arrest Charles and François de Guise. The rebels were massacred.

Ambon: see AMBOINA.

Ambridge, borough (pop. 13,865), W Pa., on Ohio R., NW of Pittsburgh. Has steel plants. Site was once Indian village. HARMONY SOCIETY had communistic settlement Economy here 1825–1906.

Ambrose, Saint, 340?–397, bishop of Milan, Doctor of the Church, b. Trier. As governor in NW Italy, he won much esteem; the people insisted on his being made bishop (374). He administered the diocese ably, refusing to bow to the emperors: he opposed the Arianism favored by Valentinian II, persuaded Gratian to outlaw heresy, and made Theodosius I do penance for a massacre of rebellious citizens of Salonica. His brilliant religious writing molded classic learning in a Christian context. His name is also associated with the type of plain song called Ambrosian chant, and he wrote hymns (many ascribed to him are spurious). He was one of the chief "founders" of the Middle Ages. Feast: Dec. 7.

Ambrosian Library, public library (founded c.1605), Milan, rich in Greek and Latin texts and incunabula.

Amchitka (ämchĭt'kù), island, 40 mi. long, off W Alaska, one of ALEUTIAN ISLANDS.

Amen, Egyptian god: see AMON.

amendment, in law, alteration of provisions of legal document (STATUTE or CONSTITUTION). In parliamentary law also, proposed changes of bill or motion. In judicial procedure, correction of errors. Amendment to Constitution of the United States requires approval of two thirds of each house of Congress, ratification by three quarters of states.

Amenemhet (ä''měněm'hět, ā''–), kings of anc. Egypt of the XII dynasty. **Amenemhet I**, d. 1970 B.C., seized throne, centralized government, and humbled nobles. **Amenemhet III**, d. 1801 B.C., son and successor of Sesostris III, restored economy, reclaimed the Fayum.

Amenhotep (ä''měnhō'těp, ā''–), or **Amenophis** (ä''měnō'fĭs), kings of anc. Egypt of the XVIII dynasty. **Amenhotep I**, fl. 1557 B.C., successor to his father, Amasis I, pushed S boundary to second Nile cataract and invaded Syria. **Amenhotep II** succeeded his father, Thutmose III (1448 B.C.), kept conquests already made. **Amenhotep III** succeeded his father, Thutmose IV (c.1411 B.C.). His was an age of splendor and comparative peace. His son and successor was IKHNATON.

Amenia (ùmē'něù), town (pop. 7,546), SE N.Y., NE of Poughkeepsie near Conn. line, in farm and dairy area; founded 1788. T. L. HARRIS had his Brotherhood of New Life settlement here, 1863–67.

America [for Amerigo VESPUCCI], the lands of the Western Hemisphere–North America, Central America (sometimes Middle America), and South America. In English, America and American are often used to refer only to U.S. Martin WALDSEEMÜLLER first used the name.

American, river, rising in three forks in N central Calif., in Sierra Nevada near L. Tahoe, and flowing c.30 mi. W and SW into Sacramento R. at Sacramento. Gold discoveries (1848) along banks played important part in state's history.

Americana, all that has been printed in and about the Americas or written by Americans; usually restricted to formative period in history of the two continents. Earliest-known example is Columbus letter (1493), on discovery of West Indies. Some early American books were printed by Juan Pablos, Stephen Daye and William Bradford.

American Academy in Rome, founded 1894. Comprises schools of fine arts and classical studies for U.S. citizens. Yearly stipends are given.

American Colonization Society, organized Dec., 1816–Jan., 1817, at Washington, D.C., to transport free Negroes from U.S. and settle them in Africa. Purchase of land in Africa in 1822 led to foundation of LIBERIA. Colonization movement attacked by abolitionists, who charged that removal of free Negroes strengthened slavery in the South. Society declined after 1840.

American Falls, city (1964 pop. 2,602), SE Idaho, on Snake R., WSW of Pocatello. Actual falls well known to Oregon Trail travelers. Town grew after arrival of railroad 1892; moved ½ mi. after dam (completed 1927) created 36-mi. reservoir, a part of MINIDOKA PROJECT, on old site. New city is center of wheatgrowing region.

American Federation of Labor–Congress of Industrial Organizations (AFL–CIO), American labor organization brought about by 1955 merger of American Federation of Labor (AFL) and Congress of Industrial Organizations (CIO). The AFL, a combination of craft unions, was founded 1881, received present name 1886; was led by Samuel GOMPERS until 1924, by William Green until 1952, thereafter by George MEANY. The CIO, originally Committee for Industrial Organization, was formed 1935 by AFL affiliates to unionize mass-production workers on an industrywide basis; was expelled from AFL 1937. Led by John L. LEWIS until 1940, it was later headed by Philip MURRAY (1940–52) and by Walter REUTHER. The CIO was noted for vigorous organizational drives and for political activity through its Political Action Committee (PAC). The United Automobile Workers and United Steel Workers were prominent CIO unions. In 1955 the AFL and CIO merged, elected George Meany president. Standing committees include the Committee on Political Education (COPE). In 1957 the AFL–CIO expelled three affiliates charged with corruption. In the 1958 elections it helped defeat five out of six proposed state "right-to-work" laws (see CLOSED SHOP, OPEN SHOP, and UNION SHOP).

American Fork, city (pop. 6,373), N central Utah, on American Fork Creek, S of Salt Lake City; settled 1850 by Mormons. Poultry-raising center served by Provo R. project. Mt. Timpanogos (12,008 ft.) is near.

American Fur Company, chartered 1808 by John Jacob Astor (1763–1848) as rival to companies in Canada. Company maintained virtual monopoly, expanded from Lakes region W to Rocky Mts.

Americanization, term used to describe cultural process by which the immigrant to U.S. assimilates American speech, ideals, traditions, ways of life. Name also given to the movement fostering assimilation, which grew to crusading proportions in first quarter of 20th cent. as result of great immigration from E and S Europe from 1880 to First World War (see IMMIGRATION). Federal bureaus of education and of naturalization joined crusade and aided private Americanization groups. Passage of immigrant education legislation by states plus return of "normalcy" after First World War and, more especially, coming of the quota system of immigration caused Americanization move to subside.

American Labor party, organized in N.Y. by labor leaders and liberals in 1936, primarily to support the New Deal. Policy toward USSR caused internal strife after 1939. Anti-Communist dissenters formed LIBERAL PARTY 1944. Failing to poll 50,000 votes in 1954 N.Y. state election, American Labor party lost its place on ballot; was voted out of existence by its N.Y. state committee (1956).

American Legion, national association of veterans of First and Second World Wars, founded in Paris in 1919. Largest of veterans' associations, it exerts considerable influence on national life. Has done much work in social welfare, particularly child care; obtained benefits for veterans; attacked "subversive" or "anti-American" teachings and organizations.

American Museum of Natural History, incorporated (1869) in New York city to promote study of natural science and related subjects. Buildings on present site opened 1877; Hayden Planetarium (1935) and Roosevelt Memorial building (1936) added since.

American party: see KNOW-NOTHING MOVEMENT.

American Red Cross: see RED CROSS.

American Revolution, 1775–83, struggle by which the THIRTEEN COLONIES on Atlantic seaboard of North America won independence from Great Britain. By middle of 18th cent., differences in thought and interests had developed between colonies and mother country. STAMP ACT (1765) aroused colonial resistance as act of taxation without representation. TOWNSHEND ACTS (1767) led to such incidents as BOSTON MASSACRE (1770), burning of the GASPEE (1772), and BOSTON TEA PARTY (1773). Parliament replied with the INTOLERABLE ACTS. At CONTINENTAL CONGRESS (1774) grievances were listed in petitions to the king. Fighting began at Lexington and Concord on April 19, 1775, followed by capture of Ticonderoga from British and battle of Bunker Hill. QUEBEC CAMPAIGN (1775–76) was disastrous. DECLARATION OF INDEPENDENCE was adopted on July 4, 1776, but many colonists remained pro-British LOYALISTS. SARATOGA CAMPAIGN (1777), successful for colonists, was followed by harsh winter at Valley Forge. Aid from France helped patriot cause. In West, George Rogers CLARK estab. patriot hold on frontier. CAROLINA CAMPAIGN (1780–81) led into YORKTOWN CAMPAIGN. Surrender of Cornwallis at Yorktown in Oct., 1781, ended fighting. Treaty of Paris (1783) recognized U.S. as nation.

American Samoa: see SAMOA.

American Society for the Prevention of Cruelty to Animals (A.S.P.C.A.), estab. 1866 by Henry Bergh to shelter homeless animals, assist farmers, and cooperate in prosecution of game-law violators.

American University, The, at Washington, D.C.; coed.; chartered 1893, opened 1914 as graduate school; undergraduate college opened 1925. Program includes student research at government institutions.

American Veterans Committee (AVC), organization of veterans of Second World War, founded Jan., 1943. Opposed special privileges for veterans.

American Veterans of World War II and Korea (Amvets), organization of veterans of Second World War, founded Dec., 1944; chartered 1947.

America's Cup, international yachting trophy, named for the *America*, yacht which defeated British craft in 1851. Winner must take four of seven races. Cup won only by U.S. yachts through 1964 challenge.

americium (ămǔrǐ'shĕum), radioactive element (symbol = Am; see also ELEMENT, table). It is produced from plutonium by bombardment with neutrons. Emits alpha rays.

Americus (úmĕr'ĭkús), city (pop. 13,472), SW Ga., SE of Columbus. Industrial center in farm and timber area. Charles Lindbergh made first solo flight here. ANDERSONVILLE is nearby.

Amersfoort (ä'mŭrsfört), municipality (pop. 73,965), in Utrecht prov., central Netherlands. Old town with medieval houses, 14th-cent. water gate, 15th-cent. Gate of Our Lady. Mfg. center.

Ames, Fisher, 1758–1808, American political leader from Mass. U.S. Congressman (1789–97), a staunch Federalist and violent attacker of Jefferson.

Ames, James Barr, 1846–1910, American jurist, dean of Harvard Law School after 1895. Helped make case method popular in law study.

Ames, Oakes, 1804–73, American manufacturer, railroad promoter, and politician. U.S. Congressman (1863–73). Involved in CRÉDIT MOBILIER scandal.

Ames, city (1965 pop. 34,826), central Iowa, on Skunk R., N of Des Moines; platted 1865. IOWA STATE UNI-

VERSITY OF SCIENCE AND TECHNOLOGY is among Federal and state institutes here.

Amesbury, town (pop. 10,787), NE Mass., on Merrimack R., NE of Lawrence; settled 1654. Whittier lived here.

amethyst (ăm′ŭthĭst), variety of QUARTZ, violet to purple in color. Valued as a semiprecious gem.

Amharic (ămhä′rĭk), standard language of Ethiopia, belonging to Ethiopic subgroup of Semitic languages. See LANGUAGE (table).

Amherst, Jeffrey Amherst, Baron (ăm′ŭrst), 1717–97, British army officer. Commanded British forces in French and Indian War; captured Louisburg (1758) and Montreal (1760). Amherst, Mass. and Amherst College were named for him.

Amherst, town (pop. 10,788), N N.S., Canada. Mfg. and lumbering town in region noted for scenic beauty. Nearby are ruins of Fort Lawrence, Fort Beauséjour.

Amherst, town (pop. 10,306), W Mass., NE of Northampton; settled 1703. Emily Dickinson and Noah Webster lived here. Town, named for Lord Jeffrey Amherst, includes village of North Amherst (pop. 1,009). Seat of Univ. of MASSACHUSETTS and of AMHERST COLLEGE.

Amherstburg, town (pop. 4,452), S. Ont., Canada, on Detroit R. at entrance to L. Erie. Fort Malden built here 1796. Was British garrison town and naval station in War of 1812. Held by Americans at end of war.

Amherst College, at Amherst, Mass.; for men; opened 1821 as development of Amherst Acad. (chartered 1816), chartered 1825. Robert Frost Library dedicated 1965. Trustees administer Folger Shakespeare Memorial Library, Washington, D.C.

Amicis, Edmondo de: see DE AMICIS, EDMONDO.

amide: see AMMONIA.

Amiel, Henri Frédéric (ärē′ frädärĕk′ ämyĕl′), 1821–81, Swiss critic known for his *Journal intime,* which was published posthumously.

Amiens (ämyē′), city (pop. 105,433), cap. of Somme dept., N France, on Somme R.; historic cap. of Picardy. Old textile industry. Cathedral (begun 1220) is largest and among finest Gothic cathedrals.

Amiens, Treaty of, 1802, made by England with France, Spain, Batavian Republic. France agreed to evacuate Naples; England to give up most conquests made in French Revolutionary Wars.

Amindivi Island: see LACCADIVE, MINICOY, AND AMINDIVI ISLANDS.

amine: see AMMONIA.

amino acids, class of simple organic compounds containing carbon, hydrogen, oxygen, nitrogen, and in certain cases sulphur; when linked together in chains they form PROTEINS. Protein molecules are held together by series of peptide linkages between adjacent amino acids. In metabolism, peptide linkages are formed and broken by enzymes. Amino acids are released in the small intestine by digestion of proteins and carried in the blood stream to the cells, where they are used for growth and repair. In the cells, amino acids may be used as structural units or they may be broken down into fragments. Certain amino acids necessary in metabolism cannot be synthesized by the human body; these are called essential and must be included in the protein diet. Others, nonessential, can be synthesized by the body when needed. Every amino acid except the simplest one can occur as either of two optically active isomers; the usual isomer in nature is the L- form of the molecule. See *ill.,* p. 885.

Amiot, Joseph: see AMYOT, JOSEPH.

Amis, Kingsley, 1922–, English poet and novelist, one of the "Angry young men" of the 1950s, critical of society and themselves. His novels include *Lucky Jim* (1954), *Take a Girl Like You* (1960), and *The Anti-Death League* (1966). He surveyed science fiction in *Maps of Hell* (1960).

Amish Church: see MENNONITES.

Amman, Jost (yŏst′ äm′än), 1539–91, Swiss engraver, noted for Bible illustrations.

Amman (ämän′), city (pop. 108,304), N Jordan. cap. and royal residence, on Wadi Zerka (Jabbok R.), on Hejaz RR, and ENE of Jerusalem. Industrial and commercial center. Was biblical Rabbah (răb′ŭ) or Rabbath, cap. of Ammonites. Rebuilt as Philadelphia; has noted Roman ruins.

Ammanati, Bartolomeo (bärtōlōmä′ō äm-mänä′tē), 1511–92, Italian architect and sculptor. Worked in Venice, Florence, and Rome. As architect to Cosimo de′ Medici, he designed court façade of Pitti Palace (Florence).

Ammann, Othmar Hermann (ôt′mär, ō′mōn), 1879–1965, American civil engineer. Designed or constructed Golden Gate, George Washington, and Delaware Memorial bridges.

ammeter: see GALVANOMETER.

Ammi (ăm′ī) [Heb.,= my people], figurative name of Israel after reconciliation with God. Hosea 2.1. See LOAMMI.

Ammon (ăm′ŭn), in Bible, marauding, nomadic people living E of Dead Sea, relentlessly hostile to Hebrews. Gen. 19.38; Deut. 2.19,20,37; 23.3,4; Judges 3.13; 1 Sam. 11; 2 Sam. 10–12; 2 Chron. 20; Neh. 2.10; 4.7; Jer. 49.1–6.

Ammon, Egyptian god: see AMON.

ammonia, compound of nitrogen and hydrogen in proportion of one to three. Colorless gas with penetrating odor. Very soluble in water (household ammonia is aqueous solution); solution basic. Easily liquefied with pressure. Forms salts with acids. Used to make SAL AMMONIAC, nitric acid, soda; in REFRIGERATION; in medicine. Prepared by destructive distillation of coal, by HABER PROCESS, by treating calcium carbide with nitrogen. Occurs in air, in plant and animal decomposition products, in animal excretions. Amides are derivatives formed by replacing one or more hydrogen atoms of ammonia by organic acid radicals; amines by replacing them with alkyl groups (chains of carbon and hydrogen atoms) or aryl groups (rings of the same).

ammoniac or **gum ammoniac,** gum resin prepared from milky exudation from stem of *Dorema ammoniacum,* plant native to Iran, India, and Siberia. Used in porcelain cements and in medicine as an expectorant.

ammonite (ăm′ŭnīt), type of extinct marine mollusk related to the nautilus, common in Mesozoic era.

ammonium, radical having one nitrogen atom linked to each of four hydrogen atoms; it has a positive valence of one.

amnesia, temporary or prolonged loss of memory of events before or after the causative shock, injury, illness, or mental disease. It is usually cured by establishment of associations with the past by suggestion or hypnotism. It is distinct from aphasia, the loss of verbal usages.

Amnon [Heb.,= faithful], David's eldest son. He ravished his half sister Tamar and was killed by her brother Absalom in revenge. 2 Sam. 3.2; 13.

amoeba (ümē′bü), member of genus (*Amoeba*) of PROTOZOA. *A. proteus* (common species) of fresh waters is c.1/100 in. long. Amoeba, a single cell, has oval nucleus surrounded by granular mass, in turn surrounded by outer clear layer. Locomotion is by false feet or pseudopods formed by outpushing of clear layer with granular mass flowing into outpushings. Pseudopods also engulf food (minute animals, plants) in water; food circulates through protoplasm until digested. Sensitive to light, heat, food, and chemicals.

Amon (ä′mŏn), d. c.641 B.C., idolatrous king of Judah (c.643–c.641 B.C.). He was murdered by servants and succeeded by Josiah. Jeremiah was a contemporary. 2 Kings 21.19–26; 2 Chron. 33.20–25.

Amon (ä′mŭn), **Ammon** (ä′mŭn), or **Amen** (ä′mĕn), anc. Egyptian deity, originally a local god of Thebes often represented as a ram or as a man with ram's head. The principal temple to him was in Libyan desert. Identified by Greeks with Zeus and by Romans with Jupiter. See EGYPTIAN RELIGION.

Amor, Roman god of love: see EROS.

amortization, reduction, liquidation, or satisfaction of a debt or the sum used for this purpose. Examples are paying off mortgage or paying off debt by SINKING FUND.

Amos (ā'mŭs), book of Old Testament, written by a shepherd-prophet in time of Jeroboam II. The book falls into 3 parts: God's judgment on Gentile nations, finally on Israel; three sermons on doom of Israel; five visions of destruction, the last promising redemption.

Amoy (ùmoi'), city (pop. 224,300), Fukien prov., China; port on Amoy Isl. and mfg. center. Joined with hinterland since 1957 by Yingtan-Amoy RR. Treaty port, opened 1842. Seat of Amoy Univ.

ampelopsis (ăm"pĭlŏp'–), woody vines of genus *Ampelopsis,* including pepper vine of S U.S. Berries are blue, purple, yellow, or orange in various species.

Ampère, André Marie (ăm'pēr; ädrā' märē āpēr'), 1775–1836, French physicist, mathematician, natural philosopher. Worked in electrodynamics, derived Ampère's law, studied relationship of electricity and magnetism.

ampere [for A. M. Ampère], electrical unit of current strength and measurement unit of rate of current flow. Current intensity (in amperes) determined by dividing volts (electromotive force) by ohms (resistance).

amphibian (ămfĭ'bēŭn), cold-blooded vertebrate animal of class Amphibia, intermediate between fish and reptiles. Typical metamorphosis is from gill-breathing aquatic larva to partially terrestrial lung-breathing adult. See FROG; NEWT; SALAMANDER; TOAD.

amphibious warfare (ămfĭ'bēŭs), the combined use of land and sea forces in warfare. Known from the time of the ancient Greeks, it is in modern war also supported by air power. In Second World War many special vessels were made for landing tanks, supplies, and men in shallow water. Amphibious warfare used in Pacific and in invasion of Europe.

Amphilochus (ămfĭ'lŭkŭs), in Greek legend, one of the EPIGONI; he fought in Trojan War.

Amphitrite (ămfĭtrī'tē), in Greek religion, queen of the sea; wife of Poseidon and mother of Triton.

Amphitryon (ămfĭ'trēŭn, –ŏn"), in Greek legend, husband of Alcmene. In Amphitryon's absence, Zeus assumed his form and visited Alcmene; she bore him Hercules, whom Amphitryon accepted as his son.

amplitude modulation (AM), radio transmission and receiving system. Carrier wave has constant frequency, varies in amplitude (strength). See FREQUENCY MODULATION.

Amritsar (ŭmrĭt'sŭr), city (pop. 325,747), NW Punjab, India. Founded 1577 by Ram Das, 4th guru [Hindustani = teacher], it is center of Sikh religion. Mfg. of silks and carpets. In Amritsar massacre of April, 1919, hundreds of Indian nationalists were killed and thousands wounded by British forces.

Amru-l-Kais (kīs'), 6th cent., Arabian poet. Subjective, formally perfect verse is esteemed by Arabs as model for erotic poetry. Included in MUALLAQAT.

Amsterdam (ăm'stùrdăm", Dutch ämstùrdäm'), municipality (pop. 866,290), and city, constitutional cap. and largest city of the Netherlands, in North Holland. Situated mainly on S bank of the IJ and connected by canals with the North Sea and the Rhine delta, it is a major port and a great commercial, intellectual, and artistic center. Stock exchange and diamond-cutting industry are important. Amsterdam is built on wooden piles; some 400 bridges cross numerous concentric and radial canals. Chartered in 1300, it joined the Hanseatic League in 1369 and the United Provs. in 1578. Large influx of refugees from all nations (notably French Protestants and Spanish and Portuguese Jews) contributed to rapid growth after late 16th cent. Birthplace of Spinoza and residence of Rembrandt, Amsterdam reached apex as cultural center in 17th cent. It

was taken by the French in 1795; served as cap. of kingdom of Netherlands under Louis Bonaparte; was declared cap. under 1814 constitution. Actually, the government is at The Hague; sovereigns are merely sworn in at Amsterdam. German occupation in the Second World War brought severe hardship. Of the large Jewish population only a few survived. Points of interest include Oude Kerk [old church], built c.1300; weighhouse (15th cent.); city hall (16th cent.); Rijks Mus. (has Dutch masters); Univ. of Amsterdam (1632; reorganized 1876).

Amsterdam, industrial city (pop. 28,772), E central N.Y., on Mohawk R., NW of Albany. Carpets and rugs made since mid-19th cent. Fort Johnson, home of Sir William Johnson, is near.

Amu Darya (ä'mōō där'yù), river, 1,577 mi. long, central Asia. Ancient name is Oxus.

amulet, object worn as charm to ward off evil influences, also used as protective emblem on walls and doors. Belief in amulets common to many cultures; today is most widespread among primitive societies, but has also survived in modern civilization (e.g., rabbit's foot). Materials of amulets vary from teeth of animals to precious stones and may bear engravings of symbols.

Amundsen, Roald (rō'äl ä'mōōnsùn), 1872–1928, Norwegian polar explorer. Commanded first negotiation of Northwest Passage (1903–6). First to reach South Pole (1911). Flew over North Pole with Lincoln Ellsworth (1926). Died in attempt to rescue a former associate, Umberto Nobile.

Amur (ämōōr'), Chinese *Hei-lung-kiang* (hā'–lōōng'–jëäng'), river, 1,767 mi. long, NE Asia. Formed by junction of Shilka and Argun at Russo-Manchurian border; follows border for 1,100 mi.; turns NE near Khabarovsk and empties into Tatar Strait opposite Sakhalin isl. Important transport artery during ice-free summer months.

Amurath: see MURAD.

amylase: see DIASTASE.

Amyot, Jacques (zhäk' ämyō'), 1513–93, French humanist, translator of Plutarch's *Lives* (1559).

Amyot or Amiot, Joseph (zhôzěf' ämyō'), 1718–1794?, French Jesuit missionary in China. He was one of first Europeans to make Chinese literature, antiquities, and customs known to Europe and also was an early authority on Manchu language.

Anabaptists [from Gr.,= rebaptizers], name applied in scorn to those 16th-cent. Protestant sects which rejected infant baptism and insisted on baptism of believers only. A convert, if baptized in infancy, was rebaptized. Persecuted for preaching separation of Church and state, they were disunited. Luther opposed them. Chief leaders were Thomas Munzer and John of Leiden. Group under Menno Simons became MENNONITES. Descendants of Jacob Hutter estab. HUTTERISCHE COMMUNITY (1874) in S.Dak.

Anabasis (ùnä'bùsĭs) [Gr.,= going up, i.e., to the sea], famed Greek prose history by XENOPHON of retreat of the Ten Thousand from Persia (c.399 B.C.).

Anacharsis (ănùkär'sĭs), fl. c.600 B.C., Scythian philosopher. Many maxims are attributed to him.

Anacletus, Saint: see CLETUS, SAINT.

Anaconda (ănŭkŏn'dù), city (pop. 12,054), SW Mont., NW of Butte; laid out 1883. Chosen by Marcus DALY for smelter of Anaconda Copper Mining Co. Most of state's copper, gold, and silver concentrated and smelted here.

anaconda, nonvenomous South American snake, mostly aquatic, partially arboreal, related to boa constrictor, python. Largest is water boa (to 37 ft.).

Anacostia (ănùkŏs'tēù), river rising near Bladensburg, Md., and flowing c.24 mi. to Potomac R. at Washington, D.C.

Anacreon (ùnăk'rēŭn, –ŏn), fl. c.521 B.C., Greek lyric poet, whose work celebrates the joys of wine and love.

Anadarko (ăn'ŭdär'kō), city (pop. 6,299), SW Okla., on Washita R., SW of Oklahoma City. Center of cotton, grain, livestock, and oil area. Annual Indian exposition. "Indian City," with replicas, is SE.

Anadyr (ŭnŭdĭr'), river, 700 mi. long, RSFSR. Flows from extreme NE Siberia into Bering Sea. Coal and gold deposits along shores.

anae-, for words beginning thus: see ANE-.

Anaheim, city (pop. 104,184), S Calif., SE of Los Angeles; founded 1857 by Germans as experiment in communal living. Industrial center in citrus-fruit and walnut area. Popular tourist center since opening (1955) of amusement park Disneyland.

Anahuac (ănŭwäk'), resort and fishing city (pop. 1,985), SE Texas, at mouth of Trinity R., E of Houston, in rice, cattle, and oil area. Scene of two clashes (1832, 1835) between Anglo-American settlers and Mexican officials.

Anáhuac (änä'wäk) [Aztec,= near the water], geographical term in Mexico, today referring specifically to part of central plateau comprising Pánuco and Lerma river systems and lake basin of Valley of Mexico.

Anakim (ăn'ŭkĭm) or **Anakims,** in Bible, a race of giants inhabiting Hebron at time of conquest of Canaan. Practically extirpated by Joshua and Caleb. Num. 13.22,28,33; Deut. 1.28; 9.2; Joshua 11.21; 14.15; 15.13,14; 21.11; Judges 1.20.

analysis, chemical: see CHEMISTRY; ASSAYING.

Ananias (ăn'ŭnī'ŭs). 1 Man who, with his wife Sapphira, kept back part of gift to church and lied about it. He was rebuked by Peter and fell dead. Acts 5.1–11. Name became term for a liar. 2 High priest at Jerusalem, Roman sympathizer. Acts 23.2–5. 3 Christian who took care of the newly converted Paul. Acts 9.10–22. 4 One of THREE HOLY CHILDREN.

anaphylaxis, hypersensitive state which may develop after introduction of a foreign protein (or other antigen) into the body tissues. When an anaphylactic state exists, a second dose of this same protein will cause a violent reaction (allergic reaction). Anaphylaxis results from the production of specific antibodies in the tissues; the violent reaction is produced by the neutralization of antigens by antibodies in the tissues. Anaphylaxis differs from IMMUNITY; in immunity, antibodies circulate in the blood and neutralize antigens without producing a violent reaction. See also ALLERGY.

Anarajapura: see ANURADHAPURA.

anarchism (ăn'ŭrkĭzŭm), theory that the state should be abolished and replaced by free association of groups (no private property). Differs from SOCIALISM in considering the state an intrinsic evil. Philosophic and literary anarchy appeared early (e.g., Zeno of Citium, medieval religious groups), political later (e.g., Anabaptists, Levelers). Modern anarchism outlined by William GODWIN and P. J. PROUDHON. Violent tone introduced by BAKUNIN, resisted by KROPOTKIN. Anarchism suppressed in Russia by Communists. In modern Spain it was a strong force particularly in syndicalist movement. In U.S. it was a political force only briefly, but its violence (Haymarket Square riot, assassination of McKinley) brought a law barring anarchists from country. A leading American anarchist was Emma Goldman.

Anatolia, the Asiatic part of TURKEY. A mountainous peninsula between the Black Sea (N), Aegean Sea (W), and Mediterranean (S), it comprises 97% (287,-117 sq. mi.; pop. 25,470,195) of all Turkey. The name sometimes designates all ASIA MINOR.

anatomy, study of body structure and structural relationships. Includes study of body tissues (histology), of structure of various animal forms (comparative anatomy), and of prenatal development (embryology). International nomenclature estab. 1895.

Anaxagoras (ăn"ŭksă'gŭrŭs), c.500–c.428 B.C., Greek philosopher. Held that an all-pervading mind (nous) governed creation of order by combining particles to make the physical world.

Anaximander (ŭnăk"sĭmăn'dŭr), c.611–c.547 B.C., Greek philosopher. Thought that the primary source of all things was the "boundless," an inchoate mass, separated to make the physical world by rotary motion begun by the nous (world mind).

Anaximenes (ăn"ŭksĭm'ĭnĕz), 6th cent. B.C., Greek philosopher, who taught that air was basic universal substance.

Anceschi, Luciano (lōōchä'nō änchĕs'kē), 1911–, Italian writer. Editor of a literary review; known for his poetry. criticism. translations.

Anchieta, José de (zhōōzä' dŭ änshē'tŭ), 1530–97, Portuguese missionary in Brazil, a Jesuit, called first Brazilian writer.

Anchises (ăn-kī'sēz, ăngkī'sēz), in Greek legend, Trojan hero; father of Aeneas by Aphrodite.

Anchorage (ăng'kŭrĭj), city (pop. 44,237), S central Alaska, at head of Cook Inlet; founded 1914 as hq. of Alaska RR. State's largest city. Now fishing center, market and supply point for gold-mining regions to N; metropolis for Matanuska Valley coal mining and farming; air-traffic center of Alaska. Petroleum one of chief industries; large iron-ore deposits SW of city. Seat of Alaska Methodist Univ.; Elmendorf Air Force Base is nearby. City devastated by earthquake in March, 1964.

anchovy (ăn'chōvē), small fish of herring family. Spanish and Italian anchovies (Engraulis encrasicholus) cured by using fermentation; Norwegian or Swedish sprats or brislings (genus Clupea) without it.

Ancona (ängkō'nä), city (pop. 103,310), cap. of Ancona prov., chief city of the Marches, central Italy; Adriatic port. Settled by Syracusan Greeks 4th cent. B.C.; medieval maritime republic; passed under direct papal rule 1532. Byzantine-Romanesque cathedral (11th–13th cent.): Arch of Trajan.

Ancren Riwle (äng'krŭn rē'ōōlŭ, rōōl', äng'krŭn) [Mid. Eng.,= anchoresses' rule], anonymous tract written (c.1200) for three ladies about to enter hermitage. Rare example of Middle English prose.

Ancyra: see ANKARA, Turkey.

Andalusia (ăndŭlōō'zhŭ, –shŭ), Span. Andalucía, region, SW Spain, on the Mediterranean and the Atlantic, crossed by Sierra Nevada and Sierra Morena and by Guadalquivir R. Cities: Seville, Granada, Córdoba, Cádiz, Málaga, Huelva. The climate is subtropical, the soil partly very fertile, producing cereals, fruit, olives. Cattle and horse raising. Copper, iron, zinc, and lead mines have been exploited since anc. times. Settled by Phoenicians (11th cent. B.C.), then by Greeks, Carthaginians, Romans, Andalusia was conquered by the Moors (A.D. 711), under whom it reached greatest prosperity. It was reconquered by Castile in 13th cent., except GRANADA, which fell in 1492.

Andalusia (ăndŭlōō'shŭ, –shŭ), city (pop. 10,263), S Ala., near Fla. line S of Montgomery, in farm and pine area; settled c.1830.

Andaman and Nicobar Islands (ăn'dŭmŭn, nĭkōbär'), territory (3.215 sq. mi.; pop. 63,500), India, in Bay of Bengal; cap. Port Blair. Lumber and copra.

Andersen, Hans Christian, 1805–75, Danish poet, novelist, and writer of fairy tales. After poverty-ridden, unhappy early years and failure of early writings, he gained success with a novel, Improvisatoren (1835). In same year appeared Eventyr, first of many volumes of fairy tales that were to make him revered and beloved all over the world. Among his stories are "The Ugly Duckling," "The Brave Tin Soldier," "The Little Mermaid," and "The Red Shoes."

Andersen Nexo, Martin, Dan. Nexø, 1869–1954, Danish novelist. His proletarian novels (e.g., Pelle the Conqueror, 4 vols., 1906–10) did much to improve social conditions in Denmark.

Anderson, Carl David, 1905–, American physicist. Shared 1936 Nobel Prize in Physics for discovery of POSITRON. Codiscoverer of MESON.

Anderson, Elizabeth Garrett, 1836–1917, English physician. Opened hospital, first in England to be staffed by women physicians. Her efforts led to opening of British medical examinations to women.

Anderson, Dame Judith, 1898–, Australian actress, originally named Frances Margaret Anderson. Came to U.S. 1918. Noted as an actress of tragedy in *Macbeth* (1937 and 1941) and in Robinson Jeffers's *Medea* (1947).

Anderson, Marian, 1902–, American Negro contralto. Her first great successes were in Europe. Was first Negro to sing with the Metropolitan Opera. Appointed (1958) alternate delegate to UN General Assembly.

Anderson, Maxwell, 1888–1959, American dramatist. Was a journalist until the success of play written with Lawrence Stallings, *What Price Glory* (1924). Plays (some in blank verse) include *Elizabeth the Queen* (1930), *Winterset* (1935), *High Tor* (1937), *Joan of Lorraine* (1946), *The Bad Seed* (1954).

Anderson, Robert, 1805–71, American army officer, defender of Fort SUMTER.

Anderson, Sherwood, 1876–1941, American author. Self-educated, he wrote in a strongly American, naturalistic vein short stories (e.g., *Winesburg, Ohio,* 1919, *The Triumph of the Egg,* 1920), novels (e.g., *Poor White,* 1920, *Dark Laughter,* 1925), and autobiographical volumes.

Anderson. **1** Industrial city (pop. 49,061), E central Ind., on White R., NE of Indianapolis; platted 1823. Anderson Col. is here. Moravian Indian mission was nearby 1801–6. Mounds State Park, with many Indian mounds, is near. **2** City (pop. 41,316), NW S.C., between Saluda and Savannah rivers, SW of Greenville, in farm, cotton, and livestock area; founded 1826.

Andersonville, village (pop. 263), SW Ga., NNE of Americus. In **Andersonville Prison** (now state park) here, tens of thousands of Union soldiers confined (1864–65) in Civil War. Conditions were so bad that over 12,000 died. Nearby is Andersonville Natl. Cemetery.

Andersson, Karl Johan, 1827–67, Swedish explorer in area of South-West Africa and Bechuanaland. Reached L. Ngami; explored Kubango R.

Andes (ăn′dēz), mountain system, over 4,000 mi. long, South America, paralleling Pacific coast. Stretching from Tierra del Fuego N to VENEZUELA, Andes form one of world's great mountain masses, only Himalayas exceeding them in height. On border between ARGENTINA and CHILE, in Patagonia, are high glacier-fed lakes with noted resorts. Farther N are ACONCAGUA (considered highest peak) and Tupungato separated by USPALLATA PASS. Controversial reports from recent expeditions call OJOS DE SALADO the highest peak. Central Andes broaden in BOLIVIA and PERU, and on plateau and in valleys Inca civilization had its home. Lake Titicaca and volcanoes here. Ranges narrow again in ECUADOR, then divide in COLOMBIA–W range running along coast, E range into Venezuela. Andes influence communication, climate, weather, and life of all South America. Copper, silver, tin are mined in several areas.

Andhra Pradesh (än′drŭ prä′däsh), state (106,052 sq. mi.; pop. c.35,980,000), India; cap. Hyderabad. Created 1956 from Telugu-speaking portions of MADRAS and HYDERABAD states. Includes N part of COROMANDEL COAST. Although mountainous in the Eastern Ghats, area is largely a plain. Rice, cotton, and sugar cane are raised.

Andizhan (ăndĭzhăn′, Rus. ŭndyēzhän′), city (1965 est. pop. 159,000), E central Uzbek SSR, in Fergana Valley. Cotton and silk production.

Andorra (ăndô′rŭ), small state (191 sq. mi.; pop. c.11,000), SW Europe, in E Pyrenees between France and Spain; cap. Andorra la Vella. Catalan-speaking population engages in sheep raising and smuggling. Nominally, Andorra has been under joint suzerainty of Spanish bishops of Urgel and rulers of France since the Middle Ages, but actually it is governed by a council and a syndic.

Andover (ăn′dōvŭr), town (pop. 15,878), NE Mass., near Merrimack R., SSE of Lawrence; settled 1643. PHILLIPS ACADEMY, often called Andover, and Abbot Academy are here. Former Andover Theological Seminary now at Newton Center.

Andrade, Olegario Víctor (ōlägä′ryō vēk′tōr ändrä′dhä), 1839?–1882, Argentine romantic poet, journalist, called national poet because of patriotism.

Andrassy, Julius, Count (ŏn′dräsh-shē), Hung. *Andrássy Gyula,* 1823–90, Hungarian statesman. Leading figure in revolution of 1848–49; returned from exile 1858; negotiated creation of AUSTRO-HUNGARIAN MONARCHY 1867. As prime minister of Hungary he fostered Magyar supremacy over Slavic and other minorities. As foreign minister of Austria-Hungary (1871–79) he signed alliance with Germany (1879). His son, **Count Julius Andrassy,** 1860–1929, Austro-Hungarian foreign minister in 1918, tried unsuccessfully to secure separate peace with Allies. Later led Hungarian royalists.

André, John (än′drē), 1751–80, British spy in American Revolution. Hanged after negotiating with Benedict ARNOLD for betrayal of West Point.

Andrea del Sarto: see SARTO, ANDREA DEL.

Andreanof Islands: see ALEUTIAN ISLANDS.

Andree, Salomon August (ändrä′), 1854–97, Swedish polar explorer. Aeronautical engineer, first to attempt arctic exploration by balloon. Entire expedition lost.

Andreev, Leonid Nikolayevich: see ANDREYEV.

Andreini (ändräē′nē), family of Italian actors, celebrated in COMMEDIA DELL′ ARTE. **Francesco Andreini,** 1548–1624, excelled as the Capitano. His celebrated wife, **Isabella Andreini,** 1562–1604, player in his troupe, the Gelosi, was well-educated and beautiful. Heroines she played were later called Isabella. Her son, **Giovanni Battista** or **Giambattista Andreini** (jämbät-tēs′tä), 1579?–1654, managed the Fedeli troupe. **Virginia Andreini,** 1583–c.1628, his wife, was noted both for acting and beauty.

Andrew, Saint [Gr.,= manly], one of Twelve Disciples; brother of Peter. Mat. 4.18; 10.2; Mark 3.18; 13.3; Luke 6.14; John 1.40–42; 6.8,9; 12.22; Acts 1.13. Traditionally a missionary in Asia Minor, Macedonia, S Russia. When martyred, he is said to have died on X-shaped cross (St. Andrew's cross). Andrew is patron of Russia and of Scotland (Union Jack has white St. Andrew's cross on blue field). Feast day Nov. 30.

Andrew II, d. 1235, king of Hungary (1205–35). Signed Golden Bull, the "Magna Carta of Hungary" (1222; expanded 1231). Father of St. Elizabeth of Hungary and of Bela IV.

Andrewes, Lancelot, 1555–1626, Anglican bishop of Chichester, Ely, and Winchester. A learned preacher, he helped translate Authorized version of Bible and led High Church party opposed to Puritanism.

Andrews, Roy Chapman, 1884–, American naturalist and explorer, director of American Mus. of Natural History (1935–42). Specialist in water mammals of Alaska, Malayan seas, and Asiatic coast, he also led expeditions to study fossil and living animals and plants in central Asia.

Andrews, city (pop. 11,135), W Texas, in Llano Estacado, NW of Midland. Once a prairie cow town, it grew rapidly in 1950s with oil production. Ranching and truck farming.

Andreyev or **Andreev, Leonid Nikolayevich** (lyĭünyĕt′ nyĭkŭl′ŭvich ŭndrä′ŭf), 1871–1919, Russian author. A revolutionist and friend of Gorki, he turned against Bolshevism in 1917 and died in Finland. *The Seven Who Were Hanged* (1908; Eng. tr., 1909) is a story of idealistic revolutionists. Other works reflect a morbid, negative view of society, as the short novel *The Red Laugh* (1905; Eng. tr., 1905) and the dramas *King Hunger* (1907; Eng. tr., 1911) and *He Who Gets Slapped* (1916; Eng. tr., 1921).

Andric, Ivo (ē'vō än'drĭch), 1892–, Yugoslav writer and diplomat. His work includes poetry, essays, short stories, and novels, e.g., *The Bridge on the Drina* (1945), *Bosnian Chronicle* (Eng. tr., 1963), and *The Woman from Sarajevo* (1945). Awarded the 1961 Nobel Prize in Literature.

Andromache (ăndrŏ'mŭkē), in Greek legend, Trojan wife of Hector and mother of Astyanax. After Trojan War she was abducted by Neoptolemus and later married Hector's brother Helenus.

Andromeda (ăndrŏ'mŭdŭ), in Greek religion, Ethiopian princess; daughter of Cepheus and Cassiopeia. Poseidon, angered by claim that she was more beautiful than Nereids, sent sea monster appeasable only by sacrifice of king's daughter. She was rescued by Perseus, who married her.

Andronicus, Livius: see LIVIUS ANDRONICUS.

Andros, Sir Edmund, 1637–1714, British colonial governor in America. Bitterly criticized as governor of N.Y. (1674–81) for highhanded methods. Made governor of Dominion of New England 1686, deposed by colonials 1689. Governor of Va. 1692–97.

Andros (ăn'drŏs), Aegean island (145 sq. mi.; pop. 12,-928), off Greece, second largest and northernmost of CYCLADES; chief town and port, Andros (pop. 3,028). Silk, fruits, wine; manganese.

Androscoggin (ăndrŭskŏg'ĭn), river, c.171 mi. long, formed in NE N.H. Flows S, E, and S again through W Maine to join Kennebec R. near Bath. Important for logging and power.

Androuet du Cerceau (ădrōō-ā' dü sĕrsō'), family of French architects. Founded by **Jacques Androuet** (zhäk) c.1520–c.1584, a leader in introducing Italian Renaissance style into France. His son **Baptiste Androuet du Cerceau** (bätēst'), c.1545–1590, designed Pont-Neuf (Paris). Another son, **Jacques Androuet du Cerceau,** c.1556–1614, worked on Tuileries. Both worked on Louvre.

Andrusov, Treaty of, 1667, peace treaty between Russia and Poland. Smolensk and Seversk provinces and Ukraine E of Dnieper (incl. Kiev) passed to Russia.

Aneirin: see ANEURIN.

anemia, condition resulting from reduction in number or in hemoglobin content of red blood corpuscles. Causes include loss of blood, excessive destruction of red corpuscles, or inadequate blood formation owing to deficiency of iron or of antianemic factor of liver or to bone marrow malfunction.

anemometer: see WIND.

anemone (ŭnĕm'ŭnē) or **windflower,** perennial plant of genus *Anemone.* Some have showy flowers, e.g., the poppy anemone of florists, and the PASQUEFLOWER and fall Japanese anemone of gardens. Among wild kinds is spring-flowering wood anemone. Rue anemone is *Anemonella thalictroides.*

aneroid barometer: see BAROMETER.

anesthesia (ănĭsthē'zhŭ), loss of sensation induced by drugs. General anesthesia causes unconsciousness; diethyl ether (commonly called ether), nitrous oxide (laughing gas), and cyclopropane are the most widely used general inhalation anesthetics; chloroform is now little used. General anesthesia can also be produced by intravenous injection of barbiturates. Local anesthesia affects area around site of application; cocaine was first used, but has now been replaced by other less toxic drugs (including novocaine and procaine). Spinal anesthesia is produced by injection of local anesthetic beneath spinal cord membranes; anesthesia below the level of the injection is complete, there is no effect above, and the patient can remain conscious. Muscle relaxants are used in certain types of surgery; these drugs include curare and its derivatives. Refrigeration can be used to produce anesthesia when blood circulation must be reduced. Extensive heart and brain surgery can be carried on at body temperatures ten or more degrees Fahrenheit below normal; metabolic rate is so much reduced that cells are not damaged by the lack of circulating blood. Various types of anesthesia are frequently used in combination; a skilled anesthetist is present at every major operation in the U.S. Anesthetics are also used in the treatment of certain types of mental illness. Anesthesia pioneers include C. W. LONG, W. T. G. MORTON, Sir J. Y. SIMPSON, Horace WELLS.

Aneto, Pico de (pē'kō dā änä'tō), Fr. *Pic de Néthou* or *Pic d'Anethou,* peak, 11,168 ft. high, NE Spain, near French border; highest of Pyrenees.

Aneurin or **Aneirin** (ă'nyōōrĭn, ä'nīrēn), fl. c.600, Welsh bard whose reputed writings are contained in a 13th-cent. manuscript *Book of Aneirin.*

aneurysm (ăn'yōōrĭzŭm), localized dilation of an artery, commonly the aorta. May be congenital or caused by syphilis, high blood pressure, arteriosclerosis, infection, penetrating injury. Weakened artery may burst resulting in internal hemorrhage and death. Only treatment is surgical replacement of aneurysm by arterial graft or by nylon or dacron tube.

Angara or **Angaran shield,** area of Precambrian rocks comprising much of eastern Soviet Union. Probably remained since early Paleozoic era, above level of invading seas.

Angara (äng"gürä', Rus. ŭn-gürä'), river, 1,134 mi. long, S central Asiatic RSFSR. It rises in L. Baikal, flows N to join the Yenisei above Strelka; navigable between Irkutsk and Bratsk. Area yields iron, coal, and gold. Hydroelectric stations on river.

angel [Gr.,= messenger], bodiless, immortal spirit, limited in knowledge and power. In traditional belief of Judaism, Christianity, and Islam, good angels are accepted as intermediate beings between God and man, living in heaven, able to visit earth in visible or invisible form—sometimes depicted with wings. Hierarchy given in three choirs in descending order: seraphim, cherubim, thrones; dominions, virtues, powers; principalities, archangels, angels. The Bible tells of guardian angels protecting nations or individuals (Dan. 10.13,20; Mat. 18.10); appearing in crises (e.g., wrestling with Jacob, Gen. 32.24–32), at the Annunciation to Mary (Luke 1.28–38), and at the Resurrection (Mat. 28.2–7). Angels of hell, dark angels, or devils, are the evil counterpart of heavenly host; they lead man into evil ways and are headed by SATAN (or Lucifer). Famous literary depictions are in Milton's *Paradise Lost* and Dante's *Divine Comedy.* See also ARCHANGEL; CHERUB; SERAPH.

Angel Falls, perpendicular waterfall, almost 5,000 ft. high, SE Venezuela, in Guiana Highlands.

angelica (ănjĕl'ĭkŭ), perennial herb (*Angelica*). Compound leaves effective in herb gardens. Roots and fruits yield oil used in perfume and liqueurs.

Angelico, Fra (frä änjĕl'ĭkō), 1387–1455, Florentine painter of religious subjects. His many extant works include frescoes in convent of St. Mark's, Florence.

Angel Island, W Calif., in San Francisco Bay; discovered 1775. Was U.S. army base 1863–1946. Radar and missile site estab. here 1952.

Angell, James Burrill, 1829–1916, American educator, editor, and diplomat. Left teaching in 1860 to edit Providence *Journal,* but returned to education to be president of the Univ. of Vermont (1866–71) and the Univ. of Michigan (1871–1909). Minister to China (1880–81) and to Turkey (1897–98). His son, **James Rowland Angell,** 1869–1949, was educator and psychologist. Taught psychology at Univ. of Chicago (1894–1920) and was dean (1911–18) and acting president (1918–19). President of Yale Univ. 1921–37. After 1937 he was educational counselor to the National Broadcasting Company.

Angell, Sir Norman, 1872?–, British internationalist, valiant fighter for peace. Renowned for *The Great Illusion* (1910), arguing futility of war because of economic interests of nations. Many later books. Received 1933 Nobel Peace Prize. Original name was Ralph Norman Angell Lane.

Angels Camp, city (pop. 1,121), central Calif., E of Stockton; founded 1848 after gold was discovered in Mother Lode. Said to be locale of Twain's Jumping Frog story.

Angelus (ăn'jūlŭs), family name of ISAAC II, ALEXIUS III, and ALEXIUS IV, Byzantine emperors.

Angelus Silesius (ăn'jūlŭs sīlē'zhŭs), pseud. of **Johannes Scheffler** (yōhän'ŭs), 1624–77, German poet. After conversion to Catholicism he wrote deeply mystical poems, the best of their period.

Angerman, Swed. *Ångermanälven* (ông'ürmänĕl'vün), river, 280 mi. long, rising in N central Sweden and flowing into Gulf of Bothnia at Harnosand. It is a main logging artery.

Angermanland, Swed. *Ångermanland,* historic province, NE Sweden. Now divided between Vasternorrland and Vasterbotten provinces.

Angers (äzhä'), city (pop. 115,252), cap. of Maine-et-Loire dept., W France, on Maine R., historic cap. of Anjou. Dates from pre-Roman times. Cathedral (12th–13th cent.), medieval castle, museum.

Angevin (ănjŭvĭn), name of two medieval dynasties and their several branches.

First Angevin dynasty, originated 10th cent. with counts of ANJOU. Geoffrey Plantagenet (see GEOFFREY) conquered NORMANDY 1144. His son became king of England as Henry II and founded Angevin or Plantagenet dynasty of English kings (see list of kings at end of article ENGLAND). Count Fulk V of Anjou (see FULK) also became king of Jerusalem, which passed to his younger son, Baldwin III, and to Baldwin's heirs (see JERUSALEM, LATIN KINGDOM OF).

Second Angevin dynasty, main line, collateral branch of Capetian dynasty; originated 1246 when Louis IX granted Anjou in appanage to younger brother Charles (see CHARLES I of Naples); ruled PROVENCE from 1246 and kingdom of NAPLES from 1266 until deposition of JOANNA I (1381).

Second Angevin dynasty, collateral lines. In Naples: CHARLES III, LANCELOT, and JOANNA II, lineal descendants of Charles II of Naples through a younger son, ruled 1381–1435. Succession was contested by Duke Louis of Anjou and his heirs (see LOUIS, kings of Naples; RENÉ). They made good their claim to Provence but not to Naples, which eventually was seized by Alfonso V of Aragon (1442). Their extinction (1486) left the French crown their heir. In Hungary and Poland: see CHARLES I of Hungary; LOUIS I of Hungary and Poland.

Anghiera, Pietro Martire d' (märtē'rä däng-gyä'rä), 1457?–1526, Italian geographer and historian. Moved to Spain in 1487. From explorers and navigators (esp. Columbus, Vespucci, Magellan) he learned latest information about explorations in his time. Wrote *De orbe decades octo* (1530).

angina pectoris (ănjī'nŭ pĕk'tŭrĭs), disease marked by chest pain radiating down patient's left arm. Caused by obstruction of coronary arteries, resulting in lack of oxygen to heart muscle. Differs from coronary THROMBOSIS in that complete closing off of coronary arteries does not occur. Angina is not fatal; it is treated with drugs that dilate the coronary arteries.

Angkor Thom (äng'kôr tôm'), ruined cap. of KHMER EMPIRE, W Cambodia, Indo-China. Among ruins of temples and royal palace are rows of huge seated stone figures. Most ornate carvings are those on the Bayon, temple of Siva or, more probably, of Lokesvara.

Angkor Wat, great temple of anc. Khmer Empire, Cambodia. The moat-surrounded, richly carved temple contains a shrine of Vishnu. It is probably the largest religious structure in the world.

Angles: see ANGLO-SAXONS; EAST ANGLIA; MERCIA; NORTHUMBRIA.

Anglesey or **Anglesea** (both: äng'gŭlsē), island county (275 sq. mi.; pop. 51,700), NW Wales. Shows traces of prehistoric occupation. Chief occupations are agr., sheep-raising, and fishing. Holyhead is terminus of packet service to Dublin.

Anglican Communion, body of churches in communion with Church of England, including Protestant Episcopal Church of America, Scottish Episcopal Church, and Church of Ireland. In 1955 the Church of England in Canada became the Anglican Church of Canada. The Communion embraces a diversity of congregations ranging from extreme "low church" (more or less evangelical) to extreme "high church" called Catholics or Anglo-Catholics).

Anglo-Egyptian Sudan: see SUDAN.

Anglo-Saxon Chronicle, compilation of the annals of English history from start of Christian era, probably begun by Winchester monks c.891 under supervision of Alfred the Great. Of several extant versions, the Peterborough Chronicle continues to 1154.

Anglo-Saxon literature, literary writings in Old English. Many early poems, though composed after English conversion to Christianity, retain paganism, materials, or somber tone of old Germanic tradition (e.g., the epic BEOWULF; WIDSITH; and "Deor," earliest English lyric). Hymn of CAEDMON first religious poem. CYNEWULF and his school adapted saints' lives and homilies; "The Dream of the Rood" notable for vividness and religious intensity. Later poets often paraphrased parts of Bible to produce stirring poems like epic fragment of *Judith.* Usual metrical form is alliterative, four-stress line broken into two half-lines. Literary prose began with translations from Latin by King ALFRED, who probably also directed ANGLO-SAXON CHRONICLE. Finest original prose was in homilies of ÆLFRIC.

Anglo-Saxons, name given Germanic-speaking people who settled in England at end of Roman rule. Angles probably came from Schleswig late 5th cent. and formed foundations for kingdoms of East Anglia, Mercia, and Northumbria. Saxons, a Germanic tribe, settled in England at same time; kingdoms of Sussex, Wessex, and Essex were outgrowths of their settlements. Jutes, probably from area at mouth of the Rhine, settled in Kent and Isle of Wight. Term "Anglo-Saxons," denoting non-Celtic settlers of England, dates from 16th cent. Now more loosely used to denote any people (or their descendants) of British Isles, including Danes and Normans.

Angmagssalik (ängmäg'sälĭk), trading post, E Greenland coast, S of Arctic Circle. Strategic radio meteorological station estab. 1925.

Angola or **Portuguese West Africa,** overseas province (with CABINDA 481,351 sq. mi.; pop. c.4,840,720) of Portugal, SW Africa, on Atlantic Ocean; cap. Luanda. A vast tableland rising abruptly from a narrow coastal strip, then sloping gradually E toward the Congo and Zambezi basins. Land is mostly desert or savanna; country is Africa's leading producer of coffee. Livestock raising and fishing important. Diamonds exported; deposits of iron ore, petroleum, manganese, and copper. The population is mainly Bantu-speaking. Portuguese settled Angola in late 15th cent. Country supplied most of the slaves shipped to Brazil (17th-19th cent.), and the region was virtually depopulated. Colony of Angola became an overseas province 1951, and in 1960s civil uprisings occurred when promised reforms failed to improve conditions.

Angora, Turkey: see ANKARA.

Angostura, Venezuela: see CIUDAD BOLÍVAR.

angostura bark (äng"gŭstū'rŭ), bitter bark of a South American tree, *Cusparia.* It is used in **angostura bitters** to flavor cocktails.

Angoulême, Margaret of or **Marguerite d':** see MARGARET OF NAVARRE.

Angoulême (ägōōlĕm'), city (pop. 48,166), cap. of Charente dept., W France, on Charente R. Brandy distilleries. Seat of counts of Angoulême, 9th–16th cent.; cap. of Angoumois prov. till 1789.

Angren (ŭn-gryĕn'), city (1965 est. pop. 69,000), E Uzbek SSR. Largest lignite-mining center in central Asia.

Angstrom, Anders Jons (än'dûrs yûns' ŏng'strûm), 1814–74, Swedish physicist. Studied light, spectrum analysis.

angstrom unit (äng'strŭm) [for A. J. Angstrom], length unit ($\frac{1}{100,000,000}$ cm) for wave lengths of light.

Anguier, François (fräswä' ägyä'), 1604–69, French sculptor. He and his brother, **Michel Anguier** (mēshěl), 1614–86, also a sculptor, studied in Rome under Algardi. A third brother, **Guillaume Anguier** (gēyōm'), 1628–1708, a painter, was director of the Gobelin factory.

Angus, earls of: see DOUGLAS, ARCHIBALD.

Angus, maritime county (874 sq. mi.; pop. 278,370), E Scotland; co. town Forfar. Mainly agr., also has jute and linen milling. Historic remains include Glamis Castle. Formerly called Forfarshire.

Anhalt (än'hält), former German state, East Germany. Formed enclave in former Prussian Saxony prov. Was ruled until 1918 by princely house descended from Albert the Bear. Joined German Empire in 1871.

Anhwei or **An-hui** (both: än-hwě'), province (c.56,000 sq. mi.; pop. c.31,500,000), E central China; cap. Hofei. The N half, watered by Hwai R., is in N China plain where wheat, kaoliang, and soybeans are raised. The Yangtze R. flows through the S half, which has rice and barley as chief crops. Tea is grown in SW. Coal and iron ore are mined. Part of N Anhwei was transferred (1955) to Kiangsu prov.

anhydride (änhī'drīd), nonmetallic oxide which forms acid with water. Also refers to metallic oxide which forms base with water.

Aniakchak (änēăk'chăk), volcano, W Alaska, in Aleutian Range, on Alaska Peninsula; crater more than 6 mi. in diameter. Erupted 1931.

aniline (ăn'ŭlĭn), colorless, oily liquid, compound of carbon, hydrogen, nitrogen; a basic amine. Molecule consists of a benzene ring with an amino group attached to a carbon of the ring (replacing a hydrogen atom). Used as starting substance in making dyes. Prepared by reduction of nitrobenzene. See *ill.*, p. 106.

animal, member of animal (as distinct from plant) kingdom. Animals require organic food; green plants can manufacture food from inorganic substances (see PHOTOSYNTHESIS). Animals have more highly developed nervous systems, sense organs, locomotion; adapted for securing, ingesting, digesting food. Classification of some microscopic forms disputed. See also INVERTEBRATE; VERTEBRATE; ZOOLOGY. See *ills.*, pp. 116, 118, 329, 347, 512, 656, 657, 1136.

animism, belief that all objects in world have consciousness and some personality. These "spirits" must be propitiated or outwitted. They may include spirits of the dead, leading to ancestor worship; or there may be a general, nonpersonalized spirit akin to the manito of the American Indian. Animism, prevalent in early cultures, has tended to disappear with growth of organized religions, but remains part of Japanese Shinto. See IDOL; SHAMAN.

anise (ăn'ĭs), annual plant, *Pimpinella anisum*. Flower clusters yield aniseed of commerce. Oil from leaves and seeds used as perfume and flavoring. **Anisette** is anise-flavored liqueur.

Anjou (än'jŏo, Fr. äzhŏo'), region and former duchy, W France, roughly coextensive with Maine-et-Loire dept.; historic cap. Angers. Drained by Loire, it is fertile and has excellent vineyards. Early counts of Anjou (see ANGEVIN dynasty) acquired Saumur, Touraine, Maine, Normandy and acceded to English throne with Henry II (1154). Anjou was confiscated (1204) by Philip II of France; became appanage of royal house; was raised to duchy 1360.

Ankara (äng'kärä), city (pop. 650,067), cap. of Turkey, central Anatolia; known anciently as Ancyra, later as Angora. An important town from Hittite times and a provincial cap. under the Romans, it later sank into insignificance until it replaced Constantinople as Turkish cap. in 1923. Except for its old citadel it is a com-

pletely modern city. Its university was founded 1925. Ankara was the scene of Tamerlane's victory over BAJAZET I (1402). The region is famed for its longhaired goats and the production of Angora wool or mohair.

Anking (än'chĭng'), commercial city (pop. 105,300), Anhwei prov., China, on Yangtze R. Became treaty port 1902. Called Hwaining from 1912 to 1949.

Ann, Cape, NE Mass., N of Mass. Bay. Noted for old fishing villages, resorts, and artists' colonies (esp. GLOUCESTER and ROCKPORT).

Anna (Anna Ivanovna), 1693–1740, empress of Russia (1730–40), cousin and successor of Peter II. Ruled autocratically through her German favorites. Intervened in War of the POLISH SUCCESSION; campaigned against Turkey (1736–39). Ivan VI succeeded her.

Anna [Gr.,= Heb. HANNAH]. **1** Aged prophetess who hailed Jesus' presentation at the Temple. Luke 2.36–38. **2** In Tobit, the mother of young Tobias.

Anna Comnena (kŏmně'nù), b. 1083, d. after 1148, Byzantine princess and historian; daughter of Alexius I. Plotted against her brother JOHN II, seeking to put her husband on the throne. Discovered, she was pardoned and retired to a convent to write the *Alexiad*, a history covering the reign of Alexius I and the First Crusade.

Anna Ivanovna: see ANNA, empress of Russia.

Annam (ŭnăm'), former state (c.58,000 sq. mi.), in central Vietnam; cap. Hué. Between Tonkin (N) and Cochin China (S). Its 800-mile coast is on China Sea. Crops include rice (insufficient for Annam's needs), cinnamon, cocoa, and cotton. Even before Chinese invasion of Annam (c.214 B.C.), the Annamese had been under influence of Chinese culture for c.2,000 years. Chinese rule lasted until 1428, when the Annamese estab. independent kingdom. After 1558 Annam was split between two dynasties of Hué and Tonkin; united again 1802 under the Hué. Maltreatment of French missionaries by native officials led to France's military campaigns (begun 1858); result was estab. of French protectorate over Annam in 1884. Annam divided by Geneva Agreements of 1954; area N of 17° parallel became part of Democratic Republic of Vietnam, rest part of South Vietnam.

Annapolis (ùnăp'ùlĭs), city (pop. 23,385), state cap., central Md., on S bank of Severn R. near its mouth on Chesapeake Bay SSE of Baltimore. Business and shipping center of agr. area with boatyards and seafood industry. Settled c.1648 by Va. Puritans, it became provincial cap. 1694. Was important colonial social and commercial center. First newspaper in Md. pub. here 1745. Annapolis Convention (held here 1786) led to Federal Constitutional Convention. Seat of SAINT JOHN'S COLLEGE and UNITED STATES NAVAL ACADEMY. Some of finest Georgian architecture in U.S. is preserved. Most famous structure is State House (1772–79), oldest state capitol in continuous use in U.S. and meeting place of Congress (1783) where Washington resigned as commander in chief of Continental army. Also has McCubbin House, where Thomas Jefferson and James Madison lived (1783–84) and Old Treasury building (c.1695).

Annapolis, river, N.S., Canada, rising NE of Annapolis Royal in a valley noted for apple orchards. Flows c.75 mi. into **Annapolis Basin,** tidal arm of Bay of Fundy (c.25 mi. long, 3–5 mi. wide).

Annapolis Convention (1786), interstate convention called by Virginia to discuss a uniform regulation of commerce. Resulted in the calling of the Federal Constitutional Convention.

Annapolis Royal, town (pop. 800), W N.S., Canada, on Annapolis R. Founded as Port Royal by de Monts (1605), it was destroyed by Samuel Argall in 1614 and later rebuilt by the French. Changed hands between French and English until 1710, when it was captured by New Englanders under Francis Nicholson. Cap. of N.S. to 1749. Ruins of fort in Fort Anne Natl. Park (c.30 acres; estab. 1917).

Annapurna (ŭn-nŭpŏŏr'nù), mountain, Nepal, in Himalayas. Annapurna I (26,502 ft.), the higher of its two peaks, was climbed 1950 by French expedition led by Maurice Herzog. Annapurna II is 26,041 ft. high.

Ann Arbor, city (pop. 67,340), S Mich., on Huron R., W of Detroit, in fruitgrowing area; laid out 1824. Grew as farm trade center. Seat of Univ. of MICHIGAN; has several museums. Indian mounds in area.

Annas, Jewish high priest, who questioned Jesus. Non-Bible sources call him retired high priest. Was Caiaphas' father-in-law. John 18.13,24; Acts 4.6–22.

Anne, Saint [from Heb. Hannah], in tradition, mother of the Virgin, wife of St. Joachim. She is not mentioned in Scripture. Patroness of Quebec (Ste Anne de Beaupré) and Brittany (Sainte-Anne-d'Auray). Feast: July 26.

Anne, 1665–1714, queen of England, Scotland, and Ireland (1702–7), later first queen of Great Britain (1707–14); last Stuart ruler. Her reign, one of transition to parliamentary government, dominated by War of SPANISH SUCCESSION (1702–13). Many victories won by duke of MARLBOROUGH (whose wife was long favorite of the queen), but high cost of war source of friction between Tories and Whigs. None of Anne's children survived her and, by Act of Settlement (1701), George I succeeded to the throne. Despite personal mediocrity, her reign was marked by intellectual awakening, popularization of Palladian architecture, and by growth of empire and parliamentary government and of the political power of the press.

annealing, process for rendering materials (e.g., glass, metals) less brittle, more ductile, by relieving internal stress. Accomplished by heating, then cooling slowly and uniformly. See TEMPERING; HARDENING.

Annecy (änsē'), city (est. pop. 33,114), cap. of Haute-Savoie dept., E France, on scenic L. Annecy. Seat of bishops of Geneva after 1535; birthplace of St. Francis of Sales. Picturesque old city crossed by canals; medieval castle of counts of Geneva.

Anne de Beaujeu (dù bōzhŭ'), c.1460–1522, regent of France for her brother, Charles VIII, after death of Louis XI (1483). Arranged Charles's marriage with Anne of Brittany.

annelid: see EARTHWORM; LEECH.

Anne of Austria, 1601–66, queen of France, daughter of Philip III of Spain; married Louis XIII (1615). Neglected by husband; persecuted by Richelieu. Her regency (1643–61) for her son, Louis XIV, was dominated by MAZARIN, disturbed by Fronde.

Anne of Brittany, 1477–1514, queen of France as wife of Charles VIII (1491–98) and of Louis XII (1499–1514); duchess of Brittany (1488–1514). Struggling to keep Brittany independent from invading French, she married by proxy (1490) Maximilian of Austria (later Emperor Maximilian I). Maximilian's dilatoriness and the use of force by France forced her to annul marriage. Her two subsequent marriages led to union of France and Brittany.

Anne of Cleves (klēvz), 1515–57, queen of England, fourth wife of Henry VIII. Henry married her (1540) for political purposes under influence of Thomas CROMWELL, but had marriage nullified same year.

Anne of Denmark, 1574–1619, queen consort of James I of England.

annexation, formal act asserting a state's sovereignty over newly incorporated territory (generally areas not inhabited by civilized peoples, areas settled by nationals of annexing power, areas already under protectorates, or conquered territory). The governing body of annexing power must ratify the act. Consent of all interested powers necessary for recognition in international law.

Anniston, city (pop. 33,657), NE Ala., ENE of Birmingham, in iron-mining region of Appalachian foothills; founded 1872 as "company town." U.S. Fort McClellan is nearby.

annual, plant which germinates, flowers, seeds, and dies within one year (e.g., marigold and zinnia), as distinguished from BIENNIAL and PERENNIAL plants.

Annunzio, Gabriele D': see D'ANNUNZIO, GABRIELE.

anode: see ELECTRODE and ELECTROLYSIS.

Anoka (ūnō'kù), city (1965 pop. 11,529), E Minn., on Mississippi at confluence of Rum R., NNW of Minneapolis; settled 1844. At first a trading post and lumber town, later a farm trade center.

Anouilh, Jean (zhä' änōōē'yù), 1910–, French dramatist, known for modern adaptations of classical stories. His plays include *Antigone* (1942), *The Waltz of the Toreadors* (1952), *The Lark* (1953), *Becket* (1959), and *L'Orchestre* (1962).

Ansbach (äns'bäkh), city (pop. 33,237), cap. of Middle Franconia, W Bavaria. Produces cars, motors, chemicals. Grew around 8th-cent. abbey; residence from 1331 of Franconian branch of the HOHENZOLLERN dynasty. Passed to Prussia 1791; to Bavaria 1806. Has Romanesque church (12th–15th cent.).

Anschluss (än'shlōōs) [Ger.,= junction], term applied to the project of union between Austria and Germany. Though forbidden by the peace treaties of 1919, it was advocated in Austria by both Socialists and National Socialists and became a reality when Hitler annexed Austria to Germany (1938–45).

Anselm, Saint (än'sĕlm), 1033?–1109, archbishop of Canterbury (1093–1109), Doctor of the Church, b. Italy. As abbot of Bec in Normandy, he gained wide reputation before succeeding his friend and master Lanfranc as archbishop. He stoutly upheld the papal claims in the quarrel over power to appoint bishops (see INVESTITURE) and had long quarrels with Kings William II and Henry I. His theological writings (e.g., *Monologium* and *Cur Deus Homo?*) were influential. Offered ontological proof of existence of God—that the fact that the human mind can conceive of an Infinite Being necessarily means that such a Being must exist. Feast: April 21.

Anshan (än'shän'), city (pop. c.600,000), Liaoning prov., China; on branch of South Manchurian RR. Steel center.

Ansky, pseud. of Solomon Rapoport, 1863–1920, Yiddish poet and playwright, b. Russia. Author of DYBBUK.

Anson, Adrian Constantine (Cap Anson), 1851–1922, American baseball player-manager. Four times National League batting champion.

Anson, George Anson, Baron, 1697–1762, British admiral. On voyage (1740–44) around world inflicted much damage on Spanish shipping. As first lord of the admiralty helped reorganize naval administration.

Anson, city (pop. 2,890), W central Texas, NNW of Abilene; settled c.1880. Once a cow town, now shipping point for agr. region. Oil wells and refinery in area. Ruins of Fort Phantom Hill, frontier outpost built 1851, are SE.

Ansonia, city (pop. 19,819), SW Conn., on Naugatuck R., NW of New Haven; settled from Derby 1651.

ant, cosmopolitan social insect, order Hymenoptera. Three body sections; narrow constriction between thorax and abdomen; usually black or various shades of brown, red, yellow. Majority nest underground, others in decaying trees or plants; some make paper nests. Colonies (dozens to hundred thousands) usually include one or more queens (egg-laying, usually winged females); female wingless workers, usually sterile; and fertile males, usually winged. Males and females swarm in nuptial flight; males die; female sheds wings, and for rest of life (up to 15 years) can lay fertilized eggs. Workers live 4 to 7 years. Adult ants eat chiefly liquids of plants and animals; colonies often have parasites, sometimes enslave other species. TERMITE is miscalled white ant.

Antaeus (äntē'ùs), in Greek mythology, giant; son of Poseidon. He became stronger when touching earth (his mother, Gaea). Hercules overcame him by lifting him into the air.

Antakya, Turkey: see ANTIOCH.

Antalya (äntälyä'). city (pop. 50,908). SW Turkey; a Mediterranean seaport. Silk mfg.; chrome and manganese deposits nearby. Known anciently as Attaleia or Attalia and later as Adalia.

Antar (äntär'), fl. 600, Arabian warrior and poet. Rose from slave to tribal chief. Represented in MUALLAQAT. Hero of popular Arabic romance *Antar*.

Antarctica, continent of 5,000,000–6,000,000 sq. mi. surrounding South Pole. Encircling waters, sometimes called Antarctic Ocean, challenge navigation. Roughly circular outline broken by Ross and Weddell seas and Palmer Peninsula, c.600 mi. from South America, the only relatively near land. Coasts circled by pack ice hundreds of miles wide ending in sheer ice cliffs. Giant mountain ranges (peaks over 15,000 ft.) surround perpetually ice-capped central plateau. Highest average altitude and severest climate of any continent. Discovered by whalers, explored by 19th-cent. voyages of Palmer, Biscoe, Weddell, Ross, and others. Exploration impeded until 20th cent. technology made possible Amundsen, Scott, and U.S. naval expeditions (led by Byrd). Territorial claims by many nations conflicted. In 1959 Argentina, Australia, Belgium, Chile, France, Great Britain, Japan, New Zealand, Norway, South Africa, USSR, and the U.S. signed a treaty; they agreed to use Antarctica only for peaceful purposes and recognized no existing territorial claims. Preliminary surveys (1955–57) prepared the way for U.S. participation in researches of the International Geophysical Year (1957–1958); Byrd headed another preliminary expedition, Operation Deep Freeze, part of the U.S. contribution to Antarctic exploration extending into the IGY. During the IGY, the U.S. joined other countries in studying from Antarctic bases the weather, atmosphere, icecap, underlying rock, and surrounding waters. **Antarctic regions,** extending beyond Antarctic Circle (lat. 66° 17′ S) to lat. 50° S, are inimical to human life: have only mosses, lichens, algae, and support no year-round animal life except small wingless insects, microscopic organisms, and penguins. In summer, whales, seals, birds, and other penguins inhabit coast and sea. Once temperate or tropical, continent may again be habitable in millions of years, say some scientists.

anteater, name for sundry insect-eating animals; more accurately applied to a toothless group, order Edentata, of Central and South America. Great anteater or ant bear (*Myrmecophaga*) has long, nearly round head and snout, sticky tongue, coarse-haired body (c.4 ft. long), sharp claws, and long broad tail. Collared or lesser anteater (*Tamandua*) is half as large, short-haired, yellowish and black, and arboreal. Two-toed (*Cyclopes*) is squirrel-sized with silky yellow fur. See also PANGOLIN and ECHIDNA.

antelope, hoofed ruminant mammal, order Artiodactyla, family Bovidae or, in some classifications, family Antilopidae. True antelopes confined to Asia and Africa. African include bushbuck, waterbuck, lechwe, marshbuck, impala or palla, kudu, nyala, springbuck, bongo, dik-dik, klipspringer, ELAND, GNU, Nilgai or blue bull, four-horned antelope, and black buck in India. See also GAZELLE; PRONGHORN; ROCKY MOUNTAIN GOAT.

antelope brush, low deciduous shrub (*Purshia tridentata*) of deserts and arid slopes in W U.S. Important browsing plant for cattle and deer.

antenna (äntĕn'ŭ) or **aerial** (âr'ēŭl), in radio, system of wires or metal bars to project or intercept radio waves. Radio waves of a particular wave length are best projected or intercepted by an antenna wire having a corresponding length, equal to the wave length of the radio wave or to a fraction of it. Directional antennas transmit or receive best only in certain selected directions. A loop is the simplest directional antenna.

Specially shaped antennas are needed for the specific circuit requirements of television transmission and reception.

anthem, sacred choral composition. Form arose in the Anglican church as English counterpart of the Latin motet. Important names in its history are Thomas Tallis, William Byrd, Henry Purcell, Handel, and Mendelssohn. Term also used for any hymn of praise or jubilation; hence, "national anthem."

Anthemius of Tralles (änthē'mēŭs, träl'ēz), 6th cent., Greek architect and mathematician. With Isidorus of Miletus he built the church of HAGIA SOPHIA in Constantinople, A.D. 532–37.

Anthony, Saint (ăn'tŭnē, –thŭnē), 251?–356, Egyptian hermit. In the desert he resisted temptations of devil. Colony of hermits grew about his retreat. Called the founder of monasticism. Feast: Jan. 17.

Anthony, Marc, Roman soldier: see ANTONY.

Anthony, Susan B(rownell) (ăn'thŭnē), 1820–1906, American reformer, leader of woman-suffrage movement. Founder of Daughters of Temperance. Coorganizer (1863) of Women's Loyal League to support Lincoln's government, especially emancipation policy. With Elizabeth Cady Stanton she secured first laws in N.Y. giving women rights over their children and property, and with Mrs. Stanton organized Natl. Woman Suffrage Association. She helped compile a history of the woman-suffrage movement and was president (1892–1900) of the Natl. American Woman Suffrage Association.

Anthony of Padua, Saint, 1195–1231, Portuguese Franciscan. In a vision he received the child Jesus in his arms, and is usually so depicted in art. Canonized 1232. Invoked to find lost articles. Feast: June 13.

anthracene (ăn'thrŭsēn), colorless, crystalline solid with blue fluorescence, melting at 217°C. and boiling at c.350°. Molecule consists of three interlocking benzene rings, side by side; central ring shares two carbon atoms with each of the outside rings; thus there are 14 carbon atoms. Source is coal tar; its derivatives are used in producing certain dyes. It is first member of **anthracene series** of aromatic hydrocarbons. See *ill.*, p. 106.

anthrax, infectious bacterial disease of animals transmissible to man by contact. Causative bacillus may exist as spore for years. Koch proved relation of bacillus to the disease; Pasteur developed method of vaccinating sheep and cattle against it.

anthropology (ănthrŭpŏl'ŭjē), science of man and his works. Concerned with the origin, development, and varieties of mankind and CULTURE, emphasizing data from nonliterate peoples. Physical and cultural anthropology are the two major divisions. Cultural anthropology includes ARCHAEOLOGY, the study of extinct cultures; ethnology, the study of living cultures; and linguistics. Physical anthropology deals basically with human evolution.

anthropometry (ănthrŭpŏm'ŭtrē), measurement of human body and its parts for studies in race classification, growth and human paleontology. Now supplemented by genetic interpretations and environmental studies.

Antibes (ätēb'), town (est. pop. 27,064), Alpes-Maritimes dept., SE France; Mediterranean port. It includes Juan-les Pins (zhüä'-lä-pē') and other resorts on the French Riviera.

antibiotic (ăn"tēbĭŏ'tĭk) name for several chemical substances that destroy or inhibit growth of certain microorganisms. Mostly obtained from fungi and bacteria; some are synthesized. R. J. Dubos prepared (1939) gramicidin and tyrocidine, first antibiotics applied medically. Penicillin, isolated (1928) by Sir Alexander Fleming, was used widely after Sir H. W. Florey and others proved it (1940) to be effective and nontoxic. Other antibiotics used in treatment of human disease include streptomycin, discovered by S. A. Waksman and associate (1943); chloramphenicol; neomycin; the tetracyclines. Indiscriminate use of antibiotics in treatment of disease is dangerous, for disease-causing bacteria may develop resistance. Hospital infections with antibiotic-resistant staphylococci can cause serious problems; kanamycin is effective against some of these strains. Careless use of antibiotics can also interfere with development of natural immunity. Continuing studies of other bad effects show them to include anaphylactic shock (see ANAPHYLAXIS), gastrointestinal disturbances, blood diseases, skin rashes; some fatalities have occurred. Antibiotics are also used to promote growth of livestock and crop plants and to preserve food. See also SULFA DRUGS.

antibody, specific substance produced by tissues when stimulated by an antigen (e.g., bacteria, toxins, foreign proteins) and capable of neutralizing or giving immunity against the specific antigen.

Antichrist, in Christian belief, person who will lead forces of evil on earth against ultimately victorious forces of good. 1 John 2.18–22; 4.3; 2 John 7. Often identified with Beast of Revelation; wrongly linked to Satan. Christians have tended to call opponents of their particular beliefs the Antichrist.

Anti-Comintern Pact: see COMINTERN and AXIS.

Anti-Corn-Law League, organization formed 1839 to work for repeal of English CORN LAWS. Its leading figures were Richard COBDEN and John BRIGHT.

Anticosti, island (pop. 532), 135 mi. long, 10 to 30 mi. wide. E Que., Canada. at head of Gulf of St. Lawrence. Main industry lumbering. Discovered by Cartier 1534. Granted to Jolliet and long held by his heirs. Returned to Canada 1774. Privately owned since 1895.

anticyclone [opposite of a cyclone], area of high barometric pressure, roughly circular, with wind blowing spirally outward (clockwise in Northern hemisphere, counterclockwise in Southern hemisphere). Associated with fair weather.

antidote: see POISON.

Antietam campaign (ăntē′tŭm), Sept., 1862, of Civil War. In invasion of Md. and Pa., R. E. Lee sent Stonewall Jackson to take Harpers Ferry and moved toward Hagerstown. Harpers Ferry taken Sept. 15, but Gen. G. B. McClellan on Sept. 14 stopped Lee, who fell back to Sharpsburg (c.9 mi. W of South Mt.), behind Antietam Creek. Sept. 17 was bloodiest day of war, a Union victory only in that Lee was stopped.

antifreezing solution, aqueous solution with freezing point below that of water used in automobile cooling systems. Solutions include alcohol (evaporates rapidly); salt (formerly used; highly corrosive); glycerin or glycerol (sluggish at low temperatures); and ethylene glycol (acts upon rubber).

antifriction metal, ALLOY used to line machinery bearings when ball bearings are not used. Consists of soft matrix in which hard particles are embedded. See also BABBITT METAL.

antigen: see ANTIBODY.

Antigone (ăntĭ′gŭnē), in Greek legend, daughter of Oedipus. When CREON forbade burial of her brother POLYNICES, she defied him and performed the funeral rites. Creon ordered her buried alive.

Antigonish (ăn′tĭgōnĭsh′), town (pop. 4,344), NE N.S., Canada. on West R. and NE of Truro. Seat of St. Francis Xavier Univ. (R.C.; for men and women; 1853) which has promoted a noted cooperative here.

Antigonus (ăntĭ′gŭnŭs), rulers of anc. Macedon. **Antigonus I** (Cyclops), 382?–301 B.C., general of Alexander the Great and ruler in Asia. He tried to rebuild the entire empire, but in the wars of the DIADOCHI he was defeated and killed at Ipsus (301). His son, Demetrius I, conquered Macedonia. Demetrius' son, **Antigonus II** (Gonatas), c.320–239 B.C., took Macedon 276, rebuilt the state and amid much warfare briefly united Greece. Succeeded by Demetrius II. **Antigonus III** (Doson), d. 221 B.C., was regent for Demetrius' son, PHILIP V, but proclaimed himself king

(227). Aided the Achaean League against Cleomenes and rebuilt power in Greece.

Antigua (ăntē′gwŭ), city (pop. 21,984), S central Guatemala, a commercial and tourist center. Founded 1542 to succeed Ciudad Vieja as cap. In 18th cent. had much splendor. Earthquakes caused removal of cap. to Guatemala City (1776).

Antigua (ăntē′gwŭ), island (area and pop. with Barbuda and Redonda 171 sq. mi.) in LEEWARD ISLANDS, principal island of Antigua presidency (1963 pop. 61,664); cap. St. John's. Discovered by Columbus 1493, settled by British 1632. Member of Federation of The WEST INDIES until federation was dissolved in 1962. In 1967 became one of WEST INDIES ASSOCIATED STATES.

antihistamine, any substance which reduces the physiological effect of HISTAMINE in tissues, excepting those substances which act by producing a physiological effect opposite to and independent of the histamine. See also ALLERGY.

Anti-Lebanon, mountain range between Syria and Lebanon, rising to Mt. HERMON. Name also Anti-Liban.

Antilles: see WEST INDIES.

Anti-Masonic party, American political organization which rose after the disappearance in W N.Y. in 1826 of William Morgan. The Masons were said, without proof, to have murdered him, and in reaction local organizations arose to refuse support to Masons for public office. At Baltimore, in 1831, Anti-Masons held first national nominating convention of any party and issued first written party platform. Helped in 1834 to form Whig party.

antimatter, matter comprising the antiparticles that are counterparts of the elementary particles of ordinary matter. The antiparticle of the ELECTRON is the positron; cosmic ray decay products may be antiparticles, and antiparticles may be made artificially. Antiparticles are short-lived, reacting with ordinary particles to annihilate each other. See also QUANTUM THEORY; PROTON; NEUTRON; NEUTRINO.

antimetabolite: see METABOLITE.

antimony (ăn′timō′nē), silver-white crystalline element (symbol = Sb [L. *stibium*]; see also ELEMENT, table), with properties of metal and nonmetal. Forms stibine, a poison gas, with hydrogen; combines readily with oxygen, sulphur, phosphorus, and the halogens. Used in making BABBITT METAL, BRITANNIA METAL, TYPE METAL, castings, batteries, and medicines. Chief ore is STIBNITE. Detected by MARSH'S TEST.

antinomianism (ăntĭnō′mēŭnĭzŭm) [Gr.,= against law], belief in Christianity that Christians, redeemed by Christ and justified by faith, need not follow the moral law (esp. that of the Old Testament). Considered heretical by majority from early Christian days to accusation of Anne Hutchinson in colonial Mass. Only large sect to hold the doctrine was that of ANABAPTISTS.

Antinoüs (ăntĭ′nōŭs), c.110–130, favorite of Emperor Hadrian, b. Bithynia. Notable for his youthful beauty, he was drowned in the Nile. Hadrian honored his memory by naming cities after him and having him deified.

Antioch or **Antakya** (äntäkyä′), town (pop. 45,848), S Turkey, on Orontes R., at foot of Mt. Silpius. Founded c.300 B.C. by Seleucus I. At crossing of routes from the Euphrates to the sea and from El Bika to Asia Minor, it soon became one of world's largest trade centers. Here followers of Jesus were first called Christians. City is one of three ancient patriarchates: seat of a Melchite, a Maronite, and a Jacobite patriarch. Fell to Persians 538 and to Arabs 637. Was under Byzantine Empire 969–1085 and under Seljuk Turks 1085–98. Taken 1098 by Crusaders, it became virtually independent fief of Latin Kingdom of Jerusalem under BOHEMOND I and successors. Fell to Mamelukes of Egypt 1268 and to Ottoman Turks 1516. Transferred to Syria 1920 but restored to Turkey 1939. Modern

Antioch 46 Antwerp

Antioch occupies mere fraction of ancient city, remains of whose walls, aqueduct, theater, and castle survive. Excavations here and at near-by Daphne have yielded splendid mosaics. An early find was Great Chalice of Antioch, held by many to be Holy Grail.

Antioch, city (pop. 17,305), W Calif., on San Joaquin R., NE of Oakland; founded 1849–50. A processing center in farm region.

Antioch College, at Yellow Springs, Ohio, near Dayton; coed.; chartered 1852, opened 1853. Horace Mann, first president, envisioned program of combined intellectual and social development. Work-study program, which requires about five years, was estab. 1921.

Antiochus (ăntī'ūkŭs), kings of anc. Syria. **Antiochus I** (Soter), d. c.261 B.C. (reigned 280–c.261 B.C.), was son of Seleucus I. **Antiochus II** (Theos), d. 247 B.C. (reigned c.261–247 B.C.). Rivalry with PTOLEMY II ended with marriage to Ptolemy's daughter Berenice, but warfare followed his death. **Antiochus III** (the Great), d. 187 B.C. (reigned 223–187 B.C.), son of Seleucus II, tried to restore crumbling Seleucid empire. An ally of Philip V, he won much territory, but was crushed by the Romans at Thermopylae (191) and Magnesia (190). **Antiochus IV** (Epiphanes), d. 163 B.C. (reigned 175–163 B.C.), son of Antiochus III, successor of his brother, Seleucus IV. Attempted to Hellenize Judaea, arousing MACCABEES. His invasion of Egypt was thwarted by the Romans.

antiparticle: see ANTIMATTER.

Antipas: see HEROD.

Antipater (ăntī'pŭtŭr), d. 319 B.C., Macedonian general under Alexander the Great, regent in Macedon (334–323 B.C.). Opposed PERDICCAS and later held the kingdom together. After his death came wars of the DIADOCHI.

Antipater, in Bible: see HEROD.

antipodes, places diametrically opposite on earth, thus separated by half the global circumference.

antipope, one supposed to be pope but not subsequently recognized by Holy See. See, e.g., GUIBERT OF RAVENNA; LUNA, PEDRO DE; COSSA, BALDASSARRE.

Anti-Saloon League, U.S. organization working for prohibition of sale of alcoholic liquors. Founded in Ohio 1893. Wielded great political influence.

anti-Semitism, antipathy toward Jews. Pre-19th-cent. anti-Semitism, largely religious, was expressed in persecutions, expulsions, and restrictions (see GHETTO). Motivation may be religious, economic, social, political, or ethnic. In 20th cent. it culminated in doctrine of "Aryan" superiority in NATIONAL SOCIALISM. Hitler exterminated c.6,000,000 European Jews between 1939 and 1945.

antiseptic, agent applied externally to inhibit the growth of or destroy microorganisms. Some examples are alcohol, iodine, dilute carbolic acid, sunlight, and hot water. Antiseptics are used usually to check bacteria in rooms, on surfaces, furnishings, bedding. Influenced by Pasteur's theory that microorganisms cause infection, LISTER was first to use antiseptic in surgery. Modern techniques founded on asepsis (absence of pathogenic organisms).

antislavery movement: see ABOLITIONISTS; SLAVERY.

Antisthenes (ăntĭs'thĭnēz), b. 444 B.C., d. after 371 B.C., Greek philosopher, founder of the school of the Cynics.

Anti-Taurus, Turkish mountain range: see TAURUS.

antitoxin: see TOXIN.

Anti-Trust Act: see CLAYTON ANTI-TRUST ACT; SHERMAN ANTI-TRUST ACT.

Antium, Italy: see ANZIO.

Antofagasta (äntōfägä'stä), city (pop. 214,090), N Chile; a Pacific port. Its founding by Chileans (1870) in Bolivian territory was a cause of war (see PACIFIC, WAR OF THE). Nitrates and copper are chief exports.

Antoine, André (ädrä' ätwän'), 1858–1943, French theatrical manager. His own companies, Théâtre Libre (formed 1887) and Théâtre Antoine (formed 1897),

presented works of naturalist school. His work became a model for experimental theaters.

Antonello da Messina (äntōnĕl'lō dä mäs-sē'nä), c.1430–1479, Italian painter, influenced by Flemish art, influential on Venetian painting.

Antonescu, Ion (yôn äntōnĕ'skoō), 1882–1946, Rumanian marshal and dictator. Appointed premier 1940; forced abdication of Carol II in favor of King MICHAEL; brought Rumania into AXIS camp; gave Hitler virtual control of country. Arrested 1944; executed.

Antonines (ăn'tŭnīnz), name used for several 2d-cent. Roman emperors including Antoninus Pius, Marcus Aurelius, and Commodus.

Antoninus, Wall of, ancient Roman wall built across N Britain in reign of Antoninus Pius–probably A.D. 140–42. It was 37 mi. long.

Antoninus Pius (äntōnī'nŭs pī'ŭs), A.D. 86–A.D. 161, Roman emperor (138–161). Adopted by HADRIAN, he succeeded and administered the empire well. Succeeded by his adopted son, MARCUS AURELIUS.

Antonioni, Michelangelo, 1912–, Italian film director. His films (e.g., L'Avventura, La Notte, L'Eclisse, The Red Desert) are expressionistic portrayals of naturalistic themes.

Antony or Marc Antony, Latin Marcus Antonius, c.83 B.C.–30 B.C., Roman political leader and general. A dashing young soldier of good family, he became a protégé of Julius Caesar, and as tribune he (with Cassius) vetoed the bill to strip Caesar of his army. After serving as Caesar's lieutenant in the Civil War against Pompey, he gained power from the victory. Caesar was assassinated in 44 B.C., and Antony roused the people against the conspirators responsible. He formed an uneasy alliance with Octavian (later AUGUSTUS), was embroiled in trouble trying to gain the province of Gaul assigned to him, and was a member of the Second Triumvirate (Octavian, Lepidus, Antony). He and Octavian defeated the republicans at Philippi (42 B.C.), and in the proscription that followed Antony brought about the death of his enemy Cicero. Antony undertook to rule Asia. In Rome his wife, Fulvia, intrigued against Octavian, but she died, and Antony married Octavian's sister, Octavia. The alliance went on. Antony had, however, already met Cleopatra and fallen under her sway; he ruled from Alexandria in great luxury. Octavian grew impatient, and Antony was deprived of power. Civil war followed. Antony and Cleopatra were defeated in the naval battle at Actium (31 B.C.) and fled to Alexandria. When Octavian approached, Antony committed suicide. He is known to English-speaking people largely through Shakespeare's Julius Caesar and Antony and Cleopatra. Also Marc or Mark Anthony.

Antrim, county (1,098 sq. mi.; pop. 273,923), N. Ireland. County town is BELFAST, a major British port and industrial center. Region mainly agr. with fishing and cattle breeding. E part of county mountainous. N coast has formation known as GIANT'S CAUSEWAY.

Antung (än'dŏong'), former prov. (c.24,000 sq. mi.), Manchuria, NE China; cap. was Tunghwa. Created in 1945, it became part of Liaoning prov. in 1954. **Antung** city (pop. c.360,000), SE Liaoning prov., is at the mouth of the Yalu R. Industrial center. Opened 1907 as treaty port.

Antwerp (ăn'twŭrp), Flemish Antwerpen, Fr. Anvers, province (1,104 sq. mi.; est. pop. 1,482,169), N Belgium. It is a cultivated plain drained by Scheldt R. and Albert Canal. Population is largely Flemish-speaking. The province was part of the duchy of BRABANT. Its cap. is **Antwerp** (est. pop. 243,426; with suburbs 657,485), on the Scheldt. Rivaled only by Rotterdam as largest sea and transit port of continental Europe, Antwerp is also a world diamond center and the seat of the oldest stock exchange (founded 1460). It has oil refineries, automobile plants, flourmills, shipyards. Its churches and museums contain treasures of Flemish art. Rising into

SMALL CAPITALS = cross references. Pronunciation key on inside end pages. Abbreviations: p. 2.

prominence with the decline of Bruges and Ghent, Antwerp was by the 16th cent. the commercial and financial hub of Europe. Its prosperity suffered when it was sacked by mutinous Spanish troops (the "Spanish Fury," 1576), and again when it resisted for 14 months before surrendering to Alexander Farnese (1584–85). The peace of Westphalia (1648) closed the Scheldt to navigation. Antwerp was reduced to insignificance until 1863, when Belgium redeemed from the Dutch the right to collect a toll on Scheldt shipping. The city suffered in both world wars. Captured by British troops in Aug., 1944, it became a vital Allied supply base and was heavily damaged by German rocket weapons. Antwerp was the home of Rubens and birthplace of Sir Anthony Van Dyck. Christophe Plantin (16th cent.) made city a printing center. Among its many splendid buildings are the Gothic Cathedral of Notre Dame and the old guild houses on the Groote Market [market place]. The zoological garden has long been world famous.

Anubis (ánū'bĭs), Egyptian god of the dead. He is depicted as a jackal-headed man.

Anuradhapura (únōō'rädúpōō'rú), town (pop. c.22,-500), N Ceylon. On the site of an ancient cap. (4th cent. B.C.–8th cent. A.D.) of Ceylon. A great Buddhist center, it has ruins of large stupas and the Brazen Palace. Buddhist pilgrims visit bo tree, grown from slip of tree at Buddh Gaya. Also called Anarajapura.

Anvers, Belgium: see ANTWERP.

Anville, Jean Baptiste Bourguignon d' (bōōrgēnyō' dävēl'), 1697–1782, French geographer and cartographer. Noted for accurate maps of ancient geography; had largest collection of maps, atlases, and geographic material in France. Made more than 200 maps.

Anyang (än'yäng'), city (pop. c.135,000), Honan prov., China. Coal-mining center. Cap. of Shang dynasty. Excavations have revealed rich Bronze Age culture.

Anza, Juan Bautista de (hwän'boutēs'tä dä än'sä), 1735–88, Spanish explorer and official in Southwest and Far West, founder of San Francisco, b. Mexico. Governor of New Mexico 1777–88.

Anzengruber, Ludwig (lōōt'vĭkh än'tsúngrōō"búr), 1839–89, Austrian author of successful folk plays. *Das vierte Gebot* [the fourth commandment] is considered one of first naturalistic plays.

Anzhero-Sudzhensk (únzhĕ"rú-sōōjĕnsk'), city (1965 est. pop. 119,000), SW Asiatic RSFSR, on Trans-Siberian RR. One of largest coal-mining centers of Kuznetsk Basin.

Anzio (än'tsyō), Latin *Antium*, town (est. pop. 15,-217), Latium, central Italy, on Tyrrhenian Sea. Bathing resort since Roman times; important Roman ruins. Scene of fierce fighting between Allied beachhead forces and Germans, Jan.–May, 1944. Birthplace of Nero.

Aomori (äōmō'rē), city (pop. 202,211), extreme N Honshu, Japan; chief port of N Honshu. **Aomori** prefecture (3,719 sq. mi.; pop. 1,426,606) has rich timber lands.

Aosta, Val d' (väldäō'stä), autonomous region (1,260 sq. mi.; pop. 99,754) NW Italy, on French and Swiss borders. Includes Gran Paradiso and Italian slopes of Mont Blanc, Matterhorn, Monte Rosa; many resorts. Most of pop. speaks French dialect. The capital is **Aosta** (pop. 30,127), near junction of Great and Little St. Bernard roads.

Apache Indians, North American Indian tribes of the Southwest, speaking Nadene languages (see LANGUAGE, table). Divided into many groups. Chiefly known for fierce opposition (late 19th cent.) to white intrusion into N.Mex. and Ariz. Notable leaders were Geronimo and Cochise.

Apalachee Bay (ăpúlăch'ē), a Gulf of Mexico arm, NW Fla., S of Tallahassee.

Apalachicola (ăp"úlăchĭkō'lú), city (pop. 3,099). NW Fla., SW of Tallahassee, on Apalachicola Bay (land-

locked harbor, bridged 1935), at mouth of Apalachicola R.; founded c.1820. Seafood (oysters, shrimp). Position after 1830 as one of country's largest cotton-shipping ports ruined by Civil War blockade.

Apalachicola, river, NW Fla., formed by junction of Chattahoochee and Flint rivers at Ga. line. Flows c.90 mi. S to Apalachicola Bay. Navigable.

apartheid (úpärt'hīd) [Afrikaans,= apartness], policy of racial segregation in Republic of South Africa advocated and implemented by Nationalist party governments of prime ministers D. F. Malan, J. G. Strijdom, H. F. Verwoerd, and B. J. Vorster. In 1961 South Africa withdrew from British Commonwealth rather than change its policy.

apatite (ăp'útīt), calcium phosphate mineral containing fluorine, chlorine, or both. Colorless when pure; impure colored types sometimes cut as gem stones. Used in making phosphorus fertilizers.

ape, usual name for primates most closely resembling man (GORILLA, CHIMPANZEE, ORANGUTAN, GIBBON). These have 32 teeth and a vermiform appendix. All lack external tails or cheek pouches; all but gibbon lack ischial callosities (bare patches on the buttocks). Stand semierectly; brain structure similar to man. Name was once used for tailless monkeys or as a synonym for monkey.

Apeldoorn (ä'púldōrn), municipality (pop. 112,235), and town, Gelderland prov., E central Netherlands. Rail junction; has varied mfg. Nearby are royal summer palace of Het Loo and several sanatoriums.

Apelles (úpĕl'ēz), fl. 4th cent. B.C., Greek painter, the most celebrated of antiquity, but now known only through descriptions of his works. Court painter to Philip and Alexander.

Apennines (ä'púnīnz), mountain system traversing entire Italian peninsula. Mts. of Sicily are a continuation. Highest peak (9,560 ft.) in Gran Sasso d'Italia group. Extensive pastures. Forests (chestnut, birch, oak, pine) much reduced by erosion.

aphasia: see AMNESIA.

aphid (ä'fĭd, ăf'ĭd) or **plant louse,** parasitic insect, also called green fly and blight. Injures vegetation. Species seen on field plants is soft-bodied, green, with long legs, antennae, two pairs membranous wings (some wingless). Reproductive cycle varies with species; commonly, fertilized eggs laid in fall hatch in spring or summer into stem mothers. These reproduce by PARTHENOGENESIS; several similar nonsexual generations may follow. Eventually a winged, sexually perfect generation is produced; these mate and migrate to other host plants to continue cycle. Some species are enslaved by ants, which feed upon the sweet honeydew the aphids produce. Numbers are reduced by other insects. fungi, damp weather. See also GALL.

Aphrodite (ăfrúdī'tē), in Greek religion, Olympian goddess of love. beauty, and fertility; wife of Hephaestus. Daughter of Zeus and Dione or of the sea into which blood of Uranus fell. Mother of Eros by Ares, of Aeneas by Anchises, and of Priapus by Dionysus. As goddess of fertility she is closely linked with ADONIS. Known also as Aphrodite Urania; her worship may have been imported from Orient, and she is akin to Astarte or Ishtar. Identified with Roman Venus. By awarding Aphrodite APPLE OF DISCORD, Paris won Helen and thus caused Trojan War.

Apia (äpē'ú), town (pop. 19,023), cap., chief port of W Samoa, on N coast of Upolu isl.

Apicius, Marcus Gabius (úpĭsh'ús), fl. 1st cent. A.D., Roman gourmet. He squandered his fortune on feasts. Cookbook *Apicius* is probably a century later.

Apo, Mount (ä'pō), active volcano, 9,690 ft. high, on S Mindanao; highest peak of the Philippines.

apocalypse (úpŏk'úlĭps) [Gr.,= uncovering], type of ancient Hebrew and Christian prophetic literature, usually written in veiled symbolism and inspired by visions (e.g., FOUR HORSEMEN OF THE APOCALYPSE). The biblical REVELATION is often called simply the Apocalypse.

Apocrypha (ŭpŏk'rĭfŭ) [Gr.,= hidden things], appendix to Authorized Version of Old Testament containing following books or parts of books: 1 and 2 ESDRAS; TOBIT; JUDITH; ESTHER 10.4–16; WISDOM; ECCLESIASTICUS; BARUCH; Dan. 3.24–90 (see DANIEL and THREE HOLY CHILDREN); Dan. 13 (see SUSANNA); Dan. 14 (see BEL and THE DRAGON); Prayer of Manasses (see MANASSEH 2); 1 and 2 MACCABEES. All but Prayer of Manasses, 1 and 2 Esdras considered canonical by Roman Catholics (Council of Trent, 1546). Protestants regard Apocrypha valuable for instruction but not canonical (see OLD TESTAMENT). For Jewish and Christian works resembling biblical books but not included in Western or Hebrew canon, see PSEUDEPIGRAPHA.

Apodaca, Juan Ruiz de (hwän' rōōēth' dä äpōdhä'kä), 1754–1835, last viceroy of New Spain (1816–21).

Apollinaire, Guillaume (gēyŏm' äpōlēnâr'), 1880–1918, French poet, b. Rome. Of illegitimate birth, he was christened Wilhelm Apollinaris de Kostrowitzky. His bizarre, exquisite poems (*Alcools*, 1913; *Calligrammes*, 1918) and his surrealistic drama, *Les Mamelles de Tirésias* (1918), were influential experiments. His art criticism promoted cubism.

Apollinarianism (ŭpŏlĭnâ'rēŭnĭzŭm), popular heretical doctrine of Apollinaris or Apollinarius (c.315–c.390) of Laodicea. Taught Christ possessed Logos in place of human mind. Anticipated MONOPHYSITISM.

Apollo (ŭpŏ'lō) or **Phoebus Apollo** (fē'bŭs), in Greek religion, Olympian god of light, music, poetry, pastoral pursuits, and prophecy. As god of music, the lyre was sacred to him (he was father of ORPHEUS). He was also god of healing and father of Asclepius. Identified with Helios as the sun-god. Son of Zeus and Leto, he (with twin sister ARTEMIS) was born in DELOS. At his temple in DELPHI, he was god of prophecy. Later he was best known as god of music and poetry, attended by MUSES. The **Apollo Belvedere** (bĕl"vĭdēr'), a marble figure in the Vatican, Roman copy of Greek original in bronze, is one of the best-known statues in the history of art.

Apollodorus (ŭpŏl"ōdôr'ŭs), fl. c.415 B.C., Athenian painter, reputedly first to use light and shadow.

Apollonius of Perga, fl. 247–205 B.C., Greek mathematician of Alexandrian school. Treatise on conic sections included work of Euclid and others.

Apollonius of Tralles: see FARNESE BULL.

Apollonius Rhodius (rō'dēŭs), 3d cent. B.C., epic poet, librarian at Alexandria, author of *Argonautica*.

Apollyon (ŭpŏl'yŭn), Greek name of the destroying angel. Rev. 9.11. See SATAN and HELL.

Apopka, Lake (ŭpŏp'kŭ), central Fla.; fishing. Winter Garden is on S shore.

apoplexy or **stroke,** result of cerebral hemorrhage, thrombosis, or other damage to blood vessels of brain. Often accompanied by coma and followed by partial paralysis, loss of speech, mental changes. Aftereffects, sometimes permanent, are often temporary, abating as normal blood flow to brain is restored. The term stroke is also used for other circulatory disorders, including certain types of heart malfunction.

apostle, in religion, one of the earliest missionaries of Christendom. The chief 12: PETER, ANDREW, JAMES (the Greater), JOHN, THOMAS, JAMES (the Less), JUDE (or Thaddeus), PHILIP, BARTHOLOMEW (may be same as Nathanael), MATTHEW, SIMON, and MATTHIAS (replacing JUDAS ISCARIOT). Traditional list of Twelve Disciples includes Judas and not Matthias, list of Twelve Apostles includes Matthias and not Judas. Number originally symbolic of 12 tribes of Israel. St. PAUL is always classed a chief apostle though not of the 12. Name given to others (e.g., BARNABAS). For Apostles' Creed, see CREED; see also DIDACHE.

Apostle Islands, group of over 20 islands, off N Wis., in SW L. Superior. Notable wave-eroded cliffs. Madeline, the largest, has ferry from Bayfield and includes town of La Pointe (pop. 130). French had trading post here 1693–98 and 1718–59. American Fur Co. had post in early 19th cent.

Apostolic Constitutions: see CONSTITUTIONS, APOSTOLIC.

apostolic succession, in some Christian churches, belief that the position of the apostles of Christ has been transmitted from generation to generation in unbroken succession so that the bishops of today are the true inheritors of the power of the apostles. This is stoutly denied in churches that do not recognize any episcopacy. The apostolic succession is to be distinguished from the doctrine of Petrine supremacy (see PAPACY).

Apoxyomenus (ŭpŏk"sēŏm'ĭnŭs) [Gr.,= scraping one's self], Roman copy in marble of a bronze statue by LYSIPPUS. Represents an athlete cleaning himself.

Appalachia, region extending from N Ala. to W N.Y. and taking its name from Appalachian Mts. An economically depressed area, it became a special target of anti-poverty program through Appalachian Regional Development Act (1965).

Appalachian Mountains (ăpŭlā'chŭn), general name for numerous groups of elevations in E North America, extending SW from St. Lawrence valley in Quebec prov., Canada, to Gulf Coast plain in Ala., and rising to 6,684 ft. in Mt. MITCHELL. They include WHITE MOUNTAINS, GREEN MOUNTAINS, CATSKILL MOUNTAINS, ALLEGHENY MOUNTAINS, BLUE RIDGE, BLACK MOUNTAINS, GREAT SMOKY MOUNTAINS, CUMBERLAND PLATEAU, and other ranges. Formed mainly by folding, they consist largely of sedimentary rocks and are much worn down. W portions, less rugged than E portions, are largely plateau formations of horizontal rock structure. Have yielded coal, iron, petroleum, and gas. Crossed by few passes, system was barrier against westward expansion. Has beautiful scenery and many resorts.

Appalachian Trail, for hikers, extending 2,050 mi. along ridges of Appalachian Mt. system from Mt. Katahdin, Maine, to Mt. Oglethorpe, N Ga. Planned by forester Benton MacKaye. Constructed 1921.

appeal, process by which a superior court reviews errors allegedly committed by a lower court. If case had a jury trial the jury's determinations of fact are usually deferred to, while matters of law (i.e., mistakes in legal rules) are fully reviewed; if trial had no jury, errors both of law and of fact (erroneous interpretation of evidence) may be reviewed.

appendix, vermiform, in man, outgrowth (c.3 in. long) of large intestine, in lower right abdomen, probably vestigial remnant. Infection may result in **appendicitis,** usually making imperative the removal of appendix; use of cathartics entails risk of rupture of appendix and spread of infection (see PERITONITIS).

Appenzell (ä'pŭntsĕl), canton, NE Switzerland. Mostly meadowland; textile mfg. Ruled by abbots of St. Gall after 11th cent.: rebelled 1403; joined Swiss Confederation 1411. In 1597 Appenzell split into two independent half cantons. Ausser-Rhoden (94 sq. mi.; pop. 48,920; cap Herisau) accepted Reformation. Inner-Rhoden (67 sq. mi.; pop. 12,943) remained Catholic; its cap., **Appenzell** (pop. 5,082), has noted embroidery mfg.

Appert, Nicolas (nēkôlä' äpâr'), known also as **François Appert** (fraswä'), 1750–1814?, French originator of an acceptable method of canning food.

Appia, Adolphe (äp'pyä), 1862–1928, Swiss stagelighting theorist. First to use intensity, color, and mobility of light to estab. mood and atmosphere of a play.

Appian (ă'pēŭn), fl. 2d cent., Roman historian. His history of Roman conquests reproduces documents and sources otherwise lost. Of 24 books, in Greek, only VI–VII and XI–XVII are fully preserved.

Appian Way, Latin *Via Appia,* road built under Appius Claudius Caecus (312 B.C.). Connecting Rome with Brundisium, it was chief highway to Greece and the provinces in Asia.

apple, best-known and commercially most important fruit of temperate zones and its tree, *Pyrus malus,* member of rose family. Cultivated from prehistoric times. Long lived and easy to grow. North America leads in apple production. See CRAB APPLE; *ill.,* p. 858.

Appleby, John Francis, 1840–1917, American farmer, inventor of Appleby knotter used on grain binders.

Appleby, county town (pop. 1,751), Westmorland, England; site of historic Appleby Castle.

apple of discord, in Greek mythology, a golden apple inscribed "for the fairest," thrown by uninvited ERIS among guests at wedding of Peleus and Thetis. It was claimed by Aphrodite, Athena, and Hera. Paris, selected to decide, chose Aphrodite, who offered him the fairest of women, Helen. His abduction of Helen caused TROJAN WAR.

Appleseed, Johnny: see CHAPMAN, JOHN.

Appleton, Daniel, 1785–1849, American publisher, founder of a large publishing house.

Appleton, Sir Edward Victor, 1892–1965, English physicist. Won 1947 Nobel Prize in Physics for studies of ionosphere which led to development of radar.

Appleton, city (pop. 48,411), E Wis., on Fox R. near its exit from L. Winnebago, in dairy and livestock region; settled 1830s. Had nation's first hydroelectric plant (1882). Seat of LAWRENCE UNIVERSITY.

Appomattox (ăpŭmă'tŭks), town (pop. 1,184), S central Va., E of Lynchburg, near source of Appomattox R. R. E. Lee surrendered to U.S. Grant at nearby **Appomattox Courthouse,** April 9, 1865. Retreating from Petersburg and Richmond, Lee was cut off here by P. H. Sheridan and yielded. This was end of war, as other Southern armies followed suit. Site of surrender now Appomattox Court House Natl. Historical Park.

Apponaug, R.I.: see WARWICK.

apprenticeship, system of learning a trade by paying with years of work for instruction from one skilled in the trade. Known in ancient world, the system was also part of medieval guild system. Apprenticeship less widespread after Industrial Revolution, but it survives in highly skilled trades. Typically apprentice becomes journeyman (working for master for wages), finally master.

appropriation, allotment by legislature of money for specific purpose. In U.S. no money may be drawn from Treasury without appropriation, and no appropriation may be made for more than two years.

APRA: see HAYA DE LA TORRE, VÍCTOR RAÚL; PERU.

Apra Harbor or **Port Apra,** on W coast of Guam, WSW of Agana. Only good harbor on island, it is port of entry closed to foreign vessels except by permit. U.S. naval base is here.

apricot, a tree, *Prunus armeniaca,* and its orange-colored fruit. It is a commercial crop in California.

Apries (ā'prē-ēz), king of anc. Egypt (588–569 B.C.), of the XXVI dynasty. Succeeded Psamtik II and sought to recover Syria and Palestine from NEBUCHADNEZZAR. Murdered during a rebellion led by Amasis II.

April: see MONTH.

Apsheron, Azerbaijan SSR: see BAKU.

Apuleius, Lucius (ā"pyōōlē'ŭs), fl. 2d cent. A.D., Latin writer. His romance, *The Golden Ass* or *Metamorphoses,* strongly influenced the later novel.

Apulia (ŭpū'lēŭ), Ital. *Puglia* (pōō'lyä), region (7,469 sq. mi.; pop. 3,409,687), S Italy, occupying southernmost third of Italian E coast; cap. Bari. In anc. times only N part of region was called Apulia. Cities: Bari, Brindisi, Foggia, Taranto, Lecce. Wine, olives, almonds, corn are grown despite scarcity of water. Sheep and goat raising. Conquered (11th–12th cent.) from Byzantines by Normans, who made it a powerful duchy, it later became part of kingdom of Naples.

Aqaba (ä'käbä), port on Gulf of Aqaba, arm of the Red Sea. Jordan's only access to the sea. Egypt mounted anti-Israel blockade of gulf in May, 1967.

Blockade broken with Israeli capture of Sinai Peninsula in hostilities in June, 1967.

Aquae Sextiae: see AIX-EN-PROVENCE.

aquamarine, transparent BERYL with blue to blue-green tint. Found in Brazil, Ceylon, Germany, Siberia, and U.S. Similar to emerald save for color.

aquarium, tank, bowl, artificial pond, or museum for aquatic animals and plants, preferably rectangular, with no copper, brass, zinc, or galvanized iron in contact with water. Tanks with new wood or concrete should be filled with water and changed at intervals for several weeks before putting in fish. Green aquarium plants are valuable oxygenators. A properly set up and unpolluted aquarium rarely needs complete change of water, only replacement of loss by evaporation.

Aquarius [Lat.,= water bearer], 11th sign of ZODIAC.

aqueduct (ă'kwŭdŭkt), channel or trough conveying water, usually fresh water to a city. First used probably in Mesopotamia; greatly developed later by Romans. Aqueduct to present Mexico city built by Mayas before Spanish Conquest. Aqueducts carry water to many large U.S. cities from great distances.

Aquidneck, R.I.: see RHODE ISLAND, isl.

Aquila or **Aquila degli Abruzzi** (ä'kwēlä dā'lyē äbrōōt'-sē), city (pop. 56,314), cap. of Aquila prov. and of Abruzzi e Molise region, S central Italy, below Gran Sasso d'Italia. Medieval architecture.

Aquila Ponticus (pŏn'tĭkŭs), 2d cent., Jewish translator of Old Testament from Hebrew into Greek. Much used by Jews. No complete specimen exists.

Aquilegia: see COLUMBINE.

Aquileia (äkwēlā'yä), town (est. pop. 3,557), Friuli-Venezia Giulia, NE Italy, near Adriatic. Founded 181 B.C.; important Roman stronghold; see of patriarchate, 6th–18th cent. Early Romanesque basilica has splendid mosaic floor. Grado, on nearby island, is bathing resort.

Aquinas, Saint Thomas: see THOMAS AQUINAS, SAINT.

Aquitaine (ăk'wĭtān), former duchy, SW France; historic cap., Bordeaux. Frontiers shifted often. A Roman prov., it passed to Visigoths (5th cent.), then to Franks (507), and was a kingdom (781–838) under Charlemagne's son Louis, and grandson Pepin. Late in 9th cent. it emerged as duchy, enfeoffed to French crown. It grew powerful and came to include most of SW and S central France. Second marriage (1152) of ELEANOR OF AQUITAINE started French-English struggle over duchy; Hundred Years War gave France victory. See also GUIENNE; GASCONY.

Ar, chemical symbol for element ARGON.

Arabia, peninsula (c.1,000,000 sq. mi.; pop. c.9,000,-000), SW Asia, between Red Sea and Gulf of Aqaba on W and Persian Gulf and Gulf of Oman on E. Bounded on S by Arabian Sea and Gulf of Aden. Occupied by SAUDI ARABIA, YEMEN, Kuwait, Oman, British protectorates of Aden, Bahrein, Qatar, and Trucial Øman, and British colony of Aden. Mainly desert; more habitable areas in HEJA, NEJD, and the SW (only section fit for extensive agriculture). Pastoral nomads raise goats and sheep. Rich oil fields (exploited by European and American firms) are in E. Much of ancient Arabia was divided between domains of Ma'in and SHEBA. Ethiopia twice held S coast (HADRAMAUT) and Yemen (300–378, 525–70). In 7th cent. dynamic faith of MOHAMMED the Prophet unified Arab tribes, inspiring them to conquer neighboring states. OMAYYAD caliphate conquered Persia but was checked in E by Byzantines and in W by defeat in battle of Tours, France (732). After removal of seat of caliphate from Medina to Damascus, Arabia again lost political cohesion. Nominally ruled after 1517 by Ottoman Turks, harassed 18th–19th cent. by WAHABI movement. Turkish rule was broken during First World War by IBN SAUD and HUSEIN IBN ALI.

Arabian art and architecture: see MOSLEM ART AND ARCHITECTURE.

Arabian music, influenced by pre-Islamic, Persian, Greek, and other traditions, sounds sparse by Western standards as it knows neither harmony nor orchestration. Chief instrument is lute. Melodies employ scales which include intervals smaller than the half step. Melodic formulas rather than individual notes are raw material of composer. Choice of formulas is dictated by melody type, called *maqam*, of which there are several. Similarly, there are rhythm types.

Arabian Nights: see THOUSAND AND ONE NIGHTS.

Arabian Sea, NW part of Indian Ocean, lying between Arabia and India.

Arabic language, Semitic language, one of most widely spoken languages in the world. See LANGUAGE (table).

Arabic literature. Golden age of lyric poets (Amru-l-Kais, Antar, Zuhair) lasted from 4th to 7th cent. It was marked by personal odes about love, fighting, and hunting, with references to power of God. These survive only in the collections MUALLAQAT, HAMASA, and MOFADDALIYAT. KORAN supplanted poetry (decried by Mohammed) until Arabic-Persian cultural renascence under Abbasids at Baghdad (8th–9th cent). New court poetry of Abu-l-Atahiya and Abu Nuwas soon became precious, as in poetry of Hariri (11th cent.). Prose romances, notably THOUSAND AND ONE NIGHTS, superseded poetry. They show Hindu and Persian influence but are essentially Arabic in form. Bukhari, Tabari, Masudi, Ibn Khaldun, and Ibn Batuta are noted for historical and geographical writing. Omayyad Spain fostered vigorous Arabic literature; its great philosophers were Avempace, Averroës, and Ibn Tufail. Since 1300 there has been little Arabic literature that has attracted wide interest in the non-Arabic world.

Arabistan: see ARABIA.

Arab League, union of Arab states formed 1945; hq. at Cairo. Intended to promote cooperation, it was instrument of joint Arab action in 1948 war with Israel. Recognized by UN as regional organization 1958. Treaty for joint defense and economic cooperation signed 1952. After 1954 dominated by Egypt. Creation of United Arab Republic in 1958 meant virtual end of league as unifying force in Arab affairs. Members at end of 1966 were Algeria, Iraq, Jordan, Kuwait, Lebanon, Libya, Morocco, Saudi Arabia, Sudan, Syria, Tunisia, United Arab Republic, Yemen.

Arabs, people of related groups considering themselves of Arabic race, generally speaking Arabic, and mostly Moslem (although there are Arabic Christians in Israel, Jordan, Lebanon, and Syria). Arabic-speaking Jews (chiefly in N Africa), Kurds, Berbers, Copts, and Druses are generally excluded from the term. Major countries are Egypt, Iraq, Lebanon, Saudi Arabia, Sudan, Syria, Tunisia, and Yemen. Arabic-speaking communities are found in Madagascar, along E African Coast, and E to Indonesia. Socially Arabs are divided into the settled Arab and the nomadic BEDOUIN. Cultural and linguistic ties were reinforced by expansion of Islam (7th–13th cent.). First World War shattered Ottoman dominance over Arab world. Resistance to subsequent European control and the long-standing Arab desire for reunification led to Pan-Arabism. After Second World War Pan-Arabism found concrete expression in the ARAB LEAGUE, UNITED ARAB REPUBLIC, wars against Israel, and Baath political party.

Aracaju, city (pop. c.115,700), NE Brazil; port on Sergipe R. near the Atlantic. Exports sugar and cotton.

Arachne (ŭrăk'nē) [Gr.,= spider], in Greek legend, girl who challenged Athena to a trial of skill in weaving. The goddess changed her into a spider.

Arad (äräd'), city (est. pop. 114,494), W Rumania, on Mures R. and near Hungarian border. Commercial and mfg. center (flour, leather, machinery). Has large Hungarian, Serbian, and German minorities.

Aradus (ăr'ŭdŭs), islet and town on Anc. Phoenicia, the modern Ruad, N of Tripoli off Syrian coast, most important of N Phoenician centers. Called Arvad in Old Testament. 1 Chron. 1.16; Ezek. 27.8,11.

Arafat (äräfät'), granite hill, Saudi Arabia, near Mecca. Shrouded in many legends, it is a site for prayers during annual pilgrimage to Mecca.

Arafura Sea (ärŭfoo'rŭ), part of the Pacific between Australia and New Guinea.

Aragats, Mount (ärŭgäts'), or **Mount Alagez** (ŭlŭgyôs'), extinct volcano, 13,435 ft. high, Armenian SSR. Astrophysical research center.

Aragon, Louis (lwē' ärägŏ'), 1897–, French journalist, poet, and novelist. Onetime Dadaist and surrealist and later a Communist. Called poet of the French resistance in Second World War.

Aragon (ä'rŭgŏn), Span. *Aragón*, region and former kingdom, NE Spain, in E Pyrenees and Ebro plain. Chief cities: Saragossa, Huesca, Teruel. Region is arid and sparsely populated, but irrigated areas yield cereals, wine, olives, sugar beets. Sheep and cattle raising. Kingdom was created (1035) out of W part of Navarre for Ramiro I. It grew at expense of emirate of SARAGOSSA and was united, by personal union, with Catalonia after 1137. Union with Castile after 1479 through marriage of Ferdinand and Isabella.

Aragon, house of, family which ruled in Aragon, CATALONIA, MAJORCA, SICILY, the kingdom of NAPLES, SARDINIA, ROUSSILLON, ATHENS, and other lands in Middle Ages; founded by RAMIRO I. Aragon and Catalonia were in personal union after 1137, but the other territories were generally ruled separately by branches of the house. Alfonso V, who conquered Naples in 1442, temporarily united all Aragonese dominions. The marriage of Ferdinand II of Aragon with Isabella of Castile led to union of the two kingdoms. In their grandson, Emperor CHARLES V, the houses of Aragon and Castile were merged with that of Hapsburg.

Araguaia (ärägwī'ŭ), river, rising at border of Goiás and Mato Grosso states, Brazil. Flows c.1,300 mi. generally northward into the Tocantins. The isl. of Bananal, formed by two arms of rivers is one of largest fresh-water islands in the world.

Araish, El: see LARACHE.

Arakan (ärŭkăn'), regional division (c.16,000 sq. mi.; pop. c.1,225,000), W Burma, along Bay of Bengal; chief city is Akyab. Area was annexed by Burma 1783, and ceded 1826 to the British.

Arakcheyev, Aleksey Andreyevich (ŭlyĭksyā' ŭndrā'-yĭvĭch äräkchā'ĕf), 1769–1834, Russian general, minister of war for Alexander I. A cruel but efficient administrator, he made valuable military reforms.

Aral Kara-Kum: see KARA-KUM.

Aral Sea (ä'rŭl, Rus. ŭräl'), inland sea (c.25,659 sq. mi.), USSR, in Kazakh SSR and Kara-Kalpak ASSR. Fed by Amu Darya and Syr Darya rivers, it has no outlet, and is shallow, slightly saline. Fisheries.

Aram (ā'răm), an anc. people and their country, roughly identified with Syria. Their language a form of Aramaic. Bible records constant contacts between Hebrews and Aram.

Aram, Eugene, 1704–59, English philologist, hanged after discovery that he had murdered (1745) his friend Daniel Clark. This story was used for a poem by Thomas Hood, a novel by Bulwer-Lytton.

Aramaic (ärŭmā'ĭk), Semitic languages of Syria, flourishing in the centuries before and after Christ. See LANGUAGE (table).

Aranha, Oswaldo (ùzhväl'dō ùrä'nyù), 1894–1960, Brazilian statesman. Ambassador to U.S. (1934–38); foreign minister (1938–44); president of UN General Assembly (1947).

Aran Islands or **Arran Islands** (both: är'ùn), in Galway Bay, Co. Galway, Ireland. The three islands are Inishmore, Inisheer, and Inishmaan. They are barren, and living conditions are primitive.

Aranjuez (äränghwäth'), town (pop. 27,251), Madrid prov., central Spain, in New Castile, on Tagus R. Its palace, a royal residence since 16th cent., was rebuilt 1727.

Aransas Pass (ûrăn′zŭs), city (pop. 6,956), S Texas, NE of Corpus Christi; settled 1890. A Gulf port on a deepwater ship channel going through Harbor Isl. and through pass between St. Joseph Isl. and Mustang Isl. (Port Aransas). Resort and fishing center.

Arany, John (ŏ′rōnyŭ), Hung. *Arany János,* 1817–82, Hungarian epic poet, author of *Toldi* (1846).

Arapaho Indians (ûrăp′ûhō), North American Indians, of Algonquian-Mosan linguistic stock. Thought to be most closely related to Cheyenne and Blackfoot (see LANGUAGE, table). The three main divisions are Gros Ventre (allied with Blackfoot), Southern Arapaho (allied with Cheyenne), and Northern Arapaho (considered the parent group). Ceremonial societies for different age groups are notable.

Arapaho Peak, N central Colo.: see FRONT RANGE.

Ararat (ă′rŭrăt), region, E Turkey and E Armenian SSR, called Massis in Armenian, Aghri (or Egri) Dagh in Turkish, Koh-i-nuh in Persian. Identical with Armenia in many ancient records; Assyrians called it Urartu. Mt. Ararat (16,916 ft.) highest peak in Turkey, traditional landing place of Noah's ark (Gen. 8.4).

Aras, anc. *Araxes,* river rising in E Turkey and flowing E to Kura R. and Caspian Sea. Border between Iran and USSR and Turkish and Russian Armenia.

Araucanian Indians (ă″rōkā′nēŭn, ă″rŭ–), South American people occupying much of present Chile at time of Spanish Conquest (1540). Opposition to Spanish under Pedro de VALDIVIA gave Araucanian leaders, Lautaro and CAUPOLICÁN, fame immortalized in epic of ERCILLA Y ZÚÑIGA. Resistance to whites ended in Chile in war of 1880–81. Araucanians who fled earlier to Argentina were subjugated 1883. Chief language: Mapuche.

Araunah (ărō′nŭ), man who sold his threshing floor to David who erected altar there. Site, on Mt. Moriah, later used for Temple. 2 Sam. 24.15–25. Ornan: 1 Chron. 21.14–30; 2 Chron. 3.1.

Arbela (ärbē′lŭ), town, anc. Assyria (modern Erbil). Near here (at Gaugamela) Alexander the Great defeated Darius III (331 B.C.).

arbitration, industrial, method of settling disputes between employer and employees by seeking and accepting decision of third party. May be compelled by government or may be voluntary, as in U.S., although U.S. government may intervene in strikes affecting public welfare. See TAFT-HARTLEY LABOR ACT.

arbitration, international, method of peacefully settling international disputes. Parties agree in advance to abide by decision of an arbitral tribunal, which may be an individual, a neutral country, or an organization such as UN's Internatl. Court of Justice. If parties do not agree in advance to be bound, the process is called conciliation.

Arblay, Madame D': see BURNEY, FRANCES.

Arbogast (är′bŭgăst), d. 394, Frankish general in Roman service. After murder of VALENTINIAN II (392), he set up puppet emperor, Eugenius, but both were defeated by THEODOSIUS (394).

Arbon (ärbō′), town (pop. 12,287), Thurgau canton, NE Switzerland, on L. of Constance. Has automobile factory and machine works.

arborvitae (är″bŭrvī′tē), evergreen tree or shrub (*Thuja*), with scalelike leaves, fanlike branchlets, and small cones. There are many garden forms of American arborvitae or northern white cedar (*Thuja occidentalis*), and less hardy Oriental species (*T. orientalis*). Wood of western red cedar (*T. plicata*) used in interiors and to make shingles and doors.

Arbuckle Mountains, range of old mountains, S Okla., with average altitude of 700 ft. and interesting geological formations. Platt Natl. Park is in area (see NATIONAL PARKS AND MONUMENTS, table).

Arbuthnot, John (ärbŭth′–, är′–), 1667–1735, English writer, court physician to Queen Anne. In satirical pamphlets on "John Bull" (1712), he created that character. Friend of Swift. See also SCRIBLERUS CLUB.

Arbutus, city (pop. incl. Halethorpe-Relay, 22,402), NE Md., a suburb SW of Baltimore.

arc, in electricity, highly luminous, intensely hot path formed when two electrodes (rods composed of charcoal, copper, or magnetite), originally touching and transmitting electric current, are pulled a short distance apart and current still flows between them. Formerly used for LIGHTING. Principle is used in WELDING and to generate heat in electric furnaces. For mercury-arc lamp see MERCURY.

arc, in geometry, a curved line or any part of it, in particular a portion of the circumference of a circle.

Arcade, Calif.: see ARDEN.

Arcadia (ärkā′dēŭ), region ⅴf anc. Greece in mid-Peloponnesus, inhabited by a pastoral people.

Arcadia, city (pop. 41,005), S Calif., ESE of Pasadena, in an area of orange and walnut groves and nurseries. The Santa Anita race track is here.

Arcadius (ärkā′dēŭs), c.377–408, Roman emperor of the East (395–408), son and successor of Theodosius I. His brother Honorius inherited the West. During his reign ALARIC I invaded Greece and was expelled (395–96) by Stilicho.

Arcagnolo: see ORCAGNA.

Arcaro, George Edward (Eddie Arcaro), 1916–, American jockey. In 31-year career finished first in 4,779 races. Only jockey to win Kentucky Derby five times. Twice took racing's triple crown (Kentucky Derby, Preakness, Belmont Stakes).

Arcas (är′kŭs), in Greek myth: see CALLISTO.

Arcesilaus (ärsēs″ûlā′ŭs), c.316–c.241 B.C., Greek philosopher, who taught that knowledge could not be distinguished from opinion.

Arch, Joseph, 1826–1919, English labor leader, instrumental in enfranchising agr. workers.

archaeology (ärkēŏ′lŭjē), scientific study of the relics of man found in deposits and ruins. To find, interpret, and preserve materials which delineate prehistoric life and supplement the documentary material of historic eras, modern archaeologists work with various experts and technicians and are often sponsored by museums, organizations, and societies which publish and maintain collections of their findings. Such materials had long been collected, but excavations at HERCULANEUM and POMPEII in the 18th cent., and the discovery of the ROSETTA STONE, inspired systematic research into the historic past. In 1832 C. J. Thomsen showed that cultural stages may be defined according to principal materials used for weapons and implements. These stages, the PALEOLITHIC PERIOD, NEOLITHIC PERIOD, BRONZE AGE, and IRON AGE, indicate the condition of a people, rather than divisions of time. Study of such prehistoric finds as at LA TÈNE and of remains of barrow, KITCHEN MIDDEN, LAKE DWELLING, various mounds, and MEGALITHIC MONUMENTS, have been enhanced by the study of existent aboriginal groups. See GEOLOGIC ERAS, table.

archaeopteryx (är″kēŏp′tŭrĭks), ancient bird. Fossil remains indicate it to be link between ancient reptiles and modern birds.

Archangel (ärk′–), Rus. *Arkhangelsk* (ûrkhän′gĭlsk), city (1965 est. pop. 303,000), RSFSR, on mouth of Northern Dvina; White Sea port (ice-free July–Sept.). Chief sawmilling center of USSR. Founded 1583 as Novo-Kholmogory after CHANCELLOR had landed here; renamed 1716. Major supply port in both World Wars; occupied 1918–20 by Allies and White Army.

archangel (ärk′–), chief ANGEL, differing from other angels only in importance. Best known are MICHAEL, GABRIEL, RAPHAEL.

Archean: see PRECAMBRIAN ERA.

Archeozoic era: see PRECAMBRIAN ERA.

Archer, William, 1856–1924, English critic. Translated Ibsen; helped G. B. Shaw; wrote popular play *The Green Goddess* (1921); was influential as London *World* dramatic critic.

Archer, the, in astrology: see ZODIAC.

archery. An important military skill in ancient and medieval times, shooting with bow and arrow was revived as sport (c.1676) by Charles II of England. Archers try to hit inner circle (or "bull's eye") of target composed of concentric circles.

Arches National Monument: see NATIONAL PARKS AND MONUMENTS (table).

archil or **orchil,** blue, red, or purple dye extracted from varieties of LICHEN called orchella weeds. Sold as powder (cudbear), wet paste (archil), or drier paste (persil).

Archimedes (ärkĭmē'dēz), 287–212 B.C., Greek mathematician, physicist, inventor. Nine of his famous treatises on geometry and hydrostatics survive. **Archimedes' principle:** a solid body immersed in liquid is buoyed up by a force equal to weight of liquid it displaces. Used in determining ship displacement and specific gravity of substances. Applies also to gases, e.g., "lifting" force of balloons. Attributed to Archimedes also is machine known as **Archimedes' screw,** a cylinder inside which a continuous screw extends full length to form spiral chamber. By placing lower end in water and revolving screw, water is raised. Principle applied also in spiral conveyors and some high-speed tools.

Archipelago (ärkĭpĕ'lŭgō), ancient name of AEGEAN SEA, later applied to its numerous islands, and finally to any cluster of islands.

Archipenko, Aleksandr (ŭlyĭksändr' ärkĭpĕng'kō), 1887–1964, Russian sculptor in America. Known for abstract figures, often based on the female nude.

archons (är'kŏnz, –kŭnz) [Gr.,= leaders], in anc. Greek cities; officers of state. In Athens there were nine; after serving they entered the AREOPAGUS. After 487 B.C. they were chosen by lot.

Arco, resort village (pop. 1,562), SE Idaho, WNW of Idaho Falls, on Big Lost R. Hq. for Craters of the Moon Natl. Monument (see NATIONAL PARKS AND MONUMENTS, table). A U.S. atomic-reactor testing station is near. First U.S. city lighted by atomic energy.

Arcole (är'kōlā), village, NE Italy, SE of Verona. Here Bonaparte defeated Austrians 1796.

Arctic Archipelago, large Canadian islands in Arctic Ocean. Franklin dist., Northwest Territories.

Arctic Ocean, sea, roughly circular, from North Pole to lat. c.70°N, nearly landlocked (by Greenland, Canada, Alaska, USSR, Norway), c.5,400,000 sq. mi. Has many islands, fringe of small seas and bays. Communicates widely with Atlantic, with Pacific only through Bering Strait. In ocean is the world's widest continental shelf, stretching N from Siberia; and similar shelf extending N from North America which drops off near the pole at the deepest part (14,070 ft.) of Bering Sea. Ice drifts S and W into northernmost Atlantic shipping lanes, but more seriously from W Greenland fjords. Arctic currents give NE shores of North America and Asia much colder climate than NW shores of Europe and North America (warmed by North Atlantic Drift, Gulf Stream, Japan Current). Aerial study has increased knowledge of drifts, ice floes, water depths, and ocean floor. Observation reveals warming of Arctic. Cooperative researches during the International Geophysical Year (1957–58) contributed much new knowledge. U.S. nuclear-powered submarines including the *Nautilus* and *Skate* conducted extended and deep underwater investigations, opening new avenue of research.

arctic regions, northernmost area of earth, centered about North Pole and Arctic Ocean. Extends more than one third way to equator. Weather boundary varies seasonally, set arbitrarily at Arctic Circle (lat. 66°17'N). Under "midnight sun" temperatures mount, vegetation appears. Abundant animal life (including seal, walrus, whale, many fish, water fowl, sea birds) supports ESKIMO tribes. Viking explorers were followed by those seeking NORTHWEST PASSAGE and

NORTHEAST PASSAGE (16th, 17th cent.). Hardships, negative results discouraged exploration until late 18th cent. North Pole first reached by Robert Peary 1909. Discovery that shortest air routes ("great circle") between capitals and commercial centers of N Hemisphere lie over Arctic Ocean replaced individual exploration with cooperative enterprise. Natural resources and strategic military value led to national settlement and exploitation in which USSR has been most consistently active. As part of U.S.–Canadian defense, construction was begun in 1955 on a 3,000-mi. radar network—Distant Early Warning (DEW) Line—stretching from Alaska to Baffin Isl.; extension across Greenland was begun 1959. During International Geophysical Year (1957–58) various nations set up some 300 arctic stations for research purposes. Successful voyages under the icecap since 1958 by U.S. nuclear-powered submarines have enhanced strategic importance of area.

Arcturus (ärktyōōr'ŭs), orange-colored first magnitude star of constellation Boötes, also Alpha Boötis. Diameter c.20,000,000 mi.; c.35.5 light years from earth.

Ardashir I (ärdäshēr'), d. 240, king of Persia (226?–240). Reunited Persia and founded Sassanian dynasty (see SASSANIDAE). Name another form of Artaxerxes.

Ardebil (ärdübēl'), town (pop. c.23,000), NW Iran; market center. Russians took city 1828; removed fine library to St. Petersburg.

Ardèche (ärdĕsh'), department (2,145 sq. mi.; pop. 248,516), S France, in Vivarais; cap. Privas.

Arden, city (pop. 73,352 including Arcade), N central Calif., NE of Sacramento.

Arden, Forest of, N Warwickshire, England. Most of Shakespeare's *As You Like It* is laid here.

Ardennes (ärdĕn'), department (2,028 sq. mi.; pop. 300,247), NE France; cap. Mézières.

Ardennes, wooded plateau, 1,600–2,300 ft. high, N France, SE Belgium, N Luxembourg, E and S of Meuse R. Wild, craggy landscape. Agr., cattle raising. Population mostly Walloons. Cities: Liège, Namur, Verviers, Spa. Traditional battleground; BATTLE OF THE BULGE fought here in Second World War.

Ardmore. 1 City (pop. 20,184), S Okla., near Red R. and Arbuckle Mts., SSE of Oklahoma City; settled 1887. Commercial and processing center of rich farm area which also produces livestock, oil, and asphalt. **2** Residential area, E Pa., suburb W of Philadelphia.

area, in geometry, extent of surface measured in some unit (e.g., square feet or acres). Formulae for simple plane figures and simple solids (a = altitude; b = base; s = side; r = radius; l = slant height):

Plane figures	Area
triangle	$ab/2$
parallelogram	ab
rectangle	ab
square	s^2
circle	πr^2

Solids	Total area
right circular cylinder	$2\pi r(r+a)$
right circular cone	$\pi r(r+l)$
sphere	$4\pi r^2$

Arecibo (äräsē'bō), town (pop. 69,879), N Puerto Rico, on coast. Industrial center in agr. region.

Areopagite: see DIONYSIUS THE AREOPAGITE, SAINT.

Areopagus (ärēŏ'pŭgŭs), rocky hill NW of the Acropolis of Athens, sacred meeting place of prime council of Athens, the **Areopagus,** which arose out of council of elders and had judicial and legislative functions. Declined after 487 B.C.

Arequipa (äräkē'pä), city (pop. 156,657), S Peru; founded by Francisco Pizarro 1540. Commercial hub of S Peru and N Bolivia, it also draws tourists.

Ares (â'rēz), in Greek mythology, Olympian god of war; son of Zeus and Hera; either husband or lover of Aph-

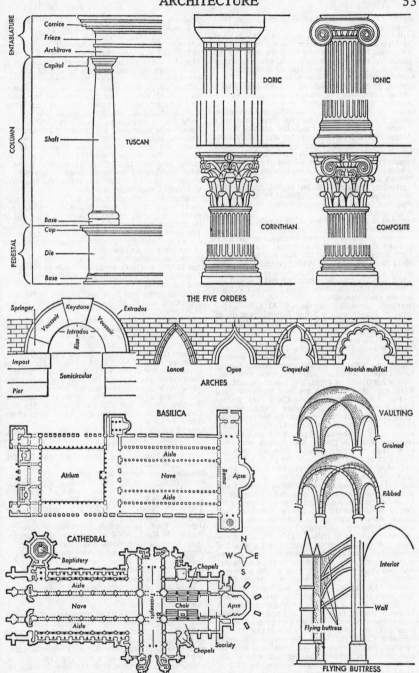

THE FIVE ORDERS

ENTABLATURE — Cornice, Frieze, Architrave

COLUMN — Capital, Shaft, Base

PEDESTAL — Cap, Die, Base

TUSCAN

DORIC

IONIC

CORINTHIAN

COMPOSITE

ARCHES

Springer, Keystone, Extrados, Voussoir, Intrados, Rise, Voussoir

Impost

Pier

Semicircular

Lancet

Ogee

Cinquefoil

Moorish multifoil

BASILICA

Atrium

Aisle

Nave

Aisle

Bema

Apse

VAULTING

Groined

Ribbed

CATHEDRAL

Baptistery

Aisle

Nave

Aisle

Transept

Chapels

Choir

Apse

Sacristy

Chapels

N W E S

FLYING BUTTRESS

Interior

Wall

Flying buttress

rodite. He favored the Trojans in the Trojan War. Identified with Roman Mars.

Arethusa (ărĭthū'sù), in Greek mythology, nymph loved by Alpheus. She fled from him and was changed into a fountain, but he caught her; hence the story that Alpheus river flows beneath sea from Greece to reappear in fountain of Arethusa in harbor of Syracuse.

Aretinian syllables: see GUIDO D'AREZZO.

Aretino, Pietro (pyä'trō ärätē'nō), 1492–1556. Italian satirist, adventurer who wrote for hire, called by Ariosto the "scourge of princes."

Arezzo (ärāt'tsō), city (pop. 74,245), cap. of Arezzo prov., Tuscany, central Italy. An Etruscan, later a Roman, town (famous for red-clay Arretine vases), Arezzo became a cultural center in late Middle Ages. Birthplace of Guido d'Arezzo, Petrarch, Aretino, Vasari. Much medieval and Renaissance architecture.

Argand burner (är'gănd), introduced principle of admitting air to interior of flame. Modern gas and oil burners based on this principle.

Argelander, Friedrich Wilhelm August (frē'drĭkh vĭl'hĕlm ou'gŏost är'gùländùr), 1799–1875, German astronomer, noted for star catalogue, *Bonn Durchmusterung* (1862).

Argenson (ärzhăsō'), French noble family, prominent in the public service in the 18th cent. Among them were **René Louis de Voyer de Paulmy, marquis d'Argenson** (rùnä' lwē dù vwäyä' dù pōlmē', märkē'), 1694–1757, foreign minister (1744–47), and his brother, **Marc Pierre de Voyer de Paulmy, comte d'Argenson** (märk' pyĕr', kōt'), 1696–1764, who as secretary of war (1743–57) reformed the army and founded the École militaire. Both brothers were friends of Voltaire and the Encyclopedists.

Argenteuil (ärzhätù'ē), city (pop. 82,321), Val-d'Oise dept., N France, on the Seine; industrial suburb of Paris. Convent where Heloise was prioress destroyed in French Revolution.

Argentia, N.F.: see PLACENTIA BAY.

Argentina (ärjùntē'nù), republic (1,072,745 sq. mi.; 1960 est. pop. 20,959,100), S South America between Andes and Atlantic; cap. BUENOS AIRES. Second largest South American nation, extends from subtropics 2,300 mi. S to TIERRA DEL FUEGO. Also claims FALKLAND ISLANDS, which are held by British, and part of Antartica. Bordered by Chile (W), Bolivia (N), Paraguay, Brazil, Uruguay (NE), Atlantic (SE). Consists of four regions. In W are Andes (crossed by TRANSANDINE RAILWAY; one of highest peaks in W hemisphere, Aconcagua) and Andean piedmont. Latter is grazing and farming area (esp. sugar cane and wine grapes). Principal cities are TUCUMÁN and MENDOZA. In N are plains of CHACO and Mesopotamia, sparsely populated area whose main products are cotton, MATE, and QUEBRACHO. In S is PATAGONIA, also sparsely populated, area of arid plateaus noted for sheep grazing and oil production. In center, between Andes and Atlantic, is the Pampa (see PAMPAS), where Argentina's population and wealth are concentrated. At mid-19th cent. Pampa was still relatively undeveloped and unsettled home of GAUCHO. Defeat of Indians (1878–79) and development of refrigeration for meat opened a period of immigration and economic progress. Now one of great beef-producing areas of the world; large wheat and corn crops grown. Chief cities are the great port of Buenos Aires, at mouth of Río de la Plata; ROSARIO, LA PLATA, SANTA FE, and BAHÍA BLANCA, also ports; the resort city of MAR DEL PLATA, and CÓRDOBA on W edge of Pampa. Population largely of European descent (esp. Italian and Spanish). Native Indians found only in NW. First European explorers: Juan Díaz de SOLÍS (1516), MAGELLAN (1520), Sebastian CABOT (1527–30). Buenos Aires founded by Pedro de MENDOZA (1536), abandoned after Indian attacks, refounded from ASUNCIÓN by GARAY (1580), made cap. of Spanish vice-royalty (1776). From 1810 to 1816 successful struggle for inde-

pendence led by generals BELGRANO, PUEYRREDÓN, and, most importantly, SAN MARTÍN. Civil war followed, lasted until dictatorship of Juan Manuel de ROSAS (1829–52). He was deposed by URQUIZA (1852), and new constitution was adopted (1853). This document (with major amendments in 1860, 1866, 1898) remained in effect until 1949, but Argentina continued to suffer political instability and military coups. Argentine-Chilean boundary dispute settled 1902; perpetual peace symbolized by CHRIST OF ANDES. Argentina remained neutral in First World War, belatedly entered Second World War and became charter member of UN. From 1946 to 1955 Juan PERÓN maintained a dictatorship supported by workers, nationalists, clericals, and army. He lost church and some labor support and was overthrown by army. Pres. Arturo Frondizi (1958–62) was succeeded by Arturo Illia (1963–66), but both failed to solve problem of continued political strength of peronists. In 1966 military overthrew Illia and made Gen. Juan Carlos Ongania president.

Arginusae, battle of (ärjĭnū'sē), 406 B.C., last Athenian naval victory in the PELOPONNESIAN WAR, off the Arginusae Isls., near Asia Minor. A storm at the end of the battle caused several Athenian ships to founder. The eight commanders' failure to rescue the crews caused the assembly to inflict the harsh punishment of execution for six of them.

Argirocastro, Albania: see ARGYROKASTRON.

Argo (är'gō), in Greek mythology, ship in which the Argonauts sailed to find the GOLDEN FLEECE.

argol: see TARTAR.

Argolis (är'gùlĭs), region or anc. Greece, in NE Peloponnesus, around Argive plain; dominated by city of Argos.

argon (är'gŏn), colorless, odorless, tasteless, inert gaseous element (symbol = Ar; see also ELEMENT, table). Occurs in air and some volcanic gases. Used in electric-light bulbs, electric signs.

Argonaut (är'gùnôt") [Gr.,= sailor on Argo], in Greek mythology, one of band led by JASON who went to Colchis in quest of GOLDEN FLEECE. Among the voyagers were Argus, Orpheus, Hercules, and the huntress Atalanta. Voyage was interrupted for a year while they tarried on Lemnos. The ship safely passed the Symplegades (floating cliffs) and also SCYLLA and CHARYBDIS, and the mariners escaped the wiles of the Sirens' singing.

Argonne (är'gŏn, Fr. ärgôn'), hilly and wooded region, NE France, in Champagne and Lorraine. French repulsed Prussians here at Valmy 1792. In First World War the Meuse-Argonne sector was carried by U.S. troops Sept.–Nov., 1918.

Argos, in Greek legend: see ARGUS.

Argos (är'gŏs, –gùs), city of anc. Greece, NE Peloponnesus, near modern Nauplia. Center of Argolis, it struggled with Sparta and rivaled Athens and Corinth. Taken by Sparta (c.494 B.C.). Flourished under Rome after 146 B.C.

Arguello, Point, promontory, extending W into the Pacific, SW Calif., WNW of Santa Barbara. Vandenburg Air Force Base, missile test center, is nearby.

Argun (ärgōon'), river, c.1,000 mi. long, NE Asia, a headstream of the Amur. Forms part of border between USSR and Manchuria.

Argus (är'gùs) or **Argos** (är'gŏs, –gùs), in Greek myth. **1** Hundred-eyed monster, also called Panopes, set by Hera to guard Io. **2** Son of Phrixus. Builder of the ARGO and an Argonaut.

Argyll, dukes of, earls of, and marquesses of, Scottish nobles: see the family name, CAMPBELL.

Argyllshire (ärgĭl'shĭr) or **Argyll,** maritime county (3,124 sq. mi.; pop. 59,345), W Scotland; co. town Inverary. Includes numerous islands of Inner Hebrides. Wild and mountainous, has agr. on coast only. One of chief sheep-raising areas of British Isles. Iona has remains of ancient monastic center.

Argyrokastron (äryērô'kästrôn), Albanian *Argirokastra*, town (est. pop. 13,100), S Albania, on Drin R. Its old castle was rebuilt (19th cent.) by Ali Pasha.

Arhus, Denmark: see AARHUS.

aria, air or melody, especially an accompanied solo in an opera, oratorio, or cantata. The *aria da capo* has a contrasting, usually shorter, middle section followed by a repetition of the first section.

Ariadne (ărēăd'nē), in Greek legend, Cretan princess, daughter of Minos and Pasiphaë. With her help Theseus killed Minotaur and escaped from Labyrinth. He took her with him but deserted her at Naxos.

Arianism, heretical movement arising from teaching of Arius (c.256–336), a Libyan theologian, priest in Alexandria. He advanced the doctrine that before the general creation God had created and begotten a Son, the first creature, but neither eternal nor equal with the Father. This idea spread, and the unity of Christendom was threatened by the resultant conflict. Emperor Constantine called the First Council of NICAEA, where ATHANASIUS vigorously opposed Arius and won a victory. Arianism was condemned, but the matter had become political as well as religious. Arius, condemned locally in 321 and anathematized by the council, was brought back from exile (335). The conflict went on, with whole groups of bishops being exiled by emperors favoring one or the other party. The Arians split into three groups, mutually antagonistic. Finally the doctrines favored by Athanasius and Rome triumphed. Theodosius made Catholicism the state religion. Arianism had, however, been carried to the Goths and Vandals, and it survived in Africa until the 6th cent., in Visigothic Spain until the 7th. Contrary to popular belief, Arianism had nothing to do with the split between Eastern and Western Churches or with Protestantism.

Arias de Ávila, Pedro (pä'dhrō ä'ryäs dä ä'vēlä), known as **Pedrarias** (pādhrä'ryäs), c.1440–1531, Spanish colonial administrator. Sent (1514) as governor of Darien, he had BALBOA executed, was notoriously cruel. Extended Spanish dominions; founded Panama city (1519). Went to Nicaragua (1526) and held power until death.

Arias de Saavedra, Hernando (ērnän'dō ä'ryäs dä sävä'drä), known as **Hernandarias** (ērnändä'ryäs), 1561–1634, b. Asunción. First American-born governor of Río de la Plata prov., he was able administrator.

Arica (ärē'kä), city (pop. c.46,000), N Chile, Pacific port won from Peru in War of the Pacific (1879–84). In settlement of Tacna-Arica controversy (1929), Chile was required to furnish port facilities to Peru. Important for mineral exports, district is now a free zone.

Ariège (äryēzh'), department (1,893 sq. mi.; pop. 137,192), SW France, in Pyrenees; cap. Foix.

Aries [Lat.,= ram], first sign of ZODIAC.

Arikara Indians (ûrī'kûrū), North American tribe, formerly on Missouri R., of Caddoan linguistic family of Hokan-Siouan stock (see LANGUAGE; table). Semisedentary, they hunted buffalo and grew maize.

Ariminum: see RIMINI, Italy.

Arion (ûrī'ûn), fl. late 7th cent. B.C., Greek poet, inventor of the DITHYRAMB.

Ariosto, Ludovico (lōōdōvē'kō äryōs'tō), 1474–1533, Italian epic and lyric poet, famous for his *Orlando Furioso* (1532), epic treatment of the Roland story, a sequel to the unfinished poem of BOIARDO. Written for his patrons, the Este family, *Orlando Furioso* combines irony and grandeur and is called the greatest Renaissance poem.

Ariovistus (â"rēōvī'stŭs), fl. 58 B.C., Germanic chieftain, leader of the Suebi. Came to dominate much of GAUL, and in 60 B.C. became a friend and ally of Rome, but his power threatened Roman rule in Gaul, and Caesar defeated and drove him out (58).

Aristarchus of Samos (är"īstär'kŭs, să'mōs), 3d cent. B.C. Greek astronomer of Alexandrian school. One of

first to conclude that earth moves around sun and to state causes of day and night and of change of seasons.

Aristarchus of Samothrace, c.217–c.145 B.C., Greek scholar, librarian at Alexandria. An innovator in scientific scholarship. His recension of Homer is responsible for good texts that survive.

Aristides (ărīstī'dēz), d. c.468 B.C., Athenian statesman and general. Ostracized by Themistocles, he was recalled and commanded the fleet in victory over the Persians at Plataea (479 B.C.). Later organized Delian League. Called Aristides the Just.

aristocracy (är"īstŏk'rūsē), in political science, government by best in interest of all. Aristocracy usually has rested on landed possessions and inheritance. In the West the bourgeoisie was in late Middle Ages a royal weapon against it. Aristocracy sometimes (as in anc. Rome and 18th-cent. England) rested on wealth.

Aristogiton: see HARMODIUS AND ARISTOGITON.

Aristophanes (är"īstŏf'unēz), b. c.448, d. after 388 B.C., greatest Greek poet of COMEDY. His plays, only full samples of the Greek Old Comedy, mix political, social, and literary satire. Among surviving eleven plays are: *The Clouds, The Wasps, The Birds, Lysistrata,* and *The Frogs.*

Aristotle (är"īstŏt"ûl), 384–322 B.C., Greek philosopher, b. Stagira. Most eminent pupil of Plato, he was later tutor to Alexander the Great and then head of the Peripatetic school of philosophy in the Lyceum at Athens. His chief extant works are the *Organon* (lectures on logic), *Metaphysics, Physics, Nichomachaean Ethics, Eudemian Ethics, On the Soul* (*De Anima*), *Politics, Rhetoric, Poetics,* and *Constitution of Athens.* He accepted the Platonic idea of a Divine Form, but otherwise he taught that form and matter were inseparable. Goodness for him lay in the adequate performance of whatever function a thing or being was best suited for—in the case of men use of reason. Aristotle was a close observer of physical fact and was to some extent the founder of Western scientific thought. Aristotle's teaching had great force in the Arab world and on medieval scholasticism.

arithmetic, elementary and anc. branch of mathematics. Includes calculation (concrete, practical, or elementary arithmetic) and theory of numbers, which is also called higher arithmetic. Both deal with number behavior in four basic operations—addition, subtraction, multiplication, division—and operations involving exponents. Higher arithmetic generalizes number concept to include complex numbers, quaternions, tensors, abstract entities.

Arius, theologian: see ARIANISM.

Arizona, state (113,909 sq. mi.; pop. 1,302,161), SW U.S.; admitted 1912 as 48th state; cap. and largest city PHOENIX. One of Rocky Mt. states. Colorado R. forms most of W line. N Ariz. is part of Colorado plateau, with forests, isolated mountains, dry plains, and canyons (incl. GRAND CANYON). To S are hot desert plains striated by N–S mountain chains. Spanish (esp. Coronado in 1540) first explored region. Missions founded by Eusebio Kino in 1690s. Became part of U.S. by Treaty of GUADALUPE HIDALGO (1848) and GADSDEN PURCHASE (1853); made a territory 1863. Intermittent warfare with the Apache troubled region 1861–86. By 1870s mining and ranching flourished. State's history has been shaped by scarcity of water; many irrigation projects permit agr. Region abounds in minerals (copper, silver, molybdenum, gold). Increased mfg. (esp. electronics equipment and consumer goods) after Second World War. Warm, dry climate and scenic wonders have made tourism important. Federal projects aid large (c.83,400) Indian population.

Arizona, University of, at Tucson; land grant, state supported; coed.; chartered 1885, opened 1891. Has 20 extension centers.

ark, in Bible. **1** Boat built by NOAH to save his family and some animals from Deluge. Gen. 6–9; Luke 17.27;

Heb. 11.7; 1 Peter 3.20. **2** Wooden chest, overlaid with gold, known as Ark of the Covenant, sacred symbol of early Hebrews, representative of God. Touching it was a desecration punishable by death. Its presence implied victory, so was carried into battle by poles thrust through rings on its sides. Taken by Philistines, it brought them disaster and was sent back to Israel. Brought by David to Jerusalem, placed in Temple by Solomon. Since lost from view. Possibly held tables of Ten Commandments. Ex. 25.10–21; Num. 10.33–36; Deut. 10.1–5; Joshua 3, 4, 6; 1 Sam. 4–7; 2 Sam. 6; 15.24,29; 1 Kings 8.3,9; 1 Chron. 13; 15–16.6; 2 Chron. 5; Jer. 3.16; Heb. 9.4.

Arkansas (är'kůnsô), state (53,104 sq. mi.; pop. 1,786,272), central and SW U.S.; admitted 1836 as 25th state (slaveholding); cap. and largest city LITTLE ROCK. Other major cities are FORT SMITH, PINE BLUFF, HOT SPRINGS, TEXARKANA. Bounded on E by Mississippi R. The Arkansas R. flows SE from mountains of N and W, between Ozark plateaus (see OZARK MOUNTAINS) and OUACHITA MOUNTAINS, down to Mississippi plains of S and E. Also has SAINT FRANCIS R., WHITE RIVER, OUACHITA R., and RED RIVER. Economy dominated by agr. (esp. cotton, soybeans, corn, rice). Minerals include petroleum, bauxite, stone, coal, natural gas. Lumbering still important in this heavily wooded state. Spanish under De Soto were probably first white men in area, 1541–42. French trading center estab. at ARKANSAS POST 1686. As part of French territory of Louisiana, region was ceded to Spain (1762) and back to France before passing to U.S. with Louisiana Purchase. Became territory 1819, after cotton boom. Seceded from Union May, 1861; readmitted 1868. Reconstruction period turbulent. Depression of 1930s hurt cotton economy; many farmers left. Second World War brought further population loss, as men went to war factories elsewhere. War promoted new industries within state (esp. aluminum). Resistance to attempted desegregation of Little Rock public schools in 1957 claimed world-wide attention.

Arkansas (ärkän'zùs, är'kůnsô"), river rising in the Rockies of central Colo. and flowing c.1,459 mi. SE, across Colo., Kansas, Okla., and Ark., to the Mississippi between Memphis, Tenn., and Vicksburg, Miss. Bridged at Royal Gorge canyon (granite walls rise sharply to over 1,000 ft.), Colo. Receives Cimarron and Canadian rivers in Okla. Passes through Wichita (Kansas), Tulsa (Okla.), and Little Rock (Ark.). Flood-control, irrigation, and power project on river and its tributaries includes John Martin Dam (Colo.); Keystone, Dardanelle, Blue Mountain, Nimrod dams (Ark.); Fall River Dam (Kansas); Hulah, Tenkiller Ferry, Wister, Oologah, and Great Salt Plains dams (Okla.). Cotton, rice, wheat, sugar beets, and fruit are grown in river's valley. There are also oil refining and coal mining.

Arkansas, University of, mainly at Fayetteville; land grant, state supported; coed.; chartered 1871, opened 1872; called Arkansas Industrial Univ. until 1899. Sponsor of Oak Ridge Inst. of Nuclear Studies at Oak Ridge, Tenn. Medical Center and technology campus are at Little Rock.

Arkansas City (ärkän'zůs), city (pop. 14,262), S Kansas, SSE of Wichita at junction of Arkansas and Walnut rivers. It is in an agr. and oil area.

Arkansas Post (är'kůnsô"), community, SE Ark., on Arkansas R., SE of Pine Bluff; founded by French as trading post 1686. Oldest white settlement in state and first territorial capital. Confederate stronghold until captured by Gen McClernand 1863.

Arkansas State College, near Jonesboro; coed.; chartered 1909, opened 1910; called State Agr. and Mechanical Col. 1925–33.

Arkhangelsk, RSFSR: see ARCHANGEL.

Arklow, urban district (pop. 5,387), Co. Wicklow, E Republic of Ireland, on St. George's Channel. Fishing port and resort.

Arkwright, Sir Richard, 1732–92, English inventor. His construction of a spinning machine (patented 1769) an early step in the INDUSTRIAL REVOLUTION.

Arlberg (ärl'běrk), pass, 5,946 ft. high, W Austria, near Arlberg peak. Arlberg Tunnel is 6½ mi. long.

Arles (ärl), city (pop. 42,353), Bouches-du-Rhône dept., SE France, in Provence, on Rhone delta. Silk mfg., wine trade. A flourishing Roman town (Arelas) and the metropolis of Gaul under late empire, it became the cap. of medieval kingdom of Arles and was the site of many Church councils and a center of Provençal culture. Roman remains include huge arena, theater. Church of St. Trophime was begun 11th cent.

Arles, kingdom of, formed 933 when Rudolph II united his kingdom of Transjurane BURGUNDY with the kingdom of PROVENCE or Cisjurane Burgundy. Emperor Conrad II joined it to Holy Roman Empire in 1033. Government by imperial vicars was nominal; France, Savoy, Switzerland, and Burgundy held actual control over component territories. After the dauphin (later Charles VI of France) was made vicar in 1378, the kingdom survived only in theory.

Arlington, Henry Bennet, 1st earl of, 1618–85, English courtier. Under Charles II was a secretary of state and member of CABAL ministry.

Arlington. 1 Residential town (pop. 49,953), E Mass., suburb SW of Boston; settled c.1630. **2** Town (pop. 8,317), SE N.Y., suburb E of Poughkeepsie. Seat of VASSAR COLLEGE. **3** City (pop. 44,775), N Texas, E of Fort Worth, in agr. area; founded nearby 1873, moved to railroad 1876. Arlington State Col., branch of Agr. and Mechanical Col. of Texas, is here.

Arlington Heights, village (1965 pop. 40,622), NE Ill., NW of Chicago. Has race track.

Arlington National Cemetery, 408 acres, N Va., on Potomac R. opposite Washington, D.C.; estab. 1864, extended 1889 and 1897. Here are graves of c.60,000 war dead, tomb of Unknown Soldier, and marble amphitheatre. Cemetery is part of "Arlington," former estate of Custis and Lee families.

Arliss, George, 1868–1946, English actor. Had his first great success (1911) in the title role of *Disraeli;* won acclaim later for film portrayal of role. Was popular for portrayals of the suave villain, notably in *The Green Goddess.*

Arlon (ärlô'), Flemish *Aarlen,* town (est. pop. 13,-721), cap. Luxembourg prov., SE Belgium.

Armada, Spanish (ärmä'dù), 1588, fleet launched by Philip II of Spain against England; called also Invincible Armada. Consisting of 130 ships and c.30,000 men, and commanded by duke of Medina Sidonia, it was to go to Flanders and from there convoy the army of Alessandro Farnese to invade England and seize the throne for Philip. The Armada set out from Lisbon in May, was delayed at Coruña, and in July, at Plymouth, found the English fleet, under Charles Howard (later earl of Nottingham). Among the English captains were Sir Francis Drake, Sir John Hawkins, and Sir Martin Frobisher. Forced up the English Channel, the Armada suffered losses in several engagements, but escaped north with favorable wind. Only half the fleet reached home; the rest was dispersed by storms off Ireland and its crews killed or captured.

armadillo (ärmùdĭl'ô), mammal of order Edentata, found from Patagonia northward to parts of S and SW U.S. Armor of bone and horny material almost covers head and body; tail has bony rings. Is omnivorous but eats chiefly insects. Nine-banded armadillo (*Dasypus*) is the only U.S. species. Flesh palatable.

Armageddon (–gĕd'ùn), great battlefield, to be site of final conflict between powers of good and evil. Rev. 16.16. Name may come from MEGIDDO.

Armagh (ärmä'), inland county (449 sq. mi.; pop. 117,-580), N Ireland. Mainly a farming region, also noted for its linen. County town is **Armagh,** urban district (pop. 9,982), religious center of Ireland. St. Patrick was bishop here 5th cent. Seat of Roman Catholic and Protestant archbishoprics.

Armagnac (ärmänyäk'), region and former county, SW France, in Gascony; historic cap. Auch. Produces brandy. Added to royal domain 1607.

Armagnacs and Burgundians, opposing factions in 15th-cent. France. Their struggle arose out of rivalry of Louis d'ORLÉANS and JOHN THE FEARLESS of Burgundy. After Louis's murder (1407) his followers were led by BERNARD VII, count of Armagnac—hence their nickname. The Burgundians—followers of John the Fearless—were strong in Paris, where the radical CABOCHIENS supported them. Civil war broke out (1411) and merged after 1415 with the HUNDRED YEARS WAR. In 1418 the Burgundians seized Paris and massacred the Armagnacs; in 1419 the Armagnacs murdered John the Fearless. The Burgundians now became full allies of England, while the Armagnacs, led by the dauphin (later Charles VII), represented the national party.

armature. 1 Part of electric GENERATOR and MOTOR. Coil of wire that rotates in magnetic field between opposite magnetic poles and cuts magnetic lines of force between them, generating current in coil. **2** Piece of iron or steel, called a keeper, placed between or across poles of magnet to prevent decrease in magnetic property.

Armavir (ärmûvēr', Rus. ŭrmŭvēr'), city (1965 est. pop. 131,000), Krasnodar Territory, SW European RSFSR, on Kuban R. A railroad junction, it has machine and tool plants.

Armenia (ärmē'nēŭ), region and former kingdom of Asia Minor. Roughly includes E Turkey and ARMENIAN SOVIET SOCIALIST REPUBLIC. Tradition says kingdom was founded in region of Lake Van by Haig or Haik, descendant of Noah. A battleground of Assyrians, Medes, and Persians, it became a Persian satrapy c.6th cent. B.C. Conquered 4th cent. B.C. by Alexander the Great; later ruled by Seleucus I. Was independent kingdom from 189 B.C. to 69 B.C., when it fell to Rome. Armenia is oldest Christian state. After 3d cent., when region was under Persian rule, Armenian Christians suffered much persecution. Enjoyed autonomy 885–1046 under the native Bagratids. Reconquered 1046 by the Byzantines, who were ousted by Seljuk Turks. Pushed westward, an Armenian group estab. kingdom of Little Armenia in CILICIA. Greater Armenia was occupied 1386–94 by Tamerlane. All Armenia was under Turkish rule by 16th cent., but E Armenia was claimed also by Persia, who lost it to Russia in 1828. Congress of Berlin (1878) gave some Armenian territory to Russia, but much of it was restored 1921 to Turkey. Armenians were sporadically massacred by the Turks 1894–1915. Treaty of Brest-Litovsk (1918), which made Russian Armenia independent under German auspices, was superseded by Treaty of Sèvres (1920) which created independent Greater Armenia (comprising Turkish and Russian parts), but in same year Communists proclaimed Russian Armenia a Soviet Republic. With Russo-Turkish treaty (1921) marking present boundaries Armenian independence was ended.

Armenian Church, group that split from the orthodox Christians in 4th cent. and accepted (5th cent.) some doctrines of MONOPHYSITISM. Liturgical language is Classical Armenian. From 1198 to 1375 the Cilician Armenians were reunited with the Holy See. The authority of the American branch of the Church was transferred from the Catholicate in Soviet Armenia to the Independent Armenian Catholicate in Beirut in 1957.

Armenian language, subfamily of Indo-European languages. See LANGUAGE (table).

Armenian literature. First work (c.5th cent.), a translation of Bible, became standard of Classical Armenian. Armenian Church fostered literature, mostly saints' lives and histories. Among secular works were translations of Aristotle and the romance of Alexander. History of Moses of Khorni is main source on pre-Christian Armenia. Catholicos Narses IV, 12th cent. prelate and poet, had unexcelled literary style. In 12th cent. vernacular came into use for contemporary topics. In 18th cent. Mechitar, Catholic Armenian monk, founded monastic literary community at Constantinople. The Mechitarists, now centered at Venice, publish works in Armenian.

Armenian Soviet Socialist Republic, constituent republic (11,500 sq. mi.; 1965 est. pop. 2,164,000), USSR, in S Transcaucasia, bordering on Turkey and Iran; cap. Erivan. Mountainous (highest peak Mt. Aragats, 13,435 ft.); good pastures. Valleys are artificially irrigated. Main products are wine, cotton, wool, copper. Hydroelectric power from L. Sevan. A part of ancient ARMENIA, territory was taken by Russia from Persia in 1828.

Armentières (ärmätyēr'), town (est. pop. 24,940), Nord dept., N France, on Lys R. Famous for First World War song, *Mademoiselle from Armentières.*

Arminius (ärmĭ'nēŭs), d. A.D. 21?, leader of the Germans. When Romans pushed E from the Rhine, Arminius, ex-Roman citizen and soldier, gathered a great force and destroyed the army of P. Quintilius VARUS. Rome never again tried to conquer E of Rhine. In German he is Hermann.

Arminius, Jacobus, 1560–1609, Dutch Reformed theologian (originally Jacob Harmensen), professor at Leiden after 1603. **Arminianism,** his teaching, as fully formulated by Simon Episcopius (1622), opposed a strict Calvinist doctrine of predestination and favored a doctrine of election based on divine foreknowledge. The Wesleys adopted this teaching.

armor, protective covering in warfare for persons, horses, vehicles, naval vessels, and aircraft. Body armor was known to many peoples, and metal armor became elaborate in the Middle Ages. Increased emphasis on mobile warfare and introduction of firearms (16th cent.) greatly reduced importance of armor, but in 20th cent. the tank and armor plate for ships and aircraft became important.

Armorica: see BRITTANY.

Armory Show, international exhibition of modern art held 1913 at the 69th Regiment Armory, New York city. It sensationally introduced modern art into America and helped to change the direction of American painting.

Arms, John Taylor, 1887–1953, American etcher, noted for studies of medieval architecture.

Armstrong, Edwin Howard, 1890–1954, American engineer. Radio contributions include regenerative circuit; superheterodyne circuit (basis for design of most receivers); superregenerative circuit; development of workable frequency modulation (FM).

Armstrong, Henry, 1912–, American boxer. In 1938 held three boxing titles (featherweight, welterweight, and lightweight) simultaneously.

Armstrong, John, 1758–1843, American army officer, U.S. Secretary of War (1813–14). Held responsible for disasters in War of 1812; resigned in disfavor.

Armstrong, Louis ("Satchmo"), 1900–, American jazz trumpeter, singer, and band leader.

Armstrong, Samuel Chapman, 1839–93, American educator and philanthropist. A major general of the Union army, he later helped found (1868) and was head of Hampton Normal and Agricultural Inst. (now Hampton Inst.).

army worm, striped green, black, and yellow larva of phalaenid moth; in North America is found E of Rocky Mts. Moving in hordes, they ravage crops; controlled by poisoning and trapping in ditches.

Arnaud, Henri (ärē' ärnō'), 1641–1721, Savoyard pastor, leader of WALDENSES at home and in exile.

Arnauld (ärnō'), French family involved in JANSENISM. Also Arnaut, Arnault. **(Marie) Angélique (de Sainte Madeleine)** (äzhälēk'), 1591–1661, was abbess of PORT-ROYAL. Under the influence of St. Francis de Sales, she reformed her abbey. Later DUVERGIER DE

HAURANNE led her to adopt Jansenist ideas. Her younger brother, **Antoine Arnauld** (ätwän'), 1612–94, was a Jansenist controversialist, author of *De la fréquente communion* (1643), collaborator in famous Port-Royal textbooks. His older brother, **Robert Arnauld d'Andilly** (rōbĕr', dädēyē'), 1588–1674, translated religious writings and wrote poetry.

Arnhem (är'nŭm), municipality (pop. 130,399) and city, cap. of Gelderland prov., E Netherlands; a port on the Lower Rhine. Industrial center. Dates from 10th cent.; long a residence of dukes of Gelderland. In Second World War British air-borne troops suffered tragic defeat here (Sept., 1944).

Arnhem Land, aboriginal reservation, area 31,200 sq. mi., Northern Territory, Australia, on a peninsula W of Gulf of Carpentaria. Large bauxite deposits.

arnica, any yellow-flowered perennial of genus *Arnica*. Medicinal preparations made from some for the treatment of wounds and bruises.

Arnim, Achim von (äkh'ĭm fŭn är'nĭm), 1781–1831, German romantic writer. Published, with brother-in-law Clemens BRENTANO, collection of folk songs, *Des Knaben Wunderhorn* [the boy's magic horn] (1806–8). *Isabella von Ägypten* (1812; Eng. tr., 1927), a short novel, is his best-known work. His wife, **Bettina von Arnim** (bĕtē'nä), 1785–1859, is also known under her maiden name, Elisabeth Brentano. A friend of Beethoven and, supposedly, of Goethe, she wrote the unreliable *Goethe's Correspondence with a Child* (1835; Eng. tr., 1837).

Arno, Peter, 1904–, American cartoonist. Joined staff of the *New Yorker* magazine 1925.

Arno (är'nō), river, 150 mi. long, Tuscany, central Italy. Flows past Florence and Pisa into Ligurian Sea.

Arnold, Benedict, 1741–1801, American Revolutionary general and traitor. Took part in QUEBEC CAMPAIGN and SARATOGA CAMPAIGN. Plot to betray West Point to British failed with capture of John ANDRÉ. Arnold escaped and fought for British.

Arnold, H(enry) H(arley), 1886–1950, American general, chief of Army Air Forces (1941–46). Called Hap or Happy Arnold.

Arnold, Matthew, 1822–88, English poet and critic; son of Thomas Arnold. Inspector of elementary schools 1851–86, he became (1857) professor of poetry at Oxford. Believed poetry should be objective, but his own poetry showed romantic pessimism (e.g., "Dover Beach"; elegy for A. H. Clough, "Thyrsis"; "The Scholar Gypsy"). Also wrote long narrative poems and many lyrics. His criticism was based on classical standards; he particularly deplored the "Philistines," the 19th-cent. English middle class, and advocated a new culture based on understanding the best that had been thought and said in the world.

Arnold, Thomas, 1795–1842, English educator; father of Matthew Arnold, grandfather of Mrs. Humphry Ward. As headmaster at Rugby (1827–42) he revivified English public school system by reforms (adding mathematics, modern languages, and modern history to curriculum; introducing monitorial system; encouraging independent thought). Also classical scholar and historian, and an eloquent, effective preacher.

Arnold of Brescia (brĕ'shù), c.1090–1155, Italian reformer. A priest and a pupil of Abelard, he criticized the Church for owning any property at all. This idea was condemned at the Synod of Sens (1140). In Rome after 1145, he took the part of the commune, pleading for liberty and democracy. Excommunicated in 1148, he was forced from power by Adrian IV (1155) and executed as a political rebel.

Arnoldson, Klas Pontus (kläs' pôn'tùs är'nôldsōn), 1844–1916, Swedish journalist and pacifist. Shared 1908 Nobel Peace Prize with Fredrik Bajer.

Arnold von Winkelried: see WINKELRIED.

Arnolfo di Cambio (ärnōl'fō dē käm'byō), c.1245–c.1310, Italian architect and sculptor. Designed the Baptistry, Palazzo Vecchio, and the basic portion of Santa Maria del Fiore in Florence.

Arnulf (är'nŭlf), c.850–899, last Carolingian emperor (896–99); natural son of Carloman of Bavaria. Was proclaimed king of East Franks (887) after leading rebellion which deposed his uncle Charles III. Defeated Normans 891. Invaded Italy 894 and 895 on request of Pope Formosus, who crowned him emperor at Rome (896).

Aroostook (ùrōōs'tòŏk), river, c.140 mi. long, rising in N Maine and winding E to St. John R. in N.B. Gives name to a county famous for potatoes.

Aroostook War, brief conflict, 1838–39, between Maine and New Brunswick over disputed U.S.–Canadian border. Full-scale war averted through agreement reached in March, 1839. Boundary settled by WEBSTER-ASHBURTON TREATY.

Arp, Jean (Hans), 1887–1966, French sculptor and painter connected with *Blaue Reiter*, Dada, and surrealism. He consistently created novel and abstract forms in various media.

Arpad (ôr'päd), c.840–907?, chief of the MAGYARS, whom he led into Hungary in 895. His descendants ruled Hungary till 1301.

Arpino, Cavaliere d': see CESARI, GIUSEPPE.

arrack, spirits distilled chiefly in Far East from fermented juices (e.g., palm toddy) or grains. Primitive methods of distilling yield injurious raw spirits.

Arran, earls of: see HAMILTON, JAMES; STUART, JAMES.

Arran, wild rocky island (165 sq. mi.; pop. 3,705), Buteshire, Scotland; hunting and fishing resort.

Arran Islands, Ireland: see ARAN ISLANDS.

Arras (äräs'), city (est. pop. 36,242), cap. of Pas-de-Calais dept., N France; historic cap of Artois. Flourished in late Middle Ages (famed for TAPESTRY). Renaissance city hall; cathedral (18th cent.); Abbey of St. Vaast (18th cent.; now museum); 17th-cent. citadel.

Arras, Treaty of. 1 Treaty, 1435, by which Charles VII of France, at heavy costs, secured the alliance of Philip the Good of Burgundy against England. **2** Treaty, 1482, between Louis XI of France and representatives of the Netherlands, regarding succession to MARY OF BURGUNDY; ratified 1483 by Mary's widower, Archduke Maximilian (later Emperor Maximilian I). Burgundian territories remained under Maximilian's regency for his son Philip (later Philip I of Castile), but France incorporated the duchy of Burgundy and Picardy and held Artois and Franche-Comté as dowry of MARGARET OF AUSTRIA, Maximilian's daughter, who was betrothed to the dauphin. Treaty of SENLIS (1493) restored dowry to Hapsburgs after CHARLES VIII married Anne of Brittany instead.

Arrebo, Anders (än'ùrs ä'rùbō), 1587–1637, Danish poet, bishop of Trondheim, author of the *Hexaemeron* (1661), narrative poem which introduced the alexandrine meter to N Europe.

arrest, seizure and detention of a person according to civil or criminal law. Civil arrest, used mostly in cases of contempt of court, always requires a warrant. Criminal arrest may be made without a warrant by any person present when a crime is committed or by an officer who reasonably suspects someone of having recently committed a felony. In some cases, release may be through habeas corpus; otherwise release usually can be obtained through bail. Evidence seized through improper arrest is inadmissible at trial. Diplomatic personnel and members of legislature (during sessions only) are exempt from arrest.

Arrhenius, Svante August (sfän'tù ou'gŭst ärä'nēùs), 1859–1927, Swedish chemist. Won 1903 Nobel Prize in Chemistry for ionization theory; worked on osmosis, toxins.

arrowhead, aquatic plant (*Sagittaria*), having white flowers and leaves that are shaped like arrowheads. Grown in aquariums, ponds, and bogs. Tubers were used as food by North American Indians.

arrowroot, edible, easily digested starch extracted from certain plants. True or West Indian arrowroot from a maranta (*Maranta arundinacea*), often grown as house plant for its decorative foliage. See also TAPIOCA.

arrowwood, any of several woody plants, notably of HONEYSUCKLE family, formerly used for making arrows.

Arsaces (är′sùsēz), fl. 250 B.C., founder of the Parthian dynasty, the **Arsacidae** (–sā′sĭdē″), which ruled Persia c.250 B.C.–A.D. 226.

arsenic (är′sùnĭk), chemical element (symbol = As; see also ELEMENT, table). Known in three forms (see ALLOTROPY): silver-gray crystalline, metallike, brittle solid; black, amorphous form; yellow, crystalline solid. Related to nitrogen and phosphorus. Used in making pigments, weed killers, insecticides (PARIS GREEN), poison gas; in dyeing textiles, in tanning, and in medicine. It is a strong poison. Its presence in compounds is detected by MARSH'S TEST.

arsenopyrite (är′sĭnōpī′rīt), metallic mineral, silvery to steel-gray. Composed of iron, arsenic, and sulfur.

Arsonval, Arsène d' (ärsĕn′ därsōväl′), 1851–1940, French physicist, physician. Pioneer in electrotherapy; originated term *diathermy*.

Artaxerxes (är″tùzûrk′sēz), Persian *Ardashir*, kings of the Achaemenid dynasty of anc. Persia. **Artaxerxes I,** d. 425 B.C. (reigned 464–425 B.C.), succeeded his father, XERXES I. Because of trouble in Egypt and Bactria and warfare with Greeks weakness of Persia said to appear in his reign. Judaism revived in his time. **Artaxerxes II,** d. 358 B.C. (reigned 404–358 B.C.), son and successor of Darius II. CYRUS THE YOUNGER tried to seize the throne but was killed at Cunaxa (401). A revolt of satraps was put down. The cult of MITHRA was revived. **Artaxerxes III,** d. 338 B.C. (reigned 358–338 B.C.), son of Artaxerxes II. Gained throne by general massacre of the family, and continued policy of terror, destroying Sidon and reducing Egypt. He was finally poisoned.

Artem (ürtyôm′), city (1965 est. pop. 64,000), Maritime Territory, NE Asiatic RSFSR. Coal-mining center.

Artemis (är′tùmĭs), in Greek legend, goddess (Roman Diana), virgin huntress with virgin attendants; daughter of Zeus and Leto, twin sister of APOLLO. She was goddess of the wild. By loosing a boar she caused CALYDONIAN HUNT. She visited punishments on Actaeon, Agamemnon, and Niobe. She was also a protector of women (temple at Ephesus was center of this cult). Complementary to Apollo, she was the goddess of the moon and the night.

artemisia: see WORMWOOD.

Artemovsk (ürtyô′mŭfsk), city (1965 est. pop. 74,-000), E central Ukraine. Industrial center in Donets Basin, it has metal-working and mining-equipment plants; known since 1476 for salt mines. Called Bakhmut until 1924.

arteriosclerosis, hardening and thickening of arterial walls sometimes caused by the deposition of calcium, or lipids (e.g., cholesterol). Hypertension is both a cause and a result of arteriosclerosis; other causes are thought to include diet and heredity. Arteriosclerosis may result in damage to any organ, particularly brain, heart, or kidneys. A restricted-fat diet has proved effective.

artery, vessel carrying blood from heart to body tissues in CIRCULATION OF THE BLOOD. Largest arterial branch leaving heart is the aorta.

Artesia (ärtē′zhù), city (pop. 12,000), SE N.Mex., W of Pecos R., N of Carlsbad. In an oil, farm, and live-stock area, it has artesian wells.

artesian well (ärtē′zhùn), in the strictest sense, a well made by drilling into a porous, water-bearing layer between two impervious strata. The water rises as a result of hydrostatic pressure dependent on the slope and rainfall. However, the term artesian is usually applied to any deep, drilled well from which water can be pumped.

Artevelde, Jacob van (yä′kôp vän är′tùvĕldù), c.1290–1345, Flemish statesman. Caught in the conflict between EDWARD III of England and PHILIP VI of France, Artevelde, as head of the city government of Ghent, negotiated a commercial treaty with England (1338) and obtained recognition of Flemish neutrality. In 1340 he secured support of Flemish towns for Edward. He was killed in a riot. His son, **Philip van Artevelde,** 1340–82, led the weavers' rebellion against the count of Flanders (1381), captured most of Flanders, but was defeated and slain by the French at Roosebeke.

arthritis, inflammation of joints. Often refers to rheumatoid arthritis, chronic, crippling, systemic disorder of unknown cause, characterized by pain and swelling, symmetrically located in hands, knees, feet. Muscle weakness, stiffness, and eye lesions occur. Rheumatoid arthritis usually occurs after age 40, and more frequently in women. Intensified by stress.

arthropod (är′thrŭpŏd″), member of phylum of invertebrate animals called Arthropoda (more species than all other animal groups combined). Includes CRUSTACEAN; SPIDER and relatives; CENTIPEDE; MILLIPEDE; INSECT; and extinct TRILOBITE. They have segmented bodies, jointed appendages, horny outer skeleton. Respiratory organs are gills or trachea.

Arthur: see ARTHURIAN LEGEND.

Arthur, dukes of Brittany. **Arthur I,** 1187–1203, posthumous son of Geoffrey, second son of Henry II of England. Succeeded his mother, duchess Constance, 1196. His claim to England was passed over (1199) in favor of his uncle JOHN, but he was invested by Philip II of France with all the French fiefs of the deceased Richard Cœur de Lion. In the ensuing warfare with John, Arthur was captured (1202), imprisoned at Rouen, and probably murdered. His brother-in-law succeeded him in Brittany as Peter I. **Arthur III,** 1393–1458, was known as comte de Richemont before his accession in 1457. As constable of France in the Hundred Years War, he captured Paris from the English (1436); led in reconquest of Normandy.

Arthur, Chester Alan, 1830–86, 21st President of the United States (1881–85). Collector of the port of New York (1871–78); his removal by Pres. Hayes defied the Conkling machine. His nomination for Vice President placated that group. Succeeding to the presidency after Garfield's assassination, Arthur had an honest, efficient, dignified administration. Supported civil service reform act of 1883; vetoed Chinese exclusion bill violating a treaty with China; prosecuted STAR ROUTE trials.

Arthurian legend, vast body of medieval story centering about King Arthur of Britain. First references to him, early as c.600, indicate that Arthur was historically a British leader in Anglo-Saxon invasion, but *Historia* (1137?) of GEOFFREY OF MONMOUTH makes him head of magnificent court and master of Europe. Meanwhile the legend had developed, with traditional Irish hero stories joining those of Welsh (see MABINOGION), Cornish, and North Britons. The expanded stories of Arthur were transmitted (before the year 1000) to the Bretons, who spread the tales over Western Europe. After Geoffrey came the chronicles of WACE, then of English LAYAMON. More important, the romances *Perceval* by CHRESTIEN DE TROYES and *Parzifal* by WOLFRAM VON ESCHENBACH became sources of PARSIFAL story. Early in the 13th cent. GOTTFRIED VON STRASSBURG composed his *Tristan,* first great version of TRISTRAM AND ISOLDE romance, which became attached to Arthurian legend. The third main theme, the knightly quest for Holy GRAIL, also developed. In England, Arthurian legend flourished in *Sir Gawain and the Green Knight* (see PEARL, THE) and the *Morte d'Arthur* of Sir Thomas MALORY. The full, later legend has Arthur, King Uther Pendragon's illegitimate son, show his royal blood by drawing a sword from a stone. His own sword, Excalibur, is given him by the Lady of the Lake; he keeps grand court with knights around honored Round Table at Camelot. When fatally wounded by his treacherous nephew (or son) Sir Mordred, Arthur is taken by three queens to the isle Avalon, whence he will return to save his people. Other characters in the legends are: Sir Launcelot of the Lake, gallant but faithless knight, lover of Arthur's queen; Elaine of Astolat, hopelessly in love with Launcelot; Elaine, daughter of Pelles, mother (by Launcelot) of the pure Sir Galahad, leader of Grail quest; Sir Gawain, Arthur's nephew, an ideal knight; Guinevere, Arthur's faithless queen, mistress of Launcelot; Sir Kay, churlish foster brother of Arthur; Merlin, great court magician; Morgan le Fay, Arthur's sister, an enchantress; and Sir Percivale (Parsifal).

artichoke, name for two different edible plants. Fleshy base of flower head and scales of the globe (or French) artichoke (*Cynara scolymus*) are eaten as salad or vegetable. It is a commercial crop in California. **Jerusalem artichoke** (*Helianthus tuberosus*) is a perennial sunflower with tuberous roots, potatolike but starchless, and grown for human food, stock feed, and as a source of inulin which yields levulose sugar.

artificial insemination, technique of artificially injecting semen from a male into a female to facilitate FERTILIZATION. It is widely used in propagation of cattle, especially to produce many offspring from one bull. Sometimes used in humans when normal fertilization is impossible.

artificial lung, mechanical device for inducing respiration. Used in asphyxia or comatose state resulting from drowning, strangulation, electric shock, gas inhalation, or a foreign body in the respiratory tract. In one device. the iron lung, patient lies in an airtight cylinder, head protruding. Air pumped rhythmically in and out of cylinder causes patient's chest to expand and deflate, simulating breathing.

artificial respiration, maintenance of breathing by artificial means. Mechanical devices are iron lung, respirator, pulmotor. Common hand method is the back pressure arm lift method. For both adults and children, mouth-to-mouth method is now preferred by American Red Cross. This method involves clearing throat of foreign matter and then breathing rythmically into mouth while applying slight pressure against patient's rib cage.

Artigas, José Gervasio (hōsä' hĕrvä'syō ärtē'gäs), 1764–1850, national hero of Uruguay. Typical gaucho of BANDA ORIENTAL, he championed Uruguayan independence from Spain, from Buenos Aires, and from Brazil. Exiled after annexation by Brazil (1820).

artillery, term originally applied to all projectiles employed in war, but later limited to certain types of heavy guns and troops serving them. Use of artillery against fortifications ended security of medieval castle. Artillery is now almost entirely mechanized and may be fixed or mobile.

art nouveau, art movement centered in Europe in the 1890s; called *Jugendstil* in Germany, *Modernismo* in Spain. Its exponents chose symbolic, exotic, or "decadent" themes. The style was richly ornamental, with a characteristic whiplash linearity. Outstanding designers of *art nouveau* include the English graphic artist, Aubrey Beardsley; the Belgian architects, Henry Van de Velde and Victor Horta; the French architect and designer of the metro entrances, Hector Guimard; and the American designer, Louis Comfort Tiffany.

Artois (ärtwä'), region and former province, N France, in Pas-de-Calais dept.; historic cap., Arras. Agr., coal mines, and textile mfg. Annexed from Flanders to France (12th cent.), it passed to Burgundy (14th cent.) and to Hapsburgs (1493). It was conquered by France in 1640 and formally ceded by Spain to France in 1659. A battleground in many wars, particularly in First World War.

arts and crafts, term for that general field of applied designing in which hand fabrication is dominant. The term was invented in England in the late 19th cent.

as a label for the current movement directed toward the revivifying of the decorative arts. Chief influence behind this movement was William MORRIS.

Art Students League of New York, art school, founded 1875 in New York city by a group of students; self-governing. A board of control elected annually by members selects noted artists to serve as teachers.

Artzybashev, Mikhail Petrovich (mĕkhûyĕl' pĕtrô'vĭch ärtsĭbä'shĕf), 1878–1927, Russian author. He leaped into fame with the sensational novel *Sanine* (1907; Eng. tr., 1914). Emigrated after October Revolution. Father of **Boris Artzybasheff,** 1899–1965, American illustrator of books and periodicals.

Aruba: see CURAÇAO.

arum, any plant of Araceae family. Grows mostly in tropical swamps; some found in temperate zones. Characterized by an inflorescence comprising a spike bearing small flowers and a modified leaf (spathe) surrounding it. Family includes calla lilies, monstera, philodendron, caladium, and elephant ears. *Colocasia esculenta* is chief ingredient of POI in Hawaii. Jack-in-the-pulpit and skunk cabbage are well-known varieties of the U.S.

Arundel, Henry Fitzalan, 12th earl of (ä'rŭndŭl), c.1511?–80, English statesman. Powerful Catholic noble, he helped bring Mary to the throne.

Arundel, Thomas Howard, 2d earl of, 1585–1646, first great English art collector. First a privy councilor, later earl marshal of England. **Arundel Marbles** are his collection of ancient sculptures donated 1667 to Oxford Univ. **Arundel Collection** of manuscripts is in British Mus. **Arundel Society** (1849–97) reproduced works of famous artists. **Arundel Club,** founded 1904, reproduces in photogravure privately owned art works.

Arundel (ä'rŭndŭl), municipal borough (pop. 2,614), Sussex W, England. Arundel Castle (12th cent.), seat of dukes of Norfolk, overlooks town.

Arvada (ärväd'ů), town (pop. 19,242), N central Colo., near Denver, in farm area.

Arvida (ärvē'dů), city (pop. 14,460), S Que., Canada, on Saguenay R. and W of Chicoutimi. Large quantities of aluminum are produced here.

Aryabhatta (är'yûbhŭt'ů), fl. 5th cent., Hindu mathematician, astronomer. One of first known users of algebra. Writings include rules of arithmetic, plane and spherical trigonometry; solutions of quadratic equations.

Aryan, name used by Hindus to designate themselves and other speakers of Indo-Iranian languages. Came to be used also as substitute for Indo-European to denote family of languages or even of races. So-called Aryan race, alleged to have spoken parent tongue, was idealized by unscientific racists.

aryl: see RADICAL.

As, chemical symbol of the element ARSENIC.

Asa (ä'sù) [Heb.,= physician], d. c.870 B.C., king of Judah (c.911–c.870 B.C.); a "good" king, zealous in abolishing idols. Succeeded by Jehoshaphat. 1 Kings 15.8–24; 2 Chron. 14–16.

asafetida (ăs'ůfĕt'ĭdů), ill-smelling gum resin from stem and roots of an Oriental parsnip of genus *Ferula*. Sometimes used as laxative and, in 70% tincture of alcohol, as sedative for spasm and hysteria.

Asama, Mount (äsä'mä), or **Asama-yama** (–yä'mä), peak, 8,340 ft. high, central Honshu, Japan. Active volcano.

Asbestos, town (pop. 11,083), SE Que., Canada, NW of Sherbrooke. Asbestos is mined in the area.

asbestos, any magnesium silicate mineral fibrous in structure and resistant to acid and fire. Often forms veins in other rock; probably results from metamorphism. Found in Canada, South Africa, U.S. It can be ground to make cement, woven into cloth, pressed into plasterboard. Used in pipe covering, fire-fighting equipment, shingles, etc.

Asbjornsen, Peter Christian (äs'byûrnsùn), Nor. *Asbjørnsen,* 1812–85, Norwegian folklorist.

Asbury, Francis, 1745–1816, American Methodist bishop, b. England. As missionary (1771) he promoted circuit rider system. Became bishop 1784.

Asbury Park, city (pop. 17,366), E N.J., on Atlantic coast E of Trenton; founded 1869. Resort with beach, boardwalk, and convention hall.

Ascalon (ăs′kŭ-), variant of ASHKELON.

Ascension, island in the S Atlantic, part of the British St. Helena Colony. A small island with few inhabitants, it is a naval station. Georgetown is the main settlement.

Ascension Island, Caroline Isl.: see PONAPE.

Asch, Sholem or **Shalom** (shō′lŭm ăsh′, shä′–), 1880–1957, Yiddish novelist and playwright, b. Poland, naturalized in U.S. 1920. Among novels are *The Nazarene* (1939), *A Passage in the Night* (1953), *The Prophet* (1955). Main themes are Jewish massacres under CHMIELNICKI; difficulties of Jewish immigrants in adjusting the New World; common spiritual heritage of Judaism and Christianity.

Aschaffenburg (äshä′fŭnbŏŏrk), city (pop. 51,998), NW Bavaria, on Main R. Manufactures precision and optical instruments, textiles, and paper. Anc. Roman garrison city; summer residence of Archbishops of Mainz after 9th cent.

Ascham, Roger (ăs′kŭm), 1515–68, English humanist, an outstanding scholar in Latin and Greek. Served as tutor (1548–50) to Princess Elizabeth and Latin secretary to Queen Mary (1553–58). Wrote *Toxophilus* (1545; on archery) and *The Scholemaster* (1570; a treatise on teaching Latin).

Asclepiades of Bithynia (ŭsklēpēăd′ēz, bĭthĭn′ēŭ), c.124 B.C.–40 B.C., Greek founder of influential school of medicine in Rome and pioneer in humane treatment of the mentally ill.

Asclepius (ăsklē′pēŭs), Latin *Aesculapius*, legendary Greek physician and god of medicine; son of Apollo and Coronis. Sick treated at his temples. Serpent and cock sacred to him.

ascorbic acid: see VITAMINS.

Ascot, village, Berkshire, England. Nearby Ascot Heath has annual horse races held since 1711.

Asenath (ăs′ŭnăth), Egyptian wife of Joseph. Gen. 41.-45, 50–52; 46.20. Their marriage is subject of story of Joseph and Asenath, one of PSEUDEPIGRAPHA.

Asgard (ăs′gärd) [Norse,= home of gods], Norse Olympus, home of 12 chief gods (Aesir).

ash, in botany, any tree or shrub of genus *Fraxinus*, e.g., white ash (*Fraxinus americana*), American timber tree with strong wood, black ash (*F. nigra*), and blue ash (*F. quadrangulata*). Mountain ash and prickly ash are not true ashes.

ash, in chemistry, solid residue of combustion; composition depends on substance burned. Wood yields carbonates and oxides of metals in plant tissues, e.g., potassium carbonate (potash). From fused mineral residue of coal (clinker), brick and cinder block are made. Iodine is extracted from burned seaweed called kelp or varec.

Ashanti (ŭshän′tē), region, central Ghana, Africa; inhabited by the Ashanti (c.800,000). Tribe formed Ashanti Confederacy c.1697. A series of Anglo-Ashanti wars in 19th cent. resulted in defeat (1896) and annexation (1901) by British coastal settlements. Confederation restored with limited powers 1935; incorporated into Gold Coast colony 1946. Region noted for goldwork; cacao and hardwoods grown. Chief city is Kumasi.

Ashby-de-la-Zouch (–zōōch′, –zōōsh′), urban district (pop. 7,425), Leicestershire, England. Figures in Scott's *Ivanhoe*. Mary Queen of Scots held in Ashby Castle 1569.

ashcan school: see EIGHT, THE.

Ashdod, ancient city of Philistines, between Jaffa and Gaza, of military importance in wars between Egypt and countries to N. Seat of the worship of Dagon, it was destroyed by the Maccabees. Now a village

called Esdud. 1 Sam. 5.1; Joshua 15.47; 2 Chron. 26.6; Neh. 4.7; 13.23; Isa. 20.1; Jer. 25.20.

Ashe, Arthur, 1943–, American tennis player. National intercollegiate singles and doubles champion, 1965; U.S. Davis cup player 1965, 1966, 1967.

Asheboro (ăsh′bŭrŭ), town (pop. 9,499), central N.C., S of Greensboro, in piedmont; founded 1779. Prehistoric Keyauwee Indian burial ground is near.

Ashendene Press, founded 1895 by Sir C. H. St. John Hornby; a leader in the 19th-cent. revival of English printing. Its edition of Dante (1909) is outstanding.

Asher (ăsh′ŭr), son of Jacob, ancestor of one (Asher) of 12 tribes of Israel. Tribe occupied NW Palestine. Gen. 30.13; Deut. 33.24; Joshua 19.24–31; Judges 5.17,18; Aser: Luke 2.36; Rev. 7.6.

Asheville, city (pop. 60,192), W N.C., on French Broad and Swannanoa rivers, on plateau in Blue Ridge; founded after 1791. A resort near Great Smoky Mtns. Natl. Park and Pisgah Natl. Forest, it is also financial, distribution, and retail center for W N.C. Birthplace of Thomas Wolfe and home of many well-known writers.

Ashi, Rab (ä′shē), 352–427, Hebrew scholar of Babylon; chief editor of TALMUD.

Ashingdon, battle of: see ASSANDUN, BATTLE OF.

Ashkelon (ăsh′kŭ–) or **Ascalon** (ăs′–), ancient city of Philistines on Mediterranean coast, between Jaffa and Gaza; center of worship of goddess Astarte. Played important role in Crusades. Also in Bible, Askelon, Eshkalon.

Ashkenazim (–năz′–), term referring to the German Jews as distinguished from Sephardim, the Jews of Spain and Portugal.

Ashkhabad (ŭshkhúbät′), city (1965 est. pop. 226,000), cap. of Turkmen SSR, on Trans-Caspian RR, near Iranian border. Cotton and silk mills.

Ashland. 1 Industrial city (pop. 31,283), E Ky., on terraces along Ohio near influx of Big Sandy R. and NW of Huntington, W.Va.; settled 1786. Rail and river shipping point in a coal, natural gas, and timber area. "Traipsin' Woman's Cabin," scene of annual American Folk Song Festival, is nearby. **2** City (pop. 17,419), N Ohio, NE of Mansfield, in farm area; laid out 1815. Seat of Ashland Col. **3** City (pop. 9,119), SW Oregon, W of Klamath Falls near Calif. line; founded 1852. A lumbering center and shipping point for farm and orchard area and a resort with mineral springs. Southern Oregon Col. is here. Holds annual Shakespeare festival. **4** Town (pop. 2,773), central Va., N of Richmond; settled 1848. RANDOLPH-MACON COLLEGE is here. Birthplaces of Patrick Henry and Henry Clay and girlhood home of Dolly Madison are nearby. **5** City (pop. 10,132), N Wis., port of entry on Chequamegon Bay of L. Superior; settled 1854. Father Allouez had mission nearby 1665. Iron ore and granite shipped. Seat of Northland Col.

Ashley, Anthony Ashley Cooper, Baron: see SHAFTESBURY, ANTHONY ASHLEY COOPER, 1ST EARL OF.

Ashley, William Henry, c.1778–1838, American fur trader, U.S. Representative from Mo. (1831–37). After 1821 he sent expeditions to upper Missouri R. region and into Green R. valley.

Ashley, river: see CHARLESTON, S.C.

Ashokan Reservoir, N.Y.: see CATSKILL AQUEDUCT.

Ashtabula (ăsh″tŭbū′lŭ), city (pop. 24,559), NE Ohio, on L. Erie at mouth of Ashtabula R., NE of Cleveland; settled c.1801. A receiving port for ore on St. Lawrence Seaway and a rail center.

Ashtaroth (ăsh′tŭrŏth). **1** Hebrew form of ASTARTE. **2** A city of Bashan was named Ashtaroth. Joshua 9.10; 12.4; 13.12,31; 1 Chron. 6.71.

Ashton, village (pop. 1,242), E Idaho, NE of Idaho Falls near Wyo. line; settled 1900. Center of timber and farm area served by MINIDOKA PROJECT. Also tourist gateway to Yellowstone and Grand Teton natl. parks.

Ashtoreth (ăsh′tŏrĕth), Hebrew form of ASTARTE.

Ashur-bani-pal, Assyrian king: see ASSUR-BANI-PAL.

Ashurnasirpal II (ä″shŏŏrnä′zĭrpäl), d. 860? B.C., king of anc. Assyria (884–860? B.C.). Conquered westward to the Mediterranean and estab. administration of empire. His palace at Nimrud was excavated.

Ash Wednesday: see LENT.

Asia, world's largest continent. Its boundary with Europe lies along Ural Mts., Ural R., and Greater Caucasus. Thus defined, Asia, including Ceylon and the islands of Japan, the Philippines, and Indonesia, has an area of c.16,700,000 sq. mi., and a population of c.1,600,000,000 (more than half the world's total). In W separated from Europe by the Bosporus, the Dardanelles, and Aegean Sea, in NE separated from N America by Bering Strait. Suez Canal breaks Asia's connection with Africa. Washed on S by Gulf of Aden and Arabian Sea, on E by China Sea, Yellow Sea, Sea of Japan, Sea of Okhotsk, and Bering Sea, and on N by Arctic Ocean. Westernmost part of Asia is ASIA MINOR. Some of the world's mightiest ranges (Himalayas, Karakorum, Kunlun, Tien Shan, Hindu Kush) are in E central Asia. Major rivers are the Ob, Yenisei, and Lena in Siberia; the Amur, Yellow, Si, Mekong, Salween, and Irrawaddy of E and SE Asia; and the Brahmaputra, Ganges, Indus, Tigris, and Euphrates in S and SW Asia. The continent ranges through all climatic extremes. The lands of Asia are as follows: in SW Asia are Turkey, Syria, Lebanon, Israel, Jordan, Iraq, Iran, and the states of the Arabian peninsula (such as Saudi Arabia, Yemen, and Kuwait); in S are Afghanistan, Pakistan, India, Ceylon, and the Himalayan states of Nepal, Sikkim, and Bhutan; in SE are Burma, Thailand, Indonesia, the Philippine Islands, Cambodia, Laos, Vietnam, Malaya, and Borneo (including N Borneo, Sarawak, Brunei); in E are China (and offshore Taiwan), Korea, Japan, and Mongolian People's Republic. In the vast N of Asia is the USSR.

Asia Minor, peninsula, extreme W Asia; called also Anatolia. It is bounded by the Black Sea, the Bosporus, the Sea of Marmara, and the Dardanelles (N); the Mediterranean (S); and the Aegean Sea (W). A high plateau, it is crossed by mountains, notably the TAURUS near the S coast, and is roughly identical with Asiatic TURKEY. Asia Minor, in close touch with Greece and Mesopotamia, was the chief meeting place of the ancient Orient and Occident. After the decline of the Hittites, the Greeks colonized coastal Ionia, coming in contact with Lydia, Phrygia, and more especially Troy. Conquest of Asia Minor by the Persians led to the Persian Wars. Divided into several small rival states in Hellenistic times, it was reintegrated by the Romans, but was subject to almost constant invasions under the Byzantine Empire and finally fell to the Ottomans in the 13th–15th cent.

Asiatic cholera: see CHOLERA.

Asimov, Isaac (ă′zŭmŏf), 1920–, American biochemist and writer, b. Russia. His works include scholarly scientific studies, science-fiction (e.g., *I, Robot,* 1950), science for the layman (e.g., *The Genetic Code,* 1963; *The Noble Gases,* 1966; *The New Intelligent Man's Guide to Science,* 1967), and books for high school students.

Aske, Robert: see PILGRIMAGE OF GRACE.

Askelon (ăs′kŭ-), variant of ASHKELON.

Asmara (äsmä′rä), city (pop. c.131,800), cap. of Eritrea, NE Africa. Alt. c.7,300 ft. Linked to port of Massawa by railroad and aerial cableway. Light industry, livestock and agr. processing.

Asmodeus (ăs″mōdē′ŭs), demon of Hebrew story, important in book of Tobit (3.6; 8).

Asoka (ŭsō′kŭ), d. 232 B.C., Indian emperor (c.269–c.232) of MAURYA empire. Domain included most of India and Afghanistan. Abandoned wars of conquest after conversion to Buddhism. Held great Buddhist convocation (c.250 B.C.), during which the Pali canon was finally codified.

Aso-san (ä′sō-sän), group of five volcanic cones, central Kyushu, Japan. Only the central cone is active. Crater floor is 37.2 mi. in circumference.

asp, popular name of poisonous snake (probably either Egyptian cobra or horned viper), known as instrument in story of Cleopatra's suicide.

Aspadana: see ISFAHAN, Iran.

asparagus (ŭspär′ŭ–), perennial garden vegetable (*Asparagus officinalis*). Its tender shoots are eaten in spring. Feathery foliage sometimes used by florists but more popular decorative species include SMILAX and asparagus fern.

Aspasia (ăspā′zhŭ), 5th cent. B.C., Greek courtesan; beautiful, learned mistress of Pericles.

Aspen, city (pop. 1,101), S central Colo., SW of Leadville; founded c.1879. Once a rich silver camp, it is now ski resort. Has annual music festival.

aspen: see POPLAR.

Aspern (äs′pŭrn), eastern suburb of Vienna, Austria. Scene of Austrian victory over Napoleon I in 1809.

asphalt (ăs′fôlt), brownish-black natural mixture of hydrocarbons used in road making, roofing, waterproofing, in making paints and varnishes. Varies from solid to semisolid, has great tenacity, melts when heated.

asphodel (ăs′fŭdĕl″), hardy stemless plant (*Asphodelus*) with showy flower spikes. The ancient asphodel sacred to Persephone belongs to the genus *Asphodeline.*

aspirin, simple nontoxic drug (acetylsalicylic acid), effective in relieving minor pain and in reducing fever. It is used as a sedative, but may be dangerous in excessive dosages, especially to children. Important in arthritis therapy.

Aspropotamos, Greek river: see ACHELOUS.

Asquith, Herbert Henry: see OXFORD AND ASQUITH, HERBERT HENRY ASQUITH, 1ST EARL OF.

ass, smaller animal of HORSE genus, known in domesticated state as the donkey; male is called a jack or jackass, female a jennet or jenny. Hardy and surefooted, it has large head, small hoofs, short mane and tail, long ears. The diminutive burro is common pack animal in W U.S., Mexico. Ass was probably domesticated by c.4000 B.C. in Mesopotamia and Egypt. Several breeds have been used to breed the MULE.

Assab, town (pop. c.5,000), S Eritrea, Ethiopia; port on Red Sea. Officially annexed by Italy 1882; modern Italy's first territorial acquisition in Africa.

Assam (ăsăm′), state (84,899 sq. mi.; pop. c.11,850,-000), NE India; cap. Shillong. Includes the NORTH-EAST FRONTIER AGENCY. Rugged terrain with fertile valleys of the Brahmaputra and Surma. Cherrapunji in SW reputedly has world's heaviest rainfall (c.500 in. annually). India's only important oil producing region; rice, tea, and jute grown. Lumbering is important. Suffered Burmese invasions from 13th to early 19th cent. Became part of British India 1826. A section in SW incorporated into East Pakistan 1947. In 1961 Nagaland state was formed from the Naga Hills–Tuensang Frontier division. Partially occupied 1962 by Chinese.

Assandun, battle of (ä′sŭndŭn), victory (1016) of the Danes under CANUTE over the English, at what is now Ashingdon, in SE Essex.

Assassin (ŭsă′sĭn) [Arabic,= under the influence of hashish], European name for member of secret order of SHIITES, which ruthlessly murdered enemies. Founded c.1090, flourished in Syria and Persia. Grand master, Sheikh al-Jabal, known in W Europe as Old Man of the Mountain, was absolute ruler.

assaying, in metallurgy, process of determining content of a specific metal in an ore or alloy. To obtain representative sample, often several samples are crushed and mixed. "Wet" assay (using liquid reagents) determines weight of metal; "dry" or fire assay yields metal in pure state.

Asser, Tobias Michael Carel (tōbē′äs mē′khäl kä′rŭl äs′ŭr), 1838–1913, Dutch statesman and jurist. For

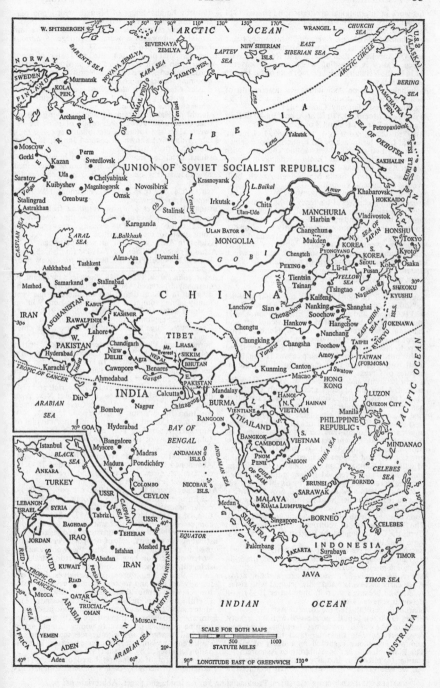

his work in international arbitration, he shared 1911 Nobel Peace Prize with Alfred Fried.

Assideans: see HASIDIM.

Assiniboine (ŭsĭn'ŭboin), river, c.600 mi. long, rising in SE Sask., Canada, and flowing SE into SW Man. to join Qu'Appelle R., then SE and E to Red R. at Winnipeg. Valley is a leading wheat area. Discovered 1736 by the Vérendryes, it became route of fur traders and settlers westward.

Assiniboine, Fort, on Assiniboine R., near mouth of Souris R., Man., Canada. Fur-trading post built 1794 by North West Company. Closed 1821.

Assiniboine, Mount, 11,870 ft. high, on Alta.–B.C. line, Canada, in Rocky Mts. and S of Banff.

Assisi (äs-sē'zē), town (est. pop. 24,853), Umbria, central Italy; birthplace of St. Francis. Above saint's tomb are two superimposed Gothic churches, with frescoes by Cimabue and Giotto. Medieval in atmosphere, Assisi has many churches, including cathedral and (outside town) Santa Maria degli Angeli, built around Porziuncola chapel.

Associated Press: see NEWS AGENCY.

association, psychological tendency to link words and ideas consciously or unconsciously. In free association, a basic psychoanalytic technique, the patient voices all thoughts, however apparently trivial or disconnected, to reveal conflict areas, repressed desires, traumatic events; psychoanalyst observes manifest content and accompanying somatic reactions which expose attempted suppression of material.

Assuan, Egypt: see ASWAN.

Assur, anc. Assyrian city: see ASSYRIA.

assurance: see INSURANCE.

Assur-bani-pal (ä"sōōr-bä'-nē-päl) or **Ashur-bani-pal** (ä"shōōr–), d. 626? B.C., king of anc. Assyria (669–633 B.C.), son and successor of Esar-Haddon. Under him Assyria reached height of glory in riches, art, and learning (his library was famous). He conquered Egypt and set Necho in power but later lost power there to Necho's son, Psamtik I. Put down revolt led by his brother, but power of empire was fading. Identified with Osnapper or Asnappar of Bible, Sardanapalus of Greeks.

Assyria (ŭsĭ'rēŭ), anc. empire of W Asia, originating around Ashur on upper Tigris R., with cap. later at Calah (also called Nimrud), where excavation has yielded rich collection of 7th-cent. ivories. At first a small Semitic city-state; had brief fame in 12th cent. B.C. under TIGLATH-PILESER I. Real importance began in 9th cent. with conquests of ASHURNASIRPAL II, who set up an imperial administration. Later kings (SHALMANESER III, TIGLATH-PILESER III, and SARGON) gained hegemony in the Middle East. SENNACHERIB consolidated the holdings, and ESAR-HADDON (reigned 681–668 B.C.) defeated the Chaldaeans and won power in Egypt. Under his successor, ASSUR-BANI-PAL (reigned 669–633 B.C.), Assyria reached its height of learning, art, and splendor. Yet Egypt broke away, and decline was rapid. Soon after his death Nineveh was sacked (612 B.C.). The Babylonian empire returned briefly to power, and Cyrus the Great founded the Persian Empire, and Assyria was absorbed.

Assyrian Church: see NESTORIAN CHURCH.

Assyrian language, Semitic language of anc. times, in Akkadian group. See LANGUAGE (table).

Astaire, Fred, 1899–, American dancer and film actor. After early success in vaudeville, teamed with sister, Adele, and became known in films (after 1933) as a debonair song-and-dance man.

Astaroth (ăs'tŭrŏth), Hebrew form of Astarte.

Astarte (ăstär'tē), Semitic goddess of fertility, beauty, and love. She was the most important Phoenician goddess, corresponding to Ishtar (also to APHRODITE), and was sometimes regarded as goddess of moon. The Bible refers to her as Ashtaroth or Ashtoreth.

astatine (ăs'tŭtēn), radioactive element (symbol = At; see also ELEMENT, table). Was first produced in

1940 by bombardment of bismuth with alpha particles in cyclotron. It is a HALOGEN.

Astell, Mary (ăs'tŭl), 1666–1731, English author and feminist. Advocated a woman's college in *Serious Proposal to the Ladies* (1694–97).

aster, perennial plant (often called wild aster) of genus *Aster,* with small daisylike flowers. Most important garden varieties derived from North American fall-blooming species and grown in Europe as Michaelmas daisies. China aster (*Callistephus*) is a popular garden annual with larger heads of ray flowers, ranging from white and pink to purple.

asteroid or **planetoid,** minor planet revolving around sun. Over 1,600 recognized; orbits of most lie between Mars and Jupiter. Ceres (diameter c.480 mi.), largest and first known, discovered Jan. 1, 1801, by Piazzi. See *ill.,* p. 1017.

asthma, condition marked by labored breathing. Allergy frequent cause; specific agent can be determined by skin tests. It is sometimes caused by psychosomatic factors.

Asti (äs'tē), city (pop. 60,217), Piedmont, NW Italy; famous sparkling wine.

astigmatism, defect of vision resulting from irregularities in the surface of the lens or of the cornea in the eye. It can be corrected by wearing lenses ground to compensate for the irregularities.

Astolat, in ARTHURIAN LEGEND: see GUILDFORD.

Aston, Francis William, 1877–1945, English chemist. Won 1922 Nobel Prize in Chemistry for discovery of a number of isotopes in nonradioactive elements.

Astor, John Jacob, 1763–1848, American merchant, b. Germany. Chartered AMERICAN FUR COMPANY. Richest man in U.S. at death; left fortune that has kept family name prominent. His great-grandson, **William Waldorf Astor,** 1st Viscount Astor, 1848–1919, American-British capitalist, moved to England in 1890. Contributed huge sums to public causes. His elder son, Waldorf Astor, married **Nancy Witcher (Langhorne) Astor, Viscountess Astor,** 1879–1964, British political leader, b. Va. As Conservative, the first woman to sit in Parliament. In late 1930s began with her husband to take a large part in politics through the "Cliveden set"—named after Astor country home.

Astoria (ăstôr'ēŭ). **1** Commercial, industrial, and residential section of NW Queens borough of New York city; settled 17th cent. as Hallet's Cove and renamed for John Jacob Astor. **2** City (pop. 11,239), NW Oregon, on Columbia R. near its mouth. Activities of American fur-trading post estab. here 1811 under John Jacob Astor helped estab. American claim to Oregon. Post sold to British in War of 1812. Restored to U.S. 1818, but trade remained in British hands. Abandoned briefly, Astoria was refounded 1843 by overlanders. Grew as seagoing and river port. Has fishing fleet and lumber and flour mills.

Astrakhan (ă'strŭkăn"), city (1965 est. pop. 342,000), SE European RSFSR; port on Volga delta. Fishing, caviar processing; transshipment point for Baku oil. Cap. of a Tatar khanate until 1557, when Ivan IV conquered it. Oriental in character, city has kept old kremlin, with cathedral, monastery, and palace.

astrakhan (ăs'trŭkŭn), pelt of newborn Persian lamb, used like fur in garments; also the woolen fabric woven on a cotton base to resemble true astrakhan.

astringent, substance that contracts body tissue and canals thus reducing excessive discharges. Used externally on skin and mucous membranes, internally for relieving peptic ulcer, gastric acidity, diarrhea. Useful astringents include mineral compounds (e.g., alum) and vegetable extracts (e.g., tannic acid).

astrolabe (ăs'trŭlāb), instrument formerly used to determine positions of heavenly bodies. Simple astrolabe had suspended disk with degrees marked on circumference and movable pointer at center. In navigation superseded by sextant (18th cent.).

astrology, form of divination based on theory that movement of heavenly bodies influences human affairs. Its lore is very old and was basis for ancient knowledge of astronomy. In Middle Ages it was associated with alchemy and occult sciences. After Copernicus, astrology and astronomy diverged. In astrology a horoscope is a map of the heavens at time of birth, using chart of the zodiac; the "house" or sign in the ascendant at time of one's birth is said to determine his temperament, tendencies to disease, and liability to certain fortunes or calamities.

astronautics, or space guidance, research in all aspects of space flight. Includes ballistics, ROCKET design and guidance, electronics, space biology, astrophysics, and astronaut flight training. Konstantin TSIOLKOVSKY is generally considered the founder. Among the problems is the developing of fuels that yield high thrust from little fuel weight. Present fuels are liquid or solid. Under consideration are nuclear and solar power, ion and plasma propulsion, and photon, or light, engines. Another problem is the developing of a fixed reference system for navigation in space. See also SATELLITE, ARTIFICIAL; SPACE TRAVEL.

astronomy, scientific study of the heavenly bodies. Arose from need for designating time intervals; was early associated with astrology. Theoretical contributions stem from Greeks including Thales, Pythagoras, Eratosthenes, and Aristarchus of Samos. Earth-centered view of HIPPARCHUS and other Alexandrian Greeks, preserved in *Almagest* of Claudius PTOLEMY, was displaced in 16th cent. by sun-centered view of COPERNICUS, which was supported by observations of GALILEO, Tycho BRAHE, and KEPLER. Astronomical knowledge was advanced by scientists including Edmund Halley, Sir William and Sir J. F. W. Herschel, C. G. Abbot, Einstein, G. E. Hale, Sir James Jeans, Sir A. S. Eddington, Harlow Shapley, Otto Streuve, and Edwin Hubble and also by application of physics (astrophysics) in studies of radiation, light, and composition of heavenly bodies. See also ASTEROID; COMET; COSMOGONY; METEOR; MOON; PLANET; STAR; SUN. See *ill.*, 1017.

Asturias (ästōō'ryäs), region, NW Spain, on Bay of Biscay. Historic cap. Oviedo. Coal, iron, zinc mines, steel mills; cattle raising; fishing. Chief port: Gijón. Reconquest of Spain from Moors was begun by Christian nobles who had held out in Asturian mountains. Kingdom of Asturias was joined with Leon in 10th cent.

Astyages (ăstī'ŭjēz), last king of Media (584–c.550 B.C.). His father Cyaxares stormed Nineveh. His grandson, Cyrus the Great, overthrew him and founded the Persian Empire.

Astyanax (ŭstī'ŭnăks), in Greek legend, son of Hector and Andromache. Slain by Greeks at Troy.

Asunción (äsōōnsyōn'), city (1962 est. pop. 305,160), cap. of Paraguay, on Paraguay R.; port and commercial center. Has many small industries. Founded 1536 or 1537, Asunción was most important town in Rio de la Plata region until rise of Buenos Aires.

Aswan or Assuan (both: äswän'), city (pop. c.48,-000), Upper Egypt, at First Cataract of the Nile. Nearby is the Aswan Dam (completed 1902). More than a mile long, the dam and the barrages of Asyut are chief means of storing irrigation water for Nile valley. Aswan High Dam (begun 1960, first stage finished 1964), is c.5 mi. S of old dam and upon completion will expand irrigation, flood control, river navigation, and hydroelectric power production. Many archaeological sites in Nubia, such as ABU-SIMBEL, will be submerged.

Asyut (äsüt') anc. *Lycopolis*, largest city (pop. c.133,-500) of Upper Egypt; trade center in Nile valley. Nearby is Asyut barrage (for irrigation).

At, chemical symbol of the element ASTATINE.

Atacama, Desert of (ätäkä'mä), arid region, c.600 mi. long, N Chile, c.2,000 ft. above sea level, between Pacific coastal range and Andes. Has no vegetation, but is rich in nitrate and copper. ALMAGRO was first

European to cross it (1537). Passed from Bolivia to Chile in War of the Pacific.

Atahualpa (ätäwäl'pä), d. 1533, last Inca of Peru. Successfully rebelled against HUÁSCAR (who shared rule with him), took whole empire. Francisco Pizarro imprisoned Atahualpa (1532) and in spite of offer of a roomful of gold as ransom had him put to death.

Atalanta (ătülän'tù), in Greek legend, huntress who joined Calydonian hunt and Argonaut voyage. She ran a race with each suitor, on condition that winner should marry her but loser should die. Hippomenes (hǐpō'mǐnēz) won by dropping three apples; Atalanta paused to pick them up.

Ataturk, Kemal (kěmäl' ätätürk'), 1881–1938, Turkish leader, founder of modern Turkey; known before 1934 as Mustafa Kemal or Kemal Pasha. An army officer, he took part in the Young Turk revolution of 1908, distinguished himself in First World War; after Turkey's collapse organized the Nationalist party and army in E Anatolia. After the Greek landing at SMYRNA (1919), he convoked Nationalist congresses at Erzerum and Sivas, was outlawed by the Allied-controlled government at Constantinople, and set up a rival government at Ankara. The signing of the Treaty of SÈVRES by the Constantinople government made the split with Ankara final. Kemal expelled the Greeks from Anatolia in a brilliant campaign (1921–22), which earned him the title Ghazi [victorious]; abolished the sultanate (1922); secured honorable peace at the LAUSANNE CONFERENCE (1923); and served as president of the Turkish republic for four terms (1923–38). Ruling dictatorially, he carried out a drastic program of Westernization and reform which changed the face of TURKEY.

Ataulf (ä'täülf), d. 415, Visigothic king (410–15). Led VISIGOTHS from Italy into S Gaul (412), later into N Spain. Married GALLA PLACIDIA.

atavism (ă'tŭvĭzùm), random combination of recessive traits resulting in reappearance of a genetic characteristic lacking in preceding generation (e.g., hair color).

ataxia (ùtăk'sēù), lack of muscular coordination resulting in erratic body movements. Permanent ataxia results from damage to the central nervous system; alcoholic intoxication causes transient ataxia.

Atbara (ätbä'rù), town (pop. c.40,000), NE Republic of the Sudan, at junction of Atbara R. and Nile. Hq. of Sudan railway system.

Atchafalaya (ùchä'fùlī'ù), river branching in E La. from Red R. near its junction with the Mississippi, and flowing c.170 mi. S through several lakes to Atchafalaya Bay of Gulf of Mexico. Navigable. Flood-control projects completed 1965.

Atchison, city (pop. 12,529), NE Kansas, on Missouri R., NE of Topeka; settled 1854. Grew as wagontrain, river, and rail terminal. Now wholesale and mfg. center. Mt. St. Scholastica Col. and St. Benedict's Col. are here.

Ate (ā'tē) [Gr.,= folly], in Greek religion, personification of infatuation leading to folly.

Athabascan (äthùbäs'kùn), also Athapascan or Athapaskan (both: äthùpäs'kùn), linguistic family belonging, with Haida and Tlingit, to the Nadene stock. Widely distributed among Indian tribes of W Canada and W U.S. See LANGUAGE (table).

Athabaska, river, rising in W Alta., Canada, in Columbia snow field of Canadian Rockies and flowing c.800 mi. N and NE to L. Athabaska.

Athabaska, Lake, 3,058 sq. mi., c.200 mi. long, 5–35 mi. wide, NE Alta. and NW Sask., Canada. Receives Athabaska and Peace rivers in SW, drains NW into Great Slave R., thence via Mackenzie R. into Arctic Ocean. On edge of Laurentian Plateau, it is connected to Churchill R. by canoe route. Fort Chipewyan, at W end of lake, built 1788. Lake surveyed and mapped by Philip Turnor 1790–92.

Athabaska, Mount, 11,452 ft. high, W Alta., Canada, on edge of Columbia Icefield and surrounded by Athabaska and Saskatchewan glaciers.

Athabaska Pass, 5,736 ft. high, W Alta. and E B.C., Canada, from headwaters of Athabaska R. across Continental Divide to Columbia R. Discovered c.1811, it became route to Columbia R. country.

Athaliah (ăth″ŭlī′ŭ), died c.841 B.C., queen of Judah (c.846–c.841 B.C.); daughter of Ahab and Jezebel, wife of Jehoram of Judah. She succeeded her murdered son, Ahaziah of Judah. Killed in coup d'état in favor of JEHOASH 2. She is subject of Racine's *Athalie.* 2 Kings 11; 2 Chron. 22–23.

Athanagild (ŭthä′nŭgĭld), d. 567, Visigothic king of Spain (554–67). Helped into power by Byzantines, to whom he ceded part of S Spain. Later fought Byzantines, Franks, Basques. Held splendid court at Toledo. Father of Brunhilda and Galswintha.

Athanasius, Saint (ăthŭnā′zhŭs), 295–373, patriarch of Alexandria, Doctor of the Church. Distinguished himself at First Council of NICAEA by eloquent opposition to ARIANISM and fought it later steadfastly. He was exiled five times. When he fled to Rome, he gained the aid of Pope Julius I. A vigorous administrator in his patriarchate, he was also a gifted writer against Arianism and helped to shape the statement of Catholic doctrine. Feast: May 2. The **Athanasian Creed** was not by him but by a Western writer of the 6th cent. It is an exact statement of Catholic belief on the Trinity and the Incarnation. Sometimes called Quicunque Vult.

Athapascan or **Athapaskan:** see ATHABASCAN.

atheism, rejection of belief in any God or gods. The position of atheists is essentially negative. It has appeared from ancient times, when Socrates was condemned to death for his disbelief. Atheism has been current in both East and West, but was perhaps most blatantly put forward in the 19th cent. by Robert G. Ingersoll. Generally speaking, disbelievers in Christianity, Buddhism, and Hinduism have adopted AGNOSTICISM rather than atheism.

Athelstan or **Æthelstan** (both: ăth′ŭlstŭn, –stăn″), d. 939, king of the English (924–39). Grandchild of ALFRED, built up state on foundations laid by him. Issued laws that attempted to impose royal authority on customary law.

Athena (ŭthē′nŭ) or **Pallas Athena** (pă′lŭs), Olympian goddess of wisdom, patron of arts of peace and war, ruler of storms, and guardian of Athens, a virgin goddess, sprung from the forehead of Zeus. She is usually shown wearing helmet and aegis with head of MEDUSA. Parthenon was her temple, Panathenaea her festival. Identified with Roman Minerva.

Athenagoras (ăthĕn′ăgŏräs), 1886–, Archbishop of Constantinople, New Rome, and Ecumenical Patriarch of the Eastern Orthodox Church (1949–); his given name was Aristokles Spirou. Elected Archbishop of Greek Orthodox Church of North and South America 1931. Became U.S. citizen in 1939 but gave up American citizenship to become Ecumenical Patriarch in 1949. Met with Pope Paul VI in the Holy Land in 1964, the first meeting between heads of the Roman Catholic and Orthodox churches since 1438. In 1967 met with Pope Paul in Turkey in further recognition of the growing reconciliation of the two churches.

Athenodorus: see LAOCOÖN.

Athens (ăth′ĭnz), Gr. *Athenai,* city (pop. 627,564; greater Athens with port PIRAEUS and other cities, 1,852,709), cap. of Greece, on the plain of Attica. It is cultural, religious (focus of Greek Orthodox Church), and industrial (textiles, machine-tool plants, utilities) center of country. Many tourists come to view remains in city that was fountainhead of Western civilization. Early history is mixed with legend (e.g., story of Theseus as consolidator of cities of Attica, account of early kings). Aristocratic archons held power when Solon presumably began reforms in 594 B.C. A period of tyrants under Pisistratus and his sons Hippias and Hipparchus lasted until 510 B.C., when CLEISTHENES founded the democracy that was to persist in the period of greatness. In the period of the PERSIAN WARS (500–449 B.C.) small Athens emerged, under hero leaders such as MILTIADES, THEMISTOCLES, and CIMON, as a great naval power, and the DELIAN LEAGUE became practically an Athenian empire. Architecture, art, and literature rose to astonishing height in the Golden Age under Pericles (5th cent. B.C.). The Parthenon was built; SOCRATES spoke his philosophy; Greek drama was founded with AESCHYLUS, SOPHOCLES, and EURIPIDES. In later decline this glory went on with PLATO and ARISTOTLE, ARISTOPHANES and the orator DEMOSTHENES. In the long-drawn PELOPONNESIAN WAR Athens was finally conquered by SPARTA. Recovery after defeat in 404 B.C. was rapid but transitory, and in the 4th cent. Athens was subjected by PHILIP II of Macedon and his son, ALEXANDER THE GREAT. When Roman greatness grew Athens became a provincial cap., and attempts to regain power resulted in humiliation (notably the sack by Sulla, 86 B.C.). Yet the tradition of Athens affected Rome and even more affected the Byzantine Empire, under which it fell. With the fall of that empire Athens passed (1205) to a French nobleman and became a duchy, later prosperous in Catalan hands (under house of Aragon). A brief renascence under the rule of Florentine nobles, the Acciajuoli, in the late 14th and early 15th cent. was followed by decline under Ottoman rule after 1458. When Greece was freed, Athens became the cap. of independent Greece and gradually grew to its present position. It retains relics of the past. On the ACROPOLIS are the Parthenon, the Propylaea, and the Erechtheum. The American School has excavated and reconstructed parts of the agora (market place).

Athens. 1 City (1964 pop. 13,652), N Ala., near Tenn. line N of Birmingham, in farm area; settled 1814. Sacked and occupied by Federals (1862), recaptured by Gen. N. B. Forrest (1864). Athens Col. is here. **2** City (1963 pop. 41,059), NE Ga., on Oconee R., ENE of Atlanta, in piedmont area. Founded 1801 as site for Univ. of GEORGIA. City's industries depend chiefly on local cotton. Many fine classic revival houses. **3** City (pop. 16,470), SE Ohio, SE of Columbus on bluffs overlooking Hocking R., in coal-mine area. Surveyed 1795–96 by Ohio Co. of Associates as university site and settled soon after. Seat of OHIO UNIVERSITY. **4** City (pop.12,103), E Tenn., between Knoxville and Chattanooga, in farm area; laid out 1821. **5** Town (pop. 1,086), S W.Va., NE of Princeton and near Va. line. Concord Col. is here.

athlete's foot: see RINGWORM.

Athlone, Godart van Ginkel, 1st earl of: see GINKEL.

Athlone (ăthlōn′), urban district (pop. 9,624), Co. Westmeath, Ireland, on Shannon R. Athlone Castle (13th cent.) was of strategic value in early Irish history.

Athol (ăth′ŭl), town (pop. 11,637), N Mass., W of Fitchburg; settled 1735.

Atholl or **Athole** (both: ăth′ŭl), mountainous district, 450 sq. mi., N Perthshire, Scotland.

Athos (ăth′ŏs, ā′thŏs) or **Akte** (äk′tä), easternmost peninsula of CHALCIDICE, NE Greece; c.40 mi. long, 1½–7 mi. wide. It forms the autonomous state of the Greek Orthodox monks of **Mount Athos,** or Hagion Oros [Holy Mountain], rising c.6,000 ft. at S tip of peninsula. The community, founded 10th cent., consists of 20 convents. Under direct rule of the patriarch of Constantinople, it has always enjoyed virtual independence. No female, human or animal, is admitted. Libraries contain a wealth of Byzantine manuscripts.

Atkinson, Henry, 1782–1842, American army officer, general commander in BLACK HAWK WAR.

Atlanta, city (pop. 487,455), state cap. (since 1868), NW Ga., near Appalachian foothills. Largest city; cultural, industrial, transportation, and commercial center of state; a leading city of South. Mfg. of textiles, foodstuffs, automobiles, steel products. Hardy Ivy settled here in 1833. Town founded 1837 as Terminus (end of a rail line) and renamed 1845. Important as a Confederate supply and communications center, it fell to W. T. SHERMAN on Sept. 2, 1864 (see ATLANTA CAMPAIGN). He burned it (Nov. 15) before his march to the sea. Conventions and expositions in 19th and 20th cent. drew attention to city's strategic distributory position. Federal penitentiary (1899) here is widely known. Here are High Mus. of Art, building with *Cyclorama of the Battle of Atlanta*, and Oakland Cemetery (with Civil War dead). Nearby is U.S. Fort McPherson. Seat of ATLANTA UNIVERSITY SYSTEM, EMORY UNIVERSITY, GEORGIA INSTITUTE OF TECHNOLOGY, Oglethorpe Col., Gammon Theological Seminary, Woodrow Wilson Col. of Law, and Atlanta Law School.

Atlanta campaign, May–Sept., 1864, of Civil War. W. T. Sherman gathered Union armies near Chattanooga with two aims—to destroy J. E. Johnston's army and to capture Atlanta. By flanking actions he forced Johnston from successive positions to Chattahoochee R. Here J. B. Hood counterattacked but failed to stop advance, and retired to Atlanta. After Union army cut communications, Confederates abandoned city Sept. 1. Sherman occupied it Sept. 2.

Atlanta University System (organized 1929) includes four schools which have some facilities in common. Atlanta Univ. (coed.; 1865) is graduate school; Atlanta Univ. School of Social Work (coed.; 1920) was affiliated 1938; Morehouse Col. (for men; 1867) and Spelman Col. (for women; 1881) are undergraduate units. Clark Col. (coed.; 1869), Morris Brown Col. (coed.; 1881), and Interdenominational Theological Center (coed.; 1958) are also affiliated.

Atlantic Charter, program of peace aims, jointly enunciated by Prime Minister Winston Churchill of Great Britain and Pres. F. D. Roosevelt of U.S. on Aug. 14, 1941. Aims incorporated in UN declaration of 1942.

Atlantic City, city (pop. 59,544), SE N.J., a seaside resort and convention center SE of Philadelphia and SSW of New York city, on Absecon Beach (10-mi. sand bar). Was fishing village before 1854. First boardwalk built 1870. Has large municipal auditorium and amusement piers.

Atlantic Ocean, second largest ocean, est. area 31,830,-000 sq. mi., extends in S-shape from arctic to antarctic regions between the Americas, Europe, and Africa. Connected with the Pacific by Panama Canal, and (through Mediterranean) with Red Sea by Suez Canal. Chief western arms: Hudson and Baffin bays, Gulf of Mexico, Caribbean Sea. Chief eastern arms: Baltic and North seas, Bay of Biscay, the Mediterranean, Gulf of Guinea. Shortest trans-Atlantic distance is between Dakar, Africa, and bulge of Brazil. More large rivers drain into it than into any other ocean. Surface waters of trade-wind belts attain highest oceanic salinity known. Chief currents: North and South Equatorial, Brazil, Guinea, and GULF STREAM, which meets Labrador Current in Grand Banks off Newfoundland, forming heavy fogs. Gulf Stream then bends eastward to form part of NORTH ATLANTIC DRIFT. This area, part of busiest shipping lane in world, is patrolled for icebergs by U.S. coast guard. A submarine ridge extends from E Greenland to N Scotland, bearing telegraph cable network. Mid-Atlantic ridge, 300–600 mi. wide, from Iceland almost to Antarctic Circle, rises to average height of c.10,-000 ft. It is center of volcanic activity and earthquakes; a few of its peaks emerge as islands. Chief Atlantic deeps are Milwaukee Depth (30,246 ft.) near the Bahamas and Nares Deep (27,972 ft.) near Puerto Rico. An 800-mi. canyon in ocean floor between Bermuda and Azores was discovered in 1952.

Atlantis, in Greek legend, large island in western sea. Plato, who describes it as a Utopia, tells of high civilization there until its destruction by earthquake.

Question of its actual existence has provoked much speculation. One theory holds that it was the part of the island of Thera that sank into the Aegean Sea after a great earthquake c.1500 B.C.

Atlas (ăt'lŭs), in Greek religion, Titan. After the downfall of Titans he was condemned to hold up sky.

Atlas Mountains, mountain system of NW Africa, extending c.1500 mi. NE from Morocco through Algeria to Cape Bon in Tunisia. Source of phosphates.

Atlin Lake, 308 sq. mi., 66 mi. long, 2–6 mi. wide, NW B.C. and S Yukon, Canada. On E shore is Atlin village, hq. of gold-mining region.

atmosphere, gaseous envelope around earth, probably extending at least 600 mi. Lower layer (troposphere) extends to limiting boundary (tropopause) and decreases in height from c.10 mi. at equator to c.5 mi. at poles; above lies stratosphere, first reached by Auguste Piccard in balloon ascent (1931). Within troposphere, air is mixed by ascending and descending currents; temperature decreases c.1°C. per 500-ft. altitude increase; air is composed of nitrogen (78.09%), oxygen (20.95%), and small amounts of argon, carbon dioxide, and other gases, and also containing water vapor and dusts. Air pressure decreases with altitude (see BAROMETER); standard pressure at sea level is 14.7 lb. per sq. in. (called an atmosphere); c.$\frac{9}{10}$ of mass of atmosphere is within 10 mi. above sea level. Above stratosphere is the IONOSPHERE. See *ill.,* p. 311.

atoll: see CORAL.

atom, according to modern atomic theory, smallest particle of matter which has the characteristic chemical properties of an element. Formerly the atom was considered the indivisible unit of matter; now known to have an internal structure. Fundamental subatomic particles are proton, having unit positive charge and MASS NUMBER 1; neutron, having neutral charge and mass number 1; electron, having unit negative charge and negligible mass. Protons and neutrons of atom are concentrated in central nucleus, which has positive charge and almost all of the mass of the atom. Because extranuclear electrons are equal in number to nuclear protons, atom is neutral. Ions are atoms or groups of atoms with electrical charge; ions are formed from atoms by gain or loss of electrons. Atoms of different elements differ in weight (ATOMIC WEIGHT or MASS NUMBER) and in number of protons and electrons (this number indicated by atomic number; see PERIODIC LAW). Chemical properties of different elements determined by differing electron arrangements. Chemically, all atoms of an element react the same; sometimes differ in mass (see ISOTOPE). Atoms of same or different elements are joined in molecules. Discovery of ELECTRON and RADIOACTIVITY essential to modern concept of atom. Other subatomic particles have been discovered (see MESON; POSITRON). Among contributors to knowledge of atom: N. H. D. BOHR, W. H. BRAGG, W. L. BRAGG, James CHADWICK, Owen CHAMBERLAIN, P. A. CHERENKOV, John DALTON, Albert EINSTEIN, Enrico FERMI, I. M. FRANK, D. A. GLASER, ROBERT HOFSTADTER, MAX von LAUE, Tsung dao LEE, Lise MEITNER, R. A. MILLIKAN, R. L. MÖSSBAUER, H. G. J. MOSELEY, Wolfgang PAULI, Max PLANCK, Baron RUTHERFORD, Erwin SCHRÖDINGER, Emilio SEGRÈ, I. Y. TAMM, Chen Ning YANG. See also ATOMIC BOMB; ATOMIC ENERGY. See *ill.,* p. 781.

atomic bomb, weapon deriving explosive force from conversion of matter into ATOMIC ENERGY by fission process. Bomb is exploded by assembling several pieces of fissionable uranium 235 or plutonium metal into a compact mass, so that neutrons spontaneously emitted split more fissionable atoms and are not dissipated into the surrounding space. If the assembled mass exceeds critical mass, the rate of fissions in the chain reaction rapidly increases and an explosion occurs. Destruction is produced by intense heat, shock wave, and lingering radioactivity. Explosive yield of an atomic bomb is measured in equivalents in thousands of tons of T.N.T. First bombs produced at Los Alamos, N.Mex., by U.S.; used against populations of HIROSHIMA and NAGASAKI in closing days of Second World War. Large and small bombs are made for varying military uses. See also HYDROGEN BOMB.

atomic energy is produced by fission or by fusion of atomic nuclei; in either process, matter is converted into energy. By experimenting with cyclotron, U.S. scientists (1939) confirmed splitting (fission) of uranium nucleus by Germany. Roosevelt named committee to investigate military uses of atomic energy. In 1942 a group under Fermi achieved, in an atomic pile (NUCLEAR REACTOR) of graphite and uranium, the first self-sustaining nuclear chain reaction; this is the fission process. In a chain reaction, a fissionable element is bombarded with neutrons. Uranium 235 (isotope of mass number 235) and plutonium are the fissionable elements most commonly used. A fissionable atom captures a neutron, becomes unstable, and splits, yielding two smaller atoms, more neutrons, and a quantity of energy. The total mass produced is less than the original mass of the fissionable atom; the difference appears as energy. The released neutrons split other atoms, extending the fission process; the rate of the chain reaction is controlled by absorbing some neutrons in nonfissionable material. The fission process is used in the atomic bomb and for POWER production in the nuclear reactor. Energy yield appears in nuclear reactor as heat; this is converted to usable power by conventional engines or turbines. Fusion may be accomplished by any of several processes. In one type of fusion process, two deuterons collide and fuse to form a helium 3 (isotope of mass number 3) nucleus, a neutron, and a quantity of energy. Here also, the total mass yielded is less than the original mass and the difference appears as energy. The fusion process is used in the HYDROGEN BOMB. Controlled nonexplosive fusion for power production has not yet been achieved. TRACER studies and cancer treatment are among the peacetime atomic energy research projects in medicine and biology. UN devised plan for international control of research and production independent of Security Council. This was favored by Western powers, opposed by USSR, which wanted prohibition and destruction of existing bombs, then control by group with limited powers, regulated by Security Council. Negotiations became deadlocked. Later U.S. proposals for aerial and ground team inspection of bomb production and tests were rejected by USSR. See *ill.*, p. 781.

Atomic Energy, International Conference on the Peaceful Uses of. Set up under UN auspices to encourage free exchange of nonmilitary nuclear data among scientists. The first conference (1955) and the second (1958), both held in Geneva, Switzerland, made public much formerly secret information. A third conference was held in 1964.

Atomic Energy Commission, United States, five-man control group, estab. 1946, to channel the uses of atomic energy to peaceful ends. Members are appointed by President with consent of Senate.

atomic number: see PERIODIC LAW.

atomic theory, holds that matter is made up of minute particles, atoms. John Dalton (19th cent.) revived ancient (5th cent. B.C.) theory of atom, accepted early idea of indivisibility (no longer held), and believed that atoms of any element are same in size and weight and unite chemically in simple numerical ratios to form compounds. Mendelejeff and Arrhenius contributed to theory. Modern theory based on discovery of ELECTRON and RADIOACTIVITY. See *ill.*, p. 781.

atomic weight, ratio of weight of atom of element to the weight of an atom of carbon (C = 12). Hydrogen (H = 1) and oxygen (O = 16) formerly used as standards. Atomic weight determined by quantitative analysis. Relative proportions by weight of different elements in a compound are determined. Relative proportions are expressed in lowest numerical ratio. From ratio, atomic weights can be computed. Atomic weight of element having atoms of different weights (see ISOTOPE) is an average.

atonality, absence of a functional center, the tonic, in a musical composition (see TONALITY). Complete avoidance of a tonic is exceedingly difficult to maintain, since the listener is inclined to create one arbitrarily. Atonal writing began after c.1908 as a rejection of 19th-cent. musical heritage and employs various means of destroying the old system of tonal relationship: chords built on fourths, chord clusters, tone rows, ignoring of vertical relationships (see SCHOENBERG, ARNOLD). Main representatives are Schoenberg and his followers Alban Berg, Ernst Krenek, and Anton Webern.

Atonement, Day of, Heb. *Yom Kippur,* most solemn Jewish holiday, late Sept. or early Oct. (10th day of the 7th month, Tishri). Day of penitence, fasting, and meditation when prayers for forgiveness of sins are offered. Liturgy ushered in with the prayer, Kol Nidre.

ATP (adenosine triphosphate), complex organic compound vital in METABOLISM. Comprises units of adenine (compound of carbon, hydrogen, nitrogen), ribose (a sugar), and three phosphate groups. ATP is formed in most energy-yielding biochemical reactions and is transfer agent for phosphate groups needed by living cells to use energy. It is involved in functioning of muscles and nerves; in reactions of carbohydrates, proteins, fats, and nucleic acids; and in plant photosynthesis.

Atreus (ā'trēus), in Greek legend, king of Mycenae; father of Agamemnon and Menelaus. He slew three sons of his brother Thyestes and served them to him at a feast. The fourth son of Thyestes killed him.

atropine (ăt'rŭpēn, –pīn), poisonous alkaloid discovered in belladonna (deadly nightshade) by P. L. Geiger (1833). Used to dilate pupil of eye and as antispasmodic, narcotic, and pain reliever.

Atropos, one of the FATES.

attar of roses, fragrant essential oil, known also as otto of roses and rose oil, used in making perfume. Extracted chiefly from petals of damask rose (*Rosa damascena*) by distillation with water or steam, or by enfleurage (absorbing floral oil with another oil). Bulgaria is major supplier. In France cabbage rose (*Rosa centifolia*) is used.

Attica (ă'tĭkŭ), region of E central anc. Greece, around ATHENS. According to legend its four tribes founded by Ion and combined as a state by Theseus.

Attila (ă'tĭlŭ), d. 453, king of the HUNS (c.434–53), called the Scourge of God. He extorted tribute from Rome, but in 450 emperors Marcian and Valentinian III refused to pay. The same year Valentinian's sister Honoria secretly offered herself in marriage to Attila, who demanded half the Western Empire as dowry. Turned down, he invaded Gaul but was defeated by AETIUS at Châlons (451). In 452 he invaded N Italy but abandoned his plan to take Rome, according to some because of the plea of Pope LEO I, but more probably because of a shortage of supplies. Accounts of his savagery, though based on fact, are probably exaggerated.

Attis (ă'tĭs) or **Atys** (ā'tĭs), Phrygian fertility god. Like Adonis, he died and was resurrected yearly.

Attleboro (ăt'ŭlbŭrŭ), city (pop. 27,118), SE Mass., NE of Providence, R.I.; settled 1634. Jewelry industry began in 1780.

Attlee, Clement R(ichard) (ăt'lē), 1883–, British statesman and LABOUR PARTY leader. A former social service worker, held posts in 1924 and 1929 Labour governments. Became party leader 1935. Was deputy prime minister (1942–45) in Churchill's wartime coalition cabinet. Made prime minister (1945) while attending POTSDAM CONFERENCE. His government nationalized much industry, began national health service, ended Palestine mandate and control of India, and strengthened ties with U.S. Stress on rearmament caused opposition within Labour party. After loss to Conservatives in 1951 elections, Attlee became opposition leader. In 1955 he was succeeded by Hugh Gaitskell and was made Earl Attlee.

Attu, island, c.35 mi. long, off W Alaska, westernmost of ALEUTIAN ISLANDS. Extremely rugged, it rises more than 3,000 ft. Japanese occupied it 1942. U.S. forces landed May, 1943, and retook island in three weeks of bloody fighting. Air base was then estab. here.

Atwater, Wilbur Olin, 1844–1907, American chemist, founded first American agr. experiment station at Wesleyan Univ. (1875). Became first director of Dept. of Agr. Office of Experiment Stations 1888. Co-inventor of respiration calorimeter used for measuring human metabolism.

Atwater, city (1963 pop. 11,105), central Calif., NW of Merced, in farm area; founded 1888. Castle Air Force Base is near.

Atwood, George, 1746–1807, English mathematician and physicist. Invented Atwood's machine, a device for measuring acceleration of falling bodies.

Atys: see ATTIS.

Au, chemical symbol of the element GOLD.

Aube (ōb), department (2,327 sq. mi.; pop 255,099), NE France, in Champagne; cap. Troyes.

Auber, Daniel François (frāswä′ ōbĕr′), 1782–1871, French composer, known chiefly for his comic opera. Among his works are *Fra Diavolo, Le Domino noir,* and *La Muette de Portici* (also called *Masaniello*).

Aubert de Gaspé, Philippe: see GASPÉ, PHILIPPE AUBERT DE.

Aubigné, Théodore Agrippa d' (tāōdôr′ ägrēpä′ dō-bēnyä′), 1552–1630, French poet and Huguenot soldier. His reputation rests on *Les Tragiques,* a powerful, partly satirical, partly epical poem.

Aubrey, John, 1626–97, English antiquary and biographer, author of *Lives of Eminent Men* (pub. 1813; later called *Brief Lives*).

Auburn or **Lissoy,** village, Co. Westmeath, Ireland; scene of Goldsmith's *Deserted Village.*

Auburn. 1 City (pop. 16,261), E Ala., SW of Opelika, in a livestock, timber, and cotton area; settled c.1836. AUBURN UNIVERSITY is here. **2** City (pop. 5,586), N central Calif., NE of Sacramento, on fork of American R.; settled 1848 after gold discovery. *Placer Herald* published here since 1852. New Orleans Hotel made famous by Bret Harte. **3** City (pop. 24,449), SW Maine, on Androscoggin R. opposite Lewiston. White settlement began c.1786 on site of former Indian village. Nearby Mt. Apatite is source of apatite and feldspar. **4** Residential town (pop. 14,047), S central Mass., S of Worcester; settled 1714. Name changed from Ward 1837. **5** City (pop. 35,249), W central N.Y., in Finger Lakes region, on outlet of Owasco L. and WSW of Syracuse; settled 1793. Auburn State Prison and homes of W. H. Seward and Harriet Tubman are here. **6** City (pop. 11,933), W Wash., between Seattle and Tacoma; settled 1855. A rail junction and farm trade center.

Auburn University, at Auburn, Ala.; land grant, state supported; coed. after 1892; opened 1856 as East Alabama Male Col.; reorganized 1872 as Alabama Agr. and Mechanical Col.; renamed Alabama Polytechnic Inst. 1899, Auburn Univ. 1960. Sponsor of Oak Ridge Inst. of Nuclear Studies in Tennessee.

Aubusson, Pierre d' (pyĕr′ dōbüsō′), 1423–1503, French cardinal, grand master of Knights Hospitalers. Defended Rhodes heroically against Turks (1480).

Aubusson (ōbüsō′), town (est. pop. 5,595), Creuse dept., central France. Famous tapestry and carpet manufacture dates from 15th cent.

Aucassin et Nicolette (ōkäse′ ĕ nēkōlĕt′) medieval French love story in prose and verse (probably 13th cent.). The original music, to which verses were to be sung, has been preserved. Many English translations.

Auch (ōsh), town (est. pop. 16,382), cap. of Gers dept., SW France; wine, brandy trade. Archiepiscopal see from 9th cent.; was cap. of Armagnac and of Gascony. Cathedral contains magnificent stained glass.

Auckland (ôk′lŭnd), city (pop. 141,000; metropolitan pop. 413,100), N North Isl., New Zealand, in hot-springs area; founded 1841. Former cap. (1841–65) and chief port of dominion. Exports dairy products, hides, and timber. Has shipyards, a sugar refinery, and canneries. Seat of Auckland Univ. Col., and museum with collection of Maori art.

Aude (ōd), department (2,449 sq. mi.; pop. 269,782), SE France, in Languedoc; cap. Carcassonne.

Auden, W(ystan) H(ugh) (ô′dŭn), 1907–, Anglo-American poet, b. England. Leader of left-wing literary group at Oxford, he wrote (with Isherwood) verse plays: *The Dog beneath the Skin* (1935), *The Ascent of F 6* (1936), *On the Frontier* (1938). Perhaps better known are lyrics such as those in *Collected Poetry* (1945).

Audenarde, Belgium: see OUDENARDE.

Audubon, John James (ô′dŭbŏn), d. 1851, American ornithologist. Birth date and place disputed (New Orleans, 1780, or Aux Cayes, Haiti, 1785). Came to U.S. in 1803. His bird-banding experiments near Philadelphia (c.1803) were first in America. Married Lucy Bakewell (1808); lived mostly in Henderson, Ky., during 1808–20, changing occupation frequently, observing birds. Taught drawing in New Orleans. On 1826 trip to England he secured publication of *The Birds of America* and *Ornithological Biography* (with William MacGillivray). Later, in New York he began with John Bachman *The Viviparous Quadrupeds of North America,* completed by his sons, Victor Gifford Audubon and John Woodhouse Audubon. National Association of Audubon Societies devoted to preserving and studying American wildlife publishes *Audubon Magazine.*

Audubon, residential borough (pop. 10,440), SW N.J., SE of Camden.

Aue, Hartmann von: see HARTMANN VON AUE.

Auenbrugger, Leopold (lä′ōpōlt ou′ŭnbrŏog′ŭr), 1722–1809, Viennese physician, pioneer in use of percussion in diagnosing chest diseases.

Auerstedt (ou′ŭrshtĕt), village, East Germany, in former state of Saxony-Anhalt, central Germany. Here the French Marshal Davout defeated Prussians on same day that Napoleon I triumphed at Jena (Oct. 14, 1806).

Augeas (ôjē′ŭs), in Greek legend, king who owned 3,000 oxen. Hercules, commanded to clean in one day the Augean stables, untouched for 30 years, did so by turning rivers Peneus and Alpheus through them.

Augier, Émile (āmēl′ ōzhyä′), 1820–89, French dramatist and satirist. Best-known comedy is *Le Gendre de M. Poirier* (1854), written with J. Sandeau.

Augsburg (ouks′bŏŏrk), city (pop. 200,236), cap. of Swabia, W Bavaria, on Lech R. Textile center of S Germany. Founded by Augustus 15 B.C. as Augusta Vindelicorum; free imperial city 1276; prominent member of Swabian League (1488–1534). Home of Fugger family and birthplace of Holbein, it was a major commercial, banking, and cultural center in 15th–16th cent. Is rich in architectural beauty.

Augsburg, League of, defensive alliance formed 1686 against Louis XIV of France by Emperor Leopold I with Sweden, Spain, Bavaria, Palatinate, and other German states. Transformed into GRAND ALLIANCE (1689) after adherence of Holland, England, Savoy.

Augsburg, Peace of, 1555, temporary settlement within Holy Roman Empire of conflicts arising from the Reformation. Chief principle: *Cuius regio, eius religio*—i.e., each prince was to determine whether Lutheranism or Catholicism was to prevail in his lands. All Church property held by abbots or bishops who had changed their faith after 1552 was to be forfeited by them.

Augsburg Confession: see CREED.

Augsburg Interim: see REFORMATION.

August: see MONTH.

Augusta (ôgŭs′tû). **1** City (pop. 70,626), E Ga., at head of navigation on Savannah R. (levees). Large cotton market and important industrial center. Also winter resort with mild climate. Laid out 1735 as trading post by James Oglethorpe. Changed hands many times; finally fell in 1781 to Continentals under Andrew Pickens and Light-Horse Harry Lee. Was cap. of Ga. 1785–95. Site of largest Confederate powder works in Civil War. Here are Paine Col., Univ. of Ga. School of Medicine, Woodrow Wilson's boyhood home, and many old Georgian and classic revival houses. **2** City (pop. 21,680), state cap., SW Maine, on Kennebec R., NE of Portland. Traders visited site before Plymouth Co. estab. trading post 1628. After Fort Western was built (1754), settlement grew with shipping and shipbuilding. A dam (1837) stimulated mfg. J. G. Blaine's home now governor's mansion.

Augustana College (ô″gŭstăn′ù), at Sioux Falls, S.D.; coed.; opened 1860 as seminary in Chicago, chartered 1865; had various names and sites as it followed Scandinavian pioneers W.

Augustine, Saint (ô′gŭstĕn, –tĭn; ôgŭ′stĭn), 354–430, Doctor of the Church, b. Tagaste, N Africa. Though reared as a Christian by his mother, St. Monica, he became a Manichaean. In Milan as a teacher of rhetoric, he was attracted by the teachings of St. Ambrose and again became a Christian (387). Returned to Tagaste, became a hermit, was later (396) made bishop of Hippo. Brought immense learning to bear on exposition of Christian doctrine and in arguments against Manichaeism, Donatism, and Pelagianism. Theologians, both Catholic and Protestant, have drawn on his works heavily and considered him master of theology. Among lay readers his autobiographical *Confessions* and his *City of God* (a profound view of the actual and the ideal in Christian society) are still very popular. Feast: Aug. 28.

Augustine of Canterbury, Saint, d. c.605, first archbishop of Canterbury. A Roman Benedictine sent with some monks to England by Pope Gregory I, he gained the favor of King Æthelbert of Kent. Introduced to England Roman rites and calendar which later triumphed over Celtic forms introduced in the N. The "apostle of England." Feast: May 28 or (in England) May 26.

Augustinians, Roman Catholic religious orders. The canons regular (Augustinians, or Austin canons) use an old rule of St. Augustine. Austin friars are a different group dating from 13th cent.

Augustus, 63 B.C.–A.D. 14, first Roman emperor. Grandnephew of Julius CAESAR, he was adopted and made heir by Caesar, without his knowledge. Originally Octavius (Caius Octavius), he became on adoption Octavian (Caius Julius Caesar Octavianus). After Caesar was assassinated he gained power in Rome and allied himself with Antony and Lepidus in the Second Triumvirate. He and Antony defeated the republicans under Brutus and Cassius at Philippi (42 B.C.). He and his lieutenant, Agrippa, drove the pirate forces of Sextus Pompeius from the sea, then after differences with Antony (see ANTONY) defeated that general and Cleopatra at Actium (31 B.C.). Augustus then was master of the Roman world. The senate showered titles on him, including *imperator* [general; from it comes word *emperor*] and *augustus* [revered]. He reformed administration, solidified Roman holdings (his only reverse was defeat of his general Varus by German leader Arminius), and beautified the city (he is said to have claimed that he found Rome of brick and left it of marble). Roman roads were extended and improved. Architecture flourished, and he was a patron of Vergil, Ovid, Livy, and Horace in the age of literature called Augustan. He imposed the Pax Romana [Roman peace] on the known civilized world. His stepson, Tiberius, succeeded him.

Augustus, kings of Poland. **Augustus I:** see SIGISMUND II (Sigismund Augustus). **Augustus II** (the Strong), 1670–1733, as Frederick Augustus I, elector of Saxony (1694–1733), was elected to succeed John III on the Polish throne (1697). Opportunistic, he became a Catholic, granted the Polish nobility unprecedented privileges, and allied himself with Russia and Denmark against CHARLES XII of Sweden (see NORTHERN WAR). Charles forced him to renounce the Polish crown in favor of STANISLAUS I (1706), but after Charles's defeat at Poltava (1709) Augustus recovered Poland (1716). Among his innumerable mistresses and illegitimate offspring were Maria Aurora von KÖNIGSMARK and her son, Maurice de Saxe. His son **Augustus III,** 1696–1763, succeeded him as elector of Saxony as Frederick Augustus II and claimed Poland from Stanislaus I, who had been reelected on Augustus II's death. After The War of the POLISH SUCCESSION he was elected Polish king (1736). As son-in-law of Emperor Joseph I, he claimed the Hapsburg lands in the War of the AUSTRIAN SUCCESSION, but he changed sides in 1742. In the SEVEN YEARS WAR (1756–63) he fled Saxony and took residence in Poland. Indolent, he left the government to Count BRÜHL.

auk (ôk), swimming, diving bird of N Atlantic, Pacific; related to puffin. Legs set far back on body. Auk is clumsy on land, where it nests. Flightless great auks, largest species, once abundant in N Atlantic, were killed off (c.1844) for flesh, feathers, oil. Least auklet (c.6½ in.), common in Bering Sea, is smallest. Largest surviving (16–18 in.) is razor-billed auk.

Aulie-Ata: see DZHAMBUL.

Aulis (ô′lĭs), small port of ancient Greece, in Boeotia. Here Greek fleet was becalmed on way to Troy; resumed sail after sacrifice of IPHIGENIA. Recent archaeological discovery is the temple of Artemis.

Aurangzeb (ôr′ŭngzĕb″), 1618–1707, Mogul emperor (1659–1707) of India, son of Shah Jehan. Won throne by defeating his brothers and imprisoning his father. Brought empire to greatest extent by military conquests. Intensely devoted to Islam, he destroyed Hindu temples and mortally offended the Sikhs.

Auray (ôrā′), town (est. pop. 8,159), Morbihan dept., NW France, in Brittany. Famous pilgrimage shrine of Sainte-Anne-d'Auray is 4 mi. N.

Aurelian (ôrē′lĕŭn), c.212–275, Roman emperor (270–75). After succeeding Claudius II, he defended the empire vigorously against barbarians and ambitious rulers (notably Zenobia of Palmyra); consolidated rule once again in Britain, Gaul, Spain, Egypt, Syria, and Mesopotamia; and revived the glory of Rome.

Auriesville, village, E central N.Y., near Amsterdam. Site of Roman Catholic shrine to St. Isaac Jogues and other Jesuit Martyrs of North America, killed by Iroquois.

Aurignac (ôrēnyäk′), village, S France, SW of Toulouse. Its caves contain relics of prehistoric man (Aurignacian period; see PALEOLITHIC PERIOD).

Aurillac (ôrēyäk′), town (est. pop. 22,224), cap. Cantal dept., SE central France, in Auvergne. Industrial center with 18th-cent. church, picturesque houses.

Auriol, Vincent (vĕsä′ ôryôl′), 1884–1966, president of the French republic (1947–54); a moderate socialist.

aurochs (ôr′ŏks), name for now extinct European wild ox or urus (*Bos primigenius*), large, blackish-brown, and believed ancestor of European domestic cattle. European bison often called aurochs.

Aurora (ürō′rù, ôrō′–), in Roman religion, goddess of dawn, identified with Greek Eos.

Aurora. 1 Residential city (pop. 48,548), N central Colo., E of Denver. Farming and mfg. Nearby are Lowry Air Force Base and large U.S. army hospital. **2** City (pop. 63,715), NE Ill., W of Chicago, on Fox

R.; settled 1834. Has mfg. and large railroad shops. Aurora Col. is here.

aurora borealis (bŏ̄"rēä'lĭs, -ā'lĭs) and **aurora australis** (ôstrā'lĭs), luminous displays of N and S Hemispheres respectively, called also northern and southern lights. Visible in a variety of colors and forms over areas near geomagnetic poles, they extend to altitudes from c.35 to c.600 mi. Believed to result from collisions of charged particles from sun with gases of upper atmosphere. Occurrence correlated with sunspot activity and magnetic storms. See *ill.*, p. 311.

Au Sable (ôsa'bŭl), river rising in several branches which unite in Crawford co., N Mich., and flowing c.80 mi. S and E to L. Huron N of Saginaw Bay.

Ausable, river, NE N.Y., formed at Au Sable Forks village by junction of two branches rising in Adirondacks. Flows c.20 mi. NE to L. Champlain S of Plattsburgh. Above Keesville (stone-arch bridge, 1842) is **Ausable Chasm** (c.2 mi. long; 20-50 ft. wide; 100–200 ft. deep), with waterfalls, rapids, curious rock formations.

Auschwitz, Poland: see OSWIECIM.

Ausonius (Decimus Magnus Ausonius) (ōsō'nēŭs dĕs'-ĭmŭs), c.310–395, Latin poet, a prefect of Gaul and consul (379). He pictures contemporary society.

Aussig, Czechoslovakia: see USTI NAD LABEM.

Austen, Jane, 1775–1817, English novelist. A clergyman's daughter, she lived a quiet life, and her novels of social comedy have a small stage, though they are made masterpieces by her observation, witty characterization, and sparkling, polished style. Published in her lifetime were *Sense and Sensibility* (1811), *Pride and Prejudice* (1813), *Mansfield Park* (1814), *Emma* (1816). *Northanger Abbey* (satire on the romances of Mrs. Radcliffe), written early, appeared with *Persuasion* in 1818. Little known in her day, Jane Austen later became one of the best-known and best-loved English novelists.

Austerlitz (ô'stŭrlĭts, ou'-), Czech *Slavkov u Brna,* small town, Czechoslovakia, E of Brno. Here, on Dec. 2, 1805, Napoleon I won the most brilliant victory of his career over the Russians and Austrians under emperors Alexander I and Francis II ("battle of the three emperors"), thus forcing Austria out of the war.

Austin, John, 1911–60, British philosopher. His major thesis is that through analysis of ordinary language we gain knowledge of the realities of the world this language talks about.

Austin, Mary (Hunter), 1868–1934; American author. Much of her fiction reflects her interest in the Spanish and Indian Southwest, as does her best play, *The Arrow-Maker* (1911), and her autobiography, *Earth Horizon* (1932).

Austin, Moses, 1761–1821, American pioneer. Secured grant from Spanish to settle 300 families in Texas. His son, **Stephen Fuller Austin,** 1793–1836, took up plans when his father died and estab. settlements between Brazos and Colorado rivers. Opposed SANTA ANNA and thus forwarded Texas Revolution.

Austin, Warren R(obinson), 1877–1962, U.S. Representative at the UN (1946–53).

Austin. 1 City (pop. 27,908), SE Minn., on Cedar R. and near Iowa line, SW of Rochester; settled 1853. Industrial and commercial center of rich farm region. **2** City (pop. 186,545), state cap., S central Texas on Colorado R. Laid out 1838 as Waterloo; voted as site of cap. of republic 1839 and renamed for S. F. Austin. Became temporary state cap. after annexation to U.S. 1845; made permanent cap. 1870. Grew to industrial city after 1920s, with power and flood-control projects on Colorado R. and urgencies of Second World War. Massive capitol (1888) most prominent of state buildings. Seat of Univ. of TEXAS, St. Edward's Univ., Austin Presbyterian Theological Seminary, and Huston-Tillotson Col. Has O. Henry's house, Elisabeth Ney's former studio (both museums), and old French embassy. In hills nearby are many scenic areas (esp. Barton Springs). Bergstrom

Air Force Base is nearby, and ranch of L.B. Johnson is to W near Stonewall.

Austin canons: see AUGUSTINIANS.

Australasia (ôstrŭlā'zhŭ, –shŭ), islands of S Pacific. Largest are Australia, New Zealand, New Guinea.

Australia, island continent between Indian and Pacific oceans. Nearly as large as continental U.S., it spans c.2,400 mi. from E to W and c.2,000 mi. from N to S. With the island state of TASMANIA, it forms the Commonwealth of Australia, a British dominion (2,-971,081 sq. mi.; pop. 10,061,222, excluding aboriginals). The five continental states are QUEENSLAND, NEW SOUTH WALES, VICTORIA, SOUTH AUSTRALIA, and WESTERN AUSTRALIA. NORTHERN TERRITORY and AUSTRALIAN CAPITAL TERRITORY (containing Canberra, the federal cap.) are areas under direct federal control. Australia owns Territory of Papua (see PAPUA, TERRITORY OF), Norfolk Isl., and Australian Antarctic Territory; holds under UN trusteeship the Territory of New Guinea (see NEW GUINEA, TERRITORY OF) and NAURU (jointly with the United Kingdom and New Zealand). The W half of the Australian continent is an arid plateau (important for large iron and gold fields) while extreme NE area js tropical jungle. In the east are the Great Dividing Range and the Murray R. The main coal-mining state is New South Wales. Staple products are wool and grain. Australia is noted for its distinctive animal life which includes the kangaroo and the platypus. The continent was first sighted in the early 17th cent. by the Portuguese and the Spaniards. In 1770 Capt. James Cook claimed the E coast for Great Britain, and in 1829 the whole continent was brought under British rule. Federation of the former Australian colonies was achieved in 1901. Executive power is vested in a governor-general (representing the British crown) and a cabinet headed by a prime minister. Parliament consists of a Senate and a House of Representatives. See map, p. 72.

Australian aborigines, homogeneous ethnic group of nomadic hunters (c.70,000) on Australian mainland, mostly in N and NE, with Arnhem Land the largest reservation. Primitive material culture with complex religious and social organization. Invented boomerang.

Australian Alps, mountain ranges, SE Australia, comprising S part of Great Dividing Range. Mt. Kosciusko (7,328 ft.) is highest peak in Australia.

Australian Antarctic Territory, comprising the islands and territory (except Adélie Land) between long. 45°E and 160°E and below lat. 60°S. Claimed in 1933 by Australia.

Australian Capital Territory (939 sq. mi.; pop. 46,070), SE Australia, within New South Wales; contains Canberra, cap. of Commonwealth of Australia. Ceded 1911 by state to commonwealth. Area was called Federal Capital Territory until 1938.

Austral Islands: see TUBUAI ISLANDS.

Austrasia (ôstrā'zhŭ), Frankish kingdom (6th–8th cent.), comprising E France, W Germany, Netherlands; cap. Metz. For history, see MEROVINGIANS.

Austria, Ger. *Österreich,* federal republic (32,375 sq. mi.; est. pop. 7,215,000), central Europe, traversed by Danube, bounded by Yugoslavia and Italy (S), Switzerland and Liechtenstein (W), Bavaria and Czechoslovakia (N), and Hungary (E); cap. Vienna. Its nine provinces—VORARLBERG, TYROL, SALZBURG, CARINTHIA, STYRIA, UPPER AUSTRIA, LOWER AUSTRIA, BURGENLAND, and VIENNA—are largely self-governing and are represented in the upper chamber of the federal bicameral parliament. Population is predominantly Roman Catholic and German-speaking. The ALPS, covering three quarters of the country, rise to 12,530 ft. in the HOHE TAUERN. Largely agricultural—yet not self-sufficient in major food staples—Austria also has industries (metallurgy, machinery, chemicals, textiles), concentrated mainly in the Vienna basin and at LINZ, STEYR, and GRAZ. Mineral resources include iron, manganese, copper, lead, zinc, petroleum (at Zisters-

AUSTRALIA

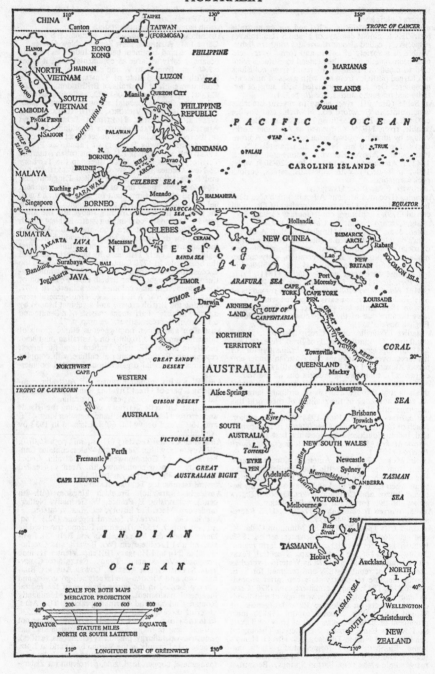

dorf), and salt. The area of present Austria was inhabited by Celts when it was conquered by Rome (15 B.C.–10 A.D.). It was overrun after the 5th cent. by Huns, Goths, Lombards, and Bavarians; conquered 788 by Charlemagne; reconquered 955 from the Magyars by Otto I; and attached as Eastern March to Bavaria 955–76. In subsequent history, the word *Austria* has four distinct meanings: (1) Austria proper, i.e., Upper and Lower Austria, including Vienna. This was ruled from 976 as margraviate (after 1156, duchy) by the house of Babenberg, and acquired in 1251 by OTTOCAR II of Bohemia. In 1276 Ottocar had to cede Austria, along with Styria, Carinthia, and CARNIOLA, to RUDOLF I of Hapsburg, in whose family it remained until 1918 (raised to archduchy 1453). (2) With the rise of Hapsburg greatness, the term *Austria* came to designate the house of Hapsburg or Austria, which ruled the HOLY ROMAN EMPIRE from 1438 to 1806 and at one time held an hereditary empire which embraced the world (see HAPSBURG). The chief historic importance of Austria proper in that period was as bulwark against Turkish onslaughts, which culminated and ended with the siege of Vienna in 1683. The house of Austria lost its primacy in German affairs in the THIRTY YEARS WAR and the wars of the 18th cent. As a result, it concentrated, especially under MARIA THERESA and JOSEPH II, on internal consolidation of its hereditary lands and on eastward expansion (esp. in POLAND and Balkans). Thrice defeated in the French Revolutionary and Napoleonic Wars (see FRANCIS II, emperor), it nevertheless emerged in 1815 from the CONGRESS OF VIENNA as leader of the GERMAN CONFEDERATION. (3) Shortly before the dissolution of the Holy Roman Empire, Francis II assumed the title "Francis I, emperor of Austria." The Austrian Empire, which is the third meaning of the term, consisted after 1815 of, roughly, German-speaking Austria, Bohemia, Moravia, S Poland, Lombardy, Venetia, Carniola, Istria, Dalmatia, and the separate kingdom of Hungary, with Croatia and Slavonia. The Revolution of 1848 drove METTERNICH from power but Emperor FRANCIS JOSEPH soon restored absolutism. In the Italian War of 1859 Austria lost Lombardy; the AUSTRO-PRUSSIAN WAR of 1866 cost it Venetia and eliminated it from German affairs. In 1867 a general reorganization of the empire resulted in the creation of the AUSTRO-HUNGARIAN MONARCHY, which collapsed at end of First World War. (4) In Nov., 1918, German Austria was proclaimed a republic. The Treaty of SAINT-GERMAIN (1919) fixed the boundaries of present Austria–i.e., the German-speaking remnant of the Austrian Empire–a small country of 6,000,000 people (a third of whom lived in the capital), stripped of its former raw materials, food, and markets. Chronic bankruptcy, unemployment, and political unrest resulted. The three-cornered struggle among Socialists, clerico-fascists, and National Socialists led to the establishment in 1934 of a corporative, authoritarian regime under Chancellor DOLLFUSS and his successor, SCHUSCHNIGG. The growth of local Nazism, German pressure, and Western appeasement resulted in the occupation of Austria by Germany in 1938. It was fully incorporated into the Reich in 1940. Conquered in 1945, Austria was restored as a republic and subjected to four-power occupation. Foreign troops left in 1955 with conclusion of peace treaty, which declared Austria a sovereign and neutral power. Austria was governed by a Catholic Socialist coalition from 1945 until 1966 when the conservative People's party won an absolute majority in Parliament. Austria was admitted to UN 1955; joined the Council of Europe 1956, the European Free Trade Association 1960.

Austrian Succession, War of the, 1740–48, European war precipitated by succession of MARIA THERESA of Austria to the Hapsburg lands by virtue of PRAGMATIC SANCTION. Her succession was challenged by the elector of Bavaria (later Emperor CHARLES VII), PHILIP V of Spain, and AUGUSTUS III of Poland and Saxony, while FREDERICK II of Prussia claimed part of SILESIA. Prussia opened war by invading Silesia, was joined (1741) by France, Spain, Bavaria, Saxony; made separate peace 1742; reentered war 1744; made final separate peace 1745 (Treaty of Dresden). England, then at war with Spain (see JENKINS'S EAR, WAR OF) supported Austria, as did Holland and Sardinia. Saxony went over to Austrian side 1743. Bavaria withdrew from war at death of Charles VII (1745). Notable military events up to 1745: Prussian victory at MOLLWITZ (1741); capture of Prague by Franco-Bavarians (1741); occupation of Bavaria and recapture of Prague by Austrians (1742); English victory at DETTINGEN (1743); French victory at FONTENOY (1745); Prussian victory at HOHENFRIEDBERG (1745). By Treaty of Dresden Prussia obtained most of Silesia but promised to support election of Maria Theresa's husband as emperor (Francis I). The remaining belligerents fought on inconclusively in N Italy, Low Countries, America and India until Treaty of AIX-LA-CHAPELLE of 1748.

Austro-Hungarian Monarchy or **Dual Monarchy,** the Hapsburg empire from the constitutional compromise (*Ausgleich*) of 1867 between AUSTRIA and HUNGARY until its fall in 1918. Rulers: FRANCIS JOSEPH (1867–1916), CHARLES I (1916–18). Empire was divided into Cisleithania (lands W of Leitha R.), including Austria proper, Bohemia, Moravia, Austrian Silesia, Slovenia, and Austrian Poland; and Transleithania, including Hungary, Transylvania, CROATIA, and part of Dalmatia. Cisleithania was ruled by emperor of Austria, Transleithania by king of Hungary (both dignities being united in the same monarch); each elected its own parliament and had its own cabinet and customs regime. A three-man common cabinet governed foreign policy, defense, imperial finances. Economically an organic whole, empire was torn and eventually broken up by nationalist aspirations of its many minorities, notably Czechs, Poles, Serbs, Italians, Rumanians. Threatened by pan-Slavism (spearheaded by Serbia and supported by Russia), Austria-Hungary concluded alliance with Germany (1879), joined also by Italy (1882; see TRIPLE ALLIANCE AND TRIPLE ENTENTE). The annexation of BOSNIA AND HERCEGOVINA (1908) envenomed relations with Serbia and Russia. The assassination of Archduke FRANCIS FERDINAND precipitated the First World War, Austria-Hungary surrendered Nov. 3, 1918. The Treaties of Versailles, Trianon, and Saint-Germain fixed boundaries of successor states.

Austronesian (ôs"trōnē'zhùn, –shùn), name sometimes used for the Malayo-Polynesian languages.

Austro-Prussian War or **Seven Weeks War,** June 15–Aug. 23, 1866, between Prussia, allied with Italy, and Austria, seconded by Bavaria, Württemberg, Saxony, Hanover, Baden, and several smaller German states. Provoked by BISMARCK with object of expelling Austria from GERMAN CONFEDERATION. Austro-Prussian dispute over administration of SCHLESWIG-HOLSTEIN served as pretext. Prussia quickly overran German states, crushed Austrians at SADOWA. Austrian victories over Italians at Custozza and Lissa proved useless at Peace of Prague (Aug. 23, 1866): Austria had to cede Venetia to Italy. Prussia demanded no territory from Austria but annexed Hesse-Kassel, Hanover, Frankfurt. NEW NORTH GERMAN CONFEDERATION was estab. under Prussian leadership. War paved way for founding of German Empire in 1871.

Auteuil (ōtû'ē), section of Paris, France, near Bois de Boulogne. Famous racecourse.

authentic modes, in music: see MODE.

autogiro (ô'tōjī'rō) or **gyroplane** (jī'rüplän), first aircraft to depart from Wright brothers type. Overhead airfoils, rotated by aerodynamic forces arising from craft's propulsion by ordinary engine and propeller, provide principal lift; wing area much reduced. Inventor, Juan de la CIERVA. Generally superseded by HELICOPTER.

Autolycus (ôtŏ'lĭkŭs), fl. 4th cent. B.C., astronomer and mathematician of Pitane in Aeolis. His treatise on revolving sphere is possibly the oldest completely preserved Greek work on a mathematical subject.

automation, in industry, application of FEEDBACK principles, whereby a mechanical system automatically observes and regulates its own performance, thus eliminating the need for human control. In an automated system, measuring instruments continuously observe the various processes and indicate performance irregularities as they arise; to produce a product with the exact desired qualities (dimensions, ingredients, etc.) the production processes must sometimes be adjusted. A computer programs the necessary adjustments on the basis of data obtained from the measuring instruments. Automation is most widely used in continuous-flow production systems, including the industrial manufacture of chemicals, foodstuffs, and pharmaceuticals. Automation is also applied to various types of piece-part production, including the manufacture of screws and other small hardware. Assembly of several parts, as in the assembly of an automobile body, presents more difficulties but can be successfully automated. Automation has found considerable application in various packaging procedures, including canning, fiber boxing, Cellophane wrapping, and bottling processes. Automation can be applied to services as well as to production. Systems for warehouse distribution of bulk articles have been automated: conveyor belts used in conjunction with electric eyes or pressure gauges are integrated by a computer into a fully automated system. Similarly, a dial telephone switchboard utilizes automation principles in distributing thousands of calls.

automaton: see ROBOT.

automobile. Probably the first self-propelled vehicle was a steam-driven, three-wheeled carriage introduced 1769 in Paris by Nicolas Joseph Cugnot. In early 19th cent. attempts to operate steam road carriages failed in England because of excessive tolls and restrictive legislation (e.g., the Red Flag Act). In Germany, INTERNAL-COMBUSTION ENGINE was used in 1885 by Karl Benz to operate vehicle; improved engine built by Gottlieb Daimler c.1885. Internal-combustion models manufactured in U.S. during 1890s by Charles Duryea, J. Frank Duryea, Elwood Haynes, Henry Ford, Ransom E. Olds, and Alexander Winton. By 1903 Detroit was becoming U.S. automotive center. Free growth of the industry was threatened by patent granted (1895) to George Selden for gasoline car. Manufacturers licensed by Selden formed association (1903) to control manufacture. Independents, led by Henry Ford, opposed this; U.S. Circuit Court of Appeals ruled (1911) Selden's patent valid but applicable to two-cycle engines only. Steam-driven cars thereafter were rapidly displaced by gasoline models; electric models retain limited use for local delivery trucks.

automobile racing, sport in which specially constructed, high-speed automobiles race on outdoor or indoor tracks. Started 1894 in France, 1895 in U.S. Indianapolis Speedway meet first held 1911. Famous drivers include William K. Vanderbilt, Barney Oldfield, Edward V. Rickenbacker, Wilbur Shaw. Sports car racing, first popular in Europe, spread in U.S. after 1947. Stock car racing also recent development. World drivers' championship now based on *Grand Prix* road racing events. Champions include Stirling Moss, Jack Brabham, Jim Clark.

autonomy (ôtŏn'ůmē), in political sense, limited self-government, short of independence. The objective test of autonomy is whether group can legislate for itself. Mother state may simply permit or formally delegate this right. It sometimes is prelude to complete sovereignty.

autumn crocus: see MEADOW SAFFRON.

Auvergne (ōvĕr'nyů), region and former province, central France, in the Massif Central, in Cantal, Puy-de-Dôme, Haute-Loire depts.; historic cap., Clermont (now Clermont-Ferrand). Auvergne mts. culminate in Mont-Dore and Puy de Dôme. Stock raising, dairying in mountains; agr. in valleys. Mineral springs and spas. Auvergnats descend from Celtic Arverni, whose leader Vercingetorix led Gallic revolt against Caesar. Region passed to English (1154) as part of Aquitaine; later was incorporated in several stages into French royal domain.

Auxerre (ōsĕr'), town (est. pop. 26,583), cap. of Yonne dept., NE central France; trading center for Chablis wines. Fine medieval architecture: Church and Abbey of St. Germain; Gothic cathedral.

auxins, plant hormones which regulate amount, type, and direction of plant growth. Auxin derivatives are used to force fruit production from unfertilized flowers. Other derivatives are used as herbicides; they kill weeds by causing disordered growth of the weed cells.

Avacha (ŭvä'chù) or **Avachinskaya Sopka** (ŭvä'chĭnskĭŭ sŏp'kŭ), active volcano (8,981 ft.), Asiatic RSFSR, on S Kamchatka peninsula.

avalanche (ăv'ŭlănch), sliding mass of snow, ice, rock, mobilized by weight added to unstable mass or by tremors.

Avalon (ăv'ŭlŏn), in Celtic mythology, island of the happy otherworld. See ARTHURIAN LEGEND.

Avalon, city (pop. 1,536), S Calif., on SANTA CATALINA; founded 1888. Center of island's resort and sport activities.

Avalon Peninsula, 3,579 sq. mi., SE N.F., Canada, most densely populated part of the province. Deeply indented at center by Conception Bay (N) and St. Mary's Bay (S).

Aveiro (ävä'rō), city (pop. 16,430), cap. of Aveiro dist., Beira Litoral, NW Portugal. Notable fishing port since 16th cent. Partially built over water, called "Portuguese Venice."

Avellaneda (äväyänä'dhä), city (pop. c.150,000), Buenos Aires prov., Argentina; industrial city, usually considered part of greater Buenos Aires.

Ave Maria (ä'vä märē'ä) [Latin,= hail, Mary], Roman Catholic prayer in Latin to the Virgin. Much set to music (notably by Schubert, Gounod). The English version, *Hail, Mary,* one of the most common of Catholic prayers.

Avempace (ā'vùmpäs, ä"vĕmpä'thä), Arabic *Ibn Bajja,* d. 1138, Spanish-Arabian Aristotelian philosopher.

Avenches (äväsh'), Latin *Aventicum,* small town, Vaud canton, W Switzerland. Flourished 1st cent. B.C.–2d cent. A.D. as chief town (pop. c.80,000) of Helvetia. Numerous Roman remains.

Avenzoar (äv"ùnzō'ùr, –zōär') or **Ibn Zohr** (ĭb'n zōr'), c.1090?–1162, Arabian physician, pioneer in experimental medicine.

average, any of certain statistical measures expressing numerically the characteristics of a group of figures. Strictly, simple average of a group of figures equals their sum divided by the number of figures in the group. See also MEAN; MEDIAN; MODE.

Avernus (ùvûr'nùs), Ital. *Averno,* small crater lake, Campania, S Italy, near Cumae. Sulfuric vapors and gloomy aspect led Romans to regard it as entrance to hell; name was later used for hell itself.

Averroës (ùvĕr'ōēz), 1126–98, Spanish-Arabian philosopher, primarily an interpreter of Aristotle. Highly influential in Jewish and Christian thought.

Avery Island, c.2 mi. in diameter, S La., in sea marshes and swamps, SW of New Iberia. Has water-bird (esp. egret) sanctuary and Jungle Gardens (rare plants). Rock-salt mining began c.1791.

Aveyron (ävärō'), dept. (3,386 sq. mi.; pop. 290,442), S central France in Guienne; cap. Rodez. Occupies old county of Rouergue.

aviary, enclosure for confining birds. Food, perches, flying space, nesting sites, material provided. Known in Roman times, aviaries are now mostly in public parks, zoos.

aviation, term applied broadly to all activities, facilities, and enterprises related to flying. Leonardo da Vinci first studied flight scientifically. Flight first achieved (1783) in lighter-than-air craft (see BALLOON). Among pioneers in heavier-than-air flight: Sir George Cayley (mechanics-of-flight analysis, 1809–10); W. S. Henson (foreshadowed modern monoplane, 1842); John Stringfellow (power-driven model plane, said to be first to fly); F. H. Wenham (devised wind tunnel, 1866); Alphonse Penaud (with Paul Gauchot designed amphibian monoplane, 1878); Clément Ader (his bat-fashioned monoplane flew, 1890); Sir Hiram S. Maxim (steam-driven plane, 1894); Samuel P. LANGLEY and Otto LILIENTHAL. First man-carrying, motor-driven airplane flight was by Orville Wright, repeated by Wilbur Wright (Dec. 17, 1903, Kitty Hawk, N.C.). Louis BLÉRIOT flew English Channel (1909). Glenn Curtis built first flying boat (1912). After First World War, aviation grew in importance. First N Atlantic crossing was by A. C. Read in U.S. Navy flying boat (May, 1919). John Alcock and A. W. Brown flew Newfoundland–Ireland (1919); Ross Smith, London–Australia (1919). Richard E. Byrd and Floyd Bennett flew Spitsbergen–North Pole (1926). Charles A. Lindbergh flew the Atlantic solo (1927). Hermann Köhl, J. C. Fitzmaurice, and G. von Hünefeld flew Ireland–Newfoundland (1928). Charles Kingsford-Smith was first to fly Pacific (1928), San Francisco–Australia with two stops. Clyde E. Pangborn and Hugh Herndon flew from Japan to Washington state nonstop (1931). Wiley Post and Harold Gatty flew round the world (1931). Post circled world solo (1933). Howard Hughes and four companions circled world (1938). Amelia Earhart Putnam was first woman to fly Atlantic as passenger (1928) and solo (1932). U.S. air transport chiefly of mail until, after 1930, passenger carrying became profitable. Pan American Airways (later Pan American World Airways) began transpacific air-mail service in 1934; added passenger service with San Francisco-to-Manila China Clipper. First transatlantic passenger service begun 1939 by Pan American. Second World War saw Army Air Transport Command and Navy Air Transport Service pioneer in global air routes. Col. David C. Schilling of USAF made first nonstop transatlantic jet flight (1950). Charles F. Blair, Jr., made first solo flight across North Pole (1951). Two U.S. S-55 helicopters made first transatlantic helicopter flight (1952). Jet airliners are in general domestic and intercontinental service. See also AIRPLANE; AIR POWER; AIRSHIP; HELICOPTER; JET PROPULSION. See ill., p. 368.

Avicebron: see IBN GABIROL, SOLOMON BEN JUDAH.

Avicenna (ăvĭsĕn'ŭ), Arabic Ibn Sina, 980–1037, Persian philosopher and physician. Sought to reconcile Aristotelian thought with Islam. Known also in the West for his Canon of Medicine.

Avignon (ävēnyō'), city (pop. 72,717), cap. of Vaucluse dept., SE France, in Provence. Wine trade, silk mfg. See of popes during "Babylonian captivity," 1309–78, and of several antipopes during Great Schism, 1378–1408. City was bought (1348) by Clement VI from countess of Provence; remained papal property until annexed by France (1791). Landmarks: 14th-cent. papal palace, Basilica of St. Peter, fragment of 12th-cent. bridge.

Ávila, Gil González de: see GONZÁLEZ DE ÁVILA.

Ávila (ä'vēlä), town (pop. 26,809), cap. of Ávila prov., central Spain, in Old Castile; birthplace of St. Theresa. Medieval walls; cathedral.

Ávila Camacho, Manuel (mänwĕl' ä'vēlä kämä'chō), 1897–1955, president of Mexico (1940–46).

Aviz, Port. Avis (both: ŭvēsh'), village, central Portugal. Granted (c.1162) to branch of Knights of Calatrava, which became the separate Order of Aviz. Mas-

ter of order became King John I of Portugal, establishing dynasty of Aviz (1383–1580).

Avoca or **Ovoca** (both: ŭvō'kŭ), river of Co. Wicklow, Ireland, formed by union of Avonmore R. and Avonbeg R. (Thomas Moore's "Meeting of the Waters").

avocado (äv"ŭkä'dō), broad-leaved evergreen tree (Persea), grown in Calif. and Fla. for pear-shaped, oil-rich fruit (alligator pear) often used in salads. Called in Spanish aguacate.

avocet (ăv'ŭsĕt), wading bird with long legs, webbed feet, slender upward-curving bill. It is related to snipe and stilt. North and South America, Europe, and Australia each have one species. North American "blue shanks," hunted for food, are rare E of Mississippi.

Avogadro, Amadeo (ämädä'ō ävōgä'drō), 1776–1856, Italian physicist, a count. Avogadro's law: equal volumes of gases under same pressure and temperature have same number of molecules. Avogadro's number (6.02×10^{23}): number of molecules in gram molecular volume of gas.

Avon (ä'vŭn, äv'ŭn) [Celtic,= river], name of several rivers in England. **1 Bristol Avon** or **Lower Avon** rises in Gloucestershire and flows 75 mi. through Wiltshire and Somerset, past Bath and Bristol, to the Severn. **2 East Avon,** in Wiltshire and Hampshire, flows 48 mi. past Salisbury to the English Channel. **3 Upper Avon,** in Northamptonshire, Leicestershire, Warwickshire, and Worcestershire is most famous. Flows 96 mi. past Rugby, Warwick, and Stratford-on-Avon to the Severn.

Awolowo, Obafemi (ôbä'fämē äwōōl"ōwō'), 1909–, Nigerian statesman, a Yoruba chief. Politically active in 1940s, he founded Action Group, a new political party, in 1950. Minister of local government for the Western Region (1952–54), he became its first premier (1954). Elected to house of representatives of Nigeria 1959, where he became leader of opposition. Placed under restriction in political unrest in 1962; freed later in year after military coup.

Axel: see ABSALON.

Axis, coalition of states headed by Germany, Italy, and Japan, 1936–45, in Second World War. Original Italo-German accord of 1936 became full alliance 1939 and was acceded to by Japan in Berlin Pact of 1940, to which Hungary, Rumania, Bulgaria, Slovakia, and Croatia adhered later. The related Anti-Comintern Pact of 1936 (see COMINTERN), between Germany and Japan, later included Berlin Pact nations, Spain, Finland, and others.

Axminster, rural district (pop. 14,350), Devonshire, England. Its famous carpets now made at Wilton.

Axum, Ethiopia: see AKSUM.

Ayacucho (äyäkōō'chō), city (pop. 22,000), S Peru. Defeat of Spanish by Sucre here (1824) secured Peruvian independence, marked triumph of revolution in South America and guaranteed independence from Spain.

Ayala, Ramón Pérez de: see PÉREZ DE AYALA.

Aydelotte, Frank (ā'dŭlŏt), 1880–1956, American educator. Was president of Swarthmore Col. 1921–40, director of Inst. for Advanced Study at Princeton 1939–47.

Ayer, Alfred Jules, 1910–, British philosopher. His Language, Truth, and Logic (1936) helped found school of LOGICAL POSITIVISM. Other works include The Foundations of Empirical Knowledge (1940) and Philosophy and Language (1960).

Ayer (âr), town (pop. 14,927), N Mass., E of Fitchburg; settled before 1670. U.S. Fort Devens is near.

Ayesha (Aisha) (ī'shù, ä'ïshä"), d. 678, Mohammed's favorite wife; Abu Bakr's daughter. Fomented unsuccessful revolt during caliphate of ALI.

Aylesbury (ālz'bûrē), county town (pop. 27,891) of Buckinghamshire, England; agr. market and industrial center for upper Thames valley; famed for its ducks.

Aymara (īmärä'), South American Indians inhabiting L. Titicaca basin. Although subjugated by the Inca in 15th cent. and by Pizarro brothers (1538), they continue to dominate region.

Aymé, Marcel (märsĕl' ämä'), 1902–, French writer of satirical and humorous novels.

Aymer of Valence (ā'mŭr, vŭlĕns', vălăs'), d. 1260, bishop of Winchester. Half brother of King Henry III of England, he was elected at the king's order. Hostility towards him important factor in BARONS' WAR.

Ayodhya, India: see FYZABAD.

Ayolas, Juan de (hwän'dä äyō'läs), d. 1537?, Spanish conquistador, explorer of Río de la Plata region (esp. Paraguay); lieutenant of Pedro de MENDOZA.

Ayrshire (âr'shĭr) or **Ayr**, maritime county (1,132 sq. mi.; pop. 342,855), SW Scotland. N Ayrshire has iron and oil deposits, varied industry. S and central Ayrshire is agr.; Ayr cows are famous. Country of Robert Bruce and Burns. The county town, **Ayr** (âr), burgh (pop. 45,297), on the Firth of Clyde, is heart of the Burns country and has Burns memorials.

Ayub Khan, Mohammad (mŭhä'mĭd ä'yŏ̄b kän), 1907–, president of Pakistan. Served as defense minister 1954–56, became president after coup d'état in 1958; confirmed in office 1960. Instituted land reforms and fought corruption. In 1962 new constitution was promulgated, and martial law ended.

Ayuthia or **Ayutthaya** (both: äyŏ̄ot'hĭä), town (pop. 33,187), S Thailand, on Menam R.; trade center. Was Siamese cap. (c.1350–1767).

azalea: see RHODODENDRON.

Azaña, Manuel (mänwäl' äthä'nyä), 1880–1940, Spanish republican statesman. As premier (1931–33, 1936), he pressed for social reforms. President of Spain 1936–39. Fled to France near end of Civil War.

Azariah (ăzŭrī'ŭ), one of THREE HOLY CHILDREN. Greek form is Azarias.

Azerbaijan (ä"zŭrbījän'), region and former province (41,160 sq. mi.), extreme NW Iran. Aras R. in N separates it from Azerbaijan SSR. Mainly mountainous with fertile lowlands yielding grain and fruit. Chief city is TABRIZ. In remote times region was dominated by kings of Van and Uratu (in Armenia). Settled by Medes before 8th cent. B.C.; became a province in Persian empire. Supposedly birthplace of Zoroaster. Persian Atropates estab. himself as independent king here after 328 B.C. Region again became part of Persia in 3d cent. A.D. Converted to Islam in 7th cent. by Arabs, who brought it under caliphate. Dominated by Seljuk Turks 11th–12th cent., conquered in 14th cent. by Tamerlane. Ruled by shahs from early 17th to early 19th cent., when N part was ceded to Russia. Remainder was organized as a Persian province, which was divided 1938 into Third and Fourth provs. In 1941 Soviet troops occupied the region, withdrawing after a Soviet-supported autonomous local government had been estab. Separatist movement suppressed in 1946.

Azerbaijan (ä"sŭrbījän'), constituent republic (33,436 sq. mi.; 1965 est. pop. 4,590,000), USSR, bordering Iranian Azerbaijan in E; cap. BAKU. Includes E ranges of Greater and Lesser Caucasus; hot, arid Kura valley; subtropical Lenkoran lowland and oil-rich Apsheron peninsula on Caspian coast. Chief products: oil, cotton, grapes, tea, fruit, tobacco. Sheep raising in mountains. Population largely Turkic Azers or Azerbaijani-Shiite Moslems of Persian culture. Region ceded by Persia to Russia (1813, 1828). For earlier history, see preceding article.

Azikiwe, Benjamin Nnamdi (nämdē' äzēkē'ōōä"), 1904–, Nigerian statesman; educated in U.S. Premier of E Nigeria 1954–59. Appointed governor-general of Federation of Nigeria 1960, named president of Republic of Nigeria 1963. An educator and journalist, he has written on economics, anthropology, history, and politics.

Azores (ŭzôrz', ā'zôrz), Port. *Açores* (ŭsô'rĭsh), islands (888 sq. mi.; pop. 327,480), in N Atlantic, administratively part of Portugal. São Miguel is largest island. Chief cities: Ponta Delgada (on São Miguel), Angra do Heroísmo (Terceira isl.), Horta (Fayal isl.). Products: grain, fruit, wine. Islands were known by 1351; colonized by Portuguese in 1445.

Azorín: see MARTÍNEZ RUIZ, JOSÉ.

Azov (ā'zŏv, Rus. ŭzôf'), city (pop. 39,800), S European RSFSR; fishing port near mouth of Don and Sea of Azov. Strategic fortress until late 18th cent. Peter the Great took it from khan of Crimea 1696, had to return it 1711. Definitively secured by Russia 1774. Ancient Greek colony of Tanais was near by. The **Sea of Azov**, Latin *Palus Maeotis*, is a N arm (c.14,000 sq. mi.) of the Black Sea, with which it is connected by the Kerch Strait. Fed by the Don and Kuban, it has important fisheries. Rostov-on-Don, Taganrog, Kerch are chief ports. SIVASH SEA is a W branch.

Aztec (ăz'tĕk"), Indian people dominating central Mexico at time of Spanish Conquest. Arrived in Valley of Mexico from N in 12th cent.; nomadic until founding of their cap., TENOCHTITLÁN (c.1325; present Mexico city). Created a composite civilization based on TOLTEC and Mixteca-Puebla heritage. Among their accomplishments were a stone wheel or calendar stone, weaving, sculpture, engineering, metalwork, music, picture writing. Agr. well advanced; education almost universal. Political and social life based on caste system (nobility; priesthood; military and merchant). Civilization fell before Spanish under Hernán CORTÉS. See also MONTEZUMA; CUAUHTÉMOC.

Aztec Ruins National Monument: see NATIONAL PARKS AND MONUMENTS (table).

Azuela, Mariano (märyä'nō äswä'lä), 1873–1952, Mexican novelist. Experiences with Villa's revolutionary forces gave material for *Los de abajo* (1915).

azurite (äzh'ŭrīt), mineral, the blue basic carbonate of copper, an important copper ore. Occurs in monoclinic crystals and in masses. Crystals used for ornament are found in SW U.S. and in France.

Azusa (ŭzōō'sŭ), city (pop. 20,497), S Calif., E of Pasadena, in San Gabriel valley; founded 1887. Shipping and industrial center in citrus-fruit area.

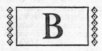

B

B, chemical symbol of element BORON.

Ba, chemical symbol of element BARIUM.

Baade, Walter, 1893–1960, German astronomer. He devised two categories for stars, population I (young) and population II (old), according to their evolutionary patterns. His calculations led to doubling of cosmic-distance scale, i.e., distance between extragalactic bodies.

Baal (bā'ŭl), plural **Baalim** (bā'ŭlĭm [Semitic,= possessor], term used in Old Testament for gods or god of Canaan. Term originally used for local gods, e.g., Baal-peor [Heb.,= Baal of Peor], but later Baal became chief deity, the source of life and fertility. Fertility rites and human sacrifice at high places were part of worship. Cult practice in Israel, but as Hebrew monotheism grew, was denounced and its temples and high places were destroyed. Synonymous with evil—hence Beelzebub (see SATAN). Other forms of Baal: Bel (in Babylonian religion); endings in Tyrian names (e.g., Jezebel, Hannibal).

Baalbek (bäl'bĕk), town, Lebanon, N of Damascus. Has ruins of great ancient city devoted to worship of Baal or Bel, the sun-god, hence called in Greek Heliopolis [city of the sun]; notable in Roman days.

Baal-peor (-pē'ôr), local god of Peor. Practices of his worship were especially abominable to the Hebrews, hence his name became a symbol of all shameful cults. Num. 25; Deut. 4.3; Ps. 106.28; Hosea 9.10. Under form of Belphegor, this was name of a devil in Middle Ages; Machiavelli used it in his *Belfagor.*

Baal-Shem-Tov (bäl-shĕm'-tōv') [Heb.,= he who has the power of invoking the miraculous name of Deity], 1699–1760, b. Russia; real name Israel ben Eliezer. Charismatic leader of the HASIDIM. Taught that religion consists of joy and sincerity, with prayerful activity making possible a mystical bond between man and God, even for the unlearned.

Baal-zebub: see BAAL and SATAN.

Baarle-Hertog, Belgium: see BAERLE-DUC.

Baasha (bā'äshŭ), d. c.886 B.C., king of Israel (c.909–c.886 B.C.). Murdered Nadab and royal family to make himself king. 1 Kings 15.27–16.7; 2 Chron. 16.

Babar: see BABER.

Babbitt, Irving, 1865–1933, American teacher, vigorous critic of romanticism, a stanch advocate of new "humanism" based on classical traditions.

Babbitt metal, silver-white ANTIFRICTION METAL alloy, originally of tin, antimony, and copper, later also of varying composition. Developed by Isaac Babbitt (1799–1862), American inventor.

Babcock, Stephen Moulton, 1843–1931, American agr. chemist. Babcock test (1890) for percentage of butterfat in milk advanced the dairy industry.

Babel, Isaac Emmanuelovich (ē'säk ŭmänōōä'lŭvĭch bä'bŭl), 1894–1941, Russian author, one of the "fellow travelers," famed for his concise, realistic stories of the ghetto and the revolution, notably *Odessa Tales* (1923–24), *Red Cavalry* (1926; Eng. tr., 1929), *Benya Krik* (1927; Eng. tr., 1935).

Babel (bā'bŭl), city where Noah's descendants (who spoke one language) tried to build tower to heaven. For this presumption they lost ability to speak intelligibly to each other. Gen. 11.1–9. Some see in this an explanation of world's many languages.

Baber or Babar (both: bä'bùr), popular name of Zahir-ed-din Mohammed, c.1482–1530, founder of MOGUL empire of India; descendant of Tamerlane. Invaded India from Afghanistan, conquering nearly all N India (1525–26). Was a distinguished poet and cultured monarch; his autobiography is greatest of his literary works.

Babeuf, François Noël (fräswä' nôĕl' bäbŭf'), 1760–97, French revolutionist. Argued for economic and social as well as political equality. After brief imprisonment he formed a group to forward economic equality and communism. After the Directory banned the group, a plot (the Conspiracy of the Equals) was made to overthrow the government. It was betrayed, and Babeuf was executed. A political socialist, he is often considered a forerunner of Karl Marx.

Babington, Anthony (bä'bĭngtùn), 1561–86, English conspirator. Plotted murder of Queen Elizabeth and freeing of MARY QUEEN OF SCOTS. Proof against him was used to bring about Mary's execution.

Babism (bä'bĭzùm), religion of 19th-cent. Persian sect, founded 1844, when Mirza Ali Mohammed of Shiraz was proclaimed Bab ed-Din (gate of faith), successor to Moses, Christ, and Mohammed. Doctrines from Sufism, Gnosticism, Shiite Islam. The sect rebelled unsuccessfully 1848; the Bab was executed 1850. Babism supplanted by Bahaism.

Babits, Michael (bô'bĭch), Hung. *Babits Mihály,* 1883–1941, Hungarian writer and editor of influential literary weekly, *Nyugat.*

baboon, large, chiefly terrestrial monkey (genus *Papio*) of Africa, Arabia. Face doglike, canine teeth large, limbs powerful; medium tail is carried arched. Travels in packs; eats scorpions, insects, other animals, plant food. Most are yellowish or brown. MANDRILL and chacma are large baboons.

Babson, Roger Ward, 1875–1967, American statistician. Founded Babson Statistical Organization (1904), which publishes business statistics. Founded Babson Institute (1919) to train business executives.

baby: see INFANT.

Babylon (bä'bĭlùn), city of anc. Mesopotamia, on the Euphrates; center of Babylonia. HAMMURABI founded its greatness, which was destroyed by SENNACHERIB but revived in later period. Under NEBUCHADNEZZAR (d. 562 B.C.) it reached a height of luxury that made it fabulous; its Hanging Gardens were considered one of the wonders of the world. After capture by Persians (538 B.C.) it declined.

Babylon, residential and resort village (1964 pop. 12,-299), SE N.Y., on Long Isl., on Great South Bay ESE of Hempstead. Popular surfing area.

Babylonia (bäbĭlō'nēù), anc. Mesopotamian empire, centered on Babylon. Name sometimes used to include all S Mesopotamia with city-states (Lagash, Akkad, Erech, Ur) that flourished 3d millennium B.C. Historically limited to first dynasty of BABYLON estab. by HAMMURABI (c.1750 B.C.) and to Neo-Babylonian era after fall of Assyrian Empire (612 B.C.). Learning (cuneiform writing derived from Sumerian), commerce, architecture flourished. At-

SMALL CAPITALS = cross references. Pronunciation key on inside end pages. Abbreviations: p. 2.

77

Babylonian captivity 78 bacteria

tacks by Hittites and nomadic Kassites (17th cent. B.C.) caused decline, but Babylonia again flowered under the Assyrian empire. A revolt was put down by SENNACHERIB (c.689 B.C.), but afterward Nabopolassar estab. (625 B.C.) Babylonian independence, and the empire grew to new and greater splendor under NEBUCHADNEZZAR. After conquest by Persians under Cyrus the Great (538 B.C.) Babylonia declined. Its contributions to art, science, and other aspects of civilization were incalculable.

Babylonian captivity: see CAPTIVITY and PAPACY.

Babylonian religion. The religion of the whole Tigris-Euphrates valley was really one, with many local gods. Dominant gods were determined by dominant cities (e.g., when Babylon was paramount, Marduk, or Bel or BAAL, was king of gods). Priests were very powerful. The rich mythology of Babylon, further elaborated by Assyria, was preserved in cuneiform writing on clay tablets. It included stories of creation of world, of flood covering whole world, journey of Ishtar to underworld, and legends of gods and heroes. Babylon was indebted to Sumerian culture for its religion, and its great towers (suggesting BABEL) were reminiscent of Sumerian worship of high places.

baby's-breath, garden perennial, *Gypsophila paniculata,* marked by delicate panicles of small white blooms.

Bacchae (bắkē) or Bacchantes (bŭkăn'tēz, bŭkănts', bắkŭnts), in Greek and Roman religion, female worshipers of DIONYSUS or BACCHUS. Their secret rites, performed in frenzied ecstasy, involved the thyrsus, the myrtle, drinking, and sweet wild music. Also called Maenads.

Bacchanalia (băkŭnā'lēŭ) [Latin], in Roman religion, festival in honor of BACCHUS. Originally religious, it became a drunken orgy and was outlawed.

Bacchantes: see BACCHAE.

Bacchus (bă'kŭs), in Greek and Roman mythology, god of wine, identified with DIONYSUS; also god of vegetation and fertility. His rites were orgiastic.

Bacchylides (băkī'lĭdēz), fl. c.470 B.C., Greek lyric poet, b. Ceos; contemporary of Pindar.

Baccio; see BANDINELLI, BARTOLOMEO.

Bach (bäkh), German family of distinguished musicians beginning with **Hans Bach,** c.1580–1626, a Thuringian violinist who was called The Player. Two of his grandsons were **Johann Christoph Bach,** 1642–1703, a composer and organist at Eisenach, and **Johann Ambrosius Bach,** 1645–95, a violinist at Eisenach and father of Johann Sebastian Bach (see separate article). One of his grandsons, **Wilhelm Friedemann Bach** (frē'dümän), 1710–84, was an organist, composer, and musical director at Halle.

Bach, Alexander, 1813–93, Austrian statesman; created baron 1854. Minister of interior 1849–59. Instituted reactionary "Bach system" of bureaucratic control, centralization, and Germanization of Hapsburg empire, along with beneficial reforms, e.g., abolition of internal tariff barriers.

Bach, Johann Sebastian, 1685–1750, German composer, b. Eisenach. Became organist at Arnstadt (1703) and at Mülhausen (1707); court organist and chamber musician at Weimar (1708), musical director (1714); musical director at Cöthen (1717); cantor at Leipzig (1723) until his death. Few of Bach's works were published during his lifetime, hence exact dates cannot be fixed for all of them, but most of them can be placed in their proper period. At Arnstadt and Mülhausen he began a series of organ works which culminated in the great works of Weimar period—the Passacaglia and Fugue in C minor, most of the noted preludes and fugues, the 45 chorale-preludes of *Das Orgelbüchlein.* At Cöthen he produced instrumental works, e.g., the English and French Suites, the Two-Part and Three-Part Inventions, *The Well-Tempered Clavier,* Book I, the unaccompanied violin sonatas, and the Brandenburg concertos. Great works of the Leipzig period include the St. John Passion, the Magnificat, the St. Matthew Passion, the Mass in B Minor,

The Well-Tempered Clavier, Book II, and the *Clavierübung* (including the Six Partitas, the Italian Concerto, and the Goldberg variations). His last work was *The Art of the Fugue* (1749). Despite his many secular compositions, Bach is regarded primarily as a church composer.

Bache, Benjamin Franklin (bäch), 1769–98, American journalist; grandson of Benjamin Franklin. Founded Philadelphia *General Advertiser* (later the *Aurora*) in 1790. Denounced Federalists; arrested under Sedition Act; released on parole. His son, **Franklin Bache,** 1792–1864, physician and chemist, prepared (with G. B. Wood) the first 11 editions of *The Dispensatory of the United States* (1st ed., 1833). His cousin, **Alexander Dallas Bache,** 1806–67, was an educator and physicist. He influenced development of free education in Philadelphia. Estab. (1839) first magnetic observatory in North America; reorganized U.S. Coast Survey; founded Natl. Acad. of Sciences.

Bache, Jules Semon, 1861–1944, American financier and art collector. His collection, which includes works by Raphael and Titian, is in the Metropolitan Mus.

bachelor's button: see CORNFLOWER.

Baciccio, Il: see GAULLI, GIOVANNI BATTISTA.

bacillus: see BACTERIA.

Back, Sir George, 1796–1878, British explorer in N Canada. Explored Great Fish R. (now Back R.) in Northwest Territories (1833–35). Explored the arctic coast of Canada (1836–37).

backbone: see SPINAL COLUMN.

Backbone Mountain, peak, 3,360 ft. high, NW Md., in Alleghenies; highest elevation in state.

Bacon, Delia Salter: see BACON, LEONARD.

Bacon, Francis, 1561–1626, English philosopher and statesman. Advanced slowly under Elizabeth but swiftly under James I from knight (1603) to lord chancellor (1621). Pleaded guilty 1621 to accepting bribes, was barred from office, and spent the rest of his life in retirement. His shrewd, concentrated *Essays* (1597) are his most popular works. Inductive method of modern experimental science was his tremendous contribution to philosophy. Of his projected reorganization of all human knowledge, *Instauratio Magna,* he completed two parts, *The Advancement of Learning* (1605; expanded as *De Augmentis Scientiarum,* 1623) and *Novum Organum* (1620). *The New Atlantis* (1627) describes a utopia based on scientific principles.

Bacon, Leonard, 1802–81, American Congregational minister, pastor for 41 years of First Church of New Haven, and noted antislavery leader. His sister, **Delia Salter Bacon,** 1811–59, was an author. She held that Shakespeare's plays were written by group including Francis Bacon.

Bacon, Nathaniel, 1647–76, leader of Bacon's Rebellion, 1676, popular revolt in colonial Va. Uprising precipitated by failure of governor, Sir William BERKELEY, to defend frontier against Indian attacks. Rebellion collapsed after Bacon's death.

Bacon, Roger, c.1214–1294?, English scholastic philosopher, a Franciscan, called the Admirable Doctor. A learned teacher at Oxford, he pugnaciously entered into many quarrels with other learned men and was in constant trouble. In modern times Friar Bacon has been celebrated chiefly for his interest in natural science, experiments, and direct observation. He considered science as complementary to, not opposed to, faith. His best-known works are the *Opus majus, Opus minor,* and *Opus tertium.* Because he wrote works on alchemy, many others on alchemy and magic have been attributed to him. The claim that he invented gunpowder is false, and the idea that he had a telescope or microscope is highly improbable.

Bacon's Rebellion: see BACON, NATHANIEL.

bacteria, minute unicellular organisms, usually classified as plants (class Schizomycetes) of division of thallophytes called fungi. Sometimes classified with blue-green algae as separate division of plant kingdom.

SMALL CAPITALS = cross references. Pronunciation key on inside end pages. Abbreviations: p. 2.

Rod-shaped (bacillus), round (coccus), spiral (spirillum) are typical forms; range from c.½₂₅₀,₀₀₀ in. to ½₂₅₀ in. long; reproduce chiefly by transverse fission. When conditions do not favor growth and multiplication, some bacteria produce resistant spores. Aerobic bacteria need free oxygen, anaerobic do not. Parasitic (or pathogenic) bacteria cause such diseases as tuberculosis, diphtheria, cholera, typhoid fever, pneumonia, tetanus, gangrene, anthrax, tularemia. Some bacteria attack tissues directly; some produce poisonous toxins. Vaccination induces immunity to some diseases. Useful bacteria outnumber harmful; NITROGEN-FIXING BACTERIA and NITRIFYING BACTERIA help enrich soil, as do decay bacteria. See *ill.*, p. 116.

bacteriophage (băk'tĕr'ē̇ûfāj), ultramicroscopic particle destructive to bacteria; much simpler than cell; similar to virus and gene. Composed of nucleic acid and protein. Can be seen in electron microscope. One particle infects bacterial cell; it disarranges cell metabolism, causing cell to produce bacteriophage particles instead of normal cell contents; eventually, cell splits open, releasing many new bacteriophage particles. Several bacteriophages recognized; each acts only on specific bacteria. Also called phage.

Bactria (băk'trĕû), ancient Greek kingdom of central Asia (now N Afghanistan and E Iran); cap. was Bactra (modern BALKH). As satrapy of Persian Empire, it was taken 328 B.C. by Alexander the Great. Later under Seleucidae. Declared independence in 240 B.C. and became powerful Greco-Bactrian state. Fell c.130 B.C. to nomadic Sakas.

Badajoz (bädhähôth'), city (pop. 102,882), cap. of Badajoz prov., W Spain, in Estremadura, on Guadiana R. Seat of a Moorish emirate (1022–94), reconquered by the Christians 1228. In Peninsular War it resisted French siege (1808–9), fell to French 1811, was liberated by Wellington 1812. Large 13th-cent. cathedral; ruins of Moorish citadel.

Badakhshan, USSR: see MOUNTAIN-BADAKHSHAN.

Badalona (bädhälō'nä), city (pop. 112,179), Barcelona prov., NE Spain, in Catalonia. Mediterranean port and industrial suburb of Barcelona. Nearby are anc. tombs and 15th-cent. monastery.

Bad Axe, river of SW Wis. flowing SW to Mississippi R. nearly opposite Minn.-Iowa line. Near its mouth Black Hawk was defeated (1832).

Bad Ems, Germany: see EMS.

Baden (bä'dùn), former German state, SW Germany, on right bank of the Rhine from the Main to Lake Constance; former cap. Karlsruhe. Divided after Second World War, between French-occupied state of Baden and American-occupied state of Württemberg-Baden; in 1952 it became part of new state of BADEN-WÜRTTEMBERG. Landscape, esp. NECKAR valley and BLACK FOREST, is famed for its beauty. Agr., wine growing; industries in N. Until French Revolution Baden had no political unity, consisting of several petty margraviates; the bishoprics of Mainz, Speyer, Strasbourg, and Constance; the Mannheim-Heidelberg dists. of Rhenish PALATINATE; and the BREISGAU, under Hapsburg rule. In 1771 the margraviates of Baden-Baden and Baden-Durlach were united under the same branch of the old house of ZÄHRINGEN. Margrave Charles Frederick, an ally of Napoleon, was raised to grand duke (1806) and by 1810 had acquired the entire state. Prussian troops helped to suppress Revolution of 1848. Baden sided with Austria in Austro-Prussian War (1886); joined German Empire 1871; became republic 1918.

Baden or **Baden-bei-Wien** (–bī-vĕn), city (est. pop. 22,000), Lower Austria. Hot sulfur springs; resort.

Baden, town (pop. 13,949), Aargau, N Switzerland, on the Limmat. Noted for sulfur baths since antiquity. Meeting place of Swiss diet 1424–1712. For treaty signed here 1714, see UTRECHT, PEACE OF.

Baden-Baden, city (pop. 39,764), Baden-Württemberg, West Germany, in Black Forest. Fashionable spa.

Baden-bei-Wien: see BADEN, Lower Austria.

Baden-Powell of Gilwell, Robert Stephenson Smyth Baden-Powell, 1st Baron (bā'dùn-pōul), 1857–1941, British soldier, founder (1908) of the Boy Scouts.

Baden-Württemberg (bäd'ún-vûrt'ùmbĕrk), state (13,-803 sq. mi.; est. pop. 7,726,900), West Germany, bordering on France (S) and on Switzerland (W); cap. Stuttgart. State came into existence 1952 by merger of former states of Baden and Württemberg and the prov. of Hohenzollern.

badger, carnivorous mammal of family Mustelidae. Broad, heavy body; rather long snout; sharp claws; shaggy fur, usually gray and brownish with black and white markings. Include *Meles* of Europe and Asia; *Taxidea* of America; ferret badger (*Helictis*) and sand or hog badger (*Arctonyx*) of Asia.

Bad Godesberg (bät' gôdùsbĕrk), town (pop. 57,442), North Rhine-Westphalia, West Germany, on the Rhine. Resort famous for radioactive mineral springs. Scene of meeting between Hitler and Neville Chamberlain in 1938 (see MUNICH PACT).

Bad Homburg: see HOMBURG.

Bad Ischl, Austria: see ISCHL.

Badlands, arid plateau, c.120 mi. long and 30–50 mi. wide, SW S.Dak., E of the Black Hills. Has fantastic scenery and deposits of prehistoric fossils. The Badlands Natl. Monument occupies part of region.

badminton (băd'mĭntùn), game played by two or four persons, in which a shuttlecock–small, cork hemisphere with feathers attached–is volleyed over a net. Light, gut-string rackets are used. Probably originated in India. Popular in England in 1870s, taking name from seat of duke of Beaufort.

Bad Nauheim (bät nou'hĭm), town (pop. 13,062), Hesse, West Germany, in Taunus Mts. World-famous health resort for heart diseases.

Badoglio, Pietro (pyä'trō bädō'lyō), 1871–1956, Italian field marshal. Conquered Ethiopia (1935–36); succeeded Mussolini as premier (1943–44); signed armistice with Allies (1943).

Bad Pyrmont, Germany: see PYRMONT.

Baduila, king of Ostrogoths: see TOTILA.

Baeck, Leo, 1873–1956, German rabbi and philosopher of religion, b. Prussia, d. London. Spokesman of Jews in Germany during Hitler regime. Expositor of philosophical foundations of the Jewish religion in his *Essence of Judaism* (1923).

Baeda: see BEDE.

Baedeker, Karl (bā'dùkùr), 1801–59, German publisher, founder of Baedeker guidebooks.

Baekeland, Lee Hendrik (bāk'länd), 1863–1944, American chemist, b. Belgium. Invented and manufactured photographic paper, rights to which he sold to Eastman 1899. Invented BAKELITE.

Baer, Karl Ernst von, 1792–1876, Estonian biologist. Considered a founder of modern embryology. He discovered mammalian ovum in 1827 and originated theory of embryonic germ layers.

Baerle-Duc (bärlù-dük'), Flemish *Baarle-Hertog*, town Antwerp prov., NE Belgium. A possession since 1479, now an enclave in S Netherlands. The sovereignty of outlying districts disputed by Dutch was settled (1959) in favor of Belgium by Internatl. Court of Justice.

Baeyer, Adolf von (ä'dôlf fün bā'yùr), 1835–1917, German chemist. Won 1905 Nobel Prize in Chemistry for work on organic dyes and hydrocarbon ring formation. Discovered molecular structure of indigo.

Baffin, William, c.1584–1622, British arctic explorer. Failed to find Northwest Passage but discovered Baffin Bay and Baffin Isl.

Baffin Bay, arm of Arctic Ocean between Greenland and Arctic Archipelago. Connects with the Arctic by Smith Sound and with the Atlantic by Davis Strait. Labrador Current brings many icebergs, making navigation hazardous. Site of U.S. military bases.

Baffin Island, 197,754 sq. mi., largest and most easterly of Arctic Archipelago, Franklin dist., Northwest Territories, Canada, in Arctic Ocean opposite W

Greenland. It is geographically a N continuation of Labrador, separated from mainland by Hudson Strait. Interior has fresh-water lakes; mountains in E. Population largely Eskimo. Trading and Royal Canadian Mounted Police posts. First visited by Frobisher 1576–78.

Bagdad, Iraq: see BAGHDAD.

Bagehot, Walter (bǎj'ǔt), 1826–77, English social scientist and critic. Among his books are *The English Constitution* (1867), *Lombard Street* (1873; on banking), *Physics and Politics* (1875; pioneer analysis of relations of natural and social sciences), and *Literary Studies* (1879). He was editor of *Economist* 1860–77.

Baghdad or **Bagdad** (both: bǎg'dǎd, bägdäd'), city (pop. 656,399), cap. of Iraq, on the Tigris and 25 mi. N of the Euphrates. From Sumerian times site was center for desert travel and trade. Founded A.D. 763 by MANSUR, city became great commercial center, reaching its height under HARUN-AL-RASHID. Its glory is reflected in many tales of *Thousand and One Nights*. City declined after Harun's death and temporary removal of caliphate to Samarra. Sacked by Mongols (1258) and destroyed by Tamerlane (1400) and by Ismail (1524). Later fell prey to warring Turks and Persians. By 1638, when it became part of Ottoman Empire, city had only c.14,000 people. Few antiquities remain, but city is still partly enclosed by ancient wall. Captured 1917 by British forces. Became cap. of Iraq 1920. City is major shipping point, a rail and air terminus.

Baghdad Pact: see CENTRAL TREATY ORGANIZATION.

Baghdad Railway, connecting Haidarpasha (opposite Istanbul), Turkey, with Basra, Iraq. Branch lines to N Iran, USSR, Israel, Lebanon, and Syria. Begun with German capital (1896), it aroused protests of England (which saw in it a threat to its Indian Empire) and others. Work was suspended and then resumed (1911) when the line became a factor leading to First World War. Last link between Mosul and Samarra completed 1940 with British funds.

Bagnell Dam, central Mo., on Osage R., SW of Jefferson City; built 1929–31. One of state's largest power dams (148 ft. high; 2,543 ft. long), it also forms L. of the OZARKS.

bagpipe, musical instrument of anc. origin. Called the musette in 18th-cent. France. Now chiefly associated with Scotland. Consists of a leathern bag with either bellows or tube to inflate it: chanters or chaunters (melody pipes having finger holes); and drones, each of which produces one sustained tone.

Bagration, Piotr Ivanovich, Prince (pyô'tǔr ēvä'nǔvĭch bägrätēŏn'), 1765–1812, Russian general. Commanded an army at BORODINO; mortally wounded.

Bagrationovsk, RSFSR: see EYLAU.

Baguio (bä'gēō), resort city (pop. 35,177; alt. c.5,000 ft.), NW Luzon, the Philippines. Summer cap. of the republic and a gold-mining center.

bagworm, larva of certain moth family species destructive to forest and shade trees in E U.S. Growing larva travels in silken covering; passes pupa stage in this bag (sometimes leaf-covered) fastened to twig. Adult female emerges partly, male fertilizes eggs. Female lays eggs inside bag; then dies.

Bahaism (bä'hä'izǔm bǔnä'–), religion founded 1863, when Baha Ullah (a Persian originally named Mirza Hussein Ali), announced himself prophet succeeding the Bab (see BABISM). Bahaists believe in simple living, universal education, unity of all religions, world peace, equality of men and women. Religion spread in 20th cent. (U.S. center Wilmette, Ill.; administrative center of world faith Haifa, Israel).

Bahama Islands or **Bahamas** (bǔhä'mǔz), archipelago (c.5,400 sq. mi.; 1962 est. pop. 138,749), c.700 islands and islets, beginning c.50 mi. off SE Florida, extending c.600 mi. SE almost to Haiti. Governed as British crown colony; cap. NASSAU on New Providence Isl. Winter resort. Spanish visited islands, but English settled them in 17th cent. and imported

Negroes. Islands were haunt of pirates (17th–18th cent.), notably Blackbeard; of blockade runners in Civil War; of rum runners during prohibition era in U.S. Used as U.S. military bases in Second World War.

Bahawalpur (bǔhä'wǔlpoōr"), city (pop. c.84,000), cap. of Bahawalpur division, West Pakistan. Was cap. of the princely state of Bahawalpur; acceded to Pakistan in 1947. Commercial center.

Bahia or **Baía** (both: bäē'ǔ), state (c.216,000 sq. mi.; pop. 5,990,600), E Brazil; cap. SALVADOR, port on Todos os Santos Bay, once chief city of Brazil. SE Bahia is one of great cacao-growing regions of world. State also produces sugar, oil, and minerals.

Bahía Blanca (bäē'ä bläng'kä), city (pop. 115,000), SE Argentina, Atlantic port. Offers access to S Pampa, oilfields of Neuquén, Patagonian lakes.

Bahrein Islands (bärän'), archipelago (c.200 sq. mi.; pop. 143,213), off Arabia, in Persian Gulf. Ruled by Arab sheik; under British protection since 1861. Claimed by Iran. Important for oil production since 1932. Chief port and cap. is Manamah.

Bahr-el-Abiad: see WHITE NILE.

Bahr-el-Azraq: see BLUE NILE.

Bahr-el-Ghazal (bär'-ĕl-gäzäl'), region, SW Republic of the Sudan. Disputed by Mahdist and Anglo-Egyptian forces in 19th cent. Bahr-el-Ghazal R., c.145 mi. long, flows E to the Bahr-el-Jebel to form WHITE NILE.

Bahr el-Huleh (bär' ĕl-hoō'lä), lake, NE Palestine. Jordan R. headwaters flow through it. May be same as Waters of Merom (site of great victory). Joshua 11.

Bahr-el-Jebel (–jĕ'bĕl), river, section of WHITE NILE, S Republic of the Sudan. Flows from border of Uganda, where it is known ae the Albert Nile, c.594 mi. N to join the Bahr-el-Ghazal and form the White Nile.

Baía, Brazil: see BAHIA.

Baia (bī'ä), Latin *Baiae*, village, Campania, S Italy, on Bay of Naples. Celebrated resort in ancient times. Remains of Roman baths.

Baikal (bīkäl'), lake, area 12,162 sq. mi.; RSFSR, in SE Siberia; largest fresh-water lake of Asia, deepest lake in world (5,710 ft.).

Baikie, William Balfour (bä'kē), 1825–64, Scottish explorer in W Africa, a philologist. Opened Niger R. to trade and translated Scriptures into Hausa.

Baikonur, town (est. pop. less than 10,000), central Kazakh SSR, c.100 mi. NE of Aral Sea. Site of Soviet space and rocket-testing center.

bail, release from prison of a person awaiting trial, on the deposit of a security, which is to be forfeited in case of failure of the accused to surrender at an appointed time. Bail is usually granted in all civil arrests, but is sometimes refused in criminal cases (e.g., that of a murder charge).

Baile Átha Cliath, Ireland: see DUBLIN.

Bailey, Liberty Hyde, 1858–1954, American botanist and horticulturist. Influential in estab. horticulture as respected science.

Baillie Scott, Mackay Hugh, 1865–1945, English architect influential in introducing to the Continent the English reform of domestic architecture.

Bailly, Jean Sylvain (zhä' sēlvĕ' bäyĕ'), 1736–93, French astronomer and politician. Won distinction as scientist before his election as president of National Assembly (1789); mayor of Paris 1789–91. Permitted National Guard to fire upon demonstrators (July 17, 1791). Arrested 1793; guillotined.

Baily, Francis, 1774–1844, English astronomer; helped found Royal Astronomical Society. First observed (1836) spots of light, now called Baily's beads, seen on edge of Sun's disk during eclipse.

Bain, Alexander, 1818–1903, Scottish philosopher and psychologist, long associated with the Univ. of Aberdeen.

Bainbridge, William, 1774–1833, American naval officer. As commander of U.S. vessel, insult offered him by dey of Algiers contributed greatly to American declaration of war against BARBARY STATES.

Bainbridge, city (pop. 12,714), extreme SW Ga., on Flint R., SSW of Albany; founded 1823. Trade and industrial center in farm area.

Baird, John Logie, 1888–1946, Scottish inventor. First to demonstrate true television (1926), and, in 1928, transatlantic and color television.

Baja California (bä'hä) [Span.,= lower California], peninsula, NW Mexico, between Gulf of California and Pacific. N is state of Baja California (cap. MEX-ICALI), S is territory of Baja California Sur (cap. LA PAZ). N experienced recent rapid growth, but S is largely unpopulated. Mining (gold, silver, copper). Mexicali valley produces cotton. N attracts many U.S. tourists.

Bajazet (bäjüzĕt'), Ottoman sultans; also spelled Baya-zit, Bayazid. **Bajazet I,** 1347–1403, reigned 1389–1402. Conquered E Anatolia; defeated Christian army at NIKOPOL (1396). His siege of Constantinople (1402) was interrupted by the invasion of TAMERLANE, who defeated him at Ankara (1402) and reputedly carried him in an iron cage (really a palanquin). **Bajazet II,** 1447–1513, reigned 1481–1512; put down the revolt of his brother Djem, who fled and eventually died in custody of Charles VIII of France (1495). The sultan lost Cilicia to the Egyptian Mamelukes (1491) and warred unsuccessfully against Venice (1499–1503), but he furthered Ottoman culture and rebuilt Constantinople after an earthquake (1509).

Bajer, Fredrik (frädh'rĭk bī'ûr), 1837–1922, Danish pacifist and writer. Helped to found Internatl. Peace Bureau at Berne (1891). Shared 1908 Nobel Peace Prize with K. P. Arnoldson.

Bakacs, Thomas: see BAKOCZ, THOMAS.

Bakelite (bā'kŭlīt), trade name for synthetic resin (amber or colorless unless dyed) made by heating under pressure the product of reaction between phenol and formaldehyde. Used in making many small molded articles (e.g., drinking glasses) and for many purposes. Invented by Leo Hendrik Baekeland (1863–1944).

Baker, Sir Benjamin, 1840–1907, English civil engineer. Helped build London's underground railway, Firth of Forth and Tower bridges, and Aswan Dam.

Baker, George Pierce, 1866–1935, American educator (Harvard, 1888–1924; Yale, 1925–33). At Harvard instituted in 1906 the 47 Workshop, a laboratory for the playwright and for experimental production which pioneered in educational theater. Works include *Dramatic Technique* (1919).

Baker, Newton D(iehl), 1871–1937, U.S. Secretary of War (1916–21). Much criticized at first, he was later praised for his direction of First World War.

Baker, Sir Samuel White, 1821–93, English explorer in Africa. Discovered Albert Nyanza 1864.

Baker, city (pop. 9,986), NE Oregon, SSE of Pendleton, in Powder R. valley; laid out 1865 after gold discovery (1861–62). Trade center of agr. and lumber area. Gold, silver, and copper are mined; stone quarries.

Baker Island, coral islet, area 1 sq. mi., central Pacific near equator, S of Howland Isl. Claimed 1857 by U.S., colonized 1935 by Americans from Hawaii, placed under Dept. of Interior 1936.

Baker Lake, 1,029 sq. mi., Keewatin dist., Northwest Territories, Canada, near Chesterfield Inlet. At W end is Royal Canadian Mounted Police post.

Bakersfield, city (pop. 56,848), S central Calif., NNW of Los Angeles at S end of San Joaquin valley; laid out 1869. Gold discovered in area 1855, and petroleum 1899. Silver, borax, and tungsten mines and oil refineries in vicinity. Ships citrus fruit.

Bakewell, Robert, 1725–95, English livestock breeder, agriculturist. His success in breeding livestock for meat contributed to 18th-cent. population explosion. Introduced progeny test for selective breeding.

Bakhchisarai (bäkh"chĕsŭrī'), city (pop. 10,900), Ukrainian SSR, in S Crimea; historic cap. of khanate of Crimea (15th cent.–1783). Has palace of khans, built 16th cent. In RSFSR until 1954.

Bakhmut, Ukraine: see ARTEMOVSK.

Bakhtiari (bäkh"tēä'rē), mountainous region of SW Iran. Chief home of nomadic Bakhtiari tribe, famed for warlike behavior. Region became important with discovery of oil in late 19th cent. Tribe played decisive part in revolution of 1908–9.

baking soda: see SODA.

Bakocz or **Bakacs, Thomas** (bŏ'kôts, bŏ'kŏch), Hung. *Bakócz* or *Bakács Tamás,* c.1442–1521, Hungarian statesman and cardinal. Of unbounded ambition, he rose from servile origin to chancellor and archprimate of Hungary. In 1514 the nobles ignored his call for a crusade and the peasants who volunteered revolted against the aristocracy. John Zapolya suppressed the rebellion and peasants were reduced to serfdom. Bakocz died enormously rich.

Bakst, Lev Nikolayevich (lyĕf' nyĭkŭlī'ûvĭch bäkst'), 1868–1924, Russian painter. Created settings and costumes for Diaghilev's ballet company.

Baku (bäkōō'), cap. of Azerbaijan, USSR, on Caspian Sea. Greater Baku (1965 est. pop. 1,147,000) includes Apsheron peninsula, which extends c.40 mi. into Caspian Sea and contains 15% of world's petroleum reserves. The chief oil center of USSR, Baku has a large port and many cultural institutions. First mentioned 8th cent. A.D., it had Zoroastrian shrines of constantly burning fires (from oil and gas wells). Ceded by Persia to Russia 1806. Oil industry began late 19th cent.

Bakunin, Mikhail (mēkhüyĕl' bŭkōō'nyĭn), 1814–76, Russian anarchist. Young aristocrat turned revolutionist, he was exiled (1849) to Siberia, but escaped. In First International after 1868 he was opposed by Marxists, who expelled him (1872). He believed "anarchism, collectivism, and atheism" would give man complete freedom and advocated violent revolution.

Bakwanga, town (pop. c.39,000), central Republic of the Congo. Mining center for industrial diamonds. In 1961 was cap. of secessionist state of South Kasai.

Balaam (bā'lûm), prophet hired by King of Moab to curse the Hebrews. By order of God he was forced to bless them instead. Later seduced Jews to evil practices, for which he was killed. Num. 22–24; 31.8, 16; 2 Peter 2.15,16; Rev. 2.14.

Balak (bā'lăk), king of Moab who hired Balaam to curse the Hebrews. Num. 22–24.

Balakirev, Mili (Alekseyevich): see FIVE, THE.

Balaklava (bä"lŭklä'vû), section of Sevastopol, S Ukrainian SSR, in Crimea; fishing and limestone quarrying. Famous for allied victory (1854) in Crimean War and for suicidal charge of an English light-cavalry brigade, celebrated by Tennyson.

balalaika: see STRINGED INSTRUMENTS.

Balance, the, in astrology: see ZODIAC.

balance, instrument to measure MASS or weight. Equal-arm (beam) balance simplest; based on LEVER principle. Beam is suspended at its center on knife-edge at right angles to it; pans of equal weight are suspended at each end, equidistant from fulcrum (point of support). Pointer is at zero when beam is in equilibrium. Object to be weighed is put in one pan, standard weights in other until balanced. Platform balances may be equal- or unequal-arm types. Spring balance (from which object is suspended) measures force of gravity at certain point on earth's surface. TORSION BALANCE, which depends on twisting of a wire or thread, is not strictly a balance. See SCALES.

balance of payments, relation between all payments in and out of a country over a given period. It is outgrowth of concept of BALANCE OF TRADE, which it includes (known as current account), as well as private foreign loans and interest, loans and grants by governments and international organizations, and movements of gold. An adverse balance of payments may affect stability of a nation's currency; INTERNA-

TIONAL MONETARY FUND estab. to deal with such problems.

balance of trade, difference between exports and imports of a country. Mercantilists believed country should have favorable balance of trade, i.e., an excess of exports over imports. Though refuted by Adam Smith and David Hume, this idea is still widely held. See also BALANCE OF PAYMENTS.

Balanchine, George, 1904–, American choreographer and ballet dancer. Performed in Russia 1921–24 and with Diaghilev's Ballet Russe in Paris 1924–28. In U.S. since 1933; founded School of American Ballet 1934. Directed Metropolitan Opera ballet 1934–37 and New York City Ballet 1948–.

Balard, Antoine Jérôme (ätwän' zhärōm' bälär'), 1802–76, French chemist. Discovered bromine; extracted sodium sulphate from sea water.

Balassa, Baron Balint (bä'lint büläs'ù, bö'lösh-shö), 1551–94, Hungarian poet, regarded as the creator of Hungarian lyric poetry.

Balaton (bä'lùtòn, Hung. bö'lötôn), Ger. *Plattensee,* lake (c.230 sq. mi), W Hungary, largest in Central Europe. Fisheries; vineyards; resorts.

Balbo, Italo (ē'tälô bäl'bō), 1896–1940, Italian Fascist leader and aviator. Took part in March on Rome (1922); became minister of aviation 1929, governor of Libya 1933. Died in plane accident.

Balboa, Vasco Núñez de (vä'skô nōō'nyäth dä bälbō'ä) c.1475–1519, Spanish conquistador, discoverer of Pacific. After reaching DARIEN (1510), he won friendship of Indians, who accompanied him on epic march across isthmus (1513). Claimed Pacific and all shores washed by it for Spain. Pedrarias had him beheaded for treason.

Balboa, town (pop. 3,500), Panama Canal Zone, Pacific port. Administration hq. of zone and canal; port for Panama city.

Balch, Emily Greene, 1867–1961, American economist and sociologist. She shared the 1946 Nobel Peace Prize with John R. Mott.

Balchen, Bernt (bäl'kùn), 1899–, Norwegian-American aviator. Headed arctic search for Amundsen and Ellsworth (1925) and joined their 1926 expedition. Chief pilot of Byrd's antarctic expedition, 1928–30.

bald cypress, tree of family Taxodiaceae, a deciduous or evergreen conifer of Far East, SE U.S., and Mexico. In the Everglades a common variety standing in water produces "knees" which project from roots upward above the water.

Balder (bôl'dùr), Norse god of light; son of Odin and Frigg. One legend says that, invulnerable to everything but mistletoe, he was killed by a mistletoe dart made by Loki.

Baldovinetti, Alessio (äläs'syô bäldō vēnēt'tē), c.1425–1499, Italian painter and decorative artist of the early Florentine Renaissance.

Baldung, Hans (häns' bäl'dōōng), c.1484–1545, German religious and mythological painter, surnamed Grien or Grün because of his predilection for green.

Baldwin, Latin emperors of Constantinople (see CONSTANTINOPLE, LATIN EMPIRE OF). **Baldwin I,** 1171–1205, count of Flanders and a leader of the Fourth Crusade, was elected emperor in 1204. Captured in battle with the Bulgarians (1205), he died in captivity. Succeeded by his brother, Henry of Flanders. **Baldwin II,** 1217–73, succeeded his brother ROBERT OF COURTENAY (1228). JOHN OF BRIENNE was regent till 1237. He sold part of the True Cross to Louis IX of France and pawned his son with the Venetians to get funds for his tottering throne, but in 1261 MICHAEL VIII stormed Constantinople and Baldwin was forced to flee.

Baldwin, kings of Jerusalem. **Baldwin I,** 1058?–1118, brother of GODFREY OF BOUILLON, whom he accompanied on First Crusade. Took title king 1100; consolidated the Latin states; gained the chief ports of Palestine. His cousin and successor, **Baldwin II** (Baldwin du Bourg), d. 1131, fought the Turks in N Syria

and made Tyre and Antioch dependent on his crown. **Baldwin III,** 1130–62, son of FULK of Anjou, reigned 1143–62. The decay of Latin power in the East had begun. Edessa fell to the Moslems (1144); the Second Crusade failed; and Sultan NUREDDIN seized N Syria (1154). His nephew, **Baldwin IV** (the Leper), c.1161–85, spent his whole reign (1174–85) defending the kingdom against SALADIN. Disabled by leprosy, he made Guy of LUSIGNAN his lieutenant, but withdrew the commission and had his five-year-old nephew crowned (1183) as **Baldwin V** (d. 1186), with RAYMOND, count of Tripoli, as regent.

Baldwin, Abraham, 1754–1807, American statesman. U.S. Representative from Ga. (1789–99); U.S. Senator (1799–1807). A founder of present Univ. of Georgia.

Baldwin, James, 1924–, American author, whose works about Negroes and Negro-white relations include novels (e.g., *Go Tell It on the Mountain,* 1953), non-fiction (e.g., *Notes of a Native Son,* 1955; *The Fire Next Time,* 1963), and a play, *Blues for Mr. Charlie* (1964).

Baldwin, Matthias William, 1795–1866, American industrialist, founder of Baldwin Locomotive Works.

Baldwin, Robert, 1804–58, Canadian statesman, leader of movement for representative government in Canada. In the assembly he led opposition group and effected alliance with French in Lower Canada. In 1842 he joined with Louis H. LAFONTAINE to form a coalition government. Second Baldwin-LaFontaine ministry (1848–51), often called the "great ministry," accomplished reform of local government in Ontario, promoted judicial and educational reforms.

Baldwin, Stanley, 1867–1947, British statesman. Conservative party leader 1923–37, he was three times prime minister. Broke 1926 general strike. During his third government the League of Nations declined, Fascist powers rose, and Edward VIII abdicated.

Baldwin. 1 City (pop. 30,204), SE N.Y., on S shore of Long Isl., S of Mineola. A summer resort on Baldwin Bay. **2** Borough (pop. 24,489), SW Pa., S of Pittsburgh, in bituminous-coal region.

Baldwin Park, city (pop. 33,951), S Calif., E of Los Angeles, in San Gabriel valley; settled 1870.

Baldwyn, town (pop. 2,023), NE Miss., N of Tupelo, in dairy and poultry-farm area. Brices Cross Roads Natl. Battlefield Site, where Gen. N. B. Forrest routed Union force June 10, 1864, is nearby.

Bâle, Switzerland: see BASEL.

Balearic Islands (bălēä'rĭk), Span. *Baleares,* archipelago in W Mediterranean, forming a province (1,936 sq. mi.; pop. 443,327) of Spain; cap. Palma. Chief islands: Majorca, Minorca, Iviza. Agr., fishing, tourist trade. Export of majolica ware, silver filigree. Inhabited since prehistoric times. the islands were occupied by Iberians, Phoenicians, Greeks, Carthaginians, Romans, Byzantines; conquered by Moors 8th cent. A.D.; made a kingdom 11th cent.; conquered by Aragonese 13th cent. See also MAJORCA.

Balenciaga, Cristóbal (bälěnsëä'gú), 1895–, Spanish fashion designer. Opened Paris salon 1937. Designs are known for classic line and elegance.

Balewa, Alhaji Sir Abubakar Tafawa (älhä'jē äbōō'-bäkär'' täfä'wä bälěwä'), 1912–66, Nigerian statesman. Appointed first prime minister of Federation of Nigeria 1957, assassinated during military coup d'état 1966.

Balfour, Arthur James (bäl'fōōr), 1848–1930, British statesman. Held many posts. As foreign secretary, issued (1917) Balfour Declaration pledging British support for a Jewish national home in Palestine. Devoted to cause of international peace.

Bali (bä'lē), island (c.2,243 sq. mi.; pop. including offshore islets 1,782,529), Lesser Sundas, E Indonesia, E of Java across Bali Strait. Exports rice, coffee, copra, tobacco, teakwood. Dutch first landed 1597, estab. rule 1849. Island became province of republic of Indonesia 1950.

Balikesir (bä"likĕsēr'), city (pop. 61,145), NW Turkey. Rail junction; agr. center. Has a large annual fair.

Balinese music, chiefly a survival of pre-Islamic music of Java, using the tonal systems of JAVANESE MUSIC. The orchestra of tuned percussion instruments is called a *gamelan.* Each type of dance or drama has its own *gamelan.* Basic instruments include bronze or bamboo xylophones, gongs, flutes, fiddles, rattles, and cymbals. Little use is made of notation; compositions are learned by rote. See *ill.,* p. 733.

Baliol, John de (bä'lēŭl), d. 1269, English baron, founder of Balliol Col., Oxford. A regent for Alexander III of Scotland, he was removed from office for treason. His third son, **John de Baliol,** 1249–1315, king of Scotland (1292–96), claimed the throne at the death of MARGARET MAID OF NORWAY. EDWARD I of England supported him, over ROBERT I, in return for feudal overlordship and he was crowned. Renounced (1296) his oath of fealty, was defeated, and surrendered to Edward. Retired to France 1299. His son, **Edward de Baliol,** d. 1363, king of Scotland, invaded Scotland (1332) with aid of Edward III and defeated supporters of DAVID II. After David's return from France (1341), he never held power.

Balkan Peninsula, SE Europe, extending S from Danube and Sava rivers. Bounded by Black Sea (E); Bosporus, Sea of Marmara, Dardanelles, Aegean Sea (S); Ionian and Adriatic seas (W). Comprises ALBANIA, BULGARIA, continental GREECE, SE RUMANIA, European TURKEY, most of YUGOSLAVIA. Very mountainous, it contains the DINARIC ALPS, the RHODOPE mts., and the **Balkans,** a range of N Bulgaria, culminating at 7,785 ft. in Yumrukchal and crossed by Shipka Pass.

Balkan Wars, 1912–13, two short wars for possession of European Turkey. In the first war Serbia, Bulgaria, Greece, and Montenegro expelled the Turks from all their European holdings except Constantinople (1912). The territorial settlement made by the Great Powers in 1913 disappointed Serbia, which was cut off from the Adriatic by the creation of independent Albania. Serbia now demanded Bulgaria cede the larger part of Macedonia, thus precipitating the Second Balkan War. Rumania, Greece, and Turkey joined Serbia against Bulgaria, which was defeated and lost territory to all its enemies in the Treaty of Bucharest (1913). Balkan Wars heightened nationalism and prepared way for First World War.

Balkh (bälkh), town (pop. 10,000), N Afghanistan. Was cap. of ancient BACTRIA. Taken 653 by Arabs, sacked 1221 by Jenghiz Khan. Population mostly Uzbek.

Balkhash (bŭl-khäsh'), city (1965 est. pop. 72,000), SE Kazakh SSR, on N shore of L. Balkhash; founded 1929. Railroad terminus; port; copper-smelting center. The saline **Lake Balkhash** (6,680 sq. mi.) stretches for 375 mi. between Kazakh Hills (N) and desert (S). Fed by Ili R., it has no outlet.

Balkis, name given in Koran to the queen of Sheba.

Ball, John, d. 1381, English priest; an instigator of the Peasants' Revolt under Wat TYLER.

ballad (bä'lŭd), narrative poem of unknown authorship, intended to be sung, preserved by oral tradition among people culturally homogeneous. Often written in ballad stanza—two lines of four and three stresses each alternating to rhyme *abcb.* Sometimes there is an additional, unchanging refrain of a line or two, but a common *incremental repetition* involves dialogue repeated with minor changes to tell the story. British ballads were collected by Francis Child, American ones by Louise Pound, Carl Sandburg, and John and Alan Lomax. Popularly, the word *ballad* applies to any narrative poem; and in music, to a simple, sentimental song, not a folk song.

ballade (bäläd'), in literature, verse form (developed from French in 14th–15th cent.), composed of four stanzas, the last called the *envoy* being shorter than the others.

Ballarat (băl'ŭrăt'), city (pop. 53,680), Victoria, Australia; founded 1851. Once a noted mining center. Woolen mills.

ball bearings: see BEARINGS.

ballet, solo or ensemble dancing of drama set to music. First ballet was *Ballet comique de la Reine,* given 1581 at the court of Catherine de' Medici. It developed in France as a court entertainment until c.1708, when first ballet was commissioned for public performance. Thereafter choreographic notation came into being, movements became more elevated and costumes less cumbersome. Pierre Beauchamps estab. the five positions; Carlo Blasis designed the *attitude.* The *prima ballerina* emerged after 1832; dancing *sur les pointes* and the standard tutu were introduced. After 1909 modern ballet with its emphasis on ensemble production was born through the efforts of Sergei DIAGHILEV of Russia.

Ballinger, Richard Achilles (băl'ĭnjŭr), 1858–1922, U.S. Secretary of the Interior (1909–11). Center of controversy over handling of natural resources.

Balliol College: see OXFORD UNIVERSITY.

ballistics (bŭlĭ'stĭks), science of motion and propulsion of projectiles. Includes processes and motion while force and guidance are applied, and also unpowered motion in trajectory (resultant of inertia, gravity, air friction). Important in artillery, rocketry.

balloon, aircraft lacking propulsive system, obtaining lift from lighter-than-air gas in containers. J. M. and J. É. Montgolfier of France credited with invention (1783). Pilâtre de Rozier, using hot-air-filled balloon attached to ground, first man to make balloon ascent (1783). Also in 1783 Robert brothers and J. A. C. Charles ascended and traveled 27 mi. in hydrogen-filled balloon. Balloons carried messages in siege of Paris (1870). Observation balloons used in First World War; in Second World War balloons held by cables were used in air defense. As sport in early 20th cent. ballooning was stimulated by annual international racing. Today balloons are used mainly as aids to scientific studies.

balm: see LEMON BALM; for bee balm, see OSWEGO TEA.

balm of Gilead, name for several unrelated plants: historic Old World *Commiphora meccanensis,* a small evergreen tree (referred to in Jer. 8.22), and the source of commercial balm of Gilead; American balm of Gilead, a poplar.

Balmoral Castle (bălmŏr'ŭl), royal residence in Braemar, Aberdeenshire, Scotland. Built by Queen Victoria 1854.

balsa, deciduous tree (*Ochroma*), native to tropical America. Its very light wood (also called corkwood) is used in airplane construction, in life preservers and floats, and for insulating purposes.

balsam, resin of various trees, including commercial and tolu balsam of South America, Mecca balsam or BALM OF GILEAD, copaiba, and CANADA BALSAM. For the herbaceous balsam plant, see IMPATIENS.

Balthazar: see WISE MEN OF THE EAST.

Baltic provinces and **Baltic states,** countries bordering on extreme E coast of Baltic Sea. See COURLAND; LIVONIA; ESTONIA; LATVIA; LITHUANIA.

Baltic Sea, arm of Atlantic Ocean, indenting N Europe, surrounded by Sweden, Finland, USSR (incl. Baltic states), Poland, Germany, and Denmark. Area c.155,-500 sq. mi. (incl. gulfs of Bothnia, Finland, and Riga). Many islands (see DENMARK). Connected with North Sea by ORESUND and Great and Little BELT (by way of Kattegat and Skagerrak); KIEL CANAL is a more direct connection. Other canal systems link it with White Sea and Volga R. Generally shallow; important fisheries. Chief ports: Copenhagen, Stettin, Gdynia, Danzig, Leningrad, Helsinki, Stockholm.

Baltimore, Baron: see CALVERT, GEORGE.

Baltimore, city (pop. 939,024), N Md., on Patapsco R. near Chesapeake Bay. State's largest city; commercial and industrial center; important seaport.

Major industries include shipbuilding, sugar and food processing, petroleum and copper refining, printing, and mfg. of apparel, chemicals, aircraft, missiles, electronic equipment. Exports large amounts of coal, grain. Site first settled early 17th cent.; provincial assembly authorized building of Baltimore 1729. Fine harbor made it important shipping center. Shipbuilding thrived early, bringing fame with clipper ships of early 1800s. Continental Congress met here 1776–77. In 1814 F. S. Key wrote *Star-spangled Banner* during defense of Fort McHENRY here. National Road aided city's rapid growth after War of 1812. BALTIMORE & OHIO RAILROAD begun 1828. City held violent pro-Southern sympathies in Civil War. Important shipbuilding and supply point in both World Wars. Seat of The JOHNS HOPKINS UNIVERSITY, Loyola Col., Mt. St. Mary's Col., Morgan State Col., Col. of Notre Dame of Maryland, St. Mary's Seminary and Univ., Medical School of Univ. of Maryland, Peabody Inst., The Maryland Inst.. Walters Art Gall., Baltimore Mus. of Art, and Enoch Pratt Free Library. Points of interest include Mt. Vernon Place (with Washington Monument), Druid Hill Park, first Roman Catholic cathedral in U.S., Westminster Churchyard (with grave of E. A. Poe), and Pimlico race track. Has symphony orchestra.

Baltimore & Ohio Railroad, first railroad in U.S. open for public traffic (1830). Rapid decline of Baltimore after trans-Allegheny traffic had gravitated toward Erie Canal in N.Y. led to its construction. Successful trial in 1830 of the *Tom Thumb,* built by Peter Cooper, brought introduction of steam locomotives. Railroad was important life line in operations of the Civil War. Merged with Chesapeake & Ohio Railway 1963.

Baltimore Highlands, Md.: see LANSDOWNE.

Baluchi (bŭlōō'chĕ), Western Iranian language of Indo-Iranian subfamily of Indo-European languages. See LANGUAGE (table).

Baluchistan (bŭlōō'chĭstăn), arid region in SE Iran and W Pakistan. Iranian section was formerly a separate province; since 1938 a part of Kerman Prov. Pakistani region (c.134,000 sq. mi.) was added 1946–47 to Pakistan.

Baluchitherium, extinct Miocene rhinoceros. Largest land mammal known, it measured c.18 ft. at shoulder, weighed c.10 tons.

Balue, Jean (zhä'bälü'), c.1421–1491, French cardinal and statesman, adviser to Louis XI. Conspired with Charles the Bold of Burgundy against Louis, who had him imprisoned (1469–80), allegedly in an iron cage. Freed by papal intervention.

Balzac, Honoré de (ônôrä' dù bälzäk'), 1799–1850, French novelist. His greatest work, "La Comédie humaine," is a vast edifice of partly interconnected novels and short novels, recreating French society of his time and picturing in precise detail individuals of every class and profession. Among best-known novels are *Eugénie Grandet* (1833), *Le Père Goriot* (1835), *La Cousine Bette* (1847), *Le Cousin Pons* (1847). Balzac wrote some masterly short stories but failed in his attempts at drama.

Balzac, Jean Louis Guez de (zhä' lwē' gā'), 1597?–1654, French writer. Helped shape French prose style.

Bamako (bämäkō'), city (pop. c.131,900), cap. of Republic of Mali, W Mali, on upper Niger R. River port and rail junction, exporting cotton, peanuts, kapok, and shea-nut oil.

Bamberg (bäm'bĕrk), city (pop. 75,116), Upper Franconia, NE Bavaria, on Regnitz R. Industrial center, has silk mills, breweries. Now an archiepiscopal see, it was cap. of a powerful prince-bishopric until 1802. Splendid 13th-cent. cathedral contains tomb of Pope Clement II. Episcopal palaces from 16th and 18th cent.

Bamboccianti: see LAER, PIETER VAN.

Bamboccio, Il: see LAER, PIETER VAN.

bamboo, a woody perennial grass of warm and tropical regions. It has rounded, hollow, jointed stalks, is usually treelike but occasionally low or climbing. Wood used for construction, furniture, utensils, and paper. Chief commercial species is *Bambusa arundinacea.* A few species are native to the S U.S., e.g., cane or cane reed, *Arundinaria gigantea.*

Bamburgh, village, Northumberland, N England, on North Sea. Cap. of anc. Bernicia and, for a time, of Northumbria.

Banaba: see OCEAN ISLAND.

banana, tropical palmlike plant (*Musa*) and its long, fleshy fruit, usually yellow or red skinned. An important commercial crop. Fruit is edible raw or cooked and is rich in carbohydrates. Other banana species are plantain, the fruit of which is cooked as a vegetable in the tropics, and MANILA HEMP.

Bananal Island: see ARAGUAIA, river.

Banaras: see BENARES.

Banat (bä'nät'), term originally used for several military frontier provs. of Hungary and Croatia; governors had title *ban.* The former **Banat of Temesvar** (tĕ'mĕshvär'), a fertile plain between Danube, Theiss, and Mures rivers, was an integral part of Hungary; chief city Temesvar (see TIMISOARA). Partitioned 1920 between Yugoslavia and Rumania.

Banbury, municipal borough (pop. 20,996), Oxfordshire, England. Still produces famous cakes. Banbury Cross of the nursery rhyme destroyed in 1602; new one built in 19th cent.

Bancroft, Edward, 1744–1821, American Revolutionary spy. Operated as secret agent to American commissioners in France, but also reported their movements to British.

Bancroft, George, 1800–1891, American historian and statesman, author of monumental *History of the United States* (10 vols., 1834–74). As Secretary of the Navy, he estab. U.S. Naval Academy at Annapolis. Minister to Britain 1846–49. An antislavery Democrat, he supported Lincoln in Civil War. Minister to Prussia 1867–74. Revised and extended editions of the *History* (6 vols.; 1876, 1883–85) won high praise.

Bancroft, Hubert Howe, 1832–1918, American publisher and historian. Collected materials on all W America, culminating in Bancroft Library of Univ. of California. Collection has some 60,000 volumes of books, manuscripts, transcripts, and personal narratives. He edited and published a history (39 vols., 1874–90), reissued (1882–90) as *The Works of Hubert Howe Bancroft.*

Bancroft, Marie Effie Wilton, Lady, 1839–1921, English actress and manager (1865–85) together with her husband, Squire Bancroft (1841–1926). They introduced realism to the English stage in the plays of Thomas Robertson and by using the innovations of Mme Vestris.

Bancroft, village (pop. 2,615), SE Ont., Canada, on York R. and WSW of Ottawa. Uranium mines.

band, in music, a group of musicians playing chiefly upon wind instruments. Present-day band originated from military ensembles used for marches. First significant band in America was the U.S. Marine Band, founded 1798. In 1854 the concert band developed. The bands and band music of Sousa and Franko Goldman have been most important in the U.S. Modern bands usually include the chief brass, wood-wind, and percussion instruments, while concert bands and jazz bands may employ strings and harp.

Banda, Hastings Kamuzu, 1902–, Malawi political leader. Educated in South Africa, U.S., and Great Britain, he was medical doctor in London after Second World War. In 1958 returned from Ghana to lead Nyasaland African Congress in a campaign against the Federation of Rhodesia and Nyasaland. Imprisoned 1959; released 1960; became prime minister of a self-governing Nyasaland Feb., 1963.

Banda Oriental (bän'dä ōryäntäl') [Span.,= eastern shore, i.e., of the Río de la Plata], region, S Uruguay.

Term applied to Uruguay in Spanish colonial period. Most of Uruguayan population and agr. concentrated here.

Bandar, India: see MASULIPATAM.

Bandaranaike, Sirimavo (sērēmä'vō bändränī'kē), 1916–, prime minister of Ceylon (1960–65). Her husband, S. W. R. D. Bandaranaike, was prime minister until his assassination in 1959; she was elected to office 1960.

Bandar Shah (shä'), town, N Iran, on Caspian Sea. Terminus of Trans-Iranian RR.

Banda Sea (bän'dä), part of Pacific Ocean, bounded by S Moluccan isls. of Indonesia.

Bandelier, Adolph Francis Alphonse, 1840–1914, American archaeologist, b. Switzerland. Carried on field researches in N.Mex., Peru, and Bolivia.

Bandelier National Monument: see NATIONAL PARKS AND MONUMENTS (table).

Bandello, Matteo (mät-tā'ō bändě'lō), 1485–1561, Italian story-teller, a priest, author of *novelle* in the manner of Boccaccio.

Bandera (bändâ'rû), village, SW Texas, on Medina R., NW of San Antonio. Founded by Mormons 1854, later a Polish settlement. A ranch and farm center.

Bandinelli, Bartolomeo (bärtōlōmä'ō bändēnēl'lē) or **Baccio** (bät'chō), 1493?–1560, Florentine sculptor and painter, follower of Michelangelo.

Bandung (bän'dŏong), city (pop. 972,566), W Java, Indonesia, SE of Djarkarta. An industrial center and tourist hub. The **Bandung Conference,** held here April, 1955, by 29 nations of Asia and Africa planned economic and cultural cooperation and opposed colonialism. Communist China important in the conference.

baneberry, perennial plant (*Actaea*), with compound leaves, clusters of small white flowers, and poisonous but handsome white, red, or black berrylike fruits. Also called cohosh.

Banér, Johan (yōō'hän bänâr'), 1596–1641, Swedish general in Thirty Years War. Succeeded Gustavus Adolphus in command of Swedish forces in Germany (1632). Routed at Nördlingen 1634. Restored Swedish prestige by victory at Wittstock (1636).

Banerjea, Surendranath (sōōrĕn'drŭnät bä'nûrjē), 1848–1926, Indian nationalist; founder of Indian Association, a predecessor of the Indian Natl. Congress.

Banff (bămf), popular summer and winter resort village (pop. 4,101), SW Alta., Canada, on Bow R. in the Rocky Mts. Here is Canadian Pacific RR station for Banff Natl. Park (2,564 sq. mi.; estab. 1887). Has annual winter carnival. Park has hot sulfur springs.

Banffshire or **Banff,** county (630 sq. mi.; pop. 46,400), NE Scotland; co. town Banff. Largely agr., it has fishing villages along the rolling fertile coast. Fine whisky distilled. Scene of many battles between Scots and Norse invaders, it was later torn by religious strife after the Reformation.

Bangalore (băn-gûlôr'), city (pop. 778,977), SE Mysore, India; cap. and commercial center of Mysore. Has remains of Tippoo Sahib's palace. Rail hub and industrial center. Seat of Tata Inst. of Science.

Bangka (băng'kä), island (c.4,611 sq. mi.; pop. 251,-639), Indonesia, in Java Sea SE of Sumatra. Major tin producer since c.1710.

Bangkok (băng'kŏk"), city (est. pop. 1,330,153), cap. of Thailand and of Phra Nakhon prov., SW Thailand, on Chao Phraya R., near Gulf of Siam. Chief port of Thailand. In 1782 succeeded Ayuthia as Thai cap. Seat of several international organizations, notably Southeast Asia Treaty Organization. Officially called Krung Thep.

Bangor (băng'gûr), municipal borough (pop. 23,865), Co. Down, N. Ireland. Scene of annual yachting regatta. Has remains of an abbey founded c.555.

Bangor (băng'gôr), city (pop. 39,912), S Maine on Penobscot R. at mouth of Kenduskeag, opposite Brewer; settled 1769. A 19th-cent. shipping and ship-

building city; now commercial and industrial center and gateway to resort and lumber area. Occupied by British in War of 1812. Dow Air Force Base is W.

Bangor (băng'gôr), municipal borough (pop. 13,977), Caernarvonshire, Wales. Seat of Univ. Col. of North Wales. Cathedral dates from 15th–16th cent.

Bangorian Controversy, in Church of England. Bishop Benjamin Hoadly, of Bangor, Wales, denied (1717) that Christ delegated authority to church. Opposed by William Law and others in ensuing controversy.

Bangui (bäng-gē'), city (pop. c.237,970), cap. of Central African Republic; port on Ubangi R. Founded 1890. Administrative and communications center. Large textile complex was begun 1965.

Bangweolo (băng-wēō'lō) or **Bangweulu** (–wāōō'lōō), lake, 60 mi. long, 25 mi. wide, N Zambia. Discovered 1868 by Livingstone. Important fishing area.

Banja Luka (bän'jä lōō'kä), city (pop. 50,463), Bosnia, N Yugoslavia; seat of pashas 1583–1638. Orthodox cathedral, 16th-cent. mosque, ruins of Roman baths.

Banjermasin or **Bandjermasin** (both: băn"jûrmä'sĭn), city (pop. 214,096), cap., chief port of Indonesian Borneo. Exports oil, rubber, and spices.

banjo: see STRINGED INSTRUMENTS.

Bankhead, Tallulah (Brockman), 1903–, American actress. Since her debut in 1918, her flamboyant personality has won her fame in England and U.S. in plays (e.g., *The Little Foxes*), films (e.g., *Lifeboat*), and on radio and television.

banking, financial transactions through institutions primarily devoted to accepting deposits and making loans. Practiced in ancient Egypt and Greece and developed by the Romans, large-scale banking during the late Middle Ages came to be dominated by Italian banking families financing transactions involving the papacy and the wool trade. Modern banking developed in 18th and 19th cent. First bank in U.S. was founded at Philadelphia 1781. The BANK OF THE UNITED STATES was the subject of political controversy. An act in 1863 set up the national banks, but banks of deposit continued under state charters and grew in number. In 1913 the FEDERAL RESERVE SYSTEM was set up to regulate unstable banking system. After Second World War banking institutions were estab. to advance credit and further investment on an international scale.

Bank of England, popularly known as the Old Lady of Threadneedle Street, founded (1694) by William Paterson as commercial bank. Bank Charter Act of 1844 set up present system. Issue department issues bank notes; banking department handles other functions (e.g., national debt). Nationalized 1945.

Bank of France, central bank of France, estab. 1800 by Napoleon. Exercises central banking functions and is also largest commercial bank. Depository of government funds; has sole right to issue notes.

Bank of the United States. Against opposition of the Jeffersonian party the Federalists under Alexander HAMILTON estab. a central bank, the Bank of the United States (1791–1811). Its conservative policies were unpopular, and it was not rechartered, but after financial difficulties in the War of 1812, the second Bank of the United States was given (1816) a 20-year charter. Under Nicholas BIDDLE it prospered, but was viewed as a tool of Eastern moneyed interests by the followers of Andrew JACKSON. It was a chief issue of the 1832 election and Jackson, successful, took government deposits from it in 1833.

bankruptcy, discharge of liabilities of a debtor wholly or partially unable to meet his obligations. Bankruptcy laws are designed to distribute the bankrupt's assets equitably among his creditors and to discharge him from further liability. Bankruptcy is regulated by both federal and state laws. The present federal law, enacted 1898, has been extensively amended.

Banks, Sir Joseph, 1743–1820, British naturalist. Collected (on round-the-world voyage with Capt. Cook and other travels) many previously unknown plants.

SMALL CAPITALS = cross references. Pronunciation key on inside end pages. Abbreviations: p. 2.

Long influential in activities of Kew Gardens and Royal Society.

Banks, Nathaniel Prentiss, 1816–94, American politician and Union general in Civil War. U.S. Congressman before and after war. Governor of Mass. 1858–60. Helped Grant open the Mississippi by capture of PORT HUDSON, July, 1863.

banksia [for Sir Joseph Banks], genus of Australian evergreen trees and shrubs. Called also honeysuckle trees or Australian honeysuckle.

Bankside, locality by the Thames, in Southwark metropolitan borough, London, England. Amusement center 16th–17th cent.; Globe Theatre and other places associated with Shakespeare were here. Palace of bishop of Winchester and the CLINK were also here.

Bannack, ghost town, SW Mont., W of Dillon; founded with gold discovery 1862. First town in Mont., it was territorial cap. 1864–65. Declined when richer Virginia City fields attracted miners. Also called East Bannack and Bannack City. Now state park.

Banning, resort city (pop. 10,250), S Calif., E of Riverside, in mountainous fruitgrowing area.

Bannister, Roger Gilbert, 1929–, British runner, first man to run the mile in less than 4 min. On May 6, 1954, at Oxford, England, ran mile in 3:59.4.

Bannockburn, moor on Bannock R., Stirlingshire, Scotland. Site of Battle of Bannockburn June 23–24, 1314, in which Robert the Bruce defeated the English under Edward II and estab. himself on the Scottish throne.

Bantam fowl: see POULTRY.

Banting, Sir Frederick Grant, 1891–1941, Canadian physician, noted for research. Shared 1923 Nobel Prize in Physiology and Medicine for isolating INSULIN.

Bantry Bay, inlet of the Atlantic, 21 mi. long and 4 mi. wide, in Co. Cork, Ireland; one of Europe's best natural anchorages.

Bantu (băn'tōō"), ethnic and (principally) linguistic group of Africa, numbering c.50,000,000. They are a Negro people inhabiting all the continent S of the Congo except extreme SW. There are several hundred Bantu languages and dialects, including Luganda, Zulu, and Swahili. Bantu itself is merely a group in the larger family of Niger-Congo languages. See LANGUAGE (table). Highly developed Bantu states included Buganda. In 19th cent. several additional confederations developed, e.g., Zulu and Basuto. Matabele is also a well-known Bantu tribe.

Banville, Théodore de (tãŏdôr' dü bävēl'), 1823–91, French poet; one of PARNASSIANS. His work includes *Odes funambulesques* (1857) and *Occidentales* (1869).

banyan (băn'yùn), tree (*Ficus benghalensis*) of fig genus, native to India. Its branches put forth numerous aerial roots, which on reaching the ground, enlarge to form many trunks.

baobab (bā'ō–), gigantic tree (*Adansonia digitata*) of Senegal. Its fruit is edible and the bark yields rope and cloth.

baptism, rite of purification, commonly in Christian countries performed with the use of water, either by immersing the person, pouring water on him, or sprinkling. It was derived from Jewish custom; converts to Judaism were formally baptized. At the time of the purification in Christian churches a formal statement is made, and the person is made in many cases a member of the church or, in some cases, has his faith renewed. In more formalistic churches infants are baptized and at the time given their names (christening). In other churches baptism is given only to those who are old enough to have attained the "age of reason." A few Christian groups refrain from any ceremony of baptism. Generally baptism is believed to remove all stains of sin. Baptism by blood (or baptism by fire) is the grace conferred on a martyr who was not formally baptized but died in performing a good deed, particularly in defense of the helpless. Baptism by desire is the grace conferred on those who love God or simply love the good but have not had formal baptism.

Baptists, denomination of Christians who hold that baptism is only for believers and only by immersion. Separatists under John Smyth formed (c.1608) in Amsterdam first English Baptist congregation. First group in London estab. 1611. First American church founded (1639) by Roger Williams in Providence, R.I. Baptist churches are congregational, with nongoverning general associations–American Baptist Convention, Southern Baptist Convention, Natl. Baptist Convention, U.S.A., and many other associations.

bar, the, originally court or system of courts. Persons authorized to conduct trials known collectively as the bar, hence lawyers collectively. The distinction between the pleader before the court (barrister, advocate, counselor at law) and the agent merely advising the client (solicitor, attorney) has disappeared in U.S. but is retained in England.

Bar, Confederation of, union formed 1768 at Bar, now in W Ukraine, by Polish nobles to oppose interference of Catherine II of Russia in Polish affairs. Defended rights of landed gentry and tried to impose Roman Catholicism on non-Catholics in right-bank Ukraine, then under Polish rule. Opposed by Stanislaus II, elected Polish king 1764 with Catherine's sponsorship. In 1770 confederation declared Stanislaus deposed. Aided by France and Turkey, it fought against Russia until 1772 (First Polish Partition).

Bara, Theda, 1890–1955, American film actress, whose real name was Theodosia Goodman. Became overnight sensation (1915) as first screen "vamp" (from the film, *The Vampire*).

Barabbas (bùrăb'ùs), notorious bandit whom mob demanded be released from punishment, demanding instead the death of Jesus. Mat. 27.15–18; Mark 15.6–14; Luke 23.13–25; John 18.39,40.

Baraboo (băr'ùbōō), city (pop. 7,660), central Wis., on Baraboo R., NW of Madison; founded before 1850. Manufacturing and farm trade center. Ringling Brothers' circus began here. Circus World Mus. opened 1959.

Barak (bā'răk) [Heb.,= lightning], leader who joined Deborah in fighting Jabin and Sisera. Judges 4–5.

Baranof Island (bā'rùnôf), off SE Alaska, in ALEXANDER ARCHIPELAGO; over 100 mi. long, 1,607 sq. mi. in area. Named for Aleksandr Baranov. On it is SITKA.

Baranov, Aleksandr Andreyevich (bùrä'nôf), 1746–1819, Russian trader, chief figure during Russian control in Alaska. Virtual governor of Russian activities in North America (1799–1817).

Baranovichi (bùrùnôvyĕ'chĕ), city (1965 est. pop. 75,000), SW Byelorussian SSR. Railway junction.

Barany, Robert (rō'bert bä'ränĕ), 1876–1936, Austrian physician. Won 1914 Nobel Prize in Physiology and Medicine for work on vestibular apparatus of ear.

Barataria Bay (bărŭtăr'ēŭ), SE La., S of New Orleans, cut off from Gulf of Mexico by islands. Was base of pirates under Jean LAFITTE. Now shrimping center.

Barbados (bärbā'dōz), island (166 sq. mi.; 1965 est. pop. 245,352), West Indies; cap. Bridgetown. Winter resort. Claimed by British from 1605. Declared its independence 1966.

Barbara, Saint, 3d or 4th cent., virgin martyr, supposed to have been killed by her father for being a Christian. Feast: Dec. 4.

Barbarossa (bärbŭrōs'ŭ), surname of Algerian corsair Khair ad-Din (c.1483–1546). His brother, Koruk, or Aruj (c.1474–1518), seized Algiers from the Spanish (1518), and Barbarossa put Algeria under Turkish suzerainty. As admiral of the Turkish fleet, he twice defeated Andrea Doria and ravaged the coast of S Europe (1533–44).

Barbarossa, Frederick: see FREDERICK I, emperor.

Barbary Coast, waterfront area of San Francisco, Calif., in years after 1849 gold rush. Open gambling, prostitution, and gangsterism won it world notoriety. Named after pirate coast of N Africa.

Barbary States, term used for the N African states of TRIPOLITANIA, TUNISIA, and ALGERIA (and usually also MOROCCO), which were semi-independent under Turkish rule from 16th cent. onward. Rulers derived revenue from large-scale piracy on Mediterranean shipping. European powers launched punitive expeditions against them but generally relied on payment of tribute as a means of protection. The U.S. joined in this system. The insult offered by the dey of Algiers to William BAINBRIDGE, taking U.S. tribute to Algiers, led to the TRIPOLITAN WAR. French capture of Algiers (1830) marked the end of piracy in the region.

barbecue (bär'bŭkū), in U.S., open-air political or social gathering, where carcass or large joints of meat are roasted whole. Barbecued meat may also be smaller cuts, basted with spicy sauce.

Barber, Samuel, 1910–, American composer. Despite experimentation with modern techniques, his music is conservative. Among his works are two *Essays for Orchestra; Adagio for Strings;* a ballet, *Medea;* two symphonies; *Andromaque's Farewell* for voice and symphony; operas *Vanessa* and *Anthony and Cleopatra.*

Barberini vase: see PORTLAND VASE.

barberry, spiny shrub (*Berberis*), used for hedges. Some have bright autumn foliage; others, less hardy, are evergreen. Berries are red or black. Common barberry (*Berberis vulgaris*) is a wheat rust host.

Barberton, city (pop. 33,805), NE Ohio, on L. Anna, SW of Akron. A farm trade center with mfg.

Barbey d'Aurevilly, Jules (zhül' bärbā' dōrvēyē'), 1809–89, French author. His novels and short novels (notably *Les Diaboliques,* 1874), laid in his native Normandy, are remarkable for vigorous style, psychological realism, and morbid imagination. He also was an intransigent critic and polemicist.

Barbizon school, informal school of French landscape painting which flourished c.1830–1870. Barbizon village, near the forest of Fontainebleau, was a favorite resort of a group of painters who, by painting from nature in rebellion against the prevalent classical tradition, helped pave the way for the later realists and impressionists. The group included Théodore Rousseau, Corot, Millet, and Daubigny.

Barbon, Praise-God: see BAREBONE, PRAISE-GOD.

Barbosa, Ruy or **Rui** (both: rōō'ē bärbô'sü), 1849–1923, Brazilian philosopher of law, noted jurist, member of World Court.

Barbour, John, c. 1320–1395, Scottish poet and churchman. *The Bruce* (1375) chronicles deeds of ROBERT I.

Barbuda: see ANTIGUA.

Barbusse, Henri (ärē' bärbüs'), 1873–1935, French author. Best known for *Under Fire* (1916; Eng. tr., 1917), a realistic story of World War I.

Barca, surname of Carthaginian family, which included HANNIBAL.

Barcelona (bärthälō'nä), city (pop. 1,665,116), cap. of Barcelona prov., in Catalonia, NE Spain, on Mediterranean. Second largest city, largest port, chief commercial and industrial center of Spain. Machinery mfg. Flourished under Romans and Visigoths, fell to Moors (8th cent.) and to Charlemagne (801). Counts of Barcelona acquired all CATALONIA and parts of S France. Marriage of Count Raymond Berengar IV with heiress of Aragon united Catalonia and Aragon (1137). Barcelona became royal residence, powerful trade and banking center. Univ. founded 1450. City declined after unification of Spain, was center of Catalan separatism and various radical movements. A modern city, Barcelona also has medieval landmarks: Gothic cathedral, city hall, exchange, Church of Santa María del Mar.

Barclay de Tolly, Mikhail, Prince (mĕkhüyēl', bŭrklī' dŭ tô'lyē), 1761–1818, Russian field marshal, of Scottish descent. Commanded Russian forces against Napoleon (1812), adopted strategy of retreat into heart of Russia. Replaced by Kutuzov after defeat at Smolensk (August) but resumed command 1813.

Bard, Samuel, 1742–1821, American physician, active in developing institution which became medical school of Columbia Univ. Writings include midwifery text, works on pathology and medical education.

Bard College, near Annandale-on-Hudson, N.Y.; founded 1860 as St. Stephen's Col. for men. Rechartered 1935; coed. after 1944. Was affiliated with Columbia Univ. 1928–44.

Bardeen, John, 1908–, American physicist. Shared with W. H. Brattain and William Shockley the 1956 Nobel Prize in Physics for work in developing the transistor.

Bardia, town (pop. c.4,000) E Libya, port on Mediterranean. Strongly defended by the Italians during Second World War; captured by British Nov., 1942.

Bardstown, city (pop. 4,798), central Ky., SSE of Louisville, in rich farm area; settled 1775. Center of early missionary work in Mississippi valley and of institutions founded by Bishop J. B. M. David. Taken in Civil War (Sept., 1862) by Bragg's Confederates. Stephen Foster may have written *My Old Kentucky Home* in one house.

Barebone or **Barbon, Praise-God** (both: bär'bŏn), 1596?–1679, English lay preacher, member of Cromwell's nominated parliament (1653). This called Barebone's Parliament, though his part was insignificant.

Barents Island: see SPITSBERGEN.

Barents Sea, arm of Arctic Ocean, N of Norway and European RSFSR. Warmed by remnants of the North Atlantic drift, it has ice-free ports.

Barentz or **Barents, Willem,** d. 1597, Dutch navigator. Noted for extent of exploration and accuracy of charts in search for Northwest Passage.

Barge Canal: see NEW YORK STATE BARGE CANAL.

Bargello (bärjĕl'lō), 13th-cent. palace in Florence, Italy, which is now the national museum. Includes famous works by Donatello and Michelangelo.

Barham, Richard Harris (bär'm), pseud. **Thomas Ingoldsby** (ĭn'glŭlzbē), 1788–1845, English humorist, a clergyman, author of *The Ingoldsby Legends* (prose and verse parodies of medieval and modern tales).

Bar Harbor, town (pop. 3,807), S Maine, on MOUNT DESERT ISLAND, SE of Bangor; settled 1763. One of New England's most famous resorts, it began developing as summer resort in 19th cent. Ferry runs to Yarmouth, N.S., in summer. Acadia Natl. Park is near.

Bar-Hebraeus, Gregorius (bär-hēbrē'ŭs), 1226–86, Syrian scholar, catholicos of Jacobite church. Noted for Syriac chronicle of the world since Adam and for commentaries on Aristotle.

Bari (bä'rē), city (pop. 323,060), cap. of Apulia, S Italy; Adriatic seaport. Center of fertile agr. area. Founded by Romans; conquered from Byzantines by Normans 1071; port of embarkation during Crusades. Has Romanesque Basilica of St. NICHOLAS of Bari (shrine of pilgrimage), cathedral, medieval castle. University founded 1924.

Baring-Gould, S(abine) (bā'rĭng-gōōld'), 1834–1924, English novelist, folklorist, hymn writer, a clergyman, best known for words of hymn *Onward, Christian Soldiers* (1865).

barite (bâ'rīt), **barytes** (bŭrī'tēz), or heavy spar, mineral, barium sulfate. Almost insoluble. Used to test for sulfate, as source of barium, and to make paint and lithopone (white pigment).

Barito (bärē'tō), river, c.550 mi. long, in S Borneo; rises near Sarawak, flows generally S to Java Sea.

barium (bā'–), silvery-white active, poisonous metallic element (symbol = Ba; see also ELEMENT, table). Divalent, alkaline earth; resembles calcium. Oxidizes in air; ionizes in solution; with water, forms hydroxide, liberates hydrogen. Forms many compounds used in ceramic industry, medicine, etc. Barium carbonate and sulfate found in nature; free metal obtained by electrolysis of molten chloride. Gives green FLAME TEST in Bunsen burner.

barium sulfate: see BARITE.

Bar-jesus or **Elymas** (ĕl'ĭmăs), sorcerer blinded by St. Paul for trying to mislead a prospective Christian. Acts 13.4–12.

Bar-jona (-jō'–) [Aramaic,= son of Jonah], patronymic of St. Peter. Mat. 16.17.

bark, covering of stems and roots, best developed in woody plants. Comprises outer layer of cork and inner layer (called bast) of phloem or food-conducting tissue separated from the wood by the cambium. Bark yields TANNIN, latex (see RUBBER), dyes, and cork (see CORK OAK).

bark (bärk), three-masted sailing vessel with fore- and mainmasts square-rigged and mizzenmast fore-and-aft-rigged. Modern bark may be as large as 6,000 tons. A four-master bark has its aftermast fore-and-aft-rigged. Barkentine has three masts, with foremast square-rigged, others fore-and-aft rigged.

Barka, Mehdi ben, 1920–, Moroccan nationalist leader. Elected president of Natl. Consultative Assembly 1956. Formed opposition party in 1959; later went into exile. His kidnaping in October, 1965, caused French-Moroccan rift. His alleged kidnapers were sentenced in absentia by a Paris court in 1967.

bark cloth, primitive fabric made by many peoples from soft inner bark of certain tropical and subtropical trees. It is often elaborately decorated. Tapa cloth is a fine kind made in Pacific isls.

Barker, Harley Granville-: see GRANVILLE-BARKER.

Barking, London borough since 1965 (est. pop. 178,-910); includes parts of the former municipal boroughs of Barking and Dagenham.

Barkla, Charles Glover (bär'klŭ), 1877–1944, English physicist. Won 1917 Nobel Prize in Physics for discovery of characteristic X rays of elements.

Barkley, Alben W(illiam), 1877–1956, Vice President of the United States (1949–53). Was Democratic Representative (1913–27), Senator (1927–49, 1955–56) from Ky.

Bar Kokhba, Simon (kŏk'bŭ) [Aramaic,= son of the star], d. A.D. 135, self-proclaimed Messiah and leader of last Jewish revolts against Rome (132–135). He took the messianic epithet Simon bar Koseba (after town of Koseba in Judah).

Barlaam and Josaphat (bär'läŭm, jō'sŭfăt), popular romance found in many languages. A Christianized version of the Buddha legend (c.980) by Euthymius, a Georgian monk, and later elaborated, it tells of the conversion to Christianity of a young Indian prince, Barlaam, by the hermit Josaphat.

Barlach, Ernst (ĕrnst' bär'läkh), 1870–1938, German sculptor and graphic artist. His simple, angular, compact forms convey intense emotion and compassion for humanity.

Bar-le-Duc (bär-lŭ-dük'), town (est. pop. 16,609), cap. of Meuse dept., NE France; historic cap. of county (later duchy) of Bar (united with Lorraine in 15th cent.). Exports famed preserves, jellies.

barley, cereal grass (*Hordeum vulgare*), probably one of earliest cereals cultivated by man. Matures quickly, hence has a wide range, including high altitudes. Used for stock feed, malting, flour; until 16th cent., was chief breadstuff of Europe.

Barlow, Joel, 1754–1812, American poet and diplomat, one of CONNECTICUT WITS. His best-known poetic works are the epic *The Vision of Columbus* (1787; rev. ed., *The Columbiad,* 1807) and the mock eulogy *The Hasty Pudding* (written 1793). In France from 1788 as a commercial agent, he wrote *Advice to the Privileged Orders* (1792) and an able critique of the French Constitution of 1791. As U.S. consul in Algiers he arranged important treaties. Died of exposure on a diplomatic mission to Napoleon at the time of the retreat from Moscow.

Barmecides: see HARUN-AL-RASHID.

Barmen, West Germany: see WUPPERTAL.

Barnabas, Saint (bär'nŭbŭs), apostle, missionary, companion of Paul and Mark. Acts 4.36,37; 9.27; 11.22–15.41; 1 Cor. 9.6; Gal. 2.1,9,13; Col. 4.10. Among

Christian PSEUDEPIGRAPHA is an epistle attributed to him. Named in Canon of Mass. Feast: June 11.

barnacle, marine crustacean usually attached to rocks, stones, seaweed, wharf piles, ships, and marine animals. Shell-like plates cover adult's body. Usually has six pairs of plumelike legs, which are plied to draw food to mouth. Larva is free swimming.

Barnard, Edward Emerson (bär'nûrd), 1857–1923, American astronomer, pioneer in astronomical photography. Discoverer of Jupiter's fifth satellite and 16 comets.

Barnard, Frederick Augustus Porter, 1809–89, American educator, a mathematician. Professor, Univ. of Alabama (1837–54); professor, Univ. of Mississippi (1854–56), president (1856–58), chancellor (1858–61). As president of Columbia Col. (1864–89) he expanded the curriculum, supported sciences, extended elective system, fostered School of Mines. Advocated equal educational privileges for men and women; Barnard Col. named for him.

Barnard, Henry, 1811–1900, American educator, a leader in reform of common schools in Conn. and R.I. Chancellor of the Univ. of Wisconsin (1858–60), president of St. John's Col., Annapolis (1866–67), and first U.S. commissioner of education (1867–70).

Barnard College: see COLUMBIA UNIVERSITY.

Barnardo, Thomas John, 1845–1905, British social reformer, pioneer in care of destitute children; instrumental in securing passage of child welfare legislation.

Barnato, Barnett (bärnä'tō), 1852–97, South African financier, b. London; originally named Barney Isaacs. Made a fortune by buying up and exploiting worked-out Kimberley diamond mines. Later combined his interests with those of Cecil Rhodes.

Barnaul (bŭrnŭ̄ōol'), city (1965 est. pop. 382,000), S central RSFSR, on Ob R. Rail junction on Turkistan-Siberia RR in a cotton-growing region.

Barnave, Joseph (zhōzĕf' bärnäv'), 1761–93, French revolutionist. An extremist, he was sent in 1791 to bring fugitive royal family back from Varennes and turned monarchist. He supported Mirabeau, led FEUILLANTS, and was guillotined.

Barnburners, radical element of Democratic party in N.Y. (1843–48), opposed to HUNKERS. Name arose from story of Dutchman who burned his barn to get rid of rats, implying that Barnburners would destroy corporations and public works to do away with their abuses. Group also opposed extension of slavery. United with FREE-SOIL PARTY in 1848.

Barnegat Bay (bär'nŭgăt), Atlantic arm, c.30 mi. long, E N.J., entered via inlet between Long Beach isl. and Island Beach peninsula. Lighthouse built 1858 by Gen. George G. Meade; replaced by lightship 1930.

Barnes, London: see RICHMOND-UPON-THAMES.

Barnet, London borough since 1965 (est. pop. 318,-000); includes the former municipal borough of Finchley and urban districts of Hendon, Barnet, East Barnet, and Friern Barnet.

Barnett, Ross Robert, 1898–, governor of Mississippi. An ardent segregationist, in 1962 he defied Federal court order requiring the Univ. of Mississippi to admit Negro student James Meredith. Federal marshals ensured admission, but rioting followed.

Barnett, Samuel Augustus, 1849–1913, English clergyman and social worker. Opened Toynbee Hall (first settlement house) in 1884.

Barneveldt, Johan van Olden: see OLDENBARNEVELDT.

Barnstable (bärn'stŭbŭl), resort town (pop. 13,465), SE Mass., on Cape Cod; settled c.1638. Includes villages of Barnstable, HYANNIS, and Osterville (pop. 1,094).

Barnum, Phineas Taylor, 1810–91, American showman. Gained fame (1842) with his American Museum in N.Y., publicized by extravagant advertising and containing exhibits of freaks. Major attractions included "Gen. TOM THUMB." Managed U.S. tour of singer Jenny LIND. His circus ("The Greatest Show on Earth"), soon an American institution, opened 1871. Merged (1881) with J. A. Bailey's, circus continued under name Barnum and Bailey.

Barnwell, city (pop. 4,568), SW S.C., SSW of Columbia; settled 1798. Burned by Sherman's army 1865.

Barocci or **Baroccio, Federigo** (fādārē'gō bārôt'chē, –chō), c.1530–1612, Italian painter, active in Urbino. His mature works show baroque traits.

Baroda (bùrō'dù), former native state, Gujarat, India. Became independent kingdom under the Gaekwars in 18th cent. Its chief city, **Baroda** (pop. 295,304), has a palace and several colleges, and cotton-textile industry.

Baroja (y Nessi), Pío (pē'ō bārō'hä ē nē'sē), 1879–1956, Spanish novelist of Basque origin, prominent in GENERATION OF '98. Best known abroad for his trilogy *La lucha por la vida* [the struggle for existence] (1904).

barometer, instrument for measuring atmospheric pressure. Invented (1643) by Torricelli, who used column of water in tube 34 ft. long. This was replaced by mercury barometer, using 3-ft. mercury-filled glass tube (sealed at one end) supported vertically with open end under surface of mercury in container exposed to atmospheric pressure. Standard pressure at sea level (14.7 lb. per sq. in.) holds mercury in tube to height of 29.92 in. (space above mercury is vacuum). Height of column varies with change in air pressure; slight changes occur continually. Air pressure diminishes with altitude, the barometer reading dropping roughly 1 in. each 900 ft. until at c.3.5 mi. above earth's surface air pressure is about one half that at sea level; at c.10 mi. above earth, pressure is c.10% that at sea level, and it diminishes ultimately to zero. **Aneroid barometer** is metal box partially exhausted of air, its surface reacting to outside air pressure which registers on dial face.

Baron or **Boyron, Michel** (bärō or bwärō), 1653–1729, first great French actor; protégé of Molière.

Baron, Salo Wittmayer, 1895–, Jewish historian, b. Galicia. Became professor at Columbia 1930. His chief work is the multi-volume *Social and Religious History of the Jews.*

Barons' War, 1263–67, phase of the English struggle between king and barons. Henry III reasserted his power in 1261. Barons led by Simon de MONTFORT resorted to arms. Failed to estab. power of the nobles but helped prepare for constitutional developments of reign of EDWARD I.

baroque (bùrōk'), in architecture and decoration, a grandiose, richly ornamented, often extravagant style which originated in Italy in late 16th cent. as reaction against classicism. Reaching its height throughout Europe a century later, it was dethroned by 18th-cent. classic revival. Epitomized in Rome in Bernini's colonnades in St. Peter's Square and in works by Borromini and Vignola. In France the style culminated under Louis XIV and gave way to ROCOCO under Louis XV. It flourished in Germany and Austria, and reached extremes in Spain in work of Churriguera.

baroque, in music, a style that prevailed from the last decades of the 16th cent. to the first decades of the 18th cent. A revolt against POLYPHONY produced the accompanied recitative and opera; with these came the use of the FIGURED BASS. By the end of the era, TONALITY had replaced church modes (see MODE). Contrapuntal writing was resumed midway in the era, but with a harmonic basis. Idiomatic writing, with attention to characteristics of instruments and voices, was a feature of baroque music. Opera, ORATORIO, and CANTATA were the principal vocal forms. Instrumental music of the baroque era included SONATA, CONCERTO, and OVERTURE. The FUGUE, chorale prelude, and toccata were forms of late baroque.

Barotseland: see ZAMBIA.

Barquisimeto (bärkēsēmä'tō), city (pop. 199,691) NW Venezuela; founded 1552. A commercial center on Pan American Highway, it ships cattle.

Barr, Alfred Hamilton, Jr., 1902–, American art historian, has organized many major exhibitions at the Museum of Modern Art, New York. His books on Matisse and Picasso are standard references.

barracuda (bärùkōō'dù), elongated fish of tropical and subtropical seas. It has a long snout, large sharp-edged teeth, projecting lower jaw. Swift and voracious, it kills other fish and is often a hazard to human bathers.

Barranquilla (bärängkē'yä), city (pop. 498,301), N Colombia, Caribbean port near mouth of Magdalena R.; founded 1629. Has sugar refineries and textile mills.

Barras, Paul, vicomte de (bärä'), 1755–1829, French revolutionist. At first a Jacobin, he turned against Robespierre on 9 THERMIDOR; led in Thermidorian reaction. Was chief member of DIRECTORY; supported Bonaparte on 18 Brumaire (1799). Notoriously corrupt and immoral.

Barrault, Jean-Louis (bärō'), 1910–, French actor and director. Notable as Hamlet in Gide's translation and as the mime in the film *Children of Paradise* (1944).

Barre (bä'rē), city (pop. 10,387), central Vt., SE of Montpelier. Town of Barre (pop. 4,580) organized 1793. Granite quarrying began after War of 1812. Goddard Col. is at nearby Plainfield.

Barre des Écrins (bär' dāzäkrē'), peak, 13,461 ft. high, SE France; highest of Dauphiné Alps.

barren grounds, arctic prairie region of NW Canada, NW of Hudson Bay and E of the Mackenzie basin. Geologically part of the LAURENTIAN PLATEAU, it has large areas of bare rock, few trees, and limited vegetation. The many lakes and streams contain fish, and musk oxen are found in the N. Vast herds of caribou cross the area seasonally. Barren grounds first crossed by Samuel Hearne 1770–71.

Barrès, Maurice (mōrēs' bärēs'), 1862–1923, French novelist. From his early advocacy of egoism, expressed in the trilogy *Le Culte du moi* (1888–91), he turned to ardent nationalism. *Les Déracinés* [the uprooted] (1897) is typical of his lucid, powerful style.

Barrett, Elizabeth: see BROWNING, ELIZABETH.

Barrie, Sir J(ames) M(atthew) (bä'rē), 1860–1937, British author. Novels laid in his native Scotland (e.g., *The Little Minister,* 1891; *Sentimental Tommy,* 1896) were followed by plays (e.g., whimsy: *Quality Street,* 1901; *The Admirable Crichton,* 1902; fantasy: *Peter Pan,* 1904; comedy: *What Every Woman Knows,* 1908; and tragicomedy: *Dear Brutus,* 1917).

Barrie, city (pop. 21,169), S Ont., Canada, on W shore of L. Simcoe, in mixed farming and dairying area.

Barrier Reef, Australia: see GREAT BARRIER REEF.

Barrington, residential and resort town (1965 pop. 16,390), E R.I., SE of Providence; settled c.1670, included in Mass. until 1746.

Barron, James, 1769–1851, U.S. naval officer. Court-martialed as commander of CHESAPEAKE, frigate involved in famous incident in 1807. Mortally wounded Stephen Decatur in duel in 1820.

Barrow, Isaac, 1630–77, English mathematician, theologian. Helped lay foundation for Newton's development of differential calculus.

Barrow, Sir John, 1764–1848, British geographer, promoter of arctic exploration. Founder of Royal Geographical Society (1830).

Barrow, village (pop. 1,314), N Alaska, NE of Wainwright, near POINT BARROW. Main trade center of N Alaska and largest Eskimo settlement. Federal hospital.

Barrow, river of Ireland, rising in the Slieve Bloom mts. and flowing 119 mi. to Waterford Harbour.

barrow, in archaeology, mound built over burial area. Usually composed of earth and stone or timber. Found chiefly in W Europe, dating from Neolithic period.

Barrow, Point, Alaska: see POINT BARROW.

Barrow-in-Furness (-fûr'nŭs), county borough (pop. 64,824), on SW coast of FURNESS peninsula, Lancashire, England; one of Britain's chief engineering cities. Has immense steelworks, smelters.

Barry, Sir Charles, 1795–1860, English architect, best known for houses of Parliament, London.

Barry, John, 1745–1803, U.S. naval officer and hero in American Revolution, b. Ireland.

Barry, Philip, 1896–1949, American dramatist. Notable stage successes include *White Wings* (1926), *Holiday* (1928), *The Animal Kingdom* (1932), and *The Philadelphia Story* (1939).

Barry, municipal borough (pop. 42,039), Glamorganshire, Wales; a great coal exporting port of Britain.

Barrymore, family of actors. The first, **Maurice Barrymore** (real name Herbert Blythe), 1847–1905, was English. In U.S. (1875), joined Augustin Daly's stock company. Acted in Modjeska's company with his wife, **Georgiana Drew Barrymore,** 1856–93, American actress, one of the great comediennes of her day. Her oldest son, **Lionel Barrymore,** 1878–1954, noted character actor, appeared on stage in *Peter Ibbetson, Pantaloon,* and *Macbeth,* in films (notably in *A Free Soul*), and on radio (famed for Dickens' *Christmas Carol* from 1936). His sister, **Ethel Barrymore,** 1879–1959, actress of dignity and warmth, achieved stardom (1901) in Clyde Fitche's *Captain Jinks of the Horse Marines* and continued on the stage in such plays as *The Corn Is Green.* Their brother, **John Barrymore,** 1882–1942, tempestuous matinee idol after 1903 debut, appeared on stage (notable as Hamlet in 1922), in films, and on radio. The three Barrymores appeared together in film *Rasputin and the Empress* (1932).

Barsabas: see JOSEPH BARSABAS.

Barstow, city (pop. 11,644), SE Calif., NNE of San Bernardino, on dry Mojave R.; founded in 1880s as silver-mining town. Outfitting point for Death Valley expeditions. Has railroad shops and California Inst. of Technology interplanetary tracking station. U.S. Marine Corps supply center is nearby.

Bart, Jean (zhä' bär'), 1650–1702, French naval hero. A privateer from 1672, he was ennobled and created rear admiral (1696) by Louis XIV, as reward for spectacular exploits in War of the Grand Alliance. Noted for his naive bluntness.

Bartas, Guillaume de Salluste du: see DU BARTAS.

Barth, Heinrich (hīn'rĭkh bärt'), 1821–65, German explorer. Traveled throughout Levant and N Africa 1845–47; explored L. Chad region, and studied the Islamic culture of W Africa.

Barth, Karl, 1886–, Swiss Protestant Reformed theologian; one of leading thinkers of 20th-cent. Protestantism. Minister and professor in Germany from 1921 to 1935, when he was expelled by Hitler. Later taught at Basel. His dialectical theology seeks to reassert principles of the Reformation. Believes that central concern of theology should be revelation of God in Jesus Christ. Among major works is *Church Dogmatics* (vols. I–IV, 1932–62).

Bartholdi, Frédéric Auguste (frädärĕk' ōgüst' bärtōldē'), 1834–1904, French sculptor. Best-known works are *Lion of Belfort* and Statue of LIBERTY.

Bartholin, Kaspar (1655–1738), Danish physician, credited with discovering the glands of Bartholin in the vagina and a duct of one of the salivary glands.

Bartholomew, Saint, one of the Twelve Apostles. May be same as NATHANAEL (Nathanael given name, Bartholomew patronymic). Legendary missionary to India and Armenia. Feast: Aug. 24.

Barthou, Louis (lwē' bärtōō'), 1862–1934, French foreign minister (1934). Assassinated with King ALEXANDER of Yugoslavia.

Bartimaeus (-mē'ŭs), blind man cured by Jesus. Mat. 20.29–34; Mark 10.46–52; Luke 18.35–43.

Bartlesville, city (pop. 27,893), NE Okla., on Caney R., N of Tulsa; founded c.1877 on site of old trading post. Distribution center for oil and agr. region.

Bartlett, Robert Abram (Captain Bob), 1875–1946, American arctic explorer, b. Newfoundland. Noted especially for exploring and scientific work in Greenland. Made annual arctic cruises from 1925 to 1941.

Bartok, Bela (bä'lū bär'tôk), 1881–1945, Hungarian composer, pianist, collector of folk music (which greatly influenced his own compositions). He played and lectured in Europe and America. Among his principal works: six string quartets; three orchestral suites; a set of progressive piano studies, *Mikrokosmos;* Music for Two Pianos and Percussion; and concertos and rhapsodies for violin and for piano.

Bartolomeo, Fra (frä' bärtōlōmā'ō), 1475–1517, Florentine Renaissance painter of religious subjects.

Barton, Clara, 1821–1912, American humanitarian. Nurse to Civil War soldiers. Organized American Natl. Red Cross (1881); served as its president until 1904.

Barton, Elizabeth, 1506?–1534, English prophetess, called the Maid of Kent or the Nun of Kent. After prophecies highly critical of Henry VIII's divorce from Katharine, she was tried, induced to confess, and executed for treason.

Bartow, city (pop. 12,849), central Fla., SSE of Lakeland, in phosphates and citrus-fruit region. Settled mid-19th cent. on site of Seminole War fort.

Bartram, John, 1699–1777, pioneer American botanist. In 1728, in Philadelphia, he established the first botanical garden in U.S. His son, **William Bartram,** 1739–1823, was a naturalist. His *Travels* (1791) written after he explored SE U.S. served Wordsworth, Coleridge, and others as a source of descriptions of the American wilderness.

Baruch, Bernard M(annes) (bŭrōōk'), 1870–1965, U.S. government adviser on economics.

Baruch, in Western canon, book of Old Testament; placed in Apocrypha in AV. Named for Jewish prince Baruch (fl. 600 B.C.), faithful scribe of Jeremiah. Jer. 32.12–16; 36; 43.3,6; 45. Book contains: message from exiled Jews to those at home; well-known Messianic allusion (3.37); words of consolation; letter of Jeremiah (sometimes called Epistle of Jeremy). For Apocalypse of Baruch, see PSEUDEPIGRAPHA.

barytes: see BARITE.

Barzun, Jacques (zhäk' bär'zŭn), 1907–, American historian and teacher, b. France. Began teaching at Columbia in 1928; was made dean of the graduate faculties in 1955, provost and dean of faculties in 1958. He is also known as a critic of literature and the arts.

basalt (bŭsôlt'), common fine-grained extrusive rock (see LAVA), dark gray to black. The crust, or outer shell, of the earth under ocean basins is composed of basalt, as are the Columbia R. plateau and Iceland flows.

base, chemical compound that, by theory of ION, yields hydroxyl (OH) ions in aqueous solution. Described also as HYDROXIDE of metal or of positive RADICAL. OH ion has a negative charge, tastes bitter, feels soapy, turns red litmus blue. In solution bases conduct electricity, react with acids (NEUTRALIZATION); strong bases (alkalis) ionize freely.

baseball, "national game" of U.S. derived from English cricket and rounders. Commission headed by A. G. Mills reported (1907) that Abner Doubleday created the modern game at Cooperstown, N.Y., in 1839, though the question has been hotly disputed. Professional baseball's two major leagues (ten teams each) are the National (organized 1876) and the American (organized 1901). Since 1903, winners of these leagues have met in the World Series. The sport's greatest stars have been elected to Natl. Baseball Hall of Fame and Mus., built at Cooperstown 1939. See *ill.,* p. 1033.

Basedow, Johann Bernhard (yōhän' bĕrn'härt bä'zŭdō), 1723–90, German educator. Emphasized realistic teaching, including physical education, manual training, nature study.

Basel (bä'zŭl), Fr. *Bâle*, canton, N Switzerland, bordering on France and Germany; in English also spelled Basle. Crossed by Rhine R. (navigable from here) and by Jura mts. Population is Protestant, German-speaking. Canton has been divided since 1833 into two independent half cantons—Basel-Land (165 sq. mi.; pop. 148,282), with cap. at Liestal, and Basel-Stadt, coextensive with city of **Basel** and suburbs (14 sq. mi.; est. pop. 211,500), on the Rhine. Commercial, industrial, and intellectual center; seat of Bank for Internatl. Settlements and Swiss Industries Fair. Univ. was founded 1459. A Roman colony, Basel became a bishopric in 7th cent. A free imperial city from 11th cent., it joined the Swiss Confederation in 1501 and in 1523 accepted the Reformation. (The prince-bishops of Basel, expelled from the city, continued to rule their vast territory from DELÉMONT until 1792.) The oppressive regime of the city patriciate led to civil troubles (1831–33) and the secession of Basel-Land. Among notable buildings are the cathedral (founded 1019) and the 16th-cent. city hall, with a Holbein collection. Erasmus and Holbein the Younger lived here. Euler and the Bernoulli family were born here.

Basel, Council of, 1431–49, council of Roman Catholic Church. A primary reason for its being summoned was trouble with the Hussites, and an agreement called the Compactata was drawn up (1433) and later split the Hussites (with the Utraquists rejoining the Church). The council is, however, remarkable chiefly for trying to put in practice the conciliar theory already advanced at the Council of Constance—the theory that ultimate authority resides in the general council, not the pope. Pope EUGENE IV early ordered it dissolved, but tried to compromise with the council, which instituted a process against the pope. He denounced the council in a bull (*Doctoris gentium,* 1437). The council deposed him and elected AMADEUS VIII of Savoy (antipope Felix V). Eugene, who summoned the Council of FERRARA-FLORENCE, had the support of most rulers. Though the French adopted many ideas of the council and many reforms proposed were adopted by the Church, the council failed. Felix V resigned in favor of Eugene's successor, Nicholas V, and the conciliar theory died with the council.

Bashan (bā'–), in Bible, region E of Jordan R., known for cattle and sheep. Num. 21.33; Deut. 3; 2 Kings 10.33; Ps. 22.12; 68.15; Amos 4.1.

Bashkir Autonomous Soviet Socialist Republic (bŭsh-kēr') autonomous state (55,444 sq. mi.; 1965 est. pop. 3,693,000), E European RSFSR, partly in S Urals; cap. Ufa. Agr., timber, minerals (iron, copper, manganese, gold, chromium, lead, bauxite, petroleum). Bashkirs (24% of pop.) are Moslem, Turkic-speaking people, tributary to Russia since 1556; rest of population mainly Russians (40%) and Turko-Tatars.

Basil, Saint: see BASIL THE GREAT, SAINT.

Basil, Byzantine emperors. Basil I (the Macedonian), c.813–86. Boon companion of Emperor MICHAEL III, whom he persuaded to make him coemperor (866) and whom he ordered slain (867). Capable, he reformed finances and the law code, and restored Byzantine military prestige. He strove vainly to prevent a schism of E and W churches and restored IGNATIUS OF CONSTANTINOPLE to the patriarchate (867). **Basil II,** c.958–1025, was co-ruler with his brother Constantine VIII after the reigns of usurpers NICEPHORUS II (963–69) and JOHN I (969–76). He suppressed the revolts of the landowners, revived laws of ROMANUS I, annexed Bulgaria (1018), and extended his empire to Caucasus. Called Bulgaroktonos, "Bulgar slayer."

Basil III, grand duke of Moscow: see VASILY III.

basil (bă'zŭl), tender herb or shrub of genus *Ocimum.* Cultivated for aromatic leaves used as seasoning.

Basilian monks (bŭzǐ'lĕŭn), monks of the Eastern Church, following the rule of St. BASIL THE GREAT. They live in collections of small cells without central government. The reformation by St. THEODORE OF STUDIUM (9th cent.) revitalized the order. Noted monasteries (hermitages) are at Mt. Athos and Mt. Sinai.

Basilicata (bäzēlēkä'tä), region (3,856 sq. mi.; pop. 648,085), S Italy; cap. Potenza. Other cities: MELFI, Matera. Poor, arid soil. Sheep and goat raising. Comprising parts of anc. Lucania and Samnium, region fell to Lombards, Byzantines; annexed (11th cent.) to Norman duchy of Apulia.

Basilius Valentinus, mythical 15th-cent. monk. Johannes Thölde of Frankenhausen, Germany, claimed his books were translations from Latin of the monk's work. His *Currus triumphalis antimonii* (1604) led to use of antimony for fevers.

Basil the Great, Saint (bä'zĭl, bā'–), c.330–379, Greek churchman, one of the Greek Fathers, Doctor of the Church, bishop of Caesarea in Cappadocia; brother of St. Gregory of Nyssa. He wrote most of the two rules for the Basilian monks. As aid and successor to Eusebius, he helped estab. orthodoxy over ARIANISM. Greatly influenced St. BENEDICT.

Baskerville, John, 1706–75, English type designer, printer for Cambridge Univ. after 1758. Introduced influential "modern" type faces. His books are large, with wide margins and excellent paper and ink.

basketball. Played by two opposing teams of five players each on regulation court 94 ft. long, 50 ft. wide. Originated (1891) in U.S. by James Naismith, physical director of Y.M.C.A. college, Springfield, Mass. Most popular spectator sport in U.S. National Basketball Association (professional), eight teams in two sections, formed in 1949.

Basket Makers, early Indian people of U.S. Southwest, dating possibly from c.1500 B.C. Had great skill in making baskets; developed from nomadic hunters to farmers; lived in pit houses. Succeeded by ancestors of Pueblo Indians.

Basking Ridge, town (pop. 2,438), N N.J., near Passaic R., SW of Morristown; settled early 18th cent. Gen. Charles Lee captured by British here 1776.

Basle, Switzerland: see BASEL.

Basov, Nikolai G., 1922–, Russian physicist. Shared 1964 Nobel Prize in Physics for work on lasers and masers and for contributions to the field of quantum electronics.

Basque Provinces (băsk), Basque *Euzkadi,* Span. *Vascongadas,* region, N Spain, S of Bay of Biscay, bordering in NE on France. Chief cities: Bilbao, San Sebastián, Vitoria. Iron, lead, copper mines; shipyards; fisheries. Majority of pop. are **Basques,** fervidly Catholic people of peasants, shepherds, and fishermen. There are c.1,650,000 Basques in Spanish Navarre and Basque Provs.; c.200,000 in SW France (Labourd, Soule, and Lower Navarre dists.); c.250,000 in S America and rest of world. Possibly descended from Cro-Magnon man, they antedate anc. Iberian tribes of Spain. Their language is related to no other. Before Roman conquest of Spain and Gaul, Basque pop. extended further N and S than now. Core of Basque country fought off Romans, Visigoths, Moors, and Franks. Basque victory at RONCESVALLES threw off short-lived overlordship of Charlemagne (778). In GASCONY the duchy set up by Basques in 601 fell apart in 9th cent., but in 824 the Basque kingdom of NAVARRE was founded; under SANCHO III it united nearly all Basques (1000–1035). Basques lost independence as Castile acquired Guipúzcoa (1200), Álava (1332), Vizcaya (1370), and most of Navarre (1512), but they retained their old democratic rights. Their assemblies at GUERNICA remain famous. In 1873 Basque privileges were abolished after Basques' pro-Carlist stand in Carlist wars. The three Basque Provs. were granted autonomy in 1936. They stoutly resisted Franco, who revoked autonomy after conquering them in 1937.

Basra (bŭs′rŭ), city (pop. 164,623), SE Iraq, port on the Shatt el Arab, 75 mi. from Persian Gulf. Founded A.D. 636 by Caliph Omar, declined during Abbasid caliphate. Railroad link to Baghdad revived its importance. Many oil refineries.

Bas-Rhin (bä-rē′), department (1,848 sq. mi.; pop. 770,-150), E France, in Alsace; cap. Strasbourg.

Bass, Sam (bås), 1851–78, American desperado. Train robber in S.Dak. and Texas. Career provided material for frontier ballads.

bass, name for various fresh-water and marine fish, valuable as game and food. Most important are sea-bass family (Serranidae) and sunfish family (Centrarchidae). Common sea bass (*Centropristes striatus*) along U.S. coast from Massachusetts to N Florida. Sometimes classed as sea bass and sometimes as separate family (Moronidae) are striped bass or rockfish (*Roccus saxatilis* or *R. lineatus*); white bass (*R. chrysops*); yellow bass (*Morone interrupta*); white or silver perch (*M. americana*).

Bassano, Jacopo (yäkō′pō bäs-sä′nō), c.1515–92, Venetian painter, b. Bassano. His real name was Da Ponte. Perhaps the first Italian genre artist. His son and follower was **Leandro Bassano** (lään′drō), 1558–1623.

Bassano, town (pop. 815), E Alta., Canada, SE of Calgary. Huge Bassano or Horseshoe Bend Dam is just S on the Bow R.

Bassano (bäs-sä′nō), city (est. pop. 28,753), Venetia, NE Italy, on Brenta R. Free commune in Middle Ages; under Venice 1402–1797. Home of Da Ponte family of painters (surnamed BASSANO) and of famous Remondini printing plant (17th-18th cent.). Palaces and churches recall past glory. Scene of Bonaparte's victory over Austrians 1796.

Basses-Alpes (bäs-zälp′), department (2,698 sq. mi.; pop. 91,843), SE France, in Provence; cap. Digne.

Basses-Pyrénées (bäs″-pēränä′), department (2,978 sq. mi.; pop. 466,038), SW France; cap. Pau.

Basses-Terre (bästēr′) port (pop. 13,978), cap. of Guadeloupe dept., French West Indies.

Basseterre, town (pop. 15,897), St. Christopher, cap. of colony of St. Christopher-Nevis-Anguilla, West Indies.

Bassett, John Spencer, 1867–1928, American historian. Founder (1902) of *South Atlantic Quarterly.* His many works on American history include *The Federalist System, 1789–1801* (1906) and *The Life of Andrew Jackson* (1911).

Bassompierre, François, baron de (fräswä′ bärō′ dù bäsōpyēr′), 1579–1646, marshal of France. Served under Henry IV; later fought Huguenots (1621–22, 1627–28). His opposition to Richelieu caused his imprisonment in Bastille (1631–43). Wrote memoirs.

bassoon: see WIND INSTRUMENTS.

Bass Strait (bås), channel, 80–150 mi. wide, between Tasmania and Victoria, Australia. Its discovery by George Bass in 1798 destroyed belief that Tasmania was part of Australian continent.

basswood: see LINDEN.

bast: see BARK.

bastard, person born out of wedlock, illegitimate child. It is legally presumed that any child born to a married woman is the child of her husband. The latter has the burden of proof if he contests his paternity on the ground of physical impossibility. Attitudes toward illegitimacy have varied greatly under different social conditions. Under English common law illegitimate children had few rights. Rights now given by statutes. In U.S. state laws on illegitimacy vary greatly; generally subsequent marriage of parents legitimizes child, and some states provide special judicial proceedings for legitimation.

Bastard of Orléans, French general: see DUNOIS, JEAN, COMTE DE.

Bastia (bästē′ä), town (pop. 50,117), NE Corsica, France; on Tyrrhenian Sea. The chief commercial center of Corsica, Bastia was its cap. until 1791. Citadel.

Bastian, Adolf (ä′dôlf bäs′tyän), 1826–1905, German anthropologist. His concept of "elemental ideas," common to all mankind but varying according to "folk ideas" of given area, foreshadow culture-area theory.

Bastidas, Rodrigo de (rōdhrē′gō dä bästē′dhäs), c.1460-1526, Spanish conquistador in Colombia. Discovered mouth of Magdalena (1501), founded Santa Marta (1525).

Bastien-Lepage, Jules (zhül′ bästyē′-lùpäzh′), 1848–84, French painter of figures in the open air.

Bastille (bästēl′), former state prison in Paris, France. Begun as fortress c.1369; demolished 1789. Fouquet, Man with the Iron Mask, and Voltaire were imprisoned here. Despite horror stories, most political prisoners were treated mildly. On July 14, 1789, a Parisian mob, protesting Necker's dismissal, stormed Bastille. The date, marking outbreak of French Revolution, became national holiday of republican France.

Bastogne (bästō′nyù), town (est. pop. 5,400), Luxembourg prov., SE Belgium, in Ardennes. During BATTLE OF THE BULGE, U.S. troops held encircled town until relieved by U.S. 3d Army (Dec., 1944.)

Bastrop, industrial city (pop. 15,193), NE La., NNE of Monroe. Founded c.1845, it grew after discovery of natural gas 1916.

Basutoland: see LESOTHO.

bat, mammal of order Chiroptera. Found in most temperate and tropical regions, it is only mammal with power of true flight. Wing is membrane stretched between elongated bones of four fingers, extending in most bats along body from forelimbs to hind limbs to tail. Thumb is small, clawed, free of membrane. Chiefly nocturnal, they have some sight; avoid collision in flight by emitting sounds which are reflected back by any object in their path; these sounds are of too high a frequency for human ears. In temperate climates, some bats hibernate in caves in winter; some migrate. Fruit bat is also called flying fox.

Bataan (båtän′, bätä-än′), peninsula and province (157 sq. mi.; pop. 111,680), W Luzon, Philippines, forming W shore of Manila Bay. After fall of Manila in Second World War, U.S. troops (first led by Gen. MacArthur and later by Lt. Gen. Wainwright) made a gallant stand here Jan.–April, 1942.

Batalha (bùtä′lyù), town, Estremadura, W central Portugal, S of Leiria. John I built its famous Dominican monastery and church to commemorate victory of Aljubarrota (1385).

Batalpashinsk, RSFSR: see CHERKESSK.

Batavia, Indonesia: see DJAKARTA.

Batavia, city (pop. 18,210), W N.Y., WSW of Rochester, in farm area. Laid out 1801 by Holland Land Co. agent.

Batavian Republic, 1795–1806. The United Provs. of the Netherlands, occupied by French in the French Revolutionary Wars, were reconstituted as the Batavian Republic in 1795, remaining under French tutelage. In 1806 Napoleon made it into kingdom of Holland for his brother Louis.

Bates, Henry Walter, 1825–92, English naturalist, explorer of upper Amazon with A. R. Wallace. In 1859 returned with 8,000 new species of animals. First to state plausible theory of mimicry.

Bates, Herbert Ernest, 1905–, English author. His best-known novel is *Fair Stood the Wind for France* (1944), a tale of the Royal Air Force. He is pre-eminently a short-story writer, widely anthologized.

Bath, county borough (pop. 80,856) and city, Somerset, England, on the Avon. Romans discovered warm springs here 1st cent. A.D.; built elaborate walls and baths. In Chaucer's time, it had become wool and cloth town. Became famous spa in 18th cent., with Beau Nash as social arbiter. John WOOD and his son planned streets and buildings such as the Royal Crescent, Assembly Rooms (destroyed in 1942 air raid), and Circus. Now residential and resort town with mfg. and quarrying. Abbey founded 1499.

SMALL CAPITALS = cross references. Pronunciation key on inside end pages. Abbreviations: p. 2.

Bath. 1 City (pop. 10,717). SW Maine, on W bank of Kennebec R.; settlement began c.1670. An important shipbuilding center since early days, it flourished during First and Second World wars with building of destroyers. **2** Village (pop. 6,166), S N.Y., NW of Elmira, in farm area; settled 1793. Has U.S. veterans' administration center. **3** Town (1966 pop. 281), E N.C. on Pamlico R., SE of Washington; settled c.1690 on Indian village site. Oldest town in state, it was cap. of province of N.C. **4** Town, W. Va.: see BERKELEY SPRINGS.

Bath, Order of the, British order of knighthood. Estab. 1725 as military order, in 1847 opened also to civilians.

Bathory (bä'tôrē), Hung. *Báthory,* Pol. *Batory,* Hungarian noble family. **Stephen Bathory,** 1477–1534, voivode of Transylvania (1529–34) was the father of STEPHEN BATHORY, king of Poland, and of **Christopher Bathory,** 1530–81, prince of Transylvania (1575–81). Christopher's son **Sigismund Bathory,** 1572–1613, was recognized as hereditary prince of Transylvania by Rudolf II (1594). Probably insane, he abdicated 1596, but soon afterward returned to power, with Bocskay's help, as vassal of the sultan. He briefly abdicated again in 1599, and definitively in 1601 (in favor of Rudolf). Other members of the family include **Elizabeth Bathory,** d. 1614, celebrated as a werewolf (she is said to have slaughtered 600 virgins to renew her youth by bathing in their blood), who died in prison, and **Gabriel Bathory,** 1589–1613, prince of Transylvania (1608–13), murdered by rebellious nobles.

Bath-sheba (băth-shē'bù), wife of Uriah the Hittite. David caused Uriah's death to marry her. She bore him Solomon. 2 Sam. 11; 12; 1 Kings 1; 2; Mat. 1.6.

Bathurst, town (pop. c.32,900), cap. of Gambia; port on the Atlantic at mouth of Gambia R. Founded by British 1816. Exports peanuts, beeswax, palm kernels, and hides.

bathysphere: see DIVING.

Batista (y Zaldívar), Fulgencio (fōolhĕn'sēō bätē'stä ē söldē'var), 1901–, president of Cuba (1940–44; 1952–58). Military coup brought him to power in 1933; after exile in U.S. 1945–49 he led successful coup in 1952 but, unable to put down revolutionary movement led by Fidel CASTRO, fled to Dominican Republic in Jan., 1959. Later settled in Madeira.

Batlle y Ordóñez, José (hōsā' băt'yä ē ôrdō'nyäs), 1856–1929, president of Uruguay (1903–7, 1911–15). Fought anarchy which prevailed after independence; championed social reforms embodied in constitution of 1917.

Batoche (bätösh'), village, central Sask., Canada, S of Prince Albert. Hq. of Louis RIEL in Riel's Rebellion.

Baton Rouge (băt'ùn rōozh'), city (pop. 152,419), state cap. (since 1849), SE La., partly on high bluffs along E bank of Mississippi R.; built 1719 as French fort. Strategically located, it was occupied in turn by French, Spanish, English, and Americans in 18th and early 19th cent. Taken by Farragut in Civil War (May, 1862); Confederate attempt to recapture it failed (Aug., 1862). A deepwater port served by rail and air, it is distribution and commercial center in area producing oil, natural gas, cotton, sugar, fruit, vegetables, cattle, and dairy products. Oil refining is chief industry. Seat of LOUISIANA STATE UNIVERSITY AND AGRICULTURAL AND MECHANICAL COLLEGE and Southern Univ. and Agr. and Mechanical Col. Old capitol (1882), built in Gothic style of original (burned in Civil War), still stands.

Batory: see BATHORY.

Battenberg (bä'tùnbûrg), princely family issued from morganatic marriage of Alexander, younger son of Louis II of Hesse-Darmstadt, and countess Julia von Hauke, created princess of Battenberg 1858. Their oldest son, Louis, an admiral in British service, was created marquess of Milford Haven, married a granddaughter of Queen Victoria, anglicized his name to Mountbatten in First World War; father of Earl

Mountbatten, grandfather of Philip, duke of EDINBURGH. Alexander's second son was Prince ALEXANDER of Bulgaria. A third son, Henry, married Beatrice, daughter of Queen Victoria; their daughter, Victoria Eugenie. married Alfonso XIII of Spain.

Battersea, part of WANDSWORTH London borough since 1965; site of 200-acre Battersea Park and Royal Festival Hall (built 1951).

Battery, the, park at S tip of Manhattan isl., New York city. Castle Clinton, fort built 1808–11 as defense for New York harbor, became Castle Garden amusement hall (scene of Jenny Lind's American debut 1850). Was later immigration station (1855–90), and aquarium (1896–1941). Estab. as Castle Clinton Natl. Monument 1950.

battery, unpermitted intentional touching by an aggressor—directly or indirectly—of any part of another person. Either a criminal or civil action can result. Consent, the most important defense, is assumed for customary contacts.

battery, electric, commonly describes electric CELL; more correctly means group of cells used as source of electric current. **A** or **filament battery** provides current to heat FILAMENT in vacuum tube of radio. **B battery** is the source of current in plate circuit; produces needed voltage on plates of vacuum tubes. Usually consists of small dry cells connected in series; also may be of storage type. **C battery** is used in grid circuit of tube (see TUBE, VACUUM) to create bias (usually negative) on grid of tube. **Storage battery** is a much used current source, e.g., in automobile; has electric cells in series (see ELECTRIC CIRCUIT; *ill.,* p. 322).

Battle, rural district (pop. 30,558), Sussex E., England, NW of Hastings. Scene of 1066 battle which resulted in death of Harold and elevation of Norman conqueror as WILLIAM I of England. Has ruins of **Battle Abbey,** founded by William after his victory. **Battle Abbey Roll,** which was kept here, supposedly listed William's noble battle companions. Its authenticity is doubtful.

Battle above the Clouds: see CHATTANOOGA CAMPAIGN.

Battle Creek, city (pop. 44,169), S Mich., SW of Lansing, at junction of Kalamazoo and Battle Creek rivers; settled 1831. A farm trade center known for cereal and health foods. Health Reform Institute (founded 1866 by Seventh-Day Adventists) was reorganized 1876 by Dr. J. H. Kellogg into present Battle Creek Sanitarium. Has veterans' administration center.

Battleford, town (pop. 1,627), W Sask., Canada, on North Saskatchewan R. at mouth of Battle R. NW of Saskatoon. Cap. of Northwest Territories 1876–83. Prominent in Riel's Rebellion.

Battle of the Bulge, name given in Second World War to the last German offensive on Western front (Dec., 1944–Jan., 1945). On Dec. 16 Germans under von Rundstedt in surprise attack broke through American front in Belgian Ardennes, creating a "bulge" in Allied lines. Allied counterthrusts turned German offensive into rout by mid-January. U.S. troops suffered heavy casualties. Defense of BASTOGNE was a notable episode.

Battle of the Spurs. 1 Victory, 1302, near Courtrai, Belgium, of Flemish towns over French army sent by Philip IV; so called for trophy formed by spurs of fallen French. **2** Victory, 1513, at GUINEGATE, of Henry VIII of England over French; possibly so called for speedy flight of French cavalry.

Batu Khan (bä'tōo kän), d. 1255, Mongol leader, grandson of Jenghiz Khan. Commander of the Mongol army assigned to the conquest of Europe; his host was known as the GOLDEN HORDE.

Batum (bütōōm'), city (1965 est. pop. 96,000), cap. of Adzhar ASSR, Georgian SSR, on Black Sea. Connected by pipe lines with Baku; major oil-refining center. Ceded by Turkey to Russia 1878.

Baucis: see PHILEMON AND BAUCIS.

Baudelaire, Charles (shärl' bōdlâr'), 1821–67, French poet. His neurotic, eccentric personality led him along a road of poverty, misunderstanding, excesses, and disease. A perfectionist, he labored for years on his one volume of verse, *Les Fleurs du Mal* [flowers of evil] (1857), six poems of which were condemned as obscene by a court. Other works include remarkable literary and art criticism and exceptionally fine translations of Poe, to whom he felt great affinity. His influence on all subsequent poetry is immeasurable. There are several English translations of his poems.

Baudette (bôdet'), village (pop. 1,597), N Minn., on Rainy R. (bridged) at Canadian line; settled c.1910. U.S. air force radar station is nearby.

Baudouin (bōdōōĕ'), 1930–, king of the Belgians (1951–); son and successor of LEOPOLD III.

Bauer, Louis Agricola, 1865–1932, American magnetician. Influential in international coordination of work in terrestrial magnetism. Founded and edited *Terrestrial Magnetism and Atmospheric Electricity*.

Bauhaus (bou'hous), art school in Germany. It revolutionized art training by combining the teaching of pure arts with the study of crafts. Founded in 1919 at Weimar with Walter GROPIUS as director, it stressed functional craftsmanship in every field with a realization of the industrial problems of mass production. In 1933 closed by the German government.

Bauhin, Gaspard (gäspär' bōĕ'), 1560–1624, Swiss botanist. He classified plants by genus and species, anticipating the binomial system of Linnaeus.

Baum, L(yman) Frank (bôm), 1856–1919, American author of juvenile books laid in imaginary magic land of Oz (e.g., *The Wonderful Wizard of Oz*, 1900).

Baumann, Oskar (bou'män), 1864–99, Austrian explorer in Africa. Traveled up Congo R.; accompanied parties to Mt. Kilimanjaro and L. Victoria.

Baumé, Antoine (ātwän' bōmä'), 1728–1804, French chemist. Invented a graduated hydrometer, discovered various important industrial processes.

Bausch, Edward (boush), 1854–1944, American inventor. Worked on kinetoscope, camera, microscope.

Bautzen (bou'tsŭn), city, (est. pop. 40,858), East Germany, in former state of Saxony, SE Germany, on the Spree. Machine, textile, chemical mfg. Napoleon I defeated Russo-Prussian forces nearby (1813).

Baux, Les (lä bō'), ruined medieval town near Arles, SE France. Was seat of powerful feudal family. Impressive ruins. Bauxite, first discovered here, is named for Les Baux.

bauxite, hydrate of ALUMINA, with other oxides. A claylike, earthy mineral, white to red or brown. Chief source of aluminum and its compounds.

Bavaria, Ger. *Bayern*, state (27,239 sq. mi., pop. 9,731,-000), West Germany; cap. MUNICH. Rises in S to Bavarian Alps (highest peak ZUGSPITZE) along Austrian frontier; BOHEMIAN FOREST forms E frontier with Czechoslovakia. Danube and Main are chief rivers. State consists of Bavaria proper, i.e., Upper Bavaria (cap. Munich) and Lower Bavaria (chief city Landshut) in S; Upper, Middle, and Lower FRANCONIA (with BAYREUTH, BAMBERG, NUREMBERG, WÜRZBURG) in N; SWABIA (cap. AUGSBURG) in W; Upper PALATINATE (cap. REGENSBURG) in NE. Rich in agr. and forests; also has mfg. (machinery, textiles, beer, toys), resorts and spas for tourists. Roman Catholicism is predominant except in N. Until early 19th cent. Bavaria did not include Franconia and Swabia, which have separate histories. Conquered by Romans 15 B.C., the region was made a duchy 6th cent. A.D. by an invading Germanic tribe (Baiuoarii). Under Carolingians 788–911; under GUELPHS 1070–1180 (with interruptions); under WITTELSBACH dynasty 1180–1918. Austria, Carinthia, and Upper Palatinate were detached (976) from original duchy to curb power of dukes. Wittelsbach fiefs (incl. Rhenish PALATINATE) were long divided among various branches of family, fully united only in 1799. Duke MAXIMILIAN I received Upper Palatinate and electoral rank (1623; see ELECTORS). Enlarged and raised to kingdom (1806), Bavaria emerged from Congress of

Vienna with present territory and Rhenish Palatinate (1815). Sided with Austria in Austro-Prussian War (1866), with Prussia in Franco-Prussian War (1870–71); joined German Empire 1871. As chief German state after Prussia, it retained special position and separatist tendencies. Republic set up Nov., 1918; joined Weimar Republic after unsuccessful Communist revolution (1919). All Bavaria under U.S. occupation after 1945, except for Rhenish Palatinate and LINDAU dist., which were detached and occupied by France. New constitution adopted 1946. Joined Federal Republic of [Western] Germany 1949. Kings of Bavaria: MAXIMILIAN I, LOUIS I, MAXIMILIAN II, LOUIS II, OTTO I, LOUIS III.

Bavarian Succession, War of the, 1778–79. Elector Maximilian III having died childless in 1777, Bavaria passed to the elector palatine, Charles Theodore, who recognized Austria's claim to Lower Bavaria and part of Upper Palatinate. Prussia protested. Ensuing campaign, spent entirely in provisioning the armies, has been called the Potato War. At the Congress of Teschen (1779) Austria renounced its claims.

Bax, Sir Arnold, 1881–1953, English composer. His works, which reflect Wagner and Debussy, include several tone poems, e.g., *The Garden of Fand*, seven symphonies, instrumental and vocal compositions.

Baxter, Gregory Paul, 1876–1953, American chemist. Chairman (1930–47) of Internatl. Committee on Atomic Weights.

Baxter, Richard, 1615–91, English nonconformist clergyman. A supporter of Cromwell, yet a moderate, he sought under Charles II to keep dissenters in Church; after Act of Uniformity (1662) withdrew from Church of England, but continued preaching despite persecution. Wrote *The Saints' Everlasting Rest* (1650).

Baxter Springs, city (pop. 4,498), SE Kansas, near Okla. and Mo. lines S of Pittsburg; settled c.1850. A rail center for zinc- and lead-mine area. W. C. Quantrill's Confederate guerrillas massacred 87 men here 1863.

Bay, Ohio: see BAY VILLAGE.

bay or sweet bay: see LAUREL.

Bayamo (bäyä'mō), city (pop. 143,487), SE Cuba. Founded 1513, it is an agr. center.

Bayamón (bäyämon'), town (pop. 15,109), NE Puerto Rico, near coast. Mfg. center. Has oil refinery.

Bayar, Celal (bäyär'), 1884–, Turkish statesman, president of Turkey (1950–60).

Bayard, Pierre du Terrail, seigneur de (bā'ürd, Fr. pyĕr' dü tĕrī'yü sänyûr' dü bäyär'), c.1474–1524, French hero, *le chevalier sans peur et sans reproche* [the knight without fear or blame]. Fought in Italian Wars; fell in battle.

Bayard, Thomas Francis (bī'ürd), 1828–98, American statesman. Was U.S. Senator from Delaware (1869–85), U.S. Secretary of State (1885–89), and U.S. ambassador to Great Britain (1893–97), first to hold that rank.

Bayard (bā'ürd), Ital. *Baiardo*, in chivalric romance, a spirited bay horse, able to fit his size to his rider. Appears in 12th-cent. French epic *Renaud de Montaubon* and in tales of Roland.

Bayazid or Bayazit: see BAJAZET.

bayberry, American shrub (*Myrica pennsylvanica*), native to the eastern seacoast of U.S. It is often cultivated for its handsome aromatic foliage. Its gray, waxy berries are used in winter bouquets and in making candles. California bayberry (*Myrica californica*) is evergreen and treelike.

Bay City. 1 City (pop. 53,604), S Mich., on Saginaw R. near its mouth on Saginaw Bay, NNE of Saginaw; settled 1837. Port for Great Lakes and ocean shipping, it has shipyards, commercial fishing, coal mines, and refineries. **2** City (pop. 11,656), S Texas, SW of Houston, near Colorado R. Shipping and industrial center for oil, rice, poultry, and livestock region.

Bayer, Johann (yō'hän bī'ûr), 1572–1625, German astronomer, known for system of designating stars of a

CONSTELLATION (using Greek letters with constellation names) and for star chart, *Uranometria* (1603).

Bayeux (bäyû'), town (est. pop. 10,077), Calvados dept., N France, in Normandy. Noted for its lace industry. Fine Gothic cathedral. In Bayeux mus. is the **Bayeux tapestry**, an embroidery chronicling the Norman conquest of England in 1066; it is worked on coarse linen, 230 ft. by 20 in. Its date is disputed.

Bay Islands, archipelago, off N coast of Honduras, in Caribbean. Garrisoned by British 1848–59.

Bayle, Pierre (bäl), 1647–1706, French rationalist philosopheŕ, long resident in Rotterdam. Chief work was *Dictionnaire historique et critique* (1697).

Bayley, Richard, 1745–1801, American physician, known for scientific account of yellow fever epidemic of 1795 in New York city.

Bayliss, Sir William Maddock (bā'lĭs), 1860–1924, English physiologist, pioneer (with Starling) in evolving theory of hormone action after discovering secretin.

Baylor University, at Waco, Texas; coed.; chartered and opened 1845 by Baptists at Independence; moved and absorbed Waco Univ. 1886. Fine Robert Browning collection.

Bayonne (bäyŏn'), city (est. pop. 32,575), Basses-Pyrénées dept., SW France, in Basque country, on Adour R. near Bay of Biscay; fortified seaport. Bayonet invented here in 17th cent. Gothic cathedral, museums of fine arts and Basque folklore.

Bayonne (bäyŏn'), city (pop. 74,215), NE N.J., on peninsula SSW of Jersey City, between New York harbor and Newark Bay. Dutch traders came c.1650; British took over 1664. Has U.S. Naval dry dock, supply depot. Oil refineries (here since 1875) are supplied by pipeline from SW.

Bay Psalm Book, hymnal used in Mass. Bay colony, entitled *The Whole Book of Psalms Faithfully Translated into English Metre;* first book printed (1640, by STEPHEN DAYE) in the Thirteen Colonies.

Bayreuth (bīroit'), city (pop. 59,544), cap. of Upper Franconia, NE Bavaria. Textile, metal, and food mfg. Founded 1194; under HOHENZOLLERN family 1248–1807. Residence of Richard WAGNER 1872–83; celebrated for annual music festivals. Wagner and Liszt are buried here.

Bay Shore, city, SE N.Y., on S shore of Long Isl. Fishing and duck-hunting center on Great South Bay. Ferry to Fire Isl.

Baytown, city (pop. 28,159), S Texas, at head of Galveston Bay, E of Houston. Formed 1947 by combining Goose Creek, Pelly, and Baytown. Oil port on Houston ship channel.

Bay Village or **Bay**, city (pop. 14,489), NE Ohio, a suburb W of Cleveland.

Bazaine, Achille (äshĕl' bäzĕn'), 1811–88, marshal of France. In Franco-Prussian War he allowed Germans to lock up his army at Metz and eventually capitulated (1870). MacMahon's attempt to relieve Metz led to disaster of Sedan. Condemned for treason (1873), Bazaine escaped abroad.

Bazán, Emilia Pardo: see PARDO BAZÁN.

Bazargic, Bulgaria: see TOLBUKHIN.

B battery: see BATTERY, ELECTRIC.

Be, chemical symbol of the element BERYLLIUM.

Beach, Moses Yale, 1800–1868, American journalist. After buying the New York *Sun* (1838) from his brother-in-law, Benjamin Day, he rivaled James Gordon Bennett in hustling for news, speeding transmission, widening coverage. Helped found the New York Associated Press and was first to have European edition of a U.S. paper and to syndicate articles.

beach grass or marram grass, perennial grass of genus *Ammophila*. Helps to control shifting sands.

Beacon, industrial city (pop. 13,922), SE N.Y., on E bank of Hudson R. opposite Newburgh; settled 1663, formed 1913, when Fishkill Landing and Matteawan villages united. Here are Mt. Beacon (with incline 'railway) and Matteawan State Hospital.

Beaconsfield, Benjamin Disraeli, 1st earl of: see DISRAELI, BENJAMIN.

Beadle, George Wells, 1903–, American geneticist. Shared with Joshua Lederberg and E. L. Tatum 1958 Nobel Prize in Medicine and Physiology for work with Tatum establishing that genes in bread mold transmit hereditary characters by controlling specific chemical reactions.

Beagle, 235-ton vessel on which Charles DARWIN made world cruise (1831–36).

Bean, Roy, c.1825–1903, American frontiersman. Justice of the peace—self-styled "law west of the Pecos" —at Vinegaroon (later renamed Langtry), Texas. Meted out justice in his saloon, the "Jersey Lily," named for actress Lillie Langtry.

bean, name for various genera and species of the legume family. Prolific, adaptable, and easily grown, beans have been from prehistoric times an important food crop for humans and cattle. Some are grown for forage and cover crops. Both pods and seeds of snap or string beans are edible while only seeds of kidney and lima beans are eaten. Scarlet runner bean is an ornamental. See also CAROB; FRIJOLE; SOYBEAN.

Bear, river rising in NE Utah in Uinta Mts., flowing c.350 mi. in circuitous course N and NW through Wyo. and Idaho, S into Utah again to enter Bear River Bay of Great Salt L.

bear, mammal of family Ursidae of order Carnivora, found almost exclusively in N Hemisphere. Feet are plantigrade, claws nonretractile, fur thick and shaggy, tail very short, and body clumsy appearing. Some run at 25–30 mi. an hour speed; excepting heavy grizzly bears, most climb trees. Bears eat fruits, roots, honey, insects, fish, carrion, and infrequently mammals. Where winters are cold they hibernate. Young, usually twins, are born during winter in undeveloped state.

Bear, Great and **Little:** see URSA MAJOR and URSA MINOR.

bearberry, trailing woody plant (*Arctostaphylos uva-ursi*) of N Hemisphere. Evergreen, astringent leaves and red berries. Often used as ground cover.

Beard, Charles A(ustin), 1874–1948, American historian. As professor (1904–17) at Columbia Univ., he broadened history teaching to embrace civilization. Helped found New School for Social Research. Widely known for *An Economic Interpretation of the Constitution* (1913), *The Rise of American Civilization* (2 vols., 1927), *America in Midpassage* (1939), and *The American Spirit* (1943), written in collaboration with his wife, Mary (Ritter) Beard, 1876–1958.

Beard, Daniel Carter, 1850–1941, American illustrator, naturalist, a founder of Boy Scouts of America (1910).

Beardsley, Aubrey (Vincent), 1872–98, celebrated English black-and-white illustrator. Art editor of the *Yellow Book*, 1894–96.

Beardstown, city (pop. 6,294), W central Ill., NW of Springfield, on Illinois R. (high levee); settled 1819. A rail, trade, and shipping center for fruit and farm area. Lincoln won Armstrong murder case here.

bearings, in general, machine parts supporting a shaft, and intended to minimize FRICTION. Generally made of ANTIFRICTION METAL, such as BABBITT METAL. Since friction generates heat, bearing efficiency depends largely upon lubrication. High-speed machinery usually fitted with ball bearings (these and roller bearings known as antifriction bearings). Bearings should fit so shaft turns freely but cannot otherwise move to set up vibration. Thrust bearings designed to resist forces in shaft along direction of its length, as in a ship's propeller shaft.

Bear Island: see SPITSBERGEN.

Bear Mountain. 1 Peak, 2,316 ft. high, NW Conn., in Salisbury town; one of state's highest points. **2** Peak, 1,284 ft. high, SE N.Y., overlooking Hudson (bridged), in Palisades Interstate Park. Sports facilities.

SMALL CAPITALS = cross references. Pronunciation key on inside end pages. Abbreviations: p. 2.

Béarn (bāärn'), region and former province, SW France, in Basses-Pyrénées dept.; historic cap. Orthez, later Pau. Agr., cattle breeding. Viscounty of Béarn passed (13th cent.) to counts of FOIX, thence, along with Navarre, to houses of Albret (1494) and Bourbon (1572); inc. into France 1620.

beat generation, group of negativist American writers and artists, born between the world wars, who became influential during the 1950s. Essentially anarchic in philosophy, members of the group, called beatniks (term coined by Herb Caen, San Francisco columnist), reject tradition. They seek intense experiences with beatific illumination modeled on some Eastern religions (e.g., Zen Buddhism), sometimes with use of drugs. Their movement, beginning in San Francisco, drew wide attention with the free-verse poem "Howl!" (1955–56), by Allen GINSBERG. Other writers are Lawrence Ferlinghetti, Gregory Corso, and Jack Kerouac.

beatification: see CANONIZATION.

Beatitudes (bēăt'–) [Latin,= blessing], blessings spoken by Jesus at opening of Sermon on Mount. Mat. 5.3–12. Luke 6.20–26.

Beaton, Cecil, 1904–, English photographer, writer, and scene designer. His real name is Walter Hardy.

Beaton or Bethune, David (both: bē'tùn), 1494–1546, Scottish churchman, cardinal of the Roman Church. Arranged marriage of James V and Mary of Guise. Failed to gain regency for Mary Queen of Scots. Murdered as reprisal for execution of George WISHART.

Beatrice (bēăt'rĭs), city (pop. 12,132), SE Nebr., on Big Blue R., SSW of Lincoln; founded 1857 on old Oregon Trail. Trade and industrial center for grain, dairy, and livestock area. Homestead Natl. Monument of America is nearby.

Beatrice Portinari (bē'ūtrĭs; bäätrē'chä pōrtēnä'rē), 1266–90, Florentine lady believed to be the Beatrice named in the writings of Dante.

Beatty, David Beatty, 1st Earl (bē'tē), 1871–1936, British admiral. Aided in defeat of German fleet at Jutland 1916. Commanded British fleet 1916–19 and was first sea lord 1919–27.

Beauce (bōs), flat region, N France, SW of Paris; chief city Chartres. The "granary of France," it is covered with wheat fields.

Beauchamp, English noble family: see WARWICK, GUY DE BEAUCHAMP, EARL OF.

Beaufort, Edmund: see SOMERSET, EDMUND BEAUFORT, 2D DUKE OF.

Beaufort, Henry (bō'fûrt), c.1377–1447, English prelate and statesman; half brother of Henry IV. Chancellor from 1403 to 1404. After Prince Henry became Henry V, he again served as chancellor (1413–17). Swung English influence (1417) to elect Pope Martin V. Was chancellor (1424–26) in regency for Henry VI. Became a cardinal in 1426 and was a papal legate. Crowned Henry VI king of France in Paris, 1431.

Beaufort, Margaret, countess of Richmond and Derby, 1443–1509, English noblewoman; mother of Henry VII. Founded Christ's Col. and St. John's Col., Cambridge. Patron of Caxton.

Beaufort (bū'fûrt), city (pop. 6,298), S S.C., on Port Royal Isl. (one of SEA ISLANDS), SW of Charleston; founded 1711. On Inland Waterway, it is a tourist center and canning and shipping point for agr. and fishing area. State's second oldest town. Held by Union forces after Nov., 1861. U.S. Marine base is S.

Beaufort Sea (bō'fûrt), part of Arctic Ocean, between N Alaska and Arctic Archipelago of Canada.

Beauharnais, Alexandre, vicomte de (ălĕksä'drŭ vēkōt' dù bōärnä'), 1760–94, French general in American Revolution and in French Revolutionary Wars. Guillotined in Reign of Terror. His widow, Josephine de Beauharnais, married Napoleon I (see JOSEPHINE). Alexandre's and Josephine's son, Eugène de Beauharnais (üzhĕn'), 1781–1824, served as general under Napoleon, who made him viceroy of Italy in 1805. Capable administrator. Retired to Munich after Napoleon's

downfall. His sister, **Hortense de Beauharnais** (ôrtãs'), 1783–1837, married Louis BONAPARTE, whom Napoleon made king of Holland (1806–10); mother of Napoleon III and the duc de Morny.

Beauharnois (bōhär'nwä), city (pop. 8,704). S Que., Canada, on S shore of L. St. Louis, SW of Montreal. **Beauharnois Canal,** opened 1843 on S side of St. Lawrence R. to bypass rapids, was superseded by Soulange Canal on N side in 1899. New Beauharnois Canal, begun 1930 for power development, was subject of political scandal. Province bought plant as public-ownership enterprise in 1945. Enlarged canal forms part of St. Lawrence Seaway.

Beaujeu, Anne de: see ANNE DE BEAUJEU.

Beaujolais (bōjôlä'), hilly region, Rhône dept., E central France; famous for light red wine. Once the fief of lords of Beaujeu.

Beaumarchais, Pierre Augustin Caron de (pyĕr' ōgüstē' kärō' dù bōmärshä'), 1732–99, French dramatist, at first a watchmaker by trade. His sparkling comedies. *Le Barbier de Séville* (1775) and *Le Mariage de Figaro* (1784) are famous in their own right and as sources for operas by Rossini and Mozart. Beaumarchais was chronically engaged in litigation, about which he wrote many witty pamphlets, and also was in the secret service of the monarchy. His dealings with Silas DEANE and Arthur LEE led to the estab. of his mock firm, Hortalès & Cie, which furnished arms to the American revolutionists (1776–77). Repayment was delayed until 1835, when the U.S. Congress made a grant to his heirs. Another costly venture was a 70-vol. edition of Voltaire (1784–90).

Beaumont, Francis (bō'mŏnt), 1584?–1616, English dramatist. *The Woman Hater* (1607) and *The Knight of the Burning Pestle* (c.1608) shows some influence of John FLETCHER, his collaborator (probably 1607–13) on *Philaster, A King and No King,* and other romantic tragicomedies.

Beaumont, William, 1785–1853, American physician, author of work (1833) which revolutionized knowledge of digestive process. Observations based on case of Alexis St. Martin, victim of stomach wound leaving an opening to exterior of body.

Beaumont, city (pop. 119,175), SE Texas, on Neches R. (arm of Sabine-Neches Waterway), ENE of Houston; settled c.1825. Industrial and transportation center with modern deepwater port. Shipbuilding important in Second World War. Lamar State Col. of Technology is here.

Beaune (bōn), town (est. pop. 13,175), Côte-d'Or dept., E France, in Burgundy. Wine center. Once a residence of dukes of Burgundy. The Hôtel Dieu hospital (founded 1443) contains Roger van der Weyden's *Last Judgment.* Romanesque church with Flemish tapestries; Hôtel de la Rochepot (c.1501).

Beauport, town (pop. 9,192), S Que., Canada, on St. Lawrence R. and NE of Quebec. One of oldest communities in Canada, settled 1634. French repulsed Wolfe's attacks here (1759) in Quebec campaign.

Beauregard, Pierre Gustave Toutant, 1818–93, Confederate general. Commander in NE Va., second in command at first battle of Bull Run. Defended coast of S.C. and Ga., and supported R. E. Lee in Va., especially at Petersburg. Stronger as engineer than as field commander.

Beauséjour, Fort, national park in SE N.B., Canada, (81 acres; estab. 1926), WNW of Amherst, N.S. Built 1751–55 by French; captured in 1755 by British and American troops under Gen. Monckton.

Beauvais (bōvä'), town (est. pop. 26,756), cap. of Oise dept., N France. Until Second World War a tapestry mfg. center. War damage virtually wiped out center of town, a gem of medieval architecture. Famous cathedral (partly damaged) was begun 1227 as highest building in Christendom; choir vault (154 ft.; highest of Gothic vaults) fell in 1284 but was reinforced; nave uncompleted.

Beauvoir, Simone de (sĭmôn' dù bōvwär'), 1908–, French novelist and essayist, leading existentialist writer. Her works include *The Second Sex* (1949; Eng. tr., 1953) and *The Mandarins* (1954; Eng. tr., 1956), a novel. Three volumes of autobiography appeared 1958–65.

Beaux-Arts, École des: see ÉCOLE DES BEAUX-ARTS.

Beaver. 1 Wheat-shipping town (pop. 2,087), extreme NW Okla., on North Canadian R. in Panhandle; first settled (by squatters) c.1880. Was cap. (1887) of Territory of CIMARRON. 2 Residential borough (pop. 6,160), W Pa., NW of Pittsburgh near junction of Beaver and Ohio rivers; laid out 1791. Site of Fort McIntosh (1778), first U.S. military post N of Ohio R.

beaver, rodent, family Castoridae, of Europe, North America. Has thick fur, round head, small ears, scaly, flattened tail (c.10 in. long, c.6 in. wide), webbed hind feet, and body c.30 in. long. Weighs 40–50 lb. Tail is used as rudder when swimming, for support while gnawing tree, or to slap water to warn other beavers of danger. American beaver *Castor canadensis* usually builds twig and mud "lodges" with underwater entrances. If water is too shallow, makes dam of tree trunks or mud. *C. fiber* found in small numbers in parts of Europe. See *ill.,* p. 1136.

Beaverbrook, William Maxwell Aitken, 1st Baron, 1879–1964, British statesman and newspaper owner. A Canadian, he amassed a fortune before going to England. After 1917 his newspapers (*Daily Express, Sunday Express,* and *Evening Standard*) thundered out his imperialist views. Held several posts in Churchill's wartime cabinet 1940–45.

Beaver Dam, locality, S Ont., Canada, S of St. Catherines. Scene of a British victory, June 24, 1813, in War of 1812.

Beaver Dam, city (pop. 13,118), SE Wis., on Beaver Dam L., SW of Fond du Lac; settled 1841.

Beaver Falls, city (pop. 16,240), W Pa., on Beaver R., NW of Pittsburgh; settled c.1793. Seat of Geneva Col.

Beaver Island, 13 mi. long, c.3–6 mi. wide, off N Mich., in L. Michigan NNW of Charlevoix (connected by ferry and plane). Largest of Beaver Archipelago; has lakes, beaches, and a harbor at St. James village. Inhabitants mainly fishermen. J. STRANG had Mormon settlement here 1847–56.

Beaverlodge, town (pop. 897), W Alta., Canada, W of Grande Prairie. Area of uranium mines.

Bebel, August (ou'gŏŏst bä'bùl), 1840–1913, German Socialist. Helped found German Social Democratic party (1869); promoted its union with Lassallean socialists (1875).

Bebington, municipal borough (pop. 52,202), Cheshire, W England, on the Mersey near Birkenhead. Part of the port of Liverpool. Composed of Bromborough and Eastham, both very old, and Port Sunlight, industrial town.

Bec (bĕk), former Benedictine abbey, N France, in Normandy, S of Rouen. Founded 11th cent. Lanfranc taught here, Anselm was abbot. Fell into ruin after suppression in French Revolution.

Beccafumi, Domenico di Pace (dōmā'nēkō dē pä'chä bĕk-käfoo'mē), 1486–1551, Italian mannerist painter, sculptor, and engraver. Active mainly in Siena.

Beccaria, Cesare Bonesana, marchese di (chā'zärä bō-näzä'nä märkā'zä dē bĕk-kärē'ä), 1738–94, Italian economist, jurist, and criminologist. Brought about local economic reforms, stimulated penal reform throughout Europe. Influenced utilitarians; application of mathematics to economics anticipated work of Adam Smith.

Béchamp, Pierre Jacques Antoine (pyèr' zhäk' ätwän' bäshä'), 1816–1908, French chemist, first to prepare aniline from nitrobenzene.

Becher, Johann Joachim (yō'hän yō'äkhĭm bä'khùr), 1635–82, German chemist, cofounder of PHLOGISTON THEORY.

Bechuanaland: see BOTSWANA.

Beck, Dave, 1894–, American labor leader, president of Internatl. Brotherhood of Teamsters (1952–58). After congressional hearings on union corruption, he was convicted of larceny (embezzling union funds) in 1957 and of income tax evasion in 1959. After the failure of several appeals, he began serving his sentence in 1962. James R. Hoffa succeeded him as president of the teamsters.

Beck, Theodric (or Theodoric) Romeyn, 1791–1855, American physician, author of standard work (1823) on medical jurisprudence.

Beckenham, London: see BROMLEY.

Becker, Carl Lotus, 1873–1945, American historian. Professor (1917–41) at Cornell Univ. Books include *The Declaration of Independence* (1922) and *The Heavenly City of the Eighteenth-Century Philosophers* (1932).

Becket, Thomas: see THOMAS À BECKET, SAINT.

Beckett, Samuel, 1906–, French author, b. Ireland. Was a friend of James Joyce. Writes in French. Known for such existentialist plays as *Waiting for Godot* (1952), *Endgame* (1958), *Krapp's Last Tape* (1959), and *Happy Days* (1961). His novels include *Molloy* (1951), *Malone Dies* (1951), and *Watt* (1958). His own translation of his *Stories and Texts for Nothing* appeared 1967.

Beckford, William, 1760–1844, English author of an oriental romance, *Vathek* (written in French; first pub. in English, 1786), and of travel books.

Beckley, city (pop. 18,642), S W.Va., N of Bluefield, in coal area; chartered 1838.

Beckmann, Max, 1884–1950, German expressionist painter, active successively in Berlin, London, Amsterdam, and New York.

Bécque, Henry (ärē' bĕk'), 1837–99, French dramatist. *Les Corbeaux* (1882; Eng. tr., *The Vultures,* 1913) and *La Parisienne* (1885; Eng. tr., 1913), the first successful French naturalistic plays, influenced later drama.

Bécquer, Gustavo Adolfo (gōōstä'vō ädôl'fō bä'kĕr), 1836–70, one of major 19th-cent. Spanish lyric poets. Author of sensuous *Rimas* [rhymes] and prose *Leyendas* [legends].

Becquerel, Antoine César (ätwän' säzär' bĕkùrĕl'), 1788–1878, French physicist. Pioneer in electrochemistry; studied telegraphy, magnetism. His son Alexandre Edmond Becquerel (älĕksä'drù ĕdmō'), 1820–91, also a physicist, professor at the Muséum d'Histoire naturelle, studied light, photochemistry, phosphorescence; invented phosphoroscope. Antoine Henri Becquerel, 1852–1908, son of Alexandre Edmond, discovered radioactivity in uranium and shared with the Curies the 1903 Nobel Prize in Physics.

Bedaresi, Yedaya ben Abraham Penini (bädär'sē), 1270–1340, Hebrew poet and Jewish philosopher of Provence. Best known for his didactic poem "Examination of the World," depicting sorrows of the world and the greatness of the spirit juxtaposed.

bedbug, bug of order Hemiptera found over most of world. Common species *Cimex lectularius* is flat, reddish-brown, c.⅕ in. long; unpleasant odor; eats only blood. Attacks man, other mammals, poultry.

Beddington and Wallington, London: see SUTTON.

Beddoes, Thomas Lovell, 1803–49, English poet. The grotesque is contrasted with lyric beauty in his poems (e.g., *The Improvisatore,* 1821) and plays (e.g., *The Bride's Tragedy,* 1822; and *Death's Jest-Book,* 1850).

Bede (bēd) or Baeda (bē'dù), 673?–735, English historian; Benedictine monk called Venerable Bede and St. Bede. Writings are summary of learning of his time. Best known for *Ecclesiastical History of the English Nation,* in Latin, often translated.

Bedford, dukes and earls of: see RUSSELL, family; JOHN OF LANCASTER.

Bedford, England: see BEDFORDSHIRE.

Bedford. 1 City (pop. 13,024), S Ind., S of Bloomington; laid out 1826. Has limestone quarries. 2 Town (pop. 10,969), E Mass., NW of Boston; settled c.1637. Hanscom Air Force base, a space research center, and veterans' hospital are here. Pre-Revolutionary houses. 3 Town (pop. 3,636), S N.H., SW of Manchester; settled 1737 on grants made to King Philip's War soldiers and heirs. 4 Residential city (pop. 15,223), NE Ohio, SE of Cleveland; settled c.1813 on Moravian settlement (1786) site. 5 Agr. borough (pop. 3,696), S Pa., on Juniata R. branch, SE of Johnstown; settled c.1750. Site of fort (c.1757) where Washington reviewed troops in Whisky Rebellion 1794. Bedford Springs, resort, is near. 6 Town (pop. 5,921), S central Va., between Roanoke and Lynchburg, in farm area; founded 1781. Nearby is "Poplar Forest" (1806–9; restored), Jefferson's country home.

Bedfordshire or Bedford, county (473 sq. mi.; pop. 380,704), S central England. Most of flat fertile area is market garden for nearby London. Luton, largest town, has modern engineering and automobile plants; known for mfg. of lace and straw plait. County town is **Bedford,** municipal borough (pop. 63,317), a market center on Ouse R. Has memorial chapel to John Bunyan, who preached here. Bedford School (estab. 1552) is one of England's largest public schools.

Bédier, Joseph (zhŏsĕf' bādyā'), 1864–1938, French authority on medieval literature. *Les Légendes épiques* (4 vols., 1908–13) developed a new theory of the origin of the great medieval romances.

Bedlam [i.e., Bethlehem], oldest English insane asylum, estab. c.1400 in Lambeth borough (London); after 1930 near Croydon.

Bedloe's Island: see LIBERTY ISLAND.

Bedouin (bĕ'dōō̆ĭn), camel-breeding, pastoral nomads of Semitic stock in Arabia. They speak Arabic, believe in Islam, are organized in tribes.

bee, insect of order Hymenoptera. There are c.20,-000 species. Bees are solitary, social, or parasitic (in nests of other bees). Best-known social bees are the honeybee, especially *Apis mellifera* (or *mellifica*), of Old World origin, and the bumblebee, of the genus *Bombus.* Honeybees are invaluable agents of pollination and producers of honey and beeswax. Honeybee colony has a single queen (who mates once in her lifetime and lays countless eggs), thousands of sexually undeveloped workers, and a few hundred males (drones). Workers build wax cells, make honey, clean and defend hive, feed queen and larvae; life span is only about six weeks during active season. Bees are known to communicate with one another by signs and patterned behavior (e.g., a bee upon returning to the hive will "dance" to indicate the location of a new nectar source). Use of bee's lancet (sting) on a human or animal usually kills insect. Stingless bees live in tropics. See *ill.,* p. 512.

bee balm: see OSWEGO TEA and LEMON BALM.

Beebe, William (bē'bē), 1877–1962, American scientist, explorer, author. Noted as curator of ornithology at New York Zoological Society and for underwater explorations in a bathysphere.

beech, large, deciduous tree (*Fagus*) of N Hemisphere. Edible nuts and smooth gray bark. Valued for timber and for landscaping (especially copper and purple varieties of European beech). American and European beeches are dominant forest trees, particularly noticeable in the Mid-West.

Beecham, Sir Thomas, 1879–1961, English conductor. He introduced the operas of Richard Strauss into England and was a champion of the music of Delius.

Beecher, Lyman, 1775–1863, American Protestant minister in N.Y., Conn., and Mass. President (1832–52) of Lane Theological Seminary, Cincinnati. A founder (1816) of the American Bible Society and preacher of temperance. One daughter was Harriet Beecher STOWE. One of his sons was **Henry Ward Beecher,** 1813–87, American Congregational minister, one of the great speakers of his time; pastor after 1847 of Plymouth Church, Brooklyn. Championed reforms

(antislavery, woman suffrage). He was the center of a trial resulting from Theodore Tilton's accusing Beecher of adultery; the jury disagreed.

Beech Grove, residential town (1964 pop. 12,632), central Ind., SSE of Indianapolis; settled 1902.

beef, flesh of CATTLE, prepared for food. A chief product of MEAT PACKING industry in many countries.

Beefeaters, popular name for YEOMEN OF THE GUARD and Yeoman Warders of the Tower of London. They wear colorful 16th-cent. uniforms.

Beelzebub (bēĕl'zĭbŭb), in Bible: see SATAN.

beer, one of oldest known alcoholic beverages. Brewing processes are similar in various countries but beer varies in color, flavor, alcoholic content (usually 3–6%). Mash of crushed malt (usually barley) and cereal adjuncts is heated and agitated, then the liquid is boiled with hops, cooled, liquid yeast is added, and fermentation is allowed to take place. Ale, in England, means any light-colored beer; in U.S. it is a pale, strongly hopped beverage. Porter is a strong, dark ale; stout is darker, stronger, and maltier than porter.

Beerbohm, Sir Max, 1872–1956, English satirist, caricaturist. Contributor to *Yellow Book,* dramatic critic of the *Saturday Review.* Mordant satire shown in caricatures, in novel *Zuleika Dobson* (1911), and in sketches, literary and graphic.

Beernaert, Auguste (ȯgüst' bârnärt', bâr'närt), 1829–1912, Belgian statesman, prominent in Hague Peace Conferences of 1899 and 1907. Shared 1909 Nobel Peace Prize with Estournelles de Constant.

Beers, Clifford W(hittingham), 1876–1943, American founder of mental hygiene movement. Wrote autobiographical *A Mind That Found Itself* (1908).

Beersheba (bērshē'bŭ) [Heb.,= seven wells or well of the oath], town, S Israel, SW of Jerusalem. In Bible times Beersheba was the S extremity of Palestine, Dan was N extremity; hence the expression "from Dan to Beersheba." Especially associated with Abraham, Hagar, Isaac, and Elijah. Gen. 21.31; 26.33; Joshua 19.1,2; Judges 20.1; 1 Chron. 21.2; 2 Kings 23.8; 2 Chron. 19.4; Neh. 11.30.

beet, vegetable (*Beta vulgaris*), cultivated for its edible roots. Other varieties grown for edible leaves (e.g., Swiss chard), for cattle (e.g., mangel-wurzel), and one, sugar beet, for beet sugar.

Beethoven, Ludwig van (bā'tōvŭn), 1770–1827, German composer, b. Bonn. Was a solo pianist, but his growing deafness made a career as a virtuoso impossible. Most critics divide his compositions into three periods: the early years, lasting until 1802, when he was still mostly writing in the classic tradition; the middle period, lasting until 1816, when, although already beset with deafness, he wrote some of his greatest music, e.g., the Third (or Eroica) Symphony, the Fifth Symphony, the Sixth (or Pastoral) Symphony, the Fifth (or Emperor) Piano Concerto, and his one opera *Fidelio;* and the last years, beginning in 1817, when most of his music was composed in total deafness. Belonging to this final period are the Ninth Symphony, the *Missa Solemnis,* and the last five string quartets. Beethoven wrote much chamber music—16 string quartets; 10 sonatas for violin and piano, including the Ninth (or Kreutzer) Sonata; and 32 sonatas for piano. His orchestral compositions include a violin concerto, five piano concertos, and nine symphonies. Beethoven is regarded as the last of the classic and the first of the romantic composers.

beetle, insect of order Coleoptera (includes c.200,-000 species). Most species are characterized by two pairs of wings; the modified front wings form thickened wing covers protecting body and membranous hind wings. Metamorphosis is complete; larva usually called a grub. Majority are terrestrial; few families aquatic. See BOLL WEEVIL; POTATO BEETLE; FIREFLY; JAPANESE BEETLE; JUNE BEETLE; LADYBIRD; SCARAB; TUMBLEBUG; WIREWORM; WEEVIL. See also *ill.,* p. 512.

SMALL CAPITALS = cross references. Pronunciation key on inside end pages. Abbreviations: p. 2.

Beeville, city (pop. 13,811), S Texas, NNW of Corpus Christi; settled 1830s. Former cow town, it is trade center of oil, cattle, and agr. area.

Beggars of the Sea: see GUEUX.

beggar-tick: see BUR MARIGOLD.

beggarweed, any of a number of plants of the leguminous genus *Desmodium. D. purpureum* is grown in S U.S. for forage and for green manure.

Beghards (bĕg'ûrdz), religious associations of men, first known (1220) at Louvain, later widespread in Netherlands, Germany, France, and Italy. Organization was like that of BEGUINES. Charged by Council of Vienne (1311) with teaching that a man may attain such perfection that no later action of his may be considered sinful. Beghards lasted until 15th cent.

begonia, tropical perennial of genus *Begonia.* Showy single or double flowers (e.g., wax and tuberous types), succulent stems and leaves, often richly colored (e.g., rex begonias). Grown in beds and pots.

Begovat (byĕgô'vät), city (pop. 41,700), E Uzbek SSR, on Syr Darya R. Industrial center with large iron and steel mills. Site of Farkhand Dam and hydroelectric plant.

Beguines (bāgēn'), religious associations of women estab. in the Low Countries in 12th cent. They took no vows and lived by no rule, but did charitable work. In 13th and 14th cent. their communities (beguinages) came into disrepute and most were dissolved. After 16th cent. there was resurgence in Belgium, where today, as in Holland, the remaining few are almshouses (esp. for spinsters). See also BEGHARDS.

Beham (bā'häm), name of two German Renaissance artists. **Hans Sebald Beham** (sā'bält), 1500–50, known primarily as an engraver, was influenced by Dürer and later by Italian art, as was his brother, **Barthel Beham** (bär'tŭl), 1502–40, well known as a portrait painter.

Behan, Brendan (bē'hän), 1923–64, Irish dramatist whose uninhibited life is echoed in his play on prison life, *The Quare Fellow* (1956); his farce, *The Hostage* (1958); his autobiography, *The Borstal Boy* (1958); and in short stories and poetry.

Behar: see BIHAR.

behaviorism, explanation of human behavior entirely as physiological response to environmental stimuli. Introduced by J. B. Watson, 1912; based on mechanistic concepts of Democritus, Epicurus, and Thomas Hobbes; supported by conditioned-reflex experiments of Pavlov and Bekhterev. Watson denied value of introspection and consciousness as unscientific concepts, saw all mental processes as bodily movements (even when the movements cannot be observed); thus verbal thinking is subvocal speech. Behaviorists considered that all emotions—aside from fear, love, and rage—are learned by conditioning and can be unlearned. Behaviorism was especially influential in the U.S. between the world wars. Behavioristic theory has much influence on other schools of modern psychology.

behemoth (bē'hĭmŏth) [Heb.,= plural of *beast*], animal mentioned in Job 40.15–24, possibly the hippopotamus (there are various theories).

Behistun (bāhĭstōōn') or **Bisutun** (bēsōōtōōn'), village, W Iran, E of Kermanshah. Nearby is mountainous rock with cuneiform inscriptions and bas-relief depicting Darius I. In 1835 Sir Henry Rawlinson scaled rock and copied writings, thus making it possible to decipher the Assyrian text and provide key for study of ancient Mesopotamia.

Behn, Aphra (bän), 1640–89, English playwright and author of romances. Her works, witty, coarse, and vigorous, include *Oroonoko* (1688), a precursor of the novel as it developed in the 18th cent.

Behrens, Peter (pā'tŭr bā'rŭns), 1868–1940, German architect, influential in the evolution of modern architectural style. Emphasized utilitarian aspect of design in his buildings in Berlin. Taught Le Corbusier, Walter Gropius, and Mies van der Rohe.

Behring, Emil Adolph von (ā'mĭl ä'dôlf fŭn bâr'ĭng), 1854–1917, German physician, pioneer in serum therapy. Won 1901 Nobel Prize in Physiology and Medicine for demonstrating immunization against diphtheria (1890) and tetanus (1892) by antitoxin injections.

Behrman, S(amuel) N(athaniel) (bâr'mŭn), 1893–, American dramatist. Studied with George Pierce Baker. His writings include sophisticated comedies (*Biography,* 1932; *No Time for Comedy,* 1939; *But for Whom Charlie,* 1964), film scripts, and biographies.

Beida (bā'du), city (pop. c.32,000), N Libya. Built since 1961 as administrative center of Libyan government to unify services from co-capitals Tripoli and Bengasi.

Beira (bā'rŭ, bā'rû), historic province, N central Portugal, S of the Douro; old cap. Coimbra. Now occupied by provs. of Beira Alta, Beira Baixa, and part of Beira Litoral. Largely mountainous with agr., vineyards, and olive groves. Was long contested between Portugal and Castile.

Beira (bā'rä), city (pop. c.50,000), E central Mozambique; port and beach resort on the Indian Ocean. Founded 1891 as terminus of railroad into interior. Copper, tobacco, tea are among exports.

Beirut or **Beyrouth** (both: bārōōt'), anc. *Berytus,* city (pop. c.400,000), cap. of Lebanon; port on Mediterranean at foot of Lebanon range. Ancient Phoenician trade center. Flourished under Seleucids, Romans, and Byzantines. Captured 635 by Arabs. Taken 1110 by Crusaders, it remained part of Latin Kingdom of Jerusalem until 1291. Controlled by Druses under Ottoman Empire. In 19th cent. it was a storm center of revolt of Mohammed Ali of Egypt. Seat of important American university.

Beisan (bāsän') town, Israel, in Jordan valley, c.300 ft. below sea level. Site of biblical BETH-SHAN. Has ruins dating from c.1500 B.C.

Beja (bā'zhŭ), town (pop. 15,685), S Portugal, cap. of Beja dist. and Lower Alentejo prov. Important trade and mfg. center. Founded by Romans; used by Moors as fortress city until reconquered by Portuguese in 1162. Citadel and monastery (14th cent.).

Bejapur, India: see BIJAPUR.

Béjart or **Béjard** (both: bāzhär'), French family of actors, a successful troupe associated (after 1643) with MOLIÈRE. Included Joseph (c.1616–1659), sisters Madeleine (1618–72; Molière's mistress) and Geneviève (1624–75), brother Louis (1630–78), and Madeleine's sister or daughter, Armande Grésinde (c.1640–1700; Molière's wife 1662). Absorption of two rival troupes resulted (1680) in COMÉDIE FRANÇAISE.

Beke, Charles Tilstone (bēk), 1800–1874, English traveler and author. Mapped much of Ethiopia, compiled vocabularies of 14 languages or dialects.

Bekescsaba or **Csaba,** Hung. *Békéscsaba* (bā'kĕshchô'bŏ), city (est. pop. 51,000), SE Hungary, in a silk-raising and tobacco-growing dist. Textile mfg.

Bekesy, Georg von (gā'ôrk fŭn bĕk'ĭshē), 1899–, American biophysicist, awarded 1961 Nobel Prize in Medicine and Physiology for research on cochlea of inner ear.

Bekhterev, Vladimir Mikhailovich (vlŭdyĕ'mĭr mēkhī'lŭvĭch byĕkh' tyĭrĭf), 1857–1927, Russian neurologist, psychologist. He studied localization of functions in brain areas and applied his study of conditioned reflexes in dogs to interpretation of human behavior. His emphasis on physiological nature of psychic phenomena influenced behaviorists.

Bel, deity of BABYLONIAN RELIGION; a form of BAAL. For Bel in Bible, see BEL AND THE DRAGON.

Bela IV (bē'lŭ, bā'lŭ), 1206–70, king of Hungary (1235–70). Defeated by Mongols at Mohi 1241; invited foreigners to settle depopulated country after Mongols withdrew. His last years disturbed by rebellion of son, later King Stephen V.

Bel and the Dragon, name given to Daniel 14 in Western canon, a chapter placed in the Apocrypha in AV. Verses 1–22 tell how Daniel brilliantly outwitted the priests of the idol Bel. Verses 23–42 tell of a dragon or great beast who was worshiped as a god. Daniel killed the dragon and was thrown into the lions' den but was protected by God.

Belasco, David, 1853–1931, American theatrical manager. As independent producer (after 1895) was famous for lighting and lavish and realistic scenic effects. Prolific playwright (notably in collaboration with James A. Herne), he created stars and vehicles (mostly adaptations) for them. Built Stuyvesant, later Belasco, Theatre 1907.

Belaya Tserkov (tsĕr′kŭf), city (1965 est. pop. 84,000), N central Ukrainian SSR. Hq. of Ukrainian Cossacks in 17th cent. Mazeppa was born here.

Belém (bŭlän′), city (pop. 402,170), cap. of Pará state, NE Brazil, on the Pará, chief port and metropolis of Amazon basin. Founded in 17th cent., city reached peak of prosperity in wild-rubber boom of early 20th cent. Sometimes called Pará.

Belfast, county borough (pop. 416,094), cap. of N. Ireland, in Co. Antrim and Co. Down; county town of Co. Antrim. Has 8½-mi.-long harbor navigable to largest ships and great shipyards. Center of Irish linen industry; has mfg. of aircraft, tools and machinery, yarn, clothing; seat of Queen's Univ. and Protestant cathedral. Parliament House at Stormont, a suburb.

Belfast (bĕl′făst), city (pop. 6,140), S Maine, on Penobscot Bay opposite Castine; settled 1770. Sacked by British, 1779 and 1814. Shipping and shipbuilding port in 19th cent. Has fish canneries and poultry farms.

Belfort (bûfôr′, bĕ–, bĕl–), city (pop. 48,070), cap. of Territory of Belfort (235 sq. mi.; pop. 109,371), E France. Strategic fortress commanding Belfort Gap between Vosges and Jura mts. Huge statue, *Lion of Belfort,* by Bartholdi, commemorates resistance to siege (1870–71) in Franco-Prussian War. Belfort remained French when rest of Alsace went to Germany (1871).

Belgian Congo: see CONGO, REPUBLIC OF THE.

Belgium (bĕl′jŭm), Flemish *België,* Fr. *Belgique,* kingdom (11,775 sq. mi.; est pop. 9,179,000), NW Europe, bounded by North Sea and Netherlands (N), Germany and grand duchy of Luxembourg (E), and France (W); cap. Brussels. Constitutional monarchy; bicameral legislature. Nine provinces—Antwerp, Brabant, East Flanders, West Flanders, Hainaut, Liège, Limburg, Luxembourg, Namur—are semi-autonomous. Belgian Congo, long a valuable colony, gained independence (1960) as the Republic of the Congo. Low-lying, except for the ARDENNES mts. in S, Belgium is crossed by the MEUSE and SCHELDT rivers and by a dense network of canals and railroads. Truck farming and cattle raising are important, but Belgium is one of the world's most intensely industrialized countries. Mining (coal, zinc, iron) and steel and chemical industries are concentrated in Sambre and Meuse valleys, at MONS, CHARLEROI, NAMUR, and LIÈGE. West Flanders and Hainaut have a huge textile industry, notably at Courtrai and Tournai. BRUSSELS, BRUGES, and MALINES are famed for their lace. ANTWERP and GHENT are major ports. Belgium is a leading nation in shipping and transit trade. Despite industrialization, the old cities of Belgium have retained many treasures of medieval architecture and art. A language border running, roughly, E-W through Brussels divides the Flemish-speaking north from the French-speaking south (see also WALLOONS); German is spoken in EUPEN and MALMÉDY dists. The Church, with the archbishop of Malines as primate, plays a leading role in overwhelmingly Catholic Belgium. As sovereign state, Belgium dates only from 1831. It is named after the Belgae, a people of ancient GAUL. The cradle of the Carolingian dynasty, the region (except Flanders) was comprised in LOTHARINGIA and later in the duchy of Lower Lorraine, which by the 12th cent. had broken up into the duchies of BRABANT and LUXEMBOURG, the county of HAINAUT, and lesser feudal states. The history of these and of FLANDERS constitute the medieval history of Belgium. By the 15th cent. all of present Belgium had passed to the dukes of BURGUNDY. The death of MARY OF BURGUNDY (1482) opened three centuries of Hapsburg rule (see NETHERLANDS, AUSTRIAN AND SPANISH). In 1797 the area was annexed by France. The Treaty of Paris (1815) gave it to the Netherlands, but in 1830 Belgium rose against WILLIAM I and proclaimed its independence. LEOPOLD I, of the house of Saxe-Coburg-Gotha, was chosen king (1831); Anglo-French intervention stopped warfare with the Dutch (1832); peace was signed in 1839. Rapid industrialization under LEOPOLD II brought grave social problems. Belgian neutrality was violated by Germany in both world wars. In the First World War Belgian forces under ALBERT I fought beside the Allies even though Belgium was occupied by the Germans (1914–18). In the Second World War LEOPOLD III surrendered Belgium on May 28, 1940, after disastrous campaign; the government continued the fight from London. German occupation brought a reign of terror. After liberation (1944), war-scarred Belgium recovered quickly. The king's fitness to govern was a burning issue until Leopold abdicated in favor of his son BAUDOUIN (1951). In 1947 Belgium, the Netherlands, and Luxembourg formed a customs union, which became (1960) the BENELUX Economic Union. Belgium joined the UN (1945) and the North Atlantic Treaty Organization (1949). An early advocate of the European Community, Belgium belongs to the European Common Market.

Belgorod (byĕl′gŭrŭd), city (1965 est. pop. 114,000), SW European RSFSR, on Northern Donets R. Railroad junction in agr. region. Center of Muscovite southern defense against Crimean Tatars in 17th cent.

Belgorod-Dnestrovsky (byĕl′gŭrŭd-dŭnyĕstrôf′skē), Rumanian *Cetatea-Alba,* Turkish *Akkerman,* city (pop. 21,600), S Ukraine. Port on mouth of Dniester. Founded as Tyras by Greek colonists 7th cent. B.C. Under Turks 1484–1812.

Belgrade (bĕl′grād), Serbo-Croatian *Beograd,* city (pop. 587,899), cap. of Yugoslavia and of Serbia, on the Danube and the Sava. Seat of univ. (founded 1863), of Orthodox patriarch, and of archbishop (R.C.). The "key to the Balkans," it has been a strategic fortress since Roman times. Became cap. of Serbia in 12th cent.; repulsed Turks 1456; fell to Turks 1521; was stormed 1688, 1717, and 1789 by Austrians, who held it briefly (1717–39). Turkish garrison withdrew 1867. Occupied by Austrians in First World War, by Germans in Second World War.

Belgrano, Manuel (mänwäl′ bĕlgrä′nō), 1770–1820, Argentine revolutionist, member of first patriot governing junta (1810). Commander of Army of the North (1812–14; 1816–19), he was succeeded by San Martín.

Belgravia, fashionable section of London, surrounding Belgrave Square.

Belial (bē′lĕŭl), name applied to SATAN.

Belinsky, Vissarion Grigoryevich (vĭsŭryôn′ grĭgôr′yŭvĭch byĭlyĭn′skē), 1811–48, Russian writer. The founder of modern Russian literary criticism and a liberal, he championed Dostoyevsky and Gogol.

Belisarius (bĕlĭsär′ēŭs), c.505–565, Byzantine general under Justinian I. Suppressed *Nika* rebellion (532). Defeated Vandals of Africa (533–34). Led expedition to recover Italy from Ostrogoths (535–40; 544–48); took Naples, Rome, Milan, Ravenna. Handicapped by political intrigue; replaced by NARSES 548. Drove Bulgarians from Constantinople (559). Briefly disgraced and imprisoned (562).

Belize (bŭlēz′), city (pop. 38,383), cap. and chief port of British Honduras, at mouth of Belize R.

Belknap, William Worth, 1829–90, U.S. Secretary of War (1869–76). Evidence that he had indirectly taken bribes led to his resignation; impeached, but not convicted by Senate.

Bell, Alexander Melville, 1819–1905, Scottish-American educator. Taught elocution in Edinburgh 1843–65; created a visible alphabet with symbols representing every vocal sound. His son was **Alexander Graham Bell,** 1847–1922, American scientist, inventor of telephone. Improved education for deaf, carrying forward the work of his father. In 1865 conceived idea of transmitting speech by electric waves; developed principle in 1875 and transmitted first sentence 1876. Organized Bell Telephone Co. in 1877. Estab. Volta Laboratory, where first successful phonograph record was produced. Invented photophone to transmit speech by light waves, audiometer, induction balance to locate metallic objects in body, wax recorders for phonographs, and tetrahedral kite. Influenced founding of *Science* (1880). Estab. Astrophysical Observatory at Smithsonian Inst. and founded Aerial Experiment Association.

Bell, Andrew, 1753–1832, British educator. In Madras, India, he devised MONITORIAL SYSTEM.

Bell, Sir Charles, 1774–1842, Scottish anatomist and surgeon, first to distinguish between motor and sensory functions of nerves. His brother **John Bell,** 1763–1820, was a founder of modern blood vessel surgery.

Bell, Gertrude Margaret Lowthian, 1868–1926, English expert on Near East, traveler, author. Invaluable as liaison officer of Arab Bureau in Iraq and assistant political officer, largely responsible for selection of Feisal I as king.

Bell, John, surgeon: see BELL, SIR CHARLES.

Bell, John, 1797–1869, American statesman. U.S. Representative from Tenn. (1827–41); U.S. Senator (1847–59). Leader of conservative Southern element. Presidential candidate of CONSTITUTIONAL UNION PARTY 1860, he unintentionally helped elect Lincoln.

Bell, city (pop. 19,450), S Calif., SE of Los Angeles.

bell, in music, a percussion instrument consisting of a hollow vessel usually cup-shaped, set into vibration by a blow from a clapper within or from a hammer without. A set of bells tuned to the intervals of the major scale is called a chime. A set with chromatic intervals is called a carillon. The bells of a carillon are stationary, are struck from without by a hammer, and are played from a keyboard. Carillon making developed in the Low Countries, reached its peak in the 18th cent., declined, revived at end of 19th cent., when English bellmakers rediscovered the tuning secrets used by 17th cent. craftsmen. In England, carillon playing was less popular than change ringing. In this practice a group of ringers, using a set of bells tuned to the diatonic scale, ring the bells by swinging them in full circle in various stated orders. Bells are of ancient origin and have been used in all major religions except Islam.

belladonna, Old World perennial (*Atropa belladonna*), in NIGHTSHADE family. Grown for narcotic poison (ATROPINE) used medicinally.

belladonna lily: see AMARYLLIS.

Bellaire. 1 City (pop. 11,502), E Ohio, on Ohio R. below Wheeling, W.Va.; settled c.1802. Has coal mines. **2** City (pop. 19,872), SE Texas, a suburb SW of Houston.

Bellamy, Edward (běʹlûmĭ), 1850–98, American writer of novels and short stories, now known chiefly for *Looking Backward, 2000–1887* (1888). This utopian romance, presenting the triumphant socialistic state of A.D. 2000, had great influence then and later.

Bellarmine: see ROBERT BELLARMINE, SAINT.

Bellay, Joachim Du: see DU BELLAY, JOACHIM.

Belle-Alliance (bělʹ-älyäsʹ), village near Waterloo, Belgium: see WATERLOO CAMPAIGN.

Belleau Wood (běʹlō, bělōʹ), forested area, N France, E of Château-Thierry. Here U.S. troops stopped German advance in First World War (June, 1918).

Bellefontaine (bělfounʹtĭn), city (pop. 11,424), W central Ohio, N of Springfield; laid out 1820. Trade and rail center for farm area. Varied industries. Campbell Hill or Hogue's Hill, state's highest point (1,550 ft.), is near.

Bellefontaine Neighbors, city (pop. 13,650), E Mo., a suburb N of St. Louis; founded c.1819.

Bellefonte, borough (pop. 6,088), central Pa., NE of Altoona; laid out 1795. Named, according to legend, by Talleyrand during his visit 1794–95. A resort and farm trade center with limestone quarries.

Belle Fourche, river rising in NE Wyo. and flowing c.290 mi. NE and E past Belle Fourche, S.Dak., to Cheyenne R. in W central S.Dak. U.S. project provides flood control and irrigation. Keyhole Dam on river, and Belle Fourche Dam on tributary.

Belle Glade, town (pop. 11,273), SE Fla., near S tip of L. Okeechobee, WSW of West Palm Beach; founded c.1925. Trade and processing center for truck and cattle area.

Belle-Isle, Charles Fouquet, duc de (shärlʹ fōōkäʹ dükʹ dü běl-ēlʹ), 1684–1761, marshal of France. Noted for epic retreat from Prague (1742) in War of the Austrian Succession.

Belle Isle, Strait of, 10–15 mi. wide, c.35 mi. long, between N.F. and Lab., Canada, N entrance to Gulf of St. Lawrence.

Bellerophon (bŭlěʹrŭfŏn″, –fŭn), in Greek legend, hero who slew the CHIMERA. He accomplished this task with aid of winged horse Pegasus. Grown proud, he tried to fly to heaven on Pegasus, but was thrown and blinded—according to one legend, killed.

Belleville, city (pop. 30,655), S Ont., Canada, on L. Ontario. Port with mfg. of machinery and optical equipment. Seat of Albert Col.

Belleville. 1 City (pop. 37,264), SW Ill., SE of East St. Louis, in coal, clay, and sand area. Scott Air Force Base is ENE. **2** Town (pop. 35,005), NE N.J., on Passaic R., N of Newark; settled c.1680, set off from Newark 1839.

Bellevue. 1 City (1966 pop. 17,496), E Nebr., on Missouri R., S of Omaha. State's oldest town; trading post in early 19th cent. and site of Presbyterian Indian mission in '40s and '50s. **2** City (pop. 8,286), N Ohio, SW of Sandusky; settled 1815. Rail center. Seneca Caverns are nearby. **3** Residential borough (pop. 11,412), SW Pa., NW of Pittsburgh; settled 1802. **4** Residential city (pop. 12,809), W Wash., opposite Seattle on E side of L. Washington. Bridge to Seattle.

Bellevue Hospital, in New York city. Operated by Dept. of Hospitals of the City of New York; developed from a "Publick Workhouse and House of Correction" commissioned 1734. Medical college, first in U.S., founded 1860; nursing school, 1873. Became associated with Columbia Univ. (1882), New York Univ. (1882), Cornell Univ. (1898), and the New York Univ.–Post Graduate Medical School (1948).

Bellflower, city (pop. 45,909), S Calif., NE of Long Beach; founded 1906. Has some light industry.

bellflower or **campanula** (kămpănʹūlu), plant of genus *Campanula* with bell- or star-shaped flowers, often blue. Species for rock gardens and borders include Canterbury bells, a biennial; HAREBELL; and the edible rampion.

Bell Gardens, city (1965 pop. 28,779), S Calif., a suburb SE of Los Angeles.

Bellingham, city (pop. 34,688), NW Wash., on Bellingham Bay, near Canada. Settled 1852 as Whatcom, it merged with three adjoining towns 1903. Distributing and processing center for dairy, poultry, truck area. Has coal mines.

Bellini (běl-lēʹnē), family of Venetian painters of the Renaissance. **Jacopo Bellini** (yäʹkōpō), c.1400–1470, was father and teacher of Giovanni and Gentile. **Giovanni Bellini** (jōvänʹnē), c. 1430–1516, became teacher of Giorgione and Titian. Serenity, majesty, and luminous color characterize his works, which include altarpieces in the Frari and San Zaccaria, Venice; *Feast of the Gods* (Natl. Gall., Washington, D.C.); *St. Francis* (Frick Coll., New York). **Gentile Bellini** (jäntē'lä), 1429–1507, painted contemporary Venetian life and used Turkish subjects after visit to Constantinople.

Bellini, Vincenzo (vēnchän'tsō bĕl-lē'nē), 1801–35, Italian operatic composer. Among his operas are *Norma* and *La sonnambula* (both 1831).

Bellinzona (bĕl-lēntsō'nä), town (pop. 13,435), cap. of Ticino, S Switzerland, on Ticino R. Has several churches and castles dating from 13th-16th cent.

Bell Island (pop. 12,281), 6 mi. long and 3 mi. wide, SE N.F., Canada, in Conception Bay. Large reserves of iron ore.

Bellman, Carl Michael, 1740–95, Swedish writer of drinking songs, pastorals, and comic songs.

Bellmawr (bĕlmär'), residential borough (pop. 11,-853), SW N.J., SSE of Camden.

bell metal: see BRONZE.

Bellmore, residential town (pop. 12,784), SE N.Y., on SW Long Isl., SSW of Levittown. Varied mfg.

Bello, Andrés (ändräs' bä'yō), 1781–1865, South American intellectual leader, b. Venezuela. After 19 years in London (1810–29), he went to Chile, became leader in education. Wrote poems, works on grammar and law; forwarded American intellectual independence from Europe.

Belloc, Hilaire (bĕl'ŏk), 1870–1953, British author, b. France. Poet, essayist, biographer, he wrote from a Roman Catholic viewpoint; friend of G. K. Chesterton.

Bellotto, Bernardo (bĕrnär'dō bäl-lôt'tō), 1720–80, Venetian architectural and landscape painter, also called CANALETTO, after his uncle and teacher.

Bellow, Saul, 1915–, American novelist, b. Quebec, of Russian Jewish parents. Best known for *The Adventures of Augie March* (1953) and *Herzog* (1964), both long novels set in Chicago and marked with a concern for the individual in an indifferent society. Other works include the novels *Seize the Day* (1956) and *Henderson the Rain King* (1959) and a play, *The Last Analysis* (produced 1964).

Bellows, George (Wesley), 1882–1925, American painter and lithographer. His work is marked by a direct, unself-conscious realism.

Bellows Falls, village (pop. 3,831), SW Vt., on Connecticut R., in town of Rockingham. One of first canals in U.S. built around falls here, abandoned after coming of railroad (1849), and rebuilt as part of hydroelectric power project (1926–28). First bridge over Connecticut R. built here 1785.

Bellwood, village (1965 pop. 22,821), NE Ill., W of Chicago.

Belmont. 1 Residential city (pop. 15,996), W Calif., SSE of San Francisco; laid out 1851. The Col. of Notre Dame is here. **2** Town (pop. 28,715), E Mass., a suburb NW of Boston; settled 1636. **3** City (1966 pop. 4,718), S N.C., W of Charlotte. Seat of Belmont Abbey Col.

Belmonte, Juan (hwän' bĕlmōn'tä), 1892–1962, Spanish bullfighter.

Belo Horizonte (bĕl' ōrēzônt') city (pop. 693,328), cap. of Minas Gerais, E Brazil. A planned city built to replace Ouro Prêto as state cap. (1895). The center of a rich mining and agr. region, it also manufactures steel and textiles.

Beloit (bīloit'), city (pop. 32,846), S Wis., on Rock R. at Ill. line, SSE of Madison; founded c.1837. Noted for winter sports. Seat of Beloit Col.

Belorussia (byĕ"lŭrōō'sēŭ) or **Belorussian Soviet Socialist Republic,** constituent republic (80,154 sq. mi.; 1965 est. pop. 8,570,000), W European USSR; cap. Minsk. Other important cities are Gomel, Vitebsk, Brest, Mogilev, and Gradno. Mainly lowland, drained by Dnieper, Western Dvina, Niemen. Pripet Marshes in S. Agr.; chemical, textile, machinery, peat industries. Population is 81% Belorussian, a Slavic group

influenced by Polish culture. Eastern Orthodoxy is major religion, but there are also Roman Catholics. Region was part of Kievan Russia from 9th cent.; conquered by LITHUANIA 14th cent.; passed to Russia through Polish partitions of 1772–95. Treaty of Riga (1921) gave W part to Poland. Belorussian SSR, founded 1919, joined USSR 1922. W part was occupied by Soviet forces 1939 and incorporated into Belorussian SSR. Belorussia suffered severly from German occupation in Second World War. Its Jewish population (c.8%) was virtually annihilated. Joined UN 1945. Also spelled Bielorussia or Byelorussia; it is sometimes (erroneously) called White Russia.

Belovo (byĕ'lŭvŭ), city (1965 est. pop. 114,000), Asiatic RSFSR, in S central Siberia. One of largest industrial centers of Kuznetsk Basin; steelworks and zinc plants.

Belsen (bĕl'zŭn), village, West Germany, in Lower Saxony. Site of notorious concentration camp during Hitler regime.

Belshazzar (bĕlshäz'ŭr), in Bible, son of Nebuchadnezzar, last king of Babylon. At his riotous feast, handwriting appeared on the wall and was interpreted by Daniel as sign of doom. That night Babylon fell to Cyrus. Dan. 5. According to Babylonian cuneiform records, Belshazzar was the first-born son of Nabonidus and with him coregent of Babylonia.

Belt, Great, and **Little Belt,** shallow straits connecting Kattegat with Baltic Sea. Great Belt, c.10 mi. wide, separates Zealand and Fyn isls., Denmark. Little Belt, ½-c.20 mi. wide, between Fyn and Jutland, is crossed by railroad and road bridge.

Belteshazzar (–shäz'–), in the book of DANIEL, Babylonian name of the prophet.

Belton. 1 City (pop. 4,897), W central Mo., S of Kansas City. Carry Nation lived and is buried here. **2** City (pop. 8,163), central Texas, NNE of Austin. A market center. Seat of Mary Hardin-Baylor Col.

Belvedere (bĕl'vŭdēr), a gallery and court of the Vatican, Rome, containing the *Apollo Belvedere* and the *Laocoön;* built 1490. A palace by this name in Vienna houses the Mus. of History and Art.

Belvidere, city (pop. 11,223), N Ill., on Kishwaukee R., E of Rockford; founded 1836. A farm trade center.

Bely, Andrei (ŭndrä' byĕ'lē), pseud. of Boris Nikolayevich Bugayev, 1880–1934, Russian poet, a leading symbolist. Besides poetry (collected in *Symphonies,* 4 vols., 1901–8), he wrote rich, masterful novels, notably *The Silver Dove* (1910) and *Petersburg* (1912). Influenced early Soviet literature.

Bembo, Pietro (pyä'trō bĕm'bō), 1470–1547, Italian humanist, cardinal of the Roman Church, secretary of Leo X. Arbiter of literary taste. His editions of Petrarch and Dante helped estab. Tuscan dialect as literary language of Italy.

Bemis Heights, battle of: see SARATOGA CAMPAIGN.

Benaiah (bĕnä'yŭ), heroic warrior, loyal follower of David and Solomon. 2 Sam. 8.18; 20.23; 23.20–23; 1 Kings 2.25,34; 1 Chron. 11.22–25; 18.17; 27.5,6.

Benalcázar, Sebastián de (sävästyän' dä bänälkä'thär), c.1479–1551, Spanish conquistador. Accompanied Columbus on third voyage (1498), served in Darien and Nicaragua, then joined Pizarros in conquest of Peru (1532). From 1533 to 1550 was active in conquest of present Ecuador and Colombia.

Benares (bŭnä'rĭz) or **Banaras** (bŭnä'rŭs), city (pop. 355,777), Uttar Pradesh, India, on Ganges R. Visited by c.1,000,000 Buddhist, Hindu, and Moslem pilgrims annually. Rail hub and trade center.

Benavente (y Martínez), Jacinto (häthĕn'tō bā"nävän'tä ē märtē'nĕth), 1866–1954, Spanish dramatist. Notable works are the farce *Los intereses creados* (1907; Eng. tr., *Bonds of Interest,* 1917) and the rural drama *La malquerida* (1913). Awarded 1922 Nobel Prize in Literature.

Ben Barka, Mehdi: see BARKA, MEHDI BEN.

Ben Bella, Ahmed, 1918–, Algerian statesman. Joined Algerian nationalist movement after Second World War. Twice taken by French; released 1962. Gained control of government and was elected premier 1962 and president 1963. Overthrown June, 1965, in coup led by Houari Boumedienne.

Benbow, William, fl. 1825–40, English pamphleteer. Introduced theory of the general strike.

Benchley, Robert (Charles), 1889–1945, American humorist. The drama critic of *Life* (1920–29) and the *New Yorker* (1929–40), he is remembered for gently sardonic articles, collected in *Of All Things* (1921), *My Ten Years in a Quandary* (1936), and other volumes. He wrote, directed, and acted in humorous film shorts.

Bend, city (pop. 11,936), W central Oregon, on Deschutes R., S of The Dalles at E foot of Cascade Range; laid out 1904. Resort and industrial and commercial center of farm and livestock area.

Benda, Julien (zhülyē′ bädä′), 1867–1956, French novelist and critic. A humanist, he attacked the philosophy of Bergson.

Ben Day process: see DAY, BENJAMIN.

Bender (bĕn′dŭr), Rumanian *Tighina*, Rus. *Bendery*, city (1965 est. pop. 55,000), S Moldavian SSR, in Bessarabia. Conquered by Turks 1538. Residence of CHARLES XII of Sweden 1709–13.

Bendigo (bĕn′dĭgō), municipality (metropolitan pop. 41,140), Victoria, Australia; founded 1851. Formerly important mining town, now wheat-trading center.

bends: see AEROEMBOLISM.

Benedetti, Vincent, Comte (vĕsä′ kōt′ bänädĕt′tē), 1817–1900, French ambassador to Prussia (1864–70). His interview with William I at Ems was published by Bismarck in an altered version (see EMS DISPATCH) which precipitated Franco-Prussian War.

Benedetto da Majano or **Maiano** (bänädĕt′tō dä mäyä′nō), 1442–97, Florentine Renaissance sculptor.

Benedict, Saint, d. c.547, Italian monk, founder of the Benedictines, b. Norcia (or Nursia). Became a hermit at Subiaco, where monks gathered around him. Later founded first Benedictine monastery, at MONTE CASSINO, and created the Rule of St. Benedict, the chief rule of Western monasticism. Feast: March 21.

Benedict XIII, antipope: see LUNA, PEDRO DE.

Benedict XIV, 1675–1758, pope (1740–58), b. Bologna; originally named Prospero Lambertini. He was renowned for learning, for patronizing art, and for protecting Eastern Catholic rites from Latinization.

Benedict XV, 1854–1922, pope (1914–22), b. Genoa; originally named Giacomo della Chiesa. In First World War, he kept the Vatican neutral and strenuously tried to restore peace.

Benedict, Ruth (Fulton), 1887–1948, American anthropologist. Student and colleague of Franz Boas at Columbia Univ. Contributed to enlarging scope of anthropology through work on concept of culture motif and relation of personality to culture. Her works include *Patterns of Culture* (1934). Margaret Mead edited a collection of her works (1959).

benedictine (bĕnŭdĭk′tēn), sweet, brown LIQUEUR originated in 1510 by Benedictine monks in France.

Benedictines, monks of the Roman Catholic Church, estab. at MONTE CASSINO by St. BENEDICT, whose rule they follow. Unlike earlier groups they stress communal living, and their abbeys are like homes of Christian families with abbots as fathers. Their waking hours are devoted principally to worship and work—chiefly manual work, though the Benedictines did much to preserve learning through the early Middle Ages. Many notable missionaries were Benedictines (e.g., St. Augustine of Canterbury, St. Boniface), and with urging of Pope Gregory I (a Benedictine himself) and others, the abbeys were spread across Europe as outposts of civilization. Among these were St. Gall, Fulda, Solesmes, Monserrat, and St. Albans. Later reforms created new orders within the general Benedictine family—the CLUNIAC ORDER,

the CISTERCIANS, and the TRAPPISTS (Cistercians of the Stricter Observance).

benefice, in canon law, a position in the Church which has attached to it a source of income; also that income itself. The value of benefices led to many abuses and frequent conflict between secular and ecclesiastical authorities in the Middle Ages.

Bene Israel (bä′nē) [Heb.,= sons of Israel] anc. Jewish community of Bombay, India; now mainly resettled in Israel.

Benelux Economic Union of Belgium, the Netherlands, and Luxembourg. Preceded by Benelux customs union (1948). The present union was estab. by treaty in 1958; provides for abolition of trade and travel restrictions, coordination of economic policies. The nations act as one trading unit.

Benes, Eduard, Czech *Beneš* (bĕ′nĕsh), 1884–1948, Czech statesman. Chief collaborator of T. G. Masaryk, he was foreign minister (1918–35), premier (1921–22), president of the republic (1935–38; 1945–48), and leader of the National Socialist (i.e., liberal) party. The Franco-Czech alliance and LITTLE ENTENTE were mainly his work. Exiled after the MUNICH PACT, he headed the Czech provisional government at London during Second World War; was reelected president of liberated Czechoslovakia; resigned after Communist coup d'état of 1948.

Benét, Stephen Vincent (bĕnā′), 1898–1943, American author. American historical and folk materials are the basis for his long Civil War poem, *John Brown's Body* (1928); poems for children, *A Book of Americans* (1933 with his wife, Rosemary Benét); his unfinished epic *Western Star* (1943); and distinguished stories such as "Johnny Pye and the Fool-Killer" and "The Devil and Daniel Webster." His brother, **William Rose Benét,** 1886–1950, poet and critic, wrote lyrics and ballads and a verse autobiography, *The Dust Which is God* (1941). He edited the *Saturday Review of Literature* (which he helped found in 1924) and the collected poems and prose of his wife, Elinor Wylie.

Benevento (bĕnŭvĕn′tō), city (pop. 54,744), Campania, S Italy. Was important Roman town on Appian Way; cap. of powerful Lombard duchy (6th–11th cent.); later under papal rule. Many Roman remains. Church of Santa Sofia (8th cent.).

Ben Ezra: see IBN EZRA, ABRAHAM BEN MEIR.

Bengal (bĕng-gôl′), region in NE India and E Pakistan, on Bay of Bengal. Mostly in Ganges-Brahmaputra delta between Bihar and Assam. Himalayan forests in N, Sundarban jungles in S. The British took Bengal from Mogul empire in 1764. Divided 1947 between India and Pakistan. **East Bengal,** province (54,501 sq. mi.; pop. 50,844,000), is coextensive with E Pakistan; cap. Dacca. Includes large jute-growing area. **West Bengal,** state (30,775 sq. mi.; pop. 34,970,000) of India; cap. Calcutta. Includes former native state of Cooch Behar. Contains the Hooghlyside industrial complex. Coal is mined and petroleum is exploited.

Bengal, Bay of, arm, c.1,300 mi. long and c.1,000 mi. wide, of Indian Ocean, with India on W and Burma and Malaya on E.

Bengali (bĕngäl′ē), Eastern Indic language of the Indo-European family. See LANGUAGE (table).

Bengasi or **Benghazi,** city (pop. c.136,640), NE Libya; joint cap. with Tripoli. Mediterranean port; communications and light industrial center. Founded c.15th cent.; came under Italian rule 1911. Captured by British during Second World War.

Benguela (bĕn-gĕ′lŭ), town (c.26,000), W Angola, on the Atlantic Ocean. Formerly a slave-trading port.

Ben-Gurion, David (bĕn-gōō′rĭŏn), 1886–, Israeli statesman, b. Poland. Fled to Palestine after pogroms of 1905 and became a Zionist. In First World War helped organize Jewish Legion in support of British. Leader of Mapai party, he became first prime minister of Israel in 1948. Resigned seven times before retiring in 1963. Broke with Mapai in 1965 and formed new party, but lost in general election.

Benhadad (-hă′dăd), kings of Damascus. **1** Fl. 890 B.C., ally of Asa of Judah against Baasha of Israel. 1 Kings 15.17–20. **2** Fl. 854 B.C., continued traditional enmity with Israel and defeated Ahab and Jehoshaphat. Murdered and succeeded by Hazael. 1 Kings 20; 22; 2 Kings 8.15. **3** Fl. 800 B.C., son of Hazael. Defeated by Jehoash of Israel. 2 Kings 13.25; Amos 1.4.

Benicia (bŭnĭsh′ŭ), city (pop. 6,070), W Calif., a port on Carquinez Strait, NE of Oakland; founded 1857. Was state cap. 1853–54.

Beni Hassan (bĕ′nĕ hä′sän), village, central Egypt, on the Nile. Has 39 rock-cut tombs of XII dynasty of ancient Egypt.

Benin (bĕnēn′), city (pop. c.100,000) and former native state, SW Nigeria. Was flourishing kingdom when discovered by Portuguese in 1485. Became rich through trade in ivory, pepper, palm oil, and slaves. Famous for bronze and ivory art.

Benjamin, youngest son of Jacob and Rachel, eponymous ancestor of one of 12 tribes of Israel. Tribe occupied E central Palestine. Tribesmen were noted archers. Famous son of house of Benjamin was Saul. Gen. 35.18; 42–46; 49.27; Num. 1.36; 13.9; 26.38–41; 34.21; Deut. 33.12; Joshua 18.11–28; Judges 3.15; 20–21; 1 Chron. 8.40; 12.2; 2 Chron. 14.8; 17.17.

Benjamin, Asher, 1773–1845, American architect. His books popularized details of Late Colonial style.

Benjamin, Judah Philip, 1811–84, Confederate statesman and British barrister, b. Virgin Isls. Ably defended Southern policy as U.S. Senator (1853–61). In Southern government he was successively attorney general, secretary of war, and secretary of state. Known in North as "the brains of the Confederacy." On its collapse in 1865, he escaped to England, where he became prominent lawyer.

Benjamin of Tudela (tŏōdā′lä), d. 1173, Jewish traveler. Account of his 14-year journey from Spain to China depicts social and cultural conditions of 12th cent.

Ben Macdhui or **Ben Muich-Dhui** (măkdŏō′ē), peak, 4,296 ft. high, Aberdeenshire, Scotland; second highest peak in Scotland.

Benn, Gottfried (gôt′frĕt bĕn′), 1886–1956, German poet and critic. His early works (e.g., *Der Vermessungsdirigent,* 1919) were strongly expressionistic. Later poems (e.g., *Statische Gedichte,* 1948) and his autobiography (1950) reflect agony and conflict of Nazi era. Also wrote prose works on esthetics and politics.

Bennet, Henry: see ARLINGTON, HENRY BENNET, 1ST EARL OF.

Bennett, (Enoch) Arnold, 1867–1931, English novelist. Naturalistic novels, many about the "Five Towns" potteries district in his native Staffordshire; notable is *The Old Wives′ Tale* (1908). Also wrote journals (3 vols., 1932–33), short stories, and plays.

Bennett, Floyd, 1890–1928, American aviator. In 1926, with Byrd, flew nonstop Spitsbergen to North Pole and return, first flight over either pole. Appointed second in command of Byrd's antarctic expedition, but died of pneumonia contracted on *Bremen* rescue flight.

Bennett, James Gordon, 1795–1872, American journalist, b. Scotland. Coming to the U.S. in 1819, he won fame as a reporter. He founded (1835) the New York *Herald,* which he made a phenomenal popular success, increasing the field of news (e.g., with financial news, with reports of foreign correspondents, with accent on detailed accounts of crimes and sensations), using the telegraph and other means to speed reporting, and employing illustrations. In 1867 he relinquished control of the *Herald* to his son, James Gordon Bennett, 1841–1918, who also founded the *Evening Telegram* and London and Paris daily editions of the *Herald.* He stressed international news and attention-getting "stunts" (e.g., financing Stanley's

expedition to Africa to find David Livingstone and G. W. De Long's Arctic expedition). He helped found Commercial Cable Co. Also a yachtsman, he gave a trophy for international yacht races.

Bennett, John Coleman, 1902–, American clergyman, b. Canada. Professor at Union Theological Seminary from 1943; became president 1964.

Bennett, Richard Bedford, 1870–1947, Canadian prime minister (1930–35), leader of Conservative party. Urged preferential tariff for the empire, and saw policy adopted 1932.

Ben Nevis (nē′vĭs, nĕv′ĭs), peak, 4,406 ft. high, Inverness-shire, Scotland; highest peak in Great Britain. NE side has precipice of more than 1,450 ft.

Bennington, town (pop. 13,002), SW Vt., N of Williamstown, Mass.; chartered 1749, settled 1761. Includes villages of Bennington, North Bennington, and Old Bennington. Shaft (300 ft. high) commemorates battle of Bennington in SARATOGA CAMPAIGN; marked site of Catamount Tavern where Green Mountain Boys met; Old First Church 1805; restored 1937). Stoneware made from late 18th to late 19th cent. Seat of BENNINGTON COLLEGE.

Bennington College, at Bennington, Vt.; for women; chartered 1925, opened at North Bennington 1932. Has program of self-dependent education; ability in arts is stressed.

Benoît de Sainte-More or **Benoît de Sainte-Maure** (bŭnwä′ dŭ sĕt-môr′), fl. 1165, French TROUVÈRE. His *Roman de Troie,* a romance based on Dares and Dictys, became source of medieval version of the Trojan legend, notably of TROILUS AND CRESSIDA.

Benoni, city (pop. c.140,790), S Transvaal, Republic of South Africa, on the WITWATERSRAND. Gold-mining center; iron and brass foundries.

Bensenville, village (1965 pop. 12,212), NE Ill., NW of Chicago, in truck-farm area. O'Hare Internatl. Airport is nearby.

Benson, Ezra Taft, 1899–, U.S. Secretary of Agriculture (1953–61). Marketing specialist; executive secretary of Natl. Council of Farmer Cooperatives (1939–44). Official in Mormon Church.

Bent, Charles, 1799–1847, American frontiersman. Led expeditions on Santa Fe Trail. Member of famous trading firm. His brother, **William Bent,** 1809–69, also a trader and frontiersman, was long the manager of BENT'S FORT.

bent grass, any species of genus *Agrostis,* slender, delicate grasses. Grown for pasture, hay, lawn (e.g., creeping bent, established by planting stolons).

Bentham, George (bĕn′thŭm), 1800–1884, English botanist, a great systematist.

Bentham, Jeremy, 1748–1832, English philosopher, the early exponent of utilitarianism. Trained for the law, he reflected legal influence in his carefully written works on society, jurisprudence, ethics, economics, and general theories of mankind and man's conduct. His best-known work is *An Introduction to the Principles of Morals and Jurisprudence* (pub. 1789, but privately printed 1780).

Bentinck, William: see PORTLAND, WILLIAM BENTINCK, 1ST EARL OF.

Bentivoglio (bän′tĕvō′lyō), Italian noble family, powerful in 15th-cent. Bologna. Its greatest member, Giovanni II, held splendid court and beautified city.

Bentley, Eric (Russell), 1916–, American drama critic, b. England. Works include *The Playwright as Thinker* (1946), *What Is Theater?* (1956), *The Life of the Drama* (1964), and translations of the plays of Bertolt Brecht and Luigi Pirandello. Became professor at Columbia 1953.

Bentley, Richard, 1662–1742, English philologist, generally considered greatest of English classical scholars. His exposure of a 14th-cent. forgery, *The Epistles of Phalaris,* gained notice.

Benton, Thomas Hart, 1782–1858, American statesman. U.S. Senator from Mo. (1821–51) and U.S. Representative (1853–55). Supported currency measures to benefit common man; drew up Pres. Jackson's Specie Circular (1836). Supported all legislation favoring Western development and aiding settlers. Opposed extension of slavery. His grandnephew is **Thomas Hart Benton,** 1889–, American painter. Dramatized American themes (notably in his murals) with characterizations of popular types.

Benton. 1 City (pop. 10,399), central Ark., SW of Little Rock; founded c.1834. Bauxite is processed. **2** Town (pop. 3,074), SW Ky., SE of Paducah. Annual singing festival held here since 1884.

Benton Harbor, resort city (pop. 19,136), SW Mich., on L. Michigan at mouth of St. Joseph R. opposite St. Joseph city; settled c.1840. Center of state's fruit industry and a mineral-spring resort. House of David (founded 1903), a religious colony, has business and farm holdings. Extension center of Mich. State Univ. is here.

bentonite: see CLAY.

Bent's Fort, noted trading post of the American West, on Arkansas R. in present SE Colo., E of La Junta. The successful trading company headed by Charles Bent and Ceran St. Vrain estab. post here in 1828 after founding it near by in 1826. Fort (often called Bent's Old Fort) completed 1833. On the mountain branch of Santa Fe Trail, it dominated trade with Indians, Mexicans, Americans. Kit Carson hunted here 1831–42. American troops used it briefly in Mexican War. Tradition says that manager William Bent blew it up. He built Bent's New Fort further downstream in 1852 or 1853, leased it to U.S. in 1860. Fort destroyed by flood shortly thereafter and replaced by new army fort.

Benue (bān'wā), river, N Nigeria, chief tributary of the Niger, joining it at Lokoja. In the rainy season lower course is navigable.

Ben Yehudah, Eliezer (ĕlĭē'zŭr bĕn" yĕhōō'dä), 1858–1922, Jewish scholar and leader. Settled in Palestine in 1881. Compiled the *Dictionary of Ancient and Modern Hebrew* (16 vols.).

Benz, Carl, 1844–1929, German engineer, credited with building first automobile powered by internal combustion engine.

Benzedrine, drug used to stimulate higher nerve centers; it produces euphoria, reduces appetite.

benzene (bĕn'zēn) or **benzol** (bĕn'zōl), colorless liquid, aromatic odor, boils at 80.1°C., solidifies at 5.48°C. Molecule has six carbons arranged in ring, with one hydrogen attached to each. Six carbon-carbon bonds make up the hexagonal (six-sided) ring. Three additional carbon-carbon bonds (each bond consists of a pair of electrons) oscillate and are equally shared among the six bond positions around the periphery of the ring. Thus the **benzene ring** is said to be conjugated or resonant. By convention, the benzene molecule is diagrammed as a hexagon of alternate single and double bonds; more correctly but less conveniently, the molecule could be diagrammed as a hexagon of single bonds supplemented by a dotted line all around (to indicate the uniform distribution of electrons). Any or all of the hydrogens may be replaced by other chemical groups or radicals; compounds which include one or more benzene rings are said to be aromatic. Benzene is used to make dyes, explosives, synthetic drugs, perfumes, lacquers, and as an organic solvent. Derivatives are carbolic acid, picric acid, and aniline. Benzene is first compound in the **benzene series** whose successive members differ by increment of one carbon and two hydrogen atoms. Second member is TOLUENE, third is XYLENE. See *ill.,* p. 106.

benzine (bĕn'zēn), colorless inflammable liquid mixture of hydrocarbons chiefly of methane (not benzene) series; obtained from petroleum by fractional distillation. Used as cleaning agent, organic solvent; used in some dyes and paints.

benzoate of soda: see SODIUM BENZOATE.

benzoic acid (bĕnzō'ĭk), solid, crystalline, organic acid. Used as antiseptic, as starting point for organic syntheses, in making dyes.

benzoin (bĕn'zoin), balsamic RESIN, dried exudate from pierced bark of benzoin tree (*Styrax*). Used in perfumery, incense, and in medicine.

benzol: see BENZENE.

Ben-Zvi, Yizhak (yĭtsh'häk bĕn-tsvē'), 1884–1963, Israeli statesman, president of Israel 1952–63, b. Russia. An active Zionist, he emigrated to Palestine 1907 and worked closely with Ben-Gurion. He was a historian and noted student of Jewish ethnology. Succeeded as president by Zalam Shazar.

Beograd, Yugoslavia: see BELGRADE.

Beowulf (bā'ŭwŏŏlf), oldest English epic, probably composed early 9th cent. in Northumbria or Mercia. Materials for poem come mainly from folk tale and Scandinavian history; the events take place in Denmark and Sweden. In first part the young hero combats and kills water monster Grendel and then Grendel's mother; in second, at end of a long, honorable life, he conquers a dragon, dies, and is given a hero's funeral. Written in strongly accentual, alliterative verse.

Berakhayh ben Natronai, Hanakdan (bĕrŭkī'ŭ bĕn nätrōnī' hänäk'dän), 12th- or 13th-cent. Jewish fabulist in N France. Composed over 100 fox fables in rhymed prose; probably influenced by PANCHATANTRA.

Béranger, Pierre Jean de (pyēr' zhā' dù bārāzhā'), 1780–1857, French poet, author of many popular songs. Like Burns he fitted his verse to existing melodies. Many of his songs helped to further the Napoleonic legend.

Berar, India: see MADHYA PRADESH.

Berat (bĕrät'), town (pop. 15,700), S central Albania, probably on site of anc. Antipatrea. Has 13th-cent. Byzantine citadel, 15th-cent. mosque.

Berbera (bûr'bŭrŭ), city (pop. c.22,000), N Somali Republic, NE Africa, on Gulf of Aden. USSR loan granted in 1962 to construct deepwater port facilities. Gypsum deposits nearby.

Berbers, aboriginal peoples of N Africa. Moslems, they speak Arabic and Hamitic tongues. Most are mountain farmers; some are oasis farmers and merchants; others are camel nomads.

Berceo, Gonzalo de (gônthä'lō dā bĕrthä'ō), 1180?–1265?, Spanish poet, Benedictine monk. His are the earliest-known poems in vernacular.

Berchtesgaden (bĕrkh'tùsgä"dùn), winter and summer resort, S Bavaria, in Bavarian Alps. Favorite residence of Hitler, who built a retreat on the Obersalzberg.

Berchtold, Leopold, Graf von (lā'ōpôlt gräf fün bĕrkh'tôlt), 1863–1942, Austro-Hungarian foreign minister (1912–15). Directed the policy which precipitated First World War after assassination of Archduke FRANCIS FERDINAND.

Berdichev (byĭrdyĕ'chĭf), city (1965 est. pop. 59,-000), NW Ukrainian SSR. Site of fortified Carmelite monastery (founded 1627). Center of Jewish Hasidism after 1780.

Berdyaev, Nicholas (bĕrdyĭ'ŭf), 1874–1948, Russian Orthodox religious philosopher, in exile from Russia after 1922. Early a Marxist, he later stressed the need for spiritual meaning and direction in individual life and in history.

Berdyansk (bĕr"dyänsk), city (1965 est. pop. 82,000), SE Ukraine, port on Sea of Azov. Mfg. of agr. and road machinery, electrical equipment; health and sea resort. Founded 1827 as Kutur-Ogli; renamed Novo-Nogaysk 1830, Berdyansk 1842. Called Osipenko 1939–58.

Berea or **Beroea** (both: bērēū'), Greek name of three places in Bible. **1** Syrian camp. 2 Mac. 9.4. **2** See VEROIA, Macedonia. **3** See ALEP, Syria.

Berea (bûrē'ŭ), city (pop. 16,592), NE Ohio, SW of Cleveland; settled 1809. Has stone quarries. Baldwin-Wallace Col. is here.

Representations of the benzene molecule, C_6H_6. C marks a carbon atom and H marks a hydrogen atom. The bonds between carbon and carbon make a six-sided ring; this is shown by solid lines. The first figure shows by the dotted line the shifting of the three additional bonds. The other two show a study of the bonds as if they were in a static position. At the right is the usual representation of the benzene ring.

① OH   ② NH_2 ③ NO_2 ④ CH_3 ⑤ CH_3 O_2N NO_2 NO_2

⑥ CH_3 CH_3 ⑦ CH_3 CH_3 ⑧ CH_3 CH_3

⑨   ⑩ COOH   ⑪ COOH   ⑫ CN

⑬ $\dfrac{[O]}{[H]}$ ⑭ O O   ⑮ NH_2 O O

⑯   ⑰   ⑱

① phenol, or hydroxybenzene, C_6H_5OH. A hydroxyl group has replaced one hydrogen. ② aniline, or aminobenzene, $C_6H_5NH_2$. ③ nitrobenzene, $C_6H_5NO_2$. ④ toluene, or methylbenzene, $C_6H_5CH_3$. ⑤ trinitrotoluene (T.N.T.), $C_6H_2CH_3(NO_2)_3$. ⑥, ⑦, ⑧ three isomers of xylene, or dimethylbenzene, $C_6H_4(CH_3)_2$. ⑨ naphthalene, $C_{10}H_8$. ⑩ β-naphthoic acid, $C_{10}H_7COOH$. ⑪ α-naphthoic acid, $C_{10}H_7COOH$. ⑫ α-naphthonitrile, $C_{10}H_7CN$. ⑬ anthracene, $C_{14}H_{10}$. On oxidation it becomes ⑭ anthraquinone. If anthraquinone undergoes reduction it again becomes anthracene. ⑮ α-aminoanthraquinone. ⑯ cholic acid, a steroid bile acid. The ring system common to all steroids is shown in white. ⑰ cholesterol, another steroid. ⑱ methylcholanthrene.

Berea College, near Berea, Ky.; coed; founded 1855 as one-room district school. Chartered 1866; became college 1869. Students work at school-owned businesses (e.g., bakery, dairy farm, printing shop, hotel) to help pay expenses. Campus includes forest lands.

Berengar II (bĕ'rĭng-gùr), d. 966, marquis of Ivrea. Made himself king of Italy in 950. His designs on Adelaide led to intervention of Emperor OTTO I. He swore fealty to Otto (952) but continued his intrigues until Otto imprisoned him (963).

Berengar of Tours, c.1000–1088, French theologian, head of the cathedral school at Tours. He was widely known as a dialectician, but his views on the Eucharist were considered radical and suspect by some theologians though approved by others (Leo IX and Gregory VII early defended him). A very bitter quarrel with LANFRANC led Berengar to an angry reply rejecting authority. This was condemned, and Berengar was declared a heretic, but was reconciled with the Church before his death. Also Bérenger, Berengarius.

Berenice (bĕrŭnī'sē), members of royal family of Egypt. **1** B. c.340 B.C.; d. 281 or 271 B.C., consort and half sister of Ptolemy I. **2** C.280–246 B.C., daughter of Ptolemy II, wife of ANTIOCHUS II. She and her infant son were murdered by Laodice, the former wife of Antiochus II, before her brother, Ptolemy III, arrived with aid. **3** C.273–221 B.C., a Cyrenian wife of Ptolemy III; joint ruler with her son, Ptolemy IV, who had her murdered. The constellation Berenice's Hair is named for her.

Berenice, Jewish princesses. **1** fl. 6 B.C., niece of Herod the Great, wife of his son Aristobulus who was executed for treason. Herod Agrippa I was their son. Her second husband was also executed. A pawn in the intrigues of the court, she later settled in Rome. **2** b. A.D. c.28, daughter of Herod Agrippa I. A beautiful woman, involved in intrigue, and devoted to her brother, Herod Agrippa II. Married three times, she became the mistress of Titus, who, on becoming emperor, sent her away for reasons of state.

Berenson, Bernard (bĕ'rŭnsùn), 1865–1959, American art critic, b. Lithuania, grad. Harvard, 1887. Authority on Italian art, especially of the Renaissance.

Berezina (bĕrĕzē'nŭ), river, 365 mi. long, Belorussia; tributary of Dnieper. Scene of heroic, costly crossing of Napoleon's fleeing army (Nov., 1812).

Berezniki (bĭryĕznyĭkĕ'), city (1965 est. pop. 132,-000), E European RSFSR, port on Kama R. One of main industrial centers of Urals; chemicals.

Berg, Alban (bĕrk), 1885–1935, Austrian composer. He used the 12-tone technique invented by his teacher, Arnold Schoenberg. Although he met violent opposition, his opera *Wozzeck* (1925) attained considerable success. Among other compositions are a *Lyric Suite* (1926) for string quartet; a violin concerto (1936); an unfinished opera, *Lulu.*

Berg, former duchy (before 1380, county), NW Germany; chief city Düsseldorf. Under dukes of JÜLICH 1348–1521; under dukes of CLEVES 1521–1609; under Wittelsbachs (Palatinate line) 1666–1806. Raised to grand duchy (1806) by Napoleon I in favor of Joachim Murat. To Prussia 1815.

Bergamo (bĕr'gämō), city (pop. 118,694), cap. of Bergamo prov., Lombardy, N Italy. Textile mfg. Ruled by Venice 1427–1797. Romanesque cathedral; baptistery; Renaissance Colleoni chapel. Birthplace of Donizetti.

bergamot (bûr'gŭmŏt), citrus tree (*Citrus bergamia*). Fruit, an orange, yields oil for perfumes and eau de Cologne. Wild bergamot is related to OSWEGO TEA.

Bergen (bûr'gŭn, Nor. bĕr'gùn), city (pop. 115,848), SW Norway, on the Vagen and the Pudde Fjord—both inlets of North Sea. Main shipping center and second largest city of Norway. Founded c.1070, it was chief city and royal residence of medieval Norway, an episcopal see, and a cultural center. HANSEATIC LEAGUE created c.1350 one of its four great foreign establishments here and dominated the city until 1560. In Second World War German naval installations were heavily bombed. Anc. buildings (mostly restorations) include Haakon's Hall, a 12th-cent. palace; cathedral (13th cent.); Rosenkrantz Tower (16th cent.). Seat of a university. Its theater gained international importance in 19th cent. through association with Ibsen and Bjornson. Annual international music festival.

Bergen, N.J.: see JERSEY CITY.

Bergenfield, residential borough (pop. 27,203), NE N.J., NE of Hackensack.

Bergen op Zoom (bĕr'gùn ôp zōm'), municipality (pop. 37,337) and town, North Brabant prov., SW Netherlands; a North Sea port on the Eastern Scheldt. Once strongly fortified, it was often besieged in the wars of the 16th–18th cent.

Berger, Victor Louis, 1860–1929, American Socialist leader and Congressman, b. Austria-Hungary. First Socialist member of Congress (1911–13). Sentenced to 20-year prison term for sedition; decision reversed by U.S. Supreme Court in 1921.

Bergerac, Cyrano de: see CYRANO DE BERGERAC.

Bergh, Henry, 1811–88, American philanthropist. Founded American Society for the Prevention of Cruelty to Animals (1866) and helped Elbridge T. Gerry estab. Society for the Prevention of Cruelty to Children (1875).

Bergius, Friedrich (frēd'rĭkh bĕr'gēŏos), 1884–1949, German chemist. Transformed coal into liquid fuel, wood into sugar. Shared 1931 Nobel Prize in Chemistry.

Bergman, Ingmar, 1918–, Swedish film director, writer, and producer. Noted for fluid impressionism in films such as *Wild Strawberries, The Virgin Spring, The Seventh Seal,* and *The Magician.*

Bergman, Ingrid, 1915–, Swedish actress. Began her career in Swedish films. Lived in U.S. 1939–49. Appeared in such films as *For Whom the Bell Tolls, Gaslight,* and *Anastasia;* lauded for stage portrayal in *Joan of Lorraine* 1946.

Bergman, Torbern Olof (tŏŏr'bùrn ŏo'lôv bĕr'yùmän), 1735–84, Swedish chemist, physicist, naturalist. Developed theory of chemical affinity, improved chemical analysis and rock classification, worked in crystallography.

Bergmann, Ernst von (ĕrnst fùn bĕrg'män), 1836–1907, German surgeon, introducer (1886) of steam sterilization of instruments and dressings.

Bergson, Henri (ärĕ' bĕrgsō'), 1859–1941, French philosopher, long a professor at the Collège de France. He opposed prevailing positivistic thought by accenting the dualism between the dynamic *élan vital* [life force] and resistant matter. Man knows matter through intellect, but, more important, knows through intuition how the *élan vital* operates and also discovers the true nature of time, which is duration in terms of life experience, not a mathematically clocked measurement. He won the 1927 Nobel Prize in Literature for his philosophical works.

Beria, Lavrenti Pavlovich (bĕ'ryä), 1899–1953, Russian Communist leader. Tried and executed for acts committed while head of NKVD (Russian secret police; later MVD), 1938–53.

beriberi (bĕ'rĕbĕ'rē), disease caused by thiamine deficiency, affecting nervous and gastrointestinal systems. May result from improper diet, poor absorption or utilization of thiamine by system, or increased need for vitamins (as in pregnancy).

Bering, Vitus Jonassen (vē'tŏos yō'näsùn bā'rĭng), 1681–1741. Danish explorer in Russian employ. Planned and carried out with government support notable expedition to map Siberian arctic regions. Died on Bering Isl. after leading expedition to Alaska.

Bering Island, off Kamchatka, extreme NE Asiatic RSFSR, in Bering Sea, largest of KOMANDORSKI ISLANDS. Here Vitus Bering was wrecked and died.

Bering Sea, northward extension of Pacific between Siberia and Alaska, c.878,000 sq. mi. Screened from Pacific by Aleutian Isls., navigable only after late May; connected with Arctic Ocean by Bering Strait, navigable only after late June. Contains several islands owned by U.S. and USSR. Bering voyages revealed fur-seal wealth, and from mid-18th cent. unregulated slaughter threatened their extinction. Protection of seals became subject of **Bering Sea Fur-Seal Controversy** (1886), international dispute over pelagic (open sea) sealing. Court of arbitration in 1893 declared against U.S. claim to control all of Bering Sea, and damages were paid to seized Canadian vessels. In 1911 international agreement gave U.S. supervision of seal summering places in Pribilof Isls., prohibited pelagic sealing, and forbade altogether the killing of sea otters. For several years sealing stopped completely and later resumed under careful restrictions.

Bering Strait, waterway between NE Asia and NW North America. Connects Arctic Ocean and Bering Sea. Narrowness (c.50 mi.) makes it plausible place of American Indian entry into America.

Berkeley, George (bär'klē), 1685–1753, British philosopher, b. Ireland; bishop of Cloyne after 1734. Going beyond the teachings of Locke, he argued for what has been called subjective idealism—the theory that all qualities exist only in the mind, that matter does not exist apart from its being perceived, and that the observing mind of God makes possible the continued apparent existence of material objects. Tried unsuccessfully to found a college to convert American Indians to Christianity. Among his works are *New Theory of Vision* (1709), *Treatise concerning the Principles of Human Knowledge* (1710), *Dialogues* (1713).

Berkeley, Sir William, 1606–77, British colonial governor of Va. A tyrant, his negligence brought on rebellion led by Nathaniel BACON. Removed from office after exacting bloody vengeance.

Berkeley (bûrk'lē). **1** City (pop. 111,268), W. Calif., on E shore of San Francisco Bay N of Oakland. Originally part of Peralta family's Rancho San Antonio (granted 1820); bought 1853 by Americans. A suburban and educational center, with part of Univ. of CALIFORNIA located here. Has aquatic park. **2** City (pop. 18,676), E Mo., a suburb NW of St. Louis.

Berkeley Springs, town (pop. 1,138), W.Va., in E Panhandle, NW of Martinsburg; chartered 1776 as Bath, still its official name. Warm springs have made town a health resort from colonial days.

berkelium (bûrk'lēŭm), radioactive element of ACTINIDE SERIES (symbol = Bk; see ELEMENT, table). Discovered 1950 by G. T. Seaborg and others at Univ. of California. Produced by bombarding isotope of americium with helium ions in cyclotron; has half-life of 4.8 hours.

Berkey, Charles Peter, 1867–1955, American geologist. A consultant on many engineering projects in New York city. From 1922 on staff of American Mus. of Natural History.

Berkhamstead, formerly also **Great Berkhamstead,** urban district (pop. 13,048), Hertfordshire, England. Site of 11th-cent. royal castle.

Berkley, city (pop. 23,275), SE Mich., a suburb NW of Detroit.

Berkman, Alexander, 1870?–1936, anarchist, b. Vilna, came to U.S. c.1887. Unsuccessful attempt to kill Henry Clay Frick (1892) caused 14 years of imprisonment. He and Emma GOLDMAN long associated, were arrested for obstructing the draft (1917) and deported to Russia (1919). Disappointed with USSR, he left and later committed suicide.

Berkshire (bärk'shĭr, –shŭr, bûrk'–) or **Berks,** inland county (725 sq. mi.; pop. 503,357) in Thames R. basin, England; co. town Reading. Largely agr., has dairying and hog raising. At Windsor is famous royal castle.

Berkshire Hills (bûrk'shēr), W Mass., region of wooded hills with many streams, small lakes, resorts, and country homes. A S extension of Green Mts., name is used loosely, referring sometimes to all W Mass. highlands, sometimes to that portion separated from main range of Taconic Mts. by valley. Pittsfield, North Adams, Great Barrington, and Lenox are main towns. Mt. Greylock (3,491 ft.) is state's highest peak. Chief rivers are Housatonic, Westfield.

Berkshire Symphonic Festival, summer music festival, featuring the Boston Symphony Orchestra, held since 1937 at "Tanglewood" near Lenox, Mass.

Berlage, Hendrik Petrus (berlä'gù), 1856–1934, Dutch architect and writer, whose Amsterdam Stock Exchange and various publications had great influence on 20th-cent. architecture.

Berle, Adolf A(ugustus), Jr. (bûr'lē), 1895–, U.S. Assistant Secretary of State (1938–44).

Berlichingen, Götz von (gûts fün bĕr'lĭkhĭng-ùn), c.1480–1562, German knight, adventurer. Led rebellious peasants in PEASANTS' WAR. His memoirs inspired Goethe's drama, *Götz von Berlichingen* (1773).

Berlin, Irving, 1888–, American composer of over 1,000 popular songs, b. Russia. His songs are of many types, e.g., the jazzy *Alexander's Ragtime Band* (his first great success, 1911); the nostalgic *White Christmas;* the patriotic *God Bless America.* He has written music for many musical comedies and films.

Berlin, Sir Isaiah, 1909–, English political scientist, b. Russia. Explored Tolstoy's view of irresistible historical forces in *The Hedgehog and the Fox* (1953); attacked determinist and relativist theories of history in *Historical Inevitability* (1954).

Berlin, Ont.: see KITCHENER.

Berlin (bûr''lĭn, Ger. bĕrlēn'), city, former cap. of Germany and Prussia, on the Spree and Havel rivers; an enclave within German Democratic Republic (East Germany). Divided (1945) into four occupation zones; the Soviet sector, known as East Berlin (pop. 1,082,349), is now cap. of German Democratic Republic; the British, American, and French zones constitute West Berlin (pop. 2,211,000). Until Second World War Berlin was second largest city of Europe and political, economic, and cultural center of Germany. It remains a major inland port and communications center with much mfg. Originating in two Wendish villages, Berlin and Kölln (merged 1307), city rose as member of Hanseatic League; became cap. of Brandenburg (15th cent.) and of Prussia (1701). Occupied by Austria (1757), Russia (1760), France (1806–8), Berlin emerged from its conflicts as a center of German national feeling. Became seat of North German Confederation (1866); underwent phenomenal growth after becoming cap. of Germany (1871); flourished as cultural cap. of Weimar Republic until 1933. Much bombed in Second World War; most severely damaged by artillery during capture by Russians (May, 1945). City was divided at POTSDAM CONFERENCE into four occupation zones under joint Allied military government. Mounting friction between Russia and Western Allies resulted in 1948 withdrawal of Russians from joint governorship and split of Berlin into two separate cities. During Soviet blockade of West Berlin in 1948–49 the city was supplied by vast airlift. Though Russia lifted blockade, lesser incidents continued, among them workers' riots in E Berlin in 1953, which were put down by Soviet tanks. Soviet efforts (from 1955) to end Berlin's occupation status and force withdrawal of Western forces led to fruitless international negotiations and resulted in barrier erected 1961—the Berlin "wall," which could be crossed only with special permission. West Berlin prospered while East Berlin suffered depression; but later, economic conditions in East Berlin improved.

Berlin. 1 Industrial town (pop. 11,250), central Conn., SSW of Hartford; settled 1686. **2** Town (pop. 2,046), Md., Eastern Shore, ESE of Salisbury; settled in early

19th cent. Stephen Decatur born here. **3 City** (pop. 17,821), NE N.H., in White Mts. at Androscoggin falls and E of St. Johnsbury, Vt.; settled 1821. In heavily forested region, was early site of pulp and paper mills. Winter sports center.

Berlin, Conference of, 1884–85, meeting of all European nations, U.S., and Turkey to consider problems arising from penetration of Africa. Called by Bismarck ostensibly to consider free trade and navigation on the Congo and Niger. Conference recognized claims of the International Association, private corporation of King Leopold II of Belgium, to most of Congo and Britain's title to S Nigeria.

Berlin, Congress of, 1878, called by signatories of Treaty of Paris of 1856 to revise Treaty of SAN STEFANO, which Russia had forced on Turkey. Bismarck, acting as "honest broker," was chairman. Other outstanding figures were Disraeli, A. M. Gorchakov, Andrassy. Principal decisions included recognition of Serbia, Montenegro, and Rumania as independent states; threefold division of BULGARIA; assignment of BOSNIA AND HERCEGOVINA to Austro-Hungarian administration; and revision of the boundary between Greece and Turkey.

Berlin Decree, issued in Berlin, Nov. 21, 1806, by Napoleon I in answer to British blockade of commercial ports. Declared British Isles under blockade; initiated CONTINENTAL SYSTEM.

Berlin Pact: see AXIS.

Berlioz, Hector (bĕrlēōs'), 1803–69, French romantic composer, whose ideas of orchestral coloring influenced many later composers. His first important work was the *Symphonie fantastique* (1830). In next decade he wrote the symphonies *Harold in Italy* and *Romeo and Juliet.* His outstanding dramatic works are *The Damnation of Faust, The Trojans.*

Bermondsey, London: see SOUTHWARK.

Bermuda (bûrmū'dú), British crown colony (c.21 sq. mi; 1964 est. pop. 48,040), comprising some 300 coral islands (c.20 inhabited), c.650 mi. SE of N.C.; cap. HAMILTON, on largest island, Bermuda. Year-round resort. Discovered by Spaniard. Juan de Bermúdez (1515), it was uninhabited until colonists under Sir George Somers were wrecked here (1609).

Bermuda grass, a grass (*Cynodon dactylon*) used for pasture and lawn in the S U.S. It is resistant to heat and drought.

Bermuda Hundred, fishing village, SE Va., on peninsula at junction of Appomattox and James rivers, NNE of Petersburg; founded 1613. Union Army of the James bottled up here after defeat at DREWRYS BLUFF, 1864.

Bern (bûrn, Ger. bĕrn) or **Berne** (Fr. bĕrn), most populous canton (2,658 sq. mi.; pop. 889,523) of Switzerland. Comprises Bernese Alps or Oberland, with JUNGFRAU and other peaks; Mittelland [midlands], in N foothills of Alps; and Seeland [lake country], in the NW, including Biel and Bernese Jura. Agr., dairying, tourist trade in Oberland and Mittelland; watchmaking in Seeland. Pop. mostly Protestant and—except in Jura—German-speaking. History of canton is largely that of its cap., **Bern** or **Berne** (est. pop. 167,400), since 1848 also cap. of Switzerland, on Aar R. Founded 1191; became free imperial city 1218; joined Swiss Confederation 1353; soon became its leading member; conquered AARGAU (1415) and VAUD (1536); accepted the Reformation (1528). Autocratic urban aristocracy governed until 1798, when French revolutionary armies sacked city and dismembered Bernese state. At Congress of Vienna (1815) Berne did not recover Aargau and Vaud but received Bernese Jura (former bishopric of Basel). Liberal cantonal constitution adopted 1831. Largely medieval in architecture, Bern has 15th-cent. cathedral, quaint arcaded streets, fountains. Modern buildings include federal palace, museums, univ. (founded 1834). Seat of Universal Postal Union, International Copyright Union, and other international agencies.

Bernadette, Saint (bûrnûdĕt'), 1844–79, French saint. whose visions of the Virgin in a grotto caused Lourdes to become a major Roman Catholic shrine. A poor and unlettered girl (Bernadette Soubirous), she was severely challenged by the skeptical both within the Church and outside before she was allowed to retreat to a quiet convent at Nevers. Canonized 1933. Feast: April 16.

Bernadotte, Count Folke (fôl'kù· bĕrnädôt'), 1895–1948, Swedish internationalist; nephew of King Gustavus V. Appointed UN mediator in Palestine (1948), he was assassinated by a Jewish extremist in Jerusalem. Ralph Bunche succeeded him.

Bernadotte, Jean Baptiste Jules: see CHARLES XIV, king of Sweden.

Bernalillo (bûrnûlē'yō), town (pop. 2,574), NW N.Mex., N of Albuquerque in lumber and farm area; settled 1698 by Spanish. Nearby was site of Coronado's hq., 1540–42.

Bernanos, Georges (zhôrzh' bĕrnänōs'), 1888–1948, French author. His novels, such as *Sous le soleil de Satan* (1926; Eng. tr., *The Star of Satan*) and *Journal d'un curé de campagne* (1936; Eng. tr., *The Diary of a Country Priest*), reflect deep mysticism. Though a monarchist and Catholic, Bernanos attacked Franco's policy in the Spanish civil war in *A Diary of My Times* (1938). *Dialogue des Carmélites* (1949) serves as libretto for opera by Poulenc.

Bernard, Saint: see BERNARD OF CLAIRVAUX, SAINT, and BERNARD OF MENTHON, SAINT. For the two Alpine passes, see SAINT BERNARD.

Bernard VII, d. 1418, count of Armagnac, constable of France; father-in-law of Charles d'ORLÉANS. Led Armagnac faction (named for him) after Charles's capture in 1415. Killed in Paris massacre (see ARMAGNACS AND BURGUNDIANS).

Bernard, Claude (klōd bĕrnär'), 1813–78, French physiologist, a founder of experimental medicine through work on digestive process and vasomotor mechanism.

Bernardin de Saint-Pierre, Jacques Henri (zhäk' ärē' bĕrnärdē' dù sē-pyēr'), 1737–1814, French author. Strongly influenced by Rousseau, he is best known for the charming prose idyl *Paul et Virginie* (1788).

Bernardo del Carpio (bĕrnär'dō dĕl kär'pyō), hero of medieval Spanish legend, counterpart of French Roland; supposedly nephew of Alfonso II.

Bernard of Clairvaux, Saint (bûr'nùrd, bûrnärd', klârvō'), 1090?–1153, French churchman, Doctor of the Church. In 1115 he founded a Cistercian monastery at CLAIRVAUX, where he remained as abbot the rest of his life, refusing high church offices. Nevertheless, holiness of life, immense capacity of mind, force of character, and burning eloquence made him the most powerful figure of his day. He sought peace among the rulers of Western Europe and had a hand in many political affairs. He led the successful fight to seat Pope INNOCENT II and was the adviser of Pope Eugene III. His vigorous attacks brought condemnations of ABELARD and ARNOLD OF BRESCIA. His preaching launched the Second Crusade. Bernard was notable also for his charity and his protection of the weak (e.g., the Jews of the Rhineland) from the powerful. Today his greatest importance lies perhaps in his writings, which include many superb sermons and profound and well-written treatises on the Christian life, theology, and mysticism (e.g., *On the Steps of Humility and Pride; On the Love of God; On Grace and Free Will; On Conversion; On Consideration;* and a life of St. Malachy). He probably did not write *Jesu, dulcis memoriae.* Feast: Aug. 20.

Bernard of Menthon, Saint (mätō'), 11th cent., Savoyard churchman, founder of the Alpine hospices in both of the SAINT BERNARD passes. Feast: May 28.

Bern Convention: see COPYRIGHT.

Berne, Switzerland: see BERN.

Bernese Alps, Switzerland: see BERN, canton.

Bernhard of Saxe-Weimar, 1604–39, Protestant general in THIRTY YEARS WAR. Captured Regensburg 1633;

was routed at Nördlingen 1634; entered French pay 1635; defeated imperials at Breisach (1638).

Bernhardt, Sarah (bûrn'härt, Fr. bĕrnär'), 1844–1923, stage name of Rosine Bernard, French actress. Superb performances at the Comédie Française 1872–80, e.g., in *Phèdre* and *Hernani*, earned her the title "divine Sarah." She appeared often in Sardou plays and toured Europe and U.S. (after 1880). After 1895 she managed the Théâtre Sarah Bernhardt, where she played Hamlet (1899) and appeared in Rostand's *L'Aiglon*, written for her in 1901. She made two silent films (1912) and continued acting even after a leg amputation in 1915.

Berni, Francesco (fränchä'skō bĕr'nĕ), 1497?–1535, Italian humorous poet, a priest, author of revision of the *Orlando Innamorato* of Boiardo.

Bernicia, Anglian kingdom, estab. 547. In late 6th cent. united with Deira to form Northumbria.

Bernina (bĕrnē'nä), Alpine mountain group on Swiss-Italian border, SE Switzerland, culminating in the Piz Bernina at 13,304 ft. The Bernina pass, 7,645 ft. high, is crossed by road and railroad.

Bernini, Giovanni Lorenzo (jōvän'nē lōrĕn'tsō bĕrnē'nē), 1598–1680, Italian baroque sculptor and architect. Carved the graceful Apollo and Daphne (Borghese Gall., Rome). Other works include royal staircase in Vatican, colonnades of elliptical plaza before St. Peter's Church, and the bronze baldachin and tombs of popes Urban VIII and Alexander VII within.

Bernoulli or **Bernouilli** (both: bĕrnōōyē'), name of family distinguished in mathematics and other sciences. After leaving Antwerp the family settled in Basel, Switzerland. **Jacob, Jacques,** or **James Bernoulli** (zhäk), 1654–1705, wrote treatise on theory of probability (1713), discovered Bernoulli's numbers. A professor at Basel, he was succeeded by his brother **Jean, Johann,** or **John Bernoulli** (zhä, yō'hän), 1667–1748, known for work in integral and exponential calculus. His son **Daniel Bernoulli** (dänyel'), 1700–1782, a mathematician and physician, solved equation known as Bernoulli's equation and advanced the kinetic theory of gases and fluids.

Bernstein, Eduard (ä'dōōärt bĕrn'shtīn), 1850–1932, German socialist. In Social Democratic party after 1872, he went into exile 1878, chiefly in England, returned 1901 to become leader of "revisionism." His *Evolutionary Socialism* (1898; Eng. tr., 1909) denies Marxist concepts of intensified class struggle and inevitable world revolution.

Bernstein, Henry (ärē' bĕrnstīn'), 1876–1953, French dramatist, author of comedies and dramas. *The Thief* (1906; Eng. tr., 1907) was most successful among his plays performed in America.

Bernstein, Leonard (bûrnstīn'), 1918–, American composer, conductor, and pianist; studied with Fritz Reiner and Serge Koussevitzky. First American-born musical director of the New York Philharmonic Orchestra (1958–). Compositions include symphonies, a Friday evening synagogue service, ballets, and musical comedies.

Bernstorff, Johann Hartwig Ernst (yohän' härt'vĭkh, bĕrns'tôrff), 1712–72, Danish statesman, of German origin. As foreign minister (1751–70) he kept Denmark at peace, negotiated exchange of Oldenburg for ducal Holstein with Russia. Dismissed through influence of STRUENSEE. His nephew, **Andreas Peter Bernstorff,** 1735–97, was Danish foreign minister (1773–80) and chief minister (1784–97). Kept Denmark neutral in French Revolutionary Wars; undertook social, economic, and educational reforms.

Beroea (bērē'ù), the same as BEREA.

Berra, Lawrence Peter (Yogi Berra), 1925–, American baseball player and manager. Played with N.Y. Yankees. Voted American League's most valuable player 1951, 1954, 1955.

Berrien Springs (bĕr'ēŭn), village (pop. 1,953), SW Mich., on St. Joseph R., SE of Benton Harbor. Seat of Andrews Univ.

Berruguete, Alonso (älōn'sō bĕr-rōōgä'tä), c.1480–1561, Spanish court artist to Charles V. Studied with Michelangelo. Known for the expressive torsion of his manneristic figures.

Berry, Charles, duc de (shärl' dük' dù bĕrē'), 1778–1820, younger son of Charles X of France. Fought with Condé against French Revolution. His assassination caused reaction against liberals. His wife, **Caroline Fernande Louise, duchesse de Berry** (kärōlēn' fĕrnäd' lwēz' düshēs'), 1798–1870, attempted in 1832 to win French throne for her son, later known as Henri, comte de Chambord. Temporarily imprisoned.

Berry, Martha McChesney, 1866–1942, American educator, founder of school for underprivileged mountain children at Mt. Berry, Ga., in 1902.

Berry (bĕrē'), region and former province, central France; historic cap. Bourges. Dry plateau (cattle raising), except fertile Indre and Cher valleys. Bought by French crown c.1100; duchy-appanage of various princes of the blood 1360–1601.

berry: see FRUIT.

Bertha of the Big Foot: see BERTRADA.

Berthelot, Pierre Eugène Marcelin (pyĕr' ûzhĕn' märsùlē' bĕrtùlō'), 1827–1907, French chemist. A founder of modern organic chemistry, he pioneered in producing synthetic organic compounds; also worked in thermochemistry and explosives.

Berthier, Louis Alexandre (lwē' älĕksä'drù bĕrtyä'), 1753–1815, marshal of France. Served in American Revolution and as chief of staff under Napoleon I. Was created prince of Neuchâtel and Wagram. Welcomed return of Bourbons. Committed suicide (or was killed) when Napoleon debarked from Elba.

Berthollet, Claude Louis, Comte (klōd' lwē' kōt' bĕrtōlā'), 1748–1822, French chemist. Stated theories of chemical equilibrium and of double decomposition of salts; analyzed ammonia. Discovered that chlorine is a bleach, carbon purifies water, and potassium chlorate has detonating properties.

Bertillon system (bùrtĭl'yùn), first scientific method of criminal identification, developed by Alphonse Bertillon (1853–1914), based on classification of body measurements.

Bertrada or **Bertha of the Big Foot,** d. 783, Frankish queen, mother of Charlemagne.

Bertrand de Born or **Bertran de Born,** c.1140–c.1214, French troubadour of Limousin. Some of his 40 surviving poems commemorate his part in the struggles between Henry II of England and his sons.

Berwick, James Fitz-James, duke of (bĕr'ĭk), 1670–1734, marshal of France; illegitimate son of James II of England and Arabella Churchill (Marlborough's sister). Fought at the BOYNE and in War of Spanish Succession (took Barcelona 1714). Killed in War of Polish Succession. Author of memoirs.

Berwick (bĕr'ĭk) or **Berwickshire** (bĕr'ĭkshĭr), agr. maritime county (457 sq. mi.; pop. 22,441), SE Scotland; co. town Duns. Separated from England by the Tweed, was long scene of border strife.

Berwick (bûr'wĭk), industrial borough (pop. 13,353), E Pa., on Susquehanna R., SW of Wilkes-Barre; settled 1783. Site of Fort Jenkins (1777).

Berwick-on-Tweed (bĕr'ĭk), municipal borough (pop. 12,166), Northumberland, England, on N side of mouth of Tweed. A leading border town, contested by England and Scotland until made officially English 1885.

Berwyn, city (pop. 54,224), NE Ill., W of Chicago; founded 1890.

beryl (bĕr'ĭl), very hard silicate of beryllium and aluminum. Gem varieties are EMERALD (green), AQUAMARINE (blue), and morganite (pink).

beryllium (bùrĭl'lēùm) or **glucinum** (glōōsĭ'nùm), rare, steel-white, metallic element (symbol = Be, sometimes Gl; see also ELEMENT, table). Resembles magnesium;

forms some compounds. Lightest stable metal, very hard, brittle; alloys used in aircraft and rockets; oxide used in atomic energy reactors. Inhalation of dust may cause berylliosis, a serious disease.

Berzelius, Jons Jakob, Baron (bürzē'lēŭs), 1779–1848 Swedish chemist. Developed modern chemical symbols; prepared table of atomic weights; analyzed many compounds; discovered selenium, thorium, cerium.

Besançon (bŭzãsŏ'), city (pop. 95,642), cap. of Doubs dept., E France, in Franche-Comté. Watch mfg. Archiepiscopal see. Free imperial city until incorporation (1648) into Franche-Comté (then Spanish). After French annexation the cap. of Franche-Comté and a university were transferred from DÔLE to Besançon (1676). Medieval and Renaissance architecture. Birthplace of Victor Hugo.

Besant, Annie (Wood) (bē'zŭnt), 1847–1933, English theosophist and social reformer. Advocated free thought, Socialism. She and Charles Bradlaugh edited the *National Reformer* and for publishing a pamphlet on birth control (1877) were tried on charges of immorality and acquitted. In 1889 she became a disciple of Mme Blavatsky. She lived in India and furthered the Indian nationalist cause. President of the Theosophical Society after 1907, she wrote much on religion. In 1926–27 she introduced her protégé, Jiddu Krishnamurti, in England and America as the new Messiah (he later declined the honor).

Besant, Sir Walter (bĭzănt'), 1836–1901, English writer and reformer, author of novels on social problems, criticism, biographies, works on London.

Beskids, range of Carpathians, along Polish-Czech border. Highest peak at 5,658 ft.

Bessarabia (bĕsŭrā'bēŭ), region of SE Europe, bounded by the Dniester, Danube and Pruth rivers and the Black Sea. Cities: Kishinev, Izmail, Belgorod-Dnestrovsky. Largely a fertile agr. steppe and grazing land (grain, tobacco, fruit, wool). Always a border country, it was part of Roman Dacia; was invaded by Goths, Petchenegs, Cumans, Mongols; fell to Moldavia 14th cent.; to Turks 16th cent.; to Russia 1812. Congress of Paris (1856) gave S Bessarabia to Moldavia; Congress of Berlin (1878) restored it to Russia. Rumania annexed the entire prov. 1918, was forced to return it to Russia 1940, reoccupied it 1941–44, ceded it formally 1947. Larger part now incorporated with Moldavian SSR, except for S part, which was added to Ukraine.

Bessarion (bĕsä'rēŭn), 1395?–1472, Byzantine humanist in Renaissance Italy; made a cardinal 1439, patriarch of Constantinople 1463. Notable for his learning, he introduced neoplatonic ideas into Italy.

Bessel, Friedrich Wilhelm (frēd'rĭkh vĭl'hĕlm bĕs'ŭl), 1784–1846, German astronomer. Made first authenticated measurement of distance of a star (1841).

Bessemer, Sir Henry: see BESSEMER PROCESS.

Bessemer, industrial city (pop. 33,054), N central Ala., SW of Birmingham; founded 1887 as mining town.

Bessemer process (bĕs'ŭmŭr), industrial process for making steel from cast iron (pig iron). Oxygen of air blown through molten iron oxidizes impurities in it, oxidation heat raising temperature of mass and keeping it molten during operation. Efficiency of process depends upon large steel container (Bessemer converter) lined with silica and clay or with dolomite. To make steel of desired properties, another substance, often spiegeleisen, is usually added to molten metal once oxidation is complete. Basic principle of process invented by **Sir Henry Bessemer,** 1813–98, who erected Bessemer Steel Works at Sheffield, England.

Bessenyei, George (bĕ'shĕnyä), 1747–1811, Hungarian dramatist and writer. Helped make Hungarian a modern literary language.

Best, Charles Herbert, 1899–, Canadian physiologist, developer with Banting of insulin treatment of diabetes. Author of works on physiology.

Betancourt, Romulo (rō'mōōlō bĕtäncōŏr'), 1908–, president of Venezuela (1945–48, 1959–64). He in-

stituted major reforms and became a leader of the anti-Communist left in Latin America.

beta ray: see RADIOACTIVITY.

betatron: see PARTICLE ACCELERATOR.

Betelgeuse (bē'tŭljōōz, bĕ'–, bē'tŭljûz) [Arabic,= shoulder of the giant], bright star in constellation Orion, also called Alpha Orionis. First star whose diameter (c.360,000,000 mi.) was measured with Michelson interferometer (1920). A variable red super-giant, it is c.270 light-years from earth.

betel nut (bē'–), fruit of a palm (*Areca catechu*). Chewed with leaf of betel pepper smeared with lime, it is narcotic stimulant for many Eastern peoples.

Bethabara (–ăb'ŭrŭ), place on Jordan R., near Dead Sea, where John was baptizing when Jesus came to him. Called Bethany in RV. John 1.28.

Bethany (bĕth'ŭnē). **1** Village at the foot of Mt. Olivet, E of Jerusalem. Home of Lazarus, Martha, and Mary, and often visited by Jesus. Ascension took place near by. Mark 11.1, 11; John 11; Mat. 21.17; 26.6; Mark 14.3; Luke 19.29; 24.50. **2** See BETHABARA.

Bethany, city (pop. 12,342), central Okla., WNW of Oklahoma City. Bethany Nazarene Col. is here.

Bethany College, near Bethany, W.Va.; coed; chartered 1840; opened 1841 by Alexander Campbell.

Bethe, Hans Albrecht (bā'tŭ), 1906–, American physicist. Developed theories on atomic properties and on origin of solar and stellar energy. Directed theoretical physics division, Los Alamos Atomic Bomb Project, 1943–46.

Bethel (bĕth'ŭl) [Heb.,= house of God], ancient city, N of Jerusalem. Here Abraham built altar, Jacob had vision of ladder reaching to heaven, and Samuel often visited. Jeroboam tried to make it a religious capital to rival Jerusalem and set up a golden calf for worship. Thus it became associated with idolatry and was denounced by later prophets. Gen. 12.8; 35.1–15; Judges 20.26, 27; 1 Kings 12.26–33; Amos 3.14. Bible says name originally Luz; the modern town is called Beitin.

Bethel, borough (pop. 23,650), SW Pa., S of Pittsburgh, in industrial area.

Bethesda (–thĕz'–), pool in Jerusalem said to have miraculous healing powers. John 5.2–9. May be same as pool recently discovered in NE corner of city.

Bethesda (būthĕz'dŭ), city (pop. 56,527), W central Md., a suburb NW of Washington, D.C. Here are research centers of many natl. health institutes and natl. naval medical center. In city are villages of Chevy Chase (pop. 2,405) and Chevy Chase Section Four (pop. 2,243).

Beth-horon (–hō'–), name of two neighboring towns between Lydda and Jerusalem. 2 Chron. 8.5. Scene of two historic victories—one by Joshua and one by Judas Maccabeus. Joshua 10.10–14.

Bethlehem (bĕth'lĕŭm) [Heb.,= house of bread or house of Lahmu, a goddess], Arabic *Beit Lahm,* town pop. (c.120,000), S central Palestine, just S of Jerusalem, now in Jordan, birthplace of Jesus and renowned Christian shrine. The inhabitants, largely Christian, depend on pilgrims for livelihood. In Old Testament, scene of book of Ruth and home of David. In A.D. 330 Constantine erected basilica on traditional site of the Nativity. Church standing there today is shared by monks of Greek, Latin, and Armenian rites. Manger where Jesus was born is said to have been in grotto under church. Bethlehem's older name was Ephrath or Ephratah. Gen. 35.16–20; 48.7; 1 Sam. 16; 17; 2 Sam. 23.13–17.

Bethlehem, industrial city (pop. 75,408), E Pa., on Lehigh R., N of Philadelphia; settled 1740–41 by Moravians. Mfg. of wearing apparel and steel products; sitc of Bethlehem Steel Corp. Its Bach Choir has international renown. Seat of LEHIGH UNIVERSITY and MORAVIAN COLLEGE.

Bethlehem Royal Hospital: see BEDLAM.

Bethlen, Gabriel (bĕth'lŭn, bĕt'lĕn), Hung. *Bethlen Gábor,* 1580–1629, prince of Transylvania (1613–29).

A Protestant, he allied himself with FREDERICK THE WINTER KING and invaded Hungary, of which he was elected king (1620). After Frederick's defeat he made peace with Emperor Ferdinand II and renounced the royal title (1621). He ruled Transylvania wisely, encouraged law and learning.

Bethlen, Count Stephen, Hung. *Bethlen István,* 1874–1950?, Hungarian premier (1921–31). Though a royalist, he prevented the return of King Charles (Emperor CHARLES I) to avoid military intervention of Little Entente. Sought revision of Treaty of Trianon. His death in a Russian prison was reported but not confirmed.

Bethmann-Hollweg, Theobald von (tā'ōbält fŭn bāt'-män-hôl'väk), 1856–1921, chancellor of Germany (1909–17). Famed for calling guarantee of Belgian neutrality a "scrap of paper" (1914). Overthrown in 1917 for his efforts to negotiate peace.

Bethnal Green, London: see TOWER HAMLETS.

Bethpage, village (pop. 20,515 including Old Bethpage), SE N.Y., on W Long Isl., SE of Hicksville.

Bethsaida (–sā'ĭdů) [Heb.,= house of fish], birthplace of Peter, Andrew, and John. Near, or on, Sea of Galilee, exact location uncertain. Mat. 11.21; Mark 6.45; 8.22; Luke 10.13; John 1.44; 12.21.

Beth-shan (–shăn') or **Beth-shean** (–shē'ŭn), anc. fortress in Jordan valley, principal strategic point of E Palestine. Modern name: Beisan.

Bethune, David: see BEATON, DAVID.

Bethune, Mary McLeod (mŭkloud' bŭthŭn'), 1875–1955, American Negro educator. Founded (1904) Daytona Normal and Industrial Inst. for Negro Girls (now Bethune-Cookman Col.); president 1904–42.

Bettendorf, industrial city (1965 pop. 17,264), E Iowa, on Mississippi R. (bridged), E of Davenport; settled c.1840.

Betterton, Thomas, 1635?–1710, English actor, manager. In William D'Avenant's company (1661–68) became leading actor of the Restoration stage. A great Hamlet and Mercutio, he played many Shakespeare roles in adaptations by Dryden, Shadwell, and himself. An actor-manager from 1668, he opened Haymarket Theatre 1705. His wife, **Mary Saunderson Betterton,** d. 1711, was the first woman to play Shakespeare's heroines.

Betti, Ugo (ōō'gō bāt'tē), 1892–1953, Italian jurist and dramatist. Among his best-known plays is *Il diluvio* [the flood] (1943).

Beulah, allegorical name for Israel. Isa. 62.4, 5.

Beuthen (boi'tůn) or **Bytom,** city (est. pop. 192,000), SW Poland (since 1945), formerly in Upper Silesia. Mfg. center of Katowice mining region.

Bevan, Aneurin (ůnī'rĭn bě'vun), 1897–1960, British political leader. Former coal miner and a trade unionist; became minister of health (1945) for Labour government's system of socialized medicine. On return of Churchill government (1951) became left-wing leader within LABOUR PARTY.

bevatron: see PARTICLE ACCELERATOR.

Beveland, North, and **South Beveland** (bā'vůlänt), two islands (combined area 170 sq. mi.), Zeeland prov., SW Netherlands, in the Scheldt estuary. Connected by railroad with mainland and with Walcheren. Agr., livestock raising. Kortgene is chief town of North Beveland and Goes of South Beveland.

Beveridge, Albert J(eremiah), 1862–1927, U.S. Senator (1899–1911) and historian. Supported policies of Theodore Roosevelt. Wrote biographies of John Marshall and Lincoln.

Beveridge, William Henry, 1879–1963, British economist. In government service 1908–19, he set up labor exchanges and devised wartime food rationing. Director of London School of Economics 1919–37 and master of Univ. Col., Oxford, 1937–45. In noted government reports, proposed full social security system for all citizens (1942) and planned spending to insure full employment (1944).

Beverley, municipal borough (pop. 16,024), administrative center of E. Riding of Yorkshire, England. Famous 13th-cent. minster contains "chair of peace" which gave right of sanctuary.

Beverly. 1 City (pop. 36,108), NE Mass., NNE of Salem; settled 1626. Had New England's first successful cotton-weaving mill (1789). Among its old houses is John Cabot house (1781). Was summer home of O. W. Holmes and his son. **2** City (pop. 3,400), W N.J., on Delaware R., W of Burlington. Was site of Civil War camp and hospital.

Beverly Hills, city (pop. 30,817), S Calif., within confines of Los Angeles, W of Hollywood; planned 1906. Home of many film and TV stars.

Bevin, Ernest (bě'vůn), 1881–1951, British trade-union and political leader. Merged unions to make powerful Transport and General Workers' Union. Was minister of labor in wartime cabinet 1940–45. As Labour government foreign minister (1945 until his death) his policy toward USSR was uncompromising. His Palestine policy criticized by Arabs and Jews.

Bewick, Thomas (bū'ĭk), 1753–1828, English wood engraver, noted for illustrations of Beilby's *History of British Birds.*

Bexley, London borough since 1965 (est. pop. 214,-950); includes former municipal boroughs of Bexley and Erith and urban districts of Crayford and part of Chislehurst and Sidcup.

Bexley, city (pop. 14,319), central Ohio, within confines of Columbus. Capital Univ. is here.

Beyle, Henri: see STENDHAL.

Beyrouth: see BEIRUT.

Beza, Theodore (bē'zů), Fr. *Théodore de Bèze* (tāō-dôr' dů běz'), 1519–1605, French reformer and Calvinist theologian, friend and aid of Calvin, of whom he wrote a biography. A distinguished classical scholar, he aided the edition of the Greek and Latin versions of the New Testament.

Bezer (bē'zůr), town, E of the Jordan. One of the cities of refuge. Deut. 4.43; Joshua 20.8; 21.36.

Béziers (bāzyā'), city (pop. 73,538), Hérault dept., S France. Wine and spirits trade. Population was massacred (1209) after Simon de Montfort captured city in Albigensian Crusade.

Bezruc, Petr, Czech *Bezruč* (pět'ůr běz'rŏŏch), pseud. of Vladimir Vasek, 1867–1958, Czech poet, author of nationalistic *Silesian Songs* (1903).

Bezwada (bĭzwā'dů), city (pop. 233,634), Andhra Pradesh, India, near Kistna R. delta. Transportation, administration, trade, and religous center.

Bhabha, Homi J(ehangir) (bä'bä), 1909–66, Indian physicist, b. Bombay. In 1948 became chairman of Atomic Energy Commission of India.

Bhagavad-Gita (bŭg'ůvůd-gē'tů) [Sanskrit,= Song of the Lord], Sanskrit poem, part of the MAHABHARATA. Exalted and often translated statement of Hindu beliefs.

Bhamo (bä'mō, bůmō'), town (pop. 9,817), cap. of Bhamo prov., Burma, on Irrawaddy R. Farthest point up-river reached by steamers, it is market town. Ruby mines.

Bhascara (bŭs'kůrů), called **Acarya** (ůchär'yů), b. 1114, Hindu mathematician, astronomer, first to give systematic exposition of decimal system.

Bhatpara (bŭtpä'rů), city (pop. 134,916), West Bengal state, India. In Hooghlyside industrial complex.

Bhave, Vinoba (vĭnōbů bä'vä), 1895–, Indian religious figure, social worker, and Sanskrit scholar. Disciple of Gandhi, Bhave was widely accepted as his successor. In 1951 founded Bhoodan (land-gift) movement.

Bhils (bēlz), people (more than 1,00,000) who inhabit parts of West Pakistan and W central India, esp. S Rajasthan and Gujarat states. Speak Bhili, an Indo-European language (see LANGUAGE, table); their culture is affected by, but not absorbed into, Hinduism.

Bholan Pass: see BOLAN PASS.

Bhopal (bō'päl), former state, central India. Became part of Madhya Pradesh in 1956. **Bhopal,** city (pop.

102,333), cap. of Madhya Pradesh. Trade center with textile mfg.

Bhubaneswar (boōbănĕ'swär), city (pop. 163,562), cap. of Orissa state, India. Was center of Sivaism and cap. of Kesaris dynasty from 5th to 10th cent. Has remains of c.500 shrines.

Bhutan (boōtän'), Indian protectorate (c.18,000 sq. mi.; pop. c.700,000) in E Himalayas, between India and Tibet; cap. Punaka. Formerly under dual control of a spiritual and a temporal ruler; since 1907 under a maharaja. Mahayana Buddhism is main religion. Largely mountainous and forested. Mineral resources are silver, iron, and mica. In 1949 India assumed Britain's former role in subsidizing Bhutan and directing its foreign affairs. After Chinese Communist forces occupied Tibet in 1950, Bhutan became a point of contest between China and India. King Jigme Dorij Wangchuk (enthroned 1953) abolished slavery and the caste system, emancipated women, and initiated land reform.

Bi, chemical symbol of the element BISMUTH.

Biafra: see NIGERIA.

Biafra, Bight of (bëä'frù), innermost bay of Gulf of Guinea, W Africa; extends from Niger delta to Gabon.

Bialik, Chayim Nachman (byä'lĕk), 1873–1934, Hebrew poet and translator, b. Russia. In addition to his own lyrical, elegaic, and liturgical composition, he translated works of Cervantes, Shakespeare, Schiller, and Heine into Hebrew.

Bialowieza (byäwŏvyĕ'zhä), Rus. *Byelovezhskaya Pushcha,* large forest, E Poland and W Belorussia. Favorite royal hunting preserve; national park since 1921. Has aurochs, boar, deer.

Bialystok (byäwĭs'tôk), city (est. pop. 134,000), NE Poland, cap. of Bialystok prov. Textile center.

Biard, Pierre (byär), c.1567–1622, French Jesuit missionary in North America. Headed first Jesuit mission to Canada (1611). His *Relation de la Nouvelle France* (1616) has much historical value.

Biarritz (bē'ùrĭts, Fr. byärēts'), city (est. pop. 22,922), Basses-Pyrénées dept., SW France, on Bay of Biscay near Spanish border. Fashionable resort.

Bibiena or **Bibbiena, Galli da** (gäl'lē dä bēbyä'nä), family of Italian artists of 17th and 18th cent. Founder, **Giovanni Maria Galli da Bibiena** (jōvän'nē), 1625–65, painted altarpieces for churches in Bologna. A son, **Ferdinando Galli Bibiena** (fĕrdēnän'dō), 1657–1743, most famous of family, was known throughout Europe for architectural views, theatrical designs, and decorations for court festivities. Rest of family noted also as decorative artists.

Bible [Gr.,= the books], name used by Christians for their Scriptures, for them a holy guide of faith and conduct. For composition and canon of the Bible, see OLD TESTAMENT; NEW TESTAMENT; APOCRYPHA; PSEUDEPIGRAPHA; articles on individual books. Traditional Christian view is that the Bible was written under the guidance of God and is, therefore, all true, literally or under the veil of allegory. Interpretation of the Bible is one of the chief points of difference between Protestantism, which believes that individuals have the right to interpret the Bible for themselves, and Roman Catholicism, which teaches that individuals may read the Bible only in accord with interpretation of the Church. Among extant manuscripts of the Bible are the Codex Vaticanus (Greek, 4th cent.), at the Vatican; Codex Sinaiticus (Greek, 4th cent.) and Codex Alexandrinus (Greek, 5th cent.), at the British Mus.; and Codex Bezae (Greek and Latin, 6th cent.) at Cambridge, England. First great translation of the whole Bible into Latin was the Vulgate of St. Jerome. The Bible, with Latin text, was the first book to be printed on the press of Johann GUTENBERG. In England there were from Anglo-Saxon times vernacular versions of parts of the Bible, mostly the four Gospels and the Psalms. Great names in the history of the English Bible are:

John Wyclif (d. 1384), whose name is borne by two translated versions; William Tyndale (d. 1536), whose New Testament (1525–26) was the first English translation to be printed; Miles Coverdale (d. 1569), who was responsible for the Great Bible (1539), the first to be issued by the crown (in the name of Henry VIII). Greatest of all English translations was the Authorized (AV) or King James Version (1611), made by a committee of churchmen led by Lancelot Andrewes. The Douay, or Rheims-Douay, Version was published by Roman Catholic scholars at Rheims (New Testament, 1582) and Douai, France (Old Testament, 1610), since extensively revised. In the 19th cent., the Authorized Version was revised from the original tongues by the Church of England and appeared as the English Revised Version and American Revised Version (both: RV). English translations begun in the 20th cent. include the Revised Standard Version (Protestant; pub. 1952) and the American Roman Catholic Confraternity of Christian Doctrine. Translations have been important in the histories of other literature besides English (e.g., Luther's translation).

Bible societies, nonsectarian Protestant groups for printing and dissemination of Scriptures. Canstein Bible Society estab. 1710 in Germany. In England societies formed 1780 and 1804. In U.S., American Bible Society estab. 1816. Group called Gideons, International (estab. 1898) places Bibles in hotel rooms. In 1946 United Bible Societies united more than 20 national groups.

Biblical Antiquities, Book of: see PSEUDEPIGRAPHA.

bibliography. The listing of books is of ancient origin. Lists of clay tablets have been found at Nineveh. Library at Alexandria had subject lists of its books. Modern bibliography began with invention of printing. Efforts at universal bibliography resulted in Konrad von Gesner's *Bibliotheca universalis* in 1545. There are lists of publications of publishing houses (e.g., *Trade List Annual,* British *Reference Catalogue of Current Literature*); subject bibliographies (e.g., Sabin's *Dictionary of Books Relating to America*); lists of works of individual authors; monthly lists of books in English (*The Cumulative Book Index*); and many special bibliographies (e.g., *The Cambridge Bibliography of English Literature* and *Literary History of the United States*). Another aspect of bibliography deals with the analysis of the printings of books.

Bibliothèque nationale (bēblēôtĕk' näsyônäl'), national library of France (with over 6,000,000 books), in Paris. Originated when early French kings made collections of writings. Building erected 1854–75 under direction of Henri Labrouste; remodeling was done 1932–39. Branch at Versailles.

Bibracte (bĭbrăk'tē), town in Gaul, cap. of the Aedui. Here Caesar defeated the Helvetii (58 B.C.). Autun was built not far away to replace it.

bicameral system, governmental system dividing legislative function between "upper" and "lower" houses (e.g., U.S. Senate and House of Representatives). Formerly reflected differences in property qualification for suffrage; two chambers now express differences in function and principle of representation.

bicarbonate: see CARBONATE.

bicarbonate of soda: see SODA.

Bichat, Marie François (märē' fräswä' bēshä'), 1771–1802, French anatomist and physiologist. His study of tissues was basis of modern histology.

bichloride of mercury: see CORROSIVE SUBLIMATE.

Bickerstaff, Isaac, pseudonym used by Jonathan Swift, and later by Richard Steele in the *Tatler.*

bicycle, two-wheeled vehicle propelled by pedals. Developed in Scotland c.1839 from earlier machines operated by thrust of rider's feet upon ground. By the 1880s developments included larger front wheel, hollow-steel frame, ball bearings, tangential metal spokes. Safety bicycle, with equal-sized wheels and sprocket chain drive, was first manufactured c.1885 in England; it displaced other models following introduction of pneumatic tire (c.1888). Later improvements include freewheel, coaster brake, and hand brake. Cycling fad in '80s and '90s stimulated road construction.

Bidault, Georges (zhôrzh' bēdō'), 1899–, French statesman. Leader of French underground, postwar premier (1949–50), several times foreign minister. Led terrorist opponents of Algerian independence, forced to flee France 1962. After 4-yr. exile in Brazil he moved to Belgium in mid-1967.

Biddeford (bĭd'ĭfûrd), city (pop. 19,255), SW Maine, at Saco R. falls opposite Saco.; settled c.1630. Biddeford Pool at mouth of Saco is resort.

Biddle, well-known family of Philadelphia. **James Biddle,** 1783–1848, U.S. naval officer, was commander of *Ontario* and took formal possession of Oregon country for U.S. in 1818. **Nicholas Biddle,** 1786–1844, as president of BANK OF THE UNITED STATES (1823–36), was a chief target of Jacksonians. **George Biddle,** 1885–, American painter, did notable frescoes in Dept. of Justice Bldg., Washington, D.C. **Francis Beverley Biddle,** 1886–, U.S. Attorney General (1941–45), was judge at Nuremberg trials.

Biddle, John, 1615–62, founder of English Unitarianism. Persecuted for his *Twelve Arguments Drawn Out of Scripture* (c.1645) and *Two-fold Catechism* (1654).

Biedermeier (bē'dûrmīûr), a style of furniture and decorations originating in Germany in the early 19th cent.; named for a humorous character in verses by Ludwig Eichrodt. A simplified and less expensive form of French Empire, Directoire, and 18th-cent. English styles. Cabinets are severe in line and surface, while chairs and sofas have curved lines.

Biel (bēl) or **Bienne** (byĕn), city (pop. 59,216), Bern canton, W Switzerland, on L. of Biel. Watchmaking center. Museum has relics of lake dwellings found in **Lake of Biel,** at foot of Jura mts. Contains Isle of St. Pierre (now a peninsula), made famous because of association with J. J. Rousseau.

Biel-. For Russian names beginning thus, see BEL-.

Bielefeld (bē'lūfĕlt), city (pop. 172,469), North Rhine–Westphalia, West Germany. Mfg. of linen, silk, cars.

Bielsko-Biala (byĕl'skô byä'wä), Ger. *Bielitz,* city (est. pop. 81,000), Katowice prov., S Poland, on Biala R. Railway junction; textile industry and varied mfg. Formerly called Bielsko, joined (1950) with Biala to form single city.

Bienne, Switzerland: see BIEL.

biennial, plant normally living but two years. Produces leaves and roots first year, flowers and seeds second. Some ANNUAL and PERENNIAL plants in certain circumstances can behave as biennials, and certain biennials can act as perennials. Canterbury bells, hollyhock, and foxglove are examples of biennials.

Bienville, Jean Baptiste le Moyne, sieur de (zhä' bätēst' lü mwän' syûr' dü byĕvĕl'), 1680–1768, colonizer and governor of Louisiana for France, b. Canada. Aided colonizing plans of brother, sieur d'IBERVILLE. Founded Mobile in 1710 and New Orleans in 1718.

Bierce, Ambrose (Gwinett), 1842–1914?, American author, b. Ohio. After service in the Union army in the Civil War, he settled in San Francisco where he was a journalist (except for years of intense literary productivity in London, 1872–76) until 1896, becoming the literary arbiter of the West Coast. Later he was a Washington correspondent. His style is terse and vigorous in short stories (as in *Tales of Soldiers and Civilians,* 1891, where his occasional interest in the macabre is reminiscent of Poe), literary essays, bitter satires (as in *Fantastic Fables,* 1899), or verse. In 1913, tired and disillusioned, he went to Mexico, where he disappeared.

Bierstadt, Albert (bēr'stät), 1830–1902, American painter of Western scenes, b. Germany.

Big Ben, bell in Parliament tower (Westminster Palace), London. Name also given huge tower clock.

Big Bend National Park: see NATIONAL PARKS AND MONUMENTS (table).

Big Bethel, locality near Fort Monroe, Va., scene of early battle of Civil War, June 10, 1861. E. W. Pierce led Union brigade against J. B. Magruder's Confederate encampment and was repulsed.

Big Black River, rising in N central Miss. and flowing c.330 mi. SW to Mississippi R. below Vicksburg.

Big Blue River, rising in SE Nebr. near Aurora and flowing c.300 mi. E and SE to join Kansas R. near Manhattan, Kansas. Tuttle Creek Dam is near mouth.

Big Dipper: see URSA MAJOR and URSA MINOR.

Bigelow, John, 1817–1911, American author and diplomat. Noted for diplomatic service in France during Civil War, preventing her recognition of Confederacy. Author of life of Benjamin Franklin.

Biggs, E(dward) Power, 1906–, English-American organist. Through recitals, broadcasts, and recordings, he has done much to make great organ music familiar to the American public.

Bighorn, river, 461 mi. long, formed near Riverton, W central Wyo., by confluence of Wind and Popo Agie rivers. Flows N between Absaroka Range and Bighorn Mts. into Mont., where it receives Little Bighorn R. and flows NE to Yellowstone R. Boysen Dam, NNE of Riverton, and Yellowtail Dam S of Hardin, Mont., are parts of MISSOURI RIVER BASIN PROJECT. Other projects in Bighorn basin include Riverton project on WIND R. and SHOSHONE PROJECT..

bighorn or **Rocky Mountain sheep,** wild sheep (*Ovis canadensis*) of W North America, once plentiful. Grayish-brown, with whitish patch on hindquarters, it is a heavy animal, with curling horns on male, short spikes on female. Alaskan forms are Dall's or white sheep (*O. dalli*) and Stone's or black sheep. See *ill.,* p. 1136.

Bighorn Mountains, part of Rocky Mts., N central Wyo., extending N of Mont. border E of Bighorn R. Range rises to 13,165 ft. in Cloud Peak.

Bigler Lake: see TAHOE, LAKE.

Big Manitou Falls (măn'ĭtŏŏ), 165 ft. high, NW Wis., in Black R. Highest falls in Wis.

Bignonia (bĭgnō'nĕŭ), genus of woody vines, especially cross vine or trumpet flower (*Bignonia capreolata*), which has orange-red trumpet-shaped blossoms and compound leaves. Native to the S U.S., it is grown in greenhouses in the North and in milder areas out-of-doors.

Bigod, Hugh: see NORFOLK, HUGH BIGOD, 1ST EARL OF.

Bigot, François (bēgō'), d. after 1760, intendant of New France (1748–59), b. France. His corrupt administration paved way for English conquest.

Big River: see FORT GEORGE, river, Que.

Big Sandy, river rising in W Tenn., N of Lexington, and flowing c.65 mi. NNE to Kentucky Reservoir of Tennessee R.

Big Sandy River. 1 River formed at Louisa, Ky., by junction of Tug Fork and Levisa Fork. Is part of Ky.–W.Va. line and flows N to Ohio R. at Catlettsburg, Ky. **2** River rising in W central Tenn., N of Lexington, and flowing generally NNE to Kentucky L. of Tennessee R.

Big Sioux (sŏŏ), river rising in NE S. Dak. and flowing 420 mi. S to Missouri R. at Sioux City, Iowa. Part of Iowa–S.Dak. line in its lower course.

Big Spring, city (pop. 31,230), W central Texas, NW of San Angelo; founded 1881. Spring, now dry, long known. A trade and rail center for farm and livestock area. Oil discovered 1928. Webb Air Force Base is SW.

Big Stone Gap, town (pop. 4,688), extreme SW Va., near Ky. line NW of Bristol. A mountain resort in Cumberlands coal district. Southwest Virginia Mus. has regional collections.

Big Stone Lake, narrow lake, c.25 mi. long, on Minn.–S.Dak. line, once outlet of glacial L. AGASSIZ. Minnesota R. has its source in lake.

Bihar or **Behar** (bēhär'), state (67,113 sq. mi.; pop. 4,645,042), NW India; cap. Patna. Ranchi is chief administration center. Agr. area in N drained by

Ganges R. Chief crops are rice, maize, wheat, sugar cane, jute and tobacco. Major source of India's mineral wealth (mica, copper, coal, iron). Bihar was heart of Magadha empire and scene of Buddha's early life; BUDDH GAYA is anc. Buddhist center. Its history after 17th cent. is linked with that of Bengal.

Bihari (bēhär'ē), Eastern Indic language of the Indo-European family. See LANGUAGE (table).

Bijarpur or **Bejapur** (both: bījä'pŏŏr), town (pop. 65,-734), Maharashstra state, India. Cap. of Deccan kingdom of Bijarpur (15th–17th cent.). Cotton ginning.

Bijns, Anna (bīns), c.1494–1575?, Flemish religious poet. Also wrote robust satires.

Bika, El: see LEBANON.

Bikaner: see RAJASTHAN.

Bikini (bēkē'nē), uninhabited atoll comprising 36 islets, central Pacific, one of the Marshall Isls. U.S. atom-bomb tests were made here in 1946.

Bilaspur (bēläs''pŏŏr'), former principality, Himachal Pradesh state, India, in the W Himalayas. Site of Bhakra dam on Sulej R.

Bilbao (bēlbä'ō), city (pop. 325,828), cap. of Vizcaya prov., N Spain, near Bay of Biscay. Chief city of Basque Provinces, second-largest port of Spain. Steel mills, shipyards. Iron mines near by.

Bildad, second and least consoling of Job's comforters. Job 8; 18; 25; 42.9.

Bilderdijk, Willem (bīl'dürdīk), 1756–1831, Dutch poet. In exile (1795–1806), he returned to the Netherlands under Louis Bonaparte (whom he tutored in Dutch). His poetry is uneven but at its best of a high order.

bile, alkaline fluid formed in liver. In man, stored in gall bladder (pear-shaped sac under liver), then passes through bile ducts into small intestine. Aids in emulsification, digestion, and absorption of fats and in carrying off bile pigments and other excretions. Obstruction of flow may result in digestive disturbances and JAUNDICE.

Bilhah (bīl'hů), Rachel's maid, Jacob's concubine, mother of Dan and Naphtali. Gen. 29.29; 30.1–8; 35. 22,25; 46.25.

bilharziasis: see SCHISTOSOMIASIS.

Billerica (bīlrī'kú), town (pop. 17,927), NE Mass., on Concord R., S of Lowell; settled 1637. Was one of John Eliot's "praying Indian" towns. Has railroad shops. Includes village of Pinehurst (pop. 1,991).

billiards, game played with tapered, leather-tipped stick (cue) and usually three ivory balls on oblong, cloth-covered slate table with raised and cushioned edges. In England table is 6 ft. by 12 ft. with six pockets; in U.S. table is 5 ft. by 10 ft., pocketless. Pool is played on a table with pockets (usually six), and with 15 balls and a cue ball. Variants of billiards were popular in France in 16th cent., similar game played earlier. Willie Hoppe considered world's greatest player.

Billings, John Shaw, 1838–1913, American surgeon and librarian. Medical inspector in Civil War. Began *Index Catalogue* of Surgeon General's Library and *Index Medicus.* Helped to create New York Public Library.

Billings, Josh, pseud. of Henry Wheeler Shaw, 1818–85, American author of humorous sketches in exaggerated New England and N.Y. rural dialect; also a popular lecturer.

Billings, William, 1746–1800, American composer, first American professional musician, b. Boston. He chiefly composed hymns and other church music.

Billings, city (pop. 52,851), S Mont., on Yellowstone R.; founded 1882 by Northern Pacific RR. Shipping center with oil refineries. Served by Huntley irrigation project. Seat of ROCKY MOUNTAIN COLLEGE.

Billingsgate, wharf and fish market district of central London, named for old city gate. Also name given coarse language once used by fish porters here.

bill of exchange: see DRAFT.

Bill of Rights, 1689, in British history, a great instrument of the constitution. Incorporated by statute the Declaration of Rights accepted by William and Mary and registered results of struggle between Stuart kings and Parliament. Gave inviolable civil and political rights to people and political supremacy to Parliament. Act of SETTLEMENT supplemented it 1701.

Bill of Rights, in U.S. history: see CONSTITUTION.

Billy the Kid, 1859–81, American outlaw, cattle rustler in N. Mex. Real name was William H. Bonney. Shot by a sheriff.

Biloxi (bĭlŭk'sē), city (pop. 44,053), SE Miss., on peninsula between Mississippi Sound and Biloxi Bay. Resort and boatbuilding center. First white settlement in lower Mississippi valley was estab. 1699 across bay at Old Biloxi (now Ocean Springs) by French under Iberville. Transferred to Mobile area 1702 by Bienville. New Biloxi, on present city's site, founded 1719 and cap. of La. until 1722. Has U.S. veterans' hospital and Keesler Air Force Base. Nearby is "Beauvoir," Jefferson Davis's last home. Ship Isl., off coast, was site of Union fort in Civil War and has served as U.S. naval base.

Biloxi Bay, arm of Mississippi Sound, c.17 mi. long, 1–3 mi. wide, SE Miss. Receives Biloxi R. Bridged from Biloxi to Ocean Springs.

bimetallism, monetary system using both gold and silver (coined at fixed ratio) as a standard. Usual in Western countries until Britain adopted gold standard by acts of 1798 and 1816. Subject of political controversy in U.S. until 1910.

Biminis (bī'mĭnēz), island group, part of Bahama Isls. Good fishing in nearby waters.

binary system, in mathematics, numerical notation system with base 2. For development of system, see DECIMAL SYSTEM. Practical importance stems from development of digital computer.

Binet, Alfred (älfrĕd' bēnā'), 1857–1911, French psychologist. With Théodore Simon, he devised (1905–11) tests for human intelligence, revised by others and widely used.

Bing, Rudolf, 1902–, Austrian opera manager. Was general manager of Glyndebourne operatic festivals 1934–49. Became general manager of Metropolitan Opera in 1950; restaged numerous operas, engaging directors of the legitimate theater.

Bingen (bĭng'ûn), city (pop. 18,048), Rhineland-Palatinate, West Germany, on Rhine R. Center of famous wine district. Fortified by Romans 1st cent. B.C. Member of Hanseatic League from 1254. Nearby, on a rock in the Rhine, is the Mäuseturm, where according to legend Archbishop Hatto of Mainz was devoured by mice for his evil deeds.

Bingham, George Caleb, 1811–79, American genre painter. Active in Missouri politics.

Bingham, Hiram, 1789–1869, American Congregational missionary, b. Vt. Went (1819) to Hawaiian Isls. Developed writing from Hawaiian language. His son, **Hiram Bingham,** 1831–1908, b. Honolulu, was missionary (1857–64) in Gilbert Isls. His son, **Hiram Bingham,** 1875–1956, was archaeologist and statesman. U.S. Senator from Conn. 1925–33. Discovered "lost" Inca cities of Vitcos and Machu Picchu.

Bingham, Seth, 1882–, American organist and composer. Has written for orchestra, for organ in combination with other instruments, and for organ alone (e.g., *Pioneer America,* 1928; *Pastoral Psalms,* 1938; *36 Hymn and Carol Canons,* 1952).

Bingham Canyon or **Bingham,** town (pop. 1,516), N central Utah, in canyon of Oquirrh Mts. SW of Salt Lake City. At first a Mormon farm (1848), it became roaring mining town in 1860s. Open-pit copper mine here largest in North America.

Binghampton (bĭng'ûmtûn), industrial city (1966 pop. 69,435), S N.Y., at junction of Chenango and Susquehanna rivers, E of Elmira; settled 1787. Grew after Chenango Canal connected it to Utica 1837. Largest of Triple Cities (others are Endicott and Johnson City), noted for shoes. A university center

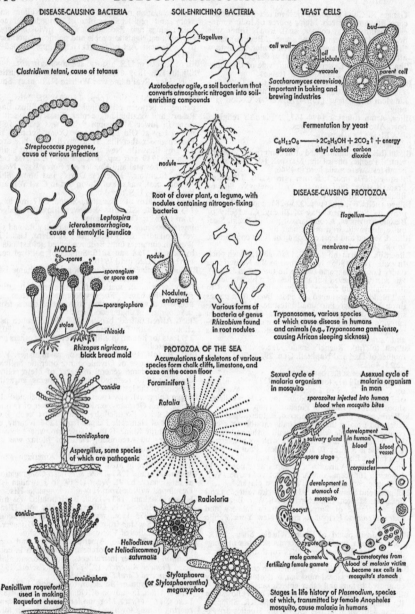

DISEASE-CAUSING BACTERIA

Clostridium tetani, cause of tetanus

Streptococcus pyogenes, cause of various infections

Leptospira icterohaemorrhagiae, cause of hemolytic jaundice

MOLDS

spores
sporangium or spore case
sporangiophore
stolon
rhizoids

Rhizopus nigricans, black bread mold

conidia
conidiophore

Aspergillus, some species of which are pathogenic

conidia
conidiophore

Penicillium roqueforti, used in making Roquefort cheese

SOIL-ENRICHING BACTERIA

flagellum

Azotobacter agile, a soil bacterium that converts atmospheric nitrogen into soil-enriching compounds

nodule

Root of clover plant, a legume, with nodules containing nitrogen-fixing bacteria

nodule

Nodules, enlarged

Various forms of bacteria of genus *Rhizobium* found in root nodules

PROTOZOA OF THE SEA

Accumulations of skeletons of various species form chalk cliffs, limestone, and ooze on the ocean floor

Foraminifera

Rotalia

Radiolaria

Heliodiscus (or *Heliodiscomma*) *saturnalia*

Stylosphaera (or *Stylosphaerantha*) *megaxyphos*

YEAST CELLS

bud
cell wall
oil globule
vacuole
parent cell

Saccharomyces cerevisiae, important in baking and brewing industries

Fermentation by yeast

$$C_6H_{12}O_6 \longrightarrow 2C_2H_5OH + 2CO_2\uparrow + energy$$
glucose   ethyl alcohol   carbon dioxide

DISEASE-CAUSING PROTOZOA

flagellum
membrane

Trypanosomes, various species of which cause disease in humans and animals (e.g., *Trypanosoma gambiense*, causing African sleeping sickness)

Sexual cycle of malaria organism in mosquito

Asexual cycle of malaria organism in man

sporozoites injected into human blood when mosquito bites

salivary gland
spore stage
development in human blood
blood vessel
red corpuscles
development in stomach of mosquito
oocyst
zygote
male gamete fertilizing female gamete
gametocytes from blood of malaria victim become sex cells in mosquito's stomach

Stages in life history of *Plasmodium*, species of which, transmitted by female *Anopheles* mosquito, cause malaria in humans

Microorganisms are living things too small to be seen with the naked eye. They are found in great numbers in the air, soil, and water. Some are very useful to man; a few types are harmful.

of the State Univ. of NEW YORK, including Harpur Col.. is here.

Binh Dinh (bǐng' dǐng'), city (pop. 21,900), central S Vietnam; cap. of Binh Dinh prov. Old Annamese cap.

Binswanger, Ludwig, 1881–, Swiss psychiatrist, pioneer in existential psychoanalysis.

Bío-Bío (bē'ō-bē'ō), river, c.240 mi. long, rising in Andes of central Chile and flowing NW to Pacific.

biochemistry, science concerned with chemical processes in living organisms and with their organic products, also called biological or physiological chemistry. Includes studies of photosynthesis, metabolism, digestion, absorption, biological oxidation. Deals also with chemistry of proteins, carbohydrates, fats, vitamins, hormones, enzymes, blood. Biochemical genetics is concerned with chemical processes of gene action.

biology, science of living things. Broadly divided into BOTANY and ZOOLOGY, it includes plant and animal cytology (cell study), histology (tissue study), anatomy or morphology, physiology, embryology, ecology, genetics, evolution, paleontology, and systematics. Microbiology is the scientific study of microscopic forms of life, including protozoa, bacteria, algae, fungi, and viruses.

Bion (bī'ŭn), fl. 2d cent.? B.C., Greek bucolic poet, an imitator of Theocritus.

biophysics, science of the mathematics and physics of biology. Paper chromatography, electron microscopy, and X-ray crystallography are among the methods used.

Birch, Reginald (Bathurst), 1856–1943, American illustrator of children's books, notably *Little Lord Fauntleroy.*

birch, deciduous tree or shrub of genus *Betula,* widely found in N Hemisphere. Paper or canoe birch (*Betula papyrifera*) and gray birch (*B. populifolia*) are native American trees with white bark. Yellow birch (*B. lutea*) important for timber in NE U.S. Others yield oil of wintergreen, birch beer extract.

Bird, Robert Montgomery, 1806–54, American author. Wrote verse plays for tragedian Edwin Forrest. Also wrote several novels; *Nick of the Woods* (1837) was a tremendous popular success.

Bird, William: see BYRD, WILLIAM (b. 1542 or 1543).

bird, warm-blooded, egg-laying vertebrate (class Aves) covered with FEATHERS, forelimbs modified into WINGS, tail skeleton telescoped to a stump. Four-chambered heart like mammals; body temperature 2° to 14° higher; relatively large brain; keen sight; acute hearing; little sense of smell; believed evolved from reptiles. Adapted for FLIGHT—body weight reduced by horny bill instead of jaws and air sacs in hollow bones; heavy parts located for balanced flight. Feathers renewed in MOLTING; male more vividly colored, aggressor in courtship, superior singer. Most birds build NEST for eggs. Birds valued for insect, weed seed destruction; many scavenge. Bills adapted to food habits. See also MIGRATION OF ANIMALS. See *ill.,* p. 118.

bird of paradise, any of several birds of New Guinea and adjacent islands. Male has bright plumage, elongated tail feathers, ruffs on wings and neck.

bird-of-paradise flower, perennial herb (*Strelitzia reginae*) of banana family native to S Africa. Cultivated in California and Hawaii for its birdlike blue and orange flower.

bird sanctuary: see WILDLIFE REFUGE.

Birdseye, Clarence, 1886–1956, American inventor of quick food-freezing process. Did research on dehydration of foods and on incandescent reflector lamps.

Bird Woman: see SACAJAWEA.

Birkbeck, Morris, 1764–1825, English pioneer in U.S. Undertook, with George Flower, scheme to create a settlement in Ill. The two fell out, but undertaking resulted in founding of Albion.

Birkeland, Olaf Christian (ō'läv krĭs'tyän bēr'kŭlän), 1867–1917, Norwegian physicist. Developed (with

Samuel Eyde) electric-arc process for nitrogen fixation; worked on magnetics.

Birkenhead, county borough (pop. 141,683), Cheshire, England; port opposite Liverpool at mouth of the Mersey. Has grain milling, steel mfg., shipbuilding.

Birmingham (bŭr'mǐng-ùm), second largest English city (pop. 1,105,651), Warwickshire; a great industrial center. Covers 80 sq. mi. Has iron and coal nearby and is noted for mfg. of automobiles, bicycles, guns, and electrical apparatus. Has noted city orchestra. Seat of Anglican and Roman Catholic cathedrals and Univ. of Birmingham.

Birmingham. 1 Industrial city (pop. 340,887), N central Ala., in Jones Valley near S end of Appalachian system; founded 1871. Largest city in state, leading iron and steel center of South. Area's iron, coal, limestone supply its factories. Mfg. also of textile products, chemicals, cement. Important trade and rail center, connected with Mobile by Black Warrior-Tombigbee system. Integration attempts after 1954 brought violence. Seat of BIRMINGHAM-SOUTHERN COLLEGE, Howard Col., Miles Col., and medical center of Univ. of Alabama. **2** City (pop. 25,525), SE Mich., suburb N of Detroit on River Rouge; settled 1819.

Birmingham-Southern College, at Birmingham, Ala.; coed.; formed 1918 by merger of Southern Univ. (opened 1859 at Greensboro) and Birmingham Col. (opened 1898). Merged with Birmingham Conservatory of Music 1953.

Birnam, village, Perthshire, Scotland. Nearby Birnam Hill once covered by Birnam Wood of witches' prophecy in *Macbeth.*

Birney, James Gillespie, 1792–1857, American abolitionist. Edited the *Philanthropist.* Advocated political action and was leader in LIBERTY PARTY, which nominated him for presidency in 1840 and 1844.

Birobidzhan (bē"rŭbējän') or **Jewish Autonomous Oblast,** administrative division (13,900 sq. mi.; 1965 est. pop. 172,000), RSFSR, in SE Siberia, on Manchurian border; cap. Birobidzhan (1965 est. pop. 43,000). Agr., timber, gold, iron. Oblast was formed 1934 to give Soviet Jewish population home territory. Jewish population increased after Second World War, but there has been emigration from area since 1958.

birth control, methods of voluntarily limiting births. Limitation of sexual intercourse and mechanical and chemical contraceptives are included. Organized birth-control movement began in England where the writings of Malthus stirred interest in overpopulation. Clinics were opened in the U.S. through efforts of Dr. Marie Stopes and Margaret Sanger. Movement much opposed by church groups, particularly the Roman Catholic Church, as violation of the order of nature. Nevertheless contraception became much more widespread in Western countries in 20th cent.

birthmark, pigmented lesion of the skin, commonly congenital. Moles, flat or raised above skin surface, may become malignant if irritated constantly. So-called "port-wine stains" and "strawberry marks" involve blood vessels.

birthstone: see MONTH.

birthwort, common name for shrubs and vines of Aristolochiaceae family. Found chiefly in warm regions. Varieties in U.S. include Virginia snakeroot, pelican flower.

Bisayas, Philippine Islands: see VISAYAN ISLANDS.

Bisbee (bǐz'bē), city (1965 pop. 9,272), SE Ariz., SE of Tucson, near Mexican border. City built in two steep canyons after copper deposits discovered (c.1876). Cattle raising and mining.

Biscay, Bay of, arm of the Atlantic, indenting coast of W Europe from Ushant isl., off Brittany, France, to Cape Ortegal, NW Spain. Chief ports: Brest, Nantes, Bordeaux, Bilbao, Santander.

Biscayne Bay, inlet of Atlantic Ocean, SE Fla. Miami and Miami Beach are on its shores.

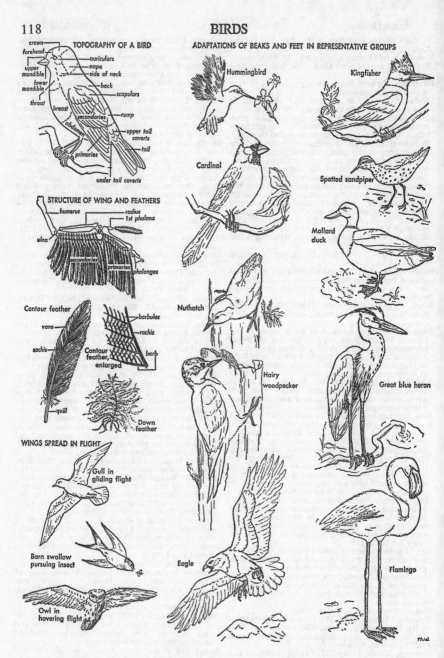

TOPOGRAPHY OF A BIRD

crown
forehead
auriculars
nape
side of neck
upper mandible
lower mandible
back
scapulars
throat
breast
secondaries
abdomen
rump
upper tail coverts
tail
primaries
under tail coverts

STRUCTURE OF WING AND FEATHERS

humerus
radius
1st phalanx
ulna
secondaries
primaries
phalanges

Contour feather
vane
rachis
barbules
rachis
Contour feather, enlarged
barb
quill
Down feather

WINGS SPREAD IN FLIGHT

Gull in gliding flight
Barn swallow pursuing insect
Owl in hovering flight

ADAPTATIONS OF BEAKS AND FEET IN REPRESENTATIVE GROUPS

Hummingbird
Kingfisher
Cardinal
Spotted sandpiper
Mallard duck
Nuthatch
Hairy woodpecker
Great blue heron
Eagle
Flamingo

A bird is a warm-blooded, egg-laying, vertebrate animal covered with feathers and gifted with wings. Birds have keen sight and acute hearing, little sense of smell. Bills and feet are variously specialized.

Bischof, Karl Gustav, 1792–1870, German chemist and geologist. Studied terrestrial heat and flammable gases in mines; perfected safety lamp.

Bischoff, Theodor Ludwig Wilhelm (tä′ōdŏr lōŏt′vĭkh vĭl′hĕlm bĭ′shôf), 1807–82, German physiologist. Authority on blood and embryology.

Biscoe, John, d. 1848, British navigator. Discovered ENDERBY LAND (1831–32); voyage was chief basis for British claims to Antarctica.

Bishop Hill, village (pop. 164), NW Ill., SW of Kewanee; founded 1846 by Swedish religious dissenters under Eric Janson. Had communistic base. Celibacy and poor financial management led to its failure.

Bishop's University: see LENNOXVILLE.

Bishops' Wars, two brief campaigns of the Scots against Charles I of England, 1639–40. Opposing his attempt to impose episcopacy, COVENANTERS pledged return to Presbyterianism. Resisting Charles's armies, they invaded England and forced him to sign Treaty of Ripon. See PURITAN REVOLUTION.

Bisk (bĕsk), city (1965 est. pop. 175,000), Altai Territory, SW Asiatic RSFSR, port on Biya R. and terminus on spur of Turkistan-Siberia RR. Agr. center.

Biskra (bĕskrä′), city (pop. 52,511), Algeria; an oasis in Sahara. French military post since 1844; site of anc. Roman military base, *Vescera*. Winter resort.

Bismarck, Otto, Fürst von (bĭz′märk, Ger. ō′tō fürst′ fün bĭs′märk), 1815–98, German statesman. Creator of the German Empire; premier of Prussia 1862–90; chancellor of Germany 1871–90; called the "iron chancellor." After dissolving parliament for opposing his armaments budget (1862), he used the SCHLESWIG-HOLSTEIN question as pretext for war on Denmark (1864). Friction with Austria over administration of conquered Danish territories enabled him in turn to eliminate Austria from German affairs through the AUSTRO-PRUSSIAN WAR (1866) and to reorganize Germany under Prussian leadership in the NORTH GERMAN CONFEDERATION. Bismarck deliberately provoked the FRANCO-PRUSSIAN WAR (1870–71) by publishing the EMS DISPATCH. In Jan., 1871, WILLIAM I of Prussia was proclaimed emperor of GERMANY. Having achieved unification by war, Bismarck sought to consolidate it by peace. In complete control of domestic and foreign policy, he allied Germany with Austria (1879) and Italy (1882), conciliated Russia, acted as arbiter of Europe. In his struggle against the Church (see KULTURKAMPF) he failed. Socialism prospered despite stringent antisocialist laws, adopted 1878 (allowed to lapse after 1890). In 1883 he introduced a series of pioneering social security and labor laws, designed to weaken the socialist appeal. German commerce, industry, and colonies expanded rapidly. Dismissed in 1890 by WILLIAM II, who resented his supremacy, Bismarck vigorously criticized William's policies during his retirement. Wrote reminiscences (Eng. tr., 1898).

Bismarck, city (1963 pop. 30,584), state cap., S central N.Dak., on hills overlooking Missouri R. Lewis and Clark camped nearby, 1804–5. At first called Edwinton; renamed for Germany's chancellor. Boomed as river port and rail center and as supply point for Black Hills gold mines (1874). Became territorial cap. 1883. Now distributing point for large springwheat, livestock, and dairy region.

Bismarck Archipelago, volcanic group, area 19,200 sq. mi., SW Pacific, part of Territory of New Guinea (see NEW GUINEA, TERRITORY OF). Includes NEW BRITAIN (largest island), NEW IRELAND, LAVONGAI, ADMIRALTY ISLANDS, Duke of York Isls., Vitu Isls., and Mussau Isls. Became a German protectorate in 1884, mandated to Australia in 1920, came under UN trusteeship 1947.

Bismarck Sea, SW arm of Pacific Ocean, NE of New Guinea. In 1943 a Japanese naval force was destroyed here by U.S. aircraft.

bismuth (bĭz′mŭth), silvery-white, reddish-tinged, crystalline, brittle element ·(symbol = Bi; see also ELE-

MENT, table). Grouped with nitrogen, phosphorus, etc., in periodic system; more strongly metallic than others. Expands on solidification. Used in low-melting-point alloys (e.g., Wood's metal, casting alloys), in cotton printing, cosmetic manufacture; insoluble compounds used in medicine and fluoroscopy.

bison, hoofed short-horned mammal related to domestic cattle, with heavily mantled shoulders sloping to hindquarters. Two species of genus *Bison:* European or wisent (miscalled aurochs; once abundant, surviving now only in reserves);· American bison (buffalo), now protected on national and state refuges.

Bissagos Islands: see PORTUGUESE GUINEA.

Bissau (bĭsou′), town (pop. c.25,000), cap. of Portuguese Guinea, in the Geba estuary, on the Atlantic. Founded late 17th cent. as slave-trading center; free port since 1869; became cap. in 1942. Exports include hardwoods, copra, rubber.

Bisschop, Simon: see EPISCOPIUS, SIMON.

Bisutun: see BEHISTUN.

Bithynia (bĭthĭ′nēŭ), anc. country of NW Asia, in present Turkey. Independent Thracian state became autonomous part of Persian Empire and after the death of Alexander the Great was independent kingdom (3d–1st cent. B.C.), warring against the Seleucids and others until King Nicomedus IV willed it to Rome (74 B.C.). Long joined with Pontus as a colony, Bithynia declined after the time of Hadrian.

Bitolj (bē′tōlyù), Macedonian *Bitola,* formerly *Monastir,* city (pop. 49,101), Macedonia, S Yugoslavia. Became bishopric 11th cent.; conquered by Turks 1395; developed into military and commercial center. Noted for its many mosques, churches, and bazaar.

Bitter, Karl Theodore Francis, 1867–1915, American neoclassical sculptor, b. Austria. Completed major commissions in New York, Philadelphia, Chicago, and Wis.

bittern, migratory marsh bird, heron family. American species (called "stake driver" for booming call) is widespread in E North America. Mostly nocturnal, it eats frogs, fish, insects. Is 2–3 ft. tall, brown and yellow, with striped foreneck.

Bitterroot, river rising in SW Mont. and flowing c.120 mi. N between Bitterroot Range and Sapphire Mts. to join Clark Fork near Missoula. U.S. project irrigates area near Hamilton.

Bitterroot Range, part of Rocky Mts., on Idaho-Mont. line. Main range runs NW and SE; includes Trapper Peak and El Capitan. S part, known also as Beaverhead Mts., sometimes said to include spur rising to 10,961 ft. in Mt. Garfield.

bitters, spirituous liquor (to 40% alcohol) containing bitter principles, e.g., angostura bark; used as flavoring (as in cocktails), and as appetizers and digestives.

bittersweet, name for two vines: *Celastrus scandens,* native to North America, which bears clusters of orange-red fruits; and bitter or woody nightshade (*Solanum dulcamara*), a poisonous plant native to the Old World (with scarlet berries).

bitumen (bĭtū′mŭn), natural mineral substances, essentially mixtures of hydrocarbons, including ASPHALT and PETROLEUM. See also COAL.

Bitzius, Albert: see GOTTHELF, JEREMIAS.

bivalve (bī′vălv″), mollusk of class Pelecypoda, with two shells joined by muscle at a hinge (e.g., clam, mussel). Internal organs joined to two siphons—one to ingest oxygen and food, one to exude waste.

Biwa (bē′wä), lake, c.40 mi. long, 2–12 mi. wide, largest in Japan, in S Honshu.

Bizerta (bĭzûr′tù), Fr. *Bizerte,* city (pop. c.44,680), Tunisia. Its port and naval base are on Mediterranean and L. of Bizerte (lagoon, 50 sq. mi.). Anciently a colony of Tyre, it was successively held by the Romans, Vandals, Arabs, Moors, Spaniards, and Barbary pirates. In 1881 occupied by French who improved and fortified the harbor. A German base in Second World War, it was heavily bombed. French troops were evacuated from French naval base in 1963 after clash with Tunisian troops.

Bizet, Georges (zhôrzh' bēzā'), 1838–75, French composer. His opera, *Carmen* (based on a story by Mérimée), became immensely popular though not successful when first performed. He also composed other operas: *Les Pêcheurs de perles* and *La Jolie Fille de Perth.* Among non-operatic compositions are suites for Daudet's *L'Arlésienne,* a Symphony in C.

Bjerknes, Vilhelm Friman Koren (byĕrk'nĕs), 1862–1951, Norwegian physicist. His work in meteorology and on electric waves helped develop wireless telegraphy. Evolved polar-front theory of cyclones with his son, **Jakob Aall Bonnevie Bjerknes** (ôl' bô'nùvē), 1897–, U.S. citizen in 1946. Became professor of meteorology, Univ. of California, 1940.

Bjornson, Bjornstjerne (byûrn'styĕrnŭ byûrn'sôn), Nor. *Bjørnstjerne Bjørnson,* 1832–1910, Norwegian writer. His dramas, novels (many of peasant life), and epic poetry won him repute as foremost Norwegian poet and novelist, second as dramatist only to Ibsen. Among his novels are *Arne* (1858) and *The Fisher Girl* (1868). Dramas include *Sigurd Slembe* (1862), *The Bankrupt* (1875). Awarded 1903 Nobel Prize.

Black, Greene Vardiman, 1836–1915, American dentist, noted as teacher, author, and originator of methods and instruments.

Black, Hugo LaFayette, 1886–, Associate Justice of U.S. Supreme Court (1937–).

Black, Jeremiah Sullivan, 1810–83, U.S. Attorney General (1857–60) and U.S. Secretary of State (1860–61). Persuaded Pres. Buchanan to send supplies to Fort Sumter.

Black, Joseph, 1728–99, Scottish chemist, physician. Discovered carbon dioxide, studied latent heat. Taught medicine at Glasgow (1756–66) and Edinburgh (from 1766).

Blackbeard, d. 1718, English pirate whose real name was probably Edward Teach or Thatch. Probably originally a privateer, preyed on West Indies and Atlantic coast 1716–18. Killed by British.

Black Belt, term loosely applied to belt across central S.C. and Ga., and also to black-soil areas in Ala., Miss., and other states.

blackberry, thorny plant (*Rubus*) with juicy, black fruits, eaten raw or used in jams or preserves.

blackbird, in North America a perching bird allied to bobolink, meadow lark, grackle, oriole. Red-winged blackbird common in E U.S.; yellow-headed, tricolored red-winged, Brewer's blackbird known to West; rusty blackbird winters in U.S. European blackbird is a thrush.

black body, in physics, theoretical body that ideally absorbs all and reflects none of the radiant energy falling on it. Experimentally, closest approximation is hollow internally blackened metal cylinder with slit at one end.

Blackburn, county borough (pop. 106,114), Lancashire, England; a cotton-weaving center. James Hargreaves invented the spinning jenny here (c.1765).

Black Canyon of the Gunnison National Monument: see NATIONAL PARKS AND MONUMENTS (table).

black codes: see RECONSTRUCTION.

Black Country, highly industrialized region, mostly in Staffordshire, but also in Worcestershire and Warwickshire, England. Produces coal, iron, and steel. Wolverhampton and West Bromwich are leading cities.

Black Death: see PLAGUE.

black earth or **chernozem** (châr'nùzĕm"), variety of soil rich in organic matter (HUMUS), generally a modified type of LOESS.

Blackett, Patrick Maynard Stuart (blă'kĭt), 1897–, English physicist. Won 1948 Nobel Prize in Physics for work in improving and extending use of Wilson cloud chamber and for discoveries concerning cosmic rays.

black-eyed Susan, North American wild herb (*Rudbeckia hirta*), having yellow daisylike blossoms with dark brown centers. Maryland state flower.

Blackfeet Indians: see BLACKFOOT INDIANS.

black fly, small vicious fly with gauzy wings, short legs, humped back. Females of many species suck blood. Black flies like heat and strong light; swarms are often seen in sunlight. Most attach eggs to underwater plants or rocks; larvae live in flowing water; adult emerges from water in air bubble.

Blackfoot, city (pop. 7,738), SE Idaho, SSW of Idaho Falls, between Blackfoot and Snake rivers near their junction; founded 1878. In an agr. area served by Minidoka and Fort Hall projects. Fort Hall Indian Reservation is near.

Blackfoot Indians, tribes formerly around upper Missouri and Saskatchewan rivers and W to the Rockies, of Algonquian linguistic family. Three main branches (Siksika or Blackfoot proper, Piegan, and Blood) were in no way connected politically, but they were united by the sense of being one people with common enemies. Allied with Atsina (see GROS VENTRE INDIANS) and Sarsi Indians, hostile to other groups and whites. They gained wealth from fur trade, but their nomadic Plains culture was destroyed with disappearance of buffalo. Elaborate rituals include the sun dance and the vision quest. Also called Blackfeet.

Black Forest, Ger. *Schwarzwald,* mountain range in Baden-Württemberg, SW Germany. It is covered by dark pine forests; rises to 4,905 ft. in Feldberg. Chief resorts: Baden-Baden and Wildbad. Clock and toy industries.

Black Friday. In 1868 a small group of American financial speculators, including Jay GOULD and James FISK, sought support of Federal officials in drive to corner gold market. Attempt failed when government gold was released for sale. Drive culminated in day of panic when thousands were ruined—Friday, Sept. 24, 1869, popularly called Black Friday. Other days of financial panic have also been called Black Friday.

black gum, sour gum, or **pepperidge,** ornamental tree (*Nyssa sylvatica*), of E North America. In autumn the foliage is bright red. This and other *Nyssa* species are also called tupelo.

Black Hand, name and symbol used by criminal or terrorist groups. Flourished in Sicily in late 19th cent.; carried to U.S. See also CAMORRA and MAFIA.

black haw, a VIBURNUM (*Viburnum prunifolium*), native to E North America. Bluish-black, edible berries.

Black Hawk War, conflict between Sac and Fox Indians and U.S. in 1832. Treaty imposed on Indians in 1831 compelled removal from Ill. Return in April, 1832, of an Indian group under Black Hawk (1767–1838) resulted in armed conflict; most of Black Hawk's party destroyed by force under command of Henry Atkinson.

Black Hills, mountains, SW S.Dak. and NE Wyo. They cover c.6,000 sq. mi. between Belle Fourche R. and Cheyenne R., rising amid semiarid plains to altitudes of 5,000 ft. and over. Forests of yellow pine, black from a distance, gave hills their name. Many features preserved in Mt. RUSHMORE Natl. Memorial, Wind Cave Natl. Park, and Jewel Cave and Devils Tower Natl. Monuments (see NATIONAL PARKS AND MONUMENTS, table). Indians lost hold after gold discovery (1874); white settlement boomed after 1876. Area also yields uranium, feldspar, mica, and silver. Highest point is Harney Peak (7,242 ft.).

Black Hole of Calcutta: see CALCUTTA.

black lead: see GRAPHITE.

blackleg or **blackquarter,** acute, infectious disease of cattle, sometimes of sheep. Caused by *Clostridium feseri,* it produces swellings on back and legs and is generally fatal.

black letter: see TYPE.

Blackmore, Richard Doddridge, 1825–1900, English novelist, author of *Lorna Doone* (1869).

Black Mountain, 4,145 ft. high, E Ky., in Cumberlands near Lynch. State's highest peak.

Black Mountains, highest range of Appalachian system and spur of Blue Ridge, W N.C., rising to 6,684 ft. in Mt. MITCHELL.

Blackmur, R(ichard) P., 1904–65, American critic and poet. His critical writings include *The Double Agent* (1935) and *Language as Gesture* (1952).

Blackpool, county borough (pop. 152,133), Lancashire, England; resort on the Irish Sea.

Black Prince: see EDWARD THE BLACK PRINCE.

blackquarter: see BLACKLEG.

Black River. 1 River rising in SE Mo. and flowing c.300 mi. SE, then SW, to White R. near Newport, Ark. Partly navigable. Clearwater Dam is near Piedmont. **2** Name often given to short stream formed after Tensas R. joins Ouachita R. in NE La. Flows c.70 mi. S to Red R. **3** River, N N.Y., rising in Adirondacks and flowing c.120 mi. SW, NNW, and WSW to inlet of L. Ontario W of Watertown. Falls provide power for factories. **4** River rising in Chequamegon Natl. Forest, central Wis., and winding c.160 mi. S and W to Mississippi R. at La Crosse.

Black Sea, anc. *Pontus Euxinus,* inland sea (c.160,000 sq. mi.; max. depth c.7,360 ft.), connected with Mediterranean by Bosporus, Sea of Marmara, and DARDANELLES. Enclosed by Bulgaria, Rumania, USSR, Turkey. Chief ports: Odessa, Batum, Constanta. Receives Danube, Dnieper, Don rivers. The Sea of Azov is one of its arms.

black snake, nonpoisonous snake of E U.S. Adults dull black, 5–6 ft. long. Seizes prey (small animals) in mouth, pressing it to ground to kill. Pilot black snake of NE U.S. has shiny black scales.

Blackstone, Sir William, 1723–80, English jurist. His *Commentaries on the Law of England* (1765–69) influential in England and the U.S.; long used as authority and sole reading matter for young lawyers.

Blackstone, river rising near Worcester, Mass., and flowing c.50 mi. SSE to Woonsocket, R.I. Continues SE to Pawtucket, where it becomes Seekonk R., and S to head of Providence R. at Providence.

blackthorn or **sloe,** thorny plum tree (*Prunus spinosa*), of Europe, Asia, N. Africa. Blue fruits used in brandy, sloe gin. Limbs used for canes in Ireland.

Black Tom, part of Jersey City, N.J., called also Black Tom Isl. Here, in July, 1916, German saboteurs demolished a munitions plant.

Black Warrior, navigable river rising in N central Ala. and flowing c.178 mi. generally SW to Tombigbee R. near Demopolis.

Black Watch or **Royal Highlanders,** Scottish infantry regiment. Name comes from their dark kilts. Formed 1739 to watch Scottish rebels and keep peace.

Blackwell, Elizabeth, 1821–1910, American physician, b. England; first woman in U.S. to be granted medical degree (1849). Helped to found (1857) New York Infirmary and Col. for Women, first nurses' school in U.S., and London School of Medicine for Women. Her brother, **Henry Brown Blackwell,** 1825–1909, was an abolitionist and, with his wife, Lucy STONE, worked for woman suffrage. Their daughter, **Alice Stone Blackwell,** 1857–1950, edited (1881–1917) the *Woman's Journal,* suffrage organ. **Antoinette Louisa (Brown) Blackwell,** 1825–1921, sister-in-law of Elizabeth Blackwell and H. B. Blackwell, was a Unitarian minister and a worker for woman suffrage.

bladder, urinary, muscular sac in pelvis. Urine secreted by kidneys enters bladder by two tubes (ureters) and is conveyed out of body by another tube (urethra).

bladderwort, carnivorous aquatic or bog plant (*Utricularia* and related genera), equipped with small bladderlike organs to trap minute animal life.

Bladensburg, town (pop. 3,103), W central Md., on Anacostia R. NE of Washington, D.C.; chartered 1742. Here British defeated Americans (Aug. 24, 1814) before capturing Washington. Stephen Decatur mortally wounded by James Barron in duel here.

Blaeu, Willem Janszoon (vǐ'lŭm yän'sŏn blou'), 1571–1638, Dutch cartographer, printer. Founded unusually fine printing establishment in Amsterdam.

Blagonravov, Anatoli Arkadyevich (ŭnŭtô'yĕ ärkädä'-yĕvĭch blägŏnrä'vof), 1894–, Soviet rocket expert. He is responsible for much of Soviet research program in astronautics.

Blagoveshchensk (blŭgŭvyĕsh'chĭnsk), city (1965 est. pop. 114,000), RSFSR, in extreme E Siberia, on Amur R. and on spur of Trans-Siberian RR. Agr. center.

Blaine, James G(illespie), 1830–93, American politician. U.S. Representative from Maine (1863–76); speaker of House (1869–75). U.S. Senator (1876–81). U.S. Secretary of State (1881, 1889–92). First called "plumed knight" in 1876 Republican convention, where improper influence he had used in case of a railroad in Ark. prevented his nomination. Nominated in 1884, he was largely defeated for President by "rum, Romanism,and rebellion" epithet used to characterize Democrats by New York minister supporting him. As Secretary of State, he fostered closer U.S.–Latin American relations, brought about first Pan American Congress (see PAN-AMERICANISM).

Blaine. 1 Village (1965 pop. 15,544), SE Minn., a suburb N of Minneapolis. **2** Tourist and farm-trade city (pop. 1,735), NW Wash., on Strait of Georgia; settled 1858. Site of Peace Arch on Canadian border.

Blair, Francis Preston, 1791–1876, American journalist and politician. Founder (1830) of Washington *Globe.* A leader in KITCHEN CABINET. Helped found Republican party; adviser to Pres. Lincoln. Blair House, his Washington residence, is now government property. His son, **Francis Preston Blair,** 1821–75, was a political leader in Mo. and a Union general in Civil War. His regiment of "Wide Awakes" helped keep Mo. loyal to Union. Served with distinction in Vicksburg, Chattanooga, and Atlanta campaigns. U.S. Senator (1871–73). An older brother, **Montgomery Blair,** 1813–83, was U.S. Postmaster General (1861–64). As first U.S. solicitor in Court of Claims (1855–57) he was counsel for Scott in Dred Scott Case.

Blair, city (pop. 4,931), E Nebr., on bluffs overlooking Missouri R., NNW of Omaha; founded 1869. Farm trade center and seat of Dana Col.

Blairstown, township (pop. 1,797), NW N.J., on Paulins Kill, E of Delaware Water Gap. Summer resort. Blair Academy is here.

Blake, Eugene Carson, 1906–, American Protestant clergyman. Served as stated clerk of United Presbyterian Church 1951–66 and president of Natl. Council of Churches 1954–57. Figured prominently in civil rights activities. Elected general secretary of World Council of Churches 1966.

Blake, Robert, 1598–1657, English admiral. Without naval training, had brilliant career after 1649. Estab. British power in Mediterranean 1654. Helped develop Commonwealth navy.

Blake, William, 1757–1827, English artist and poet. An engraver, he (with the assistance of his wife, Catherine Boucher) engraved powerful illustrations for editions of various authors (Edward Young, Cowper, Dante, Thomas Gray, the book of Job) and for all his own volumes of poetry except *Poetical Sketches* (1783). His poems show the same fusing of metaphysical vision and strong, simple line as his engravings. *Songs of Innocence* (1789) and *Songs of Experience* (1794) have many haunting and familiar short poems (e.g., "Piping down the Valleys Wild," "The Tiger"). Except for lyric bits, the "Prophetic Books" (*The Book of Thel,* 1789; *America,* 1793; *The Book of Urizen,* 1794; *The Book of Los,* 1795; *Milton,* 1804; *Jerusalem,* 1804) are less familiar to general readers; in them he developed his own mythology and religion, so that they have a more limited appeal.

Blakelock, Ralph Albert, 1847–1919, American landscape painter, known for melancholy effects.

Blakeslee, Albert Francis, 1874–1954, American botanist. Discovered sexual reproduction in bread molds.

Work on the inheritance and distribution of Jimson weed (*Datura*) yielded information on chromosome action, genic balance, evolution. Used colchicine, an alkaloid, to produce polyploid plants.

Blanc, Louis (lwĕ′ blä′), 1811–82, French socialist. His *Organisation du travail* (1840) outlined social order based on principle, "From each according to his abilities, to each according to his needs." Leader in the revolution of 1848, he was disappointed when his plan for social workshops was sabotaged; fomented unsuccessful workers' uprising; fled to England, staying until 1871.

Blanc, Mont: see MONT BLANC.

Blanca Peak: see SANGRE DE CRISTO MOUNTAINS.

Blanchard, Jean Pierre (zhä′ pyĕr′ bläshär′), or **François Blanchard** (fräswä′), 1753–1809, French balloonist. Reputed inventor of parachute (1785). With Dr. John Jeffries, he made (1785) first English Channel crossing by air.

Blanche of Castile (kästēl′), 1185?–1252, queen of Louis VIII of France, regent during minority of her son Louis IX and after his departure on Crusade (1248). Capable and authoritarian.

Blanco, Cape, SW Oregon, SW of Roseburg, projecting W into Pacific. State's westernmost point.

Bland-Allison Act, 1878, passed by U.S. Congress to provide for freer coinage of silver. Original bill offered by Rep. Richard P. Bland met Western demands for free, unlimited coinage of silver. Sen. William B. Allison offered amended version. Act required U.S. treasury to purchase $2,000,000–$4,000,000 worth of silver bullion each month at market prices for coinage into silver dollars, which were made legal tender for all debts. Neither free-silver nor gold-standard forces were satisfied, but act remained law until passage of SHERMAN SILVER PURCHASE ACT of 1890.

Blanding, city (pop. 1,805), SE Utah, S of Abajo Mts. and N of San Juan R.; settled by Mormons 1905. Natural Bridges and Hovenweep Natl. Monuments are near (see NATIONAL PARKS AND MONUMENTS, table).

Blane, Sir Gilbert, 1749–1834, Scottish physician, known for introducing lime juice to prevent scurvy and advancing sanitary measures in British navy.

blank verse: see PENTAMETER.

Blanqui, Louis Auguste (lwĕ′ ōgüst′ blänkē′), 1805–81, French revolutionist and radical thinker. A leader in February Revolution of 1848. Exiled (1864–70) in Brussels, he opposed Napoleon III, and was instrumental in his deposition. The Commune of Paris of 1871 was largely his creation, though Thiers had him arrested shortly before its proclamation. Freed in 1879. His social theories influenced Marx. Chief work: *Critique sociale* (1869).

Blantyre, town (pop. including its twin town of Limbe, c.62,600), S Malawi, in the Shiré highlands. David Livingstone estab. mission here 1876. Commercial and industrial center of the country.

Blarney, village, Co. Cork, Ireland. Castle (15th-cent.) contains Blarney stone, supposed to bestow persuasive powers on those who kiss it.

Blasco Ibáñez, Vicente (vēthän′tä blä′skō ēbä′nyäth), 1867–1928, Spanish novelist, b. Valencia, best known for *The Four Horsemen of the Apocalypse* (1916), a novel of First World War.

Blasket Islands, group of rocky islets off Co. Kerry, SW Ireland. Stronghold of last Irish chieftain to surrender to Cromwell.

blast furnace, structure for smelting, i.e., for extracting metals from ores. Principle involves removing oxygen from metal oxide to obtain metal. Furnace for iron is chimneylike, narrowing at top and bottom. Ore, coke, and flux are fed into top; hot air piped into bottom passes up through the mass. Coke oxidizes to carbon dioxide, which great heat changes to carbon monoxide; this reduces the ore, taking on oxygen and forming carbon dioxide, which is piped off. Molten iron descends to crucible at bottom of furnace and is separated from slag.

blasting, fragmentizing of rock or other material by explosive discharged within it or against it. Four steps in modern blasting: drilling holes to receive charge, placing charge, tamping hole, and igniting or detonating charge. Explosives used include black powder, dynamite, and ammonium nitrate.

Blaue Reiter, der (der blou′ŭ rī′tĕr) [the blue rider], German expressionist group in Munich, 1911–14. Named for painting by Kandinsky. Group included Marc, Kandinsky, Klee, and Macke.

Blavatsky, Helena Petrovna (blŭvät′skē), 1831–91, Russian theosophist and occultist. After traveling widely, she went (1873) to New York where she founded (1875) the Theosophical Society. After 1879 she made her hq. at Madras, India. Her *Isis Unveiled* (1887) is the textbook of her disciples.

blazing star or **gay-feather,** a North American perennial (*Liatris*), with racemes of purple or white feathery flowers.

bleaching, process of whitening by chemicals or sunlight, commonly applied to textiles, paper pulp, flour, fats, hair, feathers, wood, and other materials. Chemical methods include oxidation, reduction, and adsorption; textiles have long been sun bleached. Chloride of lime, invented 1799, was first of modern chemical bleaches. Javelle water and other chlorine mixtures are common domestic bleaches.

Bled, resort town, Slovenia, N Yugoslavia, in the Julian Alps. Former royal castle is nearby.

bleeding heart, perennial (*Dicentra spectabilis*), native to Japan. A spring-flowering garden plant with drooping, deep pink heart-shaped blooms.

Blekinge, Swed. *Blekinge län*, county (1,173, sq. mi.; pop. 144,498) and historic province, SW Sweden, on the Baltic coast; cap. Karlskrona. Cultivated valleys make it "the garden of Sweden." Conquered from Denmark 1658.

Blenheim (blĕn′ŭm), Ger. *Blindheim*, village, W Bavaria, on the Danube E of Ulm. Between Blenheim and nearby Höchstädt Marlborough and Prince Eugene defeated French and Bavarians under Tallard in major battle of War of Spanish Succession (1704).

Blenheim Park, estate, Oxfordshire, England; seat of the dukes of Marlborough, awarded to first duke for victories in War of the Spanish Succession.

Blennerhassett, Harman, 1765–1831, Anglo-Irish pioneer in America, an associate of Aaron Burr. Advanced money to Burr for Western schemes. Taken into custody after Burr's arrest, but released. In 1798 he bought part of Blennerhassett Island, in the Ohio, near Parkersburg, W.Va., and Belpre, Ohio. Here he built mansion and laboratory.

Blériot, Louis (lwĕ′ blārēō′), 1872–1936, French aviator and inventor. First to fly English Channel in heavier-than-air machine (July 25, 1909).

Blessington, Marguerite, countess of, 1789–1849, Irish beauty and intellectual who set up a brilliant salon in Kensington (1822). Wrote novels and a journal.

Blest Gana, Alberto (älbĕr′tō blĕst′ gä′nä), 1830–1920, Chilean novelist, generally considered greatest of 19th-cent. Spanish American realists. His masterpiece is *Martín Rivas* (1862).

Bleuler, Paul Eugen, 1857–1939, Swiss psychiatrist, neurologist. Introduced term SCHIZOPHRENIA in 1911. His theories of its causes are classic.

Bligh, William, 1754–1817, British admiral. Chiefly remembered for mutiny on his ship, the BOUNTY, 1789. Was governor of New South Wales 1805–8.

blight, sudden, severe plant disease or the agent causing it. Caused chiefly by bacteria, viruses, or fungi, blights wither and kill plants without rotting them.

blindness, lack or loss of sight. May result from injury or certain diseases including cataract, glaucoma. See also COLOR BLINDNESS; BRAILLE SYSTEM.

Blind River, town (pop. 4,093), S Ont., Canada, on N shore of L. Huron ESE of Sault Ste Marie. Uranium-mining center.

Bliss, Eleanor Albert, 1899–, American bacteriologist, authority on sulfa drugs.

Bliss, Porter Cornelius, 1833–85, American diplomat and adventurer. Explored Gran Chaco for Argentine government. Imprisoned as suspected spy in Paraguay, released on demand of U.S.

Bliss, Tasker Howard, 1853–1930, American army officer and statesman. Appointed chief of staff of U.S. army (1917), he helped work out mobilization plans. Delegate to Paris Peace Conference.

blister beetle: see CANTHARIDES.

Blitzstein, Marc, 1905–64, American composer. Wrote music for stage and screen; known particularly for his operas, e.g., *The Cradle Will Rock* (1937) and *No for an Answer* (1941).

Blixen, Karen, Baroness: see DINESEN, ISAK.

Bloch, Ernest (blŏk), 1880–1959, Swiss-American composer. Most work has intense Hebraic feeling, (e.g., the Hebrew rhapsody *Schelomo,* 1916). Among other works are an opera, *Macbeth;* a *concerto grosso* for string orchestra and piano.

Bloch, Felix, 1905–, American physicist, b. Switzerland. Shared 1952 Nobel Prize in Physics for developing method of measuring magnetic fields in atomic nuclei.

Bloch, Konrad E., 1912–, American biochemist, b. Germany. Shared 1964 Nobel Prize in Physiology and Medicine for discoveries concerning the mechanism and regulation of cholesterol and fatty acid metabolism.

Bloch, Marc, 1886–1944, French historian, an authority on medieval feudalism. He met death as a leader of French resistance in Second World War. Among his works are *The Historian's Craft* (Eng. tr., 1953) and *Feudal Society* (Eng. tr., 1961).

blockade, use of naval vessels to cut off access to a coast, usually to prevent neutral shipping from trade with the enemy. The Declaration of Paris (1856) provided that blockades be announced to all affected parties and be legal only if effective and enforced against all neutrals.

block book, book with each page printed from a separate wood block. European examples (about middle of 15th cent.) were crude, inexpensive (e.g., *Biblia pauperum*). Chinese examples (earliest in 8th cent.) often beautiful.

blockhouse, small fortification, usually temporary, serving as a post for a small garrison. Its use dates probably from 15th cent. Typical structure in U.S. had two stories, the second overhanging. Modern version is PILLBOX.

Block Island, 7 mi. long and 3½ mi. wide, off S R.I., at E entrance to Long Isl. Sound between Point Judith, R.I., and Montauk Point, N.Y.; coextensive with New Shoreham town (1966 pop. 527). Visited by Adriaen Block in 1614, settled 1661. Murder here of John Oldham precipitated Pequot War (1637). Long a popular resort.

Blocksberg, Germany: see BROCKEN.

Blodgett, Katharine Burr, 1898–, American chemist. Worked on tungsten filaments, monomolecular layers. Made nonreflecting glass by coating glass with layers of barium stearate.

Bloemfontein (blōōm'fŏntān″), city (pop. c.145,273), cap. of Orange Free State, Republic of South Africa. Judicial center of republic. Seat of university, two colleges. Transportation hub.

Blois (blwä), town (est. pop. 28,190), cap. of Loiret-Cher dept., central France, on the Loire. Thibaut the Cheat, 1st count of Blois, acquired Chartres and Touraine (10th cent.); successors added Champagne and Brie. Blois itself was assigned to cadet branch of family, sold to duke of Orleans 1397, Incorporated into royal domain 1498. Famous Renaissance château was residence of several kings and queens of France; scene of murder of Henri de Guise 1588. The Treaties of Blois (1504–5) were a temporary settlement of the ITALIAN WARS.

Blok, Aleksandr Aleksandrovich (ülyĭksän'dŭr ülyĭksän'drŭvĭch blôk′), 1880–1921, greatest of Russian symbolist poets. He achieved fame through the cycle *Verses about the Lady Beautiful* (1904). Embracing the Revolution of 1917, he wrote *The Twelve* (1918), a powerful epic poem.

Blondel, François (fräswä' blŏdĕl′), 1617–86, French architect. Designed triumphal arch, Porte Saint-Denis, Paris. His nephew, **Jacques François Blondel,** 1705–74, was also an eminent architect.

Blondel, Maurice, 1861–1949, French Catholic philosopher. Like Bergson, he was anti-rationalist, but did think the rational proofs for the existence of God were valid. He held that action could not be satisfied with a finite good and could only be fulfilled in God.

Blondel de Nesle (Fr. blŏdĕl′ dŭ nĕl′), fl. late 12th cent., French troubadour, a favorite of Richard I. According to legend, found Richard in prison by singing song known only to two of them and was able to effect his rescue.

blood, circulating fluid which brings food and oxygen to body tissues and carries off carbon dioxide and other wastes. In man, consists of fluid plasma containing substances essential for CLOTTING OF BLOOD, hormones, and several types of cells including red and white CORPUSCLES. Recognition of blood groups and RH FACTOR important in BLOOD TRANSFUSION. See also CIRCULATION OF THE BLOOD. See *ills.,* pp. 656–57.

blood clotting: see CLOTTING OF BLOOD.

blood poisoning: see SEPTICEMIA.

blood pressure, pressure of blood on walls of blood vessels, especially arteries. Depends on heart action, arterial elasticity, capillary resistance, and volume and viscous quality of blood. Max. pressure during contraction of heart (systole); min. during relaxation (diastole). Normal systolic range 100–140 mm. of mercury; normal diastolic range 60–90. Persistent high pressure (hypertension) often associated with obesity, arteriosclerosis, kidney disorders.

bloodstone or **heliotrope,** green CHALCEDONY spotted with red JASPER, used as a gem.

blood transfusion, transfer of blood from one person or animal to another. For safe transfusion blood of donor and recipient must belong to groups which when mixed do not cause clumping or agglutination of red blood cells. Classification of human blood based on agglutinating substances present. Four major groups designated by Karl LANDSTEINER as O, A, B, AB. In Jansky system groups they are respectively designated as I, II, III, IV; in Moss system as IV, II, III, I. Persons having group O blood are called universal donors; those having AB blood, universal recipients. Blood should be tested also for RH FACTOR, which varies independently, and for organisms causing such diseases as syphilis, malaria, or serum hepatitis.

Bloody Assizes: see JEFFREYS OF WEM, GEORGE JEFFREYS, 1ST BARON.

Bloomer, Amelia Jenks, 1818–94, American reformer. Edited (1848–54) *Lily,* a reform organ. In 1851 adopted dress now known as Bloomer costume.

Bloomfield, Leonard, 1887–1949, American linguist. His masterpiece, *Language* (1933), a standard text, is a clear statement of linguistic principles which are now axiomatic, notably that language study must always be centered in the spoken language, that definitions used in grammar should be based on forms of the language, and that a given language at a given time is a complete system of sounds and forms which exist independently of the past.

Bloomfield. 1 Town (pop. 13,613), N Conn., N of Hartford; settled c.1642. **2** Town (pop. 51,867), NE N.J., NW of Newark. Seat of Bloomfield Col. and Seminary.

Bloomgarden, Solomon, pseud. **Yehoash** (yĕhō'äsh), 1870–1927, Yiddish poet, b. Lithuania; came to America in 1910. Translated Old Testament from

Hebrew into Yiddish. Name also spelled Blumen-garten.

Bloomington. 1 City (1965 pop. 37,791), central Ill., SE of Peoria; settled 1822. Important rail, commercial, and industrial center in rich farm and coal area. Seat of Illinois Wesleyan Univ. Lincoln made famous "lost speech" to first Republican state convention here 1856. **2** City (1965 pop. 42,058), S central Ind., SW of Indianapolis; settled 1818. Seat of INDIANA UNIVERSITY. Limestone quarries in area. **3** City (1965 pop. 66,542), SE Minn., SSW of Minneapolis.

Bloomsburg, industrial town (pop. 10,655), E Pa., on Susquehanna R., SW of Wilkes-Barre; settled 1772 on site of Indian village. Only municipality incorporated as a town in the state.

Bloomsbury, residential district, central London, England. Has British Mus., Univ. of London, and many squares (e.g., Bedford, Russell, Bloomsbury). Many artists, writers, and students live here.

Bloomsbury group, social and literary group whose activities centered around Bloomsbury Square, London; active in first quarter of 20th cent. Members included Lytton Strachey, Virginia Woolf, E. M. Forster, V. Sackville-West, Roger Fry, Clive Bell, and J. M. Keynes.

Blount, William, 1749–1800, American statesman. Governor of Territory South of the River Ohio (present Tenn.) 1790–96. Involved in plan to help British conquer West Florida.

Blow, John, 1649–1708, English composer, organist at Westminster Abbey, chiefly remembered for his church music and for his masque *Venus and Adonis*. Henry Purcell was his pupil.

Blow, Susan Elizabeth, 1843–1916, American educator, follower of Froebel. Opened first successful public kindergarten (1873) in U.S.

blowfly, blue-green winged insect, also called blue-bottle or greenbottle fly. Bite may cause infected sores in farm animals; larvae are scavengers.

Bloy, Léon (lãō′ blwä′), 1846–1917, French author. A Roman Catholic and social reformer, he savagely attacked social conventions in essays, pamphlets, letters, and novels.

Blücher, Gebhard Leberecht von (blōō′kŭr, Ger. gĕp′-härt lā′bŭrĕkht fŭn blü′khŭr), 1742–1819, Prussian general in Napoleonic Wars. Played crucial part in allied victory at Leipzig (1813) and in WATERLOO CAMPAIGN. Created prince of Wahlstatt in 1814.

bluebell: see HAREBELL; VIRGINIA COWSLIP; SQUILL.

blueberry, hardy shrub of genus *Vaccinium*. Varieties of low-bush blueberry (*Vaccinium angustifolium*) cultivated commercially for blue or black edible berries. High-bush blueberry or whortleberry (*V. corymbosum*) valued for brilliant autumn foliage. Blueberries need acid soil.

bluebird, migratory bird of North America, a thrush. In East male is c.7 in. long; blue upper plumage, cinnamon-red breast, white underneath. Related are mountain, Western, azure, and chestnut-backed bluebirds. Symbol of elusive happiness in Maeterlinck's *Blue Bird*.

bluebonnet, spring-blooming lupine (*Lupinus texensis*), with sky-blue flowers. State flower of Texas.

Bluefield, city (pop. 19,256), extreme S West Va., adjacent to Bluefield, Va.; settled 1777. Shipping point for coal area and seat of Bluefield Col.

Bluefields, Caribbean port (pop. 17,649), SE Nicaragua, on Bluefields Bay. An early pirate resort, it became cap. of British protectorate over MOSQUITO COAST (1678). Nominally returned to Nicaragua (1850), it was finally annexed (1894) by Zelaya.

bluefish, stout-bodied, delicately flavored food fish (*Pomatomus saltatrix*), of warm waters of Atlantic and Indian oceans. Adults weigh 10 to 25 lb. Deep bluish, tinged with green above, silver below.

bluegrass, a grass species of genus *Poa* with bluish-green leaves. Used for pasture, hay, and lawns. Best

known is Kentucky bluegrass (*Poa pratensis*), in region noted for racehorses.

Blue Island, residential and industrial city (1966 pop. 21,986), NE Ill., S of Chicago; settled 1835. Has railroad yards and canneries.

blue jay, bird of central and E North America, allied to crow, raven, magpie. Grayish violet-blue upper parts and crest; blue wings and tail, black and white markings; black-collared neck; gray to white under parts; raucous cry, also musical notes.

blue laws, legislation aimed at rigid, minute control of public and private morals. Term originated with Loyalist clergyman, Samuel A. Peters, who in 1781 described "Blue Laws" of Conn. (17th-cent. laws printed on blue paper) with exaggeration but some truth. Strict laws against Sabbath breaking, drunkenness, and sexual misconduct were common in American colonies. Many blue laws revived in 19th and 20th cent.; now unevenly enforced.

Blue Mountains, wooded range, NE Oregon and SE Wash., c.8,500 ft. high, in midst of basin lands.

Blue Nile, Arabic *Bahr-el-Azraq*, river, c.950 mi. long, rising in L. Tana, NW Ethiopia, and flowing through the Sudan to join with the White Nile at Khartoum to form the NILE.

Blue Point, village, SE N.Y., on S Long Isl., near Great South Bay and WSW of Patchogue. Gives name to blue-point oysters.

blueprint. Plans drawn to scale on translucent material, then placed on paper treated with mixture of ferric salts and exposed to strong light. Ferric salts unprotected by drawing react to give blue color; salts under drawing wash away in water, leaving white lines.

Blue Rider: see BLAUE REITER, DER.

Blue Ridge, range of Appalachian system, W of the piedmont, extending from NW Md. just above Harpers Ferry, W.Va., SW through Va. and N.C. into N Ga. Rises to c.5,000 ft. in S. Famous for scenery, e.g., Skyline Drive section in Va. which traverses Shenandoah Natl. Park. Blue Ridge Parkway connects Shenandoah and Great Smoky Mts. natl. parks.

blues, type of song with melancholy text set to mournful tune. Grew from Negro work songs and spirituals. Typical song is W. C. Handy's *St. Louis Blues* (1914).

Blues and Greens [names derived from colors of circus charioteers], political factions in the Byzantine Empire in 6th cent. The Greens usually upheld MONOPHYSITISM; the Blues, orthodoxy. Both joined in the *Nika* sedition against Justinian I and Theodora (532). The empress saved the day by ordering Belisarius to put the rebels down by force; c.30,000 were killed.

bluestocking, representative of 18th-cent. English "conversation groups" of intellectuals; later only a woman of the groups, hence an intellectual woman. Famous early bluestockings were Elizabeth Montagu, Elizabeth Carter, Hannah More.

bluestone, slate-colored sandstone used as building stone. Term also used for BLUE VITRIOL.

bluet or **quaker-ladies,** small North American wild flower (*Houstonia caerulea*), with blue, yellow-eyed blooms.

blue vitriol or **bluestone,** common blue crystalline hydrous copper salt (cupric sulphate or copper sulphate). Produced when white anhydrous salt crystallizes from aqueous solution. Occurs in nature in chalcanthite. Used in copperplating; as dye mordant.

Bluffton, village (pop. 2,591), NW Ohio, between Lima and Findlay, in farm and limestone area; settled 1833. Has large Mennonite population and Bluffton Col.

Blum, Léon (lãō′ blŏōm′), 1872–1950, French Socialist statesman. Headed first Popular Front government (1936–37; coalition of Socialists, Radical Socialists, Communists); passed important labor reforms. Arrested by Vichy govt. 1940; defended himself courageously at RIOM trial; held prisoner by Germans until 1945. Briefly headed Socialist cabinet 1946–47. A moderate in his later years.

Blume, Peter (blŏŏm), 1906–, American painter, b. Russia. Treats social themes and problems in fantastic yet realistic manner.

Blumenbach, Johann Friedrich (yōhän' frē'drĭkh blŏŏ'-münbäkh), 1752–1840, German comparative anatomist and physical anthropologist. Notable craniometric studies. Proposed fivefold scheme of race classification.

Blumengarten, Solomon: see BLOOMGARDEN, SOLOMON.

Blunt, Sir Anthony Frederick, 1907–, English art historian. Became director of the Courtauld Inst. of Art in 1947 and in 1952 became also Surveyor of the Queen's Pictures. His writings include *Art and Architecture in France, 1500–1700* (1953).

Blunt, George William, 1807–78, American hydrographer. His company published *Bowditch's Navigator* and *Blunt's Coast Pilot,* copperplates and copyrights for which were later purchased by U.S. Hydrographic Office. Instrumental in reforming U.S. Lighthouse Service.

Blunt, Wilfrid Scawen (skō'ĭn), 1840–1922, English poet, author of *The Love Sonnets of Proteus* (1880). Advocated Irish, Indian, and Egyptian home rule.

Blytheville, city (pop. 20,797), NE Ark., near Mississippi R., ENE of Jonesboro; settled c.1853. Trading and industrial center of state's richest cotton area; soybeans and feed crops also grown. Blytheville Air Force Base is SE.

B'nai B'rith (bnā' brĭth) [Heb. = sons of the Covenant]. Jewish fraternal and service organization, founded 1843 in New York city. Spread throughout U.S., Canada; also represented in other countries. Devoted to charitable undertakings, including hospitals and disaster relief. B'nai B'rith Anti-Defamation League influential in opposing religious and racial discrimination. Has Hillel Foundation on university campuses.

Boabdil (bŏŭbdēl'), d. 1538. last Moorish king of Granada in Spain (1482–92). Defeated by Ferdinand and Isabella; fled to Morocco.

boa constrictor (bō'ŭ kŭnstrĭk'tùr), nonpoisonous constrictor snake of Central and South America; of anaconda and python family. Rarely over 15 ft. long. Agile climber.

Boadicea (bō'ŭdĭsē'ù), d. A.D. 62, British queen of the Iceni (of Norfolk). Led revolt against the Romans. On defeat she took poison.

Boanerges (bō'ŭnûr'jēz) [Gr.,= sons of thunder], name given by Jesus to James and John. Mark 3.17.

Boas, Franz (bō'äz), 1858–1942, American anthropologist. Taught at Columbia Univ. (1896–1936). His approach was independent of theoretical preconceptions and was marked by a rigorous methodology. He did significant work in physical and cultural anthropology and in linguistics.

Boaz (bō'äz), Ruth's husband, ancestor of David. Ruth 2; 3; 4; Booz: Mat. 1.5; Luke 3.32.

Bobbio (bôb'bēō), small town. Emilia-Romagna, N central Italy, SW of Piacenza. The monastery founded here by St. Columban in 612 was oldest in N Italy, flourished as cultural center 9th–12th cent.

bobcat, small lynx (*Lynx rufus*) of U.S., S Canada, parts of Mexico. Powerful, usually nocturnal hunter. Known also as bay lynx, red lynx, wildcat. See *ill.,* p. 1136.

bobolink, in N U.S. and Canada name of American songbird related to blackbird, oriole. Called reed bird and rice bird in South. Insectivorous in North; as they migrate, they gorge on rice and become so fat they are hunted as game. Winter in South America.

Bobruisk (bŭbrŏŏ'ĕsk), city (1965 est. pop. 115,000), SE Byelorussian SSR, port on Berezina R. Railroad junction.

bobwhite, American game bird of same family as pheasant and partridge. Eastern bobwhite c.10 in. long; male plumage brown, black, white; female brown, buff. Eats insects, weed seeds. Male whistles "bob-white" to attract female.

Boca Tigris: see CANTON, river.

Boccaccio, Giovanni (jŏvän'nē bŏk-kät'chyō) 1313–75. Italian poet and storyteller, b. Paris. Educated at Certaldo and Naples. Recalled to Florence 1341, where he won Petrarch's friendship. His chief work is the DECAMERON, one of the world's great books. Other works include a biography of Dante; the prose romances *Filocolo* (c.1340) and *La Fiammetta* (c.1344); *Filostrato,* upon which Chaucer drew for his *Troilus and Criseyde;* and the *Corbaccio,* a verse satire on women.

Boccherini, Luigi (bôk-kĕrē'nē), 1743–1805, Italian composer. He wrote more than 400 works, including 4 cello concertos, about 90 string quartets, and about 125 string quintets.

Boccioni, Umberto (ōōmbēr'tō bŏt-chō'nē), 1882–1916, Italian futurist painter and sculptor.

Bochum (bō'khōŏm), city (pop. 347,459), North Rhine-Westphalia, West Germany; a center of RUHR dist.

Böcklin or Boecklin, Arnold (both: är'nŏlt bûk'lēn), 1827–1901, Swiss painter who attempted to express an idealistic philosophy through art.

Bocskay, Stephen (bôch'kĭ), Hung. *Bocskay István,* 1557?–1606, Hungarian noble. Was voivode (1604–6) and prince (1605–6) of Transylvania. Aimed to secure Transylvanian independence from Austria and Turkey. In 1604 he led revolt, supported by Turkey, against Emperor Rudolf II's attempt to reimpose Catholicism on Hungary. The Treaty of Vienna (1606), which he negotiated, guaranteed religious freedom and legalized the threefold partition of HUNGARY (confirmed by treaty between Austria and Turkey).

Bode, Boyd Henry, 1873–1953, American educator, professor of education at Ohio State Univ. (1921–44).

Bode, Johann Elert (yō'hän ā'lĕrt bō'dù), 1747–1826, German astronomer. Compiler of *Uranographia* (1801; star maps and catalogue of stars and nebulae).

Bode, Wilhelm von, (vĭl'hĕlm, fûn), 1845–1929, German art historian and museum director. Under his supervision the Berlin Mus. grew into one of the world's greatest collections.

Bodel, Jehan (zhä' bōdĕl'), b. c.1165, French trouvère. *Le Jeu de Saint-Nicolas,* a mystery, is first long play entirely in French. He died a leper.

Bodensee: see CONSTANCE, LAKE OF.

Bodenstein, Andreas Rudolf: see CARLSTADT.

Bodh Gaya, India: see BUDDH GAYA.

Bodin, Jean (zhä' bōdē'), 1530–96, French social and political philosopher. He made comparative historical studies in law; later wrote *Les Six Livres de la république* (1576), which considered sovereignty as a general characteristic of all states.

Bodleian Library (bŏd'lĕùn), at Oxford Univ. Original library destroyed; replaced in 17th cent. through efforts of Sir Thomas Bodley, who left a fund for its maintenance. Receives a copy of every book published in Great Britain.

Bodley, Sir Thomas, 1545–1613, English scholar and diplomat, organizer of the BODLEIAN LIBRARY.

Bodmer, Johann Jakob (yō'hän yä'kôp bōd'mùr), 1698–1783, Swiss critic. Founded with Johann Jakob Breitinger the critical journal *Diskurse der Mahlern,* which attacked French classicism and paved the way for Klopstock, Goethe, and Schiller. Translated *Paradise Lost;* edited *Nibelungenlied.*

Bodoni, Giambattista (jämbät-tē'stä bōdō'nē), 1740–1813, Italian printer. Like Baskerville and Didot a leader in producing "modern" type faces. Indifferent to quality of text, editing, and proofreading, Bodoni produced stately quartos and folios of impressive appearance.

body snatching, stealing dead bodies. Before legal provision for supplying needs of medical schools, traffic in cadavers was profitable. Snatchers known as resurrectionists; their activities in 18th and early 19th cent.

SMALL CAPITALS = cross references. Pronunciation key on inside end pages. Abbreviations: p. 2.

increased public opposition to dissection and led to violence.

Boecklin, Arnold: see BÖCKLIN, ARNOLD.

Boehler, Peter (bû'lŭr), 1712–75, German-born missionary of the Moravian Church in America (1738–42, 1753–64). Worked in Ga.; later founded Nazareth and Bethlehem, Pa., and other settlements. In England (1747–53) he was made bishop.

Boehm, Martin (bām), 1725–1812, American evangelical preacher, b. Pa. Became (1759) Mennonite bishop, but later with P. W. OTTERBEIN founded United Brethren in Christ and was elected bishop (1800).

Boehme or **Böhme, Jakob** (bē'mŭ, Ger. bû'mŭ), 1575–1624, German mystic. His religious teaching, based on the belief that God is manifest in all aspects of creation and that evil results when one aspect (e.g., man) attempts to become the whole, was highly influential in England and the Continent.

Boeotia (bēō'shŭ), region of anc. Greece, N of the Gulf of Corinth; chief city, THEBES. A confederacy of cities was formed in the Boeotian League (7th cent. B.C.), dominated by Thebes until Athens after many battles broke up the confederacy in 457 B.C. Shortly afterward Thebes returned to power with Epaminondas' victory over Sparta at Leuctra (371 B.C.), and all Boeotia shared with Thebes the defeats by Philip II and Alexander the Great. Athenians generally considered Boeotians dull-witted clods, though Hesiod and Pindar belonged to the region.

Boer (bôr, boōr) [Dutch,= farmer], inhabitant of South Africa of Dutch descent. The Boer language is Afrikaans (see LANGUAGE, table).

Boerhaave, Hermann (boōr'hävù), 1668–1738, Dutch physician and chemist, introducer of clinical teaching at Univ. of Leiden.

Boer War: see SOUTH AFRICAN WAR.

Boethius, Anicius Manlius Severinus (bōē'thēŭs), c.475–525, Roman philosopher. A consul and a minister of Theodoric, he was accused of treason. While in prison awaiting death he wrote *De consolatione philosophiae* [the consolation of philosophy], which has been highly regarded by thoughtful readers from his time to this. Also wrote an influential treatise on music.

bog, very old lake without inlet or outlet which becomes overgrown with vegetation. SPHAGNUM and PEAT obtained from bogs. Acid medium of bogs forms natural preservative for remains of animals and plants of earlier times. Typical bog plants are orchids, cranberry, pitcher plant, and sun dew.

Bogalusa (bōgŭloō'sù), city (pop. 21,432), E La., near Pearl R., NE of Baton Rouge; founded 1906 by lumber interests. Has pine nurseries. Scene of racial strife in 1965.

Bogart, Humphrey (DeForest), 1899–1957, American film actor. Achieved success in *The Petrified Forest* (stage, 1934; film, 1936) and thereafter gave notable performances in such films as *Casablanca, To Have and Have Not,* and *The African Queen.*

Bogert, Marston Taylor, 1868–1954, American organic chemist. Noted for syntheses of complex benzene ring hydrocarbons.

Boghazkeui (bō"gäzkû'ē), village, N central Asiatic Turkey, chief center of Hittite Empire 1400–1200 B.C. Hugo Winckler found here (1906–14) its principal archives.

bog iron ore: see LIMONITE.

Bogomils (bō'gōmĭlz), earliest (10th cent.) group of the CATHARI. Flourishing in Bulgaria and the Balkans, they were distinguished not only by dualistic religious beliefs but also by political nationalism and resentment of Byzantine culture. Various subgroups were called Babuns, Phundaits, and Patarenes. They spread to Italy and converted the ALBIGENSES. Opposition of Christian churches weakened the Bogomils, who were wiped out by the triumph of Islam (15th cent.).

Bogorodsk, RSFSR: see NOGINSK.

Bogotá (bōgōtä'), city (pop. 1,697,311; alt. 8,661 ft.), central Colombia; cap. and largest city of country. Founded (1538) by Jiménez de Quesada to succeed center of Chibcha culture. In a broad valley of E Andes, it was difficult of access before air transportation. Called by Alexander von Humboldt (1801) the Athens of America. After independence from Spain, Bogotá was cap. of Greater Colombia until dissolution of union (1830). Organization of American States founded here 1948.

Bogotá, Act of: see ORGANIZATION OF AMERICAN STATES.

Bohemia, Czech *Čechy,* historic province (20,368 sq. mi.; pop. 6,039,087), W Czechoslovakia; cap. PRAGUE. Separated from Bavaria by the BOHEMIAN FOREST, from Saxony by the ERZGEBIRGE, and from Silesia by the SUDETES, it is a fertile, hilly region, drained by the Elbe and Moldau rivers. Industries include mining (coal, silver, copper, lead, radium, uranium), especially in the Erzgebirge; textile and glass mfg.; heavy industries (centered in Prague region); brewing (notably at Pilsen). Many resorts (e.g., Carlsbad, Marienbad). Since the expulsion, after 1945, of most of German-speaking minority, population is overwhelmingly Czech. Bohemia takes its name from the probably Celtic Boii, whom Czech settlers displaced during 1st–5th cent. A.D. Temporarily subjugated by the Avars and later by MORAVIA, and Christianized by SS. CYRIL AND METHODIUS, it became a duchy of the Holy Roman Empire under ST. WENCESLAUS (d. 936). Later dukes of the PREMYSL dynasty acquired Moravia and most of SILESIA, and in 1198 OTTOCAR I took the title king. The vast conquests of OTTOCAR II proved ephemeral, and in 1306 the Premyslide line became extinct. Under the Luxembourg dynasty, particularly under Emperor CHARLES IV, Bohemia had its golden age. Charles's Golden Bull (1356) gave the kings of Bohemia the rank of ELECTORS. In the 15th cent. the HUSSITE WARS brought Bohemia into chaos. GEORGE OF PODEBRAD (d. 1471) restored peace, but he was the last native ruler. The crown passed first to the kings of Hungary (see JAGIELLO), and in 1526 to the house of HAPSBURG, which ruled it until 1918. Religious tension continued. When in 1618 Emperor Matthias abrogated religious freedom (granted 1609), the Bohemian diet in defiance deposed their Hapsburg king (later Emperor FERDINAND II) and elected FREDERICK THE WINTER KING. These events led directly to the THIRTY YEARS WAR (1618–48). The Protestant defeat at the WHITE MOUNTAIN (1620) ended Czech freedom. Bohemia became a Hapsburg crownland (1627) and was subjected to rigorous Germanization. Czech nationalism flared up in the Revolution of 1848, but was crushed in 1849. Later concessions to Czech demands for equal status in the AUSTRO-HUNGARIAN MONARCHY were insufficient; Czech disaffection was one of the causes of Austria's defeat in First World War. With the realization of Czech independence in 1918, the history of Bohemia became that of CZECHOSLOVAKIA.

Bohemian Forest, Czech *Český Les,* Ger. *Böhmerwald,* thickly wooded mountain range along border of Bohemia, Czechoslovakia, and Bavaria, Germany. S section called *Šumava* in Czech. Highest point, Arber (4,780 ft.), is in Bavaria.

Bohemond I (bō'hùmónd), c.1056–1111, prince of Antioch (1099–1111), a leader in First Crusade; son of ROBERT GUISCARD. Swore fealty to ALEXIUS I but, upon capturing Antioch, made himself prince (1098). Defeated by Alexius (1108), he acknowledged him as overlord but retired and made TANCRED regent.

Böhm, Dominikus (dômē'nēkoōs bûm'), 1880–1955, German architect. His Catholic churches strongly influenced 20th-cent. ecclesiastical architecture.

Böhme, Jakob: see BOEHME, JAKOB.

Böhmerwald: see BOHEMIAN FOREST.

Bohol (bôhôl'), island (1,491 sq. mi.; pop. 665,270), Philippines, N of Mindanao and between Cebu and Leyte. Produces rice, hemp, and manganese.

SMALL CAPITALS = cross references. Pronunciation key on inside end pages. Abbreviations: p. 2.

Bohr, Niels Henrik David (nĕls' hăn'rĕk dä'vĕdh bōr), 1885–1962, Danish physicist. Won 1922 Nobel Prize in Physics for concept of structure of atom; reconciled this with quantum theory. Assisted in atomic-bomb research in U.S. (1938–39; 1943–45). Instrumental in founding Inst. of Theoretical Physics, Copenhagen.

Bohun (bōŏn), English noblemen of Norman descent. **Henry de Bohun,** 1st **earl of Hereford,** 1176–1220, was one of barons who forced King John to accept Magna Carta (1215). **Humphrey V de Bohun,** 2d **earl of Hereford** and 1st **earl of Essex,** d. 1275, led barons of Welsh Marches who returned (1263) to side of Henry III in BARONS' WAR. **Humphrey VII de Bohun,** 3d **earl of Hereford** and 2d **earl of Essex,** d. 1298, was constable of England and a leader of barons who forced Edward I to sign confirmation of the charters 1297. **Humphrey VIII de Bohun,** 4th **earl of Hereford** and 3d **earl of Essex,** 1276–1322, was one of lord ordainers attempting to curb Edward II in 1310. Aided in execution of Piers GAVESTON.

Bohuslän, Swed. *Bohuslän* (bōō'hüslĕn), historic province, SW Sweden, conquered from Denmark 1658.

Boiardo or **Bojardo, Matteo Maria** (mät-tä'ō mä-rē'ä bōyär'dō), 1441?–1494, Italian poet, count of Scandiano. Wrote the unfinished *Orlando Innamorato,* based on the Roland story. The poem was revised satirically by Francesco Berni, and the story was continued by ARIOSTO in *Orlando Furioso.*

Boïeldieu, François Adrien (bwäldyû'), 1775–1834, French composer, master of *opéra comique,* composer of *Le Calife de Bagdad, La Dame blanche.*

boil or **furuncle,** painful infected nodule in the skin, caused by microbes, commonly STAPHYLOCOCCUS AUREUS. Scrupulous cleanliness limits spread of infection; treatment includes application of moist heat, antibiotics and sometimes lancing and draining by physician. See also CARBUNCLE.

Boileau, Nicolas (nēkôlä' bwälō'), 1636–1711, French critic and poet. His verse treatise on poetics (1674) made him foremost spokesman of CLASSICISM. His poetic repute rests on *Le Lutrin* (1683), a mock epic, and on his *Satires* and *Épîtres.* Full surname Boileau-Despréaux.

boiler, steam-generating device consisting of fire box (furnace to burn fuel) and boiler proper (enclosed vessel where heated water becomes steam). Common types: fire-tube boiler (hot gases in tubes heat outside water) and water-tube boiler (water in tubes heated by outside gases). Safety valve prevents explosions.

boiling point, temperature at which substance changes from liquid to gas with bubbling called "boiling." Under constant pressure each substance has specific boiling point; lowering pressure lowers boiling point, and vice versa. When substance is at boiling point, there is no increase in temperature until VAPORIZATION is complete.

Boisbaudran, Paul Émile Lecoq de (pôl' ämēl' lûkôk' dü bwäbōdrä'), 1838–1912, French chemist. Discovered elements GALLIUM, SAMARIUM, and DYSPROSIUM; made contributions to field of spectroscopy.

Boisbrûlés (bwäbrülä') [from Fr.= burnt wood], name given part-Indian descendants of fur traders in W Canada. Important group in Red River Settlement and in Riel's Rebellion.

Boise (boi'sē), city (pop. 34,481), state cap., SW Idaho, largest city of state, on Boise R. Gold rush and estab. of military post in 1863 led to its founding. Became territorial cap. 1864. Grew as mining center, but with building of Arrowrock Dam (1911–15) began to draw wealth from orchards and fields. BOISE PROJECT increased agr. yield. Now important trade, transportation, and food-processing center.

Boise, river, SW Idaho, rising in three forks in mountains E of Boise. Flows NW, past Boise and Caldwell, to Snake R. at Oregon line. First explored by W. P. Hunt in 1811; called Reed's R. in early days for John Reed, fur trader from Astoria, who, near river's mouth, estab. post where he was killed, 1814. Used today in BOISE PROJECT.

Boise, Fort, fur-trading post, SW Idaho. Founded 1834 on Boise R. by Hudson's Bay Co. to rival Fort Hall. Moved 1838 to Snake R. near Boise R. mouth. Abandoned 1855.

Boise project, SW Idaho and E Oregon, in the Boise, Payette, and Snake river valleys, irrigating c.350,000 acres. Arrowrock division, between Boise and Snake rivers, is served by Arrowrock and Boise River dams in Boise R., three Deer Flat dams that create L. Lowell with canal from Boise R., and Anderson Ranch Dam in South Fork of Boise R. Payette division, between Boise and Payette rivers, is served by Deadwood Dam in Deadwood R., Black Canyon Dam in Payette R., and Cascade Dam in North Fork of Payette R. Power is produced at Anderson Ranch, Black Canyon, and Boise River dams, with some power supplied to Minidoka and Owyhee projects.

Boisguilbert, Pierre le Pesant, sieur de (pyĕr' lü püzä' syûr' dü bwägĕlbĕr'), 1646–1714, French economist. Argued that mass consumption was as important as mass production, and urged income tax.

Bois-le-Duc, Netherlands: see 's HERTOGENBOSCH.

Boito, Arrigo (är'rēgō bō'ētō), 1842–1918, Italian composer and librettist. His only significant opera is *Mefistofele.* More important are his librettos for Verdi's *Otello* and *Falstaff.*

Bojardo, Matteo Maria: see BOIARDO.

Bojer, Johan (yō'hän boi'ür), 1872–1959, Norwegian novelist, dramatist, noted for portrayal of Norwegian contemporary life, as in *The Power of a Lie* (1903), *The Great Hunger* (1916), *The Last of the Vikings* (1921).

Bok, Edward (William), 1863–1930, American writer. b. Netherlands; editor of the *Ladies' Home Journal* (1889–1919). His best book is autobiographical, *The Americanization of Edward Bok* (1920). He is buried at Iron Mt., Fla., near the Singing Tower he endowed.

Bokhara, Uzbek SSR: see BUKHARA.

Boksburg, city (pop. c.76,900), S Transvaal, Republic of South Africa, on the WITWATERSRAND. Gold- and coal-mining center.

Bol, Ferdinand (fĕr'dïnänt bôl), 1616–80, Dutch painter, studied with Rembrandt in Amsterdam.

Bolan Pass or **Bholan Pass** (both: bōlän'), Baluchistan region, West Pakistan; c.60 mi. long, rises to c.5,880 ft. Used by railroad. Historic route for invading India.

Boleslaus (bō'lüslôs), kings of Poland. **Boleslaus I** (the Brave), Pol. *Bolesław Chrobry,* c.966–1025 (reigned 992–1025), was the first Polish ruler to call himself king. He campaigned successfully against Germany, Bohemia, and Kiev but failed to unite all N Slavs under Polish rule. **Boleslaus III,** 1085–1138 (reigned 1102–38), reunited Poland by conquering his brother's share. By a treaty with Emperor Lothair II he was invested with Pomerania and Rügen as fiefs of Holy Roman Empire (1135).

Boleyn, Anne, 1507?–1536, queen consort of Henry VIII; his second wife and mother of Elizabeth. Henry divorced Katharine of Aragon to marry her. The marriage was generally unpopular; his ardor cooled; and she was executed for alleged adultery.

Bolgari: see BULGARS, EASTERN.

Bolingbroke, Henry of: see HENRY IV (England).

Bolingbroke, Henry St. John, Viscount: see ST. JOHN, HENRY.

Bolívar, Simón (sēmōn' bōlē'vär), 1783–1830, South American revolutionist, called the Liberator, b. Caracas. Participating in revolution against Spain from 1810, he was defeated (1812, 1815) but had liberated the N (Colombia, Venezuela, Ecuador, Panama) by 1822. Met in secret with SAN MARTÍN at Guayaquil (1822); San Martín withdrew from W campaign leaving Bolívar in command of army that won final triumph over royalist forces at Ayacucho (1824). Elected president of Venezuela (1819), also (Dec. 1819) president of Greater Colombia (present Colombia, Venezuela, Ecuador, Panama). He also organized government for liberated Peru and Bolivia. At the meeting he called at Panama (1826) to promote a united Spanish America, little was accomplished, but the meeting was beginning of Pan-Americanism. He resigned the presidency in 1830 and died of tuberculosis shortly thereafter. Hated by many during his lifetime for his tyrannical dictatorship, he is today revered as greatest of Latin American heroes.

Bolivia (Span. bōlē'vyä), republic (412,772 sq. mi.; 1964 est. pop. 3,519,532), W South America, one of two inland countries on continent. Legal cap. is SUCRE, but LA PAZ is political and commercial center. E section is tropical, N portion set in rain forests drained by rivers of Amazon basin, S part merging into the CHACO. The W section is Andean; one cordillera traces border of Chile, the other runs N-S through the center of Bolivia. In the SW is an extensive salt plain, and in the NW the great basin of L. Titicaca. On the high windswept plateau (Altiplano) between mountain ranges and in mountain valleys are the chief centers of population, industries, and transportation. Bolivia has some of the richest mines in the world—tin, silver, copper, wolframite, bismuth, antimony, zinc, lead, gold. Important mining towns are POTOSÍ and ORURO. Cities of COCHABAMBA and Tarija are agr. and commercial centers. There were Indian civilizations on the plateau long before the Inca became dominant, and today a large percentage of the Bolivian people are pure Indian. Spanish conquest began in 1538, when Gonzalo and Hernando Pizarro came in successful search for mineral wealth. Spanish poured in and developed mines, textile mills, and great landed estates, all with Indian labor. As part of the *audiencia* of Charcas, it was attached to viceroyalty of Peru until 1776, then to that of La Plata. Revolution against Spain began in 1809, but independence was gained only by victory of Sucre at Ayacucho (1824). Bolívar drew up a constitution; Upper Peru became Bolivia, Chuquisaca became Sucre. Because the boundaries of the *audiencia* of Charcas were vague and because all the republics were ambitious, Bolivian history has been plagued by disastrous border wars; a Bolivian attempt to re-unite Peru and Bolivia failed in 1839; war with Chile (1879–84; see PACIFIC, WAR OF THE) cost Bolivia the nitrate-rich coastal province of Atacama; trouble with Brazil over the Acre region led to Brazil's getting valuable wild-rubber forests (1903); a long-drawn-out dispute over the Chaco led to war (1932–35), in which Paraguay was the victor and Bolivia had to give up large claims. Minerals continued to be the chief basis of Bolivia's international trade, and petroleum found in SE Bolivia brought new railroad development. Demand for tin and wolfram in Second World War spurred economy. Bolivia declared war on Axis (1943) and joined UN (1945). From 1952 to 1964 the government was controlled by radical political party that nationalized the tin mines and instituted a program of agrarian reform. In 1964 a military junta took power, headed by Gen. René Barrientos Ortúno, who was elected president in 1966. In 1967 army patrols were harried by sporadic, but light, left-wing guerrilla activity.

Bollandists (bŏl'ŭndĭsts), group of Jesuits in Belgium, formed by Jean Bolland (17th cent.) and famous for compiling the *Acta sanctorum*, still being brought up to date.

Bolley, Henry Luke, 1865–1956, American plant pathologist. He discovered cause of potato scab, methods of preventing oak smut, bunt of wheat, and other diseases, and developed rust-resistant wheat and wilt-resistant flax.

boll weevil, snout beetle causing large yearly losses to cotton crop. Eggs are laid in holes made in bolls; larvae eat growing cotton fibers.

bollworm, name for two cotton pests: pink bollworm, larva of gelechiid moth, which feeds on blossoms, lint, and seeds; and cotton bollworm (corn earworm), larva of phalaenid moth, which burrows in bolls and also attacks corn, tomatoes, and tobacco.

Bologna, Giovanni da (jōvän'nē dä bōlō'nyä), 1524–1608, Flemish sculptor whose real name was Jean Bologne or Boulogne. Identified chiefly with the Italian Renaissance. Famous for his *Flying Mercury* and *The Rape of the Sabines* (Florence).

Bologna (bōlō'nyä), city (pop. 475,664), cap. of Emilia-Romagna, N central Italy. Cultural and commercial center. Of pre-Roman origin, city passed (8th cent.) under papal rule, but a strong free commune was estab. in 12th cent. Guelph-Ghibelline strife enabled several families to seize power over city in 14th–15th cent., Bentivoglio family being most notable. Papal rule, restored 1506, lasted (except during 1797–1815) until unification of Italy (1860). The famous Univ. of Bologna originated (11th cent.) with Roman law school and made city into one of main centers of medieval learning. Painting flourished 15th–17th cent. with Francia, the Carracci, Guido Reni. Seriously damaged in Second World War, Bologna retains many fine medieval palaces and churches. Its two leaning towers and its arcaded streets are characteristic.

Bolsena (bôlsä'nä), village, Latium, central Italy, near site of second VOLSINII, on a crater lake. Has 12th-cent. castle, a cathedral, and several medieval buildings.

Bolshevism and Menshevism (bōl'shŭvĭzŭm, bōl'–, mĕn'–shŭvĭzŭm), the two main branches of Marxist SOCIALISM in Russia from 1903 to 1918. In 1903 the Russian Social Democratic party split into two wings. The *Bolsheviki* [majority members], led by LENIN, advocated immediate revolution and establishment of dictatorship of the proletariat. The *Mensheviki* [minority members], led by PLEKHANOV, held that before reaching socialism Russia must pass through an intermediary democratic or bourgeois regime, like the rest of Europe. Bolsheviks favored a small, disciplined party; Mensheviks sought to appeal to masses and to cooperate with "bourgeois" parties. Within the Social Democratic party, which in theory remained united, the Bolsheviks soon lost their numerical superiority. In the RUSSIAN REVOLUTION of 1917 the Mensheviks cooperated with the Kerensky regime, which the Bolsheviks overthrew in Nov., 1917. The Communist party, formed 1918, absorbed or "liquidated" the remaining Mensheviks.

Bolton or **Bolton-le-Moors** (-lù-mōōrz'), county borough (pop. 160,887), Lancashire, England; textile center. Connected with Manchester by canal.

Boltwood, Bertram Borden, 1870–1927, American chemist, physicist. Discovered that radium is disintegration product of uranium, intermediate is ionium, and ultimate product is lead. Developed theories that led to discovery of isotopes and had bearings on origin of elements. Taught at Yale.

Boltzmann, Ludwig, 1844–1906, Austrian physicist; made contributions to kinetic theory and to statistical mechanics. The Stefan-Boltzmann law of radiation of a BLACK BODY bears his name.

Bolzano (bôltsä'nō), Ger. *Bozen*, city (pop. 89,070), cap. of Bolzano prov., Trentino–Alto Adige, N Italy, in S Tyrol. Tourist and health resort. Its position on Brenner road made it important medieval trade center. Population largely German-speaking.

Boma, town (pop. c.32,000), W Republic of the Congo; port on Congo estuary. A railhead, it exports timber, bananas, cacao, palm products. Cap. of Belgian Congo until 1929, when cap. was moved to Leopoldville.

bombax, family of deciduous trees (Bombacaceae) found chiefly in American tropics. Important commercially are BAOBAB, BALSA, and KAPOK.

Bombay (bŏmbā'), former province (190,700 sq. mi.), W India, on Arabian Sea. Includes former Portuguese colonies of Goa, Saman, and Diu. In 3d cent. B.C. Bombay was part of Maurya empire. Under Moslem control 13th–17th cent. Portugal was leading foreign power in 16th cent., but Great Britain predominated from 17th cent. Baroda and Kolhapur were largest of several former native states absorbed 1947. In 1956 parts of Hyderabad, Madhya Pradesh, and the princely states of Kutch and Saurashtra were absorbed. In 1960 Bombay was divided into the new states of GUJARAT and MAHARASHTRA. **Bombay**, city (pop. 4,146,491), former cap. of Bombay prov., now cap. of Maharashtra. A major port and industrial center, was hq. of British East India Co. (1668–1858). Cotton-textile industry; petroleum refinery; atomic reactor; hydroelectric stations.

Bomoseen, Lake (bōmŭsēn'), 7½ mi. long and 1½ mi. wide, W Vt., W of Rutland; largest lake wholly within Vt. Popular summer resort.

Bon, Cape (bŏn) or **Ras Addar**, headland, NE Tunisia, jutting into Mediterranean. German forces in N Africa surrendered here to Allies in May, 1943.

Bona Dea (bō'nŭ dē'ŭ), in Roman religion, a fertility goddess worshiped only by women.

Bonanza Creek, stream of the Yukon flowing into Klondike R. at Dawson. Famous in gold-rush days.

Bonaparte (bō'nŭpärt), Ital. *Buonaparte* (bwōnäpär'tä), family name of NAPOLEON I. His father, **Carlo Buonaparte**, 1746–85, a lawyer in Ajaccio, led pro-French party in Corsica. His mother, **Letizia** or **Laetitia Ramolino Bonaparte**, 1750–1836, "Madame Mère," was noted for her stoic virtues. She retired to Rome after Napoleon's fall. Their eldest son, **Joseph Bonaparte**, 1768–1844, was king of Naples (1806–8) and of Spain (1808–13); inefficient on both thrones. Lived mainly at Bordentown, N.J., from 1815–1841; died in Italy. His brother **Lucien Bonaparte**, 1775–1840, helped Napoleon in coup d'état of 18 BRUMAIRE but opposed establishment of empire. Retired to Rome; created prince of Canino by pope. His sister **Elisa Bonaparte**, 1777–1820, married Felice Bacciochi (an infantry captain). Napoleon made her princess of Lucca (1805), grand duchess of Tuscany (1809). Intelligent administrator. Another brother, **Louis Bonaparte**, 1778–1846, king of Holland (1806–10), married Hortense de BEAUHARNAIS. Deposed by Napoleon for defying Continental System. Died in Italy. **Pauline Bonaparte**, 1780–1825, Napoleon's favorite sister, was beautiful but frivolous. Accompanied her first husband, Gen. Leclerc, to Haiti; married Camillo Borghese, a Roman noble, 1803; was made princess of Guastalla 1806. Another sister, **Caroline Bonaparte**, 1782–1839, married Joachim MURAT, was queen of Naples (1808–15), intrigued against Napoleon. Fled to Austria after Murat's execution. Youngest brother, **Jérôme Bonaparte**, 1784–1860, king of Westphalia (1807–13), was extravagant and irresponsible. Early marriage (1803) with Elizabeth PATTERSON, on a visit to U.S., was annulled on pressure by Napoleon. Later married a princess of Württemberg. Returned to France 1847, lived at court of Napoleon III. Among second generation of family, NAPOLEON II (duke of Reichstadt) and NAPOLEON III were most important. Other members also gained prominence. **Charles Lucien Bonaparte**, 1803–57, prince of Canino, son of Lucien, noted ornithologist, lived in U.S. 1824–33, wrote *American Ornithology* (4 vols., 1825–33). **Pierre Napoléon Bonaparte**, 1815–81, another son of Lucien, entered French politics, supported Napoleon III, and killed a journalist during a quarrel (1870) but was acquitted of murder. Notoriously immoral. **Napoléon Joseph Charles Paul Bonaparte**, 1822–91, son of Jérôme, was known as Prince Napoleon or, familiarly, Plon-Plon. At the court of Napoleon III he advocated a liberal policy. His sister, **Mathilde Bonaparte**, 1820–1904, was prominent at Napoleon III's court. Napoleon III's only son, **Napoléon Eugène**

Louis Jean Joseph Bonaparte, 1856–79, the Prince Imperial, was killed fighting the Zulus as a member of the British army. The claim to the Bonapartist succession passed to the descendants of Jérôme by his second marriage. From Jérôme's marriage with Elizabeth Patterson the American branch of the family is issued: **Jerome Napoleon Bonaparte**, 1805–70, and his son, **Charles Joseph Bonaparte**, 1851–1921, U.S. Secretary of the Navy (1905–6) and Attorney General (1906–9). He was active in antitrust suits and was among founders of National Municipal League.

Bonar Law, Andrew: see LAW, ANDREW BONAR.

Bonaventure (bŏnŭvĕn'chŭr) or **Bonaventura, Saint**, bōnäväntōō'rä), 1221–74, Italian-French scholastic theologian, a cardinal, Doctor of the Church, called the Seraphic Doctor, b. near Viterbo. At Univ. of Paris he studied under Alexander of Hales, then taught until he was made general of the Franciscans (1257) and cardinal bishop of Albano (1273). Early works in theology and philosophy were largely devoted to reconciling Aristotelian learning with Augustinian Christianity. Later writings are guides to mysticism, bringing the mystical tradition of St. Bernard of Clairvaux to full flower. Feast: July 14.

Bonaventure Island, 2½ mi. long and ¾ mi. wide, E Que., Canada, in Gulf of St. Lawrence N of Percé Rock. Largest bird sanctuary on N Atlantic coast.

Bonavista Bay, NE N.F., Canada. Irregular bay filled with islands; has many fishing villages on its shores. Bonavista Peninsula (S) ends in Cape Bonavista (S entrance to bay), reputed landfall of Cabot in 1497. Bonavista town is on S shore.

Bond, Carrie Jacobs, 1862–1946, American song writer. The popularity of such songs as *I Love You Truly, Just a-Wearyin' for You*, and *A Perfect Day* earned her a fortune.

Bond, Thomas, 1712–84, American physician. With Benjamin Franklin, he helped estab. at Philadelphia the first hospital in U.S. (1752).

Bond, William Cranch, 1789–1859, and a son **George Phillips Bond**, 1825–65, American astronomers, pioneers in celestial photography. Both were associated with Harvard Observatory.

bond, in finance, formal contractual obligation issued in writing by governments or corporations in return for loans. Bears interest and comes to maturity after definite period. They are important money-raising device; U.S. issued bonds to finance both World Wars.

Bond Street, street in London noted for elegant shops. Fashionable residential street 18th–early 19th cent.

Bône (bōn), city (pop. c.164,844), NE Algeria, Mediterranean port. Exports iron and phosphates. Once a Carthaginian colony and cap. of Numidian kings. Flourished as Hippo Regius in Roman times and was episcopal see of St. Augustine.

bone, hard tissue composing SKELETON of most adult vertebrates. Permeated with microscopic canals and sheathed by fibrous membrane. Long bones contain marrow, important in forming blood corpuscles.

bone meal, ground bone used (because of phosphorus and nitrogen content) as fertilizer and feed.

boneset or **thoroughwort**, perennial North American herb (*Eupatorium perfoliatum*), with terminal clusters of small, white flowers in late summer.

Bo'ness, burgh (pop. 10,194), West Lothian, SE Scotland, on the Firth of Forth; industrial center. Name is contraction of Borrowstounness. James Watt's first condensing steam engine built at adjacent Burn Pitt Colliery in 1765.

Bonham (bŏn'ŭm), city (pop. 7,357), NE Texas, NE of Dallas. Processes cheese, cotton, and truck crops. U.S. veterans' hospital is here, and replica of Fort Inglish is near.

Bonheur, Rosa (bŭnŭr'), 1822–99, French painter of animals. Her *Horse Fair* is in the Metropolitan Mus.

Bonhoeffer, Dietrich (dē'trĭkh bôn'hŭfŭr), 1906–45, German Protestant clergyman. Early influenced by thinking of Karl Barth. A fierce critic of tyranny of

Natl. Socialism, he was a leader in the church's resistance to the regime. Headed influential, secret theological school from 1935 until it was closed by Gestapo in 1940. Arrested 1943; hanged 1945, a few days before his prison was liberated. Writings include *The Cost of Discipleship* (Eng. tr., 1948) and *Prisoner for God* (Eng. tr., 1953).

Bon Homme Richard: see JONES, JOHN PAUL.

Boniface, Saint (bŏn'ĭfŭs, –fās), c.675–754? English missionary called the Apostle of Germany, a monk originally named Winfrid. Leaving England in 718, he soon devoted himself to the task of converting pagan Germany, which he and his companions almost completed in his lifetime. He founded many bishoprics and many abbeys (including Fulda). He was made bishop (722), missionary archbishop (732), and archbishop of Mainz (745). He was killed by pagans in Friesland. Feast: June 5.

Boniface VIII, 1235–1303, pope (1294–1303); originally named Benedetto Caetani; successor of Celestine V. Boniface tried to assert papal authority but was not successful. He interfered unsuccessfully in Sicily, further muddied the waters of the quarrel of GUELPHS AND GHIBELLINES, and was involved in a bitter struggle with PHILIP IV of France. Boniface tried to stop Philip from collecting illegal taxes from the clergy, issuing the bull *Clericis laicos* (1296), but he was forced to agree with Philip. New trouble caused the pope to thunder forth in the bulls *Ausculta fili* (1301) and *Unam sanctam* (1302; the most extreme statement ever made of the duty of princes to be subject to the pope), but the king sent a deputation to depose Boniface. After Sciarra Colonna, one of the deputies, struck Boniface, the enraged people of Anagni drove the French out. Boniface died soon afterward. Philip forced Pope CLEMENT V to repudiate the acts of Boniface. Boniface, an able canon lawyer, issued a code called the *Sext.*

Boniface (bŏn'ŭfăs), d. 432, Roman general, governor and count of Africa. His refusal to obey his recall (427) led to warfare with imperial government. Made truce with Rome when Vandals under Gaiseric invaded Africa. Defeated by Vandals at Hippo (430), he was recalled to Italy by Galla Placidia to help her against AETIUS. Boniface defeated Aetius but died of wounds.

Bonifácio, José (zhŏōză' bônēfä'sēō), 1763?–1838, Brazilian statesman, scientist, author, whose full name was José Bonifacio de Andrade e Silva. Returning to Brazil in 1819 after studying in Europe, he became leader of the movement for the independence of Brazil from Portugal.

Bonington, Richard Parkes (bŏn'–), 1802–28, English landscape painter known for his water colors.

Bonin Islands (bō'nĭn), Jap. *Ogasawara-gunto,* volcanic island group (40 sq. mi.; 1960 pop. 213), N Pacific, c.600 mi. S of Tokyo. Largest is Chichi-jima, site of U.S. naval base. Marcus Isl. (1 sq. mi.) lies to E. Under U.S. administration since 1945.

Bonivard, François de: see BONNIVARD, FRANÇOIS DE.

Bonn (bôn), city (est. pop. 141,929), provisional cap. of Federal Republic of Germany, in North Rhine-Westphalia, on the Rhine. Dates from Roman times. Residency of electors of Cologne 1263–1794. Passed to France 1801, to Prussia 1815. Univ. founded 1784. In 1948–49 delegates from parts of Germany occupied by France, Great Britain, and the U.S. met here and drafted constitution for Federal Republic of Germany.

Bonnard, Pierre (pyĕr bônär'), 1867–1947, French post-impressionist painter and engraver.

Bonneville, Benjamin Louis Eulalie de (bŏn'vĭl), 1796–1878, American army officer, trader in Far West, b. France. Colorful figure who failed as fur trader but helped open Rocky Mt. country.

Bonneville Dam, NW Oregon, on Columbia R., c.40 mi. E of Portland; built 1933–43 by U.S. Corps of Engineers. One of key dams in river, it is used for navigation, flood control, and power. Over-all length: 2,690 ft.; height: 197 ft.

Bonnie Prince Charlie: see STUART, CHARLES EDWARD.

Bonnivard or **Bonivard, François de** (fräswä' dù bônēvär'), c.1493–1570, Swiss hero of Byron's "The Prisoner of Chillon." Supported Geneva's revolt against Charles III of Savoy, who imprisoned him twice (1519–21, 1530–36). Freed when Bernese stormed CHILLON castle. Wrote chronicle of Geneva (published 1831).

Bonpland, Aimé Jacques Alexandre (āmä' zhäk' älĕksä'drù bôplä'), 1773–1858, French naturalist and author of works on Mexican and South American plants collected on travels with Humboldt.

Bontempelli, Massimo (mäs'sēmō bōntĕmpĕl'lē), 1878–1960, Italian novelist and critic. His fiction is bizarre and intellectual.

book, collection of written material, usually considered to have some sort of unity of thought in the contents (e.g., the divisions of anc. manuscripts); primarily today a written work of substantial proportions, printed and bound in a unit of one or more volumes. Volumes are still commonly graded by sizes with names derived from the number of times the original sheet on which the type is printed has been folded—folio, quarto, octavo (very popular modern size) and duodecimo. Papyrus fragments in Egypt preceded the regular organized manuscript book. The Greeks and Romans wrote books mainly on large papyrus rolls of varying size, though in the later period parchment was also used. The method of making books by binding collections of leaves came in the 2d cent. A.D. Vellum, a type of parchment, was popular with the monks who copied and produced the medieval books (some of these made very beautiful by illumination). Many manuscript books were made, but it was the introduction to Europe of PRINTING in the 15th cent. that made large-scale production possible. The development of books and printing thereafter was rapid and diverse. The book has been the primary dispenser of human knowledge. Making and selling of books today involves many specialized skills (editing, designing, printing, selling).

bookbinding, the art and skill of encasing a book (either manuscript or printed) in protective covering. The protective covering of ancient parchment rolls, unattached to the rolls, is not considered as bookbinding, which first arose in the Middle Ages, when boards were used to protect vellum sheets. Some medieval bindings are exquisite. The principle of folding and sewing sheets in small lots was same in the monasteries as in the modern bindery. After coming of printing to Europe, demand for bookbinder's work increased rapidly. The basic skills remain the same today, although machine binding has replaced hand binding to a large degree. The sheets are normally sewn together, and the covering is fastened on. In fine hand binding, the covering is made partly on the book itself; in machine binding, it is completed separately and glued on. Popular covering materials are heavy paper, boards covered with cloth or paper, vellum, leather (esp. morocco and calfskin), and imitation leather. With the development of mass-production processes and new materials, new methods of binding have become popular. "Perfect" binding uses glue without sewing. In other cases holes are punched through the pages and plastic fasteners (usually hinged) or spiral wire bindings are inserted.

Booker T. Washington National Monument: see WASHINGTON, BOOKER T.

Book of Common Prayer, service book of Church of England and other Anglican churches. Derived from breviary and missal, the first was published 1549; Thomas Cranmer's revision incorporated 1552. Suppressed under Queen Mary, restored under Elizabeth, suppressed (1645–60) under Commonwealth and Protectorate, it was again made official and compulsory by Act of Uniformity (1662). Protestant Episcopal Church adopted first U.S. revised version in 1789.

Book of Concord, collection of authoritative confessions of faith of Lutheran Church, published 1580.

Book of Kells: see KELLS, Co. Meath, Ireland.

Book of the Dead, Egyptian religious text, probably estab. in final form in 7th-6th cent. B.C., though charms, formulas, and other parts may be found in inscriptions as early as 16th cent. B.C.

Boole, George, 1815–64, English mathematician, logician. Known for theory of invariants and especially for works on logic. Boolean algebra named for him.

boomerang, curved throwing stick used as weapon. Small boomerang (1½ to 2 ft.), used only for sport, describes circle and returns to thrower. Large or war boomerang does not return. Though best known as Australian, boomerang has been used in many civilizations.

Boone, Daniel, 1734–1820, American frontiersman, b. near Reading, Pa. In March, 1775, as advance agent for Transylvania Co., he blazed WILDERNESS ROAD and founded Boonesboro (or Boonesborough) on Kentucky R. Captured by Indians in 1778 but escaped. Moved to Missouri after land titles in Ky. were invalidated. His adventures became well known through so-called autobiographical account by John FILSON.

Boone, city (pop. 12,468), central Iowa, NNW of Des Moines, on Des Moines R.; laid out 1865 by the railroad; nearby town of Boonesboro (founded 1851) annexed 1887. Industrial and mining center.

Boonesboro, locality, central Ky., on Kentucky R. and SE of Lexington. Named for Daniel BOONE who built fort here 1775 for TRANSYLVANIA COMPANY. Was Transylvania cap. for time; had Indian attacks.

Boonville, city (pop. 7,090), central Mo., on Missouri R., W of Columbia, in grain and livestock area; laid out 1817. Union troops won Civil War battle near here, June 17, 1861.

Boötes (bō-ō′tēz) [Gr.,= plowman], northern constellation; contains bright star Arcturus. Among earliest constellations recorded.

Booth, name of English family prominent in SALVATION ARMY. **William Booth,** 1829–1912, was an evangelist in London. There he and his wife, Catherine Mumford Booth (1829–90), estab. the Christian Mission which became (1878) the Salvation Army. A son, **Bramwell Booth,** 1856–1929, succeeded his father as general in 1912. Another son, **Ballington Booth,** 1859–1940, was commander in Australia and then in U.S. (1887–96). In 1896 with his wife he withdrew to found VOLUNTEERS OF AMERICA. A daughter of William Booth, **Emma Moss Booth-Tucker,** 1860–1903, with her husband jointly commanded the Army in U.S. (1896–1903). Another daughter, **Evangeline Cory Booth,** 1865–1950, was commander in Canada (1895–1904), commander in U.S. (1904–34), and general (1934–39).

Booth, Charles, 1840–1916, English social investigator, pioneer in social survey method. Headed group making exhaustive statistical study of London poverty (*Life and Labour of the People in London,* 17 vols., 1891–1903).

Booth, Edwin: see BOOTH, JUNIUS BRUTUS.

Booth, Evangeline Cory: see BOOTH, family.

Booth, Junius Brutus, 1796–1852, English actor of Shakespearean roles. After 1821 he lived in U.S. He was surpassed by his son **Edwin Booth,** 1833–93, first great American tragedian. Gentle actor of grace and rare restraint, he toured extensively with his father and achieved success (1857) with his debut in N.Y. as Richard III. Notable was his 100-night run of *Hamlet.* Toured England and built the Booth Theatre (N.Y., 1869), presenting Shakespeare there until his bankruptcy in 1873. Also founded the Players Club. Appeared last as Hamlet in 1891. Elected to Hall of Fame 1925. His career temporarily ceased (1865) when his brother, **John Wilkes Booth,** 1838–65, assassinated Abraham LINCOLN. A Confederate sympa-

thizer, unlike his family, Booth first plotted to abduct Lincoln, a plan which failed. On Good Friday, April 14, 1865, learning Lincoln would attend that evening's performance of *Our American Cousin* in Washington, he plotted (with accomplices) simultaneous assassination of Lincoln, Vice Pres. Johnson, and Secretary of State Seward. Seward was seriously wounded, while Johnson was spared. Booth entered the presidential box in Ford's Theater, shot Lincoln, vaulted to the stage (breaking his leg), and escaped on horseback. Found in a barn after two weeks' hysterical searching, Booth was shot (either by himself or his pursuers) and the barn was burned. See also M. E. SURRATT.

Booth, William: see BOOTH, family.

Boothbay, town (pop. 1,617), S Maine, S of Wiscasset; settled c.1680. Grew as shipping, shipbuilding, and fishing center. Now resort and artists' colony. **Boothbay Harbor,** town (pop. 2,252), was settled c.1630 and set off, 1889. Has summer theater.

Boothia Peninsula, northernmost tip of N Canada, Franklin dist., Northwest Territories, connected with mainland by Isthmus of Boothia. Discovered and explored by Sir John Ross (1829–33). Expedition of Sir John Franklin (1847–48) ended in tragedy. Also explored by Roald Amundsen (1903–5).

Booth-Tucker, Emma Moss: see BOOTH, family.

Bootle, county borough (pop. 82,829), Lancashire, England; port adjacent to Liverpool. Has tanning, engineering, and flour milling.

Booz (bō′ŏz), same as BOAZ.

Bopp, Franz (fränts′ bôp′) 1791–1867, German philologist, who demonstrated relationship of Indo-European languages in his *Vergleichende Grammatik* [comparative grammar] (1833–52).

boracic acid: see BORIC ACID.

borage, common name of herbs, tropical shrubs, and trees of Boraginaceae family. Most are native to Mediterranean area. North American varieties include VIRGINIA COWSLIP and species of FORGET-ME-NOT and HELIOTROPE.

Borah, William Edgar, 1865–1940, U.S. Senator from Idaho (1907–40), Republican. Notable for independent stands; major interest in foreign policy. Opposed League of Nations, but advocated disarmament. Opposed both economic monopoly and extension of governmental powers.

Borah, Mount, or **Borah Peak** [for W. E. Borah], 12,-662 ft. high, central Idaho, in Lost River Mts. Highest point in state.

borax, hydrated crystalline salt of sodium, boron, oxygen. Used as antiseptic, for cleaning textiles and metal surfaces, and in making glass, enamels, shellacs, ceramic glazes. In large doses it is toxic. In **borax bead test,** borax heated on loop to form "bead," then dipped in substance to be analyzed and reheated. Metals give bead different colors, e.g., cobalt, blue; copper, blue or green.

Borchgrevink, Carsten Egeberg (kär′stŭn ā′gŭbĕr′ bôrk′grä″vĭngk), 1864–1934, Norwegian antarctic explorer. Emigrated to Australia. Took part (1894) in first landing on Antarctica. Commanded (1898) first expedition to winter on continent.

Bordeaux, Henri, duc de: see CHAMBORD, HENRI, COMTE DE.

Bordeaux, Henry (ärē′ bôrdō′), 1870–1963, French novelist. Wrote popular stories with moral tone.

Bordeaux (bôrdō′), city (pop. 249,688), cap. of Gironde dept., SW France, on the Garonne; historic cap. of Aquitaine and Guienne. Seaport (accessible from Atlantic through Gironde R.); export center for wines from Bordeaux region. University founded 1441. As Burdigala, was provincial cap. under Romans; became archiepiscopal see in 4th cent. Under English rule 1154–1453. Temporary cap. of France 1914, 1940. Handsome 18th-cent. architecture. Montaigne and Montesquieu were magistrates in Bordeaux.

Bordeaux mixture, a FUNGICIDE, containing copper sulfate and lime and used as a spray or as a dust.

Borden, Gail, 1801–74, American inventor and surveyor. He patented (1856) a process for evaporating milk. Founder of Borden Milk Co.

Borden, Lizzie Andrew, 1860–1927, New England spinster, accused of killing father and stepmother (1892). Trial ended with verdict of not guilty.

Borden, Sir Robert Laird, 1854–1937, Canadian prime minister (1911–20). Led Canada through First World War. Helped define new status of self-governing dominions in British Empire.

Bordentown, city (pop. 4,974), W N.J., on Delaware R. between Trenton and Burlington and at W end of old Delaware and Raritan Canal; settled 1682. Partly destroyed by British, 1778. Clara Barton's school (built 1739) is Red Cross memorial.

Border, the, in British history, region about the boundary between England and Scotland, former scene of much strife. The wild country figures in legends, folklore, and the Border ballads.

Bordet, Jules (zhül' bôrdā'), 1870–1961, Belgian serologist and immunologist. Helped devise complement fixation technique later used in Wassermann test and discovered whooping cough bacillus. Won 1919 Nobel Prize in Physiology and Medicine for work in immunity.

Bordone, Paris (pä'rēs bôrdō'nä), 1500–1571, Venetian painter of portraits and of religious and mythological scenes; pupil of Titian.

bore, influx of tidal water into a river with wavelike front upstream from the wide mouth. Retarded by river current, it builds up a tidal wave.

Boreas (bō'rēŭs), in Greek legend, north wind; son of Astraeus and Eos.

Borel, Félix Édouard Émile (fālĕks' ādwär' āmēl' bôrĕl'), 1871–1956, French mathematician. Noted for his work in infinitesimal calculus and calculus of probabilities.

Borenius, Tancred, 1885–1948, art historian and teacher, b. Finland; active in England.

borer, common name for animals that penetrate organic tissue, e.g., corn borer (beetle), shipworm (mollusk), hookworm, hagfish and lamprey (fish). Method of penetration varies with each animal.

Borger (bôr'gŭr), city (pop. 20,911), extreme N Texas, NE of Amarillo, in the Panhandle and near Canadian R. Grew after oil discovery (1925).

Borges, Jorge Luis (hôr'hä lwēs' bôr'hās), 1899–, Argentine poet, critic, and short-story writer. One of great Spanish-American writers, known as exponent of *Ultraísmo* advocating use of bold images. A collection of his works appeared 1967 as *A Personal Anthology.*

Borghese (bôrgā'zā), Roman noble family. Among its members were Pope PAUL V, several cardinals, and many prominent citizens.

Borghese, Villa (vēl'lä bôrgā'zā), summer palace in Rome, commissioned by Scipione Cardinal Borghese, built by Vasanzio 1613–15. Now an art museum.

Borgia (bôr'jä), Span. *Borja* (bôr'hä), Spanish-Italian noble family. Among members were Pope CALIXTUS III, Pope ALEXANDER VI, and St. FRANCIS BORGIA. **Cesare Borgia** (chā'zärä), c.1475–1507, younger son of Alexander VI, was an outstanding figure of Renaissance. Cardinal at 17, he resigned after murder of his elder brother (in which he probably took part); entered politics. Allied himself with Louis XII of France, who created him duke of Valentinois, and with his father's encouragement made himself master of Romagna, duchy of Urbino, and other places (1499–1502). He then lured his chief enemies to castle of Sinigaglia, where he had them strangled (1502). His father's death (1503) and JULIUS II's election to papacy ruined his ambitions. Julius forced him to restore his possessions to the Papal States, and Louis XII turned against him. He found asylum with his brother-in-law, the king of Navarre, in whose service he died fighting. Vicious, ruthless, but of superior intelligence and vision, he was the model for Machiavelli's *Prince.*

His sister was **Lucrezia Borgia** (lōokrä'tsyä), 1480–1519. Her first marriage (1492–97) ended in annulment; her second husband, Alfonso of Aragon (a natural son of Alfonso II of Naples) was murdered by her brother Cesare in 1500. In 1501 she was married to Alfonso d'Este, who became duke of Ferrara in 1505. Once removed from family influence, Lucrezia won wide esteem through her beauty, kindness, piety, despite unfounded rumors of her crimes and vices. Her brilliant court included Ariosto.

Borglum, Gutzon (John Gutzon de la Mothe Borglum) (bôr'glŭm), 1867–1941, American sculptor. The gigantic Mt. Rushmore Natl. Memorial in S.Dak. is his best-known work. Borglum had not finished the monument when he died; it was completed by his son, Lincoln Borglum.

boric acid or **boracic acid,** white, crystalline, weakly acidic compound of boron, hydrogen, oxygen. Used as antiseptic (in solution), in pottery glazing, as fireproofing agent, and in making enamels. Poisonous if taken internally.

Borinage (bôrēnäzh'), region, S Hainaut, Belgium, surrounding Mons and extending W to French border. Important coal-mining district.

Boris, rulers of Bulgaria. **Boris I,** d. 907, ruled as khan 852–89. Baptized 864, he introduced Christianity of Greek rite among Bulgarians. **Boris III,** 1894–1943, tsar (1918–43), son and successor of Tsar FERDINAND. Set up royal dictatorship (1935); forced Rumania to restore S DOBRUJA (1940); joined Berlin Pact (1941; see AXIS). Died mysteriously soon after visiting Hitler. Succeeded by small son, Simeon II.

Boris Godunov: see GODUNOV, BORIS.

Borislav (bŭrēsläf'), city (pop. 28,500), W Ukrainian SSR, in Carpathian foothills. Center of oil region and of richest ozocerite deposits in Europe.

Borlange, Swed. *Borlänge,* city (pop. 26,820), Kopparberg prov., central Sweden, on Dal R. New industrial city, chartered 1944. Ironworks and paper mill among largest in Sweden.

Born, Max, 1882–, British physicist, b. Germany. Known for research in quantum mechanics. Shared with Walther Bothe 1954 Nobel Prize in Physics for developing method of very accurate time measurement.

Börne, Ludwig (lōōd'vĭkh bûr'nŭ), 1786–1837, German journalist, of Jewish origin, whose real name was Löb Baruch. With a generally satirical tone, he attacked censorship and encouraged liberalism. He and Heine are considered initiators of the Young German many movement.

Borneo, island (268,969 sq. mi.; pop. c.2,750,000), SW of the Philippines; largest of Malay Archipelago and third largest in world. Largely jungle and mountainous. Iron, copper, diamonds are mined, and there are great oil fields. Interior is inhabited mainly by Dyaks; the coastal areas by Malays, Javanese, and Chinese. The Portuguese visited Borneo in 1521, preceding the Dutch and the English. In 19th cent. the Dutch established their control over W, S, and E Borneo. In 1949 these territories became part of Indonesia. They are now called Kalimantan. Indonesia has more than two thirds of the island, the remainder being SABAH, BRUNEI, SARAWAK.

Bornholm, island (227 sq. mi.; pop. 48,-373), Denmark, in Baltic Sea, 24 mi. off Swedish coast. Low tableland, rocky and steep on N and W coasts. Agr., fishing; granite, kaolin. Chief town and port is Ronne.

Bornu (bôr'nōō), former sultanate, NE Nigeria, S and W of L. Chad. Divided at end of 19th cent. among Great Britain, France, and Germany; German portion mandated to Britain in 1922.

Borobudur or **Boroboedoer** (both: bō'rōbōōdōōr'), ruins of a Buddhist monument, Java, Indonesia. Within intricately carved truncated pyramid is a seated Buddha. Dates from 8th and 9th cent.

Borodin, Aleksandr (Porfirevich) (ŭlyĭksän′dŭr bôrô-dyĕn′), 1833–87, Russian composer. Though a chemist and physician, he belonged to the Russian FIVE. Chief works are two symphonies; a tone poem, *In the Steppes of Central Asia;* an opera, *Prince Igor.*

Borodino (bŭrŭdyĭnô′), village, RSFSR, W of Mozhaisk. Here in 1812 Russians under Kutuzov made heroic stand against Napoleon's advance on Moscow. Battle cost c.108,000 casualties.

Boroimhe, Brian: see BRIAN BORU.

boron (bō′rŏn), chemical element (symbol = B; see also ELEMENT, table), a brownish to yellow crystalline solid or an amorphous powder. Forms organic and inorganic compounds. Not found free in nature.

Borough, Stephen, 1525–84, English navigator. Master of first ship to round North Cape (1553) and reach Russia by arctic route. Thus direct trade relations became possible.

borough-English, a rule or custom in parts of England whereby land descended to the youngest son in preference to his older brothers. Abolished 1925.

Borromean Islands, Italy: see MAGGIORE, LAGO.

Borromeo, Charles: see CHARLES BORROMEO, SAINT.

Borromini, Francesco (fränchă′skō bōr-rōmē′nē), 1559–1677, Italian baroque architect. Designed San Carlo alle Quattro Fontane, Rome, a church noted for its undulating rhythm within a basically geometric plan. His innovations in palace and church design had tremendous influence in Italy and N Europe.

Borrow, George Henry, 1803–81, English writer. A wide wanderer, he distributed Bibles on the Continent and became a friend of the gypsies. Among his extraordinary books are *The Bible in Spain* (1843), *Lavengro* (1851), and *The Romany Rye* (1857).

Borstal system, method intended to rehabilitate delinquents (between ages of 16 and 21) by stressing good conditions, physical and vocational training. Originated 1902 at Borstal Prison, Kent, England.

Boru, Brian: see BRIAN BORU.

Borysthenes: see DNIEPER, river of USSR.

Bos, Jerom: see BOSCH, HIERONYMUS.

Bosanquet, Bernard (bō′zŭnkĭt), 1848–1923, British idealistic philosopher.

Bosch, Carl (bôsh), 1874–1940, German chemist. Shared 1931 Nobel Prize in Chemistry for adapting HABER PROCESS to achieve mass production.

Bosch, Hieronymus (hērôn′ĭmŭs bôs′), or **Jerom Bos** (yä′rôm bôs′), c.1460–1516, Flemish painter of fantasies peopled with diabolical little figures. A favorite of Philip II of Spain. Principal works still in Spain.

Boscoreale (bôs′kōräälä), town (est. pop. 16,774), Campania, S Italy, at foot of Vesuvius. Celebrated collection of silverwork (1st cent. A.D.) unearthed here in 1895 is now in the Louvre.

Bose, Sir Jagadis Chandra (jŭgä′dēs chŭn′drŭ bōs), 1858–1937, Indian physicist noted for research in plant life. He showed that plant responses to stimuli are in many ways similar to animal responses; he invented crescograph, for measuring plant growth.

Bosnia and Hercegovina (bōz′nĕŭ, hĕrtsŭgōvē′nŭ), autonomous republic (19,735 sq. mi.; pop. 3,274,886), W central Yugoslavia; cap. Sarajevo. Consists of Bosnia (N), with Sarajevo, and Hercegovina (S), with Mostar. Crossed by Dinaric Alps and Sava R., it is largely forested and agr. Area produces lignite and iron ore. The inhabitants are Serbs and Croats of Catholic, Moslem, and Orthodox faiths. Settled by Serbs in 7th cent., Bosnia appeared as kingdom in 12th cent.; occasionally acknowledged kings of Hungary as overlords; annexed Hercegovina from Serbia late 14th cent.; fell to Turkey 1463. Peasants, held in serfdom by Moslem landlords, rebelled 1875. Serbia and Russia intervened in their favor (see RUSSO-TURKISH WARS). Congress of Berlin (1878) placed Bosnia and Hercegovina under Austro-Hungarian administration but left it, in theory, under Turkish overlordship. Full annexation by Austria-Hungary (1908)

nearly brought war with Serbia and Russia, but German mediation in 1909 ended the crisis to Austria's satisfaction. Archduke Francis Ferdinand's assassination at Sarajevo precipitated First World War. Annexed by Serbia 1918, region became one of Yugoslavia's constituent republics 1946.

Bosporus (bŏs′pŭrŭs), strait, 20 mi. long, 1,800 ft. wide at its narrowest, separating European and Asiatic Turkey and joining Black Sea with Sea of Marmara. Istanbul lies on both shores. See also DARDANELLES.

Bossier City (bō′zhŭr), city (pop. 32,776), NW La., on Red River, NNE of Shreveport. Has railroad shops and processing plants. Site of Confederate Fort Smith is here; Barksdale Air Force Base is S.

bossism, in U.S. history, system of political control centered about one powerful figure (boss) and an organization of lesser figures (machine). Depends on manipulation of voters. Important in mid-19th cent. when newly arrived immigrants ignorant of American ways crowded cities. Often corrupt. Among famous bosses were TWEED in N.Y. city and James Curley in Boston.

Bossuet, Jacques Bénigne (bôsüä′), 1627–1704, French preacher and writer. A canon at Metz, then long tutor to the son of Louis XIV at court (1670–81), and finally bishop of Meaux, he was one of the most celebrated of all French preachers, his panegyric sermons and his funeral orations for the great being particularly notable. He wrote religious polemics in favor of Gallicanism, against the Protestants, and against the quietism of Fénelon. His *Discourse on Universal History* (1681) is a study of the hand of God in human history. His literary style is noted for vigorous purity, simplicity, and flashing eloquence.

Boston, municipal borough (pop. 24,903), Lincolnshire, England. Once an important port, now fishing center. John COTTON and other founders of Massachusetts Bay Colony sailed from here 1633.

Boston, city (pop. 697,197), state cap., E Mass., at head of Boston Bay. Largest New England city, major financial and cultural center, leading U.S. port, and important market for fish and wool. Industries include publishing, food processing, and mfg. of shoes, textiles, machinery, electronic equipment. Settled 1630 as main colony of MASSACHUSETTS BAY COMPANY, it was early center of Puritanism with vigorous intellectual life. Public library estab. 1653; colonies' first newspaper, *News-Letter,* pub. 1704. Important in prelude to Revolution (see BOSTON MASSACRE; BOSTON TEA PARTY; FANEUIL HALL; ADAMS, SAMUEL; REVERE, PAUL. Battle of BUNKER HILL was fought here, June 17, 1775, and city was besieged until March, 1776. After Revolution Boston prospered through world shipping and textile and shoe mfg. on New England rivers. Influence of rich and conservative Beacon Hill and Back Bay (patronized arts and letters, backed reformers, esp. the ABOLITIONISTS), persisted long after industrial growth brought many immigrants (mostly Irish at first). City annexed nearby towns and cities, e.g., Roxbury and West Roxbury (with BROOK FARM), Dorchester (where Richard Mather was minister), CHARLESTOWN. Landmarks include 17th-cent. house where Paul Revere lived, Old North Church, Old South Meetinghouse, Boston Common, King's Chapel (1785; birthplace of American Unitarianism), Boston Light (1716; oldest lighthouse in U.S.). At U.S. naval shipyard here is restored U.S.S. *Constitution.* Has Boston Symphony Orchestra (founded 1881), Boston Mus. of Fine Arts (1870), Boston Public Library (1852), NEW ENGLAND CONSERVATORY OF MUSIC, Boston Athenaeum (1807), and New England Medical Center. Seat of BOSTON PUBLIC LATIN SCHOOL, BOSTON UNIVERSITY, SIMMONS COLLEGE, Emerson Col., Emmanuel Col., and Northeastern Univ. HARVARD UNIVERSITY is mainly at nearby Cambridge. Prudential Center, a civic and commercial complex, opened 1965.

Boston College, near Chestnut Hill, Mass.; partly co-ed.; opened 1863.

Boston ivy or **Japanese ivy,** woody vine (*Parthenocissus tricuspidata*), popular for wall coverings. Its three-lobed leaves turn vivid red in the autumn.

Boston Massacre, 1770, pre-Revolutionary incident in which five members of rioting crowd were killed by British soldiers sent to Boston to maintain order and enforce TOWNSHEND ACTS.

Boston Mountains, NW Ark. and E Okla. N of Arkansas R., part of Ozark plateau, rising to c.2,400 ft. White R. has its source here.

Boston Public Latin School, at Boston, for boys; opened 1635; one of oldest free public schools in U.S.

Boston Tea Party, 1773, caused by retention of tea tax after repeal of TOWNSHEND ACTS. Group of indignant colonists, disguised as Indians, threw tea from three ships into Boston harbor.

Boston University, at Boston; coed.; founded 1839, chartered 1869. Has schools of theology, law, and medicine.

Boswell, James (bŏz'wŭl), 1740–95, British biographer, b. Scotland, author of *The Life of Samuel Johnson, LL.D.* (1791), one of the most celebrated biographies of all time. A Scottish lawyer, he traveled widely on the Continent and spent much time in London. He met Johnson in 1763, became a member of the Johnson circle, and in his biography noted minutely all the doings and sayings of the literary dictator. Among Boswell's other works are his *Account of Corsica* (1768) and *The Journal of a Tour in the Hebrides with Samuel Johnson, LL.D.* (1785; complete ed., 1936). His manuscripts and papers, most of them recovered in 20th cent. by Col. Ralph H. Isham, have yielded in published form *Private Papers* (18 vols., 1928–34), *Boswell's London Journal, 1762–1763* (1950), and other volumes.

Bosworth Field, Leicestershire, England. Scene of battle (1485) in which Richard III was killed and the crown passed to his victor, Henry VII.

botanic garden, place in which plants are grown for display and scientific study. Performs diversified functions, e.g., plant breeding, maintenance of libraries and herbariums, administration of educational programs, research. Botanic gardens are found in or near most large cities.

botany, scientific study of plant life. Botany and zoology together comprise science of BIOLOGY. Beginnings of plant classification found in work of Aristotle but system of binomial nomenclature established by Linnaeus marked greatest progress in systematics. Among those who contributed to the growth of botany: Robert Brown, A. P. de Candolle, Hugo de Vries, Asa Gray, Nehemiah Grew, John Ray, Lamarck, Mendel, Hugo von Mohl, Julius von Sachs. See *ills.,* pp. 858, 859.

Botany Bay, inlet, New South Wales, Australia, just S of Sydney. Named by Capt. Cook and the botanist Sir Joseph Banks. Though Australia's first penal colony was often called Botany Bay, its actual site was Sydney.

Botev, Khristo (khrĭ'stō bō'tĕf), 1848–76, Bulgarian poet and patriot, a leader of the revolution against Turkey (in which he was killed).

botfly, hairy fly with parasitic larvae. Horse botfly eggs, laid on horse, mule, donkey hair, are carried by tongue or lips, to mouth, and migrate to stomach, attaching to lining. Ox warble flies (heel fly; bomb fly) lay eggs on cattle, other animals; larvae migrate through skin, cause swellings (warbles). Sheep botfly or gadfly attacks sheep, goats, deer, sometimes man. Mosquitoes and other insects carry eggs of one species to humans.

Botha, Louis (bō'tŭ), 1862–1919, South African soldier and statesman. Led Boers in South African War, but after 1902 favored working with the British. Premier of the Transvaal, 1907–10, and of Union of South Africa, 1910–19. In First World War he led forces which took German South-West Africa.

Bothe, Walther (väl'tŭr bō'tŭ), 1891–1957, German physicist. During World War II he worked on German atomic energy research. Shared with Max Born the 1954 Nobel Prize in Physics for developing method of very accurate time measurement.

Bothnia, Gulf of, northernmost portion of Baltic Sea, between Finland and Sweden.

Bothwell, James Hepburn, 4th earl of, 1536?–1578, Scottish nobleman; third husband of MARY QUEEN OF SCOTS. After murder of RIZZIO (1566), Mary trusted only Bothwell. Accused of murdering her husband, Lord DARNLEY, Bothwell was acquitted in rigged trial and married Mary, 1567. Scottish aristocracy attacked him and forced Mary to give him up. Fled to Denmark, was imprisoned, and died insane.

bo tree or **pipal,** fig tree (*Ficus religiosa*) of India, sacred to Buddhists. An ancient specimen grows at Anuradhapura.

Botswana (bŏtswä'nŭ), formerly **Bechuanaland** (bĕchōōä'nŭ–), independent country (c.220,000 sq. mi.; pop. c.543,105), S central Africa; cap. Gaberones. Mainly arid plateau, with Kalahari desert in S and E. The Okavango R. in NW leads into swamps and L. Ngami. Cattle, sheep, and goats exported; mineral exports include manganese, asbestos, gold. Some ranching and irrigated farming. Francistown, on railroad, is commercial center. Bushmen, the original inhabitants, live mainly in Kalahari desert; majority of people are of Sotho origin. Robert Moffat and David Livingstone traveled through the region in 19th cent., and it came under British protection in 1885. Protectorate gained independence in Sept., 1966, with Seretse Khama as first president.

Böttger, Johann Friedrich (yō'hän frē'drĭckh bût'khŭr), 1682–1719, German chemist, originator of Dresden china. Developed various glazes and perfected white porcelain.

Botticelli, Sandro (sän'drō bôt"tĭchĕl'lē), c.1444–1510, Florentine painter of the Renaissance; a pupil of Fra Filippo Lippi. Famous are his *Spring* and *Venus.*

botulism (bŏt'ŭlĭzŭm), food poisoning caused by toxin produced by a bacillus (*Clostridium botulinum*). Toxin attacks nervous system; fatal respiratory paralysis common sequel unless antitoxin serum is given.

Botvinnik, Mikhail Moiseevich (mēkhŭyĕl' bŏt'vēnyĭk), 1911–, Russian chess champion. Became chess master at age 16. From 1931 to 1953 was USSR champion seven times. World champion 1948–56, 1958–60, 1961.

Bouaké (bwä'kä, bwäkä'), town (pop. c.70,000), central Ivory Coast. Commercial and industrial center; textile and sisal production; chrome mined nearby.

Boucher, François (fräswä' bōōshä'), 1703–70, French painter. Famous for boudoir decorations, he was the most fashionable painter of his day. Became director of Gobelins factory.

Boucher de Crèvecœur de Perthes, Jacques (zhäk', dù krěvkûr' dù pěrt'), 1788–1868, French writer and archaeologist whose researches demonstrated the antiquity of man. See PALEOLITHIC PERIOD.

Bouches-du-Rhône (bōōsh'-dü-rōn'), department (2,026 sq. mi.; pop. 1,248,355), SE France, in Provence; cap. Marseilles. Includes Rhone delta, CAMARGUE.

Boucicault, Dion (bōō'sĭkō), 1822?–1890, British playwright, actor; in U.S. after 1853. Among his more than 300 plays and adaptations (in many of which he acted) are *The Octoroon* (1859), *The Colleen Bawn* (1860), and *Rip van Winkle* (1865).

Boucicaut (bōōsěkō'), c.1366–1421, marshal of France; real name: Jean Le Meingre. Captured by Turks at NIKOPOL 1396. Ransomed, he helped in defense of Constantinople 1399. Governor of Genoa 1401–7. Died in England after capture at Agincourt (1415). Wrote ballads, other poems.

Boudin, Eugène Louis (ûzhĕn' lwĕ' bōōdĕ'), 1824–98, French landscape and marine painter.

Boudinot, Elias (boō'dĭnŏt), 1740–1821, American Revolutionary statesman. Member of Continental Congress (1777–78, 1781–84). Supported the Constitution. Director, U.S. mint (1795–1805).

Bougainville, Louis Antoine de (lwē' ätwän' dù boōgēvēl'), 1729–1811, French navigator. Made voyage around the world (1767–69), rediscovering Solomon Isls., largest of which is named for him. In American Revolution fought Hood at Martinique. Wrote *Description d'un voyage autour du monde.*

Bougainville (boō'gŭnvĭl), volcanic island (c.3880 sq. mi.; pop. 51,764), S Pacific, largest of SOLOMON ISLS. Exports copra, ivory nuts, green snail, cocoa, and tortoise shell.

bougainvillea (boō"gŭnvĭl'ēù), woody vine (*Bougainvillea*) of tropical America, cultivated in S and W U.S. for their showy red or purple bracts that enclose flowers.

Bougie (boōzhe'), city (pop. c.63,000), NE Algeria; port on the Mediterranean. Anc. port, it was refounded by Berbers in 11th cent., became cultural center for NW Africa. Occupied successively by Spanish, Turks, and French. N terminus of pipeline from the Sahara.

Bouguereau, Adolphe William (ädôlf' boōgŭrō'), 1825–1905, French academic and sentimental painter.

Bouillon, Godfrey of: see GODFREY OF BOUILLON.

Bouillon, Henri de la Tour d'Auvergne, vicomte de Turenne, duc de (ärē' dù lä toōr' dôvēr'nyù, vēkôt' dù türēn' dük dù boōyō'), 1555–1623, marshal of France and Protestant leader; a grandson of Anne de Montmorency. Acquired duchy of Bouillon by marriage. Briefly a member of regency council under Marie de' Medici, he retired to his duchy after quarrel with queen. His older son, **Frédéric Maurice de la Tour d'Auvergne, duc de Bouillon** (frädärēk' mōrēs'), c.1605–1652, French general, took part in the CINQ MARS conspiracy but was pardoned. He espoused Catholicism, sided with the princes during Fronde, lost his principality of Sedan to France. TURENNE was his brother.

Bouillon, town (pop. 2,830), Luxembourg prov., S Belgium, in the Ardennes. Its ancient castle belonged to Godfrey of Bouillon, who sold it to bishop of Liège 1095. In 15th cent. town and environs passed to William de la Marck, whose heirs assumed titles duke of Bouillon and prince of Sedan. Bouillon was annexed to France 1678–1815.

Boulanger, Georges (zhôrzh' boōläzhä'), 1837–91, French general, "the man on horseback." Minister of war, 1886–87; leader of nationalist reactionary movement—Boulangism—which foreshadowed fascism. Won overwhelming victory at polls 1889. A military coup d'état seemed imminent, but Boulanger lost his nerve, fled to Belgium, and killed himself.

Boulanger, Nadia, 1887–, French teacher of composition, professor at the Paris Conservatoire after 1945. Many American composers studied under her (e.g., Aaron Copland, Virgil Thomson).

Boulder, city (pop. 37,718), N central Colo., NW of Denver on Boulder Creek; laid out 1859. A mineral spring resort and the rail and trade center of mining and farming area. Seat of Univ. of COLORADO and Natl. Center for Atmospheric Research. U.S. atomic energy plant is nearby.

boulder, any large rock fragment, either formed from bedrock below or transported by water or ice.

Boulder City, city (pop. 4,059), S Nev., W of Hoover Dam near L. Mead. Built by U.S. as hq. for dam; made self-governing municipality 1958. Tourist center.

boulder clay, unstratified mixture of clay, sand, gravel, and boulders left by retreating glacier.

Boulder Dam: see HOOVER DAM.

Boulle or Buhl, André Charles (both: ädrä' shärl' boōl'), 1642–1732, French cabinetmaker who created a distinctive furniture style roughly similar to Louis XIV and Regence design. Excelled in marquetry.

Boulogne-sur-Mer (boōlô'nyù-sür-mēr'), city (pop. 49,281), Pas-de-Calais dept., N France; por on English Channel. From here the Romans sailed A.D 43 to conquer Britain. Statue of Our Lady of Boulogne, in cathedral, is object of pilgrimages.

Boulton, Matthew (bōl'tùn), 1728–1809, English engineer and manufacturer, partner from 1775 of James Watt in production of steam engines. New British copper coinage estab. 1797 by Boulton.

Boumedienne, Houari (hwä'rē boōmûdyēn'), 1923–, Algerian soldier and political leader. Was early member of National Liberation Front (FLN). Rose through ranks to become army chief of staff. After Algerian independence in 1962, he became minister of defense and first vice president. In June, 1965, he deposed Pres. Ben Bella and set up a revolutionary council with himself as chief of state. His government joined with the Arab nations in their war against Israel in mid-1967.

bouncing Bet: see SOAPWORT.

Boundary Peak, 13,140 ft. high, SW Nev., in White Mts. near Calif. line. Highest point in Nev.

Bound Brook, borough (pop. 10,263), N central N.J., on Raritan R., NW of New Brunswick; settled 1681. Site of Cornwallis victory (April, 1777).

Bountiful, city (pop. 17,039), N central Utah, N of Salt Lake City, in irrigated truck-farm area; settled 1847 by Mormons. Has early Mormon chapel.

Bounty, British naval ship, scene of noted mutiny (1789) while on long trading voyage in the Pacific. Capt. William BLIGH and 18 of crew were set adrift in small boat; sailed c.4,000 mi. to Timor. Some mutineers settled on PITCAIRN ISLAND.

bounty, premium paid by state to encourage production or export of favored goods, or as substitute for protective TARIFF. Usually direct cash payments, but may take such form as tax exemptions or rebates. Money payments formerly made to induce army enlistment. Rewards for killing destructive animals also called bounty.

Bourassa, Henri (boōräsä'), 1868–1952, Canadian political leader; grandson of Louis Joseph Papineau. Led powerful opposition (Nationalist) party in Quebec. Opposed diplomatic entanglements with U.S. and Great Britain; also against participation in First World War.

Bourbon (boōrbō'), royal family which ruled in France, Spain, the Two Sicilies, and Parma; a cadet branch of the Capetians. Takes its name from castle in Bourbonnais (now Allier dept.), whose first lord was Adhémar, a 9th-cent. noble. In 1272 Robert of Clermont, sixth son of Louis IX of France, married the heiress of Bourbon. His son Louis was 1st duke of Bourbon. His descendant, **Charles, duc de Bourbon** (shärl', dük' dü), 1490–1527, constable of France, treacherously went over to Emperor Charles V (1523); was killed while leading imperial troops in sack of Rome. His lands were confiscated; his title discontinued. A younger son of the 1st duke founded line of Bourbon-Vendôme. **Antoine de Bourbon** (ätwän'), 1518–62, duke of Vendôme, became king of Navarre by marrying JEANNE D'ALBRET. From his brother Louis descend the houses of CONDÉ and CONTI. Antoine's son became (1589) the first Bourbon king of France as HENRY IV. His direct descendants ruled FRANCE (except from 1792 to 1814) until 1830, when Charles X was deposed, and died out in 1883 with Henri, comte de CHAMBORD. The younger branch of Bourbon-Orléans (see ORLÉANS, family) gave France King Louis Philippe and inherited claim to throne. The house of Bourbon-Spain, Span. *Borbón,* began in 1700 with accession of Louis XIV's grandson, PHILIP V, on Spanish throne. The succession in SPAIN was contested (19th cent.) by CARLISTS against ISABELLA II. Alfonso XIII was deposed in 1931. The house of Bourbon-Sicily, sprung from the Spanish line, was founded (1759) by FERDINAND I of the TWO SICILIES and ceased to rule when Francis II abdicated (1861).

The house of **Bourbon-Parma** was founded (1748) by a younger son of Philip V of Spain. Robert (1848–1907), 5th duke of PARMA and Piacenza, was deposed in 1860. He had 18 children, among them Empress ZITA of Austria and Sixtus of Bourbon-Parma.

Bourbonnais (bŏŏrbônä'), region and former province, central France, in Allier and Cher depts.; historic cap. Moulins. Other towns: Vichy, Montluçon. Appanage of dukes of BOURBON until 1527.

Bourbon-Parma, Bourbon-Sicily, and **Bourbon-Spain:** see BOURBON, family.

Bourdelle, Émile Antoine (ämēl' ätwän' bŏŏrdĕl'), 1861–1929, French sculptor. Studied under Rodin.

Bourgelat, Claude (klōd' bŏŏrzhülä'), 1712–79, French founder of organized veterinary medicine; persuaded government to estab. first school of veterinary medicine at Lyons 1761.

Bourg-en-Bresse or **Bourg** (bŏŏrk-ä-brĕs'), town (est. pop. 26,699), cap. of Ain dept., E France, chief town of Bresse; a gastronomic mecca.

Bourgeois, Léon (lāō' bŏŏrzhwä'), 1851–1925, French statesman, social philosopher. Premier 1895–96. Early advocate of League of Nations; won 1920 Nobel Peace Prize. Chief work: *Solidarité* (1896).

bourgeoisie (bŏŏrshwäzē'), name applied to citizens of French towns and subsequently to middle class in all nations. Known in feudal times as Third Estate. If defined as mercantile or trading class, bourgeoisie has existed since earliest history and was powerful in ancient Rome. In eclipse in early Middle Ages, merchants later won contest with nobles. They turned increasingly to principles of constitutionality and natural rights against claims of divine right and promoted English, French, and American revolutions. MARX used term to denote class of modern capitalists (see MARXISM). As industrial change progressed, class expanded and differences within it became more distinct. Term *bourgeois* is often used to imply materialism and lack of culture.

Bourges (bŏŏrzh), city (pop. 60,632), cap. of Cher dept., central France; historic cap. of Berry. Arms and clothes mfg. Important in Roman times; early archiepiscopal see. University founded 1463, abolished in French Revolution. Cathedral and house of Jacques Cœur are glorious examples of French Gothic. See also PRAGMATIC SANCTION OF BOURGES.

Bourget, Paul (pôl' bŏŏrzhā'), 1852–1935, French writer. Catholic and conservative, he is noted for critical essays and for novels of psychological analysis (*Le Disciple,* 1889; *Le Démon de midi,* 1914).

Bourget, Le (lü), suburb of Paris, France; one of city's airports. Lindbergh landed here 1927.

Bourget, lake, c.11 mi. long, Savoie dept., E France. Aix-les-Bains is on its scenic shore.

Bourguiba, Habib (häbēb' bŏŏrgē'bü), 1903–, Tunisian statesman. Formed New Constitution party (1934) which led drive for Tunisian independence from France. Often imprisoned, he was finally released in 1954 to partake in negotiations which led to Tunisian autonomy 1954 and independence 1956. Elected premier 1956, chosen president by constituent assembly 1957, and elected president 1959.

Bourinot, Sir John George (bŏŏ'rĭnō"), 1837–1902, Canadian historian, known for standard works on the Canadian government.

Bourne, Francis (bôrn), 1861–1935, English Roman Catholic churchman, archbishop of Westminster (1903–35); made a cardinal 1911.

Bourne, Hugh (bŏŏrn), 1772–1852, English evangelist. Held outdoor revivals despite ban by Wesleyan Conference. Estab. Primitive Methodists 1810.

Bourne (bôrn), resort town (pop. 14,011), SE Mass., crossed by Cape Cod Canal S of Plymouth. Includes village of BUZZARDS BAY.

Bournemouth (bôrn'mŭth), county borough (pop. 153,965), Hampshire, England; popular resort and fine arts center on Poole Bay.

Boutens, Pieter Cornelis (bou'tüns), 1870–1943, Dutch lyric poet.

Bouts, Dierick or **Thierry** (dē'rĭk bouts', tyĕ'rē), c.1410–1475, Netherlands painter, famous for landscape backgrounds of his altarpiece panels.

Boutwell, George Sewall (bout'–), 1818–1905, U.S. Secretary of the Treasury (1869–73). His preoccupation with reduction of the national debt led to neglect of more important problems.

Bouvier, John (bŏŏvēr') 1787–1851, American jurist, b. France. His *Law Dictionary* (1839), often revised, is still standard in U.S.

Bouvines (bŏŏvēn'), village, Nord dept., N France, near Lille. Scene of victory (1214) of Philip II of France over King John of England, Emperor Otto IV, and count of Flanders.

Bovet, Daniele (bōvä'), 1907–, Italian pharmacologist, b. Switzerland. Won 1957 Nobel Prize in Medicine and Physiology for work leading to development of sulfa drugs, antihistamines, and muscle relaxants.

Bow, Clara, 1905–65, American film actress. The "It" girl of the 1920s, her films included *Mantrap, Dancing Mothers, Red Hair, It,* and *Wings.* She retired in 1933.

Bow, N.H.: see CONCORD.

Bow (bō), river of S Alta., Canada. Rises on E slope of the Rockies and flows 315 mi. SE through superb mountain scenery of Banff Natl. Park, past Calgary, to join Belly R., forming the South Saskatchewan R. On the Bow is the Bassano or Horseshoe Bend Dam.

bow and arrow. Usage probably dates from Paleolithic period; widely used until advent of gunpowder. Romans used mounted archers; infantry in Middle Ages were armed with bow and arrow. Crossbow, or bow on a stock, was much stronger than ordinary bow; longbow, of Welsh origin, was lighter and quicker and became predominant in Europe.

Bow Bells (bō), in church of St. Mary-le-Bow in mid-London. Traditionally only a person born in sound of Bow Bells is a true Londoner, a "cockney."

Bowditch, Nathaniel, 1773–1838, American navigator, mathematician. Corrected some 8,000 errors in Moore's *Practical Navigator;* new edition (*The New American Practical Navigator*) appeared under his name. His son **Henry Ingersoll Bowditch,** 1808–92, was a physician noted as authority on public health and on chest diseases. **Henry Pickering Bowditch,** 1840–1911, grandson of Nathaniel Bowditch, was known for work at Harvard Univ. in experimental physiology and medical education.

Bowdler, Thomas (boud'lür, bŏd'–), 1754–1825, English editor. His prudish textual expurgations (especially of Shakespeare) gave rise to term *bowdlerize.*

Bowdoin College, at Brunswick, Maine; for men; chartered 1794, opened 1802. Alumni include Hawthorne, Longfellow, and Franklin Pierce.

bowel: see INTESTINE.

Bowen, Elizabeth, 1898–, Anglo-Irish writer, author of subtle novels (e.g., *The House in Paris,* 1936; *The Death of the Heart,* 1938) and books of short stories (e.g., *Ivy Gripped the Steps,* 1946), all distinguished by their purity of style. *Bowen's Court* (1912) is about her family and home in Ireland.

bower bird, any of several species of birds native to Australia and New Guinea. Build stick-grass bower or arbor for play, courtship display. Gardener bower bird makes lawn around bower and decorates with bright objects. Nests are outside bowers.

Bowery, the (bou'ürē), section and street of lower Manhattan, New York city, between Chatham Square and Astor Place E of Broadway. Street was once a road to farm of Gov. Stuyvesant (buried at St. Mark's-in-the-Bouwerie). By 1860s section had many fine theaters; later became notorious for saloons and dance halls, and finally for derelicts.

Bowie, James (bŏŏ'ē), c.1796–1836, hero of Texas revolution who died at the ALAMO. Legend says bowie knife was named after him or his brother, Rezin Bowie.

Bowie, William, 1872–1940, American geodesist. Helped develop theory of isostasy, which deals with gravitational equilibrium of earth's crust.

bowlegs (*genu varum*), deforming curvature of legs, generally the result of rickets in early life.

Bowles, Samuel, 1797–1851, American newspaper proprietor; founded Springfield (Mass.) weekly *Republican*. His son, **Samuel Bowles,** 1826–78, who joined paper at 17 and took control at 25, made it (1845) a morning daily. He and an exceptional staff made the *Republican* one of the country's most influential newspapers. His son, **Samuel Bowles,** 1851–1915, gave close editorial direction to the paper, but wrote little himself. **Chester B(liss) Bowles,** 1901–, grandson of Samuel Bowles (1826–78), was governor of Conn. (1949–51), U.S. ambassador to India (1951–53), U.S. Representative (1959–60), and Undersecretary of State (1960–61).

bowling, sport played by rolling heavy ball to knock-down bottle-like pins on indoor alley. Originated in Germany, probably as Christian rite. Dutch introduced game in America, where it became popular in 19th cent. Standardized as 10-pin game in 1895, when American Bowling Congress was founded.

Bowling Green. 1 City (pop. 28,338), S Ky., on Barren R., SSW of Louisville; founded 1780. A shipping and market center in agr. area. Occupied by Confederates in Civil War until Federals forced their retreat 1862. Seat of Western Kentucky State Col. Nearby are Lost River Cave, reputed hideout of James brothers and Gen. J. H. Morgan, and ruins of Shaker settlement. **2** City (pop. 13,574), NW Ohio, SSW of Toledo, in farm area; settled 1833. Seat of BOWLING GREEN STATE UNIV.

Bowling Green State University, near Bowling Green, Ohio; coed.; chartered 1910 as a normal school, opened 1914; became college 1929, university 1935.

Bowman, Isaiah, 1878–1950, American geographer, b. Ontario. Led expeditions to South America. Territorial adviser to Pres. Wilson at Versailles conference, to Dept. of State in Second World War. President of Johns Hopkins Univ. 1935–48.

Bowring, Sir John, 1792–1872, British statesman and linguist. Governor of Hong Kong (1854), where he precipitated war with China. Known for translations from many languages.

box, evergreen shrub of genus *Buxus* of Asia and Europe. Common box (*Buxus sempervirens*), slow growing, prized for clipped hedges in S U.S.

Boxer Uprising or **Boxer Rebellion,** Chinese revolt (1899–1900) against widening interests of the foreign powers in China. Led by a secret society called I Ho Ch'üan [fists of righteousness and harmony] or the Boxers, with support of dowager empress, Tz'u Hsi. Revolt was crushed by the joint foreign forces of Britain, France, Italy, Germany, Austria, Russia, U.S., and Japan. China was forced in 1901 to agree to payment of huge indemnity, to permit stationing of foreign troops in Peking and approach to it through Tientsin, and to amend commercial treaties to the advantage of the foreign nations. China became, in effect, a subject nation.

boxing, sport of fighting with the fists, an ancient sport, included in original Olympic games. Marquess of Queensberry's rules (introduced 1865) became standard by 1889. Boxers today fight in a ring, a roped-off area about 20 ft. square. Professional boxing in U.S. largely controlled by rulings of National Boxing Association and various state athletic commissions.

Boyacá (bōyäkä'), locality, N central Colombia, where Bolívar defeated the Spanish (1819).

Boyce, William, 1710–79, English organist, composer. Compiled *Cathedral Music* (3 vols., 1760–78).

Boyce Thompson Institute for Plant Research, estab. 1924 at Yonkers, N.Y. through gifts of William Boyce

Thompson. Institute is known for research in many branches of botany; fine library; arboretum.

boycott [from Irish land agent, Capt. Charles C. Boycott], concerted economic or social ostracism of an offender (individual, group, nation, or product) to express disapproval or effect coercion. Used in labor disputes and as a weapon in political and racial issues.

Boyd, Belle, 1844–1900, Confederate spy in Civil War. Operated in Shenandoah Valley (1862).

Boyd, Louise Arner, 1887–, American arctic explorer. She led series of explorations for scientific study of E coast of Greenland. In 1955 she flew with photographic expedition over North Pole.

Boyd Orr, John: see ORR, JOHN BOYD ORR, 1ST BARON.

Boyle, Richard, 1st earl of Cork, 1566–1643, Irish statesman. Improved land, estab. ironworks, founded towns, created trade. As lord high treasurer of Ireland (1631) his opposition to Irish program of earl of STRAFFORD was a major cause of latter's downfall. His son, **Roger Boyle, 1st earl of Orrery,** 1621–79, was a statesman and writer who attempted to keep peace by supporting regime able to govern. Royalist until 1647, served Puritans until restoration of Charles II. Author of rhymed-verse tragedies. His brother **Robert Boyle,** 1627–91, a British chemist, was the first to distinguish between element and compound. He defined chemical reaction and analysis. *Boyle's law* states that at a constant temperature, the volume of confined gas decreases in proportion to increase in pressure.

Boylston, Zabdiel, 1679–1766, American physician. He introduced in U.S. inoculation against smallpox during Boston epidemic of 1721.

Boyne, river of Ireland, flows 70 mi. NE through Co. Kildare and Co. Meath to the Irish Sea near Drogheda. William III defeated James II in the battle of the Boyne, 1690.

Boynton Beach, city (pop. 10,467), SE Fla., S of West Palm Beach.

Boyron, Michel: see BARON, MICHEL.

Boy Scouts, world-wide, nonmilitary organization of boys over 12 years old; founded 1908 by Sir Robert Baden-Powell; inc. in U.S. 1910. Similar movements in U.S. led by Dan Beard and Ernest Thompson Seton. Program designed to better mental, moral, physical development, increase knowledge of outdoors, train for citizenship.

Boys Town, village (pop. 997), E Nebr., founded by Mgr Edward J. Flanagan as community for homeless and abandoned boys.

Bozeman, John M. (bōz'mŭn), 1835–67, American pioneer. Found short route in 1862–63 from Bannack, Mont., to Colo., lying E of Bighorn Mts., known as **Bozeman Trail.** In 1865–66 U.S. government estab. forts to guard it; after FETTERMAN MASSACRE part of trail was abandoned.

Bozeman, city (pop. 13,361), SW Mont., SE of Butte; founded 1864 by J. M. Bozeman. Center of farm and livestock area and gateway to Yellowstone Natl. Park. Montana State Univ., part of Univ. of MONTANA, is here.

Bozeman Trail: see BOZEMAN, JOHN M.

Bozen, Italy: see BOLZANO.

Bozzaris, Marco or **Markos** (bôt'särēs), c.1788–1823, Greek hero in War of Independence. Defended Missolonghi against Turks (1822–23); defeated superior Turkish army at Karpenisi but fell in battle.

Br, chemical symbol of the element BROMINE.

Brabant (brŭbänt'), former duchy, now divided among the Belgian provs. of ANTWERP and of Brabant (1,268 sq. mi.; est. pop. 2,085,294; cap. Brussels) and Dutch prov. of NORTH BRABANT. The duchy emerged from the duchy of Lower Lorraine (12th cent.). Louvain was its cap. until Brussels superseded it (15th cent.). The textile industries and commercial enterprise of its cities gave medieval Brabant extraordinary prosperity. The cities were granted virtual self-government by the dukes, who in 1356 granted a charter, known as *Joyeuse Entrée,* which forbade the dukes to declare war, conclude alliances, or coin money without consent of an assembly or estates (in force until 1789). Brabant passed to the dukes of Burgundy in 1430. For its history after 1477, see NETHERLANDS, AUSTRIAN AND SPANISH.

Brac, Serbo-Croatian *Brač* (bräch), Ital. *Brazza,* Adriatic island (152 sq. mi.), Croatia, NW Yugoslavia; chief town Supetar (San Pietro).

Bracegirdle, Anne, 1663?–1748, English actress. A pupil of Betterton and the favorite of Congreve, whose comedies were written for her.

bracken or **brake,** tall, coarse FERN (*Pteridium*) of wide distribution. Often becomes weedy. See *ill.,* p. 859.

Brackenridge, Hugh Henry, 1748–1816, American author, b. Scotland. His satirical and picaresque novel, *Modern Chivalry* (6 vols., 1792–1805; rev. ed., 4 vols., 1804–7) pictures backwoods life and expresses moderate democratic views.

Bracton, Henry de, d. 1268, English jurist, author of *De legibus et consuetudinibus Angliae* [on the laws and customs of England].

Braddock, Edward, 1695–1755, British general in French and Indian Wars. Mortally wounded in disastrous expedition to capture Fort Duquesne from French; more than half his force was lost.

Braddock, industrial borough (pop. 12,337), W Pa., on Monongahela R., SE of Pittsburgh; settled 1742. Has steel plants. Gen. Edward Braddock defeated by French and Indians here 1755. Site of Whisky Rebellion protest (Aug. 1, 1794).

Bradenton (brä′dŭntŭn), city (pop. 19,380), SW Fla., S of St. Petersburg, on Tampa Bay at mouths of Braden and Manatee rivers; founded 1878. Shipping point for citrus fruit and vegetables. Natl. memorial here commemorates De Soto's landing in Fla.

Bradford, Andrew: see BRADFORD, WILLIAM (1663–1752).

Bradford, Gamaliel (gŭmā′lēŭl), 1863–1932, American biographer, noted for "psychographs" (short psychological portraits), collected in volumes such as *Confederate Portraits* (1914), *Union Portraits* (1916), and *Damaged Souls* (1923).

Bradford, John, 1749–1830, pioneer printer of Ky. Founded *Kentucky Gazette* (1787), first Ky. newspaper. Helped found Transylvania Univ.

Bradford, Roark, 1896–1948, American writer, b. Tenn. Biblical stories seen through Negro eyes in *Ol′ Man Adam an′ His Chillun* (1928) were the source of Marc Connelly's play *The Green Pastures* (1930).

Bradford, William, 1590–1657, governor of Plymouth Colony. Succeeded John Carver as governor in 1621 and remained governor for most of his life, being reelected 30 times. Was largely responsible for success of colony. Wrote *History of Plimoth Plantation.*

Bradford, William, 1663–1752, British printer in the American colonies. Set up the first press in Philadelphia and helped found first colonial paper mill (1690). Estab. first New York city newspaper, The *Gazette* (1725). His son, **Andrew Bradford,** 1686–1742, founded the *American Weekly Mercury,* first Pa. newspaper (1719). Imprisoned for criticism of council and assembly, he creditably defended own case for freedom of press. His nephew, **William Bradford,** 1722–91, estab. the Philadelphia *Weekly Advertiser.* A patriot in the American Revolution, he was printer to First Continental Congress and as a major was so badly wounded at Princeton that he did not regain health.

Bradford, county borough (pop. 295,768), Yorkshire, England. A center of the worsted-milling industry, it also has varied mfg.

Bradford, city (pop. 15,061), NW Pa., SE of Jamestown, N.Y., near N.Y. line; settled c.1823. City grew after oil discovery c.1871.

Bradlaugh, Charles (brăd′lô), 1833–91, English social reformer, champion of woman suffrage, birth control, and trade unionism.

Bradley, Francis Herbert, 1846–1924, English philosopher, a fellow at Merton Col., Oxford. An absolute idealist, he challenged contemporary metaphysical theories with the assertion that true reality is perfect changeless experience (as in *Appearance and Reality* 1893).

Bradley, James, 1693–1762, English astronomer. Discovered aberration of light and nutation (nodding) of earth's axis. Astronomer royal from 1742.

Bradley, Omar (Nelson), 1893–, U.S. general. Led U.S. 1st Army in invasion of Normandy (1944); vastly aided defeat of Germany in Second World War. Chairman of joint chiefs of staff (1949–53).

Bradshaw, George, 1801–53, English map engraver and the originator of railway guides.

Bradstreet, Anne (Dudley), c.1612–1672, American poet, b. England; daughter of Thomas Dudley. First American woman to devote herself to writing. Early poems in *The Tenth Muse Lately Sprung up in America* (1650). Her husband, **Simon Bradstreet,** 1603–97, b. England, was colonial governor of Mass. (1679–86, 1689–92).

Brady, James Buchanan, 1856–1917, American financier and philanthropist, called "Diamond Jim" Brady. Had massive collection of jewelry. Funds he gave founded Urological Institute at Johns Hopkins Hospital, Baltimore.

Brady, Mathew B., 1823–96, American pioneer photographer. Known for his many photographs of Lincoln and for his photographic record of the Civil War. *Gallery of Illustrious Americans* published 1850.

Braga, Teófilo (tēô′fïlô brä′gŭ), 1843–1924, Portuguese intellectual and political leader, influential through his literary criticism and his teaching. A republican and anticlericalist, he served as first president of Portuguese republic (1910–11).

Braga, city (pop. 42,636), cap. of Braga dist., Minho prov., NW Portugal. Flourished in Middle Ages as see of powerful bishops. Old cathedral.

Bragança or **Braganza** (both: brŭgän′zŭ), town (pop. 8,141), cap. of Bragança dist., Trás-os-Montes prov., NE Portugal. Castle was seat of royal family of Braganza.

Braganza (brŭgän′zŭ), royal house that ruled PORTUGAL from 1640 to 1910 and BRAZIL (as independent empire) from 1822 to 1889. ine founded by 1st duke of Braganza, a natural son of John I of Portugal. In 1640 his descendant expelled Spanish and became king as John IV.

Bragg, Braxton, 1817–76, Confederate general. Led A. S. Johnston's 2d Corps in battle of Shiloh. Unsuccessfully invaded Ky. (1862). In CHATTANOOGA CAMPAIGN he won at Chickamauga, but was thoroughly defeated by Grant in Nov., 1863.

Bragg, Sir William Henry, 1862–1942, English physicist. For studies, using X-ray spectrometer, of X-ray spectra and crystal structure, he shared 1915 Nobel Prize in Physics with his son, **Sir William Lawrence Bragg,** 1890–, who in 1938 became director of Cavendish Laboratory, Cambridge.

Bragg, Fort: see FAYETTEVILLE, N.C.

Brahe, Tycho (tī′kô brä), 1546–1601, Danish astronomer. By improving instruments and making exact observations of planets and stars, he paved way for discoveries of Kepler and other astronomers. On island of Ven built famed castle, Uranienborg, and observatory, Stjarneborg.

Brahma, supreme deity: see HINDUISM.

Brahman or **Brahmin:** see HINDUISM.

Brahmaputra (brämŭpoō′trŭ), river, c.1,700 mi. long, rising in SW Tibet and flowing through India and E Pakistan to join the Ganges. Lower course, called Jamuna, is sacred to Hindus.

Brahma Samaj (brä′mŭ sŭmäj′) [Hindi,= society of god], influential Indian religious organization founded 1828 by Rammohun Roy. Essentially Hindu, but without idolatry and discrimination against women and lower castes.

Brahms, Johannes (yōhän'ús brämz'), 1833–97, German composer, b. Hamburg. Among his closest friends were Robert and Clara Schumann. By 1863 he was earning his living as a composer and settled in Vienna. He wrote in every form except opera. Among his works are: sonatas and short pieces for the piano; the popular Hungarian Dances; chamber music; many lieder; the *Academic Festival Overture;* the *German Requiem;* and four concertos—two for piano, one for violin, and a double concerto for violin and cello. His four symphonies (1876–85) are ranked among the greatest in symphonic literature.

Brahui (brä'hōōē), Dravidian language of Baluchistan. See LANGUAGE (table).

Braid, James, 1795?–1860, English surgeon. First to use the term HYPNOTISM. He showed that hypnotic state is induced by suggestion. His work led to scientific study of the unconscious.

Braila (brŭē'lä), city (est. pop. 119,466), SE Rumania, in Walachia, on lower Danube. Exports grain.

Braille, Louis (brāl', Fr. lwē' brī'yú), 1809?–1852, French inventor of printing and writing system for the blind. Blinded after he was three, he studied and taught at the Institution nationale des Jeunes Aveugles, Paris. The **Braille system,** evolved from Charles Barbier's method, has 63 combinations of six raised points.

brain, mass of nerve tissue in skull. In man, center of nervous system occupying entire cranium. Includes cerebrum, controlling consciousness, sensation, and voluntary actions; cerebellum, coordinating muscular activity; and medulla oblongata, controlling all involuntary activity and connecting brain with spinal cord.

Brainerd, city (pop. 12,898), central Minn., on Mississippi R., N of St. Cloud near Cuyuna iron range; settled 1870. An industrial and commercial center in lumber and lake-resort area.

Braintree, industrial town (pop. 31,069), E Mass., SSE of Boston; settled 1634. Included Quincy until 1792. Holdup and murders for which Sacco and Vanzetti were executed occurred in South Braintree, April 15, 1920.

Brain Trust, designation for academic group, advisers to F. D. Roosevelt as governor of N.Y. and in first years as President.

brake, in botany: see BRACKEN.

brake, device to retard or stop motion of mechanical body. Friction used to resist motion, changing kinetic to heat energy. Simple types are wood or shoe pressed against wheel rim with force applied through pedal and multiplied by levers; rope wound around axle and pulled taut to brake; metal bands fitted around drum attached to wheel and controlled by levers. Mechanical automobile foot brake regulates bands of metal around outside of drum attached to axle; emergency brake attached to shoes that press outward from inside of drum. Force applied to pedals transmitted by levers, cables, or hydraulic cylinder and piston arrangement. Hydraulic brakes generally used on automobiles; air brakes on railroad cars, buses, and trucks. Electric motor often used to brake electric machines.

Brakelond, Jocelin de: see JOCELIN DE BRAKELOND.

Brakpan, city (pop. c.93,050), S Transvaal, Republic of South Africa. Gold- and coal-mining center.

Bramah, Joseph (brām'ú, brä'–), 1748–1814, English mechanician and inventor, who patented a safety lock (1784) and the HYDRAULIC PRESS (1795).

Bramante, Donato (dönä'tō brämän'tä), 1444–1514, Italian Renaissance architect and painter. His buildings in Rome are considered the most characteristic examples of high renaissance style—particularly the circular Tempietto in the courtyard of San Pietro in Montorio.

Bramantino (brämäntē'nō), c.1465–c.1535, Lombard painter, architect; pupil and imitator of Bramante.

Brampton, town (pop. 18,467), S Ont., Canada, NW of Toronto. It is noted for its greenhouses.

bran: see GRAIN.

Brancusi, Constantin (brän'kōōsh), 1876–1957, Rumanian sculptor. His work is abstract and symbolic.

Brand, Sebastian: see BRANT, SEBASTIAN.

Brandeis, Louis Dembitz (brän'dīs), 1856–1941, Associate Justice of U.S. Supreme Court (1916–39), known for judicial liberalism.

Brandeis University, at Waltham, Mass.; coed.; chartered and opened 1948. Graduate school of arts and sciences estab. 1953.

Brandenburg (Ger. brän'dûnbōŏrk), former province of Prussia, E Germany; historic cap. Potsdam. Berlin, though situated in it, was administratively separate. Flat, sandy, and forested, the region is drained by the Havel, Spree, and Oder rivers. Other cities: Frankfurt-an-der Oder, Brandenburg, Cottbus. SPREE FOREST, in Lower LUSATIA, is inhabited by WENDS, remnants of Slavic people which held the region until its colonization and Christianization by Germans. ALBERT THE BEAR, made first margrave in 1134, became effective ruler after last Wendish prince made him his heir. His descendants (the Ascanians) ruled until 1319; various princes succeeded them until in 1417 the margraviate was given to the house of HOHENZOLLERN. Margraves also held rank of ELECTORS. Reformation was introduced in 1539. In the 17th cent. Brandenburg gained much territory (notably CLEVES, duchy of PRUSSIA, E POMERANIA) and rose in prestige under FREDERICK WILLIAM, the Great Elector, whose son in 1701 took the title king of Prussia as FREDERICK I. Later history of Brandenburg is that of Prussia. Became a state of German Democratic Republic 1949 but was abolished as administrative unit 1952.

Brandenburg, city (pop. 70,632), East Germany, on Havel R. Has mfg. (trucks, textiles, machinery). The Slavic Brennabor, it was conquered 12th cent. by Albert the Bear and gave its name to his margraviate.

Brandes, Georg (Morris Cohen) (brän'dús), 1842–1927, Danish literary critic. Exerted an invigorating influence on Danish thought. Wrote widely on various literatures. His brother **Carl (Edvard Cohen) Brandes,** 1847–1931, was a critic and dramatist.

Brando, Marlon, 1924–, American actor. Achieved stage fame in *A Streetcar Named Desire* (1947). Films include *The Wild One, On the Waterfront,* and *The Fugitive Kind.*

Brandon, Charles: see SUFFOLK, CHARLES BRANDON, 1ST DUKE OF.

Brandon, city (pop. 28,166), SW Man., Canada, on Assiniboine R. and W of Winnipeg. Center of wheatraising area, it has extensive trade in farm products and machinery. Here are dominion experimental farm and Brandon Col. (Baptist; 1899).

Brandt, Sebastian: see BRANT, SEBASTIAN.

Brandt, Willy, 1913–, German politician. A Social Democrat, he fled Germany after Hitler took power but kept contact with German underground. Served in Bundestag 1949–57. Elected mayor of West Berlin in 1957, vice chancellor of Federal Republic of Germany in 1966.

brandy, strong alcoholic spirit distilled from wine or from marc, the residue of the wine press, which yields strong but inferior product. Made in many lands; most noted, called cognac, made from white grapes in Charente district of France. Brandy is also made from fruits (e.g., peach brandy), grains, and fermented sugar cane.

Brandy Station, trading center, NE of Culpeper, Va., scene of greatest cavalry battle in Civil War, June 9, 1863. First clash of Gettysburg campaign.

Brandywine, Battle of, in American Revolution, fought Sept. 11, 1777, along Brandywine Creek, near Chadds Ford, SE Pa. British under Sir William Howe defeated Washington and continued advance on Philadelphia.

Branford, borough (pop. 2,371), in Branford town (pop. 16,610), S Conn., on Long Island Sound E of New Haven; settled 1644. Grew as shipping and fishing center. Has small industries. Pre-Revolutionary houses.

Brannan, Sam(uel), 1819–89, pioneer in Calif. Founded first Calif. newspaper (1847). Organizer and first president (1851) of Committee of Vigilance.

Branner, Hans Christian, 1903–, Danish writer. Early work dealt with the irrational fears of childhood, as in *The Child Playing on the Shore* (1937). Later work employing complex Freudian themes expressed in symbols include *The Riding Master* (1949), *The Judge* (1952), and *Nobody Knows the Night* (1955).

Branner, John Casper, 1850–1922, American geologist. Created model department of geology for Ark. Long associated with Stanford Univ. as professor, vice president, president.

Branson, resort city (pop. 1,887), SW Mo., near Ark. line S of Springfield. Nearby are noted limestone formations and Table Rock Dam.

Brant, Joseph, 1742–1807, war chief of Mohawk Indians. Aided British in American Revolution. Led Indian forces in Cherry Valley massacre (1778).

Brant, Brandt, or **Brand, Sebastian** (säbäs'tyän bränt'), 1458–1521, German poet. His chief work is *Das Narrenschiff* [the ship of fools], a series of satirical and moralizing poems (Eng. tr., 1944).

brant or **brant goose,** wild sea goose. American brant breeds in arctic regions, winters along Atlantic coast, rarely inland; black head, neck, tail; brownish gray back; grayish white under parts; eats eelgrass. Black brant migrates to Pacific coast. White brant is snow goose; prairie brant is American white-fronted goose.

Brantford, city (pop. 55,201), S Ont., Canada, on Grand R. SW of Hamilton; a leading mfg. city of Canada (farm and electrical equipment, machinery, furniture, paper). Named for Mohawk chieftain Joseph Brant. Hq. of Six Nations and seat of Indian Inst.

Branting, Hjalmar (yäl'mär brän'tǐng), 1860–1925, Swedish statesman and Social Democratic leader, three times premier (1920, 1921–23, 1924–25). Shared 1921 Nobel Peace Prize with C. L. Lange.

Brantôme, Pierre de Bourdeille, seigneur de (pyěr' dù bŏŏrdä'yù sänyûr' dù brätôm'), 1540?–1614, French author, a courtier and soldier of fortune. His *Vies des hommes illustres et grands capitaines* and *Livre des dames* (Eng. tr., *Lives of Fair & Gallant Ladies,* 1933) form a racy account of his time.

Braque, Georges (zhôrzh' bräk'), 1882–1963, French painter. In 1905 joined the fauvists, in 1907 with Picasso launched cubism. Best known for still lifes.

Bras d'Or Lakes (brä dôr'), arm of the Atlantic (360 sq. mi.; 44 mi. long, up to 20 mi. wide), extending into Cape Breton Isl., N.S., Canada. Area was scene of early aviation experiments.

Brasenose College: see OXFORD UNIVERSITY.

Brasidas (brä'sǐdùs), d. 422 B.C., Spartan general. Won victories over Athens in Peloponnesian War, including that at Amphipolis, in which he was killed.

Brasilia (bräzēl'yä), city (pop. 141,172), cap. of Brazil, in Federal Dist., central Brazil. Inaugurated 1960.

Brasov (bräshôv'), Ger. *Kronstadt,* Hung. *Brassó,* city (est. pop. 133,532; large Hungarian and German minorities), central Rumania, in Transylvania. Food, textile, machinery mfg.; lumber. Founded 13th cent. by Teutonic Knights. Has Gothic cathedral (14th cent.), remains of medieval city wall, 17th-cent. citadel.

brass, name for various alloys of copper (60%–90%) and zinc (10%–40%). Properties vary with proportion of two metals; hardness varies with amount of zinc. Can be beaten, rolled into sheets, drawn into wires, machined, cast.

Brasso, Rumania: see BRASOV.

Brasstown Bald, peak, 4,784 ft. high, N Ga., in the Blue Ridge of the Appalachians near N.C. line; highest point in Ga.

brass wind instruments: see WIND INSTRUMENTS.

Bratianu, Ion (brütlä'nŏŏ), 1864–1927, Rumanian premier (1909–11, 1914–18, 1922–27). Governed dictatorially; prevented accession of Carol II (1927).

Bratislava (brä'tēslä'vä), Ger. *Pressburg,* Hung. *Pozsony,* city (est. pop. 242,000), cap. of Slovakia, Czechoslovakia, on the Danube, near Austrian and Hungarian borders. Large river port; varied industries; univ. (founded 1919). Dates from Roman times. Usual meeting place of Hungarian diet 1526–1848. Passed to Czechoslovakia 1918. Rich in historical buildings. Treaty of PRESSBURG signed here 1805.

Bratsk, city (1965 est. pop. 107,000), S central Asiatic RSFSR, on Angara R. A new industrial center, it grew rapidly after 1955 when construction of a huge hydroelectric station began (completed 1965).

Brattain, Walter H(ouser), 1902–, American physicist. Shared with John Bardeen and William Shockley the 1956 Nobel Prize in Physics for work in developing the transistor.

Brattleboro, town (pop. 11, 734), SE Vt., on Connecticut R., E of Bennington; chartered 1753. Grew near Fort Dummer, estab. 1724 to protect settlers. Winter sports center and hq. of Holstein-Friesian cattle breeders' association. Rudyard Kipling lived nearby.

Braun, Carl Ferdinand (kärl fēr'dēnänt broun), 1850–1918, German physicist. Shared with Marconi the 1909 Nobel Prize in Physics for work on wireless telegraphy.

Braunschweig, Germany: see BRUNSWICK.

Brauwer, Adriaen: see BROUWER, ADRIAEN.

Brawley, city (pop. 12,703), SE Calif., SSE of Salton Sea, in Imperial Valley agr. area; settled 1902.

Bray, Thomas, 1656–1730, English clergyman. He founded the Society for Promoting Christian Knowledge (1699) and the Society for the Propagation of the Gospel in Foreign Parts (1701).

Bray, parish, Berkshire, England, on Thames R. Ballad about the vicar of Bray often supposed to describe Simon Aleyn, vicar of Bray 1540 to 1588.

Brazil (brùzĭl', Port. *Brasil,* republic (3,287,842 sq. mi.; pop. 70,967,185), E South America; full name the United States of Brazil; cap. BRASILIA. Largest South American country, occupies nearly half of continent. Bordered by Venezuela, Guyana, Surinam, Fr. Guiana (N); Colombia, Peru (W); Bolivia, Paraguay, Argentina, Uruguay (SW); Atlantic (E). Populated coastal areas contrast with huge, undeveloped interior. Consists of five regions. North (states of Amazonas, Acre, PARÁ) includes great AMAZON basin with tropical rain forests. Famous for wild rubber, it also yields other forest products. Large manganese deposits. BELÉM and MANAUS are chief river ports. Region is mostly undeveloped and unsettled. Central West (states of GOIÁS and MATO GROSSO) is also undeveloped. Mainly high plains, it also includes lowlands of Paraguay basin. Produces livestock, coffee, and wheat. New capitol, Brasilia, was built here in order to spur development of interior. Northeast (states of MARANHÃO, PIAUÍ, CEARÁ, RIO GRANDE DO NORTE, PARAÍBA, Sergipi, PERNAMBUCO, Alagoas) includes coastal area producing sugar and cotton. Grazing area inland, subject to severe drought, is great poverty-stricken area of Brazil. Principal cities are ports of RECIFE, FORTALEZA, MACEIÓ, NATAL. East (states of BAHIA, MINAS GERAIS, Espirito Santo, RIO DE JANEIRO) is source of over half of Brazil's agr. production; produces coffee (world leader in coffee), tropical fruits, cacao, sugar cane, tobacco, livestock and dairy products. Gold and diamonds are mined here. Huge iron deposits exist, and a steel mill has been built at Volta Redonda. Principal city is beautiful former cap., port of RIO DE JANEIRO. Other important cities are SALVADOR (port) and BELO HORIZONTE (commercial center). South (states of SÃO PAULO, PARANÁ, SANTA CATARINA, RIO GRANDE DO SUL) competes with East as economic center. Produces coffee, cotton, cereals, mate, livestock, and forest products. São Paulo is second largest city in Brazil and greatest industrial center. Major ports are SANTOS and PORTO ALEGRE. Brazilians are proud of their "race" (an amalgamation of Indian, Negro, and various white strains). Portuguese is official language. Although Vicente Yáñez PINZÓN and possibly others had visited the coast earlier, the Portuguese CABRAL is usually considered the "discoverer" (1500). The first permanent settlement was at São Vicente in São Paulo state (1532). Portuguese settlement was slow even after the coming of Martin Alfonso de SOUSA as governor. French Huguenots had to be driven from Rio de Janeiro harbor (1567), and the Dutch held the Northeast until they were driven out in 1654. Portuguese tried unsuccessfully to press claims in the S to present Uruguay and Paraguay. With the Napoleonic invasion of Portugal, King John VI fled (1807–8) to Rio de Janeiro, which became the cap. of the Portuguese Empire. After Napoleon's defeat, John returned to Portugal, leaving his son as regent in Brazil. In 1822 that son proclaimed Brazil independent (at Ipiranga) and became Emperor Pedro I. He had to abdicate in favor of his son, Pedro II, who reigned 1831–89. Brazil grew as a modern nation, though wars with Argentina and with Paraguay (see TRIPLE ALLIANCE, WAR OF THE) brought little benefit to Brazil. The abolition of slavery (1888) helped bring on bloodless revolution that made Brazil a republic 1889). Immigration, the expanding coffee market, and the short wild-rubber boom (which caused trouble with neighbors, e.g., in ACRE) brought wealth to Brazil in late 19th and early 20th cent. Later, particularly under the presidency of Getulio VARGAS (1930–45, 1952–54), stress was laid on industrial expansion. Brazil joined the Allies in both world wars and joined UN (1945). After Vargas's forced resignation and his suicide an interim government was ended when Juscelino Kubitschek became president (served 1956–61). Jañio Quadros, elected to ·succeed him, resigned, making João Goulart president. In 1964 Goulart was overthrown by the army and Gen. Castelo Branco put in his place. Artur da Costa e Silva elected president 1966.

Brazil nut, seed of a tall tree (*Bertholletia excelsa*) of tropical America. Borne in large pod, the nuts have a hard brown shell and sweet white meat.

brazilwood, bright red wood of tropical trees of genus *Caesalpinia*. It is used for cabinetwork.

Brazoria (brŭzôr'ĕù), town (pop. 1,291), S Texas, on Brazos R., SSW of Houston; founded 1820s. A thriving port in S. F. Austin's colony and later center of plantations, it declined and was abandoned after present town (a farm market center) was built.

Brazos (brăz'ùs), river rising in "draws" in E N.Mex. and NW Texas. Double Mountain Fork (main headwater) and Salt Fork unite, are joined by Clear Fork. Flows more than 800 mi. SE through Waco to Gulf of Mexico at Freeport. Brazos water used for city reservoirs, irrigation, flood control, and power. Dams include Possum Kingdom, Whitney, Waco, and Proctor.

Brazosport, Texas: see FREEPORT.

Brazza, Pierre Paul François Camille Savorgnan de (sävôrnyä' dù bräzä'), 1852–1905, Franco-Italian explorer. Naturalized in France (1875) and sent by foreign office to establish French influence in Equatoria. Founded Brazzaville (1880). Estab. French protectorate over Bateke territory.

Brazza, Adriatic island: see BRAC, Yugoslavia.

Brazzaville (brä'zùvîl), industrial city (pop. c.133,-700), cap. of Congo Republic; port on Stanley Pool of Congo R. opposite Kinshasa (Leopoldville). Connected by rail with seaport of Pointe Noire. Founded 1880 by French explorer Brazza, it became cap. of

French Equatorial Africa. In Second World War was center of Free French forces in Africa.

Breadalbane, John Campbell, 1st earl of: see CAMPBELL, JOHN, 1ST EARL OF BREADALBANE.

breadfruit, tropical tree (*Artocarpus altilis*) and its fruit, a staple food in tropics. When baked, the fruit resembles bread.

Bread Loaf Mountain, 3,823 ft. high, W Vt., E of Middlebury. Middlebury Col. holds summer session in writing and languages nearby.

breadroot or **Indian breadroot**, perennial pealike plant (*Psoralea esculenta*), of North American prairies. Valued by Indians for edible, starchy roots.

Breakspear, Nicholas: see ADRIAN IV.

breakwater, structure protecting harbor from full force of waves and providing quieter ship anchorage. Artificial breakwaters may be rock or concrete-block mound, rock foundation and masonry superstructure, or superstructure from sea floor.

Breasted, James Henry, 1865–1935, American Egyptologist. Taught (1894–1933) at Univ. of Chicago; director Haskel Oriental Mus. and Oriental Inst. of Univ. of Chicago. His important archaeological research in Egypt and Mesopotamia was basis for many publications.

breathing: see RESPIRATION.

Brébeuf, Jean de (zhä' dù bräbûf'), 1593–1649, French Jesuit missionary and martyr in North America. Canonized in 1930.

Brecht, Bertolt (bĕr'tôlt brĕkht'), 1898–1956, German dramatist and poet. In the late 1920s he began to develop his expressionist, so-called epic theater. *The Threepenny Opera* (1928), with music by Kurt Weill, reflects Brecht's social views. Under National Socialism, Brecht went into exile in the U.S. A Marxist, he lived from 1948 as a theater director in East Berlin, and received the Stalin Peace Prize in 1954. His later works include *Mother Courage and Her Children* (1941) and *The Caucasian Chalk Circle* (1955).

Breckenridge, Hugh Henry, 1870–1937, American painter, a noted teacher of art.

Breckenridge, Sophonisba Preston, 1866–1948, American pioneer social worker, educator, author. Left career as lawyer to enter social work at Hull House, Chicago. After 1902 taught at Univ. of Chicago, holding chairs in social economy and public welfare. Works include *Family Welfare in a Metropolitan Community* (1924) and *Women in the Twentieth Century* (1933).

Breckinridge, John, 1760–1806, American statesman. Advised Pres. Jefferson on KENTUCKY AND VIRGINIA RESOLUTIONS. Spokesman of Western interests in Senate (1801–5). U.S. Attorney General from 1805 until his death. His grandson, **John Cabell Breckinridge**, 1821–75, was Vice President of the United States (1857–61). Presidential candidate of Southern Democratic faction (1860) and a Confederate general.

Brecknockshire (brĕk'nôkshîr) or **Brecon** (brĕk'ùn), inland county (733 sq. mi.; pop. 55,544), S Wales. Mountainous region, rising to 2,910 ft. in Brecon Beacons. Chief occupations are sheep grazing and dairy farming; there is also coal and iron mining, and woolen mfg. County town, **Brecknock** (pop. 5,797), has cathedral dating from 11th cent.

Breda (brädä'), municipality (pop. 115,782) and town, North Brabant prov., SW Netherlands. Machine plants; rayon mfg. Surrender of Breda's heroic garrison to Spanish (1625) was painted by Velázquez.

Breda, Compromise of, 1566: see GUEX.

Breda, Declaration of, 1660: see CHARLES II, king of England.

Breda, Treaty of, 1667: see DUTCH WARS.

Bredero, Gerbrand Adriaenszoon (hĕr'bränt ädrëän'-zōn brä'dĕrō), 1585–1618, Dutch dramatist and poet, a master of comedy and realism.

breeding of plants and animals to improve breed, variety, or strain probably began as propagation of specimens with desirable qualities (selective breeding). Scientific breeding arose after Gregor Mendel's promulgation of laws of inheritance. New breeds and varieties are HYBRIDS or the product of breeding individuals in which mutations have occurred. See GENETICS; HEREDITY.

Breed's Hill: see BUNKER HILL, BATTLE OF.

Bregenz (brā'gĕnts), city (pop. 21,428), cap. of Vorarlberg prov., W Austria on L. of Constance. Lake port and rail center; has hydroelectric plant; textile mfg. Bregenz Forest is nearby.

Breisgau (brīs'gou), region, Baden-Württemberg, West Germany. Held by Hapsburgs 1368–1805.

Breitenfeld (brī'tŭnfĕlt"), village, East Germany, in former state of Saxony, near Leipzig. Scene of victory of Swedes over imperials in two battles (1631 and 1642) in Thirty Years War.

Breitmann, Hans (brīt'män), pseud. of Charles Godfrey Leland, 1824–1903, American author of poems in German-American dialect, printed in *Graham's Magazine* while he was its editor, collected as *Hans Breitman's Ballads*, 1869. Founded and edited *Continental Monthly* and wrote many works under his own name.

Bremen (brĕ'mŭn, Ger. brā'mŭn), state (156 sq. mi.; pop. 704,300), West Germany, on North Sea about mouth of Weser R. Its fortunes are those of its cap., the free Hansa city of **Bremen** (pop. 507,952), second largest German port and an industrial and commercial center. Created in 845, the archdiocese of Bremen originally included all Scandinavia, Iceland, Greenland. City of Bremen itself was virtually independent from archbishops as its importance grew. Entered HANSEATIC LEAGUE 1358; accepted the Reformation; became free imperial city 1646. Trade was spurred by founding of BREMERHAVEN (1827). "Republic and Hansa city" of Bremen joined German Empire (1871), Weimar Republic (1919), and Federal Republic of Germany (1949). Gothic city hall, with statue of Roland (erected 1404 as symbol of city's freedom) and Cathedral of Sankt Petri (begun 1043) still stand.

Bremerhaven (brā'mŭrhä"fŭn), city (pop. 130,492), West Germany, in Bremen; North Sea port on mouth of Weser R. Founded 1827 as transatlantic port.

Bremerton (brĕm'ŭrtŭn), city (pop. 28,922), NW Wash., SW of Seattle on arm of Puget Sound. U.S. naval installations and hospital are here.

Breneman, Abram Adam (brĕ'nŭmŭm), 1847–1928, American chemist and educator. Discovered process named for him for preventing corrosion of iron.

Brennan, William J(oseph), Jr., 1906–, Associate Justice of U.S. Supreme Court (1956–).

Brenner Pass (brĕ'nŭr), Ital. *Brennero* (brĕn'nārō), in Tyrolean Alps, 4,495 ft. high, on Austro-Italian border. Highway built 1772; railroad 1867.

Brent, Margaret, 1600–1671?, American feminist. First woman in Maryland to hold land in her own right, she was executrix of Gov. Calvert's estates and acted as attorney for Lord Baltimore.

Brent, London borough since 1965 (est. pop. 296,030); includes former municipal boroughs of Wembley and Willesden.

Brentano, Clemens (brĕntä'nō), 1778–1842, German romantic poet; brother of Bettina von Arnim. Author of fairy tales and stories such as *Geschichte vom braven Kasperl und dem schönen Annerl* (1817; Eng. tr., *Honor*, 1847), but best known for collaboration with Achim von ARNIM on folk-song collection *Des Knaben Wunderhorn* (1806–8).

Brentano, Elisabeth: see ARNIM, BETTINA VON.

Brentano, Franz, 1838–1917, German psychologist, professor of philosophy at Vienna (1874–1880). Set out to estab. psychology as a distinct science based on empirical findings.

Brentford and Chiswick, London: see HOUNSLOW.

Brentwood. 1 City (pop. 12,250), E Mo., a suburb W of St. Louis. **2** Town (pop. 15,387), SE N.Y., on central Long Isl., N of Bay Shore. Josiah Warren

had utopian community Modern Times here, 1851–c.1860. **3** Residential borough (pop. 13,706), W Pa., S of Pittsburgh.

Brescia (brā'shä), city (pop. 185,012), cap. of Brescia prov., Lombardy, N Italy. Industrial center (steel, machinery). Of pre-Roman origin; independent commune in Middle Ages. Flourishing school of painters in 16th cent. (G. B. Moroni, Moretto). Roman remains; medieval, Renaissance, and baroque churches.

Breslau (brĕs'lou) or **Wroclaw** (vrôts'wäf), city (est. pop. 469,000), SW Poland (since 1945), former cap. of Lower Silesia, on the Oder, Became episcopal see 1000, cap. of duchy of SILESIA, under Piast dynasty, 1163. Sacked by Mongols 1241. To Bohemia 1335; under Hapsburgs 1526–1742. Became major commercial and industrial center in 19th cent., with metals, textile, and food industries; now one of most highly developed industrial regions of Poland.

Bresse (brĕs), region, E France, between Saône and Ain, in Ain dept.; chief town Bourg-en-Bresse. Agr., poultry, wine. Pond-dotted Dombes dist. is being drained. Ceded to France by Savoy (1601) and incorporated into Burgundy prov.

Brest, city (pop. 136,104), Finistère dept., NW France, on an inlet of Atlantic into tip of Brittany. Chief French naval station. Harbor created 1631 by Richelieu.

Brest, formerly **Brest-Litovsk** (brĕst'-lĭtôfsk'), city (1965 est. pop. 88,000), Belorussia, on Western Bug R. Rail, water transportation center; strategic fortress. Passed to Russia in third Polish partition (1795); fortified 1831; held by Germans in both World Wars; to Poland 1921; to USSR 1945. Union of Polish Orthodox and Roman Catholic churches (1596) and Treaty of BREST-LITOVSK (1918) were signed here.

Brest-Litovsk, Treaty of (-lĭtôfsk'), March 1918, separate peace treaty signed by Soviet Russia and the Central Powers at BREST, USSR, following armistice of Dec., 1917. Trotsky was chief Russian negotiator. Russia recognized independence of Poland, Baltic states, Georgia, Ukraine; permitted German occupation of Belorussia; ceded Kars, Ardahan, Batum to Turkey. Later Germany demanded large indemnity. General armistice of Nov., 1918, nullified this treaty.

Brétigny, Treaty of (brätĕnyē'), 1360, short-lived truce between England and France in HUNDRED YEARS WAR; signed at Brétigny near Chartres. John II of France promised English 3,000,000 gold crowns as ransom and ceded nearly half of France.

Brethren, German Baptist sect, popularly known as Dunkards, Dunkers, or Tunkers. Name derived from German "to dip," baptism being by immersion. Sect evolved from German Pietism and migrated to Pa. in 1719. It opposes war, practices the simple life, and stresses obedience to Christ rather than to creeds. There are five denominations in the U.S., of which largest is Church of the Brethren.

Breton, André (ädrā' brŭtô'), 1896–1966, French poet, novelist, critic. First a Dadaist, he was later a leading surrealist.

Breton, Nicholas (brĕt'ŭn), 1551?–c.1623, prolific English poet and miscellaneous writer. *The Passionate Shepherd* (1604) his best-known work.

Breton literature (brĕ'tŭn), in the Celtic language of Brittany, until the 19th cent. consisted mainly of popular plays (some dating back to c.1500), songs, and stories. Collection of these, as well as a cultivated literature, began mid-19th cent. Outstanding Breton poets include Auguste Brizeux (1803–58), author of collection *Telen Arvor* [the harp of Armorica] (1844), and Jean Pierre Calloc'h (1888–1917), whose poems show piety, love of the sea, and fascination with death. The 19th and 20th cents. have seen a renewed interest in Breton language and literature.

Bretonneau, Pierre (pyĕr' brŭtônō'), 1778–1862, French physician. His treatise on diphtheria established its identity; he performed first successful tracheotomy for diphtheria 1825. Stated germ theory of disease later established by Pasteur.

Breton Sound, inlet of Gulf of Mexico, SE La., between Breton Isl. (now Breton Natl. Wildlife Refuge) and Mississippi R. delta.

Breton Succession, War of the, 1341–65. Duke John III of Brittany having died childless, the succession was contested by his brother, Jean de Montfort, who was backed by England, and by CHARLES OF BLOIS, who had married a niece of the late duke and was backed by France. Charles's death at the battle of Auray (1364) decided the issue, which had merged with the Hundred Years War. France recognized the Monfort heir as ruler of Brittany in the treaty of Guérande 1365.

Bretton Woods Conference, name commonly given to United Nations Monetary and Financial Conference, held in July, 1944, at Bretton Woods, N.H. Conference resulted in creation of International Monetary Fund, to promote monetary cooperation, and of International Bank for Reconstruction and Development.

Breuer, Josef (yō′zĕf broi′ŭr), 1842–1925, Austrian physician, whose therapy and theory, developed by Freud, became psychoanalysis.

Breuer, Marcel Lajos (broi′ŭr), 1902–, architect, b. Hungary. Associated with Bauhaus group. Partner of Walter Gropius 1937–42. Designed Whitney Mus. of American Art, New York (opened 1966).

Breughel, family of painters: see BRUEGEL.

Breviary of Alaric (ă′lŭrĭk), Visigothic code of Roman law issued (506) by Alaric II for his Roman subjects in Spain and S Gaul.

Brewster, Sir David, 1781–1868, Scottish physicist. Notable research on polarization of light. Invented dioptric system of improved lighthouse illumination; said to have invented kaleidoscope.

Brewster, William, 1567–1644, Pilgrim Father. Though no minister, he was real leader of the church in Plymouth Colony.

Brezhnev, Leonid Ilyich (lāyō′nĕd ĭlyĕch′ brāzh′nĕf), 1906–, Russian Communist leader. Became chairman of the presidium of the Supreme Soviet 1960 and was titular president of the Soviet Union until 1964. Became first secretary of the central committee of the Communist party 1964.

Brezina, Otokar (ô′tôkär bzhĕ′zĭnä), Czech *Březina,* 1868–1929, Czech lyric poet, leader of the symbolist school. His real name was Vaclav Jebavy.

Brian Boru or **Brian Boroimhe** (both: brī′ŭn or brēn′, bŭrōō′ or bŭrō′), 940?–1014, high king of Ireland. A local king, he subjugated all Ireland. Annihilated coalition of Norse and his Irish enemies at Clontarf in 1014, but was murdered soon after. His victory broke Norse power in Ireland, but destroyed unity he had achieved.

Briand, Aristide (ärēstēd′ brēä′), 1862–1932, French statesman, 10 times premier between 1909 and 1921. Originally a Socialist, he later was attacked by left and right for his liberalism. As foreign minister (1925–32) he was chief architect of LOCARNO PACT and KELLOGG-BRIAND PACT. Advocated international cooperation and United States of Europe. Shared 1926 Nobel Peace Prize with Stresemann.

Briarcliff Manor, residential village (1965 pop. 6,788), SE N.Y., SE of Ossining. Briarcliff Col. is here.

Brice, Fanny, 1891–1951, American actress and comedienne, whose real name was Fannie Borach. She was skilled at caricature and satire. Starred in the *Ziegfeld Follies* after 1910 and was known for creation and portrayal (on radio after 1936) of "Baby Snooks."

bridal wreath: see SPIRAEA.

Bride, Saint: see BRIDGET, SAINT.

bridge, roadway spanning body of water. Developed from primitive log or vine across stream to arched stone structures of 2000 to 4000 B.C., the longer Roman arches, and modern steel bridges. Beginning in mid-19th cent., wooden bridges of early U.S. were largely superseded by cast and wrought iron bridges. Development of Bessemer process of converting cast iron into steel revolutionized bridgebuilding. Use of TRUSS led to vast modern structures including paneltruss bridge (braced parallel trusses supporting road on transverse beams); center-swing bridge (revolves on pier midstream to permit passage of tall ships); cantilever (long spans, usually supported by two piers and two abutments); suspension bridge (a roadway suspended by cables anchored to piers on each bank); vertical lift (truss-type span suspended between steel towers by wire ropes); and bascule or quadrant bridge (rigid, truss-type bridge resting free on one bank and mounted on heavy quadrant on other, to permit lifting clear of water). See also DRAWBRIDGE; PONTOON; VIADUCT.

bridge, card game, developed from whist, played with 52 cards by four players paired as partners. An old form of bridge was played in Middle East in 19th cent. The term *bridge* now usually means contract bridge, a form developed by Harold S. Vanderbilt of New York in 1925. Another form is auction bridge.

Bridgeburg, Ont.: see FORT ERIE.

Bridge of Sighs, covered stone bridge in Venice, Italy, built in 16th cent. to connect ducal palace with prison. Prisoners were led over bridge after trial in palace.

Bridgeport. 1 City (pop. 2,906), extreme NE Ala., on Tennessee R., ENE of Huntsville. Russell Cave Natl. Monument (see NATIONAL PARKS AND MONUMENTS, table) is near. **2** City (pop. 156,748), SW Conn., on Long Island Sound SW of New Haven; settled 1639. State's chief industrial city (ammunition, firearms, plastics, machinery, electrical equipment). Barnum Inst. of Science and History commemorates showman who lived here. Birthplace of "Gen. Tom Thumb" (C. S. Stratton) and seat of Univ. of Bridgeport.

Bridger, James, 1804–81, American fur trader, one of most famous of MOUNTAIN MEN. Guided many expeditions in Northwest. Founded Fort Bridger on Oregon Trail in 1843.

Bridger, Fort: see FORT BRIDGER STATE PARK.

Bridges, Calvin Blackman, 1889–1938, American geneticist. Proved chromosome theory of heredity; formulated theory of genic balance; studied gene positions in salivary chromosomes of *Drosophila* (fruit fly or vinegar fly).

Bridges, Harry (Alfred Renton Bridges), 1900–, American labor leader in maritime industry, b. Australia. His 1950 conviction for perjury for swearing at naturalization hearing that he had never been a Communist was set aside (1953) by U.S. Supreme Court. Also won subsequent trial on same charge, and Justice Dept. gave up fight to deport him.

Bridges, Robert (Seymour), 1844–1930, English poet laureate after 1913. Wrote lyrics, long poems (e.g., *The Testament of Beauty,* 1929), verse dramas, criticism; published poetry of Gerard Manley Hopkins.

Bridget, Saint, 453?–523?, Irish holy woman. Little is known of her except that she founded a monastery at Kildare and that she is buried at Downpatrick with fellow patrons of Ireland, Patrick and Columba. Also Brigid and Bride. Feast: Feb. 1.

Bridget of Sweden, Saint, c.1300–1373, Swedish nun. A noblewoman and a mother of eight children, she retired to become a nun after the death of her husband. She had celebrated visions, and as a result of one of them founded a new order (the Bridgettines). She lived her last years in Rome (except for pilgrimage to Palestine) and was adviser to popes. Also Birgitta. Feast: Oct. 8.

Bridgeton, city (pop. 20,966), S N.J., SE of Salem; settled 1686. Has glassworks and canneries.

Bridgetown, city (pop. 94,000), cap. of Barbados, West Indies. Tourist resort.

Bridgewater, town (pop. 10,276), E Mass., S of Brockton; settled 1650. Residential community with some mfg.

Bridgman, Laura, 1829–89, New England teacher of sewing, first blind deaf-mute to be successfully educated (by Dr. S. G. Howe of Perkins Inst.).

Bridgman, Percy Williams, 1882–1961, American physicist. Won 1946 Nobel Prize in Physics for high pressure experimentations. Wrote extensively on philosophy of modern science.

Brie (brē), region, Marne and Seine-et-Marne depts., N France, E of Paris; chief city Meaux. Rich farm district, famous for cheese.

Brieg (brēk) or **Brzeg** (bzhĕk), city (est. pop. 27,000), SW Poland (since 1945), formerly in Lower Silesia, on the Oder. A trade and mfg. center and river port. Seat of principality under PIAST dynasty 1311–1675. Has several historic buildings.

Brienne, Étienne Charles Loménie de: see LOMÉNIE DE BRIENNE, ÉTIENNE CHARLES.

Brienz (brēĕnts'), resort town (est. pop. 2,861), Bern canton, Switzerland, on NE shore of scenic L. of Brienz (11 sq. mi.). Woodcarving.

Brieux, Eugène (üzhĕn' brēü'), 1858–1932, French dramatist. Wrote on family life and social themes. Well-known plays are *La Robe rouge* (1900) and *Les Avariés* (1901; produced in U.S. as *Damaged Goods*).

Briey (brēä'), town (est. pop. 3,443), Meurthe-et-Moselle dept., NE France. Center of Lorraine iron-ore basin.

brig, two-masted, square-rigged, sailing vessel, once popular in coastal trade. Length varies from 100 to 115 ft.; tonnages go up to 350. Smaller brigantine has a fore-and-aft mainsail and square topsail on the mainmast.

Briga: see BRIGUE AND TENDE.

brigandage, robbery, blackmail, kidnaping, and plundering by armed bands. Arises from bad economic, political, or social conditions or in a chaotic society as after war or in frontier settlements. Many brigands are romantic figures, as Robin Hood, Jesse James.

Briggs, Le Baron Russell, 1855–1934, American educator. A professor of English at Harvard, he was later dean of Harvard Col. (1891–1902) and president of Radcliffe Col. (1903–23).

Brigham, Albert Perry, 1855–1932, American geographer. His *Geographic Influences in American History* (1903) had wide influence.

Brigham or **Brigham City,** city (pop. 11,728), N Utah, N of Ogden. Founded 1851 as Box Elder; name changed 1856. Center of farm area served by Ogden R. project.

Brigham Young University, at Provo, Utah; coed.; opened 1875 as academy, became university 1903. Extension centers at Lake City and Ogden, at Idaho Falls, Idaho, and Los Angeles, Calif.

Bright, Sir Charles Tilston, 1832–88, English engineer. Among cables he laid were first from Ireland to Scotland (1853) and Ireland to Newfoundland (1858).

Bright, John, 1811–89, English statesman and orator; son of Quaker cotton miller. He and Richard COBDEN were greatest 19-cent. champions of the middle class. Noted for laissez-faire views, support of FREE TRADE, and fight for repeal of CORN LAWS.

Bright, Richard: see BRIGHT'S DISEASE.

Brighton, county borough (pop. 162,757), Sussex East, England, on English Channel. Became fashionable resort under patronage of prince of Wales (later George IV), who built the Royal Pavilion.

Bright's disease, any of several forms of kidney inflammation. Symptoms include albumin in urine, dropsy, high blood pressure. Described 1827 by **Richard Bright,** 1789–1858, English physician noted for clinical observations.

Brigue and Tende (brēg, tãd), Ital. *Briga* and *Tenda,* small districts (202 sq. mi.; pop. 2,848), Alpes-Maritimes dept., SE France. Ceded to France by Italy in Treaty of Paris of 1947.

Brill or **Bril,** two Flemish artists, brothers. **Mattys Brill** (mä'tĭs), 1550–83, and **Paul Brill,** 1554–1626, both worked in Rome. The latter was important in the development of classical landscape painting.

Brill, A(braham) A(rden), 1874–1948, American psychiatrist, b. Austria. One of the earliest, most active exponents of psychoanalysis in practice, teaching, and writing, he was first translator of many major works of Freud and Jung.

Brillat-Savarin, Anthelme (ätĕlm' brēyä'-sävärē'), 1755–1826, French lawyer, economist, and gastronomist, famous for *La Physiologie du goût* (1825), published in English as *The Physiology of Taste.*

Brill's disease, mild type of typhus fever. First described, though not identified, by Nathan Edwin Brill, 1860–1925, American physician.

Brindisi (brēn'dēzē), Latin *Brundisium,* city (pop. 70,084), cap. of Brindisi prov., Apulia, S Italy; Adriatic port. Important Roman naval station; embarkation port for Crusaders. One of two columns marking end of Appian Way still stands.

Brinvilliers, Marie Madeleine d'Aubray, marquise de: see POISON AFFAIR.

Brion, Admiral de: see CHABOT, PHILIPPE DE.

Brisbane, Albert (brĭz'băn), 1809–90, American social theorist. An advocate of the ideas of Charles FOURIER, he was instrumental in founding of Fourierist communities at BROOK FARM and Red Bank, N.J.

Brisbane (brĭz'bŭn), city (pop. of the metropolitan area, 567,000), cap. of Queensland, Australia; port on Brisbane R. above its mouth on Moreton Bay. Area was settled 1824 as a penal colony. Seat of Univ. of Queensland (1909). Exports textiles, wool, meat, gold, sugar, and coal.

Briseis (brīsē'ĭs), slave girl of Achilles. His wrath when Agamemnon stole her from him forms main story of the *Iliad.* See also CHRYSEIS.

Brissot de Warville, Jacques Pierre (zhäk' pyĕr' brēsō' dù värvēl'), 1754–93, French revolutionist and pamphleteer, leader of the GIRONDISTS. Also wrote on French-U.S. relations, founded abolitionist society, and originated phrase later made famous by Proudhon: "Property is theft." Guillotined.

Bristol, John Digby, 1st earl of, 1580–1653, English diplomat. Ambassador to Spain 1611–24; offended Charles I and was imprisoned 1626–28. Released by Parliament, he became a moderate leader. As such, was increasingly unpopular and again jailed, 1642. Was royalist in civil war and died in exile. His son, **George Digby, 2d earl of Bristol,** 1612–77, was secretary of state to Charles II in exile and returned to England after Restoration.

Bristol, county borough (pop. 436,440), Gloucestershire, England, on the Avon near mouth of the Severn. A major port, it is a center for export of grain and petroleum products and an industrial center (engineering; mfg. of aircraft, chocolates, tobacco). Early transatlantic steamship built here 1838. The Cabots sailed (1497) from Bristol for American discoveries. Birthplace of Thomas Chatterton and Robert Southey.

Bristol. 1 Industrial city (pop. 45,499), central Conn., SW of Hartford; settled 1727. Mfg. of clocks since 1790; American Clock and Watch Mus. is here. **2** Fishing town (pop. 1,441), S Maine, SSE of Damariscotta; settled c.1626. Resort town. Pemaquid peninsula has reproduction of tower of Fort William Henry (built here 1692). **3** Industrial borough (pop. 12,364), SE Pa., on Delaware R., NE of Philadelphia; settled c.1681. Friends Meetinghouse dates from c.1710. **4** Town (1965 pop. 15,716), E R.I., on Narragansett Bay (connected by bridge to Portsmouth), SE of Providence; passed to R.I. from Plymouth Colony 1746. Port was base for slave trading and privateering in early 19th cent. Harbor now used chiefly by pleasure craft. Nearby monument marks site where King Philip fell. **5** Industrial city (pop. in Tenn., 17,582; in Va., 17,144), on Tenn.-Va. line ENE of Kingsport, Tenn., in mountains; settled 1749 as Sapling Grove. Separate municipalities united economically. King Col. is here, in Tenn.; Bristol Caverns are nearby.

Bristol Avon: see AVON 1, river, England.

Bristol Channel, inlet (length 85 mi.; max. width 43 mi.) of the Atlantic separating Wales and SW England. It is approach, via the Severn, to Bristol.

Britain, conventional name of Great Britain before Germanic invasions of 5th–6th cent. It then became ENGLAND, WALES, and SCOTLAND. Successive waves of migration or invasion were mainly from S and E to N and W. Before 6th cent. B.C. Celtic invasions from continent brought Iron Age culture to British Bronze Age settlements. Brisk trade with Continent developed. Last Celtic invaders (c.75 B.C.) introduced the deep plough and coining of money. First Roman invaders under Julius CAESAR (55 B.C.) found Celtic tribal organization as in Gaul, including DRUIDS. By A.D. 85 Emperor Claudius and his successors had conquered Britain S of the Clyde despite such resistance as revolt of BOADICEA. Risings in N caused building of HADRIAN'S WALL (c.121–127 A.D.) and Wall of ANTONINUS (c.140–142 A.D.) as frontier ramparts. Former became N boundary of Roman occupation. First half of 3d cent. was Roman heyday in Britain, with number of towns whose gridiron plan and architecture were Roman and whose language was probably Latin. ROMAN ROADS, mainly military, radiated from Londinium (London). Decline of Rome and three-sided invasions by Saxons and Irish progressively weakened defense. In mid-5th cent. an appeal to Rome for further military aid failed, Roman officials were withdrawn, and warring tribal kings gradually took over. Christianization lessened invasion pressure in N and W, but Saxon raids in E were heavier. ANGLO-SAXONS and Jutes began to settle in England and Celtic tribal culture revived. Residue of Roman influence remained in place names, architectural ruins, and in force of tradition.

britannia metal, silvery-white alloy of tin, copper, antimony; sometimes also with bismuth, lead, zinc.

Britannicus (brĭtă'nĭkŭs), A.D. 41?–A.D. 55, Roman prince, son of Claudius I and Messalina. Set aside in favor of Nero, son of his stepmother, Agrippina, he was apparently poisoned later.

British Cameroons: see NIGERIA; CAMEROONS.

British Columbia, province (359,279 sq. mi.; with water surface 366,255 sq. mi.; pop. 1,626,082), W Canada; cap. VICTORIA. Many islands (e.g. Vancouver and Queen Charlotte) lie off the indented W Pacific coastline. VANCOUVER is largest city and chief port. Other cities are NEW WESTMINSTER, NORTH VANCOUVER, and TRAIL. Province is mountainous with interior broken by numerous lakes annd rivers. Drained by FRASER, COLUMBIA, KOOTENAY, PEACE, and SKEENA rivers. Population is centered in S and on Vancouver Isl. Lumbering is major industry, supplemented by mining (copper, lead, zinc, silver, gold). Kitimat (town in NW) is an aluminum-smelting center. Other industries include fishing, mfg. of chemicals, food processing and shipbuilding. The area was first explored by white men (Pérez, Hecceta and Quadra, Cook, Meares) in late 18th cent. England gained control when Spanish claims were relinquished in Nootka Convention (1790). Capt. George Vancouver charted coast 1792–94, and Sir Alexander Mackenzie reached Pacific coast by land 1793. Trading posts estab. by North West Co. and Hudson's Bay Co. Boundaries defined with Alaska (1825, 1903) and the U.S. (1846). Crown colonies on Vancouver Isl. (1849) and the mainland (1858) were united 1866 and became province 1871. Gold strikes brought scattered settlement which greatly increased after Canadian Pacific RR reached Vancouver.

British Columbia, University of: see VANCOUVER.

British Commonwealth of Nations, voluntary association of the United Kingdom of Great Britain and Northern Ireland and certain former dependencies which are now sovereign states. Legal recognition given by Statute of Westminster (1931). System of trade agreements gives preferential treatment to members. Question of continued viability of Com-

monwealth raised by Britain's request for admission to European Common Market. Term also used to include countries still under British administration (see BRITISH EMPIRE).

British East Africa, inclusive term formerly used for KENYA, UGANDA, TANGANYIKA, and ZANZIBAR.

British East India Company: see EAST INDIA COMPANY, BRITISH.

British Empire, at its height (late 19th-early 20th cent.) greatest empire of the world. First colony was Newfoundland (1583). Foundations of empire laid in early 17th cent. by formation of CHARTERED COMPANIES. Desire for trade and to settle overseas led to scattered settlements by various groups. These were consolidated into colonies (by agreement or conquest) under London colonial office, with Parliament imposing taxes. Theories of MERCANTILISM were implanted by NAVIGATION ACTS. Refusal of colonists' demands for freedom in government and trade resulted in loss of the Thirteen Colonies in American Revolution (1775–83). Conquests of Ceylon, Malta, Cape of Good Hope increased British sea power. Change in attitude was shown by Reform Bill (1832), abolition of slave trade (1833), and free trade policy (1842–46); trend to self-government of settled colonists led to Canada becoming first dominion, 1867. Emigration to Australia and New Zealand was for development, not exploitation. Queen Victoria proclaimed empress of India 1877; Burma added 1885. In late 19th-cent. European colonial race, British enlarged holdings in Africa, gained power in Egypt, and acquired Malaya, Borneo, part of New Guinea, and many Pacific islands. By 20th cent. Britain controlled nearly one quarter of world. New dominions were Australia, New Zealand (1907), Union of South Africa (1910). IMPERIAL CONFERENCE held this association together through First World War. Egypt again made independent in 1923. with British given control of Suez Canal. Britain given (1920) mandates over Tanganyika, Iraq (released 1932), and Palestine (released 1948). Dominion status given Irish Free State in 1921; Ireland withdrew from Commonwealth in 1949. Statute of Westminster (1931) created BRITISH COMMONWEALTH OF NATIONS, recognizing by law equal and independent status of dominions with common allegiance to crown. After Second World War, trend to self-government and Commonwealth status advanced rapidly. In 1948 Palestine mandate was given up, Burma became an independent republic, Pakistan and Ceylon were made dominions. India became a republic within the Commonwealth 1949. United Kingdom still administers colonies, protectorates, trust territories, and dependencies throughout world. These include: Brunei and Hong Kong in E Asian waters; Gibraltar in Mediterranean; Falkland Isls., Bermuda, and St. Helena in Atlantic area; Bahamas, Barbados, and other islands of West Indies; Fiji, Pitcairn, Tonga, British Solomon Isls., Gilbert and Ellice Isls. in Pacific. Outstanding impact of British Empire has been the dissemination of European ideas and British political institutions throughout a large part of the world.

British Guiana: see GUYANA.

British Honduras (hŏndŏō'rŭs), British crown colony (8,867 sq. mi.; 1964 est. pop. 103,000), Central America; cap. Belize. Region probably entered by Cortés 1524, but the founding of Belize is credited to British buccaneers (17th cent.), and logwood cutters were early settlers. Woods still a main product. Spain contested British ownership, which is now disputed by Guatemala. The anti-British People's United party gained control of the country in 1954 after the first election by popular vote. Internal self-government was introduced in 1964.

British Isles: see GREAT BRITAIN; IRELAND.

British Museum, national repository, London, for treasures in literature, science, and art; estab. by act of Parliament 1753, opened 1759. It has collections of Sir Robert Bruce COTTON and Sir Hans Sloane, HARLE-

IAN LIBRARY; royal libraries of George II and George III, Egyptian basalt slab (ROSETTA STONE); the ELGIN MARBLES; and the Codex Sinaiticus. Sir Anthony Panizzi began printing of the library's catalogue.

British New Guinea: see PAPUA, TERRITORY OF.

British North America Act, constitution of dominion of Canada, sketched at Quebec Conference of 1864, passed by British Parliament in 1867 to take effect July 1, 1867. Gives enumerated powers to local (provincial) legislatures with residual powers left to the dominion. Interpretation by privy council has extended scope of provincial power of "property and civil rights," and a doctrine of "emergency powers" was invented for dominion use in time of war. Power of amendment is nominally vested in British Parliament which, in practice, acts only on request of Canadian Parliament. Act makes both French and English official languages in Quebec, in Parliament, and in courts; and guarantees separate tax-supported schools for Catholics and non-Catholics in Quebec and some other provinces.

British North Borneo: see SABAH.

British Somaliland: see SOMALILAND.

British thermal unit (B.T.U.), amount of heat required to raise temperature of 1 lb. of water at maximum density 1°F. One B.T.U. equals: 251.9 calories; 778.26 foot-pounds; 1055 joules; 107.5 kilogram-meters; 0.0002928 kilowatt-hours.

British Togoland: see GHANA; TOGOLAND.

British West Africa, former inclusive term for the British colonies of Cameroons, Gambia, Gold Coast, Nigeria, Sierra Leone, and Togoland.

British West Indies: see VIRGIN ISLANDS, BRITISH; WEST INDIES.

Brittany (brĭt'ŭnē), Fr. *Bretagne,* region and former province, NW France, a peninsula between English Channel and Bay of Biscay, comprising Ille-et-Vilaine, Côtes-du-Nord, Finistère, Morbihan, and Loire-Inférieure depts. Irregular, rocky coast; hilly interior. Agriculture, fishing are main occupations. Excepting Rennes, the historic cap., all chief towns are ports: Nantes (on Loire R.), Saint-Nazaire, Brest, Saint-Malo, Lorient. A part of ancient Armorica, region was conquered by Caesar, received its modern name when settled by fugitive Britons (c.500). Breton still spoken in Lower (i.e., western) Brittany. Breton history was a long struggle for independence—first from Franks (5th–9th cent.), then from dukes of Normandy and counts of Anjou (10th–12th cent.), finally from England and France. ARTHUR I, an ANGEVIN, was recognized as duke 1196; after his murder, PETER I succeeded. Extinction of direct line led to War of the BRETON SUCCESSION. The marriages of ANNE OF BRITTANY led to personal union (1491) and formal incorporation (1532) with France. Breton autonomism revived in 19th cent. Local traditions have been kept alive.

Britten, Benjamin, 1913–, English composer. His works includes choral music, e.g., *A Ceremony of Carols, War Requiem, Cantata Misericordium;* operas, e.g., *Peter Grimes, Billy Budd, Noye's Fludde;* songs; chamber music; symphonic works, e.g., *Young People's Guide to the Orchestra, Cello Symphony;* concertos.

Britton, John, 1771–1857, English antiquary and topographer. Wrote famous descriptions of landscapes and buildings. Influential in movement to preserve ancient monuments.

Britton, Nathaniel Lord, 1859–1934, American botanist, was first director of New York Botanical Garden.

Brixham (brĭk'sŭm), urban district (pop. 10,679), Devonshire, England; seaport. William III landed here 1688.

Brizeux, Auguste: see BRETON LITERATURE.

Brno (bŭr'nô), Ger. *Brünn,* city (est. pop. 314,000), cap. of Moravia, Czechoslovakia. Major mfg. center (textiles, machinery, arms). Seat of Czechoslovak supreme court; univ. (founded 1919). Large German-speaking pop. expelled 1945. Brno's charter, granted 1229, was a model of medieval liberal town government. Battle of AUSTERLITZ fought nearby 1805. Old city includes cathedral (15th cent.), Spielberg fortress (long a celebrated political prison), many fine Gothic and baroque churches and public buildings.

Broadbent, Sir William Henry, 1835–1907, English physician. Contributed (1890–97) to clinical knowledge of heart and pulse; described progressive cerebral hemorrhage (Broadbent's apoplexy).

Broad Brook, Conn.: see EAST WINDSOR.

broadcasting, public transmission by radio and television of sound and pictures. Radio broadcasting dates in U.S. from 1920; advertising "time" first sold in 1922; tentative network coast-to-coast hookup in 1924. By 1927 the two major networks had stations so numerous as to cause traffic problems and need for legislation (see FEDERAL COMMUNICATIONS COMMISSION). See also FREQUENCY MODULATION; TELEVISION.

Broad River, rising in W N.C., S of Asheville, and flowing 143 mi. SE, then S through S.C. to the Saluda, forming the Congaree near Columbia.

Broads, the, region of lakes and lagoons connected by rivers, in Suffolk and Norfolk, England; notable as yachting center.

Broadway, avenue in N.Y., extending N from Bowling Green. It leads into roads that go as far as Albany. It is, however, known primarily as a symbol of the N.Y. theater. The avenue itself carries much commercial traffic and is also tied to the financial center. Points of interest along it include Trinity Church. St. Paul's Chapel, Woolworth and Flatiron buildings, and Columbia Univ.

Broca, Paul (pôl brôkä'), 1824–80, French pathologist, anthropologist, and neurosurgeon. Localized center for articulate speech in left frontal lobe of brain. Originated methods of classifying hair and skin color and establishing ratio of brain to skull.

broccoli (brŏk'ŭlē), garden vegetable (*Brassica oleracea italica*) with loose, green, leafy, edible flower clusters. Derived from wild cabbage.

Brocéliande, Forest of (brōsālēäd'), in Arthurian legend, the home of Merlin in Brittany, France. Forest of Paimpont, SW of Rennes, is a remnant.

Broch, Hermann (hĕr'män brôkh'), 1886–1951, Austrian novelist. His trilogy *The Sleepwalkers* (1931–32) has a style reminiscent of James Joyce.

Brock, Sir Isaac, 1769–1812, British general, Canadian hero of War of 1812. Upon outbreak of war joined forces with Tecumseh, captured post at Detroit and gained control of upper lakes, thereby earning name of "hero of Upper Canada." Successfully defended Queenston Heights, where he was mortally wounded.

Brocken (brôk'ŭn) or **Blocksberg** (blôks'bĕrk), peak, 3,747 ft. high, East Germany, in former province of Saxony; highest peak of Harz mts. Legend makes it meeting place of Walpurgis Night or Witches' Sabbath.

Brockton, city (pop. 72,813), E Mass., S of Boston; settled c.1700, set off from Bridgewater 1821. Shoe and leather-products mfg. Annual fair since 1874.

Brockville, town (pop. 17,744), S Ont., Canada, on St. Lawrence R., below Thousand Isls. in rich dairy region. River port and summer resort.

Brockway, Zebulon Reed, 1827–1920, American penologist, advocate of prison reforms, superintendent (1876–1900) of pioneer reformatory at Elmira, N.Y.

Brocton, village (pop. 1,416), SW N.Y., near L. Erie SW of Dunkirk, in grape area. T. L. Harris's short-lived community of Brotherhood of New Life was here.

Brod, Max (mäks' brôd), 1884–, German author, b. Prague, of Jewish parentage. Wrote numerous novels and dramas, many of them on Jewish problems, but is best known for biographies of Heinrich Heine (1936) and Franz Kafka (1937). Was friend of KAFKA and edited his diaries. Resides in Israel.

Broderick, David Colbreth, 1820–59, American politician. Fought with William M. GWIN for Democratic party control in Calif. Killed in famous duel.

Brogan, Denis William, 1900–, British historian and political scientist. His writings include *The American Political System* (1933), *Politics in America* (1954), and *America in the Modern World* (1960).

Broglie (broi), French noble family of Piedmontese origin. **François Marie, duc de Broglie** (fräswä' märē', dük dü), 1671–1745, marshal of France, received ducal title from Louis XV. His son, **Victor François, duc de Broglie** (vēktôr', 1718–1804, marshal of France, distinguished himself in Seven Years War; was created a prince of Holy Roman Empire. In 1792 he commanded émigré forces against revolutionary France. His great-grandson, **Albert, duc de Broglie** (älbēr'), 1821–1901, was French premier (1873–74; 1877); wrote important historical works on 18th cent. Two of his grandsons became distinguished physicists: **Maurice, duc de Broglie** (mōrēs'), 1875–1960, noted for works on X rays and atomic physics; and **Louis Victor, prince de Broglie** (lwē', prēs'), 1892–, who won the 1929 Nobel Prize in Physics for his theory of the wave character of electrons.

Broken Hill, municipality (pop. 31,351), New South Wales, Australia. Principal center of silver, lead, and zinc mining in Australia since 1884.

broker, one who negotiates sale between two parties. He takes no responsibility in transaction, but brings two together and at conclusion of deal is paid a commission. Brokers useful in estab. trade connections in large industries and may also deal in property (e.g., real estate, stock brokers).

Bromberg, Poland: see BYDGOSZCZ.

brome grass, large, coarse grass of genus *Bromus*. Smooth brome (also called Hungarian or awnless brome) and rescue grass are used for forage and pasture. Many species have barbed fruits.

bromide (brō'mīd), compound of bromine and another element (except oxygen), salt of hydrobromic acid. Widely distributed in nature. Sodium and potassium bromides used as sedatives; silver bromide used in photography. In aqueous solution, hydrogen bromide is hydrobromic acid.

bromine (brō'mēn), active, nonmetallic element (symbol = Br; see also ELEMENT, table). Brownish-red liquid; vapor has suffocating odor. Member of HALOGEN family; less active than fluorine or chlorine, more active than iodine. Corrosive. Compounds occur in sea water, mineral springs, common salt deposits. Solidifies at −7°C.; boils at 58.8°C.

Bromley, London borough since 1965 (est. pop. 305,-540); includes former municipal boroughs of Beckenham and Bromley and urban districts of Orpington, Penge, and part of Chislehurst and Sidcup.

bronchoscope, instrument inserted into lungs through windpipe and bronchial tubes to examine them internally. Used also to remove foreign bodies and obstructions.

Bronk, Detlev Wulf, 1897–, American biologist. President of Johns Hopkins from 1949 to 1953, he became president of Rockefeller Institute for Medical Research in 1953.

Brontë, Charlotte (brŏn'tē), 1816–55, **Emily Jane Brontë,** 1818–48, and **Anne Brontë,** 1820–49, English novelists and poets. Life in the parsonage in Haworth, Yorks., caused them to live in an imaginary world and write imaginative literature as children. Later the three sisters produced *Poems* (1846) under pseudonyms of Currer, Ellis, and Acton Bell. Emily's poems were particularly notable, as was her novel, *Wuthering Heights* (1847). Anne wrote novels *Agnes Gray* (1847), *The Tenant of Wildfell Hall* (1848). Generally best known was Charlotte, whose novels—*Jane Eyre* (1847), *Shirley* (1849), *Villette* (1853) and *The Professor* (1857, but earliest written)—won her fame that gladdened last year of her life as wife of Arthur Bell Nicholls.

Brontosaurus (brŏntŭsô'rŭs), largest vegetarian dinosaur, probably semiaquatic, length c.70 ft., weight over 30 tons; long neck and tail.

Bronx, the, borough (land area 41 sq. mi.; pop. 1,424,-815), of NEW YORK city, SE N.Y. On peninsula NE of Manhattan isl. and S of Westchester co.; rimmed by Hudson, Harlem, and East rivers on W and S and by Long Island Sound on E. Settled 1641 under Dutch West India Co. Linked to Manhattan and Queens by bridges and tunnels. Mainly residential, with some industry. Numerous parks include Bronx, with noted zoological park and botanical garden; Van Cortlandt, with Van Cortlandt House (1748); and Pelham Bay, with Orchard Beach. Seat of FORDHAM UNIVERSITY, parts of NEW YORK UNIVERSITY (with Hall of Fame) and of HUNTER COLLEGE OF THE CITY UNIVERSITY OF NEW YORK, Manhattan Col., and N.Y. State Univ. Maritime Col. Has Yankee Stadium and Edgar Allan Poe cottage.

Bronx, river of SE N.Y., issuing from Kensico Reservoir in Westchester co. and flowing c.20 mi. SSW through borough of Bronx, New York city, to East R.

bronze, alloy of copper and tin or copper and certain other metals. Sometimes silver, aluminum, zinc, or lead added for brilliance or hardness. Harder and more resistant than brass, zinc, and copper. Used for gun metal and bell metal; also for machine bearings, valves, roofs, cornices, ornaments, and funerary urns and caskets. Ideal for casting art works, engraving, and repoussé work. Used by Egyptians, Greeks, Etruscans, Romans. Renaissance Italy noted for bronze doors of Ghiberti and others; 18th-cent. France for furniture mounts.

Bronze Age, prehistoric period, characterized by use of bronze for tools and artifacts. It followed the Neolithic and preceded the Iron Age, but did not reach all places at the same time. Egypt and SW Asia were in the Bronze Age by 2500 B.C.; Britain c.2000 B.C. The W Hemisphere had no true Bronze Age. Copper was known before bronze, and that period is sometimes termed the Copper Age. Horses and cattle were first used as draft animals in the Bronze Age. Important inventions—arch, wheel, potter's wheel.

Bronzino, Il (ēl brōntsē'nō), 1503–1572, Florentine Mannerist painter, whose real name was Angelo di Cosimo Allori. Portraitist at court of the Medici.

Brooke, Alan Francis, 1st **Viscount Alanbrooke,** 1883–1963. British field marshal. Was commander in chief of British Home Forces 1940–41 and chief of imperial general staff 1941–46.

Brooke, Sir Charles Johnson: see BROOKE, SIR JAMES.

Brooke, Sir Charles Vyner: see BROOKE, SIR JAMES.

Brooke, Fulke Greville, 1st **Baron,** 1554–1628, English poet, patron of letters, and statesman, author (as Fulke Greville) of philosophical poems and *Life of the Renowned Sir Philip Sidney* (1652).

Brooke, Sir James, 1803–68, English rajah of Sarawak on Borneo. After aiding local sultan to suppress rebel tribes he was made rajah (1841). Succeeded by his nephew, **Sir Charles Johnson Brooke,** 1829–1917, who abolished slavery and aided prosperity. His son, **Sir Charles Vyner Brooke,** 1874–1963, ceded Sarawak to Great Britain as a crown colony 1946.

Brooke, John Mercer, 1826–1906, American scientist and naval officer. Invented first device for sampling ocean floor. In Confederate navy, he planned conversion of *Merrimac* into iron-clad *Virginia;* invented Brooke gun.

Brooke, Rupert, 1887–1915, English poet. His poetry, *Poems* (1911) and *1914 and Other Poems* (1915), shows the dashing romanticism that made Brooke a legendary figure. Died on Skyros in First World War.

Brook Farm, experimental community on a 192-acre farm at West Roxbury, Mass. Founded 1841 by transcendentalists George and Sophia Ripley to combine "plain living and high thinking." The members shared manual labor and intellectual life. Nathaniel Hawthorne was a member, R. W. Emerson and Margaret

Fuller visitors. Influenced by Albert Brisbane, Brook Farm in 1844 became a Fourierist community. The uninsured central phalanstery burned in 1846, and the group, unable to survive the financial disaster, disbanded the following year.

Brookfield. 1 Village (pop. 20,429), NE Ill., a suburb WSW of Chicago. Has noted Chicago Zoological Park (Brookfield Zoo). **2** City (pop. 19,812), SE Wis., a suburb W of Milwaukee. Publishing and printing.

Brookhaven National Laboratory, Brookhaven, N.Y., one of oldest atomic energy testing and research centers in U.S. Opened in 1948, it is operated under government sponsorship by group of universities.

Brookings, city (pop. 10,558), E S.Dak., on Big Sioux R., N of Sioux Falls. Farm trade center. Seat of SOUTH DAKOTA STATE UNIVERSITY

Brookings Institution, at Washington, D.C.; chartered 1927 as consolidation of Inst. for Government Research (founded 1916), Inst. of Economics (1922), and Robert S. Brookings Graduate School of Economics and Government (1924). Finances and publishes research in economic, governmental, and international problems.

Brookline (brŏok′lĭn), town (pop. 54,044), E Mass., a suburb W of Boston; settled 1638. Included in Boston as "Muddy River" until 1705. Birthplace of Amy Lowell and Pres. J. F. Kennedy.

Brooklyn. 1 Town (pop. 3,312), E Conn., ENE of Willimantic on Quinebaug R.; settled c.1703. Gen. Israel Putnam lived and is buried here. Includes East Brooklyn village (pop. 1,213). **2** Borough (land area 71 sq. mi.; pop. 2,627,319) of NEW YORK city, SE N.Y., on SW end of Long Isl. adjoining Queens borough. Settled 1636–37 by Walloons and Hollanders; hamlet of Breuckelen estab. c.1646. Became Brooklyn under English, absorbed various settlements (e.g., Flatbush, 17th-cent. Dutch village, now residential section) until it became coextensive with Kings co. Became New York City borough 1898. Separated from downtown Manhattan by East R. (many bridges, e.g., BROOKLYN BRIDGE, and tunnels), from Staten Isl. by Narrows of New York Bay (with VERRAZANO-NARROWS BRIDGE). Though largely residential, borough is important industrial area, with shipbuilding, brewing, and mfg. of machinery, textiles, paper products, chemicals. Important port with extensive waterfront facilities, including Bush Terminal (New York Naval Shipyard, commonly Brooklyn Navy Yard, closed 1966). Seat of BROOKLYN COLLEGE OF THE CITY UNIVERSITY OF NEW YORK, Polytechnic Inst. of Brooklyn, PRATT INSTITUTE, SAINT JOHN'S UNIVERSITY, St. Joseph's Col. for Women, Junior Col. of the Packer Collegiate Inst., LONG ISLAND UNIVERSITY, St. Francis Col., and Brooklyn Inst. of Arts and Sciences. Here are CONEY ISLAND, Sheepshead Bay (resort center with fishing craft, seafood restaurants), historic Brooklyn Heights, Prospect Park (scene of fighting in battle of LONG ISLAND), Marine Park, New York Aquarium, Floyd Bennett Field (U.S. Navy), and U.S. Fort Hamilton (built 1831). Walt Whitman lived and wrote here. **3** Village (pop. 10,733), NE Ohio, suburb S of Cleveland.

Brooklyn Bridge, SE N.Y., bridge (1,595 ft.; suspension) across East R. between Manhattan and Brooklyn. Built (1869–83) by Roebling and son.

Brooklyn Center, village (1965 pop. 30,108), SE Minn., a suburb N of Minneapolis.

Brooklyn College of The City University of New York, coed.; opened 1930 by merging Brooklyn branches of City and Hunter colleges. Graduate division estab. 1935.

Brooklyn Park, village (1965 pop. 14,785), SE Minn., a suburb N of Minneapolis.

Brookneal, town (pop. 1,070), S Va., SE of Lynchburg; settled c.1790. Tobacco is grown. Nearby is "Red Hill," Patrick Henry's last home and burial place.

Brook Park, village (pop. 12,856), NE Ohio, a suburb SW of Cleveland.

Brooks, Phillips, 1835–93, American Episcopalian clergyman. Influential as preacher at Trinity Church, Boston, 1869–91. Made bishop of Mass. 1891. Wrote *O Little Town of Bethlehem.*

Brooks, Van Wyck (wĭk), 1886–1963, American critic. Wrote critical biographies (e.g., *The Ordeal of Mark Twain,* 1920) and works on the force of Puritanism in American thought. His series *"Makers and Finders: a History of the Writer in America, 1800–1915,"* began with *The Flowering of New England* (1936), stressed need for finding a "usable past."

Brooks Range, N Alaska, separating Yukon R. basin from watershed of Arctic Ocean. Embraces many mountain chains; height averages 5,500–6,500 ft.

Brooksville, city (pop. 3,301), W Fla., N of Tampa, in timber, citrus-fruit, and limestone area. Nearby are Devil's Punch Bowl, an arid sink, and Weeki Wachee Spring, emptying c.100,000 gal. a minute to form navigable river flowing to Gulf of Mexico.

broom, shrubs of two related genera, *Cytisus* and *Genista.* Yellow or white (in *Cytisus,* purple also), pealike flowers. Common or Scotch broom is *Cytisus scoparius.* Florists' genista is *C. canariensis.*

Brophy, Truman William, 1848–1928, American dentist. Devised widely used operation for cleft palate and harelip.

Brosse, Salomon de (sälōmō′ dů brôs′), 1571–1626, French architect of Luxembourg Palace. Built hunting chateau which was later to become nucleus of Versailles palace.

Brouwer or **Brauwer, Adriaen** (äd″rēän′ brou′wŭr), c.1606–1638, Flemish painter of spirited genre and rustic scenes. Influenced by Hals and van Ostade.

Browder, Earl Russell, 1891–, American Communist leader. Opposition to his policies resulted in his removal from Communist party (1946).

Brown, family of bankers in U.S. **Alexander Brown,** 1764–1834, b. Ireland, became wealthy in Baltimore as an international banker. Took sons into partnership. Firm was for a generation leading institution of its kind in U.S. One son, **George Brown,** 1787–1859, helped found Baltimore & Ohio RR.

Brown, Alexander Ephraim, 1852–1911, American inventor of hoisting and conveying machines that revolutionized ore and coal handling on Great Lakes.

Brown, Charles Brockden, 1771–1810, first professional American novelist. His most popular Gothic novel, *Wieland* (1798), somewhat foreshadowed the psychological novel in its treatment of abnormal behavior. Other novels were *Edgar Huntly* (1799) and *Ormond* (1799).

Brown, Elmer Ellsworth, 1861–1934, American educator. A teacher of education in Mich. and Calif., he later was U.S. commissioner of education (1906–11). Chancellor of New York Univ. (1911–33).

Brown, Ford Madox, 1821–93, English historical painter, closely affiliated with the Pre-Raphaelites.

Brown, George, U.S. banker: see BROWN, family.

Brown, George, 1818–80, Canadian journalist and statesman, b. Scotland. Founded Toronto *Globe* (1844) which became most powerful political journal in Upper Canada. Elected to the assembly (1851), he led "Clear Grits" faction, which opposed influence of French Canadians in that body. Played important role in movement for confederation.

Brown, John, 1800–1859, American abolitionist. Following sack of LAWRENCE, Kansas (1856), he led retaliatory slaughter of five proslavery men on banks of Pottawatamie R. As step preliminary to liberating Southern slaves he captured U.S. arsenal at Harpers Ferry, Va. (now W.Va.) on Oct. 16, 1859. Arsenal was retaken and Brown was hanged.

Brown, John Carter, 1797–1874, American book collector and philanthropist. Donated library of early Americana to Brown Univ. (named for his father).

Brown, Moses, 1738–1836, American manufacturer. Estab. first water-powered cotton mill in America (1790) with Samuel Slater.

Brown, Robert, 1773–1858, Scottish botanist and botanical explorer. He collected plants in Australia. In 1827 he observed BROWNIAN MOVEMENT and in 1831 he discovered the cell nucleus.

Brown, William Hill, 1765–93, American writer, probable author of a novel, *The Power of Sympathy* (1789), long ascribed to Sarah Wentworth Morton.

brown coal: see LIGNITE.

Brown Deer, village (pop. 11,280), SE Wis., on Milwaukee R., N of Milwaukee.

Browne, Hablot Knight, pseud. **Phiz,** 1815–82, English illustrator of many of the novels of Charles Dickens. Also contributed popular cartoons to *Punch.*

Browne, Robert, c.1550–1633, English clergyman, leader of separatists called Brownists. He preached nonconformity, and his treatises are regarded as first expression of CONGREGATIONALISM.

Browne, Sir Thomas, 1605–82, English author, a physician. His *Religio Medici* (written c.1635), a private confession of faith, and *Hydriotaphia: Urne-Buriall* (1658), reflections on death and immortality, show his convolute, inimitably fine prose style.

Brownell, Herbert, Jr., 1904–, U.S. Attorney General (1953–57). Chairman of Republican Natl. Committee (1944–46). Managed Thomas E. Dewey's 1944 and 1948 presidential campaigns.

Brownfield, town (pop. 10,286), NW Texas, in Llano Estacado SW of Lubbock. Oil and cattle spurred growth.

brown hematite: see LIMONITE.

Brownian movement, irregular movement shown by minute solid particles suspended in fluid; continuous, vibratory, unrelated to outside disturbances. Estab. by Robert Brown. Upholds kinetic molecular theory that matter is composed of particles (see MOLECULE) in constant vibratory motion. Suspended particles are buffeted by molecules of liquid or gas. Because the particles are so small, the number of molecular impacts is small; thus the effect of the impacts is an erratic movement and not an equilibrium.

Browning, Elizabeth Barrett, 1806–61, English poet, wife of Robert BROWNING. She defied her own invalidism and her tyrannical father to marry him (1846) and go to Italy. Already known as a poet, she later produced *Sonnets from the Portuguese* (1850); *Casa Guidi Windows* (1851), and *Aurora Leigh* (novel in verse, 1856).

Browning, John Moses, 1855–1926, American inventor of an automatic pistol, a machine gun, and an automatic rifle.

Browning, Orville Hickman, 1806–81, U.S. Secretary of the Interior (1866–69), U.S. Senator from Illinois (1861–63). His *Diary* important source for Lincoln and Johnson administrations.

Browning, Robert, 1812–89, English poet. Developed dramatic monologue as literary form for psychological portraits in verse, e.g., "My Last Duchess," "Fra Lippo Lippi," and "Andrea del Sarto." In longer poems such as *Sordello* (1840), *Dramatis Personae* (1864), and *The Ring and the Book* (1868–69), he displays the same insight, expressed in skillful, compressed style, later an important influence on 20th-cent. poetry. Also wrote lyric poems and poetic dramas. Married Elizabeth Barrett in 1846 after romantic courtship; they lived in Italy until her death (1861).

Browning, town (pop. 2,011), NW Mont., E of GLACIER NATIONAL PARK, in ranch and oil area. Hq. and trade center of Blackfeet Indian Reservation.

Brownists, followers of Robert BROWNE.

Brownlow, William Gannaway (broun'lō), 1805–77, itinerant Methodist preacher, known as the "fighting parson," governor of Tenn. (1865–69), a union sympathizer. His harsh Reconstruction program left Tenn. broken and impoverished.

Brown-Séquard, Charles Édouard (broun'-säkär'), 1817–94, Franco-American physiologist, pioneer in study of internal secretions and rejuvenation.

Brownson, Orestes (Augustus), 1803–76, American reformer. A vigorous writer on social and religious topics, he went through several phases of belief. At first a Presbyterian, he later became a Universalist, a Unitarian minister, head of a church he founded, a transcendentalist, and finally a Roman Catholic. He agitated for workingmen's rights, fought social evils, and wrote books and edited magazines to promote these causes.

brownstone: see SANDSTONE.

Browns Valley, village (pop. 1,033), W Minn., on S.Dak. line, NW of Ortonville; settled 1866. Farm trade center. Controversial skeleton (Browns Valley man) discovered nearby 1934.

Brownsville. 1 City, Fla.: see WEST PENSACOLA. **2** City (pop. 48,040), extreme S Texas, on Rio Grande R., S of Corpus Christi. Fort Taylor founded here 1846 by Gen. Zachary Taylor, who fought battles of Palo Alto and Resaca de la Palma coming to its aid after Mexican War began. Renamed (1846) for defender, Major Jacob Brown. Fort Brown, held briefly by Union in Civil War and prominent in Mexican border clashes, was active until 1944. One of chief cities of rich irrigated area, it also has oil and natural gas industries. A busy ocean port (deepwater channel finished 1936) across river from Matamoros, Mex.

brown thrush: see THRASHER.

Brown University, The College of, at Providence, R.I.; for men; chartered 1764 as Rhode Island Col. at Warren, opened 1765. Moved 1770; renamed 1804. Pembroke Col. (for women, 1891) is affiliated. Notable is John Carter BROWN Library.

Brownwood, city (pop. 16,974), central Texas, SE of Abilene. Industrial center with railroad shops. Seat of Howard Payne Col. Nearby L. Brownwood used for irrigation and recreation.

Bruce, celebrated Scottish family. Descended from 11th-cent. Norman duke, Robert de Brus, who aided William I in conquest of England. In struggle following death of MARGARET MAID OF NORWAY, Bruces claimed succession to the throne. Robert the Bruce was claimant to throne in 1290, rivaled by John de BALIOL. His grandson was famous Robert the Bruce, ROBERT I of Scotland. Edward Bruce, brother of Robert I, was crowned king of Ireland in 1316. Youngest son of Robert I succeeded him as DAVID II. Succeeded by his nephew ROBERT II, first STUART king.

Bruce, earls of Elgin: see ELGIN, THOMAS BRUCE, 7TH EARL OF.

Bruce, Sir David, 1855–1931, British bacteriologist, authority on cause of undulant fever and African sleeping sickness. See BRUCELLOSIS.

Bruce, James, 1730–94, Scottish explorer in Africa. Traveled mainly in North Africa. Visited Ethiopia; rediscovered source of Blue Nile (1770).

Bruce, Stanley Melbourne, 1st Viscount Bruce of Melbourne, 1883–, Australian statesman. As prime minister (1923–29) promoted relations with the empire. Was Australian delegate to League of Nations. High commissioner for Australia in London 1933–45.

Bruce, William Speirs, 1867–1921, Scottish explorer, authority on polar regions. Led Scottish Natl. Antarctic Expedition (1902–4); discovered Coats Land.

brucellosis (broōsĭlō'sĭs) or **undulant fever,** disease of domestic animals and man caused by bacteria. In animals it is also known as contagious abortion. It is transmitted to man in infected meat and milk or by contact. Quarantine, slaughter, and a vaccine are used in veterinary control.

Bruch, Max (broōkh'), 1838–1920, German composer, known for his Violin Concerto in G Minor and his variations on *Kol Nidre* for cello and orchestra.

Brücke (brük'ů) [Ger.,= bridge], German expressionist art movement lasting from 1905 to 1914. Founded in Dresden by Kirchner, Schmidt-Rottluff, and

---

SMALL CAPITALS = cross references. Pronunciation key on inside end pages. Abbreviations: p. 2.

Heckel. Nolde, Pechstein, and Otto Mueller joined later. Their art tended toward the intense and primitivistic in color and form.

Bruckner, Anton (brŏŏk'nŭr), 1824–96, Austrian romantic composer. He wrote nine symphonies, several Masses and a *Te Deum*, and one string quartet.

Brudenell, James Thomas: see CARDIGAN.

Bruegel, Brueghel, or **Breughel** (all: brū'gŭl), family of Flemish genre and landscape painters. The foremost, **Pieter Bruegel** (pē'tŭr), c.1525–69, portrayed in vibrant colors the whole living world of field and forest in which gay, robust peasants are at work and play, as in *The Harvesters* (Metropolitan Mus.). In his *Carrying the Cross* (Vienna) and *Massacre of the Innocents* (Brussels) he showed horrors of the Inquisition in a Flemish village. A son, **Pieter Bruegel** the younger, 1564–1637, was known as Hell Bruegel for his pictures of the infernal regions. His brother, **Jan Bruegel** (yän), 1568–1625, called Velvet Bruegel, painted landscapes and flowers. Shared his father's popularity.

Bruges (brŏŏzh, Fr. brüzh), Flemish *Brugge*, city (est. pop. 52,200), cap. of West Flanders, NW Belgium; linked by canal with Zeebrugge. Once the greatest port of N Europe, it is now a quiet city, famed for its medieval architecture, quaint canals, bridges, convents, and churches. It has lace and beer mfg. and a printing industry. An early and typical Flemish commune, Bruges became (late 12th cent.) the chief port and a major wool-mfg. center of Flanders. It held extensive political privileges, and its government passed gradually from the patricians to the chief guilds—weavers, fullers, shearers, dyers. Leading the Flemish rebellion against Philip IV of France, Bruges defeated the French in the BATTLE OF THE SPURS (1302). It became the chief warehouse of the HANSEATIC LEAGUE, reached its height as international port in the 14th cent., but foreign competition to the Flemish wool industry and the rise of Antwerp soon caused its decline (15th cent.), and its ports silted up. Bruges was the cradle and remains a treasure house of Flemish art. Among its many Gothic buildings are the Cloth Hall, with a famous belfry and carillon; the city hall; the cathedral; the Church of Notre Dame, with the tomb of Charles the Bold; and the Chapel of the Precious Blood, a major place of pilgrimage. The Hospital of St. John (12th cent.) contains masterpieces of Hans Memling.

Brugmann, Karl (kärl' brŏŏk'män), 1849–1919, German philologist of the "neogrammarian" school which argued that scientific rules of linguistics do not admit of exceptions. His comparative grammar of Indo-European languages is still standard.

Brühl, Heinrich, Graf von (hīn'rĭkh gräf' fŭn brül'), 1700–1763, Saxon statesman; chief minister to AUGUSTUS III of Poland and Saxony. Dictated disastrous policy in Seven Years War; allegedly amassed huge fortune through fraud.

Brumaire (brümâr'), second month of FRENCH REVOLUTIONARY CALENDAR. Coup d'état of 18 Brumaire (Nov. 9–10, 1799), overthrew DIRECTORY and established CONSULATE under Napoleon.

Brummel, Valeri, c.1935–, Russian track star. Set world high jump record three times. Won high jump gold medal at 1964 Olympics.

Brummell, George Bryan (Beau Brummell), 1778–1840, wealthy Englishman; noted for fine clothes. Intimate of the prince regent (later George IV).

Brundisium: see BRINDISI.

Brunehaut, Frankish queen: see BRUNHILDA.

Brunei (brŏŏnī'), sultanate (c.2,225 sq. mi.; pop. 83,869), NW Borneo. Cap. Brunei (pop. c.16,000) is major port. Became British protectorate 1888. Did not join Federation of Malaysia in 1963.

Brunel, Sir Marc Isambard (brŏŏnĕl'), 1769–1849, English engineer and inventor of machinery. Constructed Thames tunnel, assisted by his son, **Isambard Kingdom Brunel,** 1806–59, English engineer and authority

on railway traction and steam navigation, and designer and constructor of ocean steamships.

Brunelleschi, Filippo (fēlēp'pō brŏŏnĕl-lĕs'kē), 1377–1446, first great architect of the Italian Renaissance, a Florentine. In competition (1401) for bronze doors for Florence baptistry his design placed second to that of Ghiberti. Most famous work is octagonal ribbed dome of Florence cathedral. Other works include Pazzi chapel, churches of San Lorenzo and Santo Spirito, and the Ospedale degli Innocenti (foundling hospital).

Brunhild (brŏŏn'hĭld), **Brünnehilde** (brün''ühĭl'dŭ), or **Brynhild** (brĭn'hĭld), in Germanic mythology, mighty female warrior. In the NIBELUNGENLIED, as queen of Iceland, she is defeated by SIEGFRIED, whose death she contrives. In the VOLSUNGASAGA, as Brynhild, chief of the Valkyries, she is loved by Sigurd, but when he deserts her, she contrives his death and destroys herself on his funeral pyre. In Wagner's *Ring of the Nibelungs,* she is Brünnehilde, a Valkyrie (see NIBELUNGEN).

Brunhilda (brünhĭl'dŭ) or **Brunehaut** (brünō'), 534?–613, Frankish queen, wife of SIGEBERT I of Austrasia. Played leading part in the bloody war (567–613) against Neustria following the murder of her sister Galswintha by CHILPERIC I of Neustria. Put to horrible death by Clotaire II of Neustria.

Brüning, Heinrich (hīn'rĭkh brü'nĭng), 1885–, German chancellor (1930–32), leader of Catholic Center party. Passed drastic, unpopular financial decrees; dissolved Hitler's storm troops (1932). Pres. Hindenburg dismissed him abruptly and appointed Papen his successor. Brüning left Germany 1934, became professor at Harvard Univ. 1937. Returned to Germany 1952.

Brünn, Czechoslovakia: see BRNO.

Brünnehilde, another spelling for BRUNHILD.

Brunner, Emil (ä'mēl brŏŏ'ŭr), 1889–1966, Swiss Protestant theologian, professor of theology at Univ. of Zurich. His theological position was associated with that of Karl Barth, with some disagreement. Challenged liberal Protestantism and taught that Christian faith arises from encounter of man and God as He is revealed in Bible. Essence of his thought contained in his *Dogmatics* (3 vols., 1950–62).

Bruno, Saint (brŏŏ'nō), c.1030–1101, German monk; founder (1084) of CARTHUSIANS at Grande Chartreuse. Feast: Oct. 6.

Bruno, Giordano (jōrdä'nō brŏŏ'nō), 1548–1600, Italian philosopher. A Dominican, he was accused of heresy and left the order to become a wandering scholar and teacher. In his metaphysical works he challenged all dogmatic authority, maintaining that each man's view of the world is relative to his position, that any absolute truth is beyond statement, and that possible knowledge is unlimited. He believed that the world is composed of irreducible elements (monads), which operate under laws of relationship governed by a pantheistic principle. He returned to Venice, where he was convicted of heresy and burned at the stake—a martyr of freedom of thought. Bruno's influence on later philosophy, especially that of Spinoza and Leibniz, was profound.

Brunswick, dukes of: see CHARLES WILLIAM FERDINAND; FREDERICK WILLIAM.

Brunswick (brŭnz'wĭk), Ger. *Braunschweig,* former state, central Germany, surrounded by former Prussian provs. In 1946 larger part incorporated into state of LOWER SAXONY, West Germany; the rest into Saxony-Anhalt, East Germany. Agr.; mining in foothills of Harz (silver, copper, lead, iron). Duchy of Brunswick emerged 12th cent. from remnants of domains of HENRY THE LION, who retained only the territories of Brunswick and Lüneburg (roughly, modern Brunswick and Hanover). The Guelphic house repeatedly divided into several branches, notably those of Brunswick-Lüneburg (after 1692 electors of HANOVER) and of Brunswick-Wolffenbüttel, or Bruns-

SMALL CAPITALS = cross references. Pronunciation key on inside end pages. Abbreviations: p. 2.

wick proper. Duchy was part of the kingdom of Westphalia under Jérôme Bonaparte (1807–13); joined German Empire 1871; became republic 1918; joined Weimar Republic 1919. Its early cap., Wolfenbüttel, was replaced in 1753 by **Brunswick** city (pop. 240,431), now in Lower Saxony on the Oker, a commercial and mfg. center (machinery, beer). Chartered 12th cent., it later joined the Hanseatic League. Notable landmarks (all more or less damaged in Second World War) include the 12th-cent. cathedral, with Henry the Lion's tomb, and the famous 15th-cent. fountain named for Till Eulenspiegel, who lived here. Former Richmond Palace has fine art museum.

Brunswick. 1 City (pop. 21,703), SE Ga., on Atlantic coast SSW of Savannah; founded 1771–72. Sheltered harbor for freighters and shrimping fleet. SEA ISLANDS (offshore) and city are resorts. U.S. naval air station is nearby. **2** Town (pop. 15,797), S Maine, on Androscoggin R., W of Bath; settled 1628 as trading post. Fort Andros (1688) destroyed by Indians; Fort George (1715) dismantled. Harriet Beecher Stowe wrote *Uncle Tom's Cabin* here, and Hawthorne's first novel, *Fanshawe*, printed here. Seat of BOWDOIN COLLEGE. **3** Village (pop. 11,725), N Ohio, a suburb SSW of Cleveland.

Brusa, Turkey: see BURSA.

Brush, George de Forest, 1855–1941, American painter known for realistic paintings of American Indians and, later, for Italianate portraits and family groups.

Brussa, Turkey: see BURSA.

Brussels (brŭ'sŭlz), Flemish *Brussel,* Fr. *Bruxelles,* city (est. pop. 170,086; with suburbs, 1,065,921), cap. of Belgium and of Brabant prov. Officially bilingual (French and Flemish). Administrative seat of European Economic Community. Major commercial, industrial, and cultural center. Lace mfg. best-known industry. Dating from 10th cent., Brussels replaced Louvain as cap. of Brabant in 15th cent. and was the seat of the Spanish, later Austrian, governors of the Netherlands (16th–18th cent.). Frequently besieged in the wars of that period, Brussels twice fell to the French in the French Revolutionary Wars (1792, 1794), was Wellington's hq. in the Waterloo campaign (1815), and became the cap. of independent Belgium in 1830. It was occupied by the Germans in both world wars (1914–18, 1940–44) but suffered no physical damage. On its historic center, the Grand' Place, are the city hall (14th–17th cent.); the Renaissance Maison du Roi or Broodhuis, meeting place of the old States-General; and the 18th-cent. royal palace and parliament building. Other notable buildings include the Gothic Church of St. Gudule. The general aspect, however, is modern. The Univ. of Brussels was founded 1834.

Brussels sprouts, garden vegetable (*Brassica oleracea gemmifera*) with small, edible heads or sprouts along the stem. Derived from wild cabbage.

Brut, Brute, or **Brutus,** a Trojan, legendary first king of Britain, descendant of Aeneas. His name gave title to long poems by Wace and Layamon.

Bruttium (brŭ'tēŭm), anc. region of S Italy, roughly present Calabria (the "toe" of the "boot"), inhabited in 8th cent. B.C. by native Bruttii and Lucani and Greek colonists. Sybaris and Crotona became important cities of Magna Graecia. After Roman conquest (3d cent. B.C.), Rhegium was favored.

Brutus, surname of anc. Roman family. The semi-legendary **Lucius Junius Brutus,** fl. 510 B.C., was the brother of Lucrece and helped to end the TARQUIN dynasty. He is said to have killed his sons for plotting a restoration of the Tarquins and was honored as founder of the republic. Centuries later **Marcus Junius Brutus,** 85? B.C.–42 B.C., was the principal assassin of Julius Caesar. A partisan of Pompey, he was pardoned by Caesar after the battle of Pharsala and held high office, but joined Cassius in the successful plot to murder Caesar (44 B.C.). Antony fulminated against him and, with Octavian (later Augus-

tus), defeated him at Philippi (42 B.C.). Brutus committed suicide. His character has been much disputed from that day to this. A kinsman, **Decimus Junius Brutus,** d. 43 B.C., also a member of the conspiracy, was besieged in Gaul by Antony and was killed.

Bruyn, Barthel Bartholomaeus (bär'tŭl bärtŏlōmä'ŏōs broin), 1493–1555, German Renaissance painter.

Bryan, William Jennings, 1860–1925, American political leader. U.S. Representative from Nebr. (1891–95). Advocated free coinage of silver. Famous "Cross of Gold" speech led to Democratic presidential nomination in 1896. Nominee again in 1900 and 1908. As Secretary of State under Pres. Wilson (1913–15), he aided in passing reform measures. In later years Bryan diligently defended religious FUNDAMENTALISM, especially in famous SCOPES TRIAL. A man of integrity, a masterful orator of imposing appearance, he was idolized by the masses (esp. in West).

Bryan, city (pop. 27,542), E central Texas, NW of Houston; founded 1865. Agr. area with variety of light industry.

Bryansk (brēänsk'), city (1965 est. pop. 267,000), W European RSFSR, on Desna R. Transportation center; ironworks and machine plants. Passed to Muscovy by Lithuania in 16th cent.

Bryant, William Cullen, 1794–1878, American romantic poet, b. Mass. Famed when he was a youth for poetry (e.g., "Thanatopsis" and "To a Waterfowl"), he was a lawyer until he became after 1825 a journalist in New York—associate editor, later editor and part owner of free-trade, antislavery *Evening Post.* Among later nature poems are such familiar and widely loved verses as "The Death of the Flowers" and "To the Fringed Gentian." He also translated the *Iliad* and the *Odyssey* in blank verse.

Bryaxis (brīăk'sĭs), 4th cent. B.C., Greek sculptor. Helped decorate the Mausoleum at Halicarnassus.

Bryce, James Bryce, Viscount, 1838–1922, English historian, statesman, diplomat, and jurist. Noted for wide knowledge and ability to combine deeply scholarly writing with full, active life. Well known are his *History of the Holy Roman Empire* (1864) and his commentary, *The American Commonwealth* (1888), a classic interpretation of American way of life. Ambassador to U.S. 1907–13. In law, his *Studies in History and Jurisprudence* (1901) is major work because of its wide view of liberal principle.

Bryce Canyon National Park: see NATIONAL PARKS AND MONUMENTS (table).

Bryher, 1894–, legal name of Mrs. Kenneth Macpherson, nee (Annie) Winifred Ellerman, English author of historical novels (e.g., *Beowulf,* 1948; *The Player's Boy,* 1953; *Gate to the Sea,* 1958) and her autobiographical memoir, *A Heart to Artemis* (1962).

Brynhild, another spelling for BRUNHILD.

Bryn Mawr College, near Bryn Mawr, Pa.; for women; opened 1885 by Society of Friends. Modeled on group curriculum plan at Johns Hopkins Univ. Had early graduate school for women. Graduate school now coed.

Brythonic (brĭthŏ'nĭk), branch of Celtic languages of Indo-European family, including Welsh, Breton, and Cornish (now extinct). See LANGUAGE (table).

Brzesc: see BRIEG.

bubble chamber: see WILSON CLOUD CHAMBER.

Buber, Martin (bōō'bĕr) 1878–1965, Jewish theologian and philosopher, b. Vienna. He taught at the Univ. of Frankfurt-am-Main (1924–33) and the Univ. of Jerusalem (1938–51). He was greatly influenced by the mysticism of the Hasidim and by Kierkegaard's Christian existentialism. The main tenet of Buber's theology, as developed in his book *I and Thou,* is that the relationship between God and man and between man and the world should be one of direct response and dialogue. His thinking had great impact on such 20th-cent. Christian theologians as Tillich and Niebuhr.

bubonic plague: see PLAGUE.

Bucaramanga (bōō"kärämän'gä), city (pop. 229,748), N central Colombia, in E Andes; founded 1622. Became coffee and tobacco center after 1880.

buccaneer: see PIRACY.

Bucephalus (būsĕ'fŭlŭs), horse of Alexander the Great, hence, any horse noted for fire and speed.

Bucer or **Butzer, Martin** (bū'sŭr, bŏŏt'sŭr), 1491–1551, German Protestant reformer. Influenced by Luther's preaching, he joined (1523) Reformation movement at Strasbourg. Promoted Protestant education, brought about (1536) Wittenberg Concord on doctrine of the Eucharist. Spent his last years in England, where he taught at Cambridge and exerted influence on the Church of England.

Buchan, Alexander (bŭ'kŭn, –khŭn), 1829–1907, Scottish meteorologist. Curator, Royal Society of Edinburgh library and museum. Responsible for founding Ben Nevis observatory (1883).

Buchan, John, 1st Baron Tweedsmuir (twēdz–mŭr), 1875–1940, Scottish author and statesman. Wrote adventure novels (e.g., *The Thirty-nine Steps,* 1915; *Greenmantle,* 1916; *The Three Hostages,* 1924) and biographies. Governor general of Canada 1935–40.

Buchanan, Franklin (būkă'nŭn), 1800–1874, American naval officer. First superintendent (1845–47) U.S. Naval Academy. Joined Confederate navy; became ranking officer. Defeated by David G. FARRAGUT at Mobile Bay (Aug. 5, 1864).

Buchanan, George, 1506–82, Scottish humanist, tutor to Mary Queen of Scots and her son James VI. Works include Latin poems, plays, and treatises.

Buchanan, James, 1791–1868, 15th President of the United States (1857–61), b. Pa. U.S. Congressman from Pa. (1821–31); U.S. Senator (1834–45); Secretary of State (1845–49). As minister to Great Britain (1853–56) he helped draw up OSTEND MANIFESTO. As President (Democrat), he attempted to keep proslavery and antislavery factions in balance, was opposed by extremists on both sides. In 1860 he maintained that no state had the right to secede, but that he had no power to coerce seceding states; his view that the Federal government could use force in protecting Federal property made Federal forts in Southern states of paramount importance. Many recent historians consider Buchanan's constitutional views sound; all admire his valiant efforts for peace.

Buchanan, village (1966 pop. 2,160), SE N.Y., on E Bank of Hudson R., SW of Peekskill. Has atomic power plant.

Bucharest (bōō'kŭrĕst) or **Bucuresti** (bŏŏkŏŏrĕsht'), city (est. pop. 1,236,065), cap. and chief commercial and mfg. center of Rumania, in Walachia. Seat of patriarch of Rumanian Orthodox Church. Univ. (founded 1864). Became residence of Walachian princes 15th cent.

Buchenwald (bōō'khŭnvält"), village, East Germany, in former state of Thuringia, in Buchenwald forest. Site of notorious concentration camp during Hitler regime.

Buchman, Frank (Nathan Daniel) (bŏŏk'mŭn), 1878–1961, American evangelist, leader of Oxford Group (Buchmanites). In 1921 he preached "world-changing through life-changing" at Oxford Univ. Initiated (1938) Moral Re-armament (MRA) movement.

Buchner, Eduard (ä'dōŏärt bōŏkh'nŭr), 1860–1917, German chemist. Won 1907 Nobel Prize in Chemistry for establishing yeast enzymes as cause of alcoholic fermentation and discovering zymase (part of yeast enzyme system).

Büchner, Georg (gä'ŏrk bükh'nŭr), 1813–37, German author, a medical student and radical agitator. In his brief life he produced several bold, powerful works —a drama, *Danton's Death* (1835; Eng. tr., 1928); a comedy, *Leonce and Lena* (1850; Eng. tr., 1928); the fragments of a tragedy, *Wozzeck* (1850; Eng. tr., 1928), from which Alban Berg derived his opera; and a short novel, *Lenz.* His brother was **Ludwig Büchner** (lōŏt'vĭkh), 1824–99, German philosopher.

He protested against idealist metaphysics with a philosophy of extreme materialism.

Buck, Leffert Lefferts, 1837–1909, American civil engineer. Designed Williamsburg Bridge (New York city), Columbia river railroad bridge (Pasco, Wash.), and many others.

Buck, Pearl S(ydenstricker), 1892–, American novelist. Like her parents and her first husband (John Lossing Buck, from whom she was divorced) she was long a missionary in China. Her novels, notably *The Good Earth* (1931), picture life in China; she has contributed to understanding between races and peoples in many works and has written for and worked with children. Awarded 1938 Nobel Prize in Literature.

buckeye, tree or shrub of genus *Aesculus* of N Hemisphere. It bears clusters of red, white, or yellow flowers in late spring and large spiny fruits. Ohio is called Buckeye State after Ohio buckeye.

Buckingham, dukes of (Stafford line): see STAFFORD.

Buckingham, George Nugent Temple Grenville, 1st marquess of: see GRENVILLE, GEORGE.

Buckingham, George Villiers, 1st duke of (vĭl'yŭrz), 1592–1628, English nobleman, a royal favorite. Arrived at English court in 1614 as James I was tiring of Robert Carr. Rose rapidly and by 1620 was dispensing king's patronage. Received credit for preventing unpopular marriage of Charles I to Spanish Infanta. Urged war with Spain and promoted Charles's marriage to Henrietta Maria of France. Remained favorite after Charles came to throne. After failure of several expeditions, he was increasingly unpopular. King dissolved Parliament to prevent action against duke. Killed by a discontented naval officer. His son, **George Villiers, 2d duke of Buckingham,** 1628–87, was strong royalist in civil war. Served Charles II in exile but intrigues and his marriage to Mary Fairfax, daughter of Puritan lord, caused estrangement. Regained favor after Restoration and became one of most powerful courtiers. His temper, recklessness, and dissoluteness kept his career stormy. Was member of the Cabal. Dismissed 1674, regained favor 1684 in spite of earlier opposition to James II. A scholar with exquisite tastes, he patronized science and learning. Wrote poetry, religious tracts, and plays (including *The Rehearsal,* 1671).

Buckingham, town (pop. 7,421), SW Que., Canada, in lumbering and farming region. Has large chemical industry.

Buckingham Palace, London residence of British sovereigns since 1837. It was originally built by the duke of Buckingham in 1703. Palace has more than 600 rooms.

Buckinghamshire (bŭ'kĭng-ŭmshĭr), **Buckingham,** or **Bucks,** inland county (749 sq. mi.; pop. 486,183), S central England; co. town, Aylesbury. Region includes chalky Chiltern Hills and richly agr. Vale of Aylesbury. Southern boundary is the Thames. County has Roman and pre-Roman remains.

Buck Island Reef National Monument: see NATIONAL PARKS and MONUMENTS (table).

Buckland, town (pop. 1,664), NW Mass., in hills W of Greenfield. Mary Lyon was born and taught here.

Buckle, Henry Thomas, 1821–62, English historian. Projected panoramic history of civilization. Two volumes, *History of Civilization in England* (1857–61), caused sensation. His scientific method and broad approach influenced later historiography.

Buckner, Simon Bolivar, 1823–1914, Confederate general. Surrendered Fort Donelson to Grant (1862). Later commanded in Ky., Tenn., and La.

Bucks, England: see BUCKINGHAMSHIRE.

Bucksport, town (pop. 3,466), S Maine, on E bank of Penobscot R., S of Bangor; settled 1762. Partly burned by British in 1779 and in War of 1812. Grew as port in 19th cent.

buckthorn, thorny shrub or small tree (*Rhamnus*). Common buckthorn (*Rhamnus cathartica*) used for hedges. Cascara sagrada comes from *R. purshiana.*

buckwheat, annual plant (*Fagopyrum sagittatum*), widely grown for its three-cornered fruit, valued for buckwheat flour. Also used as poultry and stock feed.

Bucuresti, Rumania: see BUCHAREST.

Bucyrus (būsī'rŭs), city (pop. 12,276), N central Ohio, on Sandusky R., NE of Marion; settled 1819. Trade and industrial center in farm area.

bud, in lower plants and animals a protuberance from which a new organism develops. In seed plants, a growing point containing rudiments of flowers, leaves, and shoots. See also BUDDING and CUTTING.

Budaeus: see BUDÉ, GUILLAUME.

Budapest (bōō'dŭpĕst"), city (est. pop. 1,875,000), cap. of Hungary, on both banks of Danube; formed 1873 by union of Buda and Obuda (right bank) with Pest (left bank). Obuda and Pest stand near site of two Roman towns, destroyed by Mongols 1241. Buda was founded as a fortress (13th cent.), became a royal residence (14th cent.), flourished as intellectual center under Matthias Corvinus. All three cities declined under Turkish occupation (1541–1686), but Buda revived through royal favors in 18th cent. The univ. founded 1635 at Trnava by Peter Pazmany was transferred to Buda 1777, to Pest 1784. Pest, rebuilt along modern lines in 19th cent., became a leading commercial and artistic center and was, until 1914, the leading grain market of Europe. Machine, textile, and chemical mfg. developed after First World War. One of the finest cities of Europe, Budapest was 70% destroyed during 14-week siege by Russians in Second World War (1944–45). Center of popular uprising against Hungarian Communist regime 1956.

Buddha (bōō'dŭ) [Sanskrit,= the enlightened one], title of Siddhartha Gautama, c.563–483 B.C., Indian religious leader, founder of Buddhism. Son of a ruler of area N of Benares, he at the age of 29 renounced luxury, became an ascetic. "The great enlightenment" gave him principles of religion. He and disciples spread the faith.

Buddh Gaya or **Bodh Gaya** (both: bōōd' gä'yä), village, Bihar, India. Here Buddha achieved enlightenment under a bo tree. Relics of Buddhist art.

Buddhism (bōōd'īzŭm), system of philosophy and ethics founded by Buddha; one of the great religions of the world. Its beliefs were in origin closely related to Brahmanism (see HINDUISM), but had less formalism and a greater emphasis on self-denial and compassion. The "four noble truths" of Buddha are: existence is suffering; the origin of suffering is desire; suffering ceases when desire ceases; the way to reach the end of desire is by following the "noble eightfold path." This path comprises right belief, right resolve (to renounce carnal pleasure, harm no living creature, and the like), right speech, right conduct, right occupation or living, right effort, right contemplation or right mindedness, and right ecstasy. The final goal of the religious man is to escape from existence into blissful nonexistence—nirvana [Sanskrit,= annihilation]. Individual man is made up of elements that existed before him, that separate at his death, and that may be recombined in a somewhat similar fashion. It is from this chain of being that man seeks to escape by religious living. These "salvation" doctrines were spread rapidly by Buddhist monks and for a short time Buddhism reached a great height in India under Asoka (3d cent. B.C.). It later died out in India, but persisted in Ceylon and in Burma in its simpler, "purer" form (Hinayana or Theravada). It entered China in 1st cent. A.D. and later spread to Japan through Korea. Here it developed into Mahayana, which accepts a number of divine beings and has incorporated many aspects of local religion. In Tibet Buddhism became LAMAISM. Various sects and movements have arisen in Buddhism, one being ZEN BUDDHISM, which grew very strong in Japan.

budding, a form of GRAFTING in which scion is a bud. Used chiefly for roses and some fruits.

Budé, Guillaume (gēyôm' büdä'), 1467–1540, French scholar, known also as Budaeus. One of greatest French humanists and scholars, he was a towering figure of the Renaissance. He persuaded Francis I to found Collège de France, used textual criticism in study of Roman law, and helped to establish philology. He fostered Greek learning in France and wrote on various classical subjects.

Budge, (John) Don(ald), 1915–, American tennis player. In 1938 won American, Australian, French, British singles championships.

Budweis (Ger. bŏŏt'vīs), Czech *České Budějovice,* city (est. pop. 64,000), SW Bohemia, Czechoslovakia. on the Moldau. Produces beer, pencils, enamelware. Fine medieval and baroque architecture.

Buel, Jesse, 1778–1839, American agriculturist and journalist. His model farm was widely imitated later. Defeated for governor of N.Y. in 1836.

Buell, Don Carlos, 1818–98, Union general in Civil War. Supported Grant in Tenn.; saved the day at Shiloh. Forced Braxton Bragg to leave Ky. Criticized and removed from command, he withdrew entirely from the war.

Buena Park (bwā'nŭ), city (pop. 46,401), S Calif., SE of Los Angeles. Processes citrus fruit.

Buenaventura (bwä"nävän tōō'rä), city (pop. 96,708), W Colombia, Pacific port; founded c.1540. Original town was burned by Indians and resettled on island in bay. Exports coffee, platinum, gold, and hides.

Buena Vista, resort town (pop. 1,806), central Colo., on Arkansas R., W of Colorado Springs; founded 1879. Once the center of rich silver-mining area, it raises livestock and grain.

Buenos Aires (bwā'nŭs ī'rēz), city (pop. c.3,875,000); cap. of Argentina, in federal district, N Argentina, on right bank of Río de la Plata. A metropolis of Latin America, Buenos Aires is the chief port and financial, industrial, and social center of Argentina. Founded by Pedro de Mendoza (1536), it was abandoned (1541) because of hostility of Indians and resettled (1580) by Juan de Garay. It became cap. of viceroyalty of Río de la Plata in 1776. British invasions in 1806–7 were repulsed by LINIERS. The cabildo deposed the viceroy and established junta (1810). Centralist-federalist struggle in Argentina ended by making Buenos Aires paramount. The city was detached from its province and was federalized (1880). Nearby Buenos Aires prov. (cap. LA PLATA) is rich in cattle and grain.

Buffalo. 1 City (1966 pop. 481,453), W N.Y., on L. Erie and Niagara R.; laid out 1803 under Holland Land Co. Major Great Lakes port, important rail focus, and one of largest grain distributors in U.S. Produces flour, iron, steel, chemicals, autos, aircraft, missiles, and electrical equipment. Burned by British in War of 1812. Growth rapid after opening of Erie Canal (1825). Pres. McKinley was assassinated and Theodore Roosevelt took presidential oath here in 1901 during Pan-American Exposition. Presidents Cleveland (became mayor 1882) and Fillmore lived here. Seat of State Univ. of New York at BUFFALO, Canisius Col., D'Youville Col., aeronautical laboratory of Cornell Univ., Albright Art Gall., and Buffalo Mus. of Science. Has buildings by Louis Sullivan and F. L. Wright. **2** City (pop. 2,907), N Wyo., SSE of Sheridan; founded c.1880. Trade center for resort area. L. De Smet is N.

buffalo, common name for American bison, but accurately applied only to certain related oxlike mammals of Asia, Africa. Asiatic water buffalo (*Bubalus*) or Indian buffalo stands c.5 ft. at shoulder, with spreading, backward-curving horns. Pygmy buffalo (*Anoa*) is wild ox of Celebes. Cape buffalo (*Syncerus*) is in S Africa.

Buffalo, State University of New York at, state supported; coed.; chartered and opened 1846 as medical school; college of arts and science opened 1913. Was Univ. of Buffalo (private) until 1962.

buffalo berry, hardy North American shrub (*Shepherdia argentea*). Silvery foliage; female plant bears edible, yellow or scarlet berries.

Buffalo Bill, 1846–1917, American plainsman, scout, and showman; real name William Frederick Cody. Organized Buffalo Bill's Wild West Show in 1883; toured with it for many years.

buffalo fish, name for several fish of sucker family, chiefly in Mississippi valley rivers and lakes. Flesh bony and coarse, but commercially important as food.

buffalo grass, important range grass (*Buchloe dactyloides*) of plains regions. It is sod forming.

Buffon, Georges Louis Leclerc, comte de (zhôrzh' lwĕ' lüklĕrk' kôt' dü büfô'), 1707–88, French naturalist, author. Devoted life to *Histoire naturelle* (44 vols., 1749–1804).

Bug (boog), river, c.500 mi. long, E Europe. Rises E of Lvov, NW Ukraine, flows N along Polish-Ukrainian border, then NW into the Vistula near Warsaw. Canal connection with the Dnieper. Also called Western Bug.

Bug or **Southern Bug,** Rus. *Yuzhny Bug,* river, 533 mi. long, Ukraine. Rises NW of Khmelnitsky and flows SE into Black Sea. Used for grain transport March–Dec.

bug, accurately only insect of order Hemiptera. Head has structure for piercing and sucking. Those with wings have two pairs. See *ill.,* p. 512.

Buganda: see UGANDA.

Bugayev, Boris Nikolayevich: see BELY, ANDREI.

Bugge, Sophus (sō'fōōs bōō'gù), 1833–1907, Norwegian philologist. Edited Norse runes and poems of the *Eddas* (1881–89; 2d series, 1896).

bugle, brass wind musical instrument, consisting of a conical tube coiled once upon itself. Chiefly used for military bugle calls, such as taps or reveille. Key and valve bugles developed in 19th cent.

Buhl, André Charles: see BOULLE, ANDRÉ CHARLES.

buhrstone (bûr'–) or **burrstone,** any hard, rough-surfaced, siliceous rock which can be used for grinding.

Buisson, Ferdinand Édouard (fĕrdēnă' ādwär' büĕsô'), 1841–1932, French educator. He became professor of pedagogy at the Sorbonne in 1886 and was a member of chamber of deputies 1902–14 and 1919–24. An ardent pacifist, he attended (1867) first congress of International Peace League. With Ludwig Quidde he received 1927 Nobel Peace Prize.

Bujumbura (boojumboo'rù), formerly **Usumbura** (oosoombōo'rä), city (pop. c.47,300), cap. of Burundi; port on L. Tanganyika. Light industry. Coffee and cotton are exported. Germans estab. military post here 1899. Name was changed 1964.

Bukavu (bookä'voo), city (pop. c.60,500). E Republic of the Congo; port on L. Kivu. Administrative, commercial, and communications center; cap. of former Kivu prov. Coffee, hides, quinine, and cement produced. Founded 1901 as Costermansville.

Bukhara (bŏkä'rù), city (1965 est. pop. 95,000). W Uzbek SSR; also spelled Bokhara. Karakul and silk processing. Bokhara rugs originally named after city. One of oldest cities of TURKISTAN and long a center of Islamic culture, it was cap. of emirate of Bukhara, which comprised parts of Uzbekistan, Tadzhikistan, and Turkmenistan. Ruled by despotic Uzbek princes after 16th cent., emirate was forced to accept Russian suzerainty in 1873. Last emir deposed 1920. City has splendid mosques and palaces (9th–17th cent.).

Bukhari (bookhärē'), d. 870, Arabic scholar and Moslem saint, whose collection of traditional sayings of Mohammed is highly respected in Islam.

Bukharin, Nikolai Ivanovich (nyĭkülī' ēvä'nùvĭch bookhä'rēn), 1888–1938, Russian Communist. Chief party theoretician after Lenin's death. Purged and executed in treason trials of 1936–38.

Bukovina (bookùvē'nù), region, E Europe, in W Ukraine and NE Rumania; chief town Chernovtsy (Ukraine). Traversed by Carpathians and by upper Pruth R., it produces timber, grain, livestock. Mixed pop. includes Rumanians, Ukrainians, Russians, and Magyars. Region was the nucleus of the old principality of Moldavia. Ceded by Turkey to Austria

1775; to Rumania 1919. N part (c.2,140 sq. mi.; est. pop. 774,000) ceded to USSR 1940; reoccupied by Rumania 1941–44; formally ceded to USSR 1947. S part (c.1,890 sq. mi.; est. pop. 500,000) forms a historic prov. of Rumania.

Bulawayo (boolawä'yō), city (pop. c.210,900). SW Rhodesia. Major rail hub; important industrial and commercial center. Founded by British 1893

bulb, thickened fleshy plant bud, usually formed under soil. Carries plant over from one season to another. Examples are tulip, hyacinth, lily. The CORM, TUBER, and RHIZOME are not true bulbs.

bulbul (bool'bool), name for a number of species of thrushlike birds of Africa and Asia. The bulbul of Persian poetry was probably a nightingale.

Bulfinch, Charles, 1763–1844, American architect. Elegance of his structures in Boston places them among best of early American architecture. Designed Boston statehouse (1799); University Hall, Harvard Univ. (1815); First Church of Christ, Lancaster, Mass. (1816–17); and Mass. General Hospital (1820). Worked on Capitol at Washington, 1818–30.

Bulfinch, Thomas, 1796–1867, American author, popularizer of mythology in *The Age of Fable* (1855).

Bulganin, Nikolai Aleksandrovich (nyĭkülī' ŭlyĭksän'drùvĭch boolgä'nĭn), 1895–, Russian Communist leader. Helped plan defense of Moscow 1941; later was given rank of marshal; minister of armed forces 1947–49; vice premier of USSR 1949–53; premier 1953–58; succeeded by KHRUSHCHEV.

Bulgari: see BULGARS, EASTERN.

Bulgaria (bŭlgâ'rēù), republic (42,818 sq. mi.; est pop. 8,144,000). SE Europe, on Balkan Peninsula, bounded by the Black Sea (E). Turkey and Greece (S), Yugoslavia (W), and Rumania (N); cap. Sofia. Chief port: Varna. An agr. country, crossed by Balkan mts. and drained by Danube, Struma, and Maritsa rivers, Bulgaria cultivates cereals. Minerals (iron, copper, zinc) and oil. First two five-year plans (1949–57) emphasized growth of heavy industry Pop. is mainly Greek Orthodox, with some Moslems. Expulsion of Turkish minority (c.250,000) began 1950. Occupying ancient THRACE and MOESIA, country was conquered A.D. 660 by a group of Eastern BULGARS, who later merged with older Slavic settlers and adopted their language. Their khan Krum exacted tribute from Byzantine Empire (9th cent.); BORIS I introduced Christianity; SIMEON I enlarged territory, took title tsar. Subjugated by Byzantium 1018–1186, Bulgaria again became an empire (with cap. at Trnovo) under Ivan I; reached its height under IVAN II; became tributary to Serbia 1330; was annexed by Turkey after defeats at Kossovo (1389) and Nikopol (1396). Cruel suppression of revolt under Stefan STAMBULOV (1876; "Bulgarian atrocities") gave Russia an excuse for war on Turkey (1877–78). Greater Bulgaria, set up by Treaty of SAN STEFANO, was reduced by Congress of BERLIN and divided into three parts: N Bulgaria, as principality under nominal Turkish overlordship; E RUMELIA, as Turkish province with autonomous rights; and MACEDONIA, under direct Turkish rule. ALEXANDER of Battenberg, first prince of Bulgaria, annexed E Rumelia 1885; his successor, FERDINAND of Saxe-Coburg-Gotha, proclaimed full independence 1908, took title tsar. Bulgarian claims to Macedonia led to BALKAN WARS of 1912–13, in which Bulgaria first won, then lost, much territory. One of Central Powers in First World War, it lost S DOBRUJA and outlet to Aegean Sea by Treaty of NEUILLY. The regime of Premier STAMBULISKI was followed by two military dictatorships (1923–26, 1934–35) and a royal dictatorship under BORIS III (1935–43). In Second World War, Bulgaria joined the AXIS (1941) and occupied parts of Yugoslavia, Greece. In Sept., 1944, Russia declared war and invaded Bulgaria. A pro-Russian coalition cabinet took power but was soon replaced by a Communist regime. The monarchy was abolished 1946. Bulgarian peace treaty (ratified 1947) allowed Bulgaria to keep S Dobruja (ceded by Rumania 1940). A WARSAW TREATY nation, Bulgaria was admitted to the UN in 1955.

Bulgarian, language of Slavic subfamily of Indo-European languages. See LANGUAGE (table).

Bulgars, Eastern, people. probably speaking a Turkic language. who had a powerful state in E European Russia, along Middle Volga (8th–13th cent.). Their cap., Bulgari or Bolgari, was near Kazan. Conquered by Mongols 1237. A branch of the people moved west and merged with Slavs in Bulgaria.

Bulge, Battle of the: see BATTLE OF THE BULGE.

Bull, Ole (ō'lù), 1810–80, Norwegian violinist. He toured Europe and America, playing mostly his own compositions and Norwegian folk music.

Bull, the, in astrology: see ZODIAC.

bull [Latin *bulla* = leaden seal], solemn official pronouncement of the pope. In modern times encyclicals (letters to all bishops) tend to be more employed for authoritative doctrinal statements, whereas bulls are confined to the expression of more practical decisions (e.g., convocation of council, approval or condemnation).

bull bat: see NIGHTHAWK.

bullfighting, national sport of Spain, also popular in Latin America. Conducted in arena, or *plaza de toros.* The matador, who kills the bull, is assisted by *banderilleros,* who enrage bulls by stabbing them with darts, *picadores,* who jab bulls with lances, and *toreros,* who distract bulls by waving red flags.

bullfinch, any of several European songbirds of finch family, often caged. Common species is woodland bird; blue-gray upper plumage, tile red below.

bullfrog, largest North American frog; aquatic with fully webbed toes. Common bullfrog (*Rana catesbiana*) E of Rocky Mts. Deep bass cry or croaking.

bullhead, name for several species of genus *Ameiurus* of catfish family, found in sluggish waters. Commonest is brown bullhead or horned pout (12 to 18 in. long); others are black and yellow bullheads. Name also for some species of sculpin family (large-headed, toothed fish).

Bullinger, Heinrich (hīn'rĭkh bōō'lĭngŭr), 1504–75, Swiss Protestant reformer. Successor to Zwingli in Zurich in 1531, he and Calvin agreed to Consensus Tigurinus (1549) by which Swiss theology turned from Zwinglian to Calvinist theory.

Bullitt, William C(hristian), 1891–1967, American diplomat; first U.S. ambassador to USSR (1933–36); ambassador to France (1936–41).

Bull Moose party: see PROGRESSIVE PARTY.

Bullock, William A., 1813–67, American inventor. His printing press, first to feed automatically from a continuous roll of paper, revolutionized the industry.

Bull Run, small stream, NE Va., c.30 mi. SW of Washington, D.C., scene of two important Civil War battles, July 21, 1861, and Aug. 29–30, 1862. In **first battle of Bull Run,** first major clash of war, Federals under Irvin McDowell attacked Confederates under P. G. T. Beauregard. They met resistance of T. J. Jackson standing "like a stone wall," and were forced into retreat, a rout ending only at defenses of Washington. Victory cheered South, and spurred North to greater efforts. **Second battle of Bull Run,** was culmination of R. E. Lee's strategy to prevent reinforcement of John Pope's army by G. B. McClellan along Rappahannock R., where Stonewall Jackson had driven it. James Longstreet, after attack by Pope, counterattacked and drove Federals back across Bull Run. In pursuit Jackson was stopped at Chantilly, Sept. 1, 1862, and Pope withdrew to Washington. Both battlefields included in Manassas Natl. Battlefield Park.

Bülow, Bernhard, Fürst von (bērn'härt fürst' fūn bü'lō), 1849–1929, chancellor of Germany (1900–1909). His aggressive policies (notably in Morocco) isolated Germany and paved way for First World War.

Bülow, Hans von, 1830–94, German pianist and conductor; student of Liszt. Directed premières of *Tristan* and *Die Meistersinger* and propagated German music, particularly that of Brahms.

bulrush, sedge of genus *Scirpus,* often with grasslike leaves. Grown in aquatic or bog gardens. Bulrush in which Moses was hidden (Ex. 2.3) was papyrus.

Bultmann, Rudolf (rōō'dôlf bōōlt'män), 1884–, German Protestant biblical scholar and theologian. In 1940s he raised the still controversial question of the New Testament and mythology. His demythologizing is a reinterpretation of the biblical message mainly in the light of Heidegger's existential philosophy.

Bulwer-Lytton, Edward George Earle Lytton, 1st **Baron Lytton,** 1803–73, English novelist and playwright. Among his many popular novels (some historical) are *Eugene Aram* (1832), *The Last Days of Pompeii* (1834), *Rienzi* (1835). Particularly well known among his plays are *The Lady of Lyons* (1838), *Richelieu* (1838). The son born to his unhappy marriage was **Edward Robert Bulwer-Lytton, 1st earl of Lytton,** 1831–91, who wrote under the pseud. **Owen Meredith.** A diplomat and statesman, viceroy of India, he is best remembered for his verse, notably *Lucile* (1860).

Buna rubber: see RUBBER, SYNTHETIC.

Bunau-Varilla, Philippe Jean (fēlēp' zhä' bünō-värēyä'), 1859–1940, French engineer, prominent in PANAMA CANAL controversy. Organized second French canal-building company; sold it to U.S.; then engineered PANAMA revolution of 1903. As minister of Panama to U.S. negotiated Hay-Bunau-Varilla Treaty, which gave control of Canal Zone to U.S.

bunchberry or **dwarf cornel,** low North American and Asiatic perennial (*Cornus canadensis*), related to dogwood. White-bracted flowers and red berries.

Bunche, Ralph (Johnson), 1904–, American internationalist. The first Negro to be a division head in Dept. of State (1945), he became director of UN Trusteeship Division (1946) and UN undersecretary for special political affairs (1958). Awarded 1950 Nobel Peace Prize.

Bundestag (bōōn'dĕs-täkh), lower house of the parliament of Federal Republic of Germany.

Bunin, Ivan Alekseyevich (ēvän' ŭlyĭksyä'yĭvĭch bōō'nyĭn), 1870–1953, Russian author. A noted poet, he is best known for his short stories, especially *The Man* (or *The Gentleman) from San Francisco* (1916), and the autobiographical novel *The Well of Days* (1930; Eng. tr., 1933). Resided abroad after 1919. Awarded 1933 Nobel Prize in Literature.

Bunker Hill, battle of, in American Revolution, June 17, 1775, actually fought on neighboring Breed's Hill, Charlestown, Mass. British victory failed to break the triumphant ring of patriots besieging Boston.

Bunsen, Robert Wilhelm (bŭn'sŭn), 1811–99, German scientist. Studied organic arsenic compounds, photochemistry. Evolved method of gas analysis; with Kirchhoff discovered cesium and rubidium, using spectroscope; invented Bunsen electric cell. Known for **Bunsen burner:** hollow tube fitted around flame, with base opening to admit air; produces smokeless, nonluminous, high-temperature flame.

Bunshaft, Gordon, 1909–, American architect. As chief designer for the architectural firm of Skidmore, Owings & Merrill, he was responsible for the Lever building, New York (1952). Designed Beinecke Library for Yale Univ. (1963).

bunt: see SMUT.

bunting, small, plump bird of finch family. American buntings include indigo bunting; painted bunting or nonpareil; snow bunting; dickcissel. Baywinged bunting is really vesper sparrow.

Buntline, Ned, pseud. of **Edward Zane Carroll Judson,** 1822?–1886, American adventurer, editor of sensational magazine (*Ned Buntline's Own*), author of trashy novels that preceded dime novels. Lynched for murder, he was cut down alive (1846). Introduced

Buffalo Bill as actor in his *The Scouts of the Plains* (1872).

Buñuel, Luis (lwĕs bōōn'üĕl), 1900–, Spanish film director. Collaborated with Salvador Dali on early surrealistic films, notably *Un Chien andalou* (1928). In the 1930s and 1940s his films were realistic, often documentary. Later films, e.g., *Viridiana* (1961), are filled with symbolism of moral connotation.

bunya-bunya (bŭn'yù), large Australian tree (*Araucaria bidwillii*). Its seeds provide a staple food of native tribes.

Bunyan, John, 1628–88, English author, notable for his *Pilgrim's Progress from This World to That Which Is to Come* (1678). Spiritual fervor permeates his works, which unite eloquence of the Bible and vigorous realism of common speech. An evangelistic layman, he was long in prison for unlicensed preaching. Other works include *Grace Abounding to the Chief of Sinners* (1666), a spiritual autobiography.

Bunyan, Paul, Gargantuan hero of "tall tales" of American lumber camps from Mich. to the West Coast. He was aided in his feats by Babe, the Blue Ox.

Buonaparte: see BONAPARTE and NAPOLEON I.

Buonarroti, Michelangelo: see MICHELANGELO BUONARROTI.

Buraimi (bōōrī'mī), name of several oases between Oman and Saudi Arabia, SE Arabia. Region is disputed by Oman and Saudi Arabia.

Burbage, Richard (bûr'bĭj), 1567?–1619, leading tragedian of his day. Original player of Shakespeare's Hamlet, Lear, Othello, and Richard III. His father, James Burbage, d. 1597, built London's first permanent theater 1576; it was later moved and became the Globe Theater.

Burbank, Luther, 1849–1926, American plant breeder. He developed the Burbank potato, Shasta daisy, and many other new plant varieties.

Burbank, city (pop. 90,155), S Calif., N of Los Angeles; laid out 1887. Has motion picture and television studios. Heavy mfg.

Burchell, William John (bûr'chùl), 1782?–1863, English explorer and scientist. Made vast collections in Africa of natural and meteorological objects. Discovered many animal and plant species.

Burchfield, Charles, 1893–1967, American painter, known as a painter of Victorian mansions, false-front stores, and other relics of the late 19th cent. His work is marked by subtlety of color and a slightly ironic realism.

Burckhardt, Jacob Christoph (yä'kôp krĭs'tôf bŏŏrk'härt), 1818–97, Swiss historian, a founder of cultural history. His works include the classic *Die Kultur der Renaissance in Italien* (1860).

Burckhardt, John Lewis (bûrk'härt), 1784–1817, explorer, b. Switzerland. Sponsored by English association promoting African discovery. Posing as learned Moslem, was first Christian to reach Medina.

Burckmair, Hans: see BURGKMAIR, HANS.

burdock, coarse, weedy biennial (*Arctium*), naturalized in North America. Rounded, many-seeded burs.

Burdwan (bûrdwän'), town (pop. 75,376), S West Bengal, India. A group of 108 Siva linga temples (1788) is nearby. Cutlery mfg. Also spelled Bardwan.

Burgas (bōōr'gäs), city (est. pop. 101,975), E Bulgaria; a Black Sea port.

Burgenland (Ger. bōōr'gùnlänt), province (1,530 sq. mi.; pop. 271,001), E Austria, bordering on Hungary; cap. Eisenstadt. Hilly region, indented by Neusiedler L. Wine growing. Territory transferred from Hungary to Austria by treaties of 1919 and 1920. SOPRON, its leading town, was returned to Hungary by plebiscite (1921).

Bürger, Gottfried August (gôt'frĕt ou'gŏŏst bür'gùr), 1747–94, German poet. Credited with reviving the German ballad, he is best known for "Lenore" (1773), widely translated and highly influential.

Burgess, (Frank) Gelett, 1866–1951, American humorist, illustrator of his own stories and articles; best

known for quatrain "The Purple Cow" and for originating the terms *goop, bromide,* and *blurb.*

Burgess, John William, 1844–1931, American political scientist; educ. at Amherst and in Germany. Helped create faculty of political science at Columbia Univ. Wrote much on political science and U.S. history.

Burgh, Hubert de: see HUBERT DE BURGH.

Burghley or Burleigh, William Cecil, 1st Baron, 1520–98, English statesman, chief adviser of Queen Elizabeth. Rose to power 1548, but was not in favor with Mary I. Reappointed by Elizabeth; served her for 40 years. Responsible for execution of Mary Queen of Scots and solidification of Protestantism. His policy contributed to growth of industry and commerce and to rise of England as a leading European power.

Burgkmair or Burckmair, Hans (both: häns' bŏŏrk'mīur), 1473–1531, German painter and engraver of Augsburg, influenced by Dürer.

burglary, at common law, breaking and entering a dwelling house at night with intent to commit a felony; by statutes in many states of U.S. extended to mean all breaking and entering. Breaking involves only a slight use of force (e.g., turning a key) or by entry through fraud, threat, or conspiracy.

Bürglen (bürk'lùn), town (est. pop. 3,200), Uri canton, Switzerland. Alleged birthplace of William Tell.

Burgos (bōōr'gōs), city (pop. 84,098), cap. of Burgos prov., N Spain, in Old Castile. Cap. of Castile until 1087, when Toledo replaced it. Gothic cathedral, founded 1221, among finest in S Europe.

Burgoyne, John (bûrgoin'), 1722–92, British general. Helped plan SARATOGA CAMPAIGN, but led poorly equipped army, untrained for frontier fighting. Surrendered at Saratoga, Oct. 17, 1777.

Burgundians, in French medieval history: see ARMAGNACS AND BURGUNDIANS.

Burgundy (bûr'gùndē), Fr. *Bourgogne,* region and former province, E France, in Yonne, Côte-d'Or, Saône-et-Loire, and Ain depts.; historic cap., Dijon. Agr.; wine growing (particularly in Chablis region and Côte-d'Or). Cities: Dijon, Beaune, Auxerre, Chalon-sur-Saône, Mâcon. In history, the term "Burgundy" often designated much wider areas. A part of Roman Gaul, it was peacefully settled (5th cent. A.D.) by the Germanic Burgundii, who founded the **First Kingdom of Burgundy.** This comprised SE France and W Switzerland. Conquered by the Franks (534), it was repeatedly partitioned under the Merovingians and Carolingians, though it survived in name. Two kingdoms emerged in the 9th cent.: Cisjurane Burgundy or PROVENCE in the south; Transjurane Burgundy in the north. These were united (933) in the kingdom of Arles or **Second Kingdom of Burgundy** (see ARLES, KINGDOM OF). A smaller area (roughly, present Burgundy) was created (877) as the **duchy of Burgundy,** which from the 11th cent. was ruled mostly by princes of the French royal house. In the 14th and 15th cent., Burgundy had its golden age under dukes PHILIP THE BOLD, JOHN THE FEARLESS, PHILIP THE GOOD, and CHARLES THE BOLD, who acquired the Low Countries, FRANCHE-COMTÉ, and other territories. The wealthiest state of W Europe and one of the great powers, Burgundy also was a center of art and culture. In the Hundred Years War Burgundy sided with England against France from 1415 until 1435, when its alliance with France turned the tide. (See also ARMAGNACS AND BURGUNDIANS.) The defeat and death (1477) of Charles the Bold left MARY OF BURGUNDY the heir. Through her, the Low Countries passed to the Hapsburgs (see NETHERLANDS, AUSTRIAN AND SPANISH), but the duchy itself was seized by Louis XI, who made it into a French prov.

Buriat-Mongolia, RSFSR: see BURYAT AUTONOMOUS SOVIET SOCIALIST REPUBLIC.

Buridan, Jean (byōō'rĭdùn, Fr. bürĕdä'), fl. 1328, French scholastic philosopher, rector of the Univ. of Paris. A follower of William of Occam, he held man's will enables him to choose the greater good and to suspend choice in order to reconsider. He is credited (probably falsely) with using the figure of "Buridan's ass"—an unfortunate animal midway between identical bundles of hay and starving to death because he cannot decide which bundle to eat.

Burkburnett (bûrkbûrnĕt′), city (pop. 7,621), N Texas, N of Wichita Falls, near Red. R.; settled 1907. Oil strike (1918) changed town into oil-mad community and population soared. Now handles farm produce and cattle.

Burke, Edmund, 1729–97, British statesman and political writer, b. Dublin. Was a member of Dr. Johnson's circle. Strong Whig opponent of William Pitt, in famous speeches he advocated wiser policy in America. Exposed injustices in India by instigating long trial of Warren HASTINGS 1785–94. His opposition to French Revolution led to break with Whigs 1791. Advocate of many practical reforms, he feared political reform.

Burke, John, 1787–1848, Irish genealogist. Issued a publication which became British annual, *Burke's Peerage,* edited by his son, **Sir John Bernard Burke,** 1814–92, also publisher of *Burke's Landed Gentry.*

Burke, Robert O'Hara, 1820–61, Irish explorer of Australia. Crossed continent from Menindee to Gulf of Carpentaria; died from famine on return.

Burleigh, William Cecil, 1st Baron: see BURGHLEY.

Burleson, Albert Sidney (bûr′lŭsŭn), 1863–1937, U.S. Postmaster General (1913–21). His strict control of communications in First World War aroused the ire of businessmen, labor unions, liberals.

burlesque (bûrlĕsk′) [Ital.,= mockery], form of entertainment that achieves its comic effect through caricature and distortion. Dramatic burlesque includes such plays as Gay's *Beggar's Opera* and Fielding's *Tom Thumb.* American burlesque began 1865 as a variety show characterized by broad comedy; the name now more often refers to "strip-tease" shows, which were at their height c.1920–c.1937.

Burlingame, Anson (bûr′ling-găm), 1820–70, American diplomat who contracted **Burlingame Treaty** (1868), a pact of friendship between China and U.S. based on Western principles of international law. One clause encouraged Chinese immigration; resulting friction led to policy of CHINESE EXCLUSION.

Burlingame, residential city (pop. 24,036), W Calif., on San Francisco Bay, SSE of San Francisco.

Burlingame Treaty: see BURLINGAME, ANSON.

Burlington, town (pop. 47,008), S Ont., Canada, on L. Ontario NE of Hamilton. Residential town in fruit-growing and highly industrialized area.

Burlington. 1 City (1965 pop. 33,285), SE Iowa, on four hills overlooking Mississippi R., SSW of Davenport; platted 1833 on sites of Indian village and trading post. Shipping and mfg. center with railroad shops and docks. Was temporary cap. of Wisconsin Territory (1837) and Iowa Territory (1838–40). Annual Tri-State Fair. **2** Town (pop. 12,852), E Mass., NW of Boston; settled 1641. Has pre-Revolutionary meetinghouse. **3** City (pop. 12,687), W N.J., on Delaware R. between Trenton and Camden; settled 1677 by Friends. Grew mainly as port. Was cap. of West Jersey 1681–1702; alternate cap. with Perth Amboy of united Jerseys until 1790. Benjamin Franklin printed first colonial money here 1726; first N.J. newspaper printed here 1777. Has Friends' school (1792; now Y.W.C.A.) and meetinghouse (1784). Birthplace of James Fenimore Cooper. **4** Industrial city (pop. 33,199), N N.C., E of Greensboro, on Haw R. **5** City (pop. 35,531), NW Vt., on L. Champlain, S of St. Albans; chartered 1763. Largest Vt. city, it is an industrial center and seat of Univ. of VERMONT, with Trinity Col.; MIDDLEBURY COLLEGE is nearby. Ethan Allen spent last years here and is said to be buried in the vicinity.

Burma, Union of, republic (261,000 sq. mi.; pop. c.20,000,000), SE Asia; cap. Rangoon. Bordered by Bay of Bengal, East Pakistan, and India on W, Tibet on N, and China, Laos, and Thailand on E. Densely populated valley of Irrawaddy R. is surrounded by mountains extending from E Himalayas; its delta is a great rice-growing area. Rich mineral resources include oil, tungsten, tin, silver, and gems (sapphire, ruby, and jade). Rice, teak, and oil are chief exports. Population comprises Mongoloid groups of Nagas, Shans, Chins, and Mons; the Burmese, who center around MANDALAY and Irrawaddy R., moved S from Tibet before 9th cent. Anawratha estab. Burmese supremacy 1044 with cap. at PAGAN. He introduced Hinayana Buddhism, the main religion today. His dynasty fell 1287 to Kublai Khan. The Shans, who obtained rule as tributaries of China, maintained it until 1546, when Burmese dynasties arose. Burma was annexed piecemeal (1824, 1852, and 1885) to British India. It received quasi-dominion status 1937. Occupied by Japan in Second World War. In 1948 Burma became a sovereign republic and joined UN. Internal strife was aggravated by presence of Chinese Nationalist troops who moved into Burma in 1950. In 1962 Premier U Nu was arrested by military government under Gen. Ne Win, who previously had ruled 1958–60. Burma is divided into Lower Burma (with divisions of Mandalay, Pegu, Arakan, and Tenasserim) and Upper Burma (including semi-autonomous CHIN HILLS, and constituent units of SHAN, KACHIN, and KAYAH).

Burman and **Burmese,** Sino-Tibetan languages. See LANGUAGE (table).

bur marigold, weedy plant (*Bidens*), of daisy family. Burlike fruits. Also called tickseed, beggar-ticks.

Burmese or **Burman.** See LANGUAGE (table).

Burne-Jones, Sir Edward, 1833–98, English painter and decorator, an eminent exponent of Pre-Raphaelitism. Drew his material from the medieval period. His designs for stained glass were executed by the firm of William Morris.

Burnet, David Gouverneur (bûr′nĭt, bùrnĕt′), 1788–1870, provisional president of Texas (1836). Drew up Texas declaration of independence from Mexico.

Burnet, Sir Frank Macfarlane, 1899–, Australian physician. An authority on viruses, he contributed to development of immunity against influenza. Shared 1960 Nobel Prize in Physiology and Medicine.

burnet (bûr′nĭt), hardy perennial herb (*Sanguisorba*). White or greenish flowers. Leaves used in salads.

Burnett, Frances (Eliza) Hodgson, 1849–1924, American author, b. England, in U.S. after 1865. Among her children's books are *Little Lord Fauntleroy* (1886), *Sara Crewe* (1888), *The Secret Garden* (1911).

Burney, Frances (Fanny), later **Madame D'Arblay,** 1752–1840, English novelist, daughter of Dr. Charles Burney, member of the Samuel Johnson circle. Notable for characterizations, her novels of home life and society include *Evelina* (1778) and *Camilla* (1796). Her diaries and letters give an interesting account of English life and culture from 1786 to 1840.

Burnham, Daniel Hudson, 1846–1912, American architect and city planner. With his partner John W. Root he designed the 20-story Masonic Temple Building in Chicago. Their plan for the Chicago World's Fair of 1893 had enormous influence on contemporary civic design. Planned Baguio in Philippines.

Burnham, Sherburne Wesley, 1838–1921, American astronomer at Lick (1888–92) and Yerkes (from 1893) observatories. Compiled *General Catalogue of Double Stars* (1906); wrote *Measures of Proper Motion of Stars* (1913).

burning bush or **wahoo,** handsome North American deciduous shrub (*Euonymus atropurpureus*). Yellow autumn foliage and purple pods with scarlet seeds. Scriptural burning bush (Ex. 3.2) was a thorn.

Burns, John, 1858–1943, British socialist. With Ben Tillett and Tom Mann, led 1889 London dock strike.

Burns, Robert, 1759–96, Scottish poet. Son of a poor but intelligent farmer, he read both Scottish and

English poetry at home. Unsuccessful at farming and given to dissolute life, Burns accepted patronage of several women. To finance emigration to Jamaica with Mary Campbell he published *Poems, Chiefly in the Scottish Dialect* (1786), an immediate success. On Mary's death he married Jean Armour, failed again as a farmer, and became an exciseman at Dumfries (1791). His brief lyrics, such as "Auld Lang Syne" and "Comin' thro' the Rye," are among the most familiar in the English language. Longer poems include "Tam o' Shanter" and "The Cotter's Saturday Night." His use of dialect brought freshness and raciness into English poetry. Simplicity, humor, spontaneity, and genuine emotion are marks of his greatness.

Burnside, Ambrose Everett, 1824–81, Union general in Civil War. Won prestige by N.C. coastal campaign. Commanded Army of Potomac until defeat at Fredericksburg. Transferred to Dept. of the Ohio (1863); in 1864 commanded under Meade and Grant in Va.

Burr, Aaron, 1756–1836, American political leader. U.S. Senator (1791–97). Tied with Thomas Jefferson in election of 1800 for presidency; elected Vice President by House of Representatives. Killed Alexander HAMILTON in duel in 1804. Burr's plan for colonization in the Southwest led to his trial for treason in 1807; acquitted, he left for England, but after 1812 practiced law in N.Y.

Burrell, George Arthur (bŭ'rŭl), 1882–1957, American chemical engineer, specialist on petroleum. He discovered helium in Texas, invented Burrell gas detector and Burrell pipette.

Burritt, Elihu, 1810–79, American worker for world peace, "the learned blacksmith." Supported William LADD in plans for international organization.

burro: see ASS.

Burroughs, Edgar Rice, 1875–1950, American novelist, creator of character Tarzan in *Tarzan of the Apes* (1914).

Burroughs, John, 1837–1921, American naturalist. He traveled far from his farm at Esopus, N.Y., to Alaska and the West Indies to gather material for his poetic nature essays (collected in *Wake Robin,* 1871; *Locusts and Wild Honey,* 1879). Later books, such as *Time and Change* (1912), are more philosophical. Also a poet, he wrote (1867) one of the early books to evaluate the work of his friend Walt Whitman.

burrstone: see BUHRSTONE.

Bursa (bŏŏr'sä), city (pop. 153,866), NW Turkey, near the Sea of Marmara; also known as Brusa or Brussa. Silk and carpet mfg. Ancient Prusa was a flourishing city of Bithynia. Captured by Orkhan 1326; cap. of Ottoman Turks 1326–1402 when it was sacked by Tamerlane. Has fine mosques, tombs of early sultans.

bursitis, inflammation of bursae, tiny fluid sacs that reduce friction of bones in joints. Caused by injury or irritation; treated with rest, heat, antibiotics, X-ray therapy, or cortisone.

Burt, William Austin, 1792–1858, American inventor of solar compass, equatorial sextant, and typographer (an ancestor of the typewriter).

Burton, Harold Hitz, 1888–1964, Associate Justice of U.S. Supreme Court (1945–58). U.S. Senator from Ohio (1941–45).

Burton, Sir Richard Francis, 1821–90, English explorer, writer, linguist. Journeyed in various Moslem disguises to Mecca and Medina (1853), in Arabic guise to Harar, Ethiopia (1856). Explored in Africa and Brazil. Wrote accounts of his travels, translated *Arabian Nights* (16 vols., 1885–88).

Burton, Robert, 1577–1640, English clergyman, author of *The Anatomy of Melancholy* (1621; several times enlarged), a vast, wide-ranging treatise.

Burundi (bŏŏrŭn'dē), republic (10,747 sq. mi.; pop. c.2,650,000), E central Africa; cap. Bujumbura. Formerly part of Belgian colony of Ruanda-Urundi. Interior is plateau region with L. Tanganyika on W. Mainly agr.; coffee and cotton exported. Country

achieved independence July, 1962, after UN-supervised election and joined UN same year. The Watutsi king was chosen monarch. Great political unrest followed independence, and in late 1966 the king was deposed in a military coup, and the country was declared a republic.

Bury, John Bagnell (byŏŏ'rē), 1861–1927, Irish historian, authority on East Roman Empire. His chief works treat Greek, late Roman, and Byzantine history. He also edited Gibbon's *Decline and Fall.*

Bury, Richard de: see RICHARD DE BURY.

Buryat Autonomous Soviet Socialist Republic (bŏŏr-yät'), autonomous state (135,637 sq. mi.; 1965 est. pop. 761,000), RSFSR, in S Siberia; cap. ULAN-UDE. Mountainous, heavily forested, rich in metals (tungsten, molybdenum, gold, tin, mercury, iron). Population is c.50% Buryat-Mongols (see MONGOLS), mostly herdsmen. Annexed by Russia 17th cent. Formerly called Buriat-Mongolia or Buryat-Mongol ASSR; present name adopted 1958.

Busch, Adolf (bŏŏsh'), 1891–1952, German-Swiss violinist. He organized the Busch string quartet and the Busch Chamber Players, both outstanding in the performance of chamber music. His brother, **Fritz Busch,** 1890–1951, was a conductor of opera and symphony and led the Glyndebourne Festivals in England.

Busch, Wilhelm (vĭl'hĕlm bŏŏsh'), 1832–1908, German cartoonist, painter, and poet. His humorous illustrated poems are simply drawn and highly spirited and have become a national tradition in Germany.

Büsching, Anton Friedrich (büsh'ĭng), 1724–93, German geographer, educator. Noted for *Neue Erdbeschreibung* (10 vols., 1754–92); six volumes translated into English as *A New System of Geography* (1762).

Bush, Vannevar, 1890–, American electrical engineer, physicist, and administrator. He was president of Carnegie Institution (1939–55), director of Office of Scientific Research and Development in Second World War, first chairman of the Research and Development Board set up after the war. Designed calculating devices and a differential analyzer, an early type of analog computer. Author of works on technical subjects and on the wider significance of research.

bushido (bŏŏshēdō') [way of the warrior], code of honor of feudal Japan which governed the general conduct of the SAMURAI. Codified in 17th–18th cent.; stresses loyalty and self-sacrifice for one's superior and one's honor.

Bushire (bŏŏshēr'), city (pop. c.30,000), SW Iran, on island in Persian Gulf. Chief port of Iran.

bushmaster, largest New World venomous snake, of pit viper family. Found in Central and South America.

Bushmen, a people of southern Africa, seldom over 5 ft. Nomadic hunters, they live in grass dwellings in temporary clearings. Their language resembles that of Hottentots.

Bushnell, Horace, 1802–76, American Congregational minister. Minister at North Church, Hartford, Conn., 1833–59. His repudiation of austerity of Calvinism and his stress on presence of the divine in humanity and nature helped shape liberal Protestant thought.

bushrangers, gangs of escaped convicts and adventurers who terrorized rural areas of Australia in 19th cent. Later groups attacked gold convoys.

Busoni, Ferruccio (fär-rōōt'chō bōōzō'nē), 1866–1924, Italian pianist and composer. He transcribed for piano much of Bach's organ music.

Bustamante, Antonio Sanchez de (äntō'nyō sän'chäs dä bōōstämän'tä), 1865–1951, Cuban authority on international law. Drew up a code of international private law.

butane, simple hydrocarbon, a gas, obtained by cracking of petroleum. It is used as a fuel. Molecule has four carbon and ten hydrogen atoms. Butane can exist as either of two structural isomers. In *n*-butane, the four carbons are arranged in a chain; in isobutane, one central carbon is bound to the other three.

butcher bird: see SHRIKE.

Bute, John Stuart, 3d earl of, 1713–92, English Tory prime minister (1761–63). Confidant of George III, endorsed his aims of supremacy of monarchy, destruction of Whig monopoly, end of war with France. Unpopular Treaty of Paris after declaration of war on Spain (1762) led to his resignation.

Bute, island and county, Scotland: see BUTESHIRE.

Butenandt, Adolf (ä'dôlf bōō'tünänt), 1903–, German biochemist. Determined structure of progestin, a female sex hormone; isolated and named androsterone, a male sex hormone. Declined 1939 Nobel Prize in Chemistry because of Nazi doctrines.

Buteshire (būt'shir) or **Bute,** insular county (218 sq. mi.; pop. 15,129), in the Firth of Clyde, W Scotland; co. town Rothesay. ARRAN and Bute largest islands. Agr. chief occupation; cattle and sheep raised; fishing. Scenery and bracing climate attract tourists.

Butler, Irish noble family. **Thomas Butler, 10th earl of Ormonde,** 1532–1614, was first of family to become Protestant. Supported movement against Shane O'Neill and had bitter quarrel with earl of Desmond. Made lieutenant general in Ireland 1597. **James Butler, 12th earl and 1st duke of Ormonde,** 1610–88, was most powerful royalist influence in Ireland during Puritan Revolution. Succeeded earl of Strafford in command of army in Ireland and defeated rebels. Made lord lieutenant 1643. Gave up office after concluding peace with Parliament 1647. Proclaimed Charles II as king of Ireland 1649. After 1660 was again lord lieutenant. Attacked by duke of Buckingham and then earl of Shaftesbury, he was removed from office by intrigue 1684. His son, **Thomas Butler, earl of Ossory,** 1634–80, distinguished himself in naval battles with the Dutch 1665, 1672. Was lieutenant general in Ireland after 1665. His son, **James Butler, 2d duke of Ormonde,** 1665–1745, supported William III and fought at battle of the Boyne. Was lord lieutenant of Ireland (1703–6, 1710–13) and commander in chief of army. Involved in plot to prevent accession of George I, he was impeached 1715. Fled to France, took part in Jacobite rising 1715, and spent rest of his life in exile.

Butler, Benjamin Franklin, 1795–1858, American lawyer, U.S. Attorney General (1833–38). Also served as Secretary of War (1836–37).

Butler, Benjamin Franklin, 1818–93, American politician and Union general in Civil War. Commander in capture of New Orleans and military governor of city (1862), unpopular with Southerners. In U.S. Congress (1867–75), as radical Republican, was supporter of Reconstruction policy and a leader in impeachment of Pres. Johnson.

Butler, James: see BUTLER, family.

Butler, John, 1728–96, Loyalist commander in American Revolution. Organized troop called Butler's Rangers. Defeated Zebulon Butler in Wyoming Valley (1778); Indian allies perpetrated Wyoming Valley massacre. His son, **Walter Butler,** 1752?–1781, also a Loyalist officer, fought with his father and led Cherry Valley massacre (1778).

Butler, Joseph, 1692–1752, English theologian, bishop of Bristol and later of Durham. His *Analogy of Religion, Natural and Revealed, to the Constitution and Course of Nature* (1736) was written to combat deism in England.

Butler, Nicholas Murray, 1862–1947, American educator, president of COLUMBIA UNIVERSITY (1902–45). Largely responsible for expansion of Columbia Col. into Columbia Univ. For his efforts in behalf of international peace he shared the 1931 Nobel Peace Prize.

Butler, Pierce, 1866–1939, Associate Justice of U.S. Supreme Court (1923–39). Opposed New Deal laws.

Butler, Samuel, 1612–80, English satiric poet, whose mock-heroic poem *Hudibras* (parts I–III, 1663–68) is a travesty mocking Puritan hypocrisy.

Butler, Samuel, 1835–1902, English author, painter, composer. His years in New Zealand as a sheep rancher are reflected in the scene of his imaginary *Erewhon;* or, *Over the Range* (1872) and *Erewhon Revisited* (1901). An amateur, he sparred with Darwin in several volumes (e.g., *Evolution Old and New,* 1879). His novel, *The Way of All Flesh* (1903), amounted to an attack on Victorian family life.

Butler, Thomas: see BUTLER, family.

Butler, Walter: see BUTLER, JOHN.

Butler, Zebulon, 1731–95, American colonial leader. Military leader of Conn. settlers in Wyoming Valley. Defeated by Loyalists under John Butler in 1778.

Butler, city (pop. 20,975), W Pa., N of Pittsburgh; settled c.1800. In a coal, gas, oil, and limestone area.

Butor, Michel (mēshĕl' bütôr'), 1926–, French writer of essays and novels, e.g., *La Modification* (1957) and *Degrés* (1960). His *Mobile* (1962) is an impression of the U.S. In collaboration with composer Henri Pousseur he wrote an opera, *Votre Faust* (1962–65), in which the audience chooses the outcome.

Bütschli, Otto (ô'tō büch'lē), 1848–1920, German zoologist. Studied mitosis and invertebrate development. Proposed theory (1878) that protoplasm is foamlike fluid.

Butte (būt), city (pop. 27,877), SW Mont., SSW of Helena; founded 1862. First a gold, then a silver town, it gained real importance with copper discovery (c.1880) and formation of Marcus Daly's Anaconda Copper Mining Co. Bitter battles of "Copper Kings" and big labor struggle of 1912–14 centered about deposits. Mining still dominates city, which produces nearly all state's copper and most of its gold and silver. Also the commercial center of farm and livestock area and seat of Montana Col. of Mineral Science and Technology, part of Univ. of MONTANA.

butte, isolated hill, steep-sided and flat-topped, a remnant after erosion of surrounding areas. Common in U.S., as in Badlands and the SW.

butter, nourishing dairy product made by agitating cream or milk to unite the fat globules. Cows' milk is generally the basis, but that of goats, sheep, and mares has been used. Exclusively farm made until c.1850, it has become increasingly a factory product. The use of a starter culture of bacteria has generally replaced natural fermentation of cream; sweet (unsalted) butter is made of sweet cream. Clarified butter (called ghee in India) is much used in Eastern lands. Dietary value is due to the high easily digested fat and vitamin A content.

butter-and-eggs or **toadflax,** weedy perennial (*Linaria vulgaris*) introduced to U.S. from Eurasia. Yellow and orange flowers resemble small snapdragons.

buttercup or **crowfoot,** any *Ranunculus* species with yellow flowers and deeply cut foliage. Often weedy, but a few, e.g., florists' ranunculus and creeping buttercup, are grown for cutting and in gardens.

Butterfield, Herbert, 1900–, English historian. His works include *The Whig Interpretation of History* (1931), *George III, Lord North, and the People* (1948), and *Origins of Modern Science* (1949).

butterfly, insect of group comprising, with moths, order Lepidoptera. Broad membranous scaled wings. Four-stage life cycle: egg, larva, pupa, adult. Bodies more slender and smoother than in moths, antennae enlarged at tip (in moths, often feathery, rarely knobbed), when at rest wings held vertically (in moths horizontally), chiefly diurnal (moth largely nocturnal). See *ill.,* p. 512.

butterfly flower or **poor-man's-orchid,** showy annual (*Schizanthus*). Grown in greenhouse or garden.

butterfly weed or **pleurisy root,** handsome MILKWEED (*Asclepias tuberosa*) of U.S. Often cultivated for its terminal clusters of bright orange flowers.

Butterick, Ebenezer, 1826–1903, American inventor of standardized paper dressmaking patterns. Marketed first stiff-paper patterns for shirts in 1863. In 1869 started fashion magazine, later the *Delineator.*

butternut, deciduous North American tree (*Juglans cinerea*), also called white walnut, and its fruit, an edible nut. Dye from nut husks used by early settlers.

buttons, knoblike appendages on clothing, either for ornament or fastening. First became important in 13th cent., though used occasionally in Greece and Rome. In 16th cent. their increasing magnificence led many Puritans to use hook-and-eye fastenings in protest. Innumerable materials, from wood, metal, shell, and bone to gems and coins, have been used.

buttonwood: see PLANE TREE.

Butyl rubber: see RUBBER, SYNTHETIC.

Butzer, Martin: see BUCER, MARTIN.

Buxar (bŭksär'), village, W Bihar, India. British won Bengal by defeat of Nawab of Oudh here (1764).

Buxtehude, Dietrich (dē'trĭkh bŏŏks″tühōō'dü), 1637–1707, Swedish organist at Lübeck. Chiefly composed choral preludes, passacaglias, and fugues for organ.

Buxton, Sir Thomas Fowell, 1786–1845, English reformer. As member of Parliament led in abolishing (1833) slavery in British colonies.

Buxtorf, Johann (yō'hän bŏŏks'tôrf), the elder, 1564–1629, Swiss Hebraist at Univ. of Basel. Compiled dictionary of biblical Hebrew (1624). His concordance to Hebrew Bible was completed by his son **Johann Buxtorf,** the younger, 1599–1664, also professor of Hebrew at Basel. His son **Johann Buxtorf III,** 1645–1714, was professor of Semitic languages at Basel.

Buys-Ballot, Christoph Heinrich Diedrich (bois'-bälō'), 1817–90, Dutch meteorologist. Strove to organize standard system for representing meteorological findings. Formulated Buys-Ballot's law: if one stands with his back to wind, low pressure area is to his left. Reverse is true in S Hemisphere.

Buzau (bōōzŭ'ōō), city (est. pop. 51,075), SE Rumania. Oil refineries, foundries; mfg. of knitwear.

buzzard, name for certain hawks and vultures. In S U.S. are turkey VULTURE or turkey buzzard, black vulture or black buzzard. Red-tailed, red-shouldered, broad-wing hawks called buzzards.

Buzzards Bay, inlet of the Atlantic, 30 mi. long and 5–10 mi. wide, SE Mass., connected with Cape Cod Bay by Cape Cod Canal and bounded on SE by Elizabeth Isls. **Buzzards Bay,** village (pop. 2,170), seat of Cape Cod Canal administration, is in Bourne town. Massachusetts Maritime Academy is here.

B.V.: see THOMSON, JAMES, 1834–82.

Byblos (bĭb'lŭs), city of anc. Phoenicia, a port near present Beirut, Lebanon; biblical Gebal (modern Jebail). It was a center for worship of Adonis. Because of its papyri, it was the source of the Greek word for book (and English words such as Bible, bibliography). Trade existed between Byblos and Egypt as early as c.2800 B.C.

Bydgoszcz (bĭd'gôshch), Ger. *Bromberg*, city (est. pop. 250,000), NW Poland, on Bydgoszcz Canal (part of Oder-Vistula waterway), cap. of Bydgoszcz prov. Trade center. Passed to Prussia 1772; restored to Poland 1919. Lignite and salt deposits nearby.

Byel-. For Russian names beginning thus, see BEL-.

bylini (bĭlē'nē), Russian narrative and heroic poems which were handed down by word of mouth from 11th cent. and began to be collected and studied in 18th cent. The largest cycle has Prince Vladimir of Kiev and the fabulous warrior Ilya of Murom as central figures. Among other cycles, that of Novgorod is most important.

Byng, George: see TORRINGTON, GEORGE BYNG, VISCOUNT.

Byng, John, 1704–57, British admiral; son of Viscount Torrington. Was shot for abandoning his task after defeat by French while attempting to relieve Minorca (1756). Sentence caused much indignation.

Byng, Julian Hedworth George, 1st Viscount Byng of Vimy, 1862–1935, British general. In First World War Canadian troops under his command stormed (1917) Vimy Ridge. Served as governor general of Canada 1921–26.

Bynner, Witter, 1881–, American poet. Noted for lyrics of his own, from *Grenstone Poems* (1917) to *New Poems* (1960), and for his ability to catch the cadences of other cultures, as in *The Jade Mountain* (with Kiang Kang-hu, 1929). He also wrote with Arthur Davidson Ficke a satiric literary hoax, *Spectra* (1916).

Byrd, Richard Evelyn (bûrd), 1888–1957, American aviator and polar explorer. Took part in notable polar and transatlantic flights from 1925, being first man to fly over both North and South Poles. Led expeditions to Antarctica (1929, 1933). In 1933 from base at Little America he moved 123 mi. closer to South Pole to spend several winter months alone making observations. Led three government expeditions to Antarctica (1939–40, 1946–47, 1955–56). In 1955 he was placed in charge of all Antarctic activities of U.S. Due mainly to his efforts, U.S. navy organized (1955–59) Operation Deep Freeze. Byrd's explorations form much of basis for U.S. Antarctic claims. His brother was **Harry Flood Byrd,** 1887–1966, U.S. Senator from Va. (1933–65). A conservative Democrat, he was in frequent opposition to Democratic administrations.

Byrd, William, b. 1542 or 1543, d. 1623, English composer and organist. He composed both Anglican and Roman Catholic church music; also music for the virginal and other instruments. Also Bird, Byrde.

Byrd, William, 1674–1744, American colonial writer, planter, and government official. He inherited "Westover" and wide lands in Va., built up the largest library in the colonies, and wrote wise and witty journals and diaries, selections from which were published after his death.

Byrnes, James F(rancis), 1879–, American political leader. Represented S.C. in the House (1911–25) and the Senate (1931–41) and was Associate Justice of U.S. Supreme Court (1941–42). In Second World War was director of economic stabilization (1942) and director of war mobilization (1943–45). He was U.S. Secretary of State (1945–47) and governor of S.C. (1951–55).

Byron, George Gordon Noel Byron, 6th Baron (bī'rŭn), 1788–1824, English romantic poet, epitome of the romantic in his irregular life and his emotion-charged poetry. Lame from birth, left fatherless in 1791, he grew to be a dark, handsome man, beloved by and contemptuous of women. Lord Byron's name was linked with those of various women before and after his ill-fated marriage (1815–16) to Anne Isabella Milbanke. In 1819 he formed a liaison with Countess Teresa Guiccioli. Restlessly wandering about the Continent, he was fired by various causes and died while working for Greek independence. He wrote long romances and stories in verse such as *Childe Harold* (1812–18), *The Giaour* (1813), *The Bride of Abydos* (1813), *Manfred* (1817), *Mazeppa* (1819), and *Cain* (1821; much criticized for skepticism toward religion). He was also a master of satire, as in *English Bards and Scotch Reviewers* (1809), *The Vision of Judgment* (1822), and his masterpiece, *Don Juan* (1819–24). Shorter pieces (e.g., *The Prisoner of Chillon*) and lyrics are familiar works today.

Bytom, Upper Silesia: see BEUTHEN.

Bytown, Ont.: see OTTAWA.

Byzantine architecture (bī'zŭntĕn, –tīn, bĭzăn'tĭn), style of building which developed after Byzantium (Constantinople) had been made cap. of the Roman Empire (A.D. 330). It crystallized in Ravenna and Constantinople and spread through Greece and the Balkans to Asia Minor, and ultimately to Russia. The style was the product of Roman methods of construction modified by the use of colorful materials and adornments. Under Justinian (527–65) it achieved its first definitive expression in the Church of San Vitale at Ravenna and the renowned HAGIA SOPHIA. The second phase of the style, in which Eastern influences became apparent, is represented by SAINT MARK'S

CHURCH at Venice. In its later phases, Byzantine architecture became more ornate in design and decoration, as in Moscow cathedral.

Byzantine art, an art blended of Hellenistic and Oriental traditions which flourished under the Byzantine Empire. It began to develop in the 2d cent. A.D., reaching its first Golden Age c.330. Except for the interruption caused by iconoclasm, the style persisted until the fall of Constantinople in 1453. It emphasized decorativeness, neglecting plasticity in favor of flat-line harmony. Sculpture was characterized by flat, even relief, with delicate, lacy designs. Mosaics reached a high point in 6th-cent. churches built in Ravenna.

Byzantine Empire, successor state to the Roman Empire (see ROME), also called Eastern or East Roman Empire; named for its cap., CONSTANTINOPLE, the anc. Byzantium. The division of the Roman Empire into East and West became permanent in 395, although after the fall of West Rome (476) the Eastern emperors claimed succession to the entire Roman world. The core of the Byzantine Empire was Asia Minor and the S Balkan Peninsula. Throughout its 1,000 years of existence, the empire was beset by foreign invaders—Goths, Huns, Avars, Persians, Bulgars, Slavs, Arabs, Normans, Seljuk Turks, Serbs, the French, Italians, and Ottoman Turks. Its boundaries shifted according to military fortunes and to the vigor of central authority. Religious controversy played a major part in Byzantine history and was frequently interwoven with party strife (see BLUES AND GREENS; NESTORIANISM; MONOPHYSITISM; MONOTHELETISM, ICONOCLASM; PHOTIUS; ORTHODOX EASTERN CHURCH). With all its weaknesses, dissensions, court intrigues, and corruption, the empire possessed astonishing powers of recuperation and survival; it carried on the Graeco-Roman civilization, blended with Oriental influences, at a time when the West was in chaos. The first era of recuperation came under JUSTINIAN I, who recovered Italy and Africa, codified ROMAN LAW, and encouraged Hellenism. Byzantine art and architecture entered their most glorious period (6th cent.). His suc-cessors lost most of ITALY to the Lombards, and Syria, Palestine, Egypt, Africa, and Sicily to the Arabs. The reign of IRENE saw the coronation of Charlemagne as emperor of the West (800), and the schism between the Roman and the Eastern Church followed soon afterward, effectively destroying Roman universality. A new period of splendor and vigorous government was inaugurated by BASIL I (9th cent.) but ended with the Turkish victory at MANZIKERT (1071). After a brief resurgence under ALEXIUS I, a century of decay ended with the breakup of the empire under the impact of the Fourth Crusade (1204; see CRUSADES). However, the Latin Empire of CONSTANTINOPLE proved even less stable than the surviving Byzantine splinter states of NICAEA, TREBIZOND, and EPIRUS; in 1261 MICHAEL VIII of Nicaea recaptured Constantinople and restored the empire. For two centuries the ever-shrinking state held out against the Ottoman Turks, vainly begging the West for aid. At last, after a desperate defense under CONSTANTINE XI, Constantinople fell to Mohammed II (1453), and Turkey fell heir to Byzantium. The modern era is generally reckoned from that day.

Byzantine music, now regarded as an independent musical culture that flourished between the 4th and 15th cent., reached its golden age in the 7th cent. Although some Greek instruments were used, the organ was most important. Almost all extant Byzantine music is liturgical. Its principal form was the hymn; texts were usually biblical. Byzantine chant attempted to depict melodical meaning of the words. Notation was originally only a series of symbols serving to remind the singer of a melody he already knew. Later a staffless notation indicating starting note and subsequent intervals of a melody was used.

Byzantine rite: see ORTHODOX EASTERN CHURCH.

Byzantium (bĭzăn′shēum), anc. city, on site of present Istanbul; trade center founded by Greeks 667 B.C. Taken by Rome (A.D. 196), it was chosen by Constantine I (330) as site for CONSTANTINOPLE, later cap. of Byzantine Empire.

C, chemical symbol of the element CARBON.

Ca, chemical symbol of the element CALCIUM.

Caaba: see KAABA.

Cabal (kŭbăl′), inner group of advisers to Charles II of England. Their initials form the word—Clifford of Chudleigh, Ashley (Lord Shaftesbury), Buckingham (George Villiers), Arlington (Henry Bennet), and Lauderdale (John Maitland).

cabala or **cabbala** (both: kă′bŭlù) [Heb.,= reception], general term for Jewish mysticism; esoteric system of interpreting the Scriptures. Beginnings traditionally ascribed to Moses. Its speculations first appeared in Talmudic times (c.100–500 A.D.) and reflected a strong Neoplatonic influence, especially in its doctrine of emanation and transmigration of souls. Taught that all originates in God, that evil is the result of removal from God. The Hebrew letters were supposed to have magical powers. At various times the doctrine was taken up by Christians and referred to as a proof of the dogma of the Trinity. Principal texts are *Sefer Yezira* [book of creation] and *Zohar* [book of splendor]. *Zohar* was written by Moses de Leon (fl. 13th cent.), who attributed it to Simon ben Yohai (fl. 2d cent.).

cabbage, leafy garden vegetable (*Brassica oleracea capitata*) with white, green, or red leaves. It is derived from wild cabbage and allied to KALE, BRUSSELS SPROUTS, CAULIFLOWER, and BROCCOLI.

Cabell, James Branch (kă′bùl), 1879–1958, American novelist. Some novels (notably *Jurgen,* 1919) are set in imaginary medieval land (Poictesme). Also author of critical essays. Wrote both as Branch Cabell and James Branch Cabell.

Cabet, Étienne (ātyĕn′ kăbā′), 1788–1856, French utopian socialist and reformer. In exile (1834–39) in England, he wrote description of ideal society, *Voyage en*

Icarie (1840). Urged state control of all economy and social life. Founded several communistic settlements in U.S. Settlers called Icarians.

Cabeza de Vaca, Álvar Núñez (äl'vär nōō'nyäth käbā'thä dä vä'kä), c.1490–c.1557, Spanish explorer. Wandered through American Southwest (1534–36) after shipwreck off Texas coast. Deposed as governor of colony in Paraguay (1544).

Cabinda, Portuguese enclave (2,794 sq. mi.; pop. c.50,000), W Africa; administered from Angola; chief town is Cabinda. Hardwoods, coffee, rubber, and cacao are produced.

cabinet, in U.S. government, see *ill.*, p. 163.

Cabiri (kŭbī'rī), Greek fertility gods, worshiped with mysteries at Samothrace.

Cable, George Washington, 1844–1925, American author of romantic stories and novels of La. (e.g., *Old Creole Days,* 1879; *The Grandissimes,* 1880). His later years were devoted to social reform.

cable. Once a term for fibrous rope and now applied to transoceanic telegraph message; to telephone-telegraph line of intertwisted strands in insulating sheath; to chain, heavy rope, or plaited wire used to anchor, moor, or tow ships; to twisted wire rope with many engineering uses; to wire conveying electricity from source to consumer; and to intercity coaxial telephone, telegraph, and television line. The coaxial cable (which permits simultaneous transmission of many signals) consists of a copper tube through the center of which extends a copper wire held in place by insulating disks; a number of such units are enclosed in insulating material.

Cabochiens (käbōshyĕ'), faction composed of Parisian tradespeople, led by Simon Lecoustellier, called Caboche, a skinner. In 1411 they sided with Burgundians in civil war between ARMAGNACS AND BURGUNDIANS, seized control of Paris in 1413, passed radical reforms (*ordonnance cabochienne*). Soon suppressed by Armagnacs.

Cabot, John, fl. 1461–98, English explorer, probably b. Genoa, Italy. Under patent granted by Henry VII, he sailed W from Bristol (1497), presumably seeking access to riches of Far East, and reached North American coast. He set out on second exploratory expedition (1498) whose fate is unknown. English claims in North America were based on his discovery. His son, **Sebastian Cabot,** b. 1483–86?, d. 1557, was explorer in Spanish service (1512–48). Explored (1526–30) Río de la Plata country; later reentered English service; as governor of Muscovy Co. was responsible for commercial treaty with Russia.

Cabral, Pedro Alvares (äl'vŭrĩsh käbräl'), c.1460–1526?, Portuguese navigator. Commanded fleet destined for India (1500), went far west of his course, reached coast of Brazil which he claimed for Portugal. Finally reached Calicut but roused native ire by high-handed practices in trade and religion. His landing in Brazil, accidental or prearranged, was not the first European visit to Brazil, though the question of discovery is still argued.

Cabrillo, Juan Rodríguez (hwän rōdhrē'gäth käbrē'lyō), d. 1543, Spanish conquistador, discoverer of California (1542), b. Portugal. Site of his landing is now Cabrillo Natl. Monument.

Cabrillo National Monument: see CABRILLO, JUAN RODRÍGUEZ.

Cabrini, Saint Frances Xavier (kübrē'nē), 1850–1917, American nun, b. Italy; first U.S. citizen to be canonized (1946). Founded Missionary Sisters of the Sacred Heart of Jesus, and after coming to the U.S. (1889) worked with the poor and the sick. Feast: Dec. 22.

cacao (kŭkā'ō), tropical American tree (*Theobroma cacao*), bearing pods containing cocoa beans of commerce. After drying, the seeds are screened, roasted, and skinned, resulting in clean kernels known as cocoa nibs, which are made into various products, e.g., edible CHOCOLATE and cocoa, and cocoa butter, used medicinally and in cosmetics. Exported mainly from

South and Central America, western Africa, and West Indies.

Caccini, Giulio (jōō'lyō kät-chē'nē), c.1550–1618, Italian singer and composer. Composed *Euridice* (1600), one of first operas on record.

Cáceres (kä'thärãs), city (pop. 48,005), cap. of Cáceres prov., W Spain, in Estremadura. Cork mfg. Roman and Moorish walls and towers remain.

Cache (käsh), river rising in hills of SE Mo. and flowing c.213 mi. SE into E central Ark. to join White R.

cactus, succulent plant, either small or treelike, of family Cactaceae, native to New World. It is characterized by fleshy green stem (leaves inconspicuous or absent), showy flowers, and colorful fruit, often edible (e.g., PRICKLY PEAR) and is adapted to high temperatures and arid regions. Among the cacti are NIGHT-BLOOMING CEREUS, cholla, PEYOTE, and Christmas cactus.

Cadamosto or **Cada Mosto, Luigi da** (lwē'jē dä kädämō'stō), 1432?–1488, Venetian navigator in Portuguese service, from about 1454. Left a valuable record of Portuguese activity in Canary Isls., and may have been discoverer of Cape Verde Isls. (1456 or 1457).

Cadbury, George, 1839–1922, English manufacturer and social reformer; set up (with brother Richard) model village which influenced European model housing projects.

Caddoan (kä'dōŭn), linguistic family of North America, believed by some to be a part of the Hokan-Siouan linguistic stock. Some suggest that Caddoan is most closely related to Iroquoian. See LANGUAGE (table).

Cade, Jack, d. 1450, English rebel, leader of uprising in S England in 1450. Grievances were mainly political. Rebels defeated royal army and entered London. Government pardoned (and so dispersed) Cade's men, but executed him.

Cadillac, Antoine de la Mothe (kä'dīläk, Fr. ätwän' dü lä mōt' kädēyäk'), c.1658–1730, French colonial governor of territory of Louisiana (1713–16), founder of Detroit (1701).

Cadillac (kä'dīläk), city (pop. 10,112), N Mich., on L. Cadillac, SSE of Traverse City, in farm area; settled c.1871. Indian mounds and winter sports area nearby.

Cádiz (Sp. kä'dēth), city (pop. 124,479), cap. of Cádiz prov., SW Spain, in Andalusia; Atlantic port and fortified naval base. Founded c.1100 B.C. by Phoenicians as Gadir, taken by Carthage c.500 B.C. Continued to flourish under Romans, who took it 3d cent. B.C. and called it Gades. Reconquered from Moors by Castile (1262), it prospered again after discovery of America. In 1587 Drake burned Spanish fleet in Cádiz harbor; in 1596 Essex devastated the city. During Peninsular War Cádiz successfully resisted French siege 1810–1812, was seat of Spanish Cortes.

cadmium (käd'mēŭm), metallic element (symbol = Cd; see also ELEMENT, table). White, lustrous, very malleable and ductile; like tin in physical properties, zinc in chemical. Forms oxide, hydroxide, carbonate, chloride, sulphide. Occurs in nature in compounds. Used to make low-melting-point alloys.

Cadmus, in Greek legend, son of Agenor and founder of Thebes. He introduced alphabet to Greece.

Cadogan, William Cadogan, 1st Earl, 1675–1726, British general, diplomat. Friend of duke of MARLBOROUGH, aided him in War of the SPANISH SUCCESSION.

Cadoudal, Georges (zhôrzh' kädōōdäl'), 1771–1804, French royalist conspirator. Leader of counterrevolutionists in Vendée and of plot (1803) to oust Bonaparte. Cadoudal was executed, as was the duc d'ENGHIEN, who was unjustly linked to the plot.

caduceus (kŭdū'sēŭs), wing-topped staff, with two snakes winding about it, carried by Hermes. As symbol of fertility, wisdom, and healing, it appeared early in Babylonia. Hermes' staff was carried by Greek heralds and ambassadors and became a Roman symbol of truce and neutrality. By regulation, the caduceus has since 1902 been insignia of medical branch of U.S. Army.

Secretary of State (1789)

Department of State (1789)
  Agency for International Development
  Peace Corps
  U.S. Mision to the UN

Secretary of the Treasury (1789)

Department of the Treasury (1789)
  Bureau of Customs
  Bureau of Engraving and Printing
  Bureau of the Mint
  Bureau of Narcotics
  Internal Revenue Service
  U.S. Coast Guard
  U.S. Secret Service

Attorney General (1789)

Department of Justice (1870)
  Office of the Solicitor General
  Bureau of Prisons
  Community Relations Service
  Federal Bureau of Investigation (F.B.I.)
  Immigration and Naturalization Service
  U.S. Attorneys
  U.S. Marshals

Postmaster General (1829)

Post Office Department (1872)

Secretary of the Interior (1849)

Department of the Interior (1849)
  Bureau of Indian Affairs
  Bureau of Land Management
  Bureau of Reclamation
  Federal Water Pollution Control
    Administration
  Geological Survey
  National Park Service
  U.S. Fish and Wildlife Service

Secretary of Agriculture (1889)

Department of Agriculture (1889)
  Commodity Credit Corporation
  Rural Electrification Administration

Secretary of Commerce (1903)

Department of Commerce (1903)
  Bureau of International Commerce
  Bureau of the Census
  Business and Defense Services Administration
  Economic Development Administration
  Environmental Science Service Administration
  Maritime Administration
  National Bureau of Standards
  Patent Office

Secretary of Labor (1913)

Department of Labor (1913)
  Manpower Administration

Secretary of Defense (1949)

Department of Defense (1949)
  Joint Chiefs of Staff
  Department of the Army
    Secretary of the Army
  Department of the Navy
    Secretary of the Navy
  Department of the Air Force
    Secretary of the Air Force

Secretary of Health, Education, and Welfare (1953)

Department of Health, Education, and Welfare (1953)
  Administration on Aging
  Food and Drug Administration
  Office of Education
  Office of Vocational Rehabilitation
  Public Health Service
  Social Security Administration
  Welfare Administration

Secretary of Housing and Urban Development (1965)

Department of Housing and Urban Development (1965)
  Federal Housing Administration
  Renewel Projects Administration

Secretary of Transportation (1966)

Department of Transportation (1966)

The cabinet is a creation of custom and tradition, going back to George Washington's first administration. The first of what came to be known as cabinet meetings was held in 1791. In 1792 several meetings were held, and by 1793 the term "cabinet" was first applied to the President's group of advisers. The first cabinet consisted of Thomas Jefferson, Secretary of State; Alexander Hamilton, Secretary of the Treasury; Henry Knox, Secretary of War; and Edmund Randolph, Attorney General.

The cabinet is composed of the heads of the 12 executive departments of the Federal government and the U.S. ambassador to the UN. They are appointed by the President, with the advice and consent of the Senate, and are responsible, individually and not as a body, solely to the President, who may remove them at will. It is the purpose of the cabinet to advise the President.

Listed here, in order of seniority, are the cabinet officers, with the 12 executive departments they head. Some, generally the better known, of the principal

bureaus and offices of the various departments are also listed. Dates indicate when the offices were established or reached cabinet status and when the various executive departments were created by Congress.

Cabinet status and rank as an executive department were often not conferred until years after the office and department had actually begun to function. Thus the Postmaster General and his department existed since the beginning of the republic, but the Postmaster General was not made a member of the cabinet until 1829, and the Post Office Department did not become an executive department until 1872.

Prior to the organization of the Department of Defense in 1949, the Secretary of War (1789; renamed the Secretary of the Army in 1947) and the Secretary of the Navy (1798) had cabinet status.

The Department of Commerce was originally (1903–13) The Department of Commerce and Labor. In 1913 all labor activities of the Department were transferred to the Department of Labor newly created at that time.

Cadwaladr or **Cadwallader** (both: kădwä'lùdùr), semilegendary British king, leader against Anglo-Saxons in 7th cent.

Cædmon (kăd'mùn), fl. 670, first English Christian poet and first English poet known by name. BEDE, *Ecclesiastical History*, tells how Cædmon, lay brother in abbey of Whitby, was divinely inspired to compose his first work, a brief hymn, and gives Latin version. Other poems described by Bede not extant.

Caen (kä), city (pop. 91,336), cap. of Calvados dept., N France, in Normandy. Textile and lace mfg. Favorite residence of William the Conqueror. Center of heavy fighting (1944) in the Second World War. William's castle and the university (founded 1432) were destroyed, but the famous Abbaye aux Hommes [men's abbey], with William's tomb, the Abbaye aux Dames [ladies' abbey], and the Church of St. Nicholas were preserved. All three are gems of 11th-cent. Norman architecture.

Caerleon (kärlē'ûn), urban district (pop. 4,184), Monmouthshire, England. Has extensive remains of Roman fortress Isca. Village often identified with Camelot of Arthurian legend.

Caermarthenshire or **Carmarthenshire** (both: kùrmär'-dhùnshĭr), maritime county (920 sq. mi.; pop. 167,-736), S Wales. Largest of Welsh counties, it is mostly hilly. Chief occupations are agr. and grazing, but industrial coal field of S Wales extends into SE corner. Also has metal and textile mfg. The county town, **Caermarthen** or **Carmarthen** (pop. 13,249), has castle that was once hq. of Welsh chieftains.

Caernarvonshire or **Carnarvonshire** (both: kùrnär'vùnshĭr, kär–), maritime county (569 sq. mi.; pop. 121,-194), NW Wales. Region is largely mountainous; Snowdon (3,560 ft.) is highest peak in England and Wales. Sheep farming and quarrying (from world's largest slate quarries) are the chief industries. County town is **Caernarvon** or **Carnarvon** (pop. 8,998), where the prince of Wales is invested. Its castle is fine example of a medieval fortress.

Caesalpinus, Andreas (än'drēus sēsälpī'nùs), Latinized from **Andrea Cesalpino**, 1519–1603, Italian botanist and physiologist. He described in part the circulation of blood and developed the first classification of plants according to their fruits.

Caesar (sē'zùr), name used by a patrician family of Rome. The careers of Julius Caesar and the adopted Augustus led to giving the name an imperial character. It was in the later Roman empire the title given to the subemperor, who would presumably later become the emperor. The title reappeared later as the German *Kaiser* and the Russian *Czar* or *Tsar.*

Caesar, (Caius) Julius, 102? B.C.–44 B.C., Roman statesman, one of the most renowned military commanders in world history. He came of a noble family and married Cornelia, the daughter of Cinna, colleague of Caesar's uncle by marriage, MARIUS, whose party he joined. In the hour of Sulla's triumph Caesar was proscribed. On Sulla's death he began his political career in earnest, becoming the champion of the people against the senate. As pontifex maximus he instituted important reforms in the calendar, creating the Julian calendar. He divorced his second wife, Pompeia, who was involved in a scandal with Clodius, and said "Caesar's wife must be above suspicion." He later married Calpurnia. After service in Spain he returned to Rome (60 B.C.) and organized the First Triumvirate, with POMPEY and CRASSUS. He mediated between his colleagues and himself took command in Gaul, where his prosecution of the GALLIC WARS (58 B.C.–49 B.C.) estab. his reputation as one of the great military commanders of all time. He ended by a journey of conquest in Britain, where he planted Roman power. Again in Gaul, he put down the uprising led by Vercingetorix and made Roman power secure. In 54 B.C. his daughter Julia, wife of Pompey, died, and from that time on rivalry between Pompey, who became the champion of the senatorial party, and Caesar, the popular leader, grew. The death of Crassus set the two face to face (53 B.C.). The senate, fearing Caesar's power, moved to take away his army command. He agreed to submit if Pompey would surrender his. This reply caused the senate to demand (quite illegally) that he disband his army immediately. Two tribunes, Marc ANTONY and CASSIUS, vetoed the bill and fled to Caesar. He made the fateful decision to defy the senate and signalized it by leading his army across the small river Rubicon (49 B.C.). Civil war began. Caesar marched triumphantly to Rome, then pursued Pompey until he conquered him on the plain of Pharsala in Greece (48 B.C.). He followed the defeated Pompey to Egypt and there had a love affair with Cleopatra. From Egypt he went to Pontus and defeated Pharnaces II with an easy victory recorded in his words "Veni, vidi, vici" [I came, I saw, I conquered]. Returning to Rome, he exercised the dictatorial powers granted him, though he refused the title of king, preferring to remain only consul, dictator, and general (44 B.C.). His social reforms won popular support, but his enemies and some of his followers resented his autocratic rule. A conspiracy was formed against him, largely by men he had befriended, most notably M. Junius BRUTUS, Cassius, Casca, and Cimber. Just as he was preparing to leave to conduct war against Parthia, he was stabbed to death in the senate on the Ides of March (March 15), 44 B.C. His will left his money and power to his grandnephew Octavius, who was to become Emperor Augustus after he and Marc Antony had avenged Caesar's murder. The character and achievements of Julius Caesar are still hotly debated by scholars. His military and literary gifts (his *Gallic Wars* and *Civil War* are masterpieces) are unquestioned, but whether he was a purely self-seeking opportunistic lover of power, a man dedicated to the redemption of the poor and rejected, the patriot restoring the glory of Rome, or something else is still an open question.

Caesarea (sēsùrē'ù), name given to various anc. cities to honor the Roman Caesars. Among the most important were: Caesarea in Mauretania, a flourishing trade center (on the site of present Cherchel, Algeria) until sacked by the Vandals in the 5th cent.; Caesarea Mazaca or Caesarea of Cappadocia (on the site of present Kayseri, Turkey), a trade center and residence of Cappadocian kings; Caesarea Palestinae, in S Palestine, the capital of Herod the Great and scene of massacre of Jewish citizens by Romans (A.D. 66); and Caesarea Philippi, in N Palestine, at foot of Mt. Hermon, built by Philip the Tetrarch. Jesus was in the vicinity, but there is no proof that He entered the city.

caesarean section: see CESAREAN SECTION.

Caesarion: see PTOLEMY XIV.

Caffa, Ukraine: see FEODOSIYA.

caffeine, alkaloid in coffee, tea, kola nut, cocoa. Acts as a stimulant and diuretic. In tea, known as theine. Can be synthesized from uric acid.

Cagayan (kägī'ùn) or **Rio Grande de Cagayan,** river, 220 mi. long, in central Luzon, Philippines.

Cage, John, 1912–, American composer. He has experimented with such new techniques of composition and sound production as "prepared" piano, superimposed radio programs, even silence, as in *4 Minutes and 33 Seconds* (1954), silent music for piano.

Cagliari (kä'lyärē), city (pop. 194,046), cap. of Sardinia, Italy; Mediterranean port. Roman remains; medieval castle.

Cagliostro, Alessandro, Conte (älēs-sän'drō kōn'tä kälyō'strō), 1743–95, Italian adventurer; real name Giuseppe Balsamo. Traveled all over Europe posing as physician, magician, alchemist. Popular at Louis XVI's court. Implicated in Affair of the DIAMOND NECKLACE; acquitted but banished from France. Condemned by Roman Inquisition as heretic and sorcerer (1789); died in prison.

Caguas (kä'gwäs), town (pop. 65,098), E Puerto Rico; industrial and agr. center.

Cahaba (kŭhô'bủ), deserted village, S central Ala., SW of Selma. State cap. 1819–26.

Cahaba, river flowing from mountains NE of Birmingham c.200 mi. SW and S to Alabama R. near Selma.

Cahan, Abraham (kän), 1860–1951, American Jewish journalist and socialist leader, b. Vilna, a founder and editor in chief of the Jewish *Daily Forward*.

Cahokia (kủhô'kẻủ), village (pop. 15,829), SW Ill., a suburb SSW of East St. Louis. State's first permanent settlement; named for tribe of Illinois Indians. French estab. mission here 1699 and later a fur-trading post. With Kaskaskia became one of chief French centers in upper Mississippi valley. Taken by British 1765 and by Americans under G. R. Clark 1778. Has several 18th-cent. buildings.

Cahokia (kủhô'kẻủ), village (pop. 794), SW Ill., on the Mississippi just below East St. Louis. First permanent settlement in Ill., it was named for a tribe of ILLINOIS INDIANS served by French mission estab. here 1699. Became one of chief French centers in upper Mississippi valley; taken by British 1765 and by Americans under Clark 1778. Has several 18th cent. buildings.

Cahors (kȧhôr'), town (est. pop. 15,834), cap. of Lot dept., S central France, on Lot R.; historic cap. of Quercy. Major medieval banking center; Cahorsin moneylenders rivaled Lombards and Jews. Old town contains medieval cathedral, palaces, and fortifications.

Caiaphas (kā'yủfủs), high priest who presided at council that condemned Jesus to death. Also at trial of Peter and John. Mat. 26.57–68; John 11.47–54; 18.24; Acts 4.6; Mark 14.53–65; Luke 22.66–71.

Caicos Islands: see TURKS AND CAICOS ISLANDS.

Caillaux, Joseph (zhôzĕf' kãyō'), 1863–1944, French minister of finance (1899, 1906, 1913–14, 1925, 1926) and premier (1911–12). Introduced income tax (1906); reached peaceful settlement of Morocco crisis with Germany (1911), unpopular with nationalists; resigned 1914 after his wife murdered Gaston Calmette, a journalist who had attacked his private life. (She was acquitted.) Caillaux's pacifist sentiments led to his arrest (1917), imprisonment, and trial for correspondence with the enemy. Restored to citizenship 1925; later served as senator.

Caillié, René (rủnã' kãyã'), 1799–1838, French explorer in Africa. First European to visit Timbuktu and return.

Cain, farmer son of Adam and Eve. Known as world's first murderer for killing of brother Abel. Gen. 4.

Cairngorm, group of mountains (includes Ben Macdhui, Braeriach, and Cairngorm, peaks all over 4,000 ft.), forming part of the Grampians, Scotland. Name also given yellow or brown quartz found here.

Cairns, city (pop. 23,800), Queensland, Australia, on Trinity Bay. Chief sugar port of Australia.

Cairo (kī'rō), Arabic *El Kahirah* [the victorious], city (pop. c.3,518,200), N Egypt, at head of Nile delta, cap. of the United Arab Republic and largest city of Africa. Commercial, mfg., and transportation center of Egypt. Near its site was the anc. Roman city of Babylon, and across the river was Memphis, cap. of anc. Egypt. Founded 969 by the Fatimite general Jauhar. Unsuccessfully attacked by Crusaders in 12th cent. Ruled by the Mamelukes from 13th to early 16th cent. and by the Ottoman Turks, 1517–1798. Occupied by Napoleon (1798–1801) and by the British (1882–1936). Mosque of El Azhar houses world's most important Moslem university, founded 972. Seat of Mus. of Antiquities and Royal Library. The great citadel was built c.1179 by Saladin.

Cairo, residential and industrial city (pop. 9,348), extreme S. Ill., WSW of Paducah, Ky., on levee-protected tongue of land between Mississippi and Ohio rivers. Rail, highway, and river shipping point and distributing center for large, fertile farm area. Federal depot in Civil War. Flood-control project has lessened danger from rising river waters.

Cairo Conference, Nov. 22–25, 1943, meeting of U.S. Pres. Roosevelt, British Prime Minister Churchill, and Chinese Generalissimo Chiang Kai-shek at Cairo, Egypt. They pledged war against Japan until her unconditional surrender, and until she foreswore territorial gains and promised freedom of territory gained by her since 1895, notably Korea.

caisson (kā'sủn, –sŏn), in engineering, a chamber of steel, wood, or concrete used in constructing foundations or piers in or near water. Types of caissons include open (sunk, and then filled with concrete), pneumatic (air pressure prevents entry of water at cutting edge below, and airtight deck of chamber above is high enough to permit workers under it), and camel (water-filled chamber attached to sunken ship and emptied by compressed air or pump).

caisson disease: see AEROEMBOLISM.

Caithness (kāth'nĕs), county (686 sq. mi.; pop. 27,-345), N Scotland. Coastline is rocky, and much of the county treeless moorland. The county town, Wick, is an important herring fishing center. Dounreay, Britain's first large nuclear breeder reactor, is located here.

Caius, John (kēz), 1510–73, English physician. Endowed and enlarged Gonville and Caius College of Cambridge Univ.

Cajal, Santiago Ramón y: see RAMÓN Y CAJAL.

Cajamarca (kähämär'kä), city (pop. c.37,000; alt. c.9,000 ft.), N Peru. Here Francisco Pizarro captured Atahualpa.

Cajetan, Saint (kä'jủtän, kä"yätän'), 1480–1547, Italian churchman active in the Catholic Reformation. He advocated communities of priests living in poverty among the people. Founder of congregation of the Theatines. Feast: August 7.

Cajetan (kä'jủtän) [Latin,= from Gaeta], 1469?–1534, Italian churchman; originally named Giacomo de Vio. Made the general of the Dominicans (1508), he became a cardinal (1517). He tried to keep Luther in the Church and opposed the divorce of Henry VIII from Katharine of Aragon. Noted as a scholar.

Cajuns: see ACADIA.

Calabria (kälä'brēä), region (5,828 sq. mi.; pop. 2,044,-287), S Italy, forming "toe" of Italian boot; cap. Reggio di Calabria. Mountainous, arid, economically backward. Agr., grazing, fruit growing, sericulture. Anc. BRUTTIUM, the region was renamed Calabria in Middle Ages. Conquered by Normans in 11th cent.; later shared history of kingdom of NAPLES.

caladium (kủlä'dẻủm), tropical American plant (*Caladium*). Colorful foliage marked with white, purple, or rose. Popular summer bedding and pot plant.

Calais (Fr. kälä'), city (pop. 70,372), Pas-de-Calais dept., N France; a Channel port on Strait of Dover. Held by England 1347–1558. Edward III, who captured it in 1347, promised to spare the town if six prominent citizens offered their lives. The mayor and five others volunteered; the king relented. Monument by Rodin commemorates the event.

Calais (kăl'ĭs), city (pop. 4,223), SE Maine, on St. Croix R. opposite St. Stephen, N.B.; settled 1779. On St. Croix Isl. in river below Calais, Champlain and the sieur de Monts planted short-lived colony 1604.

Calamity Jane, c.1852–1903, American frontier character. Maiden name was Martha Jane Canary; origin of nickname is obscure. Lived in Deadwood, S.Dak. Went into show business.

Calamy, Edmund, 1600–1666, English Presbyterian preacher, a leader of Puritan thought. Ejected from ministry by Act of Uniformity (1662).

Calatrava (käläträ'vä), ruined village, central Spain, near Ciudad Real. Original seat of powerful military religious order of **Knights of Calatrava,** founded 1158 by Cistercians as defense against Moors. Order declined after 13th cent.

Calcasieu (kăl'kủsōō'), river rising in W central La. and flowing c.215 mi. S through L. Charles and Calcasieu

L. (20 mi. long) to Gulf of Mexico. Partly navigable; connects with Intracoastal Waterway.

calceolaria (kăl″sēōlâr′ēŭ) or **slipperwort,** herbaceous or shrubby plant (*Calceolaria*), with showy pouch-shaped flowers. Most species South American.

calcite (kăl′sīt), common mineral (calcium carbonate), usually white; its hexagonal crystals show perfect cleavage. Some forms of calcite are CHALK, LIME-STONE, MARBLE, MARL, and STALACTITE.

calcium (kăl′sēŭm), silvery-white, relatively soft, active metallic element (symbol = Ca; see also ELEMENT, table). Classed with strontium and barium as metal of alkaline earths. Reacts with water and several elements, forming many compounds. Occurs in nature in widely distributed compounds. Is constituent of most plant and animal matter. Essential for strong bones and teeth; functions in regulation of heart beat and in blood clotting.

calculating machine, device to perform mathematical processes. Simple calculators include SLIDE RULE, ABACUS, and counting rods of John NAPIER. Probably the first adding machine using geared wheels was made by Blaise Pascal 1642. G. W. von Leibniz mechanism multiplied by repeated addition, using stepped wheel (c.1672); commercial version to add, subtract, multiply, and divide, was devised by C. X. Thomas 1820. Later in 19th cent. F. S. Baldwin in U.S. patented type more compact than stepped drum; later it was redesigned by W. J. R. Monroe. Key-driven machine was patented in 1850. D. E. Felt patented key-driven calculator (later developed into comptometer) in 1887. W. S. Burroughs patented key-set adding machine with crank 1888. Calculating machines are now electrically powered. See also COMPUTER.

calculus (kăl′kyŭlŭs), in higher mathematics, any advanced method, using a notation system peculiar to itself, to solve problems. Familiar calculi are the differential and integral. Basically the differential calculus deals with problems concerning rate of change, e.g., acceleration considered as rate of change of velocity with time. The integral calculus constructs relationships of variables from rates of change, e.g., area under a plane curve. In symbolic logic, term often denotes a specific system or class of systems.

calculus or **stone,** in medicine, deposit of mineral salts as a hard concretion of stone in body. Common sites are gall and urinary bladders, kidney, joints, and salivary ducts.

Calcutta (kălkŭt′tŭ), city (pop. 2,926,498), cap. of West Bengal, India, on Hooghly R. Chief port of E India and major industrial center. Founded 1690 by the British. Fell 1756 to the nawab of Bengal, who killed most of the garrison by overnight imprisonment in a small room, the notorious "black hole." Retaken 1757 by Clive. Cap. of India 1833–1912. Seat of Univ. of Calcutta and Indian Mus.

Calder, Alexander Stirling (kôl′dŭr), 1870–1945, American sculptor. His son, **Alexander Calder,** 1898–, is an abstract sculptor, best known for his "mobiles" and "stabiles."

Calderón Bridge (käldärōn′), over Lerma R., E of Guadalajara, Mexico, scene of battle (1811) in Mexican revolution against Spain.

Calderón (de la Barca), Pedro (pä′dhrō käldärōn′ dä lä bär′kä), 1600–1681, Spanish dramatist of enormous scope; last important figure of Golden Age. Wrote classical comedies, philosophical dramas, and one-act religious plays. Best known for *La vida es sueño* [life is a dream]. Court poet from 1622, he took holy orders 1651.

Caldwell, Erskine, 1903–, American author of realistic stories and novels, especially about the rural South as in *Tobacco Road* (1932; successfully dramatized) and *God's Little Acre* (1933).

Caldwell. 1 City (pop. 12,230), SW Idaho, on Boise R., W of Boise; founded 1883 on Oregon Trail camping ground. Processing and shipping point for farm, dairy, and livestock area in Boise project. The Col. of Idaho is here. **2** Borough (pop. 6,942), NE N.J.,

NW of Montclair; settled before 1785. Birthplace of Grover Cleveland now a museum.

Caleb, warrior-champion of Israel's God and chief spy sent into Canaan. When given his choice of land, Caleb, though past 80, chose region still strongly fortified by Canaanites and drove them out. Num. 13.6; 14; 32.12; Joshua 14.6–14. Name associated with tribe in S Palestine. 1 Sam. 30.14; 1 Chron. 2.18,19,42,46, 48,49.

Caledonia (kă″lĭdō′nēŭ), Roman name for part of Britain lying N of the Firths of Clyde and Forth. Modern rhetorical use usually refers to all Scotland.

Caledonian Canal, waterway (length 60 mi.), running from Moray Firth to Loch Linnhe, Scotland. Opened in 1847, it is little used now.

calendar, system of reckoning time, usually based on recurrent natural cycle, e.g., seasons and moon's phases. Since length of solar year is 365 days 5 hr. 48 min. 46 sec. and of lunar year (12 months of 29½ days) is 354 days 8 hr. 48 min., solar and lunar reckonings must be harmonized. Because the year is not exactly divisible by months and days, practice arose of making arbitrary divisions and inserting (intercalating) extra days or months. Gregorian calendar widely used today evolved from Roman calendar as reformed (45 B.C.) by Julius Caesar. In Julian calendar April, June, September, and November had 30 days; February, 28 days (29 days every fourth year, leap year); and other months, 31 days. In computation of month, days were counted backward from the Kalends (first day), the Ides (fifteenth day of March, May, July, October and thirteenth day of other months), and the Nones (eighth day before the Ides); hence Jan. 10 was fourth of Ides of January. Since Julian year of 365 days 6 hr. was too long, by the 16th cent. the vernal equinox was displaced from March 21 to March 11. Gregory XIII ordained that 10 days be dropped in 1582 and years ending in hundreds be leap years only if divisible by 400. The non-Roman Catholic countries were slow in accepting the Gregorian (New Style) calendar; it was adopted in England in 1752 and by the Eastern Church in the 20th cent. Christian ecclesiastical calendar was based on the belief that Jesus' resurrection was on a Sunday, hence Easter should fall on Sunday. First Council of Nicaea (325) decreed that Easter be the Sunday following the first full moon after the vernal equinox; today date varies from astronomical reckoning because certain factors of lunar period were not considered. Chronology is a major problem in ancient and medieval history because years were commonly identified by rulers. Era system of computing years from fixed date, e.g., birth of Christ, simplifies chronology. Calendars used today include Jewish calendar (12 months plus intercalary month seven times in 19 years) and Moslem lunar calendar with c.33 years to every 32 in Gregorian calendar. See also FRENCH REVOLUTIONARY CALENDAR.

calendula (kŭlĕn′dūlŭ), annual plant (*Calendula*), also called pot marigold. Has yellow to orange flower heads. The marigold of Shakespeare's time.

calf, golden, idol made by Israelites on several occasions (e.g., by Aaron during absence of Moses. Ex. 32). Jeroboam placed one at Bethel and one at Dan. 1 Kings 12.26–32. Calf (or bull) worship recalls cults of Apis in Egypt, Minotaur in Crete.

Calgary (kăl′gŭrē), city (pop. 249,641), S Alta., Canada, on Bow R. near foothills of Rocky Mts. A trade, rail, and industrial center of S Alta., it has oil refineries, meat-packing plants, and grain elevators. The city began 1875 as a fort of the Northwest Mounted Police.

Calhoun, John Caldwell (kăl″hōōn′), 1782–1850, American statesman and political philosopher. A "war hawk" as U.S. Representative from S.C. (1811–17). U.S. Secretary of War (1817–25); Vice President of U.S. (1825–32). Directed passage of S.C. ordinance of NULLIFICATION (1832). U.S. Senator (1832–43, 1845–50); U.S. Secretary of State (1844–45). Leading defender of minority Southern cause against commercial, industrial North. Calhoun held that the Constitution estab. a government of concurrent majorities composed of the state governments and the Federal government, with states enjoying rights of veto (or nullification) and secession.

Calhoun, city (pop. 3,587), NW Ga., NNW of Atlanta, on Oostanaula R. Destroyed by Gen. Sherman in Civil War. Site of Cherokee cap., New Echota, is nearby.

Cali (kä'lē), city (pop. 637,929), W Colombia; founded 1536 by Benalcázar; industrial and sugar center.

calico, name for plain-weave, cheap cotton cloth, usually printed; derived from Calicut cloth, fabric first imported into England from India, c.1830.

Calicut (kä'lĭkŭt"), city (pop. c.192,485), Kerala, India; port on Arabian Sea. Visited 1498 by Vasco da Gama. Once famed for calico.

California, state (158,693 sq. mi.; pop. 15,717,204), W U.S.; admitted 1850 as 31st state; cap. SACRAMENTO. Third largest state by area, first by population, as estimated 1964. Bordered S by Mexico, W by Pacific (1,200-mi. coast), SE by Colorado R. Major ports (largest cities) are LOS ANGELES, SAN FRANCISCO, OAKLAND, SAN DIEGO. State has striking topographical, climatic contrasts. Central Valley (drained by Sacramento and San Joaquin rivers) is walled on W by COAST RANGES, E by CASCADE RANGE and SIERRA NEVADA (highest elevation Mt. Whitney). Coast Range is subject to tremors, sometimes earthquakes, has heavy rainfall in N, where giant redwoods grow, is much drier in S. In SE lie vast wastes, notably the MOJAVE DESERT with DEATH VALLEY, in contrast to lush, irrigated IMPERIAL VALLEY. Water supply and control are acute problems (most extensive irrigation in U.S.). Although agr. is second to industry as basis of its economy, Calif. leads U.S. in cultivation of fruits and vegetables. Fishing, winemaking, defense industries (aircraft, ordnance, missiles, electrical instruments) are important; also processing of food and minerals (esp. mineral fuels). Major center of motion-picture and television production and of space-age research. A pleasant climate, national parks and forests, and beautiful beaches attract tourists. Early exploration included voyages of Juan R. CABRILLO (1542), Sir Francis DRAKE (1579), Sebastián VIZCAÍNO (1602). Spanish colonizing began 1769, when Gaspar de Portolá estab. colony on San Diego Bay. Franciscans founded string of missions. Gradually outsiders arrived by sea and overland. First Americans came 1816, followed by trappers and J. A. SUTTER, but the colonization was largely Mexican until 1840s. Last Mexican governor expelled 1845, and republic set up at Sonoma under influence of J. C. Frémont 1846. Area finally ceded to U.S. by Treaty of Guadalupe Hidalgo (1848). Gold strike of 1848 brought rush of settlers. First transcontinental railroad completed 1869. Large-scale Oriental immigration in late 19th and early 20th cent. Real-estate boom of 1920s, promise of work in 1930s, and employment opportunities of Second World War brought influx of settlers, a continuing trend. The state suffered severe floods 1964 and devastating forest fires 1965.

California, Gulf of, arm of Pacific, c.700 mi. long, c.100 mi. wide, NW Mexico. Separates peninsula of Lower California from Sonora and Sinaloa. Pearl diving and deep-sea fishing are important.

California, Lower: see BAJA CALIFORNIA.

California, University of, at nine campuses; land grant, state supported; coed.; chartered 1868, opened 1869 to succeed private Col. of California. At Berkeley are Lawrence Radiation Laboratory, the main library, and extensive museum system. Los Angeles campus (UCLA), inc. 1919, has noted theater department and cancer and brain research institutes. At La Jolla is Scripps Inst. of Oceanography (estab. 1901, transferred to university 1912). At San Francisco are Medical Center and Hastings Col. of the Law. Other campuses are at Davis, Irvine, Riverside, Santa Barbara, and Santa Cruz. University operates Lick Observatory.

California Institute of Technology, at Pasadena; for men; founded 1891 as Throop Polytechnic Inst.; called Throop Col. of Technology 1913–20. Research facilities include jet propulsion laboratory (in conjunction with NASA) and Guggenheim Aeronautical Laboratory.

californium, highly radioactive chemical element (symbol = Cf; atomic no.= 98; see also ELEMENT, table); first produced (1950) in the cyclotron at the Univ. of California.

Caligula (kulĭg'yoŏlu) [little boots], nickname of Caius Caesar Germanicus, A.D. 12–A.D. 41, Roman emperor (A.D. 37–A.D. 41). The son of Germanicus, he got his name from wearing military boots when he was a small boy with his father on the Rhine. He succeeded Tiberius as emperor. An illness had apparently affected his mind, and his rule was one of senseless cruelty and despotism. He was finally assassinated, and Claudius I succeeded him.

caliphate (kä'lĭfät), in Islam the office of the caliph (kä'lĭf), head of the theocratic organization as the agent of God. When Mohammed the Prophet died, Abu Bakr was chosen as first caliph. He was succeeded by Omar, Othman, and Ali (the Orthodox caliphs). After Ali's death, Islam split. The Omayyad family became caliphs at Damascus, but were not recognized by the Shiites, who in 750 won the caliphate for the descendants of Ali (the Abbasid family), who ruled from Baghdad. One Omayyad escaped to Spain, where later the Western Caliphate or Caliphate of Córdoba was set up, to last until 1031. A third rival line was supported by the Fatimites in Africa from 909 to 1171. When the Mongols took Baghdad (1258), the Abbasids fled to Egypt, where they nominally continued the caliphate until the Ottomans took Egypt (1517) and Selim I appropriated the title of caliph. This title was used by the Ottoman rulers of Turkey until it was abolished in 1924. See also IMAM.

Calixtines, another name for UTRAQUISTS.

Calixtus I, Saint (kulĭk'stus), c.160–c.222, pope (c.217–222). Rejected Montanism. Supposedly martyred. Also Callixtus, Callistus. Feast: Oct. 14.

Calixtus II, d. 1124, pope (1119–24). As archbishop of Vienne, he convened a synod (1112) to excommunicate Emperor Henry V. Calixtus triumphed over Henry's antipope Gregory VIII, came to an agreement with Henry in the Concordat of Worms (1122), and called the First Lateran Council.

Calixtus III, 1378–1458, pope (1455–58), a Spaniard named Alonso de Borja. Aided John Hunyadi in his fight against the Turks and tried to organize a crusade against them. He struggled with Alfonso V of Aragon. Estab. Borgia family in power in Italy.

Call, Richard Keith, 1791–1862, territorial governor of Fla. (1836–39, 1841–44). Led campaign against SEMINOLE INDIANS.

call, in banking, money deposited with bank or loaned by it, returnable on demand. With reference to stocks, call money may be capital either for a new concern or for an estab. one to cover part of new issue of shares.

calla (kăl'ŭ), South African fleshy-rooted perennial (*Zantedeschia*). It has small flowers in a showy spathe; white in common calla lily, yellow or pink in others. Wild calla (*Calla palustris*) is bog plant of N Temperate Zone.

Callao (käyou'), port (pop. 161,286), W Peru, just W of Lima; notable Pacific port.

Calleja del Rey, Félix María (fä'lēks märē'ä kälyä'hä dĕl rā'), 1750–1826, Spanish general, viceroy of New Spain (1813–16), conde de Calderón. Successfully repressed beginning of revolution against Spain led by Hidalgo y Costilla.

Calles, Plutarco Elías (plootär'kō ālē'äs kä'yäs), 1877–1945, Mexican statesman, president (1924–28). Many objectives of revolution of 1910 were consolidated in his administration—agrarian and educational reforms, public works, army reorganization. Later turned conservative, ran Mexico through puppet presidents, undoing much of his former work, and was exiled (1936) for opposing reforms of Lázaro Cárdenas.

Callias (kă'lēŭs), fl. 449 B.C., Athenian statesman. Supposed to have negotiated the Peace of Callias, an agreement which set up "spheres of influence" for Persia and Athens. Peace between the two lasted a half century.

Callicrates (kŭl'krŭtēz), 5th cent. B.C., Greek architect. With Ictinus, he built the Parthenon (447–432 B.C.).

Callimachus (kŭlĭm'ŭkŭs), fl. c.265 B.C., Hellenistic poet, critic. Among his more than 800 extant works are a literary catalogue and *Aetia*, a collection of legends.

Calliope (kŭlī'ōpē) [Gr.,= beautiful of voice], in Greek mythology, greatest of MUSES, patron of epic poetry and eloquence; mother of ORPHEUS by Apollo.

calliopsis: see COREOPSIS.

Callirrhoë (kŭlĭr'ōē), wife of ALCMAEON.

Callisto (kŭlĭ'stō), in Greek legend, virgin attendant of Artemis. She bore a son, Arcas, to Zeus. As punishment she was transformed into a bear. Zeus later transferred them both to heaven, where she became Ursa Major and Arcas became Arcturus.

Calloc'h, Jean Pierre: see BRETON LITERATURE.

Callot, Jacques (zhäk' kälō'), 1592–1635, French engraver and etcher. Studied in Rome. Famous for ability to group crowds in a small space, as in the splendid series *Miseries of War*.

Calmar, Sweden: see KALMAR.

Calmette, León Charles Albert (lāō' shärl' älbĕr' kälmĕt'), 1863–1933, French physician, bacteriologist. Founded and directed Pasteur institutes at Saigon and Lille. Affiliated with Paris Pasteur Inst. from 1917. Discovered a snake bite serum and, with Alphonse Guérin, introduced a tuberculosis vaccine.

calomel (kă'lŭmĕl", –mŭl), white crystalline powder of mercury and chlorine. Former household remedy used as purgative and to eliminate parasitic worms; safer drugs are now used.

Calonne, Charles Alexandre de (shärl' älĕksä'drŭ dŭ kälōn'), 1734–1802, French statesman; controller general of finances (1783–87). His spending policy, designed to restore public credit, ended in disaster and hastened FRENCH REVOLUTION.

calorie, metric unit of heat measurement. Small calorie (gram-calorie): heat required to raise temperature of 1 gm. water at maximum density 1°C. Large Calorie (kilogram-calorie): heat required to raise temperature of 1 kg. of water at maximum density 1°C. Specific heat is number of calories needed to raise temperature of 1 gm. of any substance 1°C. In physics and chemistry term *calorie* usually means small calorie; in dietetics large Calorie used to indicate amount of heat energy food can yield. **Calorimeter** determines number of calories given off by substance in combustion or other chemical reaction, measured by rise in temperature of given quantity of water.

Calpurnia (kălpûr'nēŭ), d. after 44 B.C., third wife of Julius Caesar, to whom she was married in 59 B.C. In story she is the model of the faithful, long-suffering wife.

Calumet, village (pop. 1,139), extreme N Mich., on Keweenaw peninsula, in copper region. Grew after development of Calumet and Hecla copper mine.

Calumet City, city (1964 pop. 27,420), NE Ill., a suburb S of Chicago near Ind. line. L. Calumet, just N, connects with L. Michigan.

Calumet Park, village (1965 pop. 10,037), NE Ill., a suburb S of Chicago.

Calvados (kälvädōs'), department (2,198 sq. mi.; pop. 480,686), N France, in Normandy; cap. Caen. Gives name to strong apple brandy.

Calvary (kăl'vŭrē) [Latin,= a skull] or **Golgotha** (gŏl'-gŭthŭ) [Heb.,= a skull], place outside wall of Jerusalem where Jesus was crucified. Mat. 27.23; Mark 15–

22; Luke 23.33; John 19.17–20. Church of the Holy Sepulchre now stands on traditional site, but scholars disagree as to exact location.

Calvé, Emma (kälvā'), 1858–1942, French operatic soprano. Sang at the Metropolitan Opera, New York, 1893–1904. Carmen was one of her famous roles.

Calvert, George, 1st **Baron Baltimore,** c.1580–1632, British colonizer. In 1632 he was granted territory N of Potomac R. which became province of MARYLAND. His grandson, **Charles Calvert,** 3d **Baron Baltimore,** 1637–1715, succeeded to proprietorship in 1675. His arbitrary rule was overthrown by revolt in 1689.

Calvin, John, 1509–64, French Protestant theologian of Reformation, b. Noyon. A man learned in theology and law, he experienced (1533) "sudden conversion"; leaving Catholicism, he became a hunted Protestant leader. In 1536 began work at Geneva. Banished in 1538, he preached at Basel and Strasbourg until welcomed back to Geneva in 1541. His monumental *Institutes of the Christian Religion* (1536) sets forth fundamental Calvinist theology. This diverged from Catholic doctrine in such fundamental ways as rejecting papal authority, accepting justification by faith alone, and rejecting the Catholic sacramental system. Calvin held that the Bible is sole source of God's law, and man's duty is to interpret it and preserve order in the world: this aim he set out to realize in Geneva by founding the government solely on religious law. From his teachings grew one of the most important of Christian religious systems, **Calvinism.** Broadly, Calvinism is the system in the Protestant "Reformed churches" (see PRESBYTERIANISM) as distinct from those professing Lutheran doctrines; distinctions are in the Eucharist and doctrine of predestination. It differs basically from Catholicism in holding that redemption is for elect alone, the free gift of God not to be won by good works. Calvinism characterized the Covenanters in Scotland, the Puritans in England and in New England, and the Huguenots in France. The extension of Calvinism to all spheres of human activity was extremely important in a world emerging from agrarian, medieval economy into a commercial, industrial era because the development of a successful industrial economy was stimulated by the Christian virtues of thrift, industry, sobriety, and responsibility that Calvin preached as essential to the achievement of God's reign on earth.

Calvin, Melvin, 1911–. American organic chemist and educator. Director of bio-organic division of Lawrence Radiation Laboratory at the Univ. of California. For studies of chemical reactions when plants assimilate carbon dioxide, he won 1961 Nobel Prize in Chemistry.

Calvinistic Methodist Church, Protestant denomination. Originated (1735–36) in Wales, where it kept strong as a movement. Separated from Established Church 1811; adopted confession of faith 1823. In U.S. united (1920) with Presbyterian Church.

Calvo, Carlos (kär'lōs käl'vō), 1824–1906, Argentine diplomat and historian, writer on international law. Principle known as **Calvo Doctrine** would prohibit diplomatic intervention to enforce private claims before local remedies have been exhausted. **Calvo Clause,** found in constitutions, treaties, statutes, and contracts, is concrete application of his doctrine.

Calydon (kăl'ĭdŭn), ancient city of S Aetolia, Greece. It was scene of legendary **Calydonian hunt,** successfully led by Meleager, prince of Calydon, against a wild boar loosed by Artemis to destroy city for neglect of a sacrifice. Among the hunters were Jason, Castor and Pollux, Theseus, and Atalanta.

Calypso (kŭlĭp'sō), nymph in the *Odyssey*. Lived on isl. of Ogygia, where Odysseus stayed seven years.

calyx (kā'lĭks), outer ring of typical FLOWER parts, made up of sepals which are usually green and leaf-like or united into a tube. Often colored if COROLLA is absent (e.g., buttercup).

cam, in engineering, a part which causes a connecting part to move in an irregular but exactly timed and repeating manner. Cams are rotating or sliding pieces of precise irregular shape, and the connecting part moves along the irregular surface of the cam. Cams are used in the valve gear of automobile engines, in automatic lathes.

Cam or Granta, river of England rising in Essex and flowing NE past Cambridge to the Ouse.

Camacho, Manuel Ávila: see ÁVILA CAMACHO.

Camagüey (kämägwā'), city (pop. c.110,000), E central Cuba; commercial center of agricultural region producing cattle and sugar.

Camargue (kämärg'), island, SE France, in the Rhone delta. Intensive cattle ranching.

Camarillo (kä″múrē′yō), town (pop. 2,359), S Calif., E of Oxnard. Shipping center for farm area. Main campus of St. John's Col. is here.

camass or camas (kăm′ús), hardy bulbous plant (*Camassia*), with spikes of dark blue or white flowers. Native to W North America, found in moist soils. Some species grown in gardens.

Cambacérès, Jean Jacques de (zhä′ zhäk′ dù kōbäsārēs′), 1753–1824, French revolutionist and legislator. Second consul (1799–1804); archchancellor of the empire under Napoleon I. Created duke of Parma 1808. Prepared CODE NAPOLÉON.

Cambay, Gulf of, inlet of the Arabian Sea, between Bombay and Saurashtra states.

Cambellton, town (pop. 9,823), N N.B., Canada, on Restigouche R. near head of Chaleur Bay. Starting point for fishing and hunting trips.

Camberwell, London: see SOUTHWARK.

Cambio, Arnolfo di: see ARNOLFO DI CAMBIO.

cambium (kăm′bēùm), thin layer of tissue between bark and wood of stem, most developed in trees. It is the growth area that causes increase in diameter of stems.

Cambodia (kămbō′dēú), constitutional monarchy (c.67,000 sq. mi.; pop. c.4,952,000), SE Asia; cap. Phnom Penh. Bordered on N by Laos, on E by South Vietnam, on S by Gulf of Siam, and on W by Thailand. Situated on saucer-shaped plain drained by Mekong R., and surrounded by mountains. Rice is grown in S. TONLE SAP is important for fisheries. Hinayana Buddhism is state religion. Industry based mostly on processing natural products. Prominent during rise of KHMER EMPIRE in 6th cent., Cambodia fell prey to Siam and ANNAM 15th–19th cent. King of Cambodia appealed 1854 for French intervention; French protectorate estab. 1863. Became part of Union of Indo-China 1884. French-Siamese treaty of 1907 restored W provinces. Achieved independence 1955 and joined UN. Invaded early 1954 by Communist Vietminh troops. The 1954 Geneva agreement provided for the withdrawal of all foreign troops from Cambodia. King Norodom Sihanouk abdicated 1955 and became premier. Economic and military ties with U.S. severed 1963, and diplomatic relations 1965.

Cambodian art. Pre-Khmer (pre-7th cent.) art, such as the *Harihara* of Andet and shrines at Sambor and Kornpong Thom, was influenced by Indian Gupta art. Classical period (8th–13th cent.) of Cambodian art of Khmer Empire evolved from Hindu and Buddhist iconography. Step-pyramid plan and profuse sculpture of great temple complexes at Angkor Wat and Angkor Thom were involved in symbolization of "world mountain." Modeled with sensuous subtlety, cult images had closed or half-closed eyes, full lips set in sweet smile. Cambodian culture merged with that of Siam after 14th cent., but distinctive forms survived in music and dance.

Cambon, Paul (pôl′ käbō′), 1843–1924, French ambassador to England (1898–1920). One of chief framers of Triple Entente. His brother, **Jules Cambon** (zhül), 1845–1935, was made ambassador to U.S. 1897; mediated peace preliminaries of Spanish-American War. Ambassador to Spain 1902–7, Germany 1907–14.

Cambrai (käbrä′), city (est. pop. 29,567), Nord dept., N France, on Escaut (Scheldt) R. Old textile center;

cambric first manufactured here. Ruled by bishops until seized by Spain (1595); to France 1677.

Cambrai, League of, 1508–10, alliance of Emperor Maximilian I, Pope Julius II, Louis XII of France, Ferdinand V of Aragon, and several Italian states against Venice. French routed Venetians at Agnadello (1509), but in 1510 Julius II made peace with Venice and formed HOLY LEAGUE against France.

Cambrai, Treaty of, or **Ladies' Peace:** see ITALIAN WARS.

Cambria (kăm′brēů) [from Welsh *Cymry* = Welshmen], ancient name of Wales.

Cambrian Mountains, a name for mountains of Wales.

Cambrian period (kăm′brēùn, kăm′–), first period of PALEOZOIC ERA. Large continental areas lay under shallow seas; thus Cambrian rocks are mostly sedimentary with thickness up to 13,000 ft. in Appalachian region. For the first time fossils of marine invertebrates were abundant—TRILOBITE, brachiopods, snails, sponges. No vertebrate fossils yet discovered, but possibility is not excluded. See GEOLOGIC ERAS, table.

Cambridge (kām′–), municipal borough (pop. 95,358), co. town of Cambridgeshire, England, on Cam R. The seat of CAMBRIDGE UNIVERSITY, it is an ancient market town retaining much medieval atmosphere. Has many old churches, including St. Benedict's (10th cent.), St. Edward's (mostly 15th cent.), and Church of the Holy Sepulchre, one of four Norman round churches in England.

Cambridge. 1 City (pop. 12,239), Md., Eastern Shore, on Choptank R., SE of Annapolis, in farm area; founded 1684. A fishing and yachting port and canning (sea food, vegetables) center. **2** City (pop. 107,-716), E Mass., on Charles R., NW of Boston; settled 1630. Seat of HARVARD UNIVERSITY, Radcliffe Col., and MASSACHUSETTS INSTITUTE OF TECHNOLOGY. Washington took command of troops here, July 3, 1775. Was first seat of Mass. constitutional convention of 1780. Longfellow, J. R. Lowell (their homes are preserved), Mary Baker Eddy, and other notables buried in Mt. Auburn Cemetery. Also an industrial center, with research organizations. Printing and publishing dates from 17th cent., when Stephen Daye estab. here first American printing press. **3** Industrial city (pop. 14,562), E central Ohio, ENE of Zanesville, in farm, coal, natural gas, and clay area; settled 1798.

Cambridge Bay, government post and weather station, SE shore of Victoria Isl., Northwest Territories, Canada.

Cambridge Platform, constitution for government and discipline in Congregational churches; adopted (1648) by synod at Cambridge, Mass. Group in Conn. adopted (1708) new centralizing Saybrook Platform.

Cambridge Platonists, school of philosophy at Cambridge Univ. in the late 17th cent. Reacting to mechanism of Thomas Hobbes, the Platonists revived idealism. Among them were Robert Grenville, Ralph Cudworth, Henry More, and John Norris.

Cambridgeshire or Cambridge, inland county (864 sq. mi.; pop. 279,025), E England; co. town Cambridge. Isle of Ely, northern section of county, is separate administrative unit. Area is mostly fenland, with chalky East Anglian range (including Gogmagog Hills) in south. Efforts to reclaim the fens, dating back to Romans, completed by vast drainage project 1653. Region has since been agr. Ely, with its famous cathedral, has been an important ecclesiastical center for many centuries.

Cambridge Springs, borough (pop. 2,031), NW Pa., near L. Erie, S of Erie. Farm and resort center. Alliance Col. is here.

Cambridge University, Cambridge, England, one of two anc. English universities. Probably had beginnings in 12th cent. Residential colleges estab. by end of 13th cent; with dates of founding, they are Peterhouse or St. Peter's (1284), Clare (1326), Pembroke (1347),

Gonville (1348, refounded as Gonville and Caius, 1558), Trinity Hall (1350), Corpus Christi (1352), King's (1441), Queens' (1448), St. Catharine's (1473), Jesus (1496), Christ's (1505), St. John's (1511), Magdalene (1542); pronounced môd'lĭn), Trinity (1546), Emmanuel (1584), Sidney Sussex (1596), Downing (1800), Selwyn (1882), and Churchill (1960). Girton (1869), Newnham (1873), and New Hall 1954) are women's colleges; full degree only since 1948. University, with 19 faculties, has led in science and modern literature. Cavendish Laboratory of experimental physics here. King's College chapel, Univ. Library, Fitzwilliam Mus., and botanic gardens are noteworthy. Cambridge Univ. Press dates from 16th cent. As at Oxford University, instruction is by lecturers and tutors (called supervisors). B.A. degree is awarded on passing tripos exam (honors exam at Oxford). Initials of a degree usually followed by Cantab. from Cantabrigia, Latin name of Cambridge.

Cambyses (kămbĭ'sēz), d. 521 B.C., king of Persia, son and successor of Cyrus the Great. He disposed of his brother Smerdis, but later a false Smerdis rose to haunt him. Conquered Egypt 525 B.C., but failed in attempts to annex Ethiopia. He died, possibly by suicide.

Camden, Charles Pratt, 1st Earl: see PRATT, CHARLES.

Camden, London borough since 1965 (est. pop. 243,-360); includes former metropolitan boroughs of Hampstead, Holborn, and St. Pancras. Has British Mus., Univ. of London, Gray's Inn and Lincoln's Inn, Royal Col. of Surgeons, and Hatton Garden.

Camden. 1 City (pop. 15,823), S Ark., NNW of El Dorado, on Ouachita R.; settled 1824. Rail and river shipping point. **2** Industrial city (pop. 117,159), W N.J., on Delaware R. (bridged to Philadelphia); settled 1681. City grew as commercial, shipping, and mfg. center after arrival of railroad 1834. Walt Whitman's home and grave are here. Seat of Col. of South Jersey, campus of RUTGERS, THE STATE UNIVERSITY. **3** City (pop. 6,842), N central S.C., near Wateree R., NE of Columbia; settled c.1735. Trade and processing center in farm area. Winter resort noted for hunting and polo. Battles of Camden (Aug. 16, 1780) and Hobkirks Hill (April 25, 1781) fought nearby in Carolina campaign of American Revolution. Practically destroyed by fire in British evacuation of May 8, 1781. Taken and partly burned (Feb. 24, 1865) by part of Sherman's army in Civil War.

camel, hoofed mammal of family Camelidae, which includes true camels (Asian genus *Camelus*) and South American genus *Lama* (wild guanaco, vicuña, domesticated alpaca, llama). Arabian camel or dromedary (*Camelus dromedarius*) has one hump; Bactrian camel (*C. bactrianus*) of central Asia has two humps. Fat is stored in humps. Color varies from dirty white to dark brown; the neck is long; the ears are small, and the teeth strong. Can carry heavy loads (500–600 lb., more for Bactrian camel) and survive without water for several days (longer if juicy plants are available).

camellia (–mēl'–, –mě'–), Asiatic evergreen tree or shrub (*Camellia*), allied to the tea plant. Grown under glass or outdoors in warm regions for its beautiful flowers, single or double, in white or red shades. Leaves are glossy dark green.

Camelot (kăm'ŭlŏt), the seat of King Arthur's court in the ARTHURIAN LEGEND.

Camembert cheese (kă'mŭmbâr), a mold-ripened CHEESE.

camera, light-proof container with lens that focuses image of object on photographic plate or film (see PHOTOGRAPHY). When shutter is open, film is exposed. Many variations in parts and attachments. **Camera lucida** (lōō'sĭdŭ), optical instrument that extends virtual image of object on plane surface so outline can be traced; usually attached to eyepiece of microscope. **Camera obscura** (ŏbskyōō'rŭ), light-tight box with convex lens at one end and screen for image at other; used to make drawings. See *ill.,* p. 796.

Camerarius, Rudolph Jacob (kămûrâ'rēŭs), 1665–1721, German physician and botanist, first to present definite facts concerning sex in plants.

Cameron, Richard, d. 1680, Scottish leader of Covenanters. Opposed reestablishment of episcopacy in Scotland after Restoration. He was killed by royal troops, but Cameronian sect grew strong, forming a presbytery (1743) as Reformed Presbyterians. Most joined Free Church of Scotland (1876).

Cameron, Simon, 1799–1889, American politician. U.S. Senator from Pa. (1845–49, 1857–61, 1867–77). Notoriously corrupt U.S. Secretary of War (1861–62). Machine he created so dominated Pa. that it was not until 1936 that Democrats carried state in a national election. Definition of an "honest politician" as one who "when bought, stays bought" is attributed to Cameron.

Cameron, Verney Lovett, 1844–94, British traveler in Africa. Explored and mapped L. Tanganyika. First European to cross equatorial Africa.

Cameroon, Federal Republic of, country (183,376 sq. mi.; pop. c.5,103,000), W Africa; cap. Yaoundé. Doula is largest city and major port. Comprises former French Cameroons and S section of British Cameroons. Tropical coastal plain rises to densely forested plateau which in turn gives way to high plateau (2,500–4,500 ft.) of savanna and, in N, thorn bush. Cameroon Highlands (rising to Mt. Cameroon) extend to Nigerian border. Among major rivers are Sanaga and Nyong (flowing SW to Gulf of Guinea), Benue (flowing N and W to Nigeria), and Logone (flowing N to L. Chad). Mainly agr., Cameroon exports cacao, coffee, palm oil, cotton, and peanuts—in addition to timber, tin, and gold. Bantu peoples, many Christian, live chiefly in S; Hamitic and Semitic peoples, mostly Moslem, in N. French and English are official languages. Region came under German control in late 19th cent. (see CAMEROONS). France granted self-government to French Cameroon 1957, internal autonomy 1959, and independence 1960. Admitted to UN 1960. S section of British Cameroons became self-governing province in Cameroon 1961. Federal republic created Oct., 1961.

Cameroon Mountain, volcanic peak, 13,350 ft. high, Federal Republic of Cameroon. Highest elevation in W Africa.

Cameroons, former German colony, W Africa, between Gulf of Guinea and L. Chad. German possession of area was recognized in 1902. In 1911 parts of French Equatorial Africa were added, but these were restored in 1919, when original colony was divided into French and British mandates under League of Nations. In 1946 they became UN trust territories. British Cameroons (31,150 sq. mi.), comprised two narrow detached strips administered from Nigeria. French Cameroons (166,489 sq. mi.) was administered as a separate territory; cap. Yaoundé. In 1960 French Cameroons became Cameroon Republic; joined in 1961 by S section of British Cameroons to form the Federal Republic of CAMEROON; N section became province of Federation of Nigeria.

Camillus (Marcus Furius Camillus) (kŭmĭ'lŭs), d. 365? B.C., second founder of Rome after Gallic invasion. Elected dictator five times (396–67 B.C.).

Camisards (kämēsär'), Protestant peasants of the Cévennes, France, who rebelled against religious persecution (1702–10). Successfully used guerrilla methods against superior forces. After defection of their leader Jean CAVALIER they fought on under Roland Laporte but were slowly forced into submission.

Cammaerts, Émile (ämēl' kä'märts), 1878–1953, Belgian writer; noted for poems of Second World War.

Camões or Camoens, Luís de (both: lŏōĕsh' dù kŭmŏ'ĭsh), 1524?–80, Portuguese national poet. A tempestuous spirit, he lost an eye while soldiering in Ceuta and spent half his adult life in Portuguese possessions abroad. Although known for his sonnets and lyrics, Camões's masterpiece is *The Lusiads*

(1572), a magnificent epic that recounts Portuguese history and Vasco da Gama's first voyage.

camomile or **chamomile** (kăm'ŭmīl), perennial plant (*Anthemis nobilis*), with daisylike white or yellow flowers and aromatic, finely cut foliage. Dried flowers are source of camomile tea.

Camorra (kùmô'rù), Italian criminal association in Naples and Sicily. First appeared c.1830, grew all-powerful through intimidation, blackmail, bribery; extended terror to Italian immigrants in U.S. Action by citizens of Naples secured its dissolution (1911).

camouflage, in warfare, the disguising of objects to make them blend into surroundings or to deceive observer as to location of strategic points. Large-scale scientific camouflage developed in First World War when ships were dazzle-painted and false landscapes were created to conceal forts and factories. Camouflage grew elaborate in Second World War. Usefulness diminished with development of radar and aerial photography, though still important in guerrilla warfare.

Camp, Walter (Chauncey), 1859–1925, American football expert, long coach at Yale. Popularized All-America teams in 1890s.

Campagna di Roma (kämpä'nyä dē rō'mä), plain surrounding Rome, Italy. Malarial and arid until reclamation work of 19th and 20th cent. Flocks of grazing sheep and ruins of Roman aqueducts and tombs give landscape a special charm.

Campanella, Tommaso (tōm-mä'zō kämpänĕl'lä), 1568–1639, Italian Renaissance philosopher and poet, a Dominican. *The City of the Sun* is an account of a utopian society, recalling Plato's *Republic*. Insisted on the preeminence of faith, but foreshadowed scientific empiricism.

Campania (kämpä'nyä), region (5,250 sq. mi.; pop. 4,346,264), S Italy, between Apennines and Tyrrhenian Sea; cap. Naples. Other cities: Benevento, Salerno, Caserta. Fertile plains and hills covered with vineyards, orchards, olive groves. Conquered by Rome 4th–2d cent. B.C. In Middle Ages it was held, successively, by Goths, Byzantines, Lombards, Normans. From 1282 it shared history of kingdom of NAPLES.

campanula: see BELLFLOWER.

Campbell, Scottish noble family. **Archibald Campbell**, 5th earl of Argyll, 1530–73, fluctuated in support of Elizabeth and Mary Queen of Scots. Was lord chancellor under James VI. **Archibald Campbell, 8th earl of Argyll** and **1st marquess of Argyll**, 1607–61, was a powerful Presbyterian statesman. After surrender of Charles I to Scots, he tried to secure Presbyterian settlement in England; crowned Charles II in Scotland. Executed for treason at Restoration. His son, **Archibald Campbell, 9th earl of Argyll**, 1629?–1685, both royalist and Protestant, opposed extreme measures against the COVENANTERS. Was beheaded after leading rebellion in aid of duke of MONMOUTH. His son, **Archibald Campbell, 1st duke of Argyll**, d. 1703, was partly responsible for massacre of the Macdonalds at Glencoe (1692). **John Campbell, 2d duke of Argyll** and **duke of Greenwich**, 1678–1743, Scottish general, supported union with England. Put down rebellion of JACOBITES 1715. His brother, **Archibald Campbell, 3d duke of Argyll**, 1682–1761, commissioner for the union (1706), served as Scottish peer in the united Parliament. Consistent supporter of George I.

Campbell, Alexander, 1788–1866, American clergyman, b. Ireland. His father, **Thomas Campbell**, 1763–1854, settled in W Pa., where he and his congregation withdrew from Presbyterian Church. Alexander came to U.S. in 1809. Became leader of group, for a time (1813–20) joined to Baptists, later to be DISCIPLES OF CHRIST. Advocated return to early Christian simplicity. Founded (1840) Bethany Col. (W.Va.).

Campbell, Colin, d. 1792, Scottish architect, one of the initiators of the Neo-Palladian movement.

Campbell, John, 1st earl of Breadalbane, 1635?–1717, Scottish chieftain. Aided the Restoration. Brutally massacred Macdonald clan at Glencoe (1692) for un-

avoidable delay in taking oath of submission to William III. Joined in Jacobite rebellion (1715).

Campbell, John Archibald, 1811–89, American jurist. Associate Justice of U.S. Supreme Court (1853–61). Sought to avoid war by mediation.

Campbell, Sir Malcolm, 1885–1949, English racing enthusiast. Set speed records driving motorcycles, airplanes, automobiles, speedboats.

Campbell, Mrs. Patrick, 1865–1940, English actress, whose maiden name was Beatrice Stella Tanner. Won fame in Pinero's *Second Mrs. Tanqueray* 1893. A friend of Shaw's, she created part of Eliza Doolittle in his *Pygmalion* in 1912.

Campbell, Robert: see ROB ROY.

Campbell, Robert, 1808–94, Canadian fur trader and explorer, b. Scotland. Discovered Pelly R. 1840. Descended it in 1843 to its confluence with Lewes R. and here estab. Fort Selkirk.

Campbell, Thomas, 1763–1854: see CAMPBELL, ALEXANDER.

Campbell, Thomas, 1777–1844, Scottish poet. Wrote long poems (e.g., *Gertrude of Wyoming*, 1809), but is remembered for such shorter patriotic verse as "Hohenlinden" and "Ye Mariners of England."

Campbell, (William) Wilfred, 1861–1918, Canadian author. Known for *Lake Lyrics* (1889), volume of nature poetry. Poetical works appeared in 1923.

Campbell. 1 City (pop. 11,863), W Calif., SW of San Jose; founded 1885. Processing center in fruit and vegetable area. **2** City (pop. 13,406), NE Ohio, ESE of Youngstown. Steel mfg.

Campbell-Bannerman, Sir Henry, 1836–1908, British statesman. As prime minister (1905–08), furthered Liberal measures and autonomy for Transvaal and Orange Free State.

Campbellites: see DISCIPLES OF CHRIST.

Campbellton, town (pop. 8,389), N N.B., Canada, on Restigouche R. and W of Dalhousie; a port. Lumbering center and outfitting point for sportsmen.

Campeche (kämpā'chā), state (19,672 sq. mi.; 1963 est. pop. 185,551), SE Mexico, on Gulf of Campeche. Comprises most of W half of Yucatan peninsula. Principal ports are Carmen and Campeche (also cap.; pop. 31,272).

Camperdown (kăm'pùrdoun"), Dutch *Kamperduin*, locality near village of Kamp, North Holland prov., NW Netherlands, on North Sea. Scene of British naval victory over Dutch (1797).

Camp Fire Girls, American organization for girls 7 to 18 years old; founded 1910 by Luther H. Gulick and others. Object is "to perpetuate the spiritual ideals of the home" and to develop health and character.

camphor, volatile oil, solid at ordinary temperatures. Commercial camphor, or camphor gum, is white, crystalline, and translucent, and has a penetrating odor. Natural camphor is obtained by steam distillation of wood of the camphor tree (*Cinnamomum camphora*) native to China, Japan, and Formosa, but introduced elsewhere. Much camphor is made synthetically from a turpentine derivative. It is used especially in making celluloid, explosives, and moth preventives, and in medicine and perfumery.

Campi, Giulio (jōō'lyō käm'pē), c.1500–c.1572, Italian painter and architect, founder of school of painters at Cremona. Did altarpieces and frescoes. His pupils included his brothers, Cavaliere **Antonio Campi** (kävälyä'rä), b. before 1536, d. 1591, and **Vincenzo Campi** (vēnchän'tsō), 1532–91, portrait and still-life painter. Another brother, **Bernardino Campi**, 1522–c.1590, did colossal biblical frescoes in cupola of San Sigismundo (Cremona).

Campian, Thomas: see CAMPION, THOMAS.

Campin, Robert (käm'pĭn), 1378–1444, Flemish artist, identified with the Master of Flémalle who did *Annunciation* (Brussels). Taught Roger van der Weyden. His Merode Altar is in the Cloisters, New York.

Campinas (kämpē'nùsh), city (pop. c.179,800), E São Paulo, Brazil. An agr., transportation, and industrial center.

Campion, Edmund, c.1540–1581, English Jesuit martyr. At Oxford he was a favorite of Queen Elizabeth I, but in 1571 he fled to the Continent and later became a Jesuit. In 1580 he and Robert Persons came as missionaries to England. He converted many but was taken, tortured, and executed.

Campion or **Campian, Thomas,** 1567–1620, English poet, composer, and lutanist. He wrote Latin poetry and masques, but is most important for his lute songs.

camp meeting, outdoor religious gathering, held in summer over period of days, typical of frontier U.S. Originated c.1800 in Ky. under preaching of James McGready and spread rapidly with revival movement. Camp meetings were held by evangelical sects and were characterized by emotional fervor attendant upon "conversion."

Campobello, island, 9 mi. long, 3 mi. wide, in Passamaquoddy Bay, between Maine and N.B., Canada. Island passed to Canada in Convention of 1817. Summer home of Pres. F. D. Roosevelt is now part of internatl. park (dedicated 1964).

Campo Formio, Treaty of (käm′pō fōr′myō), Oct., 1797, French-Austrian peace treaty at end of Bonaparte's Italian campaign. Austria ceded Austrian Netherlands to France, secretly promised France left bank of Rhine. Venetian republic, despite neutrality, was dissolved: most of it (including Dalmatia) went to Austria; the Ionian Isls. to France; the rest to CISALPINE REPUBLIC.

Campos, Arsenio Martínez de: see MARTÍNEZ DE CAMPOS, ARSENIO.

Campos (käm′pôsh), city (pop. c.90,600), NE Rio de Janeiro state, Brazil, on the Paraíba near mouth; commercial center of rich agr. region.

Camrose, city (pop. 6,939), central Alta., Canada, SE of Edmonton. Has Scandinavian Lutheran college.

Camus, Albert (älbĕr′ kämü′), 1913–60, French author. Sometimes close to existentialism, he stressed absurdity of life in his essay *The Myth of Sisyphus* (1942; Eng. tr., 1955) and the novel *The Stranger* (1942; Eng. tr., 1946), but he asserted the humanist values of solidarity in the novels *The Plague* (1947; Eng. tr., 1948) and *The Fall* (1956; Eng. tr., 1957). He also wrote plays, journalistic essays, and stories. Received 1957 Nobel Prize in Literature.

Cana (kā′nù), ancient town of Galilee where Jesus performed His first miracle by turning water into wine at a wedding. John 2.1,11; 4.46,54; 21.2.

Canaan (kā′nùn). **1** Son of Ham, ancestor of the Canaanites. Gen. 9.20–27; 10.6,15,19. **2** Name given by Israelites to Palestine before they occupied it. To them it was the land promised them by God and goal of their wanderings after leaving Egypt. Gen. 12.5; Ex. 3.8; Num. 13.17,29; 14.45; 21.3; Joshua 22.11,32; Judges 1.

Canada, nation (3,851,809 sq. mi. including inland waters; pop. 18,238,247), N North America, N of U.S.; member of British Commonwealth of Nations; cap. OTTAWA. Consists of ten provinces (NEWFOUNDLAND, NOVA SCOTIA, NEW BRUNSWICK, PRINCE EDWARD ISLAND, QUEBEC, ONTARIO, MANITOBA, SASKATCHEWAN, ALBERTA, BRITISH COLUMBIA), the NORTHWEST TERRITORIES, and YUKON territory. Separated from U.S. by a 3,986.9 mi. land border and the Great Lakes. N it fronts on Arctic Ocean where Boothia Peninsula and ARCTIC ARCHIPELAGO thrust far into the Arctic. Hudson and James bays cut deeply into NE coast. Atlantic coast, broken by Gulf of St. Lawrence, is swept by Labrador Current from N and Gulf Stream from S. Pacific coast is deeply indented with many islands offshore. The LAURENTIAN PLATEAU, a rolling wooded area rich in minerals, covers c.50% of the nation. Major mountains are Canadian Rockies between Alta. and B.C. and Coast Mts. of W B.C. River and lake country is general in N Que. and Ont., the N Prairie Provs., and the N.W.T. Fertile lowlands adjoin Great Lakes and highly productive plains cover S Prairie Provs. Agr. is major industry, followed by ranching, dairying, and lumbering. Although extensive mineral resources are untouched, there is important mining of gold, copper, iron, coal, nickel, pitchblende, petroleum, and uranium. Fishing and trapping are traditionally important occupations. Water resources have been developed to power Canadian industries. Ont. and Que. are leading industrial provinces. In general population is centered in Maritime Provs. and the S areas of Que., Ont., the Prairie Provs., and B.C. Many groups are represented, notably French (esp. in Que., where French is accepted language), English, Scottish, Irish, and German. John Cabot explored E Canadian coast 1497 and estab. English claims. In 1534 the Frenchman, Jacques Cartier, planted a cross on Gaspé Peninsula. Quebec was estab. 1608 by CHAMPLAIN. The St. Lawrence became gateway to new French empire. Settlements were bases for fur traders, explorers, missionaries, and empire builders, among them LA SALLE, LAVAL, FRONTENAC, MARQUETTE, JOLLIET, AND VÉRENDRYE. British opposition to New France centered in ACADIA. Meanwhile HUDSON'S BAY COMPANY was building fur-trading empire in NW. Imperial contest closed with defeat of French under MONTCALM on Plains of Abraham (1759); British gained Canada by Treaty of Paris (1763). Exploration opened up land in W. UNITED EMPIRE LOYALISTS advanced Canada. Fight for responsible government, including separate futile rebellions in 1837–38 led by W. L. MACKENZIE in Upper Canada and Louis PAPINEAU in Lower Canada, resulted in victory for democratic groups over entrenched FAMILY COMPACT. Movement for confederation resulted in the BRITISH NORTH AMERICA ACT. Territory was added as RUPERT'S LAND was purchased from Hudson's Bay Co. (1869) and B.C. joined the Union in 1871, P.E.I. in 1873, and Newfoundland in 1948. Man. became a province in 1870, and Sask. and Alta. in 1905. Mining operations developed rapidly after KLONDIKE gold rush in 1897. Organization of cooperatives (in N.S. and Prairie Provs.) and of SOCIAL CREDIT and CO-OPERATIVE COMMONWEALTH FEDERATION originated new forms to meet economic and political problems. Canada made valuable military contributions to both world wars. It is a member of the UN (1945) and North Atlantic Treaty Organization (1949).

Canada, Lower: see QUEBEC, province.

Canada balsam, yellow, oily turpentine from balsam fir. Used in preparation of slides for microscopic work, and in paints and polishes.

Canada Company, chartered in England 1826 for purpose of making settlements, represented by John GALT. Held lands on L. Huron side of S Ont., Canada, with hq. at GUELPH. Built first road from L. Ontario to L. Huron. Successful colonizing venture.

Canada First movement, party in Canada formed soon after confederation (1867) to encourage growth of nonpartisan loyalty to new dominion. Although short-lived, its ideals influenced Canadian writers and older political parties.

Canadian, river rising in E N.Mex. and flowing 906 mi. E across Texas Panhandle and most of Okla. Joined by North Canadian R. near Eufaula, Okla., where it enters Arkansas R. Has Eufaula Dam.

Canadian literature, English. Until after 1800 only notable works were recorded travels of explorers. First novelist was John Richardson, whose *Wacousta* (1832) popularized genre of national historical novel. In *The Clockmaker* (1836) T. C. Haliburton began humorous series on Sam Slick, Yankee peddler. Important novelists writing c.1900 include William Kirby, Sir Gilbert Parker, and L. M. Montgomery. After 1900, Canadian novels tended toward stricter realism but remained predominantly regional. Prominent authors were F. P. Grove and Laura Salverson. Younger novelists, concerned with national themes and social problems, are Hugh MacLennan, Morley Callaghan, and Ernest Buckler. Humorous essays of Stephen Leacock remain perennial favorites. Canadian poetry was late in developing. The long poetic drama, *Saul* (1857), by Charles Heavysege, achieved recognition. Beginning c.1880 the "Confederation school"—C. G. D. Roberts, Archibald Lampman, Bliss Carman, and Duncan Campbell Scott—began producing large body of romantic poetry. After her death Isabella V. Crawford was recognized as a genuine poet. Other poets of early 20th cent. include W. H. Drummond, John McCrae, and Robert W. Service. In 1926 Edwin J. Pratt began writing his imaginative, heroic poems. Other modern poets are Earle Birney and Dorothy Livesay (who follow tradition of Pratt), A. J. M. Smith, and A. M. Klein.

Canadian literature, French. The inspiration of almost all Canadian writing in French has been the passionate concern of French Canadians to preserve their identity. Its themes have been found in nationalism, simple lives and folkways of the habitants (French Canadian farmers), devotion to the Catholic Church, and the tie to mother France. First artistic expression of this "racial" impulse was F. X. Garneau's *Histoire du Canada* (1845–48). This classic of French Canadian nationalism inspired first nationalist poet, Octave Crémazie, and the Quebec school of writers—among them L. H. Fréchette, H. R. Casgrain, and Antoine Gérin-Lajoie. Louis Hémon's *Maria Chapdelaine* (1913) gave impetus to more realistic fiction, and there has followed a stream of works on habitant life of backwoods, farms, and villages.

Canadian Mounted Police: see ROYAL CANADIAN MOUNTED POLICE.

Canadian National Railways, government owned and operated transportation system in Canada extending from coast to coast with many branch lines in each province; unified 1923. Amalgamation of several separate private and government lines.

Canadian Pacific Railway, transcontinental transportation system in Canada, extending into U.S., privately owned and operated in competition with Canadian National Railways. Line completed to Pacific coast 1885, after PACIFIC SCANDAL.

Canadian Shield: see LAURENTIAN PLATEAU.

canal. Irrigation canals are extremely ancient. Transportation canals (level or with inclines for hauling vessels to each level) came later. Modern canals use locks (see LOCK, CANAL). Canals connect inland waterways and seas. They are used also to avoid falls and shoals. Frequently they are links in large projects for economic advance. Also used for checking erosion and draining land.

Canaletto (känälät'tō), 1697–1768, Venetian painter, whose real name was Antonio Canale or Canal. Known for his Venetian scenes. His nephew and pupil, Bernardo Bellotto (c.1720–80), architectural and landscape painter, was also called Canaletto.

Canal Zone: see PANAMA CANAL ZONE.

Canandaigua (känûndǎ'gwǔ), city (1965 pop. 10,058), W central N.Y., at N end of Canandaigua L., SE of Rochester; settled 1789. Finger Lakes resort and farm trade center, with various industries. Treaty with Iroquois Confederacy signed here 1794. Courthouse was scene of Susan B. Anthony's trial for voting 1873. Has U.S. veterans' hospital.

Canandaigua Lake: see FINGER LAKES.

canary, bird of finch family, a descendant either of wild serin finch or similar wild canary of Canary Isls., Madeira, Azores. Wild birds mostly gray or green; breeders developed both plain and variegated birds of yellow, buff, or greenish. Breed readily in captivity. Finest singers (Harz mt. and St. Andreasberg canaries) originated in Germany.

Canary Islands, group of seven islands (2,912 sq. mi.; pop. c.944,448) off NW Africa, in the Atlantic. Comprise two provinces of Spain: Santa Cruz de Tenerife (including Tenerife, largest island) and Las Palmas (including Grand Canary, most important and populous). Rugged islands of volcanic origin; highest point is over 12,000 ft. Visited since classical times. Conquered 15th cent. by Spain; frequently raided by pirates and privateers. In French Revolutionary Wars, Nelson was repulsed in 1797 at Santa Cruz. Fishing

and fish canneries; bananas, tomatoes, and potatoes are grown. Ports are coaling stations.

canasta: see RUMMY.

Canaveral, Cape: see CAPE KENNEDY.

Canberra (kän'bûrù), city (pop. 43,973), cap. of Commonwealth of Australia, in Australian Capital Territory. Site chosen 1908, city founded 1913. Succeeded Melbourne as federal cap. in 1927. Seat of Duntroon Military Col., Canberra Univ. Col. (1929), and Natl. Mus. of Australian Zoology.

Cancer [Lat.,= crab], in astrology, fourth sign of ZODIAC.

cancer or carcinoma (kärsĭnō'mà), malignant growth or tumor of unknown cause. Wildly growing epithelial cells invade surrounding tissues. Characteristic of malignancy is metastasis, the separation of malignant cells from the original growth and their distribution by way of lymphatics and blood to other parts of body. Causes of cancer are not understood. Carcinogenic (cancer-causing) factors are thought to include constant irritation of a part of the body, excessive smoking, and contact with certain complex hydrocarbons and other organic compounds. It is suspected that viruses are involved in transmission of at least some types of cancer; other theories hold that imbalance of endocrine system may be responsible. Modern cancer therapy utilizes surgery and radiation. Any lump, ulcer, or unusual bleeding from body orifice warrants examination by physician. Information offered by American Cancer Society. See also SARCOMA.

Candella, Felix, 1910–, Mexican architect, b. Madrid. Best known for his design of thin-shelled concrete vaults, often in startling shapes.

Candia (kän'dĕù), Gr. *Herakleion,* largest city (pop. 63,458) of Crete; port on the Gulf of Candia. Has unique museum of Minoan antiquities discovered at anc. Cnossus nearby.

Candish, Thomas: see CAVENDISH, THOMAS.

candle, mass of wax, tallow, paraffin, spermaceti or similar material surrounding a wick. Date of origin uncertain; in ancient writings words translated as "candle" may have meant torch or lamp. Formerly made by repeated dipping in melted material or by pouring material into molds; now are usually machine-molded. Used widely in religious ceremonies. See CANDLEMAS; HANUKKAH.

candlefish, fish of smelt family of Pacific coast from Oregon to Alaska. Flesh delicately flavored. Its oily body, if dried and supplied with a wick, will burn, hence its name. An alternative name is eulachon.

Candlemas, Feb. 2, the feast of the Purification of the Blessed Virgin. There is a procession of candles to celebrate the day, and in the Roman Catholic Church candles are blessed. In America this is "groundhog day" (see WOODCHUCK).

Candlewood Lake, artificial body of water, W Conn., N of Danbury. Made (1926) by power dam in Rocky R., near its mouth in Housatonic R. It is 15 mi. long and covers c.6,000 acres.

Candy, Ceylon: see KANDY.

candytuft, low-growing annual or shrubby perennial plant (*Iberis*), with flower clusters of various colors. It is used in borders and rock gardens.

cane: see BAMBOO; RATTAN; SUGAR CANE.

Canea (kùnē'ù), anc. Gr. *Cydonia,* modern Gr. *Khania,* city (pop. 38,467), cap. of Crete, on Gulf of Canea. One of oldest Cretan cities. Landmarks are cathedral, mosques, and old Venetian arsenal.

canella (kùnĕl'ù), small evergreen tree (*Canella winterana*) of S Florida and West Indies; it is also known as wild cinnamon. Its dried inner bark is the canella of commerce which has stimulant qualities.

cane sugar: see SUCROSE.

Caney Fork, river rising NW of Crossville, Tenn., and flowing c.144 mi. W and NW to Cumberland R. near Carthage. On it are Center Hill and Great Falls dams.

Canfield, Richard Albert, 1855–1914, American gambler. His famous gambling house in New York city was closed in 1904. Solitaire game named for him.

Can Grande della Scala: see SCALA, CAN FRANCESCO DELLA.

cankerworm, name for destructive larvae (also called measuring worms) of two geometrid moths. Both fall and spring species pupate in ground. Wingless females climb up tree trunks to lay eggs on bark; larvae feed on leaves. Shade trees can be protected by painting a ring of sticky substance around trunk, so that female cannot climb up to lay eggs.

canna, tropical perennial (*Canna*) with large leaves and spikes of red or yellow flowers. Planted in parks and formal beds in temperate regions.

cannabis: see HEMP; MARIJUANA.

Cannae (kăn′ē), anc. village, Apulia, S Italy. Hannibal defeated the Romans here in 216 B.C.

Cannes (kän), town (pop. 58,079), Alpes-Maritimes dept., SE France. Fashionable resort on Riviera.

cannibalism, consumption of flesh of an animal by member of its own species. Supernaturally significant, ritual cannibalism is most widespread among peoples of New Guinea, Central Africa, and Central Brazil. Starvation is probably least common motive.

Canning, Elizabeth, 1734–73, London servant girl, subject of a famous mystery. Disappeared for 28 days in 1753. Claimed to have been held in a garret. A gypsy woman was arrested and sentenced to hang but at second trial Elizabeth was accused of perjury and banished to America.

Canning, George, 1770–1827, English Tory statesman. As foreign minister (1807–9) planned seizure of Danish fleet (1807). After suicide of CASTLEREAGH (1822) was again foreign minister. Opposed decisions of Congress of Verona. Aided MONROE DOCTRINE by recognizing independence of Spanish colonies in America. Arranged French-Russian-British agreement resulting in Greek independence. Favored Catholic Emancipation, free trade. Prime minister 1827. His third son, **Charles John Canning, Earl Canning,** 1812–62, was noted for clemency as governor general of India in SEPOY REBELLION. Was first viceroy of India 1858–62.

Canning, Stratford: see STRATFORD DE REDCLIFFE, STRATFORD CANNING, VISCOUNT.

canning, the process of hermetically sealing cooked food for future use, was put into use in France at beginning of 19th cent. and first patented in U.S. c.1815. Glass jars were largely supplanted (except in home canning) by tin cans, patented 1810 in England, 1825 in U.S.; tin-plated steel cans have been mass produced in U.S. since 1847 and are today the basis of a huge industry. Home and commercial processes alike depend on rapid handling of sound raw materials to prevent vitamin loss, bacterial spoilage, and enzyme changes, and on sealing and cooking in containers to kill microorganisms.

Cannizzaro, Stanislao (stänĕslä′ō kän-nĕt-tsä′rō), 1826–1910, Italian chemist. He discovered cyanamide, worked to differentiate molecular from atomic weights, and obtained alcohols from aldehydes (Cannizzaro's reaction).

Cannon, Annie Jump, 1863–1941, American astronomer. As curator of astronomical photographs at Harvard, she discovered some 300 variable stars, new stars, and other stellar phenomena. Compiled bibliography of variable stars and a catalogue of stellar spectra.

Cannon, Joseph G(urney), 1836–1926, speaker of U.S. House of Representatives (1903–11). "Uncle Joe" ruled House dictatorially in interest of "Old Guard" Republicans until bill reforming House rules broke his power.

Cano, Alonso (älōn′sō kä′nō), 1601–67, Spanish artist. Carved and painted monumental altarpieces; designed façade of Granada cathedral.

Cano, Juan Sebastian del, c.1476–1526, Spanish navigator, first to circumnavigate the globe. Set out under Magellan, but at Magellan's death took command of the expedition.

canoe, long, narrow watercraft with sharp ends, propelled by paddle, small outboard motor, or sail (commonly the lateen). Long used all over the world, canoes vary in design and construction. North American Indians made them of birch bark, hides and skins, or hollowed logs. In the S Pacific, large seagoing sailing canoes with outriggers were developed for interisland journeys. The eskimo kayak, of sealskin stretched over driftwood or whalebone frame, is completely decked, with its cover fitting closely about paddler. Canoes in U.S., used mainly for sport, are made of aluminum, wood, and synthetic materials.

canon (kă′nŭn), in Christendom, term with several meanings: decree of church council (hence body of such decrees, when ratified, contribute to canon law); official list of saints (hence canonization); list of books recognized or accepted in the Bible (the canonical books, as in the Western canon); the principal part of the MASS; one of certain church officials (canons regular, uncloistered monks; canons attached to a cathedral).

canon, in music, composition in which all parts have the same melody but begin at different times. The melody may be repeated in different note values, at different pitch, backwards, or with other consistent variation. A simple canon lacking any melodic variation is called a round.

Canon City (kăn′yŭn), city (pop. 8,973), S central Colo., on Arkansas R. above Pueblo, in fruit, truck-farm, and livestock area. Laid out 1859 on site of blockhouse built (1807) by Z. M. Pike. Coal and gold mines are nearby. City is entrance to Royal Gorge.

canonization, in the Roman Catholic Church, process by which a person is officially enrolled among the saints. The method of canonization was set by Urban VIII in acts that came in force in 1634. At a "trial" in Rome, a prosecutor (popularly called *advocatus diaboli* or devil's advocate) attacks the claims proposed by his opponent (*advocatus Dei* or God's advocate) that the proposed saint had lived a holy life and was responsible for at least four miracles. To secure beatification (frequently a step toward canonization) proof of two miracles is offered. The miracles are considered pious belief, but a Catholic is not required to believe in them. A holy person may be considered a saint without formal canonization, as indeed many of the earliest and greatest saints are.

canon law, in the Roman Catholic Church, law of the church courts, based on legislation of councils, popes, and bishops (in local matters). The present great code was promulgated in 1917. It is the culmination of long development, begun with early letters of the bishops of Rome. These and later letters and pronouncements are the decretals, gathered into collections (sometimes spurious, as in the False Decretals). The greatest figure in canon law was GRATIAN, whose compilation was the basis of all later collections. Gregory IX, Boniface VIII, and John XXII issued further collections of decretals (later gathered in *Extravagantes communes*). The Council of Trent (1545–63) added much to canon law, which deals primarily with governance of the clergy and the Church, including administration of the sacraments (notably holy orders and matrimony).

Canonsburg, borough (pop. 11,877), SW Pa., SW of Pittsburgh; settled 1773. Gram of radium produced here was given 1921 to Mme Curie, who visited town. Has Log Academy (1780), oldest school building W of Alleghenies, and Black Horse Tavern (1794), site of beginning of Whisky Rebellion. Coal mines nearby.

Canopus, star in Southern Hemisphere constellation Argo Navis, second only to Sirius in apparent magnitude.

Canossa (känôs′sä), village, Emilia-Romagna, N central Italy, in Appenines. Lords of its castle (ruins) ruled much of Tuscany and Emilia in 10th–11th cent. Countess MATILDA was last of line. In Jan., 1077, castle was scene of penance by Emperor HENRY IV, who supposedly waited barefoot in the snow for three days before Pope Gregory VII, who was Matilda's guest, lifted excommunication.

Canova, Antonio (äntō'nyō känō'vä), 1757–1822. Italian sculptor, leader of the classical revival in Italy. Did statues of Napoleon and his family.

Canso, fishing town (pop. 1,151), E N.S., near entrance to Chedabucto Bay and near Cape Canso, the easternmost point of N.S. peninsula. Western terminus of a number of ocean cables.

Cantabrian Mountains (käntä'brëun), N Spain, along Bay of Biscay from Pyrenees to Cape Finisterre. Highest peak is Peña de Cerredo (8,687 ft.). Rich in coal and iron.

Cantabrigia: see CAMBRIDGE UNIVERSITY.

Cantacuzene, John: see JOHN VI, emperor.

Cantal (kätäl'), department (2,231 sq. mi.; pop. 172,977). S central France, in Auvergne; cap. Aurillac. **Plomb du Cantal** (plō"dü), 6,096 ft. high, an extinct volcano, is highest peak of Cantal mts.

cantaloupe: see MELON.

cantata, musical form developed in Italy in the baroque era. It was a short dramatic piece which in the 17th cent. took on the form of recitative and aria. In France and Italy the secular cantata prevailed; in Germany the church cantata, with choral and instrumental parts, was adopted.

Canterbury, county borough (pop. 30,376), on Stour R. at foot of N Downs, Kent, England; spiritual center of England. St. Augustine came from Rome 597 to convert English to Christianity, founded abbey here, and became first archbishop of Canterbury. Town famous in Europe as object of pilgrimage after murder of THOMAS À BECKET. Chaucer's *Canterbury Tales* based upon stories of these travelers. Magnificent cathedral embodies work of several periods and various men (notably Lanfanc and St. Anselm). City also site of St. Martin's (Mother Church of England), St. Augustine's Abbey, and other buildings.

Canterbury bells: see BELLFLOWER.

cantharides (känthä'rūdēz) or **Spanish fly,** bright green or bluish beetle, *Lytta* (formerly *Cantharis*) *vesicatoria,* chiefly of S Europe. This and others of same family often called blister beetles because of irritating effect on skin.

Canticles, another name for the SONG OF SOLOMON.

cantilever (kän'tulēvùr), beam supported rigidly at one end to carry load along free arm or at free end. Principle used widely in construction.

Cantinflas (kän'tēnfläs"), 1911–, Mexican comedian, originally named Mario Moreno. Portrays lovable raffish characters.

Cantire, Argyllshire, Scotland: see KINTYRE.

Canton, John, 1718–72, English physicist. Noted for work in hydraulics, magnetism, electricity. Invented devices for measuring electricity.

Canton (kän'tŏn'), Mandarin *Kuang-chou,* city (pop. c.1,900,000), cap. of Kwangtung prov., S China, port on Canton R. delta. Terminus of the Canton-Hankow RR, and chief industrial and cultural center of S China. Visited by Arab traders in 10th cent. In 1511 Portugal won trade monopoly, which made her first European power to have commercial contact with China. Treaty ending Opium War (1839–42) made Canton a treaty port. After occupation by British and French forces in 1856, Shameen Isl. was made foreign concession (restored to China 1946). City was seat of Kuomintang revolutionary movement.

Canton. 1 City (pop. 13,588), W central Ill., SW of Peoria, in Ill. corn belt; founded 1825. Trade and industrial center for coal and farm area. **2** Town (pop. 12,771), E Mass., SSW of Boston. Paul Revere had copper-rolling mill here. **3** City (pop. 2,562), NE Mo., on Mississippi R., NNW of Hannibal; laid out 1830. Seat of Culver-Stockton Col. **4** Village (pop. 5,046), N N.Y., on Grass R., ESE of Ogdens-

burg; settled 1799. Seat of St. Lawrence Univ. **5** City (pop. 113,631), NE Ohio, on Nimishillen Creek, SSE of Akron; laid out 1806. Important iron and steel area. William McKinley lived and was buried here.

Canton or **Pearl,** Chinese *Yueh Kiang* or *Chu Kiang,* river, c.110 mi. long, Kwangtung prov., S China. A major waterway of China, it links Canton to the sea. Its large estuary between Hong Kong and Macao is called Boca Tigris.

Canton Island, atoll (3.5 sq. mi.), central Pacific, one of PHOENIX ISLANDS. Important transoceanic air base. Claimed in 1856 by U.S. and in 1937 by Great Britain; agreement was made 1939 for joint control of Canton and nearby ENDERBURY ISLAND for 50 years.

Cantor, Georg (gä'ôrk kän'tôr), 1845–1918, German mathematician known for work on theory of numbers and development of theory of sets and arithmetic of infinity.

Canute (kûnoōt', kûnūt'), 995?–1035, king of England, Norway, and Denmark, younger son of SWEYN of Denmark. Invaded England with his father in 1013. On Sweyn's death he withdrew to Denmark. Invaded England 1015. Divided country with EDMUND IRONSIDE after battle of Assandun. On death of Edmund (1016), Canute was accepted as sole king. Gave England peace, restored Church to high place, and codified English law. Married Emma, widow of Æthelred. Succeeded to throne of Denmark 1018. After several expeditions to Norway drove out Olaf II in 1028, thus becoming ruler of three kingdoms. He made his son Harthacanute king of Denmark, and his son Sweyn king of Norway. Canute estab. friendly relations with the Holy Roman Empire.

Canute the Saint, d. 1086, king (1080–86) of Denmark. Canonized 1100.

Canyon, city (pop. 5,864), extreme N Texas, S of Amarillo in Panhandle; settled 1892. Prairie Dog Fork of Red R. formed nearby above Palo Duro Canyon, a brilliant gash in the Llano Estacado which draws many visitors. Seat of West Texas State Univ.

Canyon de Chelly National Monument: see NATIONAL PARKS AND MONUMENTS (table).

Canyonlands National Park: see NATIONAL PARKS AND MONUMENTS (table).

Canzoneri, Toni, 1908–60, American boxer. Won lightweight championship in 1930 from Al Singer; lost it 1933 to Barney Ross; regained it 1935 from Lou Ambers. Retired 1939.

Capablanca, José Raúl (hōsä' räōōl' käpäbläng'kä), 1888–1942, Cuban chess player, world champion 1921–27.

Cap de la Madeleine (käp' dù lä mädlĕn'), industrial city (pop. 26,926), S Que., Canada, on N bank of St. Lawrence R. just N of Trois Rivières.

Cape Breton Island, c.3,600 sq. mi., forming NE part of N.S., Canada, separated from main part by Gut of Canso. Bounded by the Atlantic (S and E) and the Gulf of St. Lawrence (W). Bras d'Or salt lakes occupy center of island. There are many summer lake resorts and coastal fishing villages. Sydney and Glace Bay coal fields feed important steelworks. Cabot Trail is a motor road which circles center and W part of island, commemorating its discovery by John Cabot (1497). By Peace of Utrecht (1713–14) French retained island (named Ile Royale with cap. at Louisburg), and some Acadians migrated here. Cape Breton was attached to N.S. in 1763. Was independent with cap. at Sydney 1784–1820.

Cape Canaveral: see CAPE KENNEDY.

Cape Charles, town (pop. 2,041), E Va., on Chesapeake Bay near tip of Eastern Shore peninsula. Occupied by Federal forces in Civil War.

Cape Coast, town (pop. c.35,000), cap. of Western Region of Ghana; port on the Gulf of Guinea. A Swedish fort in 17th cent. Became hq. of British in 1664, and was cap. of Ghana until superseded by Accra in 1876. Fishing.

Cape Cod, low sandy peninsula of glacial origin, 65 mi. long and 1–20 mi. wide, SE Mass.; bounded by Cape

Cod Bay (N and W), the Atlantic (E), Nantucket and Vineyard sounds (S), and Buzzards Bay (SW). Name attributed to Gosnold, who visited here 1602. Known for its summer resorts and fishing towns, e.g., Provincetown (on site where Pilgrims put in, 1620), Barnstable, Falmouth, and Hyannis. Cape Cod Canal (built 1909–14, improved 1927), c.18 mi. long, connects Cape Cod and Buzzards bays, crossing Bourne town. Otis Air Force Base is near Falmouth. Cape has fishing, cranberry cultivation, candlemaking, and boatbuilding. Cape Cod National Seashore (10,461 acres) was estab. 1961.

Cape Colony: see CAPE PROVINCE.

Cape Fear River, formed SW of Raleigh, N.C., by junction of Deep and Haw rivers and flowing c.202 mi. SE across piedmont and coastal plains to Atlantic N of Cape Fear. Navigable from Wilmington, at head of estuary, to Fayetteville. Has three locks and dams.

Cape Girardeau (jĭrär′dō), city (pop. 24,947), SE Mo., SSE of St. Louis overlooking Mississippi R.; founded 1793 as trading post. Important early port and a Civil War fort. Now an industrial and trade center. Southeast Missouri State Col. is here.

Cape jasmine: see GARDENIA.

Capek, Josef, Czech Čapek (chä′pĕk), 1887–1945, Czech author and primitivist painter. With his brother Karel he collaborated on *The Insect Play* (1921; Eng. tr., 1923), a satire produced in U.S. as *The World We Live In. Poems from a Concentration Camp* (1946) appeared after his death at Belsen. His brother **Karel Capek,** 1890–1938, won international fame with his satirical play *R.U.R.* (*Rossum's Universal Robots,* 1921; Eng. tr., 1923), which introduced the word *robot* into English. Among other works are the play *The Makropoulos Secret* (1923; Eng. tr., 1925), a novel *Krakatit* (1924; Eng. tr., 1925), and three vols. of conversations with T. G. Masaryk.

Cape Kennedy, extending into the Atlantic, E Fla., NE of Cocoa. Major U.S. missile-testing center since 1950. Most U.S. earth satellites launched from here; site of most of Mercury and Apollo manned space flights. Name changed from Cape Canaveral 1963 as memorial to Pres. J. F. Kennedy. Patrick Air Force Base is nearby. To W, separated from cape by Banana R. (lagoon), is Merritt Isl. (c.40 mi. long, c.6 mi. wide), with Merritt town (pop. 3,554), site of space-related industries.

Capella, Martianus (märshēā′nùs kủpĕ′lù), fl. 5th cent.?, Latin writer. Long allegory, *The Marriage of Mercury and Philology,* popular in Middle Ages.

Capello, Bianca (byäng′kä käpĕl′lō), 1548–87, Italian adventuress. Became grand duchess of Tuscany by marrying Francesco de' Medici (1579). Died suddenly with her husband; presumably poisoned.

Cape May, Atlantic resort city (pop. 4,477), S N.J., at end of Cape May peninsula, S extremity of N.J. A lighthouse is at Delaware Bay entrance; c.3 mi. above point cape is bisected by canal (built by Federal government 1942–43), part of N.J. Intracoastal Waterway. Cape May Point (pop. 263) has eroded nearly a fifth of a mi. in recent years.

Cape Province, officially **Cape of Good Hope Province** (277,169 sq. mi.; pop. c.5,342,720), Republic of South Africa, on Atlantic and Indian oceans; cap. Capetown. Occupies S tip of Africa. Crops include grains, tobacco, citrus fruit, and grapes (for wine). Diamonds, copper, and coal are mined. The 15th-cent. Portuguese navigator Dias was first to round Cape of Good Hope, but the Dutch were first to settle the area, founding Capetown in 1652. The late 17th cent. saw influx of French Huguenots. In 1806 the British annexed area as Cape Colony, and British settlers arrived 1820. Opposition to British rule led many of the Boer farmers to migrate north (see TREK). In South African War fierce battles were fought at Mafeking and Kimberley. With founding of Union of South Africa in 1910, the colony became a province.

caper, white-flowered shrub (*Capparis spinosa*) of Mediterranean region. Its pickled buds, called capers, are used for flavoring.

Capernaum (kủpûr′näùm) or **Capharnaum** (kủfär′–), town, NE Palestine, associated with Jesus' ministry. Mat. 8.5–22; 11.23; Mark 1.21–34; 2; Luke 4.31–40; John 2.12; 6.59.

Capetians (kủpĕ′shùnz), royal house of FRANCE, named for HUGH CAPET, who became king in 987. His direct descendants ruled until death of Charles IV (1328), when throne passed to collateral branch of VALOIS.

Capetown or **Cape Town,** city (pop. c.807,211), cap. of Cape Prov., legislative cap. of Republic of South Africa; a large port on the Atlantic, with good rail connections to the interior. Scenically located at the foot of Table Mt. and overlooking Table Bay. Here are Houses of Parliament (1886) and Univ. of Cape Town (1916). Founded 1652 by the Dutch, taken 1806 by the British. Cap. of British Cape Colony until South Africa became independent member of British Commonwealth in 1910.

Cape Verde Islands (vûrd), archipelago (c.1,557 sq. mi.; pop. c.218,000), in the Atlantic, c.300 mi. from coast of W Africa. A Portuguese overseas territory, it comprises 10 islands. Cap. is Praia (pop. c.10,000) on São Tiago. São Vicente is an oiling station. Of volcanic origin, islands export coffee, nuts, and sugar.

Cape York Peninsula, N Queensland, Australia, between Gulf of Carpentaria and Coral Sea.

Cap-Haitien (kăp′ –hä′shùn), city (pop. c. 30,000), N Haiti. Founded by French 1670, it was cap. of colonial Haiti until 1770. Commercial center and major seaport.

Capharnaum, same as CAPERNAUM.

capillarity causes part of surface of liquid in contact with solid (e.g., a glass jar) to be elevated above or depressed below rest of surface. Named for behavior of liquids in capillary tube placed perpendicularly in liquid: water rises in tube to level above that outside; mercury is depressed. Forces operating are adhesion, cohesion, surface tension.

capillary, minute vessel connecting arterial and venous systems in CIRCULATION OF THE BLOOD.

Capistrano, John of: see JOHN CAPISTRAN, SAINT.

capital. Term originally denoted interest-bearing money, now includes entire stock of goods which produce income (e.g., tools, lands). Capital may accumulate from savings or incomes, scarcity of natural materials, presence of monopolies, previous profits, speculations, or recapitalization.

capitalism, economic system characterized by private ownership of property, by profit, and by bank credit. Modern importance dates from INDUSTRIAL REVOLUTION. Capitalism stresses freedom of individual economic enterprise. In 20th cent. the capitalist structure, grown to enormous proportions, has been restricted by social reforms and government regulation.

capital levy: see INTERNAL REVENUE.

capital punishment, putting to death by the state. Once imposed even for petty crimes, its use has decreased since 18th cent., because of efforts of such men as Beccaria and Benthan. By 1966 11 states in U.S. had abolished it.

Capitol, building, Washington, D.C., c.750 ft. long, including approaches c.350 ft. wide; seat of U.S. government. Elevated site chosen by George Washington in consultation with Major L'ENFANT. Building begun in 1793; first architect was William THORNTON. Burned by British in 1814. Charles BULFINCH brought design to completion in 1830. T. U. Walter added wings and dome (c.288 ft. in height) during period 1851–65. East front extended 32 ft. and sandstone façade replaced by marble in 1960.

Capitoline Hill or **Capitol,** highest of the seven hills of anc. Rome, historic and religious center of the city. On it were the great temple of Jupiter Capitolinus, the citadel (arx) and the Tabularium, which housed the state archives. The temple, three times destroyed by fire, was last rebuilt by Domitian.

Capitol Reef National Monument: see NATIONAL PARKS AND MONUMENTS (table).

capitularies, decrees and written commands of the Merovingian and Carolingian kings of the Franks. Most important were those addressed by Charlemagne to his officers, the *missi dominici,* for administration of the empire and carrying out reforms.

Capo d'Istria, Giovanni Antonio, Count (kä"pō dē'strēä), 1776–1831, Greek and Russian statesman. b. Corfu. Entered Russian service 1809; as Russian foreign minister (1820–22) he helped Greek uprising in 1821. Elected president of Greece 1827, but aristocratic and pro-Russian leanings led to assassination.

Capone, Al(fonso) (kŭpō'nē), 1899–1947, American gang leader. b. Italy. His crime syndicate terrorized Chicago in 1920s.

Caporetto: see KOBARID.

Capote, Truman (kāpō'tē), 1924–, American author. He has written novels (e.g., *The Grass Harp,* 1951; dramatized, 1952); film scripts; a musical play; stories, articles, and travel sketches (*Selected Writings,* 1963, gives the best); and a nonfiction report of two murderers, *In Cold Blood* (1966).

Cappadocia (kăpŭdō'shŭ), anc. region of Asia Minor, now in Turkey; term is used for varying territory. The inhabitants kept some independence even under Alexander the Great, and it became a kingdom in the 3d cent. B.C. Pontus split off from it. Cappadocia became a prosperous Roman province, and name is in the Bible. Perhaps originally a Hittite territory.

Cappel, Switzerland: see KAPPEL.

Capri (kä'prē), small rocky island (est. pop. 10,519), S Italy, in Bay of Naples. Striking scenery, pleasant climate make it a tourist center. Two small towns: Capri, Anacapri. Ruins of villas of emperors Augustus and Tiberius. The Blue Grotto is here.

Capricornus [Lat.,= goat horn], 10th sign of ZODIAC.

Caprivi, Leo, Graf von (lā'ō gräf fūn käprē'vē), 1831–99, chancellor of Germany (1890–94). Succeeded Bismarck. Favored industrial interests.

Caprivi Zipfel (käprē'vē tsĭp'fūl) [Ger. *Zipfel* = tip, point] or **Caprivi Strip,** territory, 300 mi. long and 50 mi. wide, extending along N border of Botswana to Zambezi R. Part of South-West Africa.

Capsian culture: see GAFSA.

Captivity, Exile, or **Babylonian captivity,** in history of Israel, period from fall of Jerusalem (586 B.C.) to rebuilding of Temple (516 B.C.) thus lasting the 70 years prophesied for captivity. Jer. 25.11; Dan. 9.2; Zech. 7.5. After capture of city, thousands were deported to Mesopotamia; exiles kept close contact with kinsmen at home. In 538 B.C., Cyrus decreed that worship be restored at Jerusalem and that Jews might return home. The following century was a period of reintegration into a national and religious unit. See books of Ezekiel, Ezra, and Nehemiah. For "Babylonian captivity" of popes, see PAPACY.

Capua (kä'pūä), ancient city, Campania, S Italy, strategically situated on Appian Way. Opened its gates to Hannibal 216 B.C. Retaken by Romans, it became chief center of S Italy. After its destruction by the Arabs (A.D. 841), inhabitants fled to nearby Casilinum and founded modern Capua (est. pop. 17,054).

Capuchins (kä'pūchĭnz) [Ital.,= hooded ones], independent order of the Franciscans, officially Friars Minor Capuchin; founded 1525–28. Devoted to preaching and missions, they did much to forward the Catholic Reform.

Capulin Mountain National Monument: see NATIONAL PARKS AND MONUMENTS (table).

capybara (kāpĭbä'rŭ), mammal (*Hydrochoerus capybara*) of Central and much of South America. Also called water hog and carpincho. Largest living rodent (up to 4 ft. long, 75–100 lb.), it has brownish, yellowflecked hair, no tail, partially webbed feet, and is semiaquatic. It eats vegetation. Is a source of food, glove leather, and bristles.

caracal (kä'rŭkŭl) or **Persian lynx,** mammal of cat family, native to Asia, Africa. It is reddish brown with black-tufted ears, and c.3¼ ft. from nose to tip of tail. Preys on deer, hares, birds. *Lynx caracal.*

Caracalla (kărŭkä'lŭ), 188–217, Roman emperor (211–17), son of Septimius SEVERUS. Called Caracalla after his Gallic tunic; real name Marcus Aurelius Antoninus. Had to share rule with his brother Geta, but murdered him and his followers (212). Extended citizenship to all free inhabitants of the empire, presumably to increase his income. He was murdered by Macrinus, who took the imperial rule, only to be replaced by Heliogabalus.

Caracas (kŭrä'kŭs), city (metropolitan area pop. 1,-336,119; alt. 3,100 ft.), N Venezuela, cap. and largest city of country. Independence declared here 1811. Earthquake of 1812 hurt patriot cause.

Caracci, family of Italian painters: see CARRACCI.

Caracciolo, Francesco (fränchä'skō kärät'chōlō), 1752–99, Neapolitan admiral. Commanded fleet of PARTHENOPEAN REPUBLIC (1799). Summarily executed by order of Lord Nelson.

Caractacus (kŭrăk'tŭkŭs) or **Caradoc** (kŭrä'dŭk), fl. A.D. 50, British chieftain, son of Cymbeline. Fought for nine years against Romans, was captured and taken to Rome. Claudius spared his life.

Caraman, Turkey: see KARAMAN.

Carausius (kŭrô'shēŭs), d. 293, Gallo-Roman commander. Condemned by Maximian, he fled to Britain and estab. rule. Diocletian and Maximian recognized him as coemperor. Defeated by Constantius and murdered.

Caravaggio, Michelangelo Amerighi da (mēkälän'jälō ämärē'gē dä kärävä'jō), 1573–1610, Italian painter; founder of naturalist school in Rome. One of earliest masters of dramatic light and shade. In genre and religious pictures he abandoned idealization for emphasis on the character of his lowly models.

caravel (kä'rŭvĕl"), three-masted, usually square-rigged, sailing ship. It had a roundish hull with high bow and stern and was a light ship with small displacement. Its advantage over bulkier ships was important in enabling the Portuguese to open the African coast in the 15th cent. Columbus' flagship, the *Santa María,* was a typical caravel.

caraway, biennial herb (*Carum carvi*) native to Europe. Small seeds are used medicinally and for seasoning pastries and liqueurs (e.g., kümmel).

carbide, compound of carbon and one other element, not hydrogen or oxygen. Generally produced in electric furnace. Many carbides are decomposed by water to yield a gas.

carbohydrate, organic compound of carbon, hydrogen, oxygen (with hydrogen and oxygen in ratio of 2:1). Composed of one or more simple sugar molecules. Abundant in plants and animals. Important as heatenergy supplying foods and as framework of rigid biological structures. Three classes: monosaccharides, one simple sugar molecule (e.g., galactose, glucose); disaccharides, two simple sugar molecules linked together (e.g., lactose, maltose, sucrose); and polysaccharides, branched or unbranched chains of simple sugar molecules (e.g., cellulose, chitin, glycogen, starch, pectin). Linkages between sugar molecules are formed by loss of a water molecule; linkages are broken by HYDROLYSIS. See *ill.,* p. 178.

carbolic acid or **phenol** (fē'–), colorless, crystalline solid compound. Molecule is a benzene ring with a hydroxyl radical in place of one hydrogen. It is a weak acid. Corrosive and poisonous. Used as antiseptic, disinfectant, and to make resins, explosives, and dyes. See *ill.,* p. 106.

carboloy (kär'būloi), alloy of cobalt, tungsten, carbon. Harder than steel; used for cutting.

carbon, abundant, nonmetallic element (symbol = C; see also ELEMENT, table), found in all organic matter. All life on earth is based on the chemistry of carbon, hydrogen, and oxygen. Carbon forms HYDROCARBON and CARBOHYDRATE compounds. Oxidation (burning) of carbon in fuels is the source of most chemical energy; oxidation of carbon in food provides the

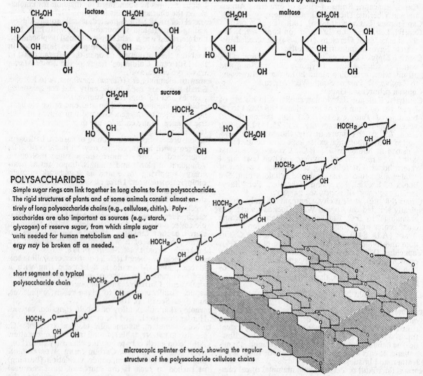

CARBOHYDRATES

Carbohydrates $(CH_2O)_n$ are organic chemical compounds containing carbon, hydrogen, and oxygen; in most carbohydrate molecules the atoms are present in the ratio of 1 carbon: 2 hydrogens: 1 oxygen.

MONOSACCHARIDES

The basic carbohydrate unit is the simple sugar molecule, the monosaccharide. There are many different simple sugars. Every one of them can exist in either a ring or a straight-chain form.

D-glucose (ring form)

D-glucose (straight-chain form)

D-fructose (ring form)

D-fructose (straight-chain form)

D-glucose (ring form)

D-glucose (ring form)

D-fructose (ring form)

DISACCHARIDES

A disaccharide is composed of a linked pair of simple sugar rings. Some of the commonest natural sugars are disaccharides. The links between the simple sugar components of disaccharides are formed and broken in nature by enzymes.

lactose

maltose

sucrose

POLYSACCHARIDES

Simple sugar rings can link together in long chains to form polysaccharides. The rigid structures of plants and of some animals consist almost entirely of long polysaccharide chains (e.g., cellulose, chitin). Polysaccharides are also important as sources (e.g., starch, glycogen) of reserve sugar, from which simple sugar units needed for human metabolism and energy may be broken off as needed.

short segment of a typical polysaccharide chain

microscopic splinter of wood, showing the regular structure of the polysaccharide cellulose chains chemical energy for biological processes. Complete oxidation yields CARBON DIOXIDE; incomplete, CARBON MONOXIDE. Carbon is in coal, wood, synthetic and natural textiles, rubber, oil (petroleum), gasoline, gaseous fuels, food, minerals, metal alloys. DIAMOND and GRAPHITE are crystalline allotropic forms. Carbonates are common in nature (e.g., LIMESTONE); STEEL contains iron and carbon. Carbon 14, the isotope of mass number 14, is used in biology in TRACER metabolism studies; carbon 14 is also important in RADIOACTIVITY DATING.

Carbon, Mount: see ELK MOUNTAINS.

Carbonari (kärbōnä′rē), secret revolutionary society in SW Europe in early 19th cent. Active in revolts in Spain, Naples, Piedmont (1820–21).

carbonate, a salt or an ester (in the case of organic carbonates) of carbonic acid. Carbonate RADICAL consists of a carbon atom bound to each of three oxygen atoms; it has two units of negative valence. Carbonates, except for ammonium, potassium, and sodium, are insoluble in water. Most decompose with heat, yielding carbon dioxide and metallic oxide. Form bicarbonates with carbonic acid. Calcium carbonate occurs in animal shells and as ICELAND SPAR, LIMESTONE, MARBLE, and STALACTITE and STALAGMITE formations. Iron carbonate (siderite) is important iron source. Potassium carbonate is POTASH; sodium, SODA. Calcium bicarbonate causes "hardness" in water.

Carbondale. 1 City (1964 pop. 18,531), S Ill., N of Cairo, in coal-mining and farm area; founded 1852. Rail division point with repair shops. SOUTHERN ILLINOIS UNIVERSITY has campus here. Memorial Day inaugurated by Gen. J. A. Logan here 1868. **2** Industrial city (pop. 13,595), NE Pa., on Lackawanna R., NE of Scranton; settled 1814.

carbon dioxide, colorless, almost odorless, gaseous compound of carbon and oxygen; formula CO_2. Heavier than air; neither burns nor supports combustion; soluble in water; can be liquefied under pressure. Occurs in ATMOSPHERE. Results from burning of carbon, hydrocarbons, and from decomposition of carbonate. Product of respiration; given off in FERMENTATION, used in photosynthesis. Causes dough to rise when formed by baking powder; gives effervescence to water when dissolved under pressure; used in fire extinguishers. Also called carbonic acid gas because aqueous solution is weak acid. Dry ice is solid CO_2.

carbonic acid, weak acid known only in solution; formed when carbon dioxide is dissolved in water. Used in carbonated beverages.

carbonic acid gas: see CARBON DIOXIDE.

Carboniferous period (kärbŭnĭ′fŭrŭs), fifth period of PALEOZOIC ERA, marked by COAL formation. In North America it is divided into Lower Carboniferous or Mississippian and Upper Carboniferous or Pennsylvanian. The Mississippian was a period of repeated submergence and rising, with vast sediment deposits, mountain making, and volcanic activity. During the Pennsylvanian warm humid climate and extensive marshes favored rapid growth of the vegetation which later became coal. As in the Mississippian crustal disturbances took place on a huge scale. Land animals included primitive amphibians and reptiles, spiders, snails, scorpions, huge dragonflies. See table, p. 406.

carbonite: see COKE.

carbon monoxide, colorless, odorless, tasteless gaseous compound of carbon and oxygen; formula CO. May cause fatal poisoning if inhaled. Lighter than air; almost insoluble in water. Used as fuel (in PRODUCER GAS, WATER GAS), and as reducing agent (oxygen remover) in obtaining certain metals from ores. Formed by incomplete combustion of carbon. Present in exhaust of gasoline engines, in illuminating gas, in furnaces when there is insufficient air.

carbon tetrachloride, compound of carbon and chlorine; nonflammable liquid used as solvent for fats, oils, and greases, and in fire extinguishers. Reacts with steam to form phosgene, a poisonous gas. Although toxic when absorbed through skin or inhaled, it is used medicinally for treating intestinal parasites.

Carborundum: see SILICON CARBIDE.

carbuncle, acute inflammatory infection of subcutaneous tissue with multiple drainage points. Usually caused by bacterial invasion. Antibiotics, systemically and directly applied, are indicated pending suppuration. See also BOIL.

carburetor (kär′byūrātŭr). **1** Gasoline-engine device for vaporizing liquid fuel before combustion. Spray type has float chamber (regulates gasoline entry) and mixing chamber (vaporizes fuel spray), with vapor and air passing over throttle valve into cylinder intake manifold. **2** Device to enrich coal or water gas, increasing illuminative power.

Carcassone (kärkäsôn′), city (est. pop. 37,035), cap. of Aude dept., S France, on Aude R. One of architectural marvels of Europe. Medieval walled city was entirely restored by Viollet-le-Duc (19th cent.). "New city" (13th cent.) lies across Aude.

Carchemish (kär′kĭmĭsh, kärkē′mĭsh), city of anc. Syria; important neo-Hittite city and trade center. Hieroglyphic inscriptions of HITTITES found here.

carcinoma: see CANCER.

Carco, Francis (fräsēs′ kärkō′), 1886–1958, French poet and novelist of the bohemian life.

cardamom (kär′dŭmŏm″), plant (*Elettaria cardamomum*), native to India and Ceylon, grown for its aromatic seeds which are used medicinally and in spices.

Cardano, Geronimo (järō′nēmō kärdä′nō), 1501–76, Italian mathematician and physician. Works include treatises on arithmetic and algebra.

Cárdenas, García López de (gärthē′ä lō′pĕth dä kär′dänäs), fl. 1540, Spanish explorer in American Southwest, discoverer of Grand Canyon.

Cárdenas, Lázaro (lä′särō kär′dänäs), 1895–, president of Mexico (1934–40). His reform program included redistribution of land on EJIDO system; expropriation of foreign-owned properties; modernization of Mexico.

Cardiff (kär′dĭf), county borough (pop. 256,270), co. town of Glamorganshire, Wales, on the Taff near its mouth on Bristol Channel; one of world's great coal shipping ports. There are also large iron and steel works, flour mills, and a fishing industry. Cardiff Castle built 1090 on site of a Roman fort. Welsh Natl. Mus. and University Col. of S Wales and Monmouthshire are in Cathays Park.

Cardigan, James Thomas Brudenell, 7th **earl of** (kär′dĭgŭn), 1797–1868, British general. In Crimean War led disastrous cavalry charge (1854) immortalized by Tennyson in *The Charge of the Light Brigade*. Cardigan jacket named for him.

Cardiganshire (kär′dĭgŭnshŭr) or **Cardigan,** maritime county (677 sq. mi.; pop. 53,564), on Cardigan Bay, S Wales; co. town Cardigan. Region is largely hilly, with fertile agr. valleys. Chief industries mfg. of woolen goods. Welsh language and customs preserved here to a large degree.

cardinal, member of the highest body of the ROMAN CATHOLIC CHURCH below the pope—the college of cardinals, having (since 1059) the duty of electing the pope and all the duties of a privy council to him. The institution grew out of the council of clerics in and around Rome who advised the pope, and the titles of cardinals still reflect this: cardinal bishops (of the sees immediately around Rome), cardinal priests and cardinal deacons (with titles from the church in Rome itself; hence the title "Cardinal of the Roman Church"). The dignity of being a cardinal is quite separate from offices in the Church hierarchy; thus the term *cardinal archbishop* means only that a man is both a cardinal and an archbishop. The maximum number of cardinals, previously set at 70 by Sixtus V, was increased to 120 by Paul VI in 1967. After the death (or in very rare instances resignation) of the pontiff, the cardinals must meet in not less than 15 nor more than 18 days to elect a new pope; they remain closeted until a candidate has been chosen and has accepted the office. Most of the cardinals have separate church offices over the world (usually arch-bishoprics); the remainder direct the affairs of the papal administration, the Curia Romana. Groups of them (with staffs) constitute the congregations for management of specific affairs—e.g., the Congregation of the Holy Office (see INQUISITION 3) and Congregation of the Propagation of the Faith (the Propaganda; in charge of missions). A cardinal heads each of the tribunals, the highest ecclesiastic courts. The secretariats, for handling of papal affairs, are also headed by cardinals (e.g., the papal secretary of state). The distinctive badge of a cardinal is a red hat, given him by the pope but never worn thereafter. Cardinals are styled "Eminence." See also PAPACY.

cardinal or **redbird,** North American songbird of finch family. The male eastern cardinal is scarlet with black throat and face, the female brown with red patches. Southern forms are the Arizona, gray-tailed, Louisiana, and San Lucas cardinals. See *ill.,* p. 118.

cardinal flower: see LOBELIA.

Cardozo, Benjamin Nathan (kärdō′zō), 1870–1938, Associate Justice of U.S. Supreme Court (1932–38). Interpreted law according to effects on society.

cards, playing: see PLAYING CARDS.

Cardston, town (pop. 2,801), SW Alta., Canada, SW of Lethbridge. Founded in mid-19th cent. by Mormons. Chief Mormon temple in Canada is here.

Carducci, Giosuè (jōzōō̄ä′ kärdōōt′chē), 1835–1907, Italian poet, professor at Bologna (1860–1904). Works include rebellious *Inno a Satana* [hymn to Satan] (1865), *Rime nuove,* and *Odi Barbare* (1877, 1882, 1889). Awarded 1906 Nobel Prize in Literature. Critical writings helped form literary taste of his age.

Carême, Marie Antoine (märē′ äntwän′ kärēm′), 1784–1833, celebrated French cook and gastronomist, chef of Talleyrand, Tsar Alexander I, George IV. Wrote extensively on culinary art.

Carew, Thomas (kürōō′), 1595?–1639?, English lyric poet, one of CAVALIER POETS, now best remembered for courtly verses on love (e.g., "Ask me no more where Jove bestows," "He that loves a rosy cheek").

Carey, Henry, 1687?–1743, English poet, musician; wrote burlesque tragedy *Chrononhotonthologos* (1734); author-composer of song *Sally in our Alley* and of burlesque opera *The Dragon of Wantley* (1737).

Carey, Mathew, 1760–1839, American publisher, bookseller, economist, b. Dublin; in U.S. after 1784. Edited magazines (notably *American Museum*), stimulated American letters. Argued for protective tariffs. His son, **Henry Charles Carey,** 1783–1879, was a leader in developing economic nationalism and an early American writer on economics.

Carey, William, 1761–1834, English Baptist missionary, one of first Protestant missionaries to India. Helped found Baptist Missionary Society (1792). Published the Bible in many Indian vernaculars.

Carey Land Act, written by Sen. Joseph M. Carey, passed by U.S. Congress in 1894. Provided for transfer of U.S.-owned desert lands to Western states on condition they be irrigated.

Caribbean Sea (kä′ribē′un, kürī′bēun), part of Atlantic. Central and South America lie to W and S; Yucatan peninsula and West Indies to N and E.

Carib Indians (kä′rib), native people originally inhabiting Lesser Antilles.

Cariboo Mountains (kä′ribōō), range, 200 mi. long, S central and E B.C., Canada. It is roughly parallel to the Rockies, extending between upper North Thompson R. and N apex of Fraser R. Mt. Titan is believed to be highest peak (c.11,750 ft.). In W foothills is Cariboo dist., scene of 1860 gold rush. Cariboo Road (built 1862–65) aided settlement of region. After extensive development, gold mining declined and was superseded by ranching and farming.

Caribou (kä′ribōō), town (pop. 12,464), NE Maine, on Aroostook R., N of Presque Isle, in potato-growing area. Winter sports center.

caribou (kä′ribōō), American name for mammal of deer family in arctic and subarctic regions. It is of same genus (*Rangifer*) as Old World REINDEER. Two main North American types: barren-ground caribou of Alaska, N Canada; woodland caribou in coniferous forests and bogs in parts of Canada.

Carignan-Salières regiment (kärēnyä-sälyēr′), largest body of French troops ever sent to New France. Arrived in Canada 1665, over 1,000 strong, to render lower St. Lawrence valley safe from Indian raids. About half the regiment remained as settlers.

carillon: see BELL.

Carinthia (kürin′thēū), Ger. *Kärnten* (3,681 sq. mi.; pop. 495,226), S Austria; cap. Klagenfurt. Predominantly mountainous; the GROSSGLOCKNER is Austria's highest point. Mining (lead, iron, zinc); agr. in fertile Drava Valley. Tourist trade. In 976 Carinthia (which then included ISTRIA, CARNIOLA, and STYRIA) was detached from Bavaria and created an independent duchy. It was acquired by Ottocar II of Bohemia 1269; fell to Rudolf I of Hapsburg 1276; became Austrian crownland (1335). After 1919 it lost minor territories to Italy and Yugoslavia.

Carleton, Guy, 1st Baron Dorchester, 1724–1808, governor of Quebec and British commander in American Revolution. Repulsed attack on Quebec in 1775; captured Crown Point in 1776.

Carleton College, at Northfield, Minn.; coed.; chartered 1866 by Congregationalists as Northfield Col.; renamed 1872 for William Carleton.

Carlisle, earls of: see HOWARD, family.

Carlisle (kärlīl′), county borough (pop. 71,112), county town of Cumberland, N England; an important rail center. Carlisle Castle, built by William Rufus in 1092, withstood many sieges, is now used as barracks. There is a 12th-cent. cathedral.

Carlisle (kärlīl′), industrial borough (pop. 16,623), S Pa., SW of Harrisburg; laid out 1751. French and Indian War expeditions (1758, 1763) were organized here. Was munitions depot in Revolution, Washington's hq. in Whisky Rebellion, and Underground Railroad stop. Attacked by Lee in Civil War. Seat of DICKINSON COLLEGE.

Carlisle Indian School, at Carlisle, Pa., 1879–1918; federally supported. It was first school of higher education for Indians estab. off a reservation.

Carlists, partisans of Don Carlos (1788–1855), second son of Charles IV of Spain, and of his successors, who claimed the Spanish throne under the SALIC LAW. Carlos's brother, Ferdinand VII, had abrogated the law of male succession in favor of his daughter, ISABELLA II. In the bloody civil war of 1836–39 Isabella's forces defeated the Carlists. Carlos's son, Don Carlos, conde de Montemolín (1818–61), and the latter's nephew, Don Carlos, duque de Madrid (1848–1909), led unsuccessful uprisings in 1860, 1869, and 1872. In 1873 full-scale civil war broke out again. The Carlists held the Basque Provinces, Catalonia, and other parts of Spain but were completely defeated by 1876. Ultrareactionaries, the Carlists supported Franco in the civil war of 1936–39.

Carloman, 751–71, younger brother of CHARLEMAGNE.

Carloman, d. 880, German king of Bavaria, Pannonia, and Moravia (876–79), king of Italy (877–79); son of Louis the German and father of Arnulf.

Carloman, d. 884, French king (879–84). Ruled jointly with his brother Louis III till 882. Checked Norman invasion at Aisne R.

Carlos. For kings thus named, see CHARLES.

Carlos, 1545–68, Spanish prince; son of Philip II by Maria of Portugal. Mentally unbalanced. Arrested by Philip's order on eve of projected flight to Netherlands; died in prison soon afterward. Hero of Schiller's tragedy *Don Carlos.*

Carlotta (kärlō′tù), 1840–1927, empress of Mexico, daughter of Leopold I of Belgium. See MAXIMILIAN.

Carlow (kär′lō), inland county (346 sq. mi.; pop. 33,-345), Leinster province, Ireland; co. town Carlow. A mostly fertile region, cattle raising, farming, and dairying are chief occupations.

Carlsbad or **Karlsbad** (kärlz'bäd), Czech *Karlovy Vary,* city (est. pop. 43,000), NW Bohemia, Czechoslovakia; famous spa. Hot mineral waters are taken for digestive diseases.

Carlsbad (kärlz'bäd), city (pop. 25,541), SE N.Mex., on Pecos R., settled 1888. Area has grazing, irrigated farming, and potash mines. Served by Carlsbad reclamation project. Carlsbad Caverns Natl. Park, in foothills of Guadalupe Mts., has stalactite and stalagmite forms; millions of bats inhabit underground chambers.

Carlsbad Decrees, 1819, resolutions of a conference of ministers of German states, convened by Metternich after murder of KOTZEBUE. Provided for press censorship, supervision of universities, suppression of liberal agitation. In force until 1848.

Carlscrona, Sweden: see KARLSKRONA.

Carlsruhe, Germany: see KARLSRUHE.

Carlstadt or **Karlstadt** (both: kärl'shtät), c.1480–1541, German Protestant reformer, whose original name was Andreas Rudolf Bodenstein. Fervent reformer and follower of Luther, he led in Wittenberg during Luther's stay at the Wartburg but was criticized for his radicalism in abolishing Catholic practices. Accused of participating in the Peasants' War he fled to Switzerland, where he became professor of theology at Basel.

Carlton Club, British political and social club. Founded 1832, it was long the center of Conservative party organization.

Carlyle, Thomas, 1795–1881, British man of letters, b. Ecclefechan, Scotland. After earning a precarious living chiefly as teacher and tutor he became the interpreter of German romanticism in his *Life of Schiller* (in *London Magazine,* 1823–24) and translation of Goethe's *Wilhelm Meister* (1824). A trenchant critic of British society, he expressed his views in a sort of spiritual autobiography, *Sartor Resartus* (in *Fraser's Magazine,* 1833–34), and in his interpretative rather than historical *French Revolution* (1837). His belief that the people could be saved from their woes by great men ("heroes") was put forth in *On Heroes, Hero-Worship, and the Heroic in History* (1841), an edition of the letters and speeches of Oliver Cromwell (1845), and a biography of Frederick the Great (1858–65). *Past and Present* (1843) contrasts 12th-cent. England with modern chaos. He had great influence on the literary world of his day, as did his wife, **Jane Welsh Carlyle,** 1801–66, a notable letter-writer.

Carman, Bliss, 1861–1929, Canadian poet. Friend of Richard Hovey, with whom he published the series *Songs from Vagabondia* (1894, 1896, 1901). Reputation rests on melodic quality of his verse and his sensuous pleasure in nature.

Carmarthen, Wales: see CAERMARTHEN.

Carmathians: see KARMATHIANS.

Carmel, Calif.: see CARMEL-BY-THE-SEA.

Carmel, Mount [Heb.= garden land], mountain, NW Israel. Extends c.12 mi. NW from plain of Esdraelon to Mediterranean Sea. Associated with prophets Elijah and Elisha. On its slopes are the tombs of Babed-din and of Abdul Baha, and a 19th-cent. Carmelite monastery. At its foot is port of Haifa.

Carmel-by-the-Sea or **Carmel** (kärměl'), city (pop. 4,580), S Calif., on Carmel Bay, S of Monterey. Artists' and writers' center; holds annual Bach festival. Father Junípero Serra buried at nearby mission.

Carmelites (kär'mŭlīts), Roman Catholic order of mendicant friars, originating apparently as hermits on Mt. Carmel, Palestine, made into a Western European order by St. Simon Stock (d. 1265). An enclosed order of Carmelite nuns was also estab. and became particularly important after the Carmelites were reformed by the Spanish mystics St. THERESA (of Ávila) and St. JOHN OF THE CROSS. Carmelites waned in 19th cent. but had spirited growth in 20th.

Carmen Sylva: see ELIZABETH, queen of Rumania.

Carmichael, city (pop. 20,455), N central Calif., ENE of Sacramento, on American R. Has boatyards and nurseries.

Carnac (kärnäk'), town (est. pop. 3,393), NW France, near Auray, in Brittany. Site of remarkable MEGALITHIC MONUMENTS, especially menhirs.

Carnap, Rudolf, 1891–, German-American philosopher; one of founders of logical positivism. In his early years he held the extreme view that the only function of philosophy is to describe and criticize the language of the particular sciences. He later modified his views, which in their original form lead to the rejection of almost all of traditional philosophy.

Carnarvon, George Edward Stanhope Molyneux Herbert, 5th earl of (kärnär'vŭn), 1866–1923, English Egyptologist. With H. CARTER he discovered the tomb of Tut-ankh-amen in 1922.

Carnarvon, Wales: see CAERNARVON.

Carnatic (kärnă'tĭk), region, SW India, on Arabian Sea. In 18th cent. it was arena of British-French struggle for supremacy in India.

carnation, perennial PINK (*Dianthus caryophyllus*), with double spice-scented flowers in white or shades of red. It is an important greenhouse crop in cold regions and a garden flower where winters are mild.

carnauba, WAX obtained from wax palm or carnauba (*Copernicia cerifera*) of Brazil. Hardest, highest-melting, natural wax known, it is used in polishes, lubricants, plastics, and carbon paper.

Carnegie, Andrew (kärnă'gē), 1835–1919, American industrialist, philanthropist, b. Scotland. Concentrated on steel production after 1873; by 1900 the Carnegie Steel Co. produced one quarter of all U.S. steel. His benefactions, totaling about $350,000,000, include Carnegie Hall (1892) in New York city, and over 2,800 libraries.

Carnegie (kärnă'gē), industrial borough (pop. 11,887), SW Pa., SW of Pittsburgh. Coal and steel town.

Carnegie Corporation of New York, foundation making grants to such worthy causes as educational institutions and libraries. Has financed studies of U.S. education and underprivileged children. Estab. 1911 as chief repository of Andrew Carnegie's wealth.

Carnegie Endowment for International Peace, foundation to promote peace by publicity, support of organizations, and the like; estab. 1910 by gift of $10,-000,000 from Andrew Carnegie.

Carnegie Institute of Technology, at Pittsburgh, Pa.; partly coed.; founded 1900, opened 1905 with funds from Andrew Carnegie, chartered 1912. Includes Margaret Morrison Carnegie Col. of Women (1906). Officially became Carnegie Mellon Univ. in July, 1967; in merger with the Mellon Inst.

Carnegie Institution of Washington, D.C., chartered 1902 and 1904, organized 1904, endowed by Andrew Carnegie and Carnegie Corp. Projects include astronomy, terrestrial and biological sciences, historical research.

Carney, Md.: see PARKVILLE.

Carniola (kärnēō'lù), Croatian *Kranj,* Ger. *Krain,* mountainous region, Slovenia, NW Yugoslavia; historic cap. Ljubljana. Passed to Hapsburgs 13th cent.; Austrian crownland until 1918. Divided between Italy and Yugoslavia after First World War; to Yugoslavia 1947. Population mostly Slovenian.

carnivorous plants: see BLADDERWORT; PITCHER PLANT; VENUS'S-FLYTRAP.

Carnot, Lazare (läzär' kärnō'), 1753–1823, French revolutionist, the "architect of victory." Trained as military engineer. Organized the republican armies and masterminded strategy in French Revolutionary Wars. Member of Directory. Later held high posts under Napoleon. Exiled 1815. His son, **Nicolas Léonard Sadi Carnot** (nēkôlä' läônär' sädē'), 1796–1832, a physicist, was a founder of modern thermodynamics. His work on relation between heat and mechanical energy anticipated that of Joule, Kelvin, and others. Another son, **Hippolyte Carnot** (ēpôlēt'), 1801–88, took part in

Revolution of 1848, was minister of education in provisional government. His son, **Sadi Carnot,** 1837–94, president of France (1887–94), was assassinated by an Italian anarchist.

Caro or **Karo, Joseph ben Ephraim,** 1488–1575, codifier of Jewish law, b. Toledo, Spain, d. Safed, Palestine. His chief work was *Shulchan Arukh* [the prepared table], which constitutes the legal and religious ordinances of traditional Judaism.

carob (kã′rŭb), leguminous evergreen tree (*Ceratonia siliqua*) native to Mediterranean region, cultivated in other warm areas. It has edible red pods. Called St.-John's-bread from belief it was "locust" eaten by St. John in the wilderness (Mark 1.6).

Carol, kings of Rumania. **Carol I,** 1839–1914, a prince of the house of Hohenzollern-Sigmaringen, was elected prince of Rumania 1866, took title king 1881. Siding with Russia in war against Turkey (1877–78), he obtained at Congress of BERLIN full independence for Rumania. Married Elizabeth of Wied (Carmen Sylva). **Carol II,** 1893–1953, had to renounce right to succession (1925). In 1930 he proclaimed himself king, dethroning his son MICHAEL. Instituted personal dictatorship 1938. Deposed in 1940 by Ion ANTONESCU, he fled with Magda Lupescu (his wife after 1947).

carol, popular hymn, especially associated with Christmas. Earliest English carols, dating from 15th cent., are polyphonic and include a refrain after each stanza.

Carol City, city (pop. 21,749), SE Fla., NW of Miami.

Carolina campaign, 1780–81, of American Revolution. After capture of Charleston, British force under Cornwallis swept N, capping success at battle of Camden, Aug. 16, 1780. Patriot defense was broken in Carolinas except for guerrilla bands. American victory at Kings Mt., Oct. 7, 1780, prefaced campaign led by Gen. Nathanael Greene which freed both Carolinas of British and set stage for YORKTOWN CAMPAIGN.

Caroline Affair. In 1837 a small steamer, the *Caroline,* owned by U.S. citizens, carried men and supplies to Canadian rebels under W. L. MACKENZIE on Navy Isl. just above Niagara Falls. On Dec. 29, 1837, British and Canadian loyalists set fire to the ship and sent her over the falls. One American was killed. Affair caused tension in U.S.–British relations but was smoothed over.

Caroline Islands, group (525 sq. mi.), W Pacific; included 1947 in U.S. Trust Territory of the Pacific Isls. under UN trusteeship. Group includes two volcanic islands (Kusaie and Ponape), three major island groups (PALAU, TRUK, YAP), and many atolls and islets. Produces trochus shell, coconuts, and sugar cane. Discovered 1526 by Spaniards; was under Spanish rule 1886–99. Sold 1899 to Germany, occupied 1914 by Japan (received mandate). In Second World War Palau and Ulithi were taken 1944 by U.S. forces.

Caroline of Anspach, 1683–1737, queen consort of George II of England. Supported Robert Walpole.

Caroline of Brunswick, 1768–1821, consort of George IV of England. Their marriage (1795) forced George, then prince of Wales, to put away his first wife, Mrs. Fitzherbert. Caroline was separated from George in 1796 but in 1820 refused to give up rights as queen. King instituted divorce proceedings, but these were later dropped.

Carolingians, dynasty of Frankish rulers, founded 7th cent. by PEPIN OF LANDEN. Ruled as mayors of the palace under MEROVINGIANS until PEPIN THE SHORT made himself king (751). His son, CHARLEMAGNE, crowned emperor in 800, brought dynasty to its zenith. After death of his son, LOUIS I, Carolingian empire was split by Treaty of VERDUN (843) among Louis's sons: LOTHARINGIA to LOTHAIR I; Germany to LOUIS THE GERMAN; France to CHARLES II. In 870 Lotharingia was divided between Louis and Charles. Arnulf was the last Carolingian emperor (d. 899); Louis the Child, the last Carolingian king in Germany (d. 911); Louis V, the last Carolingian king in France (d. 987).

Carolus-Duran (kärôlüs′-dürä′), 1837–1917, French portrait and genre painter, teacher of many famous painters. Became director of French Academy in Rome in 1905.

Carondelet, Francisco Luis Hector, barón de (kürŏndü-lĕt′), c.1748–1807, governor of Louisiana (1791–97) and West Florida (1791–95), b. Flanders. Severely taxed relations between Spain and U.S. by intriguing with Indians and Ky. frontiersmen.

Carossa, Hans (kärô′sä), 1878–1956, German poet and novelist. His autobiographical novel *Childhood* (1922) and its sequels (1928, 1941) are noted for clear graceful style. Other works include novels, discussions of literary mentors and friends (Mann, Rilke, Hesse), and volumes of poems (1938, 1949).

carp, fresh-water fish native to Asia, introduced into Europe and America. *Cyprinus carpio,* common in America, is European carp of varied form and color. It has four barbels around the mouth and a greenish or brown thick-scaled body (sometimes yellowish or silvery) with red on fins. Sometimes grows to 3 ft., 25 lb. Raised in ponds in Europe.

Carpaccio, Vittore (vĕt-tō′rä kärpät′chō), c.1450–c.1522, Venetian painter, follower of Giovanni Bellini. Depicted pageantry of 15th-cent. Venice.

Carpathians (kärpä′thēŭnz) or **Carpathian Mountains,** chain of Central Europe, in E Czechoslovakia, S Poland, W Ukraine, and N Rumania. Forming an arc c.930 mi. long, they enclose the Danubian plain in N and E. The TATRA group in the N and the Transylvanian Alps (see TRANSYLVANIA) in the S rise to 8,737 ft. and 8,361 ft. respectively. Rich in timber, minerals, mineral spas.

Carpathian Ukraine: see TRANSCARPATHIAN OBLAST.

Carpathus, Greek island: see DODECANESE.

Carpeaux, Jean Baptiste (zhä′ bätĕst′ kärpō′), 1827–75, French sculptor, a favorite of the Second Empire. His *Dance* is on the façade of the Opéra.

Carpentaria, Gulf of (kärpŭntä′rēü), arm of Arafura Sea, indenting the N coast of Australia.

Carpenter, Clarence Ray(mond), 1905–, American primatologist whose studies of apes and monkeys in Panama and Thailand are pioneer works in this field.

Carpenter, John Alden, 1876–1951, American composer. His music often depicts scenes of American life (e.g., orchestral suite *Adventures in a Perambulator,* ballet, *Skyscrapers*). He also wrote songs, symphonies, and chamber music.

Carpentersville, village (pop. 17,424), NE Ill., on Fox R., N of Elgin; settled 1834.

carpet and **rugs** were used in anc. Nineveh, and in Egypt by c.2500 B.C. Today, types include antique Orientals, European hand-woven (e.g., Aubusson, Savonnerie), Brussels, Wilton, velvet, Axminster (Oriental type), chenille or chenille Axminster, ingrain carpeting (now little used), rag and hooked rugs (often made in households), many kinds of straw and fiber mattings. Handmade Orientals have wool pile knotted by hand (up to 1,000 knots per sq. in.). European industry depended on hand looms until Erastus Bigelow's introduction of power loom, 1841. U.S. rugmaking began in colonial days.

carpetbaggers, epithet used in the South after Civil War to describe Northern adventurers who flocked S to make money and seize political power in RECONSTRUCTION period. Carpetbags held their possessions. Some came as agents of the FREEDMEN'S BUREAU. Although some were honest men, many engaged in large-scale political corruption.

Carpini, Giovanni de Piano, (jōvän′nē dä pyä′nō kär-pē′nē), c.1180–1252, Italian traveler, Franciscan monk. Sent by Pope Innocent IV to Tartary court (1245), he crossed Russia and central Asia to Karakorum, Mongolia, on horseback in c.100 days. Brought back important accounts of peoples and places.

Carpocrates (kärpŏk′rütēz), fl. c.130–c.150, Alexandrian philosopher. He and his son Epiphanes created a sect that advocated communal ownership of property, including women. The Carpocratians, related to the Gnostics, believed that corrupt man could be restored to union with the Absolute (God) by despising all created things.

Carr, Edward Hallett, 1892–, English political scientist and historian. His *History of Soviet Russia* (Vols. I–VI, 1950–59) is considered the definitive work in English on the Soviet era.

Carr, Robert: see SOMERSET, ROBERT CARR, EARL OF.

Carrá, Carlo, 1881–1966, Italian painter and writer on art; associated with futurism, cubism, and the *scuola metafisica*.

Carracci or **Caracci** (kärät'chē), family of Italian painters of Bolognese school, founders of Eclectic school. **Lodovico Carracci** (lōdōvē'kō), 1555–1619, was influenced by the Venetians. With his cousins, Agostino and Annibale, and with Anthony de la Tour, he established in Bologna an academy which tried to unite in one system the best characteristics of each of the great masters. Noted pupils included Guido Reni and Domenichino. His cousin **Agostino Carracci** (ägōstē'nō), 1557–1602, a painter of the Bologna academy, went to Rome in 1597 to collaborate with Annibale in the decoration of the Farnese Palace gallery. He executed the frescoes. His brother **Annibale Carracci** (än-nē'bälä), 1560–1609, a painter of unusual skill and versatility, assisted in decorating of the gallery.

Carrantuohill (kä"rùntōō'ùl), mountain (height, 3,414 ft.), Co. Kerry; highest peak in Ireland.

Carranza, Venustiano (vānōōstyä'nō kärän'sä), 1859–1920, Mexican statesman. Active in political life of Mexico after overthrow of Díaz (1911), he acted as president (1914–20) and contested leadership of nation with Huerta, Villa, Zapata, and Obregón. Dominant features of his reform program were incorporated in constitution of 1917: national ownership of subsoil deposits, restoration of ejido system, church and labor reforms. Constitution was never actually in force.

Carrara (kär-rä'rä), city (est. pop. 64,663), Tuscany, central Italy. Center of Italian marble industry; over 400 quarries. Constituted a duchy with MASSA. Cathedral (12th cent.); ducal palace.

Carrel, Alexis (kä'rùl), 1873–1944, American surgeon and experimental biologist, b. France. Won 1912 Nobel Prize in Physiology and Medicine for work in suturing blood vessels, transfusion, and transplantation of organs. With Charles A. Lindbergh invented mechanical heart. Carrel devised methods of keeping tissues and organs alive in nutritive solutions. Wrote *Man, the Unknown* (1935).

Carrera, Rafael (räfäēl' kärä'rä), 1814–65, president of Guatemala, a *caudillo*. Led revolt against anticlerical liberal government (1840), restored power of Church in Guatemala. Helped destroy Central American Federation and aided conservative governments in other Central American countries.

Carrera Andrade, Jorge (hôr'hä kärä'rä ändrä'dhä), 1903–, Ecuadorian lyric poet.

Carrère, John Merven (kùrâr'), 1858–1911, American architect. In partnership with Thomas Hastings, he designed New York Public Library (1911) and Senate and House office buildings in Washington, D.C.

carriage, wheeled vehicle, usually horse-drawn, dating from Bronze Age. Early forms include CHARIOT and four-wheel goods wagon. During Middle Ages in Europe wheeled vehicles were largely superseded by litters because of poor roads. Cart and wagon introduced anew c.12th cent. Use of coach spread among nobility in 16th cent. Forms developed in 18th cent. include landau, barouche, phaeton; in 19th cent., hansom cab, brougham, victoria. U.S. carriage-building trade well estab. after 1812; four-wheel buggy with open sides and folding top was popular.

Carriera, Rosalba (rōzäl'bä kär-rēä'rä), 1675–1757, Italian portrait and miniature painter. Her works are delicate in color and vivacious.

Carrière, Eugène (ûzhĕn' käryĕr'), 1849–1906, French painter and lithographer, whose figures and heads emerge from a brownish penumbra.

Carroll, Charles, 1737–1832, American Revolutionary patriot, signer of Declaration of Independence. Known as Charles Carroll of Carrollton.

Carroll, James, 1854–1907, American bacteriologist and army surgeon. As member of Yellow Fever Commission he submitted to bite of infected mosquito, contracting the fever and proving source of disease.

Carroll, John, 1735–1815, American Roman Catholic churchman, a Jesuit, b. Md.; educ. in Europe. A friend of Benjamin Franklin and an ardent patriot in the American Revolution, he is notable for his successful efforts to gain toleration for Catholics in the U.S. and to assure Catholicism a place in the republic. He was bishop (1790–1808) and archbishop (1808–15) of Baltimore.

Carroll, Lewis, pseud. of **Charles Lutwidge Dodgson,** 1832–98, English writer. Most famous works are *Alice's Adventures in Wonderland* (1865) and *Through the Looking-Glass and What Alice Found There* (1872), developed from stories he told to children of Dean Liddell (one of them named Alice). His mingling of fantasy and satirical observation has delighted generations of children and adults. A mathematician, he also wrote humorous verse; best known is *The Hunting of the Snark* (1876).

Carroll, Paul Vincent, 1900–, Irish playwright. His plays, vigorous comments on the conflicts of village life in Ireland, include *Shadow and Substance* (1937) and *The Wayward Saint* (1955).

Carrollton, city (pop. 10,973), W Ga., WSW of Atlanta, on Little Tallapoosa R. Trade center for fertile farm area. West Georgia Col. is here.

carrot, biennial plant (*Daucus carota*) with edible thickened root, rich in sugar, mineral salts, and vitamins. Cultivated for over 2,000 years. See WILD CARROT.

Carshalton, London: see SUTTON.

car sickness: see MOTION SICKNESS.

Carso, Yugoslavia: see KARST.

Carson, Edward Henry Carson, Baron, 1854–1935, North Irish politician. Opponent of Irish home rule, he denounced creation of Irish Free State (1921) but approved separation of N. Ireland.

Carson, Kit, 1809–68, American frontiersman and guide. Acted as guide for J. C. Frémont's Western expeditions of 1842, 1843–44, 1845; led Gen. Stephen Kearny's troops in trek from N.Mex. to Calif. in 1846. Noted Indian fighter.

Carson, Rachel Louise, 1907–1964, American writer and marine biologist. Her books combine scientific information with poetic description—of the sea in *Under the Sea Wind* (1941), *The Sea Around Us* (1951), *The Edge of the Sea* (1954)—and of the danger from insecticides in *Silent Spring* (1962).

Carson, Calif.: see NORTH WILMINGTON.

Carson City, city (pop. 5,163), state cap., W Nev., in Carson valley S of Reno. Laid out 1858 on site of trading post (1851), it became important with discovery (1859) of COMSTOCK LODE. Made cap. of Nev. Territory 1861; state cap. 1864. Resort and trade center for mining and agr. area.

Carson Sink, swampy area, c.100 sq. mi., W Nev., NE of Fallon. Remnant of old L. Lahontan. Carson R. disperses here. Lahontan Dam, completed 1915, saves most of the river's flow for NEWLANDS PROJECT.

Carstares or **Carstairs, William,** 1649–1715, Scottish statesman and divine. Friend and chaplain of WILLIAM III; became powerful in efforts to reconcile him with Scottish church. Under Queen Anne promoted union with England.

Carstens, Asmus Jacob (äs'mōōs yä'kōp kär'stùns), 1754–98, Danish historical painter and engraver.

Carstensz, Mount (kär'stùnz), group of peaks, W central New Guinea, in Netherlands New Guinea. Highest peak, c.16,400 ft., is highest in SW Pacific.

Cartagena (kärtähä'nä), city (pop. 242,085), N Colombia, Caribbean port; founded 1533. A treasure city of Spanish Main, it was attacked by buccaneers. Declared independence from Spain 1811. Now oil port.

Cartagena, city (pop. 129,652), Murcia prov., SE Spain; Mediterranean port and naval base. Lead, iron, zinc mines near by. Founded c.225 B.C. by Hasdrubal; chief Carthaginian base in Spain; taken by Romans 209 B.C.; sacked by Drake 1585.

Cartago (kärtä′gō), city (pop. c.18,000), central Costa Rica; founded 1563. Was political center of country until SAN JOSÉ was made cap. (1821).

Carter, Henry Rose, 1852–1935, American sanitarian. Reorganized federal quarantine service to keep yellow fever out of Southern states. Organized similar departments in Cuba and Panama.

Carter, Howard, 1873–1939, English Egyptologist. His excavations in Valley of the Kings (1906–1923), led to discovery of the tombs of Amenophis I, Merenptah, Rameses III and VI, and Tut-ankh-amen.

Carter, Mrs. Leslie, 1862–1937, American actress, whose maiden name was Caroline Louise Dudley. Associated with Belasco, she starred in several of his plays 1890–1906.

Carter, Nick, fictional detective, probably created by J. R. Coryell in 1880s. Used by F. V. R. Dey and other writers of dime novels, some of whom adopted name as pseudonym, the character continued popular in detective fiction and dramatizations.

Carteret, Sir George (kär′tûrĭt, –rĕt), c.1610–1680, British proprietor of East Jersey, part of present NEW JERSEY. His cousin, **Philip Carteret,** 1639–82, was first governor of the colony.

Carteret, John: see GRANVILLE, JOHN CARTERET, 1st EARL.

Carteret, Philip: see CARTERET, SIR GEORGE.

Carteret (kärtûrĕt′), borough (pop. 20,502), NE N.J., on Arthur Kill, SSW of Newark.

Cartersville, city (pop. 8,668), NW Ga., NW of Atlanta on Etowah R., in piedmont mining area. Near-by are Etowah Indian mounds.

Cartesian coordinates (kärtē′zhŭn) [for René Descartes], values representing the location of a point in relation to two straight lines (called axes). One axis is horizontal, the other vertical; the point is located by measuring its distance from each line along a parallel to the other line. The system can be extended, by using a third axis, into three-dimensional space; the third axis is perpendicular to the plane containing the other two. Descartes advanced generality in mathematics by showing that an infinite number of curves are referable to one system of coordinates and axes.

Cartesian philosophy: see DESCARTES, RENÉ.

Carthage (kär′thĭj), anc. city of N Africa, on the Bay of Tunis; founded (traditionally by DIDO) by Phoenicians from Tyre in 9th cent. B.C. Grew to be a mercantile city-state under an oligarchy, with explorers (e.g., Hanno) going far and wide to gather trade. Leading families contended for control. The attempt to conquer Sicily in the 5th cent. was set back by the victory of Gelon of Syracuse at Himera (480 B.C.). Later Carthaginian excursions into Sicily led to the PUNIC WARS [from Poeni, the Roman name for Carthaginians, i.e., Phoenicians]. The contest between Rome and Carthage was hotly pursued, and the greatest general involved was a Carthaginian, HANNIBAL. Nevertheless, Carthage was finally defeated in the battle of Zama (202 B.C.), and the Carthaginian commercial empire fell. The city itself was destroyed by Scipio Africanus Minor (146 B.C.). A new city was later built and was the Vandal capital (A.D. 439–533), but it was virtually destroyed by the Arabs in 698. Louis IX of France died here on crusade.

Carthage. 1 City (pop. 3,325), W Ill., near Mississippi R., E of Keokuk, Iowa; laid out 1833. Farm trade center. Jail where Mormon leader Joseph Smith was killed (1844) by mob now Mormon shrine. **2** City (pop. 11,264), SW Mo., on Spring R. near Joplin, in lead, zinc, and marble area; founded 1842. Ships farm and dairy products. Scene of Confederate victory (July 5, 1861) in Civil War. George Washington Carver Natl. Monument is at nearby Diamond.

Carthusians (kärthū′zhŭnz), Roman Catholic order of monks, noted for austerity, contemplation, and hermit life, founded by St. Bruno at La Grande CHARTREUSE. The Charterhouse in London and the Certosa at Pavia were Carthusian foundations. They manufactured first the popular liqueur that came to be called chartreuse.

Cartier, Sir Georges Étienne (kärtyä′), 1814–73, Canadian statesman. Elected to legislative assembly in 1848, he became leader of the French Canadians. Joined John A. Macdonald to form Macdonald-Cartier ministry (1857–62). Leading French Canadian advocate of confederation.

Cartier, Jacques, 1491–1557, French navigator, first explorer of Gulf of St. Lawrence and discoverer of St. Lawrence R.

Cartier-Bresson, Henri (–brüsõ′), 1908–, French photographer. Took pictures of events of world-wide importance.

cartilage (kär′tŭlĭj) or **gristle,** white, flexible, bloodless substance in skeletal system of vertebrates and in outer ear, nose, larynx, and windpipe. Forms entire skeleton of fetus.

Cartwright, John, 1740–1824, English reformer and pamphleteer. Had early naval career. Refused to fight American colonists; wrote *American Independence: the Interest and Glory of Great Britain* (1774). Called father of reform for advocacy of vote by ballot, abolition of slavery, and other reforms. His brother, **Edmund Cartwright,** 1743–1823, was the inventor of the power loom (1785) and other machines. Cooperated with Fulton in steam navigation experiments.

Carus, Paul, 1852–1919, American philosopher, b. Germany. Editor of *Open Court* and *The Monist,* periodicals devoted to philosophy and religion, in which he sought to give religion a scientific foundation.

Caruso, Enrico (kŭrōō′sō), 1873–1921, Italian operatic tenor, considered by many the greatest of all time. Made his New York debut in 1903 as the duke in *Rigoletto.* He also appeared in *La Bohème, Pagliacci,* and in many roles.

Carvajal, Francisco de (fränthē′skō dä kärvähäl′), 1464?–1548, Spanish conquistador in Mexico and Peru. Executed for opposing New Laws.

Carver, George Washington, 1864?–1943, American Negro agricultural chemist. Worked to improve economy of South; taught soil improvement, crop diversity; discovered many uses for peanuts, sweet potatoes, soybeans; devised products from cotton wastes. Birthplace, near Carthage, Mo., is natl. monument.

Carver, John, c.1576–1621, first governor of Plymouth Colony (1620–21), b. England.

Carver, Jonathan, 1710–80, American explorer of the Great Lakes and upper Mississippi R. in 1766–67. Wrote *Travels through the Interior Parts of North America in the years 1766, 1767, and 1768* (1778).

Cary, Alice, 1820–71, and **Phoebe Cary,** 1824–71, American poets, sisters. Phoebe wrote the hymn "One Sweetly Solemn Thought."

Cary, (Arthur) Joyce (Lunel), 1888–1957, English novelist. *Mister Johnson* (1939) and other early works reflect his Nigerian years as soldier and administrator. Best known are his trilogies. The first consists of *Herself Surprised* (1941), *To Be a Pilgrim* (1942), and *The Horse's Mouth* (1944); the second, of *Prisoner of Grace* (1952), *Except the Lord* (1953), and *Not Honour More* (1955).

Cary, Phoebe: see CARY, ALICE.

Casa, Giovanni della (dĕl′lä kä′zä), 1503–56, Italian author of *Galateo* (1560), a treatise on manners.

Casabianca, Louis (kä″sŭbēängkŭ), c.1752–1798, French naval officer, b. Corsica. At Aboukir Bay he commanded the *Orient,* which caught fire. Refused to quit his ship, and his young son refused to desert him. Their heroic death is subject of poem by Felicia Hemans.

Casablanca (kä″sŭblängˈkŭ), city (pop. c.965,000), Morocco, a port on the Atlantic. On site of ancient

Anfa. Destroyed 1468 and resettled 1515 by the Portuguese. Rebuilt by Mohammed XVI after 1755 earthquake. Occupied by French in 1907. In Second World War it was scene of major Allied landing (Nov., 1942) and of Roosevelt-Churchill meeting (Jan., 1943). Morocco's chief commercial and industrial center; port for large fishing fleet.

Casablanca Conference, Jan. 14–26, 1943, meeting of U.S. Pres. Roosevelt and British Prime Minister Churchill at Casablanca, French Morocco. War pledged against Axis states until their unconditional surrender. Mediation united rival French forces.

Casablanca group: see AFRO-ASIAN BLOC.

Casadesus, Robert (käsädäsüs'), 1899–, French pianist, known especially for his playing of French music. He has frequently toured the U.S., often playing his own compositions.

Casa Grande (kä'sä grän'dä), town (1965 pop. 8,483), S Ariz., near Casa Grande Mts. and SSE of Phoenix, in irrigated farm area. Named for ruined adobe tower now in Casa Grande Ruins Natl. Monument.

Casale or **Casale Monferrato** (käzä'lä mōnfär-rä'tō), city (est. pop. 38,632), Piedmont, NW Italy, on the Po. Cap. of MONTFERRAT from 1435; passed to Savoy 1703. Long an important fortress. Wine producing.

Casals, Pablo (pä'blō käsäls'), 1876–, Spanish cellist and conductor. Made U.S. debut in 1901. Served as director of music festivals in Prades, S France (1950–56), in Puerto Rico (1957–). Wrote Christmas oratorio, *El Pesebre* (1960). Considered one of the greatest cellists of all time.

Casanova de Seingalt, Giovanni Giacomo (jōvän'nē jä'-kōmō käzänō'vä dä sängält'), 1725–98, Venetian adventurer and author, an international gambler and spy. Imprisoned in Venice (1755–56), escaped and lived in Paris till 1774; became librarian to Count Waldstein at Dux, Bohemia. Wrote brilliantly on subjects ranging from poetry to theology. His remarkable memoirs (in French) stress his innumerable, perhaps partly mythical, feminine conquests.

Casas, Bartolomé de las: see LAS CASAS.

Casca (Publius Servilius Casca Longus) (käs'kü), d. c.42 B.C., one of the conspirators against Julius Caesar, first to stab him. Said to have committed suicide after defeat at Philippi.

Cascade Range, N continuation of the Sierra Nevada extending over 700 mi. through N Calif., Oregon, and Wash. into British Columbia. Parallels Pacific coast c.100–150 mi. inland. Highest summits are volcanic cones covered with snow and glaciers. Chief peaks are Mt. Shasta (14,162 ft., Calif.), Mt. Hood (11,-245 ft., highest point in Oregon and popular mountain-climbing and ski center), and Mt. Adams (12,-307 ft.), Mt. Baker (10,778 ft.), and Mt. RAINIER (14,410 ft.), all in Wash. Fir, pine, and cedar forests (many in national reserves) cover slopes. Klamath, Columbia, and Fraser rivers cut across range to Pacific.

Casco Bay, inlet of the Atlantic, SW Maine, with principal harbor at Portland. Wooded shores and islands have many summer estates and resorts.

case, in Latin INFLECTION, one of several possible forms of a given noun or adjective, the form being essential to the meaning of the word in context. In the theory of some grammarians case forms represent a fixed relationship of the word to other words in a sentence or to the speaker. The cases (in conventional order with conventional significance) are: nominative [Latin,= for naming], referring to a person performing an action; genitive [Latin,= genetic], indicating a possessor (commonly equated with English possessive); dative [Latin,= for giving], indicating the secondary recipient of an action (indirect object); accusative [Latin,= for accusing], direct recipient of an action (equated with English objective); and ablative [Latin, = for carrying off], indicating separation, cause, instrument, and location of place and time. All these have both singular and plural forms (see NUMBER); adjectives agree in case with corresponding nouns.

sixth case, the vocative [Latin,= for calling], occurs only in singular to refer to a person addressed. In many usages cases do not adhere to these conventional references (e.g., some verbs take genitive instead of accusative). The term *case* is used for noun, pronoun, and adjective inflections in other languages, some having many more cases (e.g., locative [Latin, = for placing], as in Sanskrit; instrumental, in many early and some present Indo-European languages including Russian). Cases called in English by the same name do not necessarily correspond in different languages. The case system in English is simple. Many nouns have only two cases, e.g., *man* (common) and *man's* (possessive), and a few pronouns have three, e.g., *he* (nominative), *him* (objective), *his* (possessive).

casehardening: see HARDENING.

casein (kä'sēin), complex PROTEIN and phosphorus compound. Forms c.80% of total protein in milk; enzyme rennin turns it to curds. Important in cheese making. Used in making paints, glues, plastics, and wool.

Case Institute of Technology, at Cleveland, Ohio; for men; chartered 1880, opened 1881 through bequest of Leonard Case, Jr.; called Case School of Applied Science until 1947.

Casella, Alfredo (käsĕl'lä), 1883–1947, Italian composer, pianist, conductor, and writer on music. His best-known compositions are the ballets *Il convento veneziano* and *La Giara*. Did much to promote the recognition of contemporary music.

Casement, Roger David, 1864–1916, Irish rebel. Knighted for work in British consular service. Attempted to obtain German aid for 1916 Irish rebellion. Returned in German submarine, captured, and hanged for treason. His body was returned to Dublin for burial in 1965. Irish regard him as martyr patriot.

Caserta (käzĕr'tä), city (pop. 50,810), cap. of Caserta prov., Campania, S Italy. Sumptuous 18th-cent. palace was residence of kings of Naples. Surrender of German forces in Italy to Allies signed here April 29, 1945.

Casgrain, Henri Raymond (käzgrĕ'), 1831–1904, French Canadian historian. His writings were inspired by French Canadian nationalism and by French romanticism.

cashew (kŭshōō', käsh'ōō), tropical American tree (*Anacardium occidentale*), valued for kidney-shaped cashew nut of commerce. Nuts are borne on end of fleshy stalk called cashew apple.

Cashmere, India: see KASHMIR.

Casimir (kä'sŭmēr), Polish rulers. **Casimir II,** 1138–94, duke of Cracow (1177–94). Granted privileges to nobles, who in return vested hereditary rights as rulers of Cracow in his descendants (see PIAST). **Casimir III** (the Great), 1310–70, king of Poland (1333–70). During his relatively peaceful reign he acquired most of duchy of GALICH; codified Polish law; improved the lot of the peasants and the Jews; strengthened royal power at expense of nobles; founded Univ. of Cracow. Last Polish king of Piast dynasty, he recognized overlordship of Bohemia over Silesian branch of Piasts (1335). **Casimir IV,** 1427–92, Grand Duke of Lithuania (1440–92), king of Poland (1447–92). Placed the two nations on equal footing; successfully ended war with Tuetonic Knights by Second Peace of TORUN (1466).

Casimir-Perier, Jean Paul Pierre (zhä' pôl' pyĕr' käzēmēr'-pĕryä'), 1847–1907, president of France (1894–95); grandson of Casimir Périer.

Caslon, William, 1692–1766, English type founder. His "old-style" types combine well into legible words and pages without distracting details or "color" variations. Hence printers' maxim, "When in doubt, use Caslon."

Caso, Alfonso (älfōn'sō cä'sō), 1896–, Mexican anthropologist and educator; director of National Institute of Anthropology and History after 1939.

Caspar: see WISE MEN OF THE EAST.

Casper, city (pop. 38,930), E central Wyo., on North Platte R., NW of Cheyenne; founded 1888. A rail, distributing, and processing center in oil and livestock area. City of oil booms, it tapped Salt Creek (1890), Teapot Dome, Big Muddy, and Lost Soldier (1948). Mormons estab. ferry at this Oregon Trail fording place 1847; superseded by bridge in 1850s. Nearby are Hell's Half Acre (eroded area), Independence Rock, site of Fort Caspar, and Casper Mt. (recreation area). Served by Kendrick project (Seminoe and Alcova dams), North Platte Project (Pathfinder Dam), and Missouri river basin project (Kortes Dam).

Caspian Gates: see DERBENT, RSFSR.

Caspian Kara-Kum: see KARA-KUM.

Caspian Sea, salt lake (c.163,800 sq. mi.), USSR and Iran, between Europe and Asia, at 92 ft. below ocean level; world's largest inland body of water. Max. depth c.3,200 ft.; in S. Elburz mts. rise from S (Iranian) coast; Caucasus from SW coast. Fed by Volga, Ural, Kura, Terek rivers, sea has no outlet but a high evaporation rate. Large salt deposits. Fisheries, sealeries. Chief source of black caviar. BAKU and ASTRAKHAN are main ports. Projects are under way to raise its level.

Cass, Lewis, 1782–1866, American statesman. Served as governor of Michigan Territory (1813–31), U.S. Secy. of War (1831–36), minister to France (1836–42), U.S. Senator from Mich. (1845–48, 1849–57), U.S. Secy. of State (1857–60). Was unsuccessful Democratic candidate for President in 1848.

Cassaba: see KASSABA.

Cassander (kŭsăn'dŭr), 358–297 B.C., king of Macedon, one of the DIADOCHI; son of Antipater. He managed to defeat Alexander the Great's mother, Olympias (316 B.C.), and murdered Alexander's widow, Roxana, and infant son. Cassander became the ruler in Macedonia and Greece and helped defeat Antigonus I at Ipsus (301 B.C.).

Cassandra, in Greek legend, Trojan princess; daughter of Priam and Hecuba. She learned art of prophecy from Apollo, but was never believed. As Agamemnon's slave, she was slain by Clytemnestra.

Cassano d'Adda (käs-sä'nō däd'dä), town (est. pop. 10,560), in Lombardy, N Italy. Scene of two French victories: 1705, of Vendôme over Eugene of Savoy; 1799, of Moreau over the Russians under Suvarov.

Cassatt, Mary (kùsăt'), 1845–1926, American painter and etcher. Spent most of her life in France. Greatly influenced by Manet and Degas; early allied herself with the impressionists.

cassava (kùsä'vù) or **manioc** (mă'nēŏk), tropical American plant (*Manihot esculenta*). Its roots yield cassava starch, a staple food in South America, used elsewhere in the form of TAPIOCA.

Cassel (käsĕl'), small town, N France, near Dunkirk. Scene of French victories over Flemings (1328; see PHILIP VI) and over Dutch (1677; see DUTCH WARS).

Cassel, Germany: see KASSEL.

cassia: see CINNAMON.

Cassini (käs-sē'nē), family of French astronomers and topographers, of Italian origin. Four generations successively headed observatory at Paris. **Giovanni Domenico Cassini** (jōvän'nē dōmä'nēkō), 1625–1712, organized the observatory. He discovered four satellites of Saturn and division in its ring, and determined Mars' rotation period. His son, **Jacques Cassini** (zhäk), 1677–1756, continued his work and advanced the science of earth measurement. His son, **César François Cassini** (sāzär' fräswä'), 1714–84, and grandson, **Jacques Dominique, comte de Cassini** (dōmēnēk' kôt' dù), 1748–1845, constructed a great topographical map of France.

Cassino (käs-sē'nō), town (est. pop. 21,245), Latium, central Italy, in Apennines, on Rapido R. In Second World War Germans blocked Allied advance to Rome for five months (until May, 1944) at Cassino and nearby Monte Cassino. Town virtually destroyed; now rebuilt.

Cassiodorus (kăshōdō'rùs), c.487–c.583, Roman statesman and author. Held high office under Theo-

doric the Great. Made a collection of state papers (*Variae epistolae*); wrote *History of the Goths.*

Cassiopeia (kă"sēōpē'ù), in Greek legend, mother of ANDROMEDA. She was transferred to heaven, becoming the constellation Cassiopeia (five stars in it form a rough W, called Cassiopeia's Chair).

Cassirer, Ernst (käsēr'ùr), 1874–1945, German philosopher, professor at Hamburg (1919–33), later lecturer at Oxford. His profound studies in the relationship of science and philosophy had a stimulating effect over the Western world, and his writings on the nature of the state, on aesthetics, and on the nature of meaning are influential today.

Cassites: see KASSITES.

Cassius (kă'shùs), Roman family. One member, **Quintus Cassius Longinus,** d. 45 B.C., won a reputation for greed and corruption when quaestor in Spain. He and Marc Antony vetoed the rule of the senate intended to compel Julius Caesar to surrender his army. Made an official in Spain after Caesar's triumph, he was faced with a rebellion that Caesar had to quell. Another member was **Caius Cassius Longinus,** d. 42 B.C., the Cassius of Shakespeare's *Julius Caesar.* Supporter of Pompey, he was pardoned by Caesar but was a chief figure in the successful plot to assassinate Caesar. When Antony roused the people against the conspirators, he took part with Brutus in the battle of Philippi and there committed suicide.

Cassivellaunus (kă"sĭvĭlō'nùs), fl. 54 B.C., British chief, leader against invasion of Julius Caesar, 54 B.C. Defeated, he sued for peace.

cassowary (kăs'ùwâr"ē), flightless, swift-running, pugnacious forest bird of Australia and Malay Archipelago. Smaller than the related ostrich and emu, it has dark, glossy plumage and vivid-colored, wattled neck.

Cassville, city (pop. 1,451), SW Mo., SE of Joplin; platted 1845. Ozarks resort, fishing, and shipping center. Confederate sympathizers in Mo. General Assembly met here and passed ordinance of secession 1861.

Castagno, Andrea del (ändrä'ä dĕl kästä'nyō), d. c.1457, Florentine painter, a master of realism. Frescoes in Sant' Apollonia monastery, Florence.

Castalia (kästä'lyù), spring near Delphi, Greece, on Mt. Parnassus, sacred to Apollo and the Muses.

Castalion or **Castellio, Sébastien** (kästäl'yùn, kästĕl'yō), 1515–63, French Protestant theologian, known for his defense of religious toleration in the prefaces to his Latin and French translations of the Bible (1551). His written criticisms of the execution of Servetus (1553) raised the question of toleration among Protestants. His name also appears as Castellion and Châtillon.

caste, hereditary social class. Members restricted in choice of occupation and range of social participation. Marriage outside the caste prohibited. Social status determined by caste of one's birth. In India, four chief castes (with many subdivisions): Brahmans (priests), Kshatriyas (the military), Vaisyas (farmers and merchants), Sudras (laborers). Lowest social group, the pariahs or "untouchables" are outside caste system.

Castel Gandolfo (kästĕl' gändōl'fō), village, Latium, central Italy, near Rome; possibly on site of anc. Alba Longa. Summer residence of pope.

Castellammare di Stabia (kästĕl"lämä'rä dē stä'byä), city (est. pop. 61,788), Campania, S Italy, on Bay of Naples. Navy yards. Anc. Stabiae, nearby, was Roman resort: buried A.D. 79 in eruption of Vesuvius.

Castellani, Sir Aldo, 1877–, British-Italian bacteriologist, authority on tropical medicine, and known for research in this field (esp. on sleeping sickness).

Castellio or **Castellion, Sébastien:** see CASTALION, SÉBASTIEN.

Castello or **Castelli, Bernardo** (bĕrnär'dō kästĕl'lō, –tĕl'lē), 1557–1629, Italian painter of Genoese school. Made the designs for Tasso's *Jerusalem Delivered.* His son, **Valerio Castello,** 1625–59, was a historical painter, whose best-known work is *The Rape of the Sabines* (Palazzo Brignole, Genoa).

Castellón de la Plana (kästĕlyŏn' dä lä plä'nä), city (pop. 65,918), cap. of Castellón prov., E Spain, in Valencia, near the Mediterranean. Its port, Grao, ships oranges, lemons, wine.

Castelnuovo-Tedesco, Mario (kästĕl'nwō'vō tädĕs'kō), 1895–, American composer, b. Italy. Came to U.S. in 1939. Created a personal Hebraic style in his synagogal music and Second Violin Concerto. Other compositions include a guitar concerto, operas, an oratorio, and songs to Shakespearean lyrics.

Castelo-Branco, Camilo (kämē'lō kästĕ'lō bräng'kō), 1826?–90, Portuguese romantic novelist. Works, including *Amor de perdição* (1862), are noted for stylistic beauty. Spelled his name Camillo Castello-Branco.

Castel Sant' Angelo (kästĕl' säntän'jälō) or **Hadrian's Mole,** landmark of Rome, on right bank of Tiber. Built A.D. 135–39 by Hadrian as imperial mausoleum; later converted into fortress; used as prison till 1870. Connected by secret passage with Vatican.

Castiglione, Baldassare, Conte (bäldäs-sä'rä kōn'tä kästēlyō'nä), 1478–1529, Italian author of *Libro del Cortegiano* (1528; Eng. tr., *The Courtier,* 1561), lively dialogues on Renaissance courtly ideals.

Castiglione, Giovanni Benedetto (jōvän'nē bānädĕt'-tō), 1616–70, Italian painter, portraitist, etcher of the Genoese school. Excelled at painting animals.

Castiglione delle Stiviere (dĕl'lä stēvyä'rä), small town, N Italy, NW of Mantua. Scene of Bonaparte's victory over Austrians 1796.

Castile (kästĕl'), Span. *Castilla,* former kingdom, central and N Spain. Traditionally divided into Old Castile in N, with cities of Burgos, Santander, Segovia; New Castile in S, with Madrid, Toledo, Cuenca. Contains most of the arid plateau of central Spain. The upper Duero, Tagus, and Guadiana rivers form the chief basins. Agr., sheep grazing; much erosion. Mineral resources include mercury at Almadén. Few industries. Old Castile, at first a county of kingdom of LEON, became virtually independent by 10th cent. Sancho III of Navarre acquired it 1028, made it into separate kingdom for his son FERDINAND I. Later kings expanded territory at expense of Moors (New Castile); achieved permanent union with Leon (1230); estab. authority over rebellious nobles. Marriage of ISABELLA I of Castile with Ferdinand II of Aragon (Ferdinand V of Castile) resulted in personal union of the two kingdoms (1479). Union made permanent 1516 through accession of Charles I (later Emperor CHARLES V), who suppressed *comunidades* uprisings of 1520–21. Later history is that of Spain.

Castillo de San Marcos National Monument: see SAINT AUGUSTINE, Fla.

Castine (kästēn'), town (pop. 824), S Maine, on peninsula in East Penobscot Bay. Includes Castine and North Castine villages. Plymouth Colony estab. trading post nearby after 1626. Town later changed hands several times among French, Dutch, British, and Americans. Adventurer Baron J. V. St. Castin or Castine "ruled" it for 30 years after 1667. Held by British in Revolution and War of 1812. Has Forts George (1779), Pentagoet, and Madison (1811; rebuilt in Civil War) and Maine Maritime Academy.

casting: see FOUNDING.

cast iron: see IRON.

Castle, Vernon, 1887–1918, English dancer, whose real name was Vernon Castle Blythe. Introduced many dances (e.g., "Castle walk," one-step, and "hesitation" waltz) with his wife, **Irene (Foote) Castle,** 1893–. She popularized bobbed hair and boyish figure.

Castle Clinton National Monument: see BATTERY, THE.

Castle Garden: see BATTERY, THE.

Castle Peak: see ELK MOUNTAINS.

Castlereagh, Robert Stewart, 2d Viscount (kä'sŭlrā), 1769–1822, British statesman, b. Dublin. As chief secretary for Ireland, was responsible for suppressing French-aided rebellion in 1798. Secretary of war (1805, 1807–9) during struggle with Napoleon I;

planned Peninsular War, coordinated land and sea power, and backed duke of Wellington. Resigned after political betrayal by George CANNING (with whom he fought a duel). As foreign secretary (1812–22), helped organize "concert of Europe" against Napoleon, later confirmed by QUADRUPLE ALLIANCE (1815). Advocate of moderate terms for France at Paris peace conference and Congress of VIENNA, favored policy of balance of power and ascendancy of conservative governments. Committed suicide.

Castle Shannon, borough (pop. 11,836), SW Pa., a suburb S of Pittsburgh.

Castor and Pollux, in Greek and Roman religion, twin heroes called Dioscuri [Gr.,= youths of Zeus]. Sons of Leda by Zeus or by Tyndareus. They were giants, gifted in battle, and joined Calydonian hunt and Argonaut expedition. When Castor was slain, Zeus made the brothers into the constellation GEMINI. They were highly honored in Rome. Castor was notable as a horseman; Pollux noted as a boxer. Together they were patrons of sailors. Phenomenon of St. Elmo's fire is still called Castor and Pollux.

castor oil, oil extracted from seed of castor-bean or castor-oil plant (*Ricinus communis*). Used as purgative, lubricant, leather-softener, and in brake fluids, paints, and other materials.

Castracani, Castruccio (kästrōōt'chō kästräkä'nē), 1281–1328, Italian Ghibelline leader. Made duke of Lucca (1327) by Emperor Louis IV, he sought hegemony over Tuscany and was about to conquer Florence when he died and his principality went to pieces.

Castries (kä'strēz), town (pop. 40,000), cap. of St. Lucia, West Indies. Has fine harbor.

Castriota, George: see SCANDERBEG.

Castro, Fidel (fē'dĕl kä'strō), 1927–, Cuban revolutionary leader, premier (1959–). In 1956 he launched the "26 of July" movement, which culminated with flight of Fulgencio BATISTA on Jan. 1, 1959. Castro became premier in the new government and ruled with wide authority.

Castro, Inés de (ē'nĕz dù kä'strō), d. 1355, Galician noblewoman, mistress of Dom Pedro of Portugal (later PETER I), to whom she probably was secretly married. Pedro's father, Alfonso IV, feared her influence and had her murdered. When Pedro became king he had two of her murderers put to cruel death. The tradition that he had Inés disinterred and crowned is probably untrue. Name is also spelled Inez.

Castrogiovanni, Italy: see ENNA.

Castro Valley, city (pop. 37,120), W Calif., SE of San Francisco, E of San Francisco Bay. Has light industry and farms.

Castro y Bellvís, Guillén de (gĕlyän' dä käs'trō ĕ bĕl-vēs'), 1569–1631, Spanish dramatist, author of *Las mocedades del Cid,* which inspired Corneille's *Le Cid.*

cat, small domestic carnivorous mammal related to lion, tiger, leopard, jaguar, puma. It has retractile claws and acute senses (good eyesight in dim light). Longhaired breeds include Persian (now generally includes Angora because of interbreeding), the sacred cat of Burma, and the Tibetan temple cat. Among shorthaired cats are the common short-haired, Manx (tailless), Siamese, and Abyssinian. All are genus *Felis.*

catacombs, burial places of the early Christians, arranged in extensive subterranean vaults and galleries; also used incidentally for refuge from persecution and for religious services. Those at Rome lie outside the city gates, are 22 to 65 ft. below the ground, cover an area of c.600 acres, and were built in the first five centuries. Tombs were cut into walls of narrow plastered passages, which were covered with frescoes. Most bodies were removed to churches by 8th cent. Other catacombs were in Naples, Syracuse, Paris, Alexandria, and Sousse. Catacombs discovered in vicinity of Rome in 1956 and 1959 contained frescoes of notable historical interest.

Catalan art. Although Catalonia still produces many fine artists, Catalan art as such (the religious art of Middle Ages and Renaissance) ended with 15th cent.

Elaborately painted churches, architectural sculpture, and illuminated manuscripts (notably the Bible from Farfa abbey) were in international Romanesque style. Works of more distinctly regional character culminated in gorgeous 15th-cent. religious painting (esp. of Jaime Huguet and of the Vergós family).

Catalan language, Romanic language of Italic subfamily of Indo-European languages, spoken mainly in NE Spain. See LANGUAGE (table).

catalepsy (kă'tŭlĕpsē), unconscious fit, induced by hypnosis or neurosis (can occur in schizophrenia or in hysteria). Voluntary motion and sensibility are suspended, muscles are rigid, body is cold and pale, and pulse and respiration are slow. Duration varies from minutes to days.

Catalina Island: see SANTA CATALINA.

catalogue, descriptive list of names or items, such as an alphabetical list on cards or in a book of the books in a library. Assur-bani-pal's library at Nineveh was catalogued on shelves of slate. First known subject catalogue compiled by Callimachus at the Alexandrian Library in 3d cent. B.C. Sir Anthony PANIZZI began printing of British Museum catalogue of printed books, and Charles A. CUTTER devised modern dictionary catalogue (author, title, and subject in one alphabet). In 1901 Library of Congress began printing catalogue on 3"x5" cards.

Catalonia (kătŭlō'nēŭ), Sp. *Cataluña,* historic region, NE Spain, stretching from Pyrenees southward along Mediterranean. Generally hilly; some fertile plains. Chief cities are Barcelona, Gerona, Lérida, Tarragona. Agr.; wine; olive oil. Hydroelectric power furnished by Ebro, Segre, and Cinca rivers has favored industries (textiles, machinery). Both Spanish and Catalan (akin to Provençal) are spoken. Part of the Spanish March founded by Charlemagne, medieval Catalonia was ruled by the counts of BARCELONA. Despite its dynastic union with Aragon from 1137 and with Castile from 1479, it kept its own laws and cortes until 18th cent. Peak of commercial prosperity came in 13th–15th cent., when Catalan merchants and adventurers helped the expansion of the house of ARAGON throughout the Mediterranean. Traditionally rebellious against central government, Catalonia obtained self-government in 1932–34 and in 1936–39; in the civil war it resisted Franco, who abolished its autonomy.

catalpa (kŭtăl'pŭ), ornamental tree of genus *Catalpa,* with large, heart-shaped leaves, large clusters of white flowers, and long beanlike pods. Species in North America, India, and Asia.

catalysis (kŭtă'lŭsĭs), changing speed of chemical reaction by introducing a **catalyst.** Positive catalysts increase speed of reaction; negative, decrease. In chemical catalysis, catalyst is used up in the reaction, but can be recovered as it is constantly regenerated. In physical catalysis, catalyst does not react; instead, it changes reaction conditions (e.g., particles may provide surface upon which reaction can occur). Water acts as catalyst since many compounds react only in solution. An ENZYME is a metabolic catalyst.

catamount: see PUMA.

Catania (kätä'nyä), city (pop. 379,985), cap. of Catania prov., E Sicily, Italy, in fertile plain at foot of Mt. Etna. Founded 8th cent. B.C. by Greeks; flourishing commercial center ever since. Suffered from repeated earthquakes, volcanic eruptions. Cathedral dates partly from 12th cent., univ. from 1434.

catapult, machine used to throw missiles (e.g., arrows or rocks) in medieval warfare. Widely used in warfare until invention of artillery in 14th cent. In 20th cent. principle reintroduced as means of launching aircraft from warships.

cataract, in medicine, opacity of lens of eye or its capsule. Causes include faulty development, injuries, infections, toxic states, and senility. Vision can often be restored by surgery.

catarrh (kŭtär'), inflammation of any mucous membrane accompanied by discharge, e.g., of eye, nose, or intestine. Caused by dust, fumes, bacteria, viruses.

catastrophism (kŭtăs'trŭfĭzŭm), doctrine that at intervals all living things have been destroyed by cataclysms and replaced by forms wholly different. This theory was attacked in 18th cent. by James Hutton, precursor of doctrine of UNIFORMITARIANISM.

Catawba, river: see WATEREE, river.

catbird, North American songbird and mimic related to mockingbird. It is slate gray, with black on the crown and tail and chestnut under tail coverts. It eats fruits and insects.

catchment area or **drainage basin,** area drained by a stream or other water body. Amount of water reaching stream or reservoir depends on size of catchment area, precipitation, and loss from evaporation and through absorption by soil and vegetation.

Cateau, Le (lŭ kätō), town (est. pop. 8,457), Nord dept., N France; formerly Le Cateau-Cambrésis. Matisse was born here.

Cateau-Cambrésis, Treaty of (kăbrāzē'), 1559, peace treaty among Spain, France, and England, signed at Le Cateau. From its 60-year struggle with France over hegemony in Italy (see ITALIAN WARS), Spain emerged triumphant, winning Milan, Naples, Sicily. France restored Savoy to its duke. England, though technically allied with Spain, confirmed Calais in French possession.

catechism [Gr.,= oral instruction], series of questions and answers used in teaching a religious system. Martin Luther's catechism dates from 1529. Reformed churches revere Heidelberg Catechism (1563). Presbyterians adopted Longer and Shorter Catechisms (1647, 1648). A section in Book of Common Prayer is an Anglican catechism. Peter Canisius drew up a famous Catholic catechism (1556).

catechu (kăt'tŭchōō), extract, also called cutch and black catechu, from *Acacia catechu,* tree of India and Burma. It and pale catechu, obtained from Malayan plant (*Uncaria gambir*), are used in dyeing, tanning, and medically as an astringent.

categorical imperative: see KANT, IMMANUEL.

Catena, Vincenzo di Biagio (vēnchän'tsō dē byä'jō kätä'nä), c.1470–1531, Venetian painter. With Giorgione and Titian, ranked by contemporaries as one of three great painters of the day.

catfish, scavenger fish with barbels about mouth, adipose fin, tough scaleless skin (some South American forms contain bony plates). Most larger species are palatable. The blue or Mississippi catfish weighs c.20–150 lb. The mad tom and stone catfishes have pectoral spine with poison gland.

Cathari (kă'thŭrī), name given to various groups of a religious movement that began with the Bogomils in the Balkans (10th cent.) and included the ALBIGENSES. The fundamental ideas of the Cathari were belief in a dualism (God versus Satan, good versus evil) and practice of extreme asceticism. They did not accept the Christian idea of God and rejected sacraments and the priestly hierarchy. There were two classes: the Perfect and the believers. Doctrines apparently descended from Gnosticism and Manichaeism to the Cathari through the Paulicians.

Cathay (kăthā'), medieval European name for China, popularized by Marco Polo.

Cather, Willa (Sibert), 1873–1947, American writer. Wrote novels and short stories of the Midwest (*O Pioneers!,* 1913; *My Ántonia,* 1918; *A Lost Lady,* 1923) and of historic past (*Death Comes for the Archbishop,* 1927; *Shadows on the Rock,* 1931).

Catherine: see also KATHARINE. Other spellings include Catharine, Katherine, and Kathryn.

Catherine, Saint, 4th cent.?, Alexandrian virgin martyr, traditionally supposed to have miraculously escaped dying on the wheel, only to be beheaded later. Her principal shrine is on Mt. Sinai, her attributes sword, crown, palm, wheel, and book. Her mystical marriage with Christ was popular as a subject of Renaissance art. Feast: Nov. 25.

Catherine, empresses of Russia. **Catherine I** (Martha Skavronskaya), 1683?–1727, a Livonian servant girl, was a mistress of Peter the Great before he took her as second wife (1711). Chosen his successor (1725), she ruled ably. **Catherine II** or **Catherine the Great** (Princess Sophie of Anhalt-Zerbst), 1729–96, of German birth, married the future PETER III in 1744. His worthlessness soon estranged her. She became thoroughly Russian and very popular. In June, 1762, a group of conspirators, headed by her lover Grigori ORLOV, deposed Peter and proclaimed her empress. Influenced by the Enlightenment, she planned vast reforms, but the PUGACHEV rebellion and the French Revolution drove her into reaction. A liberal law code remained a project; her charter to the nobility (1785) completed the enslavement of the serfs. Her foreign policy was imperialistic. Through her favorite, STANISLAUS II, she made Poland a Russian protectorate, then secured the major share in the Polish partitions of 1772, 1793, and 1795. She annexed the Crimea (1783) and in two wars against Turkey (1768–74, 1787–92) made Russia dominant in Near East. She began the colonization of Alaska. With her main interests in the East, she remained neutral in American and French revolutionary wars. Of versatile gifts, she wrote memoirs, comedies, stories, in French and in Russian, and encouraged birth of modern Russian literature. Among her many lovers, only Orlov and POTEMKIN were of consequence. Her son, Paul I, succeeded her.

Catherine de' Medici (dĭ mĕd'ĭchē), 1519–89, queen of Henry II of France; daughter of Lorenzo II de' Medici. Regent for her son CHARLES IX (1560–63). Sought to conciliate Protestants but later sided with Catholics. Plotted massacre of SAINT BARTHOLOMEW'S DAY (1572).

Catherine of Braganza, 1638–1705, queen consort of Charles II of England, daughter of John IV of Portugal. Dowry included Bombay and Tangier. Lived apart from court. Accused by Titus OATES of plot to poison the king (1678), but Charles protected her.

Catherine of Siena, Saint (sēē'nŭ), 1347–80, Italian Dominican nun. She early began to have visions that were to result in her *Dialogue* and *A Treatise of Divine Providence* and make her one of the greatest of Catholic mystics. Her life was one of great pain cheerfully borne, and her charitable love of mankind matched her love of God. In response to a vision, she went to Avignon and persuaded Gregory XI to end the "Babylonian Captivity" of the papacy, and later her influence was great in supporting the Roman claimant in the Great Schism. Her works were dictated for she never learned to write. Feast: April 30.

Catherine of Valois (văl'wä), 1401–37, queen consort of Henry V of England, daughter of Charles VI of France. Later married Owen TUDOR. Tudor kings descended from them.

Catherine Tekakwitha (tĕk"äkwĭth'ù), 1656–80, American Indian girl of the Mohawk tribe, a Roman Catholic noted for her austere piety.

Catherine the Great: see CATHERINE II, empress.

cathode: see ELECTRODE.

cathode ray: see ELECTRON and X RAY.

cathode ray tube, vacuum tube in which electron beams produced from hot cathode at one end are projected on fluorescent screen on other end forming visual trace or picture. See TELEVISION; RADAR; OSCILLOSCOPE.

Catholic Apostolic Church, religious community founded in England (c.1831) under Edward IRVING (hence its members are called Irvingites). Symbolism, mystery, and stress on second coming of Christ characterize the church.

Catholic Church, term meaning the universal church, adopted by many Christian sects. Generally in English when referring to the time before the Reformation it means the orthodox faith as opposed to movements pronounced heretical; when referring to the time since the Reformation, it usually means the Roman Catholic Church (sometimes also the Orthodox Eastern Church).

Catholic Emancipation, term applied to process by which Roman Catholics in the British Isles were relieved of civil disabilities dating back to Henry VIII. First concessions produced Gordon riots (1780). Most disabilities removed in 1791 for those in Great Britain who took a loyalty oath. Attempts of William Pitt and Pope Pius VII to get general repeal of the PENAL LAWS failed. In Ireland (see IRISH LAND QUESTION) agitation which forced repeal of restrictions (e.g., POYNINGS's LAW) seemed a threat to Protestant domination. Act of Union (1800) destroyed Irish Parliament; gave Ireland representation in English Parliament. After repeal of the TEST ACT (1828), growing agitation in Ireland, headed by Daniel O'CONNELL, led to Catholic Emancipation Bill (1829) sponsored by Sir Robert PEEL. Most remaining restrictions removed in 1866, 1891, and 1926. Act of SETTLEMENT still excludes Catholics from the throne, from certain civil and religious offices, and from a few university places.

Catholic League, in French history: see LEAGUE.

Catholic University of America, The, at Washington, D.C.; only U.S. pontifical university; coed.; founded 1887, opened 1889.

Catiline (Lucius Sergius Catilina) (kă'tĭlīn), c.108 B.C.–62 B.C., Roman politician. A partisan of Sulla, he was made praetor and governor of Africa. In 66 B.C. he was barred from candidacy for the consulship because he was accused of misconduct (falsely, as it turned out). Disgruntled he got up an abortive plot to murder the consuls; he and his confederates were acquitted. Running for consul in 63 B.C. he was opposed by Cicero and the conservatives and was defeated. Thereupon he concocted a conspiracy to gain power. Cicero, acting on information from Catiline's mistress, exposed the conspiracy in the first of perhaps the most famous series of orations ever delivered—the orations against Catiline. The conspirators, who even approached the ambassadors of the Allobroges, were arrested and condemned to death, though Julius Caesar urged moderation. Catiline did not surrender and was killed in battle. The question of Catiline's character and guilt is unsettled, since the only sources on him—Cicero and Sallust—are hostile.

Catlin, George, 1796–1872, American artist and traveler. Went over the West and later through Central and South America to paint Indian portraits and scenes. Many pictures in National Mus. Wrote *Manners, Customs, and Condition of the North American Indians* (2 vols., 1841) and other works.

catlinite: see PIPESTONE.

catnip or **catmint,** perennial mint (*Nepeta cataria*), with aromatic leaves often made into tea. Catnip is attractive to cats.

Catonsville (kā'tŭnzvĭl), city (pop. 37,372), N Md., a suburb W of Baltimore.

Cato Street Conspiracy: see THISTLEWOOD, ARTHUR.

Cato the Elder or **Cato the Censor** (Marcus Porcius Cato) (kā'tō), 234–149 B.C., Roman statesman. He spoke much of the austere virtues of old Rome and decried luxury, extravagance, and innovations. He had fought in the Second Punic War, and, when sent in old age to Carthage, returned to insist sternly, "Carthage must be destroyed!" He thus helped to bring on the Third Punic War, in which Carthage was destroyed. A man of great wealth, he was noted for cruelty to his servants and for niggardliness. His history of Rome is now lost, and of his extant works a treatise on farming is the best known. Also Cato Major. His great-grandson, **Cato the Younger** or **Cato Minor,** 95 B.C.–46 B.C., was also named Marcus Porcius Cato. He was known particularly for incorruptible honesty, supported by Stoicism. He opposed Julius Caesar and denounced Catiline. A supporter of Pompey, he continued the struggle against Caesar after the defeat at Pharsala and held Utica. After the crushing defeat at Thapsus, he committed suicide. Also known as Cato of Utica.

Cats, Jacob (yä'kŏp käts), 1577–1660, Dutch poet. His didactic poems made him spokesman of Dutch Calvinist culture.

cat's-eye, name for several green gems which show a line of light caused by reflection from parallel fibers within. Gems called cat's-eye include chrysoberyl, quartz, and tourmaline.

Catskill (kăt'skĭl), village (pop. 5,825), SE N.Y., on Hudson R. (Rip Van Winkle Bridge) S of Albany; settled in 17th cent. by Dutch. Gateway to Catskill Mt. resorts. Thomas Cole lived and painted here.

Catskill Aqueduct, SE N.Y., a main unit of New York city water-supply system; planned 1905. Schoharie Reservoir water sent via 18-mi. Shandaken tunnel (opened 1924) to Esopus Creek, which is dammed c.15 mi. downstream to form Ashokan Reservoir (area c.13 sq. mi.; 1916) W of Kingston. After aeration here, Catskill Aqueduct carries the water 92 mi. S, passing 1,114 ft. under Hudson R. at Storm King to Kensico Reservoir near White Plains and to Hillview Reservoir in Yonkers. Tunnels take water to New York city (steel pipe across the Narrows of New York Bay to Staten Isl.).

Catskill Mountains, range of the Appalachians, SE N.Y., W of Hudson R., to which they descend abruptly in places. Drained by Delaware R. head-streams and by Esopus, Schoharie, Rondout, and Catskill creeks. Ashokan Reservoir serves New York city. A wooded and rolling region with deep gorges and many waterfalls, it is popular summer and winter resort. Catskill Forest Preserve includes region of Rip Van Winkle legend. Highest peak is Slide Mt. (4,180 ft.).

Catt, Carrie (Lane) Chapman, 1859–1947, American suffragist. President of Natl. American Woman Suffrage Association. Led campaign for Federal suffrage amendment. Organized League of Women Voters. After 1923 she devoted efforts to peace movement.

cattail or **reed mace,** marsh perennial of genus *Typha,* with long, narrow leaves and a brown cylindrical spike of flowers used in winter bouquets.

Cattaro, Yugoslavia: see KOTOR.

cattle, domestic animals of bovine genus, probably descended from the AUROCHS; closely related to the buffalo, bison, and yak. First cattle came to W Hemisphere on Columbus' second voyage. Since mid-18th cent., have been improved by selective and scientific breeding. Chief beef breeds are the Aberdeen Angus (black Angus) and Hereford (red, with white face); for dairying, Ayrshire (red and white or brown and white), brown Swiss, Dutch Belted (black, with white midriff), Guernsey (fawn and white), Holstein-Friesian (black and white), Jersey (tan, brown, gray, or cream; sometimes varicolored); for both purposes, Devon (red to chestnut), and polled (cherry red), and shorthorn (or Durham) and the related polled (hornless) shorthorn (red, red and white, or white and roan).

Catton, Bruce, 1899–, American historian and journalist, authority on the Civil War. His works include *A Stillness at Appomattox* (1953), *This Hallowed Ground* (1956), and *The Centennial History of the Civil War* (3 vols., 1961–65). Senior editor of *American Heritage* magazine.

Catullus (Caius Valerius Catullus) (kŭtŭ'lŭs), 84?–54? B.C., Latin poet, one of greatest lyricists. Poems ascribed to him (116 extant) include many satires and epigrams as well as exquisite lyrics on his beloved (probably Clodia), called Lesbia.

Catulus (kă'chōolŭs), family of anc. Rome. An early member was **Caius Lutatius Catulus,** consul in 242 B.C., victor in the naval engagement with Carthage off the Aegates that ended the First Punic War. Another was **Quintus Lutatius Catulus,** d. 87 B.C., consul in 102 B.C. with Marius. Helped defeat the Cimbri, later opposed Marius, favoring Sulla. In the hour of Marius' triumph he committed suicide or was killed. His son, **Quintus Lutatius Catulus,** d. c.60 B.C., was consul 78 B.C. and leader of archconserva-

tives. He and Claudius put down the revolt of Lepidus. Later he violently opposed Julius Caesar.

Cauca (kou'kä), river, c.600 mi. long, rising in W Colombia and flowing N through Andes to the Magdalena.

Caucasian Gates: see DARYAL, Georgian SSR.

Caucasus (kô'kŭsŭs), mountain system, USSR, between Europe and Asia, extending c.750 mi. from Black Sea SE to Caspian Sea. Main range, the Greater Caucasus, is a majestic chain of snow-capped peaks, culminating in Mt. ELBRUS at 18,481 ft. Pierced by MAMISON, DARYAL, and other passes, it divides N Caucasia, which slopes down to Kuban steppe, from Transcaucasia. The Lesser Caucasus, S of KURA R., is extension of Iranian plateau. Pastures, forests in uplands; agr., orchards, vineyards in valleys. Many health resorts (e.g., Pyatigorsk, Kizlovodsk). Mineral resources include rich oil fields at BAKU, GROZNY, MAIKOP, manganese at Chiatura. Caucasus was known to ancient Greeks: here Prometheus was chained, Jason sought Golden Fleece. Centuries of invasions and migrations left complex ethnical structure. N Caucasia, including historic CIRCASSIA, is part of RSFSR. Transcaucasia is divided into GEORGIAN SSR, AZERBAIJAN SSR, ARMENIAN SSR. Russian penetration in 19th cent. was resisted by Moslem elements until collapse of Shamyl uprising (1859).

Cauchon, Pierre (pyĕr' kōshō'), d. 1442, bishop of Beauvais, France. President of court that convicted JOAN OF ARC (1431).

Cauchy, Augustin Louis, Baron (ōgüstĕ' lwē' bärō' kōshē'), 1789–1857, French mathematician, influential in every mathematics branch (especially theory of functions, integral and differential calculus, algebraic analysis) and also in astronomy, optics, and other fields.

caudillo (koudhĕ'yō), type of Hispanic American political leader who arose with wars of independence. Typical caudillo is usually mestizo with strong appeal to Indian and mestizo masses; has military ability; begins by championing rights of masses against wealthy white classes; later becomes oligarch himself. Famous caudillos: Rosas of Argentina, Carrera of Guatemala, Díaz of Mexico, Juan Vicente Gómez of Venezuela.

Caudine Forks (kô'dīn), narrow passes in Apennines, S Italy. Here in 321 B.C. Samnites routed Roman army, forced it to pass under sign of a yoke as humiliation.

Caughnawaga (kä'näwä"gù), village, S Que., Canada, on St. Lawrence R. opposite Lachine. Founded 1667 as refuge for Iroquois Christian converts.

Caulaincourt, Louis, marquis de (lwē' märkē' dù kōlēkōōr'), b. 1772 or 1773, d. 1827, French general. Ambassador to Russia (1807–11); aide-de-camp to Napoleon on Russian campaign; foreign minister during Hundred Days. Left remarkable memoirs of years 1812–15, first published 1933 (Eng. tr., 1935–36).

cauliflower (kô'lĭ–), garden vegetable (*Brassica oleracea botrytis*) with edible white head of flowers and flower stems. Derived from wild cabbage.

Caupolicán (koupōlēkän'), d. 1558, leader of ARAUCANIAN INDIANS who fiercely resisted Spanish Conquest of Chile.

caustic, in chemistry, substance that burns or corrodes organic materials, e.g., caustic SODA (sodium hydroxide) and caustic POTASH (potassium hydroxide). Silver nitrate, called caustic silver or lunar caustic, is used in medicine.

cautery, searing of living animal tissue by any method of burning, e.g., nitric acid, electricity. Applied usually to small lesions, such as warts.

Cauvery or **Kaveri** (kô'vùrē), river, S India; flows c.475 mi. from W Ghats to Bay of Bengal. Sacred to Hindus. Falls near Sivasamudram furnish much of the hydroelectric power in S India.

Cavafy, Constantine (käväfē'), 1863–1933, Greek poet, b. Alexandria, where he spent most of his life. His fatalistic and erotic poetry in the Greek tradition appeared posthumously (1935).

Cavaignac, Louis Eugène (lwē' ûzhĕn' kävänyäk'), 1802–57, French general. Fought in Algeria. As minister of war suppressed workingmen's rising in JUNE DAYS of 1848. Refused allegiance to Napoleon III.

Cavalcanti, Guido (gwē'dō kävälkän'tē), c.1255–1300, Italian poet, friend of Dante. His best verse is in the *Canzone d'amore*.

Cavalier, Jean (zhä' kävälyä'), 1681?–1740, French Protestant leader. Led uprising of CAMISARDS but made separate peace with government in 1704.

cavalier, in general, an armed horseman. In English civil war, Cavaliers were followers of Charles I, as against Roundheads, supporters of Parliament. Term for royalists until it was replaced by Tory.

Cavalier poets, literary group at court of Charles I of England, notable for the grace and wit of polished lyrics on love, fleeting youth and beauty. Included Herrick, Lovelace, Suckling, Carew.

Cavallini, Pietro (pyä'trō käväl-lē'nē), c.1250–c.1330, Italian painter and mosaicist, who influenced Cimabue and Giotto.

cavalry, mounted troops trained to fight from horseback. Used among the anc. Egyptians, cavalry groups were much more commonly used by the Assyrians and the Persians. Speed gave them an advantage, but this was offset by the lack of saddles (until the time of Constantine I), and Greek and Roman victories were won by well-disciplined foot troops. Cavalry was first triumphant when used by Huns, Avars, Magyars, and Mongols in invading Europe. Mounted knight became typical warrior of medieval Europe. Reintroduction of mass warfare and use of gunpowder made infantry prominent again, but cavalry was extensively used, particularly for mobile striking forces and for scouting. Cavalrymen were elite of soldiery through American Civil War. Value began to wane with introduction of automatic weapons and trench warfare and disappeared with advent of mobile tank units. In 1946 U.S. army abolished cavalry as separate arm of service.

Cavan (kă'vŭn), inland county (730 sq. mi.; pop. 56,-697), Ireland; co. town Cavan. Hilly region of lakes and bogs with cool damp climate. Agr. chief occupation, but less than a third of area is cultivated.

Cave, Edward, 1691–1754, English publisher. In 1731 he founded the *Gentleman's Magazine*. Printed in his periodical (1741–44) Samuel Johnson's parliamentary debates. Later published other works of Johnson.

cave, a hollow in earth or rock. Formed usually by chemical or mechanical action of water. Ground water dissolves or wears rock; dashing waves cut into rocky shores. Most caves are in limestone, owing to its solubility; many are famous for STALACTITE AND STALAGMITE formations. Caves of Iceland and Hawaii were caused by volcanic action.

cave art, paintings and engravings found on interior cave walls. Earliest examples date from Paleolithic times, the Magdalenian phase showing most highly developed technique. Subject matter of paintings suggests they had magical intent. Famous examples are those of lower Italy, ALTAMIRA (Spain), Dordogne (esp. at Lascaux), central Pyrenees, SE Algeria.

Cave City, town (pop. 1,418), S Ky., NE of Bowling Green, in natural gas region. Center of limestone cave region, incl. MAMMOTH CAVE NATIONAL PARK.

Cavell, Edith (kă'vŭl), 1865–1915, British nurse. Matron at Brussels hospital in First World War, she was shot by the Germans for aid to Allied prisoners.

Cavendish, pseud. of **Henry Jones,** 1831–99, English card-game expert. Formulated system for playing whist; wrote also on billiards, lawn tennis, and croquet.

Cavendish, Henry, 1731–1810, English physicist, chemist. Determined specific heats for certain substances. Did research on properties of "inflammable air" (hydrogen) that he isolated and described, on composition of air, electricity, density of earth.

Cavendish or Candish, Thomas, 1560–92, English navigator. Commanded the third voyage around the world (1586–88), ravaging Spanish towns and shipping on W coast of South America. Died during disastrous second attempt at circumnavigation.

Cavendish, William: see NEWCASTLE, WILLIAM CAVENDISH, DUKE OF.

Cavendish Laboratory: see CAMBRIDGE UNIVERSITY.

Caventou, Joseph Bienaimé (byĕnämä' kävätoo'), 1795–1877, French chemist. With P. J. Pelletier he isolated strychnine, brucine, and quinine from plants.

Caves of a Thousand Buddhas, China: see TUNHWANG.

Cave Spring, city (pop. 1,153), NW Ga., near Ala. line SW of Rome; settled 1826. Georgia School for the Deaf is near.

caviar or caviare (kä'vēär), roe (eggs) of sturgeon prepared, mainly in Russia, as table delicacy. The eggs are black, green, brown, or yellow ("gray"), and vary in size from tiny grains to pea size.

Cavite (kävē'tä), city (pop. 42,137), SW Luzon, Philippines, on small peninsula in Manila Bay. U.S. leases Sangley Point (opposite city proper) as navy base.

Cavour, Camillo Benso, conte di (kämēl'lō bän'sō kōn'tä dē kävoor'), 1810–61, Italian statesman, premier of Sardinia (1852–59, 1860–61). Chief architect of Italian unification under Victor Emmanuel II (see RISORGIMENTO).

cavy (kä'vē), name of GUINEA PIG and number of related South American rodents. Wild cavy is usually brown and has no tail. Forms include Patagonian cavy, Bolivian cavy, Peruvian cavy, restless cavy of Brazil, and CAPYBARA.

Cawdor (kô'dŭr), parish, Nairnshire, Scotland. Cawdor Castle represented by Shakespeare as scene of the slaying of Duncan by Macbeth 1040.

Cawnpore or Kanpur (both: kôn'pôr'), city (pop. 705,-400), S Uttar Pradesh, India, on Ganges R. Nana Sahib wiped out British garrison here in Sepoy Rebellion of 1857. Major trade and mfg. center.

Caxton, William, c.1421–1491, English printer. A mercer, he learned printing at Cologne. With Colard Mansion printed first book in English, *The Recuyell of the Historyes of Troye* (Bruges, 1475). He also issued first dated book printed in England, *Dictes or Sayengis of the Philosophres* (Westminster, 1477). He translated works and wrote prologues, epilogues, and additions.

Cayenne (kīen'), city (pop. 18,635), cap. of French Guiana, on island at mouth of Cayenne R. Cayenne pepper originally came from here.

Cayman Islands (kä'mŭn), archipelago (100 sq. mi.; pop. c.8,800), WEST INDIES, NW of Jamaica. Principal towns are Georgetown and West Bay.

Cayuga Indians: see IROQUOIS CONFEDERACY.

Cayuga Lake (käyoo'gŭ), 38 mi. long and 1–3½ mi. wide, W central N.Y., largest of FINGER LAKES. Joined by canal and Seneca R. to Barge Canal. Cornell Univ. and Wells Col. overlook lake.

Cb, symbol of columbium (see NIOBIUM).

C battery: see BATTERY, ELECTRIC.

Cd, chemical symbol of the element CADMIUM.

Ce, chemical symbol of the element CERIUM.

Ceará (sēûrä'), state (c.57,000 sq. mi.; pop. c.3,337,-900), NE Brazil; cap. FORTALEZA. Atlantic coastal plain produces cotton, sugar, coffee. Semiarid uplands are used for cattle and goat raising. Area suffers severely from drought.

Cebu (sāboo'), island (1,702 sq. mi.; pop. 1,350,130), one of Visayan Isls., Philippines. Agr. area. Cap. and chief port is **Cebu** (pop. 201,362), founded 1565 as San Miguel by López de Legaspi and cap. of Spanish colony until 1571. Harbor is sheltered by Mactan isl.

Cech, Svatopluk, Czech *Čech* (svä'tôploŏk chĕkh'), 1846–1908, Czech poet and novelist. An ardent pan-Slavist, he wrote lyrics and epics based on Czech history (*Zizka,* 1879; *Vaclav of Michalovce,* 1880) and country life (*The Smith of Lesetin,* 1889).

Cecil, Edgar Algernon Robert, 1st Viscount Cecil of Chelwood (sĭl'sŭl), 1864–1958, British statesman. Collaborated in draft of League of Nations Covenant. Won 1937 Nobel Peace Prize.

Cecil, Robert: see SALISBURY, ROBERT CECIL, 1ST EARL OF.

Cecil, Robert Arthur Talbot Gascoyne-: see SALISBURY, ROBERT ARTHUR TALBOT GASCOYNE-CECIL, 3D MARQUESS OF.

Cecil, William: see BURGHLEY, WILLIAM CECIL, 1ST BARON.

Cecilia, Saint, 2d or 3d cent., Roman virgin martyr, patroness of music, whose name is known in English literature through Chaucer, Dryden, and Pope. Also Cecily. Feast: Nov. 22.

Cecrops (sē'krŏps), in Greek mythology, first king of Athens, half man and half serpent. Established monogamy and first principles of law and religion.

Cedar, river rising in SE Minn., and flowing c.300 mi. SE across Iowa to Iowa R. at Columbus Junction.

cedar, name for certain trees, mostly coniferous evergreens, including northern white cedar (ARBORVITAE); red cedar (JUNIPER); southern white cedar (*Chamaecyparis thyoides*). Cedar of Lebanon (*Cedrus libani*) is native to Asia and Africa. Deodar cedar (*C. deodara*) possibly used in building Temple and house of Solomon (1 Kings 5–7).

Cedar Breaks National Monument: see NATIONAL PARKS AND MONUMENTS (table).

Cedar City, town (pop. 7,543), SW Utah, at base of Wasatch Mts. E of Escalante Desert; founded 1851 by Mormon "iron mission" sent to develop coal and iron deposits. Ranch and tourist center near Zion and Bryce Canyon Natl. Parks and Cedar Breaks Natl. Monument (see NATIONAL PARKS AND MONUMENTS, table). Col. of Southern Utah, branch of Utah State Univ. of Agr. and Applied Science is here.

Cedar Falls, city (1965 pop. 26,016), N Iowa, on Cedar R. just above Waterloo; settled 1845. Developed as milling center with coming of railroad (1861). State Col. of Iowa and Evangelical Campgrounds, scene of Interdenominational Bible Conference, are here.

Cedarhurst, residential village (pop. 6,051), on SW Long Isl., SE N.Y., SE of Jamaica.

Cedar Key, island off W Fla., NNW of St. Petersburg. Cedar Keys, group of smaller islands, are near.

Cedar Rapids, city (1965 pop. 103,545), E central Iowa, on Cedar R., NW of Davenport; settled 1838. One of state's chief commercial and industrial cities, and a distributing center for large agr. area. Coe Col. is here.

Cedron (sē'–), same as KIDRON.

Cefalù (chāfälōō'), port (est. pop. 12,775), N Sicily, Italy. Cathedral (12th cent.) is splendid example of Norman-Sicilian architecture.

celandine (sĕl'ŭndīn), Old World biennial plant (*Chelidonium majus*), naturalized in E North America. Its small yellow flowers are borne in loose clusters and the compound leaves are rounded or lobed. Alkaloids are found in the yellow juice and other parts of the plant.

Celebes (sĕ'lŭbēz), island (c.71,695 sq. mi.; pop. including offshore islands 7,079,349). Four mountainous peninsulas separated by three deep gulfs. MACASSAR in SW is chief city and port. Exports copra, coffee, and nutmeg; produces timber, coal, nickel, and iron. Discovered by Portuguese 1512, settled by them 1625 until ousted by Dutch 1660. In 1950 became part of republic of Indonesia. The Celebes Sea, to N, separates island from the Philippines.

celery, biennial plant (*Apium graveolens*) with fleshy stalks, grown largely for use in salads. Celeriac is a variety grown for edible, thickened crown.

celesta: see PERCUSSION INSTRUMENTS.

Celestina, La (lä thälästē'nä), Spanish novel in dramatic form attributed to Fernando de ROJAS. Published as *Comedia de Calisto y Melibea* (1499), it came to be

called after the principal character, La Celestina, an amusing old bawd.

Celestine I, Saint (sĕ'lŭstĭn), d. 432, pope (422–32). Asserted power of the papacy by issuing a judgment against the heresy of Nestorius and instructing his delegates to the Council of Ephesus to judge, not to discuss. Suppressed semi-Pelagianism. Feast: July 27.

Celestine V, Saint, 1215–96, pope (1294), an Italian named Pietro del Murrone. A hermit noted for ascetic holiness, he gathered followers about him (core of the later Celestines). Disagreement among the cardinals led to his being called from his mountain retreat to be made pope. Charles II of Naples took control of affairs, and the impractical pope, realizing that he was a puppet, resigned. Boniface VIII succeeded him. Canonized 1313 at instance of French king Philip IV. Feast: May 19.

Céline, Louis Ferdinand (lwē' fĕrdēnä' sälēn'), 1894–, 1961, French author; real name was Louis Ferdinand Destouches. His misanthropic novels, *Journey to the End of Night* (1932; Eng. tr., 1934) and *Death on the Installment Plan* (1936; Eng. tr., 1938), created a sensation. His misanthropy drove him to fascism.

cell, in biology, unit (usually microscopic) of structure and function of which animals and plants are composed. Protoplasm, the living matter of the cell, consists of the nucleus and CYTOPLASM; in most cells the nucleus contains a nucleolus (small, round, dense body); delicate plasma membrane functions as outer boundary of cytoplasm. Plant cells differ from animal cells in that (usually) they have a rigid nonprotoplasmic cell wall outside the plasma membrane. In growth and repair, cells multiply by dividing in two. Both plant and animal cell nuclei have major role in process of cell division; cytoplasm, controlled by nucleus, performs other cell functions. Cytology is the science of cell study. See also MITOSIS.

cell, in electricity, a source of electric current in which current flow is the result of chemical action. Cell consists of a positive ELECTRODE and a negative electrode, which conduct electricity, and an electrolyte which acts chemically upon one of the electrodes. A simple cell form is glass jar with dilute solution of sulphuric acid holding zinc and copper electrodes which are connected externally by a conductor (such as wire). Chemical action causes electrons to flow through wire from negative (zinc) plate to positive (copper) plate; this is opposite to conventional direction of flow of "electric current." Other cells are the Bunsen, Daniell, and Leclanché cells. Voltage depends on activity of substances used. Common dry cell consists of zinc cylinder enclosed at one end and lined with absorbent material, a central core of carbon, and a paste (serving as the electrolyte) of carbon granules and manganese dioxide saturated with a solution of ammonium chloride. See *ill.,* p. 322.

Celle (tsĕ'lŭ), city (pop. 57,239), West Germany, in Lower Saxony, on Aller R. Oil refineries; machinery and chemical mfg. Chartered 1294; residence of dukes of Brunswick-Lüneburg until 1705.

Cellini, Benvenuto (Ital. bänvänōō'tō chällē'nē), 1500–1571, Italian sculptor, b. Florence. As a metalworker he enjoyed the patronage of Pope Clement VII and later of Francis I of France. Famous for *Perseus with the Head of Medusa* (Florence) and for intricate metalwork, such as the gold and enamel saltcellar of Francis I. Autobiography describes escapades, enmities, and banishments.

cello or **'cello:** see VIOLIN.

celluloid, transparent, colorless substance made by treating cellulose nitrates with camphor and alcohol to form paste which can be rolled or molded. It is highly inflammable.

cellulose, polysaccharide (see CARBOHYDRATE) produced by CYTOPLASM of plant cells and forming the bulk of cell wall. It is composed of branched chains of D-glucose molecules. Absorbent cotton, jute, linen are almost pure cellulose; it forms bulk of paper, wood, wood pulp. Inert, insoluble in water, very

---

SMALL CAPITALS = cross references. Pronunciation key on inside end pages. Abbreviations: p. 2.

absorbent. Used to make guncotton, pyroxylin, celluloid, collodion, cellulose acetate, RAYON, and Cellophane. See *ill.*, p. 178.

Celsius, Anders (än'dürs sĕl'sĕŭs), 1701–44, Swedish astronomer, inventor (1742) of centigrade (or Celsius) thermometer. Made studies of aurora borealis.

Celsus, Aulus Cornelius, fl. A.D. 14?, Latin encyclopedist; his extant work, eight books on medicine.

Celt (sĕlt) **or Kelt** (kĕlt). **1** One who speaks a Celtic language or traces ancestry to area where Celtic is or recently was spoken. **2** Member of a group of peoples known from early 2d millennium B.C., who advanced to political and cultural leadership in W and Central Europe between 1200 and 400 B.C.

Celtic languages, subfamily of Indo-European languages. See LANGUAGE (table).

Cenci, Beatrice (bäätrē'chä chän'chē), 1577–99, Italian noblewoman. Imprisoned by a vicious father, she procured his murder with complicity of her stepmother, brothers, and lover. Executed after a famous trial. Subject of tragedy by Shelley.

Cenis, Mont (mō'sûnē'), Alpine pass, 6,835 ft. high, on French-Italian border. New road built 1810. Railroad tunnel, 8 mi. long, built 1871, connects Turin with Chambéry. Famous invasion route.

Cennini, Cennino (chän-nē'nō chän-nē'nē), c.1370–1440, Florentine painter. *Treatise on Painting* describes technical processes of Giotto's followers.

Cenozoic era, fifth of the five eras of geologic time; it covers 60–75 million years. It has seen the shaping of our present landscape. Mammals replaced reptiles as dominant life, and finally man appeared. See also QUATERNARY; TERTIARY; table, pp. 406–7.

censorship, official restriction of any public expression believed to threaten the governing authority or the moral order. There are two types, preventive (before material is issued) and punitive (after material is issued). Practice, known in ancient Greece and Rome, was very common in religious troubles of Reformation. Censorship of press, usual in totalitarian countries, is frowned upon in democracies except in wartime. In U.S. most censorship of movies by authorities is on grounds of obscenity. See also PRESS, FREEDOM OF THE.

census, periodic official count of persons and their condition and of resources of a country. In anc. times taken for tax, conscription purposes; now a thorough statistical review. U.S. Bureau of Census estab. 1902 in Dept. of Commerce.

centaur (sĕn'tôr), in Greek religion, descendant of Ixion, a creature half man and half horse. Centaurs lived in Thessaly. Though generally savage, some, like CHIRON, were friends and teachers of men.

Centaurus (sĕntô'rús), constellation in Southern Hemisphere known for its two stars which are closest to our solar system (c.4.3 light-years away). One, Alpha Centauri, is third brightest star in sky.

Centennial Exposition, International, held in Philadelphia from May to Nov., 1876, to celebrate 100th anniversary of Declaration of Independence. Fairmount Park was site. First U.S. world's fair, it particularly exhibited U.S. technical advance and industrial growth.

Centerdale, R.I.: see NORTH PROVIDENCE.

Center for the Performing Arts: see JOHN F. KENNEDY CENTER FOR THE PERFORMING ARTS; LINCOLN CENTER.

Center Line, city (pop. 10,164), SE Mich., a suburb NNE of Detroit.

Centerville, city (pop. 12,769), SE Ill., SSE of East St. Louis.

centigrade scale: see TEMPERATURE.

centipede (sĕn'tŭpēd), flattened, segmented, wormlike, chiefly nocturnal animal of phylum Arthropoda; related to insects. It has numerous jointed legs, the first pair bearing poison claws to paralyze prey (insects, worms). Centipedes are usually 1–8 in. long. Unlike the MILLIPEDE, the centipede does not eat plants.

Central African Republic, country (c.238,200 sq. mi.; pop. c.2,088,000), central Africa; cap. Bangui.

Former French overseas territory of Ubangi-Shari. Savanna in N, tropical forest in S, semidesert in E. Ubangi and Shari are largest rivers. Major agr. exports are cotton, peanuts, coffee, and sisal; lumbering and some mining of diamonds and gold. Country receives external economic aid, particularly from France. With no railroads, and few all-weather roads, transportation is chiefly along rivers. Official language is French; Sangho is widely spoken. Became French colony in 1894; incorporated into French Equatorial Africa 1910. Strong nationalist movement led to increased internal autonomy in 1950s. Full independence was attained 1960, when country joined UN. David Dacko was first president (1959–66).

Central America, isthmus between North and South America, also called Middle America. Includes republics of Costa Rica, Guatemala, Honduras, Nicaragua, and El Salvador. British Honduras (Belize), Panama, and some of S Mexico (Campeche, Chiapas, Tabasco, and territory of Quintana Roo) are also included in geographical area. The Organization of Central American States was formed in 1951 to help solve common problems. See map, p. 773.

Central American Federation or Central American Union, political confederation of republics of Central America (1825–38). Presidents were Manuel José Arce and Francisco Morazán.

Central Asiatic Railroad: see TRANS-CASPIAN RAILROAD.

Central Australia: see NORTHERN TERRITORY.

central bank, fiscal agent for a government which acts as support for country's banking system. Among subsidiary functions are creation and regulation of money and purchase and sale of government obligations. Central banking in U.S. is represented by FEDERAL RESERVE SYSTEM.

Central City, town (pop. 250), N central Colo., in Clear Creek Canyon W of Denver. Boomed after gold discovery 1859. Past of this "ghost town" revived in summer with play and music festival in stone opera house (1878), where in its heyday many noted players appeared.

Central Falls, industrial city (1965 pop. 18,677), N R.I., NE of Providence.

Centralia (sĕntrā'lĕŭ). **1** City (pop. 13,904), S Ill., E of St. Louis; platted 1853. Industrial and shipping center of fruit, farm, coal, and oil area. Has railroad repair shops. **2** City (pop. 3,200), N central Mo., SE of Moberly, in grain region. Scene of raid by Confederate guerrillas 1864.

Central Intelligence Agency (CIA), estab. 1947 by National Security Act. Coordinates and handles all sources of U.S. government "intelligence." Richard M. Helms was made director in 1966.

Central Park, 840 acres, largest park on Manhattan isl., New York city, between 59th and 110th streets and Fifth Avenue and Central Park West. Land was acquired by city in 1856 and improved after plans of F. L. Olmstead and Calvert Vaux. Here are Metropolitan Mus. of Art, a formal conservatory garden, a zoo, a children's zoo, an Egyptian obelisk known as "Cleopatra's Needle," the Mall, and an open-air theater (completed 1962.)

Central Powers, in First World War, the coalition of Germany, Austria-Hungary, Bulgaria, and the Ottoman Empire.

Central Provinces and Berar: see MADHYA PRADESH.

Central Treaty Organization, (CENTO). international organization formed 1955 for the military defense of the Middle East, signed by Iran, Iraq, Turkey, Pakistan, and Great Britain. Based on 1955 Baghdad Pact. Originally known as Middle East Treaty Organization, the name was changed to CENTO in 1959 when Iraq withdrew. CENTO powers are also pledged to economic and social cooperation. U.S. has close relations with the organization. Hq. are in Ankara.

Central Utah project, NE and N central Utah, planned by U.S. to carry water from Uinta Mts. across Wasatch Range to Salt L. valley by system of dams, reservoirs, aqueducts, canals. Initial phase authorized by Congress 1956; work begun 1959 near Vernal. Will provide power, water for industrial and domestic use, and irrigation for c.160,000 acres. Part of COLORADO RIVER STORAGE PROJECT.

Central Valley, town (pop. 2,854), N Calif., NNE of Redding, in farm and timber region; founded 1938 when construction was begun on Central Valley project. Nearby is Shasta L., made by Shasta Dam.

Central Valley project, central Calif., program of U.S. Bureau of Reclamation begun 1935 to use Sacramento R. waters in N to benefit San Joaquin Valley farmlands in S. Project to provide flood control, hydroelectric power, irrigation; improve navigation; supply cities and industry with water; protect Sacramento delta region from seawater; and preserve fish and wildlife. Units include SHASTA DAM and Keswick Dam (both in Sacramento R.); FRIANT DAM (in San Joaquin R.); Madera Canal, which goes 36 mi. N; Friant-Kern Canal, which goes c.150 mi. S; Delta Cross Channel to use Sacramento waters to fight soil salinity in delta; Contra Costa Canal to take Sacramento water 48 mi. to reservoir at Martinez; Delta-Mendota Canal (supplied by Delta Cross Channel) to take water c.120 mi. to supply San Joaquin; and steam power plant at Antioch. Work begun on Trinity and American rivers developments, and much more is planned. U.S. Corps of Engineers has contributed Pine Flat Dam (Kings R.) and Folsom Dam (American R.).

centrifugal force and **centripetal force:** see FORCE.

centrifuge (sĕn'trŭfūj), device using centrifugal force to separate substances of different density, e.g., liquid and solid portions of blood. Has base (or frame), motor, and rotating part which holds mixture. Cream separator is common type.

Ceos, Greek island: see CYCLADES.

cephalic index (sŭfā'lĭk), ratio of breadth of head to its length. Used in anthropological studies.

Cephalonia (sĕfŭlō'nyŭ), Gr. *Kephallenia,* island (289 sq. mi.; pop. 46,314), Greece, largest of IONIAN ISLANDS. Irregular and mountainous, it rises to 5,314 ft. in Mt. Aenos, formerly crowned with a temple to Zeus. Argostoli, port and chief town, exports currants, wine, and olive oil. Sheep raising; fishing. A member of Aetolian League, Cephalonia was ruled by Rome after 189 B.C. and by Byzantium until its occupation by Venice (1126). In 1797 it was ceded to France, and its later history is that of Ionian Isls.

cephalopod: see MOLLUSK.

Cephalus (sĕ'fălŭs), in Greek legend, husband of Procris. She followed him when he went hunting, suspecting him of infidelity, and he accidentally shot her. Later he killed himself.

Cephas (sēfŭs), Jesus' nickname for ST. PETER.

Cepheus (sē'fēŭs), constellation in Northern Hemisphere lying partly in Milky Way. Has a variable star from which a class of stars derive their name—Cepheid variables, type of pulsating star used in calculating stellar distances from earth.

Cephisodotus (sĕfĭsŏ'dŭtŭs), fl. 4th cent. B.C., two Greek sculptors. The elder was the father of Praxiteles; the younger was the son of Praxiteles.

Cephissus (sĭfī'sŭs), Gr. *Kephisos,* name of Greek rivers. **1** Rising in Parnassus and flowing 75 mi. ESE into N Euboic Gulf. **2** Rising in Mt. Pentelikon and flowing S past Athens into Saronic Gulf.

Ceram (sĕräm'), island (c.7,191 sq. mi.; pop. including offshore islands 720,169), largest of the Moluccas, E Indonesia. Mountainous. Produces copra, resin, oil.

Ceramicus Sinus (sĕrŭmī'kŭs sī'nŭs) or **Ceramic Gulf,** anc. name of Gulf of Kos or Kerme, SW Turkey, an inlet of Aegean Sea. On it was Halicarnassus.

Cerano, Il: see CRESPI, GIOVANNI BATTISTA.

Ceraunian Mountains (sĭrô'nēŭn), coastal range, S Albania, extending c.70 mi. from Greek border to Otranto Strait. Sometimes called Acroceraunian Mts.

Cerberus (sûr'bŭrŭs), in Greek religion, many-headed dog with a mane and a tail of snakes. He watched gate of Hades. The honey cake buried by the Greeks with the dead was to quiet him. His capture was one of 12 labors of HERCULES.

cerebellum: see BRAIN.

cerebral palsy: see PARALYSIS OR PALSY.

cerebrospinal meningitis: see MENINGITIS.

cerebrum: see BRAIN.

Ceres (sēr'ēz), in Roman religion, goddess of agriculture; daughter of Saturn and Ops. Identified with Greek DEMETER. Her worship included fertility rites and rites for the dead. Her most famous temple was on Aventine Hill; her chief festival was Cerealia.

Cerignola (chārēnyō'lä), city (est. pop. 54,205), Apulia, S Italy. Scene of major Spanish victory (1503) over French in ITALIAN WARS.

cerium (sēr'ēŭm), metallic element of RARE EARTHS (symbol = Ce; see also ELEMENT, table). Ductile, malleable, tarnishes in moisture. Forms oxide when heated; alloys. Compounds used to make lamp mantles, and in medicine.

Cernauti: see CHERNOVTSY, Ukraine.

Cernuda, Luis (lwĕs' thärnōō'dhä), 1904–, Spanish poet. Works include *La realidad y el deseo* [reality and desire] (1936; expanded ed., 1940).

Cernuschi, Henri (chĕrnōō'skē), 1821–96, Italian politician and economist. He went to France 1850 where he became a director of Bank of France. Strong advocate of BIMETALLISM.

Cerro de Pasco (sĕ'rō dä pä'skō), city (pop. c.19,300), central Peru. It is 13,973 ft. high (one of highest cities in world), bleak and barren, but its fabulous silver mines, discovered 1630, have made it world renowned. Copper and vanadium also mined here.

Certosa di Pavia (chārtō'zä dē pävē'ä), former Carthusian abbey in Pavia, Italy; a national monument since 1866. Built between 14th and early 16th cent., it is a masterpiece of the Renaissance, with rich marbles and profuse sculptural decorations.

cerussite (sēr'ŭsĭt), colorless, white, or gray brittle carbonate of lead, an important ore of lead.

Cervantes (Saavedra), Miguel de (sûrvän'tēz, Span. mē-gĕl' dä thĕrvän'täs sä"ävä'dhrä), 1547–1616, Spanish novelist, generally regarded as the greatest figure of Spanish literature, author of DON QUIXOTE DE LA MANCHA. As a soldier Cervantes had a highly adventurous life: a wound at the battle of Lepanto cost him his left arm; five years of captivity as a slave in Algiers ended when he was ransomed by his family. After retiring from the army (1582) he was poor and often in debt. Besides *Don Quixote,* one of the masterpieces of world literature, he wrote other fiction (e.g., *Novelas ejemplares,* 1613), a pastoral romance, and plays.

Cervera y Topete, Pascual (päskwäl' thĕrvä'rä ē tōpā'tä), 1839–1909, Spanish admiral, commander of Atlantic fleet in SPANISH-AMERICAN WAR. Blockaded (1898) by U.S. fleet at Santiago de Cuba; tried to run blockade but was utterly defeated and captured.

Cesalpino, Andrea: see CAESALPINUS, ANDREAS.

cesarean section or **caesarean section** (both: sēzā'rēŭn), removal of child from uterus through abdominal incision. Can be performed more than once.

Cesari, Giuseppe, Cavaliere d'Arpino (jōōzĕp'pä chä'zärē kävälyä'rä därpē'nō), 1568–1640, Italian late mannerist painter.

Cesis (tsä'zēz), Ger. *Wenden,* town (pop. c.13,900), N Latvia. Agr. center; paper mills. Former seat of Livonian Knights, who built its anc. castle. Also spelled Tsesis, Zehsis.

cesium (sē'zēŭm), rare, silver-white, soft, metallic element (symbol = Cs; see also ELEMENT, table). It is the most active metal, a member of ALKALI METALS, never found free in nature; cesium chloride is widely distributed in minute quantities.

Ceske Budejovice, Czechoslovakia: see BUDWEIS.

Cesky Les: see BOHEMIAN FOREST.

Cesky Tesin, Czechoslovakia: see TESCHEN.

SMALL CAPITALS = cross references. Pronunciation key on inside end pages. Abbreviations: p. 2.

cesspool, cistern made to receive sewage. Types include watertight (should be 200 ft. from surface water and 60 ft. from cistern or drinking water source), and leaching (built to allow liquid sewage to soak through). Some have drains to carry liquid sewage to adjoining ground.

Cetatea-Alba: see BELGOROD-DNESTROVSKY, Ukraine.

Cetewayo, Cetywayo (both: sĕtĭwā′ō, –wī′ō), or **Ketchwayo** (kĕchwī′ō), c.1836–1884, king of the Zulu. Determinedly resisted European advances into his territory. Defeated by British troops at Ulundi 1879.

Cetinje (tsĕ′tĭnyĕ), small town, Montenegro, Yugoslavia, near Adriatic. Grew around monastery, founded 1485; cap. of Montenegro until 1916.

Cette, France: see SÈTE.

Ceuta (syōō′tŭ), city (pop. c.73,000), Spanish enclave in Morocco, a Mediterranean port opposite Gibraltar; beyond it extends a headland, Jebel Musa, one of the Pillars of Hercules. Under Spanish rule since 1580. Technically a part of Morocco, it is administered by Spain as part of Cádiz prov.

Cévennes (sāvĕn′), mountain range, S France, limiting the Massif Central toward S and E. Mont Lozère (5,584 ft.) is highest peak. Sheep grazing, sericulture, coal mining. Much erosion.

Ceylon (sēlŏn′), anc. *Taprobane,* island (25,322 sq. mi.; pop. c.10,167,000), in Indian Ocean, SE of India. Officially named Sri Lanka, Ceylon became a dominion of British Commonwealth of Nations 1948; chief port and cap. Colombo. Mainly mountainous with broad coastal plain. Chief crops are rice, coconuts, rubber, and tea. Inhabitants mainly Singhalese. Original inhabitants were conquered in 6th cent. B.C. by Vijaya, Aryan prince of India, who estab. first Singhalese kingdom. Buddhism introduced in 3rd cent. B.C., and ANURADHAPURA became great Buddhist center. Visited by Arab traders 12th–13th cent. A.D. Portuguese won control over much of the coast in 16th cent., but were ousted by the Dutch in 1658. The British seized Dutch settlements 1795–96 and won control over kingdom of Kandy in 1815. After British rule ended, D. W. Senanayake was first premier (1948–52). S. W. R. D. Bandaranaike served from 1956 until his assassination in 1959; his widow became prime minister in 1960. She was succeeded by Dudley Senanayake, who had been premier 1952–53 and for a short time in 1960. Ceylon maintained a neutral foreign policy.

Cézanne, Paul (pôl′ sāzän′), 1839–1906, French painter who deeply influenced the course of modern art. Rejected as a student at École des Beaux-Arts, he was enabled to paint by an allowance from his banker father. Guided by Pissarro, who helped him exhibit in the first impressionist show, 1874. He reached a mature style c.1890 in still lifes and landscapes of his native Provence. He distorted natural forms by use of pure color and a new use of perspective.

Cf, chemical symbol of the element CALIFORNIUM.

Chabas, Paul Émile (pôl′ āmēl′ shäbäs′), 1869–1937, French painter. Created sensation with exhibition (1912) of his nude, *September Morn.*

Chablis (shäblē′), village, Yonne dept., N central France, in wine-growing region (white Burgundy).

Chabot, Philippe de (fēlēp′ dŭ shäbō′), also known as **Admiral de Brion** (brēō′), 1480–1543, admiral of France. Credited with originating project of a French colony in Canada.

Chabrier, Alexis Emmanuel (shäbrēä′), 1841–94, French composer. Among his works are *Joyeuse marche; Bourrée fantasque;* an opera, *Le Roi malgré lui; España.*

Chaco (chä′kō), extensive, sparsely populated lowland plain, central S America, divided among Paraguay, Bolivia, and Argentina. After Chaco War (1932–35) between Paraguay and Bolivia, treaty was signed giving Paraguay three quarters of disputed N area of Chaco and Bolivia a corridor to Paraguay R. and certain port privileges there.

Chaco Canyon National Monument: see NATIONAL PARKS AND MONUMENTS (table).

Chad, Fr. *Tchad,* republic (c.496,000 sq. mi.; pop. c.2,800,000), N central Africa; cap. Fort-Lamy. A landlocked country with forests and savanna in S, dry steppe and desert in N. L. Chad is in SW. Economy is agr. and pastoral; cotton, livestock products, and peanuts are exported. Sodium is mined; there are tungsten deposits in Tibesti mts. Peoples of N are mainly Moslem; Bantu groups in S are animist or Christian. Official language is French. Organized as a colony within French Equatorial Africa 1913, Chad became republic within French Community 1958, gained independence 1960, when it joined UN. François Tombalbaye became first premier and president.

Chad, Lake (chăd), central Africa. Bordered mainly by Nigeria and Chad. Has no outlet; major source is Shari R. Area (5,000–9,000 sq. mi.) varies with seasons.

Chadds Ford: see BRANDYWINE, BATTLE OF.

Chadwick, Florence May, 1918–, American swimmer. First woman to swim English Channel in both directions (1950, 1951).

Chadwick, George Whitefield, 1854–1931, American composer, director of the New England Conservatory of Music (1897–1931). Composer of overtures, symphonies, chamber music, and operas (e.g., *Judith*).

Chadwick, Sir James, 1891–, English physicist. Won 1935 Nobel Prize in Physics for discovery of NEUTRON.

Chadwick, Lynn, 1914–, English abstract sculptor. Known for his wire constructions.

Chaeronea (kĕrŭnē′ŭ), anc. town, Boeotia, Greece. Birthplace of Plutarch. Here Philip of Macedon defeated Athenians and Boeotians (338 B.C.), Sulla defeated Mithridates VI of Pontus (86 B.C.)

Chaffee, Adna Romanza (chä′fē), 1842–1914, U.S. army officer. Led American contingent in Boxer Rebellion. Army chief of staff 1904–6.

Chagall, Marc (märk shŭgäl′), 1889–, Russian painter, b. Vitebsk. Since 1910 he has lived mainly in France. Considered a forerunner of surrealism. He uses flower and animal symbols and draws his main subject matter from Jewish folklore.

Chahar (chä′hä′ŭr), former province (109,527 sq. mi.), N China; former cap. Changkiakow. In the S tip kaoliang, wheat, and corn are raised. Mongolian nomads inhabit remainder of Chahar, a high, barren plateau. Abolished 1952, most of Chahar was included in Inner Mongolian Autonomous Region.

Chaillé-Long, Charles (shäyā′-lông′), 1842–1917, American soldier and African explorer. Served in Civil War and Egyptian army. Explored Nile area.

Chaillu, Paul Belloni du: see DU CHAILLU.

Chain, Ernst Boris, 1906–, English biochemist. Shared 1945 Nobel Prize in Physiology and Medicine for work on penicillin.

Chaka (shä′kä), d. 1828, paramount chief (1818–28) of the Zulus in area of what is now Natal, Republic of South Africa. Also spelled Shaka.

Chalcedon (kăl′sĭdŏn, kălsē′dŭn), anc. Greek city of Asia Minor, on Bosporus, facing Byzantium.

Chalcedon, Council of, 451, fourth ecumenical council. It disposed of the heresy of EUTYCHES (which had been advanced by the scandalous Robber Synod) with the final Catholic pronouncement of the nature of Christ in the *Definition.* This, reflecting the *Tome* of Leo I, says that divine nature and human nature of Christ are distinct but inseparably united—Christ is both true man and true God. The decree of the Council that the patriarch of Constantinople should be the single head of the Eastern Church has never been accepted by the Roman Catholic Church.

chalcedony (kălsē′dŭnē), variety of quartz, transparent to translucent, with minute crystals, waxy luster. Agate, carnelian, jasper, and onyx are forms of chalcedony colored by impurities.

Chalcidice (kălsĭ′dĭsē), Gr. *Chalkidike* or *Khalkidiki,* peninsula, NE Greece, projecting into Aegean Sea from SE Macedonia; chief town Polygyros. S coast forms three peninsulas: Kassandra (anc. Gr. *Pallene*), Sithonia, ATHOS. A dry, mountainous region, it produces olive oil, wine, wheat, tobacco. Anciently famous for its timber. Named for Chalcis, which estab. colonies here (7th–6th cent. B.C.). POTIDAEA was an important city. Region was conquered by Macedon (4th cent. B.C.) and by Rome (2d cent. B.C.). Later history follows that of SALONICA.

Chalcis (kăl'sĭs), Gr. *Khalkis*, city (pop. 24,745), Greece; a port on EUBOEA. The chief city of ancient Euboea, it estab. colonies in Sicily and Chalcidice (8th–7th cent. B.C.), led revolt of Euboea against Athens (446 B.C.), and was made tributary to her (411). In 338 B.C. it came under Macedon. Aristotle died here. Called Negropont in Middle Ages.

chalcopyrite (kăl'kŭpī'rīt) or **copper pyrites**, mineral, brass-yellow with iridescent tarnish. A sulfide of iron and copper, it sometimes contains other metals. An important ore of copper.

Chaldaea or **Chaldea** (both: kăldē'ù), S portion of Tigris-Euphrates valley (Mesopotamia), but sometimes loosely used to include all Babylonia. The restored Babylonian kingdom is frequently called the Chaldaean Empire. Chaldaean or Chaldee came to be loosely used to mean astrologer or magician (e.g., Dan. 1.4) because of astronomical knowledge there.

Chaleur Bay (shŭlōōr'), inlet of Gulf of St. Lawrence, c.85 mi. long, 15–25 mi. wide, between N.B. and Gaspé Peninsula, Canada. Is submerged valley of Restigouche R., which enters at its head. Has famous fishing grounds. Discovered and named by Cartier 1534.

Chalfont (chôl'fŏnt", chäl'–), borough (pop. 1,140), SE Pa., near Doylestown. Traditional burial place of Delaware Indian chief Tamanend or Tammany.

Chalgrin, Jean François (zhã' frãswä' shälgrē'), 1739–1811, French architect. Chiefly responsible for scheme of Arc de Triomphe de l'Étoile, commissioned by Napoleon.

Chaliapin, Feodor (Ivanovich) (fyô'dùr shŭlyä'pēn), 1873–1938, Russian bass. Appeared at the Metropolitan Opera, New York in 1907 and 1921–29. An excellent actor, he was particularly known for title role in Moussorgsky's *Boris Godunov*.

chalk, a calcium carbonate mineral softer than limestone, consisting of minute marine shells. Chalk cliffs of Dover, England, date from Cretaceous period. See *ill.*, p. 116.

Chalk River, government research establishment, S Ont., Canada, on S shore of Ottawa R., W of Ottawa. Operated by National Research Council of Canada for Atomic Energy Control Board.

Challenger expedition, 1872–76, British scientific expedition which cruised in corvette *Challenger* making physical and biological surveys of Atlantic and Pacific oceans.

Challoner, Richard (chă'lùnùr), 1691–1781, English Roman Catholic bishop. Converted as a boy, he was ordained in 1716 and in 1730 returned to England, where he met many difficulties in trying to win toleration for Catholics. He was beset by anti-Catholic movements culminating in the Gordon riots (1780). A notable scholar, he revised the Douay version of the Bible and wrote and translated devotional works.

Chalmers, Thomas, 1780–1847, Scottish theologian, leader of Free Church of SCOTLAND.

Chalmette National Historical Park: see NEW ORLEANS, La.

Châlons-sur-Marne (shälō'-sür-märn'), city (est. pop. 40,659), cap. of Marne dept., NE France, on Marne R. Papermaking; brewing; wine processing.

Chalon-sur-Saône (–sōn'), town (est. pop. 37,399), Saône-et-Loire dept., E central France; inland port on Saône and Canal Central. Ships wine and grain. Cap. of Burgundy in 6th cent.

Chalukya (chä'lōōkyù), S Indian dynasty, c.550–1200. The period was one of warfare against the Cholas and defense against the Turks and Arabs who were plundering N India.

Chamberlain, Sir Austen: see CHAMBERLAIN, JOSEPH.

Chamberlain, Houston Stewart, 1855–1927, Anglo-German writer; son-in-law of Richard Wagner. His *Foundations of the Nineteenth Century* (1899; Eng. tr., 1910) was an important forerunner of National Socialist racist doctrines.

Chamberlain, Joseph, 1836–1914, British imperialist statesman. Resigned from Gladstone government (1886), opposing Irish Home Rule. Became Liberal-Unionist leader in House of Commons in 1891. As colonial secretary (1895–1903) advocated social reforms at home and empire expansion and consolidation. Unjustly blamed for acts leading to South African War (1899–1902); led in reconciling Boers after war. Favored tariff giving preference to empire; resigned to advocate tariff policy. This proposal split Liberal-Unionist-Conservative bloc and caused 1906 fall of government but was adopted in lifetime of his sons. His eldest son, **Sir (Joseph) Austen Chamberlain,** 1863–1937, began 45-year parliamentary career in 1892. Twice chancellor of exchequer (1903–6, 1919–21), he carried out in latter term his father's tariff policy. Became Conservative leader in 1921. Helped negotiate Irish Free State treaty. As foreign secretary (1924–29), his most important post, largely responsible for 1925 LOCARNO PACT. Awarded Nobel Peace Prize. His half-brother, **(Arthur) Neville Chamberlain,** 1869–1940, was chancellor of exchequer (1923, 1931–37) and succeeded Baldwin as prime minister (1937). Became symbol of appeasement of Axis powers; signed MUNICH PACT (1938). Remained in office after outbreak of Second World War but increasing opposition forced him to resign after British debacle in Norway (1940).

Chamberlain, Owen, 1920–, American physicist. For confirming the existence of the antiproton, he shared with Emilio Segre the 1959 Nobel Prize in Physics.

Chamberlain, Wilt(on Norman), 1936– American basketball player. Played at Univ. of Kansas and with the Harlem Globetrotters. Highest scorer in basketball history.

Chamberlain, city (pop. 2,598), S S.Dak., on Missouri R., SE of Pierre, in livestock and grain area. Crow Creek and Brulé Indian reservations are near.

Chamberlin, Thomas Chrowder, 1843–1928, American geologist, founder of *Journal of Geology.* Formulated PLANETESIMAL HYPOTHESIS with F. R. Moulton, on the basis of his studies of glaciation and climate.

chamber music, instrumental ensemble music with one player to a part. Most common ensembles are string quartets (viola, cello, two violins) and piano trios (piano and two strings). Considered by many the most subtle musical genre, it demands a polyphonic texture without permitting orchestral effects. Haydn, Mozart, and Beethoven wrote some of their finest music in this style. It has been the framework for experiments in atonality, percussive rhythms, and serial techniques by modern composers.

chamber of commerce, local association of businessmen organized to promote welfare of community, particularly commercial interests. First U.S. chamber of commerce estab. 1768 in N.Y. state.

Chambers, Robert, 1802–71: see CHAMBERS, WILLIAM.

Chambers, Robert, 1881–1957, American physiologist. Developed micromanipulator for dissection and injection of living cells and tissues.

Chambers, Sir William, 1723–96, English architect, foremost in his day. Proponent of Inigo Jones traditions of Palladian design, he published standard work on classic style. Chief work is Somerset House.

Chambers, William, 1800–1883, and **Robert Chambers,** 1802–71, Scottish authors, publishers. Their firm best known for *Chambers's Edinburgh Journal, Chambers's Encyclopaedia.*

Chambersburg, industrial borough (pop. 17,670), S Pa., SW of Harrisburg; settled 1730. Trade center for agr. area. Was hq. of John Brown 1859; burned by Confederates 1864. Seat of Wilson Col.

Chambéry (shäbärē'), town (est. pop. 32,139), cap. of Savoie dept., E France. Historical cap. of Savoy; archiepiscopal see.

Chambiges (shäbēzh'), family of French architects. **Martin Chambiges** (märtē'), d. 1532, helped design cathedrals of Sens, Troyes, and Beauvais. Assisted by son, **Pierre Chambiges** (pyēr'), d. 1544, who also worked on the Hôtel de Ville, Paris.

Chambly (shäblē'), town (pop. 3,737), S Que., Canada, on Richelieu R. and E of Montreal. **Fort Chambly**, built 1665, was captured and burned by Americans 1775–76; restored 1880.

Chambord, Henri, comte de (ärē' kōt' dù shäbôr'), 1820–83, French pretender, known to legitimists as Henry V; posthumous son of duc de Berry. Accompanied his grandfather, Charles X, into exile (1830). Actively claimed throne 1871–73, but lost his prospects through insistence on restoring Bourbon flag. Died childless. Claim passed to Orléans family.

Chambord, village, Loir-et-Cher dept., N central France, between Blois and Orléans. Famous for huge Renaissance château built by Francis I.

chameleon (kùmē'lyùn), small, slow-moving arboreal lizard of Africa and S Asia. Its skin color changes with feelings, varying light intensity, and temperature. The American chameleon is a small lizard of another family. See *ill.*, p. 1136.

Chamfort, Sébastien Roch Nicolas (säbästyē' rōk' nēkōlä' shäfôr'), 1740–94, French writer of maxims and epigrams.

Chaminade, Cécile (säsēl' shämēnäd'), 1857–1944, French composer and pianist. She chiefly wrote songs and piano pieces (e.g., the *Scarf Dance*).

Chamisso, Adelbert von (Chamisso de Boncourt) (ä'dùlbērt fùn shùmï'sō), 1781–1838, German poet, b. France; son of émigré nobles. His lyric cycle *Frauenliebe und Leben* was set to music by Schumann. His tale of the man who sold his shadow, *Peter Schlemihls wundersame Geschichte* (1814), has virtually passed into legend.

chamois (shä'mē), hollow-horned hoofed mammal (*Rupicapra*) related to antelope, found in Europe and E Mediterranean lands. It is about the size of a goat, light brown with black tail, and has erect hooked horns. It was the original source of chamois leather; other skins now are so named.

chamomile: see CAMOMILE.

Chamonix (shämōnē'), Alpine resort, Haute-Savoie dept., E France, base for the ascent of Mont Blanc.

Champa, kingdom of the Chams. Flourished in Vietnam 2d cent. A.D. to 17th cent. Warred with China, KHMER EMPIRE, and Annam, to whom it finally fell in 17th cent. Remnants of people were scattered.

Champagne, Philippe de: see CHAMPAIGNE.

Champagne (shämpän', Fr. shäpä'nyù), region, NE France, in Aube, Marne, Haute-Marne, Ardennes, and Yonne depts., roughly coextensive with former Champagne prov.; historic cap. Troyes. Mostly an arid plateau; agr., sheep grazing. Small fertile dist. around RHEIMS and Épernay produces nearly all French champagne wine. Acquired by house of BLOIS (11th cent.), Champagne was among most powerful fiefs of medieval France. Its counts also ruled Navarre from 1234. Louis X of France, inheriting Champagne from his mother, incorporated it with the royal domain (1314). The medieval Fairs of Champagne, particularly those of Troyes and Provins, brought together merchants from all Europe and were of immense economic importance. Large parts of Champagne were devastated in First World War.

champagne, celebrated sparkling white WINE.

Champaign (shämpän'), city (pop. 49,583), E central Ill., ENE of Springfield and adjoining URBANA, with which it is allied economically; founded 1854. A rail, commercial, and industrial center in farm area. Univ. of ILLINOIS lies between Urbana and Champaign.

Champaigne or **Champagne, Philippe de** (both: fēlēp' dù shäpä'nyù), 1602–74, French painter. Did religious paintings for Marie de' Medici and Richelieu. Later became absorbed in the Jansenist movement.

Champeaux, William of: see WILLIAM OF CHAMPEAUX.

Champlain, Samuel de (Fr. sämüēl' dù shäplē'), 1567–1635, French explorer, chief founder of New France. Estab. colony at Quebec, discovered L. Champlain, extended French claims W to Wis.

Champlain, Lake, 107 mi. long, ½–14 mi. wide, forming part of N.Y.–Vt. line and extending into Que. Lies in broad valley between Adirondacks and Green Mts. A link in Hudson-St. Lawrence waterway, lake is connected with Hudson R. by part of Barge Canal; with the St. Lawrence by Richelieu R.; with L. George by narrow channel. Has many islands, incl. ISLE LA MOTTE and VALCOUR ISLAND. Plattsburgh, N.Y., Burlington, Vt., and many resorts are on its shores. Discovered by Champlain 1609, lake was scene of battles in French and Indian War and in Revolution at CROWN POINT and TICONDEROGA, and of victory of MACDONOUGH in War of 1812.

Champollion, Jean François (zhä' fräswä' shäpôlyō'), 1790–1832, French Egyptologist. Considered the founder of Egyptology, he set (1821) the principles for deciphering Egyptian hieroglyphics by using ROSETTA STONE.

Champs Élysées (shä zälēzä'), avenue of Paris, from Place de la Concorde to Arc de Triomphe, famous for its beauty and elegance.

chance, in mathematics: see PROBABILITY.

Chancellor, Richard, d. 1556, English navigator. Sent out by English group in 1553 to seek Northeast Passage. With Stephen Borough, reached White Sea; traveled overland to Moscow to prepare way for trade. Perished on return voyage.

Chancellorsville, battle of, in Civil War, May 2–4, 1863. R. E. Lee attacked Joseph Hooker's Federals, entrenched near Chancellorsville, Va. In brilliant flank attack, Stonewall Jackson surprised and routed Federals, but was mortally wounded. On May 3–4 J. A. Early and J. E. B. Stuart drove Hooker and John Sedgwick across Rappahannock R. in defeat. This was Lee's last great victory.

chancery: see EQUITY.

chancre: see SYPHILIS.

Chandernagor (chùn''dùrnùgôr'), town (pop. 49,000), West Bengal State, India, on the Hooghly R. Ceded by the French and became part of India in 1951.

Chandigarh (chùn'dēgùr), federally administered territory (pop. c.40,000), cap. of Punjabi Subha and Hariana states, India. Designed by Le Corbusier; built largely in 1950s.

Chandler, Charles Frederick, 1836–1925, American chemist and educator. Helped estab. Columbia Univ. School of Mines (1864). A founder of the American Chemical Society, he was twice its president. Was first public health chemist (1867–73), then president of New York city board of health (1873–83).

Chandler, Raymond (Thornton), 1888–1959, American writer of "tough" detective fiction (e.g., *The Big Sleep*, 1939; *Farewell, My Lovely*, 1940). The private detective Philip Marlowe appears in all.

Chandler, Zachariah, 1813–79, U.S. Senator from Mich. (1857–75), and Secretary of the Interior (1875–77). A leading advocate of radical Reconstruction. As cabinet member, a typical Grant appointee.

Chandler, town (1965 pop. 12,181), S central Ariz., in Salt River Valley; founded 1912. In cotton and citrus fruit area. Williams Air Force Base is E.

Chandragupta: see SANDRACOTTUS.

Chanel, Gabrielle (gäbrēēl' shänēl'), 1883–, French fashion designer and perfume manufacturer. Began career as a milliner, became dress designer after 1920.

Chaney, Lon, 1883–1930, American film actor. A master of art of make-up to distort his face and body, he was noted for his work in horror films.

Changan, China: see SIAN.

Changchun (chäng'tsŏon), industrial city (pop. c.950,-000), NE China; cap. of Kirin prov. Produces heavy machinery. On South Manchurian RR, it was cap. of MANCHUKUO (1932–45) as Hsinking.

change of life: see MENOPAUSE.

change ringing: see BELL.

Chang Hsueh-liang (chäng' shüĕ-lyäng'), 1898–, Chinese general, called the Young Marshal. Succeeded his father Chang Tso-lin as military governor of Manchuria. Ousted 1931 by the Japanese. Kidnaped Chiang Kai-shek at Sian in 1936, allegedly to force him to cooperate with the Communists against Japan. Held in custody by Chiang Kai-shek since 1937.

Changkiakow (tsäng'jyä'kō), city (pop. c.425,000), Inner Mongolia, N China. Former cap. of Chahar prov. Major trade center. Formerly called Wanchuan, its Mongolian name is Kalgan.

Changpai or **Ch'ang-pai** (chäng'bī'), mountain range, mostly in NE China, partly in N Korea. Source of Yalu, Sungari, and Tumen rivers.

Changsha (chäng'shä'), city (pop. c.500,000), cap. of Hunan prov., China, port on Siang R. On Peiping-Canton RR, it is major trade and industrial center with metal refineries, glassworks, and porcelain works. Founded early 3rd cent. B.C., it is noted as literary and educational center.

Changteh or **Ch'ang-tê** (chäng'dû'), city (pop. c.85,-000), Hunan prov., China, on Yuan R. Agr. market center. Former treaty port.

Chang Tso-lin (chäng' tsō-lĭn', jäng'), 1873–1928, Chinese general. Appointed 1918 inspector general of Manchuria, which he made his private preserve. Warred constantly to extend power to N China. Chief enemy of second stage of NORTHERN EXPEDITION. Died when his train was bombed by Japanese.

Chankiang (tsän'jyäng"), Cantonese *Tsamkong,* official Chinese name of former French territory of Kwangchowan (325 sq. mi.) which was leased by China in 1898 for 99 years, but was returned 1945. Its chief city, Fort-Bayard, was renamed **Chankiang** (pop. c.269,000) and has been developed as major seaport since 1955. Industrial and trade center.

Channel Islands, Fr. *Iles Normandes,* archipelago (75 sq. mi.; pop. 104,398), off Normandy coast, France, in English Channel. Main isles are Jersey, Guernsey, Aldernay, Sark, Herm; all (but a few French owned) have belonged to Great Britain since Norman Conquest. Divided into two administrative areas: Jersey, with half the total population and chief town, St. Helier; and Guernsey, which includes all other islands. English replacing French as official language. Chiefly agr. and pastoral, isles send quantities of produce to English markets. Famous for cattle. Occupied by Germans in Second World War.

Channel Islands National Monument, Calif.: see SANTA BARBARA ISLANDS.

Channing, William Ellery, 1780–1842, American author, Unitarian minister in Boston, great preacher, lucid writer on labor problems, education, slavery, religious tolerance, and humanitarianism. His nephew, **William Ellery Channing,** 1818–1901, was author of poems for *Dial* and a biography of Thoreau. His son was **Edward Channing,** 1856–1931, historian, Harvard professor. Wrote *A History of the United States* (6 vols., 1905–25).

chansons de geste (shäsō' dù zhĕst'), epic poems of medieval France (11th–13th cent.). Oldest and most famous is *Chanson de Roland* (c.1098–1100; see ROLAND).

chant, sacred song in which several syllables of text may be sung to one sustained tone. Chant of Roman Catholic and Orthodox Christianity is called PLAIN SONG. Anglican chant, developed during the Reformation, uses harmonized melodies, English texts.

chantey or **shanty,** work song with marked rhythm, particularly one sung by sailors at work. Often has stanzas sung by leader, each followed with chorus sung by group. Similar songs also sung by shore gangs and lumbermen.

Chantilly (shätēyē'), town (est. pop. 7,065), Oise dept., N France, NE of Paris. Famous lace mfg.; racecourse. Château contains art museum.

Chanukah: see HANUKKAH.

Chanute, city (pop. 10,849), SE Kansas, on Neosho R., NW of Pittsburg; settled c.1870. Market center for agr. area, it has railroad shops and oil refineries. Site of first mission (1824–29) in state is near.

Chao Phraya (chou' präyä') or **Menam** (mănäm'), chief Thai river, c.140 mi. long. Rises near Burma-Laos border, enters Gulf of Siam through several outlets, interconnected by canals.

Chaos (kā'ŏs), in Greek religion, unfathomable space whence arose everything, earthly and divine. From it in Olympian myth came GAEA, mother of all things.

Chapala (chäpä'lä), lake, c.50 mi. long and 8 mi. wide, W Mexico, in Jalisco and Michoacán; largest in country; popular scenic resort. Fishing is important native occupation.

chaparral (chăpŭräl'), plant community of shrubs, both evergreen and deciduous, usually in regions with 10 to 20 in. annual rainfall. It is drier than forest regions but less arid than deserts. Chaparral growth exists in W and SW U.S. and may include scrub oaks, squawbush, western serviceberry, mesquite, buckthorn, and manzanita.

Chapel Hill, town (pop. 12,573), central N.C., NW of Raleigh, at edge of piedmont; founded 1792. Seat of Univ. of NORTH CAROLINA.

Chaplin, Charles Spencer, 1889–, Anglo-American film actor who writes, directs, and produces his own pictures. Discovered by Mack Sennett c.1913, Charlie Chaplin soon was famous for his baggy trousers and little mustache. Among his many films are *Easy Street, Shoulder Arms, The Kid, The Gold Rush, City Lights, Modern Times, The Great Dictator, Monsieur Verdoux,* and *Limelight.* His art is the most universal yet to appear on film.

Chapman, George, 1559?–1634, English dramatist and poet. Notable for translations of *Iliad* (1612) and *Odyssey* (1614–15). Among best plays, tragedy *Bussy d'Ambois* (1607) and comedy *All Fools* (1605).

Chapman, John, 1774–1845, American pioneer, more familiarly known as Johnny Appleseed. Wandering cultivator and promoter of apple orchards in Ohio, Ind., and Pa.

Chapman, John Jay, 1862–1933, American essayist, author of fiery works such as *Emerson and Other Essays* (1898), *New Horizons in American Life* (1932).

Chapultepec (chäpōōl'täpĕk") [Aztec,= grasshopper hill], rocky eminence in SW section of Mexico city. Occupied successively by Aztec emperors, Spanish viceroys, and later rulers of Mexico (including Emperor Maximilian). Pres. Cárdenas decreed (1937) that castle become museum and grounds a public park.

Charcas (chär'käs), Spanish colonial *audiencia* and presidency in S America, known also as Upper Peru and Chuquisaca; established 1559 and attached to viceroyalty of Peru. Transferred to viceroyalty of La Plata (1776). Roughly same as modern Bolivia.

charcoal, substance, mostly pure carbon, from destructive DISTILLATION of wood, animal matter (e.g., bone black from bones), or sugar. A smokeless fuel, it yields a large amount of heat. It is an efficient agent in ADSORPTION of solids from solution and is used in making gunpowder, in sugar refining, in purification of water and air, and in gas masks.

Charcot, Jean Martin (zhä' märtĕ' shärkō'), 1825–93, French neurologist, organizer of noted Paris clinic for nervous system diseases. He studied the treatment of hysteria by hypnosis.

Chardin, Jean Baptiste (zhä' bätēst' shärdĕ'), 1699–1779, French painter, famous for still lifes and domestic interiors. One of greatest French colorists.

Chardin, Pierre Teilhard de: see TEILHARD DE CHARDIN.

Chardzhou (chŭrjô'ŏō), city (1965 est. pop. 82,000), N Turkmen SSR; port on Amu Darya R. Shipyards

Charente (shärät'), department (2,306 sq. mi.; pop. 327,658), W France; cap. Angoulême. The **Charente** river, 220 mi. long, flows from central France past Angoulême, Cognac, and Rochefort into Atlantic.

Charente-Maritime (-märētēm'), department (2,792 sq. mi.; pop. 470,897), W France, on Atlantic coast; cap. La Rochelle. Formerly called Charente-Inférieure.

Chares (kâ'rēz, kä'–), 3d cent. B.C., Greek worker in bronze; sculptor of the COLOSSUS OF RHODES.

chargé d'affaires: see DIPLOMATIC SERVICE.

Charing Cross (chăr'ĭng), open space at W end of Strand, London. One of Eleanor Crosses (see ELEANOR OF CASTILE) erected here. Charing Cross station is busy rail terminal.

chariot (chă'rĕŭt), earliest type of carriage. Ancient form had two wheels; car usually consisted of floor and waist-high semicircular guard in front. Wheels of war chariot sometimes mounted with scythes as weapons. In Greece and Rome chariots were used primarily to carry passengers and were featured in races and processions.

Charites (kă'rĭtēz), Greek name for GRACES.

charity, public, organized relief of human disease, poverty, and misery. After Middle Ages, national and local, as well as private, agencies took over much of activity of church and guilds. First extensive state effort was Elizabethan POOR LAW of 1601. Degree to which state dispenses charity varies from country to country. Britain and Scandinavian countries are termed "welfare states" because of large governmental expenditures and extensive social welfare legislation.

Charlemagne (shär'lùmän) (Charles the Great or Charles I), 742–814, emperor of the West (800–814), king of the Franks (768–814); son of Pepin the Short. Shared kingdom with his younger brother Carloman until Carloman's death (771). Invaded Italy to support pope against DESIDERIUS; crowned king of Lombards at Pavia (774). Conquered NE Spain ("Spanish March") from Moors (778); subjugated and Christianized Saxons after long struggle (772–804); defeated Avars and Wends. In 800 he restored LEO III to papal see and was crowned emperor by him in Rome on Christmas Day, thus laying basis for HOLY ROMAN EMPIRE. To assure his succession he had his son, LOUIS I, crowned joint emperor (813). To defend and control his immense empire, Charlemagne created military frontier marches and an administrative system by which his personal representatives (*missi dominici*) made his power felt in regular inspection tours. His CAPITULARIES testify to his concern with general welfare and justice for the poor. He frequently held consultative assemblies and took personal interest in Church reform. His palace school at Aachen, founded by ALCUIN, became the cradle of the "Carolingian renaissance" of learning. He was beatified by the Church and is locally honored as a saint. Legend soon enhanced and distorted his actual achievements. Surrounded by his 12 legendary peers, he became the central figure of a cycle of medieval romances (see CHANSONS DE GESTE).

Charleroi (shärlùwä'), town (est. pop. 25,739), Hainaut prov., S central Belgium, on Sambre R. and on Charleroi-Brussels Canal. Coal-mining and steel-milling center. Important fortress 17th–18th cent.

Charles, emperors (see HOLY ROMAN EMPIRE). **Charles I:** see CHARLEMAGNE. **Charles II** (the Bald), 823–77, son of Louis, joined with his brother LOUIS THE GERMAN against his brother LOTHAIR I, whom they defeated at Fontenoy (841). Became king of West Franks (France) by Treaty of VERDUN (843); partitioned Lotharingia with Louis in Treaty of MERSEN (870). Crowned emperor 875. **Charles III** (the Fat), 839–88, inherited Swabia from his father, Louis the German. Crowned king of Italy (879), emperor (881), king of France (885). Deposed 887 after he failed to stop Norman inroads in France. **Charles IV,** 1316–78, succeeded his father JOHN OF LUXEMBURG as king of Bohemia (1346), was elected in the same year antiking to Emperor Louis IV, after whose death he made good his claim. Crowned emperor in 1355, he promulgated in 1356 the Golden Bull (see ELECTORS); added Silesia and Lusatia to his family territories; had his son WENCESLAUS elected German king (1376). His chief interest lay in Bohemia. He embellished Prague and founded Charles Univ. (1348). **Charles V,** 1500–1558, emperor (1519–58) and, as Charles I, king of Spain (1516–56); son of PHILIP I and JOANNA of Castile; grandson of Ferdinand V of Aragon, Isabella of Castile, Emperor Maximilian I, and Mary of Burgundy. The greatest of all Hapsburg emperors, he inherited an empire on which "the sun never set"–the Spanish kingdoms, Spanish America, Naples, Sicily, the Low Countries, and the Austrian hereditary lands. Born and raised at Ghent, he at first antagonized his Spanish subjects but later espoused their national traits and religious zeal and earned their loyalty. His reign was crucial in every way. A series of social uprisings ended with the victory of central authority in Spain and of the great princes in Germany (1520–25; see Juan de PADILLA; SICKINGEN, FRANZ VON; PEASANTS' WAR). The imperialist struggle with France was a Pyrrhic triumph for Spain (1521–59; see FRANCIS I and HENRY II of France; ITALIAN WARS). In his fight against Protestantism, announced at the Diet of WORMS (1521) but long delayed by war with France and Algiers, Charles seemed triumphant when he defeated the Protestant princes at Mühlberg (1547; see SCHMALKALDIC LEAGUE), but in 1555 he was forced to accept the compromise Peace of AUGSBURG and left Germany forever. He was more successful in his promotion of the Catholic REFORM, and he brought the Spanish empire to its height by the conquest of MEXICO and PERU. After his imperial coronation at Bologna (1530; he was the last German emperor crowned by a pope), Charles increasingly delegated his authority in Germany to his brother Ferdinand. After 1554 he abdicated all his titles: his son Philip II received Spain, America, Sicily, Naples, and the Netherlands; his brother became emperor as FERDINAND I. Charles himself retired in 1556 to the monastery of Yuste. **Charles VI,** 1685–1740, emperor (1711–40), and, as Charles III, king of Hungary. Before his accession he claimed the succession to Charles II of Spain (see SPANISH SUCCESSION, WAR OF THE) and in 1733 he became involved in the War of the POLISH SUCCESSION. These dynastic struggles left him with the Spanish Netherlands and Milan. Without male issue, he had a succession problem of his own. The PRAGMATIC SANCTION, by which he settled the Hapsburg lands on his daughter Maria Theresa, was challenged after his death. In his campaigns against Turkey he secured the favorable Treaty of PASSAROWITZ (1718), largely offset by the Treaty of Belgrade (1739). He was a patron of learning and of music. **Charles VII,** 1697–1745, emperor (1742–45) and, as Charles Albert, elector of Bavaria (1726–45), married a niece of Charles VI. He refused to recognize the Pragmatic Sanction, joined the coalition against Maria Theresa in the War of the AUSTRIAN SUCCESSION, and was elected emperor but lost his own Bavaria to Austrian occupation.

Charles I, 1887–1922, last emperor of Austria and, as Charles IV, king of Hungary (1916–18); grandnephew of Francis Joseph. Married Zita of Bourbon-Parma. Failed in attempt to make peace, separate from Germany, with France and Britain in First World War. Abdicated Nov., 1918, but twice sought, without success, to regain Hungarian throne by coup d'état. Died in exile on Madeira. His son Otto succeeded to his claims.

Charles, kings of England, Scotland, and Ireland, of the Stuart house. **Charles I,** 1600–1649, reigned 1625–49. Took little part in politics while his father, James I, ruled except for trip to Spain in abortive negotiations for his marriage. Upon accession, offended English opinion by his marriage to Catholic Henrietta Maria of France, sister of Louis XIII. Foreign ventures of king's favorite, duke of BUCKINGHAM, were unsuccessful. Bitter struggle between king and Parliament known as PURITAN REVOLUTION soon developed. Parliament, largely Puritan, controlled money. Charles supported bishops under William LAUD. Forced to agree to PETITION OF RIGHT 1628, Charles governed without Parliament 1629–40. Civil and religious liberties were at low point and large emigrations to America took place. Attempt to impose episcopacy in Scotland caused Bishops' Wars and king was forced to call Parliament. Long Parliament of 1640, led by John HAMPDEN, PYM, and VANE, secured itself against dissolution and brought about death of earl of STRAFFORD, abolition of Star Chamber courts, and end of arbitrary taxation. Fear of king and Catholics mounted and civil war broke out. Defeated at Marston Moor (1644) and Naseby (1645), Charles surrendered to Scottish army in 1646 and finally fell into hands of English army. Tried by a high court of justice controlled by enemies, he was convicted of treason and beheaded. His son, Charles II, 1630–85, reigned 1660–85. Fled to France 1646. At his father's death, was proclaimed king in Scotland and, accepting terms of Covenanters, was crowned there (1651). After defeat by Cromwell, escaped to Europe and lived in comparative poverty. Issued conciliatory Declaration of Breda. Aided by General MONCK, was restored 1660. Earl of CLARENDON made chief minister. Episcopacy was restored and nonconformity weakened by Clarendon Code although king favored toleration. Great London plague (1665) and fire (1666) took place during second DUTCH WAR (1664–67). CABAL ministry replaced Clarendon (1667). As result of secret Treaty of Dover (1670) with Louis XIV, Charles entered third Dutch War in 1672. It was unpopular and he was forced to approve Test Act (1673) and make peace (1674). Alliance with Louis broken by marriage of king's niece, Mary, to William of Orange. Intervened in Titus OATES affair to protect queen. Dissolved Parliament in 1681 to block passage of Exclusion Act against duke of York and ruled absolutely thereafter. Although father of children by several mistresses (e.g., Nell GWYN), he had no legitimate children and was succeeded by his brother, JAMES II. Reign was marked by gradual increase in power of Parliament, rise of political parties, advance in colonization and trade, and progress of England as a sea power. His pleasure-loving and immoral character set tone of brilliant Restoration period.

Charles, kings of France. Charles I: see CHARLEMAGNE. Charles II and Charles III (the Fat): see CHARLES II and CHARLES III, emperors. Charles III (the Simple), 879–929, son of Louis II, joint king with Eudes from 893, sole king 898–923. Ceded Normandy to ROLLO (911). Deposed and imprisoned by rebellious nobles, who made RAOUL king. Charles IV (the Fair), 1294–1328, succeeded his brother Philip V in 1322; last of direct Capetians. Charles V (the Wise), 1337–80, son of JOHN II, was regent during John's captivity (1356–60), succeeded him in 1364. As regent, dealt with JACQUERIE and reformist movement of Étienne MARCEL. During his reign, DU GUESCLIN drove English out of France (except Guienne). With his ministers, the MARMOUSETS, he strengthened royal power, founded standing army, reformed taxation. Patron of learning. His son, Charles VI (the Mad, or the Well Beloved), 1368–1422, reigned 1380–1422. Intermittently insane after 1392. France was ruled and plundered by his uncles; by his brother, Louis d'ORLÉANS; by his wife, ISABEAU OF BAVARIA. Their rivalries led to civil war between ARMAGNACS AND BURGUNDIANS; laid France open to invasion by HENRY V of England (1415). By Treaty of TROYES (1420) he named Henry his successor. His disinherited son, Charles VII (the Victorious, or the Well Served), 1403–61, repudiated the treaty. Still called dauphin (or, in derision, "king of Bourges"), he ruled indolently over what parts of France remained to him S of the Loire, but in 1429 JOAN OF ARC spurred him to action and had him crowned king at Rheims. In 1435 he won the alliance of Burgundy against England, and in 1453 he ended the HUNDRED YEARS WAR

by expelling the last English from France. He reorganized the army and, with the help of Jacques CŒUR, restored the finances. The PRAGMATIC SANCTION OF BOURGES (1438) and the suppression of the PRAGUERIE (1440) strengthened royal authority against Church and nobles. His last years were troubled by rebellions of his son, Louis XI. Charles VIII, 1470–98, son of Louis XI, reigned 1483–98. His sister, Anne de Beaujeu, regent during his minority, arranged his marriage with ANNE OF BRITTANY. In 1495 Charles began the ITALIAN WARS with the short-lived conquest of Naples. Charles IX, 1550–74, reigned 1560–74, at first under the regency of his mother, CATHERINE DE' MEDICI. Later chose COLIGNY as chief adviser, but was swayed to take part in massacre of SAINT BARTHOLOMEW'S DAY (1572). Charles X, 1757–1836, was known as count of Artois before he succeeded his brother, LOUIS XVIII, in 1824. Led powerful ultraroyalist group before his accession; appointed such reactionaries as VILLÈLE, J. A. de POLIGNAC as premiers. Liberal and capitalist forces joined to bring about JULY REVOLUTION of 1830. Charles abdicated and died in exile.

Charles, kings of Hungary. Charles I (Charles Robert of Anjou), 1288–1342, grandson of Charles II of Naples; son-in-law of Stephen V of Hungary. Elected king 1308; crowned 1310; founder of Hungarian branch of ANGEVIN dynasty. Reorganized army on feudal basis; increased city privileges. Followed dynastic foreign policy, securing succession to Poland for his oldest son, Louis I of Hungary. Charles II: see CHARLES III, king of Naples. Charles III: see CHARLES VI, emperor. Charles IV: see CHARLES I, emperor of Austria.

Charles, kings of Naples. Charles I, 1226–85, count of Anjou and Provence, youngest brother of Louis IX of France, championed the papal cause against MANFRED, was crowned king of Naples and Sicily by Pope Clement IV in 1266. Had his rival CONRADIN executed (1268). Won hegemony over Italy as leader of Guelphs; conquered Albania from Byzantium. In 1282 Sicily rebelled (see SICILIAN VESPERS) and chose PETER III of Aragon as king. War against Aragonese continued until 1302 under his son, Charles II, 1248–1309, king of Naples and count of Provence (1285–1309). Charles III (Charles of Durazzo), 1345–86, king of Naples (1381–86), was a great-grandson of Charles II. JOANNA I adopted him as heir but later repudiated him in favor of Louis of Anjou (LOUIS I of Naples). Charles invaded Naples, was crowned by the pope (1381), and imprisoned Joanna (who died by his order). Elected king of Hungary as Charles II (1385), he was murdered soon afterward.

Charles II or Charles the Bad, 1332–87, king of Navarre (1349–87). Carried on long feud with his father-in-law, John II of France. Helped suppress JACQUERIE (1358). Chosen by Étienne MARCEL to defend Paris against dauphin, he betrayed his trust.

Charles I, 1863–1908, king of Portugal (1889–1908). Yielded to British "ultimatum" (1890) which demanded cessation of Portuguese colonial expansion. His attempt to foster dictatorship under João Franco caused violent reaction. Charles and the heir apparent were shot. Manuel II succeeded him.

Charles, kings of Spain. Charles I: see CHARLES V, emperor. Charles II, 1661–1700, king of Spain, Naples, and Sicily (1665–1700), last of the Spanish Hapsburgs, saw his country weakened by wars with Louis XIV. Died childless. War of the SPANISH SUCCESSION broke out on his death. Charles III, 1716–88, son of Philip V by Elizabeth Farnese, was duke of Parma and Piacenza (1731–35) and king of Naples and Sicily (1735–59) before succeeding his half-brother Ferdinand VI as king of Spain (1759–88). Entered Seven Years War after signing FAMILY COMPACT of 1761 with France; intervened (1779) in American Revolution on American side (for territorial changes, see PARIS, TREATY OF, 1763 and 1783). With his minister FLORIDABLANCA he restored some prosperity in Spain. His son, Charles IV, 1748–1819, king of Spain (1788–1808) was dominated by Queen MARÍA LUISA and his minister GODOY. Withdrew from French Revolutionary Wars 1795, entered disastrous alliance with France (1796), which led in 1807 to PENINSULAR WAR. Palace revolution of 1808 forced him to abdicate in favor of his son, FERDINAND VII, but Napoleon I soon afterward enticed both Charles and Ferdinand to Bayonne, forced both to abdicate, and held them captive until 1814.

Charles, kings of Sweden. Charles IX, 1550–1611, youngest son of Gustavus I. Acted as regent from 1592; established Lutheranism as state religion; had his nephew, SIGISMUND III of Poland, deposed as king of Sweden (1599); accepted crown 1604. His expansionist policy involved him in wars with Poland and Denmark, which continued after his death under his son, Gustavus II. **Charles X** (Charles Gustavus), 1622–60, succeeded on the abdication of his cousin Christina (1654). Invaded Poland, took Warsaw and Cracow (1655), but was expelled after miracle of CZESTOCHOWA. Russia and Denmark having declared war, he threatened Copenhagen and forced Denmark to accept Treaty of ROSKILDE (1658), but war was resumed in same year. A regency for his son, **Charles XI,** 1655–97, ended the war in 1660 with Peace of OLIVA and Treaty of Copenhagen (confirming that of Roskilde). Charles sided with France in last of Dutch Wars and was defeated at Fehrbellin by Frederick William of Brandenburg (1675) but retained Pomerania at Treaty of Saint-Germain (1679). In 1682 he received absolute powers from the Riksdag. His son and successor, **Charles XII,** 1682–1718, was faced in 1699 by a Russo-Polish-Danish alliance which precipitated the NORTHERN WAR (1700–1721). An extraordinarily brilliant but foolhardy strategist, Charles quickly crushed Denmark, routed Peter the Great, and overran Poland, but his Russian campaign of 1708–9 ended disastrously at Poltava. Charles fled to Turkey and persuaded Sultan Ahmed III to declare war on Russia, but after the Russo-Turkish peace of 1711 he was requested to leave Turkey. Charles, residing at Bender, flatly refused and ultimately defended his house with only a handful of men against a whole Turkish army (1713). Taken a prisoner to Adrianople, he finally left in 1714. He invaded Norway in 1716 and was killed by stray bullet while besieging the fortress of Fredrikssten. His heroic failure cost Sweden its rank as a great power. **Charles XIII,** 1748–1818, king of Sweden (1809–18) and Norway (1814–18) succeeded his nephew GUSTAVUS IV. He accepted a constitution, made peace with Russia (to which he ceded Finland), France, and Denmark, and adopted as heir the French Napoleonic marshal Jean Baptiste Jules Bernadotte (1763–1844; b. Pau, France), who later succeeded him as king of Sweden and Norway styled **Charles XIV.** With the consent of Napoleon, he had agreed to his adoption by Charles XIII (1810) and actually governed in the name of the infirm king. He joined the allies against Napoleon I, played an important part in the battle of Leipzig (1813), and secured the union of NORWAY with Sweden (1814). His reign was an era of economic progress, but his hostility to the liberals made him unpopular. **Charles XV,** 1826–72, king of Sweden and Norway (1859–72), Bernadotte's grandson, was liberal and popular. His reign was one of reforms, including creation of bicameral parliament. **Charles (Philip Arthur George),** 1948–, English prince, heir apparent to British throne; son of Elizabeth II and duke of Edinburgh. Was created prince of Wales in 1958.

Charles, dukes of Lorraine. Charles IV, 1604–75, succeeded to duchy in 1624 but lost it repeatedly to Louis XIV because of his anti-French policy. He fought as a general in imperial service. His nephew, **Charles V** (Charles Leopold), 1643–90, fought successfully against the Turks at Vienna and in Hungary but never recovered Lorraine.

Charles, Jacques Alexandre César (zhäk′ äleksä′dru säzär′ shärl′), 1746–1823, French physicist. Worked in electricity and aeronautics; ascended in hydrogen balloon (1783). **Charles's law:** at constant pressure, volume of a gas is directly proportional to temperature.

Charles, river in E Mass., flowing c.47 mi. past Cambridge and Boston to Boston Bay. Harvard boat races.

Charles, Cape, E Va., S point of Eastern Shore (separates Chesapeake Bay from Atlantic Ocean) opposite Cape Henry. Ferries connect to Va. mainland.

Charles, Lake, SW La. Calcasieu R. is its inlet and outlet and connects it with Intracoastal Waterway and Gulf of Mexico. Lake Charles city on shores.

Charles Albert, 1798–1849, king of Sardinia (1831–49). To forestall revolution he granted constitution of 1848 (in force until 1947). Fought two compaigns (1848,1849) of RISORGIMENTO against Austria. Routed at Novara, he abdicated in favor of his son, Victor Emmanuel II.

Charles Augustus, 1757–1828, duke and, after 1815, grand duke of Saxe-Weimar. Friend and patron of GOETHE. Played influential role in German politics.

Charles Borromeo, Saint (böröma′ō), 1538–84, Italian churchman; nephew of Pius IV. Made a cardinal and papal secretary of state, he brought about reopening of the Council of Trent and pushed the Catholic Reform. As bishop of Milan, he rigorously reformed clerical life and education. Feast: Nov. 4.

Charlesbourg, town (pop. 14,308), S Que., Canada, on St. Charles R. just N of Quebec. One of oldest parishes in Que., settled 1659 as Bourg Royal.

Charles City, city (1965 pop. 10,419), NE Iowa, on Cedar R., NNW of Waterloo; settled c.1850.

Charles Edward Stuart: see STUART or STEWART, JAMES FRANCIS EDWARD.

Charles Martel (märtĕl′), 688?–741, Frankish mayor of the palace (714–41). United all Merovingian kingdoms under his rule. Halted Moslem invasion of Europe in battle of Tours or Poitiers (732), one of decisive battles in history. Father of Pepin the Short; grandfather of Charlemagne.

Charles Mound, hill, 1,241 ft. high, NW Ill., NE of Galena near Wis. line; state's highest point.

Charles of Blois (blwä), c.1319–1364, French prince; nephew of Philip VI. One of claimants in War of the BRETON SUCCESSION; killed at Auray. Beatified.

Charles of Valois (välwä′), 1270–1325, French prince; third son of Philip III; father of Philip VI. Sought thrones of Sicily, Byzantium, Rome, and Arles—all without success—and campaigned for Pope Boniface VIII in Italy. Took Florence 1301 and exiled Dante, who in *The Divine Comedy* placed him in Purgatory.

Charles of Viana (vēä′nä), 1421–61, Spanish prince; son of Queen Blanche of Navarre (d. 1442) and John II of Aragon. Ruled Navarre after 1442, but became involved in civil war with his father. Died soon after John had recognized him as heir.

Charles Robert of Anjou: see CHARLES I, king of Hungary.

Charles's law: see CHARLES, JACQUES ALEXANDRE CÉSAR.

Charles the Bad: see CHARLES II, king of Navarre.

Charles the Bold, 1433–77, duke of Burgundy (1467–77), son of PHILIP THE GOOD. Renewed conflict with LOUIS XI of France, whose lifelong adversary he remained. Master of Burgundy, Franche-Comté, and Low Countries, he dreamed of restoring kingdom of Lotharingia. His annexation of Lorraine and several Alsatian towns aroused the Swiss, who defeated him at Grandson and Morat (1476) and at Nancy, where he was killed. His empire fell apart after the accession of his daughter, MARY OF BURGUNDY.

Charles the Great, emperor: see CHARLEMAGNE.

Charleston. 1 City (1966 pop. 13,611), E Ill., SE of Decatur. Industrial, rail, and trade center in agr. area. Here are Eastern Illinois Univ. and Lincoln Log Cabin State Park (site of Thomas Lincoln farmhouse). **2** City (pop. 65,925), SE S.C., on p[ ] insula between Ashley and Cooper rivers at hea[ ] bay formed by them. On or in bay are Sulliva[ ] (site of Fort MOULTRIE), James Isl., Morris I[ ] SUMTER, and Castle Pinckney (fortificati[ ] 1797). State's oldest city, it has fine harb[ ] tensive coastwise and foreign trade. Varied industries, mfg., truck farming, and fishing in area. Hq. of sixth U.S. naval district (with naval hospital, shipyard, ammunition depot and SE division of U.S. Corps of Engineers. Settled 1670 by English under William Sayle, it survived Spanish and Indian threats to become major seaport and cultural center. Held by British in Revolution, 1780–82. The S.C. ordinance of secession was passed here Dec., 1860; Fort Sumter fired on April 12, 1861. Besieged by Union forces, Charleston finally fell in Feb., 1865. Old buildings and landmarks include St. Michael's Episcopal Church (begun 1752), the Battery, and Cabbage Row (original Catfish Row of DuBose Heyward's *Porgy*). Fine beaches, magnolia and cypress gardens, and annual azalea festival attract tourists. Seat of The CITADEL—THE MILITARY COLLEGE OF SOUTH CAROLINA, and Col. of Charleston. Nearby is colonial town of Dorchester. **3** City (pop. 85,796), state cap., W central W.Va., on Kanawha R. at mouth of Elk R. State's largest city and important rail and trade center for many adjacent "company" towns. Grew around site of Fort Lee, chartered as Charles Town 1794. Became permanent cap. 1885. Capitol (1932) was designed by C*a*ss Gilbert. Seat of Morris Harvey Col., Mason Col. of Music and Fine Arts, and branch of WEST VIRGINIA UNIVERSITY. West Virginia State Col. and site of Booker T. Washington's boyhood home are nearby.

Charles Town, city (pop. 3,329), W.Va., in E Panhandle SW of Harpers Ferry; laid out 1786 by George Washington's brother Charles, whose home still stands. John Brown was tried (1859) and hanged here. Near by is "Harewood," where Dolly Madison was married. City now trade center for industrial town, Ransom, and for farm and horse-breeding area. Races are held.

Charlestown. 1 Part of BOSTON, Mass., between Mystic and Charles rivers; settled 1629, included in Boston 1874. Scene of battle of BUNKER HILL, June 17, 1775. **2** Town (pop. 2,576), SW N.H., on Connecticut R., S of Claremont; settled 1740. Defended by Phineas Stevens against French and Indian attacks in King George's War.

Charles William Ferdinand, 1735–1806, duke of Brunswick (1780–1806). Prussian field marshal in Seven Years War; commander (1792–94) of Austro-Prussian armies in the FRENCH REVOLUTIONARY WARS. His son was FREDERICK WILLIAM, duke of Brunswick.

Charlet, Nicolas Toussaint (nēkŏlä′ tōōsĕ′ shärlā′), 1792–1845, French lithographer, best known for scenes of the Napoleonic Wars. Also worked in oil and water color.

Charleville: see MÉZIÈRES.

Charlevoix, Pierre François Xavier de (pyĕr′ fräswä′ zävyä′ dù shärlùvwä′), 1682–1761, French Jesuit traveler and historian. Traveled in New France 1705–9 and 1720. His *Histoire de la Nouvelle France* (1744; Eng. tr., 6 vols., 1900) is only full account of interior America in early 18th cent.

Charlevoix (shär′lùvoi), city (pop. 2,751), N Mich., on L. Michigan, NE of Traverse City; settled 1852. Resort, with fishing on L. Charlevoix. Has nuclear power plant. Vicinity rich in Indian mounds.

Charlot, Jean (zhä′ shärlō′), 1898–, American painter, b. France. A favorite subject is the Mexican Indian. Wrote *Art from the Mayans to Disney* (1939).

Charlotte (Sophia), 1744–1818, queen consort of George III of England. During king's mental illness, she was given charge of his person and household.

Charlotte (shär′lùt), city (pop. 201,564), S N.C., near S.C. line; settled c.1750. State's largest city and leading commercial and industrial center of piedmont region. Transportation hub and distribution point in cotton-growing, dairying, and farming area. MECKLENBURG DECLARATION OF INDEPENDENCE signed here May, 1775. Occupied by Cornwallis, Sept.–Oct., 1780. Here are Queens Col., Johnson C. Smith Univ., and a branch of the Univ. of NORTH CAROLINA.

Charlotte Amalie (ùmäl′yù), city (pop. c.12,900), cap. of VIRGIN ISLANDS (U.S.), on St. Thomas, founded 1673.

Charlotte Harbor, inlet of Gulf of Mexico, SW Fla. Islands at mouth. Receives Myakka and Peace rivers.

Charlottesville, city (pop. 29,427), central Va., on Rivanna R., NW of Richmond, in piedmont farm region; founded 1762. Seat of Univ. of VIRGINIA. Burgoyne's captured army quartered near here 1779–80, and Tarleton raided town 1781. Nearby are MONTICELLO; "Ash Lawn," home of James Monroe; and birthplaces of Meriwether Lewis and G. R. Clark.

Charlottetown, provincial cap. and only city (pop. 18,-318) of Prince Edward Isl., Canada, on S coast. Chief port, with steamship lines and shipbuilding. Seat of Prince of Wales Col. (1860; affiliated with Dalhousie Univ.) and St. Dunstan Univ. (affiliated with Laval Univ.). Founded as French trading post in early 18th cent. Town laid out 1768. Scene of **Charlottetown Conference** of Maritime Provs. (1864), which began Canadian confederation.

Charolais (shärôlä′), small region and former county, E central France, named for Charolles, a town in Saône-et-Loire dept. Cattle breeding. Under dukes of Burgundy 1390–1477; then under Hapsburg (Spanish) rule until annexation by Louis XIV, who incorporated it into Burgundy prov. after 1674.

Charon (kā′rŏn), in Greek mythology, ferryman of Hades, who bore newly arrived dead across the STYX.

Charpentier, Gustave (güstäv′ shärpätyä′), 1860–1956, French composer. His opera *Louise*, reflecting Parisian bohemian life, has been very popular.

chartered companies, associations for foreign trade or colonization that appeared with expansion of European national states. Chartered by the state, they had trade or settlement monopolies in specific colonial areas. Foreshadowed by English Merchants Adventurers. Notable companies were British (1600) and Dutch (1602) East India companies and Hudson's Bay Co. (1670).

Charterhouse (chär′tùrhous) [Fr.,= Chartreuse], in London, founded as Carthusian monastery 1371; became a boys' school 1611. Now a noted public school. Removed 1872 to Godalming, Surrey. Thackeray describes it in *The Newcomes*.

Charter Oak: see HARTFORD, Conn.

Chartier, Alain (älĕ′ shärtyä′), c.1385–c.1433, French poet, secretary to Charles VII. Wrote *Le Quadrilogue invectif* (1422), anti-English prose pamphlet, and the poem *La Belle Dame sans merci* (1424).

Chartism, workingmen's reform movement in Great Britain, 1838–48. "People's Charter," drafted by William Lovett and Francis Place, advocated universal manhood suffrage and other reforms.

Chartres (shär′trù), town (est. pop. 28,750), cap. of Eure-et-Loir dept., N France; chief center of BEAUCE. Magnificent Cathedral of Notre Dame epitomizes the spirit of French Gothic; its stained glass windows and sculpture are particularly famous.

chartreuse (shärtrûz′), a green or yellow LIQUEUR, originated and long made exclusively by Carthusian monks at La Grande Chartreuse, France.

Chartreuse, Grande (gräd′ shärtrûz′), mountain group (highest point 6,847 ft.), SE France, in Dauphiné Alps. The monastery, founded 1084 by St. Bruno in a high valley, was main seat of CARTHUSIANS until expulsion of order from France (1903). The monks were allowed to return in 1941. The present monastery was built in the 17th cent.

Charybdis (kùrĭb′dĭs), in Greek legend, whirlpool near rock of SCYLLA; home of a greedy monster.

Chase, Salmon P(ortland), 1803–73, American statesman. U.S. Senator from Ohio (1849–55, 1861); antislavery leader. U.S. Secretary of the Treasury (1861–64); responsible for national bank system (estab. 1863). Chief Justice of the United States after 1864. His dissenting opinion in SLAUGHTERHOUSE CASES subsequently became accepted position of the courts as to restrictive force of Fourteenth Amendment. Presided fairly over impeachment trial of Pres. Johnson. Chase earnestly sought the presidency four times, but was never nominated.

Chase, Samuel, 1741–1811, American Revolutionary patriot, signer of Declaration of Independence, Associate Justice of U.S. Supreme Court (1796–1811). Impeached in 1804 on charge of political partiality, but acquitted.

Chase, Stuart, 1888–, American writer. Investigated meat-packing industry (1917–22), and was long with Labor Bureau, Inc. Among his books are *Men and Machines* (1929), *The Economy of Abundance* (1934), *Rich Land, Poor Land* (1936), and *The Tyranny of Words* (1938).

Chase, William Merritt, 1849–1916, American painter and teacher. Known for portraits and still lifes.

Chassériau, Théodore (täödôr' shäsärēō'), 1819–56, French painter, only artist of the time to combine successfully Ingres's sense of line and Delacroix's rich color and vitality.

Chassidim: see HASIDIM.

chat, largest American warbler. Yellow-breasted chat is shy; nests in E U.S. in thickets and winters in Mexico and Central America. Long-tailed chat is in W North America. In Europe are found the wheatear, the whinchat, and the stonechat.

Chateaubriand, François René, vicomte de (fräswä' rùnä' vēkôt' dù shätōbrēä'), 1768–1848, French author. Visited U.S. 1791; émigré in England until 1800. A royalist, he was foreign minister (1823–24) and active in politics until 1830. Wrote *The Genius of Christianity* (1802; Eng. tr., 1856), including the famous extracts *Atala* and *René*. Last work was *Mémoires d'outre-tombe* [memoirs from beyond the tomb] (1849–50). A founder of French romanticism, he is noted for his rich, noble, and poetic style.

Château d'If (dēf'), castle on small If isl. off Marseilles, SE France. Built 1524; long a state prison. Scene of Dumas's *Count of Monte Cristo*.

Château Gaillard (gīär'), castle, N France, on the Seine near Les Andelys, SE of Rouen. Built 1197 by Richard I of England to protect Normandy from French; taken 1204 by Philip II. Ruins are splendid example of medieval military architecture.

Chateaugay (shätùgä'), Fr. *Châteauguay,* river rising in Chateaugay L. in Adirondacks, NE N.Y., and flowing through Quebec to St. Lawrence R. below Montreal. Strong American troops under Wade Hampton were defeated (1813) by a small Canadian-Indian force on its Quebec shores.

Château-Thierry (shätō-tyērē'), town (pop. 7,939), Aisne dept., N France, on Marne R. Focal point in second Marne battle (1918), in which last German offensive was stopped largely by U.S. troops.

Chatham, William Pitt, 1st earl of: see PITT, WILLIAM.

Chatham, city (pop. 29,826), S Ont., Canada, on Thames R., which links it to Great Lakes. Industrial center in rich farming and fruit-raising region.

Chatham, municipal borough (pop. 48,989), Kent, England, on Medway R.; major naval station. First dockyard estab. by Elizabeth I in 1588.

Châtillon, Sébastien: see CASTALION, SÉBASTIEN.

Chatrian, Alexandre: see ERCKMANN-CHATRIAN.

Chattahoochee (chătúhōō'chē), river rising in NE Ga. and flowing c.418 mi. S to join Flint R. in L. Seminole and form Apalachicola R. at Fla. line. Forms part of Ga.–Ala. and Ga.–Fla. lines. Navigable to Columbus, Ga. Columbia, Walter F. George, and Buford dams are in river.

Chattanooga (chătùnōō'gù), city (pop. 130,009), E Tenn.. on Tennessee R. near Ga. line; settled 1828 as trading post. Almost surrounded by mountains, including Missionary Ridge, Signal Mt., and Lookout Mt. First a river port, it grew with coming of railroads (1840s, 1850s. Strategically important in Civil War (see CHATTANOOGA CAMPAIGN). Nearby is Chickamauga and Chattanooga Natl. Military Park on battlefield sites. City has both Confederate and national cemeteries. Important industrial, rail, market,

and resort center for wide area yielding coal, farm produce, and timber. Mfg. of textiles, chemicals. wood and metal products. Power augmented by TVA project. Here are Univ. of Chattanooga and Rock City Gardens. U.S. Coast Guard station nearby.

Chattanooga campaign, Aug.–Nov., 1863, in Civil War. Chattanooga, as center of communications, was important Union objective. In 1863 Federals under W. S. Rosecrans drove Braxton Bragg from area. Bragg attacked at Chickamauga Sept. 19–20, but G. H. Thomas held line until ordered by Rosecrans to Chattanooga. When Bragg besieged town, U. S. Grant opposed him; with Joseph Hooker and Thomas Grant drove Confederates from Lookout Mt. in Battle above the Clouds, and then from Missionary Ridge.

Chatterjee, Bankim Chandra (bùng'kĭm chŭn'drù chä'-tûrjē), 1838–94, Indian nationalist writer. Popularized a Bengali prose style that became the vehicle of nationalistic expression. *Bandemataram* (Hail to the Mother), a song in one of his novels, became Indian national anthem.

Chatterton, Thomas, 1752–70, English poet. At 12 he was composing his "Rowley Poems," claiming that they were copies of 15th-cent. manuscripts. Came to London in 1770, failed to sell his poems, poisoned himself. His genius was recognized later.

Chaucer, Geoffrey (jĕf'rē), c.1340–1400, English poet. The few facts known of his life based mainly on official records. Page in Prince Lionel's household (1357–58), later probably in service of John of Gaunt. Captured while with Edward III's army in France (1359–60), but ransomed. By 1366 married to Philippa (de Roet?), lady-in-waiting to queen. By 1367 valet in king's household. Among frequent diplomatic missions to Continent (1370–78) were trips to Italy (1372–73, 1378). From 1374 held several official posts: comptroller of customs on wool and hides at London (1374–86) and of petty customs (1382–86), knight of the shire for Kent (1386), clerk of the king's works (1389–91). First important poems, *Book of the Duchess* (1369) and partial translation of the ROMAN DE LA ROSE, draw on French sources. From his visits to Italy until c.1385, strongly influenced by Italian literature, especially by Dante in the *House of Fame* and the *Parliament of Fowls*. His height of powers produced *Troilus and Criseyde* (c.1385–86) based on Boccaccio's *Filostrato* (see TROILUS AND CRESSIDA) and began the *Canterbury Tales* (c.1387), richly varied collection of stories represented as told by pilgrims travelling together from London to shrine of St. Thomas at Canterbury. This narrative frame and the characterization of pilgrims vividly presented in Prologue and links between tales. Chaucer is most important figure in English literature before Shakespeare. Helped to reestablish English language as vehicle for literature and introduced iambic PENTAMETER into English verse. Always acknowledged great narrative poet, only in recent times has he been recognized as one of greatest English metrists.

Chaudière (shōdyĕr'), river rising in SE Que., Canada, N of Maine-Que. line, and flowing 120 mi. NW to St. Lawrence R. above Quebec.

Chaudière Falls (shōdyĕr'), 50-ft. drop in Ottawa R., SE Ont., Canada, within city of Ottawa.

Chauliac, Guy de (gē' dù shōlyäk') c.1300–c.1370, French surgeon, author of noted work on surgery.

chaulmoogra oil (chălmōō'grù), oil from seeds of an Asiatic tree, *Taraktogenos* (or *Hydnocarous*) *kurzii.* Formerly used to treat leprosy; now largely replaced by antibiotics and sulfa drugs.

Chaumette, Pierre Gaspard (pyĕr' gäspär' shōmĕt'), 1763–94, French revolutionist. Leader of Paris commune; extremist member of CORDELIERS, after whose downfall he was guillotined.

Chaumont (shōmō'), town (est. pop. 19,346), cap. of Haute-Marne dept., NE France. Linen and cutlery mfg. For treaty signed here 1814, see QUADRUPLE ALLIANCE.

Chauncy, Charles, 1705–87, American Congregational clergyman. Minister of First Church, Boston (1727–87). Opposed revivalist preaching and led liberals in theology in the disputes following the "Great Awakening." A patriot, he set forth political philosophy of American Revolution.

Chausson, Ernest (shōsō'), 1855–1899, French composer of chamber, orchestral, and operatic music. His work combines elements of romanticism and impressionism. Best known for his Symphony in B Flat and the *Poème* for violin and orchestra.

Chautauqua (shŭtôk'wû), resort village, W N.Y., on W shore of Chautauqua L. CHAUTAUQUA MOVEMENT began here.

Chautauqua Lake, 18 mi. long, 1–3 mi. wide, SW N.Y., near L. Erie, in resort and fruit-growing area.

Chautauqua movement, adult education similar to lyceum movement. First institute estab. 1874 at Chautauqua, N.Y., as development of Methodist Episcopal summer Sunday-school institute. Developed into eightweek program of courses and lectures in arts, science, humanities, and religion. Chautauquas were formed in other communities and continued until c.1924. Assembly at Chautauqua still draws thousands each year.

Chaux-de-Fonds, La (lä shō-dů-fô'), city (pop. 38,906), Neuchâtel canton, W Switzerland; a center for making of watches.

Chavannes, Puvis de: see PUVIS DE CHAVANNES.

Chávez, Carlos (chä'väs), 1899–, Mexican composer and conductor. He has done extensive research in native Indian music, which has influenced his own writing. His works include ballets, symphonies, a piano concerto, and choral works.

Chavín de Huantar (chävēn' dä wän'tär), archaeological site, NE Peru, center of an early Andean civilization which flourished c.700–c.200 B.C.

Chayefsky, Paddy (Sydney), 1923–, American playwright. His realistic dramas for television (1955) were later made into films (e.g., *Marty*, 1956; *The Bachelor Party*, 1957) or stage drama (*The Middle of the Night*, 1956). His stage plays include *Gideon* (1962) and *The Passion of Josef D.* (1964).

Chaykovsky, Nikolai Vasilyevich (nyĭkŭlī' vŭsē'lyù-vĭch chĭkôf'skē), 1850–1926, Russian revolutionist, a leader of Chaykovsky circle (1870s), a group that advocated melding intellectual and peasant interests. He was anti-Bolshevik leader 1917–19.

Chazars: see KHAZARS.

Cheaha (chē'hô), peak, 2,407 ft. high, in Talladega Mts., E Ala.; highest point in Ala.

Cheapside, street in the City of London, most important market center of medieval London. Tournaments and some executions were held here. Mermaid Tavern was in district.

Cheb, Czechoslovakia: see EGER.

Chebeague Island: see GREAT CHEBEAGUE ISLAND.

Cheboksary (chĕbŭksä'rē), city (1965 est. pop. 163,-000), cap. of Chuvash Autonomous SSR, central European RSFSR, on the Volga. Center of agr. region.

Cheboygan (shĭboi'gŭn), city (pop. 5,859), N Mich., on S channel of Straits of Mackinac at mouth of Cheboygan R.; settled c.1845. A resort, farm-trade center, and commercial fishing port.

Chechen-Ingush Autonomous Soviet Socialist Republic (chĭchĕn'-ĭngōōsh'), republic (7,452 sq. mi.; 1965 est. pop. 983,000), SW European RSFSR, in N Caucasus; cap. Grozny. Oil fields (near Grozny), oil refineries, chemicals. Population is Russian, Chechen, and Ingush. Chechen and Ingush are Sunni Moslems speaking a Caucasian language. Chechen fought Russian conquest in 19th cent., particularly during Shamyl rebellion. Raised from oblast to autonomous republic 1936. Dissolved 1944 by USSR for alleged collaboration with Germans in Second World War. Status restored 1957 and population (deported 1944 to Kazakhstan) allowed to return.

Che-chiang, province, China: see CHEKIANG.

checkers, game for two players, played with 24 counters on board with 64 squares; known in England as draughts. Played in Europe since 16th cent.; similar game known to ancients.

Cheektowaga (chĕk"tōwä'gù), town (1964 pop. 93,-986), W N.Y., a suburb E of Buffalo; settled c.1808.

cheese, known as food since antiquity, is today made mainly from milk of cows, sheep, or goats. The making of all the varied kinds begins with coagulation of casein, the chief milk protein, by enzyme action or by lactic acid, or a combination. Hard cheeses include Cheddar (originally from England), Edam and Gouda (Holland), Emmental or Gruyère (Switzerland), and Parmesan (Italy). Stilton, Roquefort, Gorgonzola, and American brick are semihard. Soft cheeses may be either fresh (unripened), e.g., cream cheese and cottage cheese, or softened by microorganisms (which also develop flavor) in ripening: Camembert, Brie, and Limburger.

cheetah (chē'tù) or **hunting leopard,** member of cat family, native to Asia and Africa. From early times it was trained to hunt game. *Acinonyx jubatus* of Africa is about the size of a leopard and has long legs and a tawny black-spotted coat.

Chefoo (chē'fōō'), city (pop. c.227,000), Shantung prov., China, port on Pohai. Became treaty port 1858. Formerly named Yentai.

Chehalis, river, rising in SW Wash. near Willapa Hills and flowing c.115 mi. NW to Grays Harbor. Navigable lower course.

Cheka: see SECRET POLICE.

Chekhov, Anton Pavlovich (chē'kôf), 1860–1904, Russian author. His prevailing themes are man's essential loneliness and frustration and the dullness and stagnation of Russian life in his day. Sympathetic yet realistic toward his characters, he varied these themes in hundreds of masterful short stories and in the dramas *The Sea Gull* (1896), *Uncle Vanya* (1899), *The Three Sisters* (1901), and *The Cherry Orchard* (1904). Widely translated, Chekhov had immense influence on contemporary literature.

Chekiang (jū'-jyäng'), province (c.40,000 sq. mi.; pop. c.23,589,903), SE China, on East China Sea; cap. Hangchow. Includes many islands, notably Chusan Archipelago. Most fertile area is Yangtze delta, where rice, cotton, tobacco, and peanuts are grown. Also produces silk, tea, and jute. Iron, coal, and alum mined. Also spelled Che-chiang.

Chelan, Lake, c.50 mi. long, ½–1½ mi. wide, N central Wash., impounded by L. Chelan Dam. Fed by streams from Cascade Range; drained by Chelan R. **Chelan Mountains,** E branch of Cascades, run parallel to lake.

Chelmsford (chĕmz'fûrd), town (pop. 15,130), NE Mass., SW of Lowell; settled 1633. Granite quarries.

Chelsea, London, part of Royal Borough of KENSINGTON AND CHELSEA since 1965; a literary and artistic quarter.

Chelsea, city (pop. 33,749), E Mass., an industrial and residential suburb NE of Boston; settled 1624. Has printing firms and naval hospital.

Cheltenham (chĕlt'nùm), municipal borough (pop. 71,968), Gloucestershire, England. A fashionable spa near the Cotswolds, it is known for its schools and festivals of art, music, and literature.

Chelyabinsk (chĭlyä'bĭnsk), city (1965 est. pop. 805,-000), SW Asiatic RSFSR, W Siberia, in Ural foothills, on Trans-Siberian RR. A major metallurgical center of USSR, it grew rapidly after building of its first steel mill (1930).

Chelyuskin, Cape (chĭlyōō'skĭn), northernmost point (lat. 77°41'N) of Asiatic continent, on Taimyr peninsula, RSFSR. Named after 18th-cent. Russian navigator. Airfield; observation post.

chemical reaction, action taking place during change in internal molecular structure of substance, which loses characteristic properties. In some reactions, heat given off (exothermic); in some, heat absorbed (endothermic). When compound substance is broken down into constituents, it is simple decomposition. When two compounds react to form two new compounds, it is double decomposition. In replacement reactions, place of element in compound is taken by another element. In chemical combination (SYNTHESIS), elements combine to form compounds. OXIDATION AND REDUCTION are important reactions. Reaction rate depends on temperature, pressure, concentration, CATALYST, etc. EQUATION represents change.

chemical warfare, use in war of poison gases, incendiary compounds, smoke, and biological agents and development of protection against them. In First World War poison gas was used widely. Chlorine first used April 22, 1915, by Germans. In Second World War preparations for chemical warfare made by all major countries, but little resulted in part out of fear of retaliation. Chemistry contributed greatly to making of new types of incendiary bombs and to such implements as flame throwers, which use thickened gasolines (e.g., napalm).

Chemin des Dames (shmē dä däm'), road along crest between Aisne and Ailette rivers, N France. Held by Germans in First World War until they were dislodged in bitter fighting (1917–18).

chemistry, science of interaction of atoms to form new molecular combinations. These interactions, called chemical reactions, result from changes in the electron complement of atoms; nuclear changes are considered in physics. Appearance and behavior of substances are described in physical and chemical properties; changes during reactions are shown by equations. Two categories of matter are elements, represented by symbols; and compounds, represented by formulas. Composition of compounds determined by analysis: qualitative, for elements present, and quantitative, for their proportion. Organic chemistry is study of carbon compounds, and inorganic is study of other elements and compounds plus simple oxides of carbon and metallic carbonates. See also ALCHEMY; BIOCHEMISTRY.

Chemnitz (kĕm'nĭts), city (est. pop. 286,016), East Germany, in former state of Saxony, on Chemnitz R., near one of world's largest open-pit lignite mines. Leading industrial center, mfg. of machine tools, machinery, chemicals, textiles. Chartered 1143. Suffered greatly in Thirty Years War and Second World War. Renamed Karl-Marx-Stadt in 1953.

Chemulpo: see INCHON.

Chemung (shĭmŭng'), river formed near Corning, S N.Y., and flowing c.45 mi. SE, past Elmira, to Susquehanna R. near Sayre, Pa. Valley was scene of fighting in Revolutionary campaign of John SULLIVAN.

Chenab, India: see PUNJAB.

Chenango (shĭnăng'gō), river rising in central N.Y., SW of Utica and flowing c.100 mi. S and SW to Susquehanna R. Receives Tioughnioga R. at Chenango Forks.

Chengchow (chŭng'jō'), city (pop. c.766,000), cap. of Honan prov., China. Important rail center. Textile mfg. and food processing. Formerly named Chenghsien.

Chenghsien, China: see CHENGCHOW.

Chenghwa, China: see ALTAI, town.

Chengteh (chang'dû'), city (pop. c.510,000), N Hopeh prov., China. Commercial center. Was summer cap. of Ch'ing dynasty. Cap. of Jehol prov. until 1956; was formerly called Jehol.

Chengtu (chŭng'dōō'), city (pop. c.1,107,000), cap. of Szechwan prov., SW China; port on Min R. Cultural center of region since anc. times. One of the earliest (9th cent. A.D.) printing centers of China.

Chénier, André (ädrā' shänyā'), 1762–94, French poet. His pamphlets against the excesses of the French Revolutionists led to his execution. His poems range from classical lyrics, such as *La Jeune Captive, Élégies,* and *Bucoliques,* to political satires.

Chennault, Claire Lee (shĕ'nôlt"), 1890–1958, U.S. general. Formed American Volunteer Group ("Flying

Tigers") in China (1941). Headed U.S. air task force in China (1942–45).

Cheops, anc. Egyptian king: see KHUFU.

Chepachet, R.I.: see GLOUCESTER, R.I.

Chephren: see KHAFRE.

Chequamegon Bay (shĭkwä'mûgŭn), arm of L. Superior, N Wis. Visited by French explorers in 17th cent. Father Allouez founded mission on its shore 1665. Ashland and Washburn are on bay.

Cher (shĕr), department (2,820 sq. mi.; pop. 293,514), central France, in Berry; cap. Bourges. It is traversed by the **Cher** river, 200 mi. long, which flows from Massif Central NW to join Loire near Tours.

Cherbourg (shĕrbōōr'), city (est. pop. 38,262), Manche dept., NW France, on English Channel at tip of Cotentin peninsula. Fortified naval station since 17th cent.; transatlantic port since First World War.

Cherchel (shĕrshĕl'), town (pop. c.16,130), Algeria; a Mediterranean port. As Caesarea it was cap. of Mauretania. Has many relics of Roman period.

Cheremiss, RSFSR: see MARI AUTONOMOUS SOVIET SOCIALIST REPUBLIC.

Cheremkhovo (chĕrĭmkŏ'vŭ), city (1965 est. pop. 113,000), S central Asiatic RSFSR, on Trans-Siberian RR. Center of Chermkhovo coal basin.

Cherenkov, Pavel Alekseyevich (pä'vĕl' ŭlyĭksyä'ĭvĭch shĕrĕn'kŏf), 1904–, Soviet physicist. Shared with I. M. Frank and I. Y. Tamm the 1958 Nobel Prize in Physics for his discovery of Cherenkov effect (radiation accelerates electrons in water to speeds greater than that of light in same medium) that opened way to new studies of high-energy particles and cosmic radiation.

Cherepovets (chĕrĭpŭvyĕts'), city (1965 est. pop. 152,-000), NW European RSFSR, on Rybinsk Reservoir. Transportation center of VOLGA-BALTIC WATERWAY.

Cheribon (chĕrĭbŏn'), city (pop. 904,114), N Java, Indonesia. Major port and manufacturing center.

Cherkassy (chĭrkä'sē), city (1965 est. pop. 115,000), central Ukrainian SSR, port on Dnieper R. Seat of Ukrainian hetmans 1386–1694.

Cherkess Autonomous Oblast: see KARACHAI-CHERKESS AUTONOMOUS OBLAST.

Cherkessk (chĭrkĕsk'), city (1965 est. pop. 53,000), cap. of Karachai-Cherkess Autonomous Oblast, Stavropol Territory, SE European RSFSR, on Kuban R. Called Batalpashinsk 1825–1937. Mfg. of electrical equipment.

Chernigov (chĭrnyĕ'gŭf), city (1965 est. pop. 126,000), N Ukraine; agr. center and port on Desna R. One of oldest cities of Kievan state; famous for architectural monuments, many of which were destroyed in Second World War. Those remaining include Spasski Cathedral (c.1036).

Chernovtsy (chĭrnôf'tsē), Ger. *Czernowitz,* Rumanian *Cernauti,* city (1965 est. pop. 172,000), W Ukraine, on Pruth R.; railway junction. Former cap. of Bukovina.

chernozem: see BLACK EARTH.

Cherokee Indians (chĕr'ŭkē), largest and most important single tribe in SE U.S. Language is of the Iroquoian family of Hokan-Siouan stock (see LANGUAGE, table). The Cherokee Nation (estab. 1827) had a constitution providing for elected chief, senate, and house of representatives. The syllabic alphabet invented by Sequoyah gave them writing, and their material culture was high. In 1838 they were brutally removed from their homes and moved to Indian Territory where they became most important of Five Civilized Tribes. Tribe split by differing sympathies in U.S. Civil War. In 1906 tribe disbanded, and Cherokee became U.S. citizens.

Cherrapunji: see ASSAM.

cherry, name for several trees or shrubs of genus *Prunus* and their fruits, grown in home and commercial orchards. There are many varieties derived from two Old World species—*Prunus avium* (sweet cherry) and *P. cerasus* (sour cherry). Fruit is eaten raw and used in preserves, pies, and liqueurs. Flowering cherry is derived from other species and there are many varieties with showy single or double flowers. Species of American wild cherry include chokecherry, pin cherry, and wild black cherry.

Cherry Valley, village (pop. 668), E central N.Y., W of Albany. Tories and Indians led by Walter Butler and Joseph Brant burned most of the village and massacred over 40 people on Nov. 11, 1778.

Chersiphron (kûr'sĭfrŭn), Cretan architect. Traditional builder of the original Ionic temple of Artemis at Ephesus in 550 B.C.

Cherso, Yugoslavia: see CRES.

cherub (chĕr'ŭb), plural **cherubim** (–ŭbĭm), kind of angel, with seraphim attendant upon God. In old Jewish tradition described as winged creatures with human, or often, animal faces; late Christian art pictures them as plump children. Gen. 3.24; Ex. 25.18–22; 37.6–9; 1 Kings 6.23–28; Pss. 18.10; 80.1; Ezek. 10.

Cherubini, Maria Luigi (märē'ä lwē'jē kārōōbē'nē), 1760–1842, Italian composer; lived in Paris after 1788. Composed operas (e.g., *Les Deux Journées, Anacreon, Médée*) and church music.

Chesapeake, U.S. frigate, famous for her role in *Chesapeake* affair (June 22, 1807) and for her battle with British ship *Shannon* (June 1, 1813). In *Chesapeake* affair ship was fired on by British ship *Leopard* when James BARRON refused demand to search *Chesapeake* for British deserters. During battle with the *Shannon* James Lawrence reportedly issued famous last command, "Don't give up the ship!" She was, however, captured.

Chesapeake and Delaware Canal, 19 mi. long, connecting head of Chesapeake Bay near Chesapeake City, Md., with Delaware R. below Delaware City, Del. Built 1824–29; bought by U.S. 1919 and enlarged 1935–39.

Chesapeake and Ohio Canal, former waterway, c.185 mi. long, from Washington, D.C., to Cumberland, Md., running along N bank of Potomac R. Built 1828–50. Had busiest days in 1870s. Sold to U.S. 1938, estab. later as Chesapeake and Ohio Canal Natl. Monument.

Chesapeake & Ohio Railway, U.S. transportation company, with 5,091 mi. of lines in six states, Washington, D.C., and Ont., Canada. Incorporated 1878. Merged with Pere Marquette Railway Co. in 1947 and with Baltimore and Ohio RR in 1963.

Chesapeake Bay, inlet of the Atlantic (c.200 mi. long N–S, 4–40 mi. wide), cutting off Eastern Shore of Md. and Va. from mainland. Enters between Cape Henry and Cape Charles, Va. Receives Susquehanna, Patuxent, Potomac, Rappahannock, York, and James rivers. Important ports on shore are Baltimore, Norfolk, and Hampton Roads. Noted for its fishing (esp. oysters, crabs). Bridge (completed 1952) connects Kent Isl. of Eastern Shore of Md. with Md. mainland. **Chesapeake Bay Bridge-Tunnel,** linking tip of Eastern Shore of Va. (near Cape Charles) with Va. mainland (near Norfolk), was completed 1964. A bridge-tunnel-causeway complex, it stretches 17.6 mi. over and under bay's mouth. Has low-level trestle roadway, two tunnels, four man-made islands (terminals of the tunnels), and two high steel bridges near N end.

Chesapeake City, town pop. (1,104), NE Md., S of Elkton. W end of Chesapeake and Delaware Canal.

Cheselden, William (chē'zŭldŭn), 1688–1752, English surgeon who improved the kidney-stone operation and was author of works on bones and on general anatomy.

Cheshire (chē'shŭr) or **Chester,** maritime county (1,014 sq. mi.; pop. 1,367,860), W central England, co. town Chester. A low, flat, and fertile region; dairy farming extensive and Cheshire cheese famous. Estuaries of chief rivers, Mersey and Dee, form Wirral peninsula in Irish Sea. Chief industries are engineering; salt mining; shipbuilding; mfg. of railroad cars, textiles, chemicals. Communications include Manchester Ship Canal.

Cheshire, town (pop. 13,383), S central Conn., N of New Haven, in farm area; settled 1695. Cheshire Academy for boys is here.

Chesney, Francis Rawdon, 1789–1872, British soldier and explorer in Asia. Demonstrated feasibility of Suez Canal route (1829) and surveyed the Tigris and Euphrates (1835), proving their navigability.

chess [from Persian *shah* = king], game for two players each using 16 counters (a king, a queen, two rooks or castles, two bishops, two knights, and 8 pawns) on board of 64 squares. Probably originated in India. By 13th cent. chess was played all over Western Europe. Modern chess dates from 15th cent.

Chester, county borough (pop. 59,283), co. town of Cheshire, England. Site of important Roman camp, it later was last place in England to surrender to William the Conqueror (1070). Many medieval buildings survive, including cathedral with architecture from Norman to Late Perpendicular. Chester Miracle Plays originated here.

Chester. 1 City (1965 pop. 5,300), S Ill., on Mississippi R., below St. Louis; founded 1819. Shipping center for mining and quarrying area. Nearby is site of old KASKASKIA. **2** City (pop. 63,658), SE Pa., on Delaware R., SW of Philadelphia; settled c.1644 by Swedes as Uppland. Renamed by William Penn. Oldest city in state, it has shipbuilding industry dating from before Civil War. Crozer Theological Seminary and Pennsylvania Military Col. are here.

Chesterfield, Philip Dormer Stanhope, 4th earl of, 1694–1773, English statesman, author of worldly-wise *Letters to His Son* (1774; addressed to his natural son). Lord Chesterfield was rebuked in a famous letter by Samuel Johnson for belated tribute to the *Dictionary*.

Chesterton, G(ilbert) K(eith), 1874–1936, English author, convert to and apologist for Roman Catholicism. His writings include novels (e.g., *The Man Who Was Thursday,* 1908; detective fiction featuring Father Brown), wide-ranging essays, as in *Tremendous Trifles* (1909), and poetry. He also illustrated works by his friend Hilaire Belloc.

chestnut, deciduous tree of genus *Castanea* of N Hemisphere and its edible nuts borne in burs. American chestnut (*Castanea dentata*), native E of the Mississippi now nearly extinct because of chestnut blight, a fungus disease. See also CHINQUAPIN.

Chesuncook Lake (chĭsŭn'kōōk), 22 mi. long and 1–4 mi. wide, N central Maine, NE of Greenville, in hunting and fishing region.

Chevalier, Maurice (shŭvăl'yā), 1888–, French singer and film actor. As dancing partner of Mistinguette and as a star of Paris music halls, he was famous for his charm and inimitable smile.

Chevalier, Michel (mēshĕl' shŭvälyā') 1806–79, French economist, an influential advocate of industrialization and free trade. Favored form of welfare capitalism.

Cheviot (shĭv'ēŭt), city (pop. 10,701), extreme SW Ohio, a suburb WNW of Cincinnati; settled 1818.

Cheviot Hills (chĕv'ēŭt), 35 mi. range on Scotland-England border; once scene of much border strife. Celebrated in the ballad of *Chevy Chase.*

Chevreul, Michel Eugene (mēshĕl' ûzhĕn' shŭvrûl'), 1786–1889, French chemist. Became professor at the natural history museum, Paris, and was its director 1860–79. Noted for research on animal fats; discovered and named olein and stearin.

Chevreuse, Marie de Rohan-Montbazon, duchesse de (märē' dù rōä'-mōbäzō' düshĕs' dù shŭvrûz'), 1600–1679, French beauty, intimate of Anne of Austria. Intrigued against Richelieu; twice exiled. During Fronde she first opposed, then supported, Mazarin.

Chevy Chase, Md.: see BETHESDA.

Chevy Chase Section Four, Md.: see BETHESDA.

chewing gum is usually made from CHICLE, which is melted, sterilized, sweetened, flavored, and shaped into sticks or candy-coated pellets. Insoluble plastics may be mixed with, or substituted for, chicle.

Cheyenne (shĭän'), city (pop. 43,505), state cap., SE Wyo., near Colo. and Nebr. lines N of Denver. Selected as Union Pacific RR division point 1867. Became territorial cap. 1869. Cattle ranching and Black Hills gold stimulated growth in 1870s. State's largest city, it is a sheep and cattle market and center for transportation (air, highway, rail) and shipping. Annual Frontier Days celebration (since 1897). Nearby is Francis E. Warren Air Force Base.

Cheyenne, river, 527 mi. long, rising in E Wyo. and flowing NE to Missouri R. in central S.Dak., above Pierre. Has U.S. project on tributary BELLE FOURCHE; Rapid Valley project, near Rapid City; and Angostura Dam on Cheyenne itself. River's basin is in MISSOURI RIVER BASIN PROJECT.

Cheyenne Indians, North American tribe of Algonquian linguistic family. Divided (c.1830) at headwaters of Platte river into northern band (now in Mont.) and southern band (now in Okla.); both had typical Plains culture. Southern band had severe war (1861–68) with whites, marked by massacre of Indians by U.S. soldiers at Sandy Creek (1864).

Chiang Kai-shek (chěǎng" kī"-shěk', jyäng"), 1887–, Chinese generalissimo and statesman. He is also called Chiang Chung-cheng. Became prominent in Kuomintang in 1923; led the NORTHERN EXPEDITION (1926–28). Originally worked with the Communists, but broke with them in 1927. Held enormous power as Nationalist leader from 1928 to 1948. Led resistance to Japan, 1937–45. In ensuing civil war with Communists was defeated and driven from mainland. By April, 1950, retained only Taiwan (Formosa) and minor islands off the mainland. As head of Taiwan-based Nationalist government and armed forces, continues to challenge Communist rule of mainland. His wife is SOONG MEI-LING.

Chianti, Monti (mōn'tē kyän'tē), small range of Apennines, Tuscany, central Italy. Chianti wine comes from vineyards on its slopes.

Chiapas (chēä'päs), state (28,732 sq. mi.; 1963 est. pop. 1,322,811). S Mexico, on Pacific, between Isthmus of Tehuantepec and Guatemala; cap. TUXTLA. Exploitation of state's natural resources (esp. hardwoods) retarded by its inaccessibility. Airlines and Inter-American Highway have been opening country.

Chiatura (chēŭtōō'rŭ), city (pop. c.19,200), W central Georgian SSR. Large manganese production.

Chibcha (chĭb'chŭ), group of Indian tribes in E Colombian Andes, with a highly developed material culture (agr., mining of emeralds, making of gold-and copperwork, fine textiles). Two chief tribes, headed by Zaque at Tunja and Zipa at Bogotá, were conquered by Jiménez de Quesada (1536–41). Chibchan languages were probably spoken as far N as Nicaragua. Chibchan custom of gilding new rulers probably gave rise to the legend of El Dorado.

Chicago (shĭkä'gō), city (pop. 3,550,404), NE Ill., on L. Michigan. Heart of large metropolitan area, vital Great Lakes port, and busy rail, air, and highway hub. Major printing center and world-famous meatpacking city, with grain elevators and steel mills. Mfg. of machinery, electrical and electronic equipment, furniture, chemicals, clothing, autos, and metal products. Marquette and Jolliet came here 1673, and trading post was founded c.100 years later. Fort Dearborn was estab. 1803. Erie Canal speeded settling of Midwest, and Chicago was platted 1830. Harbor improvements, lake traffic, and settling of prairies brought prosperity; coming of railroads made it mid-continent shipping center. From ashes of great fire of 1871 grew a city of stone and steel. Rapidly growing industries brought thousands of immigrants and labor troubles, especially HAYMARKET SQUARE RIOT of 1886 and Pullman strikes of 1894 (see DEBS, E. V.; ALTGELD, J. P.). City's material progress was evidenced in World's Columbian Exposition of 1893 and Century of Progress Exposition of 1933–34. World's first nuclear chain reaction achieved by scientists here 1942. Opening of St. Lawrence Seaway (1959)

made it major port for overseas shipping. Notable in this Midwest cultural center are Chicago Symphony Orchestra (founded 1891), Art Inst. of Chicago (1879), Chicago Natural History Mus. (1893), Chicago Civic Opera, and Chicago Public Library. Seat of Univ. of CHICAGO, Univ. of ILLINOIS, DePaul Univ., ILLINOIS INSTITUTE OF TECHNOLOGY, LOYOLA UNIVERSITY, Mundelein Col., Roosevelt Univ., and the medical, dental, and law schools of Northwestern Univ. Landmarks include the Loop, LaSalle St. financial district, and Soldier Field.

Chicago, river, NE Ill., formed in Chicago by junction of two branches. Formerly flowed to L. Michigan; flow reversed from lake into Chicago Sanitary and Ship Canal (1900) when canal was joined to Des Plaines R., carrying Chicago's wastes to Mississippi R. Now part of Great Lakes to Gulf of Mexico waterway. River's channel has been deepened.

Chicago, University of, at Chicago; coed.; chartered 1891 (Baptist), opened 1892 with gifts from J. D. Rockefeller. Under R. M. Hutchins (1929–51), inaugurated "Chicago plan," i.e., a four-year junior college and a liberal arts university divorced from professional schools. University is notable for research and graduate work. Seat of Hutchins's "great books" program. Has Ogden Graduate School of Science, Inst. for the Study of Metals, Oriental Inst., and Enrico Fermi Inst. of Nuclear Studies. Library is rich in Lincolniana and Americana. Includes pioneer Univ. of Chicago Press (1891).

Chicago Heights, industrial city (pop. 34,331), NE Ill., S of Chicago; settled in 1830s.

Chichagof Island (chǐ'chŭgŏf), off SE Alaska, in ALEXANDER ARCHIPELAGO, N of Baranof Isl.

Chichén Itzá (chēchän' ētsä'), anc. Mayan city, occupied by the Itzá group (according to one system of dating c.514–692 and late 10th cent.–1194). Ruins, showing Classic and Post-Classic architectural styles, have been much studied by archaeologists.

Chicherin, Georgi Vasilyevich (gēôr'gē vŭsē'lyŭvĭch chēchä'rĭn), 1872–1936, Russian foreign commissar (1918–30). Prepared recognition of USSR by Great Powers at Conference of GENOA and through Treaty of RAPALLO (1922).

Chichester (chĭ'chĭstŭr), municipal borough (pop. 20,-118), Sussex West, England. Once a Roman town; was conquered by South Saxons in 5th cent. Cathedral (12th–13th cent.) has detached bell tower.

Chichi-jima: see BONIN ISLANDS.

chickadee (chĭk'ŭdē"), small North American bird related to titmouse. Black-capped chickadee is a permanent resident in much of E North America; several species are in W U.S., one in S U.S.

Chickahominy (chĭkŭhŏ'mĭnē), river of E Va., rising NW of Richmond and flowing SE c.90 mi. to the James. In Civil War there was heavy fighting along its banks (see PENINSULAR CAMPAIGN).

Chickamauga (chĭkŭmô'gŭ), city (pop. 1,824), NW Ga., S of Chattanooga, Tenn. Scene of Civil War battle in CHATTANOOGA CAMPAIGN. Chickamauga and Chattanooga Natl. Military Park is nearby.

Chickasaw (chĭk'ŭsô), city (pop. 10,002), SW Ala., within confines of Mobile. Founded 1917 as shipbuilding "company town."

Chickasaw Indians (chĭk'ŭsô), tribe of Hokan-Siouan linguistic stock, once occupying N Miss. One of the FIVE CIVILIZED TRIBES.

Chickasha (chĭk'ŭshä), city (pop. 14,866), S central Okla., on Washita R., SW of Oklahoma City, in agr. area. Seat of Oklahoma Col. for Women.

chicken: see POULTRY.

chicken pox (varicella), contagious, infectious childhood disease caused by a filterable virus. Red spots become blisters appear on various areas of body two to three weeks after exposure.

chick-pea, annual plant (*Cicer arietinum*) grown since antiquity for its edible pealike seeds in Asia, S Europe,

Mexico, and South America. It is also called *garbanzo* and gram.

chickweed, low-growing weed (*Stellaria media*) of temperate regions. Mouse-ear chickweeds are rock garden perennials of genus *Cerastium*.

Chiclayo (chĕklä'yō), city (pop. 86,904), NW Peru, on coastal desert between Andes and the Pacific. Sugar cane and rice are grown.

chicle (chĭ'kŭl), name for gum obtained from latex of sapodilla tree, a tropical American evergreen (*Achras zapota*) also grown for edible fruit. Chicle exported to U.S. for making chewing gum.

Chico (chē'kō), city (pop. 14,757), N Calif., N of Sacramento, in farm area. Seat of Chico State Col.

Chicopee (chĭ'kŭpē), industrial city (pop. 61,553), SW Mass., at junction of Chicopee and Connecticut rivers, N of Springfield; settled 1641. Includes villages of Willimansett; Chicopee; and Chicopee Falls, site of Westover Air Force Base. Col. of Our Lady of the Elms is here.

chicory or **succory,** blue-flowered herb (*Cichorium intybus*) of Europe, naturalized in North America. Root used as coffee substitute and adulterant. When blanched for winter salads, known as witloof or French endive. True endive is in same genus.

Chicoutimi (shĭkōō'tĭmē"), city (pop. 31,657), S Que., Canada, on Saguenay R. at mouth of Chicoutimi R. Hydroelectric power center; pulp, lumber, and woolen mills. Has many Roman Catholic institutions.

Chidambaram (chĭdŭm'bŭrŭm'), town (pop. 34,732), SE Madras state, India. Has remains of Dravidian art, including a statue of the dancing Siva.

chief, a leader of a clan or tribe. Hereditary succession is most common, though special qualities may aid in attainment of this status. Functions of chief may be shared by two or more persons.

Chiemsee (kēm'zä), lake, area 31 sq. mi., Bavaria, SE of Munich. An island has palace built by Louis II in imitation of Versailles.

Ch'ienfotung, China: see TUNHWANG.

Ch'ien-lung: see CH'ING, dynasty.

chigger, minute, six-legged, reddish larva of harvest mite or red bug commoner in S U.S. than in N U.S. Related to the spider, the adult has eight legs. Attacks warm-blooded mammals, including man, by attaching to the skin and gorging with blood.

Chigirin (chĭgĭrĕn'), city (1963 est. pop. 11,200), central Ukraine. Cap. of right-bank Ukraine in 17th cent.

Chignecto (shĭgnĕk'tō), isthmus connecting N.S., Canada, with the Canadian mainland.

chigoe (chĭ'gō) or **jigger,** small flea of tropical America and S U.S. Female bores into flesh of humans and animals; flea's abdomen swells forming sack wherein eggs develop; this irritation gives rise to sores and danger of infection.

Chigwell, London: see REDBRIDGE.

Chihli, China: see HOPEH.

Chihli, Gulf of, China: see POHAI.

Chihuahua (chēwä'wä), state (94,831 sq. mi.; 1963 est. pop. 1,374,358), N Mexico; cap. Chihuahua (1965 est. pop. 198,461). Largest Mexican state, it is divided into two regions with mountains in W and desert basin in N and E. Chief occupations: mining (silver, gold, copper, manganese); cattle raising; and agr. (by irrigation). First known to Spanish through Cabeza de Vaca; became state after independence from Spain. JUÁREZ, a border city, is commercial link with U.S.

Chikamatsu, Monzaemon (mōnzä'ämō chĭkä'mätsōō), 1653–1724, great Japanese dramatist, who wrote primarily for puppet stage. Influenced development of modern Japanese theater.

Child, Francis James, 1825–96, American scholar. Compiled *English and Scottish Popular Ballads* (5 vols., 1883–98).

Childe, Vere Gordon, 1892–1957, English archaeologist. An originator of the oasis theory or movement

of plants, animals, and man to areas in Mesopotamia not affected by desiccation. Recent studies have disproved his theory.

Childebert (chĭl'dŭbûrt), Frankish kings. **Childebert I,** d. 558, king of Paris (511–58). Partitioned his brother Clodomer's kingdom of Orléans with his brothers Clotaire I and Theodoric I (524), and Burgundy and Provence with Clotaire (534). **Childebert II,** 570–95, king of Austrasia (575–95) and Burgundy (593–95). Dominated by his mother, BRUNHILDA.

Childeric I (chĭl'dŭrĭk), c.436–481, Merovingian king of Salian Franks; father of Clovis I.

child labor was recognized as a social problem in late 18th-cent. England, where employment in factories became virtual slavery for the children. Factory acts of 1802 and later bettered conditions. Today almost all European countries limit the working day for children to 6–8 hr. In U.S. problem became acute after the Civil War. Congressional laws against child labor were invalidated 1918 and 1922, but Fair Labor Standards Act (1938), which set a 16-year min. age for children producing goods for interstate or foreign commerce, was upheld by Supreme Court (1941).

Children's Crusade: see CRUSADES.

child welfare. When the effects of the Industrial Revolution in exploiting CHILD LABOR were being recognized in the late 18th and early 19th cent., educators such as Rousseau, Pestalozzi, and Froebel called attention to children's special needs. The 19th cent. saw the organization of charitable institutions for orphaned, destitute, and handicapped children, and the 20th cent. saw expansion of the belief that all underprivileged and dependent children are the charge of the community. Child welfare agencies and services expanded. Notable landmarks were the British Children's Charter Act (1908), the Ohio Children's Code Commission (1911), the U.S. Children's Bureau (1912), and the United Nations Children's Emergency Fund (UNICEF, 1946).

Chile (chĭ'lē, Span. chē'lä), republic (286,396 sq. mi.; pop. 7,374,115), S South America; cap. SANTIAGO. A long (c.2,600 mi.) narrow (never more than 250 mi. wide) strip between the rugged Andes (lofty ACONCAGUA is just over the Argentine border) and the Pacific, Chile also includes outlying EASTER ISLAND and JUAN FERNÁNDEZ isls. The mainland has deserts in the N producing nitrates (see ATACAMA) and copper, exported through ANTOFAGASTA and ARICA. In the center is a long rich valley, the "garden" of Chile, where the population is concentrated (65% mestizo, 30% white, 5% Indian). Here are the cap. and other large cities (notably the port of VALPARAISO and nearby VIÑA DEL MAR). Where the Andes approach the sea in the S there is a resort area of alpine lakes near PUERTO MONTT, and further S is a region of wet, wooded islands and the southerly city, PUNTA ARENAS. Chile's S tip is in the frigid TIERRA DEL FUEGO. The predominant language is Spanish, the predominant religion Roman Catholicism—both brought by Spanish conquerors. First of these was Almagro, who in an expedition from Peru (1536) was defeated by the deserts and by fierce Araucanian Indians. Valdivia after 1540 founded Spanish cities, but resistance of the Indians was not really broken until late in the 19th cent. Chile, developed as an area of large pastoral landholdings, was a captaincy general, dependent until 1778 on the viceroyalty of Peru. The first move for independence, led by Juan Martínez de Rosas, Bernardo O'Higgins, and José Miguel Carrera, failed in the battle of Rancagua (1814), but José de San Martín led a force from Argentina through high USPALLATA PASS, and a victory at Maipu (1818) assured Chilean independence. Since the colonial aristocracy and royalist clergy were discredited the revolutionary army, a few intellectuals, and some creole landholders framed the new government, first crystallized in the constitution of 1830, which gave a base for later emergence of parliamentary government. Longstanding border disputes with Bolivia and Peru were climaxed by the War of the PACIFIC (1879–84), which gave Chile rich nitrate deposits and other minerals but left the TACNA-ARICA CONTROVERSY long unsettled; the end of a border dispute with Argentina was marked by erection of the CHRIST OF THE ANDES. Exploitation of mineral resources brought wealth and growth in commerce and transportation (e.g., the TRANSANDINE RAILWAY) but left Chile vulnerable to changes in world markets and to depressions. This has been met by industrialization (largely with hydroelectric power), mfg., and intensive use of agr. products. Chile, neutral in Second World War, joined UN 1945. Carlos Ibáñez as president (1927–31; 1952–58) used dictatorial powers. He was succeeded by Jorge Alessandri (served 1958–64). In 1964 Eduardo Frei was elected; 1965 legislative elections gave Frei's democratic reform party majority in lower house (first party to win a clear majority in a century). In July, 1967, the president signed a drastic land-reform bill into law.

Chilkoot Pass, c.3,500 ft. high, in Coast Mts. on British Columbia–Alaska boundary. Route through pass between Yukon R. valley and coast was long a monopoly of Chilkoot Indians; first white man passed through 1878. Route to the Klondike from Skagway in gold rush of 1897–98 with WHITE PASS as alternate.

Chillán (chēyän'), city (pop. c.85,000), S central Chile; founded c.1580; agr. and commercial center.

Chillicothe (chĭl''ĭkŏ'thē), city (pop. 24,957), S central Ohio, on Scioto R. and Paint Creek, S of Columbus; settled 1796. Trade, shipping, and industrial center in farm area. Cap. of Northwest Territory 1800; cap. of Ohio 1803–10 and 1812–16. Nearby are Mound City Group Natl. Monument (see NATIONAL PARKS AND MONUMENTS, table) and U.S. veterans' hospital.

Chillingworth, William, 1602–44, English theologian. Converted to Catholicism, he left that faith and took orders (1638) in the Church of England. Known for *The Religion of Protestants a Safe Way to Salvation* (1638), arguing the right of the individual to personal interpretation of the Bible, the sole source of religion.

Chillon (shĭlŏn', shĭ'lŭn, Fr. shēyŏ'), castle at E end of L. Geneva, Switzerland, built 9th–13th cent. Prison of François de BONNIVARD. Now a museum.

Chiloé (chēlōä'), island (3,241 sq. mi.) off S Chile, largest island of Chile.

Chilperic I (chĭl'pŭrĭk), d. 584, Frankish king of Neustria (561–84). With his mistress and future wife, FREDEGUNDE, he murdered his wife Galswintha (567), thus precipitating a savage feud with BRUNHILDA (Galswintha's sister) and his brother Sigebert I of Austrasia (Brunhilda's husband). The feud was inherited by his son, CLOTAIRE II.

Chiltern Hills, chalk hill range (width, 15–20 mi.; length, 45 mi.), NW of London, England.

Chiltern Hundreds, administrative districts in Buckinghamshire, England, known for the phrase "applying for the Chiltern Hundreds" (used by member of Parliament in giving up seat, since he may not resign). Reference is to stewardship of districts (now obsolete but still profitable), which no M.P. may hold.

Chimay, princesse de: see TALLIEN, THÉRÉSA.

Chimayó (chĭmīŏ'), town, N N.Mex., N of Santa Fe. Famous for blanket weaving in early 19th cent. Has El Santuário shrine (1816). Tsimajó pueblo was here or nearby.

Chimborazo (chēmbōrä'sō), inactive volcano, 20,577 ft. high, central Ecuador.

chime: see BELL.

Chimera (kĭmēr'ù), in Greek legend, monster, part lion, part goat, and part dragon. It was slain by BELLEROPHON.

Chimkent (chĭmkyĕnt'), city (1965 est. pop. 200,000), S Kazakh SSR, on Turk-Sib RR. Lead refinery, chemical plant, textile mills. Once important caravan center. Citadel stormed by Russians 1864.

chimpanzee, anthropoid ape of central and W Africa. Considered most teachable and intelligent ape: studies show they use elementary tools. Adult is 4–5 ft. tall, 150–200 lb. They swing from branch to branch in forest but do not leap. On ground they are quadrupedal.

Chimu (chē'mōō), ancient Indian civilization on desert coast of N Peru, believed to have begun c.1200 A.D.

Ch'in (chĭn), dynasty of China, which ruled from 221 to 207 B.C. Founder was Shih Hwang-ti [first emperor]. His was first dynasty to unify the country. He devised the pyramidal governmental system which lasted to the 20th cent. and sought cultural unity through the standardization of the written language and the destruction of past philosophical works. Built much of original Great Wall. Ch'in was succeeded by the Han dynasty.

Chin or **Tsin** (both: jĭn), dynasty of China, which ruled 265–420, after period of Three Kingdoms. Saw continued growth of Buddhism. Material advance was in the use of coal. The chaotic period following the collapse of Chin is known as the Six Dynasties and Sixteen Kingdoms. China was reunited under Sui dynasty (581–618).

China, republic (c.3,800,000 sq. mi.; pop. c.690,000,-000), E Asia. Cap. People's Republic of China (mainland China) is Peking—called Peiping by Nationalists; Republic of China (Nationalist China) has its headquarters on TAIWAN. Second most populous country in the world (after USSR). China's 4,000-mi. coast line fronts the Yellow, E China, and S China seas. Bounded on NE by USSR and Korea, on N by USSR and Mongolian People's Republic, on W by USSR and Afghanistan, on S by W Pakistan, India, Nepal, Sikkim, Bhutan, Burma, Laos, and N Vietnam. MANCHURIA in N is historically distinctive area. Off shore are HAINAN and Taiwan. China's climate, harsh in N and subtropical in S, is mainly temperate. Terrain is generally rugged with broad plains along rivers and coast of S China Sea. Economy is primarily agric. Mineral resources are insufficiently explored, but coal reserves are great, and tungsten is a leading export. Population essentially homogeneous. Mandarin dialects spoken in N, in S Wu, Cantonese, and Hakka spoken; written ideographs common to all dialects. The chief religions, Confucianism, Buddhism, and Taoism, are generally practiced in eclectic mixture. Hsia is traditionally first dynasty; Shang (c.1523–c.1027 B.C.) is first in documented history. Great cultural and imperialist periods were CHOU, HAN, T'ANG, SUNG, YÜAN, MING, and CH'ING dynasties. Portuguese settled Macao in 1557, but foreign trade was unimportant until 1842, when defeat of Ch'ing regime by the British in OPIUM WAR forced China to make major concessions. Regime was further weakened by Japan's success in First CHINO-JAPANESE WAR (1894–95). U.S. promotion of OPEN DOOR policy failed to prevent the antiforeign BOXER UPRISING. Success of republican revolution, led by SUN YAT-SEN, forced emperor's abdication in 1912. Sun's successor, Yüan Shih-k'ai, used repressive tactics which led to formation of rival government at Canton. China's entry into First World War on Allied side helped thwart early expansionist designs of Japan. Washington Conference (1921–22) guaranteed China's territorial integrity. After 1919 civil war raged between Kuomintang and N government (supported by war lords, notably Chang Tso-lin). Kuomintang government, estab. 1928 by Chiang Kai-shek at Nanking, won foreign recognition. The 1927 purge of Communists in the Kuomintang wing and Chiang's continued military harassment of party forced Communists, led by MAO TSE-TUNG and CHU TEH, on their 1934 LONG MARCH N to Yenan, which became their base. Second CHINO-JAPANESE WAR began 1931 with Japanese occupation of Manchuria. China's resistance steadily weakened despite Allied aid after Dec., 1941, when Japan's attack on U.S. and British bases merged Chinese war into Second World War. At war's end China regained sovereignty over all areas (except Hong Kong and Macao). The Communist-Kuomintang civil war flared anew. In 1946 natl. assembly (boycotted by Communists) adopted democratic constitution; in 1948 CHIANG KAI-SHEK became first constitutional president. In Sept., 1949, Communists proclaimed rule over all China and estab. Chinese People's Republic, with Mao Tse-tung as chairman (succeeded 1959 by Liu Shao-ch'i) and Chou En-lai as premier. Mao remained Communist party chairman. By Jan., 1950, Communist regime was recognized by USSR, Britain, and India. After April, 1950, Chiang controlled only Taiwan and minor offshore islands. China intervened 1950 in Korean war and continued on vast scale until armistice in 1953. A new constitution was adopted by the first Natl. People's Congress in 1954. Relatively little was known of internal conditions in China, but objectives of the first five-year plan (1953–57) had been substantially achieved with almost complete collectivization of agric. and nationalization of industry. Second five-year plan (begun 1958) fared far worse because of floods, locust plagues, and local discontent; agric. communes were virtually disbanded. In 1965 China exploded its first atomic device. China took part in Geneva Conference of 1954 and Bandung Conference of 1955. The pact with USSR, signed in 1950 and affirming friendship and alliance, was dramatically threatened in 1958 when China suddenly challenged USSR leadership in the Communist world. Violent suppression of revolt in Tibet in 1959, undeclared border war with India in 1962, and in some cases subversion caused China's erstwhile cordial relations with its neighbors to be moderated or reversed. In 1966–67 ideological factionalism in government flared into riots and widespread unrest. Though the Communist regime has been recognized by many other nations (notably France in 1964), its attempts to replace the Nationalist delegation at UN were still unsuccessful early in 1967. In June, 1967, China exploded a hydrogen bomb. China now divided into 21 provinces (Anhwei, Chekiang, Fukien, Honan, Hopeh, Hunan, Hupei, Kansu, Kiangsi, Kiangsu, Kwantung, Kweichow, Shansi, Shantung, Shensi, Szechwan, Tsinghai, Yünnan, and in Manchuria, Heilungkiang, Kirin and Liaoning) and five outlying autonomous regions (Inner Mongolia, Tibet, Sinkiang, Ninghsia, and Kwangsi-Chuang). See under these headings for further information.

China, Great Wall of, fortifications, c.1,500 mi. long, winding across N China from Kansu prov., to Chingwangtao, Hopeh prov., mostly on S edge of Mongolian plain. First built in CH'IN dynasty. Present form dates mainly from Ming dynasty. Since 1949 section N of Peking has been reconstructed.

china clay, a fine-textured, pure clay, consisting chiefly of the mineral kaolinite, and often called kaolin. Easily molded, it turns white when fired and is used in making fine porcelains. Sometimes used in paper making.

China Sea, western part of Pacific Ocean. Divided by Taiwan (Formosa) into EAST CHINA SEA and SOUTH CHINA SEA.

chinch bug, small hemipterous insect. *Blissus leucopterus,* feeding on sap of grains and grasses, causes huge U.S. crop losses (esp. in Mississippi, Missouri, Ohio valleys). *Blissus hirtus* is lawn pest in NE U.S.

chinchilla (chǐnchǐ'lǔ), small rodent (*Chinchilla*) of South America, living in rocky burrows in Andes of Bolivia, Chile, and Peru. Its soft gray pelt is one of costliest furs. Now raised commercially in U.S.

Chincoteague (chǐng'kútēg), town (pop. 2,131), E Va., on Chincoteague Isl.; connected to Eastern Shore by causeway and bridge. Hunting and fishing resort. Has annual wild pony roundup and auction. Chincoteague Bay, inlet of the Atlantic, extends N from island.

Chindaswinth (chǐn'dúswǐnth), d. 653, Visigothic king of Spain (642–53). Began compilation of *Forum judicum,* completed by his son RECESWINTH.

Chindwin (chǐn'dwǐn), river (c.550 mi. long) rising in hills of N Burma, chief tributary of the Irrawaddy. It is an important commercial waterway.

Chinese architecture. The classical period of Chinese building was T'ang dynasty (A.D. 618–906), but there are few surviving buildings dated before the Ming dynasty (1368–1644). Major achievement of Ming period is Forbidden City in Peking with its intricate plan and decorations of exceptional richness. Notable is the Temple of Heaven, circular structure on triple platform. Both religious and secular architecture follow one basic type, involving one-story rectangular chamber on stone platform and covered by single or several superimposed roofs of richly colored glazed tiles. The roof, which projects on brackets in upward curve beyond eaves, is supported by interior columns; walls serve merely as screens. Ancient regulations govern dimensions and number of columns. Typical temple has three parallel buildings approached by monumental steps, gateways, and buildings. A main architectural principle is harmonizing of structure with natural settings. Distinctive Chinese structures are pagoda and pailou (memorial arch with upturned tile roof).

Chinese art. Founding of Shang dynasty (c.1523 B.C.) possibly marks transition from Stone Age to Bronze Age. Cast bronze ritual vessels (with decoration varying from meager to ornate, from abstract to naturalistic) are clearest extant record of Shang, Chou, and Early Han stylistic development. Advent of Buddhism gave new impetus to sculpture; representation of Buddha and bodhisattvas focused interest on human figure. Buddhist sculpture (marked by precise modeling and linear rhythms) reached its height in early T'ang dynasty (618–906) and flourished for c.300 more years. Ancient Chinese art of painting can be traced clearly only from 4th cent. Painters used basic technique of calligraphy, relying mainly on line and silhouette. Little survives of works of T'ang dynasty, classic period of figure painting. The great art of landscape painting, which reached a peak in Sung dynasty, has continued until today a remarkable contribution to world beauty. Masterpieces were done in ink (colors or monochrome) on absorbent silk or paper. Though secular in subject, they were Buddhist or Taoist in spirit. After 12th cent. more intimate subjects appeared. Ming period produced paintings of highly decorative quality. Development of Chinese pottery roughly paralleled that of painting; perfected in Sung dynasty, it became technically elaborate in Ming. Chinese art has deeply influenced Western artists since 18th cent.

Chinese Eastern Railroad: see SOUTH MANCHURIAN RAILROAD.

Chinese exclusion. After U.S. acquired Calif., large inflow of Chinese into state was welcomed at first because of need of cheap labor. Treaty Anson Burlingame signed with China in 1868 guaranteed right of Chinese immigration, but did not guarantee right of naturalization. In following decades much anti-Chinese feeling arose in Calif. and complete ban on Chinese immigration was urged. In a treaty of 1880 China allowed U.S. some right to restrict, but not to prohibit, Chinese immigration. Chinese exclusion act of 1882 did, however, ban immigration of Chinese laborers for ten years. Later acts flatly violated 1880 treaty. In a treaty of 1894 China agreed to exclusion of Chinese laborers for ten years. When that period was up, Congress continued exclusion unilaterally until immigration arrangements of 1924 made control automatic. In 1943 the acts were repealed; an annual immigration quota of 105 was set, and citizenship privileges were extended to Chinese.

Chinese language, most important of the Sino-Tibetan languages. It includes many dialects, some mutually unintelligible. The most widely spoken is Mandarin. See LANGUAGE (table).

Chinese literature. Oldest records date from Shang dynasty (c.1523–c.1027 B.C.). Oldest surviving literature probably dates from late Chou dynasty. *Wu Ching* [five classics], traditionally associated with Confucius, includes system of divination, historical records (some are forgeries), chronology of Lu (Confucius' native state), descriptions of ritual matters, and a collection of 305 literary folk songs, occasional poems, dynastic hymns, and religious odes. The *Shih Shu* [four books] contains early statements of Confucianism, notably *Book of Mencius*. Other important early books include *Tao-te-ching* (mid-3d cent. B.C.) and works of Chuang-tze. Early Chinese wrote on strips of paper and later on silk. Invention of paper (A.D. 105) and wood-block printing (8th cent.) stimulated book production. Poetic freedom of Chou period was supplanted by minutely prescribed forms. Prosodic rules of greatest poetic era, T'ang dynasty (618–906), continued to be observed later despite pronunciation changes. Great T'ang poets, notably Li Po, Tu Fu, and Wang Wei, and the later Sung poet Su Tung-po have strongly influenced modern English poetry. Chinese poems tend to be brief, suggestive, and nonintellectual. Earliest dynastic history dates from 1st cent. B.C. Popular romances in jingling couplets or easy prose, precursors of the novel, appeared continuously, but few prior to 10th cent. survive. Drama was estab. in Yüan dynasty (1260–1368). Plays had sentimental plots and stylized performances with symbolic props. Trend toward practicality, after the literary revolution of 1919, led to writing in the vernacular, notably by Lu Hsün and Hu Shih. Poets and novelists were greatly influenced by European writers. Chinese Communist literature, after 1942, had to conform to Mao Tse-tung's concept of social realism.

Chinese music can be traced back to very ancient times, but little is known about it, since in 212 B.C., all musical books and instruments were ordered destroyed. However, certain outlines of ancient Chinese music can be ascertained. The single tone was most important and considered an attribute of the substance which produced it. Hence musical instruments were classified according to the material from which they were made—gourd (*sheng*, a free-reed instrument); bamboo (panpipes); wood (*chu*, a kind of percussion instrument); silk (various types of zither with silk strings); clay (flute); metal (bell); stone (sonorous stone); and skin (drum). Music was believed to have power over the elements and had ethical connotations. Scale of Chinese music was five-toned, roughly represented by the black keys on a piano. The various types of notation did not indicate rhythm. Ancient musical practice has given way to folk song, religious music, Western jazz, and classical music in modern China. See *ill.*, p. 733.

Chinese Turkistan: see SINKIANG.

Ch'ing (chǐng) or **Manchu** (män'jō'), last dynasty of China, ruled from 1644 to 1912. Estab. by the Manchu, a people of N China. Under Emperor Ch'ien-lung (reigned 1735–96), China reached maximum size, extending in N beyond Amur R. and in S through Indo-China. The Manchu introduced few important changes in China. One notable political innovation, however, was joint Manchu-Chinese administration of military and civic affairs. The Ch'ing strongly opposed sea-borne foreign trade but were forced by series of wars in 19th cent. (notably the OPIUM WAR) to open China's ports and give extraterritorial rights to European powers. Regime was further weakened by Japan's success in the FIRST CHINO-JAPANESE WAR (1894–95). The partitioning of China was averted by the OPEN DOOR POLICY. Efforts of Emperor Kuang-hsü in 1898 to promote reforms for strengthening China were blocked by dowager empress, TZ'U HSI. She supported the BOXER UPRISING, a vain effort to expel foreigners. Revolution of 1911 forced abdication of Henry P'U-YI.

Chingford, London: see WALTHAM FOREST.

Chinghai, province: see TSINGHAI.

Chin Hills (chin), mountain range, W Burma, bordering Assam, India. The Chin Hills district (c.10,377 sq. mi.; pop. c.250,000) is semi-autonomous.

Chinkiang (jĕn'jäng'), city (pop. c.90,000), S Kiangsu prov., China; port on the Yangtze R. Was cap. of Kiangsu 1928–49. Commercial and industrial center. Was British concession, returned 1927.

Chinnampo (chĕn'näm'pŏ'), city (pop. c.90,000), North Korea, on Korea Bay. A port for Pyongyang and an industrial center.

Chinnereth or **Chinneroth** (both: kĭn'–; –rŏth): see GALILEE, SEA OF.

Chino (chē'nō), city (1965 pop. 14,246), S Calif., E of Los Angeles; founded 1887. Processing center of diversified farm area.

Chino-Japanese War, First, 1894–95. Caused by rivalry for control of Korea. In 1885 Japan had agreed to Chinese overlordship over Korea, but in 1894 induced Korean king to reject it when a revolt broke out. In ensuing war the Japanese won a quick victory over the Chinese. Treaty of Shimonoseki gave Korea nominal independence and provided for cession of Taiwan, Pescadores Isls., and Liaotung peninsula by China to Japan. Also called First Sino-Japanese War.

Chino-Japanese War, Second, 1931–45. Caused by long-standing desire of Japan to dominate E Asia. In 1931 Japan reinforced her garrison in Manchuria, ostensibly to protect Japanese property there. After bombing of Japanese troop train near Mukden the Japanese took over all Manchuria and set up the puppet state of MANCHUKUO, attacked Shanghai, and seized Jehol prov. (1931–32). In 1935 the Japanese occupied parts of Chahar and Hopeh. A clash (July, 1937) between soldiers of the Japanese garrison at Peiping and Chinese forces, and the killing of two Japanese in Shanghai a month later, precipitated the war in earnest. Peiping, Shanghai, and Nanking (the capital) fell 1937. By 1940 Japanese had swept over the E coastal area. The Chinese, based at Chunking (temporary cap.), fought on. Japan's attack on Pearl Harbor merged the war in the Pacific into Second World War as China declared war on Axis powers. Despite Allied aid and diversion of Japanese armies, China's military position failed to improve until April, 1945. Japan capitulated Aug., 1945, formally surrendered Sept. 9, 1945. By provisions of the Cairo Declaration, Manchuria, Taiwan, and the Pescadores were restored to China. Also called Second Sino-Japanese War.

Chinon (shēnō'), town (est. pop. 6,700), Indre-et-Loire dept., central France, on Vienne R. Its imposing castle (actually a complex of three castles, built 12th–15th cent.) was a royal residence in Middle Ages. Here Joan of Arc first met the dauphin. Rabelais was born nearby.

Chinook Indians (shĭnook', chĭ'), tribe in the Columbia valley, of Penutian linguistic stock (as were nearby tribes). Had plank houses in settled villages; were skilled with canoes; traded much; and had the custom of potlatch. Chinook jargon was the lingua franca of early trade on the Northwest Coast; had Chinook, Nootka, English, and French words.

chinquapin (chĭng'kŭpĭn), chestnut species (*Castanea pumila*) of E U.S. Golden-leaved chestnut or giant chinquapin (*Castanopsis chrysophylla*) is evergreen tree of W U.S.

Ch'inwangtao (chĭng'wäng'däō), city (pop. c.186,000), NE Hopeh prov., China. Ice-free port on the Pohai.

Chioggia (kyôd'jä), city (est. pop. 48,902), Venetia, NE Italy; major fishing port on island in Adriatic near Venice. Bridge joins it to mainland. Picturesque old houses, canals. Several naval battles were fought here in "Chioggia War" between Venice and Genoa (1378–80), which ended with Venetian victory.

Chios or **Khios** (kī'ŏs), Aegean island (c.340 sq. mi.; pop. 62,233), Greece, 5 mi. W of Asia Minor; chief town and port Chios (pop. 24,053). Mountainous, it rises to 4,157 ft. in Mt. Elias. Anc. Emporio, excavated by the British School on the eastern end of Chios, offers a unique example of early Archaic Greek town; Chios was held by Persia 493–479 B.C.; then under Athenian influence; free city of Roman Empire until Vespasian's reign. From the Byzantines, it passed to the Latin Empire of Constantinople (1204), to Genoa (1261), to Turkey (1566) and to Greece (1912). Anti-Turkish revolt of 1822 ended in massacre of Chian Christians. Chios claims to be Homer's birthplace.

Chipewyan (chĭpŭwī′ŭn), trading post, NE Alta., Canada, on NW shore of L. Athabaska. Old Fort Chipewyan (built 1788), on S shore, was base for Alexander Mackenzie's expeditions in 1789 and 1793. Present post was fur trade center.

chipmunk, rodent of squirrel family. Chipmunk of E U.S. and SE Canada is of genus *Tamias*. Common Eastern chipmunk (*Tamias striatus*) is 5–6 in. long, reddish or grayish brown on top, black and white on sides, with 4–5 in. hairy, flattened tail. It eats nuts, seeds, berries, and insects; carries food in expansible cheek pouches. Winters in underground burrow provided with stores of food. Chipmunks of W North America are of genus *Eutamias*.

Chippendale, Thomas, 1718–79, English cabinetmaker. A whole general category of 18th-cent. English furniture is grouped under his name. His style is based on Queen Anne and Georgian design, but with Chinese, Gothic, and French rococo elaborations. His favorite material was dark mahogany, always without inlays. His style influenced American cabinetmakers and became a standard style in U.S.

Chippewa (chĭ′pŭwŭ), river rising in lake region of N Wis. and flowing c.200 mi. S and SW to Mississippi R. at foot of L. Pepin.

Chippewa Falls, city (pop. 11,708), W central Wis., on Chippewa R., NE of Eau Claire, in lake region; settled 1837. Commercial center for dairy and farm area.

Chippewa Indians: see OJIBWA INDIANS.

Chiputneticook Lakes (chĭpōōtnĕ′tĕkōōk), chain on Maine-N.B. border, forming international boundary for 28 mi. Source of St. Croix R.

Chirchik (chĭrchĕk′), city (1965 est. pop. 92,000), E Uzbek SSR. Industrial center with chemical and machinery plants. Hydroelectric stations.

Chiricahua National Monument: see NATIONAL PARKS AND MONUMENTS (table).

Chirico, Giorgio de (jôr′jō dā kē′rēkō), 1888–, Italian painter, b. Greece. Known mainly for his earlier works (characterized by an atmosphere of mystery) which greatly influenced early surrealist painting. Broke with surrealism in late 1920s.

Chirikov, Aleksey Ilich (ŭlyĭksyä′ ĭlyĕch′ chē′rĭkŭf), d. 1748, Russian explorer. Lieutenant of Vitus Bering on voyage leading to discovery of Alaska.

Chiron (kī′rŏn), in Greek mythology, a CENTAUR. A famous teacher, he taught Hercules, Jason, Achilles, and Asclepius. After accidentally receiving an incurable wound, he gave Prometheus his immortality. He became constellation Sagittarius.

chiropractic (kī″rŭprăk′tĭk), system of treatment by manipulation, especially of spinal column. Its purpose is to restore normal nerve function. It was originated 1895 by Daniel D. Palmer.

Chisholm Trail, route over which vast herds of cattle were driven from Texas to railheads in Kansas after Civil War. Took name from Jesse Chisholm, who, in 1866, drove his wagon, heavily loaded with buffalo hides, through Indian Territory which is now Okla. to his trading post near Wichita, Kansas. Wheels cut deeply into prairie; marked route used for almost two decades by traders and drovers.

Chishti, Muin-al-Din Muhammad (chĭsh′tē), 1142–1236, Indian Moslem saint, b. Persia. Founded a Sufi mystic order in India.

Chisinau: see KISHINEV, Moldavian SSR.

Chislehurst and Sidcup, London: see BEXLEY and BROMLEY.

chi-square test, method of determining the odds for or against a given deviation from expected statistical distribution.

Chiswick, England: see HOUNSLOW.

Chita (chĕtä′), city (1965 est. pop. 198,000), RSFSR, in SE Siberia, on Trans-Siberian RR; founded 1653. Center of a region rich in tungsten, molybdenum, gold, tin, iron, coal, lumber, cattle.

Chittagong (chĭ′tŭgŏng), city (pop. 364,205), cap. of Chittagong division, SE East Pakistan, on Karnafuli R., near Bay of Bengal. East Pakistan's largest port; jute and tea exported. Has noted Hindu temples, Buddhist ruins, and examples of Mogul art.

Chiu-chiang: see KIUKIANG.

Chiusi (kyōō′sē), Latin *Clusium*, Etruscan *Chamars*, town (est. pop. 9,157), Tuscany, central Italy. Cap. of anc. Etruria under Lars Porsena. Etruscan tombs (5th cent. B.C.); museum.

chivalry: see KNIGHTHOOD AND CHIVALRY.

chive, herb (*Allium schoenoprasum*) with globular lavender flower heads and slender tubular leaves which are used in seasoning.

Chkalov: see ORENBURG.

Chloë, Greek shepherdess: see DAPHNIS AND CHLOË.

chloral, oily, colorless liquid which results from treating absolute ethyl alcohol with chlorine. With water it forms chloral hydrate, used in medicine to produce sleep.

chlorate, salt of chloric acid, compound of metal and chlorate radical. Potassium chlorate is a colorless, crystalline oxidizing agent; used in matches, fireworks, and explosives, and as oxygen source; explosive when mixed with certain chemicals.

chloric acid, compound of hydrogen and chlorate radical ($-ClO_3$), appears only as colorless solution. It is moderately stable and a strong oxidizing agent. Salts are chlorates.

chloride, compound of chlorine and other element or radical. It is a salt formed by direct union of elements or by reaction of hydrochloric acid with base, metal, or oxide. Most form aqueous solution, conduct electricity, and are decomposed (see ELECTROLYSIS). Among uses: calcium chloride as drying agent and in refrigeration; silver chloride in photography; chloride of sulphur in vulcanizing rubber. In aqueous solution hydrogen chloride (colorless, irritating gas) is called HYDROCHLORIC ACID.

chloride of lime, white powder prepared by treating slaked lime with chlorine. Strong bleaching agent and disinfectant.

chlorine (klô′rēn), active, nonmetallic element (symbol = Cl; see also ELEMENT, table), in HALOGEN family. Greenish-yellow, poisonous gas with suffocating odor, heavier than air. Forms many compounds that occur abundantly in nature. Prepared by electrolysis of sodium chloride. Used in water purification; as disinfectant, antiseptic; to make bleaching powder, dyes, fire extinguishers, explosives; in many poison gases; in medicine.

chloroform (klô′rŭfôrm), volatile liquid, compound of carbon, hydrogen, and chlorine. Discovered 1831, it was first used as anesthetic by Sir J. Y. Simpson (1847). Solvent for fats and other organic compounds.

chlorophyll (klô′rŭfĭl″), substance that gives plants their green color and enables them to carry on PHOTOSYNTHESIS. It is contained in chloroplasts (small, oval bodies in plant cells) and chemically is similar to blood. Sunlight appears to be essential to chlorophyll formation. Certain plants lacking chlorophyll, e.g., yeasts and bacteria, live as parasites or saprophytes. Chlorophyll is used in drugs and as food coloring.

Chmielnicki or **Khmelnitsky, Bohdan** (bŭkhdän′ khmĕlnĕt′skē), c.1593–1657, hetman of the Ukraine. Stirred Cossack revolt against Polish overlordship (1648). United Ukraine with Russia (1654).

Choate, Joseph Hodges (chōt), 1832–1917, American lawyer and diplomat. Handled many famous cases in

New York city. Distinguished himself as U.S. ambassador to Great Britain (1899–1905).

Chocano, José Santos (hōsä' sän'tōs chōkä'nō), 1875–1934, Peruvian poet, a leader of *modernismo*.

chocolate is extracted from seeds of CACAO tree by complex process of grinding, heating, and blending, without removal of fat. Chocolate liquor is used in confectionery, powdered or molded chocolate in chocolate beverage, in confectionery, and cookery.

Choctaw Indians (chŏk'tô), tribe of SE U.S., of Hokan-Siouan linguistic stock. Culture similar to that of Creek Indians. They were peacefully removed to the Indian Territory in 1832. One of FIVE CIVILIZED TRIBES.

Choderlos de Laclos: see LACLOS.

Chodowiecki, Daniel Nikolaus (dä'nyĕl nē'kōlous khôdôvyĕts'kē), 1726–1801, German painter and engraver, b. Danzig. He was most popular illustrator of his day in Prussia.

choir. 1 See CHORUS. **2** Instruments of any one type in the orchestra, as brass choir, wood wind choir. **3** That part of a cathedral or abbey reserved for the singers and officiating clergy; the same area in a parish church is the chancel.

Choiseul, Étienne François, duc de (ātyĕn' fräswä' dük' dü shwäzûl'), 1719–85, French foreign minister (1758–70). Negotiated FAMILY COMPACT; annexed Lorraine, Corsica. Protégé of Mme de Pompadour.

cholera (kŏ'lŭrŭ) or **Asiatic cholera**, acute infectious disease caused by bacterium (*Vibrio cholerae* or *V. comma*). Transmitted by polluted food or water. Symptoms include watery diarrhea, vomiting, collapse. Death rate high. Vaccination gives temporary protection.

cholera infantum (ĭnfăn'tŭm), condition in infants probably resulting from severe intestinal infection by various bacteria. Symptoms resemble those of true cholera.

cholesterol (kŭlĕs'tŭrōl), principal organic sterol compound in all body tissues of higher animals, especially in brain and spinal cord. Found also in animal fats, oils, and gallstones.

Cholet (shôlā'), town (est. pop. 29,400), Maine-et-Loire dept., W France in Poitou. Linen and cotton industries. Center of fighting in wars of the VENDÉE.

Cholon (shôlô'), city (pop. 1,400,000), S Cochin China, South Vietnam, on right bank of Saigon R. Part of metropolitan Saigon since 1932. Founded c.1780 by Chinese immigrants escaping the civil disorders of Annam. Still largely a Chinese city.

Cholula (chōlōō'lä), town (pop. c.10,000), Puebla, E central Mexico. An old Toltec city, it was Aztec sacred city when Spanish came. Cortés destroyed city, built church over pyramid. Has numerous churches and is place of pilgrimage.

Chopin, Frédéric (frädārēk' shôpē'), 1810–49, composer and pianist, b. Poland of French and Polish parents, lived in Paris after 1831. Almost all his music is for solo piano. Even in his two piano concertos, the orchestra is dominated by the piano. Polish nationalism is evident in the sets of mazurkas and polonaises, while the nocturnes, waltzes, and preludes are more often elegiac. He also wrote a series of etudes, scherzos, ballades, and sonatas. His music, highly romantic, is important in the development of piano techniques. Was a lover of George Sand.

Chopin, Kate O'Flaherty (shô'păn'), 1851–1904, American author of Creole stories of La., b. St. Louis.

chorale or **choral**, any of the traditional congregational hymns of the German Protestant Church. Most early chorales were translations of Latin hymns set to folksong melodies. During the Reformation and later, German composers used the traditional tunes of chorales in writing contrapuntal works with organ accompaniment.

chorea (kōrē'ŭ) or **Saint Vitus's dance**, nervous disorder accompanied by involuntary jerking and emotional instability. Rarely occurs after puberty.

chorus. 1 In music, group of singers, usually divided into four sections—soprano, alto, tenor, and bass. A chorus performing only sacred music is called a choir. **2** In drama of ancient Greece, it arose from singing of DITHYRAMB. Became dramatic chorus, tying histrionic interludes together and commenting on action; in 6th cent. B.C. Thespis introduced the actor. Aeschylus began with chorus of 50; it later shrank (Sophocles used 12) and disappeared.

Chorzow (hô'zhôōf), Ger. *Königshütte*, city (est. pop. 153,000), S Poland. Center of KATOWICE mining and industrial region. Passed from Germany to Poland 1921.

Chosroes: see KHOSRU.

Chou (jō), dynasty of China. According to tradition ruled from 1122 to c.256 B.C., but according to some modern scholars from c.1027 to 256 B.C. Despite political disorder, the Chou era was the classical age of China: Confucius, Mencius, Lao-tze, and Chuang-tze lived then. Chou was followed by the Ch'in dynasty.

Chouans (shōō'ùnz, shwä), peasants of NW France who rose against French revolutionary government in 1793. Movement merged with royalist risings in VENDÉE, continued sporadically till 1815.

Chou En-lai (jō' ùn'-lī'), 1898–, Chinese Communist leader. Active communist since student days in France (1920–22), where he helped found the Chinese Communist party in Paris and became a founder of the organization simultaneously formed in China. Returned (1922) to China and at Canton joined Sun Yat-sen, who was then cooperating with Communists. Held high position at Whampoa Academy under Chiang Kai-shek. In 1927 he organized an insurrection in Shanghai which permitted Chiang to take the city in the Northern Expedition. Participated in the fighting (1927–33) against Chiang and in the LONG MARCH (1934–35). Became first premier and foreign minister of People's Republic of China (estab. 1949). He headed the Chinese Communist delegation to the Geneva Conference of 1954 and to the Bandung Conference (1955). Relinquished the foreign ministry in 1958. At the Twenty-Second Congress of the Communist party (1961) he openly disputed the concept of "peaceful coexistence." He was chief representative and negotiator in the Sino-Indian border war (1962–63).

Choukoutien, China: see PEKING.

Chou Shu-jen: see LU HSÜN.

Chouteau, René Auguste (rünä' ōgüst' shōōtō', shōtō'), 1749–1829, American fur trader and a founder of St. Louis (1763–64) with Pierre LACLEDE. Developed business with brother, **Jean Pierre Chouteau**, 1758–1849, fur trader and U.S. Indian agent. His son, **Auguste Pierre Chouteau**, 1786–1838, aided in the family fur trade. Another son, **Pierre Chouteau**, 1789–1865, bought interest in old American Fur Co. and expanded his business activities.

Chrestien de Troyes or **Chrétien de Troyes** (both: krätyĕ' dü trwä'), fl. 1170, French poet, author of first great literary treatments of ARTHURIAN LEGEND. Among surviving works are *Érec et Énide; Cligès; Lancelot ou Le Chevalier de la charette; Yvain ou Le Chevalier au lion;* and *Perceval ou Le Conte del Graal* (unfinished; see PARSIFAL).

Christ: see JESUS.

Christadelphians [Ger.,= brothers of Christ], religious sect founded in U.S. in 1840s by John Thomas. They show simple, early Christian faith and expect second coming of Christ to set up theocracy in Jerusalem.

Christchurch, city (pop. 149,400; metropolitan pop. 210,000), E South Isl., New Zealand; founded 1850. Canterbury Col. (1873) and School of Arts (1882) are here. Has tanneries and meat-packing plants.

Christ Church College: see OXFORD UNIVERSITY.

Christian, Danish kings. **Christian I,** 1426–81, king of Denmark (1448–81), Norway (1450–81), and Sweden (1457–64), count of Oldenburg; founder of Oldenburg dynasty of Danish kings. Also inherited Schleswig and Holstein (1460). His defeat at Brunkeberg by Sten STURE (the elder) ended his attempt to subdue Sweden (1471; see KALMAR UNION). **Christian II,** 1481–1559, king of Denmark and Norway (1513–23), king of Sweden (1520–23). His wholesale massacre of Swedish nobles at Stockholm (1520) led to rebellion. GUSTAVUS I was raised to the Swedish throne, the Kalmar Union terminated. In Denmark Christian alienated the Church and nobility by his high-handed reforms. Deposed 1523, he died a prisoner. **Christian III,** 1503–59, king of Denmark and Norway (1534–59). Broke power of Hanseatic League; established Lutheranism; declared Norway a Danish dependency. **Christian IV,** 1577–1648, king of Denmark and Norway (1588–1648). Playing a major part in THIRTY YEARS WAR, he invaded Germany as champion of Protestants (1625); was defeated by Tilly at Lutter (1626); relieved STRALSUND with Swedish help (1628). He signed a separate peace (1629) but in 1643–45 reentered the war, siding against Sweden, and lost two Norwegian provinces. **Christian V,** 1646–99, king of Denmark and Norway (1670–99). His minister GRIFFENFELD dominated his reign until 1676, made the monarchy absolute. **Christian VII,** 1749–1808, king of Denmark and Norway (1766–1808), was insane. His physician STRUENSEE held power until 1772; A. P. BERNSTORFF was chief minister from 1773. **Christian VIII,** 1786–1848, king of Denmark (1839–48). He announced new status for SCHLESWIG-HOLSTEIN (1846), thus precipitating war of 1848. **Christian IX,** 1818–1906, king of Denmark (1863–1906). Issued from cadet line of Sonderburg-Glücksburg. Annexed Schleswig to Danish crown (1863; see SCHLESWIG-HOLSTEIN). In the resulting war of 1864 with Prussia and Austria he lost Schleswig, Holstein, and Lauenburg. **Christian X,** 1870–1947, king of Denmark (1912–47) and of ICELAND (1912–44). His self-imposed seclusion during the German occupation of Denmark in Second World War made him a symbol of national resistance.

Christiana, borough (pop. 1,069), SE Pa., SE of Lancaster; settled 1691. Was a stop on Underground Railroad and scene of anti-slavery riots (1851).

Christian Catholic Church, sect founded (1896) by J. A. DOWIE (hq. Zion, Ill.). It was known for some years as Christian Catholic Apostolic Church. Members are popularly known as Zionites.

Christian Churches: see CONGREGATIONALISM; DISCIPLES OF CHRIST.

Christian Endeavor, Protestant interdenominational, international young people's association for encouraging spiritual life and Christian activities; founded 1881 by Dr. F. E. Clark.

Christiania, Norway: see OSLO.

Christianity, all doctrines and religious groups based on the teachings of Jesus Christ. Those who subscribe to any such group are called Christians. Little is definitely known of the years of early spread and nature of the teachings or of the forms of worship, and different interpretations of the known facts give one of the chief bases for the fundamental difference between "traditionalist" churches (e.g., ROMAN CATHOLIC CHURCH, ORTHODOX EASTERN CHURCH), which claim to maintain an elaborated and developed version of early doctrines and rites, and the "reformed" churches (see PROTESTANTISM), which claim to restore pristine doctrines and forms, cleansing them of false additions and developments. From the start Christianity tended to be highly organizational (in contrast to Islam and most other major religions), a tendency that developed in sporadic persecutions by Roman emperors (until toleration was proclaimed by CONSTANTINE I) and in the struggle over differences within the Church. These differences in early times centered on arguments as to the nature of Christ in relationship to the other members of the Christian Trinity. Councils were called to settle these questions, the accepted answers being deemed orthodox, the rejected ones heretical. Among the early heresies were Arian-ism, Nestorianism, and Monophysitism. Perhaps the most celebrated of the early councils was First Council of Nicaea (325). In the East the Byzantine emperors exercised much control over the Church, in the West the power of the papacy grew. From both centers Christianity was extended until it embraced all Europe, monks playing a large part in the missionary work of converting pagans. Until the rise of Islam, Christianity was also dominant in Asia Minor and N Africa. The break between the Eastern and Western churches was gradual but was more or less permanent after 1054. A main current of development in both areas was conflict between secular and church authorities. When the REFORMATION came as the most important single movement in Christian history since early days, it added a new element in the diversity of sects. Strife between the various groups, attempts at union, and various struggles to establish sound and enduring relationships between religion and the state have characterized modern Christianity. See ECUMENICAL MOVEMENT.

Christian Reformed Church. Protestant church formed 1857 by Dutch immigrants dissenting from Reformed Church in America. Name adopted 1890.

Christians, name given followers of evangelical, antisectarian preachers on American frontier. Some joined Disciples of Christ; others formed Christian Church, finally merged (1931) with Congregational Churches. See also CHRISTIANITY.

Christian Science, religion based on principles and divine laws formulated from acts and sayings of Jesus Christ by Mary Baker Eddy for Church of Christ, Scientist. Mrs. Eddy's teachings developed after her recovery of health in 1866 through reading in New Testament of healing by Jesus. Her *Science and Health* (1875) is textbook of doctrine. Church founded 1879; Mother Church, the First Church of Christ, Scientist, set up in Boston, 1892.

Christian socialism, movement begun in England in 1848 intended to advance Christian ideals in economic life in opposition to ruthless practices of industrialists. Led by Frederick Denison Maurice and Charles Kingsley, it was very active among workingmen. Its non-Marxist tradition passed to the Fabian Society, guild socialists, and Catholic groups. In U.S., Society of Christian Socialists (estab. 1889) took up the movement, as did various church groups preaching the "social gospel." Concern was with industrial social problems rather than with political socialism. Reinhold Niebuhr and Paul Tillich advocated a socialism grounded in theology, but not regarded as the contemporary equivalent of Christian witness. On the Continent, term *Christian Socialist* was given various political or labor groups directed by religious leaders.

Christiansted (krĭs′chŭnstĕd″), city (pop. 5,137), on St. Croix isl.; port of Virgin Islands (U.S.).

Christie, Agatha, 1891–, English detective-story writer. Her many popular volumes often feature the detective Hercule Poirot. Notable among them is *And Then There Were None* (1940).

Christie's, English firm of art auctioneers and appraisers, founded 1766. One of world's largest clearinghouses for art objects.

Christina, 1626–89, queen of Sweden (1632–54); daughter and successor of Gustavus II. OXENSTIERNA headed a regency until 1644. She ruled irresponsibly and eccentrically, devoting her time to intellectual pursuits. Attracted many foreign artists and scholars, including Descartes, to her court. Her refusal to marry was chiefly responsible for her abdication in favor of her cousin, Charles X (1654). She left Sweden in men's clothes, entered the Catholic Church (1655), and settled at Rome. Later attempts to regain the Swedish throne failed.

Christine de Pisan: see PISAN, CHRISTINE DE.

Christmas [Christ's Mass], feast day celebrating the birth of Jesus Christ (the Nativity), in the Western churches Dec. 25, a date almost certainly chosen for its nearness to the Epiphany (Jan. 6). Not observed earlier than A.D. 200, it grew popular in the Middle Ages, and many customs clustered about the feast, especially in English-speaking countries: the Yule log (the Yule season is simply Christmastide), gathering decorations of holly and mistletoe, the singing of carols, giving of gifts, and sending of greeting cards. The Christmas tree is a German contribution to the season; the American Santa Claus is derived from the Dutch customs in N.Y. (see NICHOLAS, SAINT).

Christmas Island (60 sq. mi.; pop. c,2,800), in Indian Ocean, W of Java. Has large deposits of phosphate of lime. Formerly part of Singapore crown colony; passed to Australia 1958.

Christmas Island, largest atoll in Pacific (c.222 sq. mi.), near equator; one of Line Isls. Discovered 1777 by Capt. James Cook, added 1919 to British colony of Gilbert and Ellice Isls. In 1950s became a British nuclear weapons testing range.

Christmas rose: see HELLEBORE.

Christ of the Andes, statue built (1904) in Uspallata Pass on Argentine-Chilean boundary to commemorate peace and boundary treaties. Dispute had arisen because crest of Andes and continental watershed did not coincide.

Christophe, Henri (ärē' krēstôf'), 1767–1820, Negro king of Haiti. A freed slave, he aided Toussaint L'Ouverture in liberation of Haiti; was army chief under Dessalines. Elected president of Haiti (1806), he disputed control of island with Pétion. Declared himself king 1811; committed suicide 1820 when revolts broke out.

Christopher, Saint [Gr.,= Christ bearer], 3d cent.?, martyr of Asia Minor. Chief legend is that when he was charitably carrying a child across a river, he felt the weight on his shoulders grow almost too great to bear and discovered that he was carrying Jesus, who carried the world in His hands. He is patron of travelers; hence the practice of wearing his medal on journeys. Feast: July 25.

Christ's College: see CAMBRIDGE UNIVERSITY.

Christ's Hospital, once a hospital (founded 1553) in London, it became a school, known as "bluecoat school" from the boys' habit. Now includes school for girls. Has been at Horsham, Sussex, since 1902.

Christ's-thorn, name for several thorny plants, especially a spiny shrub (*Paliurus spina-christi*) with hat-shaped fruit. Also called Jerusalem thorn.

Christus or **Cristus, Petrus** (both: pē'trūs krī'stŭs), fl. 1444–c.1473, Flemish painter; a follower and probably a pupil of the Van Eycks.

Christy, Edwin P., 1815–62, American showman. Estab. c.1846 a company of Negro minstrels known as Christy's Minstrels, which became the typical minstrel show with interlocutor, end men, and performers in blackface.

Christy, Howard Chandler, 1873–1952, American illustrator. Known for the "Christy girl" of posters and magazine illustrations. Also did portraits.

chromatic scale, in music: see SCALE.

chromium (krō'mēŭm), gray-white, crystalline, hard, nontarnishing metallic element (symbol = Cr; see also ELEMENT, table). Forms chromates and dichromates used as paint pigments, in dyeing, in leather tanning. Metal comparatively rare, always occurs in compounds. Used for PLATING and in several alloy steels, e.g., chromium steel, stainless steel.

chromosome (krō'mŭsōm'), form assumed by chromatin material of cell nucleus during stages of MITO-SIS and meiosis. The form and number of chromosomes depend upon the species, but chromosomes always occur in pairs (except in the case of the two sex chromosomes, which are usually similar in the female, dissimilar in the male). The alternate genes for the expression of any particular character occupy corresponding positions on each of the two chromosomes of a chromosome pair. Chromosomes are important in heredity, evolution, mutation of plants and

animals, and determination of SEX. For process of mitosis, see *ill.*, p. 329.

chromosphere (krō'mō–), rarefied layer of gases surrounding the sun and lying outside the photosphere but inside the corona. The chromosphere layer consists chiefly of hydrogen (radiating scarlet light), helium, and calcium and extends 5,000–7,500 mi.; layer 100 to 200 mi. thick at the base is known as reversing layer. Moving gases form projections (prominences) observable during eclipses or through spectroscope. Eruptive prominences burst forth in jets; cloudlike quiescent prominences extend from pole to pole.

Chronicles or **Paralipomenon** (păr"ŭlĭpŏm'ĭnŏn) [Gr., = things left out], books of Old Testament, called 1 and 2 Chronicles in AV, 1 and 2 Paralipomenon in Greek Bible and Western canon. Books contain: genealogies; history of reigns of David and Solomon; history of kingdom of Judah. Historical material parallels (and supplements) parts of Samuel and Kings.

chrysanthemum (krĭsăn'thŭmŭm), annual or perennial plant of genus *Chrysanthemum*. Late-blooming flowers, of various colors except blue or purple, range from single daisylike to large, rounded shaggy forms. Cultivated in Orient for at least 2,000 years.

Chryseis (krīsē'ĭs), in the *Iliad*, girl captured by Agamemnon. Forced by Apollo to return Chryseis, Agamemnon took Briseis from Achilles to replace her and thus aroused the wrath of Achilles.

Chrysippus (krī'sĭpŭs), c.280–c.207 B.C., Greek philosopher, who systematized Stoic philosophy.

chrysoberyl (krĭ'sŭbĕ"rĭl), a beryllium aluminate used as a gem. It is transparent to translucent and has a vitreous luster. The most valuable CAT'S-EYE is chrysoberyl. Other varieties are yellow-green chrysolite and alexandrite, which is green in natural light but red in artificial light.

Chrysostom: see JOHN CHRYSOSTOM, SAINT.

Chuang-tze (chōōäng'-tsä'), fl. 4th cent. B.C., Chinese philosopher, a follower of Lao-tze, whose doctrines he interpreted with great skill and charm.

chuck-will's-widow, bird of S U.S. allied to nighthawk and whippoorwill. Its call has the sound of its name.

Chudskoye, Lake: see PEIPUS, LAKE.

Chufut-Kale (chōōfōōt'-kŭlyĕ'), ruined fortress and town, SE Ukraine, in S Crimea, near Bakhchisarai. Center of Jewish sect of Karaites during Turkish rule (1475–1783). Last refuge of Crimean Khazars.

Chugach Mountains (chōō'găk), continuation of St. Elias Mts., S Alaska, rising to more than 13,000 ft. and bordering N shore of Prince William Sound.

Chugach National Forest (chōō'găk), S Alaska, in E part of Kenai Peninsula and along Prince William Sound. Mainly hemlock and spruce.

Chuguchak (chōōgōōchäk') or **Tarbagatai** (tärbägätī'), Chinese *Tahcheng,* town (pop. c.5,000), N Sinkiang prov., China, in Dzungaria. Center for trade with USSR. Was part of East Turkistan Republic 1944–50.

Chukchi Peninsula (chōōk'chē), NE extremity of Asia and Siberia, RSFSR, terminating in EAST CAPE. Population largely Chukchis, of Hyperborean language family; subsist on reindeer raising, fishing, fur trapping. Coal mines on Anadyr Gulf. Chukchi Natl. *Okrug* [area] (284,826 sq. mi.; 1965 est. pop. 78,000) was formed 1930.

Chulalongkorn (chōō'lälông'kôrn) or **Rama V** (rä'mä), 1853–1910, king of Siam (1868–1910). Greatly advanced Westernization begun by his father King Mongkut and thus kept Siam independent while rest of SE Asia fell subject to France and Britain.

Chula Vista (chōō'lū), city (pop. 42,034), S Calif., S of San Diego on San Diego Bay, in agr. (citrus fruit, vegetables) region.

Chungking (chōong"kĭng'), city (pop. c.1,620,000), SE Szechwan prov., China; port at junction of Kialing and Yangtze R. Commercial center of W China, also industrial center. Opened 1891 as treaty port. Wartime cap. of China (1937–46).

Chungshan (jŏong'shän'), town (pop. c.110,500), Kwangtung prov., China. Trade port on Chungshan (or Macao) isl., near Macao. Renamed Chungshan in honor of Sun Yat-sen, who was born here.

Chuquisaca: see SUCRE, Bolivia.

Chur (kŏor), Fr. *Coire,* town (pop. 24,825), cap. of Grisons canton, E Switzerland, on Plessur R. Roman settlement; early episcopal see. Temporal power of prince-bishops was ended by Reformation (1524–26). Has 8th-cent. church (restored), cathedral (12th–13th cent.), episcopal palace.

Church, Sir Arthur Herbert, 1834–1915, English chemist; discovered the mineral churchite, named for him.

Church, Frederick Edwin, 1826–1900, American landscape painter of the Hudson River School.

Church, aggregation of Christian believers; in its widest sense embracing all believers, living and dead, headed by Jesus Christ, who founded the community through his apostles. An early traditionalist division distinguishes the church militant (living Christians) from the church suffering (the dead in Purgatory) and the church triumphant (the saints in Heaven). In more usual parlance the church is the organized aspect of any sect or group of believers (e.g., the Lutheran Church, the Church of England, the Church of the Brethren, the Roman Catholic Church), but in most cases each group conceives itself to be the one true Christian body. See CHRISTIANITY.

Churches of Christ, conservative body of Protestant Christians, formerly united with Disciples of Christ. Congregational in polity, biblical in doctrine, evangelistic; one of largest U.S. denominations.

Churchill, Charles, 1731–64, English satirical poet, author of *The Rosciad* (1761), satire on actors.

Churchill, John: see MARLBOROUGH, JOHN CHURCHILL, 1ST DUKE OF.

Churchill, Lord Randolph Henry Spencer, 1849–95, British statesman. Sought to create a democratic Tory party. Resigned as chancellor of exchequer 1886 in opposition to high military spending. Father of Sir Winston Churchill.

Churchill, Winston, 1871–1947, American author of historical novels (*Richard Carvel,* 1899, *The Crisis,* 1901) and novels on social, religious, and political problems (*The Inside of the Cup,* 1913).

Churchill, Sir Winston Leonard Spencer, 1874–1965, British statesman, soldier, author. Fought in India, the Sudan, and South Africa. Elected to Parliament 1900. First lord of the admiralty in First World War (1911–15) until discredited by failure of Dardanelles campaign. Returned to office in Lloyd George Liberal government (1917–21). Conservative chancellor of exchequer 1924–29; subsequent influence as opponent of "appeasement" of Germany led to his replacing (1940) Neville CHAMBERLAIN as prime minister of coalition government seven months after outbreak of Second World War. Became symbol of British resistance. Before the entry of U.S. into war he met Pres. Roosevelt at sea (see ATLANTIC CHARTER). Twice addressed U.S. Congress. Attended series of international conferences—CASABLANCA; QUEBEC; CAIRO; YALTA; TEHERAN; POTSDAM. After Labour party victory 1945 became leader of the opposition. Conservative victory in 1951 brought him back as prime minister; retired 1955. Author of histories, biographies, and memoirs, he was awarded the 1953 Nobel Prize in Literature. Knighted 1953.

Churchill, river, N Sask. and N Man., Canada, issuing from Methy L. and flowing c.1,000 mi. SE, E, and NE to Hudson Bay at Churchill. Traverses many lakes and was famous fur-trading route. Mouth of river discovered 1619 by Scandinavian Jens Munck. Hudson's Bay Co. estab. trading post (1689) which was later abandoned and then refounded at Fort Churchill (later known as Fort Prince of Wales). Superseded c.1732 when heavy stone fort was built on W side of river's mouth. Remains of this fort now in national park. **Churchill,** port on Hudson Bay at mouth of Churchill R., was selected 1927 as terminus of Hudson Bay RR (completed 1929). Serves N Man. as grain-shipping port from mid-Aug. to mid-Oct.

Churchill College: see CAMBRIDGE UNIVERSITY.

Churchill Downs: see LOUISVILLE, Ky.

Church of Christ, Scientist: see CHRISTIAN SCIENCE.

Church of England: see ENGLAND, CHURCH OF.

Church of God: see ADVENTISTS.

Church of the Brethren: see BRETHREN.

Church Slavonic, literary language of the E and S Slavs. Like Latin in the West, it was used both in secular and religious writings. Three major forms are recognized of which the Russian has been generalized. Used today in the Orthodox Eastern Church.

Churriguera, José (chŭr"ĭgâr'ù; hōsā' chŏor-rĕgä'rä), 1665–1725, Spanish baroque artist and sculptor, b. Salamanca. Went to Madrid 1688 where he designed the catafalque for Queen María Luisa. Works include palace of Don Juan de Goyeneche. Extravagant design and capricious use of Renaissance motives led to the use of the term **Churrigueresque** (chŭr"ĕgù-rĕsk') for Spanish architecture of the late 17th and early 18th cent. The style influenced Spanish colonial work in Mexico and SW U.S.

Churubusco, battle: see CONTRERAS.

Chusan Archipelago (chŏo'sän'), Chekiang prov., China, in East China Sea. Includes main island of Chusan and c.100 lesser islands. Richest fishing ground off China coast. Puto or P'u-t'o isl. is sacred Buddhist center.

Chu Teh (jŏo'dŭ'), 1886?–, Chinese Communist leader. Trained at Yünnan military academy and in Germany and USSR. Joined the CHINESE COMMUNIST PARTY in 1922. Led the LONG MARCH (1934–35) to NW China with Mao Tse-tung. Commander in chief of all Chinese Communist forces in the Second World War and subsequent civil war; retained that post and was also named deputy chairman in People's Republic of China (founded 1949).

Chuvash Autonomous Soviet Socialist Republic (chōo-väsh'), autonomous state (7,066 sq. mi.; 1965 est. pop. 1,168,000), E European RSFSR, in Volga valley; cap. Cheboksary. Agr., forests. Population 80% Chuvash, a people of Finnic language.

Ciano, Galeazzo (gäläät'tsō chä'nō), 1903–44, Italian Fascist leader, count of Cortellazzo. Married Mussolini's daughter Edda. Foreign minister 1936–43. Helped to bring about Mussolini's fall in 1943. Arrested by Germans; executed by Fascist republic in N Italy. His diaries are a remarkable document.

Ciardi, John (chē är'dē), 1916–, American poet, translator of Dante. His poetry includes *In the Stoneworks* (1961). Also an editor, critic, and teacher.

Cibber, Colley, 1671–1757, English actor and playwright. Known for fop roles of Restoration comedy (after 1690). Manager of Drury Lane Theatre 1710–40. His play *Love's Last Shift* (1696) regarded as first sentimental comedy. Poet laureate 1730–57, attacked by Pope in *The Dunciad.* His son, **Theophilus Cibber,** 1703–58, acted in Colley's plays. Theophilus's wife, **Susannah Maria (Arne) Cibber,** 1714–66, sang in operas and acted tragic roles (e.g., Lady Macbeth and Desdemona). Handel wrote contralto arias in his *Messiah* for her.

Cibola: see MARCOS DE NIZA; CORONADO, FRANCISCO VÁSQUEZ DE.

cicada (sĭkā'dù), name for homopterous insect with wide, blunt head, prominent eyes, two pairs of membranous wings. Periodical or 17-year (13-year in S U.S.) cicada is miscalled locust. Shrill song of males caused by vibrating membranes near abdomen. Different broods mature nearly every year.

Cicero, Marcus Tullius (sĭ'sùrō), or **Tully,** 106–43 B.C., Roman orator, politician, philosopher. Consul in 63 B.C. Prosecuted Cataline. Exiled by Clodius and recalled by Pompey (58–57 B.C.). A republican, he opposed Caesar; attacked Antony in the *Philippics.* He was put to death by 2nd Triumvirate. His letters reveal Roman life; his philosophical works (*On Ends,*

On the Nature of the Gods, etc.) express his mild Stoicism and, together with his rhetorical works, reveal him as the great master of Latin prose.

Cicero, industrial town (pop. 69,130), NE Ill., a suburb NW of Chicago; founded 1857.

Cid or **Cid Campeador** (sĭd′ kăm′pĕŭdôr), d. 1099, Spanish national hero; real name Rodrigo (or Ruy) Díaz de Vivar. Served under Castilian kings, emir of Saragossa, fighting both Moors and Christians. Conquered Valencia (1094), where he ruled until death. For his chivalry, generosity, became prototype of noble Castilian warrior. Hero of *The Song of the Cid* (12th-cent. anonymous epic) and dramas by Guillén de Castro and Corneille.

cider, in Europe, is fermented juice of apples, often aged in casks; in U.S., unless qualified as "hard" cider, it is unfermented apple juice, usually pasteurized and often blended to balance the flavor.

Ciego de Ávila (syä′gō dä ä′vēlä), city (pop. c.98,000), central Cuba; a commercial center halfway between Santiago de Cuba and Havana.

Cienfuegos (syĕnfwä′gōs), city (pop. c.100,000), central Cuba, port on Caribbean. Has large and beautiful harbor. Sugar is chief product.

Cierva, Juan de la (hwän′ dä lä thyĕr′vä), 1895–1936, Spanish aeronautical engineer. Inventor of autogiro, first flown in 1923.

Cieszyn: see TESCHEN.

Cilicia (sĭlĭ′shù), anc. region of SE Asia Minor, between the Mediterranean and the Taurus range. Divided into unproductive plateau (Cilicia Trachia) and fertile plain (Cilicia Pedias). Part of the Assyrian Empire and the Persian Empire, it was later Hellenized. The cities of Tarsus and Seleucia throve under Roman and Byzantine rule. Cilicia, invaded by Arabs in the 8th cent., and in 1080 an Armenian state was set up here (later Little Armenia), to last until conquered by the Turks in 1375.

Cilician Gates (sĭlĭ′shùn), mountain pass, S Turkey, across Taurus mts., known anciently as Pylae Ciliciae, now as Gulek Bogazi. Crossed by an ancient highway from Cappadocia to Cilicia.

Cimabue, Giovanni (jōvän′nĕ chĕmäbōō′ä), d. c.1302, Florentine painter, reputedly the teacher of Giotto. Frescoes in Church of St. Francis, Assisi, are attributed to him. His work is a transition from the formalized Byzantine style to the more naturalistic 14th-cent. manner.

Cimarosa, Domenico (dōmä′nĕkō chĕmärō′zä), 1749–1801, Italian composer. *Il matrimonio segreto* is the best of his *opera buffa*. He also wrote serious operas, church music, and instrumental music.

Cimarron (sĭm″ŭrōn′), river, c.600 mi. long, rising in NE N.Mex. and flowing E, barely touching Okla. Panhandle and SE Colo., to enter Kansas. Crosses and recrosses Okla. line, then swings SE and E across Okla. to Arkansas R. just W of Tulsa.

Cimarron, Territory of, now the Panhandle of Okla. Settled by cattle ranchers. Efforts to estab. separate territory failed, and in 1890 area became part of Oklahoma Territory.

Cimber, Lucius Tillius, d. after 44 B.C., one of the conspirators against Julius Caesar. On the pretext of presenting a petition he approached Caesar, then held him as Casca stabbed him.

Cimbri: see GERMANS.

Cimmerians (sĭmĕr′ĕŭnz), anc. people who in 8th cent. B.C. moved from the Crimea to the region of Lake Van. In the late 7th cent. B.C. they swept across Asia Minor. Traditionally considered as fierce barbarians, they are actually little known in history.

Cimon (sī′mŭn) d. 449 B.C., Athenian general and statesman; son of Miltiades. In the Persian Wars he fought at Salamis and commanded in the defeat of the Persians on the Eurymedon (468 B.C.). The leader of the aristocratic party after the death of Aristides, he was exiled but later recalled.

cinchona (sĭngkō′nù), evergreen tree (*Cinchona*), native to Andes of South America. Its bark is source of

QUININE. Before Second World War, Java and India grew commercial supply; later South America cultivated wild trees.

Cincinnati (sĭnsĭnä′tē), city, (pop. 502,550), extreme SW Ohio, on Ohio R. opposite Covington, Ky.; founded 1788. State's second largest city and industrial, commercial, and cultural center for large area. Has extensive river front and good transportation facilities. Mfg. of machine tools, transportation and radar equipment, electrical machinery, and cosmetics. Busy shipping center for early settlers and first seat of Northwest Territory legislature, it was aided by opening of Ohio and Erie Canal in 1830s. Early abolitionist center and Underground Railroad station. City survived severe flood, crime waves, and riots in 1880s. Adoption of city-manager government in 1924 ended long period of political misrule. Seat of Univ. of CINCINNATI, the Athenaeum of Ohio, Our Lady of Cincinnati Col., and Xavier Univ. Has Cincinnati Symphony Orchestra (founded 1895), Taft Mus., and Eden Park (with zoo, art, and natural history museums).

Cincinnati, Society of the [Latin plural of *Cincinnatus*], formed in 1783 by officers of Continental army after American Revolution. Founded for fraternal, patriotic, and allegedly nonpolitical aims.

Cincinnati, University of, at Cincinnati, Ohio; coed.; founded 1819 as Cincinnati Col., inc. 1870 as municipal university, opened 1873. The Col. of Music of Cincinnati, Cincinnati Conservatory of Music, and Cincinnati Observatory are affiliated.

Cincinnatus (sĭnsĭnä′tùs, –nä′tùs), fl. 5th cent. B.C., semilegendary Roman hero. Consul in 460, he in 458 left his farm to become dictator, defeated the Aequi and the Volsci, and immediately returned to his farm.

cinema, film or motion picture industry. Experiments with serial photography in the 1860s led to the marketing in 1893 of the Kinetoscope (developed in the laboratories of Thomas Alva Edison) for peep-show viewing of early films at penny arcades. After 1896 moving pictures were projected on a screen by the Cinématographe of the Lumière brothers; after 1902 nickelodeons were built. In the U.S. after 1913, independent movie producers moved from New York city area to Hollywood to avoid the action of a patent company formed 1909. The star system evolved, and the work of directors such as D. W. GRIFFITH made U.S. the dominant force in the industry. Feature-length pictures were made after 1913; sound was introduced 1927 in *The Jazz Singer;* technicolor was developed after 1932 and Cinemascope and stereophonic sound after 1950. In France the newsreel was introduced c.1909 by Charles Pathé and the animated cartoon c.1905 by Emile Cohl.

cineraria (sĭn″ùrâr′–), pot plant of genus *Senecio,* with daisylike flower clusters above big leaves.

Cinna, Lucius Cornelius (sĭ′nù), d. 84 B.C., Roman statesman, leader of the popular party, consul (87 B.C.–84 B.C.). When Sulla left Italy, Cinna undertook anti-Sullan electoral reforms, and the conservatives drove him from power. He gathered an army, recalled MARIUS from Africa and took Rome, where he slaughtered Sulla's followers. Cinna was murdered in a mutiny as the civil war began. His daughter Cornelia was married to Julius Caesar.

cinnabar (sĭn′ùbär), mineral, sulfide of mercury, used chiefly as a source of mercury.

cinnamon, tropical evergreen tree (*Cinnamomum zeylanicum*) of Ceylon, and its aromatic bark. Cut-back plants produce many shoots from which commercial stick cinnamon, a flavoring, is obtained. Bark of another species, cassia bark tree, is considered inferior substitute. *C. camphora* yields camphor.

cinnamon vine: see YAM.

Cinq Mars, Henri Coëffier, marquis de (ärē′ kōĕfyä′ märkē′ dù sĕmär′), 1620–42, French conspirator. Favorite of Louis XIII; plotted with Spain against Richelieu. Executed. Subject of novel by de Vigny.

cinquefoil (sĭngk′–), plant of widely distributed genus *Potentilla*, bearing yellow flowers and foliage with five leaflets. Some species are grown in rock gardens and some are used for home remedies.

Cinque Ports (sĭngk) (Fr.,= five ports), group of maritime towns in Sussex and Kent, England. Originally five (Hastings, Romney, Hythe, Dover, and Sandwich); other places later added. For charter and other privileges, they provided ships and men against invasion before English navy was estab. Walmer Castle, near Deal, is official residence of Lord Warden. Importance declined after 1688.

Cinto, Monte (môn′tä chĕn′tō), peak (8,879 ft.), N central Corsica, France, NW of Corte.

Cintra, Port. *Sintra* (sēn′trù), town (pop. 7,340), Portugal, near Lisbon. Beautiful situation made it favorite residence of Portuguese kings. Has ruins of Moorish castle, old royal palace and monastery. By Convention of Cintra (1808) French troops under Junot were permitted to leave Portugal.

CIO: see AMERICAN FEDERATION OF LABOR–CONGRESS OF INDUSTRIAL ORGANIZATIONS.

cipher: see CRYPTOGRAPHY.

Circassia (sûrkă′shù), historic region, SE European RSFSR, between Black Sea, Kuban R., and Greater Caucasus, now in Krasnodar and Stavropol Territories. The Circassians (also known as Cherkess, Adyge, Adighe), a people of the N Caucasian language family, abandoned Christianity for Islam in 17th cent. Circassian women, famed for beauty, were prized as slaves in Turkey. Ceded by Turkey to Russia in 1829, Circassia resisted Russian conquest until 1864. They number c.178,000; of this c.30,000 live in the USSR (largely in Adyge and Karachi-Cherkess autonomous oblasts).

Circe (sûr′sē), in Greek legend, celebrated enchantress; daughter of Helios. She changed companions of Odysseus into swine, but he made her break the spell.

circle, closed plane curve each point of which is equidistant from point within called the center. Also defined as a CONIC SECTION cut by plane perpendicular to cone axis. Surface within curve also called circle, curve itself called circumference; line with each end on circumference called chord; chord through center called diameter; any line joining center with circumference called radius. For formula for area of a circle see AREA.

Circleville, city (pop. 11,059), S central Ohio, on Ohio and Erie Canal and Scioto R., S of Columbus, in farm area. Laid out 1810 within remains of circular fort allegedly erected by mound builders.

circuit, electric: see ELECTRIC CIRCUIT.

circuit rider, itinerant preacher of Methodist denomination, who served "circuit" of 20 to 40 "appointments." System, devised by John Wesley for his scattered English groups and adapted in America by Francis Asbury, greatly aided spread of Methodism.

circulation of the blood, continuous passage of blood through heart and blood vessels. Oxygenated blood is forced into general systemic circulation from left ventricle of heart through arteries into network of capillaries through whose thin walls oxygen and nutriment pass into tissues and carbon dioxide and other wastes enter blood. Deoxygenated blood returns from capillaries through veins to right auricle of heart. Blood then passes to right ventricle, from which it is pumped through pulmonary artery to lungs. After interchange of carbon dioxide and oxygen in lungs, oxygenated blood passes through pulmonary veins and left auricle into left ventricle where cycle begins anew. See *ill.,* p. 657.

circus [Latin,= circle], associated historically with chariot races and athletic contests of anc. Rome known as Circensian games. Famous *circi* were Circus Maximus, Circus Flaminius, and Circus Neronis of Caligula and Nero, at which many Christians perished. Modern circus began at end of 18th cent. as a tent show. Outstanding circus was that of P. T. BARNUM.

Cirencester (sīs′ĭtŭr, sī′rúnsĕstŭr), urban district (pop. 11,836), Gloucestershire, England. Site of Roman settlement Corinium. Royal Agr. Col. nearby.

cirrhosis, degeneration of tissue in any organ, especially of the liver. Most prevalent in middle-aged males with histories of chronic alcoholism.

Cirta: see CONSTANTINE, Algeria.

Cisalpine Republic (sĭsăl′pĭn), N Italian state created 1797 by Bonaparte through union of Cispadane and Transpadane republics, which he had set up 1796 N and S of Po R. In practice a French protectorate. Renamed Italian Republic 1802. Merged with Venetia in Napoleonic kingdom of Italy 1805.

Cisleithania: see AUSTRO-HUNGARIAN MONARCHY.

Cisneros, Francisco Jiménez de: see JIMÉNEZ DE CISNEROS, FRANCISCO.

Cispadane Republic: see CISALPINE REPUBLIC.

Cistercians (sĭstûr′shùnz), order of Roman Catholic monks founded (1098) by St. Robert, Abbot of Molesme, in Cîteaux [*Cistercium*], France. The particular stamp of the Cistercians stems from the abbacy of St. STEPHEN HARDING (after 1109). They became known as White Monks because of their white habit. The greatness of the order came with St. Bernard of Clairvaux, under whom it expanded phenomenally. In attempting to restore the early simplicity of the Benedictines, they stressed love of God, cheerful practice of austerities, and practice of manual labor, especially farming. The order became less prominent after 1400. Of later Cistercian reforms most important was that of the TRAPPISTS. The center of Cistercian communal life is the abbey. Cistercian nuns (order founded 12th cent.) lead contemplative lives, secluded from the world; a 17th-cent. reform of this order gave rise to the remarkable development of Port-Royal.

Citadel, The—The Military College of South Carolina, at Charleston; state supported; for men; chartered 1842 as The Citadel, opened 1843. Called South Carolina Military Academy 1882–1910.

Cîteaux, Côte-d'Or dept., France: see CISTERCIANS.

Cithaeron (sĭthē′rùn), Gr. *Kythairon,* mountain ridge, c.10 mi. long, central Greece, between Boeotia (N) and Attica and Megaris (S). Rises to 4,623 ft. Scene of many mythical events; sacred to Dionysus.

citrange, citrus-fruit hybrid from cross between sweet and trifoliate oranges. Hardier than orange.

citric acid (sĭ′trĭk), white, crystalline organic acid with tart taste, found in fruits. With alkaline earths and metals, it forms citrates used as laxatives. Acid used as antalkali, in calico printing, in soft drinks (as lemon juice substitute). May be prepared by fermenting sugar.

citron, small evergreen tree (*Citrus medica*), native to tropical Asia and related to other citrus fruit trees. Rind of its large lemon-shaped fruit, when candied and preserved, is used in confectionery and cookery.

citrus fruits: see CITRANGE; CITRON; GRAPEFRUIT; KUMQUAT; LEMON; LIME; ORANGE; TANGERINE.

Città Vecchia (chĕt-tä′ vĕk′kyä), **Città Notabile** (nōtä′bĕlä), or Maltese **Mdina** (ùmdĕ′nä), town, central Malta. Former cap. of Malta, has old palace of grand masters of Knights Hospitalers.

City College, The, of The City University of New York, estab. 1847 as the Free Academy, called Col. of the City of New York 1866–1929; coed. Uptown center includes schools of education, liberal arts, and technology; Bernard M. Baruch School of Business and Public Administration is downtown.

city government, political administration of urban areas. In U.S. generally, incorporated urban areas were given freedom in local matters, with a mayor and council as administrators. In 20th cent., complexity increased, efficiency waned, and reform movements (e.g., for commission form or for city manager) arose. Where state lines cut through metropolitan area other forms grew (e.g., Port of N.Y. Authority).

City of David, epithet of BETHLEHEM, the birthplace of David, and of JERUSALEM, his capital.

SMALL CAPITALS = cross references. Pronunciation key on inside end pages. Abbreviations: p. 2.

City of Refuge National Historical Park: see NATIONAL PARKS AND MONUMENTS (table).

city planning of urban centers is to secure healthful living conditions, convenient communications, and beauty. Begun in anc. times; much practiced in Europe in 17th and 18th cent. Legislation enabling U.S. cities to carry out planning projects enacted in late 19th cent. Most important example in U.S. is Washington, D.C., planned by L'Enfant 1791. A modern planning problem is integration of all communications into single mechanism.

City Point, Va.: see HOPEWELL.

city-state, autonomous neighborhood as a political and social unity, normally a single city or town with the surrounding countryside. At the dawn of history in Mesopotamia it was the normal type of organized life, and the Babylonian and Assyrian empires grew out of the cities. City-states have been known at various times and in various lands, but the most celebrated were those of ancient Greece, which cradled Western civilization. Though the modern idea of democracy stems from them (particularly from Athens) they were by no means all democracies; more commonly they were monarchies or oligarchies. Other famous examples of the city-state were the free imperial cities of the Holy Roman Empire and many of the Italian states in the Renaissance.

Ciudad (syōōdhädh′) [Span.,= city]. For cities beginning thus but not so listed, see under following name; e.g., for Ciudad Juárez, see JUÁREZ.

Ciudad Bolívar (syōōdhädh′ bōlē′vär), city (pop. c.85,-000), E Venezuela, port on Orinoco; founded 1764 as Angostura.

Ciudad Real (thyōōdhädh′ rääl′), city (pop. 19,728), cap. of Ciudad Real prov., central Spain, in New Castile. Medieval walls; Gothic cathedral.

civet (sĭ′vĭt) or **civet cat,** mammal of family Viverridae, related to cats. Both sexes have scent pouch (near anus) which yields fatty secretion used in Orient as perfume base; much of commercial supply comes from African civet (*Civettictis*). Oriental civet (*Viverra*) found in India and SE Asia.

civil defense, government activities designed to protect citizens from enemy attack. Comprises warning and protection and rescue functions; grew in proportion to use of aircraft in modern warfare. Principal U.S. civil defense agency estab. 1951; functions transferred to Defense Dept. 1961.

Civilian Conservation Corps (CCC), organization (estab. 1933; abolished 1942) to provide useful work and vocational training for unemployed young men. Aided nation by conservation of natural resources.

civil law, the law governing private affairs in contrast to public law and criminal law. In a restricted sense, signifies a modern legal system (see CODE) based on Roman law, especially as formulated in *Corpus Juris Civilis* and revived by law scholars in 11th and 12th cents. Civil law prevails on Continent, Latin America, and Westernized countries of Asia. Contrasts with COMMON LAW, usual in English-speaking countries (only La. and Quebec have civil law).

civil rights, rights a state's inhabitants enjoy by law. The term is broader than "political rights," which devolve from the franchise and are usually held only by citizens. In U.S., civil rights are thought of as specific rights guaranteed in the Constitution (e.g., freedom of speech, the rights to due process of law, equal protection under the law). An organization devoted to the protection of individuals' civil rights is the American Civil Liberties Union. In U.S. history, the term *civil rights* has been more specifically used to refer to the movement to extend rights fully to Negroes. Civil Rights Acts of 1866, 1870, 1871, 1875 granted such basic freedoms as rights to sue, give evidence, hold property. No further Federal legislation until act of 1957, which estab. investigatory Commission on Civil Rights and clarified role of Federal district courts in civil rights cases. Acts of 1957 and 1960 attempted further to protect voting

and other rights. Sweeping provisions of Civil Rights Act of 1964 included more effective guarantee of right to vote; prohibition of discrimination in public accommodations and businesses, in public facilities such as parks, libraries, hospitals, schools; guarantee of equal employment. Voting rights act passed in 1965 suspended literacy tests and other devices found to be discriminatory and provided for the appointment of Federal registrars in states and counties where such devices were used in 1964 and where less than half of eligible voters were registered or voted in 1964. See also INTEGRATION.

civil service, body of persons employed in the civil administration of a government (not including the military or elected officials). Term first used for British administrators in India, later for British home officials. It became popular in U.S. with rising demand for reforming the system after the Civil War. A Civil Service Commission was set up (1871) but was allowed to lapse and was restored by Pendleton Act (1883) only after Pres. Garfield was killed by a disappointed office seeker. Commission draws up rules to give positions on merit in certain classifications; the number of classified posts has constantly been increased. The British tradition of separation of civil service from politics has been adopted in U.S., notably by the Hatch Act (1940) forbidding officeholders to contribute to political campaigns. Civil service and official party tend to interpenetrate in totalitarian countries.

civil war, in English history: see PURITAN REVOLUTION; ROSES, WARS OF THE.

civil war, in Roman history: see MARIUS and SULLA; POMPEY and CAESAR, JULIUS.

Civil War, in U.S. history (1861–65), conflict between Northern states (Union) and Southern states in secession (see CONFEDERACY), also called the War between the States or the War of the Rebellion. Many contributing causes included sectional rivalry, moral campaign of ABOLITIONISTS, and especially quarrel concerning Federal control *vs.* STATES' RIGHTS. When compromise failed, conflict loomed. Election of Abraham Lincoln as President, and secession of Southern states (1860–61), precipitated war. When on April 12, 1861, P. G. T. Beauregard ordered Confederates to fire on Fort Sumter, hostilities began. In 1861 opening battles were Confederate victories. Irvin McDowell was defeated by Beauregard at first battle of BULL RUN, July 21. In 1862 G. B. McClellan's PENINSULAR CAMPAIGN was foiled by R. E. Lee. However, Lee's ANTIETAM CAMPAIGN was checked by McClellan in September. Lincoln then issued EMANCIPATION PROCLAMATION. Year closed with Union defeat at Fredericksburg, Dec. 13. The next year saw Confederate victory over Joseph Hooker at Chancellorsville, May 2–4, marred by death of Stonewall Jackson. Then Lee undertook the GETTYSBURG CAMPAIGN, that marked the down turn of Confederate fortunes. Meanwhile Northern navy had successfully blockaded Southern coast, under D. G. Farragut captured New Orleans (April 28, 1862), and ended day of wooden battleships (see MONITOR AND MERRIMAC). CONFEDERATE CRUISERS, built or bought in England, in turn caused great loss to Northern shipping. In West, U. S. Grant won great victory at Fort DONELSON (Feb., 1862), followed by drawn battle at Shiloh on April 6–7. Union gunboats on the Mississippi opened way for Grant's successful VICKSBURG CAMPAIGN. The Confederate general Braxton Bragg, checked by G. H. Thomas at Chickamauga in CHATTANOOGA CAMPAIGN (1863), was driven back to Ga. Grant moved against Lee in WILDERNESS CAMPAIGN (May–June, 1864), forcing him toward Richmond, and laying siege to PETERSBURG. W. T. Sherman won ATLANTA CAMPAIGN (May–Sept., 1864), and made his march to the sea. After victory of P. H. Sheridan at FIVE FORKS, April 1, 1865, Confederates evacuated Richmond on April 3. His retreat blocked, Lee surrendered to Grant at Appomattox Courthouse, April

9, 1865. Victory was marred by assassination of Pres. Lincoln. But seceding states, after trials of RECONSTRUCTION, were readmitted, and Union was saved, with slavery abolished.

Civitali, Matteo (mät-tä′ō chĕvētä′lē), 1436–1501, b. and worked in Lucca; one of the major sculptors of the 15th cent. outside Florence.

Civitavecchia (chē′vētä-vĕk′kēä), city (est. pop. 37,-545), Latium, central Italy, on Tyrrhenian Sea; port of Rome. Arsenal built by Bernini; citadel by Bramante and Michelangelo.

Cl, chemical symbol of the element CHLORINE.

Clackmannanshire (klăkmă′nŭnshĭr) or Clackmannan, smallest county (pop. 41,391) of Scotland, at head of Firth of Forth; co. town Clackmannan. Coal mining; also dairy farming, sheep raising.

Claflin, Tennessee, 1845–1923, lecturer on woman suffrage; sister of Victoria WOODHULL.

Clair, René (klâr′), 1898–, French film director. His films, filled with sophisticated wit and fantastic satire, include Sous les toits de Paris, À nous la liberté, Le Million, The Ghost Goes West, and Beauty and the Devil. Elected to French Academy 1962.

Clairaut, Alexis Claude (älĕksēs′ klōd′ klērō′), 1713–65, French mathematician, noted for work on differential equations and curves, geodesy, and astronomy.

Clairton, city (pop. 18,389), SW Pa., on Monongahela R., SE of Pittsburgh. Steel mfg.

Clairvaux: see VILLE-SOUS-LA-FERTÉ.

clam, bivalve mollusk with muscular foot for burrowing in sand or mud. Shell valves are hinged, movable; the mantle, a skin fold of body, secretes shell and with gills carries on respiration; cilia of gills cause water current (bearing food and oxygen) to enter one siphon and exit (with wastes) through other. The hard or round clam (adult of little neck or cherry stone) is widely eaten.

clan, social grouping based on common, unilateral descent of its members. Includes number of families and is included in larger tribal organization. Unlike family, descent is traced through one parent. Within clan, family relations are extended beyond biological lines, and in some clans marriage to fellow member is prohibited or discouraged.

Clapham, Sir John Harold, 1873–1946, English political scientist and economic historian. Noted for An Economic History of Modern Britain (2d ed., 3 vols., 1931–38).

Clapham, residential district, SW London, England.

Clapperton, Hugh, 1778–1827, British explorer, b. Scotland. One of first Europeans to travel through HAUSA STATES.

Clare or Clara, Saint, 1193?–1253, Italian nun, founder of the Franciscan nuns or Poor Clares. Proclaimed (1958) by Pope Pius XII as patron saint of television. Feast: Aug. 12.

Clare, John, 1793–1864, English bucolic poet, called the English Burns.

Clare, John Fitzgibbon, 1st earl of, 1748–1802, Irish statesman; lord chancellor of Ireland. Hated by the Irish for advocating union with Britain.

Clare, Richard de: see PEMBROKE, RICHARD DE CLARE, 2D EARL OF.

Clare, county (1,231 sq. mi.; pop. 73,710). Munster prov., Ireland; co. town Ennis. Broken, hilly region, with bogs and lakes and rugged coastline. Fishing and farming are chief occupations; much of land barren. Has relics of anc. peoples.

Clare College: see CAMBRIDGE UNIVERSITY.

Claremont. 1 City (pop. 12,633), S Calif., E of Los Angeles; settled 1886. The CLAREMONT COLLEGES are here. 2 City (pop. 13,563), SW N.H., on Sugar R. near its junction with Connecticut R., S of Lebanon; settled 1762.

Claremont Colleges, The, at Claremont, Calif.; founded 1925; known until 1961 as Associated Colleges at Claremont. Included are Pomona Col. (inc. 1887, opened 1888; coed.), Scripps Col. (chartered 1926, opened 1927; for women), Claremont Men's

Col. (chartered and opened 1946), Harvey Mudd Col. (inc. 1955, opened 1957; coed.), Pitzer Col. (founded 1963; for women), and Claremont Graduate School and Univ. Center (founded 1925; coed.).

Claremore, city (pop. 6,639), NE Okla., NE of Tulsa; settled in late 19th cent. A health resort, with mineral springs. Has memorial to native son Will Rogers and U.S. Indian hospital.

Clarence, George, duke of, 1449–78, son of Richard, duke of York. Joined Richard, earl of WARWICK, in rebellions against his brother Edward IV, 1469–70. Arrested for treason and thrown into the Tower (1478); allegedly drowned in a butt of malmsey wine. Prominent character in Shakespeare's Richard III.

Clarence, Lionel, duke of, 1338–68, third son of Edward III of England. Governor of Ireland 1361–67; presided at assembly adopting notorious Statute of Kilkenny, forbidding all dealings between the English in Ireland and the Irish.

Clarendon, Edward Hyde, 1st earl of, 1609–74, English statesman and historian. A monarchist, he aided Charles I and went into exile with Charles II, whose chief adviser he became. At Restoration became lord chancellor. Favored religious toleration. Unsuccessful in diplomacy and disliked at court, he was removed from office (1667), fled England, and died in exile. Wrote History of the Rebellion. His daughter, Anne, married James II.

Clarendon, George William Frederick Villiers, 4th earl of, 1800–1870, English statesman. Three times foreign secretary, in CRIMEAN WAR kept together French alliance with England.

Clarendon, city (pop. 2,172), extreme N Texas, ESE of Amarillo in Panhandle. Settled by ministers and intellectuals in golden days of cattle ranching in 1870s, it was known as "Saints' Roost." Moved to railroad 1887. Now processes and ships cattle, grain, and cotton.

Clarendon, Constitutions of, 16 articles signed in 1164 by Great Council of HENRY II. Important in development of English law; extended jurisdiction of civil over church courts. THOMAS À BECKET later repudiated them, and his quarrel with Henry ended with his murder (1170).

Clarendon Code, English statutes adopted by Cavalier Parliament 1661–65 to strengthen Established Church. Laws, four in number, decreased following of dissenting sects (esp. Presbyterians). Named for earl of Clarendon who opposed enactment but enforced them. Charles II unsuccessfully tried to interfere by Declaration of Indulgences, 1662 and 1672. They were largely superseded by Test Act (1673).

Clarens (klärä′), resort village, Vaud canton, SW Switzerland, on L. Geneva near Montreux. Residence of Byron. Scene of Rousseau's Nouvelle Héloïse.

clarinet: see WIND INSTRUMENTS.

Clark, Alvan, 1804–87, and his son, Alvan Graham Clark, 1832–97, American manufacturers of astronomical lenses, noted also for discoveries of celestial bodies.

Clark, Champ, 1850–1921, American legislator. U.S. Representative from Mo. (1893–95, 1897–1921); speaker of House (1911–19). Cooperated with George Norris in successful fight in 1910 to curtail powers of J. G. CANNON as speaker.

Clark, George Rogers, 1752–1818, American Revolutionary general, conqueror of Old Northwest. Captured Vincennes from British in 1779. Led expeditions against Indians in present Ohio. His brother, William Clark, 1770–1838, was a leader of the LEWIS AND CLARK EXPEDITION and later served as governor of Missouri Territory (1813–21).

Clark, Sir Kenneth MacKenzie, 1903–, English art historian, director of the Natl. Gall., London (1934–45), professor at Oxford, and chairman of the arts council of Great Britain (1955–60).

Clark, Mark (Wayne), 1896–, American general. Commanded in N Africa and Italy in Second World War.

Was UN supreme commander in Korea (1952–53). President of The Citadel (1953–).

Clark, Tom (Campbell), 1899–, Associate Justice of U.S. Supreme Court (1949–67). He was Attorney General of U.S. 1945–49. He resigned seat on Supreme Court when his son Ramsey Clark was appointed Attorney General.

Clark, William: see CLARK, GEORGE ROGERS.

Clark, William Andrews, 1839–1925, U.S. Senator and copper magnate. Struggled with Marcus DALY for control of copper and of political forces in Mont. Elected Senator in 1901 after his election in 1899 had been challenged.

Clark College: see ATLANTA UNIVERSITY SYSTEM.

Clarkdale, town (pop. 1,095), central Ariz., on Verde R., NE of Prescott; founded after 1915 to smelt copper from nearby mines. Many Verde valley Indian ruins are near, incl. those in Tuzigoot and Montezuma Castle Natl. Monuments (see NATIONAL PARKS AND MONUMENTS, table).

Clarke, James Freeman, 1810–88, American religious writer, a Unitarian minister, associated with Transcendentalists.

Clarke, John, 1609–76, one of founders of R.I., b. England. Founded Portsmouth (1638) with Anne HUTCHINSON and William CODDINGTON. Chief figure in obtaining R.I. charter of 1663.

Clark Fork, river, c.325 mi. long, part of Columbia R. system, rising in SW Mont. near Butte and flowing N, NW past Missoula to Pend Oreille L. in Idaho Panhandle. PEND OREILLE R., flowing W from lake, is sometimes called part of Clark Fork.

Clarksburg, city (pop. 28,112), N central W.Va., SSE of Wheeling on West Fork of Monongahela R.; chartered 1785. Industrial and shipping center for coal, oil, and natural gas area. Was important Union supply post in Civil War. Stonewall Jackson born here; his birthplace is preserved.

Clarksdale, city (pop. 21,105), NW Miss., on Sunflower R., SSW of Memphis, Tenn., in rich cotton area; settled 1848 on site of Indian fortification. Processing and distributing center. Annual cotton festival.

Clarkson, Thomas, 1760–1846, English abolitionist. Helped Wilberforce abolish British slave trade (1807).

Clarksville. 1 City (pop. 3,919), NW Ark., near Arkansas R., ENE of Forth Smith; settled c.1820. Region produces fruit, coal, and natural gas. Col. of the Ozarks is here. **2** City (pop. 22,021), NW Tenn., on Cumberland R. at mouth of Red R., NW of Nashville, in agr. area. Market and processing center. Nearby are Dunbar Cave and Fort Campbell.

Clark University, at Worcester, Mass.; coed.; chartered 1887, opened as graduate school 1889, the second in U.S. Undergraduate college merged 1920.

clary: see SAGE.

classicism, in literature and art, attention to traditional and recognized forms, producing clearness, elegance, symmetry, and repose. In music it is objectivity of conception, emphasis on balance of structure, and absence of violent passions. To be contrasted with ROMANTICISM.

classic revival, widely diffused phase of taste (known as neoclassic) which influenced architecture and the arts in Europe and the U.S. during the late 18th and first half of the 19th cent. Interest in antiquity was stimulated by excavations at Pompeii and by *Antiquities of Athens* by James Stuart and Nicholas Revett. Stuart's garden temple at Hagley, England, was first example in Europe of Greek design, and the Madeleine in Paris first of Roman temple reproductions. In France, interest in ancient Rome led to the Empire style sponsored by Napoleon. In the U.S. the Greek revival achieved first expression in 1799 in the Bank of Pennsylvania, Philadelphia, by Benjamin H. Latrobe. Fusion of Greek and Roman forms brought movement to its height in c.1820. It was the dominant influence in the U.S. until it gave way to romanticist styles of Victorian period.

Claudel, Paul (pōl' klōdĕl'), 1868–1955, French poet, dramatist, diplomat. Ambassador to Japan 1921–26; to U.S. 1927–33. His poetry is influenced by Rimbaud, imbued with Catholic symbolism. Best-known are *Corona Benignitatis Anni Dei* (1914; Eng. tr., *Coronal*) and the plays *Le Partage de midi* (1906), *L'Annonce faite à Marie* (1912; Eng. tr., *Tidings Brought to Mary*), *Le Soulier de satin* (1928–29; Eng. tr.; *The Satin Slipper*), and *Un Poète regarde la croix* (1938; Eng. tr., *A Poet before the Cross*).

Claude Lorrain (klōd' lôrĕ'), 1600–1682, French painter of expansive, luminous landscapes. His real name was Claude Gelée or Gellée. Settled in Rome in 1627 under the patronage of Pope Urban VIII.

Claudian (Claudius Claudianus) (klô'dēŭn), d.404?. last Latin classic poet. Author of idyls, epigrams, and epics, including the *Rape of Proserpine*.

Claudius (klô'dēŭs), Roman emperors. **Claudius I,** 10 B.C.–A.D. 54, reigned A.D. 41–54; son of the elder Drusus and thus nephew of TIBERIUS. When Caligula was murdered, the soldiers found Claudius hiding behind a curtain, hauled him out, and made him emperor. His reign was one of consolidation and renewing of the empire. He landed in Britain and made it a Roman province. He brought about the execution of his third wife, Messalina, and his fourth wife, Agrippina II (his niece), after persuading him to name her son Nero as heir instead of his own son Britannicus, is said to have poisoned him. **Claudius II,** d. 270, reigned 268–70. Notable chiefly for defeating the Goths at Naissus (Nis) in 269, he was called Gothicus.

Clausewitz, Karl von, 1780–1831, Prussian general and writer on military strategy. Saw much active service before appointment as director of German War School 1818. His *On War* expounded doctrines of total war (war on citizens, territory, and property of enemy in every possible way) and of war as continuation of diplomacy by other means. Enormous effect on military science and tactics.

Clausius, Rudolf Julius Emanuel (rōō'dôlf yōō'lyŏos ämä'nōŏĕl klou'zyŏos), 1822–88, German mathematical physicist. Introduced concept of entropy; restated second law of thermodynamics. Developed a kinetic theory of gases and a theory of electrolysis.

Claverack, town (pop. 4,989), E N.Y., SE of Hudson, in dairy and farm area. Has courthouse in which Alexander Hamilton tried Croswell case (1804).

Claverhouse, John Graham of: see DUNDEE, JOHN GRAHAM OF CLAVERHOUSE, 1st VISCOUNT.

clavichord: see PIANO.

Clavijero, Francisco Javier (fränsē'skō hävyĕr' klävēhä'rō), 1731–87, Mexican scholar and historian, author of *The History of Mexico* (Eng. tr., 1787).

Clawson, city (pop. 14,795), SE Mich., a suburb N of Detroit. Has machine shops.

Clay, Cassius Marcellus, Jr., 1940–, American boxer. Won heavyweight championship from Sonny Liston 1964. Became a Black Muslim in 1964 and took name Muhammad Ali. Stripped of his title in 1967 after he refused induction into military service. Filed appeal after Federal judge handed down fine and prison sentence for this felony.

Clay, Clement Claiborne, 1816–82, U.S. Senator (1853–61). Member of Confederate diplomatic mission to Canada (1864) in abortive plan for peace negotiations with U.S. government. After war, imprisoned for conspiracy, but freed.

Clay, Henry, 1777–1852, American statesman. U.S. Senator from Ky. (1806–7, 1810–11, 1831–42, 1849–52). U.S. Representative (1811–14, 1815–21, 1823–25). Leader of "war hawks" prior to War of 1812. Formulated national program for internal improvement, tariff protection, and rechartering of Bank of the United States. Pushed MISSOURI COMPROMISE through the House. U.S. Secretary of State (1825–29). Opposed Jackson regime, particularly on the bank issue. NATIONAL REPUBLICAN PARTY candidate for President 1832; WHIG PARTY candidate 1844. Denouncing extremists in both North and South, asserting superior claims of the Union, Clay sponsored the COMPROMISE OF 1850. Called the Great Pacificator and the Great Compromiser.

Clay, Lucius D(uBignon), 1897–, American general. As U.S. military governor of Germany (1947–49), directed operations to overcome Berlin blockade. Served as Pres. Kennedy's special representative in Berlin 1961–62.

clay, fine-grained aluminum silicate mixed with other substances. Classed as residual if left by decay of limestone and shale or rocks containing feldspar (see KAOLINITE), or transported if moved by agent of erosion. Bentonites are very fine clays derived usually from volcanic ash. Clays are plastic when wet (hence easily shaped) and become hard when dry or fired. Important uses: making brick, tile, porcelain, china, earthenware, drainage pipes; for filtering and purifying liquids. Some clay is desirable in soil since it helps retain moisture, but an excess has many disadvantages. See also CHINA CLAY.

Clay, Mount: see PRESIDENTIAL RANGE.

Clayton. 1 City (pop. 15,245), E central Mo., a suburb W of St. Louis. **2** Resort village (pop. 1,996), N N.Y., on St. Lawrence R., NW of Watertown, in Thousand Isls. region. Sailing races held.

Clayton Anti-Trust Act, 1914, passed by U.S. Congress as amendment to clarify and supplement SHERMAN ANTI-TRUST ACT of 1890. Drafted by Henry De Lamar Clayton. Prohibited exclusive sales contracts, local price cuttings to freeze out competitors, rebates, interlocking directorates in corporations capitalized at $1,000,000 or more in the same field of business, and intercorporate stock holdings. Labor unions and agricultural cooperatives were excluded from the forbidden combinations. Act restricted use of injunction against labor; legalized peaceful strikes, picketing, boycotts. Act was basis for numerous suits against large corporations.

Clayton-Bulwer Treaty (–bŏŏl'wŭr), concluded at Washington, D.C., on April 19, 1850, between U.S., represented by Secretary of State John M. Clayton, and Great Britain, represented by Sir Henry Bulwer. U.S.–British rivalries in Central America, particularly over a proposed isthmian canal, led to treaty, which checked British expansion in Central America but prevented U.S. from building its own canal and exercising political control over it. Very unpopular, treaty remained effective until 1901 (see HAY-PAUNCEFOTE TREATY).

Cleanthes (klēăn'thēz), fl. 3d cent. B.C., Greek philosopher, head of the Stoic school after Zeno. One of the leading characters in Hume's *Dialogues Concerning Natural Religion.*

Clearchus (klēär'kŭs), d. 401 B.C., Spartan officer. Governor of Byzantium, he recruited the Greek troops who supported CYRUS THE YOUNGER and after the defeat at Cunaxa he led the retreat of the Ten Thousand (as told by XENOPHON) until he was treacherously murdered.

Clearfield, town (pop. 8,833), N Utah, S of Ogden, in irrigated farm area. Hill Air Force Base is near.

clearing, periodic settlement of bankers' claims against each other, usually done through clearinghouse associations. Clearinghouses widespread in 18th-cent. Europe. Claims usually balance out, minimizing transfer of cash. N.Y. Clearing House clears 5 times daily, handling c.$3,000,000,000. Clearing also practiced by stock and commodity exchanges.

Clear Lake, c.30 mi. long and 2–9 mi. wide, W Calif., in wooded hills NNW of San Francisco. Fishing resort. Mt. Konochti is on its W shore.

Clearwater, residential and resort city (pop. 34,653), W Fla., on Pinellas peninsula W of Tampa (linked by causeway across Old Tampa Bay); settled after Fort Harrison was estab. here 1841. Causeway extends across Clearwater Harbor to Clearwater Beach, popular recreational center.

Clearwater, river rising in several branches in N Idaho, in Bitterroot Range near Mont. line. Flows W to Snake R. near Wash. line. Gold-mining era in Idaho began after gold discovery (1860) on South Fork.

Cleaveland, Moses, 1754–1806, American pioneer. Led party to settlement in Western Reserve region of Ohio (1796), site of present Cleveland.

Cleburne, Patrick Ronayne, 1828–64, Confederate general, b. Ireland. One of ablest division commanders. Distinguished himself at Murfreesboro.

Cleburne (klē'bûrn), city (pop. 15,381), N Texas, S of Fort Worth; founded 1867. Has cotton gins, cottonseed-oil mills, dairies, and railroad shops.

Cleef or **Cleve, Joos van** (yōs' vän klāf', klā'vù), c.1485–1540, Flemish portrait painter.

Cleisthenes (klīs'thĭnēz, klīs'–), fl. 510 B.C., Athenian statesman, head of the family of Alcmaeonidae. Ruler of Athens after the exile of Hippias, he instituted democratic reforms that ended civil strife in Athens.

clematis (klĕm'–), vine or nonclimbing perennial of genus *Clematis.* Flowers are either small and clustered, bell-shaped, or anemonelike; fruits have feathery appendage. Purple-flowered Jackman clematis and white-flowered Japanese clematis are vines widely grown in North America.

Clemenceau, Georges (zhôrzh' klămăsō'), 1841–1929, French premier (1906–9, 1917–19), called "the Tiger." Defended Dreyfus passionately in DREYFUS AFFAIR. His coalition cabinet was instrumental in achieving Allied victory in First World War. He opposed Pres. Wilson at Peace Conference. Though he regarded Versailles Treaty as too lenient, he was defeated in 1919 elections because of his moderate attitude toward Germany.

Clemens, Samuel L(anghorne): see TWAIN, MARK.

Clement I, Saint, pope (A.D. 88?–A.D. 97?). Highly revered in his day, he wrote the *Epistle of St. Clement to the Corinthians* (A.D. 96?), admonishing Corinthians to stop quarreling; the tone of authority indicates the power of the bishop of Rome in the early church. This was in the 4th cent. considered as part of the Scriptures (see NEW TESTAMENT). It and other writings wrongly attributed to him are now classed as PSEUDEPIGRAPHA. Also known as Clemens Romanus or Clement of Rome. Feast: Nov. 23.

Clement III, antipope: see GUIBERT OF RAVENNA.

Clement V, 1264–1314, pope (1305–14), a Frenchman named Bertrand de Got. Appointed archbishop of Bordeaux by Pope BONIFACE VIII, he gained the favor of the French king Philip IV, who engineered his election as pope. He set up residence in Avignon, thus beginning the long "captivity" of the PAPACY. Completely under the domination of Philip, he did resist attempts to condemn Boniface VIII posthumously but he meekly did the king's bidding in dissolving the Knights Templars on unproved charges. He issued an important collection of canon law.

Clement VI, 1291–1352, pope (1342–52), a Frenchman named Pierre Roger. Kept a splendid court at Avignon. When the Black Death struck Europe he helped sufferers and tried to stem subsequent wave of anti-Semitism. He at first favored then opposed RIENZI. Despite such faults as nepotism, he was learned, likable, and eloquent.

Clement VII, antipope: see ROBERT OF GENEVA.

Clement VII, 1478–1534, pope (1523–34), originally Giulio de' Medici, a member of the MEDICI family. Was archbishop of Florence and a cardinal before becoming pope. Vacillating and timorous, he seemed unaware of the problems the Reformation posed for the church. He disagreed with Emperor Charles V, who sent troops to sack Rome (1527) and take the pope prisoner. A peace was patched up in 1529, and Clement crowned Charles. The struggle with Henry VIII of England over the king's divorce was vigorously pursued by Clement.

Clement VIII, 1536–1605, pope (1592–1605), an Italian named Ippolito Aldobrandini. He abandoned the traditional papal alliance with Spain and was friendly with Henry IV of France. Clement was noted for piety and charity.

Clement XI, 1649–1721, pope (1700–1721), an Italian named Giovanni Francesco Albani. Known for great learning. As pope, he first favored Philip V as candidate for the Spanish throne, but later was forced to recognize Philip's rival, Charles of Hapsburg. Clement sought to stamp out JANSENISM in the church, and in his bull *Unigenitus* (1713) he condemned several Jansenist doctrines.

Clement XIV, 1705–74, pope (1769–74), an Italian named Lorenzo Ganganelli, a Conventual Franciscan. Much pressure from European monarchies (esp. France and Spain) was being exerted against the Jesuits (see JESUS, SOCIETY OF). In 1773 Clement issued a brief suppressing the order.

Clement, coworker of Paul. Philip. 4.3. Traditionally identified with St. Clement.

Clément, Jacques (zhäk′ klämä′), 1567–89, French fanatic, a Dominican monk; assassin of Henry III.

Clementi, Muzio (mōō′tsēō klämĕn′tē), 1752–1832, Italian virtuoso pianist and composer. He was the first to compose in a style for piano rather than harpsichord. His studies, *Gradus ad Parnassum,* and his many sonatas are widely used.

Clement of Alexandria, d. c.215, Greek theologian, b. Athens. After conversion to Christianity he taught at Alexandria and was the first to attempt reconciling Platonic and Christian teachings. Defended orthodoxy against Gnosticism, though he apparently held that intellectual knowledge set the holder of it above other Christians (a Gnostic notion). Fragments of his work survive. Origen was his pupil.

Clemson, town (pop. 1,587), NW S.C., SW of Spartanburg. Seat of Clemson Univ.

Cleomenes (klēō′mĭnēz), kings of Sparta, **Cleomenes I,** d. c.489 B.C., helped the Athenians to oust Hippias only to find Cleisthenes an anti-Spartan leader. He is said to have killed 6,000 Argives. **Cleomenes III,** d. 219 B.C., was an energetic ruler who defeated the Achaean League, but was overcome when Antigonus III allied himself with the League (c.222 B.C.).

Cleon (klē′ŏn), d. 422 B.C., Athenian statesman. A relentless enemy of Sparta, he won a victory at Sphacteria, but was killed in the defeat at Amphipolis. He is pictured by his enemies Thucydides and Aristophanes as an unprincipled demagogue.

Cleopatra (klēŭpä′trŭ, -pä′trŭ, -pä′trŭ), 69 B.C.–30 B.C., queen of Egypt, one of the great romantic figures of history; daughter of Ptolemy XI. Married according to family custom to her brother, Ptolemy XII, she led a revolt supported by Julius Caesar. Her husband was accidentally drowned in the Nile, and she was married to her younger brother Ptolemy XIII but was the mistress of Caesar, to whom she bore a son Caesarion (Ptolemy XIV). After Caesar's death she was visited by Marc Antony, who fell in love with her. Their love affair, which for a time threatened the Roman Empire, was ended when Octavian (later Augustus) defeated their forces at Actium (31 B.C.) and later at Alexandria. Antony committed suicide, and Cleopatra, unable to move the cool Octavian, went to her death by having an asp bite her. Apparently not beautiful, she was still a fabulously alluring woman. Shakespeare's *Antony and Cleopatra* deals with her later story, G. B. Shaw's *Caesar and Cleopatra* with earlier events.

Cleopatra's Needles, popular name for two Egyptian obelisks, c.69 ft. high, originally erected at Heliopolis in c.1475 B.C. One is now in London, the other in New York.

Clergy Reserves, lands in Upper and Lower Canada set apart under Constitutional Act of 1791 "for the support and maintenance of a Protestant clergy." "Protestant clergy" was interpreted to mean clergy of Church of England. This interpretation, opposed by other Protestant denominations, became an issue in the Rebellion of 1837. In 1854 a law was passed providing for secularization of the reserves, but Anglican and Presbyterian churches retained endowments that had been granted them.

Clerk, Sir Dugald (klärk), 1854–1932, British engineer and inventor of gas engines.

Clerk-Maxwell, James: see MAXWELL, JAMES CLERK.

Clermont-Ferrand (klĕrmō′-fĕrä′), city (pop. 127,684), cap. of Puy-de-Dôme dept., SE France; historic cap. of Auvergne. Formed 1731 by merger of Clermont and Montferrand. Rubber industry (automobile tires). Clermont dates from Roman times. At Church council held here in 1095 Pope Urban II preached First Crusade. Has Gothic cathedral (12th–15th cent.); Romanesque Church of Notre Dame (12th cent.); university (founded 1854).

Cletus (klē′tŭs) or **Anacletus, Saint** (ănŭklē′tŭs), pope (A.D. 76?–A.D. 88?), a martyr. Feast: April 26.

Cleve, Joos van: see CLEEF, JOOS VAN.

Cleve, Germany: see CLEVES.

Cleveland, (Stephen) Grover, 1837–1908, 22d or 23d (see list at end of article UNITED STATES) President of the United States (two terms, 1885–89, 1893–97). Mayor of Buffalo (1882–83). Governor of N.Y. (1883–85). Cleveland as President continued his independent, reformist, but conservative course. Argued for lower tariff. Panic of 1893 struck hard blow at his second administration. He secured repeal of SHERMAN SILVER PURCHASE ACT. His tariff measures altered by Senator A. P. GORMAN, he allowed Wilson-Gorman Tariff Act to become law without his signature. Opposed by radical Democrats, especially over gold standard, which he upheld. On grounds that movement of U.S. mail was being halted by the strikers, he sent troops to PULLMAN in 1894. In foreign affairs he took a strong stand on the VENEZUELA BOUNDARY DISPUTE; refused recognition to Hawaiian government set up by Americans.

Cleveland. 1 Market city (pop. 10,172), NW Miss., NE of Greenville, in cotton area. **2** City (1965 pop. 810,858), NE Ohio, port on L. Erie at Cuyahoga R. mouth; Ohio's largest city; laid out 1796 by Moses CLEAVELAND. Grew rapidly after opening of Ohio and Erie Canal and arrival of railroad. World's greatest ore port, large Great Lakes and rail shipping point, important center of iron and steel production, and oil-refining center (J. D. Rockefeller began oil dynasty here). Mfg. of automobiles, machinery, machine tools, electrical equipment, and chemicals. Seat of CASE INSTITUTE OF TECHNOLOGY, WESTERN RESERVE UNIVERSITY, Notre Dame Col., St. John Col., John Carroll Univ. (at UNIVERSITY HEIGHTS), Ursuline Col. for Women. Has Cleveland Orchestra (founded 1918), civic center, Western Reserve Historical Society Mus., and Wade Park (with Cleveland Mus. of Art and Fine Arts Garden). **3** City (pop. 16,196), SE Tenn., ENE of Chattanooga, in farm and timber area.

Cleveland Heights, city (pop. 61,813), NE Ohio, a suburb E of Cleveland.

Cleves (klēvz), Ger. *Kleve* or *Cleve,* former duchy, NW Germany, on both sides of the Rhine; historic cap. Kleve (pop. 20,423), North Rhine-Westphalia. Originally a county; united with county of Mark 1368; raised to duchy 1417. Duke John III inherited JÜLICH, BERG, and RAVENSBERG 1521; his daughter Anne married Henry VIII of England. Extinction of male line (1609) led to complicated dynastic quarrel over succession. Treaties of 1614 and 1666 settled Cleves, Mark, and Ravensburg on Brandenburg; Jülich and Berg on Palatinate branch of Wittelsbachs.

cliff dwellers. Buildings perched on mesas and on ledges of canyon walls in the U.S. Southwest were once thought to be the work of an extinct people, but now it is known that they were built by the ancestors of the PUEBLO INDIANS as defense against nomadic tribes. The cliff dwellers were skilled farmers, employing irrigation. Many of the buildings are now in national parks and monuments.

Clifford of Chudleigh, Thomas Clifford, 1st Baron, 1630–73, English Catholic statesman, member of

Cabal ministry of Charles II. Knew of secret clauses in Treaty of Dover pledging reestablishment of Catholicism in England. Forced to resign by passage of Test Act (1673) and committed suicide.

Cliffside Park, suburban borough (pop. 17,642), NE N.J., near Hudson R., NE of Newark.

Clifton, industrial city (pop. 82,084), NE N.J., ESE of Paterson.

climacteric: see MENOPAUSE.

climate, sum total of weather elements over long period. Elements include temperature, precipitation (see RAIN), HUMIDITY, WIND, barometric pressure. Latitude is primary factor, modified by secondary influences (e.g., relation to water and land; altitude; topography; prevailing winds; OCEAN CURRENTS; cyclonic-storm prevalence). Climatic zones include equatorial zone (see DOLDRUMS); subtropical (tradewind belts; horse latitudes); intermediate, prevailing-westerlies region; and polar zone. Subtropical-intermediate transition belt (Mediterranean type) found on continental west coasts. Climatic types combining latitude and secondary items: continental (sunny with low humidity, except at equator; temperature extremes), marine (slight temperature changes; much rain on windward side of mountainous islands; coastal or littoral; and mountain or plateau. Climatology is study of climate and its relation to plant and animal life.

Climax, village (pop. 1,609), central Colo., SW of Denver. One of world's largest molybdenum deposits is mined nearby.

climbing perch, spiny-finned, perchlike, fresh-water, walking fish (genus *Anabas*), of India and SE Asia. Adult is c.10 in. long, dark brown, with a blunt, hard head, thick skin, and scales. It walks and climbs by using its tail, fins, and spines on fins. It can breathe atmospheric oxygen.

Clinch, river formed by juncture of two forks in SW Va. and flowing c.300 mi. SW across E Tenn. to Tennessee R. Impounded by Norris Dam, it flows into Watts Bar Reservoir. Important in TENNESSEE VALLEY AUTHORITY.

clinic, institution providing medical diagnosis and treatment for ambulatory patients. Clinics are maintained by hospitals, public and private organizations, or groups of physicians. They evolved from dispensaries which supplied free drugs to the poor; in England these date from late 17th cent., in U.S. first estab. 1786 in Philadelphia by Benjamin Rush.

Clink, former district on the Bankside in Southwark, London, England; site of the famous prison.

Clinton, George, 1739–1812, American statesman. First governor of N.Y. (1777–95) under new state constitution; managed trade and public welfare problems ably. Opposed Federal Constitution. Was Vice President of United States 1805–12. His nephew, **De Witt Clinton,** 1769–1828, was mayor of New York city for ten annual terms between 1803 and 1815; promoted public education and city planning. Sponsored Erie Canal. Unsuccessful presidential candidate 1812. Governor of N.Y. (1817–21, 1825–28).

Clinton, Sir Henry, 1738?–1795, British general in American Revolution. In supreme command in America 1778–81. Captured Charleston, S.C., 1780.

Clinton. 1 Resort town (pop. 4,166), S Conn., on Long Island Sound E of New Haven; settled 1663. Monument commemorates school which opened here 1702, moved, and later became Yale University. **2** City (pop. 7,355), central Ill., N of Decatur, in farm area. Abraham Lincoln argued many law cases here. **3** City (1965 pop. 33,331), E central Iowa, on Mississippi R., NE of Davenport. Industrial and rail center in rich agr. area, it grew as a lumber-producing city in 1880s. **4** Town (pop. 1,647), SW Ky., near Mississippi R., SW of Paducah; platted 1826. On old site of Columbus city (now moved), Confederate stronghold in early Civil War. **5** Industrial town (pop. 12,848), E central Mass., near Wachusett Reservoir; settled 1654. **6** City (pop. 9,617), W central Okla.,

on Washita R., W of Oklahoma City; founded 1903. Agr. shipping center. Clinton-Sherman Air Force Base is SW. **7** Town (pop. 7,937), NW S.C., S of Spartanburg; settled c.1809. Seat of Presbyterian Col.

Clio, Muse of history: see MUSES.

clipper, fastest type of sailing ship. Long and narrow, it had the greatest beam aft of center and carried, besides topgallant and royal sails, skysails and moonrakers. Originated in the U.S., the Baltimore clippers were but forerunners of the real clipper begun with the *Ann McKim* (completed Baltimore 1832). This type was perfected by Donald McKay of Boston who built the *Flying Cloud,* the *Glory of the Seas,* and the *Lightning.* The clippers dominated long-distance commerce, cutting time and vying in famous races. The clipper at first outran the rival steamship, but in the 1860s the improved steamship began to win out over all sailing ships.

Clisson, Olivier de (ôlēvyä′ dü klēsō′), 1336–1407, constable of France. Defeated Ghent insurgents at Roosebeke (1382). One of MARMOUSETS, he used his position to amass a huge fortune.

Clitheroe (clĭdh′ûrō), municipal borough (pop. 12,-147), Lancashire, N England. Market town with weaving and paper mills; quarrying. Small Norman keep is a war memorial.

Clive, Catherine, 1711–85, English singer and actress, of Irish descent. Notable in comedies by Cibber, Gay (*Beggar's Opera*), and Coffey. Kitty Clive also sang in Handel's *Samson* 1742. Was a friend of Johnson, Fielding, and Horace Walpole.

Clive, Robert, Baron Clive of Plassey, 1725–74, British soldier and statesman. In service of East India Company he won a series of victories (culminating in Plassey, 1757). He destroyed French power in India by his military genius. Twice governor of Bengal, he brought Behar and Orissa under British control as well as CALCUTTA. Fought corruption and promoted reform. On return to England (1767) was charged with acceptance of large gifts in India; finally acquitted but committed suicide. See *Essay on Clive* by T. B. Macaulay.

clock, instrument for measuring and indicating time. First wheel clock is believed to date from 6th cent., first weight-driven clock from 9th cent. Until 17th cent. there were few mechanical clocks except in cathedral towers, monasteries, and public squares. Smaller, lighter types constructed after coiled spring came into use c.1500. Invention of pendulum clock (c.1656) attributed to Christiaan Huygens. Clocks with long cases to conceal pendulums or weights date from mid-17th cent.; forerunners of grandfather clocks. Electric clocks, first made in 19th cent., extensively used after c.1930. The latest and most precise developments in timekeeping are in the field of electronic and atomic instruments. The first atomic clock was developed 1948. Until 19th cent. clockmaking industry centered chiefly in France and England; later Germany and U.S. became leading producers. Among well-known clocks are astronomical clock with elaborate mechanical devices in cathedral of Strasbourg; clock in tower of British Houses of Parliament, with 13½-ton bell known as Big Ben; and clock in Metropolitan Life Insurance Building, New York city, with four dials, each 26½ ft. in diameter.

Clodia (klō′dēŭ), fl. 1st cent. B.C., Roman beauty; sister of Publius Clodius. As notable for her immorality as for her appearance, she is supposed to have murdered her husband. She is believed to have been poet Catullus' Lesbia.

Clodion or **Claude Michel** (klōdēō′, klōd mēshĕl′), 1738–1814, French rococo sculptor.

Clodius (Publius Clodius Pulcher) (klō′dēŭs), d. 52 B.C., Roman politician. In 62 B.C., disguised as a woman, he took part in the Bona Dea mysteries in the house of Julius Caesar, thus causing Caesar to divorce his wife. Made tribune of the people in 58 B.C., he proved to be a demagogue. His gang of hired ruffians changed the complexion of Roman politics, and he was killed by a rival gang hired by Milo.

Cloisters, the, museum of medieval art, Fort Tryon Park, New York city; a branch of Metropolitan Mus. of Art, opened May, 1938. Four French cloisters, 12th-cent. Romanesque chapel, and chapter house contain 600–700 examples of medieval art. Collection (gathered by George Grey Barnard) was given to the Metropolitan by John D. Rockefeller, Jr.

Clonmacnoise (klŏnmăknoiz′), historic religious center, Co. Offaly, Ireland. Has interesting ruins, including abbey founded by St. Kieran c.548.

closed shop, open shop, and union shop. A closed shop hires only union members. A union shop is restricted to unionized employees, but employees are not required to join union until after initial period of employment, usually 30 days. An open shop is not restricted to unionized employees. A form of union security, closed or union shops were adopted by most U.S. unions after 1840, but judicial decisions usually negated provisions until creation of NLRB (1935). Taft-Hartley Act (1947) banned closed shop but permitted union shop. Many states, however, have banned closed shop by so-called "right-to-work" laws.

Clotaire (klōtâr′), Frankish kings. **Clotaire I,** d. 561, became king of Soissons at the death of his father, Clovis I (511). With his brothers THEODORIC I and CHILDEBERT I he conquered Thuringia and Burgundy. Their deaths left him sole king of the Franks by 558. His grandson, **Clotaire II,** 584–629?, succeeded his father CHILPERIC I as king of Neustria (584), his mother FREDEGUNDE acting as regent. In 613 he put BRUNHILDA to death, became king of all Franks.

clothes moth, name for several moths of family Tineidae; adults of commonest ones are yellowish or buff, c.⅓ in. long. Larvae feed on wool, furs, other animal products. Fumigation, spraying fabrics with chemicals, cleaning, airing, and cold storage of garments help prevent damage.

Clotho, one of the FÁTES.

cloth of gold has been made since anc. times, esp. in the East; in medieval Europe, it was much used ceremonially. Gold thread for weaving and embroidery is prepared either as very fine wire or by wrapping a core yarn with thin metal (lamé).

Clotilda, Saint, Frankish queen: see CLOVIS I.

clotting of blood, process of blood coagulation in which red and white corpuscles and blood platelets are caught in network of fibrils consisting of fibrin. Fibrin forms when skin is broken. Normal clotting time about four minutes; prolonged in HEMOPHILIA.

cloud, dense suspension in air of water droplets or ice particles condensed (from water vapor in air cooled below dew point) around nuclei of microscopic atmospheric dust particles. Usually air is cooled by upward movement and expansion; sometimes by reduced air pressure aloft, or mixing of warmer and cooler air currents. Air may rise by convection (from intense ground heat); by cold-air wedge at ground forcing warm air aloft; or by mountain range deflecting air flow upward. Classification of clouds (based on Luke Howard's work, 1803, and proposed by International Meteorological Commission in 1929): high clouds, 20,000 ft. or over (cirrus, cirrocumulus, cirrostratus); middle clouds, 6,500–20,000 ft. (altocumulus, altostratus); low clouds, 6,500 ft. or below (stratocumulus, stratus, nimbostratus); vertical-development clouds, 1,600–20,000 ft. (cumulus, cumulonimbus).

cloud chamber: see WILSON CLOUD CHAMBER.

Cloud Peak: see BIGHORN MOUNTAINS.

Clouet, Jean (zhä′ klooä′), called **Janet** or **Jehannet,** c.1485–1540, court painter to Francis I of France. Probably of Flemish origin. His son **François Clouet** (fräswä′), c.1510–c.1572, was court painter to Francis I, Henry II, Francis II, and Charles IX. Both excelled in precision of draughtsmanship.

Clough, Arthur Hugh (klŭf), 1819–61, English poet, friend of literary figures of his day. He is best re-

membered for his lyric, "Say not the struggle naught availeth"; and for Matthew Arnold's poem on his death, "Thyrsis."

clove, evergreen tree (*Eugenia caryophyllata*) native to the Molucca Islands, and also its unopened flower bud, an important spice. The dried nail-shaped buds are used whole or ground to flavor confections and ham. They yield a volatile oil used medicinally and in perfumes.

clover, leguminous forage and hay plant and cover crop, of genus *Trifolium*, native to northern regions. Common species are red, crimson, and white or Dutch clovers, and alsike (*Trifolium hybridum*). Characterized by three-lobed leaves, clover was emblem of Ireland from which shamrock was derived.

Clovis I (klō′vĭs), c.466–511, Frankish king (481–511), founder of Frankish monarchy (see MEROVINGIANS). Rose from tribal chieftain to sole leadership of Salian Franks by dint of patience and murder; conquered most of Gaul and SW Germany by defeating Romans (486, at Soissons), Alemanni (496), Burgundians (500), Visigoths (507, at Vouillé). His wife, St. Clotilda, a Burgundian princess, encouraged his conversion to Christianity, but he was baptized only after 496, in fulfillment of a vow made in battle against Alemanni.

Clovis. 1 City (1966 pop. 11,461), S central Calif., NNE of Fresno. Trade center in farm and vineyard area. **2** City (pop. 23,713), E N.Mex., N of Hobbs near Texas line; settled 1907. Commercial and processing center of agr. area and important rail division point. Stockyards. Cannon Air Force Base is W.

clubfoot (talipes), foot deformity resulting from changes in joints of ankle and foot which arise from muscle defect. Lord Byron had this affliction. It can often be corrected if treatment (surgery or manipulation) is begun early enough in childhood.

club moss, low evergreen plant, of the genera *Lycopodium* and *Selaginella*, related to ferns but with small needlelike or scalelike leaves. Species of *Lycopodium*, also called ground pine and ground cedar, grow in moist, shaded places. Yellow spores of running pine, *Lycopodium clavatum*, sold as lycopodium powder or vegetable sulfur for medicinal uses. Most *Selaginella* species are tropical but some are found in temperate regions.

clubroot, slime mold disease of cabbage and other plants of mustard family. Attacks roots, causing malformation and preventing normal plant growth.

Cluj (kloozh), Ger. *Klausenburg,* Hung. *Kolozsvár,* city (est. pop. 166,428), W Rumania. Chief trade and cultural center of Transylvania; metallurgical industry. Univ. founded as Jesuit academy by Stephen Bathory (1581). Dating perhaps from Roman times and a free city from 1405, Cluj has kept many historical buildings of 14th–18th cent. Population over 50% Hungarian.

Cluniac order, medieval group of Benedictines, centering in the abbey of Cluny, France; founded 910. In the 10th, 11th, and early 12th cent. the Cluniac monks were a potent force, greatly forwarding the reforms in the church that were to reach a climax with Gregory VII; working for reforms in general Christian life; and promoting independence of the church from lay control. Their centralized organization increased their power, and they were criticized as rich and arrogant; in the 12th cent. they lost in rivalry with the Cistercians.

Cluny (Fr. klünē′), former abbey, E France, NW of Mâcon. Founded 910; center of Cluniac order. Abbey church dates partly from 10th cent.

Cluny Museum, 14th- and 15th-cent. structure in Paris, housing collection of medieval and Renaissance art objects. State-owned since 1842.

Clusium: see CHIUSI, Italy.

cluster, in astronomy, group of stars, probably of common origin, moving at same rate in same direction. More than 300 open, or galactic, clusters are catalogued. About 100 globular clusters are known, the nearest being over 20,000 light years away; in them the stars, numbering many thousands, appear to be densely massed.

clutch, device for controlling power transmission from the drive shaft to another working part, usually without interrupting the rotation of the drive shaft. Commonly consists of friction plates pushed together by springs. Less common are cone clutch, with cone fitting into end of flywheel; band clutch, with expanding segments; and magnetic fluid clutch.

Clyde, river of SW Scotland rising in S Lanarkshire and flowing N and NW for c.100 mi. to heart of Scotland's greatest industrial belt. Britain's major shipbuilding center. Glasgow, Clydebank, and Greenock are the main ports. At Dumbarton, river widens into the **Firth of Clyde** (64 mi. long), rimmed by small ports and summer resorts.

Clydebank, shipbuilding burgh (pop. 49,654), Dumbartonshire, Scotland, on the Clyde below Glasgow. *Queen Mary* and *Queen Elizabeth* built here.

Clymene (klī′mŭnē), in Greek mythology. **1** Daughter of the Titan Oceanus, wife of Iapetus, and mother of Atlas, Prometheus, and Epimetheus. **2** Nymph, wife of Helios and mother of Phaëthon.

Clytemnestra (klī″tŭmnē′strŭ), in Greek legend, daughter of Leda and Tyndareus, half sister of Helen. Wife of Agamemnon, she was mother of ORESTES, Electra, and Iphigenia. When she and her lover Aegisthus slew Agamemnon, Orestes in revenge slew both lovers.

Cm, chemical symbol of the element CURIUM.

Cnidus or **Cnidos** (both: nī′dŭs), anc. Greek city of Asia Minor, in present SW Asiatic Turkey. The town had the famous statue by Praxiteles, the Aphrodite of Cnidus.

Cnossus or **Knossos** (both: nŏ′sŭs), anc. city near the N coast of Crete. Occupied long before 3000 B.C., it was center of the MINOAN CIVILIZATION, which is known chiefly through excavations of the Cnossus palace by Arthur Evans; legendary home of Minos.

Co, chemical symbol of the element COBALT.

Coachella Valley (kō″ŭchĕl′ŭ), arid region, SE Calif., N of Salton Sea. Irrigated by artesian wells and Coachella Canal (completed 1948), which brings water from ALL-AMERICAN CANAL. Truck crops, dates, citrus fruits, and alfalfa grown in region.

coagulation, collection into a mass and precipitation of minute particles of a substance that was dispersed through another substance. In a colloidal solution it results from neutralization of charges on colloidal particles; they remain together on collision and form a precipitate.

Coahuila (kōäwē′lä), state (58,067 sq. mi.; 1963 est. pop. 974,179), N Mexico, on N bulge of Rio Grande, S of Texas; cap. SALTILLO. Mountains in E Coahuila have quantities of largely unexploited mineral resources. Lumbering and coal mining are important. Cattle raising is chief occupation in NE. Border city, PIEDRAS NEGRAS, is across Rio Grande from Eagle Pass, Texas. LAGUNA DISTRICT lies in S part with TORREÓN its chief city. Exploration of territory began in middle of 16th cent. Joining of Texas and Coahuila (1830) was contributing factor to Texas Revolution (1835–36). Joined to Nuevo León in 1857, Coahuila became independent state in 1868.

coal, fuel of plant origin composed of carbon with varying amounts of mineral matter. There is a complete series, differing in content of carbon, moisture, and volatile substances: peat is lowest in carbon, and it is followed by lignite or brown coal, bituminous, semibituminous, and anthracite (nearly pure carbon). Coal beds or seams occur in sedimentary rocks, having originated from vegetation growing in slowly submerging swampland. Weight of overlying deposits helped the conversion into coal, the greater the pressure the higher the grade of coal produced. Most coal was formed during the Carboniferous period.

coal gas is obtained in destructive distillation of soft coal as by-product from coke preparation. Composition varies. Used as fuel, illuminant.

coal tar, product of destructive DISTILLATION of coal. Upon distillation it yields coal-tar crudes that form starting point for syntheses of dyes, drugs, explosives, flavoring, perfumes, paints, etc.

coast guard, special U.S. naval force assigned to seaboard duties such as suppressing smuggling, assisting vessels in distress, and providing protection and aid for maritime commerce and air commerce over the sea. Formed in 1915 by the union of the Revenue Cutter Service (estab. 1790) and the Life Saving Service. In 1939 the Lighthouse Service was merged with the coast guard, and the Bureau of Marine Inspection and Navigation was added in 1942. The coast guard is under the Treasury Dept. but comes under the navy in wartime or for such periods as the President directs. The motto is *Semper Paratus* [Latin,= always ready]. The women's reserve active in Second World War was called the SPARS. The U.S. Coast Guard Academy at New London, Conn., trains officers for the coast guard.

Coast Mountains, range; border between NW B.C., Canada, and S Alaska. Extend c.1,000 mi. parallel to Pacific coast. Mt. Waddington, 13,260 ft., is highest peak. Sometimes confused with COAST RANGES.

coast protection. Means of protection against encroachment of sea include dikes, levees, sea walls, and groins. Extending below low-water mark, sea walls, usually of masonry, have slanted or concave front to deflect wave back into sea and often a front apron to prevent undermining. Perpendicular to shore line, from low-water to high-water level, groins are low walls, usually wooden, to slow up current.

Coast Ranges, series of mountain ranges along Pacific coast of North America, extending S from St. Elias Mts. in Alaska through B.C. and U.S. into Mexico c.800 mi. S of border. In U.S. they are usually considered to include Olympic Mts. in Wash.; Coast Range in Oregon; and Diablo, Santa Lucia, San Rafael, and Santa Monica ranges, N portion of Peninsular Range, and San Gabriel, San Bernardino, and San Jacinto mts. in Calif. Geologically young (formed by upheaval and composed mainly of granitic rock), they are rugged and well wooded.

Coatesville, city (pop. 12,971), SE Pa., on Brandywine Creek, W of Philadelphia, in farm area; settled c.1717. Steel mfg. U.S. veterans' hospital is here.

coaxial cable: see CABLE.

Cobalt, town (pop. 2,209), E Ont., Canada, NE of Sudbury. Center of rich silver district, discovered 1903. Valuable cobalt ores also mined.

cobalt, silvery-white, lustrous, magnetic metallic element (symbol = Co; see also ELEMENT, table). Chemically active, it forms many compounds. Used in pigments. Occurs alone rarely; found in meteoric metal, in ores with other metals. Used in steel alloys and in CARBOLOY. It is essential in permanent magnets used in radio, telephone, and television receivers and electric generators. Cobalt 60, the radioactive isotope of mass number 60, is produced by bombarding the normal isotope of mass number 59 with neutrons; one neutron is added to the nucleus, making it unstable. Cobalt 60 is used in medicine (cancer treatment) and in detecting flaws in metal castings. The **cobalt bomb** can be produced by encasing an atomic or hydrogen bomb in a shield of normal cobalt; the nuclear bomb explosion would release neutrons which would convert the normal cobalt 59 to cobalt 60. The highly radioactive cobalt 60 particles would spread throughout the atmosphere of the earth, considerably raising the level of radiation and endangering all life. No nation has yet exploded a cobalt bomb.

cobaltite (kō′bôltīt), opaque, silver-white mineral of pyrite group, composed of cobalt, arsenic, and sulfur. An important ore of cobalt.

Cobb, Howell, 1815–68, American statesman. U.S. Congressman from Ga. (1843–51, 1855–57); Secretary of the Treasury (1857–60). Chairman of convention in Montgomery which organized Confederacy

Cobb, Irvin S(hrewsbury), 1876–1944, American writer of humorous stories, many about his native Kentucky and the character Old Judge Priest.

Cobb, Lee J., 1911–, American actor. After early work with Group Theatre (1935–37) he won success as a character actor on stage in *Death of a Salesman* and in films.

Cobb, Tyrus Raymond (Ty Cobb), 1886–1961, American baseball outfielder. Had .367 lifetime batting average, won more batting championships than anyone in baseball history (1907–15, 1917–19). Holds records for most hits (4,191), stolen bases (892), games, runs, and many others.

Cobbett, William, 1763?–1835, British journalist and reformer. After resigning from army went to U.S. (1792); in effective pamphlets championed Federalists against pro-French Republicans. On return to England became radical working class leader and apostle of agrarianism. After flight to U.S. due to the Gagging Bills (1817), returned to become central figure in English agitation for parliamentary reform. After Reform Bill of 1832, he was elected to Parliament. *Rural Rides* (1830) most famous of his many books.

Cobden, Richard, 1804–65, English statesman, a major influence in repeal of CORN LAWS. Guided policy of Anti-Corn Law League with John BRIGHT, Sir Robert PEEL, Lord John RUSSELL. Helped keep England out of Schleswig-Holstein affair (1864). Negotiated "Cobden Treaty" for reciprocal tariffs with France (1859–60). Favored Union in U.S. Civil War.

Cobequid: see TRURO, N.S.

Cóbh (kōv) [Irish,= cove], seaport (pop. 5,266), Co. Cork, Ireland, on Great Isl. in Cork Harbour. An important transatlantic port, it is also a resort and home of oldest yacht club in the world. Called Queenstown after Queen Victoria's visit (1849), it was renamed Cóbh 1922.

Coblenz or **Koblenz** (both: kō'blĕnts), city (est. pop. 96,823), Rhineland-Palatinate, West Germany, at confluence of Rhine and Moselle; former cap. of Rhine Prov. Important wine trade; mfg. of machinery, furniture, pianos. Founded 1st cent. B.C. by Drusus as Confluentes. Under archbishops of Trier from 11th cent. until capture by French in 1794. Passed to Prussia 1815. Occupied by Allied troops 1919–29. Among ancient buildings is Church of St. Castor, founded 9th cent. Ehrenbreitstein fortress, across the Rhine, became part of Coblenz 1937.

Cobleskill, village (pop. 3,471), E central N.Y., W of Albany; settled 1752. Howe Caverns are nearby.

Cobourg, town (pop. 10,646), S Ont., Canada, E of Toronto; a port on L. Ontario; summer resort.

cobra, poisonous snake of Africa and Asia. Common cobra of India and Egypt, often used by snake charmers, and Asiatic king cobra or hamadryad (14–18 ft. long) spread their hoods when angered. Some African forms spit poison.

Coburg (kō'bûrg, Ger. kō'bŏŏrk), city (pop. 44,886), Upper Franconia, N Bavaria, on Itz R. Metal, glass, ceramics, First mentioned 1056. For history, see SAXE-COBURG; SAXE-COBURG-GOTHA.

coca, South American shrub (*Erythroxylon coca*). Its leaves yield cocaine.

cocaine (kōkān'), alkaloid prepared from leaves of coca shrub. It is a habit-forming drug used as local anesthetic and illegally as narcotic.

Cochabamba (kōchäbäm'bä), city (1965 est. pop. 95,000; alt. c.8,400 ft.), cap. of Cochabamba dept., W central Bolivia, in agr. area.

Cochin, Charles Nicolas (shärl' nēkôlä' kôshē'), 1715–90, French engraver, designer, writer on art, and painter to the French court.

Cochin (kō'chĭn'), former princely state (1,493 sq. mi), SW India, now part of Kerala state. Cochin, town (pop. 29,881), is chief port; visited 1502 by Vasco da Gama. Cochin was captured by the Dutch in 1663, and by the British in 1795.

Cochin China (kō'chĭn), historic region (c.26,500 sq. mi.) of South Vietnam. Chief city is Saigon. Bounded by Cambodia on N, China Sea on E and S, and Gulf of Siam on W. Mainly an alluvial plain drained principally by Mekong R. One of world's great rice-growing regions. Population is largely Annamese, but includes Cambodians, Chams, and Chinese. Area was part of anc. Khmer Empire. Annamese became masters of the country by mid-18th cent. Ceded to France mid-19th cent. Constituted 1946 as independent republic within Federation of Indo-China. In 1949 joined Annam and Tonkin in state of VIETNAM, included in South Vietnam by Geneva Agreements, 1954. Later divided into several provinces.

cochineal (kōchĭnēl'), scarlet dye from extract of bodies of female scale insect found on some cacti.

Cochrane, Thomas: see DUNDONALD, THOMAS COCHRANE, 10TH EARL OF.

Cock or **Kock, Hieronymus** (both: hē"ûrō'nĭmŭs kôk'), 1510–70, Flemish painter and engraver. In Antwerp he was first great publisher of prints; made numerous plates after Bruegel, Bosch, and Floris.

Cockaigne or **Cockayne, Land of** (both: kōkān'), in medieval tales a legendary country where finest food and drink are to be had for the taking.

cockatoo, name for various crested woodland parrots of Australia. Among them are the pink cockatoo, some white birds with yellow or scarlet on crests, and some with dark plumage.

Cockcroft, Sir John Douglas, 1897–, English physicist; became director of British Atomic Energy Establishment (1946). Shared 1951 Nobel Prize in Physics with T. S. Walton for transmuting atomic nuclei with accelerated atomic particles.

Cockerell, Charles Robert (kōk'ûrŭl), 1788–1863, English architect, archaeologist, and writer. He excavated temples at Bassae, Aegina, and other sites. In architecture, he was a notable exponent of the classical revival.

cockfighting, sport of pitting gamecocks against each other. Popular in anc. Persia, Greece, and Rome and recently in Asia, Latin America, and parts of U.S. Jousts usually held on small circular stage. Gamecocks placed beak to beak, then released. Cock is defeated when he refuses to fight or is unable to fight.

cockle, marine bivalve mollusk. Shell is marked by ridges radiating from the hinge. It lives in sand or mud and eats microscopic sea life. Some species move about in water; others dig into bottom. Majority of species are in tropical and subtropical waters; one (*Cardium edule*) eaten in Europe.

cocklebur, coarse annual plant of genus *Xanthium*, a persistent weed with oval burs, also called clotbur. See *ill.*, p. 858.

cock of the plains: see SAGE GROUSE.

Cockran, W(illiam) Bourke, 1854–1923, American politician, b. Ireland. U.S. Representative from N.Y. (1887–89, 1891–95, 1904–9, 1921–23); supported organized labor, opposed restrictions on immigration.

cockroach, orthopterous insect of world-wide distribution (c.1,200 species), abundant in tropics. Omnivorous and mainly nocturnal, it has a flat, oval, usually brownish body, long antennae, large eyes, unpleasant odor (glandular secretion). Croton bug found in NE U.S., wood cockroach in E U.S.

cockscomb, annual plant (*Celosia argentea cristata*), with showy red or gold, rounded, ruffled, or feathery flower spikes, used as an EVERLASTING.

Cocoa, city (pop. 12,294), E Fla., on Indian River (lagoon), ESE of Orlando, in citrus-fruit area. Causeway leads to Merritt Isl., Cocoa Beach, and CAPE KENNEDY. Patrick Air Force Base is near.

cocoa, cocoa butter, and **cocoa nibs:** see CACAO.

coconut, fruit of coco palm (*Cocos nucifera*), a tree widely scattered through tropical regions. Mature trees may yield 75–200 nuts a year. The nut, encased in a thick fibrous husk, has a hard shell surrounding its white, edible meat, and contains a nutritious milk. Shredded kernels of nuts are used in confectionery. Of world value in commerce is oil extracted from dried fruit kernels (known as copra). A sweet liquid, obtained from flower buds, is distilled to make arrack or boiled down for its sugar. Coir (coarse fibers from nut husks) is made into brushes, matting, and ropes.

Cocteau, Jean (zhä' kôktō'), 1891–1963, French author. A versatile spokesman for modernism in all arts, he wrote poetry, fiction, dramas, operatic librettos; directed moving pictures; and excelled as draftsman. His best-known works are the novels *Le Grand Écarte* (1923; Eng. tr., 1925) and *Les Enfants terribles* (1929; Eng. tr., 1930); the drama *La Machine infernale* (1934; Eng. tr., 1936); the films *The Beauty and the Beast* (1947) and *Orpheus* (1949). Many of his drawings have appeared in books. Elected to French Academy in 1955.

Cocx, Gonzales: see COQUES, GONZALES.

cod, food fish abundant in N Pacific and N Atlantic. It lays eggs in mid-ocean, feeds on marine life, and weighs 10–35 (rarely 75) lb. Chief fisheries are in Norway, Newfoundland, and Mass.

Cod, Cape: see CAPE COD.

Coddington, William, 1601–78, one of founders of R.I., b. England. Founded Portsmouth (1638) with Anne HUTCHINSON. Founded Newport (1639) with John CLARKE. Governor of united towns (1640).

code, in communication: see CRYPTOGRAPHY; MORSE CODE.

code, body of legal rules expressed in fixed and written authoritative form as contrasted with customary law (including common law). *Corpus Juris Civilis* gave term meaning of an entire legal system. *Code Napoléon* outstanding example of such codes. Official collections of statutes also called codes (e.g., the criminal code).

codeine: see OPIUM.

Code Napoléon or **Code Civil,** first modern law CODE, compiled by a commission 1800–1804, promulgated by Napoleon I; a milestone in development of civil law (modern Roman law).

codling moth (kŏd'–) or **codlin moth,** small moth with larva (called apple worm) enormously damaging to apple crop. It also attacks other fruits. Often it has two or three generations a year; eggs are laid on developing fruit. Larva eats into apple and remains there until ready to pupate; then it bores out, making hole. Cocoon develops on bark. Orchards are protected by spraying insecticides. *Carpocapsa pomonella.*

cod-liver oil, yellowish fixed oil from liver of codfish. Rich in vitamins A and D, it was once widely used in diets for treatment and prevention of rickets and malnutrition. Synthetics now used instead.

Codrington, Sir Edward, 1770–1851, British admiral. Commanded combined British, French, and Russian fleets in victory at Navarino (1827) which made possible the success of Greek war of independence.

Cody, William Frederick: see BUFFALO BILL.

Cody (kō'dē), city (pop. 4,838), NW Wyo., on Shoshone R., in livestock, farm, and dude-ranch area; settled in 1890s. Has oil refineries. Named for W. F. Cody (Buffalo Bill); has historical center with his memorabilia and a gallery with notable collection of art of Old West. Tourist center for Yellowstone Natl. Park to W. Shoshone Canyon and Shoshone project are near.

Coello, Alonso Sánchez (älōn'thō sän'chäth kōĕl'yō), c.1531–c.1588, Spanish court painter to Philip II.

Coello, Claudio (klou'dyō), c.1642–1693, Spanish baroque painter, famous for the monumental altarpiece for the sacristy of the Escorial.

Cœur, Jacques (zhäk' kûr'), c.1395–1456, French merchant prince. Chief adviser to Charles VII, founder of French trade in Levant. Amassed fabulous fortune; financed final campaigns of Hundred Years War. Imprisoned and fined millions of dollars on concocted charge of poisoning Agnès SOREL (1453). Escaped to Rome; died campaigning against Turks.

Coeur d'Alene (kûrdûlän'), city (pop. 14,291), N Idaho, on Coeur d'Alene L., W of Coeur d'Alene Mts. Founded 1877, it grew after discovery (1882)

of lead and silver and mining boom of 1884. Still a mining, lumbering, and farming area.

Coeur d'Alene Lake, c.24 mi. long, N Idaho. E of Spokane, Wash. Impounded by Coeur d'Alene Lake Dam on Spokane R.; fed by Coeur d'Alene and St. Joe rivers.

Cœur de Lion: see RICHARD I, king of England.

coffee, beverage made from seeds of a small evergreen tree, the Arabian coffee tree (*Coffea arabica*), native to tropical Africa and from certain other species of *Coffea.* After roasting to develop flavor and aroma, the "beans" are ground. Exhilarating effects result from CAFFEINE content. Coffee was known in Ethiopia before A.D. 1000, in Arabia (whence it spread to Egypt and Turkey) by the 15th cent.; it had reached most of Europe by mid-17th cent. In North America coffee became a staple beverage after the Boston Tea Party. Production of instant coffee, experimented with as early as 1838, began in 1867.

cofferdam, temporary barrier (wood or steel), a protection against water, used in construction of dams, bridges, etc. In water deeper than 30 ft. CAISSON is generally used instead.

Coffeyville, city (pop. 17,382), SE Kansas, on Verdigris R. near Okla. line, SE of Wichita; settled 1869. Flourished after discovery (1902) of oil and gas in area. Now trade center in farm and oil area. Notorious Dalton gang shot down here 1892.

Cognac (kônyäk'), town (est. pop. 19,000), Charente dept., W France, on Charente R. Export center for French brandy (named for town). A Huguenot stronghold in 16th cent., was birthplace of Francis I.

Cogswell, Joseph Green, 1786–1871, American librarian and bibliographer. Helped found Astor Library in New York city, for which he prepared alphabetical and analytic catalogue.

Cohan, George M(ichael), 1878–1942, American playwright, actor. Began in vaudeville with his family. Writer, producer, and director, he was most often star, playing in 20 musicals after 1901. Songs (e.g., *Give My Regards to Broadway, You're a Grand Old Flag*) and plays exemplified favorite themes—Broadway and patriotism. *Over There* became song classic of First World War. Dramatized mystery novel *Seven Keys to Baldpate* (1913).

Cohasset (kōhăs'ĭt), resort town (pop. 5,840), E Mass., on S shore of Massachusetts Bay E of Hingham; settled c.1647. Had first U.S. lifeboat service. Lighthouse maintained since 1850. Has summer theater.

Cohen, Hermann, 1842–1918, German Jewish philosopher, b. Coswig, d. Berlin. Founder of neo-Kantian Marburg School, teacher of Ernst Cassirer. Wrote commentaries to Kant and estab. his own system of philosophy. His *Religion der Vernunft aus den Quellen des Judentums* (1919) builds religion upon ethics and rejects all mythical theology.

Cohen, Morris Raphael, 1880–1947, American philosopher, b. Russia. He taught at the Col. of the City of New York 1912–38 and at the Univ. of Chicago 1938–42. Known for his use of Socratic irony. Influential books were *Reason and Nature* (rev. ed., 1953) and *Law and the Social Order* (1933).

Cohn, Ferdinand (fĕr'dĕnänt kōn'), 1828–98, German botanist, known as a founder of science of bacteriology.

Cohoes (kŭhōz'), industrial city (pop. 20,129), E N.Y., N of Albany at junction of Mohawk and Hudson rivers and on Barge Canal; settled 1665 by Dutch. Van Schaick mansion (1735) has historic relics.

Coimbatore (kwĭmbùtôr'), town, Madras, India. Commands approach to Palghat Gap, Eastern Ghats. Important in 18th-cent. wars between the British and Mysore sultans.

Coimbra (kwēm'brù), city (pop. 50,168), cap. of Coimbra dist., W central Portugal; old cap. of Beira. Important in Roman days; flourished through Moorish times and after its conquest by Ferdinand I of Leon

(1047). Cap. of Portugal until 13th cent. Has fine 12th-cent. cathedral. Famous univ., founded by King Diniz, was moved from Lisbon to Coimbra in 1306.

coin: see MONEY.

Coire, Switzerland: see CHUR.

Coke, Sir Edward (kŏŏk), 1552–1634, English jurist, one of England's most eminent lawyers. Solicitor general and speaker of House of Commons before becoming attorney general 1593. Was severe prosecutor. Made chief justice of common pleas 1606; became champion of Parliament against king. Upheld supremacy of common law and enunciated doctrines of personal liberty. Enmity of James I, Baron Ellesmere, and Francis Bacon caused his dismissal in 1616. Elected to Parliament again 1620; leader of popular party and important in drafting Petition of Right (1628). Writings include *Institutes*.

Coke, Thomas, 1747–1814, English clergyman and early bishop of Methodist Episcopal Church in America.

Coke, Thomas William: see LEICESTER OF HOLKHAM, THOMAS WILLIAM COKE, EARL OF.

coke, fuel made by destructive DISTILLATION of soft coal. Its by-products are ammonia, coal tar, and illuminating gas. Used in blast furnace and to make WATER GAS.

Colbert, Jean Baptiste (zhä' bätēst' kôlbĕr'), 1619–83, French statesman, chief adviser to Louis XIV after 1661. Procured conviction of Nicolas FOUQUET. The greatest exponent of MERCANTILISM, he protected industries by subsidies and tariffs, regulated prices and quality of goods, built modern road and canal network, and developed navy and colonization.

Colchester (kôl'chĭstûr), municipal borough (pop. 65,-072), Essex, England, on Colne R. Once a great pre-Roman city, it has a Norman castle housing Roman antiquities. Colne oyster fisheries important.

colchicine (kôl'chĭsēn), plant alkaloid used chiefly in genetics experiments. It interferes with the separation of nuclei in cell division, and the resulting cells have chromosome numbers that are multiples of the normal number.

Colchis (kôl'kĭs), anc. country on the Black Sea and in the Caucasus, noted for forest products. In Greek legend it was the home of Medea and the land where Jason sought the Golden Fleece.

cold, catarrhal infection of upper respiratory tract, frequently with fever. Attributed to filterable viruses, colds usually last 3 to 10 days.

Colden, Cadwallader (kôl'dûn), 1688–1776, colonial scholar and political leader of N.Y., b. Ireland, of Scottish parents. Lieutenant governor of N.Y. after 1761. He was botanist of the Linnaean system, which was mastered also by his daughter, **Jane Colden,** 1724–66, who prepared a scientific illustrated work on flora of New York. She married William Farquhar (1759).

cold frame, low, sun-heated structure with transparent cover, sunk into ground. Used for starting seeds early, to propagate cuttings, and to winter nonhardy plants. Hotbed is similar but soil is heated by stable manure, steampipes or electricity.

cold sores, fever blisters, or **herpes** (hûr'pēz), manifestations of an acute virus infection which can affect various parts of body. Invasion of virus believed to occur in most persons during infancy and childhood, either as a systemic or severe local infection. Reappearance of blisters is triggered by such factors as sunlight, menstruation, food allergies.

Cold Spring Harbor, village (pop. 1,705), SE N.Y., on N shore of Long Isl., W of Huntington. Early whaling port. Has noted marine biological station and a Carnegie Inst. department of genetics.

Coldstream, burgh (pop. 1,227), Berwickshire, Scotland. Troops raised here (1659–60) to restore Charles II were later called Coldstream Guards, one of guards regiments of the royal household.

cold type, preparation of matter for printing using typewriter, special keyboard machine, or photocomposition, instead of metal (hot type) used in letterpress composition.

cold war, struggle for power and prestige since Second World War between Western powers and Communist bloc. With European recovery, main focus of struggle shifted to Middle East, Africa and Asia. Cold war often took form of East-West competition for allegiance through economic aid; but there were also ideological struggles within the Communist world between China and USSR. Broadcasts of Radio Free Europe to Soviet-bloc countries were a strong weapon in cold war.

Coldwell, Major James, 1888–, Canadian political leader, b. England. Became national leader of CO-OPERATIVE COMMONWEALTH FEDERATION in 1942.

Cole, G(eorge) D(ouglas) H(oward), 1889–1959, English economist. Advocated guild socialism; later returned to his original Fabianism; headed (1939–46) Fabian Society as chairman and became president 1952. His many books include *History of Socialist Thought* (6 vols., 1953–58).

Cole, Thomas, 1801–48, American landscape painter, b. England; a leader of the HUDSON RIVER SCHOOL.

Cole, Timothy, 1852–1931, American wood engraver, b. London. Became known for fine reproductions of great European paintings which appeared for many years in *Scribner's* (later the *Century*) magazine.

Coleridge, Samuel Taylor, 1772–1834, English romantic poet, critic, and philosopher. With Robert Southey he planned a utopian community in America ("pantisocracy") which did not materialize. After publication of his *Poems on Various Occasions* (1796), he and William WORDSWORTH collaborated on *Lyrical Ballads* (1798). His experiments in language and subject (Coleridge's "The Rime of the Ancient Mariner" treated the supernatural) and the prefaces to later editions made it germinal in the English Romantic movement. Coleridge's later poems of music and fantasy include "Dejection: an Ode" (1802), "Christabel," and "Kubla Khan" (both published 1816). Coleridge lectured (most notably on Shakespeare), traveled, and wrote, but finally, addicted to drugs first taken for pain, he moved (1816) to the home and care of Dr. James Gillman at Highgate. He published poetry, essays from his periodical *The Friend* (1809–10), a drama, literary criticism in *Biographia Literaria* (1817), and important philosophical and religious treatises. He also continued the brilliant conversations which echo in the writings of Charles Lamb and other friends. His eldest son, **Hartley Coleridge,** 1769–1849, wrote poetry and critical biographies. S. T. Coleridge's daughter, **Sara Coleridge,** 1802–52, edited some of her father's works, wrote *Phantasmion* (1837; a fairy tale).

Colet, John (kŏl'ĭt), 1467?–1519, English humanist, friend of Erasmus, associate of Sir Thomas More, Grocyn, and Linacre. After years at Oxford was dean of St. Paul's, London (1505–19), and planned St. Paul's school. With Erasmus and William Lily wrote Eton Latin grammar. Urged Church reform but died in the Church before the Reformation.

Colette (kôlĕt'), pen name of Sidonie Gabrielle Claudine Colette Goudeket, 1873–1954, French author. Famous for analytical studies of women, such as *Chéri* (1920; Eng. tr., 1929) and *La Chatte* (1933; Eng. tr., 1936). With her first husband, Willy (pseud. of Henri Gauthier-Villars), she collaborated on the famous *Claudine* stories.

Colfax, town (pop. 1,934), central La., on Red R., in timber and farm area; founded c.1870. Had race riot (1873) when Negroes tried to assume parish offices.

Colgate University, at Hamilton, N.Y., near Syracuse; for men; chartered 1819, opened 1820 as Hamilton Literary and Theological Inst., a Baptist seminary; renamed Madison Univ. 1846, Colgate Univ. 1890.

colic (kŏl'ĭk), intense pain caused by spasmodic contraction of a hollow organ, especially stomach or intestine. In infants it may follow a large or improper feeding or constipation.

Coligny, Gaspard de (gäspär' dù kōlēnyē'), 1519–72, French Protestant leader, admiral of France; nephew of Anne de Montmorency. With Louis I de Condé, commanded Huguenots in Wars of RELIGION; negotiated peace in 1570. Became favorite adviser to Charles IX, thus arousing enmity of Catherine de' Medici. Was first victim in the celebrated massacre of SAINT BARTHOLOMEW'S DAY.

Colima (kōlē'mä), state (2,010 sq mi.; 1963 est. pop. 184,801), W Mexico, on Pacific; cap. Colima (pop. c.29,000); founded 1523. State includes Revilla Gidgedo isls.

Colins, Colin, or **Colyn, Alexander** (kōlē'), c.1527–1612, Flemish sculptor. He executed most of the reliefs in marble on the tomb of Maximilian I at Innsbruck.

Coliseum: see COLOSSEUM.

collective bargaining, in labor relations, negotiating procedure between two parties—union and management—for determining working conditions without dealings with individual workers. Employer's refusal to bargain collectively was made illegal by 1935 National Labor Relations Act. Unions were similarly restrained by 1947 TAFT-HARTLEY Act.

collective farm, agr. producers' cooperative. In USSR collectivization was obligatory after 1929; all lands were confiscated. By 1938, 99.3% of cultivated land was collectivized. Collectivization was begun by Stalin to modernize agr., secure reliable food supply, and free capital and labor for industry. Amalgamation of collective farms (*kolkhozy*) into still larger units was begun in 1950. Commune of Communist China similar but more strictly organized; puts greater emphasis on collective living; each commune supports a complete military unit. Among the collective farms in Israel best known is *kibbutz* (commune). Living is communal; all work crews are run by elected foremen.

Collège de France (kôlĕzh' dù frãs'), founded in Paris 1529 by Francis I. Has always been independent and free from supervision. Lectures are open to the public without fee, no examinations are given, and no degrees are granted.

College Park. 1 City (pop. 23,469), NW Ga., a suburb S of Atlanta. Georgia Military Academy is here. **2** City (pop. 18,482), W central Md., suburb NE of Washington, D.C. Part of Univ. of MARYLAND is here.

Colleges of the Seneca, The, at Geneva, N.Y.; corporate title after 1943 of Hobart Col. (for men, 1822) and William Smith Col. (for women, 1908). Share faculty, classes coed.

College Station, city (pop. 11,396), E central Texas, SE of Bryan. Seat of TEXAS AGRICULTURAL AND MECHANICAL UNIVERSITY.

Collegeville, borough pop. 2,254), SE Pa., NW of Philadelphia. Seat of Ursinus Col.

Colleoni, Bartolomeo (bärtōlōmä'ō kôl-lāō'nē), 1400–1475, Italian CONDOTTIERE, generalissimo of Venetian forces from 1454. Equestrian statue by VERROCCHIO.

Collier, Jeremy, 1650–1726, English clergyman, nonjuring bishop (1713), best known for his *Short View of the Immorality and Profaneness of the English Stage* (1698).

Collier, John, 1884–, American social worker and author, commissioner of Indian Affairs (1933–45). Wrote on the American Indian.

Collingdale, borough (pop. 10,268), SE Pa., SW of Philadelphia.

Collingswood, residential borough (pop. 17,370), SW N.J., near Camden; settled 1682.

Collingwood, Robin George, 1889–1943, British philosopher. He believed that philosophy should be rooted in history rather than in formal science. He upheld an expressionist theory of art sometimes known as the Croce-Collingwood theory.

Collingwood, town (pop. 8,385), S Ont., Canada, at S end of Georgian Bay. Lake port with large shipyard, grain elevator, and dry dock.

Collins, Edward Trowbridge, 1887–1951, American baseball infielder. Had .333 lifetime batting average, holds record most years (25) in major leagues.

Collins, Michael, 1890–1922, Irish leader of the SINN FEIN. Organized guerrilla warfare which forced British to sue for peace. Joined Arthur GRIFFITH in setting up the Free State (1921). He was assassinated.

Collins, (William) Wilkie, 1824–89, English novelist, best known today for two mystery stories, *The Woman in White* (1860) and *The Moonstone* (1868). Friend of Dickens.

Collins, William, 1721–59, English lyric poet. Wrote odes, notably, "Ode to Evening" and "Ode, Written in the Beginning of the Year, 1746" (beginning "How sleep the brave").

Collinsville, city (pop. 14,217), SW Ill., E of St. Louis, Mo., in coal and farm area; settled 1817.

Collodi, Carlo (kär'lō kōl-lō'dē), pseud. of **Carlo Lorenzini** (lōräntsē'nē), 1826–90, Italian writer, author of *Pinocchio: the Story of a Puppet* (1880, 1883), a children's classic, widely translated.

collodion (kŭlō'dēŭn), alcohol-ether solution of PYROXYLIN. When exposed to air, liquid evaporates, leaving thin, colorless, elastic film.

colloid (kŏ'loid), substance dispersed in solvent as particles too small to be seen but larger than molecules. It is not a true SOLUTION for the particles are not of molecular size, do not pass through certain membranes, have only slight effects on freezing and boiling points, and are observable with ultramicroscope; not SUSPENSION, for particles are invisible and do not settle on standing. Milk is an example. COAGULATION and ADSORPTION are characteristic of colloids. See also DIALYSIS.

collusion, conspiracy to defraud a person of his legal rights or to obtain some objective by misusing the forms of law. Collusion between husband and wife, or between either and a third party, is a bar to DIVORCE.

Colman, Norman Jay, 1827–1911, American agriculturist and lawyer. First Secretary of U.S. Dept. of Agr.

Colmar or **Kolmar** (kôl'mär), city (pop. 52,355), cap. of Haut-Rhin dept., E France, in Alsace. Textile mfg. Made free imperial city 13th cent.; annexed by Louis XIV 1673. Old section keeps medieval architecture. St. Martin's Church (13th cent.) contains painting by SCHONGAUER. Museum, in 13th-cent. convent, has Isenheim altarpiece by GRÜNEWALD.

Cologne (kùlōn'), Ger. *Köln* or *Köln am Rhein*, city (pop. 718,346), in state of North Rhine–Westphalia, West Germany, situated on the Rhine. A religious, historical, and commercial center, it is a major rail junction and river port. Metallurgy; mfg. of textiles, chemicals, eau de Cologne. Founded A.D. 50 by Romans as Colonia Agrippinensis. Episcopal see from 4th cent.; archbishopric since time of Charlemagne. As princes of Holy Roman Empire, archbishops ruled strip of land on W bank of the Rhine; ranked third among ELECTORS. Their constant feud with citizens of Cologne led to transfer of electoral residence to nearby Brühl and later (1263) to Bonn. A free imperial city from 1474 and a member of Hanseatic League, Cologne flourished as commercial center until 16th cent. It was seized by the French 1794. Archbishopric was secularized 1801. Annexed to Prussia as part of Rhine Province (1815), Cologne developed into largest transit port and depot of NW Germany. Industrial Deutz, on right river bank, was united with Old Cologne, on left bank. Among buildings that escaped major damage in air raids of Second World War are the famous cathedral (begun c.1248; completed 1880, after original plans), containing relics of the WISE MEN OF THE EAST, and the Church of St. URSULA. Cologne is the center of N German Catholicism. The university was founded 1388.

Coloma (kŭlō′mù), village, N central Calif., on American R., NE of Sacramento. Monument and park recall discovery of gold at Sutter's Mill here in 1848 by J. W. Marshall.

Colomb or **Colombe, Michel** (both: mĕshĕl′ kôlō′), c.1430–1512, French sculptor, a master of the early French Renaissance.

Colomb-Béchar (kôlō′-bĕshär′), town (pop. c.43,000), W Algeria. Founded as French military post 1905. Coal mined nearby.

Colombia (kōlŏm′byä), republic (455,335 sq. mi.; pop. 17,482, 420), NW South America; cap. BOGOTÁ. Bordered by Caribbean (NW), Pacific (SW), Peru and Educador (S), Brazil (SE), Venezuela (NE). The only nation on the continent with both Pacific and Atlantic coasts, Colombia consists of mountains and uplands in W and lowlands in E. The E, which includes the tropical rain forests of the Amazon basin (S) and the grasslands (llanos) of the Orinoco basin (N), contains two thirds of the land of Colombia, but is underdeveloped and sparsely populated. Cattle are raised on the grasslands. In the W the Andes are divided into three ranges by the valleys of the CAUCA and MAGDALENA rivers, where the wealth and population of Colombia are concentrated. Here are the principal cities: Bogotá, Tunja, BUCARAMANGA, CÚCUTA, MEDELLÍN, MANIZALES, and CALI. The main ports are BUENAVENTURA on the Pacific and BARRANQUILLA, CARTAGENA, and SANTA MARTA on the Atlantic. Coffee is the chief product, but oil, gold, platinum, and emeralds are also important. Conquered by JIMÉNEZ DE QUESADA and others, the region was the core of the Spanish colony and viceroyalty of New Granada, which included Panama and most of Venezuela. Revolution against Spain began in 1810 (see NARIÑO, ANTONIO) and ended with the victory of Bolívar at Boyacá (1819). Bolívar set up the republic of Greater Colombia (including Venezuela and Ecuador), but separatist movements broke it, and after 1830 Colombia (sometimes called New Granada) was a reduced nation. It was subject to political quarrels (particularly between federalists and centralists) and strong men (*caudillos*) arose. In the late 19th and early 20th cent. industries grew. A major political problem was that of the PANAMA CANAL, which resulted in 1903 in the independence of PANAMA from Colombia. In the Second World War Colombia joined the Allied side in 1943 and later became a member of the UN. In 1957, after much instability and political violence, the two major parties agreed to divide the seats in the legislature and alternate control of the presidency for the next 16 years. Carlos Lleras Restrepo, a Liberal, was elected president in 1966 in accord with the agreement.

Colombo (kŭlŭm′bō), city (pop. c.488,000), cap. of Ceylon, on Indian Ocean; Ceylon's main port. Rubber, tea, coconut fiber, and copra are exported. Successively the center of Portuguese, Dutch, and British rule in Ceylon from 1565 to 1948. Site (1950) of Colombo Plan conference.

Colombo Plan for Cooperative Economic Development in South and Southeast Asia, estab. 1951 by nations of British Commonwealth; U.S. later became largest donor. Gives educational and technical assistance, donates food and equipment. Plan extended to 1971.

Colón (kōlōn′), city (pop. c.58,000), Panama, at Caribbean end of Panama Canal; thriving commercial center exporting tropical fruits and woods. Cristobal, within zone, is American residential district.

colon, in anatomy: see INTESTINE.

Colonia (kōlō′nyä), city (pop. c.15,000),cap. of Colonia dept., S Uruguay, on Río de la Plata; resort and small port in agr. district. Founded by Portuguese (1680), it was secured by Spanish after bitter fighting.

Colonial Conference, British: see IMPERIAL CONFERENCE.

Colonial National Historical Park: see NATIONAL PARKS AND MONUMENTS (table).

colonial preference: see TARIFF.

Colonna (kōlōn′nä), noble Roman family, prominent 12th–16th cent. Though traditionally Ghibelline and antipapal, produced one of most successful advocates of papal authority in Pope MARTIN V. **Sciarra Colonna** (shär′rä), d. 1329, helped French capture Pope Boniface VIII, whose face he slapped. **Vittoria Colonna, marchesa di Pescara** (vēt-tō′rēä, dē pāskä′rä), 1492–1547, Italian poet, was known for religious poetry and for verses lamenting death of her husband, Ferrante d'Avalos.

colony, any noncontiguous territory of a state subject to its jurisdiction. Classified as colonies of settlement, where colonists try to recreate features of the home government, or colonies of exploitation, estab. to bring profit from natural resources or commercial prospects. Colonies have played important part in European diplomacy and international relations since 18th cent. In 20th cent. many colonies have been placed under international supervision as mandates or trusteeships. See TRUSTEESHIP, TERRITORIAL.

color, property of light that depends on wave length. Apparent color of object depends on wave length of light it reflects. Object that reflects all wave lengths appears white; one that reflects none, black. Dispersion occurs when sunlight passes through glass prism, producing solar spectrum. Speed at which color travels depends on wave length. Primary colors of light or spectrum are red, green, and blue; they can produce, in combination, all colors. Primary pigments are red, yellow, and blue. Any two colors that produce white when mixed are complementary colors. Light causes different color cones in human retina to react, making color perception possible. See also, LIGHT; PROTECTIVE COLORATION; SPECTRUM; VISION.

Colorado, state (104,247 sq. mi.; pop. 1,753,947), W U.S.; admitted 1876 as 38th state; cap. and largest city DENVER. Other main cities are BOULDER, COLORADO SPRINGS, and PUEBLO. A Rocky Mt. state, crossed by Continental Divide; plains in E section. COLORADO, Platte, ARKANSAS, and RIO GRANDE rivers rise in mountains. Agr. (sugar beets, potatoes, fruits, feed crops); mining (coal, uranium, molybdenum, vanadium, gold, silver, lead, zinc, copper); livestock raising. Area N of Arkansas R. and E of Rockies came to U.S. in Louisiana Purchase (1803), remainder from Mexico (1848), Texas (1850). Penetrated by French, Spanish, and MOUNTAIN MEN, but became known mainly through explorations of Z. M. PIKE, S. H. LONG, J. C. FRÉMONT. Boomed with discovery of gold (1859), declined, boomed again with silver (1875). Tourist trade important. Suffered severe floods 1965.

Colorado. 1 River, rising in N Colo. at Continental Divide and flowing SW through Colo., Utah, and Ariz. (including GRAND CANYON), then between Nev. and Ariz., between Ariz. and Calif., thence to Mexico and into Gulf of California. Great river of SW U.S., c.1,450 mi. long, it drains c.8% of U.S. area aided by the rivers Gunnison (in Colo.), Green (Utah), San Juan, Little Colorado, and Gila (Ariz.). Mouth seen by Francisco de Ulloa 1539, lower part explored by Hernando de Alarcón 1540. Sometimes called Grand R. above entrance of Green R. Used for power and irrigation, especially by means of Colorado river storage project, Colorado-Big Thompson project, Hoover Dam, Davis Dam (forms L. Mohave), Imperial Dam, All-American Canal, Parker Dam, and Glen Canyon Dam. **2** River rising in NW Texas in Llano Estacado, fed by "draws" in E N.Mex. Flows c.840 mi. SE through Austin to Matagorda Bay. Floods brought legislation on flood control, power, and irrigation. Of three boards, Lower Colorado River Authority (1934) is most active, with Buchanan, Roy Inks, Alvin J. Wirtz, Marble Falls, and Mansfield or Marshall Ford dams. Central Colorado

River Authority active in construction of small irrigation dams. Upper Colorado River Authority responsible for Concho R. branches, with San Angelo Dam.

Colorado, University of, at Boulder; state supported; coed.; chartered 1861, opened 1877. Has medical center at Denver. Operates High Altitude Observatory at Climax.

Colorado-Big Thompson project, constructed 1938–56 by U.S. to divert headstreams of Colorado R. E across Continental Divide to irrigate and supply power to NE Colo. Water diverted by several dams, including Granby Dam on Colorado R. and Green Mountain Dam on Blue R. Water stored in Granby Reservoir, Shadow Mountain L., and Grand L., then pumped through Alva B. Adams Tunnel to fall down E slope of Continental Divide into Big Thompson R., tributary of South Platte. Diversion dams near Fort Collins and Estes Park; power plants at Green Mountain Dam and Estes Park.

Colorado National Monument: see NATIONAL PARKS AND MONUMENTS (table).

Colorado potato beetle: see POTATO BEETLE.

Colorado river storage project, multipurpose plan undertaken by U.S. in 1956 to control flow of upper Colorado R. and tributaries and aid development of upper Colorado R. basin. States involved are Wyo., Utah, Colo., Ariz., and N.Mex. Series of dams will regulate stream flows, provide reservoirs and power; water will be used for irrigation, industrial and domestic purposes. Four major units are GLEN CANYON DAM on Colorado R., FLAMING GORGE DAM on Green R., NAVAJO DAM on San Juan R., and proposed Curecanti dams on Gunnison R. Includes CENTRAL UTAH PROJECT.

Colorado School of Mines, at Golden; state supported; mainly for men; chartered 1874. Pioneer mining and engineering school of university grade. Has one of world's largest mineral collections.

Colorado Springs, city (pop. 70,194), central Colo., at foot of Pikes Peak, S of Denver; founded 1871. Residential city and health resort near Manitou Springs. Gold, silver, and coal mines are in region. Garden of the Gods, area of curiously eroded rock formations, adjoins city on NW. Seat of Colorado College. Nearby is UNITED STATES AIR FORCE ACADEMY.

Colorado State University, at Fort Collins; land grant, state and Federal supported; coed.; chartered 1870, opened 1879 as agr. college; assumed present name 1957.

color blindness (Daltonism), inability to recognize colors, especially red and green. It is usually a congenital defect occurring in 5% to 10% of men, less than 1% of women.

Colosseum or **Coliseum** (both: kŏlŭsē'ŭm), common name of Flavian Amphitheater in Rome, near SE end of Forum. Built A.D. c.75–80; largely preserved; most imposing of existing Roman antiquities. Huge four-storied oval held c.45,000 spectators. Arena was scene of gladiatorial combats.

Colossians (–lŏsh'–), epistle of New Testament written to Christians of Colossae and Laodicea by St. Paul. Emphasizes centrality of Christ to counter the attractions of certain false ideas and practices. Among well-known passages are 1.24–29; 2.12–15; 2.20–3.4.

Colossus of Rhodes (kŭlŏ'sŭs), large bronze statue of the sun god, Helios, in Rhodes harbor; one of the seven wonders of the anc. world. Built by Chares, 292–280 B.C., it fell in an earthquake in 224 B.C.

Colquhoun, Patrick (kŏ'hōōn'), 1745–1820, British economist and statistician. Made statistical estimates of distribution of national income which long influenced economic and social reformers.

Colt, Samuel, 1814–62, American inventor of a breech-loading pistol (patented 1835), which became so popular that Colt grew to be a generic term.

Colton, city (1966 pop. 19,470), S Calif., a suburb S of San Bernardino; founded 1875. Processes and ships fruit, vegetables, and dairy products.

coltsfoot, Eurasian perennial plant (*Tussilago farfara*), naturalized in North America. Has yellow flowers, later downy fruits and large leaves.

Colum, Padraic (pä'drĭk kō'lŭm), 1881–, Irish-American poet, dramatist, b. Ireland; in U.S. after 1914. His wife was Mary (Maguire) Colum (1887?–1957), Irish-American critic.

Columba or **Columcille, Saint** (kŏlŭmkĭl'ē), 521–97, Irish churchman. Founded monastery schools at Derry (545), Durrow (553), and Kells (c.554). Went with companions in 563 to Iona and later converted N Scots to Christianity. Buried with St. Patrick and St. Bridget at Downpatrick. Feast: June 9.

Columban, Saint (kŭlŭm'bŭn), c.540–615, Irish missionary to the Continent. Founded many notable abbeys, including Luxeuil and Bobbio. His followers founded others, all notable for learning. Feast: Nov. 21 (in Ireland Nov. 23).

Columbia. 1 Rural town (pop. 2,163), E Conn., W of Willimantic; settled c.1695. Here Eleazar Wheelock estab. Indian charity school which became Dartmouth Col. **2** City (pop. 7,117), S Miss., WSW of Hattiesburg, on Pearl R., in agr. area. **3** City (pop. 36,650), central Mo., NNW of Jefferson City; laid out 1821. Trade center of farm and coal area. Univ. of MISSOURI and STEPHENS COLLEGE are here. **4** Industrial borough (pop. 12,075), SE Pa., on Susquehanna R. below Harrisburg; settled 1730. **5** City (pop. 97,433), state cap., central S.C., at head of navigation on Congaree R. Trading post was nearby in early 18th cent. Site chosen for new state cap. 1786; legislature first met here 1790. Burned by Sherman's army on night of Feb. 17, 1865. Now state's largest city and important trade and commercial center in heart of rich farm region. Seat of Univ. of SOUTH CAROLINA, Allen Univ., Benedict Col., Columbia Col., and U. S. veterans' hospital. Woodrow Wilson's boyhood home is here. Nearby is Fort Jackson. **6** City (pop. 17,624), central Tenn., on Duck R., SSW of Nashville; settled 1807. Trade and processing center of farm and phosphate-mining area. Has J. K. Polk house. Race riot and trials of 1946 drew wide interest.

Columbia, river, c.1,210 mi. long, rising in Columbia L., SE British Columbia. Flows c.460 mi. NW and S to enter U.S. (after receiving Kootenai R.). Continues S through Wash. (receives waters of Clark Fork–Pend Oreille system from Rockies), W, S through Columbia plateau. Turns W after being joined by Snake R., forms Oregon-Wash. line to the Pacific. Cuts through Cascade and Coast ranges, forming beautiful gorges. Commands one of the great U.S. drainage basins. Discovered 1792 by Robert GRAY and named for his ship. Reached by land in LEWIS AND CLARK EXPEDITION in 1805; in 1807 by David THOMPSON. River was focus of American settlement that created Oregon. Supports extensive fisheries (mainly salmon). Irrigation began early (esp. for orchards). Considerable progress has been made toward goals of flood control, navigation improvement, irrigation, and power. In 1966 six U.S. dams were completed or under construction, including GRAND COULEE DAM (key unit of COLUMBIA BASIN PROJECT), Chief Joseph Dam, BONNEVILLE DAM, THE DALLES Dam, McNary Dam, and John Day Dam. Columbia River Treaty, signed 1964 by U.S. and Canada, provides for joint development of flood control and power resources. Bridge (4.1 mi. long) across the mouth of the river was completed 1966.

Columbia, District of: see DISTRICT OF COLUMBIA.

Columbia basin project, central Wash., U.S. development to provide irrigation, power, flood control. Its key unit, GRAND COULEE DAM, provides power and pumps Columbia R. waters into a series of lakes, reservoirs, canals. Irrigation, begun 1946, will water more than a million acres.

Columbia Heights, city (1965 pop. 23,283), SE Minn., a suburb N of Minneapolis.

Columbia University, in Manhattan borough of New York city; founded 1754 as King's Col. by grant of George II. First president was Samuel JOHNSON; succeeded by Myles COOPER and W. S. JOHNSON. Closed during Revolution and reopened 1784 as Columbia Col. It moved to Morningside Heights under Seth Low, and greatly expanded under Pres. N. M. BUTLER (1902–45). Gen. Eisenhower president 1948–53. Named Columbia Univ. 1896 and Columbia Univ. in the City of New York 1912. Columbia Col. remains as undergraduate school for men. Other divisions: school of medicine (1767), absorbed into Col. of Physicians and Surgeons (1807) and into the university 1891; school of law (1858); school of engineering (1896), including school of mines (1864); graduate faculties—political science (1880), philosophy (1890), pure science (1892), architecture (1896), journalism (1912; endowed by PULITZER), business (1916), dental and oral surgery (1917), library service (1926), and international affairs (1946). Includes Teachers Col. (1888), Barnard Col. for women (1889), Col. of Pharmacy (1892), School of Social Work (affiliated 1940). School of General Studies, adult undergraduate college, estab. 1947. Columbia operates East Asian, European, and Russian institutes; botanical and biological field stations at Irvington-on-Hudson; Lamont Geological Laboratory at Palisades, N.Y.; and is affiliated with BELLEVUE HOSPITAL. Notable presidents include Charles KING and F. A. P. BARNARD. In 1953 Grayson Kirk became president. Columbia Univ. Press founded 1893.

Columbine, stock servant character or soubrette of COMMEDIA DELL' ARTE. Usually Harlequin's beloved.

columbine, perennial plant of genus *Aquilegia,* with spurred blossoms and delicate foliage. Wild red and yellow *Aquilegia canadensis* native to E North America; blue and white *A. caerulea* to W U.S. Garden sorts are evolved from European species.

columbium: see NIOBIUM.

Columbus, Christopher, 1451–1508, discoverer of America, b. Genoa, Italy. After much supplication he gained royal support in Spain and sailed from Palos with three ships, *Santa María, Pinta,* and *Niña.* He landed on Watling Isl., Oct. 12, 1492. On a second expedition (1493), his discoveries included Puerto Rico, Virgin Isls., Jamaica. During a third voyage (1498), he discovered the mouth of the Orinoco R. in Venezuela. His administration of a colony in Hispaniola resulted in his return to Spain (1500) in chains. A fourth expedition (1502), an attempt to regain prestige, reached the coast of Honduras but was forced back by hardships. He died in poverty, almost forgotten.

Columbus. 1 City (pop. 116,779), W Ga., at head of navigation on Chattahoochee R., WSW of Macon. Founded 1828 as trading post on site of Creek Indian village. Was busy river port until railroads came in 1850s. Supply point in Indian war of 1836, Mexican War, and Civil War. Taken by Federals in April, 1865. Hydroelectric plants of 20th cent. aided industrial growth. Important industrial and shipping center with textile mills, food-processing plants, and factories mfg. cotton-ginning machinery. Chattahoochee R. Barge Canal (opened 1964) links with Intracoastal Waterway. U.S. Fort Benning is nearby. **2** City (1963 pop. 24,782), S central Ind., on East Fork of White R., SSE of Indianapolis; settled 1820. Farm trade center. Bakalar Air Force Base is nearby. **3** City (pop. 24,771), NE Miss., on Tombigbee R. near Ala. line; settled 1817. Trade, processing, and shipping center of cotton, livestock, dairy, and timber area. Has marble works. Franklin Academy (1821) was first free school in state. Seat of MISSISSIPPI STATE COLLEGE FOR WOMEN. Columbus Air Force Base is N. **4** City (pop. 12,476), E central Nebr., in prairie region at junction of Loup and Platte rivers; founded 1856. Rail, mfg., and trade center for livestock, dairy, and grain area. Hq. of Loup River

power project. **5** Village (pop. 307), SW N.Mex., just N of Mexican border. After Mexican irregulars under Francisco (Pancho) VILLA raided village in 1916, Pres. Wilson ordered Gen. Pershing's punitive expedition into Mexico. **6** City (pop. 471,316), state cap., central Ohio, on Scioto R. Laid out as cap. 1812. Coming of feeder canal (1831) to Ohio and Erie Canal, Natl. Road (1833), and first railroad (1850) stimulated growth. Rail and highway focal point, important industrial and trade center of farm region, chief producer of mine and mill machinery in U.S. Mfg. also of aircraft and automobile parts. Here are OHIO STATE UNIVERSITY, Capital Univ. (at BEXLEY), Col. of St. Mary of the Springs, Battelle Memorial Inst., Columbus Gall. of Fine Arts. Has Confederate cemetery.

Columbus Day, commemoration of discovery of America. Celebrated Oct. 12 throughout most of U.S., parts of Canada, and several Latin American nations.

Columcille, Saint: see COLUMBA, SAINT.

Colyn, Alexander: see COLINS, ALEXANDER.

coma (kō'mù), deep insensibility from which person cannot be roused. It may be caused by brain injury, toxic conditions, shock, sunstroke, hemorrhage, or epilepsy.

Comanche Indians, tribe in N and W Texas and W Okla. after 17th cent., of Shoshonean group of Uto-Aztecan linguistic family. Nomads with a typical Plains culture, they were fiercely hostile to whites. See LANGUAGE (table).

Combaconam or **Combaconum,** India: see KUMBAKONAM.

Combe, William, 1741–1823, English satirist, author of doggerel verse for "Dr. Syntax" series illustrated by Thomas Rowlandson (1812–21).

Combes, Émile (āmēl' cōb'), 1835–1921, French premier (1902–5). Initiated separation of Church and state; abolished religious education.

combine, agricultural machine, usually operated by one man, which reaps and then threshes grain. The cleaned grain accumulates in the combine; the straw is returned to the field. The combine has increased large-scale wheat farming, esp. in the U.S.

combining weight, of an element, is computed by dividing atomic weight by its valence.

combustion, burning or rapid oxidation of a substance, liberating heat and light. Kindling temperature must be reached before substance will burn. In **spontaneous combustion,** substance bursts into flame without apparent cause; usually because there is slow oxidation, without heat loss, until kindling temperature is reached. **Heat of combustion** of a fuel is total amount of heat evolved from burning a given amount of it.

COMECON: see COUNCIL FOR MUTUAL ECONOMIC ASSISTANCE.

Comédie Française (kōmādē' frāsāz') or **Théâtre Français** (tāä'trù frāsā'), state theater of France. Estab. 1680 by royal decree (see BÉJART), company was given an annual grant and a theater. Closed during the Revolution; Napoleon revived it 1803.

comedy, a light, amusing play or other work so presented as to please and amuse. European comedy originated in anc. boisterous choruses and dialogue of the rites of Dionysius in Greece. From these developed dramas such as Aristophanes and Menander wrote; later Plautus and Terence imitated Menander. In England the tradition of the interlude blended with that of Latin classic comedies in 16th-cent. Romantic comedy, culminating in the plays of Jonson and Shakespeare. In France Molière combined classical influence with COMMEDIA DELL' ARTE. Reaction against the bawdy English Restoration comedies of Congreve, Wycherley, and others resulted in sentimental comedy, followed by satirical plays of Goldsmith and Sheridan. Only in late 19th cent. did true comedy appear in the works of Wilde, Shaw, Chekhov; in 20th cent., comedy includes works by such diverse authors as Pinero, Barrie, O'Casey,

Comenius   234   communicable diseases

Coward, even the nihilistic dramas of Beckett and Ionesco. In the U.S. the popular musical comedy derives from the successes of Gilbert and Sullivan.

Comenius, John Amos (kŏmē′nēŭs), Czech *Jan Amos Komenský*, 1592–1670, Czech educator, a Moravian churchman. Advocated relating education to everyday life, a universal system with equal opportunities for women, and teaching in vernacular.

comet, heavenly body traveling in orbit around sun. Usually consists of head of cloudy brightness within which lie one or more bright nuclei from which materials, driven away from sun by radiation pressure of sun's light, form a sweeping tail, sometimes over 100,-000,000 mi. long. Periods for covering known orbits range from 3.3 to several thousand years. Periodic comets are officially designated by year of closest approach to sun, followed by Roman numeral indicating order of passage.

Comines, Commines, or **Commynes, Philippe de** (fēlēp′ dü kōmēn′), c.1447–c.1511, French historian and diplomat. Served Charles the Bold of Burgundy and, after 1472, Louis XI and Charles VIII of France. His *Mémoires* (many translations) are outstanding for penetrating analysis of men and motives.

Cominform (kŏ′mĭnfôrm), Communist Information Bureau, estab. 1947 by Communist parties of USSR, E European satellites, France, and Italy. Membership was voluntary, decisions not binding; its stated aim was to exchange party experiences. Dominated by Russia, it expelled Yugoslavia 1948 for insisting on autonomy; dissolved itself 1956 in effort to reconcile Tito.

Comintern (kŏ′mĭntûrn) [from Communist International] or **Third International,** estab. 1919 at Moscow to give Communists leadership of world socialist movement. Gaining strength in the 1920s, it became means of Soviet control over other Communist parties. In 1936 Germany and Japan formed Anti-Comintern Pact, renewed 1941 with enlarged membership. In 1943 USSR dissolved Comintern to reassure its allies in Second World War.

Commager, Henry Steele (kŏ′mĭjŭr), 1902–, American historian, professor at Columbia and later at Amherst. His writings, often in collaboration, are extensive. Probably best-known is *The Growth of the American Republic* (with S. E. Morison, 1930).

Commandments, Ten: see TEN COMMANDMENTS.

commando, small military raiding unit organized (1940) by British in Second World War, akin to U.S. Army ranger units. First used by Boers in South African War.

commedia dell' arte (kŏm-mä′dēä dĕl-lär′tä), form of comedy in Italy in 16th–18th cent. Using improvised dialogue and masked characters (e.g., HARLEQUIN, COLUMBINE, SCARAMOUCHE, PANTALOON, *Il Capitano, Il Dotore*) in satiric song, dance, farce, it gave rise to traditional pantomime characters, to prototypes and comic situations seen even today.

Commerce, United States Department of, organized 1903 as Dept. of Commerce and Labor; separated from Dept. of Labor in 1913. Includes Bureau of the Census, Coast and Geodetic Survey, Bureau of Foreign and Domestic Commerce, Weather Bureau, Patent Office, and Civil Aeronautics Administration.

commercial law, body of laws governing business transactions. Beginnings of modern commercial law coincide with opening of large-scale commerce in the late Middle Ages. Strongly influenced by Roman law. Estab. in England in the mid-16th cent. as "law merchant" and was administered by special courts; later under royal courts but in the 18th cent. made a part of the common law and in this form adopted in the U.S., while on the Continent commercial law remains separate with special courts. Most states of U.S. have enacted the Uniform Commercial Code in an effort to prescribe the same rules for all commercial transactions.

commercial paper, comprehensive term for all kinds of short-term negotiable instruments calling for pay-

ment of money and usable as collateral. Normally only includes instruments used in commerce in place of money (e.g., drafts, bills of lading).

Commines, Philippe de: see COMINES.

commissar (kŏ′mĭsär), in the USSR, head of an administration or commissariat, similar to a minister in Western Europe.

Committee for Industrial Organization: see AMERICAN FEDERATION OF LABOR–CONGRESS OF INDUSTRIAL ORGANIZATIONS.

Commodus (kŏ′mŭdŭs), 161–92, Roman emperor (180–92), son and successor of Marcus Aurelius. Licentious, vulgar, vain, proud of his physique, he was well hated, finally murdered.

common law, legal system of England, originally (13th cent.) so called because, as law of the king's courts, it represented the common custom of the realm, not the local or manorial law; more precisely, that part of the English legal system not reduced to statutes and not arising from equity, maritime law, or other special branches. It is law arising from customs and created by judges to meet problems, unlike modern civil law (based upon the code and the statute). Common law followed in British Commonwealth of Nations (except Quebec) and the U.S. (except La., Puerto Rico, Virgin Isls.).

Common Market, Arab, economic union of Arab League member states. Estab. 1964 by treaty between United Arab Republic, Iraq, Jordan, Kuwait, and Syria, effective Jan., 1965.

Common Market, Central American (CACM), formally known as the General Treaty of Central American Economic Integration, estab. 1961 by treaty ratified by El Salvador, Guatemala, Honduras, and Nicaragua (1961) and by Costa Rica (1963). Formed to stimulate industry and trade by providing free trade, expanding communications and transportation systems, unifying currencies, integrating economic and financial policies. See also LATIN AMERICAN FREE TRADE ASSOCIATION.

Common Market, European: see EUROPEAN COMMUNITY.

Common Market, Latin American, economic organization of Latin American nations, agreed upon at conference of American presidents in Punta del Este, Uruguay, in April, 1967. LATIN AMERICAN FREE TRADE ASSOCIATION and Central American COMMON MARKET to be basis of new economic group scheduled to become effective in 1970.

Commons, House of: see PARLIAMENT; WESTMINSTER PALACE.

Commonwealth of Australia, British dominion including continental AUSTRALIA and TASMANIA.

commune: see COLLECTIVE FARM.

Commune of Paris, March–May, 1871, government set up in Paris at end of FRANCO-PRUSSIAN WAR, in opposition to government of Adolphe THIERS at Versailles. (Paris had had communal government earlier, a notable occasion being in French Revolution.) Original issue was the Parisians' refusal to accept humiliating peace terms from Prussia. When *Versaillais* troops began siege of Paris (while the Prussians stood by as neutrals), the Commune fell under the sway of leftist extremists, who shot hostages (including archbishop of Paris), burned Tuileries, city hall, palace of justice. On May 28 the *Versaillais* entered Paris. In subsequent reprisals more than 17,000 people, including women and children, were executed.

communicable diseases, diseases caused by microorganisms and transmissible from an infected person or animal to another. They are known also as infectious diseases. Commonly they are called contagious if transmissible by contact with victim of disease or infected objects or secretions. They may be spread also by substances taken into body, e.g., cholera; by bite or sting of infected animal or disease carrier, e.g., rabies, malaria; by contamination of wound, e.g., tetanus. Preventive measures include vaccination, inoculation,

SMALL CAPITALS = cross references. Pronunciation key on inside end pages. Abbreviations: p. 2.

quarantine, disinfection. An endemic disease is one always present in a given locality. Disease may become epidemic if many persons lack immunity or if infectious agent is unusually virulent.

communication, transmission and reception of message between two persons or more. Basic forms: signs (sight), sound (hearing; see LANGUAGE). Reduction of message to writing was a fundamental step in social evolution, the beginning of recorded history. Save for limited devices (carrier pigeons, smoke signals, heliograph, etc.) speed of early communication was only as fast as man could travel. Invention of TELEGRAPH, RADIO, TELEPHONE, TELEVISION made almost instantaneous communication possible. The use of communications satellites such as Telstar has greatly expanded communication. Federal Communications Commission regulates radio and television in U.S.; international phases are directed by Office of Transport and Communications, Dept. of State. UN maintains Internatl. Telecommunications Union (ITU) to promote international cooperation in that field.

Communications Satellite Corporation (Comsat), private body under jurisdiction of Federal Communications Commission, estab. 1963. It may construct, own, and operate itself or in cooperation with other authorized bodies, particularly the U.S. government, a network of communications satellites.

communion, in Christianity, partaking of bread and wine to commemorate the Last Supper, when Jesus gave bread and wine to his disciples. Called formally Holy Communion. Some—among them all Roman Catholics—believe that the substances actually become the body and blood of Christ. Others believe that the sacrament of Holy Communion—receiving the bread and wine—is symbolic, but all believe that through partaking the believer arrives at communion with Christ in faith. The belief that actual change takes place is called the doctrine of transubstantiation; the belief that the real presence of Jesus is blended with the bread and wine is the doctrine of consubstantiation. Other sects hold to the simplest sort of communion. The bread and wine are sometimes taken separately, sometimes together. The sacrament is called the Eucharist among Catholics and some others.

communism, political and social philosophy, based upon the teachings of Karl Marx. Its fundamental principle is that property should be held in common and not individually. The standard examples of governments that are Communist are those of the USSR and China—in ideological conflict in 1967. Various other states are more or less allied in thought to one or the other of these countries: in Europe, Poland, Czechoslovakia, Hungary, Rumania, Yugoslavia, Bulgaria, and Albania; and in Asia, notably North Vietnam. In the Americas the prominent Communist government is that of Cuba.

Communism, Mount, 24,590 ft., Tadzhik SSR, in the PAMIR; highest peak in USSR. Originally called Garmo Peak, renamed Stalin Peak 1933, and Mt. Communism 1962.

communistic settlements, communities practicing common ownership of goods. Existed in ancient and medieval times, and flourished again in 19th-cent. America. Some were religious (e.g., Amana Society, Shaker communities, Oneida Community); others nonreligious and utopian (e.g., New Harmony, Brook Farm, several Fourierist communities, and settlements by Cabet).

Communist party, in China. Founded 1921, under strong Comintern influence until mid-1930s. Formally allied with Kuomintang in 1924, it maintained alliance on insistence of USSR until driven underground in 1927 by Chiang Kai-shek. First rural soviet estab. in 1927 in Kiangsi prov. By 1935 MAO TSE-TUNG was in full control; a Chinese Red Army was recruited. Driven by Chiang, it trekked N on LONG MARCH (leaders incl. MAO, CHU TEH, CHOU EN-LAI, and LIN PIAO) and estab. hq. at YENAN in

Shensi prov. In the face of Japanese aggression (see CHINO-JAPANESE WAR, SECOND), the Communists obtained limited truce from Chiang; the truce broke down in 1941, but Communist guerrillas remained the only really effective force against the Japanese in N China. After the Second World War civil war flared anew. Chiang was driven to offshore Taiwan, and People's Republic of China was estab. in 1949. The Communist party became the center of government administration. (See also CHINA.)

Communist party, in USSR, officially the Communist Party of the Soviet Union (CPSU). With a strictly selected and trained membership (in 1965) of over 10,800,000 in 300,000 units, the party exercises all effective power within USSR. The central committee, directed by the presidium (formerly Politburo), is the party's highest body. MARXISM, which developed in Russia during 1880s, split (1903) into factions of BOLSHEVISM AND MENSHEVISM. The view of G. V. PLEKHANOV that conditions in Russia were not ripe for socialism until capitalism and industrialization had sufficiently progressed was adopted by the Menshevists. Under LENIN, Bolsheviks demanded disciplined, centralized revolutionary elite rather than a mass party, and this principle remains as basis of CPSU. Party gained power after 1917 revolution when Lenin and TROTSKY ousted opposition groups and imposed party dictatorship. After Lenin's death in 1924, STALIN emerged as leader. A time of oppression, Stalinist period (1930–53) was marked by massive collectivization of farms to strengthen party in rural areas. A series of purges accused former leaders of treason (e.g., Trotsky, BUKHARIN, ZINOVIEV, KAMENEV, RYKOV) and led to their exile or execution. In a struggle for power after Stalin's death, the "anti-party" group, including MALENKOV and MOLOTOV, was purged. KHRUSHCHEV became first secretary of the central committee and chairman of the council of ministers (in fact, premier). He initiated policy of de-Stalinization. In 1964 Khrushchev was succeeded by BREZHNEV as leader of the central committee and by KOSYGIN as chairman of the council of ministers, or premier. CPSU is dominant power in world Communist movement.

Communist party, in U.S., part of world-wide political movement of Communism. First organized 1919. With decline of I.W.W., party became leading revolutionary organization in U.S., having as its avowed aim the overthrow of capitalism and establishment of a dictatorship of the proletariat. Communists led many industrial strikes in 1920s and exploited weaknesses of American democracy. In 1935, following Comintern's new line, party began "cooperating" with liberal groups, and, boring from within, gained control of many organizations (e.g., many trade unions). With the Nazi attack on Russia in June, 1941, party turned from condemnation of the Second World War as "imperialist" to support of war as "democratic." Following the war cooperation with "progressive" capitalism ended. With the onset of the "cold war," Pres. Truman and Congress took steps to keep Communists out of U.S. government employment and to eliminate their influence in union activity. The Alger Hiss trials (1949, 1950) and the trials and convictions of top Communists served more widely to publicize conspiratorial and subversive nature of U.S. Communism. Party membership, always small, has been drawn mainly from groups that are discriminated against in U.S. society, idealists, and direct-action trade unionists. Its political influence extended to AMERICAN LABOR PARTY and PROGRESSIVE PARTY of 1948. Soviet attacks on Stalin and action in Hungary (1956) brought factional splits and resignations. In June, 1961, U.S Supreme Court upheld registration provisions of McCarran Act and ordered party to comply with them.

community chest, cooperative organization of citizens and social welfare agencies in a city for the purpose of raising and allocating funds for charity.

commutator: see GENERATOR.

Commynes, Philippe de: see COMINES.

Comnenus (kŏmnē'nùs), dynasty of Byzantine emperors (reigned 1057–59, 1081–1185): ISAAC I, ALEXIUS I, JOHN II, MANUEL I, Alexius II, Andronicus I. Family founded empire of TREBIZOND (1204–1461).

Como (kō'mō), city (pop. 82,070), Lombardy, N Italy, at SW end of Lake Como. Silk mfg. Founded as Roman colony; independent commune by 11th cent.; conquered 1335 by Milan, after long struggle. Cathedral (14th–18th cent.); town hall (1215). **Lake Como,** Ital. *Lago di Como* or *Lario*, c.30 mi. long, ½–2½ mi. wide, is formed by Adda R. in foothills of Alps. Celebrated scenery; many resorts (Bellagio, Cadenabbia, Cernobbio, Menaggio, Tremezzo).

Comodoro Rivadavia (kōmōdhō'rō rēvädhä'vyä), town (pop. c.30,000), SE Argentina; oil production center.

Comoro Islands (kŏ'mùrō), French overseas territory, (c.838 sq. mi.; pop. c.206,480), volcanic archipelago in the Mozambique Channel; cap. Moroni (pop. c.10,000). Agr. and lumbering. Chose to remain within the French Republic in 1958.

Compactata: see UTRAQUISTS.

compass. 1 In mathematics, an instrument for making circles and measuring distances; usually it consists of a pivot leg and a pencil or pen leg or of two pointed legs. **2** In navigation, an instrument for determining direction. Mariner's compass consists of freely suspended magnetic needle which in earth's magnetic field indicates N and S poles. "Boxing the compass" is naming in order the 32 points starting from north (N, N by E, NNE, etc.). Flux-gate or gyro flux-gate compass contains gyroscopic stabilizer and is useful in airplanes. Declination or variation at any point on earth's surface is difference in angular degrees between direction to N magnetic pole and direction to N geographic pole.

Compiègne (kōpēä'nyù), town (pop. 22,325), Oise dept., N France, NE of Paris. Château, rebuilt 18th cent., often a royal residence. Joan of Arc was captured (1430) while defending the town. In a railroad car in near-by Forest of Compiègne were signed the armistice of 1918, which ended the First World War, and the French-German armistice of 1940.

complex, term indicating group or system of ideas originating in a mind as a result of an experience or set of experiences of high emotional content. Although repressed from consciousness, it affects subsequent mental activity and behavior. Undue dominance of a complex over an individual causes psychopathic condition.

composition, in primitive and medieval law, prevention of retribution for acts of violence by payment of money to injured person or his family. Marks transition from vendetta system to system of criminal law where socially dangerous acts are concern of the state rather than of family unit. A well-known instance of composition is the Old English wergild, payment made by a murderer to the victim's family. Term also refers to agreement between insolvent debtor and creditor, whereby the creditor takes some portion of his debt and waives the rest.

Compostela, Santiago de, Spain: see SANTIAGO DE COMPOSTELA.

compound, homogeneous chemical combination of two or more elements in definite proportion by weight. Has properties distinct from those of its constituents. Can be decomposed by heat and CHEMICAL REACTION. A compound is indicated by a formula showing symbols of constituent elements in proper proportion. A compound is composed of molecules, all of which are identical and made up of atoms of two or more different elements. A mixture differs from a compound in that constituents do not join chemically, but instead retain original properties, are not in fixed proportions, and may be separated by mechanical means.

compression, external stress applied uniformly to object or substance, causing decrease in volume. Gas is compressed easily, solids less easily, liquids slightly if at all. When molecules of gas are brought together

under specific compression and temperature conditions, liquefaction occurs. Principle is used in commercial preparation of gases, e.g., liquid oxygen, helium, propane. Compression of fuel is essential to functioning of internal combustion engine.

Compromise of 1850. Annexation of Texas to U.S. and addition of new territory at close of Mexican War aggravated North-South tension over extension of SLAVERY into territories. WILMOT PROVISO was source of contention. Compromise measures, largely originating with Stephen A. DOUGLAS, were sponsored in U.S. Senate by Henry CLAY. Measures proposed admission of Calif. as free state; organization of New Mexico and Utah territories without mention of slavery, but with provisions for SQUATTER SOVEREIGNTY; settlement of Texas boundary claims; prohibition of slave trade in D.C.; a more stringent fugitive slave law. Daniel Webster, through speech on March 17, 1850, enhanced passage of the proposals. More important, however, was the death of President Zachary TAYLOR and the succession of Millard FILLMORE, a supporter of the Compromise. They were passed as separate bills in Sept., 1850. Compromise was hailed as a final solution to slavery question in territories, but issue arose again in 1854 (see KANSAS-NEBRASKA BILL).

Compton, Arthur Holly, 1892–1962, American physicist, helped develop atomic bomb. Shared 1927 Nobel Prize in Physics for his discovery of the **Compton effect:** increase in the wave lengths of X rays on collision with electrons of atoms of low atomic weights. His brother **Karl Taylor Compton,** 1887–1954, physicist, president of Massachusetts Institute of Technology 1930–48, is known for his work on radar, photoelectricity, ionization of gases, ultraviolet spectroscopy, and electric arcs.

Compton, city (pop. 71,812), S Calif., NNW of Long Beach; settled 1867.

Compton-Burnett, Ivy, 1892–, English novelist. Her many works, relying almost entirely on conversations, include *Men and Wives* (1931) and *The Mighty and Their Fall* (1961).

Compton effect: see COMPTON, ARTHUR HOLLY.

compurgation, in medieval law, legal defense by oath of the accused, supported by oaths of other persons that they believed that he swore truthfully. Found in early Germanic law and in English church law.

computer, apparatus which can perform a sequence of calculations without human aid; developed from CALCULATING MACHINE (which can perform only one operation at a time, not sequences). There are two types of computer, digital and analog. Digital computer carries out mathematical operations with variables expressed in apparatus as numbers, usually in binary system (0, 1, 10, 11, 100, 101, 110 in binary system correspond to 0, 1, 2, 3, 4, 5, 6 in decimal system). Binary system numbers are recorded in computer electromechanically (e.g., as a series of electric off-on switches) or electronically (e.g., as a series of temporary magnets, each magnetized in one of two possible directions). Modern digital computers are usually electronic; circuits are arranged to duplicate processes of mathematics carry out the desired operations upon the binary numbers. In analog computer, quantities and dimensions represent the variables; numbers are not used by the apparatus in the mathematical operations. The differential analyzer of Vannevar Bush was an early analog computer capable of solving differential equations; the solution was obtained by rotating a series of calibrated interlocking wheels, preset to express the interrelationships of the variables. Modern analog computers are electronic; current, resistance, voltage, capacitance, are among quantities used. Circuits are set up to represent interrelationships of the variables in the particular problem; varying one quantity causes others to vary accordingly (e.g., following Ohm's law) and solution can be determined. All computers, digital and analog, have input (for supply of known data in terms usable by computer), output (to express problem answers), storage unit (to record intermediate data), arithmetic unit (containing logical circuits for carrying out mathematical operations), and programing unit (to control sequence of operations). Functions of these units tend to become less specific, e.g., certain programing sequences may be preserved in storage unit for use in solving later problems. Computers are important in research and engineering, particularly in aircraft and rocket design and navigation. Computers are used in industry; in AUTOMATION, computers plan sequences of operations for automated machinery.

Comsat: see COMMUNICATIONS SATELLITE CORPORATION.

Comstock, Ada Louise, 1876–, American educator. Dean of Smith Col. 1912–23; president of Radcliffe 1923–43.

Comstock, Anthony, 1844–1915, American moral crusader. Secured New York state and Federal legislation against obscene matter. Organized New York Society for the Suppression of Vice.

Comstock, Daniel Frost, 1883–, American physicist, inventor of technicolor process for photography.

Comstock Lode, richest known silver deposit, W Nev., on Mt. Davidson in the Virginia Range. Discovered in 1857 by Ethan Allen Grosh and Hosea Ballou Grosh, who died before recording claims. In 1859 Henry Tomkins Paige Comstock laid claim to lode; later disposed of holdings for insignificant sums. Lode became scene of feverish activity, with VIRGINIA CITY its "capital." Great fortunes were made. By 1898 lode was virtually abandoned.

Comtat Venaissin: see VENAISSIN.

Comte, Auguste (ōgüst' kōt') 1798–1857, French philosopher, apostle of positivism, a philosophical system completely rejecting metaphysics and relying instead on the findings of modern positive sciences. This he first began to develop when contributing (1818–24) to the publications of Saint-Simon. His final aim was to so reform society that all men might live in harmony and comfort. He ranked sociology (a term he invented) as greatest of the sciences. His *Course of Positive Philosophy* (1830–42) set forth the system later elaborated in other of his works and developed to a more inclusive scale by followers all over the world in the late 19th cent.

Comus (kō'mŭs), in late Roman legend, god of mirth, shown as a winged youth bearing torch and drinking cup. Lover of song, dance and wine, a follower of Dionysus.

Comyn, John (kŭ'mĭn), d. c.1300, Scottish noble. Known as Black Comyn, he became (1286) one of six guardians of realm. Signed treaty by which MARGARET MAID OF NORWAY was to marry eldest son of Edward I of England. On Margaret's death claimed throne, but submitted to Edward. Meanwhile pushed claim of John de BALIOL, who was crowned in 1292. His son, **John Comyn,** d. 1306, aided de Baliol against Edward I. Murdered by Robert Bruce or his followers.

Conakry (kō'nŭkrē), city (pop. c.112,158, including Iles de Los), cap. of Republic of Guinea, SW Guinea, on Atlantic. A deepwater port, commercial center, and rail terminus, it exports bauxite, aluminum, and agr. products. Textile mfg. Also spelled Konakry.

Conanicut Island: see JAMESTOWN, R.I.

Conant, James Bryant, 1893–, American educator, a chemist. Professor of organic chemistry at Harvard (1919–33). President of Harvard (1933–53). In Second World War chairman of Natl. Defense Research Committee. Made U.S. High Commissioner for Germany 1953; ambassador 1955–57. Conducted study of U.S. public high school 1957–62. His controversial reports on teacher training have stimulated reform.

concentration camp. In 1933 National Socialist Germany set up forced-labor camps where political undesirables (mainly Jews and Communists) were held without legal procedure. In Second World War concentration camps existed throughout German-held

Europe. Some (e.g., Majdanek and Oswiecim in Poland) had gas chambers where 6,000,000 (mostly Jews and Poles) were exterminated. Countless others died of mistreatment. Among largest camps in Germany were Buchenwald, Dachau, Belsen. The term is now also used to mean forced-labor camps confining political prisoners.

Concepción (kōnsĕpsēōn'), city (1960 est. pop. 167,-468), cap. of Concepción prov., S central Chile, near mouth of Bío-Bío. Founded by Valdivia in 1550, it is now one of Chile's largest cities and a major shipping center through its port, Talcahuano. Attacks by Araucanian Indians in first years and recurrent earthquakes (1570, 1730, 1751, 1939, 1960) have plagued city.

Concepción del Uruguay (dĕl ōorōōgwī'), city (pop. c.40,000), NE Argentina, on Uruguay R., one of commercial centers of the Argentine Mesopotamia.

concertina: see ACCORDION.

concerto, musical form dating from early baroque period. The *concerto grosso,* in which a group of solo instruments alternated with a larger ensemble, was standardized by Corelli and Vivaldi. The form of the classical concerto—three movements, for solo instrument and orchestra—was developed by Mozart.

conch (kŏngk), name for certain marine mollusks with spiral univalve shells, especially those of families Strombidae and Cassididae. Some are called cameo or helmet shells. Conches eat live animal food and also scavenge. Shells, ranging from white to red, are often made into ornaments.

conciliation: see ARBITRATION, INTERNATIONAL.

Concini, Concino (kōnchē'nō kōnchē'nē), d. 1617, Florentine adventurer, favorite of MARIE DE' MEDICI, who made him marshal of France and marquis d'Ancre. Succeeded Sully as chief minister (1611). Notorious for his greed and his spy system. Assassinated by order of Louis XIII. His wife, Leonora Galigaï, was beheaded and burned for sorcery (1617).

Concord. 1 (kŏng'kŭrd) Residential city (pop. 36,-208), W central Calif., ENE of Oakland, in oil and farm region; settled c.1852. U.S. naval ammunition depot is nearby. **2** Town (pop. 12,517), E Mass., on Concord R., NW of Boston; settled 1635. Scene of Revolutionary battle on April 19, 1775 (see LEXINGTON AND CONCORD, BATTLES OF) marked by D. C. French's *Minuteman.* Houses where Emerson, the Alcotts, Hawthorne, and Thoreau lived are preserved. Old Manse (1765) is public shrine; Sleepy Hollow Cemetery has graves of many famous residents. Thoreau's Walden Pond is S. Town includes village of West Concord. **3** City (pop. 28,991), state cap. (since 1816), S central N.H., on Merrimack R. above Manchester; settled 1725–27. Famous for granite, it also has printing and other industries. St. Paul's School and Franklin Pierce's house (now a museum) are here. Mary Baker Eddy was born at nearby Bow. **4** (kŏn'kôrd") City (pop. 17,799), central N.C., NE of Charlotte near edge of piedmont, in livestock and grain area; settled 1796. Gold discovery nearby in 1799 started N.C. gold rush. Seat of Barber-Scotia Col.

Concord, river, NE Mass., short tributary of Merrimack R., which it joins at Lowell. Colonial militia fired some of first shots of Revolution at British over its bridge at Concord, April 19, 1775.

concordat (kŏnkôr'dăt), contractual agreement between pope, in his spiritual capacity, and temporal authority of a state, regulating points of conflict between Church and state. The earliest concordat (see WORMS, CONCORDAT OF) was concluded in 1122. The Concordat of 1516, with France, abolished the PRAGMATIC SANCTION OF BOURGES but was revoked in 1561. Concordats, common since 19th cent., determine method of appointing bishops and define status of religious schools, orders, and property. Best known are the LATERAN TREATY with Italy (1929) and the **Concordat of 1801** between Pius VII and Bonaparte, which restored the Roman Church in France. In 1905 France repudiated it and separated Church and state.

Concorde, Place de la (pläs′ dù lä kōkôrd′), world-famous square (85,000 sq. yds.) of Paris, France. Designed by Gabriel and built 1755–92.

Concordia (kŏngkôr′dhyä), city (pop. c.56,000), NE Argentina, port on Uruguay R. opposite Salto, Uruguay. One of chief towns of the Argentine Mesopotamia, it exports meat, mate, quebracho, and grain.

concrete music: see ELECTRONIC MUSIC.

concretion (kŏnkrē′shùn), rounded mass occurring in sedimentary rock and differing from it in composition (e.g., flint nodules in chalk).

Condé (kōdā′), French princely family, cadet branch of house of BOURBON. It originated with **Louis I de Bourbon, prince de Condé** (lwē′ dù bōōrbō′), 1530–69, Protestant leader and general. He took part in conspiracy of AMBOISE (1560), commanded Huguenots in Wars of Religion, fell at Jarnac. His great-grandson **Louis II de Bourbon, prince de Condé,** known as **the Great Condé,** 1621–86, won major victories at Rocroi (1643) and, in Thirty Years War, at Freiburg (1644), Nördlingen (1645), Lens (1648). In the FRONDE he turned against his government, taking command of the army of princes in 1651 and of the Spanish army in 1653. Defeated by Turenne, notably in Battle of the Dunes (1658), he was pardoned in 1659 by Louis XIV, for whom he fought successfully in the Dutch War. He was the brother of Armand de CONTI and of Mme de LONGUEVILLE. His great-grandson, **Louis Joseph de Bourbon, prince de Condé** (zhōzěf′), 1736–1818, formed the "army of Condé" against the French revolutionary forces (dissolved 1801). He was the grandfather of the duc d'ENGHIEN.

condensation, in physics, change in state of substance from gas to liquid. Velocity and distance between molecules of gas are so decreased by heat withdrawal that substance condenses. Dew, fog, and clouds are formed as a result of condensation of water vapor in atmosphere.

condenser, device to increase capacity of conductor for receiving and holding greater electrical charge. LEYDEN JAR is a simple type. Principle is induction. Used in telephone, radio, and ignition system of automobile. Apparatus causing condensation of gas is also called a condenser.

Condillac, Étienne Bonnot de (kōdēyäk′), 1715–80, French philosopher, a priest. He started from Locke's ideas and stressed that all psychological processes in an individual are derived from sensations, and that general ideas are built by experience through the medium of language. This sensationalism, expounded in his *Traité des sensations* (1754), was much discussed and influenced later psychologists. His attempts to arrive at exact terms for social and economic concepts had a clarifying effect in French thought.

condor (kŏn′dùr), South American vulture which nests on Andean peaks. California condor or vulture (now rare) lives in North American coastal ranges; it is one of largest birds of prey, with wingspread of 9–10 ft.

Condorcet, Antoine Nicolas, marquis de (kōdôrsä′), 1743–94, French philosopher, mathematician, and revolutionist. He was a friend of most of the leading intellectuals of his day. He made valuable contributions to the mathematical theory of probabilities. An enthusiastic supporter of the revolution, he was active politically until he protested the persecution of the Girondists. He was denounced and went into hiding. There he completed his great philosophical work, a historical sketch outlining the progress of man to the French Revolution, which he thought would usher in perfection of human state. Captured by his enemies, he died mysteriously and immediately.

condottiere (kôndôt-tyä′rä), leader of mercenary soldiers in Renaissance Italy. Condottieri hired their own bands, fought for highest bidder, often changed allegiance. Well-known condottieri were Muzio Attendolo Sforza, Colleoni, Sir John de Hawkwood.

conducting, in music, art of unifying the efforts of a number of musicians playing ensemble. Until c.1600 the conductor was primarily a time-beater, using a roll of music as a baton. In the baroque era the group was at first led by the harpsichordist, later by the first violinist, even today called the concertmaster. The nonplaying conductor, using a baton, appeared in the 19th cent. Beethoven, Mendelssohn, and Wagner often conducted; Hans von Bülow was the first of the modern virtuoso conductors.

conduction. 1 Transfer of heat energy from one part of substance to adjoining part, from molecule to molecule. Substances that readily transfer heat are conductors, e.g., metals; those that do so slowly are insulators, e.g., nonmetals, fluids. **2** Transfer of charge of electricity from one point to another. Metals are good conductors; nonmetals are insulators. Electric wires are insulated to prevent escape of charge during conduction.

cone, reproductive structure of most conifers. Male (staminate) and female (ovulate) cones are borne on same tree, but hard, woody ovulate cones are the ones commonly seen. Egg cells produced by ovulate cones are fertilized by pollen from staminate cones; after fertilization, ovulate cone functions as a seed-bearing structure. Among largest are the 10–20 in. cones of sugar pine in W U.S.; most are 1–6 in. long. See *ill.,* p. 859.

cone, in mathematics, a surface (called a conical surface), generated by a moving line (generator) which passes through a given point (vertex) and continually intersects a given fixed curve (directrix). A cone is also the solid bounded by such a surface.

Conecuh, river: see ESCAMBIA, river.

Conemaugh (kŏn′úmô″), river of SW Pa. rising in Alleghenies and flowing c.45 mi. NW to branch of Allegheny R. U.S. projects include Conemaugh River Dam.

Conestoga wagon, freight-carrying vehicle originated in Conestoga region of Pennsylvania c.1725. Used by farmers and later in commerce with frontier settlements until c.1850. Large wagons, drawn by six horses, carried up to eight tons. Bottom of the wagon box curved upward at both ends; white hood over wagon was protection against elements.

coney: see CONY.

Coney Island (kō′nē), famous beach resort and amusement center of S Brooklyn borough of New York city, on the Atlantic. Attractions include 2-mi. boardwalk and New York Aquarium.

Confederacy or **Confederate States of America** (1861–65), government estab. by Southern states of U.S. which seceded from Union. When Pres. Lincoln was elected, seven states seceded–S.C., Ga., La., Miss., Fla., Ala., and Texas. Provisional government was set up at Montgomery, Ala., and constitution drafted. After firing on Fort Sumter and Lincoln's call for troops, four more states joined–Ark., N.C., Va., and Tenn. Richmond, Va., became capital, and Jefferson DAVIS and Alexander H. STEPHENS were elected president and vice president. Judah P. BENJAMIN was outstanding member of cabinet. Story of Confederacy was story of loss of CIVIL WAR. Its citizens bore privations and invasion with bravery and courage, loyal to end. Refused recognition by England and France, which did recognize Northern blockade of Southern ports. Volunteers were insufficient; conscription used but opposed. Financial troubles were heavy from start, and paper money became worthless. Mounting Union victories made end inevitable. Confederacy fell after Lee's surrender in April, 1865.

Confederate cruisers. In Civil War, Confederacy set out to destroy North's merchant marine. Of some 18 cruisers *Florida, Alabama,* and *Shenandoah* were outstanding. *Florida* took some 60 prizes before her capture in 1864. *Alabama* took almost 70, causing over $6,000,-000 damage as settled in ALABAMA CLAIMS. She was sunk by U.S.S. *Kearsarge,* June, 1864. *Shenandoah* took 38 prizes; she reverted to U.S. Raids caused decline of nation's merchant marine.

Confederate States of America: see CONFEDERACY.

Confederation, Articles of, in U.S. history, ratified in 1781 and superseded by Constitution of U.S. in 1789. Proved unsatisfactory because of subordinate position occupied by central government; Congress was dependent upon states for funds and execution of its decrees. Government commanded little respect because of weaknesses. Most significant achievement was Ordinance of 1787.

confederation, Canadian: see BRITISH NORTH AMERICA ACT.

Confederation of the Rhine, league of German princes, formed 1806 under protection of Napoleon I. Members included Bavaria, Württemberg, Saxony, Westphalia, Baden. Confederation broke apart in 1813.

Confessing Church, German Protestant movement. Founded 1933 by Martin NIEMOELLER in opposition to Nazi-sponsored "German Christian Church." Later driven underground by Nazis.

confession, formal admission of criminal guilt, usually made in the course of examination by the police, by the prosecutor, or at the trial. To be admissible it must be made voluntarily—not induced by torture, threat, or promises—and given by one advised of right to counsel.

confirmation, in Christianity, formal affirmation of faith, linked to baptism or, in some cases, replacing it to mark entrance into the church. Among Catholics it is performed by a bishop with laying on of hands and anointing with chrism. In W Europe and the New World it is usually conferred after a person has reached the "age of discretion"; in the East it may be given at any age. The Jewish ceremony at which a 13-year-old boy may be confirmed and at which he becomes a bar mitzvah (adult) is also called Bar Mitzvah; the usage is now extended to a similar ceremony for girls.

conflict of laws, situation arising when the law of more than one territorial unit may be applied to a case, as where a contract is made in one place, with intention of performing at another, with litigation at a third. In Europe this is frequently called private international law. In the U.S. the variance of laws from state to state makes urgent the determination of which state's law controls a dispute (choice of law) and when one state must respect a final decision made by another's court. Choice of law is controlled by the law of the territory having closest connection with the transaction from which the suit arose. The U.S. Constitution compels one state to treat as valid a judgment rendered in another state which had proper jurisdiction.

Confucius (kŭnfū'shŭs), Chinese *K'ung Fu-tse,* c.551–479? B.C., Chinese ethical teacher. His life is surrounded by legend, but it is known that he was born in the feudal state of Lu, that he was a public official, and that he and his followers urged social reform. In the midst of warfare, corruption and tyranny, he urged a system of morality and statecraft to bring about peace, justice, and universal order. His teachings became the basis of the moral system of **Confucianism** (kŭnfū'shŭnĭzŭm), which was of course based on earlier ideas and was developed in some of the most important works of CHINESE LITERATURE, including the *Analects* (sayings of Confucius and his disciples), classic works supposedly edited by Confucius, and the writings of Mencius. The basic moral principle of the system is the maintenance of *jen* (roughly, sympathy) between men by keeping right relationships: treat those who are subordinate to you as you would be treated by those in positions superior to yours. This is the Confucian Golden Rule. Filial piety is heavily stressed and became more dominant as the system endured, but Confucianism created a universal pattern for government, with emphasis on the middle way, avoidance of extreme. Originally atheistic, Confucianism was later colored by religious ele-

ments from earlier beliefs, and the hierarchy of relationships was capped by Shang-Ti [ruler of heaven], the superior of earthly rulers. Confucius was himself deified. Confucianism was triumphant by the 1st cent. A.D. Though it had to contend with TAOISM and BUDDHISM and was often eclipsed by them, the actual system of government continued with Confucian principles. In the Sung dynasty (960–1279), the system was revised as Neo-Confucianism, opposing the meditation and quietism of the other religions by stress on improvement through acquiring knowledge. This remained dominant until the 20th cent. though it gradually rigidified the system of respectful relationship into an approval of the existing social order.

Congaree (kŏng'gûrē), river, central S.C., formed by junction of Broad and Saluda rivers at Columbia. Flows 52 mi. SE to Wateree R., forming Santee R.

congestion or **hyperemia,** excessive accumulation of blood in part of body. May result from exercise, inflammation, or circulatory weakness.

Congo, river, c.3,000 mi. long; 2d longest in Africa. Drainage basin (c.1,467,000 sq. mi.) includes much of W central Africa. Its upper course, from its rise in the Zambia-Katanga border area to STANLEY FALLS, is called the Lualaba. In its lower course it broadens into STANLEY POOL, on which are Brazzaville and Kinshasa (Leopoldville), beyond which begin Livingstone Falls; here the river drops 852 ft. in 220 mi. Its estuary forms part of the Angola border. Much of the Congo is navigable. Ocean-going vessels can reach Matadi, 95 mi. upstream, where there is a railroad to Kinshasa. Its mouth was discovered 1482 by the Portuguese navigator Diogo Cão. Livingstone explored area around upper course 1866–71, Sir Henry Stanley made first known descent to the mouth 1874–77.

Congo, Belgian: see CONGO, REPUBLIC OF THE.

Congo, kingdom of the, historic W African state, whose territory is now included in the Republic of the Congo, the Congo Republic, and Angola. The Congo ruler, baptized King John I, made an alliance with Portugal, and in 1491 a small Portuguese mission was estab. at Mbanza. During reign of his son, Alfonso, appeals were made in vain to Portugal to stop slave raiding. In 1548, with arrival of Jesuits, name of cap. was changed to São Salvador; by 1690 São Salvador was deserted and in ruins.

Congo, Republic of the, country (c.905,000 sq. mi.; pop. c.15,300,000), central Africa; cap. Kinshasa (formerly Leopoldville). Comprises 12 provs. (the former provs. of Leopoldville, Équateur, Orientale, Kasai, Kivu, Katanga) and the autonomous cap. city. Formerly Belgian Congo. Mainly within Congo R. basin; in E is Central Rift, containing lakes Tanganyika, Kivu, Edward, and Albert, as well as Ruwenzori Mts. Dense equatorial forest in N, savanna and woodlands to S. Vast natural resources include animal life and timber, oil palm and rubber, cotton, and coffee. Major producer of industrial diamonds and cobalt; other minerals include copper, tin, uranium, and gold. Kinshasa, Lubumbashi (Elisabethville), and Kisangani (Stanleyville) are major cities. Matadi, on Congo R., is principal port. River transportation supplemented by good rail and road network. Most Congolese are Bantus; Pygmies, among area's earliest inhabitants, are today nomadic hunters in Ituri forest. French is official language. Portuguese explorers arrived in 15th cent., and by 17th cent. there was heavy slave trade. Journeys of David LIVINGSTONE and H. M. STANLEY revealed territory's economic wealth and evoked interest of King Leopold II of Belgium. In 1885 he organized Congo Free State as his personal estate. In 1908 the Belgian parliament took over the Congo from their king, creating the Belgian Congo. Belgian attempts to suppress nationalists led in 1959 to riots; the Brussels Conference (1960) agreed to immediate independence, which was granted June, 1960. Army mutiny and social upheaval swept the country, and Belgium sent troops to protect its nationals. Upon secession of mineral-rich Katanga under Moise TSHOMBE, the central Congolese (under Pres. Joseph KASAVUBU and Prime Minister Patrice LUMUMBA) appealed to the UN. In Sept., 1960, Col. Joseph MOBUTU led a successful army coup, but Kasavubu remained president. Lumumba was captured fleeing to Stanleyville; and after his murder a new government was set up in Aug., 1961, with Cyrille Adoula as prime minister. Fighting broke out in Katanga in Sept. between UN and Katanga forces. On his way to negotiate with Tshombe, UN Secretary General Dag Hammarskjöld was killed in an air crash. By Jan., 1963, the Katanga secession was ended, but fighting broke out in Stanleyville area. In Nov., 1964, Belgian paratroopers entered Stanleyville, and by 1965 had routed rebels; in Nov., 1965, Mobutu overthrew government a second time and became president. In July, 1967, violence flared again in Kisangani (formerly Stanleyville) and Bukavu in an uprising of foreign mercenaries and rebellious Congolese troops.

Congo Free State: see CONGO, REPUBLIC OF THE.

Congo Republic, country (c.139,000 sq. mi.; pop. c.826,000), W Africa; cap. Brazzaville. Known as Middle Congo of French Equatorial Africa until 1958. Tropical climate; mainly equatorial forest. Congo-Ubangi river system leads to Atlantic. Agr. and lumbering produce timber, palm products, peanuts, rubber, tobacco, coffee. Minerals include lead, iron ore, phosphate, and gold; also petroleum. Hydroelectric project on the Kouilou R. was begun 1961 to develop an aluminum industry. Railroad from Pointe Noire to Brazzaville connects with navigable rivers in NE. People largely Bantu; some Pygmies in N. Official language is French. Region was early part of kingdom of the Congo. Area explored by Portuguese in 15th cent.; French trading posts estab. in 17th cent. Then called French Congo, territory was renamed Middle Congo and in 1910 became a colony in French Equatorial Africa. Colony granted internal autonomy 1956; became the Congo Republic (1958) within the French Community and gained full independence in 1960, the same year it joined the UN. Fulbert Youlou was first president from 1960 to 1963 when he was succeeded by Alphonse Massamba-Débat.

Congregationalism, type of Protestant organization in which each local church has free control of its own affairs. It has no bishops or presbyteries. Movement arose in 16th and 17th cent. in England in revolt of SEPARATISTS against formalized worship and state control of Established Church. Robert BROWNE published in 1582 first exposition of Congregational principles. Pilgrims brought Congregationalism to America in 1620. Cambridge Platform was adopted (1648), and Congregationalists took leading part in GREAT AWAKENING. Natl. Council of Congregational Churches of the U.S. formed 1871; in 1931 it merged with Christian Church to form General Council of the Congregational and Christian Churches of the U.S. This group united in 1957 with the Evangelical and Reformed Church to form UNITED CHURCH OF CHRIST.

Congress, Library of: see LIBRARY OF CONGRESS.

Congress of Industrial Organizations: see AMERICAN FEDERATION OF LABOR–CONGRESS OF INDUSTRIAL ORGANIZATIONS.

Congress of Racial Equality (CORE), organization founded 1942 in Chicago by James FARMER and others. Active in movement to obtain full INTEGRATION of Negroes into American society.

Congress of the United States, legislative branch of Federal government, instituted in 1789 by Article 1 of U.S. Constitution, which prescribes its membership and defines its powers. Congress is composed of two houses, the Senate and the House of Representatives. The Senators, two from each state, have six-year terms and were chosen by the state legislatures until 1913, when the Seventeenth Amendment, providing for their direct popular election, went into force. The terms of one third of the Senators expire every two years. A Senator must be at least 30 years old, not less than nine years a U.S. citizen, and a resident of the state in which he is elected. The Vice President of the United States presides over the Senate, voting only in case of a tie. Representatives are apportioned to the states according to their populations in the Federal census, every state being entitled to at least one Representative. Representatives are chosen for two-year terms, and the entire body comes up for reelection every two years. A Representative must be 25 or older, at least seven years a U.S. citizen, and an inhabitant of the state in which he is elected. The presiding officer of the House, the speaker, is elected by the members of the House. The two houses have an equal voice in legislation, though revenue bills must originate in the House of Representatives. The Senate, regarded as the more powerful body, must ratify all treaties and confirm important presidential appointments. The proceedings of each house are recorded in the *Congressional Record.*

Congreve, William, 1670–1729, English Restoration dramatist; known for his four cynical, witty comedies—*The Old Bachelor* (1693), *The Double Dealer* (1693), *Love for Love* (1695), and his masterpiece *The Way of the World* (1700). He also wrote a tragedy, *The Mourning Bride* (1697), popular in its day. With Dryden, Vanbrugh, and others he was attacked for immorality by Jeremy Collier.

conic section (kŏ′nĭk), any curve made by intersection of a right circular conical surface and a plane. These curves are the CIRCLE, ELLIPSE, PARABOLA, HYPERBOLA. If plane passes through vertex, result is a point, straight line, or pair of intersecting lines; these are called degenerate conic sections.

conifer (kŏ′nĭfûr), tree or shrub of order Coniferales, usually evergreen and cone-bearing, e.g., PINE, SPRUCE, CYPRESS, SEQUOIA.

Coninxloo or **Koninksloo, Gillis van** (gĭl′ĭs vän kō′nĭngkslō), 1544–1607, Flemish landscape painter, important for transmitting a Venetian type of landscape to the North.

Conjeeveram (kŭnjē′vûrûm), city (pop. 84,810), E Madras, India. Sacred to Hindus; known as Benares of the South. As cap. of Pallava empire (3d–8th cent.), it was a Brahmanical and Buddhist center. Its anc. name was Kanchi or Kanchipuram.

conjunctivitis, inflammation of membrane covering inside of eyelids and front of eyeball. Infectious forms caused by microorganisms include gonococcal conjunctivitis (see GONORRHEA) and pinkeye.

Conklin, Edwin Grant, 1863–1952, American zoologist. Chief interest was evolution. Helped organize marine biology laboratory at Woods Hole, Mass.

Conkling, Roscoe, 1829–88, American politician. U.S. Representative from N.Y. (1859–63, 1865–67); U.S. Senator (1867–81). When Pres. James A. GARFIELD ignored him in appointing a collector of the port of New York, this Old Guard leader and Republican state "boss" resigned from the Senate in protest.

Connally, John (Bowden), 1917–, governor of Texas (1963–). When Pres. J. F. Kennedy was assassinated in Dallas on Nov. 22, 1963, Connally was accompanying him and was wounded by assassin.

Connaught (kŏ′nôt), province (6,611 sq. mi.; pop. 419,-221), W Ireland; comprises counties MAYO, SLIGO, LEITRIM, ROSCOMMON, and GALWAY. Was an ancient kingdom of Ireland. Has some agr., but poor soil.

Conneaut (kŏ′nēŏt″), city (pop. 10,557), extreme NE Ohio, on L. Erie NE of Cleveland near Pa. line; settled 1799. Important ore-receiving port and coal-loading center. Has varied industries.

Connecticut, state (5,009 sq. mi.; pop. 2,535,234), NE U.S., one of Thirteen Colonies; cap. and largest city HARTFORD. BRIDGEPORT and NEW HAVEN among important cities. Bounded S by Long Isl. Sound. Highlands rise gently from coastal plains of Sound, divided by CONNECTICUT R. and its valley, drained E by THAMES R., W by HOUSATONIC R. Though noted for its rural loveliness and shore resorts, the state is mainly industrial: mfg. of aircraft engines, machinery, rubber goods, textiles, metal and brass products (clocks, typewriters, hardware), electrical equipment, firearms; printing and publishing. New London and Groton are submarine-building centers. Farming yields dairy and poultry products, broadleaf tobacco, truck. Hartford is major insurance center. Connecticut R. discovered 1614 by Adriaen Block. Pilgrims of Plymouth Colony estab. trading post 1633; soon absorbed by Puritans from Mass. Bay. FUNDAMENTAL ORDERS adopted 1639. New Haven colony was included under 1662 royal charter. Had semi-liberal religious system, with Congregationalism as official faith. Chief supply area for Continental Army in American Revolution and one of first states to ratify U.S. Constitution. Hurt by Embargo Act of 1807, War of 1812; resentment led to HARTFORD CONVENTION. New state constitution (1818), which disestab. Congregationalism, was in effect until 1965. Mfg. grew steadily after decline of shipping and influx of cheap immigrant labor. Host of inventors included Eli Whitney. Two world wars greatly expanded industry.

Connecticut, river rising in Connecticut Lakes in extreme N N.H. and flowing c.380 mi. S along Vt.–N.H. line, then across Mass. and Conn., past Springfield and Hartford, to Long Isl. Sound at Old Saybrook. Upper course used for power. Great damage done by 1938 and 1955 floods and hurricanes. Connecticut River Flood Control Compact, approved 1953, plans local protective works.

Connecticut, University of, mainly at Storrs village, in Mansfield; land grant, state supported; coed.; chartered and opened 1881 as Storrs Agr. School; became college 1893, university 1939. Schools of insurance, law, and social work at Hartford; schools of medicine and dentistry to be at Farmington; branches at Stamford, Torrington, and Waterbury.

Connecticut College, at New London; for women; chartered 1911 as Thames Col., opened 1915. Men admitted for graduate work under auspices of Connecticut Col. for Men (1959).

Connecticut Lakes, four lakes, N N.H.; source of headstreams of Connecticut R.

Connecticut Reserve: see WESTERN RESERVE.

Connecticut Wits or **Hartford Wits,** literary group (late 18th–early 19th cent.), mostly Yale men. Attacked anti-Federalists. Representative were Joel BARLOW, Timothy DWIGHT, Theodore DWIGHT, John TRUMBULL.

Connellsville, city (pop. 12,814), SW Pa., on Youghiogheny R., SE of Pittsburgh; settled c.1770. Produces coal and coke. H. C. Frick was attacked here during Homestead Strike (1892).

Connelly, Marc(us Cook), 1890–, American dramatist. Wrote Pulitzer Prize play, *The Green Pastures* (1930), based on Roark Bradford's *Ol' Man Adam an' His Chillun.*

Connemara (kŏnùmä'rù), wild, mountainous region, W Co. Galway, Ireland. Has many lakes and streams.

Connersville, city. (pop. 17,698), E. central Ind., on Whitewater R., ESE of Indianapolis. Fur-trading post estab. here 1808. Rail center.

Conning Towers, Conn.: see GROTON.

Connolly, James, 1870–1916, Irish republican leader and socialist. In U.S. (1903–10) helped to organize the I.W.W., but for Ireland believed that the nationalist cause came before socialism.

Connolly, Maureen, 1934–, American tennis player, first woman to hold (1953) four major tennis titles—U.S., British, Australian, French—at one time. Also won U.S. championship in 1951 and 1952, British in 1952 and 1954. Retired 1955.

Conon (kŏ'nŏn), d. after 392 B.C., Athenian commander in the Peloponnesian War. The fleet under his command was defeated at Aegospotamos (405 B.C.), but later with Persian help he defeated the Spartans off Cnidus (394 B.C.). When Persian favor turned toward Sparta, Conon's fortune fell.

Conowingo Dam, NE Md., on Susquehanna R., NE of Baltimore; completed 1928. Used for power, it is 4,648 ft. long, 102 ft. high. Here is Conowingo hamlet. Conowingo L. extends 14 mi. N.

Conrad, rulers of Holy Roman Empire. **Conrad I,** d. 918, duke of Franconia, elected German king 911. Unable to impose his authority on great feudal dukes. Designated his ablest foe, Henry the Fowler (Henry I), as successor. **Conrad II,** c.990–1039, duke of Franconia, elected German king 1024, crowned emperor 1027. Suppressed several revolts of his vassals; annexed kingdom of ARLES or Burgundy (1033); intervened energetically in Italian troubles (1026–27, 1035–37); promoted lesser nobility and officials of low birth to affirm his authority in Germany and Italy. **Conrad III,** c.1093–1152, German king (1138–52); nephew of Henry V and founder of the HOHENSTAUFEN dynasty. Antiking to LOTHAIR II from 1127. Warred against Guelphs (see GUELPHS AND GHIBELLINES). Took part in Second Crusade. **Conrad IV,** 1228–54, German king (1237–54), king of Sicily and Jerusalem (1250–54); son of Emperor FREDERICK II. Several antikings challenged his rule in Germany after 1246 and in Italy after 1251, in both cases at the behest of Pope INNOCENT IV, his implacable enemy, who excommunicated him in 1254. His son CONRADIN was the last of the Hohenstaufen to rule.

Conrad, d. 1192, king of Jerusalem (1192), marquis of Montferrat, leader in Third Crusade. Saved Tyre from the Saracens and became its lord (1187). Sought to displace Guy of LUSIGNAN as king by marrying Isabella, daughter of Amalric I. Acknowledged king, he was mysteriously assassinated. Title passed to two later husbands of Isabella–Henry, count of Champagne (reigned 1192–97), and Amalric II.

Conrad, Joseph, 1857–1924, Polish-born English novelist, originally Teodor Jozef Konrad Korzeniowski. A sailor, he became an officer in the British merchant fleet and a British citizen; after retirement in 1894 wrote novels and short stories in English, with notable, fluid style. Among his novels (laid mostly in South Seas, Malaya, and Indonesia) are *Almayer's Folly* (1895), *An Outcast of the Islands* (1896), *The Nigger of the "Narcissus"* (pub., 1897, as *The Children of the Sea*), *Lord Jim* (1900), *Typhoon* (1903), *Victory* (1915), *The Arrow of Gold* (1919). Most celebrated short story "Youth." His chief theme is demoralizing effect of isolation.

Conradi, Hermann (hĕr'män kônrä'dē), 1862–90, German author, leading exponent of naturalist school. Best known for *Lieder eines Sünders* [songs of a sinner] (1887) and *Adam Mensch* (1889).

Conradin (kŏn'rŭdĭn), 1252–68, duke of Swabia, last legitimate Hohenstaufen; son of Conrad IV. Claimed Sicily after death of his uncle MANFRED. Defeated by Charles of Anjou (Charles I of NAPLES) at Tagliacozzo; beheaded at Naples.

Conrad the Red, d. 955, duke of Lorraine (944–53). Conspired against his father-in-law, Otto I, allied himself with invading Magyars (954), but later submitted and died fighting Magyars on Lechfeld.

Conrad von Hötzendorf, Franz, Graf (fränts' gräf' kôn'rät fün hüt'sündôrf), 1852–1925, Austro-Hungarian field marshal. Chief of staff 1906–11, 1912–17.

Conscience, Hendrik (kôsēäs'), 1812–83, Flemish novelist, a founder of modern Flemish literature. His works include historical novels (e.g., *The Lion of Flanders,* 1838) and stories of village life (e.g., *Ricke ticke tack,* 1851).

conscientious objector, person who, on grounds of membership in a pacific sect or personal ethical views, passively resists state authority, especially military service. U.S. and Britain allowed objectors of recognized sects to enter non-combat service, but segregated or imprisoned others.

consciousness, in general a person's awareness of the environment; more specifically, the manner in which he is aware. Freudian psychology distinguishes the conscious (actual awareness), preconscious (memories and associations not present in the conscious but available to recall without interference from emotional or other resistances), and unconscious (store of experience not recognized by individual and not available to the conscious unless various resistances are overcome). Other psychologists define consciousness as the sum of self-understood activities that constitutes individual personality.

conscription, compulsory enrollment of personnel for service in armed forces. Obligatory service was known in early days of Greece and Rome, but first modern national conscription law was adopted in French Revolutionary Wars. In 19th cent. practice was adopted by most European nations. Great Britain accepted conscription in First World War. In U.S. conscription dates from Civil War. See SELECTIVE SERVICE.

conservation of energy: see ENERGY.

conservation of natural resources, prevention of waste of man's physical environment, including wildlife, timber, fertile topsoil, and pasture. Conservation long practiced in Europe, was forwarded in U.S. by creation of a U.S. commissioner of fish and fisheries (1871), a forestry bureau (1891), the National Conservation Commission (1909), and the National Park Service (1916). Theodore Roosevelt and Gifford Pinchot outstanding leaders. New Deal forwarded conservation with CCC, TVA, and water-control programs.

Conservative party, British political party, continuation of TORY group which began at end of 17th cent. Name first popularized in 1830. Tory reformers George CANNING and Robert PEEL killed old reactionary Tory party by Reform Bill of 1832. Party split over corn laws issue, 1846. Returned to power 1874–80, revitalized by "Tory democracy" and imperialism program of DISRAELI. In office 1885–1905 (with two brief intervals), it split over tariff reforms of Joseph CHAMBERLAIN, with consequent Liberal ascendancy until First World War coalition. Aside from Labour victories in 1924 and 1929 party maintained leadership 1922–29 and was dominant power in national government 1931–40 despite appeasement policies. Second World War brought new coalition under Conservative Winston Churchill. After 1945–51 Labour government, Conservatives returned to power under Churchill, continued under Anthony Eden (1955–57), Harold Macmillan (1957–63), and Sir Alec Douglas-Home (1963–64). Then Labour returned to power. In local elections in April, 1967, the Conservatives gained control of the Greater London Council for first time in 33 years.

Conshohocken (kŏn″shŭhŏ′kŭn), industrial borough (pop. 10,259), SE Pa., on Schuylkill R., NW of Philadelphia; laid out 1830.

Considérant, Victor Prosper (vēktôr′ prōspâr′ kŏsēdärä′), 1808–93, French social theorist and reformer, follower of Fourier.

conspiracy, agreement of two or more persons to commit a criminal or unlawful act, with some overt words or acts to that end. In medieval England conspiracy was only a combination to abuse judicial procedure; later meaning was broader. Some acts lawful when done by an individual are illegal if the aim of a conspiracy. Under this doctrine labor unions were long prosecuted for strikes but later legislation in Great Britain (1875) and U.S. (Norris-LaGuardia Act, 1932) halted this practice.

Constable, John, 1776–1837, English painter, famous for landscapes. *The Hay Wain* created sensation 1824 at Louvre and is said to have profoundly impressed Delacroix. Used broken color with freedom extraordinary in his day. Admired classical painting but worked directly from nature.

Constance, 1154–98, consort of Emperor HENRY VI; mother of Emperor FREDERICK II. Her nephew, William II of Sicily, named her as his successor, but the Sicilians crowned TANCRED instead. Warfare resulted between Tancred and Henry, who was crowned at Palermo after Tancred's death (1194).

Constance, Ger. *Konstanz,* city (est. pop. 51,243), Baden-Württemberg, West Germany, on L. of Constance. Textile, clothing mfg. Founded as Roman fort 4th cent. A.D.; episcopal see from c.580; made free imperial city 1192. Here in 1183 Emperor Frederick I recognized LOMBARD LEAGUE. At Council of Constance John Huss was burned (1415). In 1548 Charles V punished Constance for joining SCHMALKALDIC LEAGUE by abrogating its freedom and awarding it to Austria. City passed to Baden 1805; bishopric was secularized 1802–3; diocese was abolished 1827. Among many historical buildings are 11th-cent. minster and Dominican convent where council was held.

Constance, Council of, 1414–18, council of the Roman Catholic Church, in part considered ecumenical. It was called to end the Great SCHISM, which had produced three rival popes: GREGORY XII (since considered canonical, i.e., legal), John XXIII (see COSSA, BALDASSARRE), and Benedict XIII (see LUNA, PEDRO DE). It also was intended to reform the Church and end heresy. The conciliar theory (that councils are superior to the pope) was actively advanced, and the council was organized on national lines. Gregory resigned, John and Benedict were deposed, and MARTIN V was named pope. Measures of reform were adopted but were rather inconsequential. John Huss, who had come to the council with a safe-conduct of Emperor SIGISMUND, was nevertheless burned at the stake for heresy (1415), as was JEROME OF PRAGUE the next year. The rulings on the power of councils were never effective.

Constance, Lake of, Ger. *Bodensee,* lake, 208 sq. mi., bordered by Switzerland, Germany, and Austria. Formed by the Rhine, it divides near Constance into two arms. Remains of lake dwellings have been found.

Constans (kŏn′stănz), Roman and Byzantine emperors. **Constans I,** b. 320 or 323, d. 350; youngest son of Constantine I. Shared empire with his brothers CONSTANTINE II and CONSTANTIUS II upon his father's death (337). His vices and extortions led to his murder. **Constans II,** 630–68, Byzantine emperor (641–68). Forbade discussion of MONOTHELETISM; arrested and banished Pope Martin I. Fought Moslems successfully; reorganized imperial administration. Was assassinated.

Constant (de Rebecque), Benjamin (bēzhämē′ kŏstä′ dù rübĕk′), 1767–1830, French author and political theorist, b. Switzerland. His liaison with Mme de STAËL (1794–1809) was a tempestuous one. An advocate of constitutional monarchy, he generally opposed but occasionally supported both Napoleon and the Bourbons. His reputation as a writer rests on the introspective and quasi-autobiographical short novel *Adolphe* (1816). The novel *Cécile* was first published 1951.

Constant, Paul Henri Benjamin, baron d'Estournelles de: see ESTOURNELLES DE CONSTANT.

Constanta (kônstän′tsä), city (est. pop. 118,803), SE Rumania, in Dobruja; chief Rumanian Black Sea port. Oil pipeline to Ploesti. Founded 4th cent. A.D. by Constantine I.

Constantine (kŏn′stŭntēn, –tīn), Roman and Byzantine emperors. **Constantine I** (the Great, 288?–337, son of CONSTANTIUS I and St. HELENA. Though proclaimed emperor on his father's death at York (306), he was content with the title Caesar until the death of GALERIUS (310), which left four contestants for the imperial office. In the ensuing struggle, Constantine and LICINIUS joined against MAXENTIUS and MAXIMIN, whom they overwhelmed in 312. They then ruled as co-emperors (Constantine in the West, Licinius in the East) until they fell out in 324; Licinius lost his life in the struggle, leaving Constantine sole emperor. Constantine, already attracted by Christianity, had allegedly seen a flaming cross in the sky as the sign by which he would conquer just before his crucial victory at the MILVIAN BRIDGE (312). In 313 he and Licinius established toleration for Christianity by the Edict of Milan. His interest in Christianity continued, though he was baptized only on his deathbed, and in 325 he convened the epoch-making Council of NICAEA. In a reign of peace he rebuilt the empire on a basis of absolutism. He shifted his cap. to CONSTANTINOPLE (330), which he dedicated to the Virgin. At his death he divided the empire among his sons CONSTANS I, CONSTANTIUS II, and **Constantine II,** 316–40, who received Britain, Gaul, and Spain. Feeling cheated in the division, he warred with Constans I, but was killed while invading Italy. **Constantine IV** (Pogonatus), d. 685, Byzantine emperor (668–85). Answered annual naval attacks of Moslems with GREEK FIRE; ceded land S of the Danube to Bulgars after being defeated by them (679); called Third Council of CONSTANTINOPLE (680). **Constantine V** (Copronymus), 718–75, Byzantine emperor (740–75). Able administrator. His rigorous support of ICONOCLASM caused Pope Stephen III to transfer Rome to protection of Pepin the Short. **Constantine VI,** b. c.770, Byzantine emperor (780–97). His mother IRENE was regent, then co-empress (792). In 797 she took advantage of his unpopularity to have him deposed and blinded. **Constantine VII** (Porphyrogenitus), 905–59, Byzantine emperor. His reign (912–59) was interrupted by usurpation of ROMANUS I (919–44). Fostered learning and legal reform. Was a scholar and assiduous writer. **Constantine XI** (Paleologus), d. 1453, last Byzantine emperor (1448–53). Proclaimed union of E and W churches to secure aid from West against Turks (1452). No help came. In 1453 he defended Constantinople for two months against the 20 times superior army of Mohammed II. Died fighting when Turks stormed city.

Constantine, kings of the Hellenes. **Constantine XII,** 1868–1923, was king 1913–17, 1920–22. Opposed Premier VENIZELOS in First World War; forced to abdicate by Allied pressure (1917). Recalled in 1920, he was again deposed after the Turks defeated the Greeks at Smyrna. **Constantine XIII,** 1940–, appointed regent in 1964, succeeded to throne a few months later upon the death of his father, King Paul. Formally cooperated with military junta that seized power in 1967, but urged return to constitutional government.

Constantine, fortified city (pop. c.223,260), E Algeria; major trade center. Originally a Carthaginian settlement. As Cirta it was cap. of Numidia and vital shipping point in Roman grain supply. Destroyed A.D. 311 in civil war; rebuilt by Constantine I. Taken 1837 by the French.

Constantine, Donation of, document supposed to be a grant by Constantine I of great temporal authority in Italy to the pope. It actually was forged, presumably to enhance papal territorial claims by giving them a greater antiquity. In practice it had no great effect, but it was important in giving Lorenzo Valla the chance to demonstrate critical methods in proving it false, and his firm, clear argument is called the beginning of modern textual criticism.

Constantine the African, c.1020–c.1087, translator of Arabic works (esp. on medicine) into Latin.

Constantinople, former capital of the Byzantine and Ottoman empires (for modern city, see ISTANBUL). Founded by and named for CONSTANTINE I at ancient BYZANTIUM as new cap. of Roman Empire (A.D. 330), it shared the glory and vicissitudes of the Byzantine Empire, which was finally nearly identical with the city and environs. Only three of many sieges were successful: by the army of the Fourth Crusade (1204), by MICHAEL VIII (1261), and by Sultan MOHAMMED II (1453). Built upon seven hills on the Bosporus and surrounded by a triple wall of fortifications, it was the largest city of medieval Europe, a barbed fortress enclosing a sea of magnificent pal-

aces and gilded domes and towers. At its greatest period (10th cent.) it had c.1,000,000 inhabitants. The Church of HAGIA SOPHIA, the sacred palace of the emperors, the huge hippodrome, and the Golden Gate were its best-known monuments. Its artistic and literary wealth before it was sacked (1204; 1453) was almost inconceivable. Nearly depopulated when it fell to the Turks, it soon revived under the Sultans (whose court was called the Sublime Porte) as a great European center. After the First World War it was occupied by the Allies (1918–23). Ankara replaced it as Turkish cap. in 1923.

Constantinople, Councils of, 2d, 5th, 6th, and 8th ecumenical councils of the Roman Catholic Church. **1** Convened (381) by Emperor Theodosius I to confirm the acts of the First Council of Nicaea, it is said to have composed the final Nicene Creed. Declared St. Gregory Nazianzen bishop of Constantinople and appointed his successor when he died. On death of St. Meletius made Flavian of Antioch president, thus prolonging Antiochene schism. Declared against various heresies, and made bishop of Constantinople second only to the pope. **2** Convened (553) by Emperor Justinian I and dominated by him, it condemned the Nestorian writings called the Three Chapters and seems also to have declared Pope Vigilius deposed. Its canons are lost. **3** Convened (680) by Emperor Constantine IV, it condemned the heresy of MONOTHELETISM and condemned several churchmen as Monothelites (including HONORIUS I—a point much discussed). The Oriental Council of 692, called by Justinian II, is considered in the East a continuation of this council, but is called in the West the Trullan Synod [from Trullo, the dome of the palace]. It made the Apostolic Constitutions binding. **4** Convened (869) at the suggestion of Emperor Basil I, it confirmed the condemnation of PHOTIUS and the restoration of St. IGNATIUS OF CONSTANTINOPLE. It is not recognized by the Orthodox Church, which recognizes instead the council of 880 that supported Photius. The two councils mark the bitter division of Eastern and Western churches.

Constantinople, Latin Empire of, 1204–61, feudal empire established in S Balkans and Greek archipelago by leaders of Fourth Crusade (see CRUSADES). It was modeled on Latin Kingdom of JERUSALEM. BALDWIN I, HENRY OF FLANDERS, ROBERT OF COURTENAY, JOHN OF BRIENNE, and BALDWIN II were rulers. It deteriorated at once after its creation, beset by Greek rulers of NICAEA and EPIRUS, by the Bulgars under IVAN II, by the Turks, and by internal discord. Constantinople was taken by MICHAEL VIII, who restored the Byzantine Empire (1261), but Venice retained most of Greek isles; ATHENS passed to Catalans; Achaia was kept by VILLEHARDOUIN family.

Constantius (kǔnstän'shǔs), name of several Roman emperors. **Constantius I,** c.250–306, was a general who put away St. Helena (mother of CONSTANTINE I) to marry the daughter of Maximian and become (293) subemperor under Maximian. He was successful as commander in Gaul and Britain. When Diocletian and Maximian abdicated (305), he and Galerius became emperors, but the next year he died at York. Constantine took up his claim. **Constantius II,** 317–61, was son of Constantine I. After 337 he shared the empire with his brothers, CONSTANS I and CONSTANTINE II. Constantine was killed in 340, Constans I murdered in 350. Constantius put down revolt and held sole rule. He advocated ARIANISM. Trouble in Gaul and in Persia caused Constantius to rely on his cousin and general Julian (JULIAN THE APOSTATE), but Julian's men revolted against Constantius, who died on the journey to quell them. **Constantius III,** d. 421, was a general of Honorius. After the murder of his rival ATAULF, he married Ataulf's widow and the emperor's sister, GALLA PLACIDIA. In 421 he became joint emperor but died in a few months.

Constellation, U.S. frigate, launched in 1797. Won victories over French frigates *Insurgente* (Feb., 1799) and *Vengeance* (Feb., 1800). Rebuilt *Constellation* became ship with longest period of service in navy when she saw duty as flagship of U.S. Atlantic fleet in Second World War. Preserved at Baltimore.

constellation (kŏnstĭlă'shŭn), originally a configuration formed by a group of stars. The meaning was later extended to refer to 88 areas (boundaries officially estab. 1928) filling sky, in terms of which heavenly bodies are located. Brighter stars are designated (according to Bayer's system), usually in order of brightness, by Greek letters and Latin genitive of constellation in which they lie, e.g., Alpha Tauri, brightest star in Taurus. See also ZODIAC.

Constitution, U.S. 44-gun frigate, nicknamed *Old Ironsides,* launched 1797; perhaps the most famous U.S. naval vessel. Won great sea battle with British vessel *Guerrière* on Aug. 19, 1812. Rebuilt by public subscription in 1925; maintained at Boston navy yard.

constitution, the fundamental principles of government in a nation, either implied in its laws, institutions, and customs or embodied in one document or in several. In the first category is the British constitution; it is termed *flexible,* for it may be modified by an ordinary act of Parliament or by judicial decisions. The **Constitution of the United States** is classified as *rigid*—one that has superior sanction to ordinary laws of the land and that is subject to a gradual process of AMENDMENT. Statutory elaboration and judicial construction (see SUPREME COURT, UNITED STATES, and MARSHALL, JOHN) have been erected on the base of the written document drawn up at the FEDERAL CONSTITUTIONAL CONVENTION (1787). The Constitution (see *The* FEDERALIST; MADISON, JAMES), was signed on Sept. 17, 1787, and ratified by the required number of states (nine) by June 21, 1788, superseded original charter of U.S. in force since 1781 (see CONFEDERATION, ARTICLES OF) and estab. system of Federal government which began to function in 1789. The Constitution's brevity and its general statement of principles have, by accident more than by design, made possible the extension of meaning that has fostered growth. There are but seven articles and a Preamble; 25 amendments have been adopted. The Preamble's first words, "We the People of the United States," have been used against STATES' RIGHTS advocates. Another phrase of the Preamble, "to . . . promote the general Welfare," has been used to uphold much recent social legislation. The articles set up the legislative, executive, and judicial branches of government and provide for their powers; they also handle problems of the relationships of the states to the Federal government. The first nine amendments, which constitute the Bill of Rights (Tenth Amendment generally considered a part), were added within two years as a result of widespread feeling that Constitution insufficiently guaranteed individual liberties. Remaining amendments provide for matters ranging from income tax to presidential succession.

Constitutional Convention: see FEDERAL CONSTITUTIONAL CONVENTION.

Constitutional Union party, in U.S. history, organized just before election of 1860. Recognized "no political principle but the Constitution of the country, the union of the states and the enforcement of laws." Ticket of John Bell and Edward Everett carried Ky., Tenn., and Va. in the election, which was won by Lincoln.

Constitution Island, N.Y.: see WEST POINT.

Constitution of the United States: see CONSTITUTION.

Constitutions, Apostolic, late 4th-cent. compilation of rules for clergy and laity in the Church, supposedly by the Apostles, but actually including apocryphal letters and most of the Didache. Declared binding by the continuation of the Third Council of CONSTANTINOPLE.

constructivism, Russian art movement founded c.1913 by Vladimir Tatlin (1885–1956), related to SUPREMATISM. Sculptural works had an architectonic emphasis, reflecting the technological society in which they were created. Naum Gabo and Antoine Pevsner

gave new impetus to Tatlin's art of abstract constructions in 1917.

consubstantiation: see COMMUNION.

consul, title of two chief magistrates of anc. Rome. Office supposed to have originated 510 B.C. and was the supreme office in the republic, with control over the army and the treasury as well as civil affairs. Consular elections were the crucial points of political life. At first only patricians could be consuls, but after 367 B.C. plebeians were eligible. Normally a man served as quaestor, aedile, and praetor before running for the consulate. The Roman years were identified by the names of the consuls. Office became nominal under the Roman Empire.

consular service, body of agents maintained by a government at foreign ports and trade centers to protect its nationals and their interests. Deals only with local officials of foreign government. In U.S. Rogers Act of 1924 united consular and diplomatic services in Foreign Service of Dept. of State. Consuls and consulates enjoy immunity and EXTERRITORIALITY.

Consulate, 1799–1804, French government established after coup d'état of 18 BRUMAIRE. The three consuls were Bonaparte (see NAPOLEON I), Cambacérès, and C. F. Lebrun. Bonaparte, the actual ruler, was made First Consul for life in 1802, emperor in 1804.

Consumers' League, National, estab. in U.S. (1899) to forward movement begun (1890) in England to educate consumers to buy only goods made under good working conditions.

consumption, in economics, use of wealth to satisfy needs or destruction to create new wealth. Production and consumption, closely linked, form the foundation of modern capitalist economy.

consumption, in medicine: see TUBERCULOSIS.

contagious abortion: see BRUCELLOSIS.

contagious diseases: see COMMUNICABLE DISEASES.

contempt of court, in basic meaning interference with the functioning of a court. Criminal contempts are those that lessen the dignity of a court or tend to limit a judge's freedom of action (e.g., defying a judge or creating disorder in courtroom). Civil or constructive contempts are primarily injuries to private parties occasioned by disobeying a decree or court order.

Conti (kōtē'), French princely family, cadet branch of house of Bourbon. Founded by **Armand de Bourbon, prince de Conti** (ärmä' dü bōōrbō'), 1629–66, brother of the Great CONDÉ, whom he at first assisted during the FRONDE. Reconciled with the court (1653), he married a niece of Mazarin and held a command in war against Spain. A protector of Molière. Later turned to mysticism, lived in retirement. His great-grandson, **Louis François de Bourbon, prince de Conti** (lwē' fräswä'), 1717–76, fought with distinction in War of the Austrian Succession but displeased Mme de Pompadour and lost favor at court. Sided with parlement against Maupeou. Friend of Rousseau.

continent, largest unit of land mass. The continents are Eurasia (Europe and Asia), Africa, North America, South America, Australia, and Antarctica. Including fringe islands, they comprise c.29% of the total surface of the earth. Average land height in all is c.2,700 ft. above sea level, with highest known point Mt. Everest, over 29,000 ft. According to isostatic theory the floor under the oceans and extending under continents is composed of heavy basaltic rock and the continents are of lighter granitic rock; the balance between continent heights and ocean depths is called isostasy.

Continental Congress, 1774–89, Federal legislature of Thirteen Colonies and later of U.S. in American Revolution and under Articles of Confederation. First Continental Congress (Sept. 5–Oct. 26, 1774) sent petitions of colonial grievances to the king. Second Continental Congress, meeting May 10, 1775, created Continental Army and adopted Declaration of Independence on July 4, 1776. Though Congress under Articles of Confederation was shackled by weaknesses of Federal structure, it passed Ordinance of 1787.

Continental Divide, "backbone" of a continent. In North America the great ridge of the Rocky Mts. separates streams flowing W from those flowing E. Sometimes called Great Divide, a name occasionally used for the whole Rocky Mt. system.

continental drift, the slow moving apart of the continents attributed to convection currents in a plastic zone within the earth. Evidence supporting this theory includes the fitting together of continental margins (W coast of Africa and E coast of S America), paleomagnetism, and earth movement along rift in mid-Atlantic ridge.

Continental System, scheme of economic warfare adopted by Napoleon I against England. Began with BERLIN DECREE (1806); intensified by MILAN DECREE (1807) and other measures. All trade with Britain was forbidden, even to neutrals. Britain replied with OR-DERS IN COUNCIL, seizure of neutral Danish fleet, and bombardment of Copenhagen. English naval supremacy made enforcement of system impossible. Russian refusal to abide by system led to Napoleon's disastrous 1812 campaign.

continuous creation: see UNIVERSE.

contour, in geography, the physical configuration of an area, represented on maps by contour lines drawn through points of equal elevation above sea level at specified vertical distances apart (contour intervals).

contrabassoon: see WIND INSTRUMENTS.

contraception: see BIRTH CONTROL.

contract, agreement binding parties to it to perform, or to refrain from, some specific act or acts. Form usually an offer submitted by one party and accepted by the other in a reasonable time or in a stipulated period by word or act, explicitly or implicitly. To make a valid contract the parties must be mentally sound and of legal age and must be acting with free will. It must also comply with the Statute of Frauds; certain classes of contracts must be in writing and signed. In some American states all contracts must involve a consideration (something of value, however slight, even a promise to do something) given by one party to induce the other to perform. Failure to perform contractual obligation is called breach of contract and creates a right to damages in the injured party.

contraction, in physics: see EXPANSION.

contraction, in writing: see ABBREVIATION.

Contreras (kōntrā′räs), village, central Mexico, near Mexico city. On Aug. 19–20, 1847, American forces under Gen. Winfield Scott fought Mexican forces under Santa Anna here and at Churubusco in one of most important battles of Mexican War.

convection, form of heat transmission in liquids and gases. It depends on decrease of density with rise in temperature. Hotter parts of fluid move through rest. When liquid is heated in a container, the hotter part rises to the surface and its place is taken by cooler part. Thus convection current is started. Heat is transferred from point to point in fluids by this current. Convection currents that are set up when the earth's atmosphere is heated by warm land areas cause cloud formation and rain.

conversion, in psychology: see DEFENSE MECHANISM; HYSTERIA.

convict labor, use of prisoners as laborers on public works such as highways. Convicts are also trained to particular skills and are rehabilitated for their return to ordinary life and given ability to use those skills to their advantage. The use of convicts as laborers comes from anc. times.

convulsion, spasmodic muscular contraction. May accompany toxic conditions and nervous disorders. In young children it may result from tetany or sudden high fever. Stimulating mechanism is obscure.

Conway, Sir Martin (Baron Conway of Allington), 1856–1937, English mountain climber, an art critic. Led exploring expeditions to Spitsbergen (1896–97) and the Bolivian Andes (1898).

Conway, Thomas, 1735–c.1800?, Irish soldier of fortune, general in Continental Army in American Revo-

lution. Gave name to Conway Cabal (1777), intrigue to remove Washington as army commander in favor of Horatio Gates. Letter by Conway criticizing Washington was basis of abortive and cloudy scheme.

Conway, city (pop. 9,791), central Ark., NNW of Little Rock; settled c.1865 near site of French trading post. Trade center of farm and cotton area. Hendrix Col. is here.

Conway Cabal: see CONWAY, THOMAS.

cony or coney, name for rabbit (Oryctolagus) and its fur; for pika (Ochotona), small high-altitude rodent of both hemispheres; and for hyrax (Procavia), herbivorous, hoofed animal of Arabia, Syria, Africa.

Cooch Behar, India: see BENGAL.

Cook, Frederick Albert, 1865–1940, American explorer. Accompanied various polar expeditions. Claimed scaling of Mt. McKinley (1906) and reaching of North Pole (1908). Accused of fraud by Robert E. Peary, deprived of honors, but remained controversial figure. Later he was involved in oilfield swindle; was imprisoned (1925–30).

Cook, James, 1728–79, English explorer and navigator. Circumnavigated globe (1768–71) while charting transit of Venus; also explored New Zealand and E Australian coasts. On expedition to S Pacific (1772–75), he disproved rumor of great southern continent and prevented scurvy by dietary and hygienic measures. Led futile search for Pacific-Atlantic passage through North America. Rediscovered Sandwich Isls. (1778). Killed by Hawaiian natives.

Cook, Thomas, 1808–92, English founder of travel agency which bears his name. His most spectacular achievement was transport of 18,000 men up the Nile in 1884 for attempted relief of Gen. Gordon.

Cook, Mount, 12,349 ft. high, on W South Isl., New Zealand; highest in New Zealand.

Cooke, Jay, 1821–1905, American financier. Marketed Civil War loans of Federal government. Failure in financing of Northern Pacific Railway helped precipitate panic of 1873.

Cookeville, town (pop. 7,805), N central Tenn., E of Nashville; founded 1854. Trade and industrial center of farm area. Tennessee Technological Univ. is here.

Cook Islands, formerly Hervey Islands, New Zealand territory (c.84 sq. mi.; pop. 18,174), in S Pacific. Lower group comprises Rarotonga, Mangaia, and six coral islands. Export copra, fruits, pearl shells. Some of the islands were discovered by Capt. James Cook 1773, some by John Williams 1823. Northern or Manihiki group comprises Manihiki Penrhyn, and other isls. Both groups covered by New Zealand since 1901.

Coolidge, Calvin, 1872–1933, 29th or 30th (see list at end of article UNITED STATES) President of the United States (1923–29). Governor of Mass. (1919–20). Decision to use militia in a Boston police strike in 1919 brought national prominence. Vice President of U.S. (1921–23); became President after death of Warren G. Harding. Known for his New England simplicity and personal honesty; had strong popular backing. Opposed agr. price-fixing and strongly favored laissez-faire policy toward business, economy in government, and tax cuts.

Coolidge, city (1965 pop. 5,012), S central Ariz., SE of Phoenix and in Casa Grande valley; laid out 1925. Irrigated by Coolidge Dam, it has diversified farming. Casa Grande Natl. Monument is nearby.

Coolidge Dam, E Ariz., on Gila R., SE of Globe; built 1927–28 for irrigation and power. It is 920 ft. long, 249 ft. high. Forms San Carlos Reservoir irrigating 100,000 acres (half are Indian lands) around Florence, Casa Grande, and Coolidge.

coolie labor, unskilled Asian laborers. In 1830s and 1840s many Indian and Chinese laborers were taken to British and French colonies on five-year contracts. Practice continued, and coolies were taken to Latin America, U.S., and Canada. Conditions of contract and of work were bad. Chinese labor, much used in building railroads in U.S., shut out by Chinese Exclusion Act of 1888.

cooling system. Many processes and engines while operating require cooling. Cylinder heat generated by internal-combustion engines damages parts if not counteracted, usually by circulating water or air. Blast furnaces, cupolas, gas generators, casting molds, etc., are cooled by water. Rapidly moving machinery is often cooled and lubricated by oil bath. Radial airplane engines expose maximum cylinder surface to cooling effect of air flow. Air-conditioning systems maintain desirable conditions of temperature, humidity, and cleanliness of the air indoors.

Coomaraswamy, Ananda Kentish (ä″nŭndä′ kĕn′tĭsh kōōmä″rŭswä′mē), 1877–1947, art historian, b. Ceylon. Largely responsible for great Far Eastern collection of Boston Mus. of Fine Arts.

Coon, Carleton Stevens, 1904–, American anthropologist and archaeologist. Engaged in field work and anthropological research (1925–39) in Arabia, the Balkans, and in N Africa, where he discovered (1939) remains of a Neanderthal man.

Coon Rapids, village (1965 pop. 26,412), SE Minn., on Mississippi R., NNW of Minneapolis.

Cooper, Alexander: see COOPER, SAMUEL.

Cooper, Anthony Ashley: see SHAFTESBURY, ANTHONY ASHLEY COOPER, 1ST EARL OF.

Cooper, (Alfred) Duff, 1890–1954, British statesman, a Conservative. Served after 1935 as secretary of state for war, then as first lord of the admiralty in the coalition cabinet, resigning in 1938 to protest the Munich Pact. Was later minister of information under Churchill and ambassador to France (1944–47). Author of distinguished biographies. Created Viscount Norwich of Aldwick in 1952.

Cooper, James Fenimore, 1789–1851, American novelist, the first to gain world reputation. Son of a wealthy landowner, who founded Cooperstown on Otsego L. on the N.Y. frontier, he spent five years in naval service, then became a country gentleman. Entering on a literary career when he was 30, he wrote more than 50 works. Of his many novels, best loved are his adventure stories of frontiersmen and Indians, notably the *Leatherstocking Tales,* named for the frontiersman Natty Bumppo, or Leatherstocking (in order of the narrative: *The Deerslayer,* 1841; *The Last of the Mohicans,* 1826; *The Pathfinder,* 1840; *The Pioneers,* 1823; *The Prairie,* 1827); his sea stories (e.g., *The Pilot,* 1823; *The Red Rover,* 1828); and his historical novels, especially on the American Revolution (e.g., *The Spy,* 1821; his first success). An apologist for American democracy, he changed when he returned after several years (1826–33) in Europe and severely criticized the shortcomings of U.S. democracy in action. His satires, polemics, even novels (e.g., *Homeward Bound* and *Home as Found,* both 1838), earned him enemies and attacks so violent that he brought successful suits for libel. The trilogy called *Littlepage Manuscripts* (*Satanstoe,* 1845; *The Chainbearer,* 1845; and *The Redskins,* 1846) is fiction tracing the conflict in N.Y. state between the propertied and the landless classes. His nonfiction works include a vigorous history of the U.S. navy (1839).

Cooper, Myles, c.1737–1785, second president of King's College (now Columbia Univ.), b. England. A Loyalist, he fled to England in 1775.

Cooper, Peter, 1791–1883, American inventor, industrialist, and philanthropist. Built the *Tom Thumb,* first railway locomotive to be used successfully on an American railroad (1830). Helped develop national and international telegraph. Led in securing public school system in New York city. COOPER UNION was built to provide education for working classes. Cooper was GREENBACK PARTY presidential candidate 1876.

Cooper, Samuel, 1609–72, one of the greatest English miniaturists. His brother, **Alexander Cooper,** d.1660,

was for many years miniature painter at the court of Queen Christina of Sweden.

Cooper, Thomas, 1759–1839, American scientist, b. London, an associate of Joseph Priestley. Also was a Jeffersonian in politics; convicted of violating Alien and Sedition Acts. Taught at Dickinson Col. and Univ. of Pennsylvania. President of South Carolina Col. 1820–34.

Cooper, river: see CHARLESTON, S.C.

cooperative movement, voluntary association of people for any desired end, usually nonprofitmaking economic enterprises. Consumers' cooperatives are organized for wholesale or retail distribution of products. Cooperatives have operated in many fields —banking, housing, insurance, medicine, and marketing of agr. produce. Producer cooperatives, in which workers own the enterprise, are relatively few. Robert Owen in 19th cent. advocated cooperation, which became a movement in Britain with founding (1844) of the Rochdale Society. Cooperatives are numerous and highly successful in Scandinavian countries. Movement slow in U.S. until after First World War.

Co-operative Commonwealth Federation, Canadian political party, popularly known as CCF. Founded (1932) at Calgary, Alta., by representatives from farmer, labor, and socialist parties (largely of the W provinces) with aim of establishing a planned cooperative commonwealth in Canada. Regina Manifesto, issued 1933 at the party's first annual convention, outlines aims which include socialization of finance, social ownership of public utilities, and various welfare measures. J. S. Woodsworth was its first leader. M. J. Coldwell succeeded him. In 1944 the party secured a majority in Saskatchewan legislature and estab. first CCF government in Canada. CCF is represented in other provincial legislatures and in Canadian House. In 1961 CF united with Canadian Labor Congress to form New Democratic Party.

Cooperstown, village (pop. 2,553), E central N.Y., SSE of Utica, on Susquehanna R. and Otsego L. Founded by William Cooper, who brought his family here 1787. James Fenimore Cooper lived here and described region in *Leatherstocking Tales.* Has Fenimore House; Indian museum; Farmers' Mus.; Natl. Baseball Hall of Fame and Mus., recalling purported founding of baseball here by Abner DOUBLEDAY.

Cooper Union, in Manhattan borough of New York city; coed.; chartered and opened 1859. Founded by Peter Cooper. Pioneered with evening art and engineering schools; day schools added in 1900. Abraham Lincoln made famous speech here in 1860.

Coorg (kōōrg), former state (1,593 sq. mi.), SW India. Now part of Mysore.

Coornhert, Dirck Volckertszoon (dŭrk vôl′kŭrtzōn kōrn′härt), 1522–90, Dutch humanist. He wrote comedies and morality plays. A supporter of religious toleration.

Coos (kō′ŏs), island, the modern Kos. Acts 21.1.

Coosa (kōō′sù), navigable river, NW Ga. and E Ala. Formed by headstreams at Rome, Ga.; winds c.282 mi. W and S to join Tallapoosa R. and form Alabama R. above Montgomery. Three power dams in lower course.

coot, marsh bird of North America and Europe, related to the rail and crane. American coot or mud hen or marsh hen is slaty gray with black head and neck and white-marked wings. It swims and dives well; the feet are partially webbed.

copal (kō′pŭl), resin from certain tropical trees, a source of hard-surfaced lacquers and varnishes.

Cope, Edward Drinker, 1840–97, American paleontologist. His collection of fossil mammals now in American Mus. of Natural History. He believed that organisms evolved by trying to attain higher state of being.

Copeau, Jacques (zhäk′ kôpō′), 1879–1949, French theatrical producer and critic. Director of influential Théâtre du Vieux-Columbier in Paris 1913–24; director of Comédie Française 1940–49.

Copenhagen (kō̇pŭnhä′gŭn), Dan. *Kφbenhavn*, city (pop. 721,381; with suburbs 1,348,454), cap. of Denmark, on E Zealand and N Amager isls. and on the Oresund. Major fishing and naval port; commercial, industrial, cultural center. Shipyards; metallurgy; mfg. of Copenhagen ware. First fortified in 12th cent. and chartered 1254, Copenhagen became Danish cap. 1443. It resisted a long Swedish siege (1658–59). Treaty of Copenhagen (1660) confirmed Treaty of ROSKILDE. In 1807 the city was bombarded and nearly destroyed by the British, neutral Denmark having refused to surrender its fleet. Occupied 1940–45 by the Germans in Second World War, the city was bombed by the Allies, but only the shipyards suffered damage. One of the handsomest cities of Europe, it has many famous landmarks, including the picturesque houses along the Nyhavn arm of the harbor; Kongens Nytorv, the central square, with the 17th-cent. Charlottenborg palace; Amalienborg Square, enclosed by four palaces—the present royal residence; the Cathedral Church of Our Lady; and Christiansborg palace (18th cent.), housing the Rigsdag, on moated Slotsholm isl. Most of the historic buildings were restored after 1807. University was founded 1479.

Copenhagen, battle of, 1801, naval engagement of the French Revolutionary Wars. Neutral Denmark having refused to comply with British rules on neutral navigation, an English fleet was sent into the Baltic under admirals Sir Hyde PARKER and Horatio NELSON. The Danish fleet, caught at the roadsteads of Copenhagen, was defeated after a hard battle.

Copernicus, Nicholas (kō̇pûr′nĭkŭs), 1473–1543, Polish astronomer, founder of Copernican system on which modern astronomy is based. In his famed treatise *De revolutionibus orbium coelestium* (published 1543), he described the sun as the center of great system, with earth revolving around it.

Copiague (kō″pāg′), town (pop. 14,081), SE N.Y., on S shore of Long Isl., E of Amityville.

Copland, Aaron, 1900–, American composer. His music has been influenced by jazz and other American types. He has written concert music in all forms and music for the films and radio. His ballets include *Billy the Kid* (1938), *Rodeo* (1942), and *Appalachian Spring* (1944). Among his important orchestral works are *El Salón México* (1936), *Connotations* (1962), and *Music for a Great City* (1964).

Copley, John Singleton (kŏp′lē), 1738–1815, American portrait painter, b. Boston. Settled c.1774 in London, where he enjoyed many honors. His reputation today rests mainly on his early American portraits, rather than on the more polished works of his English period.

Coppard, A(lfred) E(dgar), 1878–1957, English short-story writer (e.g., *Adam and Eve and Pinch Me,* 1921) and lyric poet (e.g., *Cherry Ripe*, 1935). His work is distinguished by fantasy and wit.

Coppée, François (fräswä′ kôpā′), 1842–1908, French Parnassian poet, noted for poems of sympathy for the underprivileged, as *Les Humbles* (1872).

Copper, river rising in Wrangell Mts., SE Alaska, and flowing c.300 mi. S through the Chugach Mts. to Gulf of Alaska. Copper taken by Indians from deposits near upper river attracted Russians and Americans. Copper River and Northwestern RR (built 1908–11) from Cordova to great Kennecott mine partly followed lower river; was abandoned 1938. Water flow interrupted after earthquake in 1964.

copper, common, malleable, ductile, relatively soft metallic element (symbol = Cu; see also ELEMENT, table). It is a good conductor, changes slowly in air, and resists dilute acids. Salt water causes it to corrode. Used in roofing; for utensils, coins, metalwork; in making electrical apparatus and wires; in alloys. Occurs free and in combination; refined by electrolysis. It was one of first metals known to man. See also BRONZE AGE.

Copper Age: see BRONZE AGE.

copperas (kŏ′pŭrŭs) or **green vitriol,** ferrous sulphate, a hydrous compound of iron, sulphur, and oxygen. It is a green, crystalline, water-soluble salt.

Copperbelt, mining region, N central Zambia; extension of mineral-rich Katanga. Produces copper, lead, zinc, and cobalt.

Copper Cliff, town (pop. 3,600), S Ont., Canada, SW of Sudbury. Large nickel smelters.

copperhead, poisonous snake of E U.S. It is 2–3 ft. long; has coppery head; body is brown with hourglass-shaped chestnut markings above, pinkish white with dark spots below. Bite is not often fatal. *Agkistrodon mokasen.*

Copperheads, in Civil War, reproachful term for Northerners sympathetic to South. Especially active in Ill., Ind., and Ohio. KNIGHTS OF THE GOLDEN CIRCLE was Copperhead secret society.

Coppermine, river, Mackenzie dist., Northwest Territories, Canada. Rises N of Great Slave L. and flows 525 mi. NW to Coronation Gulf in Arctic Ocean.

copper pyrites: see CHALCOPYRITE.

Coppet (kôpā′), village, Vaud canton, SW Switzerland, on L. Geneva. Château was residence of Mme de Staël.

copra: see COCONUT.

Copt (kŏpt), member of native Christian group in Egypt that resisted conversion to Islam through the centuries. The **Coptic language** (now extinct) was the form of Egyptian spoken in early Christian times (see LANGUAGE, table). The **Coptic Church** officially holds to MONOPHYSITISM, which was declared a heresy by Orthodox and Roman Catholics in 451. It is in communion with the Church of Ethiopia, and its head, the patriarch of Alexandria, names the head of the Ethiopian church (the abuna). The ritual languages are Greek, Coptic, and Arabic. A few "Catholic Copts" are in communion with the pope.

Coptic art, Christian art in the upper Nile valley of Egypt. Reached its mature phase in late 5th and 6th cent.; its later development was marked by influence of Islamic art.

copyright, statutory property right in works of literature, art, and the like, comprising exclusive right of owner to dispose of his property as he wishes and forbid unauthorized use. Slight common law protection of literary property was extended by English copyright act (1710), allowing control for 28 years in all. This act was model for first U.S. statute (1790). Present U.S. statute as originally enacted (1891) offered copyright for 28 years with single renewal, but gave only limited protection to English language works printed outside U.S. The Bern Convention (effective 1887) was adopted by many countries (not including U.S.) for mutual copyright recognition. UNESCO brought about new Universal Copyright Convention (at Geneva) 1952. U.S. acceptance was effective in 1955, and U.S. statute was amended to conform; Russia and most Communist countries do not adhere.

Coquelin, Benoît Constant (bŭnwä′ kŏstä′ kôklē′), 1841–1909, French actor. Acted for Comédie Française, his greatest role being Cyrano de Bergerac. Played with Bernhardt in *L'Aiglon.*

Coques or **Cocx, Gonzales** (gŏnzä′lĕs kŏks′), 1614–84, Flemish portrait painter. He excelled in painting diminutive portraits and family groups.

Coquilhatville (kôkēlätvēl′), city (pop. c.51,500), W Republic of the Congo; port on the Congo R. Cap. of former Équateur prov. City founded 1883 by H. M. Stanley.

coquilla nut (kōkē′yù), hard fruit of Brazilian palm (*Attalea funifera*), used in cabinet work and for small turned articles. Tree yields stiff fiber used in brooms and ropes.

coral, small marine invertebrate usually living in a colony. The individuals, known as polyps, each consist of a jellylike body surrounded by a skeleton. They live only in warm seas, and exist in great variety. As a colony produces new polyps, the older members die and new layers build up on the dead skeletons. Wave action may pile up the coral material, helping to form **coral reefs.** A fringing reef is separated from the shore by a narrow lagoon; a barrier reef is farther out, enclosing a wide, deep lagoon around an island or islands; an atoll is a ring-shaped coral reef surrounding a circular lagoon which lacks central islands. Coral fragments (many-colored) are much used in jewelry and bric-a-brac.

Coral Gables, residential city (pop. 34,793), SE Fla., just SW of Miami. Planned and built at height of Fla. land boom of 1920s. Seat of Univ. of MIAMI. Nearby is Tropical Park race track.

Coral Sea, SW arm of the Pacific, E of Australia and SE of New Guinea, W of New Hebrides and New Caledonia. Battle of aircraft carriers here in 1942 ended by checking S expansion of the Japanese.

coral snake, poisonous snake of W Hemisphere, related to cobra. Found chiefly in Mexico, Central and South America. Two species in U.S.: coral or harlequin snake (*Micrurus fulvius*) of SE U.S. is c.2½ ft. long, with small blunt head, body ringed with bands of black and of red, with narrow yellow bands on either side of black; Sonoran coral snake (*M. euryxanthus*) found from Arizona to N Mexico.

Corbett, James J(ohn), 1866–1933, American boxer. "Gentleman Jim" won heavyweight championship (1892) by defeating John L. Sullivan (21 rounds) in first heavyweight bout in which gloves were used instead of bare fists. Lost title (1897) to Robert Fitzsimmons.

Corbin, city (pop. 7,119), SE Ky., NW of Middlesboro. Rail center and coal-shipping point on old Wilderness Road in Cumberland Plateau. Levi Jackson Wilderness Road is nearby.

Corbulo (kôr'byōōlú), d.A.D. 67, Roman general. Under Claudius, Corbulo as legate in Germany built a still-used Meuse-Rhine canal. Later in Asia he defeated the Parthians at Artaxata and Tigranocerta. Still later his successes in Asia caused the jealousy of Nero, who forced him to commit suicide.

Corby, urban district (pop. 36,322), Northamptonshire, England. Iron-mining and steel-mfg. center, situated on one of world's largest ironstone fields.

Corcoran, William Wilson, 1798–1888, American financier and art collector. Donor of Corcoran Gall. of Art, Washington, D.C., opened 1897.

Corcyra, Greek Ionian island: see CORFU.

Corday, Charlotte (shärlôt' kôrdä'), 1768–93, French assassin. A sympathizer of GIRONDISTS, she gained admission to MARAT on false pretext, stabbed him in his bath. She was guillotined.

Cordele (kôrdēl'), city (pop. 10,609), S central Ga., SSW of Macon; founded 1888. A shipping, commercial, and processing center in farm area.

Cordeliers (kôrdúlyä'), France revolutionary club. Instrumental in destruction of GIRONDISTS (1793). Its early leaders, DANTON and DESMOULINS, were displaced by extreme leftists MARAT and HEBERT. Suppressed by Robespierre 1794.

Cordier, Andrew W(ellington) (kôr'dẽur), 1901–, American diplomat and educator. Served as expert at UN Charter conference in San Francisco in 1945 and as adviser to UN in various capacities 1946–62. Became dean of Columbia Univ. Graduate School of Internatl. Affairs 1962.

Cordilleras (kôrdĭl'ŭrúz), general name for mountain systems of W North America, from N Alaska through Canada, U.S., Mexico, and Panama. In U.S. they include Rocky Mts., ranges of Great Basin, Sierra Nevada, and Coast Ranges. In South America the range from Panama to Cape Horn is known locally as Cordillera de Los Andes.

cordite: see POWDER.

Córdoba, Francisco Fernández de: see FERNÁNDEZ DE CÓRDOBA, FRANCISCO.

Córdoba, Gonzalo Fernández de: see FERNÁNDEZ DE CÓRDOBA, GONZALO.

Córdoba (kôr'dōvä), city (pop. c.588,000), cap. of Córdoba prov., central Argentina; cultural and commercial center on E flank of Sierra de Córdoba at W margin of Pampa; founded 1573. Dam on Río Primero furnishes hydroelectric power for industries. Popular tourist and health resort. University founded 1613.

Córdoba, city (pop. c.33,000), Vera Cruz, E Mexico; founded 1618. Agr. area produces coffee, sugar, cotton, tropical fruits. Treaty establishing independence of Mexico was signed here (1821).

Córdoba or Cordova, city (pop. 210,630), cap. of Córdoba prov., S Spain, in Andalusia, on Guadalquivir R. Flourished under Romans; reached zenith as seat of Moorish emirate (later caliphate) under OMAYYAD dynasty (756–1031). Fell to emir of Seville 1078; to Ferdinand III of Castile 1236. Never regained its former glory but remained famous for its gold, silver, leather crafts. From Omayyad period, when Córdoba was a center of Moslem and Jewish cultures, dates the great mosque (begun 8th cent.), which became a cathedral in 1238. Birthplace of Seneca, Lucan, Averroës, Maimonides.

Cordova (kôrdō'vù), town (pop. 1,128), S central Alaska, on Prince William Sound, ESE of Anchorage. Founded as terminus of Copper River and Northwestern RR to Kennecott copper mine, it declined with closing of mine and railroad (1938). Has commercial fishing. Area struck by earthquake 1964.

Cordova, Spain: see CÓRDOBA.

CORE: see CONGRESS OF RACIAL EQUALITY.

Corelli, Arcangelo (ärkän'jälō kōrĕl'lē), 1653–1713, Italian composer and violinist. He developed the *concerto grosso*. Best known of his many sonatas are his variations on the air, *La Follia*.

Corelli, Marie (kúrĕl'ē), 1855–1924, English novelist. Her popular novels (e.g., *Thelma*, 1887; *The Sorrows of Satan*, 1895) were written in lush, often flamboyant prose. She was Queen Victoria's favorite novelist.

coreopsis (–ŏp'–) or **tickseed,** annual or perennial of genus *Coreopsis*, with yellow or yellow-red daisylike flowers. Some forms called calliopsis.

Corfu (kôr'fŏŏ, –fū), Gr. *Kerkyra,* Latin *Corcyra,* island (229 sq. mi.; pop. 99,092), Greece, second largest of Ionian Islands, separated by a narrow channel from Greek and Albanian coast. Rises to c.3,000 ft. at Mt. Pantokrator, but is largely a fertile agr. lowland. Livestock raising; fishing. Corfu has been identified with Scheria, home of Phaeacians in Homer's *Odyssey.* It was colonized by Corinth (8th cent. B.C.), and with Corinth helped found Epidamnus (see DURAZZO). Rivalry with Corinth over its control led to an alliance with Athens and helped precipitate PELOPONNESIAN WAR (431–404 B.C.). In 229 B.C. Corfu passed to Rome. It was seized repeatedly from the Byzantines by ROBERT GUISCARD and his successors; was held by Venice 1386–1797; shared later history of IONIAN ISLANDS. It passed to Greece in 1864. Briefly occupied by Italy in 1923 and in Second World War. The island's cap., Corfu (pop. 26,991), is an important commerical port and tourist resort.

Cori, Carl Ferdinand (kôrē), 1896–, and **Gerty Theresa (Radnitz) Cori,** 1896–1957, American biochemists, who shared (with Houssay) the 1947 Nobel Prize in Physiology and Medicine for research on carbohydrate metabolism and enzymes. Both were associated with Washington Univ. from 1931.

coriander, aromatic herb (*Coriandrum sativum*). Yields oil used as flavoring, in medicine, and in liqueurs.

Corinna (kúrĭn'nú), fl.c.500? B.C., Greek poet of Tanagra. Fragments of her verse, mythological in theme, remain.

Corinth, Lovis (lô'vẽs kô'rĭnt), 1858–1925, German painter and graphic artist, most important of the German impressionists.

Corinth (kŏ'rĭnth), Gr. *Korinthos,* city (pop. 15,892), Greece, in NE Peloponnesus; a port on Gulf of Corinth. Trades in silk, olive oil, fruits. Founded 1858 after destruction of Old Corinth by earthquake; rebuilt after another quake (1928). Old Corinth, 3 mi. SW of modern city of Corinth, is now a village. Strategically situated and protected by the ACROCORINTHUS, it was a wealthy, powerful, and cultured city of ancient Greece. A Dorian town existing from Homeric times, it became under PERIANDER and his successors a flourishing seapower and colonized Syracuse, Corfu, Potidaea. Rivalry with Athens and alliance with Sparta brought on the PELOPONNESIAN WAR (431–404 B.C.). After the Macedonian occupation Corinth led the ACHAEAN LEAGUE until its conquest and destruction by Rome (146 B.C.). Caesar restored it and reestablished the ISTHMIAN GAMES. Held by VILLEHARDOUIN family in the 13th cent., later by various Italian princes, Corinth fell to Turkey (1458), and to Venice (1687). Turkey recovered it 1715; lost it to Greek insurgents 1822. The Gulf of Corinth, an inlet of the Ionian Sea, 80 mi. long, 3–20 mi. wide, lies between central Greece (N) and the Peloponnesus (S), which are connected by the Isthmus of Corinth, 20 mi. long, 4–8 mi. wide. The isthmus is crossed by the ancient Isthmian Wall, repeatedly restored by Byzantine emperors to defend the Peloponnesus. Parallel to wall runs the Corinth Canal (built 1881–93; damaged in Second World War), which connects Gulf of Corinth with Saronic Gulf.

Corinth, city (pop. 11,453), extreme NE Miss., near Tenn. line NNE of Tupelo, in livestock and farm area; founded c.1855. Strategic rail center in Civil War, it was abandoned to Gen. Halleck's Union army in May, 1862, after battle of Shiloh. Gen. Rosencrans repulsed Confederates under Gens. Van Dorn and Price here, Oct. 3–4, 1862.

Corinth, Gulf of: see CORINTH, Greece.

Corinth, Isthmus of: see CORINTH, GREECE.

Corinthians (kŭrĭn'thēŭnz), epistles of New Testament written to Christians at Corinth by St. Paul. First Corinthians, written probably early in A.D. 55, is one of longest and most important of epistles. It covers various aspects of Christian conduct, counsels against factionalism, incest, litigation, sensuality, and answers questions on marriage and celibacy. Contains many famous passages, e.g., institution of Eucharist (11.17–34); an eloquent panegyric on Christian love (13). Second Corinthians is shorter, written perhaps within a year of the other. Contains Paul's defense of his mission, citing his authority, and accounting for his actions.

Coriolanus (kô'rēùlā'nùs), legendary Roman patrician. The story goes that Coriolanus offered to give state grain to the starving people in return for abolition of the tribunate of the people. He was expelled from Rome. Joining the Volscians in an attack on Rome (possibly 491? B.C.), he was moved by the tears of his wife and his mother to spare the city. The frustrated Volscians killed him. The story is used for Shakespeare's play. Plutarch wrote Coriolanus' life.

Coriolis effect, tendency for any body moving on or above the earth to drift sideways because of earth's rotation. Affects ocean currents, winds, projectiles.

Cork, Richard Boyle, 1st earl of: see BOYLE, RICHARD.

Cork [Irish,= swamp], maritime county (2,881 sq. mi.; pop. 330,106), S Ireland, Munster Prov.; largest Irish county. Has rocky coastline with several bays and harbors. Interior has both mountains and fertile valleys. Farming, fishing, and dairying main occupations. Mfg. (automobiles, rubber goods, paint, textiles, and whisky) mostly around co. town, Cork, county borough (pop. 77,860), on Lee R. near Cork Harbour. Occupied by the Danes (9th cent.), Cromwell (1649), and Marlborough (1690). Harbor entrance is fortified; Cobh and Passage are important ports, and Haulbowline and Spike Isls. are military and naval depots. Exports mainly farm produce, cloth, and fish. Site of Univ. Col. and two cathedrals.

cork oak, evergreen oak (Quercus suber), native to Mediterranean region. Its thick but light bark or cork is used to make many things (e.g., bottle stoppers, life preservers, insulating material).

Corliss, George Henry, 1817–88, American inventor and international authority on steam-engine.

corm, short, thickened underground stem, resembling but distinguished from a bulb. Roots grow from a corm's base. The gladiolus and crocus form corms.

cormorant (kôr'mûrûnt), large aquatic bird, an expert swimmer, related to the gannet and pelican, found in temperate or tropical areas, usually on the sea, but also on inland waters. Plumage is thick, usually dark; the body is 2–3 ft. long; the feet are webbed; the long bill is hooked. Cormorants are used in the Orient to catch fish.

corn, in agr., name given to leading grain crop of a region. In England, it means WHEAT, in Scotland and Ireland, OATS. Grain called corn in America is Indian corn or maize (Zea mays), a grass, domesticated and cultivated long before white man's arrival. In U.S. it is a leading grain crop. Much improved by scientific breeding; most corn grown in U.S. is HYBRID, from seed produced by a cross of two pure lines. Sweet corn used as foodstuff; field corn, to make starch and sugar and as grain feed and fodder.

corn, in medicine, cone-shaped horny growth of the epidermis. Growing downward, it presses on nerve endings causing pain. Corns appear most frequently on toes as a result of friction caused by ill-fitting shoes.

Cornaro, Caterina (kätärĕ'nä kôrnä'rō), 1454–1510, queen of Cyprus, a celebrated Venetian beauty. Ruled from death of husband, James II of Cyprus (1473), until 1489, when Venice recalled her and annexed the island. Portrait by Titian (Uffizi, Florence).

Cornaro, Luigi or Ludovico, 1467–1566, Venetian nobleman. Advocate of temperance in diet. His Discorsi della vita sobria (1558) has been often reissued and translated.

Corn Belt, term applied to that part of U.S. where soil and climate are best suited to raising corn and corn-fed livestock. Corresponds more or less to W part of Midwest; heart is in Ill. and Iowa.

corn borer or European corn borer, small moth, in its larval stage a serious pest to corn. Probably reached U.S. from S Europe c.1910; found near Boston 1917. Often attacks other plants, e.g., dahlia.

corn ear-worm: see BOLLWORM.

Corneille, Pierre (pyĕr' kôrnä'yù), 1606–84, French dramatist, master of classical tragedy. Le Cid (1637), his masterpiece, is based on Spanish sources (see CID). Among his other plays, the most successful are the tragedies Horace (1640), Cinna (1640), and Polyeucte (1643), and the comedy Le Menteur (1643). In grandiose, dignified style, Corneille exalts the will, subordinating passion to duty. He lived to see Racine replace him in popular favor.

cornel: see BUNCHBERRY; DOGWOOD.

Cornelia, fl. 2d cent. B.C., Roman matron, daughter of Scipio Africanus Major, wife of Ti. Sempronius Gracchus, mother of the Gracchi. Devoted herself to her children after her husband's death, raising them well. When asked by a wealthy lady about her jewels, Cornelia pointed at her sons, saying, "These are my jewels!"

Cornelius, first Gentile converted by Peter; traditionally first bishop of Caesarea. Acts 10.

Cornelius, Peter von, 1783–1867, German painter who helped revive art of fresco painting. Did fresco decorations in the Glyptothek. Favorite themes were religious or philosophical.

Cornell, Ezra, 1807–74, American capitalist, founder of Cornell Univ. A founder and director of the Western Union Telegraph Co. (formed 1855). His son, Alonzo B. Cornell, 1832–1904, was governor of N.Y. (1880–83), associate of Roscoe Conkling.

Cornell, Katharine, 1898–, American actress. Since 1916 has appeared in plays such as The Green Hat, The Barretts of Wimpole Street, and Candida, all produced and directed by her husband, Guthrie McClintic.

Cornell University, mainly at Ithaca, N.Y.; land grant, state and private support; coed.; chartered 1865, opened 1868. Named for Ezra Cornell; first president was A. D. White. Has U.S. plant, soil, and nutrition laboratory; Savage school of nutrition; and nuclear physics laboratory. Operates aeronautical laboratory at Buffalo, agr. experiment stations at Geneva and Ithaca, and radar station for space exploration in Puerto Rico. Medical college is in New York city; affiliated with Bellevue Hospital, New York Hospital, and Memorial Hospital for Cancer and Allied Diseases. Has colleges of agr. and home economics, school of industrial and labor relations, and veterinary college—all affiliated with the State Univ. of New York.

corner, the securing of all or nearly all the supply of any commodity so that buyers must pay exorbitant prices; may be unintentional or planned. U.S. Supreme Court held in 1913 that a corner in a commodity entering into general use or into interstate commerce is illegal.

Corner Brook, city (pop. 25,185), W N.F., Canada, on Bay of Islands. Has large paper mills.

cornet: see WIND INSTRUMENTS.

cornflower, annual plant (Centaurea cyanus) with blue, purple, pink, or white flower heads. Also called bachelor's button, ragged sailor, bluebottle.

Corning, James Leonard, 1855–1923, American neurologist; introduced spinal anesthesia (1885).

Corning. 1 City (pop. 2,041), SW Iowa, WSW of Creston, in farm, livestock, and dairy area; platted 1855. Icarian communist settlement was here 1858–98 (see CABET, ÉTIENNE). **2** City (pop. 17,085), S N.Y., NW of Elmira on Chemung R., in dairy region; settled 1788. Famous for glass industry (begun 1868).

Cornish, rural town (pop. 1,106), SW N.H., near Connecticut R., N of Claremont. A resort and art colony. Summer house of Augustus Saint-Gaudens now a museum. S. P. Chase born here.

Cornish, Brythonic language of Celtic subfamily of Indo-European languages. See LANGUAGE (table).

Corn Islands, two islands off E Nicaragua, in the Caribbean. Leased to U.S. in 1916 in Nicaragua Canal Project.

corn laws, regulations dating from 1361 restricting export or import of grain, especially in England. Laws of 1791 and 1815 forbade import unless prices were high. Food costs rose. Resentment led to Anti-Corn-Law League's campaign and repeal of laws by Robert Peel, 1846.

Corno, Monte, Italy: see GRAN SASSO D'ITALIA.

Cornplanter, c.1740–1836, half-breed chief of the Seneca Indians. Fought for British in New York in American Revolution.

cornucopia (kôr″nŭkō′pēŭ) [Latin,= horn of plenty], in Greek religion, broken-off horn of goat Amalthaea, which filled with whatever food or drink owner desired. It is symbol of plenty.

Cornwall (kôrn′wôl), maritime county (1,365 sq. mi.; pop. 341,746), SW England; co. town Bodmin. Peninsula ending in promontory Lands End, region is lowlying plateau with market and dairy farms in fertile valleys. County includes Scilly Isles, famous for flower exports. Cornish tin mines known early to Greek traders. History distinct from rest of England. Cornish tongue did not die out until 18th cent. Great fishing center and important source of china clay. Mild climate and picturesque coast attract tourists.

Cornwall, manufacturing city (pop. 43,639), SE Ont., Canada, on St. Lawrence R. and St. Lawrence Seaway and SE of Ottaway. Linked by bridge to Massena, N.Y.

Cornwallis, Charles Cornwallis, 1st Marquess, 1738–1805, British general. Led fateful CAROLINA CAMPAIGN in American Revolution. Defeat in YORKTOWN CAM-

PAIGN ended fighting. Later was governor general of India and viceroy of Ireland.

corolla (–rŏl′–), part of FLOWER, usually brightly colored and just within CALYX. May be united as in morning glory or separate petals as in rose.

Coromandel Coast (kŏrōmän′dùl), E coast ◆f Madras and Andhra Pradesh, India, between Point Calimere and Kistna R. delta. Name probably derives from Cholomandalam, i.e., land of the Cholas, an ancient empire.

Corona (kùrō′nù), city (pop. 13,336), S Calif., WSW of Riverside; estab. 1886. Processes citrus fruits.

corona (kùrō′nù), envelope surrounding sun (outside the chromosphere), believed to consist of fine particles luminous from their own light and reflected sunlight. Pale yellow inner corona is ringed by pearly white halo of outer corona, visible during total eclipse and also by means of coronagraph.

Coronado, Francisco Vásquez de, c.1510–1554, Spanish explorer in America. Unsuccessfully sought fabled wealth of Seven Cities of Cibola and QUIVIRA, but expedition acquainted Spanish with Pueblo Indians and opened Southwest.

Coronado (kô″rùnä′dō), city (pop. 18,039), S Calif., on peninsula on W side of San Diego Bay. Wellknown beach resort. U.S. naval ordnance laboratory is here.

coronary thrombosis: see THROMBOSIS.

coronation, ceremony of crowning sovereign on accession to throne. Has origins of great antiquity and ritual; usually has some religious as well as political significance (e.g., anointing with oil). In England medieval pageantry retained. English rulers crowned at Westminster Abbey since 1066. **Coronation Stone,** on which Scottish kings were crowned at Scone, was brought to Abbey in 1296 by Edward I and is now part of the coronation chair. Traditionally Jacob's "pillow," it was long Stone of Destiny of Irish kings before removal to Scotland. Stolen 1950 by Scottish nationalists but soon returned.

Coronea (kŏr′ùnē′ù), town of anc. Greece, in Boeotia, NW of Thebes. Here in 447 B.C. Athenians were defeated by Thebans, and in 394 B.C. Spartans won a hollow victory over Thebans and Athenians.

Corot, Jean Baptiste Camille (zhä′ bätēst′ kämē′yù kôrō′), 1796–1875, French painter, associated with Barbizon school. His landscapes are of two styles: one sunlit, solidly constructed pictures of France and Italy; the other misty, poeticized forests. Also famous for paintings of women.

corporal punishment, physical chastisement of an offender, as in capital punishment, flogging, mutilating, or branding. Known from the dawn of history, it was opposed by humanitarians in 18th cent., and generally punishments have become less severe.

corporation, organization enjoying legal personality for purpose of carrying on certain activities. Most corporations are businesses organized for profit by subscribers who raise capital by selling STOCK, though other types (religious, municipal) exist. Modern corporation characterized by separation of management and ownership. Known in ancient Rome, but modern corporations developed with spread of commerce in Renaissance and growth of industry in 18th and 19th cent. In U.S. most operate under state charters. As a legal person corporation may hold property, carry on business, and even commit crimes. Increasing power and narrowing of control to a few owners by holding companies (organized to control shares in other corporations) has caused opposition and some restriction by law.

corporation tax: see INTERNAL REVENUE.

corporative state, governmental economic system, organized with guilds (or corporations) of employers and employees; thus combines capitalism and syndicalism. Corporative state gives government unlimited control over economic life. Spain and Portugal have modified corporative system.

SMALL CAPITALS = cross references. Pronunciation key on inside end pages. Abbreviations: p. 2.

Corpus Christi (kôr′pŭs krĭs′tē) [Latin,= body of Christ], feast of the Roman Catholic Church, celebrated on the Thursday after Trinity Sunday (or on the following Sunday) to commemorate institution of the Eucharist. In many countries the day is marked with great processions and with much show of flowers.

Corpus Christi, city (pop. 167,690), S Texas, on Corpus Christi Bay at entrance of Nueces Bay (inlet at mouth of Nueces R.). Bay was discovered by Spanish 1519. Trading post estab. here 1840; land claimed by Texas and Mexico. Boomed in Mexican War. Captured briefly by U.S. navy in Civil War. Grew as natural gas and petroleum center after recovering from 1919 hurricane. Deepwater channel completed 1926; has high-level bridge over harbor entrance. Seat of Univ. of Corpus Christi and U.S. naval hospital.

Corpus Christi College: see CAMBRIDGE UNIVERSITY and OXFORD UNIVERSITY.

corpuscles, cells carried in body fluids, especially blood plasma. Red blood corpuscles, yellowish biconcave disks containing hemoglobin (protein combined with iron and carrying oxygen), en masse give blood its red color; c.5,000,000 are normally found per cu. mm. of human blood. Several types of white corpuscles exist in blood and lymph, totaling 5,000 to 10,000 per cu. mm. in blood. In the human body, the main types are lymphocytes, of uncertain function; monocytes, functioning in repair of tissues and engulfing microorganisms not attacked by lymphocytes and granulocytes; and granulocytes (c. 70% of total), subdivided into three types (neutrophiles, eosinophiles or acidophiles, and basophiles). Leucocytes capable of destroying microorganisms, which they engulf by amoeboid movement, are called phagocytes. See *ill.,* p. 656.

Corpus Juris Civilis (kôr′pŭs jōō′rĭs sĭvī′lĭs), most comprehensive code of Roman law, compiled (529–35) under Justinian I, by commission of jurists headed by TRIBONIAN. Four parts are the Codex or Code (collection of imperial constitutions), the Digest of Pandects (selections from classical jurists), the Institutes (textbook of elementary rules), and the Novels or Novellae (constitutions later than the Codex). *Corpus* was main source of modern CIVIL LAW.

Correggio (kŭrĕ′jō), 1494–1534, Italian baroque painter, b. Correggio. His real name was Antonio Allegri. Greatly influenced Italian art of the 16th and 17th cent. by bold use of foreshortening and soft, moving contrasts of color, light, and shade. His most famous work is the grand fresco, *Assumption of the Virgin,* on the cupola of Parma cathedral.

Corregidor (kŭrĕ′gĭdôr″), fortress island, area c.2 sq. mi., off BATAAN peninsula of Luzon, Philippines. First fortified by the Spanish, its defenses were further strengthened by U.S. after 1898. In Second World War it was scene of hopeless fighting by U.S. troops before their surrender in May, 1942.

Corrèze (kôrĕz′), department (2,273 sq. mi.; pop. 237,926), S central France, in Limousin; cap. Tulle.

Corrientes (kôrēĕn′tĕs), city (pop. 112,725), cap. of Corrientes prov., NE Argentina, port on Paraná R. in cattle and agr. district.

corrosion: see RUSTING.

corrosive sublimate, mercuric chloride, or **bichloride of mercury,** deadly poisonous chemical compound comprising one atom of mercury and two atoms of chlorine. In very dilute solution it is used as antiseptic. Prepared by sublimation from mixture of mercuric sulfate and sodium chloride.

Corsica (kôr′sĭkŭ), Fr. *Corse,* island (3,367 sq. mi.; pop. 275,465), a department of Metropolitan France, in Mediterranean, SE of France and N of Sardinia. Its cap., Ajaccio, and Bastia are the chief towns and ports. Largely mountainous (Monte Cinto is c.8,879 ft.). Olive oil, wine, timber are main exports. Poor communications. Large areas are wild, covered by undergrowth (*maquis*), offering ideal hideout to bandits. Blood feuds and banditry were traditional until sup-

pression in 20th cent. Outside chief towns an Italian dialect is spoken. Corsica was seized in turn by the Romans (3d cent. B.C.), Vandals (5th cent. A.D.), Arabs (9th cent.), Pisans (1077), and Genoese (1312). In 1755 Pasquale PAOLI successfully rebelled against Genoa, but French intervention led in 1768 to cession of Corsica to France The Bonapartes, including Napoleon I, originated here. In 1794 Paoli returned, expelled French, united Corsica with British crown; but in 1796 France recovered it. In Second World War German-Italian occupation (1942–43) was ended by local rebellion aided by Free French task force.

Corsicana (kôrsĭkä′nŭ), city (pop. 20,344), E central Texas, SSE of Dallas. Its commerce and small industries depend largely on cotton (long dominant), beef cattle, dairy products, poultry, and oil of area. First important commercial oil well (1895) and first refinery (1898) of Texas were here.

Corte Real, Gaspar (gŭshpär′ kôr′tù rēäl′), c.1450–1501?, Portuguese explorer. Made two voyages seeking Northwest Passage. May have discovered Greenland (1500) and touched North America. Lost on second voyage. His brother, Miguel Corte Real, was lost searching for him.

Cortés, Hernán, or **Hernando Cortez** (ĕrnän′ kôrtäs′, hĕrnän′dō kôrtĕz′), 1485–1547, Spanish conquistador, conqueror of Mexico. After service in Hispaniola and Cuba, he went (1519) under a commission of the Cuban governor Diego de Velázquez to conquer Mexico. There he was aided by a Spanish survivor of an earlier expedition and by an Indian girl, Malinche (renamed Marina on becoming Christian). He won over some peoples subordinate to the Aztec empire and got the help of Tlaxcalans after defeating them. His march on the Aztec cap., Tenochtitlán, ended triumphantly when Emperor Montezuma received him as a descendant of the god Quetzalcoatl. Cortés made Montezuma hostage and governed through him. He had, however, renounced allegiance to Velázquez and in 1520 had to return to the coast to defeat a force sent by Velázquez under Pánfilo de Narváez. While he was gone the Spanish under Pedro de Alvarado were driven from Tenochtitlán. Cortés rallied his forces and in 1521 besieged and took the city, destroying the Aztec empire. In 1524–26 he led an expedition to Honduras, putting the last puppet Aztec emperor, Cuauhtémoc, to death en route. He returned to find the governing power taken from him and though he was made marqués del Valle de Oaxaca he was not able to reestablish power in long wrangles with other administrators. He died in Spain, neglected by the court.

Cortes (kôr′täs), representative assembly in Spain. Local cortes originated in 12th–13th cent. in Leon, Castile, Aragon, Catalonia, Navarre, Valencia; continued to 19th cent., though much curtailed after Spanish unification (15th cent.). Local cortes were composed of three estates: clergy, nobles, burghers. First all-Spanish Cortes met at Cádiz 1812. Since then, its status as parliament has been affected by frequent constitutional changes. The current single-chamber Cortes has lost effective legislative power.

Cortez, Hernando: see CORTÉS, HERNÁN.

Cortez (kôr′tĕz′), town (pop. 6,764), SW Colo., in fruit, grain, and livestock area; founded 1887. Nearby are MESA VERDE NATIONAL PARK, Yucca House Natl. Monument (see NATIONAL PARKS AND MONUMENTS, table), and several Indian reservations.

Cortina d'Ampezzo (kôrtē′nä dämpĕd′zō), Alpine resort, NE Italy, in heart of Dolomites.

cortisone, hormone of the cortex of the adrenal gland; its effects are not clearly understood. It is used in treating allergy, arthritis, leukemia, and inflammation. Produced synthetically.

Cortland, city (1965 pop. 19,523), central N.Y., S of Syracuse, in farm area; settled 1791.

Cortona, Pietro da (pyä′trō dä kôrtō′nù), 1596–1669, major Italian baroque painter and architect, b. Cortona, whose real name was Pietro Berrettini. His exuberant ceiling painting (1633–39) in the Barberini Palace, filled with swirling clouds and figures, was one of the most influential baroque decorative schemes.

Cortot, Alfred (kôrtō'), 1877–1962, French pianist and conductor, authoritative interpreter of Chopin. For many years he played trios with Jacques Thibaud, violinist, and Pablo Casals, cellist.

Coruña, La (kŭrŭ'nü, Sp. lä kōrōō'nyä), city (pop. 195,-519), cap. of La Coruña prov., NW Spain, in Galicia; Atlantic port. Of pre-Roman origin; flourished as port and textile center in Middle Ages; sacked by Drake 1598. Scene of Peninsular War battle in which Sir John Moore was mortally wounded (1809). Also spelled Corunna in English.

corundum (kŭrŭn'dŭm), a mineral, aluminum oxide. The finer varieties are used as gems, the coarser as abrasives. Emery is impure corundum. The chief corundum gems are ruby and sapphire.

Corunna, Spain: see CORUÑA, LA.

Corvallis (kôrväl'ĭs), city (pop. 20,669), NW Oregon, on Willamette R., SSW of Salem; settled 1846. In fertile fruit and dairy valley, it also has lumber industry. Seat of OREGON STATE UNIVERSITY.

Corvinus, Matthias: see MATTHIAS CORVINUS.

Corwin, Thomas, 1794–1865, U.S. Secretary of the Treasury (1850–53). Was U.S. Representative (1831–40, 1859–61), governor of Ohio (1840–42), U.S. Senator (1845–50), minister to Mexico (1861–64).

Coryate, Thomas (kôr'ēāt), 1577?–1617, English traveler. His *Crudities* (1611) reports his journey that covered much of the Continent.

Corydon (kôr'ĭdŭn), town (pop. 2,701), S central Ind., WSW of Louisville, Ky.; laid out 1808. Processing center in farm area. Was territorial cap. 1813–16, then state cap. until 1825. Scene of skirmish (July 9, 1863) in Civil War. Wyandotte Cave is near.

Cos, island in the Dodecanese: see KOS.

Cosenza (kôzĕn'tsä), city (pop. 72,723), Calabria, S Italy. Chief city of anc. Brutii. Alaric I is said to be buried here under Busento R., which was temporarily diverted from its course. Medieval castle built by Emperor Frederick II. Cathedral.

Cosgrave, William Thomas (kŏz'grāv), 1880–1965, Irish statesman. After Sinn Fein split (1922) he stood by Free State. Was president of executive council of Ireland 1922–32. After defeat by De Valera, was opposition leader until his resignation in 1944.

Coshocton (kŭshŏk'tŭn), city (pop. 13,160), central Ohio, NNE of Zanesville, in agr. and industrial area; laid out 1802. Flood-control dams are nearby.

cosmetics to enhance personal appearance have been used since prehistoric times. The ancient Egyptians, Greeks, Romans used them; in Middle Ages, known beauty aids were supplemented by those brought home by Crusaders. Renaissance saw beginning of lavish use, which continued until virtual disappearance of make-up in 19th cent. Revival came at turn of century; manufacture of cosmetics is now huge industry. Highly important in theater and television. Government surveillance against harmful products and fraudulent advertising continues to increase.

cosmic rays, radiation of unknown origin coming to earth from outer space, carrying large amounts of energy and able to penetrate nearly all substances. Primary rays believed to be chiefly protons; many of these collide with air particles. The nuclei of atoms destroyed in collisions break into particles which probably become secondary cosmic rays. Tertiary and quaternary rays said to be formed similarly.

cosmogony (kŏzmŏ'gŭnĕ), any theory of the origin of the world, of man, and of the universe in a philosophic, scientific setting. See NEBULAR HYPOTHESIS; PLANETESIMAL HYPOTHESIS.

cosmos (kŏz'mŭs), garden annual of genus *Cosmos* with crimson, pink, white, or orange flowers.

cosmotron: see PARTICLE ACCELERATOR.

Cossa, Baldassarre (bäldäs-sär'rä kôs'sä), c.1370–1419, Neapolitan churchman, antipope as John XXIII in the Great SCHISM. When he was a cardinal he deserted the cause of Gregory XII and supported the Council of PISA, intended to end the schism between Rome and Avignon popes. When Antipope Alexander V died, Cossa was elected (1410). He courted the favor of Emperor SIGISMUND and aided Louis II of Anjou against Lancelot (an ally of Gregory) in Naples. He convened the Council of CONSTANCE under pressure from Sigismund and reluctantly promised to abdicate if his rivals would. They did, but he fled and tried to maintain his position. He was forced to return and was held prisoner until 1418.

Cossa, Francesco, or **Francesco del Cossa** (fränchä'skō dĕl kôs'sä), c.1435–1477?, Italian painter, identified with the schools of Ferrara and Bologna.

Cossacks (kŏ'säks), peasant-soldiers of several regions in Russia who until 1918 held certain privileges of self-government in return for military service. They were descended from fugitive serfs who settled frontier steppes in 16th and 17th cent. and defended them against Turks and Tatars (see DON COSSACKS; ZAPOROZHE COSSACKS). Their prominence in naval revolts of 17th–18th cent. cost them many privileges. Cossacks took important part in conquest and colonization of new territories (e.g., SIBERIA, KUBAN). Before 1917 their 11 communities numbered c.4,000,000. Most of them fought against the Bolsheviks in civil war of 1918–20.

Costa, Isaäc da (ē'sä-äk dä kôs'tä), 1798–1860, Dutch poet. Of an aristocratic Jewish family, he entered (1822) the Reformed Church, and much of his poetry is fervently Christian.

Costa Mesa (kŏs'tŭmä'sŭ), residential city (1966 pop. 66,396), S Calif., ESE of Long Beach.

Costa Rica (kŏ'stŭ rē'kŭ) [Span., = rich coast], republic (19,650 sq. mi.; 1964 est. pop. 1,413,531), Central America, between Nicaragua (N) and Panama (S); cap. SAN JOSÉ. The NE area is a broad jungle plain, the NW is jungles and low mountains. The heart of the country is the central plateau, which has on it San José, CARTAGO (founded 1563), Heredia, and Alajuela. Few Indians survived the Spanish conquest, and as a result a system of small landholdings rather than large plantations developed. Part of the captaincy general of Guatemala before gaining independence from Spain, Costa Rica was later part of Iturbide's empire (1821–23) and a member of the Central American Federation (1823–38). Coffee, introduced in the 19th cent., became the dominant crop. In 1874 M. C. Keith founded Limón and developed banana plantations on the Caribbean coast (many now abandoned because of leaf blight). The plateau cities, linked by rail and highway, are connected with the Pacific port, Puntarenas. Costa Rica is traditionally democratic and has been active in Pan-American organizations. On the Allied side in Second World War; joined UN 1945. After disputed election and revolt in 1948–49, democratic procedures were restored. In 1966 José Joaquín Trejos Fernandez was elected president.

Costa y Martínez, Joaquín (hwäkēn', märtē'näth), 1846–1911, Spanish jurist, economist, and sociologist. Founded Liga Nacional to promote agr. reform in Spain.

Coster, Charles de: see DE COSTER, CHARLES.

Coster, Laurens Janszoon: see KOSTER, LAURENS JANSZOON.

Costermansville: see BUKAVU.

Côte-d'Or (kōt-dôr'), department (3,392 sq. mi.; pop. 387,869), E France, in Burgundy; cap. Dijon. World-famed vineyards.

Cotentin (kôtätē'), peninsular region of Normandy, N France, projecting into English Channel; roughly identical with Manche dept. Historic cap. Coutances; chief towns are Cherbourg, Saint-Lô. Agr., applé orchards.

Côtes-du-Nord (kôt'dü-nôr'), department (2,787 sq. mi.; pop. 501,923), NW France, in Brittany; cap. Saint-Brieuc.

Cöthen, Germany: see KÖTHEN.

Cotman, John Sell, 1782–1842, English landscape painter, best known for water colors and drawings.

Cotopaxi (kōtōpäk'sē), active volcano, 19,344 ft. high, N central Ecuador.

Cotswold Hills, broken limestone plateau in Gloucestershire, England, extending c.50 mi. NE from Bath. Crest is Thames-Severn watershed. Region famous for Cotswold sheep and picturesque houses.

Cotte, Robert de (rôběr' dü kôt'), 1656–1735, French architect, succeeded J. H. Mansart as architect to Louis XV.

Cotton, (Thomas) Henry, 1907–, British golfer. Won British Open (1934, 1937, 1948), Professional Golfers' Association of America (1932, 1939, 1946) championships, many others.

Cotton, John, 1584–1652, Puritan clergyman in England and Mass. Bay Colony. Getting into difficulty as Puritan vicar of St. Botolph's, Boston, Lincolnshire, he migrated (1633) to America. The city of Boston renamed to honor him. Responsible for exile of Anne Hutchinson and expulsion of Roger Williams. Helped mold Congregational Church.

Cotton, Sir Robert Bruce, 1571–1631, English antiquarian. His collection of books, manuscripts, coins, and antiquities now is in British Museum.

cotton, most important of vegetable fibers, used from prehistoric times in many lands. The plant, a perennial of genus *Gossypium*, bears capsules (bolls) containing seeds, surrounded by downy white or creamy fibers easily spun into thread. Usually grown as annual; thrives in temperate climate with well-distributed rainfall, as in U.S. COTTON BELT, where upland varieties are mainly grown; in W U.S., sea-island and American-Egyptian cotton are grown. U.S., USSR, India, China, Mexico are chief producers. Bolls were long hand picked; machine picking, now increasing, is aided by use of chemical to rid plants of leaves before stripping bolls. BOLL WEEVIL is most harmful of many insect pests and diseases. Cotton mfg., a huge industry, esp. in Great Britain and U.S., involves cleaning, ginning, carding, and spinning in order to get thread strong enough for weaving. Innumerable commodities, in addition to textiles, are made from cotton. Fibers yield cellulose; seeds, containing c.20% oil, yield **cottonseed oil**, used in refined state in cookery, as ingredient of margarine and cosmetics, and in crude state as industrial raw material.

Cotton Belt, term applied to part of U.S. formerly devoted mainly to cotton. Area included N.C., S.C., Ga., Ala., Miss., La., Ark., Okla., Texas, and sections of Va., Ky., Tenn., Fla., and Mo. Mainly diversified crops now, though cotton still important. Texas now main cotton grower, and it is also grown in Calif., Ariz., and N.Mex.

cotton gin (jĭn), machine for separating cotton fiber from seeds. Roller gin known from ancient times. Saw gin invented 1793 by Eli Whitney consisted of revolving toothed cylinder which pulled lint through grate. Modern mechanized adaptation has series of circular saws which draw fiber through grid.

cottonmouth: see WATER MOCCASIN.

cottonwood: see POPLAR.

Cottrell, Frederick Gardner, 1877–1948, American chemist, authority on nitrogen fixation, mineral fertilizers. Devised Cottrell dust precipitator for removing solids from flue gases by means of high-potential electric current.

Cotulla (kùtü'lù), city (pop. 3,960), SW Texas, on Nueces R., SW of San Antonio. Tourist stop on Pan American Highway.

Coucy, Robert de (rôběr' dù kōōse'), d. 1311, French architect who helped build Rheims cathedral.

Coucy-le-Château-Auffrique (kōōse'-lù-shätō'-ōfrěk'), village, Aisne dept., N France. Ruins of medieval fortress and castle.

Coué, Émile (kōōā'), 1857–1926, French psychotherapist known for formula, "Day by day, in every way, I am getting better and better."

cougar: see PUMA.

Coughlin, Charles Edward (kŏ'glĭn), 1891–, Roman Catholic priest in U.S., b. Canada. Bitterly opposed New Deal policies through press and radio.

Coulanges, Numa Denis Fustel de: see FUSTEL DE COULANGES, NUMA DENIS.

coulomb (kōō'lŏm), quantity of electricity that current of one AMPERE transfers in one second. **Coulomb's law:** force of attraction or repulsion between two charges is inversely proportional to square of distance between them and directly proportional to product. Established by **Charles Augustin de Coulomb**, 1736–1806, French physicist, for whom coulomb named.

Coulsdon and Purley, London: see CROYDON.

council, ecumenical (ē"kūmē'nĭkŭl, ē"–) [Gr.,=universal], council of Church authorities accepted by the Church as official. Their decrees are called canons if ratified by the pope. Roman Catholics recognize the following ecumenical or general councils: (1) 1 Nicaea, 325; (2) 1 Constantinople, 381; (3) Ephesus, 431; (4) Chalcedon, 451; (5) 2 Constantinople, 553; (6) 3 Constantinople, 680; (7) 2 Nicaea, 787; (8) 4 Constantinople, 869; (9) 1 Lateran, 1123; (10) 2 Lateran, 1139; (11) 3 Lateran, 1179; (12) 4 Lateran, 1215; (13) 1 Lyons, 1245; (14) 2 Lyons, 1274; (15) Vienne, 1311; (16) Constance, 1414; (17) Basel and Ferrara-Florence, 1431, 1438; (18) 5 Lateran, 1512; (19) Trent, 1545; (20) 1 Vatican, 1869; (21) 2 Vatican, 1962. The Orthodox recognize the first seven and also the continuation of 3 Constantinople (the Trullan Synod). At the time of the Great Schism the theory was advanced that the general council, rather than the pope, was supreme in the Church. The chief proponent was John Gerson, and this conciliar theory flourished at the Councils of Pisa and Constance, later failing.

Council Bluffs, city (1966 pop. 52,957), SW Iowa, on Missouri R. opposite Omaha, Nebr.; settled 1846 by Mormons on sites of trading post (1820s) and Indian mission (estab. 1838–40 by Father De Smet). Supply point in 1849–50 gold rush. Grew after being made E terminus of Union Pacific RR 1863. Now has repair shops and roundhouses and is trade and industrial center of agr. area. Levees here are part of Missouri river basin project.

Council for Mutual Economic Assistance (COMECON), international organization for coordination of economic policy in Soviet bloc. Estab. 1949 and given same international status as Common Market in 1959. Broad programs undertaken to meet challenge from Western economic associations.

Council Grove, city (pop. 2,664), E central Kansas, SW of Topeka on Neosho R., in farm and cattle area at edge of Flint Hills. Coronado said to have reached site 1541. Treaty made here with Osage Indians, 1825. Later a stop on Santa Fe Trail; trading post estab 1847. Methodist Indian mission (1849) still stands.

Council of Europe, Council of Foreign Ministers, Council of Ten, etc.: see EUROPE, COUNCIL OF; FOREIGN MINISTERS, COUNCIL OF; TEN, COUNCIL OF.

counterpoint, in music, the art of combining melodies, each of which is independent of the others, although together they form a harmonious whole. Five types of counterpoint have been defined: note against note; two notes against one; four notes against one; syncopation; and florid counterpoint, which combines the other four. See also POLYPHONY.

Counter Reformation: see REFORM, CATHOLIC.

Counts, George S(ylvester), 1889–, American educator, professor of education at Teachers College, Columbia Univ., 1927–56. He advocated teachers' unions and was president (1939–42) of American Federation of Teachers. Has taken part in liberal politics. Wrote many books on history and democracy.

Couperin, François (fräswä' kōopùrĕ'), 1668–1733, French organist, harpsichordist, and composer, called "le Grand" to distinguish him from other members of his musically prominent family. His four books of harpsichord suites influenced Bach.

Couperus, Louis Marie Anne (kōopä'rōos), 1863–1923, Dutch novelist. His works, popular at home and abroad, include a collection of four realistic novels, *The Book of the Small Souls* (1901–3).

Courant, Richard, 1888–, American mathematician, educator, b. Germany. Research included mathematical problems in physics (e.g., Dirichlet problem), function theory, and the calculus of variations.

Courbet, Gustave (gùstäv' kōorbä'), 1819–77, French painter, b. Ornans. An opponent of vested authority, whether aesthetic or political. Showed his avowed realism in his painting such works as *Funeral at Ornans* and *Painter's Studio;* won prestige but aroused much official criticism. In 1873, after participating in the Commune, he fled to Switzerland where he died in exile and poverty.

coureurs de bois (kōorûr' dùbwä') [Fr.,= wood runners], in French regime in Canada unlicensed traders who played active part in fur trade and exploration.

Courier, Paul Louis (pōl' lwĕ' kōoryä'), 1772–1825, French author and classical scholar. After the Restoration he wrote political pamphlets which place him among his nation's most brilliant stylists.

Courland or Kurland (kûr'lùnd, kōor'länt), region and former duchy, W Latvia; historic cap. JELGAVA. Conquered by LIVONIAN KNIGHTS in 13th cent. When the order disbanded (1561), its grand master became first duke of Courland, under Polish overlordship. Under Russian influence from early 18th cent., Courland was annexed by Russia in third Polish partition (1795). Became part of Latvia 1918.

Courland Lagoon: see KURISCHES HAFF.

Cournand, André F(rédéric) (kōor'nänd), 1895–, American physician, b. France. Shared with Werner Forssmann and D. W. Richards the 1956 Nobel Prize in Medicine and Physiology for work in developing technique of inserting catheter (tube) into heart; this technique makes possible better study of condition of heart in health and disease.

Cournot, Antoine August, 1801–77, French economist and mathematician; developed and applied theories of chance and probability to economics.

court, in law, the official bodies charged with adjudicating legal cases. In ancient Egypt and Babylonia courts were semi-ecclesiastic; in Greece assemblies had court functions; in Rome emerged secular complex system of courts, staffed with professional jurists. Britain since Judicature Act of 1873 has high court of justice (with divisions of chancery; probate, divorce, and admiralty; Queen's—or King's—Bench) and court of appeal. In U.S. two systems are Federal courts (district courts, circuit courts of appeals, and at head, Supreme Court) and state courts (including many types, e.g., police court, court of probate, courts of general jurisdiction, and appellate courts).

Courteline, Georges (zhôrzh' kōor"tùlĕn'), 1858–1929, French master of satire and farce. Wrote plays, novels, and tales.

Court of Justice: see EUROPEAN COMMUNITY.

Courtois, Bernard (bĕrnär' kōortwä'), 1777–1838, French chemist. He discovered and isolated iodine.

Courtrai (kōorträ'), Flemish *Kortrijk*, town (est. pop. 44,814), West Flanders, W Belgium, on Lys R. Textile center since medieval times. Scene of first BATTLE OF THE SPURS (1302). Church of Notre Dame (13th cent.) contains Van Dyck's *Elevation of the Cross.*

court tennis, believed to have been originated about 14th cent. in France, forerunner of most modern racquet games.

Cousin, Jean (zhä kōozĕ'), c.1490–c.1560, French painter. His treatise on portraiture and some of his glass paintings are attributed by some to his son and pupil, Jean Cousin, c.1522–c.1594.

Cousin, Victor, 1792–1867, French philosopher, minister of education under Louis Philippe. In that period he was practically dictator of education and philosophy. His own philosophy was eclectic in the extreme because Cousin believed that all conflicting doctrines held part of the truth ready for the intuitive eye to discern.

Cousin-Montauban, Charles Guillaume: see PALIKAO.

Cousteau, Jacques Yves (zhäk' ĕv' kōostō'), 1910–, French naval officer. With Émil Gagnan invented the aqualung 1943, founded French navy's undersea research group 1945.

Coustou (kōostōo'), family of French sculptors. **Nicolas Coustou,** 1658–1733, and brother, **Guillaume Coustou,** 1677–1746, worked at Marly and Versailles. Guillaume's son, **Guillaume Coustou,** 1716–77, was also a sculptor.

Cousy, Robert Joseph, 1928–, American basketball player. All-America (1950) at Holy Cross. One of highest scorers in Natl. Basketball Association, an all-star 12 times, became coach (1963) at Boston Col.

Couthon, Georges (zhôrzh' kōotō'), 1755?–1794, French revolutionist. Fanatic Jacobin. Shared with Robespierre, Saint-Just in triumvirate of Terror. Fell on 9 Thermidor; guillotined.

Couture, Thomas (tômä' kōotür'), 1815–79, French academic painter and teacher of art; pupil of Gros and Delacroix; taught Manet.

Couza, Alexander John: see CUZA.

Covadonga (kō'vädōn'gä), hamlet, N Spain, in Asturias. Scene (716?) of first Christian victory over Moors.

Covarrubias, Miguel (mĕgäl' kōvär-rōo'bĕäs), 1902–57, American artist, b. Mexico. Best known for his caricatures and drawings in *Vanity Fair.*

covenant (kŭ'vùnùnt) [O. Fr.,= agreement], in Bible and theology, explicit promise of God to man. In law, contract under seal or agreement by deed. In Scottish history (kŭvùnänt'), pact by opponents of episcopacy, known as COVENANTERS. Covenants in Bible are not contractual, but free promises of God: e.g., His covenants with Israel culminating in Law of Moses, and known as Old Covenant. In law, covenants follow same rules as other contracts; variously classified, all are characterized by explicit promise of covenantor to covenantee.

Covenanters, in Scottish history, groups of people bound by oath to defend Presbyterianism. Covenant of 1581 sought to combat Catholicism. Covenant of 1638 opposed innovations of Archbishop LAUD, especially use of English Book of Common Prayer. They resisted king's armies in BISHOPS' WARS (1639–40) and supported Parliament in PURITAN REVOLUTION only after acceptance (1643) of Solemn League and Covenant pledging Presbyterian state church in England and Ireland. Their power broken by Cromwell's conquest of Scotland in 1650. After Restoration, Covenanters were alternately coerced and persuaded to accept episcopacy but stubbornly resisted. Troubles ended with Glorious Revolution (1688).

Covent Garden (kŭ'vùnt), London opera house. Located in produce market district, it is on site of famous theater, built 1732 by John Rich, later managed by Kemble family. Present theater built 1858 to house opera and ballet.

Coventry (kŏv'ùntrē), county borough (pop. 305,-060), Warwickshire, England. An industrial center noted for mfg. of automobiles, airplanes, machine tools, electrical equipment. From 1678 until recently pageants of Lady Godiva and Peeping Tom were held. Entire central part of city destroyed in air raid, 1940; among buildings destroyed was 14th-cent. cathedral. City has since been rebuilt; new cathedral completed 1962.

Coventry, town (1965 pop. 19,577), W R.I., SW of Providence. Includes villages of Anthony and Washington.

cover crop, temporary crop sown to protect soil (e.g., from erosion), increase nutrients (e.g., nitrogen from legumes), or to improve texture by being plowed under. Valuable in rehabilitating land. Clover, barley, or turnips are often used.

Coverdale, Miles, 1488–1569, English translator of Bible, bishop of Exeter (1551–53). Published translation 1535. Later collaborated in Great Bible (1539) and edited "Cranmer's Bible" (1540).

covered wagon: see CONESTOGA WAGON; PRAIRIE SCHOONER.

Coverley, Sir Roger de: see ROGER DE COVERLEY.

Covina (kōvē'nù), city (pop. 20,124), S Calif., E of Los Angeles; laid out 1885. Processes citrus fruit.

Covington (kŭv'-). **1** City (pop. 60,376), N central Ky., on Ohio R. (suspension bridge to Cincinnati) where Licking R. (bridged to Newport) enters. Ferry and tavern estab. here c.1801; settled 1812. An industrial center, with railroad shops. Villa Madonna Col. and Latonia race track are here. **2** City (pop. 11,062), W central Va., NNW of Roanoke near W.Va. line, in Jackson R. valley surrounded by mountains; laid out 1819.

cow: see CATTLE.

Coward, Noel, 1899–, English playwright, actor, composer. His witty, sophisticated works include plays (e.g., *Private Lives*, 1930; *Blithe Spirit*, 1941), musicals (e.g., *Bittersweet*) and revues, songs and sketches, and films (e.g., *In Which We Serve*).

cowbird, New World bird of oriole and blackbird family. Male eastern, or common, cowbird (cow blackbird) is glossy black and c.8 in. long with brown head and breast. Most species lay eggs in other birds' nests; birds usually incubate the cowbird eggs and feed the young at expense of their own.

Cowell, Henry Dixon (kou'ŭl), 1897–1965, American composer, pianist. He experimented with new musical resources, e.g., tone clusters, often played with the fist on the piano; oriental textures, patterned after Indonesian gamelan or Japanese court music. Works include symphonies, ballets, piano music.

Cowes (kouz), urban district (pop. 16,974), Isle of Wight, England, near Southampton. Seaport, resort, and shipbuilding center, it is headquarters of the Royal Yacht Club and holds annual regattas.

Cowles, Henry Chandler (kōlz), 1869–1939, American botanist, a pioneer in plant ecology.

Cowley, Abraham (kōō'–, kou'–), 1618–67, English metaphysical poet and essayist. Precocious and versatile, he wrote *Poetical Blossoms* (1633), *The Mistress* (1647), *Poems* (1656), and several prose works, including autobiographical essays.

Cowley, Hannah: see DELLA-CRUSCANS.

cowpea or **black-eyed bean,** leguminous plant (*Vigna sinensis*), a forage and cover crop in S U.S.

Cowpens (kou'pĭnz), town (pop. 2,038), NW S.C., ENE of Spartanburg. National battlefield site marks battle (Jan. 17, 1781) of CAROLINA CAMPAIGN which resulted in British defeat and heavy losses.

Cowper, William Cowper, 1st Earl (kōō'pûr), c.1664–1723, English jurist. Took leading part in union of England with Scotland 1706. As first lord chancellor of Great Britain (1707–10) presided at trial of Henry Sacheverell.

Cowper, William (kōō'pûr), 1666–1709, English surgeon. Discovered Cowper's glands (bulbourethral glands) lying on either side of the prostate gland.

Cowper, William (kōō'pûr, kou'–), 1731–1800, English poet. Subject to melancholia, he was placed with the Unwin family at Huntingdon and later at Olney. His writings include intensely religious *Olney Hymns* (1779); *The Task* (1785). Pictures of rural life foreshadow romanticism. Also known for shorter poems, "John Gilpin," "To Mrs. Unwin," "To Mary," and his gloomy "The Castaway." Letters much admired.

Cowper's glands: see COWPER, WILLIAM (1666–1709).

cowpox, infectious viral disease of cows, related to SMALLPOX. Similar disease affects horses and sheep.

cowslip: see MARSH MARIGOLD; PRIMROSE; SHOOTING STAR; VIRGINIA COWSLIP.

Cox, David, 1783–1859, English landscape painter in watercolors, a follower of John Constable.

Cox, Jacob Dolson, 1828–1900, Union general in Civil War and American statesman. Served ably in Antietam and Atlanta campaigns. Secretary of Interior (1869–70) under Pres. Grant; advocated civil service reform, opposed spoilsmen in Republican party. Father of **Kenyon Cox,** 1856–1919, painter and art critic.

Cox, Palmer, 1840–1924, American writer-illustrator of the Brownie stories for children, b. Canada.

Coxey, Jacob Sechler, 1854–1951, American social reformer. Interested in unemployment and monetary problems. Farmer-Labor presidential candidate 1932, 1936. Led **Coxey's Army,** band of unemployed men who marched to Washington, D.C., following Panic of 1893, to petition Congress for measures which they hoped would relieve unemployment and distress. Reached Washington with c.500 men instead of the proclaimed 100,000; its leaders were arrested for walking on Capitol lawn.

coyote (kīō'tē, kī'ōt) or **prairie wolf,** small wolf (*Canis*) native to W North America, with thick, long, tawny fur and a bushy black-tipped tail. It hunts small animals and in packs attacks larger mammals. It is a scavenger and a destroyer of rodents. Cry is yelping, doglike.

Coypel (kwäpĕl'), family of French painters. **Noël Coypel,** 1628–1707, worked on decorations of royal palaces. His son, **Antoine Coypel,** 1661–1722, painted Aeneid series for Palais-Royal. Antoine's half-brother, **Noël Nicolas Coypel,** 1692–1734, and son, **Charles Antoine Coypel,** 1694–1752, were also well-known painters.

Coysevox, Antoine (kwäzvôks'), 1640–1720, French sculptor who did much of the sculpture at Versailles.

Cozens, Alexander (kŭz'ŭnz), c.1717–1786, English draughtsman, b. Russia. He invented a system of "blot" drawings which suggest landscape compositions. His son, **John Robert Cozens,** 1752–97, English watercolor landscape artist, influenced Turner and Girtin.

Cozzens, James Gould, 1903–, American novelist. Works include *The Just and the Unjust* (1942), *Guard of Honor* (1948), and *By Love Possessed* (1957).

Cr, chemical symbol of the element CHROMIUM.

Crab, the, in astrology: see ZODIAC.

crab, crustacean with broad, flat outer skeleton, short abdomen bent under body, stalked eyes, five pairs of legs (the first with claws). Crabs are chiefly marine, but some are fresh-water, some land forms. Omnivorous feeders, some are scavengers, others predatory. See also KING CRAB; HERMIT CRAB.

crab apple, type of apple tree and its small, sour fruit used in preserves and jellies. Siberian crab (*Pyrus baccata*) is widely grown. Other species and varieties, e.g., Bechtel's crab with double flowers, are grown for ornament.

Crabbe, George, 1754–1832, English poet of village life. A clergyman, he wrote of the sordid life of the very poor, accurately described in natural settings. His best-known long poem is *The Village* (1783).

Crabtree, Lotta, 1847–1924, American actress. A pupil of Lola Montez, she was a popular child actress in Calif. mining camps, singing, dancing, and reciting. From 1867 she was successful in N.Y. chiefly in burlesque and comic pieces.

Cracow (krā'kō, krā'cou), Pol. *Kraków*, city (est. pop. 513,000), S Poland on the Vistula; cap. of Poland from 14th cent. to 1595. Commercial and mfg. center; seat of Jagiellonian Univ. (founded 1364); episcopal see from c.1000. Kings of Poland continued to be crowned and buried at Cracow after fire of 1595 caused transfer of cap. to Warsaw. Cracow passed to Austria in third Polish partition (1795); was made a republic (with surrounding dist.) under protection of Austria, Russia, and Prussia by Congress of Vienna (1815); was annexed by Austria after insurrection of 1846; reverted to Poland 1919. Noted landmarks include royal castle (Wawel), rebuilt 16th cent.; 14th-cent. Gothic cathedral; 13th-cent. Church of Our Lady, with altarpiece by Veit Stoss; 14th-cent. cloth hall. A city-province, it is cap. of Cracow prov., an important industrial region; chief cities are Cracow, Tarnow, and Nowy Sacz.

Craddock, Charles Egbert, pseud. of **Mary Noailles Murfree,** 1850–1922, American novelist, author of novels and stories of Tennessee people.

Crafts, James Mason, 1839–1917, American chemist. Did research on silicon compounds, arsenic ethers, and thermometry. With Charles FRIEDEL he developed Friedel-Crafts reaction.

Craig, (Edward) Gordon, 1872–1966, English scene designer and producer; son of Ellen Terry. His poetic, abstract scene designs and productions for Ibsen's *Vikings* and Shakespeare's *Much Ado about Nothing* (1903) and *Hamlet* (Moscow Art Theatre, 1912) greatly contributed to modern, selective realism in scene design.

Craig, James: see CRAIGAVON, JAMES CRAIG, 1ST VISCOUNT.

Craig, Sir James Henry, 1748–1812, British soldier, governor in chief of Canada (1807–11), b. Gibraltar. Opposed to representative government and to French Canadians, he dissolved assembly of Lower Canada (1809). His arbitrary methods served only to consolidate and strengthen position of French Canadians.

Craigavon, James Craig, 1st Viscount (krăgă′vŭn), 1871–1940, Ulster statesman. Organized resistance against Home Rule. First prime minister of N. Ireland from 1921 until his death.

Craighead, Edwin Boone (krăg′hĕd), 1861–1920, American educator. Was president of several colleges including Tulane Univ. 1904–12.

Craigie, Sir William A., 1867–1957, British lexicographer, generally deemed the foremost lexicographer of his time, he was joint editor of *New English Dictionary* (commonly called *Oxford English Dictionary*) 1901–33 and was chief editor of *A Dictionary of American English on Historical Principles* (issued in parts after 1936; pub. as 4 vols., 1938–43).

Craik, Dinah Maria Mulock: see MULOCK.

Craiova (krăyŏ′vä), city (est. pop. 118,753), SW Rumania; historic cap. of Oltenia.

Cram, Ralph Adams, 1863–1942, American architect, an exponent of Gothic architecture. Wrote chiefly on medieval architecture and thought.

Cranach or Kranach, Lucas (both: lōō′käs krä′näkh), the elder, 1472–1553, German artist, whose real name was Müller or Sunder. Court painter to three electors of Saxony. A master of piquant line and silhouette in nudes, portraits, and religious paintings. Was a friend and supporter of Luther. His son and pupil **Lucas Cranach,** the younger, 1515–86, continued in his tradition.

cranberry, low creeping evergreen bog plant (*Vaccinium oxycoccus*), with red, tart berries used for sauces and jellies. Cultivated on commercial scale in parts of Mass., N.J., and Wis.

Cranbrook Foundation, at Pontiac, Mich.; estab. 1927. Includes schools, a church, an institute of science, and noted art academy. Most buildings designed by Eliel Saarinen.

Crandell, Prudence, 1803–89, American educator and abolitionist. Opened a school for girls in Canterbury, Conn., 1831, decided in 1833 to restrict it to Negro girls. She was arrested and tried; the judgment against her was reversed in 1834.

Crane, Hart, 1899–1932, American poet. His series of long poems, *The Bridge* (1930), uses the Brooklyn Bridge as a symbol of unity in America. Returning from Mexico by ship, he was drowned.

Crane, Stephen, 1871–1900, American novelist, journalist, poet. After his grim story *Maggie: A Girl of the Streets* (1893), his realistic Civil War novel, *The Red Badge of Courage* (1895), brought fame and thrust him into a career as war correspondent. Wrote short stories (*The Open Boat,* 1898), poetry, other works. Died in Germany of tuberculosis.

crane, large wading bird of Old World chiefly. Some are in North America, e.g., the whooping crane (nearly extinct), sandhill crane, little brown crane, and Florida crane. Cranes perform rhythmical dance in mating season.

crane, machine using free end of a fixed beam to hoist and transfer heavy loads. Actuated anciently by manual or animal power, modern cranes run by steam, electric, Diesel, and hydraulic, as well as manual power. Cranes used inside include bridge or overhead traveling crane (along steel girder spanning fixed rails). Outside cranes include the gantry (mounted on structure over operating area), the rotary, derrick, and hammerhead (steel tower supports cantilever-type truss with power generator at short end, load-carrying device at other). Locomotor crane revolves on turntable mounted on rail car, caterpillar tread, truck, or pontoons.

crane fly: see DADDY LONGLEGS.

Cranford, residential township (pop. 26,424), NE N.J., W of Elizabeth.

cranium: see SKULL.

Cranmer, Thomas (krăn′mŭr), 1489–1556, English churchman. Came to attention of HENRY VIII in 1529 by proposing method by which king could divorce Katharine of Aragon without recourse to Rome. Made Archbishop of Canterbury 1533; was subservient to king. As a regent for Edward VI, he largely determined course of English Church. Placed English Bible in churches; revised BOOK OF COMMON PRAYER 1552. Supported claim of Lady Jane Grey to throne. Under Catholic Mary I, was tried for treason, convicted of heresy, and burned at the stake.

Cranston, industrial city (1965 pop. 71,913), central R.I., SW of Providence.

crape myrtle (krăp), shrub (*Lagerstroemia indica*), with crinkled flowers, grown in S U.S.

craps: see DICE.

Crapsey, Adelaide, 1878–1914, American poet; originator of the cinquain—a delicate, compressed five-line verse, modeled on Japanese *hokku.*

Crashaw, Richard (krǎ′shô), 1612?–1649, English poet. Son of a Puritan clergyman, he became a High Churchman, then, in Europe, a Roman Catholic (1646): one of the METAPHYSICAL POETS. His verse is intensely religious, even baroque. It appeared in *Steps to the Temple* (1646) and *Carmen Deo Nostro* (1652).

Crassus (krǎ′sŭs), family of anc. Rome. **Lucius Licinius Crassus,** d. 91 B.C., political leader, chief interlocutor in Cicero's *De Oratore.* As consul in 95 B.C. he promoted Licinian Law, intended to banish from Rome all who had gained citizenship by illegal means. This restrictive measure helped to bring on the Social War. Most noted was **Marcus Licinius Crassus,** d. 53 B.C., who managed by personal charm and ambition to become the richest man in Rome. His devices were not always admirable; it is said that as a supporter of Sulla he got property of proscribed persons and also that he had an efficient fire-fighting organization that would not act until the owner of a burning building sold it to Crassus. He earned prestige by helping to defeat the revolt of Spartacus. Politically ambitious, he was consul with POMPEY in 70 B.C., but they disagreed. Julius CAESAR persuaded him to join in the First Triumvirate (Caesar, Pompey, Crassus) and held the organization together. Crassus, assigned the province of Syria, had military ambitions and undertook a campaign against the Parthians. He was routed at Carrhae (53 B.C.) and was murdered by treachery. Plutarch wrote Crassus' life.

crater (krā′tŭr), funnel-shaped depression at the vent of a volcano, or one formed by meteoric impact.

Crater Lake, c.6 mi. wide and 1,932 ft. deep. SW Oregon, in Cascade Range NNW of Klamath Falls. Deep blue lake lies in extinct volcano, encircled by lava walls. Discovered 1853. Now part of Crater Lake Natl. Park.

Craters of the Moon National Monument: see NATIONAL PARKS AND MONUMENTS (table).

crawfish: see CRAYFISH.

Crawford, Isabella Valancy, 1850–87, Canadian poet, b. Ireland. Her verse was not recognized until after her death.

Crawford, Thomas, 1813–57, American sculptor, best known for his figure *Armed Freedom* on the dome of the Capitol at Washington.

Crawford, William Harris, 1772–1834, American statesman. U.S. Senator from Ga. (1807–13). U.S. Secretary of War (1815–16) and Secretary of the Treasury (1816–25). Unsuccessful presidential candidate in 1824.

Crawford Notch, steep defile in White Mts., N central N.H., through which Saco R. flows.

Crawfordsville, city (pop. 14,231), W central Ind., S of Lafayette; settled 1822. Center of farm and livestock area. Has printing and publishing firms. WABASH COLLEGE is here.

Crayer, Gaspar de (gäs'pär dŭ krī'ŭr), c.1584–1669, popular Flemish religious and portrait painter, much influenced by Rubens.

crayfish or **crawfish,** fresh-water crustacean smaller than related, similar lobster, and found in most areas except Africa. Usually they live in ponds, streams, or swamps; a few are partially terrestrial. They eat small aquatic animals and carrion. Developing eggs are carried on female's swimming legs.

Crayford, London: see BEXLEY.

Crazy Horse, d. 1877, Indian leader, chief of Oglala Sioux. Aided Sitting Bull in defeat of Custer (1876). Surrendered in 1877 but, accused of planning a revolt, was imprisoned and then stabbed to death with a bayonet when attempting to escape.

cream of tartar, substance obtained from crystalline crust (argol), formed in wine-fermenting tanks. Argol is dissolved, decolorized, and purified and the crystalline product when dried and powdered is cream of tartar. Used in baking and to make ROCHELLE SALT and tartar emetic.

Crébillon, Prosper (prôspĕr' krābĕyō'), 1674–1762, French classical dramatist, author of *Rhadamiste et Zénobie* (1711) and *Catilina* (1748). His son, **Claude Crébillon** (klōd) (Crébillon fils), 1707–77, brought the licentious tale to perfection with *Le Sopha* (1745).

crèche: see DAY NURSERY.

Crécy (krē'sē, Fr. krāsē'), in English also spelled **Cressy,** small town, N France, N of Abbeville. Here in 1346 Edward III of England defeated Philip VI of France in a major battle of Hundred Years War. French nobles were decimated by English longbows, which appeared for first time on Continent. Among combatants were EDWARD THE BLACK PRINCE and the blind king of Bohemia, JOHN OF LUXEMBURG.

Credi, Lorenzo di: see LORENZO DI CREDI.

credit, financial system to facilitate transfer of capital from those who own it to those who can use it in expectation of profit. Modern business relies heavily on use of credit, from simple delivery of goods with later payment to gigantic loans for building or expanding a business. Little known in ancient world, credit developed with commerce. Excess credit in a community brings inflation; too little, deflation. See DEBT.

Crédit Mobilier of America (krĕ'dĭt mōbēlyā'), ephemeral construction company, connected with building of Union Pacific RR and with one of the major financial scandals in U.S. history. Led by Oakes AMES and Thomas C. DURANT, inner stockholders of Union Pacific set up Crédit Mobilier and made contracts with themselves, at profits of $7,000,000–$23,000,000. To forestall investigations or interference by Congress, Ames sold or assigned shares of stock to members of Congress at par, though shares were worth twice as much. Scandal broke during 1872 presidential campaign. Congressional investigation resulted in censures, no prosecutions.

credit union, bank estab. on cooperative basis, usually by association of members of some community or occupational group. Many in U.S. estab. with help of Credit Union National Extension Bureau (founded 1921).

creed [Latin *credo* = I believe], summary of basic doctrines of faith. Several have been of fundamental importance in Christianity. **1** The Nicene Creed, usually said to be a revision at the First Council of Constantinople (381) of the creed adopted by the First Council of Nicaea (325) to settle problems raised by Arianism. Actually the original creed was a simple statement including a declaration on the nature of Christ. The Nicene Creed may have been composed by St. Cyril of Jerusalem. In the Roman Catholic Church since the 9th cent. it has said, "the Holy Ghost . . . Who proceedeth from the Father *and the Son* (*Filioque*)." The Orthodox Church quarrels with the italicized words. **2** See ATHANASIAN CREED. **3** The Apostles' Creed, familiar in most of the more conservative Western churches, probably arose in the 2d or 3d cent. but did not reach its present form before 650. Essentially similar to the Nicene Creed (though simpler), it has two significant differences; it has the statement that Christ descended into Hell, not in the Nicene; it says "resurrection of the body," where the Nicene has "resurrection of the dead." **4** The Augsburg Confession (1530) is the official Lutheran statement, written by Melanchthon, endorsed by Luther. **5** The Thirty-nine Articles is the basic statement of faith for Anglican and Episcopal churches; its present form dates from the reign of Elizabeth I. **6** The Westminster Confession (1645–47) is a pronouncement of Calvinist doctrine in English, basic in the development of Presbyterianism and in Congregationalism.

Cree Indians, tribe, formerly located in Manitoba, of Algonquian linguistic family. One branch, the Plains Cree, moved SW into buffalo territory. Culture of the Woodland Cree (in N) like that of Ojibwa.

Creek Indians, confederacy of more than 50 Indian towns (or tribes) mostly in Ala. and Ga. and mostly of Hokan-Siouan linguistic stock. They had advanced agr. In Creek War of 1813–14, they massacred many at Fort Mims but were defeated by Andrew Jackson. Moved to the Indian Territory, they became one of FIVE CIVILIZED TRIBES.

creeper, name for various small birds with long decurved bills and usually inconspicuous plumage. True creepers (Certhiidae) are Old World family related to wrens and nuthatches; represented by one New World species, the brown creeper and its subspecies. Related are the Mexican or Sierra Madre, Rocky Mt., Sierra, and California creepers.

Crefeld, Germany: see KREFELD.

Crémazie, (Joseph) Octave (krämäzē'), 1822–79, French Canadian poet. Poems were strongly influenced by nationalism and romanticism; of great importance in French Canadian poetry.

crème de menthe, mint-flavored LIQUEUR.

Cremer, Sir William Randal (krē'mŭr), 1828–1908, English pacifist. For his efforts in behalf of international arbitration he was awarded the 1903 Nobel Peace Prize.

Crémieux, Isaac Adolphe (krämyû'), 1796–1880, French minister of justice. Abolished slavery in colonies and secured full citizen's rights for Jews of Algeria. Advocated universal Jewish emancipation and estab. French schools in the Levant.

Cremona (krämō'nä), city (pop. 76,242), Lombardy, N Italy, on Po R., in rich agr. dist. Was Roman colony; independent commune in Middle Ages; conquered by Milan 1344. Famous for violins made by Amati, Guarneri, Stradivari. Impressive main square has cathedral (12th–16th cent.), 13th-cent. town hall.

creole [perhaps from Span. = servant or child], in Latin America, native descendants of French and Spanish conquerors. In S U.S., descendants of French settlers as distinct from "Cajuns," descendants of Acadian exiles. The idea that Creole means part-Negro persons is incorrect though mixed bloods and Negroes may be called Creole.

Creon (krē'ŏn), in Greek legend. **1** Uncle of OEDIPUS. He became regent of Thebes after banishment of Oedipus. Helped Eteocles, son of Oedipus, wrest kingdom from his brother POLYNICES. Forbade funeral rites for Polynices and killed Antigone for defying him. **2** In Euripides' *Medea*, King of Corinth killed by Medea.

creosote (krē'ûsōt), volatile, heavy oily liquid, a strong antiseptic, obtained by distillation of wood tar. Active principle is guaiacol. Creosote oil is used as preservative of timber and meat.

Crépy, Treaty of (krāpē'), 1544, concluded between Emperor Charles V and FRANCIS I of France at Crépy-en-Laonnois (formerly Crespy), N France. Charles renounced claim to Burgundy; Francis renounced claims to Naples, Flanders, Artois.

Crerar, Henry Duncan Graham (krē'rär), 1888–1965. Canadian general in Second World War. After serving as chief of Canadian general staff, and in several commands, he was given command in 1944 of Canadian Army Overseas.

Crerar, John (krēr'är), 1827–89, American capitalist and philanthropist. Provided for the **John Crerar Library**, Chicago, noted scientific and technical reference library with many fine special collections.

Cres (tsûrěs'), Ital. *Cherso*, Adriatic island (130 sq. mi.), off Croatia, Yugoslavia. Ceded by Italy 1947.

Cresap, Michael (krē'săp), 1742–75, American frontiersman and soldier. Accused by some of starting Lord Dunmore's War (1774). In American Revolution he marched his company so fast to support patriots at Boston–550 mi. in 22 days–that he died of exhaustion.

Crescas, Chasdai, 1340–1412, Jewish philosopher of religion, b. Spain. His denial of free will and his doctrine of universal space influenced Spinoza.

Cresilas (krē'sĭlŭs), fl. c.450 B.C., Greek sculptor. His statue of Pericles is the earliest Greek portrait statue that has been identified.

Crespi, Giovanni Battista (jōvän'nē bät-tē'stä krā'spē), c.1575–1632, Italian painter, sculptor, and architect of the Milanese school, also called Il Cerano. Painted life of St. Charles Borromeo.

Crespi, Giuseppe Maria (jōōzěp'pā märē'ä), 1665–1747, Italian painter of the Bolognese school, known for his series of *The Seven Sacraments* (1712; Dresden) and for his spontaneous rendering of genre scenes.

Crespy, Treaty of: see CRÉPY, TREATY OF.

cress: see PEPPERGRASS; WATER CRESS.

Cressida: see TROILUS AND CRESSIDA.

Cressy, France: see CRÉCY.

Crestwood, city (pop. 11,106), E central Mo., a suburb SW of St. Louis.

Cretaceous period (krētā'shŭs), third period of the MESOZOIC ERA of geologic time. It was marked by extensive submergence and vast changes in the earth's surface and life. By middle Cretaceous a seaway extended from the Gulf of Mexico to the Arctic. Late Cretaceous saw uplift and withdrawal of the water; conditions resembling the Carboniferous prevailed, and coal deposits accumulated. Near the close of the period came the Laramide revolution, and the first generation of the Rockies was born. Cretaceous marine life included reptiles, some resembling fish and some of huge size. Dinosaurs were still dominant on land, but primitive mammals were beginning to appear. Before the end of the period such modern plant forms as willow, elm, birch, oak, and maple were abundant. See also GEOLOGIC ERAS, table.

Crete (krēt), Gr. *Krete*, largest island (3,235 sq. mi.; pop. 483,258), of Greece, in the E Mediterranean, c.60 mi. SE of mainland; cap. Canea. Extending c.160 mi. E-W, it is S limit of Aegean Sea. Candia is the largest city. Largely mountainous, it rises to

8,058 ft. in Mt. Ida. Agr. (olive oil, fruit, vegetables); wine growing; stock raising, dairying. There are iron and lignite deposits. Crete's ancient MINOAN CIVILIZATION, named after mythical King MINOS, was one of the world's oldest; it reached its height c.1600 B.C., then ended suddenly and mysteriously. Impressive remains have been found at CNOSSUS. Later Dorian settlers founded many flourishing city states, including Cnossus and Cydonia (modern Canea). Crete became an important trade center but played no vital political part in the Greek world. Conquered by Rome (68–67 B.C.) it later was held by Byzantium (except during Arab occupation, 823–961), then fell to Venice (1204) and to Turkey (1669; last two Venetian forts were ceded 1715). The Cretan insurrection of 1896–97 led to war between Greece and Turkey. Greece was utterly defeated, but the Great Powers forced Turkey to evacuate Crete (1898) and occupied the island until 1909. Union with Greece, proclaimed 1908, became official in 1913. Antimonarchist uprising by followers of VENIZELOS was suppressed after some fighting (1935). In Second World War Crete was held by the Germans (1941–44).

cretinism (krē'tĭnĭzŭm), condition, usually congenital, resulting from lack of thyroid secretion. Cretins are often feeble-minded and dwarfed.

Creusa (krēōō'sû), princess of Corinth: see MEDEA.

Creuse (krûz), department (2,164 sq. mi.; pop. 163,-515), central France, in Marche; cap. Guéret.

Creusot, Le (lù krûzō'), city (pop. 28,700), Saône-et-Loire dept., E central France, in coal-mining region. Seat of large Schneider plants (steel and munitions).

crevasse (krŭvăs'), crack in surface of a glacier caused by stresses developed as ice moves. The word is also applied to a crack in a river levee.

Crèvecœur, J. Hector St. John (krĕvkûr'), 1735–1813, American author and agriculturist, b. France. He introduced culture of European crops in America and wrote *Letters from an American Farmer* (1782).

Crewe (krōō), municipal borough (pop. 53,394), Cheshire, England; an important railway junction.

Crichton, James (krī'tùn), 1560?–1583? Scottish adventurer and scholar, called the Admirable Crichton. Attracted much attention in Italy (1579) by personal charms and scholarship; reputedly spoke 12 languages. Was killed in a street brawl.

Crick, Francis Harry Compton, 1916–, British scientist. Shared 1962 Nobel Prize in Physiology and Medicine for work in establishing structure and function of nucleic acid.

cricket, insect of order Orthoptera related to grasshopper and katydid. Typical species have long antennae and powerful hind legs. Some are winged. Most are nocturnal. They often destroy vegetation; some also eat insects. Males "chirp" by rubbing one front wing against other, causing vibration; pitch and rate vary with temperature.

cricket, national sport of England. Played with bats and ball by two opposing teams of 11 men on level, closely cut green turf preferably measuring about 525 ft. by about 550 ft., with two wickets 66 ft. apart. Cricket was played in medieval England. London Cricket Club drew up (1774) first authoritative set of rules. Marylebone Cricket Club, governing body of game, founded 1787.

Crile, George Washington (krīl), 1864–1943, American surgeon. He was an authority on thyroid operations and surgical shock and author of technical and popular scientific works.

crime: see CRIMINAL LAW, CRIMINOLOGY, JUVENILE DELINQUENCY, ORGANIZED CRIME.

Crimea (krīmē'ù), Rus. *Krim*, anc. *Chersonesus Taurica*, peninsula, Ukrainian SSR, on N shore of Black Sea, connected to mainland by PEREKOP Isthmus. It forms an oblast (9,924 sq. mi.; 1965 est. pop. 1,509,000), with Simferopol its cap. Other cities are Sevastopol, Kerch, Feodosiya, and Eupatoria. Consists of wheat and cotton-growing steppe in N; Crimean or Yaila Mts. (highest point 5,062 ft.) in

S; and subtropical littoral ("Russian Riviera"), growing fruit, wine, tobacco, with famous resorts such as Yalta. KERCH peninsula (E) has mineral wealth and heavy industries. Early inhabitants, Cimmerians, were followed in 8th cent. B.C. by Scythians. Coast was colonized by Ionian Greeks 7th cent. B.C. Ruled by a Thracian dynasty after 438 B.C., the "kingdom of the Cimmerian Bosporus" was annexed c.110 B.C. by Mithridates VI of Pontus and soon afterward by Rome. Between 3d and 13th cent. A.D. the Crimea was overrun by Goths, Huns, Khazars, Cumans, Mongols. Coast was controlled by Byzantium 6th–12th cent., then by Genoa, which set up prosperous colonies, notably at FEODOSIYA. In 1475 Crimea fell to the TATARS, whose khans were vassals to Ottoman sultans from 1478. From their cap. at BAKHCHISARAI the khans conquered ports of S Russia, pushed their raids as far as Moscow and Poland. In 1774 Catherine II forced Turkey to declare the khanate independent; in 1783 she annexed it to Russia. Many Russian, Greek, and other settlers came. The Crimea was a battleground in the Crimean War (1854–56), in both world wars, and in the Russian civil war, when in 1920 it became the last refuge of the Whites. Its status as autonomous soviet republic, created 1921, was abolished after Second World War, and it was made into an oblast of RSFSR 1945. The Tatar population, charged with aiding the Germans, was deported. In 1954 Crimea was transferred to Ukrainian SSR. The population is now largely Russian and Ukrainian.

Crimean War (krīmē′ùn), 1853–56, between Russia and allied powers of Turkey, England, France, Sardinia. General causes: see EASTERN QUESTION. Pretext: quarrel between Russia and France over guardianship of Palestinian holy places. Turkey having turned down Russian demands, Russia occupied Moldavia and Walachia, and Turkey declared war (1853). France and England joined Turkey in 1854; Sardinia in 1855. Main campaign, centered on siege of SEVASTOPOL in Crimea, was marked by futile gallantry (e.g., battle of BALAKLAVA) and scandalous condition of hospitals (which prompted the work of Florence NIGHTINGALE). Peace treaty (see PARIS, CONGRESS OF) checked Russian influence in SE Europe.

criminal law, distinct body of legal rules governing the definition and trial of crimes (acts deemed detrimental to the state), a part of public law. The state rather than a private individual seeks out and punishes the offender. In England criminal law developed out of common law; principles brought by settlers to British American colonies. In U.S. some important fundamental rules are: no act is a crime unless defined as such in law; accused is considered innocent until proved guilty; bills of attainder (legislative decrees declaring guilt without trial) and *ex post facto* laws (which define as crimes acts committed before the law was adopted) are expressly forbidden. Statutes generally define degrees of criminal acts denominated as FELONY or MISDEMEANOR according to degrees of seriousness (e.g., grand larceny, petty larceny). Crime generally requires an intent to commit, but most minor crime (e.g., traffic violations) requires no intent.

criminology, study of crime, its causes and prevention; a branch of sociology. Criminologists define crime as violation of social rules forbidden by law and susceptible to punishment. Study embraces environmental, hereditary, psychological causes; modes of investigation and conviction; and efficacy of punishment. While the greater attention is given to cause and prevention, the emphasis has shifted from punishment to rehabilitation.

crinoid (krī′noid, krī′–), marine animal, an echinoderm of class Crinoidea, related to starfish and sea urchin, and found in deep sea and tropical waters. Crinoids include sea lily and feather star. The body is usually a central disk with plumelike arms; many forms have stalks.

Cripple Creek, city (pop. 614), central Colo., SW of Colorado Springs. Discovery of gold made it one of richest camps of famous gold-mine area. Gold production declined after 1901, but some mining still carried on. Miners' strikes (1893, 1904) marked by violence.

Cripps, Sir Stafford, 1889–1952, British statesman; nephew of Beatrice Webb. Brilliant lawyer, was solicitor general in Labour government 1930–31. Expelled from Labour party 1939 for urging united front with communists; readmitted 1945. Under Churchill was ambassador to USSR (1940), lord privy seal and leader in Commons (1942), and envoy to India (1942) with self-government plan. In Labour government initiated (1945) Britain's austerity program. As minister of economic affairs and chancellor of exchequer (1947–50) virtually controlled British economy until ill health forced his resignation.

Crispi, Francesco (fränchä′skō krē′spē), 1819–1901, Italian premier (1887–91, 1893–96). Fostered colonial expansion; lost office after defeat at ADUWA.

Crispin and Crispinian, Saints, 3d cent., missionaries in Gaul martyred under Diocletian. They were brothers, both shoemakers. Feast: Oct. 25. The "Crispin Crispinian" speech in Shakespeare's *Henry V*, Act IV, refers to the feast.

Crispus, Christian converted by St. Paul. Acts 18.8; I Cor. 1.14.

Cristobal (krĭstō′bùl), Span. *Cristóbal* (krēstō′bäl), town (pop. c.800), Panama Canal Zone, near the Atlantic end of Canal; American residential quarter for Colón.

Cristus, Petrus: see CHRISTUS, PETRUS.

criticism, judging or evaluating works of art or literature. Aristotle's *Poetics* is considered the first major work of criticism. In all fields, however, canons have changed with the differing tastes of the period. By the early 20th cent., neo-humanism was rivaled by economic and sociological theories of interpretation. Psychology and semantics have strongly affected recent criticism.

Critius (krī′shùs) and **Nesiotes** (nēshēō′tēz), 5th cent. B.C., Greek sculptors during the Persian Wars.

Crittenden, John Jordan, 1787–1863, American statesman. U.S. Attorney General (1841, 1850–53). In 1855–61 term as U.S. Senator from Ky., tried to conciliate North and South by **Crittenden Compromise,** proposal to settle slavery issue through constitutional amendments, including restoration of Missouri Compromise line; plan was defeated.

Crivelli, Carlo (krēvĕl′lē), b. c.1430, d. after 1493, Venetian religious painter, active in the Marches. His *Pietà* in Metropolitan Mus.

Crna Gora, Yugoslavia: see MONTENEGRO.

Croaghpatrick (krō′äpä′trĭk), mountain, Co. Mayo, Ireland. Connected by legend with St. Patrick, its summit has long been a place of pilgrimage.

croaker, family of fishes which includes weakfish, spot, drum, whiting; named for noise they make. Valuable as food.

Croatan (krō″ùtăn′), unexplained word derived incorrectly from letters CROATOAN, which were found carved on tree of ROANOKE ISLAND in 17th cent., claimed by some to indicate that the "lost colony" had joined Indians.

Croatia (krōā′shù), Croatian *Hrvatska,* autonomous republic (21,824 sq. mi.; pop. 4,148,122), NW Yugoslavia; cap. Zagreb. W section is crossed by DINARIC ALPS; E part is agr. plain, drained by Sava and Drava rivers. Republic consists of Croatia proper, SLAVONIA, DALMATIA, most of ISTRIA. Chief cities: ZAGREB, RIJEKA, OSIJEK, SPLIT, ZADAR. Part of Pannonia prov. under Rome, region was settled in 7th cent. by Slavic Croats, who accepted Roman Catholicism (9th cent.) and set up a kingdom (10th cent.). From 1091 to 1918 (except during Turkish occupation, 1526–1699; French occupation, 1809–13; and Austrian annexation, 1849–68), Croatia was in personal union with Hungary–i.e., the kings of Hungary were also kings of Croatia, which, however, was governed by native bans and had its own diet. United with Serbia in 1918 (see YUGOSLAVIA), Croatia despite intense nationalist agitation secured autonomy only in 1939. After Germany invaded Yugoslavia (1941), Croatia was seized by the nationalist-terrorist group Ustachi and placed under Italian military control; it passed to the Germans in 1943. A large part of the people fought with the Yugoslav partisans. Croatia became a constituent republic of Yugoslavia in 1946.

Croce, Benedetto (bānädĕt'tō krō'chä), 1866–1952, Italian philosopher, historian, and critic. His broad idealistic thought is reflected in *Philosophy of the Spirit* (1902–17). Tended to relate philosophy to history and history with liberty; spoke of four aspects of spirit: the aesthetic, logical, economic, and ethical. Minister of education 1920–21; lived in retirement under Fascism.

Crocker, William, 1876–1950, American botanist, director of Boyce Thompson Inst. for Plant Research 1921–49. Known for research on plant growth.

Crockett, David (Davy), 1786–1836, American frontiersman. U.S. Representative from Tenn. (1827–31, 1833–35), known for backwoods humor. Died at the ALAMO. Supposed author of autobiographical exploits.

Crockett, town (pop. 5,356), E Texas. SSE of Palestine. in farm area; founded in 1830s. Replica of first Spanish mission (c.1690) in E Texas is near.

crocodile (krŏ'kŭdīl), large carnivorous reptile of order Crocodilia. It has tough scales on top, bony plates underneath, powerful jaws, short legs, and a vertically flattened tail. American species, inhabiting fresh (sometimes salt) water near S Fla., in West Indies, and Central and N South America, is not hostile to humans.

crocus, low plant of genus *Crocus,* with grasslike foliage and purple, yellow, or white flowers (usually goblet shaped) in spring or autumn. See also MEADOW SAFFRON; SAFFRON.

Croesus (krē'sús), d. c.547 B.C., king of Lydia after 560 B.C. He was to the Greeks a symbol of wealth. Allied himself with Egypt and Babylonia against Cyrus the Great of Persia and was defeated and captured.

Croghan, George (krō'gún), d. 1782, American Indian agent, b. Ireland. Became deputy superintendent of Indian Affairs in 1756 under Sir William Johnson. Responsible for much of Johnson's success.

Croker, Richard, 1841–1922, American politician, boss of Tammany Hall (1886–1902), b. Ireland. Abdicated after Tammany defeat in 1901 election.

Cro-Magnon man: see MAN, PREHISTORIC.

Cromarty, county: see ROSS AND CROMARTY.

Cromarty Firth, deep narrow inlet of Firth of Moray in Ross and Cromarty co., Scotland. An excellent anchorage. it was a naval base in First World War.

Crome, John, 1768–1821, English landscape painter, founder of Norwich School; often called Old Crome. Influenced by Gainsborough and Dutch masters.

Cromer, Evelyn Baring, 1st earl of, 1841–1917, British administrator and diplomat in Egypt. Was virtual ruler 1883–1907, reforming Egyptian finances, administration, and education.

Crommelynck, Fernand (fĕrnä' krômùlĕk'), 1888–, Belgian poet and dramatist, author of tragic farce *Le Cocu magnifique* (1921).

Crompton, Samuel, 1753–1827, English inventor of the mule spinner, a device used in spinning fine cotton. which combined features of Hargreaves's jenny and Arkwright's frame to produce fine yarn.

Cromwell, Oliver, 1599–1658, lord protector of England. Was strong Puritan in Parliament. Prominent in PURITAN REVOLUTION because of military ability (esp. at Edgehill 1642 and Marston Moor 1644). In struggle between largely Presbyterian Parliament and Puritan army, he proposed army reorganization (1644). Given command with Baron Fairfax; defeated Charles I at Naseby. After flight of Charles in 1645, he lost hope of dealing with king and was

leader in demand for his execution. Led cruelly punitive expedition to Ireland (1649) where he continued policy of settling English. Invaded Scotland 1650; defeated Charles II and royalist Scots. Dissolved Rump Parliament 1653; tried to replace it with feeble Barebone's Parliament appointed by himself. PROTECTORATE estab. 1653 with Cromwell as lord protector. Declined the crown 1657. New constitution (1657) strengthened his powers. Tried to build up Protestant league abroad but policy was governed by need for foreign trade. Navigation Act (1651) led to first DUTCH WAR (1652–54). War with Spain (1655–58) was over trade rights. Opinions of him vary widely. Favored religious toleration and democracy, but tolerated only Jews and non-Anglican Protestants and could not work with Parliament. His military genius and force of character are recognized but necessities of governing forced him into cruelty and intolerance. Dependence of Protectorate on him was shown when his son, **Richard Cromwell,** 1626–1712, succeeded him as lord protector, 1658. Army and Parliament struggled for power until Commonwealth was reestab. 1659. He lived abroad, 1660–80, and later in England under assumed name. A man of virtue and dignity, he was forced into a situation beyond his talents.

Cromwell, Thomas, earl of Essex, 1485?–1540, English statesman. Legal secretary to Cardinal Wolsey; avoided implication in his fall and attracted attention of Henry VIII. Carried out suppression of monasteries (some of whose wealth he received). Made lord great chamberlain 1539; negotiated Henry's marriage to Anne of Cleves to secure German alliance. This failed and he was convicted of treason and heresy and beheaded.

Cronaca, Il: see POLLAIUOLO.

Cronje, Piet Arnoldus (pēt' ärnôl'dús krōn'yä). 1835?–1911. Boer commander in Transvaal in South African War.

Cronstadt, RSFSR: see KRONSTADT.

Cronstedt, Axel Fredrik, Baron (äk'súl frä'drĭk krōōn'stĕt), 1722–65, Swedish mineralogist. Discovered nickel in niccolite; one of first to recognize importance of chemical constituents of minerals.

Cronus (krō'nús), Gr. *Kronos* [time], in Greek legend, the youngest TITAN, son of URANUS [heaven] and GAEA [earth]. He led Titans in revolt against Uranus and ruled the world. Father by RHEA of the great gods—ZEUS, Poseidon, Demeter, Hera, and Hestia. Fated to be overthrown by one of his children, he tried unsuccessfully to destroy them. Zeus later led the Olympian gods against his father in successful revolt called TITANOMACHY. He is equated with Roman Saturn.

Crook, George, 1828–90, U.S. general. An able Indian fighter, especially against Paiute and Snake Indians in Idaho, in Sioux War of 1876, and against Apaches under Geronimo. Noted for patience and integrity in dealing peaceably with Indians.

Crookes, Sir William (krōōks), 1832–1919, English chemist. physicist. He discovered thallium; invented the spinthariscope (fluorescent screen on which alpha particles from a radioactive substance produce light flashes); devised a radiometer and protective spectacles. Worked with rare earths and psychic phenomena. His **Crookes tube** made possible important discoveries in electricity and ionization.

Crookston, city (pop. 8,546). NW Minn.. on Red River L.. WSW of Grand Forks, N.Dak.; settled 1872. Northwest School of Agr. of the state university is here.

croquet (krōkā'), lawn game in which players hit wooden balls with wooden mallets through series of wire arches (9 or 10). A favorite game in Ireland in 18th cent., also popular in France, England, U.S.

Crosby, Bing, 1904–, American singer and film actor, whose real name is Harry Lillis Crosby. Became popular as a singer with dance bands after 1925. He was an enormous success on radio after 1931 and in films (e.g., *Going My Way*).

Cross, Charles Frederick, 1855–1935, English chemist. With E. J. Bevan he patented VISCOSE PROCESS (1882) of preparing artificial silk (RAYON) from cellulose.

Cross, Wilbur L(ucius), 1862–1948, American educator and public official. Professor of English at Yale (1902–30); dean of graduate school (1916–30); authority on the English novel. As Democratic governor of Conn. (1931–39), he brought about much reform legislation.

crossbow: see BOW AND ARROW.

Crothers, Rachel (krŭ'dhùrz), 1878–1958, American dramatist. Her plays included *A Man's World* (1909), *Let Us Be Gay* (1929), and *Susan and God* (1937).

Croton (krō'tùn), short river, SE N.Y., flowing partly in three branches S and SW to Hudson R. near Ossining. New Croton Dam at Croton L. impounds waters for diversion to CROTON AQUEDUCT.

Crotona (krōtō'nù), anc. city, S Italy, on E coast of Calabria, a city founded (8th cent.) by Greeks. Reached its height in 6th cent. B.C., when Pythagoras had his school here and the army, led by the athlete Milo, defeated Sybaris (510 B.C.). Declined later. Called Cotrone from Middle Ages to 1928.

Croton Aqueduct, 38 mi. long, SE N.Y., carrying water from Croton basin to New York city; built 1837–42. Begins at Croton L., follows Croton R. to Hudson R., Hudson R. to Yonkers, and crosses Harlem R. to Manhattan. Supplemented by second aqueduct (built 1885–91), c.30½ mi. long, passing under Harlem R.

Croton-on-Hudson, residential village (1966 pop. 7,039), SE N.Y., on E bank of Hudson R., NNW of Ossining; settled 1609. Stephanus Van Cortlandt Manor is here.

crow, partially migratory black bird of same family as the raven, magpie, jay, rook, and European jackdaw. American or eastern crow is c.19 in. long with wingspread of c.3 ft. It destroys injurious insects and rodents, but also eats some eggs, nestlings, and grain. It is easily tamed.

crowberry, low, alpine evergreen plant (*Empetrum*), with berrylike fruits. It is suited to rockeries.

crowfoot: see BUTTERCUP.

Crow Indians or **Absaroka,** tribe ranging chiefly about Yellowstone R., of Hokan-Siouan linguistic stock. Had typical Plains culture.

Crowley. 1 Alternate name of Visalia North, Calif.: see VISALIA. **2** City (pop. 15,617), SW La., WSW of Baton Rouge; founded 1886. Shipping, milling, and storing center for one of largest rice-growing areas in U.S. Oil and natural gas also produced.

Crown Point, town (pop. 1,685), NE N.Y., on L. Champlain N of Ticonderoga. Summer resort. Champlain supported Hurons in battle with Iroquois nearby, 1609. French fort, built 1731 at this strategic point on N.Y.-to-Canada route, was demolished 1759 in French and Indian Wars. British fort, built 1759, was captured by Green Mountain Boys (1775) but abandoned to Gen. Burgoyne in Saratoga campaign (1777). Crown Point Reservation, with recreational facilities, is here.

Croydon, London borough since 1965 (est. pop. 328,-890); includes former county borough of Croydon and urban district of Coulsdon and Purley.

Cruden, Alexander, 1701–1770, British scholar, a London bookseller and proofreader. His *Complete Concordance to the Holy Scriptures* (1737) is basis of later biblical concordances.

Cruikshank, George (krŏŏk'–), 1792–1878, English caricaturist and illustrator. Etchings include notable illustrations for *Oliver Twist*.

cruiser, large, fast, moderately armed warship, intermediate between battleship and destroyer. Modern cruisers fall in two classes: battle cruisers (in effect small battleships, representing an effort to combine maximum gun caliber, armor protection, and speed); and light cruisers (of moderate tonnage, lightly armed, and very fast).

Crusades, wars undertaken by European Christians between 11th and 14th cent. to recover the Holy Land, particularly JERUSALEM, from Islam. The movement began in France, when Pope URBAN II at the Council of Clermont (1095) exhorted Christendom to war, promising that the journey would count as full penance and that a general truce would protect the homes of the absent ones. From the crosses distributed at this meeting the Crusaders took their name. Religious motives dominated at first, but worldly considerations were never absent, and the conflict between spiritual and material aims grew increasingly serious: the nobles hoped for loot and territorial aggrandizement; the Italian cities expanded trade with the Near East; all were lured by travel and adventure. The First Crusade, 1095–99, began with the march of several undisciplined hordes of French and German peasants, led by WALTER THE PENNILESS, PETER THE HERMIT, and others. They started out by massacring the Jews in the Rhineland; incensed the Bulgarians and Hungarians, who attacked and dispersed them; reached Constantinople in shreds; crossed over to Asia Minor; and were promptly defeated by the Turks. The organized host, led by Count RAYMOND IV of Toulouse, GODFREY OF BOUILLON, BOHEMOND, and TANCRED, followed in 1097. All save Raymond and Tancred swore fealty to the Byzantine Emperor, ALEXIUS I, binding themselves to accept him as overlord of their conquests. Their victorious campaign was crowned by the conquest of Jerusalem (1099). The establishment of the Latin Kingdom of JERUSALEM and of the orders of KNIGHTS HOSPITALERS and KNIGHTS TEMPLARS followed. The Second Crusade, 1147–49, preached by St. BERNARD OF CLAIRVAUX after the fall of EDESSA (1144) was led by Emperor Conrad III and by Louis VII of France. It ended in dismal failure. In 1187 SALADIN captured Jerusalem. The Third Crusade, 1189–92, led by Emperor FREDERICK I, PHILIP II of France, and RICHARD I of England, failed to recapture the city, but Richard I negotiated a truce by which Christians were granted free access to the Holy Sepulchre. The Fourth Crusade, 1202–4, began in France but was completely diverted from its purpose by its leader, Enrico Dandolo, for the benefit of Venice. To pay for their passage, the Crusaders assisted the Venetians to recover Zara from Hungary (1202). Despite violent papal condemnation after the sack of that Christian city, the host next turned toward Constantinople, ostensibly to restore ISAAC II on his throne. In 1204 they stormed and sacked the city, divided the spoils with Venice, and set up the Latin Empire of CONSTANTINOPLE. The pathetic Children's Crusade of 1212 was preached by a visionary French peasant boy, Stephen of Cloyes. Thousands of children set out for Holy Land but instead were sold into slavery by unscrupulous skippers. Another group, of German children, made their way by land; they perished of hunger and disease. The Fifth Crusade, 1217–21, preached by Innocent III, was aimed at Egypt and failed. The Sixth Crusade, 1228–29, undertaken by Emperor FREDERICK II, was actually a peaceful visit. Frederick made a truce with the Moslems, securing the surrender of the Holy Places. Sporadic warfare soon broke out again. The Christian rout by the Egyptian MAMELUKES at Gaza (1244) led to the Seventh Crusade, 1248–54, led by Louis IX of France. Despite Louis's gallantry, the enterprise failed; his death cut short the Eighth Crusade (1270). The Ninth Crusade, 1271–72, led by Prince Edward (later Edward I of England) was abortive. In 1291 Acre, the last Christian stronghold, fell. The term *crusade* was also applied to other expeditions, sanctioned by the pope, against heretics and heathens (e.g., the WENDS, the ALBIGENSES) and, more loosely, to campaigns of the 15th–16th cent. against the Turks.

crustacean (krŭstā'shùn), animal of class Crustacea of phylum Arthropoda. Examples are CRAB, LOBSTER, SHRIMP, CRAYFISH, BARNACLE, water flea or daphnia, cyclops, pill bug, sow bug. They have jointed appendages and a horny outer skeleton. Breathing organs are gills. Colorless blood usually circulated by a heart. Some are omnivorous, some eat flesh only, some plants only. Many are parasites.

Cruveilhier, Jean (zhä' krüvēyā'), 1791–1874, French physician, pioneer in descriptive pathology.

Cruz, Juana Inés de la: see JUANA INÉS DE LA CRUZ.

Cruz, Oswaldo or Osvaldo, 1872–1917, Brazilian public health officer. Cleared Brazilian cities of smallpox, yellow fever, bubonic plague.

Cruz, Ramón de la (rämōn' dä lä krōōth'), 1731–94, Spanish dramatist. Best known for *sainetes*, one-act realistic comedies of lower-class life in Madrid. Also wrote tragedies and a Spanish version of *Hamlet*.

cryolite or kryolite (krī'ŭlīt), a mineral, fluoride of sodium and aluminum, used in making lampshades, hard glass, porcelain. Found in Greenland.

cryosurgery, use of extreme cold to kill diseased tissue instead of cutting it away. A chilling fluid (e.g., liquid nitrogen) courses through a probe inserted through a body aperture and placed against diseased tissue. May be used in such operations as tonsillectomies and brain surgery.

cryotron, tiny electronic device comprising two wires, one straight, the other coiled around it. At temperatures near absolute zero both are superconductors; when current is passed through coil, straight wire becomes semiconductor. Used in computers and instruments in artificial satellites.

cryptography (krīptŏg'grŭfē) [Gr.,= hidden writing], art of secret writing, employed from anc. times. A cryptogram is a secret message and also the form in which it is couched. The term cryptography strictly applies to translating messages into cipher or code. In enciphering, each letter of the message is replaced by another letter or figure; in encoding, syllables, words, or whole sentences are treated. The code is the agreed upon set of rules whereby messages are converted from one form to another. The art of breaking codes and ciphers without the key is called cryptanalysis. In the last few decades mathematical theory has been applied in cryptanalysis. A famous cipher was that devised by Francis Bacon (1605). In modern times official government cryptography, the solution of cryptograms, and even the general methods employed are jealously controlled by governments, since codes and ciphers are used for secret messages in peacetime as well as in war.

Crystal, village (1965 pop. 29,089), SE Minn., a suburb NW of Minneapolis.

crystal, solid having definite internal structure owing to atomic arrangement and definite external form (polyhedron bounded by natural plane surfaces) which is the manifestation of its internal structure. Crystallization is the assumption of crystal form when a substance passes from liquid or gaseous state to solid state or when it goes out of solution. Crystalline species are grouped, according to their type of symmetry, into 32 classes, which in turn are grouped into six systems: cubic or isometric, hexagonal, tetragonal, orthorhombic, monoclinic, triclinic.

Crystal Lake, resort city (1965 pop. 10,211), NE Ill., NW of Chicago, in farm area; settled 1836.

Crystal Palace, building erected in Hyde Park, London, for the Great Exhibition in 1851. Served for a time as a museum. Almost entirely destroyed by fire 1936. South Tower demolished 1940; North Tower 1941.

Cs, chemical symbol of the element CESIUM.

Csaba, Hungary: see BEKESCSABA.

Csepel (chĕ'pĕl), city, N central Hungary, on Csepel Island (30 mi. long), in the Danube. Industrial suburb of Budapest; has iron and steel works, oil refineries, munitions factories.

Ctesibius (tīsī'bēŭs), fl. 2d cent. B.C., Alexandrian Greek inventor. Reputedly first to discover and use energy of expanding air. Devised water clock, hydraulic organ, force pump.

Ctesiphon (tĕ'sĭfŏn), ruined anc. city, near Baghdad, Iraq, on the Tigris at mouth of the Diyala. Winter residence of Parthian kings, cap. of Sassanidae.

Cu, chemical symbol of the element COPPER.

Cuanza (kwän'zä), river rising in central Angola, flowing c.600 mi. NW and W to Atlantic. Hydroelectric power and irrigation potential.

Cuauhtémoc (kŏō-outä'môk), d. 1525, Aztec emperor. After the Spanish were driven from the Aztec cap., he fought valiantly until the city was taken and he was made captive. Taken along on the march to Honduras, he was hanged by order of Cortés. Also spelled Cuauhtemoctzín, Guatémoc, Quauhtémoc.

Cuba (kū'bŭ, Span. kōō'vä), republic (44,218 sq. mi.; 1965 est. pop. 7,434,200, incl. the Isle of Pines), occupying all the island of Cuba, westernmost and largest of the West Indies; cap. HAVANA (largest city). The island (c.700 mi. long, averaging 50 mi. in breadth) lies at the entrance to the Gulf of Mexico, with the Atlantic on the N, the Caribbean on the S; its W tip is 90 mi. from Key West, Fla. The chief ports besides Havana are SANTIAGO DE CUBA, MATANZAS, CIENFUEGOS, and GUANTÁNAMO. The mountains (in several groups) have deposits of iron, manganese, copper, nickel, chromium, and barite, and the forests of the interior yield timber and naval stores; but Cuba has been mainly dependent for exports on sugar, fine tobacco, and coffee. Other products are tropical fruits, henequen, sponges, hides, and winter vegetables. After discovery by Columbus (1492), Cuba was explored by the Spanish, and by 1511 a colony was firmly planted. Expeditions went out to conquer other territories (notably Mexico), and the island, "the Pearl of the Antilles," was a gathering point for Spanish treasure fleets from the New World. It was much harassed by French and English buccaneers. The native Arawak Indians soon died out, and the sugar plantations were worked with the labor of imported Negroes. The Negro element has contributed much to Cuban life. In the early 19th cent., when most of Latin America won independence from Spain, Cuba remained in the empire. There were intermittent revolts and filibustering expeditions, rising to a climax in the TEN YEARS WAR (1868–78). Spain retained control until a new revolt precipitated the SPANISH-AMERICAN WAR (1898), in which Cuba gained independence with U.S. help. Its history thereafter was dominated by the question of relationship with the U.S. and with the problem of a one-crop economy. U.S. military occupation of the island lasted until 1902, and the Platt Amendment (see PLATT, ORVILLE H.) giving the U.S. the right to intervene led to new occupations (1906–9, 1912). U.S. citizens owned many plantations and industries, and "Yankee imperialism" in Cuba was much decried in Latin America until a new basis for relationship was estab. in the administration of F. D. Roosevelt. Sugar boom in the First World War led to false prosperity ("the dance of the millions") and then almost total collapse. Diversification of agr. has been forwarded to avoid the ills of one-crop economy. Political life in Cuba has been stormy and intermittently marked by dictatorships (e.g., that of Gerardo Machado). Fulgencio BATISTA dominated the political scene for most of the years after 1933. In 1958 his dictatorial government was overthrown by the "26 of July" revolutionary army led by Fidel CASTRO. The new government executed many Batista followers and undertook reforms (including land expropriation). Relations with U.S. worsened as Castro government moved toward Communism. U.S. broke off diplomatic relations Jan., 1961; aided Cuban rebels in unsuccessful invasion, April, 1961. Major world crisis occurred 1962 when U.S. demanded and obtained withdrawal of Soviet missiles from Cuba. Despite economic problems, Castro continued to lead government in 1966.

Cubango: see OKAVANGO.

cubeb (kū′běb), dried, unripe berry of a climbing pepper plant, *Piper cubeba*, native to East and West Indies. Used medicinally and as a condiment.

cube root, see ROOT, in mathematics.

cubism, early form of ABSTRACT ART, emphasizing the breaking down of forms into angular planes, with the planes superimposed and rearranged. Developed in Paris c.1909 by Picasso and Braque. Other cubists were Gris and Léger. Highly influential in breaking old representational patterns in art.

Cuchulain (kōō′hōōlĭn, kōōkŭ′lĭn) [Irish,= the hound of Culan], Irish legendary hero of Ulster. He is central figure of Ulster legends, of which greatest is *Táin Bó Cúalnge* [the cattle raid of Cooley], wherein he defends his province singlehanded.

cuckoo (kōō′kōō), name for certain birds abundant in tropics, widespread in both hemispheres except in colder regions. They are usually insectivorous, arboreal, and have slightly decurved bills, long tails, and usually dull plumage. Many cuckoos make no nests but lay eggs in nests of other birds. Family includes ROAD RUNNER, ani, trogon, and KINGFISHER. Blackbilled and yellow-billed cuckoos of U.S. are slender, long-billed, olive-brown birds which eat destructive insects. Maynard's cuckoo and California cuckoo are other related birds. The cuckoo has featured largely in English literature as early herald of spring from Middle English "Sumer Is Icumen In," through Wordsworth, to present day.

cucumber, fruit of *Cucumis sativus,* an annual vine. It is eaten either raw or pickled.

cucumber tree: see MAGNOLIA.

Cúcuta (kōō′kōōtä), city (pop. c.137,000), NE Colombia, c.10 mi. from Venezuelan border on E cordillera of Andes, in coffee-raising region. Congress of 1821 met here to draft constitution for Greater Colombia.

Cudahy (kŭ′dŭhē), city (pop. 17,975), SE Wis., suburb SSE of Milwaukee on L. Michigan. Has meatpacking industry.

Cuenca (kwĕng′kä), city (pop. c.62,000; alt. c.8,000 ft.), S central Ecuador; founded 1557. In rich agr. basin of Ecuadorian Andes, it produces grains, subsistence crops, and cattle. Panama hats are woven here.

Cuenca, town (pop. 27,007), cap. of Cuenca prov., E central Spain, in New Castile. Medieval castle; 13th-cent. cathedral.

Cuernavaca (kwĕrnävä′kä), city (pop. 30,567), cap. of Morelos, central Mexico; popular tourist and health resort. Palace built here by Cortés now is decorated with murals by Diego Rivera. Maximilian and Carlotta frequently stayed in Cuernavaca.

Cueva, Beatriz de la (bäätrēs′ dä lä kwä′vä), d. 1541, governor of Guatemala, only woman to govern major American political division in Spanish times. Succeeded her husband, Pedro de Alvarado, to position but was killed a few weeks later in flood.

Cueva, Juan de la (hwän′ dä lä kwä′vä), 1550?–1610?, Spanish dramatist. Liberated Spanish drama from classical conventions. Best known for comedy *El infamador* (1581).

Cui, César (Antonovich): see FIVE, THE.

Cuiabá (kōōyübä′), city (pop. c.58,200), cap. of Mato Grosso state, W Brazil, at head of navigation on Cuiabá R.; founded in gold rush of 18th cent.

Culbertson, Ely (ĕ′lē kŭl′bŭrtsŭn), 1893–1955, American expert on contract bridge, b. Rumania of American-Russian parentage. Became a leading figure in the playing of bridge. After Second World War he wrote and lectured widely on world peace.

Culiacán (kōōlēäkän′), city (pop. c.49,000), cap. of Sinaloa, NW Mexico; founded 1531. It figured prominently in Spanish colonial period as point of departure for expeditions to N, notably that of Coronado (1540). Surrounding area produces tropical fruits, sugar, cotton, some minerals.

Culion (kōōlyôn′), island (150 sq. mi.; pop. 11,237), one of Calamian Isls., Philippines. Has leper colony.

Cullen, Countee, 1903–46, American Negro poet.

Cullman, city (pop. 10,883), N Ala., N of Birmingham. Shipping and trade center for cotton, timber, and dairy region. St. Bernard Col. is here.

Culloden Moor (kŭlô′dŭn), moorland, Inverness-shire, Scotland. Scene of decisive defeat (1746) of Prince Charles Edward Stuart by English troops.

Culpeper or **Colepeper, Thomas Culpeper,** 2d Baron (both: kŭl′pĕ″pŭr), 1635–89, British colonial governor of Va. (1675–83).

Culpeper, town (pop. 2,412), E central Va., WNW of Fredericksburg; founded 1759. Trade and shipping center of rich agr. area. Famous Culpeper minutemen were organized 1775.

cultivation, working soil by means of tools (e.g., hoe, spade) or machinery. Includes mixing, loosening, destroying weeds; aided by IRRIGATION and ROTATION OF CROPS.

culture, in anthropology, the way of life of a society, without implication of refinement or advanced knowledge. Culture is historically transmitted, primarily through language, and is the attribute that most distinguishes man from the animals.

Culver, resort town (pop. 1,558), N central Ind., on L. Maxinkuckee, SSW of South Bend. Culver Military Academy is here.

Culver City, residential and industrial city (pop. 32,-163), S Calif., WSW of Los Angeles; laid out 1913. Center of motion-picture industry.

Cumae (kū′mē), anc. city of Campania, Italy; oldest Greek colony in Italy. It was conquered by Samnites (5th cent. B.C.), later rose and declined under Roman control, disappeared only in 13th cent. A.D.

Cumaná (kōōmänä′), city (pop. c.73,000), NE Venezuela; port on Caribbean. Exports agr. products.

Cumans (kū′mŭnz), nomadic people of Turkic language; also called Kipchaks and, in Russian, Polovtsi. Conquered S Russia and Walachia (11th cent.); warred with Byzantium, Hungary, Kiev. After defeat by Mongols (c.1245), part of Cumans fled to Hungary, where they merged with Magyars.

Cumberland, Richard, 1732–1811, English dramatist, author of sentimental plays such as *The Brothers* (1769), *The West Indian* (1771), *The Wheel of Fortune* (1795).

Cumberland, county (1,520 sq. mi.; pop. 294,162), N England, next to Scotland; co. town Carlisle. Low in N, county is mountainous in SW and E. Scafell Pike (3,210 ft.) highest point in England. Pastoral area, with some mining, quarrying, textile mfg., and smelting. Scene of centuries of border strife between England and Scotland. The region, with Westmorland and Lancashire, known as LAKE DISTRICT, popular with 19th-cent. literary figures.

Cumberland. 1 City (pop. 33,415), NW Md., on North Branch of Potomac R., W of Hagerstown; laid out 1785. Grew around site of trading post estab. 1750 by Ohio Co. at natural gateway through Appalachians to Ohio valley. Fort Cumberland, built several years later, was base of operations for ill-fated Braddock expedition (1755) against French and Indians and site of Washington's first military hq. (1757). City became E terminus of Cumberland or NATIONAL ROAD; division point for Baltimore & Ohio RR.; and W terminus of Chesapeake and Ohio Canal. Now rail and shipping center for coal area. **2** Town (1965 pop. 23, 839), NE R.I., between Blackstone R. and Mass. line. Has Ballou Meetinghouse (c.1740).

Cumberland, river rising in Cumberland plateau, E Ky., and winding c.694 mi. SW then NW through Ky. and Tenn. to Ohio R. above Paducah, Ky. TVA authorized to market power from Wolf Creek Dam (Ky.), Dale Hollow and Center Hill dams (Tenn.). Also has Barkley (Ky.) and Cheatham (Tenn.) dams. Construction begun 1963 on Cordell Hull and J. Percy Priest dams (Tenn.).

Cumberland Gap, natural mountain pass, near point where Va., Ky., and Tenn. meet. Discovered 1750;

WILDERNESS ROAD ran through it. Gap was held by both sides during Civil War. Cumberland Gap Natl. Historical Park estab. 1955.

Cumberland House, Hudson's Bay Co. fur-trading post, on Cumberland L., near The Pas, W Man., Canada. Built 1774 by Samuel Hearne; first permanent settlement on Saskatchewan R. and the company's first interior post. Commanded fur trade and exploration routes to upper Saskatchewan and Churchill rivers.

Cumberland Island: see SEA ISLANDS.

Cumberland Plateau or **Cumberland Mountains**, SW division of Appalachian Mts. Extends NE-SW through S W.Va., SW Va., E Ky., E Tenn., and N Ala. Rises E from Great Valley of E Tenn., and slopes roughly W. Source of Cumberland and other rivers. Has coal and other minerals and beautiful forest areas.

Cumberland Presbyterian Church, branch of Presbyterian Church in U.S. It arose as revival movement in "Cumberland country" of Tenn. and Ky. Its presbytery was dissolved by synod but reorganized (1810) as independent body. Negro organization set apart (1869) as Colored Cumberland Presbyterian Church.

Cumberland Road: see NATIONAL ROAD.

Cumberland Valley, part of great Appalachian valley, N of Shenandoah Valley, extending from Potomac R. in Md. to the Susquehanna R. in Pa.

cumin (kŭm′ĭn), low annual herb (*Cuminum cyminum*) with threadlike foliage; native to Mediterranean region. Seedlike aromatic fruits used in bread, soup, and cheese; oil used in liqueurs.

Cummings, E(dward) E(stlin), 1894–1962, American poet. *The Enormous Room* (1922), in prose, concerns his war internment in France. In his lyric poems he emphasizes eccentric typography and punctuation.

Cummings, Homer S(tillé), 1870–1956, U.S. Attorney General (1933–39). Strong supporter of New Deal.

Cummington, rural town (pop. 550), W Mass., in hills E of Pittsfield. Marcus Whitman lived here; W. C. Bryant born here (his house is museum).

Cunard, Sir Samuel (kūnärd′), 1787–1865, Canadian pioneer of regular transatlantic steam navigation. With others he formed company which in 1840 initiated first regular mail service between North America and Britain. This was beginning of Cunard Line, which was united with White Star Line in 1934.

Cunaxa (kūnăk′sù), town, Babylonia, near the Euphrates; scene of victory (401 B.C.) of Artaxerxes II over Cyrus the Younger—victory only because Cyrus had been killed. The retreat of the Ten Thousand after the battle is told in the ANABASIS.

cuneiform (kūnē′ĭfôrm) [Latin,= wedge shaped], writing developed in lower Tigris and Euphrates valley, probably by Sumerians. Characters consist of arrangements of wedgelike strokes impressed on wet clay tablets. History of the script is much like that of Egyptian HIEROGLYPHIC (see also ALPHABET; INSCRIPTION). Babylonians and Assyrians used cuneiform writing extensively, but it existed outside Mesopotamia, notably in ELAM and among the HITTITES. A very late use was in the syllabary developed for Old Persian, and written in the era of the Achaemenidae, whose greatest monument is that of Darius I at BEHISTUN. Key finds have been made at Nineveh, Lagash, Erech, Tel-el-Amarna, Susa, and Boghazkeui. The Assyrian king Assur-bani-pal had a huge cuneiform library at Nineveh. Sir Henry C. Rawlinson and G. F. Grotefend were great interpreters of cuneiforms.

Cunene (kōōnā′nù), river rising in W central Angola, flowing c.750 mi. S and W to the Atlantic. Forms part of Angola–South-West Africa boundary.

Cunha, Euclides da (ā″ōōklē′dĭsh dä kōō′nyù), 1866–1909, Brazilian writer. Best-known work is account which he wrote as "on the spot" reporter of revolt in W Bahia: *Os sertões* (1902; Eng. tr., *Rebellion in the Backlands,* 1944), a study of conditions, prospects, and national soul of Brazil.

Cunha, Tristão da (trĕshtä′ō), c.1460–1514?, Portuguese navigator. Led 15 ships to India (1506); took Socotra in hope of controlling Red Sea.

Cunningham, Allan, 1784–1842, Scottish poet, collector of *The Songs of Scotland, Ancient and Modern* (1825), which includes his own "A Wet Sheet and a Flowing Sea." His son, **Sir Alexander Cunningham,** 1814–93, English archaeologist, army engineer, headed archaeological survey of India (1861–65, 1870–85).

Cunninghame Graham, R(obert) B(ontine), 1852–1936, Scottish author and political leader, whose sketches and tales reflect his life and travels in Latin America, Morocco, and Spain.

Cunobelinus: see CYMBELINE.

Cuoco, Vincenzo (vĕnchän′tsō kwô′kō), 1770–1823, Italian political philosopher. Exiled from Naples in 1799 for his part in republican revolution of that year. He predicted the gradual reunification of Italy, and his views became central to the philosophy of the Risorgimento.

Cupid [Latin,= desire]: see EROS.

cupping, former treatment for congestion, inflammation. Heated cup was applied to skin, the partial vacuum supposedly drew blood to the surface.

Curaçao (kū′rùsō, kōōräsou′), largest island (178 sq. mi.; pop. 132,055) of the Netherlands Antilles (394 sq. mi.; pop. 203,519), an autonomous region of the Netherlands, in the Dutch West Indies; cap. Willemstad. Territory has many widely separated islands, some off Venezuela (Curaçao, Bonaire or Buen Ayre, Aruba), some in NW Leeward Isls. (St. Martin—S part, St. Eustatius, Saba). Though discovered by Spanish (1499) and occupied briefly by English during Napoleonic Wars the islands have been under Dutch control since 1634. Discovery and exploitation of petroleum in Venezuela greatly increased importance of Curaçao and Aruba. The equable climate and unusual blend of Afro-Spanish-Dutch culture draw increasing numbers of tourists.

curare (kyōōrä′rē), aqueous poisonous extract of certain South American plants, used by South American Indians as arrow poison. Causes muscle paralysis. It is used in medicine to relax muscles.

curb market, originally, unorganized customary street meetings of brokers; now well organized and state regulated. Primary function is to introduce new securities, but a curb market lists both estab. securities and those which later "graduate" to stock exchange.

curculio (kûrkū′lēō), any typical snout beetle with a beak which is long and decurved in some, short and wide in others. Over 1,800 U.S. species, including serious pests: apple and plum curculios, imbricated snout beetle, many species of WEEVIL.

Curé Island, Hawaii: see KURE ISLAND.

Curia Regis: see PARLIAMENT.

Curia Romana: see CARDINAL.

Curicó (kūrēkō′), city (pop. 53,221), cap. of Curicó prov., central Chile. Founded c.1743; market for cattle and agr. produce.

Curie, Pierre (pyĕr kyōōrē′), 1859–1906, and his wife, **Marie Sklodowska Curie** (märē′ sklôdôf′skä), 1867–1934, b. Poland, French chemists and physicists. Pierre's early work was on crystallography, effects of temperature on magnetism, and piezoelectricity (form of electric polarity) discovered in crystals. Marie studied uranium, radioactive element in pitchblende. In 1898 she reported a probable new element in pitchblende; Pierre joined this research. They discovered polonium and radium (1898), isolated one gm. of radium salts (1902), and determined atomic weights and properties of both elements. They shared with Becquerel the 1903 Nobel Prize in Physics for radioactivity work. Marie Curie won 1911 Nobel Prize in Chemistry for isolation of metallic radium.

Curitiba (kōōrētē′bù), city (pop. c.361,300), cap. of Paraná state, SE Brazil. Founded in 17th-cent. gold rush. Immigration into Paraná hinterland in 20th cent. has made it center of agr. and ranch area with some mfg. Univ. of Paraná is here.

curium (kyōō′rēùm), radioactive element identified in 1944 (symbol = Cm; see also ELEMENT, table). Emits alpha particles, highly active (half life about five months).

curlew (kûr′lū), name for a number of large shore birds of both hemispheres. Among them are the long-billed curlew (rare) of E U.S.; Hudsonian and Eskimo (rare) curlews, which migrate from arctic breeding grounds to South America; bristle-thighed curlew; and some godwits and ibises.

curling, winter sport played on ice court by teams of four. Each player hurls squat, circular stone, weighing 38 lbs., at tees or fixed goals, placed 38 yds. apart. Stones nearest tee count for score.

current, electric: see ELECTRICITY.

Curran, John Philpot, 1750–1817, Irish statesman, trial lawyer, and orator. Opposed repressive policy of British in Ireland. Defended Wolfe Tone, Lord Edward Fitzgerald, and other anti-British rebels. His daughter was in love with Robert EMMET.

currant, shrub of genus *Ribes,* native to colder climates. Its tart black, red, or white berries are used for jellies and sauces. The shrub is a host of white-pine blister rust but an immune variety has been developed.

current, electric: see ELECTRICITY.

Currie, Sir Arthur William (kŭ′rē), 1875–1933, Canadian commander in First World War. Principal and vice chancellor of McGill Univ. 1920–33.

Currier & Ives, American lithographers and print publishers of scenes and events of 19th-cent. American life. Nathaniel Currier (1813–88), who founded the firm in 1835, was joined in 1857 by J. Merritt Ives, 1824–95, an artist and businessman.

Currituck Sound, arm of the Atlantic, NE N.C. and SE Va., extending c.35 mi. N from mouth of Albemarle Sound. Enclosed by barrier beaches.

Curry, John Steuart, 1897–1946, American painter. Known primarily for scenes of his native Kansas.

curry, pungent Eastern dish based on meat, fish, eggs, or vegetables, usually served with rice, and spiced with curry powder, a compound of turmeric, fenugreek, ginger, black and cayenne pepper, coriander, caraway, and sometimes other ingredients. When combined with RUE it is used to treat dyspepsia and diarrhea.

Curtea-de-Arges (kŏŏr′tää-dā-är′zhĕsh), town (est. pop. 12,000), S central Rumania; a former cap. of Walachia. Has 16th-cent. Byzantine cathedral (burial place of Rumanian kings).

Curtis, Benjamin Robbins, 1809–74, Associate Justice of U.S. Supreme Court (1851–57). Dissented in DRED SCOTT CASE. Chief counsel to Andrew Johnson at impeachment trial. His brother, **George Ticknor Curtis,** 1812–94, lawyer and writer, was one of the defense counsel in Dred Scott Case. Wrote classic Federalist interpretation of Constitution.

Curtis, Cyrus H(ermann Kotzschmar), 1850–1933, American publisher. In Philadelphia after 1876, he founded publication which became (1883) the *Ladies′ Home Journal.* Founded (1890) Curtis Publishing Co. Bought the *Saturday Evening Post* (1897), the *Country Gentleman* (1911), and several newspapers.

Curtis, George Ticknor: see CURTIS, BENJAMIN ROBBINS.

Curtis, George William, 1824–92, American author. Edited (1863–92) *Harper′s Weekly.* Campaigned against slavery and for civil service reform.

Curtis Institute of Music, in Philadelphia; founded 1924. Operates entirely on scholarship basis with faculty made up chiefly of concert artists.

curvature of the spine, abnormal curves of spinal column. Causes include faulty posture, pathological bony changes, and congenital factors. Lateral curvature (scoliosis) is more common than backward (kyphosis) or forward (lordosis).

curve, in mathematics, a line usually taken as any one-dimensional group of points (straight line is special case). In analytic geometry, plane curve is used mainly as graph of equation or function; properties of algebraic curves (i.e., those with algebraic equations) depend largely on degree of the equation; transcendental curves (nonalgebraic) are dependent on the particular function. Plane curves include CIRCLE; ELLIPSE; HYPERBOLA; PARABOLA. Twisted (skew) curve does not lie all in one plane.

Curzon, George Nathaniel, 1st Marquess Curzon of Kedleston, 1859–1925, British statesman. As viceroy of India (1899–1905) promoted reforms, pacified NW border. As foreign secretary presided at Lausanne Conference 1922–23. Paved way for Dawes Plan.

Cusa, Alexander John: see CUZA.

Cusa, Nicholas of: see NICHOLAS OF CUSA.

Cush (kŭsh), in Bible, eldest son of Ham, reputed progenitor of Hamites, who settled in NE Africa. "Land of Cush" may refer to Ethiopia. Nimrod, son of Cush, said to have settled Mesopotamia. Gen. 10.6–8; 1 Chron. 1.8–10.

Cushing, Caleb (kōō′shĭng), 1800–1879, American statesman. First U.S. commissioner to China, negotiated opening of Chinese ports to U.S. trade. U.S. Attorney General (1853–57).

Cushing, Harvey Williams, 1869–1939, American neurosurgeon, noted for brain surgery and as teacher and author. He won the 1925 Pulitzer Prize in biography for his life of Sir William Osler. Cushing′s disease, first described by him, is due to hyperactivity of adrenal glands.

Cushing, Richard James, 1895–, American Roman Catholic clergyman; made archbishop of Boston 1944 and cardinal 1958. Became director of national Catholic Welfare Conference in 1947.

Cushing′s disease: see CUSHING, HARVEY WILLIAMS.

Cushitic (kŭshĭt′ĭk), subfamily of Afro-Asiatic languages spoken mainly in E Africa. See LANGUAGE (table).

Cushman, Charlotte Saunders, 1816–76, first notable American actress. Gained fame as Lady Macbeth (1835) and as Meg Merrilies in an adaptation of Scott′s *Guy Mannering.* First in profession elected to Hall of Fame (1915).

Cushman, Pauline, 1835–93, Union spy in Civil War, known for her services in Tenn. in 1863.

Cushny, Arthur Robertson (kŭsh′nē), 1866–1926, Scottish physician and pharmacologist, noted for study of action of digitalis on heart and for text on pharmacology.

Custer, George Armstrong, 1839–76, American army officer. Youthful general in Civil War; made spectacular record. Custer′s last stand, during campaign against the Sioux in 1876, is still much debated: on the Little Bighorn on June 25, he and over 200 men were killed by the Indians. Battlefield is now a national monument in Mont. His wife, **Elizabeth Bacon Custer,** 1842–1933, devoted much of her life to upholding his memory.

Custer, city (pop. 2,105), SW S.Dak., SSW of Rapid City, in mining, timber, and livestock area. Oldest town in Black Hills, it was laid out in 1875 after gold discovery nearby. Nearby are Wind Cave Natl. Park, Jewel Cave Natl. Monument (see NATIONAL PARKS AND MONUMENTS, table), Mt. RUSHMORE, and Harney Peak.

Custer Battlefield National Monument: see NATIONAL PARKS AND MONUMENTS (table).

Custine, Adam Philippe, comte de (ädä′ fēlēp′ kŏt′ dü küstēn′), 1740–93, French general in French Revolutionary Wars. Guillotined on charge of treason after failure of 1793 campaign.

Custis-Lee Mansion, 3.47 acres, NE Va., in ARLINGTON NATIONAL CEMETERY. As Arlington House, was home of R. E. Lee; later inherited by his wife. Abandoned by Lees in Civil War; later used as hq. for Union army. Became national memorial 1955.

customs: see TARIFF.

Custozza (kŏŏstŏd′zä), village, N Italy, near Verona. Scene of Austrian victories over Sardinia (1848), and over Italy (1866).

Cut Bank, town (pop. 4,539), N Mont., NNW of Great Falls; settled 1910. One of state′s largest natural-gas fields is here. Blackfeet Reservation is W.

Cutch: see KUTCH.

Cutler, Manasseh (mùnăʹsù), 1742–1823, American clergyman, scientist, and colonizer. Wrote first systematic description and classification of New England flora. Aided in forming OHIO COMPANY OF ASSOCIATES. Helped estab. Marietta, Ohio, 1788.

Cutler, Charles A(mmi), 1837–1903, American librarian, a pioneer in cataloguing. His classification scheme, using letters instead of numbers, is basis of Library of Congress system.

cutter, small one-masted sailing vessel. Resembles a sloop but has its mast farther aft. Forward it usually carries a jib and a forestaysail. Coast Guard cutters are now power-driven.

cutting, method of plant propagation in which part of stem, leaf, or root is cut off and produces a new plant by forming buds and roots. Cuttings are made of chrysanthemums, grapes, African violets, and shrubs.

cuttlefish, marine mollusk of warm and temperate coastal waters with shield-shaped body, distinct head, well-developed eyes, and 10 arms. Its internal limy plate, the cuttlebone, is used in abrasives, fertilizers, and as source of lime for cage birds. Artist's sepia is made from a dried glandular secretion.

Cuttyhunk, Mass.: see ELIZABETH ISLANDS.

cutworm, larva of various noctuid or owlet moths. Eggs are laid in midsummer. After hatching, larva eats young shoots and roots, and in autumn goes underground, emerging in spring. Cutworms work by night, destroying more than they eat.

Cuvier, Georges Léopold Chrétien Frédéric Dagobert, Baron (zhôrzh lâôpôld′ krätyĕ′ frädärĕk′ dägóbĕr′ bärô′ küvyä′), 1769–1832, French zoologist and geologist, a founder of comparative anatomy and paleontology. He rejected theories of continuous evolution and supported catastrophism.

Cuvilliès, François de (Fräswä′ dù küvēyĕs′), 1695–1768, French architect, decorator, and engraver. Introduced ROCOCO style of decoration into Germany, and designed the Residenz-Theater (1751–53) and the Amalienburg (1733–39) in Munich.

Cuxhaven (kōōks′ häfún), city (pop. 43,700), Lower Saxony, West Germany, transatlantic port at mouth of Elbe R., c.60 mi. NW of Hamburg. Chartered 1907; transferred from Hamburg to Hanover prov. 1937.

Cuyahoga (kī″úhō′gú), river of NE Ohio, rises near Chardon, flows SW then N to L. Erie at Cleveland.

Cuyahoga Falls, residential and industrial city (pop. 47,922), NE Ohio, a suburb NNE of Akron.

Cuyp or **Kuyp** (koip), family of Dutch painters of Dordrecht. **Jacob Gerritszoon Cuyp** (yä′kŏp gĕ′rĭtzōn), 1594–c.1651, was a portrait and landscape painter. His stepbrother and pupil **Benjamin Cuyp**, 1616–52, did peasant scenes. Jacob's son and pupil **Aelbert Cuyp** (äl′burt), 1620–91, was a leading Dutch landscapist.

Cuyuna, iron range in Minn.: see MESABI.

Cuza, Alexander John (kōō′zä), 1820–73, first prince of Rumania; also known as Couza, Cusa, or Alexander John I. Elected prince of both Moldavia and Walachia 1859; recognized by Turkey as prince of united Rumania 1861. Was forced to abdicate 1866 because of his corrupt regime.

Cuzco (kōō′skō), city (pop. 78,289; alt. 11,207 ft.), cap. of Cuzco dept., S Peru. Site was probably actually occupied by pre-Incan tribes, but legend has city founded by first Incan ruler, Manco Capac. Pizarro entered it in 1533. Today's population is predominantly Indian. Cuzco is center for agr. produce and has woolen textile mills.

Cwmbran (kōōmbrän′), urban district (pop. 21,690; town pop. 30,043), Monmouthshire, W England. Created under New Town Act of 1949 to accommodate employees of nearby steelworks.

cyanide (sī′ūnīd), salt or ester of hydrocyanic (prussic) acid. Both sodium and potassium cyanide are corrosive and systemic water-soluble poisons, giving off prussic acid in presence of moisture. Used in insecticides, casehardening, electroplating. **Cyanide process** for extracting gold and silver from ore: gold

or silver dissolved in cyanide solution, then precipitated from solution by another metal.

cyanogen (sīä′nújĭn), colorless, inflammable, poisonous gas composed of carbon and nitrogen. Chemically active. **Cyanogen chloride:** poisonous liquid with low boiling point, used as poison gas.

Cybele (sĭ′bülĕ), in Phrygian religion, the Great Mother of the Gods. She rode in a chariot drawn by lions and attended by Corybantes and Dactyls. Her worship, involving fertility rites, was imported to Greece, where she was identified with Demeter and Rhea.

cybernetics, science of automatic control and communication processes in animals and machines. Basis of COMPUTER design and study of nerve network functions.

cycad, fernlike tropical or subtropical evergreen plant of order Cycadales; cycads are gymnosperms.

Cyclades (sĭ′klúdĕz), Gr. *Kyklades*, Aegean island group (1,023 sq. mi.; pop. 99,959), Greece, stretching SE from Attica and including DELOS, NAXOS, Andros, Tenos, Melos, Paros, Keos, and Syros; chief town Hermopolis (on Syros). Mountainous, with mild, dry climate, islands produce wine, fruit, olive oil, wheat, tobacco. Became Athenian dependency 479 B.C.; later belonged to Rome and Byzantium. After 1204, they formed major part of the duchy of the Archipelago, ruled by Italian nobles and by Venice until its fall to the Turks (1566). Passed to Greece 1829.

cyclamen (sĭk′–), any of a number of species of plants (*Cyclamen*) having nodding flowers with reflexed rose, white, or purple petals.

cycle (sī′kúl), in astronomy, time required to bring about recurrence of same relative positions or aspects of heavenly bodies. Important cycles include revolution of earth about sun (365 days 5 hr. 48 min. 46 sec.); revolution of moon about earth (c.29½ days); solar cycle (c.28 years), marking same relative position of earth and sun; solar ECLIPSE cycle (18 or 19 yr.); PRECESSION OF THE EQUINOXES. See SUNSPOTS.

cyclone (sī′klōn), low-pressure storm area, almost circular, with wind blowing spirally inward (clockwise in S Hemisphere, counterclockwise in N Hemisphere). Extratropical cyclone a term for large storms of temperate latitudes. See also HURRICANE; TORNADO.

Cyclops (sī′klŏps), plural **Cyclopes** (sīklō′pēz), in Greek religion, one of a group of one-eyed giants, descended from Uranus and Gaea. Some were shepherds, others worked in smithy of Hephaestus. In battle called the TITANOMACHY they forged a thunderbolt which enabled Zeus to vanquish the Titans.

cyclotron: see PARTICLE ACCELERATOR.

Cydonia: see CANEA, Crete.

cymbals: see PERCUSSION INSTRUMENTS.

Cymbeline (sĭm′bülĕn) or **Cunobelinus** (kū″nōbĭlī′nús), fl. A.D. 40, British king; wealthy and powerful ruler. Gave his name, but little else, to Shakespeare's play.

Cymru and **Cymry:** see WALES.

Cynewulf (kĭn′úwōolf), fl. late 8th cent.?, Old English religious poet of Northumbria or Mercia. *Elene* best of his four extant poems.

Cynics (sĭ′nĭks), Greek philosophers, who held that only virtue itself was to be prized and viewed all worldly goods and pleasures with contempt. This contempt they extended to mankind in general. The school was founded by Antisthenes (5th–4th cent. B.C.). A later leader was Diogenes.

Cynoscephalae (sīnúsĕ′fūlē), two hills in Thessaly; scene of the victory of Pelopidas in 364 B.C. and of Flamininus over Philip V of Macedon in 197 B.C.

Cynthiana, city (pop. 5,641), N Ky., NNE of Lexington on South Fork of Licking R., in farm area; founded 1793. Has tobacco warehouses and distillery. Scene of two raids by Gen. J. H. Morgan in Civil War. Has covered bridge (c.1837) and log house (1790) where Henry Clay practiced law.

Cypress, residential city (1966 pop. 19,005), S Calif., ENE of Long Beach.

cypress, coniferous evergreen tree. True cypress (*Cupressus*) is native to S Europe, China, and W U.S. Monterey cypress (*Cupressus macrocarpa*) native to limited region in Calif. Italian cypress of classical literature is *C. sempervirens*. Bald cypress (*Taxodium distichum*), common in swamps of SE U.S., produces upright root projections called knees. Other evergreens called cypress are of genus *Chamaecyparis*.

Cyprian, Saint (sĭ'prēŭn), d. 258, Father of the Church, bishop of Carthage. Though stern in his demands on Christians, he sturdily opposed the teachings of NOVATIAN that Christians who had lapsed under persecution should not be readmitted to the Church. In pleading for unity of the Church he estab. orthodox doctrines. Feast: Sept. 16.

Cyprus (sĭ'prŭs), Gr. *Kypros*, republic (3,572 sq. mi.; est. pop. 590,000), island in E Mediterranean; cap. Nicosia. Pop. mostly Greek, but also Turkish. A wide plain lies between two mountain ranges which rise to Mt. Olympus (6,406 ft.). Island rich in agr. products, mainly wine, wheat, olives, and tobacco. Minerals include copper, name derived from Cyprus. Excavations show neolithic culture existed 4000–3000 B.C. Ancient Cyprus ruled by many countries, including Phoenicia, Egypt, Greece, and Rome. Christianity introduced by apostles Paul and Barnabas. During Third Crusade, given (1192) to French LUSIGNAN dynasty. Later ruled by Venetians and Turks. Placed under British administration (1878), Cyprus received colonial status 1925. After Second World War violence arose from tension between Turkish nationalists and Greeks who wanted self-rule and union with Greece (*enosis*). Archbishop MAKARIOS III was Greek Cypriot leader after 1950. Agreement signed early in 1959 by Britain, Greece, Turkey provided for estab. of independent Cypriot republic within one year. Became member of British Commonwealth 1961. Strife between Greek and Turkish Cypriots again broke out 1963. UN forces sent 1964; UN appeal for ceasefire accepted Aug., 1964.

Cyrano de Bergerac, Savinien (sävēnyĕ' sĕränō' dǔ bĕrzhŭräk'), 1619–55, French author. His *Voyages to the Moon and Sun* (1657–62; Eng. tr., 1923) are two satirical, utopian romances. A swaggering personality, he was romanticized by Edmond Rostand in the drama *Cyrano de Bergerac* (1897).

Cyrenaica (sīrŭnā'ĭkŭ, sī–), region about anc. CYRENE, N Africa. Became Roman province. Name revived for Italian province.

Cyrenaics (sīrĭnā'ĭks, sĭrĭ–), members of Greek school of philosophy of 5th and 4th cent. B.C., founded by Aristippus. All were hedonistic, i.e., they held pleasure to be the highest good, but they varied in defining pleasure. Some stressed spiritual satisfactions, others advocated mere painlessness.

Cyrene (sīrē'nē), anc. port, center of anc. Cyrenaica. A Greek colony (7th cent. B.C.), it was a kingdom with much commerce (wheat, wool, silphium) and some development of art. Cyrene became powerful over other cities and held nominal independence until the marriage of Berenice (d. 221? B.C.) to Ptolemy III. Trajan's punishment of Cyrene because of Jewish outbreaks led to decline. Excavations have revealed the prosperity of Greek and Roman periods.

Cyril (of Jerusalem), Saint (sĭ'rŭl), 315?–386?, bishop of Jerusalem, Doctor of the Church. He opposed Arianism and may have been the actual author of the Nicene Creed. Feast: March 18.

Cyril (of Alexandria), Saint, d. 444, patriarch of Alexandria, Doctor of the Church. He was stern in attack on heretics and nonbelievers. His fight against NESTORIANISM came to a triumphant conclusion in the Council of EPHESUS (431). He for a time alienated the churchmen of Antioch but reached a compromise with them. His writings on the Trinity, though orthodox, contained seeds of later heresies of EUTYCHES and MONOPHYSITISM. Feast: Feb. 9.

Cyril and Methodius, Saints (–thō'–), d. 869 and 884 respectively, Greek Christian missionaries, brothers.

Sent to convert the Moravians (863), they met opposition of the German rulers and were haled back to Rome on charges of heresy. They were cleared, but Cyril died before he could return to the field. Methodius returned, was "deposed" by the Germans from the archbishopric of Moravia, and was restored by the pope. Methodius completed the Slavic translation of religious works begun by Cyril (after whom the Cyrillic alphabet is named, though he did not invent it). Feast: July 7.

Cyrus the Great, d. 529 B.C., king of Persia, who estab. rule of Achaemenidae. Herodotus says he overthrew his grandfather Astyages. He created a firm Persian Empire, including not only Media but all the Near East. Croesus of Lydia, Nabonidus of Babylonia, Amasis II of Egypt–all fell before him. He did not actually conquer Egypt but prepared for later Persian conquest there. He respected customs of conquered territories and recreated power of Jews in Palestine.

Cyrus the Younger, d. 401 B.C., Persian prince, son of Darius II, who favored him and gave him large commands. After the death of Darius he was accused of a plot against his brother, ARTAXERXES II. Pardoned, he soon began a rebellion and hired a Greek force (the Ten Thousand) to help him. He won much local help, but in battle with Artaxerxes at CUNAXA (401 B.C.) he was killed and his army defeated. See also ANABASIS; XENOPHON.

cystic fibrosis, disorder of mucus-secreting glands and sweat glands, producing duct obstruction in affected organs, chiefly the pancreas, lungs, and liver. Symptoms include digestive and respiratory embarrassment and high salt content in perspiration. Affects mainly infants and children.

Cythera (sĭthēr'ǔ), Gr. *Kythera*, island (109 sq. mi.; pop. 5,340), Greece, southernmost of IONIAN ISLANDS; chief town Kythera (pop. 469), on S shore. Cult of Aphrodite was centered here.

cytoplasm includes all living substance in a plant or animal cell except the nucleus. It consists of a semifluid matrix enclosed by a membrane. The membrane permits certain substances, but not others, to pass in or out of the cell; it is a selectively permeable membrane. In the matrix are certain cell particles with specific functions (e.g., respiration or photosynthesis). The rigid nonliving cell wall produced by some plant cells is not a part of the cytoplasm.

Cyzicus (sĭ'zĭkŭs), ancient city of Asia Minor, on Cyzicus Peninsula (modern Kapidagi Peninsula), NW Turkey; a port on Sea of Marmara. Colonized by Greeks from Miletus 756 B.C., it was a member of the Delian League and rivaled Byzantium. Alcibiades defeated Spartan fleet off Cyzicus 410 B.C.

Czajkowski, Michael (chĭkôf'skē), 1804–86, Polish novelist. Took part in Polish insurrection of 1831, later went to Turkey and as Sadyk Pasha fought in the Crimean War against Russia. Wrote novels on the life of Cossacks and South Slavs and on Polish history.

Czartoryski, Adam Jerzy, Prince (yĕ'zhĭ chärtôrĭ'skē), 1770–1861, Polish-Russian statesman, a close adviser of Alexander I. Russian foreign minister 1803–6. Improved Polish school system; persuaded Alexander to grant Polish constitution of 1815. Opposing later Russian policies, he headed the Polish provisional government of 1830–31; after failure of the insurrection he lived in exile at Paris.

Czech language (chĕk), a Western Slavic language of Indo-European family. See LANGUAGE (table).

Czechoslovakia (chĕk"ōslōväk'ĕŭ), Czech *Československo*, republic (49,362 sq. mi.; est. pop. 14,106,886), central Europe, bordering on Poland (N), USSR (E), Hungary, Austria (S), and Germany (W and N); cap. PRAGUE. Other large cities: BRNO, BRATISLAVA, OSTRAVA. (For geography, economy, and history before 1918, see articles on regions: BOHEMIA, MORAVIA, SILESIA, SLOVAKIA.) Population is largely Slavic, Czechs (66%) and Slovaks (c.29%). Small German and Magyar minorities exist. Roman Catholicism is majority religion, but there are large Protestant (esp. Hussite) and Eastern Orthodox groups. During First World War Czech units helped Allies; in 1918 Czechoslovakia emerged as independent republic from the ruins of the Austro-Hungarian Monarchy. Its creation was largely the work of its first and second presidents, T. G. MASARYK and Eduard BENES. The most favored of the Austro-Hungarian "successor states," Czechoslovakia was rich in agr. land, forests, minerals; had well-developed industries; and benefited from a liberal, democratic constitution. Its weakness lay in the disaffection of its German and Magyar minorities and the separatism of Slovakia, which were fostered by Germany and Hungary in the hope of obtaining a revision of their frontiers. Against this threat, the government relied on its alliance with France and on the LITTLE ENTENTE. The rise of Hitler and Western appeasement resulted in 1938 in the MUNICH PACT, through which Germany obtained the Bohemian borderlands; Poland and Hungary shared in the spoils. The truncated state, renamed Czecho-Slovakia, was altogether dissolved in March, 1939, when Germany created and occupied the "Protectorate of Bohemia and Moravia," while Slovakia became nominally independent. After liberation by U.S. and Russian forces in 1945, pre-Munich Czechoslovakia was restored (except for

RUTHENIA, ceded to USSR), and the German population was expelled. A coalition government held power until the Communists seized power in Feb., 1948. A constitution on Soviet model was voted. The new government enacted a program of rapid industrialization with nationalization of economy. The policies of the USSR were followed closely. Became member of the UN 1945 and joined the WARSAW TREATY 1955. The new constitution of 1960 declared the state a socialist republic.

Czernowitz: see CHERNOVTSY, Ukrainian SSR.

Czerny, Karl (chĕr′nē), 1791–1857, Austrian pianist. Best known for his technical studies for the piano.

Czestochowa (chĕn″stŭkô′vŭ), city (est. pop. 173,-000), S Poland on Wara R. Iron, textile, chemical, food industries. Chiefly famed for its monastery on Jasna Gora [mountain of light], with image of Our Lady, a major shrine of pilgrimage. In 1655 the monastery, defended by a handful of soldiers, withstood Swedish siege for 40 days. The Swedes withdrew, and the alleged miracle fired Poland to successful resistance to the invaders. Since then Our Lady of Czestochowa, venerated as the "Queen of Poland," has been a symbol of national survival.

Czolgosz, Leon F. (chŏl′gŏsh), c.1873–1901, American anarchist, assassin of Pres. McKinley.

Dabo, Leon (dä′bō), 1868–1960, American landscape and mural painter. He studied under Puvis de Chavannes.

Dabrowski, Jan Henryk (yän′ hĕn′rĭk dämbrôf′skē), 1755–1818, Polish general. Organized and led Polish legions in Napoleon's campaigns.

Dacca (dä′kŭ), city (pop. c.550,000), cap. of East Pakistan and of Dacca division, on Buri Ganga R. The industrial and commercial heart of East Pakistan. Its glory as 17th-cent. Mogul cap. of Bengal is reflected in Bara Katra palace. Formerly famous for muslins. Seat of Univ. of Dacca.

Dachau (dä′khou), town (pop. 25,592), S Bavaria, near Munich. Site of a notorious concentration camp under Hitler regime.

Dacia (dä′shù), region of Roman Empire, roughly modern Transylvania and Rumania. Its people were called Getae by the Greeks, Daci by the Romans. With advanced material culture they resisted Domitian, who in A.D. 90 paid them tribute to keep them quiet. Trajan planted colonies in Dacia (A.D. 105), and it became a Roman province until Aurelian had to withdraw the colonists. Their legacy to the area was the Romance language, Rumanian.

Da Costa, Isaäc: see COSTA, ISAÄC DA.

Da Costa, Jacob Mendez (dü kŏ′stŭ), 1833–1900, American physician, outstanding teacher, and author of works on diagnosis and functional heart disease.

Da Costa, Uriel: see ACOSTA, URIEL.

Dacron: see SYNTHETIC TEXTILE FIBERS.

Dada (dä′dä) or **Dadaism** (dä′däĭzm), international and nihilistic movement (1916–21) among European artists and writers. A doctrine of utter formlessness, it attacked all conventional standards of aesthetics and behavior, thus encouraging surrealism and other later radical movements.

Daddi, Bernardo (bĕrnär′dō däd′dē), fl. 1312–48, Italian painter of the Florentine school. First influenced by his contemporary Giotto, he soon adopted the delicate line and lyrical expression of the Sienese painters, especially the Lorenzetti.

daddy longlegs, name for harvestman (a relative of the spider) and for crane fly (an insect related to mosquito). Harvestman has small body, eight slender legs. It sucks fluids from fruits, other vegetable matter, and insects (some say it eats whole insects). Crane fly has a slender body and two pairs of wings.

Dadeville, town (pop. 2,940), E central Ala., near L. Martin SE of Alexander City, in timber and mineral area; founded 1832. A natl. military park is nearby on site of Andrew Jackson's defeat of Creek Indians (1814) at HORSESHOE BEND of Tallapoosa R.

Daedalus (dĕ′dŭlŭs), in Greek myth, builder of labyrinth for the Minotaur; father of ICARUS.

daffodil: see NARCISSUS.

Dafydd ap Gwilym (dä′vĭdh äp gwĭ′lĭm), c.1320–c.1380, Welsh poet. Introduced simpler language and new meters and wrote notable poems on nature.

Dagenham, part of BARKING and REDBRIDGE London boroughs since 1965. Huge Ford motor plant located here.

Dagestan or **Daghestan** (dägústän′), autonomous soviet socialist republic (19,410 sq. mi.; 1965 est. pop. 1,291,000), SE European RSFSR, between E Greater Caucasus and Caspian Sea; cap. Makhachkala. Mostly bare inaccessible mountains. Wine, cotton, corn in irrigated lowlands. Population, mostly Moslems, includes c.30 nationalities. Ceded to Russia by Persia 1813; native revolts until 1877.

Dagobert I (dăg'ōbûrt), d. c.639, Frankish king (629?–639). Last of MEROVINGIANS to exercise personal rule. Extended his influence over Basques and Bretons.

Dagon, Philistine god, perhaps a fish god. Probably his was a fertility cult. Judges 16.23; 1 Sam. 5.2–5; 1 Chron. 10.10.

Daguerre, Louis Jacques Mandé (lwē' zhäk' mädä' dägâr'), 1789–1851, French scene painter and physicist, inventor of the daguerreotype. With C. M. Bouton he also invented the diorama.

Dahlak Archipelago (däläk'), island group (pop. c.2,500), off Massawa, Ethiopia. Site of pearl fisheries since Roman times.

dahlia (dăl'–), tuberous-rooted perennial of genus Dahlia, native to Mexico. Widely grown for late-blooming colorful, composite flowers of many types (e.g., large Dahlmann, Friedrich Christoph (frē'drĭkh krĭs'tôf däl'män), 1785–1860, German historian. Dismissed from professorship at GÖTTINGEN for liberal views. Prominent in Frankfurt Parliament.

Dahlonega (dälŏn'ĕgù), city (pop. 2,604), N central Ga., NNE of Atlanta; settled 1828 with opening of gold mines. Seat of North Georgia Col. A U.S. mint was here (1836–61).

Dahomey (Fr. däōmā'), republic (44,695 sq. mi.; pop. c.2,250,000), W Africa, on Gulf of Guinea; cap. Porto Novo. Behind narrow sandy coast is region of interconnected lagoons with outlets to sea only at Grand-Popo and Cotonou. Agr. and stock breeding are important in savanna highlands. Exports include palm products, cotton, coffee, and peanuts. French is official language. France annexed region 1892 and incorporated it into French West Africa 1904. Country became self-governing member of French Community 1958. Independence was achieved Aug., 1960, and M. Hubert Maga became first president 1961. Civil unrest was followed by army coups in 1963 and 1965, when army chief Christophe Soglo became president and prime minister.

daibutsu (dī'bōotsōō) [Jap.,= great Buddha], Japanese name applied to colossal statues of Buddha, usually over 16 ft. in height. Most notable are those at Nara, Kamakura, and Kyoto.

Dáil Éireann (dôl' ā'rôn, dĭl' â'rùn [Irish,= diet of Ireland], popular representative body of National Parliament of republic of IRELAND. Second chamber, the Senate, has little power; prime minister responsible to Dáil. Members of first Dáil, ostensibly elected to British Parliament, estab. themselves as revolutionary body and proclaimed republic 1919.

Daimler, Gottlieb (dām'lûr), 1834–1900, German engineer, inventor, automobile manufacturer. Contributed to development of automobile industry by improving the internal-combustion engine.

daimyo or daimio (both: dīm'yō), great feudal barons of Japan. Owned vast tax-free estates (built up after 8th cent.); in 12th cent. held more power than imperial government until Yoritomo established system of centralized feudalism.

Dairen, China: see TALIEN.

dairying, industry producing, processing, and distributing milk or milk products. In U.S., 20% of gross natl. income from agriculture derived from it. Modern dairying developed with growth of urban areas. About ⅔ of production used for butter and market milk; rest for farm uses, cheese, and by-products.

daisy, name for many plants of composite family with petallike rays. True daisy of literature is English daisy (Bellis perennis), a low biennial with white, pink, or red flowers. Common white field or oxeye daisy (Chrysanthemum leucanthemum) is naturalized in U.S. from Europe. The Shasta daisy is a species of Chrysanthemum. See also MARGUERITE; PYRETHRUM.

Dakar (dùkär'), city (pop. c.380,000), cap. of Senegal. Major port on Cape Verde peninsula and westernmost point of Africa. Refueling station for sea and air traffic; connected by rail to interior. Major exports are peanuts and animal products; industries include mfg. of textiles, flour, cement, and shoes. Seat of university. From 1902 it was cap. of French West Africa. In 1958 it also became cap. of Senegal. Cap. of short-lived Mali Federation in 1958–59.

Dakin's solution, dilute (0.5%) solution of sodium hypochlorite. It is unstable, liberating chlorine, thus valuable as surgical antiseptic and for wound dressing. It was named for Henry Drysdale Dakin, 1880–1952, British-born American chemist.

Dakota Indians: see SIOUX INDIANS.

Daladier, Édouard (ādōōär' dälädyä'), 1884–, French politician. Premier (1933, 1933–34, 1938–40); war minister 1936–40. Signed MUNICH PACT (1938). He was a defendant at RIOM trial and was interned by Germans until 1945. An active Radical-Socialist deputy in Fourth Republic, he was defeated in first elections of Fifth Republic (1958).

Dalai Lama: see LAMAISM.

Dalarna (dä'lärnä") or Dalecarlia (dälùkär'lĕù), historic province of central Sweden, nearly identical with KOPPARBERG co. In 1521 peasants of Dalarna, under GUSTAVUS I, freed Sweden from Danish rule. Old rural customs and home industries have survived.

Dalcroze, Émile Jaques: see JAQUES-DALCROZE.

Dale, Sir Henry Hallett, 1875–, English scientist. Shared 1936 Nobel Prize in Physiology and Medicine for study of the action of acetylcholine as an agent in the transmission of nerve impulses.

Dalecarlia, Sweden: see DALARNA.

D'Alembert's principle. Jean le Rond d'Alembert introduced (1742) and estab. (1743) a principle of mechanics which shows that Newton's third law of motion applies to bodies free to move as well as to stationary bodies.

Dalen, Nils Gustaf (nĭls' gŭs'täv dälän'), 1869–1937, Swedish scientist. Won 1912 Nobel Prize in Physics chiefly for invention of automatic regulator for acetylene-gas lights used for railway signals, beacons, buoys.

Dalhousie, James Andrew Broun Ramsay, 1st marquess of (dălhōō'zē), 1812–60, British statesman. As governor general of India (1847–56) annexed Sikh territory of the Punjab 1849, promoted economic and social reforms, and annexed princely states with no natural heirs.

Dalhousie (dălhou'zē), town (pop. 5,856), N N.B., Canada, at mouth of Restigouche R. Fishing port and seaside resort with lumber and paper mills.

Dalhousie University: see HALIFAX, N.S.

Dali, Salvador (sälvädhôr' dä'lē), 1904–, Spanish surrealist painter. Tried futurism and cubism before he turned to surrealism. With fine draughtsmanship he expresses an irrational dream world.

Dalin, Olof von (ōō'lôv fün dälēn'), 1708–63, Swedish historian, lyric poet, and journalist, foremost literary figure of his day. Founded periodical, the Swedish Argus. Also wrote poetical satires, drama, and popular history.

Dalkeith (dùlkēth'), burgh (pop. 8,864), Midlothian, Scotland. Important grain center. Dalkeith House is seat of duke of Buccleuch.

Dallas, Alexander James, 1759–1817, U.S. Secretary of the Treasury (1814–16), b. West Indies. Restored confidence in U.S. currency during critical period. His son, George Mifflin Dallas, 1792–1864, was Vice President of the United States (1845–49). As minister to Great Britain (1856–61), he signed Dallas-Clarendon Convention (1856), which set basis for settlement of difficulties in Central America.

Dallas. 1 Borough (pop. 2,586), NE Pa., NW of Wilkes-Barre. Seat of Col. Misericordia. 2 City (pop. 679,684), N Texas, E of Fort Worth at head of Trinity R. Settled 1841; growth augmented by French from disbanded Fourierist colony at La Réunion. Developed as cotton market in 1870s; later became Southwest's financial and commercial center. Industries include oil refining, meat packing, and mfg. of machinery, textiles, aircraft and electronic equipment. Here are Univ. of Dallas, Southwestern Medical School of the Univ. of Texas, and Dallas Theatre Center (with public theater designed by F. L. Wright). Pres. J. F. Kennedy was assassinated here Nov. 22, 1963.

Dalles, The, Oregon: see THE DALLES.

Dalmatia (dǎlmā'shǔ), coastal region of Yugoslavia, extending along Adriatic from Rijeka to Kotor. Interior forms part of Dinaric Alps. Coastline, famed for beauty, has many islands, bays, and harbors. ZADAR, SPLIT, DUBROVNIK are main ports and cities. From the 10th cent. Dalmatia was divided among Croatia, Serbia, and Venice, which controlled the islands and main ports. Venetian possessions passed to Austria in 1797. In 1920 Yugoslavia received all Dalmatia except Zadar and several islands, which were given to Italy but which passed to Yugoslavia in 1947.

Dalou, Jules (zhül' dälōō'), 1838–1902, French sculptor, popular under the Third Republic.

Dalrymple, earls of Stair; Viscount Stair: see STAIR, JAMES DALRYMPLE, VISCOUNT.

Dalrymple, Alexander (dǎl'rǐmpǔl, dǎlrǐm'pǔl), 1737–1808, British hydrographer. Traveled in the S Pacific for the East India Co. For the British admiralty he collected charts, memoirs, and records and wrote accounts of the South Seas.

Dalton, John (dôl'tǔn), 1766–1844, English scientist. He revived the ATOMIC THEORY and applied the concept to a table of atomic weights and in formulating **Dalton's law:** total pressure of a mixture of gases equals sum of pressures of gases in the mixture, each gas acting independently.

Dalton, city (pop. 17,868), extreme NW Ga., in Appalachian Valley, SE of Chattanooga, Tenn. An industrial center in farm area. Confederate hq. in Civil War after CHATTANOOGA CAMPAIGN, it fell to Sherman in ATLANTA CAMPAIGN (1864).

Dalton's law: see DALTON, JOHN.

Daly, Augustin, 1838–99, American theatrical manager. A playwright and drama critic, made debut as manager with his melodrama *Under the Gaslight.* Opened his first theater 1869. Later started Daly's Theatre where he presented magnificent productions of Shakespeare and of French and German adaptations.

Daly, Marcus, 1841–1900, American copper magnate, b. Ireland. Estab. Anaconda Copper Mining Co. in Mont. and became very wealthy. His fierce and longlasting rivalry with William A. CLARK dominated Mont. politics and economy.

Daly City, residential city (pop. 44,791), W Calif., just S of San Francisco; settled 1906 by refugees of San Francisco earthquake.

Dam, Henrik (hǎn'rĕk däm'), 1895–, Danish biochemist. For identification and studies of vitamin K he shared 1943 Nobel Prize in Physiology and Medicine. Also worked on role of vitamin E in nutrition.

dam, barrier of rock, earth, masonry, concrete, timber (seldom used), or some combination, which restrains water. Rock or earth dams usually have upstream surface made watertight. Masonry and concrete dams are either gravity type (resist water only with own weight) or single- or multiple-arched type. Single-arched dams are usually constructed in narrow canyon having rock walls to withstand tremendous thrust of horizontal, upstream arch. Multiple-arched dams employ buttresses. Many modern dams serve multiple purposes—provide irrigation, aid flood control, provide power for hydroelectric plants.

Daman (dǔmän'), Port. *Damão,* former Portuguese colony (86 sq. mi.), India; cap. Daman. Consisted of a coastal section, Daman proper, and a detached inland section, Nagar-Aveli. Acquired 1558 by Portugal, it was seized by India in Dec., 1961.

Damariscotta (dǎm"ǔrǐskŏt'ǔ), resort town (pop. 1,093), S Maine, SE of Augusta. Includes Damariscotta village, on E side of Damariscotta R. Nearby are shell mounds, seemingly many centuries old.

Damascene, John: see JOHN OF DAMASCUS, SAINT.

Damascus (dǔmǎ'skǔs), Arabic *Esh-Sham,* city (pop. 408,774), S Syria, cap. of Damascus prov. and of Syrian Arab Republic, on Barada R. Dates from unknown antiquity. Successively held by Assyrians and Persians. Conquered 332 B.C. by Alexander the Great, after whose death it fell prey to other conquerors, notably Armenians. In 64 B.C. it passed to Romans under Pompey, becoming one of cities of Decapolis. On road to Damascus Paul was converted to Christianity. With Arab occupation in 635 cfty became Moslem; great Christian church built A.D. c.375 under Emperor Theodosius I, on foundations of Roman temple of Zeus, became Great Mosque. Seat of Omayyad caliphate 661–750. City prospered and became known for fine metalwork (esp. swords). Fell to Mongols under Hulagu Khan in 1260, sacked by Tamerlane in 14th cent. Was under Ottoman Turks 1516–1918. Captured 1918 by British, it was under French mandate 1920–41. Became cap. of independent Syria 1943. With the creation of the United Arab Republic in 1958, the city ceased to be cap. of Syria. Became cap. of Syrian Arab Republic in 1961.

damask (dǎ'mǔsk), fabric whose ground and pattern are of different weaves: e.g., ground may be in twill with the design in satin. True damasks, unlike brocade, are flat and reversible.

Damian, Peter: see PETER DAMIAN, SAINT.

Damien, Father (dä'mēǔn, dämyē'), 1840–89, Belgian missionary priest named Joseph de Veuster. After working as a missionary among the natives of Hawaii, he was transferred at his own request to the leper colony on Molokai, where he labored among the afflicted until he himself died of leprosy.

Damietta (dǎmēē'tǔ), city (pop. c.72,000), NE Egypt; textile center. As Tamiathis it was twice captured by the Crusaders in 13th cent. Destroyed 1250, later rebuilt by Egyptians.

Damocles (dǎ'mǔklēz), in classic legend, Syracusan at court of Dionysius. To demonstrate dangers of high estate, the ruler gave a banquet in his honor; Damocles was happy until, looking up, he saw a sword suspended above his head by a single hair.

Damodar (dä'mōdär), river rising in Bihar, India, and flowing c.370 mi. through West Bengal to join Hooghly R. Its dams supply electricity to Calcutta and the Hooghlyside industrial district.

Damon and Pythias (dā'mǔn, pǐ'thēǔs), two faithful Syracusan friends. When Pythias, condemned to death, was freed to arrange his affairs, Damon stayed as pledge. On Pythias' return, tyrant Dionysius, impressed, freed both and asked to be their friend.

damp, in mining, any of several gases. Firedamp, found in coal mines, is mostly methane and, mixed with air, is highly combustible. Afterdamp is gaseous mixture remaining after firedamp explosion. Chokedamp, mostly carbon dioxide, is imperceptible and when in quantity is dangerous to life.

Dampier, William (dǎm'pēr), 1651?–1715, English explorer and buccaneer. Fought in Dutch War (1673), managed plantation in Jamaica, took part as buccaneer against Spanish America (1679–81). Wrote masterly hydrographic treatise. As commander of expedition in S Pacific, discovered Dampier Archipelago and Dampier Strait, named New Britain as island.

Damrosch (dǎm'rŏsh), German-American family of conductors, composers, and educators. **Leopold Damrosch,** 1832–85, came to New York in 1871. He founded the New York Symphony Society in 1878. Many works of Brahms and Wagner received their first American performances under his baton. His compositions include violin concertos, cantatas, and a symphony. His son, **Frank Damrosch,** 1859–1937, supervised music in New York public schools. In 1905, he helped organize the Institute of Musical Art (later a unit of the Juilliard School). Another son of Leopold Damrosch, **Walter Damrosch,** 1862–1950, first conducted at the Metropolitan Opera. Later he conducted both the New York Philharmonic and the

New York Symphony. He directed a series of music education programs on the radio for children. His compositions include operas and choral works.

damselfish, name for several fishes of West Indies, Florida coast. Clownfish, blue devil, sergeant-major are popular aquarium fish.

damsel fly: see DRAGONFLY.

Dan [Heb.,= judge]. **1** Son of Jacob, ancestor of one of 12 tribes of Israel. Tribe finally settled in N Palestine. Samson was famous Danite. Many references in Genesis, Exodus, Numbers. **2** City at N extremity of Palestine, hence expression "from Dan to BEER-SHEBA." Jeroboam erected golden calf here.

Dan, river rising in SW Va. in piedmont and flowing c.180 mi. E to the Roanoke in S Va., twice crossing N.C. line.

Dana, Edward Salisbury: see DANA, JAMES DWIGHT.

Dana, Francis, 1743–1811, American diplomat. Accompanied (1779) John Adams to Paris and was sent (1780) to the court of Catherine the Great of Russia. Stayed there 1781–83, although he was never recognized. His son, **Richard Henry Dana,** 1787–1879, was a poet and essayist. His son, **Richard Henry Dana,** 1815–82, was an author and lawyer. Shipped as a common seaman around Cape Horn to Calif. Narrative of this voyage, *Two Years before the Mast* (1840), became a classic.

Dana, James Dwight, 1813–95, American geologist, author of standard works on geology and mineralogy and studies of volcanoes, coral, and crustaceans. He taught at Yale 1850–90. His son, **Edward Salisbury Dana,** 1849–1935, taught physics at Yale (1890–1917) and also wrote on mineralogy.

Dana, John Cotton, 1856–1929, American librarian, head of Newark Public Library (1902–29) and of Mus. (1909–29). Initiated progressive library projects.

Dana, Richard Henry: see DANA, FRANCIS.

Danaë (dă'năē), in Greek legend, daughter of Acrisius. Zeus visited her in a shower of gold, and she bore him PERSEUS.

Danaüs (dă'nāŭs), in Greek myth, brother of Aegyptus; he had 50 daughters, the Danaïds or Danaïdes, Aegyptus had 50 sons. When the sons demanded Danaïds as brides, Danaüs told each one to slay her husband. Only Hypermnestra failed to kill her husband, Lynceus.

Danbury, city (pop. 22,928) in Danbury town (pop. 38,382), SW Conn., NW of Bridgeport; settled 1685. An early military depot, it was partly destroyed in William Tryon's 1777 raid. City's hat industry dates from 1780. Noted for its annual fairs. Includes village of Germantown (pop. 2,893).

Danbury Hatters' Case, decided in 1908 by U.S. Supreme Court. The holding that hatters' union, which had instituted nation-wide boycott of products of nonunion hat manufacturer in Danbury, Conn., was subject to injunction and treble damages set precedent for interference by Federal courts in labor activities.

Danby, Thomas Osborne, earl of, 1631–1712, English statesman. One of chief ministers of Charles II. Impeached and imprisoned 1679–84, later joined Whigs in inviting William of Orange to England. Was president of the council and chief minister 1690–95.

dandelion, common, milky-juiced perennial plant (*Taraxacum officinale*), with a rosette of toothed leaves and bright yellow flower heads borne on hollow stalks. Young leaves are edible both cooked and in salad; wine made from flowers. See *ill.,* p. 858.

Dandolo, Enrico (ĕnrē'kō dän'dōlō), c.1108–1205, doge of Venice (1192–1205). Led Fourth Crusade to capture Zara and Constantinople (see CRUSADES). Of the same family was **Andrea Dandolo** (ändrä'ä), c.1307–1354, doge of Venice (1343–54). Reformed laws; wrote chronicle of Venetian history.

Danegeld (dān'gĕld"), medieval land tax, originally raised to buy off raiding Danes. First levied in England in 868; became regular tax under Æthelred the Unready. Collected by later rulers until 12th cent.

In France monks of Saint-Denis paid Danegeld in 845 and several times later.

Danelaw (dān'lô"), originally body of law which prevailed in part of England occupied by Danes after treaty of King ALFRED with Guthrum (886). Soon applied to area in which Danish law prevailed. Had four main regions: Northumbria; shires dependent on boroughs of Lincoln, Nottingham, Derby, Leicester, and Stamford; East Anglia; SE Midlands.

Daniel [Heb.,= God is my judge], prophet, central figure of book of DANIEL.

Daniel, Samuel, 1562?–1619, English poet, known chiefly for *Delia* (1592), a collection of sonnets.

Daniel, book of Old Testament. Some parts occur only in Greek and are placed in Apocrypha in AV, but are included in Western canon (see SUSANNA; BEL AND THE DRAGON; THREE HOLY CHILDREN). Book tells story of Daniel, a Jew living in 6th cent. B.C., who was taken in captivity into court of Nebuchadnezzar, where he rose to power and was called Belteshazzar. Proverbial for wisdom, he was hero of many stories, e.g., his interpretation of Nebuchadnezzar's dreams; his reading of handwriting on wall; his escape from lion's den; his apocalyptic visions. Book also tells of his three friends who faced ordeal of fiery furnace. Critics question date of book, its authorship and historical accuracy, but agree on its inspirational value as story of uncompromising faith.

Daniell, John Frederic, 1790–1845, English chemist and meteorologist. Invented a hygrometer, a pyrometer, and the **Daniell cell,** a double fluid cell with zinc and copper electrodes, a sulfuric acid solution and a saturated solution of copper sulfate, and an electromagnetic force of 1.06 volts.

Daniels, Josephus, 1862–1948, American statesman, newspaper editor, and author. Was editor in Raleigh, N.C., after 1884. U.S. Secretary of the Navy (1913–21); ambassador to Mexico (1933–41). Wrote *The Wilson Era* (1944–46). His son **Jonathan Worth Daniels,** 1902–, succeeded to editorship of Raleigh *News and Observer* in 1948.

Danielson, Conn.: see KILLINGLY.

Danilo I (Danilo Petrovich Niegosh) (dänē'lô), 1677–1735, prince of MONTENEGRO, reigned 1696–1735. Instigated massacre of Moslems (1703; "Montenegrin Vespers"); began traditional alliance with Russia against Turkey.

Danilova, Alexandra, 1906–, Russian ballerina. Was with Diaghilev's Ballet Russe 1924–29; prima ballerina of Ballet Russe de Monte Carlo 1938–58.

Danish language, North Germanic language of Indo-European family. See LANGUAGE (table).

Dannemora, village (pop. 4,835), NE N.Y., W of Plattsburgh. Clinton State Prison is here.

D'Annunzio, Gabriele (gäbrēä'lā dän-nōōn'tsyō), 1863–1938, Italian author and adventurer, a leader of the decadents. A strong nationalist, he led an expedition to free Fiume (1919) and was an early idol of fascism. Poems, novels, and plays include *Canto nuovo* [new song] (1882) and the play *Il sogno d'un tramonto d'autunno* (1898). His love affair with Eleanora Duse is described in the novel *Il fuoco* (1900).

Dansville, village (pop. 5,460), W central N.Y., SE of Geneseo, in agr. area. Here Clara Barton founded (1881) first local chapter of American Red Cross.

Dante (Alighieri) (dän'tā älēgyä'rē), 1265–1321, Italian poet, author of the DIVINE COMEDY, b. Florence. *La vita nuova* [the new life] (1292), a prose narrative with inserted lyrics, told of his love for a beautiful girl, identified by many as Beatrice Portinari. He went into exile with the White Guelphs (1302). He died in exile in Ravenna. Dante also wrote in Italian many fine lyrics and an unfinished encyclopedic work, the *Convivio.* His Latin works include an unfinished treatise (*De vulgari eloquentia*), on Italian language and poetics, and a masterful apology for world government (*De monarchia*).

Danton, Georges Jacques (zhôrzh' zhäk' dätō'), 1759–94, French revolutionist. A lawyer, he won immense popularity through his powerful oratory. As a leader of the CORDELIERS he championed the extreme left in the National Assembly and was instrumental in overthrowing the monarchy (1792). As head of the provisional republican government and minister of justice he set up the Revolutionary Tribunal and dominated the first Committee of Public Safety (1793). The rise of the extremists led by ROBESPIERRE led Danton to seek a relatively moderate course. His struggle with Robespierre was, however, personal rather than ideological. Danton gradually lost his influence. Early in 1794 he was arrested on a charge of conspiracy and, after a mock trial, guillotined.

Danube (dǎ'nūb), Ger. *Donau*, Hung. *Duna*, Serbo-Croatian *Dunav*, Rumanian *Dunarea*, river, c.1,750 mi. long, Central and SE Europe; largest in Europe after Volga. Draining c.320,000 sq. mi., it rises in the Black Forest (SW Germany) and flows generally SE through S Germany, E Austria, Hungary, NE Yugoslavia, and SE Rumania into the Black Sea. It forms sections of the Czechoslovak-Hungarian border and of the borders of Rumania with Yugoslavia, Bulgaria, and the USSR. After passing the IRON GATE it broadens steadily and at Galati it divides into a swampy delta. Its course passes Ulm (where it becomes navigable), Regensburg, Passau, Linz, Vienna, Bratislava, Esztergom, Budapest, Belgrade, Galati, and Izmail. Among some 300 affluents are the Inn, Drava, Theiss, Sava, and Pruth. A vital traffic artery, the Danube also is a link of many cultures. It was the N border of the Roman Empire; its fertile plains have attracted many invaders. In 1919 it was placed under an international commission, which was dissolved in 1940. The Belgrade convention of 1948, which the U.S., Great Britain, and France refused to sign, created a navigation commission composed of the seven riparian nations. West Germany was excluded; Austria joined it in 1960.

Danvers, town (pop. 21,296), NE Mass., NW of Salem; settled 1636. Israel Putnam was born here, and Whittier spent his later years in Danvers.

Danville. 1 City (pop. 41,856), E Ill., on Vermilion R. at Ind. line, E of Champaign; platted 1827. A commercial and industrial center in dairy farm and coal area. Abraham Lincoln had law office here for five years. **2** City (pop. 9,010), central Ky., SSW of Lexington, near Dix R.; settled 1775. A rail hub in agr. area. Seat of govt. 1784–92; Ky. constitutional conventions were held here. Seat of Centre Col. of Kentucky. TRANSYLVANIA COLLEGE is nearby. **3** Industrial city (pop. 46,577), S central Va., on Dan R., SE of Roanoke, near N.C. line; founded 1793. One of world's largest bright-leaf tobacco markets with warehouses and processing plants. Operates Pinnacles of Dan hydroelectric project. Became last cap. of the Confederacy in 1865, when Davis and his cabinet fled here.

Danzig (dǎn'sǐg), Pol. *Gdańsk*, city (pop. c.313,000), N Poland, major Baltic seaport on a branch of the Vistula; transferred to Polish administration 1945. The ancient cap. of Pomerelia, it was settled by German merchants; joined the Hanseatic League 13th cent.; passed to the Teutonic Knights 1308; became an autonomous state under Polish overlordship 1466; passed to Prussia 1793; was a free city 1807–14; was restored to Prussia 1814. It was the cap. of West Prussia prov. until 1919, when the Treaty of Versailles again made it a free city, united with Poland by a customs union and supervised by a League of Nations high commissioner. After 1935 the local National Socialist party gained control over the legislature and agitated for reunion with Germany. Hitler's demand for Danzig was the chief direct cause of Second World War. Danzig was annexed to Germany Sept. 1, 1939; it fell to the Russian army early in 1945. Construction of Polish port of GDYNIA after First World War reduced its importance as a port. Virtually destroyed in Second World War, Danzig lost all its fine medieval architecture; only the port

escaped destruction. Most of the German population was expelled about 1945 and replaced by Poles.

Daphne (dǎf'nē), in Greek myth, nymph who attracted love of Apollo. Pursued by him, she prayed for escape and was changed into a laurel tree.

Daphnis (dǎf'nǐs), in Greek literary legend, shepherd in love with a Naiad. Made blind for unfaithfulness, he played sad songs upon his shepherd's pipes and thus began pastoral melody.

Daphnis and Chloë (dǎf'nǐs, klō'ē), Greek pastoral romance attributed to one Longus of 3d cent. A.D.

Da Ponte, Lorenzo (lôrěn'dzō dä pōn'tä), 1749–1838, Italian poet and librettist, a pioneer in spreading Italian culture in the U.S. Wrote librettos for Mozart's *Così fan tutte* (1790), *The Marriage of Figaro* (1786), and *Don Giovanni* (1787). Came to U.S. in 1805, was made professor at Columbia Univ. 1830.

D'Arblay, Madame: see BURNEY, FRANCES.

Darby, John Nelson, 1800–1882, a founder of PLYMOUTH BRETHREN. He formed congregations on the Continent and in U.S. and Canada.

Darby, residential borough (pop. 14,059), SE Pa., SW of Philadelphia; settled 1682. One of state's oldest settlements, it has many colonial landmarks.

Dardanelles (därdŭnělz'), strait, c.40 mi. long, 1–4 mi. wide, connecting the Aegean with the Sea of Marmara and dividing the Gallipoli peninsula of European Turkey from Asiatic Turkey. Called the Hellespont in antiquity; scene of legend of HERO and Leander. Controlling navigation between the Black Sea and the Mediterranean, the Dardanelles and BOSPORUS straits have been important from the dawn of history. Ancient Troy prospered near W entrance of Hellespont. Xerxes and Alexander the Great crossed it by a bridge of boats (c.481 B.C.; 334 B.C.). Under the Byzantine and Ottoman empires the Straits were essential to defense of Constantinople; with the decay of Turkey (see EASTERN QUESTION), their status became an international problem. In 1841 the Great Powers agreed to close the Straits to all but Turkish warships in peacetime; reaffirmed by the Congress of Paris (1856). In the First World War the Allied GALLIPOLI CAMPAIGN failed to force the Straits. The Treaty of SÈVRES (1920) internationalized the Straits zone, but the Conference of LAUSANNE (1923) restored it to Turkey on condition of demilitarization. In 1936, by the Montreux Convention, Turkey was permitted to refortify it.

Dardanus (där'dŭnŭs), in Greek mythology, founder of Troy; son of Zeus and the Pleiad Electra.

Dardic languages, Indo-Iranian languages of NW India. See LANGUAGE (table).

Dare, Virginia, b. 1587, on Roanoke Isl., first white child of English parents born in America.

Dares Phrygius (dâ'rēz frǐ'jēŭs), supposed author of a history of Trojan War. Latin MS of 5th cent. A.D. became a very popular source for medieval stories.

Dar-es-Salaam (där'-ěs-sŭläm'), city (pop. c.150,000), cap. of Tanzania; port on the Indian Ocean. Connected by rail to L. Tanganyika. Exports sisal, copra, cotton, and minerals. Became cap. of German East Africa 1891; passed to British 1916.

Dariel, Georgian SSR: see DARYAL.

Darien (dâ"rēěn', dâ'rēēn', Span. däryän'), E part of Panama. Properly today Isthmus of Darien is that part of Isthmus of Panama between Gulf of Darien and Gulf of San Miguel, but formerly name was applied to entire isthmus. Visited by Bastidas (1501) and Columbus (1502). Arias de Ávila (Pedrarias) succeeded ENCISO as governor in 1514 and established harsh rule over entire isthmus.

Darien. 1 (dâ"rēěn') Residential town (pop. 18,437), SW Conn., near Long Island Sound E of Stamford; settled c.1641. **2** (dâ'rēĭn) City (pop. 1,569), SE Ga., fishing port on Altamaha R., NNE of Brunswick. Founded 1736 by Scotch Highlanders recruited by James Oglethorpe to supersede Spanish influence. Nearby is site of Fort King George (1721–27), first English settlement in Ga.

Darien Scheme, Scottish colonial project. Scottish Parliament chartered trading company 1695. Efforts made to estab. colony on Isthmus of Panama failed (1698–99) with loss of many lives and great losses to Scottish investors. Showed Scotland's commercial disadvantage outside British "realm."

Darío, Rubén (rōōbĕn′ därē′ō), 1867–1916, Spanish American poet, b. Nicaragua. Spent many years in diplomatic service. Was leader of MODERNISMO. His poems have elegance and grace strengthened by vigor and power, technical mastery, and achieve poetic universatility. Major works were *Azul* (1888), *Prosas profanas* (1886). *Cantos de vida y esperanza* (1905).

Darius (dûr′ŭs), kings of anc. Persia. **Darius I** (the Great), c.459–486 B.C., reigned 521–486 B.C. Succeeding his cousin Cambyses after the fall of a false claimant, he put down rebellions, then set up the administrative system under satraps (governors responsible only to him, with checks by the army and police). This system lasted even beyond the fall of the empire to Alexander the Great. Darius campaigned against the Scythians but is best remembered as the king against whom the Ionian Greek cities revolted (c.500 B.C.), thus beginning the PERSIAN WARS. His first expedition against Greece was turned back by storms, his second defeated at MARATHON (490 B.C.). Succeeded by XERXES I. **Darius II,** d. 404 B.C., son of Artaxerxes I, succeeded his half brother Xerxes II and reigned 423?–404 B.C. Succeeded by Artaxerxes II, but CYRUS THE YOUNGER claimed the throne. **Darius III,** d. 330 B.C., was raised to the throne (336 B.C.) by the eunuch Bagoas, who had murdered Artaxerxes III and his heir. Darius had Bagoas killed but could not estab. his rule firmly. His empire fell to ALEXANDER THE GREAT, who defeated his armies at Issus (333 B.C.) and Gaugamela (331 B.C.) and pursued Darius into Bactria, where he was murdered by his cousin, the satrap Bessus. Called Darius Codomannus.

Darius the Mede, in Bible, called son of Ahasuerus and king of Chaldeans after defeat of Belshazzar; exact identity unknown. Dan. 5.31; 9.1; 11.1.

Darjeeling (därjē′lĭng), resort town (pop. 33,605), N West Bengal, India, in Himalaya foothills, alt. c.7,000 ft. Tea-growing center.

Dark Ages: see MIDDLE AGES.

dark horse, in U.S. politics, a comparatively unknown man chosen by a major party as candidate for public office, especially the presidency. Usually chosen to break a deadlocked national convention. James K. Polk is probably the best-known dark horse. Others to win presidency were Pierce and Harding.

Darlan, Jean François (zhä′ fräswä′ därlä′), 1881–1942, French admiral. Important member of VICHY GOVERNMENT from 1940; received command of armed forces 1941; advocated collaboration with Germany. After Allied landing in N Africa (Nov., 1942) went over to Allies and assumed position of high commissioner in French N and W Africa. Assassinated.

Darling, river of SE Australia, 1,702 mi. long, mainly in New South Wales; longest tributary of Murray R. Explored by Charles Sturt in 1844.

Darlington, county borough (pop. 84,162), Durham, England; railroad center. Has locomotive works, iron, steel, and woolen mills. Locomotive which drew first passenger train (1825) preserved here.

Darlington, town (pop. 6,710), NE S.C., NW of Florence, in cotton region; settled 1798. Major stock-car races held here annually.

Darmstadt (därm′stät, därm′shtät), city (pop. 123,-306), former cap. of Hesse-Darmstadt (see HESSE), West Germany. Commercial center; chemical industry.

Darnley, Henry Stuart or **Stewart, Lord,** 1545–67, claimant to English throne and second husband of MARY QUEEN OF SCOTS. Son of powerful earl of Lennox, he claimed succession to Elizabeth through his grandmother, Margaret Tudor. Catholic sympathies, claim on throne, and perhaps his handsome appear-ance induced Mary to marry him (1565). He proved vicious and dissipated, and she did not make him royal consort. Joined in murder of David Rizzio (1566); was soon without friends. Plot formed to murder him, probably under earl of Bothwell. Killed under mysterious circumstances. Father of James I.

Darrow, Clarence (Seward), 1857–1938, American lawyer. After defending (1894) Eugene V. Debs during the Pullman strike, he gave up his lucrative practice to champion the "underdog." Defended many labor leaders (e.g., William J. Haywood) and over 100 persons charged with murder (e.g., Leopold and Loeb). Opposed W. J. Bryan in the SCOPES TRIAL.

darter or **anhinga** (änhĭng′gù), slender black water bird related to cormorant. Eats fish, crustaceans, reptiles, and insects, attacking with rapierlike thrust of sharp beak, whence its name.

Dartford, municipal borough (pop. 45,643), Kent, England. Wat Tyler's rebellion broke out here. An early English paper mill was built here in 1588.

Dartmoor, upland region c.20 mi. long, Devonshire, England. Includes ancient Royal Forest of Dartmoor. An important tin-mining region in Middle Ages, area is now a source of china clay and granite. In the middle of Dartmoor, near Princetown, is **Dartmoor Prison,** built 1806–09. Housed French captives in Napoleonic Wars, American captives in War of 1812. Made a civilian prison 1850 for convicts sentenced to long terms of imprisonment or hard labor.

Dartmouth, industrial city (pop. 46,966), S N.S., Canada, on Halifax harbor, connected with Halifax by ferry and bridge. City has large sugar and oil refineries and a naval base.

Dartmouth (därt′mùth), municipal borough (pop. 5,757), Devonshire, England. Site of Royal Naval Col.

Dartmouth, residential and resort town (pop. 14,607), SE Mass., on Buzzards Bay SW of New Bedford, in dairy region; settled c.1650. Nearly annihilated in King Philip's War; later rebuilt.

Dartmouth College, at Hanover, N.H.; for men; chartered 1769, opened 1770, the ninth colonial college.

Dartmouth College Case, decided by the U.S. Supreme Court in 1819. New Hampshire legislature amended (1816) the college charter to make it a public institution. Trustees, represented by Daniel Webster, argued that the state had violated a contract and won the case. The opinion rendered by John Marshall was that the U.S. Constitution prohibits a state from abridging a contract.

Darwin, Erasmus, 1731–1802, English pioneer scientist. A physician, he also wrote a long poem, *The Botanic Garden* (1789–91), and *Zoonomia* (1794–96), which anticipates evolutionary theories. His grandson **Charles (Robert) Darwin,** 1809–82, was a naturalist. He studied medicine and ministry before becoming official naturalist on the *Beagle*. His explorations, observations, and investigations led to his formulating a concept of EVOLUTION, known as DARWINISM, set forth in his *Origin of Species* (1859). A. R. WALLACE worked out a similar theory independently. His son **Sir Francis Darwin,** 1848–1925, a botanist, assisted his father; edited his biography, letters. **Sir George Howard Darwin,** 1845–1912, brother of Francis, was an astronomer and mathematician and an authority on cosmogony.

Darwin, port (pop. 9,395), cap. of Northern Territory, Australia, on inlet of Timor Sea. Originally called Palmerston, renamed for Charles Darwin. Important for its airport on Singapore-Sydney route. A key Allied base in Second World War.

Darwinism, concept of EVOLUTION set forth by Charles Darwin. Observing the tendency of organisms to increase geometrically while numbers of given species remained about stable, he deduced a struggle for survival. He emphasized individual variation within a species and survival of those with most favorable

variations, some being transmitted to offspring. This principle of natural selection is, with modifications, almost universally accepted by scientists.

Daryal (däryăl') or **Dariel** (däréēl'), gorge. c.3,940 ft. deep, Georgian SSR, in central Greater Caucasus, below Mt. Kazbek. Formed by Terek R.; traversed by road linking Ordzhonikidze with Tiflis. Famed for wild grandeur. Known in antiquity as Caucasian or Iberian Gates.

Dashava (dŭshä'vŭ), town (pop. 4,000), W Ukraine, in N Carpathian foothills. Major natural gas center; starting point of pipelines to Kiev, Moscow, Riga, and Poland.

dasheen: see TARO.

Dass, Petter, 1647–1707, Norwegian poet, author of still-popular *Norway's Trumpet*.

date, long-lived, tall palm (*Phoenix dactylifera*) and its edible, brown fruit (1–3 in. long) borne in heavy, pendent clusters. A principal food in many desert and tropical regions from early times. Trees are now cultivated in SW U.S. and Mexico.

Dathan (dä'–), rebel with KORAH and his brother Abiram against Moses. Killed by earthquake. Numbers 16.1–35.

Datia (dŭ'tēä), town (pop. 26,447), Madhya Pradesh, India. Has superb 17th-cent. Hindu palace.

dating, determination of actual or relative age of an object, phenomenon, or series of events. Geologic dating is commonly classified as absolute (establishing actual age of earth and its rocks) or relative (determining sequence of geologic events). Methods most widely used for absolute dating include those based on varved clay and radioactivity. Following incorporation of a radioactive element into a rock at the time of the rock's formation, an increase occurs in the concentration of the element's radioactive decay products. If the initial proportion of the radioactive element is given and if the necessary half lives are known, it is possible to determine how long radioactive decay has gone on in the rock and thereby to fix the date of the rock's formation. Radiocarbon dating is used to determine date of formation of carbon-containing organic residues; ratio of carbon 14 (radioactive ISOTOPE) to carbon 12 (normal isotope) in the specimen is determined. Since carbon 14 has a known half life, it is possible to estimate the date when the specimen was formed in a living organism (from carbon derived from atmospheric carbon dioxide, which has a known proportion of carbon 14).

dative: see CASE.

Daubigny, Charles François (shärl' fräswä' dōbēnyē'), 1817–78, French landscape painter, best known for his scenes of the banks of the Seine and the Oise. Usually classed with the Barbizon school, although he never lived in Barbizon.

Daudet, Alphonse (älfōs' dōdä'), 1840–97, French author. He wrote with charm and gentle satire of his native Provence in *Lettres de mon moulin* (1869) and *Tartarin de Tarascon* (1872), his most enduring works. His son, **Leon Daudet** (lāō'), 1867–1942, author, edited the royalist, rightist daily *L'Action française* and wrote valuable memoirs (6 vols., 1914–21).

Daugherty, Harry M(icajah) (dō'ûrtē), 1860–1941, U.S. Attorney General (1921–24). Accused of taking part in the scandal concerning the oil lands at Teapot Dome. The case was dismissed.

Daughters of the American Revolution, patriotic society in U.S., open to women whose ancestors aided patriot cause in Revolution. Organized 1890.

Daulatabad (doulŭtŭbäd'), village. Andhra Pradesh, India. Its 13th-cent. fortress is built atop a conical rock c.500 ft. high. The Chand Minar minaret is an outstanding example of Moslem art.

Daumier, Honoré (ōnōrā' dōmyä'), 1808–79, French lithographer, cartoonist, and painter. Satirized the bourgeois society of his day, producing c.4,000 litho-graphs, now considered masterpieces of the art. Imprisoned for 6 months in 1832 for his political cartoon *Gargantua*. Painted c.200 small canvases, including *Third-Class Carriage* (Metropolitan Mus.).

Daun, Leopold, Graf von (lä'ōpôlt gräf' fŭn doun'), 1705–66, Austrian field marshal. Drove French from Bohemia (1742) in War of Austrian Succession; defeated Frederick II of Prussia at Kolin (1757), but lost at Torgau (1760), in Seven Years War.

Dauphin (dô'fĭn), town (pop. 7.374), W Man., Canada, on Vermilion R. and NW of Winnipeg. Agr. and milling center. Riding Mountain Natl. Park is S.

dauphin (dô'fĭn, Fr. dōfĕ'), title of eldest son (sometimes grandson) of a king of France. See DAUPHINÉ; LOST DAUPHIN.

Dauphiné (dôfēnä'), region and former province, SE France, in Hautes-Alpes, Isère, and Drôme depts.; historic cap. Grenoble. In E, Alps culminate in the BARRE DES ÉCRINS. Vineyards and silkworm raising in lower districts. Cities: Grenoble, Vienne, Valence. As part of kingdom of ARLES, region was ruled by counts of Vienne, who took title "dauphin" (etymology uncertain). Dauphin Humbert II sold it to Philip VI of France (1349). Dauphiné was governed by eldest sons of French kings until accession of Louis XI, who incorporated it with France, although technically it was part of Holy Roman Empire. Title "dauphin" thenceforth was merely honorific.

Dauthendey, Max (doutĕn'dä), 1867–1918, German poet and novelist. Wrote many volumes of exotic, impressionistic verse and a number of novels and plays (e.g., *Caprices of an Empress*, 1910).

Davao (dävou'), city (pop. 133,754), SE Mindanao, Philippines, on Davao Gulf; hemp-producing center.

D'Avenant or **Davenant, Sir William** (dăv'ŭnŭnt), 1606–68, English poet, dramatist, theater manager. He produced what are considered the first English operas.

Davenport, John, 1597–1670, Puritan clergyman, b. England. Founded New Haven, Conn. (1637–38), with Theophilus EATON. Important figure in colony.

Davenport, city (pop. 88,981), E central Iowa, SE of Cedar Rapids, on Mississippi R. across from Rock Island, Moline, and East Moline (all in Ill.; the four are known as Quad Cities). Founded 1836 on site of early trading post, it prospered with arrival (1856) of first railroad to bridge Mississippi and had heavy river traffic in late 19th cent. An important rail, commercial, and industrial center, it processes and ships farm produce. Seat of St. Ambrose Col., Marycrest Col., and Palmer School of Chiropractic. Large roller-gate dam and several locks raise river's level.

David, Saint, d. 588?, patron saint of Wales, first abbot of Menevia (SAINT DAVID'S). His shrine was an important place of pilgrimage in the Middle Ages. On his feast, March 1, the national Welsh festival is celebrated.

David [Heb.,= beloved], d. c.972 B.C., shepherd boy who became king of Hebrews (c.1012–c.972 B.C.). One of greatest of Hebrew national heroes, celebrated not only for his valor as a warrior but for his ability as a ruler and for his gifts as a poet and musician as well. Among popular stories about him: his victory over Goliath, his friendship with Jonathan, his love for Bath-sheba, the revolt of his son Absalom. Many Psalms ascribed to him. Under David, Hebrews changed from loose confederation of tribes to strong national state. According to Gospels, Jesus was of House of David. 1 Sam. 17.12–1 Kings 2.12; 1 Chron. 11–29.

David, kings of Scotland. David I, 1084–1153, was king 1124–53. In struggle for English crown between Matilda (his niece) and Stephen, he fought for Matilda without success; made peace 1141. His rule was wise and momentous. **David II** (David Bruce), 1324–71, was king 1329–71. Edward III and Edward de BALIOL invaded Scotland 1332. David invaded England 1346, was captured, and held until 1357.

David or Davit, Gerard (gä'rärt dä'vĕt), c.1460–1523, painter of the early Flemish school.

David, Jacques Louis (zhäk' lwē' dävēd'), 1748–1825, French painter. His *Andromache* and *Oath of the Horatii* established him as the leading exponent of the classical reaction. His *Mme Récamier* and the *Assassination of Marat* are renowned. He was an ardent republican despite his honored position as painter to Louis XVI. Later served Napoleon.

David, Pierre Jean: see DAVID D'ANGERS.

David, Sir Tannatt William Edgeworth (dā'vĭd), 1858–1934, British geologist. As geologist for the Shackleton antarctic expedition, he led the party which first reached the south magnetic pole.

David d'Angers (dävēd' däzhā'), or Pierre Jean David (pyĕr' zhā'), 1788–1856, French sculptor. A typical work is the group on pediment of the Panthéon.

Davids, (Thomas William) Rhys (rēs), 1843–1922, English Orientalist, a leading authority on Buddhism and on Pali texts.

Davidson, George, 1825–1911, American geographer and astronomer, b. England. Staff member of U.S. Coast and Geodetic Survey (1845–95). Directed charting of Pacific coast for navigation (1850–60). Surveyed Delaware R.; mapped Philadelphia area for fortification (1860–66). Directed Survey's Pacific coast work (1867–87). Built first Pacific coast observatory in San Francisco 1879. Made valuable meteorological and astronomical studies.

Davidson, Jo, 1883–1952, American sculptor, best known for busts of famous contemporaries.

Davidson, Thomas, 1840–1900, American scholar and philosopher. Founded 1883, in London, the Fellowship of the New Life, which preceded the Fabian Society.

Davidson, town (pop. 2,573), SW N.C., N of Charlotte. Processes cotton and produces lumber. Davidson Col. is here.

Davies, Arthur Bowen (dā'vēz), 1862–1928, American painter. His romantic work includes symbolic pictures of the female nude in idyllic landscapes. Largely responsible for famous Armory Show of 1913.

Davies, Emily (dā'vĭs), 1830–1921, English feminist, founder of college which in 1869 transferred to Cambridge and became Girton Col.

Davies, Sir John (dā'vĭs), 1569–1626, English poet, author of *Nosce Teipsum* (1599; a philosophical poem), *Hymns to Astraea* (1599), and many epigrams.

Davies, Joseph E(dward) (dā'vēz), 1876–1958, American diplomat. Was ambassador to USSR (1937–38) and ambassador to Belgium (1938–40). His book, *Mission to Moscow* (1941), pictured conditions in USSR.

Dávila, Gil González: see GONZÁLEZ DE ÁVILA, GIL.

Dávila, Pedrarias: see ARIAS DE ÁVILA, PEDRO.

Da Vinci, Leonardo: see LEONARDO DA VINCI.

Davis, Alexander Jackson, 1803–92, American architect, exponent of the Greek-revival style.

Davis, Benjamin Oliver, 1877–, American general. First Negro general in U.S. army (1940). His son, Benjamin Oliver Davis, Jr., 1912–, was first Negro general in U.S. air force (1954).

Davis, Charles Henry, 1807–77, American naval officer. In Civil War he repulsed Confederate fleet near Fort Pillow (May, 1862); annihilated fleet before Memphis, captured city (June, 1862).

Davis, David, 1815–86, Associate Justice of U.S. Supreme Court (1862–77). His decision in *Ex parte Milligan* (1866), denouncing arbitrary military power, became a bulwark of civil liberty in U.S. Helped manage Lincoln's campaign for presidency.

Davis, Dwight Filley, 1879–1945, American public official and sportsman. Was Secretary of War (1925–29) and governor general of the Philippines (1929–32). Donated (1900) the Davis Cup, trophy for international tennis competition, which brought about annual Davis Cup matches.

Davis, Elmer (Holmes), 1890–1958, American journalist and radio commentator, director (1942–45) of the Office of War Information.

Davis, Henry Winter, 1817–65, American political leader. U.S. Representative from Md. (1855–61, 1863–65). Opposed Reconstruction program of Pres. Lincoln with more radical plan of his own.

Davis, Jefferson, 1808–89, American statesman, President of CONFEDERACY (1861–65). U.S. Senator from Miss. (1847–51). Secretary of War (1853–57). Again Senator (1857–61), he resigned at secession of Miss. Provisional president of Confederacy, then regular president; inaugurated Feb., 1862. Administration stormy as he assumed strong centralized power, thus weakening states' rights policy for which South had seceded. Lee surrendered without his approval. Captured and confined at Fort Monroe for two years; released 1867, never prosecuted.

Davis or Davys, John, 1550?–1605, British navigator. In seeking Northwest Passage, clarified much arctic geography N of Labrador. Discovered Falkland Isls. (1592). Lost his life in East Indies fighting Japanese pirates. Invented useful quadrant.

Davis, John William, 1873–1955, American lawyer. Served as U.S. Congressman (1911–13). Nominated as compromise Democratic presidential candidate in 1924 after two-week convention deadlock; won only 136 electoral votes.

Davis, Richard Harding, 1864–1916, American correspondent for all major wars of his era, author of travel books, romantic stories, and plays.

Davis, Stuart, 1894–1964, American painter of abstractions. Incorporated exciting jazz tempos into the vibrant patterns of his paintings.

Davis, William Morris, 1850–1934, American geographer. Global traveler, authority on land forms, prolific contributor to geographical journals, he helped advance science of physiography.

Davis, Mount, peak (3,213 ft.), SW Pa., in the Alleghenies near Md. line. Highest point in state.

Davis Cup: see DAVIS, DWIGHT FILLEY.

Davis Mountains, W Texas, SE of El Paso, rising to 8,382 ft. in Mt. Livermore (or Baldy Peak or Old Baldy). Parks and scenery attract visitors.

Davisson, Clinton Joseph, 1881–1958, American physicist. Shared 1937 Nobel Prize in Physics for demonstrations confirming Louis de Broglie's theory of wave properties of moving electrons.

Davis Strait, between Greenland and Baffin Isl., connecting Atlantic Ocean and Baffin Sea, c.200 mi. wide at narrowest point. John Davis sailed through in 1587.

Davit, Gerard: see DAVID, GERARD.

Davos (dävos'), town (resident pop. 9,588), Grisons canton, E Switzerland. Winter sports; health resort for tuberculosis.

Davout, Louis Nicolas (lwē' nēkôlä' dävoō'), 1770–1823, marshal of France, duke of AUERSTEDT, prince of Eckmühl; one of Napoleon's ablest lieutenants.

Davy, Sir Humphry (dā'vē), 1778–1829, English chemist and physicist. He investigated laughing gas; isolated sodium, potassium, calcium, barium, boron, magnesium, and strontium; did electrochemical research; established elementary nature of chlorine; and advanced theory that hydrogen is characteristic of acids.

Davys, John: see DAVIS, JOHN.

Dawes, Charles G(ates) (dôz), 1865–1951, American statesman and banker. Vice President of United States (1925–29). Shared 1925 Nobel Peace Prize for forwarding the Dawes Plan in 1924 to Reparations Commission of the Allied nations. Plan provided for reduction in payment of reparations and stabilization of German finances.

Dawes, Henry Laurens, 1816–1903, U.S. Senator from Mass. (1875–93). Sponsored Dawes Act, 1887, passed by U.S. Congress to provide for granting of individual landholdings to civilized Indians who would renounce their tribal holdings. Began the absorbing of Indians into body politic. **Dawes Commission,** commission to Five Civilized Tribes, was created by Congress in 1893. It reorganized Indian Territory by getting consent of chiefs to substitute individual for tribal land holding.

Dawes Plan: see DAWES, CHARLES GATES.

Dawson or **Dawson City,** town (pop. 881), W Yukon, Canada, at junction of Yukon and Klondike rivers. Trade center of a mining region, Dawson was a boom town in 1898 gold rush and was territorial cap. of Yukon until 1951.

Dawson Creek, village (pop. 10,946), E B.C., Canada, near Alta. border, NE of Prince George. S terminus of Alaska Highway.

Dax (däks), town (est. pop. 14,557), Landes dept., SW France, in Gascony. Famous hot mineral springs.

Day, Benjamin Henry, 1810–89, American journalist. Founded the New York *Sun* (1833) and made it a cheap popular paper before selling it (1838) to Moses Y. Beach. His son, **Benjamin Day,** 1838–1916, invented the Ben Day, or Benday, process for reproducing maps and illustrations.

Day, Clarence (Shepard), 1874–1935, American humorist, author of *God and My Father* (1932), *Life with Father* (1935), and *Life with Mother* (1937).

Day, John, 1522–84, English printer. Designed and made type, including musical notes and the first Anglo-Saxon type. Printed (under another title) first English edition of John Foxe's *Book of Martyrs* (1563).

Day, Thomas, 1748–89, English social reformer. His *History of Sandford and Merton* (3 vols., 1783–89), contrasts "natural" and conventional education.

Day, William Rufus, 1849–1923, Associate Justice of U.S. Supreme Court (1903–22). In Spanish-American War (1898) was U.S. Secy. of State and then chairman of U.S. peace commissioners.

Daye, Stephen, c.1594–1668, British settler in Mass., a locksmith, usually called first printer in English American colonies. Supervised Cambridge Press, first colonial printing plant. Published *Bay Psalm Book* (1640), first book printed in colonies. Actual printing was probably done by his son, **Matthew Daye,** c.1620–1649, a trained printer.

Day Lewis, C(ecil), 1904–, English writer, b. Ireland, author of several volumes of highly praised poetry and (under pseud. Nicholas Blake) of detective stories.

daylight-saving time, time reckoned later (usually one hour) than standard time. Adopted by federal law in U.S. as wartime measure (1918–19) and during Second World War, its use was continued as summer time at option of state and local governments by turning clocks ahead in spring and back in autumn. In 1966 Federal law directed all states to observe uniform daylight-saving time unless a state's legislature voted specifically to stay on standard time.

day nursery or **crèche,** institution for daytime care of children of working mothers. Originated 1844 in France; estab. in U.S. after 1854. Now regulated by states.

Dayton. 1 City (pop. 262,332), SW Ohio, NNE of Cincinnati on Great Miami R. at influx of Stillwater R.; settled 1796. Grew with extension of canals (1830s, 1840s) and railroads (1850s). First large city to adopt city-manager form of government (1913). Aviation center and industrial, trade, and distribution point for farm area. Mfg. of precision tools, refrigeration and lighting equipment, electric motors, auto parts. Was home of Wright brothers, who estab. research aircraft plant here. Here are Univ. of Dayton, Dayton Art Inst., and Carillon Park (with restored Wright brothers' plane and fine carillon tower). Wright-Patterson Air Force Base is ENE. **2** City (pop. 3,500), SE Tenn., on Tennessee R., NNE of Chattanooga; settled 1820. Scene of SCOPES TRIAL. William Jennings Bryan Col. is here; ANTIOCH COLLEGE is nearby.

Daytona Beach (dātō′nù), resort city (pop. 37,395), NE Fla., on Atlantic coast S of St. Augustine and on Halifax R. (lagoon), in citrus-fruit area. Founded 1870 in area first settled by Spanish Franciscans in late 16th and 17th cent. Noted for its hard, white beach, it has been scene of auto speed trials since 1903. Bethune-Cookman Col. is here.

DDT: see INSECTICIDE.

Dead, Book of the: see BOOK OF THE DEAD.

deadly nightshade: see NIGHTSHADE.

Dead River, NW Maine, rising in Chain Lakes on Canadian border and flowing NE to Kennebec R. Benedict Arnold followed its course on his march to Quebec, 1775.

Dead Sea, salt lake, on border of Jordan and Israel; c.45 mi. long, 3–10 mi. wide, c.1,300 ft. below sea level, max. depth c.1,300 ft. Lies in the Ghor, a great depression. Far saltier than the ocean, it yields minerals (esp. potash and bromides). It is the biblical Salt Sea, Sea of the Plain, and East Sea.

Dead Sea Scrolls, documents of great archaeological, historical, and paleographical value, discovered in 1947 and later in caves above the waters of the NW Dead Sea. Archaeologists have shown that the scrolls stored in jars in the first cave at Qumran were written between 1st cent. B.C. and first half of 1st cent. A.D. They include oldest extant manuscript of a biblical book (Isaiah), hymns of thanksgiving, eschatological *War between Sons of Light and Darkness,* and *The Manual of Discipline* which regulates a community resembling the ESSENES. Startling parallels in expression and thought between some Qumran scrolls and the New Testament (esp. Gospel according to St. John) have led to speculation about the Essene doctrines and early Christianity and about the possibility that Jesus and John the Baptist were Essenes.

Deadwood, city (pop. 3,045), W S.Dak., in Deadwood Gulch in Black Hills, NW of Rapid City; settled 1876 after discovery of gold here. City's boom-and-bust cycles followed fortunes of nearby gold and silver mines. Now tourist and trade center for mine, lumber, and livestock area. Has Adams Memorial Mus. and graves of Wild Bill Hickok and Calamity Jane; Deadwood Dick's cabin and grave are near.

Deadwood Dick, American frontiersman, celebrated in many dime novels. Original is supposedly Richard W. Clarke (1845–1930), an Englishman who came to the gold diggings of the Black Hills and became a scout.

deafness, partial or complete loss of hearing. Causes include infections, especially in the head; diseases, e.g., scarlet fever, syphilis; obstructions of auditory canal; and bone formation in ear labyrinth capsule. Electrical aids are commonly employed. School for education of deaf estab. 1755 in Paris by C. M. de l'EPÉE. Other pioneers in teaching deaf include A. M. and A. G. BELL, and T. H. Gallaudet and his sons. Most of the deaf can be taught to speak; others use manual alphabet.

Deak, Francis (dě′äk), Hung. *Deák Ferenc,* 1803–76, Hungarian statesman. Opposed extremism of Louis KOSSUTH during revolution of 1848–49; became leader of his nation after defeat of revolutionists. Insisted on recognition of Hungary as separate kingdom, but in union with Austria; negotiated, in cooperation with Julius ANDRASSY, creation of AUSTRO-HUNGARIAN MONARCHY (1867).

Deakin, Alfred, 1856–1919, Australian statesman. Fought for and helped estab. federation of Australian states. Was three times prime minister.

Deal, municipal borough (pop. 24,791), Kent, England. Reputed landing place of Caesar 55 B.C. One of CINQUE PORTS, it has official residence (Walmer Castle) of Lord Warden. Deal is a naval station.

Deal Island, off Eastern Shore, Md., in Tangier Sound N of Crisfield. Has seafood industry.

De Amicis, Edmondo (ädmōn′dō dä ämē′chěs), 1846–1908, Italian author of travel books and novel *Cuore: an Italian Schoolboy's Journal* (1886; Eng. tr., 1887).

Dean, Jerome Herman (Dizzy Dean), 1911–, American baseball pitcher, outstanding right-hander. With St.

Louis Cardinals (1930-38). Original name possibly Jay Hanna Dean. Later an outstanding sportscaster.

Dean, Forest of, ancient royal forest, Gloucestershire, England.

Deane, Silas, 1737–89, American Revolutionary patriot and diplomat. As diplomatic agent in France, secured commercial and military aid for colonies and recruited foreign officers.

Dearborn, Henry, 1751–1829, American general. U.S. Secretary of War (1801–9). Relieved of command of N frontier in War of 1812 because of his inaction. Fort Dearborn named for him.

Dearborn, city, (pop. 112,007), SE Mich., on River Rouge, W of Detroit; settled 1795. Early carriage making here led to automobile mfg. City grew after First World War when Henry Ford's auto plants were built. Site of Edison Inst., incl. GREENFIELD VILLAGE. Henry Ford born here; his estate, "Fair Lane," is on river. Dearborn Center of Univ. of Michigan is here.

Dearborn, Fort, U.S. army post on Chicago R., estab. 1803; named for Henry Dearborn. Site of Indian attack in 1812. Chicago grew around rebuilt fort.

death. In man, death is definite if no heartbeat is detectable by stethoscope for some time, if circulation is not backed up by cord around arm or leg, or if rigor mortis has set in. Heart may beat after breathing ceases; nervous system stimulation is possible for short time after heart stops beating, thus resuscitation sometimes possible.

Death Valley, E Calif., deep and arid basin, walled in W by Panamint Range and in E by Amargosa Range. Annual rainfall is less than 2.03 in. Summer temperatures are among world's highest. Has alkali flats, salt beds, briny pools, and colored and grotesque rocks. Badwater, 282 ft. below sea level, is W Hemisphere's lowest point. Valley named 1849 by party of gold seekers. Has yielded gold and borax. Vast desert solitude enlivened by many small animals; peculiar plants attract scientists. Panamint Indians are only group ever to be self-subsisting here. Here is Scotty's Castle, ostentatious home of adventurer Walter Scott (Death Valley Scotty). Death Valley Natl. Monument extends into SW Nev.

Deauville (dōvēl'), seaside resort, Calvados dept., N France, on English Channel.

De Bary, Heinrich Anton (hīn'rĭkh än'tōn dù bärē'), 1831–88, German botanist, authority on fungi.

debenture, document acknowledging indebtedness; in England similar to BOND.

Debierne, André Louis (ädrä' lwē dùbyĕrn'), 1874–, French chemist. He discovered actinium and worked with the Curies on radioactivity.

Deborah, Israel's only woman judge. Helped Barak defeat Sisera and free Israel from King Jabin. Song of Deborah one of great poems in Bible. Judges 4; 5.

De Bow, J(ames) D(unwoody) B(rownson), 1820–67, American editor. Began publishing monthly *De Bow's Review* 1846, which became a leading non-political journal. Also a statistician.

Debrecen (dĕ'brĕtsĕn), city (est. pop. 137,000), E Hungary. Commercial center. Historic stronghold of Hungarian Protestantism. University (chartered 1912) grew out of Calvinist college (founded 1550). Hungarian independence was proclaimed at Debrecen by revolutionary government on April 14, 1849. Formerly spelled Debreczen.

Debs, Eugene V(ictor), 1855–1926, American Socialist leader. Advocate of industrial unionism and a pacifist; imprisoned 1895 for violating injunction in strike at Pullman, Ill., and in 1918 under Espionage Act. Presidential candidate five times. Widely revered as martyr for his principles.

debt, obligation in services, money, or goods owed by one party (debtor) to another (creditor). If debtor fails to pay, a court may assign payment out of his property. In ancient times debtors unable to pay were sold into slavery, and imprisonment for debt persisted into 19th cent. Today relief is afforded by BANKRUPTCY.

debt, public, indebtedness of a government expressed in money terms. Such debts typically result from revenue deficiencies, wars, and expenses for public works or emergency projects. Modern form of debt is public loan through government bonds, treasury notes, and other instruments. Ultimate security of public debt is willingness of public to pay taxes and ability of government to collect.

Deburau or **Debureau, Jean Gaspard** (dùbürō'), 1796–1846, French pantomime performer. Famous for introduction of character PIERROT.

Debussy, Claude (klōd' dùbüsē'), 1862–1918, outstanding composer of the French impressionist movement. His piano music includes the *Suite bergamasque* (containing *Clair de Lune*); *The Children's Corner*; 24 preludes, including *La Cathédrale engloutie*; and 12 études. Among his orchestral works are *L'Après-midi d'un faune, Nocturnes,* and *La Mer.* He also wrote many songs and an opera, *Pelléas et Mélisande.*

Debye, Peter Joseph Wilhelm (dēbī'), 1884–1966, American physicist, b. Netherlands. Won 1936 Nobel Prize in Chemistry for work on structure of molecules.

decadents (dīkā'dŭntz, dĕ'kùdŭntz), name loosely applied to late 19th-cent. artists and writers who strove to express morbid and macabre elements in human emotions; often confused with French SYMBOLISTS, who influenced the movement. They were most evident in England (e.g., Oscar Wilde, Ernest Dowson, Aubrey Beardsley).

Decalogue: see TEN COMMANDMENTS.

Decameron, The (dīkā'mùrŭn), or **Il Decamerone** (ĕl dākämärō'nä) [Gr.,= 10 parts], collection of 100 charming and often licentious tales by Giovanni BOCCACCIO, written 1348–53.

decathlon (dĭkăth'lŏn), composite contest consisting of broad jump, high jump, discus throw, shot put, javelin throw, pole vault, 100-meter, 400-meter, and 1500-meter flat races, 110-meter hurdle race.

Decatur, Stephen (dĕkā'tŭr), 1779–1820, American naval officer. Became famous in TRIPOLITAN WAR. In Algerine War (1815) he forced dey of Algeria to sign treaty ending American tribute to Algeria. Responsible for toast ending, "may she always be in the right; but our country, right or wrong."

Decatur. 1 Industrial city (pop. 29,217), N Ala., on Tennessee R., N of Birmingham; founded 1820. A market, mfg., and shipping center, with shipyards. Uses TVA power. Almost destroyed in Civil War. **2** City (pop. 22,026), NW Ga., suburb E of Atlanta, at foot of Stone Mt. Seat of Agnes Scott Col. and Columbia Theological Seminary. **3** City (pop. 78,-004), central Ill., ENE of Springfield on Sangamon R. (here dammed to form L. Decatur); founded 1829. A rail, industrial, and distributing center in rich farm and livestock area. Coal deposits underlie region. Has log cabin courthouse where Lincoln practiced, library with Lincoln collection, and, nearby, site of first Lincoln home in Ill. Grand Army of the Republic was organized here April, 1866. Seat of Millikin Univ.

Decazes, Élie (ālē' dùkäz'), 1780–1860, French premier (1819–20) under LOUIS XVIII; a moderate.

Deccan (dĕ'kän"), region, S India. Historically defined as all India S of Narbada R., thus including the CARNATIC.

December: see MONTH.

Decembrist Conspiracy, military revolt at St. Petersburg, Russia, at the accession of NICHOLAS I (Dec., 1825). The plotters, belonging to liberal revolutionary societies, hoped to place Nicholas's brother Constantine on the throne and to obtain a constitution. The revolt was crushed, but it led to the spread of revolutionary doctrine and consequent police terrorism.

decimal system (dĕ'sĭmŭl), numerical notation system with base 10. Term decimal applied either to any number in system or to numbers less than 1 expressed in decimal notation. A row of digits in decimal system is a shorthand notation for an arithmetical sum. Thus, for example, the notation 543.21 stands for $5 \times (100) + 4 \times (10) + 3 \times (1) + 2 \times (1/10) + 1 \times (1/100)$ or for $5 \times (10^2) + 4 \times (10^1) + 3 \times (10^0) + 2 \times (10^{-1}) + 1 \times (10^{-2})$. In this scheme 10 is called the base. Theoretically the base may be any number. The BINARY SYSTEM uses 2 as the base. It is formed as follows: 1 (decimal system) $= 1 \times 2^0 = 1$ (binary system) $(2^0 = 1)$, $2 = 1 \times 2^1 + 0 \times 2^0$, $3 = 1 \times 2^1 + 1 \times 2^0 = 11$, $4 = 1 \times 2^2 + 0 \times 2^1 + 0 \times 2^0 = 100$, $5 = 1 \times 2^2 + 0 \times 2^1 + 1 \times 2^0 = 101$, etc. Thus the binary number consists of the coefficients of the powers of 2. To find the binary equivalent of an integral decimal, find the greatest power of 2 less than the number, and subtract it from the number. Find the greatest power of 2 less than the remainder, and subtract from the remainder. Continue until remainder is 0. Example: the binary representation of the decimal 100 is found as follows: 1) $64 = 2^6$ is highest power of 2 less than 100, 2) $100 - 64 = 36$, similarly, 3) $32 = 2^5$, 4) $36 - 32 = 4$, 5) $4 = 2^2$, 6) $4 - 4 = 0$. Hence 100 (decimal notation) $= 64 + 32 + 4 = 1 \times 2^6 + 1 \times 2^5 + 0 \times 2^4 + 0 \times 2^3 + 1 \times 2^2 + 0 \times 2^1 + 0 \times 2^0 = 1100100$ (binary notation). For book classification scheme, see Melvil DEWEY.

Decius (dē'shŭs), 201–51, Roman emperor (249–51). Sent to put down a mutiny against Philip the Arabian, he headed it instead, defeated and killed Philip, and became emperor. Persecuted the Christians vigorously. He was killed trying to repel the Goths in Moesia.

Decker, Thomas: see DEKKER, THOMAS.

Declaration of Independence, adopted July 4, 1776, by delegates of Thirteen Colonies, announcing their separation from Great Britain and making them into the United States. Written almost wholly by Thomas Jefferson. Opening paragraphs state idea of government based on theory of NATURAL RIGHTS. The most important American historical document, its combination of general principles and an abstract theory of government and its detailed enumeration of grievances and injustices make it one of the great political documents of the West.

Declaration of Rights: see BILL OF RIGHTS.

Declaration of the Rights of Man and Citizen, historic French document, drafted by Sieyès (1789), embodied as preamble of French constitution of 1791. Based on J. J. Rousseau's theories and on American Declaration of Independence, it asserted the equality of all men, the sovereignty of the people, the inalienable rights of the individual to "liberty, property, security."

declination: see COMPASS 2.

Decorah (dĭkô'rŭ), city (1966 pop. 7,054), NE Iowa, near Minn., on Upper Iowa R., ENE of Charles City. History of early Norwegian settlers preserved in museum at LUTHER COLLEGE. Limestone ice caves and natural springs nearby.

Decoration Day: see MEMORIAL DAY.

decorations, civil and military. Practice of rewarding achievements grew from medieval custom of conferring knighthood. In Great Britain this still exists in such orders as Garter, Thistle, and Bath. In Europe such orders have tended to lose feudal connotations. Among best known are Order of Golden Fleece (1429 or 1430, Austria and Spain); Dannebrog and Elephant (1219 and 1462, Denmark); Annunciata and SS. Maurice and Lazarus (1362 and 1434, Italy); papal order of Golden Spur (1559); Black Eagle, Red Eagle, and Pour le Mérite (Prussia); White Eagle and Polonia Restituta (Poland); and Legion of Honor (France). Military decorations for heroism include Croix de Guerre (France); Iron Cross (Germany); Distinguished Service Order, Royal Victoria Order, and Order of the British Empire (England); Congressional Medal of Honor (1862), Distinguished Service Cross, Distinguished Service Medal, Distinguished Flying Medal, Purple Heart (1782), and silver and bronze

stars (U.S.); and Red Star, Victory, Lenin, Suvarov, and Alexander Nevsky awards (USSR).

De Coster, Charles Théodore Henri (dù kō'stùr, Fr. shärl' tāōdôr' ārē' dù kôstēr'), 1827–79, Belgian author. His chief work, *La légende d'Ulenspiegel* (1868), is written in archaic style and based on the Germanic folk hero Till Eulenspiegel.

De Crayer, Gaspar: see CRAYER, GASPAR DE.

decree, in British and U.S. law, final decision in equitable actions, differing from a judgment (in actions at law) in being less rigid and not limited to the award of money damages. Can be more easily enforced by proceedings for contempt of court. Familiar are the injunction and the decree of divorce.

Dedham (dĕ'dùm), town (pop. 23,869), E Mass., SW of Boston; settled 1635. Oldest frame house in U.S., Fairbanks house (1636), is here. Scene of Sacco-Vanzetti trial (1921). Horace Mann practiced law here.

Dee, John, 1527–1608, British scientist and astrologer. Drew up geographical materials on newly found lands for Queen Elizabeth and urged adoption of Gregorian calendar. His interest in the occult led to accusations of sorcery and fame as a magician.

Dee, rivers in Scotland; **1** Aberdeenshire and Kincardine; famous for its beauty, flows c.90 mi. past Balmoral Castle to North Sea; **2** Kirkcudbrightshire.

Dee, river of Wales and England, flowing 70 mi. to Irish Sea. Shallow estuary is an expanse of sand at low tide.

Deep River, town (pop. 2,968), S Conn., on Connecticut R., NW of Essex. Name changed from SAYBROOK 1947 to distinguish it from Old Saybrook town, which is S.

deer, ruminant mammal of family Cervidae found over most of world except Australia. Males usually have antlers, which are shed annually. If they lack antlers (e.g., the MUSK DEER and Chinese river deer) their upper canines are long and serve as weapons. Deer are polygamous. They eat herbaceous plants, lichens, and mosses. The white-tailed deer (*Odocoileus virginianus*), a source of many necessities for American Indians and settlers, was nearly exterminated through years of slaughter but is now abundant. There are more white-tailed deer in the U.S. now than before arrival of the white man; some areas are overpopulated. See CARIBOU; ELK; MOOSE; REINDEER; WAPITI.

Deere, John, 1804–86, American manufacturer of agr. implements, pioneer maker of steel plows.

Deerfield. 1 Village (1966 pop. 17,245), NE Ill., NNW of Chicago. **2** Town (pop. 3,338), NW Mass., on Deerfield R., S of Greenfield; settled before 1670. Many inhabitants killed in Indian massacre 1704. Deerfield Academy, private secondary school for boys, is here. Town includes South Deerfield village (pop. 1,253).

Deerfield, river, c.70 mi. long, rising in S Vt. and flowing S into NW Mass., then SE to Connecticut R. near Greenfield, Mass. Furnishes power.

Deering, William, 1826–1913, American farm machinery manufacturer. He developed the first successful grain binder.

Deer Isle, island, c.10 mi. long, 6 mi. wide, in East Penobscot Bay, S Maine. Comprises towns of Deer Isle (pop. 1,129) in N and Stonington in S.

Deer Park, residential town (pop. 16,726), SE N.Y., on central Long Isl., N of Babylon. Has aircraft-instruments laboratory.

Defense, United States Department of, created 1947; reorganized 1949. James V. Forrestal, who pioneered in its organization, became first Secretary of Defense. Department guards U.S. security and coordinates activities of army, navy, and air force. Its organization has eliminated much overlapping and duplication.

defense mechanism, psychoanalytic expression indicating unconscious mode of behavior designed to ward off anticipated or imagined criticism or condemnation. These "dynamisms" include rationalization—substitution (for ego's sake) of socially acceptable for unsocial motives; repression–barring of distressing ideas from consciousness; regression–to infantile behavior, gratifications; projection–assignment to others of own ego-repudiated urges; identification–reaction to others' desires as if one's own; sublimation–redirection of libido to constructive ends; conversion–transformation of psychological conflict into actual physical symptoms.

Deffand, marquise du: see DU DEFFAND.

Defiance, city (pop. 14,553), NW Ohio, at junction of Auglaize and Maumee rivers, SW of Toledo, in farm area; settled 1790. Fort Defiance built here 1794; Fort Winchester built nearby 1812. Seat of The Defiance Col.

deflation: see INFLATION.

Defoe or **De Foe, Daniel,** 1660–1731, English writer, author of ROBINSON CRUSOE. A pamphleteer and journalist, he won the favor of William III with his poem, *The True-born Englishman* (1701), but strong anti-Tory sentiment in *The Shortest Way with Dissenters* (1702) brought imprisonment under Anne. His *Review* (1704–13) was an early and influential journal. Besides *Robinson Crusoe* (1719), he wrote *Moll Flanders* (1722), *Roxana* (1724), and hundreds of other vigorously written books and pamphlets.

De Forest, Lee, 1873–1961, American inventor. Pioneered in development of wireless telegraphy, sound pictures, television. Granted over 300 patents.

De Funiak Springs (dē fū′nēăk), town (pop. 5,282), NW Fla., NW of Panama City. Great spring in center of town forms L. De Funiak.

Degas, (Hilaire Germain) Edgar (ĕdgär′ dügä′), 1834–1917, French impressionist painter. Fanatic in his self-criticism and despairing of attaining perfection in oils, he turned in his middle life to pastels. Ballet dancers, modistes, and women at their toilet were among his favorite subjects. His later works, daring in composition, free in execution, and immensely effective in color, greatly influenced such men as Gauguin and Picasso.

De Gasperi, Alcide (älche′dä dä gä′spärē), 1881–1954, Italian premier (1945–53); led Christian Democrats.

De Gaulle, Charles: see GAULLE, CHARLES DE.

De Haven, Edwin Jesse, 1816–65, American arctic explorer. Led fruitless search for Sir John Franklin and party (1850); discovered Grinnell Land.

De Heem, Jan Davidszoon: see HEEM, JAN DAVIDSZOON DE.

Dehmel, Richard (rīkh′ärt dā′mŭl), 1863–1920, German poet. His works, some of which lean toward social themes but away from naturalism, include the collection *Erlösungen* [redemptions] (1891), *Schöne wilde Welt* [fair wide world] (1913), and the novel in verse *Zwei Menschen* [two souls] (1903).

De Hooch or **De Hoogh, Pieter:** see HOOCH, PIETER DE.

Dehra (dā′rŭ) or **Dehra Dun** (dōōn), city (pop. 116,404), NW Uttar Pradesh, India. Site of temple (1699) of Ram Rai, founder of Hindu Udasi sect.

Deira (dē′īrŭ), Anglian kingdom between the Humber and the Tyne, united (late 6th cent.) with Bernicia to form Northumbria.

Deirdre (dâr′drŭ, dēr′–), heroine of Irish story. Reared to be wife of King Conchobar of Ulster, but she fell in love with Naoise and fled to England with him and his brothers. On their return home Conchobar slew the brothers, and Deirdre died on their grave.

deists (dē′ĭsts), group of rationalists of 17th and 18th cent. who rejected formal religion and supernatural revelation but argued that the course of nature demonstrates the existence of God. There were deistic elements in the thinking of Voltaire, Rousseau, Franklin, and Jefferson. The religious orthodox called them freethinkers.

De Kalb, Johann: see KALB, JOHANN.

De Kalb, city (1963 pop. 23,103), N Ill., W of Chicago, in farm area; settled in 1830s. Seat of Northern Illinois Univ.

Deken, Agatha: see WOLFF, ELISABETH.

Dekker or **Decker, Thomas,** 1572?–1632?, English dramatist, author of *The Shoemaker's Holiday* (1600), *Old Fortunatus* (1600). Collaborated with Middleton on *The Honest Whore* (1604; Part II, 1630) and *The Roaring Girl* (1611), with Massinger on *The Virgin Martyr* (1622). Also wrote pamphlets and satirical *The Gull's Hornbook* (1609).

de Kooning, Willem (dŭ Kōō′nĭng), 1904–, American painter, b. Netherlands. In the 1940s he became a leader of the abstract expressionists.

de Kruif, Paul (dŭ krīf′), 1890–, American writer on scientific subjects. Works include *Microbe Hunters* (1926) and *Hunger Fighters* (1939).

Delacroix, Ferdinand Victor Eugène (fĕrdänä′ vēktôr′ üzhĕn düläkrwä′), 1798–1863, leading French romantic painter. Studied with Guérin but early revolted against academicism. Aroused controversy by using bright color and dynamic treatment, as in *Dante and Vergil* (c.1822), *Massacre of Scio,* and scenes of Morocco (visited 1832). As a colorist he ranks among the great French painters.

Delagoa Bay, large inlet of Indian Ocean, S Mozambique. Discovered 1502 by Vasco da Gama. British claimed area in late 19th cent. Portuguese estab. city of Lourenço Marques, named for early explorer of region.

de la Mare, Walter (dĕl′ŭmâr″), 1873–1956, English poet and novelist. His work shows rich imagination in poetry and prose. Some of his poetry is primarily for children (e.g., *Peacock Pie,* 1913). Best-known novel *Memoirs of a Midget* (1921).

Delambre, Jean Baptiste Joseph (zhä′ bätēst′ zhôzĕf′ dülä′brü), 1749–1822, French astronomer and mathematician, noted for astronomical computations and work in spherical geometry.

De Lancey (dŭ lăn′sē), family of political leaders, soldiers, and merchants prominent in colonial N.Y. **Étienne De Lancey** or **Stephen De Lancey,** 1663–1741, b. France, became one of New York city's wealthiest merchants. His son, **James De Lancey,** 1703–60, was chief justice of provincial supreme court (1733–60) and served as lieutenant governor (1753–55, 1757–60). Later members of family supported the British in American Revolution.

De Land, resort city (pop. 10,775), NE Fla., NNE of Orlando; founded 1876. Seat of Stetson Univ. Ponce de Leon Springs and Blue Springs are nearby.

Delano (dĕ′lŭnō), city (pop. 11,913), S central Calif., NNW of Bakersfield, in cotton and fruit area.

Delany, Martin Robinson (dŭlä′nē), 1812–85, American Negro leader. Furthered return of American Negroes to Africa in 1850s.

Delarey or **De la Rey, Jacobus Hercules** (yäkō′bŭs hĕr′kŭlēs dŭlärī′), 1847?–1914, Boer general in South African War.

Delaroche, Hippolyte (ēpôlēt′ dülärôsh′), 1797–1856, French historical and portrait painter, commonly called Paul Delaroche.

De la Rue, Warren (dĕ′lŭrōō), 1815–89, British scientist and inventor, a pioneer in celestial photography and inventor of a photoheliograph.

Delaunay, Robert (rō′bĕr dülōnā′), 1885–1941, French painter, founded orphism–an amalgam of fauve color, futurist dynamism, and analytical cubism–which sought to emulate the rhythms but not the appearance of nature.

Delaware, state (2,057 sq. mi.; pop. 446,292), E U.S.; one of Thirteen Colonies; cap. DOVER. WILMINGTON only large city. Occupies NE part of peninsula between Chesapeake Bay and Delaware Bay. Bordered E by the Atlantic, Delaware Bay, Delaware R. Land all low-lying, from sand dunes in S to low hills in N. Crossed by many small rivers. Ranks 49th of U.S. states in area. Industry in N and agr. in S are well-balanced. Chief crops are corn, soybeans, potatoes, grains. Poultry raising and fishing important. Industry centered around Wilmington, with mfg. of chemicals (growing out of DU PONT family enterprises), automobiles, textiles, leather goods, petroleum products. Easy laws on business incorporation bring many large corporations to state. Henry Hudson sailed into Delaware Bay 1609, followed the next year by British sea captain Sir Samuel Argall. Region was contested by Dutch and English. First Dutch settlement (1631) was short lived. NEW SWEDEN founded 1638, captured by Dutch 1655, sèized by British 1664. Transferred to William Penn 1682, it became sovereign state 1776. Led in movement to revise Articles of Confederation, was first state to ratify U.S. Constitution. Loyal to Union in Civil War despite strong segregationist sentiment, manifested again in 20th cent. in resistance to integration.

Delaware, city (pop. 13,282), central Ohio, on Olentangy R., N of Columbus; laid out 1801. Trade center in farm area, with some mfg. Seat of OHIO WESLEYAN UNIVERSITY.

Delaware, river, 315 mi. long, rising in the Catskills, SE N.Y., and flowing SE between N.Y. and Pa. to Port Jervis, then generally S between N.J. and Pa. to Delaware Bay. Trenton and Camden (N.J.), Philadelphia and DELAWARE WATER GAP (Pa.), and Wilmington and New Castle (Del.) are on its course. Chesapeake and Delaware Canal links river with other waterways. Reservoirs and dams on headstreams provide flood control. Further development planned under DELAWARE RIVER BASIN COMPACT. DELAWARE AQUEDUCT is part of New York city water supply. Washington Crossing villages (N.J. and Pa.) are at point where Washington crossed river (1776) before capture of Trenton. Creation of a national recreation area on upper river authorized 1965.

Delaware, University of, at Newark; land grant, state supported; coed.; founded 1743 as Presbyterian school, became Newark Col. 1833; called Delaware Col. 1843–1921.

Delaware and Raritan Canal, N.J., abandoned canal connecting Delaware and Raritan rivers between Bordentown and New Brunswick; completed 1834.

Delaware Aqueduct, SE N.Y., carrying water from Delaware R. basin to New York city. When completed, it will be 85-mile tunnel running from Rondout Reservoir in Sullivan co. to New York city water system at Hillview Reservoir in S Westchester co.

Delaware Bay, inlet of the Atlantic between N.J. and Del., receiving Delaware R.

Delaware City, city (pop. 1,658), N central Del., on Delaware R., S of Wilmington. Fort Delaware, on Pea Patch Isl., was Federal Civil War prison.

Delaware Indians, members of related Indian tribes, once living in region of Delaware R., later in Susquehanna valley, of Algonquian linguistic family. Called themselves Lenni-Lenape or Lenape. Friendly with Dutch; made famous treaty (1682) with William Penn. Iroquois drove them W into Ohio (1720). Defeated (1794) by Anthony Wayne. Later they moved to Kansas and Texas and were finally removed to the Indian Territory.

Delaware River Basin Compact, agreement signed 1961 by U.S. and Del., Pa., N.J., and N.Y., calling for 50-year program to utilize and develop Delaware R. basin water resources.

Delaware Water Gap, borough (pop. 554), E central Pa., where Delaware R. cuts through Kittatinny Mt., ESE of Stroudsburg. Scenic summer resort. On N.J. side of gap for which town is named is Mt. Tammany; on Pa. side is Mt. Minsi.

De la Warr, Thomas West, Baron (dĕ'lûwûr), 1577–1618, first governor of Virginia colony, b. England. Delaware was later named for him.

Delcassé, Théophile (tāôfēl' dĕlkäsä'), 1852–1923, French foreign minister (1898–1905, 1914–15), one of chief architects of Entente Cordiale and Triple Entente (see TRIPLE ALLIANCE AND TRIPLE ENTENTE).

Del City, city (pop. 12,934), central Okla., a suburb ESE of Oklahoma City.

Deledda, Grazia (grä'tsēä dālĕd'dä), 1875–1936, Italian novelist, b. Sardinia. Among novels are *Elias Portoliu* (1903), *Cenere* (1904; Eng. tr., *Ashes*, 1908), *La Madre* (1920). Won 1926 Nobel Prize in Literature.

De Lee, Joseph Bolivar, 1869–1942, American obstetrician and gynecologist. Improved obstetrical methods through his practice, teaching, and writing.

Delémont (dûlämō'), Ger. *Delsberg,* town (pop. 9,542), Bern canton, W Switzerland, in Jura. Château was residence of prince-bishops of Basel 1528–1792. Prince-bishopric, which did not include Basel itself, passed to France 1792, to Bern 1815.

De Leon, Daniel (dĕ lē'ŏn), 1852–1914, American socialist leader, b. Curaçao; came to U.S. 1872. A doctrinaire Marxist, he split the Socialist Labor party. Favored industrial rather than trade unions. Helped found the Industrial Workers of the World.

Delescluze, Charles (shärl' dûläklüz'), 1809–71, French journalist and radical leader. Often exiled and imprisoned. Led resistance of COMMUNE OF PARIS of 1871. When defeat became inevitable, he threw himself into line of fire and was killed.

Delft, municipality (pop. 76,760) and town, South Holland prov., W Netherlands, near The Hague. Famous for ceramics known as delftware. Its aspect has changed little since Jan Vermeer, who was born here, painted his famous *View of Delft*. The Gothic Nieuwe Kerk contains the tomb of William the Silent, who was assassinated at Delft.

Delhi (dĕl'lē), territory (578 sq. mi.; pop. 2,644,058), N India. Encompasses the Delhi plain, crossed by Jumna R. Hot and arid, extensive irrigation supports agr. Here are sites of several dynastic seats. Earliest center was 12th-cent. citadel of Chauhan Rajput, containing Lal Kot or Red Fort built 1052. Located just SW of Delhi city, it became nucleus of first cap. of DELHI SULTANATE in 1206. Also famous in the Delhi plain is the QUTB MINAR and tomb of Humayan built 1565–69. Old Delhi, or the cantonment area, on Jumna R.. became Mogul cap. (1638) of Shah Jehan, who built beautiful palace within the Red Fort. It contained fabulous Peacock Throne, carried off by Nadir Shah in 1739. City was held by Mahrattas from 1771; occupied 1803 by the British. Was interim cap. of India 1912–31, succeeded by adjacent city of **New Delhi** (pop. 260,272; including Old Delhi, 292,429), which was constructed to replace Calcutta as cap. Predominantly an administrative center, it is also a transportation hub and trade center.

Delhi Sultanate, Moslem state, ruling most of India 1192–1526. Founded by Mohammed of Ghor, Afghan ruler, who took Delhi in 1192. Qutb-ud-din became sultan in 1206. His dynasty (called Slave dynasty because of his slave origin) was succeeded by the Khalji (1290–1320) and Tughluc (1325–98). Sultanate was crushed in 1398 by Tamerlane.

Delian League, confederation of Greek states under leadership of Athens, with original hq. at temple of Apollo in Delos. The first Delian League, 478–404 B.C., was formed with Ionian cities to oppose the Persian kings. After the successful outcome of the PERSIAN WARS, it was made into an Athenian maritime empire that lasted until Sparta won the long-drawn PELOPONNESIAN WAR (404 B.C.). After Conon reestablished Athenian naval power at Cnidus (394 B.C.), a new league was formed (378 B.C.). This lasted, with Athenian-Theban quarrels, until dissolved by the victory of Philip II of Macedon at Chaeronea (338 B.C.).

Délibes, (Clément) Léo (dālēb'), 1836–91, French composer. He wrote several operas, of which *Lakmé* is best known, and ballets (e.g., *Coppélia*).

Delilah (dīlī'lû), courtesan hired by Philistines to betray SAMSON. Judges 16.4–20.

delirium tremens (trē'mĕnz), disordered mental state, resulting from continued alcoholic excess or from certain other disorders; tremors, hallucinations, and sleeplessness occur.

Delisle, Guillaume (gēyŏm′ dülēl′), 1675–1726, French geographer, founder of modern cartography. Noted for highly accurate world map (1700), first without errors of Ptolemy.

Delius, Frederick (dēl′yŭs), 1862–1934, English composer. His works, which combine elements of romanticism and impressionism, include an opera, *A Village Romeo and Juliet;* a choral work, *Sea Drift;* and orchestral pieces, *Brigg Fair* and *On Hearing the First Cuckoo in Spring.* He also composed chamber music, concertos, and songs.

Dell, Floyd, 1887–, American author of novels (e.g., *Moon-Calf,* 1920), plays, and studies of family life.

Della Casa, Giovanni: see CASA.

Della-Cruscans (dĕl′ŭ-krŭs′kŭnz) [from Accademia della Crusca, founded for linguistic purity, Florence, 16th cent.], group of English poets in Italy who published *The Florence Miscellany* (1785). Chief follower in England was Hannah Cowley (1743–1809).

Della Porta: see PORTA.

Della Quercia, Jacopo: see QUERCIA.

Della Robbia (dĕ″lŭ rŏ′bĕŭ, Ital. dĕl′lä rôb′byä), Florentine family of sculptors famous for enameled terra cotta or faïence. The atelier founded by **Luca della Robbia** (lōō′kä), 1400?–1482, was continued by his nephew **Andrea della Robbia** (ändrā′ä), 1435–1525?, and by Andrea's sons, **Luca II della Robbia,** c.1480–1550, **Giovanni della Robbia** (jōvän′nē), c.1469–c.1529, and **Girolamo della Robbia** (jērō′lämō), c.1488–1566. Andrea did the famous medallions on the Foundling Hospital in Florence.

Dells of the Wisconsin, usually called **The Dells,** scenic part of Wisconsin R., central Wis., near Wisconsin Dells city. River has cut gorge through c.8 mi. of sandstone, which is carved into caves, pinnacles, and curious shapes, often beautifully colored.

Delmonico, Lorenzo (dĕlmŏ′nēkō), 1813–81, famous restaurateur, b. Switzerland. Restaurant opened in New York city c.1834 offered fine European cuisine to U.S. and in its subsequent locations became world famous.

De Long, George Washington, 1844–81, American arctic explorer. Lost with most of his men in attempted dash to North Pole, under auspices of U.S. navy and private backing. Expedition proved essential facts about polar drift and that Wrangel Isl. was not southern tip of a northern continent.

Delorme, Marion (märyō′ dŭlôrm′), 1613?–1650, French courtesan, mistress of CINQ MARS, whom she sought to avenge during Fronde.

Delorme or **de l'Orme, Philibert** (fēlēbĕr′), c.1510–1570, French architect of the Renaissance. Designed the Tuileries and the château of Diane de Poitiers at Anet.

Delos (dē′lŏs), island (c.1 sq. mi.), in the Aegean off Greece, one of the Cyclades; in Greek legend the birthplace of Apollo and Artemis. Of great commercial importance in ancient times, it had the treasury of the Delian League until it was removed (454 B.C.) to Athens. Sacked by Mithridates VI of Pontus in 88 B.C., Delos never recovered.

Del Paso Heights, town (pop. 11,495 incl. Robla), central Calif., a suburb N of Sacramento.

Delphi (dĕl′fī), locality in Phocis, Greece, near foot of Mt. Parnassus, seat of Delphic oracle. Oracle, which answered all questions, public or private, arose from worship of an earth-goddess, possibly Gaea. It passed to Apollo and was his preeminent shrine, with oracle housed in temple built in 6th cent. B.C. Oracles, spoken by priestess Pythia, were interpreted in verse by a priest; answers were revered and had great influence in Greece. Delphi was unifying influence in otherwise fragmented life of Greece, meeting place of Delphic Amphictyony, and seat of Pythian games. Shrine was later despoiled by Romans under Sulla and Nero.

delphinium: see LARKSPUR.

Delray Beach, resort city (pop. 12,230), SE Fla., on Atlantic coast S of Palm Beach, in truck-farm area. Flowers are grown commercially.

Del Rio, city (pop. 18,612), W Texas, on Rio Grande opposite Ciudad Acuña, Mexico; founded 1868. Irrigated farms yield alfalfa, truck crops, and grapes (made into wine here). Ships wool and mohair from nearby ranches. Laughlin Air Force Base is E.

Delsarte, François (dĕlsärt′), 1811–71, French teacher of acting and singing. Formulated system of rules for coordination of vocal expression with body movement and emotion.

Deluge, in Bible, overwhelming flood which covered earth and destroyed every living thing except family of NOAH and creatures in ARK. Gen. 6–8; Isa. 54.9; Mat. 24.38; Luke 17.27; Heb. 11.7; 1 Peter 3.20; 2 Peter 2.5. Flood stories resembling biblical one found in folklore of many cultures, e.g., Babylonian, Greek, Indian, aboriginal Australian, American Indian.

delusion, false belief based on misinterpretation of reality. Passing delusions are not abnormal, but fixed delusions (e.g., of persecution, external influence, grandeur) characterize paranoia, schizophrenia. Social psychologists study delusions for their crucial role in development of mass hysteria.

dementia praecox: see SCHIZOPHRENIA.

Demerara, river: see GUYANA.

Demeter (dĭmē′tŭr), in Greek legend, earth-goddess of corn, harvest, and fruitfulness; daughter of Cronus and Rhea and mother of PERSEPHONE by Zeus. She and her daughter were chief figures in ELEUSINIAN MYSTERIES. Her festival, Thesmophoria, was held in autumn. Identified with Roman Ceres.

Demetrius (dĭmē′trēŭs), kings of Macedon. **Demetrius I** (Poliorcetes), c.337–283 B.C., aided his father ANTIGONUS I in the wars of the DIADOCHI until they were defeated at Ipsus (301 B.C.). Managed to get the throne of Macedon (294 B.C.), but his enemies drove him to take refuge with Seleucus I. He was father of ANTIGONUS II. **Demetrius II,** d. 229 B.C., reigned 239–229 B.C. His heir was young Philip V.

Demetrius, kings of Syria. **Demetrius I** (Soter), c.187–150 B.C., reigned 162–150 B.C.; son of Seleucus IV. A hostage in Rome, Demetrius escaped, killed his cousin Antiochus V, took the throne, but was beset by rebellion, notably that of Alexander Balas and the Maccabees. Demetrius was defeated. **Demetrius II** (Nicator), d. c.125 B.C., got the aid of Ptolemy VI against Alexander Balas, married Cleopatra (already the wife of Alexander), and took the throne in 146 B.C. Captured by Parthians (141 B.C.), he returned, regained the throne (128 B.C.), but again lost it and died fighting the Egyptians.

Demetrius, in Russian history: see DMITRI.

De Mille, Cecil B(lount), 1881–1959, U.S. film director, noted for "spectacle" films (e.g., *The Greatest Show on Earth, The Ten Commandments*). His niece, **Agnes De Mille,** 1908–, is a dancer and choreographer. Her ballets include *Rodeo,* and *Fall River Legend.* Her choreography for musical *Oklahoma!* (1943) made ballet popular on Broadway stage.

democracy [Gr.,= power of the people], government under control of the people as a whole rather than that of a class, group, or individual; by extension, in such phrases as social democracy and economic democracy, control of human institutions by and in the interest of the people. In the Greek city states democracy was confined to citizens (as opposed to slaves). The Roman Republic gave birth to popular representation; the Middle Ages, to the idea of a contract between the governed and their rulers. Modern democracy was advanced by the Puritan, American, and French revolutions. John Locke, J. J. Rousseau, and Thomas Jefferson were influential theorists. It grew with the demand for equal opportunity—at first, political and legal; later, social and economic as well. The modern democratic state has relied typically on a system of competing political parties (see ELECTION). In recent times the belief in man's capacity to govern himself has been challenged by fascism and by communism.

Democratic party, in U.S. history. Arose, under Thomas JEFFERSON, in opposition to Alexander Hamilton and Federalist party; emphasized personal liberty and limitation of powers of Federal government. Early party name of Democratic Republican yielded to Democratic by 1828. Election of Jefferson in 1800 had virtual force of a revolution; victory of radical group under Andrew JACKSON in 1828 represented second revolution. Arguments over slavery created or deepened splits within party; Civil War all but destroyed it. Party revived in disputed election of 1876. End of Reconstruction brought emergence of "solid South," a bulwark of Democratic strength thereafter, except for rare instances. With nomination of W. J. BRYAN in 1896 on a "free silver" platform, radicals again gained ascendant. His defeat posed problem of keeping together party's diverse factions—Southern and Western farmers, big-city industrial classes, a few of the wealthy. Leader appeared in idealistic liberal, Woodrow WILSON. Economic depression helped to sweep F. D. ROOSEVELT and Democrats into power in 1932, and party was again identified as reform party with New Deal. Roosevelt died in office in 1945, in fourth term, and Harry S. TRUMAN became President. In 1948, despite disaffection of the South, due to Negro civil-rights issue, and of dissidents under Henry WALLACE, Truman brought Democrats to surprising victory. Republican victory under Dwight D. Eisenhower in 1952 ended 20-year rule of Democratic party. Eisenhower was reelected in 1956, but Democrats recaptured the presidency in 1960 when John F. KENNEDY narrowly defeated Richard M. Nixon. In 1964 Lyndon B. JOHNSON, who had succeeded to the presidency upon the assassination of Kennedy, defeated Barry Goldwater by the largest popular vote margin in the history of presidential elections.

Democritus (dǐmŏk'rǐtŭs), c.460–c.370 B.C., Greek philosopher. A materialist, he held that the world was made up of tiny particles, imperceptible to the senses but indivisible and indestructible. These are atoms and by constant motion they combine to make the universe. The true nature of things can be discovered only by thought, for sense perceptions are confusing.

Demopolis, city (pop. 7,377), W central Ala., at junction of Black Warrior and Tombigbee rivers, in Black Belt; founded 1818 by Bonapartist exiles.

De Morgan, William (Frend), 1839–1917, English potter and novelist. A designer of glass and tiles, he began upon retirement to write long novels, most popular of which was his first, *Joseph Vance* (1906).

Demosthenes (dǐmŏs'thǔnēz), 384?–322 B.C., Greek orator, one of the greatest orators of all time. His fame rests chiefly on his orations against the conquering Philip II of Macedon—three *Philippics* and three *Olynthiacs* (asking aid for the city of Olynthus). Other orations are *On the Peace, On the False Legation* (against his rival, Aeschines), and *On the Crown* (a defense of himself against Aeschines). Even after Philip triumphed, Demosthenes was honored until he was exiled on obscure charges of financial corruption. Returning after the death of Alexander the Great, he failed to rebuild Greek strength and took poison when fleeing before Antipater. His speeches were used as models until 19th cent.

demotic: see HIEROGLYPHIC.

Dempsey, William Harrison (Jack Dempsey), 1895–, American boxer. Won heavyweight championship from Jess Willard (1919), lost title to James J. (Gene) Tunney (1926). Dempsey was again defeated by Tunney (1927) in fight involving controversial "long count" in seventh round.

Demuth, Charles (dā'mōōth), 1883–1935, American water-color painter. Shows influence of cubism.

Denain (dŭnĕ'), city (pop. 27,449), Nord dept., N France. Coal fields, ironworks. Scene of French victory (1712) in War of Spanish Succession.

Denbighshire (dĕn'bĕshĭr) **or Denbigh,** maritime county (668 sq. mi.; pop. 173,843), N Wales; co. town Denbigh. Largely high pastoral moorland with agr. in valleys. Coal mining, tin-plating, and mfg. around Wrexham.

Dendera (dĕn'dŭrä), town (pop. c.17,000), N Egypt on Nile. Has temple of Hathor (1st cent. B.C.).

dengue, acute, highly infectious disease, characterized by fever, muscle and bone pains, and joint inflammation. It is caused by a virus transmitted by certain mosquitoes. Sometimes epidemic in tropical regions.

Denikin, Anton Ivanovich (ŭntôn' ēvä'nŭvĭch dyĭnyē'kĭn), 1872–1947, Russian general. Commanded anti-Bolshevik forces in S Russia 1918–20.

Denis, Saint (dĕn'ĭs, dŭnē'), 3d cent.?, patron saint of France. Said to have been first bishop of Paris and to have been martyred on Montmartre. The name is a form of Dionysius. Feast: Oct. 9.

Denis, Maurice (môrēs' dŭnē'), 1870–1943, French muralist and writer on art. Spokesman for the NABIS.

Denison, industrial city (pop. 22,748), N Texas, near Red R., NNE of Dallas. Stagecoach station before Civil War; grew to importance with coming of railroad. Dwight D. Eisenhower was born here. Denison Dam is nearby.

Denison Dam, NE Texas and S Okla., on Red R., NNW of Denison, Texas; completed 1944, for flood control and power. Main dam is 165 ft. high, 17,200 ft. long. Its reservoir, L. Texoma, is one of largest artificial lakes in U.S. and is used for recreation.

Denmark, Dan. *Danmark,* kingdom (16,619 sq. mi.; est. pop. 4,773,000), NW Europe, southernmost of Scandinavian countries; cap. Copenhagen. Except for JUTLAND peninsula, on German border, Denmark consists of several Baltic isls., notably ZEALAND, FYN, FALSTER, LAALAND, LANGELAND, BORNHOLM. Overseas territories are GREENLAND and the FAEROE ISLANDS. A low-lying, highly cultivated country, Denmark specializes in dairying and stock raising and has important commercial and fishing fleets. Form of government is parliamentary democracy (see FOLKETING). Ruling house: Schleswig-Holstein-Sonderburg-Glucksburg. Reigning king: Frederick IX. Established Church is Lutheran. In the Viking Age (see VIKINGS) Danes took important part in Norse raids of W Europe. Harold Bluetooth (d. c.985) was their first Christian king. His son SWEYN conquered England, and CANUTE united Denmark, England, and Norway from 1018 to 1035. S Sweden was part of Denmark to 1658. Danish hegemony over the N was first estab. under Waldemar I and Waldemar II (12th–13th cent.); WALDEMAR IV restored Danish power but was successfully challenged by the HANSEATIC LEAGUE (14th cent.). His daughter MARGARET created (1397) the KALMAR UNION of Denmark, Sweden, and NORWAY; the union with Norway lasted to 1814, but that with Sweden never was effective and ended in 1523. The house of Oldenburg, from which the present dynasty is descended, acceded in 1448 with CHRISTIAN I, who also united SCHLESWIG and HOLSTEIN with the Danish crown. The Reformation was introduced by Christian III. Danish participation in the Thirty Years War (see CHRISTIAN IV) and the wars of FREDERICK III caused 17th-cent. Denmark to lose its leading position to Sweden. An absolute monarchy was estab. under Christian V, and colonial imperialism resulted in the creation of trade monopolies in ICELAND and the VIRGIN ISLANDS. Important social reforms (e.g., abolition of serfdom, 1788) marked the late 18th cent., especially under the ministries of STRUENSEE and A. P. BERNSTORFF. Denmark sought to maintain neutrality in the French Revolutionary and Napoleonic wars but was attacked by England and joined the French camp. As a result, the Congress of Vienna deprived it of Norway. The complex question of SCHLESWIG-HOLSTEIN led to the German-Danish war of 1848–49 and to war with Prussia and Austria in 1864, in which Denmark lost both duchies. (N Schleswig was restored to Denmark after a plebiscite, 1920.)

Of more lasting importance was the internal reform of 19th-cent. Denmark, which transformed its poor peasantry into the most prosperous small farmers in Europe. This achievement was largely due to the educational efforts of Bishop GRUNDTVIG and to the cooperative movement. Neutral in First World War, Denmark was occupied (1940–45) by German forces in Second World War. It joined the UN (1945), the European Recovery Program (1948), the North Atlantic Treaty Organization (1949), and the European Free Trade Association (1960).

Dennie, Joseph, 1768–1812, American Federalist journalist, editor of anti-Jefferson weekly.

Dennis, resort town (pop. 3,727), SE Mass., on Cape Cod NE of Yarmouth; settled 1639. Has summer theater. Town includes Dennis Point village (pop. 1,271).

density, measurement of a quantity of matter in a unit volume of a substance. It is usually expressed in grams per cubic centimeter; grams per liter, or pounds per cubic foot and is calculated by dividing the MASS by the volume occupied at standard temperature and pressure. SPECIFIC GRAVITY of solid or liquid is density compared with that of water; that of gas is compared with hydrogen or air.

Dent du Midi or **Dents du Midi** (both: dä′ dü mēdē′), Alpine mountain group, Vaud canton, SW Switzerland, rising to 10,696 ft. in Haute Cime.

dentistry, science of treatment and care of teeth and associated oral structures. Important contributions to evolution of modern dentistry made by Ambroise Paré, John Hunter, Pierre FAUCHARD, G. V. BLACK, C. A. HARRIS, and many others. Progress aided by development of X ray, local anesthetics, artificial dentures, drilling machine, and methods of preparing fillings and inlays. Specialized fields include oral surgery, orthodontia (corrective dentistry), peridontia (diseases of the gums), prosthodontia (replacement), pedodontia (problems of children).

Denton, city (pop. 26,844), N Texas, NW of Dallas, in farm area; founded 1855. Seat of North Texas State Univ. and Texas Woman's Univ. Man-made L. Lewisville (formerly L. Dallas) is near.

D'Entrecasteaux Islands (dätrükästō′), volcanic group, area c.1,200 sq. mi., off SE New Guinea, part of Territory of Papua. Named for the French navigator Entrecasteaux.

Dents du Midi, Switzerland: see DENT DU MIDI.

Denver, city (pop. 493,887), state cap., N central Colo., on South Platte R.; settled 1858. Made territorial cap. 1867. With rich gold and silver strikes of 1870s and 1880s the city boomed and became metropolis for bonanza kings. At this time H. A. W. TABOR built opera house, and Silver Dollar saloon flourished. As processing, shipping, and distributing point for agr. area, growth was steady after 1890s. Financial and administrative center of Rocky Mt. region. Mfg. of mining machinery, metal and meat products, aircraft and missile parts. Tourism important. Here are Univ. of DENVER, Loretto Heights Col., Regis Col., medical center of Univ. of Colorado, Denver Art Mus., Colorado State Historical Mus., and offices of many Federal agencies.

Denver, University of, at Denver, Colo.; coed.; chartered and opened 1864 as Colorado Seminary; reorganized as university 1880. Maintains Chamberlin Observatory.

deodar or **deodar cedar:** see CEDAR.

De Pere (dīpēr′), city (pop. 10,045), E central Wis., on Fox R., SSW of Green Bay. Father Allouez founded mission here 1671. St. Norbert Col. is across river.

Depew, Chauncey (Mitchell) (dīpū′), 1834–1928, American railroad president and orator. President (1885–99) and chairman of board (1899–1928) of New York Central lines. Noted as after-dinner speaker.

Depew, industrial village (pop. 13,580), W central N.Y., a suburb E of Buffalo.

De Predis, Ambrogio (ämbrō′jō dā′ prä′dēs), c.1455–c.1506, Milanese painter. Worked under Leonardo da Vinci and copied many of his paintings.

depression, period of economic crisis, characterized by falling prices, restricted credit, contraction of production, bankruptcies, and unemployment. Short period of fear in business community, called panic, does not occur with all depressions. Cause is disequilibrium between quantity of goods produced and ability to buy. Overproduction leads to wage cuts or dismissals, which in turn mean a further drop in purchasing power. Depressions now often countered by government action.

De profundis (dā prōfŏŏn′dēs), one of penitential psalms, Ps. 130 (or 129). See PSALMS.

Deptford, part of LEWISHAM London borough since 1965; industrial district. Noted in Elizabethan times for cattle market and royal dockyards. Christopher Marlowe was killed here.

De Quincey, Thomas (dĭ kwĭn′sē), 1785–1859, English essayist. Achieved literary eminence with his *Confessions of an English Opium-Eater* (1822). He was a prolific contributor to various journals; his "On the Knocking at the Gate in Macbeth" is well known.

Derain, André (ändrā′ dûrē′), 1880–1954, French painter; one of the fauvists.

Derbent (dyĭrbyĕnt′), city (1965 est. pop. 56,000), SE Dagestan, SE European RSFSR; Caspian fishing port. Founded 5th or 6th cent. A.D. by Persians at Iron Gates (called Caspian or Albanian Gates by ancients), a defile between Caucasus and Caspian, on a major commercial route. Ceded by Persia to Russia 1806. Remains of 6th-cent. Caucasian Wall (or Alexander's Wall), built by Persians to stem invaders from N.

Derby, Edward George Geoffrey Smith Stanley, 14th earl of (där′bē), 1799–1869, British statesman. As Whig colonial secretary he pushed through abolition of slavery 1833. Influenced by Robert PEEL he became a Conservative. Was colonial secretary (1841–45) and prime minister (1852, 1858–59, 1866–68).

Derby, England: see DERBYSHIRE.

Derby (dûr′bē). **1** Town (pop. 10,124), N central Colo., a suburb N of Denver. **2** City (pop. 12,132), SW Conn., W of New Haven; founded 1642 as trading post. Yale crew holds home races on Housatonic R. here.

Derby (där′bē, dûr′bē), famous horse race held annually since 1780 at Epsom Downs, near London, England. The name derby is also applied to other well-known horse races, notably Kentucky Derby (dûr′bē), held annually since 1875 at Churchill Downs, Louisville, Ky.

Derbyshire (där′bēshĭr) or **Derby,** county (1,002 sq. mi.; pop. 877,548), central England. Area flat in S, rising to Peak district in N. Has rich coal deposits in E section. Heavily cultivated; dairy farming and sheep raising are important. County town, **Derby,** county borough (pop. 132,325), on Derwent R., is a rail center. Also mfg. of cars (Rolls-Royce), pottery (Derby ware), textiles, and chemicals. Birthplace of Herbert Spencer. George Eliot lived here.

Derg, Lough (lŏkh′ dĕrg′), lakes, Ireland. **1** Expansion of Shannon R. (length, 23 mi.; width, 1–5 mi.) on borders of Counties Galway, Tipperary, and Clare. **2** SE Donegal. Station Isl. here, traditional place of St. Patrick's Purgatory, has extensive religious establishments and is noted place of pilgrimage.

dermis: see SKIN.

Dermot McMurrough or **Diarmuid mac Murchada** (both: dûr′mŭt mŭkmŭ′rŭ), d. 1171, Irish king who brought the English into Ireland. Banished 1166. Promised aid by Richard Strongbow and other adventurers, he returned to Ireland in 1168. With the invaders, he had conquered SE Ireland, including Dublin, by 1170.

Derna (dĕr'nâ), town (pop. c.36,000), E Cyrenaica, Libya; port and caravan center on the Mediterranean. A stronghold of Barbary pirates, it was occupied (1805) by U.S. forces in Tripolitan War. In Second World War it changed hands several times 1941–42.

Derry, Northern Ireland: see LONDONDERRY.

Derry, town (pop. 6,987), SE N.H., SE of Manchester. Robert Frost farmed and taught school here. Town includes West Derry village (pop. 4,468).

Derwent (dûr'wŭnt), rivers in England, 1 Cumberland, in the Lake District. 2 Derbyshire, tributary of the Trent. 3 Yorkshire, tributary of the Ouse.

Derwentwater, oval lake, 3 mi. long and 1 mi. wide, Cumberland, England. Formed by widening of Derwent R., it is surrounded by wooded hills. Lodore waterfalls are at upper end.

Derzhavin, Gavril Romanovich (gŭvrēl' rŭmä'nŭvĭch dyĭrzhä'vĭn), 1743–1816, Russian classical poet; poet laureate to Catherine II. His fame rests chiefly on his *Ode to God* (1784).

Desai, Morargi R. (mōrär'jē dē'sä), 1896–, Indian statesman. Took part in independence movement; served several years in prison. Chief minister Bombay state 1952–56. Federal finance minister 1958–63.

De Sanctis, Francesco (fränchäs'kō dä sängk'tēs), 1817–83, Italian literary critic, notable for *Saggi Critici* [critical essays] (1866) and *History of Italian Literature* (1871).

Desargues, Gérard (zhärär' dùzärg'), 1593–1662, French mathematician, engineer, a founder of modern geometry. He worked on conic sections and presented several theorems now named for him.

Descartes, René (rùnä' dākärt'), 1596–1650, French philosopher, mathematician, and scientist. His teachings are called Cartesian from his name in Latin (Renatus Cartesius). Studied at the Jesuit school at La Flèche and the Univ. of Poitiers; served in the army of Maurice of Nassau; retired to Holland for research and reflection (1628); accepted the invitation of Queen Christina (1649), but died soon after reaching Sweden. A mathematical genius, he worked out the treatment of negative roots and a system of notation in algebra; originated Cartesian coordinates and Cartesian curves and is said to have founded analytic geometry. He attempted to apply mathematical methods to philosophy (notably in *Discourse on Method*), and discarding authoritarian scholasticism, he founded his system on universal doubt. One thing, he says, cannot be doubted: doubt itself. The action of the mind proves reality; his motto was *Cogito, ergo sum* [I think, therefore I am]. He refined scholastic arguments for the existence of God and held God to be the link between the mechanical world of the senses and the rational world of the mind. In physical science he rejected tradition but relied on rationalization, mathematics, and logic rather than experiment. He made numerous advances in optics (notably in reflection and refraction of light), in psychology, and in physiology. His influence on modern thought is incalculable.

Deschanel, Paul (pôl' dāshänĕl'), 1855–1922, president of France (1920).

Deschutes (dāshōōts'), river rising in W central Oregon in Cascade Range and flowing c.240 mi. NNE to Columbia R. Largest tributary is Crooked R.; Used for power and irrigation. Dams in river are part of U.S. project serving Madras area.

desegregation: see INTEGRATION.

desert (dē'zŭrt), arid region, at least partly covered by sand, with scanty vegetation, limited and specially adapted animal life. High-altitude deserts, often perpetually covered with ice or snow, are not usually considered with deserts of warm regions. One fifth of world's land is desert. Largest desert regions lie between 20° and 30° N and S of equator, where mountains block trade winds or atmospheric high-pressure areas cause descending air currents and lack of precipitation. Other factors: amount of sunshine, water evaporation rate, temperature range, annual rainfall.

Europe, only continent without deserts, has semideserts around Black and Caspian Seas, in Ukraine, and in the N Caucasus. The GOBI, in Asia, is desert because of remoteness from water. The SAHARA, in Africa, is largest desert; second largest is central and W Australian desert region. North American deserts include MOJAVE DESERT, IMPERIAL VALLEY, and DEATH VALLEY. Desert plants, widely spaced, have stems and leaves adapted to lessen water loss; roots form spreading network penetrating down to 50 ft. North American desert animals include birds, mice, foxes, deer, snakes, lizards, and spiders. See also OASIS.

Desert Hot Springs, village (pop. 1,472), S Calif., E of Riverside. Mineral-springs resort. Has Hopi Indian pueblo replica. Joshua Tree Natl. Monument is near.

desertion, in military law, the abandonment of a place of duty without leave and with the intention not to return. It is punishable in war time by death. In maritime law, the abandonment of a ship by a seaman without leave. In family law, willful abandonment of the spouse or children of a marriage without consent of the other party or parties. In most states, desertion is ground for DIVORCE; in others, for separation.

De Sica, Vittorio (dāsē'kä), 1901–, Italian film actor, director, and producer. A popular actor from 1931 and director of such films as *Shoe Shine*, *The Bicycle Thief*, *Miracle in Milan*, and *Umberto D*.

Desiderio da Settignano (dāzēdä'rēō dä sēt"tēn-yä'nō), 1428–64, Florentine sculptor, known for church decorations and marble busts of women and children.

Desiderius, d. after 774, last Lombard king in Italy. Attacked Pope ADRIAN I, who appealed to Charlemagne. Charlemagne (who had married and later repudiated Desiderius' daughter) invaded Italy (773) and captured and deposed Desiderius (774).

Desiderius Erasmus: see ERASMUS.

De Sitter, Willem: see SITTER, WILLEM DE.

De Smet, Pierre Jean (dē smĕt'), 1801–73, missionary in U.S. Pacific Northwest, a Jesuit, b. Belgium. Often mediated between Indians and whites.

Des Moines (dù moin'), city (1966 pop. 206,739), state cap., S central Iowa, state's largest city, at junction of Des Moines and Raccoon rivers, in heart of Corn Belt. Estab. 1843 as Fort Des Moines; settled by homesteaders 1845. Became cap. by terms of 1857 state constitution. Adopted reform plan of city government 1907. Important industrial, transportation, and insurance center, with printing and publishing. Seat of DRAKE UNIVERSITY; Col. of Osteopathic Medicine and Surgery. GRINNELL COLLEGE is nearby. Of interest are capitol (1871–84), Des Moines Art Center, and State Historical, Memorial, and Art Building.

Des Moines, river rising in SW Minn. and flowing c.535 mi. SSE across Iowa to Mississippi R. at Keokuk.

Desmond, ancient division of Munster prov., Ireland, including present Co. Cork and Co. Kerry. The Fitzgeralds became powerful earls of Desmond.

Desmoulins, Camille (kämē'yù dāmōōlē'), 1760–94, French revolutionist and journalist, early leader of CORDELIERS. His oratory led to storming of Bastille, July 14, 1789. Executed with Danton.

Desna (dyĭsnä), river, 685 mi. long, W European RSFSR and N central Ukraine. Rises SE of Smolensk and flows past Bryansk and Chernigov into Dnieper above Kiev. Navigable for c.330 mi.

De Soto, Hernando (Span. dā sō'tō), c.1500–1542, Spanish conquistador. Explored (1539–42) present SE U.S., from Fla. to Tenn. to Okla., in unsuccessful search for treasure. He and his men were probably the first white men to see and cross the Mississippi R.; he was buried in its waters.

Despenser, Hugh le (hū' lù dĭspĕn'sùr), d. 1265, chief justiciar of England. Supported barons against Henry III, fought in Baron's War, and was killed at Evesham 1265. Two best-known members of this family were **Hugh le Despenser,** the elder, 1262–1326, and **Hugh le Despenser,** the younger, d. 1326. The elder

Despenser became chief adviser to EDWARD II. The younger Despenser later joined his father and the king. Were banished by barons 1321; returned to England 1322 and became real rulers of the kingdom. Hated by barons; were executed when Isabella returned from France and seized control 1326.

Despiau, Charles (shärl' dȧpē̄ō'), 1874–1946, French sculptor. Studied under Rodin. Best known for his bronze busts and nudes of young women.

Des Plaines (dĕs plänz'), city (1965 pop. 50,789), NE Ill., a suburb NW of Chicago on Des Plaines R.; founded in 1830s. O'Hare Internatl. Airport is S.

Des Plaines, river rising in SE Wis. and flowing c.150 mi. S and SW to join Kankakee R. near Joliet, Ill. This combined stream is Illinois R.

Des Prés, Josquin: see JOSQUIN DESPREZ.

Dessalines, Jean Jacques (zhä' zhäk' dĕsȧlēn'), c.1758–1806, Negro emperor of Haiti (1804–6), born a slave. Served under Toussaint L'Ouverture in wars of liberation. Was named governor (1804), later crowned emperor, Jacques I. Because of his despotic rule, he was murdered.

Dessau (dĕ'sou), city (est. pop. 92,455), East Germany, in former state of Saxony-Anhalt, at junction of Elbe and Mulde rivers. Formerly cap. of ANHALT. Machinery mfg. Seat of BAUHAUS school 1925–32.

Destaing, Charles Hector: see ESTAING.

de Stijl: see STIJL, DE.

destroyer, warship of 1,500 to 2,000 tons, very fast, with powerful torpedo armament, a few medium-caliber guns, and anti-aircraft artillery. Introduced in 1892, much improved in First World War. Equipped with new electronic devices, destroyers proved highly effective against submarines during Second World War and were used for convoying larger naval vessels and merchant ships. In battle, they rely on speed and maneuverability.

detective story, type of popular fiction in which the solution of a crime is traced step by step. Poe's *Murders in the Rue Morgue* is considered first modern example. The same detective often appears in a series of such stories, as do Conan Doyle's Sherlock Holmes and Frederic Dannay's and M. B. Lee's Ellery Queen. The "hard-boiled" school, started by Dashiell Hammett, involves the detective in scenes of sex and violence, notably in books by Mickey Spillane. The mystery story, an allied type, has no detective and often no crime, only an unexplained situation, as in Collins's *Woman in White*. A third form, the espionage tale, involves its hero in international politics and tension; examples are by Conrad, Graham Greene, E. Phillips Oppenheim, and, more recently, Eric Ambler and Ian Fleming among many.

detergent, strictly, any substance which when dissolved lowers the surface tension of the solvent and which also breaks up dirt clumps and holds them in suspension. Reduction of surface tension facilitates cleaning by increasing penetrating power of solvent; breakup of clumps prevents resetting on the cleaned surface and makes possible better rinsing. Soaps comprise one type of detergent but have the disadvantages of forming insoluble compounds with salts of hard water and of decomposing in acid solutions. Synthetic detergents have been produced in great quantities since 1930. See SOAP.

Detmold (dĕt'mōlt), city (pop. 31,209), in North Rhine-Westphalia, West Germany. Former cap. of LIPPE. Nearby is monument to victory of ARMINIUS over Romans.

detonator (dĕ'tȯnä"tür), type of explosive that reacts rapidly and is used to set off more inert explosives. Commonly used are fulminate of mercury mixed with potassium chlorate. Term is also applied to equipment to set off chemical detonator.

Detroit (dĭtroit'), city (pop. 1,670,144), SE Mich., on Detroit R. between Lakes St. Clair and Erie. State's largest city and major Great Lakes shipping and rail center. Industries include food processing and mfg. of automobiles, steel, chemicals, machinery, metal products. Settled 1701 by French. British took over 1760 and withstood long siege in PONTIAC'S REBELLION. American control, estab. 1796 with Jay's Treaty, was lost briefly to British in War of 1812. Territorial and state cap, 1805–47. Grew rapidly in 1830s with development of land and water transport. Importance increased after 1850s with shipping, shipbuilding, and mfg. Its early carriage industry helped Henry Ford and others to make it center of world's automobile industry. Here are Univ. of DETROIT, WAYNE STATE UNIVERSITY, Detroit Inst. of Arts, civic center (with Cobo Hall), and Belle Isle (with gardens, conservatory, aquarium, children's zoo). Has Detroit Symphony Orchestra (founded 1914). Includes cities of HAMTRAMCK and HIGHLAND PARK.

Detroit, river, flowing c.32 mi. from L. St. Clair between SE Mich. and S Ont. S into L. Erie. Forms part of international border. Has heavy commercial traffic.

Detroit, University of, at Detroit, Mich.; coed.; estab. 1877 as college, became university 1911.

Dettifoss (dĕ'tĭfȯs), fall, c.325 ft. high, in Jokulsa R., NE Iceland, the most powerful in the country.

Dettingen (dĕ'tĭngȯn), village, NW Bavaria, on Main R. Here in 1743 allies under George II of England defeated French in War of Austrian Succession.

Deucalion (dūkā'lēȯn), in Greek mythology, son of Prometheus and father of Hellen. He and his wife, Pyrrha, only survivors of a great flood, were told to cast behind them bones of their mother, the stones of the earth. These became human beings.

deuterium: see HYDROGEN.

deuterocanonical books: see OLD TESTAMENT.

deuteron: see HYDROGEN.

Deuteronomy (dūtürŏn'ümē),[Gr.,= second law], book of Old Testament, last of 5 books of Law (Pentateuch or Torah) ascribed by tradition to Moses. It gives the final words of Moses—his last instructions to his people and his blessing of them. Book ends with his death.

deutzia (dü'tsēü), ornamental shrub of genus *Deutzia*, with abundant white, pink, or purple blooms.

Deux-Sèvres (dû-sĕv'rü), department (2,337 sq. mi.; pop. 321,118), W France, in Poitou; cap. Niort.

De Valera, Eamon (ā'mûn dē" vülâ'rü), 1882–, Irish statesman, b. New York. Imprisoned (1916) for part in Easter Rebellion. Made president of Sinn Fein 1917. As head of DÁIL ÉIREANN raised funds in U.S. 1919–20. After period of virtual war against British rule, Irish Free State was estab. 1921. Opposing Free State, he left the Dáil in 1922. Nominal leader of republicans, he deplored subsequent civil war. Re-entering Dáil in 1927 with his party, the FIANNA FAIL, he became prime minister in 1938. Kept Ireland neutral in Second World War. Defeated 1948, he was returned to office 1951 and again in 1957. In 1959 he resigned as prime minister and was elected president.

developer, in PHOTOGRAPHY, solution used to prepare NEGATIVE after exposure of film. It acts on silver salts that were affected by light.

Deventer, Sir Jacob Louis van, 1874?–1922, Boer general in South African War; later fought against Germans in South-West Africa and German East Africa.

Deventer (dē'vĕntür) municipality (pop. 59,204) and town, Overijssel prov., E central Netherlands, on the Ijssel. Produces machinery, textiles, carpets. It was a medieval center of piety and learning (Thomas à Kempis and Erasmus studied here) and member of the Hanseatic League. There are many medieval and Renaissance buildings.

Devereux, Robert: see ESSEX, ROBERT DEVEREUX, EARL OF.

devil: see SATAN.

devilfish, common name for manta ray and an American species of octopus.

Devils Island, Fr. *Ile du Diable,* tiny island off French Guiana. Until 1946 used as penal colony, largely for political prisoners.

SMALL CAPITALS = cross references. Pronunciation key on inside end pages. Abbreviations: p. 2.

Devils Lake, city (1965 pop. 6,670), NE N.Dak., W of Grand Forks; settled 1882. Trade and food-processing center. Nearby salt Devils L. (c.30 mi. long; drying steadily) attracts tourists. Fort Totten Indian Reservation is near.

Devils Postpile National Monument: see NATIONAL PARKS AND MONUMENTS (table).

Devils Tower National Monument: see NATIONAL PARKS AND MONUMENTS (table).

De Vinne, Theodore L(ow) (dù vǐ'nē), 1828–1914, American printer, most famous of his day. By example and through his writings he advanced the cause of good printing.

Devolution, War of, 1667–68, between France and Spain, caused by complicated legal claim of Louis XIV to Spanish Netherlands. The French overran the Spanish Netherlands and Franche-Comté, but made peace when the United Provs. formed anti-French TRIPLE ALLIANCE with England and Sweden (see AIX-LA-CHAPELLE, TREATY OF).

Devon, county, England: see DEVONSHIRE.

Devonian period (dǐvō'nēŭn), fourth period of the PALEOZOIC ERA of geologic time. It began with the continents mainly dry; later large areas were flooded and thick sediments deposited. The OLD RED SANDSTONE was laid down. Fish in great numbers dominated marine life, among them sharks, lungfish, armored fish, and ganoids. Amphibians emerged in this period. Invertebrates included trilobites, corals, starfish, and sponges. On land, forests of giant ferns and fernlike trees appeared. See also GEOLOGIC ERAS, table.

Devonport, Devonshire, England: see PLYMOUTH.

Devonshire, Spencer Compton Cavendish, 8th duke of, 1833–1908, English statesman. Led Liberal Unionists who broke (1886) with Gladstone over HOME RULE for Ireland.

Devonshire or Devon, maritime county (2,612 sq. mi.; pop. 822,906), SW England; co. town Exeter. Surface largely hilly, rises to 2,000 ft. in Dartmoor. Has many rivers and streams. Mainly agr. and pastoral (Devonshire cream famous); there is also fishing, mining, and quarrying. Of great maritime importance in Elizabethan times, county is associated with Raleigh, Drake, Hawkins, and Grenville. Pilgrim Fathers sailed from Plymouth.

De Vos, Cornelis: see VOS, CORNELIS DE.

De Voto, Bernard (Augustine) (dù vō'tō), 1897–1955, American writer. Editor of Mark Twain manuscripts, he wrote also *Mark Twain at Work* (1942), literary criticism, and historical works, notably *Across the Wide Missouri* (1947).

Devoy, John, 1842–1928, Irish-American journalist and leader of FENIAN MOVEMENT. In U.S. founded *Irish Nation* and (1903) *Gaelic-American*. Secured American support for Irish Land League movement and 1916 rebellion. Backed Irish Free State.

dew, water formed by condensation of atmospheric water vapor as air cools (above freezing point). Dew point is temperature at which condensation begins.

Dewar, Sir James (dū'ür), 1842–1923, British chemist and physicist. He worked on properties of matter at low temperatures, liquefaction of gases; he liquefied and solidified hydrogen and was co-inventor of cordite. Invented **Dewar flask:** two flasks, one inside other, with vacuum between, silvered to cause heat reflection; keeps liquid hot or cold.

dewberry, trailing bramble of genus *Rubus,* similar to blackberry, but with earlier and larger fruit.

De Wet, Christian Rudolf (dù vĕt'), 1854–1922, Boer general, prominent in the South African War. Opposed entry of South Africa into First World War and led an unsuccessful revolt.

Dewey, George, 1837–1917, American admiral, hero of battle of Manila in SPANISH-AMERICAN WAR. Briefly boomed for President in resulting enthusiasm.

Dewey, John, 1859–1952, American philosopher and educator, long associated with Columbia Univ. His philosophy, called instrumentalism, is related to pragmatism. He held truth to be evolutionary, not fixed or eternal, and that the modes and forms of human activity are instruments for solving psychological and social problems—instruments that change with the problems. He recognized democracy as a primary source of ethical value. In education he abandoned belief in authoritarian methods and the use of rote practices, arguing for learning by experience, motivated by a sense of the student's need. This was the basic principle that underlay the 20th-cent. progressive education theory and movement. Among his many works are *Psychology* (1887), *The School and Society* (1899), *Democracy and Education* (1916), *Experience and Nature* (1925), *Art as Experience* (1934), and *Logic: the Theory of Inquiry* (1938).

Dewey, Melvil, 1851–1931, American library pioneer, originator of Dewey decimal system, a scheme of book classification using numbers 000 to 999 to cover the general fields of knowledge and narrowing the system to fit special subjects by the use of decimals. While librarian of Columbia Col., Dewey estab. first school for training librarians. Reestab. school in Albany where he was librarian of New York State Library 1889–1906. A founder of American Library Association.

Dewey, Thomas E(dmund), 1902–, governor of N.Y. (1942–55). Unsuccessful Republican presidential candidate (1944, 1948).

De Witt, Jan, and **Cornelius de Witt:** see WITT.

Dexter, Timothy, 1747–1806, American merchant and eccentric. Made a fortune by buying up depreciated Continental Congress currency, which was later reclaimed at full value. Author of *A Pickle for the Knowing Ones* (1802), remarkable for its individual spelling and absence of punctuation.

dextrin, a carbohydrate with same general formula as starch, but with a smaller, less complex molecule. It is an intermediate product in starch hydrolysis. Commercial type is powder that forms adhesive paste when mixed with water; used in adhesives and for sizing cotton cloth.

dextrose: see GLUCOSE.

Dezhnev, Cape, RSFSR: see EAST CAPE.

Dhar (där), town (pop. 23,652), Madhya Pradesh, India. Was cap. of Malwa kingdom and a center of Hindu learning 9th to 14th cent.

diabetes (dīŭbē'tēz, -bētĭs) or **diabetes mellitus** (mĕlī'tŭs), continued excessive secretion of urine caused by INSULIN deficiency. Results in excess sugar in blood and usually also in urine. Often marked by loss of weight; acidosis and coma may follow. Treated by diet and insulin injections.

Diadochi (dīǎ'dŭkī) [Gr.,= successors], generals and administrators of ALEXANDER THE GREAT who attempted to take over his empire on his death (323 B.C.). Chief among them were Antipater (and his son Cassander), Perdiccas, Antigonus I, Ptolemy I, Seleucus I, and Lysimachus. Rivalry led to a dreary succession of wars. The main events were the victory of Antipater over Perdiccas for the regency (321 B.C.); the coalition against Antigonus after Antipater's death (319 B.C.), which brought the defeat of Antigonus and his son, Demetrius I, at Ipsus (301 B.C.); and the victory of Seleucus I over Lysimachus (281 B.C.). The result was the irrevocable splitting of the empire into smaller empires, notably under the descendants of Ptolemy, Seleucus, and Antigonus.

Diaghilev, Sergei Pavlovich (sĭrgā' päv'lŭvĭch dyä'gĭlyĭf), 1872–1929, Russian ballet impresario. In Paris founded (1909) Ballet Russe with painter Bakst. choreographer Fokine. Dancers included Pavlova and Nijinsky. His principle of asymmetry and the use of music and scene design as integral parts of the dance were revolutionary.

dialect, variety of a language. In 20th-cent. scientific usage, a dialect is language of a person or group considered as it varies from that of other members of same speech community (which includes all speakers whose native language is intelligible to other—but not necessarily all other—members of the group). With increasing isolation differences may accumulate to the point of mutual unintelligibility. An example is Dutch-German speech community, extending from Flanders to Schleswig and to Styria, yet speakers of Flemish and Styrian dialects cannot understand each other. In the area there are standard languages (i.e., official Dutch and German) which are mutually unintelligible because developed from mutually unintelligible dialects.

dialectic, in philosophy, method of logical procedure, originating in the question-answer-resolution method of Socrates, developed by Plato into a method of reducing the many and the contradictory into systematic organized concepts. Kant used the term for his method of demonstrating metaphysics (as opposed to knowledge derived from phenomena). Hegel based his philosophy on the logic of dialectic, moving from thesis (statement) through antithesis (counterstatement) to synthesis (joining of the two in higher truth); he also held that this process underlay movement in history.

dialectical materialism, logical method of historical analysis which sees historical change as the result of conflicts between economic groups, notably classes, which are in turn determined by their relationships to the means of production. Derived by Marx and Engels from Hegel's dialectic, but materialistic rather than idealistic. See MARXISM.

dialysis (dīă′lĭsĭs), in chemistry, a method of separating a colloid from a substance in true solution by using a membrane permeable only to one. Molecular particles of dissolved substance pass through membrane; particles of colloid are too large.

diamond, crystallized pure carbon, valued as a gem. It is the hardest substance known, and inferior stones are used as abrasives, in certain types of cutting tools, and as phonograph needles. Earliest sources were stream gravels (see MINING). Most of the world's gem diamond supply comes from the pipes of old volcanoes in South Africa; Brazil is a source of carbonados (black diamonds). Small diamonds are also produced synthetically for use in industry.

Diamond Head, extinct crater, 761 ft. high, SE Oahu, Hawaii. Once burial grounds of anc. Hawaiians.

Diamond Necklace, Affair of the, scandal which took place in 1784–86 at the French court. An adventuress, calling herself the Comtesse de Lamotte, persuaded Cardinal de Rohan that he could gain Queen Marie Antoinette's favor by buying her a diamond necklace worth nearly $1,000,000. The necklace, assembled by two jewelers, was bought on installment by the cardinal in the queen's name. When he could not meet the payments, the jewelers brought a complaint. It was discovered that Mme de Lamotte's husband had absconded with the necklace to London (where it was broken up and sold). At the trial (1785) the cardinal was acquitted but disgraced; Mme de Lamotte was branded and imprisoned, but escaped. CAGLIOSTRO, at first suspected of complicity, was acquitted. Although the queen had no part in it, the affair revealed a moral laxity at her court which increased her unpopularity.

Diana, in Roman legend, goddess of the moon, of forests, of animals, and of women in childbirth; identified with Greek Artemis. Her temple at Aricia was a shrine of women.

Diane de Poitiers (dyän′ dü pwätyä′), 1499–1566, mistress of Henry II of France.

dianthus: see PINK.

Diarmuid mac Murchada: see DERMOT McMURROUGH.

diarrhea (dīŭrē′ŭ), frequent discharge of watery feces, resulting from irritation or nervous stimulation of intestines. Tissues and blood lose fluids and minerals which need to be replaced.

Dias, Bartolomeu (dē′ŭsh), d. 1500, Portuguese navigator. First European to round Cape of Good Hope (1488), thus opening sea route to India.

diastase (dī′ŭstās) or **amylase** (ă′mĭlās), an enzyme that converts starch to sugar and thus is important in digestion and fermentation. It is present in some plants and in saliva (as ptyalin) and pancreatic fluid (as amylopsin).

diathermy: see ELECTROTHERAPY.

diatom (dī′ŭtŏm″), microscopic plant form of algae group. Diatoms are the only algae having silicon-containing shells; each diatom species has a characteristic shell shape. Some diatoms float free in water; other types are held fast by stalks. Diatoms can exist as single cells or joined as colonies in fresh or salt water, in moist soil, and on moist surfaces of other plants. They are most abundant in arctic and other cold regions. Diatomaceous earth and the more compact rock, diatomite, are formed from shells of dead diatoms. Diatomite, found in parts of U.S., is used industrially, especially for insulating against both heat and sound.

Diaz, Armando (ärmän′dō dē′äts), 1861–1928, Italian field marshal. Routed Austrians at Vittorio Veneto and accepted their surrender (Nov., 1918).

Díaz, Bartholomew: see DIAS, BARTOLOMEU.

Díaz, Porfirio (pôrfē′rēō dē′äs), 1830–1915, Mexican statesman, a mestizo who became president (1876) and remained in power until 1911. His regime saw material prosperity in Mexico grow largely through investment of foreign capital, but oppressed masses were neglected and education stagnated. A revolution led by Madero was successful. Diaz died in exile.

Diaz de la Peña, Narciso Virgilio (dyäz′ dü lä pänyä′), 1808–76, French landscape and figure painter of the Barbizon school, b. Bordeaux.

Díaz del Castillo, Bernal (bĕrnäl′ dē′äth dĕl kästē′lyō), c.1492–1581, Spanish conquistador, author of The True History of the Conquest of Mexico (1632).

Diaz Mirón, Salvador (sälvädhōr dē′äs mērōn′), 1853–1928, Mexican poet. Precursor of MODERNISMO; his turbulent life was reflected in his early poetry.

Dibon (dī′–) or **Dibon-gad,** anc. city, E of Dead Sea, now a ruin called Dhiban. MOABITE STONE found here.

Dice, one of the HORAE.

dice [plural of die], small cubes usually made of ivory, bone, wood, similar materials. The six sides are numbered by dots from 1 to 6, so placed that sum of dots on opposite sides equals 7. Most popular dice game in U.S. is craps. Dice also used in poker dice, backgammon, parcheesi, many other games. Dice known to the ancient Egyptians and the Babylonians and were very popular among the Greeks and Romans.

Dick, George Frederick: see DICK TEST.

Dickens, Charles, 1812–70, English novelist, one of the outstanding writers of fiction in English. His childhood was poverty-stricken, and at 12 he worked in a blacking warehouse. Was a court and parliamentary reporter before he began writing sketches (first collected as Sketches by Boz, 1836). He was commissioned to write Posthumous Papers of the Pickwick Club (1836–37; connected humorous sketches) and began the long series of major novels: Oliver Twist (as book 1838), Nicholas Nickleby (1839), The Old Curiosity Shop (1841), Barnaby Rudge (1841), Martin Chuzzlewit (1843), Dombey and Son (1848), David Copperfield (1850), Bleak House (1853), Hard Times (1854), Little Dorrit (1857), A Tale of Two Cities (1859), Great Expectations (1860–61), Our Mutual Friend (1865), The Mystery of Edwin Drood (1870; unfinished). Also wrote Christmas books and stories (e.g., A Christmas Carol, 1843) and many short stories. Visit to United States in 1842 brought highly critical American Notes (1842) and section of Martin Chuzzlewit. Married Catherine Hogarth (1836) and had 10 children; separated from her in 1858, possibly because of interest in an actress, Ellen Ternan. His novels are remarkable for depicting quirks of character, for rich panoramas of social scenes, for sentimentality, for crusades against social evils (e.g., imprisonment for debt, legal delays, bad education). Edited magazines, was interested in drama and amateur theatricals.

Dickinson, Emily, 1830–86, American poet. She spent almost all of her life in Amherst, Mass., mostly in seclusion, seeing only a limited number of persons.

Whether or not she had a brief and abortive love affair is hotly argued. Certainly she began c.1862 writing the short, frequently cryptic lyrics that have made her one of America's major poets. Her fame began when Mabel L. Todd and T. W. Higginson edited and published her poems (1890, 1891). Quarreling over versions went on until T. H. Johnson's definitive editions of the poems (3 vols., 1955) and letters (3 vols., 1958) appeared.

Dickinson, John, 1732–1808, American patriot and statesman. A conservative, his *Letters from a Farmer in Pennsylvania* (1767–68) criticized Townshend Acts and recommended conciliation.

Dickinson College, at Carlisle, Pa.; coed.; founded 1773 as a grammar school, chartered and opened as Dickinson Col. 1783.

Dick test, skin test for determining susceptibility to scarlet fever. American physician, **George Frederick Dick,** 1881–, developed test and immunity serum and isolated streptococcus causing disease.

dictator, originally, a Roman magistrate appointed to rule the state in time of crisis; now, any autocrat. Modern dictators may, as head of party or personal following, seize power or take office constitutionally and later create dictatorship. A totalitarian dictatorship (e.g., under fascism or communism) generally has an official ideology, a single mass party usually led by one man, a system of terroristic police control, monopolies over communications and weapons, and a centrally directed economy.

dictionary, published list of forms of a language, with content governed by some specific purpose. Descriptive dictionaries (e.g., foreign-language dictionaries) attempt, ideally, to give objectively exact meaning of all forms of their languages. The modern dictionary of its own standard language is often prescriptive, for it attempts to establish certain forms as preferable (as in dictionary of the French Acad.). In 20th cent. American dictionary makers began to replace notions of purity (esp. based on ETYMOLOGY) by criteria of use. The sound line of English dictionaries may be said to begin with *Universal Etymological English Dictionary* (1721) and *Dictionarium Britannicum* (1730), by Nathan Bailey. Samuel Johnson used Bailey's second work to prepare *A Dictionary of the English Language* (1755). His definitions are basic in later lexicography. The next great lexicographer was an American, Noah Webster, whose *Spelling Book* appeared in 1783. His more advanced *Compendious Dictionary of the English Language* (1806) and his larger work, *An American Dictionary of the English Language* (1828), followed. Authorized publishers have made a series of skillful revisions, which have caused Webster's dictionaries to retain popularity. *The Century Dictionary,* an American work in six volumes, with encyclopedic features, was completed in 1891. In England dictionary work after Johnson progressed with John Walker's dictionary (1791), which gave special care to pronunciation, and later with that of the Philological Society, published 1884–1928 as *New English Dictionary, Oxford English Dictionary,* or *Murray's Dictionary* (for Sir J. A. H. Murray, one of the editors), in which examples of usage were collected and organized, with dates given.

Dictys Cretensis (dĭk'tĭs krētĕn'sĭs), supposed hero of Trojan War. Latin MS of his "diary" (A.D. 4th cent.) was popular source for medieval stories.

Didache (dĭ'dŭkē) [Gr.,= teaching], collection of Christian moral precepts, directions for baptism and the Eucharist, and instructions to ministers. It is in Greek, is also called in English *The Teaching of the Twelve Apostles,* and probably dates from before A.D. 100.

Diderot, Denis (dŭnē' dēdŭrō'), 1713–84, French philosopher, a leading figure of the ENLIGHTENMENT and a universal genius of the modern era. His life work was the editorship of the ENCYCLOPÉDIE (1747–72). His philosophy, scattered in numerous writings, combines extreme skepticism with bold materialism. As a playwright, he created the "bourgeois drama" with *Le*

Père de famille (1758). *La Religieuse* and *Jacques le fataliste,* novels, and *Le Neveu de Rameau,* a satire in dialogue (all pub. posthumously) are, like all his works, highly individualistic and personal in style. In his *Salons* (1759–71) he pioneered in modern art criticism. Late in life he enjoyed the patronage of Catherine II, whom he visited at St. Petersburg (1773–74).

Dido (dī'dō), in Roman legend, founder and queen of Carthage. Of several versions of her story the most famous is in Vergil's *Aeneid,* which tells how she loved Aeneas and how, when he had to leave her, she destroyed herself by jumping on a burning pyre.

Didot, François (fräswä' dēdō'), 1689–1757, Parisian printer. His son, **François Ambroise Didot** (äbrwäz'), 1730–1804, was called by Benjamin Franklin Bache "the best printer of this age and even the best that has ever been seen." Scholarly and typographic excellence of Didot's books is unquestioned. He designed some "modern" type and improved and secured adoption of Pierre Simon Fournier's "point" system of type measurement. His sons, **Pierre Didot,** 1761–1853, and **Firmin Didot** (fērmē'), 1764–1836, continued family tradition of printing excellence, choosing and editing texts conscientiously and also producing good inexpensive books for students.

Didrikson, (Mildred) Babe (dĭ'drĭksŭn), 1913–56, American athlete. Broke four records at Olympic games of 1932. Won many golf titles incl. U.S. Open 1948, 1950, 1954). Married George Zaharias 1938. Considered America's greatest woman athlete.

Didymus: see THOMAS, SAINT.

die, device for drawing wire or cutting, forming, impressing designs on materials, especially metals. Original die, called a matrix, is made by cutting recessed pattern into surface of metal block: the punch, or male die, is its counterpart in relief. Material (e.g., sheet metal) is blanked or cut out, shaped, or embossed between such dies by press lever or drop hammer, or by die casting (see FOUNDING). Metal forced or pulled through progressively smaller holes forms wires and rods. Hollow hard metal die, internally threaded, is used for cutting screw or pipe threads. Device used to emboss paper or leather is type of die.

Diefenbaker, John George, 1895–, Canadian statesman, prime minister of Canada 1957–63. Became member of Parliament 1940 and leader of Progressive-Conservative party 1956.

Diels, Otto Paul Hermann, 1876–1954, German chemist. Shared 1950 Nobel Prize in Chemistry with Alder for developing a method of synthesizing benzene ring hydrocarbons.

Diemen, Anton van (än'tōn vän dē'mŭn), 1593–1645, Dutch colonial official. Became governor general of Dutch East India Co. in 1636. Sent out Abel TASMAN on exploring voyages. Van Diemen's Land was original name of Tasmania.

Dienbienphu (dyĕn'byĕn'fōō), town, W North Vietnam. Scene of last great battle (March-May 1954) between the French and the Vietminh forces of Ho CHI MINH. With its fall, French domination of Vietnam ended.

Dieppe (dēĕp'), town (est. pop. 26,427), Seine-Maritime dept., N France, in Normandy, on English Channel. Harbor, mfg. center, and beach resort. Scene (1942) of Allied commando raid in Second World War.

Diesel engine (dē'zŭl), internal-combustion type of engine invented by Rudolf Diesel (1858–1913, German engineer). Since patented in 1892, it has developed into competitor of steam engine, steam turbine, and electric motor, particularly for marine work and for driving locomotives, trucks, electric generators, and pumps. Instead of igniting fuel by spark as in gasoline engines, it uses compression of air to raise air temperature to igniting point. Although heavier than gasoline engines, the Diesel uses cheaper fuel (crude oil). See *ill.,* p. 333.

Dies irae (dē'ās ē'rā) [Latin,= day of wrath], hymn of the Roman Catholic Church, part of the Requiem Mass, a description of the Last Judgment. Its plainsong tune has been used in instrumental music, as in Berlioz's *Symphonie fantastique*. Verdi and Mozart composed original music for it.

diet, daily intake of food. For maintenance of physical and mental health it should include adequate daily amounts of proteins (e.g., from meat, fish, eggs, legumes, milk, cheese); carbohydrates, i.e., starches (grain products, potatoes, rice) and sugar (fruits, honey, moderate amount of other sweets); fats; and a sufficient intake of minerals (calcium, phosphorus, iron, copper, iodine) and VITAMINS, as well as water. Obesity is caused by a diet with more calorie (i.e., energy) value than the body requires. Special diets are needed in certain diseases and to correct obesity or underweight.

Dietrich, Marlene, (dē'trĭkh), 1904?–, American singer and film actress, b. Berlin. First noted in *The Blue Angel* (1930). Her sultry cabaret singing enhanced her image as a *femme fatale.*

Dieulafoy, Marcel Auguste (dyûläfwä'), 1844–1920, French archaeologist. Discovered palaces of Darius and Artaxerxes at Susa while exploring in Persia (1885). Aided by his wife, **Jeanne** (or **Jane) Rachel Magre Dieulafoy,** 1851–1916.

differential, in automobile a set of gears used on driving axle (usually the rear) to divide torque of common power source (drive shaft) equally between two rear wheels, at the same time allowing each wheel to revolve at its own speed.

diffraction. Light travels in straight lines through a uniform, transparent medium. When an opaque object partly blocks its path, the rays that just pass the edges are bent slightly. This is diffraction; it occurs when light waves pass through narrow slits. Diffraction is a characteristic property of all wave motion. A **diffraction grating** is ruled with close parallel grooves; light waves reflected from a groove are diffracted in the same way as light passing through a slit; INTERFERENCE among the reflected light waves produces spectra and makes possible determination of the wavelengths of the light.

diffusion, uniform distribution of molecules of one substance through those of another in apparent contradiction to laws of gravity. Rate is inversely proportional to square root of density of diffusing gas (Graham's law). It is seen also in liquids and in some solids in contact with others.

Digby, earls of Bristol: see BRISTOL, JOHN DIGBY, 1ST EARL OF.

Digby, Sir Kenelm, 1603–65, English writer, man of affairs. Varied career included brief piracy, loyal support of king in civil war. Was agent of Cromwell to secure rights for Roman Catholics. His promotion of a panacea, "powder of sympathy," obscured his real scientific achievements.

Digest: see CORPUS JURIS CIVILIS.

digestion, conversion of food in alimentary canal into simple, soluble form which can pass into the circulation and be used by tissues. In man, it occurs chiefly by the action of SALIVA, BILE, and juices of STOMACH, PANCREAS, and INTESTINE.

Diggers, members of small English religio-economic movement (fl. 1649–50), so called because of efforts to cultivate wastelands. Offshoot of LEVELERS; favored egalitarian communism. Leader was Gerrard Winstanley (b. 1609). Colonies, estab. in Surrey, were destroyed by mob violence 1650.

Dighton, industrial town (pop. 3,767), SE Mass., on Taunton R., S of Taunton; settled 1678. Includes North Dighton village (pop. 1,167). Origin of inscriptions, probably Indian, on Dighton Rock, is uncertain.

digitalis, a drug, a powerful heart stimulant, obtained from the leaves of the FOXGLOVE plant. Sometimes the plant itself is called digitalis.

Dijon (dēzhŏ'), city (pop. 135,694), cap. of Côte-d'Or dept., E France; historic cap. of Burgundy. Chief trading center for Burgundy wine. Reached its flower under Duke Philip the Good (15th cent.). Among art treasures are funeral statues of dukes by Claus SLUTER and his disciples in former ducal palace (12th cent.; rebuilt 17th and 18th cent.); several 13th-cent. churches, including cathedral; 16th-cent. palace of justice (once housing parlement). Architecture is indebted to Flemish artists. University founded 1722.

dill, Old World annual (*Anethum graveolens*), with aromatic seeds used for pickling and flavoring.

Dillard University, at New Orleans, La.; coed.; chartered 1930, opened 1935 by combining New Orleans Univ. and Straight Col.

Dillinger, John (dĭl'ĭngŭr), 1902–34, American bank robber. In 1933 he terrorized the Midwest with an organization of criminals, killing c.16 persons before he was shot by FBI agents.

Dillon, Clarence Douglas, 1909–, American financier and public official. Served as Ambassador to France (1953–58) and Secretary of the Treasury (1961–65).

Dilthey, Wilhelm (vĭl'hĕlm dĭl'tī), 1833–1911, German philosopher. Argued for analytic psychology as base for philosophy, a central spiritual science distinct from natural sciences. He stressed history and development of ideas, to the exclusion of metaphysics.

DiMaggio, Joseph Paul (dĭmä'jēō), 1914–, American baseball outfielder for N.Y. Yankees. Estab. (1941) major league record by hitting safely in 56 consecutive games. Elected to Baseball Hall of Fame (1955).

dime novels, swift-moving, thrilling novels, mainly about American Revolution, frontier period, or Civil War. First sold in 1860 for 10 cents. Among most famous were those about DEADWOOD DICK and Nick CARTER. Quality of stories was lowered by imitators after 1880, and dime novels acquired bad name.

diminishing returns, law of, economic law that after a certain point an increase in one factor of production, with others held constant, will yield relatively decreasing returns.

Dimitrov, Georgi (gĕōr'gĕ dĭmē'trōf), 1882–1949, Bulgarian Communist leader. Arrested by Germans for alleged complicity in setting REICHSTAG on fire. Acquitted, he went to USSR and worked for Comintern. Returned to Bulgaria 1944 to head Communist party; was premier from 1946 until he died.

Dinah (dī'nù), daughter of Jacob. Gen. 30.21; 34.1–31.

Dinan (dēnä'), town (est. pop. 13,844), Côtes-du-Nord dept., NW France. A 14th-cent. château and Church of Saint-Sauveur (12th–16th cent.) are here.

Dinant (dēnä'), town (est. pop. 6,790), Namur prov., S Belgium, on Meuse R. Railroad junction; market center. Fortified since Merovingian times, it was noted in Middle Ages for metalware.

Dinard (dēnär'), town (est. pop. 8,540), Ille-et-Vilaine dept., NW France, facing Saint-Malo across inlet of English Channel. Bathing resort.

Dinaric Alps (dīnä'rĭk), mountain range, occupying about one third of Yugoslavia and part of Albania. Prolongs Alps along E coast of Adriatic; includes KARST in N. Highest peak (c.8,245 ft.) is in Albania.

D'Indy, Vincent: see INDY, VINCENT D'.

Dinesen, Isak (ē'säk dē'nùsùn), pseud. of Karen, Baroness Blixen, 1885–1962, Danish author. Notable among her works in English are the polished stories in *Seven Gothic Tales* (1934) and *Winter's Tales* (1943).

Diniz, Port. *Dinis* (dĭnēzh'), 1261–1325, king of Portugal (1279–1325). His reign was generally peaceful. A patron of literature, founder of Coimbra Univ. (originally at Lisbon), he also increased the royal domain (particularly at the expense of the Templars) and greatly encouraged farming. Nicknamed "the farmer." His queen was St. Elizabeth of Portugal.

dinosaur (dī'nùsôr), extinct land reptile of the MESOZOIC ERA, ranging in length from 2½ to c.90 ft. Some were herbivorous, others carnivorous. They died out by the end of the Cretaceous period.

Dinosaur National Monument: see NATIONAL PARKS AND MONUMENTS (table).

Dinwiddie, Robert, 1693–1770, colonial governor of Va. (1751–58), b. Scotland. Sent George Washington on unsuccessful mission to forestall French in Ohio valley in 1754. Aided Braddock's campaign.

Dio: see DION.

Diocletian (dīŭklē'shŭn), 245–313, Roman emperor (284–305), b. Salona, Dalmatia, of humble parents. An army commander, he was chosen to succeed after Numerian was murdered, and he killed the suspected murderer, Arrius Aper. Ruled jointly with Carinus, who had been joint emperor with Numerian, until Carinus was killed. Later to defend the empire with responsible officials he made MAXIMIAN joint emperor (286) and CONSTANTIUS I and GALERIUS Caesars (subemperors). This policy succeeded brilliantly: Britain was restored, the Persians were subdued, and some barbarians driven out. The empire throve. There was, however, severe persecution of the Christians; economic measures turned out badly; and the division of the empire formally instituted by Diocletian led to much warfare after he and Maximian abdicated (305). Diocletian retired to a splendid castle at Salona.

diode, two-element electron tube or semiconductor which conducts current in one direction only. Used mainly as a rectifier.

Diodorus Siculus (dīŭdô'rŭs sĭ'kūlŭs), d. after 21 B.C., Sicilian historian. Author of world history ending with Gallic Wars; in Greek, in 40 books, of which I–IV and XI–XX are fully preserved.

Diogenes (dīŏj'ĭnēz), c.412–323 B.C., Greek Cynic philosopher. Scorning material things, he lived in a tub in Athens. When Alexander the Great came to ask him what he might do for him, Diogenes answered only, "Get out of my light." He is said to have carried a lantern in daylight looking for a "man," someone who had the true human virtues.

Diogenes Laertius (lāŭr'shēŭs), fl. early 3d cent., Greek biographer. His work on philosophers from Thales to Epicurus is invaluable source of history.

Diomed (dī'ŏmĕd), **Diomede** (–mĕd), or **Diomedes** (dī'-ŏmē'dēz), in Greek legend. 1 One of the EPIGONI, prominent in the Trojan War. 2 Son of Ares who fed his horses on human flesh. HERCULES killed him.

Diomede Islands (dī'ŭmēd), group of three islands in Bering Strait between Alaska and Siberia. USSR-U.S. boundary passes between two larger islands. Group discovered by Vitus Bering.

Dion Cassius (Cassius Dio Cocceianus) (dī'ŭn kă'shŭs), c.155–235?, Roman historian, b. Bithynia. He held high imperial office but is known for his history of Rome, written in Greek and now only partly extant. Also Dio Cassius.

Dion Chrysostom (krī'sŭstŭm, krīsŏ'stŭm) [Gr.,= golden-mouthed], d. after A.D. 112, Greek sophist and rhetorician. Author of 80 extant orations.

Dione (dīō'nē), Greek earth goddess. In some legends Zeus' first mate. They shared oracle at DODONA.

Dionne quintuplets (dēŏn'), five daughters (Annette, Emélie, Yvonne, Cécile, and Marie) born to Oliva Dionne and his wife at Callender, Ont., on May 28, 1934. In 1935 the Ontario legislature made them wards of the province. Emélie died in 1954.

Dion of Syracuse (dī'ŭn), 409?–354? B.C., Greek political leader in Sicily. Brother-in-law of Dionysius the Elder, he knew Plato and philosophically favored moderate government. Led a force from Athens to overthrow Dionysius the Younger (357 B.C.) and commanded Sicily until murdered by an Athenian companion.

Dionysia (dīŭnĭ'shēŭ), in Greek religion, festivals to honor god Dionysus. Resembling the Bacchanalia, they stressed fertility rites. They advanced the dithyramb, the choral procession, and Greek drama (see COMEDY and TRAGEDY).

Dionysius (dīŭnĭ'shēŭs), tyrants of Syracuse. **Dionysius the Elder,** c.430–367 B.C., rose as representative of the poor to become tyrant (406 B.C.). He kept the people in obedience through fear of the Carthaginians. Led expeditions against Italian cities and the Carthaginians. Patronized literature and the arts. His son, **Dionysius the Younger,** fl. 368–344 B.C., succeeded him, tried to maintain popularity, but lost it to DION OF SYRACUSE (357 B.C.). After Dion's murder he regained power, but was expelled by Timoleon (344 B.C.).

Dionysius of Halicarnassus (hă''lĭkärnă'sŭs), fl. 1st cent. B.C., Greek rhetorician, historian, and critic. Author of *Antiquities of Rome.*

Dionysius the Areopagite, Saint (dīŭnĭ'shēŭs, ârēŏp'-ŭjīt), 1st cent. Athenian Christian, converted by St. Paul; traditionally first bishop of Athens and a martyr. He is sometimes confused with St. Denis (their names are different forms of the same one). In the Middle Ages some letters and treatises important in scholasticism were attributed to him; were probably written (in Greek) in 5th- or 6th-cent. Palestine. Their author is now called Pseudo-Dionysius. Feast: Oct. 9.

Dionysius the Elder: see DIONYSIUS.

Dionysius the Younger: see DIONYSIUS.

Dionysus (dīŭnī'sŭs), in Greek legend, god of fertility and wine, patron of choral song and drama; son of Zeus and Semele. His worship (said to have been imported from Thrace) was full of enthusiasm and emotionalism, as in the DIONYSIA. Pan and Silenus were his companions, and he was surrounded by the BACCHAE. His seat was supposedly at Delphi, which was sacred to him in winter; thus he achieved a sort of parity with Apollo. He was chief deity in ORPHIC MYSTERIES and shared in ELEUSINIAN MYSTERIES. As nature god he was confused with Bacchus.

Diophantus (dīŭfăn'tŭs), 3d cent., Greek algebraist, pioneer in solving a type of indeterminate algebraic equations. This work is now known as Diophantine analysis.

Dior, Christian (dēōr'), 1905–57, French fashion designer. He set up his own fashion house in Paris 1946 and in New York 1948. His innovations strongly influenced the world of fashion.

Dioscorides, Pedanius (pĭdă'nēŭs dīŭskô'rĭdēz), 1st cent. A.D. Greek physician, author of standard work on substances used in medicine.

Dioscuri: see CASTOR AND POLLUX.

dip, in stock raising, antiseptic solution to kill skin parasites. Applied by dipping animals in tank.

diphtheria (dĭfthēr'ēŭ), communicable disease caused by toxin produced by bacterium and characterized by membranous film in air passages. Incubation period is two to five days. Toxoid used for immunization. Antitoxin given after exposure and to treat disease. SCHICK TEST determines susceptibility.

diplomatic service, body of agents maintained by a government to conduct its relations with foreign nations. First ambassadors acted only on specific missions. In early Middle Ages Venice set up first permanent system of resident ambassadors in foreign caps., and permanent legations became general by end of 18th cent. Congress of Vienna (1815) adopted classification of officers now widely accepted: ambassador, minister plenipotentiary, envoy extraordinary, minister, chargé d'affaires. Diplomats enjoy "diplomatic immunity," their residences rights of EXTERRITORIALITY. One function of diplomats is to observe political, economic, and military trends subject to international restrictions barring espionage. A diplomat is responsible usually to his own foreign minister. His business is carried on with foreign minister of country to which he is accredited in form of memorandums, oral and written notes and formal notes. Diplomatic service is distinguished from CONSULAR SERVICE though often they are combined, as in U.S. under Rogers Act of 1924. Foreign Service Act of 1946 set up merit system for protection of staff.

dipper, only aquatic perching bird. Closely related to wrens. They live near cold mountain streams.

Dirac, Paul Adrien Maurice (dĭrăk′), 1902–, English physicist. Shared 1933 Nobel Prize in Physics for developing Heisenberg's theory of quantum mechanics.

direct current: see ELECTRICITY; GENERATOR.

Directory, Fr. *Directoire,* French government from 1795 to 1799. Its executive branch consisted of five directors, chosen by the two legislative chambers. Its history was marked by corruption, coups d'état, inflation, and, in 1799, military disaster. Sieyès and Barras, who were directors in 1799, helped Bonaparte in overthrowing the Directory and establishing the Consulate by the coup d'état of 18 Brumaire.

Diredawa (dē″rŭdä′wä), town (pop. c.35,000), E central Ethiopia. Formerly terminus (now at Addis Ababa) of rail line from Jibuti. Textile mfg. and rail shops.

dirigible balloon: see AIRSHIP.

Dis, Roman name for PLUTO.

disarmament, a major aim of all peace movements (see PEACE CONGRESSES). Period between wars saw calling of NAVAL CONFERENCES and DISARMAMENT CONFERENCE to restrict conventional armaments. After Second World War development of nuclear weapons made disarmament question much more urgent. UN Charter provided for formulation of disarmament plans, and control of armaments has always been major UN concern. Situation became acute when USSR, Great Britain, and France joined U.S. as nuclear powers. UN Disarmament Commission formed Jan., 1952, to deal with all disarmament issues. All subsequent discussions were complicated by distrust between East and West and basic disagreement on issues of inspection and control of disarmament process. Disarmament was discussed at 1955 Geneva Conference. Talks between U.S., Great Britain, and USSR on nuclear test-ban treaty began in 1958. Disarmament discussions were held at 1958 Geneva Conference between U.S. and USSR on surprise attacks, and by 10-nation disarmament committee formed in 1959. Problems were carried over to UN Disarmament Commission, which had 17 members after withdrawal of France. Importance of test-ban treaty agreed to by U.S., Great Britain, and USSR in 1963 overshadowed by refusal of France and Communist China to sign and by latter's progress in development of nuclear weapons, resulting early in 1966 in explosion of its third nuclear bomb.

Disarmament Conference, 1932–37. In 1926 preparatory commission for general disarmament met under League of Nations auspices at Geneva. First general conference met in Feb., 1932 (including members of League, USSR, and U.S.), and drafted plans for budgetary restrictions of armaments, limitation of armed forces, and permanent committee to advise on execution of treaty. France offered substitute draft, causing deadlock with Germany. After Germany withdrew from League, conference held sporadic meetings until indefinite postponement in April, 1937.

disciple: see APOSTLE.

Disciples of Christ or **Christian Churches,** Protestant religious body in U.S., sometimes called Campbellites. Originated in early 19th cent. through union of several dissident groups, notably those led by Thomas and Alexander Campbell and Barton Stone. Stress is on Bible alone rather than creeds as basis of faith. Group split in early 20th cent. into Churches of Christ and more progressive Disciples of Christ. Disciples of Christ changed name in 1957 to Christian Churches.

Discobolus (dĭskŏ′būlŭs) [Gr.,= discus thrower], 5th-cent. B.C. Greek statue in bronze by Myron. Only Roman copies of it in marble remain.

disease, departure from health resulting from changes in structure or function of tissues. See also COMMUNICABLE DISEASES.

disease carrier, person or animal harboring and capable of distributing to others the causative agent of a disease. Carrier may be immune to, or recovered from the disease. Famous example was cook known as Typhoid Mary. Typhoid fever and diphtheria are spread by human carriers; malaria, by mosquitoes.

disinfectant, agent which destroys organisms causing disease. Contaminated materials are disinfected by burning, boiling, sterilizing by steam under pressure, or by the use of a germicide.

Disko (dĭ′skŏ), island, area c.3,000 sq. mi., off W Greenland. Telluric iron has been found; lignite is mined. Godhavn is on S shore.

Dismal Swamp, SE Va. and NE N.C. Thought to have once covered c.2,200 sq. mi.; now reduced by drainage to less than 600 sq. mi. Bottom has organic material deposited by fallen trees and other vegetation. Visited by William Byrd (1728) and George Washington (as member of draining company). Canal (1828), now part of Intra-coastal Waterway, connects Chesapeake Bay with Albemarle Sound. L. Drummond (c.3 mi. in diameter), in center, is highest elevation. Dense forests and tangled undergrowth attract sportsmen and naturalists. Lumbering carried on with difficulty. Scene of H. B. Stowe's novel *Dred.*

Disney, Walt (dĭz′nē), 1901–66, producer of animated cartoons. Began career as cartoonist 1920; was known through "Mickey Mouse" series after 1928. His *Snow White and the Seven Dwarfs* (1938) was the first full-length animated cartoon. After 1950 he also produced adventure stories and documentaries on nature. Disneyland in Anaheim, Calif., was opened 1955.

dispensary: see CLINIC.

dispersion. 1 In chemistry, the dispersal of fine particles of one substance through another. According to size and nature of particles a dispersion is classed as a SOLUTION, COLLOID, SUSPENSION, or emulsion. **2** In physics, the separation of beam of white light by prism into various colors of SPECTRUM because of unequal refraction. For prism, see *ill.,* p. 796.

Disraeli, Benjamin, 1st **earl of Beaconsfield** (dĭzrā′lē), 1804–81, British statesman and author of Jewish descent. His novels (e.g., *Coningsby,* 1844, and *Sybil,* 1845) gave him a place in English literature. Elected to Parliament 1837; became leader of Tory protectionists. Largely responsible for REFORM BILL of 1867, which enfranchised c.2,000,000 men and benefited CONSERVATIVE PARTY. Succeeded DERBY as prime minister 1868. His second ministry (1874–80) had an aggressive foreign policy—annexation of Fiji Isls. (1874) and of the Transvaal (1877); war against Afghans and Zulus (1878–79). Purchase of controlling share of Suez Canal stock strengthened Britain in the Mediterranean. After Russo-Turkish War he induced Turkey to cede Cyprus to Great Britain. Through Congress of Berlin he reduced Russia's power in the Balkans. Favorite of Queen Victoria, he had her crowned Empress of India (1876). His twofold policy of democracy and imperialism revitalized the Tory party. His father, **Isaac D'Israeli,** 1766–1848, was an author. His best-known work is *Curiosities of Literature* (6 vols., 1791–1834).

dissenters: see NONCONFORMISTS.

dissociation, in chemistry, separation of molecules into simpler parts. It occurs at high temperatures (thermal dissociation) and when a substance dissolves (electrolytic dissociation, see ION).

distemper, in veterinary medicine, highly contagious catarrhal, often fatal disease of dogs and other animals. Can be controlled by vaccination.

distillation, process whereby a substance is changed from the liquid to the gaseous state, then condensed to liquid again, to be collected in a separate container. Used for purifying a substance, for separating substances from one another, and for breaking down a substance into fractional parts. In purifying water, for example, the impure water is heated to its boiling point and steam, the vapor thus formed, is led into condenser tubes where it is cooled and condensed to form liquid called the distillate. Impurities with higher boiling point than the water are left in the original container. "Double distilled" and "triple distilled" products have undergone further distillations. Many alcoholic beverages are distilled. In **fractional distillation** a liquid mixture of substances with different boiling points is repeatedly distilled at different temperatures and the parts or fractions obtained from each distillation are drawn off and condensed separately. This process is used in refining petroleum, yielding such fractions as gasoline, benzine, kerosene, fuel and lubricating oils, paraffin. **Destructive distillation** involves heating, out of free contact with air, materials such as wood, coal, or oil shale, and collecting separately the portions driven off. Wood thus yields acetic acid, methyl or wood alcohol, hydrocarbons, and residual charcoal. Coal yields coal gas, ammonia, coal tar, and residual coke. In **steam distillation,** steam is introduced to carry off volatile matter.

Distinguished Service Cross, Distinguished Service Medal, and **Distinguished Service Order:** see DECORATIONS, CIVIL AND MILITARY.

District of Columbia (pop. 763,956), E U.S., Federal district (c.70 sq. mi.) on E bank of Potomac R., coextensive with city of WASHINGTON, cap. of U.S. Estab. by congressional acts of 1790, 1791. Md. and Va. granted land on each side of river, including towns of Alexandria and Georgetown. Alexandria was returned to Va. 1847. Territorial government estab. 1871, present system 1878. Governed by Congress through executive board of presidential appointees. Inhabitants have no voice in local government, and no representation in Congress. Twenty-third Amendment (1961) to the Constitution gave inhabitants the right to vote in presidential elections.

dithyramb (dĭ'thĭrăm), in anc. Greece, choral lyric, a hymn to the god Dionysus. The TRAGEDY seems to have been developed from it.

Ditmars, Raymond L(ee) (dĭt'märz), 1876–1942, American naturalist and author, authority on snakes.

Diu (dē'ŏō), former Portuguese colony (20 sq. mi.), which comprises Diu isl., just S of Kathiawar peninsula, NW India. Diu town was estab. 1535. Colony annexed by India in Dec., 1961.

Dives (dī'vēz) [Latin,= rich] rich man of parable. Luke 16.19–31.

dividend, that part of a corporation's net earnings which is distributed to its stockholders. In U.S., dividends may be paid in bonds, stocks, cash, or scrip. Businesses being terminated may issue liquidation dividends.

Divine, Father, c.1882–1965, American Negro leader of Peace Mission movement, begun in Harlem section of N. Y. city. Born in Ga. as George Baker, he moved (c.1915) to North as Major M. J. Divine, later Father Divine. Many accept him as personification of God. Movement is nonsectarian and interracial.

Divine Comedy, Italian epic poem in *terza rima* by DANTE. Dante called it *Commedia* because it ended happily; *Divina* was added in the 16th cent. The narrator is led by Vergil through Hell and Purgatory, by Beatrice through Paradise.

divine right, doctrine that sovereigns derive their right to rule by birth alone, inheriting it from their ancestors, according to the law of God and of nature. A ruler claiming divine right rejects responsibility to his subjects. The theory, much argued in 17th-cent. England, ended there with the Revolution of 1688. Doctrine was epitomized by Louis XIV of France.

diving. Since the early days of his history and in all parts of the world man has developed the skill of plunging into water for pleasure and for profit (e.g., diving for pearls, coral, sponges). Yet deep-water diving was not possible until the early 19th cent. when Augustus Siebe devised diving dress for prolonged stays under water. The "open-type" dress was essentially a helmet with a pipe to supply air and a waterproof jacket. This type required that the diver stay upright, and Siebe therefore designed a less dangerous "closed-type" suit, which covered the diver entirely except for his hands. Later deep-water suits have merely been improvements on this. Waterproofed canvas, rubber, metal, and plastics are usual materials for making them. They have made possible much exploration of the ocean depths as well as recovery of valuable articles in sunken ships. Types of diving bells have also been used for investigating the underwater world—two notable examples being the bathysphere, used by Otis Barton and William Beebe off Bermuda to reach depth of 3,028 ft. (1934), and the bathyscaph, designed to reach the floor of the Marianas Trench, the greatest known ocean depth (35,800 ft.), and used by Don Walsh, USN, and Jacques Piccard (1960). Shallow water diving was a sport late in the 19th cent. and fancy diving contests are a usual part of all swimming meets, the divers being rated for precision, grace, and skill. The use of diving helmets (usually with breastplates) became popular for sport, including spear fishing, after the 1930s. Invention of the aqualung allows diving to 100 ft. or more without diving suit. See *ill.,* p. 311.

divorce, dissolution of a marriage by court judgment. Partial dissolution (divorce "from bed and board") is effected by judicial SEPARATION. Divorce is distinct from nullity of marriage, which is a decree that the marriage was originally illegal. In U.S., divorce powers belong to the individual states, and policies are varied; all attempts to reach some agreement between different laws have failed. Generally in all courts chief grounds are adultery, DESERTION, and cruelty. After decree is final both parties may remarry, and the wife is entitled to ALIMONY at the discretion of the court.

Dix, Dorothea Lynde, 1802–87, American reformer, pioneer in movement for more humane treatment of the insane.

Dix, John Adams, 1798–1879, American statesman. U.S. Senator (1845–49, Secretary of the Treasury for two months (1861), minister to France (1866–69).

Dix, Otto, 1891–, German painter and draughtsman, connected with NEW OBJECTIVITY.

Dix, Fort, U.S. army training center, SE of Trenton, N.J. Built in First World War, it was the largest army training center in U.S. in Second World War.

Dixie, song composed by Daniel Emmett in 1859, the patriotic song of the Confederacy during Civil War. Dixie now regarded as those states lying below Mason-Dixon line.

Dixon, city (pop. 19,565), N Ill., on Rock R., SW of Rockford, in farm area; founded 1830. Dixon Blockhouse site has statue of Lincoln as captain in Black Hawk War.

Dixville Notch, 2-mi. pass in White Mts., N N.H.

Diyarbakir (dēyärbĕkēr'), city (pop. 79,888), E central Turkey, on the Tigris. Commercial center. Occupies site of ancient Amida. Devastated by earthquake 1966.

Djakarta or **Jakarta** (jŭkär'tŭ), formerly **Batavia,** city (pop. 2,973,052), cap. of republic of Indonesia, NW Java. A commercial, industrial, transportation, and educational center. City comprises the old town to N (with Javanese, Chinese, and Arab quarters) and a modern residential section to S. Its port, Tanjungpriok, largest in Indonesia, exports tea, coffee, rubber, and minerals. Founded as Batavia by the Dutch in 1619, became Djakarta in 1949.

Djenné or **Jenné** (both: jĕnā'), town (pop. c.5,000), SE Mali, on Bani R. Founded 8th cent.; was market for gold, slaves, and salt by 13th cent. Fell to Mali empire c.1473. Came under French control in late 19th cent.

Djerba: see JERBA.

Djibouti: see JIBUTI.

Djilas, Milovan (mē'lŭvän jē'läs), 1911–, Yugoslav writer and political leader, b. Montenegro. A youthful revolutionary, later a high-ranking official (1945–

53), Djilas became a vice president 1953. Was ousted from Communist party positions 1954, later imprisoned. Article (Dec., 1956) hailing Hungarian revolt led to three-year prison sentence. *The New Class* (1957), an indictment of Communist bureaucracy, brought an additional sentence. Conditionally released (1961), he was rearrested 1962 for divulging state secrets in *Conversations with Stalin* and released for third time in 1967.

Dmitri (dǜmě'trē) or **Demetrius,** c.1582–1591, son of Ivan IV of Russia. He was murdered probably by order of Boris Godunov. An impostor, pretending to be Dmitri, invaded Russia (1604) with Polish aid. Boris died suddenly (1605), and the impostor was crowned tsar. He married Marina, a Polish noblewoman. In 1606 he was killed in an insurrection. Another false Dmitri appeared in 1607, was recognized by Marina as her husband, received Polish aid, and successfully invaded Russia. He was killed (1610), as were two later impostors who claimed to be Dmitri's son. Michael Romanov's election (1613) ended the confusion, known as the Time of Troubles.

DNA: see NUCLEIC ACID.

Dneprodzerdzhinsk (dǜnyě"prŭdzĭrzhěnsk'), city (1965 est. pop. 218,000), S central Ukraine, on the Dnieper R. Steel mills, chemical plants.

Dneproges (dǜnyěprǜgěs'), suburb of Zaporozhe, Ukraine, on the Dnieper, site of largest dam and hydroelectric power station in Europe (capacity up to 650,000 kw per hour). Its construction (1927–32) raised level of Dnieper 123 ft., made river navigable. H. L. Cooper was chief among American consultant engineers. Destroyed in Second World War; rebuilt 1947. Originally named Dneprostroi.

Dnepropetrovsk (dǜnyě"prŭpětrôfsk'), city (1965 est. pop. 774,006), central Ukraine. Port on Dnieper R.; rail center with heavy industries. Growth began late 19th cent. with exploitation of Donets Basin coal, Krivoi Rog iron, and Nikopol manganese. Receives power from Dneproges. Suffered in Second World War when fighting raged in area. Named Ekaterinoslav or Yekaterinoslav until 1926.

Dneprostroi, Ukraine: see DNEPROGES.

Dnieper (nē'pùr), Rus. *Dnepr,* river, 1,420 mi. long, Belorussia and Ukraine. Anc. name is Borysthenes. Rises in Valdai Hills, flows S past Smolensk, Kiev, Dnepropetrovsk, Zaporozhe (site of DNEPROGES dam), Kherson into Black Sea, describing vast bend between Kremenchug and Nikopol. Navigable in nearly entire length since construction of Dneproges; linked by canals with Bug, Niemen, Western Dvina.

Dniester (nē'stùr), Rus. *Dnestr,* river, 850 mi. long, SW European USSR. Rises in Carpathians; flows generally SE, partly along border between Ukraine and Moldavian SSR; joins Black Sea SW of Odessa. Navigable below Mogilev-Podolski. Formed Rumanian-USSR border 1918–40.

Doab (dō'äb), in India, a tract of land between two rivers. The Doab, unqualified by any names, designates tract between Ganges and Jumna rivers.

Doane, George Washington, 1799–1859, Episcopal bishop of N.J. (1832–59). Author of a number of hymns, including *Softly Now the Light of Day.*

Dobbs Ferry, residential village (1965 pop. 10,076), SE N.Y., on Hudson R. above Yonkers. Masters School is here.

Döbereiner, Johann Wolfgang (yō'hän vŏlf'gäng dǜ'bùrīnùr), 1780–1849, German chemist. He discovered similar triads of elements, a step in development of PERIODIC LAW.

Döblin, Alfred (dùblēn'), 1878–1957, German novelist. An expressionist writer, he is best known for *Berlin Alexanderplatz* (1929; Eng. tr., 1931), which shows the influence of James Joyce.

Dobrich, Bulgaria: see TOLBUKHIN.

Dobromierz: see HOHENFRIEDBERG.

Dobruja (dō'brōōjù), region, SE Rumania and NE Bulgaria. Constanta is the chief city of the Rumanian part of Dobruja; Tolbukhin of the Bulgarian part. Largely agr.; forests inland. Region was part of Roman Moesia, later of Byzantine Empire and of medieval Bulgaria. Under Ottoman rule from 15th cent. to 1878, when Congress of Berlin awarded most of it to Rumania. Bulgaria, forced to cede S Dobruja to Rumania in 1913, recovered it in 1940.

Dobson, (Henry) Austin, 1840–1921, English author of light verse in French forms (rondeau, villanelle, ballads) and of essays on 18th-cent. literature.

Dobson, William, 1610–46, English court painter to Charles I after death of Van Dyck.

dobson fly, insect of order Megaloptera, common to E North America. Adults may grow to five in. and are aquatic, nocturnal. Larvae, called hellgrammites, are much used as fishing bait.

Dobzhansky, Theodosius (dōshän'skē), 1900–, American geneticist, b. Russia. Expert on population genetics, evolution, origin of species.

Docetism (dōsě'tizùm), early Christian heretical movement, holding that Christ was not a man, but a mere phantasm who only seemed to live and to suffer. Gnostics held a similar belief.

dock, weedy plant of genus *Rumex,* widely distributed. It has small flowers and winged fruits. Common species are large curled dock, spinach dock, and canaigre (a food of Indians of SW U.S.). Species with arrowhead-shaped foliage are called sorrel, e.g., sheep sorrel of pastures.

Dodd, William E(dward), 1869–1940, American historian and diplomat, long at the Univ. of Chicago. He was ambassador to Germany (1933–37), and his diary (pub. 1941) records early days of Nazism there. He was an authority on the history of the South.

dodder, leafless parasitic plant of genus *Cuscuta,* with small flowers. Often a pest in fields of alfalfa, clover, and flax.

Dodds, Harold Willis, 1889–, American educator. Authority on economics and politics in Latin America, he has had international posts. A professor of politics at Princeton after 1927; president 1933–57.

Dodecanese (dōdě"kùnēs', –nēz, dō"dē–), island group (c.1,035 sq. mi.; pop. 123,021), Greece, in the SE Aegean, between Asia Minor and Crete; chief city Rhodes. Despite its name [12 islands], it consists of c.20 islands and islets, notably RHODES, Karpathos, Kalymnos, Patmos, Astypalaia, Kasos, Telos, Syme, Leros, Nisyros, Chalke, Kastellorizo. Mostly mountainous. Agr., livestock raising, sponge fishing. With fall of Rhodes to Suleiman I (1522), Dodecanese came under Turkish rule. Islands were occupied by Italy 1912; formally ceded to Italy 1922; awarded to Greece 1947.

Dodge, Grenville Mellen, 1831–1916, Union general in Civil War and railroad builder. Greatest achievement was as chief engineer (from 1866) in building of Union Pacific RR.

Dodge, Henry, 1782–1867, American frontiersman, governor of Territory of Wisconsin (1836–41, 1845–48), U.S. Senator (1848–57).

Dodge, Mary Mapes, 1831–1905, American editor of *St. Nicholas* magazine from 1873, author of juvenile classic *Hans Brinker; or, The Silver Skates* (1865).

Dodge City, city (pop. 13,520), SW Kansas, on Arkansas R. and on old Santa Fe Trail; laid out 1872 near Fort Dodge (1864). At first a trading post for buffalo hunters, it flourished as railhead after 1872. Wyatt Earp and Bat Masterson helped curb lawlessness in the rowdy cow town. Now a distributing center for large wheat and livestock area. St. Mary of the Plains Col. is here. City Hall is on site of Boot Hill, burial ground of early cowboys.

Dodgson, Charles Lutwidge: see CARROLL, LEWIS.

dodo, flightless forest-dwelling bird of Mauritius, extinct since late 17th cent. Although related to pigeon, it was larger than the turkey.

Dodona (dōdō'nù), in Greek religion, oldest oracle, in inland Epirus, sacred to Zeus and Dione.

Dodsley, Robert, 1703–64, English publisher, compiler of a well-known collection of plays (12 vols., 1744) and projector (with Burke) of *Annual Register* (1758).

Doeg (dō′ĕg), Edomite who massacred priests at Nob at Saul's command. 1 Sam. 21.1–9; 22.6–23.

Doenitz, Karl (dü′nĭts), 1891–, German admiral. Commanded submarine operations in Second World War; chief naval commander from 1943. Named by Hitler as his successor, he ordered unconditional surrender of Germany to Allies (May 7, 1945). Sentenced for imprisonment for 10 years at Nuremberg war-crimes trial (1946), he was released in 1956.

Doesburg, Theo van (tā′ō vän dōōs′bûrg), 1883–1931, Dutch painter, teacher, and writer. A founder of *De Stijl* magazine, he taught at the Bauhaus, influenced Gropius, and was successful in promoting the new aesthetic of simplicity and clarity.

dog, domesticated mammal (*Canis familiaris*) of the family Canidae, to which wolf, jackal, and fox also belong. Cave drawings of late Paleolithic period indicate that dogs were used for hunting by primitive man and thus were first domestic animals. Developed originally in SW Asia. Main progenitor was the wolf, as evidenced by identical dental structure of the two. More than 200 breeds exist; 115 are recognized by American Kennel Club. *Sporting dog* group includes pointers, retrievers, setters, and spaniels. *Hound* group is composed of scent hounds (e.g., beagle, foxhound, and bloodhound), which track prey by ground scent, and sight hounds (e.g., greyhound, Afghan hound, and Irish wolfhound), which rely mainly on eyesight to track prey. *Working dog* group includes such guard, herd, and sled dogs as boxer, German shepherd dog, and Siberian husky. Dogs of *terrier* group go to earth after their burrowing prey, and some are ratters. Group includes both short-legged (e.g., Scottish terrier) and long-legged (e.g., Airedale terrier) varieties. Such diminutive pets as Pekingese, Pomeranian, and Chihuahua belong to toy dog class. *Non-sporting dog* group is composed of Boston terrier, bulldog, chow chow, Dalmatian, French bulldog, keeshond, Lhasa apso, poodle, and schipperke.

dogfish, name for small sharks of several families of both hemispheres, found chiefly in temperate but also in tropical waters. Commonest is the spiny dogfish (*Squalus acanthias*), of the family Squalidae. It is 3–4 ft. long. In front of each dorsal fin is a stout spine, supplied with poison. It destroys food fish and nets.

Dogger Bank (dô′gúr, dô′–), extensive sand bank, central North Sea, between England and Denmark, covered by shallow water. It has fisheries.

dogtooth violet, adder's tongue, or **trout lily,** wild flower of genus *Erythronium,* with pendent, lilylike spring blossoms and mottled foliage.

dogwood or **cornel,** shrub or tree of genus *Cornus,* chiefly of N Hemisphere. Best known, flowering dogwood (*Cornus florida*), has white or pink flowers (botanically they are bracts), in spring. Its hard wood is used for shuttles, door handles. See also BUNCHBERRY.

Dohnanyi, Ernst von (dô′nänyē), 1877–1960, Hungarian composer, pianist, and conductor. His compositions include three operas, chamber music, concertos, piano pieces, and orchestral suites.

Doisy, Edward Adelbert, 1893–, American biochemist. Shared 1943 Nobel Prize in Physiology and Medicine for discovery of the chemical nature of vitamin K.

doldrums (dôl′drŭmz) or **equatorial belt of calms,** area just N of equator, circling earth between two trade-wind belts. Characterized by low pressure, light variable winds, squalls, thunderstorms.

Dole, Sanford Ballard, 1844–1926, American statesman of Hawaiian Isls., b. Honolulu. Became first president of republic of Hawaii 1894. Was first governor of Territory of Hawaii 1900–1903.

Dôle (dōl), town (pop. 22,022), Jura dept., E France, on Doubs R. Stronghold and cap. of Franche-Comté until conquest (1674) by Louis XIV, who transferred

the parlement and university (founded c.1422) to Besançon. Birthplace of Pasteur.

Dolet, Étienne (ātyĕn′ dôlā′), 1509–46, French scholar and printer. Wrote treatises on grammar and history and a famous commentary on the Latin language. Printed these and a translation of the Bible. He was finally accused of heresy, imprisoned, and executed.

Dolin, Anton, 1904–, English ballet dancer and choreographer, whose real name is Patrick Healey-Kay. Danced in Diaghilev company. Especially noted in productions with Alicia Markova.

Dolland, John, 1706–61, English optician. Invented achromatic lens and heliometer.

Dollfuss, Engelbert (ĕng′ûlbĕrt dôl′fŏōs), 1892–1934, chancellor of Austria (1932–34). A Christian Socialist, he opposed both National Socialists and Social Democrats, was driven into alliance with native fascists of E. R. von STARHEMBERG. After ruthlessly suppressing a Socialist rising, he made Austria a one-party, corporative state, under constitution drafted by SCHUSCHNIGG (1934). Assassinated by Austrian Nazis.

Döllinger, Johann Joseph Ignaz von (yō′hän yō′zĕf ĭg′näts fún dû′lĭng-ùr), 1799–1890, German theologian, church historian, leader of OLD CATHOLICS. Ordained (1822) as a Roman Catholic priest, he was long associated with the Univ. of Munich and a leading member (1845–52) of Catholic party in Frankfurt Parliament. Spurned dogma of papal infallibility pronounced by Vatican Council (1870) and was excommunicated in 1871. Although in sympathy with Old Catholics, he never intended a separate church to emerge from the movement and he never was formally a member of the Old Catholic Church.

dolmen (dôl′mĕn, dôl–), rough stone structure, consisting usually of two uprights and a capstone. Characteristic megalithic monument, probably erected as substitute for cave burial.

dolomite (dô′lŭmīt). **1** A mineral, calcium magnesium carbonate. **2** A carbonate rock composed chiefly of dolomite, similar to limestone but harder.

Dolomites (dô′lŭmīts), Alpine group, N Italy, famed for striking outline and vivid colors of its DOLOMITE rocks. Marmolada (10,964 ft.) is highest peak. Many resorts, e.g., Cortina d'Ampezzo.

dolphin. 1 Gregarious mammal, a toothed whale found in most oceans, sometimes in rivers. Its length is 4–30 ft., usually 5–14 ft. Pointed muzzle distinguishes dolphin from true porpoise. Common Atlantic and Mediterranean dolphin has bearlike jaws; bottle-nosed dolphin inhabits all but polar seas; killer whale or grampus (*Orcinus* or *Orca*) has a large, black and white mottled body, and it attacks seals, porpoises, fish, sea birds, and, in packs, large whales. River dolphins are found in Asia and South America. **2** Name for the coryphene, a small swift, iridescent, spiny-finned fish of warm seas.

Dolton, village (1965 pop. 22,557), NE Ill., S of Chicago, in truck-farm area.

Dom (dōm), peak, 14,923 ft. high, Valais canton, S Switzerland; highest in Mischabelhörner group.

Domagk, Gerhard (gär′härt dō′mäk), 1895–1964, German chemist, pathologist. Because of Nazi decree he declined 1939 Nobel Prize in Physiology and Medicine awarded for discovery of use of prontosil, forerunner of SULFA DRUGS.

Domenichino (dōmänēkē′nō) or **Domenico Zampieri** (dōmä′nēkō tsämpyä′rē), 1581–1641, Italian painter of the Carracci school. A baroque classicist.

Domenico Veneziano (dōmä′nēkō vānätsēä′nō), c.1400–1461, Florentine painter who introduced the technique of finishing tempera works with an oil glaze.

Domesday Book (dōmz′dä, dōōmz′dä), record of general survey of England made at order of William I, 1086. It ascertained economic resources of most of the country for purposes of more accurate taxation. Unsurpassed in medieval history for speed and thoroughness, it is invaluable historical source.

domicile, one's legal residence, the permanent home to which one has the intention of returning after a temporary absence. Question of domicile is especially important in tax laws and in legal matters concerning domestic relations.

Dominic, Saint (dŏ'mŭnĭk), 1170?–1221, Castilian churchman, named Dominic Guzmán, founder of the Dominicans. He and his bishop (of Osuna) were sent to preach to the Albigenses in S France, and did so with some success. In 1216 he was given a house at Toulouse for his growing band of preachers, and Pope Honorius III allowed him to form them into an order devoted to study and preaching. Tradition says that the first rosary was given to him by Our Lady in a vision. Feast: Aug. 4.

Dominica (dŏmĭnē'kŭ), island (290 sq. mi.; 1964 est. pop. 65,165), West Indies, in WINDWARD ISLANDS; cap. Roseau. In 1967 became one of WEST INDIES ASSOCIATED STATES. Discovered by Columbus 1493, it changed hands frequently. People, largely Negro, speak a French patois.

Dominican Republic (dŭmĭ'nĭkŭn), republic (19,129 sq. mi.; pop. 3,451,700), West Indies, occupying the E two thirds of Hispaniola; cap. SANTO DOMINGO. The island was first settled as the Spanish colony of SANTO DOMINGO, but later the W part became a French colony (present HAITI). After revolution had broken out in Haiti, Spain ceded all to France (1795), but triumphant Haitians conquered the W section (1801). The Spanish-speaking Dominicans opposed this union and there were numerous changes of domination—French, independent, Spanish, Haitian—before the Dominican Republic was estab. 1844. Even later one president planned reunion with Spain and another negotiated a treaty of annexation to the U.S., but both schemes fell through. The country had political and economic difficulties. Bankruptcy in 1905 brought a U.S. customs receivership (lasting to 1941), and U.S. marines occupied the country (1916–34). Rafael TRUJILLO MOLINA was dictator from 1930 until he was assassinated in 1961. Juan Bosch was elected president 1962, overthrown 1963 by the military. In 1965 civil war ensued between pro- and anti-Bosch factions. U.S. marines landed; a truce was arranged under Organization of American States sponsorship. Joaquin Balaguer was elected president 1966, defeating Bosch. Sugar, cacao, coffee, and tobacco are chief exports.

Dominicans (dŭmĭ'nĭkŭnz), Roman Catholic religious order, founded by St. Dominic 1216. More officially the order of Preachers (O.P.). Beginning as a band of preachers in S France, the order spread very rapidly and it is today one of the most important in the Church. Members (friars) are admitted not to specific houses but to the order as a whole. The heads of houses and of provinces are elected for set terms. Dominicans, who wear a white habit with a black mantle (worn while preaching), were formerly called Black Friars. Devoted to study, preaching and teaching, the order has supplied many eminent theologians, notably St. Thomas Aquinas. The Dominicans were prominent in the Inquisition. In the 19th cent. in France and England they forwarded social reform. The order came to the U.S. soon after 1800 (first U.S. province 1805). There is an order of contemplative Dominican nuns and a large third order (including many nuns devoted to teaching and good works).

dominion, territory controlled by a particular government. Commonly refers today to one of autonomous divisions of BRITISH COMMONWEALTH OF NATIONS.

Dominion Day, celebrated in Canada, July 1, anniversary of confederation of the provinces (1867).

dominoes, game played with pieces (most often 28) called dominoes—oblong pieces of wood, bone, or ivory, with one face blank, other marked with dots. Game introduced in Europe via Italy in 18th cent.

Domitian (dōmĭ'shŭn), A.D. 51–A.D. 96, Roman emperor (A.D. 81–A.D. 96); son of Vespasian and successor of his brother Titus. Obsessed with the idea of law and order, he became a despot. Plots against him ended when his wife had him murdered. Nerva succeeded.

Domrémy-la-Pucelle (dŏrāmē-lä-püsĕl'), village, Vosges dept., E France, in Lorraine. Birthplace of Joan of Arc, it preserves house where she was born and many other mementos of her life.

Don, river of Yorkshire, England, c.70 mi. long.

Don, river, 1,222 mi. long, S European RSFSR, rising SE of Tula, flowing SE, then SW, into Sea of Azov. Its eastward bend comes to within 40 mi. of the Volga at Stalingrad (Volga-Don canal here completed 1952). Navigable from Voronezh, accessible to seagoing vessels as far as Rostov, the Don is an important artery for grain, coal, lumber shipments. Chief tributary, the Donets, links it with industrial Donets Basin. The ancient Tanais, the Don has been a trading channel since Scythian times. In 16th cent. COSSACKS founded virtually independent republic of the Don Cossacks along its lower course. Stenka RAZIN was their most famous ataman. Gave nominal allegiance to tsar in 1614 but retained self-government until collapse of PUGACHEV rebellion (1775). Famed for their songs and choirs.

Don, river of Aberdeenshire, Scotland; c.82 mi. long. Empties into North Sea near Aberdeen.

Donaghadee (dŏn'ŭkhŭdē'), urban district (pop. 3,226), Co. Down, N. Ireland. Irish port nearest to Great Britain; connected by cable with Scotland.

Donaldsonville, city (pop. 6,082), SE La., on Mississippi R., SSE of Baton Rouge; founded 1806 as trading post. Was temporary state cap., 1830–31. Now trade center for agr. area.

Donatello (Donato di Niccolò di Betto Bardi) (dŏ-nŭtĕ'lō), c.1386–1466, Italian sculptor, major innovator in Renaissance art, b. Florence. His *St. Mark* (or *San Michele*, in Florence) marks a turning point toward a new humanistic expression. He invented technique known as *schiacciato* (shallow relief), in which he ingeniously achieved effects of spatial depth. With Brunelleschi he was one of the first Renaissance artists deeply interested in Roman antiquity. Worked for ten years in Padua. In his last years he created powerfully expressive works in his native Florence. His influence on both painting and sculpture is incalculable.

Donati, Giovanni Battista (jōvän'nē bät-tē'stä dōnä'tē), 1826–73, Italian astronomer. He pioneered in spectral analysis of comets and discovered six comets including Donati's comet (June 2, 1858).

Donatism (dŏ'nŭtĭzŭm), heretical movement of the 4th cent. in N Africa, led by Donatus of Casae Nigrae and the later Donatus the Great. In Roman persecutions they took the position that those who lapsed from the faith could not be readmitted fully to the Church. Bishops and priests who had given up sacred books to the government were, they held, traitors and had lost their sacramental powers. Opposed, they seceded from the Church and had a formidable church of their own, but they were condemned by the Synod of Arles (314). Extreme Donatists in Numidia terrorized the orthodox, but the teaching of St. Augustine destroyed the Donatist theology, and by 450 it had lost power in N Africa; eventually went to Islam.

Donatus, fl. 333, Roman grammarian; teacher of St. Jerome. His *Ars grammatica* [elements of grammar] was the standard elementary Latin grammar throughout the Middle Ages.

Donauwörth (dô'nouvûrt"), town (pop. 9,426), Swabia, W Bavaria, on the Danube. Noted for medieval architecture. In Thirty Years War city fell to Swedes 1632, to imperials 1634.

Donbas, USSR: see DONETS BASIN.

Doncaster (dŏng'kŭstŭr), county borough (pop. 86,-402), West Riding of Yorkshire, England, on the Don. Has coal mines, railroad shops, and steel mills. Nearby racecourse long estab.

Don Cossacks: see DON, river.

Donders, Franciscus Cornelius (fränsĭ'skŭs kôrnā'lĭus dôn'dûrs), 1818–89, Dutch ophthalmologist, pioneer in study of the eye and its disorders. Wrote treatise on accommodation and refraction (1864).

Donegal (dŏ'nĭgôl), maritime county (1,865 sq. mi.; pop. 113,815), Ulster prov., Ireland; co. town Lifford. Coastline irregular and indented; interior rugged and hilly (Mt. Errigal 2,466 ft.). Mainly agr. and pastoral (no large towns), but boggy soil makes farming hard. Deep-sea fishing and woolen industries important. Was anc. kingdom of Tyrconnell.

Donegan, Horace William Baden, 1900–, American Episcopal bishop. b. England; made bishop of N.Y. in 1950.

Donelson, Andrew Jackson (dŏ'nŭlsŭn), 1799–1871, American diplomat, nephew of and private secretary to Andrew Jackson. Successfully negotiated annexation of Texas.

Donelson, town (pop. 17,195), N central Tenn., ESE of Nashville on Stones R. Corn, cotton, and tobacco are grown.

Donelson, Fort, Confederate fortification on Cumberland R. at Dover, Tenn., commanding river approach to Nashville. Captured Feb. 16, 1862, by U. S. Grant, opening way for Union advance on Nashville. Now Fort Donelson Natl. Military Park.

Donets (dŭnyĕts'), river, 625 mi. long, S European RSFSR and S Ukraine, flowing generally SE into lower Don R. Navigable 140 mi. The **Donets Basin,** abbreviated as **Donbas,** SW of the river, is one of main coal-producing and industrial areas of Russia and Ukraine. Donetsk is largest of many industrial cities producing steel, heavy machinery, chemicals. Scene of heavy fighting in Second World War.

Donetsk (dŭnyĕtsk'), city (1965 est. pop. 809,000), SE Ukraine, in Donets Basin. Iron and steel mills, machinery works, and chemical plants. Founded 1870 as Yuzovka; called Stalino 1924–61.

Dongen, Kees van (kās' vän' dông'ɘn), 1877–, Dutch painter in Paris, associated with FAUVISM.

Doniphan, Alexander William (dŏ'nĭfŭn), 1808–87, American soldier. Led 3,600-mi. march into Mexico during Mexican War, taking Chihuahua and Saltillo.

Donizetti, Gaetano (gäätä'nō dōnĕdzĕt'tē), 1797–1848, Italian composer. His melodic operas range from serious to pure *opéra buffa*. Best known are: *Lucia di Lammermoor* (1835); *La Fille du regiment* (1840); *L'elisir d'amore* (1832); and *Don Pasquale* (1843).

Don Juan, legendary profligate, said to be one Don Juan Tenorio of Seville. In the traditional plot, he seduces the daughter of the Seville commandant and kills her father. He invites a statue of the father to a feast; it comes, seizes and drags him to hell. Famous versions are by Gabriel Téllez (1630), Molière, Mozart, Byron, Espronceda, and Shaw.

donkey: see ASS.

Donne, John (dŭn), 1572–1631, English poet and divine; one of the greatest METAPHYSICAL POETS. His worldly, witty lyrics and verse satires, full of "conceits"—ingenious figures of speech—circulated in manuscript, according to custom. His court career, begun when he was made secretary to Thomas Egerton in 1598, was ruined by discovery of his secret marriage to Lady Egerton's niece, Anne More. Great depth of thought and philosophic doubts appear in his *Anniversaries* (*An Anatomie of the World,* 1611; *Of the Progresse of the Soule,* 1612), poems on the death of Elizabeth Drury; they are evident, too, in the prose *Pseudo-Martyr* (1610) and *Biathanatos* (written c.1618; published 1644), a qualified apology for suicide. Having abandoned Roman Catholicism in the 1590s, Donne yielded to the urging of James I and took orders in the Anglican church in 1615. As dean of St. Paul's after 1621, he became a famous preacher in an age of great preaching. His *Devotions upon Emergent Occasions,* his *Divine Poems,* and his sermons often treat of death, damnation, and decay. His poetry, printed only in 1633, had great influence on his contemporaries and, after a long period of neglect, appealed

strongly to 20th-cent. poets (e.g., T. S. Eliot and W. S. Auden).

Donnelly, Ignatius, 1831–1901, American author and political reformer. His *Atlantis: the Antediluvian World* (1882; rev. ed., 1949) argued that ATLANTIS was seat of world's original civilization. He championed underdog; helped found Populist party.

Donner Party (dŏ'nŭr), group of emigrants to Calif. who in winter of 1846–47 met with tragedy. Prominent in group were two families named Donner. In Oct. party was trapped by snow in passes at what is now Donner L. in the Sierra Nevada; survivors were driven to cannibalism before rescue. Only about half of party reached Calif. **Donner Lake** is today a popular mountain resort, near Truckee. Nearby **Donner Pass** has U.S. weather observatory.

Donnybrook, suburb of Dublin, Ireland; site of famous fair, suppressed 1855 because of disorderliness.

Donora, borough (pop. 11,131), SW Pa., on Monongahela R., SSE of Pittsburgh. Has zinc, iron, and steel works.

Don Quixote (de la Mancha) (dōn' kēhō'tä dä lä män'chä, Eng. dŏn kwĭk'sŭt), romance satirizing chivalry, masterpiece of Miguel de CERVANTES SAAVEDRA and one of the great works of world literature (first part pub. 1605, and, after a spurious continuation by Alonso Fernández de Avellaneda, second part pub. 1615). Don Quixote, a country gentleman mounted upon the nag Rosinante, tries to perform deeds he has read about in chivalric romances, all for the sake of his lady Dulcinea, a country girl. He is aided by his peasant squire, Sancho Panza. The story is full of absurd situations, but expresses the tragic contrast between harsh reality and the aspirations of a noble if deluded idealist.

Dooley, Thomas Anthony, 1927–61, American physician. In 1954 supervised care for refugees from North Vietnam.

Doolittle, Hilda, pseud. **H. D.,** 1886–1961, American poet, abroad after 1911, one of the IMAGISTS, wife of Richard Aldington.

Doomsday Book: see DOMESDAY BOOK.

Doon (dōōn), river of Ayrshire, Scotland. Robert Burns sang of its beauties.

Door Peninsula, NE Wis., between Green Bay and L. Michigan. Crossed by waterway at Sturgeon Bay. Visited 17th cent. by French. Has cherry growing.

Doppler, Christian Johann (krĭs'tyän yō'hän dô'plŭr), 1803–53, Austrian physicist and mathematician. **Doppler's principle:** as distance between source of sound or light and observer becomes less or greater, frequency of waves received increases or decreases respectively. Effect called **Doppler effect.** Examples: rise in pitch of sound with decreased distance between source and observer; in light, this causes shift of color toward violet end of spectrum.

Dorcas or **Tabitha,** Christian woman raised from dead by St. Peter. She sewed for the poor. Acts 9.36–43.

Dorchester, Guy Carleton, 1st Baron: see CARLETON, GUY.

Dorchester, municipal borough (pop. 12,266), county town of Dorsetshire, England. on Frome R. Thomas Hardy lived in Dorchester, which is Casterbridge of his novels. Has Roman remains.

Dorchester, Mass.: see BOSTON.

Dordogne (dôrdô'nyŭ), department (3,561 sq. mi.; pop. 375,455), SW France, in Périgord; cap. Périgeux. It is crossed by the **Dordogne** river, 305 mi. long, rising in Auvergne mts. and joining the Garonne N of Bordeaux to form the Gironde.

Dordrecht (dôr'drĕkht) or **Dort** (dôrt), municipality (pop. 88,031) and town, South Holland prov., SW Netherlands, on Lower Merwede R. Rail junction, river port; mfg. of machinery and chemicals. Chartered 1220, it was the scene of William the Silent's proclamation as stadholder (1572) and of the Synod of Dort 1618–19; see REMONSTRANTS). Has 14th-cent. Gothic church (Groote Kerk).

Doré, Gustave (güstäv' dôrā'), 1832–83. French illustrator, engraver, painter, and sculptor. He particularly excelled in weird, fantastic scenes.

Dore, Mont, France: see MONT-DORE.

Doremus, Robert Ogden, 1824–1906. American chemist, inventor, and physician. Helped found first New York Medical Col. (now defunct). Expert on toxicology.

Doria, Andrea (ändrä'ä dō'rēä), c.1468–1560. Genoese admiral and statesman. Fought in French service in ITALIAN WARS until 1528, when he suddenly went over to Emperor Charles V. Helped Charles capture Tunis (1535) but failed at Algiers (1541). Virtual dictator of Genoa, yet preserved republican institutions.

Dorians, members of one of the traditional branches of the Greek peoples, supposedly the last comers (probably 1100–950 B.C.), Sparta and Crete were Dorian centers. The Dorian dialect was considered harsh by Athenians but gave rise to the choral lyric. Doric style is one of great simplicity.

Dormont, residential borough (pop. 13,098). SW Pa., SSW of Pittsburgh; settled c.1790.

dormouse, small, squirrellike nocturnal rodent of the Old World. Lives in bushes and trees, feeding on nuts and acorns and hibernating in winter. The family includes a number of genera, e.g., *Glis, Muscardinus, Dryomys. Eliomys,* and *Glirulus.*

Dorpat, Estonia: see TARTU.

Dorr, Thomas Wilson, 1805–54, leader of Dorr's Rebellion (1842) in R.I. Urging universal manhood suffrage, Dorr's party estab. its own government, resorted to arms. New state constitution of 1843, liberalizing voting requirements, was result.

Dorset, Charles Sackville, 6th earl of: see SACKVILLE, CHARLES.

Dorset, Thomas Sackville, 1st earl of: see SACKVILLE, THOMAS.

Dorset, town (pop. 1,150), SW Vt., N of Manchester; settled 1768. Artists' and writers' resort. Conventions that led to independent Vt. held here 1775 and 1776.

Dorsetshire or **Dorset,** maritime county (973 sq. mi.; pop. 309,176), S England; co. town Dorchester. Rolling country crossed by chalk ranges, it has fine harbor at Poole and agr. in fertile valleys. Sheep raising and dairy farming chief occupations. Marble quarried. Pre-Roman remains include large earthwork, Maiden Castle. Thomas Hardy wrote of region in "Wessex" novels.

Dort, Netherlands: see DORDRECHT.

Dortmund (dôrt'mŏont), city (pop. 623,305), North Rhine-Westphalia, West Germany. A major industrial center of the RUHR, on Dortmund-Ems Canal.

Dorval, city (pop. 18,592), S. Que., Canada. on S shore of Montreal Isl. and on St. Lawrence R. Site of Montreal internatl. airport.

Dorylaeum (dôrilē'úm), city of N Phrygia, now in NW Turkey. An important trade center in Roman times, it later declined. Here (1097) Crusaders defeated the Seljuk Turks.

Dos Passos, John (Roderigo), 1896–. American novelist. Noted for his kaleidoscopic presentation of American life in biographies plus headlines plus narration (*Manhattan Transfer,* 1925; the trilogy *U.S.A.* —*The 42nd Parallel,* 1930; *Nineteen Nineteen,* 1932; *The Big Money,* 1936). He was antiwar and represented disillusionment with the U.S. in *Three Soldiers* (1921). Later he became more radical as shown in the series of novels *U.S.A.* Still later he retreated from this position to a more sober view in the trilogy *District of Columbia. The Shackles of Power* (1966) is a study of Jefferson.

Dosso Dossi (dôs'sō dôs'sē), 1479?–1542, Italian painter of the Ferrarese school. He was influenced by Giorgione, Titian, and Raphael.

Dost Mohammed (dōst'), 1793–1863, emir of Afghanistan. Fought against the British in first Afghan War (1839–42). Later tried to play Russian interests against the British.

Dostoyevsky, Feodor Mikhailovich (fyô'dúr mĕkhī'lùvĭch dŭstùyĕf'skē), 1821–81, Russian novelist, one of the giants of modern literature. He won his first success with *Poor Folk* (1846). Arrested 1849 for membership in a Fourierist circle, he was sentenced to death; while he was waiting for death, his sentence was commuted to hard labor in Siberia. The shock of the experience and the hardship of Siberian life (described in *The House of the Dead,* 1862) aggravated his epilepsy and caused him to turn to religion. He returned to St. Petersburg 1859. His chronic financial difficulties were increased by his passion for gambling. His novels are characterized by deep psychological insight; compassion for all men, even the vilest of whom he thought capable of redemption; and morbid preoccupation with guilt and crime. His greatest novels are *Crime and Punishment* (1866), *The Idiot* (1868). *The Possessed* (1872), *The Brothers Karamazov* (1879–80). *Notes from the Underground* (1864) and other short novels are equally powerful. All his major works are translated by Constance Garnett and others.

Dothaim (dōtha'īm) or **Dothan** (dō'thăn), anc. city, central Palestine; on site of modern Tell Dotham, Jordan. Nearby Joseph was sold into slavery, Syrians were blinded at Elisha's prayer. Gen. 37.17; 2 Kings 6.13; Judith 4.6; 7.3,18; 8.3.

Dothan (dō'thún), city (pop. 31,440), SE Ala., near Chattahoochee R. and Fla. line, in farm and timber area. U.S. Fort Rucker is NW.

Dou, Dow, or **Douw, Gerard** or **Gerrit** (all: dou), 1613–75, Dutch genre and portrait painter of Leiden, a pupil of Rembrandt.

Douai (dōōä'), town (pop. 47,639), Nord dept., N France, in Flanders. Coal mining; machinery. Here Philip II of Spain estab. college where Douay Bible was prepared (1609). Taken by Louis XIV 1667; capitulated to Marlborough (1710), retaken (1712), and restored to France by Peace of Utrecht. Rebuilt in 18th cent.; most old buildings still stand.

Douaumont (dōō-ōmō'), fort on VERDUN battlefield, NE France. Now a national memorial. Its cemetery has graves of 300,000 French soldiers killed in battle.

double bass: see VIOLIN.

Doubleday, Abner, 1819–93, alleged originator of BASEBALL, a Union general in Civil War. Said to have created game 1839 at Cooperstown, N.Y.

Double Tenth: see WUCHANG, China.

Doubs (dōō), department (2,031 sq. mi.; pop. 384,-881), E France, in Franche-Comté; cap. Besançon. The **Doubs** R., c.260 mi. long, rises in the French Jura, flows NE, makes loop into Switzerland, then continues SW to join Saône near Chalon.

Doughty, Charles Montagu (dō'tē, dou'tē), 1843–1926, English traveler, author of *Travels in Arabia Deserta* (1888).

Doughty, Thomas (dou'tē), 1793–1856, American painter of the Hudson River school.

Douglas, Scottish noble family, divided into two branches. **William de Douglas, lord of Douglas,** d. 1298, was first to take title. Joined William Wallace revolt 1297, was captured, and died in Tower of London. His son, **Sir James de Douglas, lord of Douglas,** 1286?–1330, was called Black Douglas or Douglas the Good. Deprived of his estates by Edward I, became terror of border. Joined Robert I, fought at Bannockburn, and was a regent of Scotland. After death of Robert I, started for Palestine to bury king's heart but was killed in Spain. His nephew, **William Douglas, 1st earl of Douglas and Mar,** 1327?–1384, added lands to family holdings. His son, **James Douglas, 2d earl of Douglas and Mar,** 1358?–1388, married daughter of Robert II. Killed at battle of Otterburn. His uncle, **Archibald Douglas, 3d earl of Douglas,** 1328?–1400?, was illegitimate son of Sir James de Douglas. Acquired large estates. At his death, family most powerful in Scotland. His son, **Archibald Douglas, 4th earl of Douglas,** 1369?–1424, married daughter of Robert III 1390. Fought against Henry IV and Henry V. Tried and acquitted for murder of heir to Scottish throne. Joined the French and was killed at Verneuil. His son, **Archibald Douglas,** 5th **earl of Douglas,** 1391?–1439, was twice imprisoned by James I who feared his power. After James's death (1437) he was most powerful man in Scotland. His son, **William Douglas,** 6th **earl of Douglas,** 1423?–1440, was beheaded (together with his brother) by advisers of James II and family power was temporarily broken. Succeeded by his great-uncle, **James Douglas,** 7th **earl of Douglas,** 1371?–1443. His son, **William Douglas,** 8th **earl of Douglas,** 1425?–1452, reunited family estates by marrying his cousin. His brother, **James Douglas,** 9th **earl of Douglas,** 1426–88, rebelled twice (1452, 1455) against James II, was defeated, and fled to England. Captured 1483, spent rest of his life in prison. With him, power of older or "Black" Douglas branch ended. Younger or "Red" Douglas branch descended from illegitimate son of William Douglas, 1st earl of Douglas and Mar, and Margaret Stuart, countess of Angus. **Archibald Douglas,** 5th **earl of Angus,** 1449?–1514, was chancellor of Scotland 1493–98. In revolt against James III 1487–88, earned nickname of Bell-the-Cat by capture of king's favorite. Father of Gawin Douglas. His grandson, **Archibald Douglas,** 6th **earl of Angus,** 1489?–1557, married Margaret Tudor, sister of Henry VIII and widow of James IV, and attempted to gain control of her son, James V. She divorced him 1528 and he fled to England. Returned 1542 and was restored to power. His grandnephew, **Archibald Douglas,** 8th **earl of Angus,** 1555–88, supported his uncle, the earl of Morton, and opposed James Stuart, earl of Arran.

Douglas, Clifford Hugh, 1879–1952, English social economist, author of theory of Social Credit.

Douglas, David, 1798–1834, Scottish botanist, one of the first travelers in Oregon country and Calif. The Douglas fir (or spruce) is named for him.

Douglas, Gawin (gä′win) or **Gavin** (găv′ĭn), 1474?–1522, Scottish poet and churchman. Member of the powerful Douglas family, he was involved in political disputes after 1515. A major poet of the Chaucerian tradition, his works include *The Palace of Honour, King Hart,* and a translation of the *Aeneid* (one of first classical translations into English).

Douglas, James, 2d duke of Queensberry: see Queensberry, James Douglas, 2d duke of.

Douglas, James, 2d earl of Douglas and Mar: see Douglas, family.

Douglas, James, earls of Douglas: see Douglas, family.

Douglas, James (d. 1581): see Morton, James Douglas, 4th earl of.

Douglas, Sir James, 1803–77, Canadian fur trader and colonial governor, b. Scotland. In 1846 he succeeded to command of Hudson's Bay Co. territory W of the Rockies. Appointed governor of Vancouver Isl. (1851) and also became governor of new colony of British Columbia in 1858. Retired 1864.

Douglas, Sir James de Douglas, lord of: see Douglas, family.

Douglas, John Sholto: see Queensberry, John Sholto Douglas, 8th marquess of.

Douglas, (George) Norman, 1868–1952, English writer, best known for novel *South Wind* (1917) and sketches in *Old Calabria* (1915).

Douglas, Paul H(oward), 1892–, American economist and U.S. Senator (1948–66) from Ill., b. Salem, Mass.; an authority on wages and social security.

Douglas, Stephen A(rnold), 1813–61, American statesman. U.S. Representative from Ill. (1843–47); U.S. Senator (1847–61). Responsible for squatter sovereignty aspects of Compromise of 1850 and Kansas-Nebraska Bill; championed popular sovereignty as way of settling North-South controversy peacefully. Lincoln-Douglas debates featured his 1858 campaign for reelection; at Freeport, on Aug. 27, 1858, he asserted that people of a territory could exclude slavery. Freeport doctrine made him anathema to Southern Democrats. Democratic national convention of 1860 nominated him for President, but Southern delegates

broke away. In election he won only 12 electoral votes, but stood second in popular votes. Long in the shadow of the Lincoln legend, Douglas, it is now held, was one of few men in his era with truly broad national vision.

Douglas, William: see Douglas, family.

Douglas, William O(rville), 1898–, Associate Justice of U.S. Supreme Court (1939–). A liberal, he was a member of the Security and Exchange Commission (1934–39) and its chairman (1937–39).

Douglas, city (1965 pop. 12,370), SE Ariz., at Mexican line. Grew about copper smelter (1900). Ranching center in an area of gypsum and tungsten mines and limestone quarries.

Douglas and Mar, earls of: see Douglas, family.

Douglas fir or **Douglas spruce,** huge coniferous evergreen (*Pseudotsuga taxifolia*) of W North America. Named for David Douglas, it is not a true fir or spruce. Wood valued for construction.

Douglas-Home, Sir Alexander Frederick, 1903–, British Conservative party leader. After entering Parliament 1931 he held various government and cabinet posts, including that of foreign secretary (1960–63). Was prime minister 1963–64.

Douglas Point, Ont., Canada: see Kincardine.

Douglass, Frederick, c.1817–1895, American abolitionist, son of slave mother. Escaping in 1838, he took surname from Scott's *The Lady of the Lake*. At Rochester, N.Y., estab. and edited *North Star* for 17 years in abolitionist cause.

Douglas spruce: see Douglas fir.

Douhet, Giulio (jōo′lyō dōōă′), 1869–1930, Italian military theorist, a general. Held that command of air could win a war despite land and sea power.

Doukhobors: see Dukhobors.

Doumer, Paul (pôl′ dōōmâr′), 1857–1932, president of France (1931–32). Assassinated.

Doumergue, ·Gaston (gästō′ dōōmĕrg′), 1863–1937, president of France (1924–31). Headed a rightist coalition cabinet in Feb.–Nov. 1934.

Doura: see Dura.

Dounreay, village, Caithness, Scotland. Britain's first large-scale nuclear breeder reactor opened here 1959.

Douro (dō′rōō) or **Duero** (dōōā′rō), river, c.475 mi. long, Spain and Portugal; Douro is Port., Duero Span. name. Rises in N central Spain, flows generally W into Atlantic beyond Oporto. Hydroelectric plants.

Douw, Gerard: see Dou.

Dove, Arthur Garfield, 1880–1946, American painter, a precursor of the abstract expressionists.

Dove, Heinrich Wilhelm (dō′vū), 1803–79, German physicist, whose studies included earth's surface heat, climatology, induced electricity, and polarized light.

Dove (dŭv), river rising in Derbyshire, England, and forming much of Derbyshire-Staffordshire border. Its water-course was a haunt of Izaak Walton. Glen of Dovedale celebrated by artists and poets.

dove, name for certain smaller birds of pigeon family; name often used synonymously with pigeon. European rock dove is probably ancestor of domesticated pigeons. Mourning dove is native to North America.

Dover, municipal borough (pop. 35,248), on a bay beneath chalk cliffs, Kent, England. Chief of Cinque Ports; an important port for travel to the Continent. Was important naval base in First World War and constant target of German long-range guns in Second World War. Subterranean caves and tunnels in the cliffs, once used by smugglers, were shelters 1940–44. Noteworthy are Shakespeare Cliff and Dover Castle.

Dover. 1 City (pop. 7,250), state cap., central Del., on St. Jones R., S of Wilmington; settled 1683. Shipping and canning center in rich farm and fruit area. Varied industries. Statehouse (partly built 1722) has been capitol since 1777. Seat of Delaware State Col. Dover Air Force Base is SE. **2** City (pop. 19,131), SE N.H., at falls of Cocheco R. near junction with Piscataqua R.; settled 1623. Almost destroyed by Indian raids. Lord Saye and Sele had large holdings here, 1633–41.

Has 17th-cent. garrison house. **3** Industrial town (pop. 13,034), N central N.J., NW of Morristown; settled 1722. Grew as iron center on old Morris Canal. **4** City (pop. 11,300), E Ohio, on Tuscarawas R., SSW of Canton, in coal and fire-clay area; laid out 1807 and settled by Germans. Atwood and Dover dams are near.

Dover, Strait of, separates England from France and connects English Channel with North Sea. Width 21 mi. between Dover and Cape Gris-Nez near Calais. In 1588, Spanish Armada received its first serious check here. Called Pas de Calais by French.

Doves Press, founded 1900, major contributor to revival of the art of fine bookmaking. Founded by T. J. Cobden-Sanderson and Emery Walker, its masterpiece was the Doves Bible (1903).

Dovrefjell (dô'vrŭfyĕl), rough plateau of central Norway, culminating in Snohetta (Nor. Snøhetta; 7,498 ft. high) and dividing country in two.

Dovzhenko, Aleksandr (ŭlyĭksän'dŭr dŏvzhĕn'kō), 1894–1956, Soviet film director. A great innovator in film techniques, he was acclaimed for *Arsenal* (1929) and *Earth* (1930). After *Earth* was denounced as "counter-revolutionary," Dovzhenko produced films more agreeable to the regime.

Dow, Gerard: see Dou.

Dow, Lorenzo, 1777–1834, American evangelist, who introduced camp meetings into Ireland and England.

Dowie, John Alexander (dou'ē), 1847–1907, founder of Christian Catholic Church in Zion, Ill. Scotland. In Australia became interested in faith healing. Came to U.S. (1888); founded church in Chicago (1896) and community in Zion, Ill. (1901). Deposed as leader in 1905.

Down, maritime county (952 sq. mi.; pop. 267,031, excluding Belfast, which is partly within county), Ulster prov., N. Ireland; co. town Downpatrick. Coastline indented by Strangford Lough and Dundrum Bay; beautiful Mourne Mts. rise in south. Area extensively cultivated (oats, potatoes, wheat, and flax). There are many linen mfg. towns.

Downers Grove, village (1964 pop. 22,612), NE Ill., WSW of Chicago; settled 1832.

Downey, June Etta, 1875–1932, American psychologist. As professor at Univ. of Wyoming, she contributed much to the field of personality testing.

Downing, Andrew Jackson, 1815–52, American horticulturist, rural architect, and landscape gardener, author of many books on gardening and landscaping. He planned the grounds of the Capitol, the White House, and the Smithsonian Institution in Washington, D.C.

Downing College: see CAMBRIDGE UNIVERSITY.

Downing Street, London. Located here are important British government offices, including foreign office. No. 10 and No. 11 are office and residence of prime minister (also called first lord of the Treasury). Figurative use of term means government in power.

Downpatrick (dounpă'trĭk), urban district (pop. 4,219), co. seat of Co. Down, N. Ireland. Has long been a religious center and place of pilgrimage as tomb of Ireland's saints—Patrick, Colomba, and Bridget of Kildare. Holy wells of Struell nearby.

Downs, the, low chalk hills, SE England. N. Downs range in Surrey and Kent separated by the WEALD from S. Downs in Sussex. Excellent sheep pasturage.

dowry, property a woman brings to her husband at marriage. Institution apparently originated in marriage gift made by family of the bride to the groom, estab. as custom in many peoples from earliest days. Known to Greece, Rome, India, medieval Europe, and modern civil-law countries. Generally on divorce the husband must return dowry.

Dowson, Ernest (Christopher) (dou'-), 1867–1900, English lyric poet, one of the best-known poets of the decadents. Perhaps most familiar of his delicate, highly musical poems is that with the refrain "I have been faithful to thee, Cynara! in my fashion." A Roman Catholic, he also wrote religious poetry. His brief, wretched life was ended by tuberculosis.

doxology, sacred hymn of praise. Best-known doxologies of Christian church are "Gloria in Excelsis," "Gloria Patri," and Thomas Ken's "Praise God from Whom All Blessings Flow," sung to the tune *Old Hundred* from the Genevan Psalter.

Doyle, Sir A(rthur) Conan, 1859–1930, English author, creator of Sherlock Holmes, most celebrated of all fictional detectives. Among detective stories are *A Study in Scarlet* (1887), *The Adventures of Sherlock Holmes* (1892), and *The Hound of the Baskervilles* (1902). Also wrote historical romances such as *The White Company* (1891). Doyle in later life was a spiritualist.

Doylestown, borough (pop. 5,917), SE Pa., N of Philadelphia; settled 1745. Trade center of dairy and farm area.

D'Oyly Carte, Richard (doi'lē kärt), 1844–1901, English impresario of Gilbert and Sullivan operas. Built Savoy Theatre in 1881.

Drachenfels (drä'khŭnfĕls), cliff, 1053 ft. high, on the Rhine, S of Bonn, W Germany. Legendary scene of Siegfried's triumph over the dragon. Ruins of Drachenburg castle, on top of cliff, date from 12th cent. Popular excursion point.

Draco or **Dracon,** Athenian political figure and law codifier. Said to have assigned death penalty for many offences; hence Draconian means harsh.

Dracula: see STOKER, BRAM.

Dracut (drä'kŭt), textile town (pop. 13,674), NE Mass., on Merrimack R., N of Lowell; settled 1664.

draft. Similar to a check and sometimes called bill of exchange, it was originally devised to give credit to customer who intended to pay in future. Came to be used to pay foreign debts because it avoided risk of transmitting money. Normally used in commercial transactions.

draft riots, in Civil War. Nation-wide opposition to Union conscription act of March 3, 1863, broke into bloody riots in New York city (July 13–16, 1863). Huge mob overpowered police and militia, seized Second Ave. armory, set fires, and assaulted abolitionists and Negroes. Damage over $1,500,000, with est. 1,000 casualties.

Draga, queen of Serbia: see ALEXANDER, king of Serbia.

Drago, Luis María (lōōĕs' märē'ä drä'gō), 1859–1921, Argentine statesman, jurist, and writer on international law. His protest against coercion of Venezuela by Great Britain, Germany, and Italy (1902) became known as the **Drago Doctrine** (a corollary to Monroe Doctrine). It set forth principle that no public debt should be collected from sovereign American state by armed force or through occupation of American territory by foreign power. Modified form was approved at Hague Conference (1907).

dragon, mythical beast, usually represented as huge fire-breathing reptile. Its description varies, but it is usually a composite of many animals. Legends telling of hero's great victory over dragon are widespread. Often associated with evil, dragon can be benevolent. Sometimes used as national symbol.

dragonfly, large insect of order Odonata, which includes also the damsel fly. Found in most parts of world, they are numerous in South America and Japan. Eggs are laid in or near water, and nymphs (the young) are aquatic. Metamorphosis is incomplete. Adults have four membranous wings; some surpass swallow in flying speed and agility. They eat larvae and adult insects. See *ill.,* p. 512.

dragon's blood, red resin obtained from certain plants, including *Dracaena draco.* Used in photoengraving.

drainage, in mining, accomplished by causing surface or subterranean water to flow by gravity into reservoirs or sumps dug at lowest level, whence it is usually pumped out.

drainage basin: see CATCHMENT AREA.

Drake, Edwin Laurentine, 1819–80, American oilwell driller. He sank the first U.S. well to strike oil, Aug. 27, 1859.

Drake, Sir Francis, 1540?–1596, English navigator, admiral, first Englishman to circumnavigate world (1577–80). From 1572 commanded marauding expeditions against Spain, taking rich booty from treasure ships and Spanish possessions in the Americas for treasury of Queen Elizabeth, who finally knighted him and openly recognized his exploits. Commanded sea forces against rebellious Ireland; destroyed a Spanish fleet at Cádiz (1587) and participated in destruction of the Armada (1588). Died of dysentery during last and unsuccessful expedition against Spanish West Indies.

Drake, Joseph Rodman, 1795–1820, American poet. Wrote "The Culprit Fay" and, with Fitz-Greene HALLECK, satirical verse.

Drakensberg (drä'kùnzbûrg), mountain range, South Africa. Extends 700 mi. from Cape Province to the Transvaal. Rises along the Natal-Lesotho border to over 11,000 ft.

Drakes Bay, inlet of the Pacific, W Calif., NW of San Francisco. Point Reyes, with national seashore, forms its outer arm. Visited by Drake, 1579.

Drake University, at Des Moines, Iowa; coed.; chartered, opened 1881 by Disciples of Christ; named for F. M. Drake.

Drammen (drä'mùn), city (pop. 30,925), SE Norway, on Drammen R. and at head of Drammen Fjord. Wood products. **Drammen river,** c.25 mi. long, SE Norway, empties into Drammen Fjord, a branch of Oslo Fjord. Lumber mills; hydroelectric plants.

Draper, Charles Stark, 1901–, American engineer. Noted for work in gyroscopic, computing, and inertial guidance systems used in long-range missiles.

Draper, John William, 1811–82, American scientist, philosopher, and historian, b. England. He helped organize medical school of New York Univ., taught chemistry and physiology there, and became its president 1850. Conducted important research on radiant energy. His works include *Human Physiology* (1856), containing the first published microphotographs; *History of the Intellectual Development of Europe* (1863). His son **Henry Draper,** 1837–82, taught physiology at New York Univ. (1870–82) and was a pioneer in astronomical photography and spectroscopy.

Draper, Ruth, 1884–1956, American monologist. Her character sketches ranged from tragedy to farce with only a slight change of costume and props.

draughts: see CHECKERS.

Drava or **Drave** (both: drä'vù), Ger. *Drau,* river, c.450 mi. long, central Europe; tributary of the Danube. Rises in Italian Alps; flows E through Carinthia (Austria), then SE, forming part of Hungarian-Yugoslav border, past Villach, Maribor, and Osijek.

Dravidian (drùvī'dèun), name of largest group of inhabitants of India before coming of Aryans. Also name of group in S India today presumably descended from prehistoric Dravidians.

Dravidian languages, family of languages of S India; see LANGUAGE (table). Attempts have been made to connect them with other groups.

drawbridge, movable bridge, usually over stream or river in situation requiring maintenance of waterborne traffic, but prohibiting erection of fixed bridge high enough to allow passage under it. In fortresses surrounded by ditch or moat, it was part of defense system. Common types include the lifting, bascule, and swing bridges.

Drayton, Michael, 1563–1631, English poet. Wrote sonnets, odes, longer poems (e.g., panoramic, 15,000-line *Poly-Olbion*), and plays now lost.

dream, mental activity of disputed duration, associated with sleep and commonly made up of visual images. Like hallucinations, dreams are not usually evoked by sense impressions; somatic disturbances (e.g., toothache, indigestion) and external stimuli may sometimes affect choice of forms and images in dream, but do not affect its underlying psychological content. Various types of dream interpretation vigorous among ancient, primitive, and su-perstitious peoples. Freud, an early exponent of scientific dream study, distinguished manifest content (the experienced dream-image) from latent content (meaning). Dream-images are symbols—universal, cultural, or personal (translatable through free association). Symbolism protects dreamer from recognition of attempted fulfillment of impulses that consciousness forbids. Freud believed dreams insure sleep by draining force of emotional disturbances that would waken sleeper. Jung considered them testing ground for possible future steps. Adler emphasized compensatory function.

Drebbel, Cornelis Jacobszoon (kôrnä'lĭs yä'kôp-sōn drè'bùl), 1572–1634, Dutch inventor, physicist, and mechanician who settled in England. His many inventions include "perpetual motion" machine and a diving boat (first navigable submarine).

dredging, process of underwater excavation to clear or deepen channels and entrances of harbors, docks, rivers, and canals. Modern dredging equipment divisible into four main classes. The **grab dredge,** for small operations, consists of grab buckets operated by cranes. Bucket is similar to clamshell bucket used ashore, as is the **dipper dredge** (known as boom and dipper assembly) used extensively in canal construction. **Ladder-bucket dredge,** operated usually from self-propelling vessel built with well in center open to water, consists of endless succession of buckets operating through the well and discharging, as they rise, into a chute projecting to hopper barge, or to hopper in dredge itself. **Suction dredge** used principally to remove sand and mud through flexible pipe extended to bottom, by means of centrifugal pump.

Dred Scott Case, argued before U.S. Supreme Court in 1856–57. Brought as a test case; concerned status of Dred Scott, a Negro who had lived with his master for several years in free territory. Chief Justice R. B. Taney delivered court's opinion that a Negro "whose ancestors . . . were sold as slaves" was not entitled to rights of a Federal citizen and had no standing in court, and that Missouri Compromise was unconstitutional. John McLean and B. R. Curtis dissented. Verdict further inflamed North-South controversy.

Dreiser, Theodore (drī'sùr), 1871–1945, American author. His first novel (*Sister Carrie,* 1900) was suppressed by the publisher, but his later novels (including *Jennie Gerhardt,* 1911; *The Titan,* 1914; *An American Tragedy,* 2 vols., 1925) won acclaim for their naturalism and power despite their ponderous style. He also wrote excellent short stories, autobiographical works, and, during his later interest in socialism, commentaries on Russia and America.

Drenthe (drĕn'tù), province (1,029 sq. mi.; pop. 336,-207), NE Netherlands, bordering on Germany; cap. Assen. Stock raising, dairy farming.

Dresden (drĕz'dùn), city (est. pop. 491,714), East Germany, cap. of former state of Saxony, on Elbe R. Mfg. center (machine tools, optical instruments, glass, chemicals) and large inland port. Originally a Slavic settlement; settled by Germans 13th cent.; residence of electors (later kings) of Saxony 1485–1918. Napoleon defeated allies near Dresden in 1813. For Treaty of Dresden (1745), see AUSTRIAN SUCCESSION, WAR OF THE. In late 17th and 18th cent. it became a center of the arts, outstanding for baroque and rococo architecture. Famous landmarks include Zwinger palace and museum; Hofkirche [court chapel]; cathedral. Many art treasures, including Raphael's *Sistine Madonna,* were removed to Russia. "Dresden china," despite name, was made in Meissen.

Drew, Daniel, 1797–1879, American capitalist. Bold and scheming, he helped manipulate Erie RR stock (1866–68) to defeat attempt of Cornelius Vanderbilt to gain control. Drew was bankrupt by 1876.

Drew, Louisa Lane, 1820–97, American actress, b. London. From girlhood appeared in support of era's leading actors until she married (1850) John Drew (1827–62). They co-starred at his Arch St. Theatre, Philadelphia. On his death she assumed its management. Her children were Sidney, Georgiana (see BAR-RYMORE), and **John Drew**, 1853–1927, who joined the Daly company in 1875 and acted in Shakespearean productions with Ada Rehan. Under Charles Frohman did modern comedies with Maude Adams.

Drewrys Bluff (drōō'rĕz), height on S bank of James R., E central Va., S of Richmond, scene of two battles in Civil War. Union gunboats repulsed here (May 15, 1862). B. F. Butler defeated by inferior Confederate force under Beauregard (May 16, 1864). Also called Drewry Bluff, Drury's Bluff.

Drew University, at Madison, N.J.; coed.; chartered and opened 1867 as Drew Theological Seminary; named for Daniel Drew. Became Drew Univ. with addition in 1928 of Brothers Col.

Drexel Institute of Technology, at Philadelphia, Pa.; coed.; founded 1891, opened 1892; called Drexel Inst. of Art, Science, and Industry 1894–1936.

Dreyer, Johan Ludwig Emil (drī'ŭr), 1852–1926, Danish astronomer in Great Britain, compiler of standard catalogue of nebulae and clusters (1888; supplements, 1895, 1908).

Dreyfus Affair (drā'fŭs, drī'–), began 1894 with the discovery of a schedule (the famous *bordereau*) addressed to Maj. Schwartzkoppen, German military attaché in Paris, which listed secret French documents that the writer promised to furnish. A court martial convicted Capt. Alfred Dreyfus (1859–1935) of treason on the slim evidence that the handwriting on the *bordereau* was similar to his. Dreyfus never ceased to protest his innocence, but his being both a Jew and an Alsatian weighed heavily with his bigoted judges. He was sentenced to degradation and to life imprisonment on Devils Isl. (1894). The case flared up again in 1896, when Col. Georges PICQUART discovered evidence pointing to Maj. Ferdinand Walsin ESTERHAZY as the real author of the *bordereau*. Picquart was silenced by the authorities, but in 1897 Dreyfus's brother Mathieu independently made the same discovery and energetically pressed for a new trial. The case now became a major political issue, dividing all France into two violent partisan groups for 10 years. Royalists, militarists, and (with a few notable exceptions) Catholics made up the anti-Dreyfusard camp; republicans, socialists, and anti-clericalists professed faith in Dreyfus's innocence. The anti-Dreyfusards, by dint of patriotic forgeries and pious perjuries, prevailed at first; Esterhazy was acquitted by a court martial and Émile Zola was sentenced for his article "J'accuse" (1898), which had accused the authorities of framing Dreyfus. However, when Maj. Henry, who had forged evidence against Dreyfus at the Esterhazy trial, committed suicide in 1898, revision of the Dreyfus case became imperative. The court of appeals ordered a new court martial, but surprisingly the military court at Rennes found Dreyfus guilty again (1899). Though Pres. Loubet pardoned him, agitation for complete exoneration continued until 1906, when the supreme court of appeals (a civil court) cleared Dreyfus, who was reinstated as a major. Publication of the Schwartz-koppen papers (1930) conclusively proved his innocence. The Dreyfus Affair discredited the monarchists and clericalists and hastened separation of Church and state in France.

drift, mixture of clay, sand, and boulders left by an ice sheet. Unstratified drift is also called boulder clay. Stratified drift was deposited by glacial streams. Drift will form a DRUMLIN, ESKER, MORAINE.

Driftless Area, over 10,000 sq. mi. largely in SW Wis., but also in SE Minn., NE Iowa, NW Ill. Area, untouched by continental glacier which once covered surroundings, has no glacial drifts.

Drin (drēn), largest river of Albania, c.175 mi. long, formed by White and Black Drin, which rise in Yugoslavia and join in NE Albania. Flows W and S through deep gorges into Adriatic.

Drinkwater, John, 1882–1937, English writer, author of many plays (e.g., *Abraham Lincoln,* 1918; *Bird in Hand,* 1927), biographies, poetry.

Drogheda (drô'ŭdŭ, droi'dŭ), urban district (pop. 17,-071), Co. Louth, Ireland, on the Boyne. POYNINGS'S LAW enacted here in 1494. Town taken and inhabitants massacred by Cromwell 1649. Battle of the Boyne fought near here 1690.

Drogobych (drŭgô'bĭch), city (1965 est. pop. 52,000), W Ukraine, in N Carpathian foothills; center of petroleum and natural gas fields. Under Austria 1772–1918; ceded by Poland to Ukraine 1939.

Droitwich (droit'wĭch), municipal borough (pop. 7,975), Worcestershire, England. Noted for its brine baths and salt trade.

Drôme (drōm), department (2,533 sq. mi.; pop. 304,-227), SE France, in Dauphiné; cap. Valence.

Drontheim, Norway: see TRONDHEIM.

dropsy: see EDEMA.

Droste-Hülshoff, Annette Elisabeth, Freiin von (änĕ'tŭ älē'zäbĕt frī'ĭn fŭn drôs'tŭ-hüls'hôf), 1797–1848, German poet. Writer of perceptive nature poetry; a fine short novel, *Die Judenbuche* (1842); and religious poems, *Das geistliche Jahr* (1850).

Droysen, Johann Gustav (yōhän' gŏōs'täf droi'zŭn), 1808–84, German historian. Known for *Geschichte der preussischen Politik* (14 vols., 1855–86) and biography of Yorck von Wartenburg (3 vols., 1851–52).

drug addiction, craving for drug resulting in need for increasing quantity to produce effect and in nervous disturbances when not under its influence. Chief habit-forming drugs are opium, cocaine, hashish, marijuana, alcohol, and nicotine.

drugs, substances used internally or externally for cure, alleviation, or prevention of disease. They include inorganic substances, alkaloids and other plant derivatives, and hormones, vaccines, serums, and other substances derived from animals. SULFA DRUGS and ANTIBIOTIC SUBSTANCES are valued in treating infections. Many countries list standards and tests in official PHARMACOPOEIA. U.S. legislation to safeguard users began 1906, was superseded by Federal Food, Drug, and Cosmetic Act of 1938; laws enforced by Food and Drug Administration.

druids, priests and medicine men of Celtic peoples, especially in Gaul and Great Britain. Practiced herbal medicine and ruled in ritualistic religion based on sun worship and belief in immortality of soul. They had a confederation which was politically powerful and fostered revolt against Rome. Druidic system finally yielded to Christianity. Many prehistoric ruins such as Stonehenge, once attributed to druids, appear to have other sources. Much lore has been attributed to the druids, reputed to have been magicians. Little of the legend has any evidence in fact.

drum: see PERCUSSION INSTRUMENTS.

drumlin, smooth oval hill of glacial DRIFT, elongated in the direction of ice movement.

Drummond, Thomas, 1797–1840, Scottish engineer, inventor. He took part in trigonometrical survey of United Kingdom, 1820; devised **Drummond light** (intense beam made by using incandescent properties of lime; often called limelight) to aid observations in murky weather.

Drummond (of Hawthornden), William, 1585–1649, Scottish poet. A friend of Ben Jonson, he wrote graceful sonnets, elegies, hymns (as in *Flowres of Sion,* 1623). His prose *Cypresse Grove* (1623) is on death.

Drummond, William Henry, 1854–1907, Canadian poet, b. Ireland. His verse portrays French Canadians, using habitants' own dialect of English.

Drummond, Lake: see DISMAL SWAMP.

Drummond Island: see MANITOULIN ISLANDS.

Drummond light: see DRUMMOND, THOMAS.

Drummondville, city (pop. 27,909), S Que., Canada, on St. Francis R., NE of Montreal. Textile center.

Drury Lane, London street and district; site of Drury Lane Theatre built 1663 under royal charter; rebuilt

1674 to Christopher Wren's design. Present theater designed by Benjamin Wyatt 1812.

Druses (drōō'zĭz), people of S Syria and Lebanon who inhabit hills of the Hauran, much of the Lebanon and the Anti-Lebanon. They believe in divinity of 11th-cent. Fatimite caliph, Hakim. Massacred Christians in 19th cent., fought against French control of Syria and Lebanon 1925–26 and had considerable influence in building the Lebanese republic.

Drusus (drōō'sŭs), Roman family. **Marcus Livius Drusus**, d. 109? B.C., was tribune of the people with C. GRACCHUS (122 B.C.) and led the senatorial attack on Gracchus, succeeding by dubious means. He was consul in 112 B.C. His son **Marcus Livius Drusus**, d. 91 B.C., also led the senatorial party and by generous sums of money and wholesale grant of citizenship he won the allegiance of the Italians. The senate turned against him and by withdrawing the citizenship laws provoked the SOCIAL WAR. A member of family by adoption was LIVIA DRUSILLA, mother of Nero Claudius **Drusus Germanicus** (Drusus Senior), 38 B.C.– 9 B.C., who as stepson of Augustus got an army command early and fought against Rhaetians, Gauls, and Germans. His sons were Germanicus Caesar and Claudius I. The son of his brother Tiberius was **Drusus Caesar** (Drusus Junior), d. A.D. 23, who served against the Germans, awoke the jealousy of Sejanus, and died, supposedly of poison, at the instance of Sejanus.

Dryburgh Abbey (drī'bŭrù), Berwickshire, Scotland. Founded 1150, now a beautiful ruin. Contains Sir Walter Scott's tomb.

dry cell: see CELL, in electricity.

Dryden, John, 1631–1700, English poet, dramatist, and critic. Wrote *Heroick Stanzas* (1659; in praise of Cromwell) and *Astraea Redux* (1660; welcoming Charles II) and rose to prominence as a playwright with comedies such as *Marriage-à-la-Mode* (1672); tragedies, including *The Conquest of Granada* (1670–71), *Aureng-Zebe* (1675), and *All for Love* (1677; a retelling of Shakespeare's *Antony and Cleopatra*). He was made poet laureate in 1668. Among his long poems are *Annus Mirabilis* (1667), *Absalom and Achitophel* (1681; against Shaftesbury and Monmouth), *MacFlecknoe* (1682; against Thomas Shadwell), *Religio Laici* (1682; a defense of Protestantism). But in 1687 he announced his conversion to Catholicism with *The Hind and The Panther* and on the accession of William III lost the laureateship, although he continued prominent. Two well-known shorter pieces are his "Ode to Anne Killigrew" and "Alexander's Feast." His essays are much admired for their style, and he also wrote brilliant critical prefaces, prologues, and discourses; his *Essay of Dramatick Poesy* (1668) is notable. He translated and adapted much Latin literature.

dry farming produces crops in low-rainfall areas, without irrigation. Aided by drought-resistant strains, deep soil, crop rotation, and fallowing.

dry ice, solid CARBON DIOXIDE, formed when liquefying pressure is removed and liquid is allowed to evaporate in a confined space. Some liquid becomes gas at once, drawing heat from remaining liquid, which "freezes" to solid.

drying oil, an oil (from either plants or animals), which oxidizes easily and forms resistant film when exposed to air. Used in paint, varnish, linoleum.

dry rot, fungus disease that attacks seasoned timber, often causing it to collapse. Certain fungus diseases of fruits and vegetables are also called dry rot.

Dry Tortugas (tôrtōō'gŭz), island group off S Fla., W of Key West. Named by Ponce de Leon 1513; later became pirate base. On Garden Key is noted bird refuge and Fort Jefferson Natl. Monument, largest all-masonry fortification (1846) in Western World. Group also called Tortugas.

Dual Alliance, 1879–82: see TRIPLE ALLIANCE AND TRIPLE ENTENTE.

dualism, any philosophical system that explains the universe in terms of two distinct and exclusive principles—e.g., form and matter, mind and matter, being and nonbeing. In religion, dualism usually means belief in an ultimate evil principle as well as an ultimate good principle. This appeared in striking form in Zoroastrianism, in Gnosticism, and in Manichaeism.

Dual Monarchy: see AUSTRO-HUNGARIAN MONARCHY.

Duane, James (dūän'), 1733–97, American Revolutionary statesman. Member of Continental Congress (1774–83). Helped draft Articles of Confederation.

Duane, William, 1760–1835, American journalist. Editor (1798–1822) of Philadelphia *Aurora,* leading Jeffersonian organ. Arrested under both Alien Act and Sedition Act; vindicated. His son, **William John Duane,** 1780–1865, was U.S. Secretary of Treasury (June–Oct., 1833). Replaced after refusing Pres. Jackson's request to transfer government deposits from Bank of the United States to state banks.

Duarte (dwär'tù) 1391–1438, king of Portugal (1433–38). Called the "philosopher-king," he was better known for his learning than for his indecisive statemanship. Brother of Henry the Navigator.

Duarte (dōō-ôr'tä), residential city (pop. 13,962), S Calif., ENE of Los Angeles; settled c.1841.

Du Barry, Jeanne Bécu, comtesse (zhän' bäkü' kōtĕs' dü bärē'), 1743–93, last mistress of Louis XV. Of extremely vulgar background, she was notorious for her extravagance but did not seek political influence. Guillotined in Revolution.

Du Bartas, Guillaume de Salluste (gĕyōm' dü sälüst' dü bärtäs'), 1544–90, French poet and Huguenot soldier. Wrote epic poem on creation (1578).

Dubawnt, river, Northwest Territories, Canada. Rises NE of L. Athabaska, Sask., and flows c.600 mi. NE into Baker L. at head of Chesterfield Inlet of Hudson Bay.

Du Bellay, Joachim (zhōäshē dü bĕlä'), 1522?–1560, French poet of the PLÉIADE. Wrote its manifesto, *La Defènce et illustration de la langue francoyse* (1549), and sonnet collections such as *Les Regrets* (1558), nostalgic poems of Rome.

Dubinsky, David (dōōbĭn'skē), 1892–, American labor leader, b. Poland. President 1932–66 of International Ladies Garment Workers Union, he led it into the C.I.O. in 1936, but broke with C.I.O. in 1938 and later rejoined A.F. of L. He advocated political action; helped to found American Labor Party, Liberal Party, Americans for Democratic Action. He became a vice president of AFL–CIO.

Dublin, county (327 sq. mi.; pop. 716,156), Leinster prov., Ireland. City area, including Wicklow Mts. and Liffey R., dominated by Dublin. Rural area has farming, cattle, and fishing. Has several industrial suburban towns.

Dublin, Irish *Baile Átha Cliath* (bä'lĕ ä klē'), county borough (pop. 535,488), cap. of Ireland and co. seat of Dublin Co., on Dublin Bay at mouth of Liffey R. Harbor with shipyards and docks connected with interior by rail and two canals. Chief industries brewing, distilling, linen milling, and mfg. of chemicals, soap, textiles, carpets, lace, and machinery. Site of Univ. of Dublin (or Trinity Col. founded 1591) which has famous Book of KELLS, Univ. Col. (R.C.), and Natl. Gallery of Art. Dublin Castle (c.1220) houses government offices. Leinster House seat of Irish Parliament. City became seat of English government and center of Pale 12th cent. Black Monday massacre of English residents occurred 1209. Cromwell landed here 1649 after city's surrender to parliamentarians. Dublin saw much bloodshed 19th and 20th cent.— Robert EMMET's insurrection 1803, FENIAN MOVEMENT uprising 1867, murder of Lord Cavendish 1882, and Easter Rebellion 1916. ABBEY THEATRE world famous, as are many Dublin literary figures (e.g., Swift, Yeats, and Joyce).

Dublin, city (pop. 13,814), central Ga., on Oconee R., SE of Macon. Commercial and industrial center in coastal-plain farm and timber area.

Dubna (dōōb'nŭ), town (1959 pop. 3,300), central European RSFSR, on Volga R. Founded 1956 as seat of Joint Inst. for Nuclear Research. Members include most nations of Communist bloc.

Dubnow, Simon, 1860–1941, Jewish historian, b. Russia. Wrote sociologically oriented history of the Jews.

Dubois, Guillaume (gēyōm' dübwä'), 1656–1723, French cardinal, chief adviser (1715–23) to the regent, Philippe d'Orléans. Astute diplomat.

du Bois, Guy Péne (dü bwä'), 1884–1958, American painter and art critic, b. Brooklyn, N.Y.

Du Bois, W(illiam) E(dward) B(urghardt) (dū bois'), 1868–1963, American Negro author, editor of *Crisis*, magazine of the National Association for the Advancement of Colored People. In it and in many books he advocated complete equality for the Negro in America. He died in Ghana, where he had been invited to make his home.

Du Bois (dōō'bois), city (pop. 10,667), W central Pa., in Allegheny plateau region NE of Pittsburgh; settled 1865. Commercial and industrial center of coal-mine and farm region.

Du Bois-Reymond, Emil (ā'mēl dü bwä'-rāmō'), 1818–96, German physiologist, authority on muscle and nerve action and accompanying electrical changes.

Dubos, René Jules (rünā' zhül dübō'), 1901–, American bacteriologist, b. France. He isolated gramicidin from soil bacteria.

Dubrovnik (dōō'brôvnĭk), Ital. *Ragusa*, city (pop. 22,-961), Croatia, NW Yugoslavia; Adriatic port and resort. Founded by Greek refugees c.7th cent. A.D., it became a powerful, virtually independent merchant republic (under Venetian rule 13th–14th cent.; later tributary to Turkey). Republic abolished by French (1808); awarded to Austria at Congress of Vienna (1815); included in Yugoslavia (1918). A medieval center of Serbo-Croation culture, city retains much medieval architecture; including city walls.

Dubuffet, Jean (zhä' dübüfä'), 1901–, French painter, who has created primitive, childlike, and humorous effects opposed to "good taste."

Dubuque, Julien (dübük'), 1762–1810, pioneer settler of Iowa, b. Quebec.

Dubuque (dübük'), city (pop. 56,606), NE Iowa, on bluffs above Mississippi R., E of Waterloo; organized 1837. One of state's oldest cities. Trade, industrial, and rail center; river port for agr. and dairy area. Has railroad shops and shipyards. Seat of Univ. of Dubuque, Clarke Col., Loras Col., and Wartburg Theological Seminary. Nearby are grave of Julien Dubuque (for whom town was named) and Crystal Lake Cave.

Du Cange, Charles du Fresne, sieur (shärl' dü frĕn' sÿür dü käzh'), 1610–88, French medieval scholar, compiler of *Glossarium mediae et infimae Latinitatis*, greatest collection ever made of forms of early medieval Latin and of oldest Romance.

Ducas (dü'kús), Greek family of Constantinople. Four members were Byzantine emperors—Constantine X, Michael VII, ALEXIUS V, and John III.

Duccio (di Buoninsegna) (dōōt'chēō dē bwōnēnsä'-nyä), fl. 1278–1319, Italian painter, founder of Sienese school. Only authenticated work is double altar in Siena cathedral. Rucellai Madonna (in Santa Maria Novella, Florence) is attributed to him.

Du Cerceau: see ANDROUET.

Du Chaillu, Paul (Belloni) (dü shäyü'), 1831?–1903, French-American explorer in Africa, b. probably in Paris. Backed by Philadelphia Acad. of Natural Sciences, explored Gabun country in Africa (1855–59). Published account upsetting previous ideas of region's geography. Second expedition (1863–65) visited unknown tribes, verified reports of a Pygmy race.

Duchamp, Marcel (märsĕl' düshä'), 1887–, French painter. Famous work is *Nude Descending a Staircase*, painting depicting continuous action with series of overlapping figures. Was a leader of the Dadaists.

Duchamp-Villon, Raymond (rämô' düshä'-vēyō'), 1876–1918, French sculptor; brother of the artists Marcel Duchamp and Jacques Villon.

Duck, river of central Tenn. winding c.250 mi. NW to Tennessee R. SW of Waverly. Columbia is on it.

duck, waterfowl smaller than related goose and swan. Accurately, duck refers to female and drake to male. Usually divided into three groups: river or fresh-water ducks (mallard, wood duck, black duck, teal), sea ducks (canvasback, scoter, eider, redhead), and mergansers or fish-eating ducks. Domestic meat producers are Pekin or Peking, Aylesbury, and Rouen ducks, all descendants of mallard duck. See *ill.*, p. 118.

Duck Lake, central Sask., Canada, SW of Prince Albert. Saw first encounter of Riel's Rebellion, 1885.

Ducommun, Élie (ālē' dükômü'), 1833–1906, Swiss journalist and pacifist. Organized Internatl. Peace Bureau at Berne (1891). Shared 1902 Nobel Peace Prize with C. A. Gobat.

ductless gland: see GLAND.

Du Deffand, Marie de Vichy-Chamrond, marquise (märē' dü vēshē'-shärō' märkēz' dü dĕfä'), 1697–1780, French woman of letters. Her salon was frequented by the leaders of the Enlightenment. Mme du Deffand's later years were marred by blindness, but she maintained a regular correspondence with her English friend Horace Walpole.

Dudley, John: see NORTHUMBERLAND, JOHN DUDLEY, DUKE OF.

Dudley, Joseph, 1647–1720, colonial governor of Mass. (1702–15). Unpopular because of earlier connection with rule of Sir Edmund Andros.

Dudley, Plimmon Henry, 1843–1924, American civil and metallurgical engineer, inventor of instruments for testing and ways of improving railroad beds.

Dudley, Robert: see LEICESTER, ROBERT DUDLEY, EARL OF.

duel, prearranged armed fight between two persons to settle a point of honor. Presumably arose from wager of battle (form of trial in which formal fight between accuser and accused settled the case). Duels popular in 16th-cent. France, later in England. Student duels prominent in 19th-cent. German universities, revived by Nazis. In U.S. most famous duel was that in which Aaron Burr killed Alexander Hamilton (1804). Andrew Jackson was also known as a duelist. Dueling now illegal in all Western countries.

due process of law, fundamental concept of Anglo-American law, intended to protect individuals in relation to the government. In contrast to totalitarian doctrine of overriding state supremacy, the rule of due process holds that persons may not be deprived of life, liberty, or property except by the established process of law. This guarantees protection from government acts that may be arbitrary, capricious, or unreasonable. See also FOURTEENTH AMENDMENT.

Duer, William, 1747–99, American Revolutionary patriot and capitalist, b. England. One of largest contractors supplying army during Revolution. Became Assistant Secretary of Treasury in 1789; sued by government for irregularities in his work. Imprisoned for debt. His son, **William Alexander Duer**, 1780–1858, American jurist and educator, was president of Columbia Col. (1829–42). There he estab. scientific courses not requiring Latin and increased instruction in modern languages.

Duero, river: see DOURO.

Due West, town (pop. 1,166), NW S.C., S of Greenville, in cattle, cotton, and grain area. Seat of Erskine Col. Cherokee treaty (1777), relinquishing large areas of S.C., signed nearby.

Dufay, Guillaume (gēyōm' düfä), c.1400–1474, leading composer of the Burgundian (sometimes called Netherlands) school. Created first international style by fusion of French, Italian, and English elements. Composed in every contemporary form (e.g., Masses, motets, chansons).

Dufour, Guillaume Henri (gēyōm' ārē' düfōōr'), 1787–1875, Swiss general. Led federal forces to victory over

SONDERBUND (1847). Wrote military treatises. Helped estab. International Red Cross (1864).

Dufourspitze: see ROSA, MONTE.

Dufy, Raoul (räōōl' düfē)', 1877–1953, French painter and illustrator, with decorative, calligraphic style and subtle use of brilliant color.

Du Gard, Roger Martin: see MARTIN DU GARD.

Dugdale, Richard Louis (düg'dăl), 1841–83, American social investigator, author of a study on criminality in the JUKES family.

dugong (dōō'gŏng), herbivorous aquatic mammal (Dugong or Halicore) of Red Sea, Indian Ocean, and Australian waters. Like the manatee of same order (Sirenia) it is called sea cow. Brownish or grayish, 7–9½ ft. long, it has flexible front flippers and a two-lobed, flat tail. Hunted for hide, tusks, oil, and palatable flesh, it is now scarce.

Duguay-Trouin, René (rünä' dügä'-trōōē'), 1673–1736, French admiral. Enlisted as privateer 1689. By 1709 he had captured 300 merchantmen, 20 warships. Took Rio de Janeiro 1711.

Du Guesclin, Bertrand (dügěs'klĭn, běrträ' dü gěklē'), c.1320–1380, constable of France (1370–80), one of most popular heroes of France, particularly in his native Brittany. Most notable achievement was his reconquest of English-held France (1370–74; see HUNDRED YEARS WAR).

Duhamel, Georges (zhôrzh' düämĕl'), 1884–1966, French author. Best known for novel, Cycle de Salavin (1920–32), whose "hero," Salavin, is unable to adjust himself to society.

Dühring, Eugen Karl (oigän' kärl' dü'rĭng), 1833–1921, German philosopher and economist. A positivist in the manner of Comte and Feuerbach, he made man the basis of his philosophy. Believed that capitalism should be retained, but that a strong labor movement should remove its abuses.

Duisburg (düs'bŏŏrk), city (pop. 479,615), North Rhine–Westphalia, West Germany, at junction of Ruhr and Rhine rivers. Industrial center of RUHR dist. (steel, machinery, textiles) and large inland port. Armaments industry drew very heavy bombing in Second World War.

Dujardin, Karel (kä'rúl dúzhärdē'), 1622–78, Dutch painter and etcher.

Dukas, Paul (dükäs'), 1865–1935, French composer of symphonic poem The Sorcerer's Apprentice (1897) and opera Ariane et Barbe-Bleue (1907).

Duke, James Buchanan, 1856–1925, American processor of tobacco products and benefactor of Duke Univ.

Duke University, at Durham, N.C.; coed.; opened 1838, chartered 1841 as Union Inst.; reorganized 1852 as Normal Col.; became Trinity Col. and moved to Durham 1892; renamed 1924. Tobacco culture and medical research are noted.

Dukhobors or Doukhobors (both: dōō'kübôrz) [Rus.,= spirit wrestlers], religious sect that arose among Russian peasants in 17th cent.; now more properly Christians of the Universal Brotherhood. They believe in absolute equality of men and resist all authority, civil or ecclesiastic. This attitude brought persecution in Russia. Alexander I allowed them to settle on the Sea of Azov, but later resistance to military conscription caused their removal to a barren section now in Georgian SSR. This they brought to blossom, but in 1887 military conscription again reached them. In the 1890s with the help of Leo Tolstoy and of the Quakers most of them moved to Saskatchewan, Canada. Again they created a thriving community—under the leadership of Peter Veregin after he was allowed to leave Siberia and, after his death, under his son, another Peter Veregin. Trouble with their neighbors and the government led to spectacular demonstrations, notably the "nudist strikes." A small group of more ascetic Dukhobors split from the main body as the Sons of Freedom. Latter group, nearly always in trouble with the Canadians, appealed to Russian authorities for sanctuary in 1957 and again early in 1958, claiming Canadian religious persecution. Later in 1958, Canada and British Columbia offered to pay the necessary expenses for resettling in USSR those who renounced Canadian citizenship. Some Dukhobors had presumably remained in Russia; a few are in the Paraguayan Chaco.

dulcimer (dŭl'sŭmŭr), stringed musical instrument. Consists of wooden box strung with strings which are usually struck with mallets. Oriental in origin; appeared in Europe in Middle Ages.

Du Lhut, Daniel Greysolon, sieur: see DULUTH.

Dulles, John Foster, (dŭ'lŭs), 1888–1959, U.S. Secretary of State (1953–59); grandson of John Watson Foster. Was U.S. delegate to UN General Assembly (1945–48, 1950). In 1951, as ambassador at large, negotiated peace treaty with Japan. As Secy. of State he emphasized collective security of U.S. and its allies in foreign policy and, in national defense policy, the development of forces capable of "massive retaliation" in case of attack. His brother, Allen Welsh Dulles, 1893–, was director of the Central Intelligence Agency (1953–61).

Dulong, Pierre Louis (pyěr' lwē dülŏ'), 1785–1838, French physicist and chemist. Dulong and Petit's law: specific heats of elements are inversely proportional to their atomic weights; specific heat is constant for all solid elements.

Duluth or Du Lhut, Daniel Greysolon, sieur (Fr. dü-lüt'), 1636–1710, French explorer in Canada. He won the L. Superior and upper Mississippi region for France.

Duluth, city (pop. 106,884), NE Minn., at W end (and head of navigation) of L. Superior opposite Superior, Wis. Indian settlements found here by early explorers and fur traders, incl. sieur Duluth. Permanent settlement began c.1852. Built largely on rocky bluffs overlooking lake. Became nation's chief ore shipping point, with factories and shipyards, after discovery of iron in Mesabi range. Opening of St. Lawrence Seaway made it a leading Great Lakes port for export of grain. Now the commercial, industrial, and cultural cap. of N Minn. and gateway to resort area. Col. of St. Scholastica and branch of Univ. of Minn. are here. City has civic symphony orchestra. Fond Du Lac Indian Reservation is nearby.

Dulwich (dŭl'ĭj), residential suburb, S London, England. Has a well-known public school, Dulwich Col. (opened 1619).

duma (dōō'mä), Russian representative body, esp. first through fourth imperial dumas (lower house) 1906–17; first duma estab. 1906 as result of 1905 revolution.

Dumas, Alexandre (älěksä'drü dümä'), known as Dumas père (pěr'), 1802–70, French author, partly of African descent. He wrote many historical adventure novels, notably The Three Musketeers (1844), Twenty Years After (1845), The Count of Monte Cristo (1844–45). Among his dramas La Tour de Nesle (1832) is best known. He employed many collaborators. His son, Alexandre Dumas, known as Dumas fils (fēs'), 1824–95, French dramatist and novelist, wrote La Dame aux camélias (1852; known in English as Camille; basis of Verdi's La Traviata), Le Demi-Monde (1855), Le Fils naturel [the natural son] (1858), mainly plays of moral or social theme.

Dumas, Jean Baptiste André, 1800–1884, French chemist. Notable studies include those on atomic weights and laws of substitution. In 1868 he became perpetual secretary of Academy of Sciences. His writings include Traité de chimie appliquée aux arts (8 vols., 1828–45).

Dumas, city (pop. 8,477), extreme N Texas, N of Amarillo on plains of Panhandle; founded 1892. Has extensive natural gas fields, refineries, and chemical plants.

Dumas fils: see DUMAS, ALEXANDRE (1824–95).

Dumas père: see DUMAS, ALEXANDRE (1802–70).

Du Maurier, George (Louis Palmella Busson) (dü môr'ēä), 1834–96, English artist and novelist, b. Paris.

His best-known novels are *Peter Ibbetson* (1892; made into an opera by Deems Taylor, 1931) and *Trilby* (1894). His granddaughter, **Daphne Du Maurier,** 1907–, has written popular novels, notably *Rebecca* (1938).

Dumbarton (dŭmbär'tŭn), burgh (pop. 26,335), co. town of Dumbartonshire, Scotland. Shipbuilding center, it also has mfg. of aircraft, pharmaceuticals, whisky, soap, and bricks. Chief town of ancient kingdom of Strathclyde.

Dumbarton Oaks, estate, now in Washington, D.C.; scene of a conference (1944) at which the U.S., Great Britain, the USSR, and China reached an agreement to create the United Nations. Site of institute (estab. 1940), administered by Harvard, for study in humanities (esp. Byzantine and medieval).

Dumbartonshire or **Dunbartonshire** (dŭn–), county (241 sq. mi.; pop. 184,546), W Scotland, county town Dumbarton. Bordered on E by Loch Lomond, on S by Clyde estuary, and on W by Loch Long. It is mountainous region (up to 3,000 ft.) with little agr. Cattle and sheep raised. Industries include shipbuilding and cotton mfg.

Dumdum (dŭm'dŭm), town, S West Bengal, India. Lead-nosed bullets, banned in 1899 by Hague Conference, were first made here.

Dumfriesshire (dŭmfrēs'shĭr) or **Dumfries,** border county (1,074 sq. mi.; pop. 88,423), SW Scotland. Surface largely hilly with agr. in valleys. Salmon fishing and sheep grazing important; limestone and sandstone quarried. There are many beautiful lochs. Scene of much border warfare until 18th cent. County town, **Dumfries,** burgh (pop. 27,275), includes Maxwelltown across Nith R. Has Burns's mausoleum.

Dummer, Jeremiah, 1645–1718, American silversmith. His mark is ID over a fleur-de-lis in a heart.

Dumont, suburban borough (pop. 18,882), NE N.J., NNE of Teaneck; settled 1730.

Dumouriez, Charles François (shärl' fränswä' dümōorēä'), 1739–1823, French general in French Revolutionary Wars. Victor at Valmy and Jemappes 1792. Recalled by the Convention after execution of king in 1793 but fled to Austrian camp. Advised allies in Napoleonic Wars.

dumping, selling goods below normal price or cost of production, usually an occasional practice. Frequently part of a nation's trade policy although attempts have been made to restrict it. See GENERAL AGREEMENT ON TARIFFS AND TRADE.

Dunajec (dōonä'yĕts), river, S Poland, rising in Carpathians and flowing c.156 mi. NE into the Vistula. Has large hydroelectric station at Roznow.

Dunant, Jean Henry (zhä' ĕrē' dünä'), 1828–1910, Swiss philanthropist. Brought about founding of Red Cross. Shared 1901 (first) Nobel Peace Prize with Passy.

Dunapentele (dōo'nŏpĕn"tĕlĕ), city (pop. 31,048), central Hungary on the Danube. Industrial center with iron and steel mills; mfg. of machinery, chemicals, textiles. Modern city built 1950–55. Formerly known as Stalinvarosh.

Dunbar, Paul Laurence, 1872–1906, American Negro poet, b. Ohio. Wrote *Lyrics of a Lowly Life* (1896).

Dunbar, William, c.1460–c.1520, Scottish poet strongly influenced by Chaucer. Noted for inventiveness and metrical skill. "Lament for the Makers" is one of his best-known poems.

Dunbar (dŭnbär'), burgh (pop. 4,003), East Lothian, Scotland, at mouth of Firth of Forth; resort and fishing port. Has remains of castle to which Mary Queen of Scots was abducted by Bothwell 1567. Cromwell defeated Covenanters here 1650.

Dunbar, industrial city (pop. 11,006), W central W.Va., W of Charleston.

Duncan I, d. 1040?, king of Scotland (1034–1040?). He was murdered by his general Macbeth.

Duncan, Isadora, 1878–1927, American dancer. Early failures preceded triumphs (1903–8) in Budapest, Berlin, London, and finally in U.S. A daring, dynamic innovator, she danced barefoot in flowing robes. Greatly influenced modern dance through her concert tours and schools. She died at Nice, accidentally strangled by her scarf.

Duncan, Robert Kennedy, 1868–1914, American chemist and educator. Professor at Univ. of Kansas and Univ. of Pittsburgh. His system of research fellowships in industrial chemistry was later adopted as basic plan of Mellon Inst.

Duncan, city (pop. 20,009), SW Okla., SSW of Oklahoma City; founded 1892. Supply center and marketing and processing point for oil, cattle, cotton, and farm produce.

Duncansbay Head or **Duncansby Head,** 210 ft. high, northeastern extremity of Scotland, in Caithness.

Dundalk (dŭndôk'), urban district (pop. 19,706), co. town of Co. Louth, Ireland, on Dundalk Bay of Irish Sea; seaport. Industries include milling; distilling; linen, tobacco, and shoe mfg. Railroad center with large car works.

Dundalk, city (pop. 82,428), NE Md., a suburb SE of Baltimore. U.S. Fort Holabird is here.

Dundas, town (pop. 12,912), S Ont., Canada, at head of Burlington Bay and NW of Hamilton. Head of Desjardins Canal, no longer in use. Varied mfg.

Dundee, John Graham of Claverhouse, 1st Viscount (klā'vürŭs), 1649?–1689, Scottish Jacobite chieftain and soldier, known as Bonnie Dundee. Hated by Covenanters whom he tried to suppress 1678–88. Fought for James II in Glorious Revolution; raised force to restore him but was killed in battle of Killiecrankie. Subject of ballads and novels.

Dundee (dŭndē'), independent burgh (pop. 182,959), Angus, Scotland, on Firth of Tay. Has docks and various industries. Jute mfg.; Dundee marmalade famous. Site of Univ. Col., part of Univ. of St. Andrews. City early adopted doctrines of Reformation.

Dundonald, Thomas Cochrane, 10th earl of, 1775–1860, British naval commander in Napoleonic wars. Commanded Chilean navy in liberation of Chile and Peru and Greek navy in war against Turkey 1827.

Dunedin (dŭnē'dĭn), city (pop. 72,000; metropolitan pop. 102,500), SE South Isl., New Zealand; port at base of Otago Peninsula; founded 1848. Seat of Univ. of Otago (1869). Woolen mills, iron and brass foundries.

Dunedin, Scotland: see EDINBURGH.

Dunes, Battle of the, 1658, victory of French and English under Turenne over Spanish under John of Austria and Louis II de Condé; fought near Dunkirk, France.

Dunfermline (dŭmfûr'lĭn), burgh (pop. 47,159), Fifeshire, Scotland. Residence of Scottish kings from 11th cent. Abbey is burial place of Robert I and others. Birthplace of Andrew Carnegie, town is hq. of Carnegie Trusts. Has textile mills and metal foundries.

Dunkards, Dunkers, or **Tunkers:** see BRETHREN.

Dunkirk (dŭn'kûrk), Fr. *Dunkerque,* town (est. pop. 21,136), Nord dept., N France; fishing port. Key city in struggle between France and its neighbors, Dunkirk often changed masters, passed permanently to France 1662. In 1940 (May 26–June 4) it was scene of one of most memorable naval actions in history when some 300,000 Allied troops, cut off by German advance on Channel ports, were evacuated to England. Dunkirk was left in ruins. Germans held out here against Allies until May, 1945.

Dunkirk, industrial city (pop. 18,205), SW N.Y., on L. Erie SW of Buffalo. Processes farm products.

Dunlap, William, 1766–1839, American playwright, prolific writer of Gothic romances and tragedies. Adapted many French and German works. Was theater manager (1796–1805), a founder of Natl. Academy of Design, and author of books on theater and design.

Dunlop, John Boyd, 1840–1921, Scottish veterinary; patented Dunlop pneumatic tire 1888.

SMALL CAPITALS = cross references. Pronunciation key on inside end pages. Abbreviations: p. 2.

Dunmore, John Murray, 4th earl of, 1732–1809, British colonial governor of Va. Led Indian campaign in 1774, known as Lord Dunmore's War. Opposed colonists until forced to return to England in 1776.

Dunmore, industrial borough (pop. 18,917), NE Pa., NNE of Scranton; settled 1783. Has coal mines.

Dunmore's War: see DUNMORE, JOHN MURRAY, 4TH EARL OF.

Dunn, Gano, 1870–1953, American electrical engineer of large-scale projects and designer of electrical equipment for production.

Dunne, Finley Peter, 1867–1936, American humorist, journalist. His Irish-American "Mr. Dooley" excelled in deflating politicians' pretensions.

Dunnellon, town (pop. 1,079), N central Fla., on Withlacoochee R., SW of Ocala. Rainbow Springs is nearby.

Dunnet Head, promontory, Caithness, Scotland, forming N extremity of Scottish mainland.

Dunois, Jean, comte de (zhä′ kōt′ dü dünwä′), c.1403–1468, French general, called the Bastard of Orléans; natural son of Louis d'Orléans. In charge of defense of Orléans when Joan of Arc relieved it (1429); joined Joan in subsequent campaign; took part in capture of Paris (1436).

Dunsany, Edward John Moreton Drax Plunkett, 18th **Baron** (dŭnsăn′ē, –să′–), 1878–1957, Anglo-Irish author. Plays (e.g., *A Night at an Inn,* 1916), prose tales (e.g., *A Dreamer's Tales,* 1910), and poems of Lord Dunsany are part fantasy and part satire.

Dunseith (dŭn″sēth′), city (pop. 1,017), N N.Dak., near Canadian line E of Bottineau. Internatl. Peace Garden is N.

Dunsinane (dŭn″sĭnān′), one of Sidlaw Hills, Perthshire, Scotland. Has ruins of fort, called Macbeth's Castle, supposedly scene of Macbeth's defeat by earl of Northumbria, as told by Shakespeare.

Duns Scotus, John (dŭnz′ skō′tùs), d. 1308, British or Irish scholastic philosopher, a Franciscan, called the Subtle Doctor. There is no authentic list of his works, but some are definitely known. He was the founder of Scotism, opposed to Thomism (i.e., the school of St. Thomas Aquinas) in Roman Catholicism. He denied that individuality comes from matter; said that knowledge of finite truths rests on the ultimate Truth, which is God; argued that God's possible existence, demonstrable from sense experience, involves his necessary existence; and held that the state got its sanction from consent of the people and that private property is not sanctioned by natural law.

Dunstable (dŭn′stúbúl), municipal borough (pop. 25,-618), Bedfordshire, England. Traces of Stone and Bronze ages exist. Excavations in 1926 produced relics of woman of c.2000 B.C. Whipsnade Zoo is nearby.

Dunster, Henry, c.1612–1659, first president of Harvard (1640–54), b. England.

duodecimal system, notation system corresponding to decimal system but based on 12 instead of 10. Since 12 has more factors than 10 more fractions can be expressed evenly. System common in British and American measure (e.g., inches, feet) in contrast to metric system, which has a decimal base.

Dupleix, Joseph François, marquis (zhōsĕf′ fräswä′ märkē′ düplĕks′), 1697–1763, French governor of Pondichéry, India (1741–54). Captured Madras (1746); held Pondichéry against British (1748); formed plan of establishing French supremacy in India. By armed force and by diplomacy he made himself master of the Carnatic and most of Deccan (1749–51,) but British intervention under Robert Clive and fear of war with England induced the French government to recall him. This ended last hope of French empire in India. He died in poverty.

Duplessis, Maurice LeNoblet (mōrēs′ lùnôblā′ düplēsē′), 1890–1959, premier and attorney general of Que., Canada (1936–39, 1944–59).

Du Pont (dū pŏnt′), French-American family. **Pierre Samuel Du Pont de Nemours** (dù nŭmōōr′), 1739–1817, was a French economist, one of the PHYSIO-CRATS. Also active in politics. He migrated to U.S. in 1799. His son, **Eleuthère Irénée Du Pont** (ālūtĕr′ ērānā′), 1771–1834, b. Paris, set up a powder mill near Wilmington, Del., in 1802. He developed an extensive business, which he named E. I. du Pont de Nemours & Company (firm's present name). **Samuel Francis Du Pont,** 1803–65, American naval officer, was grandson of Pierre Samuel du Pont de Nemours. In Civil War he led successful attack on Port Royal, S.C. (1861). Against his own will, he led unsuccessful attack on Charleston (1863). **Pierre Samuel Du Pont,** 1870–1954, was president of family business for many years. Under him the company developed scores of chemical manufactures, acquired many other industries.

Dupré, Jules (zhül′ düprā′), 1811?–1889, French landscape painter of the Barbizon school.

Dupré, Marcel, 1886–, French organist and composer, known for contrapuntal improvisations. Compositions include *Symphonie-Passion, La Chemin de la Croix.*

Dupuy de Lôme, Stanislas (stänēsläs′ düpüē′ dù lōm′), 1816–85, French naval engineer. Built first French armored ship. Demonstrated (1872) practicability of dirigible balloon.

Dupuytren, Guillaume, Baron (gēyōm′ bärō′ düpüētrē′), 1777–1835, French surgeon, influential as a clinical teacher and through his writings.

Duquesne (dúkān′), city (pop. 15,019), SW Pa., on Monongahela R., ESE of Pittsburgh, in coal area; settled 1789. Steel mfg.

Duquesne, Fort, on site of PITTSBURGH, Pa. Strategic position at junction of Monongahela and Allegheny rivers made it major objective in last of French and Indian Wars. Abandoned by French to British in 1758 and renamed Fort Pitt.

Duquesnoy, François (fräswä′ dükĕnwä′), 1594–1643, baroque classicist sculptor, b. Flanders, active in Rome. One of the most sought-after sculptors of his day.

Dura (dōō′rù), anc. city on the Euphrates, E of Palmyra; also called Europos, Doura, and Doura-Europus. A prominent post from the 3d cent. B.C. to the 3d cent. A.D., it fell to ruins. Excavations after 1922 gave much information on Hellenistic and Roman Mesopotamia.

duralumin (dŏorăl′yùmĭn), alloy of aluminum, copper, magnesium, manganese. Because of lightness and tensile strength, is used in aircraft.

Duran, Carolus: see CAROLUS-DURAN.

Durance (düräs′), rapid river, c.180 mi. long, SE France, rising in Dauphiné Alps and joining Rhone near Avignon. Fertile valley.

Durand, Asher B(rown) (dürănd′), 1796–1886, American painter, a founder of Hudson River school.

Durango (dōoräng′gō), state (47,691 sq. mi.; 1963 est. pop. 806,114), N Mexico; cap. Durango (pop. c.94,000). Mountains in W are rich mining area; simiarid plains to E are ranch country; farther E is fertile LAGUNA DISTRICT. Gomez Palacio is chief city. Francisco de Ivarra undertook its exploration and colonization in 1562.

Durango (dōōräng′gō), city (pop. 10,530), SW Colo., on Animas R., in ranch, oil-well, and mine area; founded 1880. Mining of carnotite ore for uranium brought boom, 1948. Mesa Verde Natl. Park is W.

Durant, Thomas Clark, 1820–85, American railroad builder, chief figure in construction of Union Pacific RR. Organized CRÉDIT MOBILIER.

Durant, city (pop. 10,467), S central Okla., near Red R., ESE of Ardmore; settled c.1870. Commercial and processing center for agr. region (peanuts, cotton). Denison Dam is SW.

Duras, Marguerite (mär-gùrēt′ düräs′), 1914–, French novelist and scenarist, b. Indochina. Her works include texts for cinema (e.g., *Hiroshima, mon amour* and *Dix heures et demie du soir en été*) and novels (e.g., *Moderato cantabile,* 1958; *L'Après-midi de M.*

Andesmas, 1962; and *Le Ravissement de Lol V. Stein,* 1964).

Durazzo (dŏŏrät′sō), Albanian *Durrës,* town (est. pop. 41,275), Albania; Adriatic port. Founded c.625 B.C. as Epidamnus, a joint colony of Corinth and Corcyra, whose quarrel over it precipitated PELOPONNESIAN WAR (431 B.C.). Renamed Dyrrhachium c.300 B.C., it passed under Epirus; fell to Rome 229 B.C.; became a major Roman naval and military base. Passing to Byzantine Empire, Durazzo was often seized by foreigners, notably by the Angevin kings of Naples, who made it a duchy in 1267, and by Venice, which held it from 1392 until its fall to the Turks in 1501. Majority of pop. accepted Islam. City has many mosques; three early Byzantine towers; Venetian fortifications.

Durban (dûr′bŭn), city (pop. c.681,492), Natal prov., Republic of South Africa; port on Natal Bay and Natal's largest city. Mfg. center, winter resort; exports fruit, manganese, chrome, coal. Seat of Univ. of Natal.

Dürer, Albrecht (äl′brĕkht dü′rŭr), 1471–1528, German artist, famous for prints and drawings of keen observation and rich detail; b. Nuremberg, where he studied with Michael Wolgemut. In 1494 he estab. own studio in Nuremberg and did woodcuts for the *Apocalypse* and *Great Passion.* Visited Venice 1505–7. During his most fertile period (1507–20) he painted several great altarpieces and created his most celebrated engravings, including *Melancholia, The Knight,* and *St. Jerome in His Study.* Visited the Netherlands 1520. Was a friend of Luther. Wrote on human proportions, perspective, geometry, and fortifications.

duress, actual or threatened violence or imprisonment to force a person, directly or indirectly, to enter into an agreement or perform some other act against his will. To void such a contract, duress must be shown to have been such as to overcome the party's mind and will. Also basis for refusing probate of a WILL.

Durfee, William Franklin (dûr′fē), 1833–99, American engineer and producer of first steel by Bessemer process in America.

Durham, John George Lambton, 1st **earl of,** 1792–1840, British liberal statesman. Promoted Reform Bill of 1832. As Governor General of Canada he prepared masterly *Report on the Affairs of British North America* (1839), supporting self-government and reforms but opposing French nationalism in Canada.

Durham (dŭ′rŭm), maritime county (1,015 sq. mi.; pop. 1,517,039), N England, one of most densely populated English counties. Has dairy farming and cattle raising, but mainly industrial (rich coal deposits) and iron, steel, chemical, and glass industries. Shipbuilding along Tyne R. Sunderland and Hartlepool are important seaports. County ruled by bishops of Durham until 1836. The county town, **Durham,** municipal borough (pop. 20,484), has 11th-cent. castle occupied by Univ. of Durham. Cathedral, begun 1093 and one of England's finest examples of Norman architecture, contains relics of St. Cuthbert.

Durham. 1 Town (pop. 5,504), SE N.H., on Oyster R., SW of Dover; settled 1635. Seat of Univ. of NEW HAMPSHIRE. Early settlement suffered in Indian wars (1694, 1704). Gen. John Sullivan's house is preserved. **2** City (pop. 78,302), N central N.C., in piedmont NW of Raleigh; settled c.1852. Prominent center for marketing and processing tobacco. Tobacco industry grew after Civil War, with J. B. Duke as leader. Seat of DUKE UNIVERSITY and North Carolina Col. at Durham.

Durkheim, Émile (ämēl′ dürkĕm′) 1858–1917, French sociologist. He held that religion and morality originate in the collective mind of society. He used anthropology and statistics to support his theories. Works include *Suicide* (1897) and *The Elementary Forms of Religious Life* (1912).

Durocher, Leo (Ernest), 1906–, baseball manager. Managed New York Giants (later San Francisco

Giants) (1948–55); coached Dodgers (1961–64); became manager of Chicago Cubs 1965.

Durrell, Lawrence, 1912–, English novelist and poet, b. India, long a foreign service officer. His novels reflect his wide travels and are distinguished by imagery and allusiveness. They include the tetralogy *The Alexandria Quartet—Justine* (1957), *Balthazar* (1958), *Mountolive* (1958), and *Clea* (1960)—and *Bitter Lemons* (1957).

Dürrenmatt, Friedrich (frē′drĭkh dür′rĕnmät), 1921–, Swiss playwright and novelist. His terse plays, short stories, and novels depict a grotesque world that is occasionally comic. His best-known plays are *The Visit* (1956) and *The Physicists* (1962).

Durrës, Albania: see DURAZZO.

Duryea, Charles Edgar (dŏŏr′yä), 1862–1938, American inventor and automobile manufacturer. With his brother, J. Frank Duryea (1870–), he built one of first practical internal-combustion automobiles.

Duse, Eleonora (dŏŏ′zŭ, Ital. ālāŏnō′rä dŏŏ′zä), 1859–1924, Italian actress. Made debut at 14 as Juliet. Later vehicles included Sardou's *Fédora,* Goldoni's *La Locandiera,* and Ibsen's *Lady from the Sea.* Her acting combined simplicity with emotional power. For some years a romantic attachment existed between Duse and Italian poet D'Annunzio.

Dushan, Stephen: see STEPHEN DUSHAN.

Dushanbe (dŏŏshän′bĕ), city (1965 est. pop. 316,000), cap. of Tadzhik SSR; major industrial and transportation center. Known as Dyushambe until 1929; called Stalinabad 1929–61.

Düsseldorf (dü′sŭldôrf), city (pop. 658,941), cap. of North Rhine-Westphalia, West Germany, at junction of Rhine and Düssel rivers. Industrial and commercial center; administrative seat of Ruhr iron and steel industry. Cap. of duchy of Berg from 1288; passed to Prussia 1815. Famous art academy estab. 1819. Birthplace of Heinrich Heine. Heavily damaged in Second World War.

dust, atmospheric, minute particles of matter (chiefly inorganic) settling from or suspended in air. Sources: city activities, blown dry earth, volcanic eruptions, ocean salt spray, organic matter (e.g., pollen), and meteorite combustion. Nuclear tests in atmosphere create radioactive dust (fallout) hazardous to all forms of life.

Dust Bowl, areas of prairie states that suffer from dust storms which carry off topsoil. Removal of natural cover of grass by overgrazing, burning over, or plowing aggravates conditions. Remedies include planting cover crops, trees, and grass to anchor soil. Areas suffered greatly in 1930s.

Dutch East India Company: see EAST INDIA COMPANY, DUTCH.

Dutch East Indies: see INDONESIA.

Dutch Guiana: see SURINAM.

Dutch Harbor: see ALEUTIAN ISLANDS.

Dutch language, West Germanic language of Indo-European family. See LANGUAGE (table).

Dutchman's-breeches, North American wild flower (*Dicentra cucullaria*) related to bleeding heart. It has drooping racemes of yellow-tipped white flowers and ferny foliage.

Dutchman's-pipe, twining vine (*Aristolochia durior*) of E U.S. It has pipelike flowers and heart-shaped leaves. Flowers can trap and later release insects.

Dutch New Guinea: see NEW GUINEA.

Dutch Reformed Church: see REFORMED CHURCH IN AMERICA.

Dutch Wars. 1 1652–54, war between English and Dutch. Marked crisis between two nations' rivalry as carriers of world trade; precipitated by English search and seizure of Dutch merchant ships and by English Navigation Act of 1651, directed against Dutch trade with British possessions. Sea fight between Robert Blake and Maarten TROMP, May, 1652, opened hostilities. Tromp's victory over Blake off Dungeness, Nov., 1652, gave Dutch control of Channel; control was broken by British victory at Portland (1653).

After victory off Gabbard's Shoal, British blockaded Dutch coast. Tromp attacked blockading fleet, July 31, 1653, and was defeated. Peace signed April, 1654. Dutch agreed to salute British flag in British seas, to pay compensation for English losses, and to submit territorial claims to arbitration. **2** 1664–67, another war between Dutch and English. Dutch had continued to threaten English commercial supremacy. In 1664 British raided Dutch colonies on African coast and took New Netherland in North America. England declared war, March, 1665. Duke of York (later James II) won battle of Lowestoft in June, 1665; in Sept., bishop of Munster, an English ally, overran E province of Netherlands, but was soon expelled. Louis XIV of France declared war on England, Jan., 1666, but took little part in war. British fleet under Monck and Prince Rupert was defeated in Four Days battle or battle of the Downs (June 1–4, 1666) by Michiel de RUYTER and Cornelis Tromp; in Aug. they defeated Dutch and destroyed shipping along Dutch coast. Charles II having let the navy fall into unprepared state, De Ruyter exacted heavy losses in raid in the Thames, 1667. In Treaty of Breda (July, 1667), trade laws were modified to favor Dutch, conquests of war were retained (English received N.Y., N.J., and Del.; Dutch kept Surinam), and English and French made mutual restoration of conquests. **3** 1672–78, first of great wars of Louis XIV of France. Aimed at destruction of Dutch rivalry to French trade and expansion of French empire. Having gained allies in CHARLES II of England, in Sweden, and several German states, Louis overran S provinces of Netherlands, May, 1672. His advance on Amsterdam was stopped when Dutch opened the dikes. De Ruyter defeated English and French fleets at Southwold Bay. Dutch peace offers having been spurned, a revolution took place, and William of Orange (later WILLIAM III of England) took over from Jan de WITT, July, 1672. In 1673 Dutch received support of Spain, the emperor, Brandenburg, Denmark, and other powers, and England made peace 1674, but French victories on land (Maastricht, Seneff, Sinzheim, Cassel, Freiburg) under Louis II de CONDÉ and TURENNE and the 1676 naval campaign of Abraham Duquesne gained peace at Nijmegen (1678–79). Maastricht was ceded to Dutch, and French restrictive tariffs were modified in their favor. In subsequent treaty with Spain, France got Franche-Comté and chain of border fortresses in return for evacuating Spanish Netherlands. In treaty with the emperor (1679), France was confirmed in possession of Freiburg and part of Lorraine.

Dutch West India Company, trading and colonizing company, chartered by Dutch republic 1621, organized 1623. Founded NEW NETHERLAND (New York). Given trading rights on African coast between Tropic of Cancer and Cape of Good Hope, on American coast between Newfoundland and Straits of Magellan. Company had almost complete power in its territory.

Dutch West Indies: see NETHERLANDS WEST INDIES.

Dutton, Clarence Edward, 1841–1912, American geologist. He served in 1875 with John W. Powell on U.S. Geological Survey in the Rocky Mt. region. He introduced the term *isostasy,* and was a pioneer advocate of the isostatic theory (see CONTINENT).

Dutton, Joseph Everett, 1874–1905, English biologist. Working in Africa, he discovered (1901) the trypanosome of sleeping sickness in human blood and named it *Trypanosoma gambiense.*

Duun, Olav (ō'läv dōōn'), 1876–1939, Norwegian novelist, author of a monumental series, *The People of Juvik* (6 novels; 1918–23).

Duveen, Joseph, 1st Baron Duveen of Millbank, 1869–1939, English art dealer. Benefactor of many museums and galleries, notably the Natl. Gall. in London. Helped form several American art collections.

Duveneck, Frank (dū'vŭnĕk), 1848–1919, American portrait and genre painter, an inspired teacher.

Duvergier de Hauranne, Jean (zhä' düvĕrzhyä' dù ōrän'), 1581–1643, French theologian, one of the molders of JANSENISM. A friend of Cornelis Jansen and of the ARNAULD family, he helped make Port-Royal a Jansenist stronghold. He had trouble with the Jesuits and with Cardinal Richelieu, who had him imprisoned (1638–42).

du Vigneaud, Vincent (dū vēn'yō), 1901–, American biochemist, known for research including chemistry of insulin, biotin, sulphur-containing amino acids, and proteins. Won 1955 Nobel Prize in Chemistry for synthesizing two hormones of pituitary gland.

Duxbury, resort town (pop. 4,727), SE Mass., on Duxbury Bay and SE of Boston. Plymouth colonists including John Alden, Miles Standish, and William Brewster settled here. Alden's house still stands.

Dvina (dvēnä') or **Northern Dvina,** Rus. *Severnaya Dvina,* river, 455 mi. long, N European RSFSR, formed near Veliki Ustyug by two affluents. Flows NW, empties into White Sea below Archangel. Navigable May–Nov., it carries much commerce. Connected with the Volga-Baltic Waterway.

Dvina or **Western Dvina,** Lettish *Daugava,* Rus. *Zapadnaya Dvina,* river, 634 mi. long, E Europe, rising in Valdai Hills, RSFSR, and flowing W through Belorussia and Latvia into the Gulf of Riga of the Baltic Sea. Navigable from Vitebsk. Connected by canal with Berezina and Dnieper.

Dvorak, Anton (än'tôn dvôr'shäk), Czech *Antonín Dvořák,* 1841–1904, Czech composer. Much of his music is nationalistic in spirit and influenced by Brahms and Wagner. He is best known for his symphony in E Minor, *From the New World,* written while he was in the U.S., and for his Slavonic Dances. He wrote nine symphonies, chamber works, a violin concerto, a cello concerto, and overtures.

dwarf, a plant, animal, or person whose size is less than normal; proportions sometimes abnormal. Among humans, dwarfism seems to result from combination of genetic factors and endocrine malfunctions.

dwarf cornel: see BUNCHBERRY.

Dwiggins, W(illiam) A(ddison), 1880–1956, American type designer, calligrapher, and book designer. Gave type and book designing fresh boldness of advertising work. Designed clean, spare type faces (notably Electra and Caledonia) for linotype composition.

Dwight, Timothy, 1752–1817, American author and educator; grandson of Jonathan Edwards. An army chaplain in Revolutionary Army, he was later a Congregational pastor at Greenfield Hill, Conn. A famous preacher and writer of verse (one of CONNECTICUT WITS), he is perhaps better known as able president of Yale (1795–1817). His grandson **Theodore William Dwight,** 1822–92, headed Hamilton Col. law school, then was sole member of Columbia School of Law, later headed it. Another grandson of Timothy Dwight (1752–1817) was **Timothy Dwight,** 1828–1916, who helped to reorganize the Yale Divinity School and, as president of Yale (1886–98), helped change it from college to university.

Dy, chemical symbol of the element DYSPROSIUM.

Dybbuk [Heb.,= making cleave], in Jewish folklore a disembodied, naked soul which seeks residence in another being. Name of drama by AN-SKI.

Dyck, Sir Anthony van: see VAN DYCK, SIR ANTHONY.

dye, substance used to color materials. Natural dyes obtained from plants (e.g., alizarin), animals (e.g., COCHINEAL), minerals (e.g., OCHER) have been largely replaced by synthetic dyes. Most of these are prepared from coal tar, from aromatic hydrocarbons such as benzene (see also ANILINE) or anthracene. Some materials can be dyed directly, others require use of MORDANT. Dyes may be acid or basic. Vat dye is so named for the method of application. Method of attachment of dye to material it colors may be chemical reaction between dye and fibers or may be absorption of dye by fiber. Dyeing was practiced centuries ago by Chinese, Persians, and Indians.

Dyer, Mary, d. 1660, Quaker martyr in Mass., b. England. Banished, she returned to Boston twice to minister to imprisoned Quakers. Arrested both times, reprieved in 1659, but hanged in 1660.

Dyersburg, city (pop. 12,499), NW Tenn., near Mississippi R., NNE of Memphis; laid out 1825. Trade center for cotton and farm region.

Dyk, Viktor (vĭk'tôr dĭk), 1877–1931, Czech writer and nationalist. He considered his novels, plays, and poems weapons in struggle to free his country.

Dykh-Tau (dĭkh"-tou'), peak, 17,054 ft. high, USSR, in central Greater Caucasus.

Dykstra, Clarence Addison (dĭk'strù), 1883–1950, American educator, civic administrator. City manager of Cincinnati 1930–37. President of Univ. of Wisconsin 1937–45. Provost of Univ. of California at Los Angeles 1945–50.

dynamics, in engineering and physics, branch of mechanics concerned with the resultant motion of bodies under the influence of one or more forces. See also STATICS.

dynamite, explosive made from nitroglycerin and a porous substance; charge is set off by DETONATOR. It was discovered 1866 by A. B. NOBEL.

dynamo: see GENERATOR.

dyne (dīn), unit of force in centimeter-gram-second system producing an acceleration in a one-gram mass of one centimeter per second for each second the force acts.

dysentery, intestinal inflammation characterized by severe diarrhea. It usually results from swallowing certain microorganisms, parasitic worms, or irritating substances. Amoebic dysentery is caused by a protozoan; bacterial, by bacillus.

Dyson, Sir Frank Watson, 1868–1939, English astronomer royal of Scotland (1905–10) and of England (after 1910). As director (1910–33) of Greenwich Observatory he expanded research and inaugurated radio transmission of Greenwich time. His studies of solar eclipses confirmed (1919) Einstein's theory of effect of gravity on light.

dysphemia: see STUTTERING.

dysprosium (dĭsprō'shĕŭm), metallic element (symbol = Dy; see also ELEMENT, table) found in certain minerals with other metals of the RARE EARTHS. It is the most highly magnetic substance.

Dzaudzhikau: see ORDZHONIKIDZE.

Dzhambul (jŭmbōōl'), city (1965 est. pop. 148,000), S central Kazakh SSR, on Turkestan-Siberia RR. Food and chemical industries. Founded 7th cent. A.D.; passed to Russia 1864. Called Aulie-Ata until 1938.

Dzungaria (zōōn-gä'rēù), Chinese *Tien Shan Pei Lu,* region (c.300,000 sq. mi.; pop. c.2,000,000) of Sinkiang prov., China. Bounded by Tien Shan on S and Altai mts. on N. Agriculture and cattle raising are chief occupations. Region passed to Chinese control mid-18th cent. Dzungarian Ala-Tau mountain chain forms boundary between Sinkiang prov. and Kazakh SSR. Name also Jungaria, Sungaria, or Zungaria.

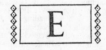

Ea (ā'ä), Sumerian water-god, widely known in Mesopotamia. Eridu was one center of his worship.

Ead-. For some Anglo-Saxon names beginning thus, see ED-; e.g., for Eadward, see EDWARD.

Eads, James Buchanan (ēdz), 1820–87, American engineer. He invented a diving bell (c.1841) to salvage wrecks in Mississippi; built fleet of Civil War ironclads, St. Louis steel-arch bridge, and system of jetties which made New Orleans an ocean port.

eagle, large diurnal predatory bird. Has keen vision, great strength and powers of flight. Related to kite, hawk, falcon; world-wide distribution. American or bald or white-headed eagle is U.S. emblem; other forms are southern and northern bald eagles, and golden or mountain eagle. Eagles eat fish, sometimes carrion. See *ill.,* p. 118.

Eagle Pass, city (pop. 12,094), W Texas, on Rio Grande R. opposite Piedras Negras, Mexico; laid out 1850 beside the border post Fort Duncan. Raises livestock, ships vegetables, and processes minerals. Linked by highway to Mexico city.

Eakins, Thomas (ā'kĭnz), 1844–1916, American painter and sculptor. Painted humble types and scenes of everyday world with uncompromising realism.

Ealing, London borough since 1965 (est. pop. 302,-385): includes former municipal boroughs of Acton, Ealing, and Southall.

Eames, Emma (āmz), 1865–1952, American soprano, b. China, of American parentage. Sang at the Metropolitan Opera, New York, 1891–1909. Among her famous roles were Aïda, Juliet, and Micaela.

Eames, Wilberforce (ēmz), 1855–1937, American bibliographer, long at New York Public Library, an expert on Americana and literature on Indians. Edited Vols. XV–XX of Sabin's *Dictionary of Books Relating to America.*

ear, organ of HEARING in mammals. External ear and auditory canal are separated by eardrum from middle ear which contains three bones (malleus, incus, stapes) and opens into EUSTACHIAN TUBE. Internal ear, labyrinth of temporal bone, contains three semicircular canals important for equilibrium. See *ill.,* p. 656.

Earhart, Amelia (âr'härt), 1897–1937, American aviator. First woman to fly Atlantic: as passenger in 1928, solo in 1932. Flew Honolulu to California, 1935. Lost in Pacific during 1937 round-the-world flight attempt. She married George Palmer Putnam in 1931.

Earle or **Earl, Ralph,** 1751–1801, American portrait and landscape painter, pupil of Benjamin West.

Early, Jubal Anderson, 1816–94, Confederate general. Prominent in battle of Chancellorsville and in Gettysburg campaign. In Wilderness campaign (1864), defeated David Hunter and Lew Wallace. Burned Chambersburg, Pa., for refusal of ransom. After defeats by P. H. Sheridan in 1864, and at Waynesboro in 1865, he was removed from command.

early man: see MAN, PRIMITIVE.

Earn, Loch (lŏkh' ûrn'), lake in Perthshire, Scotland. Ardvorlich House, on its shore, is Darlinvarach of

Scott's *Legend of Montrose*. Earn R. flows 46 mi. from the lake to estuary of the Tay.

Earp, Wyatt Berry Stapp, 1848–1920, law officer and notable gunfighter of the American West.

earth, fifth largest PLANET in the SOLAR SYSTEM and third from sun (average distance c.93,000,000 mi.). The earth rotates on its axis (which is perpendicular to plane of the equator) causing day and night. It revolves in an elliptical orbit about the sun in 365¼ days; this, with the fact that the axis is tipped 23½° to the plane of the orbit, causes change of seasons. The earth is slightly flattened at the poles, its equatorial diameter being c.7,926 mi. and polar diameter c.27 mi. less. Theory of isostasy postulates that the various segments of the earth's crust are in balance (see CONTINENT). Earth's age is estimated at from two to over four billion years. See *ills.*, pp. 311, 1017.

earthquake, trembling or shaking of earth's surface, commonly caused when rock masses slip along a FAULT. Other causes are violent volcanic activity and the collapse of roofs of caves. Seismic sea waves (erroneously called tidal waves) are caused by submarine earthquakes. See also SEISMOLOGY.

earthworm, segmented worm (phylum Annelida or Annulata) found over most of world except in deserts and cold regions; valuable to agriculture because it improves condition of soil. *Lumbricus terrestris* (common in Europe and the Americas) has no head but is sensitive to light and vibrations; it goes underground in winter, drought, and on bright days. Moves by circular and longitudinal muscles, aided by rows of bristles along sides; muscular gizzard grinds leaves and other food. Each individual produces both eggs and sperms; two worms exchange sperm cells and each worm secretes a cocoon (placed in ground) in which fertilization occurs and young develop.

earwig, popular name of rather small, mostly nocturnal insect of order Dermaptera, usually black or brown but in tropics some are brightly colored. Pincerlike organs are attached to end of abdomen. Metamorphosis is gradual. In temperate zones, they are often garden or household pests.

easement, right to make specified use of another's land, as distinguished from right to possess land. It is either a personal privilege which cannot be transferred without consent of the landowner (easement in gross), or a right attached to the land (servitude or easement appurtenant) which is transferred with sale or lease. Servitude by prescription comes from use of land for prescribed time without protest of owner; servitude by implication, from necessity of using another's land (as in drainage).

East Anglia (ăng'glĕŭ), kingdom of Anglo-Saxon England, comprising the modern counties of Norfolk and Suffolk. Settled in 5th cent. by Angles, it was one of most powerful kingdoms of late 6th cent. Became an underkingdom of MERCIA against which it later rebelled (825) to submit to Wessex. Danish invading army was quartered (865–66) in East Anglia and later conquered (869) the state entirely. Treaty of 886 made region a part of DANELAW. After 917 East Anglia was an earldom of England.

East Aurora, village (1966 pop. 6,796), W N.Y., SE of Buffalo. Elbert HUBBARD estab. Roycroft Shops here 1895.

East Avon: see AVON 2, river, England.

Eastbourne, county borough (pop. 60,897), Sussex East, England. Popular resort on the coast, the city is backed by the South Downs.

East Brooklyn, Conn.: see BROOKLYN, Conn.

East Cape, northeastern extremity of Asia, RSFSR, on Chukchi Peninsula and on Bering Strait. Official name (since 1898) is Cape Dezhnev, for Russian navigator who first reached it (1648).

East Chicago, city (pop. 57,669), extreme NW Ind., on L. Michigan, in Calumet industrial region; settled 1888. State's largest port. Has steel mfg. Indiana Harbor, its lake front, is connected with Grand Calumet R. by ship and barge canal (3 mi. long).

East China Sea or **Eastern Sea,** arm of Pacific Ocean, bounded partly by Japan, Ryukyu Isls., and China. Connected with South China Sea by Formosa Strait; opens N into Yellow Sea.

East Cleveland, city (pop. 37,991), NE Ohio, within confines of Cleveland. Nela Park, seat of General Electric's experimental laboratories, is here.

East Detroit, city (pop. 45,756), SE Mich., a suburb NE of Detroit; settled 1827.

Easter, chief Christian feast, anniversary of resurrection of Jesus Christ. Falls between March 22 and April 25 inclusive (see CALENDAR), following LENT and HOLY WEEK. Roman Catholics must perform "Easter duty" (i.e., they must receive communion at some time between Ash Wednesday and Trinity Sunday). Eastern churches have long had a different date for Easter since they do not use the Gregorian calendar.

Easter Island, island (c.64 sq. mi.; pop. c.850), in Pacific c.2,350 mi. W of Chile, to which it belongs. Has long been known for indecipherable petroglyphs and enormous stone figures whose origin is much disputed.

Eastern Empire: see ROME; BYZANTINE EMPIRE.

Eastern Ghats: see GHATS.

Eastern Question, the European problem presented by the decline and disintegration of the OTTOMAN EMPIRE after c.1700. Western powers, notably England and Prussia, took alarm at Russian expansion in RUSSO-TURKISH WARS of 18th cent. Austro-Russian plan to partition Turkey (with Constantinople and DARDANELLES going to Russia) was thwarted, but Turkish disintegration continued in 19th cent. with rise of independent Balkan states. Russian setbacks in CRIMEAN WAR (1853–56) and at Congress of BERLIN (1878) did not stop Russian influence in Balkans. Russian interference and encouragement of pan-Slavism clashed with Austro-German imperialism in East (*Drang nach Osten*), nearly caused war in crisis over BOSNIA AND HERCEGOVINA, was a major factor leading to First World War. See also KUCHUK-KAINARJI, TREATY OF; ADRIANOPLE, TREATY OF; SAN STEFANO, TREATY OF; and articles on Balkan countries.

Eastern Rumelia: see RUMELIA.

Eastern Sea: see EAST CHINA SEA.

Eastern Turkistan: see SINKIANG, China.

East Falmouth, Mass.: see FALMOUTH.

East Flanders, province (1,147 sq. mi.; est. pop. 1,-289,011), NW Belgium; cap. GHENT. Fertile soil; textile mfg. Population is mostly Flemish-speaking. For history, see FLANDERS.

East Friesland (frēz'lŭnd), region, extreme NW Germany, separated from Netherlands by the Dollart (estuary of Ems R.); chief city Emden. Region includes E FRISIAN ISLANDS, in North Sea. Became county of Holy Roman Empire 1454; duchy 1654; passed to Prussia 1744; to Hanover 1815.

East Galloway, county, Scotland: see KIRKCUDBRIGHTSHIRE.

East Grand Rapids, city (pop. 10,924), SW Mich., SSE of Grand Rapids; settled 1835.

East Haddam, resort town (pop. 3,637), S Conn., on Connecticut R.; settled c.1670. Hero Nathan Hale taught school here. Includes Moodus village (pop. 1,103).

East Ham, London: see NEWHAM.

Eastham, resort town (pop. 1,200), SE Mass., on Cape Cod between Orleans and Wellfleet; settled 1644 from Plymouth. Cape Cod Natl. Seashore hq. are here.

East Hampton, resort and residential village (pop. 1,772), SE N.Y., on E Long Isl., ENE of Southampton; settled 1648. John H. Payne house is here.

Easthampton, industrial town (pop. 12,326), W Mass., NW of Springfield; settled 1664.

East Hartford, town (pop. 43,977), central Conn., on Connecticut R. opposite Hartford; settled c.1640. Tobacco growing, aircraft mfg.

SMALL CAPITALS = cross references. Pronunciation key on inside end pages. Abbreviations: p. 2.

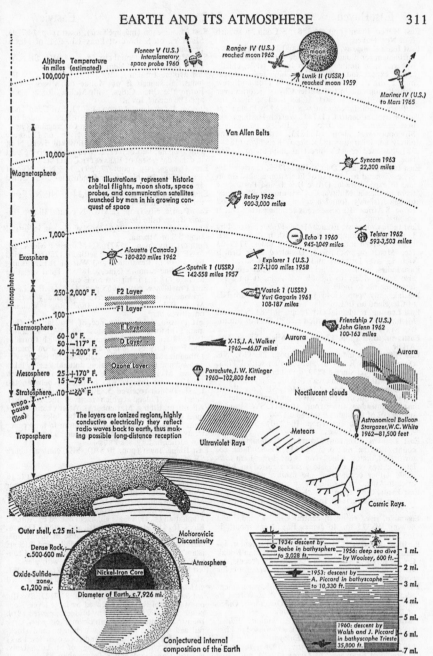

Altitude in miles   Temperature (estimated)

Pioneer V (U.S.) interplanetary space probe 1960

Ranger IV (U.S.) reached moon 1962

moon

Lunik II (USSR) reached moon 1959

Mariner IV (U.S.) to Mars 1965

100,000

10,000

Van Allen Belts

Magnetosphere

The illustrations represent historic orbital flights, moon shots, space probes, and communication satellites launched by man in his growing conquest of space

Syncom 1963 22,300 miles

Relay 1962 900-3,000 miles

1,000

Echo 1 1960 945-1,049 miles

Telstar 1962 593-3,503 miles

Exosphere

Alouette (Canada) 180-820 miles 1962

Explorer 1 (U.S.) 217-1,100 miles 1958

Sputnik 1 (USSR) 142-558 miles 1957

Ionosphere

250   2,000° F.   F2 Layer

Vostok 1 (USSR) Yuri Gagarin 1961 108-187 miles

100   F1 Layer

Thermosphere

Friendship 7 (U.S.) John Glenn 1962 100-163 miles

60   0° F.   E Layer

50   –117° F.   D Layer

40   +200° F.

X-15, J. A. Walker 1962—46.07 miles

Aurora

Aurora

Ozone Layer

Mesosphere

25   +170° F.

15   –75° F.

Parachute, J. W. Kittinger 1960—102,800 feet

Stratosphere   10   –80° F.

Noctilucent clouds

tropo-pause (line)

The layers are ionized regions, highly conductive electrically; they reflect radio waves back to earth, thus making possible long-distance reception

Astronomical Balloon Stargazer, W.C. White 1962—81,500 feet

Troposphere

Meteors

Ultraviolet Rays

Cosmic Rays.

Outer shell, c.25 mi.

Mohorovicic Discontinuity

Dense Rock, c.500-600 mi.

Atmosphere

Oxide-Sulfide zone, c.1,200 mi.

Nickel-Iron Core

Diameter of Earth, c.7,926 mi.

Conjectured internal composition of the Earth

1934: descent by Beebe in bathysphere to 3,028 ft.

1956: deep sea dive by Woolsey, 600 ft.   1 ml.

2 ml.

1953: descent by A. Piccard in bathyscaphe to 10,330 ft.   3 ml.

4 ml.

5 ml.

1960: descent by Walsh and J. Piccard in bathyscaphe Trieste 35,800 ft.   6 ml.

7 ml.

Scientific and military explorations have pierced through all levels of the atmosphere and the depths of the oceans. With the development of high-altitude rockets and man-made satellites, exploration of outer space has begun.

East Haven, town (pop. 21,388), S Conn., a suburb E of New Haven.

East India Company, British, 1600–1874, chartered by Parliament for monopoly of trade with Eastern Hemisphere. Soon limited itself to Indian trade, chiefly textile export and, after 1715, China tea. Amalgamated with its leading competitor in 1708 and grew virtually supreme in India after Clive's victories over French rivals (1748–60). It acquired territory for military establishments and was placed by Parliament under cabinet control (1774). Warren Hastings was first governor general of the Indian possessions. Monopoly was abolished 1813; activities became purely administrative 1833. Sepoy Rebellion (1857–58), hastened crown's direct assumption of Indian rule.

East India Company, Dutch, 1602–1798, chartered by States-General to aid war of liberation against Spain and to expand trade. Drove British and Portuguese from Indonesia, Malaya, Ceylon; monopolized trade of Spice Islands; founded colony at Cape of Good Hope (S Africa). Its possessions became part of Dutch colonial empire.

East India Company, French, 1664–1769, chartered by Louis XIV to compete with British trade in India. Briefly merged into Compagnie des Indes, 1719–23 (see MISSISSIPPI SCHEME). Dissolved after British victories over DUPLEIX and LALLY (1748–60).

East Indies, name used primarily for Indonesia, but also more widely to include SE Asia. It once referred mainly to India.

Eastlake, city (pop. 12,467), NE Ohio, a suburb NE of Cleveland on L. Erie.

East Lansing, residential city (pop. 30,198), S central Mich., NE of Lansing; settled c.1850. Seat of MICHIGAN STATE UNIVERSITY.

Eastlawn, town (pop. 17,652), SE Mich., SE of Ann Arbor.

East Liverpool, industrial city (pop. 22,306), NE Ohio, on Ohio R., N of Steubenville; settled 1798. Ceramics center since c.1839, it makes pottery, brick, and tile with clay from area's deposits.

East London, city (pop. c.116,056), SE Cape Prov., Republic of South Africa. River port, mfg. center.

East Longmeadow, town (pop. 10,294), SW Mass., a suburb SE of Springfield; settled c.1740.

East Los Angeles, city (pop. 104,270), S Calif., a suburb E of Los Angeles.

East Lothian (lŏ'dhĕŭn), formerly **Haddingtonshire,** county (267 sq. mi.; pop. 52,653), SE Scotland; co. town Haddington. Chief river is the Tyne. Rich lowlands extensively cultivated; sheep raised in highlands. Other occupations are fishing, coal mining, brick making, and distilling.

East Lyme, town (pop. 6,782), SE Conn., W of New London; settled c.1660. Includes Niantic village (pop. 2,788).

Eastmain, river rising in central Que., Canada, and flowing W 375 mi. to James Bay. Near mouth is 1685 Hudson's Bay Co. post.

Eastman, George, 1854–1932, American inventor, industrialist, philanthropist, founder of Eastman Kodak Co. He invented a dry-plate photographic process, devised roll film, Kodak camera, and a process for color photography.

Eastman, Joseph Bartlett, 1882–1944, U.S. government administrator. Appointed (1919) by Pres. Wilson to Interstate Commerce Commission. Director of Office of Defense Transportation (1941–44).

Eastman, Max, 1883–, American author. Edited (1913–17) the *Masses* until it was suppressed in First World War. Works include *Enjoyment of Poetry* (1913), *Enjoyment of Laughter* (1936), the autobiographical *Enjoyment of Living* (1948), and *Love and Revolution: My Journey Through an Epoch* (1965).

Eastman School of Music: see ROCHESTER, THE UNIVERSITY OF.

East Massapequa (măsŭpē'kwŭ), town (pop. 14,779), SE N.Y., on S shore of Long Isl., ESE of Massapequa.

East Meadow, residential city (pop. 46,036), SE N.Y., on W Long Isl., E of Hempstead.

East Moline (mōlēn'), city (pop. 16,732), NW Ill., industrial suburb E of Moline on Mississippi R. Forms the Quad Cities, with Moline, Rock Island, and Davenport, Iowa.

Easton. 1 Rural town (pop. 3,407), SW Conn., NW of Bridgeport; settled c.1757. Jesse Lee founded one of New England's first Methodist congregations here. **2** Industrial city (pop. 31,955), E Pa., on Delaware R. near mouths of Lehigh and Bushkill rivers, N of Philadelphia; laid out 1752. Was coal-receiving port in canal days. Seat of LAFAYETTE COLLEGE.

East Orange, city (pop. 77,259), NE N.J., NW of Jersey City, in shipping and industrial area; settled 1678. Upsala Col. is here.

East Paterson, borough (pop. 19,344), NE N.J., suburb SE of Paterson.

East Peoria, city (pop. 12,310), N central Ill., on Illinois R. opposite Peoria.

East Point, city (pop. 35,633), NW Ga., an industrial suburb S of Atlanta.

Eastport, city (pop. 2,537), SE Maine, on Moose Isl. in SE Passamaquoddy Bay; settled c.1780. Occupied by British in Revolution and War of 1812. Fishing and sardine canning (since c.1875). Tidal variation average (18 ft.) is highest on E coast.

East Providence, city (1965 pop. 44,828), E R.I., on Providence and Seekonk rivers. Originally part of Mass., it became R.I. town 1862. Roger Williams once lived here.

East Prussia, former province of Prussia, NE Germany; historic cap. KÖNIGSBERG. Was separated 1919–39 from rest of Germany by Polish Corridor and Free City of Danzig and bordered on Poland, Lithuania, Memel, and the Baltic Sea. It is a heavily wooded and largely agr. region, dotted by many lakes (as in MASURIA). At the POTSDAM CONFERENCE (1945), East Prussia was partitioned between the USSR (which received 5,830 sq. mi., incl. Königsberg) and Poland (which received the rest, incl. Allenstein, Elbing, Marienburg). After evacuation of most Germans, territory resettled by Poles and Russians. Transfers, subject to ratification in final peace treaty with Germany, are not considered final by U.S. For earlier history, see PRUSSIA.

East Ridge, town (pop. 19,570), SE Tenn., a suburb SE of Chattanooga.

East Riding: see YORKSHIRE, England.

East River, New York city, navigable tidal strait (c.16 mi. long and 600–4,000 ft. wide) connecting Upper New York Bay with Long Isl. Sound and separating Manhattan and the Bronx from Brooklyn and Queens. Connected with Hudson R. by Harlem R. at N end of Manhattan Isl. Hell Gate channel (named by Adriaen Block 1614), between Wards Isl. and Astoria, Queens, was long dangerous to ships because of strong tidal currents and rocks. Welfare, Randalls, and Rickers islands are in it. Crossed by many bridges and tunnels (subway, rail, vehicular). Lined with piers.

East Rockaway, residential village (1965 pop. 11,708), SE N.Y., on SW Long Isl. SSE of Lynbrook; settled c.1688.

East Saint Louis (lōo'ĭs), city (pop. 81,712), SW Ill., on Mississippi R. (here checked by large levees) opposite St. Louis (connected by bridges); platted 1816. Industrial center and livestock market, with large railroad yards and shops, warehouses, and stockyards. Area has coal mines and rock quarries. Parks Col. of Aeronautical Technology of St. Louis Univ. is here. Cahokia Mounds (more than 85, many of which have been excavated) are NE.

Eastview, town (pop. 24,555), SE Ont., Canada, on Rideau and Ottawa rivers. Industrial suburb of Ottawa.

SMALL CAPITALS = cross references. Pronunciation key on inside end pages. Abbreviations: p. 2.

East Whittier, town (pop. 19,884), S Calif., a suburb E of Los Angeles.

East Windsor, town (pop. 7,500), N Conn., on Connecticut R. above Hartford, in farm area. Elder Jonathan Edwards born here. Includes villages of Broad Brook (pop. 1,389) and Warehouse Point (pop. 1,936).

Eaton, Dorman Bridgman, 1823–99, American reformer. Drafted Metropolitan Health Law creating New York city's health dept. (1866) and Pendleton Act of 18883, still basis of federal civil service system.

Eaton, John Henry, 1790–1856, U.S. Senator from Tenn. (1818–29), Secretary of War (1829–31). Social snubbing of his second wife (see Margaret O'NEILL) helped disrupt Pres. Jackson's cabinet.

Eaton, Theophilus, 1590–1658, Puritan leader in Conn., b. England. Founded New Haven (1637–38) with John DAVENPORT. Governed colony there.

Eaton, William, 1764–1811, U.S. Army officer, celebrated for exploit in Tripolitan War. Devised plan to win war against Tripoli by supporting claimant to rule of Tripoli. Set off on long overland march with small band to take Tripoli from rear. War ended with truce (1805) before he arrived.

Eaton Rapids, city (pop. 4,052), S central Mich., on Grand R., SSW of Lansing, in sheep-raising area; settled 1837. National home for children of Veterans of Foreign Wars is nearby.

Eatontown, borough (pop. 10,334), E central N.J., SSE of Red Bank; settled 1670.

Eau Claire (ō′ klâr′), city (pop. 37,987), W central Wis., WSW of Wausau on Chippewa R. at mouth of Eau Claire R. Built on site of 18th-cent. trading post, it developed with lumbering. Now farm trade center in dairy area. Has varied manufactures. Branch of Wisconsin State Univ. is here.

Eau Gallie (ō gă′lē), city (pop. 12,300), central Fla., N of Melbourne on Indian River (lagoon); settled 1860.

Ebal, Mount (ē′–), central Palestine. Hebrews were cursed here for violating God's commands. Joshua built altar and monument inscribed with Mosaic law. Deut. 11.29; 27.4,13; Joshua 8.30–33.

Eber (ē′bùr), variant of HEBER.

Eberhart, Richard, 1904–, American poet. Varied in type and subject, his verse is markedly direct. His best work is in *Selected Poems, 1930–1965* (1966), and *Collected Verse Plays* (1962).

Ebert, Friedrich (frē′drĭkh ā′bùrt), 1871–1925, first president of the German republic (1919–25); a Social Democrat. Suppressed Spartacists and Kapp putsch.

Eberth, Karl, 1835–1926, German bacteriologist, anatomist. Noted the association of a bacillus with typhoid fever. Group of bacteria which includes this organism is called *Eberthella.*

Ebner-Eschenbach, Marie, Baronin von (märē′ bärō′nĭn fûn āb′nùr-ĕsh′ùnbäkh), 1830–1916, Austrian author. Her *Novellen,* famed for "poetic realism," include *The Two Countesses* (1885; Eng. tr., 1893), *The Child of the Parish* (1887; Eng. tr., 1893), and the dog story *Krambambuli* (1894; Eng. tr., 1913–15).

Éboli, Ana de Mendoza de la Cerda, princesa de (ä′nä dä mändō′thä dä lä thâr′dä, ā′bōlē), 1540–92, Spanish noblewoman. Though she supposedly had lost an eye when a girl, she was a beautiful and accomplished woman. A member of the court of Philip II, she was in love with Antonio PÉREZ. Shared Pérez's disgrace after murder of Escobedo. Spent years after 1579 in prison and enforced retirement.

ebony, handsome, dark heartwood of several tropical trees, especially of persimmon genus. Used for ornaments, tableware, inlay, piano keys.

Eboracum: see YORK, England.

Ebro (ē′brō, ā′brō), river, c.575 mi. long, NE Spain, flowing from Cantabrian Mts. SE, along foot of Pyrenees, past Saragossa, to Mediterranean. Irrigation canals; hydroelectric plants.

Eça de Queiroz, José Maria (zhōōzā′ mùrē′ù ā′sù dù kārôsh′), 1846?–1900, realistic Portuguese novelist, author of *A ilustre casa de Ramires* (1900), and *A cidade e as serras* (1901).

Ecbatana (ĕkbă′tùnù, –bùtä′nù), cap. of anc. Media, at the foot of Mt. Elvend. Later the summer residence of Persian and Parthian kings. Modern Hamadan is on the site.

eccentric, in mechanics, device by which rotary motion in one part of machine becomes longitudinal motion in another part. Cam is similarly used.

Eccles, Sir John Carew, 1903–, Australian neurophysiologist. Shared 1963 Nobel Prize in Physiology and Medicine for explanation of how messages travel over the body's nerve network.

Ecclesiastes (ĕklē″zēäs′tēz), book of Old Testament. In ancient times ascribed to Solomon. A philosophical essay, somewhat cynical in tone, it opens with theme that "all is vanity" and continues with passages in praise of wisdom and mercy. Book is example of wisdom literature (see WISDOM).

Ecclesiasticus, in Western canon, book of Old Testament; placed in Apocrypha in AV. Called also Wisdom of Jesus the Son of Sirach. Theme of book is the excellence of wisdom. Among well-known passages: praise of wisdom and protest against determinism (14.20–15.20); praise of God for works of nature (43); praise of famous men who added to Israel's glory (44–50). Example of wisdom literature (see WISDOM).

Echegaray, José (hōsā′ āchägärī′), 1832–1916, Spanish dramatist, a mathematician and economist. A common theme in his romantic realistic dramas is the clash of honor and duty. Well known are *O locura o santidad* (1876), *El hijo de don Juan* (1892), *El gran Galeoto* (1881). Shared with Mistral 1904 Nobel Prize in Literature.

Echeverría, Esteban (ästā′vän ā″chävĕrē′ä), 1805–51, Argentine romantic poet, prose writer, and revolutionary propagandist against dictator Rosas.

echidna or **spiny anteater** (ùkĭd′nù), clumsy, spiny mammal of monotreme order, with long, wormlike, extensible tongue for feeding on ants. Found in Australia, New Guinea, Tasmania. There are two genera, *Echidna* and *Zaglossus.*

echinoderm (ĭkī′nùdûrm, ĕ′kĭnù–), invertebrate marine animal of phylum Echinodermata, having a calcareous, often spiny, outer skeleton and tube feet controlled by a water-vascular system. Many forms have five or more arms. Examples of the group are STARFISH, SEA URCHIN, CRINOID.

Echmiadzin (ĕchmēädzēn′), town (1959 pop. 19,700), central Armenian SSR, W of Erivan. Dates from 6th cent. B.C.; cap. of Armenia 2d–4th cent. A.D. Called Vagarshapat until 1945. The nearby monastery, seat of the catholicos (head) of the Armenian Church, is famous for its gardens and its cathedral (traditionally dated from 4th cent.).

Echo, in Greek mythology, mountain nymph who helped Zeus in a love affair by distracting Hera with her chatter. As penalty, she could only repeat last words of someone else. In unrequited love for Narcissus, she pined away into nothing but her voice.

echo, phenomenon caused by reflection of sound waves. When wave strikes a reflecting surface, it is partly absorbed and partly reflected. When echo is reflected again and again from different surfaces the effect is called reverberation.

Eck, Johann Maier von (yō′hän mī′ùr fūnĕk′), 1486–1543, German Catholic apologist. Disputed with Martin Luther at Leipzig (1519).

Eckermann, Johann Peter (yōhän′ pā′tùr ĕ′kùrmän), 1792–1854, German scholar and author, long a secretary to Goethe. He wrote *Conversations with Goethe* (1836–48), a subjective if invaluable key to Goethe's thought.

Eckhart, Meister (mīs′tùr ĕk′härt), c.1260–c.1328, German mystical theologian. A Dominican, he awoke 14th-cent. mystical movement in Germany. He was accused of connection with the Beghards, and Pope

John XXII condemned 17 of his propositions as heretical (1329).

Eclectic school, in painting: see CARRACCI.

eclipse (ĕklīps', ĭ–), in astronomy, partial or complete obscuring of one heavenly body by another. Spherical opaque bodies cast cone-shaped shadows away from sun; when one opaque body shining by reflected light lies in shadow of another, it is eclipsed. Lunar eclipse occurs when the moon is in such a position that it is wholly or partly in the earth's shadow; it is visible from all parts of earth's surface where moon is above horizon. Maximum possible duration of a lunar eclipse c.4 hr.; maximum period of totality c.1 hr. 42 min. Solar eclipse occurs when the moon passes between the earth and the sun so that its shadow falls upon the earth; it is visible only from that part of the earth on which the moon's small shadow falls. Solar eclipse occurs only if moon and earth are close enough for moon's relatively short shadow to reach earth; it is visible at different moments at different points as moon's shadow moves eastward across face of earth. Total solar eclipse is visible about once in 400 years from any one place; maximum possible duration 7 min. 30 sec. at equator when sun is directly overhead; duration decreases as latitude increases. In true shadow (umbra), all direct sun rays are cut off; in surrounding partial shadow (penumbra) there is illumination from part of sun's face. If apex of moon's cone-shaped umbra does not reach earth, annular (ring) eclipse is observable from region on earth directly beyond apex of umbra. During total solar eclipse moon appears as dark object moving across face of sun, daylight fades, temperature drops. At totality sun's corona and prominences glow around black disk of moon. Nearly similar solar eclipses occur in cycles of c.18 years. Also important in astronomy are eclipses of Jupiter's satellites. See *ill.,* p. 1017.

ecliptic (ĕklĭp'tĭk, ĭ–), great circle in heavens which marks sun's apparent yearly course, actually the path of earth's revolution about sun. Obliquity of the ecliptic, the cause of changing seasons, is inclination at c.23.5° angle of plane of ecliptic (earth's orbit) to plane of celestial equator (imaginary extension of equator into sky).

Ecnomus, Cape: see LICATA, Sicily.

École des Beaux-Arts (ākôl' dā bōzär'), French national school of fine arts in Paris, founded 1648 by Charles Le Brun. Has three departments: painting and graphic arts, sculpture, and architecture. Free to those who pass entrance examination. Prepares students to compete for PRIX DE ROME.

ecology, scientific study of plants and animals in relation to environmental conditions, e.g., temperature, soil, light, wind, and moisture. It is also concerned with interrelations in plant and animal communities, and stages (succession) leading to final development (known as climax community or area) for a particular region. Ecology as a social science (relation of man to natural environment) developed in 20th cent.

econometrics, technique of economic analysis combining economic theory with statistical and mathematical analysis in an attempt to develop accurate economic forecasting and planning.

Economic Cooperation Administration: see EUROPEAN RECOVERY PROGRAM.

economic planning, control and direction of economic activity by a public authority, usually the state. It was practiced in various forms by governments in Egypt, Greece, and Rome, and, through guilds, in the Middle Ages. Economic management is key tenet of socialism, COMMUNISM, and fascism, but all governments have some degree of economic planning (e.g., public works). The EUROPEAN COMMUNITY organizations are attempts at economic planning on an international scale.

economics, study of the supplying of man's physical needs. It took form with growth of commerce which began in 16th cent. and gave rise to MERCANTILISM. The 18th-cent. PHYSIOCRATS advocated LAISSEZ FAIRE —allowing business to follow freely the "natural laws" of economics. The effect on economic theory of INDUSTRIAL REVOLUTION was reflected by Adam SMITH, advocate (1766) of free trade and the division of labor, and RICARDO, with his theory of diminishing returns. Early socialists, such as Saint-Simon, Proudhon, and Fourier, attacked belief in necessity of private property and competition. *Das Kapital,* by Karl Marx, appeared as the major work in socialist economics. In 20th cent. work of KEYNES has had profound influence on understanding of business cycle and on fiscal and monetary policies.

Economy, Pa.: see AMBRIDGE, Pa.; HARMONY SOCIETY.

Ecorse (ĕkôrs'), industrial city (pop. 17,328), SE Mich., on Detroit R., S of Detroit; settled c.1815.

Écrins, Barre des, France: see BARRE DES ÉCRINS.

ECSC: see EUROPEAN COAL AND STEEL COMMUNITY.

Ecuador (ĕ'kwŭdôr) [Span.,= Equator, which traverses the country], republic (108,478 sq. mi.; 1962 est. pop. 4,585,472), W South America, on Pacific; cap. QUITO. Two ranges of Andes cross the country. Many active volcanoes (including Chimborazo and Cotopaxi) and frequent earthquakes cause much damage. The highlands, with fertile intermontane valleys, support the main bulk of the population (in which the percentage of sedentary agr. Indians is high). E of the Andes is a largely unexplored wilderness of plains and rain forest, sparsely populated by "wild" Indians. W of the Andes is the hot, humid Pacific coast. Bananas, coffee, and cacao are main products. GUAYAQUIL is principal port. Francisco Pizarro sent Benalcázar into the region in 1533 to forestall Pedro de Alvarado. Unimportant in the colonial period (when it was the presidency of Quito), it was liberated from Spain by Sucre in the victory at Pichincha (1822) and was incorporated into Bolívar's republic of Greater Colombia. On dissolution of that union Ecuador became a separate republic (1830). In 1832 Ecuador gained the Galápagos Isls. A recurrent border dispute with Peru has still not been settled. The period of political stability from 1948 to 1961 was disrupted by successive military coups until 1966 when Otto Arosemena Gómez was chosen provisional president and pledged to restore democratic government.

ecumenical council: see COUNCIL, ECUMENICAL.

ecumenical movement (ĕ"kūmĕ'nĭkŭl, ĕ"–), term for a movement aimed at the unification or reunion of the Protestant churches of the world and ultimately of all Christians. The Evangelical Alliance (1846) was an early attempt in this direction, and the Federal Council of Churches of Christ (U.S.) was estab. 1908. Several world-unity conferences have been held (e.g., first meeting of the WORLD COUNCIL OF CHURCHES, 1948). The World Council of Churches is the chief instrument of ecumenicity, bringing together more than 200 Protestant, Eastern Orthodox, and Old Catholic bodies. In the U.S. progress has been made in consolidating branches within Protestant denominations (e.g. among Methodists, Lutherans, Congregationalists, and Reformed churches). Since the opening of the Second Vatican Council, the Roman Catholic Church has been increasingly involved in the quest for the reunion of all Christians.

Edam (ē'dŭm, Dutch ādäm'), town (pop. 15,946), North Holland prov., NW Netherlands, on the Ijsselmeer. Important market for famous Edam cheese.

Edda (ē'dŭ), title of two works in old Icelandic. Edda of Snorri Sturluson or *Prose Edda* was intended as a guide to scaldic poetry, has rules of that poetry as well as much mythology. *Poetic Edda,* also called Elder Edda (though compiled later) is a collection of 33 or 34 heroic lays (incomplete).

Eddington, Sir Arthur Stanley, 1882–1944, British astronomer, physicist. Contributed to study of evolution, motion, and internal constitution of stars. He was a leading exponent of the theory of relativity and a prolific author of scientific works.

Eddy, Mary Baker, 1821–1910, discoverer of principles of CHRISTIAN SCIENCE, and founder of the church based on them. In frail health from childhood, she was interested in the problem of health and faith and formulated doctrine and system which became Christian Science, dating from 1866. Her *Science and Health* appeared 1875. In 1877 she married Asa Gilbert Eddy. She planned *Manual* for conduct of church and all details of its upbuilding, and was pastor of Mother Church, Boston.

Eddystone (ĕ'dĭstŭn), lighthouse, on dangerous rocks off coast of Cornwall, England. First light here built 1696. Present structure (built 1878–82) fourth lighthouse at site.

edelweiss (ā'dŭlvīs), low-growing perennial (*Leontopodium alpinum*) of high Alps. Its small yellow flower heads are surrounded by woolly-white bracts.

edema (ŭdē'mŭ), accumulation of liquid in the tissues, frequently resulting in swelling. Caused by changes in the composition of body fluids, disorders of the blood or lymph vessels, or various heart diseases. Also called dropsy.

Eden, (Robert) Anthony, 1897–, British foreign minister. Became noted for support of League of Nations 1934–35. Foreign minister 1935–38, he resigned in opposition to Neville Chamberlain's "appeasement" of Axis. As foreign minister in Churchill's war cabinet (1940–45) during alliance of Great Britain, USSR, and U.S. On fall of Labour government (1951) he again became foreign secretary. Succeeded Churchill as prime minister (1955). Eden's policy on the Suez Canal was unsuccessful; ill-health forced his retirement in 1957. Was created earl of Avon in 1961.

Eden, name of several rivers in England and Scotland. Principal one flows 65 mi. NW from Westmorland, England, into Solway Firth.

Eden, Garden of, in Bible, first home of man. God created the garden, with its trees of knowledge and of life, as home for Adam and Eve, until, eating of forbidden fruit, they were banished. Gen. 2; 3. In Babylonia there was legend of a holy place with tree of life inhabited by a god and goddess.

Edenhall, village, Cumberland, England, on Eden R. Family seat of Musgraves, whose luck (according to legend) depended on keeping unbroken an enameled goblet taken from the fairies near St. Cuthbert's Well; basis of Longfellow's "Luck of Edenhall."

Edenton (ē'dŭntŭn), town (pop. 4,458), NE N.C., SW of Elizabeth City on Albemarle Sound. One of state's oldest towns. Townswomen had "Edenton Tea Party," boycotting English goods 1774. Historic buildings include old courthouse (1767) and St. Paul's Church (1736).

Ederle, Gertrude, (ā'dŭrlē), 1906–, American swimmer. First woman to swim English Channel (1926).

Edessa (ĭdĕ'sŭ), anc. city of Mesopotamia, modern URFA, Turkey. Center of a kingdom, later a Roman city, it was under Byzantine Empire a religious center. Fell to Arabs 639; captured by Crusaders 1097. BALDWIN I was count of Edessa before becoming king. City fell to Moslems in 1144.

Edgar or **Eadgar** (ĕd'gŭr), 943?–975, king of England (959–75). With a reign of orderly prosperity he won title of the Peaceful. He initiated widespread monastic reforms and granted practical autonomy to the Danes in England (see DANELAW) in return for their loyalty. Political unity ended with his death.

Edgar Atheling (ā'thŭlĭng), 1060?–1125?, English prince. Chosen to succeed to throne on Harold's death, but submitted (1067) to WILLIAM I. Fled to Scotland, and, after unsuccessful uprising (1069), he later settled in France. He led (1097) English expedition which dethroned Donald III and seated Atheling's nephew Edgar on Scottish throne.

Edgartown, resort town (pop. 1,474), SE Mass., on E Martha's Vineyard; settled 1642. Former prosperous whaling center.

Edgehill or **Edge Hill,** ridge on border of Warwickshire and Oxfordshire, England. Scene (1642) of first great battle of the civil war.

Edgemere, Md.: see SPARROWS POINT.

Edgeworth, Maria, 1767–1849, Irish novelist. Wrote realistic novels of Ireland, notably *Castle Rackrent* (1800), *Belinda* (1801), *The Absentee* (1812), *Ormond* (1817). Also wrote children's stories.

Edina (ĕdī'nŭ), village (1965 pop. 33,302), E Minn., a suburb SW of Minneapolis.

Edinburg, city (pop. 18,706), extreme S Texas, WNW of Brownsville, in lower Rio Grande valley. Processes meat, citrus fruit, vegetables, cotton.

Edinburgh, Philip Mountbatten, duke of (ĕ'dĭnbŭrŭ), 1921–, husband of ELIZABETH II of Great Britain. Descended from kings of Greece, Denmark, and England, he became a British citizen before his marriage in 1947. Served in British navy in Second World War.

Edinburgh (ĕ'dĭnbŭrŭ), independent burgh (pop. 468,-378), cap. of Scotland and co. town of Midlothian, near Firth of Forth. Often referred to in literature as Dunedin, it has nickname of "Auld Reekie." City is built on a series of ridges. Became burgh 1329 and capital 1437. City lost importance after English and Scottish crowns were united in 1603. After Act of Union 1707 Parliament House, now seat of Supreme Law Courts, ceased to be meeting place of national assemblies. Noteworthy are HOLYROOD palace, Norman Chapel of St. Margaret, the cathedral, Royal Botanic Gardens, and Princes St. There are several art museums, and Natl. Library has valuable manuscripts. Univ. of Edinburgh (1583) has noted medical school. City developed as center of learning and literature in 18th and early 19th cent. (*Edinburgh Review* founded 1802) and is associated with many famous men of learning. Industries—engineering, tanning, making of machine tools, chemicals and biscuits—are mostly in suburbs. Leith is city's port. Edinburgh Internatl. Festival of Music and Drama held here every summer.

Edinburghshire, county, Scotland: see MIDLOTHIAN.

Edirne, Turkey: see ADRIANOPLE.

Edison, Thomas A(lva), 1847–1931, American inventor. His early inventions include a transmitter and receiver for automatic telegraph, a system of transmitting four simultaneous messages, and an improved stock-ticker system. He invented a carbon telephone transmitter and the first successful phonograph. In 1879 he produced the first commercially practical incandescent lamp; developed complete system of electricity distribution for use with it. Later (1881–82) he developed first central electric-light power plant in world. Edison demonstrated synchronization of moving pictures and sound; produced superior storage battery; developed kinetoscope; built and ran experimental electric railroad. He held over 1,300 patents. His son. **Charles Edison,** 1890–, was U.S. Secretary of the Navy (1939–40) and governor of N.J. (1941–44).

Edisto (ĕ'dĭstō), river rising in W central S.C. and flowing c.90 mi. SE and S to the Atlantic, separating near ocean into two channels which form Edisto Isl.

Edman, Irwin, 1896–1954, American philosopher; teacher at Columbia after 1918. Achieved wide popularity, particularly in the field of aesthetics. His works include *Philosopher's Holiday* (1938) and *Philosopher's Quest* (1947).

Edmonds, Walter D(umaux), 1903–, American author of historical novels, mostly about N.Y. state, such as *Rome Haul* (1929), *Drums Along the Mohawk* (1936), *Chad Hanna* (1940).

Edmonton, city (pop. 281,027), provincial cap. (since 1905), central Alta., Canada, on North Saskatchewan R. Transportation and distribution center for Peace and Athabaska river area and for N Mackenzie region, it is an important point on Alaska Highway. Has fur trade, grain elevators, lumber and flour mills, oil refineries, woodworking and meat-packing plants, and major airport. Seat of Univ. of ALBERTA. Fort Edmonton built by Hudson's Bay Company in 1794 was one of most important trading posts in the Northwest.

Edmonton, part of ENFIELD London borough since 1965. Associated with Charles Lamb, Keats, and Cowper.

Edmund, Saint (Edmund Rich), 1170?–1240, English churchman, more properly called Edmund of Abingdon. Zealous reformer. Archbishop of Canterbury under HENRY III, with whom he vainly struggled. Feast: Nov. 16.

Edmund Crouchback: see LANCASTER, HOUSE OF.

Edmund Ironside, d. 1016, king of England (1016). Son of ÆTHELRED, he was prominent in fighting against CANUTE. On Æthelred's death, Edmund was proclaimed king although Canute received support of over half of England. Courage and bravery earned him name of Ironside. After battle of Assandun, he and Canute came to terms and partitioned England.

Edmundston, city (pop. 12,791), NW N.B., Canada, at Maine border, on St. John R. at mouth of Madawaska R. Pulp-milling center, fishing and hunting base. Settled c.1785 by Acadians as Petit Sault.

Edom (ē'dŏm), **Idumaea,** or **Idumea** (both: īdūmē'ù), mountainous country, called also Mt. Seir, given to Esau and his descendants. Extended from Dead Sea to Gulf of Aqaba. Edomites were often in conflict with their neighbors, especially the Hebrews; later they moved to S Judah and were finally subdued by the Maccabees. Gen. 32.3; Num. 20.14–22; Deut. 2.12.

Edrisi: see IDRISI.

Education, United States Office of, estab. 1867 as independent governmental agency, transferred 1869 to Dept. of the Interior, transferred 1939 to Federal Security Agency, which became (1953) the new Dept. of Health, Education, and Welfare. Created to collect and disseminate information on education and to promote better U.S. educational standards. Expanded functions now include administering funds appropriated as aids to education, conducting special studies.

Edward, kings of England. Edward I, 1239–1307, was king 1272–1307. Son of Henry III, he fought for him in BARONS' WAR (1263–67) and was responsible for triumph. Conquest of Wales was followed by long campaign against Scotland. Made notable efforts to extend English rule to all of Britain. His legal reforms (notably Statutes of WESTMINSTER) earned him name of the English Justinian. Restricted private and church courts and prohibited land grants to church without his permission. His Model Parliament (1295) marked greater representation of barons, merchants, and clergy whose resistance to war taxation forced king to confirm previous charters (e.g., Magna Carta). His promise to collect taxes only with consent of Parliament became basis of "no taxation without representation." His son, **Edward II,** 1284–1327, was king 1307–27. The dominant strains of his reign were internal dissension and the loss of Scotland. His insistence on having Piers GAVESTON at court caused rebellion of barons, who later killed Gaveston. Edward's later favorites, the Hugh Despensers, virtually ruled 1322–26. They made a truce with Robert the Bruce and recognized him as king of Scots. Queen Isabella refused to return from France while the Despensers ruled, entered an adulterous alliance with Roger de Mortimer, and invaded England (1326). The Despensers were executed and Edward forced to abdicate. Brutally mistreated, he was finally killed by henchmen of Isabella and Mortimer. His son, **Edward III,** 1312–77, was king 1327–77. Real power was held by Isabella and Mortimer until Edward seized it in 1330. He supported Edward de Baliol against Scottish king David II, but, despite his victory at Halidon Hill in 1333, Scottish question remained unsettled. HUNDRED YEARS WAR, which was to dominate his reign, began in 1337. He and his son, EDWARD THE BLACK PRINCE, took an active part in the war, the first phase of which ended with Treaty of London in 1359. War was renewed after various treaties and truces, but, like the Scottish wars, was inconclusive in Edward's reign.

Parliament, which withheld money grants and forced concessions from king, now began to take on form it was to retain. Black Death (see PLAGUE) decimated the population and brought about social changes in demands of lower classes for higher wages and social advancement. Edward quarreled with the Church, and religious unrest found a spokesman in John WYCLIF. There was rivalry between court party headed by JOHN OF GAUNT (supported by Edward's mistress Alice Perrers) and parliamentary party led by Black Prince and Edmund Mortimer. **Edward IV,** 1442–83, son of Richard, duke of York, became king (1461–70) as leader of York party (see ROSES, WARS OF) after his defeat of Lancastrians and capture of HENRY VI. Edward's disaffected cousin, earl of Warwick, fled to France and formed alliance with MARGARET OF ANJOU, queen of deposed Henry VI. They returned to England with troops and replaced Henry on throne. Their final defeat by Edward led to Henry's death in the Tower (1471) and quiet end to Edward's reign. His son, **Edward V,** 1470–83, boy king (1483), was pawn of conflicting ambitions of his uncles, Richard, duke of Gloucester, and Earl Rivers. Gloucester confined the king and his younger brother to the Tower, had them declared illegitimate, and took the throne as RICHARD III. Later, Sir Thomas More declared that they had been smothered in their sleep on Gloucester's orders. This story has been discounted as anti-York propaganda of Tudors. **Edward VI,** 1537–53, succeeded his father Henry VIII as king (1547–53) under council of regency controlled by his uncle and protector, Edward SEYMOUR, duke of Somerset. Tudor absolutism was relaxed by liberalizing treason and heresy laws. Government moved slowly towards Protestantism. Somerset's sympathy with yeomen's problems led to overthrow by his rival, John Dudley, duke of NORTHUMBERLAND. He secured ascendancy over the king and persuaded him to settle crown on Lady Jane GREY. Resulting struggle for throne ended in victory of Mary I. **Edward VII,** 1841–1910, was king 1901–10. Eldest son of Queen Victoria, he was prince of Wales for 60 years. Cooperated reluctantly in Herbert Asquith's attempt to limit veto power of House of Lords. Improved international understanding by traveling on continent, by promoting alliance with France, and by arbitration treaties with other powers. Father of George V, whose eldest son, **Edward VIII** (1894–), was king 1936. As prince of Wales he attracted attention by interest in social reform problems. The issue of his marriage to Wallis Warfield Simpson (see duchess of WINDSOR) precipitated a crisis with the cabinet headed by Stanley Baldwin. Their fear of a threat to constitutional procedure forced his abdication in 1936. As duke of Windsor he married Wallis Warfield 1937. Was governor of the Bahamas 1940–45.

Edward Nyanza, lake, area 830 sq. mi., in Great Rift Valley, E central Africa, on border of the Republic of the Congo and Uganda; alt. 3,240 ft. Connected by Semliki R. to Albert Nyanza in N.

Edwards, Jonathan, 1703–58, American theologian and metaphysician. His strict Calvinist preaching brought GREAT AWAKENING to New England. His masterpiece, *The Freedom of the Will* (1754), sets forth metaphysical and ethical arguments for determinism.

Edwards, town (pop. 1,206), W central Miss., E of Vicksburg. Battle of Champion's Hill in Grant's Vicksburg campaign fought nearby, May 16 and 17, 1863.

Edwardsville, city (pop. 9,996), SW Ill., NE of St. Louis, in coal area; settled 1800. A campus of SOUTHERN ILLINOIS UNIVERSITY is here.

Edward the Black Prince, 1330–76, son of Edward III of England. Was first duke (of Cornwall) ever created in England (1337). He fought in battle of Crécy and siege of Calais. In 1356 he won battle of Poitiers and captured John II of France. Edward III created a principality of his French holdings, and the Black Prince maintained a brilliant court at Bordeaux after 1363. He aided Peter I (of Castile and Leon) in keeping his throne against rebellious Castilians, but the taxes he was forced to levy in Aquitaine resulted in war with Charles V of France. Bad health forced him to resign his principalities in 1372. Opposed his brother, JOHN OF GAUNT, who had become virtual ruler of England with the aging of Edward III. He died before his father but his son succeeded to the throne as Richard II.

Edward the Confessor, d. 1066, king of England (1042–66). Son of Æthelred, he grew up in France and returned to succeed Harthacanute. Governed well and freed his people from heavy taxes. Strife with powerful noble, Earl GODWIN, was heightened by Edward's favor of the Normans in England. Godwin and his family were exiled (1051) but soon returned. During their absence Edward received William, duke of Normandy, and probably promised him the succession. Since both William and Harold III of Norway had claims to the English throne, Edward recognized Godwin's warlike son, HAROLD, as his heir. Crisis was resolved by the NORMAN CONQUEST. Edward's piety won him name of Confessor.

Edward the Elder, d. 924, king of Wessex (899–924). Son of Alfred and joint king with him, he played an active part in wars with the Danes. Gradually became ruler of all England S of the Humber.

Edward the Martyr, d. 978, king of England (975–78), son of Edgar. Murdered at Corfe, his body was removed to Shaftesbury. Miracles occurred there and he was regarded as a saint and martyr.

Edwin or **Eadwin** (both: ĕ'dwĭn), 585?–632, king of Northumbria (616–32). Kept from the throne by Æthelfrith, he was restored by Rædwald and became overlord of all the Anglo-Saxon kingdoms except Kent.

Eeckhout, Gerbrand van den (gĕr'bränt vän dĕn äk'-hout), 1621–74, Dutch painter and etcher; pupil and close follower of Rembrandt.

eel, edible fish of family Anguillidae of order Apodes. Common fresh-water eel (*Anguilla*) found in Atlantic waters of North America, Europe, and in Mediterranean. Minute scales embedded in skin cover snake-like body; dorsal and anal fins are continuous around tail. Females grow to c.4 ft. long; males to c.2 ft. American and European species breed in Atlantic Ocean S and SE of Bermuda. They hatch as tiny, flattened, transparent larvae which travel back to ancestral shores, developing as elvers. Females swim up rivers, while males remain near mouth. Sexually mature adults migrate to breeding grounds, reproduce, and die.

Efate: see NEW HEBRIDES.

Effen, Justus van (yōōs'tōōs vän ĕ'fŭn), 1684–1735, Dutch writer. Founded *Hollandsche Spectator* (1731–35), modeled on the journal of Addison and Steele.

efficiency: see INDUSTRIAL MANAGEMENT; MACHINE; WORK.

Effigy Mounds National Monument: see NATIONAL PARKS AND MONUMENTS (table).

efflorescence: see HYDRATE.

EFTA: see EUROPEAN FREE TRADE ASSOCIATION.

Égalité, Philippe: see ORLÉANS, family.

Egan, Pierce, 1772–1849, English sports writer, author of *Life in London* (1821) about the "man about town."

Egbert, d. 839, king of Wessex (802–39), son of an underking of Kent. He eventually secured submission of Kent, East Anglia, Mercia, and Northumbria, thus gaining overlordship of all the Anglo-Saxon kingdoms.

Eger (ā'gŭr), Czech *Cheb,* city (est. pop. 22,391), NW Bohemia, Czechoslovakia. Commercial center; lignite deposits nearby. Town hall and castle were scene of assassination of Wallenstein and his officers (1634).

Eger (ĕ'gĕr), Ger. *Erlau,* city (est. pop. 40,000), NE Hungary, on Eger R., in wine-growing region. Created bishopric by St. Stephen (now archiepiscopal see), it is called the "Rome of Hungary" for its many churches. Fortress withstood Turkish siege in 1552,

fell through treachery in 1596, was razed after Francis II Rakoczy used it in his fight against Austria.

Egeria (ējĕr'ēŭ), in Roman religion, water goddess sometimes identified with Diana and invoked as goddess of childbirth. She was adviser to King Numa. Her name used today for women who advise artists or politicians.

Egerton, Thomas: see ELLESMERE, THOMAS EGERTON, BARON.

egg: see OVUM.

Egge, Peter (pä'tŭr ĕ'gŭ), 1869–1959, Norwegian novelist. Wrote *Hansine Solstad* (1925).

Eggertsville, city (pop. 44,807), W N.Y., a suburb NNE of Buffalo.

Eggleston, Edward, 1837–1902, American author, a Methodist clergyman, circuit rider in Indiana, best known for his novel *The Hoosier Schoolmaster* (1871).

eggplant, tropical vegetable (*Solanum melongena*) widely grown for purple or white fruit.

Egham (ĕg'ŭm), urban district (pop. 30,553), Surrey, England, on the Thames. Near by are Virginia Water, an artificial lake, and RUNNYMEDE.

eglantine: see SWEETBRIER.

Eglevsky, André, 1917–, American ballet dancer. Noted for classic style and virtuosity, he has danced with Ballet Russe de Monte Carlo (1939–42), Ballet Theatre in N.Y. (1942–46), and NY City Ballet (1951–).

Eglon (ĕg'-). **1** King of Moab: see EHUD. **2** Ancient city near Lachish. Excavated 1890 by Petrie who devised here a system of dating by use of shards.

Egmont, Lamoral, count of (lä'mōräl), 1522–68, Flemish statesman, governor of Brabant and Artois. Though a devout Catholic and a loyal servant of Philip II of Spain, he intervened in behalf of the persecuted Protestants. Duke of ALBA had him and count of HOORN arbitrarily arrested (1567) and beheaded after an irregular trial. Their death stirred the Netherlanders to open rebellion. Egmont is central figure in tragedy by Goethe, with overture and incidental music by Beethoven.

ego: see PSYCHOANALYSIS.

egret (ēgrĕt), name for several heron species in both hemispheres. Slaughtered in nesting colonies for white, silky plumage (called aigrettes) used in millinery, they were nearly exterminated before they were protected by law.

Egypt, Arabic *Misr,* officially **United Arab Republic** (386,198 sq. mi.; pop. c.26,080,000), occupying NE corner of Africa and Sinai peninsula of SW Asia; cap. CAIRO, chief port ALEXANDRIA. Bounded on W by Libya and on S by ANGLO-EGYPTIAN SUDAN. Mainly a plateau, split by the Nile into Western Desert and Eastern Desert. Some 95% of population lives in fertile valley and delta of the Nile. Chief export crop is cotton; oil, salt, potash are exploited. Most important industry is cotton spinning and weaving. Some 91% of population is Moslem; 8% is Christian (Coptic); and there is small minority of Jews. Earliest known date in world history is that of adoption of Egyptian calendar in 4241 B.C. A widely accepted dating system divides Egyptian history into 30 dynasties (3400–332 B.C.). In c.3400 B.C. Menes united two earlier kingdoms to create centralized Egyptian state, with cap. at Memphis. Fall of Old Kingdom in 25th cent. B.C. was followed by dark age. Unity restored in 2160 B.C. by IX dynasty, with cap. at Thebes; Middle Kingdom reached its height in 2000 B.C. After its fall (1788 B.C.) Egypt passed under the Hyksos (apparently Semites from east), who were expelled 1580 B.C. by native founder of New Kingdom. Weakened by decline of royal power, Egypt came under rule of the Nubians in 712 B.C. and later, briefly, under the Assyrians. Returned to orderly native rule in c.663 B.C., but again came under foreign rule in 525 B.C. with conquest by Cambyses of Persia. Regained freedom in 405 B.C. by successful revolt. Alexander the Great took Egypt unopposed in 332 B.C. His brief empire faded, and Egypt fell to his general Ptolemy who became king as Ptolemy I, with cap. at Alexandria. Rising power of Rome early overshadowed Egypt, and even the wily efforts of CLEOPATRA failed to regain power for Egypt. Octavian annexed Egypt to Rome and killed Ptolemy XIV (last of the Ptolemies). Christianity was welcomed in Egypt, and several of most famous Doctors of the Church were Egyptians; Coptic Church arose out of MONOPHYSITISM. Arabic conquest (639–42) made Egypt an integral part of Moslem world. In 10th cent. Egypt fell to FATIMITE family, who founded Cairo as their capital. During period of Ayyubite dynasty (founded by Saladin) Egypt came under control of the MAMELUKES (1250–1517). Ottoman Turks conquered Egypt in 1517, but by 18th cent. their rule had become almost nominal. Napoleon's occupation of Egypt (1798–1801) was undertaken ostensibly to restore Turkish rule in region but actually to sever British trade lines with India; his withdrawal was forced by Anglo-Turkish forces. MOHAMMED ALI, who rose to power in 1805 as Egyptian pasha (governor), became founder of present royal line. With growing independence from Ottoman rule the title khedive (viceroy) was granted to ISMAIL PASHA. In First World War British (who had brought Egypt under their control 1883–1907) made it a British protectorate. Agitation by WAFD party led to granting of independence in 1923, with FUAD I as Egypt's first constitutional monarch. Anglo-Egyptian treaty of 1936 promised eventual withdrawal of all British troops. In Second World War it was defended by the British (see NORTH AFRICA, CAMPAIGNS IN); it did not declare war against the Axis until Feb., 1945. Under FAROUK I, Egypt (as member of Arab League attacked ISRAEL in 1948. Farouk was driven from his throne Aug., 1952, by an army coup headed by Gen. Mohammed Naguib, engineered by NASSER. A republic was proclaimed July, 1953. Naguib was president until Nov., 1954, when Premier Nasser took the presidency. The constitution, approved Jan., 1956, provided for a one-party system. Nasser was elected president for a six-year term. In 1956 nationalization of the SUEZ CANAL brought occupation of part of Egypt by Israeli and Anglo-French forces; they withdrew after UN intervention. In Feb., 1958, Syria and Egypt united as the United Arab Republic. Later that year Yemen joined UAR to form the short-lived United Arab States. In 1961 Syria and Yemen withdrew from union. Industry and agr., developed through Soviet technical and economic aid, were largely nationalized by 1962. New constitution was promulgated 1964. The same year the first stage of Aswan High Dam was completed. Egypt signed mutual defense pact with Syria (1966), who asked for aid in serious border skirmishes with Israel. In May, 1967, Nasser closed Gulf of Aqaba to Israeli shipping, precipitating hostilities which resulted in crushing defeat for Egypt and Arab nations involved. Gaza Strip and Sinai peninsula of Egypt taken by Israelis. Just before outbreak of fighting Egypt signed mutual defense pact with long-time rival Jordan.

Egyptian architecture reached formulation prior to 3000 B.C. Lack of wood and availability of clay and stone led to development of an architecture of massive and static quality. Immensely thick walls, containing only a few small openings, were covered with colorful pictorial and hieroglyphic carvings. Columns were confined to halls and inner courts, and supported flat stone roofs. Belief in existence after death resulted in sepulchral architecture of impressiveness and permanence. Remains of Old Kingdom (2680–2258 B.C.) are chiefly tombs of monarchs (see PYRAMID). Tombs of Middle Kingdom (2134–1786 B.C.) were tunneled out of rock cliffs. New Empire (1570–1085 B.C.) was great period of temple construction, exemplified by temple at KARNAK.

Egyptian art. Characteristic stylistic conventions appear with beginning of Old Kingdom period (3200–2258 B.C.). Relief sculpture and painting show human figure with eyes and shoulders in front view, head, pelvis, legs, and feet in profile view. Little attempt at plastic or spatial illusionism; color applied in flat tones. Sculpture in the round emphasized symmetry and minimized suggested movement. Painting served primarily as accessory to sculpture. In Middle Kingdom Period (2134–1786 B.C.) painting and sculpture became increasingly formalized. In Empire period (1570–1085 B.C.) they tended toward greater elasticity of line and boldness of design; a masterpiece of period is painted limestone bust of Queen Nefretete. Art of Saïte period (8th cent. B.C.) returned to simplicity of Old Kingdom style. Egyptian art began to decline during Ptolemaic dynasty and was eventually stifled by infiltration of Greek and Roman forms.

Egyptian language, chief language of the extinct Egyptian subfamily of Afro-Asiatic languages. See HIEROGLYPHIC; LANGUAGE (table).

Egyptian religion. Although documentary evidence on religion of ancient Egypt is rich and varied, interpretations are difficult because of its complexity and contradictions. Gods are identical and yet coexist, and contradictory myths explaining creation of world and natural phenomena were simultaneously accepted. Gods had relationship to various animals and were represented as part animal and part human—e.g., Ptah and Serapis, the great gods, with the Apis bull; Nut and Hathor, mother goddesses, with the cow; Bast, mother goddess, with the cat; and Horus, sun-god, with the hawk. Sun worship was very important in Egypt. The one attempt to establish monotheism there—the reforms of IKHNATON—was aimed at making sungod the sole deity. Horus, Ra, and Amon were sungods. Great emphasis was placed on cult of the dead; hence building of PYRAMID as tomb of king and preservation of body by embalming and mummification. There was belief in immortality of body and of vital spirit or ka. King as successor to god and himself a god was chief priest. Many Egyptian gods, notably Isis, Horus, Osiris, and Serapis, became popular in Greece and Rome.

Egyptians, Gospel of the: see PSEUDEPIGRAPHA.

Ehrenburg, Ilya (Grigoryevich) (ĕlyä′ grĭgôr′yùvˈĭch ä′rŭnbŏork), 1891–, Russian novelist and journalist. Among translated works are *The Love of Jeanne Ney* (1924); *The Tempering of Russia* (1944; reports on First and Second World Wars). Received Stalin Prize twice (1942, 1958). His post-Stalin novel *The Thaw* (1954) gave name to period of decreasing internal tensions in USSR.

Ehrlich, Paul (poul′ âr′lĭkh), 1854–1915, German bacteriologist. He shared 1908 Nobel Prize in Physiology and Medicine for work in immunology. Discovered drugs effective against syphilis.

Ehud (ē′hŭd), man who assassinated King Eglon of Moab and freed Israel from Moabite oppression. He later became a judge of Israel. Judges 3.12–30.

Eichendorff, Joseph, Freiherr von (yō′zĕf frī′hĕr fûn ī′khŭndôrf), 1788–1857, German poet. His lyric nature poems are spontaneously musical and have attracted many composers, notably Schumann. Some have passed into folklore. *Memoirs of a Good-for-Nothing* (1826; Eng. tr., 1866), a delightful short novel, shows German romanticism at its best.

Eichmann, Adolf (īkh′män), 1906–1962, German National Socialist official. Became head of Gestapo's Jewish section in 1940, overseeing deportation and mass extermination of millions of Jews. Escaped from Allies in 1945; located in Argentina by Israeli agents in 1960 and abducted to Israel. An Israeli court found him guilty of crimes against Jews and humanity, and he was hanged.

Eider (ī′dŭr), river, 125 mi. long, N Germany, separating Holstein from Schleswig. Flows W into North Sea.

Eidsvoll or **Eidsvold** (both: āts′vôl), village (pop. 11,843), Akershus prov., SE Norway. Constitution of

Norway was proclaimed by Norwegian patriots at Eidsvoll manor in 1814.

Eifel (ī'fùl), plateau, NW Germany, N of Moselle R. and E of the Ardennes. Barren area with deep valleys, extinct volcanoes, crater lakes. Highest point 2,447 ft.

Eiffel, Alexandre Gustave (ī'fùl, Fr. älĕksä'drü güstäv' äfĕl'), 1832–1923, French engineer, bridge and viaduct builder, authority on aerodynamics. He designed the **Eiffel Tower** (984 ft. high) erected for the Paris exposition of 1889.

Eight, The, group of American artists in New York, formed in 1908 to exhibit paintings. Comprised Arthur B. Davies, Maurice Prendergast, Ernest Lawson, William Glackens, Everett Shinn, Robert Henri, John Sloan, and George Luks. These men of widely different tendencies were bound by common opposition to academism and were stigmatized as "the ashcan school." They organized Armory Show of 1913 which introduced modern European art to a reluctant but curious America.

Eijkman, Christian (krīs'tyän īk'män), 1858–1930, Dutch physician. Shared 1929 Nobel Prize in Physiology and Medicine for work on cause of beriberi.

Eikon Basilike (īkŏn būsī'līkē) [Gr.,= royal image], work generally believed an autobiography by Charles I of England. Later John GAUDEN claimed authorship and started long controversy. Also Icon, Ikon.

Eildon Hills (ēl'dùn), three conical hills, Roxburghshire, Scotland. Associated with legends of Thomas of Erceldoune.

Eilshemius, Louis Michel (īlshē'mēùs), 1864–1941, American painter of numerous landscapes. His work first won notice at Armory Show of 1913.

Einaudi, Luigi (lwē'jē änou'dē), 1874–1961, president of Italy (1948–55); opponent of Fascism.

Eindhoven (īnt'hō"vùn), municipality (pop. 178,336), North Brabant prov., S Netherlands. Mfg. of electrical appliances, radios, plastics, textiles.

Einhard (īn'härd) or **Eginhard** (ä'gïnhärd), c.770–840, Frankish historian. Known for biography of Charlemagne, a prime contemporary source book.

Einhorn, David (īn'hôrn), 1809–79, Jewish theologian, b. Bavaria. Leader of Reform movement in American Judaism. His vigorous antislavery campaign during Civil War forced him to leave Baltimore, where he was rabbi.

Einsiedeln (īn'zē"dùln), town (pop. 8,792), Schwyz canton, central Switzerland. Benedictine abbey (founded 10th cent.). Its church contains sacred image of the "Black Virgin"; noted place of pilgrimage.

Einstein, Albert (īn'stīn), 1879–1955, American theoretical physicist, b. Germany. Won 1921 Nobel Prize for contributions to theoretical physics, especially for work on the photoelectric effect. He postulated (1905) light quanta or photons, comparable to energy quanta, and on these based his explanation of the photoelectric effect; he developed the quantum theory of specific heat. In 1905 he set forth his special theory of relativity on electrodynamics of moving bodies and equivalence of mass and mechanical energy. In 1911 he asserted the equivalence of gravitation and inertia and c.1916 completed the mathematical formulation of his general theory of relativity which included gravitation as a determiner of curvature of space-time continuum and represented gravitation as a field rather than a force. His mathematical expression of the theory appeared in 1950. In 1953 he announced completion of work on his unified field theory, which attempts to explain gravitation, electromagnetism, and subatomic phenomena in one set of laws. In 1939 he stressed the urgency of investigating the use of atomic energy in bombs. See *ill.,* p. 781.

einsteinium, radioactive chemical element (symbol = Es; see also ELEMENT, table). Discovered 1952 at Univ. of California, where it was produced by bombarding uranium with nitrogen nuclei.

Einthoven, Willem (vī'lùm īnt'hōvùn), 1860–1927, Dutch physiologist. Won 1924 Nobel Prize in Physiol-

ogy and Medicine for development of electrocardiograph which makes graphic records of heart action.

Eire: see IRELAND.

Eisenach (ī'zùnäkh), city (est. pop. 48,853), East Germany, in former state of Thuringia. Mfg. of cars, machine tools, electrical supplies. Birthplace of J. S. Bach; residence of Luther 1498–1501. German Social Democratic party formed here by Bebel and Liebknecht at Socialist congress of 1869. Wartburg castle is nearby.

Eisenhower, Dwight D(avid) (ī'zùnhou"ùr), 1890–, American general, 33d or 34th (see list at end of article UNITED STATES) President of the United States (1953–61), b. Denison, Texas. Chief of Allied forces in North Africa in Second World War. Made supreme commander of Allied Expeditionary Force in 1943; integrated forces in battle for Europe. Made general of the army ("five-star general") in 1944. U.S. army chief of staff 1945–48. President of Columbia Univ. 1948–53. Appointed supreme commander of Allied forces in Europe (NATO) in 1950; resigned post 1952. Successful Republican presidential candidate in 1952. Reelected 1956 (after recovery from severe illness). Moderate domestic policies have stressed balancing budget, minimizing government activities in business, agr.; however, exigencies of cold war led him to submit to Congress some of the highest peacetime budgets in the nation's history. Sent Federal troops to Little Rock, Ark., in 1957 to enforce school desegregation. In foreign affairs he sought peace through negotiation and strong Western alliance. Helped arrange truce in Korea in 1953. To bolster Middle Eastern nations against Communism, formulated so-called Eisenhower doctrine in 1957. Met European heads of state at Geneva Summit Conference in 1955; Paris Summit Conference (1960) canceled after Nikita Khrushchev accused him of treachery in permitting espionage flights over USSR. In 1961 Congress restored Eisenhower to rank of "five-star general." In 1962 Eisenhower presidential library was dedicated at Abilene, Kansas.

Eisenhower, Milton S(tover) (ī'zùnhou"ùr), 1899–, American educator. President Kansas State Col. (1943–50), Pa. State Univ. (1950–56), Johns Hopkins Univ. (1956–).

Eisenstadt (ī'zùnshtät), town (est. pop. 7,158), cap. of Burgenland, E Austria. Hayden resided here under patronage of Esterhazy family.

Eisenstein, Sergei Mikhailovich (sîrgä' mēkhī'lùvïch äzùnshtyän'), 1898–1948, Russian film director. Won world wide fame (1925) with *Potemkin.* Other films include *Ten Days That Shook the World* and *Alexander Nevsky.* Pioneered much of aesthetics of films and developed new techniques such as montage.

Eisleben (īs'lābùn), town (est. pop. 29,023), East Germany, in former state of Saxony-Anhalt, at foot of Harz mts. Copper-mining center for 750 years. Houses where Martin Luther was born and died still stand.

Eisner, Kurt (kŏort īs'nùr), 1867–1919, German Socialist. Organized revolution which overthrew Bavarian monarchy (1918); was first republican premier of Bavaria. A separatist, he opposed Prussian domination of a federal Germany. Assassinated by an anti-Semitic nationalist.

eisteddfod (āstĕdh'vŏd) [Welsh,= session], Welsh festival. Contests are held in all arts and crafts, with special emphasis on music and poetry. National Eisteddfod held annually in August; local eisteddfods held throughout year. Important in preserving Welsh language and culture.

ejido (āhē'dō) [Span.,= common land], in Mexico, agricultural land expropriated from large private holdings and distributed in communal ownership; worked cooperatively or in individual plots. First large-scale *ejido* estab. in LAGUNA DISTRICT (1936).

Ekaterinburg, RSFSR: see SVERDLOVSK.

Ekaterinodar, RSFSR: see KRASNODAR.

Ekkehard (ĕ'kùhärt), name of several monks of St. Gall, Swiss monastery. **Ekkehard I** wrote the *Waltharilied* (c.930), a Latin epic. **Ekkehard II**, fl. 10th cent., appears in Scheffel's novel *Ekkehard*. **Ekkehard IV**, fl. 11th cent., revised *Waltharilied* and contributed to chronicle of St. Gall.

Ekron (ĕ'krŏn), Philistine city on border of Judah, and ESE of Jaffa, last resting place of Ark of the Covenant before its return to Jews. 1 Sam. 5.10,11.

El. For Arabic and Spanish names beginning thus and not listed here, see second element; e.g., for El Alamein, see ALAMEIN; for El Salvador, see SALVADOR.

Elagabalus: see HELIOGABALUS.

Elah (ē'lù), **1** Died c.885 B.C., king of Israel (c.886–c.885 B.C.), successor of Baasha. He was murdered by Zimri, who succeeded him. 1 Kings 16.8–14. **2** Valley in which David slew Goliath. 1 Sam. 17.2,19; 21.9.

El Alamein, Egypt: see ALAMEIN.

Elam (ē'lùm), anc. Asiatic country, N of Persian Gulf, now in W Iran. A civilization began in 4th millennium B.C. Cap. was SUSA, and country is often called Susiana. In 18th cent. B.C. it overthrew Babylonia. Golden age came in 14th cent. B.C. Fell to ASSUR-BANI-PAL (c.645 B.C.).

eland (ē'lùnd), the largest living African antelope. Bull may be 6 ft. high at shoulder and weigh over 1,200 lb. Spiral horns extend straight upward. Several species of genus *Taurotragus*.

elasticity, ability of matter to return to original shape or volume after distortion. Elasticity is measured in the amount of force a substance can resist without permanent deformity; the elastic limit is set by the smallest force that brings this about.

Elath (ē'–), ancient port, on Gulf of Aqaba. Built by King Uzziah of Judah, lost by King Ahaz. Also appears as Eloth. Was on or near site of modern Aqaba. Modern port (begun 1948), with deep-water harbor, was cut off by Arab blockade of gulf in Middle Eastern conflict of 1967.

Elba (ĕl'bù), island (86 sq. mi.; est. pop. 29,121), off Tuscany, central Italy, in Tyrrhenian Sea; chief town Portoferraio. Iron mines. Principality 1814–15 under exiled Napoleon.

Elbasan (ĕlbäsän'), town (est. pop. 30,600), central Albania; center of fertile agr. region.

Elbe (ĕl'bù), Czech *Labe*, river, c.725 mi. long, Czechoslovakia and Germany, rising in N Bohemia and flowing NW through Bohemia, Saxony, and N Germany (past Dresden, Magdeburg, and Hamburg) into North Sea. Connected by canal system with Oder and navigable for 525 mi., it is a major European waterway. Germany repudiated (1938) its internationalization by Versailles Treaty.

Elberfeld, West Germany: see WUPPERTAL.

Elbert, Mount, peak, 14,431 ft. high, W central Colo., in Sawatch Mts.; highest peak of U.S. Rocky Mts.

El-beth-el, name given by Jacob to place at BETHEL where God appeared to him. Gen. 35.7.

Elbing (ĕl'bĭng) or **Elblag** (ĕl'blȧk), city (est. pop. 84,000), N Poland (since 1945), formerly in E Prussia, on Elbing R. Seaport near Vistula Lagoon; has shipyards, machinery and metalworks. Was member of Hanseatic League; passed to Poland 15th cent.; to Prussia 1772.

Elbrus, Mount (ĕl'brōos), highest mountain of Caucasus and Europe, NW Georgian SSR, formed by two extinct volcanic cones, respectively 18,481 and 18,356 ft. high.

Elburz (ĕlbŏŏrz'), mountains, N Iran, S of Caspian Sea. Highest is Mt. Demavend (c.18,600 ft. high).

El Cajon, residential and industrial city (pop. 37,618), S Calif., ENE of San Diego.

El Centro, city (1965 pop. 19,414), SE Calif., SSE of Salton Sea; laid out 1905. Processing and shipping center for IMPERIAL VALLEY farm produce.

El Cerrito (ĕl sùrē'tō), residential city (pop. 25,437), W Calif., on San Francisco Bay N of Berkeley.

elder or **elderberry,** deciduous tree or shrub of genus *Sambucus,* widely distributed. Common elderberry (*Sambucus canadensis*) has purple berries in late sum-

mer used to make wine and jelly. Other species, e.g., European elder (*S. nigra*), are sometimes grown for ornament.

Eldon, John Scott, 1st **earl of,** 1751–1838, English statesman and jurist. As attorney general he drew up repressive laws of 1793–98. Lord chancellor almost continuously 1801–27 and virtual prime minister 1807–12. A reactionary Tory, he opposed Catholic Emancipation and liberal reform.

El Dorado (ĕl' dùrä'dō) [Span.,= the gilded man], mythical country sought by adventurers in North and South America. Used figuratively to mean any country of wealth or land of desire.

El Dorado (ĕl dùrä'dù). **1** City (pop. 25,292), S central Ark., SSW of Little Rock; settled 1843. Oil center of state and farm-trade center. **2** City (pop. 12,523), SE Kansas, on Walnut R., ENE of Wichita, in grain and livestock area; laid out 1868. Grew as shipping and refining point after oil discovery (1915) in area.

Eldorado Mines or **Port Radium,** port, N Northwest Territories, Canada, on Great Bear L. Discovered 1930, mines yielded pitchblende and uranium oxide. Mines taken over by Canadian government 1944, closed 1960.

Eleanor Crosses: see ELEANOR OF CASTILE.

Eleanor of Aquitaine (äkwĭtän'), 1122?–1204, queen of HENRY II of England; daughter of William X, duke of Aquitaine. Her marriage to LOUIS VII of France was annulled in 1152. Shortly thereafter she married Henry, then duke of Normandy. Two of her sons became kings of England—RICHARD I and JOHN. Henry's infidelities (see ROSAMOND) caused her to estab. (1170) her own court at Poitiers. Aided her sons in an unsuccessful revolt (1173) against Henry (who confined her for many years) and helped Richard secure the throne. Her court was the scene of much artistic activity.

Eleanor of Castile (kästēl'), d. 1290, queen consort of EDWARD I of England. After her death Edward supposedly had Eleanor Crosses erected to mark stages of her funeral journey at Lincoln, Grantham, Stamford, Geddington, Northampton, Stony Stratford, Woburn, Dunstable, St. Albans, Waltham, Westcheap, and Charing. Three are extant, though restored.

Eleatic school (ēlēä'tĭk), Greek pre-Socratic school of philosophers who taught that ultimate being is permanent, change illusory. PARMENIDES was a notable Eleatic.

elecampane (ĕ"lùkămpān'), hardy Old World herb (*Inula helenium*) naturalized in U.S. It has yellow-rayed flowers. Its thick root was formerly used as cough remedy and in horse medicine.

election, organized voting to choose candidates for office. Greek officials, though occasionally elected, were more often selected by lot than elected by balloting, and in Rome the popular assemblies elected the tribunes. Popular suffrage and elections, practically abandoned in Middle Ages, have grown principally along with democracy. In England, elections, associated with parliamentary procedures from the 13th cent., were regularized after 1688 and led to the secret ballot in 1872. In the U.S., the Seventeenth Amendment provided for the popular election of Senators, the Fourteenth (1868) and Fifteenth (1870) for the enfranchisement of the Negro, and the Nineteenth (1920) for the enfranchisement of women. Certain classes of felons, some Indians, and feeble-minded are denied suffrage.

electoral college, in U.S. government, the body of electors in the states which chooses the President and Vice President. The Constitution provides that each state shall appoint a number of electors equal to the full number of the state's U.S. Senators and Representatives. Congress is authorized to count their votes. To win, a presidential candidate must have a majority in the electoral college (not necessarily a majority of popular votes). Twelfth Amendment (1804) enjoins electors to vote for President and Vice President separately and provides that, in case no candidate has a majority of the electoral vote, the House of Representatives (voting by state, with one vote for each state) shall choose the President from among the three candidates highest on electoral list. Present popular election of electors superseded earlier choice by state legislatures; prevailing general-ticket system enables a party to carry whole state if it achieves a plurality vote.

electors, in theory, the head of the HOLY ROMAN EMPIRE was elected by a number of princes called electors; until 1562 his title was king of the Romans unless he was crowned emperor by the pope. In practice, in all elections but one after 1438, a member of the house of HAPSBURG was chosen. The Golden Bull (so called because of its golden seal), issued by Charles IV in 1356, designated as upper house of the DIET the seven prince-electors: archbishops of Mainz, Trier, and Cologne; king of Bohemia; count palatine of the Rhine; duke of Saxony; margrave of Brandenburg. The palatine vote was transferred (1623) to duke of Bavaria, but in 1648 an eighth vote was created for the count palatine. A ninth vote was given to the dukes of Hanover (after 1714 also kings of England). Elections took place amid great pomp at Frankfurt.

Electra (ĭlěk'trŭ), in Greek mythology. 1 Daughter of Agamemnon and Clytemnestra. She helped her brother ORESTES avenge murder of their father by their mother. Portrayed by Aeschylus, Sophocles, and Euripides. 2 One of the Pleiades; daughter of Atlas and mother by Zeus of Dardanus. 3 Daughter of Oceanus and mother of Iris and the Harpies.

electric circuit, unbroken path along which current of electricity flows. A simple circuit can be set up with electric cell, two conducting wires (one attached to negative and one to positive pole of cell), small lamp and socket to which free ends of wires from cell are attached. When wires are made fast, circuit is "closed," lamp will light. External circuit is part in which current flows from cell along wire to lamp, through lamp, and back along other wire to cell; internal circuit is where current flows from one electrode to another through electrolyte of cell. When wires are disconnected, circuit is "open" or broken. In practice this is done by switches and fuses. Series circuit is one in which current flows through one part after another; negative electrode of one cell is connected with positive electrode of another. Resistance to flow of current in series circuit is sum of the separate resistances; voltage is sum of voltages for different parts; current strength is same throughout circuit. In parallel circuit current flows through all parts at same time; like electrodes are connected, i.e., negative with negative, positive with positive. Resistance is less than that of part having least resistance; voltage same for all parts; current strength is sum of current strengths in different parts. Parallel circuit is most commonly used. Devices connected in series must all operate at same time. Series circuit generally used for street lighting, in windings of generators and motors, and transformers when high voltages are needed. See *ill.*, p. 322.

electric eye: see PHOTOELECTRIC CELL.

electric fish, name for various fish with organs (usually from modified muscle tissue) producing electricity to kill or paralyze prey or enemies. Electric eel (*Electrophorus*), a fresh-water fish related to carp, has organs producing 450–600 volts. Others are electric ray or torpedo (species in warm waters of Europe and U.S.); fresh-water electric catfish (*Malapterurus*); and U.S. Atlantic coast marine stargazer (*Astroscopus*).

electricity [from Gr.,= amber; named by Wm. Gilbert]. Modern electron theory views matter as basically electrical and the ATOM, basic unit of matter, as composed of negative charges (electrons), positive charges (protons), and neutral charges (neutrons). Electrons move within atom in orbits around nucleus and sometimes move to another atom. Loss of an electron leaves atom positively charged; gain of an electron charges it negatively. Static electricity is concerned with nature, strength, and effect of charge on bodies; ways of charging a body include bringing it close to a charged body (see INDUCTION), rubbing a glass rod with silk, and rubbing a hard rubber rod with flannel. Capacity to receive and hold charge varies; some metals, called good conductors, pass charge on rapidly; some other materials are poor conductors (see INSULATION). In solid conductors, current flow results from short-range movement of many electrons; no electron moves around the circuit. In electrolytic and gaseous conductors, both positive and negative charges move either way from electrode to electrode. Electric current (or electron flow) is set up in a conductor when it connects cell electrodes, forming a closed electric circuit; one-direction flow called direct current; generator current (if no commutator is used) alternates directions. Current can produce magnetism (see ELECTROMAGNET); GALVANOMETER measures force and strength of current; electric MOTOR transforms electrical into mechanical energy. Heat produced in conductor depends on strength of current and resistance of conductor; light-bulb filament is heated to incandescence, as is electric ARC. Passage of current through solutions (see ION; ELECTROLYTE; ELECTROLYSIS) is important to metallurgy in various ways. Among the many who contributed to the knowledge and utilization of electricity are Henry Cavendish, Coulomb, Ohm, Joule, Galvani, Volta, Oersted, Ampère, Joseph Henry, Michael Faraday, J. C. Maxwell, Heinrich Hertz, W. T. Kelvin, T. A. Edison, A. G. Bell, Michael Pupin, and E. H. Armstrong. See *ill.*, p. 322.

electric shock, effect of passage of electric current through the body. Shocks of 1–2 amperes and 500–1,000 volts may be fatal, depending on wetness of the skin, area of contact, and constitution of victim. Burn exists at site of entry. Disturbances include muscle spasm and loss of consciousness. Thick rubber or dry clothes should be used to detach victim from current. Artificial respiration and shock therapy should be started immediately.

electrochemistry, branch of chemistry concerned with relations between chemical reactions and electricity. It deals with production of electric current by chemical means, with conductivity of solutions, ELECTROLYSIS, theory of ION and ionization, and related phenomena.

electrode (ŭlĕk'trōd), a terminal or pole of electric cell or other source of current. It may be positive (anode) or negative (cathode). In any external electric circuit the flow of electrons is from negative to positive electrode.

electrolysis (ŭlĕktrŏ'lŭsĭs), passage of electric current through conducting solution (electrolyte) with decomposition of this compound. One explanation: when a compound dissolves it undergoes DISSOCIATION, i.e., each atom either loses or gains electrons to become a charged ION. When current is introduced, positive ions move to negative pole (cathode) and each gains an electron, negative move to positive (anode) and each loses an electron, and thus they revert to atoms of the new substances formed. Principle applied in metal refining and PLATING; electrotype plates are prepared by electrolysis.

electrolyte (ŭlĕk'trŭlīt), compound which, in solution, conducts an electric current and is decomposed by it (see ELECTROLYSIS).

electromagnet, magnet in which magnetism is produced by electric current. If bar of soft iron is placed in coil of wire through which current is flowing, the iron becomes a magnet only so long as current flows. Strength depends on number of turns in coil. Electromagnets are used in electric bell, telephone, telegraph, electric generator, and motor. See *ill.*, p. 322.

electromotive force: see VOLT.

electromotive series: see METAL.

electron (ŭlĕk'trŏn), a fundamental subatomic particle. It has negative unit charge and negligible mass. Electrons move in orbits around nucleus of ATOM; valence and chemical properties of element depend on number and arrangement of extranuclear electrons. Sir J. J. Thomson showed cathode rays made of electrons; R. A. Millikan determined size of charge. See *ill.*, p. 781.

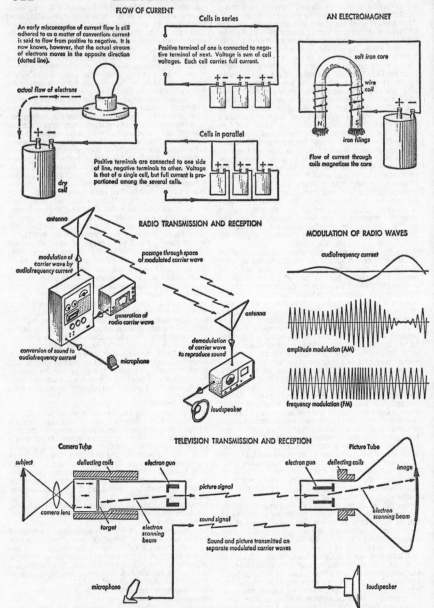

FLOW OF CURRENT

An early misconception of current flow is still adhered to as a matter of convention: current is said to flow from positive to negative. It is now known, however, that the actual stream of electrons moves in the opposite direction (dotted line).

actual flow of electrons

dry cell

Cells in series

Positive terminal of one is connected to negative terminal of next. Voltage is sum of cell voltages. Each cell carries full current.

Cells in parallel

Positive terminals are connected to one side of line, negative terminals to other. Voltage is that of a single cell, but full current is proportioned among the several cells.

AN ELECTROMAGNET

soft iron core

wire coil

N   S

iron filings

Flow of current through coils magnetizes the core

RADIO TRANSMISSION AND RECEPTION

antenna

modulation of carrier wave by audiofrequency current

passage through space of modulated carrier wave

generation of radio carrier wave

conversion of sound to audiofrequency current

microphone

antenna

demodulation of carrier wave to reproduce sound

loudspeaker

MODULATION OF RADIO WAVES

audiofrequency current

amplitude modulation (AM)

frequency modulation (FM)

TELEVISION TRANSMISSION AND RECEPTION

Camera Tube

subject

deflecting coils

electron gun

camera lens

target

electron scanning beam

picture signal

sound signal

Sound and picture transmitted on separate modulated carrier waves

Picture Tube

electron gun

deflecting coils

image

electron scanning beam

microphone

loudspeaker

Electricity flows through wires or other matter, as in a battery. By electronics, waves go through space and are received in radio and television. Study of electric currents concerns distribution of electrons; electronics deals with electromagnetic fields, which have no material existence.

electronic music, term applied to compositions which evolve through use of electronic devices for the production or transformation of sound and for its reproduction. A distinction is made between electronic music and concrete music: the former, in a strict sense, employs only sounds created electronically; the latter uses natural sounds recorded through a microphone—e.g., running steps, dripping water, human voices,—and transforms or manipulates these sounds by electronic means. The use of magnetic tape is common to all the experiments in composition and is essential for the performance of a work that is reproduced electronically by loudspeakers.

electronics (ĭlĕk″trŏ′nĭks), science that deals with use of electrons emitted from solids or liquids and made to move through a vacuum or a gas. Electrons in outer orbit of an atom of a metal can be liberated by heating the surface (thermionic emission); by allowing light to fall on certain surfaces (as in PHOTOELECTRIC CELL); by bombarding metal surface with electrons or with ions (secondary emission); and by use of intense electric field of high positive potential (high-field emission or cold-cathode effect). Electron emission also occurs in naturally radioactive substances (e.g., radium, thorium, uranium, plutonium) and in cyclotron and other atom-disintegrating machines. Edison observed thermionic emission in lamp bulb (1883). Sir J. A. Fleming utilized thermionic emission in his two-element vacuum tube, or diode; Lee de Forest produced triode (1907) which advanced radio. Radio, television, Loran, radar devices, electron microscope, betatron, cyclotron, X-ray machine and certain other medical tools are products of science of electronics. Light of neon signs and of mercury-vapor, sodium-vapor, and fluorescent lamps is produced by passage of electrons through the gas. See *ill.*, p. 322

electron microscope: see MICROSCOPE.

electron tube: see TUBE, VACUUM.

electrophorus: see VOLTA, ALESSANDRO, CONTE.

electroplating: see PLATING.

electrotherapy (ĭlĕk″trōthĕ′rŭpē), use of electricity for medical treatment and diagnosis. Galvanic (direct) current is used to destroy skin tumors and blemishes, to stimulate surface circulation, to introduce charged particles into tissues. Diathermy (use of long- or short-wave high-frequency currents) produces heat.

electrotype, in printing, a plate made by electrically coating with metal a wax or plastic mold, then pouring molten type metal over this coating.

elegy, in Greek and Roman poetry, a poem in elegiac verse (i.e., a couplet of a hexameter line followed by a pentameter line). Elegiac verse reached its height in Latin works of Catullus and Ovid. In English the elegy is a short formal poem of personal lament over death or unhappy love. There is no set pattern. Examples include Milton's "Lycidas," Shelley's "Adonais," and Whitman's "When Lilacs Last in the Dooryard Bloom'd."

element, in chemistry, substance composed of atoms, all of which are identical. Elements cannot be decomposed into simpler substances by chemical action. Each element is represented by a symbol. Listing elements in order of increasing ATOMIC WEIGHT was important step in formulation of PERIODIC LAW. Elements differ in VALENCE, boiling and melting points, density and specific gravity, hardness, specific heat, spectrum, radioactivity, compressibility, elasticity, thermal expansion, electrical conductivity. Some appear in different forms (see ALLOTROPY; ISOTOPE). Oxygen is most abundant element. Elements may be gas, liquid, or solid, and either metals or nonmetals. Some metallic elements were known to early man and alchemists discovered some. Hennig Brandt probably was first to discover a new element; in 1669 he prepared phosphorus from human urine. With production of transuranium elements with cyclotron, gaps in periodic table were filled and new elements were discovered. TRANSMUTATION OF ELEMENTS has been accomplished.

elephant, largest living land mammal, of order Proboscidea, related to extinct mammoth and mastodon. Ancestral home believed to be Egypt, from where it migrated to Asia, Europe, North and South America. Two genera living: Asiatic or Indian (*Elephas*), and African (*Loxodonta*) now found S of Sahara only. African bulls reach 11 ft. shoulder height, Asiatic c.9 ft. African elephant has larger ears and tusks; longer, more wrinkled trunk terminating in two fingerlike protuberances (one in Asiatic). Trunk conveys plant foods to mouth and sucks up water to spray into mouth. Adults mature at 25 yrs.; at 50 are old. Usually one calf born at time; gestation lasts 18–22 months. Pygmy elephant (5–7 ft. high) inhabits W Africa. Herds in both Africa and India have been much reduced by unregulated hunting.

Elephanta (ĕlĭfän′tŭ), island, area c.2 sq. mi., in Bombay harbor, Maharashtra, India. Brahmanic cave temples (8th cent.).

Elephant Butte Dam, N.Mex.: see RIO GRANDE.

elephantiasis (ĕ″lŭfăntĭ′ŭsĭs, –fŭn–), condition resulting from obstruction of lymphatic vessels and marked by edematous enlargement of affected part and thickening of skin (see EDEMA). It sometimes accompanies filariasis (disease caused by parasitic roundworms).

Elephantine (ĕ″lŭfăntĭ′nē), island, Egypt, in the Nile near Aswan. The anc. Nilometer, built to gauge the water level of the Nile, is here.

elephant's ear: see TARO.

elephant's-foot or **Hottentot bread,** twining S African vine (*Testudinaria elephantipes*), with huge edible roots.

Eleusinian Mysteries (ĕl″ūsĭ′nēŭn), principal religious mysteries of anc. Greece, held at Eleusis. Dealt with legends of Demeter, Persephone, and Dionysus, symbolized yearly decay and renewal of vegetation, and the immortality of the soul.

elevator, device for vertical transportation. Term is applied to both enclosed structures and open ones used in buildings, ships, and mines and also to continuous-belt device with buckets for handling bulk material. Power elevators, often run by steam, were used from middle of 19th cent. Elisha Graves Otis in 1853 introduced elevator with safety device in case cable should break. Sir William Armstrong's introduction of hydraulic crane (1846) led to hydraulic elevators, which began to replace steam elevators in early 1870s. Toward close of 19th cent. electric elevators came into use.

Elfsborg, Sweden: see ALVSBORG.

Elgar, Sir Edward, 1857–1934, English composer. Music composed for Queen Victoria's Diamond Jubilee (1897) brought him recognition; he was knighted in 1904. His works include a violin concerto, two symphonies, the so-called *Enigma Variations,* and the five marches, *Pomp and Circumstance.*

Elgin, Thomas Bruce, 7th **earl of** (ĕl′gĭn), 1766–1841, British soldier and diplomat. Brought to England the so-called ELGIN MARBLES from Athens. His son, **James Bruce,** 8th **earl of Elgin** (1811–63), governor general of Canada (1847–54), implemented plan for responsible government outlined by his father-in-law, the earl of DURHAM. Negotiated with U.S. the reciprocity treaty of 1854. His son, **Victor Alexander Bruce,** 9th **earl of Elgin,** 1849–1917, was viceroy of India 1894–99 and colonial secretary 1905–8.

Elgin (ĕl′jĭn), city (pop. 49,447), NE Ill., on Fox R., NW of Chicago; founded 1835. A rail, trade and industrial city; home of Elgin watch factories. Elgin Community Col. is here.

Elgin Marbles (ĕl′gĭn), ancient sculptures taken from Athens to London in 1806 by Thomas Bruce, 7th earl of Elgin. Consist of PARTHENON frieze and part of the ERECHTHEUM. They are now in British Mus.

Elginshire, county, Scotland: see MORAYSHIRE.

Elgon, Mount (ĕl′gŏn), peak, 14,178 ft. high, central Africa, on the Kenya-Uganda border; extinct volcano.

Element	Symbol	Atomic Number	Mass Number*	Atomic Weight	Melting Point In degrees Centigrade	Boiling Point	Valence
actinium	Ac	89	227		1600(†)		
aluminum	Al	13	27	26.98	659.7	2057	3
americium	Am	95	243				3, 4, 5, 6
antimony (stibium)	Sb	51	121	121.75	630.5	1380	3, 5
argon	Ar	18	40	39.948	−189.2	−185.7	0
arsenic	As	33	75	74.92	sublimes at 615		3, 5
astatine	At	85	210				1, 3, 5, 7
barium	Ba	56	138	137.34	850	1140	2
berkelium	Bk	97	247				3, 4
beryllium	Be	4	9	9.02	1278±5	2970	2
bismuth	Bi	83	209	209.00	271.3	1560±5	3, 5
boron	B	5	11	10.81	2300	2550	3
bromine	Br	35	79	79.909	−7.2	58.78	1, 3, 5, 7
cadmium	Cd	48	114	112.41	320.9	767±2	2
calcium	Ca	20	40	40.08	842±8	1240	2
californium	Cf	98	249				
carbon	C	6	12	12.011	>3550	4200	2, 4
cerium	Ce	58	140	140.13	804	1400	3, 4
cesium	Cs	55	133	132.91	28.5	670	1
chlorine	Cl	17	35	35.453	−103±5	−34.6	1, 3, 5, 7
chromium	Cr	24	52	51.996	1890	2480	2, 3, 6
cobalt	Co	27	59	58.93	1495	2900	2, 3
copper	Cu	29	63	63.54	1083	2336	1, 2
curium	Cm	96	248	245			3
dysprosium	Dy	66	164	162.51			3
einsteinium	Es	99	254				
erbium	Er	68	166	167.27			3
europium	Eu	63	153	152.0	1150±50		2, 3
fermium	Fm	100	252				
fluorine	F	9	19	19.00	−223	−188	1
francium	Fr	87	223				1
gadolinium	Gd	64	158	157.26			3
gallium	Ga	31	69	69.72	29.78	1983	2, 3
germanium	Ge	32	74	72.60	958.5	2700	4
gold	Au	79	197	197.0	1063	2600	1, 3
hafnium	Hf	72	180	178.49	1700(†)	>3200	4
helium	He	2	4	4.003	−272	−268.9	0
holmium	Ho	67	165	164.93			3
hydrogen	H	1	1	1.0080	−259.14	−252.8	1
indium	In	49	115	114.82	156.4	2000±10	3
iodine	I	53	127	126.90	113.7	184.35	1, 3, 5, 7
iridium	Ir	77	193	192.2	2454	>4800	3, 4
iron	Fe	26	56	55.85	1535	3000	2, 3
krypton	Kr	36	84	83.8	−156.6	−152.9	0
lanthanum	La	57	139	138.91	826		3
lawrencium	Lw	103	257				
lead	Pb	82	208	207.19	327.43	1620	2, 4
lithium	Li	3	7	6.940	186	1336±5	1
lutetium	Lu	71	175	174.97			3
magnesium	Mg	12	24	24.31	651	1107	2
manganese	Mn	25	55	54.94	1260	1900	2, 3, 4, 6, 7
mendelevium	Mv	101	256				
mercury	Hg	80	202	200.59	−38.87	356.58	1, 2
molybdenum	Mo	42	98	95.94	2620±10	4800	3, 4, 6
neodymium	Nd	60	142	144.24	840		3
neon	Ne	10	20	20.183	−248.67	−245.9	0
neptunium	Np	93	237				4, 5, 6
nickel	Ni	28	58	58.71	1455	2900	2, 3
niobium	Nb	41	93	92.91	2500±50	3700	3, 5
nitrogen	N	7	14	14.0067	−209.86	−195.8	3, 5
nobelium	No	102	253				
osmium	Os	76	192	190.2	2700	>5300	2, 3, 4, 8
oxygen	O	8	16	16.000	−218.4	−182.86	2
palladium	Pd	46	106	106.4	1549.4	2000	2, 4
phosphorus	P	15	31	30.974			3, 5
platinum	Pt	78	195	195.09	1773.5	4300	2, 4
plutonium	Pu	94	242				3, 4, 5, 6

* The mass number value given is that of the stable (nonradioactive) isotope most common in nature. For elements having no stable isotope, the mass number of the isotope having the longest half life (slowest rate of radioactive decay) is given in italics.

†Computed.   > Greater than.

ELEMENTS (continued)

Element	Symbol	Atomic Number	Mass Number*	Atomic Weight	Melting Point	Boiling Point	Valence
					In degrees Centigrade		
polonium	Po	84	209	210			
potassium	K	19	39	39.102	63.3	760	1
praseodymium	Pr	59	141	140.91	940		3
promethium	Pm	61	145				3
protactinium	Pa	91	231	231			
radium	Ra	88	226	226	700	1140	2
radon	Rn	86	222	222	−71	−61.8	0
rhenium	Re	75	187	186.22	3167±60		
rhodium	Rh	45	103	102.91	1966±3	>2500	3
rubidium	Rb	37	85	85.47	38.5	700	1
ruthenium	Ru	44	102	101.1	2450	2700	3, 4, 6, 8
samarium	Sm	62	152	150.35	>1300		2, 3
scandium	Sc	21	45	44.96	1200	2400	3
selenium	Se	34	80	78.96	217	688	2, 4, 6
silicon	Si	14	28	28.09	1420	2355	4
silver	Ag	47	107	107.870	960.8	1950	1
sodium	Na	11	23	22.991	97.5	880	1
strontium	Sr	38	88	87.62	800	1150	2
sulfur	S	16	32	32.06	See SULFUR		2, 4, 6
tantalum	Ta	73	180	180.95	2996±50	c. 4100	5
technetium	Tc	43	99				6, 7
tellurium	Te	52	130	127.60	452	1390	2, 4, 6
terbium	Tb	65	159	158.92	327±5		3
thallium	Tl	81	205	204.37	302	1457±10	1, 3
thorium	Th	90	232	232.04	1845	4500	4
thulium	Tm	69	169	168.93			3
tin	Sn	50	120	118.70	231.89	2270	2, 4
titanium	Ti	22	48	47.90	1800	>3000	3, 4
tungsten (wolfram)	W	74	184	183.85	3370	5900	6
uranium	U	92	238	238.03	c.1133		4, 6
vanadium	V	23	51	50.94	1710	3000	3, 5
xenon	Xe	54	132	131.30	−112	−107.1	0
ytterbium	Yb	70	174	173.04	1800		2, 3
yttrium	Y	39	89	88.91	1490	2500	3
zinc	Zn	30	64	65.37	419.47	907	2
zirconium	Zr	40	90	91.22	1857	>2900	4

* The mass number value given is that of the stable (nonradioactive) isotope most common in nature. For elements having no stable isotope, the mass number of the isotope having the longest half life (slowest rate of radioactive decay) is given in italics.

† Computed. > Greater than.

El Greco: see GRECO, EL.

Eli (ē'lī), high priest and judge of Israel, teacher of boy Samuel. 1 Sam. 1–4.

Eli, Eli, lama sabachthani? (ē'lī, lä'mû säbăk'thûnī; ā'lĕ, lä'mäsäbäkh'thänē) or **Eloi, Eloi, lama sabachthani?** (ē'loi; ä'loi) [Eli, Eloi: Heb. or Aramaic,= Lord; lama sabachthani?: Aramaic,= why hast thou forsaken me?], cry of Jesus on the cross. Mat. 27.46; Mark 15.34. Seemingly a quotation of Ps. 22.1.

Elia: see LAMB, CHARLES.

Eliakim (ēlī'ŭkĭm), king of Judah: see JEHOIAKIM.

Elias, Greek form of ELIJAH.

Elihu (ēlī'hū) [Heb.,=he is my God], last of Job's comforters to speak. Job 32.2–37.24.

Elijah (ēlī'jù) or **Elias** (ēlī'ùs) [Heb.,= God's God], fl. c.875 B.C., Hebrew prophet. His mission was to destroy cults of Baal brought into Israel by Jezebel, wife of King Ahab. He is the hero of many stories (e.g., his raising of widow's son from the dead; his contest of faith with priests of Baal; his being fed by ravens; his experience of the still, small voice on Mt. Horeb). He departed from earth in a chariot of fire, leaving his sacred mantle and the continuation of his work to his disciple Elisha. Elijah appeared in the Transfiguration. He is prominent in the Koran. 1 Kings 17–19; 21.17–29; 2 Kings 1–2; Mal. 4.5; Mat. 11.14; 16.14; 17.3; Luke 4.25; John 1.21; James 5.17.

Elijah ben Solomon, 1720–97, Jewish scholar. Known as the Gaon [excellence] of Vilna. Opposed Hasidic movement among Jews of Poland and Lithuania.

Eliot, Charles W(illiam), 1834–1926, American educator, president of Harvard Univ. (1869–1909). Under his guidance many changes were made—e.g., introduction of elective system—the university grew, and standards were raised. Eliot also fostered development of Radcliffe Col. He was later a member of the General Education Board, a trustee of the Carnegie Foundation for the Advancement of Teaching, and an emissary abroad of the Carnegie Endowment for Internatl. Peace. He edited The Harvard Classics to further adult education.

Eliot, George, 1819–80, English novelist, real name Mary Ann or Marian Evans. She defied convention to live a happy life with George Henry LEWES, mentor of her literary career. Her novels picture middle-class life in realistic terms with stern moral interest: in Adam Bede (1859), The Mill on the Floss (1860), Silas Marner (1861), Middlemarch (1871–72), Daniel Deronda (1876). Also wrote Romola (1862–63) and Felix Holt (1866). After Lewes's death she married John W. Cross (1880).

Eliot, Sir John, 1592–1632, English statesman. Promoter of PETITION OF RIGHT (1628), he refused to submit to Charles I and died in prison.

Eliot, John, 1604–90, English missionary in colonial Mass., called the Apostle to the Indians. Estab. villages for Christian natives, translated (1661–63) Bible into an Algonquian Indian language (first Bible printed in North America).

Eliot, T(homas) S(tearns), 1888–1965, English poet and critic, b. St. Louis, Mo.; studied at Harvard, the Sorbonne, and Oxford. His poetry, highly influential and much imitated, is complex, with allusions and references in intellectual, often difficult language. His early poetical works (e.g., *Prufrock and Other Observations,* 1917; *The Waste Land,* 1922) express disillusion and despair over modern life. He became a British subject and an Anglo-Catholic in 1927. Later poetry included *Ash Wednesday* (1930) and *Four Quartets* (1935–42). His plays (e.g., *Murder in the Cathedral,* 1935; *The Cocktail Party,* 1950) attempted to revitalize verse drama. His critical essays did much to revive interest in the literature of the 16th and 17th cent. The more recent of them were collected in *On Poetry and Poets,* 1957. Awarded the 1948 Nobel Prize in Literature.

Elis (ē′lĭs), region of anc. Greece, W Peloponnesus, noted for horses and for games at OLYMPIA.

Elisabethville: see LUBUMBASHI.

Elisavetgrad, Ukrainian SSR: see KIROVOGRAD.

Elisha (ēlī′shù) or **Eliseus** (ĕlĭsē′ŭs) [both: Heb.,= God is salvation], fl. 875 B.C., Hebrew prophet. He continued the work of ELIJAH under successors of Ahab. His miracles include raising of the dead boy, curing of Naaman's leprosy, and timely aid to widow in debt. 1 Kings 19.16–21; 2 Kings 2.9; 13.14–21; Luke 4.27.

Elizabeth, Saint, mother of St. John the Baptist and cousin of the Virgin MARY. Luke 1. Feast: Nov. 5.

Elizabeth, Saint, 1207–31, daughter of Andrew II of Hungary, wife of Louis II of Thuringia; noted for devotion to the needy.

Elizabeth, 1837–98, empress of Austria and queen of Hungary, consort of Francis Joseph; a Bavarian princess. Her life was marked by tragedy, notably the death of her son, Archduke RUDOLF, and her own assassination by an Italian anarchist at Geneva.

Elizabeth, 1709–62, empress of Russia (1741–62); daughter of Peter I and Catherine I. Gained throne by deposing IVAN VI. Rid Russia of German influence; successfully warred against Prussia in SEVEN YEARS WAR. Founded Moscow Univ. Her nephew, Peter III, succeeded her.

Elizabeth, 1876–1965, queen of Belgium, consort of ALBERT I; a Bavarian princess. Revered for her hospital work in First World War.

Elizabeth, 1596–1662, queen of Bohemia and countess palatine, consort of FREDERICK THE WINTER KING; daughter of James I of England. Nicknamed "Queen of Hearts" for her beauty. After her husband's defeat (1620) she lived in poverty in Holland; returned to England 1661. Among her 13 children were Prince RUPERT and SOPHIA, electress of Hanover.

Elizabeth I, 1533–1603, queen of England (1558–1603). Daughter of HENRY VIII and Anne BOLEYN, she was declared illegitimate after her mother's execution. Parliament reestab. her in succession in 1544. Imprisoned as rallying point for discontented Protestants, she regained freedom by outward conformity to Catholicism. On her succession England's low fortunes included religious strife, a huge government debt, and failure in wars with France. Her reign took England through one of its greatest eras. It produced such men as Shakespeare, Spenser, Francis Bacon, and Walter Raleigh. It saw the country united to become a first-rate European power with a great navy. It saw commerce and industry prosper and colonization begin. Her Tudor concept of strong rule and need for popular support helped her select excellent counselors. She reestab. Anglicanism and measures against Catholics grew harsher. Important measures enacted included stabilization of labor conditions, currency reforms, poor laws, and acts to encourage agr., commerce, and mfg. Elizabeth began a policy

of peace and her series of diplomatic maneuvers eventually defeated Spain and stalemated France. Treaty of Edinburgh (1560) started policy of supporting Protestant lords against Catholics. After abdication of MARY QUEEN OF SCOTS from Scottish throne, Elizabeth gave her refuge, kept her prisoner, and executed her only after plots to seat Mary on English throne. By marriage negotiations with Francis, duke of Alençon and Anjou, she secured (1572) defence alliance against Spain and, later, French aid for the Dutch against Spain, who now emerged as England's main enemy. Philip II of Spain, whose offer of marriage Elizabeth had refused in 1559, planned Spanish Armada expedition as reprisal against English raids on Spanish shipping. Defeat of Armada broke power of Spain. Vain, fickle in bestowing favors (see 2d earl of ESSEX and earl of LEICESTER), prejudiced, vacillating, and parsimonious, she was also highly aware of responsibility of rule and immensely courageous.

Elizabeth II, 1926–, queen of Great Britain (1952–), eldest daughter of GEORGE VI. She married (1947) Philip Mountbatten, duke of Edinburgh. They visited Canada and U.S. in 1957 and 1959. They have three children: Prince Charles (1948–), Princess Anne (1950–), and Prince Andrew (1960–). Her mother, **Elizabeth,** 1900–, queen consort of George VI, is the daughter of the 14th earl of Strathmore.

Elizabeth, 1843–1916, queen of Rumania, consort of Carol I; a German princess. Wrote extensively, under pseud. Carmen Sylva, in German, French, English, Rumanian. Her works include *Pensées d'une reine* (1882); *The Bard of Dimbowitza* (1891; Rumanian folk tales).

Elizabeth, city (pop. 107,698), NE N.J., S of Newark, on Newark Bay and Arthur Kill (Goethals Bridge to Staten Isl.). Area purchased from Indians 1664; called Elizabethtown until 1740. Was home and provincial cap. of Gov. Philip Carteret; assembly met here, 1668–82. School that became Princeton Univ. was founded 1747. Scene of several Revolutionary clashes; many buildings were burned 1780. Expansion of industry (esp. machine production, oil refining, shipbuilding) in 19th cent.; a Singer sewing-machine plant was estab. 1873. Has Elias Boudinot's house (c.1750), Belcher Mansion (before 1750), and Nathaniel Bonnell House (before 1682). Alexander Hamilton and Aaron Burr once lived here.

Elizabeth City, town (pop. 14,062), NE N.C., port of entry on Pasquotank R., N of Albemarle Sound; founded 1793. Agr. trade and shipping center, with boatyards; gateway to sportsmen's resort area. A U.S. Coast Guard air station is nearby.

Elizabeth Farnese (färnā′sā), 1692–1766, queen of Spain, second wife of PHILIP V; niece of duke of Parma. She dominated her weak husband; secured Naples and Parma for her sons Charles and Philip.

Elizabeth Islands, chain forming SE boundary of Buzzards Bay, off SE Mass. Cuttyhunk (discovered 1602, settled 1641) is farthest W; Naushon (nô′shŭn), 7 mi. long, is largest.

Elizabeth of Valois (välwä′), 1545–68, queen of Spain, third wife of Philip II; daughter of Henry II of France. She had been originally promised to Philip's son CARLOS, but the story of a tragic love between her and Carlos is unfounded.

Elizabethton, town (pop. 10,896), NE Tenn., E of Johnson City, one of earliest settlements in Tenn. Sycamore Shoals Monument commemorates organization of WATAUGA ASSOCIATION 1772, Richard Henderson's Cherokee treaty 1775, and formation of Revolutionary force. An industrial and textile center.

Elizabethtown. 1 City (pop. 9,641), central Ky., S of Louisville; settled 1780. Trade center for farm (esp. tobacco and grain) and limestone area. Thomas Lincoln once lived here. Union garrison captured here by Gen. J. H. Morgan, Dec., 1862. Area's Indian mounds have yielded artifacts. Fort Knox is N. **2** Early name of ELIZABETH, N.J.

elk, member of deer family, genus *Alces* (or *Alce*), found in reduced numbers in parts of N Europe and Asia. Smaller but similar to American MOOSE.

Elkader (ĕlkä'dŭr), town (pop. 1,526), NE Iowa, on Turkey R., NW of Dubuque. Ruins of Communia, a cooperative town settled c.1850, are nearby.

Elk Grove Village, village (1964 pop. 13,155), NE Ill., a suburb NW of Chicago.

Elkhart, industrial city (pop. 40,274), N Ind., at junction of Elkhart and St. Joseph rivers, E of South Bend, in farm area; settled 1832. Has railroad shops and yards.

Elkhorn, river rising in N Nebr. and flowing c.333 mi. SE to Platte R. WSW of Omaha.

Elkhorn Tavern: see PEA RIDGE.

Elkins, Stephen Benton, 1841–1911, American statesman. U.S. Secretary of War (1891–93). As U.S. Senator from W.Va. (1895–1911), he was the author of the Elkins Act of 1903 against REBATE system.

Elk Island National Park, central Alta., Canada, E of Edmonton; estab. 1913. Canada's chief fenced preserve of buffalo and other prairie animals.

Elk Mountains, range of Rocky Mts., W central Colo. Its highest point, Castle Peak (also called Mt. Carbon), rises to 14,265 ft. SW part called West Elk Mts.

Elkton. 1 City (pop. 1,448), SW Ky., ESE of Hopkinsville near Tenn. line, in tobacco, livestock, and farm area. Birthplace of Jefferson Davis marked by memorial park and monument. **2** Town (pop. 5,989), NE Md., NE of Baltimore; founded 1681. Until state changed marriage laws (1938), town was Gretna Green of Eastern states.

Ellesmere, Thomas Egerton, Baron, 1540?–1617, lord chancellor of England. He took part in trial of Mary Queen of Scots (1586) and was a favorite and adviser of Queen Elizabeth. Originally a friend of the 2d earl of Essex, he was a witness against him at the trial which resulted in his execution. Retained by James I, he upheld James's harsh policy toward Puritans and was severe to Catholics. He was a man of learning and an incorruptible judge.

Ellesmere Island, 77,392 sq. mi., largest of Queen Elizabeth Isls., Franklin dist., Northwest Territories, Canada, in Arctic Ocean opposite NW Greenland. Most northerly of Arctic Archipelago; largely covered by ice cap in SE.

Ellet, Charles, 1810–62, American civil engineer, noted bridge and canal builder. During Civil War he designed and built ramboats that helped capture Memphis by sinking Confederate gunboats. His flood control plan for Mississippi and Ohio rivers (1853) was reprinted (1927–28) for use of Congress.

Ellice Islands (ĕl'ĭs) or **Lagoon Islands,** group of nine atolls (9.5 sq. mi.; est. pop. 5,039), S Pacific; with Gilbert Isls. constitutes British colony. Most important are Funafuti and Nanumea. Discovered 1764. Main export is copra.

Ellicott, Andrew, 1754–1820, American surveyor. As surveyor of capital at Washington, he issued a revised city plan (1792). Surveyed U.S.–Fla. boundary (1796–1800) and Ga.–S.C. boundary (1811–12).

Ellington, Duke (Edward Kennedy Ellington), 1899–, American jazz pianist and composer.

Elliot, Daniel Giraud, 1835–1915, American zoologist, authority on birds of Near East and Europe. His works include *Review of the Primates* (3 vols., 1912).

Elliott Lake, district (pop. 13,179), S Ont., Canada, W of Sudbury. Center of large uranium-mining area.

ellipse (ĭlĭps'), closed CONIC SECTION (other than circle). Can be defined analytically as closed plane curve of which sum of distances between any point on curve and two fixed points (foci) is same for all points of curve.

Ellis, Havelock, 1859–1939, English psychologist. A qualified physician, his major work, *Studies in the Psychology of Sex* (1897–1928), greatly influenced the public attitude toward sex problems.

Ellis Island, SE N.Y., in Upper New York Bay, SW of Manhattan isl.; c.27 acres. Government property

since 1808. Nation's chief immigration station 1892–1943. Part of Statue of Liberty Natl. Monument since 1965.

Ellison, Ralph (Waldo), 1914–, American Negro novelist and teacher. Works include the distinguished novel *The Invisible Man* (1952; rev. ed., 1961), *Shadow and Act* (1964, collected essays), and many more short stories, lectures, and essays.

Ellora (ĕlō'rŭ), village, Maharashtra, India. Has Hindu, Buddhist, and Jain rock and cave temples 5th–13th cent.), which extend over a mile. The Kailasa, temple of Siva carved from a single mass of rock, is one of India's greatest architectural treasures.

Ellsworth, Henry Leavitt, 1791–1858, American agriculturist who worked to promote agricultural research and aid to farmers.

Ellsworth, Lincoln, 1880–1951, American explorer. Financial supporter and associate of Roald Amundsen in arctic aviation ventures. Flew over North Pole in 1926. Accomplished first flight over Antarctica in 1935. In 1939 he flew into interior Antarctica, viewing and claiming for U.S. land (named American Highland) hitherto unseen.

Ellsworth, Oliver, 1745–1807, American statesman. Advanced "Connecticut compromise" at FEDERAL CONSTITUTIONAL CONVENTION. Chief Justice of the United States (1796–99).

Ellwood City, industrial borough (pop. 12,413), W central Pa., NW of Pittsburgh near Ohio line; settled 1890. Mfg. of metal products. Limestone deposits in area.

elm, deciduous tree of genus *Ulmus* of wide distribution. Among North American species are American or white elm (*Ulmus americana*), a favorite shade tree, and slippery elm (*U. fulva*). Elm wood is hard and durable. The Dutch elm disease, caused by a fungus carried by beetles, has exterminated many plantings in U.S. of both American and European species.

Elman, Mischa (ĕl'mŭn), 1891–1967, Russian-American violinist. After his debut in New York (1908), he toured widely in Europe and the U.S.

Elmhurst, residential city (1963 pop. 40,329), NE Ill., W of Chicago, in truck-farm area; settled 1843. Seat of Elmhurst Col.

Elmina (ĕlmē'nŭ), town (pop. c.10,000), Ghana, on Gulf of Guinea; earliest European settlement on the Gold Coast. Founded by Portuguese, who lost it to the Dutch in 1637; purchased from them by the British in 1872.

Elmira, city (pop. 46,517), S central N.Y., on Chemung R., W of Binghamton near Pa. line; settled 1788. Distributing and mfg. center. Burial place of Mark Twain and seat of Elmira Col. Elmira State Reformatory (see Z. R. BROCKWAY) and Arnot Art Gall. are here. Annual glider contest held nearby.

Elmo, Saint: see PETER GONZALEZ, SAINT.

Elmont, residential city (pop. 30,138), SE N.Y., on W Long Isl., E of Jamaica. Belmont Park race track is nearby.

El Monte, city (pop. 13,163), S Calif., E of Los Angeles; founded 1842.

El Morro National Monument: see NATIONAL PARKS AND MONUMENTS (table).

Elmwood, city (pop. 1,882), N central Ill., WNW of Peoria, in coal and farm area. Birthplace of Lorado Taft, whose statue *Pioneers of the Prairies* is here.

Elmwood Park, village (pop. 23,866), NE Ill., a suburb NW of Chicago.

Elohim (ĕlōhēm', ĕlō'hĭm), Hebrew word for God. Actually plural of *elōh* but often used as singular.

Eloi, Eloi, lama sabachthani?: see ELI, ELI, LAMA SABACHTHANI?

Elon College (ē'lŭn), town (pop. 1,284), N central N.C., E of Greensboro. Elon Col. is here.

Eloth (ē'lōth), the same as ELATH.

El Paso (ĕl pă'sō), city (pop. 276,687), W Texas, on Rio Grande opposite JUÁREZ, Mexico. Much international traffic (rail, highway, air). Largest U.S.–Mex. border city; its long past is bound with that of Juárez. Both are in region once known as El Paso del Norte to which missionaries, soldiers, and traders came in 17th cent. Missions were founded at YSLETA and elsewhere, but main settlement was Juárez. First El Paso house not built until 1827. After U.S.–Mex. border was estab. and railroad arrived (1881), settlement grew and city became great commercial center. Vineyards irrigated by Elephant Butte Dam yield prized Paso wine. Diversified industries include copper and oil refining. Attracts tourists, but international trade is most important. Texas Western Col. of the Univ. of Texas, U.S. Fort Bliss, and army hospital are here. Biggs Air Force Base is NE.

Elphinstone, George Keith, 1746–1823, British admiral. In wars of American and French revolutions, he was noted for the reduction of Charleston (1780) and the capture of Capetown (1795).

El Reno, city (pop. 11,015), central Okla., near North Canadian R., WNW of Oklahoma City; settled 1889. Marketing and shipping center with railroad shops. U.S. reformatory and Fort Reno are nearby.

El Segundo (ĕl sĭgŭn'dō), industrial city (pop. 14,219), S Calif., on Santa Monica Bay SW of Los Angeles; founded 1911 as oil town.

Elsheimer, Adam (ä'däm ĕls'hīmùr), 1578–1610?, German painter. He painted chiefly biblical and mythological pictures notable for landscape backgrounds and light effects. His *Good Samaritan* (Louvre) is one of his well-known works.

Elsinore (ĕl'sĭnôr"). Dan. *Helsingør*, city (pop. 26,658), NE Zealand, Denmark; a port on the Oresund opposite Halsingborg. Flourished until 1857 as toll-collection station for ships passing through Oresund. Kronborg castle (built 1577–85; restored 1635–40) is sometimes used for performances of Shakespeare's *Hamlet*, which is laid in Elsinore.

Elssler, Fanny (ĕl'slùr), 1810–84, Austrian dancer. Made her debut in 1833 and was popular in London, Paris, and U.S. Her forte was folk dancing.

Eluard, Paul (pôl' älwär'), 1895–1952, French poet. Was long associated with surrealism, later with Communism. Among his volumes of poetry are *Mourir de ne pas mourir* (1924), *Poésie et vérité* (1942), *Au rendez-vous allemand* (1945). Was active in anti-German resistance during Second World War.

Elvehjem, Conrad Arnold (ĕlvä'ùm), 1901–, American biochemist. His research led to use of niacin (part of vitamin B complex) in treating pellagra. He discovered that copper is essential to hemoglobin formation and made many other valuable contributions.

Elvend or **Elwend** (both: ĕlvĕnd'), mountain, c.11,600 ft. high, W Iran, SW of Hamadan. It bears cuneiform inscriptions of Darius and Xerxes.

Elwood, city (pop. 11,793), central Ind., NNW of Anderson; platted 1852. Processes and ships tomatoes. grain, and livestock. W. L. Willkie born here.

Ely, Richard Theodore, 1854–1943, American economist who helped popularize study of economics. A founder of American Economic Association and an early leader of Christian socialism in U.S.

Ely, city (pop. 4,018), E central Nev.; settled 1868. Trade center for state's rich copper-mining area. Lehman Caves Natl. Monument (see NATIONAL PARKS AND MONUMENTS, table) and Wheeler Peak are near.

Ely, City of, urban district (pop. 9,815), Isle of Ely, England, NNE of Cambridge. Ely cathedral (begun 1083), one of largest in England, has architecture of varied periods. Within its grounds are Tudor palace of the bishop, a theological college, and King's Grammar School, founded by Henry VIII.

Ely, Isle of, administrative county (372 sq. mi.; pop. 89,112), E England; administrative center is March. Region of extensive fens, now drained for agr. Historically a part of CAMBRIDGESHIRE.

Elymas (ĕ'lĭmäs), the same as BAR-JESUS.

Elyria (ĭlēr'ēù), city (pop. 43,782), N Ohio, on Black R., WSW of Cleveland; settled 1817. Farm trade center.

Élysee (älēzā'), palace in Paris, France. Built 1718. Official residence of French presidents since 1873.

Elysian fields (ĭlī'zhŭn) or **Elysium** (ĭlī'zhēùm) in Greek religion, happy otherworld for heroes favored by the gods. Identified with Isles of the Blest or Fortunate Isls., and. in Vergil, part of underworld.

Elzevir, Louis (ĕl'zùvùr, –vēr), 1540–1617, Dutch publisher, whose name also appears as Elsevier and Elzevier. The business he founded in 1583 at Leiden was continued by his descendants until 1712, and the name is still used. They owned presses and type and hired good editors and printers to turn out legible inexpensive books. Because of types designed for the house by Christopher van Dyck, the type known in English-speaking countries as "old-style" is called "Elzevir" on the Continent.

Emancipation, Edict of, March 3, 1861 (N.S.), edict by which Alexander II freed all Russian serfs (c.22,000,000—one third of total pop.). Provisions for peasants' purchase of land were complex and cumbersome, made private ownership of land nearly impossible until belated reform of STOLYPIN (1906).

Emancipation Proclamation. Despite insistence of abolitionists, Pres. Lincoln, in early Civil War, did not issue edict freeing slaves lest it alienate loyal border states. But on July 22, 1862, he read a draft to his cabinet. After successful Antietam campaign he issued preliminary edict, and on Jan. 1, 1863, the formal Emancipation Proclamation. It did not free all slaves in U.S., but only those in states in rebellion "as a fit and necessary war measure for suppressing said rebellion." Designed to deplete Southern manpower reserve in slaves and to enhance Union cause abroad.

embalming (ĕmbä'mĭng), treatment for preserving a corpse. Practiced by ancient peoples, notably Egyptians. Bodies can now be preserved indefinitely.

Embargo Act of 1807, passed Dec. 22, 1807, by U.S. Congress in answer to British ORDERS IN COUNCIL restricting neutral shipping and to Napoleon's opposing CONTINENTAL SYSTEM. Forbade all international trade to and from American ports in attempt to persuade England and France of the value and rights of a neutral commerce. In Jan., 1809, prohibition was extended to inland waters and land commerce to halt trade with Canada. England and France stood firm, and enforcement of act was difficult, especially in New England. Acts replacing it effectually dissolved whole purpose of embargo.

embezzlement, misappropriation of another's property by a wrongdoer who is in lawful possession. Since common law considered only "felonious taking" as larceny, the misuse of funds by the legal administrator for selfish ends is covered in England and U.S. by statutes making embezzlement a distinct crime or enlarging definition of larceny to include it.

embolism, any condition resulting from presence in blood vessel of an obstruction (called embolus). THROMBOSIS (due to blood clots) is one type of embolism. Aeroembolism is due to presence of undissolved gas in blood stream; it can result from rapid changes in atmospheric pressure.

embroidery, ornamental needlework in thread, fiber, or leather thongs, applied to a fabric or to leather. As an art it is probably older than weaving; primitive peoples used embroidered skins. From ancient times, the East has produced rich embroideries; the art came to Europe through Byzantine influence. From 12th to 14th cent., church embroidery (e.g., altarcloths, vestments) flourished; later, secular embroidery, such as that on the rich costumes of Elizabethan England, reached its height. Advent of machinery caused decline of embroidery as an art.

embryo (ĕm'brēō), name for developing young of animal and plant. Embryology is the scientific study of development up to hatching or birth. Exact dura-

GENERALIZED DIAGRAMS OF MITOSIS IN A BODY CELL OF AN ANIMAL

Early prophase	Later prophases	Metaphase	Anaphase	Telophase	Daughter cells

Chromatin material forms a network of fine threads | Individual chromosomes form, and each splits lengthwise | Chromosomes continue to shorten and thicken | Spindle fibers form, and chromosomes line up at equator | Half of each chromosome moves toward nearest pole of spindle | New nuclear membrane forms around each chromosome group | Division of cytoplasm is completed; the two daughter cells have the same hereditary factors

REPRESENTATIVE STAGES IN MEIOSIS IN A GERM CELL OF AN ANIMAL

Chromatin material is in form of thin twisted thread | Homologous chromosomes pair off; diploid number here is eight | Paired chromosomes twist about each other | Paired chromosomes split lengthwise, forming tetrads | Tetrads line up at equator in first meiotic division | Two cells take form, each with four diads | Members of each diad separate in second meiotic division | Four gametes form, each with haploid number of chromosomes

FERTILIZATION OF AN EGG CELL

membrane
egg
nucleus
head of sperm
tail of sperm
entrance cone
aster
head of sperm
centrosome
fusing of egg and sperm nuclei

VARIOUS STAGES IN THE DEVELOPMENT OF A BIRD

shell
inner shell membrane
shell membrane
yolk
chalaza
albumen
air cavity
embryo

Hen's egg

yolk
blood vessels
embryo

Embryo about 5 days old

Embryo about 10 days old

Embryo about 15 days old

EMBRYOS OF THREE ANIMALS AT COMPARABLE STAGES OF DEVELOPMENT
(after Häckel)

Fish

Tortoise

Rabbit

Embryology is the science that tells of the development of animals from the union of single cells to the time of hatching or birth. Divisions known as cleavage begin soon after fertilization. The resulting hollow ball of cells develops layers which soon shift in relative position and are transformed into the various tissues of the early embryo.

tion of embryo stage is not well defined; in mammals the young in later prenatal stages is called fetus. In all animal reproduction involving union of sperm and egg cells, a series of cell divisions begins soon after fertilization; succeeding stages vary. In many forms, a blastula, a hollow ball consisting of one layer of cells, develops and later becomes two-layered cuplike gastrula; in higher forms, a third cell layer develops. Various body parts develop from each layer. In vertebrates, ectoderm forms brain, nerves, and skin; endoderm forms digestive organs; mesoderm, the third layer forms bone and muscle. See *ill.*, p. 329.

Emden (ĕm'dŭn), city (pop. 42,858), Lower Saxony, West Germany, chief city of East Friesland; a North Sea port at mouth of Ems R. and on Dortmund-Ems Canal. Shipyards, herring fisheries. Dates from 10th cent., had large merchant fleet in 16th cent.

emerald, green gem variety of BERYL. The finest come from South America. Oriental emerald is a variety of corundum.

Emerson, Ralph Waldo, 1803–82, American essayist, poet, and philosopher, b. Boston. Educated at Harvard for the Unitarian ministry, he became pastor of the Old North Church, Boston, in 1829 but retired in 1832 because of doctrinal difficulties. A trip to Europe broadened his acquaintance with the literary world of his day and wide reading in English, Continental, classic, and Oriental literature stimulated his thought. Settling in Concord, Mass., he, Thoreau, Margaret Fuller, and other friends soon made it a center of American TRANSCENDENTALISM. In *Nature* (1836) he set forth his belief in the mystical unity of nature. Noted as a lecturer, he called for American intellectual freedom in his Phi Beta Kappa address at Harvard (*The American Scholar,* 1837). In his address at the Harvard Divinity School in 1838 he asserted that the individual finds redemption and truth in his own soul and intuition. He developed this theme in lectures (which were yearly more famous) based on the *Journal* he had kept since Harvard days and in his related *Essays* (1st series, 1841; 2d series, 1844), among which were "The Over-Soul," "Compensation," and "Self-Reliance." Some of his short lyrics, such as "Brahma," and "The Concord Hymn," are familiar to many Americans. Later works include *English Traits* (1856; lectures after a trip to England in 1847), *Representative Men* (1850), *The Conduct of Life* (1860), and other collections of lectures.

emery: see CORUNDUM.

Emesa: see HOMS, Syria.

Emigrant Aid Company, formed 1854 to promote organized antislavery immigration to Kansas from the Northeast. Name associated exclusively with New England Emigrant Aid Co., though other Kansas aid societies were subsequently formed. Founder Eli Thayer received 10% of all money he collected. Amos A. Lawrence was treasurer. Company sent out 1,240 settlers. Natl. Kansas Committee, formed at Buffalo, N.Y., 1856, as joint endeavor of aid societies, divided over problem of how to handle proslavery excesses. Whole movement was virtually ended by 1857. The movement, although it did little toward making Kansas a free state, captured public attention and engendered much bitterness and hate.

Emilia-Romagna (āmē'lyä-rōmä'nyä), region (8,542 sq. mi.; pop. 3,646,507), N central Italy, extending S from Po R.; cap. BOLOGNA. Other cities: FERRARA, FORLÌ, MODENA, PARMA, PIACENZA, RAVENNA, REGGIO NELL' EMILIA, RIMINI. Fertile agr. plain; few industries. Annexed to Sardinia 1860. For earlier history see articles on individual cities; ROMAGNA.

Eminescu, Mihail (yĕmēnĕ'skŏō), 1850–89, foremost Rumanian poet, whose last name was originally Iminovici. His poetry has been widely translated.

Emin Pasha (ā'mĭn pä'shä), 1840–92, German explorer in Africa, originally named Eduard Schnitzer. Served 1876–78 in the Sudan as a medical officer; became governor of Equatoria prov. 1878. Cut off

by the Mahdist uprising in 1885, he returned to Mombasa with H. M. Stanley in 1889.

Emmanuel, in Bible: see IMMANUEL.

Emmanuel. For Byzantine and Portuguese rulers thus named, see MANUEL.

Emmanuel College: see CAMBRIDGE UNIVERSITY.

Emmanuel Philibert, 1528–80, duke of Savoy (1553–80), called Ironhead. In Spanish service, he fought the French, who had occupied Savoy; won a brilliant victory at Saint-Quentin (1557); recovered Savoy at Treaty of Cateau-Cambrésis (1559). An energetic reformer, he restored his duchy to prosperity, shifted his cap. to Turin, made Savoy an Italian rather than French state.

Emmaus (ĕm'äŭs), place near Jerusalem where Cleopas and another disciple met the risen Christ. Luke 24.13.

Emmaus (ĕmä'ŭs), industrial borough (pop. 10,262), E central Pa., S of Allentown; settled c.1740 by Moravians. Birthplace of Moravian church in U.S.

Emma Willard School, at Troy, N.Y.; for girls; founded and opened 1814 in Vermont as Middlebury Seminary, chartered 1819. Moved and called Troy Female Seminary 1821–92.

Emmental (ĕ'mŭntäl), valley of Emme R., Bern canton, Switzerland. Produces fine cheese.

Emmet, Robert, 1778–1803, Irish patriot. After an unsuccessful attempt at a French-aided uprising in Ireland (1803), he was captured and hanged. He made a stirring speech from the scaffold and became a great hero of Irish patriots.

Emmitsburg, town (pop. 1,369), N Md., near Pa. line NE of Hagerstown; founded around convent estab. 1809 by Mother Seton (who is buried here). Seat of St. Joseph Col.

Emory University, at Atlanta, Ga.; coed.; chartered as Emory Col. 1836, opened 1837 at Oxford; renamed 1915, moved 1919. Emory-at-Oxford, a four-year junior college, opened 1929 at original site.

emotion, term loosely used synonymously with feeling. In psychology: a response (to stimuli) involving physiological changes and tending to stimulate further activity. Fear, love, anger (primary responses) are roused directly by external stimuli, indirectly through memory, and expressed variously according to individual and to culture. Psychosomatic medicine has shown that tension from unrelieved emotions may cause physical disorders.

Empedocles (ĕmpĕ'dŭklēz), c.495–c.435 B.C., Greek philosopher. Held that universe was made up of particles of earth, air, fire, and water, and motion was basis of change.

emphysema, pathological or physiological enlargement or overdistension of air sacs of lungs. Usually chronic, it can be localized or diffuse. Symptoms are breathing difficulty, cough with sticky sputum, and bluish skin. A progressive disorder, it can occur with advanced age or as result of long-standing respiratory ailments.

Empire State Building, in central Manhattan, New York city, on Fifth Ave. between 33d and 34th streets, built 1930–31. Tallest building in the world; 1,250 ft. high, 102 stories.

Empire style, manner of interior decoration evolved in France from Directoire style and identified with reign of Napoleon I. Roman forms were used to emphasize grandeur of Napoleonic era, and symbols of imperial pomp added to traditional classic motifs. Staple wood was mahogany, but rosewood and ebony also used. Brass and ormolu mounts were chief ornaments. Style fell into disuse c.1840. Simplified form was adopted in England and U.S.; a German bourgeois adaptation is Biedermeier.

empiricism, philosophical doctrine that all knowledge is derived from experience. Opposed to RATIONALISM, it denies innate ideas and a priori truth and stresses generalizations based only on observation (experience). Basic to scientific method, it dominated British philosophy from Francis Bacon to John Stuart Mill.

employment bureau, establishment for bringing together the employer offering work and the employee seeking it. In England the first employment bureau was opened 1855; a national system was established 1909. France has had public employment agencies since 1916. In the U.S. the first state regulation of private agencies was in Mass. in 1848. Regulations requiring licensing have been enacted in 41 states. The U.S. government has operated employment offices since 1907. In 1918 the Employment Service of Dept of Labor was estab. The state agencies, brought directly under Federal operation in 1942, were turned back to the states in 1946.

Emporia, city (pop. 18,190), E central Kansas, between Neosho and Cottonwood rivers, SW of Topeka; founded 1857. Rail center and chief commercial city of large livestock, farm, and oil area. Has grain elevators, stockyards, varied mfg. William Allen White made Emporia *Gazette* famous. The Col. of Emporia is here.

Empson, William, 1906–, English critic and poet. His *Seven Types of Ambiguity* (1930), a study of the meanings of poetry, is a classic of modern criticism.

Ems or **Bad Ems** (bät′ĕms′), town (pop. 9,237), Rhineland-Palatinate, West Germany, on Lahn R. It is one of Europe's oldest watering places.

Ems, river, c.208 mi. long, NW Germany, rising near Paderborn and flowing NW into North Sea near Emden. Wide mouth is called the Dollart Much of its course is paralleled by the Dortmund-Ems Canal. Oil and natural gas were discovered after 1940 in the Emsland (region along river's lower course).

Ems dispatch, July 13, 1870, incident leading to Franco-Prussian War. The Spanish throne had been offered to a Hohenzollern prince. France having protested, the prince refused the offer. But the French ambassador Benedetti, meeting William I of Prussia at Ems, demanded assurance that no Hohenzollern should ever seek the Spanish throne. William turned him down flatly but politely. Seeking to goad France into declaring war, Bismarck published the interview in skillfully altered language, with complete success.

emu (ē′mū), large flightless bird of Australia, related to cassowary and ostrich. A swift runner, it is 5–6 ft. tall. It is almost extinct.

emulsion: see SUSPENSION.

Encarnación (ĕngkärnäsyōn′), city (pop. c.40,000), SE Paraguay. Port on Paraná R. and commercial center for agr. region.

encephalitis lethargica: see SLEEPING SICKNESS.

Encina or **Enzina, Juan del** (both: hwin′ dĕl änthē′nä), 1469?–1530, Spanish dramatist, musician, poet, a priest. Adapted Italian humanist culture to Spanish verse.

Enciso, Martín Fernández de (märtē′ fĕrnän′däth dā ĕnthē′sō), fl. 1509–19, Spanish conquistador and geographer. Refounded colony in Darien (1509), but was replaced by Pedrarias (1514). Wrote commentary on flora and fauna in New World.

Encke, Johann Franz, 1791–1865, German astronomer, director (from 1825) of Berlin Observatory. Noted for studies of comet orbits and for calculation of earth's distances from sun based on transits of Venus.

enclosure of land: see INCLOSURE.

encomienda (änkōmyän′dä), system of tributary labor adapted in Spanish America, modeled on that imposed in Spain on conquered Moors. It permitted conquistadors receiving land grants from crown to exact tribute from Indians living thereon. In return Indians received the protection of owner and subsistence rights on the land. See also REPARTIMIENTO.

encyclical: see BULL.

encyclopedia, either a general compendium of knowledge in all fields or a work which aims to be comprehensive in some one field. *Natural History* of Pliny the Elder is often considered the most ancient encyclopedia because it aimed at encompassing all knowledge. Various medieval scholars attempted to make all knowledge available to less informed. Example of

modern encyclopedia–including alphabetical arrangement of material and bibliographies–was set by John Harris (c.1667–1719) in his *Lexicon technicum* (1704). *The Encyclopaedia Britannica* was first published in 1771. Famous French ENCYCLOPÉDIE was completed in 1772. The German *Brockhaus' Konversations-Lexikon* was first issued in 1796–1808. On this was based *The Encyclopaedia Americana,* edited by Francis Lieber (13 vols., 1829–33). Since that time many extensive later editions and new similar works have appeared in various countries. *The Columbia Encyclopedia* (1935; 3d ed., 1963) was the first general one-volume one in English, although others had become popular in Europe. Examples of a large group of specialized works are *The Encyclopedia of the Social Sciences* and *The Encyclopedia of Islam.*

Encyclopédie (äsĕklōpādē′), French encyclopedia, in 28 vols., edited by DIDEROT, published 1751–72. D'ALEMBERT, coeditor until 1758, wrote "Preliminary Discourse"; other collaborators included MONTESQUIEU, QUESNAY, J. J. ROUSSEAU, VOLTAIRE. Banned by the government in 1759, it was clandestinely printed with the secret tolerance of the police chief. The emphasis of the *Encyclopédie* is on science, crafts, mechanics; it contains no biographic articles. Its outlook is deliberately rationalist and materialistic. It had great influence on European learning.

Endecott or **Endicott, John,** c.1588–1665, first governor of Mass. Bay colony (1628–30).

endemic disease: see COMMUNICABLE DISEASES.

Enderbury Island, area 2.3 sq. mi., Phoenix Isls., central Pacific, near CANTON ISLAND; under Anglo-American control since 1939.

Enderby Land, area in Indian Ocean sector of Antarctica. Claimed by British because of John Biscoe's discovery (1831); not visited again until 1929.

Enders, John Franklin, 1897–, American bacteriologist. Shared with T. H. Weller and F. C. Robbins the 1954 Nobel Prize in Medicine and Physiology for successfully growing poliomyelitis virus in tissue culture (outside a living organism).

Endicott, John: see ENDECOTT, JOHN.

Endicott, village (1966 pop. 17,473), S central N.Y., on Susquehanna R. and W of Binghamton and Johnson City, with which it forms the Triple Cities; settled c.1795. Mfg of shoes.

endive (ĕn′dīv; Fr. ēdēv′), salad plant (*Cichorium endivia*) with crisp curly or broad leaves; related to chicory. Commonly blanched.

endocrine gland: see GLAND.

endogamy: see MARRIAGE.

En-dor, village, Palestine, S of Mt. Tabor. Here Saul consulted famous witch. 1 Sam. 28.7; Ps. 83.10.

Endymion (ĕndī′mēun), in Greek legend, shepherd of Mt. Latmos, loved by Selene (the moon). He was given immortality and eternal sleep.

energy, in physics, defined usually as ability to do work. Electrical, heat, mechanical, atomic, and chemical energy are mutually transmutable. Law of conservation of energy holds that, since mass and energy are interconvertible, their total in a closed system is constant. **Potential energy** is work capacity of a body that depends on its position; **kinetic energy** is work capacity of a body that depends on its motion.

Enesco, Georges (zhōrzh ĕnĕs′kō), 1881–1955, Rumanian composer, violinist, and teacher. Works include two Rumanian rhapsodies for orchestra.

Enfantin, Barthélemy Prosper, 1796–1864, French Socialist, leader of movement started by SAINT-SIMON, which Enfantin made into religious group.

Enfield, London borough since 1965 (est. pop. 270,-140); includes former municipal boroughs of Edmonton, Enfield, and Southgate. Site of Royal Small Arms factory which makes Enfield rifles.

Enfield, town (pop. 31,464), N Conn., on Connecticut R. at Mass. line; settled c.1680. Part of Mass. until 1749. Site of Shaker settlement (c.1780–1915) is now state prison farm.

Engadine (ĕng'gŭdēn), upper part of Inn R. valley, Grisons canton, E Switzerland. BERNINA group rises at S end. Many tourist and health resorts, e.g., St. Moritz, Pontresina. Pop. largely Romansh-speaking and Protestant.

Engelberg (ĕng'ŭlbĕrk), village, Obwalden half-canton, central Switzerland. Winter and summer resort. Has 12th-cent. Benedictine abbey.

Engels, Friedrich (frē'drĭkh ĕng'ŭls), 1820–95, German socialist, cofounder (with Karl MARX) of Marxist COMMUNISM. His first major work was *The Condition of the Working Class in England in 1844* (1845). After organizing revolutionary movements in Europe (1845–50) and collaborating with Marx on several works, notably the *Communist Manifesto* (1848), he lived in England; compiled 2d and 3d vols. of *Das Kapital*, using Marx's drafts and notes. Known also for *Landmarks of Scientific Socialism* (1878), *The Origin of the Family, Private Property, and the State* (1884). See DIALECTICAL MATERIALISM and MARXISM.

Engels (ĕn'gĭls), city (1965 est. pop. 116,000), S central European RSFSR; port on Volga. Cap. of former German Volga Autonomous SSR (1924–41). Called Pokrovsk until 1931.

Enghien, Louis Antoine Henri de Bourbon-Condé, duc d' (lwē ätwän' ärē' dù bōōrbō'-kōdä' dük dägē'), 1772–1804, French prince. Emigrated with his father, Louis Henri Joseph de Condé. Unjustly suspected by Napoleon of participation in conspiracy of CADOUDAL, he was kidnaped from Baden, court-martialed, and shot within few hours.

engine: see DIESEL ENGINE; INTERNAL-COMBUSTION ENGINE; STEAM ENGINE; *ill.,* p. 333.

engineering, science dealing with design, construction, and operation of structures, machines, engines, and other devices used in industry and everyday life. Until Industrial Revolution engineering embodied only civil engineering (construction of tools, roads, bridges, etc.) and military engineering (construction of fortifications, engines of war, etc.); afterward mechanical engineering developed separately for design and construction of machinery. Vast field of modern engineering includes aeronautical, agricultural, chemical, civil, electrical, geological, industrial or management, marine, mechanical, and metallurgical engineering, and engineering physics.

England, John (ing'glŭnd), 1786–1842, Irish-American churchman, b. Ireland. Catholic bishop of Charleston, S.C. after 1820, he was a devoted American, interested especially in the needs of the Negroes.

England, largest political division (all figures without Monmouthshire: 50,327 sq. mi.; pop. 43,430,972) of the island of Great Britain in the British Isles. It is bounded on the W by WALES, on the N by SCOTLAND (above Solway Firth). Cut off from continent of Europe by English Channel, Straits of Dover, and North Sea, England's growth was determined by defensibility from attack, mild climate, and geographic accessibility by S ports and E and W river estuaries. The 40 historic political divisions, the counties or shires (some subdivided to make 50 administrative units), are Bedfordshire, Berkshire, Buckinghamshire, Cambridgeshire, Cheshire, Cornwall, Cumberland, Derbyshire, Devonshire, Dorsetshire, Durham, Essex, Gloucestershire, Hampshire, Herefordshire, Hertfordshire, Huntingdonshire, Kent, Lancashire, Leicester, Lincoln, Middlesex, Monmouth (often included in Wales), Norfolk, Northamptonshire, Northumberland, Nottinghamshire, Oxfordshire, Rutland, Shropshire, Somerset, Staffordshire, Suffolk, Surrey, Sussex, Warwickshire, Westmorland, Wiltshire, Worcestershire, and Yorkshire. S and SE are low and fertile; marshy NE has been mostly reclaimed. W is rough country, ending in peninsula of Cornwall. N of the Humber the Pennine Chain leads to scenery of Lake District and to Scotland. For the last 200 years England's chief wealth has derived from great industries of the Black Country (based on coal and iron fields N of large Midlands plain), from the industrial centers of

Lancashire and Yorkshire, and from shipping and mfg. of leading cities—London (capital), Manchester, Liverpool, Leeds, Sheffield, Birmingham, Bristol, Bradford, and Hull. In 19th cent. England led the world in exports of manufactures. A limited monarchy, England is joined with Scotland and N. Ireland in the United Kingdom of Great Britain and N. Ireland. Legislative and actual sovereignty reside in PARLIAMENT. Executive authority, nominally vested in the crown, lies with a cabinet responsible to parliament. The established church is the Church of England. Education Act of 1944 attempted coordination of all secondary and public schools. Oxford and Cambridge are the two oldest and most noted of England's universities. *Celt and Roman, Saxon and Dane.* For history of these early invaders and settlers, see BRITAIN. By 865 the Danes (term for all Norse invaders) had conquered England until resistance by ALFRED and his successors finally ended the DANELAW. New invasions led to CANUTE becoming Danish ruler of all England in 1016. The ANGLO-SAXONS had important effects on English culture—they developed Christianity, stimulated trade and the growth of towns, and brought central government from tribal chieftainships to a monarchy controlling executive and judicial powers. Period was ended by the NORMAN CONQUEST in 1066. *Feudal England.* Norman king William I marked a new point in English history. His strong rule and efforts at centralization were typified in DOMESDAY survey. Political and military FEUDALISM were introduced. Under his successors baronial wars produced noted English constitutional document, the MAGNA CARTA (1215). Increased royal holdings in France led to the first Anglo-French struggles and to the HUNDRED YEARS WAR (1337). Subsequent dynastic Wars of the ROSES were ended by accession of Henry VII (1485) of family of Tudor, with whom modern English history begins. *Tudor and Stuart.* Tudor period was a glorious one. REFORMATION introduced by Henry VIII, ran parallel with the flowering of the Renaissance. Trade expanded. Succession to throne was a vital issue in reigns of Edward VI Mary I, ELIZABETH I. STUART period, introduced by James I, was dominated by PURITAN REVOLUTION, culminating in civil war (1642). Parliamentarian victory led to execution of CHARLES I (1649) and to the Protectorate under Oliver CROMWELL. Reaction against puritanism was shown by the Restoration of CHARLES II. Supremacy of parliament final after overthrow of James II by the Glorious Revolution of 1688 and the accession of WILLIAM III and Mary. WHIG and TORY party government developed under Sir Robert Walpole. Colonial expansion and rivalries led to wars of European alliances, mainly with France. Tudors, Stuarts and Cromwell continued conquest of Ireland. Under Queen ANNE Scotland was joined to England by Act of Union in 1707. For later history see GREAT BRITAIN and BRITISH EMPIRE. *In a World of Industry.* England's leadership in INDUSTRIAL REVOLUTION in 19th cent. was derived from industrial Midlands. Attendant depressions produced CHARTISM. Expanding trade caused enormous growth of cities. Second World War brought huge damage from air raids. Postwar period saw development of welfare state, nationalization of key industries, loss of England's financial supremacy to U.S.

The royal rulers of England since William the Conqueror have been: *Norman*—William I, 1066–87; William II, 1087–1100; Henry I, 1100–1135. *Stephen*—Stephen, 1135–54. *Plantagenet*—Henry II, 1154–89; Richard I, 1189–99; John, 1199–1216; Henry III, 1216–72; Edward I, 1272–1307; Edward II, 1307–27; Edward III, 1327–77; Richard II, 1377–99. *Lancaster*—Henry IV, 1399–1413; Henry V, 1413–22; Henry VI, 1422–61 and 1470–71. *York*—Edward IV, 1461–70 and 1471–83; Edward V, 1483; Richard III, 1483–85. *Tudor*—Henry VII, 1485–1509; Henry VIII, 1509–47; Edward VI, 1547–53; Mary I, 1553–58; Elizabeth I, 1558–1603. *Stuart*—James I, 1603–25; Charles I,

STEAM ENGINE

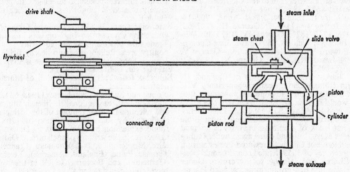

Labels: drive shaft, steam inlet, steam chest, slide valve, flywheel, piston, cylinder, connecting rod, piston rod, steam exhaust

GASOLINE ENGINE

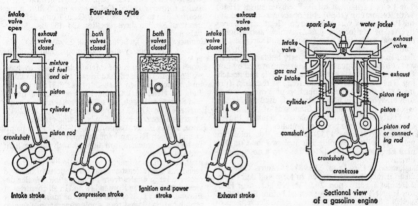

Four-stroke cycle

intake valve open — exhaust valve closed — mixture of fuel and air — piston — cylinder — crankshaft — piston rod

both valves closed

both valves closed

intake valve closed — exhaust valve open

Intake stroke — Compression stroke — Ignition and power stroke — Exhaust stroke

A Diesel engine may be either a four-cycle or a two-cycle engine. It differs from the gasoline engine chiefly in that air alone is compressed, the amount of compression is much greater, and a spray of oil rather than gasoline provides the inflammable material for the power stroke.

spark plug — water jacket — intake valve — exhaust valve — gas and air intake — exhaust — cylinder — piston rings — camshaft — piston — piston rod or connecting rod — crankshaft — crankcase

Sectional view of a gasoline engine

GAS TURBINE ENGINE

air intake — fuel — combustion chamber — exhaust gases — compressor — moving blades — stationary blades — drive shaft — moving buckets

The steam engine is an external-combustion engine. On the other hand, the gasoline engine, Diesel engine, and gas turbine are internal-combustion engines, since the combustion process must take place within the confines of the working mechanism.

1625–49 (executed 1649; Commonwealth and Protectorate, 1649–60; Charles II in exile); Charles II, 1660–85; James II, 1685–88. *Orange*–William III, 1688–1702, and Mary II, 1688–94. *Stuart*–Anne, 1702–14. *Hanover*–George I, 1714–27; George II, 1727–60; George III, 1760–1820; George IV, 1820–30; William IV, 1830–37; Victoria, 1837–1901. *Saxe-Coburg-Gotha*–Edward VII, 1901–10. *Windsor*–George V, 1910–36; Edward VIII, 1936; George VI, 1936–52; Elizabeth II, 1952–.

England, Church of, official church of England. Its break with Roman Church came when Henry VIII withdrew from allegiance to pope and announced that the king would be head of English church; this move was confirmed by Act of Supremacy of 1534. Henry suppressed monasteries and authorized Great Bible (1539). First Book of Common Prayer was adopted 1549. Under Mary, England came again under Catholic communion, but Elizabeth restored Protestantism. Act of Supremacy of 1559 defined constitutional position of Church and relation to the crown. Under James I rising tide of Puritanism necessitated Hampton Court Conference (1604), where king upheld estab. doctrine. Under Charles I measures of Archbishop Laud against Calvinists contributed to civil war (1642). The Long Parliament estab. Presbyterianism (1646). With Restoration (1660) episcopacy was restored and the Prayer Book was made the only legal service book by Act of Uniformity (1662), which also required episcopal ordination of all ministers. Thereafter, despite many internal controversies, the Church held firm. In polity, High Church party holds to ritualism and APOSTOLIC SUCCESSION, and is contravened by Low Church party which emphasizes the Bible and preaching. The archbishop of Canterbury is the chief (primate) of the church; archbishop of York is second to him. Worship is liturgical; creeds used are Nicene, Apostles', and Athanasian. Standards of doctrine are in Thirty-nine Articles, Book of Common Prayer, Catechism, and two books of homilies.

Engleheart, George, 1752–1829, English miniature painter, pupil of Reynolds. His nephew **John Cox Dillman Engleheart,** 1784–1862, was also a noted miniaturist.

Englewood. 1 City (pop. 33,398), N central Colo., industrial suburb S of Denver, in farm and dairy area. **2** Residential city (pop. 26,057), NE N.J., near Hudson R., NNE of Hoboken; settled before Revolution.

English Channel, Fr. *La Manche* = the sleeve; arm of the Atlantic, 350 mi. long and 21 mi. to c.150 mi. wide, between France and England, connecting with North Sea at E end. Main islands are Isle of Wight and Channel Isls. Train-ferry service from Paris to London opened 1936. Tunneling Channel has long been discussed. First crossed by balloon 1785; by airplane 1909. First to swim across was Matthew Webb 1875. Channel has important fisheries. Ports include Plymouth, Southampton, Portsmouth, Folkestone, and Dover (England), and Cherbourg, Le Havre, and Calais (France).

English horn: see WIND INSTRUMENTS.

English language, language prevalent in U.S. and much of Canada, in British Isles, in Australia and New Zealand, in much of South Africa, and in a few other places. Today the most widely scattered of great speech communities, English is probably native tongue of more people than any other except North Chinese and is used extensively as an auxiliary language. There are many dialect areas. Today's English is continuation of language of 5th-cent. invaders of Britain (see ANGLO-SAXON LITERATURE). This Old English (to c.1050) was followed by Middle (to c.1450; see MIDDLE ENGLISH LITERATURE) and that by Modern, with no discontinuity, even during French hegemony. Between the period of Old and Modern the cultural center shifted, however, so that the basis of the standard literary language was no longer the Wessex dialect but that of London. Modern vocabulary includes words derived from earliest English and words from

Latin Christianity, Scandinavian settlers, Norman French, and from classical languages. Language most closely related to English is Frisian. See LANGUAGE (table).

Enid, city (pop. 38,859), N central Okla., NNW of Oklahoma City; settled 1893 on U.S. land office site. Trade and processing center for wheat, cattle, and poultry area. Refines oil from nearby fields. Phillips Univ. is here. Vance Air Force Base is SSW.

Enisei, river, USSR: see YENISEI.

Eniwetok (ĕnīwē′tŏk), circular atoll of Marshall Isls., central Pacific; comprises 40 islets. Site of U.S. atomic and hydrogen bomb tests (1948–54).

Enlightenment, the rationalist, liberal, humanitarian, and scientific trend of thought of the 18th cent. Foreshadowed by scientific revolution of 17th cent., it found expression in such works as Diderot's ENCYCLOPÉDIE; in the writings of such men as Diderot, Voltaire, Montesquieu, J. J. Rousseau (France), Hume, Thomas Paine (England, America), Lessing, Kant (Germany), and Beccaria (Italy); in the reforms of such "enlightened despots" as Frederick II of Prussia, Catherine II of Russia, and Emperor Joseph II; and in the American and French revolutions.

Enna (ĕn′nä), city (est. pop. 29,130), central Sicily, Italy; formerly called Castrogiovanni. Sulfur mines nearby. Fell to Syracuse 396 B.C., to Rome 258 B.C.; center of Sicilian slave rebellion 135–132 B.C. Medieval citadel.

Ennius, Quintus (kwĭn′tŭs ĕn′nēŭs), 239–169? B.C., father of Latin poetry and a dramatist, author of the epic *Annales*.

Enoch (ē′nŭk), father of Methuselah. Said to have walked with God, and, like Elijah, to have been taken up into heaven. Gen. 5.18–24; Luke 3.37; Heb. 11.5; Jude 14. Henoch: 1 Chron. 1.3. For Book of Enoch and Secrets of Enoch, see PSEUDEPIGRAPHA.

Enschede (ĕn′skhŭdä), municipality (pop. 134,281), Overijssel prov., E Netherlands. Textile center.

Ensor, James Ensor, Baron, 1860–1949, Belgian painter and etcher. His capricious compositions, filled with fantasy and sarcasm, are flooded with intense light and strong color.

entail, restriction of inheritance to a limited class of descendants for at least several generations in order to preserve large estates from disintegration. Similar devices were known in Roman law and in all countries of Europe. In the U.S. entails are for the most part either prohibited or limited to a single generation. See also PRIMOGENITURE.

Entebbe (ĕntĕ′bŭ), town (pop. c.11,000), S Uganda, on NW shore of Victoria Nyanza. Seat of British administration until cap. was moved to Kampala after Ugandan independence in 1962. Internatl. airport is here.

Entente: see TRIPLE ALLIANCE AND TRIPLE ENTENTE; LITTLE ENTENTE.

Entente Cordiale: see TRIPLE ALLIANCE AND TRIPLE ENTENTE.

Enterprise, city (pop. 11,410), SE Ala., NW of Dothan; founded 1884. Diversified agr. U.S. Fort Rucker is nearby.

Entrecasteaux, Joseph Antoine Bruni d' (dätrŭkästō′), 1739–93, French navigator. In command of expedition to search for La Pérouse (1791–92), he explored coast of New Caledonia, Tasmania, and New Holland, and located several island groups including D'Entrecasteaux Isls.

Entrecasteaux Islands, D', Territory of Papua: see D'ENTRECASTEAUX ISLANDS.

entropy: see THERMODYNAMICS.

Enver Pasha (envär′ päshä′), 1881–1922, Turkish general. Prominent in Young Turk revolution (1908). Led Turkey into First World War, holding virtually dictatorial powers. Was killed while leading anti-Soviet expedition in Bukhara.

envoy: see DIPLOMATIC SERVICE.

Enzina, Juan del: see ENCINA, JUAN DEL.

Enzio (än'tsē̄ō) or **Enzo** (än'tsō), c.1220–72, king of Sardinia (1238–49); natural son of Emperor Frederick II. Spent his last 22 years in dungeon as prisoner of Guelphs.

enzyme (ĕn'zīm), organic compound produced by plant or animal cells which causes chemical change in substance on which it acts. An enzyme consists of a specific protein alone or combined with a smaller nonprotein organic molecule. Often the nonprotein component is derived from a vitamin. Enzyme action believed to be catalysis but differs from nonbiological catalysis in that it is more specific, has optimum temperature and acidity, and the effect of changing enzyme concentration is not always predictable by simple chemical theory. Enzymes catalyze digestion, oxidation, muscle contraction, other metabolic processes. Series of enzymes carry out series of metabolic processes, where the product of one process is the substrate of the next. Under proper conditions, tissue pastes carry out normal metabolic sequences in laboratory glassware. Ordinarily, the intermediates are produced and metabolized too rapidly for biochemical analysis. Metabolism is studied by selectively poisoning the action of single enzymes, causing an accumulation of the intermediate which is the particular enzyme's substrate. By determining beforehand the effect of particular poisons on particular isolated enzymes, it becomes possible to understand entire metabolic sequences.

Eocene epoch, first epoch of the TERTIARY PERIOD and Cenozoic era of geologic time. The early part is usually distinguished as the Paleocene. During these epochs North America assumed practically its present outline. The Eocene was marked by submergence of the Atlantic and Gulf coastal plains (as far north as S Ill.), and, in the west, of the Great Valley of California. Paleocene mammals were primitive, but in the Eocene proper ancestors of modern mammals appeared, including Eohippus, the "dawn horse."

Eohippus: see HORSE.

Eos (ē'ŏs) [Gr.,= dawn], Greek personification of dawn, daughter of Hyperion and Theia. Mother of the winds and the stars and of MEMNON. She was Aurora to the Romans.

Epaminondas (ĭpă"mĭnŏn'dŭs), d. 362 B.C., Greek general of Thebes, who defeated the Spartans at LEUCTRA (371 B.C.). Killed after winning at MANTINEA (362).

Épée, Charles Michel, Abbé de l' (shärl' mēshĕl' äbā' dŭ läpā'), 1712–89, French Jansenist. Developed manual system of communications for deaf-mutes.

Épernay (āpĕrnā'), town (pop. 21,222), Marne dept., NE France, in Champagne, on Marne R. A center of champagne industry.

Ephesians (–fē'–), epistle of New Testament, traditionally written by St. Paul to Christians of Ephesus from his captivity at Rome (A.D. c.60). Main theme of letter is unity in Christ. Most poetical of epistles, it contains famous metaphor of the Christian as a soldier. Some critics think this was a general letter intended for many churches.

Ephesus (ĕ'fŭsŭs), anc. Ionian Greek city, in modern Turkey; a wealthy seaport. Recent excavations reveal Roman Empire remains and support its claim as leading Roman city. Temple of Diana (Artemis) was one of Seven Wonders of the World. Later it was a Christian center. City, home of Mary, mother of Jesus, in later years, visited by Pope Paul VI in 1967.

Ephesus, Council of, 431, third ecumenical council called to deal with NESTORIANISM. St. CYRIL of Alexandria was the leader of the faction that after a struggle succeeded in exiling Nestorius and condemning his doctrines. The council declared Mary might be called the Mother of God, since God and Christ were one person, a doctrine further defined later by the Council of CHALCEDON. For the Robber Synod (Latrocinium) of Ephesus, see EUTYCHES.

ephod (ē'fŏd, ĕ'fŏd), sacred linen garment worn by high priests of Israel; apparently somehow used in divina-

tion. Ex. 28; Judges 8.27; 17.5; 18.14; 1 Sam. 2.28; 14.3; 22.18; 23.6,9; 30.7; Hosea 3.4.

Ephraim (ē'frŭm), son of Joseph, ancestor of one of 12 tribes of Israel. Tribe occupied region around Shiloh. Gen. 41.52; 46.20; 48.14–20; Joshua 16; 1 Chron. 7.20. Samuel was of house of Ephraim.

Ephrata (ĕ'frŭtŭ), industrial borough (pop. 7,688), SE Pa., NE of Lancaster, in farm area. Semimonastic religious community, Ephrata Cloisters, was settled (c.1728–33) here by Seventh-Day Baptists. Was famous for music; estab. early printing press.

Ephratah (ĕ'frŭtŭ) or **Ephrath:** see BETHLEHEM.

epic, a long, exalted narrative poem on a serious subject, centered about a heroic figure. Epics are often classed as those by various unknown poets using legends of the founding or expanding of a nation (BEOWULF and ROLAND) and those conceived and composed by one mind (Vergil's *Aeneid*, Milton's *Paradise Lost*). The Greek ILIAD and ODYSSEY embrace both groups. Some epics embody the ideals of a nation, e.g., the Finnish KALEVALA and the LUSIADS of Camões.

Epictetus (ĕpĭktē'tŭs), b. A.D. c.60, Roman Stoic philosopher who taught that good is within oneself and advocated the brotherhood of man.

Epicurus (ĕpĭkū'rŭs), 341–270 B.C., Greek philosopher. Defined philosophy as the art of making life happy, with intellectual pleasure or serenity the only good. Taught that physical pleasure was good, but in moderation. Denied the existence of the gods. See also LUCRETIUS.

Epidaurus (ĕpĭdô'rŭs), anc. city, NE Peloponnesus, Greece. To the temple of Asclepius here came many health seekers.

epidemic disease: see COMMUNICABLE DISEASES.

Epigoni (ĕpĭg'ŭnī) [Gr.,= the offspring], in Greek legend, sons of the SEVEN AGAINST THEBES. Led by Adrastus, they conquered Thebes ten years after the first attempt and gave the kingdom to THERSANDER.

epigraphy: see INSCRIPTION.

epilepsy, chronic cerebral disorder characterized by periodic convulsive attacks (fits) with loss of or impairment of consciousness. Seizures vary in frequency, duration, intensity. Most cases begin in youth.

Epimetheus (ĕpĭmē'thĕŭs, –thŭs) [Gr.,= afterthought], in Greek religion, Titan. Brother of Prometheus, who warned him against marrying PANDORA—but in vain.

Épinal (āpēnäl'), town (est. pop. 28,688), cap. of Vosges dept., E France, in Lorraine. Famous for *images d'Épinal*—popular colored portrayals of melodramatic events long printed here.

Épinay, Louise de la Live d' (lwēz' dŭ lä lēv' dāpēnā'), 1726–83, French patroness of letters, friend of Diderot and Grimm. She was a benefactress of J. J. Rousseau, who broke with her in 1757 and calumnied her in his *Confessions.*

epinephrine: see ADRENALINE.

Epiphania: see HAMA, Syria.

Epiphany (ĭpĭ'fŭnē) [Gr.,= showing], a prime Christian feast, celebrated Jan. 6; called also Twelfth Day, Little Christmas, and Manifestation of Christ to the Gentiles. Its eve is TWELFTH NIGHT. It commemorates three events–baptism of Jesus (Mark 1), visit of Wise Men to Bethlehem (Mat. 2), and miracle at Cana (John 2). Feast is more ancient than Christmas and technically more important, ranking after Easter and Whitsunday. The term *epiphany* (without capital letter) means a manifestation (usually of divine power) or a moment of intuitive perception.

epiphyte: see AIR PLANT.

Epirus (ĕpī'rŭs), anc. country of W Greece, on Ionian Sea. Reached its height in 3d cent. B.C. under PYRRHUS. Sided with Macedon against Rome, was sacked (167 B.C.), and passed under Roman rule. In A.D. 1204, as result of Fourth Crusade, an independent state, the **despotat of Epirus,** was set up here by a branch of Angelus family. It became nominally dependent on the empire of NICAEA (c.1246), passed to

Serbs and Albanians (14th cent.) and to Turks (15th cent.).

Episcopal Church, Protestant, in the United States of America, in communion with the Anglican church. Services in America were first held (1607) in Jamestown, Va. In 1689 King's Chapel was opened in Boston, and Trinity Church in N.Y. city. Col. of William and Mary was founded 1693, King's Col. (now Columbia Univ.) 1754. After Revolution American Anglicans organized, with Samuel Seabury first bishop (1784). First General Conference (1789) approved name of church, and adopted constitution and revised Book of Common Prayer. Church spread rapidly in U.S. Standards of doctrine are Apostles' and Nicene creeds and Thirty-nine Articles.

Episcopius, Simon (ēpĭskŏ'pēŭs), 1583–1643, Dutch theologian; originally named Bisschop or Bischop. As leader of Arminians or REMONSTRANTS, he formulated in his *Institutiones theologicae* (1650) the doctrines of Jacob Arminius.

epistemology (ĭpĭ"stŭmŏ'lŭjē), branch of philosophy devoted to theories of knowledge, its origin and nature. Empirical epistemology teaches that all knowledge comes from experience; rationalistic epistemology holds that the mind contributes innate ideas.

epistle, in the Bible, a letter of the New Testament. Those traditionally ascribed to St. Paul are Romans, 1 and 2 Corinthians, Galatians, Ephesians, Philippians, Colossians, 1 and 2 Thessalonians, 1 and 2 Timothy, Titus, Philemon, and Hebrews. The Catholic, or General, Epistles are James, 1 and 2 Peter, 1, 2, and 3 John, and Jude. This classification is traditional. There is an Epistle of Jeremiah in Baruch.

Epping Forest, NNE of London, England, the anc. Royal Waltham Forest. Originally included all Essex. Has been a 5,600-acre public park since 1882.

Epsom and Ewell (yōō'ŭl), municipal borough (pop. 71,177), Surrey, England. DERBY and OAKS horse races are run on Epsom Downs.

Epstein, Sir Jacob (ĕp'stīn), 1880–1959, British sculptor, b. New York city. Settled in England c.1906; knighted 1954. Studied under Rodin. Influenced by vorticism and African art. Famous for bronze portraits and carvings for architecture.

equal temperament, in music, a system of tuning based on the arbitrary division of the octave into 12 equal semitones. The octave is the only acoustically correct interval; other tones of scale are adjusted or tempered so that, in keyboard instruments, a single key can represent two tones—for example, both F sharp and G flat. Scale thus derived is called a tempered scale. Bach supported this system with his *Well-Tempered Clavier,* containing preludes and fugues in all major and minor keys.

equation. 1 in mathematics, a statement of the equality of two quantities or algebraic expressions. If equation contains only numbers, it is called numerical; if it has letters as well as numbers, literal; if literal equation is true for all values of the variable, it is called an identical equation; if not, it is called a conditional equation. To solve equation, obtain value or values of variables which satisfy it. **2** in chemistry, an equation represents a reaction, the first member of the equation consisting of the formulas for the reacting substances and the second member the formulas for the resulting products. An arrow ($\longrightarrow$) is used instead of an equals sign and its direction shows the direction in which the reaction is proceeding. In physics, equations are means of expressing fundamental relationships.

equatorial belt of calms: see DOLDRUMS.

Equatorial Guinea: see SPANISH GUINEA.

equinox (ē'kwĭnŏks), in astronomy, either of two points of intersection of ECLIPTIC and celestial equator. Night and day are of equal length over entire earth on dates when sun's center crosses celestial equator southward (vernal equinox, about March 21) or northward (autumnal equinox, about Sept. 23). See also PRECESSION OF THE EQUINOXES. See *ill.,* p. 1017.

equites (ĕ'kwĭtēz) [Latin,= horsemen, knights], original cavalry of the Roman army, later selected (to number 3,600) on basis of wealth. By the 1st cent. B.C. had become the influential capitalist class.

equity, principles of justice developed by chancellor and court of chancery in England to make up for inadequacies of common law. Equity originally drew many of its principles from Roman and canon law. Contest with common law was important in 16th and 17th cent. In 1875 common law and equity amalgamated by Judicature Acts in England. In U.S. most states have also done away with distinction between equity and common law.

Er, chemical symbol of the element ERBIUM.

era of good feelings, phrase applied to period 1817–23 in U.S. history, when, the Federalist party having declined, there was little open party feeling. Under the surface, however, vast sectional issues and personal rivalries were shaping themselves to break loose in campaign of 1824.

Erasistratus (ĕrŭsĭ'strŭtŭs) 3d cent. B.C., Greek physician, a founder of medical school at Alexandria.

Erasmus (ĭrăz'mŭs) or **Desiderius Erasmus** (dĕsĭdēr'ēŭs), 1469?–1536, Dutch humanist. A Catholic priest and teacher, he had great influence after 1500. Acquainted with most scholars of the day, he was the broadest of humanists. Edited Greek and Latin works, including those of Church Fathers. Wrote satires (*The Praise of Folly,* 1509; *The Education of a Christian Prince,* 1515). His position with regard to the Reformation caused enmity of Luther.

Erastus, Thomas (ĭră'stŭs), 1524–83, Swiss physician and theologian, b. Lüber, Lieber, or Liebler. Opposed Calvinist doctrine and punitive power of church. Term **Erastianism** represents approval of dominance of civil authority in punitive matters, and, by extension, dominance of state over church.

Erato, Muse of the poetry of love: see MUSES.

Eratosthenes (ĕrŭtŏs'thŭnēz), c.275–c.195 B.C., versatile Greek scholar, head of Alexandria library. Especially noted for measuring circumference and tilt of earth and for map of known world.

Erbil (ĕr'bĭl), town (pop. c.26,000), NE Iraq. On site of anc. ARBELA, it has an old Turkish fort.

erbium (ûr'bēŭm), rare metallic element (symbol = Er; see also ELEMENT, table; metals of the RARE EARTHS).

Ercilla y Zúñiga, Alonso de (älōn'sō dä ĕrthĭ'lyä ē thōō'nyĕgä), 1533–94, Spanish author of epic poem, *La Araucana,* about Araucanians, whom he had fought.

Erckmann-Chatrian (ĕrkmän'-shätrēä'), joint authorship of Émile Erckmann (āmēl'), 1822–99, and Alexandre Chatrian (älĕksä'drü), 1826–90. They wrote historical romances and plays set in native Lorraine, e.g., *Madame Thérèse* (1863) and *L'Ami Fritz* (1864; adapted into a play 1877).

Erebus (ĕ'rĭbŭs) [Gr.,= darkness], in Greek mythology, gloomy part of underworld on way to Hades.

Erebus, Mount, volcanic peak, c.13,000 ft. high, on Ross Isl., in the Ross Sea off Antarctica. Discovered 1841 by Sir James C. Ross.

Erech (ē'rĕk) or **Uruk** (ōō'rŏok), anc. Sumerian city of Mesopotamia, on Euphrates, near Ur; long the cap. of Lower Babylonia. The site has been excavated.

Erechtheum (ĭrĕk'thēŭm), Ionic temple on the Acropolis, Athens; built c.421–405 B.C., probably by Mnesicles. On S portico is Porch of the Caryatids, six draped female figures supporting the entablature on their heads.

Erechtheus (ĕrĕk'thūs), ancient mythological king of Athens; son of Hephaestus and Gaea. Often confused with ERICHTHONIUS. Erechtheus is said to have founded worship of Athena and built the Erechtheum.

Erenburg, Ilya (Grigoryevich): see EHRENBURG.

Eretria (ĕrē'trēü), anc. city of Greece, on Euboea. Mother-city of colonies in N Aegean, it supported the Ionian revolt against Persia (499 B.C.). Darius I destroyed it (but not permanently) in 490 B.C.

Erfurt (âr′fŏŏrt), city (est. pop. 184,819), East Germany, in former state of Thuringia, on Gera R. Former cap. of Thuringia; industrial and horticultural center. Bishopric of Erfurt, founded 741 by St. Boniface, passed to electors of Mainz 1664, to Prussia 1802. Was scene of Congress of Erfurt (1808), where Napoleon I and Alexander I renewed their alliance of 1807. Univ. of Erfurt (1392–1816) had Luther as student. Erfurt Program, adopted by German Social Democrats at party congress of 1891, marked triumph of Marxist doctrines over those of Lassalle. Erfurt's cathedral (12th cent.) and Church of St. Severus (13th cent.) are notable.

erg, unit of work and energy in centimeter-gram-second system. It is the work done by one DYNE acting through distance of one centimeter. A joule is 10,000,000 ergs.

Erhard, Ludwig (âr′härdt), 1897–, German statesman; introduced currency reform 1948, spurring German economic recovery. A Christian Democrat, he succeeded Adenauer as chancellor 1963, was reelected 1965, defeated 1966.

Eric, kings of Sweden. **Eric IX** (The Saint), d. 1160. Forcibly converted Finland to Christianity. Murdered by a Danish pagan, he became patron saint of Sweden. **Eric XIV,** 1533–77, reigned 1560–68. In conflict with nobility, he had Nils Sture and other powerful nobles assassinated. His unpopularity and soon evident insanity led to his deposition and imprisonment.

Erichthonius (ĕrĕkthō′nēŭs), in Greek legend, half man, half serpent; often identified with ERECHTHEUS.

Ericsson, John (ē′rĭksŭn), 1803–89, Swedish-American inventor and marine engineer, b. Sweden. Chiefly remembered as designer and builder of the *Monitor* (see MONITOR).

Ericsson, Leif: see LEIF ERICSSON.

Eric the Red, fl. 10th cent., Norse chieftain, discoverer and colonizer of Greenland. Vainly resisted the introduction of Christianity there by his son, Leif Ericsson.

Eridu (ā′rĭdōō), anc. Sumerian city of Mesopotamia, near the Euphrates, not far from Ur. It perhaps was in existence c.5000 B.C. Excavations yield objects of god Ea, who was worshiped here.

Erie, city (pop. 138,440), NW Pa., on L. Erie SW of Buffalo; laid out 1795. Only Pa. port on Great Lakes, it is busy shipping point and mfg. city. Fort Presque Isle, built here 1753 by French, was rebuilt 1760 by English and destroyed 1763 in Pontiac's Rebellion. At Crystal Point, Perry's fleet was launched before victory over British 1813. *Wolverine,* early iron warship, was assembled (1843) here. Seat of Gannon Col., Mercyhurst Col., and Villa Maria Col.

Erie, Lake, 241 mi. long, 30–57 mi. wide, fourth in size and shallowest of the Great Lakes. Lies c.572 ft. above sea level, maximum depth 210 ft., area 9,930 sq. mi. Bordered N by Ontario; S and E by N.Y., Pa., and Ohio; W by small portion of Mich. Detroit R. is inlet from L. Huron; Niagara R. is outlet to L. Ontario. Navigation between Lakes Huron and Erie follows natural channel; between Lakes Erie and Ontario it uses Welland Canal. N.Y. State Barge Canal and Hudson R. connect lake with the Atlantic. Subject to violent storms, it is partially ice-bound and largely closed to navigation from mid-Dec. to about end of March. Principal U.S. ports include Buffalo, N.Y.; Erie, Pa.; Cleveland and Toledo, Ohio; and Detroit, Mich. First white man to see lake was probably Louis Jolliet (1669). Forts and trading posts were built on shores. French and Indian Wars gave Britain control. At close of War of 1812 U.S.–Canadian boundary was estab. to run about through center of lake. The **Battle of Lake Erie,** fought Sept. 10, 1813, at Put in Bay, ended in British defeat by U.S. fleet under O. H. PERRY and U.S. control of lake.

Erie Canal, artificial waterway, extending from Albany to Buffalo and connecting the Hudson with L. Erie. Authorized by N.Y. in April, 1817; completed 1825. Later converted into NEW YORK STATE BARGE CANAL. The Erie furthered New York city's financial develop-

ment, opened Eastern markets to farm products of the Great Lakes region, fostered immigration to Old Northwest, helped create numerous large cities.

Erie Indians, sedentary tribe of Hokan-Siouan linguistic stock, in region E and S of L. Erie in 17th cent. Enemies of the Iroquois Confederacy, they were almost exterminated after 1656.

Erie Railroad. Incorporated 1832 as New York and Erie Railroad Co. Struggle for control among railroad barons after Civil War, with victory for Jay Gould, was main phase of company's unstable financial history in 19th cent. Beginning as a short N.Y. railroad, it had by 1880 branch lines to Chicago, and E terminus at Jersey City. Reorganized 1895 as Erie Railroad Co. and reorganized again in 1941. On Oct. 15, 1960, the Erie merged with the Delaware, Lackawanna and Western to form the Erie-Lackawanna RR.

Erigena, John Scotus (skō′tŭs ĕrĭj′ĭnŭ), c.810–880, scholastic philosopher. Identified philosophy and theology and made a four-fold division of nature, a creative cycle that begins and ends with God.

Erin (ĕr′ĭn, ēr′ĭn), poetic name of IRELAND.

Erinyes (ĕrĭn′ē-ēz) or **Furies,** in Greek religion, goddesses of vengeance. Named Alecto (ŭlĕk′tō), Megaera (mējē′rŭ), Tisiphone (tĭsĭf′ōnē). Born from blood of Uranus which fell on land. Usually described as three crones, winged, with snakes as hair, they avenged wrongs perpetrated on blood relatives. Euphemistically, also called Eumenides [favorable ones], their title in the chorus in the *Eumenides* of Aeschylus.

Eris (ē′rĭs) [Gr.,= discord], in Greek legend, female personification of strife. In revenge for not being invited to a wedding, she threw the APPLE OF DISCORD.

Erith, London: see BEXLEY.

Eritrea (ĕrĭtrē′ŭ), autonomous state of Ethiopia (c.48,350 sq. mi.; pop. c.1,200,000), NE Africa, on Red Sea; cap. Asmara. Desert coastal strip adjoins rugged interior plateau. Inhabited by pastoral nomads of Ethiopian descent. Products are coffee, cotton, grains, hides, and sisal. Eritrea was virtual possession of Ethiopia until 16th cent., when it fell to Ottoman Turks. Divided among local chieftains from 17th to mid-19th cent. Became Italian colony in 1890. British troops expelled the Italians in April, 1941. In 1949 the UN awarded most of Eritrea to Ethiopia; federated with Ethiopia in 1952 as autonomous province; became integral part of Ethiopia in 1963.

Erivan (ĕrĭvän′), Armenian *Yerevan,* city (1965 est. pop. 633,000), cap. of Armenian SSR since 1920, on Zanga R.; mfg. of machine tools, electrical equipment, chemicals. Known in 7th cent. A.D.; cap. of Armenia under Persian rule; after 15th cent. passed back and forth between Persia and Turkey; ceded by Persia to Russia 1828.

Erlach, Johann Bernhard Fischer von: see FISCHER VON ERLACH, JOHANN BERNHARD.

Erlander, Tage Fritiof (tä′gŭ frĭt′yŭf ĕr′ländŭr), 1901–, Swedish prime minister (1946–). Extended welfare state and preserved Sweden's neutrality.

Erlangen (ĕr′läng-ŭn), city (pop. 60,378), Middle Franconia, N Bavaria, on Regnitz R. Has important mfg. of medical equipment (X-ray machines, hearing aids). Under margraves of Bayreuth-Kulmbach (house of Hohenzollern) from 1402; to Prussia 1792; to Bavaria 1810. University was founded at Bayreuth 1742, transferred to Erlangen 1743; Schelling and Schleiermacher taught here. City was rebuilt after a fire (1706), has baroque architecture.

Erlanger, Joseph (ûr′läng-ŭr), 1874–1965, American scientist. Shared 1944 Nobel Prize in Physiology and Medicine for work in physiology (esp. nerve action).

Erlau: see EGER, Hungary.

Ermak, Cossack leader: see YERMAK.

ermine (ûr′mĭn), name for various species of weasel and their fur. Fur trappers use name weasel for North American skins and stoat for chief species (*Mustela erminea*) of N Europe and Asia. The pelts (the most valuable white with black markings) make wraps, coats, and trimmings; black tails are used in Europe with ermine robes of royalty.

Ermine Street, early Roman road in Britain said to have extended from London to Lincoln.

Erne, river of Ireland and N. Ireland, flowing 72 mi. from Lough Gowna to Donegal Bay in the Atlantic.

Ernest I, 1784–1844, duke of Saxe-Coburg-Gotha; brother of Leopold I of Belgium, uncle of Victoria of England, father of Victoria's consort, Albert. Succeeded to Coburg 1806; acquired Gotha 1826.

Ernst, Max (mäks' ērnst'), 1891–, German surrealist painter. Was a Dadaist in his early period.

Eros (ĭ'rŏs, ē'rŏs) [Gr.,= love], in Greek mythology, god of love. He is the force of love in all its manifestations. Pictured by some as one of oldest gods, born from Chaos. Associated with Dionysus in Orphic Mysteries, he was worshiped as Protogonos, first-born. More usually, he was called son of Ares and Aphrodite and pictured as winged youth or child armed with bow and arrows. Identified with Roman Cupid or Amor. For his own love story, see PSYCHE.

erosion, wearing away of the earth's surface by running water, waves, glaciers, wind. Streams transport rock fragments formed by weathering, and these particles serve as cutting tools. Sea coasts are worn back by waves and the rock waste they carry. A glacier erodes by grinding boulders against its bed. In arid regions wind is an important erosive agent, transporting sand as dunes.

ERP: see EUROPEAN RECOVERY PROGRAM.

Errigal, Mount (ĕrĕgôl'), 2,466 ft. high, Co. Donegal, Ireland; highest point in the county.

Erskine, Thomas, 1st Baron Erskine, 1750–1823, British jurist. A great trial lawyer, he defended Thomas Paine's *The Rights of Man* against charge of sedition. Caused liberal revision of libel laws.

Ervine, St. John (Greer) (sĭn' jŭn, ûrvĭn), 1883–, British author, b. Ireland. Best known for plays (e.g., *Jane Clegg,* 1911), he has also written novels and biographies, notably of Oscar Wilde (1951) and G. B. Shaw (1956).

Erwin, cotton-mill town (pop. 3,183), central N.C., S of Raleigh. Sherman's army unsuccessfully attacked by Confederates in 1865 near here.

Eryri, Wales: see SNOWDON.

erysipelas (ĕrŭsĭ'pŭlŭs, –ĭis, ĭrŭ–), acute febrile disease attended by inflammation of skin and underlying tissues. Results from invasion of break in skin by hemolytic streptococcus.

Eryx (ē'rĭks), ancient city, W Sicily, Italy. Long a bone of contention between Carthage and Syracuse; destroyed by Carthaginians c.260 B.C. Cyclopic walls and Phoenician inscriptions remain.

Erzberger, Matthias (mätē'äs ĕrts'bĕrgûr), 1875–1921, German statesman, leader of Catholic Center party. Headed delegation which signed armistice of Nov., 1918. Assassinated by a nationalist.

Erzerum or **Erzurum** (both: âr'zùrōōm), city (pop. 90,-069), NE Turkey, in Armenia. Agr. trading center. Long of strategic and commercial importance.

Erzgebirge (ĕrts'gŭbĭr''gù) or **Ore Mountains,** Czech *Krušné Hory,* mountain range of Bohemia (Czechoslovakia) and Saxony (Germany), extending c.95 mi. SE from the Elbe. Highest point, Mt. Klinovec (Ger. *Keilberg),* in Czechoslovakia, is at 4,064 ft. Important silver and iron mines exploited 16th-19th cent., notably at JACHYMOV. Now uranium, wolframite, lead, tin, copper, and sulfur are mined. Among the many spas, CARLSBAD and MARIENBAD are best-known. Intensive mfg. (textiles, machinery). Czech part of Erzgebirge was annexed by Germany in 1938, but was restored in 1945.

Erzurum, Turkey: see ERZERUM.

Es, chemical symbol of element EINSTEINIUM.

Esaias (ēzā'yùs), variant of ISAIAH.

Esar-Haddon (ē''sär-hä'dùn), king of Assyria (681–668 B.C.), son of SENNACHERIB. Put down revolts, defeated the Chaldaeans; secured the N frontier from the

Medes and Scythians; conquered Egypt (673–670); curbed Elam. He rebuilt Babylon. Succeeded by Assur-bani-pal.

Esau (ē'sô), [Heb.,= hairy], son of Isaac, tricked out of his inheritance by his twin, Jacob. He settled on Mt. Seir. As ancestor of Israel's enemies, the Edomites, he is called EDOM. Gen. 25–28; 32; 33; 36; Deut. 2.4,5; Joshua 24.4; Jer. 49.7–22; Heb. 12.14–17.

Escambia (ĕskăm'bēù), river rising in SE Ala. (called Conecuh [kŭnē'kù] there). Flows 231 mi. SW, then S through NW Fla. to Escambia Bay, which is an arm of Pensacola Bay.

Escanaba (ĕskùnô'bù), resort city (pop. 15,391), W Upper Peninsula, N Mich., on inlet of Green Bay NE of Menominee; settled 1852. Rail, lumber, and fishing center. Ships much ore.

escarpment or **scarp,** a long cliff, bluff, or steep slope. It is usually the result of erosion or of geologic faulting; often both causes are involved.

Escaut (ĕskō'), French name of SCHELDT river.

Esch, town (pop. 28,135), grand duchy of Luxembourg, on Alzette R. Steel center.

Eschenbach, Wolfram von: see WOLFRAM VON ESCHENBACH.

Eschweiler (ĕsh'vīlûr), city (pop. 38,005), North Rhine-Westphalia, West Germany, near Aachen. Center of a soft-coal basin; iron and steel mills.

Escondido (ĕskûndē'dō), city (pop. 16,377), S Calif., N of San Diego; in agr. valley (citrus fruit, grapes, dairy goods); laid out 1885. To E is monument commemorating Mexican War battle (1846).

Escorial (ĕskō'rēùl, Span. äskōrēäl') or **Escurial,** former royal residence near Madrid, Spain. Built 1563–84, it comprises massive palace, monastery, church; contains royal tombs. Decorated by noted artists; has fine library and collection of Spanish painting.

Esdraelon (ĕs'drūē'lûn) fertile plain, central Palestine, drained by Kishon R., extending from SE foot of Mt. Carmel to Jordan valley. In ancient times a battleground, especially around MEGIDDO (see also GILBOA). Called also plain of JEZREEL or of Megiddo.

Esdras (ĕz'–) [Gr. from Heb. Ezra], name given in Western canon to four books of Old Testament and PSEUDEPIGRAPHA. Esdras 1 and 2 are same as AV EZRA and Nehemiah; Esdras 3 and 4 are pseudepigrapha, called, in Apocrypha of AV, Esdras 1 and 2. In Greek Bibles, Ezra and Nehemiah together are called 1 Esdras and pseudepigrapha are called 2 and 3 Esdras. Pseudepigrapha are (1) Greek translations of portions of 2 Chron., Ezra, and Nehemiah, and (2) an account of visions of Ezra.

Esenin, Sergei Aleksandrovich: see YESENIN.

Esher (ē'shûr), urban district (pop. 60,586), Surrey, England. Wolsey's Tower, remains of "Esher Place" occupied by Cardinal Wolsey, is here.

Esk, name of several rivers in Scotland. N and S Esk in Midlothian join and enter Firth of Forth; Black and White Esk of Dumfriesshire join and enter Solway Firth; and N and S Esk of Kincardine and Angus flow into the North Sea.

esker (ĕs'kûr), long, narrow, winding ridge of stratified DRIFT. Eskers resemble abandoned railway embankments; probably were deposited by streams flowing beneath a retreating ice sheet.

Eshkol, Levi, 1895–, Israeli statesman, b. Russia. He emigrated to Palestine 1913 and became active in Zionist affairs. Minister of finance (1952–63), he succeeded David Ben-Gurion as premier and minister of defense 1963.

Eski Krim or **Eski Krym:** see STARY KRYM.

Eskilstuna (ĕ'skĭlstü''nä), city (pop. 59,882), SE Sweden. Center of Swedish cutlery industry.

Eskimo (ĕ'skùmō), native inhabitant of the arctic and subarctic regions of North America. Estimated Eskimo pop. c.55,000. Despite their wide dispersal they are highly uniform in language, physical type, and culture; Mongoloid features point to an Asiatic origin. The ingenuity of their material culture is essential to survival in the Arctic.

Eskimo-Aleut, linguistic family consisting of Aleut, spoken on Aleutian Isls. and Kodiak Peninsula, and Eskimo, spoken from N Siberia E to Greenland.

Eskisehir (ĕskē'shĕhĕr), city (pop. 153,096), W central Turkey; probably identical with ancient Dorylaeum. Export center for meerschaum, chromium, magnesite; agr. market; railroad junction; cotton and tile mfg. Mineral springs.

espalier (ĕspăl'yŭr), tree (usually a fruit such as apple or pear) or vine trained to grow flat against wall or trellis. Plants so trained take up little space and are ornamental (often fan or fork shaped).

Espartero, Baldomero (bäldōmā'rō ĕspärtā'rō), 1793–1879, Spanish general. After his victory over the CARLISTS in civil war of 1836–39 he was created duque de la Victoria. As regent he ruled dictatorially (1841–43), was forced to flee by an uprising. Served as premier 1854–56.

Esperanto: see UNIVERSAL LANGUAGE.

Espinel, Vicente Martínez (vēthän'tä märtē'nĕth äs-pēnĕl'), 1550–1624, Spanish poet, novelist, musician. Composed for the guitar. Introduced 10-line stanza.

espionage, clandestine securing of information, particularly the seeking of data about one nation for the benefit of another. By First World War all great powers except the U.S. had espionage systems. First U.S. espionage agency was the Office of Strategic Services, created 1942. Revelation of massive espionage activity in the U.S. led to National Security Act of 1947, creating the CENTRAL INTELLIGENCE AGENCY and the Natl. Security Agency. Espionage now relies heavily on surveillance by high-altitude planes with sensitive photographic equipment. Earth-orbiting satellites will be important in future.

Espírito Santo, state (c.15,200 sq. mi.: pop. c.1,888,-700), E Brazil on Atlantic Ocean; cap. Vitoria. Produces coffee, sugar, lumber. Mineral resources are largely untapped.

Espiritu Santo: see NEW HEBRIDES.

Espronceda, José de (hōsā' dä äsprōnthä'dhä), 1808–42, Spanish romantic poet and revolutionary. Best known for *El diablo mundo* (1841).

Espy, James Pollard (ĕ'spē), 1785–1860, American meteorologist. Developed a convection theory of storms. His work in War and Navy departments laid basis for scientific weather forecasting.

Esquimalt (ĕskwī'môlt), W suburb of Victoria, on Vancouver Isl., B.C., Canada. Here is chief naval station and naval dockyard in W Canada.

Esquirol, Jean Étienne Dominique (zhä ätyĕn' dômē-nēk' ĕskülrōl), 1772–1840, French psychiatrist. Among first to recognize emotional basis of mental disorder. he was a leader in the reform of mental institutions.

Essad Pasha (ĕ'sät pä'shä), 1863–1920, Albanian dictator (1914–16). Expelled the king (William, prince of Wied), who had appointed him premier. Defeated by the Austrians (1916); was assassinated.

Esseg, Yugoslavia: see OSIJEK.

Essen (ĕ'sŭn), city (pop. 710,805), North Rhine-Westphalia, West Germany. Center of Ruhr dist.; seat of KRUPP steel works. Chief source of electric power for Germany; one of world's great industrial cities.

Essenes (ĕ'sēnz), Jewish religious sect, known also as *Therapeutai* [healers]. Rejected sacrificial temple cult, practiced ceremonial purity, abstained from eating meat. The people of the DEAD SEA SCROLLS were probably related to the Essenes.

essential oils: see OILS.

Essex, Robert Devereux, 2d earl of (dĕ'vŭrōō), 1567–1601, English nobleman, favorite of Queen Elizabeth. His position involved him in rivalry with Sir Walter RALEIGH. He arranged (1590) the queen by his secret marriage to Sir Philip Sidney's widow. Advised by Francis Bacon he entered politics, hoping to seize power from the aging Lord Burghley. Elizabeth, wary of his demands, conferred power on Robert Cecil.

Made lord lieutenant of Ireland (1599), Essex was sent there to quell rebellion of earl of Tyrone. He failed, was confined on his return to England, and later banned from court. He unsuccessfully tried to oust opposing party and estab. his own party about queen in 1601. He was arrested, Elizabeth signed the death warrant, and he was executed. His son, **Robert Devereux, 3d earl of Essex,** 1591–1646, was restored (1604) to his estates by James I. He fought with royal army in first Bishops' War and later commanded parliamentary forces. After failure and disgrace in 1644, he relinquished his command.

Essex, kingdom of Anglo-Saxon England. Probably settled in early 6th cent., it eventually included modern counties of Essex, London, Middlesex, and most of Hertfordshire. Having early accepted Christianity the kingdom lapsed into heathenism until reconverted by Cedd in 7th cent. Long dominated by MERCIA, Essex joined other kingdoms in 9th cent. in submitting to Wessex and became an earldom. Became part of DANELAW in 886; was later retaken (917) by Edward the Elder of Wessex. Its most famous later earl was Byrhtnoth, defeated (991) at Maldon.

Essex, county (1,400 sq. mi.; est. pop. 1,026,180), E England, on N bank of Thames estuary; co. town Chelmsford. SW portion became part of Greater London in 1965. Chief products are fish, oysters, fruits, vegetables. Has mfg. of chemicals, machinery, textiles, cement. Popular coastal resorts.

Essex. 1 Industrial town (pop. 4,057), S Conn., on Connecticut R., W of New London; settled 1690. Once an important shipping and shipbuilding center. **2** City (pop. 35,205), NE Md., a suburb E of Baltimore. **3** Town (pop. 7,090), NW Vt., on Winooski R., E of Burlington; chartered 1763. Includes Essex Junction village (pop. 5,340).

Essex Junction, Vt.: see ESSEX, Vt.

Essex Junto, group of New England merchants, so called because many of them were from Essex co., Mass. Opposed radicals in Mass. in American Revolution and supported the Federalists. Later encouraged disaffection of Hartford Convention.

Essling, battle of: see ASPERN.

Esslingen (ĕs'lĭng-ŭn), city (pop. 77,209), Baden-Württemberg, West Germany, on Neckar R. Noted for wines; machine, textile mfg. Free imperial city from 1219; passed to Württemberg 1803. Swabian League was founded here 1488. Has 13th-cent. castle.

Essonnes (ĕsôn'), department, N France, in Île-de-France; cap. Évry. Formed 1964; formerly part of Seine-et-Oise dept.

Established Church: see ENGLAND, CHURCH OF; SCOTLAND, CHURCH OF; IRELAND, CHURCH OF.

Estaing, Charles Hector, comte d' (shärl' ĕktôr' kôt' dĕstĕ'), 1729–94, French admiral. Commanded French fleet sent to aid American revolutionists, 1778–80. His planned attack on Newport, R.I., was undone by a storm (1778). Cooperated with Benjamin LINCOLN in unsuccessful attack on Savannah (1779). Was guillotined as a royalist.

estate. 1 In law of property, term describing ownership interest in real or personal property (e.g., estate for years, life estate). **2** In constitutional law, an organized class given a separate voice in government in Middle Ages and later. Three estates were nobility, clergy, commons (townspeople of substance, bourgeoisie, "third estate"). By extension "fourth estate" means newspapers.

Estates-General: see STATES-GENERAL.

Este (ĕ'stä), Italian noble family; branch of the GUELPHS. Derives name from town of Este, near Padua. Ruled FERRARA (1240–1597; from 1471 as dukes) and MODENA (1288–1796; from 1452 as dukes). Court of the Este family at Ferrara in 15th–16th cent. was a major center of literature and art. **Isabella d'Este,** 1474–1539, wife of Francesco GONZAGA, and her sister **Beatrice d'Este,** 1475–97, wife of Ludovico SFORZA, were brilliant ladies of the Renaissance and patronesses of Leonardo and Ariosto. Their brother, **Alfon-**

so d'Este I, 1476–1534, dûke of Ferrara and Modena (1505–34), also was a lavish patron. In the Italian Wars he sided first with France against Pope Julius II (who in 1510 declared him forfeit of his fiefs), later with Emperor Charles V against Pope Clement VII (who had to reinstate him in 1530). He was the second husband of Lucrezia BORGIA. His brother, **Ippolito I, Cardinal d'Este** (ēp-pô'lētō), 1479–1520, was long the patron of Ariosto, who dedicated *Orlando furioso* to him. Alfonso's son, **Ippolito II, Cardinal d'Este,** 1509–72, built the famous Villa d'Este at Tivoli, near Rome. The direct male line of dukes died out 1597; in 1598 Pope Clement VIII incorporated Ferrara into Papal States, despite claims of cadet line, which retained Modena. Deposed by Bonaparte 1796, last duke died 1803. His daughter married Archduke Ferdinand of Austria, a son of Emperor Francis II, who founded line of Austria-Este. Their descendants were dukes of Modena, Massa, and Carrara 1815–59.

ester, compound formed by a reaction, esterification, between alcohol and organic acid; a molecule of water is also produced. Esters are heated with sodium (sometimes potassium) hydroxide to form soaps; this is saponification. Fats (solid) and vegetable or animal oils (liquid) are esters of certain organic acids with the trihydric alcohol, glycerol (see FATS AND OILS); SOAP is made commercially from fats. Esters are used for flavoring and in making explosives (e.g., NITROGLYCERIN), paints, perfumes.

Esterhazy (ĕ'stürhä″zē), Hung. *Esterházy.* Hungarian noble family; princes of Holy Roman Empire since 1687. Best-known are **Paul Anton, Fürst Esterhazy von Galantha** (gä'läntä). d. 1762, and his brother and successor to the title, **Nikolaus Joseph, Fürst Esterhazy von Galantha,** 1714–90, because of their patronage of Haydn, who was in their service 1761–90. Nikolaus Joseph was extremely lavish with his immense wealth, built the famous château of Esterhaz on the Neusiedler Lake, endowed Haydn with handsome pension in his will.

Esterhazy, Ferdinand Walsin (Fr. fĕrdēnä′ välsĕ′ ĕstĕräzĕ′), 1847–1923, French army officer, claiming membership in old Hungarian Esterhazy family. His guilt in selling military secrets to Germany was pinned on Captain Dreyfus (see DREYFUS AFFAIR). Fled to England 1898 and confessed the following year.

Estes Park (ĕs'tēz), resort town (pop. 1,175), N central Colo., in Rockies NNW of Denver; settled 1859. Hq. for Rocky Mt. Natl. Park (see NATIONAL PARKS AND MONUMENTS, table). Two dams and power plants of COLORADO–BIG THOMPSON PROJECT are in area.

Esther, book of Old Testament. It tells of a Jewish girl, named originally Hadassah, who became queen of Persian king Ahasuerus (Xerxes). A wicked courtier, Haman, tried to incite a massacre of the Jews, but Esther, with aid of her uncle Mordecai, saved her people. The feast of Purim commemorates this. Chapters 10.4–16 are in Apocrypha in AV but are in Western canon.

Estherville, city (1966 pop. 8,092), N central Iowa, NNW of Emmetsburg on West Fork of Des Moines R.; settled 1857. Shipping, processing, and trade center for agr. area. Site of Fort Defiance (1862) is preserved nearby.

esthetics: see AESTHETICS.

Estienne, Étienne (ātyĕn'), Latin **Stephanus,** family of printers and scholars in Paris and Geneva. **Henri Estienne,** d. 1520, was a printer in Paris by 1502. His son, **Robert Estienne,** b. 1498 or 1503, d. 1559, printed scholarly works, many edited by himself. Specialized in editions of classical authors, dictionaries—his own Latin thesaurus (1531) is a masterpiece—and critical editions of the Bible. Geofroy Tory designed his printer's mark (the Olive Tree) and Claude Garamond designed some of his type faces. A Protestant, he found himself in trouble and moved to Geneva (1550). His brother **Charles Estienne,** c.1504–1564, took over the Paris shop in 1551. Educated in medicine and in the classics, he wrote on many subjects. Got out an

early French encyclopedia, a treatise on dissection, and *Praedium rusticum* [country property]. Robert's son, **Henri Estienne,** 1531?–1598, was the greatest scholar of the family. He took over the Geneva business, and though his books were not so good typographically as his father's, he brought out editions of Greek and Latin works notable for accuracy and textual criticism. He compiled a notable *Thesaurus Graecae linguae* (1572). Championed the use of French as a literary language. Trouble with Geneva authorities, begun by his satirical *Apologie pour Herodote* (1566), forced him to leave Geneva and later caused imprisonment. Became wandering scholar.

Estonia, Estonian *Eesti,* republic (17,429 sq. mi.; est. pop. 1,221,000), NE Europe, bounded by RSFSR (E), Latvia (S), and Baltic Sea (N and W); cap. Tallinn. Its inclusion (1940) into USSR is not recognized by U.S. A generally flat, dairy-farming country, it also has shale oil, timber, fisheries. Estonians speak a Finnic language, are mostly Lutherans. Country, part of historic LIVONIA, was ruled by Livonian Knights from 13th cent.; passed to Sweden 1561; was conquered by Russia 1710 (formally ceded by Sweden 1721). Descendants of German knights formed ruling class till 1917. Independence from Russia was proclaimed 1918; peace treaty with Russia was signed 1920. Democratic rule ended 1934, when Pres. Konstantin Päts began authoritarian regime. USSR secured military bases 1939 and in 1940 occupied Estonia and made it constituent Soviet republic. Occupied by Germany 1941–44. Retaken by Soviet Union; economy now integrated with that of USSR.

Estournelles de Constant, Paul Henri Benjamin, baron d' (pôl' ārē' bĕzhämĕ' bärō' dätōŏrnĕl' dü kôstä'), 1852–1924, French diplomat and pacifist. Shared 1909 Nobel Peace Prize with Auguste Beernaert.

Estrées, Gabrielle d' (gäbrēĕl' dĕsträ'), 1573–99, famous beauty, mistress of Henry IV of France.

Estremadura (ĕshtrŭmŏŏ'dŏŏ'rŭ), region, SW Portugal, former province, now divided among provs. of Estremadura (cap. Lisbon), Ribatejo, and a small part of Beira Litoral. Tagus R. flows through fertile valley. Agr., orchards, vineyards, forests.

Estremadura (ĕshtrŭmŭdŏŏ'rŭ), Span. *Extremadura,* region (16,059 sq. mi.; pop. 1,378,777), W central Spain, bordering on Portugal. Cities: Badajoz, Cáceres. Arid tableland except for fertile Tagus and Guadiana valleys. Sheep grazing, hog raising.

Estremoz, Port. *Estremôs* (ĕshtrŭmôsh'), town (pop. 9,932), Évora dist., Upper Alentejo prov., Portugal. Famous for white marble and pottery. Castle was built by King Diniz.

Eszek, Yugoslavia: see OSIJEK.

Esztergom (ĕ'stĕrgôm), Ger. *Gran,* city (pop. 23,065), N Hungary, on the Danube. Birthplace of St. Stephen; seat of archprimates of Hungary since 1198. Has beautiful domed cathedral (built 19th cent.). Primate's palace contains museum and rich library. Also a warm-spring spa.

Eteocles (ētē'ŏklēz), in Greek legend, son of Oedipus. He defended kingdom of Thebes, usurped from his brother, POLYNICES, in war of SEVEN AGAINST THEBES.

Ethan [Heb.,= strong], a wise man. 1 Kings 4.31; title of Ps. 89. May be same as Ethan of 1 Chron. 2.6.

ethane, simple hydrocarbon, a gas, obtained from petroleum by a high-temperature decomposition process (cracking). Molecule consists of two carbon and six hydrogen atoms. Ethane molecule less one hydrogen becomes ethyl radical.

ethanol: see ETHYL ALCOHOL.

Ethel–. For some Anglo-Saxon names beginning thus, see ÆTHEL–; e.g., for Ethelbald, see ÆTHELBALD.

ether. 1 In chemistry, type of organic compound; molecule consists of an oxygen atom linking two identical or different alkyl radicals. Popularly, term means ethyl ether, in which the alkyl radicals are both ethyl groups; used as an anesthetic. **2** In physics and astronomy, theoretical medium formerly postulated as transmitting energy phenomena with wave properties (e.g., light, radio, magnetic attraction) through vacuum. Experiments to detect actual presence of ether have all failed. Modern theory states that energy transmission through vacuum can be explained in several ways; energy waves and energy particles are useful alternate concepts. Einstein dispensed with ether in his relativity theory.

Etherege, Sir George (ĕth'ŭrĭj), 1634?–1691, English Restoration dramatist, author of witty, licentious comedies of manners.

Ethical Culture movement, originating in Society for Ethical Culture founded in New York city (1876) by Felix Adler. It stresses ethical factor in life, apart from theological or metaphysical considerations. The society holds religious services; it lays emphasis on education and pioneered in kindergarten and adult education. In England, Stanton Coit founded society (1887). Internatl. Union of Ethical Culture Societies estab. 1896.

ethics, study and evaluation of human conduct in light of moral principles. Historically, various theories have developed as to man's conscience and responsibility for his actions. The intuitionists (e.g., ROUSSEAU) hold that conscience is innate and instigates moral action. Empiricists (e.g., COMTE, LOCKE, John Stuart MILL) instead explain it as a by-product of experience. Some philosophers seek an absolute ethical criterion in religion. Idealists (e.g., PLATO, KANT) see basis of ethics in metaphysics. Some (e.g., HEGEL, MARX) teach that the state is the arbiter of morals, others (e.g., DEWEY, Felix ADLER) that the individual controls.

Ethiopia (ēthēō'pēă) or **Abyssinia** (ăbĭsĭ'nēŭ), empire (c.457,000 sq. mi.; est. pop. c.22,200,000), E central Africa; cap. Addis Ababa. Comprises low-lying deserts and mountainous plateau, rising to 15,158 ft. at Ras Dashan. In NE is Tana L., source of Blue Nile. Economy primarily agr.; exports include coffee, grains, hides, and gold. Rail lines link Addis Ababa to Jibuti, and Agordat to Massawa. Communication is primarily by air. Official language is Amharic; English main foreign language. According to tradition empire was founded c.1000 B.C. by Menelik I, Solomon's first son, born to queen of Sheba; records go back only to 1st cent. A.D. From 1st to 6th cent. cap. was at AKSUM, which traded with Mediterranean and Near East areas. In 4th cent. the king was converted to Coptic Christianity. Rise of Islam (7th cent.) deprived Ethiopia of its coast and encircled it with hostile neighbors. Period of chaos followed, but order was restored in 13th cent., when new dynasty was founded. Portuguese embassies and missionaries arrived in 16th cent. Emperor was converted to Roman Catholicism, but Coptic Church was fully restored mid-17th cent. and all foreigners expelled. Civil strife of next two centuries ended 1889, when Menelik II became dominant with help of Italy. Claiming that Menelik had agreed to estab. of protectorate, Italy invaded Ethiopia 1895. Decisive battle of Aduwa compelled Italy to recognize Ethiopia's independence. HAILE SELASSIE, who ascended throne in 1930, faced renewed Italian threat, culminating in full-scale invasion (1935). Economic sanctions imposed against Italy by League of Nations were soon abandoned. Ethiopia was incorporated into Italian East Africa until 1941, when it was liberated by British troops. Unification with ERITREA was finally achieved 1952. Constitution of 1955 extended franchise and provided for liberal reforms. Unsuccessful coup in 1960 by officials dissatisfied with slow pace of reform brought strengthening of economy and educational system, but little political change. Ethiopia instrumental in estab. of Organization of African Unity in 1962.

Ethiopic (ēthēōp'ĭk), subgroup of Semitic languages. See LANGUAGE (table).

ethnology: see ANTHROPOLOGY.

ethyl (ĕ'thĭl), in chemistry, organic radical of carbon and hydrogen. Consists of two linked carbon atoms, one attached to three hydrogen atoms and the other attached to two; ethyl radical attaches itself to other groups with the fourth VALENCE of the carbon carrying two hydrogens.

ethyl alcohol, ethanol, or **grain alcohol,** colorless liquid alcohol; molecule consists of an ethyl radical attached to a hydroxyl radical. It has a strong affinity for water and mixes completely in all ratios. Absolute alcohol is pure ethyl alcohol, free of water. Absolute alcohol is 200 proof; one unit of proof is equal to one half a percent. Ethyl alcohol is prepared by the fermentation of carbohydrate, e.g., starch or sugar, in the presence of yeast. An enzyme in yeast is essential to the fermentation process. Ethyl alcohol is used as industrial solvent; biological preservative; to make essences, tinctures, medicines; as fuel. It is denatured by addition of poison.

ethylene (ē'thĭlēn), colorless gas with faint odor, sweet taste. Forms explosive mixture with oxygen. Used in illuminating gas, as anesthetic, to bring out color of citrus fruit. It is an unsaturated HYDROCARBON with two carbon atoms joined by double bond; each carbon holds two hydrogen atoms. It is first member of the ethylene (called also olefine or olefin) series; each member has one double bond and has alkyl radicals replacing one or more of the four hydrogens; each member has twice as many hydrogens as carbons. Lower members, gases; middle, liquids; higher, solids.

Étienne, family of printers: see ESTIENNE.

Etna or **Aetna** (ĕt'nŭ), active volcano, 10,700 ft. high, on E coast of Sicily, Italy. Shape and height of central cone often changed by eruptions. There are c.260 lesser craters. Its densely populated, fertile base is subtropical; the top has snow most of the year. Observatory at 9,650 ft. First known eruption 475 B.C. Those of 1169 and 1669 were particularly destructive.

Eton (ē'tŭn), urban district (pop. 3,901), Buckinghamshire, England. Chiefly known for **Eton College,** largest famous English public school, founded by Henry VI in 1440. Unlike other similar schools, Eton is controlled by elected student representatives. Closely allied with King's Col., Cambridge. Many outstanding Englishmen educated here. Since Second World War more scholarships granted to poorer students. Has annual cricket match with Harrow.

Etowah, river rising in N Ga. in the Blue Ridge and flowing c.150 mi. SW to Rome to join Oostanaula R. and form Coosa R. Allatoona Dam (flood control and power), near Cartersville, was first project in plan for development of Alabama-Coosa river system.

Etruria (ĭtrōō'rēŭ), anc. land, W Italy, now Tuscany and W Umbria. See ETRUSCAN CIVILIZATION.

Etruscan civilization (ĭtrŭ'skŭn), highest civilization in Italy before rise of Rome. Modern research upholds Herodotus that the Etruscans came from Lydia, Asia Minor, in 12th cent. B.C. In language and culture they differed from other Italians. Their wealth was based partly on knowledge of metalworking. They made fine pottery and improved agr. The oligarchical Etruscan cities (e.g., Tarquinii, Caere, Veii, Clusium) formed a loose confederacy. By 500 B.C. their civilization was at its height and included the Umbrian cities and part of Latium. In 5th and early 4th cent. B.C. Rome beat them back, capturing Veii after long struggles (396 B.C.). Invading Gauls in N aided disintegration.

Ettrick Forest, former woodland and royal hunting ground famous in legend, Selkirkshire, Scotland.

Ettrick Water, river of Selkirkshire, Scotland, flowing c.32 mi. from Capel Fell NE to the Tweed.

Etty, William, 1787–1849, English painter. Studied under Sir Thomas Lawrence; influenced by Venetians. Known for his voluptuous nudes.

etymology, historical derivation of linguistic forms, especially words. Study had prestige for centuries because of an accepted theory that knowledge of the history of a word made its meaning clearer. This study revealed the regular relations of sounds in Indo-European languages (as in Grimm's law). In 20th cent. linguists continued to use etymology to learn how meanings change, but they came to consider that the meaning of a form at a given time must be understood without reference to its history if it is to be understood at all.

Eu, chemical symbol of the element EUROPIUM.

Euboea (ūbē'ū), Gr. *Evvoia,* Aegean island (c.1,467 sq. mi.; pop. 166,097), Greece, off Boeotia and Attica; chief city CHALCIS (connected with mainland by drawbridge across EURIPOS). Island is mostly mountainous. Agr., cattle raising. Euboea belonged to Athenian empire from 506 B.C.; passed to Macedon 338 B.C.; to Rome 194 B.C. After the Fourth Crusade it passed to Venice (1209), which lost it to the Turks in 1470. Its Venetian name was Negropont.

eucalyptus (ūkŭlĭp'tŭs) **or gum tree,** large tree or shrub of genus *Eucalyptus,* native to Australia and Asia. Some, e.g., blue gum and red gum, are widely planted on W coast of U.S. Various species yield timber and medicinal oils.

Eucharist: see COMMUNION.

Eucken, Rudolph Christoph (oi'kŭn), 1846–1926, German philosopher. His "activism" stressed experience as the source of value. Awarded 1908 Nobel Prize in Literature.

Euclid (ū'klĭd), fl. c.300 B.C., Greek mathematician famous for his *Elements,* a collection (postulates, rules, theorems, problems) forming basis of Euclidean geometry and important in number theory. It is still commonly used as standard text for Euclidean geometry. See GEOMETRY.

Euclid, city (pop. 62,998), NE Ohio. within confines of Cleveland; settled 1798. Natl. American Shrine of Our Lady of Lourdes is here.

Eudes (ūdz, ûd) **or Odo,** c.860–898, French king (888–98); great-uncle of Hugh Capet. As count of Paris he defended his city against the Normans (885–87).

Eudoxus of Cnidus (ūdŏk'sŭs, nīdŭs), 408?–355? B.C., Greek astronomer and mathematician, credited with calculating length of solar year and discovering certain parts of Euclidean geometry.

Eugene III, d. 1153, pope (1145–53), a CISTERCIAN, friend of BERNARD OF CLAIRVAUX. His rule was disturbed by Arnold of Brescia. Eugene promoted the disastrous Second Crusade.

Eugene IV, 1383–1447, pope (1431–47). Opposed antipapal acts of Council of BASEL, but was driven by Roman rebellion to exile at Florence (1434). He ordered the council to convene at Ferrara, but leaders at Basel refused to obey and declared Eugene deposed. Meanwhile Council of FERRARA-FLORENCE met.

Eugene, city (pop. 50,977), W Oregon, on Willamette R., S of Salem; settled 1846. Processing and shipping center of lumber and farm area. Seat of Univ. of OREGON.

Eugene of Savoy, Prince, 1663–1736, French general in imperial service; son of a prince of Savoy-Carignano and of Olympe MANCINI. Louis XIV having refused him a commission, he entered service of Emperor Leopold I (1683). Defeated Turks at Zenta (1697) and Belgrade (1717), making possible victorious Treaty of PASSAROWITZ (1719). In War of the SPANISH SUCCESSION he shared in victory of Blenheim with Marlborough (1704); defeated French at Oudenarde (1708) and Malplaquet (1709); negotiated Peace of Rastatt (1714). His only major defeat was inflicted on him by his cousin Vendôme (Cassano, 1705).

eugenics (ūjĕ'nĭks), study of methods to improve human race physically and mentally through control of mating and heredity by society. It is directed toward discouraging propagation by unfit and encouraging it in the fit. Some states have laws relating to sterilization of mental defectives, but many problems are involved in carrying out such laws. Future problems of eugenics have been considered in novels of social criticism, e.g., *Brave New World* (1932) by Aldous Huxley and *Nineteen Eighty-Four* (1949) by George

Orwell. Probably the greatest immediate hope lies in education and in bettering the environment.

Eugénie (Fr. ûzhānē') (Eugenia María de Montijo de Guzmán), 1826–1920, empress of the French, consort of Napoleon III; a Spanish noblewoman famed for her beauty. Fled to England in 1870.

Euhemerus (ūhē'mŭrŭs), fl. 300 B.C., Greek philosopher, b. N Africa. He held that the gods were all deified men (euhemerism).

Eulenburg, Philipp, Fürst zu (fē'lĭp fürst tsōō' oi'lŭnbōōrk), 1847–1921. German diplomat, confidant of William II. In 1906 a scandal concerning him weakened respect for the government.

Eulenspiegel, Till (oi'lŭn-shpē'gŭl), N German peasant clown of the 14th or 15th cent., immortalized all over Europe by chapbooks describing his tricks, particularly on upper class persons. Subject of tone poem by Richard Strauss and of literary treatment by De Coster. Also spelled Tyl Ulenspiegel.

Euler, Leonhard (lā'ônhärt oi'lŭr), 1707–83, Swiss mathematician. A founder of higher mathematics, known especially for work on calculus of variations, trigonometry, and analytic mathematics and mechanics. His work in astronomy, hydrodynamics, and optics was also notable. Eulerian equation and Euler's formula named after him.

Euler-Chelpin, Hans von (häns fŭn oi'lŭr kĕl'pĭn), 1873–1964, Swedish chemist, b. Germany. He shared 1929 Nobel Prize in Chemistry for work on sugar fermentation and chemistry of enzymes.

Eumenides: see ERINYES.

Eunice (ūnī'sē, ū'nĭs) [Gr.,= good victory], mother of Timothy; a Christian. 2 Tim. 1.5; Acts 16.1.

Eunice, town (pop. 11,326), S central La., WSW of Opelousas, in cotton, rice, and oil area; founded 1894.

Eunomia, one of the HORAE.

euonymus (ūōn'ĭmŭs) **or spindle tree,** shrub or vine of genus *Euonymus.* Some are evergreen and some have winged stems and brilliant autumn foliage and fruits. See also BURNING BUSH.

Eupatoria (ūpŭtô'rēŭ), Rus. *Yevpatoriya,* city (1965 est. pop. 66,000), Ukrainian SSR, in W Crimea; Black Sea port. Founded 1st cent. A.D.; named for Eupator, king of Pontus. Occupied by allies in Crimean War, by Germans in Second World War. Old section contains ruins of Tatar fortress, 16th-cent. mosque. A variant spelling is Evpatoriya.

Eupen (oi'pŭn), town (est. pop. 14,692), Liège prov., SE Belgium. Mfg. of steel products, heavy machinery, and woolens. Districts of Eupen and MALMÉDY (c.380 sq. mi.; pop. 60,000) were transferred from Germany to Belgium by Treaty of Versailles (1919). Population is predominantly German-speaking.

Euphrates (ūfrā'tēz), river of SW Asia, rising in E Turkey. Flows c.1,675 mi. through Syria to Iraq, where it irrigates date plantations and merges with TIGRIS R. in SHATT EL ARAB. With Tigris it watered Mesopotamia, birthplace of early civilization.

Euphrosyne, one of the GRACES.

euphuism (ū'fūĭzŭm), in English literature, a highly artificial style derived from the *Euphues* (1578) of John Lyly. Has come to mean any high-flown style.

Eurasia (yōōrā'zhŭ, –shŭ), land mass comprising continents of Europe and Asia.

Euratom: see EUROPEAN COMMUNITY.

Eure (ûr), department (2,331 sq. mi.; pop. 361,904), N France, in Normandy; cap. Évreux.

Eure-et-Loir (ûr-ā-lwär'), department (2,293 sq. mi.; pop. 277,546), N France, in Beauce; cap. Chartres.

Eureka (ūrē'kŭ), city (pop. 28,137), NW Calif., on Humboldt Bay WNW of Redding; founded 1850. Fishing and lumbering center in redwood and sequoia region.

Eureka Springs, resort city (1963 pop. 1,681), NW Ark., NNE of Fort Smith, in Ozarks near Mo. line; settled 1879. Has mineral springs. Carry Nation began organization of a prohibitionist school here.

Euric (yōō'rĭk), d. c.484, Visigothic king of Spain (466–c.484). Conquered nearly all Iberian peninsula and part of Gaul; made Toulouse his cap.; issued first code of Visigothic law.

Euripides (yōōrī'pĭdēz), b. 480 or 485 B.C., d. 406 B.C., Greek tragic poet. Author of perhaps 92 plays, 18 extant. Most important: *Alcestis, Medea, Hippolytus, Andromache, Trojan Women, Electra, Iphigenia in Tauris, Iphigenia in Aulis,* and *Bacchae.* A realist, with an interest in contemporary people and problems and with an iconoclastic attitude toward the gods. Used the *deus ex machina* [god from a machine] to resolve a play's problem.

Euripos (yōōrī'pŭs), strait, 130 ft. to 1 mi. wide, between Euboea and Greek mainland.

Europa (yōōrō'pŭ), in Greek religion, Phoenician princess; daughter of Agenor or Phoenix. Zeus, in guise of bull, took her to Crete, where she bore him Minos. She later married king of Crete.

Europe, continent (with adjacent islands c.4,000,000 sq. mi.; pop. c.610,000,000), a vast peninsula of the Eurasian land mass. Separated from Asia by Ural mts., Ural R., Caspian Sea, Caucasus, Black Sea, Bosporus, and Dardanelles; from Africa by Mediterranean Sea and Strait of Gibraltar. It is washed in the N by the Arctic Ocean (incl. Barents Sea, White Sea), in the W by the Atlantic, with which the Irish, North, Baltic, Mediterranean, and Black Seas are connected. A huge mountain chain (Pyrenees, Alps, Carpathians, Balkans, Caucasus) crosses continent from W to E. Highest points: Mt. Elbrus (18,481 ft.), Mont Blanc (15,781 ft.). Between the mountainous Scandinavian peninsula and this chain extends the great European plain—largely fertile soil, with steppe, forest, lake, and tundra dists. in E and N. S of the mountain chain are the fertile Po and Danubian plains and the mountainous Balkan, Italian, and Iberian peninsulas. Among chief rivers are (from E to W) the Volga, Don, Dnieper, Danube, Oder, Elbe, Rhine, Loire, Garonne, and Tagus. Climate, though greatly varied, is subject to moderating prevailing westerly winds. The states of Europe, grouped here by geographic regions, are: E Europe—USSR (incl. Lithuania, Latvia, Estonia) and Poland; SE Europe—Rumania, Hungary, Yugoslavia, Albania, Bulgaria, Greece, Turkey; Scandinavia—Sweden, Norway, Denmark, Finland; Central Europe—Austria, Czechoslovakia, Germany (now split into E and W Germany), Switzerland, Liechtenstein; W Europe—Belgium, Netherlands, Luxembourg, France, Monaco; S Europe—Italy, San Marino, Vatican City, Spain, Portugal, Andorra; British Isles—United Kingdom of Great Britain and Northern Ireland, republic of Ireland; and Iceland. Turkey and USSR lie only partly in Europe.

Europe, Council of, international body, estab. 1949, hq. Strasbourg, France, to promote greater unity and to deal with humanitarian, cultural, and social problems. Members are Austria, Belgium, Cyprus, Denmark, France, West Germany, Great Britain, Greece, Iceland, Ireland, Italy, Luxembourg, the Netherlands, Norway, Sweden, Switzerland, and Turkey. Estab. a European Court of Human Rights 1958 to protect individuals against arbitrary government action.

European Atomic Energy Community: see EUROPEAN COMMUNITY.

European Coal and Steel Community: see EUROPEAN COMMUNITY.

European Community, term covering network of organizations estab. by France, West Germany, Belgium, Luxembourg, the Netherlands, and Italy since Second World War to promote European unity. It developed out of revulsion for nationalistic excesses and from desire to prevent another war. First came **European Coal and Steel Community** (ECSC), estab. 1952. Member nations pledged to create single European market in coal and steel, lifting restrictions on exports and imports. ECSC provided pattern of European organization—independent executive (High Authority); Council of Ministers representing member states; Court of Justice; and supervisory Common Assembly, now European Parliament, of representatives from member states. Short-lived **European Defense Community** followed, patterned on ECSC but rejected by France in 1954. Treaties of Rome (1957) estab. **European Atomic Energy Community** (Euratom), to coordinate development of Europe's nuclear energy resources, and **European Economic Community** (Common Market, EEC). EEC provides for estab. of customs union and complete economic union over 12-year period. Members are to eliminate internal tariff barriers and trade restrictions, to create uniform tariff system for imports from other countries, and to allow free movement of labor and capital; social security systems and wage rates are to be standardized; industrial conversion is to be financed by a European investment bank. Members' overseas territories to benefit from tariff cuts and six-nation investment pool. EEC progress was slowed after 1963 by French Pres. de Gaulle's opposition to its supranational aspects. In 1967 Britain again planned to apply for EEC membership.

European corn borer: see CORN BORER.

European Court of Human Rights: see EUROPE, COUNCIL OF.

European Defense Community: see EUROPEAN COMMUNITY.

European Economic Community: see EUROPEAN COMMUNITY.

European Free Trade Association (EFTA), trading bloc organized 1960 on Great Britain's initiative to meet economic threat of Common Market (see EUROPEAN COMMUNITY). EFTA provided for reduction of tariffs and quotas among members but, unlike Common Market, did not set up single tariff against outside world. Members are Great Britain, Sweden, Norway, Denmark, Austria, Switzerland, and Portugal, known as "outer seven." However, when Great Britain applied to join Common Market in 1961, several other EFTA members followed suit.

European Monetary Agreement, agency of ORGANIZATION FOR ECONOMIC COOPERATION AND DEVELOPMENT, it replaced European Payments Union (EPU) in 1958. Facilitates settlement of balance of payments accounts by providing for convertibility of currencies of member states and by simplifying EPU procedures for settlement of accounts, notably by providing short-term credit facilities.

European Organization for Nuclear Research (CERN), estab. 1954, to coordinate non-military nuclear research among European states. Active in creation of European Space Research Organization (1962).

European Parliament: see EUROPEAN COMMUNITY.

European Payments Union: see EUROPEAN MONETARY AGREEMENT.

European Recovery Program, name popularly given project instituted at Paris Economic Conference (July, 1947) to foster post-war economic recovery in certain European countries. Took form when U.S. Secretary of State George C. Marshall—for whom program was also called Marshall Plan—urged (June, 1947) integration of U.S. economic aid to European countries. The Economic Cooperation Administration (ECA) administered program 1948–51; activities then transferred to Mutual Security Agency.

europium (yōōrō'pēŭm), metallic element of rare earths (symbol = Eu.; see also ELEMENT, table).

Europos or **Europus:** see DURA.

Eurydice, nymph, wife of ORPHEUS.

Eurymedon (yōōrī'mŭdŏn), small river of anc. Pamphylia, S Asia Minor. Here in the Persian Wars Cimon defeated the Persians (c.467 B.C.).

eurythmics (yōōrĭdh'mĭks) [as if Gr.,= good rhythm], system of musical training through harmonious bodily movements; first advanced by Émile Jaques-Dalcroze. Method begins with a set of gymnastics in response to music. Finally, student is able to improvise an interpretation, through gesture language, of an entire composition. System has influenced ballet and acting.

EUROPE

Eusebius of Caesarea (ūsē'bēŭs sēzŭrē'ŭ) or **Eusebius Pamphili** (păm'fĭlĭ), c.263–339?, church historian, b. Palestine. Bishop of Caesarea Palestinae. Works include *Ecclesiastical History*.

Eustace II (ū'stĭs), d. 1093, count of Boulogne, kinsman by marriage of Edward the Confessor. Over his visit to England (1051) Earl Godwin of Wessex broke with Edward. His great-grandson, **Eustace IV,** d. 1153, count of Boulogne, was the son of Stephen of England. Died before his father.

Eustachi, Bartolomeo (bär"tōlōmä'ō ā"ōōstä'kē), d. 1574, Italian anatomist, discoverer of many structures recorded in remarkable drawings (1552, published 1714). Discoveries include **Eustachian tube** (ūstā'kēŭn, –shŭn), the auditory canal equalizing air pressure between throat and middle ear.

Euterpe, Muse of music or of lyric poetry: see MUSES.

Eutin: see LÜBECK.

Eutyches (ū'tĭkēs), c.378–c.452, archimandrite in Constantinople, sponsor of Eutychianism, the first phase of MONOPHYSITISM, and leader of opponents of NESTORIANISM. His chief doctrine was that Christ's humanity was absorbed in his one divine nature. His teachings were denounced and he was deposed (448), but the so-called Robber Synod at Ephesus (449) reinstated him. At the synod St. Flavian, who opposed Eutyches, was manhandled and died. Theodoret was deposed. The Council of CHALCEDON annulled Robber Synod and ended Eutychianism.

Evald, Johannes: see EWALD, JOHANNES.

Evangelical Alliance, association of Evangelical Christians, not of churches but of individuals from many denominations and countries. Estab. (1846) in London; in 1923 the largest association became known as the World's Evangelical Alliance.

Evangelical and Reformed Church: see UNITED CHURCH OF CHRIST.

Evangelical Church: see EVANGELICAL UNITED BRETHREN CHURCH.

Evangelical United Brethren Church, Protestant denomination, merger (1946) of Evangelical Church and United Brethren in Christ. Both bodies grew from evangelistic efforts. Former estab. (1807) under Jacob Albright, Lutheran convert to Methodism; latter founded (1800) by P. W. Otterbein and Martin Boehm. Church has episcopal government and Arminian doctrine, and stresses individual responsibility. In 1967 the denomination united with the Methodist Church to become the United Methodist Church.

evangelist (from Gr.,= Gospel), title first given to SS. Matthew, Mark, Luke, and John. Now used for Protestant preachers who preach personal conversion. See also CAMP MEETING; GRAHAM, BILLY; REVIVAL, RELIGIOUS.

Evans, Sir Arthur John, 1851–1941, English archaeologist. Excavating in Crete (1898–1935), he discovered the remains of a civilization which he named Minoan.

Evans, Herbert McLean, 1882–, American anatomist and embryologist, discoverer of vitamin E.

Evans, Lewis, c.1700–1756, colonial surveyor and geographer, b. Wales. His detailed maps of the middle colonies were used by migrating colonists and by Braddock. He drew attention to Ohio, suggested how to wrest it from French.

Evans, Luther H(arris), 1902–, American librarian and political scientist. Librarian of Congress 1945–53. Director General of UNESCO 1953–58. Appointed director of Internatl. and Legal Collections of Columbia Univ. in 1962.

Evans, Maurice, 1901–, Anglo-American actor-manager. Noted for interpretations of Shakespeare and G. B. Shaw.

Evans, Oliver, 1755–1819, American inventor of grain-handling machinery and pioneer builder of high-pressure steam engines. He built the first steam river dredge in America.

Evans, Mount: see FRONT RANGE.

Evanston, residential city (pop. 79,283), NE Ill., on L. Michigan N of Chicago; settled 1826. Seat of NORTHWESTERN UNIVERSITY and Seabury–Western Theological Seminary. Once home of Frances E. Willard; hq. of Woman's Christian Temperance Union.

Evansville, city (pop. 141,543), extreme SW Ind., on Ohio R., WNW of Owensboro, Ky.; settled 1817. Shipping and commercial center for agr. region. Coal mines in area. Evansville Col. is here.

evaporation, conversion of liquid to gas at temperature below boiling point; rate depends on amount of exposed surface and on humidity. Molecules at surface bound into air, are prevented from returning by collision with molecules of air and resulting deflection. Increased energy of molecules depends on heat drawn from surrounding substances, e.g., the skin is cooled when liquid evaporates from it.

Evarts, William Maxwell, 1818–1901, American lawyer and statesman; grandson of Roger Sherman. Counsel for U.S. in several important legal cases. As U.S. Secretary of State (1877–81) he formulated U.S. position that any isthmian canal must remain under American control.

Evatt, Herbert Vere (vēr, ē'vŭt), 1894–1965, Australian statesman. Judge of Australian High Court 1930–40; served as foreign minister 1941–49. President of UN General Assembly 1948–49, he was noted for upholding rights of small nations.

Eve [Heb.,= life], in Bible, first woman, Adam's wife. Led by serpent to eat forbidden fruit from tree of knowledge, she tempted Adam to eat. Both exiled from the Garden of Eden in punishment. Gen. 2–4; 2 Cor. 11.3; 1 Tim. 2.13.

Evelyn, John (ēv'ŭlĭn, ēv'lĭn, ēv'lĭn), 1620–1706, English diarist and miscellaneous writer. His diary, first published in 1818, offers much information on late 17th-cent. life.

evening primrose, plant of genus *Oenothera,* native to North America. Yellow flowers open in evening.

Evenki National Okrug (ĕvyĕn'kē), administrative division (287,644 sq. mi.; 1965 est. pop. 11,000), Krasnoyarsk Territory, N central Asiatic RSFSR; cap. Tura. Has coal and salt. Native Evenki, a Tungus-Manchurian people numbering c.30,000, raise reindeer, trap fur, and fish.

Everest, Sir George (ē'vŭrĭst), 1790–1866, British surveyor, b. Wales. Worked on trigonometrical survey of India (1806–43). Mt. Everest named for him.

Everest, Mount, peak, 29,141 ft. high, on Tibet-Nepal border, in the Himalayas; highest point on earth. Named for Sir George Everest. Tenzing Norkay of Nepal and Sir Edmund Hillary reached summit in 1953. In 1958 the Chinese laid claim to the peak.

Everett, Edward (ēv'rĭt, ē'vŭrĭt), 1794–1865, American orator and statesman. U.S. Representative from Mass. (1825–35); adopted conservative attitude on slavery question. Governor of Mass. (1836–39). U.S. Senator (1853–54). In Civil War he traveled throughout North speaking for Union cause. Delivered principal oration at Gettysburg on same occasion that called forth Pres. Lincoln's address.

Everett. 1 City (pop. 43,544), E Mass., an industrial suburb N of Boston; settled c.1643. **2** City (pop. 40,-304), NW Wash., on Puget Sound at mouth of Snohomish R., NNE of Seattle; settled c.1890. Port and commercial center with lumber mfg. Paine Field air force base is N.

Everglades, subtropical area, c.5,000 sq. mi., covering most of S. Fla., S of L. Okeechobee. Sedge and water stretch 100 mi. from lake to Florida Bay at peninsula's tip. Water flows S from central Fla. to lake, overflows into Everglades. Underlying oolitic limestone rims area as retaining sea wall. Surface is no more than few ft. above sea level and dotted by hammocks (islandlike masses of vegetation). Overdrainage aimed at reclaiming solidly packed black muck for agr. led to great fires in 1939. Only lake border actually is farmed. In SW part is Everglades Natl. Park, which also includes sandy beaches, mangrove forests, subtropical and rare flora and fauna. After severe drought in 1961, fires destroyed thousands of acres in whole area. N of park is Seminole Indian reservation.

evergreen, term often used as synonym for CONIFER, but properly applied to all plants that bear green leaves throughout the year.

Evergreen Park, village (pop. 24,178), NE Ill., a suburb SSW of Chicago.

everlasting or **immortelle,** name for certain plants with papery or chaffy flowers which on drying retain their shape and color. Often thus used in winter bouquets are COCKSCOMB; GLOBE AMARANTH; STRAWFLOWER.

Everyman, late 15th-cent. morality play in English, counterpart of Dutch play *Elckerlijc.* Which is the original has been disputed. Summoned by Death, the hero, Everyman, can persuade none of his friends—Beauty, Kindred, Worldly Goods—to go with him, except Good Deeds.

Evesham (ēv'shům, ē'shùm), municipal borough (pop. 12,608), Worcestershire, England, on Avon R. in productive fruit and vegetable region. Simon de Montford slain in battle here 1265.

Évian (āvyā') or **Évian-les-Bains** (-lä-bĕ'), resort, Haute-Savoie dept., E France, on L. Geneva. Mineral spa.

evidence, facts introduced before a judicial body to aid it in assessing the truth of disputed matters other than disputes over legal doctrine. Such facts include documents and testimonial evidence of witnesses under oath. Introduction of particular evidence is controlled by legal rules: evidence may be excluded by the judge on the grounds that it is irrelevant (having no bearing on the case), immaterial (having no direct connection with substance of the case), or incompetent (outside the knowledge of the witness; e.g., hearsay evidence). The duty of proving particular facts is allocated between opposing parties. As a general rule, each party in a civil suit must prove its affirmative contentions; in criminal suits, the burden of proof rests on the prosecution.

evolution, concept that animals and plants developed by gradual, continuous change from earlier forms. This concept, known as organic evolution (in contrast to inorganic evolution or origin of the physical universe) conceives of life as having arisen from simple primordial protoplasmic mass, probably in sea. Evolutionary concepts appeared in early Greece; during 15 centuries of Christian era under Church restraint, none developed until glimpses of later evolutionary theory began to appear after mid-16th cent. Invention of microscope and classification studies contributed to development. Charles Darwin, after 20 years of gathering evidence, formulated evolutionary theory later known as DARWINISM (similar work was done independently by Alfred Russel Wallace). Darwin presented his theory in 1859, when first edition of his *Origin of the Species* appeared. Influence of theory upon scientific thought and philosophy incalculable. The concept was later enlarged by the growth of science of genetics, based on Mendel's laws of inheritance and extended through the work of T. H. Morgan, H. J. Muller, and others.

Évora (ĕ'vôrů), town (pop. 24,787), cap. of Évora dist. and Upper Alentejo prov., S Portugal. The Ebora of Roman times, it has impressive ruins ("temple of Diana"). Commercial center under Moors; captured by Portuguese 1166. Cathedral (12th cent.); former Jesuit univ. (1559–1758) now a high school.

Evpatoriya, Ukrainian SSR: see EUPATORIA.

Évreux (āvrû'), town (pop. 23,647), cap. of Eure dept., N France, in Normandy. Counts of Évreux were also kings of NAVARRE 1349–1425. Cathedral (14th–17th cent.) is noted for stained glass windows.

Evtushenko, Evgeny: See YEVTUSHENKO, YEVGENY.

Ewa Beach (ē'wä), town (pop. 2,459), Hawaii, on S coast of Oahu, just W of entrance to Pearl Harbor. A U.S. naval air station is nearby.

Ewald, Georg Heinrich August von (gā'ôrk hīn'rīkh ou'gŏŏst fŭn ā'vält), 1803–75, German Orientalist and philologist, an authority on Hebrew and the Bible. He was one of the seven professors of the Univ. of Göttingen who protested the revocation of the Hanoverian constitution (1837).

Ewald, Johannes (ā'väl), 1743–81, Danish romantic poet. Author of dramas *Rolf Krage* (1770; first original Danish tragedy), and *The Fishermen* (1779; containing the Danish national anthem). Name also spelled Evald.

Ewbank, Thomas, 1792–1870, American inventor and writer, b. Durham, England. Employed his own patents for tinning lead in pioneer manufacture of tubing. As U.S. commissioner of patents he improved greatly handling of claims. Wrote (1842) authoritative work on hydraulic and other machines for raising water.

Ewe (ē'vē), Negro tribe, numbering over 800,000, W Africa, especially SE Ghana, S Togo, and S Dahomey. Partition of German Togoland after First World War divided the Ewe between British and French trusteeships. Reunification has been their goal for many years.

Ewell, Richard Stoddert (ū'ùl), 1817–72, Confederate general. Supported Stonewall Jackson in Shenandoah Valley (1862). Succeeded Jackson in command (1863) and ably led Lee's advance in Gettysburg campaign. Fought in Wilderness campaign (1864), and defended Richmond (1865).

Ewing, Sir James Alfred, 1855–1935, Scottish engineer and physicist. His research in magnetism disclosed phenomenon of hysteresis, and he advanced the knowledge of crystalline structure of metals. His studies of earthquakes in Japan were significant.

Ewing, Thomas, 1789–1871, American statesman. Served as U.S. Senator from Ohio (1831–37, 1850–51), Secretary of the Treasury (1841), first Secretary of the Interior (1849–50).

Excalibur: see ARTHURIAN LEGEND.

Excelsior Springs, city (pop. 6,473), W Mo., NE of Kansas City; founded 1880. Health resort (mineral springs). Frank and Jesse James lived nearby.

excess profits tax: see INTERNAL REVENUE.

exchange, mutual transfer of goods, money, or services. Barter replaced in modern society by money and price system. Value of exchanged items set mainly by market demand. In commerce, an exchange is a place where trading goes on, such as a STOCK EXCHANGE.

Exchequer, Court of (ĕkschĕ'kůr), British governmental agency. Originated after Norman Conquest as a financial committee of the Curia Regis. By end of 13th cent. the court of appeal was separated from the exchequer or treasury. After 1830 a single Court of Exchequer emerged as court of appeal intermediate between common-law courts and House of Lords. The Judicature Act of 1873 made it the exchequer division of the high court of justice.

excise: see INTERNAL REVENUE.

excommunication, formal expulsion of a person from a religious community, particularly notable in Judaism (e.g., expulsion of Spinoza) and Roman Catholicism. Elaborate Catholic form involves pronouncement of anathema and public exclusion from Church and was important in Middle Ages.

excretion, elimination of useless matter by living organism. In man, organs that form excretions include skin, lungs, kidneys, and large intestine.

Exe (ĕks), stream of Somerset and Devonshire, England, flowing from Exmoor to the English Channel.

executive, one who carries out plans of another person or group. In government it refers to all who execute laws, as well as to chief administrative officer. Separation of powers in U.S. is modified in practice: President performs many judicial and legislative

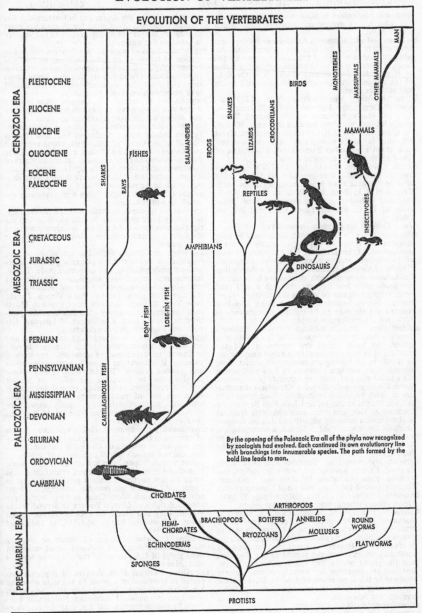

EVOLUTION OF THE VERTEBRATES

By the opening of the Paleozoic Era all of the phyla now recognized by zoologists had evolved. Each continued its own evolutionary line with branchings into innumerable species. The path formed by the bold line leads to man.

functions. Distinction is often made between executive who makes policy and administration which carries it out.

executors and administrators. An executor is the person designated in a will to carry out its provisions. An administrator is appointed for same purpose by the court, if there is no capable executor named or living or if a person dies without a will. It is the duty of the administrator to collect the decedent's assets and settle his debts.

Exeter (ĕk'sûtûr), county borough (pop. 80,215), co. town of Devonshire, England, on Eve R. Industrial, agr., and marketing center of SW England. Strategically located, town was besieged by Danes, William the Conqueror, Yorkists, and religious factions. Great cathedral is classic example of 14th-cent. architecture; chapter house has **Exeter Book,** MS volume of Old English poetry, compiled c.1000.

Exeter, town (pop. 7,243), SE N.H., SW of Portsmouth. Rev. John Wheelwright settled here 1638 after banishment from Mass.; town organized 1639. Cap. of N.H. in Revolution. PHILLIPS EXETER ACADEMY and 17th-cent. garrison house are here. Birthplace of D. C. French, Lewis Cass, and William Ladd.

Exeter College: see OXFORD UNIVERSITY.

exile, expulsion of a national from his country by government, or voluntary departure usually to avoid punishment. Ostracism, exile for ten years by vote of population, was common in Greek city-states. Growth of national states, along with the theory that ties between them and their citizens are indissoluble, has made exile less frequent although it still may occur during civil war or under a dictatorship. "Government-in-exile"—person or group living outside a country but claiming to be rightful government—is 20th-cent. international concept.

existentialism (ĕgzĭstĕn'shŭlĭzŭm, ĕksĭ–). Although there are three main developments of this philosophic school, the basic beliefs are commonly held—the problem of human existence is the major one; reason, by itself, is an inadequate method of explanation; anguish is an emotion common to men confronting life's problems; and morality demands participation. Soren Kierkegaard developed a Christian existentialism in which anguish is relieved by transcendent faith in God. Martin Heidegger and Jean Paul Sartre deny existence of God and stress man's absolute freedom to choose, with resulting anguish and despair. Jacques Maritain has approached a Christian existentialism, based upon St. Thomas Aquinas, in which desire to be and fear of nothingness are rendered powerless by faith in God.

Exmoor, high moorland, Somerset and Devonshire, England. Largely a wasteland, with hills, valleys, and wooded glens, underlain by slate and sandstone. Grazing ground for sheep and small Exmoor ponies.

Exmouth (ĕks'mouth), urban district (pop. 19,740), Devonshire, England; port and summer resort.

Exodus (ĕk'sŭdŭs), book of Old Testament, second of books of Law (Pentateuch or Torah), ascribed by tradition to Moses. Some of the most important events of biblical history occur in Exodus, e.g., the deliverance of the Hebrews in Egypt from bondage, the institution of Passover, the parting of the Red Sea, and the giving of the Ten Commandments. In the last part are directions for worship. A most solemn moment is the appearance of God to Moses in the burning bush revealing His name as I Am.

exogamy: see MARRIAGE.

expanding universe: see UNIVERSE.

expansion, in physics, increase in volume resulting from temperature increase; contraction is reverse. When heat is applied, rate of vibration and distance between molecules increases; increased volume results. Degree of expansion is specific property of each liquid and solid; amount per unit volume per one-degree temperature rise is coefficient of cubical expansion. Coefficient of linear expansion is increase

per unit of length per degree rise in temperature. Expansion coefficient about same for all common gases at ordinary temperatures; Kelvin scale of temperature is based on this number.

expatriation, loss of nationality, either general (as in cession of territory) or individual; may or may not be voluntary; U.S. forbids expatriations in wartime. In some cases it results in statelessness. Many countries still hold that voluntary expatriation cannot take place without state's permission.

Exploits, largest river of N.F., Canada, rising in Long Range and flowing NE to Exploits Bay. Grand Falls and Bishop's Falls have hydroelectric plants.

explosive, substance undergoing decomposition or combustion rapidly with evolution of heat and production of large volume of gas, which exerts enormous sudden pressure causing blasting of rocks, etc. Some explosives are not truly explosive but are mixtures of substances which undergo very rapid combustion; others are compounds which liberate much energy during rapid decomposition. Most high explosives are prepared from nitric acid. Some high explosives are set off by a DETONATOR.

exponent (ĕk'spōnŭnt), in mathematics, a number, letter, or algebraic expression written above and to the right of another number, letter, or expression called the base. Exponent indicates power to which base is to be raised.

exposition, term usually applied to exhibitions or fairs organized to reflect cultural progress, promote international understanding, and encourage trade. Today, international expositions emphasize scientific and technological innovations, but fine and industrial arts still have their place. London, Paris, Vienna, Zurich, New York, Chicago, San Francisco, Brussels, Montreal, and Seattle are among cities that housed expositions or world's fairs. The Bureau of Internatl. Expositions, Paris, regulates world's fairs.

expressionism, term used generally to describe any art work in which representation of nature is subordinated to expression of emotion. In modern painting it characterizes much postimpressionism and various schools (Brücke, Blaue Reiter, Neue Sachlichkeit). In literature the effort to project spiritual actualities rather than naturalistic records of events was of most importance in the drama and the novel. Outstanding among expressionist playwrights of period after First World War was the German Georg Kaiser.

exterritoriality or **extraterritoriality,** privilege of alien of exemption from local jurisdiction in foreign country. Applies to officials of UN while performing duties; and to a nation's official personnel and residences, public vessels in port, and sometimes armed forces. Nonofficial residents have enjoyed exterritoriality in many foreign countries, custom persisting longest in Egypt and China. It was resented, however, and legal reforms led to abolition. China in First World War abolished rights of Central Powers, in Second World War of Italy and Japan. In 1924 USSR abandoned rights, followed by Britain and U.S. in 1943, and France in 1946.

extortion, unlawful obtaining of money or property through wrongful use of authority or of office. In most states of U.S., wrongful use of fear or force is also unlawful.

extradition (ĕkstrŭdĭ'shŭn), delivery of a person suspected or convicted of a crime by the state where he has taken refuge to the state asserting jurisdiction over him. International extradition is normally governed by special treaties, and it is usual for neighboring countries to grant extradition more readily than countries remote from each other. Without treaty, extradition is not an obligation, though asylum may be refused. The first U.S. treaty with an international extradition clause was Jay's Treaty (1794). In the 19th cent. many extradition treaties were concluded by Western nations. Usually extradition for political crimes is excluded, though a nation may refuse asylum to a political fugitive. In the U.S., Congress has estab. a uniform law for state-to-state extradition; it provides that any person properly charged shall be extradited.

extrasensory perception: see PSYCHICAL RESEARCH.

extraterritoriality: see EXTERRITORIALITY.

Extremadura, Spain: see ESTREMADURA.

extreme unction: see SACRAMENT.

extroversion and **introversion,** terms introduced by C. G. Jung for opposed psychological types. The extrovert's general activity or drive (libido) is directed toward external world, the introvert's upon himself. Everyone has both tendencies, with one generally dominant as a result of both temperament and environment. Extreme extrovert behavior becomes an irrational flight from self, the acting out of feelings in society, as in hysteria. Extreme introvert retreats into inner world, with fantasies displacing reality. Jung saw schizophrenia as introvert's psychosis.

Eyck, Hubert van (hoi′brĕkht vän īk), c.1370–1426, and **Jan van Eyck** (yän), c.1390–1441, Flemish painters, brothers, outstanding artists of their time in N Europe. Their descriptive realism resulted in an astounding minuteness of detail and in unusually fine differentiations between textures and kinds of atmospheric light. Their altarpiece in the church of St. Bavo in Ghent was completed by Jan in 1432. The wedding picture of *Giovanni Arnolfini and his Bride* (Nat. Gall., London) is signed by Jan and dated 1434.

Eyde, Samuel (sä′mōŏĕl ā′dū), 1866–1940, Norwegian engineer, co-developer of Birkeland-Eyde process for nitrogen fixation.

eye, organ of vision consisting of eyeball that encloses transparent media. Outer fibrous layer of eyeball comprises white, opaque sclera at back and sides and transparent cornea in front. Vascular, pigmented middle layer consists of chorioid (or choroid) under the sclera; iris, behind cornea and perforated by pupil; and ciliary body connecting chorioid and iris rim. Inner layer, the retina, has many optic nerve fibers on its surface; these respond to light and color. Transparent media consist of lens behind iris, jelly-like vitreous humor between retina and lens, and aqueous humor between lens and cornea. See *ill.,* p. 657.

eyeglasses, device to improve vision or protect eyes. Convex lenses suggested 13th cent. by Roger Bacon; concave, used in 14th cent. Bifocals, with upper part for viewing distant objects and lower for near objects, invented by Benjamin Franklin. Trifocals later developed. Contact lenses, shaped to fit eye and worn under eyelid, first used 1887; popularity increased after 1930s because of improved grinding and fitting techniques.

Eyja Fjord (ā′ù fyôrd″), longest fjord in Iceland (37 mi.), on N coast. At its head is Akureyri.

Eylau (ī′lou) or **Bagrationovsk** (bùgrǔ″tyĕŏ′nǔfsk), town (est. pop. 5,000), RSFSR (since 1945), formerly in East Prussia. Here, in Feb., 1807, Napoleon I fought a bloody but indecisive battle against Russian and Prussian forces (in which Prince Bagration distinguished himself). Formerly called Preussisch Eylau.

Eyre, Lake (âr), shallow salt lake, area 3,430 sq. mi., NE South Australia; frequently dry.

Ezechiel: see EZEKIEL.

Ezekias (ĕzükī′ùs): see HEZEKIAH.

Ezekiel or **Ezechiel** (both: ēzē′kēĕl) [Heb.,= God strengthens], book of Old Testament, an account of the prophetic career of the priest Ezekiel (fl. 592 B.C.). Central point is the fall of Jerusalem, what goes on before being prophetic of doom, the rest inspired by hope of restoration. Among famous passages are chapters 18, 21, 26–28, 31–32, 37.

Ezekiel, Mordecai Joseph Brill, 1899–, American agr. economist; director of economic division of UN Food and Agricultural Organization 1947–50. Pioneered in price forecasting for farm products.

Ezel, Estonian SSR: see SAAREMAA.

Ezra [Heb.,= help] and **Nehemiah** (nēùmī′ù) [Heb.,= consoled by God], in AV, books of Old Testament; called 1 and 2 ESDRAS in Western canon; a single work in Hebrew canon. Ezra (fl. after 460 B.C.) was a priest and scribe; Nehemiah (fl. 444 B.C.) was cupbearer to Artaxerxes I and later governor of Jerusalem. Books tell of return of Jews to Palestine from captivity. Important events are the reading of the Law to the assembled people, the signing of a covenant, and the completion of the wall.

Ezzelino da Romano (ĕt″sālĕ′nō dä rōmä′nō), 1194–1259, Italian Ghibelline leader, lord of Verona, Vicenza, Padua. A supporter of Emperor Frederick II, he dominated N Italy after 1237; was excommunicated by Pope Innocent IV 1254; suffered defeat shortly before his death. Reputedly a cruel tyrant; mentioned in Dante's *Inferno.*

F, chemical symbol of element FLUORINE.

Faber, Frederick William (fā'bùr), 1814–63, English theologian, adherent of the Oxford movement; friend of J. H. Newman. Founded community at Birmingham which became the Oratory of St. Philip Neri (1848) and an oratory at London (1849).

Fabian Society, influential English socialist society, developed 1884 out of the Fellowship of the True Life (1883). Among its outstanding exponents were G. B. Shaw and Sidney and Beatrice Webb. Fabians repudiated the Marxist class struggle, believing in natural development of socialism. They helped found the British Labour Party in 1900.

Fabius (fā'bēŭs), family name of several Romans. **Quintus Fabius Maximus Rullianus** (kwĭn'tŭs, măk'sĭmŭs rŭlēā'nŭs) or **Rullus** (rŭ'lŭs), d. c.291 B.C., renowned as a general for his victory over Etruscans, Samnites, and allies at Sentinum (295 B.C.). His descendant, **Quintus Fabius Maximus Verrucosus** (vĕrōōkō'sŭs), d. 203 B.C., opponent of HANNIBAL in the Second PUNIC WAR, was called Cunctator (kŭngk'tŭtôr) [Latin,= delayer] because of his tactics, which have given the term Fabian to any waiting policy. Tired of his masterly inaction, the Romans replaced him as consul and were defeated at Cannae.

fable, short moral story, often one in which characters are beasts or inanimate objects. One of oldest collections is Indian PANCHATANTRA. Fables of AESOP were earliest to be written down. In medieval times began satirical series about REYNARD THE FOX. Great French fabulist was LA FONTAINE. John Gay and Dryden continued the beast fable in England. The fable as story with a lesson goes on in the 20th cent. (e.g., James Thurber, *Fables for Our Time,* 1940).

fabliau (fablēō'), plural **famliaux,** short comic, often bawdy tale in verse satirizing middle- or lower-class characters. Popular in medieval France.

Fabre, Jean Henri (zhā ãrē' fä'brŭ), 1823–1915, French entomologist and author, known for observations and studies of insect behavior. Chief work is *Souvenirs entomologiques* (10 vols., 1879–1907); English translations of parts of this work include *The Life of the Spider* (1912); *The Wonders of Instinct* (1918); *The Marvels of the Insect World* (1938).

Fabriano, Gentile da: see GENTILE DA FABRIANO.

Fabricius, Hieronymus (hĭŭrŏ'nŭmŭs), 1537–1619, Italian anatomist, teacher of William Harvey at Padua.

Fabritius, Carel (kärl fäbrēt'sēŏōs), 1622–54, Dutch painter; pupil and worthy follower of Rembrandt.

facsimile (făksĭ'mŭlē), in communication, a radio or wire transmission system for pictures and other graphic matter. By light-beam and photoelectric-cell arrangement light and dark areas of material are translated into transmittable tones; receiver reproduces them on chemically treated paper.

factory acts: see LABOR LAW.

Facundo Quiroga, Juan: see QUIROGA, JUAN FACUNDO.

fading, in radio, irregular variation in strength and quality of received signal. Chief cause considered changing altitude and density of Kennelly-Heaviside layer; transmitted wave reflects unevenly, arrives out of phase. Automatic volume control corrects.

Faenza (fään'tsä), city (est. pop. 49,834), Emilia-Romagna, N central Italy, in Romagna. Renaissance cathedral and palace. Richly colored ceramics, called faïence, made here since 12th cent.

Faeroe Islands or **Faroe Islands** (both: fâ'rō), Dan. *Faerørne,* Faeroese *Føroyar,* group of 21 volcanic islands (c.540 sq. mi.; pop. 34,596), in N Atlantic Ocean, between Iceland and the Shetlands; Danish crown possession. Stromo (with cap., Thorshavn) and Ostero isls. are largest. Transferred from Norway to Denmark 1814; under British protection in the Second World War; obtained home rule 1948. Faeroese language is a survival of Old Norse, akin to Icelandic. Fish and wool are main exports.

Fages, Pedro (pä'dhrō fä'häs), fl. 1767–96, Spanish governor of Alta Calif. (1782–91). Notable for encouraging colonization, agr., and missionary work.

Fahrenheit, Gabriel Daniel (fä'rŭnhīt, Ger. gä'brēĕl dä'nyĕl fä'rŭnhīt), 1686–1736, German physicist. He devised Fahrenheit TEMPERATURE scale and substituted mercury for alcohol in thermometer.

Fair, A. A.: see GARDNER, ERLE STANLEY.

fair. Before transportation and marketing developments made distribution of goods to all markets easy, marketing opportunities arose from religious observances which brought widely separated people together. Markets or fairs of this kind developed in Greece and Rome. Their advantages multiplied during the Middle Ages in Europe, the greatest period being the 13th–14th cent. Always a business institution for buying, selling, and bartering, they declined under competition with continuous marketing; a few (e.g., at Leipzig) survived. The typical American fair (e.g., at Danbury, Conn.) is dissimilar, being an exhibition of farm and home products ranked by judges for excellence.

Fairbairn, Sir William (fâr'bârn), 1789–1874, Scottish engineer, builder of iron ships and railroad bridges.

Fairbanks, Douglas, 1883–1939, American film actor, whose real name was Douglas Elton Ulman. After 1915 he made such swashbuckling films as *The Mark of Zorro, Robin Hood,* and *The Thief of Bagdad.* He was married (1920–35) to Mary Pickford.

Fairbanks, Thaddeus, 1796–1886, American inventor of the platform scale, patented 1831.

Fairbanks, city (pop. 13,311), central Alaska, on Tanana R., NNE of Anchorage. Transportation, distribution, and financial center for Tanana R. area and all of inland Alaska. Grew as mining camp after 1902 gold discovery; town increased in importance with coming of Alaska RR. Richardson Highway from Valdez on coast reaches Fairbanks, which became terminus of ALASKA HIGHWAY in Second World War. Was U.S. army air base in war. Eielson Air Force Base and Univ. of ALASKA are nearby.

Fairborn, city (pop. 19,453), SW Ohio, NE of Dayton. Wright-Patterson Air Force Base is nearby.

Fairchild, David Grandison, 1869–1954, American botanist. He organized and then directed division of plant exploration and introduction in U.S. Dept. of Agriculture. His works include *The World Was My Garden* (1938); *The World Grows Round My Door* (1947).

SMALL CAPITALS = cross references. Pronunciation key on inside end pages. Abbreviations: p. 2.

350

Fair Employment Practices Committee (FEPC), estab. 1941 during Second World War to eliminate discriminatory employment practices. Suspended 1946 for lack of funds. A few states have estab. similar bodies.

Fairfax, Thomas Fairfax, 6th Baron, 1693–1781, British proprietor of Northern Neck of Va. Claim to land between Rappahannock and Potomac rivers, disputed by Va., confirmed in 1745.

Fairfax, town (pop. 13,585), NE Va., W of Washington, D.C. In old courthouse are wills of George and Martha Washington. Mount Vernon, Gunston Hall (1755–58), and Pohick Church (1774) are in county. George Mason Col. of Univ. of Virginia is here.

Fairfax of Cameron, Thomas Fairfax, 3d Baron, 1612–71, English soldier-statesman. Commanded New Model Army that crushed Charles I in 1645. Fearing military dictatorship, he opposed Cromwell. Was instrumental in return of Charles II to the throne (1660).

Fairfield. 1 City (pop. 15,816), N central Ala., suburb W of Birmingham. Planned as industrial city, it was founded c.1910. **2** City (pop. 14,968), W Calif., NE of San Francisco; founded 1859. Travis Air Force Base is nearby. **3** Industrial town (pop. 46,183), SW Conn., on Long Island Sound W of Bridgeport; settled 1639. Scene of Pequot War battle (1637). British burned much of it in Revolution. Fairfield Univ. is here. **4** City (1966 pop. 11,587), SE Iowa, E of Ottumwa. Trade center. First annual Iowa State Fair held here in 1854. Seat of Parsons Col.

Fair Haven, town (pop. 2,378), W Vt., W of Rutland. First slate quarry in Vt. was opened here 1839.

Fairhaven, residential and resort town (pop. 14,339), SE Mass., at mouth of Acushnet R. opposite New Bedford; settled 1670. Boatbuilding.

Fairhope, resort town (pop. 4,858), SW Ala., on E coast of Mobile Bay; founded 1894–95 by followers of Henry George.

Fair Isle, small rocky island off N Scotland. Known for knitted hosiery of bright, many-colored designs. Also a famous bird migration station.

Fair Labor Standards Act: see WAGES AND HOURS ACT.

Fair Lawn, borough (pop. 36,421), NE N.J., near Passaic R., NE of Paterson.

Fairleigh Dickinson University, at Rutherford, Teaneck, and Madison, N.J.; coed.; inc. and opened 1942 as junior college, became four-year college 1948, university 1956. Extension center at Wayne.

Fairmont, city (pop. 27,477), N central W.Va., where West Fork and Tygart rivers form Monongahela; in bituminous-coal area; founded 1843. Valley Falls are nearby.

Fair Oaks: see PENINSULAR CAMPAIGN.

Fairview Park, city (pop. 14,624), NE Ohio, a suburb W of Cleveland.

fairy, in folklore, one of a variety of supernatural beings having magical powers. Although usually represented as mischievous, capricious, and, at times, demonic, fairies could also be loving and bountiful. Belief in fairies has existed since earliest times, but concept and description varies widely, ranging from tiny old men to beautiful enchantresses; from the Arabic jinni to the Scandinavian troll, the Germanic elf, and the English pixie. Great adapters of popular fairy tales were Charles Perrault, the brothers Grimm, and Hans Christian Andersen.

Faisal: see FEISAL.

Faiyum, Egypt: see FAYUM.

Faizabad, Uttar Pradesh, India: see FYZABAD.

Falange (fä-län'hä), Spanish political party, founded 1933 as Falange Española Tradicionalista by José Antonio Primo de Rivera. Based on FASCISM; emphasized Spanish national tradition. Sided with Insurgents in civil war of 1936–39; merged with Carlist militia by Franco 1937. Grew weaker after 1941; cabinet organization of 1957 left party powerless; when new constitution was approved in 1966 party ceased to exist.

Falashas (–lä'–) [Ethiopic,= emigrant], group of Abyssinians of Jewish affinity.

falcon (fôl'kŭn, fô'kŭn), name for numerous species of long-winged, swift birds of prey, found throughout the world. They have strong hooked, notched bills and eat birds, small mammals, and insects. Duck hawk (American variety of Old World peregrine), pigeon hawk, sparrow hawk, and prairie falcon are American falcons. The female of some species is trained for **falconry,** hunting birds and small animals for masters. Known to ancient Chinese, Persians, Egyptians.

Falconet, Étienne Maurice (ätyen' môrēs' fälkōnā'), 1716–91, French sculptor; pupil of Lemoyne.

Faliero or **Falier, Marino** (märē'nō fälyä'rō, fälēēr'), 1274–1355, doge of Venice (1354–55). Joined in plot against patricians to overthrow oligarchic government and make him dictator. Plot was discovered, Faliero and accomplices executed.

Falkberget, Johan (yōhän' fälk'běrgù), 1879–, Norwegian novelist. Wrote of miners in *Lisbeth of Jarnfjeld* (1915), trilogy *Christianus Sextus* (1927–35), and *Night Bread* (1940).

Falkirk (fôl'kûrk), burgh (pop. 38,043), Stirlingshire, Scotland. In mining and mfg. region, it has aluminum and casting works. Has annual stock fairs. English defeated Scots here 1298; Gen. Hawley defeated by Prince Charles Edward's Jacobites here 1746.

Falkland, Lucius Cary, 2d Viscount (fôk'lŭnd), 1610?–1643, English statesman and literary figure. Represented Charles I in attempts to make peace with Parliament. He supposedly let himself be killed in battle rather than fight either king or Parliament.

Falkland Islands (fô'klŭnd), islands, S Atlantic, c.300 mi. E of Strait of Magellan. Ownership disputed by Argentina and Great Britain. Group administered as British crown colony (4,700 sq. mi.; pop. 2,701); cap. Stanley. Spanish name *Islas Malvinas.*

Falkner, William: see FAULKNER, WILLIAM.

Fall, Albert Bacon, 1861–1944, U.S. Secretary of the Interior (1921–23). Convicted in 1929 for his part in TEAPOT DOME conspiracy.

Falla, Manuel de (mänwěl' dä fäl'yä), 1876–1946, Spanish composer. Notable among his compositions are *La vida breve,* an opera; *Nights in the Gardens of Spain,* for piano and orchestra; the ballets *El Amor Brujo* and *The Three-Cornered Hat.*

Fallada, Hans (häns' fä'lädä), pseud. of Rudolf Ditzen, 1893–1947, German novelist. Best remembered for novel, *Little Man, What Now?* (1932; Eng. tr., 1933).

fallen arches: see FLAT FOOT.

Fallen Timbers, state historical monument. Commemorates battle won 1794 by Anthony Wayne in NW Ohio at rapids of Maumee R., SW of Toledo. Victory hastened collapse of Indian resistance in area and secured northwest frontier.

Fallières, Armand (ärmä' fälyěr'), 1841–1931, president of France (1906–13). Under him law of separation of Church and state was carried out; Dreyfus Affair was concluded (1906).

falling star: see METEOR.

fall line, boundary between upland region and coastal or tidewater plain. Marks place where rivers drop to plain in falls or rapids. Since falls supply water power for industries, fall-line cities rival ports in economic importance.

Fallopius (fŭlō'pēŭs), 1523–62, Italian anatomist, noted teacher at Padua. His discoveries include **Fallopian tubes** leading from ovaries to uterus.

fallout, atmospheric radioactive material resulting from nuclear explosions; it is distributed throughout all of earth's atmosphere and it eventually falls to earth. It can cause various diseases (e.g., leukemia, bone cancer) and also genetic damage. The fallout concentration in the atmosphere is gradually increasing. In U.S., Natl. Committee on Radiation Protection and Measurements establishes standards for maximum permissible human exposure to fallout and other radiation dangers, but medical and scientific knowledge of radiation effects does not permit definite conclusions. See ATOMIC BOMB; HYDROGEN BOMB; STRONTIUM.

Fall River, industrial city (pop. 99,942), SE Mass., on Mt. Hope Bay at mouth of Taunton R.; settled 1656. Excellent harbor. First cotton mill built 1811; mfg. of textiles later declined.

Falls Church, residential town (pop. 10,192), NE Va., W of Washington, D.C. The Falls Church was built 1767–69 on site of earlier church (1734).

Falmouth (făl′mŭth), municipal borough (pop. 15,427), Cornwall, England; port and fishing town. Has excellent harbor guarded by two castles. Unusually warm climate; subtropical plants thrive.

Falmouth. 1 Town (pop. 5,976), SW Maine, on Casco Bay N of Portland; settled c.1632. Site of early settlement which was nearly destroyed by British 1775; its nucleus set off as Portland 1786. Town includes Falmouth Foreside village (pop. 1,062). **2** Resort town (pop. 13,037), SE Mass., on SW Cape Cod; settled c.1660. Attacked by British in Revolution and War of 1812. Otis Air Force Base is NNE. Includes Woods Hole village, site of marine biological laboratory and Oceanographic Inst. (maintains research ship *Atlantis*), and East Falmouth village (pop. 1,655).

False Decretals (dĭkrē′tŭlz), collection of partly spurious documents treating of canon law, published c.847–852 probably in France. Compiler called himself Isidore Mercator (hence term Pseudo-Isidorian Decretals). By incorporation in GRATIAN the False Decretals received authority in medieval canon-law texts. One of the great forgeries of history, they were first exposed by Nicholas of Cusa and Juan de Torquemada (15th cent.).

false imprisonment, complete restraint upon a person's liberty of movement against his will and without legal justification, either by a private person or by an official improperly issuing a warrant for arrest. Redress is given by civil action for money damages. Release may be had through HABEAS CORPUS.

Falstaff (fôl′stăf), famous jovial companion of Prince Hal (later Henry V) in Shakespeare's *Henry IV.* Also leading character in Shakespeare's *Merry Wives of Windsor.* Verdi used the character in his opera *Falstaff* (1893).

Falster (fäl′stŭr), island (198 sq. mi.; pop. 46,662), S Denmark, in the Baltic Sea; cap. Nykobing.

Falun (fä′lŭn), town (pop. 18,745), central Sweden, co. seat and industrial center of KOPPARBERG co. Oldest Swedish industrial company was organized in 12th cent. to operate its copper mine, now exhausted.

Famagusta (fämägōō′stä), city (est. pop. 38,000), on E Cyprus; chief port of island. Seat of Venetian governors (15th–16th cent.); thought to be main scene of Shakespeare's *Othello.* Ruins include so-called Tower of Othello, 13th-cent. Gothic cathedral, and Venetian governors' palace. A British naval base, it was bombed in Second World War.

family, social group consisting of parents and their children. Other close relatives may be added, forming "extended" or "joint" family, especially important in pastoral or agr. economies. Hebrew and Roman law gave the father almost complete control over the family. In modern times the family unit has been affected by the legal equalization of women (beginning in 19th cent.), removal from the family of economic tasks, and state interest in children's education. The changed relationships of the members of the family to each other and to the community are thought to contain the germ of many psychological and sociological maladjustments.

Family Compact. 1 Name of three agreements (1733, 1743, 1761) between French and Spanish branches of Bourbon family. The last provided for Spanish entry into Seven Years War on French side. **2** Term popularly applied to small, powerful group of men who dominated government of Upper Canada from late 18th cent. to the beginnings of responsible government under the Baldwin-LaFontaine ministry (1848–51). Opposition movement developed into the Reform party. Religious differences embittered the struggle, since the Family Compact (term first appeared c.1828) was composed almost entirely of members of the Church of England. Chateau Clique was name given to similar powerful group in French Lower Canada.

Fanariots: see PHANARIOTS.

Faneuil Hall (făn′l, făn′yŭl), public market and hall given to Boston by merchant Peter Faneuil, 1742. Burned 1761, then rebuilt; enlarged by Bulfinch, 1806. Called "the cradle of liberty" because of Revolutionary meetings held here.

Fanfani, Amintore (ämēntō′rä fänfän′ē), 1908–. Italian statesman, a Christian Democrat. Four times premier, in 1962 he gained support of Socialist party; urged cooperation with parties of left.

Fannin, James Walker (fă′nĭn), 1804?–1836, hero in Texas Revolution, b. Ga. Distinguished himself in first victories of 1835. Captured after evacuating Goliad, shot on Santa Anna's orders.

Fanning, Edmund, 1769–1841, American trader and explorer. Discovered Fanning Isl., Washington Isl., and other islands (1783). Became agent for group of New York city merchants to promote and organize South Sea trading expeditions.

Fanning Island, atoll (c.15 sq. mi.; pop. 369), central Pacific, one of Line Isls., NW of Christmas Isl. Added 1916 to British colony of Gilbert and Ellice Isls. British cable relay station here.

Fantin-Latour, Ignace Henri Jean Théodore (fätēlätōōr′), 1836–1904, French painter and lithographer. Best known for portrait groups of famous contemporaries. Influenced by Courbet.

Faraday, Michael (fă′rŭdā″), 1791–1867, English scientist. He developed the first dynamo, the precursor of modern dynamos and generators. From his discovery of electromagnetic induction stemmed the development of electrical machinery for industry. He formulated laws of electrolysis.

Farallon Islands (fä′rŭlŏn), group of small, rocky islands in the Pacific, W of San Francisco, Calif.

farce, light comic theatrical piece in which the characters and events are exaggerated to produce broad, simple humor, as in slapstick comedy. Plautus and Terence wrote Latin comedies which are farces, but term is derived from medieval French *farces.* Shakespeare, Molière, Gay, and Fielding wrote comedies which are farces or have large farcical elements.

Far East, a term applied to China, Korea, Japan, and the Far Eastern area of the RSFSR. In a more extended sense it also includes the Philippine Islands, Indonesia, Burma, Pakistan, India, Ceylon, Thailand, Malaya, Cambodia, Laos, Vietnam, Tibet, Bhutan, Nepal, Sikkim, and Mongolia.

Far Eastern Republic: see SOVIET FAR EAST.

Far Eastern Territory: see SOVIET FAR EAST.

Farel, Guillaume (gĕyōm′ färĕl′), 1489–1565, French reformer. He did much to secure acceptance of the Reformation in Geneva (1535) and thereafter was a confidant and consultant of Calvin.

Farewell, Cape, southernmost point of Greenland, on Egger Isl.

Fargo, William George, 1818–81, American pioneer expressman. Helped found American Express Co. (1850). By 1852 he and Henry Wells organized Wells, Fargo & Co. to handle express service between New York and San Francisco.

Fargo, city (1965 pop. 49,572), E N.Dak., on Red R., E of Jamestown; settled 1871. Rail center and river port, largest city in state, and major distributing point of livestock, wheat, and farm region. NORTH DAKOTA STATE UNIVERSITY OF AGRICULTURE AND APPLIED SCIENCE and Concordia Conservatory of Music are here.

Faribault (fă′rĭbō), city (pop. 16,926), SE Minn., S of Minneapolis at confluence of Cannon and Straight rivers, in farm area; platted 1854. Alexander Faribault, French fur trader, built post here 1826. Became Episcopal center with work of J. L. Breck and Bishop H. B. Whipple. Turkeys are raised and processed.

Faridun: see FERID ED-DIN ATTAR.

Farley, James A(loysius), 1888–, American political leader, U.S. Postmaster General (1933–36, 1937–40). As Democratic Natl. Committee chairman, he managed successful 1932 and 1936 F. D. Roosevelt presidential campaigns.

Farm Credit Administration (FCA), agency supervising loans to farmers and agricultural cooperatives; part of U.S. Dept. of Agriculture 1939–53. Federal Farm Loan Act of 1916 estab. land banks as centralized source of farm-mortgage credit. In 1933 FCA took over land banks, and additional farm credit measures were taken, though original plan that farm-credit system would be cooperatively owned was not achieved.

Farmer, Fannie Merritt, 1857–1915, American expert on cookery, editor of *The Boston Cooking School Cook Book* (1896). Her cooking school emphasized accuracy of measurement.

Farmer, James, 1920–, American Negro leader in civil rights movement. A founder of the Congress of Racial Equality, he served as its national chairman (1942–44, 1950) and national director (1961–66).

Farmer, Moses Gerrish, 1820–93, American inventor. Installed country's first electric fire-alarm service in Boston (1851); developed incandescent electric lamps (1858–59) twenty years before Edison.

Farmer-Labor party, in U.S. history, political organization formed 1920 by former members of the older Progressive party together with farm and labor representatives, chiefly from Middle West. Advocated socialistic program. Party particularly strong in Minn. Dissolved 1924, reorganized later, but lost strength as New Deal incorporated some of its reforms.

Farmers Branch, city (pop. 13,441), N Texas, just NW of Dallas, in farm area.

farming, in taxation, the collection of taxes through private contractors. Tax farmers pay a lump sum; difference between that sum and sum actually collected is their profit or loss. Practiced since ancient times (e.g., by publicans in Rome), the system was most fully applied in 18th-cent. France, where indirect taxes were collected by the farm general (a body consisting of 40 financiers). Notorious for extortion, some 30 farmers general were executed in French Revolution.

Farmington. 1 Town (pop. 10,813), central Conn., SW of Hartford; settled 1640. Miss Porter's School and Hill-Stead Mus. are here. Includes Unionville borough (pop. 2,246). **2** Town (pop. 23,786), NW N.Mex., on San Juan R., NNE of Gallup; settled 1876. Distribution point for Navajo Indian reservation and trade center of oil, farm, and ranch region. Natural gas and uranium produced. Aztec Ruins and Chaco Canyon Natl. Monuments (see NATIONAL PARKS AND MONUMENTS, table) are nearby.

Farmville, town (pop. 4,293), S central Va., on Appomattox R., ESE of Lynchburg. Tobacco market and processing point in farm and timber area. Hampden-Sydney Col. is nearby.

Farnborough, urban district (pop. 31,437), Hampshire, England. Site of important RAF stations, it includes part of Aldershot military camp. Empress Eugenie lived here (1881–1920) and is buried (with Napoleon III) in crypt of church she built.

Farne Islands, group of islets off Northumberland coast, England. Sheltered St. Cuthbert in 7th cent. Scene of Grace Darling's heroism at wreck of *Forfarshire* in 1838.

Farnese (färnā´zā), Italian noble family, long prominent in Rome, which ruled duchy of PARMA and PIACENZA 1545–1731. Duchy was created out of papal lands by Pope PAUL III (Alessandro Farnese) in favor of his natural son Pierluigi. Pierluigi's son and heir Ottavio married MARGARET OF PARMA. Their son, Alessandro

Farnese, 1545–92, duke of Parma and Piacenza (1586–92), fought under his uncle, John of Austria, at Lepanto (1571) and in the Netherlands. Succeeding John as Spanish governor of the Netherlands (1578), he took Tournai, Maastricht, Breda, Bruges, Ghent, and Antwerp from the rebels, thus securing continued possession of S Low Countries for Spain. In 1509 he led an army to support the Catholic LEAGUE against Henry IV of France. He relieved Paris (1590) and Rouen (1592), but died from a wound. After male line of family died out (1731), ELIZABETH FARNESE in 1748 secured Parma and Piacenza for her son Philip, founder of the line of Bourbon-Parma.

Farnese Bull, sculptured group attributed to Apollonius of Tralles and his brother Tauriscus of 1st or 2d cent. B.C. Shows Dirce being tied to an infuriated bull. A copy in Naples national museum was formerly in Farnese Palace.

Farnese Hercules, marble statue by Glycon, Athenian sculptor of 1st cent. B.C. Once in the Farnese Palace, now in Naples national museum.

Farnesina (färnāzē´nä), Renaissance villa, Rome, Italy. Built 1508–11 by Peruzzi. Frescoes by Raphael and pupils.

Farnsworth, Philo Taylor, 1906–, American inventor. Demonstrated television system (1927); developed Orthicon or dissector tube, an all-electronic (no moving parts) device for scanning the scene to be transmitted.

Farnumsville, Mass.: see GRAFTON.

Faro (fä´rō), town (pop. 19,094), cap. of Faro dist. and Algarve prov., S Portugal; seaport. Exports fish and cork.

Faro, Swed. *Fårö*, island (40 sq. mi.), N Gotland prov., E Sweden, separated from Gotland by Faro Sound. Has lighthouse and anc. ruins.

faro (fä´rō) [for *Pharaoh*, from old French card design], gambling game played with pack of 52 cards. First played in France and England, especially popular in American gambling houses in 19th cent.

Faroe Islands: see FAEROE ISLANDS.

Farouk I (färōōk´), 1920–65, king of Egypt (1937–52), son and successor of Faud I. After long opposition of Wafd party to monarchy, revolt led by Mohammed Naguib and Gamel Abdal NASSER forced Farouk's abdication. Monarchy was abolished with the estab. of republic in July, 1953.

Farquhar, George (fär´kŭr, –kwŭr), 1678–1707, British Restoration dramatist, b. Ireland. Best known of his licentious, somewhat sentimental comedies is *The Beaux' Stratagem* (1707).

Farragut, David Glasgow, 1801–70, American admiral, hero of New Orleans and Mobile Bay in Civil War. Commanding West Gulf Blockading Squadron (1862), he boldly sailed up the Mississippi past Forts St. Philip and Jackson to defeat Confederate flotilla, enabling B. F. Butler to take New Orleans. In 1864 he moved on Mobile. Forcing defenses in Mobile Bay, he defeated Franklin Buchanan, thus closing last Gulf port of Confederate blockade-running. The outstanding naval commander in war, honored by rank of admiral, created for him in 1866.

Farrar, Geraldine (fŭrär´), 1882–1967, American operatic soprano; pupil of Lilli Lehmann. Sang at the Metropolitan Opera, New York, 1906–22. Her most famous roles were in *La Bohème, Madame Butterfly,* and *Carmen.*

Farrell, James T(homas) (fä´rŭl), 1904–, American novelist. Wrote realistically of Chicago's Irish population, as in the *Studs Lonigan* trilogy (1923–35), the "Danny O'Neill" series (e.g., *The Face of Time,* 1953), and *The Silence of History* (1963)

Farrell, city (pop. 13,793), W central Pa., on Shenango R. at Ohio line and adjoining Sharon. Rail center with steel and iron mfg.

Fars (färs) or **Farsistan** (färsĭstän´), region (68,319 sq. mi.; pop. 1,494,649), SW Iran, corresponding to Seventh Prov. Almost identical with ancient Persis, nucleus of Persian Empire. Chief city is Shiraz, chief port Bushire.

farsightedness, vision defect in which far objects, but not near ones, may be easily seen. Caused by shortness of eyeball from front to back, resulting in light focused behind the retina. Corrected by eyeglasses with convex lenses.

Farsistan, Iran: see FARS.

fascism (fă'shĭzŭm). In narrower sense, Fascism was political and economic system in Italy under MUSSOLINI; developed after 1922, lasted until Italy's defeat in Second World War. In a wider sense, the term *fascism* has been applied rather loosely to similar ideologies elsewhere; e.g., to NATIONAL SOCIALISM in Germany, and to Franco's regime in Spain. Fascism in general has been negative reaction against socialism and democratic equalitarianism, its roots reaching back to reaction of ruling classes against French Revolution. It plays upon national pride and prejudice and often exploits ANTI-SEMITISM, and sets itself up as champion of law and order against threat of mob rule. In Italy particularly social unrest was mixed with nationalist dissatisfaction over poor fruits of victory after First World War. Governmental paralysis enabled Mussolini to become premier by a show of force. He posed as strong-armed savior of Italy from anarchy and Communism. With strong organization and party militia, the Black Shirts, he set up a dictatorship. Use of Roman fasces as emblem gave regime name Fascist. Fascism differed from Communism in two respects: it followed Darwinian theory of survival of fittest, making youth and struggle paramount; and its organization was based on representation by classes, making CORPORATIVE STATE. Masses were won by paternalistic methods of works and relief, but real power was in hands of élite.

Fashoda: see KODOK.

Fashoda Incident (fŭshŏ'dŭ), 1898, diplomatic dispute between France and Great Britain caused by rivalry for control of upper Nile region. While British troops under Kitchener were quelling Mahdist revolt in N Sudan, a French–Ethiopian party led by J. B. Marchand entered S Sudan and took town of Fashoda (now Kodok). Upon British insistence the French withdrew from area and in March, 1899, yielded their claims to upper Nile region. Peaceful settlement mainly due to efforts of Delcassé.

fat: see FATS AND OILS.

Fatehpur Sikri: see FATHPUR SIKRI.

Fates, in Greek mythology, three goddesses who controlled lives of men; daughters of Zeus and Themis. Known as Moerae or Moirai; they were Clotho, who spun web of life, Lachesis, who measured its length, and Atropos, who cut it off. Roman Fates were called Parcae (see PARCA) and Germanic, NORNS.

Fathers of the Church, orthodox Christian writers of early times (See PATRISTIC LITERATURE). One of many groupings distinguishes eight Doctors of the Church: (Greek Church) St. Basil the Great, St. Gregory Nazianzen, St. John Chrysostom, St. Athanasius; (Latin Church) St. Ambrose, St. Jerome, St. Augustine, St. Gregory the Great.

fathometer, marine device for measuring depth of water. It radiates sound through ship's bottom, then receives echo from ocean floor; elapsed time indicates depth.

Fathpur Sikri or **Fatehpur Sikri** (both fŭtŭpŏŏr' sĭk'rē), deserted ancient city, Uttar Pradesh, India. Founded 1569 by Akbar, was Mogul cap. until 1584. A masterpiece of Moslem architecture and unique in India as a nearly intact Mogul city.

fatigue, in engineering, change which takes place in materials subjected to repeated stress and which eventually causes them to break or otherwise fail.

fatigue, in physiology, decreased ability or inability of tissue or organ to respond to stimulus because of continual stimulation without adequate rest. Believed to result from accumulation of waste products and using up of nutritive material in cells.

Fatima (fă'tĭmù), 606?–632, daughter of Mohammed by his first wife. Wife of Ali, mother of Husein; reputedly the ancestress of Fatimites.

Fátima (fă'tēmù), hamlet, W Portugal, near Leiria. Nearby shrine of Our Lady of the Rosary became a great Roman Catholic center of pilgrimage after apparitions of Virgin Mary to shepherd children in 1917.

Fatimite (fă'tĭmīt) or **Fatimide** (fă'tĭmĭd), family claiming to hold the CALIPHATE on basis of alleged descent from FATIMA, a daughter of Mohammed the Prophet. In c.904 Obaidallah, leader of Syrian Shiite group, went to NW Africa, where he was hailed as the longawaited Mahdi. In 909 he claimed the caliphate in opposition to the Abbasids. Conquered Cyrenaica and Libya. His successors consolidated his empire and conquered Sicily, W Arabia, Palestine, and Syria. Cairo became Fatimite cap. with conquest of Egypt in 969. The sixth Fatimite caliph, Hakim, proclaimed 1020 that he was a reincarnation of God; his claim is still espoused by DRUSES. Fatimite rule officially came to an end when SALADIN entered Cairo in 1171.

fats and oils, esters of organic acids (of fatty-acid series) with glycerin, a trihydric alcohol. The three acids linked to glycerin may be identical or may differ. Fats are solid; oils, liquid. Derived from both plants and animals. Vegetable oils are obtained by cold pressing of cleaned fruits or seeds; this is followed by warm pressing which yields industrial grades. Vegetable fats are usually made by hydrogenation of oils: hydrogen is brought into contact with heated oil in presence of catalyst. Fats and oils in the diet are an energy source; cod-liver oil contains vitamins A and D. Soap is made commercially by heating fats with sodium (or potassium) hydroxide. Fats and oils of the ester type are not found in PETROLEUM. See also ESTER; OILS.

Fauchard, Pierre (pyĕr' fōshär'), 1678–1761, French dentist, a founder of modern dentistry.

Faulhaber, Michael von (mĭkh'äĕl fŭn foul'häbùr), 1869–1952, German cardinal, archbishop of Munich, an unflinching opponent of the Nazis.

Faulkner or **Falkner, William,** 1897–1962, American novelist, b. Miss. His major novels and stories probe the anguish of the Deep South since the Civil War, showing family decay and social change in his mythical town of Jefferson, Yoknapatawpha Co. He was awarded 1949 Nobel Prize for Literature. His best-known works are *The Sound and the Fury* (1929), *As I Lay Dying* (1930), *Sanctuary* (1931), *Light in August* (1932), *Absalom, Absalom!* (1936), *The Unvanquished* (1938), *The Hamlet* (1940), *Go Down, Moses* (1942), *Intruder in the Dust* (1948), *Requiem for a Nun* (1951), *A Fable* (1954), *The Town* (1957), *The Mansion* (1959), *and The Reivers* (1962). In 1966 his *Essays, Speeches and Public Lectures* were edited by J. B. Merriwether. *The Wishing Tree* (1967) is a story for children.

fault, in geology, a fracture in the earth's surface, with displacement on one side of the fault plane relative to the other. This displacement may be horizontal, vertical, or oblique, or both horizontal and vertical. The immediate cause of faults is stretching and compression of the earth's crust; the remote causes are probably the same as those of folding, since faulting and folding alike are involved in mountain making. Faults are responsible for most earthquakes.

faun (fôn), in Roman religion, creature similar to Greek SATYR, half man and half goat.

Faunus (fô'nùs), in Roman religion, popular god of nature, protector of farmers and herdsmen, identified with Greek PAN. He was attended by many little fauns.

Faure, Élie (ālē' fōr'), 1873–1937, French art historian. Related history of art to progress of human culture.

Faure, Félix (fălĕks' fōr'), 1841–99, president of France (1895–99). His term was marked by the Dreyfus Affair.

Fauré, Gabriel (gäbrēĕl' fōrä'), 1845–1924, French composer. His works include nocturnes and barcarolles for piano, chamber music, operas, a Requiem, and songs.

Faust (foust) or **Faustus** (fô′stŭs), in German legend, a learned doctor who sold his soul to the devil (Mephistopheles) in exchange for youth, knowledge, and magical power. Supposedly based on the life of one Dr. Johann Faust (d. 1541), the subject has been used in literature since 1570. The *Volksbuch* of Johannes Spies (1587), an early version, was the basis of Marlowe's *Dr. Faustus* (1593). GOETHE wrote a masterpiece on Faust (treated also by other authors, including Thomas Mann). Musical treatments of the legend include those by Berlioz, Gounod, Liszt, and Boito.

Fausta (fô′stŭ), d. c.326, wife of Constantine I, daughter of Maximian, mother of Constantine II, Constantius II, and Constans I. Constantine I is supposed to have had her murdered after discovering that she had brought about the murder of his son Crispus through false accusations.

Faustina (fôstī′nŭ), name of two Roman empresses. **Faustina,** the elder, c.104–141, was wife of Antoninus Pius. **Faustina,** the younger, c.125–176, was wife and companion of Marcus Aurelius. Called *Mater Castrorum* [mother of camps].

Faustus: see FAUST.

fauvism (fō′vĭzŭm) [Fr. *fauve* = wild beast], name adopted by group of French painters including Matisse, Derain, Roualt, Vlaminck, Dufy, and Braque after 1905 for an art movement which preceded cubism. Essentially an expressionistic movement, marked by bold distortion and vivid color used for emotive effect.

Favre, Jules (zhül′ fä′vrŭ), 1809–80, French statesman. A republican, he was a leading opponent of the July Monarchy and of Napoleon III. Served in provisional governments of 1848 and 1871.

Fawkes, Guy: see GUNPOWDER PLOT.

Fay, Charles Ernest (fā), 1846–1931, American mountain climber, known as "dean of American mountain climbing." First president (1902–8) American Alpine Club. Mt. Fay in Canadian Rockies named for him.

Fay, Sidney Bradshaw, 1876–, American historian. Asserted that responsibility for First World War rested with all powers involved, but that Austria, Serbia, and Russia were primarily to blame.

Fayetteville (fā′ĕtvĭl). **1** City (1965 pop. 26,279), NW Ark., in Ozarks NNE of Fort Smith; founded 1828. Canning and farm trade center. Univ. of ARKANSAS is here. U.S. veterans' hospital is nearby. Captured by both sides in Civil War; battles fought in area include PEA RIDGE. **2** City (1964 pop. 51,022), S central N.C., at head of navigation on Cape Fear R., SSW of Raleigh; founded 1739. Market center in cotton, tobacco, and timber area. Was state cap. 1789–93; state convention ratified U.S. Constitution 1789. Occupied by Sherman, who destroyed arsenal 1865. U.S. Fort Bragg, Pope Air Force Base, and SAINT ANDREWS PRESBYTERIAN COLLEGE are nearby. **3** Town (pop. 6,804), S central Tenn., SSE of Nashville on Elk R. near Ala. line, in farm area. Nearby is site of Camp Blount, scene of troop-mustering (1813) for Andrew Jackson's campaign against Creek Indians.

Fayum or **Faiyum** (both: fīyōōm′), fertile region, N Egypt, W of the Nile. Produces cereals, fruits, sugar cane, and cotton. Rich in archaeological remains, it has yielded many 8th-cent. papyri in ancient Egyptian and Arabic. Chief city, Fayum (pop. c. 117,800), is trade and rail center; cotton spinning.

Fe, chemical symbol of the element IRON.

Fear, Cape, promontory on Smith Isl., off SE N.C., at mouth of Cape Fear R. Lighthouse. Lightship off Frying-Pan Shoals (extend c.20 mi. to sea).

Feather, river, rising in N Calif. in the Sierra Nevada and flowing c.80 mi. S into Sacramento R. above Sacramento. Basin was rich source of gold. Feather R. project (begun 1957) is key unit of vast plan to move available water from N Calif. to S. Will provide flood control, irrigation, power. Includes OROVILLE DAM.

feathers, skin outgrowths characteristic only of birds. Considered modified scales, they grow in definite areas called feather tracts or pterylae; each feather develops from papilla of cells of both layers of the skin embedded in a pit; blood supply nourishes it until feather is grown, then discontinues. Contour or body feathers consist of shaft bearing barbs with small barbules that have microscopic interlocking projections. Down feathers lack projections. Bristles are modified feathers. See *ill.,* p. 118.

February: see MONTH.

February Revolution, 1848, French revolution which overthrew LOUIS PHILIPPE (abdicated Feb. 24) and set up Second Republic. Caused by increasingly reactionary policy of king and his chief minister, GUIZOT, and by dissatisfaction of workers, whose condition had deteriorated in Industrial Revolution. Provisional government, which included Lamartine and LEDRU-ROLLIN, was predominantly bourgeois and moderate. At first, concessions were made to the radicals: right to work was guaranteed, national workshops (planned by Louis BLANC) were created. Deliberate sabotage and eventual dissolution of workshops led to JUNE DAYS rebellion, which was bloodily suppressed. After completion of republican constitution Louis Napoleon was elected president (Dec., 1848; see NAPOLEON III). February Revolution set off similar outbreaks in most of Europe; all were eventually suppressed.

February Revolution, 1917: see RUSSIAN REVOLUTION.

Fécamp (fēkä′), town (pop. 18,201), Seine-Maritime dept., N France; fishing port on English Channel. Famous for benedictine liqueur invented here by monks. Abbey church is a splendid example of 12th-cent. Norman architecture.

Fechner, Gustav Theodor (fĕkh′nŭr), 1801–87, German philosopher, founder of psychophysics.

Federal Art Project: see WORK PROJECTS ADMINISTRATION.

Federal Aviation Agency, executive agency created 1958 by Congress. Duties include regulation of air commerce and of both civilian and military aircraft, control of air space, development of aids to navigation, and promulgation of safety regulations. Incorporated into U.S. Department of Transportation 1966.

Federal Bureau of Investigation, division of U.S. Dept. of Justice, created 1908, given present name 1935. J. Edgar HOOVER is director. FBI investigates Federal law violations.

Federal Capital Territory: see AUSTRALIAN CAPITAL TERRITORY.

Federal Communications Commission, independent executive agency of U.S. government estab. by Federal Communications Act of 1934. Replaced Federal Radio Commission (estab. 1927). FCC has jurisdiction over all radio and television activities.

Federal Constitutional Convention, in U.S. history, held at Philadelphia, May to Sept., 1787. Under Articles of Confederation the central government was too weak to be effective, incapable of enforcing obligations entered into with foreign nations, impotent to quell internal disorder or maintain economic stability among the states. The wealthy and conservative class and the investors in Western territories favored a stronger central government. All states except R.I. sent delegates to convention. George Washington presided. Convention's only real division lay between smaller states, wishing to retain their power, and larger states, wishing to have power fall where population and wealth lay. Disagreement centered on composition of new Congress. A compromise measure proposed by Oliver Ellsworth finally won approval; this provided for Congress as it is now constituted. James Madison was chief drafter of Constitution; Gouverneur Morris also worked on it. Document went to states for ratification. Despite opposition, a sufficient majority to make Constitution binding had ratified it by the end of June, 1788.

federal government: see FEDERATION.

Federalist, The, series of 85 essays, sometimes called **The Federalist Papers,** written 1787–88. Written by Alexander Hamilton, James Madison, and John Jay to explain and urge adoption of the Federal Constitution, then before the states for decision. Widely published in newspapers, they helped greatly to secure the Constitution's adoption.

Federalist party, in U.S. history. When political division appeared in Pres. Washington's cabinet the party that emerged to champion views of Alexander HAMILTON was Federalist party. It was conservative, favoring a strong centralized government, encouragement of industries, attention to needs of great merchants and landowners, and establishment of a well-ordered society. Pro-British in foreign affairs. Geographically, it was concentrated in New England, with strong element in Middle Atlantic states. After Democratic victory of 1800, Federalist party remained powerful locally, but leadership passed to reactionaries, rather than moderates. Federalist opposition to EMBARGO ACT OF 1807 and to War of 1812 resulted in HARTFORD CONVENTION. Successful issue of war ruined party; by election of 1824 it was virtually dead.

Federal Power Commission, independent executive agency of U.S. government estab. by Federal Water Power Act of 1920. Commission controls activities of privately-operated hydroelectric and natural-gas projects on navigable rivers and public lands. Also supervises various parts of Federal hydroelectric projects.

Federal Reserve System, central banking system of the U.S., established 1913. Each of 12 reserve banks (at Boston, N.Y., Philadelphia, Cleveland, Richmond, Atlanta, Chicago, St. Louis, Minneapolis, Kansas City, Dallas, San Francisco) serves a national region. All national banks belong to this system and must maintain reserves on deposit with their regional reserve banks. The operation of the reserve system is on a non-profit basis. System seeks to maintain sound national monetary and credit conditions; it has markedly improved American banking.

Federal Theatre Project: see WORK PROJECTS ADMINISTRATION.

Federal Trade Commission (FTC), U.S. government commission (set up 1914) serving to check monopolies, prevent fraudulent advertising, investigate doubtful business practices, and preserve competition. Its attempts at legal enforcement of its cease-and-desist orders, in cases where violations are observed, have frequently been frustrated by differing court interpretations of the intent and phrasing of antitrust laws. It now seeks to obtain voluntary adoption of its recommendations wherever possible.

Federal Writers' Project: see WORK PROJECTS ADMINISTRATION.

federation, union of states in which sovereignty is divided between federal government and component state governments. The central power acts upon individuals and upon states. Its powers usually include war, coinage, foreign relations, and commerce. There are federal governments in U.S., Canada, Australia, Switzerland, West Germany. Confederation, as in U.S. 1781–89, represents a looser form of cooperation. Federal government may strengthen local self-government, but may also encourage local interests.

Federation of Malaysia: see MALAYSIA, FEDERATION OF.

Fedor. For Russian rulers thus named, see FEODOR.

feeble-mindedness, state of arrested mental development. In U.S. three degrees are recognized: idiots (I.Q., 0–25) who have mental age up to three years, need constant supervision; imbeciles (I.Q., 26–50), mental age 3–7 years, can learn simple tasks, rarely reading; morons (I.Q., 51–70), mental age 8–12 years, can do manual labor as complex as operation of lathe or sewing machine under supervision. Less than 10 percent show physical defects: cretinism, stunted growth owing to underactive thyroid gland; Mongolism, mongoloid appearance caused by unknown influence on embryo; microcephalia, small skull, receding forehead, resulting from fetal injury; hydrocephalia,

large head, protruding forehead, cause unknown, high infant mortality rate. Disease, glandular disturbance, birth injury, as well as heredity cause mental deficiency. In U.S. only 10 percent of feeble-minded are in institutions.

feedback, in mechanics and electronics, arrangement for returning part of output to input to render a system self-regulatory. For example, a governor on an engine reduces fuel supply when predetermined limit is exceeded. In radio a feedback loop amplifies or decreases output signal (makes circuit oscillatory). Feedback is used widely in AUTOMATION.

Fehling's solution (fā'lǐngs) is used to test for glucose, fructose, and other reducing agents. Discovered by Hermann von Fehling (1812–85) German chemist. Two solutions, cupric sulphate and alkaline Rochelle salt, are combined just before use; when heated with reducing agent red precipitate forms.

Fehmgericht: see VEHMGERICHT.

Feijóo y Montenegro, Benito Geronimo: see FEYJÓO.

Feininger, Lyonel (fī'nǐng-ùr), 1871–1956, American painter. Went to Germany 1887. Associated with the Blaue Reiter; taught at the Bauhaus 1919–32. Returned to U.S. 1937.

Feisal or **Faisal** (both: fī'sùl), kings of Iraq. **Feisal I,** 1885–1933, reigned 1921–33. In 1916 joined T. E. Lawrence in Arab revolt against Turkey. Became king of Syria in 1920 but deposed in same year by the French. Won Iraqi throne with British support. **Feisal II,** 1935–58, succeeded his father, Ghazi I, in 1939. Abdul Ilah was regent until 1953; both were killed during a military coup in July, 1958, and republic was established.

Feisal, Ibn al Saud (ībûn äl säōod), 1905–, king of Saudi Arabia. Was premier and foreign minister (1957–61) and premier again in 1962. Succeeded his brother, King Saud, in 1964 and then abolished premiership, becoming, in effect, absolute ruler.

Feith, Rhijnvis (rīn'vǐs fīt), 1753–1824, Dutch romantic poet, novelist, and dramatist.

Feke, Robert (fēk), c.1705–c.1750, early American portrait painter, b. Oyster Bay, N.Y. Worked in Newport, New York, Philadelphia, and Boston.

feldspar or **felspar,** common mineral of many varieties; composed of any of three silicates (potassium-aluminum silicate, sodium-aluminum silicate, or calcium-aluminum silicate), separately or mixed. Feldspar has clean cleavage planes in two directions. It is colorless when pure but occurs in pinkish, red, white, gray, and other colors. As constituents of granite and other crystalline rocks the feldspars form part of the earth's crust.

Felix V, antipope: see AMADEUS VIII.

Felixstowe (fē'lǐkstō), urban district (pop. 17,254). Suffolk East, England. It is a fishing port, seaplane base, and summer resort (yachting).

Feller, Robert William Andrew (Bob Feller), 1918–, American baseball pitcher. Right-handed ace of Cleveland Indians (1936–56). Shares major league record for most strikeouts in one game (18, against Detroit Tigers, 1938). Pitched 3 no hitters.

Fellini, Federico (fĕl-lē'nē), 1920–, Italian film director. Directed own scripts, which were noted for montage of poetic lyricism and irony; they include *Nights of Cabiria, La Strada, Juliet of the Spirits* (all starring his wife, Giulietta Masina), *La Dolce Vita,* and *8½.*

felony, grave crime, in contrast to a misdemeanor, or petty crime. Felonies in Great Britain and U.S. are usually tried by jury and carry with them as possible consequences imprisonment, loss of citizenship, or (for an alien) deportation.

felspar: see FELDSPAR.

Feltham, London: see HOUNSLOW.

Felton, William Harrell, 1823–1909, American political leader. After Civil War he was leading independent Democrat of Ga., opposing reactionary machine politics. U.S. Representative (1875–81). His second wife, **Rebecca Latimer Felton,** 1835–1930, was first woman to enter U.S. Senate, serving briefly in 1922 by appointment.

Femgericht: see VEHMGERICHT.

feminism, movement for political, social, and educational equality for women and men. Prior to Industrial Revolution women had no personal or property rights. Early leaders in England such as Mary Astell and Mary WOLLSTONECRAFT pleaded in vain. In U.S. active feminist movement dates from 1848 convention at Seneca Falls, N.Y., where Elizabeth Cady STANTON, Lucretia MOTT, and others issued a declaration of independence for women. Sparked by leaders such as Mrs. Stanton and Susan B. ANTHONY, movement spread rapidly. See also WOMAN SUFFRAGE.

fencing, sport of attack and defense with foil, épée, saber by two opponents. These three modern weapons are descendants of old dueling swords. Fencing is included in Olympics. Amateur Fencers League of America (1891) regulates sport in U.S.

Fénelon, François de Salignac de la Mothe (frãswä' dü sälēnyäk' dü lä môt' fãnülõ'), 1651–1715, French theologian and author, archbishop of Cambrai. Wrote *Télémaque* (1699) for young duke of Burgundy, his pupil. Defended QUIETISM.

Feng Yü-hsiang (füng' yü' hsyäng'), 1880–1948, Chinese general, called the Christian General. Held military positions under Ch'ing dynasty. Fought Wu P'ei-fu and Chang Tso-lin. 1920–26, for control of N China and Manchuria. In 1927 he joined Chiang Kai-shek in the NORTHERN EXPEDITION. A Nationalist government figure, he later became leader of dissident faction opposing Chiang Kai-shek.

Fenian movement (fē'nēun), Irish secret revolutionary society (organized c.1858) for independence from England by force. Under James Stephens (1825–1901), the main appeal in Ireland was to the nonagrarian population and was opposed by the Catholic Church. Risings and terrorism led first to suppression by the British but finally to their attention to Irish problems. In U.S. John O'Mahony was the leader of embittered Irish emigrants whose attempts to invade Canada increased Anglo-American tension at end of Civil War—although Fenian raids fostered Canadian confederation. By 1914 Fenian influence was drawn into the new SINN FEIN organization founded by a former Fenian.

Fenichel, Otto, 1897–1946, Austrian psychoanalyst; in U.S. after 1937. Writings include *The Psychoanalytical Theory* (1945).

fennel, Old World herb (*Foeniculum vulgare*) with fine, licorice-scented foliage and seeds used to flavor sauces, bread, liqueurs. Finochio or sweet fennel (*F. dulce*) has bulbous-based stalk eaten like celery.

Fens, the, district W and S of the Wash, England. Includes parts of Bedford, Norfolk, Cambridge, Huntingdon, and Lincoln counties. Extending c.70 mi. from N to S and c.35 mi. from E to W, it is traversed by several streams. Originally a swampland; Romans attempted drainage and built roads. First effective drainage developed by Cornelius Vermuyden (Dutch) in 17th cent. District now has fertile soil and is largely cultivated.

Fenton, Reuben Eaton, 1819–85, U.S. Senator from N.Y. (1869–75). Fought with Sen. Roscoe Conkling over distribution of patronage; Conkling won.

Feodor (fyô'dùr), tsars of Russia. **Feodor I,** 1557–98, son of Ivan the Terrible, reigned 1584–98. Dominated by his brother-in-law and successor, Boris GODUNOV. **Feodor II,** 1589–1605, succeded his father Boris Godunov; was killed the same year at accession of first false DMITRI. **Feodor III,** 1656–82, succeeded his father Alexis 1676. Crippled; energetic reformer. His brother Ivan V and half-brother Peter I jointly succeeded him. Name sometimes appears as Theodore.

Feodosiya (fä"üdô'sēü), city (1965 est. pop. 56,000), Ukraine; port on Black Sea. Exports grain; health resort. Founded 6th cent. B.C. by Greek colonists as Theodosia; known as Caffa or Kaffa in Middle Ages, when Genoese had flourishing colony here, from

which they virtually monopolized Black Sea trade. Fell to khan of Crimea 1475, to Russia 1783. Twice occupied by Germans in Second World War. Ruins of Genoese fortifications.

Ferber, Edna, 1887–, American novelist, playwright, author of novels (e.g., *So Big,* 1924; *Show Boat,* 1926, later a musical), stories, and, with George S. Kauffman, *Stage Door* (1936) and other plays.

fer-de-lance (fâr"dù-lãs'), poisonous snake, c.5–6 ft. long, related to bushmaster and rattlesnake and found in tropical America and some of West Indies. It hunts at night.

Ferdinand, emperors, kings of Hungary and Bohemia. **Ferdinand I,** 1503–64, younger brother of Emperor CHARLES V, was brought up in Spain at court of his grandfather Ferdinand the Catholic. Charles gave him Austria (1521), had him crowned German king (1531), put him in charge of German affairs, and abdicated in his favor (1558). Meanwhile, Ferdinand had inherited Hungary and Bohemia from his brother-in-law, LOUIS II of Hungary (1526). In Hungary, he fought against rival claimants JOHN I and JOHN II, whom Sultan SULEIMAN I was supporting. Eventually, Ferdinand kept NW Hungary and the royal title but had to pay tribute to sultan. In Bohemia, Ferdinand vigorously pushed the Catholic Reform and established Hapsburg absolutism by abolishing most of local liberties (1547). In Germany he dealt with the PEASANTS' WAR and other rebellions and negotiated the Peace of AUGSBURG (1555). His grandson **Ferdinand II,** 1578–1637, succeeded his cousin MATTHIAS as king of Bohemia (1617) and Hungary (1618) and as emperor (1619). In 1619 the Bohemian nobles rebelled against him (because of his strong anti-Protestant stand) and elected FREDERICK THE WINTER KING. Thus the THIRTY YEARS WAR began. Ferdinand defeated Frederick (1620). His generals won major victories, but Ferdinand's Edict of Restitution (1629) provoked renewed opposition. He almost certainly instigated the murder of WALLENSTEIN (1634). The war reached its conclusion under his son, **Ferdinand III,** 1608–57, who succeeded him as king of Hungary (1626) and Bohemia (1627) and as emperor (1637). Under him the war took a disastrous turn, and he reluctantly accepted the Peace of WESTPHALIA (1648).

Ferdinand, 1793–1875, emperor of Austria (1835–48). Was subject to fits of insanity. A council of state, dominated by METTERNICH, governed in his name. Fled Vienna after outbreak of 1848 revolution; abdicated in favor of nephew Francis Joseph.

Ferdinand, 1861–1948, tsar of Bulgaria (1908–18); a prince of Saxe-Coburg-Gotha. Was chosen to succeed Alexander of Battenberg as prince of Bulgaria (1887); took advantage of Young Turk revolution (1908) to declare full independence of Bulgaria and proclaim himself tsar. First triumphed, then lost, in BALKAN WARS (1912–13). In First World War he joined Central Powers (1915). Was forced to abdicate in favor of his son, Boris III. Died in Germany.

Ferdinand II, king of Aragon: see FERDINAND V, Spanish king of Castile.

Ferdinand, kings of Portugal. Ferdinand I, 1345–83, nicknamed "the Handsome" and "the Inconstant"; reigned 1367–83. Leonor Teles, whom he married after securing dubious annulment of earlier marriage, had a baleful influence on his reign. He fought three unsuccessful wars against Henry II and John I of Castile. In 1382 he abandoned his ally, John of Gaunt, and made peace with John I, to whom he gave his daughter and heiress Beatrice in marriage. Portugal would thus have gone to Castile after his death if a revolution had not given the throne to John of Aviz (see JOHN I of Portugal). **Ferdinand II,** 1816–85, oldest son of Ferdinand, duke of Saxe-Coburg-Gotha, was titular king of Portugal (1837–55) through his marriage with MARIA II.

Ferdinand, 1865–1927, king of Rumania (1914–27). Joined Allies in First World War (1916); annexed Bessarabia (1918); intervened in Hungary to break up

Communist government of Bela Kun (1919); acquired Transylvania and SE Hungary in peace treaties. Agr. reforms and universal suffrage were introduced during his reign. His consort was MARIE of Rumania. Succeeded by grandson MICHAEL.

Ferdinand, Spanish kings. **Ferdinand I** (the Great), d. 1065, king of Castile (1035–65) and Leon (1037–65); son of Sancho III of Navarre. Reduced Moorish emirs of Saragossa, Badajoz, Seville, and Toledo to vassalage. Divided his kingdom among three sons. **Ferdinand III,** 1199–1252, king of Castile (1217–52) and Leon (1230–52). Crusaded successfully against Moors. Canonized a saint of Roman Church (1671). **Ferdinand IV,** 1285–1312, king of Castile and Leon (1295–1312). Conquered Gibraltar. **Ferdinand V or Ferdinand the Catholic,** 1452–1516, king of Castile and Leon (1474–1504); king of Aragon (as Ferdinand II, 1479–1516), king of Sicily (1468–1516), king of Naples (1504–16); son of John II of Aragon. Married ISABELLA I of Castile (1469), shared kingship of Castile with her until her death (1504), when he became regent for his daughter JOANNA. The Catholic Kings, as Ferdinand and Isabella are called, completed the reconquest of Spain from the Moors by taking GRANADA (1492); expelled JEWS and Moors from Spain (1492; 1502); instituted Spanish INQUISITION; financed expedition of Christopher COLUMBUS (1492); divided world with Portugal by Treaty of TORDESILLAS (1494). Their reign thus was crucial in the history of the world as well as of Spain. Ferdinand also took a leading part in the ITALIAN WARS and annexed most of NAVARRE (1512). His grandson, Emperor CHARLES V, inherited the Spanish empire from him. **Ferdinand VI,** b. 1712 or 1713, d. 1759, king of Spain (1746–59); son of Philip V and Marie Louise of Savoy. Sent his stepmother Elizabeth Farnese into retirement. Kept Spain neutral in Seven Years War. **Ferdinand VII,** 1784–1833, king of Spain (1808–33). Deposed his father CHARLES IV, but was lured to Bayonne by Napoleon I, who forced him to renounce throne in favor of Charles IV, who in turn was forced to resign his rights to Napoleon (1808). Imprisoned in France until 1814, when he was restored to Spanish throne. He disappointed his liberal supporters by abolishing constitution of 1812. A revolution in 1820 forced him to reinstate it, but in 1823 French military intervention (sanctioned by Holy Alliance) restored him to full authority, and he revoked the constitution once more. He set aside the Salic law to give the succession to his daughter ISABELLA II; the Carlist Wars resulted (see CARLISTS). During his reign Spain lost its colonies on N and S American mainland.

Ferdinand, kings of the Two Sicilies. **Ferdinand I,** 1751–1825. In 1759 he became king of Naples as Ferdinand IV, of Sicily as Ferdinand III, succeeding his father, who had become king of Spain as Charles III. Promoted absolutism under influence of Queen MARIE CAROLINE and Sir John ACTON. Suppressed PARTHENOPEAN REPUBLIC (1799), but after joining Third Coalition against Napoleon I (1805) he lost Naples to French (1806–15). After his restoration he styled himself king of the Two Sicilies as Ferdinand I (1816), ruled despotically. **Ferdinand II,** 1810–59, reigned 1830–59. During revolutionary outbreaks of 1848–49, he ordered bombardments of Messina and Palermo, thus earning nickname "King Bomba." Was notorious among liberals as a reactionary.

Ferdinand the Catholic: see FERDINAND V.

Fergana or **Ferghana** (both: fyĕrgünä'), city (1965 est. pop. 89,000), E Uzbek SSR, in Fergana Valley. Silk and cotton industries. Founded (1876) as Novy Margelan, renamed Skobelev (1907), and Fergana (1924).

Fergana Valley or **Ferghana Valley** (fĕrgä'nû), region c.8,494 sq. mi.), central Asiatic USSR, in Uzbek SSR, Tadzhik SSR, and Kirghiz SSR. Fergana Range (part of Tien Shan system) rises in NE, Pamir in S. Drained by SYR DARYA R., valley is partly desert, partly densely populated irrigated steppe (cotton, fruit). Ko-

kand is chief city. One of world's oldest cultivated regions, valley has long been a major silk-producing area, with such ancient trade centers as MARGELAN and OSH. Arabs introduced Islam 8th cent. Valley passed under rule of shahs of KHOREZM (12th-14th cent.), of Jenghiz Khan, of Tamerlane, and of Uzbek khans of KOKAND (16th–19th cent.). Russian conquest completed 1876.

Fergus Falls, city (pop. 13,733), W central Minn., SE of Fargo, N.Dak.; settled 1857. Dairy products.

Ferguson, James Edward, 1871–1944, governor of Texas (1915–17). Impeached and removed from office. His wife, **Miriam A. Wallace Ferguson,** 1875–1961, known as Ma Ferguson, became governor in 1925; served again 1933–35. Ferguson was actual, though not nominal, governor.

Ferguson, city (pop. 22,149), E Mo., NNW of St. Louis; settled c.1874.

Fergusson, Robert, 1750–74, Scottish poet, author of "Auld Reekie."

Ferid ed-Din Attar (fĕrēd' ĕdĕn' ŭtär'), d. c.1229, Persian poet; a Sufi. Known for *Mantiq ut-Tair* [language of birds], a masterful exposition of SUFISM. Also called Faridun.

Ferishtah: see FIRISHTA.

Fermanagh (fûrmä'nù), inland county (653 sq. mi.; pop. 51,613), N. Ireland, in Ulster; co. town Enniskillen. Erne R. divides county almost in half. Hilly land, largely devoted to grazing. Exports include butter, eggs, and oats. Pottery and linen are made, and some limestone and sandstone quarried.

Fermat, Pierre de (pyĕr' dû fĕrmä'), 1601–65, French mathematician, founder of modern theory of numbers and investigator of probability. Conjectured famous problem, still partially unsolved, called Fermat's last theorem.

fermentation, chemical change caused by enzyme action. Formation of lactic acid in milk and production of vinegar are fermentation. Alcoholic fermentation is most important commercially. Pasteur proved it is caused by yeast; later it was found that yeast enzyme system of which zymase is chief component is responsible. Reaction involves production of ethyl alcohol and carbon dioxide from sugars; is a source of industrial alcohol and of alcoholic beverages.

Fermi, Enrico (ĕnrē'kō fĕr'mē), 1901–54, American physicist, b. Italy. Won 1938 Nobel Prize in Physics for work on radioactive substances. He greatly aided atomic bomb project by research (1934–38) and active participation after 1939 when he came to U.S. He headed the group which in 1942 at Univ. of Chicago achieved the first self-sustaining nuclear chain reaction.

fermium, radioactive chemical element (symbol = Fm; see also ELEMENT, table). Discovered 1954 at Univ. of California, where it was produced in nuclear reactor by bombarding plutonium with neutrons.

fern, flowerless perennial plant of which there are more than 6,000 species, widely distributed, especially in tropics. They range in form from the climbing fern to the TREE FERN. Those of North America usually have green fronds (leaves) rising from a rootstalk. Reproduction is by asexual spores usually found on backs of fronds or on special frond stalks. Valued as ornamental plants for growing in shade and as house plants (e.g., Boston fern). See *ill.*, p. 859.

Fernández or **Hernández, Gregorio** (grägō'rēō fĕrnändäth, ĕrnän'däth), c.1576–1636, Spanish baroque sculptor of religious figures.

Fernández de Córdoba, Francisco (fränthĕ'skō fĕrnän'däth dä kör'dhōbä), d. 1518?, Spanish explorer. Died of wounds suffered in battle with Mayas during first invasion of Yucatan.

Fernández de Córdoba, Francisco, d. 1526?, Spanish conquistador. Sent by Pedrarias (1523) to take Nicaragua from González de Ávila, he tried to seize territory for himself; he was captured and executed.

Fernández de Córdoba, Gonzalo (gōnthä'lō), 1453–1515, Spanish general, called the Great Captain. Took part in conquest of Granada; expelled French from Naples twice (1495, 1503) during Italian Wars. First Spanish viceroy of Naples.

Fernández de Lizardi, José Joaquin (hōsā' hwäkēn' fĕrnän'däs dā lēsär'dē), 1776–1827, Mexican journalist, novelist, and dramatist, author of novel *El Periquillo Sarniento* (1816–30).

Fernández de Moratín, Leandro (lään'drō fĕrnän'däth dā mōrätēn'), 1760–1828, Spanish dramatist, author of comedies after the manner of Molière.

Fernández Navarrete, Juan: see NAVARRETE, JUAN FERNÁNDEZ.

Fernandina Beach (fûrnändē'nù), resort city (pop. 7,276), NE Fla., on Amelia Isl. at the mouth of St. Mary's R. Shrimping and fishing center. Site of Spanish fort in 1680s. Changed hands many times in 18th cent. Declared free port in 1808, it developed rapidly as base of pirates, slave traders, smugglers. Permanently captured by U.S. 1817. Fort Clinch (built 1847–61) captured by Union troops, 1862.

Fernando da Noronha (fĕrnän'dō dù nùrō'nyä), islands in Atlantic, off NE Brazil. Discovered by Portuguese (1503). Long used as a penal colony by Brazil, it is now military base.

Fernando Po: see SPANISH GUINEA.

Fernán González (fĕrnän' gônthä'läth), d. 970, count of Castile. Won virtual independence from Leon. Hero of 13th-cent. popular epic poem.

Ferndale, city (pop. 31,347), SE Mich., a suburb NNW of Detroit.

Fernel, Jean François (zhä fräswä' fĕrnĕl'), 1497–1558, French physician and author of influential works on medicine, mathematics, and astronomy.

Ferney-Voltaire (fĕrnä'-vôltĕr'), town and commune (pop. 1,275), Ain dept., E France, near Geneva. Voltaire bought seigniory 1758; lived there until 1778; founded still-flourishing pottery industry.

Ferrar, Nicholas (fĕ'rûr), 1592–1637, English theologian, founder of religious community at Little Gidding, Huntingdonshire.

Ferrara (fär-rä'rä), city (pop. 156,889), Emilia-Romagna, N central Italy. Agr. center. Its past splendor as princely cap. of the ESTE family is recalled by its palaces and works of art. It declined after passing to Papal States (1598). Notable buildings include Palazzo dei Diamanti, Schifanoia palace, 14th-cent. moated castle, Romanesque cathedral. It was the birthplace of Savonarola.

Ferrara-Florence, Council of, 1438–45, second part of 17th ecumenical council of Roman Church (see BASEL, COUNCIL OF). Chief goal at Ferrara was to end Schism of East and West. Promoted by Byzantine Emperor John VII, who hoped Christian union might save his empire from the Turks. Leading figure was Bessarion, archbishop of Nicaea. In Jan., 1439, the council moved to Florence, and in July the pope issued the bull *Laetentur coeli,* announcing the religious union of E and W churches. After the Eastern delegates went home, the party opposing union gained power. The council moved to the Lateran (1443) and devoted itself to reuniting smaller, non-Orthodox E churches and the Holy See.

Ferrari, Gaudenzio (goudän'tsēō fĕr-rä'rē), c.1480–1546, Italian religious painter, a leading member of Lombard school.

Ferrari, Guiseppe (jōōzĕp'pä), 1812–76, Italian philosopher. His philosophy of revolution encouraged the radical and liberal elements in Italy during the RISORGIMENTO. He advocated a federalized state as opposed to monarchial plan of Cavour.

Ferraris, Galileo (gälēlā'ō fär-rä'rēs), 1847–97, Italian physicist and electrical engineer. He discovered the rotary magnetic field and thereby promoted the development of alternating-current motors.

Ferrel, William (fĕ'rùl), 1817–91, American meteorologist. Worked on government coast and geodetic survey (1867–82); did research on tides, currents, winds, storms. Formulated Ferrel's law: because of earth's rotation moving bodies on earth's surface are deflected

to right in N Hemisphere, to left in S Hemisphere; deflection (zero at equator, greatest near poles) varies with velocity of motion and with latitude.

Ferrer, José (Vicente), 1912–, American actor, director, and producer, b. Puerto Rico. After his debut in 1935 he won acclaim in *Charley's Aunt* (1940) and later as Iago to Paul Robeson's Othello. Films include *Moulin Rouge* and *Cyrano de Bergerac.*

Ferrer, Vincent: see VINCENT FERRER, SAINT.

Ferrero, Guglielmo (gōōlyĕl'mō fä-rä'rō), 1871–1942, Italian man of letters and historian. Noted for works on Roman history, notably *The Greatness and Decline of Rome* (Eng. tr., 5 vols., 1907–9).

ferret. American (black-footed) ferret is largest and very rare North American weasel. It inhabits Great Plains; chief prey is prairie dog. It is c.2 ft. long, yellow-buff marked with brown, with black band across eyes, black-tipped tail, and black feet. Old World ferret is domesticated polecat (c.14 in. long) used to eliminate rats and mice. Both ferret species are of genus *Mustela* (or *Putorius*).

Ferri, Ciro (chē'rō fĕr'rē), 1634–89, Italian painter, pupil and follower of Pietro da Cortona.

Ferris wheel, huge, revolving wheel for carrying passengers in cars suspended on the wheel, built by George W. Ferris, American engineer, for World's Columbian Exposition (1893).

Ferrol, El (ĕl fĕrōl'), officially **El Ferrol del Caudillo** (dĕl koudē'lyō), city (pop. 77,748), La Coruña prov., NW Spain, in Galicia, on the Atlantic. Important naval base. Birthplace of Francisco Franco.

Ferry, Jules (zhül' fĕrē'), 1832–93, French statesman. Minister of education (1879–80, 1882); premier (1880–81, 1883–85). Established modern French educational system on secular, anticlerical basis. Built up French colonial empire in Africa, Indo-China.

ferry, a passage across water by boat, provided for the public upon payment of toll. Ferries include rowboats for transport of persons, flat-bottomed barges (carrying vehicles, persons, or animals) propelled by hand or by utilizing water currents, and power-driven ferryboats. Trains can be carried across the English Channel by ferry.

Fersen, Hans Axel, Count (häns' äk'sùl fĕr'sùn), 1755–1810, Swedish soldier. Served in French army from 1779; became a favorite of Marie Antoinette; helped to plan flight of royal family (1791) and himself drove their coach out of Paris. Made marshal of Sweden 1801. Killed by a mob after Swedish revolution.

Fertile Crescent, historic region of Near East. Area lies between the Nile and the Euphrates and Tigris rivers, and includes parts of present-day Israel, Lebanon, Syria, Jordan and Iraq.

fertility rites, magico-religious rites to insure ample food and birth of children. In primitive cultures natural phenomena, such as cycle of vegetation, were personified and symbolized in mythical marriages of earth-goddess and sun-god and birth and death of their progeny. Myths of death and resurrection of the hero-god (e.g. Adonis) were the basis of elaborate fertility rites, frequently phallic in nature. Later MYSTERIES apparently grew out of fertility rites. The sacred drama was developed from them. Survivals in disguised form abound (e.g., Maypole dance and carnivals).

fertilization, in biology, a process in plant and animal reproduction, involving union of two unlike sexual cells, or gametes (SPERM and OVUM). Process occurs in seed-producing plants after POLLINATION. Cross-fertilization, in botany, refers to fusion of sperm of one flower with ovum of another, in contrast to self-fertilization (fusion of sperm and ovum in one flower). See *ill.,* p. 329.

fertilizer, material containing nitrogen, phosphorus, potash, or other substances essential to plant growth, applied to soil or other growing medium. Fertilizers may be organic (e.g., animal manures, bone meal), or artificial (inorganic or those containing nutrients in proportions required by soil and crop).

fescue (fĕs′kŭ), annual or perennial grass (*Festuca*), used for pasture, forage, or lawns.

Fessenden, William Pitt (fĕ′sŭndŭn), 1806–69, American statesman. U.S. Representative from Maine (1841–43). U.S. Senator (1855–64, 1865–69). U.S. Secretary of the Treasury (1864–65).

Festival of Lights, Jewish festival: see HANUKKAH.

Festus, Sextus Pompeius, fl. at some time between A.D. 100 and 400, Roman lexicographer. His surviving work, *On the Meaning of Words,* an abridgment of the lost glossary of M. Verrius Flaccus, is an important source for Roman antiquities.

Fetterman, William Judd, 1833?–1866, American army officer. **Fetterman massacre** occurred when, despite his unfamiliarity with frontier conditions and methods of Indian fighting, he volunteered to lead supply party of 80 men, ignored orders not to leave trail, and was ambushed by Indians under Red Cloud. Entire party was killed.

fetus or **foetus** (both: fē′tŭs), unborn offspring of a viviparous animal, especially in later stages of development. In earlier prenatal life the offspring is called an embryo. Circulatory system is separate from maternal system; nourishment and oxygen are received through placenta.

Feuchtwanger, Lion (lē′ōn foikht′väng-ûr), 1884–1958, German author; in U.S. after 1940. Historical novels include *The Ugly Duchess* (1923), *Jud Süss* (1925; U.S. ed., *Power*), and the *Josephus* trilogy (1923–42). His last work is a biblical story, *Jephta and His Daughter* (1957).

feudalism, social order in W Europe from end of Charlemagne's empire to rise of absolute monarchies. Basic character was local, agricultural political economy. Usual unit was manor—peasants, VILLEIN or SERF, held land from lord of manor, the seigneur, who gave protection and use of land in return for personal services and dues. This was MANORIAL SYSTEM. In ideal feudal society, ownership of all land was vested in king. Under him was hierarchy of nobles, highest holding from him directly, lesser ones from them, and so on to seigneur, holding single manor. Holding was by fief, acquired by formal ceremony of INVESTITURE. Basically system rested upon unsettled conditions of time and a lord's need for armed warriors. The KNIGHT was the typical warrior. Gradations of nobility were based on both land-holding and military service. The Church had great influence in shaping feudalism; it owned much land, and its hierarchy somewhat paralleled feudal system. The system probably had its roots in disruption of decaying Roman institutions by inroads and settlements of Germans. It spread from France to Spain, to Italy, and later to Germany and E Europe. Frankish form was imposed on England by William the Conqueror (1066). System disappeared gradually with rise of monarchies that broke down local systems, but it persisted in France until French Revolution (1789), in Germany and Japan until 19th cent., and in Russia until 1917.

Feuerbach, Anselm von (än′zĕlm fŭn foi′ûrbäkh), 1829–80, German painter, leading exponent of the German classicist school. Worked in Italy.

Feuerbach, Ludwig, 1804–72, German philosopher. Abandoned Hegelianism for materialism, asserting religion is but a symbolic "dream" and philosophy is the study of man as defined by experience.

Feuillants (fŭyä′), political club of French Revolution. Formed 1791 by right-wing JACOBINS led by Barnave. Advocated constitutional monarchy, peace policy. Suppressed by Jacobins in 1792.

fever blisters: see COLD SORES.

feverfew, strong-scented perennial herb (*Chrysanthemum parthenium*), with small daisylike flowers.

fever therapy, treatment of disease by artificially produced fever. High temperature can destroy organisms causing disease without injuring patient. Original method of injecting microbes to produce fever, introduced 1917 by Wagner-Jauregg, is largely replaced

by use of electric cabinets or blankets, hot baths, radiation.

Feyjóo y Montenegro, Benito Geronimo (bānē′tō härō′nēmō fāēhō′ō ē mōntänā′grō), 1676–1746, Spanish Benedictine scholar and critic. Led in bringing Enlightenment to Spain. Feijóo is variant spelling.

Feynman, Richard P(hillips), 1918–, American theoretical physicist. Shared 1965 Nobel Prize in Physics for fundamental work in quantum electrodynamics, with consequences for the physics of elementary particles.

Fez, city (pop. c.216,000), Morocco. Located at central point on routes to Tangier, Rabat, and Marrakesh. Fez was cap. of several dynasties (8th–19th cent.). Consists of old city (founded 808), new city (founded 1276), and European suburb. Has c.100 mosques and ancient Moslem university. Noted for native industries, it gave its name to the brimless felt cap.

Fezzan (fĕzän′), region (c.220,000 sq. mi.), SW Libya. Desert plateau; population mainly in oases. Dates and grain grown; some grazing. On the trans-Saharan caravan routes. Taken by Turkey 1842; held by Italy 1911–30; occupied by France during Second World War. Murzuk is chief settlement.

Fianna Fail (fē′ŭnŭ fäl′) [Irish,= Fenians of Ireland], Irish political party (organized 1926). Led by Eamon DE VALERA, it opposed Irish Free State. In control of the government after 1932, it advocated complete separation from Great Britain. Defeated (1948) by a coalition, it returned to power in 1951 and 1957.

fiat money, inconvertible money, usually paper, made legal tender by government decree. May lead to INFLATION.

fiber, threadlike strand, usually pliable and capable of being spun into yarn. Of about 40 commercially important kinds, those of animal origin (mainly composed of protein) include silk and wool and the hair of the goat (mohair), llama (alpaca), vicuña, camel, horse, rabbit, beaver, hog, badger, sable; vegetable fibers (containing mostly cellulose) include cotton, kapok, flax, hemp, Manila hemp, istle, ramie, sisal hemp, Spanish moss; and synthetic fibers, both organic (rayon) and inorganic (nylon, Orlon). Chief natural inorganic fiber is asbestos.

Fibiger, Johannes (yōhä′nŭs fē′bēgŭr), 1867–1928, Danish pathologist. Won 1926 Nobel Prize in Physiology and Medicine for his research on cancer.

Fibonacci, Leonardo (lāōnär′dō fēbōnät′chē), late 12th, early 13th cent., Italian mathematician, also called Leonardo da Pisa. Wrote early work on algebra and arithmetic, standard for centuries; organized, extended known geometry and trigonometry.

Fichte, Johann Gottlieb (yō′hän gôt′lēp fĭkh′tŭ), 1762–1814, German philosopher and political leader. His ethical idealism was a development of Kantianism. His *Addresses to the German People* (1808) awoke liberal nationalism.

Fichtelgebirge (fĭkh′tŭlgŭbēr″gŭ), mountain range, Upper Franconia, NE Bavaria, near Czech border. Highest point 3,447 ft. (Schneeberg). Many resorts.

Ficino, Marsilio (märsē′lyō fēchē′nō), 1433–99, Florentine humanist. He translated Plato into Latin, wrote works of Platonic philosophy, and forwarded humanism as head of Cosimo de′ Medici's academy.

Field, Cyrus West, 1819–92, American promoter of first Atlantic cable. Unsuccessful attempts of 1857–58 preceded success of *Great Eastern* in laying a cable in 1866. His brother, **David Dudley Field,** 1805–94, a lawyer, worked in behalf of law reform. His codes of procedure for N.Y. were adopted by several other states; strongly influenced English Judicature Acts of 1873 and 1875. Also worked to establish a code of international law. Another brother, **Stephen Johnson Field,** 1816–99, was U.S. Supreme Court Justice (1863–97). As member of Calif. legislature in 1850s, he estab. legal recognition of mining camp usages and regulations.

Field, Eugene, 1850–95, American poet, journalist. In Chicago *Daily News* (later the *Record*) his column,

"Sharps and Flats," was popular and influential. His first book, *The Little Book of Western Verse* (1889), contains his "Wynken, Blynken and Nod," and other favorite poems.

Field, John, 1782–1837, composer and pianist, b. Dublin, settled in Russia. Chopin's nocturnes were modeled after those of Field.

Field, Marshall, 1834–1906, American merchant. As head of Marshall Field and Co. from 1881, he pioneered in modern retailing practices. Benefactor of Art Institute of Chicago, Univ. of Chicago, Chicago Museum of Natural History (formerly Field Museum of Natural History). His grandson, **Marshall Field III,** 1893–1956, devoted himself to many social projects. Backed New York city liberal newspaper *PM* (1940–48). Started Chicago *Sun* in 1941; merged it with Chicago *Times* in 1948.

Field, Stephen Johnson: see FIELD, CYRUS WEST.

Fielding, Henry, 1707–54, English novelist. Began career by writing comedies, farces, and parodies, with many attacks on Walpole's government. These helped bring about the censorship of the Licensing Act (1737), and Fielding had to give up drama. His first novel *Joseph Andrews* (1742) was undertaken to burlesque Richardson's *Pamela*. Fielding defined his novels as "comic epics in prose"; his use of satire and epic conventions was best realized in his great novel *Tom Jones* (1749). Other novels are *Jonathan Wild* (1743) and *Amelia* (1751).

Field of the Cloth of Gold, meeting ground of Henry VIII of England and Francis I of France, near Calais, France (1520); so called because of splendor of pageantry. Projected Franco-English alliance against Emperor Charles V did not materialize.

Fields, Lew(is Maurice): see WEBER, JO(SEPH).

Fields, W(illiam) C(laude), 1880–1946, American comic actor, whose real name was Claude William Dukenfield. With his rasping voice and bulbous nose he gained renown in films as raffish, swaggering drunk. Often co-starred with Mae WEST.

Fiesole, Mino da: see MINO DA FIESOLE.

Fiesole (fyā′zōlä), town (est. pop. 12,473), Tuscany, high above Florence. Once important Etruscan and Roman town (Faesulae). Has Roman theater, baths; Romanesque cathedral. Nearby Church of San Domenico has Fra Angelico paintings.

Fife or **Fifeshire,** maritime county (505 sq. mi.; pop. 320,541), Scotland, between Firths of Forth and Tay; co. town Cupar. Part of central Scottish Lowlands, well cultivated terrain rises to Lomond Hills. One of most prosperous Scottish counties, it has coal mining, linen mfg., brewing, and shipbuilding. Fife was once a Pictish kingdom. Saint Andrews, famous golfing resort, is seat of oldest Scottish university.

Fifth Avenue, famous street of Manhattan, New York city, from Washington Square to Harlem R. Business and shopping center between 34th and 59th Street; passes Empire State Building, New York Public Library, Rockefeller Center, St. Patrick's Cathedral, Metropolitan Mus. of Art, and Guggenheim Mus. From 59th to 110th streets it borders Central Park. N of park it runs through Harlem.

Fifth Monarchy Men, religious group during Puritan Revolution in England, millenarians expecting imminent second coming of Christ, who would set up fifth monarchy (earlier four being Assyrian, Persian, Greek, and Roman empires). Opposed church and civil government.

Fifth Republic: see FRANCE.

Fifty-four forty or fight, phrase commonly used by extremists in controversy with Great Britain over Oregon country. They held that U.S. rights extended to lat. 54° 40′ N, the recognized S boundary of Russian America. Phrase was used by Democrats as 1844 campaign slogan. Boundary set in 1846 at 49°.

fig, a tree (*Ficus carica*), native to Mediterranean region and long grown for its commercially valuable fruit, now cultivated in California and Gulf states. Some varieties require pollination by fig wasp before setting fruit.

figured bass, in music, a system of notation in which the notes of the bass part have figures written below them to indicate which chords are to be played. Also called thorough bass and *basso continuo*. Used much in harpsichord and organ music of baroque era. Now chiefly used as device for teaching harmony.

Fiji (fē′jē), island group (7,056 sq. mi.; pop. 374,284), S Pacific; most important British colony in the Pacific. Comprises 250 islands, of which 80 are inhabited. Main islands are Viti Levu, with Suva, cap. of colony, and Vanua Levu; gold mines on both islands. Crops include sugar cane, tropical fruits, rice, and cotton. Discovered 1643 by Tasman, annexed 1874 by Great Britain. Missionaries arriving in 1835 helped abolish cannibalism. Fijians, of Melanesian origin, make up only c.40% of population. Indian laborers, imported 1879–1916 under indenture system, are chiefly engaged in sugar industry.

filament, in incandescent lamp, threadlike wire (usually tungsten) wound in center of bulb, which becomes hot when current runs through it. In vacuum tube an uncoiled filament is used.

filament battery: see BATTERY, ELECTRIC.

Filaret, Vasily Drosdov: see PHILARET, VASILY DROSDOV.

filariasis, parasitic tropical disease caused by certain nematode worms; they attack tissues and can cause swelling by plugging lymph vessels.

filbert: see HAZEL.

Filchner, Wilhelm (vĭl′hĕlm fĭlkh′nŭr), 1877–1957, German explorer, geophysicist. Estab. magnetic stations in China and Tibet; led German antarctic expedition (1910–12) which discovered Luitpold Land.

Filene, E(dward) A(lbert) (filēn′, fī–), 1860–1937, American merchant. As president of Boston firm of William Filene's Sons he pioneered in scientific methods of retail distribution.

filibuster, in 17th cent., buccaneer who plundered Spanish colonies in New World. In 19th cent., adventurer who led privately organized armed forays into friendly countries; e.g., from U.S. into Cuba and Mexico. Term now denotes obstructionist tactics in legislative bodies.

Filipino: see PHILIPPINE ISLANDS.

Fillmore, Millard, 1800–1874, 13th President of the United States (July, 1850–March, 1853). U.S. Representative from N.Y. (1833–35, 1837–43); promoted high tariff of 1842. Vice President of U.S. (1849–50); succeeded to presidency on death of Zachary Taylor. Signed Compromise of 1850; tried to enforce Fugitive Slave Act. Upheld nonintervention in foreign disputes and approved treaty opening Japan to Western commerce. Unsuccessfully strove to make Whigs a national party to conciliate sectional struggle. Hoping to unite North and South, he joined KNOW-NOTHING MOVEMENT; its presidential candidate in 1856.

Fillmore, city (pop. 1,602), W central Utah, NW of Richfield; settled 1851 by Mormons. Nominal territorial cap. 1851–56; briefly seat of legislature.

film, photographic: see PHOTOGRAPHY.

Filson, John, c.1747–1788, Kentucky pioneer, b. Pa. Author of *Discovery, Settlement, and Present State of Kentucke* (1784), containing alleged autobiography of Daniel Boone. Boone's subsequent high reputation mainly stems from this work.

filtration: see WATER.

fin, locomotive organ of fish consisting of cartilaginous or bony rays covered by thin tissue. In some (e.g., eel) single fin extends from back around tail along ventral surface. Majority have one, two, or three dorsal fins, a tail fin, an anal fin (called median or unpaired fins). Paired fins are pectoral (behind gills) and pelvic (position varies; sometimes lacking). Some (e.g., salmon, catfish) have adipose fin (fatty tissue without support) behind dorsal fin.

finch, member of largest bird family (Fringillidae). Finches have cone-shaped bills and eat chiefly seeds. Among the finches are SPARROW, GROSBEAK, CANARY,

GOLDFINCH, BULLFINCH, chaffinch, indigo BUNTING, JUNCO, purple finch, hawfinch.

Finchley, London: see BARNET.

finder. The discoverer of lost property is treated differently in various countries. In many states of U.S. he has the right to retain it against all but the owner, unless it is found embedded in the ground or in a private area, in which case the owner of the place where found has prior right. In other states (e.g., N.Y.) he is obligated to deliver it to the police, although he becomes the owner if the article is not claimed within a fixed period. In most countries the finder must deliver found property to the police but is entitled to a reward from the owner.

Findlay (fĭn'lē), city (pop. 30,344), NW Ohio, on Blanchard R., S of Toledo; laid out 1821. Major farm trade and industrial center; seat of Findlay Col.

Fine Gael (fĕn gāl'), Irish political party. More conservative on welfare issues than its rival, Fianna Fail, it succeeded in forming coalition government (1954–56) under John A. Costello.

Fingal: see FINN MAC CUMHAIL.

Fingal's Cave, unusually beautiful cavern, on Staffa Isl., Inner Hebrides, Scotland. Associated with many legends. Mendelssohn composed an overture called *The Hebrides* or *Fingal's Cave.*

Finger Lakes, W central N.Y., group of long, narrow glacial lakes in N-S valleys, in scenic resort and agr. (fruits, esp. grapes for wine) region between Geneseo and Syracuse. From W to E lakes are Conesus; Hemlock; Canadice; Honeoye; Canandaigua (kănŭndā'gwû), c.15 mi. long; Keuka (kū'kû), c.18 mi. long; Seneca, extending c.35 mi. N from Watkins Glen to Geneva, with U.S. army depot on E shore; Cayuga, the longest; Owasco (ōwä'skō), c.11 mi. long; Skaneateles (skĭnēăt'lŭs), c.15 mi. long with Skaneateles village (pop. 2,291) at N end; and Otisco.

fingerprint, an impression of the inside of the end of a finger or thumb, used for identification because the arrangement of lines is thought to be unique with each person. First practical classifications of fingerprints were those of Sir Francis Galton and Juan Vucetitch in 1891.

Fini, Tommaso di Cristoforo: see MASOLINO DA PANICALE.

Finiguerra, Maso or **Tommaso** (mä'zō, tôm-mä'zō fēnēgwĕr'rä), 1426–64, Florentine goldsmith and engraver, who probably introduced copperplate engraving process into Italy.

Finistère (fēnēstâr'), department (2,714 sq. mi.; pop. 749,558), NW France, at the tip of Brittany; cap. Quimper.

Finisterre, Cape, rocky promontory, extreme NW Spain, on Atlantic. Here English navy twice defeated French (1747, 1805).

Fink, Albert, 1827–97, American engineer, b. Germany. Designed a truss bridge known by his name. After Civil War he helped regulate Southern railway freight rates.

Fink, Colin Garfield, 1881–1953, American electrochemist. Invented drawn tungsten filament, insoluble anode for copper electrolysis, and process for smelting and refining tin ores. Produced corrosion resistant alloys; contributed to commercial application of chromium, tin plating. He devised methods for restoring metal objects for the Metropolitan Mus. of Art.

Fink, Mike, 1770?–1823?, American frontier hero, river boatman. A notable shot and fighter, he is said to have ended by shooting one companion and being shot by another.

Finland, Finnish *Suomi,* republic (117,882 sq. mi., with water surface 130,085 sq. mi.; pop. 4,509,000), N Europe; cap. Helsinki. Bounded in W and S by the Gulf of Bothnia and Gulf of Finland (branches of Baltic Sea); in NW by Sweden and Norway; in N and E by USSR. Central and S Finland is covered by thousands of interconnected lakes. N section (a part of LAPLAND)

rises to 3,500–4,000 ft. Third of population is agr., although only c.9% of land is arable. Forests cover c.70% of area; timber and timber products form chief exports. Major part of economic life is carried on by cooperatives. Most Finns are Lutherans. There is a small Swedish-speaking minority. Conquered and Christianized by Sweden (12th cent.), Finland was made a grand duchy (16th cent.), and was ceded by Sweden to Russia in 1809. With its own parliamentary constitution, Finland enjoyed semi-independence as Russian grand duchy, though Russian rule was tightened after 1890. Full independence was proclaimed in 1917. Communists were defeated in civil war by Marshal MANNERHEIM; republic was established 1919. Land reforms made 90% of farmers independent. After outbreak of Second World War, Russia demanded demilitarization of Finnish fortification facing Leningrad (Mannerheim Line) and cession of military bases. Finland refused, and Russian troops invaded Finland (Nov., 1939). Despite heroic and, at first, successful resistance, Russia won the war and by the peace treaty of March, 1940, obtained part of Karelian Isthmus, Vyborg, and other border sections. To recover its territories, Finland joined in the German attack on Russia (1941). Forced to capitulate in Sept., 1944, it kept its promise to expel German troops. N Finland suffered much in resulting German-Finnish warfare. Peace treaty between Finland and principal Allies (except U.S., which had not been at war with Finland) was signed at Paris in 1947. In addition to territories ceded in 1940, Finland ceded Petsamo and leased Porkkala area to USSR. USSR returned Porkkala to Finland 1956. Finland admitted to UN 1955; became associate member of European Free Trade Association 1961. In 1966 Communists were included in coalition cabinet for first time since 1948.

Finlay, Carlos Juan, or **Charles John Finlay,** 1833–1915, Cuban physician of Scotch and French blood. In 1881 he suggested that yellow fever is carried by the mosquito. Reed Commission of 1900 undertook experiments which proved this theory.

Finlay, river of N B.C., Canada, rising in Stikine Mts. and flowing c.250 mi. SE to join Parsnip R. at Finlay Forks and form chief tributary of the Peace.

Finletter, Thomas Knight, 1893–, U.S. Secretary of the Air Force (1950–53).

Finney, Charles Grandison, 1792–1875, American theologian and educator. Broadway Tabernacle, New York city, organized for him in 1834. President of Oberlin Col. 1851–65. His revivalist preaching and writings set tone of "Oberlin theology."

Finnish language, Uralic language spoken by c.3,000,-000 people. See LANGUAGE (table).

Finn mac Cumhail, Fionn mac Cumhail, or **Finn Mac-Cool** (all: fĭn' mŭkōōl'), a central hero in the Irish legend of OSSIAN and the original of Macpherson's Fingal. Said to have led a corps of Fenian fighters in 3d-cent. Ireland.

Finnmark (fĭn'märk), county 18,799 sq. mi.; pop. 71,-726) N Norway, forming northernmost part of Scandinavian peninsula; cap. Vadso. NORTH CAPE is on one of numerous islands off coast. A plateau rising to barren glaciated mountains, Finnmark is largest and least populated county of Norway. Fishing, reindeer raising (mainly by Lapps) are main sources of livelihood.

Finno-Ugric languages, subfamily of Uralic languages. See LANGUAGE (table).

finochio: see FENNEL.

Finsbury, part of ISLINGTON London borough since 1965. Site of Bunhill Fields (Bunyan, Blake, Defoe, and Isaac Watts buried here), John Wesley's chapel and house, Sadler's Wells Theatre (home of English ballet).

Finsen, Niels Ryberg (nēls rü'bĕr fĭn'sùn), 1860–1904, Danish physician. Won 1903 Nobel Prize in Physiology and Medicine for method of treating certain diseases with ultraviolet rays.

Finsteraarhorn (fin"stûrär'hôrn"), peak 14,032 ft. high, Switzerland; highest of the Bernese Alps.

Fiorenzo di Lorenzo (fyōrän'tsō dē lōrän'tsō), b. c.1440, d. after 1521, Italian painter, b. Perugia. May have been master of Perugino.

fir, tall, coniferous evergreen tree (*Abies*), widely distributed. North American kinds include balsam fir, silver fir, and red and white firs.

Firbank, (Arthur Annesley) Ronald, 1886–1926, English writer. His mannered short novels (e.g., *Vainglory*, 1915) appeal to a small but appreciative audience.

Firdausi (fûrdou'sē) (Abul Kasim Mansur), c.940–1020, Persian poet, author of *Shah Namah* (great Persian epic, which set standard for Persian poetry).

fire. For nature of fire, see COMBUSTION and FLAME. There is no record of any human community without use of fire, an exclusively human property. Ideas of indispensability and mysterious force have made fire a sacred object (in Zoroastrianism and other sun-worshiping religions it is a god). In Greece, fire in colony was kindled from that of mother city as tie between them. In Rome, cult of Vesta, goddess of hearth, was strong. Story of Prometheus, the fire bringer, is a great Greek myth. Greek philosophers regarded fire as one of the four elements.

fire apparatus, devices to combat fire or escape from it. Fire-fighting apparatus is designed to remove one or more of the conditions essential to burning: fuel, oxygen, and heat. For ordinary combustible materials (wood, paper, cloth), water is commonly used, serving to cool burning substance and help exclude oxygen. Since water spreads fires of liquid (e.g., gasoline, alcohol, oil, paint) and electrical types, they require chemicals. Soda (sodium bicarbonate) and acid are used in indoor extinguishers; when extinguisher is inverted, soda and acid mix, releasing carbon dioxide which smothers fire. Addition of chemical detergents to water gives it greater penetrating power and this mixture is used for both forest fires and indoor fires (liquid, electrical, or ordinary). Foam-type extinguishers emit carbon dioxide foam from a cylindrical container. Vapor-type extinguishers include those of liquid carbon tetrachloride, which forms heavy vapor shutting off oxygen; and liquid carbon dioxide under pressure, which flakes upon release, vaporizes, and forms layer of gas over fire. Numerous chemicals are used in dry form. Sprinkler systems, from which excessive heat automatically releases water, are employed in many buildings. Motorized equipment includes pumping engines, hook-and-ladder trucks, searchlight apparatus, rescue wagons, smoke ejectors, water towers, chemical apparatus, and salvage weapons. Fireboats are used at sea and on water fronts.

firebrick, heat-resistant brick used in construction of kilns, furnaces, ovens, and fireplaces, especially in metalworking industries. Firebrick should not fuse below 1600° C. and should resist chemical decomposition. Its composition varies according to intended use.

fire clay, a clay high in percentage of silica and alumina, and offering great resistance to heat. Used in making firebrick and metalworking utensils such as crucibles and retorts.

firedamp: see DAMP.

fire-eaters, in U.S. history, term applied by Northerners to Southern proslavery extremists before Civil War. Led by R. B. Rhett and W. L. Yancey, they urged secession as early as 1850.

fire extinguisher: see FIRE APPARATUS.

firefly, luminescent carnivorous beetle (often called lightning bug) of family Lampyridae, more numerous in tropical than in temperate regions. Light organs on abdomen are several layers of small cells acting as reflectors and a lower layer of luminescent or photogenic cells, all permeated by nerves and by air tubes permitting oxidizing of luciferin in presence of enzyme called luciferase. Color of light (yellow, greenish, bluish, or reddish) varies with species, as do intensity and intervals between flashes. Light believed to be related to attraction between sexes. Males, females, larvae, and eggs of some forms emit light.

Fire Island, SE N.Y., c.30 mi. long, off S shore of Long Isl., between Great South Bay and the Atlantic. Has several resorts and a lighthouse (1858). Ferries from mainland. Bridge at E end (1959) and one at W end (1964) connect it with Long Isl. Fire Island Natl. Seashore (839 acres; estab. 1964) includes island's sunken forest.

fire lands: see WESTERN RESERVE.

Firenze, Italy: see FLORENCE.

fireproofing, method of making combustible materials resistant to fire. Usually it is a treatment with solution or coating which merely retards ignition. Wood can be impregnated with ammonium phosphate solution; paints can be made fire-retardant by using certain pigments (antimony oxide and calcium carbonate) or chlorinated resins, chlorinated oils, chlorinated paraffins. Asbestos and cement are mixed to make fireproof board. Fireproof doors are made of steel or of wood pressed between metal covering sheets; sometimes they are closed by automatic devices to check spread of fire. Hollow clay tile, brickwork, gypsum, plaster, and concrete are fire-resistant building construction materials. Steel fails rapidly above 1000° F. and must be protected when used in construction; very heavy slow-burning timber is sometimes used. Textiles are made flameproof by being dipped in or brushed with certain chemical solutions. Asbestos, which is noncombustible and a nonconductor of heat, is used for insulation, roofing, and many other purposes and the fibers can be woven into flexible cloth used in many products.

Firestone, Harvey Samuel, 1868–1938, American manufacturer of rubber products.

fireworks: see PYROTECHNICS.

Firishta or **Ferishtah** (both: fĭrĭshtä'), c.1560–c.1620). Indian Moslem historian. Wrote history of Moslems in India from 10th cent.

Firkins, Oscar W., 1864–1932, American literary critic, professor at the Univ. of Minnesota.

first aid. The immediate treatment of a patient in case of emergency while awaiting the arrival of a physician is often a means of saving life and also may result in a better and more rapid recovery. Prevention of further injury is important. Essential knowledge includes that of the proper bandage for a wound; that of the treatment of bleeding, fracture, sprain, dislocation, fainting, bites and stings, burns and scalds, poisoning (in all such cases call doctor), sunstroke, and heat exhaustion; and that of the method of artificial respiration for drowning and asphyxia. See also Red Cross literature.

Asphyxia. Symptoms: blue color; gasping; unconsciousness. Treatment: remove cause, e.g., a foreign body or gas; use artificial respiration.

Bites. Symptoms: wound. Treatment: apply pressure bandage between heart and wound. Clean wound. Use antivenin for snake bite. Rabies vaccination treatment is absolutely necessary after bite of rabid dog; see physician.

Bleeding. Symptoms: external wound; pallor; weakness if internal. Treatment: local pressure; temporary tourniquet for severe arterial bleeding.

Burns. Symptoms: redness; blistering; charring. Treatment: Leave burn clean and dry. Apply thick dry bandage to ease pain and prevent infection. Caution: treat for shock.

Dislocation. Symptoms: pain; swelling; deformity of the joint. Treatment: rest; cold or hot wet applications. Caution: do not move patient.

Drowning. Treatment: artificial respiration. Mouth-to-mouth method is now recommended for adults and children.

Fainting. Symptoms: pallor; cold; rapid pulse. Treatment: elevate legs. When conscious, give stimulants.

Foreign body in eye. Symptoms: pain; redness; tears. Treatment: wash out with clean water; remove with clean cloth. Caution: do not touch cornea, the eyeball covering over pupil and iris.

Fracture. Symptoms: pain; deformity of bone. Treatment: splint the whole limb. Caution: do not move until splint is in place. Treat for shock.

Heat exhaustion. Symptoms: pale, clammy skin; weakness; subnormal temperature. Treatment: rest; stimulants. Caution: no cold application to skin.

Poisoning. Symptoms: corrosive stain around mouth from irritants; depression from narcotics. Treatment: give emetic or soothing liquids (e.g., eggs, milk, or food oils) according to poison. Call physician.

Shock. Symptoms: pallor; cold; weak breathing; weak pulse. Treatment: head low; warmth; stimulants; treat cause of shock. Caution: do not move; avoid contact if electric shock.

Sprain. Symptoms: pain; swelling. Treatment: rest, cold wet applications.

Sunstroke. Symptoms: headache; unconsciousness; fever; red, dry, hot skin. Treatment: rest; cool applications to skin; cool drinks. Caution: no stimulants.

Wound. Treatment: remove foreign body; apply clean dressing and bandage. Caution: treat for bleeding and shock.

firth or **frith,** name applied to an estuary in Scotland. For Firth of Clyde, see CLYDE.

Firuzabad (fĭrŏō'zŭbäd"), ruined city, S Iran, S of Shiraz. Has palace built by Ardashir I.

Fischart, Johann (yōhän' fĭ'shärt), 1548–c.1590, German satirist. Wrote an imitation of Rabelais, *Geschichtsklitterung* (1575), and religious satires.

Fischer, Emil (ä'mĕl fĭ'shür), 1852–1919, German organic chemist. Won 1902 Nobel Prize in Chemistry for work on structure and synthesis of sugars, purines, and purine base derivatives, e.g., caffeine.

Fischer, Hans (häns), 1881–1945, German organic chemist. Won 1930 Nobel Prize in Chemistry for studies of chlorophyll and synthesis of hemin (salt of a constituent of hemoglobin).

Fischer von Erlach, Johann Bernhard (yō'hän bĕrn'härt fĭ'shür fün ĕr'läkh), 1656–1723, Austrian architect. His baroque buildings, notably the Karlskirche and Schönbrunn palace, give a definite stamp to Vienna.

Fish, Hamilton, 1808–93, American statesman. U.S. Representative from N.Y. (1843–45); U.S. Senator (1851–57). U.S. Secretary of State (1869–77); one of ablest to hold that office. Greatest achievement was bringing about treaty of Washington (see WASHINGTON, TREATY OF); accomplished amid great difficulties. Settled VIRGINIUS affair. Long chairman of board of trustees of Columbia Col. His son, **Hamilton Fish,** 1849–1936, was long a Republican leader in N.Y. His son, **Hamilton Fish,** 1888–, was a U.S. Representative from N.Y. and isolationist leader.

fish, aquatic gill-breathing vertebrate animal with fins, skin with mucous glands and usually scales or plates, and no distinct neck. Lamprey and hagfish (cyclostomes) are primitive, elongated creatures without paired fins, attaching themselves by suctorial mouths to larger fish on whose tissues they feed. Cartilaginous fish (including shark and ray) are more highly developed. Highest in scale are bony fish (those with true bone in skeleton), which includes most fresh-water and marine species. Whale shark (said to reach 50 ft. length) is largest living fish; smallest is goby (c.⅔ in. long) of Philippines. Fish move by contracting body muscles, moving fins, and expelling water through gill slits (giving thrust). They eat plankton, aquatic animals, plants, and refuse. See CLIMBING PERCH; ELECTRIC FISH; FIN; FLYING FISH; GILL. See *ill.,* p. 1136.

Fishbein, Morris, 1889–, American physician, editor. Edited *Hygeia,* the publication of the American Medical Association 1924–50. Writings include *Modern Home Medical Adviser* (rev. ed., 1953).

Fisher, Geoffrey Francis, 1887–, archbishop of Canterbury (1945–61), an educator for 21 years, bishop of Chester (1932–39), of London (1939–45). Active in ecumenical movement.

Fisher, John (Saint John Fisher), 1459–1535, English cardinal, a very learned man. Opposed divorce of Henry VIII and Katharine of Aragon, and was imprisoned (1534). Pope Paul III in defiance made Fisher a cardinal (1535). Bishop Fisher was beheaded. Canonized by Roman Church 1935. Feast: July 9.

fisher, large species of marten (genus *Martes*) of N U.S. and Canada. It is over 3 ft. long and the beautiful fur is brown shading to black. It hunts other mammals and robs traps by night. Also called pekan, black cat, and Pennant's marten.

Fisher, Fort, Confederate outpost on peninsula between the Atlantic and Cape Fear R., defending port of Wilmington, N.C., in Civil War. Taken by Adm. D. D. Porter and Gen. A. T. Terry on Jan. 15, 1865.

fisheries. From earliest times and almost universally fisheries have had industrial and commercial importance. Largest grounds are in N Atlantic off Labrador and Newfoundland, yielding cod, herring, mackerel, haddock, and bluefish. U.S. is now the fifth largest fishing nation in the world, preceded by Japan, China, Peru, and the USSR. Fishing on the high seas is subject to international agreements. Treaties covering rights of Americans to fish on entire Atlantic coast date from Treaty of Paris (1783); final agreement was made 1910 by North Atlantic Coast Fisheries Arbitration at The Hague. In 1882 Great Britain, Germany, France, Denmark, and Belgium signed North Sea Fisheries Convention, and other pacts in 1901 and 1904, ending lawlessness in that area. Pacific has been subject of many controversies, e.g., Japanese right to fish in Siberian waters, and celebrated BERING SEA FUR-SEAL CONTROVERSY. New problems are raised when nations ask for extension of limits of territorial waters.

Fishers Island, SE N.Y., c.8 mi. long, off NE tip of Long Isl. and SE of New London, Conn. Summerresort and residential area. Has U.S. Coast Guard station.

fish hawk: see OSPREY.

Fisk, James, 1834–72, American financial buccaneer. Manipulation of Erie RR stock by him and Jay Gould wrecked the road. Fisk had a part in BLACK FRIDAY scandal.

Fiske, Bradley Allen (fĭsk), 1854–1942, American naval officer and inventor. Aide for naval operations (1913–16). Invented electric range-finder and other instruments for shipboard use.

Fiske, John, 1842–1901, American philosopher and historian; b. Edmund Fisk Green. In early lectures and books he sought to reconcile orthodox belief with science. Later he lectured and wrote many popular books on American history of years 1000–1865.

Fiske, Minnie Maddern, 1865–1932, American actress, on stage from childhood. A great interpreter of intellectual drama, she excelled with Ibsen. Also won fame as Becky Sharp and Tess of the D'Urbervilles, although she was best loved as a comedienne. A talented director, she opened Manhattan Theatre 1901.

Fisk University, at Nashville, Tenn.; coed.; founded 1865 for Negro education, opened 1866, chartered 1867.

fission, in physics: see ATOMIC ENERGY.

fit: see CONVULSION; EPILEPSY.

Fitch, (William) Clyde, 1865–1909, American playwright. Among more than thirty popular plays were his psychological studies (*The Girl with the Green Eyes,* 1902; *The Truth,* 1907; *The City,* 1909) and historical romances (e.g., *Beau Brummel,* 1890).

Fitch, John, 1743–98, American inventor, believed to be first to invent American steamboat. Unable to commercialize his invention and robbed of recognition, he committed suicide.

Fitchburg, industrial city (pop. 43,021), N Mass., on N branch of Nashua R., N of Worcester; settled c.1730.

Fittig, Rudolf, 1835–1910, German organic chemist. Discovered lactones and, with others, constitution of phenanthrene and piperine. With C. A. WURTZ, he devised Wurtz-Fittig reaction, a method of synthesizing aromatic hydrocarbons.

Fitzgerald, Irish noble family. **Maurice Fitzgerald,** d. 1176, Anglo-Norman invader of Ireland, aided Dermot McMurrough and acquired vast Irish landholdings. From his sons descend the two branches of the Fitzgeralds, the earls of Kildare and the earls of Desmond. **Thomas Fitzgerald,** 10th **earl of Kildare,** 1513–37, rebelled against the pro-English Ormondes in 1534 and was hanged with five of his uncles. To avenge his death **Gerald Fitzgerald,** 15th **earl of Desmond,** d. 1583, made allies of his relatives in Kildare. Was defeated in life-long fight against pro-English Butlers of Ormonde. **James Fitzgerald,** 20th **earl of Kildare** and 1st **duke of Leinster,** 1722–73, defeated attempts to divert surplus Irish revenues to the Crown. His son, **Lord Edward Fitzgerald,** 1763–98, Irish patriot, fought (1779–81) in American Revolution in British army from which he was later expelled for republicanism. Joined United Irishmen in French-aided rebellion and was captured (1798) by the English.

FitzGerald, Edward, 1809–83, English poet, translator and adapter of the Persian *Rubáiyát* of Omar Khayyam in four English versions (1859, 1868, 1872, and 1879), all widely acclaimed.

Fitzgerald, F(rancis) Scott (Key), 1896–1940, American writer. He reflected his own jazz-age "lost generation" of the 1920s in his novels—*This Side of Paradise* (1920), *The Beautiful and the Damned* (1922), *The Great Gatsby* (1925), *Tender is the Night* (1934), and *The Last Tycoon* (unfinished, 1941)—and in his short stories.

Fitzgerald, Gerald, earl of Desmond; James and **Thomas, earls of Kildare;** and **Maurice:** see FITZGERALD, family.

Fitzgerald, city (pop. 8,781), S central Ga., near Ocmulgee R., ENE of Albany; founded 1895 as colony for aging Union veterans. Processing and shipping center for agr. (cotton, peanuts, tobacco) area. Jefferson Davis taken prisoner by federal troops near here.

Fitzgibbon, John: see CLARE, JOHN FITZGIBBON, 1ST EARL OF.

Fitzherbert, Maria Anne, 1756–1837, wife (1785–95) of George IV. The marriage, illegal under English law, was ignored when the then prince of Wales married Caroline of Brunswick.

Fitzmaurice, Henry Charles Keith Petty: see LANSDOWNE, HENRY CHARLES KEITH PETTY FITZMAURICE, 5TH MARQUESS OF.

Fitzmaurice, William Petty: see SHELBURNE, WILLIAM PETTY FITZMAURICE, 2D EARL OF.

Fitzpatrick, Thomas, c.1799–1854, American trapper, fur trader, and guide, one of greatest of MOUNTAIN MEN, b. Ireland.

Fitzroy, Robert, 1805–65, British meteorologist and naval officer. Commanded H.M.S. Beagle on Charles Darwin's expedition. Later, with Board of Trade, he instituted storm warnings, daily weather forecasts. Invented a barometer.

Fitzsimmons, Robert, 1863–1918, British boxer. Won heavyweight championship 1897 by defeating James J. Corbett, lost title 1899 to James J. Jeffries.

Fiume, Yugoslavia: see RIJEKA.

Five, The, group of Russian composers: Mili Balakirev (1837–1910), RIMSKY-KORSAKOV (1844–1908), BORODIN (1833–87), MOUSSORGSKY (1839–81), and César Cui (1835–1918). Considered founders of the Russian National school. Drew on Russian history (Moussorgsky, *Boris Godunov*), literature (Balakirev, symphonic poem *Tamara*), folk music and folklore (Borodin, *Polovtzian Dances* in opera *Prince Igor*).

Five Civilized Tribes, inclusive term for portions of Cherokee, Chickasaw, Choctaw, Creek, and Seminole tribes settled in E Okla. Were officially recognized as domestic dependent nations, with constitutional governments modeled on those of American states. This status was lost after Civil War because of support rendered to Confederacy.

Five Forks, crossroads near Dinwiddie Courthouse, SW of Petersburg, Va., scene of last important battle of Civil War, April 1, 1865; a Union victory.

Five Nations: see IROQUOIS CONFEDERACY.

Five-Year Plan, Rus. *Pyatiletka,* program adopted 1928 with primary objective of industrializing USSR. Subsequent plans became standard feature of Soviet economy. Many nations now imitate this procedure.

Fizeau, Armand Hippolyte Louis (ärmä' ēpôlēt' lwē' fēzō'), 1819–96, French physicist; first to measure velocity of light in air. Also studied polarization of light, expansion in crystals, Doppler effect.

flag, piece of light, colored material, plain or bearing a device, of any shape, but often oblong or square, used as ensign, standard, or signal, or for decoration. It is generally attached by one edge. The attached part is the hoist; the piece from it to the free end, the fly; and the quarter next to the staff and to the top, the canton. Symbolic standards were used in earliest times (biblical references to them are many), and early flags usually had a religious significance. The Dannebrog of Denmark, red ensign, swallow-tailed, bearing a white cross, is oldest existing flag. In medieval times many different kinds of flags were used, from the gonfalon, resembling the Roman labarum and vesillum, to pennons, banderoles, and guidons. On Jan. 1, 1776, the first flag of the U.S. was raised by George Washington at Somerville, Mass. On June 14, 1777, Congress delineated general form of present U.S. flag. This was revised in 1818 to provide that 13 alternate red and white stripes, denoting original 13 colonies, remain fixed and a white star be added to the blue union for each state on its admission to the Union. The 49th star was added for Alaska, the 50th, for Hawaii. International code flags enable mariners to communicate in spite of language barrier. Armies and navies the world over use flags for signaling. Special codes govern display of flags, e.g., yellow flag is sign of infectious disease, and inverted national ensign is signal of distress.

Flag Day, anniversary of adoption of American flag in 1777. In 1895, June 14 was set in U.S. as Flag Day. It is not a legal holiday.

flagellants (flǎ'jŭlŭnts, flŭjĕ'lŭnts), groups of Christians who practiced public flagellation as a penance. Appeared as a movement in 12th cent. in N Italy. It was put down by the church, but there were later occasional flare-ups (e.g., at time of Black Death, 1348–49). In 1349 Pope Clement VI prohibited the practice. Most important heretical sects were the Bianchi of Italy and France (1399) and a group led by Karl Schmid or Schmidt in Thuringia (1414). There was a short-lived rebirth of practice within the Church after the Reformation. In Spanish America flagellant orders persisted; in New Mexico the Penitentes still practice secret rites.

flageolet: see WIND INSTRUMENTS.

Flagg, James Montgomery, 1877–1960, American painter and magazine illustrator. Made posters as official artist for N.Y. state during First World War.

Flagler, Henry Morrison, 1830–1913, American capitalist. Early associate of John D. Rockefeller. His backing of Fla. developments was chiefly responsible for state's growth as winter playground.

Flagstad, Kirsten (fläg'stät), 1895–1962, Norwegian soprano. First appeared at the Metropolitan Opera, New York, in 1935 in Wagner's *Die Walküre*. She was considered the greatest Wagnerian soprano of her time.

Flagstaff, city (1965 pop. 24,592), N central Ariz., near San Francisco Peaks NE of Prescott, in lumbering and ranching area; founded 1881. Nearby Sunset Crater, Walnut Canyon, and Wupatki Natl. Monuments (see NATIONAL PARKS AND MONUMENTS, table) attract tourists. Lowell Observatory and Arizona State Col. are here.

Flaherty, Robert J(oseph) (flǎ'ûrtē), 1884–1951, American explorer and film producer. His *Nanook of the North* (1922) was the first full-length documentary film.

Flamand, François: see DUQUESNOY, FRANÇOIS.

flame, result of chemical reaction of a gas heated above kindling temperature with another gas, usually oxygen (see COMBUSTION); heat and light are produced. Luminosity is usually caused by foreign matter; shape of flame is commonly a hollow cone. BUNSEN BURNER increases heat by mixing gas with air before igniting. **Flame test** is used to identify metals. Salt of metal introduced into Bunsen burner flame produces a characteristic color: barium, yellow-green; calcium, reddish-orange; copper, bluish-green; potassium, violet; lithium, crimson; sodium, yellow; strontium, red.

Flaming Gorge Dam, NE Utah, in deep canyon of Green R. near Wyo. line; built 1958–64. Major unit of COLORADO RIVER STORAGE PROJECT, it is 495 ft. high, 1,270 ft. long. Regulates flow of upper river, provides power. Its reservoir extends c.91 mi. upstream.

flamingo (flùmĭng'gō), large, gregarious wading bird. Found in marshes and lagoons of both hemispheres; it has vermilion plumage with black-edged wings. Rare American flamingo nests in Bahamas and other islands. See *ill.*, p. 118.

Flaminian Way, principal Roman road to Cisalpine Gaul, 215 mi. long, built by C. Flaminius (220 B.C.).

Flamininus, Titus Quinctius (tī'tùs kwĭngk'shùs flǎmĭnī'nùs), c.230–175 B.C., Roman general, known as Liberator of Greece. Defeated Philip V of Macedon at Cynoscephalae (197 B.C.). Crushed Sparta (195) and forced king of Bithynia to give up Hannibal.

Flaminius, Caius (kā'ùs flùmĭ'nēùs), d. 217 B.C., Roman statesman, general, constructor of Circus Flaminius and Flaminian Way.

Flamsteed, John (flăm'stēd), 1646–1719, English astronomer, compiler of noted star catalogue. First astronomer royal.

Flanagan, Hallie (Ferguson), 1890–, American dramatic director. Was production assistant to G. P. Baker at Harvard, director of the Federal Theater Project.

Flanders, former county in the Low Countries, extending W of Scheldt R. along North Sea; now divided between Belgium (see EAST FLANDERS; WEST FLANDERS) and France. In Belgian Flanders, Flemish is spoken by most inhabitants (Flemings). A county from 862, Flanders soon came under overlordship of France (though later acquisitions in the E were held in fief from the Holy Roman Empire). Direct line of counts died out 1191 and was succeeded by counts of HAINAUT. The cities, notably GHENT, BRUGES, YPRES, and COURTRAI, enjoyed virtual independence. Their cloth industry (which is still important) was the largest in Europe (13th cent.), but intense industrialization brought such modern problems as economic crises and class war. In the chronic struggle between the French kings and the counts of Flanders the lower classes generally sided with the *Clauwaerts* (supporters of the counts), the upper classes with the *Leliaerts* (supporters of the kings). Routed at Bouvines (1214), the *Clauwaerts* triumphed in the BATTLE OF THE SPURS (1302). However, despite the efforts of Jacob and Philip van ARTEVELDE, the French party won out eventually at Roosebeke (1382). In 1384 PHILIP THE BOLD became count of Flanders. Under his successors (see BURGUNDY) Flemish commerce and art reached their flower, but industry declined and local liberties were curtailed. The death of MARY OF BURGUNDY (1482) brought Flanders under Hapsburg rule (for subsequent history until 1797, see NETHERLANDS, AUSTRIAN AND SPANISH). Annexed by France in 1797 and awarded to the Netherlands in 1815, Flanders became part of Belgium in 1830 and was divided into two provinces. It has long been a traditional battleground. In Second World War, Battle of Flanders began with German invasion of Low Countries (May 10, 1940) and ended with Allied evacuation at Dunkirk (June 4, 1940).

Flanders, French, region and former province, N France, on North Sea, bordering on Belgium; historic cap. Lille. Rich coal fields; industries. Part of county of Flanders until incorporated into France (1668). Flemish is still widely spoken.

Flandrin, Jean Hippolyte (zhä' ēpôlēt' flädrē'), 1809–64, French painter, a follower of Ingres. Best known for religious paintings.

Flatbush: see BROOKLYN, New York city borough.

flatfish, fish of order Heterosomata with compressed body and, in adult form, both eyes on same side of head. Larvae are bilaterally symmetrical at first; asymmetry of adult involves skeletal and digestive changes, migration of one eye. Includes flounder, halibut, sole, plaice, turbot, fluke.

flat foot, condition of human foot in which entire sole rests on ground. This depression of the arches is caused by distorted alignment of bones forming longitudinal arch, which extends from heel to toes on inner side of foot, and transverse arch extending across foot in metatarsal region. Distortion usually results from muscle weakness and consequent straining and stretching of ligaments.

Flathead, river rising in three forks. North Fork rises in SE British Columbia, flows SE; Middle Fork rises in Mont. near Continental Divide, flows NW; South Fork rises NW of Helena, Mont., flows N. Joined near Coram, Mont., united stream flows c.240 mi. S through Flathead L., then W and S to Clark Fork. Has Hungry Horse Dam and Kerr Dam (power, irrigation).

Flathead Indians, tribe of Mosan linguistic family in Bitterroot river valley, W Mont. In 19th cent. After introduction of the horse, adopted Plains area culture. Suffered heavily in wars with Blackfoot.

Flathead Lake, 30 mi. long, NW Mont., in midst of mountains. Many small islands. Flathead R. flows through it.

Flattery, Cape, NW Wash., at entrance to Juan de Fuca Strait; discovered 1778 by Capt. James Cook. Makah Indian Reservation is nearby.

Flaubert, Gustave (güstäv' flôbĕr'), 1821–80, French novelist. An untiring stylist striving for complete objectivity and exactitude of expression, he produced *Madame Bovary* (1857), *Salammbô* (1862), *Éducation sentimentale* (1869), *The Temptation of St. Anthony* (1874), *Three Tales* (1877; including "A Simple Heart" and "St. Julian the Hospitaler"), and *Bouvard et Pécuchet* (1881), an unfinished satire.

Flavian (flǎ'vēùn), epithet given to three Roman emperors, Vespasian, Titus, and Domitian.

flax, annual plant (*Linum usitatissimum*), grown for its fiber and seed. A plant domesticated in man's early history, it was chief source of textile fiber, but is now largely replaced by other fibers. Still grown in USSR, in Belgium for fine LINEN, and in U.S. and Argentina for flaxseed, the source of linseed oil. Other flax species are grown in gardens.

Flaxman, John, 1755–1826, English neoclassical sculptor and draughtsman. Made designs for Wedgwood pottery, outline figure drawings from Greek vases, and memorial sculptures in Westminster Abbey.

flea, wingless, leaping insect. Mouth parts of the adult can pierce skin and suck blood of mammals and birds. Dog flea and cat flea also attack man. Human flea is abundant in warmer parts of Europe and Asia. Flea parasitic on rodents transmits bubonic PLAGUE. Order Siphonaptera. CHIGOE is a flea. See *ill.*, p. 512.

Flecker, James Elroy, 1884–1915, English writer of poetry (e.g., *The Golden Journey to Samarkand,* 1913) and plays (e.g., *Hassan,* 1922).

Fleet Prison, former London jail. Rebuilt several times, finally demolished 1845–46. Mainly notable for incarceration of debtors. "Fleet marriages," clandestine and irregular, performed here by debtor clergymen. System abolished under George II.

Fleet Street, center of journalism in London. Named for Fleet R., now an underground sewer. Most major British newspapers have offices here.

Flémalle, Master of: see CAMPIN, ROBERT.

Fleming, Sir Alexander, 1881–1955, Scottish bacteriologist. He shared 1945 Nobel Prize in Physiology and Medicine for work on penicillin, which he discovered. He also discovered lysozyme.

Fleming, Sir John Ambrose, 1849–1945, English engineer. Led in introducing electric light, telephone, radio into England; invented a thermionic tube.

Flemington, borough (pop. 3,232), W central N.J., W of New Brunswick; settled c.1730. Scene of Hauptmann's trial (1935) for kidnaping and murder of Charles A. Lindbergh, Jr.

Flemish [adjective for Flanders], Germanic language (see LANGUAGE, table), very closely allied to Dutch. The distinction is made on a more or less political basis, the Flemings being the Germanic-speaking people of Belgium (in earlier days, those of Flanders). Dutch and Flemish literature have maintained affinity to the present day, with Flemish authors contributing notably. The great period of Flemish painting (1400–1600) began with the brothers Van Eyck. After the 18th cent. Flemish painting, sculpture, and architecture generally showed decided French influence. In music, the Flemish school flourished between 1450 and 1600. Its members included most of the period's great composers, such as Josquin Desprez.

Flemming, Arthur Sherwood, 1905–. American public administrator. After serving as U.S. Secretary of Health, Education, and Welfare (1958–61), he became president of Univ. of Oregon. In 1966 he was named president of National Council of Churches.

Flensburg (flĕns′bŏŏrk), city (pop. 93,046), Schleswig-Holstein, West Germany; a port on Baltic Sea. Shipbuilding, rum distilleries.

Fletcher, Giles, the elder, 1548–1611, English writer and diplomat. An envoy to Russia in 1588, he published *Of the Russe Common Wealth* (1591), which was suppressed. Wrote sonnet sequence *Licia* (1593). His son **Phineas Fletcher,** 1582–1650, was a poet whose allegory of the human body, *The Purple Island* (1633), shows the influence of Spenser. His brother, **Giles Fletcher,** the younger, b. 1585 or 1586, d. 1623, was also a poet, influenced by Spenser. His *Christ's Victory and Triumph* (1610) is a baroque devotional work.

Fletcher, John, 1579–1625, English dramatist. Collaborated with Francis BEAUMONT on many plays, perhaps with Shakespeare on two, and with Philip MASSINGER and others. His own plays (e.g., *The Island Princess,* 1622; *Rule a Wife and Have a Wife,* 1624) were ingenious, extravagant, facile, and popular.

Fletcher, John Gould, 1886–1950, American poet. *Preludes and Symphonies* (1922) typifies imagist verse. Later work (e.g., *XXIV Elegies,* 1935; *Burning Mountain,* 1946) shows more exacting forms.

Fletcher, Phineas: see FLETCHER, GILES.

Flettner, Peter: see FLÖTNER, PETER.

Fleurus (flürüs′), town (pop. 7,718), Hainaut prov., Belgium. Scene of Protestant victory in Thirty Years War (1622); of French victory in War of the Grand Alliance (1690); and of a decisive French victory in French Revolutionary Wars (1794).

Fleury, André Hercule de (ädrä′ ĕrkül′ dù flûrē′), 1653–1743, French cardinal, chief minister to Louis XV. Virtually ruled France, 1726–43. Restored finances, strove for peace, but was unwillingly drawn into wars of Polish and Austrian successions.

Flexner, Simon, 1863–1946, noted pathologist; director (1920–35) of Rockefeller Inst.

flicker, large North American woodpecker, the only brown woodpecker. Northern or yellow-shafted flicker has many local names (e.g., yellowhammer, high hole). Southern form is similar. In flight the white rump patch is prominent. Red-shafted flicker found in W U.S.

flight, sustained progress through air by aircraft or animal. Science of flight included in study of aerodynamics, the physics of air (and other gases) in motion. Balloons and airships inflated with lighter-than-air gas stay aloft by ARCHIMEDES' PRINCIPLE. Airplanes, autogiros, helicopters, and gliders sustained by forward motion, their airfoils developing lifting air pressure on under surfaces and reduced air resistance on upper surfaces. Engine-driven craft are pulled or pushed by propellers (air screws) or jets. Mechanical flight was first suggested by natural flight of birds. The leading edge of the slightly concave wings of birds is rather sharp and feathers are small and close-fitting, so streamlined surface meets the air. On trailing edge of each wing the interlocking of larger feathers forms surface that simulates action of ailerons of plane. In all of three general types of bird flight—flapping, soaring, gliding—principal flight feathers overlap so that air pressure on underside of wing causes feathers to form airtight surface; on upstroke feathers part enough to allow some air to pass through, thus reducing pressure against which wings must work. Form and size of wings and speed of flight vary; most bird flight ranges from 10 to 60 mi. an hour. See SPACE TRAVEL; *ill.,* p. 368.

Flinck, Govert (gō′vârt flĭngk′), 1615–60, Dutch painter; a student of Rembrandt.

Flinders, Matthew, 1774–1814, English naval captain and hydrographer, noted for his charting and coast surveys of Australia and Tasmania (1795–99, 1801–3). W. M. Flinders Petrie was his grandson.

Flinders Island: see FURNEAUX ISLANDS.

Flinders Petrie, Sir William Matthew: see PETRIE.

Flin Flon, town (pop. in Man. 10,546; in Sask. 558), on Man.-Sask. border, Canada, NW of The Pas. Mining and smelting center (copper, zinc, silver, gold, cadmium).

Flint, county, Wales: see FLINTSHIRE.

Flint, city (pop. 196,940), S Mich., on Flint R., NW of Detroit; settled 1819 as fur-trading post on site of Indian village. Mfg. of automobiles, foundry and dairy products, structural steel. Here are Flint Col. of the Univ. of Michigan, Flint Inst. of Arts, and General Motors Inst.

Flint, municipal borough (pop. 13,690), Flintshire, Wales. Castle was scene of Richard II's submission to Bolingbroke in 1399.

Flint, river rising S of Atlanta, Ga., and winding c.330 mi. SE and SW. Empties into L. Seminole, impounded by Jim Woodruff Dam on Apalachicola R. Navigable to Bainbridge. Valuable power source.

flint, variety of QUARTZ often found in chalk and limestone. Since it was easy to chip, primitive man made tools and weapons of flint. It was long used with steel for fire making and to discharge flintlock guns.

Flintridge, Calif.: see LA CANADA.

Flintshire or **Flint,** county (256 sq. mi.; pop. 149,888), NE Wales; co. town Mold. Uplands devoted to pasturage; farming in fertile valleys. Has rich coal and metal deposits and mfg. of textiles, paper, and chemicals.

Flodden, hill, Northumberland, England; scene of battle of Flodden Field (1513) where English defeated Scots under James IV, who was killed. Battle is described in Scott's *Marmion.*

flogging: see CORPORAL PUNISHMENT.

Flood, in the Bible: see DELUGE.

flood plain, level land along lower course of large river formed by deposition of sediment during floods. Often extensive, extremely fertile.

Flor, Roger de, d. c.1306, German soldier of fortune, b. Italy. Led band of Spanish adventurers (Catalan company) in service of Byzantium; defeated Turks but oppressed native population and was assassinated. His followers set up duchy of Athens (1311).

Flora [from Latin,= flower], Roman goddess of flowers. Her temple was near the Circus Maximus.

Floral Park, residential village (1965 pop. 17,762), SE N.Y., on W Long Isl. near Mineola.

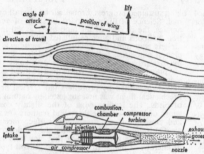

FLIGHT

The flight of any craft heavier than air requires means of lift for raising the machine into the air, means of thrust for moving the machine horizontally, and means of control for navigating the machine. In the conventional airplane these requirements are fulfilled by wings, propellers, and various control surfaces.

THE AIRFOIL.

The airfoil is specially shaped for particular application to flight. One familiar form is the airplane wing. When a wing passes through air, an area of low pressure develops on the top surface and an area of higher pressure is formed on the bottom surface. The net effect is a force called lift, which tends to draw the airfoil upward into the area of lower pressure. The slight upward tilt of the airfoil is its "angle of attack" (shown diagrammatically above the airfoil); this determines maximum lift for a given air speed.

JET PROPULSION

The turbojet engine is essentially an open-ended tube in which the reaction principle is utilized to provide forward thrust. Air is drawn in, compressed, and forced into a combustion chamber. Here fuel is injected, and, after combustion, the resultant hot gasses pass through a turbine and are exhausted at great speed from the nozzle. The reaction of this exhaust on the jet causes forward motion.

TYPE FOR FLIGHT

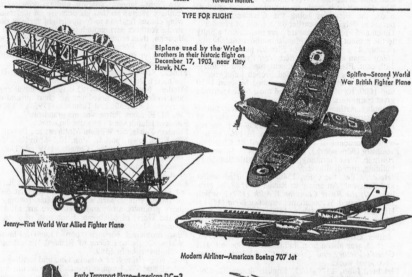

Biplane used by the Wright brothers in their historic flight on December 17, 1903, near Kitty Hawk, N.C.

Spitfire—Second World War British Fighter Plane

Jenny—First World War Allied Fighter Plane

Modern Airliner—American Boeing 707 Jet

Early Transport Plane—American DC-3

Modern American Helicopter

Flying Fortress—Second World War American Bomber

Supersonic Bomber American "Hustler" B-58 A

Florence, Ital. *Firenze,* city (pop. 362,459; with suburbs 454,963), cap. of Tuscany, central Italy, on Arno R. Of Roman origin, it rose to prominence after 1200, when it gained autonomy and grew into a commercial and cultural center of world importance. Despite civil strife between GUELPHS AND GHIBELLINES —later between Black and White Guelphs—Florence waged successful warfare against rival cities, notably PISA, which it absorbed within its growing territories. The silk, wool, and jewelry industries brought enormous wealth. In the 15th cent. the MEDICI family of merchants and bankers took the power, but the republican constitution was ostensibly retained. Twice exiled (1494–1512, 1527–30), the Medici were both times restored through foreign intervention; in the first of these revolutions SAVONAROLA and MACHIAVELLI played leading parts. In 1569 Cosimo I de' Medici was made grand duke of Tuscany (for later history, see TUSCANY). Florence was the cap. of Italy 1865–70. The cradle and chief jewel of the Italian RENAISSANCE, Florence saw an enormous outburst of creativeness in the 14th–16th cent.: Dante, Boccaccio, Fra Angelico, Brunelleschi, Donatello, Da Vinci, Raphael, Michelangelo, and Cellini are among the best-known of the many geniuses who were born or worked in Florence. Probably the world's greatest repository of art, Florence abounds in famous churches, palaces, museums, and monuments. Among these are the Gothic Cathedral of Santa Maria del Fiore; the near-by baptistery, with doors by Ghiberti; the churches of Santa Croce, Santa Maria Novella, and San Lorenzo; the Palazzo della Signoria (city hall) and the near-by Loggia; the UFFIZI, Strozzi, and Pitti palaces; and the BARGELLO. Each of these contains works by the most famous Renaissance artists. Many historic buildings suffered in Second World War; all bridges except the famous Ponte Vecchio were blown up. Severely damaged by floods 1966.

Florence. 1 City (pop. 31,649), NW Ala., on Tennessee R. near MUSCLE SHOALS and Wilson Dam; laid out 1818. In cotton and mineral area; power from Muscle Shoals spurred growth of industry **2** City (pop. 38,164 including Graham), S Calif., a suburb SE of Los Angeles. **3** City (pop. 24,722), NE S.C., near Pee Dee R., ENE of Columbia; founded c.1853. Industrial, rail, and trade center. Supply point and site of prison camp in Civil War. National cemetery is nearby.

Florence, Council of: see FERRARA-FLORENCE, COUNCIL OF.

Flores, Indonesia: see SUNDA ISLANDS.

Florey, Sir Howard Walter, 1898–, Australian pathologist. He shared 1945 Nobel Prize in Physiology and Medicine for work on penicillin.

Florianópolis (flō″rēŭnä′pŭlĭs), city (pop. c.98,500), cap. and chief port of Santa Catarina state, SE Brazil, on Santa Catarina Isl.; founded 1700.

Florida, state (58,560 sq. mi.; pop. 4,951,560), extreme SE U.S.; admitted 1845 as 27th state (slaveholding); cap. TALLAHASSEE. MIAMI, TAMPA, JACKSONVILLE, SAINT PETERSBURG are other large cities. Low peninsula, washed on E by Atlantic, W by Gulf of Mexico. FLORIDA KEYS stretch S, separated from Cuba by Straits of Florida. E coast has sand bars, islands; inland are pine and palmetto flatlands. Rolling panhandle and swamps in NW, EVERGLADES in S; interior abounds in lakes (e.g., OKEECHOBEE). SAINT JOHNS R. chief waterway. Climate mainly subtropical. Tourism is chief industry, but agr. (citrus, truck, sugar cane), mining (phosphates), cattle raising, commercial fishing, lumbering, food processing are important. Mfg. of machinery, electrical and transportation equipment expanding. Region discovered by PONCE DE LEÓN 1513; de NARVÁEZ and DE SOTO followed. Spanish colonization began 1565 when MENÉNDEZ DE AVILÉS drove out French and founded SAINT AUGUSTINE. Colony ceded to England 1763; returned to Spain 1783 (see WEST FLORIDA CONTRO-VERSY). Sold to U.S. in 1819. Became territory (with present boundaries) 1822. Wars with SEMINOLE INDIANS impeded development. Fla. seceded from Union Jan., 1861; readmitted 1868. Growth of railroads, drainage of Everglades, and land booms aided development in 20th cent. After Second World War mfg. (esp. aeronautics industries) expanded rapidly. CAPE KENNEDY became famous space center. Despite control projects, state remains vulnerable to hurricanes.

Florida, village, NE Mo., SW of Hannibal, in farm area. Mark Twain was born here; birthplace now a museum.

Florida, ship: see CONFEDERATE CRUISERS.

Florida, Straits of, SE and S of Fla., between Florida Keys and Cuba. Here the Gulf Stream passes from Gulf of Mexico to the Atlantic.

Florida, University of, at Gainesville; land grant, state supported; coed.; chartered and opened 1853 at Ocala; moved 1906. School of Inter-American Studies is here. Operates Florida State Mus.

Florida Agricultural and Mechanical University, at Tallahassee; land grant, state supported; coed.; founded for Negro education, chartered and opened 1887.

Floridablanca, José Moñino, conde de (hōsä′ mōnyē′nō kōn′dä dä flōrē′dhäbläng′kä), 1728–1808, Spanish statesman. As ambassador to Rome he secured suppression of Society of Jesus (1773). As premier (1776–92) he consolidated absolutism, pushed program of economic reform, promoted peace, but was drawn into war with England in American Revolution.

Florida Keys, chain (c.135 mi. long) of small coral and limestone islands or reefs, forming S tip of Fla. Separated from mainland by Florida Bay and from Cuba by Straits of Florida. Many are habitable. Key West, with city of KEY WEST, and Key Largo (largest, c.30 mi. long) are best known. Noted for commercial fisheries, resorts, and tropical vegetation. Most are joined to mainland by highway opened 1944, replacing railroad destroyed in 1935 hurricane.

Florida Southern College, at Lakeland; coed.; founded and opened 1885.

Florida State University, The, at Tallahassee; coed.; chartered 1851, opened 1857 as Florida State Col. for Women; renamed 1947.

Florina, Greece: see PHLORINA.

Florio, John (flō′rēō), 1553?–1625, English author, best remembered for his translation (1603) of the essays of Montaigne.

Floris, Frans, c.1517–1570, Flemish painter and etcher. Studied in Liège and Rome; influenced by Italian mannerists. Had large school in Antwerp; William of Orange was a patron.

Florissant, city (pop. 38,166), E Mo., suburb N of St. Louis on Missouri R. Settled 1785 by French, it was later called St. Ferdinand by Spanish. Has Church of St. Ferdinand (1821) and Jesuit St. Stanislaus Seminary (1823, rebuilt 1840–49). Father De Smet was ordained here, 1827.

Florit, Eugenio (ĕōōhä′nyō flōrēt′), 1903–, Cuban poet, b. Madrid. His work reflects preoccupation with mystical values.

flotation process, method of separating economic mineral from powdered ore. Air bubbled through a mixture of powdered ore, water, and dissolved chemicals rises to form surface froth. Desired minerals cling to bubbles which are drawn off; waste material settles to bottom.

Flötner or Flettner, Peter (pä′tŭr flŭt′nŭr, flĕt′nŭr), c.1485–1546, German medalist and craftsman, a pioneer of German Renaissance.

Flotow, Friedrich von (flō′tō), 1812–83, German composer of operas, of which *Martha* is best known.

flotsam, jetsam, and ligan (flŏt′sŭm, jĕt′sŭm, lī′gŭn), in maritime law, goods lost at sea, distinguished from wreck, goods which come to shore. Flotsam refers to goods floating on surface, jetsam to those thrown overboard and generally partly submerged. Ligan (or lagan) designates goods which go down with a ship, or sunken goods marked with a buoy. The return of such is obligatory; flotsam and jetsam are returned only upon claim by owner. Rules of salvage apply.

flounder: see FLATFISH.

Flower, George, 1788–1862, pioneer settler of Ill., b. England. With Morris Birkbeck, undertook settlement scheme which led to founding of Albion, Ill.

flower, specialized part of a seed plant containing organs of reproduction. Outermost parts are usually green sepals of CALYX, within which are the often showy, colored petals of the COROLLA. Innermost are the organs of reproduction: the male organs (or stamens) bear powdery pollen, and the female organ (the pistil or pistils) is enlarged at the base to form the ovary containing eggs. Some flowers have both stamens and pistil, others are unisexual. Fruit and seed develop after POLLINATION, which results in fertilization of the egg. See *ill.*, p. 858.

flowering maple: see ABUTILON.

flowering quince, spiny, Asiatic shrub (*Chaenomeles*), with early spring flowers ranging from white to red. Yellowish fruits, similar to related quince, are sometimes used in preserves. Certain species are also called Japanese quince or japonica.

Floyd, John Buchanan, 1807–63, U.S. Secretary of War (1857–60) and Confederate general. In quarrel over Fort Sumter, and because of irregularities in War Dept., he resigned by request and became secessionist. Equally incompetent in war, he was removed from command after his defeat at Fort Donelson.

fluke, fish: see FLATFISH.

fluorescence, emission of light of visible color from substance stimulated by light waves or other means. Light is given off only during stimulation. Rock fluorescence known for many years. Sir George G. Stokes named fluorescence and discovered it can be induced by ultraviolet light. Stokes's law states: wave length of fluorescent light is (with few exceptions) greater than that of the exciting radiation. Visible light, infrared, X rays, radio waves, cathode rays, friction, heat, or pressure can all cause fluorescence. Fluorescent lights are long, sealed, glass tubes with electrode at each end; argon and small amount of mercury are inside tube. Inner surface of tube is coated with fluorescent powders; when electric discharge is maintained through mercury vapor, ultraviolet light so produced causes excitation of coating, producing fluorescent light.

fluorine (floo'ŭrēn), most active nonmetallic element (symbol = F; see also ELEMENT, table); yellowish, poisonous, corrosive gas. It is a member of HALOGEN series. Its compounds are used in metallurgy, in etching, and also in making insecticides. It does not occur free in nature. Fluoridation of drinking water is recommended by dentists to prevent tooth decay; opposition by certain groups has limited this use of fluorides.

fluorite (floo'ŭrīt) or **fluorspar** (floo'ŭrspär), a mineral, calcium fluoride, varied in color. Used as a flux in metallurgy; also in preparation of hydrofluoric acid, opal glass, and enamel.

fluoroscope (floo'rŭskōp), device used in medical diagnosis. Bismuth salts are given to patient, who is placed between screen and X-ray source; since X rays cannot penetrate salts, course of bismuth through alimentary canal is seen.

fluorspar: see FLUORITE.

Flushing (flŭ'shĭng), Dutch *Vlissingen*, municipality (pop. 28,414), Zeeland prov., SW Netherlands; a port on S coast of Walcheren isl. Terminus for boats crossing English Channel; oil refineries, shipyards, machinery and metallurgical plants. One of first Dutch towns to rebel against Spain (1572), Flushing has strategic position at mouth of Scheldt R. British took it from French 1809, from Germans 1944.

Flushing: see QUEENS, New York city borough.

flute: see WIND INSTRUMENTS.

Fly, largest river of New Guinea, rising in NW and flowing c.800 mi. into Gulf of Papua.

fly, name for many winged insects; accurately only for all members of the order Diptera, including housefly, gnat, midge, and mosquito. One pair of wings is functional; vestiges of second pair, knobbed threadlike structures called halteres, aid in balancing. Many flies are disease carriers and crop destroyers; some parasitize harmful insects. See *ill.*, p. 512.

flycatcher, name for various members of Old World songbird family, Muscicapidae. For some members of New World tyrant flycatcher family (Tyrannidae), see KINGBIRD; PEEWEE; PHOEBE.

Flying Dutchman, according to sailors, ominous apparition of a ship seen near Cape of Good Hope. The legend of its blasphemous captain, doomed to sail forever, is used in Wagner's *Der fliegende Holländer*.

flying fish, name for various gliding fish of warm seas, usually traveling in schools. In some only the pectoral or anterior paired fins are enlarged and winglike as in members of genus *Exocoetus*, usually c.1 ft. long, seen in N Atlantic. Others (Catalina flying fish, *Cypselurus*, c.18 in. long) have enlarged pelvic or hind paired fins. After swimming rapidly in water, then "taxiing" along surface propelled by tail movements, they rise into air, sometimes to 25 ft.

flying saucer: see UNIDENTIFIED FLYING OBJECTS.

flying squirrel, name chiefly for certain nocturnal tree squirrels of Asia, North America, and Europe. Using furry skin fold around body which spreads parachutelike, they glide, rather than fly, from heights. Tail is used as rudder. North American tree squirrel (*Glaucomys*) is 9–14 in. long.

flywheel, heavy, metal wheel attached to drive shaft of an engine or other machine; its weight is concentrated at the circumference. It has a large rotational inertia; thus small irregularities in power supply do not change speed of rotation. Equalizes velocity of engine. See *ill.*, p. 333.

Fm, chemical symbol of element FERMIUM.

Foch, Ferdinand (fĕrdēnä' fôsh'), 1851–1929, marshal of France. In First World War, stopped Germans at the Marne (1914); became chief of French general staff (1917); headed Allied supreme command 1918.

focus, in optics, point of convergence of rays after reflection by mirror or refraction by LENS is real focus. Virtual focus is imaginary point from which rays seem to have diverged after reflection by convex mirror or refraction by diverging lens.

foetus: see FETUS.

fog, cloudlike aggregation of water droplets immediately above land or water. If light, usually called mist. Forms when moisture content of air increases above saturation point (e.g., when cold air is in contact with warm body of water or warm rain) or when air cools below dew point, causing radiation fog (earth at night after losing heat by radiation cools adjacent air), advection fog (warm air flows on cold surface), and upslope fog (ascending air expands, cools).

Fogazzaro, Antonio (äntō'nyō fōgät-tsä'rō), 1842–1911, Italian poet and novelist, known for his *Piccolo mondo antico* (1896), a study of an agnostic wife's relations with her devout husband.

Foggia (fôd'jä), city (pop. 122,271) Apulia, S Italy. Important communications center and wheat market. By anc. custom grain is stored in huge holes dug in the squares of the city.

Foix (fwä), town (pop. 6,466), cap. of Ariège dept., S France, on Ariège R. Counts of Foix rose to great power after 11th cent., acquired BÉARN 13th cent., inherited NAVARRE 1479. Their titles and lands passed by marriage to house of ALBRET 1494. Foix was incorporated into French royal domain 1607.

Fokine, Michel (mēshĕl' fōkēn', Rus. fō'kyĭn), 1880–1942, American choreographer and ballet dancer, b. Russia; a founder of modern ballet. Worked with Sergei DIAGHILEV. He created c.70 ballets including *The Dying Swan* (for Pavlova), *Les Sylphides*, *Petrouchka*, and *Scheherazade*.

Fokker, Anton Herman Gerard (än'tŏn hĕr'män gā'-rärt fŏ'kŭr), 1890–1939, American aircraft manufacturer, b. Java. His factories in Germany built famed First World War triplanes and biplanes. Came to U.S. in 1922 and was later naturalized.

fold, in geology, a bend in stratified rocks, which normally are horizontal (see STRATIFICATION). Arches are called anticlines; troughs, synclines. Folds are often formed far below the surface and are exposed by erosion. The top of an anticline may be eroded till only the worn-down stumps remain. The cause of folding is related to compression of the earth's crust involved in mountain building.

Folengo, Teofilo (tāō'fēlō fōlĕng'gō), 1496–1554, Italian burlesque poet, a Benedictine monk. Wrote *Baldus,* a burlesque of chivalric romance.

Folger, Henry Clay, 1857–1930, American capitalist and collector of Shakespeariana. With help of his wife, Emily Jordan Folger, acquired one of the largest collections. Endowed **Folger Shakespeare Library,** Washington, D.C., dedicated 1932, administered by trustees of Amherst Col.

folic acid: see VITAMINS.

Folkestone (fōk'stŭn), municipal borough (pop. 44,-129), Kent, England, on the Channel; summer resort and seaport.

Folketing (fōl'kŭting), national parliament of Denmark; elected by direct universal suffrage.

folklore, in its widest extent, body of oral traditions, art, and superstitions of any society. It includes folk dances, folk songs, folk tales, and folk medicine. Its study was originally domain of the antiquarian, but rise of European romanticism and of nationalism made this a serious pursuit. Folk tales have been collected, and folk heroes (e.g., Robin Hood in England, the Cid in Spain, and Paul Bunyan in U.S.) have received much attention. Today anthropologists regard folk tales as imaginative expression by a social group of its desires, attitudes, and cultural values. Almost every country now has a folklore society.

folk school, form of adult education originated in Denmark by Bishop Nikolai Grundtvig in mid-19th cent. Idea was to stimulate intellectual life of young adults of rural Denmark, foster patriotism and religion, and provide agricultural and vocational training. First school estab. 1844.

folkways, term coined by William Graham Sumner (c.1907) to define more clearly the patterning of behavior usually denoted as custom. Included traditions, laws, manners, usages, mores, and the like, which make up the culture of a group.

Follen, Charles (Karl Theodor Christian Follen) (fŏ'lŭn), 1796–1840, American educator, b. Germany. Appointed to Harvard faculty in 1825, he taught first course in German offered in America. Later became identified with reform movements. His wife, **Eliza Lee (Cabot) Follen,** 1787–1860, influential as a writer in Unitarian movement, led in antislavery and feminist causes.

Folsom, city (pop. 3,925), central Calif., on American R., ENE of Sacramento, in farm area; founded 1855. Was on road to gold fields. Terminal of first steam railroad in Calif. Folsom Dam, unit of Central Valley project, is nearby.

Folsom culture, early North American culture known through artifacts first found near Folsom, N. Mex. The findings suggest the presence of man in North America c.10,000 or more years ago.

Fonda, Henry, 1905–, American actor. Successful on stage (e.g., *Mr. Roberts*) after 1929 and in films (e.g., *Grapes of Wrath, Young Mr. Lincoln,* and *Twelve Angry Men*) after 1935.

Fond du Lac (fŏn' dŭ lăk"), industrial city (1966 pop. 34,180), E central Wis., at S end of L. Winnebago, NNW of Milwaukee, in resort region; settled c.1835. Was French fur-trading post in late 18th cent. and lumbering town in 19th cent.

Fonseca, Gulf of (fōnsā'kä), inlet of Pacific, c.50 mi. long and 30 mi. wide, Central America. Harbor shared by Nicaragua, Honduras, and Salvador. Rights for Nicaragua Canal given to U.S. by Nicaragua disputed by other nations.

Fontaine, Pierre François Léonard (fōtĕn'), 1762–1853, French architect, associate of Charles PERCIER, with whom he fostered Empire style in France.

Fontainebleau (fōtĕnblō'), town (pop. 19,915), Seine-et-Marne dept., N France, SE of Paris. The vast Forest of Fontainebleau was a favorite hunting ground of French kings. In the magnificent Renaissance palace, built by Francis I, Pope Pius VII was imprisoned (1812–14) and Napoleon I abdicated (1814).

Fontainebleau, school of, group of 16th-cent. artists who decorated the royal palace at Fontainebleau in a style akin to Italian MANNERISM. The major figures of the group were Rosso and Primaticcio, Italian painters invited to France by Francis I.

Fontaine-de-Vaucluse: see VAUCLUSE, village.

Fontana, Domenico (dōmā'nēkō fōntä'nä), 1543–1607, Italian architect, who played leading part in rebuilding of Rome. Designed Lateran palace and parts of the Vatican; helped finish dome of St. Peter's.

Fontana, Prospero (prō'spärō), 1512–97, Italian painter. Worked mainly in Bologna. His daughter **Lavinia Fontana,** 1552–1614, Italian mannerist painter in Bologna and Rome.

Fontana, city (pop. 14,659), S Calif., W of San Bernardino; settled 1905.

Fontane, Theodor (tä'ōdōr fōntä'nù), 1819–98, German author. He is best known for his ballads and for the novels *L'Adultera* (1882), *Irrungen, Wirrungen* (1888; Eng. tr., *Trials and Tribulations*), and *Effi Briest* (1895; Eng. tr., 1913–15).

Fontanne, Lynn: see LUNT, ALFRED.

Fontenelle, Bernard le Bovier de (bĕrnär' lù bôvyä' dù fōtùnĕl'), 1657–1757, French author. His *Entretiens sur la pluralité des mondes* (1686) is a model of scientific popularization.

Fontenoy (fōn'tùnoi, Fr. fōtùnwä'), village, Hainaut prov., Belgium, SE of Tournai. Here in 1745 French under Maurice de Saxe won celebrated victory over British and allies under duke of Cumberland in War of Austrian Succession.

Fontenoy or **Fontenoy-en-Puisaye** (fō"tùnwä'-ä-pwēzä'), village, N central France. near Auxerre. Reputed site of a battle in which Charles II of France and Louis the German checked their brother, Emperor LOTHAIR I (841). Battle led to Oath of STRASBOURG and Treaty of VERDUN. Also known as Fontenay, Fontanet, or Fontenailles.

Fonteyn, Dame Margot, 1919–, English ballerina; real name Margaret Hookham. In Sadler's Wells Ballet (after 1934) and Vic-Wells Ballet she was outstanding in *The Sleeping Princess, Giselle, Cinderella, Sylvia,* and *Firebird.*

Foochow (fōō'jō'), city (pop. c.600,000), cap. of Fukien prov., China, on Min R. Major commercial and industrial center. City dates from T'ang dynasty (A.D. 618–906). Became treaty port after Opium War (1839–42). Was largest tea-exporting center in mid-19th cent.

food adulteration, the intentional debasement of quality of foods offered for sale, has been dealt with from consumer's standpoint only since mid-19th cent., when new knowledge made close analysis possible. First British food law passed in purchaser's interest came in 1860; in U.S., Pure Food and Drugs Act of 1906, often amended and later superseded, came only after stormy campaign. Federal and local regulations now govern content, handling, labeling, and advertising of food, drugs, and cosmetics, and certain aspects of importation and interstate traffic.

Food and Agriculture Organization (FAO), agency of UN. Estab. in Oct., 1945; under UN in Dec., 1946. FAO contributes to expanding world economy by bettering rural conditions, improving production and distribution, and raising level of nutrition.

food poisoning, any of a number of illnesses marked by gastrointestinal disturbances and caused by eating

SMALL CAPITALS = cross references. Pronunciation key on inside end pages. Abbreviations: p. 2.

food contaminated by poisonous substances. The term "ptomaine poisoning" is now generally replaced because ptomaines (produced by action of decay bacteria on proteins) are not known to cause illness. Substances causing food poisoning include inorganic chemicals; organic substances derived from animals and plants (e.g., certain mushrooms); and bacterial toxins, especially toxins produced by species of *Staphylococcus*, *Salmonella*, and *Clostridium* (see BOTULISM).

food preservation has been practiced since remotest times; early products of experiment were cheese, butter, wine, bacon, parched grain. Advances came with scientific investigation (notably by Pasteur) of causes of putrefaction. Basic preserving processes include dehydration, freeze-drying, atomic radiation, heating (as in CANNING and PASTEURIZATION), refrigeration (both freezing and chilling), exclusion of air (hermetic sealing and coating with paraffin), use of such agents as salt, vinegar, sugar, smoke, alcohol, and saltpeter. These methods are also used in combination. Use of chemicals is generally limited by legislation.

foot, organ in most higher vertebrates, used chiefly for support and locomotion. In man seven bones form heel; five parallel metatarsals form long arch and their lower ends form transverse arch. Each toe has three phalanges except great toe, which has two. See also FLAT FOOT. See *ill.*, p. 656.

foot and mouth disease or **hoof and mouth disease,** communicable virus disease of cattle and other cloven-footed animals. It causes great losses to cattle industry and is more prevalent in Europe and South America than in U.S. It is characterized by eruption of blisters on mucous membranes, especially of mouth, feet, and udder. Control is by slaughter and deep burial of infected animals, disinfection of area occupied, and strict quarantine.

football, in U.S., game played by two opposing teams of 11 men on level field 100 by 53½ yd. Game originally developed from Greek *harpaston*. American football similar to rugby, dating from 1823 in England. Rutgers and Princeton played (1869) first intercollegiate football game in America at New Brunswick, N.J. Organized professional football in U.S. dates from 1920. See *ill.*, p. 1033.

Foote, Andrew Hull, 1806–63, American naval officer. In Civil War he gave brilliant support to Union army in victories at Fort Henry, Fort Donelson, and Island No. 10, and was made rear admiral but had to retire because of injuries.

Foote, Henry Stuart, 1804–80, U.S. Senator (1847–52), governor of Miss. (1852–54). Fought states' rights doctrines in the Senate and later opposed Jefferson Davis in Confederate congress; supported Republicans after the war.

Foote, Lucius Harwood, 1826–1913, American minister to Korea (1883–84), first regular diplomat from a Western power to that country.

foot-pound: see WORK.

Foot Resolution, offered 1829 by Samuel A. Foot in U.S. Senate. Instructed committee on public lands to inquire into limiting of public-land sale. Jacksonian Democrats, encouraging migration W, opposed resolution; New England manufacturing interests, demanding a ready labor supply, backed it. Advocates of states' rights identified themselves with interests of West. Touched off dramatic debates of 1830 between Robert HAYNE and Daniel WEBSTER.

Foppa, Vincenzo (věnchän'tsō fôp'pä), c.1427–c.1515, Italian painter, founder of Lombard school. Worked in Pavia and Milan.

Foraker, Joseph Benson (fôr'ŭkùr), 1846–1917, American political leader. U.S. Senator from Ohio (1897–1909). Old Guard Republican; accused of accepting retainers from Standard Oil Co.

foraminifera (fŭră"mŭnĭ'fùrù), members of an order of protozoa most of which have a shell. They inhabit all oceans, and there are a few species in fresh and brackish water. Discarded skeletons of genus *Globigerina*

form on ocean bottom a deposit which solidifies into chalk.

Forbes, James David, 1809–68, Scottish physicist and pioneer glaciologist. Discovered polarization of radiant heat.

Forbes, John, 1710–59, British general in French and Indian Wars. Captured Fort Duquesne 1758.

Forbes-Robertson, Sir Johnston, 1853–1937, English actor. On stage from 1874, he appeared with the Bancrofts and Henry Irving. Excelled as Hamlet.

Forbidden City, China: see CHINESE ARCHITECTURE.

force, in physics, is commonly defined as any "push" or "pull" acting on a body or as that effort acting to change its state of motion (i.e., its acceleration or direction of movement) or state of rest. Forces are measured in pounds, grams, or kilograms, depending upon system of weights used. For every force there is an equal and opposite force. Both direction and magnitude enter into effect of a force upon a given body. Forces can produce rotation of certain bodies, e.g., of a lever bar free to revolve about its center. A rotating part is acted upon by centrifugal force, i.e., a force acting to make it fly off at a tangent from its path around the center. This force must be balanced, if equilibrium is to be maintained, by a centripetal force, i.e., a force acting in the opposite direction and toward the center, holding the body in its regular path. Forces acting on the various parts of structures and machines are factors determining stress and strain and STRENGTH OF MATERIALS. Certain force measurements are based on velocity imparted to a given mass in a certain unit of time. The DYNE is unit of force in cgs (centimeter-gram-second) system; in English system it is the poundal. See also GRAVITATION; MAGNETISM; PRESSURE; VOLT.

force bill, popular name for several laws in U.S. history, notably act of March 2, 1833, and Reconstruction acts of 1870 and 1871. First force bill, passed in response to ordinance of NULLIFICATION of S.C., empowered Pres. Jackson to use army and navy, if necessary, to enforce laws of Congress, specifically the tariff measures at issue. In second set of force bills, radical Republicans strengthened their Reconstruction program by imposing severe penalties on those Southerners who tried to obstruct it. Act of May 31, 1870, penalized anyone preventing qualified citizens (in this case Negroes) from voting, and placed congressional elections under exclusive Federal control. Act of April 20, 1871, inspired by activities of Ku Klux Klan, declared acts of armed combinations tantamount to rebellion and empowered President to suspend privilege of habeas corpus in lawless areas.

Ford, Edsel Bryant: see FORD, HENRY.

Ford, Ford Madox, 1873–1939, English author. As editor of literary reviews he greatly influenced modern writing. Taught English to Joseph Conrad, collaborated with him. Originally Ford Madox Hueffer.

Ford, Henry, 1863–1947, American industrialist, pioneer automobile manufacturer. An inexpensive, standardized car, resulting from mass production, helped make Ford world's largest automobile producer. Had employee profit-sharing plan; opposed union organization until 1941. Estab. FORD FOUNDATION. His son, **Edsel Bryant Ford,** 1893–1943, was president of Ford Motor Co. 1919–43. **Henry Ford II,** 1917–, succeeded his grandfather as president in 1945. Became board chairman in 1960.

Ford, John, 1586–c.1640, English dramatist, author of verse plays, including *'Tis Pity She's a Whore* (1633). Collaborated with Dekker, Rowley, and others.

Ford, John, 1895–, American film director, originally named Sean O'Feeney. Noted especially for spectacular scope of his Westerns. Among his many films are *The Informer*, *The Grapes of Wrath*, *How Green Was My Valley*, and *The Quiet Man*.

Ford, Worthington Chauncey, 1858–1941, American historian and editor. He was chief of the manuscripts division of the Library of Congress (1902–9) and editor of the Mass. Historical Society (1909–29).

Works he edited include the writings of George Washington (14 vols., 1889–93) and of John Quincy Adams (7 vols., 1913–17). Joint editor of *Winnowings in American History* (15 vols., 1890–91), together with his brother, **Paul Leicester Ford,** 1865–1902. He edited many early U.S. writings, including those of Thomas Jefferson (10 vols., 1892–99), and wrote biographies (notably *The True George Washington,* 1896) and novels (e.g., *Janice Meredith,* 1899; *The Honorable Peter Stirling,* 1894).

Ford Foundation, incorporated 1936 with funds from Henry Ford and Edsel B. Ford for general purpose of advancing human welfare. Greatly expanded program was inaugurated in 1950 with five main aims: to support activities directed toward world peace; to secure greater allegiance to basic principles of freedom and democracy; to advance economic well-being of people everywhere; to promote educational and cultural activities; and to support scientific study. Autonomous subsidiary, the Fund for the Republic, estab. 1951 to study civil liberties and individual freedom in U.S.

Fordham University (fôr′dŭm), at four sites in New York city; partly coed.; founded 1841 as St. John's Col., chartered 1846 as university; renamed 1907. Exchange program with Union Theological Seminary began 1966.

Ford Island, Hawaii: see PEARL HARBOR.

Forefathers' Day, celebrated by New Englanders Dec. 21, to commemorate landing of Pilgrims in 1620 on Plymouth Rock. It was first observed in 1769.

foreign aid, military, technical, and financial assistance given usually on intergovernmental level. U.S. foreign aid began with lend-lease in Second World War. In expectation that foreign aid would be financed by loans from INTERNATIONAL BANK FOR RECONSTRUCTION AND DEVELOPMENT and INTERNATIONAL MONETARY FUND, U.S. aid at first took form of *ad hoc* emergency grants under no central organization. In 1948, U.S. launched EUROPEAN RECOVERY PROGRAM (Marshall Plan) for reconstruction of Western Europe. Emphasis there shifted later from economic to military aid. Needs of underdeveloped nations led to Truman's POINT FOUR PROGRAM. Mutual Security Act of 1951 covered in a single act of Congress the continuation of military and economic aid and technical assistance on a world-wide basis. Aid was administered by Mutual Security Agency. Internatl. Cooperation Administration (ICA) was estab. 1955. Military aid was to be administered by Dept. of Defense. U.S. aid has since increasingly taken form of loans, with emphasis on underdeveloped areas. The Agency for International development (AID) was created in Dept. of State, replacing ICA, Food for Peace program, and Development Loan Fund. Soviet aid began in 1950s but lags behind that of U.S. In percent of national income, France contributes largest amount of foreign aid to underdeveloped nations. On smaller scale, Britain provides aid for former colonies. Several UN agencies are concerned with foreign aid. In 1961 Organization for Economic Cooperation and Development was formed to coordinate and centralize giving of foreign aid.

foreign exchange, methods of adjusting payment of debts between two areas using different currency systems. Rate of exchange is price in local currency of one unit of foreign currency. It is determined by relative supply and demand of the currencies in the foreign exchange market.

Foreign Legion, French volunteer infantry regiment, created 1831 for pacification of Algeria, where it is normally stationed. Enlisted men are mostly foreigners. Important in French colonial expansion, Legion also fought gallantly in First World War. Renovated and reorganized after 1946, Legion fought in Indo-China until 1954 and later in Tunisia, Morocco, and Algeria.

Foreign Ministers, Council of, informal body set up at Yalta Conference Feb., 1945, by U.S., British, and

Russian ministers. France was admitted 1946. After POTSDAM CONFERENCE, group met in London, then in Moscow in late 1945. It decided on certain peace treaties, an 11-power Far Eastern Commission and Council for Japan, and an atomic energy commission within UN. It steered Paris peace conference of 1946 and subsequent decisions, but at Moscow and London in 1947 it failed to draft peace treaties with Germany and Austria. Revived June, 1949, at Paris, it achieved ending of Soviet blockade of Berlin. Berlin Conference (Jan.–Feb., 1954) failed to reunite Germany; resulted in calling of GENEVA CONFERENCE. The ministers discussed disarmament and German unity at Geneva (Oct.–Nov., 1955) but reached no accord. Meeting at Geneva again (May–Aug., 1959), they failed to settle problems of Germany and Berlin but agreed on establishment of a ten-nation disarmament council. In 1963 British, U.S., and Russian ministers met in Moscow and reached a partial nuclear test-ban agreement which was signed by 106 nations.

foreign missions: see MISSIONS.

Forel, Auguste or **August** (ōgüst′ fôrĕl′), 1848–1931, Swiss psychiatrist and entomologist. As a boy he began his studies of ants on which he wrote a number of books and which later influenced his approach to psychiatry. He promoted humane treatment of the insane and contributed to study of hypnotism and of sexual problems.

Forel, François Alphonse (fräswä′ älfôs′), 1841–1912, Swiss physician and naturalist. He taught anatomy and physiology at Univ. of Lausanne and studied Swiss glaciers and lakes.

Foreland, North, and **South Foreland,** headlands of Kent, England. Both are chalk cliff formations. Defeat of Dutch in 1666 associated with Forelands.

Forester, C(ecil) S(cott), 1899–1966, British author of superior adventure stories, notably those about naval hero Horatio Hornblower.

Forest Grove, city (pop. 5,628), NW Oregon, W of Portland, in farm, lumber, and dairy area; founded 1849. Seat of Pacific Univ.

Forest Hill, town (pop. 20,489), S Ont., Canada, residential suburb of Toronto.

Forest Hills, see QUEENS, New York city borough.

Forest Park. 1 Town (pop. 14,201), NW Ga., SSE of Atlanta. **2** Village (pop. 14,452), NE Ill., a suburb W of Chicago; founded 1857.

Forfarshire: see ANGUS, county.

forgery, willful fabrication or alteration of a written document (private or public—e.g., birth or marriage certificate) with the intent fraudulently to injure the interests of another. In the U.S. forgery ordinarily is a state crime, but to send forged documents through the mail may constitute Federal crime.

forget-me-not, plant (*Myosotis*) with small flowers, usually blue, used in borders and rock gardens.

forging, working metals by heating, then hammering and rolling. Metal is heated to red or white heat in forge; charcoal and coke are usual fuels. Heated metal is removed with tongs to anvil, hammered to desired shape, and thrust into water for tempering. Like founding, forging was practiced prehistorically, probably first in Asia. Early importance of metals is indicated by names Bronze Age and Iron Age.

Forli, Melozzo da: see MELOZZO DA FORLÌ.

Forlì (fôrlē′), city (pop. 91,146), Emilia-Romagna, N central Italy, in Romagna. Free commune from 11th cent.; later a principality; passed to Papal States 1504. Citadel (14th cent.); art gallery.

formaldehyde (fôrmăl′dŭhīd), the simplest ALDEHYDE, a gas with suffocating odor. Molecule consists of a carbon atom doubly bound to an oxygen atom and also singly bound to each of two hydrogen atoms. Formaldehyde is used to make dyes, certain plastics, resins; subject to POLYMERIZATION. **Formalin,** 40% water solution of formaldehyde, used as antiseptic, disinfectant, biological preservative.

formic acid, colorless, corrosive organic acid, lowest member of fatty-acid series. It is a compound of hydrogen, carbon, and oxygen. Found in red ants, sting of bees, and other insects.

Formosa: see TAIWAN.

Formosa Strait, Chinese *Tai-wan Hai-hsia,* arm of Pacific Ocean, between China's Fukien coast and Taiwan. Links the East and South China seas. Contains the Pescadores. Also called Strait of Formosa.

formula, in chemistry, a written expression which indicates elements, in proportion by weight, making up one molecule of a chemical COMPOUND. Formula of water is H_2O: symbol $H = $ hydrogen, $O = $ oxygen; subscript 2 shows that there are 2 atoms of hydrogen. Formula also shows that 2 parts of hydrogen by weight (2 × its ATOMIC WEIGHT of 1) and 16 parts of oxygen (1 × 16) are combined to form 18 parts by weight of water. Structural formula shows arrangement of atoms.

formula, in mathematics and physics, a statement in symbols of relationship between certain quantities. Quantities are expressed usually by letters, relationships by algebraic symbols.

Forres (fŏ′rĭs), burgh (pop. 4,780), Morayshire. Scotland; resort town with mfg. of textiles and chemicals. Part of Shakespeare's *Macbeth* is set here.

Forrest, Edwin, 1806–72, American actor, first national idol of the American theater. Debut (1826) as Othello established him as great tragedian, though he was often criticized for ranting. Violent rivalry with MACREADY and demonstrations instigated by Macready and Forrest adherents culminated in the Astor Place riot (1849), but failed to dim Forrest's reputation as an actor.

Forrest, John Forrest, 1st Baron, 1847–1918, Australian explorer and statesman. Led coastal expedition from Perth to Adelaide (1870). Surveyor general of Western Australia (1883); first premier (1890–1901).

Forrest, Nathan Bedford, 1821–77, Confederate general. Commanded cavalry units in Tenn. (1862–63); in N Miss., where his victories menaced Sherman's communications; and again in Tenn. (1864) under J. B. Hood. Probably greatest Confederate cavalryman, he is the hero of many legends in South. To him is attributed the formula for victory: "Git there fustest with the mostest men."

Forrestal, James V(incent) (fŏ′rĭstäl), 1892–1949, U.S. Secretary of the Navy (1944–47) and first Secretary of Defense (1947–49).

Forrest City, city (1964 pop. 12,032), E central Ark., at foot of Crowley's Ridge, NNW of Helena; settled c.1868. Rail and trade center in peach-growing area.

Forssmann, Werner (vĕr′nŭr fôrs′män), 1904–, German physician. Shared with A. F. Cournand and D. W. Richards the 1956 Nobel Prize in Medicine and Physiology for work in developing technique of inserting catheter (tube) into heart; this technique makes possible better study of condition of heart in health and disease.

Forster, E(dward) M(organ), 1879–, English novelist. Lived in Italy, India, Egypt. His novels are noted for crisp style and subtle irony: *Where Angels Fear to Tread* (1905), *The Longest Journey* (1907), *A Room with a View* (1908), *Howards End* (1910), *A Passage to India* (1924). Also wrote short stories, essays, and literary criticism.

Forsyth, Alexander John, 1769–1843. Scottish inventor of first workable percussion cap for ignition of gunpowder in firearms.

Forsyth, John, 1780–1841, American statesman. U.S. Senator from Ga. (1818–19, 1829–34); supported Pres. Jackson in nullification controversy in Ga. U.S. Secretary of State (1834–41).

forsythia (–sĭth′ĕ), Old World shrub (*Forsythia*) with abundant yellow flowers appearing in spring before the leaves.

Fort, Paul (pōl′ fôr′), 1872–1960, French symbolist poet, noted for use of "rhythmical prose," as in *Ballades françaises* (1897).

Fortaleza (fôrtúlä′zú), city (pop. c.514,800), cap. of Ceará state, NE Brazil; Atlantic port, founded 1609.

Long a center of great sugar plantations; today important also for cotton.

Fortas, Abe, 1910–, Associate Justice of U.S. Supreme Court (1965–).

Fort Beauséjour National Park: see BEAUSÉJOUR, FORT.

Fort Benton, city (pop. 1,187), N central Mont., at head of navigation on Missouri R. and NE of Great Falls. Grew around fur-trading post (1846). Reached by steamboat in 1859, it became supply point for gold seekers and cattlemen.

Fort Bridger State Park, SW Wyo., E of Evanston and on Blacks Fork of Green R. The supply post, founded 1843 by James BRIDGER, was held by Mormons 1853–57, then leased by U.S. as fort until 1890.

Fort Collins, city (pop. 25,027), N Colo., N of Denver and on Cache la Poudre R.; settled around fortification (1864–71). Trade, processing, and shipping center of farm area (grain, sugar beets, livestock). Seat of COLORADO STATE UNIVERSITY. Several dams of COLORADO-BIG THOMPSON PROJECT are nearby.

Fort Davis, village (pop. 1,080), W Texas, SE of El Paso in Davis Mts.; settled near frontier army post (1854–91). A key post in defense of W Texas, it is now a national historic site. City is ranching center popular with vacationers. McDonald Observatory (1932; Univ. of Texas and Univ. of Chicago) is on nearby Mt. Locke.

Fort-de-France (fôr-dù-fräs′), city (pop. 85,281), cap. of Martinique dept., French West Indies; chief port of island. It exports sugar and rum.

Fort Dodge, city (1966 pop. 29,654), central Iowa, on Des Moines R., NNW of Des Moines; settled c.1846. Fort Clarke estab. here 1850, named Fort Dodge (for Henry Dodge) 1851, abandoned 1853. Rail, distributing, and industrial center in agr. (corn, poultry, hogs) and mining (gypsum) area.

Fort Donelson National Military Park: see DONELSON, FORT.

Fort Edward, village (pop. 3,737), E central N.Y., on Hudson R. at confluence of Champlain division of Barge Canal. Fort built 1755 to guard portage between Hudson R. and L. Champlain. Occupied briefly by Burgoyne 1777.

Fort Erie, town (pop. 9,027), S Ont., Canada, on Niagara R. (bridged) opposite Buffalo, N.Y. Has steel mills, gold refineries, mfg. of aircraft and auto parts. Some U.S. firms have branch units here. Fort built 1764 by British. Taken by Americans in War of 1812 and successfully defended in 1814. Merged 1931 with Bridgeburg.

Fortescue, Sir John, c.1394–c.1476, English jurist and chief justice of the Court of King's Bench 1442–60. His writings were significant in the development of English constitutional law.

Fort Frances, town (pop. 9,481), W Ont., Canada, on Rainy R. opposite International Falls, Minn. Hunting and camping center with paper, pulp, and lumber mills. Built as Hudson's Bay Co. post.

Fort Frederica National Monument: see SEA ISLANDS.

Fort George, river, central and W Que., Canada, longest river (c.550 mi.) flowing into Hudson Bay from the East. Formerly called Big R.

Fort Gibson, town (pop. 1,407), E central Okla., on Grand R. near junction with Arkansas R., NE of Muskogee. Founded 1824 to protect traders on Santa Fe Trail. Natl. cemetery and dam nearby.

Forth, river of Scotland. Flows c.50 mi. from Stirlingshire to Alloa. **Firth of Forth** extends c.50 mi. from Alloa to North Sea and is 1–19 mi. wide. Crossed at Queensferry by cantilever railroad bridge (5,330 ft. long). Rosyth, on bay, is a naval base. Several other rivers flow into the firth.

Fort Howard, Md.: see SPARROWS POINT.

fortification, defense structure for protection from enemy attack. May be permanent or improvised in field in wartime. By Middle Ages, walled city and castle were common, but walls failed to withstand artillery, which appeared c.15th cent. Subsequent fortifications featured posts for defenders' artillery and a far-flung defense perimeter around main fortress. Extensive systems of intricate fortification were used in Europe during two World Wars. Increased mobility of warfare has led to reemphasis of temporary or improvised fortifications designed to delay invaders until reinforcements arrive.

Fort Jefferson National Monument: see DRY TORTUGAS.

Fort-Lamy (fôr-lämē'), city (pop. c.91,700), cap. of Chad Republic, at confluence of Shari and Logone rivers. Founded 1900; important air base in Second World War. Trade, industrial, and commercial center.

Fort Lauderdale (lô'dúrdāl), city (pop. 83,648), SE Fla., on Atlantic coast N of Miami; settled around Seminole War fort (c.1837). On navigable canal to L. Okeechobee, it is interwoven with c.270 mi. of natural and artificial waterways. Large beach and yachting resort. Port Everglades and Seminole Indian reservation are nearby.

Fort Lee, borough (pop. 21, 815), NE N.J., on Hudson R., W terminus of George Washington Bridge; settled c.1700. Fort here abandoned Nov. 20, 1776, by Gen. Greene after British took Fort Washington (across river). Early center of motion-picture industry.

Fort Livingstone, post of Northwest Mounted Police, W Man., Canada, near Swan R. Hq. for mounted police and cap. Northwest Territories 1875–77.

Fort McHenry National Monument and Historic Shrine: see McHENRY, FORT.

Fort Madison, city (pop. 15,247), SE Iowa, on Mississippi R. (bridged), SSW of Burlington; settled 1833. Rail, commercial, and industrial center in agr. area. Fort Madison, U.S. trading post, was here 1808–13.

Fort Matanzas National Monument: see SAINT AUGUSTINE, Fla.

Fort Myers, city (pop. 22,523), SW Fla., on Caloosahatchee R. near Gulf of Mexico. Grew around Fort Harvie, built 1841 in Seminole War and held by Federals in Civil War. Ships citrus fruit, vegetables, flowers, fish, and cattle. T. A. Edison wintered and experimented here.

Fort Nelson, settlement and government post, N B.C., Canada, on Alaska Highway and Fort Nelson R., N of Dawson Creek. Hudson's Bay Co. post here estab. c.1800.

Fort Oglethorpe, town (pop. 2,251), extreme NW Ga., SSE of Chattanooga, Tenn. Chicamauga and Chattanooga Natl. Military Park is nearby.

Fort Peck Dam, NE Mont., in Missouri R. above mouth of Milk R. Built 1933–40 to control floods and improve navigation, it is used also for irrigation and power by MISSOURI RIVER BASIN PROJECT. One of world's largest earth-filled dams, it is 21,026 ft. long and 250 ft. high.

Fort Pierce, city (pop. 25,256), SE Fla., on Indian River (lagoon), here connected with the Atlantic by inlet. Grew around fort (1838). With good harbor and rail facilities, it ships fruit, vegetables, fish, and lumber. Halpatiokee Swamp is W.

Fort Pulaski National Monument: see PULASKI, FORT.

Fortress Monroe: see MONROE, FORT.

Fort Smith, city (1964 pop. 64,196), NW Ark., on Arkansas R. at Okla. line; founded 1817 as one of first U.S. military posts in Louisiana Territory and center of law and order for regions to W until 1890. Fort is now a national historic site. City is major industrial center of state and rail and trade center for farm and livestock area. U.S. Fort Chaffee is nearby.

Fort Stockton, city (pop. 6,373), W Texas, on plateau W of Pecos R., in farming area. Grew around army post founded 1859 at nearby Comanche Springs (once camp site for Indians and overlanders).

Fort Sumner, village (pop. 1,809), E N.Mex., NNE of Roswell. Nearby are Alamagordo Dam, grave of Billy the Kid, and ruins of Fort Sumner (1862).

Fort Sumter National Monument: see SUMTER, FORT.

Fort Thomas, residential city (pop. 14,896), N central Ky., on Ohio R., E of Newport. U.S. army post (1887) was here.

Fortuna: see TYCHE.

Fortunate Isles or **Isles of the Blest,** in classical and Celtic legend, islands in Western Ocean, eternal home of souls of favored mortals. Long thought to be Canary or Madeira Isls.

Fortunatus (Venantius Honorius Clementianus Fortunatus), d. c.600, last Gallic Latin poet, author of the hymn *Vexilla Regis prodeunt.*

Fortune, Robert, 1813–80, British botanist. He introduced in England the kumquat and many other plants which he collected in the Orient. His experiments led to the growing of tea in India.

Fort Union National Monument: see NATIONAL PARKS AND MONUMENTS (table).

Fort Walton Beach, resort town (pop. 12,147), NW Fla., on Gulf of Mexico E of Pensacola. Grew around fort built here in Seminole War.

Fort Wayne, city (pop. 161,776), NE Ind., where St. Joseph and St. Marys rivers form Maumee R. Strategic point of water transport between Great Lakes and Ohio R. Miami Indians had their chief town here before French founded trading post (c.1680) and fort (1697). Taken by British 1760, fort was held briefly by Indians in Pontiac's Rebellion. Anthony Wayne subdued Indians and built fort that bore his name. After War of 1812 town grew with fur trade. Today one of state's largest cities and a major rail, shipping, and industrial center. Seat of St. Francis Col. and Concordia Senior Col.

Fort William, city (pop. 45,214), W Ont., Canada, on NW shore of L. Superior at mouth of Kaministikwia R. With twin city, Port Arthur, is W Canadian lake port and shipping center with one of world's largest coal docks. Terminus of Canadian Natl. and Canadian Pacific railways. Has grain elevators and paper, pulp, lumber, and flour mills, foundries, machine shops, and shipyards. Fort Kaministiquia built here 1717, and Fort William estab. 1801 as post of North West Co.

Fort William, burgh (pop. 2,715), Inverness-shire, Scotland, on Loch Linnhe; tourist center for Highlands. Fort (built by General Monck 1655; rebuilt 1690) was twice beseiged by Jacobites, whose relics are in a museum. Has important aluminum industry.

Fort Worth, city (pop. 356,268), N Texas, at junction of Clear and West forks of Trinity R. and W of Dallas; settled 1843. Army Fort Worth estab. 1847. Was cowtown after Civil War. Railroad (1876) aided growth and helped estab. city as meat-packing center. Enriched by oil and gas industries in 20th cent. During Second World War aircraft assembly was added to its diverse and growing industry. Seat of TEXAS CHRISTIAN UNIVERSITY, Texas Wesleyan Col., and Southwestern Baptist Theological Seminary. Has symphony orchestra, Scott Theater, and Amon Carter Mus. of Western Art. Carswell Air Force Base is WNW.

Forty Fort, residential borough (pop. 6,431), NE Pa., on Susquehanna R., N of Wilkes-Barre. Settled 1772 on site of Forty Fort, from which militia of WYOMING VALLEY marched (1778).

Fort Yukon (yōō'kŏn), village (pop. 701), NE Alaska, at junction of Yukon R. and Porcupine R.; early fur-trading post.

Foscolo, Ugo (ōō'gō fō'skōlō), 1778–1827, Italian poet and patriot. His novel *The Last Letters of Jacopo Ortis* (1796–1802; Eng. tr., 1818), modeled on Goethe's *Werther,* stirred Italian hearts for generations. His "graveyard" poem *Sepolcri* (1807) is notable.

Fosdick, Harry Emerson, 1878–, American clergyman. Pastor Park Ave. Baptist Church (1926) and its successor, interdenominational Riverside Church, New York, from 1930 to his retirement in 1946. Noted for Modernist stand in controversies of 1920s. His voluminous writings include *A Great Time to Be Alive* (1944) and *The Living of These Days: An Autobiography* (1956).

Fosse Way (fŏs), Roman road in England, supposed to have linked present Exeter, Bath, Cirencester, Leicester, and Lincoln.

fossil, organic remains or impressions preserved in sedimentary rocks from the geologic past. Favorable conditions included burial in asphalt, mud, or other materials which prevent decay. Fossilization is usually confined to skeletons or hard parts, but entire mammals of the late Pleistocene have been found frozen in ice. Footprints of land animals and tracks of marine invertebrates are regarded as fossils. Petrified wood and other petrified plant and animal remains form when original structure is replaced by minerals.

Foster, John Watson, 1836–1917, American diplomat. Minister to Mexico (1873–80), Russia (1880–81). Secretary of State (1892–93). Represented U.S. in arbitration of Bering Sea Fur-Seal Controversy.

Foster, Stephen Collins, 1826–64, American composer. His knowledge of the Negro was gained from minstrel shows, for which he wrote many of his songs. Wrote for Edwin P. CHRISTY, but despite the popularity of his songs, died in extreme poverty. Among his best-loved songs are *Oh! Susannah* (1848), *Camptown Races* (1850), *Old Folks at Home* (1851), *My Old Kentucky Home* (1853), *Jeanie with the Light Brown Hair* (1854), and *Old Black Joe* (1860).

Foster, William Z(ebulon), 1881–1961, American Communist leader. Three-time presidential candidate.

Fostoria, city (pop. 15,732), NW Ohio, SSE of Toledo; estab. 1854 by union of Risdon and Rome villages. Industrial, trade, and shipping center for livestock and grain area.

Fothergill, John (fŏ'dhûrgĭl), 1712–80, English physician, a Quaker, noted for his London practice, for botanic garden at Upton, Essex, and for work to improve jails and sanitation.

Fotheringhay (fŏdh'ŭring-gā), village, Northamptonshire, England. Castle was birthplace of Richard III and scene of Mary Queen of Scots' execution.

Foucauld, Charles Eugène de (fōōkō'), 1858–1916. French missionary priest. A former army officer and explorer in N Africa, he became a Trappist. Settled as a hermit among the Tuareg in the Sahara and was killed during a tribal revolt. After his death several congregations grew up which were inspired by his writings, and devoted to a life of prayer, poverty, and friendship among the poor.

Foucault, Jean Bernard Léon (zhā' bĕrnär' lāō' fōōkō'), 1819–68, French physicist. He determined velocity of light in air; found that speed of light in other media is reduced in proportion to index of refraction. He devised the Foucault PENDULUM.

Fouché, Joseph (zhôzĕf' fōōshā'), 1759–1820, French police minister (1799–1802, 1804–10); created duke of Otranto 1809. A lifelong opportunist, he sided with every party in power from the French Revolution through the Bourbon restoration. Through his private spy system he discovered the CADOUDAL plot (1804), thus earning a return to favor. Sometimes considered the father of the modern police state, he created a ruthlessly efficient system of criminal and political police. After his second dismissal (because of secret dealings with England) he held several high posts but never regained his power.

Foucquet: see FOUQUET.

Fouillée, Alfred (fōōyā'), 1838–1912, French philosopher. Developed motor theory of consciousness, making ideas agents of change and progress.

founding or **casting,** shaping of metals by melting and pouring into molds. Foundry is place where this is done. Sand or loam mold (held to desired form by wooden pattern) used to cast iron or steel. Pattern is made slightly large to allow shrinkage when metal solidifies. Rapid cooling increases hardness of casting. Metal molds are used in type founding and also in die-casting.

Fountain City, town (pop. 10,365), E central Tenn., a suburb N of Knoxville.

Fountains Abbey, ruined 12th-cent. abbey, West Riding of Yorkshire, England, SW of Ripon.

Fountain Valley, city (1965 pop. 13,099), S Calif., SW of Santa Ana, in citrus-fruit area.

Fouqué, Friedrich, Freiherr de la Motte- (frē'drĭkh bärōn' dù lä môt'-fōōkā), 1777–1843, German romantic poet, best known for the fairy tale *Undine* (1811).

Fouquet or **Foucquet, Jean** or **Jehan** (all: zhā' fōō-kā'), c.1420–c.1480, founder of 15th-cent. school of French painting which shows influence of Van Eycks and early Florentines.

Fouquet or **Foucquet, Nicolas** (nēkōlä'), 1615–80, French statesman, superintendent of finance (1653–61). Mismanaged treasury, accumulated huge private wealth. Denounced by Colbert and resented by Louis XIV for his ostentatious entertainments, he was brought to trial (1661) and sentenced (1664) to banishment. The king "commuted" the sentence to life imprisonment. Fouquet was a patron of La Fontaine and Molière.

Fouquier-Tinville, Antoine Quentin (ätwän' kätē' fōōkyā-tēvēl'), 1746–95, French revolutionist, chief prosecutor in Revolutionary tribunal during REIGN OF TERROR. Guillotined after fall of Robespierre.

Fourcroy, Antoine François, comte de (ätwän' fräswä' kôt dù fōōrkrwä'), 1755–1809, French chemist. Pioneer in animal and plant chemistry; collaborated in reforming chemical nomenclature.

Four Forest Cantons, Ger. *Vier Waldstätten,* cantons of UNTERWALDEN, SCHWYZ, URI, and LUCERNE; first Swiss communities to win freedom. Lake of the Four Forest Cantons is called in English Lake of LUCERNE.

Four Freedoms. In message to Congress (Jan. 6, 1941) Pres. F. D. Roosevelt stated that Four Freedoms should prevail throughout world—freedom of speech and expression, freedom of worship, freedom from want, and freedom from fear. These were substantially incorporated in ATLANTIC CHARTER.

Four-H or **4-H clubs,** organizations under Dept. of Agr. for boys and girls in rural areas. They aim to improve methods of agr. and home economics and to promote good citizenship. Name is derived from fourfold purpose of improving head, heart, hands, health.

Four Horsemen of the Apocalypse (ùpŏk'ùlĭps), allegorical figures in Bible. Rev. 6.1–8. Rider on white horse has many interpretations—one is that he represents Christ; rider on red horse is war; rider on black horse is famine, and rider on pale horse, death.

Fourier, Charles (shärl' fōōryä'), 1772–1837, French social philosopher. Projected social utopia organized in small economic units (phalanxes) in which work would be divided according to natural inclination. Doctrine of Fourierism spread to America under auspices of Prosper Considérant, Albert Brisbane, Horace Greeley. BROOK FARM was for a time Fourierist; most successful community was at Red Bank, N.J.

Fourier, Jean Baptiste Joseph, Baron (fōō'rēā", Fr. zhā' bätēst' zhôzēf' bärō' fōōryä'), 1768–1830, French mathematician and physicist. Noted for research on heat and numerical equations; he originated Fourier's theorem on vibratory motion and Fourier series which provided method for representing discontinuous functions by trigonometric series.

Four Lakes, S Wis., chain of lakes (Mendota, largest; Monona, Waubesa, Kegonsa). Madison is between first two. Univ. of Wisconsin is on Mendota.

Fournier, Alain-: see ALAIN-FOURNIER.

Fournier, Pierre Simon (fōōrnyä'), 1712–68, Parisian type founder. Devised first point system for measuring type. Wrote *Manuel typographique* (1764–66).

Fourteen Points, formulation of a peace program, presented by U.S. Pres. Woodrow Wilson in address before Congress on Jan. 8, 1918. Message was intended to reach people and liberal leaders of Central Powers as a seductive appeal for peace, in which purpose it was successful, and to provide a framework for peace discussions. Message made Wilson moral leader of the Allies, but after the Armistice opposition to the points quickly crystallized, and actual treaty (see VERSAILLES, TREATY OF) represented a compromise or defeat of many of them.

Fourteenth Amendment, to the U.S. Constitution (1868). Section 1 established the basis of U.S. citizenship and forbade states to abridge privileges and immunities of U.S. citizens, to deprive any person of life, liberty, or property without DUE PROCESS OF LAW, or to deny any person equal protection of law. The U.S. Supreme Court used Section 1 extensively to limit restrictive state legislation (e.g., the states were forbidden to favor or suppress any religious establishment). The Supreme Court after 1954 ruled that color is not a legal basis to deprive persons of rights otherwise enjoyed by the community, such as access to public facilities like parks and schools. In 1967 the court voided an amendment to the California state constitution that would have allowed racial discrimination in the disposal of property.

fourth dimension: see SPACE TIME.

Fourth of July, Independence Day, or **July Fourth,** U.S. patriotic holiday par excellence, commemorating adoption of Declaration of Independence. Observance began during American Revolution.

Fourth Republic: see FRANCE.

Fowke, Gerard (fouk), 1855–1933, American archaeologist. Noted for study of the Ohio valley. Investigated aboriginal remains in E U.S. (1885–88, 1891–93). Explored Vancouver Isl. (1898). Made ethnological studies in Hawaiian Isls. (1920).

fowl: see POULTRY.

Fowler, H(enry) W(atson), 1858–1933, English lexicographer. He and his brother, F. G. Fowler, collaborated on *The King's English* (1906) and on an abridgment of *Oxford English Dictionary* (1911). After F. G. Fowler died in 1918 H. W. Fowler completed alone *A Dictionary of Modern English Usage* (1926).

Fowliang (fō'lyäng'), city (pop. c.110,000), NE Kiangsi prov., China, on Chang R. Celebrated porcelain center. Founded 6th cent. Formerly known as Kingtehchen (Ching-te-chen).

Fox, Charles James, 1749–1806, English Whig statesman and orator. Disliked by George III, he was a friend of the prince of Wales (George IV). Opponent of Lord North, he attacked British policy in the American war. Was foreign secretary for brief periods (1782, 1783, 1806). Supported repeal of Poynings's Law in 1782. Opposed William Pitt by demanding British nonintervention in French Revolution. Urged abolition of slave trade (passed in 1807 after his death) and political freedom for dissenters.

Fox, George, 1624–91, English founder of Society of FRIENDS. He turned from organized religion to direct, personal relationship with God through "inward light" of Christ and began to preach in 1647. Despite persecutions and imprisonments he won many followers. Plan of organization was set up in 1668, with first London Yearly Meeting in 1671. His writings include his noted journal (1694; preface by William Penn).

Fox or Foxe, Luke, 1586–1635, English explorer. Sought Northwest Passage; explored W shore of Hudson Bay, satisfied himself there was no passage through it (1631).

Fox, Margaret, 1833–93, American spiritualist. She claimed connection with spirit world and toured U.S. and Europe with her sisters. In 1888 she admitted that effects were fraudulent.

Fox, river, c.176 mi. long, rising in central Wis. and flowing SW to within c.1½ mi. of Portage, on Wisconsin R., with which it is connected by ship canal. Thence flows NE to Green Bay, at Green Bay city. Drains L. Winnebago. Above lake it is known as Upper Fox R., below lake as Lower Fox. Route of early explorers, missionaries, traders into Wis. and Northwest. Jolliet and Marquette were first Europeans to

reach Mississippi R. by way of Fox-Wisconsin portage 1673. Principal tributary is the Wolf R.

fox, predatory intelligent animal of dog family. Fur is usually long and thick; tail bushy, and longer than the wolf's. It eats small animals, berries, and fruits. Red fox (*Vulpes*) inhabits parts of Europe, Asia, N Africa, most of U.S., and Canada. Usually the coat is reddish, the tail white-tipped, the ears black-tipped. Silver, black, and cross fox (yellowish to pale orange) are color phases which may appear in any red fox litter. Breeders have developed platinum fox. Arctic fox has circumpolar range. Gray fox found over most U.S. and through Mexico to N South America.

Foxboro, town (pop. 10,136), SE Mass., SW of Boston; settled 1704.

Foxe, John, 1516–87, English clergyman, author of *Book of Martyrs.* In Strasbourg appeared (1554; in Latin) story of Protestant martyrs to c.1500. At Basel appeared (1559) first complete edition. John Day issued (1563) first complete English edition; its purpose was to praise Protestant martyrs of Mary's reign.

Foxe, Luke: see FOX, LUKE.

foxglove, Old World biennial or perennial plant of genus *Digitalis.* It has handsome, spirelike spikes of purple, pink, or white bell-shaped flowers in early summer. Its leaves yield the drug digitalis.

Fox Indians: see SAC AND FOX INDIANS.

Fox Islands: see ALEUTIAN ISLANDS.

Foxx, James Emory (Jimmy Foxx), 1907–, American baseball player. Led American league in home runs in four seasons. Career total of 534 home runs.

Foyle, river of Co. Tyrone, N. Ireland. Its navigable estuary is called Lough Foyle.

Fr, chemical symbol of the element FRANCIUM.

Fracastoro, Girolamo (jērō'lämō fräkästō'rō), 1483–1553, Italian physician, authority on epidemic diseases. He wrote a poem on syphilis from which the disease takes its name.

fracture, a breaking, especially of a bone. Types include simple, in which overlying skin is unbroken; compound, in which broken bone communicates with external wound; and greenstick, in which one side of bone is broken, other side bent.

Fra Diavolo (frä" dēä'vōlō) [Ital.,= brother devil], 1771–1806, Neopolitan bandit and soldier whose real name was Michele Pezza. Taking up the cause of the Bourbon rulers of Naples, he fought the French, who captured and hanged him. Auber's opera, *Fra Diavolo,* is in no way historical.

Fragonard, Jean Honoré (zhä ōnôrä' frägônär'), 1732–1806, French painter. Studied with Chardin and Boucher. Painted scenes of love and gallantry for the French court.

Framingham, industrial town (pop. 44,526), E Mass., on Sudbury R. WSW of Boston; settled 1650. FRAMINGHAM STATE COLLEGE is here.

Framingham State College, at Framingham, Mass.; coed.; chartered 1838, opened 1839 at Lexington; moved 1853; a normal school until 1930. Until 1964 called Massachusetts State Teachers Col. (for women). Oldest existing U.S. school for teachers and first under state control, it was estab. by Horace Mann.

Franca (frän'cä), city (pop. c.100,000), São Paulo state, SE Brazil, in center of rich coffee-growing area. Important for mfg. and export of shoes since c.1885; also has mfg. of rubber goods, textiles, beverages.

France, Anatole (änätôl' fräs'), pseud. of **Jacques Anatole Thibault** (zhäk', tēbō'), 1844–1924, French author. The style of his early works is charming and ironic, as in *Le Crime de Sylvestre Bonnard* (1881), *Le Livre de mon ami* (1885), *Thaïs* (1890), *La Rôtisserie de la Reine Pédauque* (1893), *Le Lys rouge* (1894). Following the Dreyfus Affair, in which he supported Zola, he turned to political satire with *Penguin Island* (1908) and *La Révolte des anges* (1914). Awarded 1921 Nobel Prize in Literature.

France, republic (212,659 sq. mi.; pop. 46,520,271), W Europe, bordering on English Channel (N), Atlantic

Ocean (W), Spain (SW), Mediterranean (S), Italy, Switzerland, Germany (E), Luxembourg, and Belgium (NE); cap. Paris. Called Metropolitan France, it is the chief member of the FRENCH COMMUNITY, consists of the 94 departments of continental France and the is-land-department of CORSICA. Its central natural fea-ture is the MASSIF CENTRAL. N of that rugged moun-tain mass and the LOIRE R. extend the fertile Paris basin, drained by the SEINE and MARNE, and the hilly landscapes of NORMANDY and BRITTANY. W and SW of the Massif Central the Aquitanian plain, drained by the GARONNE and DORDOGNE, stretches to the Atlantic and the PYRENEES; S of the Massif is the coastal plain of LANGUEDOC. A chain of mountains parallels the E border—the ARDENNES, VOSGES, and JURA, and the ALPS of SAVOY, DAUPHINÉ, and PROVENCE (highest point MONT BLANC). Despite extreme administrative centralization, the old provinces (abolished 1789) re-tain striking diversity and are basic cultural, economic, and geographic units—e.g., ALSACE, AUVERGNE, Brit-tany, CHAMPAGNE, GASCONY, TOURAINE). Nearly self-sufficient in agr., France is a country of small, inde-pendent farmers and many small towns. Only Paris, Marseilles, Lyons, Toulouse, and Nice have more than 250,000 inhabitants. Wine and luxury articles are among chief exports. Natural resources include coal (NORD dept.), iron (LORRAINE), hydroelectric power (RHONE valley). Lille, Saint-Étienne, Roubaix, Cler-mont-Ferrand, Le Creusot, Grenoble, Nîmes, Nantes, and Bordeaux are important industrial centers. Le Havre, Rouen, Cherbourg, Saint-Nazaire, Nantes, Bordeaux, Marseilles, and Toulon are the chief ports. Though some German, Flemish, and Basque are spok-en in border regions, as well as Breton in lower Brit-tany, Latin culture predominates, as does Roman Ca-tholicism. Separation of Church and state dates from the struggle of 1905–6.
Medieval France. Roman conquest of GAUL was com-pleted by Caesar 51 B.C. A Christian, Latin, highly civilized, prosperous country by the 5th cent. A.D., Gaul was suddenly reduced by Germanic invaders to chaos and barbarism. The FRANKS, emerging as sole masters under CLOVIS I, ruled Gaul as part of their empire under the dynasties of the MEROVINGIANS (481–751) and CAROLINGIANS (751–987). CHARLES MARTEL saved Gaul from Arabic conquest; CHARLEMAGNE gave it an era of order and cultural rebirth; the trea-ties of VERDUN (843) and MERSEN (870) made France a separate kingdom; the decline of Carolingian rule hastened the establishment of FEUDALISM and the MA-NORIAL SYSTEM. Powerful feudal lords easily usurped the authority of the weak kings. In 987 began the dy-nasty of the direct Capetians (Hugh Capet, Robert II, Henry I, Philip I, Louis VI, Louis VII, Philip II, Louis VIII, Louis IX, Philip III, Philip IV, Louis X, John I, Philip V, Charles IV). Their rule was a patient uphill struggle for control over the nobles and robber bar-ons, extension of the royal domain, and revival of commerce; in this they were aided by the rising urban bourgeoisie. The reform of the CLUNIAC ORDER, the prestige of the SORBONNE, and its leading role in the CRUSADES gave France cultural supremacy in medieval Christendom. These gains were lost in the HUNDRED YEARS WAR with England, which devastated France and nearly ended its national existence (1337–1453). The VALOIS kings, aided by such heroes as DU GUES-CLIN and JOAN OF ARC, emerged victorious; LOUIS XI (reigned 1461–83) created a new, unified France under a strong royal authority.
From Renaissance to Revolution. The later Valois kings—CHARLES VIII, LOUIS XII, FRANCIS I, Henry II, Francis II—wasted much effort on their imperial-istic struggle with Spain (see ITALIAN WARS); under the last Valois—Charles IX, Henry III—France bled in bitter civil strife (see RELIGION, WARS OF). Never-theless, French culture in the 16th cent., stimulated by the Renaissance, went through a golden age which continued through the 17th cent. HENRY IV, first Bourbon king, ended the civil war and restored pros-

perity. The reigns of LOUIS XIII (1610–43) and LOUIS XIV (1643–1715), parts of which were dominated by cardinals RICHELIEU and MAZARIN, made France a nearly absolute monarchy and in a series of costly wars raised it to the chief power of Europe. But the quest for glory strained the treasury and drained the people. Louis XV's wars were no less ruinous but brought no glory; LOUIS XVI's intervention in the American Revolution made France bankrupt. At the same time the bourgeoisie had risen to prosperity and increasingly resented an antiquated system which re-stricted its economic activities (see MERCANTILISM), drained it through an iniquitous and inefficient fiscal system, misspent the revenues, and to some extent barred it from the government. This, rather than royal absolutism—which in fact was limited by custom and law—was the chief factor leading to the revolution of 1789.
Modern France. The vast upheaval that shook Eu-rope from 1789 to 1815 is covered in the articles FRENCH REVOLUTION; FRENCH REVOLUTIONARY WARS; NAPOLEON I. France emerged from it a uniform bu-reaucratic state, dominated by its bourgeoisie, whom the Industrial Revolution brought into its own. The Bourbon Restoration was shortlived (see LOUIS XVIII; CHARLES X). The July Revolution of 1830 set up the monarchy of LOUIS PHILIPPE, overthrown in turn by the FEBRUARY REVOLUTION of 1848. The Second Re-public was changed into the Second Empire by NA-POLEON III (1852), whose rule ended disastrously in the FRANCO-PRUSSIAN WAR (1870). French prosperity and colonial expansion continued under the Third Re-public (1871–1940), but political disunity was a con-stant source of instability. Weakened by First World War and unable to deal with ensuing crises, France was forced to capitulate (1940) in Second World War. Germany occupied part of France; the rest was ruled by subservient VICHY GOVERNMENT until late 1942, when all France came under German occupation. Gen. Charles de GAULLE headed the Free French movement from London. Liberated in 1944, war-scarred France recovered slowly. Governed alter-nately by left-center and right-center party coalitions, France under the Fourth Republic (estab. 1946) eventually came to terms with W Germany and with nationalists in INDO-CHINA, TUNISIA, and MOROCCO but was unable to control inflation at home or re-bellion in ALGERIA. The crisis in Algeria was the immediate cause of collapse of the Fourth Republic (1958). Granted plenary powers, de Gaulle became premier. Under the constitution for the Fifth Repub-lic the presidency was made stronger, the bicameral legislature weaker. Algeria was granted independence in 1961. Constitutional changes (1962) provided direct election of president; de Gaulle was chosen a second time in 1965. France participated in the European Recovery Program (1948); joined North Atlantic Treaty Organization (1949) and announced withdrawal from it (1966). Belongs to UN, Euro-pean Coal and Steel Community (1952), Western European Union (1955), and European Atomic En-ergy Community (1957). Although a Common Mar-ket member, France opposed rapid European political integration. In May, 1967, government by decree in economic and social fields was voted for six months; one of first decrees issued gave workers a share of profits and ownership of industry.
Francesca da Rimini (fränsĕ'skŭ, Ital. fränchä'skä dä rē'mēnē), 13th-cent. heroine of tragic verse. Her love for Paolo, brother of her crippled husband, was im-mortalized in Dante's *Divine Comedy*.
Franceschi, Piero de': see PIERO DELLA FRANCESCA.
Francesco del Cossa: see COSSA, FRANCESCO.
Franche-Comté (fräsh-kōtä'), region and former prov-ince, E France, in Haute-Saône, Doubs, and Jura depts.; historic cap. Dôle (until 1676), later BESANÇON. A mountainous region (JURA in E, VOSGES in N), it has forests, pastures, agr. Mfg. of clocks, machinery,

plastics. Free County of Burgundy or Franche-Comté was created 9th cent.; passed with kingdom of Arles to Holy Roman Empire 1034. Philip the Bold of Burgundy acquired it by marriage (15th cent.); through his daughter, Mary of Burgundy, it passed to the Spanish Hapsburgs, but it retained considerable autonomy. A battleground in the Wars of Religion and the Thirty Years War, it was twice laid waste. Louis XIV conquered it twice (1668, 1674) and obtained its cession from Spain in 1678.

Francia (frän′chä), c.1450–1517, Italian painter of early Bolognese school. Influenced by Perugino and Raphael.

Francia, José Gaspar Rodríguez (hōsä′ gäspär′ rōdrē′gäs frän′syä), 1766–1840, dictator of Paraguay (1814–40) and creator of national independence, known as El Supremo. By keeping Paraguay from foreign intercourse he stimulated internal growth and strong nationalistic spirit.

Franciabigio (frän″chäbē′jō), 1482–1525, Florentine painter. Collaborated on several works with his master, Andrea del Sarto.

Francis, Saint (Francis of Assisi), 1182?–1226, founder of the Franciscans, one of the greatest of Christian saints, b. Assisi, Italy. His original name was Giovanni di Bernardone, but he was called Francesco [Frenchman] from his father's travels in France. Was briefly a soldier, but at 22 he turned from worldly things and became devout. In 1209 he set out to preach, and from the first he won others by his humility, his joyful poverty, his singular devotion to other men, and his religious fervor. A little group of men gathered about him, and they went to Rome, where they were permitted to form a band of friars. These new Franciscans went about Italy, and soon they were preaching in foreign lands. Francis went abroad too and was in the Holy Land when dissension in the order led to his return. He held an assembly (1221), at which, with typical self-abnegation, he laid down command. He went on preaching and leading an ascetic life, and he wrote the rule for his order. In 1224 in a vision he received the stigmata (painful wounds corresponding to the wounds of the crucified Christ). He was well loved in his time and mourned throughout Italy when he died. Stories clustered about his holy, simple life, some of them later collected in *The Little Flowers of St. Francis;* very familiar are the stories of his preaching to the birds and of his taming a wolf at Gubbio by gentleness. He may have written the joyous appreciation of nature called *Hymn of the Sun.* Feast: Oct. 4.

Francis, emperors of the Holy Roman Empire. **Francis I,** 1708–65. Married MARIA THERESA 1736; elected emperor 1745 (see AUSTRIAN SUCCESSION, WAR OF THE). Earlier, he had been duke of LORRAINE (1729–37) and grand duke of TUSCANY (1737–65). Ruled ably in Tuscany, but left imperial government largely in hands of Maria Theresa. Father of Joseph II, Leopold II, Marie Antoinette. **Francis II,** 1768–1835, succeeded his father Leopold II as emperor and king of Hungary and Bohemia (1792). Was defeated four times in FRENCH REVOLUTIONARY WARS (1797, 1801) and in wars against NAPOLEON I (1805, 1809). Took title emperor of Austria as **Francis I** in 1804; dissolved Holy Roman Empire in 1806. Gave his daughter Marie Louise in marriage to Napoleon (1810). Joined new coalition against Napoleon 1813; presided over Congress of VIENNA (1814–15). With his minister METTERNICH he dominated HOLY ALLIANCE and German Confederation. His son Ferdinand succeeded him.

Francis, kings of France. **Francis I,** 1494–1547, son-in-law of Louis XII, reigned 1515–47. Resuming ITALIAN WARS, he won at MARIGNANO (1515). He lost in imperial election of 1519 to CHARLES IV, his life-long rival. Despite failure to win English alliance at FIELD OF CLOTH OF GOLD he attacked Charles (1521), was routed and captured at Pavia (1525). Having, in his words, "lost all save life and honor," he obtained freedom by signing Treaty of Madrid (1526), in which he

renounced territorial claims. His creation of the League of Cognac (with Pope Clement VII, Francesco !I Sforza, Venice, and Florence) precipitated a second war (1527–29), which ended, unfavorably, with the Treaty of Cambrai. A third war (1536–38) was inconclusive. In 1542, in alliance with SULEIMAN I of Turkey, he again attacked Charles (allied with Henry VIII). Peace with Charles (1544: see CRÉPY, TREATY OF) and with Henry (1546) confirmed his previous failures. A typical Renaissance monarch, unscrupulous, spendthrift, and dissolute, Francis also was a patron of arts and letters. Da Vinci, Cellini, and Rabelais were among his protégés. His grandson **Francis II,** 1544–60, son of Henry II, reigned 1559–60. Married Mary Queen of Scots (1558). Government was in hands of Charles and François de GUISE. Reprisals against conspiracy of AMBOISE enraged Protestants.

Francis, kings of the Two Sicilies. **Francis I,** 1777–1830, reigned 1825–30. His rule was reactionary and corrupt. **Francis II,** 1836–94, reigned 1859–61. Fought against RISORGIMENTO. His capitulation at Gaeta to Victor Emmanuel II (1861) led to proclamation of united Italy.

Francis, c.1554–1584, French prince, duke of Alençon and Anjou; youngest son of Henry II of France. One of suitors for hand of Elizabeth of England. In 1580 William the Silent offered him the rule of Netherlands (then in rebellion against Spain). He accepted, set sail from England in 1582, but was expelled by his subjects and lost Elizabeth's support when he tried to obtain absolute power (1583). His death opened French succession to Henry of Navarre (Henry IV).

Francis II, 1435–88, duke of Brittany (1458–88). Sought to preserve Breton independence from France. Joined League of Public Weal against LOUIS XI, who forced him to sign Peace of Ancenis (1468). Died shortly after his rout by Charles VIII (1488), who eventually married his daughter ANNE OF BRITTANY.

Francis Borgia, Saint (bôr′jü), 1510–72, Spanish Jesuit, third general of his order (1565–72). A member of the Borgia family, he was great-grandson of Pope Alexander VI and was duke of Gandia and a wealthy courtier of Emperor Charles V. After his wife's death (1546) he went to join St. Ignatius Loyola in Rome to become a Jesuit. Gave money to build the Roman College. After ordination in 1551, he built up the order and took charge of foreign missions (including those to America). As general of the Society of Jesus, he sent missionaries to N and E Europe and did much to promote the Catholic Reform. Edited the Jesuit rule and the *Spiritual Exercises.* Feast: Oct. 10.

Franciscans (frănsĭ′skŭnz), members of the religious orders following the rule of St. FRANCIS (approved by the pope 1223). They include three organizations of friars: the Friars Minor (formerly called Observants; they use the abbreviation O.F.M.), the Friars Minor Capuchin (see CAPUCHINS), and the Friars Minor Conventual. The Franciscans began as friars living in absolute poverty without property, but later generations relaxed this custom, and there were recurrent moves within the order to return to "pure" poverty. These caused some dissension, particularly that led by zealots called Spirituals; briefly they were very powerful in Italy, and one of their heroes was pope as CELESTINE V, but had to abdicate. In 1322 the pope settled the matter by putting Franciscans on the same basis as other orders as to property holding. Later another move toward primitive practice produced the Observants, who were made independent in 1517. Friars wishing still more strict observance of the rule became the Capuchins in 1525. The Franciscans were prominent at the medieval universities and contributed to scholasticism. They also were vigorous missionaries and did much work in many parts of the New World. St. CLARE, a follower of St. Francis, founded an order of Franciscan nuns (also called Poor Clares). There are also many members of the third order, both men and women, some living as laymen in the world, others in religious communities.

Formerly the Franciscans were called the Gray Friars, but their habit now is typically brown.

Francis Ferdinand, 1863–1914, Austrian archduke, heir apparent of his great-uncle, Emperor Francis Joseph. Was assassinated, with his wife, by a Serbian nationalist at Sarajevo (June 28). Serbia's partial rejection of resulting Austrian ultimatum led to First WORLD WAR.

Francis Joseph, 1830–1916, emperor of Austria (1848–1916), king of Hungary (1867–1916); nephew of FERDINAND, who abdicated in his favor. Subdued Hungary and defeated Sardinia (1849), but lost Lombardy in Italian War of 1859, Venetia in AUSTRO-PRUSSIAN WAR of 1866. Reorganized in 1867, his empire became the AUSTRO-HUNGARIAN MONARCHY. His private life was beset by the tragedies of his wife, ELIZABETH; his brother, MAXIMILIAN of Mexico; his son, Archduke RUDOLF. Charles I succeeded him.

Francis of Sales, Saint, 1567–1622, Savoyard Roman Catholic preacher, Doctor of the Church. Of an aristocratic family, he joined the priesthood contrary to his father's wishes and rose to become bishop coadjutor (1599) and bishop (1602) of Geneva. With St. Jane Frances de Chantal he founded the Order of the Visitation for women. His eloquent sermons moved to religion and converted many Protestants. Their burden was love of God and love of man. Two treatises *L'Introduction à la vie dévote* and *Treatise on the Love of God* are masterpieces of religious writing. Feast: Jan. 29.

Francis Xavier, Saint (zā'vyùr), 1506–52, Basque Jesuit missionary, called the Apostle to the Indies. Friend of St. IGNATIUS OF LOYOLA, with whom he and five others formed the Society of JESUS; he was ordained with Ignatius (1537). He spent last 11 years of his life as missionary in India and Far East. Feast: Dec. 3.

francium (frăn'sēŭm), rare radioactive element (symbol = Fr; see also ELEMENT, table), an alkali metal. Half life of longest-lived isotope is 21 min.; it decays by beta emission. Discovered 1939 by Marguerite Perey as disintegration product of actinium.

Franck, César (säzär' frăk'), 1822–90, Belgian-French composer and organist. Much of his finest music was for organ. Among his most significant works are the Symphony in D Minor; *Variations symphoniques* for piano and orchestra; *Les Béatitudes*, oratorio; a violin sonata; also wrote for organ and piano.

Franck, James, 1882–1964, American physicist, b. Germany. Shared 1925 Nobel Prize in Physics for discovery of laws governing effect of impact of electron on atom. Noted for later work on photosynthesis.

Francke, August Hermann, 1663–1727, German Protestant minister, leading exponent of German Pietism.

Franco, Francisco (fränthē'skō frän'kō), 1892–, Spanish generalissimo and dictator. Became chief of Insurgent government 1936 (see SPAIN and SPANISH CIVIL WAR). Combined fascist and traditional elements in his authoritarian rule. Kept Spain out of Second World War despite commitments to Mussolini and Hitler. By law of succession (1947), he restored Spanish monarchy and retained position of regent, pending actual installment of a king.

Franco-German War: see FRANCO-PRUSSIAN WAR.

Franconia (frăngkō'nēŭ), Ger. *Franken,* duchy of medieval Germany. Created 9th cent., it extended from W bank of the Rhine eastward along Main R. Emperor Otto I broke it up into two nominal duchies—W or Rhenish Franconia (incl. archbishoprics of Mainz and Speyer, free cities of Frankfurt and Worms, Rhenish Palatinate, landgraviate of Hesse) and E Franconia (incl. bishoprics of Würzburg and Bamberg, margraviates of Ansbach and Bayreuth, free city of Nuremberg). Titular dukes of W Franconia furnished Franconian or Salian dynasty of emperors (1024–1125; see HOLY ROMAN EMPIRE). In E Franconia the ducal title, long in disuse, was revived by bishops of Würzburg (15th cent.). E Franconia passed to Bavaria in 1803–15 and was later divided into the provinces of

Lower Franconia (cap. Würzburg), in the Main valley, NW Bavaria; **Middle Franconia** (cap. Ansbach), in hilly region of N Bavaria, with Nuremberg, Fürth, and Erlangen; and **Upper Franconia** (cap. Bayreuth), which includes the wooded Frankenwald plateau and the Fichtelgebirge, in NE Bavaria.

Franconia Mountains, range in White Mts., NW N.H., rising to 5,249 ft. in Mt. Lafayette. To W is **Franconia Notch,** c.6-mi. pass, with Old Man of the Mountain or the Profile ("Great Stone Face" of Hawthorne's story) and the Flume (chasm, c.60 ft. high), Tramway (1938) mounts Cannon Mt. near Echo L. **Franconia** town (pop. 491), NW of notch, is resort.

Franco-Prussian War or **Franco-German War,** July 19, 1870–Jan. 28, 1871. By his publication of EMS DISPATCH, Bismarck deliberately goaded the aggressive French government into declaring war on Prussia, which was joined by the other German states. A brilliant campaign, led by H. K. B. von Moltke, resulted in French rout at Sedan, where NAPOLEON III was captured (Sept. 1). French resistance continued under a provisional government but became useless after surrender of BAZAINE at Metz (Oct. 27). Paris, however, resisted Prussian siege until Jan., 1871, despite growing famine, and refused to accept preliminary peace signed at Versailles (see VERSAILLES, TREATY OF, 1871) until May, when COMMUNE OF PARIS was suppressed by regular French forces. Chief results of war were creation of German Empire under William I of Prussia (proclaimed at Versailles on Jan. 18, 1871); cession of Alsace-Lorraine to Germany; establishment of Third Republic in France.

Frank, Anne (fränk), 1929–45, Dutch Jewish girl. Her diary, written while in hiding from the Nazis, is a moving account of the reactions of a sensitive girl to contemporary conditions (*The Diary of a Young Girl,* 1947; Eng. tr., 1952; dramatized in 1956 as *The Diary of Anne Frank*). She died in the Belsen concentration camp.

Frank, Ilya Mikhailovich (ŭl'yä mēkhī'lŭvĭch fränk), 1908–, Soviet physicist. Shared with P. A. Cherenkov and I. Y. Tamm the 1958 Nobel Prize in Physics for studies of CHERENKOV effect that opened way to new studies of high-energy particles and cosmic radiation.

Frank, Jacob, c.1726–1791, Jewish sectarian and adventurer, b. Podolia. Real name was Jankiev Lebowicz. Influenced by extravagant doctrines of Sabbatai Zevi, he posed as a Messiah and was excommunicated. Many of his followers were later converted to true Catholicism.

Frankel, Charles, 1917–, American philosopher. Became teacher at Columbia 1939. Concerned with social philosophy, philosophy of history, and value theory. In 1965 he became Assistant Secretary of State for Educational and Cultural Affairs.

Frankel, Zacharias, 1801–1875, Jewish theologian. Head of conservative rabbinical seminary of Breslau. Stressed historical continuity in Judaism.

Frankenstein: see SHELLEY, MARY.

Frankfort. 1 City (pop. 15,302). W central Ind., SW of Lafayette; laid out 1830. Trade and processing center for farm and livestock area. Has railroad shops. **2** City (pop. 18,365), state cap. (since 1792), N central Ky., on both sides of Kentucky R.; settled 1779. City organized by Gen. James Wilkinson 1786. Trade and shipping center for blue-grass area and major whisky-distilling center. Here are Kentucky State Col., present capitol (1909). old capitol (1827–30), Liberty Hall (1796, perhaps designed by Thomas Jefferson), and cemetery with graves of Daniel and Rebecca Boone.

Frankfurt (frängk'fûrt, Ger. frängk'fŏŏrt) or **Frankfurt-am-Main** (äm-mīn'), city (pop. 623,172), Hesse, West Germany, on Main R. Historic, cultural, mfg., commercial, financial, and publishing center; river port. Produces chemicals, pharmaceutical articles, machinery, electrical equipment, clothing. Seat of university (opened 1914). Founded on site of Roman settlement; a royal residence under Carolingians; free imperial city from 1372; site of imperial elections from 1356 (see ELECTORS). Emperors-elect were crowned at Church of St. Bartholomew, then proceeded amid medieval pageantry to banquet at city hall, the Römer. Semiannual fairs, first mentioned 1240, brought city prosperity. Jews played important part until Nazi regime; Rothschild family originated here. Frankfurt accepted Reformation (1530), belonged to Schmalkaldic League (1536–47), was seat of diet of GERMAN CONFEDERATION (1815–66). In 1848–49 the Frankfurt Parliament met here at Church of St. Paul to plan unification of Germany; it adopted a federal constitution (excluding Austria) and offered imperial crown to FREDERICK WILLIAM IV of Prussia, whose refusal caused the failure of the whole scheme. Having sided with Austria in Austro-Prussian War, Frankfurt was annexed by Prussia (1866) and incorporated into Hesse-Nassau prov. After Second World War, when it was severely damaged, Frankfurt became hq. of U.S. occupation forces. Its historic landmarks, including the Römer, the Catholic Church of St. Bartholomew, the Protestant Church of St. Paul, and the house where Goethe was born, have been largely rebuilt.

Frankfurt, Treaty of, 1871: see VERSAILLES, TREATY OF, 1871.

Frankfurt-an-der-Oder (–än-dĕr-ō′dŭr), city (est. pop. 56,356), East Germany, in former state of Brandenburg, on Oder R. Mfg. of machinery, textiles, frankfurter sausages.

Frankfurter, Felix, 1882–1965, Associate Justice of U.S. Supreme Court (1939–62), b. Austria. Had long public record in support of liberal tradition.

frankincense, resin of E African and Arabian tree of genus *Boswellia*. It is gathered in lumps for use in incense for religious ceremonies—a use it has had since Old Testament times (Ex. 30.34).

Frankland, Sir Edward, 1825–99, English chemist. He evolved the theory of valence; made studies of flame, luminosity, and gases; discovered helium. His work on water purification was continued by his son **Percy Faraday Frankland** (1858–1946).

Franklin, Ann Smith, 1696–1763, American printer. Succeeded her husband, James Franklin, Benjamin Franklin's brother, in commercial printing business. Published Newport, R.I., *Mercury,* and printed legal documents, paper money of R.I., and almanac series.

Franklin, Benjamin, 1706–90, American statesman, printer, scientist, and writer, b. Boston. Went to Philadelphia as printer (1723). His common-sense philosophy and wit won attention, especially that of *Poor Richard's Almanack,* published 1732–57. Helped estab. (1751) present Univ. of Pennsylvania. Experiment with kite in a thunderstorm proved identity of lightning and electricity. Deputy postmaster general of colonies (1753–74). Proposed plan of union for colonies at ALBANY CONGRESS (1754). Agent for several colonies in England before American Revolution. Helped draft Declaration of Independence, which he signed. Successful diplomatic agent to France for new republic. Chosen commissioner (1781) to negotiate peace with Great Britain. Popular figure in France and England. Took part in Federal Constitutional Convention (1787). His autobiography is well known. His natural son, **William Franklin,** c.1730–1813, last royal governor of N.J., sided with Loyalists in American Revolution.

Franklin, Christine Ladd-: see LADD-FRANKLIN, CHRISTINE.

Franklin, Edward Curtis, 1862–1937, American chemist. Taught at Univ. of Kansas (1888–1903) and Stanford (1903–29). An authority on liquid ammonia, he was chemical warfare expert in First World War.

Franklin, Sir John, 1786–1847, British explorer in N Canada. Led two expeditions into arctic regions (1819–22, 1825–27). Set out in 1845 to seek Northwest Passage. Entire expedition of 129 men lost. More than 40 rescue parties subsequently sought traces of expedition, gaining immense geographical knowledge.

Evidence of expedition's tragic fate finally discovered in 1850s. Evidence found by McClintock showed Franklin had sighted passage.

Franklin, William: see FRANKLIN, BENJAMIN.

Franklin, William Suddards, 1863–1930, American physicist; worked on theory of alternating currents.

Franklin, provisional district: see NORTHWEST TERRITORIES, Canada.

Franklin. 1 Village (pop. 446), SE Idaho, NW of Preston at Utah line; founded 1860 by Mormons. Idaho's first permanent settlement. **2** City (1966 pop. 11,292), S central Ind., S of Indianapolis; laid out 1822. Franklin Col. is here. **3** Town (pop. 10,530), SE Mass., near R.I. line SW of Boston; settled 1660. Birthplace of Horace Mann. **4** Town (1965 pop. 8,051), central Tenn., on Harpeth R., SSW of Nashville. Scene of Civil War fight in 1864. **5** City (pop. 10,006), W central Wis., SSE of Eau Claire.

Franklin, State of, government (1784–88) formed by inhabitants of Washington, Sullivan, and Greene counties in present E Tenn. after N.C. ceded (June, 1784) to U.S. its western lands. Government under John Sevier passed out of existence when terms of its officers expired.

Franklin and Marshall College, at Lancaster, Pa.; for men; estab. 1787 as Franklin Col.; merged 1853 with Marshall Col. (1836) and reorganized.

Franklin D. Roosevelt Lake: see GRAND COULEE DAM.

Franklin Institute, in Philadelphia; for the promotion of mechanic arts; chartered and opened 1824, first of its kind in U.S. Named for Benjamin Franklin. An important research center, it includes Fels Planetarium, applied-science museum, technical library, Bartol Research Foundation (physics, now housed at Swarthmore Col.), and Biochemical Research Foundation. Has published journal since 1826; makes awards for work in physical sciences.

Franklin Park, village (pop. 18,322), NE Ill., a suburb NW of Chicago.

Franklin Square, residential city (pop. 32,483), SE N.Y., on W Long Isl., SW of Garden City.

Franks, group of Germanic tribes which by the 3d cent. A.D. had settled along the Rhine (Salian Franks in N, Ripuarian Franks in S). Salian Franks moved into Gaul in 4th cent. A.D. as Roman allies. Their leader CLOVIS I united all Franks under his kingship (481), accepted Christianity, founded dynasty of MEROVINGIANS. He and his successors conquered most of W and central Europe, but the Frankish empire was usually divided into several kingdoms, notably NEUSTRIA, AUSTRASIA, and BURGUNDY. In 8th cent. began rule of CAROLINGIANS, which culminated under CHARLEMAGNE. After Treaty of MERSEN (870), kingdom of W Franks became France; that of E Franks, Germany.

Franz, Robert (fränts′), 1815–92, German composer of about 350 lieder, intimate songs, which have some of the feeling of folk song.

Franz Josef Land (fräns′ jō′zŭf, fränts′ yō′zĕf), archipelago, c.8,000 sq. mi., in the Arctic Ocean, N of Novaya Zemlya. Claimed by USSR 1926. Its 85 islands include settlements and government observation stations, but are 90% covered by ice interspersed with poor lichen vegetation. Discovered by Karl Weyprecht and Julius van Payer (1873); explored by Fridtjof Nansen (1895–96) and others.

Franz Joseph: see FRANCIS JOSEPH.

Frascati (fräskä′tĕ), town (est. pop. 14,740), Latium, central Italy, in Alban Hills near site of anc. Tusculum. Noted for its wine and its fine Renaissance villas (e.g., Villa Aldobrandini, Villa Torlonia).

Frasch process, method of extracting sulfur from deposits. Three concentric pipes are sunk in bed; water heated above melting point of sulfur is sent down outer pipe. air under pressure down inner and sulfur is forced to surface through middle pipe. Process was named for Herman Frasch, 1851–1914, German-born American chemist who also devised methods for refining paraffin and for preparing industrial chemicals.

Fraser, Simon, 1776–1862, Canadian explorer and fur trader. Explored Fraser R. to its mouth while establishing trading posts for North West Co.

Fraser, chief river of B.C., Canada. Rises on W slope of the Rockies and flows c.350 mi. NW to Prince George, then c.500 mi. S and W to the Strait of Georgia S of Vancouver. Chief tributaries are Nechako, Quesnal, Thompson, Chilcotin, Blackwater and Lillooet rivers. Navigable to Yale, c.80 mi. from the mouth. Above this is scenic Fraser R. canyon. Discovered 1793 by Alexander Mackenzie and named for fur trader Simon Fraser. Gold discovered on upper reaches 1859, after which Cariboo Road opened area to settlement.

Fraserburgh (frä′zŭrbŭrŭ), burgh (pop. 10,462), Aberdeenshire, Scotland. Has a fine harbor and is one of chief herring fishing centers in Scotland.

fraternal orders, social organizations offering members a fellowship reminiscent of code and spirit of medieval guild. Local "lodges," in such orders as FREEMASONRY (oldest in the U.S.) and the Odd Fellows, use symbolic rituals. Orders may be restricted to one sex only, or may be mixed. See also GRANGER MOVEMENT.

fraud, willful misrepresentation intended to deprive another person of some right. "Actual" fraud requires intent to deceive another to his hurt, while a "constructive" fraud is a presumption of overreaching conduct arising when a profit is made from a relation of trust. Fraud generally constitutes only a tort, but may result in the crime of false pretenses. Fraud may also be interposed as defense in a suit based on a contract to which the defendant was fraudulently induced to assent.

Frauenfeld (frou′ŭnfĕlt), town (pop. 14,702), cap. of Thurgau canton, N Switzerland. Aluminum and food industries. Has 11th-cent. castle.

Fraunhofer, Joseph von (yō′zĕf fŭn froun′hōfŭr), 1787–1826, German optician and physicist. Studied and mapped the dark lines in solar spectrum called Fraunhofer lines.

Fray Bentos (frī băn′tōs), city (pop. c.15,000), SW Uruguay, port on Uruguay R.; founded 1859 as Independencia. Has large meat-packing plants.

Frayser's Farm: see SEVEN DAYS BATTLES.

Frazer, Sir James George, 1854–1941, Scottish classicist and anthropologist, known especially for *The Golden Bough* (1890), a study of magic and religion.

Fréchette, Louis Honoré (fräshĕt′), 1839–1908, French Canadian poet. First Canadian poet whose works were crowned by French Academy. His verse shows genuine feeling for nature and for heroic history of French Canada.

Fredegunde (frĕ″dŭgŭn′dŭ), c.545–597, Frankish queen. Married CHILPERIC I of Neustria after inducing him to murder his wife Galswintha (567). Resulting feud with BRUNHILDA of Austrasia continued until 613 under her son CLOTAIRE II.

Frederica, town (pop. 863), S central Del., SSE of Dover. At nearby Barratt's Chapel annual services commemorate formation of Methodist Episcopal Church.

Frederick, emperors and German kings. **Frederick I** or **Frederick Barbarossa** [Ital.,= red beard], c.1122–1190, of the house of HOHENSTAUFEN, succeeded his uncle Conrad III as German king (1152), pacified Germany by proclaiming a general land peace (1152), and was crowned emperor by Pope ADRIAN IV (1155). In four subsequent campaigns in Italy he struggled against the papacy (notably ALEXANDER III) and the cities of Lombardy (see LOMBARD LEAGUE). Though victorious at first, he was excommunicated by Alexander, defeated at Legnano (1176), and forced to accept the Lombard League's demands in the Peace of Constance (1183). He succeeded, however, in breaking the power of his Guelphic rival, HENRY THE LION, in 1180–81. In 1189 he set out on the Third Crusade. He drowned in Cilicia. Legend has him still alive, awaiting German unification in the KYFFHÄUSER. His grand-

son, **Frederick II,** 1194–1250, was the son of Emperor HENRY VI and of Empress CONSTANCE. Pope Innocent III invested him with Sicily (1197) and promoted his election as antiking to OTTO IV (1212). He was crowned king at Aachen after Otto's formal deposition (1215) and emperor at Rome (1220). His long-delayed crusade (1228–29), actually a state visit, resulted in the peaceful cession of Jerusalem, Nazareth, and Bethlehem to the Christians and his own coronation as king of Jerusalem. This treaty was denounced by Pope GREGORY IX and soon broken by the Moslems. Sporadic warfare between emperor and pope flared into a life-and-death struggle in 1239 and Gregory excommunicated the emperor. The struggle reached its culmination under INNOCENT IV, who declared Frederick deposed and excommunicated (1245). Frederick died of dysentery while the war was turning in his favor. It was left for his son CONRAD IV and his grandson CONRADIN to see the final downfall of their house and the triumph of the papacy. An Italian by birth and temperament, Frederick left German affairs largely to his sons Henry (whom he had imprisoned in 1235 after a rebellion) and Conrad IV. Henry made sweeping concessions to the German princes, and under Conrad Germany fell into anarchy. In Sicily, Frederick promoted far-seeing legal and fiscal reform and expanded commerce and industry. His universal gifts made him a patron and student of medicine, mathematics, astronomy, and poetry. His court at Palermo was of oriental splendor. **Frederick III,** 1415–93, duke of Styria (1435–93) and of Austria (1457–93), became head of the house of HAPSBURG at the death of his cousin Albert II. Elected German king (1440) and crowned emperor (1452), he overcame his many rivals and enemies by dint of sheer indolence and longevity. Through his marriage policy he came near to realizing his motto, AEIOU (*Austriae est imperare orbi universo:* "it is Austria's destiny to rule the whole world"). The marriage of his son MAXIMILIAN I with MARY OF BURGUNDY was indeed the cornerstone of Hapsburg world power.

Frederick III, 1831–88, emperor of Germany, king of Prussia (March–June, 1888); son of William I, father of William II. He was a liberal and a patron of art and learning. His consort, Victoria, daughter of Queen Victoria of England, was known after his death as Empress Frederick.

Frederick, Danish kings. **Frederick III,** 1609–70, king of Denmark and Norway (1648–70). Lost Skane, Halland, and Blekinge to Sweden in Treaties of Roskilde (1658) and Copenhagen (1660). His minister GRIFFENFELD drew up "King's Law" (*Kongelov*), which made Denmark an absolute hereditary monarchy (1665). **Frederick IV,** 1671–1730, king of Denmark and Norway (1699–1730). Joined alliance with Poland and Russia against Charles XII of Sweden in NORTHERN WAR. In peace treaties of 1720–21 he renounced claims to S Sweden but obtained ducal Schleswig. Consolidated absolutism, reduced corruption. **Frederick V,** 1723–66, king of Denmark and Norway (1746–66). His reign was period of commercial prosperity. **Frederick VI,** 1768–1839, king of Denmark (1808–39) and of Norway (1808–14). After English attack on Copenhagen (1807) he allied himself with Napoleon I and was punished at Congress of Vienna by transfer of Norway to Sweden. **Frederick VII,** 1808–63, king of Denmark (1848–63). The vexed SCHLESWIG-HOLSTEIN question caused trouble throughout his reign. **Frederick VIII,** 1843–1912, king of Denmark (1906–12) was the father of Christian X of Denmark and Haakon VII of Norway. **Frederick IX,** 1899–, king of Denmark (1947–), succeeded his father, Christian X.

Frederick, kings of Prussia. **Frederick I,** 1657–1713, elector of Brandenburg (1688–1713), was crowned first king of PRUSSIA in 1701. **Frederick II** or **Frederick the Great,** 1712–86, succeeded his father, FREDERICK WILLIAM I, in 1740. Despised by his father as effeminate esthete (he cultivated music, philosophy, and poetry), he spent a miserable youth. In 1730 he planned to flee abroad and barely escaped execution as a deserter. As soon as he became king, Frederick showed unexpected qualities of leadership and decision. With a spurious claim on parts of SILESIA, he opened the War of the AUSTRIAN SUCCESSION with a surprise attack on Maria Theresa 1704. Disregarding his allies, he twice concluded separate peace treaties with Maria Theresa (1742, 1745), securing Silesia. This war and the SEVEN YEARS WAR (1756–63) made Prussia the foremost military power of Europe and established Frederick as one of the great military geniuses of all time. Seconded by a brilliant general staff which included his brother prince Henry, Johann Carl von Winterfeldt, SCHWERIN, SEYDLITZ, and ZIETEN he developed a new concept of troop mobility in the field. He also was the prime mover for the first partition of POLAND (1772), which vastly increased his kingdom. The War of the BAVARIAN SUCCESSION (1778–79) and his creation of the Fürstenbund [league of princes] (1785), thwarted the schemes of Emperor JOSEPH II. A "benevolent despot," he promoted important legal and social reforms. His stormy friendship with VOLTAIRE is well known, as are his philosophical midnight suppers at Sans Souci. His writings, mostly in French, are collected in Œuvres de Frédéric le Grand (33 vols., 1846–57). His poetry is mediocre, his prose excellent. Though idolized by German nationalists, he despised German cultural aspirations. His philosophy was skeptical and materialistic. A champion of religious tolerance, he disliked all religions. He composed passable flute concertos and other music. Childless, he was succeeded by his nephew, Frederick William II. **Frederick III:** see FREDERICK III, emperor of Germany.

Frederick I, c.1372–1440, elector of Brandenburg (1417–40); as Frederick VI, burgrave of Nuremberg. Emperor Sigismund rewarded his good services by investing him with Brandenburg, of which he was the first Hohenzollern ruler.

Frederick, electors palatine. **Frederick III (the Pious),** 1515–76, reigned 1559–76. Inclining toward Calvinism, he caused HEIDELBERG CATECHISM to be drawn up (1563). **Frederick IV,** 1574–1610, reigned 1592–1610. Promoted and headed PROTESTANT UNION. **Frederick V:** see FREDERICK THE WINTER KING.

Frederick III (the Wise), 1463–1525, elector of Saxony (1486–1525). Founded Univ. of Wittenberg (1502). A protector of Luther, he gave him asylum at the Wartburg but himself remained a Catholic.

Frederick, city (pop. 21,744), NW Md., near Monocacy R., SE of Hagerstown; settled 1746. Processing center of farm area, with canneries and milk-receiving stations. Here are Hood Col., homes of Barbara Frietchie and R. B. Taney, and Francis Scott Key's grave.

Frederick Augustus, rulers of Saxony. **Frederick Augustus I** and **Frederick Augustus II,** electors: see AUGUSTUS II and AUGUSTUS III, kings of Poland. **Frederick Augustus III,** 1750–1827, elector (1763–1806), became king of Saxony as **Frederick Augustus I** in 1806 after concluding a separate peace with Napoleon I. Napoleon also made him titular duke of Warsaw (1807–14). He abandoned his alliance with Napoleon too late to avoid losing half his kingdom to Prussia at the Congress of Vienna (1815).

Frederick Barbarossa: see FREDERICK I, emperor.

Frederick Henry, 1584–1647, prince of Orange; son of William the Silent. As stadholder of the Netherlands (1625–47) he secured (1635) French and Swedish alliance in Thirty Years War; captured 's Hertogenbosch (1629), Maastricht (1632), and Breda (1637) from Spaniards. In 1631 stadholderate of United Provs. was made hereditary in his family. His rule is known as "The Golden Age of Frederick Henry" because of its great artists (Rembrandt, Frans Hals) and scientists, and the commerce, prosperity, and prestige of the Netherlands.

Frederick Louis, 1707–51, prince of Wales, eldest son of George II of England. His opposition to the king

was furthered by Bolingbroke and William Pitt. Father of George III.

Fredericksburg, city (pop. 13,639), E Va., on Rappahannock R., N of Richmond; settled 1671. Farm trade center. Seat of Mary Washington Col. of Univ. of Virginia. Here are Mary Washington's home (1772–89); "Kenmore," home of George Washington's sister; Rising Sun Tavern (c.1760); James Monroe's law office; and home of J.P. Jones. Nearby is Fredericksburg and Spotsylvania County Battlefields Memorial Natl. Military Park, commemorating Civil War battles of Fredericksburg, CHANCELLORSVILLE, Wilderness, and Spotsylvania Courthouse (see WILDERNESS CAMPAIGN). George Washington Birthplace Natl. Monument, including WAKEFIELD, and STRATFORD, home of Lee family, are ESE.

Fredericksburg, battle of, in Civil War, fought Dec. 13, 1862, at Fredericksburg, Va. A. E. Burnside, aiming for Richmond, sent his Union troops across Rappahannock R. in frontal assault on James Longstreet's impregnable position. A severe Union defeat, with losses of over 12,000.

Fredericksburg and Spotsylvania County Battlefields Memorial National Military Park: see NATIONAL PARKS AND MONUMENTS (table).

Frederick the Fair, c.1286–1330, German antiking (1314–26), duke of Austria. Elected by Hapsburg party as rival king to Emperor LOUIS IV. Renounced his rights in 1326.

Frederick the Great: see FREDERICK II, king of Prussia.

Frederick the Winter King, 1596–1632, king of Bohemia (1619–20), as Frederick V elector palatine (1610–20). The Protestant diet of Bohemia chose him king after deposing FERDINAND II. The expected help from his father-in-law, James I of England, did not materialize, and he was disastrously defeated at the White Mountain (1620). Nicknamed the Winter King for his short tenure, he was stripped of all his territories. Through his daughter Sophia he was grandfather of George I of England.

Frederick William, kings of Prussia. **Frederick William I,** 1688–1740, reigned 1713–40; known as the soldier-king. Laid foundation for Prussian greatness by creating efficient army and administration. Notoriously avaricious, he left surplus in treasury, avoided warfare. His tastes were coarse, and he despised his gifted heir, FREDERICK II. **Frederick William II,** 1744–97, nephew of Frederick II, reigned 1786–97. Defeated in French Revolutionary Wars, he made separate peace in 1795. Shared in Polish partitions of 1793, 1795. An amateur cellist, he was a patron of Mozart. His son, **Frederick William III,** 1770–1840, reigned 1797–1840. He accepted the harsh Treaty of TILSIT (1807) after his defeat at Jena by Napoleon I. Though weak and vacillating, he had the aid of such men as Karl vom und zum STEIN, K. A. von HARDENBERG, and SCHARNHORST, who reformed the Prussian state and prepared the way for the Prussian "War of Liberation" against Napoleon (1813–14). Joining the Holy Alliance in 1815, he became increasingly reactionary. His elder son, **Frederick William IV,** 1795–1861, reigned 1840–61. A romanticist, mystic, and half-hearted liberal, he crushed the revolution of March, 1848, and turned down the imperial crown offered him by the FRANKFURT Parliament (1849), arguing that a monarch by divine right could not receive authority from an elected assembly. His scheme for a German union was prevented by Austria in the Treaty of OLMÜTZ (1850). In 1857 his mental unbalance necessitated the regency of his brother and successor William I.

Frederick William, known as **the Great Elector,** 1620–88, elector of Brandenburg (1640–88). Secured E Pomerania and other territories at Peace of Westphalia (1648); rebuilt his devastated state after Thirty Years War; obtained full sovereignty over Prussia at Peace of OLIVA (1660). His victory over Charles XI of Sweden at Fehrbellin (1675) in third Dutch War increased his prestige. His son became king of Prussia as Frederick I (1701).

Frederick William, 1771–1815, duke of Brunswick; son and successor of CHARLES WILLIAM FERDINAND. Dispossessed of his duchy by Napoleon (1806), he seized it in a dashing raid of his free corps, the "Black Brunswickers" (1809), but soon had to flee to England. Was killed in the Waterloo campaign.

Fredericton, city (pop. 19,683), provincial cap. (since 1788), S central N.B., on St. John R. and NW of St. John; founded 1785 by United Empire Loyalists. Seat of Univ. of New Brunswick (provincially supported; coed.; opened 1800). Hunting and fishing center with lumbering and mfg. of wood and leather products.

Frederikshaab (frĭdh'rĭks-hôp), district (pop. 1,817) and town (pop. 1,038), SW Greenland. Settlement founded 1742; has radio and meteorological station.

free association: see ASSOCIATION; PSYCHOANALYSIS.

Free Church of Scotland: see SCOTLAND, FREE CHURCH OF.

Freedmen's Bureau, U.S. government agency, estab. by act of March 3, 1865, under name "bureau of refugees, freedmen, and abandoned lands," to aid and protect newly freed Negroes in South after Civil War. Organized under War Dept., bureau provided relief work for both blacks and whites in war-stricken areas, regulated Negro labor, managed abandoned and confiscated property, and supported education for Negroes. In its relief and educational activities bureau compiled an excellent record, often marred, however, by excesses of its local agents. Ultimately, bureau became little more than a political machine, organizing the black vote for Republican party. Work of bureau was discontinued in 1869, but its educational activities were carried on for another three years.

freedom: see LIBERTY.

freedom of the press; freedom of speech: see PRESS, FREEDOM OF THE; SPEECH, FREEDOM OF.

free enterprise, system in which ownership and control of means of production and distribution remain in private hands. See CAPITALISM.

Freehold, borough (pop. 9,140), E central N.J., ENE of Trenton; settled c.1650, called Monmouth Courthouse 1715–1801. Battle of MONMOUTH took place nearby. Philip Freneau lived here.

Freeman, Douglas Southall, 1886–1953, American editor and historian. Author of Pulitzer Prize-winning biographies of Robert E. Lee and George Washington.

Freeman, Edward Augustus, 1823–92, English historian. Major work was History of the Norman Conquest (6 vols., 1867–79). Others included History of Sicily and The Ottoman Power in Europe.

Freeman, Mary (Eleanor) Wilkins, 1852–1930, American author. Wrote on New England life as in A New England Nun and Other Stories (1891).

Freeman's Farm, battle of: see SARATOGA CAMPAIGN.

Freemasonry, teachings and practices of the secret fraternal order of Free and Accepted Masons. Not restricted to stoneworkers, it retains much of the spirit and code of the medieval masons' guild. Charity is enjoined on Masons and practiced by them. Custom is the supreme authority in the order, and its teachings include obedience to the law of the land. There has been strong opposition to such secret societies (see ANTI-MASONIC PARTY). The order–always an independent national group–has had adherents in many parts of the world, George Washington and Goethe among them.

Freeport. 1 City (pop. 26,628), NW Ill., WNW of Rockford; settled 1835. Trade and mfg. center in farm and dairy region. Battle with Black Hawk's Indian forces occurred nearby 1832. Douglas expounded famous "Freeport doctrine" in Lincoln-Douglas debate here 1858. **2** Town (pop. 4,055), SW Maine, on Casco Bay NE of Portland; settled c.1700. Papers which estab. Maine as independent state signed here 1820. **3** Village (1965 pop. 38,429), SE N.Y., on S shore of Long Isl., SSE of Hempstead; settled c.1650. Resort and deep-sea-fishing center with varied industries. **4** City (pop. 11,619), SE Texas, at mouth of Brazos R., S of Houston, in farm,

oil, and natural-gas region. Port with chemical industries, commercial fishing. Center of Brazosport industrial area. Federal sea-water purification plant opened 1961. Intracoastal Waterway crosses Brazos R. here. Historic VELASCO annexed 1957.

Freer, Charles Lang (frēr), 1856–1919, American art collector and industrial capitalist. Gave his collection and the building which houses it to Smithsonian Institution of Washington, D.C. Freer Gallery of Art is best known for its collection of works of Whistler and of Oriental masters.

freesia, fragrant flower (Freesia) native to S Africa. Grown from corms, largely in greenhouses, for winter and spring cutting. Five to seven white or yellow tubular blossoms are borne near tip of stem.

free silver. Free coinage of silver became a popular proposal in U.S. soon after panic of 1873 and a major political issue in the next quarter century. Hard times of 1873–78 stimulated advocacy of cheap money; GREENBACK PARTY flourished in local elections. Inflationists, not getting paper-money expansion, turned to silver. Silver-mining interests also wanted silver coinage. BLAND-ALLISON ACT of 1878 and SHERMAN SILVER PURCHASE ACT of 1890 represented compromises. POPULIST PARTY demanded free silver. Nomination of W. J. BRYAN in 1896 made free silver major issue of presidential campaign. McKinley's victories of 1896 and 1900, coupled with increasing gold supplies and returning prosperity, minimized free silver as a political issue.

Free-Soil party, in U.S. history, a political party born 1847–48 out of rising opposition to extension of slavery into territories newly acquired from Mexico. In 1848, vote for its ticket gave N.Y. to the Whigs, made Zachary Taylor President. Following Compromise of 1850 element in party known as BARNBURNERS returned to Democratic party, but radical antislavery men kept organization alive until 1854, when new Republican party absorbed it.

freethinkers, those who reach religious conclusions by reasoning, rejecting supernatural authority and ecclesiastical tradition. Name used in England c.1713 to denote esp. deists. In France it was associated with Voltaire and the Encyclopedists. In U.S. chief groups founded were American Rationalist Association, American Secular Union, and Freethinkers of America.

Freetown, city (pop. c.127,900), cap. of Sierra Leone; port on the Atlantic. Founded 1788 by the British as settlement for liberated slaves. Cap. of British West Africa (1808–74). Exports diamonds, iron ore, coffee, and cocoa. Seat of Fourah Bay Col., founded 1827, declared university college 1960.

free trade, commerce without restrictive duties. Domestic free trade is customary, but international commerce is frequently subjected to taxation. Theoretical basis for free trade is territorial division of labor: each region producing what it can most cheaply and best. In England, Adam Smith endorsed free trade, which was furthered by repeal of CORN LAWS; U.S. and many European states, however, have followed policies of protection. Trade barriers increasingly viewed as promoting international discord; in Europe, attempts are being made to further free trade. See EUROPEAN COMMUNITY; TARIFF.

free verse or vers libre (vĕr' lē'brŭ), term loosely used for rhymed or unrhymed verse made free of conventional and traditional limitations and restrictions in regard to metrical structure. Cadence, especially cadence of common speech, is often substituted for rhythmical meter. Writers of free verse include Whitman, Pound, Amy Lowell, H.D., John Gould Fletcher, and T. S. Eliot.

freezing: see MELTING POINT; REFRIGERATION.

Frege, Gottlob, (gôt'lōp frā'gŭ), 1848–1925, German philosopher and mathematician; a founder of modern logic. He demonstrated that all mathematics could be derived from logical principles and definitions and believed that verbal concepts were expressible as symbolic functions with one or more variables.

Freiberg (frī'bĕrk), city (est. pop. 46,567), East Germany, in former state of Saxony. Was long a lead-and silver-mining center. Has mining academy (founded 1765). Today mines lead and zinc and produces optical equipment.

Freiburg, Switzerland: see FRIBOURG.

Freiburg im Breisgau (Ger. frī'boŏrk ĭm brīs'gou), city (pop. 130,228), Baden-Württemberg, West Germany, near Black Forest. Archiepiscopal see; seat of university (founded 1457). Founded 1120; passed to Hapsburgs, with rest of Breisgau, 1368. Scene of French victory over imperials in Thirty Years War (1644). Held by France 1677–97 and 1744–48; passed to Baden 1805. Has splendid Gothic cathedral (begun in 12th cent.).

Freising (frī'zĭng), city (pop. 24,633), Upper Bavaria, on Isar R. Mfg. of agr. machinery, brewery implements, textiles. Founded 724. Prince-bishopric until 1803; diocese was united with that of Munich 1817. Cathedral was started in 8th cent.

Fréjus (frāzhüs'), town (est. pop. 13,500), Var dept., SE France, near Mediterranean. With Fréjus-Plage, on sea, is well-known Riviera resort. Preserves Roman ruins and cathedral with 5th-cent. baptistery.

Frelinghuysen, Frederick Theodore (frē'lĭnghī"zŭn), 1817–85, U.S. Secretary of State (1881–85). Urged reciprocity agreements with Latin America; generally carried on a patient, pacifistic policy.

Fremantle, principal port (pop. 30,600) of Western Australia, SW of Perth, at mouth of Swan R. and at terminus of Trans-Australian RR; founded 1829. Exports wheat, wool, fruit, and flour.

Frémont, John Charles (frē'mŏnt), 1813–90, American explorer, soldier, and political leader. His enthusiastic reports of explorations in West did much to publicize that region. Prominent in liberating Calif. from Mexico; governor there in 1847 until his quarrel with S. W. Kearny. U.S. Senator (1850–51). Republican candidate for President in 1856. Removed from command of Western Dept. in Civil War. Lost fortune in railroad venture (1870). Governor of Arizona Territory (1878–83). The Pathfinder, as he was called, is one of most controversial figures of Western history. His wife, **Jessie Benton Frémont,** 1824–1902, daughter of Thomas H. Benton, encouraged and aided her husband. Wrote accounts of her experiences to support household when their fortune was lost.

Fremont. 1 City (pop. 43,790), W Calif., N of San Jose. Mission San Jose de Guadalupe (1797) is here. **2** City (pop. 19,698), E central Nebr., on Platte R., WNW of Omaha; founded 1856. Trade and shipping center for grain-growing, dairying, and grazing prairie area. Seat of Midland Lutheran Col. **3** City (pop. 17,573), N Ohio, on Sandusky R., SE of Toledo. Industrial and trade center. Croghansville and Lower Sandusky settled after War of 1812, united 1829, named Fremont 1849.

Fremont Peak: see WIND RIVER RANGE.

Fremy, Edmond (ĕdmō' frāmē'), 1814–94, French chemist. Director of Mus. of Natural History in Paris 1879–91. His work on iron, steel, fats, and sulfuric acid was applied industrially.

French, Daniel Chester, 1850–1931, American sculptor. Executed first commission *The Minuteman* (Concord, Mass.) at age of 23. Among other works is the heroic Lincoln in Lincoln Memorial, Washington, D.C.

French Academy, first and chief constituent of the INSTITUT DE FRANCE. Founded 1635 by Cardinal Richelieu; suppressed 1793; reinstated 1803. Its chief aim was the governance of French literary effort, grammar, orthography, and rhetoric. Its dictionary (1694; 8th ed., 1932–35) and grammar (1932) are noted for conservatism. Another function is the awarding of prizes. Its 40 members (often called "the forty immortals") are self-perpetuating; elections may be vetoed by head of state. Members include mostly literary men but also other eminent Frenchmen, such as ecclesiastics and military men. Among prominent authors who failed to be admitted were Molière, Rousseau, Balzac, Stendhal, Flaubert.

French and Indian Wars, 1689–1763, name given to North American colonial wars between England and France in late 17th and 18th cent., roughly linked to wars of European coalitions. Ultimate aim was domination of eastern part of continent; wars were marked by capture of seaboard strongholds and Western forts and attacks on frontier settlements, including Indian border warfare. First war was King William's War, corresponding to European War of the GRAND ALLIANCE (1688–97), marked principally by frontier attacks on British colonies. Queen Anne's War (1701–13) corresponded to the War of the SPANISH SUCCESSION. King George's War (1744–48) was connected with War of the AUSTRIAN SUCCESSION. Last and most important conflict, called simply French and Indian War (1754–60), was linked to SEVEN YEARS WAR. British captured French forts in the West, Lord AMHERST captured Louisburg (1758), and Quebec fell to the British (see ABRAHAM, PLAINS OF). Treaty of Paris (1763) ended French control in Canada and the West.

French Broad River, rising in W N.C. in the Blue Ridge and flowing c.210 mi. N, WNW past Asheville into Tenn., joining Holston R. to form Tennessee R. near Knoxville. Douglas Dam forms L. Douglas.

French Cameroons: see CAMEROONS.

French Community, estab. by constitution of Fifth Republic (1958), superseding French Union. Originally consisted of Metropolitan France (France proper), twelve overseas territories (including Algeria and African and Polynesian territories), and four overseas departments (French Guiana, Guadeloupe, Martinique, Réunion). Member states were self-governing, but were represented through the institutions of the community in matters of common interest such as foreign policy, defense, finance. In 1960 all African states became independent, six choosing to retain membership and six to maintain "special relations." In 1962 Algeria won independence and ended its affiliation. Community's institutions are now only consultative.

French Congo: see FRENCH EQUATORIAL AFRICA.

French East India Company: see EAST INDIA COMPANY, FRENCH.

French Equatorial Africa, former French federation, W central Africa. Its four constituent territories were GABON, Middle Congo (now CONGO REPUBLIC), CHAD, and Ubangi-Shari (now CENTRAL AFRICAN REPUBLIC); cap. was Brazzaville. Little interest was shown in area until France founded Libreville in 1849; French authority over whole area was estab. 1894. Separate territories voted to become autonomous republics within French Community 1958; independence achieved for each state 1960.

French Guiana: see GUIANA.

French Guinea: see GUINEA, republic.

French horn: see WIND INSTRUMENTS; also *ill.,* p. 1062.

French India, former French overseas territory in India. Comprised five settlements: Pondicherry (or Pondichéry) and Karikal on Coromandel Coast, Madras, Yanaon (or Yanam) in Andhra Pradesh, Mahé on Malabar Coast, Kerala, and Chandernagor near Calcutta. CHANDERNAGOR was ceded 1952 to India. The others, under Indian administration since 1954, were ceded to India by treaty 1956 with formal transfer in 1962; now administered as PONDICHERRY special territory.

French Indo-China: see INDO-CHINA.

French language, Romance language. See LANGUAGE (table).

French Lick, resort town (pop. 1,954), S Ind., SSW of Bedford. Was French trading post in colonial times. Has sulfur springs.

Frenchman Bay, inlet of the Atlantic, S Maine, extending inland between Mt. Desert Isl. and mainland.

French North Africa, originally general name for ALGERIA, former French MOROCCO, and TUNISIA.

French Polynesia, overseas territory (c.1,554 sq. mi.; pop. c.75,000) of France, in S Pacific. Comprises Society, Marquesas, Tubai, Tuamotu, and Gambier islands. Cap. Papeete (pop. 18,057), on Tahiti. Exports copra, vanilla, and phosphates; tourism. French construction of nuclear test site begun 1966.

French Revolution, political upheaval which began in France in 1789 and which affected the whole world. Historians differ widely as to its "causes"—some see it as an intellectual movement, born from the liberal ENLIGHTENMENT of the 18th cent.; some, as a rebellion of the underprivileged classes against feudal oppression; some, as the assertion of the new capitalist bourgeoisie against an outdated and restrictive social and economic system. It is now generally held that the oppressive features of the *ancien régime* have been much exaggerated. The immediate cause of the revolution was without doubt the bankrupt state of the public treasury. The wars of the 17th and 18th cent., an iniquitous and inefficient system of taxation, waste, and intervention in the American Revolution had resulted in a gigantic public debt, which neither NECKER, nor CALONNE, nor LOMÉNIE DE BRIENNE was able to reduce. As last resort, LOUIS XVI called the STATES-GENERAL, which, it was hoped, would pass the necessary fiscal reforms. It convened at Versailles on May 5, 1789. From the start, the deputies of the third estate, joined by many members of the lower clergy and by a few nobles, pressed for sweeping political and social reforms that far exceeded the assembly's powers. Defying the king, they proclaimed themselves the National Assembly (June 17) and took an oath not to separate until a constitution had been made. The king yielded, but his dismissal of Necker led to the storming of the BASTILLE by an excited mob (July 14). Louis XVI, ever anxious to avoid bloodshed, gave in once more: Necker was recalled; the commune was estab. as city government of Paris; the National Guard was organized. On Aug. 4 the Assembly abolished all feudal privileges. Rumors of counterrevolutionary court intrigues were exploited by extremist demagogues, and on Oct. 5 a mob marched on Versailles and forcibly moved the royal family and the Assembly to Paris. Honoré de MIRABEAU, foreseeing the uncontrolled revolution that the king's weakness was about to unleash, tried to restore strength to the executive branch, but the Constituent Assembly (as the National Assembly was now called) drafted a constitution which reduced the executive to impotence (1791; its preamble was the famous DECLARATION OF THE RIGHTS OF MAN). Anticlerical legislation was capped when the clergy was required to take oaths to civil authority (1790), a measure which alienated many pious rural districts from the Revolution. The king decided to join those nobles who had already fled abroad (émigrés), but his flight (June 20–21, 1791) was arrested at Varennes. Brought back to Paris, Louis accepted the new constitution. In the Legislative Assembly the republican GIRONDISTS and the extreme JACOBINS and CORDELIERS gained the upper hand. "Liberty, Equality, Fraternity" became the watchword. Meanwhile, the émigrés were inciting other European courts to intervene. The Declaration of PILLNITZ played into the hands of the Girondists, who hoped that a foreign war would rally the nation to the republican cause. With the declaration of war on Austria (April 20, 1792) the FRENCH REVOLUTIONARY WARS began. Early reverses led to rumors of treason by the king and, particularly, Queen MARIE ANTOINETTE. A mob stormed the Tuileries palaces and massacred the SWISS GUARDS (Aug. 10, 1792); all police power was seized by the Paris commune (dominated by DANTON and MARAT); the Assembly suspended the king and ordered elections for a new body, the National Convention; and hundreds of royalist prisoners were killed in "spontaneous" mobs in the September Massacres. The Convention on Sept. 21 abolished the monarchy, set up the First Republic, and proceeded to try the king for treason. Louis's execution (Jan., 1793) led to royalist uprisings, notably in the VENDÉE, and was followed by the REIGN OF TERROR, in which ROBESPIERRE and his associates triumphed in turn over the more moderate Girondists and over his rivals Danton and HÉBERT. The republican constitution never became active; the Committee of Public Safety and the Revolutionary Tribunal reigned supreme. Robespierre's final excesses frightened the Convention into the coup d'état of 9 THERMIDOR (July 27, 1794), which resulted in his execution and in a period of relative reaction. Under the new constitution of 1795 the DIRECTORY came into existence. Its rule, which was marked by corruption, intrigues, run-away inflation, and bankruptcy, was ended by Bonaparte's coup d'état of 18 BRUMAIRE (Nov. 9, 1799). With the establishment of the CONSULATE (followed 1804 by Napoleon's empire), the victory of the moneyed bourgeoisie became final. Together with the French Revolutionary and Napoleonic wars, the French Revolution tore down the medieval structure of Europe and opened the paths of 19th-cent. liberalism.

French Revolutionary calendar, official calendar of France, 1793–1805. It was computed as from Sept. 22, 1792. Year was divided into 12 months of 30 days—Vendémiaire, Brumaire, Frimaire, Nivôse, Pluviôse, Ventôse, Germinal, Floréal, Prairial, Messidor, Thermidor, Fructidor; the 5 remaining days, called sansculottides, were feast days; in leap years the extra day (last of year) was Revolution Day. Months were divided into three decades; every 10th day (*décadi*) was day of rest. Example: 18 Brumaire of year VIII = Nov. 9, 1799.

French Revolutionary Wars, 1792–1802, general European war precipitated by the FRENCH REVOLUTION. The Declaration of PILLNITZ was used by the revolutionists as pretext for declaring war on Austria (April, 1792). Meeting little resistance at first, allied Austrian and Prussian armies invaded France, but the cannonade of VALMY proved a turning point. Late in 1792 the French overran the Austrian Netherlands, crossed the Rhine into Germany, and seized Savoy and Nice from Sardinia, while the National Convention proclaimed its determination to carry the revolution to all Europe. This and the execution of Louis XVI led to the formation of the First Coalition (Austria, Prussia, England, Holland, Spain). In the emergency, the Committee of Public Safety was created in France (see REIGN OF TERROR) and a *levée en masse* (universal conscription) was ordered. Guided by Lazare CARNOT, the committee raised new armies which, by the end of 1793, had driven the allies from France. The French again took the offensive in the Low Countries (1794). Holland, transformed into the BATAVIAN REPUBLIC, made peace in 1795, as did Prussia and Spain (Treaties of Basel, 1795). Against Austria and Sardinia, Carnot now evolved a plan of three-pronged attack: Jourdan was to advance SE from the Low Countries; Moreau was to strike at S Germany; Bonaparte was to strike at Piedmont and Lombardy, cross the Alps, and join Jourdan and Moreau. Only the Italian campaign, where one victory followed another (see NAPOLEON I) was completely successful and ended with the Treaty of CAMPO FORMIO (1797). England alone stayed in the war. Bonaparte's hope to strike at England by way of Egypt and India failed utterly and resulted in the destruction of the French fleet at Aboukir (1798). French interference in Italy, Switzerland, and Egypt led to the Second Coalition (England, Russia, Austria, Turkey, Portugal, Naples). Hastening back to France from Egypt, Bonaparte estab. himself as First Consul and set about to repair French losses in Italy and Switzerland. Faulty cooperation between the Austrians and Russians facilitated the victory of Masséna over the Russians at Zurich (Sept., 1799), followed by Suvarov's epic retreat across the Alps and the defection of Russia from the coalition. In 1800 Bonaparte crossed the St. Bernard and routed the Austrians at Marengo. Moreau's victory at Hohenlinden (Dec., 1800) demolished Austrian resistance. Austria consented to the Peace of LUNÉVILLE (1801) and the Second Coalition collapsed. England continued the war alone, expelling the French from Egypt and destroying the neutral Danish fleet (see COPENHAGEN, BATTLE OF), but after Pitt's retirement it also made peace with France and its allies (Spain and Batavian Republic) in the Treaty of AMIENS (1802). Peace was shortlived, for in 1803 began the Wars of NAPOLEON I.

French Sudan: see MALI. republic.

French Union: see FRENCH COMMUNITY.

French West Africa, former federation comprising territories of Dahomey, French Guinea, French Sudan, Ivory Coast, Mauretania, Niger, Senegal, and Upper Volta. Created 1895 with Dakar as cap.; dissolved 1958.

French West Indies: see WEST INDIES.

Freneau, Philip (frēnō'), 1752–1832, American poet. A Revolutionary prisoner on brig *Aurora,* he wrote "The Prison Ship." Was a Jeffersonian journalist, but his fame rests on lyrics ("The Wild Honeysuckle," "The Indian Burying Ground," "Eutaw Springs.")

frequency: see RADIO FREQUENCY; SOUND; VIBRATION; WAVE.

frequency modulation, radio transmitting and receiving system, called FM in contrast to older AM system (amplitude modulation). FM reduces static; improves fidelity. Amplitude of carrier wave is constant; its frequency varies.

Frescobaldi, Girolamo (jĕrō'lämō fräskōbäl'dē), 1583–1643, Italian organist and composer, organist at St. Peter's in Rome between 1608 and 1643. He wrote toccatas, fugues, and other works for organ.

Fresnel, Augustin Jean (ōgüstē' zhä' frȧnĕl') 1788–1827, French physicist, engineer. His researches on light phenomena, notably INTERFERENCE and POLARIZATION, lent support to wave theory of light.

Fresno (frĕz'nō), city (pop. 133,929), S central Calif., NNW of Bakersfield; founded 1872. Rail, processing, and marketing center for agr. area (grapes, raisins, figs, cotton). Fresno State Col. is here.

Freud, Sigmund (froid, Ger. zēk'mōont froit'), 1856–1939, Austrian psychiatrist, founder of PSYCHOANALYSIS. Freud treated hysteria using hypnosis methods developed by Joseph Breuer. This work by Freud marked beginning of psychoanalysis, revealed that symptoms of hysteria, traceable to early psychic trauma, represent undischarged emotional energy (conversion). Freud differed with Breuer over Freud's growing conviction that undefined energy causing conversion was sexual. Freud subsequently replaced hypnosis with free ASSOCIATION. His theories roused bitter antagonism. He was joined in 1906 by Eugen Bleuler, Jung, and Adler, but later Jung and Adler formed their own schools (1911–13) in protest against Freud's emphasis on infantile sexuality and the OEDIPUS COMPLEX. Basic structure of analysis is still Freudian and disagreement is in emphasis on concepts largely originated by Freud. After 1923 he used psychoanalytic theory in cultural studies. He greatly influenced anthropology, education, art, and literature.

Frey and **Freyja** or **Freya** (frī, frī'yŭ, frä'ä), Scandinavian deities (brother and sister) of fertility, love and matrimony, and light and peace. Frey's chief shrine was at Upsala, Sweden. Freyja is often confused with goddess FRIGG.

Freycinet, Louis Claude Desaulses de (dùsōls' dù fräsēnā'), 1779–1842, French marine officer. Commanded, and edited findings of, scientific expedition to South Pacific on the *Uranie* (1817–20).

Freyre, Gilberto (jĕlbĕr'tō frä'rù), 1900–, Brazilian sociologist and anthropologist, known for social history of plantation system in NE Brazil.

Freytag, Gustav (gŏō'stäf frī'täk), 1816–95, German author. His most lasting works include the comedy *The Journalists* (1855; Eng. tr., 1888) and the novels *Debit and Credit* (1855; Eng. tr., 1856) and *The Lost Manuscript* (1864; Eng. tr., 1865).

Friant Dam, central Calif., in San Joaquin R., E of Fresno; completed 1942. It is 320 ft. high. 3,430 ft. long. Forms Millerton L. It and Madera and Friant-Kern canals are part of CENTRAL VALLEY PROJECT.

friar's balsam, a tincture of BENZOIN, storax, aloes, and tolu balsam. Used medicinally for wounds, sores, sometimes for sore throat.

Fribourg (Fr. frēboōr'), Ger. *Freiburg,* canton (645 sq. mi.; pop. 159,194), W Switzerland, on N slopes of Bernese Alps. Agr., cattle raising, cheese production (Gruyère). City of **Fribourg** (pop. 32,583), its cap., on Sarine R., was founded 1157, joined Swiss Confederation 1481. Largely Catholic, it is an episcopal see and has a Catholic university and a cathedral (14th–15th cent.).

Frick, Ford Christopher, 1894–, American commissioner of baseball. Elected comissioner of Natl. Baseball League 1934. Became commissioner of major league baseball 1951.

Frick, Henry Clay, 1849–1919, American capitalist. Key figure in coke industry. Engineered expansion of Carnegie Steel Co. Largely responsible for antiunion policy of steel industry. His New York city mansion, together with art collection and large endowment, was willed to public as a museum.

friction, resistance between surfaces moving against one another. Factors on which it depends include nature of surfaces in contact, magnitude of force holding them together (including gravity), their weight, their chemical natures, and the attractive force between different materials. So-called **coefficient of friction:** quotient obtained by dividing the value of force necessary to move one body over another at constant speed by weight of the moving body. Coefficient varies with type of surface though weight of body is constant, but it is constant for any two given kinds of materials. **Fluid friction** is observed in flow of liquids and gases. It is affected by increased velocities and streamlining is attempt to minimize it.

Frida, Emil Boluslav: see VRCHLICKY, JAROSLAV.

Friday: see WEEK.

Fridley, city (1965 pop. 24,789), SE Minn., a suburb N of Minneapolis.

Fried, Alfred Hermann (frēt), 1864–1921, Austrian pacifist. Settled in Berlin. where he devoted himself to movement for international arbitration. Shared 1911 Nobel Peace Prize.

Friedel, Charles (shärl frēdĕl'), 1832–99, French chemist, mineralogist, co-developer of Friedel-Crafts reaction for production of hydrocarbons and ketones.

Friedlaender, Walter (frēd'lĕndùr), 1873–1966, American art historian, b. Berlin. A noted author on art of the 16th and 17th cent.

Friedland (frēt'länt), Czech *Frýdtlant,* town, N Bohemia, Czechoslovakia. Castle was seat of duchy awarded to Wallenstein in 1625.

Friedland or **Pravdinsk** (präv'dyĭnsk), town, RSFSR, formerly in East Prussia. Renamed on transfer to USSR (1945). Napoleon's victory at Friedland over Russians led to Treaty of Tilsit (1807).

Friedländer, Max J. (frēd'lĕndùr), 1867–1958, German art historian and museum director. Noted specialist on 15th- and 16th-cent. Dutch painting.

Friedrich, Caspar David (käs'pär dä'fĕt frē'drĭk), 1774–1840, German romantic landscape painter of melancholy and symbolic compositions.

Friedrichshafen (frē'drĭkshä''fún), town (pop. 32,319), Baden-Württemberg, West Germany, on L. of Constance. Mfg. of machine tools, motors. As home of Zeppelin works, greatly damaged in Second World War.

Friendly Islands: see TONGA.

SMALL CAPITALS = cross references. Pronunciation key on inside end pages. Abbreviations: p. 2.

Friends, Society of, religious body originating in England in 17th cent. under George Fox. He believed that a person needed no spiritual intermediary but could find understanding and guidance through "inward light" supplied by Holy Spirit. Fox's followers were known as Religious Society of Friends, popularly called Quakers because they trembled with emotion in meetings. Refused to worship in Established Church, to take oaths, and to bear arms in war. They rejected social and official titles and used "plain" forms of address (notably "thee" and "thou"). Mission effort took them to Asia, Africa, and America. Persecuted in New England, they found refuge in R.I. and in colony estab. (1682) for them by William Penn in Pa. In 1827 they split into "Hicksites" under Elias Hicks, who stressed inner guidance, and "Orthodox" group, with guidance by church elders. Meetings of Friends are periods of silent meditation, only those urged by "Inner Light" offering prayer or exhortation. Friends are noted for activity in education and social welfare. The American Friends Service Committee and the Service Council of the British Society of Friends were jointly awarded the 1947 Nobel Peace Prize.

Friern Barnet, London: see BARNET.

Fries, John, c.1750–1818, American rebel. Stirred Pennsylvania Germans into uprising (called Fries's Rebellion) against assessors and collectors of Federal property taxes (1799). Arrested, sentenced to death, but pardoned by Pres. John Adams.

Friesland (frēz'lŭnd) or **Frisia** (frĭ'zhù), province (1,325 sq. mi.; pop. 495,720), N Netherlands; cap. Leeuwarden. Comprises several of W FRISIAN ISLANDS. Intensive dairying and cattle raising. Frisians, a Germanic people, were conquered by Franks in 8th cent.; they have preserved their language. Medieval Frisia, under counts of HOLLAND, extended from Scheldt R. in W to Weser R. in E. After 1433 Frisians defied authority of their successive new masters—the dukes of Burgundy, Duke Albert of Saxony, and the Hapsburgs—until they were subdued by Emperor Charles V (1523). Friesland joined the United Provs. 1579. It appointed its own stadholders until 1748, when its stadholder, Prince William IV of Orange, became sole and hereditary stadholder of the Netherlands. EAST FRIESLAND, in Germany, had a separate history after 1454.

Friesz, Othon (ôtô' frēēs'), 1879–1949, French painter. Calligraphic style was influenced by impressionism.

frigate (frĭ'gĭt), originally a long, narrow type of vessel propelled by oars or sails in the Mediterranean. Now denotes a warship, with raised quarterdeck and forecastle, of about the same tonnage as the destroyer.

Frigg or **Frigga,** in Germanic mythology, wife of Woden. Originally an earth-goddess, she became confused with Scandinavian Freyja and thus was worshiped as goddess of fertility and love. From her likeness to Venus, the Latin day of Venus became in Germanic-speaking countries *Frigg's day* or *Friday*.

frijole (frēhō'lē), used mostly in plural **frijoles,** in Mexico and Spanish American countries, any cultivated bean of genus *Phaseolus;* in particular, small black bean second only to maize as article of diet.

Frisia: see FRIESLAND.

Frisian Islands (frĭ'zhùn), chain of islands off North Sea coast of Netherlands, Germany, and Denmark. W Frisian Isls., belonging to Netherlands, include Texel, Vlieland, Tershelling, Ameland. E Frisian Isls., in Germany, include Norderney, Borkum. N Frisian Isls., off Schleswig-Holstein, Germany, and S Jutland, Denmark, include Sylt, Föhr, Romo. Fishing, cattle raising are important on all the islands. Many bathing resorts.

Frisian language, Germanic language of Frisian Isls. and nearby coasts, the language most like English. See LANGUAGE (table).

Frithjof (frēt'yôf), hero of Icelandic saga (late 13th or early 14th cent.). Swedish poet Esaias Tegner used legends of him in *Frithjof's Saga* (1825).

Friuli (frēōō'lē), historic region, NE Italy and NW Yugoslavia, between E Alps and Adriatic. Includes a fertile plain and part of KARST region. Chief cities: Udine, Gorizia (both in Italy). Once a Lombard duchy (6th–8th cent.), Friuli was later divided into county of Gorizia (E) and county of Friuli (W). W Friuli (with Udine) passed to patriarchs of Aquileia (11th cent.), to Venice (1420), and to Austria (1797). Gorizia passed to Austria in 1500. Italy received W Friuli in 1866 and the rest in 1919, but by the Italian peace treaty of 1947 E Friuli (except Gorizia) was ceded to Yugoslavia, where it forms part of Slovenia. The remaining Italian part of Friuli was merged with what is left of VENEZIA GIULIA to form the autonomous province of **Friuli-Venezia Giulia** (vānā'tsyä jōō'lyä) (2,948 sq. mi.; pop. 1,205,222); cap. Udine.

Friulian, Rhaeto-Romanic language spoken in NE Italy. Similar to Romansh of Switzerland, but has been influenced by Venetian speech. See LANGUAGE (table).

Froben, Johannes (yōhä'nŭs frō'bùn), 1460–1527, German printer in Basel. He employed Erasmus as editor and the then unknown Hans Holbein as designer.

Frobenius, Leo (lā'ō frōbā'nēōōs), 1873–1938, German archaeologist and anthropologist, authority on prehistoric art and culture (esp. African).

Frobisher, Sir Martin (frō'bĭshùr), 1535?–1594, English mariner. Licensed by Queen Elizabeth, backed by merchants, he made three fruitless voyages (1576, 1577, 1578) to arctic regions seeking Northwest Passage. Commanded a ship in Sir Francis Drake's West Indies expedition (1585). Knighted for role in defeat of Spanish Armada (1588). Discovered (1576) **Frobisher Bay,** arm of the Atlantic, 150 mi. long, 20–40 mi. wide, cutting into SE Baffin Isl., Northwest Territories, Canada. There is a trading post and an air base at its head.

Froding, Gustaf, Swed. *Fröding* (frù'ding), 1860–1911, Swedish lyric poet.

Froebel, Friedrich Wilhelm August (frā'bùl, frō–, Ger. frē'drĭkh vĭl'hĕlm ou'gōost frù'bùl), 1782–1852, German educator and founder of KINDERGARTEN system. In 1837 he founded first kindergarten and in 1849 first kindergarten training school. His educational system, based on unity of nature, or God, reflects influence of Fichte and Schelling. He stressed importance of pleasant surroundings, self-activity, and physical training in child development. Most important work is *Menschenerziehung* (1826; Eng. tr., *The Education of Man*, 1877).

frog, amphibian living usually in quiet fresh water or woods. Skin is smooth, usually green or brown, often spotted. Most frog species hibernate underwater in mud over winter and lay eggs (which are fertilized as they are laid) in early spring. Gelatinous covering secreted by female causes eggs to adhere in mass, giving buoyancy, protection. In 3–10 days, small tadpole hatches; by summer's end metamorphosis from fish-like form to lung-breathing, tailless, carnivorous adult is completed (except in BULLFROG). Growth to adult size takes several years. Edible U.S. frogs include leopard, pickerel, and green frogs, common and southern bullfrogs, and Oregon red-legged frog. See also TREE FROG. See *ill.*, p. 1136.

Frohman, Charles, 1860–1915, American theatrical manager and producer. Bronson Howard's *Shenandoah* (1889) made him a successful producer. Known for ability to develop talent, he launched stars (e.g., Julia Marlowe, Maude Adams, Ethel Barrymore) and playwrights (e.g., Clyde Fitch, Barrie, Rostand). Headed Theatrical Syndicate of 1890s.

Froissart, Jean (zhä' früwäsär'), c.1337–1410?, French chronicler, poet, and courtier. His chronicle covers history of W Europe from early 14th cent. to 1400, i.e., first half of Hundred Years War. Historically it suffers from inaccuracy and unobjectiveness, but in literary merit ranks high and brings whole era to life.

Standard English translation is by John Bourchier, Lord Berners.

Fromm, Erich, 1900–, German-American psychoanalyst, author, and teacher; in U.S. after 1934. Fromm holds that industrial society imbues man with sense of isolation and doubt about meaning of life. Works include *Escape From Freedom* (1941) and *Beyond the Chains of Illusion* (1962).

Fronde (frôd), 1648–53, series of outbreaks in France during minority of Louis XIV. Caused by rivalry between Parlement of Paris and royal authority (as championed by MAZARIN); by the discontent of the great nobles; by the excessive fiscal burden of the people. The **Fronde of the Parlement,** 1648–49, began with the Parlement's refusal to register a fiscal edict. The court retired to Rueil; government forces under Louis II de CONDÉ blockaded Paris until a compromise peace was arranged. The arrest of the overbearing Condé, by Mazarin's orders, precipitated the much more serious **Fronde of the Princes,** 1650–53. Although Condé was released and Mazarin left for voluntary exile (1651), Condé with the support of several powerful nobles and the provincial parlements of S France waged open warfare on the government and even concluded an alliance with Spain, then at war with France. Defeated at the Faubourg Saint-Antoine (1652), he was given shelter in Paris through the intervention of Mlle de MONTPENSIER. His arrogance soon alienated the Parisians, and the Fronde disintegrated. In 1653 Mazarin returned to Paris, but Condé continued to wage war at the head of a Spanish army until the Peace of the PYRENEES (1659).

Frondizi, Arturo, 1908–, president of Argentina (1958–62). A liberal and an antiperonist, he supported a policy of economic austerity.

Frontenac, Louis de Buade, comte de (frŏn'tĭnăk), 1620–98, French governor of New France (1672–82, 1689–98). Dealt successfully with Indians, encouraged explorations, and aided in establishment of forts. Sought to restrain British in French and Indian Wars. Reestab. **Fort Frontenac,** on site of Kingston, Ont., Canada, in 1696. La Salle was made commandant of original fort (1673). Its capture by British in 1758 gave them control of L. Ontario.

frontier, borderland, in various senses. May be used to mean actual border between two countries or region about an international boundary. In U.S. history, however, it means border area of white settlement, vital in conquest of land between Atlantic and Pacific. Theory that frontier was a governing factor (if not the governing factor) in developing U.S. civilization as distinct from that of other nations was announced by F. J. Turner in 1893. Thesis is that American democracy was shaped by the frontier, by the contest of settler with wilderness. In the contest man learned self-reliance; he became assured of equality with other men and resentful of class distinctions and any attempt at civic and social coercion. Belief that the frontier shaped American thought and character is now almost universally accepted. It has been pointed out, however, that other factors (e.g., industrialization) were of telling weight, that individualism on the frontier has been perhaps overemphasized, and that the frontier farming community was possibly not as classless as has been pictured.

Front Range, part of Rocky Mts., extending c.300 mi. SE and S from SE Wyo. through central Colo. to Arkansas R. near Canon City. Stretches along E edge of Rockies and faces Great Plains. Includes Laramie Mts. and most of Rocky Mt. Natl. Park. In Colo. it forms part of Continental Divide. PIKES PEAK is in S part. Other peaks include Grays Peak (14,270 ft.), Mt. Evans (14,264 ft., with Inter-Univ. High Altitude Laboratory on summit), Longs Peak (14,255 ft.), Mt. Meeker (13,911 ft.), Arapaho or Arapahoe Peak (13,506 ft) with large glacier, and James Peak (13,-260 ft.) partly cut by Moffat Tunnel.

Front Royal, town (pop. 7,949), N central Va., on S Fork of Shenandoah R., S of Winchester. Skyline

Caverns (calcite formations) are nearby at N entrance of Shenandoah Natl. Park where Skyline Drive begins. In Shenandoah Valley campaign Stonewall Jackson routed Union troops here (1862).

Frost, Robert, 1874–1963, American poet, b. San Francisco; in New England after 1885. Won recognition while in England, where *A Boy's Will* (1913) and *North of Boston* (1914) appeared; was famous after return to U.S. Later volumes of lyrical, dramatic, and reflective poems include *West-running Brook* (1928), *Steeple Bush* (1947), and *In the Clearing* (1962).

frost or **hoarfrost,** feathery ice deposit caused by direct condensation of water vapor in crystalline form on surfaces at below-freezing temperatures. Frost-occurrence factors: topography, altitude, latitude, relation to land and water. Killing (to vegetation) frosts occur variously (Sept. 1–June 1 in Rocky Mt. region; Dec. 1–Mar. 1 along Gulf coast, parts of Calif., Ariz.).

Froude, James Anthony (frōōd), 1818–94, English historian. Wrote voluminously on many historical and biographical topics. Major work is *The History of England from the Fall of Wolsey to the Defeat of the Spanish Armada* (12 vols., 1856–70).

Froude, William, 1810–79, English engineer and naval architect. First to use model hulls experimentally, he improved ship design to reduce friction, increase stability.

fructose (frŏŏk'tōs), **levulose** (lĕ'vūlōs), or **fruit sugar,** simple SUGAR, a CARBOHYDRATE, found in honey and fruits; it is an isomer of GLUCOSE. It is one of the two components of the disaccharide, sucrose. See *ill.,* p. 178.

Frug, Simeon Samuel (sĭmyŏn' sŭmŏŏĕl' frŏŏk), 1860–1916, Russian-Jewish lyrical poet. Took up Zionist themes.

fruit, fully developed seed-producing organ of a FLOWER. Botanically it is the ripened ovary. Seedlike fruit (see GRAIN) of grasses is commonly called seed, and many food fruits are popularly called vegetables (e.g., beans, tomatoes). Fleshy fruits include the pome (e.g., apple, pear), berry (raspberry), and drupe (cherry, peach). See also NUT. See *ill.,* p. 858.

fruit fly, name for certain insects of family Trypetidae whose larvae bore through fruits and other plant parts. Damagers of North American fruit include apple or blueberry maggot, currant and gooseberry fruit fly, cherry fruit fly. Mexican, West Indian, and papaya fruit flies are serious pests farther south. Mediterranean fruit fly is a pest in many areas. Fruit (or vinegar) flies of genus *Drosophila* are much used in genetic research.

Fruitridge, Calif.: see SOUTH SACRAMENTO.

fruit sugar: see FRUCTOSE.

Frunze (frŏŏn'zĕ), city (1965 est. pop. 360,000), cap. of Kirgiz SSR, on branch of Turk-Sib RR. Mfg. of machinery and textiles. Founded 1846 as Uzbek fortress; taken by Russians 1862, and renamed Frunze 1926.

Fry, Christopher, 1907–, English dramatist. His verse plays, often compared in style to those of the Elizabethans, include *The Lady's Not for Burning* (1949), *Venus Observed* (1950), *A Sleep of Prisoners* (1951), and *The Dark Is Light Enough* (1954).

Fry, Elizabeth (Gurney), 1780–1845, English prison reformer and philanthropist. Worked to improve conditions of women in Newgate prison; her methods tried in other prisons.

Fry, Roger (Eliot), 1866–1934, English art critic and painter. Helped to introduce postimpressionists to England.

Frydlant: see FRIEDLAND, Czechoslovakia.

Frye, Northrop, 1912–, Canadian literary critic, professor at the Univ. of Toronto. His writings include *Anatomy of Criticism* (a synoptic work, 1957), *Fables of Identity* (1963), and *Natural Perspective* (1965).

Fuad I (fŏŏäd'), 1868–1936, first king of modern Egypt (1917–36), son of deposed khedive, Ismail Pasha. Became sultan in 1917, acquired title of king in 1922. Autocratic rule opposed by Wafd party. Succeeded by his son Farouk I.

Fuchs, Sir Vivian Ernest (fŏŏks'), 1908–, British explorer and geologist, led first overland crossing (1957–58) of Antarctic via South Pole. Knighted in 1958.

fuchsia (fū'shù), tropical American shrub (*Fuchsia*), with graceful, pendulous flowers in various shades of red and purple. Grown outdoors in mild climates and as pot or summer bedding plant elsewhere.

fuel, any substance which undergoes chemical or atomic change to produce usable heat or power. COMBUSTION is essential principle for all non-nuclear fuel forms; rapid oxidation of carbon and hydrogen produces heat energy (see HYDROCARBON; CARBOHYDRATE). Chemical fuels are valued in terms of heat (calories or B.T.U.) that a unit weight can produce. Nuclear fuel produces usable heat in a NUCLEAR REACTOR; here matter is converted to energy which appears as heat. Used as atomic fuels are fissionable atoms, which can be split into fragments (with a smaller total mass than the unsplit atom) and a quantity of energy. See also ATOMIC ENERGY; HEAT; PLUTONIUM; POWER; URANIUM.

fuel cell, simple, efficient device for converting chemical energy into electrical energy by reacting (burning) a fuel with oxygen. Both fuel and oxygen are supplied from outside, and therefore the device, unlike a storage battery, does not run down. Used in spacecraft because of high electricity production at low cost in weight.

Fuertes, Louis Agassiz (fūĕr'tēs), 1874–1927, American artist and naturalist. He is known for his paintings of birds which appeared in leading American ornithological works and for murals and habitat groups in the American Mus. of Natural History.

Fuessli, Johann Heinrich: see FUSELI, HENRY.

Fugger (fŏŏ'gûr), German family of merchant princes at Augsburg. Its fortune reached its zenith with Jacob Fugger II (1459–1525), who held a virtual monopoly in the mining and trading of silver, copper, and mercury. He lent immense sums to Emperor Maximilian I and financed the election of Charles V, who ennobled the family and granted them sovereign rights over their vast land holdings. Owning merchant fleets and palatial establishments throughout Europe, the Fuggers were also noted patrons of art and learning. Their fortunes declined with the Hapsburgs, whose wars they financed.

fugitive slave laws, in U.S. history, Federal acts of 1793 and 1850 providing for return between states of escaped Negro slaves. As Northern states abolished slavery they relaxed enforcement of 1793 law; abolitionism brought the UNDERGROUND RAILROAD. Many Northern states passed personal liberty laws allowing fugitives jury trial; others forbade state officials to help capture alleged fugitive slaves or to lodge them in state jails. As a concession to the South, COMPROMISE of 1850 incorporated a more rigorous fugitive slave law. Required "all good citizens" to help execute it; heavily penalized anyone aiding fugitive slaves; denied fugitive jury trial and right to give testimony. New personal-liberty laws of Northern states contradicted 1850 legislation; abolitionists fearlessly defied it. Trials of fugitive slave cases increased sectional hostility. Congress repealed both acts in 1864.

fugue (fūg) [Fr., from Ital.,= flight], in music, a composition in which the basic principle is imitative counterpoint of several voices. The theme (subject) is stated in each voice successively and reappears from time to time throughout the composition. The peak of fugue writing was reached with J. S. Bach's *Art of the Fugue,* a collection of some 20 fugues and canons based on the same subject. Fugue writing neglected after Beethoven, but modern composers show renewed interest in it.

Fujiyama (fŏŏ"jēyä'mä) or **Mount Fuji,** sacred mountain, 12,389 ft. high, central Honshu, Japan; highest point in Honshu. Symmetrical cone with dormant volcanic crater at summit.

Fukien (fŏŏjyĕn'), province (c.46,00 sq. mi.; pop. c.13,680,000), SE China, on Formosa Strait; cap. Foochow. Largely mountainous. Chief rivers are Min and Lung. Amoy is only port which can accommodate large vessels. Lumbering and fishing important. Once a great tea center. Extensive iron, coal, and manganese deposits are scarcely exploited. Located opposite Taiwan, area has maintained large numbers of troops since 1950.

Fukuoka (fŏŏkŏŏ'ōkä), city (pop. 647,122), cap. of Fukuoka prefecture, N Kyushu, Japan; port on Hakata Bay. Largest city on Kyushu. Textile center. Seat of five universities and three noted shrines.

Fulani (fŏŏlä'nē), people of W Africa. Numbering c.7,000,000, they are of mixed Negro and Berber origin. They embraced Islam in 11th cent., and both as a sedentary and as a nomadic people have played important part in the history of W Africa.

Fulbright, James William, 1905–, U.S. Senator from Ark. (1945–). Gained international reputation from the Fulbright Act (1946), which provided for exchange of students and teachers between U.S. and many other countries. Chairman of Senate Foreign Relations Committee (1959–).

Fulda, Ludwig (lŏŏt'vĭkh fŏŏl'dä), 1862–1939, German playwright. His works include *Der Talisman* (1893) and *The Pirate* (1911; adapted by S. N. Behrman 1942). Also translated Ibsen, Molière, Shakespeare, and Spanish dramatists.

Fulda (fŏŏl'dä), city (pop. 45,216), Hesse, West Germany, on Fulda R. Grew around Benedictine abbey founded 744 by St. Boniface. From here Christianity spread through central Germany. Abbots held temporal power under Holy Roman Empire; became prince-bishops 1752. Secularized 1802, Fulda passed to Electoral Hesse in 1815. Still an episcopal see, Fulda is meeting place of annual conference of Catholic bishops of Germany. Historic buildings include baroque cathedral, where St. Boniface is buried, and Church of St. Michael (9th cent.).

Fulham, included in HAMMERSMITH London borough since 1965. Has a palace of the bishops of London.

Fulk (fŭlk), 1092–1143, king of Jerusalem (1131–43), count of Anjou (1109–29). Journeyed to Holy Land 1120 and again 1129, when he made over Anjou to his son Geoffrey IV (Geoffrey Plantagenet). Married daughter of Baldwin II of Jerusalem, whom he succeeded as king.

Fuller, George, 1822–84, American portrait, figure, and landscape painter.

Fuller, Henry Blake, 1857–1929, American author. His novels are divided into romantic novels laid in Europe (e.g., *The Chevalier of Pensieri-Vani,* 1890) and realistic works about the Chicago scene (e.g., *The Cliff-Dwellers,* 1893). He also wrote short stories.

Fuller, John Frederick Charles, 1878–, English soldier. A military analyst and proponent of mechanized warfare, he greatly influenced military thinking on the Continent.

Fuller, (Sarah) Margaret, 1810–50, American writer. Translated Eckermann's *Conversations with Goethe* (1839), was a feminist (*Woman in the Nineteenth Century,* 1845), editor 1840–42 of *Dial* (see TRANSCENDENTALISM), and critic. In Rome she married Marchese Ossoli and supported the revolution of 1848–49; both drowned in shipwreck on way to U.S.

Fuller, Melville Weston, 1833–1910, Chief Justice of the United States (1888–1910). Leaned toward strict construction of Constitution.

Fuller, R(ichard) Buckminster, 1895–, American architect and engineer, designer of revolutionary technological devices to solve the problems of modern living. Invented the geodesic dome.

Fuller, Thomas, 1608–61, English writer, a moderate Anglican clergyman, compiler of antiquary *Worthies of England* (1662), author of *History of the Holy Warre* (1639) and *The Holy State and the Profane State* (1642).

fuller's earth, a sedimentary clay which has the property of absorbing basic colors. Chiefly used in clarifying petroleum and refining edible oils.

Fullerton, city (pop. 56,180), S Calif., SE of Los Angeles; founded 1887.

fulminate (fŭl′mĭnāt), commonly a name for explosive, crystalline mercury salt of fulminic acid, used as detonator when mixed with potassium chlorate.

Fulton, Robert, 1765–1815, American inventor, engineer, painter. His *Clermont*, launched in 1807, though not first steamboat in America, was first to be commercially successful in American waters.

Fulton. 1 City (pop. 11,131), central Mo., NE of Jefferson City, in farm area; founded 1825. Seat of Westminster Col. **2** City (pop. 14,261), N central N.Y., on Oswego R., NNW of Syracuse.

Fulvia (fŭl′vēū), d. 40 B.C., Roman woman. Her third husband was Marc ANTONY. She led an unsuccessful revolt against Augustus (40 B.C.).

fumitory, Old World herb (*Fumaria officinalis*) with red-tipped purplish flowers. It is naturalized in North America. Climbing fumitory or Allegheny vine (*Adlumia fungosa*) is a North American vine.

Funafuti: see ELLICE ISLANDS.

Funchal (fōōnshäl′), city (pop. 43,706), chief city of Madeira isl., Portugal. Port and resort. Cathedral built 15th cent.

function, in mathematics, rule which associates with each given value of a variable (domain of the independent variable) a definite value of a second variable (range, or image, of the dependent variable). For example, the distance a body falls is a function of the time it is allowed to fall.

fundamentalism, conservative religious movement in Protestant denominations early in 20th cent. Aim was to maintain traditional interpretations of Bible and fundamental doctrines of faith against what they considered threat of scientific discoveries. Such doctrines were the Virgin birth, physical resurrection of Christ, infallibility of Scriptures, substitutional atonement, and physical second coming of Christ. There were bitter controversies. In 1925, William Jennings Bryan, a fundamentalist leader, won state's case in famous SCOPES TRIAL.

Fundamental Orders, in U.S. history, basic law of Conn. colony, 1639–62. Contained preamble and 11 orders, including voting restrictions. Placed welfare of community over that of individual.

Fundy, Bay of, inlet of the Atlantic (100 mi. long, 60 mi. wide at entrance), between U.S. (NE Maine) and Canada. In its upper arms, Chignecto Bay and Minas Basin, its tides or bore rise to 70 ft. Some flatlands have been diked off and reclaimed. Annapolis Royal, on N.S. shore, is oldest settlement in Canada. St. John, N.B., is chief port.

Fundy National Park, 80 sq. mi., S N.B., Canada, on Bay of Fundy and NE of St. John; estab. 1948.

Fünfkirchen, Hungary: see PECS.

fungicide, chemical used to destroy fungi. Sprayed or dusted on plants, or applied to seeds, soils, woods, or fabrics. Sulfur, copper (Bordeaux or Burgundy mixture), and organic mercury compounds are used to destroy or prevent fungus diseases of plants.

fungus (fŭn′gŭs), plural **fungi** (fŭn′jī), simple plant lacking true roots, stems, and leaves and belonging like algae to lowest division of plant kingdom. Unlike algae the fungi have no chlorophyll and must get food from living or dead organic matter. Certain fungi are cultivated to obtain the ANTIBIOTIC SUBSTANCES they produce. Types of fungi include MOLD; MUSHROOM; YEAST. BACTERIA are sometimes classed as a type of fungi. See *ill.*, p. 859.

Funk, Casimir (kä′zĭmēr fōōngk′), 1884–, American biochemist. Pioneer in the study of vitamins.

Funston, Frederick, 1865–1917, U.S. general. Captured Emilio AGUINALDO in 1901. Commanded occupying troops at Veracruz in 1914.

fur, hairy covering of an animal, especially the skins of such animals as have thick, soft, close-growing hair next to the skin itself and coarser protective hair above it. Term *fur* extends to dressed sheep and lamb skins prepared for wearing with hair kept on and (usually) curled (persian lamb, karakul, astrakhan, and mouton). Since prehistoric days man has used furs for clothing. Some of the more prized furs are sable, marten, mink, ermine, and chinchilla. Staple fur of great fur-trading days in North America was beaver. Fur trade reached its peak in wilderness of North America and Asia from 17th to early 19th cent. Effect in opening wilderness was even more striking in Canada. Important fur-trading companies were HUDSON'S BAY COMPANY, NORTH WEST COMPANY, and AMERICAN FUR COMPANY. Advance of settlement, depletion of beaver and other fur-bearing animals, and decline in importance of beaver hat ended day of fur trader in 1840s in U.S. and S Canada. Later threat of extinction of fur seal led to BERING SEA FUR-SEAL CONTROVERSY. Preparation and sale of furs remains, however, a very considerable business; fur farming has become in U.S. and Canada a major industry in 20th cent.

furfural (fûr′fûrăl″) or **furfuraldehyde,** ALDEHYDE produced from corncobs. It is a colorless, oily liquid with aromatic odor. Used as a solvent and in making deodorants, disinfectants, preservatives.

Furies, goddesses of vengeance: see ERINYES.

Furka (fōōr′kä), road, central Switzerland, linking Uri and Valais cantons. Built 1864–66, it crosses Furka Pass, 7,971 ft. high. A rail line goes through Furka Tunnel.

Furman University, at Greenville, S.C.; coed.; opened 1827 at Edgefield as Furman Academy and Theological Inst. Moved 1851 and rechartered under present name.

Furneaux Islands (fûr′nō), group in Bass Strait between Tasmania, to which it belongs, and Australia; discovered 1773. Largest is Flinders Isl. Sheep, dairy products, tin.

Furness, hilly peninsula of Lancashire, England. In SW are rich iron mines and great steelworks which center at Barrow-in-Furness.

Fürth (fûrt), city (pop. 98,643), N central Bavaria, on Regnitz R., near Nuremberg. Mfg. center; has toy and glass industries.

Furtwängler, Adolf (ä′dôlf fōōrt′věng-lùr), 1853–1907, German archaeologist, authority on antique sculpture, vases, and gems.

furuncle: see BOIL.

furze, spiny Old World shrub (*Ulex europaeus*), also called gorse. It has scalelike leaves and fragrant yellow pealike flowers. Often used as sand binder in the U.S.

fuse, electric, safety device in electric circuit; when current exceeds safe amount, fuse breaks circuit, stopping flow of electricity.

Fuseli, Henry (fū′zĭlē), 1741–1825, Anglo-Swiss artist, b. Zurich; also called Johann Heinrich Fuessli or Füssli. Famous for drawings ranging from neoclassical to demonic. Was a friend of William Blake.

fusel oil (fū′zŭl), colorless liquid with disagreeable odor and taste. It is a mixture of higher alcohols found as a contaminant; it is a by-product in the production of ethyl alcohol by fermentation. Fusel oil causes temporary headaches when present as a contaminant in alcoholic beverages.

Fushun (fōō′shŭn′), city (pop. 985,000), NE Liaoning prov., China. Major industrial center. The Fushun coal mine is one of the largest in the world.

fusion, in physics: see ATOMIC ENERGY; HEAT; HYDROGEN BOMB; MELTING POINT.

Füssli, Johann Heinrich: see FUSELI, HENRY.

Fust, Johann, d. 1466, printer at Mainz. Johann Gutenberg, unable to repay Fust's loans, had to give Fust his press and types. Fust and his partner, Peter Schöffer, were first to print in colors and among the first to use Greek type (1465). Issued first dated book (1457).

Fustel de Coulanges, Numa Denis (nümä' dŭnē' füstĕl' du kŏŏlãzh'), 1830–89, French historian. His *Ancient City* (1864) traced growth of Greek and Roman institutions; *Histoire des institutions politiques de l'ancienne France* (6 vols., 1888–92) stressed the Roman instead of German origins of feudalism.

futurism, Italian movement in art and literature launched 1909 by poet Marinetti to glorify dynamism of the machine age.

Fyn (fün), island (1,149 sq. mi.; pop. 376,872), Denmark, in Baltic Sea, between Little Belt (W) and Great Belt (E); chief city Odense. Second largest Danish island. Fertile lowland; it has dairy farming and cattle breeding.

Fyne, Loch (lŏkh fīn'), arm of Firth of Clyde, Argyllshire, Scotland. Famous for its herring fisheries. Leading city on Loch is Inverary.

Fyt, Jan (yän' fīt'), 1611–61, Flemish animal painter and etcher. Collaborated with Rubens and Jordaens.

Fyzabad or **Faizabad** (fī'zúbăd), town, Uttar Pradesh, India, joint municipality with Ajodhya (total pop. 82,497). Fyzabad was cap. (1724–75) of kingdom of Oudh. Ajodhya or Ayodhya was cap. of kingdom of Kosala (7th. cent. B.C.) and is sacred to Hindus.

Ga, chemical symbol of the element GALLIUM.

Gaberones, town, cap. of Botswana. In 1965 it became administrative cap. of Bechuanaland, which until that time had been administered from Mafeking, Republic of South Africa.

Gabès (gä'bĕs), city (est. pop. 24,420), SE Tunisia, on the Gulf of Gabes, an arm of the Mediterranean. Fishing port; date-producing oases nearby.

Gabirol: see IBN GABIROL, SOLOMON BEN JUDAH.

Gable, Clark, 1901–60, American film actor. After his film debut in 1930, he became symbol of rugged American male with his performance in *It Happened One Night* (1934). Best-remembered role was Rhett Butler in *Gone With the Wind* (1941).

Gablonz, Czechoslovakia: see JABLONEC NAD NISOU.

Gabo, Naum (noum' gä'bō), 1890–, American sculptor, b. Russia; brother of Antoine Pevsner. A leader of constructivism, he worked after 1921 in Germany, Paris, and London. Came to U.S. 1946. Has executed much nonobjective sculpture in transparent plastics.

Gabon (gäbô'), republic (c.102,300 sq. mi.; pop. c.454,000), W Africa; cap. LIBREVILLE. Coastal lowlands; some mountains in N; country lies mostly within Ogoué R. basin. Chief export is tropical hardwoods. Mineral wealth includes manganese, petroleum, uranium, iron ore, and gold. Official language is French. Portuguese explored Gabon coast in 15th cent. Dutch, English, and French carried on slave trade. The French explored region after 1847, and in 1885 Congress of Berlin recognized French rights. In 1890 it became part of French Congo; was later part of French Equatorial Africa. Became autonomous republic within French Community 1958 and achieved independence 1960, when it was admitted to UN. Leon M'Ba became first president and retained post after political unrest in 1964.

Gabriel (gā'–) [Heb.,= man of God], archangel, the divine herald. In Bible he appears to Daniel, to Zacharias, and to the Virgin Mary in the Annunciation. Dan. 8.16; 9.21; Luke 1.19,26,27. Christian tradition makes Gabriel the archangel trumpeter of the Last Judgment. 1 Thes. 4.16. In Islam, Gabriel revealed the Koran to Mohammed. Feast: March 24.

Gabriel, Jacques Ange (zhäk' äzh gäbrēĕl'), c.1698–1782, French architect, who designed Place de la Concorde (Paris) and finished Petit Trianon (Versailles).

Gabrieli, Giovanni (gäbrēä'lē), 1557?–1612, Italian organist and composer. His music shows the beginnings of baroque techniques; thus, his *Sonata pian' e forte* employs the baroque use of contrasts in dynamics and contains elements of modern orchestration.

Gabrilowitsch, Ossip (ô'sĭp gäbrĭlô'vĭch), 1878–1936, Russian-American pianist and conductor. Conductor of the Detroit Symphony Orchestra, 1918–36.

Gad, son of Jacob, ancestor of one of 12 tribes of Israel. Tribe settled in GILEAD. Gen. 30.11; 35.26; 49.19; Num. 2.14; 13.15; 32.1,2,34; Deut. 3.12; 33.20; Joshua 13.24; 1 Chron. 5.18,26; 12.8,14.

Gadames: see GHADAMES.

Gadara (gä'–), anc. city, SE of Sea of Galilee, in the Decapolis. The "country of the Gadarenes"–or Gergesenes or Gerasenes–given in Bible as scene of miracle of the possessed swine probably refers not to this city but to obscure town on E shore of Sea of Galilee. Mat. 8.28; Mark 5.1; Luke 8.26.

Gadda, Carlo Emilio (kär'lō ämē'lēō gäd'dà), 1893–, Italian writer. Among his novels are *Il castello di Udine* (1934) and *Quer pasticciaccio brutto de via Merulana* (1957).

Gaddi (gäd' de), family of Florentine artists. **Gaddo Gaddi** (gäd'dō), c.1260–c.1333, painter and mosaicist, was probably an associate of Cimabue and Giotto. His son, **Taddeo Gaddi,** c.1300–c.1366, was godson and pupil of Giotto, whom he assisted for 24 years. Also painters were Taddeo's sons, **Agnolo Gaddi,** c.1350–1396, and **Giovanni Gaddi,** d. 1383.

gadolinium (gädúlī'nēŭm), rare metallic element of RARE EARTHS (symbol = Gd; see also ELEMENT, table).

Gadsden, James, 1788–1858, American railroad promoter and diplomat. Urged reconstruction of railroad from South to the Pacific. Minister to Mexico (1853–56); negotiated GADSDEN PURCHASE. Recalled for exceeding instructions.

Gadsden, industrial city (pop. 58,088), NE Ala., near Lookout Mts., NE of Birmingham; founded c.1840. Alabama City annexed 1932. Iron, coal, limestone, sand, clay, and timber in area.

Gadsden Purchase, strip of land purchased (1853) by U.S. from Mexico. Pres. Franklin Pierce wanted to insure U.S. possession of Mesilla Valley near the Rio Grande–most practicable route for southern railroad to the Pacific. James GADSDEN negotiated purchase. Area of c.30,000 sq. mi., purchased for $10,000,000, now forms extreme S N.Mex. and Ariz. S of the Gila.

Gadshill (gädz'hĭl), low hill, Kent, England. Scene of Falstaff's robberies in Shakespeare's *Henry IV.*

Gaea (jē'ù) [Gr.,= earth], Greek earth-goddess; daughter of Chaos, mother of Uranus and Pontus. Mother by Uranus of Cyclopes and Titans, by Pontus of five sea-deities. Worshiped as mother of all things, a counselor of gods and men. Oracles of Delphi and Olympia traced their origin to her.

Gaelic (gā'lĭk), Celtic languages spoken in Ireland (Irish), Highland Scotland (Scottish or Scottish Gaelic), and on the Isle of Man (Manx). Erse is sometimes a synonym for Gaelic. See LANGUAGE (table).

Gaelic literature, literature of Gaelic-speaking Ireland and Scotland. Irish literature is divided into Old Irish (before 900), Middle Irish (until 1350), Late Middle or Early Modern Irish (until 1650), and Modern Irish (from 1650). Old Irish works survive in Middle Irish copies (e.g., Book of Leinster). Middle Irish literature consists of two groups of romances or sagas: the Red Branch or Ulster cycle has pagan heroes (e.g., Cuchulain) and simple style; the Fenian cycle, later and more romantic, includes Christianity in the time of the poet OSSIAN. In the 16th and 17th cent. the rise of modern Irish prose culminated in the work of Geoffrey Keating (d. 1650?), and the bardic tradition gave way to less formal meters in a poetic revival. Gaelic poetry in Ireland declined in and after Cromwell's time and again when the 19th cent. potato famine struck Ireland. Since the 16th cent. Scottish Gaelic literature has been separate. The 1745 rebellion of Charles Edward Stuart led to an outburst of poetry by such men as Alexander Macdonald. Controversy over *Ossian* of James MACPHERSON renewed interest in Gaelic, and some Highland writers have used it in the 19th and 20th cent. In the late 19th cent., in Ireland, the Gaelic League and Douglas Hyde led a successful Gaelic revival.

Gaeta (gää'tä), city (est. pop. 19,188), S Latium, central Italy; Mediterranean port on Gulf of Gaeta. Long a stronghold of kingdom of Naples. On its fall to Victor Emmanuel II of Sardinia after long siege (1860–61), the kingdom of Italy was proclaimed.

Gaffney, city (pop. 10,435), NW S.C., NE of Spartanburg near N.C. line, in cotton, grain, and peach region; settled early 19th cent. Seat of Limestone Col. Kings Mountain Natl. Military Park is nearby.

Gafsa (gäf'sù), anc. *Capsa*, town (pop. 24,345), S central Tunisia, in an oasis. Exports phosphates, dates, and olives. Surrounding region has yielded artifacts of an upper Paleolithic culture (Capsian) of N Africa and S Europe.

Gagarin, Yuri Alekseyevich (yōō'rē ŭlyĭksyä'vĭch gägä'rĭn), 1934–, Russian astronaut (cosmonaut), first man in space. Made first manned orbital flight April 12, 1961.

Gage, Thomas, d. 1656, English traveler. Lived and traveled among Indians of Central America (1625–37). Wrote *The English-American: His Travail by Sea and Land* (1648).

Gage, Thomas, 1721–87, British general. Commanded British forces in North America (1763–75). As governor of Mass. (1774–75) he enforced coercive measures on eve of American Revolution.

gag rules, procedural rules in force in U.S. House of Representatives from 1836 to 1844. Southerners, aided by Northern Democrats, secured their passage to prevent discussion of antislavery proposals in the House. Repealed following John Quincy Adams's successful fight to secure right of petition. Their effect was to strengthen cause of abolitionists.

Gagry (gä'grē) or **Gagra**, city (1959 pop. 13,700), Abkhaz Autonomous SSR, NW Georgia, on Black Sea. Subtropical health resort.

Gaillard, David DuBose (gā'lùrd), 1859–1913, American army engineer. Directed construction of central division of Panama Canal, including excavation of Culebra (now Gaillard) Cut, most difficult portion of undertaking.

gaillardia (gālär'–), annual or perennial plant (*Gaillardia*) of W U.S. It has showy red or yellow daisy-like flower heads, used for cutting.

Gaines's Mill: see SEVEN DAYS BATTLES.

Gainesville. 1 City (pop. 29,701), N central Fla., SW of Jacksonville; founded c.1854. First settlement made 1830, just before Seminole War. Seat of Univ. of FLORIDA. **2** City (pop. 16,523), N central Ga., near Chattahoochee R., NE of Atlanta, in piedmont. Trade and industrial center of poultry-farm area. Brenau Col. is here; Riverside Military Academy is near. **3** City (pop. 13,083), N Texas, on Elm Fork of Trinity R., NNW of Dallas; founded 1850 on California Trail. Was riotous cow town and stopping point on Chisholm Trail. Today is a farm-processing and oil-refining city.

Gainsborough, Thomas (gänz'bùrù), 1727–88, English portrait and landscape painter. Began as apprentice to a London silversmith. At peak of career his popularity rivaled that of Reynolds. Famous for elegance of his portraits (esp. of women), which have a light and airy quality. Greens and blues predominate in his work. Among famous paintings is *The Blue Boy* (Huntington Art Gall., San Marino, Calif.).

Gainsborough, urban district (pop. 17,276), Lincolnshire, England, on Trent R. It is St. Ogg's of George Eliot's *Mill on the Floss*. Town estab. very early; Old Hall supposedly built by John of Gaunt.

Gaiseric (gī'sùrĭk) or **Genseric** (gĕn'sùrĭk, jĕn'–), c.390–477, king of the VANDALS (428–77). Invaded Roman Africa from Spain (429); took Carthage 439; won control of Mediterranean through his pirate fleets; sacked Rome 455. When he made peace with Zeno (476), he held N Africa, Sicily, Sardinia, Corsica, Balearic Isls.

Gaitskell, Hugh Todd Naylor, 1906–63, British politician and leading Labour party theorist. During Second World War served in ministry of economic warfare and on board of trade. Entered Parliament 1945 and became chancellor of the exchequer 1950. Succeeded Clement Attlee as Labour party leader 1955. Supported moderation of party policies.

Gaius (gā'ùs, gī'–), 2d cent. A.D., Roman jurist, known for his *Institutes*, a legal textbook used in the compilation of the Corpus Juris Civilis.

galactose, simple SUGAR, a CARBOHYDRATE, occasionally found in nature. It is an isomer of GLUCOSE. Galactose molecule is one of the two components of the disaccharide, lactose. See *ill.*, p. 178.

Galahad, Sir: see ARTHURIAN LEGEND.

Galápagos Islands (gùlä'pùgōs) [Span.,= tortoises], Pacific archipelago (3,029 sq. mi.; pop. c.2,000), c.650 mi. W of Ecuador, to which they belong. Discovered in 1535, the islands have biological interest. Visited by Charles Darwin (1835).

Galatea (gälùtē'ù), in Greek mythology, beautiful statue made by the sculptor PYGMALION. Aphrodite granted his prayer that it might come to life.

Galati or **Galatz** (gäläts'), city (est. pop. 111,906), E Rumania, in Moldavia; a major port on lower Danube. It was the seat of Danube Navigation Commission from 1856 to 1939.

Galatia (gùlä'shù), anc. territory of central Asia Minor, in the present Turkey (around Ankara). So called from its inhabitants, the Gauls, who conquered it in 3d cent. B.C. and increased territory to extend from Bithynia and Pontus on N to Pamphylia on S. Their advance was checked c.230 B.C. by Attalus I of Pergamum. Fell to Romans 189 B.C., became Roman province 25 B.C. Chief city was Ancyra (present Ankara.).

Galatians (gùlä'shùnz), epistle of New Testament, written by St. Paul to Christians of central Asia Minor. The Galatians had acquired the belief that rigid obedience to the Law of Moses was the means of salvation. This, Paul thought, would vitiate the whole of Christian freedom won for men on the Cross. He states that man is justified in the sight of God by faith, rather than by adherence to the Law. This doctrine is of great importance in Christian theology.

Galatz, Rumania: see GALATI.

galax (gā'lǎks"), low-growing evergreen plant (*Galax aphylla*), native to mountain woods from Va. to Ga. Its spikes of white flowers and heart-shaped leaves are used by florists.

galaxy (gǎ'lŭksĕ), type of system of stars and nebulae; usually comprises thousands of millions of stars and many nebulae and is in the form of a disk. The universe contains many galaxies; our sun is located in the galaxy called the MILKY WAY SYSTEM.

Galba (Servius Sulpicius Galba) (gǎl'bû), 3 B.C.–A.D. 69, Roman emperor. An able soldier, he was proclaimed emperor on Nero's death (68) but soon was killed in a rebellion. Otho became emperor.

Galbraith, John Kenneth, 1908–, American economist, U.S. Ambassador to India (1961–63). His works include *American Capitalism: The Concept of Countervailing Power* (1952), *The Great Crash: 1929* (1955), *The Affluent Society* (1958), and *The New Industrial State* (1967).

Galdhoppigen: see JOTUNHEIM.

Galdós, Benito Pérez: see PÉREZ GALDÓS, BENITO.

Galeed (gǎ'lĕĕd) or Mizpah (mĭz'pû), cairn, raised by Jacob and Laban to mark their covenant. So-called "Mizpah benediction" given here was mutual warning, not a blessing. Gen. 31.44–55. Also called Jegarsahadutha.

Galen (gā'lŭn), c.130–c.200, physician of Greek parentage, systematizer of contemporary medical learning. His authority was almost undisputed until the 16th cent. He wrote many treatises; about 83 of his medical works are extant.

Galena, city (pop. 4,410), extreme NW Ill., on Galena R. near Mississippi R.; settled c.1820. Region, rich in lead and zinc deposits, frequented by French miners in early 18th cent. From 1807, when U.S. took mines under its protection, to 1860s, busy river port and center of NW Ill. and SW Wis. lead area. Now trade and shipping point of dairying region. Home of U. S. Grant is state museum.

galena (gŭlē'nù) or lead glance, lustrous, blue-gray crystalline mineral, an important ore of lead and in some areas of silver. It is chiefly lead sulfide, but often contains silver and sometimes copper, zinc, or other elements.

Galena Park, city (pop. 10,852), S Texas, industrial suburb E of Houston.

Galerius (gùlēr'ĕùs), d. 310, Roman emperor (305–10). Appointed Caesar by Diocletian in 293, he succeeded (305) to empire in the East when Constantius I succeeded in the West. After Constantius' death, Galerius recognized Severus as coemperor, but after they were defeated by the troops of Maxentius, he supported Licinius. A confused fight for power was still going on when Galerius died.

Galesburg, city (pop. 37,243), W Ill., WNW of Peoria, in farm, livestock, and coal area; founded 1836. Trade, rail, and industrial center with railroad shops. Seat of KNOX COLLEGE, scene of Lincoln-Douglas debates. Town and college founded by N.Y. Presbyterians under G. W. Gale. Carl Sandburg's birthplace preserved.

Galiani, Ferdinando (färdēnän'dō gälyä'nē), 1728–87, Italian economist. His *Della moneta* [on money] (1750), and *Dialogues sur le commerce des blés* (1770), set forth modern theory of value and historical approach to economics.

Galich (gä'lĭch). Ukr. *Halych*, Pol. *Halicz*, city (1959 pop. 4,800), NW Ukraine, on Dniester. Seat of dukes of Przemysl from c.1134, it later became cap. of duchy of Galich, which in 1188 was united with Vladimir (see VLADIMIR-VOLYNSKI). In 13th cent. Galich-Vladimir (which then included GALICIA and VOLHYNIA), extended E to Kiev. Under Tatar overlordship from 1245, duchy was partitioned in 1366 between Poland and Lithuania. City, now insignificant, has medieval remains.

Galicia (gŭlĭ'shù), Pol. *Galicja*, Ukr. *Halychyna*, historic region, now in SE Poland and W Ukraine. Pol-ish section covers Rzeszow and larger part of Cracow prov. Ukrainian section includes Lvov, Stanislov, and Tarnopol oblasts. Originally the duchy of GALICH and Vladimir, it passed to Poland 1366, to Austria 1772. Polish population enjoyed limited autonomy 1861–1918. A battleground during the First World War, Galicia was contested by Poland and Ukrainian republic 1918–20. Poland secured all Galicia and was confirmed in possession by Treaty of Riga with USSR (1921). Most of E Galicia was incorporated (1939) into Ukraine, an act upheld by Polish-Soviet Treaty of 1945.

Galicia, historic region, NW Spain, bordering on Atlantic Ocean and on Portugal. Largely mountainous; drained by Miño R. Fishing, cattle raising, agr. Chief cities: Santiago de Compostela, La Coruña, Vigo, El Ferrol, Pontevedra. Galician dialect, akin to Portuguese, has a great literary past. Region was conquered from Moors by kings of Asturias 8th–9th cent.

Galigaï, Leonora: see CONCINI, CONCINO.

Galilee (gǎ'lĭlē), agr. region, N Palestine, chief scene of ministry of Jesus. The lake, countryside, and towns —Cana, Capernaum, Tiberias, Nazareth—are repeatedly referred to in the Gospels. Jesus was called the Galilean. Joshua 20.7; 21.32; 1 Kings 9.11; 2 Kings 15.29; Isa. 9.1; Mat. 26.69; John 7.52.

Galilee, Sea of, fresh-water lake, 13 mi. long, 3–7 mi. wide, NE Palestine. It has fisheries. In Old Testament called Chinnereth or Chinneroth; in New Testament called Galilee, Gennesaret, or Tiberias. Modern Arabic name is Bahr Tabariyeh. In Jesus' time there were nine flourishing towns on its shores.

Galilei, Vincenzo (vēnchän'tsō gälēlā'ē), c.1520–91, Italian singer, writer, and composer; father of Galileo. A pioneer of the baroque era, he was one of the first to compose recitatives.

Galileo (gä"ilē'ō), It. *Galileo Galilei*, 1564–1642, Italian astronomer, mathematician, and physicist whose investigation of natural laws laid the foundations of modern experimental science. He formulated mathematically many physical laws and is credited with conclusions foreshadowing Newton's laws of motion. Constructed the first complete astronomical telescope (1609). His astronomical discoveries confirmed Copernican theory of solar system which he supported in his dialogue on the two chief systems of the world (published 1632). He was forced by the Inquisition, however, to abjure belief that earth moved about sun.

Galion, city (pop. 12,650), N central Ohio. W of Mansfield, in farm area; settled c.1819.

Galitzin or Galitsin: see GALLITZIN.

Gall (gôl), c.1840–1894, war chief of Sioux Indians. Refused to accept treaty of 1868 confining him to reservation. Joined Sitting Bull in defeat of Custer (1876). Surrendered at Poplar, Mont., and became farmer on reservation.

gall (gôl), abnormal growth of plant tissue produced by stimulus of external agent. Common agents are bacteria and insects (e.g., certain aphids, midges, moths wasps, beetles). Usually each species produces the same type of gall even on different hosts. Galls are source of tannin and of good quality permanent ink

Galla Placidia (gä'lù plùsĭ'dèù), c.388–450, West Roman empress; daughter of Theodosius I. Long a hostage among Visigoths, she married ATAULF (414) but was returned to her brother HONORIUS after Ataulf's death. Her second husband through her influence was made coemperor as CONSTANTIUS III. After 425 she was regent for her son VALENTINIAN III.

Gallas, Matthias, Graf von (mätě'äs gräf' fün gä'läs), 1584–1647, Austrian field marshal in Thirty Years War. Sided with emperor against his superior, WALLENSTEIN; succeeded to Wallenstein's command and to most of his duchy of Friedland. Won major victory at NÖRDLINGEN (1634).

Gallatin, Albert (gä'lùtĭn), 1761–1849, American statesman and financier, b. Switzerland. Member, U.S. Congress (1795–1801). As U.S. Secretary of the Treasury (1801–14), he reshaped country's financial policy from Federalist to Jeffersonian principles. Key figure in negotiating Treaty of Ghent. Authority on banking and finance.

Gallatin, town (pop. 7,901), N Tenn., NE of Nashville near Cumberland R.; founded 1802. Tennessee walking horses bred here. Town, with Union garrison, captured Aug., 1862, by Gen. J. H. Morgan.

Gallatin, river, SW Mont., rising in NW Yellowstone Natl. Park and flowing c.125 mi. N between Madison and Gallatin ranges, then NW to join Madison and Jefferson rivers at Three Forks of the Missouri. Irrigation.

Gallaudet, Thomas Hopkins, 1787–1851, American educator of the deaf. Founded (1817) first free school for deaf in Hartford, Conn. His son, Thomas **Gallaudet,** 1822–1902, an Episcopal priest, did missionary work among the deaf; founded St. Ann's Church for Deaf Mutes in New York city. A younger son, **Edward Miner Gallaudet,** 1837–1917, opened school for deaf mutes in Washington, D.C., which became Gallaudet Col.

gall bladder: see BILE; *ill.,* p. 657.

Galle, Johann Gottfried (yō′hän gôt′frēt gä′lŭ), 1812–1910, German astronomer. He discovered the planet Neptune from calculations of Leverrier.

Galle (gäl), city (pop. 55,848), SW Ceylon, port on Indian Ocean. Marketing and shipping center under Portuguese, Dutch, British, and native rule.

Gallegos, Rómulo (rō′mōōlō gäyä′gōs), 1884–, Venezuelan novelist, president of Venezuela (Feb.–Nov., 1948). Best-known novel is *Doña Bárbara* (1929; Eng. tr., 1931).

galleon (gä′lĕŭn), type of ocean-going sailing vessels used by Spanish in 15th and 16th cent. They were cumbersome three-masted, square-rigged ships with high bow and stern, the latter ornamented with carvings. They were much used to bring goods from the Americas.

galley, type of long, narrow vessels of anc. and medieval times, propelled usually by oars, sometimes by sails. Earliest type was sometimes 150 ft. long with 50 oars, decked at bow and stern but otherwise open. Benches along sides were for chained rowers (slaves, prisoners), while center was for cargo. Usual number of banks of oars was three (triremes); smaller biremes had two banks. Galleys allegedly grew to as many as 40 banks; these were abandoned for smaller vessels by 1st cent. B.C. When used for war, sides were raised to protect rowers. Romans used hooks for grappling and carried bridges for boarding other vessels. French and Venetians used galleys in the Mediterranean until 17th cent.

gallic acid, colorless, crystalline solid organic acid usually obtained from tannins. Used as astringent and disinfectant.

Gallicanism (gä′lĭkŭnĭzŭm), theory that the French monarch had special rights in the Roman Catholic Church in France. It was put forward with the doctrine that the pope was subordinate to the ecumenical council (the conciliar theory), which emerged from the Univ of Paris during the Great SCHISM and was confirmed by Charles VII in the Pragmatic Sanction of Bourges (1438). Francis I repealed the act after the Concordat of 1516 in which the papacy surrendered rights of appointment. The concordat was revoked in 1561, and the struggle resumed. LOUIS XIV in his trouble with INNOCENT XI had an assembly of bishops pass the "Four Gallican Articles of 1682," putting both councils and kings above the pope. Innocent XII managed to quiet the trouble in 1693, and Louis abandoned Gallican theory. Its effect was felt later in Jansenism, in the Revolutionary Civil Constitution of the Clergy, and in clauses added by Napoleon to the Concordat of 1801. Gallicanism has been impossible since the enunciation of papal infallibility of the Vatican Council (1869).

Galli-Curci, Amelita (gäl′lē-kōōr′chē), 1882–1963, Italian-American coloratura soprano. Made her American debut (Chicago, 1916) as Gilda in *Rigoletto;* sang with the Chicago Opera Co. until 1926 and with the Metropolitan, New York, 1926–30.

Gallic Wars (gä′lĭk), campaigns of Caesar as proconsul of GAUL (58–51 B.C.). His first task was to prevent the Helvetii from entering SW Gaul. Next the Aedui asked his help against the German ARIOVISTUS. In 57 he pacified Belgica. In 56 he attacked the Veneti. In 55 he went to the Low Countries and crossed the Rhine. In 54 he invaded Britain. Next, some Belgian tribes led by AMBIORIX raised a revolt which Caesar dispersed. In 53 all central, E, and N Gaul revolted under VERCINGETORIX. With incredible speed and brilliant tactics Caesar crossed the Alps and stifled the uprising. The prime source is his own commentary, *The Gallic Wars.*

Galli da Bibiena: see BIBIENA, GALLI DA.

Gallieni, Joseph Simon (zhôzěf′ sēmō′ gälyänē′), 1849–1916, French general. As military governor of Paris early in First World War, he vitally contributed to victory of the Marne (Sept., 1914), sped troops from Paris to front in commandeered taxicabs. Made marshal posthumously (1921).

Gallienus (gä″lĭē′nŭs), d. 268, Roman emperor, colleague of his father, VALERIAN (253–60), and alone (260–68). Dissolution of the empire started in his reign.

Gallipoli (gŭlĭ′pŭlē), Turkish *Gelibolu,* city (pop. 12,-956), European Turkey; a port near the neck of the Gallipoli Peninsula, which extends c.60 mi. to the SW between the Aegean Sea and the Dardanelles. Peninsula was scene of **Gallipoli Campaign,** April, 1915–Jan., 1916, First World War Allied expedition to gain Dardanelles, capture Constantinople, and make contact with Russia through Black Sea. Idea of forcing Straits was originally Winston Churchill's. A naval expedition having failed (March), British troops landed on peninsula, French on Asiatic shore. Allies, whose cooperation was poor, were prevented from joining by stubborn Turkish resistance and had to withdraw.

Gallitzin (gŭlĭt′sĭn), Rus. *Golytsin,* Russian princely family; also spelled Galitzin, Galytzin. Vasily **Vasilyevich Gallitzin** (věsě′lyē vŭsě′lyŭvĭch), d. 1619, helped to enthrone first false Dmitri. **Vasily Vasilyevich Gallitzin,** 1643–1714, lover and adviser of SOPHIA ALEKSEYEVNA, was banished to Siberia by Peter I (1689). **Boris Alekseyevich Gallitzin** (bŭrēs′ ŭlyĭksyä′ĭvĭch), 1654–1714, tutor of Peter I, helped him to depose Sophia. **Dmitri Mikhailovich Gallitzin** (dŭmē′trē měkhī′lŭvĭch), 1665–1737, diplomat and general, was exiled by Empress Anna for seeking to limit her power (1730). **Dmitri Alekseyevich Gallitzin,** 1735–1803, Russian ambassador to Paris (1765–73), was a friend of Diderot and Voltaire. His son, **Demetrius Augustine Gallitzin,** 1770–1840, became a Roman Catholic, went to America. Ordained 1795; worked in SW Pennsylvania as frontier missionary; was known as Father Smith. Founded Catholic colony of Loretto near Gallitzin, Pa. **Aleksandr Nikolayevich Gallitzin** (ŭlyĭksän′dŭr nyĭkŭlī′ŭvĭch), 1773?–1844, was minister of education under Alexander I; a liberal. **Nikolai Dmitreyevich Gallitzin** (nyĭkŭlī′ dŭmē′trēŭvĭch), 1856–1925, became premier 1916, proved unable to stem revolutionary tide.

gallium (gä′lĕŭm), silver-gray metallic element (symbol = Ga; see also ELEMENT, table), widely distributed in small quantities. Since it is liquid over a wide temperature range it is sometimes used in high-temperature thermometers.

Galloway, Joseph, c.1731–1803, American colonial leader. Urged conciliation and written constitution as means of avoiding conflict prior to American Revolution and later remained loyal to the king.

Galloway, district of SW Scotland, comprising Wigtownshire and Kirkcudbrightshire. Black, hornless Galloway cattle bred here.

gallstone: see CALCULUS, in medicine.

Gallup, George Horace, 1901–, American public opinion statistician, originator of the Gallup poll. Founded (1935) American Institute of Public Opinion.

Gallup, town (pop. 14,089), NW N.Mex., on Puerco R. near Ariz. line; founded c.1879. Rail and trade center in coal-mine area. Ships wool and livestock. In heart of Indian country with reservations and pueblos nearby.

Galois, Évariste (ävärēst' gälwä'), 1811–32, French mathematician. He contributed to theories of equations, numbers, and functions and was a pioneer in establishing theory of groups in algebraic solutions.

Galswintha (gälswĭn'thù), d. 567, Frankish queen, sister of BRUNHILDA and wife of CHILPERIC I, by whom she was murdered.

Galsworthy, John, 1867–1933, English novelist and dramatist. Many plays concern social problems (e.g., *Strife,* 1909). Novels portray the limited social consciousness and viewpoint of upper-middle-class families of Victorian era. Many are grouped in three trilogies, *The Forsyte Saga* (1922), *A Modern Comedy* (1928), *The End of the Chapter* (1934). Received 1932 Nobel Prize in Literature.

Galt, John, 1779–1839, Scottish novelist, founder of CANADA COMPANY (1826). Novels and stories portray Scottish country life. His son, **Sir Alexander Tilloch Galt,** 1817–93, was a Canadian statesman, b. England. A leader for confederation of Canadian provinces. As minister of finance (1858–62, 1864–66) he defended protective tariff. Dominant member of Halifax Fisheries Commission. First Canadian high commissioner in London (1880–83).

Galt, industrial city (pop. 27,830), S Ont., Canada, on Grand R. and NW of Hamilton.

Galton, Sir Francis (gôl'tùn), 1822–1911, English scientist, founder of eugenics (term coined by him); cousin of Charles Darwin.

Galuppi, Baldassare (bäldäs-sä'rä gälōōp'pē), 1706–85, Italian composer of oratorios, chamber music, and operas. Immortalized in Browning's poem "A Toccata of Galuppi's."

Galvani, Luigi (lwē'jē gälvä'nē), 1737–98, Italian physician. He observed that leg muscle cut from a frog contracts when touched with two different metals; he realized that electricity caused the contraction. Galvani held that the muscle was the electricity source; Volta correctly said the metals were. Controversy stimulated development of physiology.

galvanizing, term commonly used for process of coating a metal (usually iron or steel) with zinc, which resists oxidation and moisture. Methods include dipping, electroplating, and baking.

galvanometer, instrument for determining presence of a current in a conductor, the direction of flow, and strength of current. It is based on Hans C. Oersted's discovery that magnetic needle is deflected by passage of electric current along a conductor; magnetic needle tends to turn at right angles, the extent of turn being, in general, dependent upon strength of current. Modern galvanometers have fixed magnet and movable coil. Ammeter is a form of galvanometer with scale to indicate number of amperes. Voltmeter is moving-coil galvanometer which has high-resistance coil and which indicates number of volts of current—the greater the electromotive force of the current, the greater the deflection of the needle.

Galveston (gäl'vùstùn), city (pop. 67,155), on Galveston Isl., SE Texas. Island lies across Galveston Bay (inlet of Gulf of Mexico) entrance. Spanish knew it early; probable scene of Cabeza de Vaca's shipwreck (1528). Explored late 18th cent., later outlaw country (esp. for pirates of Jean Lafitte). Settled in 1830s, city progressed despite yellow fever, hurricanes, and Union occupation (briefly in 1862). Sea wall built after 1900 hurricane. Connected to mainland by long causeways. Processes and ships cotton, sulfur, rice, and flour; has oil refining, shipbuilding, fishing, and shrimping. Beach resort. Univ. of Texas medical school is here.

Gálvez, José de (hōsä' dā gäl'vĕth), 1720–87, Spanish colonial administrator, visitor general to New Spain (1765–72). Upon return to Spain was responsible for two important changes in Spanish colonial policy: more liberal trade policy to replace earlier narrow mercantilism; system of intendancies. His brother, **Matías de Gálvez** (mätē'äs), 1717–84, was Spanish colonial administrator; viceroy of New Spain (1783–84). Matías's son, **Bernardo de Gálvez,** c.1746–1786, became Spanish governor of Louisiana in 1777. Aided patriot cause in American Revolution. After Spain declared war on England (1779), he captured Baton Rouge and Natchez (1779), Mobile (1780), and Pensacola (1781). Succeeded his father as viceroy.

Galway (gôl'wä), maritime county (2,293 sq. mi.; pop. 149,800), W Ireland, in Connaught. Lough Corrib divides the county; W is Connemara, with picturesque mountains, and E a rolling plain. The Shannon is chief river, and Aran Isls. chief islands. Industries mainly agr. and fishing. The county town is **Galway,** urban district (pop. 21,989) on N side Galway Bay. Galway was first incorporated by Richard II. Has good harbor and exports agr. produce, salmon, herring, marble, woolen goods. Site of University Col.

Galway Bay, inlet of the Atlantic, 30 mi. long and 23 mi. wide at entrance on W Ireland coast, in counties Galway and Clare. Aran Isls. at entrance.

Gama, Vasco da (vä'skō dù gä'mù), c.1469–1524, Portuguese navigator, first European to reach India by sea (1497–99). Voyage around Africa made wealth of Indies accessible to Europe and made possible growth of Portuguese wealth and empire. On second voyage (1502) he estab. Portuguese power in Indian waters and on African coast by harsh methods.

Gamaliel (gùmā'lēùl) [Heb.,= recompense of God], president of Sanhedrin at Jerusalem and teacher of Paul. Grandson of Hillel. Advocated leniency toward Christians. Acts. 5:34, 22:3.

Gambetta, Léon (lāō' gäbĕtä'), 1838–82, French statesman. In FRANCO-PRUSSIAN WAR (1870–71) organized French resistance in provinces. Played important part in creation of Third Republic, was premier 1881–82. Republican and anticlerical, he steered mid-course between radicals and royalists, advocated revenge against Germany.

Gambia (găm'bēù), country (c.4,000 sq. mi.; pop. c.324,000), W Africa, on the Atlantic; cap. Bathurst. A narrow enclave in Senegal, it comprises Bathurst and St. Mary's isl. and the area bordering both banks of the Gambia R. for c.200 mi. above its mouth. A former British colony and protectorate. Exports peanuts. Largely inhabited by Negro Moslem tribes. The Portuguese, who estab. settlements here in mid-15th cent., were succeeded by the British in early 17th cent. Present boundaries estab. 1888. Country achieved self-government in 1963, independence 1965, when it was admitted to UN. Uncertainty about boundaries has caused difficulty with Senegal.

Gambier Islands (găm'bēr) or **Mangareva** (män″gärä'vä), coral group, S Pacific Ocean; part of FRENCH POLYNESIA. Mangareva is largest and most important island. Discovered 1797 by the British, annexed 1881 by France. Produces copra and coffee.

gamboge (gămbōj'), reddish yellow gum RESIN (from tree sap) used as paint pigment and as a purgative.

Gambrinus (gămbrī'nùs), mythical Flemish king, to whom is attributed invention of beer.

game laws. In U.S. common protective devices include prohibition against lake and river pollution, designation of closed season, limitation of age, size, and sex of game hunted, requirement of license, prohibition of sale or possession of game beyond a certain period after season closes, and prohibition of transportation or sale outside state.

games, theory of, group of mathematical theories first developed by John von Neumann. It applies statistical logic to choice of strategies where two or more are available; applicable to military problems, economics, and sociology.

gamma globulin, protein fraction of human blood plasma that contains most antibodies in the circulating blood. When pooled from diverse groups of the adult population, resulting mixture contains high concentrations of antibodies against most infections in a given area. Used as IMMUNITY measure, especially for measles and hepatitis.

gamma ray: see RADIOACTIVITY.

Gammer Gurton's Needle, second extant English comedy, acted c.1553 at Christ's Col., Cambridge. Once attributed to John Still (later bishop of Bath and Wells), but more probably by William Stevenson, fellow of the college.

Gamow, George (gä'mŏf), 1904–, Russian-American physicist and author; noted for application of nuclear physics to stellar evolution.

Gander, airport, E N.F., Canada. Important air base in Second World War; Newfoundland converted it to civilian international airport 1945.

Gandhara (gŭndä'rŭ), historic region of West Pakistan on middle Indus R. A part of the Persian Empire, it was conquered 327 B.C. by Alexander the Great. Part of ancient Bactria. Noted for sculpture of Hellenistic period.

Gandhi, Indira (ĭndē'rŭ gän'dē), 1917–, Indian prime minister; daughter of Jawaharlal Nehru. Active in social and relief work. She led Indian Natl. Congress 1959–60 and became executive board member of UNESCO in 1961. Became first Indian woman prime minister in 1966 on the death of Lal Bahadur Shastri.

Gandhi, Mohandas Karamchand (mō"hŭndäs' kŭ"rŭmchŭnd gän'dē), 1869–1948, great Indian leader. Educated in India and London; admitted to the bar in 1889. While in South Africa he fought for rights of Indians in that country. Returned 1915 to India and began working for India's independence. Gave up Western ways to lead life of abstinence in accordance with Hindu ethics; advocated revival of home industries (esp. cloth weaving). Asserting man's unity under one God, he preached Christian and Moslem scriptures along with the Hindu; vigorously espoused abolition of untouchability. Several times leader of INDIAN NATIONAL CONGRESS he opposed British policy with *Satyagraha* [Sanskrit,= truth force] or, in English, nonviolent resistance. Imprisoned 1930 for violating state salt monopoly by publicly extracting salt from sea water, but released 1931 to attend London conference on India. Called the Mahatma [great souled], he was so widely revered that he could exact political concessions by threatening "fasts unto death." Called for *Satyagraha* in 1942, when the British rejected offer to cooperate in war if India were freed at once; interned until 1944. A major figure in conferences leading to India's freedom (1947), he was deeply disappointed by the partition of India. Shot fatally on Jan. 30, 1948, by a Hindu who blamed him for the partition.

Gandzha, Azerbaijan SSR: see KIROVABAD.

Ganges (găn'jēz), river, c.1,560 mi. long, in N India and E Pakistan, rising in Himalayas in N Uttar Pradesh and flowing to Bay of Bengal; most sacred Hindu river. Especially holy bathing sites at Allahabad and at Benares.

gangrene, death of a part or area of tissue; it is caused by local stoppage of circulation, usually resulting from disease or injury. The affected part must be surgically removed or the condition will spread.

Ganivet, Angel (än'hĕl gän'ēvĕt), 1865–98, Spanish writer. His *Idearium español* (1897) had enormous influence on the Generation of '98.

gannet (găn'ĭt) or **solan goose** (sō'lŭn), large white sea bird related to pelican. Common gannet of N Atlantic dives for fish from high in air to deep in water. Boobies are related tropical sea birds.

Gannett, Henry, 1846–1914, American geographer. Chief geographer of U.S. Geological Survey after 1882; improved system of census taking. His efforts

led to establishment of U.S. Board of Geographical Names (1890); he served as chairman until 1910.

Gannett Peak, Wyo.: see WIND RIVER RANGE.

Ganymede (găn'ĭmēd), in Greek mythology, beautiful boy seized by Zeus to be his cupbearer.

Garamond, Claude (gă'rŭmŏnd; Fr., klōd' gärämō'), d. 1561, Parisian designer and maker of printing types. His designs were used by the Estiennes and Bodoni and were used as a base for designs used by the Elzevir family. His roman and italic types were the first to be primarily designed for metal type, not imitated after handwriting. His roman also helped make roman standard rather than black letter. Modern Garamond types do not closely resemble his.

Garay, Juan de (hwän' dù gärī'), c.1528–83, Spanish conquistador in South America. Refounded Buenos Aires (1580) from Asunción.

Garbo, Greta, 1905–, American film actress, whose real name is Gustafsson, b. Sweden. Noted for her beauty and as a tragic heroine, she won fame in such films as *Anna Christie, Queen Christina, Camille,* and *Ninotchka.*

Garborg, Arne Evensen, 1851–1924, Norwegian poet and novelist. Championed use of Landsmaal, the language of the peasants.

García (y Iñigues), Calixto (kälēk'stō gärsē'ä ē ēnyē'gēs), 1836–98, Cuban revolutionist, leader in Ten Years War and Spanish-American War. Elbert Hubbard's essay *A Message to Garcia* has made his name famous.

García, Manuel del Popolo (mänwĕl' dĕl pōpō'lō gärthē'ä), 1775–1832, Spanish tenor, teacher, impresario, and composer. His opera company included his wife, his son, and his daughter, Maria MALIBRAN. He was first to produce opera in Italian in New York. His son, **Manuel Patricio García** (pätrē'thyō), 1805–1906, inventor of the laryngoscope, taught in Paris and London. Jenny Lind was his pupil.

Garciá Calderón, Francisco (gärsēä' käldärōn'), 1883–1953, Peruvian writer. Lived in France for many years. Wrote (in French) *Latin America: Its Rise and Progress* (Eng. tr., 1913), a conservative interpretation.

García Gutiérez, Antonio (äntō'nyō gärthē'ä gōōtyĕr'rĕth), 1813?–84, Spanish playwright. Author of *El trovador* and *Simón Bocanegra,* both adapted for opera by Verdi.

García Lorca, Federico (fädhärē'kō gärthē'ä lôr'kä), 1898–1936, Spanish poet and dramatist. Author of *Romancero gitano* [gypsy balladeer] (1929) and *Bodas de Sangre* [blood wedding] (1938). Major poet of his generation. Shot by Falangists just after outbreak of Spanish civil war.

García Moreno, Gabriel (gäbrēĕl · gärsē'ä mōrā'nō), 1821–75, president of Ecuador (1861–65, 1869–75). Ardent Roman Catholic and able administrator, he is remembered for religious fanaticism and despotism. Murdered by liberal assassins.

Garcilaso de la Vega (gärthēlä'sō dä lä vā'gä), 1503?–1536, Spanish courtier and poet. Successfully adapted Italian 11-syllable line to Spanish.

Garcilaso de la Vega (gärsēlä'sō dä lä vā'gä), 1539?–1616, Peruvian historian; son of Spanish conquistador and Incan princess; called the Inca. Writings (notably *Royal Commentaries of Peru*) tell of conquest of Peru and legends of the Inca.

Gard (gär), department (2,271 sq. mi.; pop. 435,482), S France, in Languedoc, on Mediterranean; cap. Nîmes.

Garda, Lake (gär'dä), Ital. *Lago di Garda* or *Benaco,* lake (143 sq. mi.; 32 mi. long), N Italy, between Lombardy and Venetia. Fed by Sarca R., drained by the Mincio. N tip, with Riva di Trento, is Alpine resort. Shores are dotted with vineyards, resorts.

Garden, Alexander, c.1730–1791, Scottish naturalist. Discovered and classified congo eel and mud eel. The gardenia was named for him.

Garden, Mary, 1877–1967, American operatic soprano, b. Scotland. She made her U.S. debut (New

York, 1907) with the Manhattan Opera Co. as Thaïs. Other famous roles were Louise, Mélisande, Salomé.

Gardena (gärdē'nà), city (pop. 35,943), S Calif., an industrial suburb S of Los Angeles.

Garden City. 1 City (pop. 11,811), SW Kansas, on Arkansas R., WNW of Wichita; founded 1878. Trade and mfg. center in farm (grain, sugar beets, alfalfa) and dairy region. **2** Residential city (pop. 38,017), SE Mich., NW of Dearborn. **3** Village (1965 pop. 24,661), SE N.Y., on W Long Isl., NW of Hempstead; founded 1869. Printing and publishing. Residential and retailing community planned by A. T. Stewart. Seat of Adelphi Univ.

garden city, community surrounded by a rural belt, owned by inhabitants, with predetermined maximum population and area. Scheme originated as preventative of urban crowding following Industrial Revolution. Original proponents were Robert Owen, James Silk Buckingham, and Charles Fourier. A number of such cities have been built since 1851 in England and America, but outside of England most such cities have become simply satellite suburbs of a larger industrial city, rather than communities whose industries have a self-sufficient labor force.

Garden City Park, town (pop. 15,364 incl. Herricks), SE N.Y., on W Long Isl., NE of New Hyde Park.

Garden Grove, residential city (pop. 84,238), S Calif., a suburb SE of Los Angeles; founded 1877.

gardenia, subtropical shrub (*Gardenia jasminoides*) also known as Cape jasmine. It has fragrant white flowers and glossy evergreen leaves. Grown outdoors in mild regions, as house plant in cold areas.

Garden of the Gods: see COLORADO SPRINGS.

Gardiner, Sir Christopher, fl. 1630–32, personage in early history of Mass. Bay colony. When Puritans arrived at Mass. Bay to found colony (1630), they found him and a young woman. Later discovered to be agent of Sir Ferdinando Gorges, whose claims to Mass. he aided.

Gardiner, Samuel Rawson, 1829–1902, English historian. Wrote a thorough, careful history of Puritan Revolution in England, covering years 1603–60. Also edited constitutional documents of Revolution. Editor (1891–1901) *English Historical Review.*

Gardiner, city (pop. 6,897), SW Maine, on Kennebec R., S of Augusta; founded 1760. First technical school in U.S. estab. here 1823 by Benjamin Hale. E. A. Robinson spent his youth here.

Gardiners Island, c.3,000 acres, SE N.Y., in Gardiners Bay between two flukelike peninsulas of E Long Isl.; settled 1639 by Lion Gardiner.

Gardner, Erle Stanley, 1889–, American lawyer, author of detective stories about fictional lawyer Perry Mason; writes other detective fiction under pseudonym A. A. Fair.

Gardner, Ernest Arthur: see GARDNER, PERCY.

Gardner, Isabella Stewart, 1840–1924, American art collector. Her collection and Fenway Court, which houses it, were willed to Boston as a museum.

Gardner, Percy, 1846–1937, English classical archaeologist and author of works on Greek art, history, and coins. While professor of archaeology at Oxford (1887–1925) he built up the archaeology department and its library and collections. His brother **Ernest Arthur Gardner,** 1862–1939, was director of British School of Archaeology at Athens (1887–95), professor of archaeology (1896–1929) and vice chancellor at Univ. of London, and author of works on Greek art and history.

Gardner, city (pop. 19,038), N central Mass., NNW of Worcester; settled 1764. Furniture mfg. since c.1805.

Garfield, James A(bram), 1831–81, 20th President of the United States. U.S. Representative from Ohio (1863–80). Elected President in 1880 after being chosen by Republicans as compromise candidate. By appointing J. G. Blaine, political foe of Roscoe CONKLING, as Secretary of State, Garfield declared war with most important faction of his party. He won first battle by getting his appointee for New York port collectorship approved. Began prosecution of STAR ROUTE frauds. Constantly harassed by office seekers, he was shot by one of them, Charles J. Guiteau, on July 2, 1881; on Sept. 19 he died. Chester A. Arthur succeeded to presidency.

Garfield, industrial city (pop. 29,253), NE N.J., on Passaic R., NNE of Passaic.

Garfield Heights, city (pop. 38,455), NE Ohio, suburb SE of Cleveland; founded 1904.

garfish, marine fish with long, slender body and long, pointed, toothed beak. It is found in most temperate and warm waters. Sometimes it enters rivers. Some of the 50 known species reach length of 5–6 ft. Swift and predatory, they swim near surface.

Garibaldi, Giuseppe (jōōzĕp'pä gärēbäl'dē), 1807–82, Italian patriot and soldier, hero of the RISORGIMENTO; b. Nice. Fled abroad after taking part in an unsuccessful republican plot (1835); fought in civil wars of Brazil and Uruguay (1835–46); returned to Italy and fought with Sardinian forces against Austria (1848–49) and with Mazzini's Roman republic against French interventionists (1849). Renouncing his republican ideal, he gave support to the policy of CAVOUR and VICTOR EMMANUEL II. In 1860, with Victor Emmanuel's connivance, he led 1,000 volunteer "Red Shirts" in spectacular conquest of Sicily and Naples. After handing his conquests over to Victor Emmanuel, who thus became king of Italy, Garibaldi retired to his home on Caprera isl. He twice attempted to conquer the Papal states, but was stopped by Italian troops at Aspromonte (1862) and by French and papal troops at Mentana (1867).

Garigliano (gärēlyä'nō), name of LIRI R., S central Italy, below junction with Rapido R.; empties into Tyrrhenian Sea. Scene of bitter fighting (1943–44) during battle for CASSINO.

Garland, Augustus Hill, 1832–99, American lawyer, U.S. Attorney General (1885–89). In *Ex parte Garland* (1867), Garland, a former Confederate, won plea to resume practice before U.S. Supreme Court.

Garland, Hamlin, 1860–1940, American writer of stories of the Middle Western prairie country. Wrote *Main-travelled Roads* (1891; stories), novels, and autobiographical classic, *A Son of the Middle Border* (1917).

Garland, Judy, 1922–, American singer and film actress. Among her notable films (after 1935) are *The Wizard of Oz, Meet Me in St. Louis, A Star Is Born.* Has made concert tours.

Garland, town (pop. 38,501), N Texas, industrial suburb NE of Dallas. Center for electronics research and production of electronic equipment.

garlic, perennial herb (*Allium sativum*), native to Europe and closely related to onion. The bulb is used as food flavoring.

Garmisch-Partenkirchen (gär'mĭsh-pär"tŭnkĭr'khùn), town (pop. 23,938), Upper Bavaria. Winter resort at foot of ZUGSPITZE.

Garmo Peak, USSR: see COMMUNISM, MOUNT.

Garneau, François Xavier (gärnō'), 1809–66, French Canadian historian. His *Histoire du Canada* (3 vols., 1845–48; 2d ed., with added material, 1852) covers Canadian history to union of two Canadas. Later editions by author's grandson brought work up to date. History has influenced and stimulated French Canadian literature, especially poetry.

Garner, John Nance, 1868–, Vice President of the United States (1933–41).

garnet, name given to a group of widely distributed crystalline minerals some of which are gems. They are commonly red and are double silicates.

Garnett, Richard (gär'nĭt), 1835–1906, English librarian and author. Served at the British Mus. with distinction. Wrote biographies (of Carlyle, Emerson, Milton, Coleridge, and others), essays, and critical works. His son, **Edward Garnett,** 1868–1937, was a critic who encouraged many great writers. His wife, **Constance**

(Beach) **Garnett,** 1862–1946, made widely read translations from the Russian. Their son, **David Garnett,** 1892–, was a partner in the Nonesuch Press and wrote the fantastic short novel, *Lady into Fox* (1923), and other works. *The Golden Echo* (1953) and *Flowers of the Forest* (1955) are his autobiography.

Garnett, city (pop. 3,034), E Kansas, SSW of Lawrence; founded 1856. E. L. Masters born here.

Garnier, Jean Louis Charles (gärnyä'), 1825–98, French architect, who built the Paris Opéra.

Garnier, Marie Joseph François, 1839–73, French explorer and naval officer usually known as Francis Garnier. Accompanied Doudart de Lagrée's expedition through Indo-Chinese area unfamiliar to Europeans (1866–68). Captured Hanoi on Tonkin expedition (1873). Wrote accounts of experiences.

Garnier, Tony, 1869–1948, French architect and city planner, influential in 20th-cent. design.

Garofalo, Il (ēl gärō'fälō), 1481–1559, Italian painter of Ferrarese school. Real name was Benvenuto Tisi or Tisio. Worked in Ferrara, Bologna, and Rome.

Garofalo, Raffaele, 1851–1934, Italian jurist and criminologist; helped found school of Italian positivists.

Garonne (gärôn'), river, c.400 mi. long, SW France, rising in Pyrenees. It flows NE to Toulouse, then swings NW, and below Bordeaux joins the Dordogne to form the GIRONDE.

Garonne, Haute, France: see HAUTE-GARONNE.

gar pike, fresh-water fish of E and S U.S., Central America, Mexico, West Indies. It has a cylindrical body, platelike scales, snoutlike jaws, sharp teeth. Flesh is unpalatable. Gars eat more useful fish. Garfish is name sometimes given to salt-water gar.

Garrett, João Batista de Almeida: see ALMEIDA GARRETT.

Garrick, David, 1717–79, English actor and manager. Was long associated with Charles Macklin and Margaret (Peg) Woffington at Covent Garden. Friend of Diderot and of Samuel Johnson, Oliver Goldsmith, and others in "The Club." His formal debut (1742) as Richard III made him London's idol; he was equally at home in contemporary drama. His simple manner of acting swept the declamatory school from the stage. As manager of Drury Lane 1747–76, he made important stage reforms.

Garrison, William Lloyd, 1805–79, American abolitionist. Founded the *Liberator* (1831), in which paper he waged uncompromising antislavery campaign for 35 years. Although a nonresistant and a believer in moral persuasion, his militant style antagonized many. His opposition to political action divided abolitionists. A founder of American Anti-Slavery Society (1833), its president 1843–65. Opposed Civil War until Emancipation Proclamation.

Garrison Dam, W central N.Dak., in Missouri R. S of Garrison; completed 1962. Key structure of MISSOURI RIVER BASIN PROJECT, it is 11,300 ft. long, 210 ft. high. Provides flood control and power.

Garry, Fort, early trading post on site of present city of Winnipeg, Man. Founded 1821. Until city was founded (1860s), it was seat of authority in Manitoba region. Louis Riel captured it in rebellion of 1869. Sold in 1882, it was torn down except for the gate. Lower Fort Garry, on Red R., 19 mi. below Fort Garry, was built 1831 and still stands.

Garter, Order of the, oldest and most important order of knighthood in England. Instituted c.1346 by Edward III, it was originally limited to 26 members. Motto is *Honi soit qui mal y pense* [evil be to him who evil thinks]. Title is abbreviated K.G.

garter snake, common harmless North American snake, usually c.2 ft. long. Common form of NE U.S. varies, but usually is blackish or brownish with three yellow stripes. Young born alive in litters of 30 to 65. Ribbon snake is a garter snake found in wet places.

Garvan, Francis Patrick, 1875–1937, American lawyer; dean of Fordham Univ. law school (1919–23). As alien property custodian (1919) for U.S. govern-

ment, he organized foundation to develop seized German patents.

Garvey, Marcus, 1887–1940, American Negro leader, b. Jamaica. Plans for an African settlement ended when he was charged with fraud.

Gary, Elbert H(enry), 1846–1927, American industrialist, a lawyer. Chairman of board of directors of U.S. Steel Corp. (1903–27). Helped found GARY, Ind. Promoted employee benefits, but refused labor union recognition and insisted on the open shop.

Gary, Romain (rōmē' gärē'), 1914–, French author, b. Vilna, of Russian parents. Author of *The Roots of Heaven* (1958) and other novels.

Gary, city (pop. 178,320), NW Ind., on L. Michigan SE of Chicago in Calumet industrial region. On U.S. Steel Corp. land, city was chartered 1906. State's second largest city and one of nation's leading steel producers midway between iron-ore beds of NW and coal areas of E and SE.

gas. 1 In general usage, any substance appearing in gaseous state at ordinary temperature and pressure; may be compound, element, or mixture. POISON GAS is used in chemical warfare, in insecticides, fumigation; LAUGHING GAS in anesthesia. Illuminating gases include air gas, natural gas. 2 In physics, one of the three states of matter, i.e., that state in which a substance is without definite shape or volume. Gases are classed with liquids as fluid. Molecules of gas move faster and are farther apart than those of liquids or solids. Cohesion between molecules is small; when not confined gas is capable of unlimited DIFFUSION. Volume can be reduced by compression; gases undergo liquefaction after being cooled below critical temperature. At constant temperature volume of gas decreases in direct proportion to increase in pressure (Boyle's law). At fixed volume, increase in pressure and in temperature are directly proportional. Dalton's law deals with mixtures of gases. At constant pressure, volume of gas is directly proportional to temperature. Kelvin temperature scale is used in calculating changes in volume and pressure on gases when temperature change is involved. Avogadro discovered that there are same number of molecules in equal volumes of gases under standard conditions. Volume of one molecular weight of any gas under standard conditions is 22.4 liters. When gas diffuses into a liquid and is held there it is said to have undergone absorption.

Gasca, Pedro de la (pä'drō dä lä gä'skä), c.1485–1567?, Spanish colonial administrator. A priest and lawyer, he was sent to Peru (1547), where he restored order. Repealed New Laws of Las Casas.

Gascoigne, George (gäskoin'), c.1539–1577, English poet. First essay on prosody in English was his *Posies of George Gascoigne* (1575). Wrote first English prose comedy, *Supposes* (1566), a translation from Ariosto. Also wrote *The Steel Glass* (1576), an early attempt in English at formal satire.

Gasconade (gäskünäd'), river rising in S Mo. in the Ozarks and flowing c.265 mi. NE to the Missouri near Gasconade, E of Jefferson City.

Gascony (gä'skünē), Fr. *Gascogne*, region and former province, SW France, in Landes, Gers, Hautes-Pyrénées, Basses-Pyrénées, Lot-et-Garonne, Tarn-et-Garonne, Haute-Garonne, Gironde, and Ariège depts.; historic cap. Auch. Agr., fishing, cattle raising, winegrowing, brandy mfg. (in Armagnac dist.) are main occupations. Basque is still spoken in old Basque provs., notably in and around Bayonne. Part of Roman Aquitania, region was inhabited by BASQUES, who created duchy of Vasconia or Gascony in 7th cent. A.D. Duchy fell into anarchy in 9th cent.; was united in 11th cent. with AQUITAINE, whose later history it shared. Recovered by France at end of Hundred Years War, Gascony consisted of several fiefs, held mainly by the counts of ARMAGNAC and of FOIX and the lords of ALBRET; all these passed, through marriage and inheritance, to Henry of Navarre, who after becoming king of France as Henry IV incorporated them into the royal domain (1607).

gas engine: see INTERNAL-COMBUSTION ENGINE.

Gaskell, Elizabeth (Cleghorn Stevenson), 1810–65, English novelist. Known especially for *Mary Barton* (1848) and *Cranford* (1853; a charming tale of British village life). She also wrote a controversial biography of Charlotte Brontë (1857).

gasoline, volatile fuel oil obtained by fractional distillation of petroleum, by cracking (thermal decomposition) heavier petroleum hydrocarbons, from natural gas, and synthetically by polymerization of lighter hydrocarbons obtained from coal or some other source. Chief uses are as gas-engine fuel and as organic solvent.

Gaspar: see WISE MEN OF THE EAST.

Gasparri, Pietro (pyä′trō gäspär′rē), 1852–1934, Italian cardinal. Directed great codification of canon law and received cardinal's hat from Pius X (1907); as papal secretary of state in First World War, worked for peace; under Pius XI concluded LATERAN TREATY 1929.

Gaspé, Philippe Aubert de (fēlēp′ ōbĕr′ dú gäspä′), 1786–1871, French Canadian author, whose writings give a historical picture of customs in early Quebec.

Gaspee (gä′spē″, gäspē′), British revenue cutter, burned (June 10, 1772) at Gaspee Point in Narragansett Bay, R.I. Ship sent to enforce revenue laws; burning was act of defiance by colonists.

Gaspé Peninsula (gäspä′), tongue of land (150 mi. long, 60–90 mi. wide), E Que., Canada, extending E into the Gulf of St. Lawrence between St. Lawrence R. (N) and Chaleur Bay (S). **Gaspé Bay** is a deep inlet at E end of the peninsula. The resort and market village of **Gaspé** (pop. 2,603) is near the head of the bay. **Cape Gaspé** is at the E end of the peninsula. Population (chiefly French Canadian) is scattered in villages along coast. Fishing, the major industry, is supplemented by lumbering, pulp milling, and some agr. Excellent hunting and fishing is found in the heavily forested and mountainous interior. Tourists have been attracted by the charm of picturesque villages and fine scenery.

Gasperi, Alcide de: see DE GASPERI, ALCIDE.

Gassendi, Pierre (gäsädē′), 1592–1655, French materialist philosopher and scientist. Opposed Aristotelian authority; as vigorous rival of Cartesian school, revived atomic theory; sought to reconcile mechanism and theology.

Gasser, Herbert Spencer (gă′sŭr), 1888–1963, American physiologist. Shared 1944 Nobel Prize in Physiology and Medicine for work on electrophysiology of nerves. Director of Rockefeller Inst. 1935–53.

Gasset, José Ortega: see ORTEGA Y GASSET, JOSÉ.

Gastein (gä′stīn), valley and resort area in Salzburg, W central Austria. Bad Gastein, a fashionable bathing place, has radium thermal springs; its water is also piped to Bad Hofgastein. By Gastein Convention (1865) Austria assumed administration of Holstein, Prussia that of Schleswig.

Gastonia, industrial city (1966 pop. 45,429), W N.C., W of Charlotte, in piedmont. Textile mfg. Kings Mountain Natl. Military Park is SW.

gastric juice: see STOMACH.

gastropod: see MOLLUSK.

Gat: see GHAT.

Gatchina (gä′chĕnŭ), city (pop. 37,000), RSFSR, SSW of Leningrad. Developed around imperial summer residence (built 1766–81). Palace (now museum) looted by Germans in Second World War.

Gate City, trade town (pop. 2,142), SW Va., near Tenn. line WNW of Bristol; settled late 18th cent. Natural Tunnel (100–200 ft. high, 130 ft. wide, c.900 ft. long) is nearby.

Gates, Horatio, 1727–1806, American Revolutionary general, b. England. National hero after success of SARATOGA CAMPAIGN. Commanded Carolina campaign until disgraceful defeat at Camden, S.C. (1780).

Gates, Sir Thomas, fl. 1585–1621, British colonial governor of Va. (1611–14). One of grantees in original charter to found colony.

Gateshead (gäts′hĕd), county borough (pop. 103,332), Durham, England, on Tyne R. opposite Newcastle. Has locomotive works, railroad shops, shipbuilding, and mfg. of glass, iron goods, cables and chemicals. Nearby are coal mines and grindstone quarries.

Gath, Philistine city, on borders of Judah; birthplace of Goliath; refuge of David during years when he was outlawed. 1 Sam. 5.8; 17.4; 21.10; 2 Chron. 26.6.

Gatineau, river of SW Que., Canada, flowing from the Laurentians 230 mi. S to Ottawa R. at Hull.

Gatlinburg, town (pop. 1,764), E Tenn., SE of Knoxville near foot of Mt. Le Conte in Great Smoky Mts. Natl. Park. Popular resort. Park hq. are nearby.

Gatling, Richard Jordan, 1818–1903, American inventor of Gatling multiple-firing gun, precursor of machine gun. His name gave rise to slang word *gat*.

Gatti-Casazza, Giulio (jōō′lyō gät′tē-käzät′sä), 1869–1940, Italian operatic manager. Director of La Scala Opera Co., Milan, 1898–1908; director of Metropolitan Opera, New York, 1908–35.

Gatun Lake, artificial lake (alt. 85 ft.; area 163.38 sq. mi.), Panama Canal Zone, formed by impounding of Chagres R. Used as part of canal route. Gatun Dam, 1½ mi. long, 115 ft. high, controls level of lake.

gaucho (gou′chō), cowboy of Argentine pampa, typically a mestizo, a skillful horseman, lover of adventure. Played important part in national life of Argentine (also Uruguay and Paraguay) 18th–19th cent. Glorified in José Hernández' *Martín Fierro*.

Gaudeamus igitur (gou″dää′mōōs i′gitōor″) [Latin,= let us rejoice therefore], student song; based on songs dating back to at least 13th cent. Present variant forms did not appear in print until 18th cent. Probably originated in parodies of, and borrowings from, religious songs. Brahms used its tune in his *Academic Festival Overture*.

Gauden, John (gô′dŭn), 1605–62, English bishop, who claimed authorship of the EIKON BASILIKE (1649).

Gaudier-Brzeska, Henri (ärē′ gōdyä′-bùrzĕskä′), 1891–1915, French sculptor, the chief exponent of vorticism in sculpture.

Gaudi i Cornet, Antonio (äntō′nyō gôdē′ ē kôr′nĕt), 1852–1926, Spanish architect, noted for his aesthetic audacity and innovations in building technology. His undulating façades resemble sculptural configurations.

Gauguin, Paul (pôl′ gōgĕ′), 1848–1903, French painter, b. Paris. At 35 he gave up a successful banking career to devote himself to art. Allied himself with impressionists and contributed to their last exhibition (1886). During next five years spent some time in Martinique, Brittany, and Arles (with Van Gogh). In 1891 went to Tahiti where he painted some of his finest pictures; except for one brief trip to France spent rest of his life in South Seas. Died in Marquesas Isls. His paintings, neglected in his time, are now highly prized. His figure compositions, gorgeous in color, place him among the great postimpressionists. Also did wood carvings.

Gaul (gôl), Latin *Gallia*, anc. name for the land S and W of the Rhine, W of the Alps, and N of the Pyrenees. The name was extended by the Romans to include N Italy. The name is derived from its settlers of the 4th–3d cent. B.C.—invading Celts, called Gauls by the Romans. Julius CAESAR conquered Gaul in the GALLIC WARS (58–51 B.C.). He is the best ancient source and has immortalized its three ethnic divisions, Aquitania, Gaul proper (central France), and Belgica. It was rapidly Romanized.

Gaulle, Charles de (shärl dù gōl′), 1890–, French general and politician. Opposed 1940 armistice and fled to England; organized "Free French" forces. With Gen. GIRAUD he became co-president of French Committee of Natl. Liberation at Algiers in 1943. Despite coolness of U.S. government he ousted Giraud from the committee, which in June, 1944, proclaimed itself provisional government of France. De Gaulle was elected president of France in 1945 but, having lost leftist support, resigned (1946). In 1947 he organized a rightist movement, Reunion of the French People

(RPF), which he disbanded 1953 after setback. Convinced of his mission, he retired until 1958, when he was made premier with power to rule by decree for six months. A new constitution greatly increased powers of presidency to which de Gaulle was elected 1958, 1965. By building nuclear force, recognizing Communist China, and withdrawing France from the North Atlantic Treaty Organization, he hoped to restore French prestige and independence of action.

Gaulli, Giovanni Battista (jōvän'nē bät'tēs'tä gäōōl'lē), 1639–1709, Italian painter, called Il Baciccio, noted for his frescoes; influenced by Bernini and Correggio.

Gaunt, John of: see JOHN OF GAUNT.

Gaur (gour), anc. city of West Bengal, India. Center of Moslem culture from 1198 to late 16th cent. Has fine Golden Mosque. The Kadam Rasul Mosque (1530) is erected over supposed relics of Mohammed.

Gauss, Christian (gous), 1878–1951, American educator, dean of Princeton Univ. from 1925 to 1945.

Gauss, Karl Friedrich (kärl frē'drĭkh gous'), 1777–1855, German mathematician and astronomer. He made important contributions to theory of numbers, solving of binomial equations, geometry of curved surfaces, and method of least squares, and also in geodesy. He pioneered in applying mathematical theory to electricity and magnetism. Unit of intensity of magnetic field was called gauss until 1932 when gauss was applied to unit of magnetic induction. One of greatest mathematicians of all time.

Gautama: see BUDDHA.

Gautier, Émile Félix (āmēl' fālēks' gōtyā'), 1864–1940, French geographer. Authority on Algiers, the Sahara, and French African possessions.

Gautier, Théophile (tāōfēl' gōtyā'), 1811–72, French poet, novelist, and critic. His aesthetic creed, illustrated in the carefully tooled poems of Émaux et camées [enamels and cameos] (1852), influenced the Parnassians. His best-known novels are Mademoiselle de Maupin (1835) and Le Capitaine Fracasse (1863).

Gavarnie, Cirque de (sērk' dù gävärnē'), gigantic natural amphitheater in central Pyrenees, SW France. From its bottom, at c.5,740 ft., it rises in concentric circles and is enclosed by crests over 9,000 ft. high. The famous Brèche de Roland is a cleft in one of crests. Nearby is a waterfall 1,385 ft. high.

Gaveston, Piers (pērz' gă'vùstùn), d. 1312, favorite of EDWARD II of England. Had great influence with Edward and in his absence acted as regent. His greed and arrogance aroused the barons' hostility; they twice banished him and then put him to death.

Gavle, Swed. **Gävle** (yĕv'lŭ), city (pop. 55,947), co. seat of Gavleborg co., E Sweden; a Baltic Sea port. Produces wood pulp, textiles, tobacco, chemicals. Chartered 1446; oldest and largest city of Norrland.

Gavleborg, Swed. **Gävleborgs län,** province (7,612 sq. mi.; pop. 293,395), E central Sweden; on Gulf of Bothnia; cap. GAVLE. Abundant timber supplies sawmills and papermills.

gavotte, originally a peasant dance of the Gavots, inhabitants of the Gap region, France; introduced at court of Louis XIV; used by Lully in ballets and operas, by Bach and Couperin in keyboard suites.

Gawain, Sir: see ARTHURIAN LEGEND; PARSIFAL.

Gay, John, 1685–1732, English playwright and poet. Friend of wits and courtiers of his day, he is famous for realistic, satiric Beggar's Opera (1728), a ballad opera still revived. Also wrote verse, The Shepherd's Week (1714), and essays, Trivia (1716).

Gaya (gī'ŭ), city (pop. 133,700), Bihar, India. Has noted Vishnuite temple. Buddh Gaya, site of Buddha's enlightment, is nearby.

gay-feather: see BLAZING STAR.

Gay Head, resort town (pop. 103), SE Mass., on W tip of Martha's Vineyard; settled 1669. Has lighthouse (1799) on beautiful, high clay cliffs.

Gay-Lussac, Joseph Louis (zhôzĕf lwē gā'-lüsäk), 1778–1850, French chemist and physicist. Discovered cyanogen; made advances in industrial chemistry; collaborated in isolating boron; invented alcoholometer, hydrometer; discovered Charles's law independently. **Gay-Lussac's law** of combining volumes: volumes of gases that interact to give gaseous product are in ratio of small whole numbers to each other and each has similar relation to volume of product.

Gayoso de Lemos, Manuel (mänwĕl' gīō'sō dā lā'mōs), c.1752–1799, Spanish governor of Louisiana (1797–99). Intrigued to separate American West from U.S.

Gaza, Theodore (gā'zù, gä'zù), c.1398–c.1478, Greek scholar and humanist of the Renaissance. When Turks attacked Constantinople, he went to Italy. His Greek grammar was printed (1495) by Aldus Manutius.

Gaza (gā'–) or **Ghuzzeh** (gŭ'–), town (pop. c.100,-000), NE Egypt, near the Mediterranean; in anc. times a town of commercial importance, modern Gaza is principal city of the **Gaza Strip** (pop. c.251,-960), a coastal area under Egyptian rule since 1949. Area occupied (1956–57) by Israel during Sinai campaign. UN polices border and supports Arab refugee camps. Region again taken by Israel in hostilities in June, 1967.

Gazel, Al-: see AL-GAZEL.

gazelle (gùzĕl'), graceful antelope of genus Gazella. Number of species are found chiefly in Africa, also in central and SW Asia and India. They are small (2–3 ft. high) and fleet, usually fawn color, but some are marked with black and white.

gazetteer, originally one who wrote gazettes; now a dictionary of geographical names (of a region, of certain classes, or of the world). First used in its modern sense after publication of Lawrence Echard's geographical index, Gazetteer's or Newsman's Interpreter (1703). Such lists have been made since the 6th cent., but general gazetteers date only from the 19th cent. Well-known gazetteers include Johnston's (Scotland, 1850), Blackie's (Scotland, 1850), Bouillet's (France, 1857), Ritter's (Germany, 1874), Longman's (England, 1895), Garollo's (Italy, 1898), Lippincott's (U.S., 1865; latest revised issue The Columbia Lippincott Gazetteer of the World, 1952).

Gaziantep (gä"zĕäntĕp'), formerly **Aintab** (īntäb'), city (pop. 124,097), S Turkey. Textile mfg. Taken by Saladin 1183. Fell after six-month siege (1920–21) to the French in occupation of region, but it was returned to Turkey 1921.

Gazira, region, central Republic of the Sudan, lying between the White Nile and Blue Nile. Irrigation works, built after 1925, opened part of region to agr. Works nationalized 1950. Most of Sudan's cotton grown here. Also Gezira.

Gd, chemical symbol of the element GADOLINIUM.

Gdansk: see DANZIG.

Gdynia (gùdĭn'yŭ), city (est. pop. 161,000), N Poland; a Baltic seaport on Gulf of Danzig. Constructed after 1924 to end Poland's dependence on Danzig. Now an important commercial port and railway center; has metal, machinery, and food industries.

Ge, chemical symbol of the element GERMANIUM.

gearing, in a machine, device for transmitting motion by means of teeth or friction wheels. **Spur gearing** utilizes wheels with teeth at right angles to their shafts. **Bevel gearing,** accomplished by inclined tooth edges, transmits motion to shafts intersecting drive shaft. **Screw or worm gearing** transmits by screwlike action. **Friction gearing** transmits motion, without use of teeth, by friction of two surfaces in contact.

Geary, John White (gēr'ē), 1819–73, American politician, Union general in Civil War. As governor of "bleeding" Kansas (1856–57), he helped bring peace to territory. Governor of Pa. 1866–73.

Gebal (gē'–), biblical name of BYBLOS.

Geber (gā'bùr, jēbùr) or **Jabir** (jä'bùr, jä'bēr), fl. 8th cent., Arabian alchemist, physician. Authenticity of many works on alchemy supposedly written by him is disputed. Modern studies show that Latin translations attributed to him were probably written c.1100 or later. These works influenced development of medieval alchemy and indicated use of laboratory experimentation. They maintained that all metals are composed of mercury and sulfur and are transmutable into gold.

Gedaliah (gĕdŭlī'ŭ), governor of Jews not carried off in Captivity. He was treacherously murdered. Day of death still observed as Jewish fast. Jer. 40–41.

Geddes, James, 1763–1838, American engineer. Surveyed canal routes between Great Lakes and Hudson R. (1808) and from Chesapeake to Ohio rivers (1827). Was engineer for Erie and Champlain canal systems.

Geddes, Norman Bel, 1893–1958, American scenic designer. *The Miracle* was popular work. Originated modernistic style in shop-window displays.

Geddes, Sir Patrick, 1854–1932, Scottish biologist and sociologist. Interested in the evolution of sex, he sought to relate biological knowledge with civic welfare and to city planning.

Gedeon (gĕ'dēun), same as GIDEON.

Geelong, city (metropolitan pop. 88,160), Victoria, Australia, on inlet of Port Phillip Bay. Principal exports are wool, wheat, meat, and hides.

Geertgen tot Sint Jano (hâr'tyŭ tôt' sĭnt yäns'), fl. latter half of 15th cent., Dutch painter.

Gehenna: see HELL.

Gehrig, (Henry) Lou(is) (loo gâ'rĭg), 1903–41, American baseball infielder. As first baseman (1925–39) of N.Y. Yankees, estab. major-league record of playing 2,130 consecutive league games. Had lifetime batting average of .340, batted .361 in seven world series. Four times won American League most-valuable-player award.

Geiger, Abraham (ä'brähäm gī'gŭr), 1810–74, German rabbi, Semitic scholar, foremost exponent of the reform movement, a chief rabbi of Berlin and from 1870 head of academy for Jewish science.

Geiger counter (gī'gŭr), instrument for detection and quantitative determination of ionizing particles, such as beta rays and cosmic rays. Variously designed, it usually consists of a thin metal cylinder (forming one electrode) and a needle (or a thin wire as the other electrode) enclosed by glass tube in which a gas is also sealed. Current passes from electrode to electrode when the counter is near radioactive substances. Emanations, however faint, ionize the gas, allowing current to jump gap and close circuit, activating audible indicator. Instrument named for Hans Geiger (1882–1945), German physicist.

Geijer, Erik Gustav (ā'rĭk gŭs'täv yĭ'ŭr), 1783–1847, Swedish historian and poet. Leader in revival of national literature. Known for his *History of the Swedes* (Eng. tr., 1845).

Geijerstam, Gustaf af (äv yä'yŭrstäm), 1858–1909, Swedish novelist, author of realistic studies of peasant life and of "problem novels."

geisha (gā'shŭ), Japanese female entertainer. Trained from childhood in singing, dancing, and repartee, a geisha works under contract for a geisha house, a place of relaxation for businessmen and politicians. Her status varies; she may or may not be a courtesan; she may marry. Many live luxuriously and wield considerable political influence.

Geissler tube (gīs'lŭr), a gas discharge tube in which light is produced when electricity is passed through gas in the tube. It is used in spectroscopy. It was named for **Heinrich Geissler,** 1814–79, German mechanic and inventor.

Gela (jē'lŭ), city (pop. 43,200), SW Sicily, Italy, on Mediterranean; founded c.688 B.C. by Greek colonists. Reached its height under tyrants Gelon and Hippocrates (5th cent. B.C.). Modern Gela (known as Terranova di Sicilia until 1927) was founded by Emperor Frederick II in 1230. Poet Aeschylus died here.

Gelasius II (jĭlā'shēus), d. 1119, pope (1118–19), elected in protest against weakness of PASCHAL II in struggle with Emperor Henry V over INVESTITURE. Thrown in prison by emperor's party, he was delivered by the people, but advance of Henry with an army forced Gelasius to flee to Gaeta, then to France. Henry set up Gregory VIII as antipope.

gelatin, a type of animal protein. It is obtained from supporting structures of vertebrates. Pure product is brittle, transparent, colorless, odorless, tasteless; it dissolves in hot water, congeals when cold. It swells to an elastic mass in cold water. Some of its many uses are: in making confectionery, jellied soups, and molded meats and salads, in preserving meat and fruit, in electrotyping, photography, waterproofing, dyeing, as bacteriologic culture medium, coating for pills and capsules, and emulsifying agent. Glue and size are impure forms. AGAR is vegetable gelatin.

Gelderland, Guelderland, or **Guelders** (gĕl'dŭrlŭnd, gĕl'dŭrz), province (1,939 sq. mi., pop. 1,384,459). E and central Netherlands; cap. Arnheim. Drained by Ijssel, Lower Rhine, and Waal rivers, which enclose fertile agr. lowland in SW. Duchy of Gelderland was conquered by Charles the Bold of Burgundy 1473; passed to Hapsburgs after his death; joined United Provs. of Netherlands 1579. Part of province, including ducal cap., Geldern, was ceded to Prussia 1715.

Gelibolu, Turkey: see GALLIPOLI.

Gellée, Claude: see CLAUDE LORRAIN.

Gellius, Aulus (jĕl'yŭs), fl. 2d cent., Latin writer, a lawyer; author of *Noctes Atticae*, a collection valuable for its quotations from lost works.

Gelon (jē'lŏn), d. 478 B.C., Greek Sicilian ruler. Tyrant of Gela, he ruled Syracuse (485–478 B.C.), dominating Greek Sicily. In 480 he crushed the Carthaginians under Hamilcar. He was succeeded by HIERO I.

Gelsenkirchen (gĕl'zŭnkĭr"khŭn), city (pop. 376,956), North Rhine–Westphalia, West Germany, adjoining Essen; a major industrial and coal-mining center of Ruhr dist. Has several moated castles.

gem, substance of mineral or organic origin used for adornment. Beauty, rarity, and durability determine value. Beauty depends mainly on optical properties, which impart luster, color, and fire; durability or HARDNESS. Other properties include form of crystal, index of refraction, cleavage, type of fracture. Gems most prized are DIAMOND, RUBY, SAPPHIRE, EMERALD, PEARL (organic); some semiprecious stones are AQUAMARINE, AMETHYST, GARNET, TOURMALINE, TOPAZ, TURQUOISE, MOONSTONE, JADE, CHRYSOBERYL.

Gemara: see TALMUD.

Gemini [Latin, = twins] (jĕ'mĭnē), third sign of ZODIAC. The twins were Castor and Pollux.

Geminiani, Francesco (fränchä'skō jämēnyä'nē), d. 1762, Italian violinist and composer of music for strings. He wrote on methods of playing stringed instruments (e.g., *The Art of Playing the Violin*).

Gemistus, Georgius (jôr'jŭs jŭmi'stŭs), c.1355–c.1450, Greek Platonic philosopher. He led Cosimo de' Medici to found the Florentine Academy and inspired the study of Plato that characterized the Italian Renaissance.

Gemniczer, Wenzel: see JAMNITZER.

gender, in grammar, subclassification of a form class (or part of speech) in which members of the subclass have characteristic features of agreement with other words. The term *gender* is usually restricted to such a classification of nouns or nounlike words and is not usually considered to include NUMBER. In French *la viande* [the meat] and *le vin* [the wine] are distinguished by *la* and *le* as different genders, *la* being feminine, *le* masculine (because most French nouns referring to females are feminine, most referring to males are masculine). German, Russian, and Latin have three genders—masculine, feminine, and neuter. A two-gender distinction between animate and inanimate is widespread (as in Algonquian languages). English nouns may be divided into gender classes according to personal pronoun used to refer to them; these do not match sex classes (e.g., *she* for *ship*). The grammatical device of concord or agreement is bound up with gender distinctions; thus in Romance languages adjectives "agree" with the corresponding nouns in being masculine or feminine.

gene (jēn), fundamental unit in transmission of hereditary characters in plants and animals. Genes are believed to be contained within chromosomes and to control development of specific morphological characters by control of biochemical reactions. Composed of NUCLEIC ACID. See also GENETICS.

General Agreement on Tariffs and Trade (GATT), specialized agency of UN. Estab. 1948, its members are pledged to reduce tariffs and other barriers to international trade, and to eliminate discriminatory treatment in international commerce. Only exceptions to GATT rules involve BALANCE OF PAYMENTS difficulties. The 1964 round of negotiations, known as Kennedy round, resulted in agreement (May, 1967) to reduce tariffs by one third over 5-yr. period and in other liberalizations.

General Land Office, estab. 1812 in U.S. Treasury Dept. and transferred in 1849 to U.S. Dept. of the Interior. Managed and disposed of public domain. Emphasized conservation of remaining public land after 1900. Consolidated in 1946 with Grazing Service into Bureau of Land Management.

general strike, cessation of work by all or a majority of workers in a region. The motive is economic if the strike is directed against employers, political if it seeks to eventuate in governmental concessions or governmental overthrow. It has been advocated by syndicalists and anarchists, and has been a powerful weapon of European labor.

Generation of '98, Spanish literary and cultural movement that flourished for two decades after the end of the Spanish-American War. Characterized by literary experimentation, critical reassessment of Spanish culture, and political liberalism, it included Machado, Ganivet, Unamuno, Azorín, Ortega y Gassett, Baroja, Valle Inclán, Benevente y Martínez, and Pérez de Ayala.

generator, machine for changing mechanical into electrical energy, using principle of electromagnetic INDUCTION. Simple generator consists of coil of wire rotating between two magnetic poles; as turning coil cuts magnetic lines of force, electric current is generated in coil, from which metal strips (brushes) lead current into closed circuit. Turning coil cuts lines of force first in one direction then another, so current flows first in one then another direction (AC or alternating current). One-direction current (DC or direct current) obtained by using device called commutator, but current remains pulsating. Commercial generators avoid pulsation by use of more complicated structure involving so-called ARMATURE. In dynamo, the ELECTROMAGNET is commonly used.

Genesee (jěnŭsē′), river, rising in N. Pa. in the Alleghenies and flowing c.158 mi. N through N.Y. to L. Ontario at Rochester. Beautiful and fertile valley. Flood control dam near Mt. Morris, N.Y.

Geneseo, farm trade village (1966 pop. 4,415), W central N.Y., on Genesee R., SSW of Rochester; settled c.1790. State Univ. Col. at Geneseo is here.

Genesis (jě′nŭsĭs) [Gr.,= origin], first book of Old Testament, first of the five books of Law (the Pentateuch or Torah), ascribed by tradition to Moses. It is a religious account of the creation of the world and of man, of man's first fall from grace, of the great Deluge. It tells the stories of the great religious patriarchs: Noah, Abraham, Isaac, and Jacob–who later became Israel. Book ends with story of Joseph and the migration of Jacob's family to Egypt. For religious conceptions derived from opening chapters, see SIN and GRACE. Importance of Genesis in Jewish and Christian thought is inestimable.

Genesis, Little: see PSEUDEPIGRAPHA.

Genêt, Edmond Charles Édouard (zhŭnā′), 1763–1834, French minister to U.S. (1793–94), known as Citizen Genêt. Welcomed by pro-French Jeffersonians, his efforts to raise troops against Spanish Florida and to commission privateers against British commerce were not approved by Pres. Washington. His recall was demanded.

Genet, Jean (zhā), 1910–, French playwright. His dramas of revolt against society include *The Balcony* (1957) and *The Blacks* (1959). *Miracle of the Rose,* a novel, appeared 1967.

genetics (jŭnĕ′tĭks), scientific study of heredity. The basis of the science was the work of Gregor MENDEL rediscovered in 1900 independently by Hugo De Vries, K. E. Correns, and Erich Tschermak-Seysenegg. Mendel's principles were modified and extended by discovery of CHROMOSOME and GENE as physical basis of transmission of hereditary characters; by discoveries such as those related to tendency of certain characters to be inherited together, of some characters to be sexlinked, and of interaction of different genes to determine presence of characters. Work of T. H. Morgan and his followers on *Drosophila melanogaster* (fruit fly) was important to progress of genetics. Biochemical genetics describes gene action in chemical terms; NUCLEIC ACID is the active stuff of gene. See also HEREDITY; MUTATION. See *ill.,* p. 329.

Geneva (jŭnē′vù), Fr. *Genève,* canton (109 sq. mi.; pop. 259,234), SW Switzerland, at SW tip of L. of Geneva, almost entirely surrounded by French territory. Rural section produces fruits, vegetables, wine. Its cap., **Geneva** (pop. 176,183), lies on both sides of the Rhone, which emerges here from the lake. It is a cultural and financial center, mfg. machinery and watches. Included in Roman Gaul, Geneva early became an episcopal see, shared history of first and second kingdoms of BURGUNDY and passed to Holy Roman Empire 1033. Though citizens won extensive rights of self-rule (1387), these rights were increasingly encroached on by the dukes of Savoy, whose representatives shared the authority with the bishops. In alliance with Swiss cantons of Fribourg and Bern, the citizens expelled the bishops in 1533 and accepted the Reformation, preached by Guillaume Farel, in 1535. Under CALVIN Geneva became the focal point of the Reformation. An attempt by Charles Emmanuel I of Savoy to recapture the city was repulsed (1602). Huguenot refugees contributed to growing prosperity of Geneva, which was a cosmopolitan intellectual center by the 18th cent. Under French occupation 1798–1814, Geneva joined Switzerland as a canton 1815. It is the seat of the Internatl. Red Cross, the Internatl. Labor Organization, and several UN bodies. The huge Palais des Nations housed the League of Nations until it was taken over by the UN. Univ. of Geneva originated with academy founded by Calvin. Historic monuments include cathedral, city hall. Its fine parks and splendid situation make Geneva a cosmopolitan resort. It is the birthplace of J. J. Rousseau. The **Lake of Geneva** or **Lake Leman,** between Switzerland and France, is 45 mi. long, 2–9 mi. wide. The Rhone is its main feeder and only outlet. N (Swiss) shore is bounded by vineyards and orchards and dotted with resorts. From S (French) shore rise the French Alps. Scenery has been celebrated by many writers.

Geneva (jŭnē′vù), city (pop. 17,286), W central N.Y., at N end of Seneca L. and SE of Rochester, in farm region; settled 1788. Trade center with nurseries. Seat of Hobart and William Smith Colleges (see COLLEGES OF THE SENECA, THE).

Geneva, Lake, c.8 mi. long, SE Wis., near Ill. line. Shores have summer homes and camps of religious and social organizations.

Geneva, Lake of: see GENEVA, Switzerland.

Geneva Arbitration: see ALABAMA CLAIMS.

Geneva Conference. 1 International conference held at Geneva, Switzerland, April–July, 1954. Chief participants: U.S., USSR, Great Britain, France, Communist China, N Korea, S Korea, Vietnam, Vietminh party, Laos, Cambodia. Conferees agreed on armistice and political settlement in Indo-China (see VIETNAM, LAOS), but reached no agreement on transforming armistice in Korea into permanent peace. **2** "Summit Conference" held at Geneva in July, 1955, by U.S.,

British, French, and Russian heads of state. U.S. suggested mutual aerial inspection and exchange of information on military establishments; Russia gave priority to weapons reduction. Conferees agreed to increase cultural and economic exchanges and issued directives for foreign ministers' conference in Geneva; this meeting (Oct.–Nov., 1955) ended in deadlock. See also FOREIGN MINISTERS, COUNCIL OF; DISARMAMENT.

Genevieve, Saint, d. 512, patron saint of Paris, a nun said to have averted an attack of Attila on Paris. Feast: Jan. 3.

Genghis Khan: see JENGHIZ KHAN.

genie, an older name for JINNI.

Génissiat Dam, France: see RHONE.

genista: see BROOM.

genitive: see CASE.

Genk (khĕngk), city (est. pop. 54,924), Limburg prov., E Belgium, on Albert Canal. Commercial center with coal mines nearby.

Gennesaret (gĕnĕ'sŭrĕt): see GALILEE, SEA OF.

Genoa, Ital. *Genova,* city (pop. 824,474), cap. of Liguria, NW Italy, on the Mediterranean. Chief Italian port; industrial center with shipyards, mfg. of automobiles, airplanes. City flourished under Romans; became free commune, governed by consuls, c.10th cent. Its growth as a commercial and Mediterranean power brought wars with Pisa and Venice (13th–14th cent.) in which Genoa acquired colonies and trading privileges from Spain to the CRIMEA; its expansion was largely financed by a group of merchants who in 1408 founded a powerful bank, the Banco San Giorgio. After 1339 the republic (which came to include most of Liguria) was governed by doges elected for life. The foreign possessions were gradually lost, and internal strife made possible intervention by France and Milan. Genoese power was briefly revived by Andrea DORIA (16th cent.), but his rule was followed by periods of Spanish, French, and Austrian control. Austrians were expelled 1746, but in 1768 Genoa lost Corsica to France. Annexed to France in 1805, Genoa and Liguria were united in 1815 with the kingdom of Sardinia. Notable buildings include Cathedral of San Lorenzo (rebuilt 1100) and the doges' palace. The harbor section is picturesque. University (1812) was originally a Jesuit college. Birthplace of Christopher Columbus, Mazzini, Paganini.

Genoa (jŭnō'ů). **1** City (pop. 1,009), E central Nebr., on Loup R., NW of Lincoln, in prairie region; settled 1857 by Mormons. Pawnee village has been excavated nearby. **2** Village (pop. c.150), extreme W Nev., SW of Carson City; founded c.1849 as Mormon station. Post on early road to Calif., it was first permanent settlement in state and for a time provisional cap. of Territory.

Genoa, Conference of, 1922, international conference held at Genoa, Italy, to discuss economic reconstruction of Europe after First World War. Main item was Russian debt, which the Soviets had repudiated. Some progress was made, but announcement of German-Soviet Treaty of RAPALLO cut negotiations short.

genocide, intentional destruction by a government of racial, religious, ethnic, or national group. Term was coined in 1944, but the acts it describes are found frequently in history. In 1945 the Nurenberg Tribunal listed persecution on racial or religious grounds as a crime. Genocide was made an international crime by a UN convention (concluded 1949) which so designated it and described it in detail.

gens (jĕnz), ancient Roman family group, counterpart of clan or sib in other societies. Descent was traced in male line only, from common ancestor worshiped by all. Marriage within gens was discouraged.

Genseric: see GAISERIC.

Genth, Frederick Augustus (gĕnt), 1820–93, German-American chemist and mineralogist. Came to U.S.

1848. Identified 23 new minerals including genthite, named for him.

gentian (jĕn'shùn), perennial or annual plant of widely distributed genus *Gentiana,* bearing predominantly blue flowers, usually in autumn. Two species native to E North America are fringed gentian (*Gentiana crinita*), a biennial and difficult to grow, and bottle, or closed, gentian (*G. saponaria*). Others are prized for rock gardens.

Gentile da Fabriano (dä fäbrëä'nō), c.1370–1427, Italian painter, first great representative of Umbrian school. Retained gilt ornament and glowing color of early Umbrian painters. Influenced Venetians. Masterpiece is *The Adoration of the Magi.*

Gentileschi, Orazio (ōrä'tsēō jäntēlä'skē), c.1562–1647, Florentine mural and portrait painter. In 1626 settled in England at invitation of Charles I. His daughter **Artemisia Gentileschi** (ärtämē'zyä), c.1597–c.1651, was a renowned portraitist.

gentlemen's agreement, in business, an informal, private, usually verbal agreement among rivals as to prices charged, goods handled, or areas served. They are outlawed in the U.S. by antitrust legislation. In U.S. and Japanese history the gentlemen's agreement was the understanding arrived at (1907) in the administration of Theodore Roosevelt, with Ishii the Japanese negotiator. It provided that Japan should stop emigration of Japanese workers to the U.S. and the U.S. should halt discrimination against Japanese. The U.S. immigration laws of 1924 automatically ended this agreement.

Gentz, Friedrich von (frē'drĭkh fŭn gĕnts'), 1764–1832, German publicist. Conducted polemics against Napoleon; became Metternich's secretary 1812. The brain of the Holy Alliance, he was secretary at congresses of Vienna, Aachen, Troppau, Laibach, Verona.

geodesy, study of the dimensions, mass, weight, and elasticity of the earth. **Geodetic surveying** is the theory and practice of determining points and making measurements on the earth's surface involving dimensions so large that the earth's curvature must be taken into account.

Geoffrey IV, known as **Geoffrey Plantagenet** (plăntăj'ùnĕt) [O.Fr.,= sprig of broom; he usually wore a sprig in his helmet], 1113–51, count of Anjou (1129–51); son of FULK. Married MATILDA, daughter of Henry I of England (1128); claimed Normandy in her name and completed its conquest 1144. Went on crusade with Louis VII (1147). His son became Henry II of England.

Geoffrey of Monmouth, c.1100–1154, British author. His *Historiae regum Britanniae* (1137?), an important source for Arthurian legend, is probably a mixture of chronicle, folktale, and fiction.

Geoffroy Saint-Hilaire, Étienne (ātyĕn' zhôfrä' sētēlĕr') 1772–1844, French zoologist. Proposed in *Philosophie Anatomique* (2 vols., 1818–22) that all animals conform to a single plan of structure.

geography, science that observes, catalogues, analyzes, correlates facts of area differentiation on earth's surface. First systematic study was Greek: Aristotle demonstrated world's sphericity, delimited its habitable parts; Strabo's interest in human adaptation to physical setting enlarged scope of study beyond mathematical relationships; study culminated in Ptolemy. Arabs carried learning through Middle Ages. Marco Polo's travels, growing Eastern trade, and exploration voyages revived geographic interest beyond Moslem world. The 16th and 17th cent. textbooks (Varenius) and maps (Mercator) formulated sound theoretical geography. Modern era began late 18th cent. with Alexander von Humboldt and Karl Ritter. Two basic methods of approach are systematic and regional. Systematic approach was spurred by growth of physical and social sciences; regional approach integrates results of systematic method, focuses them on specific place or area—meeting demand for inventory of resources of newly discovered regions. These approaches are actually interdependent. Two branches of geography are physical and human (or cultural). First, based on physical sciences, studies features of world's surface in relation to cosmic influences; climate, land form, soil are examined as to origin, classified as to distribution; flora and fauna are brought into areal pattern. Human (economic, social, political) geography studies man's relation to environment, also his conscious adaptation of himself to it and it to his needs. Geography integrates data of other sciences in terms of areal differentiation. Cartographers, gazetteer compilers, scientific expeditions, university studies, Federal agencies, and geographic institutes promote modern geographic knowledge.

Geological Survey, United States, bureau organized under Dept. of the Interior (1879) to explore surface and geological structure of country, investigate natural resources, classify public lands, and issue papers, bulletins, and maps based on surveys.

geologic dating: see DATING.

geology (jēō′lŭjē), the science of the earth with respect to its structure, rocks, surface features. Its branches include petrology, structural geology, geomorphology, physiography, cosmology, paleontology, and economic and historical geology. Geologic history includes four grand divisions or eras: PRECAMBRIAN, PALEOZOIC, MESOZOIC, CENOZOIC. Each is supposed to have marked a new stage in life development, and to have ended with profound structural changes. The geologic cycle, repeated again and again, consists of a period of mountain building, followed by one of erosion and, in turn, by renewed uplift. Time elapsed since deposition of the oldest known rocks is probably at least three and one half billion years. See *ill.,* p. 774; see also GEOLOGIC ERAS, table.

geometry, branch of mathematics dealing with space properties and relations of figures in space. Elementary, Euclidean, axiomatic geometry includes plane (study of figures lying entirely in one plane), solid (three-dimensional figures), and spherical (figures drawn on spherical surface). Analytical geometry includes geometric relations between curves, using algebraic relations between equations corresponding (by coordinate system) to curves; descriptive geometry includes study of reproducing solid figures on a plane; differential geometry includes theory of properties of figures describable in terms of calculus. Modern geometry includes study of non-Euclidean spaces, Riemannian geometry, and topology.

geomorphology, study of origin and evolution of earth's topographic features. Developed after 1890 as a result of William M. Davis's concept of the geomorphic cycle, theory that land forms pass through a series of well-organized stages in an inorganic evolution.

Geophysical Year, International: see INTERNATIONAL GEOPHYSICAL YEAR.

geopolitics, study of relationship between physical environment and politics, first emphasized by Aristotle. School of geopolitical determinists became especially prominent in Germany in 19th cent. Geopolitical theories, e.g., *lebensraum* [living space], were adopted by Nazi Germany to rationalize regime.

George, Saint, 4th cent.?, patron of England, perhaps a soldier in the imperial army who died for the faith in Asia Minor. Ancient patron of soldiers, he was adopted in medieval England. In old plays and art St. George is the slayer of the dragon (the tale was popularized in *The Golden Legend*). His red cross appears on the Union Jack.

George, kings of Great Britain and Ireland. George I (George Louis), 1660–1727, was king 1714–27. Great-grandson of James I, he was the first British sovereign of house of HANOVER under Act of SETTLEMENT. His indifference to government led to first real cabinet and rise of the Whigs to power. Quadruple Alliance guaranteed Hanoverian succession in 1718. His son, **George II** (George Augustus), 1683–1760, was king 1727–60. More active in government, in War of AUSTRIAN SUCCESSION he was last British king to lead troops in person. His wife, CAROLINE OF ANSPACH,

furthered long dominancy (1721–42) of Robert WALPOLE. Whigs united behind policy of William PITT (the elder) in SEVEN YEARS WAR (1756–63). King's grandson, **George III** (George William Frederick), 1738–1820, was king 1760–1820. Ended long Whig control by securing Pitt's resignation in 1761. Wanting to rule personally, he found amenable minister (1770–82) in Lord North whose policy of coercion led to AMERICAN REVOLUTION. Notable Tory ministry of the younger William Pitt (1783–1801) saw the end of royal attempts to control the ministry. His reign saw changes effected by Industrial Revolution; a flowering of arts and letters. King's insanity led to regency (1811) of his son, **George IV** (George Augustus Frederick), 1762–1830, who was king 1820–30. Ruling through Tory ministers, he was the leader of a profligate society and was personally hated. Succeeded by William IV. **George V** (George Frederick Ernest Albert), 1865–1936, king 1910–36, was the second son of Edward VII. Interested in empire affairs, he visited India in 1911. In 1917 he gave up all German titles and changed the name of the royal house from Saxe-Coburg-Gotha to Windsor. His second son, **George VI** (Albert Frederick Arthur George), 1895–1952, became king in 1936 upon the abdication of Edward VIII, his brother. With Elizabeth, his consort, he made state visits to France (1938), Canada and U.S. (1939), and South Africa (1947). In Second World War he visited bombed areas, inspected war plants, and toured theaters of war. His elder daughter, Elizabeth II, succeeded him.

George V, 1819–78, last king of Hanover (1851–66). Sided against Prussia in Austro-Prussian War; lost Hanover to Prussia. He was blind.

George, kings of the Hellenes. George I, 1845–1913, second son of Christian IX of Denmark, was elected 1862 to succeed Otto I on Greek throne. Introduced democratic constitution (1863); acquired Thessaly and part of Epirus (1881) and Crete (1908). Was assassinated. His grandson was **George II,** 1890–1947. Reigned 1922–23; exiled 1923–35; restored 1935. Countenanced dictatorship of METAXAS. In exile during Axis occupation of Greece in Second World War; returned 1946 after plebiscite had decided in favor of monarchy. Civil war with Communists continued under his brother Paul, who succeeded him.

George, David Lloyd: see LLOYD GEORGE, DAVID.

George, Henry, 1839–97, American economist, founder of the single-tax movement. He believed a single tax on land would meet all costs of government and even leave a surplus. Wrote *Progress and Poverty* (1879). Candidate for mayor of New York city 1886.

George, Stefan (shtā′fän gâôr′gŭ), 1868–1933, German poet. Influenced by the French symbolists, he perfected a style of classic, polished beauty and hardness which raised him to the position of major poet and had tremendous influence on the younger generation. His lyric cycles include *Algbaig* (1892), *Die Bücher der Hirten* [book of the shepherds] (1895), *Das Jahr der Seele* [the soul's year] (1897), *Das neue Reich* [the new kingdom] (1928). His thinking was influenced by Nietzsche.

George, river of N Que., Canada, flows 365 mi. N into Ungava Bay on Hudson Strait.

George, Fort, B.C., Canada: see PRINCE GEORGE.

George, Lake, 33 mi. long and 1–3 mi. wide, NE N.Y., in foothills of the Adirondacks and S of L. Champlain, into which it drains. Center of resort area. Discovered and named Lac du Saint Sacrement by Isaac Jogues, 1646; renamed by Sir William Johnson, 1755. At S end is Lake George village (pop. 1,026). Has ruins of Fort William Henry (1755) and Fort George (1759). Lake is on water route between Hudson and St. Lawrence rivers. Area was scene of much fighting in French and Indian and Revolutionary wars.

George Junior Republic, community at Freeville, N.Y., founded 1895 by W. R. George, and similar communities elsewhere, for neglected and maladjusted

Time	Geologic Development	Life Forms

CENOZOIC ERA. Age of mammals and modern seed plants. The era slated c.62 million years.* The epochs Paleocene through Pliocene are sometimes classed as Teritary period, and the subsequent time as Quaternary period.

Time	Geologic Development	Life Forms
Recent Began c.25,000 years ago.	Most glaciers melted and lands became warm. Deserts formed in parts of world.	Neolithic man developed after last glacial age, at least 20,000 B.C. Beginnings of civilization: pottery, community life, agriculture, domestication of animals. Copper and Bronze Ages began 5000–2000 B.C. and Iron Age 3000–800 B.C.
Pleistocene epoch or Ice age Began c.1 million years ago.	Glaciers covered parts of Americas, Europe, and Asia four or five times; disappeared from N.Y. c.38,000 years ago and from Sweden c.12,000 years ago. Great Lakes formed when ice last disappeared. Erosion in nonglacial regions; volcanoes on Pacific coast.	Four species elephants in North America, including mastodon and mammoth; also camels, sabretooth tiger. Camels and horse survived glacial eras but died out in U.S. before advent of man. Beginning extinction of mammals and rise of man: Java, Peking, Heidelberg, Neanderthal, Cro-Magnon (known for cave paintings).
Pliocene epoch Began c.13 million years ago, lasted c.12 million years.	Land still rose; volcanoes on Pacific coast and inland. At end of era, Sierras, Cascades, Rockies, Appalachians lifted. Climate increasingly cooler and drier.	Horse evolved almost to modern form; mastodons migrated from Old World to W North America. Manlike apes: gibbon, gorilla. Beginning of Old Stone Age: earliest implements of man, antedating any skeleton of man himself thus far discovered.
Miocene epoch Began c.25 million years ago, lasted c.12 million years.	In mid-era, great mountain making: Sierras and Rockies rose again, as well as Himalayas, Andes, and Alps. Volcanic activity in W U.S. Climate cooler and drier.	Modern birds. Horse further developed; camels abundant and varied. Great ape in Europe. Cooler climate reduced forests and resulted in more plains. More modern trees.
Oligocene epoch Began c.36 million years ago, lasted c.11 million years.	Erosion continued; volcanoes on Pacific coast and in parts of Europe. North America increasingly emergent; N Atlantic coast and most of Pacific coast dry land.	Mammals dominant: cat and dog families supreme; three-toed horse; mastodon; true carnivores. Primates walked erect; primitive anthropoid ape.
Paleocene and Eocene epochs Began c.63 million years ago, lasted c.27 million years.	Mountain building continued in early period, followed by erosion. Atlantic and Gulf coasts partly submerged. Climate mild in most of world, but with seasonal changes.	Modern birds. Primitive mammals: Eohippus (early horse, c.1 ft. high), ancestors of cat, dog, elephant, camel; small primates. Vegetation fairly modern: seed-bearing plants.

MESOZOIC ERA. Age of reptiles; lasted c.167 million years.*

Time	Geologic Development	Life Forms
Cretaceous period Began c.135 million years ago, lasted c.72 million years	Greatest submergence of continents; 50% of North America submerged. Most of world chalk supply formed, chiefly from limy skeletons of foraminifera. Coal and oil in W U.S. At end of era, Rockies elevated, Andes formed, seas retreated. Climate generally mild but a cold age late in period.	Dinosaurs included Tyrannosaurus and armored, horned, and duck-billed forms. At close of period dinosaurs became extinct. Marsupials and primitive placental mammals evolved. Flowering plants appeared: deciduous trees became dominant. Sequoias widely distributed.
Jurassic period Began c.181 million years ago, lasted c.46 million years.	Pacific coastal region of North America submerged during most of period; deposition of sediments (esp. red beds) and volcanic matter. At close of period vast disturbances formed Sierra Nevada, Cascade, and coastal ranges. Gold-quartz veins formed in Sierras. In E North America land continuously elevated and eroded. Period best defined in Europe; rich fossil beds.	Reptiles dominated land, sea, air (winged reptile, pterosaur). Chief land animals dinosaurs. First bird (archaeopteryx). Modern insects: bees, moths, flies. Cycads dominant plant life; also conifers, ginkos, tree ferns.

* All figures vary widely among authoritative sources.

Time	Geologic Development	Life Forms

MESOZOIC ERA (continued)

Time	Geologic Development	Life Forms
Triassic period Began c.230 million years ago, lasted c.49 million years.	Marked erosion of mountains in E North America; at close of period, complex faulting and tilting known as Palisade disturbance. Parts of W U.S. invaded by sea; waters retreated late in period. Climate mild; aridity and semiaridity widespread but some areas were moist.	Vertebrate animals included fresh-water fishes, aquatic reptiles (e.g., ichthyosaur), and dinosaurs (many bipedal) which became dominant life by mid-period. Forests chiefly conifers and cycads; also ferns, tree ferns, scouring rushes.

PALEOZOIC ERA. Age of invertebrates and marine forms; lasted c.400 million years.*

Time	Geologic Development	Life Forms
Permian period Began c.280 million years ago, lasted c.50 million years.	Lands rose, swamps dried up, and some deserts formed. Widespread aridity. Salt beds formed in Kansas, Germany, and USSR. At end of period, world-wide mountain making. Glaciation in Southern Hemisphere.	Reptiles (four-legged, not large, and mostly sprawling) developed in number and variety. Spore-bearing ferns and conifers survived aridity.
Carboniferous period (in North America, Mississippian and Pennsylvanian) Began c.345 million years ago, lasted c.60 million years.	Lands flooded several times. Almost 80% of world's coal beds formed from marshy vegetation—in U.S., especially in Pa. Mountains formed in North America, Europe, and Asia. At end of era E North America largely dry. Air warm and moist.	Fish abundant. First reptiles. Insects, larger than at any other period: giant dragonflies, c.800 species cockroaches. Tree ferns, scale trees, primitive conifers; first seed plants.
Devonian period Began c.405 million years ago, lasted c.60 million years.	About 40% of U.S. under water at times, but emerged gradually and completely. North America connected with Europe by land bridge. Volcanic activity. Second upthrusting of Appalachian chain. At close of period E coast rose while W sank. Climate mild.	Age of fishes: marine and armored; also lungfish. Primitive land vertebrates (amphibians); wingless insects and spiders. Ferns, mosses, horsetails; forests of tree ferns. Primitive evergreens.
Silurian period Began c.245 million years ago, lasted c.20 million years.	Seas flooded inland basin of North America; great salt beds deposited in E U.S. Mountains eroded, but Appalachians continued high and volcanic. In late period, lands emerged almost completely; arid deserts formed in E U.S.	Sea scorpions most distinctive; also mollusks, corals (reefs), primitive vertebrate fish. Animals similar to scorpions, possibly the first air-breathing forms. Beginnings of land plants.
Ordovician period Began c.500 million years ago, lasted c.75 million years.	Fully half of North America covered by seas periodically. Greatest deposition of limestones, marbles, and slates. Great disturbances at end of period; Taconics (N.Y.) thrust up. No sharp gradations in climate.	Great numbers of marine animals; some corals, gastropods, clams. Continued dominance of marine invertebrates. First primitive, fishlike vertebrates.
Cambrian period Began c.600 million years ago, lasted c. 100 million years.	Seas covered much of world; conditions unstable, with many periods of uplifts. Highlands mostly leveled. Climate generally mild.	Marine invertebrates: trilobites dominant; primitive snails; first shells. Calcareous marine algae. Lichens in some regions.

PRE-CAMBRIAN TIME. Began 4,500–5,000 million years ago.* Includes three eras.

Time	Geologic Development	Life Forms
1. AZOIC TIME	Formation of the earth; lands and seas developed.	No life forms.
2. ARCHEOZOIC ERA	Much volcanic activity. Mountain ranges formed, then eroded to hills. Minerals deposited.	Rudimentary life forms probably existed.
3. PROTEROZOIC ERA	Iron, copper and other metallic ores deposited. Glacial periods at least twice. At end of period, volcanic disturbances in North America, followed by erosion of mountains.	Simple marine life: probably soft-bodied wormlike animals; algae.

* All figures vary widely among authoritative sources.

adolescents. Community is self-governing, but all must work. Schooling is provided.

George of Podebrad (pǒ'dyěbrät), 1420–71, administrator (1452–58) and king (1458–71) of Bohemia. Came to power as leader of UTRAQUISTS. Was excommunicated by Pope Paul II (1466); expelled MATTHIAS CORVINUS, whom Catholic nobles had proclaimed king in 1469. Restored peace and prosperity to Bohemia.

George of Trebizond (trě'bǐzǒnd), c.1396–1486, Greek scholar, b. Crete. He took part in revival of learning in Italy. Translator of Aristotle and Plato.

Georgetown, city (metropolitan area pop. c.162,000), cap. and largest city of Guyana; port on Demerara R.

Georgetown. 1 Residential section (since 1895) of WASHINGTON, D.C., on Potomac R. near confluence of Rock Creek; settled c.1665. Was part of land granted by Md. in 1790 to U.S. for national cap. Has many fine old houses and GEORGETOWN UNIVERSITY. **2** Village (pop. 2,674), SW Ohio, near Ohio R., SE of Cincinnati; laid out 1819. Birthplace of U. S. Grant is at nearby Point Pleasant. **3** City (pop. 12,261), E S.C., at head of Winyah Bay, c. 15 mi. from the Atlantic, where Pee Dee, Waccamaw, Black, and Sampit rivers enter bay; founded c.1734. Resort and shipping center. Church of Prince George dates from 1740s. **4** City (pop. 5,218), central Texas, N of Austin; founded 1848. Seat of Southwestern Univ.

Georgetown University, in Georgetown section of Washington, D.C.; mainly for men; founded 1789 by John Carroll, chartered 1815; inc. 1844. Has notable law and medical schools, School of Foreign Service, and Inst. of Language and Linguistics.

George Washington Birthplace National Monument: see WAKEFIELD.

George Washington Bridge, vehicular suspension bridge over Hudson R. between Manhattan borough of New York city and Fort Lee, N.J.; main span is 3,500 ft. long; constructed 1927–31. Lower deck completed 1962.

George Washington Carver National Monument: see CARVER, GEORGE WASHINGTON.

George Washington University, The, at Washington, D.C.; coed.; chartered 1821 as Columbian Col., opened 1822, became university 1873, renamed 1904.

Georgia, USSR: see GEORGIAN SOVIET SOCIALIST REPUBLIC.

Georgia, state (58,876 sq. mi.; pop. 3,943,116), SE U.S.; last founded (1733) of Thirteen Colonies; cap. and largest city ATLANTA. Other major cities are SAVANNAH, COLUMBUS, AUGUSTA, MACON, ALBANY. Bounded E by SAVANNAH R. and the Atlantic. CHATTAHOOCHEE R. and SAINT MARYS R. (rising in OKEFENOKEE SWAMP) form part of boundary. Coastal plains in S rise to piedmont plateau to mountains in N. Agr. (peanuts, pecans, cotton, corn, tobacco, peaches, truck), mfg. (aluminum, pulpwood products, chemicals). Rich in minerals, the state leads as producer of kaolin clay; also has marble, granite, limestone. Hernando DE SOTO crossed Ga. c.1540; Spanish later estab. missions on SEA ISLANDS. Possession of area contested by Spanish and English. Savannah founded 1733 by J. E. OGLETHORPE, who assured English control by defeating Spanish at Bloody Marsh 1742. Flourished as royal colony after 1754. Tory and patriot sentiment divided in Revolution; British held most of state. First Southern state to ratify U.S. Constitution, but early took strong states' rights stand. Seceded from Union Jan., 1861; suffered in Civil War from Atlanta campaign of W. T. SHERMAN. Political and racial conflict followed depression of 1930s. Liberal governorship of Ellis G. Arnall (1943–47) brought reforms. Ga. led deep South in integration of public schools 1961.

Georgia, Strait of, channel, c.150 mi. long, between mainland of B.C. and Vancouver Isl., Canada, connecting Puget Sound and Queen Charlotte Sound. Forms part of inland waterway to Alaska.

Georgia, University of, at Athens; land grant, state supported; coed.; chartered 1785 as first state-supported college in U.S., opened 1801. Maintains a marine biology laboratory on Sapelo Isl.

Georgia Institute of Technology, at Atlanta; state supported; coed.; chartered 1885, opened 1888.

Georgian Bay, NE arm of L. Huron, S Ont., Canada (120 mi. long, c.50 mi. wide), separated from main part of lake by Saugeen Peninsula and Manitoulin Isl. Connected to L. Ontario by Severn R., L. Simcoe, and Trent Canal. The **Georgian Bay Islands National Park** (3,458 acres; estab. 1929) includes 30 islands in the bay.

Georgian Military Road, highway (c.129 mi.), S central USSR, in Greater Caucasus, between Ordzhonikidze and Tiflis. Built by Russians 1799–1863, it passes through DARYAL gorge.

Georgian Soviet Socialist Republic or **Georgia,** constituent republic (c.26,311 sq. mi.; 1965 est. pop. 4,-515,000), USSR, W Transcaucasia; cap. Tiflis. Extending S from Greater Caucasus, it borders on Black Sea in W, on Turkey in S. KURA and RION are chief rivers. Climate and vegetation vary from subtropical coastal region of MINGRELIA in W to high mountain crest and dry Kura steppe in E. Fruit, tea, tobacco, silk, wine are grown in warmer districts. Manganese at Chiatura. Mfg. of machinery and chemicals; iron and steel works. GEORGIAN MILITARY ROAD and OSSETIAN MILITARY ROAD are major traffic routes. Batum, Poti, Sukhum are chief ports. Main political subdivisions are ABKHAZ ASSR, ADZHAR ASSR, S OSSETIA. About two thirds of pop. are Georgians, speaking a S Caucasian language. Minorities include Armenians, Ossetians, Abkhazians, Azerbaijanians. Georgian church is one of oldest Orthodox Eastern foundations. Known in antiquity as COLCHIS (in W) and Iberia (in E). Georgia became a kingdom c.4th cent. B.C., with cap. at MTSKHET. Persian Sassanidae ruled it 3d–4th cent. A.D.; branch of Armenian Bagratid dynasty 6th–19th cent., with interruptions caused by numerous invasions. Greatest flowering under Queen Thamar (12th-13th cent.). Pressed by its Moslem neighbors, Georgia accepted Russian overlordship in 18th cent. Last king abdicated 1801. Additional territories ceded by Turkey between 1803 and 1829. Briefly independent after 1917, Georgia became soviet republic 1921.

Georgian style, in English architecture of the reigns (1714–1820) of George I, George II, and George III. Based on principles of Andrea Palladio introduced into England by Inigo Jones and Sir Christopher Wren. Emphasized classic correctness, which made symmetry the essential feature. Typical Georgian house was brick structure with courses and cornices of white stone and trimmings of white painted woodwork. Corridors in interiors were an innovation. Notable examples of public architecture of the period include St. James's Club, by Robert Adam; Somerset House, by Sir William Chambers; Bank of England, by Sir John Soane; and St. Martin's-in-the Fields, by James Gibbs. American buildings of the period, closely resembling their English prototypes, are usually called Colonial.

Georgiaville, R.I.: see SMITHFIELD.

Gera (gā'rä), city (est. pop. 98,399), East Germany, in former state of Thuringia. Former cap. of principality of REUSS (Younger Line). Textile center.

geranium, name for widely grown house and bedding plant of genus *Pelargonium,* native to S Africa. Many varieties have showy flowers; others are grown for their scented leaves. Native American wild geranium or crane's-bill belongs to the genus *Geranium.*

Gérard, François Pascal Simon, Baron, 1770–1837, French portrait and historical painter, a favorite pupil of David. Appointed Court painter to Louis XVIII (1814).

Gerard, James Watson (jŭrärd'), 1867–1951, U.S. ambassador to Germany (1913–17).

Gerbert: see SYLVESTER II, pope.

Gerhard, William Wood, 1809–72. American physician. First to distinguish clearly between typhoid and typhus fever (1837).

Gerhardt, Charles Frédéric, 1816–56, French chemist. Revived theory of acid radicals, which he called theory of residues, made contributions to organic chemistry, and aided development of atomic weight theory.

Géricault, Jean Louis André Théodore (zhä' lwē' ädrä' tāōdôr' zhärēkō'), 1791–1824, French painter, who helped to introduce romanticism into France. In 1819 he exhibited his famous *Raft of the Medusa* (Louvre), which brought violent protests from classical artists.

Gering (gĕr'ĭng), city (pop. 4,585), W Nebr., on North Platte R. opposite Scottsbluff; founded 1887. Scotts Bluff Natl. Monument is nearby.

Gérin-Lajoie, Antoine (zhärē'-läzhwä'), 1824–82, French Canadian author. Most popular works are two novels which idealize simple life of French Canadian habitants.

Gerizim (gĕ'rŭzĭm), mountain, Jordan. The Samaritans still consider it the only proper place of worship; 300-year-old Samaritan temple was destroyed by Maccabean leader, John Hyrcanus, c.130 B.C.

Gerlachovka, Czechoslovakia: see TATRA.

germ, any disease-causing microscopic organism. Includes pathogenic forms of bacteria, protozoa, molds, viruses, and rickettsia. Germ theory of disease was accepted in 19th cent., largely through Pasteur's experiments. Lister's successful use of ANTISEPTIC methods to reduce infection strengthened theory. See DISINFECTANT.

German, Sir Edward, 1862–1936, English composer. Known for incidental music to plays, e.g., *Henry VIII*, *Nell Gwynn*, and for light operas. Knighted 1928.

German Confederation, 1815–66, estab. by Congress of Vienna. Membership consisted of the sovereign states and free cities of Germany; the emperor of Austria; the king of Denmark (as duke of Holstein and Lauenburg); the king of Hanover; and the king of the Netherlands (as duke of Luxembourg). The federal diet, which met at Frankfurt under presidency of Austria, was reduced to impotence through unanimity rule; suspended 1848–50, when the FRANKFURT Parliament was meeting, it resumed under Austrian leadership after Treaty of OLMÜTZ. AUSTRO-PRUSSIAN WAR led to dissolution of the confederation and establishment of NORTH GERMAN CONFEDERATION.

German East Africa, former German colony, area c.370,000 sq. mi., E Africa. Divided into three parts after First World War. Kionga was annexed to Mozambique, and Tanganyika and Ruanda-Urundi became mandated territories held by Great Britain and Belgium, respectively Dar-es-Salaam was cap.

Germanic languages, subfamily of Indo-European, of which English and German, standard language of Germany, are members. See LANGUAGE (table).

Germanic laws, customary laws of the Germans before and after Roman invasion. Mostly known through codes adopted (5th–9th cent.) after Germanic tribes had invaded Roman Empire. Since law then applied to the person rather than the territory or governmental unit. there were codes for the Germans themselves (called *leges barbarorum*) and, in S Europe, other codes for Romans under German rule (*leges Romanorum*). Although all except the Anglo-Saxon were in Latin and all imitated the form of the Roman law code, the *leges barbarorum* are now accepted as incorporating much of the older Germanic customary law. They are largely concerned with penal law and particularly with COMPOSITION for personal injuries. Some of the more important codes, however, show strong Roman influence. The Visigoths in Spain had a series of notable codes: that of King Euric (5th cent.), *the Breviary of Alaric* (or *Lex Romana Visigothorum*) in 506, and the *Lex Visigothorum* or *Liber iudiciorum* (later translated as the *Fuero juzgo* and applying to Goths and Romans alike) of c.654. Notable also was the *Edictum Rotharis* (643), which with a collection of

Italian legislation of the Holy Roman Empire became the basis for the later renaissance of Roman law in Italy.

Germanic religion. Tacitus' *Germania* and *Beowulf* are our best sources on it. It was polytheistic, with "Olympian" and underworld gods. Its principal gods were Woden, Tiw, Frey and Freyja, and an earth-goddess. Sacrifices, oracles, and fertility rites were practiced. Mythology was not highly developed, but there was much story-telling, and from later works (such as NIBELUNGENLIED) mythical ideas can be gained. Ideas of death and afterworld were similar to those of the Greeks. In Iceland, sources of its mythology are the Eddas, the oldest direct material on Germanic myth. Norse mythology differs from that of other Germanic peoples because of Christian influence, isolation of Old Norse, and longer development of the system.

Germanicus Caesar (jûrmă'nĭkŭs), 15 B.C.–A.D. 19, Roman general; son of Drusus Senior, nephew of TIBERIUS. Fought well against the Germans, but was replaced by his brother Drusus. Later poisoned, supposedly by Piso, governor of Syria. Claudius I was his brother, Agrippina II and Caligula, his children.

germanium (jûrmă'nēŭm), rare, gray, brittle metallic element (symbol = Ge; see also ELEMENT, table). It resembles tin and lead and occurs in a few minerals. Germanium crystal can rectify electricity and convert light into electrical energy. Germanium is used in transistors, in very high-powered photoelectric eyes, and, with silicon, in lenses for infrared equipment.

German language, a Germanic language. See LANGUAGE (table).

German measles: see MEASLES.

German New Guinea: see NEW GUINEA, TERRITORY OF.

German Reformed Church: see UNITED CHURCH OF CHRIST.

Germans, groups of people in Europe of related language and culture. They gave rise to the present cultures of Scandinavia, Germany, Austria, Switzerland, the Low Countries, and England. They lived in N Germany and along the Baltic Sea, expanding S, SE, and W in the early Christian era. Prime sources for their culture and distribution are works of Caesar and Tacitus. The Teutons and Cimbri whom Marius defeated in 102–101 B.C. may have been Germans. Germans became increasingly troublesome to the Roman Empire; attacks were made by the VANDALS in the W and by the OSTROGOTHS in the E. The Germans probably retained a certain ethnic solidarity until the 2d or 3d cent., but later broke up into many peoples. Chief among these were the ALEMANNI, the FRANKS, the ANGLO-SAXONS, the Burgundii (see BURGUNDY), the LOMBARDS, the SAXONS, and the VISIGOTHS. The Scandinavians, a large group, included the Icelanders, who produced the first Germanic literature (see OLD NORSE LITERATURE).

German silver or **nickel silver,** silver-white alloy of copper, zinc, nickel in varying proportions. Hard, tough, and resistant to corrosion, it is used in tableware and in heating coils.

German Southwest Africa: see SOUTH-WEST AFRICA.

Germantown. 1 Town, Conn.: see DANBURY. **2** Residential section of Philadelphia, Pa., on Wissahickon Creek; settled c.1683 by Dutch and Germans. Early American center of printing and publishing. Annexed to Philadelphia 1854. British quartered here after battle of Brandywine; Washington's attack on camp (Oct. 4, 1777) failed. Has Howe House and other colonial buildings.

German Volga Republic, former autonomous state (c.18,000 sq. mi.), central European RSFSR, along lower Volga. Settled under Catherine II by German colonists 1762; made German Autonomous SSR 1924. Dissolved 1941 after German invasion of USSR; its German population (c.440,000) was deported to Siberia.

Germany, Ger. *Deutschland,* country of N Central Europe, stretching from the Baltic Sea and the

North Sea on the N to the Alps on the S. In 1949, pending a final peace settlement, two separate republics were formed: (1) Federal Republic of [West] Germany (95,744 sq. mi.; pop. 53,975,600; provisional cap. Bonn), under U.S., British, and French occupation until 1955, consisting of the states of BADEN-WÜRTTEMBERG, BAVARIA, BREMEN, HAMBURG, HESSE, LOWER SAXONY, NORTH RHINE-WESTPHALIA, RHINELAND-PALATINATE, SAARLAND, and SCHLESWIG-HOLSTEIN; and of W Berlin, which has a special status; and (2) [East] German Democratic Republic (41,479 sq. mi.; pop. 16,116,713; cap. E Berlin), under Russian occupation until 1955, consisting of the states of BRANDENBURG, MECKLENBURG, SAXONY, Saxony-Anhalt, and THURINGIA. In 1952 the old divisions were replaced by 15 administrative districts (including E Berlin). N Germany is generally level and low lying. Central Germany, with the HARZ mts. and Thuringian Forest, and S Germany, with the mountains of SWABIA and FRANCONIA and the Bavarian Alps (highest peak, ZUGSPITZE) are generally mountainous and forest-covered. The RHINE, WESER, ELBE, ODER, and DANUBE are the principal rivers. The heaviest industrial concentrations are in the NW (N Rhineland and RUHR dist., with Cologne, Düsseldorf, and Essen); at Berlin; and in Saxony (with Leipzig, Dresden, and Chemnitz). Other major commercial and industrial centers: Munich, Stuttgart, Nuremberg (S); Frankfurt, Mannheim (W); Dortmund, Duisburg (NW); Hanover, Magdeburg (N); and the port cities of Hamburg, Bremen, Kiel, and Lübeck. For its huge metallurgical industry Germany depends largely on Ruhr coal and on imported ores. Other major industrial products are textiles, chemicals, electrical machinery. Germany lost some of its chief industrial, mining, and agr. districts in 1945, when the Saar and the E provinces of SILESIA, POMERANIA, and EAST PRUSSIA were detached. The Saar was returned in 1957 to become the tenth state of the Federal Republic. A large percentage of the population is engaged in agr. In W Germany, Protestants have a slight majority over Catholics, Catholicism prevailing in the S and W. E Germany is predominantly Lutheran.

Germany before 1871. In antiquity, Germany was inhabited by a number of Germanic tribes (see GERMANS). Rome conquered (1st cent. B.C.–1st cent. A.D.) the regions along the Rhine and parts of S Germany, but further conquest was stopped at the battle of TEUTOBURG FOREST (A.D. 9). In the 4th–5th cent. German tribes invaded the Roman Empire, while the Slavs occupied the lands E of the Elbe. The FRANKS soon subjugated other German tribes and created a vast empire in Germany and Gaul (see also MEROVINGIANS; CAROLINGIANS; CHARLEMAGNE). Christianization of Germany, begun by St. BONIFACE, was completed in the 12th–13th cent. with the German colonization of the lands E of the Elbe (see WENDS; TEUTONIC KNIGHTS). From divisions of the Frankish empire (9th cent.) came a separate kingdom under LOUIS THE GERMAN. Weakened by foreign invaders (Norsemen, Slavs, Magyars) and by the rise of powerful feudal princes (the dukes of FRANCONIA, SWABIA, BAVARIA, SAXONY, and LOTHARINGIA), the kingship recovered authority under HENRY I and OTTO I (crowned as emperor, 962). German history then overlapped with that of the HOLY ROMAN EMPIRE. The feudal structure of Germany proved persistent. The great "stem duchies" were broken up by the emperors in the 10th–12th cent., but still lesser principalities and free cities made Germany a loose federation over which the emperors presided with varying degrees of effectiveness. After the Thirty Years War (1618–48) imperial control was nominal, and within the federal structure arose two powerful rival states—AUSTRIA (i.e., the far-flung, multinational Hapsburg empire) and the modern, centralized kingdom of PRUSSIA. Austro-Prussian rivalry was temporarily in-

terrupted by Napoleon I, who swept aside the Holy Roman Empire (1806) and created the CONFEDERATION OF THE RHINE. The Congress of Vienna (1814–15) reduced the number of sovereign German states but retained the federal structure by creating the GERMAN CONFEDERATION. The liberal-nationalist revolution of 1848 was easily suppressed and the FRANKFURT Parliament vainly sought to create a unified Germany. However, under the leadership of BISMARCK, Prussia eliminated Austria from German affairs (see AUSTRO-PRUSSIAN WAR, 1866), and at the end of the FRANCO-PRUSSIAN WAR William I of Prussia was proclaimed emperor of Germany (1871). The new empire, increased by ALSACE and LORRAINE, was united by a common ruler, a federal diet (Reichstag), and a customs union (see ZOLLVEREIN), but it remained a confederation of kingdoms (Prussia, Bavaria, Württemberg, Saxony), grand duchies (Baden, Hesse, Saxe-Weimar, Mecklenburg), lesser principalities, and Hanseatic cities (Hamburg, Bremen, Lübeck).

From Bismarck to Hitler. In half a century, Germany had evolved from a feudal, disunited, socially and industrially retarded area into the chief military and economic power of the Continent. The phenomenal speed of industrial and commercial expansion continued after 1871 and, combined with the program of colonial and naval expansion under WILLIAM II, became a serious threat to England. As long as Bismarck held power (i.e., until 1890) the government sought peaceful relations with its neighbors, but William II's aggressive diplomacy helped bring about the First World War (1914–18). Germany in 1914 was at the peak of prosperity. By 1918, it was exhausted by the war. A Social Democratic revolution forced the abdication of William II and the conclusion of an armistice. In 1919 Germany accepted the harsh Treaty of VERSAILLES and adopted the republican constitution drafted at Weimar. The "Weimar Republic" retained the federal structure of the empire, with some minor territorial adjustments. It was beset from the beginning by extremist agitation (both nationalist and Communist), mass unemployment, and a currency inflation that wiped out the nation's savings. Pres. Ebert, who steered a middle course, was succeeded by HINDENBURG. After 1925 came economic recovery, while the foreign policy of STRESEMANN restored Germany as a great power. However, the world economic crisis that began in 1929 again plunged Germany into near-bankruptcy. Both Communism and NATIONAL SOCIALISM made great electoral gains. By 1932 Hitler's party was the largest single party in the Reichstag; in Jan., 1933, disunion among his opponents made possible the appointment of HITLER as chancellor.

Third Reich and Collapse. Within a year, Hitler estab. absolute dictatorship, virtually abolished the powers of the state governments, and reduced all German life to Nazi control. Repudiating the Treaty of Versailles, he began a program of intensive rearmament, remilitarized the Rhineland (1936), and annexed Austria (March, 1938). Allied with Fascist Italy from 1936 (see AXIS), Germany interfered in the Spanish civil war of 1936–39, and was allowed by the Western Powers to seize part of Czechoslovakia in Sept., 1938 (see MUNICH PACT). Bohemia and Moravia were annexed altogether in April, 1939, along with the Memel dist., and Germany began to demand DANZIG and part of the POLISH CORRIDOR. After concluding a nonaggression pact with the USSR (Aug., 1939), Germany invaded Poland and began Second World War. Despite spectacular victories up to 1942, the war ended with Germany's unconditional surrender in May, 1945, and left German cities in ruin. According to decisions made at the YALTA and POTSDAM conferences, Germany was divided into four occupation zones; Berlin, under four-power occupation, received special status. Dissension between the USSR and the West paralyzed the Allied control council, from which the USSR withdrew in 1948. The REPARATIONS question was a major factor in the failure to arrive at a general peace treaty. The Soviet blockade of W BERLIN (1948–49) widened the rift between E and W Germany, which in 1949 became two separate republics. W Germany, supervised by a three-power Allied High Commission, became a federal, parliamentary democracy. It received virtual sovereignty in 1952 and full scvereignty when, by ratification of the PARIS PACTS (1955), it became a member of the Western European Union and the North Atlantic Treaty Organization. Industry, freed of Allied restrictions in 1952, recovered rapidly, and W Germany regained its position as a major industrial power, becoming a member of the European Coal and Steel Community (1952), the European Atomic Energy Community and European Economic Community (1957). Both major parties, the Christian Democratic Union (CDU) and Social Democrats (SPD) pursued policy of alignment with West, a policy firmly pursued by chancellors ADENAUER and ERHARD. In 1955, the USSR gave full recognition to E Germany. Soviet troops remained by mutual agreement of the two Communist governments, and a re-armed E Germany joined the WARSAW TREATY. A wall sealing off E from W BERLIN, erected in 1961 by E Germany, caused new tensions. In the mid-1960s, however, W German policy toward E Europe and the nations recognizing E Germany grew less tense. In 1966 Kurt Georg Kiesinger became chancellor and succeeded in strengthening Germany's relations with France and opened new communications channels with E Germany.

germination, in a seed, the growth of the embryo (after period of dormancy) and emergence of young plant from seed. Suitable conditions of temperature, moisture, and oxygen are necessary. Seed viability ranges from a few days to (rarely) 400 years or more. Use of germination tested seed prevents planting of old or inferior seed.

Germiston (jûr'mĭstŭn), city (pop. c.214,393), S Transvaal, Republic of South Africa, on the Witwatersrand. Gold is mined and processed.

Gérôme, Jean Léon (zhä' lāŏ' zhärōm'), 1824–1904, French historical and genre painter.

Gerona (hārō'nä), town (pop. 32,784), cap. of Gerona prov., NE Spain, in Catalonia. Textile mfg. Heroically resisted French in Peninsular War 1808–9. Notable Gothic cathedral.

Geronimo (jŭrŏ'nŭmō), c.1829–1909, chief of a Chiricahua band of the Apache Indians. Terrorized Ariz. by brutal raids in 1880s.

Gerry, Elbridge (gĕ'rē), 1744–1814, American statesman. Supported patriot activities before and during American Revolution. Opponent of strong central government. Had a part in XYZ AFFAIR. Governor of Mass. (1810, 1811); Vice President of U.S. (1813–14). Name used by opponents in political practice called **gerrymander** (jĕ'rĕmăn"dŭr), rearrangement of voting districts so as to favor party in power. Origin of term, though not origin of practice, was in such an arrangement made in Mass. when Elbridge Gerry was governor.

Gers (zhĕr), department (2,429 sq. mi.; pop. 182,264), SW France, at foot of Pyrenees, in Armagnac region of Gascony; cap. Auch.

Gershom ben Juda (gûr'shŭm bĕn jōō'dŭ), 960–1040, rabbi, religious poet in Mayence, Germany. Organized Rhenish Jewish communities; banned polygamy among Franco-German Jews.

Gershon, Levi ben: see GERSONIDES.

Gershwin, George, 1898–1937, American composer. Songs from his musical comedy scores (e.g., *Embraceable You* and *The Man I Love*) are masterpieces of their kind. His principal larger compositions are *Rhapsody in Blue* (1923), the classic example of symphonic jazz; Piano Concerto in F (1925); *An American in Paris* (1928); and *Porgy and Bess* (1935), a folk opera.

Gerson, John (Jean Charlier de Gerson) (gûr'sŭn), 1363–1429, French ecclesiastical statesman and a notable mystic, teacher, philosopher, preacher. With Pierre d'AILLY (his teacher at Paris), he sought to end the Great SCHISM by advancing the conciliar theory (basically, doctrine that councils are superior to the pope; later declared heretical) for Council of Pisa. Attended Council of CONSTANCE, and helped to end the schism and condemn John Huss. Wrote much and, as chancellor of the Univ. of Paris, opposed teaching of Occam and began change to realism.

Gersonides (gûrsŏ'nĭdēz) or **Levi ben Gerson** (lē'vī bĕn gûr'shŭn), 1288–1344, philosopher, b. Provence. Follower of AVERROËS. Bible commentator and perhaps inventor of camera obscura.

Gersoppa, Falls of (gûrsŏ'pŭ), cataract of Sharavari R., Mysore, India. Highest of four cascades is c.830 ft.

Gesenius, Wilhelm (vĭl'hĕlm gāzā'nyŏōs), 1786–1842, German orientalist. Noted for his Hebrew grammar and dictionary, which have appeared in many editions, including English.

Gesner, Konrad von, 1516–65, Swiss scientist. His *Historia animalium* (5 vols., 1551–58, 1587) is one of the foundations of modern zoology. Other works include a philological study of 130 languages.

Gessner, Salomon (zä'lōmôn gĕs'nŭr), 1730–88, Swiss poet, landscape painter, and etcher. His poems and "idyllic prose pastorals" (e.g., *The Death of Abel,* 1758) were very popular and had great influence on European literature.

Gestalt (gŭshtält'), school of psychology which interprets phenomena as organized wholes rather than as aggregates of distinct parts and which maintains that the whole is greater than the sum of its parts. The term Gestalt was coined in Germany by Christian von Ehrenfels. Other noted contributors to Gestalt psychology included Kurt Koffka, Wolfgang Köhler, Max Wertheimer. Early experimentation led to the laws of membership character (i.e., each element of a pattern through its dynamic participation in that pattern alters its individuality), and of *Prägnanz,* the dynamic attribute of self-fulfillment in all structured wholes. Structural correspondence between sensory and extrasensory mental processes was postulated.

Gestapo: see SECRET POLICE.

Gesta Romanorum (jĕ'stŭ rō"mŭnô'rŭm) [Latin,= deeds of the Romans], medieval collection of Latin stories, each tale characterized by a moral.

gestation: see PREGNANCY.

Gethsemane (gĕthsĕ'mŭnē), olive grove or garden, near foot of Mt. of Olives, E of Jerusalem, scene of the agony and betrayal of Jesus. Mark 14.32–50; Mat. 26.36–56.

Gettysburg (gĕ'tĕzbûrg), borough (pop. 7,960), S Pa., near Md. line SW of York; laid out c.1780. Named for James Gettys, grantee of land from William Penn. Seat of Gettysburg Col. and Lutheran Theological Seminary. Gettysburg Natl. Military Park is shrine of Civil War battle (see GETTYSBURG CAMPAIGN). At dedication of national cemetery here Abraham Lincoln delivered the Gettysburg Address Nov. 19, 1863. Home of D. D. Eisenhower.

Gettysburg campaign, June–July, 1863, of Civil War. After victory at Chancellorsville, R. E. Lee undertook second invasion of North via Shenandoah Valley into S Pa. At Chambersburg he learned Army of Potomac under G. G. Meade was concentrating N of Potomac. Two armies met just W of Gettysburg. On July 1 Federals were driven to Cemetery Hill, S of town. Meade, in strong position, consolidated forces. On July 2 Confederates failed in assaults both on Union left at Round Top and Little Round Top and on its right at Cemetery Hill. On July 3 Lee sent Longstreet with G. E. Pickett's division in famous charge against Union center; it was beaten back. On July 4 Lee withdrew. Confederate defeat, turning point of war.

Geulincx, Arnold (gû'lĭngks), 1624–69, Belgian Cartesian philosopher; a founder of occasionalism. He argued that God is the sole active power and therefore there is no interaction between finite things.

geyser (gī'zŭr), a hot spring that intermittently erupts steam and hot water. Geysers occur only in New Zealand, Iceland, Yellowstone Park. Some build up cones of mineral matter about their vents.

Geysir (gā'sĭr), hot spring, SW Iceland, W of Reykjavik. Eruptions (at intervals of several weeks) last c.20 minutes. Max. height of jet is 200 ft.; max. temperature 180 F. Neighborhood has many hot springs. English name *geyser* derives from Geysir.

Gezelle, Guido (gĕ'dô khǔzĕ'lǔ), 1830–99, Flemish lyric poet, a Roman Catholic priest, b. Bruges; forerunner of the Flemish literary revival.

Gezer (gē'–), natural fortress, Palestine, on ridge overlooking the road between Jerusalem and Jaffa. In Bible, important in the wars of Joshua, David, and the Maccabees. Scene of important excavations.

Gezira: see GAZIRA.

Ghadames or **Gadames** (both: gùdä'mĕs), town (est. pop. 5,146), NW Libya. A Sahara oasis and caravan center.

Ghana (gä'nä), anc. Negro kingdom, centered in bend of Niger R., W Africa. Founded c.4th cent. A.D., it prospered from trade in gold, slaves, and salt. The rulers of the kingdom were Fulani. Kingdom declined after an Almoravide invasion in mid-11th cent.

Ghana, republic (c.91,690 sq. mi.; pop. c.7,500,000), W Africa, on the Gulf of Guinea; cap. Accra. Comprises the former crown colony of Gold Coast, former trusteeship territory of British Togoland, and former British protectorates of Northern Territories and Ashanti. Has swampy regular coast, forested and savanna interior. Cacao, hardwoods, manganese, diamonds, gold, and bauxite produced. Vast potential for hydroelectric power in Volta R. project begun 1962. Deepwater ports at Tema and Takoradi; adequate road network; limited rail and air service. Official language is English. Among main peoples are Ashanti, Fanti, Ga, and Ewe; majority is Christian or animist, some are Moslem. Portuguese estab. fort at Elmina in 1482. British crown colony created 1874. Under 1951 constitution, Kwame NKRUMAH was elected first premier. Independence within the British Commonwealth granted 1957; former Togoland Trust Territory included. Ghana became a republic July, 1960. A leader in pan-African movement, Ghana formed Union of African States in 1961 with Guinea and Mali. In Jan., 1964, Ghana officially became a one-party state. In Feb., 1966, the military ousted Nkrumah and took control of the government.

Ghardaia, town (est. pop. 48,080), E Algeria; chief town of the Mzab. Founded 11th cent.

Ghat or **Gat** (both: gät), walled town (est. pop. 3,929), SW Libya; an oasis in the Sahara.

Ghats (gôts, gäts), two mountain ranges of S India. Eastern Ghats extend c.1,000 mi. along E coast and merge in S with Western Ghats, which parallel W coast for c. 1,000 mi, with Palghat Gap as only major break. Mt. Dodabetta (8,760 ft.) in the Nilgiri Hills of Kerala state is highest point.

Ghazali, Al-: see AL-GAZEL.

Ghazni (gŭz'nē), town (pop. c.25,000), central Afghanistan. Flourished under Turkish Ghaznivid dynasty (962–c.1155), founded by Mahmud of Ghazni, whose domain reached from the Caspian to the Ganges. Held by the British in Afghan Wars (1839–42).

ghee: see BUTTER.

Ghelderode, Michel de (mĕshĕl' dù gĕldùrôd'), 1898–1962, Belgian dramatist. Wrote in French. Utilized biblical themes, medieval customs, modern grotesqueries. His plays include *Barabbas* (1928) and *Pantagleize* (1929).

Ghent (gĕnt), Flemish *Gent*, Fr. *Gand*, city (est. pop. 157,834; with suburbs 232,975), cap. of East Flanders prov.; historic cap. of Flanders, N Belgium, at confluence of Scheldt and Lys rivers and at focus of a canal network. Second largest port and chief textile and steel center of Belgium; episcopal see; seat of university (founded 1816); art center. City grew around ruins of fortress built on a small island (9th cent.). A major cloth-mfg. center by the 13th cent., it witnessed bitter social strife between the "lesser folk" and the rich bourgeoisie. Under Jacob and Philip van ARTEVELDE Ghent led Flanders in struggle against the French. Ghent's liberties were curtailed by Philip the Good after an insurrection (1453); Mary of Burgundy restored them through the Great Privilege, signed at Ghent (1477). Emperor Charles V, who was born and reared at Ghent, abrogated its liberties after another rebellion (1540). By the Pacification of Ghent, signed here 1576, the provinces of the Netherlands allied themselves with William the Silent to drive out the Spanish. Capture of Ghent by Alessandro Farnese (1584) completed Spanish reconquest of Flanders. Among landmarks of Ghent are ruins of Abbey of St. Bavon (631?) and of castle of the counts (begun 867); Cathedral of St. Bavon (10th–16th cent.); cloth hall (16th cent.); and 14th-cent. belfry, with famous carillon. Flemish painting flourished here in 15th cent. with Hugo van der Goes and the brothers Van Eyck. The **Treaty of Ghent,** signed here Dec. 24, 1814, ended War of 1812 between U.S. and Great Britain. Provision for restoring territories and places taken by either party represented diplomatic victory for U.S.

Gheorghiu-Dej, Gheorghe (gäôr'gä gäôr'gyü-däzh), 1901–65, Rumanian Communist leader. Premier (1952–54); first secretary of central committee of Rumanian Communist party (1955–61). He became head of both state and party in 1961 and directed country away from economic dependence on USSR.

Gherardesca, Ugolino della: see UGOLINO DELLA GHERARDESCA.

ghetto (gĕ'tō), originally street or sector of city enclosed by walls and gate in which Jews were compelled to live. Earliest ghettos were in Italy, 11th cent. In 1870 the last ghetto, in Rome, was abolished. During Second World War the Germans set up ghettos in E Europe, from which Jews were transported to extermination camps. Term now used loosely to denote section where a minority group lives in large numbers.

Ghibellines: see GUELPHS AND GHIBELLINES.

Ghiberti, Lorenzo (lōrän'tsō gēbĕr'tē), c.1378–1455, Florentine sculptor. In 1401 he won competition for bronze doors of Florence baptistery. His superb panels on N and S doors show scenes from life of Christ and Old Testament.

Ghilan, Iran: see GILAN.

Ghirlandaio or **Ghirlandajo, Domenico** (both dōmä'-nēkō gērländä'yō), 1449–94, Florentine painter. Studied with Baldovinetti and later taught Michelangelo. Magnificent frescoes in Santa Trinità and Santa Maria Novella (both in Florence) are famous for contemporary portraits and settings. His son **Ridolfo Ghirlandaio** (rēdôl'fō), 1483–1561, was also a painter. He was esteemed by Leonardo da Vinci and by Raphael.

Ghor (gôr) or **Ghur** (gōōr), mountainous region, W central Afghanistan. Powerful Moslem dynasty was estab. here in 12th cent.

Ghose, Aurobindo (ōrōbĭn'dō, gōsh'), 1872–1950, Indian nationalist leader and mystic. Advocate of nonviolent resistance, important student of VEDANTA philosophy. Called honorifically Sri Aurobindo.

ghost dance, central ritual of messianic religion instituted by Paiute Indian, Wovoka. It included dancing, shaking, and hypnotic trances. After 1887 spread among Western tribes.

Ghur, Afghanistan: see GHOR.

Ghuzzeh: see GAZA.

Giacometti, Alberto (jäcōmĕt'tē), 1901–66, Swiss sculptor and painter of elongated, emaciated human figures.

Giacosa, Giuseppe (jōōzĕp'pä jäkō'zä), 1847–1906, Italian dramatic poet. His plays include *Tristi amori* (1888) and *La Dame de Challant* (1891; written for Bernhardt). With Luigi Illica, he wrote librettos for Puccini's *La Bohème, Tosca,* and *Madame Butterfly.*

giant, manlike being of great size and strength. Giants appear in mythology of various peoples (Greeks, Germans, Celts). No evidence of such beings is known. Gigantism in humans results from over-secretion in childhood of growth hormone of anterior lobe of pituitary gland.

Giant Mountains: see RIESENGEBIRGE.

Giant's Causeway, headland on N coast of Co. Antrim, N. Ireland, extending 3 mi. along coast. Thousands of basaltic columns form three natural platforms. Built, according to legend, for giants to cross to Scotland.

Giauque, William Francis (jēōk'), 1895–, American chemist. Won 1949 Nobel Prize in Chemistry for studies of properties of substances at extremely low temperatures. He is codiscoverer of the second and third isotopes of oxygen.

Gibbon, Edward, 1737–94, English historian, author of *The History of the Decline and Fall of the Roman Empire.* It was conceived on a visit to Rome. Appearing in six volumes (1776–88), it met wide acclaim. Standard edition is J. B. Bury's (7 vols., 1896–1900). Gibbon also wrote an autobiography.

gibbon (gĭ'bŭn), smallest of anthropoid apes (genera *Hylobates* and *Symphalanga*) found in SE Asia and East Indies. Gibbons have slender bodies and very long arms; they travel through trees with speed and agility and on ground often walk erect. They live in family groups and are monogamous.

Gibbons, James, 1834–1921, American cardinal. Became bishop of Baltimore (1877), cardinal (1886). Notable for praising the blessings of American democracy for the Church. He persuaded the pope to lift the ban on the Knights of Labor.

Gibbons, Orlando, 1583–1625, English composer and organist, the last of the great Tudor composers. His works include madrigals, English anthems and services, and music for strings and for the virginal.

Gibbs, James, 1682–1754, English architect, distinguished exponent of GEORGIAN STYLE.

Gibbs, Josiah Willard, 1839–1903, American mathematical physicist, known especially for contributions in field of thermodynamics.

Gibbs, Oliver Wolcott, 1822–1908, American chemist. Taught at Col. of the City of New York (1849–63) and Harvard (1863–87), where he became dean. Noted for work on cobalt compounds and platinum.

Gibraltar (jĭbrôl'tŭr) town (pop. c.26,400, including garrison), constituting a British crown colony. Located at NW end of Rock of Gibraltar (one of PILLARS OF HERCULES), a peninsula of S Spain at E end of Strait of Gibraltar. Strait connects the Atlantic and the Mediterranean. Gibraltar Bay, an inlet of the Strait, has safe enclosed harbor of 440 acres. Rock, 2¾ mi. long and ¾ mi. wide, rises to height of 1,408 ft. Of Jurassic limestone, its caves have produced valuable archaeological finds. Has been an English possession since 1704. Town is a free port and serves as a port of call; a strategic air and naval base, its civilian population is kept small. Underground tunnels built in Second World War. Since 1945 Spain has renewed its claims on Gibraltar. In response to a UN resolution in Dec., 1966, a plebiscite was announced for Sept., 1967, to determine whether colony would remain under British rule.

Gibson, Althea, 1927–, American tennis player. First Negro to win major tennis championship. Won (1957, 1958) both U.S. women's and British women's singles championships. Retired 1958.

Gibson, Charles Dana, 1867–1944, American illustrator, a leading exponent of black-and-white art in America. Creator of Gibson Girl.

Gibson, W(ilfred) W(ilson), 1878–1962, English poet of Georgian group. Wrote poetry reflecting the struggles of the common man (e.g., *Daily Bread,* 1910).

Giddings, Franklin Henry, 1855–1931, American sociologist. Based explanation of social phenomena on principle of "consciousness of kind."

Giddings, city (pop. 2,821) S central Texas, E of Austin; founded 1872 by Wends. Nearby Serbin was (1855) first Wend settlement in Texas.

Gide, André (ädrä' zhēd'), 1869–1951, French author and intellectual leader. Of Calvinist background, he projected the conflict between the wish for self-fulfillment and the barriers of convention into semi-autobiographical fiction, such as *L'Immoraliste* (1902; Eng. tr., 1930), *Strait Is the Gate* (1909; Eng. tr., 1924), and *The Counterfeiters* (1926; Eng. tr., 1927). His lucid, gemlike style also illuminates his journals (1939; Eng. tr., 4 vols., 1947–51). Awarded 1947 Nobel Prize in Literature.

Gide, Charles (shärl), 1847–1932, French economist, expert on monetary problems. Played important role in cooperative movement.

Gideon (gĭ'dēŭn) or **Gedeon** (gē'–), judge of Israel. Called by an angel of the Lord to free Israel from Midianite oppressors, he won a spectacular victory with only 300 men. He was strong opponent of Baal cult. Judges 6–8; Heb. 11.32. Jerubbaal: Judges 6.30–32; 7.1. Jerubbesheth: 2 Sam. 11.21.

Gideons, givers of Bibles: see BIBLE SOCIETIES.

Gideonse, Harry D(avid) (gĭ'dēŭnz), 1901–, American educator, president of Brooklyn Col. 1939–67.

Giedion, Sigfried (gĭ'dēŭn), 1893–, Swiss architectural historian of the modern movement; author of *Space, Time and Architecture* (1941).

Gielgud, Sir John (gĭl'gŏŏd), 1904–, English actor. Made his stage debut with the Old Vic in 1921. Has played Hamlet (his greatest role) many times since 1929 in U.S. and England.

Giers, Nikolai Karlovich (nyĭkûlī' kär'lŭvĭch gēyĕrs'), 1820–95, Russian foreign minister (1882–95). Unable to keep German alliance, he turned to France (1892) setting the stage for Triple Entente (see TRIPLE ALLIANCE and TRIPLE ENTENTE).

Gies, William John (gīz), 1872–1956, American biological chemist. Helped found School of Dentistry at Columbia Univ. and the American Association of Dental Schools. Edited *Journal of Dental Research* (1919–36).

Giessen (gē'sûn), city (pop. 58,178), Hesse, West Germany in Upper Hesse, on Lahn R. Seat of well-known Protestant university 1607–1945. Academy for medical research founded here 1949.

Gijón (hēhōn'), city (pop. 127,602), Oviedo prov., N Spain, in Asturias; Atlantic port on Bay of Biscay. Exports minerals. Fishing; mfg. Dates from pre-Roman times.

Gila (hē'lû), river, rising in mountains of W N.Mex. and flowing c.650 mi. W across all of Ariz., to Colorado R. at Yuma, Ariz. Early peoples in "Valley of the Sun" farmed by irrigation. Near head is U.S. "unimproved" Gila Wilderness Area. Has irrigation dams in N.Mex., COOLIDGE DAM and Painted Rock Dam in Ariz. Lower Gila and tributaries have other projects, notably in SALT RIVER VALLEY.

Gila Cliff Dwellings National Monument: see NATIONAL PARKS AND MONUMENTS (table).

gila monster (hē'lû), a species of *Heloderma,* only genus of poisonous lizards. Found in deserts of SW U.S. It averages c.18 in. long. Tuberclelike scales cover the skin and the stout, clumsy body is black with a marbled pattern of orange or pink, yellow, or dull white. The tail is a food reservoir. Poison glands are in lower jaw; grooved teeth (carrying venom) are far back in mouth. Mexican gila monster is black and yellow.

Gilan or Ghilan (both: gēlän'), region, NW Iran, between Elburz Mts. and Caspian Sea. Held by Russia 1722–32. Was a Soviet republic 1920–21. Produces fish, rice, fruit, and silk.

Gilberd, William: see GILBERT, WILLIAM.

Gilbert, Cass, 1859–1934, American architect. Built the 60-story Woolworth Building, New York, and Supreme Court Building, Washington, D.C.

Gilbert, Charles Kendall, 1878–1958, American Episcopal bishop. Editor of the *Churchman* (1912–18); suffragan bishop of N.Y. (1930–46); bishop (1947–50).

Gilbert, Grove Karl, 1843–1918, American geologist. He was appointed senior geologist when the U.S. Survey was created in 1879 and published many reports, including a notable one on extinct Lake Bonneville.

Gilbert, Sir Humphrey, 1537?–1583, English soldier, navigator, and explorer; half brother of Sir Walter Raleigh. Knighted (1570) for Irish campaign services. His *Discourse* (1576), arguing existence of Northwest Passage, long motivated English exploration. Claimed Newfoundland for Queen Elizabeth and assumed authority over fishermen's colony already there (1583). Lost on return voyage.

Gilbert, John, 1897–1936, American film actor. Famous on silent screen in romantic leads. Films include *The Count of Monte Cristo, The Big Parade, The Merry Widow,* and *Flesh and the Devil.*

Gilbert or Gilberd, William, c.1540–1603, English scientist and physician, noted for pioneer studies of magnetism described in his *De magnete* (1600; Eng. tr., 1893, 1900).

Gilbert, Sir W(illiam) S(chwenck), 1836–1911, English playwright and poet. Wrote amusing, cynical *Bab Ballads* (1869). In 1871 he began his long collaboration with composer Arthur Sullivan, resulting in popular satiric operettas: *Trial by Jury* (1875), *H.M.S. Pinafore* (1878), *The Pirates of Penzance* (1879), *Patience* (1881), *Iolanthe* (1882), *Princess Ida* (1884), *The Mikado* (1885), *Ruddigore* (1887), *The Yeomen of the Guard* (1888), *The Gondoliers* (1889).

Gilbert and Ellice Islands (ĕl'ĭs), British colony (375 sq. mi.; pop 46,186), central and S Pacific, estab. 1915 and placed under Western Pacific High Commission at Suva, Fiji; cap. Tarawa. Includes GILBERT ISLANDS, ELLICE ISLANDS, OCEAN ISLAND, FANNING ISLAND, WASHINGTON ISLAND, CHRISTMAS ISLAND, and part of PHOENIX ISLANDS. Chief exports of colony are copra and phosphate.

Gilbert Islands, group of atolls (144 sq. mi.; pop. 34,434), central Pacific, part of GILBERT AND ELLICE ISLANDS, a British colony. Discovered by Capt. Byron 1764, became voluntary British protectorate 1892. Occupied by Japanese 1941 and regained by U.S. 1943 after fierce fighting at Tarawa and Makin.

Gilboa (–bō–), ridge, between Israel and Jordan, on E side of plain of Esdraelon. Here Saul and Jonathan were defeated and killed. 1 Sam. 28.4; 31; 2 Sam. 1.21.

Gilder, Richard Watson (gĭl'–), 1844–1909, American editor, poet, editor of *Century* magazine.

Gildersleeve, Virginia (Crocheron), 1877–1965, American educator. She was dean of Barnard Col. (1911–47) and only woman member of U.S. delegation to the UN founding conference in San Francisco in 1945.

gilds: see GUILDS.

Gilead (gĭl'ĕăd), mountainous region, NE of Dead Sea; allotted to Reuben, Gad, and Manasseh. Noted for spices, myrrh, and balm. Also called Mt. Gilead and Land of Gilead.

Giles, William Branch (jīlz), 1762–1830, American statesman. Anti-Federalist U.S. Representative from Va. (1790–98, 1801–03); U.S. Senator (1804–15). Opposed Albert Gallatin and James Monroe.

Gilgamesh (gĭl'gŭmĕsh), in Babylonian legend, king of Erech. Hero of Gilgamesh epic (c.2000 B.C.), which tells of his adventures with his friend Enkidu (half bull, half man) and his futile search for immortality after Enkidu's death.

Gill, Sir David (gĭl), 1843–1914, Scottish astronomer, astronomer royal of Cape of Good Hope (1879–1907); a leader in use of photography in star cataloguing.

Gill, Eric (Rowland), 1882–1940, English sculptor and wood engraver. Some of best work is religious sculpture. His books give his views on art and life.

Gill, Theodore Nicholas, 1837–1914, American zoologist and taxonomist. Classified many families of fishes and mammals.

gill (gĭl), respiratory organ of many aquatic animals. In fish, gill is chief respiratory organ throughout life. Blood in tiny vessels permeating gill filaments absorbs oxygen, releases carbon dioxide; filaments are attached to the outer edge of cartilaginous or bony branchial (or gill) arch. Projections from inner edge of arch are gill rakers; these are present except in fish eating whole fish or other large food and serve to strain food from water which enters mouth and leaves through gill clefts. Similar gills are also present in larval amphibians. In higher vertebrates, gills have disappeared through evolution, but derivatives remain as parts of windpipe, of tongue, of larynx. Gills different in structure are found in invertebrates (crustaceans, echinoderms, mollusks, water insects).

Gillette, William, 1853–1937, American actor and playwright. Permanently associated with *Sherlock Holmes* —play and stage character he created after the Conan Doyle character.

Gilliam, David Tod, 1844–1923, American gynecologist. Originated the Gilliam operation for displacement of the uterus (1899).

Gillmore, Quincy Adams, 1825–88, Union general in Civil War. Known especially for service as commander of Dept. of the South (1863–64, 1865).

gillyflower: see STOCK; WALLFLOWER.

Gilman, Charlotte Perkins, 1860–1935, American feminist, reformer, and writer; great-granddaughter of Lyman Beecher. Edited *Forerunner.*

Gilman, Daniel Coit, 1831–1908, American educator. He helped to found Sheffield Scientific School at Yale. After serving 1872–75 as president of Univ. of California, he became first president (1875–1901) of Johns Hopkins Univ. He was president of Carnegie Inst. of Washington, 1902–4.

Gilmer, Thomas Walker, 1802–44, U.S. Secretary of the Navy (Feb., 1844). His death from gun explosion while on the *Princeton* with other government officials raised question of succession to presidency in event of wholesale death of public officials.

Gilson, Étienne (ātyĕn' zhēlsō'), 1884–, French philosopher and historian. Primarily an historian of philosophy, he is also one of leaders of the Catholic Neo-Thomist movement.

Gil Vicente: see VICENTE, GIL.

Gimbel, Adam, 1815–96, American merchant, founder of a family of merchants and philanthropists, b. Bavaria. His sons furthered the Gimbel department store business in Philadelphia, New York city, and many other cities.

gin [archaic *geneva,* from Dutch from O. Fr. from Latin; = juniper], spirituous liquor distilled chiefly from fermented cereals and flavored with juniper berries. Types include London, sloe (flavored with sloe instead of juniper), dry (distilled several times), "Old Tom," which is sweetened for use as a liqueur.

ginger, tropical perennial plant (*Zingiber officinale*) and its rootstalk, a commercially important spice. It is marketed as preserved or green ginger, mostly in China, or as dried or cured ginger. It is used in cookery and medicine; the oil flavors ginger ale.

Ginkel, Godart van, 1st earl of Athlone (vän gĭng'kŭl, äthlōn'), 1644–1703, Dutch general in service of WILLIAM III of England. In War of Grand Alliance he was commander in chief in Ireland (1690–91); captured Ballymore and Athlone, defeated forces of James II at Aughrim, and took Limerick.

ginkgo (gĭngk'gō) or **maidenhair tree,** deciduous tree (*Ginkgo biloba*), with fan-shaped leaves. It is native to China but widely planted elsewhere for shade and ornament. Ginkgo trees are either male or female; usually only male trees are used as plantings, since female trees produce very foul-smelling fruit. The ginkgo is a survivor of a group of trees that existed in geologic times. See *ill.*, p. 859.

Ginsberg, Allen, 1926–, American poet of the BEAT GENERATION, author of *Howl* (1955–56) and other poems.

ginseng (jĭn′sĕng″), perennial herb (*Panax*) of North America and Asia. Asiatic ginseng (*Panax schinseng*) has long been prized by Chinese as a panacea. Demand for ginseng led to cultivation of a substitute for export, the American *P. quinquefolius.*

Ginzberg, Asher: see ACHAD HAAM.

Ginzberg, Louis, 1874–1953. Jewish talmudical scholar, b. Lithuania. Professor at Jewish Theological Seminary, New York; collected legends of the Jews.

Gioberti, Vincenzo (vĕnchän′tsō jōbĕr′tē), 1801–52, Italian statesman; a priest and philosopher. Premier of Sardinia 1848–49. Advocated at first a federation of Italian states under papal arbitration; later a unified, constitutional monarchy.

Gioia or **Gioja, Melchiorre** (both: mälkyôr′rä jō′yä), 1767–1829, Italian economist, an early advocate of unification of Italy. An opponent of Adam Smith, he insisted on economic duty of the state.

Giolitti, Giovanni (jōvän′nē jōlēt′tē), 1842–1928, Italian premier (1892–93, 1903–5, 1906–9, 1911–14, 1920–21). A leftist but no Socialist, he favored labor unions, promoted social reform, opposed participation in First World War and Fascism.

Giono, Jean (zhä′ jônō′), 1895–, French novelist. His pastoral novels, such as *Colline* (1920; Eng. tr., *Hill of Destiny,* 1929), were followed by an account of his pacifism (*Refus d'obéissance,* 1937). His recent novels are tales of man's struggle against fate, e.g., *Le Hussard sur le toit* (1951; Eng. tr., *The Horseman on the Roof,* 1954) and *Le Bonheur fou* (1957).

Giordano, Luca (lōō′kä jōrdä′nō), 1632–1705, Neapolitan painter, pupil of Ribera and Cortona. Executed frescoes in Naples, Florence, Madrid and Toledo.

Giordano, Umberto, 1867–1948, Italian composer of operas (e.g., *Andrea Chénier, Madame Sans-Gêne*).

Giorgio, Francesco di (fränchä′skō dē jōr′jō), 1439–1502, Italian artist, b. Siena. Paintings show influence of Filippo Lippi. Did sculpture for choir of Siena cathedral. Was also an engineer and architect.

Giorgione (jōrjō′nä), c.1478–1510, Venetian painter, fellow student of Titian under Giovanni Bellini. A great innovator, he initiated fusion of forms and subordination of local color to the pervading tone. His works have luminous color and poetic sensibility. Extant works include *Concert champêtre* (Louvre) and *Venus and Cupid in a Landscape* (Natl. Gall., Washington, D.C.).

Giotto (jôt′tō), c.1266–c.1337, Florentine artist. Tremendously influenced course of European painting. Turned from Italo-Byzantine conventionalism to study of nature, achieving lifelike, expressive faces and illusion of movement. Tradition says he was a pupil of Cimabue. Most famous works are the 38 biblical frescoes in Scrovegini (Arena) Chapel, Padua.

Giovanni da Bologna: see BOLOGNA, GIOVANNI DA.

Giovanni delle Bande Nere: see MEDICI, GIOVANNI DE' (under MEDICI, *Younger line*).

Giovanni di Paolo (jōvän′nē dē pä′ōlō), c.1403–1483, major Italian painter of the Sienese school.

gipsy: see GYPSY.

giraffe (jĭräf′), ruminant mammal (genus *Giraffa*) of Africa living in open country S of Sahara. The tallest animal, it may be 18 ft. from hoof to crown and can outrun most enemies. Its short horns are covered with skin and hair. It is protectively colored with large sandy to chestnut angular spots, closely spaced. It eats chiefly acacia and mimosa leaves, using extensible tongue and mobile lips; can live without water for long intervals.

Girard, Stephen (jĭrärd′), 1750–1831, American merchant, banker, and philanthropist, b. France. A merchant in Philadelphia, he set up a bank, and helped finance U.S. in War of 1812. Bequeathed money to found Girard College, free educational institution for poor white orphan boys.

Girard, city (pop. 12,997), NE Ohio, on Mahoning R., NNW of Youngstown; settled c. 1800. Steel mfg.

Girard College, at Philadelphia, Pa.; for fatherless boys; a home, secondary school, and junior college. Opened 1848 with bequest from Stephen Girard.

Giraud, Henri Honoré (ärē′ ōnôrā′ zhērō′), 1879–1949, French general. Captured by Germans in both world wars, he escaped both times. In 1942 he landed with the Allies in N Africa; succeeded Darlan as high commissioner. With his rival de GAULLE, he briefly was co-president of the French Committee of Natl. Liberation (1943). He remained in command of the Free French forces until 1944.

Giraudoux, Jean (zhä′zhērōdōō′), 1882–1944, French novelist and dramatist. Among his novels is *Suzanne et le pacifique* (1921). His plays, imaginative commentaries on modern society, include adaptations of myths and legends (*Tiger at the Gates,* 1935) and fantasies (*The Madwoman of Chaillot,* 1945).

Girl Scouts, organization founded 1912 at Savannah, Ga., by Mrs. Juliette Gordon Low (who had been a leader of Girl Guide troops in England), to promote good citizenship, sociability, and outdoor life among girls from 7 to 17.

Gironde (zhērōd′), department (4,141 sq. mi.; pop. 935,448), SW France, in Guienne; cap. Bordeaux. Includes Bordeaux wine region. Crossed by the **Gironde,** estuary c.45 mi. long and 2–7 mi. wide. formed by junction of Garonne and Dordogne rivers c.14 mi. N of Bordeaux; great artery of wine trade.

Girondists (jĭrŏn′dĭsts), Fr. *Girondins,* group of moderate republicans in French Revolution; so called because early members were mostly deputies from Gironde dept. (1791). Among leaders were Brissot de Warville, Vergniaud, Condorcet, Dumouriez. In June, 1793, the Jacobin and Cordelier extremists expelled the Girondists from the Convention and had their leaders executed. The assassination of Marat by Charlotte Corday brought further persecution. Joined by the royalists, the Girondists rose in revolt in the provinces, but their efforts were drowned in blood.

Girtin, Thomas, 1775–1802, English water-colorist. He was among first to abandon the tinted drawing and to paint directly in water color.

Girton College: see CAMBRIDGE UNIVERSITY.

Girty, Simon (gûr′tē), 1741–1818, American frontiersman, known as the Great Renegade. Joined British in 1778. Led or participated in many savage Indian raids; known for his cruelty.

Gish, Lillian, 1896–, and **Dorothy Gish,** 1898–, American actresses; sisters. Won renown in early films, playing separately or together in such films as *The Birth of a Nation, Broken Blossoms, Way down East, Orphans of the Storm, The White Sister,* and *Romola.* Lillian Gish was successful later on the N.Y. stage.

Gissing, George, 1857–1903, English author. His novels (best known is *New Grub Street,* 1891) were influenced by Dickens and the French naturalists. Wrote semiautobiographical *Private Papers of Henry Ryecroft* (1903).

Gist, Christopher (gĭst), c.1706–1759, American frontiersman. Explored Ohio valley region for Ohio Co. (1750). Served as guide on Braddock's expedition (1755).

Giulio Romano (jōō′lyō rōmä′nō), c.1492–1546, Italian artist, whose real name was Giulio Pippi. Favorite pupil of Raphael, some of whose Vatican frescoes he completed. Architect to duke of Mantua (1524) and briefly of St. Peter's.

Giusti, Giuseppe (jōōzĕp′pä jōō′stē), 1809–50, Italian nationalist poet, known for anti-Austrian satires and polemics.

Gizeh or **Giza** (both: gē′zŭ), market town (pop. c.276,200), Egypt, on Nile opposite Cairo. Pyramid of Khufu (Cheops) and great Sphinx are nearby.

Gjellerup, Karl Adolf (yĕ′lŭrōŏp), 1857–1919, Danish poet and novelist. Early novels are largely autobiographical; later writings show influence of Buddhism. Shared with Henrik Pontoppidan the 1917 Nobel Prize in Literature.

Glace Bay (glās), coal-mining town (pop. 24,186), Cape Breton Isl., N.S., Canada, on NE coast. Good harbor and large fishing fleet.

glacial periods (glā'shŭl), times in past geologic history when owing to excessively cold climate great ice sheets extended over the land. Most recent ice invasion occurred in Pleistocene. See GEOLOGICAL ERAS, table.

glacier, slowly moving ice mass formed from accumulated snow. Chief types are valley, piedmont, and continental. Valley glaciers are ice tongues which start in mountain snow fields and follow stream valleys. A piedmont glacier forms when valley glaciers unite. Greenland and Antarctica now have the only continental ice sheets (see PLEISTOCENE EPOCH). Ice is an important agent of erosion and transportation, having shaped the present topography of Canada and much of N U.S. See also DRUMLIN, ESKER, MORAINE.

Glacier Bay National Monument: see NATIONAL PARKS AND MONUMENTS (table).

Glacier National Park, 521 sq. mi., SE B.C., Canada, in Selkirk Mts.; estab. 1886. Illecilliwaet Glacier one of outstanding features.

Glackens, William (James), 1870–1938, American landscape and genre painter and illustrator. First exhibited with The EIGHT. His work shows influence of French impressionists.

Gladden, Washington, 1836–1918, American Congregational clergyman. Leading modernist theologian and early proponent of the Social Gospel. Pastor in Columbus, Ohio, 1882–1918.

gladiolus (glădēō'lŭs), tender cormous-rooted plant (*Gladiolus*), native to Africa. It has sword-shaped leaves and long stalks of flowers of many pastel as well as vivid colors.

Gladkov, Feodor Vasilyevich (fyô'dŭr vŭsĕ'lyŭvĭch glŭtkôf'), 1883–1958, Russian author. Famed for novel *Cement* (1926; Eng. tr., 1929), describing post-revolution reconstruction.

Gladstone, William Ewart, 1809–98, British statesman, dominant personality of the Liberal Party 1868–94. As chancellor of exchequer (1852–55, 1859–66), he promoted free trade and fairer tax distribution. Was prime minister four times—1868–74, 1880–85, 1886, 1892–94. He achieved notable reforms—Irish land act, changes in civil service, vote by secret ballot, abolition of the sale of army commissions, parliamentary reform, and educational expansion. Constant advocacy of Irish HOME RULE ended his last ministry. A great orator and a master of finance, he was deeply religious and discussed politics in high moral terms.

Gladstone, city (pop. 14,502), W Mo., a suburb N of Kansas City; founded 1878.

Glamis (glämz; in Shakespeare glä'mĭs), parish and village, Angus, Scotland. Macbeth was thane of Glamis; castle here wrongly claimed as scene of Duncan's murder. Birthplace of Elizabeth, queen consort of George VI.

Glamorganshire (glŭmôr'gŭnshĭr) or **Glamorgan,** maritime county (813 sq. mi.; pop. 1,227,828), S Wales, on Bristol Channel; co. town Cardiff. Has rich coal deposits in N, dairy farming and cattle grazing on coastal plain. Great mineral wealth (iron and copper) make it one of chief industrial areas of British Isles. Severe industrial depression struck area in 1920s; conditions now improved. Cardiff and Swansea important ports.

gland, organ which forms a SECRETION from material extracted by its cells from body fluids. Varies from single cell to many cells, or system of tubes uniting into a duct (e.g., salivary glands, breasts). Hormones, secretions of endocrine (ductless) glands (e.g., thyroid, parathyroids, pituitary, adrenals) are taken up directly by the blood. Some glands (e.g., testis, ovary,

liver, pancreas) produce both a hormone and a secretion which flows from a duct.

Glarus (glä'rŭs), canton (264 sq. mi.; pop. 40,148), central Switzerland, S of the Wallensee; cap. Glarus (pop. 5,852). Mountainous and pastoral; hydroelectrical and textile industries. Glarus joined Swiss Confederation 1352. Inhabitants are mainly German-speaking Protestants.

Glaser, Donald Arthur, 1926–, American physicist. Awarded 1960 Nobel Prize in Physics for inventing the bubble chamber (1952) to observe tracks of moving subatomic particles.

Glasgow, Ellen (glăs'gō), 1873–1945, American novelist, b. Va. Among her realistic novels are *Barren Ground* (1925), *The Romantic Comedians* (1926), and *Vein of Iron* (1935). *A Certain Measure* (1943) contains her critical prefaces. Her autobiography, *The Woman Within*, was published in 1954.

Glasgow (glăs'gō, –kō), city (pop. 1,054,913), Scotland, on the Clyde. Largest city in Scotland, it lies mostly in Lanarkshire, but its suburbs are partly in Renfrewshire and Dumbartonshire. Most important seaport in Scotland, it has huge shipyards, metalworks, and mfg. of steel, chemicals, carpets, textiles, tobacco, and machine tools. Univ. of Glasgow, founded 1451, has faculties of the arts, medicine, theology, law, engineering, and nuclear research.

Glasgow. 1 City (pop. 10,069), S central Ky., E of Bowling Green; founded 1799. Trade center for timber, oil, livestock, and farm area. Has tobacco warehouses. **2** City (pop. 6,398), NE Mont., on Milk R., WNW of Wolf Point; founded 1888. Lively cow town on Northern Pacific RR in 19th cent. Now center of agr. and livestock area served by Milk R. project. Fort Peck Dam and Glasgow Air Force Base are near.

Glaspell, Susan (glăs'pĕl), 1882–1948, American writer. A novelist, she became interested in the Provincetown Players (after her marriage to George Cram Cook) and wrote plays (e.g., *Alison's House*, 1930).

Glass, Carter, 1858–1946, U.S. Secretary of the Treasury (1918–20), U.S. Senator from Va. (1920–46). Active in framing of Federal Reserve System.

Glass, Hugh, fl. 1822–33, trapper in American West. Experience while on expedition in Missouri river country of being mauled by a grizzly bear, left for dead, and dragging himself 100 mi. to Fort Kiowa is told in John G. Neihardt's *Song of Hugh Glass.*

Glassboro, borough (pop. 10,253), SW N.J., SSW of Camden; settled 1775. Farm trade center with glassworks. Glassboro State Col. here was scene of summit conference June, 1967, between Pres. Lyndon Johnson and Premier Alexei Kosygin after Middle Eastern war.

glass snake, legless burrowing lizard of genus *Ophisaurus* of S and central U.S. It averages c.2 ft. long; shiny body is gray or greenish brown, sometimes striped, above; the sides are darker with light lines; ventral surface is whitish. Its long tail breaks easily from body; new, usually shorter, tail without real backbone grows to replace it. The glass snake has eyelids, ear openings, broad tongue; eats insects, worms, and small snakes.

Glastonbury, municipal borough (pop. 5,796), Somersetshire, England. Place of many legends. One tells that Joseph of Arimathea founded England's first Christian church here. He rested his staff, which rooted and grew into Glastonbury thorn. Another says Glastonbury is Isle of Avalon of Arthurian legend. Abbey dates from 8th cent.

Glastonbury, town (pop. 14,497), central Conn., on Connecticut R. below Hartford; settled c.1650. Has several 17th-cent. houses. Gideon Welles born here.

Glatz (gläts) or **Klodzko** (kwôts'kô), city (est. pop. 25,000), SW Poland (since 1945), formerly in Lower Silesia on Glatzer Neisse R. Trade and mfg. center; slate quarries. Founded in 10th cent. The **Glatzer Gebirge** (glä'tsŭr gŭbĭr'gŭ), a range of the Sudetes, rises to 4,672 ft. at Czech border. For **Glatzer Neisse R.,** see NEISSE.

Glauber, Johann Rudolf, 1604–68, German alchemist. Made important contributions to analytical chemistry. Compounds he helped prepare included **Glauber's salt,** common name for hydrated sodium sulfate. Compound of sodium, sulfur, oxygen, and water. it effloresces in moist air. Mined in Europe and SW U.S.; also prepared synthetically. Used in dyeing. in industry, and as mild laxative.

glaucoma (glôkō′mŭ), eye disease marked by increased pressure within eyeball and often resulting in impaired vision or blindness.

Glaucus (glô′kŭs), in Greek legend, sea-god who loved SCYLLA.

Glazunov, Aleksandr (Konstantinovich) (ŭlyĭksändr′ gläzōō′nôf), 1865–1936, Russian composer. He wrote eight symphonies, a piano and a violin concerto, ballets, and chamber music.

Gleiwitz (glī′vĭts) or **Gliwice** (glĭvē′tsĕ), city (est. pop. 147,000), SW Poland (since 1945), formerly in Upper Silesia. It is a center of the KATOWICE mining region.

Gleizes, Albert Léon (älbĕr′ lāō′ glēz′), 1881–1953, French cubist painter and illustrator.

Glen Canyon Dam, N central Ariz., in Colorado R. just S of Utah; built 1956–64. One of world's largest concrete dams and key unit of COLORADO RIVER STORAGE PROJECT, it is 700 ft. high, 1,560 ft. long. Regulates flow of upper Colorado R. and tributaries; provides power. Forms L. Powell (extends 186 mi. upstream). Glen Canyon Bridge (700 ft. high, 1,271 ft. long; completed 1959) is one of world's highest steel-arch bridges.

Glencliff, Tenn.: see WOODBINE.

Glencoe, residential village (pop. 10,472), NE Ill., NNW of Chicago; settled 1836.

Glencoe (glĕnkō′), valley of Coe R., Argyllshire, Scotland, overhung by lofty mountains. Macdonald clan massacred here by the Campbells in 1692.

Glen Cove, city (1965 pop. 25,048), SE N.Y., on N shore of Long Isl., N of Mineola; settled 1668. Webb Inst. of Naval Architecture is here.

Glendale. 1 City (1965 pop. 30,760), S central Ariz., NW of Phoenix, in Salt River Valley; founded 1892. In agr. region (lettuce, melons, other truck crops) irrigated by Salt R. project. Luke Air Force Base is near. **2** City (pop. 119,442), S Calif., a suburb N of Los Angeles; laid out 1887 on site of first Spanish land grant in Calif. (1784). Has Forest Lawn Memorial Park Cemetery, with graves of many film celebrities. **3** City, Tenn.: see WOODMONT.

Glendale, battle of: see SEVEN DAYS BATTLES.

Glendora, city (1966 pop. 29,513), S Calif., E of Los Angeles, in citrus-fruit area; founded 1887.

Glendower: see OWEN GLENDOWER.

Glen Ellyn, village (1964 pop. 18,620), NE Ill., W of Chicago; platted 1851. Maryknoll Seminary is here.

Glenn, John Herschel, Jr., 1922–, first American astronaut to achieve orbital flight, Feb. 20, 1962.

Glen Rock, borough (pop. 12,896), NE N.J., NNE of Paterson; settled c.1710.

Glen Rose, city (pop. 1,422), N central Texas, SW of Fort Worth. Health and vacation resort with mineral springs. Dinosaur tracks found in limestone nearby.

Glens Falls, city (pop. 18,580), E central N.Y., on Hudson R., NNE of Saratoga Springs; settled 1762. C. E. Hughes born here.

Glenview, village (1966 pop. 23,521), NE Ill., a suburb NNW of Chicago. Has dairy research center.

Glenwood Springs, resort city (pop. 3,637), NW Colo., on Colorado R., NE of Grand Junction; laid out 1883. Has mineral springs.

glider, engineless aircraft similar to airplane, using gravity and natural air currents to obtain forward motion. Otto Lilienthal demonstrated (1890–96) superiority of curved over flat surfaces. Other pioneers: Percy Pilcher, England; Henri Farman, France; Oc-

tave Chanute and John J. Montgomery, U.S. Chanute first used movable plane parts to obtain stable flight. Wright brothers added landing skids. Troop-transport gliders towed by airplanes were used in Second World War invasions.

Glière, Reinhold (Moritzovich) (rīn′hŏlt glēĕr′), 1875–1956, Russian composer. Music is nationalistic. Most popular of his many works are the ballet *The Red Poppy* and the Third Symphony, *Ilya Mourometz.*

Glinka, Mikhail (Ivanovich) (mēkhŭyĕl glīn′kä), 1804–57, first of the Russian nationalist composers. Known for his operas, *A Life for the Tsar* and *Russlan and Ludmilla.*

Glittertind, mountain of Norway: see JOTUNHEIM.

Gliwice, Poland: see GLEIWITZ.

Globe, city (1965 pop. 6,299), E Ariz., in foothills near Pinal Mts.; settled 1876. Grew with silver boom; later became copper center. Copper, silver, gold, and asbestos still mined. Apache Indian reservation is nearby.

globe, spherical body used to illustrate the earth (terrestrial globe) or sky (celestial globe). Terrestrial globe represents sizes and shapes of continents without distortion of shape, mistakes in relative area, or inaccuracy of angles and direction, except that while globes are spheres, earth's equatorial diameter exceeds the polar one by 27 mi. Probably oldest globe was made by Crates, Greek geographer, 2d cent. B.C. First modern globes made by Martin Behaim (1492), by Leonardo da Vinci soon after. On celestial globes star positions correspond to actual ones on sky; if globe is in correct position a line drawn from its center to any star on surface, if extended, focuses actual star.

globe amaranth, annual plant (*Gomphrena globosa*) with chaffy dome-shaped flowers in various colors. Used as an EVERLASTING.

globeflower, perennial (*Trollius*) of N temperate regions with white, yellow, orange, or purple blooms, similar to buttercups but larger.

Globe Theatre, London playhouse, built 1598. Most of Shakespeare's plays were first presented here. Puritans destroyed it in 1644.

Glocester (glŏs′tŭr), rural town (1965 pop. 4,142), NW R.I., on Conn. line WNW of Providence. Nearby Chepachet village has monument to T. W. Dorr, leader of Dorr's Rebellion, who gathered his men here.

glockenspiel: see PERCUSSION INSTRUMENTS.

Glogau (glō′gou) or **Glogow** (gwô′gŏŏf), town (est. pop. 8,300), SW Poland (since 1945), formerly in Lower Silesia, on the Oder. Cap. of principality of Glogau under Piast dynasty (1249–1506); passed to Prussia 1745.

Glomma (glŏ′mä), chief river of Norway, rising in highlands S of Trondheim Fjord and flowing c.375 mi. S into the Skagerrak. Large falls at Sarpsborg furnish power for industrial concentration.

Gloria in excelsis (ĕksĕl′sĭs) [Latin,= glory in the highest], the *Angelic Hymn* or greater doxology, anc. Christian hymn; an amplification of Luke 2.14. In the Roman Mass it follows the *Kyrie;* in Anglican communion it is just before the benediction. Omitted from both services at certain seasons.

Glorious Revolution, in English history, the events of the years 1688–89 resulting in deposition of JAMES II. His overt Catholicism and the birth of a Catholic heir united Tories and Whigs in opposition. Seven nobles invited William of Orange and his consort Mary, Protestant daughter of James, to come to England's aid. After Bloodless Revolution they ruled jointly as WILLIAM III and Mary II. Their acceptance of the Bill of Rights assured ascendancy of parliamentary authority over royal absolutism.

glory lily, tropical tuberous-rooted climbing plant (*Gloriosa*), with lilylike yellow and red flowers.

glossolalia [Gr.,= speaking with tongues], distinctive utterances of persons speaking an unidentifiable language under the inspiration of the Holy Spirit. On the first day of Pentecost, tongues of fire descended on the gathered disciples, who then spoke and were understood by the many people from other lands—each in his own language. This recalls the prophecy of Joel that the followers of the Lord shall see visions and prophesy. Examples of such spontaneous utterances have continued to today down through such diverse groups as 13th-cent. Franciscans, Jansenists, and Irvingites. The phenomenon of glossolalia continues to puzzle theologians.

Gloucester, Gilbert de Clare, earl of: see GLOUCESTER, RICHARD DE CLARE, 7TH EARL OF.

Gloucester, Humphrey, duke of (glŏ'stŭr), 1391–1447, English nobleman; son of Henry IV. Fought for his brother (Henry V) in France and served (1420–21) as regent of England during Henry's absence. After the accession of the infant Henry VI, he was powerful in the regency and (after 1435) heir to the throne. His influence waned and in 1447 he was arrested on charges of plotting Henry's death. He died in custody. A patron of Oxford Univ., his gift of books formed nucleus of the Bodleian Library.

Gloucester, Richard de Clare, 7th earl of, 1222–62, English nobleman. He vacillated between support of Henry III and baronial party. Gloucester and his rival, Simon de MONTFORT, were most powerful political figures of the time. His son, **Gilbert de Clare,** 8th **earl of Gloucester,** 1243–95, was first a leader of the barons under Simon de Montfort. Henry III surrendered to him (1264) after the battle of Lewes. He later aided the accession of Edward I (1272) and married (1290) Edward's daughter. His son, **Gilbert de Clare, 9th earl of Gloucester,** 1291–1314, was several times regent of England and was killed at Bannockburn.

Gloucester, Robert, earl of, d. 1147, English nobleman; illegitimate son of Henry I. Earldom created c.1121 for him. Refused to claim throne at his father's death (1135) and supported STEPHEN. Later quarreled with him, declared for MATILDA (Robert's half-sister), and was leader of the Angevin party.

Gloucester, Thomas of Woodstock, duke of, 1355–97, English nobleman; seventh son of Edward III. Was a leader (1388) of baronial opposition to his nephew, RICHARD II. Made peace with the king (1389), but later intrigues caused his arrest and conviction for treason. Was probably killed at king's command.

Gloucester, England: see GLOUCESTERSHIRE.

Gloucester, city (pop. 25,789), NE Mass., on Cape Ann; settled 1623. At head of excellent Gloucester Harbor (protected by breakwater), it was once important shipbuilding center; first schooner said to have been built (1713) here. Now fish-processing center. Summer resort and artists' colony since late 19th cent. Hammond Mus. has art collections. Bronze *Fisherman* is memorial to Gloucestermen lost at sea.

Gloucester City, city (pop. 15,511), SW N.J., on Delaware R., SW of Camden, in industrial area. Settled 1682 by Irish Quakers on site of Fort Nassau (built 1623 by Dutch).

Gloucestershire or **Gloucester** (glŏ'stŭrshĭr), county (1,255 sq. mi.; pop. 1,000,493), W England. Includes Cotswold Hills (sheep grazing) in E; fertile Severn valley (dairy farming) in center; and Forest of Dean in W. Mfg. centered around Bristol. Rich in ecclesiastical remains. County town is **Gloucester,** county borough (pop. 69,867), on Severn R., an industrial city and site of a cathedral.

Gloversville, city (pop. 21,741), E central N.Y., NW of Amsterdam; settled c.1760. Glove mfg. since late 18th cent.

glowworm, name for luminescent larva and wingless female of certain beetles or fireflies chiefly of families Lampyridae and Phengodidae. Common European glowworm is wingless female of beetle *Lampyris noctiluca;* cells of abdominal segments emit greenish light.

Glubb, Sir John Bagot, 1897–, British soldier. Commanded (1939–56) Arab Legion of Jordan until

pressure of Arab public opinion during Sinai campaign forced his dismissal by Hussein I.

glucinum: see BERYLLIUM.

Gluck, Christoph Willibald von (krĭs'tôf vĭ'lēbält), 1714–87, operatic composer, b. Bavaria, studied in Prague and Italy. His early operas were in Italian tradition. With *Orfeo ed Euridice* (1762) he began his reform of opera, giving greater unity to text and music and emphasizing simplicity. To Ranieri Calzabigi, librettist of *Orfeo* and of *Alceste* (1767), he credited much of his new operatic style. *Iphigénie en Tauride* (1779) is considered his masterpiece.

glucose, dextrose, or **grape sugar,** simple SUGAR most common in plants and animals. It is a white, crystalline solid CARBOHYDRATE. There are a number of other simple sugars with the same numerical formula (6 carbon atoms, 12 hydrogen, 6 oxygen); these are structural isomers of glucose. Glucose occurs in two forms having different optical properties. Only D-glucose is found in plants and animals; the other optical isomer is the form having mirror-image structure, L-glucose. Glucose is a component of the disaccharides LACTOSE, MALTOSE, and SUCROSE. Presence of glucose is shown by test with FEHLING'S SOLUTION. See *ill.,* p. 178.

glue: see ADHESIVE.

gluten (glōo'tŭn), mixture of proteins, tough, elastic, tasteless. Present in cereals, it is found in larger amounts in northern wheat. It gives dough adhesiveness. Cereals having little gluten (e.g., rice) cannot be made into bread because the dough cannot rise.

glycerol, glycerin, or **glycerine,** colorless, odorless liquid ALCOHOL, used in perfume, cosmetics, some inks, explosives, antifreeze mixtures, and in medicine. It is a by-product of soapmaking.

glycogen (glī'kŭjĕn), form of carbohydrate stored in animal cells; also called animal starch. It is made of branched chains of D-glucose molecules. Some animal cells convert glucose into glycogen for storage, usually in the liver. It resembles plant starch in physical properties. See CARBOHYDRATE.

Glyptothek (glüp"tōtāk'), museum in Munich, founded by Louis I of Bavaria. Designed by Leo von Klenze, built 1816–30. Destroyed in Second World War, but collection (ancient and modern sculptures) was saved.

Gmelin, Leopold (lā'ōpôlt gŭmā'lĭn), 1788–1853, German chemist. Taught at Univ. of Heidelberg; noted for works on chemistry of digestion; discovered potassium ferrocyanide.

Gnadenhutten (jīnä'dŭnhŭ"tŭn), rural village (pop. 1,257), E central Ohio, on Tuscarawas R., W of Steubenville. State memorial marks site of Gnadenhutten massacre (1782) of some 96 Christian Indians by white men.

gnat (năt), name for various small flies of order Diptera. BLACK FLY is pest to humans and most other warm-blooded animals. Several fungus gnat species injure mushrooms and various greenhouse plants. Potato scab gnat bores through tubers; gall gnats and midges damage plants.

Gneisenau, August, Graf Neithardt von (ou'gŏost gräf' nīt'härt fŭn günī'zŭnou), 1760–1831, Prussian field marshal. Won fame in Napoleonic Wars for his defense of Kolberg (1807); was Blücher's chief of staff 1813–15.

gneiss (nīs), rock which shows alternating light and dark bands. May result from metamorphism of igneous and sedimentary ROCK.

Gneist, Rudolf von (roo'dôlf fŭn günīst'), 1816–95, German jurist. Tried to reform the Prussian constitution and to make administration a cooperative function of citizens, local officials, and central administration.

Gniezno (günyĕz'nô), Ger. *Gnesen,* town (est. pop. 47,000), Poznan prov., W central Poland. Legendary cradle and first cap. of Polish nation; metropolitan see of Poland since 1000 (transferred to Poznan 1821). Under Prussian rule 1793–1919.

SMALL CAPITALS = cross references. Pronunciation key on inside end pages. Abbreviations: p. 2.

Gnosticism (nŏ'stĭsĭzŭm) [from Greek *gnosis* = knowledge], religious and philosophical movement, arising in the Hellenistic era. Its fundamental doctrine was that salvation is to be obtained through knowledge rather than through faith or good works. Gnostics generally accepted a strong dualism of good and evil and adopted many magical practices. Some Jewish sects (the Essenes and Therapeutae), affected by Gnosticism, rejected the Old Testament idea of God as Righteousness and substituted that of Divine Wisdom. Early Christian Gnostics rejected the Jewish foundations of Christianity and the Old Testament. Redemption through Wisdom (Sophia) was the basis of the complex doctrines of Valentinus and other 2d cent. Gnostics. They divided men into three classes: the Gnostics, sure of salvation; non-Gnostic Christians who might be saved through faith in Christ; and all others, who are incapable of salvation. Gnosticism merged with MANICHAEISM. The MANDAEANS are the only surviving Gnostic sect. The movement had a great effect on early Christianity by forcing the new religion to define doctrines in declaring Gnosticism heretical. Present knowledge of the movement is based on Coptic texts and wisdom literature of the PSEUDEPIGRAPHA. Of the 13 volumes of extremely valuable Gnostic manuscripts discovered by Egyptians in 1945, 12 were finally made available to scholars at the Coptic Mus. (Egypt) in 1956.

gnu (nōō), S African antelope resembling the ox. White-tailed gnu (genus *Connochaetes*) or black wildebeest is believed extinct in wild state. It is dark brown or blackish; long hair tufts stand erect on muzzle, and hang from throat and between forelegs; the broad head has horns and an upright mane. Males stand c.4 ft. high at the shoulder. Brindled gnu (genus *Gorgon* or *Connochaetes*) or blue wildebeest exists in small herds; it is bluish gray with brown on the sides, larger than the white-tailed gnu and with a narrower head.

Goa (gō'ŭ), former Portuguese colony (1,268 sq. mi.), W India, enclave on Arabian Sea. Founded by Alfonso de Albuquerque. Its original cap., Old Goa, is site of St. Francis Xavier's tomb. New Goa or Pangim was built (1842) to replace Old Goa as cap. Invaded and annexed by India Dec., 1961.

goat, ruminant animal with hollow horns, related to sheep. Probably it was domesticated in Persia from wild bezoar goat or pasan. True goats belong to genus *Capra*, family Bovidae; they are raised for milk, wool, flesh. Milk goats are common in Old World and are increasing in U.S.

Goat Island, N.Y.: see NIAGARA FALLS.

goatsbeard, tall perennial plant (*Aruncus sylvester*), with handsome spikes of small white flowers. The unrelated purple goatsbeard, better known as salsify or oyster plant (*Tragopogon porrifolius*), is grown as a vegetable for its edible roots.

Gobat, Charles Albert (shärl älbĕr' gōbä'), 1843–1914, Swiss statesman. He helped found an international peace bureau. Shared 1902 Nobel Peace Prize.

Gobelins, Manufacture nationale des (gōbŭlĕ'), state-controlled tapestry manufactory in Paris. Founded as dye works in mid-15th cent. by brothers, Gilles and Jehan Gobelin. Purchased 1662 by Louis XIV. Famous Gobelin tapestries include the set based on Raphael's frescoes in Vatican.

Gobi (gō'bē), Mandarin *Sha-mo*, sandy desert, area 500,000 sq. mi., in China and Mongolia; average alt. c.4,000 ft. Winds have stripped off most of its soil. Small number of pastoral Mongols inhabit scanty grasslands. Many paleontological finds have been made here.

Gobineau, Joseph Arthur, comte de (zhōzěf' ärtür' kŏt' dü gōběnō'), 1816–82, French author and diplomat. *The Inequality of Human Races* (1853–55; Eng. tr., 1915) was an early and influential attempt at proving the supremacy of the "Nordic race."

God, the divinity of the great monotheistic religions, Judaism, Christianity, and Islam. In the Old Testa-

ment the most celebrated form of his name was the ineffable (not to be spoken) name represented by the four letters transcribed as YHWH (the tetragrammaton). The origin of this is unknown; the reconstruction *Jehovah* is mistaken, and the form *Yahweh* is not now widely accepted. Because the name was ineffable the Hebrews used substitutes such as *Adonai* [my Lord] and *Elohim* (a plural form). *El* is not related to *Elohim* but is connected with *Allah*, used by Arabs (Moslem and Christian) as the name for God. The general conception of God in all three religions is that of a Being infinite, all powerful, all good, all creating, all knowing, loving but judging mankind, transcendent over and immanent in the world. He is often treated as a personality, though not necessarily in an anthropomorphic sense. The 19th-cent. rationalists argued that the Hebrew God was originally simply the chief of many gods and that He absorbed the attributes of His fellow divinities. Gradually He was considered as more and more powerful until He became the one God (though still preferring the Hebrews). In recent times in the Western world the term God has come to be applied to any overriding universal concept (such as the world soul or the Absolute). Scholasticism produced several demonstrations of the existence of God that are still current. One is the argument from First Cause: every effect in the world has its cause but this chain must lead back to the primary cause of the whole existing universe, which must have been itself both cause and effect (i.e., God). The cosmological argument is that the relations extant in the world must have their base in some independent, absolute existence (God), since all that is in the world is relative. The teleological argument is that the world operates on a great plan and toward set ends; therefore a master planner (God) must exist. The ontological argument is that since the human mind can reach the highest conception, which is God, that conception must have existence, for if not there could be a higher conception—one including existence. In the Western world the word god written without a capital letter is used for all the gods of polytheism (see MYTH).

Godavari (gōdä'vŭrē), river, c.900 mi. long, rising in the Western Ghats, Maharashtra, India. It empties into the Bay of Bengal. It is sacred to Hindus.

Goddard, Henry Herbert, 1866–1957, American psychologist, research director (1906–18) at Training School, Vineland, N.J., for retarded children. He was noted for systematic hereditary studies, especially for *The Kallikak Family* (1912).

Goddard, P(aul) B(eck), 1811–66, American physician and scientist. After Daguerre's work in photography became known, Goddard experimented with sun photography and discovered (1839) that a bromine vapor heightened impression on silver plate.

Goddard, Robert H(utchings), 1882–1945, American physicist and rocket expert. Designed and built early high-altitude rockets. Successfully fired (1926) world's first liquid-fuel rocket.

Godden, Rumer, 1907–, Anglo-Indian novelist. Her works include *Black Narcissus* (1939), *The River* (1946), stories for children, and essays and reminiscences of life in India, all written in subtle, fine style.

Gödel, Kurt, 1906–, American mathematician, logician, b. Czechoslovakia. Known for Gödel's theorem concerning inconsistency of sets of axioms and the consequences of this in logic.

Godesberg: see BAD GODESBERG.

Godey, Louis Antoine (gō'dē), 1804–78, American publisher, owner of first famous and successful woman's magazine, *Godey's Lady's Book.*

Godfrey of Bouillon (bōōyō'), c.1058–1100, duke of Lower Lorraine, leader of First Crusade. Elected king of Jerusalem, which he helped capture, but took title "protector of the Holy Sepulchre." His brother Baldwin succeeded him.

Godhavn (gôdh'houn), district (pop. 878) and town (pop. 584), W Greenland on Disko Isl. Town.

founded 1773, is a fishing base; has arctic research station (estab. 1906 by Univ. of Copenhagen).

Godiva, Lady (gōdī'vŭ), 1010?–1067, the wife of Leofric, earl of Mercia and lord of Coventry. Legends claim she rode naked through the town to get her husband to lower heavy taxes of the people. The only man who looked became known as Peeping Tom.

Godkin, E(dwin) L(awrence), 1831–1902, American editor, b. Ireland. His fearless and perceptive criticism made the *Nation* and the New York *Evening Post,* which he edited, influential in reform.

Godolphin, Sidney Godolphin, 1st earl of, 1645–1712, English statesman. By financial ability as lord treasurer aided victories of Marlborough (with whom he was politically associated after marriage of their children). Queen Anne dismissed him in 1710.

Godoy, Manuel de (mänwäl' dā gōdoi'), 1767–1851, Spanish statesman. Favorite of Queen MARÍA LUISA; chief minister to CHARLES IV after 1792. Favored war on revolutionary France, but made peace 1795. *Principe de la Paz* [prince of the peace] was one of many titles showered on him. The corruption of his regime and his increasing subservience to France led to his overthrow by Ferdinand VII (1808).

God Save the King (or Queen), English national anthem. Both words and music of uncertain origin. Tune was first sung publicly 1745.

Godthaab (gôt'hôp), town (pop. 3,181), cap. of S Greenland and of Godthaab dist. (pop. 4,306); a port on Godthaab Fjord of SW Greenland. Founded 1721 by Hans Egede, it was first Danish colony in Greenland. Has foreign consulates.

Godunov, Boris (bŭrēs' gŭdŏōnôf'), c.1551–1605, tsar of Russia (1598–1605). A favorite of Ivan IV, he ruled Russia as regent during reign of Feodor I (1584–98). He probably had Feodor's brother DMITRI murdered (1591). Chosen successor to Feodor, Boris ruled capably but lost popular support. He died during the false Dmitri's invasion of Russia. His son, Feodor II, lost his throne to the impostor. Boris's life is the subject of a drama by Pushkin, basis of Moussorgsky's opera.

Godwin or **Godwine** (both: gŏd'wĭn), d. 1053, English statesman. Earl of Wessex, he was chief adviser to Canute and most powerful earl in England. After king's death he supported claims to throne of Harthacanute. Opposed the French favorites of Harthacanute's successor, Edward the Confessor, and was exiled (1051). Invaded England (1052) and regained his former importance.

Godwin, William, 1756–1836, English author and political philosopher. His materialism pervaded his anarchistic tract, *An Enquiry concerning the Principles of Political Justice and Its Influence on General Virtue and Happiness* (1793) and also his novel *The Adventures of Caleb Williams* (1794). In 1797 he married Mary Wollstonecraft. Their daughter, Mary, became wife of SHELLEY.

Godwin-Austen, Mount, or **K2,** peak, 28,250 ft. high, Kashmir, in Karakorum range; second highest in world.

Godwine: see GODWIN (d. 1053).

Goebbels, (Paul) Joseph (poul' yō'zĕf gŭ'bŭls), 1897–1945, German National Socialist (Nazi) propaganda minister (1933–45), an able orator and writer. Worked on principles of self-justification of power and inculcating "the big lie" by varied repetition. Died by suicide when Berlin was being conquered.

Goerdeler, Carl Friedrich (kärl' frē'drĭkh gûrd'lûr), 1884–1945, German civil servant, a leader of resistance to Hitler. Executed Feb., 1945.

Goering or **Göring, Hermann Wilhelm** (hĕr'män vĭl'-hĕlm gŭ'rĭng), 1893–1946, German National Socialist (Nazi) leader. An air force hero of First World War, he joined the party early. President of Reichstag from 1932, he became in 1933 air minister for Germany and Prussian premier. He founded the Gestapo (secret police), which he headed until 1936; directed German economy with dictatorial powers, 1937–43 (invented slogan "guns instead of butter"); was designated by

Hitler as successor (1939). Also boasted such unique titles as "imperial marshal," "imperial master of the hunt." In Second World War he was responsible for initiating total air war. Excessively fond of pomp and pageantry, he amassed fabulous wealth and art collection. Surrendered to U.S. troops 1945. Chief defendant at Nuremberg war-crimes trial (1945–46); sentenced to death but took poison before scheduled hanging.

Goes, Hugo van der (hōō'gō vän dĕr gōōs'), d. 1482, Flemish painter. Realism and rich detail mark portraits and Portinari altarpiece (c.1476: Uffizi).

Goethals, George Washington (gō'thŭlz), 1858–1928, U.S. army engineer. Chief engineer of Panama Canal (1907–14). Governor of Canal Zone (1914–16).

Goethe, Johann Wolfgang von (yō'hän vôlf'gäng fŭn gŭ'tù), 1749–1832, German poet, dramatist, novelist. His universal genius also embraced other fields, notably science. After a happy childhood in Frankfurt, he studied the law at Leipzig and later at Strasbourg, where he came under the spell of the STURM UND DRANG movement. In 1773 he won recognition with his drama *Götz von Berlichingen* (see BERLICHINGEN, GÖTZ VON). While a lawyer at Wetzlar (1772), he fell unhappily in love with Charlotte Buff; he overcame his despair by writing *The Sorrows of Young Werther* (1774), an epistolary novel of morbid sensitiveness. It made him famous overnight. In 1775 he accepted an invitation to the court of Charles Augustus, duke of Saxe-Weimar, where he remained for the rest of his life. For 10 years he served the duke as chief minister. Goethe's first trip to Italy (1786–88) fired his enthusiasm for the classical ideal. His drama *Egmont* (1788) still shows traces of *Sturm und Drang,* but the drama *Iphigenie auf Tauris* (1779, rewritten 1787), *Römische Elegien* (1788), and the domestic epic *Hermann und Dorothea* (1797) are pure products of classicism. His two great novels, *Wilhelm Meisters Lehrjahre* (1796) and *Die Wahlverwandtschaften* [elective affinities] (1809), aside from their intrinsic merit, showed the way for the German novel of character development and the German psychological novel. His friendship with SCHILLER, begun in 1794, had a stimulating effect on both men. In 1808 he published the first part of his life work, FAUST, completed shortly before his death. Increasingly aloof in his old age, Goethe became more and more the Olympian divinity, to whose shrine at Weimar all Europe flocked. Literary products of his later years include *Dichtung und Wahrheit* (1811–33), his charming autobiography, and *Westöstlicher Diwan* (1819), a collection of exquisite lyrics inspired by readings of Persian poets. Goethe attached equal importance to his scientific and his poetic work. His discovery of the intermaxillary bone in man (1784) was important to the theory of evolution; his work in botany showed great intuitive insight; his *Zur Farbenlehre* (1810) was a stubborn attack on Newton's theory of light. His philosophy, greatly influenced by Spinoza, was a mystic pantheism. Most of his best-known works have been translated into English, as have been many of his lyrics and ballads.

Gog, leader who, according to prophecy, will come from land of Magog, attack Israel, and be defeated. Ezek. 38–39. Rev. 20.8 warns of Gog and Magog.

Gogarty, Oliver St. John (gō'gûrtē),1878–1957, Irish writer and wit. A surgeon and a senator of the Irish Free State (1922–36), he was the Buck Mulligan of James Joyce's *Ulysses.*

Gogebic (gōgē'bĭk), range, c.80 mi. long, extending W from W Upper Peninsula, N Mich., into N Wis. Known for its iron content.

Gogebic, Lake, c.12 mi. long, N Mich., W Upper Peninsula, in resort and iron-ore region.

Gogh, Vincent van (văn gō', Dutch, vĭnsĕnt' vän khôkh'), 1853–90, postimpressionist painter, b. Netherlands. Decided to become a painter only 10 years before his death. His early pictures were dark, but after moving in 1886 to Paris, where he met Pissarro,

Degas, and Gauguin, he began to paint the brilliantly colored and dynamic pictures that later made him famous. Despite periodic fits of insanity he succeeded in producing works of extraordinary intensity.

Gogmagog (gŏg'măgŏg), low chalk hills, Cambridgeshire, England.

Gogol, Nikolai Vasilyevich (nyĭkŭlī' vŭsē'lyŭvĭch gô'gŭl), 1809–52, Russian author. Won his first success with stories about rural life in Ukraine. His most famous tales include the short story "The Overcoat" (1842) and a satiric novel *Dead Souls* (1842), both written in a grotesquely humorous style which made him a founder of the great school of Russian realism. His fame as a dramatist rests on *The Inspector General* (1836), a satire of provincial officialdom.

Goiás (goiäsh'), state (c.247,900 sq. mi.; pop. c.1,-954,900), central Brazil; cap. Goiânia (pop. c.153,-500). On landlocked plateau, it has rivers in both Amazon and Paraná systems. Part of state was voted (1956) as location of new Federal Dist.

goiter: see THYROID GLAND.

Gokcha: see SEVAN.

Gokhale, Gopal Krishna (gō'päl krĭsh'nŭ gōkä'lä), 1866–1915, Indian nationalist leader and reformer. A moderate, he founded the Servants of India Society.

Golan (gō–), one of the cities of refuge, E of the Jordan. Deut. 4.43; Joshua 20.8; 21.27; 1 Chron. 6.71.

Golconda (gŏlkŏn'dŭ), deserted city, Andhra Pradesh, India. Became cap. of Moslem sultanate of Golconda in 1512. Declined after conquest by Aurangzeb in 1687. Famed diamond trade made Golconda a by-word for wealth.

gold, metallic element (symbol = Au [Latin *aurum*]; see also ELEMENT, table). Very ductile and malleable, it can be beaten into gold leaf. It is a good conductor of electricity and is chemically inactive. Usually it is hardened by being alloyed with other metals. The gold content of an alloy is stated in carats (a carat being 1⁄24 by weight of the total mass; because of this "pure" gold is 24 carats fine). Gold is a favored metal for the backing of currency. The quest for gold has had an important and colorful place in history. Chief producers are Union of South Africa, USSR, Canada, and U.S.

Goldberg, Arthur, 1908–, American labor lawyer, jurist and diplomat. Was U.S. Secretary of Labor (1961–62) and Associate Justice of U.S. Supreme Court (1962–65). Resigned to become U.S. Ambassador to UN.

Goldberg, Rube, 1883–, American cartoonist. Known for his panels showing fabulously involved machinery for simple operations.

Goldberger, Joseph, 1874–1929, American medical research worker, discoverer of cause of pellagra.

Gold Coast: see GHANA.

Golden, resort city (pop. 7,118), N central Colo., just W of Denver, in area yielding coal, gold, clay, farm produce; founded 1859. Territorial cap. 1862–67. Seat of COLORADO SCHOOL OF MINES. Grave of Buffalo Bill is on nearby Lookout Mt.

Golden Ass, The, Latin novel: see APULEIUS, LUCIUS.

Golden Bough, The: see FRAZER, SIR JAMES GEORGE.

golden bull. 1 In history of Holy Roman Empire: see ELECTORS. **2** In Hungarian history: see ANDREW II.

Golden Emperor: see HUANG TI.

Golden Fleece, in Greek legend, magic fleece of a ram that had carried Phrixus, son of Athamas, from Boeotia to the safety of Colchis. There fleece was hung in a wood guarded by a dragon. JASON and Argonauts took it after fulfilling tasks set by King Aeëtes.

Golden Gate, strait, 5 mi. long and 1–2 mi. wide, W Calif., between San Francisco Bay and the Pacific. **Golden Gate Bridge** (built 1933–37) crosses strait from San Francisco to Marin co. One of world's longest suspension bridges (4,200 ft. span across strait; overall length 9,266 ft.).

golden glow, double-flowered yellow variety of a North American coneflower (*Rudbeckia laciniata*).

Golden Horde, Mongol host, so called because of magnificence of the camp of its leader BATU KHAN. Their empire (see TATARS) was founded in mid-13th cent. and comprised most of Russia, with cap. at Sarai (near modern Volgograd). At first tributary to Great Khan at Karakorum, Golden Horde took part in Kublai Khan's conquest of S China. Islam became official religion after 1314. Ascendancy of grand duke of Moscow after 1380 brought decline; after 1405 empire broke up into independent khanates of Astrakhan, Kazan, Crimea, Sibir.

Golden Horn: see ISTANBUL.

Golden Legend, The, popular collection of saints' lives written in the 13th cent. by JACOBUS DE VORAGINE; originally entitled *Legenda sanctorum*.

goldenrod, perennial plants of large North American genus *Solidago*. Their spikes or panicles of fluffy yellow (rarely white) flowers brighten fields and roadsides in late summer. Goldenrod pollen now rarely considered a cause of hay fever.

Golden Rule, a saying of Jesus, "As ye would that men should do to you, do ye also to them likewise." Luke 6.31; Mat. 7.12.

Golden Valley, village (1965 pop. 21,248), SE Minn., a suburb W of Minneapolis.

Goldfield, town (pop. 148), SW Nev., S of Tonopah. Gold discovery here of 1902 brought a rush in 1903. Peak production was reached 1910, then fell off rapidly.

goldfinch, name for several finches of Europe and America. North American eastern goldfinch (thistle bird or wild canary) is olive yellow, but in spring the male becomes vivid yellow and black. There are several forms in W U.S.

goldfish, fresh-water fish of carp and minnow family, used in aquariums and ponds. It was domesticated from wild form in China centuries ago; reverts to type upon escape. Bizarre varieties are bred.

Goldie, Sir George (George Goldie Taubman), 1846–1925, British colonial administrator. Through his Royal Niger Company, chartered 1886, he extended British power over hinterland of Nigeria.

Golding, William, 1911–, English novelist. Best known for his allegorical *Lord of the Flies* (1954), the nightmarish adventures of English schoolboys stranded on a desert island.

Goldman, Edwin Franko, 1878–1956, American bandmaster. Organized Goldman Band (1918), for which he wrote many marches. Author of books on band techniques.

Goldman, Emma, 1869–1940, American anarchist, b. Russia. Her speeches attracted wide attention; she was imprisoned for advocating birth control (1916) and for obstructing the draft (1917). She was deported (1917) to Russia, which she left in 1921.

Goldmark, Karl, 1830–1915, Austrian composer. His style is melodious, his orchestration rich and colorful. Works include two violin concertos and a symphony, *Rustic Wedding.*

Goldoni, Carlo (kär'lō gōldō'nē), 1707–93, Italian dramatist. He wrote real and witty comedy to replace *commedia dell' arte* on Italian stage. His plays include *La bottega del caffè* (1751) and *La locandiera* (1753). His memoirs (1787) are in French.

Goldsboro, city (pop. 28,873), E central N.C., near Neuse R., SE of Raleigh, in coastal plains region; settled c.1840. Important bright-leaf tobacco market and trade, processing, and shipping center for timber, livestock, and farm area. Seymour Johnson Air Force Base is SSE.

Goldsborough, Louis Malesherbes, 1805–77, American naval officer. In Civil War, commanded North Atlantic Blockading Squadron in support of successful expedition against N.C. coast (1862).

Goldschmidt, Richard Benedikt, 1878–1958, American geneticist, b. Germany. His research in sex determination and gene theory did much to unify evolutionary theory.

Goldsmith, Oliver, 1730?–1774, English poet, dramatist, and novelist, b. Ireland. Unsuccessful as physician, he turned to writing. Fame, won with "Chinese letters" of *The Citizen of the World* (1762), grew with poems *The Traveller* (1764) and *The Deserted Village* (1770). He wrote one novel, *The Vicar of Wakefield* (1766; a masterpiece of domestic literature), and popular comedies (notably *She Stoops to Conquer,* 1773). The anonymous children's classic *Little Goody Two-Shoes* (1765) is sometimes attributed to him. Eccentric but lovable, he was a close friend of Reynolds, Burke, Garrick, and Samuel Johnson.

gold standard: see BIMETALLISM; MONEY; INTERNATIONAL GOLD STANDARD.

Goldstein, Kurt, 1878–, American neurophysiologist, b. Germany. Authority on psychological effects of brain damage. Works include *Aftereffects of Brain Injuries in War* (1942).

Goldwater, Barry Morris, 1909–, U.S. Senator from Ariz. (1953–65). A conservative, he was Republican presidential candidate in 1964.

Goldwater, Robert, 1907–. American art historian. Became director of the Mus. of Primitive Art, New York, in 1957.

Goldwyn, Samuel, 1882–, American film producer, originally named Goldfish. Goldwyn Pictures Corp. organized 1916; later merged with L. B. Mayer to become Metro-Goldwyn-Mayer.

golem (gō'lŭm) [Heb.,= embryo], in Jewish legend, robot of clay given life by means of a charm or *shem* [Heb.,= name, or the name of God]. Most famous one, ascribed to 16th-cent. Rabbi Löw of Prague, is background of play by Leivick.

golf, game played with specially made clubs and balls on outdoor course called links. Game identified with Scotland, where it has been popular since 15th cent. Royal and Ancient Golf Club of St. Andrews, Scotland, founded 1754, became international shrine of golf; its basic rules accepted throughout the world. U.S. Golf Association, founded 1894, governing body of game in U.S. Standard golf course, usually more than 6,000 yd. around, is divided into 18 holes of varying length.

Golgi, Camillo (kämĕl'lō gôl'jē), 1844–1926, Italian physician, noted as neurologist and histologist. Shared 1906 Nobel Prize in Physiology and Medicine for work on structure of nervous system. He described the Golgi apparatus, part of the ultrastructure of cells, having secretory function.

Golgotha (gŏl'gŭthù), the same as CALVARY.

Goliad (gō'lĕăd), city (pop. 1,782), S Texas, on San Antonio R. SE of San Antonio. Spanish mission moved here 1749 from Lavaca Bay (Goliad then La Bahia). Captured twice (1812, 1821) by filibusters from U.S. Texans regained it in Texas Revolution. Col. J. W. FANNIN and his troops were captured (March 20, 1836) by Mexicans during evacuation of Goliad and massacred (March 27). Restored mission and presidio ruins now in state park.

Goliardic songs (gōlĕär'dĭk), Late Latin poetry written by "wandering scholars." The origin of the name is uncertain. Songs, resembling medieval hymns in form but not in content, were usually licentious and attacked the church. Number of vagabond scholars grew so great as to become a plague in the 13th cent., but it is no longer thought that they actually organized a burlesque religious order. Church began (c.1230) to take strong measures against them, and they gradually declined.

Goliath (gōlī'ŭth), Philistine giant, killed by young David. 1 Sam. 17; 21.9; 22.10; 2 Sam. 21.19.

Gollancz, Sir Hermann (gō'lŭnts), 1852–1930, English rabbi; Semitist at Univ. Col., London, 1902–24.

Gomberg, Moses, 1866–1947, American chemist, b. Russia. Internationally known for research in or-

ganic chemistry. Taught at Univ. of Michigan 1893–1936.

Gombos, Julius, Hung. *Gömbös Gyula* (gŭm'bûsh dyŏō'lŏ), 1886–1936, Hungarian premier (1932–36); authoritarian and anti-Semitic. Favored national brand of fascism but opposed German expansion.

Gomel (gō'mĭl), city (1965 est. pop. 216,000), SE Belorussia. Light industry. Dates from 12th cent.; to Russia in first Polish partition (1772). Jewish pop. (c.40%) was largely exterminated by the Germans in Second World War.

Gómez, Juan Vicente (hwän' vēsän'tä gō'mĕs), 1857–1935, ruler of Venezuela (1908–35), a *caudillo*. Of Indian and white parentage, he grew up as nearly illiterate cattle herdsman. Supported Cipriano Castro (1899), then replaced Castro as president (1908). Ruled Venezuela—not always as president—until his death. Though tyrannical, he was honest and industrious and improved his country economically, largely through encouraging foreign investments.

Gomorrah or **Gomorrha,** city, destroyed with SODOM.

Gompers, Samuel (gŏm'pŭrz), 1850–1924, American labor leader, b. London. Helped found (1881) the Federation of Organized Trades and Labor Unions, which became (1886) the American Federation of Labor, of which he was president, except for 1895, until his death. He rejected cooperative business plans and socialist or radical programs, maintaining that the just aims of labor were simply shorter hours, more wages, and greater freedom. Wrote autobiographical *Seventy Years of Life and Labor* (1925).

Gomulka, Wladyslaw (gŭmōōl'kŭ), 1905–, Polish Communist; party leader (1943–48, 1956–). Charged with nationalist deviations, he was ousted from party 1949. Resuming political leadership after Poznan riots (1956), he continued close ties with Soviet Union but estab. greater freedom for Poland.

Gonaïves (gônäēv'), city (1965 est. pop. 14,000), NW Haiti; port on Gulf of Gonaïves. In 1804 Haitian independence was proclaimed here, and DESSALINES, first of the Negro emperors, was crowned.

Gonçalves Dias, Antonio (äntô'nyō gônsäl'vĭsh dē'ûsh), 1823–64, Brazilian romantic poet.

Goncharov, Ivan Aleksandrovich (ēvän' ŭlyĭksän'drŭvĭch gŭnchŭrôf'), 1812–91, Russian novelist; author of *Oblomov* (1858).

Goncourt, Edmond (Huot) de (ĕdmō' üō' dù gōkōōr'), 1822–96, and **Jules (Huot) de Goncourt** (zhül), 1830–70, French authors, brothers. Together, in their own nervous, telegraphic style, they wrote art criticism, naturalistic novels, as *Renée Mauperin* and *Germinie Lacerteux* (both 1864), and the famous *Journal des Goncourt* (9 vols., 1887–96), an intimate picture of Parisian society. Edmond founded the Goncourt Academy to award annual prizes for fiction.

Gondar (gŏn'dùr), town, NW Ethiopia. Cap. of Ethiopia from c.1650 until 1867, when it was almost destroyed in civil war.

Gondola, Giovanni: see GUNDULIC, IVAN.

gong: see PERCUSSION INSTRUMENTS.

Góngora y Argote, Luis de (lwēs' dä gōn'gōrä ē ärgō'tä), 1571–1627, last great Spanish poet of the Golden Age, a priest. His manneristic verse gave rise to *Gongorism,* equivalent to euphuism in English.

gonorrhea (gŏnùrē'ù), an infectious venereal disease caused by gonococcus. It is commonly transmitted to genital organs by direct contact; may spread to adjacent structures or be carried to other parts of body by lymphatic system. Gonococcus, transmitted to infant at birth from genital tract of mother, sometimes causes conjunctivitis and blindness (preventable by silver-nitrate treatment, now hospital routine for every newborn infant). Gonorrhea is treated with penicillin and sulfa drugs.

Gonville and Caius College: see CAMBRIDGE UNIVERSITY.

Gonzaga (gōntsä'gä), Italian princely family. Senior line ruled MANTUA 1328–1627 (first as captains general, from 1433 as marquesses, from 1530 as dukes) and acquired MONTFERRAT in 1536. After its extinction (1627) it was succeeded by a younger line, which by marriage had acquired the French duchies of NEVERS and RETHEL; this in turn became extinct 1708. Another branch ruled GUASTALLA (1539–1746). Many rulers of Mantua were lavish patrons of art and letters, notably Francesco Gonzaga, d. 1519, who married Isabella d'ESTE. In the Italian Wars he preserved Mantuan independence with difficulty, siding first with Venice, then with France, then with Pope Julius II.

Gonzales (gǔnză'lĭs), city (pop. 5,829), S central Texas, near Guadalupe R., E of San Antonio; founded 1825 as administrative center of Green De Witt's colony. Men of Gonzales dispersed Mexican cavalry in first battle of Texas Revolution, Oct. 2, 1835; nearby park encloses battlefield.

Gonzalez, Richard A(lorzo) (Pancho Gonzalez), 1928–, American tennis player. Won (1948–49) U.S. championship. Outstanding professional player 1949–61. Professional champion 1954–61.

González de Ávila. Gil (hēl' gŏnthä'lĕth dä ä'vēlä), d. 1543, Spanish conquistador. Conquered Nicaragua (1522); his claims usurped by Francisco Fernández de Córdoba (1523).

González de Ávila, Gil, 1578?–1658, Spanish historian. Royal chronicler of Castile and Indies, he wrote history of the Church in Spanish colonies.

González Prada, Manuel (mänwěl' gōnsä'les prä'dä), 1848–1918, Peruvian writer and political reformer. Influenced later leaders of APRA movement.

Gooch, George Peabody, 1873–, English historian. An editor of Cambridge History of British Foreign Policy, 1783–1919 (3 vols., 1922–23). His History and Historians in the Nineteenth Century (1913; 2d ed., 1946) is among best in modern historiography.

Good Hope, Cape of: see CAPE PROVINCE.

Goodhue, Bertram Grosvenor, 1869–1924, American architect. Evolved a distinctive style for his ecclesiastical work, which was Gothic in form yet permeated with a modern spirit.

Goodland, city (pop. 4,459), NW Kansas, NW of Hays, near Colo. line. Mt. Sunflower (4,026 ft. high), state's highest elevation, is SSW.

Goodman, Benny (Benjamin David Goodman), 1909–, American clarinetist and dance band leader. In 1934 he organized his own orchestra, which became nationally famous. His contributions to the development of swing music earned him the title "king of swing." He also appeared as solo clarinetist with many symphony orchestras and in chamber ensembles.

Goodnews Bay, inlet of Kuskokwim Bay, SW Alaska.

Goodnight, Charles, 1836–1929, Texas cattleman, a pioneer in improving cattle breeds. He laid out Goodnight cattle trail to Wyoming in 1866.

Goodrich, Samuel Griswold, pseud. Peter Parley, 1793–1860, American editor and writer of juvenile stories. His Peter Parley Tales were sugar-coated moralistic stories of instruction. Edited periodicals, including The Token and juvenile Robert Merry's Museum.

Goodspeed, Edgar Johnson, 1871–1962, American Greek scholar. Principally known for his new translation of the Bible: The New Testament—an American Translation (1923) and The Complete Bible—an American Translation (with J. M. P. Smith, 1930).

Good Thief or Penitent Thief, the thief crucified with Jesus who did not mock Him but accepted Him; Jesus promised him Paradise that day. Luke 23.39–43. His feast is March 25. Tradition names him Dismas or Desmas, the other thief Gesmas.

Goodwin Sands, 10 mi. stretch of shoals and shifting sands, off E coast of Kent, England. Formerly scene of many shipwrecks, Sands were supposedly once a fertile isle, property of Godwin, earl of Wessex.

Goodyear, Charles, 1800–1860, American inventor, originator of rubber vulcanization (1839; patent 1844). His son Charles Goodyear, 1833–96, was pioneer in use of sewing machine for shoe manufacturing.

Goole, municipal borough (pop. 18,875), West Riding of Yorkshire, England; a port. Shipbuilding; passenger lines to the Continent.

goose, wild and domesticated bird related to duck and swan. Accurately, goose is the female, gander the male. Common Canada or wild goose of North America migrates in V-shaped flocks in spring and autumn. Other wild geese are BRANT, the blue, the snow, and the white-fronted or laughing geese. Domestic are Toulouse or gray goose, African and Embden geese, and oriental breeds.

Goose Bay, village, SE Labrador on Goose Bay. Has large air base and radio station built in the Second World War for transatlantic transport.

gooseberry, shrub (Ribes) of temperate regions and its fruit, a berry used in preserves. It is related to the currant and is a host to white pine blister rust.

Goose Creek, Texas: see BAYTOWN.

Goosport (gäs'pôrt), town (pop. 16,778), SW La., suburb NE of L. Charles, in oil and sulfur area.

gopher (gō'fŭr) or pocket gopher, burrowing rodent of North America and Central America. In U.S. chief genera are western (Thomomys) and eastern (Geomys) gophers. Gophers are gray, buff, or dark brown and 7–14 in. long. They have fur-lined pouches opening on outside of cheeks for carrying food and nesting material. They live and forage mostly underground, feeding on roots and tubers.

Gorboduc (gôr'bŭdŭk), legendary early British king who created murderous strife by dividing his realm between two sons. The story is treated in early English tragedy (1562) by Thomas Norton and Thomas SACKVILLE.

Gorchakov, Aleksandr Mikhailovich, Prince (ŭlyĭksän'-dŭr mēkhī'lŭvĭch, gŭrchŭkôf'), 1798–1883, Russian foreign minister (1856–82). Sought to nullify Treaty of Paris which closed Crimean War. Though friendly to Prussia and hostile to Austria, kept Russia neutral in Austro-Prussian and Franco-Prussian wars and helped form THREE EMPERORS' LEAGUE. Opposed Russo-Turkish War of 1877–78; represented Russia at Congress of BERLIN.

Gordian I (Marcus Antonius Gordianus Africanus) (gôr'dēŭn), d. 238, Roman emperor. Ruled (238) with his son, Gordian II, 192–238, who was killed in Carthage. The father committed suicide. Gordian II's son, Gordian III, c.223–244, was emperor (238–44).

Gordian knot: see GORDIUS.

Gordin, Jacob Mikhailovich, 1853–1909, American writer of Yiddish plays, b. Russia.

Gordion: see PHRYGIA.

Gordium, anc. city of Asia Minor, cap of PHRYGIA c.1000–800 B.C.

Gordius (gôr'dēŭs), legendary king of Phrygia and founder of Gordium. Pole of his wagon was tied to yoke with intricate knot. Oracle said that he who untied it would rule all Asia. Alexander the Great severed it with his sword. Hence the figure "to cut the Gordian knot," meaning to solve a perplexing problem with one bold stroke.

Gordon, Charles George (Chinese Gordon), 1833–85, British soldier and administrator. Commander of Chinese army that suppressed the Taiping Rebellion. Was governor of Egyptian Sudan 1877–80. Trying to crush power of the Mahdi, he was killed in the siege of Khartoum. Popular indignation at his death was partial cause of fall of Gladstone government in 1885.

Gordon, Lord George, 1751–93, English agitator, responsible for the tragic Gordon riots in London (June 2–7, 1780). Protestant demonstration against removal of civil restrictions from Catholics; became an orgy of destruction and plunder.

Gordon, John Brown, 1832–1904, Confederate general and Ga. statesman. Served brilliantly in Wilderness campaign and Shenandoah Valley (1864). A leader in Ga. politics after war; U.S. Senator (1873–80, 1891–97), governor (1886–90).

Gordon, Leon, 1830–92, Russian-Hebrew novelist and poet, leader in renaissance of Hebrew culture.

Gordon riots: see GORDON, LORD GEORGE.

Goremykin, Ivan Longinovich (ĕvän' lŭn-gē'nŭvĭch gôrylmĭ'kĭn), 1839–1917, Russian statesman. His conservative policies and mishandling of the first Duma resulted in his dismissal from premiership. Again premier (1914–16), he was killed by the Bolsheviks.

Goren, Charles Henry, 1901–, American bridge expert and author. Point count bidding system popularized by him made him world's best-known contract bridge player. Won 26 U.S. titles, world champion 1950, 1957.

Gorenko, Anna Andreyevna: see AKHMATOVA, ANNA.

Gore Range: see PARK RANGE.

Gorgan (gôrgän') or **Jurjan** (jŏorjän'), town (pop. c.25,000), N Iran, E of the Caspian. In area known as Hyrcania in anc. times. Birthplacè of Aga Mohammed, founder of Kajar dynasty (1794–1925). Formerly known as Asterbad.

Gorgas, William Crawford (gôr'gŭs), 1854–1920, American disease and sanitation expert, surgeon general of U.S. (1914–19). Cleansed Havana and the Canal Zone of yellow fever.

Gorges, Sir Ferdinando (gôr'jĭz), c.1566–1647, British colonizer, proprietor of Maine. A leading figure in Plymouth Co. Conducted long struggle with Mass. Bay and Salem colonies over patent rights.

Gorgons (gôr'gŭnz), in Greek myth, female monsters. Winged and snake-haired, the three hideous creatures turned to stone all men who looked on them. MEDUSA, only mortal one, was killed by Perseus.

Gorham, town (pop. 3,039), NE N.H., at confluence of Androscoggin and Peabody rivers; settled c.1805. Resort within sight of Presidential Range.

Gori (gô'rē), city (1959 pop. 35,200), central Georgian SSR, at confluence of Bolshoy Liakhvi and Kura rivers; railroad junction. Known 7th cent. as Tontio; passed to Russia 1801. Birthplace of Stalin.

gorilla, anthropoid ape (genus *Gorilla*) native to W equatorial Africa. Largest of the great apes, males reach 5–6 ft. in height, and weigh 300–600 lb. Usually terrestrial, they walk on all fours, hands doubled under. They are chiefly vegetarian. Females and young sleep in tree platform nests; males sleep at base. They are now protected.

Göring, Hermann Wilhelm: see GOERING.

Gorizia (gôrēt'sēä). Ger. *Görz,* city (pop. 41,854), Friuli-Venezia Giulia, NE Italy, in FRIULI, on Isonzo R. Under Austria 1500–1918. Bitterly contested in First World War.

Gorki, Maxim (mŭksyēm gôr'kē), pseud. of Aleksey Maximovich Pyeshkov, 1868–1936, Russian author. After years of vagabondage, he began writing in 1892. Among his early short stories, "Twenty-six Men and a Girl," "Chelkash," and "Malva" are well known in English, as are his novels *Foma Gordeyev* (1899) and *Mother* (1907) and his drama *The Lower Depths* (1902). A Marxist from his youth, he sought social realism in his descriptions of the outcasts of society, in whom he saw the hope of the future. Living abroad after 1905, he returned to Russia in 1928, where he was given the highest honors. Late novels include *The Artamanov Affair* (1925; Eng. tr., *Decadence,* 1927) and *The Life of Klim Samgin* (1927–36; Eng. tr., in four separate vols., 1930–38), covering the whole revolutionary period from 1880 to 1934. He also wrote *My Childhood* (1913; Eng. tr., 1915) and *Reminiscences* (Eng. tr., 1946).

Gorki or **Gorky,** formerly **Nizhni Novgorod** (nyēzh'nyē nôv'gŭrŭt), city (1965 est. pop. 1,085,000), central European RSFSR, on right bank of Volga and mouth of Oka R. Major transportation and industrial center (rolling stock, heavy machinery, electric equipment, chemicals). Univ., technical schools. Founded 1221 as outpost by prince of Vladimir; became seat of a principality 1350; fell to Moscow 1393. Site of famous annual fairs 1817–1930. Renamed 1932 for Maxim

Gorki, who was born here. Old section contains 1,3thcent. kremlin, with palace and two cathedrals.

Gorky, Arshile (ärshēl' gôr'kē), 1904–48, American nonobjective painter, b. Armenia; influenced many abstract expressionists.

Görlitz (gûr'lĭts), city (est. pop. 92,351), East Germany, in former state of Saxony, on Görlitzer Neisse R. Chief city of Lusatia, it has lignite mines, textile and brewing. Cap. of duchy of Görlitz, passed to Saxony 1635, to Prussia 1815. After Second World War part of city placed under Polish administration. Jakob Boehme lived here. For **Görlitzer Neisse river,** see NEISSE.

Gorlovka (gôr'lŭfkŭ), city (1965 est. pop. 337,000), E central Ukrainian SSR, in Donets Basin. Major coal-mining and industrial center.

Gorman, Arthur Pue, 1839–1906, U.S. Senator from Md. (1881–99, 1903–6). Led in making Wilson-Gorman Tariff Act of 1894 a high-tariff act.

Gorno-Altai and **Gorno-Altaisk,** RSFSR: see MOUNTAIN-ALTAI.

Gorno-Badakhshan, Tadzhik SSR: see MOUNTAIN-BADAKHSHAN.

Gorostiza, José (hōsā' gōrōstē'zä), 1901–, Mexican poet. One of Mexico's foremost poets, his work is marked by technical brilliance and subjectivity.

gorse: see FURZE.

Gorton, Samuel, c.1592–1677, one of founders of R.I., b. England. He settled Warwick (1642), where he preached unorthodox religious views.

Görz: see GORIZIA, Italy.

Gorzow Wielkopolski: see LANDSBERG AN DER WARTHE.

Gosforth (gŏz'fûrth). **1** Village, Cumberland, England; site of famous Viking cross. **2** Urban district (pop. 27,072), Northumberland, England; coal-mining center. George Stephenson built his first locomotive here in 1814.

goshawk (gŏs'hôk), fearless, relentless hawk of Old World and North America. Eastern goshawk male is c.22 in. long, female c.24 in. As adults both have black crown, white stripe over red eye, blue-gray upper parts, and white, gray-barred lower parts. Western goshawk has darker plumage. Goshawks destroy poultry and game birds.

Goshen (gō'–), fertile part of Egypt occupied by Israelites during bondage. Gen. 47.6; Ex. 8.22; 9.26.

Goshen. 1 City (pop. 13,718), N central Ind., on Elkhart R., ESE of South Bend; settled c.1830. Distribution point in farm and dairy area. Has Amish and Mennonite colonies. Seat of Goshen Col. **2** Village (1965 pop. 4,175), SE N.Y., SE of Middletown; settled 1712. Famed as trotting center.

Goslar (gôs'lär), city (pop. 40,222), Lower Saxony, West Germany, at N foot of Harz mts. Mining center since its foundation in 10th cent. (formerly silver; now copper, lead, zinc, iron, sulfur). A favorite residence of early German emperors. A free imperial city until 1802, it was awarded to Hanover 1815, transferred to Brunswick 1941. City has preserved its medieval character. Much Romanesque and Gothic architecture (notably the 11th-cent. Kaiserhaus, built for Henry III).

Gosnold, Bartholomew (gŏz'nōld), fl. 1572–1607, English explorer and colonizer. Explored coast from Maine to Narragansett Bay (1602). Commanded *God Speed* in first settlement of Va. (1606).

Gospel [M.E.,= good news; cf. *evangel* from Gr.,= good news], one of the four biographies of Jesus in New Testament. The gospels are named MATTHEW, MARK, LUKE, and JOHN. First three called SYNOPTIC GOSPELS because of their apparent relationship. Word also used by Jesus and by St. Paul to refer to the message of redemption. Solemn reading of the Gospel of the day is a special feature of liturgy of many churches. Formerly a book of the Gospels was used instead of Bible for the oath in courts in Christian countries. Illumination of the Gospels became an art (e.g., the Lindisfarne Gospels, the Book of Kells). For apocryphal Gospels, see PSEUDEPIGRAPHA.

Gosport (gŏs'-), municipal borough (pop. 62,436), Hampshire, England; port on Portsmouth Harbour.

Gossaert or **Gossart**: see MABUSE, JAN DE.

Gosse, Sir Edmund W(illiam), 1849–1928, English poet, critic, and literary biographer.

Gota, Swed. *Göta älv*, river, 56 mi. long, SW Sweden, draining Vanern lake into the Kattegat. Forms part of **Gota Canal**, 240-mile system of rivers, lakes, and canals, from Goteborg to Stockholm.

Gotaland or **Gotarike**: see SWEDEN.

Goteborg (Swed. yûtûbör'yù) or **Gothenburg** (gō'thùn-bûrg), Swed. *Göteborg*, city (pop. 408,436), SW Sweden, co. seat of Goteborg and Bohus co.; a seaport at mouth of Gota R. on Kattegat. Second largest city of Sweden; shipyards, machinery mfg. Seat of Lutheran bishop. Founded 1619, city was planned by Dutch architects and retains many stately old buildings. University was founded 1887.

Gotha (gō'thù, Ger. gō'tä), city (est. pop. 56,386), East Germany, in former state of Thuringia. Mfg. center; long a center of geographic research and publishing. *Almanach de Gotha*, reference work on European royalty and nobility published here from 1764. Passed to Ernestine line of Wettin dynasty 1485; cap. of Saxe-Gotha 1640-1826; cap. of Saxe-Coburg-Gotha 1826–1918. Historic buildings include ducal palaces (17th and 18th cent.).

Gotham (gō'tùm), village, Nottinghamshire, England. Inhabitants reputed to do ridiculous things (e.g., trying to drown an eel). Stories may stem from efforts to prevent King John from living there. Hence, Gotham (gō'thùm), name for New York city, first used by Washington Irving and others in *Salmagundi Papers*.

Gothenburg: see GOTEBORG.

Gothic architecture, style dominant in Europe from late 12th cent. to 15th cent. It used elements of ROMANESQUE ARCHITECTURE (see also NORMAN ARCHITECTURE), but it was notable for use of pointed arch and ribbed vault (an early example was the abbey at St.-Denis). Buildings were made higher, with thinner vaults and walls. Flying buttresses (masonry arches leaning on parts of the outer walls to counteract pressure of the vaults) gave more stability to the skeleton structure. A flowing, soaring effect is the hallmark of Gothic. It is notably shown in the French High Gothic of the Amiens cathedral. High towers, pinnacles, much sculpture, and stained-glass windows were part of Gothic design. French Late Gothic (or Flamboyant) churches had lacelike ornament. In England builders preferred length to height, stressed elaborately ribbed vaults and frequently used central towers. Examples of English Gothic are the cathedrals at Salisbury, Lincoln, and Canterbury. German Gothic cathedrals frequently have broken silhouette. In Spain the Gothic churches are heavily decorated and have smaller windows. See *ill.*, p. 53.

Gothic language, East Germanic language. Earliest literary remains in any Germanic tongue are in Gothic Bible of Ulfilas. See LANGUAGE (table).

Gothic revival, a 19th-cent. style of architecture and decoration imitating arts of Middle Ages. Reached its peak in c.1850. In England it gained support of the Church and many medieval structures were restored. Came into conflict with classic revival, with respective exponents taking sides in "battle of the styles." A triumph for Gothicists was building of Houses of Parliament in Perpendicular Gothic in 1840. Revival of interest in arts and crafts, with medieval work as inspiration, was led by William Morris. Movement spread to France, where Viollet-le-Duc became its chief exponent, and to U.S., where it was influenced by Victorian taste.

Gothic romance, type of novel popular in late 18th-cent. England; it soon spread to Germany and the U.S. Against medieval "Gothic" background, melodrama with supernatural horrors filled works by Horace Walpole (*The Castle of Otranto*, 1764), M.

G. Lewis, Anne Radcliffe, Mary Shelley (*Frankenstein*, 1818), and C. B. Brown.

gothic type: see TYPE.

Goths: see OSTROGOTHS; VISIGOTHS.

Gotland (gôt'lùnd), Baltic island, SE Sweden, off coast of Kalmar co. With several smaller islands it forms a county (1,245 sq. mi.; pop. 54,209). Agr., fishing. For its colorful history, see article on its cap., WISBY.

Gottfried von Strassburg (gôt'frēt fŭn shträs'bŏork), fl. 13th cent., German poet. Ranks among greatest medieval writers for his epic *Tristan* (c.1210), which breaks off before the parting and death of the lovers (see TRISTRAM AND ISOLDE). The poem was concluded by Ulrich von Türheim and Heinrich von Freiberg.

Gottheil, Gustav (gôt'hīl), 1827–1903, American reform rabbi, b. Prussia. Prepared first American Jewish hymnal.

Gottheil, Richard James Horatio, 1862–1936, American orientalist. Taught Semitic languages at Columbia Univ. from 1886. President of the American Federation of Zionists.

Gotthelf, Jeremias (yärämē'äs gôt'hĕlf), 1797–1854, Swiss author whose real name was Albert Bitzius; a Protestant clergyman. A forerunner of German naturalism, he crusaded against the materialism of his time in the novels *Uli der Knecht* [Ulric the farmhand] (1840) and *Uli der Pächter* [Ulric the tenant] (1849), written partly in Swiss-German idiom.

Göttingen (gŭ'tĭng-ùn), city (pop. 78,448), Lower Saxony, West Germany, in Hanover, on the Leine R. Mfg. of optical and precision instruments. Its famous university was founded 1737 by Elector George Augustus (later George II of England). When King Ernest Augustus revoked Hanoverian constitution (1837), seven professors (incl. Jakob and Wilhelm Grimm) protested and were summarily dismissed. In late 19th cent. university became a world center for study of mathematics and physics.

Gottsched, Johann Christoph (yō'hän krĭs'tôf gôt'shät), 1700–1766, German poet and critic. As professor at Leipzig, he dominated the literary scene of the German Enlightenment, advocated classical drama on French model. His influence waned after the attacks of Bodmer and Lessing.

Gottwald, Klement (klämûnt' gôt'vält), 1896–1953, Czechoslovak Communist leader. Succeeded Benes after coup in 1948; made Czechoslovakia a satellite of USSR.

Gottwaldov (gôt'väldôf), city (est. pop. 62,000), Moravia, Czechoslovakia, formerly Zlin (renamed 1949). The center of the Czech shoe industry (now nationalized), it was developed as a model factory community by the Bata family of shoe manufacturers.

Götz von Berlichingen: see BERLICHINGEN, GÖTZ VON.

Goucher College, at Towson, Md.; for women; inc. 1885, opened 1888 by Methodists.

Gouda (gou'dù, Dutch khou'dä), municipality (pop. 46,273), South Holland prov., W Netherlands. Pottery mfg.; cheese trade. Has Gothic city hall.

Goudy, Frederic William, 1865–1947, American type designer. The most prolific type designer in history (Kennerley, Deepdene, and Garamont are among more than 100 faces), he also wrote about his craft.

Goujon, Jean (gŏozhŏ'), c.1510–c.1566, French Renaissance sculptor, known for decorations in low relief for buildings. Associated with Pierre Lescot, architect of the Louvre.

Gould, Benjamin Apthorp, 1824–96, American astronomer. Helped estab. longitude department of U.S. Coast Survey; first to use Atlantic cable to coordinate U.S. and European observations. Founded *Astronomical Journal* (1849). He organized national observatory and meteorological service for Argentine government.

Gould, Jay, 1836–92, American capitalist. Helped defeat Cornelius Vanderbilt for control of ERIE RAILROAD. He and James FISK caused BLACK FRIDAY panic. Later, Gould controlled four Western railroads. His son, **George Jay Gould,** 1864–1923, inherited all his father's holdings and, through daring policies, seemed to have a transcontinental system in his grasp. By 1918 he had lost control of his railroads.

Gounod, Charles (shärl' gōōnō'), 1818–93, French composer. He wrote church music, e.g., *La Rédemption* and *Messe à Sainte Cécile,* but his fame rests chiefly on his operas *Faust* and *Romeo and Juliet.*

gourd (gōrd), fruit of vinelike tender annual plants of several genera related to cucumber, melon, and pumpkin. The dried cleaned fruit shells have been used from ancient times as drinking cups, dippers, bowls, etc., in tropical and Asiatic countries. In U.S. they are mostly grown for decoration.

Gourgues, Dominique de (gōōrg'), c.1530–1593, French soldier and adventurer. Avenged massacre of Huguenot colony of Jean RIBAUT by slaughtering Spanish garrison on Fla. coast (1568).

Gourlay, Robert Fleming (gōōr'lē), 1778–1863, Scottish writer and agitator. Came to Upper Canada in 1817. Led agitation against control of land grants by Family Compact. Banished from province (1819). Sentence was nullified in 1842. Wrote account of Upper Canada (1822) and autobiographical work (1843).

Gourmont, Remy de (rúmē' dù gōōrmō), 1858–1915, French critic. Chief apologist for SYMBOLISTS.

gout, disease characterized by joint inflammation, much uric acid in blood, and deposits of sodium urate crystals about joints. It tends to recur.

Gouverneur (gŭvùrnōōr'), village (pop. 4,946), N central N.Y., on Oswegatchie R., S of Ogdensburg; laid out 1787. Named for Gouverneur Morris, whose mansion is still here.

Govan (gŭ'vùn), parish, Lanarkshire, suburb of Glasgow, Scotland. Has extensive shipbuilding yards and mfg. of chemicals, asbestos, and machine tools.

government ownership: see PUBLIC OWNERSHIP.

Government Printing Office, United States, authorized by joint Congressional resolution (1860), purchased for $135,000 (1861). Its activities, defined by the Printing Act of 1895, include executing orders of Congress and the various Federal offices for printing and binding, distributing government publications, and reprinting documents for public purchase.

Governors Island, c.173 acres, in Upper New York Bay, S of Manhattan isl. Bought 1637 from Indians by the Dutch. Present name adopted 1784 because colonial governors lived there. Historic landmarks include Fort Jay (early 19th cent.) and Castle Williams (military prison; built 1807–11). A U.S. army base since 1794, it was turned over to U.S. Coast Guard 1966.

Gower, John (gou'ùr, gôr), d. 1408, English poet, contemporary and friend of Chaucer. Author of *Confessio Amantis* (c.1390; collection of tales in English verse illustrating Seven Deadly Sins) and of other poems in English, French, and Latin.

Gower (gou'ùr), peninsula, c.15 mi. long and 5 mi. wide, Glamorganshire, Wales, SW of Swansea.

Gowrie, earls of: see RUTHVEN, family.

Goya (y Lucientes), Francisco José de (fränthē'skō hōsä' dä gō'yä ē lōōthēän'tēs), 1746–1828, Spanish artist, b. near Saragossa. Gained royal notice with his witty scenes of popular life for tapestry designs. As court painter to Charles III and Charles IV, he did candidly realistic portraits. Most Madrid notables, including the duchess of Alba, posed for him. Mordant social satire fills the three series of etchings: *Caprichos, Proverbios,* and *Tauromaquia* [bullfight]. The great *Desastres de la guerra* [disasters of war] is a terrifying series of etchings, suggested by Peninsular War. At 70 he retired to his villa, which he decorated with macabre paintings, such as *Saturn Devouring his Children* (Prado). Spent last years in Bordeaux. Generally conceded to be greatest painter of his time.

Goyen, Jan Josephszoon van (yän' yō'zùfsōn vän gō'yún), 1596–1656, Dutch landscape painter, one of first to subordinate detail to atmospheric effect.

Gozzano, Guido (gwē'dō gōt''tsä'nō), 1883–1916, Italian poet. Called a successor to D'Annunzio. His volumes of verse include *La via del rifugio* (1907) and *I colloqui* (1911).

Gozzi, Carlo, Conte (kär'lō kōn'tä gôt'tsē), 1720–1806, Italian dramatist. He defended the *commedia dell' arte* against Goldoni. His *Fiaba dell' amore delle tre melarance* (1761) inspired Prokofiev's *The Love for the Three Oranges,* and his *Re Turandot* (1762) was made into an opera by Puccini. His brother **Gasparro Gozzi** (gä'spärō), 1713–86, stimulated critical interest in Dante.

Gozzoli, Benozzo (bänôt'tsō gôt'tsōlē), 1420–97, Florentine painter, whose real name was Benozzo di Lese. Assisted Fra Angelico, whose influence is seen in his decorative style. Famous for frescoes in San Gimignano and in Campo Santo, Pisa.

GPU: see SECRET POLICE.

Graaf, Reinier de (rīnēr dù gräf'), 1641–73, Dutch physician, noted for studies on pancreatic juice and generative organs. He discovered the follicles of the ovary known as Graafian follicles, which contain maturing ovum.

Graça Aranha, José Pereira da (zhōōzä' pĕrā'rù dù grä'sù ärä'nyù), 1868–1931, Brazilian novelist.

Gracchi (grä'kī), two Roman statesmen and reformers; brothers, sons of CORNELIA. **Tiberius Sempronius Gracchus,** d. 133 B.C., the elder, alarmed by the growth of wealth of the few, stood for tribunate in 133 B.C. as an avowed reformer. He passed the Sempronian Law (see AGRARIAN LAWS), to redistribute public lands. At the next election he renominated himself, and the senate postponed the election. In a great riot the following day he was murdered. **Caius Sempronius Gracchus** (kā'ùs), d. 121 B.C., publicly committed himself to avenging his brother and completing his work. Elected tribune (123 B.C.), he initiated a series of remarkable social reforms. He was reelected (122) and proceeded with further schemes, checking the power of consuls and senate. In 121 he was defeated. When repeal of his measures was proposed, riots ensued and he was killed.

grace, in Christian theology, free favor of God towards men necessary for their salvation. Natural graces (e.g., gift of life) are distinguished from supernatural graces, by which God makes man (depraved through original sin) capable of enjoying eternal life. Supernatural grace, keystone of the whole Christian theological system, is usually defined as actual grace, which turns the soul to God, or sanctifying grace, which perpetuates this conversion. Most theologies, except CALVINISM, distinguish prevenient grace, which makes man's will free, from cooperating grace, by which God assists to salvation the free man who seeks it. Grace may be so powerful that a man cannot escape conversion (efficacious grace), or it may be of lesser strength so that a man can reject it though always sufficient for conversion if he accepts it (sufficient grace). As to the means of grace, there is serious cleavage regarding the SACRAMENT. Catholics hold the sacrament actually confers grace; Protestants that it is the sign, not the means, of grace. Certain Christian systems have developed other ideas of grace (e.g., the Society of FRIENDS, who deny original sin). A blessing or benediction is sometimes called grace (notably in grace before and after meals, universally advocated by Christians).

Graces, Greek goddesses, daughters of Zeus. Usually three—Aglaia (äglä'ù), Thalia (thäl'ù), and Euphrosyne (ūfrōs'inē). They were personifications of beauty and charm. Called Charites by Greeks and Gratiae by Romans.

Gracián, Baltasar (bältäsär' gräthyän'), 1601–58, Spanish philosopher, scholar, satirist, a Jesuit, notable for epigrams. Among his works is *El criticón,* 1651–57.

grackle, name for some members of family of New World orioles and blackbirds. Purple or common grackle of Atlantic coast is black with metallic hues, iridescent in sun. It eats grain and insects and is a cannibalistic nest robber. Bronze grackle found inland, W to Rocky Mts., Florida and boat-tailed grackles in S U.S.; great-tailed or jackdaws in Texas and Mexico.

Graeae or **Graiae** (both: grē'ē), in Greek mythology, three sisters of the Gorgons. Personifications of old age, they shared one eye and one tooth.

Graecia Magna: see MAGNA GRAECIA.

Graefe or **Gräfe, Albrecht von** (both: äl'brĕkht fŭn grä'fü), 1828–70, German ophthalmologist, noted for eye surgery and as a teacher. His father, **Karl Ferdinand von Graefe** (kärl fĕr'dĕnänt), 1787–1840, was a pioneer in plastic surgery.

Graetz or **Grätz, Heinrich** (both: hīn'rĭkh grĕts'), 1817–91, German Jewish historian and exegete. His *History of the Jews* (11 vols. 1853–75), translated into several languages, had strong influence on Jewish historiography.

Graf or **Graff, Urs** (öörs), c.1485–1528, Swiss wood engraver, etcher, painter, and goldsmith, influenced by Dürer and Hans Baldung.

graft or **transplant,** in surgery, tissue or organ replacing part which is nonfunctional or lost. Body tends to reject any foreign tissue. Grafting patient's own skin to cover scars has long been successful. Organs can sometimes be grafted between identical twins. Sections of some tissues can be processed and preserved so as to be acceptable to another body (e.g., bones, blood vessels, corneas). Synthetic material (plastic, orlon, dacron) is used for replacing tubes in heart. Severed limbs have also been rejoined.

grafting, method of propagation in which two parts of closely related plants are united so that they grow as one. The scion (a bud or shoot) united with the stock retains its own characteristics. Either seedlings or mature trees may be grafted. The method is particularly important in growing fruit, notably in orange and grapefruit groves.

Grafton. 1 Town (pop. 10,627), S central Mass., SE of Worcester; settled 1718 on site of Indian village. Includes Farnumsville village (pop. 1,041). **2** City (pop. 5,885), NE N.Dak., on Park R., NNW of Grand Forks, in Red R. valley wheat region. Shipping and processing center for grain, potatoes, sugar beets, and livestock.

Graham, Billy (William Franklin Graham), 1918–, American evangelist. His revival campaigns in U.S. and abroad drew huge crowds, attracted much attention.

Graham, James: see MONTROSE, JAMES GRAHAM, 5TH EARL and 1ST MARQUESS OF.

Graham, Martha, 1893?–, American dancer and choreographer; a leading figure in modern dance. With Denishawn company after 1916; she made independent debut 1926, organized company 1929, began tours 1939. Her works include *Frontier* and *Appalachian Spring*.

Graham, Robert Bontine Cunninghame: see CUNNINGHAME GRAHAM, ROBERT BONTINE.

Graham, Thomas, 1805–69, Scottish chemist. He distinguished between colloids and crystalloids, and discovered DIALYSIS. His research on diffusion led to **Graham's law:** rate of diffusion of gas is inversely proportional to square root of density.

Graham, Calif.: see FLORENCE.

Graham Coast: see PALMER PENINSULA.

Grahame, Kenneth, 1859–1931, English writer of children's books, author of *The Wind in the Willows* (1908), a classic.

Graham Island, 2,485 sq. mi., largest of Queen Charlotte Isls., W B.C., Canada, in the Pacific Ocean.

Graham Land: see PALMER PENINSULA.

Graham of Claverhouse: see DUNDEE, JOHN GRAHAM OF CLAVERHOUSE, 1ST VISCOUNT.

Grail, Holy, a feature of medieval legend and literature. Appears variously as a chalice, cup, or dish and sometimes as a stone or caldron into which a bleeding lance drips blood. Identified by Christians as chalice of the Last Supper. The Grail would be revealed only to a pure knight; Grail Quest appears in different stories.

In Arthurian legend purest knight is variously Parsifal or Galahad. Legend has features of Christian story, Celtic myth, and ancient fertility cults.

grain, name for cereal grasses, certain other plants (e.g., buckwheat), and their edible fruits, which whole or ground supply the main food of man and some domestic animals. Principal grain crops are wheat, Indian corn, oats, barley, rye, and rice; all staple grain crops were domesticated in Neolithic period. In preparing the seedlike fruits of these plants for many uses the husk, outer coat, or bran is removed. To make whole-wheat flour part of the bran is removed; for graham flour whole grain is used.

grain alcohol: see ETHYL ALCOHOL.

Grain Coast, name formerly applied to coast of W Africa in the area of Liberia; named for early exports of seeds of melegueta peppers, known as "grains of Paradise."

Grainger, Percy (Aldridge), 1882–1961, Australian-American pianist, composer; disciple of Edvard Grieg, whose music he often played. Known for his adaptations of folk music, e.g., *Molly on the Shore, Shepherd's Hey, Mock Morris,* and *Country Gardens.*

Gram, Hans Christian Joachim (gräm, Dan. häns krĭs'tyän yō'äkĭm gräm'), 1853–1938, Danish physician. He developed a differential staining method useful in identification and classification of bacteria. Bacteria that retain the dye after immersion in decolorizer are Gram positive; others, Gram negative.

Gramont or **Grammont, Philibert, comte de** (fēlēbĕr' kŏt' dü grämō'), 1621–1707, French courtier. Exiled by Louis XIV, he was prominent at court of Charles II of England (1663–64). His brother-in-law, Anthony HAMILTON, wrote the celebrated *Mémoires du comte de Grammont,* a racy and thoroughly amoral account of his time.

Grampians, mountain system, cutting NE–SW across central Scotland, separating Highlands from Lowlands. Highest peak is Ben Nevis (4,406 ft.). Wild, magnificent scenery on N side; deer forests on more gently sloping S side.

Gran, Hungary: see ESZTERGOM.

Granada (gränä'dhä), city (pop. 40,092), W Nicaragua, on L. Nicaragua; founded 1524. Was long stronghold of landed aristocracy. Controls extensive commerce on lake.

Granada, city (pop. 157,833), cap. of Granada prov., S Spain, in Andalusia, picturesquely situated in view of the Sierra Nevada. It became in 1238 the cap. of the kingdom of Granada, the last Moorish foothold in Spain, and flourished as a center of Moslem art and culture. Long torn by feuds among the noble families, notably the Zegris and Abencerrages, the kingdom fell to Ferdinand and Isabella of Castile during the reign of Boabdil. The city itself fell in 1492 after a long siege. Its Moorish fortress, the ALHAMBRA, is its most famous monument. Near by is the imposing palace of Emperor Charles V. The late Gothic and plateresque cathedral (16th cent.) is adjoined by a chapel containing the tombs of Ferdinand and Isabella.

Granados (y Campiña), Enrique (ēnrĕ'kä gränä'dōs ē kämpē'nyä), 1867–1916, Spanish composer. *Goyescas,* a set of piano pieces which later formed the basis for an opera of the same name, is his best-known work. It was inspired by paintings and tapestries of Goya.

Granby, city (pop. 31,463), S Que., Canada, on North Yamaska R. and E of Montreal. Has textile mills and mfg. of furniture and rubber products.

Grand Alliance, War of the, 1688–97, war between France and the powers of the League of AUGSBURG, known as Grand Alliance after 1689. Louis XIV had been promised the support of James II of England, who however was overthrown by William III. French support of counterrevolution in Ireland was frustrated by William's victory at the Boyne (1690). On the sea, also, England was victorious at La Hogue (1692), but on land the French defeated the allies at Fleurus (1690), Namur (1692), Neerwinden (1693), and Marsaglia (1693). The Treaty of RYSWICK ended the war, which in America was known as King William's War (see FRENCH and INDIAN WARS).

Grand Army of the Republic, organization estab. by Union veterans of Civil War. First post formed at Decatur, Ill., April 6, 1866; first national encampment at Indianapolis, Nov. 20, 1866. Aims were to preserve friendships, honor fallen comrades, aid widows and handicapped, and increase pensions. Members were mostly Republicans; added to that party's strength until 1900. Parallel Southern group, United Confederate Veterans, was founded in 1889. The 83d and last G.A.R. encampment met Aug. 28–31, 1949, at Indianapolis.

Grand Bank, town (pop. 2,703), S N.F., Canada, on SE shore of Fortune Bay. Important base for Grand Banks fisheries.

Grand Banks, submarine plateau off SE N.F., Canada, c.50 mi. E of Cap Race. Extends NE–SW c.300 mi. and is c.200 mi. wide, with depths of 20–100 fathoms. Mostly in the Labrador Current, with E edge in Gulf Stream. Meeting of warm and cold air results in persistent fogs. Probably most important cod-fishing region in world. Fishing endangered by icebergs.

Grand Canal. 1 Chinese *Yün-ho* [transit river], longest canal of China and one of the longest of the world, c.1,200 mi. long. Extends from Peking to Ningpo. Largest sections completed in Sui dynasty (581–618) in reign of Yang Ti (605–17). Reconstructed and extended 13th–14th cent. Silting and roads have reduced canal's importance. **2** see VENICE.

Grand Canyon, gorge, c.1 mi. deep, 4–18 mi. wide, and 217 mi. long, of Colorado R., NW Ariz. Visible strata show long record of geologic changes from Archeozoic era to present. Varicolored layers, steep and embayed rims, isolated towers, mesas, and other eroded rock forms in chasm catch light of sun and shadow and glow with changing hues of intense beauty. Discovered by G. L. de Cárdenas 1540; boat party taken through by J. W. Powell 1869. Much of canyon now included in Grand Canyon Natl. Monument, with Toroweap Point, and Grand Canyon Natl. Park.

Grand Coulee, city (pop. 1,058), E Wash., on Columbia R., WNW of Spokane. Work base for **Grand Coulee Dam,** built 1933–42. Key unit in COLUMBIA BASIN PROJECT and one of world's largest concrete dams (550 ft. high, 4,173 ft. long), it has great power-producing capacity. Dam impounds Franklin D. Roosevelt L. (recreation area).

Grand Detour, village, N Ill., SW of Rockford on Rock R. Founded 1835 by Leonard Andrus, who was associated with John Deere in making first Grand Detour steel plow here 1837.

Grande Prairie (grăd prā″rē'), city (pop. 8,352), W Alta., Canada, NW of Edmonton. Business center for Peace R. valley farming area. Northern Winter Carnival held here annually.

Grand Falls. 1 Town (pop. 3,983), W N.B., Canada, on St. John R. Falls here attract many visitors. Has large hydroelectric development. **2** Town (pop. 6,605), central N.F., Canada, on Exploits R. and NW of St. John's. Has large paper mills and hydroelectric plant.

Grand Falls, spectacular waterfalls of upper Hamilton R., S Labrador. River drops 245 ft., then flows 12 mi. through canyon over series of rapids in a total fall of 1,038 ft. Discovered 1839 by John McLean of Hudson's Bay Co., but forgotten and rediscovered 1891.

Grand Forks, city (1964 pop. 38,230), E N.Dak., at Minn. line and junction of Red and Red Lake rivers; settled 1871. Was early trading post. Processing and distributing center for spring-wheat, livestock, and farm area, it has grain elevators and flour mills. Univ. of NORTH DAKOTA is here. Grand Forks Air Force Base is W.

Grandgent, Charles Hall (grăn′jŭnt), 1862–1939, American philologist and distinguished student of Italian language and Italian literature.

Grand Haven, city (pop. 11,066), SW Mich., on L. Michigan at mouth of Grand R. Resort and commercial fishing center. Its lake port ships sand and gravel.

Grand Island. 1 City (pop. 25,742), S Nebr., on Platte R., WNW of Lincoln; settled 1857 by Germans. Horse, mule, and cattle market; rail, mfg., and shipping center for farm, and dairy area. **2** Town (1965 pop. 10,774), NW N.Y., comprising group of islands in Niagara R., NW of Buffalo.

Grand Island, N Mich., in L. Superior N of Munising; one of largest Mich. islands (c.13,000 acres). Wooded area, it is a resort with game refuge.

Grand Isle, town (pop. 2,074), SE La., on Grand Is. at mouth of Caminada Bay. Hq. of Jean Laffite's corsairs, who engaged in smuggling and piracy here in early 19th cent. Treasure is supposedly buried here. Ruins of Fort Livingston are nearby. Town is fishing and truck-farming center.

Grand Junction, resort city (pop. 18,694), W Colo., at junction of Gunnison and Colorado rivers near Utah line; founded 1881. Shipping and processing center of ranch and farm area. Colorado Natl. Monument is nearby.

Grand Lake. 1 Lake, c.2 mi. long, N central Colo., at W edge of Rocky Mt. Natl. Park and in Colorado-Big Thompson project. Resort; has annual yacht race. **2** Lake, Okla.: See GRAND RIVER DAM.

Grand Manan, island (pop. 2,564), c.16 mi. long and c.7 mi. wide, S N.B., Canada, in Bay of Fundy near entrance to Passamaquoddy Bay. Summer resort and fishing center. Settled after Revolution by Loyalists; claims disputed by U.S. until 1817.

Grand Marais (mûrā′), resort village (pop. 1,301), NE Minn., on L. Superior NE of Duluth; settled on site of Indian village. Early fur-trading post. U.S. Coast Guard station is here.

Grand'Mère (grä″mĕr'), city (pop. 15,806), S Que., Canada, on St. Maurice R. and NNW of Trois Rivières. Here are hydroelectric station, paper and woolen mills, and lumbering.

Grand Portage (pôr′tǐj), nine-mi. stretch of land, in extreme NE corner of Minn. Overland link (between L. Superior and widening of Pigeon R.) in water highway used by fur traders and explorers. Area is now Grand Portage Natl. Monument.

Grand Prairie, industrial city (pop. 30,386, N Texas, a suburb just W of Dallas.

Grand Pré (grăn′ prā, Fr. grä prā′), agr. village, N N.S., Canada, on Minas Basin. Old village, founded nearby c.1675, was early home of Acadians and of Evangeline, heroine of Longfellow's poem. Statue to her by L. P. Hébert.

Grand Rapids. 1 City (pop. 177,313), W central Mich., on Grand R., NW of Lansing. Several Indian villages and a trading post were here. Distribution, wholesale, and industrial center for area yielding fruit, farm produce, and gypsum. Furniture industry began 1859. Mfg. also of business machines, automobile bodies and parts, aircraft instruments, machinery, and metal products. Has furniture museum and symphony orchestra. Here are Calvin Col. and extension centers of Univ. of Michigan and Michigan State Univ. **2** Village (pop. 7,265), N central Minn., near Mesabi iron range NW of Duluth, in region of woods, lakes, and streams; settled 1877. North Central School of Agr. of Univ. of Minnesota is here.

Grand River. 1 River, 165 mi. long, S Ont., Canada, flows into L. Erie at Port Maitland. Navigable for 70 mi. from mouth. **2** Former name of the OTTAWA river, E Ont. and W Que., Canada.

Grand River. 1 River: see COLORADO river **1. 2** River rising in SW Iowa near Creston and flowing c.215 mi. SE through NW Mo. to Missouri R. near Brunswick. **3** River rising in S Mich. and flowing c.260 mi. NW, and W past Lansing and Grand Rapids (head of navigation) to L. Michigan at Grand Haven. Longest river in state. **4** River rising in SW N.Dak.

and flowing c.209 mi. ESE through S.Dak. to Missouri R. near Mobridge. Has Shadehill Dam. part of Missouri R. basin project. 5 River, Okla.: see NEOSHO, river; GRAND RIVER DAM.

Grand River Dam, NE Okla.. in Grand R. (local name of NEOSHO R.). NE of Tulsa. Completed 1941. it is 6,500 ft. long and 145 ft. high. Also called Pensacola Dam. Impounds Grand L.. recreation area.

Grand Saline (sùlēn'). city (pop. 2,006). extreme NE Texas, E of Dallas. Has one of largest salt mines in U.S.

Grandson (gräsō'). town (est. pop. 2,100). Vaud canton. Switzerland, on L. of Neuchâtel. Here Swiss defeated Charles the Bold 1476. Also spelled Granson.

Grand Teton National Park: see TETON RANGE.

Grand Traverse Bay, arm of L. Michigan, c.32 mi. long and c.10 mi. wide, indenting NW Mich.

Grandview, city (pop. 6,027). W Mo., S of Kansas City. Richards-Gebaur Air Force Base is nearby.

Grange, Harold (Red Grange), 1904–, American football player. Famous running back (called "the galloping ghost") for Univ. of Illinois in early 1920s. Professional star with Chicago Bears (1925–35).

Grangemouth, burgh (pop. 18,860), Stirlingshire, Scotland, on the Forth estuary. Has extensive docks and shipyards.

Granger, Francis (grän'jùr), 1792–1868, American political leader. Defeated as Anti-Masonic party nominee in 1830 and 1832. Later became a leader of conservative Whigs.

Granger movement, American agrarian movement taking its name from the Natl. Grange of the Patrons of Husbandry, organization founded in 1867 by Oliver H. Kelley and others. Local units were called granges and the members grangers. Expanded rapidly after Panic of 1873. Though originally estab. for social and educational purposes, local granges became political forums, channels of protest against economic abuses; sought correction partly through cooperative enterprises. Their political activity secured passage in Ill., Wis., Minn., and Iowa of so-called Granger laws, dealing with railroad and storage rates. So-called Granger Cases challenged constitutionality of these laws (see MUNN VS. ILLINOIS). Inadequacy of state regulation led to demands for national legislation. After 1876 other groups led agrarian protest and granges returned to being social organizations.

Grangesberg, Sweden: see KOPPARBERG.

Grangeville, city (pop. 3,642). N central Idaho, SE of Lewiston; settled 1876. Important outfitting point in 1898 gold rush. Now tourist center.

Granicus (grùnī'kùs), anc. name of small river of Mysia, Asia Minor; now the Turkish Kocabas. Here Alexander the Great defeated Persians in 334 B.C., and Lucullus defeated Mithridates VI in 73 B.C.

granite, hard igneous rock of coarse structure, commonly containing quartz, feldspar, mica. It takes a high polish, and is used for buildings, monuments.

Granite City, industrial city (pop. 40,073). SW Ill., on Mississippi R.. N of East St. Louis. Rail center. U.S. army depot is here.

Granite Peak, 12.799 ft. high, S Mont., in Absaroka Range NE of Yellowstone Natl. Park; highest peak in Mont.

Graniteville, village (pop. 1,017), W central S.C., near Savannah R.. W of Aiken. Founded 1846 as state's first mill town by William GREGG. Kaolin quarries.

Granjon, Robert (grän'jùn, Fr. rōbĕr' gräzhō'), fl. 1545–88, French designer of type. Worked in Paris, Lyons, Antwerp, and Rome. Created *caractères de civilité*, intended as a French equivalent of italic; though beautiful, they lost out in competition with more legible italic. He is honored by having a later type face named for him.

Gran Paradiso (grän" pärädĕ'zō), mountain, 13,323 ft. high, NW Italy, in Alps S of Aosta. Is the highest peak entirely in Italian territory.

Gran Quivira National Monument: see NATIONAL PARKS AND MONUMENTS (table).

Gran Sasso d'Italia (grän säs'sō dētä'lyä), mountain group, Abruzzi, S central Italy, highest of the Apennines. Culminates at 9,557 ft. in Monte Corno or Corno Grande.

Granson, Switzerland: see GRANDSON.

Grant, Ulysses S(impson), 1822–85, commander in chief of Union army in Civil War, 18th President of the United States (1869–77); originally named Hiram Ulysses Grant. Captured Fort Henry and Fort Donelson in 1862, then fought controversial battle of Shiloh. VICKSBURG CAMPAIGN (1862–63) was great success. Became supreme commander in the West, Oct., 1863. After CHATTANOOGA CAMPAIGN, became commander in chief, March, 1864. Directed WILDERNESS CAMPAIGN (1864) against Lee. Accepted Lee's surrender at APPOMATTOX COURTHOUSE (1865). His campaigns were successful largely because he practiced elementary military doctrine that destruction of enemy's main armies was principal objective in warfare. Made a full general in 1866. Served as Secy. of War ad interim (1867–68), replacing Stanton. Was successful Republican candidate for President in 1868; reelected 1872. Was possibly the most ill-fitted man for that office nation ever had. Punitive radical Reconstruction program was pushed with new vigor; monetary legislation favorable to commercial and industrial interests was passed (see GREENBACK). Grant, though honest himself, associated with disreputable politicians and financiers. In foreign affairs, however, much was accomplished by Secretary of State Hamilton Fish. Grant's *Personal Memoirs* (2 vols., 1885–86) are among the great military narratives of history.

Granta, river, England: see CAM.

Grantham (grän'tùm, grän'thùm), municipal borough (pop. 25,030), Lincolnshire, England. Here Richard III condemned duke of Buckingham to death (1483) and Cromwell won first victory over royalists (1643). Site of George Hotel described in Dickens's *Nicholas Nickleby.*

Grants, town (pop. 10,274), W central N. Mex., W of Albuquerque on San Jose R.; settled 1882. Boomed with discovery (1950) of uranium deposits.

Grants Pass, city (pop. 10,118), SW Oregon, WNW of Medford on Rogue R. Commercial center of irrigated region (flower bulbs, fruits, nuts, vegetables, dairy products). Oregon Caves Natl. Monument is S.

Granville, Antoine Perrenot de (ätwän' pĕrùnō' dù grä-vĕl'), 1517–86, cardinal, statesman in service of Emperor Charles V and King Philip II of Spain; b. Besançon, France. As chief adviser to MARGARET OF PARMA (1556–64), he brought Spanish troops and Inquisition into Netherlands. His unpopularity stirred up rebellion and necessitated his recall.

Granville, John Carteret, 1st Earl, 1690–1763, British statesman. Ambassador to Sweden (1719–20), he mediated treaties ending the Northern War. Secretary of state 1721–24, he clashed with Robert Walpole and became (1730–42) leader of the opposition which brought about Walpole's downfall. Became unpopular for favoring George II's Hanoverian policies. Was president of the privy council 1751–63.

Granville, village (pop. 2,868), central Ohio. ENF of Columbus; settled 1805. Seat of Denison Univ

Granville-Barker, Harley Granville, 1877–1946, dramatist, actor, critic, producer of plays of old masters and new writers (Shaw, Galsworthy, Schnitzler). Wrote plays and *Prefaces to Shakespeare* (1927–45)

grape, woody vine of genus *Vitis,* widely cultivated in N Hemisphere, and its fruit. Varieties of *Vitis vinifera* are native to Mediterranean region and have been cultivated there from ancient times (now also grown in Calif.). They are used for making most WINE and are source of the RAISIN. In U.S. grapes grown E of the Rockies are hybrids or are derived from native species.

grapefruit or **pomelo,** citrus fruit (*Citrus paradisi*), related to orange and lemon, and originally native to SE

Asia. The large globular fruit grows in bunches and weighs up to 4–5 lb. Fla., Texas, and Calif. lead in U.S. production.

grape hyacinth, bulbous plant of genus *Muscari,* bearing clusters of dainty blue or white flowers in spring.

grape sugar: see GLUCOSE.

graphite (grä'fīt), allotropic form of CARBON, also called plumbago and black lead, soft and greasy with metallic luster. It is used in "lead" of pencils, stove polish, some paints, and as a lubricant.

Grasmere, village, Westmorland, England. Dove Cottage, Wordsworth's home 1799–1808, now a museum. De Quincey and Coleridge also lived here. Grave of Wordsworth, his family, and Hartley Coleridge.

Grass, Günter (gün'tŭr gräs'), 1927–. German writer of poems, dramas, farces, and novels. He is best known for *The Tin Drum* (1959), a novel of the Second World War, recounting the adventures from conception to early manhood of a boy who purposely remained a dwarf.

grass, any plant of important and widely distributed family Gramineae. Grasses, which have hollow, jointed stems and bladelike leaves, include hay and pasture grasses, the cereals (see GRAIN), sugar cane, and bamboo.

Grasse, François Joseph Paul, comte de (kōt' dü gräs'), 1722–88, French admiral. Played crucial part in YORKTOWN CAMPAIGN of American Revolution by blockading York and James rivers, thus bottling up Cornwallis at Yorktown.

Grasse (gräs), town (pop. 22,187), Alpes-Maritimes dept., SE France, in hills above Cannes, in a flower-growing dist. Center of French perfumery industry.

grasshopper, name for leaping insect of order Orthoptera. Common grasshoppers and locusts belong to short-horned grasshopper family. Long-horned family includes katydid, meadow grasshopper, Mormon, sand, and cave or camel crickets. Most grasshoppers have firm but flexible forewings, membranous underwings, powerful jumping legs, and strong jaws. Many are herbivorous, some carnivorous.

Grassi, Giovanni Battista (gräs'sē). Italian zoologist. Demonstrated (1898) that female *Anopheles* mosquito carries plasmodium of malaria in its digestive tract.

Grassmann, Hermann Günther (hĕr'män gün'tŭr gräs'-män), 1809–77, German mathematician and Sanskrit scholar. Formulated the linguistic law that in Indo-European bases, especially in Sanskrit and Greek, successive syllables may not commence with aspirates.

grass-of-Parnassus, perennial plant (*Parnassia*) with green-veined white flowers. Grows in damp places.

Gratian (grä'shŭn), 359–83, West Roman emperor (375–83). Ruled with his brother, VALENTINIAN II. In 378 he made Theodosius I emperor of the East. He took St. Ambrose as adviser and attacked paganism. In 383 he was assassinated by MAXIMUS.

Gratian, fl. 1140, Italian founder of the science of CANON LAW, a monk who taught at Bologna. His great work, the *Decretum,* or *Concordia discordantium canonum,* appeared c.1140. A private synthesis, it was used by later popes and became the kernel of the *Corpus juris canonici.*

Grattan, Henry, 1746–1820, Irish patriot statesman. Through his fight to repeal Poynings's Law (1782) the Irish Parliament regained power to initiate legislation. Gained Catholics the right to vote in Ireland (1793) and consent for them to sit in Parliament. This latter right was overruled by George III, thus encouraging the Rising of '98.

Gratz, Barnard (gräts), 1738–1801, American merchant, b. Upper Silesia. With his brother Michael Gratz (1740–1811) he estab. firm that acquired land in Ohio, Ky., Ind., and Ill. for pioneer settlement and ran boats on Ohio R. Michael's daughter, Rebecca Gratz, 1781–1869, known for her philanthropies in Philadelphia, is remembered chiefly as probable prototype of Rebecca in Scott's *Ivanhoe.*

Grätz, Heinrich: see GRAETZ, HEINRICH.

Gratz, Rebecca: see GRATZ, BARNARD.

Graubünden, Switzerland: see GRISONS.

gravel, rock fragments rounded by water, coarser than sand and classed according to size as pebble, cobble, or boulder gravel. Quartz is commonest constituent. Used in road building and in concrete.

Gravelines (grävlēn'), small Channel port, Nord dept., N France. Scene of Spanish victory over French (1558) during last phase of Italian Wars.

Gravenhage, 's, Netherlands: see HAGUE, THE.

Graves, Robert (Ranke), 1895–, English poet, critic, and novelist, best known for historical novels, such as *I, Claudius* (1934). Interested in myth (both in fiction and socio-religious history).

Gravesend (grāv'zĕnd'), municipal borough (pop. 51,-388). Kent, England, on S bank of the Thames. Has long been official reception place of London's distinguished visitors and starting place of expeditions. Station of pilots and customhouse officers. Has shipbuilding and mfg. Hq. of Royal Thames Yacht Club. Grave of Pocahontas.

Graves's disease: see THYROID GLAND.

gravitation. Law of gravitation states that all bodies in universe have a mutual attraction for one another. This attractive force is in direct proportion to product of masses of bodies concerned and varies inversely as square of distance between them. Gravitation constant is force exerted by a body with mass of 1 gm. upon another body with same mass at a distance of 1 cm. Law of gravitation was first stated by Isaac Newton but work of Johannes Kepler contributed to it, and experiments of Cavendish helped to establish its universality. **Gravity,** although commonly used synonymously with gravitation, is more accurately defined as that force operating between other bodies and the earth. This force is the cause of a body's having weight; the force is considered to act upon the whole body at a definite point (the center of gravity) within the body. The force of gravity varies slightly in different places, therefore the weight also varies accordingly. Gravity gives to a falling body a uniform acceleration; the value for this acceleration generally used as a standard is 32 ft. per second per second at sea level.

Gray, Asa, 1810–88, American botanist and taxonomist. As Harvard professor and through his writing, he helped popularize study of botany. He was author of *Manual of the Botany of Northern United States* (1848) known in numerous revisions.

Gray, Elisha, 1835–1901, American inventor. Invented telautograph for transmitting handwriting and line drawing 1888. Independently developed means to transmit human voice shortly after Bell received patent.

Gray, Robert, 1755–1806, American sea captain, discoverer of Columbia R. (1792). First American to circumnavigate globe (1787–90).

Gray, Thomas, 1716–71, English poet. Most familiar of his works is "An Elegy Written in a Country Churchyard" (published 1751). His earlier poems, such as "On A Distant Prospect of Eton College" (published 1747), were influenced by classical modes; his later poems, such as "The Descent of Odin" (1768), by Old Norse literature. He refused the laureateship in 1757.

Gray Eminence: see JOSEPH, FATHER.

grayling, game fish related to salmon, found chiefly in clear, cold, fresh waters of N Hemisphere. It has a high dorsal fin, is usually vivid with mixed purples and blues, sometimes marked with other colors. Its flesh is delicious. Generic name *Thymallus* refers to wild thyme odor. Common grayling (*Thymallus thymallus*) found in European rivers.

Grays Harbor, a Pacific inlet, W Wash., at mouth of Chehalis R. Aberdeen and Hoquiam are on its shore.

Gray's Inn: see INNS OF COURT.

Grayson, town (pop. 1,692). NE Ky., SW of Ashland. Nearby are Carter and Cascade limestone caves and several natural bridges.

Grays Peak: see FRONT RANGE.

SMALL CAPITALS = cross references. Pronunciation key on inside end pages. Abbreviations: p. 2.

Graz (gräts), city (pop. 243,500), cap. of Styria, SE Austria, on Mur R. Second largest city of Austria. Metallurgy; mfg. of machinery. Has Gothic cathedral, several medieval churches (13th–15th cent.), 16th-cent. Landhaus [provincial parliament], museum. Kepler taught at Graz univ. (founded 1585).

Graziani, Rodolfo (rōdōl'fō grätsēä'nē), 1882–1955, Italian marshal. Governed Ethiopia (1936–37), Libya (1940–41). Briefly imprisoned for treason (1950).

greasewood, spiny shrub (*Sarcobatus vermiculatus*) native to alkali soils of W U.S. Leaves are eaten by cattle and hard yellow wood is used as fuel.

Great Australian Bight, wide bay of Indian Ocean, indenting S coast of Australia.

Great Awakening, wave of religious revivals in American colonies in middle of the 18th cent. It began in N.J. under the evangelical preaching of Gilbert Tennent. In New England, where the Congregationalists played a leading role, it was stirred by Jonathan Edwards. It was spread by the tour (1739–41) of George Whitefield and by the preaching of Samuel Davies among the Presbyterians of Va. It led to missionary work among Indians by Samuel Kirkland and others. It also caused bitter disputes that resulted in doctrinal changes; swayed social and political thought; and served to build up intercolonial relations and to create a democratic spirit in religion.

Great Barrier Reef, 1,250 mi. long, largest coral reef in world, in Coral Sea, forming natural breakwater for coast of Queensland, Australia. Contains islets with coral gardens and unusual marine life.

Great Barrington, town (pop. 6,624), SW Mass., on Housatonic R., in Berkshires near N.Y. line; settled 1726. Resort. Includes Housatonic village (pop. 1,307).

Great Basin, interior region of W U.S., between Rocky Mts. and Sierra Nevada, extending SE to Colorado Plateau and SW to Sonoran Desert. Its more than 200,000 sq. mi. comprise most of Nev., W half of Utah, parts of Idaho, Oregon, and SE Calif. Its rugged N–S ranges are divided by deep, flat valleys. Altitude varies from thousands of feet above sea level to 280 ft. below in Death Valley. Little rain falls, streams do not reach ocean (e.g., Humboldt R., Carson R.), and most lakes are saline. In some early geological age N part was covered by Bonneville (Great Salt L. is remnant) and Lahontan lakes. J. C. Frémont explored parts of basin (1843–45) and gave it its name. Yields minerals and has grazing lands.

Great Bear Lake, c.175 mi. long, 25–110 mi. wide, N central Mackenzie dist., Northwest Territories, Canada. Drained W by Great Bear R. (flows c.100 mi. to Mackenzie R.). ELDORADO MINES on E shore. Waters open about four months of year. Discovered by North West Company traders c.1800. Fort Franklin built on SW shore by Sir John Franklin 1825.

Great Belt: see BELT, GREAT.

Great Bend, city (pop. 16,670), central Kansas, on Arkansas R. and old Santa Fe and Chisholm trails; settled 1871. Trade and shipping center for grain region. Oil and natural gas resources tapped in 1930s.

Great Berkhampstead: see BERKHAMPSTEAD.

Great Britain, largest of the British Isles. Politically the name is given to England, Scotland, and Wales since Act of Union of 1707. With NORTHERN IRELAND they form the United Kingdom (which earlier included all of IRELAND). Island was originally called BRITAIN. For history, see ENGLAND, SCOTLAND (until 1707), and WALES (until 1282).

The Growth of Empire. After 1707 Union the government remained as described under England. Founding of BANK OF ENGLAND (1694) showed growing English dominance of world trade and finance. After victories over Holland and France and success in War of the AUSTRIAN SUCCESSION and SEVEN YEARS WAR, the empire was expanded in late 18th cent. under the Georges; Britain's predominance was confirmed in India by Robert Clive and Warren Hastings; in North America by the conquests of James Wolfe. Loss to empire through the AMERICAN REVOLUTION was soon made up by settlements in Australia and New Zealand and by victories in FRENCH REVOLUTIONARY WARS and over NAPOLEON I. Period saw growth of cabinet and party government under such leaders as Sir Robert WALPOLE and William PITT. Rapid internal changes were caused by the INDUSTRIAL REVOLUTION. Irish grievances were only intensified by union with England (1800).

Commercial Leadership of the World. In the reign of VICTORIA (1837–1901) prosperity reached a peak. REFORM BILLS brought political reforms, and economic legislation removed the worst social abuses. Pressure from the new LIBERAL PARTY ended slavery (1832). The CORN LAWS were repealed in 1846. Robert Peel's advocacy of free trade split the CONSERVATIVE PARTY. A policy of colonial representative self-government contrasted with further conquests in INDIA. Britain's commercial interests led to OPIUM WAR with China (1840); its European diplomacy to participation in CRIMEAN WAR. Dominating statesmen of late 19th cent. were Liberal William GLADSTONE and Conservative Benjamin DISRAELI. Problems of empire expansion (see BRITISH EMPIRE) led to SOUTH AFRICAN WAR. Creation of the civil service improved government administration. The growth of trade unions increased the power of labor.

Before the Second World War. The reigns of Edward VII and George V saw tariff and social reforms, reduction of the power of the House of Lords by LLOYD GEORGE, the TRIPLE ALLIANCE and TRIPLE ENTENTE, FIRST WORLD WAR, and the Treaty of VERSAILLES. Problems mounted—reparations, WAR DEBTS, and new relation with Irish Free State. The LABOUR PARTY won its first victory (1924). 1931 saw a government crisis and a world-wide depression from which Britain recovered only slowly. Premiership of Neville CHAMBERLAIN (1937–40) saw policy of preferential tariffs maintained, decline of LEAGUE OF NATIONS, appeasement of Axis by MUNICH PACT (1938), delayed rearmament, pact with Poland, Soviet-German accord, and outbreak of Second World War.

The Second World War and Social Change. After British defeat in Norway, Winston CHURCHILL became war-time coalition prime minister. DUNKIRK was followed by widely destructive air bombings of Britain. Outstanding military leaders were Bernard Montgomery, Archibald Wavell, and Lord Louis Mountbatten. After increasing aid from U.S. the ATLANTIC CHARTER was proclaimed in 1941. Britain took part in international conferences of CASABLANCA, CAIRO, MOSCOW, TEHERAN, and YALTA. Living standards were lowered drastically. German surrender (1945) was followed by a Labour government headed by Clement Attlee. Britain withdrew from India (1948), turned over problem of PALESTINE to UN, and signed a 50-year pact with France, Belgium, Luxembourg, and the Netherlands. Programs of nationalization of industry, socialized medicine, and housing and educational reforms were started. After termination of LEND-LEASE large U.S. loans (see EUROPEAN RECOVERY PROGRAM) failed to stop depletion of Britain's dollar reserve and devaluation of the pound. Conservatives returned to office (1951) under Churchill, Eden (1955), and Macmillan (1957). Economy was deeply affected by loss of closed markets and industrial holdings in former possessions after formation of BRITISH COMMONWEALTH OF NATIONS. Britain helped (1959) form European Free Trade Association and applied (1961) for membership in Common Market, but was refused. Application for entry was again made in 1967. Conservatives were defeated (1964, 1965) by Labour party under Harold WILSON. Labour government faced severe economic problems aggravated by instability of pound sterling. Elizabeth II opened (1956) world's first nuclear power station. For list of British rulers see ENGLAND.

Great Chebeague Island (shĭbēg′) or **Chebeague Island,** SW Maine, in Casco Bay. Resort and residential island (c.2,000 acres). Chebeague Is. village on E shore.

Great Divide: see CONTINENTAL DIVIDE.

Great Dividing Range, general name for mountains and plateaus roughly paralleling E and SE coasts of Australia. Includes Australian Alps.

Great Falls, city (pop. 55,357), N central Mont., largest city in state, on Missouri R. opposite mouth of Sun R. and near falls for which city is named. Founded 1883 by Paris Gibson with help of J. J. Hill to be industrial city. Highly industrialized and center of extensive hydroelectric power development. Communications center and market for farm and livestock area and Sun R. project. Col. of Great Falls is here. Nearby are Giant Springs and Malmstrom Air Force Base.

Great Fish, river: see BACK, SIR GEORGE.

Great Glen, depression extending NE–SW across Scotland. Traversed by CALEDONIAN CANAL.

Great Lakes, five fresh-water lakes, central North America, between Canada and U.S. Stretching 1,160 mi., they are L. SUPERIOR, L. MICHIGAN (entirely in U.S.), L. HURON, L. ERIE, and L. ONTARIO, out of which flows SAINT LAWRENCE R. French traders first saw lakes in c.1612. War of 1812 ended long English-French struggle for region, and settlement was fast. Erie Canal opening in 1825 accelerated commerce. Huge quantities of iron ore, grain, coal, oil, steel, and manufactured products are shipped out from April until Dec. when winter closes most ports. Shipbuilding and fishing are major industries. The lakes are linked to the Atlantic by SAINT LAWRENCE SEAWAY AND POWER PROJECT, to Hudson R. by N.Y. State Barge Canal, and to Mississippi R. and Gulf of Mexico by Illinois R. waterway. Low water level in recent years threatens navigation and power plants.

Great Meadows: see NECESSITY, FORT.

Great Miami: see MIAMI, river.

Great Mother of the Gods, in ancient religions, Mother Earth, goddess of motherhood and of wild things, the symbol of fertility. She was worshiped under many names—Gaea, Rhea, Demeter, Artemis, and Aphrodite in Greece; Magna Mater and Bona Dea in Rome; Cybele in Phrygia; Isis in Egypt; Astarte in Phoenicia; and Ishtar in Babylonia and Assyria. See FERTILITY RITES.

Great Neck, residential village (1965 pop. 10,306). SE N.Y., on N shore of Long Isl.; settled c.1634. UNITED STATES MERCHANT MARINE ACADEMY is nearby.

Great Northern Peninsula or **Petit Nord Peninsula,** NW part of N.F., Canada, extending 170 mi. NNE from Bonne Bay (SW) and White Bay (E) to Cape Bauld (N). Long Range Mts. lie along W coast.

Great Ouse, river, England: see OUSE 1.

Great Plains, high, extensive grasslands of W U.S. and Canada; generally level, treeless, semiarid. Bounded W by Rocky Mts., S by Llano Estacado and South Plains of Texas Panhandle, E by level prairies of Mississippi valley. In U.S. they include W parts of N.Dak., S.Dak., Nebr., Kansas, Okla.; E parts of Mont., Wyo., Colo., N.Mex.; and NW Texas. Plateau's elevation slopes gently from 6,000 ft. on W to the 2,000 ft. of prairies on E. Flowing E are the rivers Platte, Republican, Kansas, Arkansas, Cimarron, and Canadian rivers. Wheat raising on this natural grazing land has caused some drought.

Great Rift Valley, geological FAULT system of E Africa and SW Asia, marked by chain of lakes. Ranges in elevation from 1,300 ft. below sea level (Dead Sea) to 6,000 ft. above in S Kenya.

Great Salt Lake, N Utah, W of Wasatch Range. Fed by Weber, Jordan, and Bear rivers, it is largest lake W of Mississippi R. (c.1,000 sq. mi. and average depth of c.13 ft., but dimensions vary). A remnant of ancient L. Bonneville. Some islands become peninsulas in low water. Salt content varies from 20 to 27%; only brine shrimp survive extreme salinity.

Commercial salt is extracted. To W are dead wastes of salt desert, now used for auto races. Railroad cutoff from Ogden to Lucin (completed 1903) crosses lake. Explored 1825 by James Bridger.

Great Salt Plains Dam, NW Okla., in Salt Fork (Arkansas R. tributary); 6,010 ft. long, 72 ft. high, completed 1941. Built for flood control and wildlife refuge.

Great Sand Dunes National Monument: see NATIONAL PARKS AND MONUMENTS (table).

Great Schism: see SCHISM, GREAT.

Great Slave Lake, 11,170 sq. mi., S Mackenzie dist., Northwest Territories, Canada, 300 mi. long and 30–140 mi. wide. Drained at W end by Mackenzie R. Discovered 1771 by Samuel Hearne. Gold found in 1930s on N shore and town of Yellowknife estab. as mining center. Receives the Hay (SW) and the Mackenzie (S), which is called **Great Slave** or **Slave River** between L. Athabaska and Great Slave L.

Great Smoky Mountains, part of Appalachian system, W N.C. and E Tenn., between Asheville and Knoxville, and between French Broad and Little Tennessee rivers. Loftiest range E of Black Hills and one of earth's oldest uplands. Includes Great Smoky Mts. Natl. Park, a resort area with lakes and streams. Clingmans Dome (6,642 ft.) is highest peak; 15 other peaks are over 6,000 ft.

Great South Bay, protected bay with several inlets from the Atlantic, SE N.Y., between S shore of Long Isl. and Outer Barrier. Extends c.45 mi. from inlet near Rockaway Beach to Moriches Bay. Shores have resorts and beaches. Crossed by several bridges.

Great Stone Face: see FRANCONIA MOUNTAINS.

Great Whale, river, rising in N central Que., Canada, and flowing 365 mi. W to Hudson Bay.

Great Yarmouth, Norfolk, England: see YARMOUTH.

Greb, Harry, 1894–1926, American boxer. In 1922 won light heavyweight title from Gene Tunney; took middleweight crown 1923.

Grebe, John Josef (grē′bē), 1900–. American physical chemist. b. Germany. Best known for work on quantum theory and for a period table for fundamental nuclear particles.

grebe (grēb), diving bird related to loon and found on lakes and oceans over most of world. It has short wings, a vestigial tail, smooth plumage, and long, individually webbed toes. Grebes swim and fly well, but walk clumsily. Nests are on floating vegetation or fastened to water plants.

Greco, El (ĕl grē′kō), c.1541–1614, Greek painter in Spain, b. Candia, Crete; real name was Domenicos Theotocopoulos. Studied in Venice. Settled 1577 in Toledo, where he painted the famous *View of Toledo* (Metropolitan Mus.). In his own day he enjoyed little popularity, but modern criticism ranks him among the greatest artists of all time. Typical paintings have elongated, distorted figures and vibrant color contrasted with subtle grays; pervading tone is one of religious ecstasy. Works are best seen in Toledo, Madrid, and the Escorial.

Greece, Gr. *Hellas* or *Ellas,* kingdom (51,182 sq. mi.; pop. 8,388,553), SE Europe, in S Balkan Peninsula and on islands in surrounding Ionian and Aegean seas (largest EUBOEA and CRETE; others, variously grouped: see CYCLADES, DODECANESE, IONIAN ISLANDS, SPORADES). Continental Greece is cut sharply into two sections at the Isthmus of Corinth. S portion is the Peloponnesus, with Patras as its largest center. More populous and prosperous N has most of the cities, notably the cap., ATHENS, and the ports, PIRAEUS (part of Greater Athens), SALONICA, and KAVALLA. The country is hilly to mountainous, cut by short rivers, some with very fertile valleys. Though predominantly agr., Greece, a food-importing country, concentrates on export crops (tobacco, olive oil, raisins, currants, dried figs, wine) to pay for essential imports (incl. meat, wheat, flour). The soil is badly eroded due to centuries of goat and sheep raising. Greece also exports sponges and some minerals (iron ore, magnesite, chromite, emery). Population is mainly Greek Orthodox.

Ancient Greece. The region had seen the rise and fall of splendid civilizations (see MINOAN CIVILIZATION, MYCENAEAN CIVILIZATION) before Greek-speaking peoples migrated in waves and thoroughly entrenched themselves. Traditional branches of the Greeks are Aeolians, Ionians, and Dorians, who supposedly arrived at different times, the last coming before 1000 B.C. In the mountain-divided lands they developed many independent CITY-STATES, which engaged in a constant succession of wars and alliances. Most important of these were to be Athens, SPARTA, THEBES, and CORINTH. Even before the era celebrated in the poems of Homer the Greeks had looked to the sea and had begun to spread colonies across the Mediterranean that were ultimately to create a net of city-states from the Ionian shores of Asia Minor to Sicily, S Italy, and even to S France and Spain (see MAGNA GRAECIA). All the cities were united by a feeling of being Hellenes; they had common shrines (as at DELPHI) and common celebrations (as the OLYMPIC GAMES). Nevertheless, political disunity was so strong that even when the Persians threatened the Ionian cities there was only a half-hearted union to oppose them in the PERSIAN WARS (500–449 B.C.). When the war was successful the greatest period of Greek history was begun. The city-states, and Athens in particular, felt a surge of cultural development scarcely equaled in world history. Prosperity came to Athens with the aid of the DELIAN LEAGUE, and the age of Pericles was one of glory. Drama and poetry, art, architecture, and philosophy flourished, and Greece became the fountainhead of later Western civilization. The list of great men whose words still echo is astonishing, and the list continued to grow after political misfortune set in: Aeschylus, Sophocles, Euripides, Aristophanes, Phidias, Socrates, Plato, and Aristotle are all well known to all the West. Though Athens lost to Sparta in the PELOPONNESIAN WAR (431–404 B.C.), Athenian thought prevailed. Even in politics, though the city-states varied from monarchy to aristocracy, oligarchy, and tyranny, the idea of democracy was born in Greece. Sparta's short-lived triumph was followed by the hegemony of Corinth and of Thebes, but all soon yielded to the conquest of PHILIP II of Macedon at Chaeronea (338 B.C.). Ironically, this defeat made it possible for Philip's son, ALEXANDER THE GREAT, to carry Greek civilization across the known world. While Greece itself fell prey to wars and conquest (despite the efforts of the Achaean League and the Aetolian League), HELLENISTIC CIVILIZATION spread, and though the Romans by 146 B.C. had reduced Greece to a political cipher, they looked up to the Greeks as bearers of civilization. When the Roman Empire was split (A.D. 395), the E portion, the BYZANTINE EMPIRE, was thoroughly Greek in tradition.

Medieval and Modern Greece. Greece was not an important factor in Byzantine history, and was frequently overrun by barbarians. In the 11th cent. began the Turkish inroads and Norman attacks. The Fourth Crusade led (1204) to disintegration of the empire and creation of the Latin Empire of Constantinople. When the Byzantine Empire was restored (1261–1453), only parts of Greece were recovered, European rulers holding the rest until all fell to the Turks (by 1456). Greece was unimportant in the Ottoman Empire. With the awakening of nationalism in the early 19th cent. the Greeks dreamed of independence and in 1821 commenced a rebellion that, with the leadership of the Ypsilantis and the aid of European liberals, succeeded. In 1827 CAPO D'ISTRIA became president of a Greece whose independence was assured by the battle of Navarino (1827), and wide recognition (1832). Civil struggles continued, and the Bavarian king imposed on the Greeks, OTTO I, was finally deposed (1862) and succeeded by GEORGE I.

A war with Turkey (1896–97) to obtain Crete was unsuccessful, but later international pressure forced incorporation of Crete into Greek territory (1913). In the following decades Venizelos and Zaïmis were the leading statesmen. Greece gained SE Macedonia in Balkan Wars (1912–13). In the First World War King CONSTANTINE insisted on neutrality, refusing to join the Allies even after the Salonica campaigns. Venizelos led a movement that forced Constantine to abdicate in favor of his son, ALEXANDER. After the war Greece was awarded W Thrace by the Treaty of Neuilly and most of European Turkey by the Treaty of Sèvres, but the latter award was subsequently modified. Greece invaded Asia Minor and was defeated by the Turks under Ataturk (1922). The Conference of Lausanne restored E Thrace to Turkey. A supplementary agreement provided for exchange of national minorities under League of Nations supervision: Turkish and Bulgarian minorities left Greece, and nearly 1,500,000 Greeks from Asia Minor were settled in Greece. After the death of Alexander (1920), Constantine had returned as ruler but was deposed again in 1922. His successor, GEORGE II, was deposed in 1923. Following the collapse of the strife-ridden republic (1924–35), George II was restored (1935) but in 1936 a dictatorship was set up under METAXAS. In the Second World War Greece repulsed an Italian invasion (1940) but was subsequently invaded and occupied (1941–44) by the German army. Within the Greek resistance forces royalist and Communist-led contingents battled one another. Economically exhausted after the liberation (1944), Greece was also beset by civil war. George II was recalled by plebiscite (1946), but the Communist-led opposition set up a rival government (1947). Under the "Truman Doctrine" (1947) the U.S. gave economic and military aid to the anti-Communist forces, whose campaign against the Communists was completed by 1950. In 1947 George II died and was succeeded by his brother PAUL. A member of the UN since 1945, Greece entered the North Atlantic Treaty Organization in 1951, signed defense pact with Turkey and Yugoslavia in 1954, entered the Common Market as associate member in 1962. Its relations with Turkey and Great Britain were strained over CYPRUS dispute. In 1964 Constantine XIII became king on the death of his father, Paul I. Right-wing military junta assumed governmental power in April, 1967, and installed rigid controls over Greek life. King gave formal approval, but urged return to constitutional government.

Greek Anthology, collection of Greek epigrams or short poems, including poetry down to the decay of Byzantium. Edited and added to successively by ancient and medieval scholars; versions of 10th and 14th cent. most used.

Greek architecture began with advent of the Dorians in Greece (before 1000 B.C.) and was evolved between 10th and 6th cent. B.C. The Heræum at Olympia, most ancient temple yet discovered, illustrates beginning of Doric style. Chief Greek works were produced between 700 B.C. and Roman occupation (146 B.C.). Great age was reign of Pericles, in which architects Callicrates, Mnesicles, and Ictinus flourished and in which the perfected Doric order appeared in PARTHENON and PROPYLAEA. The Greeks laid masonry without mortar but with joints cut to great exactness. Colors and gilding were used to emphasize decorative sculpture. The Ionic order, evolved in Greek colonies of Asia Minor, was used extensively at Miletus. It appeared after 500 B.C. in Greece proper, where its only great example is the ERECTHEUM. Latest and most ornate Greek style, Corinthian order (mid-4th cent. B.C.), was little used. After shift of power from Greece proper to Asia Minor, Hellenistic architecture arose (4th–3d cent. B.C.) with florid elements, more complicated design, and a new emphasis on city planning. The

Romans doubtless acquired their concepts of monumental civic design from Hellenistic architects.

Greek art may be said to have begun with pottery making (c.900–700 B.C.), marked by abstract, mathematical systems of design. New interest in representation arose between 700 and 600 B.C. Sculpture emerged as dominant artistic form in archaic period (c.625–480 B.C.) with statues of nude walking youths, *kouroi*, which suggest Egyptian prototypes, and draped female figures, which suggest Near Eastern influence. Painters of archaic period depicted many mythological and contemporary scenes as decoration for vases; outstanding masters were Euthymides and Euphronius. Early classical or transitional period (c.480–450 B.C.) tried to find balance between naturalism and abstraction. Classical period or Golden Age (c. 450–400 B.C.) aimed to represent the ideal human being, both in form and in character. Significant sculptures of the period are from Athenian Acropolis. In late classical period (400–300 B.C.) emphasis on emotion was increased (esp. in sculptures of Scopas). Among great sculptors who flourished 500–300 B.C. were Praxiteles, Lysippus, Myron, Cresilas, Timotheus, and Bryaxis; the painters included Apollodorus, Zeuxis, Parrhasius, and Apelles. Hellenistic period was last phase of Greek art; its best-known masterpiece is *Victory of Samothrace* (Louvre) and *Lacocoön* (Vatican).

Greek Church: see ORTHODOX EASTERN CHURCH.

Greek fire, inflammable substance, a "liquid" fire, said to have been invented by Callinicus of Heliopolis who, at Constantinople in reign of Constantine Pogonatus, used it to set fire to enemy ships. Byzantine Greeks used it in early Middle Ages. Chemical nature not known, but probably contained sulphur, various easily inflammable materials, and a substance (e.g., lime) which reacts with water to produce heat.

Greek language, Indo-European language. Modern Greek is derived from the standard Greek (or Koine) of Hellenistic world. The New Testament is written in a form of this. See LANGUAGE (table).

Greek music. Music in ancient Greece was evidently a highly developed art. Few examples are extant, but something about it can be learned from secondary sources, e.g., the third book of Plato's *Republic* and writings on musical theory by Aristoxenus of Tarentum (fl. 4th cent. B.C.). Early Greek music was inseparable from poetry and dancing and was attributed an emotional and moral influence. Chief instruments were the oboe-like aulos (used in festivals of Dionysus) and a kind of lyre called the kithara (sacred to Apollo). Notation was indicated by letters. There were two such systems, one vocal and one instrumental. Its melodic system was based upon the MODE. Early in Greek music's history, its relation to physics was recognized.

Greek religion. Sources and history of Greek myth are subject of much argument and conjecture. Religious beliefs in ancient Greece were complex and often contradictory. There was a basic animism, but it was complicated by confusion with local deities. Even in Homer's time, when gods were pictured anthropomorphically, no code of ethics or morals was connected with them. Cults of mortal heroes were common from earliest times. Later, heroes and gods became inextricably mixed in legends. Characteristics and stories of the great gods were drawn from many sources; some stemmed from early worship of the Greeks outside the peninsula, some came from Minoan and Mycenaean civilizations, and some were brought in from Asia and Egypt. ZEUS was ruler of OLYMPIAN gods, whose home was Mt. Olympus but who wandered freely about the world. There were also underworld gods. These dwelt in Hades, ruled by Pluto and PERSEPHONE. The underworld and the cycle of vegetation were the base for ELEUSINIAN MYSTERIES. Other MYSTERIES, such as ORPHIC MYSTERIES were connected with worship of DIONYSUS. Mysteries were important for their strong ethical and moral teachings, and their priests were exalted, as were those of the great oracles

(see ORACLE; DELPHI). By 5th cent. B.C. literal belief in gods was fading in minds of the educated, and dematerialization of gods into great forces enabled poets and philosophers to picture a cosmos in which moral struggle was paramount.

Greek revival: see CLASSIC REVIVAL.

Greeley, Horace, 1811–72, American newspaper editor, founder of New York *Tribune* (1841). Sought to provide for laboring classes a cheap paper that would be both clean and intelligent. Staff included distinguished talent; his editorials made paper widely known. Supported protective tariff; other causes he advocated included many social reforms. The *Tribune* was popular in the West; many had acted upon Greeley's advice, "Go West, young man, go West." One of first editors to join Republican party. His humanitarian hatred of war often embarrassed Lincoln's administration; at end of Civil War he advocated amnesty for all Southerners. Though an early supporter of U. S. Grant, Greeley encouraged growth of LIBERAL REPUBLICAN PARTY. Party's unsuccessful candidate for President in 1872.

Greeley, city (pop. 26,314). N Colo., NNE of Denver near South Platte R. Rail. trade. and processing center for irrigated farm area. Cooperative Union Colony founded here 1870 by agent of Horace Greeley.

Greely, Adolphus Washington, 1844–1935, American army officer and arctic explorer. Commanded U.S. expedition to establish one of chain of international circumpolar meteorological stations (1881). Rescued with few survivors (1884). Noted builder of army telegraphic communications. Directed relief operations after San Francisco earthquake. Awarded Congressional Medal of Honor (1935).

Green, Duff, 1791–1875, American journalist and politician. His paper, the *United States Telegraph,* supported Pres. Jackson until Green turned to support of J. C. Calhoun and to defense of South on slavery and tariff issues. Later was diplomatic agent to Texas and Mexico.

Green, George, 1793–1841, English mathematician. He worked on equilibrium of fluids and was first to introduce potential as applied to theories of magnetic and electric fields.

Green, Henry, pseud. of Henry Vincent Yorke, 1905–, English novelist, an industrialist. His novels, somewhat experimental in style, and both comic and sympathetic, include *Living* (1929), *Loving,* (1948), and *Nothing* (1950).

Green, Hetty (Howland Robinson), 1835–1916, American financier. Managed inherited fortune so shrewdly that she was considered greatest woman financier in the world.

Green, John Richard, 1837–83, English historian. His *A Short History of the English People* (1874) stressed social rather than political change.

Green, Julian, 1900–, French writer, of American origin. Studied in U.S. Author of somber psychological tales (*The Closed Garden,* 1927; Eng. tr., 1928), journals (1938–39; Eng. tr., *Personal Record*), and reminiscences (*Memories of Happy Days,* 1942).

Green, Matthew, 1696–1737. English poet. author of *The Spleen* (1737), witty praise of contemplative life.

Green, Paul, 1894–. American author. b. N.C. His plays (e.g. *In Abraham's Bosom,* 1926), short stories, and novels treat Negro and folk life; historical pageants (e.g. *The Lost Colony,* 1937; *The Common Glory,* 1948) deal with American history.

Green, Samuel Swett, 1837–1918, American librarian. One of the founders and president (1891) of American Library Association; author of *The Public Library Movement in the United States, 1853–1893* (1913).

Green, Seth, 1817–88, pioneer American pisciculturist, credited with making large-scale fish breeding practical. He transplanted Atlantic shad to Pacific.

Green, Thomas Hill, 1836–82, English neo-Hegelian philosopher. Asserted that consciousness made knowledge possible, thus setting idealism against prevailing empiricism and sensationalism. His *Prolegomena to Ethics* (1883) was an influential book.

Green, William, 1873–1952, American labor leader, president of American Federation of Labor (1924–52).

Greenaway, Kate, 1846–1901, English illustrator of children's books and water-color painter. Her illustrations influenced children's clothing.

greenback. In 1862 U.S. government first issued, on a temporary basis, legal tender notes (popularly called greenbacks) which were placed on a par with notes backed by specie. By end of Civil War such notes were outstanding to amount over $450,000,000. In accordance with Funding Act of 1866 Secretary of State Hugh McCulloch began retiring them. Hard times in 1867 led to demand that currency should be inflated rather than contracted; Congress suspended retirement. In 1868 a compromise left greenbacks to amount of $356,000,000 in circulation. Law creating them was declared constitutional in later LEGAL TENDER CASES. Following Panic of 1873 agrarians wanted currency inflated with more greenbacks. Conservatives triumphed with Resumption Act of 1875, which fixed Jan. 1, 1879, as date for redeeming greenbacks in specie. Congress provided in 1878 that greenbacks then outstanding ($346,681,000) remain permanent part of currency.

Greenback party, in U.S. history, political organization formed in years 1874–76 to promote currency expansion. Members were principally Western and Southern farmers; stricken by Panic of 1873, they wanted inflated currency because it would wipe out farm debts contracted in times of high prices. Failing to capture the Democratic party in 1874, Greenback party nominated Peter Cooper for President in 1876; got only 81,737 votes. In 1878, however, the Greenback-Labor party, representing a union of labor and greenback supporters, polled over 1,000,000 votes and elected 14 Representatives to Congress. Party dissolved after 1884 election. Many members later became Populists.

Green Bay, city (pop. 62,888), NE Wis., NE of Appleton, at mouth of Fox R. on Green Bay. Here Jean Nicolet estab. trading post 1634. Oldest permanent settlement in state (1701). Became fur-trading center and was occupied in turn by French (1717), British (1761), and Americans (1816). First Wis. newspaper estab. here 1833. One of best of Great Lakes harbors and a rail center, it has heavy shipping, large wholesale and jobbing trade, and thriving industries. Extension center of Univ. of Wisconsin is here. Home of professional football's Green Bay Packers.

Green Bay, W arm of L. Michigan, c.100 mi. long, indenting NE Wis. and along Mich. Upper Peninsula.

Greenbelt, city (pop. 7,479), W central Md., suburb ENE of Washington, D.C.; chartered 1937. Planned and built by U.S. government as model community.

Greenbrier, river, rising in E W.Va. and flowing c.175 mi. SW, parallel to Va. line. Joins New R. near Hinton.

greenbrier: see SMILAX.

Greencastle, city (pop. 8,506), W central Ind., NE of Terre Haute; founded c.1823. Seat of DePauw Univ.

Greene, Graham, 1904–, English writer. His early "entertainments" or thrillers include *Orient Express* (1942) and *Ministry of Fear* (1943). A Roman Catholic convert, he also wrote novels on the moral relation of man to God; these include *Brighton Rock* (1938), *The Power and the Glory* (1940), *The Heart of the Matter* (1948), and *The End of the Affair* (1951). Among other works are plays (e.g., *The Potting Shed,* 1957; *The Complaisant Lover,* 1959), short stories, essays, and film scripts (e.g., *The Third Man,* 1950; *Our Man in Havana,* 1960).

Greene, Nathanael, 1742–86, American Revolutionary general. Commander in CAROLINA CAMPAIGN.

Greene, Robert, 1558?–92, English dramatist, poet, miscellaneous writer. His short romantic "novels" (e.g. *Pandosto,* 1588) were popular. His plays, pseudo-historical in tone, include *Friar Bacon and Friar Bungay*

(1594) and *James IV* (1598). Among his many didactic tracts, those on cony-catching show sordid London underworld.

Greeneville, town (pop. 11,759), NE Tenn., SW of Johnson City, in farm and tobacco area. Cap. of State of FRANKLIN 1785–88. Here are Andrew Johnson Natl. Historic Site (his home, tailor shop, grave), monument to Gen. J. H. Morgan (killed here in Civil War), and Tusculum Col. Davy Crockett was born at nearby Limestone.

Greenfield. 1 City (pop. 9,049), central Ind., F of Indianapolis; settled 1828. J. W. Riley born here; his house is restored. Brandywine Creek is in memorial park. **2** Industrial town (pop. 17,690), NW Mass., near junction of Deerfield and Connecticut rivers; settled 1686. E terminus of Mohawk Trail. **3** City (pop. 17,636), SE Wis., suburb SW of Milwaukee.

Greenfield Village, reproduction of early American village estab. 1933 by Henry Ford at Dearborn, Mich., as part of Edison Inst. About a typical New England village green are grouped public buildings and other structures, including Edison's Menlo Park workshop, Noah Webster's birthplace, Stephen Foster's home, Luther Burbank's birthplace, Wright brothers' shop and home. Mills and craft shops illustrate early methods.

Green Hills, Tenn.: see WOODMONT.

greenhouse, enclosed glass house used for growing plants in regulated temperatures and humidity. In size range from lean-to type attached to home to large commercial buildings or hothouses for growing flowers and vegetables out of season.

Greenland, Dan. *Grønland,* Danish island (c.840,000 sq. mi.; pop. 33,113), lying largely within Arctic Circle, between Canada (W) and Iceland (E); max. length 1,660 mi., max. width 684 mi. Geologically part of Canadian shield, Greenland is covered by an ice sheet (c.14,000 ft. thick in some places) ringed with mountains, except for c.132,000 sq. mi. of coastland. Numerous glaciers (Humboldt is largest), which "calve" icebergs, debouch into coastal fjords. Over 90% of pop. lives on warmer W coast. Natives are mostly of mixed Danish and ESKIMO ancestry. Danish ministry for Greenland estab. 1955; governor appointed in Denmark and provincial council govern. Cap. Godthaab. Other settlements are Godhavn, Julianehaab. Chief resources are minerals (esp. cryolite at Ivigtut; also lignite and graphite). Agr. and sheep grazing are limited to SW, but Peary Land supports musk oxen. There are cod and halibut fisheries, and seals and walruses are hunted. Island was discovered and settled (c.982) by ERIC THE RED, but it fell into neglect in 14th and 15th cent. and was not rediscovered until 16th cent. Then coast was charted by seekers of Northwest Passage. Modern colonization was begun (1721) by a Norwegian missionary, Hans Egede. Greenland was explored and mapped by many arctic explorers in 19th and 20th cent. In 1951 U.S. and Denmark signed agreement for the common defense of Greenland. U.S. has constructed military bases (notably at THULE) under the North Atlantic Treaty Organization. Danish constitution of 1953 gave Greenland equal status with all other parts of the kingdom.

Greenland Sea, arm of Arctic Ocean, off NE coast of Greenland. Main outlet of Arctic Ocean to Atlantic. Due to ice it is rarely open to navigation.

Green Mountain Boys, popular name of partisan armed bands in present Vt. Defended region against New York control in NEW HAMPSHIRE GRANTS controversy. Chief leader was Ethan ALLEN. In American Revolution they captured Ticonderoga in 1775 and won victory at Bennington in 1777.

Green Mountains, range of the Appalachians extending N and S through Vt. and rising to 4,393 ft. at Mt. Mansfield. Generally low and rounded, peaks are well forested with fertile valleys and many streams (water power). Resort area noted for scenic beauty. Has Long Trail and Appalachian Trail. Mountains yield marble and granite.

Greenock (grē'nŭk, grĭ'-). burgh (pop. 74,578). Renfrewshire, Scotland, on S shore of Firth of Clyde. A port. it has shipbuilding and varied mfg. Birthplace of James Watt.

Greenough, Horatio (grē'nō), 1805–52, American sculptor and writer. b. Boston. Worked in Florence 1829–51. His colossal statue of Washington is in Smithsonian Inst.

Green River. 1 River rising in central Ky. and flowing 370 mi. WNW to Ohio R. near Evansville, Ind. **2** River, 730 mi. long, rising in W Wyo. in Wind River Range and flowing through W Wyo. and E Utah, with loop in NW Colo., to Colorado R. in SE Utah. Largest tributary of the Colorado, it receives Yampa, White. Blacks Fork. Duchesne, Price, and San Rafael rivers. Extensive irrigation and power development planned as part of COLORADO RIVER STORAGE PROJECT. FLAMING GORGE DAM is one of major units.

Greensboro, city (pop. 119,574), N central N.C., E of Winston-Salem, in piedmont; settled 1749. State's second largest city and regional financial. insurance, and distribution center. Mfg. of textile, tobacco products. electrical and electronic equipment. Seat of AGRICULTURAL and TECHNICAL COLLEGE, Bennett Col., Greensboro Col., Guilford Col., and branch of Univ. of NORTH CAROLINA. Nearby Guilford Courthouse Natl. Military Park is on site of battle fought (March 15. 1781) in CAROLINA CAMPAIGN.

Greensburg, city (pop. 17,383), SW Pa., SE of Pittsburgh; settled 1782. Seat of Seton Hill Col. Col. Henry Bouquet defeated Indian warriors of Pontiac nearby in 1763. opening W Pa. for settlement.

Greenville. 1 City (pop. 41,502), W central Miss., on L. Ferguson, adjoining Mississippi R. With deepwater harbor, it is trade. processing, and shipping center of Mississippi-Yazoo delta (producing cotton, soybeans, oats, and corn). **2** Town (pop. 22,860), E N.C., on Tar R., ESE of Raleigh; founded 1786. Important bright-leaf tobacco market and agr. trade and wholesale center, with lumber industry. East Carolina Col. is here. **3** City (pop. 10,585), W Ohio, NW of Dayton, in farm area; laid out 1808. Gen. Anthony Wayne built Fort Greenville here 1793 and negotiated Treaty of Greenville 1795 with Indians, who ceded large part of Old Northwest to U.S. **4** City (pop. 66,188), NW S.C., in piedmont near Blue Ridge and on Reedy R., WSW of Spartanburg; laid out 1797. One of major industrial and commercial centers of SE U.S., it has textile mills and farm-produce processing and packing plants. Center of mill-town region. FURMAN UNIVERSITY and Bob Jones Univ. are here. **5** City (pop. 19,087), E Texas, NE of Dallas, in blackland cotton region; settled 1846.

green vitriol: see COPPERAS.

Greenwich (grĭ'nĭj), London borough since 1965 (est. pop. 233,440); includes former metropolitan borough of Greenwich and part of Woolwich. Located here are Royal Naval Col., Greenwich Hospital (on the site of a former palace where Henry VIII. Mary I, and Elizabeth I were born), and the Natl. Maritime Mus. The Royal Observatory was located until 1946 on a hill in Greenwich Park selected by Sir Christopher Wren. Geographic longitude is still figured from the prime meridian here.

Greenwich, residential and resort town (pop. 53,793), SW Conn., on Long Isl. Sound. Purchased from Indians 1640. Raided by British 1779. Here is house (1731) from which Gen. Israel Putnam traditionally escaped from British. Seat of Rosemary Hall and Greenwich Acad. Printing and publishing. engineering research. and some mfg. Includes villages of Greenwich. Riverside. Quaker Ridge (has Audubon Nature Center). Old Greenwich, and Cos Cob.

Greenwich Village, residential district of lower Manhattan. New York city, extending roughly from 14th St. S to Houston St. (hou'stŭn), from Washington Square W to Hudson R. Separate village in colonial period. it was later exclusive residential area; gained renown c.1910 as home and workshop of nonconformist artists. writers. and theater people. Lingering aura of bohemianism still found in old houses along narrow. crooked streets. Its restaurants. coffee houses. nightclubs. theaters. little shops. and semiannual outdoor art exhibit attract many visitors.

Greenwood. 1 City (pop. 20,436). W central Miss., on Yazoo R.. ENE of Greenville: settled 1834. Important processing, marketing. and shipping center of cotton region. **2** City (pop. 16,644), W S.C., WNW of Columbia; settled 1824. Processing center of cotton. corn. and peach region. Lander Col. is here. Buzzard Roost hydroelectric development is nearby on Saluda R.

Greenwood Lake, resort village (1965 pop. 1,479), SE N.Y.. SSE of Middletown; founded c.1750. Nearby are lake of same name (crosses N.Y.–N.J. line) and Sterling Forest Gardens.

Greet, (Sir Philip) Ben, 1857–1936, English actor and theatrical manager. Initiated outdoor productions of Shakespeare (1886); toured England and U.S.

Gregg, Josiah, 1806–50, American trader, historian of Sante Fe Trail. Wrote *Commerce of the Prairies* (1844), classic of American frontier history.

Gregg, William, 1800–1867, "father of Southern cotton manufacture." Estab. Graniteville, S.C. (1846), first Southern mill town.

Gregorian chant: see PLAIN SONG.

Gregory I, Saint (the Great), c.540–604, pope (590–604), Doctor of the Church. A Roman prefect, he gave his property to the Church and became a monk. Though he resisted each promotion, his abilities carried him finally to the papacy. His rule was notable for the firmness with which he defended his office and Rome, attacking Donatism in Africa, refusing to recognize the patriarch of Constantinople as ecumenical (an act that helped split East and West), treating with attacking Lombards (592) after the imperial exarch failed to act. Gregory did much to shape the history of the Church for centuries; he encouraged the spread of monasticism, made laws for the lives of the clergy, and sent missionaries to England. He wrote much and well (commentaries on Job; saints' lives; *Pastoral Care*) and contributed to development of Gregorian chant or PLAIN SONG. Feast: March 12.

Gregory VII, Saint, d. 1085, pope (1073–85) (Hildebrand; Ital., *Ildebrando*). A Benedictine, he became a notable figure under Pope Gregory VI, and under Leo IX launched the Hildebrandine reform, aimed at correcting chief Church abuses of simony, lay INVESTITURE, and violation of clerical celibacy. As chief figure in the curia under Leo's successors, he transferred papal election from the Romans to the college of cardinals and formed an alliance with the Normans of S Italy. A powerful antireform party grew among laymen who feared church domination; with this ambitious German King HENRY IV sided. Hildebrand, made pope (1073) as Gregory VII, pressed his reform and sent papal legates throughout Europe enforcing his decrees. The quarrel between Henry and Gregory came to an open break in 1076. The pope excommunicated Henry, who, losing his support, humbled himself before Gregory at Canossa. In 1080 the two again fell out. Henry, again excommunicated, set up GUIBERT OF RAVENNA (Clement III) as antipope. Gregory's appeal to the Christian world failed, and when the German civil war ended Henry marched into Italy. He took Rome (1083) and Gregory retired into the Castel Sant' Angelo. The Normans under ROBERT GUISCARD rescued him but they were quickly expelled from Rome. Gregory went with them; he died in Salerno after a year of exile. His last words were said to be, "I have loved justice and hated iniquity, therefore I die in exile." His extreme assertion of papal prerogative and devotion to reform made him one of the most powerful and greatest of the popes. He was canonized in 1728. Feast: May 25.

Gregory IX, 1143?–1241, pope (1227–41); nephew of Innocent III. He excommunicated Emperor FREDERICK II for delaying to fulfill his vow to go on crusade (1227). Imperialists in Rome then revolted, and the pope fled to Viterbo and Perugia. Later, in a struggle over Italian liberties Gregory again excommunicated Frederick and ordered his dethronement. Frederick prevented German publication of the bulls and blocked a general council. Gregory died as Frederick was about to attack Rome.

Gregory XI, 1330–78, last French pope (1370–78). (Pierre Roger de Beaufort). He received prophetic warnings from St. Bridget of Sweden and St. CATHERINE OF SIENA to remove papacy from Avignon to Rome, but Avignon court was opposed and Italy inhospitable. He defeated Bernabò Visconti of Milan with hired aid of Sir John de Hawkwood (1374). A struggle with Milan and Florence ensued, ending with the interdict on Florence. Gregory finally consented to Catherine's pleas and moved to Rome (1376–77). Gregory first condemned Wyclif. Elections after his death began the Great SCHISM.

Gregory XII, c.1327–1417, pope (1406–15). He agreed before his election during course of Great SCHISM to resign if Avignon antipope Benedict XIII (Pedro de LUNA) would also resign. The agreement failed, and Gregory created four new cardinals despite agreement against new creations. But the cardinals united in convoking the Council of Pisa (1409), which declared pope and antipope deposed, and elected a new antipope, Alexander V. After years of confusion the Council of CONSTANCE recognized Gregory as canonical pope, after which he resigned.

Gregory XIII, 1502–85, pope (1572–85), best known for his reformed Gregorian CALENDAR. He was prominent in the Catholic Reform and at Council of TRENT (1545, 1559–63). As pope, he proposed deposition of Queen Elizabeth, refused to compromise with German Protestants, and held public thanksgiving at Rome for the massacre of St. Bartholomew's Day (having been told it was suppression of a rebellion). Issued new edition of the canon law. His government of Papal States was execrable.

Gregory XVI, 1765–1846, pope (1831–46); a conservative, much denounced by European liberals. His most famous act was condemnation of LAMENNAIS (1832).

Gregory, Augusta (Persse) Gregory, Lady, 1859–1932, Irish author and playwright. A founder of the ABBEY THEATRE, she devoted many years to managing and directing it and writing for it. Her journals are a vivid source of Irish literary history.

Gregory, Horace, 1898–, American poet. His work includes *Chelsea Rooming House* (1930) and *Medusa in Gramercy Park* (1961). With his wife, Marya Zaturenska, he wrote *A History of American Poetry 1900–1940* (1946).

Gregory, James, 1638–75, Scottish mathematician. He invented a reflecting telescope and a photometric mode of measuring the distance of stars.

Gregory Nazianzen, Saint (nāzēăn'zĭn), c.330–390, Cappadocian theologian, Doctor of the Church. An intimate of St. Basil the Great, he was chosen bishop of Constantinople (379), but on the failure of the First Council of Constantinople, he retired. Feast: May 9.

Gregory of Nyssa, Saint (nĭs'ŭ), d. 394, bishop of Nyssa, Cappadocia (after 371); brother of St. BASIL THE GREAT; one of great orthodox Catholic writers on Trinity, redemption, grace. Feast: March 9.

Gregory of Tours, Saint, 538–94, French historian, bishop of Tours (from 573), author of *History of the Franks.* Feast: Nov. 17.

gremlin, in American folklore, malicious gnome, first heard of during Second World War as causing unexplainable mechanical failures.

Grenada (grĭnä'dŭ), island (133 sq. mi.; 1964 est. pop. 93,000), West Indies, in WINDWARD ISLANDS;

cap. St. George's. In 1967 became one of WEST INDIES ASSOCIATED STATES.

grenadine: see POMEGRANATE.

Grenfell, Sir Wilfred (Thomason), 1865–1940, English Protestant medical missionary. Served 40 years in Labrador and Newfoundland among fishermen and Eskimo.

Grenoble (grŭnô'blŭ), city (pop. 156,707), cap. of Isère dept., SE France. on Isère R.; historic cap. of Dauphiné. Hydroelectric center of France. Mfg. (paper, cement); electrical industries. Famous university estab. 1339. Among notable buildings are cathedral (12th–13th cent.). Church of St. André (13th–14th cent., with tomb of Bayard), and Renaissance palace of dauphins. Birthplace of Stendhal. Grande CHARTREUSE is nearby.

Grenville, George, 1712–70, British prime minister (1763–65). Initiated unpopular prosecution of John Wilkes and caused unrest in America by ill-advised STAMP ACT (1765). His son, **George Nugent Temple Grenville, 1st marquess of Buckingham,** 1753–1813, Whig member of Parliament (1774–79), opposed Lord North's policy of coercion of the American colonies. His brother, **William Wyndham Grenville, Baron Grenville,** 1759–1834, was William Pitt's foreign secretary 1791–1801. In 1806 he formed the "ministry of all the talents" which abolished the slave trade.

Grenville, Sir Richard, 1542?–1591, English naval hero. Commanded fleet carrying first colonists to ROANOKE ISLAND in 1585. On an expedition to capture Spanish treasure ships in 1591, his ship *Revenge* became separated from the rest of the fleet. He tried to break through the Spanish line, fought 15 ships, and was mortally wounded.

Grenville, William Wyndham Grenville, Baron: see GRENVILLE, GEORGE.

Gresham's law (grĕ'shŭmz), economic principle that "bad money drives out good," i.e., when debased money is in concurrent circulation with money of high value in terms of precious metals, the good money disappears. Named for Sir Thomas Gresham (1519?–1579), English merchant and financier.

Gretna, city (pop. 21,967), SE La., suburb S of New Orleans on Mississippi R.; founded early 19th cent.

Gretna Green or Gretna, village, Dumfriesshire, Scotland, on English border. Famous as a place of runaway marriages 1754–1856.

Grétry, André Ernest (ädrä' ĕrnĕst' grätrē'), 1741–1813, French composer, master of the *opéra comique*. His masterpiece is *Richard Cœur-de-Lion.*

Greuze, Jean Baptiste (zhä' bäptēst' grŭz'), 1725–1805, French genre and portrait painter. Sentimental and moralistic works; praised by Diderot.

Greville, Fulke: see BROOKE, FULKE GREVILLE, 1ST BARON.

Grévy, Jules (zhül grävē'), 1807–91, president of France (1879–87); a moderate republican.

Grew, Joseph C(lark), 1880–1965, American diplomat. U.S. ambassador to Japan from 1932 until Pearl Harbor. he was earlier ambassador to Turkey (1927–32) and twice served as Undersecretary of State (1924–27, 1944–45).

Grew, Nehemiah, 1641–1712, English botanist, physician. He practiced medicine in London and made important microscopic studies of plants. His observations of sex in plants were probably the first.

Grey, Charles Grey, 2d Earl, 1764–1845, British prime minister (1830–34). Put through Wilberforce's act to abolish African slave trade (1807). Secured passage of Reform Bill of 1832 by forcing William IV to threaten to create enough Whig peers to carry it in the House of Lords. His grandson, **Albert Henry George Grey, 4th Earl Grey,** 1851–1917, English statesman, was liberal member, House of Commons (1880–86); opposed Home Rule Bill of 1886. Governor general of Canada (1904–11).

Grey, Lady Jane, 1537–54, candidate for the throne of England; greatniece of Henry VIII. Married to the son of duke of Northumberland who persuaded Edward VI to name her as his successor. Unwillingly proclaimed queen (1553), she was imprisoned after nine days and Mary I became queen. Her father joined Wyatt's rebellion and she was beheaded.

Grey, Zane, 1875–1939, American writer of many Wild West tales (e.g., *Riders of the Purple Sage,* 1912).

Greylock, Mount: see BERKSHIRE HILLS.

Grey of Fallodon, Edward Grey, 1st Viscount (fǎ'-lōdŭn), 1862–1933, British statesman. Foreign secretary (1905–16), he worked long but fruitlessly to avert war in Europe.

Griboyedov, Aleksandr Sergeyevich (ŭlyĭksän'dŭr sĭrgā'uvĭch grĕbŭyĕ'dŭf), 1795–1829, Russian playwright, author of *The Misfortune of Being Clever* (1825; Eng. tr., 1914), a satire on Moscow society.

Gridley, Charles Vernon, 1844–98, U.S. naval officer. To him Adm. Dewey said, "You may fire when you are ready, Gridley," at Manila in 1898.

Grieg, Edvard (ĕd'vär grēg'), 1843–1907, Norwegian composer. He often used Norwegian folk themes in his music. Apart from the Piano Concerto in A Minor, his most successful work was in the small forms—songs and piano and chamber music. His suites for Ibsen's *Peer Gynt* are very popular.

Grien, Hans Baldung: see BALDUNG, HANS.

Grierson, Sir George Abraham, 1851–1941, Irish philologist. He directed compilation of the great *Linguistic Survey of India* (19 vols., 1894–1927).

Griffenfeld, Peder Schumacher, Count (pā'dhŭr shōō'mäkhŭr, grĭ'fŭnfĕlt), 1635–99, Danish statesman; created count 1673. Secretary to Frederick III, 1665–70; chief minister to Christian V, 1671–76. Introduced absolute monarchy; centralized administration; promoted trade, industry, peace. Opposition of nobles and army led to his fall and trial on trumped-up treason charges. Death sentence was commuted to life imprisonment.

Griffes, Charles Tomlinson (grĭ'fĭs), 1884–1920, American composer. His best-known works combine elements of romanticism and impressionism (e.g., *The Pleasure Dome of Kubla Khan* and *The White Peacock*).

Griffin, Eugene, 1855–1907, American electrical engineer. Made first extensive investigation (1886–88) of use of electricity in U.S.; was instrumental in developing streetcar system.

Griffin, city (pop. 21,735). W central Ga., SSE of Atlanta, in farm and cotton area; laid out 1840.

griffin, in anc. and medieval mythology, animal represented as a cross between lion and eagle. Conspicuous in Assyrian and Persian sculpture. In heraldry it symbolizes vigilance. Origin traced to Hittites.

Griffith, Arthur, 1872–1922, Irish statesman, founder of SINN FEIN. Served cause by propaganda in his newspapers. Commanded revolution in De Valera's absence. First president (1922) of Free State.

Griffith, David Wark, 1880–1948, American film director and producer. Began (1908) association with Biograph Company as scenarist and actor, then as director. Evolved many film techniques (e.g., cross-cutting, flashback, fade-in, fade-out, close-up, juxtaposition). His experiments were summed up in first notable long American film, *Birth of a Nation* (1915). His films include *Intolerance, Broken Blossoms, Orphans of the Storm,* and *Way Down East.*

Griffith, residential town (1964 pop. 12,810), extreme NW Ind., SW of Gary; settled c.1891.

Grignard, Victor (vĕktôr' grēnyär'), 1871–1935, French chemist. Shared 1912 Nobel Prize in Chemistry for discovery of **Grignard reagent,** halogen compound used with other substances to synthesize a wide variety of organic compounds.

Grijalva, Juan de (hwän' dā grēhäl'vä), d. 1527, Spanish explorer. Led expedition to Yucatan (1518).

Grillparzer, Franz (fränts' grĭl'pärtsŭr), 1791–1872, Austrian dramatist. His plays, notable for power and poetic beauty, include *Der Traum: ein Leben* (1817–34); *Des Meeres und der Liebe Wellen* (1831); the posthumous *Die Jüdin von Toledo.*

Grimaldi, Francesco Maria (fränchä'skō märē'ä grēmäldē), 1618–1663, Italian physicist. First to describe DIFFRACTION and wave theory of light. Also studied and named dark areas on the moon.

Grimaldi, Giovanni Francesco (jōvän'nē fränchä'skō grēmäl'dē), 1606–80, Italian painter and architect, called Il Bolognese.

Grimaldi, Joseph (grĭmäl'dē), 1779–1837, English pantomime actor and clown. A master of grimace and of stagecraft, he was so popular that his songs were demanded long after his death.

Grimké, Angelina Emily (grĭm'kē), 1805–79, American abolitionist and feminist, b. Charleston, S.C. She and her sister, **Sarah Moore Grimké,** 1792–1873, settled in North and worked for freedom of slaves and woman's rights. Their nephew, **Archibald Henry Grimké,** 1849–1930, son of slave mother, was a lawyer, author, and crusader for Negro advancement.

Grimm, Friedrich Melchior, Baron (frē'drĭkh mĕl'khēŏr grĭm'), 1723–1807, French author, b. Germany. His *Correspondance littéraire* (1st complete ed., 1829–30) was a private newsletter service which throws a unique light on intellectual life of 18th-cent. Paris. He was a friend of Diderot.

Grimm, Jakob (yä'kôp), 1785–1863, German philologist; a founder of comparative philology. His chief contributions were formulation of GRIMM'S LAW; German grammar (1819–37); *German Mythology* (1835; Eng. tr., 1880–88). With his brother **Wilhelm Grimm** (vĭl'hĕlm), 1786–1859, he collected and published German folktales, world-famous as *Grimm's Fairy Tales* (1812–15).

Grimmelshausen, Hans Jakob Christoffel von (häns' yä'kôp krĭs'tôful fün grĭ'mŭlshou"zŭn), 1625?–1676, German author. His satirical *The Adventuresome Simplicius Simplicissimus* (1669) is a picaresque, partly autobiographical novel of the Thirty Years War.

Grimm's law, principle of relationships in Indo-European languages, first observed by Jakob Grimm in 1822. It shows that a process—the regular shifting of consonants in groups—took place early in the development of the Germanic languages and subsequently repeated itself in the High German languages. Grimm's law shows that Indo-European voiceless stops (k, t, p) became voiceless spirants (h, th, f) in Germanic and mediae (h. d. f) in High German; that unaspirated voiced stops (g, d. b) became voiceless stops in Germanic and then voiceless spirants in High German; and that aspirated voiced stops (gh, dh, bh) became unaspirated voiced stops in Germanic and voiceless stops in High German.

Grimsby, county borough (pop. 96,665), Lincolnshire, England, at mouth of Humber R.; largest fishing port in Great Britain. Has over 100 acres of docks.

Grindelwald (grĭn'dŭlvält), resort in Bernese Alps, Switzerland, at foot of the Eiger. Celebrated for grandeur of scenery.

Grinnell, Josiah Bushnell, 1821–91, American pioneer, clergyman, and abolitionist. Lost pastorate in Washington, D.C., after antislavery sermon. Went West following Horace Greeley's advice to him, "Go West, young man, go West!" Founded Grinnell, Iowa.

Grinnell College, at Grinnell, Iowa, near Des Moines; coed.; inc. 1847 as Iowa Col., opened 1848 by Congregationalists at Davenport. Moved 1859, merged with Grinnell Univ. (1856; founded by J. B. Grinnell), named 1909.

Griqualand: see TRANSKEIAN TERRITORIES.

Gris, Juan (hwän' grēs'), 1887–1927, Spanish cubist painter. Settled in Paris 1906. Produced mostly still lifes in oil and collage.

Griselda (grĭzĕl'dŭ), in medieval story, heroine who patiently endures many trials imposed by her husband to test her devotion.

Gris-Nez, Cape (grē-nā'), cliff near Calais, N France, projecting into Strait of Dover, 21 mi. from English coast. Lighthouse.

Grisons (grēsōnz', Fr. grēsō'), Ger. *Graubünden,* canton (2,747 sq. mi.; pop. 147,458), E Switzerland; cap.

Chur. Largest but least populated of Swiss cantons. Pastures, forests, hydroelectric stations; some agr. in valleys. ENGADINE valley and other resorts attract many tourists. German, Romansh (a Rhaetic dialect), and Italian are official languages. Part of ancient Rhaetia, region passed to Ostrogoths 493, to Franks 537. Bishops of Chur exercised considerable temporal power after 9th cent., but their control was broken after 1367 by three local leagues of towns; the Gray League gave the canton its name. Joining Swiss Confederation as allies, the leagues conquered Valtellina from Milan in 1512 (lost 1797). In the Thirty Years War the country was torn by civil war between Protestants and Catholics and by French and Spanish intervention. Forced by Napoleon to enter the Helvetic Republic (1799), Grisons became a Swiss canton (1803) after Napoleon's mediation.

gristle: see CARTILAGE.

Griswold, A(lfred) Whitney, 1906–63, American educator. A teacher of history at Yale from 1933, he served as its president 1950–63.

Griswold, town (pop. 5,728), SE Conn., NE of Norwich. Includes Jewett City borough (pop. 3,702; textiles).

Grodno (grôd′nô), city (1965 est. pop. 99,000), Belorussia, on the Niemen. Mfg. of agr. machinery, textiles, tobacco. Seat of Polish diets 1673–1793. Passed to Russia 1795, to Poland 1920, to USSR 1939.

Grofé, Ferde (grōfā′), 1892–, American composer and conductor. Used jazz idiom in his larger symphonic works; *Grand Canyon Suite* and *Mississippi Suite* are perhaps best known.

Grolier de Servières, Jean, vicomte d'Aguisy (grōl′yür, Fr. grôlyā′), 1479–1565, French collector of fine books.

Gromyko, Andrei Andreyevich (ündrā′ ündrā′üvĭch grümĭ′kŭ), 1909–, Russian diplomat. Soviet ambassador at Washington 1943–46, chief permanent delegate to UN 1946–48, chief deputy foreign minister 1949–52 and 1953–57, ambassador to England 1952–53, foreign minister 1957–.

Grongar Hill, Caermarthenshire, Wales. It is celebrated in a poem by John Dyer.

Groningen (khrō′nĭng-ün), province (898 sq. mi.; pop. 497,472), N Netherlands, on North Sea coast. Cattle raising, dairying, agr. Vast natural gas reserves discovered here in 1961. History is that of its cap., the municipality of **Groningen** (pop. 152,513), an agr.-trading center. Nominally under bishops of Utrecht from 11th cent., city joined Hanseatic League 1284; gained control over central Friesland (i.e., modern Groningen prov.); joined United Provs. 1579. University was founded 1614.

Groote, Gerard or **Geert** (khā′rärt, khärt′, khrō′tü), 1340–84, Dutch Roman Catholic reformer. A Carthusian deacon, he preached in Netherlands, founded Brothers of the Common Life (later joined with Augustinian canons), urged monastic reform. *The Following of Christ* is attributed to him by some.

Groote Eylandt (grōōt ī′lünd), area 950 sq. mi., off N Australia, largest island in Gulf of Carpentaria. Aboriginal reservation.

Gropius, Walter (väl′tür grō′pēōōs), 1883–, German architect, one of leaders of modern "functional" architecture. Headed the famous BAUHAUS, 1919–28. Set of buildings he designed for it at Dessau in 1926 is one of his finest achievements. Worked in London 1934–37; came to U.S. 1937 (at Harvard until 1953).

Gropper, William, 1897–, American painter. Contributed radical cartoons to periodicals, notably the *New Masses*. Won recognition as a painter when he first exhibited his oils in 1936.

Gros, Antoine Jean, Baron (ätwän′ zhä′, bärō′ grō), 1771–1835, French painter. A classicist, he studied with David and was important in the Napoleonic era.

grosbeak (grōs′bĕk), name used (generally in combination) for various birds, especially of finch family. They have large, conical bills and bright summer plumage, and are 8–9 in. long. Rose-breasted grosbeak, pine grosbeak, western or black-headed grosbeak, and common European grosbeak (hawfinch) are well known.

Groseilliers, Médard Chouart, sieur des (mädär′ shwär′ syür dü grôsāyā′), 1618?–c.1690, French trader and explorer in North America. Brother-in-law of Pierre E. RADISSON; his companion on journeys.

Gros Morne (grō′ môrn′), mountain, 2,651 ft. high, W N.F., Canada, in Long Range. Highest point in Newfoundland.

Gross, Chaim (khīm′ grōs′), 1904–, American sculptor, b. Galicia, now in Ukraine; to U.S. 1921. Noted for realistic carved wood figures.

Gross, Samuel David, 1805–84, American surgeon, influential as teacher and writer. He invented surgical instruments and techniques.

Grosse, Aristid V. (grō′sü), 1905–, American chemist, b. Russia. A professor at Univ. of Chicago, he worked on "Manhattan District" atomic bomb research 1940–43. Also noted for work on synthetic rubber and radioactivity.

Grosse Point (grōs′ point′), city (pop. 6,631), SE Mich., suburb NE of Detroit, on L. St. Clair. Nearby is the residential city of **Grosse Pointe Farms** (pop. 12,172). Branch of Detroit Inst. of Arts is here. Also near are villages of **Grosse Pointe Park** (pop. 15,457) and **Grosse Pointe Shores** (pop. 2,301) and the residential city of **Grosse Pointe Woods** (pop. 18,580).

Grosseteste, Robert (grōs′tĕst), c.1175–1253, English prelate; chief founder of Oxford Franciscan school. As bishop of Lincoln after 1235, he fought efforts of HENRY III to control appointments and supported reforms of Simon de Montfort; upheld the papal prerogative but censured INNOCENT IV for exactions. His studies of Aristotle were the basis for scholastic thought of THOMAS AQUINAS. Very learned, he wrote hundreds of works.

Grosseto (grōs-sā′tō), town (pop. 51,004), in Tuscany, central Italy; agr. center in reclaimed MAREMMA area.

Grossglockner (grōs′glôknür), highest peak of Austria, 12,530 ft. high, in the Hohe Tauern. First ascended 1800. The Grossglocknerstrasse, a highway rising to 7,770 ft., now crosses near peak.

Grossgörschen: see LÜTZEN.

Grosswardein, Rumania: see ORADEA.

Grosvenor Square (grōv′nür), fashionable residential square, W London. Site of American Embassy. Statue of F. D. Roosevelt erected here 1949.

Gros Ventre Indians (grō vä′trü) [Fr.,= big belly], name for two quite distinct North American Indian tribes. One was the Atsina, a detached band of the Arapaho, of Algonquian linguistic family. The other was the Hidatsa Indians, of Hokan-Siouan stock.

Grosz, George (grōs), 1893–1959, German artist, famed for bitter social satire of post-First World War drawings. Associated with Dada and the new objectivity. In 1933 he came to the U.S., where he painted landscapes, nudes, and symbolic war pictures (during Second World War).

Grote, George, 1794–1871, English historian of ancient Greece. His *History of Greece* (12 vols., 1846–56) is a classic of historical writing.

Grotefend, Georg Friedrich (gā′ôrk frē′drĭkh grō′tüfĕnt), 1775–1853, German archaeologist and philologist. Deciphered cuneiform inscriptions of Persia.

Grotius, Hugo (grō′shüs), 1583–1645, Dutch jurist, author of *De jure belli ac pacis* (1625) [concerning the law of war and peace]. The book is on natural law and is generally considered the first definitive text on international law.

Groton (grō′tün). 1 Town (pop. 29,937), SE Conn., on Thames R. opposite New London; settled c. 1650. Site of Fort Griswold (1775), taken by British 1781. Ship and submarine building. U.S. naval submarine base and U.S. Coast Guard training school are nearby. Silas Deane born here. Includes Groton borough (pop. 10,111) and villages of Conning Towers (pop. 3,457), Noank (nō′ängk) (pop. 1,116), and West

Mystic (pop. 3,268). **2** Town (pop. 3,904), N Mass., NW of Boston; settled 1655. Destroyed in King Philip's War. Seat of Groton School and Lawrence Academy.

Grouchy, Emmanuel, marquis de (ĕmänüĕl' märkē' dù grōōshē'), 1766–1847, marshal of France. Was largely responsible for Napoleon's disaster in WATERLOO CAMPAIGN through his failure to prevent the Prussians from joining the English.

ground bass (bās), short musical phrase constantly reiterated in the bass of a composition, with variations in the upper parts. Popular during baroque era; used by Purcell, Bach, and Buxtehude. Upper parts were either written out by the composer (most passacaglias and chaconnes) or were improvised by the player (English baroque "divisions upon a ground").

ground hog: see WOODCHUCK.

ground ivy, creeping perennial plant (*Glechoma hederacea*), also called gill-over-the-ground, now naturalized in North America. It has small purple flowers and rounded leaves.

ground pine: see CLUB MOSS; *ill.,* p. 859.

groundsel, common name for large, varied, widely distributed plant genus *Senecio* of daisy family. Includes such plants as golden groundsel, purple ragwort, CINERARIA, dusty miller, and german ivy. Groundsel bush (*Baccharis halimifolia*) native to U.S. coastal regions, has downy white seed heads.

ground squirrel, rodent of squirrel family. The name is used chiefly for those of genus *Citellus* (or *Spermophilus*) of North America, Europe, and Asia, and also for the African ground squirrel *Xerus,* and for the chipmunk.

grouper, carnivorous BASS of warm seas, useful as food fish. Most can change colorful markings to match background. Numerous species include coney, jewfish, and commercially important red and black groupers.

Group Theatre, organization formed 1931 in N.Y. city by Harold Clurman, Cheryl Crawford, and Lee Strasberg to present contemporary plays of social significance. At its height 1935–37, disbanded 1941.

grouse (grous), game bird of colder parts of N Hemisphere (c.25 species). It is henlike and terrestrial, and has red, brown, and gray plumage. American grouse include eastern ruffed grouse (called also partridge or pheasant), prairie chicken, SAGE GROUSE, and PTARMIGAN.

Grove, Sir George, 1820–1900, English musicographer, whose *Dictionary of Music and Musicians* (1879–89) is a standard reference work. First director of the Royal Col. of Music, 1883–94.

Grove, Robert Moses (Lefty Grove), 1900–, American baseball pitcher. In 1931 he won 31, lost 4, equaled American League record of 16 consecutive victories. In 17 years in major leagues, he won 300, lost 141, struck out more than 2,000 batters.

Groves, city (pop. 17,304), SE Texas, suburb N of Port Arthur.

Grozny (grôz'nē), city (1965 est. pop. 314,000), cap. of CHECHEN-INGUSH AUTONOMOUS SSR, RSFSR, at the foot of Greater Caucasus. It is the center of oil field, linked by pipe lines with Caspian, Black Sea, Donets Basin. Major German objective in Second World War, but Germans were stopped c.50 mi. to W (1942).

Grub Street, in London, since 1830 named Milton St. Once famous as home of poor authors, it was used as symbol of hack work by Dr. Johnson and others.

Gruenther, Alfred M(aximilian), 1899–, U.S. general, NATO chief of staff (1951–53), supreme commander of Allied forces in Europe (1953–56). Retired from active duty 1956. President of American Red Cross (1957–).

Grün, Hans Baldung: see BALDUNG, HANS.

Grundtvig, Nikolai Frederik Severin, 1783–1872, Danish writer and educator, founder of the Danish folk school.

Grünewald, Mathias (mätē'äs grü'nüvält), c.1480–1528, German religious painter. Famous for *Isen-*

heim Altarpiece (Colmar) which portrays passion of Christ with dramatic realism.

Grünwald, battle of, 1410: see TANNENBERG.

Grütli, Switzerland: see RÜTLI.

Gruyère (grüyĕr'), Ger. *Greierz,* area in Fribourg canton, Switzerland. Known for its cattle and for Gruyère cheese.

Guadalajara (gwä"dhälähä'rä), city (1965 est. pop. 1,048,351), cap. of Jalisco, W Mexico, second largest city of Mexico; modern commercial city with picturesque survivals of colonial period. Permanently settled 1542, it was later seat of *audiencia* of Nueva Galicia and center of reformists in war against Spain (1810–21) and War of Reform (1858–61). Famous for handmade glass and pottery.

Guadalajara, city (pop. 21,230), cap. of Guadalajara prov., central Spain, in New Castile, on Henares R. Nearby is battlefield where Loyalists defeated Insurgents, mostly Italian "volunteers," March, 1937.

Guadalcanal (gwä"dhälkŭnäl'), volcanic island (c.2,510 sq. mi.; pop. 2,760), S Pacific, largest of Solomon Isls. Mountains rise to c.8,000 ft. Scene of first U.S. large-scale invasion of a Japanese-held island (1942–43).

Guadalquivir (gwä"dhälkēvēr'), river, c.350 mi. long, S Spain, in Andalusia, flowing from Sierra de Cazorla SW through fertile region, past Córdoba and Seville (head of navigation), into Atlantic.

Guadalupe (Span. gwädhälōō'pä), village, W central Spain, in Estremadura. Noted for shrine of Our Lady of Guadalupe, whose cult was transferred (16th cent.) to Guadalupe Hidalgo, Mexico.

Guadalupe Hidalgo (gwädhälōō'pä ēdäl'go), shrine, central Mexico, suburb of Mexico city; one of principal shrines in Christendom. In 1531, an Indian, Juan Diego, had vision of Virgin at place renamed Guadalupe in honor of shrine in Spain; Hidalgo was added in 1810 to honor revolutionary priest, Hidalgo y Costilla. **Treaty of Guadalupe Hidalgo,** signed and ratified in 1848, ended Mexican War. In it Mexico recognized Texas as U.S. possession and ceded most of present SW U.S.; U.S. agreed to pay Mexico $15,000,000 and assumed American claims against Mexico.

Guadalupe Mountains (gwä'dùlōōp), SE N.Mex. and W Texas. In Texas are El Capitan (8,078 ft.) and Guadalupe Peak (8,751 ft.), state's highest point, W of which are salt lakes and flats.

Guadalupe Victoria (gwädhälōō'pä vēktōr'yä), 1786?–1843, Mexican general, president of Mexico (1824–29). Active in revolution against Spain from 1811, he adopted the name of the revolutionary standard (his real name, Manuel Félix Fernández).

Guadarrama, Sierra de (sē̄'rä dä gwädhärä'mä), mountain range, central Spain, N of Madrid, culminating in Peñalara peak (7,972 ft.).

Guadeloupe (gŏdùlōōp', gwä–), overseas department of the French Republic (657 sq. mi.; pop. 295,000), in Leeward Isls., West Indies; cap. BASSE-TERRE. Discovered by Columbus, 1493, it was abandoned by Spain 1604. French settled it 1635, but English contended for its ownership until 1815.

Guadiana (gwädhyä'nä), river, c.500 mi. long, central Spain and S Portugal. Flows W past Ciudad Real and Badajoz, then S, forming Spanish-Portuguese border till it empties in Gulf of Cádiz.

Guaira, La (lä gwī'rä), town (pop. c.20,000), N Venezuela, port on Caribbean.

Guam (gwäm), island (209 sq. mi.; pop. 67,044), W Pacific, unincorporated territory of U.S.; largest, most populous, and southernmost of MARIANAS ISLANDS. AGNA is seat of government. Discovered 1521 by Magellan, belonged to Spain until taken by U.S. 1898. Under Dept. of Navy until 1950. Fell to Japanese Dec. 9, 1941; regained by U.S. July, 1944, and became major air and naval base. By Organic Act of 1950 natives became American citizens and Guam came under administration of Dept. of Interior. Port of call for sea and air lines. Economy flourished after recovery from typhoon of 1962. Base of U.S. operations in Vietnam conflict in mid-1960s.

Guanabara, state (452 sq. mi.; pop. c.3,307,200), SE Brazil; cap. Rio de Janeiro. Formerly the Federal Dist.; it is mfg. area.

guanaco (gwänä′kō) or **huanaco** (hwänä′kō), wild South American mammal (genus *Lama*) of camel family of Andes. Llama and alpaca were probably domesticated from it. Its shoulder height is c.3½ ft. and it has a dark face, brown back and sides, and light under parts. Indians use its flesh, hide, bones.

Guanajuato (gwänähwä′tō), state (11,805 sq. mi.; pop. 1,883,297; average alt. c.6,000 ft.), central Mexico, on central plateau. Leading mining state of Mexico, it produces silver, gold, mercury, lead, tin, copper, opals. Principal cities are Celaya (pop. c.34.500), LEÓN, Irapuato (pop. c.35,000), Guanajuato (cap.; pop. c.25,000).

guano (gwä′nō), fertilizer of dried excrement of sea birds collected from equatorial coasts, especially Peru. Once important in manufacture of gunpowder and fertilizer; now replaced by synthetic chemicals.

Guantánamo (gwäntä′nämō), city (pop. c.125,000), SE Cuba. Large sugar center on Guantánamo Bay (with U.S. naval station).

Guaraní Indians (gwäränē′), people of Andean-Equatorial linguistic stock in S Brazil and Paraguay. Lived in patrilineal communities, practiced seminomadic agr. Called Tupí in Brazil.

Guardi, Francesco (fränchä′skō gwär′dē), 1712–93, Venetian landscape painter. Developed more brilliant style than that of his master Canaletto.

Guardia, Tomás (tōmäs′ gwär′dēä), 1832–82, president of Costa Rica almost continuously from 1870. Through repressive military dictatorship, he laid a foundation of political stability.

guardian and ward. Guardianship is the relation in which a ward—an infant, insane person, or spendthrift—and (in most cases) his property are placed under the management and control of a guardian. Generally the guardian is appointed by the court; in some countries appointed by one of the parents (in others by the father only). Prudent management of the ward's property is the duty of the guardian.

Guareschi, Giovanni (jōvän′nē gwärēs′kē), 1908–, Italian journalist and novelist. Best known as author of *The Little World of Don Camillo* (Eng. tr., 1950).

Guarini, Giovanni Battista (jōvän′nē bät-tē′stä gwärē′nē), 1537–1612, Italian poet, author of the pastoral drama *Pastor Fido* (1590), rival of Tasso.

Guarini, Guarino (gwärē′nō gwärē′nē), 1624–83, Italian architect, mathematician, and writer. His Sindone Chapel and Church of San Lorenzo, both in Turin, are major monuments of baroque architecture.

Guarneri (gwärnä′rē) or **Guarnerius**, family of violin-makers of Cremona, Italy, beginning with **Andrea Guarneri** (ändrā′ä), c.1626–1698, a pupil of Niccolò Amati. His grandnephew, **Giuseppi Guarneri** (jōōzĕp′pä), 1687?–1745, called "del Gesù" because he signed his labels with a cross and the letters IHS, was the greatest craftsman of the family.

Guastalla (gwästäl′lä), town (est. pop. 13.760) and former duchy, Emilia-Romagna, N Italy. Bought by Gonzaga family 1539; duchy from 1621; passed to Parma 1748. Napoleon I gave it to his sister Pauline (1806); it reverted to Parma on his downfall.

Guatemala (gwätämä′lä), republic (42,042 sq. mi.; pop. 4,278.341). Central America, just S of Mexico. most populous of Central American countries; cap. GUATEMALA. Tropic areas on Pacific and Caribbean coasts and jungles of Petén yield produce, but cool highlands from border of Mexico to borders of Salvador and Honduras have most of the population. Except in urban areas—notably Guatemala and Quezaltenango—the Indian patterns of life persist. The chief ports are San José and Puerto Barrios; chief exports are bananas and coffee. Near W coast is a chain of volcanoes. The Maya-Quiché had a notable civilization be-

fore the Spanish conquest under Pedro de Alvarado. The first capital was Ciudad Vieja, the second Antigua, the third Guatemala. Though a captaincy general, it was of little importance in the Spanish Empire. Gained independence in 1821 and was briefly part of Iturbide's Mexican Empire. Guatemala was the nucleus of the Central American Federation (1825–38) and since that time, under such leaders as Rafael Carrero, Manuel Estrada Cabrera, and Justo Rufino Barrios, has tried to gain hegemony in Central America. Border disputes have been numerous. In Second World War Guatemala declared war against Axis countries (1941); became member of UN 1945. After the war the government tended to be leftist in character until in 1954 Carlos Castillo Armas, with a revolutionary force. entered the country from Honduras and overthrew the government of Jacobo Arbenz Guzmán. Castillo Armas was assassinated 1957. Miguel Ydígoras Fuentes, president after 1958. initiated reforms and showed friendship to U.S. He was overthrown 1963 by the military, who ruled until 1966 when Julio César Méndez Montenegro, a reformer, was elected president. Despite new president's plea for end to civil strife, terrorism continued.

Guatemala, city (pop. 572,937). S central Guatemala, cap. and largest city of republic, in highland valley. Founded 1776 as cap. after Antigua was abandoned; rebuilt after destruction by earthquake (1917–18).

Guatémoc: see CUAUHTÉMOC.

guava (gwä′vü), small tree (*Psidium*) native to tropical America, and its fruit, a fleshy berry with many hard seeds. Guava jelly is made from the fruit. Both strawberry guava (*Psidium littorale*) with round red fruit, and common guava (*P. guajava*) are grown in Fla. and Calif.

Guayaquil (gwīūkēl′), city (pop. 506,037). W Ecuador, on Guayas R.; Pacific port and largest city of Ecuador; founded by Benalcázar 1535. Historic meeting between Bolívar and San Martín occurred here 1822.

Guaymas (gwī′mäs), city (pop. 18,890), Sonora, NW Mexico, a port on Gulf of California; a popular resort for gulf fishing. Exports agr. and fish products of area.

Gubbio (gōōb′byō), town (est. pop. 35,200), Umbria, central Italy. Anc. town of Umbrians (IGUVINE TABLES found here). Flourished in Middle Ages, first as free commune, later under dukes of Urbino. Fine ceramics made here in 16th cent. City retains much medieval architecture.

Gudbrandsdal (gōōd′bränsdäl″), valley, central Norway, extending from Mjosa L. NW to Dovrefjell. Rich agr. and timber district; horse breeding. Many valley farmers trace ancestry to saga times; population preserves own dialect, customs.

Guden (gōō′dün), Dan. *Gudenaa,* river, 98 mi. long, Jutland, Denmark. Only important Danish river; partly navigable. Flows N and NE to the Kattegat.

Gudmundsson, Kristmann, 1902–, Icelandic novelist. His romantic stories are in Norwegian and in Icelandic. Works include *The Bridal Gown* (1931) and *Winged Citadel* (1940).

Gudrun or **Kudrun**, name of principal female character of the Icelandic *Laxdaelasaga*, a stalwart heroine; also of a character in the *Volsungasaga* (corresponding to Kriemhild in the *Nibelungenlied*).

Guelderland or **Guelders,** Netherlands: see GELDERLAND.

Guelph (gwĕlf), city (pop. 33,860), S Ont., Canada, on Speed R. and NW of Hamilton; founded 1827 by John Galt. Has knitting and paper mills, meat packing, woodworking and varied mfg. in center of rich farm area. Site of Ontario Agr. Col.

Guelphs (gwĕlfs), European dynasty, tracing descent from Guelph I or Welf I (9th cent.), father-in-law of Emperor Louis I. Guelph d'Este IV (d. 1101), duke of Carinthia from 1055 and duke of Bavaria from 1070, was common ancestor of Italian house of ESTE and of the German Guelphs, who ruled Bavaria and Saxony to 1180 (see HENRY THE PROUD; HENRY THE LION). In feud with house of HOHENSTAUFEN, German Guelphs lost all but the duchy of BRUNSWICK. The line of Brunswick-Lüneburg or HANOVER ascended the British throne in the person of George I (1714). Because of Salic law of succession, Hanover was separated from British crown when Victoria became queen of England (1837). After the deposition of GEORGE V of Hanover (1866), the so-called Guelphic party sought to restore the kingdom, but with no success.

Guelphs and Ghibellines (gǐ'bŭlĕnz, –lĭnz), opposing political factions in later Middle Ages. They originated 12th cent. in the rivalry between the German Guelphs or Welfs and the Hohenstaufen emperors. (See HENRY THE PROUD; HENRY THE LION.) The name Ghibelline probably derives from the Hohenstaufen castle of Waiblingen. The struggle continued in Italy, where the Guelphs at first were the papal party in the struggle between emperors and popes. The Guelphs included many important cities (e.g., LOMBARD LEAGUE, Bologna, Florence, Genoa) and the Angevin kings of Naples. The Ghibellines included several noble families and petty tyrants, such as Ezzelino da Romano, the Della Scala of Verona, the Visconti of Milan, and several cities (e.g., Pisa, Arezzo). The cities themselves were often divided, and bloody strife resulted. The party names soon lost their original connotations, and local feuds disturbed party alignments—as in Florence, where the Guelphs split into Blacks and Whites. The names fell into disuse by the 15th cent.

Guercino (gwĕrchē'nō), 1591–1666, Italian eclectic painter; real name was Giovanni Francesco Barbieri. Work shows influence of Caravaggio and Guido.

Guericke, Otto von (ô'tō fŭn gā'rĭkŭ), 1602–86, German physicist. Made first air pump; devised Magdeburg hemispheres for demonstrating air pressure.

Guérin, Pierre Narcisse, Baron, 1774–1833, French painter, exponent of the classicism of David.

Guernica (gĕrnē'kä), historic town, Vizcaya prov., N Spain. Oak of Guernica, former meeting place of Vizcayan diet, symbolizes lost liberties of Basques. In 1937 German planes, in aid of Insurgent forces, bombed the defenseless town. The action, which provoked widespread indignation, inspired Picasso's famous painting.

Guernsey, one of the CHANNEL ISLANDS.

Guernsey cattle: see CATTLE.

Guerra Junqueiro, Abílio (äbē'lyō gĕ'rŭ zhōŏnkä'rō), 1850–1923, Portuguese poet, author of violent satiric poems and also of touching lyrics.

Guerrero (gĕrā'rō) [for Vicente Guerrero, revolutionary leader], state (24,887 sq. mi.; pop. 1,283,119), SW Mexico, on Pacific; cap. Chilpancingo (pop. c.13,000). Extremely mountainous except for narrow coastal strip around ACAPULCO. Silver works at TAXCO are famous. Prominent in war against Spain (1810–21), it was not a state until 1849.

Guerrière: see CONSTITUTION, ship.

guerrilla warfare [Span.,= little war], fighting by other than regularly organized military forces in areas occupied by enemy. Called the contribution of American Revolution to warfare. French guerrillas (called *francs-tireurs*) important in Franco-Prussian War. Theories of guerrilla warfare were perfected in China by Mao Tse-tung in 1920s and, as applied by underground forces, were highly effective in defeat of Germany in Second World War. In postwar years used extensively in conflicts in such countries as Malaya, Cypress, Cuba, and Vietnam.

Guesclin, Bertrand du: see DU GUESCLIN, BERTRAND.

Guesde, Jules, 1845–1922, French socialist whose real name was Basile. Largely responsible for formation (1905) of strongly Marxist French socialist party.

Guess, George: see SEQUOYAH.

Guest, Lady Charlotte (Bertie), 1812–95, English author, translator of MABINOGION.

Gueux (gû) [Fr.,= beggars], nickname given to the Dutch and Flemish noblemen and burghers (both Protestant and Catholic) who in 1566 signed a petition protesting against Spanish encroachments on their traditional liberties. The petition was a toned-down version

of the Compromise of Breda (1566), which pledged the signers to resist Spanish oppression. The nickname was taken up by the patriots in the ensuing struggle. Patriotic privateers chartered in 1569 by William the Silent were called Beggars of the Sea; their chief success was the raising of the siege of LEIDEN (1574).

Guevara, Antonio de (äntō'nyō dā gāvä'rä), 1480?–1545, Spanish novelist, author of didactic *Libro llamado Relox de príncipes* (1529).

Guevara, Ernest (gāvä'rä), 1928–. Cuban revolutionary and political leader. b. Argentina. Fidel Castro's chief lieutenant and director of economic policy until spring of 1965 when he dropped from public view.

Guevara, Luis Vélez de: see VÉLEZ DE GUEVARA.

Guggenheim (gōō'gŭnhīm), family of American industrialists and philanthropists. **Meyer Guggenheim,** 1828–1905. b. Switzerland, made fortune from metal smelting and refining. His son, **Daniel Guggenheim,** 1856–1930, was largely responsible for combining Guggenheim interests with the American Smelting and Refining Co. in 1901. The Daniel and Florence Guggenheim Foundation is his principal philanthropy. His brother, **Simon Guggenheim,** 1867–1941, estab. (1925), with his wife, the John Simon Guggenheim Memorial Foundation, which grants fellowships to scholars, writers, and artists. Another brother, **Solomon Robert Guggenheim,** 1861–1949, estab. foundation to increase appreciation of non-objective art. Building for Solomon R. Guggenheim Mus., New York city, was designed by Frank Lloyd Wright.

Guiana (gēä'nä), region, NE South America, roughly bounded by the Orinoco basin, the Casiquiare channel (connecting the Orinoco with the Río Negro), the Amazon basin, and the Atlantic. The narrow coastal region is rainy and hot. The vast, unexploited interior includes the Guiana Highlands as well as broad savannas and vast rain forests. The region includes SE Venezuela and part of N Brazil as well as the three countries called Guiana. Westernmost of these is **British Guiana** (see GUYANA); central is **Dutch Guiana** (see SURINAM); easternmost is **French Guiana** (23,000 sq. mi.; pop. 33,698), a department of overseas France, comprising the colony proper and the interior Territory of Inini; cap. CAYENNE. The name—and even more the name of Devil's Isl. in the colony—was made notorious as a penal colony until 1946.

Guiana Highlands, mountainous tableland, mostly in Venezuela, bounded by Orinoco and Amazon basins and coastal lowlands of British Guiana. Tablelands rise in escarpments and create magnificent waterfalls in rivers which pour over edges. Rich flora and fauna made famous in W. H. Hudson's *Green Mansions.* Minerals include iron, gold, diamonds.

Guibert of Ravenna (gwĭ'bûrt, gĕbĕr'), d. 1100, antipope as Clement III (1080–1100). Led antireform party which repudiated Pope Alexander II. HENRY IV made him archbishop of Ravenna (1072). Henry, excommunicated in 1080 by GREGORY VII, declared Gregory deposed and enthroned (1084) Guibert, who then crowned Henry emperor.

Guicciardini, Francesco (fränchä'skō gwēt-chärdē'nē), 1483–1540. Italian historian and statesman. Served Florentine government and Pope Leo X. His history of Italy during 1492–1534 (period of the Italian Wars) is masterwork of Italian historical literature of Renaissance. He was a follower of Machiavelli.

guided missile, self-propelled unmanned space or air vehicle carrying an explosive warhead; its flight path can be adjusted during flight, either by automatic self-contained controls or by distant human control. Guided missiles are powered by ROCKET or JET PROPULSION. An intercontinental ballistic missile (ICBM) is a surface-to-surface guided missile; it is rocket-propelled and its trajectory passes through empty space. One ICBM carrying a hydrogen bomb warhead can destroy any city on earth. An IRBM is an intermediate range ballistic missile and is similar to an ICBM. Air-to-surface guided missiles, released from aircraft, are used against battlefield positions. Air-to-air and surface-to-air types are used against other missiles or aircraft. Some may be launched by naval craft. International control of production and use of guided missiles has not been agreed upon. See also SPACE TRAVEL.

Guido d'Arezzo (gwē'dō därĕt'tsō) or **Guido Aretinus** (ârŭtī'nŭs), c.990–1050, Italian Benedictine monk, important in the history of musical notation. He added two lines to the two already serving as a staff, using the spaces as well as the lines. His chief contribution was the solmization syllables (a system to denote tones by syllables), called the Aretinian syllables or Guido's scale. He had observed that each line of a certain hymn began a note higher than the previous line, so, as an aid to memorizing, he named each of the tones of the hexachord (a group of six consecutive notes) after the first syllable of each line of the hymn: *Ut queant laxis; Resonare fibris; Mira gestorum; Famuli tuorum; Solve* polluti; and so on. As the octave superseded the hexachord, an additional *si* or *ti* was added; *ut* was replaced by the more singable *do*. These syllables became the basis of various systems of MUSICAL NOTATION (see also SOLFÈGE) used today.

Guido Reni: see RENI, GUIDO.

Guienne (gēĕn', gwēĕn'), Fr. *Guyenne,* region and former province, SW France; historic cap. Bordeaux. Synonymous with AQUITAINE until Hundred Years War. Largely under English rule 1152–1453.

Guilbert, Yvette (ēvĕt' gēlbĕr'), 1865–1944. French diseuse, immortalized (with her long black gloves) in the lithographs of Toulouse-Lautrec.

Guildford, municipal borough (pop. 53,977), co. town of Surrey, England. Identified with Astolat of Arthurian legend. Grave of Lewis Carroll is here.

guilds or **gilds,** economic and social groups of people in same business or craft, typical of W Europe in Middle Ages. Membership was never by class but by profession or trade. Primary functions were to control profession or trade in a locality, to set standards of workmanship and price, to protect business from capricious exactions, to prevent encroachment from other localities, and to establish status for guild members in society. Similar groups both of merchants and of craftsmen were known from early Greek times, some of them extremely powerful. Merchant guilds had vast effect on what is known as Commercial Revolution. No less important were craft guilds, which grew rapidly in 12th cent. Generally members were masters, apprentices, and journeymen. Masters owned shops and trained apprentices, bound to them. Journeymen were men who had finished training but could not attain status of masters, limited in number. Guilds reflected medieval desire for orderly society, and often dominated municipal government, e.g., LIVERY COMPANIES of London. Increasing power of nations in 15th and 16th cent. reduced power of guilds, which, by 17th cent., had withered in England, but persisted on Continent until French Revolution.

guild socialism, type of socialism developed in England, advocating industrial self-government through worker-controlled guilds; originated by A. J. Penty in 1906. Aspects of Marxism and SYNDICALISM were adopted. Control of industry was emphasized, rather than political reform. Movement eventually waned, although it influenced British trade unions.

Guilford, town (pop. 2,420), S Conn., on Long Isl. Sound E of New Haven; settled 1639. Has several summer shore communities and some of state's oldest houses, including Whitfield House (1639–40; restored 1936, now museum). Abraham Baldwin and Samuel Johnson born here.

Guilford Courthouse National Military Park: see NATIONAL PARKS AND MONUMENTS (table).

Guillaume, Charles Édouard (shärl' ädwär' gēyōm'), 1861–1938, French physicist. Won 1920 Nobel Prize in Physics for discovery of several alloys, among them invar and platinite.

Guillaume de Lorris (dù lōrēs'), c.1215–c.1278, French poet, author of first part of ROMAN DE LA ROSE.

Guimarãis or **Guimarães** (both: gē″mŭrā'ĕsh), city (pop. 23,598), Braga dist., NW Portugal. Seat of Henry of Burgundy and his son, Alfonso I of Portugal. Favorite royal residence; noted old castle.

Guimard, Hector (ĕktŏr' gēmär'), 1867–1942, French *art nouveau* architect and furniture designer. Created Paris *métro* station entrances.

Guimerà, Angel (än'zhĕl gēmärä'), 1845?–1924, Catalan poet and dramatist.

Guinea (gĭ'nē), archaic term for W coast of Africa from Angola to Senegal; included Grain Coast, Ivory Coast, Gold Coast, Slave Coast.

Guinea, Fr. *Guinée,* republic (c.95,000 sq. mi.; pop. c.3,420,000), W Africa; cap. Conakry. Low-lying tropical coastal zone gives way to savanna and then mountains in N. Major crops include coffee, pineapples, bananas, and rice; timber and quinine also produced; great mineral wealth in bauxite, iron ore, diamonds, and gold. Deepwater port of Conakry linked to interior by rail. Major tribes are Christian, Moslem, and animist. French is official language. The anc. kingdoms of Ghana, Mali, and Songhai included much of interior region. Region became French colony 1891 and in 1895 became part of French West Africa. Independence was achieved in 1958, when Guinea voted to leave the French Community. Sekou Touré was elected first president. In 1958 Ghana and Guinea signed a declaration of union and were joined by Mali in 1960 in fostering the Union of African States. Pres. NKRUMAH of Ghana given political asylum in Guinea in 1966.

Guinea, Gulf of, inlet of the Atlantic, W Africa. Extends from Cape Palmas in Liberia to Cape Lopez in Gabon.

guinea fowl, breed of domestic poultry related to the pheasant and developed from wild species of Africa. It is in demand for its delicate, but gamelike flesh.

guinea pig, domesticated form of the cavy (genus *Cavia*), descended from wild South American species. In North America it is chiefly a laboratory animal used for testing serums, antitoxins, and for experiments in genetics and nutrition.

Guinegate (gēngät'), village, Pas-de-Calais dept., N France, near Saint-Omer. Scene of two French defeats: 1479, by Archduke Maximilian, in war over Burgundian succession; 1513, by English and imperialists, in second BATTLE OF THE SPURS.

Guinevere: see ARTHURIAN LEGEND; also spelled Guenever or Guenevere.

Guinicelli or **Guinizelli, Guido** (gwē'dō gwēnēchĕl'lē, gwēntsĕl'lē), c.1230–1276?, Italian poet, called by Dante his literary father.

Guinness, Sir Alec, 1914–, English actor. Made stage debut 1934, later worked with Old Vic company. Known for comedy roles and character versatility in film and stage work (film *The Bridge on the River Kwai,* play *Dylan*). Knighted 1959.

Guipúzcoa, Spain: see BASQUE PROVINCES.

Güiraldes, Ricardo (gwērä'l'däs), 1886–1927, Argentine novelist. Wrote a classic work on the gaucho, *Don Segundo Sombra* (1926; Eng. tr., 1935).

Guiscard, Norman rulers of Sicily: see ROBERT GUISCARD and ROGER I.

Guise (gēz, gwēz), French ducal family, founded as cadet branch of house of LORRAINE by **Claude de Lorraine, 1st duc de Guise** (klōd' dù lōrĕn'), 1496–1550, whom Francis I made duke and peer. His daughter MARY OF GUISE married James V of Scotland and was the mother of Mary Queen of Scots. His sons **François de Lorraine, 2d duc de Guise** (fräswä'), 1519–63, and **Charles de Guise, Cardinal de Lorraine,** c.1525–1574, controlled French politics in the reign of Francis II, first husband of Mary Queen of Scots. Championing the Catholic cause against the Huguenots, they cruelly suppressed the conspiracy of AMBOISE (1560). After Francis's death they opposed the tolerant policy of CATHERINE DE' MEDICI and provoked the outbreak of the Wars of RELIGION (1562). François defeated the Huguenots at Dreux, but was assassinated shortly afterward. Charles negotiated for Spanish help and held power at court in 1567–70. **Henri de Lorraine,** 3d **duc de Guise** (ārē'), 1550–88, son of François, helped to plan the massacre of SAINT BARTHOLOMEW'S DAY and after 1576 formed the Catholic LEAGUE. Immensely ambitious and popular, he instigated the revolt of Paris against King HENRY III (1588) and took control of the city. After an ostensible reconciliation the king had him murdered. His brother, **Louis de Lorraine, Cardinal de Guise,** 1555–88, was killed at the same time. Leadership of the League devolved upon their brother, Charles, duc de MAYENNE. **Henri de Lorraine,** 5th **duc de Guise,** 1614–64, conspired against Richelieu (1641); fought in Naples against Spain (1647–48, 1654); later was grand chamberlain at court of Louis XIV.

guitar: see STRINGED INSTRUMENTS.

Guitry, Lucien Germain (gētrē'), 1860–1925, French actor; versatile successor of Coquelin. Also a prominent manager and director, he often acted in the plays of his actor son, **Sacha Guitry** (säshä'), 1885–1957, a witty, prolific dramatist and film director.

Guizot, François (fräswä' gēzō'), 1787–1874, French statesman and historian; leading intellectual exponent of the bourgeois monarchy of LOUIS PHILIPPE. He dominated the cabinet from 1840, was premier 1847–48. His complacency led to FEBRUARY REVOLUTION of 1848. Ranking high as historian, he wrote *Histoire de la révolution d'Angleterre* (6 vols., 1826–56); *General History of Civilization in Modern Europe* (1829–32; Eng. tr., 3 vols., 1846).

Gujarat (gōōjŭrät'), state (c.72,000 sq. mi.; pop. c.20,-620,000). India, on Arabian Sea, comprising Kathiawar peninsula; cap. Ahmedabad. Constituted 1960 from N and W portions of former Bombay state. Rice, wheat, and cotton are grown, and salt, limestone, and bauxite are mined. State is the seat of Indian cotton textile industry. Region was center of Jainism under the Hindu Anhilvada kingdom (c.755–1233).

Gulf. For names beginning thus, see second part; e.g., for Gulf of Mexico, see MEXICO, GULF OF.

Gulfport, city (pop. 30,204), SE Miss., on Mississippi Sound WSW of Biloxi, in farm area; settled 1891 as site for railroad terminus. Resort and shipping center (fine artificial harbor). Processes sea food. Has large veterans' hospital.

Gulf Stream, ocean current found (1513) by Ponce de León. It originates in Gulf of Mexico, passes through Straits of Florida, flows NE parallel to U.S. coast, separated from it by narrow "cold wall" of water. Temperature is 80°F. at beginning, drops as stream moves N. Stream slows up and spreads out, finally merges with North Atlantic Drift (lat. 40°N, long. 60°W). Stream results from general vertical circulation of ocean: cold water from N sinks down, warm water of equatorial region rises and flows N above cold current.

gulfweed, a SEAWEED of genus *Sargassum,* a brown alga of tropical waters, which commonly floats in large patches in Sargasso Sea and Gulf Stream. Sometimes called sea lentil.

Gulick, Luther Halsey (gū'lĭk), 1865–1918, American pioneer in physical education. He helped to originate game of basketball and in 1910 helped found Camp Fire Girls.

Gulistan, Treaty of, 1813, between Russia and Iran, ended Russo-Persian War begun in 1804. Persia ceded khanates forming present Azerbaijan SSR, renounced claims to Georgia, Dagestan.

gull, aquatic bird of tern family found near all oceans and many inland waters. Sea gull is a common name for herring gull (a subspecies of European gull) found on Atlantic and Pacific coasts of Canada and U.S., as well as inland. Larger and heavier than terns, gulls have webbed feet and hooked bills. They are useful as scavengers. See *ill.,* p. 118.

Gullah, distinctive dialect of the Negroes of the Sea Isls., SE U.S. Because of its great isolation, the dialect retains many Africanisms.

Gullstrand, Allvar (äl'vär gŭl'stränd), 1862–1930, Swedish ophthalmologist. Won 1911 Nobel Prize in Physiology and Medicine for study of optical images and of light refraction in eye.

gum, term for a variety of plant substances, many not true gums. True gums are complex organic materials; some are soluble in water, others are insoluble but absorb large amounts of water. Gum arabic is typical; it is used in making inks, adhesives, confections; as fabric filler; as emollient.

gum ammoniac: see AMMONIAC.

gumbo, a name for OKRA. In W U.S. it is name for black alluvial soil, sticky or soapy when wet.

Gumplowicz, Ludwig (lōōt'vĭkh gōōm'plōvĭch), 1838–1909, Austrian sociologist. Held that social development rose out of conflict, first among races, then among states, then among other social groups.

gum tree: see EUCALYPTUS; BLACK GUM; SWEET GUM.

guncotton or **nitrocellulose,** explosive formed by action of cold nitric and sulfuric acids on cotton. Burns when ignited; explodes with detonator. Used in torpedoes, in blasting (mixed with nitroglycerin), in underwater blasting and mines; in making smokeless powder.

Gundulic, Ivan (ē'vän gōōndōo'lĭch), Ital. *Giovanni Gondola.* 1588–1638, Croatian poet. Held high office in his native Dubrovnik (Ragusa). His chief work, *Osman* (1626), is an epic of the Polish-Turkish wars.

gun metal, a BRONZE, an alloy of copper, tin, and zinc in varying proportions. Originally used for making guns; now used for casting machine parts.

Gunn, J. B., 1928–, Anglo-American physicist, b. Egypt. Described the **Gunn effect,** in solid state physics, in which a high electric field applied to a crystal produces a current which oscillates at high frequencies.

Gunnarsson, Gunnar, 1889–, Icelandic novelist. Early works in Danish, later in Icelandic.

Gunnison, town (pop. 3,477), W central Colo., on Gunnison R.; laid out 1879 as silver-mining town. Western State Col. of Colorado is here.

Gunnison, river formed in W central Colo. and flowing c.180 mi. W and NW to Colorado R. at Grand Junction. Courses through Black Canyon of the Gunnison (a national monument). Some water diverted for irrigation by Gunnison Tunnel (1905–9), 30,582 ft. in length.

gunpowder, explosive mixture of potassium nitrate (75%), sulfur (10%), and carbon (15%). Formerly much used in blasting and in weapons. In guns, because of the large residue of solid matter, it has been superseded by smokeless powder. Though some have called Roger Bacon or Berthold Schwarz the inventor, it is now agreed that gunpowder was invented in Asia (probably 9th-cent. China). Introduction to Europe in 14th cent. revolutionized warfare.

Gunpowder Plot, frustrated plan to blow up the British houses of Parliament and King James I on Nov. 5, 1605, the opening day of Parliament. A rising of English Catholics was to follow. Plot was exposed by a warning to a relation of one of the plotters not to attend Parliament on that day. Guy Fawkes, a conspirator, was arrested as he entered the cellar of the House of Lords. Nov. 5 is still celebrated as Guy Fawkes Day and effigies of him are burned.

Gunsaulus, Frank Wakeley (gŭnsô'lŭs), 1856–1921, American Congregational clergyman and lecturer, president of Armour Inst. of Technology (now Illinois Inst. of Technology) after 1893.

Gunter, Edmund, 1581–1626, English mathematician and astronomer. He invented a portable quadrant, Gunter's surveyors chain, Gunter's sector or scale; discovered variation (declination) of the magnetic compass. He was probably first to use terms *cosine* and *cotangent.*

guppy or **rainbow fish,** small fish (*Lebistes reticulatus*) abundant in parts of South America. It is a popular aquarium fish. It can survive temperatures of 65°–100° F. Rainbow-colored, inch-long male has black bars and spots. Female is greenish gray, c.1½ in. long. Adults are cannibalistic. They produce 12–25 living young every few weeks.

Gupta (gōōp′tù), dynasty, c.320–c.544, of N India, founded by Chandragupta I. It saw a golden age of Hindu culture.

Gurkha (gōōr′kù), ethnic group of Nepal, of mixed Mongol-Rajput extraction and predominantly Hindu in religion. A warlike people, they serve in the armies of India and that of Great Britain.

Guryev (gōōr′yĭf), city (1965 est. pop. 96,000), W Kazakh SSR, on Ural R. and Caspian Sea. Center of Emba oil fields; linked by pipeline with Orsk.

Gustavus (gŭstä′vùs), kings of Sweden. **Gustavus I** (Gustavus Vasa), 1496–1560. His father, Erik Johansson, was a Swedish senator murdered in the Stockholm massacre (1520). Gustavus led the peasants of Dalarna in the rebellion against CHRISTIAN II of Denmark, defeated the Danes, and was elected king by the Riksdag in 1523. Thus the KALMAR UNION of Denmark, Norway, and Sweden was dissolved. Gustavus's reign was marked by the establishment of a national Protestant Church (1527) and by the Swedish-Danish victory over Lübeck (1537), which freed Sweden from economic subjection to the Hanseatic League. He reigned firmly, made the crown hereditary in the Vasa family, transformed Sweden into a modern, national state. **Gustavus II** (Gustavus Adolphus), 1594–1632, reigned 1611–32. Helped by his chancellor, Axel OXENSTIERNA, he insured internal stability by granting concessions to the nobles and ended the KALMAR WAR by buying off the Danes (1613). His resumption in 1621 of intermittent warfare with Poland gained him a large part of Livonia when a truce was made at Altmark (1629). Meanwhile, however, he had been drawn into an alliance with Christian IV of Denmark (1628) and with France (1629); to both powers he promised to intervene on the Protestant side in the THIRTY YEARS WAR. Gustavus landed in Pomerania (1630) and in a spectacular sweep through Germany defeated the imperials at Breitenfeld (1631), at the Lech (April, 1632), and at Lützen (Nov., 1632). In that last battle, he was killed. His daughter Christina succeeded him. **Gustavus III,** 1746–92, reigned 1771–92. By a coup d'état (1772) he restored the royal prerogatives lost by his predecessors. He waged successful war on Russia (1788–90). His reform policies and his autocratic tendencies earned him the hatred of the nobles, one of whom murdered him. His son and successor, **Gustavus IV** (Gustavus Adolphus), 1778–1837, joined the third coalition against Napoleon I (1805). He lost Swedish Pomerania to French occupation and Finland to Russia (1808). His despotism and mental unbalance led to his enforced abdication (1809). He died in Switzerland. **Gustavus V,** 1858–1950, reigned 1907–50. Sweden evolved toward advanced democracy and economic prosperity; kept neutral in both world wars. His son **Gustavus VI** (Gustavus Adolphus), 1882–, succeeded him in 1950.

Gustavus Adolphus: see GUSTAVUS II, GUSTAVUS IV, and GUSTAVUS VI, kings of Sweden.

Gutenberg, Johann (gōō′tùnbûrg; Ger. gōō′tùnběrk), c.1397–1468, German printer, generally considered the first European to print from movable type, though some claim that honor for Laurens Janszoon Koster, for Pamfilo Castaldi, or for some unknown. Little is known of his life. His father's name was Gensfleisch, and the name Gutenberg was derived from his mother. He is believed to have lived in Strasbourg, where he may have made his great invention in 1436 or 1437. He founded a print shop in Mainz (apparently his birthplace), where he issued the MAZARIN BIBLE. Mainz became the center of the new printing trade, but Gutenberg had to give up his press and types to Johann FUST for debt. See PRINTING and TYPE.

Guthrie, Samuel, 1782–1848, American physician. Made flintlock musket obsolete by inventing a percussion powder and a punch lock for exploding it. Discovered chloroform 1831.

Guthrie, city (pop. 9,502), central Okla., near Cimarron R., N of Oklahoma City; founded 1889 Territorial and state cap. until 1910. Now commercial center of farm and dairy area. Langston Univ is nearby.

Gutiérrez Nájera, Manuel (mänwěl′ gōōtyě′rěs nä′-härä), 1859–95, Mexican poet, showing transition from romanticism to modernism.

gutta-percha, solidified milky juice or latex of various Malayan evergreen trees (esp. *Palaquium gutta*). It is nonelastic and insoluble in water; pliable when heated in water. Of great value as insulation for submarine cables; also used in golf balls, telephone receivers, adhesives, waterproofing materials, etc.

Guttmann, Julius, 1880–1950, German Jewish scholar and historian of Jewish philosophy.

Guyana (gīän′ù) formerly **British Guiana,** British dominion (83,000 sq. mi.; 1964 est. pop. 635,743); cap. Georgetown, on the Demerara R. The population is polyglot—a few whites and Indians, many East Indians, and many Negroes. Sugar, rum, rice, hardwoods, gold, diamonds (the Mazaruni fields are rich), and bauxite are exported. British settlement in Guiana began in present Dutch Guiana by 1630, and the Dutch settled Essequibo, Berbice, and Pomeroon in present Guyana. In the course of Continental and colonial wars involving the Dutch, British, and French, the areas changed hands often, and it was not until the Congress of Vienna that the present division of the three areas was more or less fixed. Discovery of gold in British Guiana led to British expansion and to the VENEZUELA BOUNDARY DISPUTE. New constitution inaugurated in 1952 was suspended in 1953. Elections in 1957 under a changed constitution made Cheddi B. Jagan chief minister. Colony became an independent dominion 1966.

Guyenne: see GUIENNE.

Guy of Chauliac: see CHAULIAC, GUY DE.

Guy of Lusignan: see LUSIGNAN.

Guyon, Jeanne Marie Bouvier de la Motte (zhän′ märē′ bōōvyä′ dù lä môt′ güēyō′), 1648–1717, French mystic, author of works on QUIETISM. Confined by government to convent because of heretical opinions and correspondence with Miguel de MOLINOS, she was released through aid of Mme de Maintenon but was later imprisoned in Bastille (1695–1702).

Guys, Constantin (gois), 1805?–1892, French draughtsman, b. Holland. Did superb drawings in line and wash, first reproduced in *Illustrated London News*.

Guyton de Morveau, Louis Bernard, Baron (lwē běr-när′ bärō′ gětō′ dù môrvō′), 1737–1816, French chemist, lawyer. Wrote chemical section of *Encyclopédie méthodique* (Vol. I, 1786) and with Lavoisier and others systematized chemical nomenclature.

Guzmán, Martin Luis (märtēn′ lwēs′ gōōsmän′), 1887–, Mexican novelist and journalist. In *The Eagle and the Serpent* (1928) he described the Mexican revolution. Editor of *Memorias de Pancho Villa* (5 vols., 1938–51) and founder of the weekly paper *Tiempo.*

Guzmán, Nuño de (nōō′nyō dä gōōthmän′) d. 1544, Spanish conquistador. As head of first *audiencia* of New Spain (1528), he ruled so notoriously that he was forced to leave Mexico city (1959). Conquered Nueva Galicia; founded Culiacán and Guadalajara.

Guzmán Blanco, Antonio (äntō′nyō gōōsmän′ blän′kō), 1829–99, president of Venezuela. A *caudillo,* he dominated the nation 1870–88 as a benevolent despot. After overthrow of his regime, he lived in Paris.

Gwalior (gwä′lêôr), former princely state, Madhya Pradesh, India. Founded in 18th cent. by Ranaji Sindhia, a Mahratta chief. Town of **Gwalior** (pop. 300,-513) adjoins Lashkar and lies at foot of a hill fort containing ornate palaces and shrines.

Gwin, William McKendree, 1805–85, American politician. U.S. Senator from Calif. (1850–55, 1857–61). Spokesman for Calif. slavery interests. Involved in political battles with antislavery rival, David C. BRODERICK.

Gwinnett, Button, c.1735–1777, American Revolutionary patriot, signer of Declaration of Independence, b. England. His signature, one of the rarest of American holographs, is very valuable.

Gwyn or **Gwynn, Nell** (Eleanor), 1650–87, English actress, notable in comic roles. Charles II's mistress after 1669, she bore him two sons.

gymnastics, exercises for balanced development of body. In Greece the gymnasium was originally the place of training for the Olympic games. Modern gymnastics date from early 19th cent., when Ludwig Jahn estab. *Turnplätze* in Berlin. In U.S., principal gymnastics events are side and long horse, parallel and horizontal bars, rope climbing, flying rings, tumbling.

Gyor (dyûr), Hung. *Györ,* Ger. *Raab,* city (est. pop. 74,000), NW Hungary, on Raab R. Chief textile center of Hungary; mfg. of machinery. Episcopal see since 1001; 12th-cent. cathedral rebuilt in 17th cent. Scene of decisive Austrian victory over Hungarian revolutionists (1849).

gypsum (jĭp′sŭm), name for hydrated calcium sulfate. Alabaster and satin spar are varieties. Plaster of Paris is obtained from gypsum.

gypsy or **gipsy,** nomadic people numbering roughly 5,000,000, found on every continent. They are probably partly of East Indian origin and speak an Indo-Iranian language called Romany. Disinclined to assimilate, they hold to own customs. Usually depend on trading for living.

gypsy moth, European insect with larva destructive to forest and fruit trees. It appeared in U.S. c.1869 and is confined to NE portion. Adult male is yellowish brown; female whitish; dark lines mark forewings of each. Larva is c.2 in. long, dark brown or black with yellow markings and rows of blue and red tubercles bearing hairs. Air sacs on hairs make the larva buoyant; it can be carried by wind. *Porthetria dispar.*

gyroscope, rapidly rotating heavy wheel or disk which tends to resist any change in its axis of rotation, because of inertia. A force acting on axis of rotation will not change plane of rotation; it will instead cause precession, a sideways motion of the spinning axis. Precession is illustrated by the slow progression of a spinning top across a floor. Gyroscope was invented in 1852 by Foucault and was used to demonstrate earth's rotation. With later invention of electric rotor its uses grew to include giant gyroscopic ship stabilizers, directional instruments such as gyrocompass (unaffected by magnetic variations), automatic pilot for guiding aircraft, and other devices.

Gyulafehervar, Rumania: see ALBA-IULIA.

H, chemical symbol of element hydrogen.

Haag, Den, Netherlands: see HAGUE, THE.

Haakon (häˈkŭn, Nor. hôˈkoōn), kings of Norway. **Haakon I** (the Good), c.915–961, son of Harold I, was brought up as Christian at court of King Athelstan in England. Displaced his brother Eric as king c.935. Strengthened national army and fleet; sought unsuccessfully to introduce Christianity. **Haakon IV** (Haakon Haakonsson), 1204–63, a grandson of Sverre, was formally recognized as king in 1223 after overcoming rival claimants. Under him medieval Norway reached its zenith. He acquired Greenland and Iceland, carried out legal reforms, held a splendid court. He died during an expedition in the Orkney Isls. **Haakon VII,** 1872–1957, king of independent Norway (1905–57), second son of Frederick VIII of Denmark. In England during Second World War.

Haardt, Georges Marie (zhôrzh′ märē′ ärt′, härt′), 1886–1932, French explorer. Traversed Africa from Cape Town to Cairo by automobile. Led trans-Asian motor expedition.

Haarlem (härˈlŭm), municipality (pop. 172,017), cap of North Holland prov., W Netherlands, near North Sea. World center of tulip breeding and bulb industry since 17th cent. Mfg. of machinery, textiles. Chartered 1245; sacked 1573 by Spanish. Center of 17th-cent. Dutch painting: Frans Hals, Ruisdael worked here. Landmarks include Church of St. Bavo (Groote Kerk, 15th cent.) and city hall (begun 1250; former palace of counts of Holland). Formerly also spelled Harlem.

Haas, Arthur, 1884–1941, American physicist, b. Bohemia. Proposed in "tired" light theory that the bundles of light, or quanta, lose energy speeding to earth. This would explain shift in the light rays toward red end of spectrum, phenomenon that has caused difficulties for exponents of expanding universe concept.

Habakkuk or **Habacuc** (both: hŭbăˈkŭk, hăˈ–), book of Old Testament, a set of poems on the triumph of justice and divine mercy over evil. Identity and time of prophet unknown. A prophet of this name appears in story of Bel and the Dragon. Also Habbacuc.

Habana, Cuba: see HAVANA.

habeas corpus (hāˈbēŭs kôrˈpŭs) [Latin,= you may have the body], writ directed by a judge to some person who is detaining another; it commands that the person in custody shall be brought at a specified time to a specified place for a specified purpose. It was known in England as early as the 14th cent. and came to be in England and later in the U.S. the prime remedy for false imprisonment and illegal detention without a judicial hearing. The U.S. Constitution provides that the privilege of the writ shall not be suspended unless, when in cases of rebellion or invasion, public safety may require suspension.

Haber, Fritz (häˈbŭr), 1868–1934, German chemist. He won the 1918 Nobel Prize in Chemistry. The Haber process for commercial synthesis of ammonia by direct combination of hydrogen and nitrogen was his invention.

Habsburg, family: see HAPSBURG.

hackberry, deciduous tree of genus *Celtis,* widely distributed, and often grown for ornament. It has warty bark, elmlike leaves, small edible fruit.

Hackensack, city (pop. 30,521), NE N.J., on Hackensack R., ESE of Paterson. Trading post estab. here by Dutch from Manhattan, 1647. Scene of much Revolutionary activity. Residential and industrial suburb of New York since late 19th cent. Has Dutch Reformed church (1696; rebuilt 1728) and Steuben House (1739).

Hackensack, river rising in SE N.Y., W of Haverstraw, and flowing c.45 mi. S into N.J. past Hackensack and through Jersey Meadows to Newark Bay. Navigable for c.20 mi. above its mouth to New Milford.

Hackney, London borough since 1965 (est. pop. 254,-720), includes the former metropolitan boroughs of Hackney, Shoreditch, and Stoke Newington.

Hadassah (hŭdä′sù), Hebrew name of ESTHER.

Hadassah (hŭdä′sù), the women's Zionist organization of America; founded 1912 by Henrietta Szold. Maintains medical and child welfare services in Israel, educational services in U.S.

Haddam, town (pop. 3,466), S Conn., SSE of Middletown, crossed by Connecticut R.; settled 1662.

Haddington, burgh (pop. 5,506), co. town of East Lothian, Scotland. Remains of abbey church (called "Lamp of the Lothians") serve as parish church.

Haddingtonshire: see EAST LOTHIAN, Scotland.

haddock, food fish of N Atlantic similar to cod. Black lateral line runs from gill to tail. Its averages 2–4 lb., with maximum of c.17 lb. Flesh is tender, white, flaky. Smoked haddock is finnan haddie.

Haddonfield, borough (pop. 13,201), SW N.J., suburb of Camden; settled 1682. Has Indian King Tavern (1750), where first state legislature met, 1777.

Hades, Greek underworld: see HELL and PLUTO.

Hadewijch (hä′dúvïkh), fl. early 13th cent., Dutch mystical poet, a nun.

Hadfield, Sir Robert Abbott, 1858–1940, English metallurgist. For many inventions, notably manganese steel, he was knighted 1908. Works include *Faraday and His Metallurgical Researches* (1931).

Hadhramaut, Arabia: see HADRAMAUT.

Hadley, town (pop. 3,099), W Mass., on Connecticut R. opposite Northampton; settled 1659. Joseph Hooker born here; Edward Whalley and William Goffe lived here.

Hadramaut or **Hadhramaut** (both: hädrûmout′), region, S Arabia, on Gulf of Aden and Arabian Sea, occupying roughly Eastern Aden protectorate. Called Hazarmaveth in Bible.

Hadrian: see also ADRIAN.

Hadrian (hä′drêün), A.D. 76–138, Roman emperor (117–38), b. Spain. A ward of TRAJAN, he distinguished himself as commander and administrator and was named to succeed to the throne. His rule was vigorous, and he traveled about the empire, stabilizing government and beautifying cities with new architecture. He abandoned Trajan's aggressive policy in Asia, fixing the Euphrates as a boundary; had great walls built in Germany and Hadrian's Wall in Britain. In Palestine he put down the uprising under Bar Kochba and built a temple of Jupiter Capitolinus on the ruined Temple, renaming Jerusalem as Aelia Capitolina. Patronized the arts, and his regard for his favorite Antinoüs is recorded in many statues. Chose ANTONINUS PIUS as his successor. Name also appears as Adrian.

Hadrian's Mole: see CASTEL SANT' ANGELO.

Hadrian's Wall, anc. Roman wall, 73½ mi. long, across narrow part of Great Britain from Wallsend on Tyne R. to Bowness at head of Solway Firth. Built A.D. c.121–127 by Emperor Hadrian. Fragments remain of wall (6 ft. high and 8 ft. thick) and stone forts along it. British government preserves wall, one of largest Roman remains.

Hadrumetum: see SOUSSE.

Haeckel, Ernst Heinrich (ërnst′ hïn′rïkh hĕ′kùl), 1834–1919, German biologist and philosopher, an early exponent in Germany of Darwinism. His studies of marine invertebrates are well known. Although often erroneous, his theories stimulated research.

haemo-, for words beginning thus: see HEMO-.

Hafiz (häfēz′), d. 1389?, Persian poet, known for lyrics and drinking songs. Was a teacher of the Koran. Moslem critics interpret his poems allegorically.

Hafnarfjordur (häp′närfyûr″dhür), town (pop. 7,902), SW Iceland. Distribution, industrial, and fishing center; refrigeration plants, fishmeal factories, and shipyards.

hafnium (häf′nêûm), widely distributed metallic element (symbol = Hf; see also ELEMENT, table).

Hafrs Fjord or **Hafs Fjord** (both: häfs′fyôrd), inlet of North Sea, SW Norway, near Stavanger. HAROLD I won decisive victory here, 872.

Hagar (hä′gùr) [Heb.,= flight], handmaid of Sarah and mother of Ishmael by Abraham. Sent into desert because of Sarah's jealousy, she was comforted by an angel. Gen. 16: 21.9–21. St. Paul used Hagar as symbol for bondage of the Old Law. Gal. 4.25. Also Agar.

Hagen, Walter (hä′gùn), 1892–, American golfer. Won U.S. Natl. Open (1914, 1919), British Open (1922, 1924, 1928, 1929), U.S. Professional Golfers Association championships (1921, 1924–27), many other titles.

Hagen (hä′gùn), city (pop. 179,063), North Rhine-Westphalia, West Germany. Industrial center of Ruhr dist.

Hagerstown (hä′gùrztoun), city (pop. 36,660), NW Md., NW of Frederick, in agr. region of Cumberland Valley; settled 1762.

haggadah: see TALMUD.

Haggai (hä′gāī), book of Old Testament, written in Jerusalem after the return from captivity. It urges renewal of work on restoring the Temple and contains a Messianic prophecy (2.7). In Vulgate: Aggeus.

Haggard, Sir H(enry) Rider, 1856–1925, English novelist, author of romantic adventure stories (e.g., *King Solomon's Mines,* 1885; *She,* 1887).

Hagginwood, town (pop. 11,469), central Calif., N of Sacramento, in Sacramento valley.

Hagia Sophia (hä′jù sōfē′ù, hä′jù, hä′gyù) [Gr.,= Holy Wisdom] or **Santa Sophia,** originally a Christian church at Constantinople, now a museum of Byzantine art; supreme masterpiece of Byzantine architecture. On site of earlier churches (destroyed by fire) built in 360 by Constantine II and in 415 by Theodosius II. Present fireproof structure was built 532–37 by Justinian on designs of Anthemius of Tralles and Isidorus of Miletus. With Turkish conquest of city in 1453, it became a mosque. Nave is covered by lofty central dome (102 ft. in diameter, 184 ft. high) in which opens a luminous corona of 40 arched windows. All interior surfaces are sheathed with polychrome marbles and gold mosaic. Four slender minarets rise at outer corners of building. A cross surmounts the dome.

Hague, Frank, 1876–1956, Democratic political boss, mayor of Jersey City, N.J. (1917–47).

Hague, The (häg), Dutch *'s Gravenhage* or *Den Haag,* municipality (pop. 598,709), cap. of South Holland prov. and *de facto* cap. of Netherlands, near the North Sea. Seat of royal court, legislature, supreme court of justice, and foreign embassies. City is almost entirely residential. It grew around palace begun 1250 by William, count of Holland, the Binnenhof, which now houses the legislature. As residence of stadtholders of United Provs. in 17th–18th cent. it grew into a major diplomatic and intellectual center. Since First Hague Conference (1899) it also has been the center for promotion of internatl. justice and arbitration; Peace Palace (completed 1913) has housed Permanent Court of Arbitration, Permanent Court of Internatl. Justice, and, since 1945, Internatl. Court of Justice. Other landmarks include royal palace; Gevangenenpoort (14th-cent. prison, where brothers De Witt were murdered 1672); Mauritshuis (residence of John Maurice of Nassau, now a museum containing outstanding paintings by Rembrandt); 16th-cent. city hall; and Nieuwe Kerk [new church], with Spinoza's tomb.

Hague Conferences (hāg), term for the Internatl. Peace Conference of 1899 and the Second Internatl. Peace Conference of 1907, both proposed by Russia and held at The Hague. Failed to effect an arms reduction, but modified some of the rules of war. First conference estab. (1899) the Permanent Court of Arbitration, known popularly as the **Hague Tribunal.** Each member nation may appoint up to four members of a panel of judges from which arbitrators are picked when two or more nations submit a dispute for arbitration. More than 20 international disputes have been arbitrated. After First World War the Tribunal lost most of its importance to the World Court.

Hahn, Otto (ō'tō hän), 1879–, German chemist and physicist. Split the uranium atom in 1939 and discovered possibility of chain reaction. Won 1944 Nobel Prize in Chemistry for this work.

Hahnemann, Samuel (hä'nůmůn), 1755–1843, German physician, founder of homeopathy.

Hahnemann Medical College and Hospital, in Philadelphia; chartered 1848 as Homeopathic Medical Col. of Pennsylvania. United 1869 with Hahnemann Medical Col. of Philadelphia (1866–67); assumed present name 1885.

Haida Indians (hī'dů), North American Indian tribe, on Queen Charlotte Isls. and Prince of Wales Isl. Language is only one of Haida family which is part of Nadene linguistic stock. The Haida belong to Pacific Northwest culture area. See LANGUAGE (table).

Haidar Ali: see HYDER ALI.

Haifa (hī'fä), city (pop. c.174,000), NW Israel, on the Mediterranean, at foot of Mt. Carmel. Chief port of Israel; heavy industries and oil refineries.

Haig, Douglas Haig, 1st Earl, 1861–1928, British soldier. In First World War he was British commander in chief after 1915. Maintained confidence of the public despite antagonism of Lloyd George.

hail, pellets or lumps of ice, snow, or rime, falling usually over small areas in hot weather at onset of thunderstorm. A raindrop is blown upwards into a thundercloud; the raindrop freezes and becomes the nucleus of a hailstone. Hailstone nuclei are repeatedly carried up and down by turbulent winds and grow between wetting and freezing until heavy enough to fall to earth.

Haile Selassie (hī'lē sůlä'sē), 1891–, emperor of Ethiopia, originally named Tafari Makonnen; grandson of Menelik II. Was governor of several provinces during reign of Lij Yasu. When emperor became a Mohammedan, Haile Selassie (a Coptic Christian and then known as Ras Tafari) forced his deposition and put Menelik's daughter Judith on the throne, with himself as regent. Crowned emperor in 1930. During Italian invasion (1935–36) he personally led troops against the enemy. Fled to England 1936, returned in early 1941 to regain his throne. Estab. national assembly 1955. Survived unsuccessful coup against regime in 1960 and thereafter instituted numerous reforms within the government. Played active part in Pan-African movement.

Hailey, city (pop. 1,185), S central Idaho, ESE of Boise; laid out 1881. Resort with hot springs.

Haileybury, town (pop. 2,638), E Ont., Canada, N of North Bay, on L. Timiskaming. Center of mining region. Popular ski resort.

Hainan (hī'nän), island (c.13,000 sq. mi.; pop. c.3,-200,000), in South China Sea; part of Kwangtung prov., China. Separated from mainland by Hainan Strait (15 mi. wide). Chief port is Hoihow. Agr. and lumbering. Rich in mineral deposits, especially high-grade iron. Occupied 1939–45 by Japanese.

Hainaut (ĕnō'), province (1,437 sq. mi.; est. pop. 1,328,883), SW Belgium, touching France; cap. Mons. Formerly spelled Hainault. Drained by Scheldt, Sambre, and Dender rivers. Agr.; cattle raising and dairying in S. Important coal mines (Borinage dist.); metallurgy (at Charleroi); textile mfg. (at Tournai). Population is mainly French-speaking. Hainaut became a county in 9th cent., was part of Lotharingia. In 1191 Flanders passed to counts of Hainaut by marriage. Baldwin VI (as Baldwin IX, count of Flanders) became emperor of Constantinople as BALDWIN I (1204). In 1278 the two counties were separated: Flanders passed to Guy of Dampierre, a great-grandson of Baldwin; Hainaut passed to John of Avesnes, another great-grandson, who also became count of Holland. With HOLLAND, Hainaut passed to the houses of Burgundy (1433) and Hapsburg (1482). (For later history, see NETHERLANDS, AUSTRIAN AND SPANISH.) Parts of Hainaut were annexed to France 1659, 1678.

Haines, city (pop. 392), SE Alaska, on Chilkoot Inlet of Lynn Canal, SSW of Skagway. Fur-trading post estab. here 1867, U.S. army post later. Has good harbor, fishing, and lumbering. Haines Cutoff built in Second World War to connect with Alaska Highway at Haines Junction, Yukon territory, providing short land route to interior.

Haiphong (hī'fông'), city (pop. c.375,000), N. Vietnam on small island at confluence of two rivers. Major port and naval base, terminus of railway from China, and commercial center.

hair, modified skin structure, consisting of a shaft and a root which is expanded into hair bulb embedded in dermis of the skin. See *ill.*, p. 656.

Haiti (hā'tē), Fr. *Haïti* (äĕtē'), republic (c.10,700 sq. mi.; 1965 est. pop. 4,000,000), West Indies, on W third of Hispaniola (rest occupied by DOMINICAN REPUBLIC); cap. PORT-AU-PRINCE. Island (called also Haiti and SANTO DOMINGO) belonged to Spanish, but English and French buccaneers used Haiti region as a base, and French colonists developed sugar plantations with Negro slaves in 17th cent. Spain ceded Haiti (then Saint-Domingue) to France in 1697. French Revolution caused uprising of slaves, which was successful under TOUSSAINT L'OUVERTURE. Spain ceded all the island to France in 1795, but Toussaint conquered it all, and the Haitians resisted Napoleon's punitive force under Gen. Leclerc and even kept up resistance after Toussaint was captured by trickery. Independence, proclaimed in 1804, was achieved. Jacques DESSALINES and Henri CHRISTOPHE became emperors, then Alexandre Pétion, J. P. Boyer, and Faustin SOULOUQUE ruled. Political trouble continued, and financial trouble followed. The U.S. exercised customs receivership (1905–41), and U.S. naval control was strong until 1934. Haiti produces coffee, cotton, sugar, sisal, bananas, and cacao, diversification being enforced by law since the collapse of the sugar market in 1926. Mulattoes dominate the political scene, and most of the population (95% Negro) lives on bare subsistence from farms. Practice of *vodun* (voodoo) rites has been much studied. Since 1957 Pres. François Duvalier has maintained a dictatorship despite domestic unrest, opposition from other Caribbean governments, and American disapproval.

Hajj Omar (häj' ō'mär), 1797–1864, Moslem religious and military leader in W Africa. Fought the French (1857–59), conquered the kingdoms of Segu and Massina, and sacked Timbuktu. Killed during Fulani revolt in Massina.

Hakluyt, Richard (hä'klōōt), 1552?–1616, English geographer. Noted for *The Principal Navigations, Voyages, Traffics, and Discoveries of the English Nation* (3 vols., 1598–1600), called by J. A. Froude "the prose epic of the English nation."

Hakodate (häkō'dätä), city (pop. 243,012), extreme SW Hokkaido, Japan; port on Tsugaru Strait. Shipbuilding center and chief port of island.

Hakone (hä'kō'nä), resort region in Fuji-Hakone Natl. Park, central Honshu, Japan. Noted for mountains, hot springs, and Hakone Shrine (built 757).

halakah or **halacha:** see TALMUD.

Halbe, Max (mäks' häl'bů), 1865–1945, German naturalist dramatist. Best known for *Jugend* (1893; Eng. tr., *When Love Is Young*, 1904).

Halberstadt (häl'bůrshtät), city (est. pop. 44,467), East Germany, in former state of Saxony-Anhalt.

Railroad center with textile and paper mills. Fine medieval buildings include Liebfrauenkirche (12th cent.) and cathedral (13th–17th cent.).

Halcyone (hǎlsī'ūnē) [Gr.,= kingfisher], in Greek mythology, daughter of Aeolus. At death of her husband she leaped into the sea. The gods, from compassion, changed the pair into kingfishers, and Zeus forbade the winds to blow for 14 days at the winter solstice, the time when halcyons breed. Hence the expression "halcyon days," a time of tranquillity.

Haldane, John Scott (hôl'dān), 1860–1936, English scientist, known for studies in respiration and gasometry of blood, industrial hygiene, safety and health in mines. His son, **J(ohn) B(urdon) S(anderson) Haldane**, 1892–1964, is known for application of mathematics to biology and for expositions of science for the layman.

Haldimand, Sir Frederick (hôl'dĭmŭnd), 1718–91, British general and colonial governor of Quebec (1778–84), b. Switzerland.

Hale, Edward Everett, 1822–1909, American author of *The Man Without a Country* (1863); a Unitarian clergyman and influential reformer. His sister, **Lucretia Peabody Hale**, 1820–1900, wrote *The Peterkin Papers* (1880), amusing stories for children.

Hale, George Ellery, 1868–1938, American astronomer, authority on solar vortices and magnetic fields, inventor of spectroheliograph. He organized the Mt. Palomar, Yerkes, and Mt. Wilson observatories.

Hale, Lucretia Peabody: see HALE, EDWARD EVERETT.

Hale, Sir Matthew, 1609–76, English jurist, author of scholarly works on criminal law (*Pleas of the Crown*, 1678; *History of the Pleas of the Crown*, 1685).

Hale, Nathan, 1755–76, American patriot in American Revolution. Hanged by British as spy. Remembered for reputed last words, "I only regret that I have but one life to lose for my country."

Hale, Sarah Josepha (Buell), 1788–1879, American author, long editor of *Godey's Lady's Book*. "Mary Had a Little Lamb" is attributed to her.

Haleakala (hä'lää"kälä'), mountain, 10,023 ft. high, Hawaii, on Maui and in Haleakala Natl. Park. A dormant volcano with enormous crater (3,000 ft. deep, 21 mi. in circumference).

Hales, Alexander of: see ALEXANDER OF HALES.

Hales, John, 1584–1656, English clergyman and scholar, often called the Ever-Memorable. His lectures on Greek at Oxford, his preaching, and his writings won him renown.

Hales, Stephen, 1677–1761, English physiologist, a clergyman (curate of Teddington), noted for experimental studies in plant and animal physiology. He was the first to measure blood pressure.

Halethorpe, Md.; see ARBUTUS.

Ha-Levi, Judah: see JUDAH HA-LEVI.

Halévy, Élie (ālē' älävē'), 1870–1937, French historian, authority on 19th-cent. England. His masterpiece is *A History of the English People in the Nineteenth Century* (6 vols., 1912–30).

Halévy, Jacques Fromental (zhäk' frômätäl' älävē'), 1799–1862, French operatic composer. His one successful opera was *La Juive* (1835). Father-in-law and teacher of Bizet, he was the uncle of **Ludovic Halévy** (lüdôvēk', 1834–1908, author of the librettos of Offenbach's most successful operettas and, with Henri Meilhac, of the libretto of Bizet's *Carmen* (1875).

Halévy, Joseph (zhôzēf' älävē'), 1827–1908, Jewish-French Orientalist. Deciphered Sabean and Himyaritic inscriptions and argued that Sumerian literature was merely Babylonian literature in secret writing.

Halevy, Judah: see JUDAH HA-LEVI.

Halévy, Ludovic: see HALÉVY, JACQUES FROMENTAL.

Half-Way Covenant, doctrinal decision of Congregational churches in New England regarding membership in 1662. Original rule had permitted children of "converted" adults to share in covenant. New rule included also grandchildren even though their parents had not been converted. Decision, nicknamed Half-Way Covenant, caused dissension and secession.

Haliburton, Thomas Chandler, pseud. **Sam Slick**, 1796–1865, Canadian author, a jurist. His popular series of the sayings and doings of Sam Slick, Yankee peddler, were collected in *The Clockmaker* (1836) and in later volumes.

halibut, important food fish, largest of flatfish, of genus *Hippoglossus*. Two species are known, one in N Atlantic and one in N Pacific. Females sometimes weigh 500 lb., males rarely over 50 lb.

Halicarnassus (hă"lĭkärnă'sŭs), anc. city of Caria, SW Asia Minor. Widow of ruler MAUSOLUS (4th cent. B.C.) built him a great tomb (see MAUSOLEUM).

Halicz, Ukrainian SSR: see GALICH.

Halifax, Charles Montagu, earl of (hă'lĭfăks, hă'lŭ-), 1661–1715, British statesman. Wrote (with Matthew Prior) *The City Mouse and the Country Mouse* (1687). Persuaded Commons to estab. (1692) national debt. Adopted plan to found Bank of England and was made (1694) chancellor of the exchequer. First lord of the treasury 1697–99 and again in 1714.

Halifax, Edward Frederick Lindley Wood, 1st earl of, 1881–1959, British statesman. Governor general of India 1926–31. As foreign secretary (1938–40) he played a large part in negotiating the MUNICH PACT. Ambassador to U.S. 1941–46.

Halifax, city (pop. 92,511), provincial cap., S N.S., Canada, on Halifax Harbour on the Atlantic. Largest city and chief port of N.S. All-year port is main Canadian winter terminal for transatlantic shipping. Industries include oil and sugar refining, shipbuilding, and meat packing. Has large fishing fleet. Founded 1749, it became a naval base in 1758 expedition against Louisburg, in American Revolution, and in War of 1812. Important naval and air base in both World Wars. The Citadel, fortress built 1794–97, overlooks town and harbor. Seat of Dalhousie Univ. (nonsectarian; coed.; 1838) and associated or affiliated Univ. of King's Col. (opened 1790, became first Canadian university by royal charter in 1802, moved from Windsor, N.S., 1923), Nova Scotia Technical Col., and St. Mary's Col. The Halifax *Gazette* (1752), first Canadian newspaper, continues as the *Nova Scotia Royal Gazette*.

Halifax, county borough (pop. 96,037), West Riding of Yorkshire, England. Noteworthy are Akroyd museum and art gallery. Defoe supposedly wrote part of *Robinson Crusoe* here. Industries include mfg. of carpets, cotton, wool, and worsteds.

Halifax, town (pop. 370), N N.C., on Roanoke R., NE of Raleigh; settled c.1750. Site of first constitutional convention (1776) of N.C.

Hall, Charles Francis, 1821–71, American arctic explorer. Made two expeditions (1860–62, 1864–69) seeking Sir John Franklin's party. Added much to geographical knowledge of area. Led government North Pole expedition (1871).

Hall, Charles Martin, 1863–1914, American chemist, a founder of Aluminum Company of America. He discovered electrolytic process that made large-scale aluminum production possible.

Hall, Edwin Herbert, 1855–1938, American physicist. Discovered Hall effect, a difference of electrical potential transverse to the lines of current flow in a conducting medium when magnetic field is applied perpendicular to current. He contributed to study of thermal conduction in metals.

Hall, Granville Stanley, 1846–1924, American psychologist, educator. He was the first president of Clark Univ. (1889–1920). His work *The Contents of Children's Minds on Entering School* (1894) initiated the child-study movement in U.S.

Hall, James, 1793–1868, American author of works on the West, a magazine editor.

Hall, James, 1811–98, American geologist and paleontologist. His work served as a basis for later geological histories of North America.

Hall, Marshall, 1790–1857, English physician and physiologist, pioneer in study of reflex action.

Hall, Fort, trading post, SE Idaho, on Snake R. and near present Pocatello. Built 1834. Important stopping point on Oregon Trail.

Hallam, Arthur Henry (hăl'ŭm), 1811–33, English poet. Tennyson's *In Memoriam* is an elegy for him.

Halland (hä'länd), Swed. *Hallands län,* county (1,903 sq. mi.; pop. 170,201), SW Sweden, on the Kattegat; co. seat Halmstad. This area was conquered from Denmark by Charles X of Sweden, 1658.

Hallandale, town (pop. 10,483), SE Fla., on Atlantic coast N of Miami. Vegetable packing.

Halle (hä'lŭ), city (est. pop. 280,614), East Germany, cap. former state of Saxony-Anhalt, on Saale R. Transportation hub of an important salt-mining dist.; chemical and machine-building industries. Ruled in Middle Ages by archbishops of Magdeburg; accepted Reformation 1544; was awarded to Brandenburg (i.e., the later Prussia) 1648. Famous university was founded 1694; it absorbed Wittenberg Univ. 1817. First Bible Society was founded here 1710. Among many fine buildings are Gothic Red Tower and Marienkirche, on medieval market place. Birthplace of Handel.

Halleck, Fitz-Greene, 1790–1867, American poet. With Joseph Rodman Drake wrote satirical verse in "Croaker" papers. Also known for "Marco Bozzaris" and elegy on Drake.

Halleck, Henry Wager, 1815–72, Union general in Civil War. Commanded Dept. of the Missouri (1861–62). Gained unwarranted prestige from victories under his command. General in chief at Washington (1862–64); exerted little influence as military adviser to President and Secretary of War.

hallel (hŭlāl, hä'lĕl) [Heb.,= praise], sequence of Psalms (113–118) recited in Jewish liturgy on festivals except those of the New Year and Day of Atonement.

Hallelujah (hä"lŭlōō'yŭ) or **Alleluia** (ä"lŭlū'yŭ) [Heb., = praise the Lord], expression of joy in Hebrew worship. Pss. 104–6; 113; 115–17; 135; 146–50. Used in Christian liturgy, especially at Easter.

Haller, Albrecht von (äl'brĕkht fŭn hä'lŭr), 1708–77, Swiss scientist and author. Especially noted for researches in experimental physiology, he was distinguished also as botanist, writer on bibliography and medical history, poet, and novelist.

Hallet, Étienne Sulpice (ātyĕn' sülpēs' älä'), 1755–1825, French architect, known in U.S. as Stephen Hallet. Became supervisor of execution of William Thornton's design for the Capitol, Washington, D.C., but was dismissed for attempted alterations.

Halley, Edmund (hä'lē), 1656–1742, English astronomer, astronomer royal from 1720. First to predict (1682) return of a comet (Halley's comet).

Hall of Fame, national shrine estab. 1900 at New York Univ. with the aid of $250,000 donation by Finley J. Shepard. Names of 50 outstanding Americans were inscribed on bronze tablets in 1900. Other names were added later.

Halloween, Oct. 31, evening before feast of All Saints. Tales and customs concerned with witches and ghosts on Halloween are Celtic in origin.

hallucination, false sensory impression lacking external stimulus or due to misinterpretation of actual external stimulus. Most psychiatrists consider hallucinations symbolic of repressed wishes; study of an individual's hallucinations helps to reveal emotional conflicts, especially in schizophrenic patients. Some hallucinations are caused by emotional stress or great fatigue, e.g., the fata morgana or imagined oasis of desert travelers.

hallucinogenic drugs: see PSYCHOTOGENIC DRUGS.

Halmahera (hälmähä'rä) or **Jailolo** (jīlō'lō), island (c.7,565 sq. mi.; pop. c.87,500), E Indonesia, in the Moluccas, between New Guinea and Celebes. Mountainous, volcanic, lushly tropical. Island produces nutmeg, resin, sago, and rice. Discovered c.1525 by Europeans, came under Dutch control 1660.

Halmstad (hälm'städ"), industrial town (pop. 39,724), co. seat of Halland co., SW Sweden, seaport on the Kattegat. Mineral baths are near.

halo, in physics, circle of light around sun or moon, produced when light from either is refracted and reflected by atmospheric ice crystals. Most complex and brilliant when seen from near poles.

halogen (hä'lŭjŭn), member of a family of very active elements. FLUORINE is lightest, most active; in order of decreasing chemical activity the other halogens are CHLORINE, BROMINE, IODINE, and ASTATINE. All are monovalent, nonmetallic, and form negative ions.

Hals, Frans (fräns' häls'), c.1580–1666, Dutch painter, b. Antwerp. Spent most of his life in Haarlem. Painted both single and group portraits as well as studies of low-life types. His bold brushwork gives his work an air of vivacity and informality. Used heavy browns in early period; later alternated blacks and grays with brilliant color. His *Laughing Cavalier* is among widely known works. Also painters were his son **Frans Hals,** c.1618–c.1669, and his brother **Dirk Hals,** c.1591–1656, noted for festivals and drinking scenes.

Halsey, William F(rederick) (hôl'sē), 1882–1959, American admiral. Commanded naval action in South Pacific and Philippines area in Second World War. Promoted to admiral of the fleet 1945, retired 1947.

Halsingborg (hĕlsĭng'bôryŭ), Swed. *Hälsingborg,* city (pop. 77,006), Malmohus co., S Sweden, seaport on the Oresund opposite Elsinore, Denmark. Trade center and stronghold from 9th cent., it was ceded 1658 by Denmark to Sweden, seized and plundered 1676 by Danes, and regained 1710 by Sweden. Its products include copper, sugar, beer, and superphosphates. To NE is only coal field in Sweden. Formerly also spelled Helsingborg.

Halsted, William Stewart (hôl'stĕd), 1852–1922, American surgeon, professor at Johns Hopkins. His many surgical innovations include use of rubber gloves.

Haltom City (hôl'tŭm), village (pop. 23,133), N Texas, suburb N of Fort Worth.

Halych, Ukrainian SSR: see GALICH.

Halychyna: see GALICIA, Poland and Ukraine.

Halys, river of Asia Minor: see KIZIL IRMAK.

Ham [Heb.,= swarthy], son of Noah and father of Cush, Mizraim, Phut, and Canaan. Gen. 9; 10. Hamitic languages named after him; see LANGUAGE, table.

Hama (hä'mä), city (pop. c.156,000), N Syria, on Orontes R. Was Hittite center in anc. times. Called Hamath in Bible, it was renamed Epiphania by Antiochus IV. Was famed for fine textiles. Now a trade-center for grain-producing area.

Hamadan (hä'mŭdăn), city (pop. c.100,000; alt. c.6,-000 ft.), W Iran, at foot of Mt. Elvend; market center. On site of ECBATANA, cap. of Media. Traditional tombs of Esther and Mordecai are here.

Haman (hä'-), courtier of Ahasuerus. He ordered the massacre of the Jews but was thwarted by Esther and Mordecai and was hanged. Esther 3–7. Also Aman.

Hamann, Johann Georg (yō'hän gā'ôrk hä'mŭn), 1730–88), German theologian. Advocated religious immediacy, stressing importance of inner religious experience. Greatly influenced Kierkegaard.

Hamar (hä'mär), city (pop. 13,234), SE Norway, on Mjosa L. It is center of rich agr. area, with mfg. of machinery and leather goods. Founded 1152 as an episcopal see by Nicholas Breakspear (later Pope Adrian IV), it is now a Lutheran see. Remains of 12th-cent. cathedral survive, but modern city dates only from 19th cent.

Hamasa (hämä'sä), anthology of beautiful early Arabic poems, gathered by Abu Tammam (c.805–c.845).

Hamath, Syria: see HAMA.

Hambletonian (hămbŭltō'nēŭn), 1849–76, American trotting horse, foundation sire of trotting horses bearing his name. Hambletonian Stake Race for three-year-old trotters held annually at Goshen, N.Y. (1926–56), at Du Quoin, Ill. (1957–).

Hamburg (hăm'bûrg, Ger. häm'bŏŏrk), state (288 sq. mi.; pop. c.1,837,000), N Germany. It consists mainly of the free Hansa city of **Hamburg**, on the Elbe near its mouth on the North Sea. Largest German seaport; shipyards; mfg. (machinery, chemicals); fishing fleet. A cultural center, it has a university (founded 1919) and several technical and medical institutes. Founded by Charlemagne, Hamburg soon grew to commercial importance and became a free imperial city. Its alliance with Lübeck (1241) was the basis of the HANSEATIC LEAGUE. Hamburg joined the German Confederation (1815), the German Empire (1871), the Weimar Republic (1919), and the Federal Republic of [W] Germany (1949). In 1938 its outlying port, CUXHAVEN, was ceded to Prussia; in exchange, it received Altona, a port on Elbe R. Damaged severely by air raids in Second World War; post-war reconstruction was rapid. Birthplace of Brahms and Felix Mendelssohn.

Hamburg, village (1966 pop. 9,493), W central N.Y., S of Buffalo; settled c.1808. Nearby is Hamburg–Lake Shore town (pop. 11,527).

Hamden, town (pop. 41,056), S Conn., SW of Wallingford; settled c.1664. Site of Eli Whitney's arms factory is marked.

Hameln, (hä′muln) or **Hamelin** (hä′mŭlĭn), city (pop. 50,418), West Germany, in Lower Saxony, on Weser R. Scene of legend of PIED PIPER OF HAMELIN.

Hamhung (häm′hŏong′), city, North Korea. Mfg. metalware and cotton textiles. Coal mines nearby.

Hamilcar Barca (hä′mĭlkär, hŭmĭl′kär), d. 228 B.C., Carthaginian commander. Gave a good account of himself in Sicily in the First Punic War. When the peace settlement surrendered Sicily, he withdrew without submission. He ruthlessly put down an insurrection of the mercenaries (238 B.C.) and became practically dictator of Carthage. Set out (237 B.C.) to conquer Spain and was successful until he fell in battle. Father of HANNIBAL.

Hamilton, Scottish noble family. **James Hamilton**, 2d **Baron Hamilton** and 1st **earl of Arran**, 1477?–1529, grandson of King James II, was regent (1522–24) for boy king, James V, whom he helped to keep prisoner. His son, **James Hamilton**, 2d **earl of Arran**, d. 1575, joined English party as a Protestant, then French party as a Catholic. Again Protestant, he fled Scotland when Mary Queen of Scots married Darnley. Tried unsuccessfully to marry Mary to his son, **James Hamilton**, 3d **earl of Arran**, 1530–1609, who later became insane. Succeeded as head of the family by his brother, **John Hamilton**, 1st **marquess of Hamilton**, 1532–1604, nearest heir to Scottish throne after James VI. Banished after his part in murder of earl of Murray, he later enjoyed the king's favor. His grandson, **James Hamilton**, 3d **marquess** and 1st **duke of Hamilton**, 1606–49, was Charles I's chief adviser for Scottish affairs. Tried to pacify the Covenanters. Fought for the king at Preston in 1642 and was found guilty of treason by same court which condemned Charles. His brother, **William Hamilton**, 2d **duke of Hamilton**, 1616–51, was also favored by Charles I. Signed for the Scots the treaty known as the engagement with Charles in 1647.

Hamilton, Alexander, 1755–1804, American statesman, b. West Indies. Supported patriot cause and fought in American Revolution. By essays in *The FEDERALIST* he did much to get Constitution ratified. Strong exponent of centralized government. A leader of FEDERALIST PARTY. As first Secretary of the Treasury, he estab. Bank of the United States. Favored strengthening Federal government at expense of the states, tying administration more or less tightly to moneyed interests, and following a pro-British foreign policy. Though Jeffersonianism was more popular, Hamilton's vision of the future America as a wealthy, industrial land proved more accurate than Jefferson's agrarian dream. Hamilton was killed in a duel by Aaron Burr, whom he had kept from the presidency in 1800 and from the governorship of N.Y. in 1804. He left an enduring legacy to the U.S.

Publication of the Hamilton papers was begun in 1961 (ed. by H. C. Syrett).

Hamilton, Andrew Jackson, 1815–75, provisional governor of Texas (1865–66). Pursued wise and courageous course, but much of his work was undone by radical Republican plan of Reconstruction.

Hamilton, Anthony, c.1646–1720, Scottish author of the French *Mémoires du comte de Grammont* (1713?), based on the reminiscences of his brother-in-law, Philibert de GRAMONT. It is a thoroughly amoral but vastly entertaining account of the times.

Hamilton, Emma, Lady, c.1765–1815, English beauty. Mistress (and later wife) of Sir William Hamilton, ambassador to Naples, she had great influence with the queen of Naples. After 1798 she was the mistress of Horatio NELSON whose daughter she bore in 1801. There are many portraits of her by Romney.

Hamilton, Henry, d. 1796, British army officer. In American Revolution, accused of being a "hair buyer" —i.e., one who paid bounties to Indians for scalps taken in frontier raids. Captured by George Rogers Clark at Vincennes (1779).

Hamilton, James, earls of Arran, and **James, 3d marquess** and 1st **duke of Hamilton**: see HAMILTON, family.

Hamilton, James, 1786–1857, U.S. Representative (1822–29), governor of S.C. (1830–32). Presided over convention which passed nullification ordinance. Diplomatic agent in Europe for Texas (1839).

Hamilton, John, 1st **marquess**, and **William**, 2d **duke, of Hamilton**: see HAMILTON, family.

Hamilton, Sir William, 1788–1856, Scottish philosopher. Revived Scottish "common sense" school of metaphysics.

Hamilton, Sir William Rowan, 1805–65, British mathematician, b. Dublin. Worked in optics and mechanics; noted for discovery of quaternions.

Hamilton, city (pop. c.3,000) and cap. of Bermuda; chief port and center of governmental, commercial, and social life.

Hamilton, city (pop. 273,991), S Ont., Canada, on Hamilton Harbour at head of L. Ontario, SW of Toronto; laid out 1813. Lake port, rail and air center. Has steel, cotton, and knitting mills, automobile plants, and railroad shops. In fruitgrowing region. Seat of McMaster Univ. (Baptist; coed.; 1887).

Hamilton, burgh (pop. 41,928), Lanarkshire, Scotland. Rudolf Hess landed on nearby Hamilton estate after his flight from Germany in May, 1941.

Hamilton. 1 City (pop. 2,475), W central Mont., on Bitterroot R., SSW of Missoula. Marcus Daly had estate and model farm here. **2** Industrial city (pop. 72,354), SW Ohio, N of Cincinnati on Great Miami R.; settled on site of Fort Hamilton (1791).

Hamilton, river, 600 mi. long, S Labrador. Rises as Ashuanipi R. from Ashuanipi L. and flows in arc N then SE through series of lakes to the GRAND FALLS where it becomes the Hamilton. Below it flows SE to Lake Melville.

Hamilton, Mount, peak, 4,372 ft. high, W Calif., in Coast Range E of San Jose. Lick Observatory (built 1876–88) of Univ. of California has 120-in. telescope.

Hamilton College, at Clinton, N.Y.; for men. Founded 1793 by Samuel Kirkland as Hamilton-Oneida Acad.; chartered 1812 as Hamilton Col. Kirkland Col., for women, to be coordinate with Hamilton, was chartered in 1965.

Hamilton Inlet, large bay on SE Labrador coast. Rigolet, Hudson's Bay Co. post, is at its narrows.

Hamitic languages, former linguistic grouping, now discredited, of the non-Semitic languages of the Afro-Asiatic family. These were falsely thought to comprise a unitary branch opposite to Semitic.

Hamlin, Hannibal, 1809–91, Vice President of the United States (1861–65). U.S. Senator from Maine (1848–57, 1869–81). Minister to Spain (1881–82).

Hamlin, Talbot Faulkner, 1889–1956, librarian of Avery Architectural Library, Columbia Univ. Wrote several books on architecture.

Hamm (häm), city (pop. 66,305), North Rhine–Westphalia, West Germany, on Lippe R. Railroad and industrial center in Ruhr dist.

Hamm, village, grand duchy of Luxembourg. Has large American military cemetery.

Hammarskjold, Dag, 1905–61, Swedish statesman, secretary general of UN (1953–61). He greatly extended influence of UN as well as prestige of secretary general. A highly active diplomat, he initiated and directed UN role in Congo (see CONGO, REPUBLIC OF THE). Died in plane crash in Northern Rhodesia, Sept. 18, 1961; was posthumously awarded 1961 Nobel Peace Prize.

Hammerfest (hä'mûrfĕst), city (pop. 5,604), Finnmark co., N Norway, port on Kval isl.; inc. 1789. Though it is northernmost city of Europe, harbor is always ice free. It is fishing, whaling, and sealing center. Germans, who used it as naval base in Second World War, demolished it upon retreating.

Hammersmith, London borough since 1965 (est. pop. 216,940); includes the former metropolitan boroughs of Hammersmith and Fulham. St. Paul's School for boys, founded 1509 and attended by Milton and Pepys, was moved to Hammersmith in 1884.

Hammerstein, Oscar (hä'mûrstīn), 1847–1919, German-American operatic impresario. He brought many famous singers to the U.S. and introduced such operas as *Louise, Pelléas et Mélisande,* and *Elektra.* His grandson, **Oscar Hammerstein** 2d, 1895–1960, was a lyricist and librettist. His musicals (e.g., *Oklahoma!, Carousel, South Pacific*) with composer, Richard RODGERS made theatrical history; the songs are an integral part of the plot and serious elements were introduced.

Hammett, Dashiell, 1894–1961, American writer of "tough" detective stories (e.g., *The Maltese Falcon,* 1930).

Hammond, James Henry, 1807–64, governor of S.C. (1842–44). Early advocate of secession. Elected to U.S. Senate in 1857, he made famous "Cotton is King" speech there.

Hammond, John Hays, 1855–1936, American mining engineer. Employed by Cecil Rhodes in South Africa. Involved in Jameson raid (1895–96), captured and sentenced to death, released on payment of fine. Promoted many mining and hydroelectric projects. His son, **John Hays Hammond, Jr.,** 1888–1965, gained note as inventor and electrical engineer. His inventions include torpedoes for coastal defense, incendiary projectiles, telegraphic apparatus.

Hammond. 1 City (pop. 111,698), extreme NW Ind., on Grand Calumet R., SW of East Chicago, in Calumet industrial region; settled 1851. Once a slaughtering center, it now has diversified industry. **2** City (pop. 10,563), SE La., ENE of Baton Rouge, in strawberry area; settled 1855. Seat of Southeastern Louisiana Col.

Hammondsport, village (pop. 1,176), SW N.Y., at S end of Keuka L., NE of Bath. Champagne and other wines are produced. Birthplace of Glenn Curtiss and site of some of his aviation experiments.

Hammurabi (hämōōrä'bē), fl. 1792–1750 B.C., king of BABYLONIA. Founded an empire that was destroyed by Kassites. He is famous for his law code and his great political abilities.

Hampden, John, 1594–1643, English statesman; cousin of Oliver Cromwell. Popular hero of the parliamentarians after his attempted arrest (1642) by Charles I helped to precipitate the civil war.

Hampden, Walter (hăm'dŭn), 1879–1955, American actor, whose real name was Walter Hampden Dougherty. He acted in classical repertory, Ibsen, and Shakespeare. He was first seen as Cyrano de Bergerac in 1923, a role which he often repeated.

Hampden, town (pop. 4,583), S Maine, on W bank of Penobscot R. below Bangor; settled 1767. Plundered by British 1814.

Hampshire (hămp'shīr) or **Hants** (hănts), maritime county (1,649 sq. mi.; pop. 1,431,563), S England; co. town WINCHESTER. Officially Southampton since 1888, county no longer includes Isle of WIGHT. Undulating region devoted to sheep raising and dairy farming, it also has shipbuilding and large maritime trade. SOUTHAMPTON and Portsmouth major ports. Has many literary and historical associations.

Hampstead, part of CAMDEN London borough since 1965. Residential area, associated with artists and writers. On a hill above is **Hampstead Heath,** a public park of 869 acres.

Hampton, Wade, 1818–1902, Confederate general. Succeeded J. E. B. Stuart as cavalry corps commander (1864). Restored home rule as governor of S.C. (1877–79). Until 1890 he was dominant in S.C. politics.

Hampton, since 1965 part of Richmond upon Thames London borough, England, on the Thames. It is the site of **Hampton Court Palace,** built by Cardinal Wolsey in 1515 as his private residence. After his downfall, it was a royal residence until time of George II. Has an art gallery and public gardens. **Hampton Court Conference** was held (1604) to find agreement between Puritans and Established Church, with results most unsatisfactory to Puritans.

Hampton. 1 Town (pop. 5,379), SE N.H., SSW of Portsmouth; settled 1638. Henry Dearborn was born here. Nearby is Hampton Beach, seaside resort. **2** City (pop. 89,258), SE Va., port of HAMPTON ROADS, opposite Norfolk (bridge and tunnel); settled 1610 on site of Indian village. One of oldest continuous English settlements in U.S. Sacked by British 1813 and burned by Confederates 1861. Ships, crabs and oysters. Seat of HAMPTON INSTITUTE. Nearby are Langley Air Force Base, large shipyard, and Federal aeronautical research facilities.

Hampton Court Conference and **Hampton Court Palace:** see HAMPTON, England.

Hampton Institute, at Hampton, Va.; founded for Negro education; opened 1868, chartered 1870 as normal and agr. school.

Hampton Roads, roadstead, SE Va., outlet of James, Nansemond, and Elizabeth rivers into Chesapeake Bay. One of finest natural harbors and one of busiest U.S. seaports; port of Newport News, Hampton, Portsmouth, and Norfolk. In Civil War, scene of fight between ironclads MONITOR AND MERRIMAC. The **Hampton Roads Peace Conference** was a meeting to end Civil War, held Feb. 3, 1865, on board Union transport *River Queen* here. Lincoln presented Union terms. They were unacceptable to South, and meeting failed.

hamster, small rodent of temperate parts of Europe and W Asia. It has a rather broad head and large internal cheek pouches in which food is carried. Common hamster (*Cricetus cricetus*) has a thickset body c.10 in. long and a short hairy tail; gray or brown in color. Golden hamster (*Mesocricetus auratus*) is of considerable importance as a laboratory animal and pet; it is smaller, c.6 in. long. In the wild state hamsters eat small animals and vegetation in summer and grain stored underground in winter.

Hamsun, Knut (kŭnōōt häm'sōōn), 1859–1952, Norwegian novelist. His wandering life brought him twice to U.S., where he had many jobs. His best-known novels are *Hunger* (1890), *Pan* (1894), and *The Growth of the Soil* (1917). Awarded 1920 Nobel Prize in Literature.

Hamtramck (hămtră'mĭk), city (pop. 34,137), SE Mich., within confines of Detroit. Population largely Polish. Growth began c.1910 with auto industry.

Hamun-i-Helmand (hämōōn'-ē-hĕl'mŭnd), lake, area 5,000 sq. mi., on border of Iran and Afghanistan.

Han (hän), dynasty of China, which ruled 202 B.C.–A.D. c.220. Its 400 years of expansion and cultural growth were broken only by the Hsin dynasty (A.D.

c.9–A.D. c.25) which divided Early or Western Han from Later or Eastern Han. Under emperor Wu Ti (reigned 140 B.C.–87 B.C.) Han power was extended W to Sinkiang and Central Asia, N to Manchuria and Korea, and S to Yünnan, Hainan isl., and Annam. Confucianism was made basis of state and civil service examinations were introduced. First encyclopedic history produced by Ssu-ma Ch'ien, and first dictionary compiled. Buddhism was introduced. Collapse of Han was followed by c.350 years of petty states, including the Three Kingdoms and the Tsin dynasty. China eventually reunited under Sui dynasty.

Han (hän), river, c.800 mi. long, rising in Shensi prov., China, flows through Hupei prov. to join Yangtze R. at Wuhan, the tri-city area of Hankow, Hanyang, and Wuchang.

Hananiah (hănŭnī'ŭ), one of the Three Holy Children.

Hancock, John, 1737–93, American Revolutionary patriot, signer of Declaration of Independence. Advocated resistance to British. President of Continental Congress (1775–77).

Hancock, Winfield Scott, 1824–86, Union general in Civil War. Conspicuous as leader of 2d Corps at Gettysburg; foremost in repulsing Confederate attacks, notably Pickett's charge on July 3, 1863. Democratic presidential candidate in 1880.

Hand, Learned, 1872–1961, American jurist; judge of Federal District Court 1909–24, of U.S. Court of Appeals 1924–51. His published works include *The Spirit of Liberty* (1952) and *The Bill of Rights* (1958).

hand, terminal portion of arm. Human hand has eight carpal bones in wrist (carpus), five parallel metacarpals, three phalanges in each finger and two in each thumb. Actions of small hand muscles and forearm muscles permit intricate motions. Man and certain other primates have opposed thumb, with motion differing from that of other four digits, which greatly increases ability to manipulate. In evolution, greater development of central nervous system paralleled appearance of opposed thumb. See *ill.,* p. 656.

handball, indoor and outdoor game played on one-wall or four-wall court. In one-wall game, court is 20 ft. by 34 ft. In four-wall game, court is 23 ft. by 46 ft., surrounded by three walls 23 ft. high and back wall 12 ft. high. Four-wall handball, played in England and Ireland for many centuries, was introduced in U.S. in 1870s.

Handel, George Frideric, 1685–1759, German-English composer, b. Halle. After traveling through Germany and Italy, presenting his early operas, he finally settled in England in 1712. Much of his finest music is to be found in his operas, e.g., *Atalanta, Berenice,* and *Serse* (containing the tenor aria now known as *Largo*). His great oratorio, *The Messiah,* was presented in Dublin in 1742. Among other oratorios are *Samson, Judas Maccabeus,* and *Esther.* His orchestral suites, *Fireworks Music* and *Water Music,* are popular today. He also wrote many songs, sonatas, and concertos for various solo instruments and instrumental combinations, and an anthem for the coronation of George II, still used at coronations today. He was buried in Westminster Abbey.

Handy, W(illiam) C(hristopher), 1873–1958, American Negro composer. First to set down blues. His songs, such as *Memphis Blues, St. Louis Blues,* and *Beale Street Blues,* are classic examples of their type.

Hanford, city (pop. 10,133), central Calif., SSE of Fresno. Trade and processing center in San Joaquin Valley.

Hangchow (häng'jō), city (pop. c.740,000), cap. of Chekiang prov., China; port on Tsientang R. at head of Hangchow Bay, situated on scenic West Lake. Connected to Shanghai and Ningpo by rail. Famous silk-producing center. Founded A.D. 606. As cap. (1132–1276) of Southern Sung dynasty, city was center of art, literature, and scholarship.

Hanko (häng'kō), Swed. *Hangö,* city (pop. 8,152), SW Finland, icefree port on small peninsula in Baltic Sea; summer resort. Following Finnish-Russian War (1939–40) Hanko peninsula was leased to USSR as naval base. Returned to Finland 1944 in exchange for lease on Porkkala dist.

Hankow (häng'kō'), city (pop. c.750,000), Hupei prov., China; port at junction of Han and Yangtze rivers. Linked by bridge to Wuchang and Hanyang; largest city of the Wuhan conurbation, and foremost mfg. and commercial city of central China. Peking-Canton RR crosses here by ferry.

Hanna, Marcus Alonzo (Mark Hanna), 1837–1904, American capitalist and politician. Handled 1896 campaign of William McKinley for presidency. U.S. Senator from Ohio (1897–1904). A great party boss who exemplified union between business and politics for purposes of economic policy.

Hannah [Heb.,= grace], mother of Samuel. 1 Sam. 1; 2.1–26. Anna and Ann are variants of Hannah.

Hannibal [Punic,= grace of Baal], 247–182? B.C., Carthaginian general, one of the great military geniuses of all time; son of Hamilcar Barca, of the great Barca family. In the Punic Wars he succeeded his brother-in-law, Hasdrubal, as commander in Spain (221 B.C.). With a small force of picked troops he set out to invade Italy, crossed the Alps with full baggage train and elephants, and with his cavalry overran the Po valley. He wiped out a Roman force and in 217 set out toward Rome. After defeating the Romans again at L. Trasimeno, he went to S Italy and gained many allies. At Cannae (216 B.C.) he won one of the most brilliant victories of history, but he failed to get proper support from Carthage and could not take Rome. In 207 B.C. his brother Hasdrubal was defeated on the Metaurus, and Hannibal had to draw back. Recalled (203) to defend Carthage against Scipio, he was decisively beaten in the battle of Zama (202). After peace was concluded (201 B.C.), he was chief ruler in Carthage, governing well, but Rome demanded him as a prisoner, and he went into exile, finally poisoning himself to avoid being given to the Romans.

Hannibal, city (pop. 20,028), NE Mo., on Mississippi R., S of Quincy, Ill.; founded 1819. River port, rail center, and industrial city. Boyhood home of Mark Twain, who is commemorated by various structures here.

Hanno, fl. c.470? B.C., Carthaginian navigator. Supposedly explored NE coast of Africa. Hamilcar's son.

Hannover, Germany: see Hanover.

Hanoi (hä'noi), city (pop. c.650,000), cap. of North Vietnam, E Tonkin; port on Red R. A center of network of roads and waterways, with rail connections to Kunming, Peking, and Saigon. Shipping center for agr. and industrial products. Has some heavy mfg. Contains old Annamese town and modern sections. Seat of Chinese rulers of Annam 7th–15th cent. Was cap. of French Indo-China after 1902 and seat of Vietnam government 1945–46. Scene of heavy fighting between French and Vietminh forces (1946–54). Became cap. of North Vietnam 1954. Damaged in U.S. air raid bombing in Vietnam conflict in 1967.

Hanover (hä'nōvŭr), Ger. *Hannover,* former province of Prussia, West Germany, stretching from Dutch border and North Sea in NW to Harz mts. in SE. In 1946 it was incorporated into new state of Lower Saxony. Cities include Hanover, Osnabrück, Hildesheim, Emden, Lüneburg, Celle, Göttingen. Mostly agr. lowland (grain, potatoes, sugar beets). Part of old duchy of Brunswick, the region constituted the duchy of Brunswick-Lüneburg until 1692, when Duke Ernest Augustus was raised to rank of elector and his duchy became the electorate of Hanover. Personal union of England and Hanover under Hanoverian dynasty began 1714 with George I (see Hanover, House of). Hanover formed part of Jérôme Bonaparte's kingdom of Westphalia (1807–13). After restoration of its dynasty, it was raised to a kingdom

Hanover — 454 — Harar

(1815) and became member of GERMAN CONFEDERATION. Because of Salic law of succession it was separated from British crown when Victoria became queen of England (1837). Ernest Augustus, son of George III, who became king of Hanover, began his reactionary reign by rescinding the constitution but was forced to restore it in 1848. His son, George V, succeeded in 1851. As a result of his pro-Austrian stand in the Austro-Prussian War (1866) he lost his kingdom, which became a Prussian province. **Hanover** city (pop. 572,900), on Leine R., is a commercial center and has varied and important industries. The cap. of the former kingdom and province of Hanover, it became the cap. of Lower Saxony in 1946.

Hanover. 1 Borough (pop. 15,538), SE Pa., ESE of Gettysburg. First Civil War battle N of Mason-Dixon line fought here 1863. **2** Village, E central Va., NNE of Richmond. Patrick Henry lived here for many years and pleaded (1763) first important case in courthouse.

Hanover, house of, royal family, of Guelphic origin (see HANOVER, province). Succeeded to English throne by Act of Settlement (1701) through a claim based on descent from James I. The first of five Hanoverian kings of Great Britain was (1714) George I, elector of Hanover. With Victoria (1837) the crowns of Hanover and Great Britain were separated.

Hansberry, Lorraine, 1930–65, American playwright acclaimed for *Raisin in the Sun* (1959), first play by a Negro woman to be produced on Broadway, and for her last play, *The Sign in Sidney Brustein's Window* (1964).

Hanseatic League (hăn″sēă′tĭk, hăn″zē–), mercantile league of medieval German towns. It came into existence gradually. Originally a *hansa* seems to have been a company of individual traders to foreign lands. The principal establishments of Hansa companies were at WISBY, NOVGOROD, BERGEN, BRUGES, and London (see STEELYARD, MERCHANTS OF THE). To protect themselves against piracy and to overcome foreign competition and trade restrictions, the mercantile cities drew closer. In 1241 LÜBECK and HAMBURG signed a treaty of mutual protection. Some 70 other cities joined. The League was formally organized in 1358. In 1370 it forced on WALDEMAR IV of Denmark the Treaty of Stralsund, which gave it trade monopoly in Scandinavia for more than a century. After a steady decline, the league dissolved in the 17th cent., but the name "Hansa city" has lived on in Bremen, Hamburg, and Lübeck.

Hansen, Peter Andress, 1795–1874, Danish astronomer. He revised lunar theory and compiled *Tables de la lune* (1857), widely used in preparation of nautical almanacs.

Hansen's disease: see LEPROSY.

Hanson, Howard, 1896–, American composer; director (1924–64) of the Eastman School of Music. Rochester, N.Y. His works include the Second, or Romantic, Symphony; the opera, *Merrymount;* and cantata, *Song of Human Rights.*

Hanson, John, 1715–83, first "President of the United States in Congress Assembled." First President (1781–82) to serve one-year term under Articles of Confederation, but his duties were merely those of a presiding officer.

Hants: see HAMPSHIRE.

Hanukkah (hä′nŏŏkä) [Heb.,= dedication] joyous anniversary of rededication of Temple in Jerusalem in 165 B.C by the MACCABEES. Occurs in December and lasts eight days, during which time lights are kindled each evening.

Hanyang (hän′yang′), city (pop. c.500,000), Hupei prov., China, at junction of Han and Yangtze rivers. Part of WUHAN conurbation. Linked by bridge to Hankow and Wuchang. Has cotton mills, ironworks, and steelworks.

Hapeville, residential city (pop. 10,082), NW Ga., suburb S of Atlanta.

Hapsburg or **Habsburg** (both: hăps′bûrg, Ger. häps′-bŏŏrk), ruling house of AUSTRIA from 1282 to 1918. Original holdings of family, which can be traced to 10th cent., were in NW Switzerland and Alsace. Name is taken from Habsburg castle, now in ruins, in Aargau, Switzerland. By 13th cent. family held most of Upper Alsace, Switzerland, and Baden. Count Rudolf IV of Hapsburg was elected (1273) German king as RUDOLF I. He confiscated Austria, Styria, Carinthia, Carniola from Ottocar II of Bohemia (1276) and in 1282 made these duchies hereditary family possessions. SWITZERLAND was soon lost, but Tyrol was added in 1363. All Hapsburg possessions as a whole were held together by a family law and could not be alienated from family nor inherited by females. With the election of Albert II as German king (1438), the imperial office, though theoretically still elective, became vested in the house of Hapsburg (for list of Hapsburg emperors, see HOLY ROMAN EMPIRE). Three marriages made the Hapsburgs a world power: (1) that of Maximilian I with MARY OF BURGUNDY, which brought the Low Countries; (2) that of their son, Philip I, to Joanna of Castile, which gave their elder son, Emperor CHARLES V, Spain and the Spanish empire; (3) that of Philip and Joanna's younger son, Ferdinand, with Anna, sister of Louis II of Hungary and Bohemia, which in 1526 brought these two crowns to the Hapsburgs. Thus the Hapsburg empire, "where the sun never set," stretched from the Carpathians to the Philippines. In the division made by Charles V, his son Philip II received the Spanish empire, including Sicily, Naples, Milan, and the Netherlands (see NETHERLANDS, AUSTRIAN AND SPANISH); Ferdinand, as FERDINAND I, became emperor and retained Austria, Bohemia, Hungary, and various German territories. Imperial wars of the 17th cent. weakened authority and cost them Alsace, Franche-Comté, Artois, and parts of Flanders and Hainaut, but at the same time they recovered Hungary from Turkey. The Spanish branch ended in 1700 with Charles II; the resulting War of the SPANISH SUCCESSION (1701–14) forced Austria to give up its claim to Spain but gave it the Austrian Netherlands and Milan. The PRAGMATIC SANCTION made it possible for a woman, MARIA THERESA, to inherit the Hapsburg lands; in the War of the AUSTRIAN SUCCESSION (1740–48) she defended her inheritance against a coalition, losing only SILESIA. Her husband, the grand duke of Tuscany, became emperor as FRANCIS I (1745). With their son, JOSEPH II, one of the greatest Hapsburg monarchs, began the line of **Hapsburg-Lorraine.** TUSCANY was ruled by a separate branch 1790–1860; Modena, acquired by marriage, was ruled by branch of Austria-Este (see ESTE) until 1859. The main branch was continued by Leopold II and by Francis II, who in 1804 took title "Emperor of Austria" as Francis I. From this point, the history of the Hapsburgs became that of Austria and, after 1867, of the AUSTRO-HUNGARIAN MONARCHY. After the death of Emperor Charles I (abdicated 1918), the claims of the dynasty passed to his son, Archduke Otto (b. 1912).

hara-kiri (hä′rŭ-kēr′ē, hă′rŭ-) Japanese form of honorable suicide. Before 1868 was obligatory for disobedience or disloyalty to emperor. Still occasionally performed voluntarily after misfortune.

Harald: see HAROLD.

Haran (hā′răn) or **Harran** (hä′răn), anc. city of Mesopotamia, now in SE Asiatic Turkey, SE of Urfa. A trade center, seat of the temple of the Assyrian moongod, it was also the home of Abraham's family after the migration from Ur. As Carrhae in Roman times it was the scene of a disastrous defeat of Romans by Parthians (53 B.C.). Site has been excavated.

Harappan civilization: see INDUS VALLEY CIVILIZATION.

Harar or **Harrar** (both: hä′rŭr), city (pop. c.40,000), E central Ethiopia. Walled city founded 14th cent. Occupied by Egyptians 1875–85, incorporated 1887 into Ethiopia. Trades in coffee, cereals, and cotton.

SMALL CAPITALS = cross references. Pronunciation key on inside end pages. Abbreviations: p. 2.

Harbin (här'bĭn), city (pop. c.1,552,000), cap. of Heilungkiang prov., China; main port of Sungari R. and junction of Chinese Eastern RR and South Manchurian RR. Trade, mfg., and communications center. Former (1896–1924) Russian concession.

Hardanger Fjord (härdäng'ür fyôrd'), second largest fjord of Norway, penetrating 114 mi. from the Atlantic into SW Norway. At head of a S branch is Skjeggedalsfoss (waterfall, 525 ft. high); Voringfoss (535 ft. high) is near head of an E branch. The Hardangerfjell, mountain mass extending inland from fjord, rises to 6,153 ft. in the Hardangerjokel. Picturesque villages and scenery make region a favorite of tourists.

Hardee, William Joseph, 1815–73, Confederate general. An able leader in Army of Tennessee. Surrendered to W. T. Sherman in N.C. in April, 1865.

Harden, Sir Arthur (här'dŭn), 1865–1940, English biochemist. Shared 1929 Nobel Prize in Chemistry for research in alcoholic fermentation: he estab. the character of zymase and discovered that other yeast enzymes are also concerned with fermentation.

Hardenberg, Friedrich von: see NOVALIS.

Hardenberg, Karl August, Fürst von (kärl' ou'gŏost fürst' fŭn här'dŭnbĕrk), 1750–1822, Prussian minister of foreign affairs (1804–6) and chancellor (1810–22). Continued reform program begun by Karl vom und zum STEIN; abolished trade monopolies; turned feudal land into freeholds; emancipated Jews. Persuaded Frederick William III to join coalition against Napoleon (1813). After 1815 he came increasingly under the conservative sway of Metternich.

hardening, in metallurgy, any of several processes for increasing resistance of metal to penetration. An indenter made of steel, tungsten carbide, or diamond measures hardness value. A metal is harder when it has small grains; it has smaller grains when cooled fast. Methods for rapid cooling include quenching at high temperature in various liquids or insertion of metal pieces (chills) in wall of sand mold to cool small areas on surface of a casting. Cold rolling imparts hardness by stretching grains, which then resist further stress. In chemical hardening other elements are added to molten metal making an alloy. Surface of steel is casehardened by increasing its carbon content by surrounding metal with charcoal, hydrocarbon gas, or molten cyanide, and then heating.

hardening of the arteries: see ARTERIOSCLEROSIS.

hardhack or **steeplebush,** a North American spirea (*Spiraea tomentosa*) with clusters of rose or white flowers.

Hardin, city (pop. 2,789), S Mont., near confluence of Bighorn and Little Bighorn rivers; settled 1906. Trading point for Crow Indian Reservation. Custer Battlefield Natl. Monument is nearby.

Harding, Stephen: see STEPHEN HARDING, SAINT.

Harding, Warren G(amaliel) (gŭmä'lĕul), 1865–1923, 28th or 29th (see list at end of article UNITED STATES) President of United States (1921–23). U.S. Senator (Republican) from Ohio (1915–21). His noncommittal utterances in presidential campaign of 1920 (he coined the word *normalcy* to express social and economic conditions he promised the nation) helped win him election. One achievement of his administration was calling of the Washington Conference (see NAVAL CONFERENCES). He died suddenly in San Francisco, Aug., 1923. Exposure of TEAPOT DOME scandal and lesser scandals came later; as a result, his administration has been stigmatized as one of most corrupt in U.S. history.

hardness, the resistance a substance offers to being scratched. Mohs's scale (named for Friedrich Mohs) ranges from softest to hardest: talc, 1; gypsum, 2; calcite, 3; fluorite, 4; apatite, 5; feldspar, 6; quartz, 7; topaz, 8; corundum, 9; diamond, 10. The hardness of many minerals falls between those listed; e.g., barite is 3.3.

hardpan, condition of soil or subsoil in which particles become bound together in an impervious mass. It is a serious handicap to farming.

Hardy, Thomas, 1840–1928, English novelist and poet, b. Dorsetshire. Fame came in 1874 with novel *Far from the Madding Crowd.* Novels laid in his native region (which he called Wessex) include *The Return of the Native* (1878), *The Mayor of Casterbridge* (1886), *Tess of the D'Urbervilles* (1891), *Jude the Obscure* (1896). They are generally gloomy and naturalistic studies of character and environment. Adverse criticism led him to turn to poetry. His pessimism was expressed in such books as *Wessex Poems* (1898); a poetic drama. *The Dynasts* (1903–8): and *Moments of Vision* (1917, lyrics). He also wrote distinguished short stories, such as *Wessex Tales* (1888).

Hare, Robert, 1781–1858, American chemist. Invented oxyhydrogen blowpipe.

hare, mammal of North America, Europe, Asia, and Africa, formerly considered a rodent, now usually placed in order Lagomorpha. True hares (genus *Lepus*) have longer ears and hind legs than rabbits. At birth they are covered with hair and the eyes are open. Varying hare or snowshoe rabbit and jack rabbit (with ears sometimes c.½ body length) are native to North America; arctic hare has circumpolar distribution; European hare native to central and W Europe is introduced in North America.

harebell, bluebell, or **bluebell of Scotland,** slender wiry-stemmed perennial bellflower (*Campanula rotundifolia*), with dainty blue bell-shaped blossoms.

harelip, congenital cleft or split of the upper lip: occurs often with associated cleft palate. Disfigurement, speech and eating problems are present. Correctable by early surgery.

Haren, Willem van (wĭl'ŭm vän hä'rŭn), 1710–68, Dutch poet, of a noble family. His chief work was an epic poem, *Friso* (1741). His brother, **Onno Zwier van Haren** (ô'nō zvēr), 1713–79, wrote patriotic verse.

Harfleur (ärflûr'), town (pop. 7,495), Seine-Maritime dept., N France; a Channel port at mouth of the Seine. Captured 1415 by Henry V of England.

Hargeisa (härgä'sä), town (pop. c.20,000), NW Somali Republic. Commercial center of a livestock-raising region. Cap. of British Somaliland until 1960.

Hargreaves, James, d. 1778, Englishman credited with invention of spinning jenny (see SPINNING).

Hari, Mata: see MATA HARI.

Haringey, London borough since 1965 (est. pop. 257,-950); includes the former municipal boroughs of Hornsey, Tottenham, and Wood Green.

Hariri (härē'rē), 1054–1122, Arabian writer of Basra. Chief work is the popular *Makamat,* a kind of picaresque novel, consisting of 50 episodes.

Hari Rud (härē'rood'), anc. *Arius,* river, c.750 mi. long, rising in central Afghanistan; it disappears in the steppes S of Kara Kum. Forms part of Iran-Turkman SSR boundary. Called Tejend in USSR.

Harkness, E(dward) S(tephen), 1874–1940, American philanthropist. Extended philanthropies especially to colleges, hospitals, and museums.

Harkness, William, 1837–1903, American astronomer. b. Scotland. Studied terrestrial magnetism, discovered spectral line in sun's corona. Astronomical director of U.S. Naval Observatory (1894–99).

Harlan, John Marshall, 1833–1911, Associate Justice of U.S. Supreme Court (1877–1911). On the whole, a strict constructionist; known as a "dissenter." His grandson, **John Marshall Harlan,** 1899–, also Associate Justice of U.S. Supreme Court (1955–).

Harlan, city (pop. 4,177). SE Ky., SW of Lynch, in Cumberlands near Va. line; settled 1819. Shipping center for coal of Harlan co., where mines were unionized 1941 after 20 years of bitter strife between coal operators and miners.

Harlech (här'lĕkh), village, Merionethshire, Wales. Its heroic defense against Yorkists (1468) is theme of Welsh battle song, *The March of the Men of Harlech.* Has best golf course in Wales.

Harleian Library (här'lē̆ŭn), collection of manuscripts and legal documents, formed by Robert Harley, 1st earl of Oxford, and his son Edward Harley, 2d earl of Oxford. Purchased by British government in 1753; now in British Museum library.

Harlem, city (pop. 1,267), N central Mont., E of Havre. Hq. of nearby Fort Belknap Indian Reservation. Harlem Dam is part of Milk R. project.

Harlem, congested residential and business section of upper Manhattan borough of New York city, bounded roughly by Central Park and 110th St. (S), East R. (E), Harlem R. (NE), 168th St. (N), Amsterdam Ave. and Morningside Park (W). Estab. 1658 as Dutch settlement of Nieuw Haarlem. Revolutionary Battle of Harlem Heights fought nearby, Sept. 16, 1776. Largely rural until modern transportation linked it to lower Manhattan in 19th cent. Rapid influx of Negroes (1910–20) made it one of largest Negro communities in U.S. Large numbers of Puerto Ricans settled in E section.

Harlem River, navigable tidal channel c.8 mi. long. in New York city, separating Manhattan from the Bronx. With Spuyten Duyvil Creek (spī'tŭn dī'vŭl) (1-mi. ship canal) on W, it connects Hudson R. with Hell Gate channel of EAST RIVER. Bridges.

Harlequin, called earlier *Arlecchino,* stock servant character of COMMEDIA DELL' ARTE and counterpart to Columbine. An acrobat and a wit, always childlike and amorous.

Harley, Robert, 1st earl of Oxford and **Earl Mortimer,** 1661–1724, English statesman. Had great influence on Queen Anne through his cousin, Lady Masham, and was virtual prime minister 1711–14. Began SOUTH SEA BUBBLE scheme. Secretly negotiated end of War of Spanish Succession in 1713. Struggled for power with Henry ST. JOHN and was forced out of office. His library was basis of HARLEIAN LIBRARY.

Harlingen (här'lĭnjŭn), city (pop. 41,207), extreme S Texas, NW of Brownsville; founded c.1904. Processes and ships fruit, vegetables, and cotton. Linked to Intracoastal Waterway by barge canal.

Harlow, Jean, 1911–37, American film actress. notable for her beauty and spectacular appearance. Her films include *Hell's Angels, Bombshell,* and *Platinum Blonde.*

Harmas Koros, river, Hungary: see KOROS.

Harmhab (härm'hăb), d. c.1303 B.C., king of anc. Egypt. Powerful under Ikhnaton and Tut-ankhamen, he himself became king c.1342 B.C. and founder of the XIX dynasty. He suppressed corruption in government and restored prosperity. RAMSES I succeeded him. Also appears as Horemheb or Haremhab.

Harmodius and Aristogiton (härmō'dēŭs, ă"rĭstōjī'tŭn), d. c.514 B.C., Athenian patriots. Hipparchus the tyrant tried to win the affection of Harmodius away from Aristogiton and, spurned, insulted Harmodius' sister. The two friends planned to kill Hipparchus and his brother Hippias. They did kill Hipparchus but not Hippias. Harmodius was killed on the spot, Aristogiton executed. The two were regarded as heroes by liberty-loving Athenians.

Harmon, Judson, 1846–1927, U.S. Attorney General (1895–97), governor of Ohio (1909–13).

harmonica. 1 In music, the simplest of the free-reed instruments; also called the mouth organ. The reeds, set in a narrow wooden or metal case, are supplied with holes through which air is drawn or blown. Most harmonicas have only a diatonic scale. **2** Musical glasses were known and played in antiquity. Benjamin Franklin's instrument consisted of a graduated series of glass bowls fitting inside one another and supported by a spindle which revolved the edges of the bowls through a water trough. Fingertips touching the moistened edges produced the sound. Both Mozart and Beethoven composed for it.

Harmony. 1 Village (pop. 1,214), SE Minn., near Iowa line SSE of Rochester; settled in 1850s. Nearby Niagara Cave is popular tourist attraction. **2** Borough

(pop. 1,142), W Pa., NE of Zelienople. First settlement (1805) of HARMONY SOCIETY.

harmony, in music, the simultaneous sounding of two or more tones, which produces chords. The study of harmony examines chords and their relation to each other. The idea of chords was definitely estab. about the 16th cent. Before then, music was polyphonal, and although sounds resembling chords did occur, horizontal and melodic considerations took precedence over vertical or harmonic ones. In 1722, Rameau presented theories that form the basis for the highly complicated rules of harmony. During the 18th cent., the concept of TONALITY became general. Freer uses of tonality developed in the 19th cent., and the 20th cent. saw the evolution of ATONALITY and some breakdown of the old laws of harmony.

Harmony Society, religious society founded by German Separatists led by George Rapp. Harmonists held property in common and subscribed to celibacy. Several communities (Harmony, Pa., in 1805; New Harmony, Ind., in 1814; and Economy, Pa., in 1825) were created in the U.S.

Harmsworth, Alfred Charles William: see NORTHCLIFFE.

Harnack, Adolph von (ädôlf fŭn här'näk), 1851–1930, German theologian and church historian, noted for *Lehrbuch der Dogmengeschichte* (4 vols., 1886–90).

Harnett, William Michael, 1848–92, American painter of *trompe-l'œil* realistic effects in still life.

Harney, William Selby, 1800–1889, American general. Ranking cavalry officer in Mexican War, he fought brilliantly at Cerro Gordo (1847). In early Civil War he commanded Dept. of the West; his conciliatory policy lost him his command in 1861.

Harney Peak: see BLACK HILLS.

Harnosand (härnûsänd'), Swed. *Härnösand,* city (pop. 17,136), co. seat of Vasternorrland co., NE Sweden, seaport (ice-bound in winter) at mouth of Angerman R. Exports timber, tar, cellulose, and wood pulp. It is a Lutheran episcopal see. Settled in 14th cent. and inc. 1585. It was sacked 1721 by Russians.

Harold, 1022?–1066, king of England (1066), rival of WILLIAM I. Son of GODWIN, he belonged to most powerful noble family in reign of Edward the Confessor. Exiled in 1051, family returned 1052 and recovered power. Driven by winds to French coast, he was seized and forced to take oath to support William's claim to English throne. Returning home he renounced oath. In a revolt of the Northumbrians, Harold sided against his brother Tostig. Family was thus divided at death of Edward, who named Harold his heir. William at once invaded in S and Tostig, with Harold III of Norway, invaded from N. Harold defeated and killed Tostig and Harold III. Opposed William at Hastings and was killed.

Harold, kings of Norway. **Harold I** (Harold Fairhair), Norse *Harald Haarfagre,* c.850–c.933, became first king of Norway after victory at Hafrs Fjord over several petty kings (872). Many Viking rulers fled to Iceland as a result; others (e.g., ROLLO) conquered and settled Normandy. **Harold III,** Norse *Harald Hardhrádhi* [stern council], d. 1066, half-brother of OLAF II, entered Byzantine service after Olaf's defeat (1030). He returned in 1042, joined revolt against MAGNUS I, became joint ruler with Magnus 1046, sole ruler 1047. In 1066 he took part with TOSTIG in invasion of England; fell at STAMFORD BRIDGE.

Harold Bluetooth, d. c.985, first Christian king of Denmark (935–85).

Harold Harefoot, d. 1040, king of England (1037–40). Illegitimate son of Canute, he struggled with his halfbrother Harthacanute for control of England.

harp, stringed musical instrument of anc. origin, whose strings are plucked with the fingers. Modern harp consists of three parts—sound box, neck, and pillar. Strings are stretched from sound box to neck, where tuning pegs are fastened. The harp was originally diatonic. More strings were added to make it chromatic, but its capabilities were still limited. Introduction of double-action pedals (c.1810) made it possible to raise the pitch of a string either a tone or a semitone, thus increasing the possibilities of the instrument and making it popular in the orchestra.

Harper, William Rainey, 1856–1906, American educator and Hebrew scholar. He became professor of Semitic languages at Yale in 1886. In 1891 he was appointed first president of Univ. of Chicago.

Harpers Ferry, town (pop. 572), E W.Va., on bluffs at confluence of Potomac and Shenandoah rivers, c.55 mi. NW of Washington, D.C. Scene of John Brown's raid on U.S. arsenal, Oct. 16, 1859. Key to Shenandoah Valley in Civil War, it changed hands several times, being finally taken by Union forces in 1863. Site of Harpers Ferry Natl. Historic Park.

Harper Woods, city (pop. 19,995), SE Mich., suburb NE of Detroit.

harpsichord: see PIANO.

Harpy, in Greek religion, predatory monster with head of a woman and body, wings, and claws of a bird.

harpy, large bird of prey found from S Mexico to Brazil. It is 38–40 in. long.

Harran, anc. city of Mesopotamia: see HARAN.

Harrar: see HARAR.

Harriman, E(dward) H(enry), 1848–1909, American railroad executive. Gained control of several Western railroads. Attempt to control Chicago, Burlington & Quincy RR was blocked by James J. HILL. His son, **W(illiam) Averell Harriman,** 1891–, was ambassador to the USSR (1943–46), U.S. Secretary of Commerce (1946–48), and director of the Mutual Security Agency (1951–53). Governor of N.Y. (1953–59). Served as U.S. ambassador at large (1961–63, 1965–) and as undersecretary of state for economic affairs (1963–65).

Harrington, James, 1611–77, English political writer. His utopian *Commonwealth of Oceana* (1656) influenced democratic thought in America and elsewhere.

Harris, Chapin Aaron, 1806–60, American dentist, pioneer in modern dentistry, noted for writings and as founder of *American Journal of Dental Science* and of first school of dentistry.

Harris, Frank, 1856–1931, British American author, b. Ireland. Edited magazines in London and New York. Gained notoriety with biographies of Oscar Wilde and other friends and with his own autobiography.

Harris, Joel Chandler, 1848–1908, American Southern author, a newspaper editor, famous for "Uncle Remus" stories in Negro dialect.

Harris, Julie, 1925–, American actress. Achieved success on the stage in *Member of the Wedding* (1950). Created leading roles in *I Am a Camera* and *The Lark.*

Harris, Roy, 1898–, American composer; pupil of Nadia Boulanger. Among his works are *When Johnny Comes Marching Home,* an "American Overture"; Symphony for Voices, to poems by Whitman; Folksong Symphony; and a piano quintet. While he is not a strict modernist, he occasionally uses such devices as polytonality and irregular metrical patterns.

Harris, Thomas Lake, 1823–1906, American Christian mystic, b. England. Founded the Brotherhood of the New Life, 1861.

Harris, Townsend, 1804–78, American diplomat. Appointed first U.S. consul general to Japan in 1855, raised to minister in 1859. Negotiated commercial treaty (1858).

Harris, Hebrides, Scotland: see LEWIS WITH HARRIS.

Harrisburg, city (pop. 79,697), state cap. (since 1812), SE Pa., on Susquehanna R.; settled c.1710. Important rail focus; commercial and wholesale center. Steel mfg. Notable buildings include state capitol, education building (with state library), and Pennsylvania State Mus.

Harrison, Ross Granville, 1870–1959, American biologist. Noted for his discovery of a tissue culture used in studying isolated living cells.

Harrison, Wallace K(irkman), 1895–, American architect. He was coordinating architect for UN hq. and for Lincoln Center, New York.

Harrison, William Henry, 1773–1841, 9th President of the United States (1841). Governor of Indiana Territory (1800–1812); primarily responsible for opening Ohio and Indiana to white settlement. Won battle of Tippecanoe against Indians, Nov. 6–7, 1811. In War of 1812, as commander in Northwest, he won battle of the Thames (see THAMES, BATTLE OF THE). U.S. Representative (1816–19) and Senator from Ohio (1825–28). The Whigs, presenting Harrison as a rugged Westerner and using "Tippecanoe and Tyler too" as a slogan, waged first "rip-roaring" campaign in U.S. history to elect him President. He died a month after taking office. His grandson, **Benjamin Harrison,** 1833–1901, was 23rd President of the United States (1889–93). Served in Civil War. U.S. Senator (Republican) from Ind. (1881–87). As President he approved all regular Republican measures, including highly protective McKinley Tariff Act. His moderate stand on civil service reform displeased both reformers and spoilsmen. First Pan-American Conference was held in his administration (1889).

Harrison. 1 City (1964 pop. 7,015), NW Ark., in Ozarks NE of Fayetteville; settled c.1820. Nearby is Mystic Cavern. **2** Town (pop. 11,743), NE N.J., industrial suburb on Passaic R. opposite Newark. **3** Town (1965 pop. 20,433), SE N.Y., suburb of New York city, between Mamaroneck and Rye.

Harrisonburg, city (pop. 11,916), NW Va., in Shenandoah Valley NNE of Staunton; settled 1739. Processing center in poultry, dairy, and livestock area. Seat of Eastern Mennonite Col. Limestone caverns nearby.

Harrod, James, 1742–93, American frontiersman. In 1774 he founded first settlement in Ky., later named Harrodsburg in his honor.

Harrodsburg, city (pop. 6,061), central Ky., S of Frankfort; founded 1774 by James Harrod. Oldest settlement in state. Trade center in bluegrass area; livestock, grain, and tobacco grown. Resort city with mineral springs. Has replica of Fort Harrod (where state's first school was conducted) and cabin where Nancy Hanks and Thomas Lincoln were married.

Harrow or **Harrow-on-the-Hill,** London borough since 1965 (est. pop. 209,520). Seat of Harrow, one of England's great public schools.

Harsha (hûr'shǔ), c.590–647, Indian emperor. Conquered N India 606–12. His cap. at Kanauj was artistic and literary center. Turned from Hinduism to Buddhism.

Hart, Albert Bushnell, 1854–1943, American historian. Harvard professor (1883–1926) and prodigious worker, responsible for over 100 volumes written or edited by him. Editor of and contributor to "American Nation" series (28 vols., 1904–18) and *Epochs of American History* (4 vols., 1891–1926). Editor or coeditor of many series, notably *Guide to the Study and Reading of American History* (1896; revised ed., 1912), an important bibliography.

Hart, Basil Henry Liddell: see LIDDELL HART, BASIL HENRY.

Hart, Lorenz Milton: see RODGERS, RICHARD.

Hart, Moss, 1904–61, American dramatist. Collaborated with GEORGE S. KAUFMAN on *You Can't Take It With You* (1936) and other plays; wrote the books for *Lady In the Dark* (1941) and other musicals; wrote plays of his own, including *Winged Victory* (1943).

Hart, William S., 1870–1946, American stage and film actor. After a long stage career (1889–1914), he entered films and became the model of the strong, silent man of the West.

Harte, (Francis) Bret, 1836–1902, American writer. A gold seeker, teacher, and journalist, he wrote stories (e.g., "The Luck of Roaring Camp," "The Outcasts of Poker Flat"), novels, and humorous poems of the West. Last years spent in England.

hartebeest (här′tĭbēst″), name for certain African antelopes. Usually it refers to genus *Alcelaphus* (or *Bubalis)*; sometimes to *Damaliscus*, the bontebok and blesbok. The bubal hartebeest (*Alcelaphus buselaphus*) is believed by some to be extinct. It is reddish or fawn, stands c.3½ ft. at the shoulder, and has ringed, pointed, curved horns. The larger red hartebeest (*A. caama*) is native to S Africa.

Hartford. 1 City (pop. 162,178), state cap., central Conn., on Connecticut R.; settled 1635–36 on site of Dutch trading post (1633). State's largest city and commercial, industrial, and cultural center. Internationally famous for its insurance business (since 1794). Mfg. of firearms, typewriters, marine turbines and engines, tools, and brushes. Hartford *Courant*, founded 1764, is one of oldest U.S. newspapers. Birthplace of Noah Webster, John Fiske, and elder J. P. Morgan. Homes of Harriet Beecher Stowe and Mark Twain are preserved. Seat of TRINITY COLLEGE, Hartford Seminary Foundation, and Univ. of Hartford. Has old statehouse (1796; designed by Bulfinch), where Hartford Convention met, and capitol (1872). Charter Oak stood here until 1856; tradition says Conn. charter was hidden in this tree when Sir Edmond Andros demanded it (1687). **2** Town (pop. 6,355), E Vt., on Connecticut and White rivers, E of Rutland; settled 1765. Includes industrial and commercial village of White River Junction (pop. 2,546; gateway to large resort area), residential villages of Hartford and Wilder.

Hartford Convention, Dec. 15, 1814–Jan. 4, 1815, meeting of 26 delegates to consider the problems of New England in the WAR OF 1812, held at Hartford, Conn. Grew out of opposition to embargo acts and to war. It recommended that New England secession, which extremists had urged, if it came at all, should be gradual and should be executed in peaceful times. Importance of meeting is twofold: it continued the view of states' rights that was the refuge of minority groups; it virtually destroyed the Federalist party politically, since the Federalists, who had sponsored the convention, were unable to regain lost prestige.

Hartford Foundation, estab. 1942 by John A. Hartford and George L. Hartford; aims to reduce time lag between medical research findings and their clinical use.

Hartford Wits: see CONNECTICUT WITS.

Harthacanute (här′thăkŭnŭt), d. 1042, king of Denmark (1035–42) and of England (1040–42), son of Canute. Ruled in Denmark until the death of Harold Harefoot, then in England. Left throne to Edward the Confessor.

Hartlepool (härt′lē–, härt′ŭl–), municipal borough (pop. 17,674), Durham, England; a seaport. Has extensive docks and trade in coal and timber.

Hartley, David, 1705–57, English physician, philosopher. Founder of associational psychology, the theory that all consciousness results from combinations of simple sensations.

Hartley, Marsden, 1877–1943, American landscape, genre, still-life painter. One of the first Americans to practice expressionism, he exhibited with the Blaue Reiter. Also wrote poetry and criticism.

Hartmann, Eduard von (härt′män), 1842–1906, German philosopher. His philosophy of the "unconscious" (meaning forces of nature) stressed struggle in man between impulse and reason.

Hartmann, Nicolai, 1882–1950, German philosopher. Believed that the mission of philosophy was the statement of the problems of being.

Hartmann von Aue (härt′män fün ou′ŭ), c.1170–c.1220, German poet. He wrote lyrics, chivalric romances (*Erec, Iwain*), a religious legend (*Gregorius,* which inspired Thomas Mann's *The Holy Sinner*), and the idyl *Der arme Heinrich* (used by Longfellow for his *Golden Legend*).

Hartsville, city (pop. 1,712), N central Tenn., near Cumberland R., NE of Nashville; settled in early

1800s. In Civil War Gen. J. H. Morgan defeated Federals garrisoned here, Dec., 1862.

Harun-al-Rashid (härōōn-äl-räshĕd′, hä′rōōn-äl-rä′-shĭd), c.764–809, 5th ABBASID caliph (786–809). Imprisoned the Barmecides, a powerful Persian family who had helped him become caliph. Under him Baghdad was at its height as a cultural center. Figures prominently in *Thousand and One Nights*.

Harunobu (Harunobu Suzuki) (hä′rōō′nō′bōō), c.1725–1770, Japanese artist. Introduced multiple color printing with wood blocks.

Harvard, John, 1607–38, chief founder of Harvard Col. He bequeathed half his estate and his library toward the college, which was named for him.

Harvard, town (pop. 2,563), E central Mass., NW of Boston; settled 1704. Has Shaker house and Harvard Univ. observatory. Nearby is site of "Fruitlands," cooperative vegetarian community founded by Bronson ALCOTT.

Harvard, Mount: see SAWATCH MOUNTAINS.

Harvard University, mainly at Cambridge, Mass. The oldest American college, Harvard Col., for men, was founded 1636 by Mass. Bay Colony and named 1638 for John Harvard, its first benefactor; it was chartered 1650. Intended for the education of Puritan ministers, it grew to be institution of general education. Last state grant received 1823. In Pres. Charles W. Eliot's administration (1869–1909), Harvard Col. became great university. He introduced elective system; physical plant was expanded and graduate school was estab. University also includes schools of medicine (1782), dental medicine (1867), and public health (1922), all at Boston, and graduate schools of divinity (1816), law (1817), arts and sciences (1872), business administration (1908), education (1920), and public administration (1955; renamed 1966 in honor of Pres. J. F. Kennedy). Radcliffe Col., for women, is coordinate with Harvard. Classes began 1879; Society for the Collegiate Instruction of Women (known as Harvard Annex) chartered 1882; rechartered and renamed 1894. Instruction is given by Harvard faculty; since 1963 all degrees are granted by Harvard. Graduate and professional courses are coed. Harvard has one of the largest libraries in America and Fogg Mus. of Art (1894). Site of library to house papers of Pres. John F. Kennedy's administration.

harvest fish, name for family of small marine food fishes. Butterfish and whiting, found along E coast of U.S., have high commercial value. Pompano is a Pacific coast variety.

harvestman: see DADDY LONGLEGS.

Harvey, Gabriel, 1545?–1630, English poet and miscellaneous writer; friend of Spenser, bitter opponent (in pamphlets) of Thomas Nashe.

Harvey, William, 1578–1657, English physiologist, discoverer of circulation of blood and function of heart as pump. His theory was stated in 1616, published 1628. Known also for research in embryology.

Harvey, city (1965 pop. 33,230), NE Ill., a suburb S of Chicago; founded 1890. Has oil research center.

Harvey Mudd College: see CLAREMONT COLLEGES, THE.

Harwich (här′ĭj), municipal borough (pop. 13,569), Essex, England; port and chief naval station on E coast. Dovercourt Bay is popular yachting resort here.

Harz (härts), densely forested mountain range, central Germany, extending c.60 mi. between Elbe and Weser rivers and occupying parts of Lower Saxony and former Anhalt. Upper Harz, in NW, is rich in silver, iron, lead, copper; culminates in the BROCKEN. After Second World War prospecting for uranium ore began. There are many resorts.

Hasa, El (ĕl hä′sŭ), region, NE Saudi Arabia, on Persian Gulf. Extensive oil drilling.

Hasan (hä′sŭn), c.625–c.669, 5th caliph; son of Ali and Fatima (Mohammed's daughter). Succeeded Ali as caliph, 661; abdicated under Omayyad pressure. His brother, HUSEIN, took up the family cause. He is a saint of the Shiites.

Hasbrouck Heights (hăz'brŏŏk), residential borough (pop. 13,046), NE N.J., SSW of Hackensack; settled c.1685.

Hasdrubal (hăz'drŏŏbùl), name of two Carthaginian generals. **Hasdrubal**, d. 221 B.C., succeeded his father-in-law, Hamilcar Barca, as commander in Spain, increased the Carthaginian empire, founded Cartagena. He was succeeded by his brother-in-law HANNIBAL. The brother of Hannibal, **Hasdrubal**, d. 207 B.C., took command in Spain when Hannibal left for Italy. He fought against the Scipios and, to avoid a disaster, crossed the Alps to Italy. There on the Metaurus he was killed in battle (207 B.C.), and his head was thrown into Hannibal's camp. The defeat marked the beginning of Carthaginian decline.

hashish (hă'shĭsh), name used chiefly in Asia for narcotic and intoxicating substance prepared from hemp plant and sometimes limited to extract of leaves. It is chewed, smoked, or taken as liquid.

Hasidim (hăsē'dĭm) or **Assideans** (ăsĭdē'ùnz) [Heb.,= pious], originally the most rigid adherents of Judaism. The sect developed between 300 B.C. and 175 B.C. When Antiochus IV decreed that the Jews must offer sacrifices to the Greek gods, the Hasidim led the resistance. The modern sect of Hasidim was founded in Poland in 18th cent. by BAAL-SCHEM-TOV. It opposed formalistic aspects of rabbinic Judaism. Taught communion with God and emotional exaltation in prayer Achieved a wide following in Ukraine. Adherents now mainly in New York city and Israel.

Haskalah (häs'kälä") [Heb.= understanding], the Jewish Enlightenment, especially among E European Jews, begun by Moses MENDELSSOHN and continued by his school.

Haskins, Caryl Parker, 1908–. American biologist. In private industry 1935–55, during which time he was also associated with Massachusetts Inst. of Technology and Union Col. in Schenectady Became president of Carnegie Inst. in Washington, D.C 1956. Books include *Of Ants and Men,* 1939; *The Amazon, The Life History of a Mighty River,* 1943; *The Scientific Revolution and World Politics,* 1964.

Hasmoneans: see MACCABEES.

Hassam, Childe (chīld' hă'sùm), 1859–1935, American painter and etcher. His landscapes and interiors show strong influence of impressionism.

Hassan II (hä'sän), 1929–, king of Morocco (1961–) Eldest son of Mohammed V, he was appointed army chief of staff 1957. A neutralist in foreign policy, he declared Morocco a constitutional monarchy in 1963.

Hasse, Johann Adolph (hä'sù), 1699–1783, German composer. Although he wrote in all forms, he was chiefly known for operas written in the Italian tradition, e.g., *Allesandro nell' Indie* and *Arminio.*

Hasselt (hä'sùlt), city (est. pop. 38,386), cap. of Limburg prov., E Belgium.

Hassi Messaoud (hä'sē mēsäōod'), oil town (pop. c.5,000), S Algeria. Refinery built 1961; connected by pipeline to port of Bougie.

Hassler, Ferdinand Rudolph, 1770–1843, American geodesist, b. Switzerland. Helped organize U.S. Coast and Geodetic Survey. His original survey of Atlantic seacoast has not had to be repeated.

Hastings, Thomas, 1860–1929, American architect; with John M. Carrère he designed New York Public Library

Hastings, Warren, 1732–1818, first governor general of British India (1774–84). Began as clerk for East India Company (1750). His aggressive policy of judicial and financial reform rebuilt British prestige in India but met with opposition. When he returned to England after resigning he was charged with high crimes by Edmund BURKE and was impeached (1787). Was finally acquitted in 1795.

Hastings, county borough (pop. 66,346), Sussex East, England, on S coast. One of the CINQUE PORTS. Fa-

mous as scene of battle of Hastings (Oct. 14, 1066) between Normans under William the Conqueror and Saxons under HAROLD. One of history's most celebrated battles, it was won by William's smaller but better trained and equipped force after a whole day's fighting. It was first and most decisive victory of NORMAN CONQUEST.

Hastings. 1 City (1965 pop. 10,588), SE Minn., SE of St. Paul on Mississippi R. opposite junction of St. Croix; settled 1850. Farm trade center. **2** City (pop. 21,412), S central Nebr., S of Grand Island; founded 1872. Trade, rail, and industrial center for wheat area. Hastings Col. and noted regional museum are here. Nearby is a U.S. naval ammunition depot.

Haswell, Charles Haynes, 1809–1907, American engineer. Designed and built engines for first U.S. naval steamship, the *Fulton* (1857). First to use zinc plates in boilers and ships to prevent corrosion.

Hatay, Turkey: see ALEXANDRETTA, SANJAK OF.

Hathaway, Anne: see SHAKESPEARE, WILLIAM.

Hatshepsut, Egyptian queen: see THUTMOSE I.

Hatta, Mohammad, 1902–, Indonesian political leader Became first vice-president of Republic of Indonesia in 1945, its premier and defense minister in 1948 to direct fight against Dutch. Again vice-president, he resigned 1956 in dispute with Sukarno.

Hatteras, Cape (hă'tùrùs), promontory on low sandy island, off E N.C., E of Pamlico Sound. Dangerous because of frequent storms; marked by lighthouses since 1798. Cape Hatteras Natl. Seashore (24,705.23 acres; estab. 1953) has one of most extensive stretches of undeveloped seashore on the Atlantic Three islands are Hatteras, Bodie, Ocracoke, Cape Hatteras Lighthouse (1870) is operated by U.S. Coast Guard.

Hattiesburg, city (pop. 34,989), SE Miss., on Leaf R. SSE of Jackson; settled in early 1880s. Rail, trade, and industrial center of farm and timber area. Univ of Southern Mississippi and William Carey Col. are here. Camp Shelby, U.S. army training center, is nearby.

Hauff, Wilhelm (vil'hèlm houf'), 1802–27, German author. *Lichtenstein* (1826) was a popular historical novel. English translations of his tales are *Fairy Tales* (1910) and *Caravan Tales* (1912).

Haugesund (hou'gùsŏon), city (pop. 26,958), Rogaland co., SW Norway, fishing port and fish-processing center on North Sea. Nearby Viking monuments include grave of Harold I.

Haupt, Herman, 1817–1905, American civil engineer Started Hoosac tunnel in Berkshire Mts. in 1856. Chief of army road construction during Civil War Wrote *General Theory of Bridge Construction* (1851).

Hauptmann, Bruno Richard, 1899–1936, convicted kidnaper and murderer of infant son of Charles A. Lindbergh, b. Germany. Electrocuted after sensational trial at Flemington, N.J.

Hauptmann, Gerhart (gēr'härt houpt'män), 1862–1946, German poet, dramatist, novelist. After his naturalistic plays *Before Dawn* (1889) and *The Weavers* (1892), he turned to a romantic medium in the dream play *Hannele* (1893) and in *The Sunken Bell* (1897). The tragedies *Drayman Henschel* (1899) and *Rose Bernd* (1903) mark a return to realism. His novels, notably *The Fool in Christ, Emanuel Quint* (1910) and *The Heretic of Soana* (1918), show his mastery of prose. Awarded the 1912 Nobel Prize in Literature; ranks among foremost modern German writers.

Hauran (hourän'), district, SW Syria, E of Jordan R. Many caverns (once inhabited) are in mountainous NE. Region has volcanic peaks and rich lava soil. Inhabited mainly by Druses. At least part of Hauran belonged to biblical kingdom of BASHAN; it marked NE boundary of the Promised Land. Some 300 ancient towns, with buildings and furniture made of lava, have been located.

Hausa or **Haussa** (both: hou'sù), Negro people numbering over 6,000,000, chiefly in N Nigeria and S

Niger. Skilled agriculturalists and extensive traders, primarily Moslem; their language is a lingua franca in much of W Africa. Earlier organized in the seven Hausa States, independent sultanates, of which Kano was most important. Conquered by the Fulani in early 19th cent.

Hauser, Kaspar (käs'pär hou'zůr), 1812?–1833, German foundling; possibly an impostor. Appeared in Nuremberg as a "wild boy" (1828), claiming to have spent years in a dark prison hole. His intelligence developed with amazing speed, and the earl of Stanhope assumed responsibility for his education. He died of a knife wound, possibly self-inflicted. The theory that he was a son of the grand duke of Baden has not been substantiated. Subject of a novel by Jakob Wassermann.

Haushofer, Karl (kärl' hous'hōfůr), 1869–1946, German geographer, chief exponent of GEOPOLITICS. A professor at Munich, he became one of Hitler's advisers on foreign affairs. Died by suicide.

Haussa: see HAUSA.

Haussmann, Georges Eugène, Baron (ōsmän'), 1809–91, French city planner, largely responsible for layout of present-day Paris. Boulevard Haussmann named in his honor.

Haute-Garonne (ōt″-gärôn'), department (2,458 sq. mi.; pop. 594,633), S France; cap. Toulouse. S part lies in Pyrenees.

Haute-Loire (–lwär'), department (1,931 sq. mi.; pop. 211,036), S central France, in Auvergne; cap. Le Puy.

Haute-Marne (–märn), department (2,416 sq. mi.; pop. 208,446), NE France, in Champagne; cap. Chaumont.

Hautes-Alpes (ōt″zälp'), department (2,178 sq. mi.; pop. 87,436), SE France, in Dauphiné; cap. Gap.

Haute-Saône (ōt″-sōn'), department (2,075 sq. mi.; pop. 208,440), E France, in Franche-Comté; cap. Vesoul.

Haute-Savoie (–sävwä'), department (1,775 sq. mi.; pop. 329,230), E France, in Savoy; cap. Annecy.

Hautes-Pyrénées (–pēränä'), department (1,751 sq. mi.; pop. 211,433), SW France, bordering on Spain; cap. Tarbes.

Haute-Vienne (–vyěn'), department (2,145 sq. mi.; pop. 332,514), W central France; cap. Limoges.

Haute-Volta: see UPPER VOLTA.

Haut-Rhin (ō″-rē'), department (1,354 sq. mi.; pop. 547,920), E France, in Alsace; cap. Colmar.

Hauts-de-Seine (ō″-dů-sěn'), department, N France; cap. Nanterre. Formed 1964; formerly part of Seine dept.; coextensive with metropolitan area of Paris.

Havana (hůvă'nů), Span. La Habana, city (pop. c.850,000), W Cuba, cap. of Havana prov. and Cuba; largest city and chief port of the West Indies; founded c.1515. Its position has been strategic historically and commercially. After Cuban independence (1898), U.S. forces improved sanitary conditions in Havana. Industrial growth continues. Principal exports: sugar, minerals, tobacco.

Havel (hä'fůl), river in NE Germany. Flows c.215 mi. generally S to the Spree, which links it with the Oder. Navigable for over 200 mi.

Havelock, town (pop. 2,433), E N.C., SSE of New Bern. U.S. Marine Corps air station is nearby.

Havelok the Dane, English 14th-cent. metrical romance, telling the story of a prince brought up as a peasant who comes into his own.

Haverford College, at Haverford, Pa., near Philadelphia; for men; opened 1833, called school until 1856. Notable collection of Quaker literature.

Haverhill (hă'vůrĭl), industrial city (pop. 46,346), NE Mass., on Merrimack R., N of Boston; settled 1640. Was one of leading producers of shoes in U.S. J. G. Whittier's birthplace is nearby.

Havering, London borough since 1965 (est. pop. 249,-750); includes former municipal borough of Romford and urban district of Hornchurch.

Havers, Clopton, c.1650–1702, English physician, anatomist. Studied bone structure and growth. Haversian canals inside bones are named for him.

Havre (hă'vůr), city (pop. 10,740), N central Mont., NE of Great Falls on Milk R.; founded 1887. Center of cattle, sheep, wheat area served by Milk R. project.

Havre, Le (lů ä'vrů), city (pop. 183,776), Seine-Maritime dept., N France, at mouth of Seine. Chief French transatlantic port. Founded 1517.

Havre de Grace (hăv'ůr dů gräs'), city (pop. 8,510), NE Md., on Chesapeake Bay at mouth of Susquehanna R. (bridged), NE of Baltimore. Race track nearby.

Hawaii (hůwī'ē), state (6,424 sq. mi.; pop. 632,772), central Pacific, c.2,100 mi. from San Francisco; admitted 1959 as 50th state; cap. HONOLULU. Consists of eight major islands—HAWAII (largest), OAHU (most populous), MAUI, KAUAI, LANAI, NIIHAU, MOLOKAI, KAHOOLAWE—and numerous islets. Hawaiian isls., formerly the Sandwich Isls., are of volcanic origin (with some of the world's largest active and inactive volcanoes) and are edged with coral reefs. Mostly fertile with luxuriant vegetation; famous for fine climate and scenic beauty. Sugar cane and pineapples are chief crops and basis of principal industries; coffee, fruit, nuts, sisal are also grown. Coastal waters teem with fish. Extensive marine research. Tourism and military installations are important economically. Many ethnic and cultural groups are represented in population. Polynesian voyagers were first known settlers of islands. Under warring native kings when Capt. James Cook discovered them 1778, islands were united by KAMEHAMEHA I in 1810. American and European traders came, followed by missionaries in 1820. From 1842 to 1854 an American, J. P. Judd, was prime minister, encouraged reforms. Economy prospered from thriving trade with U.S. Queen LILIUOKALANI was deposed 1893, and republic set up with S. B. DOLE as president in 1894. Annexed by U.S. 1898, became U.S. territory 1900. America's entry into Second World War came with Japanese attack on PEARL HARBOR. Islands became chief Pacific outpost for U.S. forces. Postwar years brought economic and social expansion.

Hawaii, formerly Owyhee (ōwī'ē), island (4,030 sq. mi.; pop. 61,332), largest and southernmost island of Hawaii state. Made up of mountain masses of MAUNA LOA (in Hawaii Volcanoes Natl. Park), MAUNA KEA, and Hualalai. Vast lava deserts contrast with fern and bamboo forests. SE coast has black-sand beach. Cattle and sugar are chief crops. KONA is state's coffee belt and is noted for its health resorts and deep-sea fishing. W coast has City of Refuge Natl. Historical Park. HILO is chief port.

Hawaii, University of, at Honolulu; land grant, state supported; coed.; chartered 1907, opened 1908 as Col. of Agr. and Mechanic Arts; called Col. of Hawaii 1911–20. Has volcano research and marine laboratories.

Hawaii Volcanoes National Park: see NATIONAL PARKS AND MONUMENTS (table).

Hawick (hô'ĭk), burgh (pop. 16,204), Roxburghshire, Scotland. Nearby Branxholm Tower is Branksome Hall of Scott's Lay of the Last Minstrel. Woolen and hosiery mfg. center.

hawk, bird of prey of same family as eagle, kite, osprey. It is short winged and swift flying and has sharp claws and a hooked bill. Completely harmful North American hawks are sharp-shinned hawk, Cooper's or chicken hawk, GOSHAWK. Largely beneficial are American, rough-legged, broad-winged, red-tailed, and red-shouldered hawks which eat insects and rodents. Marsh hawk sometimes kills game. Name hawk is applied to some birds of FALCON family.

Hawkesbury, town (pop. 8,661), SE Ont., Canada, on Ottawa R. and W of Montreal. Has paper and lumber mills.

Hawkins or Hawkyns, Sir John, 1532–95, English mariner. In profitable slave-trading expeditions he sold African Negroes in Spanish ports. As treasurer and comptroller of the navy he improved ship construction. Fought against the Spanish Armada (1588) as did his son, **Sir Richard Hawkins,** 1562?–1622. Served under his father and Drake. Captured by Spanish while raiding South America, he was imprisoned 1597–1602. Later served in Parliament.

Hawksmoor, Nicholas, 1661–1736, English architect. Known chiefly for work done under Sir Christopher Wren and Sir John Vanbrugh. His own designs show influence of Italian baroque.

hawkweed, perennial plant of genus *Hieracium,* widely distributed, generally considered a weed but sometimes cultivated in rocky soil. It has small dandelion-like flower heads of yellow, orange, or red.

Hawley-Smoot Tariff Act, enacted 1930 by U.S. Congress. Highest protective tariff act in U.S. history. Retaliatory foreign tariffs caused sharp decline in U.S. foreign trade.

Haworth, Sir Walter Norman (härth), 1883–1950, English biochemist. Shared 1937 Nobel Prize in Chemistry for work on carbohydrates and vitamin C.

Haworth (hô'ùth, hou'–), part of Keighley, West Riding of Yorkshire, England. Has home of Brontë family, now a museum and library. All the Brontës but Anne are buried here.

hawthorn, thorny shrubs or small trees of genus *Crataegus,* particularly prevalent in E North America. Clusters of white or red flowers in spring are followed by showy, variously colored fruits sometimes used in jelly. Much used in landscaping in U.S. and England.

Hawthorne, Charles Webster, 1872–1930, American portrait and genre painter, a noted teacher.

Hawthorne, Nathaniel, 1804–64, American novelist and short-story writer, b. Salem, Mass. After graduation from Bowdoin Col. (1825) he spent years in seclusion in his home doing literary hack work and winning notice with his short stories (collected in *Twice-told Tales,* 1837; 2d series 1842). He secured a job as measurer at the Boston customhouse, then tried (1841) life at Brook Farm. He married Sophia Peabody in 1842 and through her grew to know well Emerson, Thoreau, Margaret Fuller, and other transcendentalists. His *Mosses from an Old Manse* (1846) was written in Concord. He was a surveyor of the port at Salem (1846–49) and was made consul to Liverpool by his friend Franklin Pierce. His novels, like many of his short stories, deal with the gloomy, brooding spirit of Puritanism: *The Scarlet Letter* (1850), *The House of the Seven Gables* (1851), *The Blithedale Romance* (1852; based on the Brook Farm experience), and *The Marble Faun* (1860; laid in Italy). His *Wonder-Book* (1852) and *Tanglewood Tales* (1853; named for an estate near Lenox, Mass., where he lived) are children's classics. His notebooks have been subjected to much scholarly study. Hawthorne, with his brooding symbolism and his blend of realistic detail and romantic theme, stands as a major American novelist and short-story writer.

Hawthorne. 1 City (pop. 33,035), SW Calif., a suburb SW of Los Angeles. **2** Town (pop. 2,838), W Nev., S of Walker L. U.S. naval ammunition depot is nearby. **3** Borough (pop. 17,735), NE N.J., just NNE of Paterson; settled 1850. Primarily residential.

Hay, John, 1838–1905, American author and diplomat. Assistant private secretary to Pres. Lincoln. Wrote *Pike County Ballads* (1871) and, with J. G. Nicolay, *Abraham Lincoln: a History* (10 vols., 1890). As U.S. Secretary of State (1898–1905), Hay was responsible for Open Door policy in China (1899) and for the HAY-PAUNCEFOTE TREATY.

Hay, river, rising in NE B.C., Canada, and flowing c.350 mi. across NW Alta. into Great Slave L.

hay, wild or cultivated plants (e.g., timothy, alfalfa, clover), dried and cured for livestock feed.

Haya de la Torre, Víctor Raúl (věk'tôr räōōl' ä'yä dä lä tô'rě), 1895–, Peruvian leader, founder of APRA (Alianza Popular Revolutionario Americana) party, which advocates overthrow of Peruvian oligarchy.

Hayakawa, S(amuel) I(chlye) (häyäkä'wà), 1906–, American semanticist, b. Canada; came to U.S. 1929. Books include *Language in Action* (1941), *Language, Meaning, and Maturity* (1954), and *Symbol, Status, and Personality* (1965).

Haydn, Franz Joseph (hī'dùn), 1732–1809, Austrian composer. Most of his music was written in the 29 years he was musical director for the Princes Esterhazy. The number of his symphonies is usually set at 104. Many bear nicknames, e.g., Toy, London, Surprise, and Clock. Outstanding also are symphonies No. 88 in G and No. 99 in E Flat. His early string quartets influenced Mozart. Haydn also wrote sonatas, songs, Masses, chamber music, operas, and *The Seven Last Words,* originally for orchestra, but later arranged as a choral work. His last great works were the oratorios, *The Creation* and *The Seasons.*

Haydon, Benjamin Robert, 1786–1846, English painter, whose admirers included the great literary figures of his day. His *Lazarus* is in Natl. Gall., London.

Hayes, Carlton J(oseph) H(untley), 1882–1964, American historian and diplomat. Noted especially for studies in nationalism, *Essays on Nationalism* (1926) and *The Historical Evolution of Modern Nationalism* (1931). Ambassador to Spain (1942–45), he was influential in keeping Spain neutral in Second World War.

Hayes, Helen, 1900–, American actress. N.Y. debut 1908. One of her well-known roles was the queen in Laurence Housman's *Victoria Regina* (1935–39). In 1955 the Fulton Theatre in New York city was renamed the Helen Hayes Theatre in her honor.

Hayes, Isaac Israel, 1832–81, American arctic explorer. Led expedition in search of open seaway to North Pole (1860–61). Wrote several books on his experiences.

Hayes, Patrick Joseph, 1867–1938, American cardinal (created 1924), archbishop of New York (1919–38). Organized the Catholic Charities of New York; sponsored social reform.

Hayes, Rutherford B(irchard), 1822–93, 19th President of the United States (1877–81). Served in Civil War. U.S. Representative (1865–67). Governor of Ohio (1868–72, 1876–77). In 1876 an electoral commission appointed by Congress decided disputed presidential elections in S.C., Fla., La., and Oregon in his favor and against Samuel J. TILDEN. His administration was generally conservative and efficient. Reconstruction era was ended. His conciliatory policy toward the South and his interest in civil service reform alienated important Republican party groups. An advocate of hard money, he provided for resumption of specie payments in gold.

Hayes, river of NE Man., Canada, rising NE of L. Winnipeg and flowing generally NE c.300 mi. to Hudson Bay. Chief route of Hudson's Bay Co. traders from Hudson Bay to L. Winnipeg.

hay fever, inflammation of mucous membrane of nose and eyes resulting from specific sensitivity to foreign substance, usually pollen of plants.

Hay-Herrán Treaty (hā"-ĕrän'), concerning Panama Canal, signed by U.S. Secretary of State John Hay and Foreign Minister Tomás Herrán of Colombia on Jan. 22, 1903. Provided that New Panama Canal Co. might sell its properties to U.S.; Colombia was to lease a strip of land across the Isthmus of Panama to U.S. for canal construction; U.S. was to pay Colombia $10,000,000 and, after nine years, an annuity of $250,000. U.S. Senate ratified treaty, but Colombian congress declined ratification.

Haymarket Square riot, outbreak of violence in Chicago on May 4, 1886. Demonstration for an eight-hour working day, largely staged by anarchists, caused a crowd of some 1,500 to gather at Haymarket Square. Policemen attempted to disperse the meeting; a bomb exploded and rioting ensued. Eleven persons were killed, over 100 were wounded. A trial convicted eight anarchist leaders of inciting violence; four of them were hanged. Incident was frequently used by adversaries of organized labor to discredit the waning Knights of Labor movement.

Hayne, Paul Hamilton, 1830–86, Southern lyric poet of the Charleston, S.C., group; wrote of the South and the Civil War. Edited poems of Henry Timrod.

Hayne, Robert Young, 1791–1839, American statesman. U.S. Senator from S.C. (1823–32); in famous debate of Jan., 1830, with Daniel WEBSTER, he upheld doctrines of states' rights and nullification. Governor of S.C. (1832–34).

Haynes, Elwood, 1857–1925, American automobile manufacturer and inventor, designer of one of earliest gasoline automobiles (tested 1894).

Hay-Pauncefote Treaty (hā″-pôns′fŏot), negotiated in 1901 by U.S. Secretary of State John Hay and Julian Pauncefote, 1st Baron Pauncefote of Preston, British ambassador to U.S. Replaced CLAYTON-BULWER TREATY. Estab. supremacy of U.S. in the Caribbean. Original treaty, signed Feb. 5, 1900, was ratified, with amendments, by U.S. Senate; Great Britain refused ratification. Revised treaty represented a compromise. It provided that U.S. might construct a transisthmian canal and have full control of it, retained nominally the principle of neutrality under sole guarantee of U.S., and provided that the canal be open to ships of all nations on equal terms. Panama Canal Act (1912), exempting from tolls U.S. ships engaged in coastwise trade, was protested by Great Britain as a treaty violation; Pres. Wilson secured repeal of act in 1914.

Hays, Arthur Garfield, 1881–1954, American lawyer, long counsel for American Civil Liberties Union.

Hays, Will(iam) H(arrison), 1879–1954, president of Motion Picture Producers and Distributors of America (1922–45). Administered motion-picture moral code (the "Hays Code").

Hays, city (pop. 11,947), W central Kansas, W of Salina, in farm and livestock area; founded 1867 near Fort Hays (estab. 1865, abandoned 1889). Prospered after 1936 with development of nearby oil fields. Fort Hays Kansas State Col. is here.

Hays and Harlington, London: see HILLINGDON.

Hayward, city′ (pop. 72,700), W Calif., SSE of Oakland; founded 1854. Food-processing and shipping point.

Haywood, William Dudley (Big Bill Haywood), 1869–1928, American labor leader. Helped found INDUSTRIAL WORKERS OF THE WORLD. Joined Socialist party, but was ejected for advocating violence. Imprisoned for sedition in First World War, he escaped (while awaiting a new trial) in 1921 to Russia.

Hazael (hā′zāēl, hūzā′ŭl), fl. 840 B.C., king of Damascus; murderer and successor of Benhadad **2.** In Bible, he is designated by Elijah and Elisha as God's scourge to punish Baal-worshipers. He ravaged Judah and Israel. 1 Kings 19.15; 2 Kings 8; 10.32; 12.17, 18.

Hazard, Paul (pôl′ äzär′), 1878–1944, French scholar, one of the outstanding authorities on comparative literature. He taught at the Sorbonne, Collège de France, and Columbia Univ. In 1939 he was elected to French Acad.

haze, diminished transparency of air owing to suspension in it of dust or salt particles, or water droplets. Optical haze or "shimmer" caused when unequally heated air, varying in density, refracts light unequally.

hazel, hazelnut, or **filbert,** shrub or small tree of genus *Corylus.* It is often grown for ornament but European species (*Corylus maxima*) is grown commercially for its nut crop.

Hazel Park, city (pop. 25,631), SE Mich., suburb NW of Detroit.

Hazleton, industrial city (pop. 32,056), E central Pa., SSW of Wilkes-Barre, in anthracite-coal area; settled 1870. Branch of Pennsylvania State Univ. is here.

Hazlitt, William, 1778–1830, English essayist, literary and dramatic critic. Works include *Characters of Shakespeare's Plays* (1817), *Lectures on the English Poets* (1818), *Lectures on the English Comic Writers* (1819), *Table Talk* (1821–22), and *The Spirit of the*

Age (1825). With Coleridge he led in reinterpreting Shakespeare and Elizabethan drama. His perceptive essays, such as "On Going a Journey" and "My First Acquaintance with Poets," are noted for their lucid style.

H.D.: see DOOLITTLE, HILDA.

He, chemical symbol of the element HELIUM.

Head, Sir Francis Bond, 1793–1875, British administrator in Canada. Lieutenant governor (1835–37). His reactionary policy and alliance with Family Compact estranged moderate reformers and drove W. L. Mackenzie and other radical reformers to open rebellion in 1837.

head-hunting, taking the head of a slain enemy. It occurs in many parts of the world and often is associated with attempt of the taker to gain status.

Health, Education, and Welfare, United States Department of, created 1953 by Pres. Eisenhower; Secretary has cabinet rank. Operating agencies include Public Health Service, Office of Education, Social Security Administration, and Food and Drug Administration.

hearing, sense by which sound is appreciated. Vibrations are collected by outer EAR, transmitted by eardrum to bones of middle ear, and pass to spiral tube (cochlea) of inner ear where fluid-filled sacs convey them to specialized cells in organ of Corti which generate nerve impulses reaching brain.

Hearn, Lafcadio (lăfkä′dēō hûrn′), 1850–1904, author; b. Ionian Isls. of Irish-Greek parents. Journalist-writer in U.S. 1869–90. In Japan after 1890, he became a Japanese citizen, lectured at the Imperial Univ. of Tokyo, and wrote, among several works, *Japan: An Attempt at Interpretation* (1904).

Hearne, Samuel (hûrn), 1745–92, British fur trader, explorer in N Canada. His expedition to mouth of Coppermine R. opened unknown territory.

Hearst, George (hûrst), 1820–91, American mining magnate, U.S. Senator from Calif. (1886–91). His wife, Phoebe Apperson Hearst (1842–1919), became a prominent philanthropist and donated freely to Univ. of California. Their son, **William Randolph Hearst,** 1863–1951, was a journalist and publisher. After managing the San Francisco *Examiner* for his father, he bought (1895) the N.Y. *Morning Journal* and demanded (1897) war with Spain. Outdoing other "yellow" journalists, he founded a news empire including, at his death, 18 newspapers (also magazines, motion-picture interests, and services supplying news, features, and photographs). Influential in N.Y. politics, he opposed all internationalism.

Heart, river, rising in SW N.Dak. and, after being joined by Green R., flowing c.180 mi. E to Missouri R. at Mandan. Heart Butte and Dickinson dams (irrigation and flood control) are part of Missouri R. basin project.

heart, cone-shaped, muscular organ which maintains CIRCULATION OF THE BLOOD. In man and other mammals it lies in the chest and is enclosed in a sac (pericardium). The mammalian heart consists of four chambers, two auricles lying above two ventricles; right and left sides are separated by septum which in prenatal life has opening between auricles. Diseases of the heart have attracted much medical attention in the 20th cent. (see ANGINA; THROMBOSIS). See also BLOOD; PULSE. See *ill.,* p. 657.

heart attack, markedly reduced blood supply to part of heart. Generally associated with coronary ARTERIOSCLEROSIS and THROMBOSIS, leading to occlusion of the vessels. Constant chest pain, sweating, fainting, nausea are symptoms.

heart-lung machine, device for maintaining circulation of blood and oxygen content of body when connected with the arteriovenous system. Heart contractions are halted by running a potassium citrate solution through coronary vessels. Used in open-heart surgery.

heat, form of ENERGY into which others are convertible. It is also described as the energy of motion that the molecule possesses. Sun, an atomic furnace, is man's most important source of heat; heat from all organic fuels (e.g., coal, petroleum) is derived from sun. Heat results from friction, chemical reactions, compression of substances, impact, passage of electric current over a high resistance. It is measured qualitatively by THERMOMETER; CALORIE and BRITISH THERMAL UNIT indicate amount of heat. Specific heat of substance is amount of heat needed to raise temperature of 1 gm. of the substance 1°C. Heat needed to change unit mass of substance from solid to liquid at melting point is latent heat of fusion; amount needed to change substance from liquid to gas at boiling point is heat of vaporization. Heat is transmitted by CONDUCTION, CONVECTION, and RADIATION. Relationship between mechanical energy and heat was first determined by Sir James P. Joule.

heath, in ecology. open land characterized by a few scattered trees. abundant moss cover. and numerous low shrubs. chiefly of heath family.

heather, low evergreen shrub (*Calluna vulgaris*) of Old World, with scalelike foliage and red, rose, purple, or white nodding flowers in late summer. Also known as heather, but more properly called heath, are shrubs of closely related genus *Erica*. They have needlelike leaves and bell-shaped white, rose, or yellow flowers in winter and early spring.

heatstroke: see SUNSTROKE.

heaven, in Christian theology, the state of bliss in which God is seen face to face: abode of souls of the good, reunited to their glorified bodies after the RESURRECTION. Roman Church teaches that many must prepare for heaven by suffering in purgatory. Popular notion of heaven is of place full of material delights. Islamic heaven often thought to contain fleshly pleasures, but passages of Koran describing it may be allegorical. See ELYSIAN FIELDS; FORTUNATE ISLES: VALHALLA.

Heaviside, Oliver (hě'vēsĭd), 1850–1925, English physicist. He contributed to development of telephony and predicted existence of conducting layer in upper atmosphere known as Kennelly-Heaviside layer and also as Heaviside layer.

heavy hydrogen: see HYDROGEN.

heavy spar: see BARITE.

heavy water: see WATER.

Hebbel, Friedrich (frē'drĭkh hě'bŭl), 1813–63, German dramatist. As a leading tragic poet he was concerned mainly with the tragedy of new forces repressed by obsolete ideas. His plays include *Maria Magdalena* (1844), *Herod and Mariamne* (1850), *Agnes Bernauer* (1852), and *The Nibelungs* (1862).

Hebe (hě'bē), in Greek mythology, goddess of youth; daughter of Zeus and Hera and wife of HERCULES. Identified as Juventas by Romans.

Heber (hě'bûr), man's name from which Hebrews is supposedly taken. Luke 3.35. Eber: Gen. 10.21.

Heber, city (pop. 2.936). N central Utah. SE of Salt Lake City: settled 1859 by Mormons. "Hot pots" (hot-water pools of extinct geysers) are nearby.

Hébert, Jacques René (zhäk' rŭnä' ābĕr'), 1757–94, French revolutionist. Edited a virulent paper, *Père Duchesne;* led CORDELIERS after Marat's death; promoted worship of Reason. Largely responsible, during Reign of Terror, for tightening maximum price laws and Law of Suspects. His power over Paris commune threatened position of Robespierre, who had him and his followers guillotined on a concocted charge of conspiracy. Hébert's fall marked triumph of propertied middle classes.

Hébert, Louis (ābĕr'), d. 1627, French pioneer, known as first Canadian farmer. Settled in Quebec in 1617.

Hébert, Philippe (fēlēp' ābĕr'). 1850–1917. Canadian sculptor. Most noted sculptor and monument designer of his time in Canada.

Hebrew language, Semitic language of the Canaanite subgroup. See LANGUAGE (table).

Hebrew literature. The great monuments of the early period of Hebrew literature are the OLD TESTAMENT and APOCRYPHA. parts of PSEUDEPIGRAPHA. and the DEAD SEA SCROLLS. From 2d cent. until the 6th. the TALMUD, the great anonymous encyclopedic work, and the MIDRASH were compiled. In the 4th cent. the TARGUM to the Pentateuch and to the Prophets was finished. The 6th and 7th cent. saw the development of the MASORA in Palestine, while in Babylonia commentaries on the Talmud were written until the suppression of the academies (11th cent.). Jewish literary activity then shifted to Spain, where fine poetry and philosophy were written. In the 14th cent. the great work of CABALA, the *Zohar,* appeared. Famous scholars and authors of Hebrew literature in the Middle Ages were Solomon ben Judah IBN GABIROL, RASHI, MAIMONIDES, and Joseph ben Ephraim CARO. After the 14th cent., the Jews, driven from country to country, clung to their existing literature, especially the Old Testament. Modern Hebrew literature began with Moses MENDELSSOHN. Important names of the more recent period are the novelist Solomon Yakob Abramovich, whose pen name was MENDELE MOCHER SFORIM, and the poet Hayyim Nahman BIALIK. The works of S. J. AGNON have become classics in modern Hebrew epic literature. Hebrew writers native to Israel seek inspiration in classical Hebrew past or in new life of Israel: outstanding in this group is Moshe Shamir (b. 1921). The rise of Zionism made Palestine the center of Hebrew publication. Outside of Israel. Jews usually write in the vernacular or in YIDDISH.

Hebrew music: see JEWISH LITURGICAL MUSIC.

Hebrews. For history, see JEWS; for religion, see JUDAISM.

Hebrews, epistle of New Testament. Tradition ascribes it to St. Paul, but few critics agree. It is treatise on the superiority of the new religion over the old and proclaims the ascendancy of Christ over the angels and Moses. It describes the new priesthood under Christ replacing that of Aaron and speaks of the sacrifice by Christ of himself as taking away sin. Hebrews is a call to faith, urging dynamic action in following Christ–even unto martyrdom. Its teachings are very important in history of theology.

Hebrews, Gospel according to the: see PSEUDEPIGRAPHA.

Hebrew University, at Jerusalem. First proposed 1882, formally opened 1925. Institutes of chemistry. microbiology. and Jewish studies opened 1924; school of agr. 1940; and Hebrew Univ.–Hadassah Medical School 1949. Weizmann Inst. of Science and Tel-Aviv school of law and economics merged with univ. 1950 and 1959. Noted for work on Dead Sea Scrolls and experiments in atomic and solar energy.

Hebrides (hě'brĭdēz) or **Western Islands,** group of more than 500 islands, off W and NW Scotland. Less than a fifth inhabited. Outer Hebrides, extending 130 mi., separated from mainland and from Inner Hebrides by straits of Minch and Little Minch and Sea of the Hebrides. Mild, humid climate and beautiful scenery draw tourists. Chief occupations fishing, farming, sheep grazing, quarrying, and mfg. of tweeds. Tales of Sir Walter Scott did much to make islands famous. There has been much emigration, particularly to Canada in 20th cent.

Hebrides, New: see NEW HEBRIDES.

Hebron (hě'brŭn). city (est. pop. 35,000). Jordan. SW of Jerusalem. Modern Arabic name: El-Khalil. Bible first mentions it as site where Abraham estab. family tomb. Was David's capital before Jerusalem. Hebron figured in every Palestinian war–Maccabean, Roman, and Crusaders' Also appears in Bible as Kirjath-arba and Mamre. Hebron is a shrine of Moslems and Jews.

Hecate (hě'kutē. hě'kĭt). in Greek mythology. goddess of ghosts and witchcraft. Attendant of Persephone in underworld. she could conjure up dreams and spirits of the dead. In upper world she haunted graveyards and crossroads.

Hecht, Selig (hěkt), 1892–1947, American biophysicist, pioneer in applying physiochemical principles to sensory physiology. He determined minimal quantal requirements at threshold of vision. Wrote scientific works for laymen (e.g., *Explaining the Atom,* 1947).

Hecker, Isaac Thomas, 1819–88, American Roman Catholic priest, founder (1858) of Paulist Fathers. Associated with New England transcendentalists, was converted to Catholicism (1844) and ordained priest (1849). Worked among immigrants. Founded Paulist organ, *Catholic World.*

Hector, in the *Iliad,* leader of Trojan forces in Trojan War, greatest Trojan hero; son of Priam and Hecuba, brother of Paris, husband of Andromache, and father of Astyanax. Slain by Achilles in revenge for death of PATROCLUS.

Hecuba (hē'kyōōbù), in Greek legend, queen of Troy, wife of PRIAM. After Trojan War she was taken as slave by Odysseus. She is a prominent character in two plays by Euripides.

Heda, Willem Claasz (vĭl'ùm klä̀s' hā'dä), 1594–c.1678, Dutch still-life painter.

hedge, ornamental or protective barrier of shrubs, e.g., box, privet, barberry, or yew. Formal hedges were once pruned to resemble statuary.

hedgehog, insectivorous, nocturnal, hibernating Old World mammal with spines among its hairs. American porcupine is incorrectly called hedgehog. European hedgehog is of genus *Erinaceus;* related forms are in Africa and Asia.

Hedin, Sven (Anders) (hĕdēn'), 1865–1952, Swedish explorer in central Asia. Wrote scientific and popular accounts of travels in Kunlun and Trans-Himalaya ranges, Tibet, and Sinkiang prov., China.

Hedjaz, Saudi Arabia: see HEJAZ.

Hedmark (hĕd'märk), province (10,592 sq. mi.; pop. 177,908), SE Norway; cap. Hamar. Chief forest area of Norway and a rich agr. region. Lumbering is main industry.

hedonism, philosophy that holds pleasure to be the chief goal of man. Pleasure may be variously defined —from the mere satisfaction of sensual desires (as by some Cyrenaics) to a strong belief in rationally ascetic control of desires (as in the school of Epicurus). All materialistic philosophies contain elements of hedonism (thus utilitarianism stresses the chief ethical and social aim of life as the greatest good for the greatest number).

Hedrick, Ulysses Prentiss, 1870–1951, American horticulturist, authority on fruit cultivation, and author of many works including *History of Horticulture in America to 1860* (1950).

Heem, Jan Davidszoon de (yän' dä'vĕtsōn dù häm'), 1606–84, celebrated Dutch still-life painter, known for fruit and flower pieces.

Heemskerck, Maarten van (mär'tùn vän häms'kĕrk), 1498–1574, Dutch painter; sketched Roman monuments and the construction of St. Peter's.

Hegel, Georg Wilhelm Friedrich (gā'ŏrk vĭl'hĕlm frē'drĭkh hā'gùl), 1770–1831, German philosopher, formulator of an idealistic philosophy that has had enormous influence since his day. He taught at various universities, being a professor at Jena, Heidelberg, and Berlin. His idealism, set forth in a series of books (*Phenomenology of Mind,* 1807; *Science of Logic,* 1812–16; *Encyclopedia of the Philosophical Sciences,* 1817; *Philosophy of Right,* 1821), is all-embracing and highly unified, welding together a world view with theories of ethics, aesthetics, history, politics, and religion. The system is complicated, and no brief statement does justice to it. Fundamentally he believed in an enveloping Absolute. The world soul is seen through contemplation of dialectical knowledge. In this dialectic, one concept (thesis) inevitably evokes its opposite (antithesis), and the two interact to form a new concept (synthesis), which in turn becomes a new thesis. Thus the idea of being evokes the idea of not being, and the two necessarily produce the synthesis, becoming. The universe is thus in a state of perpetual self-creation. The absolute is the active principle in this process. History also shows the progress from lower to higher manifestations of the principle. Thus cultures conflict, and the higher is triumphant. In art also different periods succeed each other.

In religion Christianity was considered as succeeding to nature religions, and Christ is the union of God and man, of spirit and matter. Various later philosophers developed differing aspects of this system. Hegelian dialectic appealed strongly to the socialists and was developed into Marxian dialectical materialism.

hegira or **hejira** (hĕjī'rù, hĕ'jĭrù), flight of the prophet MOHAMMED from Mecca, June, 622, to Yathrib (Medina). Since the foundation of Islam was laid in Medina, Mohammedan era dates from the hegira. Abbreviation A.H. is used in West with year number to mean After the Hegira.

Heiberg, Johan Ludvig (hī'bâr), 1791–1860, Danish poet, dramatist, critic, and director of the Natl. Theater. His play, *The Hill of the Elves* (1828), was very popular.

Heidegger, Martin (hī'dĕgùr), 1889–, German philosopher. Professor at Marburg (1923–28) and Freiburg (1928–33), where he became rector in 1933. He considered and adapted ideas put forward by Kierkegaard and Husserl and created a system of thought which has been labeled atheistic existentialism. Viewing man as oppressed by anguish and forlornness in his brief existence in the finite world, Heidegger rejected the conventional religious answers to man's problem and argued that by questioning man may learn the nature of existence and, accepting it, may assert his essence and destiny by "resolute decision." One of his best-known works is *Sein und Zeit* (1927). Jean Paul Sartre became his disciple.

Heidelberg (hī'dùlbĕrk), city (pop. 123,305), Baden-Württemberg, West Germany, on Neckar R., beautifully situated in region of orchards and vineyards. It is best known for its university, founded 1386. The cap. of the Rhenish PALATINATE until 1720, it was devastated by the imperials in 1622, and by the French in 1689 and 1693. The castle dates from 15th–17th cent. The **Heidelberg Catechism,** a profession of faith of German Reformed (Calvinistic) Church was drawn up at the request of Elector Frederick III and was published 1563.

Heidelberg man: see MAN, PREHISTORIC.

Heidenstam, Verner von (hā'dùnstäm), 1859–1940, Swedish lyric poet, novelist, and essayist. Opposed pessimistic realism and in his novels evoked a patriotic sense of the continuing unity of Sweden's history. Awarded 1916 Nobel Prize in Literature.

Heifetz, Jascha (yä'shù hī'fĭts), 1901–, Russian-American violinist, known for his virtuosity. Studied at St. Petersburg Conservatory with Leopold Auer. Came to the U.S. 1917.

Heijermans, Herman (hī'ùrmäns), 1864–1924, Dutch dramatist. Much of his work treated life among the Dutch Jews.

Heilbronn (hīlbrōn'), city (pop. 80,152), Baden-Württemberg, West Germany, on Neckar R. Rail junction; mfg. of metals, chemicals. Free imperial city 1281–1803. In Second World War old city was largely destroyed. Götz von Berlichingen was imprisoned (1522) in the Götzenturm, a tower built in 1392.

Heilungkiang (hā'lŭng'jyäng'), province (c.180,000 sq. mi.; pop. c.12,760,000), NE China, cap. HARBIN. Soybeans, grains, and sugar beets exported. Lumbering and mining (coal, gold). In 1949 W Heilungkiang was made part of Inner Mongolian Autonomous Region. Heilungkiang absorbed former Hingan and Nünkiang provs. in 1950, and Sungkiang in 1954.

Heine, Heinrich (hīn'rĭkh hī'nù), 1797–1856, German author, of Jewish parentage. His *Buch der Lieder* [book of songs] (1827) placed him among the greatest German poets. Lyrics have musical, folklike quality (as in "Lorelei"), often spiced with subtle irony and dissonant endings, have attracted many composers, notably Schubert, Schumann, Mendelssohn, Brahms. His prose travel sketches, beginning with *Die Harzreise* (1826), show the same mixture of lyric emotion and corrosive wit. In 1831, drawn by his revolutionary sympathies, he left Germany for Paris, where he died after eight years of tragic sickness, confined to his "mattress grave." There he wrote the verse satires *Atta Troll* and *Deutschland; Neue Gedichte* (1847) and *Letzte Gedichte* (1853), in which his verse takes on an increasingly bitter and tragic tone; prose essays on German literature and philosophy (in French); and political reports for a German newspaper. Nearly all his work has been translated into English, although his verse often defies translation.

Heisenberg, Werner (vĕr'nùr hī'zùnbĕrk), 1901–, German physicist. Won 1932 Nobel Prize in Physics for theory of quantum mechanics and discovery of allotropic forms of hydrogen.

Heiser, Victor George (hī'zùr), 1873–, American physician, authority on public health, associated with Rockefeller Foundation (1915–34). His works include *An American Doctor's Odyssey* (1936); *Toughen Up, America* (1941).

Heisman, John William, 1869–1936, American football coach. Credited with legalizing the forward pass (1906). Trophy presented annually to outstanding college football player is named for him.

Hejaz or **Hedjaz** (both: hĕjäz') region, NW Saudi Arabia, on Gulf of Aqaba and Red Sea. Mainly a mountain range and plateau, lying between coastal strip and interior desert. Holy cities of Mecca and Medina are here. Husein ibn Ali overthrew Turkish rule in 1916, but was ousted 1924 by Ibn Saud.

hejira: see HEGIRA.

Hekla (hĕk'lä), volcano, 4,937 ft. high. SW Iceland. Since 1004 many eruptions have been recorded.

Hel (hĕl), in Norse mythology, the underworld.

Held, Anna, 1873?–1918, American musical comedy actress, b. Paris. Famed for her beauty and for her tempestuous private life.

Held, Julius Samuel, 1905–, American art historian. A connoisseur of Dutch and Flemish art, he has written several books on Rubens.

Helen, in Greek legend, daughter of Leda and Zeus. From many suitors she chose MENELAUS. When PARIS awarded APPLE OF DISCORD to Aphrodite, she, in return, gave him the fairest of women, Helen, whom he carried off to Troy, thus causing TROJAN WAR. After the war Helen returned with Menelaus to Sparta. She bore him only one child, Hermione.

Helena, Saint (hĕ'lùnù), c.248–328?, mother of Constantine the Great. Converted to Christianity in 313, she is said to have gone to Jerusalem, where she found True Cross, Holy Sepulcher. Feast: Aug. 18.

Helena (hĕ'lùnù). **1** City (pop. 11,500), E central Ark., ESE of Little Rock on Mississippi R. Rail center and river port, it ships cotton, lumber, and oil. Union victory here, 1863. **2** City (pop. 20,227), state cap., W central Mont., SW of Great Falls; founded after 1864 gold discovery in Last Chance Gulch. Replaced Virginia City as territorial cap., 1874. Had rich silver strikes and still depends on mining. Ranching and agr. in Prickly Pear valley. Carroll Col. is here.

Helgoland (hĕl'gōlänt) or **Heligoland**, island, area less than 150 acres, Germany, in North Sea off the Elbe estuary. Consisting of red sandstone, it rises c.160 ft. above sea and is covered by grazing land. Once a Danish possession, it was ceded to England 1814; traded to Germany for Zanzibar 1890. It served as German naval base in Second World War; fortifications were blown up by British 1947.

Helicon (hĕ'lĭkòn), Gr. *Elikon*, mountain group, Boeotia, Greece. In Greek legend, abode of the MUSES.

helicopter (hĕ'lĭkòptùr), rotor aircraft obtaining lift and propulsion from engine-driven rotors. It differs from the autogiro, the rotor of which is moved by aerodynamic forces resulting from propulsion in the conventional manner by engine-driven propeller. Able to maneuver and hover at nearly zero ground speed, it is valuable for air-sea rescue, aeromagnetic surveying, sowing crops, traffic control, and various military uses. See *ill.*, p. 368.

Heligoland, German island: see HELGOLAND.

Heliodorus (hē'lēōdō'rùs), fl. 175 B.C., Syrian political leader. Murdered Seleucus IV in vain hope of getting the throne. In 2 Mac. 3 he is said to have been prevented by three angels from taking the treasure from the Temple at Jerusalem.

Heliogabalus (hē'lēōgā'bùlùs), c.205–222, Roman emperor (218–22). He was Varius Avitus Bassianus, a priest of the sun-god of Emesa, cousin and, according to his mother, son of CARACALLA. The troops in Syria chose him as emperor on the defeat of Macrinus, who was a usurper. He had a reign notorious for the indecency of the rites of his sun-god and of his own life. He and his mother were killed in an uprising of Praetorian guards. His cousin, Alexander Severus, succeeded. Also Elagabalus.

heliograph (hē'lēùgrăf), signaling device consisting of a mirror reflecting sunlight and shuttered to permit interruption of light beam for long and short signal flashes. Heliostat similarly reflects light beam on distant spot. Spectroheliograph, combining heliostat and spectroscope, is used by scientists to photograph sun.

Heliopolis (hēlēō'pùlis) [Gr.,= city of the sun], anc. city, N Egypt, near Cairo, center of the worship of Ra (or Re), who was long the state deity. It was under the New Empire (c.1570–c.1085 B.C.) seat of the viceroy of N Egypt. Obelisks called Cleopatra's Needles were erected here. Its schools of philosophy and astronomy flourished until founding of Alexandria.

Heliopolis, anc. Syrian city: see BAALBEK.

Helios (hē'lēòs) [Gr.,= sun], in Greek religion, sungod; son of Hyperion and Theia, husband of nymph Clymene, and father of PHAËTHON. Each day he drove a golden chariot from his palace in the E to his palace in the W. In Rhodes he was national god, and Colossus represented him. He symbolized material aspects of the sun, Apollo its spiritual aspects. In the *Odyssey* Helios shipwrecked Odysseus for eating his sacred cattle. He was called Sol by Romans.

heliotrope (hē'–), in botany, tender perennial plant (*Heliotropium arborescens*) with fragrant purple flower clusters. Commonly called garden heliotrope is a valerian (*Valeriana officinalis*).

heliotrope, in geology: see BLOODSTONE.

helium (hē'lēùm), colorless, odorless, tasteless, inert gaseous element (symbol = He; see also ELEMENT, table). Because of its lightness (only hydrogen is lighter) and noninflammability it is used in balloons and airships. Used in pressure chambers for divers and caisson workers because of low solubility in human blood. U.S. controls production. Alpha rays from decomposing atoms are helium nuclei. See *ill.*, p. 781.

hell, in Christian theology, eternal abode of those damned by God's judgment and forever denied sight of Him. It is ruled by Satan (Lucifer, the devil). Tradition and legend have made of it a place of fire and brimstone, with the damned souls undergoing physical torment. The vivid description of hell (Inferno) by Dante is known over the Western world. The Islamic idea of hell is similar to the Christian. The Sheol or Tophet of the ancient Jews was a gloomy place where the souls of the dead wander about unhappy; the name Gehenna (from Hinnom) is used in the New Testament. The Greeks believed that the souls of the dead (good and evil) went to an underworld, Hades, ruled by the god Hades (also called Pluto) and his wife Persephone. Its entrance was guarded by Cerberus, and Hades was surrounded by the river Styx, across which Charon ferried the dead. Tartarus below Hades was a place of torment for the very wicked. The Romans also called the underworld Hades and Orcus, Dis (also a name for Pluto) and Avernus. The Hel of the Icelandic *Edda* is probably a borrowing from Christianity.

Hellas, name for GREECE.

hellebore (hĕl'ù–), name for winter- or spring-blooming Eurasian perennial plants of genus *Helleborus*. The Christmas rose (*Helleborus niger*) has evergreen leaves and its flowers (usually white) resemble wild roses and often bloom in winter. Roots of North American false hellebores (*Veratrum*) yield veratrine used in insecticides.

Hellen, in Greek mythology, ancestor of Hellenes or Greeks; son of DEUCALION.

Hellenism, culture, ideals, and pattern of life of Greece, as represented in Athens at the time of Pericles; frequently contrasted with Hebraic seriousness in the Old Testament. Hellenism gave way to Hellenistic civilization in 4th cent. B.C., but any modern attempt to revive Greek ideals is called Hellenism.

Hellenistic civilization, widespread, Greek-tinctured culture that grew out of the efforts of ALEXANDER THE GREAT to spread Hellenism with his conquests across the known world. After his death (323 B.C.) the DIADOCHI estab. dynasties that helped to give that world political disunity but at the same time Greek unity of trade and learning. A new culture in art, letters, and science developed. Alexandria and Pergamum were notable centers. Physical comfort increased for the well-to-do, education was general among the wealthy. Literature grew to vast proportions and learning (as distinct from knowledge and philosophy) came into being. Though accused of being derivative and ponderous, literature had great richness. Libraries were built, anthologies compiled. Sculpture developed, and some of the most familiar statues of the present day (e.g., the Venus of Milo, the Dying Gaul) are Hellenistic. Philosophy became the field of all the educated. The triumph of Rome meant the Roman absorption of Hellenistic culture, not its extinction.

Hellespont: see DARDANELLES.

Hell Gate, N.Y.: see EAST RIVER.

hellgrammite: see DOBSON FLY.

Hellman, Lillian, 1905–, American dramatist. Her works include the tragedy, *The Children's Hour* (1934), and *The Little Foxes* (1939), *Watch on the Rhine* (1941), *The Autumn Garden* (1951), and *Toys in the Attic* (1960).

Helmand (hĕl'mŭnd), river, rising in central Afghanistan. Flows c.850 mi. SW to Hamun-i-Helmand on Iranian border. Has vital irrigation works.

Helmholtz, Hermann Ludwig Ferdinand von (hĕr'män lōōt'vĭkh fĕr'dĕnänt fŭn hĕlm'hôlts), 1821–94, German scientist. He extended the application of law of conservation of energy and formulated it mathematically; contributed to thermo- and electrodynamics. He extended Young's theory of color vision; explained lens accommodation in eye; invented ophthalmoscope.

Helmont, Jan Baptista van (yän bäptĭ'stä vän hĕl'mônt), 1577–1644, Flemish scientist. He discovered carbon dioxide, distinguished gases from solids and liquids, and is credited with introducing the term *gas* in present scientific sense.

Heloise: see ABELARD, PETER.

Helsingborg, Sweden: see HALSINGBORG.

Helsingfors, Finland: see HELSINKI.

Helsingor, Denmark: see ELSINORE.

Helsinki (hĕl'sĭngkē), Swed. *Helsingfors*, city (pop. 441,678), cap. of Finland; a Baltic seaport on Gulf of Finland. Intellectual, commercial, administrative center of Finland. Mfg. of paper, tobacco, sugar, liquor, textiles, machinery. Called White City of the North for its cleanliness and buildings of native granite. Founded 1550, it grew rapidly after cap. was moved here from Turku (1812). Outstanding sites include university (moved here from Turku 1828), railway station (designed by Saarinen), national archives, opera house, Church of St. Nicholas. Slightly damaged in the Second World War. Olympic games were held here 1952.

Helst, Bartholomeus van der (hĕlst'), c.1613–1670, Dutch portrait painter. *Banquet of the Civic Guard* (Rijks Mus.) is considered his masterpiece.

Helvellyn (hĕlvĕl'ĭn), mountain, 3,118 ft. high, Cumberland and Westmorland, England.

Helvetia (hĕlvē'shù). **1** Latin name of Switzerland; short for *Confoederatio Helvetica*. **2** Roman administrative district of Upper Germany, 1st cent. B.C.–5th cent. A.D. It occupied W part of modern Switzerland. The Helvetii, a predominantly Celtic people, tried to conquer S Gaul in 58 B.C., were defeated by Julius Caesar at Bibracte.

Helvetic Republic, 1798–1803: see SWITZERLAND.

Helvétius, Claude Adrien (hĕlvē'shùs; Fr. ĕlvāsyüs'), 1715–71, French philosopher, one of the Encyclopedists. After serving as farmer-general and as chamberlain to the queen he retired in 1751. His philosophy as set forth in *Essays on the Mind* (1758) held that all men are born with equal ability and that educational influences create distinctions. He argued that all intellectual activity arises from sensation, even the soul being at first a capacity for sensation. He regarded self-interest as the sole motive for action and influenced the utilitarians. In France he was condemned by the Sorbonne.

Hemans, Felicia Dorothea (Browne). 1793–1835, English poet, noted for sentimental poems, such as "Casabianca" and "The Landing of the Pilgrims."

hematite (hē'mŭtīt), a mineral, an oxide of iron, important as an ore. It occurs in red earthy masses and gray to black crystals.

Hemel Hempstead, municipal borough (pop. 55,164), Hertfordshire, England. Old borough, with many 17th- and 18th-cent. buildings; included since 1947 in Hemel Hempstead New Town.

Hemingway, Ernest, 1899–1961, American writer. One of the "lost generation" of expatriates in Paris after the First World War. In his laconic, direct style, underplaying emotion, he stressed courage and virility in the struggle against a mutilating environment. His novels include *The Sun Also Rises* (1926), *A Farewell to Arms* (1929), *For Whom the Bell Tolls* (1940). His vigorous short stories, such as "The Killers" and "The Snows of Kilimanjaro," are in *Men Without Women* (1927) and later volumes. His fictional novel, *Death in the Afternoon*, is about bullfighting. He settled in Cuba, where he wrote the novella *The Old Man and the Sea* (1952). He was awarded the 1954 Nobel Prize in Literature.

hemlock, name for several plants, especially coniferous evergreen trees of genus *Tsuga*, native to North America and Asia. They are popular ornamentals with small cones and flattened leaves on horizontal branches. The poison hemlock (*Conium maculatum*) by which Socrates died, a perennial meadow plant with flattened clusters of white flowers, is naturalized in North America. Similar to it is the North American water hemlock (*Cicuta maculata*).

hemoglobin: see CORPUSCLES.

Hémon, Louis (lwē' āmō'), 1880–1913, French Canadian novelist, b. France. Wrote *Maria Chapdelaine* (1913), story of pioneer life in Quebec.

hemophilia (hē'mŭfĭ'lèù, hē''–), rare disease marked by delayed CLOTTING OF BLOOD. Death sometimes results from bleeding after even minor injuries. Occurring in males only, it is transmitted as a sex-linked character only through females.

hemorrhage (hē'mŭrĭj), escape of blood from heart or blood vessels. Bleeding from arteries is red and of rhythmic flow; from veins, it is dark and of constant flow. See also HEMOPHILIA.

hemorrhoids (hĕ'mŭroidz) or **piles**, dilated veins at anus. They often result from constipation, poor circulation, and pressure on rectum.

hemp, tall annual plant (*Cannabis sativa*), native to Asia but cultivated elsewhere for its bast fiber, also called hemp, and as a source of the narcotic drug marijuana. It has large, digitately divided narrow leaves and inconspicuous male and female flower spikes on separate plants. Cordage, paper, canvas, etc., are made from the bast fiber. Dried plant parts, especially female flowers, are the source of marijuana and hashish; the U.S. government restricts its cultivation.

Hempstead, Residential village (1965 pop. 37,192), SE N.Y., on W Long Isl., WSW of Levittown; settled c.1644. Important retailing center. Hofstra Univ. is here.

Hems, Syria: see HOMS.

henbane, weedy annual Old World plant of nightshade family. Black henbane (*Hyoscyamus niger*) is naturalized in E North America. It has yellow flowers and is poisonous, especially to poultry.

Hench, Philip Showalter, 1896–1965, American physician. Authority on rheumatic diseases, he was long associated with Mayo Clinic and Mayo Foundation (of Univ. of Minnesota). He shared 1950 Nobel Prize in Physiology and Medicine for work on hormones of the cortex of adrenal glands.

Henderson, Alexander, 1583–1646, Scottish churchman. Opposed English domination of Church of Scotland. As moderator of general assembly he conferred with Charles I on Presbyterian aims of Covenanters.

Henderson, Arthur, 1863–1935, British statesman, leader of British Labour party. Awarded 1934 Nobel Peace Prize for work toward world disarmament.

Henderson, Leon, 1895–, American economist, head of Office of Price Administration (1941–42).

Henderson, Richard, 1735–85, American colonizer in Ky. Chief promoter of TRANSYLVANIA COMPANY. Important figure in early frontier expansion.

Henderson. 1 Industrial city (pop. 16,892), NW Ky., on Ohio R., S of Evansville, Ind., in oil, coal, tobacco, corn, and livestock area; founded 1797. Important tobacco-exporting center. J. J. Audubon lived here (1810–19); nearby is Audubon Memorial State Park with museum and bird sanctuary. **2** City (pop. 12,525), SE Nev., SE of Las Vegas. Grew as industrial center with availability of power from nearby Hoover Dam. **3** City (pop. 12,740), N N.C., NNE of Raleigh near S tip of Kerr L.; settled c.1811. Important bright-leaf tobacco market. Tungsten deposits nearby. **4** City (pop. 9,666), NE Texas, SE of Tyler; founded 1844. First gusher of the rich E Texas oil field brought in nearby, 1930. Shawnee Indian village site is near.

Hendon, London: see BARNET.

Hengchow, China: see HENGYANG.

Hengist and Horsa (hĕng′gĭst, hôr′sə), traditional names of two leaders of 5th-cent. Germanic invasion of Britain. Supposedly invited to help Britons against Picts and Scots, they settled in Kent.

Hengyang (hŭng′yäng′), city (pop. c.181,000), Hunan prov., China, on Siang R. Transportation center. Formerly known as Hengchow.

Henie, Sonja (sō′nyə hĕ′nē), 1913–, Norwegian-American skater. Won Olympic figure-skating championship (1928, 1932, 1936), world title (1927–36).

Henle, Jacob (yä′kôp hĕn′lə), 1809–85, German anatomist and pathologist, noted for work on microscopic structure of tissues.

Henley, William Ernest, 1849–1903, English lyric poet, critic, and editor. Best known of his poems "England, My England" and "Invictus." He wrote plays with Stevenson and edited literary reviews.

Henley-on-Thames (-tĕmz), municipal borough (pop. 9,131), Oxfordshire, England, at base of the Chilterns, on the Thames. Scene of annual Henley rowing regatta (begun 1839) in which several English and some American crews take part.

Henlopen, Cape (hĕnlō′pŭn), SE Del., at mouth of Delaware Bay opposite Cape May, N.J. Lightship.

henna, Old World tropical shrub (*Lawsonia inermis*) with small fragrant flowers. From its dried leaves henna dye is made.

Hennepin, Louis, 1640–1701?, Franciscan Recollect friar, explorer in North America. With Michel Aco he explored the upper Mississippi valley.

Henri, Robert (hĕn′rī), 1865–1929, American painter and teacher, b. Cincinnati. His teachings helped to destroy tradition of academicism and to inspire development of living art for America. One of The EIGHT, he

sponsored first exhibit in America without a jury. Excelled in dramatic portraits.

Henrietta Maria, 1609–69, queen consort of Charles I of England, daughter of Henry IV of France. Her dealings with the pope, foreign powers, and army officers increased suspicion of Charles and fear of a Catholic uprising which partly led to civil war.

Henrietta of England (Henrietta Anne), 1644–70, duchess of Orléans, called Madame; sister of Charles II of England and wife of Philippe I d'ORLÉANS. Negotiated Treaty of Dover with Charles II in behalf of Louis XIV. An unfounded rumor ascribed her sudden death to poison.

Henríquez Ureña, Pedro (pä′dhrō ānrē′kĕs ōōrā′nyä), 1884–1946, Dominican writer. Noted for critical works on Spanish-American literature. His brother, **Max Henríquez Ureña** (1885–), is also a critic. Known for study of *modernista* movement in Spanish letters.

Henry, emperors and German kings. **Henry I** or **Henry the Fowler,** 876?–936, duke of Saxony, was elected king 919 to succeed Conrad I. He won Lotharingia from allegiance to France (925), defeated the Magyars (933), built many walled towns in E border regions. His queen, St. Matilda (d. 968) founded many monasteries. His son Otto I succeeded him. **Henry II,** 973–1024, duke of Bavaria, was elected German king 1002; crowned king of the Lombards 1004; crowned emperor at Rome 1014. He and his empress, Kunigunde, were canonized saints of the Roman Church. **Henry III,** 1017–56, was crowned joint king with his father Conrad II in 1028; became sole king 1039; was crowned emperor 1046. Under him the medieval empire reached its greatest power. He supported the reforms of the CLUNIAC ORDER. In 1046 he deposed three rival claimants to the papacy at the Synod of Sutri and caused the election of a reform-minded German (Clement II). Popes Leo IX and Victor II were also his candidates (1048, 1055). His son, **Henry IV,** 1050–1106, succeeded him as king (1056). During his minority archbishops Anno of Cologne and ADALBERT of Bremen held the power. Beginning his personal rule in 1065, Henry restored his authority in the duchies, notably Saxony. His appointments of bishops in 1075 met the condemnation of Pope GREGORY VII (see INVESTITURE), whom Henry declared deposed (1076). Gregory in turn declared Henry excommunicated and deposed, and Henry, threatened with revolt, made his humiliating journey to CANOSSA, where the pope gave him absolution (Jan., 1077). Nevertheless, the German nobles elected Rudolf of Swabia antiking. Civil war resulted, and in 1080 Gregory renewed his excommunication of Henry. But Henry was now supported by a large party. Invading Italy (1081), he drove Gregory from Rome in 1084 and was crowned emperor by GUIBERT OF RAVENNA. He was forced to abdicate in 1105 by his rebellious son, **Henry V,** 1081–1125, who had the support of Pope Paschal II. The new king soon fell out with the pope over the question of lay investiture. In 1111, at Rome, he took the pope and cardinals prisoners. To obtain his release, Paschal conceded to Henry the right to invest at will and crowned him emperor. The struggle was continued with popes Gelasius II and Calixtus II until a final compromise was reached in 1122 (see WORMS, CONCORDAT OF). Henry's widow, Matilda, married Geoffrey Plantagenet. **Henry VI,** 1165–97, succeeded his father Frederick I as German king (1190) and was crowned emperor in 1191. As husband of CONSTANCE, heiress of Sicily, he took possession of that kingdom in 1194, after the death of TANCRED of Lecce. In the same year good fortune delivered RICHARD I of England into his power, whom he forced to swear fealty as vassal. He died on his way to lead a crusade to Holy Land. His son, who later became Emperor Frederick II, succeeded him in Sicily; his brother Philip of Swabia, succeeded him as German king. **Henry VII,** c.1275–1313, count of Luxemburg, was elected German king to succeed Albert I (1308). He vainly sought to restore imperial authority in Italy by ending the strife between Guelphs and Ghibellines. Crowned king of the Lombards (1311) and emperor (1312), he died in the middle of a campaign in S Italy. He was the father of John of Luxemburg.

Henry, kings of England. **Henry I,** 1068–1135, king 1100–1135, was the youngest son of William I. On death of his brother William II, he obtained crown by a coup d'état which excluded his brother Robert II, duke of Normandy, who was on crusade. Robert invaded England (1101) but was bought off by Henry. Henry invaded Normandy (1105) and imprisoned his brother for life. Was involved in a struggle with AN-SELM over investiture. His attempts to secure succession for his daughter MATILDA later led to long civil war between STEPHEN and Matilda. **Henry II,** 1133–89, king 1154–89, was son of Matilda and Geoffrey IV. Duke of Normandy, he married ELEANOR OF AQUITAINE, thus gaining vast territories in France. Invaded England and forced Stephen to acknowledge him as heir. He restored order to war-ravaged England, subdued barons, centralized power of government in royal authority, and strengthened royal courts. His long controversy with THOMAS À BECKET concerned sole jurisdiction of ecclesiastical courts over clergymen accused of crimes. Henry adopted Constitutions of Clarendon (1164) which brought such men into lay courts; Becket protested and fled to France. Soon after his return and continued insistence on ecclesiastical prerogative, Thomas was murdered by four knights in Canterbury Cathedral. Henry was forced by public indignation to do penance. During his reign he gained N counties of England from Scotland and subdued N Wales. He was also involved in family struggles–revolt of his son Henry, and intrigues of sons Geoffrey, RICHARD I, and JOHN. Richard, with Philip II of France, defeated the aged king, who died. He was the founder of ANGEVIN or Plantagenet line. **Henry III,** 1207–72, king 1216–72, was the son of John. Became king under a regency; was granted full powers in 1227. Against advice of HUBERT DE BURGH, chief justiciar and greatest power in government, he led unsuccessful expedition to Gascony and Brittany. Dismissed De Burgh in 1232 and began a reign of extravagance, absolutism, and general incapacity. Spent vast sums on futile wars in Gascony. Henry's absolutism, and his attempt to put his son Edmund, earl of Lancaster, on Sicilian throne eventually led to outbreak of BARONS' WAR (1263). Simon de MONTFORT, leader of barons, won at Lewes and summoned (1265) a famous Parliament. Another son, Edward (later EDWARD I), led royal troops to victory at Evesham, where Montfort was killed. From 1267 Edward was actually ruler and Henry king in name only. **Henry IV,** 1367–1413, king 1399–1413, was son of JOHN OF GAUNT. Opposed RICHARD II in 1387 and was one of lords appellant who ruled England for a year. After accusing duke of Norfolk of treason against Richard he was banished for six years. In the absence of Richard (whose rule was unpopular) he landed in England in 1399 and claimed throne, thus founding Lancastrian dynasty. Put down rebellions by Richard's followers, by the Scots and the Welsh, and by the Percies. Maintained prerogatives of the crown against Parliament, but he left crown enormously in debt. His son, **Henry V,** 1387–1422, king 1413–22, presided over privy council during his father's illness. As prince (Shakespeare's Prince Hal) he had led armies against Welsh Owen Glendower and been active in royal victory over the Percies. Rebellion by the Lollards continued after his accession until 1417. Determined to regain lands which he sincerely but mistakenly believed to be his, he invaded France in 1415, thus reopening HUNDRED YEARS WAR. Announced his claim to French throne and defeated the French at Agincourt. Henry conquered Normandy (1417–19) and in 1420 married CATHERINE OF VALOIS. Fell ill and died in 1422. Despite early recklessness he ruled with justice and industry; restored civil order and national spirit. His

charm, military genius, and care for less fortunate subjects made him a popular hero even though his wars left the crown heavily in debt. His son, **Henry VI,** 1421–71, king 1422–61 and 1470–71, became king when less than a year old. During his early years England was under protectorate of his uncles, John of Lancaster and Humphrey, duke of Gloucester. The English, after their defeat by Joan of Arc, attempted to protect their French interests by crowning Henry king of France at Paris (1431) but their cause became hopeless. Rebellion of Jack Cade was one of many riots showing dissatisfaction with government. Struggle between factions headed by Queen, MARGARET OF ANJOU, and Edmund Beaufort, duke of SOMERSET, and by Richard, duke of YORK, developed into dynastic battle between Lancasters and Yorkists called Wars of the ROSES. In battle of St. Albans (1455) Somerset was killed and Henry captured. York, who had been made protector and named successor to Henry (whose mind had given way), was killed in 1460 but his son Edward defeated Lancastrians and was proclaimed king as EDWARD IV in 1461. He later fled to Holland and Henry was restored briefly. Edward retook crown and Henry died in the Tower in 1471. **Henry VII,** 1457–1509, king 1485–1509, became head of house of Lancaster at Henry VI's death. Invaded England from Brittany (1485) and at battle of Bosworth Field defeated forces of RICHARD III. Married Elizabeth, daughter of Edward IV, uniting houses of York and Lancaster and founding Tudor dynasty. Sent Edward POYNINGS to Ireland in 1494 to consolidate British rule there. Peace treaty (1499) between Scotland and England was followed by marriage of Henry's daughter, Margaret, to James IV of Scotland. Henry estab. Tudor tradition of autocratic rule tempered by justice and greatly increased (1487) the powers of the court of Star Chamber. His reign saw end of Wars of the Roses and is generally considered beginning of modern English history. His son, **Henry VIII,** 1491–1547, king 1509–47, married his brother's widow, KATHARINE OF ARAGON, who bore him a daughter, Mary. His chief minister, Thomas WOLSEY, concluded an alliance with France but Henry (despite FIELD OF THE CLOTH OF GOLD) joined (1522) Emperor Charles V in war against France. England prospered internally under Wolsey (who had almost complete control). Court was a center of learning and the pope gave Henry title of "Defender of the Faith" for treatise against Luther. Henry now wished to marry Anne BOLEYN but Pope Clement VII resisted his demands for a divorce from Katharine. Wolsey's failure in the affair caused his downfall and Thomas Cromwell became chief minister. An antiecclesiastical policy was begun and subservient Thomas Cranmer became archbishop of Canterbury. Henry married Anne (1533) and was excommunicated. Papal powers were now transferred to king who became supreme head of English church. Break with Rome was complete and Church of ENGLAND was estab. Anne had one daughter, Elizabeth. The marriage ended when Anne was convicted of adultery and beheaded. Ten days later Henry married Jane Seymour who died in 1537 giving birth to Edward VI. Dealt harshly with such rebellions as the Pilgrimage of Grace. Licensed (1537) publication of Bible in English. His marriage (1540) to ANNE OF CLEVES (whom he disliked and divorced) led to execution of Cromwell. He then married Catherine HOWARD who suffered (1542) Anne Boleyn's fate. In 1543 Catherine Parr became his sixth queen. War with Scotland began again (1542) and Henry made unsuccessful attempts to unite the two kingdoms. Wales was officially incorporated into England (1536) but conquest of Ireland proved too expensive. End of his reign saw gradual move toward Protestantism. He remained immensely popular despite his advancement of personal desires under guise of public policy or moral right. His political insight, however, steadily grew better; he gave England a comparatively peaceful reign.

Henry, kings of France. **Henry I,** c.1008–1060, reigned 1031–60. He was a powerless tool of the great feudal lords. **Henry II,** 1519–59, son of Francis I, reigned 1547–59. Was dominated by Anne de Montmorency, by his mistress Diane de Poitiers, and by François and Charles de Guise. He continued his father's struggle against Emperor Charles V; recovered Calais from England (1558). Treaty of CATEAU-CAMBRÉSIS ended French pretensions to Italy (1559). He was accidentally killed in a tournament. His queen was Catherine de' Medici. His third son, **Henry III,** 1551–89, was elected king of Poland in 1573 but returned to France in 1574 to succeed his brother Charles IX. His reign was almost continually disturbed by the Wars of RELIGION. The death in 1584 of his brother Francis made him the last male member of the house of Valois. His recognition of Henry of Navarre (later Henry IV) as heir presumptive was opposed by Henri, 3d duc de GUISE, head of the Catholic LEAGUE (the "War of the Three Henrys" resulted). Having procured the murder of Guise (1588), the king was faced with a revolt of the League and was expelled from Paris. Henry of Navarre came to his aid, but Henry III was assassinated in the siege by Jacques Clément, a fanatic monk. Henry III was notorious for his vices. **Henry IV** (Henry of Navarre), 1553–1610, first BOURBON king of France, was the son of Antoine de Bourbon and JEANNE D'ALBRET. On her death he succeeded to the kingdom of Navarre (1572). He took leadership of the Huguenot (Protestant) party in 1569. His marriage in 1572 with MARGARET OF VALOIS was the occasion for the massacre of SAINT BARTHOLOMEW's DAY. Henry saved his life by abjuring Protestantism, but in 1576 he escaped from his virtual imprisonment at court and returned to Protestantism. When in 1584 HENRY III named him heir presumptive, the Catholic LEAGUE, headed by Henri, 3d duc de GUISE, refused to recognize him as heir and persuaded Henry III to send an army to force his conversion. In the resulting "War of the Three Henrys," Henry of Navarre defeated Henry III at Coutras (1587) but came to the king's support in the troubles of 1588, and after Henry III's death (1589) defeated the League forces at Arques (1589) and Ivry (1590); he was unable to enter Paris until 1594, after he had abjured Protestantism—allegedly with the remark, "Paris is worth a Mass." His war with Spain, the ally of the League, ended in 1598 with the Treaty of VERVINS. In 1598 also he established religious toleration through the Edict of NANTES. With his minister SULLY he spent the rest of his reign restoring order, industry, and trade. His slogan, "A chicken in every peasant's pot every Sunday," has remained famous. In 1600 he married Marie de' Medici, having had his earlier marriage annulled. He was stabbed to death by RAVAILLAC. His gallantry and wit, his concern for the common people, and his exploits with the ladies have become legendary. **Henry V:** see CHAMBORD, HENRI, COMTE DE.

Henry II or Henry of Trastamara (trăstùmä'rù), 1333?–1379, Spanish king of Castile and Leon (1369–79); natural son of Alfonso XI. In his struggle against his half-brother PETER THE CRUEL he was aided by Du Guesclin, Peter by Edward the Black Prince. Though defeated at Najéra (1367), he routed and killed Peter in 1369. His son JOHN I succeeded him.

Henry, Joseph, 1797–1878, American physicist, first secretary and director of Smithsonian Institution (estab. 1846). He improved the electromagnet, discovered self-inductance, and independently of Michael Faraday he discovered principle of the induced current (basic to dynamo, transformer, and many other devices).

Henry, O., pseud. of **William Sydney Porter,** 1862–1910, American short-story writer, notable for unexpected twist at end of stories. Charged with fraud in an Austin, Texas, bank, he fled to Central America, later returned to imprisonment, then lived as a writer in New York. Many stories (as in *The Four Million,* 1906) picture great-city life.

Henry, Patrick, 1736–99, American patriot and orator. Spurred colonial revolt in the South by oratory; he was responsible for the phrase, "Give me liberty or give me death." Later fought to add Bill of Rights to the Constitution.

Henry, William: see HENRY's LAW.

Henry, Cape, SE Va., at entrance to Chesapeake Bay E of Norfolk. Memorial marks approximate spot where Jamestown settlers landed April 26, 1607. Site included in Colonial Natl. Historical Park.

Henry, Fort, fortification, SE Ont., Canada, on St. Lawrence R. overlooking Kingston harbor. Built 1812, demolished 1832, rebuilt 1832–36. Prisoners' camp in both World Wars.

Henry E. Huntington Library and Art Gallery: see HUNTINGTON, COLLIS POTTER.

Henry of Burgundy, d. 1112 or 1114, count of Portugal. A brother of Eudes, duke of Burgundy, he was called by Alfonso VI of Leon to help in the fight against the Moors and was assigned a portion of land which under his son, Alfonso I, became the independent kingdom of Portugal.

Henry of Flanders, c.1174–1216, Latin emperor of Constantinople (1206–16); brother of Baldwin I. Fought successfully against Bulgarians.

Henry of Navarre: see HENRY IV, king of France.

Henry of Trastamara: see HENRY II, Spanish king.

Henry's law states that amount of gas that dissolves in liquid is proportional to pressure of gas above liquid. Named for William Henry (1774–1836), English chemist and physician.

Henryson, Robert, c.1425–c.1506, Scottish poet, imitator of Chaucer. His *Testament of Cresseid* is a sequel to *Troilus and Criseyde.* Also wrote the lively *Moral Fables of Aesop* and *Robene and Makyne.*

Henry Street Settlement: see WALD, LILLIAN D.

Henry the Fowler, German king: see HENRY I.

Henry the Lion, 1129–95, Guelphic duke of Saxony (1142–80) and Bavaria (1156–80); son of HENRY THE PROUD. Emperor Frederick I restored the two duchies to him in the hope of restoring peace between the Guelphs and the Hohenstaufen. Henry took part in Frederick's early Italian campaigns; was a leader in the Wendish Crusade of 1147; and extended his power over the Wendish lands of NE Germany, where he introduced Christianity. The growth of his power resulted in friction with Frederick, who in 1180 seized upon a pretext for confiscating Henry's fiefs. Bavaria and Saxony, last of the great German duchies, thus were subdivided into a patchwork of small principalities. Henry went into exile to England but returned 1189, recovered parts of Saxony (Brunswick and Lüneburg), and was left in possession of them by the Peace of Fulda (1190). His younger son became emperor as Otto IV.

Henry the Navigator, 1394–1460, Portuguese prince, patron of exploration; son of John I of Portugal. Founded naval arsenal, observatory, school for study of geography and navigation. His navigators explored W coast of Africa, penetrated into Sudan and Senegal, estab. slave and gold trade (but Henry in 1455 forbade kidnaping of Negroes). He also fought in Moroccan campaigns and exerted considerable political influence, but his chief importance was his contribution to art of navigation and progress of exploration.

Henry the Proud, c.1108–1139, Guelphic duke of Bavaria (1126–38) and Saxony (1137–38). He helped his father-in-law, Emperor LOTHAIR II, against the HOHENSTAUFEN. CONRAD III of Hohenstaufen defeated him in the imperial elections of 1138 and deprived him of his duchies. Henry was in the process of reconquering them when he died, leaving HENRY THE LION as his heir.

Henslowe, Philip, d. 1616, English theatrical manager, associated with Edward Alleyn. His diary contains valuable information on Elizabethan stage.

Henson, Josiah, 1789–1883, reputed original of Uncle Tom in *Uncle Tom's Cabin.* Escaped from slavery and became leader of community of escaped Negroes in Canada. Autobiography published 1849.

Henty, G(eorge) A(lfred), 1832–1902, English journalist and writer of boys' books. Wrote c.80 tales of adventure, as popular in America as in England.

hepatica or liverwort, low woodland wild flower (genus *Hepatica*) of the temperate zone. It has three-lobed leaves and white or lilac blooms in spring.

hepatitis, inflammation of the liver; it may be caused by virus or other infection, poisons, or blocking of the bile channels.

Hepburn, Katharine, 1909–, American actress. Noted for stage work (e.g., *The Philadelphia Story*) and for films (e.g., *Morning Glory* and *Dragon Seed*).

Hephaestus (hĕfē′stŭs), in Greek religion, Olympian god of fire and metalwork; son of Zeus and Hera and father of Erechtheus. He was usually represented as a bearded man, with mighty shoulders and arms, but lame. A comic figure on Olympus, he was butt of many jokes. His favorite abodes on earth were volcanic islands where he had workshops manned by the Cyclopes. As the craftsman's god he was worshipped at industrial centers such as Athens. In Trojan War he supported the Greeks. Most scholars agree that he was the husband of Aphrodite, who was unfaithful to him. Romans called him Vulcan.

Hepplewhite, George (hĕ′pŭlhwīt), d. 1786, English cabinetmaker and furniture designer. His style is marked by such details as slight tapering legs with spade feet, chair backs in shield, oval, hoop, and interlaced heart forms.

Hepworth, Barbara, 1903–, English sculptor of smooth, nonfigurative forms.

Hera (hēr′ū), in Greek religion, queen of Olympian gods, protectress of women; daughter of Cronus and Rhea, sister and wife of Zeus, and mother of Hephaestus and Ares. A jealous wife, she persecuted Zeus, his earthly mistresses, and their progeny. The Trojan Prince Paris did not award to her APPLE OF DISCORD, and she in revenge supported Greeks in Trojan War. She had especially fine temples at Argos and Samos. Romans called her Juno.

Heraclea (hĕrŭklē′ū), anc. Greek city, S Italy, not far from the Gulf of Taranto. Here Pyrrhus defeated the Romans 280 B.C.

Heraclea Pontica (pŏn′tĭkŭ), anc. Greek city, on S shore of the Black Sea, site of modern Eregli, Turkey; large commercial center (5th–6th cent. B.C.).

Heracles, another name for HERCULES.

Heraclitus (hĕrŭklī′tŭs), c.535–c.475 B.C., Greek philosopher of Ephesus. He held that the only reality is change and that permanence is an illusion. All things carry with them their opposites, and therefore being and not being are in everything and the only real state is one of transition. Heraclitus believed that fire was the underlying substance of the universe.

Heraclius I (hĕrŭklī′ŭs, hĭrā′klēŭs), c.575–641, Byzantine emperor (610–41). Recovered Syria, Palestine, and Egypt from Persia (622–28), only to see them fall to the Moslem Arabs (629–42). Favored MONOTHELETISM.

Herakleion, Crete: see CANDIA.

Heralds' College, body first chartered in 1484 by Richard III of England. Purpose is to assign coats of arms and trace lineages. Officials are called Garter king-of-arms, other kings-of-arms, heralds, and pursuivants. Officials also proclaim accession of king and attend at state occasions.

Herat (hĕrät′), anc. *Aria,* city (pop. c.100,000), cap. of Herat, NW Afghanistan, on Hari Rud R. Textile and carpet mfg. On trade route from Persia to India, it was taken by various conquerors, notably Alexander the Great and Tamerlane. Disputed by Persians and Afghans until mid-19th cent.

Hérault (ārō′), department (2,403 sq. mi.; pop. 516,-658), S France, in Languedoc; cap. Montpellier. Sète is the chief port.

herb (ûrb, hûrb), botanically any plant lacking woody tissue as distinguished from shrubs or trees. More specifically, it is a plant used either medicinally or for its flavor or scent.

herbaceous plant, an ANNUAL with soft green stem, slight woody tissue; sometimes called herb.

herbarium, collection of dried plant specimens used in study of botany. They are mounted on heavy paper and arranged according to genera. Notable herbariums in U.S. include Gray Herbarium at Harvard Univ. and those at the National Museum and the New York and Missouri botanical gardens.

Herbart, Johann Friedrich (yō′hän frē′drĭkh hĕr′bärt), 1776–1841, German philosopher, professor at Königsberg and Göttingen. He made important contributions to psychology and education. To Herbart the universe was made up of simple independent "reals" and change came from shifting relationships of these "reals" in their efforts at self-preservation. In education he emphasized the conscious effort to relate learning to the learner's former experience and stressed moral education.

Herbert, A(lan) P(atrick), 1890–, English writer and member of Parliament. Largely responsible for the bill liberalizing English divorce law (1937). Among his many books is *The Water Gipsies* (1930).

Herbert, George, 1593–1633, English religious poet and clergyman, one of the METAPHYSICAL POETS. His poems (posthumously pub. as *The Temple,* 1633) are marked by deep feeling, precise language, and metrical versatility. His elder brother, **Edward Herbert, 1st Baron Herbert of Cherbury,** 1583–1648, was a philosopher and poet. Precursor of deism, he wrote *De religione laici* (1645). In *Poems* (1665) he published secular metaphysical verse.

Herbert, Mary: see PEMBROKE, MARY HERBERT, COUNTESS OF.

Herbert, Victor, 1859–1924, Irish-American composer and conductor. He began his career playing cello; was conductor of the Pittsburgh Symphony Orchestra, 1898–1904. His operettas (e.g., *Babes in Toyland* 1903; *Mlle Modiste,* 1905; *The Red Mill,* 1906; *Naughty Marietta,* 1910; and *Sweethearts,* 1913) have been much revived.

Herbert, William: see PEMBROKE, WILLIAM HERBERT, 3D EARL OF.

Herbert of Cherbury: see HERBERT, GEORGE.

Hercegovina: see BOSNIA AND HERCEGOVINA.

Herculaneum (hûrkyōōlā′nēŭm), anc. city, S Italy, on the Gulf of Naples, at the foot of Mt. Vesuvius, on table chiefly because it was buried (along with Pompeii) by the eruption of Vesuvius in A.D. 79. Excavations have uncovered walls, statues, books, and the like in fine preservation.

Herculano de Carvalho Araújo, Alexandre (älĕshän′-drŭ ĕrkōōlä′nō dŭ kärvä′yō ŭrou′zhō), 1810–77, Portuguese historian. Known for his history of Portugal (4 vols., 1846–53) and of the Inquisition in Portugal (Eng. tr., 1926).

Hercules (hûr′kyōōlēz) or **Heracles** (hĕ′rŭklēz), most popular hero in Greek and Roman legends, famous for his extraordinary strength and courage. Son of Zeus and Alcmene, he was hated by Hera, who sought to kill him by sending two serpents to his cradle, but these he strangled; later she sent madness upon him, so that he slew his wife and children. As advised by Delphic oracle, he sought (and achieved) purification at court of King Eurystheus, who demanded of him 12 labors: killing Nemean lion, nine-headed Hydra, and man-eating Stymphalian birds; cleaning stables of Augeas; procuring golden apples of Hesperides and girdle of Hippolyte; and capturing fleet-footed Cerynean hind, mad Cretan bull, flesh-eating mares of Diomed, Erymanthian boar, cattle of Geryon, and three-headed watchdog of Hades, Cerberus. Later he joined Calydonian hunt and expedition of Argonauts. At his death he ascended to Olympus, where he married Hebe. He was widely worshiped. Hero of plays by Sophocles, Euripides, and Seneca. Most famous statue of him is *Farnese Hercules* in Naples.

Hercules, Pillars of: see PILLARS OF HERCULES.

Hercules'-club, small North American tree (*Aralia spinosa*) with a stout thorny trunk, huge compound leaves, and a large flower cluster at the top of the tree. Sometimes called devil's-walking-stick.

Herder, Johann Gottfried von (yō'hän gôt'frēt fŭn hĕr'dŭr), 1744–1803, German philosopher, poet, and critic. Studied theology and after winning attention by literary criticism he became (1776) court preacher at Weimar at the instance of Goethe, whom he influenced. He was a leader in the *Sturm und Drang* movement in German literature, a passionate opponent of the cool rationalism of 18th-cent. Enlightenment and a precursor of the romantics. Herder sought to develop a philosophy of history showing the march of man's progress. His most ambitious work was *Outlines of the Philosophy of Man* (1784–91). He did much to introduce foreign literature (notably Shakespeare, Ossian, and English and Romance folk songs) to German intellectuals and stirred interest in the science of language.

Heredia, José María (hōsā' märē'ä ārā'dhēä), 1803–39, Cuban journalist and poet. Though his poetry is classic in form, he was in temperament a romantic.

Hérédia, José Maria de, 1842–1905, French poet, b. Cuba. *Les Trophées* (1893), a collection of sonnets of classic inspiration, brings to perfection the ideals of the PARNASSIANS.

heredity (hŭrē'dĭtē), transmission, through reproductive process, of factors in plants and animals which cause offspring to resemble parents. First scientifically founded concepts, those of Gregor J. MENDEL, indicated that characters are inherited as units independently of each other. Studies of chromosomes, genes, MITOSIS, meiosis, and sex-linked characters shed light on mechanism of heredity. Constancy of transmission of hereditary characters from generation to generation does not preclude changes required by evolutionary concept since MUTATION can occur. See also GENETICS.

Hereford, England: see HEREFORDSHIRE.

Hereford cattle: see CATTLE.

Herefordshire or **Hereford** (hĕ'rŭfŭrd), county (842 sq. mi.; pop. 130,919), W England, on Welsh border. Has undulating terrain, rising to Black Mts. and Malvern Hills. Mainly agr. and pastoral region famous for orchards and cattle. Scene of border warfare with Welsh. The county town is **Hereford,** municipal borough (pop. 40,413), on the Wye. Has cathedral dating from 11th cent.; scene every third year of Festival of the Three Choirs, held other years at Gloucester and Worcester. White Cross near town marks end of great plague, mid-14th cent. Birthplace of Nell Gwyn and David Garrick.

Herero (hŭrâ'rō), Bantu people, mainly in South-West Africa. Rebelled against German rule in early 20th cent., and reprisals reduced tribe from 80,000 to 15,000. Active nationalists.

Hereward the Wake (hĕ'rĭwŭrd), fl. 1070, thane of Lincolnshire. A leader of resistance against William I, he was folk hero of conquered Anglo-Saxons.

Herisau (hā'rīzou), town (pop. 14,361), cap. of Ausser-Rhoden half canton, Appenzell, Switzerland. Embroideries, cotton textiles, machinery.

Héristal, Belgium: see HERSTAL.

Herkimer, industrial village (pop. 9,396), central N.Y., on Mohawk R., ESE of Utica; settled c.1725 by German immigrants. Gillette trial here used as plot of Dreiser's *An American Tragedy.*

hermandad (ĕrmändädh') [Span.,= brotherhood], league of towns in medieval Spain. *Hermandades* were formed as protection against lawless nobles. Ferdinand and Isabella founded the Holy Hermandad for all Spain to act as permanent police force. Local *hermandades,* greatly modified, continued to 1835. Mexican Acordada was similar organization.

Hermann, d. A.D. 21: see ARMINIUS.

Hermannstadt, Rumania: see SIBIU.

Hermaphroditus (hŭrmă"frŭdī'tŭs), beautiful son of Hermes and Aphrodite. He and nymph Salmacis became one body, with characteristics of both the male and female.

Hermes (hûr'mēz), in Greek religion, Olympian god; son of Zeus and Maia. He had great variety of functions: god of commerce, of cheats and thieves, of luck (and hence gamblers), of athletic contests, and of eloquence; messenger of the gods; and conductor of souls to Hades. Lyre and flute were his inventions. He was thought of as a merry youth with much cunning, and he inspired riotous festivals. In art he is usually shown wearing a winged hat and winged sandals and carrying the CADUCEUS. His Roman equivalent is Mercury.

Hermetic books, metaphysical works that also discuss magic, astrology, and alchemy. Authorship is attributed to Egyptian god THOTH, whom Greeks identified as Hermes Trismegistus (trĭsmùjī'stùs). Hermetical philosophy was popular in 17th cent.

Hermione (hŭrmī'ùnē), in Greek legend, only child of Helen and Menelaus and wife of Neoptolemus.

Hermitage, museum in Leningrad. Rebuilt in 19th cent. as a museum in Neo-Greek style from Catherine II's pavilion palace. Fine collection includes Dutch, Flemish, French, Italian, and Spanish paintings.

Hermitage, home of Andrew Jackson, central Tenn., near Nashville. House built 1819–31, rebuilt 1835. Jackson and wife buried here. Has church (1823) built by him.

hermit crab, crustacean with soft, asymmetrical, usually coiled abdomen. It is chiefly a marine animal but in the tropics some are largely land forms. Most hermit crabs occupy shells of snails or other gastropod mollusks, thus protecting the abdomen with a portable shelter.

Hermite, Charles (shärl ĕrmēt'), 1822–1901, French mathematician. He made valuable contributions to theory of numbers, theory of elliptic functions, and theory of equations.

Hermite, Tristan l': see TRISTAN L'HERMITE.

Hermon, Mount, on Syria-Lebanon boundary, near Israel. Highest of its three peaks rises to c.9,000 ft. Mentioned in Bible as Hermon, Sion, Senir, and Shenir. A sacred landmark in anc. Palestine, it is designated as scene of Transfiguration. Was also revered by worshipers of Baal.

Hermopolis (hŭrmŏ'pŭlĭs), city (pop. 14,402), Syros Isl., Greece, chief city and port of the CYCLADES.

Hermosa Beach, resort and residential city (pop. 16,-115), SW Calif., on Santa Monica Bay SW of Los Angeles.

Hermosillo (ĕrmōsē'yō), city (1965 est. pop. 143,-215), cap. of Sonora, NW Mexico, on Sonora R. Trading and mfg. center in tropical-fruit district.

Hernandarias: see ARIAS DE SAAVEDRA, HERNANDO.

Hernández. For some Spaniards thus named, see FERNÁNDEZ.

Hernández, José (hōsā' ĕrnän'dĕs), 1834–86, Argentine poet, author of classic of gaucho literature, *Martín Fierro* (1872).

Herndon, William Henry, 1818–91, law partner and biographer of Abraham Lincoln. Much of *Herndon's Lincoln: the True Story of a Great Life* (3 vols., 1889) ran counter to established legend.

Herne, James A. (hûrn), 1839–1901, American actor and dramatist whose real name was James Aherne. Noted for adaptation of *Hearts of Oak* (1880), written in collaboration with David Belasco.

Herne (hĕr'nù), city (pop. 115,566), North Rhine–Westphalia, West Germany; a center of Ruhr dist.

hernia or **rupture,** protrusion of any internal organ from cavity in which it is normally located. Common form is protrusion of a loop of intestine through weak point in wall of abdomen or groin.

Hero, in late Greek legend, priestess of Aphrodite in Sestos. Her lover, Leander, swam the Hellespont nightly to see her. He drowned one night, and she threw herself into sea.

Hero, mathematician: see HERON OF ALEXANDRIA.

hero, in Greek religion, dead person of note who was given reverence and worship as quasi-divine. Heroes were regarded as ghosts to be appeased, and rites were like those for underworld gods. Heroes might be actual dead men, real or imaginary ancestors, or "faded gods," those demoted to human status.

Herod, dynasty reigning in Palestine at time of Christ. Founder of family fortune was Antipater (ăntĭp'ŭtŭr), d. 43 B.C., who was in favor with Caesar after defeat of Pompey and who had gained power in Palestine by aiding Hyrcanus II (see MACCABEES). His son, Herod the Great, d. 4 B.C., gave family its name. Through Marc Antony, Herod secured title of King of Judaea (37 B.C.–4 B.C.); after battle of Actium he made peace with Octavian (Augustus). Herod married 10 times, and the various families intrigued against each other. In his last years Herod was subject to insanity and executed his sons Aristobulus (ăr"ĭstōbū'lŭs), Alexander, and Antipater. It was this Herod who was ruling at time of Jesus' birth and who ordered massacre of all small children. Mat. 2. He divided his kingdom among his sons Archelaus, Herod Antipas, and Philip. Archelaus (ăr"kēlā'ŭs), d. after A.D. 6, ruled Judaea and Idumaea (4 B.C.–A.D. 6). Mat. 2.22. Herod Antipas (ăn'tĭpăs), d. after A.D. 39, tetrarch of Galilee and Peraea, was the Herod who executed John the Baptist and who was ruling at Jesus' death. He repudiated his wife to marry Herodias (hērō'dĕŭs), daughter of his half brother Aristobulus, divorced wife of his half brother Herod Philip, and mother of Salome. Her vaulting ambition caused his ruin, and Caligula banished him (A.D. 39). Mat. 14; Mark 6; Luke 3; Acts 12. Herod the Great's son Philip, d. A.D. 34, was made tetrarch of region E of Galilee. The eldest son of Aristobulus became Herod Agrippa I, d. A.D. 44. Caligula made him king (A.D. 39) of Philip's tetrarchy and of region W of Damascus. On Claudius' accession he was made ruler of S Syria and of Palestine E and W of Jordan R. His son, Herod Agrippa II, d. c.100, was a poor ruler who alienated his subjects. St. Paul spoke before him. Acts 25; 26. After fall of Jerusalem he went to Rome. As a dynasty the Herods were neither good nor capable rulers; they depended largely on power of Rome and are usually blamed for state of virtual anarchy in Palestine as Christian era began.

Herodotus (hĕrŏ'dŭtŭs), 484?–425? B.C., Greek historian, called father of history. His work, the first comprehensive attempt at secular narrative history, marks start of Western history writing. It deals primarily with Persian Wars, but its rich diversity of contemporary information makes it an important source book on ancient Greece.

heroic couplet, a verse form: see PENTAMETER.

heroin: see OPIUM.

heron (hĕ'rŭn), large wading bird of most temperate parts of world, abundant in the tropics and subtropics. It has a long, sharp bill, long neck and legs, and large wings. Many nest in large colonies. Among American species are great and little blue herons, little green heron, black-crowned and yellow-crowned night herons, and Louisiana heron. See *ill.*, p. 118.

Heron of Alexandria (hĕ'rŏn) or **Hero,** mathematician, inventor; birth and death dates probably between 2d cent. B.C. and 3d cent. A.D. He wrote on measurement of geometric figures, studied mechanics and pneumatics, and invented many devices operated by water, steam, and compressed air.

Herophilus (hĭrŏ'fŭlŭs), fl. 300 B.C. Greek anatomist, a leader of Alexandria school of medicine.

herpes: see COLD SORES.

Herrera, Fernando de (fĕrnän'dō dā' ĕrā'rä), 1534–97, Spanish poet, notable for graceful sonnets and love lyrics, heroic odes.

Herrera, Francisco de (frănthē'skō), the elder, c.1590–1656, Spanish religious painter, a founder of naturalistic school of Seville. A teacher of Velazquez. His son, **Francisco de Herrera,** the younger, 1622–85, stud-

ied in Rome, where he painted still lifes. Designed baroque Saragossa cathedral.

Herreshoff, John Brown (hĕ'rŭs-hŏf), 1841–1915, American yacht and speedboat builder. He and his brother, **Nathaniel Greene Herreshoff,** 1848–1938, introduced radical features of design in sailing yachts after 1891. The *Gloriana* won them a reputation, and they subsequently produced five successful defenders of the *America's* Cup at their Bristol, R.I., yards.

Herrick, Robert, 1591–1674, English poet, usually called greatest of CAVALIER POETS. Took orders c.1627 and lived at Dean Prior in Devon. The volume *Hesperides* (1648) contains his *Noble Numbers* (sacred songs) and bucolic love lyrics (e.g., "Night-Piece: To Julia," song opening "Gather ye rosebuds," and "Cherry-ripe") and epigrams.

Herrick, Robert, 1868–1938, American novelist. His realistic novels include *The Web of Life* (1900), *Clark's Field* (1914), and *The End of Desire* (1932).

Herricks, N.Y.: see GARDEN CITY PARK.

Herrin, city (pop. 9,474), S central Ill., NW of Marion; settled 1818. Site of "Herrin Massacre" (1922), local clash in country-wide coal strike, which resulted in death of about 25 persons.

herring, common food fish in N Atlantic waters of North America and Europe. There are many species; common herring is *Clupea harengus,* which travels in huge schools. It is c.1 ft. long, blue above and silver on the sides. In spring or autumn it lays c.30,000 eggs, which sink to bottom and develop; young mature in three years.

Herrings, battle of the, 1429, episode in siege of Orléans. An English wagon train, led by Sir John Fastolf, repulsed a French attack at Rouvray by using wagons with herring barrels as barricade.

Herriot, Édouard (ādwär' ĕryō'), 1872–1957, French politician. As leader of Radical Socialists, he played prominent part in chamber of deputies, in cabinets, and as premier (notably 1924–25, 1932); favored conciliatory foreign policy, payment of war debts to U.S. Under German arrest 1942–45, he resumed party leadership after the war, presided over national assembly 1947–54.

Herrnhut (hĕrn'hŏōt), town (est. pop. 2,024), East Germany, in former state of Saxony. Founded 1722 by Zinzendorf as colony of Moravian Church.

Herschel, Sir William, 1738–1822, English astronomer, b. Germany, originally named Friedrich Wilhelm Herschel; pioneer systematizer of sky exploration and cataloguing of heavenly bodies. His many discoveries with reflecting telescopes which he constructed include the planet Uranus (1781). He concluded that solar system as a whole moves through space. His sister Caroline (1750–1848) worked with him. His son **Sir John Frederick William Herschel,** 1792–1871, confirmed and extended his observations and cataloguing of nebulae and double stars.

Hersey, John (hûr'sē), 1914–, American author and journalist. A former war correspondent, he wrote works on events in Second World War. They include *Hiroshima* (1946) and the novels *A Bell for Adano* (1944) and *The Wall* (1950). Later novels are *A Single Pebble* (1956), *The War Lover* (1959), *The Child Buyer* (1960, and *White Lotus* (1965).

Hershey, town (pop. 6,851), SE Pa., ENE of Harrisburg; founded 1903. Owned by Hershey company, it makes chocolate confectionery.

Herskovits, Melville Jean, 1895–1963, American anthropologist. Noted for his research throughout Africa, he pioneered studies in Negro ethnology.

Herstal (hĕr'stäl), town (est. pop. 29,849), Liège prov., E Belgium; suburb of Liège. Also known as Héristal. Mfg. of arms. Residence of early Carolingian mayors of the palace and of Charlemagne.

Herter, Christian A(rchibald), 1895–1966, American public official. Republican governor of Mass. (1953–57). U.S. Secretary of State (1959–61).

Hertford, England: see HERTFORDSHIRE.

Hertford College: see OXFORD UNIVERSITY.

Hertfordshire (här'fürdshĭr, härt–), **Hertford**, or **Herts** (härts, hûrts), inland county (632 sq. mi.; pop. 832,088), S England. Agr. county with level terrain, it produces wheat, hay, vegetables, and flowers. St. Albans an important urban center. County prominent in military history, particularly during Wars of the Roses. The county town, **Hertford**, municipal borough (pop. 15,734), was important in Saxon times. First national church council held here 673. Haileybury Col., important English public school, near here.

Hertogenbosch, 's: see 's HERTOGENBOSCH.

Herts: see HERTFORDSHIRE.

Hertwig, Oscar (ôs'kär hĕrt'vĭkh), 1849–1922, German embryologist. He discovered that fertilization consists of union of male and female germ cell nuclei.

Herty, Charles Holmes, 1867–1938, American chemist. His work on making paper from pine pulp helped to industrialize the South.

Hertz, Gustav (gŏos'täf hĕrts'), 1887–, German physicist. Shared 1925 Nobel Prize in Physics for work on effect of impact of electrons on atoms. Undertook atomic research in USSR after Second World War.

Hertz, Heinrich Rudolf (hûrts, Ger. hīn'rĭkh rōō'dôlf hĕrts'), 1857–94, German physicist. In the course of his experiments confirming J. C. Maxwell's electromagnetic theory, he produced and studied electromagnetic waves (known also as hertzian waves or radio waves).

Hertzog, James Barry Munnik, 1866–1942, South African military and political leader. Commanded a division of Boer forces in South African War 1899–1902. Organized (1913) nationalist party for independence from British Empire. Prime minister (1924–39) in coalition government with Labour party.

Hervey Islands: see COOK ISLANDS.

Hervey of Ickworth, John, Baron (här'vē, hûr'vē), 1693–1743, English statesman and memoir writer. Vice chancellor and privy councilor, Lord Hervey influenced Queen Caroline. Bitterly attacked by Pope. Author of *Memoirs of the Reign of George II.*

Herzen, Aleksandr Ivanovich (ŭlyĭksän'dŭr ēvä'nŭvĭch här'tsĭn), 1812–70, Russian revolutionary leader and writer. Lived abroad after 1847, attacking tsarist autocracy in various writings and in the influential periodical, *Kolokol* (1857–62).

Herzl, Theodor (tā'ōdôr hĕr'tsŭl), 1860–1904, Hungarian journalist, founder of modern Zionism. Aroused by the Dreyfus Affair, he devoted his life to the creation of a Jewish state, which he advocated in his booklet *Der Judenstaat.*

Hesiod (hē'sēŭd, hē'–), fl. 8th cent.? B.C., Greek poet. Little-known, self-styled Boeotian farmer; author of the didactic *Works and Days* (advice to farmers) and of the *Theogony.*

Hesperides (hĕspē'rĭdēz) [Gr.,= in the west], in Greek religion, nymphs; daughters of Atlas. On an enchanted island in the western sea they guarded tree bearing golden apples, which HERCULES took as one of his 12 labors.

Hesperus (hĕ'spŭrŭs) [Gr.,= western], anc. Greek name for Venus as evening star. As morning star it was called Phosphorus.

Hess, Germain Henri (hĕs, Fr. zhĕrmē' ärē ĕs'), 1802–50, Swiss-Russian chemist, a founder of thermochemistry. Hess's law: amount of heat liberated or absorbed in chemical reaction is constant regardless of number of stages occurring, if same original substances and end products are involved.

Hess, Moses, 1812–75, German socialist. Converted Engels to communism and greatly influenced Marx. Urged estab. of a Jewish state.

Hess, Dame Myra, 1890–1965, English pianist. Made her London debut 1907; her N.Y. debut 1922.

Hess, Rudolf (rōō'dôlf hĕs'), 1894–, German National Socialist leader. Hitler made him deputy Führer and minister without portfolio (1933). Hess created worldwide sensation by his secret airplane flight to Scotland (1941), where he was imprisoned. Of doubtful sanity, he was sentenced to life imprisonment at Nuremberg war-crimes trial (1946).

Hess, Victor Francis, 1883–1964, American physicist, b. Austria. Shared 1936 Nobel Prize in Physics for discovering cosmic rays.

Hess, Walter Rudolf, 1881–, Swiss physiologist. Shared 1949 Nobel Prize in Physiology and Medicine for work on control of organs by certain areas of the brain.

Hesse, Herman (hĕr'män hĕ'sŭ), 1877–1962, German novelist and poet, a Swiss citizen (1923). Concerned with man's spiritual loneliness, his novels include *Peter Camenzind* (1904), *Demian* (1919; Eng. tr., 1923), *Der Steppenwolf* (1927; Eng. tr., 1929), *Narziss und Goldmund* (1930; Eng. tr., *Death and the Lover*, 1932), and *Das Glasperlenspiel* (1943; complete ed., 1945; Eng. tr., *Magister Ludi*, 1949). Awarded 1946 Nobel Prize in Literature.

Hesse, Philip of: see PHILIP OF HESSE.

Hesse (hĕ'sē, hĕs), Ger. *Hessen,* state (8,150 sq. mi.; 1963 est. pop. 5,004,900), Federal Republic of [W] Germany, between Thuringia and the Rhine R.; cap. Wiesbaden. Generally hilly, agr., and forested, with famous vineyards along the Rhine. Industries are concentrated at Frankfurt (chemicals), Kassel (machinery), and Darmstadt. The Taunus area is famed for its resorts. Hesse has no historical unity. Its name is derived from the landgraviate of Hesse, which in 1247 became an immediate fief of the Holy Roman Empire. After the death (1567) of PHILIP OF HESSE, who introduced the Reformation, Hesse underwent several subdivisions among branches of the ruling family: Hesse-Kassel and Hesse-Darmstadt were the chief divisions. The rulers of the 18th-cent. Hesse improved their finances by letting mercenaries for hire (notably to the English in the American Revolution). In 1803 the landgrave of Hesse-Kassel was raised to the rank of elector; Hesse-Kassel henceforth was known as Electoral Hesse (Ger. *Kurhessen*). Napoleon I in 1806 raised the landgraviate of Hesse-Darmstadt to a grand duchy and in 1807 annexed Electoral Hesse to the kingdom of Westphalia under his brother Jérôme. The Congress of Vienna (1814–15) restored Electoral Hesse and awarded it and Hesse-Darmstadt substantial territorial gains. In 1866 Electoral Hesse, NASSAU, and the free city of Frankfurt, having all three sided with Austria in the Austro-Prussian War, were annexed by Prussia and merged in Hesse-Nassau prov., with its cap. at Kassel. Hesse-Darmstadt continued under its grand dukes until 1918 (after 1871 as a member of German Empire) and joined the Weimar Republic in 1919. After the Second World War all of former Prussian Hesse-Nassau and all of Hesse-Darmstadt E of the Rhine were consolidated into the single state of Hesse. The section W of the Rhine (called Rhenish Hesse and containing MAINZ and WORMS) was incorporated into Rhineland-Palatinate. Under occupation for some time, the territories are now part of West Germany.

Hesse-Nassau, Germany: see HESSE; NASSAU.

Hessian fly, *Phytophaga destructor,* widely distributed wheat pest, a gall gnat, said to have been carried across the Atlantic from its native Europe by Hessian troops. Most serious wheat pest in U.S.; the larvae injure plants by removing sap from stem. Control methods include late planting of seed and plowing under infected wheat. Also attacks barley, rye.

Hestia (hĕ'stēŭ), in Greek mythology, old and honored virgin goddess of the hearth and domestic life and guardian of state's welfare; daughter of Cronus and Rhea. Identified with Roman Vesta.

Heston and Isleworth, London: see HOUNSLOW.

Hetch Hetchy Valley, in Yosemite Natl. Park, central Calif., on Tuolumne R. O'Shaughnessy Dam (built 1923; enlarged 1938) turned valley into lake c.9 mi. long, supplying San Francisco with water and power.

Heuss, Theodor (hois), 1884–1963, president (1949–59), German Federal Republic; member of Free Democratic party. Author of many books on history, politics, and literature.

Hevelius, Johannes (hĭvĕ'lēŭs, Ger. yōhä'nŭs hāvā'lēōōs), 1611–87, astronomer, b. Danzig. He was a pioner in the study of the moon's surface.

Hevesy, George von (gā'ôrk fŭn hĕ'vĕshē), 1885–1966, Hungarian biophysicist and chemist. Won 1943 Nobel Prize in Chemistry for work on use of isotopes as tracers in studying chemical and biological processes.

Hevros: see MARITSA.

Hewitt, Abram Stevens (hū'ĭt), 1822–1903, American industrialist and political leader; son-in-law of Peter Cooper. Promoted advanced methods of ironmaking and steelmaking. U.S. Representative from N.Y. (1875–79, 1881–86).

hexameter: see ALEXANDRINE; VERSIFICATION.

Hexapla (hĕk'sŭplŭ) [Gr.,= sixfold], polyglot version of Old Testament made by Origen. Mainly in six columns —Hebrew text, Greek transliteration of it, and four Greek versions.

Heymans, Corneille (kôrnä'yŭ hī'mäns), 1892–, Belgian physiologist. Won 1938 Nobel Prize in Physiology and Medicine for study of regulation of respiration and blood pressure.

Heyrovsky, Jaroslav (yä'rôsläf hā'rôf"skē), 1890–1967, Czech chemist. Won the 1959 Nobel Prize in Chemistry for having devised in 1922 an electrochemical method of analysis.

Heyse, Paul (poul' hī'zŭ), 1830–1914, German realistic author. His voluminous work includes novels (*Children of the World*, 1873; Eng. tr., 1882), dramas, and *Novellen* (notably *L'Arrabbiata*, 1855; Eng. tr., *The Fury*). Was awarded 1910 Nobel Prize in Literature.

Heyward, DuBose (dŭbōz'), 1885–1940, American author, b. Charleston, S.C., author of *Porgy* (1925)— a story of Negro life, later made into a play and an opera (*Porgy and Bess;* score by George Gershwin).

Heywood, John, 1497?–1580?, English dramatist, most famous writer of the interlude, short comic dialogue (e.g., *The Play of the Weather,* 1533; *The Four P's*).

Heywood, Thomas, 1574?–1641, English playwright and actor. Of his numerous plays *A Woman Killed with Kindness* (performed in 1603) is notable.

Hezekiah (hĕzŭkī'ŭ), d. c.687 B.C., king of Judah, successor of Ahaz. Resisted two invasions of Sennacherib of Assyria; the second was ended by plague in Assyrian army. Hezekiah, one of best of Judah's kings, abolished idolatry and listened to Isaiah and Micah. 2 Kings 18–20; 2 Chron. 29–32; Isa. 36–39; Prov. 25.1.

Hf, chemical symbol of the element HAFNIUM.

Hg, chemical symbol of the element MERCURY.

Hialeah (hīŭlē'ŭ), residential city (pop. 66,972), SE Fla., NW of Miami; settled 1921. Hialeah Park race track is here.

Hibbing, village (pop. 17,731), NE Minn., on Mesabi iron range and NW of Duluth; laid out 1893. Moved to present site after 1917 to make way for world's largest open-pit iron mine.

hibernation (hī"bŭrnā'shŭn), practice among certain animals of passing part of cold season in more or less dormant state. It is believed that the habit arose as protection against cold when food was scarce, or as an alternative to migration (like migration, probably is connected with reproductive life). Hibernation is possible only for those animals able to store enough food in their bodies to carry them over until food is again available. In hibernation bodily activity is at a low ebb. Body temperature falls to nearer the temperature of the surroundings, but never to freezing point. Deepness of sleep varies; on warmer winter days, some emerge. Aestivation (dormant period of escape from heat when water is scarce) occurs chiefly among amphibians, reptiles, fishes.

Hibernia: see IRELAND.

hibiscus (hĭbĭs'kŭs), annual or perennial shrub or small tree of widely distributed genus *Hibiscus,* many of which are known as rose mallow. Variously colored flowers are large and showy (esp. in tropical forms). See also ROSE OF SHARON.

hiccup or hiccough, sharp sound associated with spasm of larynx and diaphragm and produced when inhaled air strikes closed glottis.

Hickok, Wild Bill, 1837–76, American frontier marshal in Kansas. Real name was James Butler Hickok. Known as a marksman in encounters with outlaws. Murdered in Deadwood, S.Dak.

Hickory, city (pop. 19,328), W N.C., NW of Charlotte, in Blue Ridge foothills; founded c.1846. Lenoir Rhyne Col. is here.

hickory, deciduous nut-bearing tree of genus *Carya,* chiefly native to North America. One species, the PECAN, is an important nut tree of U.S. Others include shagbark hickory (*Carya ovata*), shellbark hickory (*C. laciniosa*), and mockernut (*C. tomentosa*), all found in E and SE U.S. The pignut (*C. glabra*) has small bitter nuts. Hickory wood, hard and strong, is valued commercially for tool handles, furniture, etc.

Hicks, Edward, 1780–1849, American painter, best known for *The Peaceable Kingdom,* of which c.25 versions are extant.

Hicks, Elias, 1748–1830, American preacher of Society of FRIENDS. In schism of 1827 he led liberal separatist party called Hicksites.

Hicks, Thomas, 1823–90, American portrait painter, one of the most outstanding of his day.

Hicksville, residential city (pop. 50,405), SE N.Y., on W Long Isl.. ENE of Mineola; founded 1648.

Hidalgo (ēdhäl'gō), state (8,058 sq. mi.; pop. 1,043,-437) central Mexico. Largely mountainous, Hidalgo has plains in S and W and fertile valleys within central plateau. Mining, the main industry, has centered at PACHUCA (cap.). Conquered 1530 by Spanish, territory was not made separate state until 1869.

Hidalgo y Costilla, Miguel (mēgĕl' ēdhäl'gō ē kōstē'yä), 1753–1811, Mexican revolutionist and a national hero, a priest. Hidalgo was among the creoles who met at Querétaro to plan revolution against Spain. On Sept. 16, 1810, he issued the *grito de Dolores* which precipitated the revolt. The banner of Our Lady of Guadalupe was his standard. Initially successful in encounters with Spanish forces, he was finally defeated at Calderón Bridge, betrayed, degraded by Inquisition, and shot.

Hidatsa Indians (hēdät'sä), North American tribe, also known as the Minitari and the Gros Ventre of the River, of Siouan language family. In 18th cent. they lived on upper Missouri, in N.Dak. Were typical of "village Indians" of Plains area, cultivating corn and organizing annual buffalo hunt.

hieratic: see HIEROGLYPHIC.

Hiero (hī'ŭrō), Greek tyrants of Syracuse. Also Hieron. **Hiero I** was tyrant 478–467 B.C., succeeding his brother Gelon. He was a patron of literature and was victor over the Etruscans in a naval battle at Cumae (474 B.C.). **Hiero II,** d. c.215 B.C., was, because of his ability, chosen tyrant (c.265 B.C.). At first an ally of the Carthaginians, he saw the rising power of Rome and as an ally aided the Romans in the Punic Wars. He encouraged his relative, Archimedes, who made him great engines for warfare.

Hideyoshi (Hideyoshi Toyotomi) (hēdāō'shē), 1536–98, Japanese warrior and dictator. Rose from common soldier to succeed NOBUNAGA and by 1590 had unified Japan. Failed in his 1592 campaign to conquer China, but did subdue Korea; Japan withdrew from Korea after his death. He froze class structure by banning change of occupation, developed a maritime code, encouraged the arts, and beautified Osaka, his capital. First tolerated but later persecuted Christian missionaries.

hieroglyphic (hī"rŭglĭ'fĭk, hī"ŭrŭ–) [Gr.,= priestly carving], pictographic writings of anc. Egypt (by extension also those of Crete, Asia Minor, and Central America and Mexico). Interpretation of Egyptian hieroglyphics, begun by CHAMPOLLION, is quite complete. Hieroglyphics are conventionalized pictures used chiefly to represent meanings that seem arbitrary and are seldom obvious. Egyptian hieroglyphics were alread· ·er·

fected in the I dynasty. They began to go out of use in Middle Kingdom; in New Empire they were no longer well understood, and from 500 B.C. their use was a *tour de force.* A given hieroglyphic might be put to three uses (though very few were used for all three), i.e., as an ideogram, as a phonogram, or as a determinative. Phonograms, controlling factor in progress of hieroglyphic writing, became basis of an alphabet. A developed cursive (the hieratic) was used in the Middle Kingdom. This was later supplanted by the demotic, so conventionalized that its hieroglyphic origin was not discernible.

Hieron, tyrants of Syracuse: see HIERO.

high-bush cranberry or **cranberry bush,** name for two tall viburnum shrubs, *Viburnum opulus,* native to Europe, and the North American *V. trilobum.* Both have flat-topped white flower clusters and red berries.

High Church: see ENGLAND, CHURCH OF.

Highgate, residential suburb of London, England. Dick Whittington supposedly was resting at foot of Highgate Hill when he heard Bow Bells recalling him to London.

Highland, residential town (1963 pop. 20,354), extreme NW Ind., just S of East Chicago; settled 1850.

Highland Park. 1 City (1965 pop. 30,054), NE Ill., suburb NNW of Chicago on L. Michigan; settled 1834. U.S. Fort Sheridan is nearby. **2** City (pop. 38,063), SE Mich., within confines of Detroit; laid out 1818. Grew after Henry Ford built factory here in 1909. **3.** Residential borough (pop. 11,049), E central N.J., on Raritan R. opposite New Brunswick. **4** Town (pop. 10,411), N Texas, suburb NNW of Dallas; settled 1907 .

Highlands, mountainous country in Scotland, N of line running from Moray Firth to Dumbarton. Late Middle Ages produced clan system and dress (kilt, tartan, sporran, tam, dirk) outlawed by British in drastic suppression of Highland support of Jacobites in 18th cent. With decline of Scottish Gaelic language in 19th cent., revival of dress and use of bagpipes were allowed. Rugged beauty and persisting old customs are depicted in romantic literature.

High Point, city (1966 pop. 61,396), N N.C., SW of Greensboro, in piedmont; settled before 1750. Industrial center with mfg. of furniture and hosiery. High Point Col. is here.

High Point: see KITTATINNY MOUNTAIN.

Hightstown, borough (pop. 4,317), central N.J., ENE of Trenton; founded 1721. Seat of Peddie School for boys.

Hilbert, David, 1862–1943, German mathematician. Known for work on differential and integral equations, logic, foundations of mathematics, and number theory. Posed Hilbert's problem which related to unresolved mathematical questions.

Hildebrand: see GREGORY VII, SAINT.

Hildebrand, Adolf von (ä'dôlf fün hĭl'dübränt), 1847–1921, German sculptor and author, known for public monuments and portrait busts.

Hildesheim (hĭl'dús-hīm), city (pop. 84,695), West Germany, in Lower Saxony. Was seat of prince-bishopric until 1803; passed to Hanover 1815. Famous as historic, cultural center; has wealth of medieval architecture—11th-cent. Romanesque cathedral and the Knochenhaueramtshaus [butchers' guildhouse], built in 1529.

Hildreth, Richard, 1807–65, American historian. Chief work *The History of the United States* (6 vols., 1849–52), written from Federalist viewpoint.

Hill, Ambrose Powell, 1825–65, Confederate general. His 3d Corps initiated fighting at Gettysburg, and he directed battle on July 1, 1863. Led corps in Wilderness campaign (1864). Killed in action at Petersburg (1865).

Hill, Archibald Vivian, 1886–, English physiologist. Shared 1922 Nobel Prize in Physiology and Medicine for work on thermodynamics of muscular activity.

Hill, Daniel Harvey, 1821–89, Confederate general. Served with distinction in Peninsular campaign and

Antietam campaign (1862). Protesting Braxton Bragg's command in Chattanooga campaign, he was himself removed by Jefferson Davis.

Hill, James J(erome), 1838–1916, American railroad builder, b. Canada. His extension of St. Paul and Pacific RR to Seattle, completed 1893, was probably greatest feat of railroad building in U.S. Formed Great Northern Railway Co. in 1890. With J. P. Morgan, in 1901, he defeated E. H. Harriman in struggle for the Chicago, Burlington & Quincy.

Hill, Sir Rowland, 1795–1879, English educator. Introduced system of self-government in his school at Hazelwood in Birmingham.

Hillah or **Hilla** (both: hĭ'lù), town (pop. 51,361), Iraq, on branch of Euphrates R. Largely built of materials taken from ruins of nearby Babylon.

Hillary, Sir Edmund, 1919–, New Zealand mountain climber. He and Tensing Norkay were first men to reach (1953) the summit of Mt. Everest, highest mountain in the world.

Hillcrest Heights, town (pop. 15,295), W central Md., suburb SSE of Washington, D.C.

Hillebrand, William Francis, 1853–1925, American chemist. With U.S. Bureau of Standards from 1908. Pioneer in mineral analysis.

Hillel (hĭl'ĕl), fl. 30 B.C.–A.D. 10, Jewish scholar, b. Babylon; progressive interpreter of Jewish religious law. Patriarch in Jerusalem. found essence of Judaism in maxim, "Do not unto others that which is hateful unto thee," thus anticipating this essential teaching of Christ.

Hillgrove, town (pop. 14,669), SW Calif., SW of West Covina, in agr. region (fruit, livestock, poultry).

Hilliard, Henry Washington, 1808–92, U.S. Representative from Ala. (1845–51). A Whig, chief opponent of secession in Ala.

Hilliard, Nicholas, 1537–1619, first true miniaturist in England; court painter to Elizabeth and James I.

Hillingdon, London borough since 1965 (pop. 232,-520); includes former municipal borough of Uxbridge and urban districts of Hayes and Harlington, Ruislip–Northwood, and Yiewsley and West Drayton.

Hillman, Sidney, 1887–1946, American labor leader, b. Lithuania. Became (1915) president Amalgamated Clothing Workers, helped found C.I.O., American Labor Party, and World Federation of Trade Unions. A moderate, he promoted labor-management cooperation and sought labor support for political platforms favored by labor, especially the New Deal. Headed (1943–46) C.I.O. Political Action Committee.

Hillquit, Morris, 1869–1933, American lawyer and Socialist leader, b. Latvia, entered U.S. 1886. Led rightwing Socialists against Daniel De Leon (1897) and founded Social Democratic party, which evolved into present Socialist party; became a leading theorist.

Hillsboro, 1 City (pop. 2,441), central Kansas, NNE of Wichita, in Cottonwood valley; laid out 1879. Largely Mennonite community engaged in winterwheat and corn production. Tabor Col. is here. **2** town (pop. 2,310), S N.H., on Contoocook R., WSW of Concord; settled 1741, abandoned 1744 in Indian war. **3** Town (pop. 1,349), N central N.C., NW of Durham; settled before 1700. Early cap. of N.C. prov.; scene of disturbances in REGULATOR MOVEMENT. Birthplace of T. H. Benton. **4** City (pop. 5,474), SW Ohio, E of Cincinnati; platted 1807. Women's Temperance Crusade founded here, 1873. Several mound builders' forts are nearby.

Hilo (hē'lō), city (pop. 25,966), Hawaii, on E Hawaii, on Hilo Bay. Second largest city in state and trade and shipping center of sugar-cane, orchid, and coffee area. Lyman House (c.1839) contains Hawaiiana.

Hilprecht, Hermann Volrath (hĕr'män fōl'rät hĭl'-prĕkht), 1859–1925, American Assyriologist, noted authority on cuneiform writing. He was scientific director of four expeditions (1895–1914) to Nippur.

Hilversum (hĭl'vùrsùm), municipality (pop. 102,992). North Holland prov., W central Netherlands. Radio broadcasting center. Residential city; health resort.

Himachal Pradesh (hǐmä'chŭl prŭdäsh'), union territory (19,879 sq. mi.; pop. c.1,350,000), NW India, in Himalayas; cap. Simla. Territory formed 1948 from 30 Punjabi princely states; state of Bilaspur was absorbed 1954. Produces timber, wheat, rice, and corn.

Himalayas (hǐmä'lŭyûz, hǐmûlä'ûz) [Sanskrit,= abode of snow], Asiatic mountain system, c.1,500 mi. long, in West Pakistan, India, Tibet, Nepal, Sikkim, Bhutan, and China. Comprises two nearly parallel ranges separated by a wide valley; the N range is usually called the Trans-Himalaya. MT. EVEREST is highest peak, followed by MT. GODWIN-AUSTEN (K2) and KANCHENJUNGA. Other great peaks include NANGA PARBAT in Kashmir, ANNAPURNA in Nepal, NANDA DEVI in India, and MINYA KONKA in China. The ranges form almost insuperable barrier between Tibet and India and give rise to many great rivers, notably the Indus, Ganges, and Brahmaputra.

Himeji (hēmä'jĕ), city (pop. 328,689), S Honshu, Japan; railroad and mfg. center. Site of famous 14th-cent. castle.

Himera (hǐ'mùrù), anc. Greek city, N Sicily. Here according to tradition Gelon of Syracuse defeated the Carthaginians (480 B.C.), but in 408 B.C. Carthaginians destroyed the city.

Himmler, Heinrich (hĭn'rĭkh hĭm'lûr), 1900–1945, German National Socialist leader. Headed SS (see NATIONAL SOCIALISM) from 1929; became head of entire German police system in 1936 (see SECRET POLICE) and minister of the interior in 1943. After putting down a conspiracy against Hitler in July, 1944, he acted as virtual dictator of Germany. The most ruthless of Nazi leaders, he was responsible for the death of millions in forced-labor and extermination camps and ended up by terrorizing his own party hierarchy. He died by taking poison shortly after his arrest by the British.

Himyaritic, Semitic language. See LANGUAGE (table).

Hincks, Sir Francis, 1807–85, Canadian journalist and statesman, b. Ireland. Became editor in 1838 of Toronto *Examiner,* a Reform party newspaper. As premier in joint Hincks-Morin administration (1851–54) he sought a reciprocal trade treaty with U.S. and promoted railroad construction. Finance minister 1869–73.

Hindemith, Paul (hĭn'dûmĭth), 1895–1963, German-American composer and violist; became U.S. citizen 1946. Early compositions were often atonal; later works displayed return to tonality. Among his works are the symphony (1934) drawn from his own opera *Mathis der Maler;* a song cycle, *Das Marienleben* (1923; revised 1948); the viola concerto *Der Schwanendreher* (1935); the ballet *Nobilissima Visione* (1938); and the symphony *Die Harmonie der Welt* (1952). He lived in Zurich after 1952.

Hindenburg, Paul von (Paul von Hindenburg und Beneckendorff) (hĭn'dŭnbûrg, Ger. –bōŏrk), 1847–1934, German field marshal and president, b. Poznan (then in Prussia). In the First World War, he and his chief of staff, LUDENDORFF, routed the Russians at TANNENBERG (1914) and occupied Poland. In 1916 Hindenburg became chief commander of Central Powers. After the armistice, he led his troops back in sufficiently good order to prevent a radical revolution. Though a monarchist, he was elected president of the Reich in 1925. He was a tool in the hands of the reactionary Junker class. With Socialist help, he defeated Hitler in the presidential elections of 1932, but in Jan., 1933, largely through the intrigues of PAPEN, he was persuaded to appoint Hitler as chancellor. He continued as a figurehead till his death.

Hindenburg: see ZABRZE, Poland.

Hindi, Indian language of Indo-European family. One of the 15 official languages of India. See LANGUAGE (table).

Hinduism, Western term for religious beliefs and practices of most of the people of India. It is divided into innumerable sects and has no well-defined ec-clesiastical organization and no fixed scriptural canon, but VEDA, *Brahmanas,* and *Bhagavad-Gita* have elaborate theological commentary. Brahmanism substituted (c.550 B.C.) for Vedic religion a complex system of ritual and theosophy expounded in *Brahmanas* and *Upanishads. Brahmanas* regulate sacrifices to gods and personify moral qualities. *Upanishads,* foundation of modern Hindu philosophy, develop doctrine of a universal soul or being to which individual souls will be reunited after maya (illusion of time and space) is conquered. Buddhism and Jainism, which flourished from c.300 B.C. to A.D. c.400 in India, attacked this complex ritual and theology. However, Brahmanism adopted features of those religions and codified its own ritual in *Laws of Manu.* Several schools of interpretation of *Upanishads* appeared (see VEDANTA) and YOGA was developed. A later stage of Hinduism is represented by *Tantras* and *Puranas. Tantras* are mainly prescriptions for securing divine favor; *Puranas* comprise poems addressed mainly to Siva (or Shiva) the Destroyer and Vishnu the Preserver. These and Brahma, a remote deity who created the universe and is equated with it, form triad at center of modern Hinduism. Many cults, with widely variant practices, exist side by side. Modern Hinduism, always more than a religion, has become more flexible to adjust to problems of 20th-cent. world. Child marriage, rite of suttee, and untouchability are now illegal; status of women has risen. Still widely regarded is sacredness of animals (esp. cow and snake). Pilgrimages to sacred shrines are a marked feature of Hinduism.

Hindu Kush (hĭn'dŏŏ kŏŏsh'), mountain system, central Asia, lying mainly in NE Afghanistan and extending E to Pakistan and Kashmir. Culminates in Tirich Mir (25,426 ft). Crossed by passes (10,000–17,000 ft.) which were used by conquerors of India.

Hindu music. In the music of India, only one voice part carries the melody. The tonal system divides the octave into 22 segments, each roughly equivalent to one quarter of the whole tone of Western music. The most important scale, called *sa-grama,* closely resembles our C major scale. Melody is based on the system of *ragas* or melody types which are used as the basis of an improvisation. There are 60-odd *ragas,* each having its own rules for improvising in that *raga.* Each has its own ethical and emotional properties; each is associated with a certain season or time of day. Traditionally, a night *raga,* sung by a skilled performer at noon, could produce darkness. *Gamakas,* the ornaments or graces of *ragas,* are very important. The accompanying rhythm is based on certain constantly repeated rhythm patterns called *talas.* Among instruments used are various types of drums, the vina (in modern times, a kind of zither), and kinds of bagpipes, lutes, fiddles, oboes, trumpets, flutes, cymbals, and gongs.

Hindustan (hĭn"dŏŏstän') [Persian,= Hindu land], a term applied to various areas of India and Pakistan. Sometimes refers to region between Narbada R. and the Himalayas, but sometimes limited to mean N central India. Since partition of Indian subcontinent (1947) it has sometimes been applied to the largely Hindu state of India as opposed to Moslem Pakistan.

Hindustani (hĭndŏŏstän'ē), the spoken form of Hindi and Urdu. See LANGUAGE (table).

Hines, John Elbridge, 1910–, American Episcopal bishop. Bishop of Texas 1955–65. Became presiding bishop of Protestant Episcopal Church in 1965.

Hinesville, city (pop. 3,174), SE Ga., SW of Savannah. U. S. Fort Stewart is nearby.

Hingan (hsĭng'än'), former province (c.100,000 sq. mi.), NE China; cap. was Hailar. Part of Heilungkiang prov. since 1950.

Hingham, town (pop. 15,378), E Mass., on South Shore of Boston Bay; settled c.1633. Church (1681) is a fine example of American Gothic architecture.

Hinkle, Beatrice M(ores Van Geisen), 1874–1953, American psychiatrist. Opened first U.S. psychotherapeutic clinic (1908) at Cornell Medical Col. She wrote *The Re-Creating of the Individual* (1923).

Hinnom, valley, near Jerusalem. Despised as place of Moloch worship and dump for Jerusalem's refuse. Tophet was in the valley. In New Testament, Gehenna, a form of Hinnom, meant HELL, perhaps because of fires of Moloch or dump fires always burning there.

Hinsdale, residential village (1965 pop. 14,738), NE Ill., WSW of Chicago.

Hinshelwood, Sir Cyril Norman, 1897–, British chemist. For his studies in kinetics of gaseous reactions he shared the 1956 Nobel Prize in Chemistry.

Hinsley, Arthur, 1865–1943, English cardinal, Roman Catholic archbishop of Westminster (after 1935).

Hiouentang: see HSÜAN-TSANG.

Hipparchus, tyrant of Athens: see HIPPIAS.

Hipparchus (hĭpär'kŭs), 2d cent. B.C., Greek astronomer. Ptolemy based his geocentric theory of the universe largely on conclusions of Hipparchus whose researches are recorded in Ptolemy's *Almagest*.

Hippias (hĭp'ēŭs), 6th–5th cent. B.C., tyrant of Athens. He and his brother Hipparchus governed jointly after the death of their father PISISTRATUS until Hipparchus was killed by Harmodius and Aristogiton (c.514 B.C.). Hippias then reigned alone until overthrown by the Alcmaeonidae and the Spartans. He advised the Persians in the campaign ending at Marathon.

Hippocrates (hĭpŏ'krŭtēz), c.460–c.370 B.C., Greek physician, recognized as father of medicine. Placed medicine on scientific basis through practice of bedside observation of disease. Hippocratic writings (including those of disputed authorship) appeared in many translations; some are in Loeb Library. Hippocratic oath, administered to many graduates in medicine, is said to represent his ideals of ethical professional conduct.

Hippodamus (hĭpŏ'dŭmŭs), fl. 5th cent. B.C., Greek architect, earliest known planner of cities. Designed Piraeus (port of Athens) and Rhodes.

Hippolyte (hĭpŏ'lĭtē), in Greek mythology, queen of the Amazons; daughter of Ares. HERCULES captured her girdle.

Hippolytus, Saint (hĭpŏ'lĭtŭs), d. c.236, antipope (c.217 –235), a theologian. Urging a Neoplatonic theology rejected by the popes, he left the Church to become the first antipope. Later officially reconciled, he died a martyr in Maximin's persecution. Feast: Aug. 13.

Hippolytus, in Greek myth, son of Theseus and Antiope or Hippolyte. His stepmother, Phaedra, loved him, but, rebuffed by him, she accused him of dishonoring her. Poseidon then caused his death.

Hippomenes, in Greek legend, winner of ATALANTA.

hippopotamus (hĭpŭpŏ'tŭmŭs), herbivorous mammal (genus *Hippopotamus*) of Africa, related to pig. It has short legs, a broad body, tough gray or brown hide, and a wide mouth. Its incisors and lower canines are large tusks, a source of "ivory." Frequents water and eats aquatic plants. Pygmy hippopotamus (genus *Choeropsis*) is in W Africa.

Hippo Regius: see BÔNE, Algeria.

Hiram (hī'–). **1** Fl. 1000 B.C., king of Tyre, friend of David and Solomon. Sent magnificent gifts for Temple. 2 Sam. 5.11; 1 Kings 5; 9; 10. Huram: 2 Chron. 2; 8; 9. **2** Artisan in metals, sent to Solomon by King Hiram to work on ornamentation of Temple. 1 Kings 7.13–45. Huram: 2 Chron. 4.11–22.

Hiram College, at Hiram, Ohio, SE of Cleveland; coed.; opened 1850. Has well-known plan for intensive study of one subject for nine weeks.

Hirohito (hĕrō'hētō), 1901–, emperor of Japan. Became regent 1921. Under reign name of Showa succeeded his father Yoshihito in 1926. Publicly rejected concept of imperial divinity in 1946. Constitution of 1947 deprived him of all real power, though he remains a key symbol in Japanese life.

Hiroshige, Ando (än'dō hĕrō'shēgä"), 1797–1858, Japanese painter and color-print artist of the ukiyo-e school.

Hiroshima (hī"rōshē'mù), city (pop. 431,336), SW Honshu, Japan, port on Hiroshima Bay. Commercial center; textile mfg. Founded c.1594 as castle city on Ota R. delta. In Second World War was target (Aug. 6, 1945) of first atomic bomb, which caused c.130,-000 casualties and devastated 90% of the city. Much of the city has been rebuilt. A gutted section is set aside as a "Peace City" to illustrate effects of atomic bomb. Seat of an annual world conference against nuclear weapons since 1955.

Hirsch, Maurice, baron de (mōrēs bärō' dù hïrsh'), 1831–96, Jewish philanthropist, b. Munich. Founder of Jewish Colonization Association for the emigration of Russian Jews to Argentina and other countries (1891), Estab. an American fund for Jewish education.

His, Wilhelm (vĭl'hĕlm hïs'), 1831–1904, German biologist. Devised microtome to prepare tissue for microscopic study.

Hispaniola (hī"spänyō'lù), island (c.30,000 sq. mi.), West Indies, between Cuba and Puerto Rico. Haiti occupies W third and Dominican Republic the remainder. Discovered by Columbus 1492. In Spanish the name is Española.

Hiss, Alger, 1904–, American public official. In Aug., 1948, Whittaker Chambers charged that Hiss, while in the Dept. of State, helped to transmit confidential government documents to the Russians. After denying the charges, Hiss stood trial twice and was finally convicted of perjury (Jan., 1950) and sentenced to a five-year prison term. His appeals were denied. He was released from prison Nov., 1954.

histamine, organic compound containing carbon, hydrogen, nitrogen. Sometimes liberated in human or animal body during neutralization of foreign material (antigens) by antibodies. Histamine can cause various more or less distressing reactions in the body (see ANAPHYLAXIS). ANTIHISTAMINE can be used to neutralize histamine. See also ALLERGY.

histoplasmosis, fungal infection, varying in intensity, involving liver, lungs, spleen, lymphatic system, bone. Occurs throughout U.S., especially in Mississippi R. valley.

Hitchcock, Alfred (Joseph), 1899–, Anglo-American film director. Brilliant creator of suspense in such films as *The Lady Vanishes, Rebecca, Lifeboat, Spellbound, Dial M for Murder,* and *Rear Window.*

Hitchcock, Frank Harris, 1869–1935, U.S. Postmaster General (1909–13). Estab. parcel post and postal savings banks; promoted founding of air mail.

Hitchcock, Henry-Russell, 1903–, American architectural historian, whose writings are among the foremost in the field.

Hitchcock, Lambert, 1795–1852, American chairmaker. Village erected by his factory in Conn. was called Hitchcockville (now Riverton). The **Hitchcock chair,** now sought by collectors, is a factory product of good wood, painted black over red and often having designs stenciled in colors or bronze. Seats are of wood, cane, or rush.

Hitchcock, Thomas, Jr., 1900–1944, American polo player. Probably greatest polo player of all time, he received highest polo rating from U.S. Polo Association, a 10-goal handicap, 1922–40 (except in 1935, when he had 9-goal rating).

Hitchcock chair: see HITCHCOCK, LAMBERT.

Hitler, Adolf, 1889–1945, German dictator, founder and leader (Ger. *Führer*) of NATIONAL SOCIALISM; b. Braunau, Upper Austria, the son of an Austrian customs official. Studied at Munich; moved to Vienna 1907, where he was refused admission to art academy and spent years of utmost poverty. His violent anti-Semitism began then. In 1913 he moved to Munich. He enlisted in the Bavarian army in First World War; became a corporal, received the Iron Cross for bravery, and was gassed. After the war he and a few malcontents founded at Munich the National Socialist German Workers' party (NSDAP). Still small but well-disciplined and backed by such men as LUDEN-

DORFF, the NSDAP sought to gain control over Bavaria by a coup d'état, the so-called "beer-hall putsch" of Nov. 8–9, 1923. The plot was put down by the army, on whose support Hitler had counted; 14 Nazis were killed. Hitler was sentenced to five years at Landsberg fortress, where he wrote *Mein Kampf* [my battle], the bible of Nazism, but he was released after 13 months. The depression after 1929 helped in the spectacular growth of the NSDAP. Hitler and his propaganda chief GOEBBELS blamed all ills on Jewish capitalism, Communism, the Treaty of Versailles, and the Social Democrats and promised a millennium for pure-blooded Germans. Secretly backed by a few great industrialists (who hoped to use him as a tool for their own ends), he controlled a powerful press and a private militia. Though he lost the 1932 presidential election to Hindenburg, his party became the largest in the Reichstag. In Jan., 1933, Hindenburg appointed him chancellor. Even with his allies, the monarchist German National party, Hitler had no absolute majority in the Reichstag. To estab. his dictatorship, he outlawed the Communists, whom he accused of setting the REICHSTAG fire, and in March, 1933, an obedient Reichstag voted him dictatorial powers. Hitler placed Germany under the absolute rule of the NSDAP, which took control not only of the state but of all German life, including youth activities (through the Hitler Jugend). Within his party, he crushed opposition in the "blood purge" of 1934. Anti-Semitism was enacted into law. Concentration camps were set up to take care of all suspected enemies of the regime. Only in the churches was some opposition left alive. In 1934, 88% of the voters favored the union of the presidency and the chancellorship in the person of the Führer. Hitler's aggressive foreign policy, though long abetted by English and French appeasement (see (MUNICH PACT) led GERMANY on the road to Second World War (1939–45). Late in 1941 Hitler personally took command of the war in Russia, with disastrous results. To save Germany from total defeat, a group of high military and civil officials resolved upon assassinating Hitler. The bomb placed under his chair failed to kill him, and the conspiracy was put down ruthlessly by the police chief, HIMMLER. On April 30, 1945, with the Allies closing in from all sides, Hitler committed suicide at Berlin, together with Eva Braun, his mistress, whom he had just married. No trace of their burned bodies was found, and there are persistent though dubious rumors that Hitler actually escaped into hiding. His appointed successor, Adm. DOENITZ, arranged for the unconditional surrender of Germany a few days later.

Hittites (hĭt'ĭts), anc. people of Asia Minor and Syria, who had a culture that is still imperfectly known despite many inscriptions that have been uncovered (notably at Boghazkeui). Most inscriptions in cuneiform are in Hittite (or Kanisic) and in Babylonian, with some in Luwian, Hattian, and Hurrian (the last two not related to Hittite). One reconstruction has it that the Hittites created a powerful federation of cities in Cappadocia by c.1800 B.C., then moved S, and finally came into conflict with Ramses II of Egypt. Supposedly their state was destroyed in late 12th cent. B.C. by Thracians, Phrygians, and Assyrians. Lydia was one of the successor states.

Hittorff, Jacques Ignace (hĭ'tôrf, Fr. zhäk' ēnyäs' ētôrf'), 1792–1867, French architect, a leader of classic revival in France. Chief work is church of St. Vincent de Paul, Paris. Designed fountains for Place de la Concorde and the column in Place Vendôme (both in Paris).

Hiva Oa: see MARQUESAS ISLANDS.

hives (urticaria), skin eruption, marked by raised areas (wheals) which burn and itch, thought to be an allergic reaction. Causative agents include foods, drugs, infections. See ALLERGY.

Hjalmaren (yĕl'märŭn), Swed. *Hjälmaren*, lake, area 190 sq. mi., central Sweden. It is connected with Malaren L. and Abroga R.

Ho, chemical symbol of the element HOLMIUM.

Hoadly, Benjamin, 1676–1761, bishop of Bangor, Wales, center of BANGORIAN CONTROVERSY.

Hoar, Ebenezer Rockwood, 1816–95, American lawyer, U.S. Attorney General (1869–70). One of Grant's few excellent appointments. U.S. Senate rejected his nomination to U.S. Supreme Court in 1870.

hoarfrost: see FROST.

Hoban, James (hō'bŭn), c.1762–1831, American architect, b. Ireland. Designed and built the White House (1792–99); rebuilt it after its burning in 1814 by the British.

Hobart (hō'bŭrt), city (pop. of metropolitan area 109,200), cap. and principal port of Tasmania, Australia, on Derwent estuary; founded 1804. Seat of Univ. of Tasmania. Woolen mills.

Hobart, city (1966 pop. 20,875), extreme NW Ind., S of Gary; settled c.1849.

Hobart College: see COLLEGES OF THE SENECA, THE.

Hobbema, Meindert (mĭn'dŭrt hŏ'bŭmä), 1638–1709, great Dutch landscapist; probably studied with Jacob van Ruisdael. His woodland and village scenes are luminous and full of life. Much of work is in England, where it influenced later English landscapists.

Hobbes, Thomas, 1588–1679, English philosopher. In his works, both in Latin and in English, he set forth a rationalist materialism, which offended the religious. His view was strongly mechanistic. His best-known work, the *Leviathan* (1651), made him the first of the great English political theorists. This argues that men in their natural existence are self-seeking, brutish, and constantly at war with one another. To escape the dangers of this anarchy groups of men agree to set up an artificial body for maintaining peace. They submit absolutely to the sovereign, who is, however, obliged to protect the people and to promote truth. Hobbes implies that if the sovereign failed in this duty the citizens would have a right to revolt. In his psychology he was a strict sensationalist.

hobblebush or **wayfaring tree,** a viburnum (*Viburnum alnifolium*) of E North America. It has long straggling branches which often root at the tips.

Hobbs, William Herbert, 1864–1953, American geologist, authority on earthquakes, volcanoes, and glaciers.

Hobbs, city (pop. 26,275), SE N.Mex., near Texas line ENE of Carlsbad; founded 1907. Trade center in livestock and farm area. Hq. for rich oil fields found 1927.

Hobby, Oveta Culp, 1905–, U.S. Secretary of Health, Education, and Welfare (1953–55). Organized and directed WAC in Second World War.

Hobhouse, Leonard Trelawney, 1864–1929, English philosopher, sociologist, and journalist. He sought to show that biological and spiritual evolution were concurrent.

Hoboken (hō'bōkŭn), town (est. pop. 30,249), Antwerp prov., NE Belgium on Scheldt R. Industrial suburb of Antwerp; shipyards, metal refineries, wool-processing plants.

Hoboken (hō'bōkŭn), city (pop. 48,441), NE N.J., on Hudson R., NNE of Jersey City; settled c.1640 by Dutch. Changed title many times before John STEVENS bought site c.1800 and laid out town 1804. He built (c.1825) and ran on his estate first locomotive to pull train on tracks in U.S. Important industrial and commercial center since late 19th cent. Rail terminal and port for ocean-going vessels (with dry docks and marine shops). Access to New York city by ferry and subway under river. John Jacob Astor's home here was gathering place for noted authors. Seat of STEVENS INSTITUTE OF TECHNOLOGY.

Hobson, John Atkinson (hŏb'sŭn), 1858–1940, English economist. Criticized classical economics, holding that economic theory should be guide to social reform. His many books include *Imperialism* (1902).

Hobson, Richmond Pearson, 1870–1937, American naval officer. Gained notice by his effort to sink collier

Merrimac to block harbor of Santiago in Spanish-American War.

Hoche, Lazare (läzär' ōsh'), 1768–97, French general. Pacified VENDÉE (1794–96); failed in invasion of Ireland (1796); defeated Austrians at Neuwied (1797).

Hochelaga (hō″shŭlä′gŭ, –lä′gŭ), former Indian village, Canada, discovered by Jacques Cartier in 1535. At foot of Mt. Royal in what is now central part of Montreal. Capital of Hochelagan people, chief inhabitants of St. Lawrence valley. Excavations have unearthed early cultural remains.

Hochhuth, Rolf (rôlf hōkh′hŏŏt), 1933–, Swiss playwright, b. Germany; known for controversial work, *The Deputy* (1962), which examined the relations between Pope Pius XII and the Hitler regime. His drama *The Soldiers*, about Winston Churchill, aroused controversy in England in 1967, with the National Theater declining to perform it.

Ho Chi Minh (hō′ chē-mĭn′), 1890?–, Indo-Chinese revolutionary leader, president of the Democratic Republic of Vietnam (North Vietnam). Left his native Annam at 19 for France, where he helped to found the French Communist party. Visited the USSR (1925–27) and subsequently became a Comintern leader in Shanghai, China. Founded the Vietnam Communist party (1930). Between 1930 and 1945 he returned to Indo-China, organized and led Viet Minh (League for Independence of Vietnam), levied guerrilla warfare against the Japanese in the Second World War, and headed the VIETNAM provisional government in 1945. Warfare begun 1946 between the French and Ho's government was ended (July, 1954) by the Geneva agreements which awarded full control of Vietnam N of 17th parallel to Ho's forces. Ho is a leading figure in Asian Communist affairs. Also called Nguyen Ai Quoc.

Höchstädt (hûkh′shtĕt), town (pop. 3,256), W Bavaria, on Danube R., near battlefield of BLENHEIM.

hockey, game played on field or ice. Field hockey, played in England for several centuries, has been popular in U.S. since 1901, especially among college girls. Played on level field measuring 50 to 60 yd. by 90 to 100 yd. by two teams of 11 players. Ice hockey, played exclusively by men, originated in Canada and was probably standardized by McGill Univ. students in 1870s. Game is played on regulation ice rink 200 ft. by 85 ft. by teams of six players. See *ill.,* p. 1033.

Hodeida (hōdā′dŭ), city (pop. c.30,000), W Yemen, on Red Sea. Chief port of Yemen.

Hodgenville (hŏj′ĭnvĭl), town (pop. 1,985), central Ky., S of Louisville near Nolin R.; settled 1789. Nearby is Abraham Lincoln Birthplace Natl. Historic Site, with Lincoln's traditional birthplace cabin enclosed in memorial building.

Hodgkin, Alan Lloyd, 1914–, British research scientist. Shared 1963 Nobel Prize in Physiology and Medicine for work on how signals are generated through body nerve cells.

Hodgkin, Dorothy Mary Crowfoot, 1910–, British biochemist. Won 1964 Nobel Prize in Chemistry for work on the structure of biochemical compounds essential to the understanding and control of pernicious anemia.

Hodgkin's disease, chronic progressive disease manifested chiefly by enlargement of lymph nodes; also involved are bone marrow, spleen, and liver.

Hodler, Ferdinand, 1853–1918, Swiss painter and lithographer of symbolic, rhythmical compositions. Influenced the expressionists.

Hodmezovasarhely (hôd′mĕzûvä′shärhä), city (est. pop. 53,000), S Hungary. An agr. center; also produces machinery, textiles, and pottery.

Hoe, Richard March, 1812–86, American inventor, manufacturer of first U.S. flat bed and cylinder press, and designer (1846–47), of the first Hoe rotary press.

Hoek van Holland: see HOOK OF HOLLAND.

Hofei (hŭ′fē), city (pop. c.304,000), cap. of Anhwei prov., China. Textile center. Former name Luchow.

Hofer, Andreas (ändrä′äs hō′fŭr), 1767–1810, Austrian patriot; a Tyrolean innkeeper. Led peasants of TYROL in revolt against Bavaria (1809) and was made governor of Tyrol by the Austrians. Betrayed to the French, he was shot at Mantua.

Hoffa, James R(iddle), 1913–, American labor leader. Succeeded Dave Beck as president of Internatl. Brotherhood of Teamsters (1957). Tried for attempted extortion (1947); acquitted of attempting to bribe a Senate committee investigator (1957) and of wire tapping (1958). As protest against corrupt officials, AFL-CIO suspended teamsters' union in 1957. Hoffa was convicted in March, 1964, of tampering with a Federal jury; in July, he was convicted of wire and mail fraud and conspiracy in the use of union's pension fund. While both cases were under appeal in 1966, he was reelected president of teamsters. In March, 1967, he began to serve an eight-year prison sentence for jury tampering. In May, 1967, the Supreme Court granted him new hearing on the mail fraud charges.

Hoffmann, E(rnst) T(heodor) A(madeus) (ĕrnst′ tā′ōdōr ämädä′ŏŏs hôf′män), 1776–1822, German author, composer, and artist. Was active as conductor and as jurist. Himself an eccentric personality, he was a master of fantastic fiction, which his poetry and flashes of psychological insight raised to the highest level. His works include *The Serapion Brethren* (1819–22), *The Devil's Elixir* (1815–16), *Kater Murr, the Educated Cat* (1820–22). These and many selected tales have been translated into English. *The Nutcracker and the Mouse-King* served as basis for Tchaikovsky's ballet; three other tales were used for Offenbach's opera *Tales of Hoffmann.*

Hoffmann, Friedrich, 1660–1742, German physician; introduced Hoffmann's anodyne or compound spirit of ether. Among first to describe appendicitis and German measles. He viewed disease as a disruption of body's tonus (hence term *tonic* for his remedies).

Hoffmann, Joseph, 1870–1965, Austrian decorator and architect, influential in early 20th cent.

Hoffmann-Donner, Heinrich (hĭn′rĭkh hôf′män-dô′nŭr), 1809–94, German author of *Struwwelpeter* [slovenly Peter] (1845), widely known children's book.

Hofmann, August Wilhelm von (ou′gŏŏst vĭl′hĕlm fŭn hôf′män), 1818–92, German organic chemist. He was first to prepare rosaniline and its derivatives, thereby laying basis for aniline dye industry.

Hofmann, Hans, 1880–1966, American painter, important in abstract expressionism.

Hofmann, Joseph (hôf′mŭn), 1876–1957, Polish-American pianist. Made American debut (1887) at Metropolitan Opera House. Director (1926–38) of the Curtis Inst. of Music, Philadelphia.

Hofmannsthal, Hugo von (hŏŏ′gō fŭn hôf′mänstäl), 1874–1929, Austrian dramatist and poet. His *Electra* (1903), *Der Rosenkavalier* (1911), *Ariadne auf Naxos* (1912) and others were set to music by Richard Strauss. Also notable are his *Poems* (1903), the tragedy *Der Turm,* and his adaptation of *Everyman* (1911).

Hofstadter, Robert, 1915–, American physicist. Shared 1961 Nobel Prize in Physics with R. L. Mössbauer for investigations of internal structure of the proton and neutron.

hog: see SWINE.

Hogan, Ben (hō′gŭn), 1912–, American golfer. Won many tournaments, including P.G.A. championship (1946, 1948), U.S. Open (1948, 1950–51, 1953), Masters invitational (1951, 1953), and British Open (1953).

Hogarth, William (hō′gärth), 1697–1764, English painter and engraver. Won fame and financial security with his engravings, notably the three series *The Harlot's Progress, The Rake's Progress,* and *Marriage à la Mode,* which reveal his power as a satirist. Also made didactic prints (e.g., *Gin Lane*) to spur social reform. In his own time he won little recognition as a serious painter, although he produced some magnificent canvases, including *Shrimp Girl* (Natl. Gall., London).

Hogben, Lancelot (Thomas) (hŏg'bĕn), 1895–, English scientist and author. Known for work in genetics and endocrinology and for popular science books.

hog cholera, infectious, very contagious, often fatal virus disease of hogs. It can be prevented by vaccination.

Hogg, James, 1770–1835, Scottish poet, the "Ettrick Shepherd." Known for his rustic verse, such as *The Mountain Bard* (1807) and *The Queen's Wake* (1813).

Hoggar: see SAHARA.

Hog Island, in Delaware R., SE Pa. Was chief emergency shipyard of U.S. in First World War. Acquired by Philadelphia 1930 as airport, shipping and mfg. area.

Hogue, La (lä ôg') or **La Hougue** (lä ōōg'), harbor on English Channel, NW France, on NE coast of Cotentin peninsula. Scene of English-Dutch naval victory over French (1692).

Hohenfriedberg (hōŭnfrēt'bĕrk), Pol. *Dobromierz,* town, SW Poland (since 1945), near Breslau. Scene of decisive victory of Frederick II of Prussia over Austro-Saxon forces (1745).

Hohenlinden (hōŭnlĭn'dŭn), village, S Bavaria. Scene of French victory over Austrians (1800).

Hohenlohe-Schillingsfürst, Chlodwig, Fürst zu (klōt'vĭkh fürst' tsōō hō'ŭnlōŭ-shĭ'lĭngsfürst), 1819–1901, chancellor of Germany (1894–1900).

Hohenstaufen (hō"ŭnshtou'fŭn), German dynasty; dukes of Swabia from 1079; emperors and German kings 1138–1254; kings of Sicily 1194–1266 (see CONRAD III; FREDERICK I; HENRY VI; PHILIP OF SWABIA; FREDERICK II; CONRAD IV; MANFRED; CONRADIN). Their chief rivals were the Guelphs (see GUELPHS and GHIBELLINES), who sided with the popes.

Hohenwald, city (pop. 2,194), central Tenn., SW of Nashville. Meriwether Lewis Monument is nearby.

Hohenzollern (hō"ŭntsô'lŭrn), German dynasty, named for its ancestral castle in Swabia. Frederick of Hohenzollern (d. c.1200) became burgrave of Nuremberg 1192. His sons founded the two main lines of the house—the Swabian line (see HOHENZOLLERN, former province) and the Franconian line, which received the margraviates of ANSBACH and BAYREUTH (which later passed to separate branches) and, in 1415, the electorate of BRANDENBURG. In 1525 ALBERT OF BRANDENBURG created the duchy of Prussia, which passed to the main line of Brandenburg in 1618. Elector FREDERICK WILLIAM (reigned 1640–88) vastly increased his territories, which his son Frederick I transformed in 1701 into the kingdom of PRUSSIA. From 1871 to 1918 the Hohenzollern kings of Prussia were also emperors of Germany (William I, Frederick III, William II).

Hohenzollern, former province of Prussia, West Germany, in Swabia. After Second World War it became part of state of Baden-Württemburg. Sigmaringen is chief city. Mountainous; agr.; forestry. Zollern or Hohenzollern castle, in N, gave name to Prussia's ruling house. About 1600 territory split into two counties, later principalities, ruled by two branches of the Swabian Hohenzollern line—**Hohenzollern-Hechingen** and **Hohenzollern-Sigmaringen.** Both houses yielded their rights to Prussia 1849. Charles of Hohenzollern-Sigmaringen became king of Rumania as Carol I.

Hohe Tauern (hō'ŭ tou'ŭrn), range of E Alps, S Austria, in Salzburg, Carinthia, and E Tyrol. Rises to 12,-530 ft. in GROSSGLOCKNER.

Hokan-Siouan (hō'kŭn-sōō'ŭn), hypothetical linguistic stock of North America deriving from unproven unification of a number of Western and Eastern families.

Hokiang (hû'jyäng'), former province (c.52,300 sq. m.), NE China; cap. was Kiamusze. Created 1945 largely from Kirin prov. Included 1949 in Sungkiang prov., which was absorbed by Heilungkiang prov. 1954.

Hokkaido (hōkī'dō), island (30,132 sq. mi.; pop. 5,039,206), N Japan; cap. Sapporo. Northernmost, second largest, and most sparsely populated of major islands of Japan. Rugged interior with many volcanic peaks; most of area is forested. Ishikari R. in W is second largest in Japan. Winters are severe. Chief products are coal, lumber, paper, iron. One of world's major fishing centers. Until 1800 Ainus outnumbered the Japanese. Formerly called Yezo.

Hokusai (hō'kōōsī), 1760–1849, Japanese artist, the foremost figure of ukiyoye school. Accurately depicted Japanese scenes and contemporary life. A famous color-print series is *Hundred Views of Fuji.* His landscapes had much influence on Western art.

Holbach, Paul Henri Thiry, baron d' (ôlbäk'; also German hôl'bäkh), 1723–89, French philosopher, b. the Palatinate. A friend of Diderot, Condorcet, and Rousseau, he was an Encyclopedist. He is remembered chiefly as a stalwart opponent of all positive religion. Man, he held, was innately moral but perverted by education.

Holbein, Hans (hôl'bīn), the elder, c.1465–1524, German painter, designer of stained glass, silverpoint portraitist. His son **Ambrosius Holbein** c.1495–c.1519, is known for book illustrations and portraits. The other son, **Hans Holbein,** the younger, c.1497–1543, was an outstanding artist of German Renaissance. Spent early half of life in Basel, where he enjoyed friendship of Erasmus, whose *Praise of Folly* he illustrated and of whom he painted many portraits. In 1526 he visited England, where he painted Sir Thomas More and other eminent persons. Settled in England after brief return to Basel. Became painter to Henry VIII in 1536 and made many portraits of the king and his wives. As impressive as his paintings are numerous preliminary portrait drawings, remarkable for sensitivity of line and characterization. Among other famous works are his woodcuts, which include *Dance of Death* series and illustrations for Luther's Bible.

Holberg, Ludvig, Baron (lōōdh'vē, hōl'bĕr), 1684–1754, Danish dramatist and historian, b. Norway. One of the great figures of Danish literature, he was first to use Danish as a literary medium. *The Danish Stage* (1731) is a collection of 15 comedies.

Holborn, London: see CAMDEN.

Holbrook, Josiah (hôl'brŏŏk), 1788–1854, American educator. He founded the LYCEUM movement at Millbury, Mass., in 1826.

Holbrook. 1 Town (1965 pop. 4,481), E Ariz., on Little Colorado R., SE of Winslow; settled 1870 as cow town (Horsehead Crossing). Petrified Forest Natl. Park, Navajo and Apache reservations, and Hopi villages are nearby. **2** Town (pop. 10,104), E Mass., N of Brockton; settled 1710.

Holden. 1 Town (pop. 10,117), central Mass., suburb NNW of Worcester; settled 1723. **2** City (pop. 1,951), W central Mo., SE of Kansas City, in farm area; laid out 1857. Carry Nation lived here.

Hölderlin, Friedrich (frĕ'drĭkh hûl'dŭrlĭn), 1770–1843, German poet. Before he became insane at 36 he wrote lyric poetry of deep and intensely personal content, in classic meter and in free rhythms, which place him among the foremost German poets. Equally notable for its blending of classical and romantic elements is the epistolary novel *Hyperion* (1797–99).

holding company: see CORPORATION.

Holdsworth, Sir William Searle, 1871–1944, British legal historian. Professor at Oxford after 1922. His *History of English Law* (new ed., 9 vols., 1922–38) is a highly respected account of English legal procedure to 1875.

Holguin (ōlgēn'), city (pop. c.227,000), NE Cuba. Located in agr. region, it is commercial and transportation center.

Holinshed, Raphael, d. c.1580, English chronicler. His *Chronicles of England, Scotland, and Ireland* (1577) was source for many English history plays.

Holland, former county of the Holy Roman Empire and, from 1579 to 1795, chief member of the United Provs. of the Netherlands; historic cap. The Hague. The name is popularly applied to the entire Netherlands. Created a county in 10th cent., Holland originally also controlled ZEELAND and FRIESLAND. It was seized in 1299 by John of Avesnes, count of HAINAUT, and was ruled by his successors till 1433, when Duke Philip the Good of Burgundy wrested it from Jacqueline, countess of Hainaut, Holland, Zeeland, and Friesland. After the death of Mary of Burgundy (1482) Holland was taken over by Maximilian of Austria (later Emperor Maximilian I), who suppressed a Dutch rebellion in 1490. The ports and cities of Holland—e.g., Amsterdam, Rotterdam, The Hague, Leiden, Delft—rose to prosperity in the 15th and 16th cent., and Holland led in the struggle for Dutch independence from Spain (16th–17th cent.). Its history became virtually identical with that of the NETHERLANDS. In 1840 Holland was divided into NORTH HOLLAND and SOUTH HOLLAND provs.

Holland, city (pop. 24,777), SW Mich., near L. Michigan on L. Macatawa, SW of Grand Rapids, in dairy and poultry area; founded 1847 by Dutch. Mfg. of furnaces; tulip growing and annual tulip festival. Seat of Hope Col. and Western Theological Seminary.

Holland, Parts of: see LINCOLNSHIRE, England.

Holland House, residence of the Holland family in Kensington, London, made famous in first half of 19th cent. by hospitality of Henry Richard Vassall Fox, 3d Baron Holland. Did much for English liberalism by providing an intellectual center for scientists, writers, and statesmen.

Hollandia: see KOTABARU.

Holland Land Company, a Dutch venture active in the settlement of much of W N.Y. and some of NW Pa. Organized 1796. Company developed its holdings, planned town sites, and sold lands directly to settlers on liberal terms.

Hollar, Wenzel or **Wenceslaus** (hŏ′lŭr, –lär), 1607–77, Bohemian etcher. Works included portraits, architectural studies, still lifes, and religious scenes. Worked mainly in England.

Holley, Alexander Lyman, 1832–82, American engineer. Built first Bessemer steel plant in U.S. at Troy, N.Y.; later improved efficiency and output of system.

Holley, Robert W., 1922–, American biochemist. He determined the basic structure of RNA, the first nucleic acid for which structure was known.

Hollins College, at Hollins College, Va., near Roanoke; for women; opened 1842 as seminary; called Hollins Inst. 1855–1911.

Hollister, city (pop. 6,071), SW Calif., E of Monterey Bay. Pinnacles Natl. Monument is near.

holly, handsome evergreen or deciduous tree or shrub of widely distributed genus *Ilex* with berrylike fruits of various colors. Male and female flowers are often on different plants. English holly (*Ilex aquifolium*), with glossy spiny evergreen leaves and bright red berries, is closely associated with Christmas tradition. The similar American holly (*I. opaca*) may reach 50 ft. in the South. Other hollies include inkberry, winterberry, and commercially important MATE.

hollyhock, a tall biennial or perennial plant (*Althaea rosea*), with large leaves and showy single or double flowers of various colors.

Holly Springs, city (pop. 5,621), N central Miss., SE of Memphis, Tenn. Confederates under Gen. Van Dorn captured it, Dec., 1862, seizing Federal supplies and delaying Grant's advance on Vicksburg. Seat of Rust Col.

Hollywood. 1 Part (pop. 148,971) of Los Angeles (since 1910), S Calif.; founded in late 1880s. Center of country's motion-picture industry, although many major studios are now in nearby sections. Hollywood's first film was made c.1911. Name Hollywood now symbol for American motion-picture industry in general—its morals, manners, and characteristics. Has Sunset Strip, Grauman's Chinese theater, Hollywood Bowl, Griffith Park, and estates of many film celebrities. West Hollywood (pop. 28,870) is mainly residential. **2** City (pop. 35,237), SE Fla., on Atlantic coast N of Miami; founded 1921. Resort center; race track nearby.

Holmes, John Haynes, 1879–1964, American clergyman (undenominational), minister (1907–49) of Community Church, New York city; founder of Natl. Association for the Advancement of Colored People and of American Civil Liberties Union.

Holmes, Oliver Wendell, 1809–94, American author and physician. Professor of anatomy and physiology at Harvard, he wrote important medical papers. His poems include the familiar "Old Ironsides," "Lord of All Being, Thron'd Afar," and the witty "The Deacon's Masterpiece." Contributions to the *Atlantic Monthly* were collected as *The Autocrat of the Breakfast Table* (1858) and later volumes. His novels (e.g., *Elsie Venner*, 1861) were "medical" in his day and only recently have been hailed as the first American psychological novels. His son, **Oliver Wendell Holmes,** 1841–1935, was Associate Justice of U.S. Supreme Court (1902–32). Known as the "great dissenter," he gained the notice of the nation's liberals by his clear, forceful opinions. He believed in respecting human rights more than property rights. His writings (e.g., *The Common Law*, 1881) are much admired.

Holmes, William Henry, 1846–1933, American geologist and anthropologist. He served with U.S. Geological Survey, contributing pioneer reports on Yellowstone, Grand Canyon, and other areas. His interest in cliff dwellings of the Southwest turned him to archaeology. From 1910 to 1920 he was curator of anthropology at U.S. National Museum.

holmium (hŏl′mēŭm), metallic element of rare earths (symbol = Ho; see also ELEMENT, table).

Holofernes (hŏlŭfûr′nĕz, hōlō′–), invading general killed by JUDITH to save her city. Judith 2–13.

Holst, Gustav (hŏlst), 1874–1934, English composer. Among his compositions are *The Mystic Trumpeter* (1904), for voice and orchestra; *The Planets* (1914–16), a suite for orchestra; and *The Perfect Fool* (1920–22), an opera.

Holst, Hermann Eduard von (fūn hōlst′), 1841–1904, American historian. Main work, *The Constitutional and Political History of the United States* (7 vols., 1876–92), studies struggle to preserve Union.

Holstein, Friedrich von (frē′drĭkh fūn hōl′shtīn), 1837–1909, German civil servant, the "Gray Eminence" of the German foreign office. Holding a relatively obscure post, he was a powerful influence in shaping German foreign policy. Resigned 1906.

Holstein (hōl′stīn, Ger. hôl′shtīn), former duchy, N Germany; the part of Schleswig-Holstein S of the Eider R.; cap. Kiel. Created a county of the Holy Roman Empire in 1111, Holstein was ruled until 1459 by the house of Schauenburg, which in 1386 also received SCHLESWIG. In 1459 it passed by inheritance to Christian I of Denmark, of the house of OLDENBURG, who in 1460 estab. the relationship of Denmark, Schleswig, and Holstein as a personal union. Holstein was raised to a duchy in 1474. For subsequent history, see SCHLESWIG-HOLSTEIN.

Holstein-Friesian cattle: see CATTLE.

Holsteinsborg (hôl′stänsbôr″), district (pop. 2,331) and town (pop. 1,714), W Greenland. Town is fishing center, has canning factory.

Holston, river, NE Tenn., flowing c.115 mi. SW through Great Appalachian Valley to join French Broad R. near Knoxville and form Tennessee R. Major route of westward migration. Cherokee Dam is in it.

Holt, Joseph, 1807–94, U.S. Postmaster General (1859–60), Secretary of War (1861), judge advocate general of U.S. army (1862–75).

Holt, Luther Emmett, 1855–1924, American physician, specialist in children's diseases, author of *Care and Feeding of Children* (1894).

Holtby, Winifred, 1898–1935, English novelist and journalist. Director of *Time and Tide* after 1926. Her novel *South Riding* (1936) widely known.

Holton, city (pop. 3,028), NE Kansas, NNW of Topeka, laid out 1857 by Free Staters. Potawatamie Indian Reservation is nearby.

Holy Alliance, formed 1815, agreement among Alexander I of Russia (its sponsor) and the rulers of Austria and Prussia. Its wording, which reflects Alexander's confused mysticism, bound the sovereigns to conduct themselves according to Christian principles and was later interpreted to mean that the political status of Europe as of 1815 was divinely inspired and should remain unchanged forever. All sovereigns of Europe adhered to the alliance save three—George IV of England (who could not for constitutional reasons) and the pope and the sultan (who could not for religious reasons). The QUADRUPLE ALLIANCE of 1814, though distinct from the Holy Alliance, became soon confused with it and under the leadership of Metternich acted as its instrument. The defection of England from the Quadruple Alliance (1822) did not prevent the survival of the Holy Alliance as a spiritual climate until the Revolution of 1848.

Holy City: see ALLAHABAD; BENARES; JERUSALEM; MECCA; ROME.

Holy Cross, College of the, at Worcester, Mass.; for men; founded and opened 1843, chartered 1865.

Holy Ghost or **Holy Spirit,** in Christian doctrine, third Person of the Trinity, often defined as the aspect of God immanent in the world; the giver of faith, the Paraclete (Comforter or Strengthener). Descended upon the apostles at first Pentecost, giving them the gift of tongues (Acts 2). The dove is symbol of the Holy Ghost.

Holy Grail: see GRAIL, HOLY.

Holyhead (hŏ′lēhĕd), urban district (pop. 10,408), on Holyhead Isl., Wales, small island off W coast of Anglesey. Chief port for mail and passenger service to Dublin. Also a fishing port and resort.

Holy Island, England: see LINDISFARNE.

Holy Land: see PALESTINE.

Holy League. 1 In French history: see LEAGUE. **2** In Italian history, alliance formed 1510 by Pope Julius II with Venice, Swiss Confederation, Spain, England, Emperor Maximilian I, and others to expel LOUIS XII of France from Italy. Swiss routed French at Novara (1513), but league broke up when Julius died.

Holy Loch, inlet of the Firth of Clyde, Argyllshire, Scotland. In 1961 it became a base for U.S. nuclear submarines equipped with nuclear missiles.

Holyoke, city (pop. 52,689), SW Mass., on Connecticut R. above Springfield: settled 1745. Its industrialization began before middle of 19th cent.

holy orders: see ORDERS, HOLY.

Holy Roman Empire, political body embracing most of central Europe from 962 to 1806; "Roman" because it claimed succession to imperial Rome; "holy" because it originally claimed supremacy over Christendom. Its universality was never recognized in the E by the Byzantine emperors and only briefly in the W, where England, France, and Spain developed into separate states. A constantly evolving organism, the Holy Roman Empire was a mixture of conflicting theories and realities. CHARLEMAGNE in 800 recreated a Western Empire and sought to restore the order and unity Europe had known under Rome; this empire broke up under his successors (LOUIS I, LOTHAIR I, LOUIS II, CHARLES II, CHARLES III, ARNULF). The union of GERMANY and ITALY under OTTO I and his imperial coronation (962) created a new empire, based on FEUDALISM. Its rulers were chosen by the princes of Germany (after 1356, by a fixed number of ELECTORS) unless crowned emperor by the pope, they bore the title German king or king of the Romans. Customarily, after being crowned king at Aachen, the emperor-elect proceeded to Rome to be crowned emperor there. To keep the succession in his family, he normally had his heir elected king of the Romans in his lifetime. After 1530 the emperors-elect dispensed with coronations by the pope and were crowned at Frankfurt. The emperors exercised direct rule only over their hereditary family domains (e.g., the Saxon dynasty, over Saxony; the Hapsburg dynasty, over Austria); they also held immediate jurisdiction over the free imperial cities (e.g., Frankfurt, Regensburg, Augsburg), which they chartered in the 12th–13th cent. The rest of the empire they controlled only to the extent to which they controlled the DIET, which might even depose them. They succeeded, in the 10th–12th cent., in breaking up the powerful "stem duchies" (see GERMANY) and raised a multitude of lesser temporal and ecclesiastic princes to the rank of immediate vassals. This process was completed by FREDERICK I, who also brought to a head the long-standing rivalry between emperors and popes. One factor in that bitter struggle was that both popes and emperors claimed supremacy over Christendom—the popes in spiritual matters, the emperors in temporal matters, but with no agreement as to ultimate rights in administration and authority. From this arose the quarrel over INVESTITURE (settled 1122 by the Concordat of WORMS). Another factor was the dual role of the emperors as kings of both Germany and Italy and the dual role of the popes as both spiritual and temporal rulers. If the emperors stayed N of the Alps, they lost effective control over Italy; if they invaded Italy (as they did at irregular intervals) to reassert their authority, the popes as a rule managed to' stir up trouble in Germany, thus forcing the invader to hasten back. Frederick I lost out in his struggle against the LOMBARD LEAGUE, which had papal backing; FREDERICK II, who was also king of Sicily, shifted his center of interest to Italy, which he temporarily subdued, but after his death (1250) the papacy emerged triumphant and imperial rule over Italy was lost. After an interregnum which put Germany at the mercy of robber barons, feuding nobles, and rival kings, a new phase began with the election of RUDOLF I of Hapsburg (1273). The HAPSBURG dynasty, which became permanently entrenched after 1438, directed its primary attention to its own aggrandizement and to its hereditary domains, which under CHARLES V stretched around the entire globe, far beyond the boundaries of the Holy Roman Empire. The victory of the princes and the towns in the PEASANTS' WAR (1524–26) prolonged serfdom and feudalism for another three centuries; the REFORMATION destroyed even the religious unity of the empire and offered the German princes a pretext for rebelling against Hapsburg supremacy in the THIRTY YEARS WAR (1618–48). The Peace of WESTPHALIA dissolved the empire in all but its name. Some 300 princes obtained virtual sovereignty, limited only by vague provisions forbidding alliances directed against the emperor. Hapsburg power was further weakened by France in the wars of Louis XIV (17th cent.) and by PRUSSIA in the War of the AUSTRIAN SUCCESSION and the SEVEN YEARS WAR (18th cent.). The FRENCH REVOLUTIONARY WARS and Napoleon I swept away the empire. In 1803 the diet deposed and indemnified the majority of princes, creating a smaller number of larger states; in 1804 Francis II took the title Francis I, emperor of Austria; in 1806 the empire was dissolved. The following is a list of German kings and emperors from 919.

Saxon dynasty (919–1024): Henry I, Otto I, Otto II, Otto III, Henry II.

Salian or *Franconian dynasty* (1024–1125): Conrad II, Henry III, Henry IV, Henry V.

Lothair II (reigned 1125–37; duke of Saxony).

Hohenstaufen dynasty (1138–1254): Conrad III, Frederick I, Henry VI, Philip of Swabia (antiking: Otto IV), Frederick II, Conrad IV (antiking: William, count of Holland).

Interregnum (1254–73): Richard, earl of Cornwall and Alfonso X of Castile, rivals.

Hapsburg, Luxemburg, and other dynasties: Rudolf I (1273–91; Hapsburg); Adolf of Nassau (1292–98); Albert I (1298–1308; Hapsburg); Henry VII (1308–13; Luxemburg); Louis IV (1314–46; Wittelsbach); Charles IV (1346–78; Luxemburg); Wenceslaus

(1378–1400; Luxemburg); Rupert (1400–1410; Wittelsbach); Sigismund (1410–37; Luxemburg).

Hapsburg dynasty (1438–1740); Albert II, Frederick III, Maximilian I, Charles V, Ferdinand I, Maximilian II, Rudolf II, Matthias, Ferdinand II, Ferdinand III, Leopold I, Joseph I, Charles VI.

Interregnum (1740–42).

Charles VII (emperor, 1742–45; elector of Bavaria).

Francis I (emperor, 1745–65; ex-duke of Lorraine; husband of Maria Theresa).

Hapsburg-Lorraine dynasty (1765–1806): Joseph II, Leopold II, Francis II.

Holyrood (hŏ'lĕrōōd) [i.e., holy cross], former residence of Scottish kings, in Edinburgh. David I founded abbey here in 1128. Its Chapel Royal contains remains of several kings. Present building begun 1501; rebuilt after fire of 1650. Scene of murder of David Rizzio (1566).

Holy Sepulcher, church in Jerusalem on the supposed site of Jesus' tomb, officially the Church of the Resurrection. St. HELENA is said to have pointed out the site. Most of the church is controlled by the Orthodox, though other Christian groups have sections. In recent years steps have been taken to repair the aging edifice.

Holy Spirit: see HOLY GHOST.

Holy Week, week before Easter marked by commemoration of Jesus' passion and death. Chief days are Palm Sunday, Maundy Thursday, Good Friday, and Holy Saturday (Lent ends Saturday at noon).

Holywell (hŏ'lĕwĕl), urban district (pop. 8,459), Flintshire, Wales. Gothic chapel (place of pilgrimage for Roman Catholics) covers St. Winifred's Well, which, legend says, sprang up on the spot where St. Winifred was beheaded.

Holywood, urban district (pop 8,060) Co. Down, N. Ireland. Has ruins of 13th-cent. monastery on the site of one founded in the 7th cent.

Holz, Arno (är'nō hôlts'), 1863–1929, German poet; an influential critic and a founder of the naturalistic school.

Homayun: see HUMAYUN.

Homburg (hŏm'bŏŏrk), town (est. pop. 35,676), Hesse, West Germany. Famous spa and resort. Was cap. of landgraviate of Hesse-Homburg.

Home, Daniel Dunglas, 1833–86, American spiritualist medium. He claimed to have discovered his gifts at 13 and from 1850 on had triumphant career in U.S. and Europe. His séances produced highly physical manifestations of spirits. Many efforts were made to expose him but none was successful.

Home, Henry: see KAMES, HENRY HOME, LORD.

Home, John, 1722–1808, Scottish dramatist, author of successful tragedy *Douglas* (1756), which has speech beginning, "My name is Norval."

home missions: see MISSIONS.

homeopathy (hōmēō'pŭthē), system of medicine based on principle that disorders are cured by small doses of drugs producing in healthy people effects similar to the symptoms of the disorder. Homeopathy was originated by Samuel Hahnemann and gained great popularity (now somewhat dwindled).

Home Owners' Loan Corporation, established (1933) to refinance urban mortgage debt and stabilize depreciated real estate. HOLC lent $3,000,000,000, all of which had been liquidated by 1951.

Homer, first extant Greek poet. His actual existence debated in 19th cent., but most recent scholars say such a poet lived before 700 B.C. Legend says that he was blind and that seven cities claimed him. Narrative poems, the ILIAD and the ODYSSEY, are masterpieces of world literature and models for all later epics. The Homeric Hymns, a comic poem, and a mock epic (*The Battle of the Frogs and the Mice*) were falsely attributed to him.

Homer, Winslow, 1836–1910, American landscape, marine, and genre painter. Many of his studies of everyday life date from Civil War period when he was a popular magazine illustrator. Best known for his dramatic interpretations of the sea in water color.

Homeric Hymns (hōmĕ'rĭk), hexameter poems, complimentary to the gods, composed c.800–400 B.C., anciently attributed to Homer.

Home Rule. Desire in Ireland, long under English dominance, for autonomy. The modern movement began in 1870 and was strengthened by rise of Charles Stewart PARNELL who unified Irish party in British Parliament. Accompanied by a campaign of violence in Ireland. First Home Rule Bill introduced by Gladstone (1886) failed to pass. Second Home Rule Bill (1893) was passed by House of Commons but defeated by House of Lords. Third Home Rule Bill passed by Commons (1912) led to threats of civil war and House of Lords excluded Ulster. Bill never took effect because 1916 rebellion led to recognition of the Irish Free State with dominion status in 1921. Since 1949 Republic of Ireland has had no legal ties to Britain. N. Ireland is governed under the Fourth Home Rule Bill of 1920.

home rule, municipal, system permitting cities to draft and amend their own charters without state interference. Adopted first (1875) in Missouri and now also used in other states, it has not—because of great variation from state to state and court strictures—accomplished all that was expected of it.

Homestead. 1 City (pop. 9,152), SE Fla., SSW of Miami. Homestead Air Force Base and Everglades Natl. Park are nearby. **2** Industrial borough (pop. 7,502), SW Pa., on Monongahela R. near Pittsburgh. Iron and steel works (now largely in Munhall borough) were scene of bitter **Homestead strike** (1892). Pinkerton men, hired by Carnegie company, and strikers met in armed battle in which a number of men were killed or wounded. Strike broken when governor called out Natl. Guard.

Homestead Act, 1862, passed by U.S. Congress. It gave a quarter section of unoccupied public land to homesteader for nominal fee after five years' residence. It replaced earlier government practice of selling land for purposes of revenue. Homestead Natl. Monument of America estab. on site of one of first claims made under act.

Homestead National Monument of America: see HOMESTEAD ACT.

Homestead strike: see HOMESTEAD, Pa.

Homewood. 1 City (pop. 20,289), N central Ala., suburb S of Birmingham. **2** Village (1966 pop. 17,399), NE Ill., suburb S of Chicago; platted 1852. Washington Park race track is nearby.

homicide (hŏ'mŭsīd), taking of human life. A homicide is considered excusable if it results from an accident not amounting to culpable negligence. Justifiable homicide is defined variously but generally includes legal execution of criminals, killing committed to prevent a felony or arrest a felon, and killing in self-defense (i.e., committed by someone reasonably fearing death or serious injury at the hands of the person slain). Other homicides are criminal; if committed with malice aforethought the homicide is murder, otherwise manslaughter—though statutes in various states use different terminology.

hominy, hulled corn, coarsely broken or ground. As a pioneer food it was prepared by soaking grains in weak wood lye. Now marketed as hominy grits, also called samp.

Homma, Masaharu (mäsä'härōō hōmä'), 1888?–1946, Japanese general. Led invasion of Philippines 1941; ordered Bataan "death march." Executed 1946 as war criminal.

Homs (hôms), anc. *Emesa*, city (pop. c.127,000), W Syria, on Orontes R. and S of Hama. The Roman emperor Heliogabalus was originally a priest of Emesa temple to Baal. Aurelian defeated Zenobia here in 272. It fell to Arabs 636. Name also written Hems.

Honan (hû'nän'), province (c.65,000 sq. mi.; pop. c.46,025,000), China; cap. Chengchow. Wheat, cotton, rice, and tobacco are main crops. Coal and iron mined. Region a center of Chinese civilization since c.2000 B.C. ANYANG, LOYANG, and KAIFENG are historic cities. Area N of Yellow R. was part of Pingyuan prov. 1949–52.

Honanfu, China: see LOYANG.

Honduras (hŏndŏō'rŭs), republic (43,227 sq. mi.; 1964 est. pop. 2,163,011), Central America, bordering on Nicaragua, Salvador, Guatemala; with Carribbean and Pacific coasts; cap. TEGUCIGALPA. The N (Caribbean coast) has on its W half vast banana plantations owned by U.S. companies; principal ports are Trujillo, La Ceiba, Tela, and Puerto Cortés. S (Pacific) coast largely semiarid and unproductive; has small port of Amapala. Between the coasts are mountain ranges, ending in the E in jungles and swamps of MOSQUITO COAST. Silver mining developed Comayagua and Tegucigalpa, and silver is still exported. First visited by Columbus (1502), it was reached by Cortés (1524) and conquered and settled by Pedro de Alvarado. Gained independence from Spain (1821) then was part of Iturbide's Mexican Empire and a member of the CENTRAL AMERICAN FEDERATION (1825–38). Great Britain long controlled all the Mosquito Coast and The BAY ISLANDS, and liberation was attempted by William Walker in 1860. Foreign capital, plantation life, and conservative policies dominated Honduras from late 19th to mid-20th cent. when liberal movement reawakened. In 1965 new constitution completed and Oswald López Arellano became president.

Hone, Philip, 1780–1851, American diarist. A successful businessman, he was (1825) mayor of New York. His diary (1828–51) is an invaluable historical record.

Honegger, Arthur (hŭ'nĕgŭr), 1892–1955, Swiss-French composer. Member of The SIX. His works include five symphonies, operas, oratorios (*King David, Joan of Arc*), and songs.

Honesdale, industrial borough (pop. 5,569), NE Pa., on Lackawaxen R., NE of Scranton; settled 1803. First regular trial run of a locomotive in U.S. made here 1829. Was terminus of Delaware and Hudson Canal.

honey locust, thorny leguminous deciduous tree (*Gleditsia triacanthos*) native to E U.S. and widely planted as a shade tree. It has fragrant flowers and the fruits are long pods often used as cattle feed.

honeysuckle, ornamental shrub or vine of genus *Lonicera,* widely distributed in N Hemisphere. White, red, or purple flowers, usually fragrant, are followed by variously colored berries.

Hong Kong (hŏng' kŏng'), Mandarin *Hsiang-chiang.* British crown colony (391 sq. mi.; pop. 3,133,131). SE China, adjoining Kwangtung prov.; administrative center Hong Kong (Victoria). Comprises Hong Kong isl. (32 sq. mi.) ceded by China 1842; Kowloon peninsula (3 sq. mi.) ceded 1860; and the New Territories, on adjoining mainland area with Mirs Bay, leased 1898 for 99 years. Hong Kong is a free port and international air hub. Industrial and mfg. center. Fishing important. Occupied by Japan Dec. 25, 1941; restored to British after Second World War.

Honolulu (hŏnŭlŏō'lŏō), city (pop. 294,194), state cap., Hawaii, on SE coast of Oahu. Crossroads of the Pacific and state's economic center and chief port. City lies in narrow plain between sea and Koolau Range. Bypassed by Capt. James Cook in 1778; harbor entered c.1793 by English ship captain William Brown. History much the same as that of HAWAII after missionaries came 1820. Chief residence of Hawaiian royalty, it became permanent cap. of kingdom of Hawaii 1845 and remained cap. when U.S. annexed islands 1898. After bombing of PEARL HARBOR, became staging area for U.S. forces in Pacific. Postwar years saw rise in tourism and diversification of industry. Has sugar processing, pineapple canning, and coffee growing. Center for marine research. Here are Univ. of HAWAII, Honolulu Academy of Arts, Iolani Palace (former home of Hawaiian kings, now seat of state government), WAIKIKI beach, and PUNCHBOWL. Nearby is DIAMOND HEAD crater.

Honorius I (hŏnô'rēŭs), pope (625–38). Wrote a letter apparently supporting the heresy of MONOTHELETISM. He and the letter were condemned by the Third Council of Constantinople, but this condemnation is held not to affect the doctrine of papal infallibility because Honorius was not speaking *ex cathedra.*

Honorius II, d. 1130, pope (1124–30). As adviser to Paschal II, he concluded the Concordat of Worms (1122) with German King Henry V. Supported Lothair II, who yielded to church demands on episcopal election. Quarreled with Henry I of England.

Honorius III, d. 1227, pope (1216–27), an Italian, successor of Innocent III. He had been tutor to Frederick II, crowned him, and tried in vain to get the emperor to go on crusade.

Honorius, 384–423, West Roman emperor (395–423); son of Theodosius I. His brother Arcadius inherited the East. Honorius had his guardian STILICHO murdered in 408. He held out at Ravenna against ALARIC I (409–10) but made peace with the Visigoths in 412. In 421 he had to make his brother-in-law joint emperor as CONSTANTIUS III. His reign marked important stage in decline of Western Empire.

Honshu (hŏn'shŏō), island (c.89,000 sq. mi.; pop. 71,-354,357), central Japan, between Sea of Japan and the Pacific; largest and most important island of Japan. Largely mountainous, rises to 12,389 ft. at Fujiyama; Mt. Asama highest of active volcanoes. Chief lowland area is Kanto Plain in central part. Climate ranges from extreme cold of N to subtropical warmth of S. Frequent earthquakes. Agr. and raw-silk production are widespread. Chief industrial cities are Yokohama, Tokyo, Nagoya, Osaka, and Kobe.

Honthorst, Gerrit van (gĕr'ärt van hŏnt'hôrst), 1590–1656, Dutch portrait, genre, and allegorical painter. He brought the style of Caravaggio from Italy to Holland.

Hooch or **Hoogh, Pieter de** (both: pē'tŭr dŭ hōkh), b. c.1629, d. after 1677, noted Dutch genre painter. Typical themes are quiet domestic interiors, often with housewives and children.

Hood, John Bell, 1831–79, Confederate general. Commanded in ATLANTA CAMPAIGN. Advanced to Nashville, Tenn., where forces were virtually annihilated by G. H. Thomas. Resigned command Jan., 1865.

Hood, Raymond M(athewson), 1881–1934, American architect. Designed Daily News Building (New York).

Hood, Thomas, 1799–1845, English poet, known today especially for poems of sentiment and social protest ("The Bridge of Sighs" and "The Song of the Shirt"). Also wrote humorous verse and prose.

Hood, Mount: see CASCADE RANGE.

hoof, horny epidermal casing at end of digits of an ungulate mammal. In some animals (pig, sheep, cattle) hoof is cloven, in others (horse, zebra) solid.

Hooft, Pieter Corneliszoon (hŏft), 1581–1647, Dutch historian and poet, author of a classic history (1642, incomplete) of the Netherlands from 1555 to 1584. A fine lyric poet, he introduced into Dutch the tones of French and Italian Renaissance love poetry.

Hoogh, Pieter de: see HOOCH, PIETER DE.

Hooghly (hŏō'glē), river, c.200 mi. long, West Bengal, India; arm of Ganges R. Shipping artery to major industrial area around Calcutta. On it is town of Hooghly, founded 1537 by the Portuguese.

Hooke, Robert, 1635–1703, English scientist. He was first to formulate the theory of planetary movements as a mechanical problem. He improved astronomical instruments; devised practical system of telegraphy; invented spiral watch spring; constructed first arithmetical machine and Gregorian telescope. He described cells in plant tissues. **Hooke's law:** within the limit of elasticity, the stress on a body is in direct proportion to strain.

Hooker, Joseph, 1814–79, Union general in Civil War. Known as "Fighting Joe." Commanded Army of the Potomac; defeated at Chancellorsville (1863). Commanded ably in Chattanooga campaign.

Hooker, Richard, 1554?–1600, noted English theologian. His *Of the Laws of Ecclesiastical Polity* formulated concepts of Anglicanism and influenced civil as well as ecclesiastical government.

Hooker, Thomas, 1586–1647, Puritan clergyman in American colonies, chief founder of Hartford, Conn. (1635–36), b. England.

Hooke's law: see HOOKE, ROBERT.

Hook of Holland, Dutch *Hoek van Holland,* town, South Holland prov., SW Netherlands, on North Sea; an outer port of Rotterdam, with which it is connected by the New Waterway. Terminus for Channel crossings from Harwich, England.

hookworm (ancylostomiasis), disease in man caused by certain parasitic nematode worms lodged in intestine. Anemia results from blood sucking and bleeding. Worm eggs passed from intestine of victim develop into larva stage in warm, moist soil, then burrow into skin of persons in contact with infected soil and travel by way of body fluids to lungs and thence to pharynx where they are swallowed.

Hoorn or **Horn, Philip de Montmorency, count of** (both: hôrn), 1518?–1568, Netherlands nobleman. Joined EGMONT in protesting Spanish abuses in the Netherlands. Was beheaded after an irregular trial. He is a national hero.

Hoosac Range (hōō'sŭk), S continuation of Green Mts. in SW Vt. and NW Mass., E of the Berkshires. Pierced by 5-mi. railroad tunnel (built 1852–73).

Hooton, Earnest Albert (hōō'tŭn), 1887–1954, American anthropologist. Studied early man and primates.

Hoover, Herbert (Clark), 1874–1964, 30th or 31st (see list at end of article UNITED STATES) President of the United States 1929–33), b. Iowa. Before 1915 he engaged in world-wide mining and engineering activities. Headed food administration and war relief bureaus during and after First World War. As U.S. Secretary of Commerce 1921–29), he reorganized and expanded department. Stock market crash of 1929 ushered in an economic depression which continued throughout his administration as president. Hoover recommended extensive public works, appointed commissions to study urgent problems. Destitute farmers were aided by Federal Farm Board. RECONSTRUCTION FINANCE CORPORATION was created. Congress, which had a Democratic majority after 1930 election, passed Emergency Relief Act and created Federal home loan banks. Veterans seeking a bonus marched on Washington; Hoover ordered Federal troops to oust them from Federal property. Disarmament conferences were ineffective (see NAVAL CONFERENCES); debt moratorium which Hoover proposed in 1931 to alleviate Germany's financial situation had no practical results. Hoover left office in 1933 during serious banking crisis. Handled world food problems in 1946. Headed "Hoover Commission" (1947–49), which studied and advised on organization of the executive branch of government, and second "Hoover Commission" (1953–55), which advised on policy as well as organization.

Hoover, J(ohn) Edgar, 1895–, American administrator, director of the FEDERAL BUREAU OF INVESTIGATION (1924–).

Hoover Dam, in Black Canyon, at Nev.-Ariz. line, in Colorado R.; built 1931–36. One of world's largest, 726.4 ft high, 1,244 ft. long. Key unit of projects on Colorado R., it is one of world's largest suppliers of hydroelectric power. Irrigates areas of S Calif., Ariz. and Mexico. Also used for flood control. Forms L. Mead, resort center and world's largest man-made lake. Formerly called Boulder Dam.

Hoover Library on War, Revolution, and Peace, at Stanford Univ., Palo Alto, Calif.; estab. 1919 by Herbert Hoover. Contains mostly materials on period of First World War and afterward. Housed in Hoover Tower since 1941.

hop, perennial twining vine (*Humulus lupulus*) grown from early times for brewing purposes. The conelike

female flowers, "hops," contain lupulin, a bitter-tasting yellow powder added to beer.

Hopatcong, Lake (hōpăt'kŏn), c.8 mi. long and 3 mi. wide, N N.J., NW of Dover. Largest lake entirely in N.J. On its shores are resort villages of Landing, Mt. Arlington, and Lake Hopatcong.

Hope, Anthony, pseud. of Sir Anthony Hope Hawkins, 1863–1933, English novelist, known for his romantic *Prisoner of Zenda* (1894).

Hope, Bob, 1903–, American film actor and comedian, originally named Leslie Townes Hope. First success was on N.Y. stage (1932). Noted for his work in radio (after 1935), in films (after 1938; notably in films with Bing Crosby) and television, and after 1942 for his overseas tours to entertain servicemen.

Hopedale, town (pop. 3,987), E Mass., SE of Worcester; settled 1660. Adin Ballou had Christian communistic settlement here, 1841–c.1857.

Hopeh or **Ho-pei** (hŭ'bā'), province (c.75,000 sq. mi.; pop. c.44,434,000), NE China, on Pohai, arm of Yellow Sea. Cap. Tientsin; other chief centers are Peking, Chingwangtao, and Paoting. Crops include wheat, millet, kaoliang, and soybeans. Major coal and iron mines; heavy industry, mainly metallurgical plants, steelworks, and textile factories. Parts of former Jehol and Chahar provs. added to Hopeh 1956. Formerly called Chi and Chihli.

Hope Island: see SPITSBERGEN.

Hope Town, town (pop. c.2,631), E central Cape Prov., Republic of South Africa. Site of diamond discovery 1867.

Hopewell. 1 Borough (pop. 1,928), W central N.J., N of Trenton; settled before 1700. John Hart lived here. C. A. Lindbergh's nearby home was deeded to state 1941. **2** Industrial city (pop. 17,895), SE Va., at junction of James and Appomattox rivers; founded 1913 as munitions center. City Point (settled 1613; annexed 1926) was Grant's base of operations 1864–65. John Randolph was born here. U.S. Fort Lee is nearby.

Hophni (hŏf'nī), wicked son of Eli. See PHINEHAS.

Hopi Indians (hō'pē), tribe of Pueblo Indians, formerly called Moki, or Moqui. Almost all speak Hopi language (Azteco-Tannoan stock). They live in pueblos, practice sedentary farming (corn, beans, squash), with irrigation. The highly developed Hopi culture is typical of Southwest Indians. See LANGUAGE (table).

Hopkins, B. Smith, 1873–1952, American chemist. An expert on rare earths, he discovered, with others, the element illinium, now called PROMETHEUM.

Hopkins, Sir Frederick Gowland, 1861–1947, English biochemist. Shared 1929 Nobel Prize in Physiology and Medicine for pioneer work on vitamins. Authority on carbohydrate metabolism and muscular activity.

Hopkins, Gerard Manley, 1844–89, English poet. Followed Newman into Roman Catholicism, and became a Jesuit. By his own wish, his poetry was unpublished in his lifetime; his *Poems* (1918) were edited by his friend Robert Bridges. A relatively small body of work, his poetry is distinguished for innovations in prosody and intense use of language.

Hopkins, Harry (Lloyd), 1890–1946, American public official. Intimate friend of Pres. F. D. Roosevelt, held high posts as his special assistant.

Hopkins, Johns, 1795–1873, American financier and philanthropist. In 1867 he founded a free hospital and Johns Hopkins Univ. (opened 1876) at Baltimore.

Hopkins, Mark, 1802–87, American educator. He was professor of philosophy at Williams until his death and president of the college from 1836 to 1872. He was also president of American Board of Commissioners for Foreign Missions, 1857–87.

Hopkins, Samuel, 1721–1803, New England clergyman and theologian. He adopted doctrine of Jonathan Edwards as basis of his own, called Hopkinsianism.

Hopkins, Stephen, 1707–85, colonial governor of R.I., American Revolutionary patriot, signer of Declaration of Independence. Governor for nine years between 1755 and 1768.

Hopkins, city (1965 pop. 12,187), SE Minn., suburb SW of Minneapolis, in truck-farm and fruitgrowing (raspberries) region; settled 1853.

Hopkinson, Francis, 1737–91, American writer and musician, signer of Declaration of Independence. Considered first native American composer. Wrote political satires.

Hopkinsville, city (pop. 19,465), SW Ky., WSW of Bowling Green. Important tobacco and livestock market. Jefferson Davis Memorial Park is nearby.

Hopkinton. 1 Town (pop. 4,932), E Mass., WSW of Boston; settled 1715. **2** Rural town (1965 pop. 4,674), SW R.I. Includes villages of Ashaway and Hopkinton.

Hoppe, William Frederick (Willie Hoppe) (hŏ'pē), 1887–1959, American billiards champion. Probably greatest player in game's history. Held world three-cushion title (1936, 1940–44, 1947–52).

Hopper, DeWolf, 1858–1935, American singer and comedian. Made debut in 1879 and thereafter was popular in musicals and light opera. First recited "Casey at the Bat" in 1888.

Hopper, Edward, 1882–1967, American painter of the American scene. Used light with sharp effect.

Hoppe-Seyler, Felix (fä'lĭks hŏ'pŭ-zī'lŭr), 1825–95, German physiological chemist; taught at universities of Tübingen and Strasbourg. Noted for studies of hemoglobin, chlorophyll, and metabolism. First to prepare pure lecithin.

Hoppner, John, 1758–1810, English portrait painter, known for idealized portraits of women and children. Was a protégé of George III.

hops: see HOP.

Hoquiam (hŏ'kwĕŭm), city (pop. 10,762), W Wash., on Grays Harbor WNW of ABERDEEN; settled 1859.

Hor, unlocated mountain, on the boundary of Edom, scene of Aaron's death. Num. 20. Identified with Jebel Harun, c.4,383 ft., in SW Jordan, but it does not correspond with biblical description. The Hor of Num. 34.7 is probably Mt. Hermon.

Horace (Quintus Horatius Flaccus), 65 B.C.–8 B.C., Latin lyric poet. Vergil introduced him to MAECENAS, who became his patron. His *Satires* and *Epodes* (35–29 B.C.) established him as leading lyric poet in Rome. The *Odes, Epistles,* and *Ars Poetica,* products of his mature years at Sabine farm, display his mastery of phrase and poetic form. His verse, though it owes something to the Greek Archilochus, reflects an emancipated Roman cultivation of the arts and the true spirit of the Augustan age. His humor, good form, and polish influenced lyrical and satirical English poetry.

Horae (hŏ'rē), in Greek and Roman religion, goddesses of the seasons (usually three); daughters of Zeus and Themis. They were Irene (īrē'nē), Peace; Dice (dī'sē), Justice; and Eunomeia (ūnŏ'mēŭ), Order.

Horatius (hŏrā'shŭs), legendary Roman hero. He and two companions held Lars Porsena's Etruscan army at bay while the Romans cut down the Sublician Bridge to protect the city. He then swam the Tiber safely and was given as much land as he could plow around in a day.

Hordaland (hôr'dälän"), province (6,125 sq. mi.; pop. 223,119), SW Norway. Comprises the Hardanger Fjord region. One of the favored tourist areas of Norway.

Horeb (hŏ'rĕb), mountain, another name for Mt. SINAI. Ex. 3.1; 17.6; 33.6; Deut. 1.6, 19; 4.10, 15.

horehound, aromatic Old World perennial herb (*Marrubium vulgare*) with woolly-white foliage. Used to make horehound candy and cough and cold remedies.

Horemheb: see HARMHAB.

hormone: see GLAND.

Hormuz (hôr'mŭz") or **Ormuz,** island, off S Iran, in Strait of Hormuz between Persian Gulf and Gulf of Oman. Town of Hormuz moved here from mainland c.1300. Was center of trade with India and China. Fell to Portuguese under Afonso de Albu-

querque 1507. Recaptured 1622 by Persians with British aid.

Horn, Philip de Montmorency, count of: see HOORN.

horn, in biology, organ projecting from head of animal and used chiefly in offense and defense. Three main types among mammals: hollow, permanent, un-branched horns, each horn overlying a bone core growing on skull (as in cattle, sheep, buffalo, musk oxen, Old World antelopes, related animals); branched horns or antlers of DEER family composed of bone and usually shed annually; and that of the PRONGHORN, with characteristics of both bovine and deer types. Rhinoceros horns derive entirely from epidermis of skin of snout; probably are modified hairs. Craftsmen use horn to make many useful articles (e.g., knife handles, brush handles).

horn, in music: see WIND INSTRUMENTS.

Horn, Cape, headland, 1,391 ft. high, S Chile, most southerly point of South America, in archipelago of Tierra del Fuego. Discovered and first rounded by Willem Schouten in 1616.

hornbeam, deciduous tree of genus *Carpinus* native to N Hemisphere. American hornbeam, blue beech, or ironwood (*Carpinus caroliniana*) has strong wood used for tool handles, etc. The hop hornbeam (*Ostrya virginiana*), also called ironwood, and of same family, has wood of similar strength and value.

horned toad, lizard, several species of which live in deserts of SW U.S. and Mexico. Body (3–5 in. long) is broad and flattened, the tail short and thin, and the legs short. Spines are on the head; some scales on sides and back are sharp. It is protectively colored, usually dull grays and browns.

Hornell, city (pop. 13,907), SW N.Y., on Canisteo R., WNW of Elmira; settled 1790. Railroad shops. ALFRED UNIVERSITY is nearby.

hornet: see WASP.

Horney, Karen (hôr'nī), 1885–1952, American psychiatrist, b. Germany. She was founder (1941) and dean of American Inst. of Psychoanalysis. She modified orthodox Freudian analysis by emphasis on social factors, holding that environmental disturbances cause "basic anxiety" that forces individual to meet problems by responding with neurotic behavior (neurotic because rigid and compulsive).

Hornsby, Rogers, 1896–1963, American baseball player and manager. Had .358 lifetime batting average in 19 major-league seasons, hit (1924) .424, a 20th-cent. major-league record, was Natl. League batting champion seven times.

horoscope: see ASTROLOGY.

Horowitz, Vladimir (hŏ'rōwĭts), 1904–, Russian-American pianist, known for his technical virtuosity; son-in-law of Toscanini. Made his American debut in 1928 with the New York Philharmonic.

Horsa: see HENGIST AND HORSA.

horse. The horse family (Equidae) is now represented by only one genus (*Equus*) which includes the horse, ASS, ZEBRA, ONAGER, and QUAGGA (extinct from 1872). Evolution of the horse from its tiny primitive ancestor (*Eohippus*) occurred in North America, whence it reached the Old World over a now vanished land bridge. Horses became extinct in America about the time the Indians arrived. One of the last animals to be domesticated, the horse was probably first tamed by central Asian nomads. First used in hunting and war, it did not supersede the ox for farm work until the 19th cent. Modern draft horses owe much of their quality to the breeding of heavy chargers in the Middle Ages. The Belgian has replaced the Percheron as chief draft breed in America. The Arabian breed has the longest history; it and the thoroughbred are primarily saddle horses. All wild horses now living, except the TARPAN, are descended from tame horses.

Horse Cave, tourist town (pop. 1,780), S central Ky., just E of Mammoth Cave Natl. Park. Hidden River Cave lies under part of town.

horse chestnut, deciduous tree (*Aesculus hippocastanum*) of Mediterranean region, widely planted for ornament and shade. It has pyramidal clusters of white or salmon flowers and nonedible chestnutlike fruits.

horsefly, large, swift, hairy fly of family Tabanidae, a common pest of stock and sometimes of humans. Male sucks flower nectar; female sucks blood as well. Some transmit disease. In North America are nearly 200 species of genus *Tabanus.* Genus *Chrysops* includes smaller horseflies; some attack man. Eggs are laid on plants or stones close to water.

horse latitudes, two belts of calms (with generally fair weather) between trade winds and prevailing westerlies; about 35° N and 30° S. See CLIMATE.

horsepower, unit of power (rate of doing work) originated by James Watt. He determined experimentally that a horse can do work equal to 33,000 foot-pounds per minute; this unit is now standard in computing power generated by an engine.

horse-radish, perennial herb (*Armoracia lapathifolia*) native to S and central Europe and naturalized in North America. The grated roots are mixed with vinegar to make a sharp sauce for meats and sea food.

Horseshoe Bend, turn on Tallapossa R., near Dadeville, Ala., site of battle on March 27, 1814, in which Creek Indians were defeated by troops of Andrew Jackson. Defeat broke Indians' power. Horseshoe Bend Natl. Military Park is located here.

horseshoe crab: see KING CRAB.

horsetail, perennial rushlike plants of genus *Equisetum,* related to ferns and club mosses. They have jointed hollow stems and small scaly leaves.

Horsley, Samuel, 1733–1806, English bishop and scientist, particularly remembered for controversy (c.1783–1790) with Joseph Priestley concerning doctrine of Christ's incarnation.

Horta, Victor, 1861–1947, Belgian architect. Initiated a new architectural mode with use of ART NOUVEAU ornament and frank use of metal structure.

Horta (hôr'tù), city (pop. 7,250), cap. of Horta dist., Portugal, on Fayal isl., one of Azores.

Horthy (de Nagybanya), Nicholas (hôr'tē dù nŏ'dyùbä'-nyō), Hung. *Nagybányai Horthy Miklós,* 1868–1957, Hungarian admiral and statesman. Headed counterrevolutionary forces during Bela KUN regime; was regent of HUNGARY 1920–44. Forced by Germans to resign after trying to reach armistice with Russia, he fled to Bavaria; died in Portugal.

horticulture, a branch of agr.; includes cultivation of ornamental plants, market gardening, fruit growing, landscape gardening. Known to prehistoric peoples and in civilizations of both East and West. Formal gardening developed first in irrigated regions of Orient. Crusaders disseminated in Europe many ideas gathered from Eastern gardens. Horticulture has become a complex science; the Dept. of Agr., state experiment stations, agr. colleges, and horticultural societies in the U.S. provide information.

Horus (hō'rùs), sun-god, one of great gods of EGYPTIAN RELIGION, often identified with Amon. A popular myth tells how he avenged death of father, Osiris, aided by his mother, ISIS, and the god Thoth.

Hosanna [perhaps Heb.,= save now. Ps. 118.25,26], word shouted in greeting to Jesus as He entered Jerusalem. Mat. 21.9,15; Mark 11.9,10; John 12.13. Used in Christian worship as joyous salutation.

Hosea (hōzē'ù) or **Osee** (ōsē'), book of Old Testament, written by prophet of 8th cent. B.C. Book contains allegory comparing the idolatrous Israel to a faithless woman; sermons against moral decadence; promise that after punishment will come redemption.

Hoshea (hōshē'ù). **1** See JOSHUA. **2** Died after 722 B.C., last king of Israel (c.730–722 B.C.). A vassal of king of Assyria, he rebelled. Assyrians captured Samaria and all Israel. 2 Kings 15.30; 17.

Hospitalers: see KNIGHTS HOSPITALERS.

Host, in Roman Catholic communion: see COMMUNION.

hostage (hŏ'stĭj), person delivered by a constituted authority to another as guarantee that some stated promise will be executed or some stated loyalty upheld. In the Middle Ages the practice of giving hostages for fulfillment of treaty obligations was common and was governed by a strict code of feudal honor; this practice was generally abandoned in the 18th cent. The fundamental idea was that the hostage might be killed if the obligation was not fulfilled. By extension the seizure of civilians in an occupied country is called taking of hostages. The practice has been known since early times. In Second World War the Germans used it ruthlessly in an attempt to put down resistance movements. Germans responsible for the massacre of such hostages were tried as war criminals.

Hostos, Eugenio María de (āōōhä'nyō märē'ä dā ō'stōs), 1839–1903, Latin American philosopher, sociologist, writer, and political and educational reformer, b. Puerto Rico.

hotbed: see COLD FRAME.

hothouse: see GREENHOUSE.

Hotin, Ukraine: see KHOTIN.

Hot Springs. 1 Resort city (pop. 28,337), SW central Ark.; in Ouachita Mts. SW of Little Rock; settled 1807. City almost entirely surrounds Hot Springs Natl. Park, with 47 hot mineral springs. **2** See TRUTH OR CONSEQUENCES, N.Mex. **3** City (pop. 4,493), SW S.Dak., near Cheyenne R. and Black hills, SSW of Rapid City; settled 1879–81. Health and tourist resort with hot sulfur springs. Nearby are Jewel Cave Natl. Monument (see NATIONAL PARKS AND MONUMENTS, table) and Wind Cave Natl. Park (see BLACK HILLS). Angostura Dam is nearby. **4** Famous resort, western Va., SSW of Warm Springs, in a valley of Allegheny Mts.

Hot Springs National Park: see HOT SPRINGS, Ark.

Hotspur: see PERCY, SIR HENRY.

Hottentot bread: see ELEPHANT'S FOOT.

Hottentots (hŏ'tùntōts"), people of S and SW Africa numbering c.24,000 and resembling the Bushmen in language and physical type. They were forced into the interior by Dutch. Economy based on herding with some farming and metallurgy.

Hötzendorf, Franz Conrad von: see CONRAD VON HÖTZENDORF, FRANZ, GRAF.

Houbraken, Arnold (är'nŏlt hou'bra"kùn), 1660–1719, Dutch painter, etcher and author of *The Great Theater of Dutch Painters* (3 vols.; 1718, 1719, 1721).

Houdin, Jean Eugène Robert (zhä' ûzhĕn' rōbĕr' ōōdē'), 1805–71, French conjurer and magician. He was noted for his optical illusions and for fact that he made no claim that his devices were supernatural.

Houdini, Harry (hōōdē'nē), 1874–1926, American magician and writer. Born Erich Weiss, he took his stage name after the French magician Houdin. He was world famed for escapes from bonds and noted for his exposure of fraudulent mediums and their phenomena.

Houdon, Jean Antoine (zhä' ätwän' ōōdō'), 1741–1828, French neoclassic sculptor, famous for his portrait sculptures, which included Catherine II of Russia, George Washington, Jefferson, Franklin, Lafayette, and Voltaire.

Houghton, Richard Monckton Milnes, 1st Baron (hô'tùn, hou'-), 1809–85, English author, philanthropist, and patron of letters.

Houghton (hô'tùn), village (pop. 3,393), extreme N Mich., Keweenaw peninsula, on Portage Lake Ship Canal opposite Hancock (connected by bridge); settled 1851. Shipping, distributing, and industrial center in heart of L. Superior copper-mining region. Michigan Technological Univ. and mainland hq. of Isle Royale Natl. Park are here.

Hougue, La, France: see HOGUE, LA.

Houma (hō'mù), city (pop. 22,561), SE La., on Bayou Terrebonne SW of New Orleans, in sugarcane and oil area; founded 1834. Port on Intracoastal Waterway processing seafood.

Hounslow, London borough since 1965 (pop. 208,170); includes former municipal boroughs of Brentford and Chiswick and Heston and Isleworth, and urban district of Feltham.

Houphouët-Boigny, Felix (fäleks' ōōfwä' bwä'nyē), 1905–, president of Republic of the Ivory Coast (1960–). A medical doctor, he helped draft (1956) law which estab. political autonomy throughout the French Union. The first African to become a French minister of state (1957), he returned to Ivory Coast in 1959 to head government.

Housatonic (hōōsŭtŏn'ĭk), river rising in the Berkshires, W Mass., and flowing c.130 mi. S through Conn. to Long Isl. Sound at Stratford.

House, E(dward) M(andell), 1858–1938, American statesman. Col. House (a Texas state title) was a confidant of Pres. Woodrow Wilson. Helped to draft Treaty of Versailles, particularly concerned with drawing up of Covenant of the League of Nations.

housefly, common name of *Musca domestica*, found over most of world. It visits excrement and other filth and transports bacteria, protozoa of many diseases (typhoid fever, cholera, dysentery) in its digestive system, on hairy body, and sticky foot pads. Breeds in manure and other decaying organic matter; larvae are white maggots. It ejects a liquefying material on food before eating it.

House of Commons: see PARLIAMENT; WESTMINSTER PALACE.

House of David: see BENTON HARBOR, Mich.

House of Lords: see PARLIAMENT; WESTMINSTER PALACE.

House of Representatives: see CONGRESS OF THE UNITED STATES.

Houses of Parliament: see WESTMINSTER PALACE.

housing, the living accommodations provided for people in a community. Housing for workers during Industrial Revolution was constructed by employers on a profit basis. First housing legislation in U.S. was N.Y. tenement house law of 1867. Government housing began in First World War. Housing shortages in Europe in '20s resulted in government construction of workers' apartments. In England the GARDEN CITY was developed. In 1934, the U.S. set up the Federal Housing Administration to insure private loans and mortgages; in 1937 the U.S. Housing Authority was established. Government aid to housing was greatly extended by Housing Act of 1961. Underdeveloped nations are now undergoing shortages of urban housing.

Housing and Urban Development, United States Department of, estab. 1965. Incorporated programs of Federal Housing and Home Finance and Renewal Projects administrations. Aim is to provide long-range solutions to urban and suburban problems (e.g., slums, pollution). Robert C. Weaver was appointed first secretary.

Housman, A(lfred) E(dward), 1859–1936, English poet. A classical scholar, he edited Manilius, Juvenal, and Lucan. He is best known for his poems (e.g., in *A Shropshire Lad*, 1896), including "When I Was One and Twenty" and "Loveliest of Trees." His brother, **Laurence Housman**, 1865–1959, author and artist, is known for *Victoria Regina* (1934), dramatic biography compiled from his play cycle *Palace Plays*.

Houssay, Bernardo Alberto (bĕrnär'dhō älbĕr'tō ou'sī), 1887–, Argentine physiologist. Shared 1947 Nobel Prize in Physiology and Medicine for demonstrating role of pituitary secretion in inhibiting body's use of insulin.

Houston, Sam(uel) (hū'stŭn), 1793–1863, American frontier hero and statesman of Texas. Commanding Texas revolutionary troops, he captured Santa Anna at battle of SAN JACINTO (April 21, 1836). First president of Texas republic 1836–38; again president 1841–44. U.S. Senator 1846–59. Governor of Texas 1859–61; his refusal to join the Confederacy brought about his removal.

Houston (hū'stŭn), city (pop. 938,219), S Texas, on Gulf Coast plain NW of Galveston Bay. Harrisburg (now part of Houston) settled 1823; Houston found-

ed 1836. Cap. of Texas republic 1837–39. Grew in 19th cent. as rail and shipping center. Great expansion came with ship canal (1912–14; making it deep-water port) and development of Gulf Coast oil fields. One of main U.S. ports and largest city in South. Shipbuilding, wholesale trade, and mfg. of steel, oil-field machinery and tools, chemicals, paper. The Natl. Aeronautics and Space Administration's Manned Spacecraft Center is here for spacecraft development and astronaut training. Seat of RICE UNIVERSITY, Univ. of Houston, Texas Southern Univ., Univ. of St. Thomas, and dental school of Univ. of Texas; PRAIRIE VIEW AGRICULTURAL AND MECHANICAL COLLEGE OF TEXAS is nearby. Has Houston Symphony Orchestra, Mus. of Fine Arts, and domed stadium. Battlefield of SAN JACINTO is nearby.

Hovenweep National Monument: see NATIONAL PARKS AND MONUMENTS (table).

hovercraft: see AIR-CUSHION VEHICLE.

Hovey, Richard (hŭ'vē), 1864–1900, American poet, author of *Songs from Vagabondia* (1894; with Bliss Carman).

Howard, British noble family. First called Hereward, their career in England goes back to 10th cent. A Hereward fought against William I. His descendants were created earls of Arundel (1139), Barons Maltravers (1330), earls of Surrey and dukes of Norfolk (1483), Barons Fitzalan (1627), earls of Norfolk (1644), and Barons Herries (1884). **John Howard, 1st duke of Norfolk**, 1430?–85, adherent of the house of York in the Wars of the Roses, was killed at Bosworth fighting for Richard III. His son, **Thomas Howard, 2d duke of Norfolk**, 1443–1524, was imprisoned after Bosworth but released by Henry VII. Arranged the marriage of Margaret Tudor and James IV of Scotland. Became leading general of England and defeated (1513) the Scots at Flodden. He is the ancestor of all the living Howards in the main line. His son, **Thomas Howard, 3d duke of Norfolk**, 1473–1554, bitterly opposed Cardinal Wolsey. Supported the marriage of his niece, Anne Boleyn, to Henry VIII but later presided at her trial and execution. Remained Catholic although he conducted campaign against Pilgrimage of Grace in 1536. Accused of treason (1546), he was saved by death of Henry. Mary I released him (1553) and he led campaign against Wyatt's rebellion. His power had waned since the execution of his niece, **Catherine Howard**, 1521?–1542, queen of England, fifth wife of Henry VIII. Married in 1540, she was accused (1541) of immoral conduct and confessed. Beheaded largely to rid Henry of Howard family influence. **Henry Howard, earl of Surrey**, c.1517–1547, was the son of the 3d duke of Norfolk. A poet, he introduced new forms (chiefly blank verse) into English poetry. Arrested with his father on questionable treason charges, he was beheaded. His son, **Thomas Howard, 4th duke of Norfolk**, 1536–72, was favored by Elizabeth but jealous of the earl of Leicester. Became a candidate for the hand of Mary Queen of Scots and aroused Elizabeth's suspicions. Imprisoned (1569–70), he became involved in a Spanish plot on his release and was beheaded. His brother, **Henry Howard, earl of Northampton**, 1540–1614, was a courtier known for his great learning and lack of principle in public life. His cousin, **Charles Howard, 1st earl of Nottingham**, 1536–1624, was lord high admiral of England and commanded (1588) the forces against the Spanish Armada. **Thomas Howard, 1st earl of Suffolk**, 1561–1626, was son of the 4th duke of Norfolk. Commanded squadron that attacked Spanish treasure fleet in 1591. Became lord high treasurer in 1614. His daughter, Frances, and her husband, the earl of Somerset, were tried (1615) and convicted of the murder of Sir Thomas Overbury. Convicted (1619) of fraud and embezzlement as treasurer, Suffolk never regained power. **William Howard, 1st Viscount Stafford**, 1612–80, was the son of Thomas Howard, 2d earl of ARUNDEL. Falsely accused at the time of Popish Plot, he was convicted on false testimony of Titus Oates and others and beheaded. Other prominent Howards have included **Charles Howard, 1st earl of Carlisle,** 1629–85; **Frederick Howard, 5th earl of Carlisle,** 1748–1825, viceroy of Ireland and guardian of Lord Byron; and **Esme William Howard, 1st Baron Howard of Penrith,** 1863–1939, ambassador to U.S. 1924–30. Present head of the family is **Bernard Marmaduke Fitzalan-Howard,** 1908–, 16th duke of Norfolk, premier duke of the kingdom and hereditary earl marshal of England.

Howard, Bronson, 1842–1908, American dramatist. Among his plays are *Young Mrs. Winthrop* (1882; drama of social criticism), *The Henrietta* (1887; satire on American business), *Shenandoah* (1888; a Civil War play), and *Aristocracy* (1892).

Howard, Catherine; Charles, 1st earl of Carlisle; and **Charles, 1st earl of Nottingham:** see HOWARD, family.

Howard, Sir Ebenezer, 1850–1928, English town planner, chief founder of English garden-city movement.

Howard, Frederick, 5th earl of Carlisle: see HOWARD, family.

Howard, Henry, earl of Northampton; Henry, earl of Surrey; and **John, 1st duke of Norfolk:** see HOWARD, family.

Howard, Leland Ossian, 1857–1950, American entomologist. He profoundly influenced development of economic and medical entomology in America. Author of *The Insect Menace* (1931) and other works.

Howard, Oliver Otis, 1830–1909, Union general in Civil War. Fought in East from Bull Run through Gettysburg campaign. Commanded Army of the Tennessee in W. T. Sherman's march to sea. Advocate of Negro betterment, chief commissioner of the Freedmen's Bureau (1865–72), a founder of Howard Univ. and its president (1869–73).

Howard, Sidney (Coe), 1891–1939, American dramatist, author of *They Knew What They Wanted* (1924), *The Silver Cord* (1926), *Yellow Jack* (1934).

Howard, Thomas, dukes of Norfolk; Thomas, 1st earl of Suffolk; and **William, 1st Viscount Stafford:** see HOWARD, family.

Howard of Penrith, Esme William Howard, 1st Baron: see HOWARD, family.

Howard University, at Washington, D.C.; Federal support; coed.; founded 1867 by Gen. O. O. HOWARD of Freedmen's Bureau.

Howe, Elias, 1819–67, American inventor. He obtained (1846) first patent on a lock-stitch sewing machine.

Howe, Joseph, 1804–73, Canadian journalist and statesman. In 1828 he became editor of the *Novascotian,* which became leading journal of the province. Campaigned for responsible government, but opposed confederation. Premier of N.S. (1860–63).

Howe, Julia Ward, 1819–1910, American author. Espoused reforms—abolition, woman suffrage, and world peace. Wrote *The Battle Hymn of the Republic.* Also aided her husband, **Samuel Gridley Howe,** 1801–76, reformer and philanthropist. He organized New England Asylum for the Blind (now Perkins Institution and Massachusetts School for the Blind) and headed it for 44 years.

Howe, Richard Howe, Earl, 1726–99, British admiral. Defended English channel in Seven Years War. Commanded (1776–78) British fleet in American Revolution. Best known for victory over the French in 1794. His brother, **William Howe, 5th Viscount Howe,** 1729–1814, was a British general in American Revolution. Succeeded Gen. Thomas Gage as commander in chief (Oct., 1775). Commanded in successful battle of Long Island; defeated Washington at BRANDYWINE. Resigned 1778.

Howe, Samuel Gridley: see HOWE, JULIA WARD.

Howe, William Howe, 5th Viscount: see HOWE, RICHARD HOWE, EARL.

Howell, Francis Clark, 1908–, American anthropologist, authority on evolution of man and on pleistocene ecology.

Howell, William Henry, 1860–1945, American physiologist, authority on blood clotting and nerve fibers, author of standard physiology textbook.

Howells, William Dean, 1837–1920, American novelist and critic. A printer, journalist, and biographer, he gained recognition with the first of many travel books, *Venetian Life* (1866), written after five years as consul in Venice. Later, as editor of the *Atlantic Monthly* and *Harper's Magazine* and in such books as *Criticism and Fiction* (1891), he championed realism. Friend and editor of Mark Twain, he sponsored younger realists such as Stephen Crane and Frank Norris. His own many novels included such famous examples of realism as *A Modern Instance* (1882) and *The Rise of Silas Lapham* (1885). Also wrote short stories, plays, and volumes of reminiscences, including valuable literary ones.

Howells, William White, 1908–, American anthropologist renowned for his work in human physical variation and fossil man.

howitzer, piece of heavy ARTILLERY, differing from gun in high trajectory of its fire.

Howland Island, area 73 sq. mi., central Pacific near equator. Discovered by American traders and claimed by U.S. 1842, with Jarvis Isl. and Baker Isl. Settled 1935 by Americans, placed under Dept. of Interior 1936. A stop on air route to Australia.

Howrah (hou'rä), city (pop. 433,630), West Bengal, India, on Hooghly R. opposite Calcutta. A great industrial center, it has textile, jute, glass, and steel mfg.

Hoxha, Enver (ĕn'vùr ôh'jä), 1908–, Albanian Communist leader. Headed anti-Italian resistance in Second World War. As premier (1946–54), he kept ties with USSR, but joined Peking in rift with Moscow in 1961.

Hoy, second largest of the ORKNEY ISLANDS.

hoya, tropical climbing shrub (*Hoya carnosa*) with thick leaves and fragrant white or pink flowers.

Hoyle, Edmond (hoil), 1672–1769, English writer on games. Codified rules of whist, quadrille, backgammon, piquet, others. "According to Hoyle" has come to mean the definitive word on games. Editions of his work are kept up to date.

Hoyle, Fred, 1915–, British astronomer, author, cosmologist. Discarded his long-held steady-state theory of the universe (universe does not change its over-all character or density with time) when extragalactic radio sources indicated that the universe has changed character and is less dense than previously thought ("big-bang" theory). Wrote *Galaxies, Nuclei, and Quasars* (1965).

Hradec Kralove (hrä'dĕts krä'lôvĕ), Czech *Hradec Králové,* Ger. *Königgrätz,* city (est. pop. 60,000), E Bohemia, Czechoslovakia, on the Elbe. Battle of SADOWA or Königgrätz was fought nearby (1866).

Hrdlicka, Ales (ä'lĕsh hŭrd'lĭchkä), 1869–1943, American anthropologist, b. Bohemia. He organized division of physical anthropology at U.S. Natl. Mus. Led many expeditions. Studied supposed migration tracks of American Indian in Siberia and Alaska.

Hroswitha or **Roswitha** (rōswĭ'thú, rôsvĕ'tä), c.935–c.1002, German Latin poet, a Benedictine nun at Gandersheim. Wrote lyrics; six saints' lives, notable for naïve charm and piety; and six morality plays, intended as antidote to Terence.

Hsia (shyä), earliest and semilegendary dynasty of China. Said to have ruled either from c.2205 to c.1766 B.C., or c.1994 to c.1523 B.C. Scanty archaeological remains suggest the people had the potter's wheel, bronze weapons, and war chariots. Hsia was succeeded by Shang, the first historic dynasty of China.

Hsüan-tsang (shü'ä'-tsäng) or **Hiouentang,** 605?–664, Chinese monk. Translated Buddhist scriptures after pilgrimage to India.

Hsüan-t'ung: see P'U-YI, HENRY.

huanaco: see GUANACO.

Huancayo (wän-kī'ō), city (pop. c.50,000; alt. c.11,000 ft.), S central Peru; agr. center.

Huang Ti (hwäng' dē'), c.2698–c.2597 B.C., Chinese cultural hero and legendary ruler. Regarded as first emperor of China. Also called Yellow Emperor or Golden Emperor.

Huáscar (wäs'kär), d. 1533, Inca of Peru; son of Huayna Capac. Shared empire with half brother, Atahualpa, who had him drowned.

Huayna Capac (wī'nä kä'päk), d. 1525, Inca of Peru, last of great emperors. His decision to divide his empire by leaving recently conquered kingdom of Quito to his favorite son, Atahualpa, and the rest to his legitimate heir, Huáscar, and the resultant war between them, weakened the Inca empire and made Francisco Pizarro's conquest easier.

Hubbard, Bernard Rosecrans, 1888–1962, American priest, scientist, and explorer. Became head of Univ. of Santa Clara geology department in 1926. Made many annual scientific expeditions to Alaska. Noted for lectures, films, and books.

Hubbard, Elbert, 1856–1915, American author. His Roycroft Shops and Press promoted handicrafts and bookmaking. Wrote *Little Journeys* to homes of the great and the inspirational *Message to Garcia* (1899).

Hubbell, Carl (Owen), 1903–, American baseball pitcher. Left-handed N.Y. Giant ace won 24 consecutive games in 1936–37 seasons, won 253 major-league games.

Hubble, Edwin Powell, 1899–1953, American astronomer; director of Mt. Wilson Observatory. His studies of extragalactic nebulae were major contributions. Among his many writings are *The Realm of Nebulae* (1936) and *The Observational Approach to Cosmology* (1937).

Hubert de Burgh (dù bûrg'), d. 1243, chief justiciar of England (1215–32) under John and Henry III. After Henry assumed power in 1227 trouble increased between Hubert and king whose foreign favorites opposed him. Tried to prevent (1230) expedition to France and resisted drain of money to papacy. In 1232 he was accused of disloyalty to crown and imprisoned. Was later reconciled with the king.

Hubertusburg, Peace of (hōōbĕr'tōōsbōōrk), 1763, treaty between Austria and Prussia, at end of Seven Years War, signed at Hubertusburg castle in Saxony. Prussia retained Silesia; Saxony was restored to prewar boundaries.

Huch, Ricarda (rēkär'dä hōōkh'), 1864–1947, German novelist. Her historical novel of the Thirty Years War, *Der grosse Krieg in Deutschland* (1912–14), ranks among the best of its kind.

Huchu (hōō'jōō'), city (pop. c.120,000), Tsinghai prov., China. Chief city of Huchu Autonomous Region.

huckleberry, North American shrub of genus *Gaylussacia* of heath family. Common huckleberry (*Gaylussacia baccata*) is valued for its black edible fruit, usually picked from wild plants. Evergreen box huckleberry (*G. brachycera*) is often cultivated.

Huddersfield, county borough (pop. 130,302), West Riding of Yorkshire, England. An important textile-milling center, it also has other mfg.

Hudibras: see BUTLER, SAMUEL (1612–80).

Hudson, Henry, fl. 1607–11, English navigator and explorer. Ascended Hudson R., establishing Dutch claims to region, later explored Hudson Bay for English, both while seeking Northwest Passage.

Hudson, W(illiam) H(enry), 1841–1922, English author and naturalist, b. Buenos Aires of American parents. Wrote romances laid in South America—*The Purple Land* (1885) and classic *Green Mansions* (1904). *Far Away and Long Ago* (1918) is autobiographic.

Hudson. 1 City (pop. 11,075), E N.Y., on E bank of Hudson R. (bridged to Catskill), S of Albany; settled 1662. **2** Residential village (pop. 2,438), NE Ohio, SE of Cleveland; settled 1799 by New Englanders. Boyhood home of John Brown. Western Reserve Academy is here.

Hudson, river, c.315 mi. long, rising in NE N.Y. in L. Tear of the Clouds near Mt. Marcy in the Adirondacks and flowing generally S, forming N.Y.-N.J. line for c.17 mi. near its mouth in Upper New York Bay. Port region is called North R. Chief tributary is Mohawk R. One of the world's important highways, the Hudson is linked to the Great Lakes, L. Champlain, and St. Lawrence R. by N.Y. State Barge Canal. Tidal to Albany, head of channel for ocean-going vessels; Troy is at head of 14-ft. channel. At New York city (max. width here 4,400 ft.) Holland and Lincoln tunnels, railroad tunnel, subways, ferries, and George Washington Bridge link N.Y. and N.J. Above New York city river widens at Tappan Zee. On W bank PALISADES stretch N from N.J. Catskill Mts. descend to Hudson Valley. First explored by Henry Hudson 1609. Major highway for Indians and early settlers. Has many historic, literary, and artistic associations.

Hudson Bay, great inland sea, 850 mi. long and 650 mi. wide, area c.475,000 sq. mi., E central Canada. Lies generally SE of Northwest Territories, to which bay and islands belong. Has important cod and salmon fisheries. CHURCHILL is chief port on bay, connected to interior by Hudson Bay RR. Among rivers draining into bay are the CHURCHILL, NELSON, ALBANY, Abitibi, and SEVERN. Hudson's Bay Co. posts estab. at the rivers' mouths. Bay open to navigation from mid-July to Oct. Discovered 1610 by Henry Hudson and named for him.

Hudson Bay Railway, part of Canadian Natl. Railways system, 510 mi. long, extending from The Pas, Man., to Churchill, Man., on W coast of Hudson Bay. Built 1910–29; designed to reduce rail and sea rates from grain-producing provinces to Liverpool.

Hudson River school, 1825–75, in American landscape painting. Influenced by European romanticism. So called because the artists classified with the school were attracted by scenic beauty of Hudson R. valley. Group included Thomas Doughty, Thomas Cole, Asher B. Durand, J. F. Kensett, Frederick Church, and George Inness.

Hudson's Bay Company. Organized 1668 by English merchants and courtiers to open fur trade with Indians in Hudson's Bay region of North America and to discover Northwest Passage to Orient. Permanent charter issued 1670. French contested claim to region; warfare ended with British in control. Company was harshly criticized in middle of 18th cent. for failure to discover Northwest Passage. NORTH WEST COMPANY became chief rival. RED RIVER SETTLEMENT scheme under earl of SELKIRK brought disaster to company. Amalgamation with North West Co. in 1821 marked beginning of period of true monopoly. Governorship (1821–56) of Sir George Simpson marked peak of company's fortune. Company territory transferred to Canada (1869) by governmental order for £300,000. In 20th cent. company expanded into retail trade and mfg. of all sorts. In 1930 Canadian stores were segregated in separate organization and London portion again turned to fur trade.

Hué (hwä), city (pop. c.113,000), former cap. of Annam, South Vietnam, on Hué R. near South China Sea. Port and trade center. Has palaces of Annamese kings and their tombs.

Huelva (wĕl'vä), city (pop. 78,388), cap. of Huelva prov., SW Spain, in Andalusia, on Odiel R. near Atlantic. Exports copper and sulfur from nearby Rio Tinto mines; ships cork; has large fisheries.

Huerta, Victoriano (vĕktōryä'nō hwĕr'tä), 1854–1916, Mexican general and president (1913–14). Served under Porfirio Díaz. After successful revolution of Madero (1911), Huerta supported him until 1913, then betrayed him and was made president. His sanguinary, tyrannical rule brought trouble with U.S. and revolutions led by Carranza, Villa, and Zapata, and he was forced to resign. Died in U.S.

Huesca (wä'skä), town (pop. 24,377), cap. of Huesca prov., NE Spain, in Aragon. Dates from Roman times. Residence of kings of Aragon 1096–1118. Has Gothic cathedral.

Hügel, Friedrich, Baron von (frē'drĭkh bärōn' fŭn hü'gŭl), 1852–1925, British Catholic philosopher, b. Florence. The independent thought in his writings, stressing inner security and moral responsibility, profoundly influenced modern Catholicism.

Huggins, Charles Brenton, 1901–, American cancer researcher. Shared 1966 Nobel Prize in Physiology and Medicine for discoveries in field of hormonal treatment of prostatic cancer.

Huggins, Sir William, 1824–1910, English astronomer, pioneer in spectroscopic analysis of stars and in spectroscopic celestial photography.

Hugh Capet (kā'pĭt, kā'pĕt), c.938–996, king of France (987–96); son of HUGH THE GREAT and first of the CAPETIANS. He succeeded LOUIS V and was followed by his son ROBERT II (the Pious).

Hughes, Charles Evans, 1862–1948, American jurist and statesman. Governor of N.Y. (1907–10) and Associate Justice of U.S. Supreme Court (1910–16). Lost 1916 presidential election to Wilson in very close contest. Was U.S. Secy. of State (1921–25) and Chief Justice of the United States (1930–41).

Hughes, Howard Robard, 1869–1924, American inventor. Devised widely used, cone-shaped, oil-drilling bit.

Hughes, John Joseph, 1797–1864, American Roman Catholic clergyman; bishop coadjutor (after 1838), bishop (after 1842), and first archbishop (after 1850) of New York.

Hughes, (James) Langston, 1902–67, American Negro poet. His lyrics and songs (e.g., *The Weary Blues,* 1926; *Selected Poems,* 1959; *The Panther and the Leash,* 1967), dramas, and fiction deal with Negro problems. He was spokesman for the American Negro in his autobiographical *I Wonder as I Wander* (1956) and in *Fight for Freedom: the Story of the NAACP* (1962).

Hughes, Richard, 1900–, English writer, best known for his novel of macabre fantasy, *High Wind in Jamaica* (1929). He has also written plays, poems, short stories, and other novels (e.g., *The Fox in the Attic,* 1961).

Hughes, Thomas, 1822–96, English author of the classic of school life, *Tom Brown's School Days* (1857), which idealizes Dr. Thomas Arnold of Rugby.

Hugh le Despenser: see DESPENSER, HUGH LE.

Hugh of Lincoln, Saint, d. 1200, bishop of Lincoln (1186–1200), b. Burgundy. Spokesman of the barons (1198) in their refusal of money to Richard I, he was also in conflict with John. Noted for charity, love of the poor, and holiness. Partially rebuilt Lincoln Cathedral. Feast: Nov. 17.

Hugh of Saint Victor, 1096–1141, French or German scholastic philosopher. Headed school of the monastery of St. Victor, Paris, after 1133 and made it a center of learning and of opposition to the teachings of Abelard. Hugh himself wrote learned theological works (notably one on the sacraments) and also works on mysticism. Also Hugo.

Hugh the Great, d. 956, French duke; son of King Robert I, father of HUGH CAPET. Waived succession in favor of RAOUL; placed LOUIS IV on French throne (936), later quarreled with him; virtually ruled France after 954.

Hugo, Victor (Fr. vēktôr' ügō'), 1802–85, French poet, dramatist, and novelist. The preface to his drama *Cromwell* (1827) and the production of the tragedy *Hernani* (1830), which caused a riot, placed him at the head of the romanticists. Other plays include *Le Roi s'amuse* (1832; basis of Verdi's *Rigoletto*) and *Ruy Blas* (1838). After the tragic death of his daughter (1843), his poetry turned from the lush romanticism of earlier collections such as *Les Orientales* (1829) to the philosophic content of *Les Contemplations* (1856). Though created peer and viscount under Louis Philippe, Hugo soon turned to republicanism and ardently advocated reform. He opposed Napoleon III, fled

abroad in 1851, and took residence in Jersey (till 1855), then in Guernsey till Napoleon's fall in 1870, when he returned to Paris in triumph. In the poems of *Les Châtiments* (1853) he vituperated Napoleon III. *La Légende des siècles* (1859) is an epic evocation of history. Hugo's great novels are *Notre Dame de Paris* (1831), *Les Misérables* (1862), and *Toilers of the Sea* (1866), on which his popularity in the English-speaking world is founded.

Huguenots (hū'gŭnŏts), the Calvinist Protestants of France. Presbyterian church was founded in France at synod of 1559 and gained many followers among all classes. After the Wars of RELIGION (1562–98), Henry IV promulgated the Edict of NANTES, which gave the Huguenots complete toleration and estab. Protestantism in 200 towns. Cardinal RICHELIEU used an uprising (1621–22) against the introduction of Catholicism into Béarn as a pretext for depriving the Huguenots of all their strongholds save La Rochelle and Montauban. Another Protestant uprising (1625) led to the capture of La Rochelle by Richelieu (1628) and to the peace of Alais (1629), which stripped the Huguenots of all political power. Mounting persecution of Protestants under Louis XIV culminated in 1685 with the revocation of the Edict of Nantes. Countless Huguenots fled to England, Holland, Germany, Switzerland, and America, where they contributed substantially to civic and industrial life. In the Cévennes, the Protestant CAMISARDS long fought Louis XIV's troops (1702–10).

Huhehot, city (pop. c.314,000), cap. of Inner Mongolian Autonomous Region, NW China. Transportation and trade center. Seat of the Living Buddha until 1664. Called Kweisui prior to 1954.

Huitzilopochtli (wē"tsēlōpŏcht'lē), Aztec god of war. Human beings, especially prisoners of war, were sacrificed to him at the splendid temple of Tenochtitlán.

Huizinga, Johan (yōhän' hoi'zĭngù), 1872–1945, Dutch historian. Noted for work in cultural history of late Middle Ages, the Renaissance, and the Reformation.

Hulagu Khan (hōōlä'gōō khän'), 1217–65, Mongol conqueror; grandson of Jenghiz Khan. Sacked Baghdad 1258, but westward move was checked 1260 by Mamelukes of Egypt. His Persian khanate lasted until 1335.

Hull, Cordell, 1871–1955, U.S. Congressman (1907–21, 1923–31), Senator (1931–33), and Secretary of State (1933–44). Author of one of the first Federal income tax laws (1913) and early backer of F. D. Roosevelt. As Secy. of State consistently pursued a course making for sound international economic relations and constructive good will toward nonaggressor nations. Awarded 1945 Nobel Peace Prize.

Hull, Robert (Bobby Hull), 1939–, Canadian hockey player. Set record in 1965–66 season with Chicago Blackhawks for most goals scored in a season (54).

Hull, William, 1753–1825, American general. In command of Detroit in War of 1812, he lost it to British on Aug. 16, 1812. Court-martialed, he was saved from execution only by his Revolutionary War record.

Hull, city (pop. 56,929), SW Que., Canada, on Ottawa R.; part of city of Ottawa metropolitan center. Paper, pulp, and lumber mills; iron foundries; hydroelectric power station.

Hull, officially **Kingston-upon-Hull,** county borough (pop. 303,268), East Riding of Yorkshire, England, on the Humber. One of chief ports for Yorkshire and Lancashire, it also has extensive mfg. There are steamship lines to the Continent. It is an ocean fishing base. Town has several museums, grammar school (founded 1486), University Col., and Trinity House (estab. 1369, for sailors).

Hull House: see ADDAMS, JANE.

humanism, movement in thought in the Renaissance, characterized chiefly by a revolt against medieval religious authority and attitudes and a great spread of classical learning. The rediscovery of Greek and Latin works was a main preoccupation of scholars, and the classic secular (humanistic) attitudes were generally adopted. The new learning more or less coincided with the religious upheaval of the Reformation, and many humanists became Protestants, though others clung to the old religion. The humanists formed a sort of intellectual community, which continued from the 14th cent. until shattered by the religious struggle in the late 16th cent.; numbered among them were such men as Boccaccio, Petrarch, Pico della Mirandola, Budé, the Scaligers, Reuchlin, Ulrich von Hutten, Erasmus, John Colet, and Sir Thomas More. The term *humanism* has been used for other later movements, most particularly in the 20th cent. by F. C. S. Schiller, Irving Babbitt, and C. F. Potter. Humanism in this cent. has also been applied to philosophies that make human capacity the measure of value, especially the Continental existential movement led by Jean Paul Sartre.

Human Rights, Commission on, division of the Economic and Social Council of the United Nations. Drew up Universal Declaration of Human Rights, adopted by UN 1948. Made drafts of covenant on human rights, but U.S. refused to sign, and dispute over economic and political rights ended in stalemate.

Humayun or **Homayun** (both: hoōmä'yoōn), 1507–56, second MOGUL emperor of India (1530–56), son of BABER. Defeated by SHER KHAN in 1540, he sought refuge in Persia. Invaded India 1555 and reestab. Mogul authority. Succeeded by son AKBAR.

Humber, navigable estuary of Trent R. and Ouse R., on E coast of England. It is 40 mi. long and 1–8 mi. wide. Encroachment of sea has destroyed former ports. Hull and Grimsby are chief cities.

Humbert, kings of Italy. **Humbert I,** 1844–1900, reigned 1878–1900. Was assassinated. **Humbert II,** 1904–, received royal prerogatives of the realm 1944, succeeded his father Victor Emmanuel III on his abdication (1946). Referendum of 1946 estab. republic, and Humbert went into exile.

Humboldt, Alexander, Freiherr von (äleksän'dŭr frī'hĕr fün hoōm'bŏlt), 1769–1859, German explorer, scientist, and natural philosopher. His expedition to Cuba, Central and South America (1799–1804), noted for systematic observations, initiated era of scientific exploration. Estab. use of isotherms. In his great work on natural science, *Cosmos* (5 vols., 1845–62), he sought to formulate known facts about universe into uniform conception of nature. His brother **Wilhelm, Freiherr von Humboldt** (vil'hĕlm), 1767–1835, was Prussian minister of education (1809–10), reformed school system, founded Univ. of Berlin. In 1819 he left government service in protest against reactionary regime. A friend of Goethe and Schiller, he also wrote a work on Kavi, the ancient language of Java, important in history of philology.

Humboldt, river rising in NE Nev. and flowing W and S c.300 mi. into Humboldt Sink near Humboldt Range. Named by J. C. Frémont, it was followed by Utah emigrants bound for Calif. Rye Patch Dam, completed 1936, serves Humboldt project around Lovelock.

Humboldt Bay, land-locked inlet of the Pacific, NW Calif. Eureka is on its S shore.

Humboldt Glacier, NW Greenland, largest known glacier. It debouches into Kane Basin. E. K. Kane discovered it on his expedition of 1853–55.

Hume, David (hūm), 1711–76, Scottish philosopher and historian. He pressed the analyses of Locke and Berkeley into a determined, thorough-going skepticism. He found in the mind nothing but a series of sensations and the cause-effect relation in the natural world as apparent only because two sensations were customarily joined. Rejecting the possibility of knowledge that is certain, he fell back on common sense and faith. His essays (e.g., *Treatise of Human Nature,* 1739–40; *Essays Moral and Political,* 1741–42; *Philosophical Essays,* 1748; *An Enquiry Concerning the Principles of Morals,* 1750; *Political Discourses,* 1752) are marked by the purity of literary style that

made his *History of England* (1754–62) long standard despite errors in fact. He was patron of Rousseau in his English exile, but later the two quarreled bitterly.

humidity, water vapor content of atmosphere, primary climatic element. Measured as absolute humidity (water vapor per unit volume of natural air); relative humidity (ratio of water vapor content to water vapor-holding capacity of air at a given temperature); specific humidity (water vapor per unit mass of natural air); and mixing ratio (water vapor per dry air unit mass). Hygrometer is used to measure humidity.

Hummelstown, agr. borough (pop. 4,474), SE Pa., E of Harrisburg; founded c.1740. Indian Echo Cave is nearby.

hummingbird, small perching bird of New World. Most of c.750 species and subspecies are native to Central and South America. They have brilliant plumage with a metallic sheen and long, slender, sometimes curved bills. In seeking insects and nectar of flowers they carry on cross pollination. Giant hummer of Andes (c.8½ in. long) is largest; smallest, Helena's hummingbird of Cuba (c.2½ in. long). See *ill.,* p. 118.

humour, according to anc. theory, one of four body fluids (blood, phlegm, black bile, and yellow bile) which control man's health and temperament. Hippocrates postulated that glands controlled the delicate balance of the humours; imbalance resulted in disease and pain. In literature, especially in comedies of Elizabethan and Renaissance periods, a humour character was one in whom a single passion predominated.

Humperdinck, Engelbert (hüm'pŭrdĭngk), 1854–1921, German composer and teacher. Apart from the opera *Die Königskinder,* he is known chiefly for his first opera, *Hansel and Gretel* (1893).

Humphrey, George M(agoffin), 1890–, U.S. Secretary of the Treasury (1953–57). President of M. A. Hanna Co., steel mfg. firm, Cleveland (1929–52).

Humphrey, Hubert (Horatio), 1911–, Vice President of the U.S. (1965–). U.S. Senator from Minn. 1949–64.

Humphreys, Andrew Atkinson, 1810–83, American army engineer, Union general in Civil War. Known for topographic and hydrographic survey of Mississippi delta (1850–61).

Humphreys, David, 1752–1818, American diplomat and poet. Active in U.S. service abroad. One of the CONNECTICUT WITS. His poetry is largely patriotic and didactic.

Humphreys, Joshua, 1751–1838, American ship designer, responsible in 1790s for successful frigates (*United States, Constitution,* and others).

Humphreys Peak: see SAN FRANCISCO PEAKS.

Hunan (hoō'nän'), province (c.79,000 sq. mi.; pop. c.34,296,029), S central China; cap. Changsha. Watered by Siang, Yuan, and Tzu rivers which drain through Tungting L. into Yangtze R. Rice is outstanding crop. Leading producer of antimony and mercury; gold, lead, zinc, tungsten, tin also mined. Timber and paper mills. Traditionally known as Siang. Since 1952 three autonomous reserves have been estab. for Yao and Miao peoples in the hills of W and S.

Hundred Days, March 20–June 28, 1815, period of attempt by NAPOLEON I to rebuild empire after return from Elba. See also WATERLOO CAMPAIGN.

Hundred Years War, 1337–1453, between England and France. Basic cause: the kings of England, who as dukes of GUIENNE were vassals of the French kings, opposed the centralizing policies of the French crown and showed increasing reluctance to do homage to France for their continental possessions. Contributing causes: claim of EDWARD III to the French crown as a grandson of Philip IV; territorial disputes between Edward and PHILIP VI of France; English-French rivalry in Flanders; Philip's support of Scotland against England. First phase of war (1337–60) began when Edward proclaimed himself king of France. Allied with the Flemings under Jacob van ARTEVELDE, he defeated the French navy at Sluis (1340); routed the French at CRÉCY (1346); took CALAIS (1347); and routed and captured JOHN II of France at Poitiers (1356). The Treaty of BRÉTIGNY (1360) gave England Calais and W and SW France. Second phase of war (1369–73) was brought on by the oppressive taxation of EDWARD THE BLACK PRINCE and resulted in the reconquest by DU GUESCLIN of most of the lost French territories. After a period of quiescence, HENRY V of England renewed the war in 1415. Victorious at AGINCOURT, he later won the alliance of PHILIP THE GOOD of Burgundy (1419) and in 1420, by the Treaty of TROYES, was recognized by Charles VI as regent and heir of France. The dauphin (later CHARLES VII) refused to accept his disinheritance, and desultory warfare recommenced after Charles VI's death (1422). By 1429 the English and Burgundians were masters of nearly all France N of the Loire, but in that year JOAN OF ARC appeared, relieved besieged ORLÉANS, defeated the English at Patay, and saw Charles VII crowned at Rheims. The tide turned, and in 1435, when by the Treaty of ARRAS Burgundy passed over to the French camp, the final phase of the war began. The French reconquered Paris (1436), Normandy (1449–50), and all Guienne but Bordeaux (1449–51). The capture of Bordeaux (1453) left only Calais in English hands. England, torn by the Wars of the Roses, made no attempt at reconquest and henceforth turned its interest to sea power rather than to expansion on the Continent. France, laid waste and reduced to anarchy by the war, recovered under Charles VII and Louis XI, who took advantage of the virtual destruction of the feudal class to rebuild a centralized monarchy. The Hundred Years War saw the transition from medieval to modern warfare (artillery) and from feudalism to the first awakening of national consciousness.

Hunedoara (hōōnädwä'rä), Hung. *Vajdahunyad*, city (est. pop. 49,087), W Central Rumania. Major industrial center with iron and steel industry.

Hungabee (hŭng'gŭbē), mountain, E B.C., in L. Louise district of Canadian Rockies; 11,305 ft. high. First climbed in 1903.

Hungarian language, Uralic language of the Ugric branch. See LANGUAGE (table).

Hungary, Hung. *Magyarország,* republic (35,912 sq. mi.; pop. c.10,055,000), SE Europe, in the Danubian plain; cap. Budapest. E of the Danube the Great Hungarian Plain (Hung. *Alföld*) extends beyond the border to the Carpathians; W of the Danube are the Little Alfold, with L. BALATON, and the Bakony, Vertes, and Mecsek mts. Present frontiers, except for minor changes in 1947, were estab. by Treaty of TRIANON (1920), which stripped Hungary of two thirds of former area (incl. its Adriatic coast). Though it has mineral resources (coal, manganese, bauxite, petroleum) and industrial concentrations (esp. at Budapest, Gyor, Miskolc), Hungary is predominantly agr. (wheat, maize, livestock, poultry, wine). Irrigation has reduced the former PUSZTA to a small area around Debrecen. Chief industrial products: textiles, machinery, metal products, chemicals. Population is c.68% Catholic, c.27% Protestant (mainly Calvinist). Part of the Roman provinces of Pannonia and Dacia, Hungary was later conquered by the Huns, Ostrogoths, Avars, and (9th cent.) MAGYARS. Magyar expansion in W was halted by Emperor Otto I at the Lechfeld (955). St. STEPHEN, first king of Hungary, completed the Magyars' Christianization. A feudal society came into being. The power of the magnates (great nobles), who were to play a major role until 1918, was only temporarily curbed by the Golden Bull of ANDREW II (1222). Hungary was occupied by the Mongols in 1241–42. In 1301 the ARPAD dynasty died out. The kingship was elective, but dynastic ties influenced the royal elections. Hungary was ruled after 1308 by the ANGEVIN dynasty and after 1386 by other foreign houses (mostly in personal union with Bohemia and Poland; see esp. JAGIELLO dynasty). The

double marriage treaty of 1515 (see ULADISLAUS II) prepared the advent of HAPSBURG rule in 1526. Medieval Hungary reached its zenith under LOUIS I (14th cent.) and under MATTHIAS CORVINUS (15th cent.), whose reign interrupted that of the Jagiellos. John HUNYADI successfully led the resistance against Turkish conquest, but the defeat and death of Louis II at MOHACS (1526) plunged Hungary into chaos. Ferdinand of Austria (see FERDINAND I, emperor) contested the succession with the Zapolya family (see JOHN, kings of Hungary), and in 1541 Turkey annexed most of the country. The resulting threefold partition of Hungary (confirmed by treaty, 1606) lasted until the reconquest of Turkish Hungary by the Hapsburgs after 1683: W Hungary remained under the Hapsburgs, who kept the royal title; central Hungary was a Turkish province; TRANSYLVANIA, ruled by its own princes, shifted its allegiance back and forth between the sultans and the emperors. By 1711, the rebellion of Francis II RAKOCZY having failed, all Hungary and Transylvania was firmly under Hapsburg control. Religious freedom had been guaranteed by the treaty of 1606 between BOCSKAY and the emperor. The peasantry, subjected to serfdom after its rebellion of 1514, was freed in 1781 by Emperor Joseph II. Magyar opposition to Hapsburg rule remained strong and flared up in the Revolution of 1848. The short-lived Hungarian republic (April–Aug., 1849) under KOSSUTH was put down by Austrian and Russian troops. Hungarian self-rule was abolished until 1867, when Hungary became a constitutional kingdom in personal union with Austria (see AUSTRO-HUNGARIAN MONARCHY). Except in CROATIA, which enjoyed some autonomy, the Slavic and Rumanian minorities (in SLOVAKIA, RUTHENIA, DALMATIA, and the BANAT OF TEMESVAR) were held in virtual subjection by Magyar nationalism. After the collapse of the Dual Monarchy in First World War, Hungary was proclaimed an independent republic (1918) and reduced by the Treaty of Trianon to its predominantly Magyar core. (Large Magyar minorities passed to Czechoslovakia, Rumania, and Yugoslavia.) The Communist dictatorship of Bela KUN (1919) was put down by Rumanian intervention, and in 1920 Hungary became a kingdom without a king, with Adm. HORTHY DE NAGYBANYA as regent. The authoritarian and reactionary regimes of premiers Bethlen and Gombos were tempered by the parliament but blocked a much-needed agrarian reform. Hungarian agitation for treaty revision met the hostility of the LITTLE ENTENTE and eventually caused Hungary to join AXIS powers in Second World War (1941). Invaded by Russia 1944), Hungary signed an armistice in Jan., 1945. Paris peace treaty (1947) confirmed the loss of Slovakian and Rumanian border lands and provided for $300,000,000 in reparations to the USSR, Czechoslovakia, and Yugoslavia. Hungary adopted a republican constitution in 1946. The governing moderate-leftist coalition introduced some land reforms. A Communist coup d'état in 1948 set up a totalitarian people's republic (1949), which forcibly collectivized farmers and raised industrial output at expense of living standard. During premiership of Imre NAGY (1953–55) renewed emphasis was placed on consumers' goods. Hungary was admitted to UN 1955. After ouster of Nagy (1955) reintroduction of the old policy and continuing intellectual ferment (see PETOFI circle) contributed to the anti-Communist uprising of Oct. 23, 1956. A coalition government under Nagy (Oct. 24–Nov. 4) appealed to the UN for aid. Janos Kadar formed a counter-government and asked USSR for military support. Soviet troops suppressed the revolution, and Kadar replaced Nagy as premier. An estimated 190,000 Hungarians fled. Gradual liberalization has since occurred, including limited economic contacts with W Germany. In 1965 Kadar resigned as premier, but retained post as party secretary. Gyula Kallai became premier.

Hungry Horse Dam, NW Mont., in South Fork of Flathead R., E of Kalispell; built 1948–53 for power, flood control, and irrigation. Major unit in Columbia R. basin program, it is 564 ft. high and 2,115 ft. long.

Hunkers, conservative faction of the Democratic party in N.Y. in the 1840s, so named because they were supposed to "hanker" or "hunker" after office. Opposed the BARNBURNERS. Generally controlling party machinery and patronage, they favored internal improvements and liberal chartering of state banks; opposed antislavery agitation.

Huns, nomadic people from N central Asia. Organized into hordes, they were indomitable horsemen living off the countries they ravaged. They first appeared 3d cent. B.C., when the Great Wall of China was built to contain them. They occupied China from 3d cent. A.D. to 581. About 372 A.D. they invaded the Volga valley and advanced W, pushing the OSTROGOTHS and VISIGOTHS before them, thus starting the waves of migrations that destroyed the Roman Empire. In 432 they forced Emperor Theodosius II to pay tribute. ATTILA, from his hq. in Hungary, levied tribute in nearly all central and E Europe but was defeated in Gaul (451). The Huns withdrew after his death, and little is known of their later movements.

Hunt, Holman, 1827–1910, English painter, a founder of the Pre-Raphaelite brotherhood.

Hunt, (James Henry) Leigh, 1784–1859, English poet, critic, and essayist. Edited weeklies *Examiner* and *Liberal;* contributed to many others. A friend of contemporary writers, he strongly influenced Keats. His lyrics (e.g., "Abou Ben Adhem," "Jenny Kissed Me"), essays, and autobiography are still read.

Hunt, Richard Morris, 1828–95, American architect, brother of William Morris Hunt; an exponent of 19th-cent. eclecticism. His Tribune Building, New York, was one of first elevator buildings.

Hunt, William Morris, 1824–79, American painter, a follower of Barbizon School. As teacher and painter in Boston he exerted wide influence on American art.

Hunt, Wilson Price, 1782?–1842, American explorer, leader of the overland expedition (1810–12) to Astoria, Oregon.

Hunter, Dard, 1883–1966, American printer. Known for researches on history and technique of papermaking. Founder of Dard Hunter Paper Mus. in 1938 at Massachusetts Inst. of Technology; moved to Appleton, Wis., 1954.

Hunter, John, 1728–93, Scottish pioneer in comparative anatomy and in surgery. His noted anatomical collection was acquired by the Royal College of Surgeons. His brother, **William Hunter,** 1718–83, was famed as obstetrician and as head of influential school of anatomy.

Hunter, Robert Mercer Taliaferro, (tŏ'lŭvûr), 1809–87, American statesman. U.S. Representative from Va. (1837–43, 1845–47); a leading states' rights Democrat. U.S. Senator (1847–61). Participated in Confederate government.

Hunter, William: see HUNTER, JOHN.

Hunter College of The City University of New York, campuses in Manhattan and the Bronx; coed.; opened 1870 as Normal Col., chartered 1888; renamed 1914.

Huntingdon, England: see HUNTINGDONSHIRE.

Huntingdon, industrial borough (pop. 7,234), S central Pa., E of Altoona; settled c.1755. Seat of Juniata Col.

Huntingdonshire or **Huntingdon,** inland county (365 sq. mi.; pop. 79,879), E central England. Mainly agr., it has some brick mfg. and brewing. County town is **Huntingdon,** municipal borough (pop. 8,812), birthplace and home of Oliver Cromwell.

hunting leopard: see CHEETAH.

Huntington, Collis P(otter), 1821–1900, American railroad builder. Helped organize Central Pacific RR. Gained for himself and partners practical control of transportation in West. President of Southern Pacific after 1890. Left most of fortune to his nephew,

Henry E(dwards) Huntington, 1850–1927. Endowed his estate at San Marino, near Pasadena, Calif., for public use. Has fine gardens and the **Henry E. Huntington Library and Art Gallery** with largest collection of incunabula in America; many rare documents, manuscripts and books, with accent on American and British past. Special art treasures are Gainsborough's *Blue Boy,* Reynolds's *Mrs. Siddons as the Tragic Muse,* and Thomas Lawrence's *Pinkie.* The library gives research fellowships and scholarships.

Huntington, Ellsworth, 1876–1947, American geographer. Accompanied expeditions to central Asia (1903, 1905–6). At Yale 1907–47, he made notable climatic and anthropogeographic studies.

Huntington, Henry Edwards: see HUNTINGTON, COLLIS POTTER.

Huntington. 1 City (pop. 16,185), NE Ind., SW of Fort Wayne near Wabash R.; settled 1831. Farm trade center and industrial city. Huntington Col. is here. **2** Town (pop. 11,255), SE N.Y., on NW Long Isl., E of Oyster Bay; settled 1653. Residential and resort suburb of New York city. Walt Whitman's birthplace is preserved. **3** City (pop. 83,627), W central W.Va., on Ohio R., WNW of Charleston; founded 1871 as W terminus of Chesapeake & Ohio RR. Commercial center and river port shipping bituminous coal. Marshall Univ. is here.

Huntington Bay, village (1963 pop. 1,405), SE N.Y., on N shore of Long Isl., N of Huntington. British captured Nathan Hale here.

Huntington Beach, city (1965 pop. 75,053), SW Calif., on Pacific coast SE of Long Beach, in truck-farm, citrus-fruit, and oil area; settled 1901.

Huntington Library and Art Gallery: see HUNTINGTON, COLLIS POTTER.

Huntington Park, city (pop. 29,920), SW Calif., suburb SE of Los Angeles; laid out 1903.

Huntington Station, town (pop. 23,438), SE N.Y., on N shore of Long Isl., S of Huntington.

Huntsville. 1 City (1964 pop. 123,519), N Ala., between Tennessee R. and Tenn. line; settled 1807. Site of constitutional convention of Ala. Territory (1819); first state legislature met here for a few months. Redstone Arsenal, rocket research center, and George C. Marshall Space Flight Center are here. **2** City (pop. 11,999), E central Texas, NNW of Houston, in timber area. Home (restored) and burial place of Sam Houston.

Hunyadi, John (hōōn'yŏdĭ), c.1385–1456, Hungarian national hero, leader of resistance against the Turks. Was voivode of Transylvania 1441–46; regent of Hungary 1446–53 (for Ladislaus V). His chief victory (together with St. John Capistran) was that of Belgrade (1456), which staved off Turkish conquest of Hungary for 70 years. Matthias Corvinus was his son.

Hunza (hōōn'zä), small kingdom (3,900 sq. mi.; pop. 15,691), in Gilgit Agency, NW Kashmir, administered by Pakistan.

Hupeh or **Hupei** (hōō'bä'), province (c.72,000 sq. mi.; pop. c.30,790,000), central China; cap. Wuchang. Largely an alluvial plain drained by Yangtze and Han rivers. The tri-city area of WUHAN (Wuchang, Hankow, and Hanyang) is at river junction. Rice, cotton, grains, and soybeans are raised. HWANGSHIH in SE is major iron and steel complex.

Hur, man who upheld hand of weary Moses during battle, thus insuring Hebrew victory. Ex. 17.12; 24.14.

Hurd, Peter, 1904–, American painter of Western scenes and types. Uses realistic style.

Hurley, Patrick Jay, 1883–1963, U.S. Secretary of War (1929–33). In Second World War he served on diplomatic missions to Russia, Middle East, China.

hurling, game popular in Ireland, played on field 80 yd. by 140 yd. by two teams of 15 players each. A corkcentered ball and wooden stick (the hurley) are used.

Huron, city (pop. 14,180), E central S.Dak., on James R., E of Pierre; laid out 1879. Shipping and trade center for livestock and grain area. Huron Col. is here.

Huron, river rising in S Mich. and flowing c.97 mi. SE to L. Erie S of Detroit.

Huron, Lake, 206 mi. long, 183 mi. wide, second largest of Great Lakes. Lying 579.79 ft. above sea level, it has maximum depth of 750 ft., area of 23,010 sq. mi. Bounded N and E by Ontario, W by Mich. Drains L. Superior and L. Michigan and empties into L. Erie. Its large Georgian Bay indents Ont.; Saginaw Bay is in Mich. Islands include Mackinac and the Manitoulins. Iron ore, grain, coal, limestone, other articles are shipped. Ports include Bay City, Alpena, and Cheboygan in Mich., and Goderich, Collingwood, and Midland in Canada. L. Huron has violent storms, and is usually icebound from about mid-Dec. until early April. Probably first of Great Lakes visited by white men, possibly by Étienne Brulé c.1612.

Huronian: see PRECAMBRIAN ERA.

Huron Indians, confederation of four North American Indian tribes, who spoke Wyandot language (Iroquoian family). Their culture was of the Eastern Woodlands area. In early 17th cent. occupied region around L. Simcoe and near Georgian Bay, Ontario. The Hurons were friendly to the French, and the confederacy was destroyed by the Dutch-supported Iroquois (1649).

hurricane, cyclone originating in doldrums (in tropics) on W side of oceans, probably from convective heating. Most frequent in late summer or autumn in N Hemisphere, late winter or spring in S Hemisphere. Called typhoon in India and China.

Hurst, city (pop. 10,165), N Texas, industrial and residential suburb NE of Fort Worth.

Hurtado de Mendoza, Diego (dyä'gō ōōrtä'dhō dä mändō'thä), 1503–75, Spanish writer, a diplomat under Charles V. Banished by Philip II to Granada, he wrote an unbiased account of the Moorish rebellion. Also wrote poetry.

Husein (hōōsīn'), c.626–680, Moslem saint of the Shiites; second son of ALI and FATIMA. On death of his brother Hasan he unsuccessfully claimed caliphate. Tomb at KERBELA is holy place for Shiites. Name also spelled Hussein.

Husein ibn Ali (ī'bŭn ä'lē), 1856–1931, Arabian leader; father of Abdullah of Jordan and Feisal I of Iraq. Led revolt against Turkish rule and made himself king of the HEJAZ in 1916. Overthrown 1924 by Ibn Saud.

Hu Shih (hōō' shŭ'), 1891–1962. A major literary figure of Republican China, he favored the movement for vernacular literature and greatly promoted writing and art in China. Ambassador to U.S. (1938–42).

Huss, John, Czech *Jan Hus* (yän' hōōs'), 1369?–1415, religious reformer. He early came under the influence of the writings of Wyclif and opposed the condemnation of Wyclif's doctrines by the Univ. of Prague (1403). He attacked abuses of the clergy, earning their hostility, but was supported by Queen Sophia and Emperor Wenceslaus, who made him rector of Univ. of Prague (1409). He incurred the hostility of archbishop of Prague who had him excommunicated by antipope John XXIII. At castle near Tabor, Huss wrote his chief works, including *De ecclesia*. Emperor Sigismund invited him to defend his views at Council of Constance (1414), but by unfair means he was condemned as heretic and burned. See HUSSITES.

Hussein: see also HUSEIN.

Hussein I (hōōsīn'), 1935–, king of Jordan (1952–), son and successor of Talal. Was deputy chief of state of the short-lived Arab Union in 1958. Married an English girl in 1961; a son, crown prince Abdullah, was born in 1962.

Husseini (Amin el Husseini) (hōōsä'nē; ämēn' ĕl), 1896?–, Arab political leader. Appointed mufti of Jerusalem in 1921. Arrested 1937 for instigation of anti-Semitic riots but escaped to Lebanon and later to Iraq. Broadcast Nazi propaganda from Berlin in Second World War. Listed as war criminal, he found asylum in Egypt 1946, later in Pakistan.

Husserl, Edmund (hōōs'ûrl), 1859–1938, German philosopher. His theories on the relationship of the conscious mind and objects—the basis of the system of *phenomenology*—have had great influence.

Hussites, followers of John Huss in Bohemia and Moravia. In 1420 they drew up Four Articles of Prague, demanding freedom of preaching, communion in both kinds for laymen and priests, limited property holding by Church, and civil punishment of mortal sin. In Hussite Wars movement divided into moderate UTRAQUISTS (some of whom in 16th cent. fused with Lutherans and were called Evangelicals) and radical TABORITES (from whom stemmed Moravian Church).

Hussite Wars, 1419–36, conflict caused by the rise of the HUSSITES in Bohemia and Moravia. Its nature was religious and national (Hussite Czechs vs. Catholic Germans) as well as social (radical TABORITES, largely recruited among peasantry, vs. moderate UTRAQUISTS, backed by Czech nobility). The Hussites took up arms in 1419 to prevent the succession of Emperor SIGISMUND to the Bohemian crown. Under the leadership of ZIZKA and, after 1425, of PROCOPIUS THE GREAT, the Hussites defeated Sigismund (1420, 1422), invaded Silesia (1425–26) and Franconia (1429–30), and repulsed several anti-Hussite crusades. Hussite delegates at the Council of BASEL accepted the so-called Compactata, by which the Utraquists were taken back into the Catholic Church (1433), but the Taborites refused to compromise. In the resulting civil war, the Taborites were routed at Lipany (1434); the Compactata were ratified and Sigismund was recognized as king of Bohemia in 1436. The later wars against GEORGE OF PODEBRAD were of primarily political nature, though Hussitism was the ostensible issue.

Hutchins, Robert Maynard, 1899–, American educator. Dean of Yale Law School 1927–29, helped organize Inst. of Human Relations at Yale. President Univ. of CHICAGO 1929–45, chancellor 1945–51; instituted "Chicago plan." Promoted "great books" program (1946). Associate director Ford Foundation 1951–54. Became president of Fund for the Republic 1954.

Hutchinson, Anne, c.1591–1643, religious leader in New England, b. England. Banished from Mass. Bay colony as antinomian heretic, she and followers founded Portsmouth, R.I. (1638).

Hutchinson, Thomas, 1711–80, colonial governor of Mass. (1771–74) and historian. Unpopular with colonists because he upheld British measures. Wrote history of Mass. Bay colony.

Hutchinson, city (pop. 37,574), S central Kansas, on Arkansas R., NW of Wichita; laid out 1871. Rail, shipping, trade, and mfg. center of wheat-growing region. Has large salt beds. Oil and natural gas wells nearby. Site of state fair.

Hutt, city (pop. 93,000), North Isl., New Zealand. Until 1951 part of Wellington. Varied heavy industry.

Hutten, Ulrich von (ōōl'rĭkh fŭn hōō'tŭn), 1488–1523, German humanist, poet, and political reformer. Wrote in Latin, later in German. Was poet laureate of Maximilian I (1517). Supported Johann REUCHLIN; joined with Franz von SICKINGEN (1519); supported Luther. Sickingen's defeat forced him into exile in Switzerland (1522).

Hutterische Community (hŏōtĕ'rĭshŭ) or **Hutterian Brethren** (hŭtĕr'ēŭn), religious communistic group founded (1874) at Tabor, S.Dak. by immigrant descendants of followers of Jacob Hutter. Closely allied with Mennonites in matters of doctrine and principles.

Hutton, James, 1726–97, Scottish geologist. He formulated the theory of UNIFORMITARIANISM as opposed to the long accepted belief known as CATASTROPHISM.

Huxley, Andrew Fielding, 1917–, British physiologist. Shared 1963 Nobel Prize in Physiology and Medicine for research on how signals are generated through body nerve cells.

Huxley, T(homas) H(enry), 1825–95, English biologist. While assistant surgeon on H.M.S. *Rattlesnake* he collected marine life in Pacific areas (1846–50). A supporter of Darwin, he wrote on evolution, and also on anatomy, physiology, and other fields of science. His grandson **Julian S(orell) Huxley,** 1887–, biologist and author, was director general of UNESCO 1946–48. His works include *The Living Thoughts of Darwin* (1939) and *Heredity East and West* (1949). Another grandson, **Aldous (Leonard) Huxley,** 1894–1963, gained early fame with satirical novels and short stories (*Crome Yellow,* 1921; *Antic Hay,* 1923; *Point Counter Point,* 1928; and *Brave New World,* 1932, depicting a repulsive Utopia). Mordant criticism of the modern world continued in *Eyeless in Gaza* (1936) and later novels, though some reflected his interest in Eastern mysticism. He also wrote travel books (e.g., *Beyond the Mexique Bay,* 1934), biography, and essays.

Huygens, Constantijn (kōnstäntīn′ hoi′gŭns), 1596–1687, Dutch poet. Noted for descriptive and satirical poems, he wrote in French, Italian, Latin, Dutch. His son, **Christiaan Huygens** (krīs′tyän), 1629–95, was a mathematician and physicist. He improved telescopic lenses and discovered a satellite and the rings of Saturn. He was first to use pendulum in clocks. **Huygens's principle:** every point on wave front of light is source of new waves.

Huysmans, Cornelis (hois′mäns), 1648–1727, Flemish painter of landscapes and religious subjects. His brother and pupil, **Jan Baptist Huysmans,** 1654–1716, also painted landscapes.

Huysmans, Jacob (yä′kōp), c.1633–1696, Flemish portrait painter, fashionable at the court of Charles II of England.

Huysmans, Joris Karl (zhōrēs′ kärl′ ūēsmäs′), 1848–1907, French novelist. His early work was naturalistic, after Zola. Becoming a Catholic convert he turned toward symbolism. His novel *À Rebours* (1884; Eng. tr. *Against the Grain,* 1922) is an embodiment of the intellectual atmosphere of his time.

Hvar (khvär), Gr. *Pharos,* Ital. *Lesina,* Adriatic island, 112 sq. mi., Yugoslavia, off Dalmatia. Chief town, Hvar, has 12th-cent. Byzantine cathedral.

Hwai (hwī), river, rising in S Honan prov., China, flows c.675 mi. E across Anhwei prov., marking boundary between N China plain and the Yangtze delta.

Hwainan (hwī′nän′), city (pop. 286,900), N central Anhwei prov., China. Estab. after 1949 as center of China's chief coal-mining region.

Hwaining, China: see ANKING.

Hwang Ho: see YELLOW RIVER.

Hwangpoo, China: see WHANGPOO.

Hwangshih (hwäng′shŭ′), city (pop. c.52,000), E Hupei prov., China, on Yangtze R. Industrial center built after 1950. Has huge steel complex.

Hyacinth, in Greek myth, beautiful youth loved by Apollo, who accidentally killed him with a discus. Flower named for him sprang up from his blood.

hyacinth, bulbous plant of genus *Hyacinthus* native to Mediterranean region and S Africa. Common or Dutch hyacinth became so popular in 18th cent. that 2,000 kinds were said to be grown in Holland. It has a single dense spike of fragrant flowers in the spring but can be made to bloom earlier indoors.

Hyannis (hīän′ĭs), resort village (pop. 5,139), SE Mass., on S shore of Cape Cod. Business center for area.

Hyatt, John Wesley, 1837–1920, American inventor of CELLULOID and of Hyatt filter for chemical purification of water while it is in motion.

Hyattsville, city (pop. 15,168), W central Md., suburb NE of Washington, D.C. Scientific research laboratories.

hybrid (hī′brĭd), term of plant and animal breeders for offspring of two different species or genera. In genetics it is usually a term for offspring of two parents differing in any genetic character.

Hyde, Douglas, 1860–1949, Irish scholar and president of Ireland, 1938–45. Founder of the Gaelic League

(1893), which revived the use of the Irish language. He also wrote much on Irish literature and history.

Hyde, Edward: see CLARENDON, EDWARD HYDE, 1ST EARL OF.

Hyde Park, 363 acres, in W London. Was once a deer park where races were held. Duke of Hamilton and Lord Mohun fought their fatal duel here. The Serpentine, artificial lake, was constructed 1733. Distinctive features of the park are Marble Arch, meeting place of soapbox orators; Rotten Row, famous bridle path; and the Albert Memorial.

Hyde Park, town (1964 pop. 14,700), E N.Y., on E bank of Hudson R., N of Poughkeepsie; settled c.1740. Franklin D. Roosevelt and Vanderbilt Mansion national historic sites are here.

Hyderabad (hī′dŭrŭbäd″), former state, India; region now constituted of states of Mysore, Maharashtra, and Andhra Pradesh. Produces cotton and grain. Cotton textiles and food processing are chief industries. Conquered in late 17th cent. by Mogul empire; Hyderabad achieved independence under the viceroy Asaf Jah in 1724. In 1948 India invaded the state and the predominantly Hindu population endorsed accession to India in a plebiscite. **Hyderabad,** city (pop. 1,255,000); cap. of Andhra Pradesh; administration, commercial, and transportation center. Was founded 1589 as cap. of Golconda kingdom.

Hyderabad (hī′dŭrŭbäd″), division (36,821 sq. mi.; pop. c.3,300,000) of West Pakistan. Central portion is an alluvial plain watered by the Indus R.; W is hilly and S forms western edge of Thar or Indian desert and the Rann of Kutch. Its cap. is the city of **Hyderabad** (pop. 434,537), formerly cap. of the Amirs of Sind. Mfg. center.

Hyder Ali or **Haidar Ali** (both: hī′dŭr ä′lē), 1722–82, Indian maharaja. Though illiterate and a Moslem, he rose to become highest military leader in Hindu state of Mysore. Seized power in 1761, made himself maharaja in 1766. Defeated the British in 1769 and 1780, but he and his son Tippoo Sahib were defeated in 1781 by Warren Hastings.

Hydra (hī′drŭ) [Gr.,= watery (snake)], in Greek mythology, water serpent with nine heads. When one head was cut off, two new ones grew. HERCULES conquered monster by burning neck after severing each head.

hydrangea (hīdrän′jŭ), ornamental deciduous shrub of genus *Hydrangea,* native to Asia and the Americas. It has flat-topped or rounded clusters of blue, white, or pink flowers. Used in landscaping and as potted plant.

hydrate (hī′drāt), substance formed by chemical combination of a compound and one or more molecules of water (number of molecules is specific for substance). This water is called water of crystallization; it is given off on heating or in some hydrates at ordinary temperatures (efflorescence).

hydraulic brake: see BRAKE.

hydraulic machine, machine actuated by motion or pressure of fluid (liquid or gas). Water under pressure is used as power agent for presses, riveters, winches, and other machines. Power derived from falling water drives TURBINE and the water wheel. Hydraulic elevator, jack, and press are based on PASCAL'S LAW. Certain machines are driven by accumulator (consisting chiefly of cylinder enclosing weighted ram) which keeps liquid at fixed pressure.

hydraulic press, hydraulic machine (also called hydrostatic press), invented by Joseph Bramah. Consists essentially of two liquid-filled cylinders of very unequal diameter, connected by pipe and each fitted with piston. Pressure exerted on smaller piston is transmitted through liquid and forces up larger piston; this is an application of PASCAL'S LAW. Hydraulic press is used in industry to shape and form metal.

hydraulics: see HYDRAULIC MACHINE; MECHANICS.

hydrazine, chemical compound, a colorless, fuming liquid, composed of nitrogen and hydrogen and having basic properties. Used as a rocket fuel.

hydrocarbon (hī″drōkär′bŭn), organic compound composed only of carbon and hydrogen, in varying proportions. Every hydrocarbon molecule is a branched or unbranched chain or ring of carbon atoms, with hydrogen atoms attached to the remaining free valences of the carbons. Hydrocarbons are classed in series of compounds of related structure; in a series, each member has a definite relation to the member preceding and the one following. Typical series are the alkanes, the alkenes, and the alkines. An alkane (saturated hydrocarbon) molecule is a chain which includes only single bonds; METHANE, ETHANE, PROPANE, and BUTANE are the simplest alkanes. An alkene (ethylenic hydrocarbon) molecule includes one double bond; ETHYLENE, propylene, and butene are the simplest alkenes. An alkine (acetylenic hydrocarbon) molecule includes one triple bond; ACETYLENE, methylacetylene, and dimethylacetylene are the simplest alkines. Other series include molecules with more than one double or triple bond. In each series, several compounds with the same numerical formula may exist; these are isomers, differing in structural arrangement (branching) and in chemical properties. Hydrocarbons containing one or more benzene rings have special qualities and are said to be aromatic; hydrocarbons without benzene rings are aliphatic. Cyclic aliphatic compounds occur; these molecules include rings which are not benzene rings. Small hydrocarbon molecules containing double or triple bonds can be linked together by opening the extra bonds and joining together the freed valences of the different molecules; this is a form of POLYMERIZATION. Synthetic rubber, certain plastics, and certain synthetic textiles are polymers produced in this way. Hydrocarbons vary in chemical activity, resist ordinary reagents, and burn in air. Many are important as fuels, e.g., gasoline, various grades of fuel oil, and kerosene are all mixtures of hydrocarbons derived from petroleum. COAL TAR is also a mixture of hydrocarbons. Many compounds are derivatives of hydrocarbons, formed by replacing one or more hydrogens with other chemical groups or radicals. See also ANTHRACENE; BENZENE; ISOMERISM; RADICAL.

hydrocephalia: see FEEBLE-MINDEDNESS.

hydrochloric acid, aqueous solution of hydrogen chloride, a strong acid of great commercial importance. It reacts with most metals, and with their oxides and hydroxides, forming chlorides. It is used for cleaning metal; in producing chlorides, glue, dyes, glucose; and in medicine. Muriatic acid is a solution of 30–35% by weight.

hydrocyanic (–sī·ă′nĭk) or **prussic** (prŭ′sĭk) **acid,** colorless, volatile, very poisonous liquid with almond odor. Water solution is a weak acid; salts are cyanides. It is used in the laboratory, as poison gas in war, and as a fumigant.

hydrodynamics: see MECHANICS.

hydroelectric power: see POWER.

hydrofoil, finlike device attached to hull of a watercraft, enabling the hull to travel above surface of water, reducing its friction. Hydrofoil vessels can travel faster than 70 mph and do not pitch and roll. Type of hydrofoil called stabilizer is used on oceangoing passenger ships to minimize wave action. First hydrofoil vessel built 1905 by Italian engineer, Enrico Forlanini.

hydrogen (hī′drŭjŭn), colorless, odorless, tasteless gaseous element (symbol = H; see also ELEMENT, table). It is the lightest known gas, explosive when mixed with air or oxygen, and burns with a hot blue flame. It is slightly soluble in water; can be liquefied under pressure; is active at high temperatures; is a powerful reducing agent; forms many important compounds. Discovered in 1766 by Henry Cavendish, it was named in 1783 by Lavoisier. Heavy hydrogen, deuterium, is isotope of mass number 2; it and its atomic nuclei (deuterons) are important in research. Tritium is the radioactive isotope of mass number 3, which is essential to explosion of hydrogen bomb.

hydrogenation of oils (hī′drŭjŭnā′shŭn), treatment of vegetable oils with hydrogen, in presence of catalyst, at high temperature under pressure. It forms a product resembling solid animal fats.

hydrogen bomb derives energy from fusion of atomic nuclei of low mass; nuclei of hydrogen isotopes are usually used. In one fusion process, two deuterons collide to form a helium 3 (isotope of mass number 3) nucleus, a neutron, and a large quantity of energy. The total mass of the two deuterons is greater than the total mass of the helium nucleus and the neutron; the difference is converted into energy. Atomic bomb is used as detonator to provide needed amount of heat to set off fusion reaction. The thermonuclear reactions involved are believed to be same as those producing heat of sun. Explosive yield of bomb is measured in megatons (i.e., equivalents in millions of tons of T.N.T.). Bomb explosion can be of terrible size; it creates a fireball several miles in diameter and a mushroom cloud many miles high, hundreds of miles across. Radioactive fallout particles, deposited from the wind-blown atomic cloud, spread across continents and poison plants and animals. Certain diseases (e.g., leukemia) and also genetic damage can result from fallout. Theoretical power yield of fusion process for peaceful use may be almost unlimited because of its great energy production and the abundance of hydrogen in atmosphere and as component of water; however, the necessary control of the fusion process has not yet been achieved. Confining the ionized fusion nuclei in a magnetic field may make possible controlled fusion and the conversion of fusion energy into power. Tests made at Eniwetok atoll advanced U.S. development of hydrogen bomb. U.S. exploded world's first hydrogen bomb in 1952; Russia exploded its first in 1953, and in 1961 exploded a 50 megaton bomb; Britain exploded its first in 1957, China its first in 1967. There is no effective defense against delivery of a hydrogen warhead bomb by an intercontinental ballistics missile. International test-ban treaty regulating nuclear devices was signed by 106 nations in 1963; in 1967 U.S., Britain, and USSR agreed on a treaty insuring peaceful uses of outer space. See also ATOMIC ENERGY; COBALT BOMB.

hydrogen-ion concentration: see ION.

hydrogen peroxide (pŭrŏk′sīd), colorless, unstable liquid with metallic taste; has two atoms of both hydrogen and oxygen. Used as bleaching agent and in cleansing wounds (germicidal value disputed).

hydrolysis (hīdrŏ′lŭsĭs), type of chemical reaction in which water (dissociated into hydrogen ions and hydroxyl ions) is involved. It is common in life processes, e.g., in digestion, food substances (carbohydrates, fats and oils, and proteins) are decomposed by action of water in presence of enzymes. Final product of hydrolysis of starch is glucose; of fats and oils, products are glycerol and fatty acids; and of proteins, amino acids. Some salts undergo hydrolysis in water solution, others do not. Some reactions involving water are not hydrolysis, e.g., when a metal and water react to form a base and liberate hydrogen. See ill., p. 885.

hydrometer (hīdrŏ′mŭtŭr), device to determine directly the SPECIFIC GRAVITY of a liquid. Usually it is a thin glass tube closed at both ends, with a bulb at one end filled with mercury or fine shot so that it will float upright in liquid being tested. Scale is so calibrated that reading at level of surface of liquid gives specific gravity. Density can be calculated from specific-gravity readings. Commercial hydrometers usually are calibrated for 20°C.

hydrophobia [from Greek,= hatred of water] (hī′′drŭfō′bēŭ) or **rabies** (rā′bēz), acute infectious disease caused by virus which affects nervous system. It is transmitted by bite of rabid animal. Spasm of pharynx on swallowing results in fear of drinking water. Pasteur developed method of preventing disease by inoculation 1884 and first used it on human patient 1885.

hydrophone, device for detecting or emitting sound under water; called transducer when used to produce sound. Used for submarine communications, sonar, and seismic investigation of ocean floor.

hydroponics, science of growing plants without soil. Set in water to which nutrients are added, many types of plants are raised commercially in this manner throughout North America.

hydrostatics: see MECHANICS.

hydroxide (hīdrŏk'sīd), term commonly used for a BASE, although some compounds with hydroxyl (OH) radical show acid properties. Others have both acidic and basic characteristics (i.e., are amphoteric); still others are neutral.

hydroxyl radical: see HYDROXIDE; RADICAL.

hyena (hīē'nû), nocturnal Old World mammal. Its front legs are longer than hind ones. It eats mostly carrion. Striped hyena of Asia Minor, Persia, India, and N Africa and brown hyena or strand wolf of S Africa both belong to genus *Hyaena.* Spotted hyena (*Crocuta*) in Africa S of Sahara is largest form (2½ ft. high at shoulder). It has a maniacal cry and is said to rob graves and steal children.

Hyères (yĕr), town (est. pop. 29,000), Var dept., SE France. Mediterranean resort. Off coast is group of islands of same name.

hygiene (hī'jēn), science of health and its preservation. Community aspects are handled by PUBLIC HEALTH and SOCIAL HYGIENE programs. Field of MENTAL HYGIENE developed after recognition of health role of mental and emotional factors.

hygrometer (hīgrŏ'mùtùr), instrument for measuring moisture content of air. In the condensing, or dew-point hygrometer, fluid in a tube is evaporated, thereby drawing heat from surrounding air; since air holds less moisture as temperature decreases, excess moisture condenses on tube. From temperatures recorded, when condensation begins, by thermometers within tube and outside it, moisture content is calculated. Other hygrometers are based on use of substance that expands or contracts as moisture varies or of substance that absorbs moisture from air with consequent weight increase. In the psychrometer moisture content is determined by difference in temperatures recorded by two thermometers, the bulb of one kept moist, the other dry.

Hyksos (hĭk'sōs), successful invaders of anc. Egypt c.1715 B.C. A Semitic people who conquered the Pharaohs of the Middle Kingdom. During a century of rule (XV–XVII dynasties) they introduced the horse-drawn chariot, foreign cultural ideas, cognizance of the outside world. They were expelled by Amasis I.

Hymen or **Hymenaeus** (hīmùnē'ùs), Greek personification of marriage, represented as beautiful youth carrying bridal torch and wearing veil.

Hymettus (hīmē'tùs), Gr. *Hymettos,* mountain group, Attica, Greece. Mt. Hymettus (3,367 ft.) famed since antiquity for its honey. Marble quarries.

hymn, song of praise, devotion, or thanksgiving, especially of a religious nature. Early Christian hymnody consisted mainly of the Psalms and other biblical texts chanted in unison. Metrical Latin hymns developed in 4th cent. Great medieval hymns include *Dies irae, Stabat Mater Dolorosa,* and *Pange lingua.* In the Reformation, the Lutheran chorale developed; Luther wrote several (e.g., *A Mighty Fortress,* which has a famous setting by J. S. Bach). Calvinism contributed the Genevan Psalter, containing the tune *Old Hundred.* The English hymn developed largely in the 18th cent. with the sacred texts of Cowper, Watts, and Wesley. An early collection of hymns in America was the *Bay Psalm Book* (pub. 1640).

Hyndman, Mount, or **Hyndman Peak:** see SAWTOOTH MOUNTAINS.

hyoscine: see SCOPOLAMINE.

Hypatia (hīpā'shù), d. 415, Alexandrian Neoplatonic philosopher, a woman renowned for beauty, learning, and eloquence. Murdered by Christian monks, supposedly at the instigation of St. Cyril of Alexandria.

hyperbola (hīpûr'bùlù), CONIC SECTION consisting of pair of symmetrical open curves. Can be defined in analytic geometry as a plane curve such that difference between distances from any point on curve to two fixed points (foci) is same for all points on curve.

Hyperboreans (hī"pùrbô'rēùnz, –bōrē'ùnz), in Greek legend, people dwelling in bliss in the Far North.

hyperemia: see CONGESTION.

Hyperion (hīpēr'ēùn), in Greek religion, Titan; son of Uranus and Gaea and father of Helios, Selene, and Eos by Theia.

hypertension: see BLOOD PRESSURE.

hypertrophy, enlargement of a body organ as result of increase in size of its cells. Accompanies increased power or effectiveness in use of the tissues involved. Includes athlete's heart and uterus enlargement in pregnancy. After surgical removal of a kidney the remaining one compensates by enlarging; such hypertrophy is associated with hyperplasia, an increase in number of cells.

hypnotism, Braid's term (1842) for animal magnetism or mesmerism (see MESMER). It is induced in a relaxed subject by monotonous repetition of words and gestures–some people are not affected. In slight hypnosis consciousness remains, actions are remembered; in deep hypnosis, sensory system and muscles are affected, supernormal feats cause no fatigue, are forgotten. Hypnosis heightens suggestibility, was used to treat and study hysteria. Briefly used by Freud in psychoanalysis, it is still used in some therapy and in study of mental activities.

hypochondria (hī"pùkŏn'drêù), the neurotic reaction marked by habitual preoccupation with health and with imagined or negligible physical defect.

Hyrcania: see GORGAN.

Hyrcanus, John (hùrkā'nùs), name of two of the MACCABEES.

hyssop (hĭs'ùp), aromatic perennial herb (*Hyssopus officinalis*) native to Old World. It has small violet-blue, white, or pink flowers. Once used as flavoring, it is now grown chiefly for ornament.

hysteria, in general usage, highly emotional and irrational conduct, reflected in bodily disturbance. Psychologists define it as a conversion NEUROSIS. Occasionally hysteria creates organic sickness (see PSYCHOSOMATIC MEDICINE). In late 19th cent., the psychological origin of hysteria was recognized, and hypnosis was used for its cure.

Hythe (hīdh), municipal borough (pop. 10,026), Kent, England; summer resort and one of CINQUE PORTS. School of Small Arms is here.

I, chemical symbol of element IODINE.

Iakovos, 1911–, American clergyman, b. Turkey. His name is Demetrios A. Coucouzis. Became primate and archbishop of Greek Orthodox Archdiocese of North and South America in 1959.

iambic pentameter: see PENTAMETER.

Iamblichus (ĭăm'blĭkŭs), d. c.330, Syrian philosopher, pupil of Porphyry at Rome. Greatly increased mystic and magical beliefs in Neoplatonism.

Iapetus (īă'pĭtŭs), in Greek mythology, Titan; son of Uranus and Gaea and husband of CLYMENE.

Iasi, Rumania: see JASSY.

Ibadan (ēbä'dan), city (pop. c.630,000), administrative center of W Nigeria. Inhabited mainly by Yoruba. Has commerce in cacao, cotton, and rubber. Cultural center; seat of Univ. of Nigeria (founded 1947).

Ibagué (ēbägä') city (pop. 163,661), W central Colombia; founded 1550; a commercial center.

Ibáñez, Vicente Blasco: see BLASCO IBÁÑEZ.

Iberia (ībēr'ēŭ), anc. name of a country in Transcaucasia, roughly E part of Georgian SSR.

Iberian Gates, Georgian SSR: see DARYAL.

Iberian Peninsula, SW Europe, comprising SPAIN and PORTUGAL, between Atlantic and Mediterranean. Separated from main continent by Pyrenees, from N Africa by Strait of Gibraltar. Named for the Iberians, anc. people believed to have migrated from Africa in Neolithic period. They merged with the Celts (who came later) into "Celtiberian" nation.

Ibert, Jacques (zhäk' ēbĕr'), 1890–1962, French composer. Works include operas, ballets, orchestral suites (*Escales*), concertos (for piano, saxophone), piano works.

Iberville, Pierre le Moyne, sieur d' (pyĕr' lü mwän' syûr' dēbērvēl'), 1661–1706, French Canadian naval officer and colonizer. Led attacks on British settlements in North America. Estab. colony in lower Mississippi valley with brother, sieur de BIENVILLE.

ibex (ī'bĕks), gregarious, sturdy, agile wild goat (*Capra*) living at snow line of mountains of Asia, Europe. It is brown or gray, 2½–3½ ft. high at the shoulder, and has long ridged horns curving backward.

ibis (ī'bĭs), wading bird of warm parts of both hemispheres. Usually it nests in colonies. Its body is c.2 ft. long; the bill is long, slender, decurved, and grooved from nostril to tip. In North America are white ibis, white-faced and eastern glossy ibises, and wood ibis (really a stork).

Ibiza, island, Spain: see IVIZA.

Ibn Batuta (ĭ'bŭn bätōō'tä), 1304?–1378?, Moslem traveler, b. Tangier. More widely traveled than any known medieval man, he wrote valuable accounts of the Near and Far East.

Ibn Ezra, Abraham ben Meir (mâr' ĭ'bŭn), 1092–1167, Jewish poet, mathematician, philosopher. In his biblical commentaries, he was a precursor of the critical approach. Inspiration for Browning's "Rabbi Ben Ezra."

Ibn Gabirol, Solomon ben Judah (ĭ'bŭn gäbē'rôl), c.1021–1058, Jewish poet and Neoplatonist in Spain. Also known as Avicebron. His *Fountain of Life* exercised great influence on Christian philosophy.

Ibn Khaldun (ĭ'bŭn khäldōon'), 1332–1406, Arab historian. In *Kitab al-Ibar* [universal history] he treats history as science and outlines philosophy of history. Deemed greatest of Arab historians.

Ibn Saud (Abdu-l-Aziz ibn Saud) (ĭ'bŭn säōod'), c.1888–1953, founded SAUDI ARABIA. Triumphed over his rival, HUSEIN IBN ALI, in 1924 and declared himself king of the HEJAZ and NEJD. Remained neutral during Second World War. A leader in anti-Zionist movement among Arab states.

Ibn Tufail (ĭ'bŭn tōofīl'), 12th-cent. Spanish-Arabian philosopher and physician. Wrote *Hayy ibn Yaqzan*, a philosophical romance. Also known as Abubacer.

Ibn Zohr: see AVENZOAR.

Ibo (ē'bō), largest tribe of SE Nigeria, numbering c.5,500,000. They live in dispersed villages in one of world's most densely populated rural regions. Many are Christian. Progressive and politically active, strong advocates of national independence, as shown by secession in 1967 of Eastern Region to become country of Biafra.

Ibrahim Pasha (ĭbrähēm' pä'shä), 1789–1848, Egyptian general; son of MOHAMMED ALI. Led Turkish forces against Wahabis in Arabia (1816–19) and rebel Greeks (1825–28). Conquered Turkish-held Syria (1832–33), but European troops forced his withdrawal 1838.

Ibsen, Henrik, 1828–1906, Norwegian dramatist, one of the outstanding figures in modern world theater. A satirical verse play, *Love's Comedy* (1862) was followed by dramatic poems *Brand* (1866) and *Peer Gynt* 1867) and a series of powerful, realistic social plays in prose (*The Pillars of Society*, 1877; *A Doll's House*, 1879; *Ghosts*, 1881; *An Enemy of the People*, 1882; *The Wild Duck*, 1884; *Rosmersholm*, 1886; *The Lady from the Sea*, 1888; *Hedda Gabler*, 1890; *The Master Builder*, 1892; *Little Eyolf*, 1894; *John Gabriel Borkman*, 1896; *When We Dead Awaken*, 1899). His uncompromising insistence in presenting natural characters in conflict with social custom and environment brought a fresh breath into the theater. G. B. Shaw was one of his disciples.

Ica (ē'kä), city (pop. c.22,000), SW Peru; commercial center for irrigated valley of Ica R.

Içá, river: see PUTUMAYO.

Icaria (īkâ'rēŭ), mountainous island (c.99 sq. mi.; pop. 9,577), near coast of Turkey but belonging to Greece, in the Sporades. Icarus is said to have fallen into the sea near here.

Icaria, idealistic society: see CABET, ÉTIENNE.

Icarus, in Greek myth. He flew too near the sun with wings made by his father, Daedalus. Wax joints of the wings melted, and he fell into the sea.

ICBM: see GUIDED MISSILE.

Ice Age: see PLEISTOCENE EPOCH.

iceberg, ice mass detached from glacier or ice sheet and floating on ocean. About one ninth of mass projects above water.

Iceland, Icelandic *Island*, republic (39,709 sq. mi.; pop. 177,292), westernmost state of Europe, occupying Iceland isl. and several smaller islands in the Atlantic just S of Arctic Circle, c.600 mi. W of Norway;

SMALL CAPITALS = cross references. Pronunciation key on inside end pages. Abbreviations: p. 2.

499

cap. REYKJAVIK. Iceland is a plateau, averaging 2,000 ft. high and culminating in vast icefields, of which VATNAJÖKULL is largest. Deep fjords indent the coast. Many of the more than 100 volcanoes are still active (highest is Mt. HEKLA). Hot springs such as the GEYSIR abound. Climate is mild and humid because of North Atlantic Drift. Iceland is only c.25% habitable, and most cities are on the coast. Island lacks timber, but has extensive grazing (sheep, horses, cattle). Agr. (hay, potatoes, turnips) is limited. Fishing is most important industry, codfish and herring constituting chief export. Iceland is governed by parliamentary democracy. Here social-security legislation is very advanced. Most citizens are Lutherans. High educational level is due to ancient tradition and ingrained civilization rather than to formal schooling. Irish monks visited Iceland before 9th cent., but abandoned it on arrival of Norse settlers (c.850–870). In 930 a general assembly, the ALTHING, was estab., and c.1000 Christianity was introduced. However, memory of paganism was preserved in literature of 13th-cent. Iceland, where OLD NORSE LITERATURE reached its greatest flowering (modern Icelandic is virtually same language as that of the sagas). Attempt of SNORRI STURLUSON to establish full control of King Haakon IV of Norway over Iceland failed, but in 1261–64 king obtained acknowledgment of his sovereignty by the Icelanders. With Norway, Iceland passed under the Danish crown (1380). In 17th and 18th cent. pirates ruined trade; epidemics and a general volcanic eruption (1783) killed many; and creation (1602) of a private trading company at Copenhagen, with exclusive rights to Iceland trade, caused economic ruin. Foreign traders were not admitted until 1854. Home rule was finally granted in 1874, and in 1918 Iceland was declared a sovereign state in personal union with Denmark. During Second World War, when British and U.S. forces were based in Iceland, the Althing assumed king's prerogatives, and on June 17, 1944, after popular referendum, kingdom of Iceland became an independent republic. Iceland was admitted to the UN in 1946, and joined in European Recovery Program and North Atlantic Treaty Organization (1949).

Icelandic language, North Germanic language. See LANGUAGE (table).

Icelandic literature. The Eddas and sagas of early Icelandic literature (see OLD NORSE LITERATURE) had a lasting effect on later writing. Literature declined after the loss of Iceland's independence (1261–64), but in the 14th cent. arose the *rimur*, a type of narrative poem. After the Protestant Reformation, religion dominated literature until the period of enlightenment (1750–1835). The romantic revival, begun in the 1830s, stressed nationalism as well as romantic elements. The classic Icelandic style was developed in 19th–20th cent. by such men as the short-story writer Jonas Hallgrimsson; the novelist Jon Thoroddsen; the poets Grimur Thomsen, Benedikt Grondal, and Steingrimur Thorsteinsson; and the dramatist Matthias Jochumsson. The historian Jon Sigurdsson helped to promote Icelandic language and literature. Realism appeared to challenge romanticism with attacks on the Church and social institutions; important in the movement were short-story writer Gestur Palsson; the Icelandic-Canadian poet Stephen G. Stephansson. A more introspective type of literature also developed. Various strains enriched Icelandic literature, as in the neo-romantic movement and "proletarian" writing. Among 20th-cent. figures have been Jon Trausti (pseud. of Gudmundur Magnusson), Sigurdur Nordal, Kristmann Gudmundson, and Halldor K. LAXNESS.

Iceland moss, a grayish paper-thin lichen (*Cetraria islandica*) of northern countries and found as far south as N U.S. It has long been used in Scandinavian countries for human food and for fodder.

Iceland spar, transparent calcite characterized by double refraction. Used for prisms of polarizing microscopes and other optical instruments.

ice plant, low, fleshy plant (*Cryophytum crystallinum*) of warm, dry, barren regions. Useful as ground cover or pot plant. Formerly combined with related herbs in genus *Mesembryanthemum*.

Ichabod (ĭ′kŭbŏd) [Heb.,= inglorious], grandson of Eli. 1 Sam. 4.21; 14.3. He was born at the hour of the capture of the Ark by the Philistines and named to commemorate unfortunate event.

Ichang or **I-ch'ang** (ē′chäng′), city (pop. c.100,000), SW Hupei prov., China, on Yangtze R. Terminus for ocean-going vessels from Shanghai.

ichneumon fly (ĭknū′mŭn), parasitic insect of N America and Europe, related to wasp. They prey on other insects but are harmless to humans.

ichthyol (ĭk′thēŏl), oleaginous compound derived from bituminous materials consisting of deposits of fossil fish. It is thick, dark brown, and has characteristic fishy odor. Formerly used in treatment of skin disorders.

Ickes, Harold L(eClaire) (ĭ′kŭs), 1874–1952, U.S. Secretary of the Interior (1933–46). Long a progressive known for his bluntness in action, he called himself a "curmudgeon."

Icknield Street (ĭk′nēld), Saxon name for an early road in Britain over Berkshire Downs and Chilterns.

Icolmkill, Inner Hebrides, Scotland: see IONA.

Icon Basilike: see EIKON BASILIKE.

Iconium (ĭkō′nēŭm), anc. city of Asia Minor, included in various regions as boundaries shifted. In Galatia when Paul visited it as a missionary. Modern Konya, Turkey is here.

iconoclasm (ĭkŏ′nōklăzŭm) [Gr.,= image-breaking], opposition to religious use of images. Use of religious pictures and statues was an early feature of Christian worship (see ICONOGRAPHY and CATACOMBS). After the 5th cent., however, images came to be associated with superstitions, and iconoclasm flourished in Monophysite center of Asia Minor and was perhaps influenced by iconoclasm of Islam, Judaism, Manichaeism, and the Paulicians. Emperors Leo III, Constantine V, Leo IV, and Leo V favored iconoclasm, but Empress IRENE restored the images. Iconoclasm was rejected at the Second Council of NICAEA. The controversy gave Byzantine art a spiritual bent, away from naturalism.

iconography (ī″kŏnŏg′-), broadly, act of representation by pictures and images, which may or may not have a symbolic as well as a literal meaning; also the study of such figural representations. Systematic investigation of the history of art has shown that each major phase or epoch has developed an iconography of its own, and the term is necessarily qualified (e.g., iconography of Egyptian deities, iconography of Napoleon, Byzantine iconography). The aim of iconographic research is to recover and express the thought behind a certain type, particularly if the type became a symbol. Christian iconography is extremely rich and varied. It began with the catacombs and developed a complex language of symbols. Every medieval artist had to learn the characters of this sacred "writing" and also the sacred "mathematics" that dictated position, group, symmetry, and number of figures in representation. The symbolic code (as in representing the Holy Ghost as a dove) has invited men to look at one thing and see the figure of another. The essence of Christian iconography lies in the expression and reading of the spiritual meaning intended in the art.

Ictinus (ĭktī′nŭs), 2d half of 5th cent. B.C., one of greatest architects of Greece. Designed PARTHENON with Callicrates as associate.

id: see PSYCHOANALYSIS.

Ida, Mount, 8,058 ft. high, central Crete; island's highest mountain. Also known as Psilorite.

Idaho, state (83,557 sq. mi.; pop. 667,191), NW U.S.; admitted 1890 as 43rd state; cap. BOISE. Other cities are POCATELLO and IDAHO FALLS. Panhandle bounded N by British Columbia; BITTERROOT RANGE (E) forms most of Mont. line; SNAKE R. part of W line. A Rocky Mt. state, Idaho changes from forested mountains N to prairies and deep canyons along

Snake R. and SALMON R., to large irrigated areas (see BOISE PROJECT; MINIDOKA PROJECT). Vast wilderness areas remain. Agr. (potatoes, wheat, sugar beets), livestock raising, lumbering, tourism (esp. SUN VALLEY). State abounds in minerals: silver (chief U.S. producer), lead, zinc, phosphate rock, antimony (sole U.S. producer). Atomic Energy Commission project near ARCO supplies power. Lewis and Clark expedition 1805 preceded rival activities of Canadian and American fur traders. Franklin was first permanent settlement 1860. Gold discovery that year brought rush of settlers. Idaho Territory set up 1863. Late 19th cent. saw growth of cattle and sheep raising, mining boom (silver and lead), arrival of railroads.

Idaho, University of, mainly at Moscow; land grant, state supported; coed.; chartered and opened 1889. Has several extension and adult education centers.

Idaho Falls, city (1966 pop. 35,711), SE Idaho, on Snake R., NE of Pocatello. Chief city of upper Snake valley (irrigated by MINIDOKA PROJECT), it is commercial and processing center of farm (potatoes, wheat, sugar beets, seed peas), livestock, and dairy area. Atomic Energy Commission's national reactor testing station is nearby.

Idaho Springs, resort city (pop. 1,480), N central Colo., just W of Denver on Clear Creek, in area of mines and hot mineral springs. Settled 1859, with first major gold strike in Colorado Rockies.

Ida Mountains (ī'dů), range, NW Turkey, SE of site of anc. Troy. Its modern name is Kazdagi. Rises to c.5,800 ft. at Mt. Gargarus.

idealism, in metaphysics, belief that the underlying reality of the universe resides in ideas, ideal forms, or an absolute. It is opposed by all types of materialism and relativistic beliefs. The classic statement of idealism was that of Plato. In modern times Hegel was the most thorough-going philosopher in his doctrines of the Absolute and the unchanging laws by which change takes place. Among later idealists Bernard Bosanquet and A. N. Whitehead may be named. Subjective idealism, represented by Bishop Berkeley, is the belief that all reality exists only in personal consciousness. Outside metaphysics the term is used in several wide senses (e.g., in art, tendency to represent things as artist thinks they should be rather than as they are).

identification, in psychology: see DEFENSE MECHANISM.

Ides: see CALENDAR.

idiocy: see FEEBLE-MINDEDNESS.

Idlewild: see QUEENS, New York city borough.

idol [Gr.], image believed to possess supernatural power because it is dwelling place of supernatural being. Represents fixation of a spiritual force in a material object. Whereas fetish or charm has inherent power, idol must be consecrated before it can be worshiped. It is animal or human in form, and is treated as though alive. Idolatry has inspired many great works of art.

Idomeneus (īdŏ'mĭnūs, –mĭnĕus), in Greek legend, aged Cretan king who led Cretan troops in the Trojan War. Caught in a storm at sea when returning home, he vowed that if the ship was saved he would sacrifice to Poseidon the first living thing he met after landing. This was his son, whom he sacrificed.

Idrisi or **Edrisi** (īdrē'sē, ĕ–), b. 1099?, d. after 1154, Arabian geographer. He compiled a description of the earth (1154), most important geographic work of the period.

Idumaea or **Idumea:** see EDOM.

Ie-jima: see OKINAWA.

Ieyasu (Ieyasu Tokugawa) (ēä'äsōō), 1542–1616, Japanese dictator, founder of TOKUGAWA shogunate. Victory over rival barons in battle of Sekigahara (1600) made him successor to Hideyoshi as supreme leader of Japan. Secured title of shogun 1603, set up cap. at Yedo (Tokyo). First tolerated, then persecuted Christian missions, but encouraged foreign trade. Name also spelled Iyeyasu.

If, Château d', France: see CHÂTEAU D'IF.

Ifni (ēf'nē), Spanish possession (c.740 sq. mi.; pop. c.50,000), NW Africa, enclave on Atlantic coast of SW Morocco; cap. Sidi Ifni (pop. c.13,000). Region is associated with Spanish fort built 1476. Morocco ceded the area to Spain in 1860; Spanish administration only nominal until 1934. Residence of governor general of Spanish Sahara until 1958. Spanish claims to territory disputed by Morocco.

Igarka (ēgär'kŭ), city (pop. 14,000), NW Asiatic RSFSR, on Yenisei R. Major lumber port with sawmills. Founded 1928; site of forced labor camps 1935–53.

Iggdrasill, another spelling for YGGDRASILL.

igloo (ĭ'glōō), dome-shaped dwelling of the Eastern Eskimo constructed from snow blocks. It is usually a temporary shelter, used when Eskimo is traveling.

Ignatius of Antioch, Saint (ĭgnā'shŭs, ăn'tēŏk), d. c.107, bishop of Antioch, Christian martyr. Wrote epistles to Christian communities to combat heresy. First to use word *Catholic;* he enjoined obedience to bishop, deacons, and presbyters. Feast: Feb. 1.

Ignatius of Constantinople, Saint, c.800–877, Greek patriarch of Constantinople. A son of Emperor MICHAEL I, he was castrated and imprisoned by LEO V (813) to prevent his accession. In 846 or 847 he was made patriarch by Empress Theodora, who approved his zeal against iconoclasm. After her banishment St. Ignatius was asked to resign, and MICHAEL III made PHOTIUS patriarch. Under BASIL I, St. Ignatius was restored and was declared legal patriarch by Fourth Council of Constantinople. Feast: Oct. 23.

Ignatius of Loyola, Saint (loiyō'lů), 1491–1556, Spanish founder of the Jesuits (see JESUS, SOCIETY OF). A courtier and then a soldier, he was converted to the religion in 1521 when recovering from wounds. At Monserrat, at Manresa, and at various other places he studied and prepared himself. In 1534 he and six companions took together vows of chastity and poverty and agreed to go to the Holy Land. War prevented their journey, but they were ordained (1537), received by the pope (1538) and kept at Rome. In 1539 Pope Paul III accepted Ignatius' *Formula,* which (called in revised form the *Constitutions*) is still the charter of the Jesuits. Ignatius was general of the order until his death. He was a leader in the Catholic REFORM, but his chief interests were foreign missions and education of boys rather than reconversion of Protestants. He was a mystic as well as a practical leader, and his *Spiritual Exercises* (begun just after his conversion) is a contemplative devotional work. His idea of the Jesuit as a "soldier of Christ" is based on St. Paul (Eph. 6.10–17). Feast: July 31.

igneous rock: see ROCK.

ignis fatuus: see WILL-O'-THE-WISP.

ignition, device for igniting an explosive mixture. Ignition system in automobiles uses electric spark which ignites compressed mixture of air and gasoline vapor in the cylinders. Necessary high-voltage current is obtained from magneto or by battery-ignition system (with engine-driven generator) and is used directly, or indirectly through storage battery. System consists of storage battery, circuit breaker, induction coil (condenser), distributor, and wiring. Low voltage from battery is increased to high voltage by flowing into primary winding of coil and setting up magnetic flux. When circuit breaker is opened low-voltage current ceases and magnetic field collapses; this induces in secondary winding of coil a high voltage which then goes to distributor for relay to spark plugs; these are "fired" in definite order to insure even movement of pistons in cylinder and smooth running of engine.

Igor (ē'gŭr), 1151–1202, Russian prince. Led unsuccessful expedition against Cumans 1185. Hero of Russian epic, *The Lay of the Host of Igor,* discovered in 1795 and attributed to 12th cent.; used by Borodin for opera, *Prince Igor.*

Igorot (īgŭrŏt'), proto-Malayan people of N central Luzon isl. They live under village-state form of organi-

SMALL CAPITALS = cross references. Pronunciation key on inside end pages. Abbreviations: p. 2.

zation and practice rice-terrace agr. Were formerly head-hunters.

Iguaçu Falls or **Iguassú Falls** (both: ēgwäsōō'), in Iguaçu R., South America. Higher and wider than Niagara, they belong partly to Argentina, partly to Brazil.

Iguala (ēgwä'lä), city (pop. c.20,000), Guerrero, SW Mexico. Famous as place where Iturbide proclaimed the Plan de Iguala, Feb. 24, 1821, which provided for Mexico's independence from Spain, for Roman Catholicism as the estab. religion, and for equality of races.

Iguana (īgwä'nù), large lizard of tropical America, West Indies, some Pacific isls. Common tropical American species is greenish (blending with the tree branches which it frequents), 3–6 ft. long, and has a crest of spiny scales from neck to tail. It eats leaves, fruit, sometimes small animals.

Iguassú Falls: see IGUAÇU FALLS.

Iguvine Tables (ĭ'gyōōvĭn), several inscribed bronze tablets discovered in 1444 at Gubbio, where most of them are still preserved. They proved helpful in understanding ancient Umbrian language and supplied information on ancient Italian religious rites.

IGY: see INTERNATIONAL GEOPHYSICAL YEAR.

Ij or **Y,** Dutch *IJ* (all: ī), inlet of the Ijsselmeer, NW Netherlands, on which Amsterdam is located. Receives Amstel R. and is connected by canals with North Sea and with Lek and Waal rivers.

Ijssel, Dutch *IJssel* (both: ī'sùl), river, 72 mi. long, E and central Netherlands. Branches from the Lower Rhine near Arnhem and flows N into the Ijsselmeer near Kampen. The Hollandsche Ijssel, in W Netherlands, branches from Lek R. and flows WSW to the Meuse just E of Rotterdam. Also Yssel.

Ijsselmeer, Dutch *IJsselmeer* (both: ī'sùlmär"), shallow fresh-water lake, N and central Netherlands. It was formed from old ZUIDER ZEE by construction of a dam (completed 1932) extending 19 mi. between North Holland and Friesland provinces. Ijssel R. is chief feeder. Large areas (293 sq. mi. in all) have been reclaimed from the former Zuider Zee since 1932. Largest is Northeast Polder (185 sq. mi.). Parts of the polders flooded in Second World War have been salvaged, and reclamation continues. Rich agr. area. Former Zuider Zee was important fishing ground.

Ikhnaton (ĭknä'tún) or **Akhenaton** (ä"kùnä'tún) [Egyptian,= Aton is satisfied], d. c.1354 B.C., king of Egypt (c.1372–c.1354 B.C.) of the XVIII dynasty, son of Amenhotep III. Beginning his reign as Amenhotep IV, he changed his name to Ikhnaton and built a new capital called Akhetaton (TEL-EL-AMARNA). He held that Aton, the sun-god, was the only god. This belief and his efforts to enforce it brought bitter opposition from the priests, unrest among the people, and rebellion in the provinces, but his period was one of the greatest of Egyptian art. His queen was NEFRETETE.

Ikon Basilike: see EIKON BASILIKE.

Ile-aux-Noix, Fort (ēl-ō-nwä'), French fort in Canada, on Île aux Noix, an island in Richelieu R., c.30 mi. SE of Montreal. Built 1759. Fort surrendered to British in 1760. Named Fort Lennox, it fell to Americans in 1775 and became base of operations against Quebec until it was evacuated in 1776. Present fortifications (now included in Fort Lennox Natl. Historic Park; 210 acres) were started in 1782 and maintained as a military post until 1870.

Ile-de-France (ēl-dù-fräs'), region and former province, N France, in Paris, Hauts-de-Seine, Val-de Marne, Seine-Saint-Denis, Val d'Oise, Yvelines, Essonnes, Seine-et-Marne, Oise, and Aisne depts; historic cap. Paris. Other cities: Beauvais, Compiègne, Fontainebleau, Soissons, Versailles. The center of the Paris basin, a fertile depression watered by the Seine, Marne, and Oise rivers, it is a vast agr. area, supplying Paris and its suburbs with fruit, vegetables, dairy products. There are many large and beautiful forests (e.g., at Fontainebleau, Compiègne, Ram-

bouillet). The cradle of the French monarchy, the region grew out of the county of Paris, whose count, Hugh Capet, became king in 987. The crown enlarged its domains, acquiring parts of Beauce, Brie, the Vexin, and other neighboring areas, and in the 15th cent. the region was made a province.

Ile de France, former name of MAURITIUS.

Ile Jésus (ēl zhäzü') or **Jesus Island,** island (93 sq. mi.; pop. 124,741), S Que., Canada, between Mille Îles R. and Rivière des Prairies. Market gardening and dairy center; suburban area of Montreal.

Iles du Salut (ēl dü sälü'), small archipelago, off French Guiana, including Devil's Island. Also Safety Islands.

Ilf, Ilya (Arnoldovich) (ēlyä' ùrnôl'dùvĭch ēlf'), pseud. of I. A. Fainzilberg, 1897–1937, Russian humorist. With Y. P. Petrov, wrote satirical works of which the best known are *The Twelve Chairs* (1928) and *Little Golden Calf* (1931).

Ilhéus (ēlyĕ'ōōs), city (pop. c.45,700), E Bahia state, Brazil; port and cacao center.

Ili (ē'lē'), river, rising in NW Sinkiang prov., China, flows c.600 mi. to Lake Balkhash, Kazakh SSR.

Iliad (ĭ'lĕùd) [from Gr. *Ilion* = Troy], Greek epic in 24 books by HOMER, telling of the wrath of ACHILLES and its consequences in the Trojan War.

Ilion: see TROY, anc. city of Asia Minor.

Ilion (ĭl'ĕún), industrial village (pop. 10,199), E central N.Y., on Mohawk R. and Barge Canal, SE of Utica. Mfg. of firearms (see REMINGTON, ELIPHALET) and typewriters.

Ilium: see TROY, anc. city of Asia Minor.

Illampú (ēyämpōō'), peak, 21,300 ft. high, E Bolivia, in Andes near L. Titicaca.

Ille-et-Vilaine (ēl'-ä-vēlēn'), department (2,697 sq. mi.; pop. 614,268), NW France, in Brittany; cap. Rennes.

Illimani (ēyēmä'nē), mountain (21,184 ft. high), E Bolivia, in Andes.

illinium: see PROMETHIUM.

Illinois, state (56,400 sq. mi.; pop. 10,081,158), N central U.S.; admitted 1818 as 21st state; cap. SPRINGFIELD. CHICAGO is the metropolis; ROCKFORD and PEORIA are other large cities. Bounded W by Mississippi R., NE by L. Michigan, S and SE by Wabash R. and Ohio R. Called the "Prairie State," it is a region of well-watered plains. Farming (livestock, corn, soybeans, wheat); mining (coal, oil, fluorspar). Meat processing, food, oil; printing and publishing; mfg. of farm machinery, metal products, chemicals. A major transportation center of Midwest. Marquette and Jolliet entered region in 1673. La Salle in 1679. French mission 1699 at CAHOKIA was first permanent settlement. Passed to British after last French and Indian War (1763). Won by U.S. in Revolution after G. R. CLARK captured Cahokia and KASKASKIA 1778. Part of Northwest Territory; became separate territory 1809. Land speculation, mob fury (see E. P. LOVEJOY, Joseph SMITH), factory of C. H. McCORMICK (1847), and railroad building of 1850s mark state's rise. Abraham Lincoln and Stephen Douglas won national attention by their debates on slavery issues in 1858. Industrial expansion followed Civil War. Farmers joined GRANGER MOVEMENT to resist domination of railroads. Labor unrest was shown by HAYMARKET SQUARE RIOT (1886) and strike at PULLMAN (1894). Opening of SAINT LAWRENCE SEAWAY AND POWER PROJECT in 1959 made Chicago major overseas shipping port.

Illinois, river formed in NE Ill. by junction of Des Plaines and Kankakee rivers. Flows c.273 mi. SW past Peoria to Mississippi R. at Grafton. Connected by canal with L. Michigan, it is important commercial and recreational waterway.

Illinois, University of, mainly at Urbana, Champaign, and Chicago; land grant, state and Federal supported; coed.; chartered 1867, opened 1868 as Illinois Industrial Univ.; renamed 1885. Pioneered in vocational education. Includes Rush Medical Col. (chartered 1837, affiliated with Univ. of Chicago 1898, transferred to the Univ. of Illinois 1941), one of oldest and best-known medical schools in U.S.

Illinois Indians, group of North American Indian tribes of Algonquian language family. In 17th cent. were scattered over S Wis., N Ill., and parts of Iowa and Mo. They were of Eastern Woodlands area culture, but also hunted buffalo. Wars with Iroquois and with Lake tribes (provoked by assassination of Pontiac) reduced Illinois Indians almost to nothing.

Illinois Institute of Technology, at Chicago; coed.; founded 1940 by merger of Armour Inst. of Technology (1892) and Lewis Inst. (1896); a Technology Center affiliate.

Illuminati (ĭloo″mĭnā′tī, –nä′tē) [Latin,= the enlightened], members of a rationalist society founded by Adam Weishaupt (after 1776) and flourishing briefly. It was connected with Freemasonry, was condemned by the Roman Catholic Church, and dissolved (1785) in Bavaria by the government. Later groups have also used the name, and the Rosicrucians call themselves Illuminati.

illuminating gas: see GAS; METHANE; NATURAL GAS.

illumination, in art, the decoration of manuscripts and books with colored and metal pictures, especially initial-letter and marginal decorations. Used in many medieval writings copied in monasteries and cathedral schools. A beautiful example is the Irish Book of Kells (8th cent.), at Trinity Col., Dublin.

Illumination, in physics: see LIGHTING; PHOTOMETRY.

illumination of streets and buildings: see LIGHTING; PHOTOMETRY.

Illyria (ĭlĭ′rēủ) and **Illyricum** (ĭlĭ′rĭkŭm). In prehistoric times Indo-European tribes (Dalmatians and Pannonians) migrated to the N and E shores of the Adriatic in region later known as Illyria. Warlike and given to piracy, they withstood Greek influence and campaigns by Macedon. Romans conquered the Illyrian kingdom and created the province of Illyricum (167 B.C.) from part of it. Later the region was Dalmatia and Pannonia. Today Illyria means the Adriatic coast N of central Albania.

Ilmen (ĭl′mủn), lake (c.400 sq. mi.), NW European RSFSR. Empties through Volkhov R. into L. Ladoga. Novgorod and Staraya Russa are near its shores.

Iloilo (ē″lō̄ē′lō), city (pop. 182,382), cap. of Iloilo prov., SE Panay, Philippines. Major port, commercial center. Seat of a junior college of the Univ. of the Philippines.

image, in optics, likeness of object produced when light rays from object are reflected from mirror or refracted by lens. A real image, one formed by light rays coming from an object and converging before producing an image, can be thrown on a screen. A virtual image formed by prolongations of rays (not by rays themselves) cannot be thrown on screen, e.g., image from plane mirror. Size of image and whether it is erect or inverted, real or virtual, depend on distance from lens and type of lens or mirror used. See *ill.*, p. 796.

imagists, Anglo-American group of poets of the 1910s who stressed concentration, hard clear images, new rhythms, and use of common speech. Led by Ezra Pound, later by Amy Lowell, the group included Richard Aldington, Hilda Doolittle, John Gould Fletcher.

imam (ĭmäm′), in Islam, leader, especially in Friday prayer at mosque. As synonym for caliph, applied by Shiites to caliphs descended from ALI. After OMAYYAD family had held caliphate for centuries, the believers in Ali's supremacy (esp. Fatimites) adopted theory that Alid caliphs were really carrying on their rule secretly and that one Alid caliph (the MAHDI) would be restored to public rule before the end of the world. The fervor of Alid followers has led to rebellions in some Moslem countries.

Imandra (ē′mủndrủ), lake (347 sq. mi.), NW European RSFSR, on Kola Peninsula. Empties into White Sea through Niva R.

imbecility: see FEEBLE-MINDEDNESS.

Imeritia (ĭmūrĭ′shủ), agr. region, W Georgian SSR, in upper Rion R. basin. Chiatura and Kutais are chief cities. Manganese and coal deposits. Independent kingdom 16th–18th cent.: annexed by Russia 1810.

immanence, in metaphysics, the presence within the natural world of a spiritual or cosmic principle, especially of the Diety. It is contrasted with transcendence.

Immanuel or **Emmanuel** [Heb.,= God with us], Isaiah's name for child who was to be a sign of Judah's deliverance. A name of Jesus. Isa. 7.14; 8.8; Mat. 1.23.

Immanuel ben Solomon, c.1265–c.1330, Hebrew satirical poet and philosopher, b. Rome. Friend of Dante.

Immermann, Karl (kärl′ ĭ′mủrmän), 1796–1840, German author. Successful as playwright in his lifetime, he survives chiefly through his novel *Die Epigonen* (1836), a satire on his contemporaries, and through short novels, e.g., *Der Oberhof.*

immigration, entrance of person into new country for purpose of establishing permanent residence; administered in U.S. by Immigration and Naturalization Service. U.S. received c.38,000,000 immigrants between 1820 and 1930, most from Europe. First move to restrict immigration was "Chinese exclusion" law (1882). Literacy requirement imposed in 1917. A quota system was set up in 1921, tightened in 1924. Quota was based on percentage of residents of a particular nationality in U.S. in 1920; Asians were almost totally excluded. So-called McCarran Act (1952) relaxed rule against Asians somewhat but strengthened "national origin" feature of earlier laws. In 1965 these national origin quotas were abolished.

immortelle: see EVERLASTING.

immunity, resistance to disease. Immunity arises from body's ability to destroy invading microorganisms and nonliving foreign organic materials by action of certain white blood corpuscles and antibodies in blood. The antibodies react in the blood stream with the invading materials (called antigens) and neutralize them. Natural immunity is due to body's inherent ability to produce certain types of antibodies. Acquired immunity may be active or passive. Active acquired immunity arises from previous infection by the specific antigen (accidentally by disease or deliberately by VACCINATION): the body acquires the ability to produce the specific antibody. Passive acquired immunity results from injection of the specific antibodies (e.g., by antitoxin injections). Antibodies are not produced in the blood; the body produces antibodies only in the tissues, from which antibodies may be released into the blood. When neutralization of antigens by antibodies occurs in the blood stream, there is no clinical reaction; immunity exists. When neutralization occurs in the tissues, a violent reaction (ANAPHYLAXIS) may occur. See also ALLERGY.

impala or **pallah,** antelope (*Aepyceros*) of E and S African bush country. It is reddish brown shading to whitish on under parts; shoulder height c.3 ft. Only male has horns (long, curved, lyre-shaped).

impatiens, touch-me-not, or **balsam,** annual or perennial plant of genus *Impatiens* with seed pods that burst at a touch when ripe. Annual garden balsams (*Impatiens balsamina*) have camellialike flowers. Wild jewelweed (*I. capensis* or *I. biflora*), native to moist soil in North America, has orange spurred flowers.

impeachment, formal accusation made by a legislature against a public official charging crime or serious misconduct. Also loosely used to describe the ensuing trial. In England, House of Commons presented articles of impeachment to House of Lords, who rendered judgment. Impeachment of Warren Hastings (1788–95) was one of last English cases. U.S. Constitution gives House of Representatives right to impeach U.S. officials (but not members of Congress). Senate tries cases; vote of two thirds of those present necessary to convict. Famous case was that of Pres. Andrew Johnson (impeached, but not convicted).

Imperial, city (1963 pop. 3,007), SE Calif., SSE of Salton Sea in Imperial Valley; founded 1902. Hq. of Imperial Irrigation District.

Imperial Beach, residential and resort city (pop. 17,-773), extreme SW Calif., S of San Diego near Mexican border. Several U.S. naval bases are nearby.

Imperial Conference, assembly of representatives of self-governing members of British Empire, held about every four years. First called Colonial Conferences (1887–1906) and dealt with defense problems. Since 1907 economic problems have been discussed. Dominion premiers now attempt to unify Empire policy. Decisions have no legal power, but are influential. Has not met formally since Second World War.

imperialism, broadly, extension of rule or influence by one people over another. Empires have existed since dawn of history, as in Egypt, Mesopotamia, Assyria, and Persian Empire. Ancient imperialism reached climax in Roman Empire and in Byzantine Empire and later Ottoman Empire. In West imperialism emerged with rise of modern national states and age of exploration and discovery; and term is normally restricted to this modern type of empire building. Through colonies European hegemony was introduced by force, with an assumed superiority over native people. Spanish and Portuguese built "trading" empires, British and French true "settlement" empires, all motivated by MERCANTILISM and later by the need for markets and raw materials created by the Industrial Revolution. Westward expansion of U.S. was strongly imperialistic in tone, though U.S. had no colonies until Spanish-American War. Term is also used specifically to denote European expansion into Asia and Africa 1884–1914, which MARXISM considered the ultimate stage of capitalism. Since 1945 most colonies have achieved independence, though Communists hold that Western nations are still imperialistic, exercising control by economic rather than political means.

Imperial Valley, low-lying area, SE Calif., in middle of old Colorado Desert. Most of region is below sea level. Rainfall is scanty, and there are sudden, extreme changes in temperature (32°F.–115°F.). Irrigation from Colorado R. (begun c.1900, hindered by floods) succeeded by 1907. About 1,000,000 acres now irrigated, especially by ALL-AMERICAN CANAL. Chief crops are fruit, alfalfa, truck crops, and cotton. Main cities are Brawley, Calexico, Calipatria, El Centro, Holtville, Imperial, and Westmorland. SALTON SEA is in valley.

impressionism, in painting, a late 19th-cent. French school. Its adherents attempted to depict quick visual impressions, often painted directly from nature. By using broken color they produced a luminous effect and were particularly successful with sunlight. Movement originated in 1870s and became popular in '90s, when most of its exponents had already left it. Most consistent impressionists were Monet, Sisley, and Pissarro. Others associated with school were Renoir and Degas. The term is used also in music for a late 19th-cent. French movement, typified in works of DEBUSSY.

impressment, enforcement of conscription. May be applied either to property or to persons in peace or war by virtue of a state's sovereign authority, except that constitutional limitations and legal regulations must be respected. In most modern democracies impressment in the historic sense of a "press gang" actually seizing and carrying an individual into service has been abandoned. Impressment of American sailors by the British was a cause of the War of 1812.

In, chemical symbol of the element INDIUM.

inbreeding, mating of closely related living things. Used to preserve desirable characteristics in the progeny of plants and animals; inbreeding reduces chances of diversity of characters. Repeated inbreeding establishes pure lines, in which both alternate genes (alleles) for each character are identical. Pure lines are useful in research where plants or animals having identical genetic make-up are required.

Inca (ĭng'kù), pre-Colombian Indian empire (c.650,000 sq. mi.; pop. c.6,000,000), centered at Cuzco, Peru. The name Inca specifically refers to emperor and is used loosely to mean his people. Founded c.1200, empire reached its greatest extent under Huayna Capac (1493–1525), who was succeeded by his sons Huascar and Atahualpa. Atahualpa won in ensuing civil war, but Spanish, under Pizarro, began (1533) conquest of empire. Through a genius for organization, the Inca had welded together many peoples speaking different languages and exercised close control. The state was responsible for welfare of subjects, and owned everything except houses and movable household goods. Taxes were collected in labor. Populations were shifted at government's discretion for economic and control purposes. The Inca were skilled in engineering and agriculture, their activities in those fields running to road, bridge, drainage, and irrigation construction, and use of fertilizer. Highly developed arts and crafts included textiles, metallurgy, and ceramics.

incest (ĭn'sĕst), sexual relations between persons to whom marriage is prohibited because of blood relationship. Degree of proscribed relationship varies from group to group; in some societies marriage between clan members is taboo; in others even brother-sister marriage is accepted (e.g., among Egyptian and Inca royalty).

Inchcolm (ĭnch'kŭm), small island in Firth of Forth, Fifeshire, Scotland. Has ruins of Abbey of St. Columba (founded 1123).

Inchon (ĭn'chŏn'), city (pop. c.402,000), South Korea, on Yellow Sea. Its ice-free harbor is the port for Seoul. Textile and steel center. Formerly called Chemulpo.

incinerator (ĭnsĭ'nŭrātùr), furnace for burning combustible refuse. Usually it consists of a brick-lined combustion chamber fitted with stationary or mechanically-operated grates, charging holes, stoking and removal openings, ducts, and valves; often there are forced-draft blowers supplying air for combustion and a flue conducted through tall chimney.

inclined plane, a simple machine, of ancient origin, using a slanted plane up which the load or resistance is moved. Work put into the machine equals the effort multiplied by length of the plane; work output is product of the load and the height of the plane. Applications include the screw, wedge, chisel, carpenter's plane, and ax.

inclosure or **enclosure,** in British history, the practice of fencing off land formerly subject to common rights. Began in 12th cent. and accompanied breakdown of manorial system. Increased with growth of Flemish wool trade and resulting monetary advantages of fenced sheep pastures after 14th cent. Reached its peak in late 17th cent. Caused shift of poor to towns. Encouraged efficient tillage and reclamation of wasteland.

income tax: see INTERNAL REVENUE.

incubator, artificially heated apparatus for hatching eggs. Crude incubators were devised in ancient times; the Chinese have long used baskets heated by layers of wheat. Modern incubators are usually operated by electricity with automatic controls for heat, air, and moisture, and devices for turning eggs. Modified smaller models are used for premature babies and for the culture of microorganisms.

incunabula (ĭn"kyōōnä'byōōlù), books of the "cradle" days of printing (15th cent.) by such printers as Gutenberg, Jenson, Caxton, and Aldus Manutius. There are many well-known European collections. Notable American collections are in Washington (Library of Congress), New York (Pierpont Morgan Library and others), Providence (John Carter Brown Library and Annmary Brown Memorial), and San Marino, Calif. (Henry E. Huntington Library).

Independence. 1 City (pop. 11,222), SE Kansas, SE of Wichita on Verdigris R. near Okla. line; founded 1869. Refining center in oil-producing area. Nearby is site of Rebel Creek battle, where Confederate detachment was wiped out by Indians. **2** City (pop. 62,328), W Mo., E of Kansas City; founded 1827. Was starting point for SANTA FE TRAIL, OREGON TRAIL, and California Trail. Hq. of Reorganized Church of Jesus Christ of Latter Day Saints. Home of H. S. Truman and site of Harry S. Truman Library.

Independence, Declaration of: see DECLARATION OF INDEPENDENCE.

Independence Day: see FOURTH OF JULY.

Independence Hall, building in Philadelphia on Independence Square. Houses LIBERTY BELL and historical museum. Scene of proclamation of Declaration of Independence and meeting place of Continental Congress and Constitutional Convention. Part of Independence Natl. Historical Park.

Independents, in religion, name given to Christian congregations claiming freedom from ecclesiastical and civil authority. In England called Brownists (see BROWNE, ROBERT) or SEPARATISTS until in 17th cent. name Independents became popular.

Independent Treasury System. Pres. Andrew Jackson secured transfer of government funds from BANK OF THE UNITED STATES to state banks, but Panic of 1837, at least partially brought on by transfer of government surplus to states, showed evils of that arrangement. Pres. Van Buren proposed an independent treasury isolated from all banks. A law to this end was passed in 1840, but the Whigs, victorious in national election, repealed it. Objections of Pres. John Tyler on constitutional grounds prevented establishment of another Bank of the United States. Following Democratic return to power, an act of Aug., 1846, ordered public revenues retained in the Treasury building and in subtreasuries (see SUBTREASURY) in various cities. Treasury was to pay out its own funds and be completely independent of banking and financial system of the nation. In practice, however, specie tended to accumulate in the Treasury to detriment of business. Civil War put strain on Treasury and proved interdependence of Treasury and banks; NATIONAL BANK was created. Old theory of absolute independence was in practice abandoned by 1898. Federal Reserve Act of 1913 marked true end of Independent Treasury.

Index or **Index librorum prohibitorum,** list of books Roman Catholics were not allowed to read without special permission of a bishop. It has been suppressed in accordance with reforms issued by Vatican II.

index, of a book or periodical, a list, nearly always alphabetical, of the topics treated. Seeks to direct reader to every subject and proper name about which any information is given in book. Indexes to periodicals are less specific; in U.S., *Poole's Index* to most widely circulated periodicals began in 1848 and was superseded in 1907 by *Reader's Guide to Periodical Literature.* Special fields of knowledge have indexes, as do some newspapers such as *The Times* of London and New York *Times.*

index number, figure showing change in price or quantity in ratio to a number taken as norm, or base, often expressed in percentage. Index of wages divided by index of cost of living is index of purchasing power, or real wages.

India, subcontinent, S Asia, cut off from most of the continent by lofty Himalayas. In it are PAKISTAN and republic of **India,** officially also called *Bharat* (1,262,-275 sq. mi.; pop. c.442,000,000); member of British Commonwealth of Nations; cap. New Delhi. Comprises 17 states and 10 centrally administered territories. Among states are Maharashtra, Madras, Kerala, Mysore, and Uttar Pradesh. SIKKIM is a protectorate. Republic is bounded NE by Burma and China, N by Tibet and Nepal, and NW by W Pakistan, with E Pakistan forming an enclave in NE India. The subcontinent is in its S half a huge peninsula jutting between Arabian Sea and Bay of Bengal. Great Indian rivers are Ganges, Brahmaputra, and Indus. Agr. output is inadequate for feeding vast population. Crops include rice, cotton, jute, and tea. Among natural resources are valuable forests (esp. teak and ebony) and deposits of mica, manganese, coal, copper, and iron. Heavy industry is centered at Jamshedpur (iron and steel), Bombay (textiles), and Calcutta (jute products). Largest cities and main ports are Bombay, Calcutta, and Madras. Much of Indian life is still largely based on CASTE system, despite official disapproval. Relief from life of poverty is found in religious rites (mainly Hindu and Moslem) and in pilgrimages to holy cities, notably Benares. Earliest known civilization was Indus valley civilization, taking root in MOHENJO-DARO and Harappa and flourishing from 3d millenium to c.1500 B.C. It was destroyed by invasions of Vedic Aryans who attacked India from NW in c.1500 B.C. and developed a Brahmanic civilization, in which basic tenets of HINDUISM were formulated. BUDDHISM and JAINISM emerged in 6th cent. B.C. Hinduism was at first the religion of MAURYA empire (325–184 B.C.), founded after Alexander the Great's invasion of N India (c.326 B.C.); but in 3d cent. B.C. ASOKA estab. Buddhism as state religion. During Gupta dynasty (A.D. 320?–c.544?) and reign of Harsha (606–47), Hindu culture enjoyed a golden age. After 8th cent., Rajputs dominated NW. Moslem power began with raids of Mahmud of Ghazni in 11th cent. and establishment (1206) of DELHI SULTANATE. MOGUL empire, founded 1526 by BABER, flourished under AKBAR, SHAH JEHAN, and AURANGZEB. Meanwhile the Portuguese had taken Goa in 1510; in 18th cent., while MAHRATTAS and SIKHS were weakening the empire, the British and French carved out colonial domains. Victories of Robert CLIVE over DUPLEIX ended all European threats to power of British East India Co. Warren HASTINGS as governor general did much to solidify Clive's gains. SEPOY REBELLION (1857) led to abolition of East India Co. and transfer of Indian rule to crown. Some steps taken toward self-government; Indians educated in new universities formed INDIAN NATIONAL CONGRESS (1885). Movement for independence became important after GANDHI assumed leadership of Congress. Desire of Congress to form united front against Britain was balked by MOSLEM LEAGUE (led by Mahomed Ali Jinnah), which agitated for separate Moslem state (Pakistan). When India became free in 1947, Congress reluctantly agreed to partition. Dominion of India became sovereign republic Jan. 26, 1950, with Jawarhalal NEHRU as prime minister. Problems facing India included overpopulation, underdeveloped economy, undereducation, and difficulty of creating national unity from diverse cultural and linguistic groups. Major foreign policy problems were border dispute with Communist China, which reached peak in 1962 with Chinese offensive against Ladakh, and struggle with Pakistan over KASHMIR, which erupted in serious armed conflict in 1965. After the death of Nehru (1964), his successors—Lal Bahadur Shastri, prime minister from 1964 until his death in 1966, and Mrs. Indira Gandhi, daughter of Nehru, who became prime minister the same year—strove to maintain India's position as leader of the neutralist countries in the face of the same severe internal problems prevailing in 1950.

Indiana, state (36,291 sq. mi.; pop. 4,662,498), N central U.S.; admitted 1816 as 19th state; cap. and largest city INDIANAPOLIS. Other large cities are EVANSVILLE, FORT WAYNE, SOUTH BEND, TERRE HAUTE. Bounded NW by L. Michigan, S and SE by Ohio R., SW by WABASH R. Farming (corn, soybeans, wheat, livestock, dairying); mining (coal, limestone, oil). Mfg. of steel, other metals, transportation equipment, electrical and other machinery, chemicals, and food products. A major transportation complex of Midwest. French estab. first permanent settlement at VINCENNES (c.1702). British took over region in 1763. Won by U.S. in Revolution after G. R. CLARK captured Vincennes 1779. Indiana Territory estab. 1800. Process of subduing Indians continued through indecisive battle of TIPPECANOE

(1811) under W. H. HARRISON. Immigration swelled after virtual dispossession of Indians following War of 1812. State hurt by Panic of 1837. Supported Union in Civil War despite activities of KNIGHTS OF THE GOLDEN CIRCLE. Rapid rise of industry in late 19th cent. found farmers and laborers fighting for their rights. State benefited by opening 1959 of SAINT LAWRENCE SEAWAY AND POWER PROJECT.

Indiana, industrial borough (pop. 13,005), W Pa., NE of Pittsburgh; settled c.1772. Chief supply and trade center for bituminous-coal-mine area in Alleghenies. Seat of Indiana Univ. of Pennsylvania.

Indian Affairs, Bureau of, created (1824) in U.S. War Dept. and transferred (1849) by act of Congress to U.S. Dept. of the Interior. Had jurisdiction over Indian trade and removal of Indians to reservations in the West. Developed primarily into land-administering agency. Now also provides educational facilities and other services.

Indianapolis, city (pop. 476,258), state cap. (since 1825) and largest city, central Ind., on White R.; settled 1820. Major grain and livestock market; commercial, transportation, and industrial center; farm-processing point. Mfg. of automobile bodies, aircraft engines, pharmaceutical products, and electronic and electrical equipment. Seat of Butler Univ., Marian Col., Indiana Central Col., Herron School of Art, and medical school of Indiana Univ. Here are home and burial place of J. W. Riley, home of Benjamin Harrison, and American Legion national hq. Annual Indianapolis Motor Speedway races are held nearby.

Indian art and architecture is essentially decorative and often highly symbolic. Historical period began c.250 B.C. with Buddhist shrines, temples, and stupas (memorial mounds), which show Persian and Greek influence. Paintings were mainly frescoes. Jain work (100 B.C.–A.D. 1300) flourished as Buddhism waned (from 3d cent.), resulting in impressive temples with pointed domes. Hindu style, which borrowed much from the Jains, is marked by pyramidal roof and great richness of detail. Finest example of late Indian Moslem style, characterized by graceful dome, arch, and minarets, is the TAJ MAHAL. As architectural decoration sculpture was more important than painting. Decorative arts (e.g., damascening and jewelry making) have been carried to perfection.

Indiana University, mainly at Bloomington; state supported; coed.; chartered 1820 as seminary, opened 1824; became college 1828 and university 1838. Regional campuses at East Chicago, Gary, Jeffersonville, Kokomo, and South Bend; university centers at Evansville, Richmond, and Vincennes. Medical school at Indianapolis. Has noted nuclear energy laboratory.

Indian breadroot: see BREADROOT.

Indian literature. An extensive written literature in vernacular languages of the subcontinent of India did not appear until 16th cent. Its development was spurred by emergence of Hindu pietistic movements which encouraged popularizing of SANSKRIT LITERATURE. Great classics, e.g., *Ramayana*, were put into popular verse form. Classical Persian poetry was basis for Urdu verse written for Mogul court. In early 19th cent. popular prose began to flourish with introduction of printing presses and establishment of vernacular schools. Literature today includes works in English and major languages of India and Pakistan. Best-known writers of modern India include Tagore, Iqbal, R. K. Narayan, Sudhin N. Ghose, and Sarojini Naidu. See PALI LITERATURE and PRAKRIT LITERATURE.

Indian music of North America is primarily a vocal art. It is entirely melodic, having no harmony or polyphony. Intonation is uncertain, resulting from the use of forced muscular tension in the vocal chords. Drums and rattles are the chief percussion instruments; wind instruments are mainly flutes and whistles. A song is considered a means of communication with supernatural powers; definite results, (e.g., victory, rain, or health) are expected. There is no system of notation; songs are handed down from generation to genera-

tion. Certain ceremonial and medicinal songs are believed to be owned by the singer and to have been received by him in a dream. Only the owner of such a song may sing it, unless he chooses to sell it and share the mystical properties that accompany it. Most love songs associated with Indians actually show strong European influence.

Indian Mutiny: see SEPOY REBELLION.

Indian National Congress, political organization of India, founded 1885. Original purpose was to make India a British dominion by constitutional means. In 1917 the militants, led by GANDHI, forced resignation of moderates and began call for *Swaraj* [complete independence]. Their chief weapon, a passive resistance campaign, was first used on large scale in 1919. Refusal to cooperate with the British in Second World War led to arrest of its leaders. Outlawed 1942–45. In conferences leading to India's independence (1947), party was forced to bow to demand of MOSLEM LEAGUE for separate state of Pakistan. Under the leadership of NEHRU (1947–64) the Congress became ruling party of India. On his death leadership passed to Lal Bahadur Shastri (1964–66), then in 1966 to Nehru's daughter, Mrs. Indira Gandhi. Party's strength was greatly weakened in elections of 1967.

Indian Ocean, third largest ocean of world, extending from India to Antarctica and from E Africa to Tasmania; stretches c.4,000 mi. along equator and c.6,000 mi. N to S. Greatest known depth, c.24,000 ft., is near Java. Its great seasonal winds (monsoon) bring rain to SE Asia. Only northern part is important for shipping.

Indianola (ĭn"dēŭnō'lù), vanished town, S Texas, on Matagorda Bay S of Port Lavaca; founded 1844. Once most bustling port in Texas, it was destroyed by hurricanes (1875, 1886).

Indian paintbrush or **painted cup,** parasitic annual or perennial plant (*Castilleja*), with many species native to W U.S. They bear flowerlike red bracts.

Indian pipe, low funguslike saprophytic woodland plant, waxy white or salmon, of genus *Monotropa*, found in North America and Asia. It has scalelike leaves and pipe-shaped flowers which form seeds.

Indian River, lagoon, c.100 mi. long, E Fla., paralleling coast and extending S from N of Titusville to Stuart. Resorts border its shores. Its fertile valley produces citrus fruit.

Indians, American, peoples who occupied North America, Middle America, and South America before the coming of the Europeans. Most authorities today believe that the Indians came into the W Hemisphere from Asia via the Bering Strait in a series of migrations (the waves accounting for many linguistic families). Common origin is taken to explain the common physical features—coarse, straight black hair, dark eyes, sparse body hair, and brownish skin color. They supposedly brought with them their Neolithic culture; most Indians made fire with a drill, had domesticated dogs, made baskets, and used stone tools. In Middle America and South America high material cultures were built up before the coming of the white man: MAYA, TOLTEC, AZTEC, INCA, and CHIBCHA. The development of powerful city-states and, in the case of the Inca, a true empire, was accompanied by a rich architectural and artistic development. Some tribes, however (e.g., those of Tierra del Fuego) had very sparse material culture. Other groups had intermediate culture, some agricultural, and some dependent on gathering, hunting, and fishing. Among the agricultural societies, maize was generally the basic crop. Anthropologists distinguish so-called culture areas (as Eastern Woodlands, Plains). In 1492 Indians N of Mexico numbered 900,000, but by 1870 they had dwindled to 300,000. In 1945, there were 400,000. In most Central and South American countries, the Indian strain predominates, and in the 20th cent. a movement for reviving and preserving Indian culture (*indianismo*) has been strong.

Indian Territory, in U.S. history, name generally applied to country set aside for Indians by Indian Intercourse Act (1834) and more particularly applied to territory to which Cherokee, Creek, Seminole, Choctaw, and Chickasaw tribes were removed between 1820 and 1845. E part of present Okla., N of Red R., became known as Indian Territory as Indians were gradually forced into settlement there. Tribes other than original five also moved there. Extinction of Territory came in 1907 with entrance of Okla. into the Union.

Indian turnip: see JACK-IN-THE-PULPIT.

Indian wars, term referring to the years of conflict between the white man and North American Indians. After 1815 U.S. government pursued policy of Indian removal to reservations more or less successfully, although removal often brought battle between regular army and Indians. The wars reached climax 1869–75, and Wounded Knee in 1890 is often considered last battle.

India-rubber tree: see RUBBER PLANT.

Indic languages, branch of Indo-Iranian subfamily of Indo-European languages. See LANGUAGE (table).

indictment (indīt'mŭnt) formal written charge of a crime made by a public prosecutor before a grand jury. The grand jury, in turn, offers the charge against the accused. A person suspected of crime may also be brought to trial by presentment (accusation issued by the grand jury though the prosecutor has not offered a formal bill of indictment) or by information (accusation made directly by prosecutor without consideration by grand jury; not permissible in capital or otherwise infamous crime). When an indictment or a presentment is approved, the foreman of the grand jury marks it "true bill."

indigo, the most important blue dye. Known in ancient India and Egypt, it was introduced into Europe in 16th cent. It is obtained from leguminous plants of genus *Indigofera* by fermentation of macerated plants; these liberate colorless indican which oxidizes to blue indigo when stirred. Adolf von Baeyer first synthesized it.

Indio, city (pop. 6,450), SE Calif., ESE of Redlands. Trade center in COACHELLA VALLEY. Joshua Tree Natl. Monument is near.

indium, silver-white, metallic element (symbol = In; see also ELEMENT, table) resembling aluminum. It is relatively soft, malleable, and ductile.

Indo-Aryan, alternate name for INDIC LANGUAGES. Broader uses on a racial basis are now obsolete.

Indo-China, former French possession, also once called French Indo-China. It has become North VIETNAM and South VIETNAM, LAOS, and CAMBODIA.

Indo-European, family of languages to which English belongs. It includes more speakers than any other family. See LANGUAGE (table).

Indo-Iranian, subfamily of Indo-European languages. See LANGUAGE (table).

Indonesia, island republic (c.574,400 sq. mi.; pop. c.95,200,000), SE Asia, comprising c.3,000 islands in Malay Archipelago; cap. DJAKARTA. Principal island groups are SUNDA ISLANDS (including JAVA, SUMATRA, and BORNEO); Lesser Sundas (including BALI and part of TIMOR); the MOLUCCAS; the RIOUW ARCHIPELAGO; and WEST NEW GUINEA (West Irian). Rice, maize, tapioca, sago, tea, and spices are grown. Forest products include rubber, quinine, palm oil, and hardwoods. Large supplies of oil, tin, and bauxite. Little industrial production. Inhabitants are chiefly Malayan and Papuan; Chinese form largest minority; Islam dominant religion. Early in Christian era, area came under influence of Indian civilization through influx of Buddhist and Hindu monks; great native empires that emerged after 7th cent. were strongly linked to Hinduism and Buddhism. Islam was introduced by Arab traders in 13th cent. By 16th cent., when Portuguese traders appeared, Indonesia had disintegrated into many small weak states. The Portuguese were soon ousted by Dutch East India Co., which succeeded also (1610–23) in removing rivalry of British East India Co. After liquidation of company (1798), area came under direct rule of Dutch government; known thereafter as Netherlands East Indies. Dutch rule was broken briefly 1811–15 when islands were occupied by the British under Raffles. Native Indonesian independence movements began early in 20th cent.; in 1927 Indonesian Nationalist party arose under leadership of SUKARNO, and in Second World War nationalists were active throughout Japanese occupation. Indonesia was proclaimed an independent republic in 1945, but the Dutch were bitterly opposed and intermittent warfare followed even after a compromise proposal for a United States of Indonesia was accepted by both sides. Indonesia became a sovereign country on Dec. 28, 1949. Called the United States of Indonesia, it comprised the nationalist-sponsored republic of Indonesia and 15 Dutch-supported states. Federation gave way in Aug., 1950, to unified republic (headed by Sukarno). Relations between the two countries continued to worsen until 1960 when they were severed. Under Sukarno's erratic rule Indonesia knew considerable political and economic instability. A revolt of dissident army officers (1956–58) which was crushed with Soviet Aid prompted him to dissolve parliament. In 1959 Sukarno restored the 1945 charter which gave executive wide powers. Indonesia opposed creation of the Federation of Malaysia, and in 1965 it resigned from the UN in protest to Malaysia's election to the UN. An attempted pro-Communist coup in late 1965 was suppressed by the army; Sukarno was left virtually powerless with responsibility being assumed by Lt. Gen. Suharto. The congress later confirmed Suharto in his emergency power. In 1967 he became acting president. In 1966 Indonesia and Malaysia agreed on principles for reaching a solution to their armed disagreements.

Indore (indôr'), former princely state, W central India; in 1956 became part of Madhya Pradesh. Was part of Madhya Bharat 1948–56. **Indore,** city (pop. 395,035), was capital of Indore maharajas; now major commercial center.

Indra (ĭn'drŭ), in Vedic religion and in Hinduism, god of war and storms, a beneficent deity of Aryan invaders of India. With rise of Brahmanism, he was displaced by trinity of Brahma, Vishnu, and Siva. See also VEDA.

Indre (ē'drŭ), department (2,666 sq. mi.; pop. 251,432), central France, in Berry, crossed by Indre R.; cap. Châteauroux.

Indre-et-Loire (ēdrălwär'), department (2,378 sq. mi.; pop. 395,210), N central France, in Touraine; cap. Tours.

induction. Electrostatic induction is the production of an electric charge on a body by bringing it near a charged body. This "charging by induction" can be done, for example, by bringing a negatively charged body near an uncharged body; negative charges in the uncharged body are repelled and some will leave the uncharged body if there is a conductor through which they can run off into the ground. If ground connection is removed before charged body is withdrawn, the originally uncharged body will be positively charged since negative charges have become less than number of positive charges. Electromagnetic induction is accomplished by movement of a conductor through a stationary magnetic field (i.e., stationary magnetic lines of force) or by movement of a magnetic field (i.e., transverse movement of magnetic lines of force) through a stationary conductor. The magnetic field may be set up by an ordinary magnet or it may be an electromagnetic field, set up by flow of current in another and entirely separate conductor. Movement of an electromagnetic field may be caused by either of two methods: by actually moving the conductor through which the current flows or by increasing or decreasing the current, causing the field to expand or shrink. Self-induction, also called electromagnetic inertia or inductance, is the setting up in a conductor of a current opposing a change of the original current, i.e., it retards both an increase and a decrease, so that current cannot be instantaneously started or stopped. See also GENERATOR; MAGNETISM; TRANSFORMER.

indulgence (ĭndŭl′jŭns). The Roman Catholic Church teaches that a sinner, forgiven through the sacrament of penance, must yet make satisfaction for his sins here or in purgatory. But Christ and his saints have by their good works earned a superfluity of satisfaction to God for human sins, and this accumulated grace is called doctrinally the Infinite Treasury of Merits. From this satisfaction the Church as God's ministry remits punishment the sinner would otherwise have to undergo. Official statement of this remission is an indulgence, which may be gained by Catholics in many ways (e.g., prayers, visiting churches). Until the Council of TRENT, there were many abuses in granting indulgences (esp. their purchase for money), and it was these abuses that LUTHER first denounced.

Indus (ĭn′dŭs), river, c.1,800 mi. long, rising in Himalayas in W Tibet. Flows through Kashmir and West Pakistan (where it is joined by Panjnad R.) to Arabian Sea. Chief river of West Pakistan. An ancient civilization (see INDUS VALLEY CIVILIZATION) flourished on its banks.

Indus Civilization: see MOHENJO-DARO.

industrial diseases: see OCCUPATIONAL DISEASES.

industrial management, the highly organized modern method of carrying on industrial operations. Growth of manufacturing required special supervision of machinery and elimination of inefficiency. The first sustained effort in this direction was made in the 1880s by F. W. Taylor of the Midvale Steel Co. The motions of workers were studied to speed up production by cutting out excess movements. Such time and motion studies of the flow of materials through the plant became a major item of inquiry, as did product design. Relations with workers became the subject of industrial psychology. Soon after 1910 U.S. firms estab. the first personnel departments, and much attention was given to improving worker morale by providing better facilities and new incentives, such as chance for advancement and, occasionally, a voice in management. Other items that have come to be the concern of management include safety devices, better sanitation, rest, eating, and recreation facilities, health insurance, and pensions. Automation has been a source of labor-management friction and the cause of many strikes since the late 50's.

Industrial Revolution. The term refers primarily to the period in English history, roughly 1750–1850, in which striking changes in economic structure were produced by transition from stable agr. and commercial society to modern industrialism. Voyages of 15th and 16th cent. opened the way for world-wide commerce. Capitalism appeared in 17th cent. Machines were made of wood and driven by water and wind power. In 18th cent. the change to steam power was made by James Watt. England became world textile center and there were such inventions as Arkwright's spinning frame (1769) and Edmund Cartwright's power loom (1783). Coke was used in iron production; coal mines and the use of steel became of paramount importance. Factories and industrial towns sprang up. In 19th cent. railroads and steamboats wrought new changes. Electricity and the gasoline engine have produced further changes. Spread has been world wide. Germany (after 1850), U.S. (after Civil War), and Japan (in 20th cent.) have been transformed by industrialism. Accompanying economic philosophy was laissez faire doctrine of Adam Smith. Later interpretations have been attempted by Karl Marx, Socialism, and the Manchester school. Industrialism has divided society into opposing classes of capital and labor, brought about world economic interdependence, and introduced many economic problems as well as causing a world-wide rise in the level of material goods.

industrial union, one composed of all the workers in a given industry, regardless of skill, craft, or occupation.

All American unions were craft unions until the 1870s. Knights of Labor, Industrial Workers of the World, and the C.I.O. have advocated organizations cutting across craft lines. An industrial union is called a vertical union (including workers of all levels of skills), as opposed to horizontal or craft unions.

Industrial Workers of the World (IWW), revolutionary industrial union, organized 1905 in Chicago. Among founders were Eugene V. DEBS, William D. HAYWOOD, Daniel DE LEON. Members were nicknamed "Wobblies." It aimed to overthrow capitalism and achieve socialism by uniting all workers, calling general strike to lock out employers, seizing industry, and setting up trade union state. It opposed arbitration and collective bargaining, concentrating on direct action. After 1908, it became organization of the unskilled, reaching peak strength of 100,000 in 1912, but diminishing rapidly after 1917.

Indus valley civilization or **Harappan civilization,** one of world's earliest high civilizations, mainly in what is today West Pakistan. Forgotten until 1922 when excavation began, it flourished c.2500 B.C. in the valley of the Indus river and its tributaries. An urban, conservative, peaceful culture, its two major cities were Mohenjo-Daro in S on Indus R. and Harappa 400 mi. to N on Ravi R. There were at least 60 other known settlements, all of which were carefully planned. The arts flourished, there was some trade with Sumer. Its pictographic writing is as yet undeciphered. The cause of its decline c.1500 B.C. is not certain, but there is evidence of prolonged flooding.

Indy, Vincent d' (vĕsä′ dĕdē′), 1851–1931, French composer; pupil of Franck. His compositions include *Symphony on a French Mountain Air* for piano and orchestra; symphonic variations, *Istar;* songs, chamber music, piano works, and three symphonies.

inertia (ĭnûr′shŭ), in physics, resistance of body at rest to being set in motion and that of body in motion to being accelerated, retarded, or changed in direction. Force must be applied to overcome it.

Inez de Castro: see CASTRO, INÉS DE.

infallibility (ĭnfăl″ŭbĭl′ĭtē), in Christian thought, inability of Church to err as a teaching authority. The idea is widely rejected by Protestants. There is disagreement as to which organ of Church is protected by God from teaching error. Orthodox hold ecumenical councils infallible; Roman Catholics agree but do not accept conciliar acts unratified by the pope. The dogma that the pope's pronouncements made ex cathedra on faith and morals are infallible was enounced by the Vatican Council (1870).

infant, human baby from birth to about two years. Development and characteristics vary greatly. Average birth weight 6½–7½ lb.; height, 20–21 in. Weight usually is doubled at 5–6 months, trebled at one year. Height increases c.5 in. in first 6 months, 8 to 10 in. by end of year. Skull bones, sutures, and posterior of two fontanels (called "soft spots") close in several weeks; larger, front fontanel at about one year. Teeth usually begin to erupt at 5–8 months; first dentition (20 teeth) complete at 24–30 months. At first human milk or substitute formula provides essential nutrients except vitamins C and D. Cereals and strained foods are added gradually. Injections immunizing against diphtheria, smallpox, and other diseases are advisable during first year. Affectionate care is needed for healthy development.

infantile paralysis: see POLIOMYELITIS.

infantry, body of foot soldiers equipped with handcarried weapons. Used in all ancient wars (see PHALANX, LEGION); importance declined with advent of light cavalry in Middle Ages. Became dominant with reappearance of mass warfare in 14th cent.; in 20th cent. strongly supported by artillery, aircraft, tanks.

infectious diseases: see COMMUNICABLE DISEASES.

inferiority complex, Adler's term for a COMPLEX of emotionally toned ideas centered on real or imaginary handicaps. Attempt to compensate for feelings of inferiority may lead to behavior aimed at proving them unjustified. Failure to compensate successfully ends in NEUROSIS. Successful compensation is directed to valuable social or personal ends.

infinity, in mathematics, term for quantity larger than any number; indicated by symbol ∞. In geometry, a position an infinite distance from the portion of space considered.

inflation and deflation. In economics inflation is often defined as increase of circulating currency beyond needs of trade; deflation, the opposite. Each involves fall or rise of purchasing power of money and corresponding rise or fall in prices.

inflection, in grammar. In most languages words can be arranged in formally similar sets, such that members of each set have a common feature (stem, root, or base), and members of different sets have features in common not included in the stem; these features are often called inflections. Examples of languages with extensive inflections are Latin, Eskimo, and Arabic; of those with few inflections, Chinese. Typical Latin noun or adjective is inflected for CASE and NUMBER; adjectives are inflected for gender. Latin verbs have overlapping categories of inflection, MOOD, VOICE, TENSE, person, and number. Some linguists distinguish between inflection and agglutination, which is inflection with relative looseness of fusion between stem and inflectional feature. In 19th cent. theory was widely held that agglutination was more primitive than inflection. This theory is now abandoned.

influenza (ĭn″flōŏĕn′zŭ), contagious, infectious disease characteristically occurring in epidemic and pandemic outbreaks. It is caused by a virus, and it is attended by rapid progressive inflammation of mucous membranes of respiratory tract.

infrared rays (ĭn″frŭrĕd′), invisible rays of wave length longer than visible light and having a heating effect.

infusorial earth (ĭn″fyŏōsô′rĕùl), name sometimes used for diatomaceous deposits built up from remains of microscopic plant life. It is not generally approved as a term.

Inge, William (ĭnzh), 1913–, American dramatist, author of *Come Back, Little Sheba* (1950), *Picnic* (1952), *Bus Stop* (1955), and *The Dark at the Top of the Stairs* (1958).

Inge, William Ralph (ĭng), 1860–1954, Anglican prelate and author, dean of St. Paul's Cathedral (1911–34). His pessimism earned him the name of "gloomy dean," which he disliked.

Ingelow, Jean (ĭn′jŭlō), 1820–97, English author of verse (e.g., "High Tide on the Coast of Lincolnshire, 1571"), novels (e.g., *Off the Skelligs*, 1872), children's books (e.g., *Mopsa the Fairy*, 1869).

Ingemann, Bernhard Severin (ĭng′ŭmän), 1789–1862, Danish poet. Poems in *Holger Danske* (1837) became popular national songs. Also wrote religious lyrics in *Morning and Evening Songs* (1839) and historical novels.

Ingermanland (ĭng′gùrmŭnländ), historic region, RSFSR, S of Gulf of Finland, between L. Peipus and L. Onega; also called Ingria. Subject to Great Novgorod, later to Moscow, in Middle Ages; conquered by Sweden 1617; restored to Russia 1702. Peter I built St. Petersburg (Leningrad) in Ingermanland.

Ingersoll, Charles Jared (ĭng′gùrsôl), 1782–1862, American political leader and author. U.S. Representative from Pa. (1813–15, 1841–49). Some of his publications urge more intellectual independence and national self-sufficiency.

Ingersoll, Robert Green, 1833–99, American orator, a lawyer. Nominated James G. Blaine for President in famous "plumed knight" speech (1876). Known as "the great agnostic"; his lectures on religion won wide attention. Called Bob Ingersoll.

Ingersoll, Simon, 1818–94, American inventor. Patented rock drill 1871.

Inglewood. 1 City (pop. 63,390), S Calif., SW of Los Angeles; laid out 1887. **2** City (pop. 26,527), N central Tenn., suburb NNE of Nashville.

Ingoldsby, Thomas: see BARHAM, RICHARD HARRIS.

Ingolstadt (ĭng′gôlshtät), city (pop. 48,389), Upper Bavaria, on the Danube. Produces textiles, automobiles. Dates from 8th cent. Unsuccessfully besieged by Gustavus II of Sweden 1632. The university, founded 1472, was transferred to Landshut in 1800, to Munich in 1826. Has 15th-cent. Gothic minster.

Ingres, Jean Auguste Dominique (zhã″ ōgüst′ dômēnēk′ ē′grü), 1780–1867, French painter, a master draughtsman and portraitist; b. Montauban. Studied with J. L. David and became bulwark of classicism in a romantic era. Lived much in Rome. Director of French Acad. in Rome 1835–40.

Ingria: see INGERMANLAND.

Ingush: see CHECHEN-INGUSH AUTONOMOUS SOVIET SOCIALIST REPUBLIC.

Inisfail (ĭ″nĭsfāl′) [Irish,= island of destiny], literary name for Ireland.

Inishowen (ĭ″nĭsh-ō′ĭn), peninsula, Co. Donegal, Ireland. Has prehistoric relics and early Christian stone crosses.

initiative and referendum, the initiating of a law by popular petition (initiative) and the referring to popular vote a law passed by the legislature (referendum). In the U.S., individual states require signatures of from 5 to 15 percent of the electorate for an initiative. The referendum is required in most states for constitutional amendments.

injection, introduction of liquid into body. Types include intradermal, into skin tissue; intramuscular, into muscle; intravenous, into vein; spinal, beneath outer membrane of spinal cord. Usually administered by means of a needle and syringe or a container which introduces fine spray into tissues. Common method for administering medical agents.

injunction, formal written order of a court commanding or prohibiting a certain act, historically developed as the main remedy in equity. It is usually granted by a judge without a jury. Originally, only prohibitive (negative) injunctions were granted, but later courts broadened the practice to include positive commands. Interlocutory injunctions are those issued while an action is pending, and tend to protect a plaintiff's interests so that the final judgment may be of use to him. A final injunction is the judgment of the court after all the evidence has been heard. In case of disobedience of an injunction, the defendant is tried for contempt of court. In labor disputes injunctions were formerly very widely used (see CONSPIRACY).

ink. India or China ink, a permanent black ink, made of lampblack or ivory black mixed with glue or gum, probably known in China from c.1200 B.C. Standard black ink containing tannic acid, probably known from 2d cent., is much used because it flows freely. Aniline dyes generally used in colored inks.

Inkerman (ĭng′kùrmŭn, Rus. ēn-kĭrmän′), E suburb of Sevastopol, RSFSR, scene of costly allied victory (1854) in Crimean War.

Inkster, village (pop. 39,097), SE Mich., suburb W of Dearborn; settled 1825.

Inland Sea, area c.3,668 sq. mi., Japan. Between Honshu on N and Kyushu and Shikoku on S. Rich in fish; has c.950 islets. Famed for scenic beauty.

Inman, Henry, 1801–46, American portrait, genre, and landscape painter.

Inn, river, 320 mi. long, rising in Engadine valley, Switzerland, and flowing NE through Austria and Bavaria, joining the Danube at Passau.

Inner Hebrides, Scotland: see HEBRIDES.

Inner Mongolian Autonomous Region: see MONGOLIA.

Inner Temple: see INNS OF COURT; TEMPLE, THE.

Inness, George (ĭ′nĭs), 1825–94, American landscape painter. Early work was in Hudson River school tradition. Later influenced by Barbizon school, but achieved free and colorful personal style. A Swedenborgian, he sought the mystical in nature. His son, **George Inness, Jr.**, 1854–1926, was a landscape and animal painter.

Innisfree, small island, Co. Sligo, Ireland, in Lough Gill. Celebrated by W. B. Yeats in his poem "Lake Isle of Innisfree."

Innocent I, Saint, d. 417, pope (401–17). Upheld supremacy of the papacy; supported St. John Chrysostom and condemned Pelagius; tried vainly to prevent Alaric's sack of Rome (410). Feast: July 28.

Innocent II, d. 1143, pope (1130–43), a Roman. Opposed by Antipope Anacletus II, Innocent won the support of Bernard of Clairvaux and Emperor Lothair II and prevailed over Anacletus' successor, Victor IV. Convened Second Lateran Council and condemned some teachings of Abelard and Arnold of Brescia.

Innocent III, b. 1160 or 1161, d. 1216, pope (1198–1216), an Italian named Lotario di Segni; one of the most prominent figures of medieval history. A learned theologian and jurist, he held the theory that supremacy of the spirit over the flesh meant that the Church ruler (the pope) should have superiority over lay rulers of states—a theory later carried to an extreme by Boniface VIII but not held in present Roman Catholic doctrine. To establish papal supremacy Innocent was active in political affairs. In the Holy Roman Empire he arbitrated the dispute of PHILIP OF SWABIA and OTTO IV in Otto's favor (1201); later favored Philip (1207–8); crowned Otto (1209) after Philip's murder, only to excommunicate him (1210) and bring about the election of FREDERICK II, who was his ward. In England, Innocent, by setting aside two claimants for the archbishopric of Canterbury and naming Stephen Langton, infuriated King John; in the quarrel Innocent put England under the interdict and formally deposed the king (1212). John submitted and received England and Ireland as a fief from the pope. Later he declared that the Magna Carta was not binding on John because extorted by force and without the knowledge of his overlord (Innocent). In France, the pope could not establish political power over Philip II but did force him to bow to canon law in the matter of a divorce. In Italy he reclaimed and reorganized papal territories and was recognized as overlord of Tuscany, but he failed to subdue N. Italian cities. Thus in all Europe he went far to put his theory of papal supremacy into effect, though history was to make his victories hollow. He promoted the Fourth Crusade and protested when the Crusaders instead of going to the Holy Land attacked the Byzantine Empire; nevertheless he recognized the Latin Kingdom of Constantinople which they set up, and by efforts to spread the Latin rite in that kingdom embittered relations between the Eastern and Western churches. Similarly he protested when the crusade he had started against the Albigenses was turned to political and economic ends by Simon de Montfort, but his protests were vain; he later urged St. Dominic's mission. Innocent was vigorous in internal Church affairs and dominated the Fourth LATERAN COUNCIL (1215). He wrote extensively and his *De contemptu mundi* [on contempt of this world] was popular in the Middle Ages.

Innocent IV, d. 1254, pope (1243–54), a Genoese. His reign was occupied chiefly in a contest with the Hohenstaufen rulers. He opposed Emperor FREDERICK II and had to flee to Lyons, where he convened a council (1245) that declared Frederick deposed. Innocent supported counterclaimants to the throne against Frederick, CONRAD IV, and MANFRED. Just before his death he supported young CONRADIN as claimant to the Sicilian throne. Heavy taxes to support these contests brought criticism on Innocent (from Robert Grosseteste among others).

Innocent VIII, 1432–92, pope (1484–92), a Genoese. Papal affairs were largely directed by his friend Giuliano della Rovere (later Julius II). He originally planned a crusade against the Turks, but later he obtained Djem, the brother of the sultan, from Pierre

d'Aubusson (who became a cardinal) and the French king, Charles VIII. Innocent threatened BAJAZET II with recognizing the captive Djem as sultan.

Innocent XI, 1611–89, pope (1676–89), an Italian, noted for his saintliness and desire for reform. Engaged in a quarrel with LOUIS XIV, who actively promoted GALLICANISM. He denounced not only Louis's Gallican statement (1682) but also revocation of the Edict of Nantes (1685). He was beatified in 1956.

Innsbruck (ĭnz′brŏŏk, Ger. ĭns′–), city (pop. 107,454), cap. of Tyrol, W Austria, on the Inn. Its beautiful situation, in the Alps, and its architectural treasures make it a favorite tourist resort. Landmarks include 16th-cent. Hofkirche, a Franciscan church, with a monument to Emperor Maximilian I by Peter Vischer; 15th-cent. Fürstenburg palace. The university was founded 1677.

Inns of Court, collective name of the four legal societies in London which have exclusive right of admission to the bar. They are Lincoln's Inn, Gray's Inn, the Inner Temple, and the Middle Temple (see also TEMPLE, THE); all date from before the 14th cent. Names come from the buildings in which masters taught law to "apprentice" lawyers.

inoculation, in strict sense, insertion of disease-causing microorganisms into human or animal body to immunize by producing a mild form of a disease or to produce disease for experimental purposes. A form of inoculation used for immunization is VACCINATION. See also IMMUNITY.

Inonu, Ismet (ĭs′mĕt′ ĕnŭnŭ′), 1884–, Turkish general. Premier under Ataturk 1923–24, 1925–37; president of Turkey 1938–50. Regained power after military coup in 1960 and became premier 1961; was forced to resign 1965.

inquest, inquiry into certain matters by body of men appointed by law. The term usually refers to the investigation conducted by a coroner's jury seeking the cause of death. In a coronor's inquest, procedure is generally like that of a grand jury. Among verdicts returnable are natural death, accidental death, suicide, and murder.

Inquisition. 1 The medieval Inquisition began c.1233 when the pope commissioned certain Dominicans to investigate the ALBIGENSES in S France. As it evolved in France, N Italy, Germany, and the Papal States (where it continued to the 19th cent.), the Inquisition soon resorted to judicial torture, but it rarely condemned accused heretics to burning; imprisonment was the usual punishment. The medieval clerical inquisitors were eager to receive abjurations of heresy and to avoid trials; sentences could be enforced only by the local authorities ("secular arm"). 2 The Spanish Inquisition, estab. 1478 by Ferdinand and Isabella, and first headed by Tomás de TORQUEMADA, was independent of the medieval Inquisition and was controlled by the Spanish kings. Originally supposed to spy out converted Jews and Moors who were insincere, it soon evolved into a form of thought police from which no Spaniard was safe. It was far better organized, harsher, and freer with the death sentence than the medieval Inquisition. Its attempted introduction into the Netherlands led to rebellion. It was driven from Naples in 1510 and was abolished in Spain in 1820. 3 In 1542 Paul III assigned the medieval Inquisition to the Congregation of the Inquisition or Holy Office. The modern Congregation of the Holy Office has the decision as to questions of faith, morals, heresy, and some matrimonial cases, and also had the duties of censorship (the Index).

insanity, in law, mental aberration or defect which may relieve a person from certain legal consequences of his acts. Criminal and civil insanity differ from concepts of mental incapacity in psychopathology (see NEUROSIS; PSYCHOSIS). There is much medical criticism of legal insanity categories. The strictest U.S. jurisdictions limit criminal insanity to ignorance of the nature of one's acts, inability to distinguish right from wrong, i.e., crimes committed in frenzy or by idiots, but paranoiacs may be judged sane. Less strict jurisdictions include PARANOIA and sudden irresistible impulse (temporary insanity). Less mental aberration is required for civil insanity; extreme deficiency of intelligence or marked defect in reason may suffice. Harmless lunatics may be placed under guardianship on application to court. Dangerous lunatics may be committed to institutions on application of close relatives or public authorities; court approval, and sometimes a jury verdict of insanity, must be given. Asylum detention may be reviewed by habeas corpus proceedings.

inscription, writing on durable material. The art is called epigraphy. Modern inscriptions are made for permanent, monumental record, as on gravestones, cornerstones, and building fronts. First writing was probably everywhere done on hard materials, mainly stones, clay, metal, bone, and ivory. When light materials were developed, it was possible to distinguish between temporary writing and permanent recording. Outside Western history epigraphy was important in New World (MAYA, TOLTEC, AZTEC) and in China. Earliest Chinese inscriptions are on bronze (c.1500 B.C.). First Sanskrit inscriptions date from some centuries later than Prakrit inscriptions of ASOKA (3d cent. B.C.). Western epigraphy began in Mesopotamia (CUNEIFORM inscriptions, probably Sumerian, c.4000 B.C.; a similar Eastern instance is epigraphy at MO- HENJO-DARO, c.3000 B.C.) and in Egypt (HIEROGLYPH- IC inscriptions from 4th millennium B.C.). Influences of Egyptian epigraphy are found everywhere in Arabian peninsula in inscriptions of 1st millennium B.C. In the Mediterranean earliest epigraphy of Greek culture appears in AEGEAN CIVILIZATION and MINOAN CIVILIZATION. From expansion of Greece through career of Rome epigraphy flourished everywhere, and inscriptions are literally innumerable. Greek influence was decisive in Italy, first in inscriptions of ETRUSCAN CIVILIZATION. There are also many inscriptions in Italic languages, notably the IGUVINE TABLES. Latin epigraphy began with religious documents, but by end of the republic it was touching every phase of life. Germanic RUNES and Celtic OGHAM writings are European alphabets used in inscriptions of the early Christian era. Modern monumental inscription is in the same tradition as Latin epigraphy.

insect, air-breathing arthropod of class Insecta, with distinct head, thorax, and abdomen, three pairs of legs, one pair of antennae. The adult usually has one or two pairs of wings. Many (e.g., BUTTERFLY, MOTH, MOSQUITO, BEE, HOUSEFLY) undergo complete metamorphosis, passing through egg, larva, pupa, and adult stages. Grasshopper and some others undergo gradual metamorphosis (the young resemble the adult). Some primitive wingless ones hatch in adult form and grow in size only Fossil records indicate that insects are earth's oldest inhabitants; c.⁹⁄₁₀ of all animals are insects; a few hundred of 600,000 known species are harmful. Many are useful for cross-pollination (see POLLINATION); some are enemies of harmful insects and some form chief food of some fish, reptiles, birds, mammals. Men eat white ants in Brazil; grasshoppers in China. Silk, honey, cochineal, and lac are insect products. See *ill.,* p. 512.

insecticide (ĭnsĕk′tŭsīd), substance used to destroy insect pests. Some insecticides are effective only against specific insects, some are toxic, some can be used only under certain conditions. They are applied by dusting, spraying, fumigating (release of a gas), or by aerosol method (insecticide and liquefied gas are packed in container and released as fine mist under gas pressure). Stomach poisons are used against chewing insects; arsenical poisons (e.g., PARIS GREEN) are the oldest widely applied stomach poisons. Others are fluorine compounds, copper salts, organic poisons, synthetics. Contact poisons (those that penetrate body covering or enter breathing pores) include compounds of sulphur and nicotine, petroleum oils, coal-tar derivatives, pyrethrum (from flowers), rotenone (from derris and

other plants), and DDT (dichloro-diphenyl-trichloroethane), which has a long-lasting residual effect.

insectivorous plants: see BLADDERWORT; PITCHER PLANT; VENUS'S-FLYTRAP.

insemination, artificial: see ARTIFICIAL INSEMINATION.

Inside Passage, natural, protected waterway, c.950 mi. long, off coast of British Columbia and SE Alaska. Threads through ALEXANDER ARCHIPELAGO. From Seattle, Wash., to Skagway, Alaska, route uses channels and straits between islands and mainland giving protection from storms and open waters of ocean. Known to early explorers. Of great scenic beauty, it is route generally used by steamers between continental U.S. and Alaska.

installment buying and selling, payment at specified intervals in set amounts for goods taken on credit. Goods belong legally to seller until fulfillment of payment. Practice originated in Paris in 19th cent. and now is applied to purchase of goods of all kinds. It is usually state regulated, and was severely curbed by the Federal government during Second World War to reduce inflation.

instinct, controversial term generally indicating an innate tendency, disposition, or drive to action rising from vital needs of an organism, expressed in activity not based on past experience. It is seen in adult insects which emerge from pupa stage after complete bodily changes but with immediate command over food-getting and reproductive structures. In mammals gregariousness is ascribed to herd instinct and maternal activities of suckling and caring for young, to parental instinct. In man instinctive action, with specific goals but no specific means of reaching them, is distinguished from reflex action with its specific response to a stimulus. However, some psychologists claim that adult human behavior is too complex, too much modified by civilization and individual intelligence to be explained adequately on the basis of instinct.

Institut de France (ĕstētü′ dü fräs′), cultural institution of the French state, founded 1795 to replace five royal academies suppressed in 1793. Subsequent reorganizations restored, within the framework of the Institut, the earlier academies, though the names of several were changed. They are: FRENCH ACADEMY; Académie des Inscriptions et Belles-Lettres (history and archaeology; originally founded 1663); Académie des Sciences (1666); Académie des Beaux-Arts (1648); Académie des Sciences morales et politiques (1795).

Institute for Advanced Study, at Princeton, N.J.; chartered 1930, opened 1933; founded by Louis Bamberger and Mrs. Felix Fuld as research and experimental center beyond the graduate level. Abraham Flexner was first director; succeeded by Frank Aydelotte (1939–47); Einstein was faculty member. Owns Gest Oriental Library.

Institutes: see CORPUS JURIS CIVILIS.

instrumental: see CASE.

instrumentalism: see DEWEY, JOHN.

instrument-landing system (ILS), ground-based radio system which provides precise guidance to airplane pilot during final approach in landing. Two intersecting radio beams provide horizontal and vertical guidance by activating visual indicator in aircraft.

insulation (ĭn″sŭlā′shŭn), use of materials to prevent passage of heat or electricity. Common heat insulators are asbestos, glass, wood, wool; all are poor heat conductors. They prevent flow of heat in either direction. Air spaces and vacuums are effective insulators. In conduction of electricity, the conductor acts as a guide for the current and must be insulated at every point of contact to prevent leakage. Ordinary wires are usually insulated by thin rubber coating wrapped with cotton.

insulin (ĭn′sŭlĭn), active principle of hormone secreted by groups of cells (islands of Langerhans) in pancreas. It regulates sugar metabolism in body and glycogen storage in liver. Banting and Best first prepared it in a form effective in treatment of diabetes.

ARTHROPODS: INSECTS OF VARIOUS ORDERS

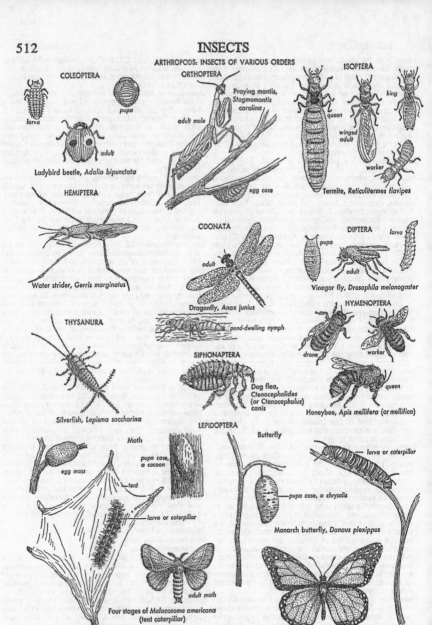

COLEOPTERA

larva

pupa

adult

Ladybird beetle, Adalia bipunctata

HEMIPTERA

Water strider, Gerris marginatus

THYSANURA

Silverfish, Lepisma saccharina

ORTHOPTERA

Praying mantis, Stagmomantis carolina

adult male

egg case

ODONATA

adult

Dragonfly, Anax junius

pond-dwelling nymph

SIPHONAPTERA

Dog flea, Ctenocephalides (or Ctenocephalus) canis

ISOPTERA

queen

king

winged adult

worker

Termite, Reticulitermes flavipes

DIPTERA

larva

pupa

adult

Vinegar fly, Drosophila melanogaster

HYMENOPTERA

drone

worker

queen

Honeybee, Apis mellifera (or mellifica)

LEPIDOPTERA

Moth

egg mass

pupa case, a cocoon

tent

larva or caterpillar

adult moth

Four stages of Malacosoma americana (tent caterpillar)

Butterfly

larva or caterpillar

pupa case, a chrysalis

Monarch butterfly, Danaus plexippus

Some insects, including the honeybee and silkworm, provide man with valuable products. Others, such as the praying mantis and dragonfly, destroy harmful insects. Certain insects, particularly the honeybee, are necessary for cross-pollination. Some harmful insects, such as the moth, silverfish, and termite, destroy goods. Flies and fleas feed on man and beast and transmit disease.

Insull, Samuel, 1859–1938, American public-utilities financier, b. England. Vindicated of charges of embezzlement and using mails to defraud following collapse (1932) of his public-utilities empire.

insurance or **assurance,** plan for guaranteeing an individual against loss out of a fund to which many individuals exposed to same risk have contributed specified sums called premiums. Amount of premium determined by law of averages calculated by actuaries. Forerunners of modern insurance found in ancient times. By middle of 14th cent., marine insurance almost universal in Europe (earliest known insurance contract made in Genoa in 1347). Life insurance began in England in 1583. Fire, burglary, and other forms of insurance were gradually added; insurance may now be obtained against any conceivable risk. Since late 19th cent. the state has entered field of social insurance (see SOCIAL SECURITY).

Insurgents, in U.S. history, Republican Senators and Representatives who in 1909–10 revolted against conservative party policies of N. W. Aldrich and J. G. Cannon. Many joined PROGRESSIVE PARTY.

integration, in U.S. history, goal of the movement to remove barriers of discrimination and segregation separating Negro from the rest of American society. Segregation, estab. in U.S. after Civil War, was maintained by terrorism and by force of social custom; laws of late 19th cent. reinforced white dominance. Serious opposition began prior to Second World War. Government wartime contracts contained "no discrimination" clauses; segregation in armed forces ended 1948. Supreme Court, moving toward principle of racial equality, took a momentous step on May 17, 1954, in case of Brown vs. Board of Education of Topeka, Kansas, when it ruled that separation in public schools is "inherently unequal." Integration struggle centered on school question. Opposition was bitter but scattered. Notable was defiance (1957) of Gov. Orval Faubus of Ark., who called Natl. Guard to prevent school integration, but Pres. Eisenhower enforced the law with Federal troops. James H. Meredith's entry into Univ. of Mississippi in 1962 was similarly achieved with protection of Federal troops. Suits for school desegregation were brought in several Northern cities in 1960–1961. Boycott of Montgomery, Ala., bus system led by Dr. Martin Luther KING in 1955–56 culminated in Supreme Court nullification of Ala. laws on bus segregation, and eventually in 1961 the Interstate Commerce Commission banned segregation in interstate transportation facilities. The "sit-in" campaign in Greensboro, N.C., in Feb., 1960, to desegregate public lunch counters spread to other cities, in both North and South. Integration groups became especially active in housing and voter-registration drives, after passage of 1964 Civil Rights Act. See also CIVIL RIGHTS; NATIONAL ASSOCIATION FOR THE ADVANCEMENT OF COLORED PEOPLE.

intelligence is usually defined as the general ability of the organism to utilize understanding gained in past experience to deal with similar or new situations. Potential intelligence is somewhat related to heredity, while environment largely determines the extent of its realization. **Intelligence tests** help determine individual ability to learn. Alfred Binet's first scale of tests (1905) inaugurated testing movement. Some psychologists doubt that such tests actually measure intelligence, but they have been valuable in education (to assign class groups and judge aptitude for high school or college) and in industry (to determine suitability for particular positions). Tests are a heterogeneous series of questions, problems, tasks, of varying difficulty to complete within a specified time. Tests are administered to a maximum of people of all ages and standardized by determining average number of questions, problems, tasks, done by any age group. Mental age is determined by those averages. **Intelligence quotient** (I.Q.) is a comparison between mental and chronologi-

cal age (M.A. and C.A.) multiplied by 100 to eliminate decimal point. Since 1920s interest in pure intelligence tests has declined and has increased in tests that measure special aptitudes and personality factors. See MENTAL TESTS; FEEBLE-MINDEDNESS.

Inter-American Conferences: see PAN-AMERICANISM.

Inter-American Highway, section, 3,400 mi. long, of PAN AMERICAN HIGHWAY system from Nuevo Laredo, Mexico, to Panama city, Panama.

Inter-American Treaty of Reciprocal Assistance: see RIO TREATY.

intercontinental ballistics missile: see GUIDED MISSILE.

interest, charge for use of money, usually percentage of principal. Simple interest computed on principal alone; compound, on principal plus unpaid interest. In 1545, England fixed legal maximum interest; higher rates were considered usury, although among certain groups all interest was condemned as usurious.

interference, in physics, effect produced under certain conditions by combination or superposition of two trains or systems of waves, especially of sound or light, in which these waves reinforce, neutralize, or in other ways interfere with each other. When, for example, two sound waves occur at same time and are in same phase, i.e., when condensations of the two coincide and hence also their rarefactions, the waves reinforce each other; if the rarefactions of one coincide with condensations of the other (i.e., if they are of opposite phase) they neutralize each other and silence results. Alternate reinforcement and neutralization (or weakening) occur when two sound waves differing slightly in frequency are superimposed; audible result is series of pulsations or beats. Light waves reinforce or neutralize each other in much the same way. Experiments of Thomas Young first illustrated interference and led to wave theory of light. Work of A. J. Fresnel showed that interference phenomena could be adequately explained only on basis of wave theory. A. A. Michelson's determinations of velocity of light are based on interference of light waves. Iridescence results from interference. **Interferometer** is instrument for measuring thickness of very thin films; when the wave length of the light used is known, the instrument indicates the thickness of the film by the nature of the interference patterns it forms. It can also measure length of an unknown light wave. Another type is used in measuring diameters of stars.

Interior, United States Department of the, organized in 1849 by act of U.S. Congress. Responsible for advancing domestic interests in U.S. Includes Indian affairs bureau (see INDIAN AFFAIRS, BUREAU OF), the GEOLOGICAL SURVEY, Bureau of Reclamation, National Park Service, Bureau of Mines, Bureau of Land Management.

Interlaken (ĭn'tûrlä́kŭn), town (pop. 4,738), Bern canton, Switzerland, between L. of Brienz and L. of Thun. With a fine view of the Jungfrau, it is a major tourist resort.

Interlingua: see UNIVERSAL LANGUAGE.

interlocking directorate, a corporation directorate, one or more of whose members serves on another corporation directorate. While this increases cooperation between the involved corporations, it may also raise prices in order to mulct consumers. Interlocking directorates are legally prohibited (by the Sherman and Clayton antitrust acts) when they lessen competition.

internal-combustion engine, type of engine operating by combustion of fuel within the cylinder of the engine. Heat energy is transformed into mechanical energy. First practical gas engine (using a combustible gas) was invented by Étienne Lenoir of France (c.1860), although earlier attempts date from 17th cent. The gasoline engine developed later was more compact and relatively light, and its use soon became widespread. In typical automobile gasoline engine, fuel is fed from storage tank by gravity or pump to CARBURETOR and mixed with air; the mixture then goes to cylinder to be compressed and ignited by electric spark (see IGNI-

TION). Resultant explosion forces piston down, transmitting through connecting rod a rotary motion to crankshaft. This activates camshaft attached to cam controlling the cylinder intake and exhaust valves. Typical four-stroke cycle (more common than two-stroke type) consists of: piston downstroke sucking in fuel; piston upstroke compressing fuel vapor, which is ignited as piston reaches top; piston downstroke transmitting force of exploding fuel vapor, leaving burned gases in chamber; and piston upstroke, expelling gases through exhaust valve, for cycle to begin again. (In single-cylinder engine, momentum of heavy flywheel after firing stroke carries through the cycle of intake, compression, and firing.) Besides carburetor, automobile engine accessories usually include water pump, timing gear, oil pump, and generator. Some types are air cooled. Many types of gasoline engines have been developed for use in aircraft. Marine engines are essentially the same as automobile engines but are more ruggedly constructed and are water cooled, and usually have forced-feed lubrication and an oil-cooling device. Oil-burning engines are similarly designed but the heavier grade fuel requires different ignition, usually by maintenance of high temperature in chamber to vaporize and ignite the oil jet. This type is being replaced by gasoline engine for small power; by DIESEL engine for larger power. The Wankel engine, named for its German inventor. Felix Wankel, uses rotary instead of reciprocal motion. An eccentrically triangular disk rotates within a cylinder that has combustion pockets. A single rotation causes intake, compression, expansion, and exhaust in each pocket.

internal revenue, taxes on goods produced and consumed within a country, also called excise taxes. First developed (17th cent.) by Holland. First use by U.S. in 1791; repealed 1802; alternately increased and all but abandoned until two World Wars. Nearly all states levy taxes on such items as tobacco, gasoline, liquor, and amusements. Some of these may be luxury taxes to discourage consumption of or raise revenue on "less essential" items. Sales taxes, or percentage of selling price, are relatively easy to collect and source of revenue for many states. Personal income taxes, legalized in U.S. by 16th Amendment (1913), are major source of Federal revenue. Corporation taxes are levied on corporations' income as well as on licensing and dividends. Excess profits tax, a wartime phenomenon, was imposed in both World Wars and in Korean war on firms' profits above peacetime level. Capital levy is taking part of actual capital of individual or business; upheld as social welfare measure but opposed as deterrent to saving. U.S. has resorted to special tax on capital gains. Land tax is oldest form of direct taxation and the chief method of collecting local revenue in U.S.; it is usually assessed on sale value of property. Inheritance taxes (in U.S., primarily a state tax) are levied on inherited property.

International. International Workingmen's Association, called International or First International, estab. 1864 in London by Karl Marx. Purpose was to unite workers of world for aims of *Communist Manifesto* (1848). Dissension caused dissolution 1874. In 1889 Second or Socialist International estab. hq. at Brussels. Comprised most Socialist parties, with leaders such as Friedrich Engels. It suffered from dissension and was torn apart by First World War. Bolshevik Revolution led to Third International or COMINTERN. Though its political significance waned, Second International (revived 1919) includes Socialist parties of many countries. TROTSKY founded Fourth International 1937.

International Atomic Energy Agency, international organization estab. 1957 under UN auspices to promote peaceful uses of atomic energy. Originating in Pres. Eisenhower's "atoms-for-peace" proposal, agency is authorized to facilitate and control the peaceful application of nuclear energy.

International Bank for Reconstruction and Development, specialized agency of UN. Estab. 1945, hq. Washington, D.C. Capital (not to exceed $21,000,-000,000) is used for loans to member states and private investors to facilitate investment, encourage foreign trade, and discharge international debts. All members of the bank must also belong to the INTERNATIONAL MONETARY FUND.

International Civil Aviation Organization (ICAO), specialized agency of UN. Estab. 1947, hq. Montreal. Objective is to promote orderly growth of international civil aviation including standarization of markings and air safety.

International Cooperation Administration: see FOREIGN AID.

International Court of Justice, principal judicial organ of the United Nations. Replaced the WORLD COURT. Consists of 15 judges named by the Hague Tribunal and ordinarily sits at The Hague. Renders judgment between states on matters of international law. Gives advisory opinions when requested to do so by the UN General Assembly.

International Criminal Police Commission (Interpol), international clearinghouse for police information; hq. in Paris.

International Development Association: see INTERNATIONAL BANK FOR RECONSTRUCTION AND DEVELOPMENT.

International Finance Corporation: see INTERNATIONAL BANK FOR RECONSTRUCTION AND DEVELOPMENT.

International Geophysical Year (IGY), 18-month period from July, 1957, through Dec., 1958, designated for cooperative study of earth and its cosmic environment by world's scientists. Studies were made of the solar system, cosmic rays, the atmosphere, earth's magnetic field, weather and climate, and the oceans. Earth satellites were launched (see SATELLITE, ARTIFICIAL); Antarctica and the arctic regions were studied.

international gold standard. Meant, until 20th cent., that monetary unit of each nation was tied to a fixed legal price for gold. System broke down after First World War and was replaced by gold-exchange standard, under which nations fix value of their currency to some foreign currency, in turn fixed to gold. Many currencies are fixed to U.S. dollar.

International Labor Organization (ILO), autonomous institution created in 1919 by Versailles Treaty to standardize and improve working conditions among laborers in member nations. First affiliated with League of Nations, it became a specialized agency of the UN in 1946.

International Law, Institute for, founded 1875, at Ghent, Belgium. Estab. for recording and study of developments in international arbitration. Awarded the 1904 Nobel Peace Prize. Reorganized in 1961.

International Monetary Fund, specialized agency of UN, estab. 1945, hq. Washington, D.C. Fund of $15,000,000,000 is used, on application of members, to purchase foreign currencies to discharge international indebtedness. It has limited power to set par values of currencies and works in close collaboration with International Bank for Reconstruction and Development.

International Peace Bureau, founded 1891, to prepare questions for peace congresses. Offices were in Bern, Switzerland, later in Geneva. Awarded 1910 Nobel Peace Prize.

International Quiet Sun Year (IQSY), 24-month period from Jan., 1964, through Dec., 1965, during which time solar flares and sunspots were at minimum. Scientists of many nations cooperated to maintain constant observation and measurement of solar phenomena.

International Red Cross: see RED CROSS.

International Refugee Organization: see UNITED NATIONS HIGH COMMISSIONER FOR REFUGEES, OFFICE OF THE.

SMALL CAPITALS = cross references. Pronunciation key on inside end pages. Abbreviations: p. 2.

international style, in architecture, phase of the modern movement that emerged in 1920s. New emphasis was given to a regularization of structure and a lightening of mass, often resulting in an austere framework surrounding great expanses of glass. Important examples are the Bauhaus (1926) at Dessau by Gropius, the Barcelona pavilion (1929) by Mies van der Rohe, and the Villa Savoye (1929–31) at Poissy by Le Corbusier. In the U.S. exponents of the style were Lescaze and Neutra.

International Telecommunication Union (ITU), UN agency, estab. 1934 by merging two existing organizations, hq. Geneva. Operates under Internatl. Telecommunication Convention (adopted 1947, effective 1949). Allots radio frequencies, furthers low rates, and perfects communications in rescue work.

Interpol: see INTERNATIONAL CRIMINAL POLICE COMMISSION.

Interstate Commerce Commission, estab. 1887 by U.S. Congress as a result of mounting indignation over railroad malpractices. Board was to regulate common carriers in interstate commerce and in foreign commerce within U.S. ICC was designed chiefly to prevent railroads from charging exorbitant rates and from engaging in discriminatory practices (e.g., the REBATE), but its activities were limited by numerous Supreme Court decisions won by railroads. Hepburn Act of 1906, however, extended commission's jurisdiction to include intraterritorial commerce and express, sleeping-car, and pipe-line (exclusive of those carrying water or gas) companies; empowered ICC upon complaint and after a full hearing to reduce rates adjudged unreasonable. Later extensions of board's jurisdiction included power to regulate communications (i.e., telephone, telegraph, and cable companies), motor carriers engaged in interstate commerce, and water-borne carriers operating coastwise, intercoastally, and upon inland U.S. waters; power to fix rates without previous complaint; power to evaluate property of common carrier companies; power to deal with labor disputes in interstate commerce. In 1950s and 1960s, ICC faced the problem of dealing with the desegregation of passenger facilities in accordance with Supreme Court decision.

intertype, trade name of machine that makes slugs, each doing work of a line of hand-set type. Similar to LINOTYPE, they have interchangeable matrices. Developed and produced by Internatl. Typesetting Machine Co. (organized 1912). See MONOTYPE.

intestine or **bowel,** tubular portion of alimentary canal extending from stomach to anus. Food mass is carried along within the intestine by contractions of muscular walls. In small intestine (tube c.23 ft. long), bile, pancreatic juice, and secretion from glands in its lining complete digestion of proteins, fats, carbohydrates; digested nutrients pass through lining into blood and lymph. Large intestine (c.5 ft. long) continues from cecum (blind portion at junction with small intestine) as ascending, transverse, and descending colon, rectum, anal canal, anus. See *ill.,* p. 657.

Intolerable Acts, name given by American patriots to five laws (including QUEBEC ACT) adopted by Parliament in 1774, limiting political and geographical freedom of colonists. Four of laws punished Mass. for BOSTON TEA PARTY.

Intracoastal Waterway, route, 2,455 mi. long, part natural, part artificial, providing protected water passage from Trenton, N.J., to Brownsville, Texas, along Atlantic and Gulf of Mexico coasts. Authorized by Congress, maintained toll free by U.S. Corps of Engineers. Minimum depth, 6.8 ft. Important works include Chesapeake and Delaware Canal, Albemarle and Chesapeake Canal, Alligator-Pungo Canal, dredging of cut from Pensacola Bay to Mobile Bay, New Orleans–Rigolets Cut, and deepening of channel between Port Arthur and Corpus Christi, Texas. Many navigable waterways connect with it, e.g., Hudson R., Erie Canal, New Jersey Intracoastal Waterway, and entire Mississippi R. system.

introversion: see EXTROVERSION.

intuitionism, any philosophy that depends fundamentally on the theory that man can perceive truth, and therefore gain knowledge, immediately, without drawing upon either experience or intellect. It has appeared throughout Western history, but was common among mystics of the late Middle Ages and the Renaissance.

Inuvik (ĭn´o͞ovĭk), village, NW Mackenzie dist., Canada, near mouth of Mackenzie R. Uranium mines.

Inverness-shire (ĭn´vûrnĕs´shĭr) or **Inverness,** maritime county (4,211 sq. mi.; pop. 83,425), NW Scotland. Largest Scottish county, it includes many of the HEBRIDES. Caledonian Canal follows Great Glen diagonally across county through several lochs. Mountainous region, it has highest peak in Great Britain (Ben Nevis, 4,406 ft.). Chief occupations are sheep grazing and fishing (herring and salmon). The co. town is **Inverness,** burgh (pop. 29,773), called "Capital of the Highlands." Inverness has museum of Highland relics and annual Highland Gathering. Castle is on site of Macbeth's castle, said to be scene of Duncan's murder.

invertebrate (ĭnvûr´tŭbrāt), any animal without a backbone. Invertebrates are divided into phyla including protozoa, sponges, coelenterates (jellyfish, sea anemone, coral), echinoderms (starfish and related forms), flatworms, roundworms, segmented worms, mollusks, arthropods. In size they range from microscopic protozoans to giant SQUID.

investiture, in FEUDALISM, ceremony by which an overlord transferred a fief to his vassal. After oath of fealty, lord "invested" him with fief, usually by giving a clod or stick or stone, or other token of land or office given. Ceremony imposed on lord duties of suzerain, chiefly protection of vassal's interests. Clerical investiture was of great importance as dispute about it was phase of struggle between Church and state in Middle Ages. Fundamental trouble lay in dual role of bishops and abbots as both spiritual and temporal lords. Always both king and pope were interested in election and installation of bishops. Quarrel was touched off by divergence between Emperor Henry IV and Pope Gregory VII. After long conflict agreement was reached by Henry V and Pope Calixtus II in Concordat of WORMS (1122), a victory for Church. In England William the Conqueror had trouble with the Church. Agreement (1107) by Henry I and Anselm gave investiture to Church, with homage to king.

involutional psychotic reactions, mental illnesses characteristically affecting people over 40 years of age who have no previous psychotic history. Symptoms include acute depression or paranoia.

Inwood, residential town (pop. 10,362), SE N.Y., on W Long Isl., SW of Hempstead.

Io (ī´ō), in Greek religion, princess of Argos, who was transformed into a heifer by Zeus to protect her from Hera's jealousy. Hera claimed the heifer and sent Argus to guard her. A gadfly drove her to Egypt, where Zeus returned her to human form. Sometimes identified with Egyptian Isis.

Ioannina (vŏä´nēnä), city (pop. 34,997), NW Greece, in Epirus: also spelled Janina, Yannina. Agr. center; silk and textile mfg. Was under Turkish rule 1438–1913. Scene of severe fighting in Second World War. Famous as residence of ALI PASHA.

iodine (ī´ŭdīn), the least active HALOGEN, it is a dark gray to purple-black, lustrous, crystalline solid element (symbol = I; see also ELEMENT, table). Undergoes SUBLIMATION when heated; its vapor is violet. It forms many compounds; is found in salt deposits and in some seaweed. Used in treating goiter, as antiseptic (in alcoholic solution and as iodoform), and in making certain drugs and dyes.

Iola (ī´ō´lŭ), city (pop. 7,094), SE Kansas, W of Fort Scott. Center of dairy, grain, and livestock area.

Ion (ī´ŭn, ī´ŏn), in Greek mythology, son of Apollo and Creusa. He became ancestor of the Ionians.

PROTOZOA

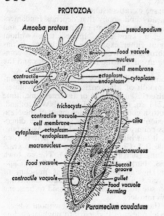

Amoeba proteus
— pseudopodium
— food vacuole
— nucleus
— cell membrane
contractile vacuole — ectoplasm — cytoplasm
endoplasm

trichocysts
contractile vacuole
cell membrane — cilia
ectoplasm
cytoplasm — endoplasm
macronucleus
— micronucleus
food vacuole
— buccal groove
contractile vacuole — gullet
— food vacuole forming

Paramecium caudatum

ROTIFERA

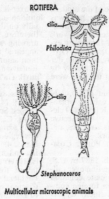

cilia
Philodina

cilia

Stephanoceros

Multicellular microscopic animals

PORIFERA—SPONGES

— skeleton

Sycon, a calcareous sponge

COELENTERATA

A colonial coelenterate

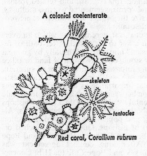

polyp
— skeleton
— tentacles

Red coral, Corallium rubrum

A free-living solitary coelenterate

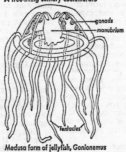

gonads
— manubrium

— tentacles

Medusa form of jellyfish, Gonionemus

A fixed solitary coelenterate

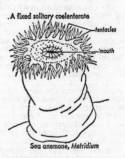

— tentacles
— mouth

Sea anemone, Metridium

PLATYHELMINTHES—FLATWORMS

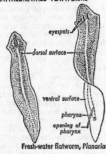

— eyespots
— dorsal surface
— ventral surface
— pharynx
— opening of pharynx

Fresh-water flatworm, Planaria

NEMATHELMINTHES—ROUNDWORMS OR THREADWORMS

Hairworm, Gordius

Ascaris lumbricoides, common roundworm parasitic in man

ANNELIDA—SEGMENTED WORMS

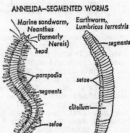

Marine sandworm, Neanthes (formerly Nereis)
head
— parapodia
— segments
— setae

Earthworm, Lumbricus terrestris
— segments
— setae
— clitellum
— setae

ECHINODERMATA

Echinoidea

dorsal view of test or skeleton of sea urchin with spines removed

side view with spines intact

Sea urchin, *Arbacia*

Asteroidea

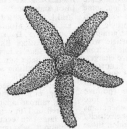

Starfish, *Asterias*

Ophiuroidea

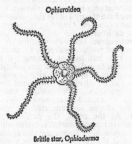

Brittle star, *Ophioderma*

MOLLUSCA

Pelecypoda

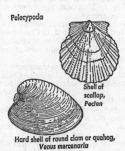

Shell of scallop, *Pecten*

Hard shell of round clam or quahog, *Venus mercenaria*

Cephalopoda

Squid, *Loligo*

Gastropoda

Edible European snail, *Helix*

ARTHROPODA

Crustacea

A marine shrimp

Blue crab, *Callinectes*

Arachnoidea

Spider and portion of web

Scorpion, *Centrurus*

Chilopoda

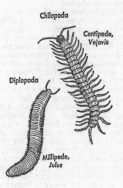

Centipede, *Vejovis*

Diplopoda

Millipede, *Julus*

ion (ī'ŏn). To explain the fact that some substances conduct current only in aqueous solution, S. A. Arrhenius advanced the theory (1887) that molecules dissociate and parts conduct. According to theory of ion, some of the molecules break up into two parts—one with positive charge, one with negative. A particle with one unit of positive charge is an atom or group of atoms that has lost an electron; a particle with one unit of negative charge has gained an electron. Some ions have several positive or negative charges. When electric current is introduced (see ELECTROLYSIS), particles with positive charge are attracted to cathode (negative pole); those with negative charge are attracted to anode (positive pole). At the poles, the particles gain or lose electrons to become neutral, combine with other atoms to form molecules. Substances that conduct electricity are called electrolytes (e.g., sodium chloride); those that do not, nonelectrolytes (e.g., sugar). Acids, bases, and salts are, in general, electrolytes. Some substances ionize when melted; important industrial processes are based on this. Acidity or alkalinity of substance in solution depends on concentration of hydrogen ions (H⁺) or hydroxyl ions (OH⁻). Indicators show which ions are present in greater concentration. Litmus is an indicator that turns red in acid solution (excess of H⁺); blue in basic solution (excess of OH⁻ ions). Hydrogenion concentration is indicated by pH.

Iona (ī'ŏ'nů) or **Icolmkill** (ī'kŏmkĭl'), island of Inner Hebrides, in Argyllshire, off W Scotland. It is c.3½ mi. long and 1½ mi. wide. At this early center of Celtic Christianity St. Columba landed in 563. It has many ancient remains. Cathedral dates from 12th or 13th cent. Cemetery reputed to be burial place of kings from several countries.

Ionesco, Eugène (ûzhěn' yŏně'skō), 1912–, French playwright, b. Rumania. His theater of the absurd portrays Western culture as stifling in its emphasis on materialism. His plays include *The Bald Soprano* (1950) and *Rhinoceros* (1959).

ion exchange, in chemistry, reversible procedure in which ions in a liquid replace ions of a solid body (immersed in the liquid), releasing the ions of the solid into the liquid. No great change in the form of the solid results. Used in water purification and in uranium production.

Ionia (ī'ŏ'něŭ), anc. Greek region of Asia Minor occupying a narrow coastal strip of what is today W Turkey and the neighboring Aegean Isls. Here Ionian Greek settlers founded colonies, presumably before 1000 B.C. Athens claimed to be mother city of them all. There came to be 12 important cities, among them Miletus, Ephesus, and Samos. After conquest by several empires came under Persian power. In 500 B.C. they revolted against Darius. Athens supported them, and the PERSIAN WARS ensued. Continued rich and important under Roman and Byzantine Empires. After the Turkish conquest their culture was destroyed.

Ionian Sea (ī'ŏ'něŭn), part of Mediterranean Sea, between SE Italy and Greece. Connected with Adriatic Sea by Strait of Otranto. In it are the **Ionian Islands,** chain (752 sq. mi.; pop. 212,573), off W Greece. They include CORFU, CEPHALONIA, ZANTE, CYTHERA, Ithaca, Paxo, Leucas. Largely mountainous. Agr., fruit growing, cattle raising, fishing, soapmaking. Islands passed from Byzantine Empire to Venice in 14th–15th cent. Though ceded by Venice to France in 1797, they were under Russo-Turkish occupation 1799–1807 and under English occupation from 1809. Treaty of Paris made them a British protectorate (1815). England ceded them to Greece 1864.

ionization: see ION.

ionosphere (ī'ŏ'nŭsfěr), a series of concentric ionized layers in upper atmosphere. It makes possible long-distance wireless communication by reflecting radio waves back to earth. Independently discovered by Oliver Heaviside and A. E. Kennelly; both entire ionosphere and a particularly highly ionized layer are

known also as Kennelly-Heaviside layer. See *ill.,* p. 311.

Ioshkar-Ola: see YOSHKAR-OLA.

Iowa, state (56,290 sq. mi.; pop. 2,757,537), N central U.S.; admitted 1846 as 29th state; cap. and largest city DES MOINES. Other cities are CEDAR RAPIDS, SIOUX CITY, DAVENPORT, and DUBUQUE. Bounded E by Mississippi R., W by Missouri and Big Sioux rivers. State is largely a rolling plain with some of world's finest agr. lands. Farming includes dairying, livestock, raising soybeans, grains, corn (chief U.S. producer). Minerals are bituminous coal, gypsum, stone; cement is leading mineral product. Food processing; mfg. of machinery (agr., industrial, electrical), railroad equipment, metal products. Region explored in 17th cent. by French and by fur traders. In late 18th cent. Indians leased land to Julien DUBUQUE, who opened lead mines. Part of Louisiana Purchase (1803). Most Indian claims abandoned after BLACK HAWK WAR (1832). Iowa Territory estab. 1838; rural civilization developed rapidly. Farmers joined GRANGER MOVEMENT, GREENBACK PARTY, and POPULIST PARTY in hard times of late 19th cent. Improved conditions lulled radicalism until depression of 1930s. In 20th cent. agr. commonwealth has generally prospered.

Iowa, river, rising in N central Iowa and flowing c.329 mi. SE across state. Joined by Cedar R. at Columbus Junction, it enters Mississippi R. between Muscatine and Burlington. Coralville Dam is major part of recent flood-control work.

Iowa, The University of, at Iowa City; state supported; coed.; chartered 1847, opened 1855. Operates Child Welfare Research Station, Lakeside Laboratory for biological sciences, a hydraulic research institute. Formerly called State Univ. of Iowa.

Iowa City, city (1965 pop. 40,467), E central Iowa, on both sides of Iowa R., SSE of Cedar Rapids; founded 1839 as cap. of Iowa Territory. Was state cap. 1846–57. Became important supply center for western trails after arrival of railroad 1855. Seat of The Univ. of IOWA. Nearby are villages of AMANA SOCIETY.

Iowa Indians, tribe of Siouan language family, formerly on the Platte R. Were presumably once part of the Winnebago people and shared culture of Eastern Woodlands and Plains areas.

Iowa State University of Science and Technology, at Ames; land grant, state and Federal supported; coed.; chartered 1858, opened 1868 as agr. college; called Iowa State Col. of Agr. and Mechanic Arts 1896–1959. Ames Laboratory of Atomic Energy Commission is here.

Ipatieff, Vladimir Nikolaevich (vlä'dyĭmĭr nyĭkŭlī'ůvĭch ēpä'tyůf), 1867–1952, Russian-American chemist. b. Moscow. Taught and directed chemical works for Russian government in First World War; came to U.S. 1931. In 1940 he founded Ipatieff Catalytic High Pressure Laboratory at Northwestern Univ. His work is important in oil refining and synthesis of artificial rubber.

ipecac (ĭ'pĭkăk"), drug obtained from dried roots and rhizomes of a tropical creeping shrub. Contains toxic, emetic alkaloids capable of destroying amoebae and occasionally used in treatment of certain parasitic diseases.

Iphigenia (ĭ"fůjůnī'ů), in Greek legend, daughter of Clytemnestra and Agamemnon. His ships becalmed at Aulis en route to Trojan War, Agamemnon sacrificed her to Artemis, but goddess rescued her and took her to Tauris as a priestess for her temple. Here she saved Orestes from sacrifice and fled with him to Greece.

Ipin or **I-pin** (e'bĭn'), city (pop. c.177,500), Szechwan prov., China, at junction of Min and Yangtze rivers. Commercial center. Formerly called Suifu and Suchow.

Ipiranga or **Ypiranga** (both: ē"pěräng'gů), stream, São Paulo, SE Brazil, where Pedro issued Grito de Ipiranga, declaring independence of Brazil from Portugal, Sept. 7, 1822.

Ippolitov-Ivanov, Mikhail (Mikhailovich) (mēkhŭyēl'ēpŭlyē'tŭf-ēvä'nŭf), 1859–1935, Russian composer; pupil of Rimsky-Korsakov. His music is nationalistic. His best-known work is his orchestral *Caucasian Sketches*. He also composed operas, choral works, and chamber music.

Ipsambul: see ABU-SIMBEL.

Ipsus (ĭp'sŭs), town, anc. Phrygia, Asia Minor, the modern Ipsili Hissar. Here ANTIGONUS I was defeated and slain by other Diadochi (301 B.C.).

Ipswich, county borough (pop. 117,325), Suffolk East, England. Town is very old and has many historical houses and buildings. Industries include shipping and mfg. of agr. machinery.

Ipswich, town (pop. 8,544), NE Mass., NNE of Salem, on Ipswich R. (crossed by bridge built 1764). Area (called Agawam) settled 1633. Has early colonial atmosphere. Historic buildings include John Whipple House (c.1640) and Platt-Bradstreet House (1666–70). Crane's Beach is here.

Iqbal, Mohammad (mŭhŏ'mĭd īkhbäl'), 1873–1938, poet, philosopher, and Indian Moslem leader. President of the Muslim League in 1926 and 1930, Iqbal was early advocate of Hindu-Moslem unity, but came to believe in the concept of an independent homeland for the Moslems of India.

IQSY: see INTERNATIONAL QUIET SUN YEAR.

Iquitos (ēkē'tōs), city (pop. c.70,000), N Peru, on Amazon, c.2,300 mi. up the river; founded 1863. Was important port in wild-rubber boom of early 20th cent.

Ir, chemical symbol of the element IRIDIUM.

Ira (ī'rŭ), chief officer of David. 2 Sam. 20.26.

Irak: see IRAQ.

Irala, Domingo Martínez de (dōmēng'gō märtē'näs dā ērä'lä), d. 1556 or 1557, first governor of Paraguay elected by free vote of colonists. Moved inhabitants of Buenos Aires to Asunción (1539).

Iran (ērän', īrän'), kingdom (636,294 sq. mi.; pop. c.20,-678,000), SW Asia; name changed from Persia in 1935; cap. TEHERAN. Bounded on N by USSR and Caspian Sea. on S by Gulf of Oman and Persian Gulf, on W by Iraq, and on E by Afghanistan and Pakistan. On great plateau surrounded by Elburz and Zagros ranges. Great salt deserts are in interior. Trans-Iranian RR links Caspian Sea with Persian Gulf. People are predominantly SHIITES in religion. Wheat and rice are grown; opium-poppy growing was prohibited in 1955. Main industrial products are carpets and rugs, but supreme source of wealth is oil. In ancient times the area was the heart of a great empire (see PERSIA). Safavid dynasty (1499–1736) reached its peak under Shah Abbas I. After brief period of Afghan rule, NADIR SHAH estab. Afshar dynasty in 1736. It was succeeded by Zand dynasty (1750–94) and by Kajar or Qajar dynasty (1794–1925), founded by Aga Mohammed Khan. In 19th cent. Iran fell under increasing pressure of European nations. Lost Caucasian lands to Russia by treaties of 1813 and 1828. Divided into British and Russian spheres of influence 1907–19. Agreement with Great Britain in 1919 ambiguously affirmed Iran's independence, while Russians withdrew in 1921. New dynasty was founded 1925 by REZA SHAH PAHLEVI, whose abdication in favor of his son MOHAMMED REZA SHAH PAHLEVI was forced by British and Russians who in Second World War had again occupied Iran. In 1946 foreign troops withdrew under terms of Teheran Declaration of 1943. Two separatist governments set up in NW region with Russian support were abolished in 1947. Nationalism, fueled by foreign occupation with help of Communist Tudeh party, strengthened the movement of MOSSADEGH, who proposed nationalization of the British-owned oil industry. He became premier in 1951. Nationalization brought stoppage of oil production and breaking of relations with Britain. Economic strains and difficulty with the shah brought Mossadegh's downfall. In 1954 a twenty-five year

agreement was signed with a consortium. Sixteen years of martial rule ended in 1957, and closer ties with the West were estab. after Mossadegh's downfall. Iran joined the Baghdad Pact (later renamed the Central Treaty Organization) in 1955. Recipient of U.S. military and economic aid, Iran, at the initiative of the shah, undertook a broad program of reform, especially agrarian reform. The constitutional monarchy has two houses of legislature.

Iranian languages, branch of Indo-Iranian subfamily of Indo-European languages. See LANGUAGE (table).

Iraq or Irak (both: ērāk'), republic (171,600 sq. mi.; pop. c.7,085,000), SW Asia; cap. Baghdad. Bordered by Turkey on N, Iran on E, Saudi Arabia on S, and Jordan and Syria on W. Roughly coextensive with anc. MESOPOTAMIA. Population concentrated on banks of TIGRIS and EUPHRATES rivers, which merge into SHATT EL ARAB. In dry SE area cotton and dates are grown; oil exploited in mountainous N. Most Iraqi are Arab-speaking Moslems. Iraq fell to Ottoman Turks in 16th cent. Supported Allies in First World War and welcomed British occupation in 1915. Was League of Nations mandate under the British 1920–32. Became kingdom under FEISAL I in 1921. Nationalist opposition increased as the British lost Middle East territory in early phase of Second World War. In 1941 the British defeated pro-Axis usurper Rashid Ali Gailani and recalled Emir Abdul Illah, regent for FEISAL II. Declared war on Axis powers 1943. Iraq joined Arab League and warred on Israel in 1948. Anti-British sentiment culminated in a military coup by Abdul Karim Kassem in 1958, assassination of the royal family, and the founding of a republic. Iraq withdrew from Middle East Treaty Organization 1959. In 1960 it claimed sovereignty over Kuwait and the Iranian portion of Shatt el Arab. Kurds, led by Mustafa al-Barzani and supported by Communists, revolted 1962; bloody strife ensued. Kassem was executed after military coup of 1963 led by Adbel Salam Aref. In 1966 Aref died in air crash and was succeeded as president by his brother Abdel Rahman Aref.

IRBM: see GUIDED MISSILE.

Ireland, John, 1879–1962, English composer. He wrote chamber music, piano pieces, orchestral works (e.g., *Symphonic Rhapsody* and *London Overture*), and songs (*Sea Fever*, the cycle *Songs of a Wayfarer*).

Ireland, William Henry, 1777–1835, English forger of Shakespearean documents and manuscripts. Exposed, he admitted hoax in *Authentic Account* (1796).

Ireland [Irish *Eire* (â'rŭ); to it are related the poetic *Erin* and, perhaps, the Latin *Hibernia*], island (32,-408 sq. mi.; pop. 4,240,165), second largest of British Isles. Lies W of Great Britain, from which it is separated by the North Channel, the Irish Sea, and St. George's Channel. At present divided into political regions—NORTHERN IRELAND (cap. Belfast) and the republic of Ireland (26,599 sq. mi.; pop. 2,814,703; cap. Dublin). Island has 32 counties and, historically, four provinces. ULSTER is divided between N. Ireland (counties Antrim, Down, Armagh, Fermanagh, Tyrone, and Londonderry) and republic (counties Monaghan, Cavan, and Donegal). Other three provinces are in republic—LEINSTER has counties Louth, Meath, Dublin, Kildare, Wicklow, Carlow, Wexford, Kilkenny, Laois, Offaly, Westmeath, and Longford; MUNSTER has Tipperary, Waterford, Cork, Kerry, Limerick, and Clare; CONNAUGHT has Leitrim, Roscommon, Galway, Mayo, and Sligo. Island has a large central plain, extremely fertile, roughly enclosed by a highland rim. In N are Mourne Mts., Sperrin Mts., and those of Antrim; in W are mountains of Connemara and Mayo; and in S are mountains of Galty, Knockmealdown, and Kerry. Heavy rains (over 80 in. annually in S) account for brilliant green grass of "emerald isle." Off W coast are many islands (including Aran and Blasket Isls.) and in interior are many lakes and wide stretches of rivers called loughs. SHANNON

R., 250 mi. long, provides electric power for much of the republic. Lagan, Foyle, Liffey, and Lee are among other rivers. Economy is mainly agr., chief products being dairy goods and flax. Fine linen and laces are world famous. Industrial activity is concentrated in Belfast area and adjoining area in the republic. Population of republic is overwhelmingly Catholic. Protestants outnumber Catholics in N. Ireland, but number of Catholics has increased in recent years, and the traditional religious difference between sections seems likely to be upset.

Ireland to 1170. Ireland was invaded before the Christian era by several Celtic tribes who left their culture. Anglo-Saxons and Romans did not affect the island. Ireland enjoyed golden age of its culture until 8th cent. when Norsemen began their raids. People were organized into clans owing allegiance to one of five provincial kings (of Ulster, Munster, Leinster, Connaught, and Meath) who in turn served high king of all Ireland at Tara. Despite constant clan fighting, literary and artistic culture flourished (see GAELIC LITERATURE). In 5th cent. St. PATRICK completed the island's conversion to Christianity. Later Irish religious leaders included St. Columba, St. Columban, and St. Bridget. In 1014 Brian Boru broke the hold of Norse invaders. There followed 150 years of freedom from foreign interference. Overlordship of Ireland was granted in 12th cent. to Henry II of England by Pope Adrian IV. English in 1170 began conquest. Anglo-Irish struggle was to continue intermittently for nearly 800 years.

Ireland to Union of 1800. Anglo-Norman rapacity in Ireland led to landlord-tenant problem. Irish were denied benefit of English law and their own law was split apart. English control lessened, however, until Henry VIII became first monarch to bring all Ireland under English control. POYNINGS'S LAW (1495) gave legislative initiative to English Parliament. By 16th cent. Irish people were sunk in desperate poverty which was to last for centuries. The Protestant English imposed the PENAL LAWS upon the Catholic Irish. In Elizabeth's reign three serious rebellions were crushed. Scotch settlers were planted in Ulster. A rebellion began in 1641 which lasted ten years, cost 600,-000 lives, and was brutally crushed by Cromwell (who massacred Irish at Drogheda). Irish support of James II led to new Penal Laws and economic exploitation after battle of the Boyne (1690). In 1782 Henry GRATTAN obtained an independent Parliament which proved ineffective. After rebellion under Wolfe TONE, England and Ireland were united (1800), and Irish were unwillingly represented in English Parliament.

Ireland under the Union, 1800–1921. Agitation led by Daniel O'Connell caused Catholic Emancipation Act to be passed in 1829. Other causes for Irish discontent persisted. Church of Ireland was not disestab. until 1869. Evils of absentee landlordism grew more serious (see IRISH LAND QUESTION). Potato blight struck Ireland in 1840s. In five years ending 1851 c.1,000,000 Irish died of starvation and disease and some 1,600,-000 emigrated, mostly to U.S. FENIAN MOVEMENT was organized. By 1870 PARNELL had arisen as a leader. HOME RULE movement was gradually superseded by SINN FEIN. Easter Rebellion of 1916 led to guerrilla warfare in 1918. English tried to suppress it with auxiliaries known as Black and Tans, who terrorized country (1920) and met increasing resistance. Irish cause was strengthened by literary and cultural revival of late 19th cent.; by such writers as G. B. Shaw, W. B. Yeats, and James Joyce; and by Abbey Theatre. *Irish Free State and the Republic.* Irish Free State was estab. (1921) as result of negotiations between British and Eamon DE VALERA. Six N Protestant counties accepted dominion status as N. Ireland. Split of Sinn Fein into right- and left-wing groups led to a period of civil war. William Cosgrave was president 1922–32. Succeeded by De Valera who estab. (1937) sovereign country of Ireland (officially Eire) associated in foreign policy with British Commonwealth of Nations.

Trade war between England and Ireland ended. In Second World War Ireland remained neutral and protested Allied military activity in N. Ireland. Outlawed Irish Republican Army continued to agitate for end of separation of N. Ireland from Eire. In 1948 De Valera was voted out of power and a coalition chose John Costello new premier. Republic of Ireland Bill of 1949 estab. independent nation. Executive power is vested in prime minister and legislative power in the DÁIL ÉIREANN. De Valera was prime minister from 1951 to 1954 (Costello held the office 1954–57) and from 1957 to 1959, when he resigned and was elected president (reelected to second term 1966). Sean Lemass succeeded him as prime minister and retired 1966 after seven-year term to be replaced by John Lynch. Ireland was admitted to UN 1955.

Ireland, Church of, the Anglican church in Ireland. Unlike the Church of England, it has been disestablished since 1869. Represents minority of population.

Irenaeus, Saint (īrīnē′ŭs), c.125–c.202, bishop of Lyons, Gaul, b. Asia Minor, author of *Against the Heresies* (against GNOSTICISM). Feast: July 3.

Irene (īrēn′, īrē′nē), 752–803, Byzantine empress (797–802). As regent for her son Constantine VI after 780, she bent all her efforts on suppression of ICONOCLASM. Constantine's misconduct led to his deposition (797); Irene had him blinded and ascended the throne. She was deposed and exiled by Nicephorus I (802).

Irene, one of the HORAE.

Ireton, Henry (ī′urtŭn), 1611–51, English parliamentarian general in Puritan Revolution; husband of Oliver Cromwell's daughter. As lord deputy of Ireland (1650) he carried on Cromwell's policy of dispossessing the Irish in favor of Englishmen.

Iriarte, Ignacio (ēgnä′thyō ēryär′tä), 1621–85, Spanish landscape painter, who often painted romantic backgrounds for paintings by Zurbaran and Murillo.

Iriarte, Tómas de (tōmäs′ dā ēryär′tä), 1750–91, Spanish poet and critic. Wrote *Fabulas literárias* (1782).

iridescence (ī″rĭdĕ′sŭns), exhibition of changing, shifting color bands by certain surfaces (e.g., in mother-of-pearl). It results from breaking up of white light and INTERFERENCE of light rays caused by irregularities in the surface.

iridium (īrī′dēŭm), rare, silver-white metallic element (symbol = Ir; see also ELEMENT, table). It resembles platinum, is very hard, and one of the heaviest elements known. Alloys are used for making standard weights and other apparatus resistant to action of atmosphere, contact points of electrical apparatus, and pen points.

Irigoyen, Hipólito (ēpō′lētō ērēgō′yän), 1850?–1933, Argentine political leader, president of the republic (1916–22, 1928–30).

Iris, in Greek religion, goddess of the rainbow; daughter of Electra and attendant of Zeus and Hera.

iris, stately perennial plant of genus *Iris* from which the fleur-de-lis is thought to have been derived. Native American irises are called blue flags. Violet-scented rootstalks of some Old World irises, especially *Iris florentina*, are sold commercially as orrisroot, which is powdered and used in perfume, sachet, etc. The bearded irises of June gardens include several thousand varieties; beardless kinds include Japanese and Siberian irises. These all have creeping rootstalks. Spanish, Dutch, and English irises are grown from bulbs.

Irish Free State: see IRELAND.

Irish Land Question. The problem of Irish land ownership, which came to a crisis in 19th cent., goes back many centuries. Feudal landholding system was imposed on Ireland in 12th cent. The Tudors, Cromwell, and William III continued land confiscations. Longterm result was creation of an absentee landlord class and of an impoverished Irish peasantry; 18th cent. Penal Laws increased difficulty of landowning by Catholics. CATHOLIC EMANCIPATION did not materially help. Hatred for England grew through great famine of 1840s and influx of speculators after Encumbered Estates Act of 1849. The violent Fenian movement, the Reform Act of 1867, and support by Gladstone led to first land act (1870). Agitation of Michael Davitt and Charles Stewart Parnell led to Land Act (1881) giving the farmer the "three F's"—fair rent, fixity of tenure, and freedom from sale. Main issue then became land purchase by the tenant. Agitation of William O'BRIEN led to Wyndham Act (1903) and Amended Land Purchase Act (1909). By 1921 Irish tenants owned two thirds of the land; the rest was confiscated by law and given to the tenants.

Irish language, one of the Goidelic branch of the Celtic subfamily of Indo-European languages. It is also called Gaelic and Erse. See LANGUAGE (table).

Irish literature: see GAELIC LITERATURE.

Irish moss, reddish or purplish seaweed (*Chondrus crispus*), found off coasts of Ireland and E U.S. When cooked it yields gelatine used as pudding or as textile sizing. See *ill.*, p. 859.

Irish Republican Army, known as IRA, nationalist organization formed by Michael COLLINS after Easter Rebellion of 1916 and trained in guerrilla and terrorist tactics. Was stronghold of opposition to Ireland's dominion status and separation of Northern Ireland in 1920s. Banned by both Irish governments after Second World War, it became a secret organization.

Irish Sea, part of the Atlantic, 130 mi. long, up to c.130 mi. wide, between Ireland and Great Britain. Connected with the Atlantic by North Channel and (on S) St. George's Channel.

Irkutsk (ĭrkōōtsk′), city (1965 est. pop. 401,000), RSFSR, in S central Siberia, on Angara and Irkut rivers and on Trans-Siberian RR. River port; mfg. of aircraft, machine tools, chemicals. Hydroelectric station nearby. Founded 1652; became cap. of E Siberia 1803. Place of exile since 18th cent.

Irnerius (ûrnēr′ēŭs), c.1055–c.1130, Italian teacher and commentator on Roman law, founder of the school of law at Bologna.

iron, silver-white metallic element (symbol = Fe; see also ELEMENT, table), lustrous, ductile, malleable, attracted by magnet. It rusts easily. Chemically active, it forms ferrous (divalent) and ferric (trivalent) compounds. The fourth most abundant element, it comprises about 5% of earth's crust. Its compounds occur in soil, sand, plants, animals. Iron in blood protein hemoglobin carries oxygen from lungs or gills to cells. Deficiency causes anemia. Three forms of commercial iron: cast iron, wrought iron, STEEL. **Cast iron** is made when pig iron, prepared in BLAST FURNACE, is remelted and poured into molds to make castings. Usually has 92–94% iron, 2–6% carbon, small amounts of silicon, sulphur, manganese, phosphorus. Used in making machine parts, ranges, stoves, pipes, radiators. **Wrought iron** is made by purifying melted pig iron in puddling furnace; relatively pure, with 0.1–0.2% carbon. Used for rivets, bolts, water pipes, chains, anchors, fire bars, ornamental ironwork.

Iron Age, period of industrial development that begins with the general use of iron and continues in the present. Beads of meteoric iron shaped by rubbing were worn in Egypt c.4000 B.C., but the oldest known hammered object is a dagger made there before 1350 B.C. Casting of iron was known in ancient Greece, where the Iron Age began c.1000 B.C. From previous times the Iron Age inherited staple farm crops, animals, wheeled vehicles, and a variety of tools and implements. Glass and pottery making, spinning, weaving, and writing developed.

ironclad, mid-19th-cent. wooden warship protected from gunfire by iron armor. Introduced by French in Crimean War, ironclads were later used in the American Civil War. They became obsolete with the introduction (1870–90) of all-metal warships.

Iron Cross: see DECORATIONS, CIVIL AND MILITARY.

Irondequoit (ĭrŏn′dĭkwoit″), town (1964 pop. 60,704), W N.Y., N of Rochester; settled 1791.

Iron Gate, narrow, mountainous gorge of the Danube, between Orsova and Turnu-Severin, on the Rumanian-Yugoslav border.

Iron Guard, Rumanian nationalistic, anti-Semitic, terrorist organization, founded 1924 by Corneliu Zelea Codreanu. Banned 1933, it carried on under different name. It helped Ion Antonescu into power (1940), but he suppressed it after a rebellion (1941).

iron lung: see ARTIFICIAL LUNG.

Iron Mask, Man with the, mysterious French prisoner of state, brought to Bastille in 1698, buried 1703 under name Marchioly. Wore black velvet (not iron) mask to prevent identification. Wild speculation as to his identity was started by Voltaire's *Age of Louis XIV*, reached fantastic proportions in Dumas Père's *Le Vicomte de Bragelonne*. Actually, most modern students agree that the Iron Mask was one Count Mattioli, secretary to the duke of Mantua, whom Louis XIV had kidnaped for political reasons; but other theories still flourish.

Iron Mountain, elevation, 325 ft. high, central Fla., N of L. Wales. Site of Singing Tower, with carillon of 71 bells, and bird sanctuary estab. by Edward Bok (who is buried here) and opened 1929.

iron pyrites: see PYRITE.

Ironton. 1 Resort city (pop. 1,310), SE Mo., SW of St. Louis, in Ozarks; founded 1857. Battle of Pilot Knob between Federals under Thomas Ewing and Sterling Price's Confederates fought nearby, Sept., 1864, resulting in temporary reverse for Price on his Missouri raid. Taum Sauk Mt. and L. Killarney are nearby. **2** Industrial city (pop. 15,745), extreme S Ohio, on Ohio R. opposite Ashland, Ky., in fruit area; founded 1848.

Ironwood, city (pop. 10,265), N Mich., extreme W Upper Peninsula, on Montreal R. at Wis. line; founded 1885 Trade center of Gogebic iron range. Has some of world's deepest mines. Indian relics nearby.

ironwood: see HORNBEAM.

Iroquoian (ĭrŭkwoi′yŭn), North American Indian linguistic family, in N.Y., Pa., E Canada, and in S U.S. (Tuscarora, Cherokee). See LANGUAGE, table.

Iroquois Confederacy or **Iroquois League** (ĭ′rŭkwoi), Indian confederation consisting of Mohawk, Oneida, Onondaga, Cayuga, and Seneca tribes; founded c.1570 by prophet Deganawidah and disciple Hiawatha; also called Five Nations. Gave name to Iroquoian linguistic family. Despite some intertribal warfare, the confederacy was tight knit, the main Onondaga village serving as meeting place of the council. Material culture, based on hunting and agr., was most advanced of Eastern Woodlands area, exhibiting also traits of SE area. Iroquois were second to no other Indians N of Mexico in political organization, statecraft, and military prowess. In second half of 17th cent. they conquered neighboring tribes and dominated area bounded by Kennebec, Ottawa, Illinois, and Tennessee rivers. Were allies of British against the French in French and Indian Wars and (excepting the Oneida) American Revolution. Sir William Johnson held their loyalty. In the Revolution Cornplanter, Red Jacket, and Joseph Brant were Iroquois leaders against the patriots. The Cherry Valley and Wyoming Valley massacres incensed Americans, and John Sullivan led a punitive expedition (1779) against them and Walter Butler, the Tory leader, defeating them near Elmira.

Irrawaddy (ĭrŭwŏ′dē), chief river of Burma, c.1,000 mi. long, rising in NW and flowing to Bay of Bengal. Chief tributary is Chindwin R.

irredentism (ĭrĭdĕn′tĭzŭm), Italian nationalist movement for annexation of *Italia irredenta* [unredeemed Italy]—the ethnically Italian territories left to Austria after 1866 (e.g., Trentino, Trieste, part of Dalmatia). Chief motive for Italian entry into First World War.

irrigation, artificial watering of arable lands. It is used chiefly in regions with an annual rainfall under 20 in., but also in areas of greater rainfall to supply the high water requirements of certain crops, e.g., rice. Irrigation has been practiced from ancient times. Methods include free-flooding of entire areas from canals and ditches; check-flooding, in which water is guided over strips of land between levees; furrow method in which water is run between crop rows; and surface-pipe and sprinkler systems. Large-scale irrigation is commonly a part of multiple-purpose water projects combining irrigation, water supply, hydroelectric power production, and flood control.

Irtysh (ĭrtĭsh'), river, 1,844 mi. long, China and USSR, chief tributary of Ob. Rises in Sinkiang, flows generally NW through W Siberia past Semipalatinsk, Pavlodar, Omsk, Tobolsk. Navigable April–Nov. Reached by Russians 1594.

Irving, Edward, 1792–1834, Scottish preacher, a founder of CATHOLIC APOSTOLIC CHURCH, whose members are often called Irvingites. His emphasis on the supernatural and on the second coming of Christ and his other teachings caused expulsion (1833) from Church of Scotland.

Irving, Sir Henry, 1838–1905, English actor and manager, originally named Brodribb. Manager (1878–1903) of London's Lyceum Theatre, where he (with leading lady Ellen Terry) dominated English stage. His productions were lavish with scenic detail; his acting was best suited to the melodramas of the day. His company often toured U.S. He was the first English actor knighted.

Irving, Washington, 1783–1859, American author, b. New York city. Began early contributing essays to periodicals, styled *Letters of Jonathan Oldstyle, Gent.* (1802–3) and after a tour in Europe joined William Irving and James K. Paulding in a series called *Salmagundi* (1807–8), and under the pseudonym Diedrich Knickerbocker he produced the comic *History of New York* (1809). Sent (1815) to England to manage the Liverpool branch of the family hardware business, he saw that fail and turned definitely to literature. Essays and stories, appearing serially and collected as *The Sketch Book of Geoffrey Crayon, Gent.* (1820) made his reputation. This was followed by others in *Bracebridge Hall* (1822) and *Tales of a Traveller* (1824). He was attached to the embassy at Madrid after 1826 and turned to writing of things Spanish: a biography of Columbus (1828), *The Conquest of Granada* (1829), and *The Alhambra* (1832). After returning to the U.S., he wrote several works on the American West: *A Tour on the Prairies* (1835); *Astoria* (1836; written with his nephew, Pierre Irving, for John Jacob Astor); and *The Adventures of Captain Bonneville, U.S.A.* (1837). Except for service as minister to Madrid (1842–46), he lived most of his later years at "Sunnyside," near Tarrytown, N.Y. (and in Irvington), now a sort of shrine to him. Completed biography of Washington (5 vols., 1855–59). One of the first American writers to receive wide recognition abroad, Irving has been held in affectionate regard by Americans for his familiar tales (e.g., "Rip Van Winkle" and "The Legend of Sleepy Hollow"). He was notable for smooth style, good humor, and playful satire.

Irving, city (pop. 45,985), N Texas, suburb WNW of Dallas.

Irvington. 1 Town (pop. 59,379), NE N.J., industrial suburb W of Newark; settled 1692. **2** Residential village (1965 pop. 5,686), SE N.Y., on E bank of Hudson R., just S of Tarrytown; settled c.1655. "Sunnyside," Washington Irving's estate, is nearby. "Nevis," once estate of Alexander Hamilton's son is Columbia Univ. biological field station.

Irwell, river of Lancashire, England.

Isaac, Byzantine emperors. **Isaac I,** c.1005–1061, first of Commenus dynasty, was proclaimed emperor by the army in 1057 but abdicated, ostensibly because of bad health, in 1059. Uncle of Alexius I. **Isaac II** (Isaac Angelus), d. 1204, proclaimed emperor by the people in 1185, was deposed and blinded in 1195 by his brother ALEXIUS III. His son, ALEXIUS IV, appealed to the host of the Fourth Crusade (see CRUSADES), which re-

stored father and son as joint emperors in 1203. Their overthrow by ALEXIUS V (1204) led to the sack of Constantinople by the Crusaders.

Isaac [Heb.,= laughter], only son of Abraham and Sarah, father of Jacob and Esau. Offered as sacrifice to God by Abraham in act of supreme faith; saved by divine intervention. Tricked into blessing Jacob instead of Esau. Lived longest and most peaceful life of all the patriarchs. Gen. 21–27; 35.29; 49.31; Amos 7.9,16; Mat. 8.11; Heb. 11.17; James 2.21.

Isaacs, Jorge (hôr'hä ē'säks), 1837–95, Colombian novelist, author of idyllic romance, *María* (1867).

Isabeau of Bavaria (ēzäbō'), 1371–1435, consort of CHARLES VI of France. In league with Burgundy, she helped bring about the Treaty of TROYES (1420), which disinherited her own son, Charles VII.

Isabel, 1846–1921, princess imperial of Brazil; daughter of Pedro II, wife of comte d'Eu. As regent, during father's absence, she signed law abolishing slavery (1888). After downfall of empire, lived in Paris.

Isabella, 1296–1358, queen consort of EDWARD II of England; daughter of Philip IV of France. Mistreated by her husband, she hated royal favorites, the Despensers. Visited France (1325), formed a liaison with Roger de MORTIMER, invaded England. King abdicated and was murdered. Isabella and Mortimer ruled until Edward III seized power in 1330.

Isabella, Spanish queens. **Isabella I** or **Isabella the Catholic,** 1451–1504, queen of Castile and Leon (1474–1504), consort of Ferdinand II of Aragon, who became Ferdinand V of Castile. Her claim to Castile was contested in civil war by JUANA LA BELTRANEJA until 1479. For the crucial reign of Ferdinand and Isabella, called the Catholic monarchs, see FERDINAND V. **Isabella II,** 1830–1904, queen of Spain (1833–68), succeeded her father Ferdinand VII under the regency of her mother MARIA CHRISTINA. Her accession was challenged by her uncle Don Carlos; the Carlist Wars resulted (see CARLISTS). She married her cousin, Francisco de Asís (1846). Her rule was troubled by continuous party conflicts and frequent rebellions. Deposed in 1868, she went into exile in France. In 1870 she abdicated her rights in favor of her son Alfonso XII.

Isabey, Jean Baptiste (zhä bäptēst' ēzäbā'), 1767–1855, French portrait painter and miniaturist. Portrayed, among others, Marie Antoinette and Napoleon III. His son, **Eugène Louis Gabriel Isabey,** 1804–86, was a marine and genre painter.

Isafjordur (ē'säfyûr''dhör), town (pop. 2,658), NW Iceland, on Isafjardardjup, an arm of the Denmark Strait. Shipping port with shrimp and fishmeal factories, shipyards, and machine shops.

Isaiah (īzā'yŭ) [Heb.,= salvation of God] or **Isaias** (īsā'yŭs), book of Old Testament. A collection of prophecies attributed to Isaiah (fl. 710 B.C.), one of major prophets. Message partly political, urging recognition of Assyrian power and opposing Egyptian alliance. Chapters 1–35 contain poetic prophecies of fate of Israel and Judah, followed by a prose section (36–39) similar to 2 Kings 18.13–20.19. The second poetic section (40–66) is a prophecy of redemption, containing Messianic allusions (40; 42; 53). Authorship of last part thought to differ from that of first. Later biblical mention includes Mat. 1.23; 4.14; 13.14.

Isaiah, Ascension of: see PSEUDEPIGRAPHA.

Isaias: see ISAIAH.

Isauria (īsô'rēŭ), anc. district of Asia Minor, N of the Taurus range, in present S central Turkey. A wild region, it was inhabited by bands who lived by depredations on land and sea traffic. They were only partially checked by the Romans and not subdued until the arrival of the Seljuk Turks.

Iscariot: see JUDAS ISCARIOT.

Ischia (ēs'kyä), volcanic island (18 sq. mi.; est. pop. 33,967), S Italy, at entrance to Bay of Naples. Health resort with warm mineral springs. Wine making.

Ischl or **Bad Ischl** (bät' ĭshŭl), town (est. pop. 12,-968), Upper Austria, in SALZKAMMERGUT. Famous spa; after 1822 summer residence of imperial family.

Ise City (ē'sä), city (pop. 99,026), S Honshu, Japan, on Ise Bay. Important Shinto center, with shrines of Ise. Called Uji-yamada until 1955.

Isère (ēzĕr'), department (3,180 sq. mi.; pop. 729,789), SE France, in Dauphiné; cap. Grenoble. Named for Isère R., tributary of the Rhone.

Iseult: see TRISTRAM AND ISOLDE.

Isfahan (ĭsfŭhän'), anc. *Aspadana*, city (pop. c.340,-000), central Iran, midway between Teheran and Shiraz. Repeatedly cap. of Persia from 11th cent. Here are Abbas I's palace and the superb imperial mosque (built 1585–1612). The Julfa quarter, originally Armenian, was founded 1605 by Shah Abbas. City endured massacres by Tamerlane (1387) and by Ghalzai Afghans (1723). Occupied by Russian troops 1916. Traditionally known for metalwork, it is now a textile center. Also spelled Esfahan.

Ish-bosheth (ĭsh-bō'shĕth, ĭsh'bōshĕth), son of Saul. Contested throne with David for 7 years. 2 Sam. 2; 3; 4. Esh-baal: 1 Chron. 8.33; 9.39.

Isherwood, Christopher (ĭ'-), 1904–, English writer; U.S. citizen in 1946. Collaborated with Auden on plays (e.g., *The Dog Beneath the Skin*, 1935; *The Ascent of F6*, 1936). Among his novels are two on Berlin (1935, 1939; reissued as *The Berlin Stories*, 1946), *Prater Violet* (1945), *Down There on a Visit* (1962), and *Down There by the River* (1967). He has also written on travel, Eastern mysticism, and for motion pictures.

Ishii, Kikujiro, Viscount (kē"kōō"jērō', ĭshē'), 1865–1945, Japanese diplomat. In 1907–8 aided in negotiating GENTLEMEN'S AGREEMENT with U.S. Negotiated Lansing-Ishii agreement (1917) with U.S., reaffirming Open Door policy in China.

Ishikari (ēshēkä'rē), river, c.225 mi. long, W Hokkaido; second largest river of Japan. Waters Ishikari lowland, a rice-producing region.

Ishim, river, 1,124 mi. long, N central Kazakh SSR and SW Asiatic RSFSR. It rises N of Karaganda and flows into Irtysh at Tobolsk. Its navigable lower course passes through Ishim Steppe, rich grain-growing region.

Ishimbay (ēshēmbī'), city (1965 est. pop. 52,000), central Bashkir Autonomous SSR. Center of Volga-Ural oil fields; refineries and machinery works. Linked by oil pipeline with Ufa. Orsk. Shkapovo.

Ishmael [Heb.,= God hears], son of Abraham and Hagar, half brother of Isaac. Sent, with Hagar, into desert because of wife's jealousy. Settled in wilderness; became noted archer. Gen. 16.4–16; 17.18–26; 21.9–21; 25.9,12–17; 28.9; 1 Chron. 1.28,29. Honored as forefather of the Arabs by Moslems who esteem him as the Hebrews do Isaac; thus, use of name Ishmael for a social outcast is unknown in Islam though common in Judaism and Christianity.

Ishpeming (ĭsh'pŭmĭng), city (pop. 8,857), N Mich., W Upper Peninsula, W of Marquette. Center of Marquette iron range. Also has marble quarries. Ski tournaments held here since 1888.

Ishtar (ĭsh'tär), in Babylonian and Assyrian religion, goddess of fertility. She corresponds to Phoenician Astarte, Greek Aphrodite, and Roman Venus. As her cult grew, Ishtar became identified with various other earth-goddesses. See GREAT MOTHER OF THE GODS.

Isidore of Seville, Saint, c.560–636, Spanish encyclopedist, bishop of Seville, best known for his voluminous *Etymologiae* or *Origines*, a compendium of knowledge.

Isidorus of Miletus (ĭzĭdô'rŭs, mīlē'tŭs), name of two architects who helped rebuild Hagia Sophia, one in A.D. 532–37, the other in A.D. 553.

Isis (ī'sĭs), in Egyptian religion, nature goddess, whose worship, originating c.1700–1100 B.C., expanded throughout Egypt and Mediterranean world. She became prototype of all goddesses, and her cult was one of most antagonistic forces met by early Christians. In mythology of Egypt she was faithful wife and sister of OSIRIS and mother of Horus. After Osiris was slain by their brother, Set, and his body scattered in pieces, Isis gathered these together; Osiris was then restored and became ruler of dead. The legend symbolizes the sun (Osiris) overwhelmed by night (Set), followed by birth of the sun of a new day (Horus) from the eastern sky (Isis). Isis was universal mother and mistress of all magic. Centers of her worship were at Memphis, Abydos, and Philae, where her cult prevailed until 6th cent. A.D. The cow was symbol of Isis.

Isis: see THAMES, river, England.

Iskander Beg, Albanian hero: see SCANDERBEG.

Iskenderun (ĭskĕn'dûrōōn), formerly **Alexandretta**, city (pop. 62,061), SW Turkey, on inlet of the Mediterranean. See ALEXANDRETTA, SANJAK OF.

Isla, José Francisco de (hōsä' fränthē'skō dä ē'slä), 1703–81, "el Padre Isla," Spanish Jesuit preacher, author of the satirical novel *Historia del famoso predicador Fray Gerundio de Campazas* (1758).

Islam (ĭs'lŭm, ĭsläm') [Arabic,= submission to God], religion of which MOHAMMED was the 'prophet; adherents are called Moslems or Muslims (popularly also Mohammedans). The latest of the three great monotheisms, it drew upon the other two (Judaism and Christianity); Abraham and Jesus are in the list of prophets preceding Mohammed. It is generally held that Jesus will return as the MAHDI at the end of the world. Islam is based on the sacred book, the Koran, revealed by God (called Allah in Arabic) to Mohammed. The concepts of God and of heaven and hell are akin to those in Judaism and Christianity. Five duties are prescribed for every Moslem: (1) At least once in his life the believer must say with full acceptance, "There is no god but God and Mohammed is his prophet." (2) He must pray five times daily, facing toward Mecca, and he must say Friday noonday prayers in the mosque. (3) He must give alms generously—above the amount absolutely prescribed by law. (4) He must keep the fast of Ramadan. (5) He must, if he can, once in his life make the pilgrimage (Hajj) to Mecca. This last provision has made the pilgrimage the greatest in the world and a great unifying force in Islam. In addition to the Koran, Islam accepts the Sunna, collections of Traditions (moral sayings and anecdotes) of Mohammed. These were collected as early as the 9th cent. by BUKHARI and others. There are contradictions in the Sunna, but they are resolved by the doctrine of Ijma, which expresses the agreement of Islam; every Moslem holds that a belief held by the greater part of Islam is infallibly true; the principle has made the religion flexible. There was early a great split in Islam between SUNNITES and SHIITES, and this has persisted. The WAHABI defection was the only important later sectarian movement among Sunnites, but many groups developed among the Shiites (e.g., Assassins, Fatimites, Karmathians). The original split was over the CALIPHATE, which was the crowning institution of the theocratic structure of Islam. Though secularism has modified the unity somewhat, in theory the civil law in Mohammedan countries is not separate from religious law; religion governs all aspects of life. There have developed some four different systems of interpretation of the law in Sunnite Islam, all regarded as orthodox. Islamic philosophy is in effect part of theology; the greatest philosopher was Al-Gazel. Rationalism and mysticism (see SUFISM) both grew up in Islam, but were equally absorbed. The spread of the religion after its founding by Mohammed was phenomenally rapid in the 7th and 8th cent., and it soon was dominant from Spain (see MOORS) to India. It is today spread across Asia to the S Pacific. prevails in N Africa (with its intellectual center at Cairo), and is still gaining converts in the rest of Africa. In 1954, Egypt, Saudi Arabia, and Pakistan led movement for annual Islamic Conference at Mecca. There are also Mohammedan groups in Europe (Albania, Bosnia, and sections of

Russia), but only scattered communities in the New World.

Islamabad (ĭs"lŭmŭbăd', ĭslăm"–), city, NE West Pakistan; 12 mi. NW of Rawalpindi. Construction of Islamabad as new cap. of Pakistan began 1960, and transfer of some administrative government offices to new city commenced 1965. Completion of major construction scheduled for 1975.

island, relatively small body of land surrounded entirely by water. As oceans form continuous water mass, continents are, strictly speaking, islands. Largest island is Greenland, followed by New Guinea, Borneo, Madagascar, Baffin Isl., Sumatra, Honshu, Great Britain. Islands are continental if created by submergence of coastal highlands with only summits left above water, or by sea's breaking through an isthmus or peninsula. Great Britain, Japanese archipelago, Sicily are continental; submarine banks show former coherence of each with mainland. Islands are oceanic if created by ascent of ocean floor, as through volcanic action, or by coral growth (atoll). In rare cases coastal island reunites with mainland.

Island No. 10, formerly a Tenn. island (not now extant) in Mississippi R. near New Madrid, Mo. Scene of Civil War campaign (March 3–April 7, 1862). A Union victory.

Islay (ī'lā, ī'lū), island (pop. 3,866) of the Inner Hebrides, off W Scotland, in Argyllshire. Agr., fishing, and distilling are chief occupations. Memorials to victims of the sinking (1918) of the *Tuscania* and *Otranto* are here.

Isle La Motte (īl" lù mŏt'), island, 6 mi. long and 2 mi. wide, NW Vt., in L. Champlain NW of St. Albans. Site of French Fort Ste Anne (built 1666), first white settlement in Vt. Abandoned long before permanent settlement began c.1788. Black marble deposits.

Isle of. For names beginning thus, see second element; e.g., for Isle of Ely, see ELY, ISLE OF.

Isle of Palms, resort town (pop. 1,186), SE S.C., on Sullivans Isl., E of Charleston. Has one of finest beaches in state.

Isle Royale National Park: see NATIONAL PARKS AND MONUMENTS (table).

Isles of Shoals, off SE N.H. and S Maine, SE of Portsmouth, N.H. Seven islands, a resort area, include Appledore, Cedar, Duck, and Smuttynose (in Maine) and Lunging, White, and Star (in N.H.).

Isles of the Blest: see FORTUNATE ISLES.

Isleta (īslĕ'tù), Indian pueblo (pop. c.1,830), central N.Mex., on E bank of Rio Grande R., S of Albuquerque; discovered 1540. Seat of a Franciscan mission from c.1621 until Pueblo revolt of 1680. Captured by Spanish 1681. Mission revitalized as San Augustín de Isleta in early 1700s. Holds annual feast of St. Augustine. PUEBLO INDIANS here are mainly prosperous farmers. Language Tanoan.

Islington, London borough since 1965 (est. pop. 259,-160); includes metropolitan boroughs of Islington and Finsbury. Residential district. Site of Pentonville Prison and Halloway Gaol for women.

Islip (ī'slĭp), town (1964 pop. 222,460), SE N.Y., on Great South Bay NE of Babylon; settled c.1665. Includes several villages, mainly resorts and residential suburbs of New York city.

Ismail (ĭsmäĕl'), 1499–1524, shah of Persia (1502–24), founder of Safavid dynasty. Made Shiism the official religion of Persia.

Ismail, Ukraine: see IZMAIL.

Ismailia (ĕs"mäĭlē'ä), city (pop. c.156,300), Egypt, at midpoint of Suez Canal. Founded 1863 by Lesseps as operational base for construction of canal. City badly damaged in Middle Eastern war in June, 1967.

Ismail Pasha (ĭsmäĕl' pä'shä), 1830–95, ruler of Egypt (1863–79), son of Ibrahim Pasha; first to bear the title khedive (viceroy). His schemes, such as building of Suez Canal, put Egypt seriously in debt, forcing him to sell his stock (c.44%) in Suez Canal to Great Britain, and to submit in 1876 to joint Anglo-French manage-

ment of Egyptian government. Deposed 1879 in favor of his son Tewfik Pasha.

Ismay, Hastings Lionel Ismay, 1st Baron, 1887–1965, British general. Chief of staff to Churchill and deputy secretary to war cabinet during Second World War. Secretary General of NATO 1952–57.

isobars (ī'sùbärz") or **isobaric lines** (ī"sùbă'rĭk), weathermap lines connecting points of equal barometric pressure. Can be used to define cyclones, anticyclones.

Isocrates (īsŏ'krŭtēz), 436–338 B.C., Greek orator, a pupil of Socrates and perhaps the greatest teacher in Greek history. *Panegyricus* was considered his most celebrated oration.

Isolde: see TRISTRAM AND ISOLDE.

isomerism (īsŏ'mùrĭzùm), in chemistry, condition in which the molecules of two or more compounds have same numbers of same atoms but different molecular arrangements. Structural isomers (ī'sùmùrz) have different structural linkages, e.g., different branching. Stereoisomerism depends not on structural linkage but on asymmetric arrangement of the molecule. Stereoisomers occur only in pairs; each pair consists of a right-handed isomer and a left-handed isomer. Optical isomerism is a form of stereoisomerism; in optical isomerism, a particular atom (not merely the whole molecule) exists in both a right-handed and a left-handed form. Crystals of optical isomers have different effects on polarized light; the two configurations are termed D- and L-. Structural isomers have different chemical properties; optical isomers are chemically identical, but other types of stereoisomers differ chemically. Isomers are common among benzene ring compounds, other hydrocarbons, sugars.

isomorphism, similarity of crystal structure between substances having different chemical compositions, e.g., magnesia (MgO) and halite (NaCl), both form cubes. Concept of isomorphism was developed c.1820 by Eilhard Mitscherlich, German chemist.

Isonzo (ēzōn'tsō), river, 87 mi. long, Yugoslavia and Italy. Fiercely contested in First World War.

isotope (ī'sùtōp), in chemistry, one of two or more elements identical in chemical activity but differing in ATOMIC WEIGHT. Weight difference probably caused by difference in number of neutrons in nucleus; identical properties result from atoms having same number and arrangement of electrons outside nucleus. Radioactive isotopes are used as tracers in research.

Israel (ĭz'rēùl) [as understood by Hebrews,= prevailing with God], in Bible, name given to Jacob as ancestor of the Hebrews, God's chosen people. The 12 tribes of Israel—Reuben, Simeon, Judah, Zebulun, Issachar, Dan, Gad, Asher, Naphtali, Benjamin, Ephraim, Manasseh—were named for 10 sons and 2 grandsons (sons of Joseph) of Jacob. For 13th tribe, see LEVI. When Hebrew kingdom was divided under REHOBOAM, N part called Israel, S part Judah.

Israel (ĭz'rēùl), republic (8,050 sq. mi.; pop. c.2,175,-000), W Asia, on the Mediterranean; cap. JERUSALEM. Boundaries are not permanently fixed; at present Lebanon is N, Syria and Jordan E, and Egypt SW. Grains are grown mainly in Galilee in N, citrus fruits in coastal area. Irrigation and dry-farming methods used in the NEGEV. Agr. cooperatives are widespread. Industrialization is being advanced, mainly at HAIFA and TEL-AVIV. Haifa and Jaffa are chief ports. For early history see PALESTINE. The nearly all-Jewish state grew out of ZIONISM. After Second World War many backed an independent state for Palestinian Jews (1945 pop. c.500,000) which would also be a homeland for surviving European Jews and Jews in Arab countries. Palestinian Arabs (1945 pop. c.1,000,000) and Arab states opposed a Jewish state and demanded independence for all Palestine, with Jews a protected minority. British decision to admit only 2,000 displaced European Jews a month, until 100,000 had been admitted, led to attacks on British military installations by Jewish secret societies. In 1947 the UN divided Palestine into a Jewish state, an Arab state, and a small international zone, including Jerusalem. Despite Arab opposition the state of Israel was proclaimed at Tel-Aviv on May 14, 1948. Ensuing war between ARAB LEAGUE countries and Israel was ended Jan., 1949, by UN mediation supervised first by Count Folke BERNADOTTE and later by Ralph Bunche. The war had increased Israel's holdings by about a half; most of the territory designated for a new Arab state was annexed by Egypt and Jordan. Many displaced Arabs confined to the GAZA STRIP. Egyptian seizure of Suez Canal precipitated the SINAI CAMPAIGN in 1956. DAVID BEN-GURION was first prime minister. Chaim Weizmann was president until his death in 1952. President Yizhak Ben-Zivi (1952–63) was succeeded by Shneour Zalam Shazar. Ben Gurion retired as prime minister in 1963 and was succeeded by Levi Eshkol. In 1964 Israel began channeling water from Jordan R. S to Negev desert. Border clashes with Jordan and Syria continued. In May, 1967, peacekeeping UN Emergency Force withdrawn from Gaza Strip at Egypt's request, and Egypt announced blockade of Gulf of Aqaba to Israeli shipping. Israel accepted action as aggression and mobilized forces. Diplomatic attempts to solve crisis failed, and on June 5 Israel launched air and land attacks against Arab forces and took Gaza Strip, Sinai peninsula, Jordanian territory to W bank of Jordan R., and Syrian highlands commanding Sea of Galilee. Israel announced intention of keeping conquered land until negotiations could be held with Arab powers.

Issachar (ĭ′sŭkŭr), son of Jacob, ancestor of one of 12 tribes of Israel. Tribe allotted land W of Jordan R. Gen. 30.18; 46.13; 49.14; Num. 1.29; 2.5; Deut. 27.12; 33.18; Joshua 19.17; 1 Chron. 7.1–5.

Isserles, Moses ben Israel (ĭ′sûrlĕs), c.1520–1572, Polish rabbi and philosopher. His additions to Caro's *Shulchan Arukh* made the code of CARO authoritative among Ashkenazic Jews. Also known as Remah.

Issus (ĭ′sŭs), anc. town, SE Asia Minor. Here in 333 B.C. Alexander the Great defeated DARIUS III.

Issyk Kul (ēsĭk′kōōl′), lake (2,690 sq. mi.), NE Kirgiz SSR, in Ala-Tau mts. Altitude c.5,280 ft.; max. depth 2,313 ft.; slightly saline.

Istanbul (ĭ′stänbōōl′, Turkish ĭstäm′bōol), city (pop. 1,466,535), Turkey, on both sides of the BOSPORUS; name was officially changed from Constantinople 1930. (For history, see CONSTANTINOPLE.) The cap. of Turkey until 1922 and still its chief commercial center and seaport, Istanbul also is the seat of a university (founded 1453; reorganized 1933) and is the see of three patriarchs (Greek Orthodox, Latin-rite Roman Catholic, Armenian). Only the European side of Istanbul corresponds to historic Constantinople. Rising on both sides of the Golden Horn, an inlet of the Bosporus, it is built on seven hills. Several miles of medieval city walls and forts still stand. The commercial quarter of Galata and the quarters of Pera (formerly reserved for foreigners) and Haskoy (Jewish quarter) are outside the walls. A famous bridge crosses the Golden Horn into Stambul, the core of the city, abutting on the Bosporus and the Sea of Marmara. In the NW are the former Greek quarter of Phanar and the Byzantine imperial palace of Blachernae. The Asiatic part of Istanbul includes Kadikoy (anc. Chalcedon) and Uskudar (also known as Scutari). The chief monument from Byzantine times is the HAGIA SOPHIA. Masterpieces of Turkish architecture include the 16th-cent. mosques of Bajazet II, Suleiman I, and Ahmed I; the Seraglio (former palace of sultans); and the Dolma Bagtche and Yildiz Kiosk (sultans' residences in 19th and 20th cent.). Istanbul is also famed for its polyglot population and its beautiful environs.

Isthmian games (ĭ′smēŭn), athletic events organized c.581 B.C. Held at Corinth in spring of first and third years of Olympiad. Contests generally like OLYMPIC GAMES, but conducted on smaller scale.

Istria (ĭ′strēŭ), Serbo-Croatian *Istra*, mountainous peninsula, c.2,000 sq. mi., projecting into N Adriatic and bounded in N by Karst plateau; chief city Pola. Population is Yugoslav and Italian. Nominal Byzantine rule ceased in 8th cent. A.D., and area was partitioned by Venice, Carinthia, the patriarchs of Aquileia, and the counts of Gorizia. By the 15th cent. Venice held the SW, Austria the NE, and by 1815 all passed to Austria. In 1919 all passed to Italy, but in 1947 most given to Yugoslavia. NW Istria passed to Trieste.

Italian East Africa, former Italian colony, comprising ERITREA, SOMALIA, and ETHIOPIA.

Italian language, one of the Romance or Romanic branch of the Italic subfamily of Indo-European languages. See LANGUAGE (table).

Italian Somaliland: see SOMALI REPUBLIC.

Italian Wars, 1494–1529. Rivalry among the states of Renaissance ITALY invited imperialist intervention of the rising national states, especially France and Spain. Alignments of Italian and foreign powers shifted constantly. In the first phase (1494–95) CHARLES VIII of France conquered Naples but was forced to abandon it by a coalition of Spain, the emperor, the pope, Venice, and Milan. In the second phase (1499–1504) LOUIS XII of France occupied Milan, Genoa, and (jointly with Spain) Naples. French-Spanish disagreement flared into warfare (1502); Louis lost at Cerignola and at the Garigliano; the Treaties of Blois (1504–5) gave Milan and Genoa to France but pledged Naples to Spain. The third phase (1508–16) consisted of three subphases: the victorious campaign of the League of CAMBRAI against Venice (1509); the formation of the HOLY LEAGUE and the expulsion of the French from Lombardy by the Swiss (1510–13); the victory of Francis I at Marignano (1515), followed by the Peace of Noyon, which restored Milan to France. The wars between FRANCIS I and Emperor Charles V opened 1521. Defeated and captured at Pavia (1525), Francis bought his freedom by the Treaty of Madrid (1526), in which he renounced all claims in Italy, Flanders, and Artois, ceded Burgundy, and surrendered his sons as hostages. Freed, he formed the League of Cognac with Pope Clement VII, Francesco II Sforza, Venice, and Florence, thus precipitating a fifth war. Charles's mutinous army sacked Rome (1527), the French invaded Naples, but the defection of Genoese sea power under Andrea Doria (1528) forced Francis to accept the Treaty of Cambrai or Ladies' Peace (1529); negotiated by Margaret of Austria, Charles's aunt, and Louise of Savoy, mother of Francis, it reaffirmed the Treaty of Madrid. Charles released French princes, and Burgundy remained in French hands. After three more wars, fought largely outside Italy, Spain retained supremacy in Italy by the Treaty of CATEAU-CAMBRÉSIS (1559).

Italic languages, subfamily of Indo-European languages. Latin superseded the other two important groups (Oscan and Umbrian) and was the only one to survive antiquity; from it the Romanic languages are derived. See LANGUAGE (table).

Italy, Latin and Ital. *Italia*, republic (116,372 sq. mi.; pop. 50,463,462), S Europe; cap. Rome. N Italy is separated by the ALPS from France, Switzerland, Austria, Yugoslavia. Central and S Italy, traversed by the APENNINES, form a boot-shaped peninsula between the Tyrrhenian and Adriatic seas and contain VATICAN CITY and SAN MARINO. Of the 19 regions making up Italy, five enjoy autonomous rights—the islands of SICILY and SARDINIA and the border regions of Val d'AOSTA, TRENTINO-ALTO ADIGE, and FRIULI-VENEZIA GIULIA. The other regions are: LIGURIA, PIEDMONT, LOMBARDY, VENETIA, EMILIA-ROMAGNA, MARCHES, TUSCANY, UMBRIA, LATIUM, CAMPANIA, BASILICATA, ABRUZZI E MOLISE, CALABRIA, APULIA. N Italy, with the fertile Po plain and the commercial and industrial centers of MILAN, GENOA, and TURIN, is the richest part of the country. Central Italy contains such historic and cultural centers as FLORENCE, PISA, BOLOGNA, RAVENNA, ROME. S Italy, with NAPLES as chief city, is scarred by poverty. The varied beauty of the Italian landscape conceals the harshness of its rocky, eroded soil, intensely and patiently worked by a frugal population. Fruit, wine, olive oil, cheese are among the exports; food staples and basic raw materials are largely imported. Industries (silk, textiles, automobiles, machinery, chemicals, luxury goods) depend largely on export markets and imported raw materials; hydroelectric power, sulphur, mercury, and marble are the only important natural resources. Roman Catholicism is the official religion of this overwhelmingly Catholic country, but freedom of worship is guaranteed.

Ancient and Medieval Italy. About the 8th cent. B.C. the Etruscans settled in N Italy, the Greeks along the S coasts (see ETRUSCAN CIVILIZATION; MAGNA GRAECIA). A Celtic invasion (4th cent. B.C.) drove the Etruscans S, until they were stopped by the SAMNITES. Italian history from the 5th cent. B.C. to the 5th cent. A.D. is largely that of rising ROME and of the Roman Empire. The barbarian invasions (5th cent.; see VISIGOTHS, HUNS, ODOACER, OSTROGOTHS) destroyed the Western Empire and Italian unity. THEODORIC THE GREAT preserved Roman institutions, but after his death the papacy alone remained a stable element. JUSTINIAN I reconquered Italy (535–54), but his successors were defeated by the LOMBARDS. Byzantine rule persisted for some time in Ravenna, the PENTAPOLIS, and along the S coast. In Rome, Pope GREGORY I resisted Lombard conquest and laid the foundation for the PAPAL STATES. The persisting Lombard threat to Rome brought the intervention of PEPIN THE SHORT (751) and CHARLEMAGNE (800), who enlarged the papal domain and estab. Frankish hegemony over Italy. After the divisions of the Carolingian empire (9th cent.), Italy gradually slipped from imperial control and fell into anarchy. The coronation of OTTO I as king of Italy (961) and Roman emperor (962) created the HOLY ROMAN EMPIRE, but despite their frequent incursions the German emperors could never establish control over Italy. S Italy, conquered by the Normans (11th cent.), passed, after a period of HOHENSTAUFEN rule, to the Angevins of Naples and the Aragonese kings of Sicily. The cities in the N (where the LOMBARD LEAGUE had defied imperial authority) and in central Italy became separate and warring states, some under princes (the VISCONTI, the SFORZA, the GONZAGA, the ESTE, the MALATESTA), some as republics. VENICE and GENOA built huge commercial empires, while merchants of FLORENCE, SIENA, and LUCCA gained power and wealth. Despite constant struggles between and within cities (see GUELPHS AND GHIBELLINES), the city-states had great prosperity, dominated European finances through their great bankers (e.g., the MEDICI), and produced the miraculous cultural flowering known as the RENAISSANCE. *Disintegration and Rebirth.* With the ITALIAN WARS, beginning 1494, Italy became the battleground of French and Hapsburg imperialism. The Treaty of CATEAU-CAMBRÉSIS (1559) gave Sicily, Naples, and Milan to Spain. The Wars of the 17th and 18th cent. completed Italian subjection to foreign rule. By 1748 Naples, Sicily, Parma, and Piacenza were ruled by branches of the Spanish Bourbons; Milan, Mantua, Tuscany, and Modena were under Austrian rule. Venice, Genoa, Lucca, still independent, were declining. The Papal States and the kingdom of SARDINIA, under the rising house of SAVOY, made up the rest. All this was swept away by the FRENCH REVOLUTIONARY WARS and the rise of NAPOLEON I, who remade the Italian map several times. The Congress of Vienna (1814–15) more or less restored the pre-Napoleonic status quo. Austria, receiving Lombardy and Venetia, held a paramount position, but could not for long suppress the nationalist movement for unification (see RISORGIMENTO). The Italy of which VICTOR EMMANUEL II became king in 1861 still lacked Venetia (acquired in AUSTRO-PRUSSIAN WAR of 1866) and Rome. Florence was the cap. In 1870 Italian troops annexed Rome; the resulting conflict with the papacy was resolved only in 1929 (see LATERAN TREATY).

Modern Italy. From 1861 to 1922 Italy was ruled under the relatively liberal Sardinian constitution of 1848 by Victor Emmanuel II, Humbert I, and Victor Emmanuel III. Italy acquired colonies (Somaliland, Eritrea, Libya), expanded industrially, and found an outlet for overpopulation in mass emigration to the Americas. Though a member of Triple Alliance with Germany and Austria, it entered First World War on Allied side (1915). At the Paris Peace Conference of 1919 it obtained S Tyrol, Trieste, Istria, part of Carniola, several Dalmatian isls., and the Dodecanese, but not all the territory it had been secretly promised. Italian seizure of Fiume (1921) was symptomatic of nationalist discontent. Political and social unrest furthered the growth of FASCISM, and in 1922 MUSSOLINI seized the power. He gradually created a totalitarian corporative state and sought to solve the problem of overpopulation through "dynamic expansion." His conquest of ETHIOPA (1935–36), his intervention in Spain (1936–39), and his seizure of ALBANIA (1939) were followed by formal alliance with Germany (1939; see AXIS). In 1940 Italy entered Second World War; by 1943 it had lost Africa and Sicily to the Allies. The king dismissed Mussolini, appointed BADOGLIO as premier, and surrendered Italy to the Allies, who eventually recognized Italy as "cobelligerent" against Germany. The Italian campaign was slow, arduous, and destructive. Rome fell in 1944; in May, 1945, the Germans surrendered. By popular referendum Italy became a republic in 1946. The 1947 peace treaty deprived Italy of its colonies, some lesser territories, and most of VENEZIA GIULIA, including TRIESTE. Italy recovered Italian sectors of Trieste 1954. Aided by UNRRA, the European Recovery Program, and land reform in the south, Italy's economy began to grow rapidly after 1950, although unemployment remained a problem in the south. Governed by a series of pro-Western coalitions, Italy joined the North Atlantic Treaty Organization (1949), European Coal and Steel Community (1952), Western European Union (1954), and European Common Market and European Atomic Energy Community (1957). Was admitted to UN in 1955. Political and economic instability prevalent in early 1960s. Political division of two decades ended 1966 when Social Democratic and Socialist parties reunited. In 1966 negotiations were completed with Austria over German-speaking minority in Trentino–Alto Adige region.

Itasca, Lake (ītȧ'skŭ), small shallow lake in NW central Minn., SSW of Bemidji. Identified by H. R. Schoolcraft as source of the Mississippi, but later geographers consider source to be above lake.

itch: see SCABIES.

Ithaca (ĭ'thĭkŭ, ĭ'thŭkŭ), Gr. *Ithake*, mountainous island (37 sq. mi.; pop. 6,521), W Greece, one of the IONIAN ISLANDS; chief town Ithaca (pop. 2,632). Famed as home of ODYSSEUS.

Ithaca, city (pop. 28,799), W central N.Y., in Finger Lakes region, on hills at S end of Cayuga L.; settled 1789. Seat of CORNELL UNIVERSITY and Ithaca Col.

Ito, Hirobumi, Prince (hērō'bōōmē, ē'tō), 1841–1909, Japanese statesman, the outstanding figure in modernization of Japan. Sent abroad 1882 to study foreign governments. Drafted constitution of 1889 in the MEIJI period of reform. Was prime minister (1892–96, 1898, 1900–1901) and first president of powerful Seiyukai party. Responsible for agreement (1905) making Korea a virtual protectorate. His assassination while Japanese resident general of Korea served as pretext for annexing.

Itsuku-shima (ētsōōkōō'shǐmä), sacred islet in Inland Sea, Japan. Site of an anc. Shinto shrine, a 9th-cent. Buddhist shrine, a 16th-cent. hall, and a huge torii (1875). Also known as Miya-jima.

Iturbide, Agustín de (ägōōstēn' dä ētōōrbē'dä), 1783–1824, Mexican revolutionist, emperor of Mexico (1822–23). Commander of royalist troops, he united with the insurgents and proclaimed the Plan of IGUALA. Instead of liberal state that separatists had planned, Iturbide had himself made emperor (1822). Forced to abdicate (1823), he fled to Europe. Returning to Mexico (1824), he was tried and shot.

Ituzaingó, battle of (ē"tōōsīn-gō'), fought in S Uruguay, Feb. 20, 1827. Argentine-Uruguayan forces defeated Brazil. Argentina and Brazil both claimed Uruguay but in peace treaty (1828), an independent Uruguay emerged as buffer state.

Itzá (ētsä'), Maya Indians of Yucatán and Petén (Guatemala), probable founders of Chichén Itzá (c.514). Moved c.1450 to L. Petén, remained there until driven from their capital, Tayasal (1697).

Iuka (īū'kū), resort town (pop. 2,010), NE Miss., near Tennessee R., SE of Corinth. Mineral springs nearby. Here on Sept. 19, 1862, Gen. Rosecrans attacked Confederates under Sterling Price, who withdrew.

Ivan II (Ivan Asen), d. 1241, tsar of Bulgaria (1218–41). Bulgaria reached its zenith under his rule. He made it the strongest Balkan power but was essentially a man of peace.

Ivan (ī'vän, ī'vůn, Rus. ēvän'), rulers of Russia. **Ivan III** (the Great), 1440–1505, grand duke of Moscow (1462–1505), expanded Muscovite state, freed Muscovy from allegiance to Golden Horde (1480). Married niece of last Byzantine emperor, claimed successorship of Moscow to East Roman Empire. His grandson, **Ivan IV** (the Terrible), 1530–84, acceded as grand duke of Moscow 1533, had himself crowned tsar 1547. Conquered Kazan (1552) and Astrakhan (1557) from Tatars, thus beginning Russia's eastward expansion, which was carried into Siberia by the Cossack YERMAK. Warfare with Poland and Sweden over Baltic Coast ended to his disadvantage (1558–82). He began and encouraged trade relations with England. At home, Ivan crushed power of boyars (high nobles), favored common people, strengthened tsarist autocracy, and estab. special corps (*Oprichnina*) to fight rebellion. The death of his first wife (1560; six others followed her) apparently affected his mental balance. He was given to alternate fits of cruel rage (in one of which he killed his eldest son) and of prayerful repentance. Two sons survived him—FEODOR I and DMITRI—but his favorite, Boris GODUNOV, inherited the actual power. **Ivan V,** 1666–96, tsar (1682–96), succeeded his brother Feodor III jointly with PETER I under regency of SOPHIA ALEKSEYEVNA. Feeble-minded, he was excluded from affairs of state. He was the father of Empress Anna, who was succeeded in 1740 by her infant grand-nephew, **Ivan VI,** 1740–64, a German by birth. In 1741 he was deposed by Empress Elizabeth, and in 1764 he was murdered in Schlüsselburg fortress on orders of Catherine II.

Ivano-Frankovsk, formerly **Stanislav** (stůnyīslä̈f'), Pol. *Stanisławów,* city (1965 est. pop. 82,000), W Ukraine. Rail center; oil refineries; carpet mfg. Founded 1662; passed to Austria 1772, to Poland 1919; included in Ukraine 1939. Called Stanislav until 1962.

Ivanovo (ēvä'nůvů), city (1965 est. pop. 389,000), RSFSR, 155 mi. NE of Moscow. Major textile center. Chartered 1328. First textile mill 1751. Called Ivanovo-Voznesensk until c.1930.

Ives, Charles, 1874–1954, American composer. In the insurance business 1898–1930, he was at the same time composing music in a modern idiom. Most of his works were unknown until 1939. Among his works are symphonies, suites (including *Three Places in New England*), sonatas, chamber music, and songs. His Third Symphony won the Pulitzer Prize in 1947.

Ives, Frederic Eugene, 1856–1937, American inventor; perfected orthochromatic and trichromatic photography, photoengraving, and optical devices. His son, **Herbert Eugene Ives,** 1882–1953, helped develop television and the wirephoto process.

Ivigtut (ē'vīgtōōt), town (pop. 123), SW Greenland. port SE of Frederikshaab. Here is world's largest cryolite mine.

Iviza, Span. *Ibiza,* island (221 sq. mi.; pop. c.37,173), one of the Balearic Isls., Spain; chief town Iviza (pop. 11,259).

ivory, type of dentine present only in the tusks (prolongations of the upper pair of second incisors) of the elephant. Africa, the principal source of supply, furnishes the best and largest tusks. The chief commercial uses are for piano keys, billiard balls, handles, and decorative objects. In art, ivory is an excellent material for miniature painting and has been used through the ages for inlay work and intricate carvings. The civilizations of Egypt, Mesopotamia, Assyria, Babylon, Greece, Rome, India, China, and Japan are represented by works in ivory. Imitations and substitutes for ivory include celluloid and vegetable ivory (tagua).

Ivory Coast, republic (c.125,700 sq. mi.; pop. c.3,340,-000), W Africa, on the Gulf of Guinea; cap. and chief port ABIDJAN. Coastal swamps merge into inland savanna. Primarily agr., it exports large quantities of coffee, as well as cocoa, rubber, cotton, and timber. Diamonds, manganese, and gold are mined. Rail connections from Abidjan to Upper Volta. Official language is French. Portuguese traded for ivory and slaves in 16th cent. French estab. protectorate in 1893. Internal autonomy in 1956 led to independence in 1960; Felix Houphouët-Boigny became first president.

ivory nut: see TAGUA.

Ivry-la-Bataille (ēvrē'-lä-bätä'yù), village near Évreux, N France, where Henry IV of France won a major victory over the League (1590).

ivy, name referring usually to English ivy but also to other climbing plants, e.g., poison ivy, Boston ivy, ground ivy. Grape ivy (*Cissus rhombifolia*) is a house plant.

Ivy League, for many years popular name for eight major Eastern colleges (Brown, Columbia, Cornell, Dartmouth, Harvard, Pennsylvania, Princeton, Yale). Formalized as an athletic group (1946); actual league formed, ties tightened in 1954.

Ivywild, town (pop. 11,065), central Colo., S of Colorado Springs, in farm area.

Iwasa Matabei (ēwä'sä mätäbä'), 1578–1650, Japanese genre and portrait painter. His works had a strong influence on later genre painters.

Iwo Jima (ē'wō jē'mů), volcanic island (c.8 sq. mi.), most important and largest of Volcano Isls., W Pacific. In S is Mt. Suribachi (extinct volcano, 546 ft. high). Sulfur mining. In Second World War the site of Japanese air base, taken in early 1945 in one of most important actions of U.S. forces.

IWW: see INDUSTRIAL WORKERS OF THE WORLD.

Ixion (īk'sēūn), in Greek mythology. He was chained to revolving, fiery wheel in Hades as punishment for his lust for Hera. Through a union with a cloud, substituted by Zeus for Hera, he became father of centaur monsters.

Ixtacihuatl (ēs"täsē'wätùl) [Aztec,= white woman], dormant volcano, 17,342 ft. high, central Mexico, near POPOCATEPETL. Known also as Sleeping Woman.

Iyeyasu: see IEYASU.

Izhevsk (ē'zhīfsk), city (1965 est. pop. 351,000), cap. of Udmurt ASSR, E European RSFSR. Steel-milling center; mfg. of machinery, tools, small arms.

Izmail (ēzmŭēl'), Rumanian *Ismail,* city (1965 est. pop. 59,000), SW Ukraine, on Danube delta and Rumanian border. Commercial center; naval base. A Turkish fortress from 16th cent., it was captured by the Russians in 1770 and 1790. Ceded to Russia 1812, it shared later history of BESSARABIA.

Izmir, Turkey: see SMYRNA.

Izmit (ī'zmēt'), city (pop. 73,488), NW Turkey, on Asiatic side of Sea of Marmara. Rich tobacco region. Founded c.712 B.C., rebuilt by Nicomedus I (264 B.C.) as his capital, NICOMEDIA.

Izu-shichito (ē'zōōshǐchǐtō), volcanic island group, extending c.300 mi. S of Tokyo Bay, Japan. O-shima is largest island.

Izvolsky, Aleksandr Petrovich (ǔlyǐksän'dŭr pĕtrô'vǐch ēzvôl'skē), 1856–1919, Russian foreign minister

(1906–10). Ended Russo-English rivalry in Middle East by establishing zones of influence (1907). After Austria annexed Bosnia and Hercegovina (1908), he prepared for war by strengthening Triple Entente.

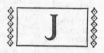

Jabbok, river of Jordan, the modern Wadi Zerka, which enters Jordan R. N of Jericho. On its S bank Jacob wrestled with angel. Gen. 32.22; Num. 21.24.

Jabesh-gilead (jā'bĕsh-gĭl'ēăd), city of Gilead. Saul saved its people from atrocities at the hands of the Ammonites. At his death the grateful city buried him.

Jabir: see GEBER, Arabian alchemist.

Jablonec nad Nisou (yä'blônĕts näd nē'sō), Ger. *Gablonz*, city (est. pop. 26,859), NE Bohemia, Czechoslovakia. Mfg. center for Bohemian glass.

jaborandi (jăb''ürăn'dē), tropical American shrub (*Pilocarpus*), yielding poisonous drug jaborandi which contains pilocarpine used in medicine.

Jabotinsky, Vladimir (yäb''ütǐn'skǐ), 1881–1940, Jewish Zionist leader, b. Russia. A militant Zionist and founder of Zionist Revisionist party (1925).

Jachymov, Czech *Jáchymov* (yä'khǐmôf), Ger. *Joachimsthal*, town, NW Bohemia, Czechoslovakia. A major mining center for radium, uranium, and lead, it also has thermal and radioactive springs. Its former rich silver mines are now little exploited. From the Joachimsthaler, a coin struck here in the 16th cent., came the words *Thaler* and *dollar*.

jackal (jă'kôl), nocturnal wild mammal (genus *Canis*) of dog family, found in SE Europe, Asia, Africa. It eats carrion, plant food, and animals. It resembles the wolf but is smaller.

jack-in-the-pulpit or **Indian turnip**, American woodland perennial (*Arisaema triphyllum*). Small flowers are borne on club-shaped spadix enveloped by purplish-striped hooded spathe and are followed by cluster of red berries. Cooked roots were eaten by Indians. Swamp jack-in-the-pulpit is *A. stewardsonii*.

Jackman, Wilbur Samuel, 1855–1907, American educator, a leader of the nature study movement in elementary schools.

jack rabbit: see HARE.

Jackson, Andrew, 1767–1845, 7th President of the United States (1829–37). Decisive victory as U.S. commander in battle of New Orleans made him the military hero of War of 1812. His popularity almost elected him President in 1824. Idol of the democratic West, an expansionist, man of action, he led what later came to be called Jacksonian democracy—government for the good of the small man, of the frontier farmer and the backwoodsman, the laborer and the mechanic of Eastern cities. His sweeping victory of 1828 led to conflict between reformers and settled proponents of order. KITCHEN CABINET was powerful; party was paramount and SPOILS SYSTEM was born. Social slights offered Margaret O'NEILL helped break up the cabinet; John C. CALHOUN provoked further estrangement through his NULLIFICATION doctrine and his resignation from the vice presidency. Jackson's fight against the BANK OF THE UNITED STATES was an important factor in election of 1832, in which he de-

feated Henry CLAY. Second administration was dominated by bank issue. Jackson sponsored Specie Circular in 1836; stipulating that all public lands must be paid for in specie, it helped hasten Panic of 1837. After presidency he retired to his estate, the Hermitage, in Tenn.

Jackson, Barbara Ward Jackson, Lady: see WARD, BARBARA.

Jackson, Chevalier, 1865–1958, American laryngologist. Perfected technique of removing foreign bodies from respiratory tract by means of bronchoscope and from digestive tract with the esophagoscope.

Jackson, Claiborne Fox, 1806–62, governor of Mo. (1860–61). Opponent of Union cause, called by him "unholy crusade." After conflict with Union troops Jackson was deposed.

Jackson, Helen (Fiske) Hunt, 1830–85, American writer, pseud. H. H. Notable for historical account of the Indian problem, *A Century of Dishonor* (1881), and novel on the theme, *Ramona* (1884).

Jackson, Robert H(oughwout), 1892–1954, Associate Justice of U.S. Supreme Court (1941–54). Granted leave (1945–46) to serve as U.S. chief counsel at Nuremberg war-crimes trial.

Jackson, Thomas Jonathan known as **Stonewall Jackson**, 1824–63, Confederate general. At first battle of Bull Run, he and his brigade won sobriquet by standing "like a stone wall." He won renown by his Shenandoah Valley campaign (1862). Supported Lee in Seven Days battles, and was largely responsible for victory in second battle of Bull Run. Ably led Confederate right at Fredericksburg (Dec., 1862). Mortally wounded at battle of CHANCELLORSVILLE. Next to Lee he was Confederacy's greatest general.

Jackson. 1 City (pop. 50,720), S Mich., on Grand R., W of Detroit; settled 1829. Industrial and commercial center in farm region dotted with lakes. Republican party founded here July 6, 1854. **2** City (pop. 144,-422), state capital, W central Miss., on Pearl R. Largest city and rail and shipping center of state, with important diverse industries centered around cotton, lumber, textiles, and gas. Laid out as state cap. 1821; legislature first met here 1822. Center of military activity in VICKSBURG CAMPAIGN and largely destroyed by Sherman, 1863. Here are old capitol (1839; new capitol occupied 1903), Millsaps Col., Belhaven Col., and Jackson State Col. Nearby is Tougaloo Southern Christian Col. City was scene of much racial violence in desegregation of interstate transportation facilities in 1961; public schools integrated 1964. **3** Town (pop. 1,746), SW S.C., near Savannah R., S of Aiken. Grew after estab. of Atomic Energy Commission's Savannah River plant in 1951. **4** City (pop. 34,376), W Tenn., on South Fork of Forked Deer R., NE of Memphis; settled 1819. Rail center (with large repair shops), industrial city with variety of mfg., and shipping point for extensive farm area. Lane Col., Lambuth Col., and Union Univ. are here. Indian mounds in vicinity. **5** Resort town (pop. 1,437), NW Wyo., NNE of Afton, near Teton Mts. and Snake R., in area of scenic beauty. Tourist and trade center for JACKSON HOLE region. S gateway to Grand Teton Natl. Park. U.S. elk refuge is nearby.

Jackson, Port, or Sydney Harbour, inlet of the Pacific, E New South Wales, Australia, forming Australia's finest harbor. Sydney on S shore connected with N suburbs by Sydney Harbour Bridge (1932) with arch span of 1,650 ft. Shipyards on Cockatoo Isl.

Jackson Hole, fertile mountain valley, c.50 mi. long, 6–8 mi. wide, NW Wyo., in Grand Teton Natl. Park. Snake R. waters valley and flows through Jackson L. (18 mi. long, 4 mi. wide). Has abundant game (elk, fish, waterfowl) as well as rare trumpeter swan.

Jacksonville. 1 City (pop. 5,678), NE Ala., N of Anniston; founded 1833. Seat of Jacksonville State Col. U.S. Fort McClellan is nearby. **2** City (pop. 14,448), central Ark., NE of Little Rock. Little Rock Air Force Base is nearby. **3** City (pop. 201,030), NE Fla., on St. Johns R. near its mouth on the Atlantic. One of South's busiest ports and a chief center of commerce, finance, and industry. Leading tourist resort. Rail, air, and highway focal point. Industries include shipbuilding, food processing, and mfg. of cigars, fertilizer, and paper, wood, and metal products. Lewis Hogans settled here 1816; city laid out 1882. Seminole War and Civil War (in which much of city was destroyed) interrupted its growth. Commerce and industry developed in late 1800s, with building of good harbor and railroads. Seat of Jacksonville Univ. Nearby are Fort Caroline Natl. Memorial, and U.S. naval air station and hospital. **4** City (pop. 21,690), W central Ill., W of Springfield; laid out 1825. One of state's oldest cities. Seat of Illinois Col. and MacMurray Col. S. A. Douglas and W. J. Bryan lived here. **5** City (pop. 13,491), E N.C., on New River, NE of Wilmington; settled c.1757. Summer resort and fishing town. Camp Lejeune (U.S. Marine Corps base) is nearby.

Jacksonville Beach, resort city (pop. 12,049), NE Fla., on Atlantic coast ESE of Jacksonville.

Jacob [Heb.,= supplanter]. **1** Son of Isaac, brother of Esau. As ISRAEL, ancestor of the Hebrews. By bargaining and trickery he gained the inheritance and blessing that Isaac intended for Esau. Jacob's life was filled with cruel disappointments (his discovery that after his years of labor to obtain Rachel, Leah was his first bride; the conduct of his wayward older sons), with spiritual revelations (his vision of the ladder to heaven; his wrestling with the angel), and with great joy (his reunion with Joseph in Egypt). Gen. 25–50; Hosea 12.2–4, 12; Mal. 1.2; Acts 7.12–16; Heb. 11. 20, 21. **2** Father of St. Joseph. Mat. 1.15, 16.

Jacob, François, 1920–, French biologist. Shared 1965 Nobel Prize in Physiology and Medicine for discoveries concerning genes.

Jacob, Max (mäks' zhäköb'), 1876–1944, French writer and painter. His poems, plays, novels, and short stories, and paintings in their extreme symbolism to some extent anticipated surrealism. He was a Catholic convert and a mystic. Died in a concentration camp.

Jacobi, Abraham (jŭkō'bē), 1830–1919, American physician, a pioneer in pediatrics. His wife **Mary Putnam Jacobi,** 1842–1906, also a physician, taught at medical schools in New York city and was the first woman member of several medical societies.

Jacobi, Friedrich Heinrich (yäkō'bē), 1743–1819, German philosopher. Argued that philosophy cannot maintain distinct realms of experience and that unity is based on faith, knowledge on intuition and reason.

Jacobi, Karl Gustav Jakob (kärl gōōs'täf yä'köp yäkō'bē), 1804–51, German mathematician, noted for his work on elliptical functions, differential determinants, and theory of numbers.

Jacobi, Mary Putnam: see JACOBI, ABRAHAM.

Jacobins (jăk'ŭbĭnz), political club of French Revolution; so called for original meeting place, a monastery of the Jacobins (Parisian name of Dominicans). Founded 1789, it first was led by such moderates as Mirabeau, Sieyès, Lafayette. Jacobins and FEUILLANTS dominated Legislative Assembly (1791–92). Split of Jacobins and GIRONDISTS occurred when Girondist majority advocated war as a means to discredit monarchy; Jacobins (mainly Parisian deputies) opposed war, advocated direct reform, became increasingly radical and republican. In the Convention the Jacobins and CORDELIERS were called the MOUNTAIN. Among their new leaders were DANTON, ROBESPIERRE. After the fall of the Girondists (June, 1793), Jacobins began REIGN OF TERROR, liquidated the extremist Cordeliers and the moderate Danton (1794), and governed dictatorially till Robespierre's fall on 9 THERMIDOR.

Jacobite Church (jă'kŭbīt), Christian church of Syria, Iraq, and India, founded (6th cent.) as part of the Monophysite heresy by Jacob Baradaeus, aided by Empress Theodora. Church is out of communion with both Roman Catholics and Orthodox. Its head is the patriarch of Antioch (at Homs), its rite is the Antiochene, its liturgical language Syriac. One group (the "Syrian Catholics") since 17th cent. has resumed relations with the pope, but keeps its practices and rite (head is another patriarch of Antioch, at Beirut). On the other hand in the 17th cent. most Malabar Christians left communion with the pope and became "Malabar Jacobites" with Antiochene rite; later a group became "Reformed Jacobites," and in 20th cent. another portion returned to communion with Rome (the "Malankarese Catholics"). The Malabar Christians who did not become Jacobites at all are "Syro-Malabar Catholics" (Chaldean rite).

Jacobites (jă'kŭbīts), adherents of exiled branch of the house of STUART after Revolution of 1688. Sought restoration of JAMES II; later advanced claims of his descendants until 1807 when direct Stuart line ended. Included many Catholics, high churchmen, extreme Tories, and the NONJURORS. Two major risings in 18th cent. are known as "the '15" and "the '45." After the death of Queen Anne (1714) Henry St. John and the 6th earl of MAR attempted intrigue and revolt to crown James Edward Stuart; he was defeated at Preston (1715). The abortive invasion of Charles Edward Stuart (Bonnie Prince Charlie), which was crushed at Culloden Moor in 1745, was the last serious action of Jacobitism as an important political force.

Jacobs, Helen (Hull), 1908–, American tennis player. Won U.S. women's singles title 1932–35, British women's singles crown 1936.

Jacobs, W(illiam) W(ymark), 1863–1943, English author, known for humorous short stories of London docks (as in *Many Cargoes,* 1896; *Snug Harbour,* 1931) and for horror tale, "The Monkey's Paw."

Jacobsen, Jens Peter, 1847–85, Danish novelist, creator of a prose style. His *Marie Grubbe* (1876) is a historical novel. Also wrote poetry.

Jacob's ladder: see PHLOX.

Jacobus de Voragine (vûrä'jĭnē), c.1230–1298, Italian hagiographer. Chiefly remembered as compiler of the GOLDEN LEGEND, he was archbishop of Genoa (1292–98) and was beatified in 1816. Also Jacobus da Varagine.

Jacopone da Todi (yäköpō'nä dä tō'dē), 1230?–1306, Italian religious poet, a Franciscan tertiary, probable author of the hymn *Stabat Mater Dolorosa.*

Jacquard, Joseph Marie (zhōsĕf' märē' zhäkär'), 1752–1834, French inventor, whose LOOM is of the greatest importance in modern mechanical figure weaving.

Jacquerie (zhäk"ûrē'), 1358, revolt of French peasants (nicknamed *Jacques*) against nobles and pillaging soldiers. Put down by Charles II of Navarre. Thousands were massacred in retaliation.

jade, name for two silicate minerals, jadeite and nephrite, used as gems, ranging in color from white to green. Jade is especially prized by Chinese and Japanese, who attribute to it magical properties.

Jadida, El (jädē′dû), city (pop. 40,464), Morocco; port on Atlantic. Seized by Portuguese 1502; recaptured by Moroccans 1769. Tourist resort; exports agr. products. Formerly called Mazagan.

Jadotville (zhädōvēl′), city (pop. c.75,000), S Republic of the Congo. Industrial and communications center of former Katanga prov. Mining and metallurgical complex producing cobalt and copper. Chemical plants.

Jadwiga (yädvē′gä), 1374–99, Polish queen (1384–99); daughter of Louis I of Hungary and Poland. Married Ladislaus Jagiello, grand duke of Lithuania (see LADISLAUS II of Poland), who accepted Christianity. She is nationally venerated as a saint.

Jael (jāl), heroine in time of Deborah. She murdered the Canaanite general, Sisera. Judges 4; 5.

Jaén (hään′), city (pop. 65,975), cap. of Jaén prov., S Spain, in Andalusia. The seat of a small Moorish kingdom, it was conquered by Castile 1246. Has imposing cathedral (16th–18th cent.), palaces, ruins of Moorish castle.

Jaffa (jä′fû), city (pop. c.50,000), Israel, on Mediterranean; chief port for Jerusalem. It often changed hands in Maccabee and Syrian battles. Destroyed by Vespasian A.D. 68. Held by Crusaders in 12th cent. Fell to Napoleon 1799 and to the British 1917. Largely inhabited by Arabs until captured by Israel in 1948. Incorporated 1950 into Tel-Aviv. It is the Japho of Joshua 19.46; Jappe in the Apocrypha; elsewhere in the Bible it appears as Joppa. Jonah departed from here for Tarshish.

Jaffe, Bernard, 1896–, American author; teacher in New York city from 1924. Works include *Crucibles* (1930; rev. ed., 1957) and *Michelson and the Speed of Light* (1960).

Jaffrey, resort town (pop. 3,154), SW N.H., near Mt. Monadnock; granted 1749.

Jagannath, India: see PURI.

Jagiello (yägē′lō) or **Jagello** (yägē′lō), Pol. *Jagiello*, ruling dynasty of Poland and Lithuania (1386–1572), Hungary (1440–44, 1490–1526), and Bohemia (1471–1526). Founded by Ladislaus Jagiello, grand duke of Lithuania, who became king of Poland as LADISLAUS II. His successors were Ladislaus III, Casimir IV, John I, Alexander I, Sigismund I, and Sigismund II. See also ULADISLAUS II and LOUIS II, kings of Hungary and Bohemia.

jaguar (jä′gwär), largest New World predatory cat (*Panthera*) ranging from SW U.S. to S central Argentina. Black spots and rosettes mark its yellow fur; occasionally an all black jaguar occurs. Males reach 6–7 ft. body length.

Jahn, Friedrich Ludwig (frē′drĭkh lōōt′vĭkh yän′), 1778–1852, German patriot; a high school teacher in Berlin. Hoped to promote national revival by organizing gymnastic associations (Ger. *Turnvereine*); became known as *Turnvater*. Imprisoned as political agitator 1819–25.

Jahve, Jahveh, Jahweh (jä′vē, –wē), modern reconstructions of anc. Hebrew name of God (which could be neither spoken nor written). Other forms are Jehovah and Yahweh.

jai alai: see PELOTA.

jail: see PRISON.

Jailolo: see HALMAHERA.

Jaimes Freyre, Ricardo (rēkär′dhō hī′mēs frä′rä), 1872–1933, Bolivian poet; exponent of *modernismo*.

Jainism (jī′nĭzûm), Indian religion held by c.2,000,000 people. Rose with Buddhism in 6th cent. B.C. as protest against Hinduism. Tradition teaches a succession of 24 Tirthankaras (saints) originated the religion; last was prophet Vardhamana, called Mahavira [the great hero] and Jina ["the victor"]. Basis of Jain doctrine is belief that everything in universe, even matter, is eternal. Spirits retain consciousness of identity through successive incarnations which are determined by cumulative effect of conduct. Nirvana–release from

body and matter–may be attained after nine incarnations. For the yati [ascetic] 12 years of self-denial earn Nirvana. For salvation all must be guided by three gems: right faith, cognition, conduct. Today some Jains do not discriminate between Hinduism and Jainism, whereas others fiercely maintain the distinction. For Jainist writings, see PRAKRIT LITERATURE.

Jaipur (jī′pōōr′), former princely state in Rajputana, India; since 1949 part of Rajasthan. Estab. in 12th cent. **Jaipur,** city (pop. 402,760), cap. of Rajasthan, was cap. of Jaipur state; financial center. Famed for jewelry, enamels, and muslins. Maharaja's palace and a university. Rajput palace is at nearby deserted city of Amber.

Jairus (jāī′–), man whose daughter Jesus raised from the dead. Mat. 9.18–26; Mark 5.22–43; Luke 8.41–56.

Jakarta: see DJAKARTA.

Jalalabad (jûlä′′läbäd′), city (pop. c.25,000), SE Afghanistan, on Kabul R. near Khyber Pass. Held by British in First Afghan War (1839–42). Trade center.

Jalapa (hälä′pä), city (pop. 51,159), cap. of Veracruz, E Mexico; agr. center and health resort.

Jalisco (hälē′skô), state (31,152 sq. mi.; pop. 2,707,499), W Mexico, on Pacific; cap. Guadalajara. Has coastal plains in W, volcanic mountains in center (L. Chapala is here), and productive plateau in E. Products are maize, wheat, fruits, minerals, timber. Explored 1522, settled 1529, Jalisco led in the liberal reform movement of 1858.

Jamaica: see QUEENS, New York city borough.

Jamaica (jûmā′kû), island (4,411 sq. mi.; 1965 est. pop. 1,766,749), the West Indies, S of Cuba and W of Haiti; cap. KINGSTON. Discovered by Christopher Columbus 1494; settled by Diego Columbus 1509. Attacked by English (1596, 1643), Jamaica was formally ceded to Great Britain 1670. Population, largely Negro, is overcrowded and unemployment is high. Products include fruits, spices, coffee, tobacco, cacao, and bauxite. Became independent dominion in 1964.

Jamaica Bay, SE N.Y., shallow inlet, c.18½ sq. mi., indenting SW Long Isl. Rockaway Inlet opens on SW to the Atlantic. Floyd Bennett Field (U.S. naval air station) is on Brooklyn shore; John F. Kennedy Internatl. Airport is on Queens shore.

Jambres: see JANNES AND JAMBRES.

James, Saint [ultimately from Jacob]. **1** One of the Twelve Apostles, called St. James the Greater, son of Zebedee; he and his brother, St. John, called BOANERGES, executed by Herod Agrippa I (Acts 12.1–2). Legend made him missionary to Spain, where he is much revered (see SANTIAGO DE COMPOSTELA). Feast: July 25. **2** One of the Twelve Apostles, called St. James the Less, son of Alphaeus. His mother, Mary, was at the Crucifixion (Mark 15.40). Sometimes identified as "brother" of the Lord and as head of the Church at Jerusalem (Acts 15; 21.18; Gal. 1.19). Epistle of James ascribed to him. Feast: May 1.

James I (the Conqueror), 1208–76, king of Aragon and count of Barcelona (1213–76). Conquered Balearic Isls. and Valencia from Moors; brought Murcia under Castilian control. In Treaty of Corbeil (1258) he and Louis IX of France renounced their respective claims to territories in S France and Spain. Wrote chronicle of his reign.

James, kings of England. James I, 1566–1625, king 1603–25, was the son of Lord Darnley and MARY QUEEN OF SCOTS. Became James VI of Scotland on his mother's abdication (1567). During his minority Scotland was ruled by regents and saw complicated struggle between pro-French Catholic party and pro-English Protestant faction. Began personal rule in 1583. Allied himself (1586) with Elizabeth and accepted calmly his mother's execution in 1587. Succeeded Elizabeth in 1603. From Hampton Court Conference (1604) grew movement which produced Authorized (King James) version of the BIBLE. Inconsistent policy toward English Catholics angered them and Protestants alike. Despite GUNPOWDER PLOT of

1605, James was suspected of favoring Catholics. His reliance on incompetent favorites (Robert Carr, earl of SOMERSET, and George Villiers, 1st duke of BUCKINGHAM) and his extravagance furthered discontent. His claims for divine right of kings led to PURITAN REVOLUTION. In 1611 he dissolved Parliament and (except for Addled Parliament) ruled without it until 1621. James acceded (1624) to wish of Commons for war with Spain. His reign saw beginnings of English colonization in North America. **James II**, 1633–1701, king 1685–88, was son of Charles I and brother and successor of Charles II. Escaped to France (1648) in Puritan Revolution. Returned to England as lord high admiral in 1660, but resigned after Test Act (1673). His marriage (1673) to MARY OF MODENA brought close ties to Catholic and imperial policies of Louis XIV and increased Whig hatred of him. His daughter Mary married Protestant prince of Orange (later WILLIAM III). Exiled after accusations of Titus Oates about the Popish plot, he was recalled in 1680. After failure of Parliament to exclude him from succession and the abortive RYE HOUSE PLOT, Charles's death brought him to throne in 1685. His unpopularity was increased by Bloody Assizes of Baron Jeffreys of Wem; by the trial of seven bishops (1688) who opposed his declaration of indulgences giving religious toleration; and by his autocratic methods with a hostile parliament. Birth of James Edward Stuart as possible Catholic heir led to Glorious Revolution of 1688. James fled to France. In 1689 he attempted to restore himself in Ireland but was defeated at battle of the Boyne (1690). Died in exile.

James, kings of Scotland. **James I**, 1394–1437, king 1424–37, was the son of Robert III. Fearful for his safety because of king's brother, Robert STUART, duke of Albany, Robert sent James to France in 1406. Captured by the English and held prisoner until 1424, he was treated as a royal guest and well educated. Before his return to Scotland he married Joan Beaufort. He brought peace to Scotland by ruthless methods, but his popularity was lessened by his vindictiveness, cupidity, and quick temper. He was assassinated by a group of nobles. Thought to be the author of a number of fine poems. His son, **James II**, 1430–60, king 1437–60, had successive earls of Douglas as regents during his minority. Allied himself with the 8th earl of Douglas (whom he later slew) and from 1449 ruled in his own right. Invaded England in Wars of the Roses and was accidentally killed. His son, **James III**, 1451–88, king 1460–88, was seized at his mother's death by Boyd family who ruled until 1469. He reigned in a turbulent period, and was murdered by nobles at Sauchieburn. His son, **James IV**, 1473–1513, king 1488–1513, was popular, and his reign was a profitable one for Scotland. Married (1503) Margaret Tudor, daughter of Henry VII of England. Relations with England deteriorated with accession of Henry VIII. James invaded England and was killed at battle of Flodden in 1513. His son, **James V**, 1512–42, king 1513–42, was the object of a struggle between his regents. Held captive, he escaped (1528) and allied himself with France against Henry VIII. Married MARY OF GUISE in 1538. War broke out with England (1542). He died shortly thereafter. **James VI**, king of Scotland: see JAMES I, king of England.

James, kinsman of St. Jude. Luke 6.16.

James, Henry, 1811–82, American student of religious and social problems, b. Albany, N.Y. He rejected the Calvinism taught at Princeton Theological Seminary and was much influenced by Swedenborgian teachings. He became a member of Fourierist circles and a friend of literary men. He spent much time in Europe and, following his own theories of education, had his sons spend much time there. One son, **William James**, 1842–1910, became one of the most eminent of American philosophers and psychologists. He was a teacher at Harvard (1872–1907), at first of physiology and anatomy, later of psychology and philosophy. He considered consciousness as active and purposeful.

Will and interest are primary, and knowledge is an instrument. The true is "only the expedient in our way of thinking." Ideas only lead the way to the objective world. For this basic theory of knowledge he borrowed from C. S. Peirce the word PRAGMATISM. In his "radical empiricism" James rejected all transcendent principles and argued that all experience is organized by "conjunctive relations," which are themselves direct experience. His works, notable for lucid and trenchant literary style, include *Principles of Psychology* (1890), *The Will to Believe* (1897), *The Varieties of Religious Experience* (1902), and *Pragmatism* (1907). His brother, **Henry James**, 1843–1916, was a celebrated American novelist and critic. Educated in the U.S. and Europe, he left Harvard Law School to write; eventually he settled in England (1876) and became a British citizen in 1915 as a gesture of his sympathies in First World War. In his fiction about the wealthy and leisured, he assumed the role of detached observer and analyst of life; he contrasted ingenuous Americans with sophisticated Europeans in such early novels as *The American* (1877), *Daisy Miller* (1879), and *The Portrait of a Lady* (1881). Reformers, revolutionaries, and political aspirants concerned him in a middle group of novels which included *The Bostonians* (1886), *The Princess Casamassima* (1886), and *The Tragic Muse* (1890). Between 1889 and 1895 he wrote several plays, all unsuccessful, followed by volumes of short stories, and later by short, powerful novels, including *What Maisie Knew* (1897), *The Spoils of Poynton* (1897), *The Turn of the Screw* (1898), and *The Sacred Fount* (1901). Returning to the international theme, James created his most subtle characterizations in his great novels *The Wings of the Dove* (1902), *The Ambassadors* (1903), and *The Golden Bowl* (1904). His extensive literary criticism (including his prefaces to reissues of his novels) has had great influence. He also wrote books on travel and autobiographical works.

James, Jesse (Woodson), 1847–82, American outlaw. In 1866 he and his brother Frank (Alexander Franklin James, 1843–1915) became leaders of gang which robbed and murdered through most of central states.

James, Thomas, 1593?–1635?, English navigator and explorer. In 1631 he explored James Bay (named for him) while seeking Northwest Passage.

James, William: see JAMES, HENRY.

James. 1 River rising in central N.Dak. and flowing c.710 mi. SSE across the Dakotas to Missouri R. near Yankton, S.Dak. Jamestown Dam (irrigation, flood control) is part of MISSOURI RIVER BASIN PROJECT. **2** River formed in western Va. and winding c.340 mi. E to Chesapeake Bay through Hampton Roads. Bridged just N of Newport News. Lower course is rich in historical associations. Here Jamestown was founded, 1607. In Civil War river was avenue of Union attempts to take Richmond (at head of navigation).

James, epistle of New Testament, ascribed by one tradition to St. James the Less. Book gives various admonitions applying mostly to everyday aspects of Christian behavior; urges Christians to "be doers of the word, not hearers only" (1.22). Scriptural source cited for extreme unction is here (5.14–15). One of later books to be accepted as canonical.

James, Protevangelium of: see PSEUDEPIGRAPHA.

James Bay, S arm of Hudson Bay, c.300 mi. long, 140 mi. wide, E central Canada, between Ont. and Que. Posts on bay include Rupert's House, Fort Albany, Moose Factory, Fort George, and Eastmain. Discovered 1610 by Hudson and named for Capt. Thomas James, who explored it 1631.

James Island: see CHARLESTON, S.C.

Jameson, Sir Leander Starr, 1853–1917, British colonial administrator and statesman in South Africa. Made famous unauthorized Jameson Raid from Rhodesia into Boer colony of Transvaal (1895).

James Peak, N central Colo.: see FRONT RANGE.

Jamestown. 1 City (pop. 41,818), W N.Y., on Chautauqua L., SW of Buffalo; founded c.1806. Its predominantly Swedish influence is reflected in cooperative community services. **2** City (pop. 15,163), SE N.Dak., on James R., W of Fargo; settled 1872, when army post was estab. to protect railroad workers. Rail, trade, and processing center of wheat, livestock, and dairy region. Jamestown Col. is here. **3** Resort town (1965 pop. 2,567), S R.I., in Narragansett Bay. It comprises Conanicut Isl. (kŭnăn´Ĭkŭt), c.9 mi. long and 1–2 mi. wide, and Dutch and Gould isls. Conanicut Isl., which includes Jamestown village (pop. 1,843), has bridge and ferry to mainland. Beavertail Light on S tip was estab. c.1750. **4** First permanent English settlement in America, SE Va., SW of Williamsburg; estab. May 24, 1607, by London Company on peninsula (now island) in James R. Suffered many hardships and, despite efficient leadership of John Smith, faced extinction. Saved by arrival of Lord De la Warr with supplies and by introduction of tobacco by John Rolfe. As cap. of Va., was seat of first representative assembly in New World, 1619; Village was restored after being largely destroyed in Bacon's Rebellion, but declined when cap. was moved to Williamsburg 1699. Has old church tower (c.1639), cemetery, and statues of Pocahontas and John Smith. Included in Colonial Natl. Historical Park.

Jamestown weed: see JIMSON WEED.

Jami (jä´mē), 1414–92, Persian poet, whose works include the collections *Haft Aurang* (poems) and *Baharistan* (short stories).

Jamitzer, Wenzel: see JAMNITZER, WENZEL.

Jammes, Francis (fräsĕs´ zhäm´), 1868–1938, French poet. Influenced by symbolists, but distinctive in his optimism and rustic simplicity, as in *De l'angélus de l'aube a l'angélus du soir* (1898). Later wrote religious verse in classical style.

Jammu and Kashmir: see KASHMIR.

Jamnia (jăm´nĕŭ), biblical *Jabneel* and *Jabneh*, anc. town (pop. 5,250), central Israel. Modern name is Yibna. A Philistine center, it was sacked by Judas Maccabeus and later rebuilt. After fall of Jerusalem, Vespasian allowed Johanan ben Zaccai to settle here as leader of the Jews. Except for short period, city remained center of Judaism until revolt of Bar Kokba in 130. Fortified by Crusaders in Middle Ages. Has a rabbinical college.

Jamnitzer, Jamitzer or **Gemniczer, Wenzel** (vĕn´tsŭl yäm´nĭtsŭr, –mĭtsŭr, gĕm´nĭtsŭr), 1508–85, leading member of a German family of goldsmiths and engravers. Adapted Italian mannerist forms.

Jamshedpur (jŭm´shĕdpŏŏr´), city (pop. 218,162), SE Bihar, India; major steel center.

Jamtland (yĕmt´länd), Swed. *Jämtlands län*, county (19,896 sq. mi.; pop. 139,918), NW Sweden, bordering on Norway; co. seat Ostersund. It consists, roughly, of historical provinces of Jamtland in N and Harjedalen in S, both conquered 1645 by Sweden from Norway. There are health and winter resorts, dairy farms, and lumber camps. Formerly spelled Jemtland.

Jamuna, river, India: see BRAHMAPUTRA.

Janacek, Leos (lä´ōsh yä´nächĕk), Czech *Janáček*, 1854–1928, Czech composer and collector of Slav folk music. Among his works are an orchestral rhapsody, *Taras Bulba;* and an opera, *Jenufa.*

Janesville, city (pop. 35,164), S central Wis., on Rock R., SE of Madison; settled 1835. Industrial and commercial center in tobacco area.

Janet: see CLOUET, JEAN.

Janet, Pierre (pyĕr´ zhänä´), 1859–1947, French physician and psychologist. He contributed greatly to knowledge of mental pathology and origins of hysteria, chiefly by use of hypnosis. He founded automatic psychology and first described psychasthenia.

Janina, Greece: see IOANNINA.

Janizaries (jä´nĭzĕ˝rēz) or **Janissaries** (–sĕ˝rēz), élite corps of old Ottoman army, recruited from forced levies of Christian youths and trained in strict discipline. Janizaries later gained enormous power and often made and unmade sultans. In 17th cent. membership became largely hereditary; conscription of Christians gradually ceased. Mahmud II liquidated them in a massacre (1826).

Jan Mayen (yän´ mī´ŭn), island (147 sq. mi.; pop. 8), Norwegian possession (since 1929) in Arctic Ocean, c.300 mi. E of Greenland. It is narrow strip of tundra, rising to 7,471 ft. in Mt. Beerenberg, an extinct volcano. Has meteorological and wireless station. Discovered 1607 by Henry Hudson.

Jannes and Jambres (jă´nĕz, jăm´brĕz), opponents of Moses. 2 Tim. 3.8. By tradition, names of Pharaoh's magicians. Ex. 7.11. See PSEUDEPIGRAPHA.

Jansen, Cornelis (kôrnā´lĭs yän´sŭn), 1585–1638, Dutch Roman Catholic theologian, professor at Louvain and bishop of Ypres. He and DUVERGIER DE HAURANNE sought to reform Christian life by returning to teachings of St. Augustine. From his posthumously published *Augustinus* (1642) grew up the movement called **Jansenism** (jănsŭnĭ´zŭm), which stressed greater personal holiness and austerity and made much of the necessity of divine grace for conversion and of predestination. The Jansenists were called "Calvinists" by their opponents, but actually they were bitter opponents of Calvinism and held that the Catholic Church was necessary to salvation. Members of the ARNAULD family became leaders in the movement, and PORT-ROYAL was its center. The Jansenists' teachings of predestination, discouragement of frequent communion for the faithful, and attacks on the Jesuits raised a storm in the Church. In 1653 some Jansenist doctrines were condemned, and in 1656 Antoine Arnauld was expelled from the Sorbonne. The able Blaise PASCAL came to Arnauld's defense. Trouble continued, complicated by the relationship of Jansenism with GALLICANISM, the use Louis XIV made of it to combat the pope. Clement XI condemned a vernacular New Testament with Jansenist notes by Pasquier Quesnel. A Jansenist declaration in 1702 that the pope's infallibility is limited to declaring propositions (and not particular statements) heretical brought matters to a head. The bulls *Vineam Domini* (1705) and *Unigenitus* (1713) practically put the Jansenists out of the Church. Port-Royal was closed, and most Jansenists fled from France. Some submitted; others founded an independent church in the Netherlands. There are Jansenist bishops of Utrecht, Haarlem, and Deventer. The first bishop of the OLD CATHOLICS was consecrated by Jansenists. The early Jansenist ideas still reverberate in some Catholic groups.

Jansky, Karl, 1906–50, American physicist; discovered that some radio waves (static) originate outside the solar system. Called the father of radio astronomy.

Janson, Nicolas: see JENSON, NICOLAS.

Janssen or **Jansen, Zacharias** (zäkhärē˝äs yän´sŭn), late 16th-early 17th cent., Dutch spectaclemaker credited with making first compound microscope c.1590.

January: see MONTH.

Janus (jä´nŭs), in Roman religion, god of "beginnings" both temporal and spatial. As spatial god he presided over gates and doors; as temporal god, over first hour of day, first day of month, and first month of year (named for him). He was represented with two bearded heads set back to back.

Japan, Japanese *Nippon,* country (142,000 sq. mi.; pop. 93,600,000), occupying an archipelago off E coast of Asia; cap. Tokyo. Main islands are HONSHU, KYUSHU, SHIKOKU, HOKKAIDO; c.1,000 smaller islands stretch from Sea of Japan to Pacific. Prior to Second World War it included KOREA, S half of SAKHALIN, KURILE ISLANDS, Formosa (see TAIWAN), PESCADORES isls., BONIN ISLANDS, Kwantung leased territory (see LIAONING), Caroline Isls., Marshall Isls., and Marianas Isls. Mountains, many volcanic, cover most of islands. Temperate climate, abundant rainfall, frequent typhoons and earthquakes. Rivers supply much hydroelectric power. Rail and coastwise shipping are chief means of transportation. Arable land, less than 20% of total area, is cultivated intensively; rice and cereals are main crops. Mineral resources meager except for coal. Fisheries highly developed. Dominant strain of people is N Asiatic or Mongoloid; AINU were among the earliest peoples. Principal religion is native SHINTO; Buddhism has many adherents. According to tradition empire was founded 660 B.C. by Emperor Jimmu, descendant of sun goddess. Reliable records date from c.400 A.D. Foundation for Japanese state was laid in 5th cent. by Yamato clan whose priest-chief later assumed role of emperor. Japan borrowed heavily from Chinese culture 6th–8th cent. By 9th cent. authority of imperial government was reduced by rising power of Fujiwara family and Buddhist priesthood. In 12th cent. YORITOMO Minamoto became master of Japan and the first to bear title of SHOGUN. First European contact made by Portuguese 1542. Christianity introduced 1549 by St. Francis Xavier. The 16th-cent. dictators NOBUNAGA and HIDEYOSHI were succeeded by IEYASU, founder of TOKUGAWA shogunate (1603–1867). Opening of Japan to West by Commodore PERRY in 1854 was a factor in overthrow of shogunate and subsequent MEIJI restoration (1868). With a policy of Westernization, Japan rapidly became a modern industrial state and military power. Constitution of 1889 created a diet consisting of house of peers and elected house of representatives. Victory in First CHINO-JAPANESE WAR (1894–95) and RUSSO-JAPANESE WAR (1904–5) estab. Japan as a world power. Annexed Korea 1910; after First World War won mandate over former German islands in Pacific. In 1931 detached Manchuria from China and estab. puppet state of MANCHUKUO. After 1937 Second CHINO-JAPANESE WAR was intensified. Signed pact with Germany and Italy in 1940. On Dec. 7, 1941, with approval of Premier Tojo, Japan struck at Pearl Harbor, Singapore, and other U.S. and British possessions (see Second WORLD WAR). Unconditional surrender on Sept. 2, 1945, followed explosion of atomic bombs in Hiroshima and Nagasaki. Allied occupation ended with peace treaty signed Sept., 1951, at San Francisco by most Allied powers. Remaining U.S. troops were withdrawn 1958. Peace treaties signed with Taiwan and India 1952, Burma 1954, USSR and the Philippines 1956, and Indonesia 1958. Admitted to UN in 1956. Democratic constitution adopted 1946. After its formation in 1955 the pro-Western Liberal Democratic party dominated politics. Present-day Japan among world's greatest mfg. and shipbuilding nations. Series of reconciliation treaties with S. Korea signed 1965.

Japan, Sea of, part of Pacific Ocean between Japan and Korea.

Japan Current or **Kuroshio** (kōōrōshē'ō) warm ocean current of the Pacific. A northward flowing branch of North Equatorial Current, it runs E of Taiwan (Formosa) and Japanese archipelago. Near lat. 35° N it divides: E branch nears Hawaiian Isls.; N branch skirts Asia coast, merges with Oyashio current.

Japanese architecture. Building art of China came to Japan with introduction of Buddhism in 6th cent. The temple Horyu-ji (near Nara) was completed c.650; it is oldest known example of wood architecture extant and is basis of all later Japanese design. Wood has always been favored material. Chief features of traditional Japanese design are interior columns, thin exterior walls of woodwork, plaster, and rice paper, and curved overhanging roofs. Pavilion called Phoenix Hall in temple at Uji represents peak of native design. Emphasis on ornamentation began in 14th cent. and became increasingly important during Tokugawa shogunate (1603–1867). Striking example of late style is group of lavishly decorated temples at Nikko. All Buddhist temples have courtyards approached by terraces and wide flights of stairs. Ac-

cessory structures include square pagoda (often omitted) and drum tower. Shinto temple (still in pre-Buddhist form) is severely simple and roofed with bark thatch. At approach to it is gateway called *torii.* Typical native dwelling, as developed in Tokugawa era, is elegantly simple. Interior is subdivided by sliding screens; main spaces have *tokonoma* (alcoves for display of flower arrangement or a painting). For public and commercial buildings Western methods are now used.

Japanese art is based on Chinese art, which was introduced in 6th cent. with Buddhism by way of Korea. Kose no Kanaoka (9th cent.), first notable native master, adopted T'ang traditions of Chinese painting. In 11th cent. Motomitsu estab. the Yamato, or native, school, which still leaned heavily on Chinese style. Painters of Tosa school (13th–14th cent.) were aristocrats, who confined their work to the court. Toba Sojo (late 12th cent.) satirically represented various personages as animals in amusing poses; he and later caricaturists expressed the people's incisive humor. Next era produced painters who worked in classic Chinese tradition, with SESSHU and JOSETSU among leading exponents. Emerging in same period was KANO school. Linked with original movements in Japanese art are Korin, whose work was Japanese in feeling, and IWASA MATABEI, HOKUSAI, HIROSHIGE, HARUNOBU, all connected with the ukiyo-e school. The 18th cent. produced the Shijo naturalistic school and the Ganku school of Chinese traditions. Mid-19th-cent. contact with European culture had negative effect on native art. Traditional method of painting requires Chinese ink and water colors, applied on paper or silk placed flat on the floor. Mounted on silk brocade or paper, pictures are of two types: *kakemono* (hanging picture) and *makimono* (scroll portraying series of scenes). Early sculptors (Chinese and Koreans) made spirited wooden images and small bronzes of Buddhist deities, which show Greco-Indian influences (7th–8th cent.). Stone sculptures are few; but exquisite ivory carvings are numerous. Among highly developed minor arts are porcelain and lacquer work, enamels, cloisonné.

Japanese beetle, name for destructive insect related to June bug. Discovered (1916) in New Jersey, it spread so widely that extermination was impossible. Adult is c.½ in. long, has a metallic green head and thorax, and brown wing covers. It skeletonizes leaves and destroys fruits and flowers. Eggs are laid in summer on ground; larvae feed on roots, winter underground, and emerge in June or July.

Japanese drama. The lyric drama, *no* or *noh,* originated in pantomimic dance performed at ancient Shinto and Buddhist festivals. Most of c.800 extant *no* plays were written in 15th cent. Restraint and symbolism characterize both acting and staging of *no;* vocal recitative is indispensable, and wooden masks are used. Farcical interlude, *kyogen* (dialogue or monologue, without music), developed along with *no* to provide comic relief. *No* appealed mainly to aristocratic tastes; by 17th cent. need for popular fare had been filled by *kabuki,* a form utilizing bizarre make-up and exaggerated stylized acting. Dramatic ballad, *joruri,* though used in *kabuki,* was adapted to and is best known in puppet plays, especially those of Chikamatsu. Translations of Western dramas were successfully introduced in late 19th cent.

Japanese literature. Japan had no written language until late 3d cent. A.D., when Chinese was introduced by Korean scholars. Early in 8th cent. a method of writing Japanese was evolved by adapting Chinese ideographs to spoken Japanese. This system was used in writing of *Kojiki* (712), sacred book of Shinto, which gives basis for myth of emperor's divine origin, but other principal works of the period were written in pure Chinese. In 9th cent. simplification of written language by use of two syllabaries opened golden age of letters. By early 11th cent. such writers as Lady MURASAKI were adding luster to literature in native language (as opposed to classical Chinese). Basic forms of JAPANESE DRAMA were evolved, 12th–17th cent. Under Tokugawa shogunate (17th–19th cent.) written language was standardized and freer verse forms (e.g., *haikai* or *hokku*) began to replace the *tanka*, the classical form. Notable authors were the poetic innovator Basho Matsura (1648–94), the playwright CHIKAMATSU, and the novelist Kyokutei Bakin (1767–1848). Modern Japanese literature reflects profound influence of Western writing, and such novelists as Yasunari Kawataba, Jiro Osaragi, and Yukio Mashima have won international respect.

Japanese music. Much of Japanese music was borrowed from other countries, especially China. Forms of sacred music include: the *gagaku*, ancient ceremonial music, brought from China, 5th cent. A.D.; Buddhist hymns dating from the 6th cent.; the *bugaku*, ceremonial dance music, imported from China in the 7th cent.; and the *kagura*, native to Japan, principally vocal, and used for the most solemn religious rites. Historically midway between sacred and secular music is the music for *no* drama (see JAPANESE DRAMA). Secular music dates from the 16th cent. with the importation of the *samisen* (a type of lute). Other instruments include the *koto* (a zither) and many kinds of flutes, oboes, drums, and gongs. Japanese scales are all five-toned. Those borrowed from China are without semitones; native scales have semitones. There is no harmony as we understand the term. Rhythm background provided by drums forms no pattern recognizable to Western ears. Western music was introduced into Japan in late 19th cent.; now integral part of the culture. See *ill.*, p. 733.

Japheth (jā'fĕth), son of Noah, ancestor of those who were to occupy the isles of the Gentiles. This was taken to mean the Mediterranean lands of Europe and Asia Minor. Gen. 5.32; 6.10; 9.27; 10.1–5.

Japho: see JAFFA.

japonica: see FLOWERING QUINCE.

Japurá (zhŭ"pŏŏrä'), river, over 1,000 mi. long, rising in Colombia as Caquetá and flowing SE across Brazil into Amazon.

Jaques-Dalcroze, Émile (zhäk"-dälkrōz'), 1865–1950, Swiss educator and composer. Developed the Dalcroze system of EURYTHMICS.

Jarmo: see MESOPOTAMIA.

Jarnac (zhärnäk'), town (pop. 4,100), Charente dept., W France. Scene of Catholic victory over Huguenots, where Louis I de Condé was killed (1569).

Jarrell, Randall, 1914–65, American poet. Among his books are *Blood for a Stranger* (1942) and *Losses* (1948). Also wrote children's books.

Jarrow, municipal borough (pop. 28,752), Durham, England, on the Tyne estuary. Industries include iron foundries and shipbuilding. Scene of labors of the Venerable Bede, who died here.

Jarvis Island, area 1.74 sq. mi., central Pacific, just S of equator, one of Line Isls. Claimed 1857 by U.S., annexed 1889 by Great Britain, settled 1935 by Americans and placed under Dept. of Interior, 1936. On air route from Hawaii to New Zealand.

jasmine or jessamine, shrub or climbing plant of genus *Jasminum* of tropical or semitropical regions. The scented flowers, mostly white or yellow, are often used in tea; the oil is used in perfumery. For Cape jasmine, see GARDENIA.

Jason, in Greek mythology, hero who claimed kingdom of Iolcus, which his uncle, Pelias, had stolen from his father, Aeson. Pelias would return it only in exchange for GOLDEN FLEECE, owned by Aeëtes, king of Colchis, where Jason led the Argonauts in ship *Argo*. He secured the fleece with aid of MEDEA, who loved him and who returned with him to Iolcus. He was also a hero of Calydonian hunt. In one legend Jason committed suicide; in another he was crushed by beam of the *Argo*.

Jasper, city (pop. 10,799), NW central Ala., NW of Birmingham, in coal-mine area; settled 1822. Processes cotton and timber.

jasper, opaque, impure cryptocrystalline QUARTZ, usually red, used as a gem.

Jasper National Park, 4,200 sq. mi., W Alta., in Canadian Rocky Mts.; estab. 1907. Game reserve and recreation center, noted for spectacular mountain scenery. Jasper is park hq. and station on Canadian National RR.

Jaspers, Karl (kärl yäs'pŭrs), 1883–, German philosopher, associated with existential school developed by KIERKEGAARD, and Heidegger. His philosophy is subjective and nonrational, stressing the difference between facts and the individual's emotional attitude toward facts. Love is considered the highest expression of existence.

Jassy (yä'sē) or **Iasi** (yäsh), city (est. pop. 126,865), E Rumania, historic cap. of Moldavia. Mfg. of textiles, machinery. Seat of Orthodox archbishop. Former large Jewish population was killed in Second World War at German instigation (1941). Has a university (founded 1860) and several fine churches in Byzantine style (15th–17th cent.). For Treaty of Jassy (1792), see RUSSO-TURKISH WARS.

Jastrow, Marcus, 1829–1903, American rabbi and Talmudic scholar, b. Poland. Author of *Dictionary of the Targumim, Talmud Babli and Yerushalmi, and the Midrashic Literature* (1903).

Játiva (hä'tēvä), town (pop. 19,896), Valencia prov., E Spain. Noted for its Spanish-Moorish castle and several fine churches and palaces. Was residence of Borgia or Boria family.

jaundice (jôn'dĭs), condition attended by yellowish discoloration of tissues and excretions resulting from bile pigments in blood. Causes include obstruction of bile duct and virus infections, damaging liver function.

Jauregg, Julius Wagner: see WAGNER-JAUREGG.

Jaurès, Jean (zhä' jŏrēs'), 1859–1914, French Socialist leader and historian. An idealist and pacifist, he advocated a peaceful revolution to obtain economic equality. Was killed by a fanatic nationalist on eve of First World War, which he desperately sought to avert. His *Histoire socialiste de la Révolution française* is an economic interpretation.

Java (jä'vǔ), island (48,842 sq. mi., pop. 63,059,575), including offshore islands), INDONESIA, S of Borneo, from which it is separated by Java Sea, and SE of Sumatra. Cultural, political, and economic center of Indonesia. Chain of volcanic mountains rises to 12,-060 ft. Produces sugar, rubber, copra, coffee, tea, quinine, and tropical woods. Sulfur, gold, and phosphates are mined in small quantities. Petroleum fields are in NE. Native arts include silver craft and batik work. A home of early man (see MAN, PREHISTORIC); remains of Java man or *Pithecanthropus erectus* found here 1891. Religion is predominantly Moslem, but Hinduism and Buddhism have strongly affected native culture. Highly developed arts include the *wayang* or shadow play employing puppets and musical accompaniment. Largest city is DJAKARTA (cap. of Indonesia); others include JOGJAKARTA and SURABAYA. Hindu colonists entered central and E Java in 7th cent. Rise of Hindu-Javanese state of Majapahit (founded 1293) marked peak of Javanese history; it ruled over much of Indonesia and Malay Peninsula. Islam, introduced in 13th cent., produced Moslem state of Mataram. Following the Portuguese, the Dutch arrived 1596; after 1619 Dutch East India Co. gradually absorbed remnants of Javanese empire. Java now constitutes three provinces of Indonesia—West, Central, and East Java.

Java man: see MAN, PREHISTORIC.

Javanese music, of uncertain origin, is remarkable in its orchestral development. It is based on two pentatonic systems—*pelog*, which has semitones, and *slendro* (or *salendro*), which is composed of whole tones.

Slendro is considered masculine, *pelog* feminine. The *gamelan,* an orchestra of tuned percussion instruments, originated in Java. See BALINESE MUSIC.

Javelle water or **Javel water** (both: zhŭvĕl′, jŭvĕl′), one of earliest bleaching solutions, first prepared at Javelle, near Paris. It is a solution of either potassium hypochlorite or sodium hypochlorite; used also as disinfectant.

Javits, Jacob K(oppel), 1904–, U.S. Senator from N.Y. (1957–).

Jawlensky, Aleksey von (youlĕn′skē) 1864–1941, Russian painter: he is associated with Kandinsky in Munich.

Jaxartes: see SYR DARYA.

Jay, John, 1745–1829, American statesman. Urged moderate policy as delegate to Continental Congress. As the Secretary of Foreign Affairs (1784–89) he recognized need of a more powerful central government; wrote five essays in *The* FEDERALIST. First Chief Justice of the United States (1789–95). American signer of Jay's Treaty. First volumes of his papers (ed. by Richard B. Morris) appeared 1967–68. His son, **William Jay,** 1789–1858, a jurist, was an active abolitionist.

jay, common name for certain birds of the crow family, found in Europe, Asia, and the Americas. Well known in America are BLUE JAY and Canada jay (often called camp robber) which is gray, with a white throat and black cap.

Jay's Treaty, concluded in 1794 between U.S. and Great Britain to settle difficulties arising mainly out of violations of Treaty of Paris of 1783 and to regulate commerce and navigation. Treaty, signed in England by John Jay and Baron Grenville, provided for British evacuation of Northwestern posts, unrestricted navigation of the Mississippi, and equal privileges to vessels in Great Britain and the East Indies, but placed severe restrictions on American trade in the West Indies. It did not allow indemnity for those Americans whose Negro slaves were carried off by Britain's evacuating armies, guarantee protection to American seamen against impressment, or secure recognition of principles of international maritime law. Therefore, it aroused indignation in America, and appropriations to carry it into effect were delayed until May, 1796.

jazz, musical style derived from American Negro folk music. Some main elements of jazz—rhythmic intensity (the beat), stressing of weak beats of the measure, repetition of short rhythmic phrases (riffs), vocal inflections like glissandos, and minute flattening of some scale degrees—seem to be indigenous to some West African tribal music. In the U.S. these elements were first incorporated into the performance of spirituals and blues but c.1900 with the rise of Negro instrumentalists this manner of performance was extended to dance music and marches (ragtime). With Louis Armstrong brilliant, improvised solo work against a band background began to displace the older ensemble style, and blues took the place of ragtime. With the growth of big bands the saxophone became the predominant solo instrument, and jazz developed into swing. In its wider application jazz includes styles sometimes lacking a stated pulsating rhythm. Highly subtle and complex improvisations on popular tunes employ new harmonic techniques, superimposed rhythms, and more angular melodies (bebop, progressive jazz).

Jean Baptiste de la Salle, Saint: see JOHN BAPTIST DE LA SALLE, SAINT.

Jean-Baptiste Vianney, Saint, 1786–1859, French parish priest, popularly known as the Curé d'Ars, from the village in which he exercised his ministry. Canonized 1925, he is patron saint of parish priests. Feast: Aug. 8.

Jean de Meun or **Meung** (both: zhã′ dŭ mũ′), d. 1305, French poet, author of second part of the ROMAN DE LA ROSE.

Jeanne d'Albret (zhän′ dälbrä′), 1528–72, queen of Navarre (1555–72); daughter of Henri d'Albret and Margaret of Navarre; mother of Henry IV of France. Unlike her turncoat husband, Antoine de Bourbon, she was a staunch Protestant.

Jeanne d'Arc: see JOAN OF ARC.

Jeanneret, Charles Édouard: see LE CORBUSIER.

Jeannette, city (pop. 16,565), SW Pa., ESE of Pittsburgh; laid out 1888.

Jean Paul: see RICHTER, JOHANN PAUL FRIEDRICH.

Jeans, Sir James (Hopwood), 1877–1946, English astronomer, mathematician, physicist. With H. A. Jeffreys he developed the tidal theory of origin of solar system. His works include *The Universe Around Us* (1929), *Through Space and Time* (1934), *Science and Music* (1937), *Physics and Philosophy* (1942).

Jebail: see BYBLOS.

Jebb, Sir Richard (Claverhouse), 1841–1905, British classical scholar. He was noted for his standard editions and translations of Greek writers and for his *Growth and Influence of Greek Poetry* (1893).

Jebus (jē′–), **Jebusi,** or **Jebusite,** name of tribe occupying Jerusalem before the Hebrews. Judges 1.21.

Jedburgh (jĕd′bûrŭ), burgh (pop. 3,647), co. town of Roxburghshire, Scotland. Border town, it suffered from Scottish-English strife; "Jedburgh Justice" (hanging first, trying after) became an unpleasant byword.

Jedda, Saudi Arabia: see JIDDA.

Jedidiah (jĕdĭdī′ŭ) [Heb.,= beloved of God], name given by Nathan to baby Solomon. 2 Sam. 12.24, 25.

Jeffers, Robinson, 1887–1962, American poet. His works, stressing modern man's alienation from nature, include *Tamar and Other Poems* (1924) and *The Double Axe* (1948). Several of his plays (esp. his adaptation of *Medea,* 1947) have been produced.

Jefferson, Joseph, 1829–1905, American actor. After 20 years as strolling player. Was famous as Bob Acres in Sheridan's *Rivals* and had particular renown in *Rip Van Winkle,* which he played first in 1859 and in the adaptation by Dion Boucicault from 1865 to 1880.

Jefferson, Thomas, 1743–1826, 3d President of the United States (1801–9), author of DECLARATION OF INDEPENDENCE, and apostle of agrarian democracy. In Va. legislature (1776–79) he laid groundwork for abolition of entail and primogeniture, for establishment of religious freedom, and for a public school system. Served as minister to France (1785–89), U.S. Secretary of State (1790–93). Growing opposition to Alexander Hamilton and his policies associated Jefferson with group called Republicans, forerunners of present DEMOCRATIC PARTY. While serving as Vice President (1797–1801), he drafted Kentucky Resolutions (see KENTUCKY AND VIRGINIA RESOLUTIONS). He was elected President following a long deadlock with Aaron Burr in the House of Representatives, largely because Hamilton considered Burr the more dangerous man and gave support to Jefferson. First President inaugurated in Washington, which he had helped to plan, he instituted a republican simplicity there. Notable achievements of his first administration were LOUISIANA PURCHASE and LEWIS AND CLARK EXPEDITION. In his second administration attempts to enforce measures such as EMBARGO ACT of 1807 brought strong opposition. In retirement at his beloved MONTICELLO, Jefferson secured the founding of Univ. of Virginia and continued his activities as scientist, architect, and philosopher-statesman. He had complete faith that a people enlightened by free education could under democratic-republican institutions govern themselves better than under any other system. Publication of the definitive edition of Jefferson's papers, under the editorial supervision of Julian P. Boyd, was begun in 1960.

Jefferson, river, rising in SW Mont., W of Yellowstone Natl. Park, and flowing c.207 mi. W and NW (as Red Rock R.), then NE (as Beaverhead R.). Becomes Jefferson R. at entrance of Ruby and Big Hole rivers, then flows E to join Madison and Gallatin rivers at Three Forks. Main headstream of Missouri R.

Jefferson, Mount: see PRESIDENTIAL RANGE.

Jefferson City. 1 City (pop. 28,228), state cap., central Mo., on S bank of Missouri R., SSE of Columbia; laid out 1822. With rail and river facilities, it is commercial and processing center of agr. area. Has railroad shops, printing and publishing houses. Seat of Lincoln Univ. **2** Town (pop. 4,550), NE Tenn., ENE of Knoxville; settled c.1810. Area has zinc mines and farms. Carson-Newman Col. is here. Cherokee Dam, just N, is part of TVA.

Jefferson Heights, town (pop. 19,353), SW La., suburb W of New Orleans.

Jefferson Medical College of Philadelphia, at Philadelphia, Pa.; coed.; estab. 1825 as part of Jefferson Col. at Canonsburg, Pa.; independent charter 1838. One of oldest U.S. medical schools.

Jefferson Memorial: see THOMAS JEFFERSON MEMORIAL.

Jeffersonville, city (1964 pop. 19,482), S Ind., at falls of Ohio R. (bridged to Louisville, Ky.); founded 1802. Diversified industry.

Jeffreys of Wem, George Jeffreys, 1st Baron, 1645?–89, English lord chancellor. In the Bloody Assizes after the duke of Monmouth's rebellion (1685) he caused c.300 to be hanged, c.800 transported, and many imprisoned or whipped.

Jeffries, James J., 1875–1953, American boxer. Won (1899) heavyweight championship from Bob Fitzsimmons, retired undefeated 1905. Returned to ring, lost title to Jack Johnson (1910).

Jegar-sahadutha: see GALEED.

Jehannet: see CLOUET, JEAN.

Jehlam: see JHELUM.

Jehoahaz (jēhō'ŭhăz) or **Joahaz** (jō'–). **1** Died c.804 B.C., king of Israel (c.820–c.804 B.C.), son of Jehu. 2 Kings 13.1–9; 14.1. **2** Fl. 609 B.C., king of Judah (c.609 B.C.), son of Josiah. Deposed and taken to Egypt by Pharaoh Necho, who made Jehoiakim king instead. 2 Kings 23.30–34; 2 Chron. 36.1–4. Shallum: 1 Chron. 3.15; Jer. 22.11.

Jehoash (jēhō'ăsh) or **Joash** (jō'–). **1** Died c.789 B.C., king of Israel (c. 804–c.798 B.C.). Successful in wars against Damascus and Judah. 2 Kings 13; 14. **2** Died c.802 B.C., king of Judah (c.841–c.802 B.C.), son of Ahaziah **2**. When his father was murdered and Athaliah seized the throne and massacred the royal family, Jehoash, a baby, was saved by his uncle and aunt, Jehoiada and Jehosheba. He was placed on throne 6 years later in coup d'état. 2 Kings 11,12.

Jehoiachin, (jēhoi'ŭkĭn), d. c.598 B.C., king of Judah (c.598 B.C.). Captured by Nebuchadnezzar; imprisoned in Babylon. Later freed and honorably treated. 2 Kings 24.6–16; 25.27–30. Also variously called Jeconiah, Jechonias, and Coniah.

Jehoiada (jēhoi'ŭdŭ), high priest. With his wife, Jehosheba, he saved the baby Jehoash and led conspiracy against Athaliah that put Jehoash **2** on the throne. 2 Kings 11; 12; 2 Chron. 22–24.

Jehoiakim (jēhoi'ŭkĭm), d. c.598 B.C., king of Judah (c.609–c.598 B.C.), successor of JEHOAHAZ **2**. Restored idol worship; burned book of Jeremiah's prophecies. Died just before Nebuchadnezzar took Jerusalem. Originally called Eliakim, took name of Jehoiakim on becoming king. 2 Kings 23.34–24.6. Jer. 36.

Jehol (zhŭ'hŭ'), Mandarin *Je-ho,* former province (c.44,000 sq. mi); cap. was Chengteh. Divided between Inner Mongolian Autonomous Region, Hopei, and Liaoning provs. 1955. Seat of Liao (Khitan) empire 10th–12th cent. Became part of Manchukuo 1932; restored to China after Second Chino-Japanese War.

Jehoram (jēhō'rŭm) or **Joram** (jō'–). **1** Died c.846 B.C., king of Israel (c.852–c.846 B.C.), successor of Ahaziah **1**. Killed in Jehu's coup d'état; last house of Ahab in Israel. 2 Kings 1.17, 3; 8; 9. **2** Died c.846 B.C., king of Judah (c.851–c.846 B.C.), son of Jehoshaphat.

His wife was ATHALIAH. Succeeded by Ahaziah **2**. 2 Kings 8.16–24; 2 Chron. 21.

Jehoshaphat (jēhō'shŭfăt) or **Josaphat** (jŏs'–). **1** Died c.851 B.C., king of Judah (c.870–c.851 B.C.), son of Asa. A "good" king, he made many religious reforms. Often allied with kings of Israel. 1 Kings 22; 2 Kings 3; 2 Chron. 17–21.1. **2** Recorder under David and Solomon. 2 Sam. 8.16; 1 Kings 4.3. **3** Father of Jehu. 2 Kings 9.2,14. Also Joshaphat. **Valley of Jehoshaphat,** a place of judgment, is traditionally the N extension of vale of Kidron on the E of Jerusalem.

Jehosheba (jēhŏ'shĕbŭ), princess of Judah; daughter of Jehoram **2**, aunt of Jehoash **2**. See JEHOIADA.

Jehovah (jŭhō'vŭ, jē–), modern reconstruction of the anc. Hebrew ineffable (to be neither spoken nor written) name of God.

Jehovah's Witnesses, sect founded in U.S. in 1872 by Charles Taze Russell and in earlier days called Russellites. Doctrine centers on second coming of Christ. Highly evangelistic, the sect considers each Witness a minister of God. Witnesses refuse to salute flag, bear arms, or participate in government. Known formally as The Watch Tower Bible and Tract Society, the group issues monthlies, *Watch Tower* and *Awake.*

Jehu (jē'hū), d. c.820 B.C., king of Israel (c.846–c.820 B.C.). Anointed king by Elisha. Jehu murdered Jehoram **1**, Ahaziah **2**, and the royal family. His speed as a charioteer is proverbial. 2 Kings 9; 10.

Jekyll Island: see SEA ISLANDS.

Jelgava (yĕl'gävä), Ger. *Mitau,* city (pop. 36,300), Latvia, SW of Riga. Agr. center; varied mfg. Founded by Livonian Knights 1266; cap. of Courland 1561–1795. Notable buildings include Trinity Church (16th cent.) and ducal palace (18th cent.).

Jellicoe, John Rushworth Jellicoe, 1st Earl, 1859–1935, British admiral. In First World War was commander in chief of the Grand Fleet (1914–16) and first sea lord (1916–17). Commanded at battle of JUTLAND. Governor general of New Zealand 1920–24.

jellyfish, popular name for the medusa, the gelatinous, umbrella-shaped, free-swimming form of marine invertebrate related to coral polyp and sea anemone. Most species pass through both medusa and polyp or hydroid stage. Jellyfish capture small animals by means of tentacles with stinging cells.

Jemappes (zhŭmäp'), town (est. pop. 12,766), Hainaut prov., W Belgium; coal-mining center. Here (1792) French defeated Austrians in one of first important battles of French Revolutionary Wars.

Jemez (hä'mäs), pueblo (pop. c.1,065), central N. Mex., W of Santa Fe. Diminished from several pueblos in 1500s to one by 1680, when PUEBLO INDIANS revolted against Spanish. Captured by Spanish in 1694. Jemez Indians rose again in 1696, killed the missionary, and fled to Navaho lands. Some finally returned and built present village c.1700. Language Tanoan. Annual feast to San Diego.

Jemima (jĕmī'–) [Heb.,= dove], first daughter of Job after his misfortune. Job 42.14.

Jemtland, Sweden: see JAMTLAND.

Jena (yā'nä), city (est. pop. 80,930), East Germany, in former state of Thuringia, on the Saale R. Industrial and cultural center. Part of the great Zeiss plant (optical and precision instruments) was removed by Soviet occupation forces after Second World War. Chartered in 13th cent., Jena later passed to Saxe-Weimar-Eisenach; was incorporated with Thuringia 1920. Napoleon I decisively defeated Prussians here 1806. Univ. of Jena (founded 1558) reached height in late 18th–early 19th cent., when Schiller, Hegel, Fichte, and A. W. von Schlegel taught here.

Jenghiz Khan or **Genghis Khan** (both: jĕng'gĭs kän'), 1167?–1227, Mongol conqueror. Succeeded his father, Yekusai, as chieftain of Mongolian confederacy. In 1206 completed conquest of Mongolia and made Karakorum his capital. Began conquest of N China in 1213; by 1215 held most of Ch'in empire. Conquered Turkistan, Transoxania, and Afghanistan and penetrated SE Europe (1218–24). His vast domains were divided among his sons and grandsons. Kublai Khan completed his conquest of China.

Jenkins's Ear, War of, 1739–41, struggle between England and Spain. Based on commercial rivalry, it led into the larger War of the Austrian Succession. Propaganda effect of claim by shipmaster Robert Jenkins that Spanish coast guards cut off his ear forced Sir Robert Walpole to declare war.

Jenkintown, residential borough (pop. 5,017), SE Pa., NNE of Philadelphia; settled 1750. Beaver Col. is nearby.

Jenné: see DJENNÉ.

Jenner, Edward, 1749–1823, English physician, originator of inoculation with cowpox virus to immunize against smallpox. He first demonstrated his method in 1796 on James Phipps.

Jenner, Sir William, 1815–98, English physician, known especially for distinguishing between typhus and typhoid fever.

Jenney, William Le Baron, 1832–1907, American architect and engineer. In 1883 built the 10-story Home Insurance Building (Chicago), generally known as first skyscraper.

Jennings, Sarah, duchess of Marlborough: see MARLBOROUGH, JOHN CHURCHILL, 1ST DUKE OF.

Jennings. 1 City (pop. 11,887), SW La., E of Lake Charles; settled 1884. Rice-milling and oil center, with machine shops and lumber industry. **2** City (pop. 19,965), E Mo., suburb NW of St. Louis.

Jensen, Johannes Hans Daniel, 1906–, German physicist. Shared 1963 Nobel Prize in Physics for research on atomic nuclei.

Jensen, Johannes V(ilhelm), 1873–1950, Danish author. Interest in biological science shown in the epic *The Long Journey* (1908–22). Created a distinctive literary form in short essays (called "myths"). Awarded the 1944 Nobel Prize in Literature.

Jenson or Janson, Nicolas, d. c.1480, Venetian printer, b. France. Excellence of designs of roman type inspired many of his successors. He produced many beautiful works after 1470. The Aldine Press used his types from 1480.

jeopardy (jĕ′pŭrdē), subjecting a person to trial for crime and hence creating a danger that he may be punished. In U.S. it is interesting chiefly for double jeopardy, prohibited by U.S. constitution, which would make a man liable for trial for the same offense more than once. If the trial was abortive (e.g., if it ended with the jury unable to reach a verdict) or if a new trial is ordered after review by a court of appeal, a new trial does not constitute double jeopardy.

Jephthah (jĕf′thŭ), judge of Israel. Because of rash vow, he had to sacrifice his daughter, an only child. Judges 11.1–12.7. Jephthae: Heb. 11.32.

Jerba or Djerba (both jĕr′bŭ), island (area 197 sq. mi.; pop. c.60,000), off SE Tunisia, in the Mediterranean. Corsair base in 16th cent. Sponge fishing.

jerboa, small, jumping rodent (2–8 in. long) of N Africa, Asia, and SE Europe. They are gregarious, nocturnal, burrowing, desert dwellers, able to live without water.

Jeremiah (jĕrĭmī′ŭ) or **Jeremias,** book of Old Testament. Tells story of Jeremiah (fl. 600 B.C.), one of the major prophets, who preached in Jerusalem under Josiah and his successors. He foresaw nothing but doom in Judah's foreign policy and urged the people to turn from futile resistance to Babylon and concern themselves with domestic reform and their own religious welfare. For such unpopular advice, he was imprisoned. Released after fall of Jerusalem (586 B.C.). Among Messianic passages in book: 14.8–9; 23.5–6; 30.9–24; 32.37–44. Other references to Jeremiah in Bible: 2 Chron. 35.25; Dan. 9.2; Mat. 2.17; Heb. 8.8. See also LAMENTATIONS; BARUCH.

Jeremy, Epistle of [Eng. form of Jeremiah] (jĕ′rĭmē), name given to sixth chapter of BARUCH.

Jerez de la Frontera (hārāth dē lä frŏntä′rä), city (pop. 134,278), Cádiz prov., SW Spain in Andalusia. Export center for sherry (named after town).

Jericho (jĕ′rĭkō), anc. city, Palestine, N of Dead Sea. Its spectacular capture by Joshua marked Hebrew entry into Canaan, the Promised Land; its fall to Babylonia centuries later marked end of kingdom of Judah. Sacked and rebuilt by many conquerors. Recent excavations reveal a walled city dating from c.8000 B.C.–c.6000 B.C., making Jericho the oldest town now known to man.

Jericho, residential town (pop. 10,795), SE N.Y., on W Long Isl., N of Hicksville, in farm area.

Jeroboam I (jĕrŭbō′ŭm), d. c.910 B.C., first king of N kingdom of Israel after it broke away from Rehoboam. Notorious for fostering idolatry and restoring worship of golden calf. 1 Kings 11.26–14.20; 2 Chron. 10; 13. **Jeroboam II,** d. c.749 B.C., king of Israel (c.789–c.749 B.C.), son of Jehoash I. During his reign the kingdom expanded northward. Amos and Hosea prophesied under him. 2 Kings 14.16,23–29.

Jerome, Saint (jâr′ŭm, jŭrōm′), c.347–419?, Christian scholar, Doctor of the Church, one of the Latin Fathers; full name in Latin Sophronius Eusebius Hieronymus. Studies (partly at Rome) made him proficient in pagan learning, but after a vision at Antioch (375) he renounced this scholarship and fled to the desert, where he devoted himself to scriptural studies. These, after he was ordained in 378, he continued under St. Gregory Nazianzen in Constantinople. Went (382) to Rome, where he became secretary to Damasus I and at the pope's request began work on a new version of the Bible. He was spiritual adviser to a number of Roman ladies, including St. Paula, who founded a monastery for him in Bethlehem. There Jerome lived from 386 to his death. His scholarly editing of Latin translations of the Bible together with some of his own translations of some portions from the Hebrew were the basis of the VULGATE. Also wrote exegetical works, tracts (often attacking the opinions of others with some violence), lives of Christian writers, and brilliant letters. Feast: Sept. 30.

Jerome, Jerome K(lapka), 1859–1927, English humorist and playwright, best known for play *The Passing of the Third Floor Back* (1907).

Jerome, William Travers, 1859–1934, American lawyer. Prominent in cause of reform in New York city. Led campaign against crime and political corruption.

Jerome of Prague, c.1370–1416, Bohemian religious reformer. With Huss (1407) he urged Bohemian control of Univ. of Prague. Defended Huss (1415) before Council of Constance, but was himself imprisoned and burned (1416) as a heretic.

Jersey, largest of the CHANNEL ISLANDS.

Jersey cattle: see CATTLE.

Jersey City, city (pop. 276,101), NE N.J., E of Newark, on Hudson R. opposite lower Manhattan (subway, ferry, tunnel connections). Commercial and industrial center and rail and transportation terminal point. Mfg. of soap, metal products, clothing, paints, audio and visual equipment. Area acquired by Michiel Pauw as Pavonia patroonship c.1629. Dutch soon set up trading posts of Paulus Hook, Communipaw, and Horsimus. Nearby Dutch village of Bergen (settled before 1620) had first municipal government in N.J., first church (Dutch Reformed), and first school (1662). Site became British 1664. Jersey town became Jersey City 1836, consolidated with Bergen and Hudson 1869, with Greenville 1873. Industrial growth began in 1840s with arrival of railroad and improvement of water transport system. Was home of Democratic boss Frank HAGUE, long-time political boss of N.J. Here are Jersey City State Col. and Saint Peter's Col.

Jerusalem, Arabic *El Kuds,* city (pop. of Israeli sector 166,301; pop. of Jordanian sector c.80,000), Israeli-Jordanian border, SE of Tel-Aviv on rocky ridge of Judaean Hills. New City was proclaimed cap. of Israel in 1950; Old City is in Jordan. Jerusalem is the Holy City of Jews and Christians and one of the chief shrines of Islam. Often called Zion in Jewish and Christian literature, it is the symbol of the City of God (Rev. 21.2). Almost all holy sites of the three faiths are in the Old City. Moslems visit the Haram esh-Sherif, a sacred enclosure, with the Dome of the Rock or Mosque of Omar (built on the old Mt. Moriah) and the Mosque of Aksa. Part of the wall of the Haram is believed to be made from stones from Solomon's Temple; this, the Wailing Wall, is revered by Jews. Christians revere especially the Church of the Holy Sepulcher which stands on the traditional site of Calvary. The Old City is surrounded by a wall built by Suleiman I (1542). E of the Old City is the valley of Kidron, across which lie the Garden of Gethsemane and the Mt. of Olives; N is Mt. Scopus, with Hadassah Medical Center, the Natl. Library, Hebrew Univ. Jerusalem is rich in both Old and New Testament associations. Churches and shrines marking sites connected with biblical and other holy persons are innumerable. City dates back to at least 15th cent. B.C. It may be the Salem mentioned in Gen. 14.18. David made it his capital after taking it from the Jebusites; Solomon glorified it with his Temple; here Judah's kings clung to their waning power; many of the great Hebrew prophets spoke in its streets. It fell in 586 B.C. to Babylonia; was rebuilt by Ezra and Nehemiah after return from exile. It was city of the Maccabees and of the Herods. Early Roman emperors were enemies of the Holy City; Titus razed its buildings and destroyed its Temple (A.D. 70). After the revolt of Bar Kokba the Romans made Jerusalem a pagan shrine called Aelia Capitolina (134). With the conversion of Constantine to Christianity, Jerusalem underwent a revival. His mother, St. Helena, is said to have discovered and restored many of its holy places. Moslems believe city was visited by Mohammed, treated it well when it fell into their hands in 637, made it their chief shrine after Mecca; but the molesting of Christian pilgrims and destruction of the Church of the Holy Sepulcher by fanatics led to the Crusades. Jerusalem fell to Crusaders in 1099 (see JERUSALEM, LATIN KINGDOM OF). In 1187, Moslems, led by Saladin, again took the city, and it was to remain almost constantly under Moslem control until it was taken by the British in First World War; was later the center of British mandate of Palestine. When the mandate ended, both Arabs and Jews were determined to control Jerusalem. After considerable fighting, the Jews surrendered the Old City but held the New. In Arab-Israeli conflict of June, 1967, Israel took Old City and placed whole city under unified administration, guaranteeing access to holy places of all faiths.

Jerusalem, Latin Kingdom of, state created in Syria and Palestine by leaders of First Crusade after conquest of Jerusalem (1099; see CRUSADES). Organized along lines of feudal theory, it consisted of the royal domain of Jerusalem (incl. subfiefs, e.g., counties of Jaffa and Ashkelon, lordships of Krak and Montreal), and of the fiefs of Antioch, Edessa, and Tripoli, over which the kings held only nominal overlordship. Kingship was elective (in theory); Assizes of Jerusalem (the law of the country) reflected ideal feudal law. In practice, royal authority was weakened by independence of feudal lords and by rise of great military orders—KNIGHTS TEMPLARS and KNIGHTS HOSPITALERS. Internal dissensions facilitated advance of neighboring Moslems. Edessa fell 1144; Jerusalem 1187; Acre, last stronghold, 1291. Reigning kings of Jerusalem were Baldwin I, Baldwin II (house of Bouillon); Fulk, Baldwin III, Amalric I, Baldwin IV, Baldwin V (Angevin dynasty). Titular kingship passed to various princes, notably Emperor Frederick II, and later was borne by kings of Cyprus.

Jerusalem artichoke: see ARTICHOKE.

Jerusalem cherry: see NIGHTSHADE.

Jervis, John, earl of St. Vincent (jär'vĭs, jûr–), 1735–1823, British admiral. His victory over a much larger

Spanish fleet off Cape St. Vincent (1797) was largely due to an unauthorized attack by Horatio Nelson. First lord of the admiralty 1801–6.

Jervis, John Bloomfield, 1795–1885, American civil engineer and railroad builder. Designed fastest locomotive of its day, the *Experiment* (1832). Port Jervis, N.Y., named for him.

Jervis Bay (jär'vĭs), inlet of the Pacific, E New South Wales, Australia. Harbor and 28 sq. mi. of peninsula sheltering it were transferred 1915 to commonwealth for a port to be linked by rail with Canberra, 85 mi. inland.

Jespersen, Otto (yĕ'spùrsun), 1860–1943, Danish philologist. First earned a name for his brilliant work in phonetics and later wrote widely known books on English language and linguistics in general.

jessamine: see JASMINE.

Jesse, father of David. Name came to symbolize the royal line and Messianic hopes involving it. Ruth 4.17–22; 1 Sam. 16.1–18; 17.12,58; 1 Chron. 2.12, 13; Isa. 11.1,10; Mat. 1.5,6; Luke 3.32. Jesus has been called Jesse's Rod and the Virgin Mary Jesse's Root. Jesus' family tree, depicted with Jesse as source, was popular subject of medieval art.

Jesselton, town (pop. 21,714), cap. of SABAH, on small inlet of South China Sea. Chief port of colony, it exports rubber. Founded 1899.

Jesuit: see JESUS, SOCIETY OF.

Jesuit Estates Act, adopted 1888 by Quebec legislature, partly to indemnify the Society of Jesus for Jesuit property confiscated after Pope Clement XIV had suppressed the society. It caused a violent controversy and was vetoed by the Canadian House of Commons.

Jesuit Martyrs of North America, designation for six Jesuit missionaries and two assistants who were beatified in 1925 and canonized in 1930 for having suffered martyrdom in 1648–49 at the hands of the Iroquois.

Jesuit Relations, reports by French Jesuit missionaries in New France. Important historical sources of French exploration and Indian conditions.

Jesus or **Jesus Christ.** The name *Jesus* is Greek for the Hebrew *Joshua* [savior]; Christ is Greek translation of the Hebrew *Messiah* [anointed]. Primary sources for life of Jesus are the four Gospels of MATTHEW, MARK, LUKE, and JOHN, and the epistles of the New Testament. The apocryphal gospels (see PSEUDEPIGRAPHA) and traditional sayings ascribed to Jesus (see AGRAPHA OF JESUS) are unreliable. Scholarly analysis of life of Jesus was not extensively begun until end of 19th cent. The facts of his career are subject to question (a small group even denying his historicity). In Christian teaching, Jesus was born of Mary, wife of Joseph, a carpenter of Nazareth, who had brought his wife to Bethlehem for the Roman tax-census. The Christian era is computed (according to a 6th-cent. reckoning) to begin with Jesus' birth, A.D. 1. Date is placed several years too late; Jesus was probably born between 8 B.C. and 4 B.C. According to the Gospels, wonderful events surrounded the birth of Jesus (e.g., the Annunciation to Mary, the appearance of the heavenly host, the adoration of the shepherds and the Wise Men). Jesus lived at a critical time in Jewish history. The Jews were restive under Roman rule as administered by the corrupt house of HEROD; Judaism was under control of the Pharisees and scribes who upheld the letter of Mosaic law. The simple people of Galilee and Judaea were eager for the promised Messiah and deliverance from Roman domination. Shortly before A.D. 30, an ascetic preacher, John the Baptist, made a stir in the Jordan valley, urging people to repent and prepare for the Messiah. Among those he baptized was his cousin Jesus. Jesus went from his baptism to solitude and meditation, thence to emerge on his three-year mission. He went about as a wandering teacher, accompanied by a small band of disciples (see APOSTLE). His extraordinary powers (see MIRA-

CLE) and his PARABLES, spoken in the language of the people instead of the pedantries of the priestly scholars, attracted great crowds. His living of the principles he taught, his denunciation of the hypocrisy of Pharisees and scribes, his preference for the company of the miserable and the oppressed, reached the hearts of the people. At the end of three years, he went with his disciples to Jerusalem for the Passover. Jerusalem was seething with unrest at this feast of Jewish independence. Jesus' arrival was marked by an outburst of Messianic enthusiasm, alarming to those in power. After he had made a scene in the Temple by driving out the usuring money-changers, the ruling clique decided to destroy this man whom they could see only as a revolutionary leader and violent reformer. They bribed one of his companions, JUDAS ISCARIOT, to betray him. Jesus ate a farewell supper with his disciples and went out of the city to pray in the Garden of Gethsemane. There he was arrested. He was rushed to trial before the ecclesiastical court of the Sanhedrin. His claims to be the Messiah and the Son of God convicted him of blasphemy, a crime carrying the death penalty in Jewish law. Since only the Roman governor (at this time Pontius Pilate) could order a man's death, the court, in turning Jesus over to Pilate, emphasized Jesus' claims of kingship, thus charging him with treason against Rome. Pilate tried to evade action, but he dared not brave popular opinion, which was now aroused against Jesus. He yielded and delivered Jesus to be crucified. Jesus died and was buried, deserted by all but his mother and a few friends. About three days later, some of the women visiting the tomb found it open and the body of Jesus gone. An angel told them that he had risen from the dead. Later they saw him and spoke with him; his disciples met with him, and many others as well. Here the Gospels end, but the book of Acts tells how, 40 days after the Resurrection, Jesus ascended into heaven in sight of his disciples. In orthodox theology, Jesus is God made man, the second person of the Trinity, born of Mary, a virgin; he was crucified to make atonement to God for man's sins; rose from the dead and ascended into heaven, and he shall come again with glory to judge the living and the dead; he founded, through his disciples, the Church to continue his work on earth. The Christian calendar revolves around Christmas (Dec. 25), the day set aside to celebrate the birth of Jesus; and Easter, with its movable feasts and fasts, commemorating the Resurrection. Though Christians disagree among themselves on many points, all agree on the inspiring nature of the Gospels and on the reality of Jesus. Incidents of his life have long been the inspiration of artists in every medium of art.

Jesus. 1 Son of Sirach, author of ECCLESIASTICUS. **2** or **Jesus Justus,** Jewish convert in Rome. Col. 4.11. **3** Greek form of JOSHUA.

Jesus, Society of, religious order of the Roman Catholic Church. Its members are called Jesuits (jĕz′wĭts, jĕzh′-ūĭts) and sign the initials S.J. after the names. Originally called *Compañia de Jésus* [Span.,= (military) company of Jesus], when founded (1534–39) by St. IGNATIUS OF LOYOLA (for founding, see article on him) and six companions. Ignatius drafted the rules which still govern the society. Training of those who enter the order is long and rigorous, involving much study. Jesuits have been particularly active as missionaries, as educators, and as scientists. Though not (as frequently asserted) founded to combat the Reformation, Jesuits were active leaders in the Catholic REFORM, laboring with some success to convert Protestants in S and W Germany, France, Hungary, and Poland in 16th and 17th cent. They also made daring attempts to reconvert England. From their beginning Jesuits have always been active in foreign missions. One of the original band, St. FRANCIS XAVIER, went as far afield as the Far East. In India, China, and Japan, Jesuit missions flourished long, and though many

were washed away in blood, the Jesuits did estab. Catholicism in the Orient. They were also active in the New World, not only creating the much-discussed reductions (Indian settlements) in Paraguay but also working in all parts of Latin America and in New France (Canada). From Quebec the "black robes" went out into the wilderness of present Canada and N U.S. to convert the Indians, even penetrating as far as Oregon. Six Jesuits and two of their lay helpers, murdered by the Indians in the 1640s, became the Jesuit Martyrs of North America (most celebrated are Isaac Jogues and Jean Brébeuf). Their zeal and solidarity and their peculiar devotion to the Holy See aroused the jealousy of some other orders and the hatred and fear of some ecclesiastical vested interests and especially of the absolute monarchs of Catholic Europe, who wanted to be free of all papal influence. The pope's power was weakened, and by 1700 the Jesuits were his chief support. They were the object of violent and concerted abuse. Some color was lent to charges of commercialism by a notable scandal. The accusations that they were given to intrigue and were lax in receiving penitents back into the Church have been hotly debated. Some of the claims against them were scurrilously false and were perhaps the basis for ridiculous statements repeated even today (e.g., that they have a secret constitution; that there are secret male and female affiliates; that they have special privileges; that they accept the doctrine that "the end justifies the means"; that they have revolutionary intentions). The princes had their way. The order was suppressed in Portugal 1759, in France 1764, in Spanish dominions 1767, and Clement XIV was compelled to dissolve the order in 1773. Frederick the Great and Catherine the Great refused to publish the papal brief, so the order continued in Russia and Prussia. It was reestablished as a world order on general demand in 1814 and has since resumed and expanded its missionary and educational work. There are notable Jesuit schools and colleges in the U.S. (e.g., Georgetown, Fordham, St. Louis universities).

Jesus College: see CAMBRIDGE UNIVERSITY; OXFORD UNIVERSITY.

Jesus Island: see ÎLE JÉSUS, Que.

jet, black variety of lignite coal. Compact, takes good polish, and is easily worked into beads and other ornaments. Yorkshire, England, is chief source.

Jethou: see CHANNEL ISLANDS.

Jethro (jĕth′rō), Midianite priest of Sinai; father-in-law of Moses. Ex. 2.21; 3.1; 4.18; 18. Reuel: Ex. 2.18; Raguel: Num. 10.29. Hobab: Judges 4.11.

jet propulsion, forward "thrust" resulting from rearward expulsion of mass of gas under high pressure generated by combustion in jet engine. Any apparatus using jet propulsion is essentially a reaction motor based on Newton's 3d law of MOTION and obtaining oxygen for combustion from the atmosphere; a jet differs from a rocket, which is a reaction motor carrying a supply of stored oxygen. A jet engine for powering a full-sized airplane was developed (1939) by Frank Whittle, an Englishman. Various types of jet engines and augmentation devices were later developed and supersonic speeds were attained and exceeded. Military jet aircraft were used in the closing days of Second World War; commercial jet aircraft in wide use in 1967. See *ill.,* p. 368.

jetsam: see FLOTSAM, JETSAM, AND LIGAN.

Jevons, William Stanley (jĕ′vŭnz), 1835–82, English economist and logician. He developed the theory, mathematically demonstrated, that value is determined by utility. Wrote *The Theory of Political Economy* (1871), *The Principles of Science* (1874).

Jewel Cave National Monument: see NATIONAL PARKS AND MONUMENTS (table).

jewelweed: see IMPATIENS.

Jewett, Sarah Orne, 1849–1909, American novelist. Her stories of Maine (e.g., *The Country of the Pointed Firs,* 1896) are fine local-color pieces.

Jewish Autonomous Oblast, RSFSR: see BIROBIDZHAN.

Jewish literature: see HEBREW LITERATURE; YIDDISH.

Jewish liturgical music. In the Bible, music making was common among the ancient Jews on all important occasions. Instruments mentioned include the *kinnor* (a lyre), the *ugab* (a flute?), and the *shofar* (a ram's horn; still used today). With the formation of the kingdom of Israel, music was systematized with a professional group of musicians in the Temple. New instruments, apparently including varieties of harp, oboe, and organ appeared. Biblical passages were chanted on set modal patterns. After the destruction of the Temple (A.D. 70), instrumental music disappeared, but some of the chants survive today. Jewish music influenced early Christian plain song. With the growing importance of the synagogue came the rise of the cantor, a singer who performed the solo chants in the service. Among North European Jews in the Middle Ages, traditional melodies were corrupted under the influence of German folk song. During the Renaissance, there was a reintroduction of ancient elements by Oriental Jews. Cantors returned to improvisation in the Oriental modes and developed a very distinct type of coloratura. In the 17th cent., this art was found all over Europe. Instruments, especially the organ, were reintroduced into the synagogue. In the early 19th cent., an extreme reform movement eliminated the cantor and set traditional Jewish hymns to the tunes of Protestant chorales. A more moderate reform retained the cantor, as well as traditional chants, but at the same time made use of new music written by Jewish composers for the synagogue. Ernest BLOCH was the leading figure in the attempt to create a Jewish national music.

Jews [from Judah], descendants of the tribes of ISRAEL, adherents of the religion of JUDAISM. Before the Second World War they numbered c.16,000,000; between 5,000,000 and 6,000,000 were massacred during the war. Only a minority of Jews speak YIDDISH. According to the OLD TESTAMENT, their ancestor was Terah of Ur of the Chaldees, from whom descended the patriarchs Abraham, Isaac, and Jacob, who considered Canaan their home. The ancient history of Israel continues with settlement of Jews in Egypt as farmers, many years before Christ. Under Ramses II they were persecuted; Moses led them out of Eygpt and, at Mt. Sinai, gave them the Decalogue. After many years in the wilderness the Jews conquered Canaan and united under Saul, their first king, who was defeated by the Philistines. The next king, David, conquered the enemies of the Jews. His son, King Solomon, built the monumental first temple. Disruption followed, and the two kingdoms then formed, Israel and Judah, warred during much of the following two centuries (935–725 B.C.). In 722 the capital of Israel was captured and the Israelites (the LOST TRIBES) were exiled. Judah went from Assyrian to Egyptian to Babylonian domination. The Temple, destroyed in 586 B.C. by the Babylonians, was rebuilt in 516 B.C. History of Jews begins with resettlement in Judea after Babylonian CAPTIVITY. The Jews were subsequently under Persian, Macedonian, Egyptian, and Syrian domination. A short period of independence under the MACCABEES ended in 70 A.D. with Roman occupation of Palestine. With the fall of the Roman Empire, Jews appeared in Western Europe, where from the 9th to the 12th cent. they enjoyed a golden age of literary activity (notably in Spain). From the time of the Crusades until the 19th cent. the Jews were persecuted and driven from many countries. The rise of capitalism improved the conditions of the Jews throughout Europe, as did the revolutionary movements of the 19th cent. The emancipation of the Jews brought forth two opposed movements: cultural assimilation, begun by Moses MENDELSSOHN, and ZIONISM, founded by Theodor HERZL in 1896. A wave of persecution starting in Russia (1881) and moving westward to France slowly abated until 1933, when with the rise to power in Germany of the Nazis, persecution of the Jews became violent. After the massacres of the Second World War, many sought refuge in Palestine, where a Jewish state (see ISRAEL) was established in 1948.

Jex-Blake, Sophia, 1840–1912, English physician, active in opening medical profession to women.

Jezebel (jĕ′–), d. c.846 B.C., wife of AHAB, mother of Ahaziah **1,** Jehoram **1,** and Athaliah. Willful and cruel, she led Israel into idolatry and persecuted the prophets. Killed in Jehu's coup d'état; her body thrown to the dogs. 1 Kings 16.31; 18; 21; 2 Kings 9.1–10, 30–37. Reference in Rev. 2.20 obscure.

Jezreel (jĕz′rēĕl), anc. city, Palestine, in plain of Esdraelon, between Megiddo and Jordan R.; residence of King Ahab, whose family is often called the house of Jezreel. 1 Kings 21.1.

Jhelum or **Jehlam** (both: jā′lŭm), anc. *Hydaspes,* river, c.500 mi. long, in Kashmir and West Pakistan; westernmost of five rivers of Punjab.

Jibuti (jĭbōo′tē), town (est. pop. c.40,000); cap. of French Somaliland, on an inlet of the Gulf of Aden. Major port on shipping lanes to Suez Canal; terminus of railway to Addis Ababa. Also Djibouti.

Jidda (jĭ′dŭ) or **Jedda** (jĕ′dŭ), city (pop. c.200,000), Hejaz, Saudi Arabia, on Red Sea; port of Mecca. Has huge influx of pilgrims.

jigger: see CHIGOE.

Jiménez, Juan Ramón (hwän′ rämōn′ hēmä′näth), 1881–1958, Spanish lyric poet. Verse characterized by technical simplicity, profundity of meaning. Known in English for tale, *Platero and I.* Won 1956 Nobel Prize in Literature.

Jiménez de Cisneros, Francisco (fränthĕ′skō hēmä′näth dä thēsnä′rōs), 1436–1517, Spanish cardinal and statesman. Archbishop of Toledo from 1495; inquisitor general from 1507. Led expedition which captured Oran (1509); founded Univ. of Alcalá; had Polyglot Bible compiled. Became regent on death of Ferdinand V (1516) but was summarily dismissed by Charles I (Emperor Charles V). Formerly spelled Ximenes.

Jiménez de Quesada, Gonzalo (gônthä′lō hēmä′näth dä käsä′dhä), c.1499–1579, Spanish conquistador in New Grenada. Exploring (1536) the Magdalena R. in search of El Dorado, he defeated Chibchas; founded Bogotá 1538. His claims, disputed by Federmann and Benalcázar, were verified by Spain 1550. A later expedition (to Orinoco R., 1569) was disastrous.

Jimson weed or **Jamestown weed,** coarse tropical annual plant (*Datura stramonium*) naturalized in North America. It has rank smelling foliage, trumpet-shaped white or purple flowers, and spiny fruits. Contains a narcotic poison similar to belladonna.

Jim Thorpe, borough (pop. 5,945), E Pa., on Lehigh R., SE of Hazleton, in resort area; settled 1815. Some of Molly Maguires were executed in local jail. Named for Jim Thorpe, who is buried here.

Jinja, town (pop. c.30,000), SE Uganda, on N shore of Victoria Nyanza; a lake port and on Kenya-Uganda RR. Sugar refineries and textile plants.

Jinnah, Mahomed Ali (mŭhŏ′mĭd ä′lē jĭ′nŭ), 1876–1948, founder of Pakistan. Admitted to the bar in England 1896, returned to India to practice law. First supported INDIAN NATIONAL CONGRESS and advocated Hindu-Moslem unity, but after 1934 (when he won control of MOSLEM LEAGUE) he agitated for separate state of Pakistan. Gained power during World War II by supporting the British; forced Congress to accept partition of India (1947). Became first governor general of dominion.

jinni (jĭnē′), plural **jinn** (jĭn), in Arabic folklore and in Moslem literature, creature like man but having certain supernatural powers, especially those of changing size and shape. Jinn may be good or evil. They appear constantly in the *Thousand and One Nights.* Also spelled genie.

jiujitsu or **jiujutsu:** see JUJUTSU.

Joab (jō'ăb), David's nephew, commander of his armies. An able administrator but often cruel, as in his killing of Abner, Absalom, and Amasa. Executed by Solomon for supporting Adonijah. 2 Sam. 2.12–32; 3.22–31; 8.16; 10.7–14; 11; 12.26; 14; 18; 19.1, 5–7; 20.7–23; 24.1–9; 1 Kings 1; 2.28–34.

Joachim, Saint (jō'ŭkĭm), in tradition, father of the Virgin, husband of St. ANNE. Feast: Aug. 16.

Joachim, Joseph (yō'äkĕm), 1831–1907, Hungarian violinist; friend of Mendelssohn, Brahms, and Schumann. Considered a master interpreter of great violin works, he composed cadenzas for violin concertos of Beethoven and Brahms.

Joachimsthal, Czechoslovakia: see JACHYMOV.

Joad, C(yril) E(dwin) M(itchinson) (jōd), 1891–1953, English rationalist philosopher.

Joahaz: see JEHOAHAZ.

Joanes, Vicente: see MACIP, VICENTE JUAN.

Joanna (jōä'nù), queens of Naples. **Joanna I,** 1326–82 (reigned 1343–81), was also countess of Provence. The murder of her husband, Andrew of Hungary (probably with her complicity) in 1345 brought recurrent warfare with Andrew's brother, Louis I of Hungary. She successively adopted Charles of Durazzo (see CHARLES III of Naples) and Louis of Anjou (see LOUIS I of Naples) as heirs. Charles imprisoned her and probably had her murdered. **Joanna II,** 1371–1435, succeeded her brother Lancelot in 1414. Her reign was beset by court intrigues and by rival claims of LOUIS III of Naples. Her successive adoptions as heirs of ALFONSO V of Aragon, Louis, and RENÉ of Anjou plunged Naples into warfare from which Alfonso emerged victorious after her death.

Joanna (the Mad), 1479–1555, Spanish queen of Castile and Leon (1504–55); daughter of Ferdinand V and Isabella I. Married PHILIP I, after whose death her insanity became apparent. She never ruled, her father being regent 1504–6; Philip I, 1506–7; her father again, 1507–16. Her son, Emperor Charles V, governed as joint ruler 1516–55.

Joanna, in Bible, wife of Herod's steward, follower of Jesus. One of those who visited Jesus' tomb and found it empty. Luke 8.3; 24.10.

Joan of Arc, 1412?–1431, French saint and national heroine, called the Maid of Orléans; daughter of a farmer of Domrémy, in Lorraine. She early began to hear "voices"—of St. Michael, St. Catherine, and St. Margaret—exhorting her to bear aid to the dauphin, CHARLES VII, then kept from his throne by the English. After many rebuffs, she was authorized by Robert de Baudricourt, military governor of Vaucouleurs, to journey to the dauphin (1429). She adopted male attire, which she was to keep till her last days. Meeting the dauphin at Chinon, she convinced him of her mission. After some more delays she was given troops, succeeded in lifting the siege of ORLÉANS, took other places along the Loire, routed the English at PATAY, and persuaded Charles to march on Rheims, where he was crowned, with Joan standing beside him (1429). She was eager to push her victories, which had turned the tide of the Hundred Years War, but the king's advisers and his indolence inclined him to negotiations with Burgundy, England's ally. After besieging Paris without success (1429), Joan in 1430 went to relieve Compiègne but was captured by the Burgundians who later sold her to the English. An irregular trial before an ecclesiastic court at Rouen, headed by Pierre CAUCHON, ended with her condemnation for heresy and sorcery (1431). She was burned at the stake. Rehabilitated in a new trial (1456), she was canonized in 1920. Feast: May 30.

João Pessoa (zhwä'ŏ pùsō'ù), city (pop. c.155,100), cap. of Paraíba state, NE Brazil; port near Atlantic, founded 1585. Exports cotton, sugar, minerals.

Joash: see JEHOASH.

Job (jōb), book of Old Testament. A dramatic dialogue concerned with problem of good and evil in the world. In prologue in heaven, plan is laid to test Job, a truly good man. Property, family, and health are taken

from him. Some friends who come to "comfort" him accuse Job of some great sin; Job protests his innocence. He learns that God's judgment is beyond man's understanding. In epilogue, all that Job lost is restored to him. Ethical problem, not explicitly resolved, suggests that suffering is not always due to sin. Parts of original text may be lost, new parts added at a later date.

Job's-tears, tall tropical grass (*Coix lacryma-jobi*) with bony, white or gray beadlike fruits.

Jocasta, mother of OEDIPUS.

Jocelin de Brakelond (jŏs'lĭn dù brăk'lŏnd), fl. 1200, English monk whose chronicle of Bury St. Edmunds (1173–1202) is simple, vigorous, vivid.

Jodhpur (jŏd'pŏŏr) or **Marwar** (mär'wär), former princely state, part of Rajasthan, India, since 1949. Estab. in 13th cent. by Rathor Rajputs, it later fell to the Mogul empire. Placed under British protection 1818. **Jodhpur,** city (pop. 180,717), cap. of former state, was founded 1459.

Joel, book of Old Testament. Joel, an otherwise unknown prophet, vividly describes plague of locusts, urges people to repent. Has Messianic prophecy (2.28–32; 3), much quoted. Peter used Joel as text. Acts 2.

joe-pye weed, tall North American perennial (*Eupatorium purpureum*) bearing pinkish or purple flower clusters in the autumn.

Joffe, Abram, 1880–1960, Soviet scientist. Noted for work on semiconductors and thermoelectric generators. Invented many devices used in radio and aerodynamics, including new type of dynamo and a powerful accumulator.

Joffre, Joseph Jacques Césaire (zhôzĕf' zhäk' săzĕr' zhô'frü), 1852–1931, marshal of France. French commander in chief in First World War until 1916; chairman of Allied War Council 1916–18. Won first battle of Marne (1914); nearly lost Verdun (1916).

Jogjakarta (jŏg"yäkär'tä), city (pop. 308,530), S Java, Indonesia, at foot of volcanic Mt. Merapi. Cultural, handicrafts, and light-mfg. center. Seat of Univ. of Gadjah Mada. Provisional cap. of Indonesia 1949–50.

Jogues, Isaac (ēzäk' zhôg'), 1607–46, Jesuit missionary and martyr in New World, b. France. Discovered L. George (1646). Murdered by hostile Mohawks. Canonized in 1930.

Johanan ben Zakkai (jōhä'nùn bĕn zä'kāī), leader of Pharisees of Jerusalem before destruction of Temple in 70 A.D. Afterwards founder of academy of Jabne (see JAMNIA) which assured continuation of Judaism.

Johannesburg (jōhä'n'ĭsbûrg), city (pop. c.1,152,525), S Transvaal, Republic of South Africa. Founded 1886 as mining settlement when surface gold was discovered. Largest city of South Africa; commercial and transportation hub; industrial center of the WITWATERSRAND. Seat of Univ. of Witwatersrand. After 1956 official policy of APARTHEID forced resettlement of large numbers of non-Europeans.

John, Saint, one of the Twelve Apostles; son of Zebedee, brother of St. James the Greater (see also BOANERGES). John was apparently the disciple "whom Jesus loved" and to whom Jesus on the cross committed the care of His mother (John 13.24; 19.26). Ancient tradition makes him the author of the fourth Gospel, three epistles, and Revelation, but this ascription has been much disputed among modern scholars. It thus may have been he who was exiled to Patmos (Rev. 1.9), and he may have died at Ephesus c.100. Called St. John the Divine (i.e., theologian), St. John the Evangelist. Feast: Dec. 27.

John VIII, d. 882, pope (872–82). Opposed St. Ignatius of Constantinople and recognized Photius as patriarch, thus temporarily reconciling E and W churches. Crowned Charles II (the Bald) and helped Charles III (the Fat) to the imperial throne.

John XII, c.937–964, pope (955–64), a Roman. Called in Otto I to help him against Berengarius, king of Italy, and was confirmed in the Patrimony of St.

Peter, but shortly turned against Otto. Otto conquered Rome and called a synod to depose John and elect an antipope, Leo VIII. John retook Rome (964) but was soon murdered. His life was immoral, his pontificate a disgrace.

John XXI, d. 1277, pope (1276–77), a Portuguese, called Petrus Hispanus and reputed to be the author of a textbook on logic. Actually 19th canonical pope named John but called himself John XXI.

John XXII, 1244–1334, pope (1316–34), a Frenchman, chosen after a delay as successor to Clement V. He quarreled with Emperor Louis IV (who was assisted by Marsilius of Padua and William of Occam). Louis invaded Italy and set up as antipope Pietro Rainalducci, who shortly had to submit to John, but the pope's claims to authority over the empire came to nothing. Because of confused numbering also called John XXI.

John XXIII, 1881–1963, pope (1958–63), an Italian named Angelo Roncalli. Papal representative in Balkans and Near East (1925–44), papal nuncio to France (1944–53). He became patriarch of Venice and cardinal 1953. Showed deep concern for church reform, promotion of peace, world social welfare (expressed in his encyclical *Mater et Magistra,* 1961), and for dialogue with other Christians. Convened Second VATICAN COUNCIL. His outstanding Christian character greatly influenced modern reform movement and spirit of renewal in the Roman Catholic Church.

John XXIII, antipope: see COSSA, BALDASSARRE.

John, Byzantine emperors. **John I** (Tzimisces), c.925–976, gained the throne by murdering Nicephorus II (969), whose anticlerical legislation he revoked. Extended Byzantine power against Russians and Arabs. **John II** (Comnenus), 1088–1143, succeeded his father Alexius I in 1118, despite the intrigues of his sister Anna Comnena to put her husband on the throne. He unsuccessfully tried to cancel Venetian commercial privileges. **John III** (John Ducas Vatatzes), d. 1254, emperor of Nicaea (1222–54), took Salonica from Latin Empire of Constantinople (1246), thus nearly completing reunion of dismembered Byzantine Empire. **John V** (Palaeologus), 1332–91, reigned 1341–76 and 1379–91. His throne was usurped during his minority by John VI and from 1376 to 1379 by his son Andronicus IV. **John VI** (Cantacuzene), c.1292–1383, usurped throne of John V (1341–55). Called Ottoman Turks to his aid and allowed Stephen Dushan to build up Serbian empire. Retired to a monastery. **John VIII** (Palaeologus), 1390–1448, reigned 1425–48. Sought to secure Western aid against Turks by agreeing to union of Eastern and Western churches at Council of Florence (1439).

John, kings of Aragon and counts of Barcelona. **John I,** 1350–95, reigned 1387–95. Patron of learning; held brilliant court. **John II,** 1397–1479, reigned 1458–79. Also inherited Sicily (1458). Married Blanche, heiress of Navarre (1425). After her death (1442) conflict broke out between John and his son, CHARLES OF VIANA, whose death in 1461 was followed by further troubles in Catalonia until 1472. John's son Ferdinand II (Ferdinand V of Castile) inherited Aragon, Catalonia, Sicily; his son-in-law, the count of Foix, inherited Navarre.

John, 1166–1216, king of England (1199–1216), youngest son of Henry II. Supported his brother, Richard I, against his father in 1189. While Richard was on the Third Crusade, he had himself declared heir and conspired to keep Richard in captivity. Succeeded Richard to exclusion of his nephew, Arthur I of Brittany. Arthur's supporters, aided by PHILIP II of France, revolted and John was finally forced to surrender most of his French possessions. Excommunicated and deposed by INNOCENT III, he surrendered England to the pope and received it back as fief (1213). Barons, intensely opposed to John, united and forced him to sign (1215) the MAGNA CARTA. Ty-

rannical, treacherous, and cruel, he is the subject of one of Shakespeare's chronicle plays.

John, kings of France. **John I** (the Posthumous), 1316, son of Louis X, lived only a few days. **John II** (the Good), 1319–64. His reign (1350–64) was troubled by HUNDRED YEARS WAR and internal disturbances, notably his quarrels with CHARLES II of Navarre and the JACQUERIE. Captured by English at Poitiers (1356), he was released by Treaty of BRÉTIGNY (1360). In 1364 one of hostages who had taken his place in England escaped; John, to save his honor, returned to England, where he died. During his absences, his son (later CHARLES V) was regent.

John, kings of Hungary. **John I** (John Zapolya), 1487–1540; son of Stephen ZAPOLYA. Voivode of Transylvania (1511–26), he was chosen king by the Hungarian nobles after Louis II's death at MOHÁCS (1526). Louis's brother-in-law, Ferdinand of Austria (later Emperor FERDINAND I) challenged the succession in a series of campaigns, but in 1529 Sultan Suleiman I intervened and set up John as puppet king. John was succeeded by son **John II** (John Sigismund Zapolya), 1540–71. Suleiman, on pretext of protecting the infant's interests, invaded Hungary in 1541 (thus beginning 150 years of Turkish rule) and made John prince of Transylvania. Deposed by the pro-Austrian party in Transylvania (1551), John was recalled in 1556 on Turkish pressure. Austro-Turkish peace of 1562 left him in possession of Transylvania, with the rest of Hungary divided between Austria and Turkey.

John, kings of Poland. **John II** (John Casimir), 1609–72. His reign (1648–68) is known in Polish history as the Deluge. Cossack rebellion under CHMIELNICKI led to war with Russia (1654–67) and cession of E Ukraine. Invasion by CHARLES X of Sweden (1655) was checked by miracle of CZESTOCHOWA, but in Peace of OLIVA John had to cede N Livonia to Sweden and to grant Elector Frederick William of Brandenburg full sovereignty over Prussia, in exchange for aid against Sweden. Abdicated in 1668; retired to a French monastery. **John III** (John Sobieski), 1624–96, reigned 1674–96. He briefly restored Polish prestige when, in 1683, he led his forces to relieve Vienna from Turkish siege. Pursuing the Turks into Hungary, he formed a Holy League with the pope, Emperor Leopold I, and Venice (1684), but he failed to wrest Moldavia and Walachia from Turkey. His death marked virtual end of Polish independence.

John, kings of Portugal. **John I** (the Great), 1357?–1433, illegitimate son of Pedro I, grand master of the Knights of Aviz. When his half-brother Fredinand I died (1383), Portugal was ruled by a regency for Ferdinand's daughter Beatrice, wife of John I of Castile. John of Aviz cooperated with Nun' Álvares Pereira in the national revolt against Spanish hegemony and in 1385 was elected king. The great victory of Aljubarrota (1385) assured Portuguese independence. John's reign, one of the most glorious in Portuguese history, was marked by an alliance with England, the beginnings of Portuguese colonial and maritime expansion, the capture of Ceuta from the Moors (1415), and the flowering of Portuguese literature. **John II** (the Perfect), 1455–95, reigned 1481–95. Asserted royal supremacy over nobles; fostered exploration (but refused to aid Columbus); signed Treaty of TORDESILLAS with Spain. Patron of Renaissance art and learning. **John III** (the Fortunate), 1502–57. His reign (1521–57) marked the height of the Portuguese empire but saw the beginning of decadence in Portugal itself. Introduced Inquisition; imported African slaves. **John IV,** 1604?–1656, duke of Braganza, descended from Manuel I and in illegitimate line from John I, became king in 1640 when Portugal cast off Spanish rule. Founder of Braganza dynasty. **John V** (the Magnanimous), 1689–1750, reigned 1706–50. **John VI,** 1769–1826, became regent for his insane mother, Maria I, in 1799. Joined second coalition against France; defeated, he accepted humiliating Treaty of Badajoz (1801). Fled to Brazil when French attacked Portugal (1807); succeeded to throne 1816; returned to Portugal 1821, leaving his son PEDRO I as regent of Brazil. In 1825 Portugal recognized Brazilian independence (proclaimed 1822). On his death, John left regency of Portugal to his daughter Isabella but left matter of succession unsettled.

John, Spanish kings of Castile and Leon. **John I,** 1358–90, reigned 1379–90; son of HENRY II. Sought to unite Portugal and Castile; defeated by Portuguese at Aljubarrota (1385). JOHN OF GAUNT challenged his succession, but made peace 1388 and married his daughter to John's heir. **John II,** 1405–54, reigned 1406–54. Left government to Alvaro de LUNA. Notable as a patron of literature.

John, in Bible. **1** See JOHN, SAINT. **2** See JOHN THE BAPTIST. **3** See MARK, SAINT. **4** See MACCABEES.

John, Augustus Edwin, 1879–1961, British painter and etcher, b. Wales. A leading portrait painter.

John, epistles of New Testament, called First, Second, and Third John; ascribed to St. John the Apostle. **1** John is homily on blending of mystical and practical religion. Discusses God as light (1.5–2.28), God as righteousness (2.29–4.6), God as love (4.7–5.12). **2** John, shortest book of Bible, warns against false teachers who deny historical reality of Jesus. **3** John is protest against a certain church leader's failure to receive teaching missionaries.

John, Gospel according to Saint, book of New Testament, traditionally ascribed to John the Apostle. A biography of Jesus in essay form, it interprets the spiritual truth of Jesus' message, e.g., in the stories of Nicodemus and of Samaritan woman and sermon on Bread of Life. It shows Jesus as completely human and yet divine and stresses the redemptive purpose of His mission. Book begins with the famous philosophical passage identifying Jesus as the Word (see LOGOS). There follow two main sections, the ministry of Jesus (1.19–12.50) and the Passion and Resurrection (13–21).

John Baptist de la Salle, Saint (säl), 1651–1719, French educator. At Rheims he formed the first order devoted solely to Christian education, Brothers of the Christian Schools (Christian Brothers; 1684). In 1685 he founded first normal school at Rheims to train his teachers. Name in French: Jean Baptiste de la Salle. Feast: May 15.

John Birch Society, ultraconservative, anti-Communist organization, founded in Dec., 1958, by manufacturer Robert Welch. Named after John Birch, an OSS captain killed by Chinese Communists (Aug., 1945).

John Bosco, Saint, 1815–88, Italian priest at Turin, founder (1841) of the Salesian order for work with boys and in foreign missions, and of Daughters of Mary Auxiliatrix, for work with girls. Feast: Jan. 31.

John Capistran, Saint (kŭpĭ'strŭn), 1385?–1456, Italian preacher, a Franciscan. Preached against the Hussites (1451) and led a wing of Hunyadi's army in great victory of Belgrade (1456). Feast: March 28.

John Carter Brown Library: see BROWN, JOHN CARTER.

John Chrysostom, Saint (krĭ'sŭstŭm, krĭsŏ'stŭm) [Gr.,= golden-mouth], c.347–407, Doctor of the Church, greatest Greek Father. Made patriarch of Constantinople (398), he undertook reforms and defied the imperial powers. Illegally deposed by Empress Eudoxia and Theophilus, bishop of Alexandria (403), he was recalled when people rioted. Later he was exiled by Arcadius. St. John's many authoritative homilies and commentaries, in excellent Greek style, had great influence.

John Crerar Library: see CRERAR, JOHN.

John Damascene, Saint: see JOHN OF DAMASCUS, SAINT.

John Day, river, NE Oregon, rising in Blue Mts. and flowing c.280 mi. W and N to Columbia R.

John Day Dam: see COLUMBIA, river.

John Fisher, Saint: see FISHER, JOHN.

John F. Kennedy Center for the Performing Arts, in Washington, D.C. Ground broken 1964 at its site on the Potomac R. upstream from the Lincoln Memorial. Edward Durell Stone designed building to house an opera, concert hall, two theaters, and a cinema. Public contributions include gifts from foreign nations.

John F. Kennedy International Airport: see QUEENS.

John Frederick I (the Magnanimous), 1503–54, elector (1532–47) and duke (1547–54) of Saxony. A member of Schmalkaldic League, he was captured by Emperor Charles V at Mühlberg (1547) and had to renounce electorate in favor of his cousin MAURICE of Saxony.

John Henry, legendary Negro strong man, celebrated in Southern American Negro ballads and "tall tales."

John Mark: see MARK, SAINT.

John Maurice of Nassau, 1604–79, Dutch general; grandnephew of William the Silent. As governor of Brazil (1636–43), for the Dutch West India Company, he conquered NE Brazil from Portuguese, built up state of Pernambuco, made broad plans for development. Subsequently held commands in Thirty Years War and Dutch Wars. His residence at the Hague is the celebrated Mauritshuis.

Johnny Appleseed: see CHAPMAN, JOHN.

John of Austria, c.1545–1578, Spanish admiral and general; natural son of Emperor Charles V. Won decisive naval victory against Turks at LEPANTO. As governor general of Netherlands (1576–78) Don John fought rebels with inconclusive success.

John of Austria, 1629–79, natural son of Philip IV of Spain. While governor of the Netherlands, he was defeated by French in battle of the Dunes (1658). Took over regency for Charles II in 1677.

John of Brienne (brēĕn'), c.1170–1237, French crusader. Became, through marriage, titular king of Jerusalem (1210); captured Damietta in Fifth Crusade (1219); became regent for the Latin emperor, Baldwin II (1228); defended Constantinople against Greeks and Bulgars (1236). Father-in-law of Frederick II.

John of Damascus, Saint, or **Saint John Damascene** (dă'mŭsēn), c.675–749, Syrian theologian, Doctor of the Church. Reared at court of the caliph in Damascus, he entered a Palestinian monastery (c.726) and spent most of his life in writing against iconoclasm and defending orthodoxy. *The Fountain of Wisdom* is his theological masterpiece.

John of Gaunt, 1340–99, duke of Lancaster; fourth son of Edward III of England. By his first marriage (see LANCASTER, HOUSE OF) he became one of most influential nobles in England. Served under his brother, Edward the Black Prince, in Hundred Years War. Aided Peter the Cruel of Castile and married his daughter. As viceroy for senile Edward III he espoused cause of court party and, for a time, ruled England. Fought (1386–88) for his claim to throne of Castile against John I. Helped keep peace between Richard II and hostile barons. His eldest son became Henry IV. By his third marriage, he was ancestor of the house of Tudor. Patron of Chaucer.

John of Lancaster, 1389–1435, duke of Bedford; son of Henry IV of England and brother of Henry V. Made protector of Henry VI (1422), he devoted himself to English affairs in France.

John of Leiden, c.1509–1536, Dutch Anabaptist leader. In revolt in Münster (1534) he set up theocracy and was leader of a communistic, chaotic state until in 1535 Anabaptists were ousted and their leaders tortured and executed.

John of Luxemburg, 1296–1346, king of Bohemia (1310–46); son of Emperor Henry VII. Was elected king after marriage with Elizabeth, daughter of Wenceslaus II of Bohemia. The blind king is best remembered for his gallant death at Crécy, where he fought as ally of Philip VI of France; he commanded that his charger be led into the thick of the fight. His son was Emperor Charles IV.

John of Procida (prŏ'chēdä), c.1225–c.1302, Italian Ghibelline conspirator. Prepared uprising of SICILIAN VESPERS (1282).

John of Salisbury (sôlz–), c.1115–1180, English scholastic philosopher. Studied at Paris and traveled much.

Was secretary to St. Thomas à Becket, and later bishop of Chartres (1176–80). His *Metalogicus* sums up the scholastic knowledge of his time; his *Polycraticus* urged independence of church and state.

John of the Cross, Saint, Span. *Juan de la Cruz*, 1542–91, Spanish mystic, founder of the Discalced Carmelites, friend of St. Theresa of Ávila. His mystical poetry and treatises have had great influence on modern Catholicism. Feast: Nov. 24.

John o' Groats House, locality in Caithness, Scotland; often erroneously named as N point of Scotland. House, now gone, was supposedly built by a Dutchman in the 16th cent.

John Scotus: see DUNS SCOTUS; ERIGENA.

Johns Hopkins University, The, at Baltimore; partly coed.; chartered 1867, opened 1876 with bequest from Johns Hopkins. Its medical school, opened 1893, connected with the noted hospital, is one of world's largest. Has continually excelled in laboratory and research work; institute for cooperative research estab. 1946. Had first university press in U.S. (1878). Includes McCoy Col. and School of Advanced Internatl. Studies.

Johnson, Andrew, 1808–75, 17th President of the United States (1865–69). Completely self-educated. A tailor in Greeneville, Tenn. U.S. Representative (1843–53); governor of Tenn. (1853–57); U.S. Senator (1857–62). Interested in securing legislation providing Western land for laboring class; as a war Democrat he vigorously supported Lincoln. U.S. Vice President (1865). As President he was denounced by radical Republicans for his RECONSTRUCTION program. After passage over his veto of bill extending life of FREEDMEN'S BUREAU, his administration was the record of one humiliation after another. His efforts to remove from office E. M. STANTON, whom he rightly suspected of conspiring with congressional leaders, led to impeachment proceedings. On Feb. 24, 1868, the House passed a resolution of impeachment against him even before it adopted 11 articles detailing the reasons for it. Most important of the charges, which were purely political, was that he had violated the TENURE OF OFFICE ACT in the Stanton affair. By a narrow margin the Senate failed to convict. Important achievement of his administration in foreign affairs was purchase of Alaska (1867), negotiated by W. H. Seward. Again U.S. Senator in 1875.

Johnson, Eastman, 1824–1906, American portrait and genre painter. Influenced by Dutch masters.

Johnson, Edward, 1881–1959, Canadian operatic tenor. He sang at the Metropolitan Opera, New York, after 1922, and was its general manager 1935–50.

Johnson, Guy: see JOHNSON, SIR WILLIAM.

Johnson, Herschel Vespasian, 1812–80, American statesman. U.S. Senator from Ga. (1848–49). Nominated by National Democrats as Vice President (1860). Opposed secession of Ga. in 1861, but in Confederate senate he upheld states' rights policies.

Johnson, Hiram (Warren), 1866–1945, American political leader, U.S. Senator from Calif. (1917–45). A founder of Progressive party; its candidate for Vice President in 1912. A Republican supporter of F. D. Roosevelt in 1932. He was a consistent isolationist and opponent of the League of Nations.

Johnson, Hugh (Samuel), 1882–1942, American army officer, government administrator. Supervised First World War draft. Head of National Recovery Administration (1933–34).

Johnson, Jack (John Arthur Johnson). 1878–1946, American boxer. Defeated Tommy Burns (1908), claimed world's heavyweight championship. Johnson definitely won title by knocking out James J. Jeffries (1910), lost championship to Jess Willard (1915).

Johnson, James Weldon, 1871–1938, American author, diplomat, and one of founders of Natl. Association for the Advancement of Colored People. His works include *Autobiography of an Ex-Colored Man* (fictional, 1912), *God's Trombones* (poems, 1927), and an autobiography (1933). His brother, **(John) Rosa-**

mond Johnson, 1873–1954, composed several hundred songs, including *Lift Every Voice and Sing* (for which J. W. Johnson wrote the words). His *Rolling Along in Song* (1937) is an anthology of American Negro songs.

Johnson, Sir John: see JOHNSON, SIR WILLIAM.

Johnson, Lyndon Baines, 1908–, 35th or 36th (see list at end of article UNITED STATES) President of the United States, b. near Stonewall, Texas. Served as Congressman from Texas 1937–49, a tenure briefly interrupted by naval service in 1941–42. Elected to U.S. Senate in 1948, he came to wield great power as majority leader (1955–60). After losing the 1960 presidential nomination to J. F. Kennedy, he accepted Kennedy's offer of the vice-presidential nomination. After being elected, he served as an American emissary to nations throughout the world and exerted important influence on presidential committees for civil rights and space activities. Upon the assassination of Kennedy on Nov. 22, 1963, he assumed the presidency. In the 1964 presidential election he won a landslide victory over Barry M. Goldwater. Johnson's "Great Society" program brought to completion many of the Kennedy administration's proposals for social legislation, including reforms in education, civil rights legislation, and Medicare. The Johnson administration faced many difficulties in foreign affairs, among them the Panama Canal dispute, the sending of American troops to DOMINICAN REPUBLIC, and the determination of President De Gaulle of France to withdraw from the NORTH ATLANTIC TREATY ORGANIZATION. Of paramount importance was the intensification of the war in VIETNAM.

Johnson, Martin Elmer, 1884–1937, American explorer and author. Photographed wildlife and native tribes on expeditions to South Sea Isls., Borneo, and particularly Africa. His wife, **Osa Helen (Leighty) Johnson,** 1894–1953, was his companion on all expeditions and co-author of accounts of their adventures.

Johnson, Philip Cortelyou, 1906–, American architect, museum curator, and historian. Collaborated on the Seagram Building, New York; one of the architects of Lincoln Center for the Performing Arts.

Johnson, Reverdy, 1796–1876, American lawyer and statesman. One of ablest constitutional lawyers of his day. U.S. Senator from Md. (1845–49, 1863–68). U.S. Attorney General (1849–50). Opposed secession. Minister to Great Britain (1868–69).

Johnson, Richard Mentor, 1781–1850, Vice President of the United States (1837–41). U.S. Representative from Ky. (1807–12, 1814–19, 1829–37); U.S. Senator 1819–29). Elected Vice President by U.S. Senate.

Johnson, Rosamond: see JOHNSON, JAMES WELDON.

Johnson, Samuel, 1696–1772, American clergyman, educator, and philosopher. He was first president (1754–63) of King's Col. (now Columbia Univ.). His son, **William Samuel Johnson,** 1727–1819, was a statesman and also president of Columbia Col. (1787–1800). Active in political affairs in Conn.; representative at Continental Congress (1784–87). U.S. Senator (1789–91).

Johnson, Samuel, 1709–84, English author. His first major work was in satiric verse, *London* (1738) and *The Vanity of Human Wishes* (1749). His *Rambler* essays appeared 1750–52. Despite extreme difficulties he published in 1755 *A Dictionary of the English Language,* which won immediate fame. His "Idler" essays appeared 1758–60, and his moralizing fable *Rasselas* in 1759. In 1763 he met James BOSWELL, his future biographer, and in 1764, with Reynolds, Goldsmith, Burke, and others he formed his famous "Club." In 1765 began his long friendship with Mr. and Mrs. Henry Thrale. He published in 1765 an edition of Shakespeare (preface and notes still highly valued). His tour of the Hebrides produced *A Journey to the Western Islands of Scotland* (1775). Last major work was *Lives of the Poets* (1779–81), full of personal but illuminating criticism. His prose is ponderous, but often incisive and always distinguished; his critical judgments were often prejudiced, but always shrewd and interesting. Johnson was dictator of literary taste in London and, because of his literary judgment and his integrity, the dominating literary figure of his age.

Johnson, Tom L(oftin), 1854–1911, American municipal reformer, mayor of Cleveland (1901–10). Fought political bosses and business interests; inspired reform movements in other cities. Served in U.S. House of Representatives (1891–95).

Johnson, Walter (Perry), 1887–1946, American baseball pitcher. Right-handed Washington Senator ace, acknowledged fastest hurler in baseball history, he won 414, lost 276 in 21 major-league seasons. His major-league records include most shutouts (113), most strikeouts (3,497), most consecutive scoreless innings pitched (56).

Johnson, Sir William, 1715–74, British colonial leader in America, b. Ireland. Influence over Indians made him a key figure in French and Indian Wars and in control of land afterwards. Founded Johnstown, N.Y. (1762). His son, **Sir John Johnson,** 1742–1830, was a Loyalist leader in American Revolution. Failed in plan to organize settlers and Indians of Mohawk region against patriots. Served in Saratoga campaign. **Guy Johnson,** c.1740–1788, Loyalist leader in colonial N.Y., b. Ireland, was son-in-law of Sir William Johnson. Superintendent of Indian affairs (1774–82). Directed raids against patriot frontier settlements in American Revolution.

Johnson, William Samuel: see JOHNSON, SAMUEL (1696–1772).

Johnson City. 1 Village (1966 pop. 20,442), S N.Y., just W of Binghamton. With Endicott and Binghamton, forms the Triple Cities. Mfg. of shoes. **2** City (pop. 31,187), NE Tenn., NE of Knoxville, in mountainous region with farms, timber, and limestone quarries; settled before 1800. Tobacco market and rail center, with railroad shops. East Tennessee State Univ. is here. **3** City (pop. 611), E central Texas, W of Austin. Birthplace of Pres. Lyndon B. Johnson.

Johnston, Albert Sidney, 1803–62, Confederate general. Commanded operations in West. Death at Shiloh (April 6, 1862) was severe loss to South.

Johnston, Joseph Eggleston, 1807–1901, Confederate general. For vital part played in first victory at Bull Run, made commander of Army of Northern Virginia. Opposed McClellan in PENINSULAR CAMPAIGN. Lost Vicksburg campaign (1863). Commanded Army of Tennessee in ATLANTA CAMPAIGN. Probably peer of R. E. Lee as defensive general.

Johnston, Mary, 1870–1936, American novelist. Her many works combining historical accuracy with stilted romance include *To Have and To Hold* (1900).

Johnston, town (pop. 17,160), W central R.I., suburb W of Providence.

Johnston Island, c.3,000 ft. long and c.600 ft. wide, central Pacific, c.760 mi. SW of Honolulu. Discovered 1807 by British, claimed 1858 by U.S. Became U.S. naval base 1941. Nuclear tests made in area 1962.

Johnstown. 1 City (pop. 10,390), E central N.Y., near Mohawk R., NW of Albany; founded 1762 by Sir William Johnson, whose home remains. Gloves are made. Elizabeth C. Stanton born here. Last Revolutionary battle in N.Y. fought nearby, Oct. 25, 1781. **2** Industrial city (pop. 53,949), SW Pa., on Conemaugh R. at mouth of Stony Creek ESE of Pittsburgh; settled 1794. A nucleus of heavy industry, with iron and steel mfg. First Kelly pneumatic converter for transformation of crude iron into steel built here, 1862. Johnstown flood (May 31, 1889) resulted in great loss of life.

John the Baptist, Saint, fl. A.D. c.29, prophet, cousin of JESUS, son of Zacharias and Elizabeth. An ascetic, he urged people to repent and prepare for the Messiah. Venerated by Christians as forerunner of Jesus, whose coming he heralded. Jesus was baptized by him before beginning His mission. At instigation of Herodias (see HEROD) and SALOME, John was beheaded. Mat.

11.1–19; 17.11–13; Mark 6.16–19; Luke 1; 3; John 1. Birthday observed June 24; feast of his beheading, Aug. 29.

John the Fearless, 1371–1419, duke of Burgundy (1404–19); son of PHILIP THE BOLD. Captured by Turks at Nikopol (1396), but ransomed. Inherited his father's feud with Louis d'ORLÉANS, whom he had murdered (1407). During the resulting struggle between ARMAGNACS and BURGUNDIANS he controlled Paris 1411–13 and again from 1418. Connived with English in Hundred Years War but continued to negotiate with Armagnacs. Assassinated during interview with the dauphin (later Charles VII). His son PHILIP THE GOOD succeeded him.

Johore (jōhôr′), state (7,330 sq. mi.; pop. c.930,000), MALAYA, at S tip of Malay Peninsula opposite Singapore; cap. Johore Bahru. Largely jungle, with great rubber plantations. Ruled by a sultan, it accepted British protectorate in 1914.

joint, in anatomy, articulation between bones. Types of joints allowing free movement are ball-and-socket (hip), hinge (knee), gliding (wrist). Joints may be immovable as in skull or permit limited movement as in spinal column.

Joinville, Jean, sire de (zhă′ sēr′ dù zhwĕvēl′), 1224?–1317?, French chronicler, biographer of Louis IX (St. Louis). Went on Seventh Crusade 1248–54. His memoirs of St. Louis are invaluable record of the king, of feudal France, and of the crusade.

Jokai, Maurice (yō′koi), 1825–1904, Hungarian novelist, a prolific, popular writer. Many novels have been translated into English (e.g., *An Hungarian Nabob; Black Diamonds*).

Jokulsa (yû′kûlsou), Icelandic *Jökulsá,* river, c.130 mi. long, rising in central Iceland and flowing N into Axar Fjord. DETTIFOSS waterfall is on it.

Joliet, Louis: see JOLLIET, LOUIS.

Joliet (jo′lēĕt″), industrial city (pop. 66,780), NE Ill., on Des Plaines R., SW of Chicago; settled 1831. River port and rail center. Limestone quarries and coal mines in area. Seat of Col. of St. Francis.

Joliette (zhôlyĕt′), city (pop. 18,088), S Que., Canada, on L'Assomption R. and NNE of Montreal. Has quarrying and steel, textile, and paper mills. Seat of Séminaire de Joliette.

Joliot-Curie, Frédéric (frädärĕk′ zhôlyô′-kürē′), 1900–1958, and **Irène Joliot-Curie** (ērĕn′) 1897–1956, French scientists. They won the 1935 Nobel Prize in Chemistry for artificial production of radioactive elements by bombarding certain nonradioactive elements with alpha particles.

Jolliet or **Joliet, Louis** (both: jō′lēĕt″, jō″lēĕt′, Fr. lwē′ zhôlyā′), 1645–1700, French explorer, b. Canada; joint discoverer with Jacques MARQUETTE of upper Mississippi R.

Jolson, Al (jōl′sún), 1888–1950, American entertainer, whose real name was Asa Yoelson. Came to U.S. c.1895. First sang his "mammy" song in blackface in San Francisco 1909. Began film work with *The Jazz Singer* (1927), the first film with dialogue.

Jonah (jō′–), **Jonas,** or **Jona,** book of Old Testament. Tells of Jonah, a prophet, who tried to avoid his mission by sailing away. His presence on ship was a curse; a violent storm arose. Jonah agreed to be thrown overboard. He was swallowed by a fish and after three days left on shore, alive and now ready to preach. Jonah's escape from fish regarded as foreshadowing resurrection of Jesus. Story alluded to later in Bible: Mat. 12.39–41; 16.4; Luke 11.29–30.

Jonah, Rabbi, or **Abu-l-Walid Merwan ibn Janah** (ä′bōolwä′lĕd mĕr′wän ī′bùn jä′nä), c.990–c.1050, Hebrew lexicographer and grammarian, b. Córdoba, Spain. His *Book of Hebrew Roots* strongly influenced later Hebrew lexicography.

Jonas, Greek form of Hebrew JONAH.

Jonathan (jŏn′–). **1** Oldest son of Saul, brave and gallant hero. Killed in battle of Mt. Gilboa. His close friendship with David is proverbial. 1 Sam. 13; 14; 18.1–4; 19.1–7; 20; 31.1,2. **2** One of the MACCABEES.

Jones, Anson, 1798–1858, last president of the Texas republic (1844–46).

Jones, Casey, 1863–1900, American locomotive engineer famous in ballad and song. Real name was John Luther Jones. His application of brakes saved passengers in crash of *Cannon Ball* express on April 30, 1900, at Vaughan, Miss.; Jones was killed.

Jones, David (Michael), 1895–, English painter and poet of Welsh descent. His works include *In Parenthesis* (on First World War, 1938) and *The Anathemata* (poems, 1952). Selected essays are in *Epoch and Artist* (1959).

Jones, Sir Edward Burne-: see BURNE-JONES.

Jones, Ernest, 1879–1958, British psychoanalyst. Credited with introducing psychoanalytical study into England and U.S. Writings include authoritative biography of Freud.

Jones, Henry: see CAVENDISH.

Jones, Henry Arthur, 1851–1929, English playwright. Some of his many successful plays (e.g., *The Liars,* 1897) contained social and moral criticism.

Jones, Howard Mumford, 1892–, American author. Professor of English at Harvard 1936–60. Wrote on American literature and culture (e.g., *The Theory of American Literature,* 1947; rev. ed., 1966). Author of the influential *Guide to American Literature and its Backgrounds since 1890* (3d ed., with R. M. Ludwig, 1964).

Jones, Inigo, 1573–1652, earliest of England's great architects. Traveled in Italy, where he closely studied Renaissance buildings of Palladio. In 1619 began his finest work, the royal banquet hall in Whitehall, London, which marked starting point for classic architecture of late Renaissance and Georgian periods in England. Designed settings for masques performed at court of James I and Charles I.

Jones, James, 1921–, American novelist. His first book was *From Here to Eternity* (1951), a powerful story of army life in Hawaii just before Pearl Harbor. *The Thin Red Line* (1962) concerns American soldiers in battle.

Jones, Jesse (Holman), 1874–1956, U.S. Secretary of Commerce (1940–45). Was director of Reconstruction Finance Corporation 1932–39, chairman of RFC board 1933–39.

Jones, John Paul, 1747–92, American naval hero, b. near Kirkcudbright, Scotland. Raided shores of British Isles in command of *Ranger* (1778). Captured frigate *Serapis* (1779) but his own ship, *Bon Homme Richard,* sank; this memorable victory was little noticed at the time. Later served in Russian navy.

Jones, Le Roi, 1934–, American Negro writer whose works include poetry (e.g., *Preface to a Twenty Volume Suicide Note,* 1961; *The Dead Lecturer,* 1964), plays (e.g., *Dutchman* and *The Slave,* 1964), a novel (*The System of Dante's Hell,* 1965), and social essays (*Home,* 1966).

Jones, Mary (Harris), 1830–1930, American labor agitator, called Mother Jones.

Jones, Owen, 1809–74, English architect and writer. His *Grammar of Ornament* (1856) is standard work on decorative arts.

Jones, Robert Edmond, 1887–1954, American scene designer; studied with G. P. Baker and Max Reinhardt. His use of color and dramatic lighting to enhance his imaginative sets began a new era of scene design. Notable designs were for *Macbeth, Richard III, Hamlet, The Green Pastures,* and for the plays of O'Neill with the Provincetown Players.

Jones, Robert Tyre, Jr. (Bobby Jones), 1902–, American golfer. Won Natl. Open (1923, 1926, 1929), Natl. Amateur (1924–25, 1927–28), British Open (1926–27). First golfer to win (1926) Natl. and British Open tournaments same year. Only golfer ever to score "grand slam"–winning (1930) Natl. Open, Natl. Amateur, British Open, and British Amateur.

Jones, Rufus M(atthew), 1863–1948, American writer on mysticism and minister of Society of Friends. A teacher at Haverford Col. (1893–1934) and a founder of American Friends Service Committee (1917).

Jones, Sir William, 1746–94, English philologist and jurist, one of greatest scholars of England. He was famous in jurisprudence and for translations from Greek and Oriental languages. He was first to suggest that Sanskrit originated from the same source as Latin and Greek, thus laying foundation for modern comparative philology.

Jones Beach, state park, 2,413 acres, on sandy island off S shore of Long Isl., SE N.Y.; estab. 1929. Has 2½ mi. of fine beaches and a marine stadium.

Jonesboro. 1 City (1963 pop. 23,944), NE Ark., in hilly region WSW of Blytheville; founded 1859. Trade and distributing center for large farm area (livestock, cotton, rice, soybeans, corn, fruit). ARKANSAS STATE COLLEGE is nearby. **2** City (pop. 3,014), W central Ga., S of Atlanta, in farm area; settled 1823. Site of battle (1864) in Sherman's Atlanta campaign is nearby. **3** Town (pop. 1,148), NE Tenn., WSW of Johnson City; laid out 1779. Oldest town in state, it was first cap. of State of FRANKLIN. Andrew Jackson admitted to law practice here, 1788. One of first abolitionist newspapers in U.S. estab. here 1819.

Jongkind, Johann Barthold (yōhän' bär'tôlt yông'kīnt), 1819–91, Dutch landscape painter and etcher. Worked mainly in France. Paintings have elements of both naturalism and impressionism.

Jonkoping, Swed. *Jönköping* (yûn'chû"pîng), city (pop. 50,941), co. seat of Jonkoping co., S central Sweden, on Vattern L.; chartered 1284. Has some of world's largest match factories (founded 1844). In 1620 Gustavus Adolphus gave it special privileges after citizens had burned it to avoid sack by Danes.

Jonquière (zhōkyĕr'), city (pop. 28,588), S Que., Canada, on Sable R., SW of Chicoutimi. Paper and pulp mills.

jonquil: see NARCISSUS.

Jonson, Ben, 1572–1637, English dramatist and lyric poet, an actor. His life and works bridge the Elizabethan and Jacobean periods. His comedies, such as *Every Man in His Humour* (1598), *Every Man Out of His Humour* (1599), were capped by *Volpone* (1606), *Epicoene* (1609), *The Alchemist* (1610), and *Bartholomew Fair* (1614). His tragedies *Sejanus* and *Catiline* were much praised in his time. His nondramatic poems showed the same neoclassic influence as his plays. Of his graceful lyrics the most familiar today is "Song to Celia" ("Drink to me only with thine eyes"). He had much influence on a group of younger poets called "the tribe of Ben." He was a friend of Shakespeare, Donne, and the other great of his age. His tomb in Westminster Abbey has the inscription "O rare Ben Jonson."

Jonsson, Einar (ā'när yōn'sôn), 1874–1954, Icelandic sculptor and painter. His work is housed in a special museum in Reykjavik, Iceland.

Joplin, city (pop. 38,958), SW Mo., at edge of Ozarks, WSW of Springfield; settled c.1840. Rail, shipping, and processing center of grain and livestock region. Dairying and fruitgrowing; lead and zinc mines in area.

Joppa, Israel: see JAFFA.

Joram (jō'–), kings of Israel and Judah: see JEHORAM.

Jordaens, Jacob (yä'kôp yôr'däns), 1593–1678, Flemish painter. Like his master Rubens he excelled in large allegorical paintings and portraits. Ranks among great masters of Flemish school.

Jordan, kingdom (c.37,500 sq. mi.; est. pop. 1,724,-800). SW Asia; cap. Amman. Formerly called Trans-Jordan or Transjordania. Bordered by Saudi Arabia on E and S and by Israel on W. Only outlet to the sea is Aqaba, port on Gulf of Aqaba. Mainly arid and mountainous. Wheat, vegetables, and fruits are grown. Country roughly corresponds to biblical lands of Edom, Ammon, Moab, and Bashan, and to the lordships of Montreal and Krak in the Latin Kingdom of Jerusalem. Under the Ottoman Empire from 16th cent. to 1918. In 1920 it was part of short-lived kingdom of Syria. Originally part of British mandate of PALESTINE, it was estab. as semi-independent emirate under ABDULLAH in 1923. Agreement of 1928 made Britain suzerain, with right to maintain garrisons. In 1946 mandate was ended and kingdom proclaimed. Treaty in 1948 provided for annual British subsidy for its famed Arab Legion. After partition of Palestine (1948) it joined other members of ARAB LEAGUE in armed attack against Israel. When truce was made in 1949 its forces held most of the Palestinian area that had been designated Arab territory by UN. Annexation in 1950 of occupied area (c.2,350 sq. mi.) was strongly resented by other Arab countries. Almost half the population is made up of Arab refugees from Palestine. Jordan had difficulties not only with Israel but also with the United Arab Republic and with Iraq formed the short-lived Arab Union. Following Abdullah's assassination, Talal was king (1951–52), to be succeeded by his son Hussein I. Treaty relationship with Britain ended after the Suez crisis. Jordan's independence was supported by U.S., Iraqi, and Saudi Arabian aid. Accepted temporary British protection following the Iraqi revolution (1958). Border clashes with Israel and unhappy diplomatic relations after Israel diverted (1964) water from Jordan R. to Negev. Mutual assistance pact signed with Egypt in 1967 after Egyptian blockade of Gulf of Aqaba to Israeli shipping. In brief Arab-Israeli war in June, Jordan lost Old City of Jerusalem and territory W of Jordan R.

Jordan, the great river of Palestine, rising in Anti-Lebanon mts. and flowing c.230 mi. S to Dead Sea. Jordan contains S half of river; N half marks part of Israel-Jordan and Israel-Syria borders. In Israel the river is used to irrigate NEGEV. Jordan valley is called the Ghor and is northernmost part of Great Rift Valley. Often mentioned in the Bible; it was scene of baptism of Christ.

Jordan, river, N central Utah, flowing c.60 mi. N, from Utah L., past Salt Lake City, to Great Salt L.

Josaphat (jŏ′sŭfăt), in Bible: see JEHOSHAPHAT.

Josaphat, in literature: see BARLAAM AND JOSAPHAT.

Joseph, Saint, husband of Mary, a carpenter of Nazareth, descended from royal line of David. Mat. 1; Luke 2; John 1.45; Mat. 13.55. Much honored by Orthodox and Roman Catholics as foster father of Jesus and chaste spouse of Mary the Virgin. Feast: March 19.

Joseph, emperors (also kings of Hungary and Bohemia). **Joseph I,** 1678–1711. His reign (1705–11) was taken up with the War of the SPANISH SUCCESSION and the rebellion of Hungary under Francis II RAKOCZY. **Joseph II,** 1741–90, son of Francis I and MARIA THERESA. Ruled Hungary, Bohemia, and hereditary Hapsburg lands jointly with his mother from 1765 till her death (1780). Succeeded Francis I as emperor 1765. A revolutionary reformer and "benevolent despot," he sought to raise the miserable condition of his people and to centralize his administration by a series of radical decrees, but his impatience undid much of his work in his own lifetime. Falling far short of his aim of abolishing hereditary and ecclesiastic privileges, he nevertheless abolished serfdom and feudal dues (1781); enabled peasants to buy land cheaply; granted wide religious tolerance (1781); abolished judicial torture; humanized the penal code; created two degrees of appeal. He took anticlerical measures, forbidding religious orders to obey foreign generals and suppressing all contemplative orders, and was unmoved by a personal visit of Pope PIUS VI. His schemes for a single land tax and for providing free food and medical care for the indigent were failures. His bullying attempts to centralize all administration provoked revolts in the Austrian Netherlands and in Hungary. His plan to annex Bavaria was frustrated by the War of the BAVARIAN SUCCESSION; his project to exchange his part of the Netherlands for Bavaria was thwarted by Frederick II of Prussia, who formed the *Fürstenbund*

[princes' league] for the purpose (1785). His anti-Turkish alliance with Catherine II of Russia brought Austria no advantage.

Joseph, 1714-77, king of Portugal (1750–77). His reign was dominated by his minister POMBAL.

Joseph, in Bible. 1 Favored son of Jacob. Sold into slavery by his jealous brothers, he was taken to Egypt. Imprisoned because of false accusation by the wife of his master (Potiphar), but released after he interpreted Pharaoh's dream. He became governor of Egypt and was reunited with his father and brothers when he helped them during a famine. Gen. 30; 37; 39–50. Story has been expanded in Joseph and Asenath (see PSEUDEPIGRAPHA) and in works of Thomas Mann. 2 See JOSEPH, SAINT.

Joseph (Chief Joseph), c.1840–1904, American Indian leader, chief of the Nez Percé Indians. Since his tribe refused to recognize land cessions made to U.S. in 1863, he undertook to lead them to Canada (1877). Forced to surrender to U.S. troops after winning several engagements, notably one at Big Hole, Mont. (battle site now a national battlefield).

Joseph, Father, 1577–1638, French Capuchin monk, confidant and agent of Cardinal Richelieu; called "Gray Eminence"; lay name François Leclerc du Tremblay. He dreamed of restoring Catholicism throughout Europe but advanced a policy of supporting Protestant states and the Turks against the house of Hapsburg. Rumor made him the cardinal's evil genius, but actually he was probably simply a tool.

Joseph Barsabas, competitor of Matthias for place among the disciples left vacant by Judas Iscariot. Matthias was chosen. Acts 1.23.

Josephine (Marie Josèphe Rose Tascher de la Pagerie), 1763–1814, empress of the French, b. Martinique. Her first husband, Alexandre de BEAUHARNAIS, was guillotined 1794, but she escaped persecution through friendship with Barras. Married Napoleon Bonaparte 1796. He ignored her many indiscretions but had marriage annulled (1809) because of her alleged sterility. Died in retirement at Malmaison.

Joseph of Arimathea, Saint (ă″rĭmŭthē′ù), man who gave body of Jesus decent burial. Mat. 27.57–61; Mark 15.42–47; Luke 23.50–56; John 19.38–42. Grateful Christendom has always honored him.

Josephus, Flavius (flă′vēùs jōsē′fùs), A.D. 37–A.D. 95?, Jewish historian and soldier. Thoroughly Romanized, he won the favor of Vespasian. Wrote *The Jewish War; Antiquities of the Jews; Against Apion* (a defense of the Jews); and an autobiography.

Joses (jō′–) [Gr.,= Heb. Joseph]. 1 Kinsman of Jesus. Mark 6.3; Mat. 13.55. 2 Brother of James the Less; may be same as 1. Mat. 27.56; Mark 15.40,47.

Josetsu (jō″sä′tsŏŏ), fl. 1425, Japanese landscape painter, a priest. His work has characteristics of Ming painting.

Joshua (jō′–) or **Josue** (jō′sŭē), book of Old Testament. Its hero is Joshua, successor of Moses as leader of the Hebrews. Moses had brought the people to edge of Canaan, the Promised Land; it was Joshua's task to lead them into the country, conquer it, and divide the land among the tribes. Well-known events of book: fall of Jericho; battle in Ajalon valley where the sun stood still. Other forms of Joshua are Hoshea, Jehoshua, Jehoshuah, Jeshua, and Jesus.

Joshua tree: see YUCCA.

Joshua Tree National Monument: see NATIONAL PARKS AND MONUMENTS (table).

Josiah (jōsī′ù) or **Josias** (jōsī′ùs), d. c.610 B.C., king of Judah (c.641–c.610 B.C.). Chief event of his reign was discovery of old book of the law, apparently Deuteronomy, in the Temple. Josiah had it read publicly and led a reform movement to concentrate worship at Jerusalem. He later fell in battle against Egypt. 2 Kings 22–23; 2 Chron. 34–35.

Josquin Desprez (zhōs′kĕn dĕprā′), c.1440–1521, Flemish composer, considered by his contemporaries as the greatest of his age. Surpassed older Flemish masters (who relied upon COUNTERPOINT) by introducing new textures.

Jostedalsbreen (yŏ'stŭdälsbrä"ŭn), glacier, area 340 sq. mi., Sogn og Fjordane co., W Norway, W of Jotunheim mts. Largest icefield on European mainland, it rises to 6,700 ft.

Josue, variant of JOSHUA.

Jotham (jŏ'-). **1** Only son of Gideon not killed by Abimelech. Told parable of the trees electing bramble as king. Judges 9.5–21. **2** Died c.731 B.C., king of Judah (c.735–731 B.C.); contemporary of Isaiah, Hosea, Micah. 2 Kings 15.5,32–38.

Jotunheim (yŏ'tŏonhäm), mountain group, central Norway, highest of Scandinavia, rising to 8,098 ft. in Galdhoppigen and to 8,138 ft. in Glittertind. JOSTEDALSBREEN glacier is W. Supports summer grazing. In Norse mythology, it was home of the giants.

Jouett, Matthew Harris, 1787–1827, American portrait painter, b. Ky. Studied with Gilbert Stuart.

Jouhaux, Léon (lāŏ' zhŏō-ŏ'), 1879–1954, French Socialist labor leader. Headed Confédération générale du Travail 1909–47, organized Internatl. Confederation of Free Trade Unions 1949. Prominent in Internatl. Labor Organization. Was awarded 1951 Nobel Peace Prize.

Joule, James Prescott (jŏōl), 1818–89, English physicist. Made studies in electricity, thermodynamics, and was first to determine mechanical equivalent of heat. Electrical unit the **joule** (joul) is named for him. It is work done in one second in maintaining current of one ampere in resistance of one ohm.

Jourdan, Jean Baptiste (zhä' bäptēst' zhŏōrdä'), 1762–1833, marshal of France. Fought in American Revolution and in FRENCH REVOLUTIONARY WARS.

journalism, collection and periodical publication of news. Includes writing for, editing, and managing such media as the NEWSPAPER and the PERIODICAL. Journalism had real beginnings at end of 18th cent. Until freedom of speech was instituted, journalism served as handmaiden of politics or a means of business. Growth of individualistic leadership in newspaper field in U.S. in 19th cent. (see GREELEY, HORACE; BOWLES, SAMUEL) in turn influenced other journalistic media. In 20th cent., power of individualistic journalist declined in the face of technological advances, growth of the news agency, vast strides in reporting techniques, broadening of education and reform, and growth of advertising. Earliest school of journalism in U.S. was estab. at Univ. of Missouri in 1908.

Jouvenet, Jean (zhä' zhŏōvŭnä'), 1644–1717, French painter, known for religious pictures. Worked in Paris studio of Charles Le Brun.

Jouvet, Louis (zhŏōvä'), 1887–1951, French actor, producer, and director. Organizing his own theater 1922), he presented plays of Molière, Cocteau, and Giraudoux. His films include *Carnival in Flanders,* *Dr. Knock,* and *Volpone.*

Jove, another name for JUPITER.

Jovellanos, Gaspar Melchor de (gäspär' mělchôr' dä hŏvělyä'nōs), 1744–1811, Spanish writer and statesman. Well known for his diary of the years 1790–1801.

Jovian (jŏ'vēŭn), c.331–364, Roman Emperor (363–64). Returned Christianity to privileged position it had enjoyed before Julian the Apostate.

Jowett, Benjamin (jou'ĕt), 1817–93, English Greek scholar, an Anglican clergyman, master of Balliol College, Oxford, and vice chancellor of Oxford, one of greatest educators England has had. His translations of dialogues of Plato are famous.

Joyce, James, 1882–1941, Irish novelist, b. Dublin; spent almost all adult life in "exile" on Continent. First published works were poems in *Chamber Music* (1907; later included with *Pomes Penyeach* and *Ecce Puer* in *Poems,* 1937). His *Dubliners* (1914) was a linked collection of stories, his *Portrait of the Artist As a Young Man* (1916) a novel that foreshadowed the two great novels that made Joyce a major figure of world litera-

ture—*Ulysses* (1922; banned in U.S. for indecency until 1933) and *Finnegans Wake* (1939). His labyrinthine prose explores many levels of meaning, both conscious and unconscious, and employs many linguistic devices, including many-faceted puns. His influence on writing has been great, though he has few direct imitators.

Juana Inés de la Cruz (hwä'nä ēnäs' dä lä krōōs'), 1651–95, Mexican poet, generally considered greatest lyric poet of colonial Spanish America. Became a nun in Mexico at 16 or 17, devoting her life to pursuit of knowledge. Her poems are marked by spontaneity and sincerity. Family name Asbaje.

Juana la Beltraneja (hwä'nä lä běltränä'hä), 1462–1530, Castilian princess. Her legal father was Henry IV of Castile; her presumed actual father, Beltrán de la Cueva, a courtier. Henry designated first his sister (later ISABELLA I), then Juana as successor. His death brought war between the two (1474–79). Juana, though aided by her husband Alfonso V of Portugal, lost and retired to a convent.

Juan de Fuca Strait (wän dŭ fū'kŭ), inlet of the Pacific, 100 mi. long and c.11–17 mi. wide, between Vancouver Isl. and Wash. state. Connects Strait of Georgia and Puget Sound with the Pacific. Discovered 1787 by Capt. C. W. Barkley.

Juanes, Juan de: see MACIP, VICENTE JUAN.

Juan Fernández (hwän' fērnän'däs), group of small islands (pop. c.900), c.400 mi. W of Valparaiso, Chile, belonging to Chile. Thought to be locale of Daniel Defoe's *Robinson Crusoe.*

Juan-les-Pins: see ANTIBES.

Juárez, Benito (bänē'tō hwä'räs), 1806–72, Mexican liberal statesman and national hero, an Indian. Led liberal opposition to conservative government of Santa Anna and was acting president during War of the Reform (1858–61). During French attempt at establishment of Mexican empire under Maximilian (1864–67), Juárez moved his capital to El Paso del Norte (now Juárez). His sturdy resistance defeated the French and destroyed the empire. Reelected president 1871, he died while suppressing a revolution led by Porfirio Díaz.

Juárez (hwä'räs), city (1965 est. pop. 385,082), Chihuahua, N Mexico, on Rio Grande opposite El Paso, Texas. Originally El Paso del Norte, it included settlements on both sides of river until close of Mexican War (1848). Name of Mexican town changed (1888) to honor Benito Juárez.

Juba (jŏō'bŭ), c.85 B.C.–46 B.C., king of Numidia. Fought for Pompey and ended his life after Caesar won at Thapsus. His young son, **Juba II,** d. A.D. c.20, was educated in Rome and reinstated as king probably first in Numidia, then Mauretania by Augustus. A very learned man, he wrote historical works.

Jubal, originator of musical instruments. Gen. 4.21.

Jubbulpore (jŭbŭlpōr'), city (pop. c.365,000), Madhya Pradesh, India. Ordnance-mfg. center.

jubilee, in Bible, a year when slaves were freed and debts forgiven. It occurred once in 50 years. Lev. 25.8–55. Name now used to mean celebration of a 50-year or longer period (e.g., Diamond Jubilee of Queen Victoria, 1897). In Roman Catholic Church name is applied to a holy year when special privileges are given by the Church for pilgrimages to Rome.

Jubilees, Book of: see PSEUDEPIGRAPHA.

Juda. 1 See JUDAH. **2** See JUDE, SAINT.

Judaea or **Judea** (both: jŏōdē'ŭ), Greco-Roman name (from Judah) for S Palestine, southernmost of Roman divisions of Palestine. At time of Christ it was part of province of Syria and a kingdom ruled by the Herods.

Judah I, 135?–220?, Jewish leader, called *ha-Nasi* [prince], editor of the Mishna (see TALMUD), president of Sanhedrin.

Judah, son of Jacob and ancestor of one of 12 tribes of Israel; a leader in family counsels, spokesman for his brothers before Joseph in Egypt. Tribe of Judah settled in S Palestine; gave its name to kingdom. Royal and Messianic line of David was of this tribe. Gen.

29.35; 35.23; 37.26; 38; 43.3; 44.14; 46.12,28; 49.8; Num. 2.3; 10.14; 13.6; 26.22; 34; Joshua 15.1; 1 Chron. 2–5. Juda: Luke 3.33; Heb. 7.14; Rev. 5.5; 7.5. Judas: Mat. 1.2.

Judah, Theodore Dehone, 1826–63, American railroad builder. Promoted idea of railroad across mountains E from Central Valley of Calif. Central Pacific RR Co. was formed, with Judah as chief engineer.

Judah, southern of the two kingdoms after division of Hebrew nation under REHOBOAM (N kingdom was Israel); cap. Jerusalem; dynasty, the house of David.

Judah Ha-Levi or **Halevy** (both: hä″lē′vī), 1085?–1140?, Jewish philosopher, foremost poet of the Middle Ages, b. Toledo. His elegy on Zion and dialogue *Kuzari* stress intimate connection between the soil and the soul of Israel.

Judaism (jōō′dūīzùm, –dē–) [from Judah; cf. Jews], religion of the Jews, oldest of the great monotheistic religions. It is the complex of law, tradition and doctrine consisting of the OLD TESTAMENT and the TALMUD. Its outstanding feature is its belief in an omnipotent God, and in his law, the TORAH, given by him to Moses, the leader of Israel, whom God had chosen as his people in the time of Abraham, the father of Israel. The great text of Judaism, the Shema, begins "Hear, O Israel: the Lord our God is one Lord" (Deut. 6.4–9). Circumcision of males is practiced as a sign of God's covenant with his people. The synagogue is primarily a place of meeting; the most elaborate feast of Judaism, the PASSOVER, is celebrated in the home. The rabbi is primarily a teacher. The principal Jewish sects of ancient times were the ESSENES, SADDUCEES, and the PHARISEES. In more modern times, the cabalists (see CABALA) and the HASIDIM are notable. In the 18th cent. appeared a new movement, Reformed Judaism. Unlike orthodox Jews, the reformed reject many of the restrictions of the Law, use the vernacular in religious ceremonies, and reduce much of the ritual. One group, the "conservatives," retains some orthodox customs. Judaism demands the recognition of God and the observance of the Law. The importance of the Law is seen in the development and preservation of the exalted ethical standards of Judaism.

Judas [Gr.,= Judah], in Bible. **1** See JUDE, SAINT. **2** See MACCABEES. **3** See JUDAS ISCARIOT.

Judas Iscariot (ĭskā′rēŭt), disciple who for 30 pieces of silver betrayed Jesus, identifying him for capture by kissing him. Judas hanged himself. Blood money went to buy potter's field, thenceforth called ACELDAMA. His place as one of the Twelve Apostles taken by Matthias. Mat. 26.20–25, 47–49; 27.3–10; Acts 1.16–20.

Judas Maccabeus: see MACCABEES.

Judas of Galilee, d. A.D. 7, leader of the ZEALOTS. Raised an insurrection against the Romans and was killed. Acts 5:37.

Judas tree: see REDBUD.

Judd, Orange, 1822–92, American agr. editor and publisher. His generosity helped estab. first experimental agr. station in U.S.

Jude, Saint [an Eng. form of Judas], one of the Twelve Apostles, also called Thaddaeus and Lebaeus. Tradition says he was martyred with St. Simon in Persia. Feast (with St. Simon): Oct. 28.

Jude, epistle of New Testament. Traditionally ascribed to St. Jude the Apostle, but many critics disagree. Book shows the danger of heresy in the church by citing examples from Old Testament.

Judea: see JUDAEA.

Judges, book of Old Testament; sequel to Joshua in biblical history, telling of the Hebrews in Canaan from death of Joshua up to time of Samuel. Tells of punishment of Hebrews by God for their apostasies and His raising up of leaders called judges to deliver them. Among these judges, mostly war heroes, were Samson, Gideon, Jephthah, Abimelech, and Deborah.

judgment, final decision of a court of law. It can be altered by a court of appeal, which rectifies error, but cannot be reconsidered from the beginning like a de-

cree. In criminal cases the judge gives a sentence in accord with the verdict of a jury. In civil cases, a judge normally awards damages (including legal costs). When a debtor fails to pay, the sheriff may seize his property.

Judith [Heb.,= the Jewess], book of Old Testament, placed in Apocrypha in AV, before Esther in Western canon. Tells of time when Palestine was occupied by foreign army led by Holofernes. Judith, a Jewish widow of great beauty, entered the enemy camp, gained the favor of Holofernes, and murdered him. The invaders, without a leader, were easily routed by the Jews. Story repeated in an Anglo-Saxon epic.

judo: see JUJUTSU.

Judson, Adoniram (ădŭnī′rŭm), 1788–1850, American Baptist missionary. Was leader of movement that led to formation of American Board of Commissioners for Foreign Missions. After two years in India as Congregational worker, he became a Baptist and transferred to Burma, where he spent most of his life as pioneer in Protestant mission work. Judson's first wife, Ann (Hasseltine) Judson (1789–1826), founded a girls' school at Rangoon. His second wife, Sarah (Hall) Boardman Judson (1803–45), translated *Pilgrim's Progress* into Burmese. His third wife, Emily (Chubbuck) Judson (1817–54), was an author, whose pseudonym was Fanny Forester. Judson wrote a Burmese grammar, Burmese dictionary, and translated the Bible into Burmese.

Judson, Edward Zane Carroll: see BUNTLINE, NED.

Jugendstil: see ART NOUVEAU.

Juggernaut, India: see PURI.

Jugoslavia: see YUGOSLAVIA.

Jugurtha (jōōgŭr′thŭ), c.156–104 B.C., king of Numidia, grandson of Masinissa. He was finally defeated after long warfare with the Romans through treachery of his father-in-law, Bocchus of Mauretania.

Juilliard School of Music (jōōl′yärd), in Manhattan borough of New York city; coed.; chartered 1926. In 1946, its two units, Juilliard Graduate School (1924) and Inst. of Musical Art (1905), were amalgamated. School is part of Lincoln Center for the Performing Arts.

Juin, Alphonse (älfōs′ zhüē′), 1888–1967, marshal of France, b. Algeria. Left Vichy government forces in N Africa to join Allies in Second World War (1942); led French forces in Italy (1943–44). Was NATO commander of central European ground forces (1951–53) and ground, air, and naval forces (1953–56). Opposed granting of independence to Algeria. At his death, Juin was the last surviving marshal of France.

Juiz de Fora (zhwēzh′ dù fô′rù), city (pop. c.125,000), S Minas Gerais state, E Brazil; industrial city.

jujube (jōō′jōōb), deciduous or evergreen spiny shrub or tree of genus *Zizyphus* of tropics and subtropics of both hemispheres. Long grown by Chinese for fruit used fresh, dried, or preserved.

jujutsu (jōōjōōt′sōō, –jīt′–) or **jiujitsu** (jōōjīt′sōō), Japanese method of defense and offense without weapons in personal encounter. Requires extensive training and detailed knowledge of anatomy. Probably imported from China, jujutsu was long exclusive property of Japanese nobility. By 20th cent. jujutsu had attracted attention in Europe, America. It was taught in U.S. Army in Second World War. Modified form called judo.

Jujuy (hōōhwē′), city (pop. c.52,000), cap. of Jujuy prov., NW Argentina, on Jujuy R.; founded 1593. Center of agr., cattle-raising, and mining region. Interesting Indian ruins nearby.

juke box: see PHONOGRAPH.

Jukes, fictitious name of a family studied through several generations by sociologists. R. L. DUGDALE concluded from study that feeble-mindedness, criminality, and degeneracy were inheritable characteristics. Theories have since been disproved.

Julia, feminine name in the family of the Caesars. **1** Died 54 B.C., daughter of Julius Caesar and wife of

Pompey. It was only after her death that warfare broke out between the two. 2 39 B.C.–A.D. 14, daughter of Augustus, wife of M. Claudius Marcellus, M. Vipsanius Agrippa, and Tiberius. Banished for gross immorality to the island of Pandataria, she died of starvation. 3 18 B.C.–A.D. 28, daughter of Julia 2 and Agrippa, also banished for immorality.

Julian, George Washington, 1817–99, American abolitionist, U.S. Representative from Ind. (1849–51, 1861–71). In later life a Liberal Republican and then a Democrat.

Juliana, 1909–, queen of Netherlands (1948–); daughter of Wilhelmina. Married (1937) Prince Bernhard of Lippe-Biesterfeld.

Julian Alps, mountain range, NE Italy and NW Yugoslavia; extends from Carnic Alps to Ljubljana region. Rises to c.9,362 ft. in Triglav, highest peak in Yugoslavia.

Julianehaab (yōōlyä′nühôp″), port and chief trade center (pop. 1,741) of Julianehaab dist. (pop. 2,407), SW Greenland. Sheep raising.

Julian the Apostate, 331?–363, Roman emperor (361–63); nephew of Constantine I. Both a scholar and an able general, he unsuccessfully tried to restore paganism, which to him meant the glory of antiquity. He did not institute systematic persecution of Christians and ruled justly and humanely.

Jülich (yü′lĭkh), former duchy, NW Germany, between Cologne and Aachen; historic cap. Jülich. At first a county, Jülich was united with county of Berg (1348) and made a duchy (1356). After extinction of Jülich line, both Jülich and Berg passed to dukes of Cleves (1521), to Palatinate-Neuburg branch of Wittelsbach dynasty (1666), to France (1806), to Prussia (1815).

Julier (yōōl′yŭr), pass, 7,507 ft. high, Grisons canton, Switzerland; connects Upper Engadine and Oberhalbstein valleys. Modern road built 1820–40.

Julius I, Saint, pope (337–52). When called upon for his opinion in the Arian controversy, he summoned a council at Rome (340). The Arians did not come, and Julius wrote them a letter, chiding them for lack of sincerity and asserting the papal claim to jurisdiction over the whole church. Feast: April 12.

Julius II, 1443–1513, pope (1503–13). As Giuliano della Rovere, created cardinal by his uncle Sixtus IV. As pope he completed work of Cesare Borgia (his enemy) of restoring Papal States to the Church. A warrior, he took a vigorous part in the Italian Wars. In 1512 Julius assembled the Fifth LATERAN COUNCIL, which condemned Gallicanism in France, abolished simony in the college of cardinals. A patron of art, he favored Raphael (for whom he sat), Michelangelo, and Bramante. He laid the cornerstone of St. Peter's.

Julius Caesar: see CAESAR, JULIUS.

Jullundur (jŭ′lŭndŭr), city (pop. 221,952), Punjab, India. Cap. of Punjab until Chandigarh was built.

July: see MONTH.

July Revolution, 1830, French revolution which deposed CHARLES X and created the bourgeois July Monarchy under LOUIS PHILIPPE. It resulted from the opposition of the propertied middle class, led by such men as THIERS, and of the radical workers in Paris to Charles's reactionary policies. The repressive, ultraroyalist July Ordinances under ministry of J. A. de POLIGNAC brought matters to a head. Revolution was over in two days.

Jumna (jŭm′nŭ), river, India. Rising in the Himalayas near Mt. Kamet, it flows c.850 mi. through Uttar Pradesh and joins the Ganges R. at ALLAHABAD.

Junagadh (jōō′nŭgäd″) or **Junagarh** (jōō′nŭgär″), former principality, India, on Kathiawar peninsula; a district of Gujarat since 1960. **Junagadh,** town (pop. 62,730), was former cap. Has Buddhist caves and Rajput forts.

Junagarh (jōō′nŭgär″) or **Junagadh** (jōō′nŭgäd″), former princely state, India, on Kathiawar peninsula; town 1956 part of Bombay state. **Junagarh,** town (pop. 62,-730), was Rajput stronghold until 15th cent.

junco or **snowbird,** bird of FINCH family. Slate-colored junco is a winter resident in E North America. About the size of a sparrow, it is dark gray with white abdomen. Other juncoes are in W and S U.S.

Junction City, city (pop. 18,700), NE Kansas, at junction of Republican and Smoky Hill rivers, W of Topeka; founded 1858. Rail and trade center of agr. and dairy area. Fort RILEY is nearby. Limestone quarries in vicinity.

June: see MONTH.

Juneau, Solomon Laurent (jōōnō′, jōō′nō), 1793–1856, French Canadian fur trader and founder of Milwaukee, Wis. Moved to fur post at Milwaukee in 1818; surveyed town site, built first store, became first mayor (1846).

Juneau (jōō′nō), city (pop. 6,797), state cap. (since 1960), in Alaskan Panhandle. Lies at foot of two peaks, Mt. Juneau and Mt. Roberts, on Gastineau Channel separating mainland from Douglas Isl.; settled 1881 as gold-rush town. Made territorial cap. 1900, began functioning as such 1906. Trade center for Panhandle area, with ice-free harbor, seaplane base, and airport. Has salmon and halibut fishing, lumbering, and tourism. Gold mining has almost ceased. Alaska Historical Library and Mus. is here.

June beetle, June bug, or **May beetle,** nocturnal blackish or mahogany-colored beetle of scarab family. Larvae (white grubs) eat underground roots.

Juneberry: see SHADBUSH.

June Days, 1848, in French history, insurrection of Parisian workers, brought on by government sabotage of national workshops established by Louis BLANC. Workers had played major part in FEBRUARY REVOLUTION, felt cheated of its fruits. Rebellion was ruthlessly put down by military in four days' fighting.

Jung, Carl Gustav (kärl gōōs′täf yōōng′), 1875–1961, Swiss psychiatrist, founded school of analytical psychology. As first president of International Psychoanalytic Association he was second only to Freud in the movement; they worked together until differences of approach caused a formal break (1913). Jung conceived of libido as primal, nonsexual energy and postulated two systems in the unconscious: the personal (repressed events of personal life) and the collective unconscious (archetypes of inherited tendencies). He introduced terms EXTROVERSION and introversion.

Jungaria, China: see DZUNGARIA.

Jünger, Ernst (yüng′ŭr), 1895–, German writer. His works seek solutions to social and political problems of his day. Among his writings are *Storm of Steel,* a novel of First World War (1919); diaries of Second World War; *Heliopolis* (1949); *Am Sarazenenturm* (1955).

Jungfrau (yōōng′frou) [Ger.,= Virgin], peak, 13,653 ft. high, Switzerland, in Bernese Alps. First ascended 1811. The **Jungfraujoch** (–yôkh″) is a mountain saddle 11,342 ft. high, highest point in Europe reached by rail. Has scientific institute and weather station.

Juniata (jōōnēä′tŭ), river of Pa., rising in Alleghenies and flowing 150 mi. E to Susquehanna R. above Harrisburg.

Junín (hōōnēn′), small town, W central Peru. Near here Bolívar aided by Sucre won first important battle (1824) in liberation of Peru from Spain.

juniper, evergreen tree or shrub of genus *Juniperus,* with berrylike fruits and needle- or scale-shaped leaves. Dwarf or pyramidal forms of the common juniper (*Juniperus communis*) of N Hemisphere are used in landscaping. Their fruits flavor gin. Wood of red cedar, a juniper (*J. virginiana*) native to E U.S., is much used for chests and closets; its oil is used in medicine and perfumery.

Junius, English political controversialist, anonymous writer of letters to London *Public Advertiser* (notably Jan., 1769–Jan., 1772) attacking the king's party and George III himself. Mystery of identity added interest to letters; most likely claimant seems to be Sir Philip Francis.

Juno (jōō'nō), in Roman religion, queen of gods; sister and wife of Jupiter. Like Greek goddess HERA, she was protector of women.

Junot, Andoche (ädōsh' zhünō'), 1771–1813, French general. Commanded French invasion of Portugal (1807); was driven out by Wellington (1808). Created duke of Abrantès by Napoleon. His wife, Laure Junot, duchesse d'Abrantès (1784–1838), was socially prominent during Restoration and left lively memoirs.

Jupiter [Latin,= God the father], in Roman religion, supreme god, also called Jove; son of Saturn and Ops and brother and husband of Juno. Identified with Olympian god Zeus.

Jupiter, in astronomy, largest PLANET (mean diameter c.88,700 mi.) of solar system. It revolves around the sun in 11.86 years at mean distance of 483,310,000 mi. in an orbit between Mars and Saturn. Mean rotation period is 9 hr. 55 min. It is enveloped by a thick atmosphere; has 12 known satellites. See *ill.*, p. 1017.

Jura (zhürä), department (1,952 sq. mi.; pop. 225,682), E France, in Franche-Comté; cap. Lons-le-Saunier.

Jura (jōō'rü), mountain range, E France (Jura and Doubs depts.) and W Switzerland (Vaud, Neuchâtel, Bern, Solothurn, and Basel cantons). Extends in parallel ridges from the Rhine R. at Basel to Rhone R. at Geneva; rises above 5,500 ft. Pine forests, pastures, agr. Watch industry in many towns (e.g., Le Locle, La Chaux-de-Fonds). Many resorts. Formed of sandstone and limestone rich in fossils. Jura gives name to Jurassic period. Mountains of S Baden-Württemberg are called the Swabian Jura.

Jurassic period (jōōrä'sĭk), second period of the MESO-ZOIC ERA of geologic time. As in Triassic period E North America was continuously elevated and subject to erosion which reduced the Appalachians to a peneplain. Deserts at first prevailed in SW U.S., but this region was later flooded from the N, and sediments were deposited. The period's close was marked by mountain making and lava intrusions in the W; to the E, by upwarping of the Appalachian peneplain. Reptiles dominated sea, land, air. Plant life included cycads, conifers, tree ferns. See also GEOLOGIC ERAS, table.

Jurieu, Pierre (pyěr' zhüryû'), 1637–1713, French Protestant theologian and Calvinist controversialist. Took refuge in Rotterdam after publication (1681) of *La Politique du clergé de France*, an attempt to preserve Huguenot liberties. Attacked Arnauld, Bossuet, and others in controversial works.

jurisprudence, study of the nature, origin, and development of law. Prevailing concept from 13th to 19th cent. was that of natural law—that laws took their sanction from a law of nature estab. by divine ordinance. In 19th cent. there grew up theories that law depends only on sovereign decree or custom of the culture, divorced from theology or morality. Other schools of thought are the historical (that law is the product of development) and the sociological (that law expresses the dominant social pattern in a nation or the community.)

Jurjan, Iran: see GORGAN.

Juruá (zhōōrwä'), river, c.2,000 mi. long, rising in E Peru, flowing generally NE through Brazil to Amazon. Important during wild-rubber boom.

jury, in Anglo-Norman times, body of men brought together to decide from personal knowledge in an inquest what the facts were. Institution gradually developed until it became before the 18th cent. the symbolic and actual protection against tyranny for all Englishmen. It was incorporated into the U.S. constitution. At present, two types of juries are used, the grand jury (in criminal cases passing preliminarily on the INDICTMENT) and the petit jury (deciding factual issues at trial). The petit jury's decision is binding on the judge as to the facts of a case if supported by substantial evidence. Selection of petit juries is essentially alike in criminal and civil trials. A group of prospective jurors (the venire) is summoned for examination. Counsel may challenge the whole group or any individuals as unfit. A grand jury usually has 12 to 23 members, a petit jury 12 (or less, according to state law). A petit jury takes an oath to reach a fair decision on evidence (the verdict). On the Continent, jury trials are restricted to criminal cases of great importance.

Jusserand, Jean Jules (zhä' zhül' zhüsürä'), 1855–1932, French diplomat and scholar. As ambassador to Washington (1902–25) he was extremely popular. Among his works are *English Wayfaring Life in the Middle Ages* (1889) and an incomplete autobiography (1933).

Jussieu (zhüsyû'), name of a French family of botanists. **Antoine de Jussieu** (ätwän' dü), 1686–1758, was director of the Jardin des Plantes, Paris, and editor of botanical works. His brother **Bernard de Jussieu** (běrnär'), 1699–1777?, was director of gardens at Trianon, Versailles, and developer of a classification system. Another brother, **Joseph de Jussieu** (zhôsěf), 1704–79, traveled in South America and introduced into Europe many plants (e.g., heliotrope) from there. A nephew, **Antoine Laurent de Jussieu** (lōrä'), 1748–1836, elaborated Bernard's system of classification in his *Genera plantarum* (1789). He was professor at the Museum of Natural History, Paris, and organized its botanical collection. His son, **Adrien de Jussieu** (ädrēě'), 1797–1853, was also professor of botany at the museum.

Justi, Karl (kärl' yōōs'tē), 1832–1912, German art historian, wrote on Winckelmann, Velásquez, and Michelangelo. Taught at Univ. of Bonn.

Justice, United States Department of, created by act of Congress in 1870. Office of U.S. Attorney General became nucleus of department. Act of 1870 also set up office of Solicitor General to represent government in Supreme Court cases and empowered creation of assistants to aid Attorney General in administering department. Department furnishes legal counsel in Federal cases, provides means for enforcing Federal laws, and officially construes laws—subject to court decisions —under which government officials act. Department consists of eight specialized divisions (e.g., Antitrust Division), three bureaus (e.g., FEDERAL BUREAU OF IN-VESTIGATION), and two boards.

Justin I, c.450–527, Byzantine emperor (518–27). Chief of imperial guard, he seized power on death of Anastasius I. He was illiterate and entrusted the government to his nephew, Justinian I.

Justinian I, 483–565, Byzantine emperor (527–65); nephew of JUSTIN I. His reign was a rebirth of imperial greatness. His generals BELISARIUS and NARSES recovered Africa from the Vandals and Italy from the Ostrogoths. The *Nika* riot, caused by discontent with heavy taxation and his hostility to Monophysitism, was crushed by the firm stand of Empress THEODORA (532). Justinian advocated caesaropapism—the supremacy of the emperor over the Church—and in 553 called the Second Council of Constantinople in an attempt to reconcile the Monophysites. His chief accomplishment was the codification of Roman law (see CORPUS JURIS CIVILIS). He also had the Church of HAGIA SOPHIA built.

Justin Martyr, Saint, A.D. c.100–c.165, Christian apologist, b. Palestine. Converted to Christianity at c.38, he was finally martyred with disciples at Rome. Two undisputed works (in Greek) remain, both philosophic defenses of Christian doctrine—the *Apology* and the *Dialogue*. Feast: April 14.

Justin Morgan, 1792–1821, American horse, foundation sire of Justin Morgan breed, which preceded Hambletonian strain as favored type of trotting horse in U.S.

jute (jōōt), annual tropical plant (*Corchorus capsularis*) grown for fiber which lies between outer bark and central wood. The fiber, widely used, is cheap, easily spun and dyed. Burlap, webbing, twines, backing yarns for carpets and linoleum, oakum, paper, etc., are made from jute. Calcutta is leading manufacturer and exporter, but the plant can be grown in any hot humid country.

Jutes: see ANGLO-SAXONS; KENT, KINGDOM OF.

Jutland, Dan. *Jylland,* Ger. *Jütland,* peninsula, N Europe, comprising continental Denmark and German SCHLESWIG N of Eider R.; bounded on N by the Skagerrak and W by North Sea. Danish Jutland, including adjacent islands, has area of 11,441 sq. mi. and pop. of 2,018,168. Dairying and cattle raising are chief occupations on fertile and densely populated E coast. Aarhus, Aalborg, and Frederickshavn are main ports here. Jutland has many lakes and is crossed by Guden R. South Jutland is name applied in Denmark to N part of former duchy of Schleswig. The **battle of Jutland,** May 31, 1916, chief naval engagement of First World War, was fought c.60 mi. W of Jutland coast; also known as battle of the Skagerrak. Although the German fleet, brilliantly commanded by admirals Hipper and Scheer, suffered lighter losses than the British (under Beatty and Jellicoe), it was forced to return to its bases and remain there.

Juvarra, Filippo (fēlēp'pō yōōvär'rä), 1678–1736, Italian architect of the late baroque period.

Juvenal (Decimus Junius Juvenalis) (jōō'vùnùl), 1st–2d cent. A.D., Roman satirical poet. His 16 savage satires, in denouncing the criminal excesses, immorality, and tyranny of the Romans, give a vivid picture of the society.

juvenile delinquency, behavior of children and adolescents which in adults would be judged criminal (see CRIME). Maximum age of juveniles is variously defined, from 14 to 21 years. Delinquency frequently arises from bad family situations, and it persists in slum neighborhoods. Though juvenile corrective institutions have been separated from regular prisons since early 19th cent., the separate judgment of youth was developed only after 1899 in the juvenile court, and the rehabilitation of delinquents, though benefit-

ing from improved psychiatric and sociological programs, is still recognizably inadequate.

juvenile literature. Before printing began, children's Latin school texts by Bede (7th cent.) and Ælfric existed, but only with Caxton's printing of Aesop's fables (1484) and the invention of the hornbook did children have their own copies. John NEWBERY, 18th-cent. publisher, first made small books expressly for children. Many 18th-cent. children's stories were didactic, as were Sunday school tales of the 19th cent. Charles and Mary Lamb on Shakespeare, the fairy tales of the brothers Grimm, and stories by Hans Christian Andersen, all before 1850, began the "children's classics" which proliferated until 1920 in England (e.g., books by Edward Lear, John Ruskin, Lewis Carroll, Robert Louis Stevenson, Rudyard Kipling) and the U.S. (e.g., works by Joel Chandler Harris, Mark Twain). Didactic series (e.g., by Horatio Alger) had begun earlier, but after 1920 they swelled into big business—series on history, biography, sports, occupations, science, and mystery, adventure, science fiction. Famous 19th-cent. illustrators (e.g., Cruikshank, Tenniel, Greenaway, Caldecott) made pictures integral to children's books (as in works of Howard Pyle, N. C. Wyeth, Arthur Rackham); today some artists also write their books (e.g., Wanda Gag, Dr. Seuss, Ludwig Bemelmans). Some animal books follow Beatrix Potter, Kenneth Grahame, and Dr. Doolittle in personifying animals; and the line between juvenile and adult reading blurs in the work of such authors as A. A. Milne, E. B. White, and T. H. White. Juvenile books are reviewed in periodicals such as *The Hornbook* (U.S.) and *The Junior Bookshelf* (Great Britain).

Jylland: see JUTLAND.

K

K, chemical symbol of the element POTASSIUM.

K2: see GODWIN-AUSTEN, MOUNT.

Kaaba or **Caaba** (both: kä'bù, kä'ùbù), most sacred building, housing the sacred Black Stone; goal of the pilgrimage to Mecca, center of Islam. Its sanctity is earlier than Islam.

Kabardian-Balkar Autonomous Soviet Socialist Republic (kùbär'dēùn-bälkär'), autonomous republic (4,826 sq. mi.; 1965 est. pop. 505,000), S European RSFSR, on N slopes of Greater Caucasus; cap. Nalchik. Includes peaks of Mt. Elbrus, Koshtan-Tau, Dykh-Tau. Kabardians, a Moslem Circassian group, support themselves by agr., stock raising.

kabuki: see JAPANESE DRAMA.

Kabul (kä'bōōl, kùbōōl'), city (pop. c.300,000), cap. of Afghanistan, on Kabul R. The political, economic, and cultural center of Afghanistan. Early cap. of Baber (1504–19), it succeeded Kandahar as cap. of Afghanistan in 1773. Figured prominently in First Afghan War (1839–42). Also spelled Kabol.

Kachin State (kùchīn'), constituent state (c.16,000 sq. mi.; pop. c.501,000) of Burma; cap. Myitkyina. Northernmost state in the Union of Burma. Many of inhabitants are Kachins or Jinghpaws, a tribal society. The state was constituted 1948 and is largely autonomous.

Kadar, Janos (yä'nôsh kä'där), 1912–, Hungarian Communist leader. Became head of secret police 1948, but was himself imprisoned 1951–54. Regaining power, he supported Nagy in 1956 revolution, then formed counter-government, which presided over Soviet suppression of the revolt. Resigned premiership 1958 but resumed it 1961.

Kaduna (kùdōō'nú), city (pop. c.150,000), admin. center of N Nigeria. Educational, sports, and communications center; textile mills.

Kaesong (kä'sŭng), city (pop. c.200,000), N South Korea. Commercial center. As Songdo, it was cap. of Korea 10th–14th cent. Divided by the 38th parallel, city was major contact point between North and South Korea 1945–51. Korean war truce talks, later transferred to PANMUNJON, were begun here.

Kaffa, Ukraine: see FEODOSIYA.

kaffir or **kaffir corn:** see SORGHUM.

Kaffirs: see KAFIRS.

Kaffraria, South Africa: see KAFIRS.

Kafirs or **Kaffirs** (both: kä'fùrz), term used only by Europeans in S Africa, referring to Bantu-speaking Negroes. Term, originally applied to people of Kaffraria, region in E Cape Prov., Republic of South Africa, is derived from Arabic word meaning infidel. First applied to Africans by Arab slave traders.

Kafka, Franz (fränts' käf'kä), 1883–1924, German novelist and essayist, b. Prague, Czechoslovakia, of a Jewish family. Among his works are *The Trial* (1925), *The Castle* (1926), and *Amerika* (1927), all translated into English. In prose remarkable for clarity and precision, Kafka presents a world at once real and dreamlike in which modern man, burdened with guilt, isolation, and anxiety, makes a futile search for personal salvation. His *Tagebücher, 1910–1923* appeared originally in English as *The Diaries of Franz Kafka* (1948–49), edited by his friend Max BROD.

Kafue (käfoo'ā), river, central Zambia; c.600 mi. long, flowing from border of Republic of the Congo to Zambezi R.

Kagawa, Toyohiko (tōyō'hēkō kä"gä'wä), 1888–1960, Japanese Christian social worker. Influential in organizing cooperatives and in labor problems. Arrested in Second World War for pacifism. Wrote poetry, novels, essays, and religious studies.

Kagera (kägē'rŭ), river, E central Africa, the remotest source of the Nile. Flows c.250 mi. N and W to Victoria Nyanza.

Kagoshima (kä"gō'shĭmä), city (pop. 296,003), S Kyushu, Japan, on Satsuma peninsula and Kagoshima Bay. Port and navy yard. Japanese rocket base since 1961. Mfg. of porcelain ware, clothing, and tinware. St. Francis Xavier landed here 1549. Was seat of Satsuma lords.

Kahn, Albert, 1869–1942, American architect, b. Germany. His firm in Detroit applied technique of mass production to architecture; designed many factories and war plants; pioneered in use of reinforced concrete and steel.

Kahn, Louis Isadore, 1901–, American architect and teacher. Influential in 1960s.

Kahoolawe (kähō'ōlävä), island (45 sq. mi.), Hawaii, SW of Maui (separated by Alalakeiki Channel).

Kaifeng (kē'fŭng'), city (pop. c.299,100), NE Honan prov., China, on Lunghai RR. Trade center and former provincial cap. Founded in 3d cent. B.C. A major political and cultural center in Chinese history. Cap. of northern Sung dynasty (960–1127).

Kailas (kīläs'), peak, c.22,280 ft. high, SW Tibet, in Himalayas. Dwelling of Hindu god Siva, it is goal of pilgrimages.

Kailua (käēloo'ŭ), city (pop. 25,622 including Lanikai [länĭkä'ē]), Hawaii, on SE coast of Oahu. Hawaiian kings lived here until royal residence was moved to Waikiki. U.S. Marine Corps air station is nearby.

Kairouan (kīrwän'), city (pop. c.40,000), Tunisia; sacred city of Islam. Founded 670, it was seat of Arab governors in W Africa until 800. First cap. of Fatimites was estab. here in 909. Has famous 9th-cent. mosque. Noted for carpet industry.

Kaisaria, Turkey: see KAYSERI.

Kaiser, Georg (gä'ôrk kī'zŭr), 1878–1945, German playwright. His plays, which he called thought dramas, have social themes. *From Morn to Midnight* (1916; produced in New York 1922), *The Corals* (1917; a trilogy), and *Gas* (1918) are translated into English.

Kaiserslautern (kī"zŭrslou'tŭrn), city (pop. 84,145), Rhineland-Palatinate, West Germany. Machine and textile mfg.

Kaiser Wilhelm Canal: see KIEL CANAL.

Kakhetia (kŭkě'shŭ, Rus. kŭkhě'tyěŭ), region, E Georgian SSR, along upper Kura R. Noted for wine; Telav is chief town. Became part of Georgia 1010. Independent 1468–1762, then joined Karthlia to form East Georgian kingdom; joined Russia 1801.

Kalahari (kä"lähä'rē), arid plateau, area c.200,000 sq. mi., Botswana and the Republic of South Africa. Thorn and sand veld cover much of area. Some grazing. Inhabited by Hottentots and Bushmen.

Kalamata (kälämä'tŭ), Gr. *Kalamai,* city (pop. 38,211), S Greece, in SW Peloponnesus; a port on the Gulf of Messenia. Fisheries, silk and cigarette mfg., distilleries. Exports olive oil.

Kalamazoo (kăl'ŭmŭzoō), city (pop. 82,089), SW Mich., on Kalamazoo R. at junction with Portage Creek; settled 1829. Industrial and commercial center in farm area (celery, peppermint, fruit). Seat of Kalamazoo Col., Nazareth Col., and Western Michigan Univ.

Kalamazoo, river rising in S Mich. and flowing c.185 mi. NW past Battle Creek and Kalamazoo to L. Michigan.

Kalaupapa, Hawaii: see MOLOKAI.

Kalb, Johann (Ger. yō'hän kälp'), 1721–80, general in American Revolution, known as "Baron de Kalb" (dē kälb), b. Germany. Mortally wounded in battle of Camden, S.C. (1780).

kale, nonheading cabbage variety (*Brassica oleracea acephala*) with curly leaves, grown for greens and, in Europe, for fodder. Sea kale (*Crambe maritima*) is N European coastal plant sometimes used as a potherb.

kaleidoscope (kŭlī'dŭskōp), cylindrical tube, one end containing two mirrors set at angle of 60° and many particles of varicolored glass which can move between two glass disks. Other end has eyepiece. When tube is rotated, glass forms many patterns, always symmetrical because of reflection in mirrors.

Kalevala (kä'lēvä"lä), Finnish national epic, a compilation of folk verses dealing with the deeds of three semidivine brothers of gigantic stature. Known to scholars as early as 1733, verses were collected in 19th cent. by Zakarias Topelius and Elias LÖNNROT. Effect on Finnish art has been great.

Kalgan, China: see CHANGKIAKOW.

Kali (kŭ'lē), in Hinduism, primarily the black goddess of death and evil, though she has other and more attractive aspects. As consort of Siva, she represents the female principle. The name was also given earlier to one of the tongues of the fire-god Agni.

Kalidasa (kä"lĭdä'sŭ), fl. 5th cent.?, Indian poet and dramatist, often regarded as greatest figure in classical Sanskrit literature. Three surviving verse dramas (including *Sakuntala*) relate fanciful or mythological tales of lovers separated by adversity but reunited by happy chance. Two epics mingle delicate descriptions of nature with battle scenes. Also wrote shorter lyrical poems.

Kalimantan: see BORNEO.

Kalinin, Mikhail Ivanovich (mēkhŭyēl' ēvä'nŭvĭch kŭlyē'nyĭn), 1875–1946, Russian revolutionist, first president of USSR (officially: president of the Soviet central executive committee 1919–38 and of the Presidium of the Supreme Soviet 1938–46).

Kalinin, formerly **Tver,** city (1965 est. pop. 306,000), RSFSR, NW of Moscow, on the Volga. An industrial center (railway cars, machinery, textiles). The seat of a powerful principality in 14th–15th cent., it was annexed to Moscow c.1486. Renamed 1933 for M. I. Kalinin. It was briefly held by the Germans in 1941 and was heavily damaged.

Kaliningrad, Russian name of KÖNIGSBERG.

Kalispel Indians: see PEND D'OREILLE INDIANS.

Kalispell (kä'lĭspĕl"), city (pop. 10,151), NW Mont., NW of Flathead L., near Glacier Nat. Park; settled 1883. Tourist and trade center of agr., fruit, and timber region. Hungry Horse Dam on Flathead R. is nearby.

Kalisz (kä'lēsh), Ger. *Kalisch,* city (est. pop. 75,000), W Poland. Mfg. of clothing, food, machinery. By Convention of Kalisz (1813) Prussia promised Russia to declare war on Napoleon I.

Kalm, Peter (pä'tŭr kälm'), 1715–79, Swedish scientist. His *Travels in North America,* recording his observations of natural history, plantations, and agriculture, was the first account of its kind by a trained scientist. It was published between 1753 and 1761; was republished in 1937. Genus *Kalmia* (mountain laurel) is named for Kalm.

Kalmar (käl'mär), city (pop. 31,425), co. seat of Kalmar co., SE Sweden, Baltic port opposite Oland isl. across Kalmar Sound. Its medieval castle, the Kalmarnahus, has withstood 24 sieges. Here in 1397 was effected the

Kalmar Union of Denmark, Sweden, and Norway under Queen MARGARET. Since kingship was elective in all three countries, a lasting union under the Danish crown proved impossible. Sweden definitively left the union in 1523 (see GUSTAVUS I). The **Kalmar War,** 1611–13, between Denmark and Sweden, took its name from the fall of Kalmar to the Danes early in the conflict. Gustavus II bought off the Danish claims at the Peace of Knared.

Kalmucks (kǎl′mŭks) or **Kalmycks** (kǎl′mǐks), Asiatic people, a branch of Oirat Mongols. They migrated from Altai region to lower Volga basin c.1636 and became vassals of Russia. To avoid Russian colonization, a large part of Kalmucks E of the Volga migrated to China in 1771, but were decimated along their arduous route. The others stayed on, clinging to their Lamaist Buddhist faith and to their traditional ways. During the Russian civil war of 1917–20 many migrated to Central and W Europe. The Kalmuck Autonomous Soviet Socialist Republic (29,315 sq. mi.; 1965 est. pop. 238,000; cap. Elista), RSFSR, was estab. 1958. Previously existed 1935–44, but was dissolved because the Kalmucks allegedly collaborated with the German invaders. Many fled to Germany and became "displaced persons"; those who remained were "resettled" elsewhere in USSR.

Kaluga (kŭlŏō′gŭ), city (1965 est. pop. 169,000), W European RSFSR, on Oka R. Machinery mfg. Scene of murder of second false Dmitri (1610). Center of action in Second World War, 1941.

Kalymnos (kä′lēmnôs), Greek island (41 sq. mi.; pop. 26,032); part of DODECANESE. Sponge-fishing center.

Kama (kä′mŭ), river, 1,262 mi. long, E European RSFSR; chief tributary of the Volga, which it joins below Kazan. Navigable about half the year, it is an important transportation route.

Kamakura (kämä′kŏō′rä), city (pop. 98,617), Honshu, Japan, on Sagami Bay. Religious center and resort. Noted for its *daibutsu*, a bronze figure of Buddha 42 ft. high, cast in 1252. Was seat of YORITOMO and his descendants (1192–1333). Government hq. of E Japan under Ashikaga Shogunate (1333–1573).

Kamchatka (kämchăt′kŭ), peninsula (135,135 sq. mi.), autonomous province, RSFSR, in NE Siberia. It separates Sea of Okhotsk (W) from Bering Sea and Pacific Ocean. Beyond Cape Lopatka (S tip) lie Kurile Isls. Petropavlovsk is main center. Two volcanic ranges, which rise to 15,666 ft. in Klyuchevskaya Sopka, enclose central valley (N–S), drained by Kamchatka R. (478 mi. long). There are hot springs, peat marshes, forests, petroleum, and coal deposits. Fishing, fur trapping, lumbering, and reindeer raising are chief occupations. The sparse population is mainly Russian, but in N part dwell native Kamchatkans and Koryaks. It was discovered 1697; conquest by Russia completed 1732. Part of Khabarovsk Territory until 1956.

Kamehameha I (Kamehameha the Great) (kämä′hämä′hä), 1758–1819, Hawaiian monarch. United the islands in 1810, estab. law and order.

Kamenets-Podolski (kä′mĭnyĭts-pŭdôl′skē), city (pop. 40,300), W Ukrainian SSR, former cap. of PODOLIA. Mfg. of agr. machinery. Joined to Poland 1430. Passed to Russia 1793.

Kamenev, Lev Borisovich (lyěf′ bûrě′sŭvĭch kä′mĭnyĭf), 1883–1936, Russian Communist leader whose real name was Rosenfeld; brother-in-law of Trotsky. One of triumvirate (with Stalin and Zinoviev) which succeeded Lenin in 1924. Joined Trotsky's opposition 1926; twice expelled from party (1927, 1932); executed after 1936 treason trials.

Kamerlingh Onnes, Heike (hī′kŭ kä′mŭrlǐng ô′nùs), 1853–1926, Dutch physicist. Won 1913 Nobel Prize in Physics chiefly for study of properties of helium.

Kames, Henry Home, Lord (hūm, kāmz), 1696–1782, Scottish judge and philosopher. His works include dissertations on Scottish law and on problems of moral and aesthetic philosophy.

Kamet (kä′mĕt), peak, 25,447 ft. high, on Tibet-India border, in Himalayas.

kamikaze (kä′mēkä′zä) [Jap.,= divine wind], typhoon that destroyed Kublai Khan's fleet, foiling his invasion of Japan in 1281. In Second World War term used for Japanese suicide pilots (esp. active at Okinawa) who crashed their planes into enemy targets, usually ships.

Kaministikwia or **Kaministiquia** (both: kùmĭ′nĭstĭ′kwēŭ), river, c.60 mi. long, rising in W Ont., Canada, and flowing S, then E to L. Superior at Fort William. Was alternate route to the GRAND PORTAGE.

Kamloops (kăm′lōōps), city (pop. 10,076), S B.C., Canada, on Thompson R. Trading post estab. here 1812. Growth spurred by Cariboo gold rush. Canadian Pacific RR reached here 1885. Center of agr. and mining area.

Kampala (kämpä′lä), city (pop. c.50,000), cap. of Uganda. Chief commercial center and site of traditional cap. of the Buganda kingdom. Seat of Univ. Col. of East Africa.

Kamperduin, Netherlands: see CAMPERDOWN.

Kanab (kùnăb′), city (pop. 1,645), S Utah, ESE of St. George near Ariz. line; settled 1864. Tourist resort and ranching center in region which includes Zion and Bryce Canyon national parks and Pipe Spring Natl. Monument.

Kanawha (kùnô′wù), river, formed in S central W.Va. and flowing c.97 mi. NW to Ohio R. at Point Pleasant. State's principal river. Charleston is on its banks.

Kanazawa (kä′nä′zäwä), city (pop. 298,972), central Honshu, Japan, on Sea of Japan. Mfg. of silk textiles, porcelain, and lacquer ware. Park has noted gardens.

Kanchenjunga (kän′chùnjōōng′gù), mountain, on Sikkim-Nepal border, in Himalayas; third highest in the world. Tallest of its five peaks is 28,146 ft. high. British expedition climbed peak in 1955. Name also spelled Kanchanjanga or Kinchinjunga.

Kanchipuram, India: see CONJEEVERAM.

Kandahar (kän′dùhär′), city (pop. c.100,000), S Afghanistan. Of unknown antiquity, was cap. of Afghanistan 1747–73. Held by British in 19th-cent. Afghan wars. Situated in fruit-growing region.

Kandinsky, Vassily (vŭsē′lyē kŭndyēn′skē), 1866–1944, Russian painter and theorist. Called the originator of abstract painting. With Franz Marc he helped found the BLAUE REITER group of artists in Munich. Taught at the BAUHAUS.

Kandy (kän′dē), city (pop. c.57,200), central Ceylon, on Kandy Plateau. Site of temple said to house one of Buddha's teeth. Market center for rich tea and rubber region. Name formerly Candy.

Kane, Elisha Kent, 1820–57, American arctic explorer. Accompanied first Grinnell expedition (1850) seeking lost Franklin party. Interest in his published account made possible second expedition (1853–55), which discovered Kane Basin.

Kaneohe (kä′näōhä), town (pop. 14,414), Hawaii, on E coast of Oahu, on Kaneohe Bay. Many anc. fishponds built by Hawaiian chiefs are in area. U.S. Marine Corps air station is on bay.

Kaneohe Bay (kä′näōhä), E Oahu, Hawaiian Isls. U.S. naval air station here.

kangaroo, vegetarian MARSUPIAL of Australia and Tasmania. The front limbs are small and the long, powerful hind limbs enable the animal to leap swiftly over the ground; the long muscular tail aids balance while leaping and is a prop when standing or moving slowly. In the large kangaroos and wallaroos (genus *Macropus*) the hind foot of adults is more than 10 in. long; in the smaller kangaroos or wallabies (members of several genera) the hind foot is 6–10 in. long. Tree kangaroos (genus *Dendrolagus*) are partially arboreal; rat kangaroos are smallest forms.

Kangting or **K'ang-ting** (both: käng′dǐng′), city (pop. c.40,000), cap. of Kantse Tibetan Autonomous Region, Szechwan prov., China. Cap of former Sikang prov.

Kaniapiskau (känyŭpĭ′skô″), river, NE Que., Canada, issues from **Kaniapiskau Lake,** on St. Lawrence-Hudson Bay watershed. Flows 450 mi. generally NNW to form Koksoak R. with Larch R.

Kankakee (kăngkŭkē'), city (pop. 27,666), E Ill., on Kankakee R., SE of Chicago. Industrial and shipping center for farm area, with varied mfg. Limestone quarries are nearby. Seat of Olivet Nazarene Col.

Kankakee, river, rising near South Bend, N Ind.. and flowing c.230 mi. SW to Kankakee, Ill.. then NW to Des Plaines R. below Joliet. There combined stream becomes Illinois R.

Kannapolis (kŭnăp'ŭlĭs), city (pop. 34,647), W central N.C., NNE of Charlotte; founded c.1905. "Company town," it produces household linens.

Kano (kä'nō), family or school of Japanese painters. Its forerunner, **Kano Masanobu** (mäsä'nōbōō), c.1453–c.1550, painted landscapes, birds, and figure pieces, chiefly in ink, with touches of palest tints. His son, **Kano Motonobu** (mōtō'nōbōō), c.1476–1559, actual founder of school, gave it its character—the subordination of color to design. The painting of **Kano Eitoku** (ä'tōkōō), 1543–90, grandson of Motonobu, is characterized by energy, ease, and inventiveness. His grandson, **Kano Tanyu** (tänyōō'), 1602–74, was so original and versatile that he really created a school of his own.

Kano (kä'nō), city (pop. 295,432) N Nigeria. Built in 16th cent. on site of 9th-cent. settlement. Flourished as caravan center in 19th cent. Now an important transport center, with international airport. Chief town of Nigeria's peanut industry and important center for leathercraft, cotton goods, and metalwares.

Kanpur: see CAWNPORE.

Kansa Indians, North American tribe of Siouan linguistic family, known also as Kansas or Kaw Indians. They were at the mouth of the Kansas R. in the 18th cent., later moved farther W, were settled on a reservation at Council Grove until 1873, then were moved to present Okla., near the related Osage Indians. Had a typical Plains culture.

Kansas, state (82,264 sq. mi.; pop. 2,178,611), central U.S.; admitted 1861 as 34th state; cap. TOPEKA. Other cities are WICHITA (largest) and KANSAS CITY. Bounded NE by Missouri R. Part of GREAT PLAINS, it rises from E alluvial prairies to semiarid high plains in W. Drained by KANSAS and ARKANSAS rivers. Leading U.S. producer of winter wheat, Kansas also grows sorghum, corn, other grains, raises cattle. Stone, petroleum, coal, natural gas, helium, and salt are major minerals. Meat packing, dairying, aircraft and cement industries; also mfg. of metal goods and lumber products. Region visited by Coronado (1541) and Juan de Oñate (1601), but claimed for France by La Salle (c.1682). Part of Louisiana Purchase (1803). Explored by Lewis and Clark expedition, Z. M. Pike, S. H. Long. Part of INDIAN TERRITORY until made separate territory under KANSAS-NEBRASKA Bill (1854). Rivalry of proslavery and antislavery factions spurred settlement (LEAVENWORTH, ATCHISON, LAWRENCE, Topeka, all founded 1854) and brought violence (see BROWN, JOHN). Free Staters' victory aided by J. H. LANE. After Civil War agr. developed, but was periodically disrupted by national depressions and natural disasters. Farmers supported POPULIST party until conditions improved, then returned to Republican party. State marked by conservative, moral tone.

Kansas, sometimes called the **Kaw,** river formed by junction of Smoky Hill and Republican rivers in NE Kansas. Flows c.170 mi. E to the Missouri at Kansas City. Drains parts of Kansas, Nebr., and Colo. Many dams, reservoirs, and levees built since heavy floods (esp. in 1951).

Kansas, University of, mainly at Lawrence; state supported; coed.; chartered 1864, opened 1866 with aid from A. A. Lawrence.

Kansas City, two adjacent cities of same name, one (pop. 121,901) in Kansas, the other (pop. 475,539) in Mo., at junction of Missouri and Kansas (or Kaw)

rivers. Each is second largest city of its state. Together they form a great commercial, industrial, transportation, cultural, and educational center, with stockyards, grain elevators, box factories, and railroad shops, and food-processing, soap, and metal products plants. Surrounding area was starting point of many westward expeditions; Santa Fe and Oregon trails passed through here. Several early 19th-cent. settlements were foundations for these present-day cities. One was Westport (in Mo.) where Confederate forces were decisively defeated on Oct. 21–23, 1864, thus ending last Confederate invasion of Far West. Kansas City, Kansas, has Univ. of Kansas Medical Center. Kansas City, Mo., has William Rockhill Nelson Gall. of Art, Atkins Mus. of Fine Arts, Rockhurst Col., and Univ. of Missouri at Kansas City. Has symphony orchestra. Political reform move in 1937 led to deposing of T. J. PENDERGAST.

Kansas-Nebraska Bill, legislation by which U.S. Congress estab. territories of Kansas and Nebraska, more properly Kansas-Nebraska Act, since it became law on May 30, 1854. Sectional conflict over slavery and over location of transcontinental railroad made territorial organization a serious problem. Southerners, wanting no free territory W of Mo., had already defeated four attempts to organize a single territory for the area. Bill, presented by Stephen A. Douglas, provided for "popular sovereignty" (see SQUATTER SOVEREIGNTY) and creation of two territories instead of one. An amendment specifically repealed Missouri Compromise. Bill caused sectional division to grow beyond reconciliation. Proslavery and antislavery forces exerted pressure to determine "popular" decision in Kansas in their own favor (see EMIGRANT AID COMPANY); result was "bleeding" Kansas. Opponents of bill founded new Republican party.

Kansas State University of Agriculture and Applied Science, at Manhattan; land grant, state supported; coed.; chartered and opened 1863.

Kansu (gän'shōō'), province (c.300,000 sq. mi.; pop. c.13,330,000), NW China; cap. Lanchow. Bordered on N by Mongolian People's Republic. Inadequate rainfall limits agr. to valleys of Yellow and Wei rivers. Oil produced at Yümen and coal mined at Lanchow; but mineral resources (oil, coal, iron, gold) largely unexploited.

Kant, Immanuel (känt), 1724–1804, German philosopher, one of the greatest figures in the history of philosophy. He lived a quiet life at Königsberg, becoming professor of logic and metaphysics at the university and quietly evolving a system of thought that influenced all succeeding philosophers in one way or another. His great works are *Critique of Pure Reason* (1781), *Foundations of the Metaphysics of Ethics* (1785), *Critique of Practical Reason* (1788), *Critique of Judgment* (1790), and *Religion within the Boundaries of Pure Reason* (1793–94). In them he set forth intricate and well-knit arguments that defy brief summary. He distinguished sharply between the things of our experience (phenomena), which can be fitted into categories of our understanding (including causality and substantiality) and things-in-themselves (noumena), which the intellect cannot actually fathom. To illustrate the failure of the intellect to deal with things-in-themselves, he set up the antinomies, logical contradictions of principles which cannot be resolved; thus, he demonstrated that space and time are infinite and that they are finite, that God exists and that he does not exist. Yet though we cannot *know* the noumenal realm, we can know that it exists. Ethics and aesthetics are grounded in it. Moral conduct rests upon the categorical imperative. One formulation of this imperative is: "Act as if the maxim from which you act were to become through your will a universal law." Faith, not knowledge, justifies belief in freedom of the will, immortality, and God—the three great problems of metaphysics whose existence cannot be estab. on theoretical grounds nor demonstrated scientifically.

Kaohsiung (gou'shoong'), city (pop. c.438,400), Taiwan. Leading port of S Taiwan. Industrial center.

Kaolack (kou'läk), city (pop. c.46,800), W Republic of Senegal, on the Saloum R.; port and rail terminus. Exports peanuts.

kaolin: see CHINA CLAY.

kaolinite (kā'ŭlīnīt), crystallized clay mineral forming main constituent of kaolin and china clay. It is a hydrous aluminum silicate resulting chiefly from weathering of feldspar.

Kapilavastu (kä"pĭlŭvä'stoo), town, S Nepal. Inscriptions show that Buddha was born nearby.

Kapitza, Peter (kä'pētsŭ), 1894–, Russian physicist, noted for research in magnetic and electrical properties of matter at low temperatures.

Kaplan, Mordechai Menachem, 1881–, American rabbi, educator, and philosopher of religion, b. Lithuania. Founder (1922) of Society for the Advancement of Judaism and of a reconstructionist movement seeking to make Judaism compatible with a secular age.

kapok (kā'pŏk, kă'–), tropical tree of Bombacaceae family and the fiber (floss) obtained from its ripe pods. Light, resilient, and resistant to water and decay, the fiber has been of commercial value since 1890s for filling and insulation. Oil from seed kernels is used for soap and as edible oil.

Kappel or **Cappel** (kä'pŭl), village, Switzerland, S of Zurich. Here ZWINGLI fell in battle (1531).

Kapteyn, Jacobus Cornelius (yäkō'bŭs kôrnā'lĭŭs käptīn'), 1851–1922, Dutch astronomer, authority on Milky Way system. Computed positions of many stars of S Hemisphere.

Kapuas (kä'pooäs), longest river of Borneo, rising on Sarawak border, flowing 710 mi. to South China Sea.

Karabakh, USSR; see MOUNTAIN-KARABAKH.

Karachai-Cherkess Autonomous Oblast (kŭrŭchī'-chĭrkěs'), administrative division (5,444 sq. mi.; 1965 est. pop. 320,000), Stavropol Territory, SW European RSFSR, in Greater Caucasus, along upper Kuban R.; cap. Cherkessk. Livestock, grain, coal. Some Cherkess, but majority of population is Karachai, Turkic-speaking Moslems, who settled here 14th cent.; conquered by Russia 1828. Region made oblast 1922, divided (1924) into Karachai Autonomous Oblast and Cherkess Natl. Okrug; latter made oblast 1928 (see CIRCASSIA). Oblast dissolved and population deported to Siberia 1943 because of alleged collaboration with Germans; reestab. 1957.

Karachi (kŭrä'chē), city (pop. c.1,916,000), West Pakistan, on Arabian Sea. After it passed to the British in 1843, it became major port of NW India. Became cap. of Pakistan in 1947, but cap. was moved to Rawalpindi in 1959. The largest city in Pakistan, it is a major port, commercial hub, and industrial center.

Karafuto, former Japanese possession: see SAKHALIN.

Karaganda (kä"rŭgŭndä'), city (1965 est. pop. 482,000), Kazakh SSR, in Kazakh Hills. Center of one of largest coal basins in USSR, developed after 1928.

Karageorge (kä"rŭjôrj', kä"räjôr'jä) [Turkish,= Black George], Serbo-Croatian *Czerny George,* 1752?–1817, Serbian patriot. An illiterate peasant, he led Serbian insurrection against Turks (1804), took Belgrade (1806), was proclaimed hereditary chief of Serbia (1808). Abandoned by his Russian allies in 1812, he fled to Austria. On his return to Serbia he was murdered at instigation of MILOSH Obrenovich. From him is descended the **Karageorgevich** (kä"rŭjôr'jŭvĭch) dynasty of Serbia and Yugoslavia–Prince ALEXANDER and Kings PETER I, ALEXANDER, and PETER II. The family was long in feud with the OBRENOVICH dynasty.

Karaites [from Heb. *Kara* = Bible], Jewish sect founded c.765 in Persia by Anan ben David. Relied only on Old Testament scriptures, rejecting Oral Law as interpreted in the Talmud. Some present-day adherents in the Crimea.

Karajan, Herbert von (käräyän'), 1908–, Austrian conductor. Named musical director of the Berlin Philharmonic 1955; served as artistic director of the Vienna State Opera 1956–64.

Karajich, Vuk Stefanovich (vook' stěfä'nōvĭch kä'-räyĭch), 1787–1864, Serbian philologist and folklorist. He adopted Serbian vernacular as his literary language, introduced phonetic spelling, and invented new letters to complete the Cyrillic alphabet. In 1847 he translated the New Testament into Serbian.

Karakalpak Autonomous Soviet Socialist Republic (kä"rŭkŭlpäk'), autonomous republic (63,938 sq. mi.; 1965 est. pop. 596,000), NW Uzbek SSR, comprising part of Ust-Urt plateau, Kizil Kum desert, and Amu Darya delta; cap. Nukus. Produces cotton and alfalfa. Population consists mostly of Turkic Karakalpaks, Uzbeks, Kazakhs–all Moslems.

Karakoram (kä"rŭkō'rŭm), mountain system, N Kashmir, extending c.250 mi. Main range (sometimes called Mustagh) has large glaciers and includes Mt. GODWIN-AUSTEN, second highest peak in world.

Karakorum (kä"rŭkō'rŭm), ruined city, Mongolian People's Republic. Was cap. of Jenghiz Khan. Nearby is site of Uigur cap. also named Karakorum.

Kara Kul (kä'rŭ kool'), mountain lake, area 140 sq. mi., Tadzhik SSR, in the Pamir, near Chinese border; alt. 12,838 ft. and depth 781 ft.

Kara-Kum (kä'rŭ koom'), two deserts, S USSR. The Caspian Kara-Kum (c.115,830 sq. mi.) is in SE Turkmen SSR, W of Amu Darya R. Crossed by Trans-Caspian RR. Here is MERV oasis. Seminomadic population raises goats, camels, karakul sheep. Sulfur mines. The Aral Kara-Kum (c.15,440 sq. mi. is in Kazakh SSR.

Karaman (kärämän') or **Caraman,** town (pop. 21,660), S Turkey, N of Taurus mts. Taken by a Turkic tribe c.1250, it became the cap. of the emirate of Karamania, a successor state of the Seljuk empire. Karamania, which once comprised most of Asia Minor, fell to the Ottoman Turks in the mid-15th cent. There are ruins of a castle and two fine college-mosques.

Karamanlis, Constantine (kôn'stäntēn kärämänlĭs'), 1907–, Greek statesman. Premier 1955–63. Signed agreement with Great Britain and Turkey 1959 establishing free Cyprus republic.

Karamzin, Nikolai Mikhailovich (nyĭkŭlī' mēkhī'lŭvĭch kŭrümzēn'), 1766–1826, Russian historian and novelist. Wrote *Letters of a Russian Traveler, 1789–90* (1792) and a history of Russia (11 vols., 1818–24).

Kara Sea, section of Arctic Ocean, between W Siberia and Novaya Zemlya. Receives Ob, Yenisei, Pyasina, and Taimyra rivers. Navigable Aug.–Sept.

Karasimbi, peak: see VIRUNGA.

Karbala, Iraq: see KERBELA.

Karelian Autonomous Soviet Socialist Republic or **Karelia** (kŭrēl'yŭ), autonomous republic (66,564 sq. mi.; 1965 est. pop. 696,000), RSFSR, between Finland and White Sea; cap. Petrozavodsk. A glaciated plateau stretching from Kola Peninsula in N to L. Ladoga and L. Onega in S, it is covered by thousands of lakes and by dense coniferous forests. Karelia has important lumber industries (paper, furniture, prefabricated houses); marble, quartzite, and porphyry quarries; iron, magnetite, and lead-zinc ores. Majority of population is Russian; the rest are Karelians and Finns, whose written languages are identical. W Karelia, conquered by Swedes in 12th cent., shared history of Finland until 1940. E Karelia, conquered by Novgorod in 13th cent., became an autonomous republic of RSFSR in 1923. Following Soviet-Finnish War (1939–40), most of the territory ceded by Finland was added to the Karelian ASSR. In 1940 it became Karelo-Finnish SSR and in 1956 again became autonomous republic of RSFSR. **Karelian Isthmus** is a land bridge 90 mi. long and 25–70 mi. wide, connecting Russia and Finland, between the Gulf of Finland and L. Ladoga. It contains the cities of Leningrad and Vyborg. Until 1940 all except its S end belonged to Finland, which built the MANNERHEIM LINE across it. The Russo-Finnish peace treaty of 1940 and the Finnish peace treaty of 1947 gave the whole isthmus to the USSR.

Karelo-Finnish Autonomous Soviet Socialist Republic or **Karelia:** see KARELIAN AUTONOMOUS SOVIET SOCIALIST REPUBLIC OR KARELIA.

Karenni States: see KAYAH STATE.

Karens (kürĕnz'), members of Thai-Chinese cultural group, one of most important minorities in Burma (esp. in Kayah State). Some are pagan, but many are Christian and Buddhist.

Karfiol, Bernard (kär'fēōl), 1886–1952, American painter, known for nudes, landscapes, portraits.

Kariba Dam (kärē'bä), in the Kariba gorge of the Zambezi R., S central Africa, on the Zambia-Rhodesia border. Completed 1959, one of world's largest dams (c.420 ft. high, c.1,900 ft. long). Its reservoir, Kariba L., covers c.2,000 sq. mi. Fishing.

Karikal: see FRENCH INDIA.

Karkonosze, Polish name of RIESENGEBIRGE.

Karlfeldt, Erik Axel, 1864–1931, Swedish lyric poet. He was posthumously awarded the 1931 Nobel Prize in Literature, which he had refused in his lifetime.

Karl-Marx-Stadt: see CHEMNITZ, Germany.

Karlovy Vary, Czechoslovakia: see CARLSBAD.

Karlowitz, Treaty of (kär'lōvĭts), 1699, between Turkey and the Holy League (Austria, Venice, Poland). Turkey ceded Hungary, Croatia, Slavonia to Emperor Leopold I; Podolia to Poland; Peloponnesus to Venice. This treaty marked beginning of decline of Ottoman empire.

Karlsbad, Czechoslovakia: see CARLSBAD.

Karlsburg, Rumania: see ALBA-IULIA.

Karlsefni, Thorfinn: see THORFINN KARLSEFNI.

Karlskrona (kärlskrōō'nä), city (pop. 33,227), co. seat of Blekinge co., S Sweden. A Baltic port built on islands and on mainland, it is hq. of Swedish navy (since 1679). Fortifications and docks are cut out of granite. Sometimes spelled Carlskrona.

Karlsruhe (kärls'rōŏŭ), city (pop. 224,045), Baden-Württemberg, West Germany, linked to Rhine by canal. Industrial city; seat of many government offices and institutes of higher learning; cultural center with well-known theaters and art galleries. Founded 1715, it was laid out in a semicircle, with streets converging radically upon ducal palace (heavily damaged in Second World War). Was cap. of Baden-Durlach 1715–71; of Baden 1771–1945. Formerly spelled Carlsruhe.

Karlstad (kärl'städ), city (pop. 43,618), co. seat of Varmland co., W central Sweden, port on Vanern L. and on Thingvalla isl. It is a Lutheran episcopal see. It has lumber, pulp, and textile mills and shipyards. Union of Norway and Sweden was severed by treaty signed here, 1905.

Karlstadt, Reformation leader: see CARLSTADT.

Karman, Theodor von, 1881–, American aeronautical engineer, b. Hungary. Known for mathematical formulas (called von Karman theory of vortex streets) used in aircraft and rocket design.

Karmathians or **Carmathians,** crypto-Moslem sect, similar to ASSASSIN sect. An independent political force, they conquered Arabia early in the 10th cent., defied Abbasid caliph, and rocked Islam (c.930) by taking the black stone from the Kaaba, keeping it 10 years. They declined after 1000.

Karnak (kär'năk), town (pop. c.11,000), central Egypt, on Nile R. Near LUXOR, it occupies part of the site of THEBES. Most notable of ancient ruins here is temple of Amon (XVIII dynasty), with its impressive Great Hall of Columns.

Karnataka, state, India: see MYSORE.

Karo, Joseph ben Ephraim: see CARO.

Karolyi, Count Julius, Hung. *Károlyi Gyula* (kä'rôlyī dyōō'lō), 1871–1946?, Hungarian premier (1931–32). Though a nationalist, he abandoned Hungarian agitation for a revision of Treaty of Trianon in an effort to obtain foreign loans. His brother, **Count Michael Karolyi,** Hung. *Károlyi Mihály* (mī'hī), 1875–1955, socialistic liberal, was Hungarian premier after abdication of Charles IV (1918). Elected president of the provisional republic (1919), he reluctantly surrendered the government to the Communists. He was Hungarian ambassador in Paris 1947–49.

Karpathos (kär'päthôs), Ital. *Scarpanto,* Greek island (111 sq. mi.; pop. 8,129); part of DODECANESE.

Karpinsky, Alexander Petrovich, 1846–1936, Soviet geologist, noted for research on paleontology, mineralogy, petrology. Completed first geologic map of European Russia. During Soviet Revolution he was influential in securing important role in new regime for Soviet Academy of Sciences, of which he was president 1916–36.

Karrer, Paul (kä'rŭr), 1889–, Swiss chemist. Shared 1937 Nobel Prize in Chemistry for work on vitamins, flavins, and carotinoids.

Karroo (kŭrōō'), name of two semiarid plateaus, W Cape Prov., Republic of South Africa. Fertile where irrigated. Citrus fruits produced; sheep, goats, and ostriches raised.

Kars (kärs), city (pop. 32,046), NE Turkey, in Armenia. Long an important fortress, it was taken by the Russians in 1828, 1855, and 1877. Kars dist. was formally ceded to Russia at Congress of Berlin (1878) but was returned to Turkey in 1921.

Karst (kärst), Ital. *Carso,* Serbo-Croatian *Kras,* barren limestone plateau, NW Yugoslavia. Characterized by deep fissures, caves (see POSTOJNA), underground channels. The name karst applies also to similar geological formations elsewhere.

Karun (kärōōn'), river, c.450 mi. long, rising in SW Iran and flowing to Shatt el Arab on Iraq border. It is probably the biblical Ulai.

Karvinna, Czech *Karviná,* city (est. pop. 66,000), N Moravia, Czechoslovakia. Industrial center of Ostrava-Karvinna coal-mining region, formerly in Austria. Disputed by Poland and Czechoslovakia (see TESCHEN).

Kasai (käsī'), former province, S central Republic of the Congo; cap. was Luluabourg. Agr. region; area rich in industrial diamonds. After independence of the Republic of the Congo in 1960, the S part of the province seceded as the Mining State of South Kasai. The republic constituted two new provinces from the province as of June, 1966.

Kasai or **Kassai,** river, S central Africa. A main tributary of the Congo, it rises in Angola and flows c.1,100 mi. N to the Congo.

Kasavubu, Joseph (käsŭvōō'bōō, käsŭ–), 1917–, Congolese political leader. An active nationalist, he was imprisoned after the uprising of 1959 but was released to attend Brussels conference in 1960. Became first president of Republic of the Congo 1960. After Col. Mobutu's coup in Sept., 1960, the Kasavubu-Mobutu regime was recognized by the UN in Nov., 1960. Second coup by Mobutu in Nov., 1965, deposed Kasavubu.

Kaschau, Czechoslovakia: see KOSICE.

Kashgar (käsh'gär), Mandarin *Su-fu,* city (pop. c.50,-000), Sinkiang prov., China, on Kashgar R. Center for caravan trade with India, Afghanistan, and USSR. Cotton and wool cloth, rugs, and jewelry mfg. Cap. of Uigur Turks and center of Manichaeism 750–840. Passed definitively to Chinese in 1760.

Kashing (gä'shǐng'), Mandarin *Chia-hsing,* town (pop. c.86,200), Chekiang prov., China, at junction of Grand Canal, Whangpoo R., and Hangchow-Shanghai RR. Silk-producing and commercial center.

Kashmir (kăshmēr', käsh'mēr), officially **Jammu and Kashmir** (jŭ'mōō), state (c.86,000 sq. mi.; pop. c.5,-000,000), NW India and NE Pakistan. Administered in two sections: Indian Kashmir (c.55,000 sq. mi.; pop. c.4,000,000) with summer cap. at Srinagar, winter cap. at Jammu; Azad (Free) Kashmir (c.31,000 sq. mi.; pop. c.1,000,000) with cap. at Muzaffrarabad. Mainly mountainous. Vale of Kashmir (valley of Jhelum R.) is most populous area; produces wheat and rice. Formerly renowned for cashmere shawls. Was under Hindu rulers until 14th cent., when it fell to Moslems who converted most of the people to Islam. Moslem rule was overthrown 1819 by Ranjit Singh, aided by the Rajput Gulab Singh (a Hindu), who became raja and his heirs the maharajas of Kashmir. After partition of India (1947) Moslem tribesmen, aided in 1948 by Pakistan forces, sought control of state; opposed by Hindu maharaja (who acceded to India) and by Indian troops which occupied most of area. Dispute was brought 1948 before UN, which effected a ceasefire early in 1949. Subsequently, repeated attempts to settle dispute in UN failed. Plans for a plebiscite were never implemented. In 1957 India formally annexed Kashmir. Pakistan continued to occupy N and W sections of Kashmir.

Kashmiri, language of Dardic branch of Indo-Iranian subfamily of Indo-European spoken principally in Kashmir. See LANGUAGE (table).

Kasimir: see CASIMIR.

Kaskaskia (käskä'skéŭ), village (pop. 97), Ill., on Kaskaskia Isl. in the Mississippi at junction with Kaskaskia R. Settled by Jesuits 1703. French had fort here 1721–55; destroyed by British 1763. George Rogers Clark took possession for U.S. in 1778. Cap. of Illinois Territory 1809–18; state cap. 1818–20.

Kaskaskia, river, rising in E central Ill., near Urbana. Flows c.325 mi. SW to Mississippi R. near Chester.

Kasner, Edward (kä'snŭr), 1878–1955, American mathematician, known especially for studies of relativity, horn angles (angle formed when two circles barely touch); introduced the term *googol* (for the number 1 followed by a hundred zeros).

Kassa, Czechoslovakia: see KOSICE.

Kassaba or **Cassaba** (käsä'bä), former name of modern Turkish city of TURGUTLU. The casaba melon was introduced here.

Kassala (käsä'lä), city (pop. c.40,612), NE Republic of the Sudan, near Ethiopian border. Cotton mart; linked by rail with Sennar and Port Sudan.

Kassel or **Cassel** (kä'sŭl), city (pop. 197,523), Hesse, West Germany, on Fulda R. Small harbor; rail hub; center of locomotive, car, machinery, textile industries; a center of armaments production during Second World War. Virtually obliterated by Allied bombings, the city has since been restored to its former beauty. Paintings of celebrated gallery (itself destroyed) were saved. Kassel was after 1567 the cap. of the landgraviate of Hesse-Kassel (raised to electorate 1803); cap. of kingdom of Westphalia 1807–13; cap. of Hesse-Nassau prov. 1866–1945.

Kassem, Abdul Karim (kässěm'), 1915–63, Iraqi general and politician. He led the military coup that in 1958 overthrew the Iraqi monarchy and estab. Kassem as premier of the new republic. An Arab nationalist, he quelled a pro-Communist uprising in 1959. He was executed in 1963 after the overthrow of his government by Col. Abdel Salam Aref.

Kasserine Pass, gap, 2 mi. wide, central Tunisia, in an extension of Atlas Mts. Key point in Allied offensive on Tunisia in Second World War.

Kassites or **Cassites,** fierce anc. people, probably of Indo-European origin. Overran and ruled Babylonia 18th–12th cent. B.C.

Kastler, Alfred, 1902–, French physicist. Won 1966 Nobel Prize in Physics for research on the energy levels of atoms which led to development of lasers, superaccurate atomic clocks, and instruments used in spacecraft to measure magnetic fields in space.

Kästner, Erich (ä'rĭkh kĕst'nŭr), 1899–, German novelist, poet, and writer of popular children's books, notably, *Emil und die Detektive* (1929). His more serious *Fabian* (1930) deals with questions of nihilism and political violence. His books were burned under the National Socialists.

Kastoria (kästôrē'ŭ), city (pop. 10,162), Macedonia, Greece, on L. Kastoria. Fur processing. Byzantine architecture, many palatial homes.

Katahdin, Mount (kùtä'dĭn), 5,268 ft. high, between branches of Penobscot R. in N central Maine. Highest point in state and N terminus of Appalachian Trail.

Katanga, former province, SE Republic of the Congo; cap. was Elisabethville. Fertile plateau and enormously rich mineral region supplying cobalt, copper, tin, radium, uranium, and diamonds. Metallurgical complexes around JADOTVILLE and Kolwezi. After Republic of the Congo received independence in 1960 Katanga seceded from the central government, and Moise Tshombe became president. Through efforts of Patrice LUMUMBA, Dag HAMMARSKJOLD, U THANT, and UN forces, secession was ended Jan., 1963. Former provincial boundaries were disbanded, and two new provinces were constituted as of June 30, 1966.

Katayama, Tetsu (tětsōō kätäyä'mä), 1887–, Japanese statesman. Leader of Social Democratic party, prime minister of coalition cabinet (1947–48).

Katayev, Valentin Petrovich (vŭlyĭntyēn' pĕtrô'vĭch kŭtī'ŭf), 1897–, Russian author. His novels *The Embezzlers* (1926), *Time, Forward!* (1932), and *The Wife* (1944), all translated into English, portray Soviet life. Also wrote popular comedies.

Katharine or **Katherine.** For some persons thus named, see CATHERINE.

Katharine of Aragon, 1485–1536, queen of England, daughter of Ferdinand and Isabella of Spain and first wife of HENRY VIII. She did not produce a male heir and her political importance waned after the collapse (1525) of the Spanish alliance. Henry, infatuated with Anne Boleyn, tried to have the marriage annulled. Pope denied the divorce, and Henry married Anne secretly. Led to English Reformation. Katharine never accepted the decision that her marriage was invalid. She was confined and died after a prolonged illness.

Kathiawar (kä'tēŭwär"), peninsula (c.25,000 sq. mi.), Gujarat, W India, between Gulf of Kutch and Gulf of Cambay.

Katkov, Mikhail Nikiforovich (mēkhŭyēl' nyĭkē'fŭrŭvĭch kŭtkôf'), 1818–87, Russian journalist. Became a reactionary and Slavophile adviser of Alexander III.

Katmai National Monument (kät'mī), dying volcanic region, S Alaska, near end of Alaska peninsula. Here are Katmai Volcano and Valley of Ten Thousand Smokes, scene of violent eruption 1912. Mt. Trident had lava flows in 1950s.

Katmandu (kätmändōō'), city (pop. c.195,000), cap. of Nepal. Founded 723, it lies at an altitude of c.4,500 ft. Originally ruled by the Newars, it became independent in 15th cent. Captured by the Gurkhas in 1768 and made their cap. City received its name from Katmandu [wooden temple] temple built in 1596. Has an elaborate palace, a college, and Sanskrit libraries.

Kato, Takaakira, Viscount (tä"kä-ä'kērä kä'tō) 1860–1926, Japanese statesman. Largely responsible for Twenty-one Demands presented to China. As prime minister (1924–25) he cut budget and army strength, sponsored manhood-suffrage law.

Katona, Joseph (kŏ'tônō), 1791–1830, Hungarian dramatist. His tragedy *Bank dan* (1821) was made into an opera by Francis Erhel (1810–93).

Katowice (kätôvē'tše), Ger. *Kattowitz*, city (est. pop. 284,000), cap. of Katowice prov., S Poland. Industrial center of important mining district (coal, iron, zinc, lead) which also contains industrial centers of Beuthen, Chorzow, Gleiwitz, and Hindenburg. Chartered 1865, it passed from Prussia to Poland 1921.

Katrine, Loch (lŏkh kăt'rĭn), lake, c.8 mi. long and 1 mi. wide, Perthshire, in the Trossachs, Scotland. Its beauty is celebrated in Scott's *Lady of the Lake.* In 1859 Loch became source of water supply for Glasgow.

Kattegat (kä'tǐgät"), strait, 137 mi. long and 37–c.100 mi. wide, between Sweden and Jutland, Denmark. It connects with North Sea through the Skagerrak, with

Baltic Sea through the Oresund, Great Belt, and Little Belt. Goteborg (Sweden) and Aarhus (Denmark) are chief ports. Also spelled Cattegat.

Kattowitz, Poland: see KATOWICE.

katydid, insect of long-horned grasshopper family. Most of c.7,000 species are green and eat plants. Produce sound by rubbing forewings together.

Katyn (kŭtīn'), village. RSFSR, W of Smolensk. Mass grave of some 4,250 Polish officers, imprisoned after Poland's defeat in 1939, was found in a nearby forest by German occupation forces in 1943. Russians, though they denied having committed the massacre, refused international investigation. They later accused Germans of the crime.

Katzenbach, Nicholas de B(elleville), 1922–. Under Secretary of State (1966–). U.S. Attorney General 1965–66.

Kauai (kou'wī), island (623 sq. mi.; pop. 27,922), part of Hawaii, separated from Oahu by Kauai Channel. Geologically oldest of Hawaiian Isls. LIHUE is main town, and NAWILIWILI HARBOR chief port. In central mountain mass are Kawaikini (5,170 ft.), highest peak, and scenic WAIALEALE. First major attempt at agr. in Hawaii made here with estab. of sugar plantation 1835. Now has sugar growing, truck farming, ranching, and tourism.

Kauffman, Angelica, 1741–1807, Swiss historical and portrait painter. As protégée of Sir Joshua Reynolds she enjoyed great success in England and Italy.

Kaufman, George S. (kôf'mŭn, kouf'–), 1889–1961, American dramatist, drama critic of the New York *Times*. His many collaborations include the musical *Of Thee I Sing* (with Morris Ryskind; score by George Gershwin, 1931), *You Can't Take It With You* (with Moss Hart, 1936), and *Stage Door* (with Edna Ferber, 1936).

Kaufmann Peak: see LENIN PEAK.

Kaukauna (kôkô'nú), industrial city (pop. 10,096), E Wis., ENE of Appleton; settled 1793. Was fur-trading post in late 18th and early 19th cent. Railroad shops, stone quarries, and factories.

Kaunas (kou'näs), Rus. *Kovno*, city (1965 est. pop. 269,000), central Lithuania. A port on the Niemen, it has food and textile mfg. A Lithuanian stronghold against the Teutonic Knights in medieval times, Kaunas passed to Russia in third Polish partition (1795). It was the provisional cap. of Lithuania 1918–40, VILNA being held by Poland. The Germans who occupied Kaunas 1941–44, massacred nearly all the Jews (c.30% of prewar population) and destroyed most of city before withdrawing. The university was formed 1922.

Kaunda, Kenneth (koun'dú), 1924–, Zambian political leader. Active in African nationalist causes; in 1953 became secretary general of Northern prov. Led agitation against Federation of Rhodesia and Nyasaland. Arrested and later released. Upon Zambia's independence in 1964, he was elected first president.

Kaunitz, Wenzel Anton, Fürst von (vĕn'tsŭl än'tôn fürst' fün kou'nïts), 1711–94, Austrian chancellor and foreign minister under Maria Theresa, Joseph II, and Leopold II. His astute diplomacy created the anti-Prussian coalition that led to the SEVEN YEARS WAR and secured a share for Austria in the Polish partition of 1772.

Kautsky, Karl Johann (kärl yō'hän kout'skē), 1854–1938, German-Austrian socialist. Was principal figure in devising the Erfurt Program, cofounder of the Independent Social Democratic party in Germany, and a dominant figure in Second International. He opposed Lenin and Bolshevism as well as those who advocated revision of Marxist doctrines.

Kavalla or **Kavala** (both: kävä'lä), city (pop. 44,517), E Macedonia, Greece; an Aegean port on the Gulf of Kavalla. Chief Greek tobacco center. Taken by Bulgaria from Turkey in first Balkan War; ceded to Greece after second Balkan War (1913).

Kaveri: see CAUVERY.

Kaverin, Veniamin Aleksandrovich (vĕnyûmēn' ûlyĭk-sän'drŭvĭch kŭvyĕ'rĭn), 1902–, Russian novelist. His work deals with the adjustment of the intellectual to Soviet society.

Kaw, river: see KANSAS, river.

Kawartha Lakes (kŭwôr'thû), group of 14 lakes in Lindsay-Peterborough area, S Ont., Canada. Popular resort region.

Kawasaki (käwä'sä'kē), city (pop. 632,975), central Honshu, Japan, on Tokyo Bay. Steel mills, shipyards.

Kaw Indians: see KANSA INDIANS.

Kay, John, 1704–64, English inventor of fly shuttle, patented 1733, important in mechanical weaving.

Kayah State (kúyä') or **Karenni State** (kúrĕ'nē), constituent state (c.4,500 sq. mi.; pop. c.83,000) of Burma. Borders on Thailand; cap. Loikaw. Inhabitants are Karens. Area produces tungsten and teak. Constituted 1948, it became largely autonomous after Karen rebellion (1948–49). Official name changed from Karenni State to Kayah State 1952.

kayak: see CANOE.

Kaye, Danny, 1913–, American film actor and comedian, originally named Kominski. First successful on the N.Y. stage (1941) with his rapid patter of nonsense talk. In films after 1944, he often played several characters in same film (e.g., *The Secret Life of Walter Mitty*).

Kayseri (kī'sĕrē), anc. *Caesarea Mazaca*, city (pop. 102,596), central Turkey. Agr. center; cotton and tile mfg. Was important in Byzantine and Seljuk empires. Also known as Kaisaria.

Kazakh Soviet Socialist Republic (käzäk') or **Kazakhstan** (kä"zäkstän'), second largest constituent republic (1,048,300 sq. mi.; 1965 est. pop. 11,985,000), S USSR, bordering on Caspian Sea (W) and China (E); its cap. is Alma-Ata. Consists of the dry Caspian and Turan lowlands, the arid Ust Urt plateau, and the Kazakh hills, and it contains the Aral Sea and L. Balkhash. In the E and S rise the Altai and Ala-Tau ranges. The Irtysh, Ural, Ili, and Syr Darya are the chief rivers. Wheat is grown in black-earth steppes of N; camels and sheep are raised in arid central section; irrigated S plains grow rubber-bearing plants, cotton, rice, fruit, and other crops. Industry is based on rich mineral resources (copper, coal, lead, zinc, iron). The Kazakhs (30% of population) are a Turkic-speaking Moslem group of warlike ancestry. Area came under Russian rule in 19th cent. Called Kirgiz Autonomous SSR 1920–25. Became constituent republic 1936.

Kazan, Elia, 1909–, American theatrical director, b. Turkey. After early training with the Group Theatre in N.Y., he received awards for directing both plays (*Skin of Our Teeth, All My Sons, A Streetcar Named Desire, Death of a Salesman*) and films (*Gentleman's Agreement, On the Waterfront*). Cofounder (1947) of Actors' Studio in N.Y.

Kazan (kúzän'), city (1965 est. pop. 762,000), cap. Tatar ASSR, E European RSFSR, near the Volga, where its port and shipyards are. Industrial and commercial center, it has mfg. of locomotives, aircraft, agr. machinery, synthetic rubber, gunpowder, and textiles. There are various cultural institutions including a university (founded 1804). Founded 1401, Kazan was cap. of a powerful khanate, which was conquered 1552 by Ivan IV. In 18th cent. it became an E outpost of Russian colonization. Of the Moslem period of Kazan little remains except the Suyumbeka tower in the 16th-cent. kremlin.

Kazanlik (kä"zänlĭk'), town (pop. 31,133), central Bulgaria, in a valley famous for its rose fields. Long a mfg. center for attar of roses.

Kazantzakis, Nikos (nī'kôs käzändzä'kĭs), 1883?–1957, Greek writer and statesman. In *The Odyssey, a Modern Sequel* (1938) he uses the further adventures of Odysseus to examine the world view of Jesus, Buddha, Lenin, Nietzsche, and others. He also wrote other novels and short tales.

Kazbek, Mount (kŏzbĕk'), peak, 16,541 ft. high, N Georgian SSR, in central greater Caucasus, above DARYAL gorge. Its glaciers give rise to Terek R. First scaled 1868.

Kazin, Alfred (kā'zĭn), 1915–, American critic. His works on American literature and culture include *On Native Grounds* (1942) and *Contemporaries* (1962). *A Walker in the City* (1951) and *Starting Out in the Thirties* (1965) tell of his life in New York city.

Kazvin or Qazvin (both: käzvēn'), city (pop. c.80,-000), NW Iran. Has textile and flour mills. Founded by King Shapur I in 3rd. cent. Was cap. of Persia 1548–98. Occupied by Russia in both world wars.

Kea or Keos, Greek island of the CYCLADES.

Kealakekua Bay (kā'ŭläkäkōō'ŭ), W Hawaii, S of Kailua. Monument to Capt. Cook, killed by natives here 1779, stands on the shore.

Kean, Edmund, 1787?–1833, English actor. His triumph (1814) as Shylock is a landmark in theatrical history. Other great roles of his brief career include Iago, Lear, and Richard III. Kean's intensity and insight made him ideal in spirited romantic roles. His son, **Charles John Kean,** 1811?–1868, was an actor whose forte was melodrama. Played opposite his wife, **Ellen Tree Kean,** 1808–80, a noted comedienne.

Kearney, Denis (kär'nē), 1847–1907, American political agitator, b. Ireland. In 1870s he inflamed Californians against Chinese labor. Formed a working-men's party which achieved reform measures.

Kearney (kär'nē), city (pop. 14,210), S central Nebr., on Platte R., SW of Grand Isl.; founded 1871. Processing, trade. industrial, and rail center in Great Plains grain and livestock area. Site of Fort Kearney (1848–71), estab. to protect Oregon Trail, is nearby.

Kearns (kûrnz), town (pop. 17,172), N central Utah, suburb just S of Salt Lake City.

Kearny, Stephen Watts (kär'nē), 1794–1848, American general in Mexican War. Commanded Army of the West. Took Santa Fe and Los Angeles; served as military governor of California territory until May, 1847. His cousin, **Lawrence Kearny,** 1789–1868, was an American naval officer Commanding East India squadron (1840–43), he opened negotiations which led to a U.S.–China commercial treaty. signed 1844. **Philip Kearny,** 1814–62, nephew of S. W. Kearny, was a Union general in Civil War. Led 1st N.J. Brigade in Peninsular campaign and second battle of Bull Run. Killed at Chantilly. Noted for courage and dash, idolized by his men.

Kearny (kär'nē), town (pop. 37,472), NE N.J., containing much of tidal wastelands between Passaic and Hackensack rivers, NNE of Newark. Has shipvards and drydocks. Meadowlands being reclaimed.

Kearsarge (kēr'särj"), Union ship in the Civil War. See CONFEDERATE CRUISERS.

Keats, John, 1795–1821, English lyric poet. Apprenticed to a surgeon (1811). he turned to poetry under the influence of Leigh Hunt and his circle. *Poems* (1817) included "On First Looking into Chapman's Homer." His long poem *Endymion* (1818) was vigorously attacked by critics. In that year began his love for Fanny Brawne; but he had developed tuberculosis, and his poor health prevented their marriage. Keats sailed to Italy in search of health in 1820 (shortly after the publication of his *Lamia, Isabella, The Eve of St. Agnes, and Other Poems*) and died there. Despite a tragically brief life, Keats is one of the greatest English poets. Among his poems are "Ode to a Nightingale," "Ode on a Grecian Urn," "To Autumn," "Ode to Melancholy," and the unfinished epic "Hyperion." "The Eve of St. Agnes" and "La Belle Dame sans Merci" are examples of romantic medievalism at its best. His sonnets include "When I have fears that I may cease to be," and "Bright star! would I were steadfast as thou art."

Keble, John (kē'bŭl), 1792–1866, English clergyman and poet. His devotional poems in *The Christian Year*

(1827), based on Book of Common Prayer, won him a professorship of poetry at Oxford. His sermon "National Apostasy," given in 1833 Newman called the beginning of OXFORD MOVEMENT. Wrote many hymns.

Keble College: see OXFORD UNIVERSITY.

Kebnekaise (kĕb'nŭkī"sŭ), glaciated peak. 6,965 ft. high, Norrbotten co., N Sweden; highest in Sweden.

Kechua: see QUECHUA.

Kecskemet, Hung. *Kecskemét* (kĕch'kĕmāt), city (est. pop. 69,000), central Hungary; center of fruit export.

Kedah (kĕ'dŭ), state (c.3,660 sq. mi.; pop. 701,643), NW MALAYA, on Strait of Malacca; cap. Alor Star. Ruled by a sultan. Has rubber plantations in S. Rice grown on coastal plain. Tin mined.

Kedesh (kē'–), one of the cities of refuge, N Palestine. It is frequently mentioned in the Bible. Also Kedesh-naphtali.

Keeler, James Edward, 1857–1900, American astronomer. Discovered many nebulae and confirmed theory that Saturn's rings are composed of meteoric particles.

Keelung or Kilung (jē'lŏŏng), city (pop. c.226,400), N Taiwan, on East China Sea. Principal port and naval base. Large chemical industry. In 17th cent., occupied first by Spaniards, later by the Dutch. Came under Chinese control 1683. Held by Japan 1895–1945.

Keene, Laura, c.1826–1873, Anglo-American actress and manager. Her most famous production was Taylor's *Our American Cousin,* given (Ford's Theater, Washington, 1865) when Lincoln was shot.

Keene, city (pop. 17,562), SW N.H., W of Manchester, in resort area; settled 1736. State Col. of Univ. of New Hampshire is here.

Keewatin (kēwä'tĭn), provisional district: see NORTH-WEST TERRITORIES, Canada.

Keewatin: see PRECAMBRIAN ERA.

Kefauver, (Carey) Estes (kē'fävŭr), 1903–63, U.S. Senator from Tenn. (1949–63). Headed Senate crime investigating committee (1950–51). Served in House of Representatives (1939–49). Unsuccessful candidate for Democratic presidential nomination in 1952 and 1956.

Keflavik (kĕp'lävĕk"), town (pop. 5,070). SW Iceland, on Faxa Bay. Major fishing port; international airport, built by U.S. in Second World War.

Keighley (kēth'lē), municipal borough (pop. 55,852), West Riding of Yorkshire, England. Products include textiles, leather, and paper.

Keita, Modibo, 1915–, African political leader, president of Republic of Mali (1959–). A strong supporter of African unity, in 1962 he led Mali into union with Ghana and Guinea.

Keitel, Wilhelm (vīl'hĕlm kī'tŭl), 1882–1946, German field marshal. Chief of combined German general staff in Second World War. Was hanged after Nuremberg war-crimes trial.

Keith, Sir Arthur (kēth), 1866–1955, British anthropologist and anatomist, authority on human evolution.

Keith, George, c.1638–1716, Scottish preacher. At first a Friend, he estab. (1684) in America Christian Quakers, separatists denounced by William Penn 1692. Ordained priest (1700) in Church of England.

Keith, George, 1693?–1778, 10th earl marischal of Scotland. A leader in the Jacobite rebellion of 1715 and the Spanish expedition to Scotland (1719), he fled to the Continent. Held various high offices under Frederick the Great. His brother, **James Francis Edward Keith,** 1696–1758, also took part in the Jacobite rebellion and fled abroad. After service in Spain and Russia he was made (1747) a Prussian field marshal and rendered great service in the Seven Years War. Killed in the battle of Hochkirch.

Keith, George Keith Elphinstone, Viscount: see EL-PHINSTONE, GEORGE KEITH.

Keith, James Francis Edward: see KEITH, GEORGE (1693?–1778).

Keith, Minor Cooper, 1848–1929, American magnate, founder of United Fruit Co. Dominated banana trade, greatly altered economic life of Central America.

Kekulé von Stradonitz, Friedrich August (frē'drĭkh ou'-gōŏst kā'kōōlā fün shtrā'dōnĭts), 1829–96, German chemist. Worked in organic chemistry, especially on benzene, for molecular structure of which he developed ring theory.

Kelantan: see MALAYA.

Keller, Gottfried (gôt'frēt), 1819–90, Swiss novelist, one of the major German prose writers. Among his chief works are the autobiographical novel *Der grüne Heinrich* (1854–55) and a collection of short novels, *People of Seldwyla* (1856–74; Eng. tr., 1929).

Keller, Helen (Adams), 1880–, American author and lecturer, blind and deaf from the age of two, grad. Radcliffe 1904. Her teacher and companion was Anne Sullivan Macy. Helen Keller gained world fame for her aid to the handicapped.

Kellermann, François Christophe de (frāswä' krēstôf' dü kēlērmän'), 1735–1820, marshal of France; created duke of Valmy 1808. He and Demouriez stopped Prussians at Valmy (1792).

Kelley, Hall Jackson, 1790–1874, American propagandist who urged settlement of Oregon.

Kelley, Oliver Hudson, 1826–1913, American agriculturist, a founder of the Natl. Grange of the Patrons of Husbandry, the central influence in the GRANGER MOVEMENT of the 1870s.

Kelley, William Darrah (dā'rü), 1814–90, U.S. Representative from Pa. (1861–90). Called "Pig Iron" Kelley for his protectionism and his allusions to iron industry of Pa. Humanitarian in his views.

Kellogg, Edward, 1790–1858, American economist. His scheme of government loans at low interest rates was backed by many radical political parties in U.S.

Kellogg, Frank B(illings), 1856–1937, American statesman. As U.S. Secretary of State (1925–29) he promoted Kellogg-Briand Pact. Was U.S. Senator (1917–23), ambassador to Great Britain (1924–25), judge of Permanent Court of Internatl. Justice (1930–35). Awarded 1929 Nobel Peace Prize.

Kellogg, city (pop. 5,061), NW Idaho, in Coeur d'Alene mining district, SE of Coeur d'Alene. Grew around Bunker Hill and Sullivan mines (discovered 1885), now combined as one of world's largest lead producers. Sunshine Mine is a leading producer of silver.

Kellogg-Briand Pact (–brēā'), agreement, signed Aug. 27, 1928, condemning war and agreeing to peaceful settlement of international differences. More properly known as the Pact of Paris. Primary moving forces were Aristide BRIAND of France and F. B. KELLOGG of U.S. Effectiveness of pact vitiated by its failure to provide for enforcement.

Kells, urban district (pop. 2,193), Co. Meath, Ireland. Has relic of an anc. monastery founded by St. Columba. Here was found the Book of Kells, beautifully illuminated manuscript of the Latin Gospels, written probably 8th cent. Now in Trinity Col. library in Dublin.

Kelly, George, 1887–, American dramatist. Wrote satirical comedies (e.g., *The Torchbearers*, 1922; *The Show-off*, 1924) and drama *Craig's Wife* (1925).

Kelly, Grace, later Grace, princess of Monaco, 1929–, American actress. After N.Y. debut (1949) in Strindberg's *The Father*, she won renown in such films as *Country Girl*. In 1956 she married Prince Rainier.

Kelly, Howard Atwood, 1858–1943, American surgeon, influential professor of gynecology and obstetrics at Johns Hopkins (1889–1919). He was also an authority on American medical history.

Kelly, William, 1811–88, American inventor. He independently discovered basic principle of Bessemer process and estab. his priority right. Conflict between Bessemer and Kelly interests was settled by consolidation of the rival companies.

Kelmscott Press, printing establishment in Hammersmith, London, founded by William MORRIS. A leader in the revival of fine bookmaking, its masterpiece was *The Works of Geoffrey Chaucer*, illustrated by Sir Edward Burne-Jones (1896).

Kelowna (kĭlō'nü), city (pop. 13,188), S B.C., Canada, on Okanagan L. SW of Vernon, in fruitgrowing region.

kelp, name for various species of brown algae, or seaweeds, found in waters along Atlantic and Pacific coasts. Some, e.g., *Macrocystis*, have fronds up to 200 ft. long; others are small. They are a source of potassium and iodine.

Kelt: see CELT.

Kelvin, William Thomson, 1st Baron, 1824–1907, British mathematician and physicist. Inventor of many improvements in transmission of messages by submarine cables, of the reflecting galvanometer, and a siphon recorder for telegraphic messages; he also contributed to thermodynamics. He coordinated the various theories of heat, established on a firm basis Joule's law of conservation of energy, and introduced the Kelvin or absolute scale of TEMPERATURE.

Kemal Pasha, Mustafa: see ATATURK, KEMAL.

Kemble, Roger, 1721–1802, English actor and manager. Father of 12 children, he founded one of England's most distinguished acting families. His eldest son, **John Philip Kemble**, 1757–1823, was educated for the priesthood, but turned to the stage. Managed Drury Lane 1788–1803 (gaining fame in Shakespearean roles opposite his sister, Sarah Kemble SIDDONS) and Covent Garden, 1803–8. A formal, stately actor, he was best in tragedy. His brother, **George Stephen Kemble**, 1758–1822, played roles such as Falstaff. His youngest brother, **Charles Kemble**, 1775–1854, excelled in comic roles. Toured U.S. (1832–34) with his elder daughter, **Fanny Kemble** (Frances Ann Kemble), 1809–93. Her debut (1829) at Covent Garden as Juliet brought her fame, which she increased in such roles as Lady Macbeth, Portia, and Beatrice. In England she wrote against slavery during U.S. Civil War. Her sister, **Adelaide Kemble**, 1814–79, was a singer, notable in Italian operatic roles.

Kemerovo (kĕ'mŭrŏ"vō), city (1965 est. pop. 351,000), RSFSR, S central Siberia, on Tom R. and branch of Trans-Siberian RR. Coal-mining center of Kuznetsk Basin, with chemical industries.

Kemi (kĕ'mē), city (pop. 28,353), NW Finland, on Gulf of Bothnia and at mouth of Kemi R. Lumber and cellulose industry.

Kemp, Will(iam), fl. 1579–1600, English comic actor and dancer, known as a player in Shakespeare's company and for his morris dance from London to Norwich (1599).

Kempe, Margery (kĕmp), d. 1438 or after, English religious enthusiast. Her autobiography, perhaps the earliest in English, was known only in part until 1934.

Kempener, Pieter de (kĕm'pünŭr), c.1503–1580, Flemish religious painter. Worked in Italy and Spain.

Kempis, Thomas à: see THOMAS À KEMPIS.

Ken, Thomas, 1637–1711, English prelate and hymn writer. Bishop of Bath and Wells, he was deprived of his see in 1691 for refusing oath of allegiance to William III. His best-known hymn is the doxology, *Praise God from Whom All Blessings Flow*.

Kenai Peninsula (kē'nī), S Alaska, jutting into Gulf of Alaska, between Prince William Sound and Cook Inlet. Kenai Mts. cross it from NE to SW. Coastal climate mild, with abundant rainfall; growing season adequate for many crops. Forest, mineral, fishing resources; good farmland in W section. Alaska RR crosses peninsula from Seward.

Kendal, Dame Madge, 1849–1935, English actress, whose maiden name was Margaret Robertson; sister of dramatist T. W. Robertson. Made debut as Ophelia in 1865. Costarred often with her husband, William Kendal (1843–1917), in productions of Shakespeare and contemporary comedies.

Kendall, Amos (kĕn'dŭl), 1789–1869, American journalist and statesman. Leading member of Pres. Jackson's KITCHEN CABINET; defended Jackson's policies in Washington *Globe*. U.S. Postmaster General (1835–40); thoroughly reorganized department.

Kendall, Edward Calvin, 1886–, American biochemist. Shared 1950 Nobel Prize in Physiology and Medicine for work on hormones of the cortex of adrenal glands. Other contributions include isolation of thyroxine, preparation (with others) of cortisone by partial synthesis, and investigations (with co-workers) of effects of cortisone and ACTH (adrenocorticotropic hormone from the pituitary gland) on rheumatoid arthritis and rheumatic fever. Associated with Mayo Clinic from 1914 and with Mayo Foundation (of Univ. of Minnesota) from 1921.

Kendall, George Wilkins, 1809–67, American journalist. Cofounder of New Orleans *Picayune* (1837). His articles during Mexican War made him first modern war correspondent.

Kendrew, John Cowdery, 1917–, English chemist. Shared 1962 Nobel Prize in Chemistry for determining molecular structure of myoglobin, the protein that carries oxygen to muscles.

Kenilworth (kĕn′ŭl-), urban district (pop. 14,427), Warwickshire, England. Has ruins of noted castle celebrated in Scott's *Kenilworth*. Built c.1120, it was later the property of Simon de Montfort and of John of Gaunt. Earl of Leicester entertained Queen Elizabeth here lavishly in 1575.

Kenites, wilderness tribe, friendly to the Hebrews, with whom they came into Palestine. Judges 1.16.

Kenmore, residential village (1966 pop. 21,146), NW N.Y., N of Buffalo; settled 1889.

Kennan, George, 1845–1924, American authority on Siberia. Explored Siberia and other parts of Russia. His articles were for many years only reliable source of information on the area. His grandnephew, **George F(rost) Kennan,** 1904–, became a diplomat and historian. Originated (1947) U.S. policy of "containment" of USSR. Became ambassador to USSR 1925, but Soviet government demanded his recall; ambassador to Yugoslavia 1961–63. His writings include *Russia Leaves the War* (1956) and *Russia and the West under Lenin and Stalin* (1961).

Kennebec (kĕn′ŭbĕk), river, flowing from Moosehead L., NW Maine, c.164 mi. S to the Atlantic, receiving the Dead, Sandy, Sebasticook, and Androscoggin rivers. Champlain explored it 1604 and 1605; in 1607 Fort St. George, short-lived colony, was estab. at its mouth. Trading posts were set up after 1625. Villages near power sites became industrial centers.

Kennebunk (kĕn′ŭbŭngk′), town (pop. 4,551), SW Maine, SW of Portland; in resort area; settled c.1650.

Kennebunkport or **Kennebunk Port** (both: kĕn″ĭbŭngk-pôrt′), town (pop. 1,851), SW Maine, on coast SE of Kennebunk; settled 1629. Summer resort, especially for authors, artists, and actors.

Kennedy, Gerald (Hamilton), 1907–, American clergyman. Became bishop of Methodist Church in the Los Angeles area in 1952. Author of *For Preachers and Others* (1964).

Kennedy, John F(itzgerald), 1917–63, 34th or 35th (see list at end of article UNITED STATES) President of the United States, b. Brookline, Mass. Enlisted in the navy and served with distinction in Second World War as commander of a PT-boat in the Pacific. Served as Congressman from Mass. (1947–52), and U.S. Senator (1953–60). Defeated Richard M. Nixon in 1960 presidential election to become the youngest man ever elected President. Domestic program, known as the New Frontier, called for Federal aid to education, medical care for the aged, aid to depressed areas, enlargement of civil rights, and an accelerated space program. In foreign affairs, Kennedy was criticized for U.S. encouragement of ill-fated invasion of Cuba (April, 1961), but was highly praised for forcing withdrawal (Oct., 1962) by USSR of offensive nuclear weapons from Cuba. He expanded aid to anti-Communist forces in Vietnam, and in 1963 he helped ease international tension through an agreement with the Soviet Union on a limited ban on nuclear testing. Also established the PEACE CORPS and an Alliance for Progress with Latin America. He was murdered on Nov. 22, 1963, in Dallas, Texas, by a hidden assassin (see OSWALD, LEE HARVEY). He was succeeded as President by Lyndon B. Johnson. **Robert F(rancis) Kennedy,** 1925–, served his brother as Attorney General (1961–64). He became U.S. Senator from New York in 1965. **Edward M(oore) Kennedy,** 1932–, became U.S. Senator from Mass. in 1962. Their father, **Joseph Patrick Kennedy,** 1888–, served as U.S. ambassador to Great Britain (1937–40). He engaged in such business activities as banking, shipbuilding, and motion-picture distribution before serving as chairman of the Securities and Exchange Commission (1934–35) and head of U.S. Maritime Commission (1936–37).

Kennedy, John Pendleton, 1795–1870, American novelist, author of *Horse-Shoe Robinson* (1835). Was a member of Congress (1838–44) and Secretary of the Navy (1852–53).

Kennedy, Cape: see CAPE KENNEDY.

Kennedy, Mount, c.14,000 ft. high, Yukon territory, Canada, in St. Elias Mts. near Alaska border. Named in honor of Pres. John F. Kennedy, 1965. Discovered in 1935, climbed for first time in 1965 by team that included Robert F. Kennedy.

Kennedy Center for the Performing Arts: see JOHN F. KENNEDY CENTER FOR THE PERFORMING ARTS.

Kennedy International Airport: see QUEENS, borough.

Kennedy round: see GENERAL AGREEMENT ON TARIFFS AND TRADE.

Kennelly, Arthur Edwin (kĕ′nŭlē), 1861–1939, American electrical engineer, b. India. His theory (advanced 1902, independently of Oliver Heaviside) that layer of ionized air in upper atmosphere deflects electromagnetic waves toward earth was later verified; the deflecting layer is called Heaviside layer, Kennelly-Heaviside layer, and ionosphere.

Kenner, town (pop. 17,037), SE La., suburb W of New Orleans. International airport and race track are nearby.

Kennesaw (kĕn′ŭsô), city (pop. 1,507), NW Ga., NW of Marietta. Nearby Kennesaw Mt. Natl. Battlefield Park was scene of Sherman's June 27 attack in ATLANTA CAMPAIGN.

Kenneth I (Kenneth mac Alpin), d. 858, traditional founder of the kingdom of Scotland.

Kennett Square, borough (pop. 4,355), SE Pa., NW of Wilmington, Del.; settled c.1705.

Kennewick, city (pop. 14,244), SE Wash., on Columbia R. near influx of Snake R., in farm and vineyard region. Grew after estab. of Atomic Energy Commission's nearby Hanford Works in Second World War.

Kenny, Elizabeth, 1886–1952, Australian nurse, originator of a system of treating infantile paralysis patients. Her method was based on use of hot, moist applications and passive exercise.

Kénogami (kānō′gŭmē), town (pop. 11,816), S Que., Canada, on Sable R. and W of Chicoutimi. Here are hydroelectric station, paper and pulp mills.

Kenora (kŭnô′rŭ), town (pop. 10,904), W Ont., Canada, at N end of L. of the Woods. Fishing, hunting, and canoeing base. Here are paper, pulp, lumber, and flour mills, boatbuilding, and fish hatchery.

Kenosha (kĭnō′shŭ), industrial city (pop. 67,899), SE Wis., on L. Michigan S of Milwaukee; settled 1835. First public school in state opened here 1849. Has branch of Univ. of Wisconsin and Carthage Col.

Kensett, John Frederick, 1818–72, American landscape painter of Hudson River school.

Kensico Reservoir, N.Y.: see CATSKILL AQUEDUCT.

Kensington and Chelsea, Royal borough of, London borough since 1965 (est. pop. 219,190); includes former metropolitan boroughs of Kensington and Chelsea. Kensington Gardens, adjoining Hyde Park, includes Long Water (the Serpentine of Hyde Park), Round Pond, and Flower and Broad Walks. Kensington Palace, former royal residence, is W of gardens. South Kensington is site of part of British Mus., Victoria and Albert Mus., Imperial Inst., Science Mus., Royal Col. of Art, Royal Col. of Science, and Albert Hall.

Kensington Rune Stone, found near Kensington, Minn., in 1898. Contains account of Norse exploration party. Authenticity of stone much disputed.

Kent, James, 1763–1847, American jurist, first professor of law at Columbia College. Chancellor Kent had great influence on law in New York and U.S., principally through his *Commentaries on the American Law* (1826–30).

Kent, Rockwell, 1882–, American painter, wood engraver, and lithographer.

Kent, maritime county (1,525 sq. mi.; pop. 1,701,083), SE England; co. town Maidstone. North Downs cross county E to W. Largely agr. and pastoral, the region has growing industry as London urban area encroaches in W. Strategic location on path to the Continent has always made Kent important. Many religious houses were estab. in Middle Ages; Canterbury was goal of many pilgrimages (Chaucer's *Canterbury Tales*). Coast was heavily fortified in First and Second World Wars against possible invasion.

Kent. 1 Resort town (pop. 6,264), W Conn., at N.Y. line SW of Torrington; settled 1738. Has Kent School for boys and Kent School for girls. **2** Industrial city (pop. 17,836), NE Ohio, NE of Akron. Settled as Franklin Mills, combined 1863 with Carthage as Kent. Seat of Kent State Univ.

Kent, kingdom of, one of the states of the Anglo-Saxon heptarchy in England. Settled in mid-5th cent. by the Jutes, perhaps under Hengist and Horsa. St. Augustine of Canterbury led first Catholic mission to England here in 597. Became a province of Mercia, then of Wessex. Was one of the most advanced areas in pre-Conquest England.

Kent, Maid of: see BARTON, ELIZABETH.

Kenton, Simon, 1755–1836, American frontiersman. Joined Daniel Boone in settlement at Boonesboro. Took part in expeditions of G. R. Clark. Participated in many Indian raids.

Kentucky, state (40,395 sq. mi.; pop. 3,038,156), S central U.S.; admitted 1792 as 15th state (slaveholding); cap. FRANKFORT. Other cities are LOUISVILLE (the largest), LEXINGTON, and COVINGTON. Bounded N by Ohio R., SW by Mississippi R., E by Big Sandy R. and Tug Fork. Hilly in E and W (coal areas); gently rolling in center, with BLUEGRASS region in N and Pennyroyal plateau in S. Chief rivers are the KENTUCKY, CUMBERLAND, LICKING, TENNESSEE, and OHIO. Famous for whisky (esp. bourbon) and horse breeding, Ky. is also a leading producer of tobacco, coal, and fluorspar. Corn, soybeans, potatoes are other major crops; other minerals are petroleum, natural gas, stone. Industry now rivals agr.; meat packing, flour and grain milling, and mfg. of household goods, electronic equipment, and metal products are important. French claimed region in 17th cent., but British gained control after French and Indian Wars in 1763. First permanent settlement, HARRODSBURG (1774). Daniel BOONE blazed WILDERNESS ROAD, founded BOONESBORO 1775. Indian raids virtually ended by 1794. Growth after War of 1812 was rapid as Ohio and Mississippi R. traffic increased. Became huge slave market for Lower South in 1840s. Remained in Union during Civil War, but supplied men to both sides. Industrial surge after war, but farmers suffered evils of one-crop (tobacco) system. The 20th cent. marked by labor troubles in mines. Compliance with 1954 Supreme Court decision on integration was general and orderly. New Tennessee Valley Authority projects in 1960s aided state's growing power supply.

Kentucky, river, formed in central Ky. and flowing c.259 mi. NW to Ohio R. at Carrollton. Buckhorn Dam is on Middle Fork.

Kentucky, University of, mainly at Lexington; land grant, state supported; coed.; opened 1865 as part of Kentucky Univ. (now Transylvania College), became state college 1878, and university 1908. Junior colleges at Ashland, Covington, Cumberland, Elizabethtown, Fort Knox, Henderson, and Prestonburg.

Kentucky and Virginia Resolutions, passed in 1798 and 1799 in opposition to ALIEN AND SEDITION ACTS. Kentucky Resolutions, written by Thomas Jefferson, denied to the Federal government powers not specifically delegated to it by the Constitution. If it did assume such powers, states had right to judge constitutionality of acts. Virginia Resolutions, written by James Madison, were somewhat milder. Resolutions were later considered first notable statement of STATES' RIGHTS theory.

Kentucky University: see KENTUCKY, UNIVERSITY OF; TRANSYLVANIA COLLEGE.

Kenya (kĕn'yŭ, kĕn'yŭ), republic (224,960 sq. mi.; pop. c.9,104,000), E Africa, on Indian Ocean; cap. Nairobi. Lies across equator. Inland highlands are bisected by Rift Valley. To the SW lies L. Victoria; to N is extremely arid region. Productive land within the highlands produces coffee, tea, sisal, grains, and sugar cane; cattle ranching. Mineral resources include soda ash, limestone, gold, copper, kyanite, asbestos. Hunting and tourism. Kiswahili and English are main languages; people primarily animist, with large Christian minority, fewer Moslems and Hindus. Coastal area was settled in 7th cent. by Arab and Persian traders in slaves and ivory. Under Portuguese control, 16th–17th cent. British expanded their influence in mid-19th cent. through British East Africa Co., and in 1895 Kenya was made a protectorate. In 1920 the leased coastal strip was named Kenya Protectorate, while rest of region became crown colony. Land pressure was leading factor in outbreak of Mau Mau terrorism in 1952. Subsequent reforms included general elections (1961), and in 1963 internal self-government became effective with Jomo Kenyatta as prime minister. Full independence achieved Dec., 1963; Kenya became a republic 1964, and Kenyatta became president. Border conflict with Somalia continued to plague government in 1967.

Kenya, Mount, extinct volcano, 17,058 ft. high, central Kenya. Tea is grown on slopes.

Kenyatta, Jomo (jō'mō kĕnyä'tŭ), 1893?–, Kenyan political leader; a member of the Kikuyu tribe. Long a campaigner for land reform and political rights for Africans. In Europe he wrote *Facing Mount Kenya* (1930), study of Kikuyu customs. Returned to Kenya and in 1947 became president of the Kenya African Union. Imprisoned 1953 by British as an instigator of Mau Mau uprising; exiled 1959 to N Kenya, where, nevertheless, he was elected president of the Kenya African National Union (1960). Released 1961, he became Kenya's prime minister in 1963 and its president in 1964.

Kenyon College, at Gambier, Ohio, near Mt. Vernon; for men; chartered and opened 1824. Founded by Philander Chase as theological seminary with some college work; assumed present name 1891; today includes divinity school.

Keokuk (kē'ŭkŭk), c.1780–1848, American Indian, chief of Sac and Fox tribes. Refused to aid British in War of 1812. Keokuk, Iowa, named for him.

Keokuk, city (pop. 16,316), extreme SE Iowa, on Mississippi R. (bridged) at foot of Des Moines R. rapids; platted 1837 on site of trading post (1829). U.S. ship canal around rapids completed 1877. Gravity dam for power forms L. Keokuk. Trade and mfg. center in farm area. Notable are cemetery (1861), grave of Keokuk, and mementos of Mark Twain's days as printer here.

Keos or **Kea,** Greek island of the CYCLADES.

Kepler, Johannes (yō'hä'nǔs kĕplǔr), 1571–1630, German astronomer, evolver of laws of planetary motion. **Kepler's laws,** summarized, are: (1) Orbit of each planet is an ellipse, of which sun's center is one of the foci; (2) Radius vector of each planet (line joining its center with that of sun) moves over equal areas in equal times; (3) Square of period of each planet's revolution around sun is proportional to cube of its mean distance from sun.

Keppler, Joseph, 1838–94, American cartoonist and founder of *Puck,* b. Vienna.

Kerak, El, Jordan: see KRAK.

Kerala (kä′rälä), state (c.15,000 sq. mi.; pop. c.16,-880,000), SW India, on Arabian Sea: cap. Trivandrum. Created 1956. Roughly coextensive with former state of Travancore-Cochin (see TRAVANCORE). In 1957 Kerala elected India's first Communist administration; it was subsequently removed. Acute shortage of food led to massive food riots in 1965–66.

Kerbela (kûr′búlú) or **Karbala** (kär-), city (pop. c.123,000), SW Iraq, at edge of Syrian Desert; cap. of Kerbela prov. Has tomb of HUSEIN, a great shrine of pilgrims of Moslem Shiite sect.

Kerch (kyĕrch), city (1965 est. pop. 114,000), Ukrainian SSR, in E Crimea; fortified Black Sea port on Kerch Peninsula. Has iron and steel mills, coking plant, shipyards, fisheries, and canneries. Founded by Greek colonists in 6th cent. B.C., it became a Genoese colony in 13th cent. Conquered by Crimean Tatars in 1475, by Russians in 1771. German-held in Second World War. A museum has Greco-Scythian antiquities. Church of St. John the Baptist dates from 8th cent. Kerch is on **Kerch Strait,** shallow channel, 25 mi. long, connecting Sea of Azov (N) and Black Sea and separating the Crimea (N) from Taman peninsula. Known to ancients as Cimmerian Bosporus.

Kerensky, Aleksandr Feodorovich (kûrĕn′skē, Rus. ülyĭksän′dŭr fyô′dŭrüvĭch kâ′rĭnskē), 1881–, Russian revolutionist. A moderate Socialist, he succeeded Prince Lvov as provisional premier in July, 1917. His vacillation enabled Lenin to overthrow his government in November (see RUSSIAN REVOLUTION). Settled in U.S. (1940).

Kerguelen (kûr′gŭlĕn), subantarctic archipelago, S Indian Ocean, French possession since 1893. Largest island, Kerguelen (or Desolation) Isl., of volcanic origin, is a whaling station.

Kerman (kĕrmän′), city (pop. c.62,000), cap. of Eighth Prov., Iran. Center of Kerman region (anc. *Carmania*). A walled city with medieval mosques, it was ravaged in 1794 by Aga Mohamad Khan.

Kermanshah (kĕrmän″shä′), town (pop. 125,439), W Iran. Founded by Sassanids in 4th cent., it became royal summer residence. Now agr. market center. Oil refinery. Nearby are famed inscriptions of BEHISTUN.

kermes (kûr′mēz), brilliant red dye extracted from adult female scale insects. Known since anc. times; now largely replaced by cochineal and synthetic dyes.

Kermit, town (pop. 10,465), W Texas, near N.Mex. line S of Odessa. Center of oil area; refineries.

Kern, Jerome, 1885–1945, American composer of musical comedies. He wrote *Sally* (1920), containing the song *Look for the Silver Lining; Sunny* (1925); *Roberta* (1933), containing *Smoke Gets in Your Eyes;* and, perhaps his greatest work, *Show Boat* (1927), containing *Ol' Man River.*

Kern, river rising in S Sierra Nevada; E Calif., and flowing c.150 mi. S and SW past Bakersfield to reservoir in N part of what was Buena Vista L. Provides power and irrigation with aid of Friant-Kern Canal (see CENTRAL VALLEY PROJECT). Gold discovered, 1853. Upper gorge (in Sequoia Natl. Park) is spectacular canyon.

kerosene, colorless, oily mixture of hydrocarbons, obtained from fractional distillation of PETROLEUM. It is also prepared from coal, oil shale, wood. It is used as illuminant, insecticide, fuel (esp. in jet aircraft).

Kerouac, Jack (JOHN KEROUAC), 1922–, American author, one of the BEAT GENERATION. His works include *On the Road* (1957), other novels, and poems (e.g., *Mexico City Blues* (1959).

Kerry, maritime county (1,815 sq. mi.; pop. 116,405), W Ireland, in Munster; co. town Tralee. Consists of mountainous peninsulas extending into the Atlantic.

Carrantuohill (3,414 ft.) is highest point in Ireland. Lakes of Killarney attract tourists. Farming, dairying, and fishing chief occupations.

Kesselring, Albert (äl′bĕrt kĕ′súlrĭng), 1885–1960, German field marshal in Second World War. Commanded in Italy 1943–45. Was sentenced to life imprisonment after war-crimes trial (1945–46), freed 1952.

Kesteven, Parts of: see LINCOLNSHIRE, England.

Keswick (kĕs′ĭk), urban district (pop. 4,752), Cumberland, England, in Lake District. Southey and Coleridge lived here, and Southey's tomb is here. Has anc. Druids' Circle nearby. **Keswick Convention** is an evangelical convention of the Church of England, held annually since 1875.

ketch, two-masted sailing vessel with its mainmast forward and its mizzen or jigger mast aft and stepped forward of the wheel or tiller.

Ketchikan (kĕ′chĭkăn″), city (pop. 6,483), SE Alaska, on Revillagigedo Isl. in Alexander Archipelago. Supply point for miners in 1890s gold rush. Now center of Alaska's fishing (salmon, halibut) and pulp industries. With good port on Inside Passage, it is distribution center for large area and attracts tourists. U.S. Coast Guard station here.

Ketchwayo: see CETEWAYO.

ketone, any organic compound containing a carbonyl group (a carbon atom doubly bound to an oxygen atom) linked to each of two alkyl or aryl radicals. ACETONE is the simplest ketone. Ketones are related in structure to aldehydes. See RADICAL.

Kettering, city (pop. 54,462), SW Ohio, suburb S of Dayton; settled c.1812.

kettledrum: see PERCUSSION INSTRUMENTS.

Keuka Lake: see FINGER LAKES.

Kewanee (kĭwä′nē), industrial city (pop. 16,324), NW Ill., SE of Rock Island, in coal, farm, and livestock area.

Keweenaw (kē′wĭnô), peninsula, extreme N Mich., jutting NE from W Upper Peninsula into L. Superior. Portage L. and ship canal cut across it, making upper portion an island and creating important waterway. Canal has bridge with one of heaviest lift spans in world (4½ million lb.). Copper center and resort. Settlements include Houghton, Hancock, Calumet.

Kew Gardens (kū), Surrey, England, on the Thames, W of London. Royal Botanic Gardens is official name. They cover 288 acres and contain thousands of species of plants, four museums, and laboratories and hothouses. Nearby is Kew Palace, once home of George III.

Key, Francis Scott (kē), 1779–1843, American poet, author of STAR-SPANGLED BANNER. Was U.S. attorney for the District of Columbia (1833–41).

Keyes, Sir Roger John Brownlow (kēz), 1872–1945, British admiral. In First World War he commanded the Dover patrol that raided Zeebrugge and Ostend. In Second World War he was director of combined operations (1940–41) and helped develop amphibious warfare.

Key Largo: see FLORIDA KEYS.

Keynes, John Maynard, 1st baron of Tilton (kānz), 1883–1946, English economist and monetary expert, studied at Cambridge. Until 1929 a classical economist believing in free economy, Keynes came to support both government large-scale economic planning and spending to promote employment. He profoundly influenced economic policy in democratic nations. Wrote *Economic Consequences of the Peace* (1919), *The General Theory of Employment, Interest, and Money* (1936).

Keyser, Cassius Jackson (kī′zŭr), 1862–1947, American mathematician, author of works in mathematics, logic, and mathematical philosophy.

Keyser, Thomas de (kī′zŭr), c.1596–1677, Dutch portrait and figure painter.

Keyser (kī′zŭr), city (pop. 6,192), W.Va., among hills in Panhandle, on North Branch of Potomac R.;

settled 1802. Was major Civil War supply base. Potomac State Col. of West Virginia Univ. is here.

Key West, city (pop. 33,956), S Fla., on island in W part of FLORIDA KEYS; settled 1822. Southernmost city of continental U.S., it is resort and fishing center. Called Bone Isl. by early Spanish sailors, for human bones they found. Here are a U.S. naval station, hospital, and fleet sonar school; U.S Coast Guard Base is at Fort Taylor (built 1844–46). Sponge pier; aquarium; and two Civil War forts. Has heterogeneous population of Cuban, Spanish, Negro, and English descent. Railroad (1912) spanning Keys from mainland was replaced by 123-mile highway (opened 1944). Plant to desalt sea water for city's use opened 1967.

Khabarovsk (khŭbûrôfsk'), city (1965 est. pop. 408,-000), RSFSR, in E Siberia, on Amur R. and on Trans-Siberian RR. Has oil refinery; auto, aircraft, agr. machinery plants. Cap. of **Khabarovsk Territory,** administrative division (309,378 sq. mi.; 1965 est. pop. 1,279,000), bounded by Yakut ASSR in W. Sea of Okhotsk in E. Manchuria in S; includes Jewish Autonomous Oblast (see BIROBIDZHAN). Stanovoi, Kolyma, and Anadyr ranges cross it SW–NE. Rich in gold, iron, coal, petroleum, and nonferrous metals. In N there is reindeer raising, seal hunting, and fur trapping. Territory founded 1938; reorganized 1953 and 1957.

Khachaturian, Aram (Ilich) (ŭräm' khä″chŭto͞oryän'), 1903–, Russian composer, of Armenian parentage. His music contains many themes from Russian folk music. Among his works are a piano concerto, a violin concerto, and the ballets *Gayane* and *Masquerade.*

Khafre (khä'frä) or **Chephren** (kĕf'rĕn), fl. 2565 B.C., king of IV dynasty of Egypt, builder of the second pyramid at Gizeh.

Khakass Autonomous Oblast (khŭkäs'), administrative division (c.24,000 sq. mi.; 1965 est. pop. 458,-000), Krasnoyarsk Territory, SW Asiatic RSFSR; cap. Abakan. Lumbering; mining (coal, iron, gold). Came under Russian control 17th–18th cent. Oblast estab. 1930. Population is largely Russian with Khakass and Ukrainian minorities.

Khama, Seretse M. (sĕrĕt'sĕ khä'mŭ), 1921–, African political leader from Botswana. Son and grandson of tribal chiefs; educated in South Africa and Great Britain. Surrendered claim to chieftainship after marrying an Englishwoman. Elected to Legislative Council 1961, became prime minister 1965 and president 1966.

Khania, Crete: see CANEA.

Khanty-Mansi National Okrug (khŭntĕ'-mŭnsĕ'), administrative division (201,970 sq. mi.; 1965 est. pop. 194,000), NW Asiatic RSFSR, in central W Siberian lowland. Lumbering, fishing, fur trapping. Population is mostly Russian, with large Khanty and Mansi minorities; both are Finno-Ugric speaking peoples. Conquered by Russia 16th–18th cent. Okrug called Ostyak-Vogul Natl. Okrug until 1940. The cap., Khanty-Mansisk (pop. 22,000), is on Ob and Irtysh rivers and has fish canneries and lumber mills.

Kharga (khär'gŭ), large oasis, S central Egypt; accessible by railroad. Produces dates, cotton, grain. Ruins of anc. temples.

Kharkov (kär'kôf), city (1965 est. pop. 1,070,000), SE Ukraine. Industrial and engineering center, major rail junction. Mfg. of machinery, electrical goods, locomotives, precision instruments, and machine tools. Seat of a university (founded 1804). Founded by Cossacks 1655–56, it grew rapidly after industrialization of S Ukraine in late 19th cent. Cap. of Ukraine 1919–34 (superseded by Kiev). Heavily damaged in Second World War.

Khartoum (kärto͞om'), city (pop. c.98,000), cap. of Republic of the Sudan, on White Nile and Blue Nile rivers. Founded in 1820s by Mohammed Ali. Razed 1885 by Mahdists, who besieged and killed Gen.

Charles GORDON. Recovered 1898 by Lord Kitchener. Mainly a commercial and educational center.

Khayyam, Omar: see OMAR KHAYYAM.

Khazars (käzärz'), anc. Turkic people, partly nomadic, who appeared in Transcaucasia in 2d cent. A.D. and subsequently settled in S Russia between the Volga and the Don (cap. at Itil). In 7th cent. they conquered the Crimea and levied tribute from E Slavs. They embraced Judaism c.740, but kept complete religious tolerance. Khazar empire fell when Sviatoslav, duke of Kiev, defeated its army, 965. Some say Khazars were ancestors of many Russian Jews. Also spelled Chazars.

Kherson (khĕrsôn'), city (1965 est. pop. 210,000), SW Ukraine, on the Dnieper, near mouth on Black Sea. Shipyards, machine shops, and metalworks. Founded 1778 by Potemkin as port and shipbuilding center. Grew in importance after 1932 with building of Dneproges power station and increase in navigation on Dnieper.

Khingan, Great (shĭng'än'), mountain range, Inner Mongolia, NE China; rises to c.8,000 ft. Connected by Ilkhuri range to its offshoot, the **Lesser Khingan,** which is mainly in Heilungkiang prov., along Amur R.

Khios, Greek island: see CHIOS.

Khiva (kē'vù), city (pop. 17,500), Uzbek SSR, near Kara-Kum desert. Mfg. of carpets. Its medieval Moslem splendor is preserved. In late 16th cent. it became cap. of **khanate of Khiva,** the successor of KHOREZM Empire, S of Aral Sea and of Amu Darya R. Independent until 1873 when it became Russian protectorate. In 1920 it was fully annexed to USSR.

Khmelnitsky, Bohdan: see CHMIELNICKI, BOHDAN.

Khmelnitsky (khmĕlnĕt'skē), city (1965 est. pop. 81,-000), W central Ukraine, in Podolia, on Southern Bug R. Machine tool, metalworking, sugar-refining industries. Passed to Russia 1793. Called Proskurov until 1954, when it was renamed for Bohdan Khmelnitsky, the Ukrainian hetman.

Khmer Empire (kùmär'), Indo-Chinese kingdom (6th–15th cent.) roughly corresponding to modern Laos and Cambodia. Declined after series of wars with the Annamese, Chams, and Siamese. Khmer civilization was largely formed by Indian influences. Its great achievement in architecture and sculpture is revealed by ruins in ANGKOR WAT and ANGKOR THOM.

Khodzhent, Tadzhik SSR: see LENINABAD.

Khokand, Uzbek SSR: see KOKAND.

Khorezm (khŭrĕ'zùm), medieval empire, the predecessor of khanate of KHIVA, central Asia, contained by Caspian and Aral seas, Amu Darya R., and Persia; cap. URGENCH. Converted to Islam by Arab conquerors in 18th cent. Under Seljuk Turks it subdued Bukhara, Samarkand, and most of Persia, 12th–13th cent. Conquered by Jenghiz Khan, 1218–24.

Khorog (khŭrôk'), city (1965 est. pop. 11,000), cap. of Mountain-Badakhshan Autonomous Oblast, SE Tadzhik SSR, in Pamir. Light industry.

Khorramshahr (kho͞orräm″shär'), town (pop. 43,850), SW Iran, at confluence of Karun and Shatt el Arab; Iran's chief port on Persian Gulf. Important in Second World War when harbor facilities expanded.

Khorsabad (khôrsäbäd'), village, NE Iraq, near Tigris R. Built on site of Assyrian city, founded 8th cent. B.C. by Sargon. Its mounds were excavated by P. E. Botta in 1842 and 1851. Cuneiform tablets in Elamite language were discovered in 1932.

Khortitsa: see ZAPOROZHE.

Khosru (khôsro͞o'), Sassanid kings of Persia. **Khosru I** (Noshirwan), d. 579, reigned 531–79. Extended rule over Bactria, Arabia, and parts of Armenia and Caucasia. Fought the Byzantine emperors. His grandson, **Khosru II** (Parviz), d. 628, was aided by Emperor Maurice in ousting usurper Bahram. Avenged murder of Maurice by taking Byzantine territory until defeated by Heraclius. Name also appears as Chosroes.

Khotin (khŭtyēn'), city (1963 est. pop. 10,800), W Ukraine, on Dniester R. Agr. market. A leading town of Moldavia in 17th–18th cent. From 1812 it shared history of BESSARABIA. Also spelled Hotin.

Khrushchev, Nikita Sergeyevich (nyĭkē′tȧ sĭrgā′ŭvĭch khrōōshchôf′), 1894–, Russian Communist leader. Joined Communist party 1918. Became first secretary of party's Moscow committee 1935 and of Ukrainian party 1938, a full member of Politburo 1939, and first secretary of party's central committee 1953. A spectacular personality and blunt talker, he emerged as undisputed leader of both state and party within five years of death of STALIN. He attacked Stalin's rule 1956 and announced a policy of "peaceful coexistence," touring U.S. in 1959. In 1960, however, he protested U.S. espionage at Paris summit meeting and attacked UN policies in Congo. He withdrew Soviet missiles from CUBA (1962) and signed test-ban treaty (1963). His policies led to bitter struggle with Communist China. Economic difficulties and continuing intraparty strife led to his peaceful removal from office in Oct., 1964.

Khufu (khōō′fōō) or **Cheops** (kē′ŏps), fl. c.2680 B.C., king of anc. Egypt, founder of the IV dynasty; builder of greatest pyramid at Gizeh. Sun boat, built for travel of his soul after death, found at Gizeh 1954.

Khulna (kōōl′nŭ), town (pop. 127,970), East Pakistan. Transportation hub and trade center of the Sundarbans.

Khyber Pass (kī′bŭr), between West Pakistan and Afghanistan; c.26 mi. long, rising to c.3,500 ft. Trade route between Kabul and Peshawar, it has road and railway. One of main routes in ancient times for invasion of India. Was vitally important to the British in 19th-cent. Afghan Wars.

Kiakhta: see KYAKHTA.

Kiamusze (jyä′mōō′sŭ), Mandarin *Chia-muszu*, city (pop. c.292,000), Heilungkiang prov., China, port on Sungari R. Food processing plants and paper mills. Cap. of former Hokiang prov.

Kiangsi (jyäng′hsē′), province (c.66,000 sq. mi.; pop. c.17,297,442), SE China; cap. Nanchang. Largely hilly and mountainous with many rivers; Kan R. valley extends N to Poyang L. Fertile soil and mild climate. Leading producer of rice and tungsten. Coal mining, lumbering, porcelain mfg. Traditionally known as Kan. area ruled (722–481 B.C.) by Chou dynasty. Named Kiangsi in Southern Sung dynasty (1127–1279). Its present boundaries date from Ming dynasty (1368–1644). Communists estab. base here after 1927 split with Kuomintang.

Kiangsu (jyäng′hsōō′), province (c.41,800 sq. mi.; pop. c.49,228,742), E China, on Yellow Sea; cap. Nanking. Consists largely of alluvial plain of Yangtze R. and includes much of its delta. One of the richest agr. regions of China and its most densely populated prov. Industry limited largely to textile mfg. (esp. Shanghai, Soochow, and Wusih). Traditionally known as Wu; named Kiangsu 1667. After 1949 administered for a time as North and South Kiangsu; province reunited 1952.

Kiangtu, China: see YANGCHOW.

Kiaochow (jyou′jō′), former German territory (c.200 sq. mi.), S Shantung prov., China; cap. TSINGTAO. Leased by Germany 1898; held by Japan 1914–22.

kibbutz: see COLLECTIVE FARM.

Kibo: see KILIMANJARO.

Kickapoo Indians, Indian tribe of Algonquian linguistic family, in SW Wis. in late 17th cent. Were of Eastern Woodlands culture, but also hunted buffalo. Joined in war against Illinois Indians (c.1769); fought against the Americans in the Revolution and the War of 1812, and supported the Sac and Fox in the Black Hawk War. Some went to Mexico (c.1852) but were later induced to return to present Okla.

Kicking Horse, river of SE B.C., Canada, rising on W slopes of the Rockies and flowing SW and NW to the Columbia. **Kicking Horse Pass,** 5,339 ft. high, NW of L. Louise, is highest point of Canadian Pacific route. Connects Bow and Kicking Horse rivers.

Kid, Thomas: see KYD, THOMAS.

Kidd, William, 1645–1701, British privateer. Commissioned as a privateer (1696), he was arrested (1699) on charges of piracy. Hanged after a probably unfair trial. Has become semilegendary as cruel Captain Kidd with huge hidden treasure.

Kidderminster, municipal borough (pop. 40,822), Worcestershire, England. Kidderminster carpets have been made here since 1735.

Kiddush (kĭ′dŭsh) [Heb.,= sanctification], anc. Hebrew ceremonial blessing recited at beginning of Sabbath and other Jewish festivals. Said over bread and wine.

kidnaping, the unlawful and wilful taking away of a person by force, threat or deceit with intent to cause him to be detained against his will. The object is usually ransom, and the victim is usually a child—though neither condition need be true. Kidnaping differs from abduction (which requires intent of sexual intercourse) and from false imprisonment which does not involve "taking away." Strong public sentiment over such cases as the kidnaping of the Lindbergh child (1932) led to Federal and state legislation.

kidney, artificial, mechanical device capable of assuming functions of kidneys. A cellophane tube is inserted into patient's artery and the blood is channeled through tube immersed in bath containing all normal blood chemicals except urea. The poisonous urea in the blood passes through tube walls into bath because of difference in concentration of the solutions.

kidneys, in the human body two reddish, bean-shaped organs c.4 in. long, lying below ribs near spine. Urine is secreted in outer zone, collects in tubules of inner part, passes through ureters to bladder and is excreted by way of the urethra. Kidneys also regulate body water level, acid-base balance, and at times even blood pressure. See *ill.*, p. 657.

Kidron (kĭd′–) or **Cedron** (sē′–), deep valley between Jerusalem and Mount of Olives.

Kiel (kēl), city (pop. 256,727), cap. of Schleswig-Holstein, West Germany. A major Baltic seaport, it was chief German naval station until 1945, when its installations were dismantled. Kiel was chartered 1242, was the seat of the dukes of Holstein, and with Holstein passed to Prussia in 1866. Its university was founded 1665. A sailors' mutiny at Kiel touched off the German revolution of 1918. Kiel is connected with the North Sea by the **Kiel Canal** (also known as Kaiser Wilhelm Canal), an artificial waterway c.60 mi. long, opened 1895. Its E terminus is on the Elbe estuary opposite Cuxhaven.

Kiel, farm trade city (pop. 2,524), E central Wis., on Sheboygan R., NE of Fond du Lac. St. Nazianz, German communistic religious colony, founded nearby in 1854.

Kielce (kyĕl′tsĕ), city (est. pop. 99,000), S central Poland. Railway and trade center; mfg. of metals, agr. machinery, chemicals. Founded 1173, it belonged to bishops of Cracow until 1789; passed to Austria (1795), to Russia (1815); reverted to Poland (1919).

Kielland, Alexander Lange (khē′län), 1849–1906, Norwegian author of novels dealing with social reform (e.g., *Skipper Worse,* 1882).

Kierkegaard, Soren, Dan. *Søren* (sŭ′rŭn kyĕr′kŭgôr), 1813–55, Danish philosopher, writer on religion. He emphasized supranational faith and absolute commitment and held that lack of faith led to despair. Although almost unknown outside Denmark in the 19th cent., Kierkegaard later exerted great influence upon Protestant theology and the philosophy of existentialism. His philosophic works include *Either/Or* (1843) and *Stages on Life's Way* (1845); his more specifically religious writings are *Works of Love* (1817) and *Training in Christianity* (1850). An extensive journal contains many of his insights.

Kiesinger, Kurt Georg (kōōrt gā′ôrg′ kē′zĭngŭr), 1904–, German lawyer and political leader. Minister-

President of Baden-Württemberg 1958–66. Became chancellor of Federal Republic of Germany 1966. A Christian Democrat, he formed a coalition government with support of Social Democrats.

Kiev (kēēf′), Ukr. *Kyyiv*, city (1965 est. pop. 1,348,-000), cap. of Ukrainian SSR, on Dnieper R. Ukraine's largest city, it is industrial (machinery, rolling stock, radio equipment, textiles), cultural, and commercial center; see of a metropolitan of Russian Orthodox Church. University was estab. 1833. A Slavic settlement on trade route between Scandinavia and Constantinople, it passed from Khazars to Varangians under Oleg in 882. It was cap. of medieval RUSSIA, but declined and became tributary to Mongols in 1240. Passed in 14th cent. to Lithuania, which was united with Poland in 1569. In 1654 Cossacks voted union of UKRAINE with Russia. Kiev changed hands several times in Russian civil war (1917–20), and was devastated in Second World War by Germans, who decimated the population. The Cathedral of St. Sophia and Lavra monastery (formerly a pilgrim's shrine), both dating from 11th cent., indicate Kiev's close link with Byzantium and its role as cradle of Christianity in Russia.

Kigoma (kēgō′mä′), town (pop. c.61,000), W Tanzania, a port on E shore of L. Tanganyika. A free port for vessels from the Republic of the Congo and terminus of railroad from Dar-es-Salaam.

Kikuyu (kĭkōō′yōō), Bantu-speaking people from Kenya, numbering over 1,000,000. Resentment over loss of land in the Kenya highlands to white settlement caused many to join political movements, of which MAU MAU was most famous.

Kilauea (kē′läwä′ů), crater, 3,646 ft. high, Hawaii, on SE slope of MAUNA LOA in Hawaii Volcanoes Natl. Park. One of world's largest active craters, it has circumference of c.8 mi. and is surrounded by volcanic rock wall 200–500 ft. high. In its floor is Halemaumau, a fiery pit.

Kildare (kĭldâr′), inland county (654 sq. mi.; pop. 64,-346), S Ireland, in Leinster; co. town Naas. Flat agr. region, with the Bog of Allen and the fertile plain of Curragh.

Kilgore, city (pop. 10,092), E Texas, W of Shreveport, La., near Sabine R.; settled 1872. Boomed after 1930 discovery of East Texas oil field.

Kilimanjaro (kĭ″līmûnjä′rō), mountain, NE Tanzania; highest in Africa. Extinct volcano cone. Its two main peaks are Mt. Kibo (19,565 ft.) and Mt. Mawenzi (17,300 ft.). Coffee plantations on lower slopes.

Kilkenny (kĭlkě′nē), inland county (796 sq. mi.; pop. 61,670), SE Ireland, in Leinster. Flat agr. region, it has a coal field around Castlecomer. Area is roughly same as ancient kingdom of Ossory. The county town is **Kilkenny,** urban district (pop. 10,158), on Nore R. Strife between two sections (Englishtown and Irishtown) may account for stories of Kilkenny cats, who ate each other up. Swift, Berkeley, and Congreve went to school here.

Killarney, urban district (pop. 6,824), Co. Kerry, Ireland. Tourist center for three Lakes of Killarney. Lough Leane has Ross Isl. and "sweet Innisfallen" of Thomas Moore's poem.

killdeer, North American PLOVER with plaintive and penetrating cry.

Kill Devil Hill National Memorial: see KITTY HAWK, N.C.

Kill Devil Hills, town (pop. 268), NE N.C., on sandy peninsula separating Albemarle Sound from the Atlantic, SSE of Kitty Hawk. Wright brothers experimented (1900–1903) with gliders and airplanes here. National memorial marks site of first sucessful flight.

Killeen, city (pop. 23,377), central Texas, SW of Waco, in farm area; settled 1882. U.S. Fort Hood is nearby.

Killian, James Rhyne, 1904–, American scientist; president of M.I.T. (1948–57). Later scientific adviser to Presidents Eisenhower and Kennedy.

Killiecrankie, Pass of (kĭlĭkrăng′kē), Perthshire, Scotland, through which flows Garry R. Battle of Killiecrankie (1689) was fought at N end of pass.

Killigrew, Thomas, 1612–83, English dramatist, a theater manager in the time of Charles II.

Killingly, town (pop. 11,298), NE Conn., bordered on W by Quinebaug R., on E by R.I.; settled c.1700. Manasseh Cutler born here. Town includes industrial borough of Danielson (pop. 4,642; chartered 1854) and South Killingly village.

Killingworth, rural town (pop. 1,098), S Conn., bordered on W by Hammonasset R., on S by Clinton; organized c.1667. Has noted church (1817) and Ely House, where Longfellow supposedly wrote "The Birds of Killingworth."

Kill Van Kull: see NEW YORK BAY.

Kilmainham (kĭlmä′ŭm), suburb of Dublin, Co. Dublin, Ireland. Parnell was imprisoned here when he signed (1882) "Treaty of Kilmainham" with the English.

Kilmer, Joyce, 1886–1918, American poet, journalist. The title poem of *Trees and Other Poems* (1914) is well known. He was killed in First World War.

Kilpatrick, William Heard, 1871–1965, American philosopher. Was professor of the philosophy of education at Teachers Col., Columbia Univ., 1918–38.

Kilpatrick, Old or **West,** village (pop. 9,393), Dumbartonshire, Scotland; one of the places claiming to be St. Patrick's birthplace.

Kilung, Taiwan: see KEELUNG.

Kilwinning (kĭlwĭ′nĭng), burgh (pop. 7,287), Ayrshire, Scotland. Traditional birthplace of Freemasonry in Scotland. Has celebrated archery meets.

Kimball, (Sidney) Fiske, 1888–1955, American architect and writer. Specialized in restoration of old houses, notably Monticello, Va. Director of Philadelphia Mus. of Art (1925–55).

Kimberley, mining city and district (pop. 5,774), SE B.C., Canada, NW of Cranbrook. Has large silver, lead, and zinc mines. Here is Sullivan Mine.

Kimberley, city (pop. c.86,295), Cape Prov., South Africa; founded 1871; diamond-cutting center. Its great diamond mines are controlled by a trust organized 1888 by Cecil Rhodes. In South African war it was besieged by Boer forces, Oct., 1899–Feb., 1900.

Kimchi, family of Hebrew grammarians and Bible commentators in Spain and France. **Joseph ben Isaac Kimchi,** 1105?–1170, poet and translator. His son **Moses Kimchi,** d. 1190, wrote a grammatical textbook. Another son, **David Kimchi,** 1160?–1235?, wrote a Hebrew grammar, **Mikhlol** [completeness], a dictionary of the Bible, and commentaries on the Old Testament which, translated into Latin, greatly influenced Christian translators, e.g., Luther.

Kim Il Sung (kē″mēlsŏong′), 1912–, North Korean political leader. Became first premier of Democratic People's Republic of Korea 1948. Moscow trained, he has pursued close ties with Communist China.

Kinabalu or **Kinibalu, Mount** (both: kĭ″nůbůlŏo′), peak, 13,455 ft. high, North Borneo; highest peak of Borneo.

Kincardine (kĭnkär′dĭn, kĭng-), town (pop. 2,841), S Ont., Canada, on L. Huron, SW of Owen Sound. Resort and mfg. town. To N is Douglas Point, site of a nuclear-power plant.

Kincardineshire (kĭngkär′dĭnshĭr) or **Kincardine,** maritime county (379 sq. mi.; pop. 48,810), E Scotland; co. town Stonehaven. Has rocky coast and mountainous interior. Sheep grazing, fishing, and quarrying are main occupations; oats and barley chief crops. County sometimes called the Mearns (mârns). Dunnottar Castle located near Stonehaven.

Kinchinjunga: see KANCHENJUNGA.

kindergarten [Ger.,= garden of children], system of preschool education. FROEBEL designed (1837) system less formal than that of elementary schools. Children's creative play instincts are used to develop cooperation and application and to prepare them for school. First kindergarten in U.S. started 1856.

Kinderhook (kĭn-), village (pop. 1,078), SE N.Y., NE of Hudson; settled before Revolution. Martin Van Buren born and buried here; to S is "Lindenwald," Van Buren home.

Kineo, Mount (kĭn'ēō), 1,789 ft. high, central Maine, on peninsula in Moosehead L. Summer resort.

Kineshma (kĕ'nyĭshmŭ), city (1965 est. pop. 93,000), W central European RSFSR; port on Volga. Known in early 15th cent.; old textile center.

King, Charles: see KING, RUFUS.

King, Clarence, 1842–1901, American geologist. He persuaded Congress to authorize 40th Parallel Survey (1867–72), of which he was chief geologist. He organized and served as first director of the U.S. Geological Survey (1879). His publications in geology were significant.

King, Ernest Joseph, 1878–1956, American admiral. Made commander in chief of Atlantic fleet (1941), and then of entire U.S. fleet. In Second World War served (1942–45) as chief of naval operations. Promoted (1944) admiral of the fleet ("five-star admiral"); retired 1945.

King, Martin Luther, 1929–, American clergyman and civil-rights leader. His policies of nonviolent action and resistance to segregation won him the 1964 Nobel Peace Prize. His *Where Do We Go From Here* (1967) discusses the future of the civil rights movement.

King, Rufus, 1755–1827, American statesman. Delegate to Federal Constitutional Convention (1787). U.S. Senator from N.Y. (1789–96, 1813–25); minister to Great Britain (1796–1803, 1825–26). Supported Federalists. His son, **Charles King,** 1789–1867, was an editor and educator. President of Columbia Col. 1849–64.

King, Thomas Starr, 1824–64, American Unitarian clergyman, lecturer, and author. Influential in keeping Calif. loyal to Union in Civil War. Wrote *The White Hills* (1860).

King, William Lyon Mackenzie, 1874–1950, Canadian statesman, prime minister for over 21 years; grandson of W. L. Mackenzie. Chosen leader of Liberal party in 1919. Served as prime minister 1921–30, except for brief interval in 1926, and again 1935–48. Concluded joint defense agreements with U.S. at beginning of Second World War. Represented Canada at important post-war international conferences.

kingbird, North American flycatcher. Eastern species, also called tyrant flycatcher and bee martin, eats some bees but chiefly noxious insects. It is dark gray above, light gray and white below with a white-banded black tail and an orange crest.

king crab or **horseshoe crab,** marine arthropod (*Limulus*) having a cephalothorax (fused head and thorax) covered by domed, horseshoe-shaped carapace, a triangular abdomen with carapace, and spinelike tail or telson. It has one pair of simple eyes, one of compound eyes, and six pairs of legs. They destroy oyster and clam beds.

kingfisher, member of family of birds most abundant in Malayan region and on Pacific isls. but found on all continents. American kingfishers, chiefly fisheaters, live near lakes, ponds, or coast; usually they have large, crested heads, long, heavy bills, and short bodies and tails. See *ill.*, p. 118.

King George's War: see FRENCH AND INDIAN WARS.

Kinglake, Alexander William, 1809–91, English traveler and historian. *Eöthen* (1844), an account of his journey to the Far East, is a classic travel book.

kinglet, any of five species of Old World warblers, similar to thrushes. Dainty and slender, soft gray in color.

King Philip's War: see PHILIP (King Philip).

King Ranch, S Texas, S and W of Corpus Christi, hq. at Kingsville. Covers c.1,000,000 acres in several divisions (Santa Gertrudis is home ranch). Has Santa Gertrudis cattle, a new breed; race horses; oil wells; and farming. Founded c.1853 by Richard King, ex-Rio Grande steamboat captain. Now managed by

grandson Robert Kleburg. Divisions made 1935, but ranch still one of world's largest.

Kings, county, N.Y.: see BROOKLYN, borough.

Kings, river rising in the Sierra Nevada, E Calif., and flowing W and SW until it almost disappears in sands of San Joaquin Valley. Some of its waters reach Tulare L. Two enormous river canyons dominate Kings Canyon Natl. Park, a mountain wilderness.

Kings, books of Old Testament, called 1 and 2 Kings in AV, 3 and 4 Kings in Western canon (1 and 2 SAMUEL called 1 and 2 Kings in Western canon). They narrate the history of the Hebrews from the death of David to the fall of Judah. Among notable events are the golden reign of Solomon and the building of the Temple; the division of the kingdom under Rehoboam into Israel (N) and Judah (S); the end of the notorious house of Ahab; and the inspiring careers of the prophets Elijah and Elisha.

Kings Bay, inlet, 14 mi. long, in NW coast of West Spitsbergen. It was base (1926) of successful polar flights by R. E. BYRD and AMUNDSEN.

Kings Canyon National Park: see KINGS, river.

King's College: see CAMBRIDGE UNIVERSITY; COLUMBIA UNIVERSITY; LONDON, UNIVERSITY OF.

King's College, University of: see HALIFAX, N.S.

King's County, Ireland: see OFFALY.

Kingsley, Charles, 1819–75, English clergyman and novelist. His views on Christian socialism were embodied in *Alton Locke* (1850). A controversy with J. H. NEWMAN led to Newman's *Apologia*. Kingsley is best known for *Westward Ho!* (1855), *Hereward the Wake* (1866), and *The Water-Babies* (1863).

King's Lynn, Lynn Regis (rē'jĭs), or **Lynn,** municipal borough (pop. 27,554), Norfolk, England. Once a major port, it dates from Saxon times.

Kings Mountain, town (1966 pop. 8,256), SW N.C., near S.C. line W of Charlotte. On crest of ridge (S of town, in S.C.) party of frontiersmen defeated (Oct. 7, 1780) British force in CAROLINA CAMPAIGN. Site now Kings Mt. Natl. Military Park.

king snake, nonvenomous, egg-laying constrictor snake of North America. Common form of E U.S. is 3–5 ft. long, black or brown with yellow or white rings or bands forming chainlike pattern. It and related milk snake are useful destroyers of rodents.

Kings Peak: see UINTA MOUNTAINS.

Kingsport, city (pop. 26,314), NE Tenn., on Holston R. near Va. line. On site of Forts Robinson (1761) and Patrick Henry (1775) and old Wilderness Road.

Kingston, city (pop. 53,526), S Ont., Canada, on N shore of L. Ontario, near head of St. Lawrence R. and at S end of Rideau Canal. Mfg. of locomotives, machinery, textiles, nylon; also food processing. Seat of Queen's Univ. (coed.; 1841) and Royal Military Col. Fort Frontenac (1673) important in French and Indian Wars. City founded 1784 by United Empire Loyalists. Used as naval base in War of 1812. Cap. of United Canada 1841–44.

Kingston. 1 City (pop. 29,260), SE N.Y., on W bank of Hudson R., S of Albany, in farm area; settled 1652 by Dutch. Burned (1777) by British, it was abandoned as first cap. of N.Y. Growth stimulated in early 19th cent. by Delaware and Hudson Canal. Has senate house (1676), meeting place of first N.Y. state legislature and now museum; old Dutch church (1659); cemetery (1661) with grave of James Clinton; and, nearby, "Slabsides," John Burroughs' former cottage. Ashokan Reservoir and Catskill Mts. are W. **2** Industrial borough (pop. 20,261), NE Pa., on Susquehanna R. opposite Wilkes-Barre; settled 1769. **3** Village, R.I.: see SOUTH KINGSTOWN.

Kingston, port (pop. c.424,000), cap. and largest city of Jamaica, the West Indies; founded 1693; made cap. 1872.

Kingston-upon-Hull, Yorkshire, England: see HULL.

Kingston-upon-Thames, Royal borough of, London borough since 1965 (est. pop. 146,450); includes former municipal boroughs of Kingston-upon-

Thames. Malden and Coombe. and Surbiton; area largely residential. with some metalworking and mfg. Site of Saxon coronations.

Kingstown, port (1963 est. pop. 20,688). cap. of SAINT VINCENT, the West Indies.

Kingsville, city (pop. 25,297), S Texas. SW of Corpus Christi; settled 1902. Hq. of KING RANCH. Processes produce of farm and oil area. Seat of Texas Col. of Arts and Industries.

Kingswood, urban district (pop. 25,419). Gloucestershire, England. Open-air chapel marks site where Wesley preached in 18th cent.

Kingtehchen, China: see FOWLIANG.

King William Island, S Franklin dist., Northwest Territories, Canada, in Arctic Ocean, an island of the Arctic Archipelago. Discovered 1831 by Sir John Ross. Sir John Franklin and party were lost here 1847–48. Roald Amundsen's winter hq. 1903–4.

King William's War: see FRENCH AND INDIAN WARS.

Kinibalu, Mount: see KINABALU, MOUNT.

kinkajou, (kǐng′kụjōo), arboreal, nocturnal mammal, related to the raccoon. Found from Brazil to Mexico.

Kinnarodden: see NORTH CAPE, Norway.

Kino, Eusebio Francisco (āōōsā′vyō fränsĕ′skō kē′nō), c.1644–1711, Jesuit missionary explorer in American Southwest, b. Segno, in the Tyrol. Tumacacori Natl. Monument near Nogales, Ariz., includes historic Spanish mission building near site first visited by Father Kino.

Kinross-shire (kǐnrŏs′-shǐr), inland county (82 sq. mi.; pop. 6,704), Scotland; co. town Kinross. Level plain surrounded by hills. Agr. is chief occupation; there is some mfg. of woolens and linen.

Kinsey, Alfred Charles, 1894–1956, American zoologist, authority on gall wasp. He later undertook highly publicized studies of human sexual behavior.

Kinsha, river, China: see YANGTZE.

Kinshasa, formerly **Leopoldville,** city (pop. c.420,000). cap. of Republic of the Congo, on Stanley Pool of Congo R.. opposite Brazzaville. River port and rail terminus. it is major commercial and mfg. center with cotton and jute mills. Seat of Lovanium Univ. City founded 1887 by H. M. Stanley and named for King Leopold II; succeeded Boma 1929 as cap. of Belgian Congo.

Kinston, city (pop. 24,819). E N.C.. on Neuse R., NW of New Bern: settled c.1740. Processes. trades. and markets tobacco. timber. livestock. and cotton.

Kintyre (kǐntīr′) or **Cantire** (kǎntǐr′), peninsula, 42 mi. long and 10 mi. wide, Argyllshire, Scotland. S extremity is 13 mi. from N. Ireland.

Kioga (kyō′gä). lake. c.80 mi. long. N central Uganda. on the Victoria Nile. Swampy and shallow; some fishing: transportation route for cotton-growing region.

Kioto, Japan: see KYOTO.

Kiowa (kī′ụwù). city (pop. 1,674). S central Kansas, near Okla. line SW of Wichita: founded 1874. Carry Nation wrecked her first saloon here 1900.

Kiowa Indians, North American tribe, occupying W Mont. in 17th cent.. later ranging through the West. Their language. a single member family, is part of Azteco-Tanoan linguistic stock. Shared Plains area culture, but had several distinctive traits, including a pictographic calendar and the worship of a stone image. Allied with the Comanche, they waged many bloody wars against whites and Cheyenne, Sioux, Navaho. and Osage. See LANGUAGE (table).

Kipchaks, Turkic people: see CUMANS.

Kipling, Rudyard, 1865–1936, English poet, novelist, and story writer, b. India. His many popular works include poems in *Departmental Ditties* (1886) and *Barrack-Room Ballads* (1892); stories in *Plain Tales from the Hills* and *Soldiers Three* (both 1888); novel *The Light That Failed* (1890); children's stories such as *The Jungle Book* (1894), *Captains Courageous* (1897), *Kim* (1901), and *Just So Stories* (1902). Familiar poems are "Mandalay," "Gunga Din," and *Recessional* (1897). He interpreted India, the army,

and British imperialism, and was England's first Nobel Prize winner in literature (1907).

Kipnis, Alexander (kǐp′nǐs). 1891–, American basso, b. Russia. Made U.S. debut in 1923; member of Metropolitan Opera 1940–46. Famous roles include Boris Godunov.

Kirby, William, 1817–1906, Canadian author. b. England. His *Le Chien d'Or,* also published as *The Golden Dog* (1877), helped popularize historical novel in Canadian fiction.

Kirby-Smith, Edmund: see SMITH, EDMUND KIRBY.

Kircher, Athanasius (ätänä′zyōos, kǐr′khùr), 1601?–1680, German Jesuit archaeologist, mathematician, biologist, and physicist. He was possibly first to hold that disease and putrefaction were caused by presence of invisible living bodies. He also perfected the aeolian harp.

Kirchhoff, Gustav Robert (gōōs′täf rō′bĕrt kǐrkh′hôf), 1824–87, German physicist. With Bunsen he worked on spectroscope, discovered cesium and rubidium. He explained Fraunhofer lines in solar SPECTRUM.

Kirchner, Ernst Ludwig (ĕrnst′ lōōt′vǐkh kǐrkh′nùr), 1880–1938, German expressionist painter and graphic artist; cofounder of the BRÜCKE group in Dresden.

Kirghiz Soviet Socialist Republic (kǐrgēz′) or **Kirghizia** (kǐrgē′zhù) or **Kirghizstan** (kǐrgēstän′), constituent republic (76,641 sq. mi.; 1965 est. pop. 2,609,000) of USSR, in central Asia, bordering on China (SE); cap. Frunze. Mountainous country in Tien Shan and Pamir systems, rising to 24,406 ft. in Pobyeda Peak; grazing in highland valleys. Crop production is mainly in FERGANA VALLEY and Issyk Kul basin. Industry is based on mineral resources (e.g.. mercury, antimony, uranium). The Kirghiz, a Moslem, Turko-Mongolian pastoral people, migrated here in 16th cent. They were formerly known as Kara Kirghiz to distinguish them from the Kazakhs (formerly called Kirghiz). With khanate of Kokand they passed to Russia in 1876.

Kirin (kē′rǐn′), Mandarin *Chi-lin*, province (c.72,000 sq. mi.; pop. c.11,300,000). NE China; cap. Changchun. Bordered by Inner Mongolian Autonomous Region on W. USSR on NE, and Korea on SE. Part of fertile Manchurian plain. watered by Sungari R. Soybeans and grain are chief crops. Vast timberlands exploited; iron. coal, gold, and lead mined. In SE is Yenpien Korean Autonomous Region (estab. 1952).

Kirjath-arba: see HEBRON.

Kirk, Grayson L(ouis), 1903–, American educator, president of Columbia Univ. (1953–). Was professor of government and of international relations.

Kirkaldy of Grange, Sir William (kûrkôl′dē), c.1520–1573, Scottish soldier and politician. Associated with brutal murder of Cardinal Beaton, he later became prominent Protestant leader to whom Mary Queen of Scots surrendered at Carberry in 1557.

Kirkcudbrightshire (kûrkōō′brēshǐr), maritime county (897 sq. mi.; pop. 28,877), SW Scotland; co. town Kirkcudbright. NW part is wild and hilly. Agr. is chief occupation: cattle grazing is important. Region is in the Galloway district.

Kirke, Sir David, 1597–1655?, French-born English merchant adventurer. Attacked the French in Canada and Nova Scotia; forced surrender of Quebec (1629). Became governor and colonizer (1638) of Newfoundland which the Commonwealth later took away from him because he was royalist.

Kirkland, Samuel, 1741–1808, American missionary to the Oneida Indians. Founded an academy which developed into Hamilton Col.

Kirkland Lake, mining town, E Ont., Canada. N of Sudbury. One of largest gold-mining centers in Canada.

Kirksville, city (pop. 13,123), N central Mo., N of Moberly: founded 1841. Trade and industrial center of agr. area. Has college of osteopathy and surgery.

Kirkuk (kǐrkōōk′), town (pop. c.120,600), NE Iraq. Its great oil fields are linked by pipeline to Mediterranean ports of Tripoli and Banias.

Kirkwall (kûrk'wôl, –wŭl), burgh (pop. 4,315), cap. of Orkney Isls., Scotland. Has a good harbor and carries on trading, fishing, and boatbuilding.

Kirkwood, city (pop. 29,421), E Mo., suburb WSW of St. Louis; laid out 1852.

Kirov, Sergei Mironovich (sîrgā' myîrô'nŭvĭch kē'rŭf), 1888–1934, Russian Communist leader, one of Stalin's closest aides. His assassination was officially laid to a Trotskyist conspiracy and led to treason trials and party purge of 1930s.

Kirov, formerly **Vyatka** (vyät'kŭ), city (1965 est. pop. 296,000), E European RSFSR, on Vyatka R. Rail junction. Mfg. of machines, tires, textiles. Place of political exile in 19th cent. Renamed Kirov 1934.

Kirovabad (kē"rŭvŭbät'), city (1965 est. pop. 166,000), W central Azerbaijan SSR. Formerly Gandja or Gandzha; cap. of a khanate under Persian suzerainty until Russian conquest in 1804. Renamed 1935. Produces copper sulphate, cotton textiles, wine.

Kirovograd (kē"rŭvŭgrät'), city (1965 est. pop. 153,-000). S central Ukraine, on Ingul R.; agr. center. Founded 1754 and named Elisavetgrad; renamed Zino-vievsk 1924, Kirovo 1936, and Kirovograd 1939.

Kirseher (kĕrshĕ'hĕr), town (est. pop. 20,200), central Turkey. Noted for carpet mfg.

Kirtland Hills, village (pop. 292), NE Ohio, NE of Cleveland; settled 1808–9. First Mormon temple built here by Joseph Smith and his followers 1833–36.

Kiruna (kē'rünä), village (pop. 27,063), Norrbotten co., N Sweden. It is center of Lappland iron-mining dist. Ore, c.70% pure, is shipped to Baltic port of Lulea and Atlantic port of Narvik (Norway).

Kisangani (kĭsängä'nē), formerly **Stanleyville,** city (pop. c.126,530), NE Republic of the Congo, on Congo R.; former cap. of Orientale prov. Terminus of river transport from Kinshasa (Leopoldville). Exports cotton and rice. Founded 1883 by H. M. Stanley. Became stronghold of Patrice LUMUMBA in late 1950s; his supporters attempted to set up a national government here in 1960. Scene of fighting and brutalities against civilians in 1964.

Kisfaludy, Charles (kĭsh'fôlōōdē), 1788–1830, Hungarian dramatist, founder of the Hungarian national drama. *Tatars in Hungary* (1819), first of his many successes, was first genuinely dramatic Hungarian play. His brother, **Alexander Kisfaludy,** 1772–1844, founded the Hungarian school of lyric poetry.

Kish. 1 Father of Saul. 1 Sam. 9.1; 10.21. Cis: Acts 13.21 **2** Uncle of Saul. 1 Chron. 8.30; 9.36.

Kish, anc city of Mesopotamia. near Babylon. Powerful in 3d millennium B.C Though a Sumerian outpost, it was a Semitic city with its own cultural style.

Kishi, Nobusuke (nōbōōs'kä kē'shē), 1896–. Japanese statesman. Was state minister in Tojo war cabinet. Foreign minister (1956–58) and premier (1958–60).

Kishinev (kĭshēnyôf), Rumanian *Chisinau,* city (1965 est. pop. 282,000), cap. of Moldavian SSR. Mfg. of food, leather, and metal products. Seat of a university (founded 1945) and the Academy of Sciences of the Moldavian SSR (founded 1961). Was cultural, spiritual, commercial and (after annexation by Russia, 1812) political center of BESSARABIA. Population was 40% Jewish until Second World War.

Kishon, river of central Palestine, flowing NW through Esdraelon to the Mediterranean. On its banks Barak defeated Sisera, Elijah slew the prophets of Baal.

Kiska, island, c.20 mi. long, off W Alaska, in Rat Isls. group of ALEUTIAN ISLANDS, between Adak and Attu. Mountainous, rising to nearly 4,000 ft. in Kiska Volcano. Occupied and garrisoned 1942 by Japanese, it was cut off 1943 by recapture of Attu, and abandoned by Japanese, Aug., 1943.

Kislovodsk (kēslŭvôtsk'), city (1965 est. pop. 84,000), S Stavropol Territory, RSFSR, in central Greater Caucasus; health resort.

Kismayu (kĭsmī'ōō), town (est. pop. c.35,000), SW Somali Republic; port. Bananas are chief export.

Kissimmee, Lake, central Fla.; one of state's largest fresh-water lakes. Entered and drained by Kissimmee R., which flows c.90 mi. S to L. Okeechobee. Has several small islands.

Kisumu (kēsōō'mōō), town, W Kenya, on E shore of Victoria Nyanza. Principal lake port; exports sisal. Formerly called Port Florence.

Kitasato, Shibasaburo (shĭbä'säbōōrō kē'täsä'tō), 1852–1931, Japanese physician, authority on infectious diseases. Discovered, simultaneously with Yersin in 1894, bacterium causing PLAGUE.

Kit Carson Peak: see SANGRE DE CHRISTO MOUNTAINS.

Kit-Cat Club, London political and literary club, active c.1700–1720. Center of Whig support for Hanoverian succession.

Kitchen Cabinet, popular name for group of intimate, unofficial advisers of Pres. Andrew Jackson. Administration policies were formed in its meetings. Members, all able journalists, included the elder Francis P. BLAIR, Duff GREEN, and Amos KENDALL. John H. Eaton of regular cabinet met with group; Martin Van Buren enjoyed its confidence.

Kitchener, Horatio Herbert Kitchener, 1st **Earl,** 1850–1916, British field marshal and statesman. As commander in chief of Egyptian army, he reconquered (1896–98) the Sudan and became its governor general. In SOUTH AFRICAN WAR he used fortified blockhouses and systematic denudation of farm lands to conquer the Boers (1900–1902). As secretary for war in First World War he expanded army from 20 to 70 divisions (1914–16). On voyage to confer with Russian leaders, he was drowned when his ship hit a mine and sank.

Kitchener, city (pop. 74,485), S Ont., Canada, in Grand R. valley W of Toronto. Important mfg. center with tanning and meat packing. Settled 1806 by Germans from Pa. Called Berlin to 1916.

kitchen midden, refuse heap left by a prehistoric community. Valuable in archaeological study.

kite, bird: see HAWK.

Kitimat, town (pop. 10,203), W B.C., Canada, at head of Douglas Channel and ESE of Prince Rupert. Aluminum smelting. Has deepwater anchorage.

Kittatinny Mountain (kĭtŭtĭn'ē), ridge of Appalachian system, extending from its junction with Shawangunk Mt.. SE N.Y.. across N.J. to join Blue Mt. in E Pa. High Point (1,803 ft. high) is highest peak in N.J.

Kittery, town (pop. 10,689). extreme SW Maine, at mouth of Piscataqua R. opposite Portsmouth, N.H.: settled 1623, inc. 1647 as first town in Maine. John Paul Jones's ship *Ranger* (1777) and Civil War vessel *Kearsarge* built here. Portsmouth Naval Shipyard is on two islands belonging to U.S. and connected with Kittery by two bridges. Nearby Kittery Point (pop. 1,259) is resort village.

Kitt Peak, 6,875 ft. high. S Ariz., in Quinlan Mts., SW of Tucson and on Papago Indian Reservation. Site of U.S. observatory with one of world's largest telescopes.

Kittredge, George Lyman, 1860–1941, American scholar; professor of English at Harvard 1896–1936. He was an authority on Chaucer, Shakespeare, the English language, balladry, and witchcraft.

Kitty Hawk or **Kittyhawk,** sandy peninsula, NE N.C., F of Albemarle Sound. Nearby is Kill Devils Hill, where Wright brothers experimented (1900–1903) with gliders and airplanes. Wright Brothers Natl. Memorial marks site of first successful flight.

Kitwe (kē'twä), city (pop. c.123,200), N Zambia. Commercial and industrial center of the Copperbelt.

Kitzbühel (kĭts'bü"hŭl), town (est. pop. 7,743), Tyrol, W Austria. Winter resort and skiing center.

Kiukiang or **Chiu-chiang** (jyō'jyäng'), city (pop. c.125,000), Kiangsi prov., China; port on Yangtze R. and rail terminus. Exports rice and tea. Former treaty port. Confucian philosopher Chu Hsi taught at White Deer Cave on Lü Shan Mt.

Kiushu, Japan: see KYUSHU.

kiva (kē'vù), underground ceremonial chamber of Pueblo Indians. Used, by men only, for secret ceremonies, lounging, and as a workshop for weaving.

Kivu (kē'vōō, kēvōō'), former province. E Republic of the Congo: cap. was BUKAVU. Borders on L. Tanganyika. Agr region: gold and tin are mined. Albert Natl. Park, vast game preserve, and Ruwenzori Mts. are in the area. Scene of strife after independence of the republic. Two provinces were constituted as of June 30, 1966.

Kivu, lake, c.60 mi. long, E central Africa, on the border of the Republic of the Congo and Rwanda. Highest (4,829 ft.) of Africa's lakes.

Kiwanis International (kĭwä'nĭs), organization of business and professional men, founded 1915. Local clubs are active in business and civic affairs.

kiwi (kē'wē), flightless bird (*Apteryx*) of New Zealand. Its wings are vestigial and it walks with back hunched. Nocturnal in habit, it hunts worms, insects, and grubs largely by scent.

Kizil or **Kyzyl** (both: kēzēl'), city (1965 est. pop. 44,000), cap. of Tuva Autonomous Oblast, SW Asiatic RSFSR, on the Yenisei. Brickyards, sawmills. Founded 1914; called Belotsarsk until 1917 and Khem-Beldyr until 1926.

Kizil Irmak (kĭzĭl ĭrmäk'), anc. *Halys*, river, c.700 mi. long, rising in N central Turkey and flowing in a wide arc to the Black Sea.

Kizil Kum or **Kyzl-Kum** (both: kēzēl' kōōm'), desert (c.116,000 sq. mi.), Kazakh SSR and Uzbek SSR, in central Asia, E of Aral Sea between Amu Darya and Syr Darya rivers. Raising of karakul sheep and camels. Deposits of coal, polymetallic ores, petroleum.

Kladno (kläd'nô), city (est. pop. 53,000), central Bohemia, Czechoslovakia. Coal mining; iron and steel plants.

Klagenfurt (klä'gùnfŏŏrt), city (pop. 69,218), cap. of Carinthia, S Austria, on Glan R., in mountain lake area. Episcopal see. Winter sports center.

Klaipeda: see MEMEL.

Klamath (klä'mùth), river, with main source in Upper Klamath L., SW Oregon. Flows c.270 mi. SW into NW Calif. and across to the Pacific. Used for irrigation.

Klamath Falls, city (pop. 16,949), SW Oregon, at S tip of Upper Klamath L.; settled c.1867. Klamath irrigation project (1900) and railroad (1909) stimulated growth. Center of area with lumbering, farming, sheep and cattle raising. Hunting and fishing region. Crater Lake Natl. Park and Klamath Indian Reservation are nearby.

Klamath Indians, North American tribe, of Penutian linguistic stock, living in 19th cent. in SW Oregon. Got food by hunting, fishing, and root digging. They were friendly to the whites but hostile towards Indians of N Calif. U.S. government announced plans to end reservation status of Klamath lands.

Klaproth, Martin Heinrich, 1743–1817, German chemist. Called the father of analytic chemistry, he recognized zirconium and uranium in minerals. worked on analyses for titanium, tellurium.

Klausenburg, Rumania: see CLUJ.

Klaypeda: see MEMEL.

Kléber, Jean Baptiste (zhä' bäptēst' kläbĕr'), 1753–1800, French general. Left in command in Egypt after Bonaparte's return to France, he defeated the Turks at Heliopolis (1800). Was assassinated by Turkish fanatic.

Klebs, Edwin (kläps), 1834–1913, German-American pathologist, pioneer in study of infectious diseases.

Klee, Paul (poul' klä'), 1879–1940, Swiss painter and graphic artist; one of the foremost figures in modern art. Famed for imagination and fantasy. He was a member of the BLAUE REITER and taught at the BAUHAUS.

Klein, Felix (fä'lĭks klīn), 1849–1925, German mathematician, noted for work in geometry, theory of functions, and programs for unifying geometry and connecting mathematics more closely with physics.

Kleist, Heinrich von (hīn'rĭkh fün klīst'), 1777–1811, German poet. His unhappy life ended in suicide. His comedy *Der Zerbrochene Krug* [the broken jug] (1806) and his serious plays such as *Penthesilea* (1808). *Das Käthchen von Heilbronn* (1810), and *Der Prinz von Homburg* (1821) rank among the finest of the German theater for their dramatic skill, emotional power, and bold poetry. He also wrote several remarkable short stories and a short novel, *Michael Kohlhaas* (1808).

Klenze, Leo von (lä'ō fün klĕn'tsù), 1784–1864, German architect. Built Glyptothek (Munich) and part of Hermitage (Leningrad).

Kleve, Germany: see CLEVES.

Klimt, Gustav (gōōs'täf klĭmt'), 1862–1918, Austrian painter, cofounder of the Vienna Secession. He was the foremost painter of ART NOUVEAU in Vienna.

Kline, Franz, 1910–62, American painter, member of the school of ABSTRACT EXPRESSIONISM.

Klinger, Friedrich Maximilian von (frē'drĭkh mäk"-sēmē'lyän fün klĭng'ùr), 1752–1831, German dramatist. His play *Wirrwarr; oder, Sturm und Drang* [confusion; or, storm and stress] (1776) gave the STURM UND DRANG period its name.

Klinger, Max (mäks'), 1857–1920, German sculptor, painter, and etcher.

Klodzko: see GLATZ, Poland.

Klondike (klŏn'dīk), region of Yukon territory, NW Canada, just· E of Alaska border. Gold strike on Klondike Creek led to Klondike stampede of 1897–98. Thousands of prospectors rushed into area, numbering c.18,000 in 1898. Since that time gold production has declined.

Klopstock, Friedrich Gottlieb (frē'drĭkh gôt'lēp klôp'-shtôk), 1724–1803, German poet. His greatest work is the epic *Messias* (1748–83). Influenced later writers.

Klosterneuburg (klōs"türnoi'bŏŏrk), outer district (pop. 22,787) of Vienna, on right bank of Danube. Its Augustinian monastery (consecrated 1163) has a noted library with many incunabula.

Kloster-Zeven, Convention of (klō'stür-tsä'fùn), 1757. Early in Seven Years War duke of Cumberland, defeated by French at Hastenbeck, capitulated at the former Benedictine abbey near Zeven (a small town NE of Bremen, Germany) and allowed the French to occupy Hanover. English government disavowed convention and dismissed Cumberland.

Kluckhohn, Clyde Kay Maben (klŭck'hōn), 1905–60, American anthropologist, known primarily for studies of the Navaho and of personality and culture.

klystron, vacuum tube used in ultrahigh-frequency electronic units. A stream of electrons directed and focused by a series of electrodes is made to pass through one or more cavity resonators. High, positively charged electric potentials on resonators modify speed of electrons. The circuit may be adjusted to provide amplification or oscillation. Widely used in microwave radar and communications equipment.

Knapp, Seaman Asahel, 1833–1911, American agriculturist and teacher. Demonstrated methods of fighting BOLL WEEVIL. This led to estab. of Farmers Cooperative Demonstration Work division in Dept. of Agr. which he headed. His son, **Bradford Knapp,** 1870–1938, carried forward his work.

Kneller, Sir Godfrey (nĕl'ùr), 1646–1723, English portrait painter, b. Germany. Succeeded Lely as court painter under the monarchs from Charles II to George I. Responsible for such works as *Ten Beauties of the Court* and 42 portraits of fellow members of the KIT-CAT CLUB.

Knickerbocker (nĭ'kùrbŏ"kùr), family name, which came to be used as a term for all early N.Y. Dutch and was immortalized by Washington Irving's pseudonym Diedrich Knickerbocker.

knight. 1 In ancient history, a noble of second class who in military service furnished own mount and equipment. In Rome knights (*equites*) ranked between senatorial class and citizens. **2** In medieval history, armed and mounted warrior belonging to nobility. With growth of FEUDALISM term applied to landholders as well as to nobility. Knighthood, in true meaning, was never hereditary but had to be earned. In late Middle Ages son of a noble served as page and as squire before being knighted. Knighthood was conferred by overlord with accolade (blow, usually with flat of sword, on neck or shoulder). Military tenure was subject to law of PRIMOGENITURE, leading to a class of landless knights. In Crusades these formed great military orders such as KNIGHTS TEMPLARS, KNIGHTS HOSPITALERS, and TEUTONIC KNIGHTS. Secular orders also grew up, e.g., orders of Garter and of Thistle in England, Order of the Golden Fleece in Burgundy. Title knight (Ger. *Ritter*, Fr. *chevalier*) was later used as noble title. In modern England knighthood is not title of nobility, but is conferred by king on commoners or nobles for civil or military achievements. Knight is addressed as Sir; a woman knighted, as Dame.

knighthood and chivalry. Ethical ideals of FEUDALISM found highest expression in 12th and 13th cent. They originated in France and Spain and spread over Continent and England. They were fusion of Christian and military ideals, with piety, bravery, loyalty, and honor as virtues. Chivalrous love glorified womanhood (finding supreme expression in cult of the Virgin) and rendered homage in noblest sense. Virtues were proved in battle and tournament. Medieval secular literature dealt primarily with knighthood and chivalry, with ARTHURIAN LEGEND and CHANSONS DE GESTE as patterns. ROMAN DE LA ROSE and work of CHRESTIEN DE TROYES also were influential. For lyric poetry of age of chivalry, see TROUBADOUR; TROUVÈRE; MINNESINGER.

Knights Hospitalers (hŏ'spĭtŭlûrz), members of the military religious Order of the Hospital of St. John of Jerusalem, called also Knights of St. John and Knights of Jerusalem. The order grew out of a hospital estab. 11th cent. to care for pilgrims in Holy Land. Reconstructed as a military order, it soon grew in wealth and power, with subsidiary establishments (preceptories) all over Europe. Its knights, with their colleagues and rivals, the Templars, took part in all the military ventures of the Latin Kingdom and of the Crusaders. After the Saracens took Jerusalem (1187) the order moved to Margat and then to Acre (1189) and was driven from the Holy Land (1291) to Cyprus. Their conquest of Rhodes (1310) and the material benefits derived from the dissolution of the Knights Templars marked the beginning of a period of increasing power. Dominating the Mediterranean, the Knights of Rhodes, as they were called, checked Moslem piracy but often turned to piracy themselves. Under Pierre d'Aubusson they heroically defended Rhodes against Mohammed II (1480), but they had to capitulate to Suleiman I in 1522. In 1530 Emperor Charles V gave them the island of MALTA, which became their fixed home. Under Jean de la Valette they defended Malta against the Turks, whose menace remained acute until the battle of Lepanto (1571). Thereafter the Knights of Malta carried on their charitable hospital work in relative peace until Napoleon seized Malta in 1798. Remnants of the order survived in Europe, and in 1879 the pope restored the office of grand master; but, as reconstituted, the order bears little relation to the old Knights of Malta. The Hospitalers were called also Knights of the White Cross for the white cross worn on their black robes.

Knights of Columbus (K.C. or K. of C.), American Roman Catholic society for men, founded 1882, at New Haven, Conn.

Knights of Jerusalem: see KNIGHTS HOSPITALERS.

Knights of Labor, American labor organization, started 1869. Organized on an industrial basis, with women, colored workers, and employers welcomed. With the motto "an injury to one is the concern of all," it championed the 8-hour day and abolition of child labor. Reached its apex in 1886, under Terence V.

Powderly, with a membership of 702,000. It collapsed from financial and factional difficulties.

Knights of Malta and **Knights of Rhodes:** see KNIGHTS HOSPITALERS.

Knights of Saint Crispin, union of shoemakers organized in 1867. At one time it was the largest trade union in the U.S. By 1878 it was defunct, many of its members having joined the Knights of Labor.

Knights of Saint John of Jerusalem: see KNIGHTS HOSPITALERS.

Knights of the Golden Circle, secret order of Southern sympathizers in North in Civil War. First "castle" estab. 1854 in Cincinnati. Active in Ky., Ind., Ohio, Ill., and Mo. Membership mostly Peace Democrats, opposed to war and increasing Federal power. In 1863 named Order of American Knights, in 1864 organized as Order of the Sons of Liberty; C. L. Vallandigham, leading Copperhead, was commander. Numbered over 200,000 in 1864; with mounting Union victories order soon dissolved.

Knights of the White Camellia: see KU KLUX KLAN.

Knights Templars, in medieval history, members of military religious order of Poor Knights of Christ, called also Knights of the Temple of Solomon. Like their rivals, KNIGHTS HOSPITALERS and TEUTONIC KNIGHTS, Templars formed in period of CRUSADES. Nucleus was band of nine knights headed by Hugh de Payens who united c.1118 for protection of pilgrims. Group increased, adopted Benedictine rule, and had quarters beside Solomon's Temple. They rapidly became one of most powerful bodies in Europe, and their dashing military exploits won great fame throughout Crusades. They held Acre till citadel fell in 1291, then retired to Cyprus. Through receipts of many gifts and lands they became wealthy, and were bankers of Europe. Their financial control aroused jealousy of Philip IV of France, who accused order of many crimes and abuses and persecuted it 1308–14. Last grand master, Jacques de Molay, was burned 1314, and order came to an end.

Knobelsdorff, Georg Wenzeslaus von (knŏ'bŭlsdôrf), 1699–1753, German architect, who designed Sans Souci (Potsdam) and State Opera House (Berlin).

Knob Lake: see SCHEFFERVILLE, Que., Canada.

Knob Noster, city (pop. 2,292), W Mo., E of Warrensburg. Whiteman Air Force Base is S.

Knossos: see CNOSSUS.

Know-Nothing movement, in U.S. history. During 1840s in Eastern cities where Roman Catholic immigrants especially had concentrated and been welcomed by Democrats, local nativistic societies formed to combat "foreign" influences and uphold "American" view. Native American party, stemming from American Republican party (formed in N.Y. in 1843), became a national party in 1845. In 1850s many secret orders grew up. All inquiries of supposed members were met with a statement to the effect that they knew nothing; hence members were called Know-Nothings. They sought to elect only native Americans to office and to estab. a 25-year residence qualification for citizenship. Allied with a Whig faction, Know-Nothings in 1854 swept Mass. and Del. polls. In 1855 they adopted name American party, yielded much of their secrecy. Slavery issue split them apart; Millard Fillmore, party candidate for President in 1856, polled small vote. Movement continued until 1860, mainly in Eastern cities and in border states among Southern Unionists.

Knox, Frank, 1874–1944, U.S. Secretary of the Navy (1940–44). Opposed to New Deal, he was appointed by Pres. F. D. Roosevelt to help create national unity in defense preparations.

Knox, Henry, 1750–1806, patriot general in American Revolution. Directed artillery in many battles. U.S. Secretary of War (1785–94).

Knox, John, 1505?–1572, Scottish religious reformer, founder of Scottish Presbyterianism. Originally a Catholic priest, he attached himself to George Wishart and became a Protestant. Preached (1549–54) in

England, was a royal chaplain briefly, and helped revise second Book of Common Prayer. After accession of Mary I he went into exile on the Continent, chiefly at Geneva where he consulted with Calvin. Scottish Protestant nobles made their first covenant in 1557 (see SCOTLAND, CHURCH OF) and invited Knox's help against Mary of Guise. After a civil war (1559–60) the reformers forced withdrawal of the French and won their freedom and dominance of the new religion. Knox, as minister of Edinburgh, tried to abolish pope's authority and condemn creeds and practices of old church. He attacked the religion of Mary Queen of Scots. Her abdication led to estab. of Church of Scotland. His single-minded zeal made him the outstanding leader of the Scottish Reformation and an important influence on the Protestant movements in England and on the Continent but closed his mind to tolerance.

Knox, Philander Chase, 1853–1921, U.S. cabinet officer. Attorney General (1901–4). Secretary of State (1909–13); protected financial interests abroad, policy attacked as "dollar diplomacy."

Knox, Fort [for Henry Knox], U.S. military reservation, 33,000 acres, N Ky., c.30 mi. SW of Louisville; estab. 1917 as training camp, made permanent post 1932. In vaults of U.S. Depository, built here by Dept. of Treasury in 1936, is stored bulk of nation's gold bullion.

Knox College, at Galesburg, Ill.; coed.; chartered 1837, opened 1841; called Knox Manual Labor Col. until 1857. Absorbed Lombard Col. (1851) in 1930.

Knoxville. 1 City (1966 pop. 8,521), S central Iowa, SE of Des Moines, platted 1845. Large U.S. veterans' hospital is here. **2** City (pop. 111,827), E Tenn., on Tennessee R.; settled c.1786. Cap. of Territory of the U.S. South of the River Ohio (1792–96) and twice state cap. (1796–1812, 1817–19). Loyal to Union in Civil War, it was held by Confederates until abandoned to Gen. A. E. Burnside's Federals, Sept., 1863. Gen. James Longstreet's attempt to recapture it (Nov.–Dec., 1863) failed. A livestock and tobacco market, it is important industrial, commercial, and shipping center for farm, marble, and coal area. Has knitting mills. Seat of Univ. of TENNESSEE. LINCOLN MEMORIAL UNIVERSITY is nearby. Nearby are Norris Dam and Great Smoky Mts. Natl. Park. Has graves of John Sevier and William Blount, Blount Mansion (1792), and Chisholm Tavern (1791).

Knut: see CANUTE.

Knutson, Paul: see PAUL KNUTSON.

koala (kōä'lủ), arboreal marsupial animal (genus *Phascolarctos*) of Australia. It is grayish, thickly furred, tailless, usually 2–2½ ft. high, and has a protuberant, curved, black nose, and large furry ears. Each foot has five toes with claws fitted for climbing and grasping. It often sleeps by day, and at night it eats leaves and shoots of certain eucalyptus trees. Mother carries single cub (c.¾ in. long at birth) in pouch for first six months; cub emerges, uses pouch two months more, and is carried in arms or on back until it is a year old. Koala is harmless and defenseless. Toy "Teddy bears" resemble koalas. See *ill.*, p. 1136.

Kobarid (kō'bärĭt), Ital. *Caporetto*, village, Slovenia, NW Yugoslavia, on Isonzo R. Passed from Austria to Italy 1919; to Yugoslavia 1947. Scene of Italian rout by Austrians 1917.

Kobe (kō'bā), city (pop. 1,113,977), S Honshu, Japan, on Osaka Bay. Leading port, rail hub, and industrial center (shipbuilding, steel mills, sugar refineries, chemical plants). Includes anc. port of Hyogo. A cultural center, it has seven colleges and universities, and many temples and shrines.

Kobenhavn, Denmark: see COPENHAGEN.

Koblenz, Germany: see COBLENZ.

Kobo-Daishi: see KUKAI.

Koch, Robert (rō'bĕrt kôkh'), 1843–1910, German bacteriologist. He developed techniques of bacteriological culture and discovered causative organisms of many infectious diseases including anthrax (1876), tu-

berculosis (1882), cholera (1884). Won 1905 Nobel Prize in Physiology and Medicine for developing tuberculin test for tuberculosis.

Kochanowski, Jan (yän kôkhänôf'skĕ), 1530–84, greatest Polish Renaissance poet. Of especial note is his Polish version of Psalms of David.

Kocher, Emil Theodor (ā'mĕl tā'ōdŏr kô'khủr), 1841–1917, Swiss surgeon. Won 1909 Nobel Prize in Physiology and Medicine for work on thyroid gland.

Kock, Hieronymus: see COCK, HIERONYMUS.

Kodaly, Zoltan (zôl'tän kô'dälĕ), 1882–1967, Hungarian composer. Worked with Bartok in collecting folk tunes and, like Bartok, used them in his compositions. Among his works are an opera, *Hary Janos;* the *Psalmus Hungaricus* and *Missa Brevis* for chorus and orchestra; and the *Dances of Galanta* for orchestra.

Kodiak Island (kō'dēǎk), c.100 mi. long. 10–16 mi. wide, off S Alaska, on Shelikof Strait. Mountainous. heavily wooded in N and E; good pasturage in S for cattle. sheep. Kokiak bear is native here. Discovered 1763 by Stepan Glotov, it had first permanent Russian settlement in Alaska, planted by Grigori Shelekhov on Three Saints Bay 1784, moved to Kodiak village later. Center of fur trade until Aleksandr Baranov moved hq. to Sitka in 1799. Salmon fishing chief occupation; Karluk R. famous for salmon run. Also fox breeding and whaling. U.S. naval station is here.

Kodok (kō'dŏk), formerly **Fashoda** (fủshō'dủ), village, W central Republic of the Sudan, on the White Nile. Scene of the FASHODA INCIDENT in 1898.

Koestler, Arthur (kĕst'lủr), 1905–, Hungarian-born author. Led adventurous life as newspaper correspondent; in England since 1941. An ex-radical, he found his chief theme in anti-Communism. Among his works are *Spanish Testament* (1937), *The Yogi and the Commissar* (1945), *The God that Failed* (1950), *The Sleepwalkers* (1959), *Janus, or the Ambiguity of Man* (1966); the novels *Darkness at Noon* (1941), *Thieves in the Night* (1946), and *The Age of Longing* (1951); and his autobiography, *Arrow in the Blue* (2 vols., 1952–54).

Koffka, Kurt, 1886–1941, American psychologist, b. Germany. A founder of GESTALT psychology, he taught at Cornell, Univ. of Wisconsin, Smith College (after 1928).

Kohala (kōhä'lủ), peninsula, Hawaii, on N tip of Hawaii island. Rich in anc. relics, including burial caves and *heiau* (temples). Kamehameha I born near Kapaau-Halaula village. Kohala Mts. rise to 5,489 ft.

Koh-i-noor, name of a diamond associated through centuries of India's history with deeds of violence. In 1849 came into possession of the British and after being recut was placed among crown jewels.

Kohler, Kaufmann, 1843–1926, American rabbi, scholar, and leader of reformed Judaism, b. Bavaria. Came to America in 1869; was president of Hebrew Union Col. in Cincinnati (1903–22). Instrumental in formation of "Pittsburgh Platform" of reformed Judaism (1885). Wrote *Jewish Theology Systematically and Historically Considered* (1918).

Köhler, Wolfgang, 1887–1967, American psychologist, b. Estonia. Among first to use apes in experiments; his work helped develop Gestalt psychology.

Kohler, village (pop. 1,524), E Wis., on Sheboygan R., WSW of Sheboygan. Scene of some of longest and most bitter labor disputes in U.S. history.

kohlrabi (kōl'rä'bē), vegetable (*Brassica oleracea gongolodes* or *B. caulorapa*) with turniplike edible swollen stems. Derived from wild cabbage.

Kokand or **Khokand** (both: kōkǎnd'), city (1965 est. pop. 126,000), Uzbek SSR, in Fergana Valley. Important city since 10th cent.; cap. of Kokand khanate from 16th cent. until Russian conquest, 1876. Textile mfg. (silk and cotton).

Kokiu or **Ko-chiu** (gōō'jō'), town (pop. c.159,700), Yünnan prov., China. Major tin mining center.

Kokomo (kō'kûmō), city (pop. 47,197), N central Ind., N of Indianapolis; settled 1840. Inventor Elwood Haynes tested first practical automobile here 1894.

Koko Nor (kōkō nōr'), Chinese **Tsinghai**, salt lake, c.2,000 sq. mi., NE Tsinghai prov., China. Largest lake of Tibetan highlands.

Kokoschka, Oskar (ôs'kär kōkôsh'kä), 1886–, Austrian expressionist painter and playwright, famous for portraits and dramatic landscapes.

Koksoak, river, NE Que., Canada, formed by Kanaipiskau and Larch rivers SW of Fort Chimo. Flows 90 mi. NE and N to Ungava Bay.

Kokura (kōkōō'rä), city (pop. 286,474), N Kyushu, Japan, port on Inland Sea. Industrial center (steel, cotton textiles, porcelain, chemicals).

kola, tropical tree (*Cola acuminata*) native to Africa and grown in warm regions for seeds known as kola (or cola) nuts. They contain caffeine, oil, and a glucoside (kolanin). Native peoples chew the fresh nuts. Some nuts are exported for use in beverages and medicine.

Kola Peninsula (kō'lù), area c.50,000 sq. mi., N European RSFSR, an E extension of Scandinavian peninsula between Barents (n) and White seas. Rich mineral deposits. Russians live along coasts, Lapps inland. MURMANSK is chief city.

Kolar Gold Fields (kōlär'), city (pop. 159,084), E Mysore, India; India's chief gold-mining center.

Kolarovgrad (kōlärōv'grät), formerly **Shumen,** city (est. pop. 70,758), NE Bulgaria. Trade and railroad center. Founded 927; strategic fortress during Turkish rule. Noted for Moslem architecture.

Kolas, Jakub (yä'kōob kō'läs), 1882–1956, Belorussian poet and novelist. His real name was Konstantin Mitskevich. His novels were devoted to moral themes, to collectivism, to war.

Kolbe, Georg (gā'ôrk kôl'bù), 1877–1947, German sculptor of introspective figures. Influenced by Rodin. During the Hitler regime he produced ideal heroes—warriors and athletes.

Kolchak, Aleksandr Vasilyevich (ûlyīksän'dùr vùsē'-lyùvîch kûlchäk'), 1874–1920, Russian admiral and counterrevolutionist. Commanded Black Sea fleet in First World War. After October Revolution of 1917 he organized anti-Bolshevik government in Siberia, was recognized by Allies, assumed dictatorship 1918.

Kolding (kôl'dĭng), city (pop. 35,101), E Jutland, Denmark; a port on Kolding Fjord (inlet of Little Belt). Shipbuilding; machinery and dairy mfg.

Kolhapur (kōlùpōōr'), former princely state (3,219 sq. mi.), Maharashtra, India. Kolhapur, city (pop. 136,835), was its cap. City occupies site of an anc. Buddhist center.

Kolin, Czech **Kolín** (kô'lēn), city (est. pop. 21,975), central Bohemia, Czechoslovakia, on the Elbe. Varied mfg. Scene of victory of Austrians under Daun over Frederick II of Prussia (1757).

kolkhoz: see COLLECTIVE FARM.

Kollar, Jan, Czech **Kollár** (yän' kô'lär), 1793–1852, Slovak poet who wrote in Czech. His ardent panSlavism is reflected in his best-known poem, *The Daughter of Slava* (1821–24).

Kölliker, Albert von (äl'bĕrt fün kû'lĭkûr), 1817–1905, Swiss anatomist and physiologist. His microscopic studies of animal tissues advanced development of embryology and histology.

Kollwitz, Käthe (Schmidt) (kä'tù shmĭt' kôl'vĭts), 1867–1945, German lithographer, best known for her superb studies of poor people. Was ardent socialist and pacifist.

Kolmar, France: see COLMAR.

Köln, Germany: see COLOGNE.

Kol Nidre: see ATONEMENT, DAY OF.

Kolomna (kùlôm'nù), city (1965 est. pop. 130,000), central European RSFSR, on Moskva R., SE of Moscow. Mfg. of locomotives and rolling stock. Founded 1177, it passed 1301 to Moscow. Strategically impor-

tant in defense of Moscow against Tatars until 16th cent.

Kolomyya (kùlûmî'yù), Ger. *Kolomea,* Pol. *Kolomyja,* city (pop. 31,300), W Ukraine, on Pruth R.; agr. machinery, textiles. Known 1240; passed to Poland 14th cent. and made a fortress; ruled by Austria 1772–1918; incorporated into Ukrainian SSR 1939.

Kolozsvar, Rumania: see CLUJ.

Kolwezi (kōlwē'zē), city (pop. c.44,000), S Republic of the Congo. A transportation center of former KATANGA prov., in a copper- and cobalt-mining region.

Kolyma (kōlē'mù), river. c.1,615 mi. long, RSFSR, in NE Siberia. Flows N into Arctic Ocean. It is partially navigable June–Oct. There are rich gold mines along upper course. **Kolyma Range** (c.6,000 ft. high) parallels E shore.

Komandorski Islands (kōmùndôr'skē), group (including Bering Island) off Kamchatka Peninsula, RSFSR, in SW Bering Sea. Foggy, composed of volcanic rock, and subject to frequent earthquakes, they are whaling and sealing base, populated mainly by Aleuts.

Komarno, Slovak *Komárno* (kô'märnô), or **Komarom,** Hung. *Komárom* (kô'märôm), city of Czechoslovakia and Hungary. Komarno (est. pop. 25,974), on left bank of the Danube, belongs to Slovakia; has machinery and textile mfg., flour mills, shipbuilding. Komarom (est. pop. 9,862), on right (Hungarian) bank, has lumber and textile industries. There are port installations on both banks. Entire city belonged to Austria-Hungary until partition in 1920.

Komi Autonomous Soviet Socialist Republic (kō'mē), autonomous republic (160,579 sq. mi.; 1965 est. pop. 950,000), NE European RSFSR, W of the N Urals; cap. Syktyvkar. Nearly half the area is permanently frozen. The sparse population is concentrated in S, where there is farming, lumbering, and stock raising. Coal mines in Pechora Basin. Inhabitants are mostly Komi, formerly called Zyrians, a Finnic people, closely related to Komi-Permyaks, also called Permyaks. Latter group lives largely in **Komi-Permyak National Okrug** (–pûrm'yàk) (12,703 sq. mi.; 1965 est. pop. 228,000), W central European RSFSR; cap. Kudymbar. Lumbering is major industry.

Komsomolsk (kùmsùmôlsk') or **Komsomolsk-on-Amur,** city (1965 est. pop. 204,000), S Khabarovsk Territory, RSFSR, in E Siberia. Industrial center of Soviet Far East; steel and lumber mills, shipyards, aircraft plants, petroleum refineries. Founded 1932.

Kona (kō'nù), district, Hawaii, on W Hawaii. State's coffee belt and favorite tourist spot, with fine deepsea fishing off coast. First American missionaries landed at Kailua Bay in 1820. City of Refuge Natl. Historical Park is at Honaunau.

Konakry: see CONAKRY.

Konev, Ivan Stepanovich (ēvän' styīpá'nùvîch kô'nyĭf), 1897–, Russian field marshal in Second World War. Took part in capture of Berlin. Supreme commander of military forces of nations allied by Warsaw Pact, 1955–60.

Konia, Turkey: see KONYA.

Königgrätz: see HRADEC KRALOVE; SADOWA.

Königsberg (kû'nĭksbĕrk), since 1945 **Kaliningrad** (kùlyē"nyĭngrät'), city (1965 est. pop. 253,000), historic cap. of East Prussia; transferred to USSR 1945; inc. into RSFSR. It is an ice-free Baltic seaport and produces freight cars, machinery, processed foods. Founded 1255 as fortress of Teutonic Knights, it joined Hanseatic League 1340. Residence of dukes of Prussia 1525–1618; coronation city of kings of Prussia from 1701. Its university, founded 1544, reached greatest fame when Kant taught there; the building, like most of the city, was destroyed in Second World War during a two-month siege by the Russians (1945). Kaliningrad, built up after war in NW section of Königsberg, has a Russian population.

Königshütte, Poland: see CHORZOW.

Königsmark, Countess Maria Aurora (märē'ä ourô'rä kû'nĭksmärk), 1666–1728, Swedish noblewoman, mistress of Augustus II of Poland and Saxony. Their son Maurice became known as Marshal de SAXE.

Koninck or **Coningh, Philips de** (fē'lǐps dù kō'nǐngk), 1619–88, Dutch landscape and portrait painter.

Koninksloo, Gillis van: see CONINXLOO, GILLIS VAN.

Konotop (kŏnŭtŏp'), city (1965 est. pop. 59,000), Ukrainian SSR, center of agr. region; mining equipment, railroad repair shops. Historical museum and archives.

Konoye, Fumimaro, Princę (fōō"mēmärō' kōnoi'), 1891–1945, Japanese statesman. Of ancient Fujiwara family. Premier 1937–39, 1940–41. Forsook liberalism to advance Japanese aggression in China. Resigned 1941 when talks with U.S. failed; succeeded by Gen. Tojo. Suicide prevented trial as war criminal.

Konstantinovka (kŭnstŭntyē'nŭfkŭ), city (1965 est. pop. 99,000), E central Ukrainian SSR, in Donets Basin. Metallurgical center; glass and chemical plants.

Konstanz, Germany: see CONSTANCE.

Konya or **Konia** (kōn'yä) city (pop. 119,841), S central Turkey. Center of rich agr. area; mfg. of carpets, textiles, leather goods. The ancient ICONIUM, it reached its peak after becoming the seat of the powerful Seljuk sultanate of Iconium or Rum, in Asia Minor (11th cent.). After the Seljuks' defeat by allied Mongols and Armenians (late 13th cent.), the territory passed to the emirs of Karaman, then to the Ottoman Turks (15th cent.). Konya remained important as religious center of the whirling dervishes, whose order was founded here in 13th cent. It has kept several medieval mosques and its old city walls. In 1832 Egyptians under Ibrahim Pasha routed Turks at Konya.

Koo, V(i) K(uiyuin) Wellington (kōō'), 1887–, Chinese diplomat, educated at Columbia Univ. At various times minister of foreign affairs and prime minister. Ambassador to France (1932–41), to Great Britain (1941–46), and to U.S. (1946–56). Elected to International Court of Justice, 1957.

Kook, Abraham Isaac, 1864–1935, Jewish scholar and philosopher, b. Latvia. Was chief rabbi of Ashkenazic community in Palestine. Taught mystical oneness of land and people of Israel.

Koolau Range (kō'ŭlou'), mountain chain, Hawaii, on Oahu, extending NW–SE and rising to 3,105 ft. in Konahuanui. Cut by two scenic passes, Nuuanu Pali and Waimanalo Pali.

Kootenai (kōō'tǐnā) (in Canada, Kootenay), river, rising in SE B.C., Canada, and flowing into NW Mont., W into N Idaho, then N to Kootenay L. in B.C. Part of Columbia R. system.

Kootenai Indians, group of North American tribes whose language is probably of Algonquian-Mosan linguistic stock. In 18th cent. they lived in N Mont., N Idaho, and SE British Columbia. Their culture was essentially that of Plateau area but after the coming of the horse, the Kootenai adopted many Plains area traits.

Kootenay Lake, SE B.C., Canada, E of the Selkirk range, an expansion of Kootenay (in U.S., Kootenai) R. To E, on Alta. line, is **Kootenay National Park,** estab. 1920.

Kooweskoowe: see ROSS, JOHN.

Kopparberg, Swed. **Kopparbergs län** (kō"pärbēryùs lĕn'), county (11,711 sq. mi.; pop. 286,309). central Sweden, virtually identical with historical DALARNA prov.; cap. FALUN. Copper mines, from which name derives, are now exhausted, but rich iron mines are worked in Grangesberg dist. in S. There are iron, steel, and lumber mills.

Köprülü, family of grand viziers: see KUPRILI.

Korah (kō'rŭ), Levite leader (with Abiram and his brother Dathan) of revolt against Moses. Rebels ended by being consumed by fire and earthquake. Num. 16; 26.9–11; Deut. 11.6. Core: Jude 11.

Koran or **Quran** (kōrän', –rän') [Arabic,= reading], sacred book of Islam; after the Bible, the world's most influential book. Moslems consider it a series of revelations by God to Mohammed. Canonical text (in classical Arabic) estab. A.H. 30 (A.D. 651–52) under

the Caliph Othman according to the 114 suras [chapters] of Zaid ibn Thabit, the Prophet's secretary. All variant texts were destroyed. Moslems memorize the Koran, consider all science a commentary on it. The Koran holds that man must surrender his will and purpose to those of the Lord, that prophets Moses, Jesus, and Mohammed are laudable, but are all under God. Recent English translations of the Koran point up the growing recognition of Islam in the U.S.

Korça or **Korçë,** Albania: see KORITSA.

Korcula (kôr'chōōlä), Ital. *Curzola,* Serbo-Croatian *Korčula,* Adriatic island, area 105 sq. mi., off Dalmatia, Yugoslavia. Chief town, Korcula (pop. c.3,000), has fine medieval cathedral and fortifications.

Korea (kôrē'u, kŭ–), Korean *Choson,* historic region (85,286 sq. mi.), E Asia. A mountainous peninsula, Korea is bordered by Korea Bay on W, Korea Strait on S, and Sea of Japan on E; its land boundaries with China and USSR are marked by Yalu and Tumen rivers. Has c.3,400 offshore islands. Principal mountain range extends along E coast, rising to 9,003 ft. at Mt. Paektu. Rich in deposits of gold, coal, iron and tungsten. Vast timberlands in N. In S and SW river valleys rice, barley, cotton, tobacco, soybeans, and vegetables are grown; soybeans and cereals are raised in N. Most Koreans are Buddhists, Confucians, or adherents of Chon-go-gyo, a mixture of Buddhism, Confucianism, Christianity, and Taoism. Recorded history began with colony at Pyongyang estab. 12th cent. B.C. by Chinese scholar Ki-tze. In 7th cent. A.D. native Silla kingdom, founded c.350, unified Korea. Occupied by Mongols 1231–60. Yi dynasty, 1392–1910, with cap. at Seoul, made Confucianism official religion. Phonetic alphabet and printing were developed in early Yi. Invasion by Japanese dictator HIDEYOSHI 1592 was repelled with Chinese aid. Made vassal state of China in early 17th cent. Long known as the Hermit Kingdom, Korea's isolation ended 1876 with forced acceptance of commercial treaty with Japan. Japan's success in First CHINO-JAPANESE WAR (1894–95) and RUSSO-JAPANESE WAR (1904–5) led to annexation of Korea 1910. In Second World War, CAIRO CONFERENCE of 1943 promised Korea independence. At war's end, country was divided into occupation zones—the Russians N and Americans S of 38th parallel. Cooperation between the two proved impossible, and in 1948 the division was formalized by the estab. of N Korean and S Korean regimes. Foreign troops withdrew by mid-1949. On 25 June, 1950, N Korea invaded S Korea, and was declared aggressor by UN Security Council (USSR was voluntarily absent). In Aug., UN forces under supreme command of Gen. MACARTHUR (replaced 1951 by Gen. RIDGWAY) came to S Korea's aid. In the first few weeks of war, N Korea pushed S to Pusan area at SE tip of peninsula. Landing at INCHON on W coast in Sept. carried UN forces to Manchurian border. Entrance of Communist China into the war in Nov. forced UN troops far below 38th parallel. which was regained early 1951 and maintained until war's end. Cease-fire negotiations at Panmunjon began July, 1951, and were concluded July, 1953. Korean partition along 38th parallel was reaffirmed. North Korea or Democratic People's Republic of Korea (47,861 sq. mi.; pop. c.10,000,000); cap. Pyongyang. After Korean war, led by KIM IL SUNG, it launched a vast industrialization and rehabilitation program. It was sharply curtailed by acute shortages in food, housing, and essential consumer goods in 1959. Population augmented by Chinese colonists and Koreans from Manchuria. Signed military pacts with USSR and People's Republic of China in 1961. South Korea or Republic of Korea (37,425 sq. mi.; pop. c.25,524,000); cap. Seoul. Traditionally agr. region, attempts to estab. adequate industrial base thwarted by limited resources and lack of power (mostly supplied from N before 1948), further aggravated by war damage and influx of refugees. Syngman Rhee was ousted after election to his 4th consecutive presidential term in 1960. In 1961 an army group seized power under Gen. CHUNG HEE PARK, who was elected president 1963 and 1967. Normal diplomatic relations with Japan estab. 1965 by treaty.

Korean war, conflict between Communist and non-Communist forces in Korea from June 25, 1950, to June 27, 1953. At end of Second World War Korea was divided at 38th parallel into N (USSR) and S (U.S.) occupation zones; rival governments estab. 1948. When North Korean forces invaded South Korea, UN authorized member nations to aid South Korea. (Gen. Douglas MacArthur commanded UN forces until 1951, when he was replaced by Gen. Matthew B. Ridgway.) Chinese Communist forces joined North Korean army Oct., 1950. Fighting after that centered around 38th parallel. Negotiations for cease-fire were begun 1951 at Panmunjom, achieved July 27, 1953.

Koritsa (kôrǐt'sù), Albanian *Korçë* or *Korça*, city (est. pop. 40,000), SE Albania. Commercial and agr. center of a fertile plain. Long claimed by Greeks, who occupied it in Balkan Wars and both world wars.

Kornberg, Arthur, 1918–, American biochemist. For his studies of enzymes involved in the natural synthesis and breakdown of nucleic acids, he shared with Severo Ochoa the 1959 Nobel Prize in Medicine and Physiology.

Kornilov, Lavr Georgyevich (lä'vùr gēyôr'gyǐvǐch kŭr-nyē'lûf), 1870–1918, Russian general. Kerensky made him commander in chief after February Revolution of 1917 but dismissed him in Sept. He refused to accept his dismissal, was arrested, escaped after the Bolshevik Revolution, and led an army of counterrevolutionary volunteers in S Russia. Forced to fall back on the Kuban, he was killed in action; succeeded by Denikin.

Korolenko, Vladimir Galaktionovich (vlŭdyē'mĭr gùlûktyŏ'nùvĭch kŭrùlyĕn'kù), 1853–1921, Russian author and liberal publicist. Known for short stories.

Koros or **Harmas Koros** (här'mŏsh kû'rûsh), river, E Hungary and W Rumania, c.345 mi. long. Formed by three headstreams rising in Transylvania and flowing W into the Theiss.

Kortrijk, Belgium: see COURTRAI.

Korzybski, Alfred (Habdank) (kôrzĭb'skĕ), 1879–1950, Polish-American scientist, b. Warsaw. Founded system of General Semantics. Wrote (1933) *Science and Sanity,* on distinction between words and objects.

Kos (kŏs, kôs), Latin *Cos,* Aegean island (111 sq. mi.; pop. 19,987), Greece, second largest of the DODECANESE, 2½ mi. off Asia Minor; chief city Kos (pop. 8,138). Important cultural center in Roman times; home of Hippocrates.

Kosala (kŏ'sùlù), ancient N Indian kingdom, c.6th–4th cent. B.C., cap. Ayodhya. Scene of much Sanskrit epic literature. The Buddha and Mahavira, founder of Jainism, taught here.

Kosciusko, Thaddeus (kŏ"sēŭ'skŏ), 1746–1817, Polish general. Fought for patriot cause in American Revolution. Champion of Polish independence, he led an unsuccessful rebellion against Russian and Prussian control (1794) and became a Polish hero.

Kosciusko, Mount (kŏzĕŭ'skŏ), 7,328 ft. high, SE New South Wales, in Australian Alps; highest peak of Australia.

kosher [Heb.,= proper, i.e., fit for use], term applied to food which complies with the Jewish dietary laws. Kosher meat is the flesh of animals which chew the cud and have cloven hoofs; both meat and fowl must be slaughtered by a specially trained pious Jew and must be salted and soaked to remove all traces of blood. Kosher fish are those which have scales (mollusks and eels are forbidden). The laws forbid cooking and eating of milk with meat and also the use of the same kitchen or table utensil for handling both meat and milk. It is widely held that many of these laws stem from the health preservation measures of ancient Palestine. See also TALMUD.

Koshtan-Tau (kŭshtän"-tou'), peak, 16,880 ft. high, USSR, in central Greater Caucasus.

Kosice, Slovak *Košiče* (kŏ'shǐtsä), Ger. *Kaschau,* Hung. *Kassa,* city (est. pop. 99,000), SE Slovakia, Czechoslovakia. Industrial center; transportation hub. Petroleum refinery and modern iron and steel center. Originally a fortress town, most frequently occupied by Austrians, Hungarians, and Turks. Has 14th-cent. Gothic Cathedral of St. Elizabeth.

Köslin (kûs'lĭn) or **Koszalin** (kŏ-shä'lĕn), city (est. pop. 51,000), NW Poland (since 1945), in Pomerania, near Baltic Sea. Produces canned fish, metal products, chemicals. Founded 1188.

Kosovo, Yugoslavia: see Kossovo.

Kossel, Albrecht (äl'brĕkht kŏ'sùl), 1853–1927, German physiological chemist. Won 1910 Nobel Prize in Physiology and Medicine for work on proteins, cells, and cell nuclei.

Kossovo, Serbo-Croatian *Kosovo* (kŏ'sôvô), autonomous region, largely mountainous, SW Serbia, Yugoslavia. Population mainly Albanian, Serbian, and Montenegrin. Under Turkish rule from 1389 until 1913 when it was divided between Serbia and Montenegro and incorporated into Yugoslavia 1918. After Second World War made autonomous region in Serbia.

Kossuth, Louis (kŏsŏŏth', Hung. kŏsh'ŏŏt), Hung. *Kossuth Lajos,* 1802–94, Hungarian revolutionary hero. One of the principal figures in the Hungarian revolution of March, 1848, he was a liberal and an extreme nationalist. When Austria prepared to move against Hungary, Kossuth became head of the government of national defense; in April, 1849, he became president of the newly proclaimed Hungarian republic. He resigned in August, when Russian troops came to aid the Austrians, and spent the rest of his life in exile.

Koster, Laurens Janszoon (lou'rùns yän'sŏn kŏ'stùr), c.1370–c.1440, Dutch sexton [*koster*], to whom some have attributed the use of movable type in printing prior to Gutenberg.

Kostroma (kŭstrùmä'), city (1965 est. pop. 202,000), central European RSFSR, on Volga. Linen milling. Annexed to Moscow 1364. Michael Romanov was elected tsar here in 1613. Has Uspenski Cathedral (c.1250).

Kosygin, Alexei Nikolayevich (ùlĕk'sä nēkŏlī'ùvĭch kŏsē'gyĕn), 1904–, Russian Communist leader. He was an aide to Stalin in the 1940s and was recognized as an expert in economics and industry under Khrushchev. In 1964 he succeeded Khrushchev as premier and chairman of the council of ministers. Held summit meeting (June, 1967) with Pres. Lyndon Johnson in Glassboro, N.J., following Arab-Israeli war.

Koszalin: see KÖSLIN.

Kotabaru, town (pop. 16,335), cap. of West Irian, N New Guinea, on Humboldt Bay. A trade center in sugar-cane area. Known as Hollandia until 1963.

Kotelny Island or **Kotelnyy Island** (both: kŏtĕl'nē), 100 mi. long, 60 mi. wide, it is largest of Anjou group of New Siberian Isls. off N Asiatic RSFSR.

Köthen (kû'tùn), city (est. pop. 37,927), East Germany, in former state of Saxony-Anhalt. Lignite mines, sugar mills, textile mfg. Until 1847 residence of dukes of Anhalt-Köthen. Formerly spelled Cöthen.

Kotka (kŏt'kä), city (pop. 30,068), S Finland; a seaport on Gulf of Finland and at southern end of *Päijänne* waterway. Main Finnish paper, pulp, and timber export center.

Kotor (kŏ'tôr), Ital. *Cattaro,* town (pop. c.5,600), Montenegro, SW Yugoslavia, on Bay of Kotor, an inlet of the Adriatic. A seaport and tourist center, it dates from Roman times. Venetian from 15th cent. till 1797, when it passed to Austria. An important Austrian naval base, it passed to Yugoslavia in 1918. Has medieval fort; 16th cent. cathedral.

Kotzebue, August von (ou'gŏŏst fŭn kŏt'sùbŏŏ), 1761–1819, German playwright, author of many. popular melodramas. After a stay in Russia he returned to

Germany as paid agent of Alexander I. His assassination by a student led to suppression of German student organizations by CARLSBAD DECREES. His son, **Otto von Kotzebue**, 1787–1846, Russian naval officer and explorer, commanded two voyages around world (1815–18, 1823–26). Discovered and explored some 400 Pacific islands and, in 1816, Kotzebue Sound, NW Alaska.

Kotzebue, village (pop. 1,290), NW Alaska, on Kotzebue Sound at tip of Baldwin Peninsula, on a tundra. Beginning as 18th-cent. Eskimo trading post, it is now one of largest Eskimo settlements.

Koublai Khan: see KUBLAI KHAN.

Koufax, Sanford (Sandy Koufax), 1935–, American baseball player. Retired 1966. Held major league record for most no-hitters pitched (4).

Koussevitzky, Serge (sĕrzh' kōōsūvīt'skē), 1874–1951, Russian-American conductor. Began his career playing the double bass. Made his conducting debut in Berlin, 1908. Was conductor of the Boston Symphony Orchestra (1924–49); director of the Berkshire Symphonic Festivals after 1936.

Kovalevsky, Sonya or **Sophie**, 1850–91, Russian mathematician. Worked on partial differential equations and wrote a famous memoir on the motion of a top.

Kovel (kō'vŭl), Pol. *Kowel*, city (pop. 24,700), W Ukraine, in Volhynia. Agr. processing center. Passed to Russia from Poland 1795; reverted to Poland 1921; was incorporated into Ukrainian SSR 1939.

Kovno, Lithuania: see KAUNAS.

Kovrov (kŭvrôf'), city (1965 est. pop. 113,000), central European RSFSR, port on Klyazma R. Machine tools, textiles, excavating machines, motorcycles.

Kowel, Ukraine: see KOVEL.

Kowloon: see HONG KONG.

Koya (kō'yä), peak, 2,858 ft. high, S Honshu, Japan. 9th-cent. Buddhist monastery on summit has 120 temples. Pilgrimage center.

Koyukuk (kúyō͞o'kōōk), river rising on S slope of Brooks Range, N Alaska, and flowing c.500 mi. SW to the Yukon near Koyukuk village.

Kozlov, RSFSR: see MICHURINSK.

Kr, chemical symbol of the element KRYPTON.

Kraepelin, Emil (krâ"pŭlēn'), 1856–1926, German psychiatrist. Concerned only with diagnostic classification of mental disease, he helped introduce scientific methods of investigation.

Krafft-Ebing, Richard von (rĭkh'ärt fŭn kräft-ā'bĭng), 1840–1902, German physician and neurologist, authority on psychological aspect of mental disorders and their medico-legal relations.

Kraft or **Krafft, Adam** (both: ä'däm kräft'), c.1455–1509, German sculptor of Nuremberg. Most famous work was Tabernacle for Church of St. Lawrence, Nuremberg.

Krak (kräk) or **El Kerak** (ĕl kĕ'räk), town (pop. c.10,-000), S central Jordan; trade center. As the ancient Kir Moab it was walled citadel of Moabites. Lordship of Krak and Montreal was one of chief baronies of Latin Kingdom of Jerusalem; Reginald de Châtillon held lordship when he attacked (1187) caravan of Sultan Saladin, provoking events that led to fall of Jerusalem. Krak fell to Saladin 1188. Town was archiepiscopal see from early Christian era until Christians expelled by Turks in 1910.

Krakatoa (kräkŭtō'ù), volcanic island, Indonesia, in Sunda Strait between Java and Sumatra. Its explosion in 1883 caused great destruction in surrounding area and scattered debris across Indian Ocean as far as Madagascar.

Krakow, Poland: see CRACOW.

Kramatorsk (krŭmŭtôrsk'), city (1965 est. pop. 135,-000), E central Ukraine, in Donets Basin. Center of heavy-machine building.

Kramer, Jack (John Albert Kramer), 1921–, American tennis player. Won (1946–47) national singles, British singles. As professional he won U.S. singles (1948), world singles (1949). Professional tennis promoter.

Kranach, Lucas: see CRANACH, LUCAS.

Krasicki, Ignacy (ĕgnä'tsē kräsēts'kē), 1735–1801, Polish writer and archbishop. Noted for prose and verse satires (including *Monachomachia*, on monastic life), fables, and novels.

Krasinski, Sigismund (kräsē'nyùskē), Pol. *Zygmunt Krasiński*, 1812–59, Polish poet, an ardent Slavophile. His works include the dramatic poems *The Undivine Comedy* (1835) and *Iridion* (1835).

Krasnodar (krŭs"nùdär'), city (1965 est. pop. 385,000), SE European RSFSR, port on Kuban R. Rail hub, industrial center (oil refineries, machinery plants, steel foundries). Founded 1794 as Ekaterinodar (after Catherine II), it became hq. of Kuban Cossacks. Renamed 1920. German-held in World War II. It is cap. of **Krasnodar Territory**, administrative division (32,800 sq. mi.; 1965 est. pop. 4,147,000), RSFSR; extends from Sea of Azov and Black Sea to KUBAN Steppe, its main agr. region. Subtropical Black Sea littoral, with health resorts, produces citrus fruits, essential oils, tea, and wine. Rich oil fields at Maikop. N section was annexed to Russia 1783; Black Sea littoral ceded by Turkey 1829; the rest, CIRCASSIA, was annexed 1864.

Krasnovodsk (krŭsnùvôtsk'), city (pop. 42,000), NW Turkmen SSR; port on Caspian Sea. Petroleum-refining center.

Krasnoyarsk (krŭsnùyärsk') city (1965 est. pop. 541,-000), RSFSR, in central Siberia, on Yenisei R. and Trans-Siberian RR. Transportation center; machinery, lumber, textile mills. Founded 1628. Cap. of **Krasnoyarsk Territory**, administrative division (928,000 sq. mi.; 1965 est. pop. 2,901,000), RSFSR; extends across Siberian steppe, forest, and tundra to Arctic Ocean. Includes TAIMYR PENINSULA and Taimyr Natl. Okrug, Khakass Autonomous Oblast, and Evenki Natl. Okrug. In arable S section dwells 94% of population (Russian, Turkic, Mongol peoples). Farther N are gold, coal, and graphite deposits. Organized 1934.

Krasnoye Selo (kräs'nùyù syĭlô'), city (pop. over 10,-000), RSFSR, SW of Leningrad. Peter III was murdered in a nearby palace in 1762. City was a summer resort for St. Petersburg society before 1917.

Kraszewski, Joseph Ignatius (kräshĕf'skē), 1812–87, Polish writer. Works include more than 600 novels; among the best known are *Countess Cosel* and *Count Bruehl*.

Krauskopf, Joseph (krous'kŏpf), 1858–1923, American rabbi and humanitarian, b. Prussia. Came to U.S. in 1872. Founder of Natl. Farm School at Doylestown, Pa.

Krautheimer, Richard (krout'hīmùr), 1897–, American art historian, b. Germany; an authority on early Christian and Byzantine architecture.

Kravchinski, Sergei Mikhailovich: see STEPNIAK, S.

Krebs, Hans Adolf, 1900–, English biochemist, b. Germany. Shared with F. A. Lipmann 1953 Nobel Prize in Physiology and Medicine for metabolism studies.

Krefeld (krā'fĕlt), city (pop. 197,140), North Rhine-Westphalia, West Germany, on the Rhine and NW of Düsseldorf. Silk and rayon mfg. (estab. 18th cent. by Frederick II); mfg. of quality steel, machinery, dyes. Formerly spelled Crefeld.

Kreisler, Fritz (krī'slùr), 1875–1962, Austrian-American violinist. Made his debut as a child prodigy. After studying medicine, then art, he returned to the violin and became world famous.

Kremenchug (krĕmĭnchōōk'), city (1965 est. pop. 121,000), central Ukraine, on the Dnieper. River and rail center with machinery and automobile mfg; hydroelectric station. Iron ore deposits nearby.

Kremenets (krĕmĭnĕts'), city (pop. 16,400), W Ukraine. Old Slavic settlement (1438); passed to Russia 1795; reverted to Poland 1921 and was incorporated into Ukrainian SSR 1939. Ruins of fortress (13th–16th cent.).

Kremer, Gerhard: see MERCATOR, GERARDUS.

kremlin, Rus. *kreml*, citadel of several Russian cities, which served as administrative and religious center and offered protection against military attacks in Middle Ages. Among most famous kremlins are those of Astrakhan, Kazan, Moscow, Nizhni Novgorod, Novgorod, and Pskov. That of Moscow, known simply as the **Kremlin**, occupies historic core of the city. Triangular in shape, it contains such structures as Uspenski Cathedral (late 15th cent.), where tsars were crowned; Arkhangelski Cathedral (14th–17th cent.), with tsars' tombs; and 300-ft. bell tower of Ivan the Great, with golden cupola. The Grand Palace, built in 19th cent., was rebuilt under Soviet regime to house supreme council (parliament) of USSR. Other buildings are used as government offices and residences for some high officials.

Kremsier (krĕm′zēr), Czech *Kroměříž*, town (est. pop. 21,942), Moravia, Czechoslovakia, on Morava R. Agr. center; sugar refineries and mfg. of agr. machinery. Site of meeting (1848–49) of first Austrian constituent parliament. Has 18th-cent. palace with large library and ceremonial hall.

Krenek, Ernst (krĕ′nĕk), Czech *Křenek*, 1900–, Austrian-American composer. Well schooled in the traditions of the past, he is at the same time an innovator (e.g., he wrote a jazz opera, *Jonny spielt auf*, 1926). He adopted (1928) the 12-tone technique which had been originated by Arnold SCHOENBERG and wrote an opera *Karl V* (1933) in it. He has also composed chamber, orchestral, choral music; some with electronic sounds.

Kretschmer, Ernest, 1888–1964, German psychiatrist. His theories correlating physical characteristics with personality types are not widely accepted.

Kreutzer, Rodolphe (kroi′tsŭr), 1766–1831, French composer and violinist. A prolific composer, he is best remembered for his 40 études for violin. Beethoven's Kreutzer Sonata is dedicated to him.

Kriloff, Ivan Andreyevich, see: KRYLOV.

Krishna (krĭsh′nù), eighth avatar of the god Vishnu, very popular in Hinduism; one of the more joyful expressions of deity.

Krishna Menon, Vengalil Krishnan (vĕngä′lēl krĭsh′nùn krĭsh′nù mĕn′ĭn), 1897–, Indian diplomat. British high commissioner for India 1947–52, delegate to UN 1952–57, and unofficial ambassador at large after 1953. Defense minister from 1957 to 1962, he was relieved after Chinese-Indian border conflict.

Krishnamurti, Jiddu (jĭ′dŏō krĭsh″nùmŏōr′tē), 1897–, Hindu religious leader. Mrs. Annie Besant met him in 1907, proclaimed him the incarnation of Maitreya, the world teacher. Toured England and America with her (1926–27), later repudiated her claims.

Kristiania, Norway: see OSLO.

Krivoi Rog (krĕvoi′ rôk′), city (1965 est. pop. 488,-000) S central Ukraine, on Ingulets R. Center of iron-mining region with enormous ore reserves. In Second World War Germans held city and destroyed most industrial installations.

Krk (kŭrk), Ital. *Veglia*, Adriatic island, area 157 sq. mi., Croatia, NW Yugoslavia, off Dalmatian coast. Chief town, Krk, has medieval walls, castle, and cathedral.

Krkonose: see RIESENGEBIRGE.

Krochmal, Nachman Kohen (näkh′män kō′hĕn krôkh′-mäl), 1785–1840, Jewish philosopher of history, b. Galicia. His chief work was *Guide to the Perplexed of Our Time* (1851).

Kroeber, Alfred Louis, 1876–1960, American anthropologist. Noted for contributions to archaeology, physical anthropology, and ethnology.

Krogh, August (ou′gŏost krôkh), 1874–1949, Danish physiologist. Won 1920 Nobel Prize in Physiology and Medicine for work on regulation of capillary blood supply in muscle.

Kroll, Leon (krōl), 1884–, American painter, perhaps best known for his studies of women.

Kromeriz, Czechoslovakia: see KREMSIER.

Kronborg: see ELSINORE.

Kronecker, Leopold (lā′ōpôlt krō′nĕ″kùr), 1823–91, German mathematician. He was a pioneer in the field

of algebraic numbers and in formulating relationship between theory of numbers, theory of equations, and elliptic functions.

Kronstadt, Rumania: see BRASOV.

Kronstadt (krōn′stät), city (pop. c.50,000), RSFSR, on island of Gulf of Finland, near Leningrad; also spelled Cronstadt. Founded 1703 by Peter I as port and fortress; now base of Soviet Baltic fleet. Port lost commercial value after dredging of deep-sea canal to St. Petersburg (1875–93). Mutinies of naval garrison played a part in revolutions of 1905 and 1917. City defended Leningrad in Second World War.

Kropotkin, Peter (krōpŏt′kĭn), 1842–1921, Russian anarchist, a prince who became interested in the peasants and renounced his title. Escaped prison in Russia and, after a three-year imprisonment in France, lived thereafter in England. Returned to Russia after Revolution, despite his opposition to Bolshevism.

Krout, John Allen, 1896–, American historian, long a professor and dean at Columbia Univ. He has written texts and scholarly works. Vice president and provost of the university 1953–62.

Krüdener, Julie de (dù krü′dùnùr), 1764–1824, Russian pietist. Before her conversion she wrote a sentimental novel, *Valérie* (1804), which caused some scandal. Later she preached her mystic faith throughout Europe. Purportedly under her spell, Alexander I of Russia created the Holy Alliance (1815).

Kruger, Stephanus Johannes Paulus (krōō′gùr), 1825–1904, South African statesman, known as Paul Kruger or Oom Paul. Played important role in history of TRANSVAAL as pioneer, soldier, farmer, and politician. With Joubert and Pretorius he negotiated Pretoria agreement with the British (1881) restoring independence to the Boer state. As president (1883–1900) he implacably opposed the policies of Cecil Rhodes. After outbreak of SOUTH AFRICAN WAR he went to Europe on futile mission to win support for the Boers. Died in Switzerland.

Kruger National Park, game reserve, c.8,000 sq. mi., NE Transvaal, Republic of South Africa. One of largest wildlife sanctuaries in world. Founded 1898.

Krugersdorp (krōō′gùrzdôrp), town (pop. c.82,750), S Transvaal prov., Republic of South Africa. Named for Paul Kruger. Industrial and gold-mining center.

Krupp (krŏōp), family of German armament manufacturers, settled in Essen since 16th cent. **Friedrich Krupp**, 1787–1826, began the modern concern with a steel plant; his son, **Alfred Krupp**, 1812–87, the "cannon king," specialized in armaments. Great financial expansion took place under his son, **Friedrich Alfred (Fritz) Krupp**, 1854–1902; under the latter's son-in-law, **Gustav Krupp von Bohlen und Halbach**, 1870–1950, the Krupp works became the center for German rearmament after 1933. His son, **Alfried Krupp von Bohlen und Halbach**, 1907–67, imprisoned for war crimes 1948. He was freed 1951, and confiscation of his property was reversed. Krupp industries have regained their position of eminence.

Krusenstern, Adam Johann von (krōō′zùnstĕrn), 1770–1846, Russian navigator and hydrographer. Circumnavigated the globe in 1803–6.

Krusevac, Serbo-Croatian *Kruševac* (krōō′shĕväts), town (pop. 22,140), Serbia, Yugoslavia, SE of Belgrade. Was a cap. of medieval Serbia.

Krusne Hory: see ERZGEBIRGE.

Krutch, Joseph Wood (krōōch), 1893–, American author, drama critic of the *Nation* (1924–50), and long a professor at Columbia Univ. He is highly regarded as a social and literary critic for such works as *The Modern Temper* (1929), *The Measure of Man* (1954), *Human Nature and the Human Condition* (1959), and the essays collected in *If You Don't Mind My Saying So* (1964). He also wrote *Samuel Johnson* (1944) and *Henry David Thoreau* (1948). Many later works deal with nature, as in *The Twelve Seasons* (1949) and *The Voice of the Desert* (1955). *More Lives Than One* (1962) is his autobiography.

Krylov, Ivan Andreyevich (ēvän' ŭndrā'ŭvĭch krĭlôf'), 1768–1844, Russian poet, celebrated for his fables. Name also appears as Kriloff.

kryolite: see CRYOLITE.

krypton (krĭp'tŏn), inert, colorless, odorless, tasteless, gaseous element (symbol = Kr; see also ELEMENT, table). It forms no known compounds.

Kuala Lumpur (kwä'lŭ lōōm'pōōr), city (pop. 316,– 230), SW Malaya; cap. of Federation of Malaysia and of Selangor. Was cap. of Federated Malay States 1898–1948, and cap. of Federation of Malaya 1948– 63. Commercial center and transportation hub.

Kuang-hsü (gwäng'hsü'), 1872–1908, emperor of China (1875–98), reign name of the grandson of Emperor Tao-kuang (reigned 1821–50). Enthroned by his aunt, dowager empress and regent Tz'ʊ HSI; began personal rule 1889. In 1898 he initiated what was known as the "hundred days of reform." Tz'u Hsi thereupon forced him to abdicate and kept him in life imprisonment while she resumed her personal rule of China.

Kuan Yin (kwän' yĭn'), in Japanese *Kwannon*, goddess of mercy in Chinese and Japanese Buddhism, honored by many images and temples. Derived from a male deity of Indian Buddhism.

Kuban (kōōbän'), river, 584 mi. long, Georgian SSR and RSFSR, rising in the Greater Caucasus and flowing N, then W into Sea of Azov and Black Sea via two arms. Kuban Steppe, a major grain region, is on lower course. After Russian annexation of the khanate of Crimea (1783), of which the area was a part, Cossacks were settled here to protect it from Circassian mountaineers. Cossacks fought against Bolsheviks in 1917. Scene of heavy fighting in Second World War.

Kubango: see OKAVANGO.

Kublai Khan (kōō'blī kän'), 1215?–1294, Mongol emperor, founded YÜAN dynasty of China (1260). Consolidated Mongol authority in China by conquering Sung dynasty (1279), but was defeated in campaigns against Japan, SE Asia, and Indonesia. Tolerated Chinese culture, improved communications, and encouraged foreign commerce. His cap. at Cambuluc (later Peking) was visited by Marco Polo.

Kuching (kōō'chĭng, city (est. pop. 56,000), W Borneo, cap. of Sarawak. Ships sago flour and pepper.

Kuchuk Kainarji, Treaty of (kōōchōōk' kīnär'jē), 1774, peace treaty between Russia and Turkey. Khanate of Crimea was declared independent, except for Kerch and several other Crimean ports on the Black Sea, which passed to Russia. Russia also gained right to intervene on behalf of the Moldavian and Walachian principalities (which, however, were restored to Turkish overlordship) and certain rights of representation on behalf of the sultan's Greek Orthodox subjects. The treaty prepared Russia's annexation of the Crimea (1783) and marked Russian ascendancy over Turkey (see EASTERN QUESTION). It was signed at village of Kainardzha, now in Bulgaria; other spellings include Kutchuk and Kainardji.

Kudrun, Germanic heroine: see GUDRUN.

kudzu (kōōd'zōō), perennial leguminous vine (*Pueraria lobata*). It is native to Japan; has broad leaves and purple flowers. Of rapid growth, it is used in S U.S. as a ground cover and forage or cover crop.

Kuhn, Richard (rĭk'ärt kōōn'), 1900–1967, Austrian chemist. Won 1938 Nobel Prize in Chemistry for work on carotinoids, vitamins, isolation of riboflavin; Nazi decree prevented his acceptance of the award.

Kuhn, Walt (kūn), 1880–1949, American painter. Known for portrait studies of circus and back-stage types. Helped assemble the famed Armory Show.

Kuibyshev (kwē'bĭshĕf), formerly **Samara** (sümä'rä), city (1965 est. pop. 948,000), E European RSFSR, river port on Volga; rail center. Mfg. of aircraft, locomotives, ball bearings, synthetic rubber, and textiles; many oil refineries. Large hydroelectric station (dedicated 1958). Founded 1586 as Muscovite stronghold, it was attacked by Nogai Tatars in 1615 and

Kalmucks in 1644; gates opened to Cossack rebels in 1670. Became chief grain center of the Volga. Seat of anti-Bolshevik government 1918. Renamed 1935. Central government (USSR) here in Second World War.

Kukai or **Kobo-Daishi** (kōō'kī, kō'bō'-dī'shē'), 774– 835, Japanese priest, scholar, and artist, founder of the Shingon sect of Buddhism. Member of Japanese embassy to T'ang China. Invented the hira-gana, a set of phonetic symbols based on Chinese ideographs.

Ku Klux Klan (kū' klŭks" klän', kōō'), name of two distinct secret societies in U.S. history. **1** Original Ku Klux Klan was organized by ex-Confederates at Pulaski, Tenn., in May, 1866, to oppose radical Republican RECONSTRUCTION, maintain "white supremacy." Absorbed many smaller groups as it spread. Its practices played upon fears and superstitions of the blacks. General organization of local Klans was effected in April, 1867; Gen. N. B. Forrest was made leader. Disbandment ordered in Jan., 1869; local organizations continued. Success in keeping Negroes from polls enabled ex-Confederates to gain political control in many states. Congressional legislation attempted to combat Klan (see FORCE BILL). In Lower South dominant group was more conservative Knights of the White Camellia. **2** Second Ku Klux Klan was founded in 1915; first meeting was held on Stone Mt., Ga. Added to "white supremacy" an intense nativism, anti-Catholicism, anti-Semitism. After 1920 it spread throughout North and South. Controlled politics in many communities. Texas, Okla., Ind., Oregon, Maine were particularly under its influence. Klan frequently took extra-legal measures, some of them extreme. Large membership of mid-1920s declined to estimated 30,– 000 by 1930. After Second World War attempt at revival failed when state after state specifically barred the order. Still existing in limited form in several Southern states, the Klan was investigated by the House Committee on Un-American Activities in 1965–66.

Kulikovo, battle of (kōōlyĭkô'vù), 1380, fought near Don R., SE of Tula, with victory for Grand Duke Dmitri Donskoi of Moscow over the Golden Horde. It made Moscow the center of strengthened resistance to Mongol domination.

Kulmbach, Hans von (kōōlm'bäkh), c.1480–1522, German painter and engraver; follower of Dürer.

Kulturkampf (kōōltōōr'kämpf") [Ger.= conflict of cultures], 1873–87, the conflict between the German government under Bismarck and the Roman Catholic Church. Bismarck saw in political Catholicism, as represented by the Center party (founded 1870), a threat to the unified German state. With a series of drastic laws he sought to intimidate the clergy and to break down the Catholic school system. His measures merely strengthened the Catholic party. In 1887, fearing the rise of socialism, Bismarck rescinded his anti-Catholic measures and reached a *modus vivendi* with Pope LEO XIII.

Kum, Qum, or **Qom** (all: kōōm), city (pop. c.80,000), central Iran, on Trans-Iranian RR. Region has large oil deposits. Shiite pilgrimage center.

Kumamoto (kōōmä'mōtō), city (pop. 373,922), W Kyushu, Japan. Agr. market town. Mfg. of bamboo ware and pottery. Important castle town in 17th cent. Seat of two universities.

Kumasi (kōōmä'sē), city (pop. c.200,000), S central Ghana; chief city of Ashanti. Center of large cocoagrowing area; rail and road junction; light industrial and commercial center.

Kumbakonam (kōōmbŭkō'nùm), city (pop. 91,643), S Madras, India, on Cauvery R.; Brahmanic cultural center. Silk and cotton weaving, jewelry making. Name also spelled Combaconam or Combaconum.

Kumbum (kōōm'bōōm'), lamasery in Hwangchung, Tsinghai prov., China. Founded c.1400. Pilgrimage center.

kumquat (kŭm'kwŏt), ornamental evergreen shrub of genus *Fortunella*, native to China and closely related to the orange. It has sweet-scented white flowers and small, orange fruits which can be eaten fresh or in preserves.

Kun, Bela (bā'lŏ kŏŏn'), 1886–1939?, Hungarian Communist. As head of coalition government of Communists and Social Democrats (1919) he set up dictatorship of the proletariat, raised Red Army, overran Slovakia. Forced out of Slovakia by Allies and defeated by Rumanian army of intervention, Kun fled abroad. It is generally thought that he died in a Russian prison or was executed after Communist party purges of 1930s.

Kunersdorf (kŏŏ'nûrsdôrf'') or **Kunowice** (kŏŏnôvē'-tsĕ), village, W Poland (since 1945), in former prov. of Brandenburg. Here Frederick II of Prussia suffered a critical defeat by Austrians and Russians (1759).

Kung, H. H., Chinese *K'ung Hsiang-hsi* (kŏŏng shyäng'shē'), 1881–, Chinese banker and Nationalist political leader before Communist conquest of mainland. Educated at Oberlin Col. and Yale Univ. Married SOONG AI-LING.

Kuniyoshi, Yasuo (yäsŏŏ-ō' kŏŏn"ēyō'shē), 1892–1953, American painter, b. Japan. His decorative work is Oriental in spirit, Western in technique.

Kunlun (kwīn'lûn'), mountain system of central Asia, between Himalayas and Tien Shan; forms N boundary of Tibet. Rises to 25,340 ft. in Ulugh Muztagh. Extends c.1,000 mi. from W to E.

Kunming (kwīn'mĭng'), city (pop. c.880,000), cap. of Yünnan prov., China. Commercial and cultural center; transportation hub with rail connections to Burma and North Vietnam. In Second World War was vital supply point at E end of Burma Road.

Kunowice, Poland: see KUNERSDORF.

Kuomintang (kwō'mĭntäng') [Chinese,= national people's party]. Organized 1912 by Sung Chiao-jen with program calling for independent republic and adherence to principles of SUN YAT-SEN. Sung was assassinated 1913, and the party was suppressed by Yüan Shih-k'ai. Party reorganized by Sun in 1914 (in Japan) and 1919. Unrecognized governments estab. in Canton in 1918 and 1921. Reorganized 1922–24 with Comintern help. At first party congress (1924), coalition including the Communists adopted constitution. CHIANG KAI-SHEK led NORTHERN EXPEDITION (1926–28) to unify the country. In 1927 Chiang and Kuomintang right wing formed government at Nanking in opposition to the party's left wing, which had moved the Canton government to Wuhan. After the purge of the Communists and the reunification of the party, the Nanking government received diplomatic recognition 1928; by 1930 all China was under the Nationalist flag. Until 1947 Kuomintang excluded minority parties from government. Civil war (1945–49) forced Nationalists to take refuge on TAIWAN.

Kuopio (kŏŏ'ôpēô), city (pop. 41,912), central Finland, on L. Kallavesi, in principal forest region of Finland and at head of Saimaa lake system. Timber industries.

Kupala, Janka (yäng'kä kŏŏpä'lä), 1888–1942, Belorussian writer. Real name Ivan Lutsevich. His early writings include a novel stressing national liberation. His poetry and plays written before 1928 reveal hostility to Communism. Later works indicate acceptance of new regime.

Kuprili (kŭprē'lē), Turkish-Albanian family, many members of which served as grand viziers; also spelled Köprülü. It rose into prominence with **Mohammed Kuprili,** 1583–1661, grand vizier of Mohammed IV from 1656. Though an upstart and illiterate, he restored some of its former prestige to the Ottoman Empire, notably by reorganizing the fleet and by his conquest of Transylvania (1658). The power of the family ended with Abdullah Kuprili (d. 1735), acting vizier from 1723.

Kuprin, Aleksandr Ivanovich (ŭlyĭksän'dŭr ēvä'nŭvĭch kŏŏ'prĭn), 1870–1938, Russian author. His novels *The*

Duel (1905) and *The Pit* (1909) are well known. Also wrote numerous short stories.

Kura (kŏŏrä'), anc. *Cyrus,* river, 940 mi. long, chief river of Georgian and Azerbaijan republics, in Transcaucasia. From Turkish Armenia it flows NE, then SE to Caspian Sea. Lower course irrigates cotton-growing plain.

Kurdistan (kûr'dĭstän", kŏŏrdĭstän'), extensive plateau and mountainous region, c.74,000 sq. mi., inhabited by Kurds or Carduchis, and occupying parts of E Turkey, Soviet Armenia, NE Iraq, and NW Iran. Ethnically related to the Persians, the Kurds are a nomadic pastoral people of several million; leading industry is carpet mfg. The majority are fanatic Sunnite Moslems. A warlike people, the Kurds have struggled for centuries for autonomy from Ottoman rule, and at the Paris Peace Conference (1919) reaffirmed claims to independence. The Treaty of Sèvres (1921) provided for a free Kurdish state, but the amending Treaty of Lausanne (1923) failed to mention Kurdistan. Kurdish revolts in Turkey (1925, 1930) and in Iran (1946) were suppressed.

Kurds: see KURDISTAN.

Kure (kŏŏ'rä), city (pop. 210,032), SW Honshu, Japan, on Hiroshima Bay. Major naval base and port.

Kure Island (kŏŏ'rä), formerly **Ocean Island,** atoll in NW part of Hawaiian group. Annexed 1886 by Hawaii. Also spelled Curé.

Kurgan (kŏŏrgän'), city (1965 est. pop. 198,000), W central Asiatic RSFSR, on Tobol R. Agr.; mfg. of chemicals, electrical machinery, buses. Founded 17th cent.; named Kurgan 1782. Anc. burial mounds nearby.

Kurhessen, Germany: see HESSE.

Kurile Islands (kŏŏ'rĭl), island chain (c.6,023 sq. mi.), Sakhalin oblast, RSFSR, in N Pacific, between Kamchatka and Hokkaido. Comprises 30 large and many small islands; mainly volcanic (38 active volcanoes), rising to 7,672 ft. Sulfur mining, hunting, and fishing. Became Japanese possession 1875; annexed 1945 by USSR in accordance with Yalta agreement.

Kurisches Haff (kŏŏ'rĭshûs häf') or **Courland Lagoon** (kŏŏr'länd), coastal lagoon, 56 mi. long. Lithuania and former East Prussia. Separated from Baltic Sea by Kurische Nehrung, a thin sandspit which leaves only a narrow opening at the Memel channel in the N. The Niemen empties into the Kurisches Haff.

Kurland: see COURLAND.

Kuropatkin, Aleksey Nikolayevich (ŭlyĭksyä' nyĭkŭlī'-ŭvĭch kŏŏrŭpät'kĭn), 1848–1925, Russian general. Minister of war after 1898, he opposed policy leading to Russo-Japanese War of 1904–5, but took command in Manchuria after its outbreak. Resigned after Russian defeat at Mukden.

Kuroshio: see JAPAN CURRENT.

Kursk (kŏŏrsk), city (1965 est. pop. 245,000), S central European RSFSR. Rail junction and mfg. center. Seat of a principality in the 11th cent., it was destroyed 1238 by Mongols and not rebuilt until 1586. Scene of heavy fighting in Second World War.

Kusch, Polykarp (kŏŏsh), 1911–, American physicist, b. Germany. Shared with W. E. Lamb, Jr., the 1955 Nobel Prize in Physics for precisely measuring certain electromagnetic properties of electron.

Kuskokwim (kŭs'kôkwĭm), river rising on NW slopes of Alaska Range, W Alaska, and flowing c.550 mi. SW to Kuskokwim Bay of Bering Sea.

Küssnacht (küs'näkht), village, Schwyz canton, Switzerland, on L. of Lucerne. A chapel commemorates legendary shooting of Gessler by William Tell.

Kutais (kŏŏtūēs') or **Kutaisi,** city (1965 est. pop. 154-000), W Georgian SSR, on Rion R. Mfg. of machinery, chemicals, textiles. Founded 6th cent. B.C., it was cap. of anc. Imeritia. Taken by Russia 1810.

Kutb Minar: see QUTB MINAR.

Kutch or **Cutch** (kŭch), district (c.17,000 sq. mi.; pop. 567,606), Gujarat state, India, bounded on N by

West Pakistan, and on W by Arabian Sea. Rann of Kutch is salt waste (9,000 sq. mi.), mainly in N.

Kutchuk Kainardji or Kutchuk Kainarji, Treaty of: see KUCHUK KAINARJI, TREATY OF.

Kut-el-Amara (kōōt'-ĕl"-ūmä'rū), town, Iraq, on the Tigris and c.100 mi. S of Baghdad; scene of bitter fighting in First World War.

Kutna Hora, Czech *Kutná Hora* (kōōt'nä hô'rä), city (est. pop. 14,665), central Bohemia. Czechoslovakia. Silver mines largely created power of medieval kings of Bohemia. After its capture by Zizka in Hussite Wars, city was for two centuries the center of Bohemian Protestantism. Its rich medieval architecture includes two Gothic churches (14th cent.) and "Italian Court," a castle once used both as a mint and as a royal residence.

Kutuzov, Mikhail Ilarionovich (mĕkhŭyĕl' ĕlūryôn'ŭvĭch kōōtōō'zŭf), 1745–1813, Russian field marshal. Fought brilliantly in Russo-Turkish Wars, replaced Barclay de Tolly as commander in chief against Napoleon (1812), and fought bloody battle of BORODINO but then resumed Barclay's Fabian tactics. Pursued *Grande Armée* into Germany and was created prince of Smolensk shortly before his death.

Kutztown (kōōts'toun), industrial borough (pop. 3,312), SE Pa.. NE of Reading; settled 1733 by Germans. A Pennsylvania Dutch festival held here annually. Crystal Cave is nearby.

Kuwait (kōōwīt', -wät'), sheikdom (c.5,800 sq. mi.; pop. c.300,000), NE Arabia, near head of Persian Gulf; cap. al-Kuwait or Kuwait (pop. c.180,000). Bordered by Iraq on N, and Saudi Arabia and Saudi-Arabian–Kuwait Neutral Zone on S. A sparsely populated, low, and sandy region. Has 20% of world's known oil reserves; major oil producer since 1946. Present dynasty founded 1756. Sought British protection 1897; was British protectorate 1899–1961. Joined ARAB LEAGUE 1961. Constitution proclaimed 1963, and Kuwait joined UN. Shekiah Sabah al-Salim al-Sabah ascended the throne 1965. Gave aid to Arab forces in Arab-Israeli war in June, 1967.

Kuyp, family of Dutch painters: see CUYP.

Kuznetsk Basin (kōōznyĕtsk'), abbreviation **Kuzbas,** richest coal basin of USSR, area c.10,000 sq. mi., RSFSR, in S central Siberia, between Kuznetsk Ala-Tau (E) and Salair Ridge. Vast reserves are of high quality and great variety. Mining centers are Anzhero-Sudzhensk, Kemerovo, and Leninsk-Kuznetski. New metallurgical industry is centered at Novokuznetsk (formerly called Stalinsk).

Kwajalein (kwä'jŭlān), atoll (c.6.5 sq. mi.; pop. 282), central Pacific, largest of Marshall Isls. District hq. of U.S. Trust Territory of the Pacific Isls. Captured 1944 by U.S. forces.

Kwakiutl Indians (kwä'kēōō'tùl), Indian tribes of Wakashan subfamily of Algonquian-Mosan linguistic stock, on N Vancouver Isl. and adjacent mainland of Canada. Their culture was typical of Pacific Northwest Coast.

Kwangchowan, China: see CHANKIANG.

Kwangsi (gwäng'hsē'), province (c.85,100 sq. mi.; pop. c.20,200,000), S China; cap. Nanning. Borders North Vietnam on S. Drained by Si R., it has fertile areas in S and E where rice, millet, and barley are grown. Lumber and tung oil produced; coal, iron, tin, and antimony mined. Good network of roads and railroads; rail connections to North Vietnam. Has large non-Chinese minority. In 1958 most of province organized into Kwangsi Autonomous Region.

Kwangtung (gwäng'doong'), province (c.89,000 sq. mi.; pop. c.35,900,000), S China, on South China Sea; cap. CANTON. Includes HAINAN isl. On its coast are foreign enclaves of MACAO and HONG KONG.

Borders Vietnam on extreme W. Subtropical climate with heavy rainfall. Largely mountainous; agr. limited to river valleys and delta lowlands, notably of Canton and Han rivers. Silk culture important. Mineral resources include coal, tungsten, and manganese. Once known as Yüeh, region ruled by China after 211 B.C. Was scene of early Kuomintang party activity.

Kwantung Territory, China: see LIAONING.

kwashiorkor (kūäshēôr'kŭr), protein-deficiency disorder of infants and children, prevalent in impoverished areas. Manifestations include retarded growth, decreased albumin in blood (resulting in body swelling), diarrhea, mental apathy, muscular atrophy, and depigmentation of skin.

Kweichow (gwä'jō'), province (c.66,000 sq. mi.; pop. c.15,570,491), SW China; cap. Kweiyang. Mainly a high plateau with many deep river valleys, notably that of the Wu. Produces rice, grain, lacquer, and timber. Rural areas inhabited by Miaos and Lolos. Chinese (80% of pop.) first settled here c.2000 years ago. Made prov. 17th cent. under Ming dynasty. Traditionally known as Kien or Ch'ien.

Kweilin (gwä'lǐng'), city (pop. c.145,100), former cap. of Kwangsi prov., China, on Kwei R. Noted for scenic beauty. Seat of Kwangsi National Univ.

Kweisui, China: see HUHEHOT.

Kweiyang (gwä'yäng'), city (pop. c.504,000), cap. of Kweichow prov., China. Industrial center.

Kyakhta or Kiakhta (both: kyäkh'tŭ), city (pop. 10,-300), Buryat Autonomous SSR, SE Asiatic RSFSR, near Soviet-Mongolian border. Anc. center of Russian trade with China and Mongolia. Called Troitskosavsk until 1935.

Kyd or Kid, Thomas, 1558–94, English dramatist, exponent of "tragedy of blood." His best-known work is *Spanish Tragedy* (printed 1592?).

Kyffhäuser (kǐf'hoizŭr), forested mountain, c.1,550 ft. high, in former state of Thuringia, East Germany. It is crowned by ruined castles of Rothenburg and Kyffhausen and by huge monument to Emperor William I. A legend, originally applied to Emperor Frederick II, has been later transferred to Emperor Frederick I (Barbarossa), who is said to be waiting in a cave of the mountain for the right time to return and restore German greatness.

kyogen: see JAPANESE DRAMA.

Kyongsong, Korea: see SEOUL.

Kyoto (kyō'tō), city (pop. 1,284,818), S Honshu, Japan, on Kamo R. Third largest city of Japan and its leading cultural center. Founded 8th cent. Cap. of Japan from 794 until 1868, when it was succeeded by Tokyo. Seat of Kyoto Univ. A center of Buddhism with many noted anc. temples and a 59 ft. statue of Buddha. Long noted for hand-crafted products (cloisonné, bronzes, damascene work, porcelain, lacquer ware).

Kyrie eleison (kĕ'rēä ālā'ēsōn) [Gr.,= Lord, have mercy], in Roman Catholic Church, prayer of the Mass, following introit, the only part of the ordinary (section that does not change with the day) said in Greek. There are many notable musical settings.

Kyushu (kyōō'shōō), island (c.13,760 sq. mi.; with offshore isls. c.14,990 sq. mi.; pop. 12,903,515), S Japan; third largest, southernmost, and most densely populated of four major islands of Japan. Connected with Honshu (just N) by tunnel under Shimonoseki Strait. Mountainous with hot springs. In N is Japan's chief coal field. Mild climate favors agr. (rice, tobacco, fruit). Extensive production of raw silk. Chief ports are Nagasaki, Moji, Kagoshima, and Sasebo. Name also spelled Kiushiu.

Kyzyl, Asiatic RSFSR: see KIZIL.

Kyzyl-Kum, Uzbek SSR: see KIZIL KUM.

L

La. For names beginning thus and not listed here, see second element; e.g., for La Guaira, see GUAIRA, LA.

La, chemical symbol of the element LANTHANUM.

Laaland or **Lolland** (both: lô′län), low island (479 sq. mi.; pop. 83,170), Denmark, in Baltic Sea, S of Zealand. Sugar beets are main crop. Nakskov and Maribo are chief cities.

Labadie, Jean de, or **Jean de la Badie** (zhä′ dù lä bädē′), 1610–74, French mystic. A Catholic priest, he became a Protestant minister (c.1650). In Holland he estab. the Labadists, a religious community dedicated to simple living, holding goods and children in common. Movement was dead by 1732.

Laban (lā′–), father of Leah and Rachel, uncle of Jacob. Gen. 24.29–60; 29–31.

Labe: see ELBE.

Labiche, Eugène (ûzhĕn′ läbēsh′), 1815–88, French playwright. His best-known comedy is the farcical *Le Voyage de M. Perrichon* (with Édouard Martin, 1860).

La Boétie, Étienne de (ätyĕn′ dù lä bôäsē′), 1530–63, French judge, remembered for his friendship with Montaigne and as author of a fiery and original attack on despotism, *Discours sur la servitude volontaire; ou, Contr′un* (Eng. tr., *Anti-Dictator,* 1942).

labor, term used both for the effort of performing a task and for the social group doing the work. In the ancient world the status of labor was low, since most physical work was done by slaves. During the feudal period, skilled artisans were influential citizens. With the introduction of machinery, status of labor was again depressed. Since 19th cent., labor has become organized (see UNION, LABOR) so as to bargain collectively with employers and to place pressure on governments. See STRIKE, CHILD LABOR, MIGRATORY LABOR, SLAVERY, AMERICAN FEDERATION OF LABOR–CONGRESS OF INDUSTRIAL ORGANIZATIONS.

labor, hours of. Until the Industrial Revolution, the work day varied from 8 to 14 hr. With the growth of capitalism and the introduction of machinery, longer hours began to prevail. The great competition for work forced workers to accept whatever conditions employers imposed. A day of 16 hr. was not uncommon, with 14 to 15 hr. the accepted working day. First law on the length of a working day was passed (1833) in England, limiting miners to 12 hr. and children under 13 to 8 hr. The 10-hr. day was legally established in 1848, and shorter hours at the same pay were achieved gradually thereafter. When American labor demanded an 8-hr. day in 1860s, the movement led to strikes and violence. Fair Labor Standards Act of 1938 set 44 hr. maximum work week (reduced to 40 in 1950) for firms engaged in interstate commerce.

Labor, United States Department of, organized in 1913 under Secretary of Labor by act of U.S. Congress. Began in 1884 as Bureau of Labor in U.S. Dept. of Interior. Department includes following major units: Bureau of Labor Statistics; Women's Bureau; U.S. Employment Service; Bureau of Labor Standards; Bureau of Apprenticeship; Wage and Hour and Public Contracts Divisions; Bureau of Veterans' Reemployment Rights.

Labor Day, holiday celebrated in U.S. on first Monday in Sept. to honor the workingman.

labor law, legislation dealing with workers. The earliest English factory law dealt (1802) with the health, safety, and morals of child textile workers. Labor unions were legalized in 1825, but agreements among their members to seek better hours and wages were punishable as conspiracy until 1871. In the U.S., the Norris-LaGuardia act (1932) outlawed the use of injunctions in labor disputes, the Wagner Act (establishing the NATIONAL LABOR RELATIONS BOARD; 1935) required employers to accept collective bargaining, and the WAGES AND HOURS ACT (1938) set up minimum standards of hours and wages in basic industries; the TAFT-HARTLEY LABOR ACT (1947) sharply modified the acts of 1932 and 1935 and introduced an 80-day injunction procedure in labor disputes affecting the national welfare. This act was much opposed by the labor organizations.

Labor Relations Act: see NATIONAL LABOR RELATIONS BOARD; TAFT-HARTLEY LABOR ACT.

labor union: see UNION, LABOR.

La Bourdonnais, Bertrand François Mahé de (bĕrträ′ fräswä′ mää′ dù lä bŏŏrdônä′), 1699–1753, French naval officer in service of French India Co. Captured Madras (1746). After a quarrel with Dupleix he was recalled, tried for treason, and acquitted.

Labour party, British political party. Founded in 1900 as result of long history of trade-union activity that became effective after Reform Bill (1867) enfranchised the urban workers. Aided by Fabian Society (founded 1883). Until 1918 it was a federation of trade unions and socialist groups, with no individual members. Split over British participation in the First World War. Ramsay MACDONALD became first Labour prime minister in 1924. After domestic reforms, recognition of USSR, and peace efforts in the Ruhr, he was overthrown over a forged letter supposedly written by Grigori Zinoviev. Labour was returned to power in 1929. Hampered by deepening economic crisis, MacDonald formed (1931) a coalition ministry and was read from the party. Moving to the left, party advocated nationalization of industries and opposition to any foreign war. By 1937 new leaders were Herbert Morrison, Ernest BEVIN and Clement ATTLEE. Intellectual leaders were Hugh Dalton and Harold Laski. Labour entered coalition government in Second World War. Won 1945 elections; Attlee became prime minister. Passed national health bill, nationalized important industries, and estab. the dominions of India and Pakistan (1947). The 1951 election restored Conservatives to power. After Attlee retired, left wing, led by Aneuran BEVAN, unsuccessfully contested leadership of Hugh GAITSKELL. On Gaitskell's death (1963) Harold WILSON became head of party and prime minister (1964).

Labrador (lă′brŭdôr″), dependency of NEWFOUNDLAND, E Canada (c.110,000 sq. mi.; pop. 13,534), at mouth of Gulf of St. Lawrence; cap. Battle Harbour. Population (largely Algonquin Indians and Eskimo) scattered along Atlantic coast with a few white settlers in fishing villages and missions (e.g., Carteret, Battle Harbour, Rigolet, Hopedale, Nain). Icy Labrador

SMALL CAPITALS = cross references. Pronunciation key on inside end pages. Abbreviations: p. 2.

582

Current and lack of transportation facilities discourage settlement. Iron ore, mined in SW lake district at headwaters of Hamilton R., led to development of the Grand Falls region, source of hydroelectric power. Probably explored by Vikings c.1000, and later by Cabot (1498), Corte Real (1500), and Cartier (1534). Became British after Treaty of Paris (1763), with jurisdiction given to N.F. 1763–64 and again in 1809. Moravian missions, estab. in 1760s, shared fur trade with Hudson's Bay Co., which virtually controlled peninsula until 1870. Claims to NE peninsula (called Ungava) settled 1927 by British Privy Council.

Labrador Current: see OCEAN CURRENTS.

labradorite (lă'brŭdŏrīt'), variety of FELDSPAR, usually gray, brown, or green. Some varieties showing color play of red, yellow, blue, green (labradorescence) are used for decorative purposes.

La Brea (lù brā'ù), area, S Calif. Asphalt pits which yielded prehistoric remains now in Los Angeles park.

Labrouste, Henri (ärĕ' läbrōost'). 1801–75, French architect; made effective use of metal construction.

La Bruyère, Jean de (zhä' dù lä brüyĕr'), 1645–96, French writer; tutor at the house of the prince de Condé. His great work is *Les Caractères* (1688), in small part translations of THEOPHRASTUS, but mainly a series of brilliant character sketches, maxims, and short essays. Though he applied his strong moral views to the contemporary scene, he was a detached observer, rather than a reformer.

Labuan (lùbōo'ùn), island (c.35 sq. mi.; est. pop. 9,200), off NW Borneo, administratively attached to British North Borneo since 1946. Victoria, chief town, is shipping center for North Borneo.

laburnum (lùbûr'nùm), small ornamental tree (*Laburnum anagyroides*), native to Europe, widely grown in U.S. It has sprays of yellow flowers in spring.

lac (lăk), resinous exudate from bodies of female scale insects from which SHELLAC is prepared. Insects feed on sap of trees, which form resinous secretion around bodies of female and young. Crude material is stick-lac. When purified and red coloring is removed, it is seed-lac from which shellac is made. Red coloring is sometimes used as dye and pigment.

Lacaille, Nicolas Louis de (nēkôlä' lwē dù läkä'yù), 1713–62, French astronomer, noted for calculations. Recorded positions of many stars of S Hemisphere.

La Canada, residential town (pop. 18,338 including Flintridge), S Calif., NW of Pasadena.

Laccadive, Minicoy, and Amindivi Islands (lă'kùdīv, mĭ'nĭkoi, ämĭndē'vī), island territory (11 sq. mi.; pop. 21,035), of India, in Arabian Sea. Group of coral atolls.

lace, patterned openwork fabric made by hand or by machine. General types of handmade laces include needlepoint, bobbin lace, tatting, and crochet work. Needlepoint, the most costly, is worked with a needle in variations of the buttonhole stitch; Venetian point or *punto in aria* developed in Italy from reticella cut-work. From the early laces patterned in France after Venetian point, developed *point de France;* among later French laces are Alençon, Argentan, and Valenciennes. Brussels is a name used for either needle-point or bobbin lace of a certain style. Pillow, bone, or bobbin lace, woven with bobbins, includes *point d'Angleterre* (similar to Flemish point), Valenciennes (fine, diamond-meshed), Mechlin (very filmy), torchon (simple and loose), Honiton (English lace with net foundation and appliqués of delicate braid), duchesse (exquisite patterns, with much raised work), Maltese (coarse), and Chantilly (delicate mesh, ornate patterns). Crocheted lace reached its finest development in Ireland. There are also knitted laces and those made by knotting (e.g., tatting, macramé). Machine-made lace dates from late 18th cent.

Lacedaemon (lăsùdē'mùn), in Greek mythology, ruler of LACONIA or Lacedaemon; son of Zeus. He gave his capital the name of his wife, Sparta.

La Chaise, François d'Aix de (fräswä' däks' dù lä shĕz'), 1624–1709, French Jesuit, confessor of Louis XIV. Held considerable influence. Père-Lachaise cemetery in Paris is named for him.

Lachaise, Gaston (läshäz'), 1882–1935, American sculptor, b. Paris. Famous for his female nudes.

Lachesis, one of the FATES.

Lachine (lùshēn'), city (pop. 38,630), S Que., Canada, on Montreal Isl., at E end of L. St. Louis; settled 1675. Iron and steel founding and mfg. of tires, wires, and tiles. Is SW terminus of **Lachine Canal** connecting L. St. Louis and St. Lawrence R. at Montreal (opened 1825).

Lachish (lā'kĭsh), anc. Amorite city, S Palestine. Captured by Joshua; later besieged by Sennacherib.

Lachute (lùshōot'), town (pop. 7,560), SW Que., Canada, on North R. and W of Montreal. Woolen and paper mills, lumbering, and dairying.

Lackawanna, city (1966 pop. 28,717), W N.Y., on L. Erie just S of Buffalo. Steel mfg.

Lackawanna, river, rising in NE Pa., and flowing c.50 mi. S–SW through anthracite region to Susquehanna R. near Pittston.

Laclede, Pierre (pyĕr' läklĕd'), c.1724–1778, French pioneer in U.S. As fur trader with René Auguste CHOUTEAU, helped found St. Louis (1763–64).

Laclos, (Pierre) Choderlos de (pyĕr' shôdĕrlô' dù läklô'), 1741–1803, French author and general. His savage novel of manners, *Les Liaisons dangereuses* (1782) had great influence.

Lac Mégantic, Que.: see MÉGANTIC.

Laconia (lùkō'nēù) or **Lacedaemon** (lăsùdē'mùn), anc. region, S Peloponnesus, Greece. On the Eurotas, the main river, stood SPARTA, the cap.

Laconia, city (pop. 15,288), central N.H., N of Concord on Winnipesaukee R. Industrial and trade center of resort region of lakes and rivers.

Lacordaire, Jean Baptiste Henri (zhä' bätēst' ärĕ' läcôrdĕr'), 1802–61, French Roman Catholic preacher. A liberal, he was a collaborator of LAMENNAIS, but after the pope condemned the liberal program, he submitted. Later he was a famed preacher at Notre Dame in Paris; joined the Dominicans (1840). Favored the Revolution of 1848 and went into exile after coup d'état of Napoleon III.

Lacoste, René (rùnä' läkôst'), 1905–, French tennis player. Won British singles (1925, 1928), U.S. singles (1926, 1927). Member of French team that won Davis Cup, 1927, 1928.

La Crosse (lù krôs'), city (pop. 47,575), W Wis., at foot of high bluffs on Mississippi R. where La Cross R. enters, in dairy area. Site of 18th-cent. French trading post. Thriving lumber industry gave way to varied mfg. Has branch of Wisconsin State Univ. and Viterbo Col.

lacrosse (lùkrôs'), national sport of Canada since 1867. Played by two teams of 10 players on grass-covered playing field 60 to 70 yd. wide by 110 yd. long. Lacrosse gained following in U.S. after 1880s, particularly in North Atlantic states. Women's lacrosse team has 12 players.

Lactantius (lăktăn'shùs), c.260–340, Christian apologist, b. Africa. Converted to Christianity, he became a member of Constantine's household. His writings on Christian doctrine and Christian history show his wide knowledge of pagan rhetoric and literature.

lactic acid, colorless organic acid, present in sour milk and formed in animals as result of muscle contraction. Usually prepared commercially by bacterial fermentation of glucose. Used in tanning and dyeing and in medicine.

lactose (lăk'tōs) or **milk sugar**, white crystalline disaccharide carbohydrate. Lactose has the same numerical molecular formula as sucrose and maltose but it differs in structure. It is found in mammalian milk and cells of mammary gland, and is important in diet of young mammals. When hydrolyzed (by acid or enzyme) lactose yields glucose and galactose. See *ill.*, p. 178.

Ladakh (lŭdäk'), region (45,762 sq. mi.; pop. 195,-431), E Kashmir, on Tibet border. Former dependency of Tibet, annexed to Kashmir mid-19th cent. Region now claimed by People's Republic of China, which occupied part of area in 1962.

Ladd, George Trumbull, 1842–1921, American philosopher. He worked in experimental psychology, then a new science to America.

Ladd, William, 1778–1841, American peace advocate. He proposed (1840) plan for a world congress and court of nations.

Ladd-Franklin, Christine, 1847–1930, American scientist, first woman student at Johns Hopkins. She developed theory of color vision, wrote *Colour and Colour Theories* (1929).

Ladies' Peace: see ITALIAN WARS.

Ladislas. For rulers thus named, see LADISLAUS; LANCELOT; ULADISLAUS.

Ladislaus, Hung. *László,* kings of Hungary. **Ladislaus I** (Saint Ladislaus), 1040–95, reigned 1077–95. Conquered Croatia 1091; compelled CUMANS to accept Christianity and allowed them to settle in certain parts of Hungary; reformed law code. Was noted for his valor and chivalry. **Ladislaus V** (Ladislaus Posthumus), 1440–57; posthumous son of the German king, Albert II. Duke of Austria by birth, he was claimed as king by the Bohemian diet and in 1445 was also elected king of Hungary, but his guardian, Emperor Frederick III, refused to let him leave his court until 1452. In 1453 he was crowned king of Bohemia and entered Hungary, but actual rule was exercised by GEORGE OF PODEBRAD in Bohemia and by John HUNYADI in Hungary.

Ladislaus, king of Naples: see LANCELOT.

Ladislaus, Pol. *Władysław,* kings of Poland. **Ladislaus I** (the Short), 1260–1333, crowned king 1320, restored unified Polish kingdom after 182 years of division. **Ladislaus II** or **Ladislaus Jagiello** (yägyĕ'lō), 1350?–1434, grand duke of Lithuania (1377–86), acceded to the Polish throne in 1386 by marrying Queen JADWIGA. He was baptized and converted Lithuania to Christianity. Though Lithuania was ruled by other members of the JAGIELLO dynasty (see WITOWT), Ladislaus' marriage was the basis of the eventual union of the Polish and Lithuanian nations. The victory over the Teutonic Knights at Tannenberg (1410) and the First Peace of TORUN (1411) were the main events of his reign. His son **Ladislaus III,** 1424–44, succeeded him in Poland and as Uladislaus I was elected king of Hungary (1440). He led two crusades against the Turks and was defeated and slain at Varna. The name also appears as Wladislaw, Wladyslav, and Wladislas.

Ladoga, Lake (lä'dōgŭ), largest lake in Europe, area c.7,000 sq. mi., S Karelo-Finnish SSR and NW European RSFSR, NE of Leningrad. Max. depth 738 ft. The Svir (from L. Onega), Vuoksi (from Saimaa lake system of Finland), and Volkhov (from L. Ilmen) are the main feeders; Neva R. is main outlet. Because of difficult navigation the S shore of L. Ladoga is paralleled by the Ladoga Canals, 100 mi. long, connecting Svir and Neva rivers. N shore belonged to Finland until its cession to USSR in 1940 (confirmed 1947). Valaam isl., in N part of lake, has famous Russian monastery dating from 12th cent.

ladybird or **ladybug,** beetle of the family Coccinellidae. It is oval, reddish, or yellow spotted with black or black spotted with red or yellow; most species eat aphids and other harmful insects. Australian ladybird was imported by U.S. to eat cottony-cushion scale which is destructive to citrus fruit. Injurious herbivorous species are the Mexican bean beetle and the squash beetle. See *ill.,* p. 512.

Lady Margaret Hall: see OXFORD UNIVERSITY.

Lady of the Lake: see ARTHURIAN LEGEND.

Ladysmith, town (pop. c.28,000), W Natal, Republic of South Africa. Named for wife of Sir Harry Smith, governor of Cape Colony. British forces were besieged here, 1899–1900, during South African War. Cotton milling, light industry.

lady's-slipper or **moccasin flower,** wild flower of genus *Cypripedium* of orchid family, native to north temperate zone. There are white-, yellow-, and pink-flowered species in North America.

Lae (lä'ē), city (pop. 65,475), E New Guinea. Founded 1927 as supply base for nearby gold fields. Now commercial center of area.

Laënnec, René Théophile Hyacinthe (rŭnā' tāôfēl' yäsĕt lääněk'), 1781–1826, French physician. He invented the stethoscope and used it in diagnosis.

Laer or **Laar, Pieter van** (both: pē'tŭr vän lär'), c.1592–1642, Dutch landscape and genre painter and etcher, called Il Bamboccio [the puppet]. The name Bamboccianti is given to Laer and artists following him in portraying genre scenes of low-class life.

Laertes (lāûr'tēz), in Greek mythology, king of Ithaca; father of Odysseus.

La Farge, John (lù färzh'), 1835–1910, American artist, writer, and worker in stained glass. A man of wide culture, he did much to create a tradition of the fine arts in America. His grandson, **Oliver La Farge,** 1901–63, a writer, is remembered for novel *Laughing Boy* (1929) and short stories based on his life-long study of American Indians.

Lafargue, Paul, 1842–1911, French socialist, son-in-law of Karl Marx. Helped found, with Jules Guesde, French Marxist socialist party.

Lafayette or **La Fayette, Marie Joseph Paul Yves Roch Gilbert du Motier, marquis de** (märē' zhôzěf' pōl' ēv' rôk zhělbĕr' dù môtyā' märkē' dù läfäyĕt'), 1757–1834, French general and statesman. Despite opposition by his government, he sailed for America in 1777 to join Washington's army. Was made major general by Congress; was wounded at Brandywine (1777) and was at Valley Forge. After a trip to France (1779–80), where he negotiated for French aid, he played a vital part in the YORKTOWN CAMPAIGN. Active in the French Revolution, he became commander of the National Guard (July 15, 1789) and in 1792 commanded an army. A moderate, he sought to save the monarchy but in his irresolution missed his opportunity, deserted his army, and was imprisoned in Austria (1792–97). His triumphal tour of the U.S. in 1824–25 has passed into legend. He also took part in the July Revolution.

La Fayette, Marie Madeleine Pioche de la Vergne, comtesse de (märē' mädùlěn' pyôsh' dù lä vĕr'nyù, kôtĕs'), 1634–92, French novelist. Mme de La Fayette's classic masterpiece, *La Princesse de Clèves* (1678), was the first French psychological novel.

Lafayette. 1 (lä"fēĕt') City (pop. 42,330), W central Ind., on Wabash R., NW of Indianapolis; laid out 1825. Mfg. city in grain and livestock area, with railroad shops. Seat of PURDUE UNIVERSITY. Battle of TIPPECANOE fought nearby. **2** (lä"fēĕt') City (1963 pop. 50,312), S central La., on Vermilion R., N of Vermilion Bay; settled in 1770s by Acadians. Commercial and shipping center for area producing sugar, rice, cattle, cotton, oil, and natural gas. Univ. of Southwestern Louisiana and Carmelite monastery are here.

Lafayette, Mount: see FRANCONIA MOUNTAINS.

Lafayette College, at Easton, Pa.; for men; chartered 1826, opened 1832.

Lafayette Escadrille (ĕskùdrīl'), group of American volunteer aviators in First World War in French air service. In Jan., 1918, outfit was reorganized in U.S. army as 103rd Pursuit Squadron.

Laffite or **Lafitte, Jean** (both: zhä' läfēt'), c.1780–c.1825, leader of a band of privateersmen and smugglers. Preyed on Spanish commerce off La. and Texas. Aided U.S. in battle of New Orleans.

La Follette, Robert M(arion) (lùfō'lĭt), 1855–1925, American statesman. Under his governorship of Wis. reform legislation known as Wisconsin Idea was instituted. As U.S. Senator (1906–25) he took courageous, independent stands; supported reform, opposed both war measures and international peace bodies. As PROGRESSIVE PARTY presidential candidate in 1924 he polled 5,000,000 votes. Known as "Fighting Bob" La

Follette. His wife, **Belle Case La Follette,** 1859–1931, was an ardent feminist and able adviser to her husband. Their older son, **Robert M(arion) La Follette, Jr.,** 1895–1953, U.S. Senator (1925–47), generally backed New Deal legislation. Another son, **Philip (Fox) La Follette,** 1897–1965, was governor of Wis. (1931–33, 1935–39).

La Fontaine, Henri (ärē′ läfōtĕn′), 1854–1943, Belgian jurist. Headed Internatl. Peace Bureau from 1907; was awarded 1913 Nobel Peace Prize.

La Fontaine, Jean de (zhä′ dů), 1621–95, French poet, author of the famous *Fables choisies* (1668–94), 12 books of c.230 fables. Their material is largely based on Aesop, Phaedrus, and other classics (see FABLE), but La Fontaine's subtle originality, exquisite charm, and perfection of verse place him among the masters of world literature. Though popular with children, his fables are essentially satires, sometimes bitter and cynical, always sophisticated; their appeal is universal. Other works include *Contes et nouvelles en vers* (1664), imitations in verse of Boccaccio and Ariosto.

LaFontaine, Sir Louis Hippolyte, 1807–64, Canadian statesman. Formed the Baldwin-LaFontaine ministry (1842–43) with Robert Baldwin. Second Baldwin-La-Fontaine ministry (1848–51) was notable for its reforms and achievement of responsible government.

Laforgue, Jules (zhül′ läfôrg′), 1860–87, French poet, one of the SYMBOLISTS.

Lafosse, or La Fosse, Charles de (shärl′ dů lä fôs′), 1636–1716, French painter. A pupil of Le Brun, he was influenced by Veronese, Correggio, and Rubens.

Lafourche, Bayou (bī′ō läfōōsh), SE La., flowing to Gulf of Mexico. Former Mississippi R. outlet, it has been cut off from river by dam at Donaldsonville.

Lagan (lä′gŭn), river of N. Ireland, rising in Co. Down and flowing 45 mi. to Belfast Lough at Belfast.

Lagash (lä′gäsh) or **Shirpurla** (shīrpōōr′lu), anc. city of SUMER, S Mesopotamia. City was flourishing by 2400 B.C. After fall of Akkad (2180 B.C.) it maintained its strength under ruler Gudea. Excavators found sculptures and thousands of tablets at the site.

Lagerkvist, Par (Fabian), (pâr′ fä′bēän lä′gůrkvīst), 1891–, Swedish poet, dramatist, and novelist. His writings reflect his interest in political and social problems; his verse has had a marked influence on Swedish poetry. Among his novels are *The Dwarf* (1944) and *Barabbas* (1950). His collected plays (*Dramatik,* 3 vols.) were published in 1956. Awarded the 1951 Nobel Prize in Literature.

Lagerlof, Selma, Swed. *Lagerlöf* (lä′gůrlûv), 1858–1940, Swedish novelist. Winner of 1909 Nobel Prize in Literature, she was also the first woman to be elected (1914) to the Swedish academy. Popular stories (many laid in Varmland prov.) are *The Story of Gosta Berling* (1891), *The Ring of the Lowenskolds* (1931), and a classic of juvenile literature, *The Wonderful Adventures of Nils* (1906).

Laghouat (läg′wät), town (pop. c.43,000), Algeria, on N edge of Sahara, SE of Amour Mts. Occupied by French 1852. Natural gas found nearby.

Lagos (lä′gŏs), city (pop. c.665,246), cap. of Republic of Nigeria. Comprises Lagos and Iddo isls. and a mainland section. Notorious slave market from 18th to mid-19th cent. Ceded 1861 to British. In 1886 Lagos and surrounding area became self-governing colony and protectorate, which in 1906 was combined with protectorate of Southern Nigeria. Made federal territory in 1954. A major lagoon harbor and rail terminus, it exports palm products, cocoa, and peanuts. Industrial and educational center.

Lagos (lä′gōōsh), city (pop. c.8,000), Faro dist., SW Portugal, in Algarve, on the Atlantic. Starting point of Portuguese explorers at the time of Henry the Navigator; now harbors important sardine and tuna fishing fleets.

Lagrange, Joseph Louis, Comte (zhôzĕf′ lwē′ kôt lä-gräzh′), 1736–1813, French mathematician and astronomer, b. Turin. He studied the nature and propagation of sound and the vibrations of strings; he

also made notable contributions in application of differential calculus to theory of probabilities and in solution of equations. He made studies of the moon and the satellites of Jupiter and made calculations of the motions of the planets. He was influential in bringing about the adoption of the decimal (metric) system of weights and measures in France.

La Grange (lù gränj′). **1** City (pop. 23,632), W central Ga., SW of Atlanta near Chattahoochee R. Industrial center which has retained its charm as beautiful residential city. Seat of La Grange Col. **2** Village (1963 pop. 16,326), NE Ill., suburb W of Chicago; settled in 1830s. Limestone quarries in vicinity.

La Grange Park, village (1963 pop. 15,430), NE Ill., suburb W of Chicago.

LaGuardia, Fiorello H(enry) (fēūrĕ′lō lùgwär′dĕů), 1882–1947, was U.S. Congressman (1917, 1923–33) and Fusion mayor of New York city (1934–45). Fought for labor reforms in Congress. Executed vast program of municipal improvement. Because of his first name jocularly called "the Little Flower."

LaGuardia Field: see QUEENS, New York city borough.

Laguna (lügō̄′nů), pueblo (pop. c.3,246), W central N.Mex., WSW of Albuquerque; estab. 1699. Keresan linguistic stock. Annual feast to San José.

Laguna, La, city (pop. c.41,731), on Tenerife isl., Canary Islands. Seat of Univ. of San Fernando.

Laguna Beach, residential and resort city (pop. 9,288), S Calif., on Pacific coast SE of Los Angeles.

Laguna District [Span.,= pond], irrigated area (c.900,-000 acres), N central Mexico. Land was redistributed (1936) on *ejido* system by Lázaro Cárdenas. After 1592 drought, settlement continued on reduced scale.

La Habra (lù hä′brů), city (1964 pop. 35,253), S Calif., SE of Los Angeles; settled in 1860s by Basque sheepherders. Citrus fruits and avocados grown.

Lahaina (lùhī′nù), town (pop. 3,423), Hawaii, on W coast of Maui, in sugar-cane and pineapple region. Was cap. of Hawaiian Isls., 1810–45, and whalers once anchored here. Site of islands' first white settlement.

La Halle, Adam de: see ADAM DE LA HALLE.

La Hire (lä ēr′), c.1390–c.1443, French commander in Hundred Years War; real name Étienne de Vignolles. Helped Joan of Arc in victory of Patay (1429).

La Hire or La Hyre, Laurent de (both: lä ēr′), 1606–56, French portrait and historical painter.

Lahontan, Louis Armand, baron de (läōtä′), 1666–c.1713, French explorer in America. His admiration of Indian life influenced European thought.

Lahontan, Lake (lùhŏn′tùn, läōtä′), extinct lake of enormous size in W Nev. and NE Calif. Brought into existence by glacial age, it vanished soon after Pleistocene epoch; several lakes in Nev. are remnants. Area rich in fossils.

Lahore (lùhôr′), city (pop. c.1,297,000), cap. of West Pakistan. Became a Mogul cap. in 16th cent.; and Sikh cap. in early 19th cent. Notable remains of Moslem art are palace of Janhangir and Shalimar gardens (1667). Punjab Univ. and famed museum of Indian antiquities are here.

Lahti (lä′tĕ, läkh′tĕ), city (pop. 63,633), S Finland. Center of Finnish furniture industry.

La Hyre, Laurent de: see LA HIRE, LAURENT DE.

Laibach (lī′bäkh), German name of LJUBLJANA, Yugoslavia. At the **Congress of Laibach,** 1821, widening of the breach between Great Britain and the powers of the Holy Alliance became apparent. The congress countenanced the suppression by Austrian forces of the insurrection in Naples.

Laie (lūē′ē), village (pop. 1,767), Hawaii, on NE coast of Oahu. Mormons came here in 1864, started cooperative sugar plantation.

laissez faire (lĕ′sä fâr′), doctrine that an economic system functions best without governmental interference. Historically it was a reaction to MERCANTILISM. First formulated by French physiocrats, doctrine was developed by Adam SMITH, who held that competition would regulate economic life more effectively than would the state. Doctrine came to be principle of classical economics and political conservatism, still adhered to by private enterprise as an antidote to socialism, but the tendency of business combinations to evolve into monopolies has made government intervention necessary to restablish competition.

Laius, father of OEDIPUS.

La Jolla (lŭ hoi'yŭ), resort and residential part of San Diego, S. Calif.; founded 1869. Beaches, sea-washed caves, and cliffs attract visitors. Seat of Scripps Inst. of Oceanography of Univ. of CALIFORNIA.

Lake, Simon, 1866–1945, American designer of submarines. His type was at first disregarded by the U.S. navy, but was used by Germans in First World War and was later adopted by the Allies.

lake, body of standing water surrounded by land. Most lakes originate in glacial action by excavation and filling in of depressions or by damming of rivers by ice or moraine. Lakes are also caused by interference in river courses, by filling in of extinct volcanic craters, by volcanic separation of parts of ocean. Lakes disappear because of detrital deposits and lowering of affluent streams in humid climate, or (in arid regions) because of greater evaporation than precipitation. World's largest lakes are Caspian Sea, L. Superior, Victoria Nyanza, Aral Sea, L. Michigan, L. Huron. World's highest lake is L. Titicaca, 12,500 ft. above sea level; lowest, the Dead Sea, 1,292 ft. below sea level.

lake, in dyeing, insoluble compound formed in the material by action between organic dye and MORDANT.

Lake Charles, city (pop. 63,392), SW La., on L. Charles at mouth of Calcasieu R., in rice, oil, and natural-gas area; settled c.1852. Deepwater port connected with Gulf of Mexico by channel. it ships petroleum products, chemicals, rice, and cotton. Seat of McNeese State Col.

Lake City, city (pop. 9,465), N Fla., W of Jacksonville near Suwannee R.; founded in 1830s as military post. U.S. veterans' hospital is here. Historic OLUSTEE is nearby.

Lake District, region (c.30 mi. in diameter) of mountains and lakes in Cumberland, Westmorland, and Lancashire, England. Has 15 lakes and some of England's highest peaks. Area a favorite resort of artists and writers. Wordsworth, Coleridge, and Southey called Lake poets; Keats, Shelley, and other poets have also lived here.

lake dwelling, habitation built over shallow waters of lake or marsh, supported by piles or artificial mounds. Prehistoric lake dwellers lived in Africa, Asia, and New World; most famous were the Neolithic inhabitants of European Alpine region.

Lake Forest, residential city (1965 pop. 13,345), NE Ill., on L. Michigan N of Chicago; settled 1835. Seat of Lake Forest Col. U.S. Fort Sheridan is nearby.

Lake George, N.Y.: see GEORGE, LAKE.

Lakehurst, borough (pop. 2,780), E N.J., SW of Lakewood. Site of U.S. naval air station with facilities for dirigibles. First used by the *Shenandoah* 1923. U.S. terminal for transatlantic airships from 1924 until the *Hindenburg* burned here, 1937.

Lakeland, resort city (pop. 41,350), central Fla., E of Tampa, in highland region; settled in 1870s. Important processing and shipping center for citrus fruit. FLORIDA SOUTHERN COLLEGE and L. Mirror are here.

Lake of the Woods, c.65 mi. long, 10–60 mi. wide, in pine forest region of N Minn., SE Manitoba, and W Ont. Fed by Rainy R. and drained by Winnipeg R. Separates Northwest Angle, northernmost land of U.S. proper (exclusive of Alaska and Hawaii) from rest of Minn. Resort region with fish and game.

Lake Placid, resort village (pop. 2,998), NE N.Y., in Adirondacks, surrounding Mirror L. and extending to S end of L. Placid (c.4 mi. long, c.1–2 mi. wide). Settled c.1850, it is a noted Eastern sports center, with bobsled run (opened 1930) on Mt. Van Hoevenberg. Site of 1932 Olympic winter games. Nearby is farm and grave of John Brown.

Lake Success, village (1965 pop. 3,176), SE N.Y., on NW Long Isl., S of Great Neck. Was temporary seat of UN, 1946–50.

Lakeview, town (pop. 10,384), S central Mich., suburb S of Battle Creek.

Lakeville, Conn.: see SALISBURY.

Lake Wales, city (pop. 8,346), central Fla., in highlands W of L. Kissimmee; platted 1911. Noted lake resort. IRON MOUNTAIN is nearby.

Lakewood. 1 City (pop. 67,126), S Calif., suburb N of Long Beach. **2** Town (pop. 19,338), N central Colo., suburb of Denver. **3** Township (pop. 13,004), E central N.J., resort in pine woods near Atlantic coast, ENE of New Hanover; settled c.1786. Georgian Court Col. is here. Nearby is former Rockefeller estate, now a state reserve. **4** City (pop. 66,154), NE Ohio, suburb W of Cleveland on L. Erie. Varied industry.

Lake Worth, city (pop. 20,758), SE Fla., on L. Worth (lagoon) S of West Palm Beach. Resort center.

Lakhnau, India: see LUCKNOW.

Lalande, Joseph Jérôme de (zhôzĕf' zhärôm' dù läläd'), 1732–1807, French astronomer, influential teacher and author, and establisher of annual Lalande Prize (1802) in astronomy.

Lalique, René (rùnä' lälĕk'), 1860–1945, French designer of jewelry and glass.

Lally, Thomas Arthur, baron de Tollendal, comte de (tômä' ärtür' bärô' dù tôlädäl' kôt' dù lälĕ'), 1702–66, French general of Irish parentage; governor of French India (1758–61). His surrender to the English at Pondichéry ended the French empire in India. After a highly irregular trial in France he was executed for treason. His son, with Voltaire's aid, secured his posthumous rehabilitation (1778).

Lalo, Édouard (ädwär' lälô'), 1823–92, French composer. His works include an opera, *Le Roi d'Ys* (1888), and *Symphonie espagnole* for violin and orchestra.

Lamaism, BUDDHISM of Tibet and Mongolia; in doctrine it is derived from Mahayana form of Buddhism, but much of its ritual is based on the erotic mysticism of tantrism and on the shamanism of Bon, Tibet's primitive animistic religion. Tradition says the religion was imported by Indian and Chinese wives of a 7th-cent. king. A later king invited an Indian monk to found monastery near Lhasa (749), beginning Red Hat sect which still exists. Another Indian monk, Atisa, in 11th cent. reformed Lamaism and tried to eliminate elements of Bon (native religion). Translation of Sanskrit writings into *Kanjur* and *Tanjur*, Lamaist scriptures, was begun. The Saskya monastery was after the conversion of Kublai Khan given temporal rule of W Tibet. Under lama [priest] Tsong-kha-pa, Atisa's sect was reformed (15th cent.) as celibate Yellow Hat order, and in 1640 its 5th Ta-lai or Dalai Lama was given temporal rule of all Tibet by Mongol prince. Hierarchical priesthood developed; palace monastery was built near Lhasa. Dalai Lama is considered divine and is believed to be reincarnated immediately on death, perpetuating succession (14th installed 1940). Second to him is the abbot Panchen Lama (or Tashi). On 2,500th anniversary (1956) of Buddha's death, Dalai Lama visited India. In 1959 Tibetan revolt against Chinese Communists, he fled to India. Panchen Lama, who returned to Tibet from China in 1952, remained in Tibet.

Lamar, Joseph Rucker (lŭmär'), 1857–1916, Associate Justice of U.S. Supreme Court 1911–16.

Lamar (lŭmär'), **Lucius Quintus Cincinnatus,** 1825–93, American statesman. U.S. Representative from Miss. (1857–60, 1873–77); U.S. Senator (1877–85). U.S. Secretary of the Interior (1885–88); Associate Justice of U.S. Supreme Court (1888–93).

Lamar, Mirabeau Buonaparte, 1798–1859, Texas statesman, b. Ga. As president of Texas (1838–41) he secured recognition of Texas independence by European countries; carried out vigorous Indian policy;

SMALL CAPITALS = cross references. Pronunciation key on inside end pages. Abbreviations: p. 2.

laid foundations of present Texas public education system; founded capital at Austin.

Lamar, city (pop. 3,608), SW Mo., NNE of Joplin; founded c.1856. H. S. Truman was born here.

Lamarck, Jean Baptiste Pierre Antoine de Monet, chevalier de (zhä bäptēst' pyĕr' ätwän' dù mônä' shùvälyä' dù lämärk'), 1744–1829, French naturalist. Noted as introducer of evolutionary theories, of term *Invertebrata,* and for classification of invertebrates. Regarded founder of invertebrate paleontology. His skill as a botanist was first shown in his *Flore français* (1778). **Lamarck's theory of evolution** is based on belief that organism passes to offspring characteristics developed because of need created by its environment. This is known as the theory of inheritance of acquired characteristics, which is no longer accepted by Western scientists.

La Marque (lùmärk'), city (pop. 13,969), SE Texas, S of Texas City; settled c.1860. Mainly residential.

Lamartine, Alphonse de (älfόs' dù lämärtēn'), 1790–1869, French poet, novelist, and statesman. Author of *Les Méditations poétiques* (1820; including well-known "Le Lac") and of *Harmonies* (1830), in which he expressed his personal lyricism in musical verse. His religious orthodoxy turned to pantheism in *Jocelyn* (1836) and *La Chute d'un ange* (1838). He wrote *Histoire des Girondins* (1847) in praise of the Girondists. After the FEBRUARY REVOLUTION of 1848, he headed the provisional government. Politically idealistic, democratic, and pacific, his moderation eventually caused his supporters to desert him. Later works include the novel *Graziella* (1849).

Lamb, Lady Caroline: see MELBOURNE, WILLIAM LAMB, 2D VISCOUNT.

Lamb, Charles, 1775–1834, English essayist. A friend from boyhood of Coleridge, he worked as a clerk at India House (1792–1825). Collaborated with his sister Mary in *Tales from Shakespeare* (1807). *His Specimens of English Dramatic Poets* (1808) estab. his reputation as a critic, and his famous *Essays of Elia* (collected 1823, 1833) marked him as the great master of the familiar literary style. Despite personal and family handicaps, he was able to give to his essays the warm, humorous quality of his personality.

Lamb, William: see MELBOURNE, WILLIAM LAMB, 2D VISCOUNT.

Lamb, Willis Eugene, Jr., 1913–, American physicist. Shared with Polykarp Kusch the 1955 Nobel Prize in Physics for their work which precisely determined certain electromagnetic properties of the electron.

Lambaréné (lämbùrēn', Fr. läbäränä'), village, W Gabon Republic. Dr. Albert SCHWEITZER founded his hospital here in 1913.

Lambert, Johann Heinrich (yō'hän hīn'rĭkh), 1728–77, German-French philosopher and scientist. He developed many concepts in mathematics and physics. His philosophical work, *Neues Organon* (1764), stressed the importance of beginning with experience and using the analytical method to investigate any theory.

Lambertville, city (pop. 4,269), W central N.J., on Delaware R. opposite New Hope, Pa.; settled c.1705. Washington set up hq. near here before crossing Delaware R.

Lambeth, London borough since 1965 (est. pop. 341,-137); includes former metropolitan borough of Lambeth and part of Wandworth, S of the Thames. Site of Lambeth Palace, chief residence of Archbishop of Canterbury and scene of Lambeth conferences. Convened decennially by the archbishop, they are the principal instruments of international Anglicanism. The ninth conference was in 1958. Here also are St. Thomas Hospital (9th cent.), Doulton ware potteries, hq. for the Royal Festival Hall, and Old Vic Theatre.

lamb's quarters, European annual weed (*Chenopodium album*) of goosefoot family, naturalized in North America. It has small green flowers and whitish leaves used for greens when young.

Lambton, John George: see DURHAM, JOHN GEORGE LAMBTON, 1ST EARL OF.

Lamennais or **La Mennais, Félicité Robert de** (fälēsētä' rόbĕr' dù lämùnä'), 1782–1854, French Roman Catholic apologist. Leader of a liberal group, he was aided by MONTALEMBERT and LACORDAIRE in founding (1830) the journal *Avenir,* which forwarded ultramontanism, opposed Gallicanism, and maintained that the Church could not be free under royal government. In clash with the royalist clergy, he appealed to Pope Gregory XVI, who condemned liberal doctrines in encyclical *Mirari vos.* Lamennais retired for two years, emerged as a non-Christian, and died outside the Church. Ironically he probably did more than any other man to end Gallicanism and forward papal power. His *Paroles d'un croyant* (1834) expresses liberal humanitarianism.

Lamentations, book of Old Testament, ascribed to Jeremiah, a series of poems mourning the fallen Jerusalem and the sin of man as the judgment of a righteous God. Chapters 1–4 are each divided into equal groups of lines; initial letters of the groups form an alphabetical acrostic in Hebrew.

La Mesa (lù mä'sù), city (pop. 30,441), S Calif., suburb E of San Diego.

Lamesa (lùmē'sù), city (pop. 12,438), NW Texas, S of Lubbock on S Llano Estacado; settled 1903. Center of agr. and cattle area with cotton gins and cottonseed oil mills.

La Mettrie, Julien Offray de (lä mētrē'), 1709–51, French physician and materialist philosopher. Explained man's mind and all his actions on a mechanical basis. Wrote *Man, the Machine* (1748).

Lamia (lä'mēù), in Greek mythology, grief-crazed woman whose name was used to frighten children. Her own children were killed by Hera, jealous of Zeus' love for her, and thereafter Lamia, envious of happy mothers, stole and killed their children.

Lamia (Gr. lämē'ä), city (pop. 21,509), E central Greece. Founded c.5th cent. B.C. as chief city of Malis; became an ally of Athens. Gave its name to Lamian War (323–322 B.C.) waged by the united Greeks against Antipater, who was besieged here.

La Mirada (lä mĭrä'dù), city (pop. 22,444), S Calif., SE of Los Angeles.

Lammermuir Hills (lămùrmūr', lä'mùrmūr) or **Lammermoor Hills** (–mōōr'), broad range of hills, East Lothian and Berwickshire, Scotland.

Lamont, Daniel Scott, 1851–1905, U.S. Secretary of War (1893–97).

Lamont, Johann von, 1805–79, German astronomer, b. Scotland. Made surveys of terrestrial magnetism in W Europe 1849–58. Published theory of magnetic decennial period (1850) and his discovery of earth currents (1862).

Lamont, Thomas W(illiam), 1870–1948, American banker. A partner of J. P. Morgan & Co. after 1910. Served abroad as U.S. financial adviser in 1920s and 1930s. Benefactor of Harvard.

La Motte-Fouqué: see FOUQUÉ.

Lampedusa (lämpädōō'zä), Mediterranean island (77 sq. mi.; est. pop. 4,065), between Malta and Tunis, belonging to Italy. Sponge and sardine fishing.

Lampman, Archibald, 1861–99, Canadian nature poet, author of *Among the Millet* (1888).

Lamy, Jean Baptiste (zhä' bätēst' lämē'), 1814–88, Roman Catholic archbishop in U.S. Southwest, b. France. Willa Cather's *Death Comes for the Archbishop* (1927) is based on his career.

Lanai (lùnī'), island (141 sq. mi.; pop. 2,115), part of Hawaii, across Auau Channel from Maui. Developed as pineapple-growing center after 1922. Mt. Palawai (3,370 ft.) is highest point.

Lanarkshire (lä'nùrkshĭr, lä'närk–) or **Lanark,** county (892 sq. mi.; pop. 1,626,317), S central Scotland. In Clyde R. valley, it has level plain in N and mountains in S. Extensive mfg. and rich mineral deposits in and near Glasgow. Central agr. region has cattle, sheep, and dairying. County town is **Lanark,** burgh (pop. 8,436), on Clyde R. New Lanark, just S. scene of social experiments by Robert Owen.

Lancashire (lăng'kŭshĭr, –shŭr), **Lancaster** (lăng'kústúr), or **Lancs** (lăngks), county (1,878 sq. mi.; pop. 5,131,- 646), NW England, on Irish Sea. E and N parts in Lake District; W and S are lowlands with rich coal and iron deposits. FURNESS separated from rest of county by Morecombe Bay. Most populous county of England with one of world's great industrial regions centered around MANCHESTER and LIVERPOOL. Has textiles (notably cotton), much mfg., and large shipyards. County also a duchy, vested in the sovereign. County town is **Lancaster**, municipal borough (pop. 48,887), on Lune R. Has textile and other mfg. and flour mills.

Lancaster, earls and dukes of: see LANCASTER, HOUSE OF; JOHN OF GAUNT.

Lancaster, John of: see JOHN OF LANCASTER.

Lancaster, Joseph, 1778–1838, English Quaker educator. In 1801 he founded a free elementary school using a type of MONITORIAL SYSTEM. Later, he came to America to lecture and promote his ideas.

Lancaster, England: see LANCASHIRE.

Lancaster. 1 City (pop. 26,012), S Calif., NNE of Los Angeles; laid out 1894. **2** City (pop. 3,021), central Ky., SSW of Lexington, in blue-grass region; settled 1798. Site of Kennedy House, said to have been used in *Uncle Tom's Cabin*, is nearby. **3** Town (pop. 3,958), central Mass., NE of Wachusett Reservoir; settled 1643. Destroyed in King Philip's War. Has one of Bulfinch's finest churches (1816–17). Luther Burbank born here. Includes South Lancaster village (pop. 1,891). **4** Residential village (1966 pop. 13,- 408), W N.Y., E of Buffalo; settled 1810. Stone quarries. **5** City (pop. 29,916), S central Ohio, SE of Columbus on Hocking R., in livestock area; founded 1800. Generals W. T. Sherman and Thomas Ewing were born here. **6** City (pop. 61,055), SE Pa., on Conestoga R., W of Philadelphia; settled c.1721. In heart of Pa. Dutch region, it is commercial center for one of most productive agr. counties in U.S. and an important tobacco market. Has large stockyard. Seat of FRANKLIN AND MARSHALL COLLEGE. Munitions center in Revolution. Continental Congress met here briefly in 1777. State cap. 1799–1812. Was W terminus of Lancaster Turnpike. Robert Fulton was born nearby. President Buchanan is buried here, and his home, "Wheatland," is a national shrine.

Lancaster, house of (lăng'kústúr), royal family of England. Title began in 1267 when Henry III gave it to his second son, **Edmund, earl of Lancaster,** 1245–96, called Edmund Crouchback from a cross he wore on crusade. He had been made titular king of Sicily in 1254 but the title lapsed. His son, **Thomas, earl of Lancaster,** 1277?–1322, opposed Piers Gaveston and the Despensers under Edward II, led the baronial party, and was executed for treason. His brother, **Henry, earl of Lancaster,** 1281?–1355, was chief adviser to Edward III in his seizure of power from his mother. His son, **Henry, duke of Lancaster** 1299?– 1361, was made duke for victories in the Hundred Years War. He died without male issue and the title passed to JOHN OF GAUNT, fourth son of Edward III, who married Henry's daughter, Blanche. His son became the first Lancastrian king as HENRY IV. Others were HENRY V and HENRY VI. Struggle with the rival house of YORK led to Wars of the ROSES.

Lancelot or **Ladislaus,** c.1376–1414, king of Naples (1386–1414); son of Charles III. His reign was consumed by his struggle with the rival claimant, Louis II of Naples, and with the antipope John XXIII.

Lancelot, Sir: see ARTHURIAN LEGEND.

Lanchow or **Lan-chou** (län'jō'), city (pop. c.699,000), cap. of Kansu prov., China, on Yellow R.

Lancret, Nicolas (nĕkōlä' läkrä'), 1690–1743, French painter, whose style is suggestive of Watteau. Painted balls, fairs, and other festivities.

Lancs, county, England: see LANCASHIRE.

Landau, Lev Davidovich (lyĕf' dŭvē'dŭvĭch lŭndou'), 1908–, Russian physicist, early a colleague of Niels Bohr. Helped develop Soviet atomic bomb; active in space research. Received 1962 Nobel Prize in Physics for theory of state of helium gas at temperature near absolute zero.

Landau, Mark Aleksandrovich: see ALDANOV, MARK.

Lander, Richard Lemon, 1804–34, English explorer. Accompanied Clapperton to the Niger in 1827. With brother John Lander, 1807–39, led expedition to determine course of lower Niger (1830–31).

Lander, town (pop. 4,182), W central Wyo., SW of Riverton on Popo Agie R.; settled c. 1870. Dude-ranch area. It is near Fort Washakie, trade center for Wind River Indian Reservation.

Landes (länd'), region of Gascony, SW France; a sandy, marshy area stretching for c.100 mi. along Atlantic coast. Sheep grazing. Part has been reclaimed through drainage and forestation. It occupies part of Gironde dept. and most of **Landes** dept. (3,614 sq. mi.; pop. 260,495; cap. Mont-de-Marsan).

land-grant colleges and universities, state institutions benefiting from provisions of Morrill Act of 1862. Hatch Act (1887) provided for research and experiment stations, Smith-Lever Act (1914) for extension work in agriculture and home economics.

Landis, Kenesaw Mountain, 1866–1944, American jurist, first commissioner of baseball (1921–44). Did much to restore public faith in baseball after 1920 "Black Sox" scandal.

Landon, Alf(red) M(ossman), 1887–, governor of Kansas (1933–37) and unsuccessful Republican candidate for President (1936).

Landor, Walter Savage, 1775–1864, English poet and essayist, known best for such poems as "Rose Aylmer" and "Past Ruined Ilion Helen Lives" and for his prose dialogues, *Imaginary Conversations* (1824– 53). His bad temper involved him in a number of celebrated quarrels.

Landowska, Wanda (ländôf'skä), 1877–1959, Polish-French harpsichordist, long resident in U.S. Made her American debut in 1923. She did much to revive interest in the harpsichord and its music.

Landsberg an der Warthe (länts'bĕrk än dĕr vär'tú) or **Gorzow Wielkopolski** (gôr'zŏŏf vyĕlkôpōl'skē), city (est. pop. 66,000), W Poland (since 1945), in former Prussian prov. of Brandenburg, on Warthe R. Trade and transportation center.

Landseer, Sir Edwin Henry (lăn'sēr), 1802–73, English animal painter, extremely popular in his day.

Lands End, promontory, Cornwall; SW extremity of England. Has granite cliffs 100 ft. high.

Landskrona (länskrōō'nä), seaport city (pop. 28,900), Malmohus co., S Sweden, on the Oresund; founded 1413. It has shipyards, flour mills, sugar refineries, and metalworks. Town was burned 1428 by Hansa merchants and devastated in 16th- and 17th-cent. wars. Its citadel was built 1540. Swedes defeated Danes in naval battle here, 1677.

landslide, slipping of a mass of rock and earth down a slope. Main cause is saturation with water, which increases weight, lessens friction. Caused also by earthquakes. Landslides dam streams and destroy forests, farm land, habitations, life, and cause floods.

Landsmaal: see NORWEGIAN LANGUAGE.

Landsteiner, Karl (kärl länt'shtīnúr), 1868–1943, American medical research worker, b. Vienna. For discovery of human blood groups, he won 1930 Nobel Prize in Physiology and Medicine. With A. S. Wiener, he identified Rh blood factor (1940).

land tax: see INTERNAL REVENUE.

Landy, John, 1930–, Australian athlete. Second man (Roger Bannister was the first) to run the mile in less than 4 min. On June 21, 1954, at international meet in Finland, he ran the mile in 3 min. 58 sec.

Lane, Franklin Knight, 1864–1921, U.S. Secretary of the Interior (1913–20).

Lane, James Henry, 1814–66, American politician, called "Liberator of Kansas." Encouraged antislavery men to emigrate to Kansas; secured Free State control of legislature. U.S. Senator (1861–66).

Lane, Joseph, 1801–81, American general in Mexican War, territorial governor of Oregon (1848–50). Also superintendent of Indian affairs there.

Lane, Sir Ralph, c.1530–1603, leader of first attempted English settlement in America, on ROANOKE ISLAND, N.C. (1585).

Lanfranc (lăn'frăngk), d. 1089, Italian churchman, archbishop of Canterbury. A theologian and scholar trained in France under BERENGAR OF TOURS, he founded the famous school at Bec and wrote (against Berengar) a widely popular treatise on transubstantiation. He was a friend of William the Conqueror, and after the Norman Conquest reluctantly became archbishop of Canterbury. A strong reformer, he did much to root out abuses in the English church.

Lang, Andrew, 1844–1912, Scottish scholar, poet, and man of letters. His anthropological theory of myth appears in *Myth, Ritual, and Religion* (1887). In collaboration with others, he wrote prose translations of the *Odyssey* (1879) and the *Iliad* (1883). Lang is perhaps best known for his collections of translations and adaptations of traditional children's stories, e.g., *Blue Fairy Book* (1885).

Lang, Cosmo Gordon, 1864–1945, English churchman, archbishop of York (1908–28), archbishop of Canterbury (1928–42). He exercised some influence in the abdication of Edward VIII.

Langdon, John, 1741–1819, American statesman. Largely responsible for N.H. ratifying Constitution as ninth state, thus making instrument effective. U.S. Senator (1789–1801).

Lange, Christian Louis (krĭs'tyän lōō'ē läng'ŭ), 1869–1938, Norwegian pacifist. Shared 1921 Nobel Peace Prize with Hjalmar Branting.

Langeland (läng'ŭlän), island (110 sq. mi.; pop. 18,-692), Denmark, in Baltic Sea, between Fyn and Laaland. Produces grain. Langeland Belt, strait, joins Great Belt and Baltic Sea.

Langensalza (läng"ŭnzäl'tsä), town (est. pop. 16,227), East Germany, in former state of Thuringia, on Salza R. Has cotton and paper mills. Scene of Prussian victory over Hanoverians 1866. Nearby Bad Langensalza has sulfur springs.

Langer, Susanne, 1895–, American philosopher. A student of Alfred North Whitehead, she has written extensively on aesthetics and other subjects. She attempted to give act the meaning that science was given through Whitehead's symbolic modes. She makes a distinction between discursive and nondiscursive symbols. The former are found in science and ordinary language and the latter in art.

Langerhans, Paul, 1849–88, German physician. Described (1869) the **islands of Langerhans.** See PANCREAS.

Langevin, Paul (pôl' läzhŭvĕ'), 1872–1946, French physicist and chemist; noted for work on the electron theory of magnetism and for research on sound devices for submarine detection.

Langlade, Augustin (ōgüstĕ' lägläd'), c.1695–c.1771, French Canadian fur trader. Estab. fur trade at Green Bay, Wis. His son, **Charles Michel de Langlade,** 1729–1800, aided in fur trading and was a leader in French and Indian Wars.

Langland, William, c.1332–c.1400, supposed author of PIERS PLOWMAN, b. probably Ledbury, near Welsh Marches; lived in London; took minor orders.

Langley, Samuel Pierpont, 1834–1906, American scientist. A pioneer in mechanics-of-flight studies and heavier-than-air flight experiments. Flew models successfully (1896), but full-scale aircraft, financed by War Dept., in 1903 could not be launched. Reconstructed in 1914, it flew. Invented bolometer (instrument for recording variations in heat radiation); pioneered in studies of infrared radiation. Helped to popularize astronomy. Secretary of Smithsonian Institution from 1887.

Langley Park, town (pop. 11,510), W central Md., suburb NNE of Washington, D.C.

Langmuir, Irving (läng'mür), 1881–1957, American chemist. Contributed to development of radio vacuum tube, introduced atomic-hydrogen arc welding. Won 1932 Nobel Prize in Chemistry for work in molecular surface chemistry; this work has important applications in immunology research. Devised methods of cloud seeding to induce rain or snow.

Langres (lä'grü). town (pop. 8,300), Haute-Marne dept., NE France, surrounded by wooded Langres Plateau. Medieval fortifications. Cutlery industry. Birthplace of Diderot.

Langtry, Lillie, 1852–1929, English actress, called the Jersey Lily; one of first socially prominent women on the stage. Noted for her beauty and liaison with Edward VII. Wilde wrote *Lady Windermere's Fan* for her.

Langtry [for Lillie Langtry], village, W Texas, on Rio Grande near mouth of the Pecos. Near old town of Langtry where "law west of Pecos," Judge Roy Bean, meted out whisky and justice at his saloon.

language, systematic human vocal communication. It is a distinctive, exclusive, and universal mark of the human species, but its origin is unknown. When languages resemble each other in a systematic way they are held to be genetically related. Though scientifically estab., such relationships have always been on the basis of sounds of the languages and the way the sounds are grouped in systematic patterns; no certainty has been attained in comparing the fundamental grammatical structures of languages. Maximal groups of related languages are called families and stocks. For a survey of the important languages by families, see tables on pp. 590–94. In the tables asterisks indicate extinct languages and locations are general.

Languedoc (lägdôk'), region and former province, S France; historic cap. Toulouse. It consists of Lower Languedoc, along Mediterranean coast, with cities of Nîmes, Montpellier, and Narbonne; of the fertile Garonne plains, with Toulouse as center (agr., wine growing); and of part of the Massif Central (incl. the Cévennes, Vivarais, and Velay). Languedoc corresponds roughly to Narbonensis prov. of Roman Gaul, the later Septimania. Its history before its incorporation into the French royal domain (1271) is largely that of the county of TOULOUSE.

langue d'oc and langue d'oïl (läg dôk', dôēl', dô'yü), names of the two principal groups of medieval French dialects, *oc* and *oïl* being their respective words for *yes*. *Langue d'oc* was spoken S of a line running roughly from Bordeaux to Grenoble. The *langue d'oïl* dialect of the Paris region gradually developed into modern French. Both *langue d'oïl* and *langue d'oc* (e.g., Provençal) dialects (*patois*) persist, however, in some rural regions.

Lanier, Sidney (lŭnēr'), 1842–81, American poet, b. Ga. A Confederate soldier, he was imprisoned and lost his health. Lanier was a musician (flutist with Peabody Orchestra, Baltimore) and devoted much attention to the relationship of music and poetry—the subject of his *Science of English Verse* (1880). His own poems show the use of musical principles as in "The Symphony" and "The Marshes of Glynn." Some of his shorter poems, notably "The Song of the Chattahoochee" and "A Ballad of Trees and the Master" have lasting popularity.

Lanikai, Hawaii: see KAILUA.

Lanka: see CEYLON.

Lannes, Jean (zhä' län'), 1769–1809, marshal of France; one of Napoleon's chief lieutenants. Fell at Essling.

lanolin (lă'nŭlĭn), greasy yellow substance from wool. It is used as ointment base, in finishing and preserving leather, in some varnishes and paints.

Lansbury, George, 1859–1940, British Labour party leader. Founded (1912) and edited the *Daily Herald*,

AFRO-ASIATIC or **HAMITO-SEMITIC LANGUAGES**	
Berber	Old Libyan*; Guanche*; Numidian*; Modern Berber: Kabyle, Rif, Shilh, Tuareg, Zenaga
Chad	Bata-Margi group, Hausa, Kotoko group, many little known languages in Nigeria
Cushitic	Beja (Bedauye); Bilin; Galla, Saho-Afar, Sidamo, Somali; Doko, Wolamo; Burungi, Mbugu
Egyptian	Ancient Egyptian*, Coptic*
Semitic	
EAST SEMITIC	
Akkadian	Assyrian*, Babylonian*; Nuzi Akkadian*
WEST SEMITIC	
Northwest Semitic	Aramaic: Old*, Biblical*, and Palestinian Aramaic*; Mandean*, Syriac*, Neo-Syriac Canaanite: Old Canaanite*, Moabite*, Phoenician*, Punic*, Ugaritic*, Old (Biblical) Hebrew*, Talmudic Hebrew*, Israeli Hebrew
Southwest Semitic	Arabic: Classical A.*, Arabian A., Egyptian A., Iraqi A., Syrian A., Western A. (incl. Andalusian* and Maltese); Southern A. (incl. Sabean* and Himyaritic) Ethiopic: Ge'ez (Classical Ethiopic)*, Amharic, Tigrē, Tigrinya

ALTAIC LANGUAGES	
West Altaic	
BULGARIC	Chuvash, Volga-Kama Bulgar (E Bulgar)*
TURKIC	
East	Chaghatay*, (Old) Uighur* (incl. Kök Turkic*), New Uighur, (Iranized) Uzbek
South (Oghuz)	Azeri (Azerbaijani), Turkish (or Ottoman Turkish or Osmanli), Turkoman (Turkmenian)
West (Kipchak)	Bashkir, Crimean Tatar, Karaim, Karakalpak, Kazakh, Kazan Tatar, Kipchak*, Kirghiz, Noghay
North	Abakan, Oyrot, Soyon, Tuva
East Siberian	Yakut
East Altaic	
MONGOLIAN	
East	Chakhar, Khalkha, Kharchin, literary Mongolian Afghanistan Mongol
North	Buryat (incl. Selenga)
West	Oirat (incl. Kalmuck)

TUNGUSIC	
Manchu	Manchurian, Udekhe
Tungus	Even (Lamut), Evenki (Tungus), Negidal

AUSTRO-ASIATIC LANGUAGES	
Mon-Khmer (SE Asia)	Cham, Khasi, Khmer (Cambodian), Mon, Nicobarese, Wa
Munda (India)	Ho, Mundari, Santali, Sora
Annamese-Muong	Muong, Vietnamese (Annamese)

CAUCASIAN LANGUAGES	
North Caucasian	
ABKHAZO-ADYGHEIN	Abkhaz-Abazin, Adyghe (incl. Kiakh or Circassian and Kabardian), Ubykh
DAGHESTANI	Avaro-Andi group, Dargwa group, Lakk, Lezghian or Samurian group
VEINAKH	Chechen, Ingush, Bats
South Caucasian (relation to N Caucasian uncertain)	
KARTVELIAN	Georgian, Laz, Mingrelian, Svan

DRAVIDIAN LANGUAGES (mainly S India)	
	Brahui (NW India) Gondi, Konda; Telugu, Tulu Kanarese, Kodagu, Malayalam, Tamil

INDO-EUROPEAN LANGUAGES	
Anatolian	Hieroglyphic Hittite*, Hittite (Kanesian)*, Luwian*, Lycian*, Lydian*, Palaic*
Armenian	Classical Armenian*, Eastern Armenian, Western Armenian
Baltic	Latvian (Lettish), Lithuanian, Old Prussian*
Celtic	
BRYTHONIC	Breton, Cornish*, Middle Welsh*, Welsh (or Cymric)
CONTINENTAL	Gaulish*
GOIDELIC	Old*, Middle*, and Modern Irish, Manx, Scots Gaelic (Scotland and Nova Scotia)
Germanic	
EAST GERMANIC	Burgundian*, Gothic*, Crimean Gothic*, Vandalic*
NORTH GERMANIC	Eastern: Old Danish*, Danish, Dano-Norwegian (Rigsmaal); Gutnish; Old Swedish*; Swedish Western: Faroese; Icelandic; Old Norse (incl. Old Icelandic)*, Norwegian (Landsmaal)

An asterisk (*) indicates a dead language. A dagger (†) represents a highly tentative listing.

WEST GERMANIC

High German	Old* and Middle* High German, standard German
	Central: Middle and Rhine Franconian, Pennsylvania Dutch, Yiddish
	Upper: Alemannic (incl. Alsatian, Swabian, and Swiss German), High Franconian; Austro-Bavarian; Lombard*
Low German	Old Saxon*, Middle Low German*, Plattdeutsch (Modern Low German)
	Old Low Franconian*, Flemish, Dutch, Afrikaans
	Anglo-Frisian: Old Frisian*, Frisian; Old English (incl. West Saxon, Kentish, and Anglian dialects)*, Middle English*, Middle Scots*, English (British, Scottish, American, Australian, New Zealand, South African English; also various creoles, e.g., Beach-la-mar, Taki-Taki)

Greek (Hellenic)

WEST GREEK	Doric*, Tsaconian; Northwest Greek*
EAST GREEK	Aeolic*; Arcado-Cyprian (incl. Mycenaean Greek = Linear B)*; Ionic (Homeric Greek)*, Attic*, Koine*, Byzantine Greek*, Modern Greek (incl. Katharevusa and Demotik)

Indo-Iranian

DARDIC or PISACHA	
(central Asia)	Kafiri, Kashmiri, Khowar, Kohistani, Romany (Gypsy), Shina
INDIC or INDO-ARYAN	Vedic*, Sanskrit*, Prakrits* (incl. Pali*)
Central Indic	Eastern Hindi: Awadhi, Bagheli, Chattisgarhi (or Laria)
	Western Hindi: Khari Boli (standard Hindustani) (literary Hindi; Urdu)
East Indic	Assamese, Bengali, Bihari (Bhojpuri, Magahi, Maithili), Oriya
NW Indic	Lahnda, Punjabi, Sindhi
Pahari	Central Pahari (Kumaoni, Garhwali), Eastern Pahari (Khas-kura or Gorkhali or Nepali), Western Pahari
Sinhalese	Sinhalese (incl. major dialect Mahl)
South Indic	Marathi (incl. major dialect Konkani)
West Indic	Bhili, Gujarati, Khandesi, Rajastani (many dialects)
IRANIAN	
East Iranian	Avestan*, Old Persian* Khwarazmian*, Ossetic, Pamir dialects, Pashto (Afghan),

IRANIAN

East Iranian (continued)	Saka (Khotanese)*, Sogdian*, Yaghnobi
West Iranian	Baluchi, Kurdish, Middle Persian (Pahlavi)*, Parthian*, Persian (Farsi), Tajiki

Italic

(NON-ROMANCE)	Faliscan*: Old*, Classical*, Vulgar*, and Medieval* Latin
	Oscan*, Sabellic*, Umbrian*
ROMANCE	Catalan (E Spain); Dalmatian*; Old French*, French (incl. Canadian French, Haitian Creole, Louisiana French); Galician (NW Spain); Old Italian*, Italian (dialects and standard Tuscan); Moldavian; Old Portuguese*, Portuguese (incl. Brazilian P.); old Provençal*, Provençal (SE France); Rhaeto-Romanic (incl. Friulian, Ladin, Romansh); Rumanian; Sardinian; Old Spanish*, Spanish (incl. American Sp. and Philippine Sp.), Judeo-Spanish (Ladino) (Sephardic)

Slavic

EAST SLAVIC	Byelorussian (White Russian), (Great) Russian, Ukrainian (Little Russian)
SOUTH SLAVIC	Old Bulgarian (Old Church Slavonic)*, Bulgarian, Macedonian, Serbo-Croatian, Slovenian
WEST SLAVIC	Czech, Kashubian*, Polabian*, Polish, Slovak, Sorbian (Wendish)

Thraco-Illyrian

(uncertain grouping)	Albanian (incl. Geg and Tosk), Illyrian*, Messapic*, Thracian*, Venetic*
Tokharian (W China)	Tokharian A (Agnean)*; Tokharian B (Kuchean)*

LUORAWETLAN or PALEOASIATIC LANGUAGES (E Siberia)

Chukchi, Kamchadal, Koryak
Possible relation: Ainu, Gilyak

MACRO-KHOISAN LANGUAGES (S Africa)

South African Khoisan

Bushman (incl. Auen, Hiechware, !kung, Naron), Hottentot (incl. Korana, Nama)

East African Khoisan

Hatsa, Sandawe

MALAYO-POLYNESIAN or AUSTRONESIAN LANGUAGES

Indonesian or Malayan

WEST	Chamorro, Formosan, Malagasy

An asterisk (*) indicates a dead language. A dagger (†) represents a highly tentative listing.

Indonesian or Malayan

WEST (*continued*) — Philippine: Bisaya, Igorot, Ilocano, Magindanao, Tagalog
Southern: Balinese, Dyak, Javnese, Makassar, Malay (Bahasa Indonesia), Sumatran, Sudanese

EAST — Aru, Savu

Melanesian — Fijian, Malo, Marovo, Mono

Micronesian — Caroline, Gilbertese, Marianas, Marshallese, Yap

Polynesian — Hawaiian, Maori, Marquesan, Rapa Nui, Rarotongan, Samoan, Tahitian, Tongan

---

NIGER-CONGO LANGUAGES

Adamawa-Eastern — Sango, Zande, many little known languages

Benue-Congo or Central Branch

BANTOID GROUP

Bantu — Bemba, Chaga, Chwana, Herero, Kamba, Kikuyu, Kimbundu, Kongo, Luba, Luganda, Ngala, Nyaruanda, Rundi, Shona, Sotho, Swahili, Swazi, Xhosa, Zulu

Non-Bantu — Bitare, Bute, Mambila, Tiv

CROSS-RIVER GROUP — Boki, Efik, Olulomo

JUKUNOID GROUP — Jukun, Kentu, Nyidu

PLATEAU GROUP — Eggon, Kambari, many little known languages

Gur or Voltaic — Lobi-Dogon group, Mossi-Grunshi group, Senufo group

Kordofanian

KATLA GROUP — Katla, Tima

KOALIB GROUP — Koalib, Laro, Otoro, Shwai, Tira

TALODI GROUP — Eliri, Lafofa, Tacho, Talodi

TEGALI GROUP — Tagoi, Tegali, Tumale

TUMTUM GROUP — Karondi, Katcha, Miri, Tumtum

Kwa — Akan (incl. Baoule, Fanti, Twi), Ewe, Fon, Gan, Ibo, Ijo, Kru group (incl. Kru and Bassa), Nupe, Yoruba

Mande

WESTERN — Bambara, Dyula, Malinke, Soninke; Kpelle, Loma, Mende

EASTERN — Dan, Mwa, Samo

West Atlantic

NORTHERN — Biafada, Fulani, Mandyak, Serer-Sin, Wolof

SOUTHERN — Bulom, Gola, Kissi, Limba, Temne

NILO-SAHARAN or SUDANIC LANGUAGES
(mainly E Africa)

Chari-Nile or Macro-Sudanic

EASTERN SUDANIC — Nilotic: Acholi, Dinka, Nuer, Shilluk; Bari, Masai, Nandi, Suk
Nubian: Nile Nubian; Kordofanian Nubian; Birked
Dagu, Barea, and other small branches

GENERAL SUDANIC — Bagirmi, Sara dialects; Moru; Mangbetu; Kreish

BERTA

KUNAMA

Fur — Fur

Koman — Ganza, Gule, Koma, Mao, Uduk

Maban — Maba, Runga

Saharan — Kanembu, Kanuri; Daza, Teda; Berti, Zaghawa

Songhai — Songhai

SINO-TIBETAN LANGUAGES

Chinese — Archaic*, Old* and, Middle* Chinese
North: Mandarin
Central: Hsiang, Wu
South: Foochow, Amoy-Swatow, Kan-Hakka, Cantonese

Thai — Laotian (Lao), Shan, Thai (Siamese)

Tibeto-Burman

BURMAN — Standard Burmese, Kachin, Karen languages, Kuki-Chin, Miao, Yao

TIBETAN — Bodo, Garo, Lepcha, Naga, standard Tibetan

URALIC LANGUAGES

Finno-Ugric

FINNIC — Balto-Finnic: Estonian, Finnish (Suomi), Karelian, Livonian, Lude, Olonecian, Vepse, Vote
Lapp
Permian: Komi (Zyrian), Votyak (Urdmurt)
Cheremiss (Mari), Mordvinian

UGRIC — Hungarian (Magyar)
Obi-Ugrian: Ostyak (Khanty), Vogul (Mansi)

Samoyedic (N Urals) — North: Nganasan (Tawgi), Yenisei-Samoyedic, Yurak
South: Ostyak-Samoyedic (Selkup), Sayan-Samoyedic

Non-Related Languages of the Old World: Andamanese, Basque, Burushaski, Elamite*, Etruscan*, Hurrian*, Iberian*, Japanese, Ket (Yenisei Ostyak), Khattian*, Korean, Ligurian*, Meroitic*, Sumerian*, Urartaean (Vannic)*, Yukaghir, each of the 96 aboriginal languages of Australia, each of the 132 Papuan languages.

An asterisk (*) indicates a dead language. A dagger (†) represents a highly tentative listing.

ALGONQUIAN-MOSAN LANGUAGES
(North America)

	Kootenai (Kutenai)
Algonquian	
CENTRAL	Algonquin, Cree, Delaware, Fox, Illinois*, Kickapoo, Menominee, Miami*, Montagnais, Naskapi, Ojibwa (Chippewa), Ottawa, Potawatomi, Powhatan*, Sauk, Shawnee
EASTERN	Abnaki, Malecite, Micmac, Mohegan*, Narragansett*, Natick*, Passamaquoddy, Penobscot, Pequot*
WESTERN	Arapaho, Blackfoot, Cheyenne
Ritwan (N Calif.)	Wiyot, Yurok
Mosan	
CHIMAKUAN	Chimakum, Quileut
SALISHAN	Bella Coola, Coeur d'Alene, Flathead
WAKASHAN	Bella Bella, Kwakiutl, Nootka

ANDEAN-EQUATORIAL LANGUAGES†
(mainly South America)

Andean	
ARAUCANIAN	Mapuche
QUECHU-MARAN	Aymará, Quechua
ZAPAROAN	Iquito, Zaparo
Equatorial	
ARAWAKAN	Arawak, Taino (Caribbean region)
TUPI-GUARANI	Guaraní, Tupí (Lingua Geral)
Jivaroan	Jívaro
Tucanoan	Tucano, Yupua

AZTECO-TANOAN LANGUAGES (W North America and Mexico)

Kiowan	Kiowa
Tanoan	
TEWA	Hano, Nambé, Pojoaque*, San Idlefonso, San Juan, Santa Clara, Tesuque
TIWA	Isleta, Sandia; Picuris, Taos
TOWA	Jemez, Pecos*
Uto-Aztecan	
AZTECOID	Cora, Huichol, Classical Nahuatl (Aztec)*, Nahuatl, Tolteca-Chichimeca
HOPIAN	Bannock, Hopi
PIMAN	Papago, Pima
SHOSHONEAN	Comanche, Shoshone
SOUTHERN CALIFORNIAN	Cahuilla, Luiseño, Tubatulabal
TARACAHITIAN	Cahita, Tarahumara, Yaqui
UTAN	Paiute, Ute
Zuni (doubtful relation)	Zuñi

ESKIMO-ALEUT LANGUAGES

Aleut, Eskimo

GE-PANO-CARIB† (Caribbean region and South America)

Cariban	Carib, Quimbaya
Gê (S Brazil)	Apinage, Chavante
Panoan	Caxibo, Conibo

HOKAN-SIOUAN LANGUAGES (North America)

Caddoan	Arikara, Caddo, Pawnee, Wichita
Hokan-Coahuiltecan	
COAHUILTECAN	Coahuilteco, Comecrudo*, Karankawa, Tonkawa
HOKAN	Barbareño Chumash, Karok, Pomo, Salinan, Shasta, Yana, Yuman group (Mohavi, Walapai, Yuma) Central America: Jicaque, Subtiaba, Tequistlatec
Iroquoian	Cayuga, Cherokee, Erie*, Mohawk, Onondaga, Oneida, Seneca, Susquehanna*, Tuscarora, Wyandot (Huron)
Keresan	Western Keresan: Acoma, Laguna Eastern Keresan: Cochiti, Santa Ana
Natchez-Muskogean	Alabama (incl. Koasati), Chickasaw, Choctaw, Creek, Natchez, Seminole
Siouan	Assiniboin, Biloxi*, Catawba, Crow, Dakota, Hidatsa, Iowa, Kansa, Mandan, Omaha, Osage, Ponca, Sioux, Winnebago
Tunican	Atakapa, Chitimacha, Tunica
Yukian	Yuki

MACRO-CHIBCHAN LANGUAGES† (Central and South America)

Chibchan	Boruca, Cara, Chibcha*, Paez
Misumalpan	Bambana, Miskito

MACRO-OTOMANGUEAN LANGUAGES (Mexico and Central America)

Chinantecan	Chinanteco
Mixtecan	Amusgo, Cuicatec, Mixtec
Otomanguean	Chiapanec, Mangue, Mazatec, Otomí, Popoloca, Trique
Zapotecan	Solteco, Zapotec (several languages)

NADENE LANGUAGES (W North America)

Athabascan	
NORTHERN	Beaver, Carrier, Chipewyan, Kutchin, Sarsi, Sekani, Slave, Yellowknife
PACIFIC	Chasta-Costa, Hupa, Mattole
SOUTHERN	Apache, Kiowa Apache, Lipsan, Navaho
Haida	Haida
Tlingit	Tlingit

An asterisk (*) indicates a dead language. A dagger (†) represents a highly tentative listing.

PENUTIAN LANGUAGES (W North America and Central America)		Oregon Penutian	Alsea, Coos, Kalapuya, Takelma
California Penutian	Costanoan*, Maidu, Miwok*, Wintun, Yokuts	Sahaptian	Cayuse, Klamath, Modoc, Nez Percé, Walla Walla, Yuma-tilla
Chinook	Chinook, Wishram	Totonacan	Tepehua, Totonaco
Mayan		Tsimshian	Tsimshian
MAYOID	Chontal, Huastec, Itzá, Maya, Tzeltal, Tzotzil, Yucatec		
QUICHOID	Aguacetee, Cakchiquel, Mam, Quiché	**Non-Related Languages of the New World:** Hundreds of the languages of South America are not yet satisfactorily classified. Many of these may belong to the families already established, or the classifications may have to be considerably changed.	
Mixe-Zoque	Huave, Mixe, Popoluca (Sierra), Zoque		

An asterisk (*) indicates a dead language. A dagger (†) represents a highly tentative listing.

the voice of British labor. Pacifist and reformer, he headed Labour party in Parliament 1931–35.

Lansdale, industrial borough (pop. 12,612), SE Pa., N of Philadelphia; settled 1857.

Lansdowne, Henry Charles Keith Petty Fitzmaurice, 5th marquess of (lǎnz'doun), 1845–1927, British statesman. As foreign secretary early in 20th cent. he tried to end England's diplomatic aloofness by alliances.

Lansdowne. 1 Town (pop. 13,134 including Baltimore Highlands), NE Md., suburb SW of Baltimore. **2** Residential borough (pop. 12,601), SE Pa., SW of Philadelphia.

Lansing, Robert, 1864–1928, U.S. Secretary of State (1915–20). Authority on international law. Advocated U.S. joining in First World War with Allies. Disapproved Covenant of League of Nations as part of peace treaty.

Lansing. 1 Village (1964 pop. 20,926), NE Ill., suburb S of Chicago; founded in 1860s. **2** City (pop. 107,870), state cap. (since 1847), S Mich., at junction of Grand and Cedar rivers; settled 1837. Development came with railroads (1870s) and automobile industry (1897). Automobiles and parts made.

Lanston, Tolbert, 1844–1913, American inventor of a typesetting machine, MONOTYPE (patented 1887).

lantana (lǎntǎ'nù), tropical shrubs of genus *Lantana. Lantana camara,* grown as bedding or greenhouse plant, has clusters of red or yellow flowers.

lanthanide series or lanthanides: see RARE EARTHS.

lanthanum (lǎn'thùnùm), relatively common metallic element of rare earths (symbol = La; see also ELE-MENT, table). It is gray-white, ductile, malleable.

Laocoön (lāŏk'ōŏn), in Greek legend, priest of Apollo who warned the Trojans not to touch wooden horse made by the Greeks in Trojan War. Two sea serpents, sent (according to different versions) by Athena, Poseidon, or Zeus, killed Laocoön and his two sons. Struggle is represented by Greek statue now in the Vatican. Pliny names Agesander, Athenodorus, and Polydorus, Greek sculptors of 1st cent. B.C., as creators of the work.

Laodicea (lāō"dǐsē'ù), anc. city of Asia Minor; under Rome a Christian center and seat of one of the Seven Churches.

Laois (lā'ĭsh) or **Leix** (lā'ĭsh, lāks), inland county (644 sq. mi.; pop. 45,062), S central Ireland; in Leinster; co. town Port Laoise. Formerly known as Queen's Co. and Laoighis. Mostly level, it has Slieve Bloom Mts. in N. Agr. and dairying are main occupations.

Laon (lä), town (pop. 21,931), Aisne dept., N France. Its famous Church of Notre Dame (12th–13th cent.; a cathedral until French Revolution) dominates the plain from a rocky height.

Laos (lā'ŏs), kingdom (c.89,000 sq. mi.; pop. c.2,000-000), SE Asia; administrative cap. Vientiane, royal cap. Luang Prabang. Bounded by China on N, Viet-nam on E, Cambodia on S, Burma and Thailand on W. Terrain rugged with dense forests, but mainly level along Mekong R. Rice is chief crop. Opium, coffee, benzoin exported. Hinayana Buddhism is state religion. Population is primarily Lao, descendants of Thai tribes which pushed S from Yünnan, China, into KHMER EMPIRE in 13th cent. Laos was subject to Siam from early 19th cent. to 1893, when sovereignty was shifted to France. Constitutional monarchy estab. 1947. Made associated state of French Union 1949. Pro-Communist Pathet Lao, formed 1951 by Prince Souphanouvong, was estab. 1953 in N by Vietminh. After Geneva Conference of 1954, French and Viet-minh troops withdrew from Laos. Attained full independence in Dec., 1954, and joined UN in 1955. A succession of coups (1960) resulted in a struggle for power by Pathet Lao, neutralists, and pro-West-ern faction. Conference convened in Geneva (1961) to secure neutrality of Laos and unified government. In 1962 coalition government under neutralist Prince Souvanna Phouma was formed.

Lao-tze or Lao-tzu (both lou'dzŭ), b. c.604 B.C., Chinese philosopher, legendary founder of TAOISM.

La Paz (lä päs'), city (1965 est. pop. 361,000), W Bolivia, *de facto* cap., largest city of Bolivia (Sucre is *de jure* cap.); founded 1548. In a narrow valley (alt. c.12,000 ft.), it lacks fuel and power and has little mfg. Chief tourist attractions are nearby Illi-mani and L. Titicaca.

La Paz, city (pop. c.13,000), Baja Calif., NW Mexico; pearl fishing center.

La Pérouse, Jean François de Galaup, comte de (dù gälō' kōt' dù lä pārōōz'), 1741–c.1788, French navigator. Led French government expedition in 1785 to explore Pacific, seeking Northwest Passage. He discovered (1787) **La Pérouse Strait,** a channel, 25 mi. wide, separating Hokkaido, Japan, from Sakhalin, USSR. Sometimes called Soya Strait.

lapis lazuli (lǎ'pĭs lǎz'yōōlī, –lē), a gem, deep blue, violet, or greenish blue, usually flecked with yellow iron pyrites. Found in Afghanistan, Chile, Siberia, Burma, U.S. Formerly made into vases, bowls; used also for beads, small ornaments.

Laplace, Pierre Simon, marquis de (pyĕr' sēmō' märkē' dù läpläs'), 1749–1827, French astronomer and mathematician, evolver of scientific form of NEBULAR HY-POTHESIS. His research on motions of heavenly bodies was published in his *Mécanique céleste* (1799–1825). His notable work in mathematics includes development of theory of probabilities.

Lapland, Finnish *Lappi,* Nor. *Lapland,* Swed. *Lapp-land,* vast region of N Europe, largely within Arctic Circle. It includes Finnmark, Troms, and part of Nordland counties (Norway); historic Lappland prov., now comprising Norrbotten and Vasterbotten coun-ties (Sweden); N Finland; and Kola peninsula (RSFSR). Region is mountainous in N, rising to 6,965 ft. in the KEBNEKAISE (Sweden), and consists largely of tundra in NE. It has extensive forests and many lakes and rivers. Its rich mineral resources include highgrade iron ore (esp. at KIRUNA, Sweden), copper (Sulitelma, Norway), nickel (Pechenga, RSFSR), and apatite (Kirovsk, RSFSR). Narvik and Murmansk are important ports. **Lapps or Laplanders,** the indigenous population (c.30,000) are concentrated mainly in Norway, where they are called Finns. Largely nomadic, they follow their reindeer herds, fish, and hunt. They are believed to have come from central Asia and to have been pushed N by other migrations. Though nominally conquered by Sweden and Norway in Middle Ages, their Christianization was not completed until 18th cent. Finno-Ugric language.

La Plata (lä plä'tä), city (pop. c.357,000), cap. of Buenos Aires prov., E Argentina, SE of Buenos Aires. Founded 1882 as cap. of prov. after Buenos Aires had been federalized. Has large meat-packing plants. Renamed to honor Eva Perón 1952, its former name was restored 1955.

La Plata, Río de: see PLATA, RÍO DE LA.

La Pointe, Wis.: see APOSTLE ISLANDS.

Laporte, Roland (rōlä' läpôrt'), 1675–1704, French leader of the CAMISARDS, known as Roland. Betrayed, he fell defending himself.

La Porte. 1 City (1966 pop. 21,917), NW Ind., SE of Michigan City; settled 1830. Resort in lake region. **2** City (pop. 4,512), S Texas, on Galveston Bay, ESE of Houston; settled 1889. Resort area with fishing.

Lapps: see LAPLAND.

Laptev Sea (läp'tyïf), section of Arctic Ocean, bounded by E Siberia (S), Severnaya Zemlya and Taimyr Peninsula (W), and New Siberian Isls. (E). Navigable in Aug. and Sept.

La Puente (lä pōōĕnt'ē), city (pop. 24,273), S Calif., E of Los Angeles; laid out 1842. Adjacent city of Industry is mfg. center of region.

lapwing, crested plover of Old World, also called green plover or pewit. It has a deep, iridescent green back, greenish-black crown and crest, black throat and upper breast, white under parts, and fawn tail coverts.

Larache (läräsh'), Arabic *El Araish,* city (pop. c.41,-900), Morocco; port on Atlantic Ocean. Captured by Christian Andalusians in 1270. Spain held it twice 1610–89, 1911–56). Exports oranges.

Laramie (lä'rŭmē), city (pop. 17,520), SE Wyo., on Laramie R., WNW of Cheyenne; settled 1868. Rail, air, trade, and industrial center for livestock and timber region. Grew with development of surrounding ranch country. Seat of Univ. of WYOMING. Nearby is site of Fort Sanders, estab. 1866 to protect Overland Trail and Union Pacific RR workers.

Laramie, river rising in N Colo. in S Medicine Bow Mts. Flows c.216 mi. NE to North Platte R. in Wyo.

Laramie Mountains: see FRONT RANGE.

larceny, unlawful taking and carrying away of the property of another with intent to deprive the owner of its use or to appropriate it to the use of the perpetrator or of someone else. Usually distinguished from EMBEZZLEMENT and from false pretenses, larceny is in some U.S. states defined to include them. Grand larceny, usually a felony, differs from petty larceny, usually a misdemeanor, as to the value of the property stolen.

larch or tamarack (tä'mŭrăk), tree of genus *Larix.* Larches are conifers of the pine family but are not evergreen. Widely distributed in N Hemisphere, they are grown for ornament and lumber. American larch or hackmatack is *Larix laricina.* Timber of *L. occidentalis* of W U.S. used in construction.

Larchmont, suburban village (1965 pop. 6,860), SE N.Y., on Long Isl. Sound between New Rochelle and Mamaroneck. Yachting center.

Lardner, Ring(gold Wilmer), 1885–1933, American short-story writer. A sports reporter, he later used the pungent idiom of the sports world in *You Know Me Al* (1916) and many other volumes of stories written in a tough and sardonic vein of humor.

Laredo (lŭrä'dō), city (pop. 60,678), SW Texas, on Rio Grande (bridged) opposite Nuevo Laredo, Mexico. Founded by Spanish in 1750s, it grew as post on road to other Texas cities. Mexican after Texas Revolution, city went to U.S. after Mexican War. A border city, it grew with ranching and farming and discovery of oil and gas. Trade center for large area on both sides of Rio Grande.

La Reine, Fort (lä rĕn'), S Man., on Assiniboine R., near the present Portage la Prairie. Built 1738 by Vérendrye.

lares and penates (lâ'rēz, pùnä'tēz), in Roman religion, household gods. Each household had one lar and two penates. The lares were also worshiped as spirits of ancestors. Penates were guardians of the storeroom and, with Vesta, guardians of the hearth.

Largillière, Nicolas de (lärzhēlyär'), 1656–1746, French portrait painter. Influenced by Rubens.

Largo Caballero, Francisco (fränthē'skō lär'gō käbälyä'rō), 1869–1946, Spanish Socialist leader. Led in overthrow of monarchy (1931). Premier of Loyalist government 1936–37. Died in Paris.

Larissa (lŭrĭ'sù, Gr. lä'rēsä), city (pop. 55,391), E Greece, on the Peneus; cap. of Thessaly. Was annexed by Macedon 4th cent. B.C.; became a Roman ally 196 B.C.

lark, member of large family of perching birds, chiefly of Old World and best known through SKYLARK. Horned larks belong to the only American species. MEADOW LARK belongs to blackbird family.

larkspur or delphinium, annual or perennial plant of genus *Delphinium* with handsome spires of flowers. Annual kinds are commonly called larkspur and are white, pink, red, or purple; perennials, known as delphinium, are usually white or blue.

Larnaca (lär'nûkù), town (est. pop. 20,000), SE Cyprus. Port trading in local products. Site of anc. Citium.

La Rochefoucauld, François, duc de (fräswä' dük dù lä rôshfōōkō'), 1613–80, French author. He described his part in the FRONDE (he was wounded at the Faubourg Saint-Antoine) in his remarkable memoirs, but his great work is *Réflexions ou sentences et maximes morales* (1665), in which he viewed selfishness (*amour-propre*) as mainspring of human behavior. His style, peerless in its hard brilliance and incisive clarity, made the maxim a major genre in French literature.

La Rochejaquelein, Henri du Vergier, comte de (ärē' dü vĕrzhyä' kōt dù lä rôshzhäkŭlē'), 1772–94, French commander of counterrevolutionary army in the VENDÉE. Fell in battle.

Larrey, Dominique Jean (dômēnēk' zhä' lärä'), 1766–1842, French military surgeon. While surgeon in chief of Napoleon's army (1792) he introduced *ambulances volantes,* light vehicles which aided wounded on battlefield and were precursors of modern ambulance.

Lars Porsena or Lars Porsenna (lärz' pôr'sùnù, pôrsĕ'nù), semilegendary king of Clusium, Etruria. Marched against Rome to reinstate the TARQUIN family (c.500? B.C.); legend says that heroism of the Romans caused him to abandon the conquest.

larva (lär'vù), term for stage between egg and pupa in life of insects with complete metamorphosis, and for nymph stage of insects with incomplete metamorphosis. It is sometimes used also for immature stages of other animals (e.g., mollusks, crustaceans, fish, amphibia). Grubs are larvae of beetle, bee, and some related insects; maggots are larvae of certain flies; mosquito larvae are wrigglers or wigglers. Larvae usually eat ravenously; many do great damage to crops, foods, etc. See *ill.,* p. 512.

larvae (lär'vē), in Roman religion, ghosts of the dead. To keep them from returning to frighten the living, rites, the Lemuria, were celebrated silently at night in May. See MANES.

larynx (lä'rĭngks), voice organ lying above windpipe. Composed of cartilages, membranes, and two elastic vocal cords extending from front to back wall. See *ill.*, p. 657.

Las. For names beginning thus and not listed here, see second element; e.g., for Las Palmas, see PALMAS, LAS.

La Salle, Jean Baptiste de: see JOHN BAPTIST DE LA SALLE, SAINT.

La Salle, Robert Cavelier, sieur de (rōbĕr′ kävúlyã′ syûr′ dǔ lä säl′), 1643–87, French explorer in North America. Commanded Fort Frontenac, developed trade, built forts. Descended the Mississippi to mouth (1682), claiming entire valley for France. Murdered by own men during third futile attempt to reach mouth of the Mississippi by sea.

Lasalle (lüsäl′) or **Ville Lasalle,** residential town (pop. 30,904), S Que., Canada, SW of Montreal and on St. Lawrence R. La Salle built fort here.

La Salle, city (pop. 11,897), N Ill., on Illinois R., NNE of Peoria, in area of coal and other minerals; laid out 1837. Mfg. of electrical equipment, cement, zinc products. Nearby is Starved Rock State Park.

Las Animas (läs ä′nēmäs), city (pop. 3,402), SE Colo., E of Pueblo. Kit Carson Mus., site of Bent's Fort.

Lascaris, Constantine (kŏn′stǔntēn lá′skúrĭs), d. 1501?, Greek grammarian. After fall of Constantinople he came to Italy. His Greek grammar (1476) was first book printed in Greek characters.

Las Casas, Bartolomé de (bärtōlōmä′ dã läs kä′säs), 1474–1566, Spanish missionary and historian, called Apostle to the Indies. Ordained a priest in Hispaniola 1510, he worked most of his life (in Hispaniola, Peru, Guatemala) for abolition of Indian slavery and for bettering the lot of all Indians. Largely through his efforts the New Laws (1542) were adopted to protect Indians in colonies. Wrote monumental *Historia de las Indias.*

Las Cruces (läs krōō′sĭs), city (pop. 29,367), SW N.Mex., on Rio Grande R., NNW of El Paso, Texas, in irrigated area (cotton, fruit, livestock); founded 1848. Nearby are historic MESILLA; New Mexico State Univ. of Agr., Engineering, and Science; and Indian village of Tortugas.

laser (lā′súr), acronym for *l*ight *a*mplification by *s*timulated *e*mission of *r*adiation; device for producing intense, coherent beam of light. After excitation by light, atoms of chromium or nitrogen return to lower energy level, emitting radiation. Used in transmitting energy and accelerating chemical reactions. See MASER.

La Serena (lä sērē′nä), resort city (pop. c.60,000), N central Chile. Founded 1544; destroyed 1549 by Indians; sacked 1680 by English filibusters. Has fine cathedral.

Lashio (läsh′yō, lùshyō′), town (pop. 56,059), Shan State, Burma. Rail terminus and trade center.

Lashkar (lŭsh′kŭr), city (pop. 300,513), Madhya Pradesh, India; commercial and rail center.

Lasker, Emanuel (ämä′nōōĕl), 1868–1941, German chess player. Won (1894) world's championship by defeating Steinitz, lost (1921) title to Capablanca.

Laski, Harold J(oseph) (lä′skē), 1893–1950, English political scientist, economist, and writer, chairman (1945–46) of the British Labour party, grad. Oxford. He was a member of the executive committee of the Fabian Society and a professor at London School of Economics and Univ. of London. His numerous books include *Reflections on the Revolution of Our Time* (1943) and *The American Democracy* (1948). He taught and lectured much in the U.S.

Laski, John (lä′skē), 1499–1560, Polish Protestant reformer. As a Roman Catholic he was archbishop of Warsaw, but left Poland because of his Calvinistic views. After influential ministry in England, he returned to lead Reformation in Poland. Name also Johannes à Lasco.

Las Palmas: see PALMAS, LAS.

Lassalle, Ferdinand (fĕr′děnänt läsäl′), 1825–64, German socialist. In contrast to Marx, he emphasized the role of the state and favored a state system of work-

ers' cooperatives. He greatly influenced the German politics of his day and helped establish (1863) the first German workers' political party, which later became the Social Democratic party.

Lassen Peak, 10,457 ft. high, N Calif., in Cascade Range. Only active volcano in U.S. outside Alaska and Hawaii, it erupted between 1914 and 1917. Was landmark for westward travelers to Calif. It is included in Lassen Volcanic Natl. Park.

Lasso, Orlando di (ōrlän′dō dē läs′sō), Latin *Orlandus Lassus,* 1532?–1594, composer, last great master of the Flemish school. He wrote in every form of the day (e.g., Masses, motets, madrigals). A contemporary of Palestrina and ranked as his equal, Lasso exhibits greater emotional intensity and pathos.

Last Supper, of Jesus and His disciples at the time of the Pasch just before His crucifixion (Mat. 26.17–30; Mark 14.12–26; Luke 22.7–39; John 13–17; 1 Cor. 11.23–29). For the sacrament, see COMMUNION and LORD'S SUPPER. It has been a favorite subject of painting; best known is that of Leonardo da Vinci.

Las Vegas (läs vä′gŭs). **1** City (pop. 64,405), S Nev., near Colorado R. Fort built here 1855 by Mormons was abandoned 1857. U.S. Fort Baker estab. 1864. Grew after arrival of railroad (1905) from sleepy desert town to largest city in Nev. Mainly resort center noted for opulent gambling casinos. Also commercial hub of ranch and mine area. Has branch of Univ of NEVADA; Nellis Air Force Base is NE. **2** City (pop. 7,790), N N.Mex., ESE of Santa Fe; settled c.1835. Sometimes called East Las Vegas, it forms community with Las Vegas town (pop. 6,028; settled c.1835), sometimes called West Las Vegas. Mountain and health resort in dude-ranch area. New Mexico Highlands Univ. and Fort Union Natl. Monument are nearby.

Latakia (lătùkĕ′ù), city (pop. c.105,000), W Syria, port on Mediterranean opposite Cyprus. Was anc. Phoenician city and the Roman Laodicea and Mare. Passed to Crusaders 1098, and thrived until retaken by Saladin 1188. Now noted for Latakia tobacco.

La Tène (lä tĕn′), anc. Celtic settlement, L. Neuchâtel, Switzerland. Tenian culture of second Iron Age, spanning period from 6th cent. B.C. to end of 1st cent. B.C., was so named for antiquities found here.

Lateran (lä′tùrùn), name of group of buildings of SE Rome facing the Piazza San Giovanni. Occupies land once belonging to the Laterani and given to the Church by Constantine. The basilica, known as St. John Lateran, is cathedral of Rome, the pope's church, and first-ranking church in Roman Catholic world. Original basilica, built perhaps before 311, was restored 5th–10th cent.; rebuilt and altered 14th–18th cent. Original Lateran palace was replaced in 16th cent. by present palace.

Lateran Councils, 9th–12th and 18th ecumenical councils of the Roman Catholic Church. **1** 1123, summoned by CALIXTUS II. Confirmed Concordat of Worms (1122) ending the INVESTITURE controversy. **2** 1139, convened by Innocent II to heal the wounds left by schism of antipope Anacletus II (d. 1138). **3** 1179, convened by ALEXANDER III after the Peace of Venice (1178) had reconciled Emperor Frederick I. Most important canon gave papal election exclusively to the cardinals. **4** 1215, convened by INNOCENT III as pinnacle of his pontificate. Its decrees included a statement of faith, definition of transubstantiation, laws for trials of clergy, arrangements for a new crusade. Made annual confession and communion at Easter time minimal requirements for church membership. **5** 1512–17, convened by JULIUS II, continued by LEO X, called to counter an attempt (1510) by Louis XII of France to revive the conciliar theory (see SCHISM, GREAT). The council ratified a papal agreement with France, the Concordat of 1516. It also republished the bull of Julius (1503) declaring that simony invalidated a papal election.

Lateran Treaty, concordat between the Holy See and Italy, signed in 1929 in the Lateran Palace by Cardinal GASPARRI for PIUS XI and by MUSSOLINI for Victor Emmanuel III. Unification of Italy (completed 1871) brought confiscation by the state of all papal possessions except a few buildings. The pope was then granted an annual indemnity, but subsequent popes refused indemnity and looked upon themselves as prisoners. These problems, called the Roman Question, were solved by the treaty, which provided for a sovereign and independent new state called Vatican City and a guarantee of the pope's inviolability by the Italian government.

Lateur, Frank: see STREUVELS, STIJN.

latex: see RUBBER.

lathe (lādh), machine tool to hold and turn wood or metal while it is cut into form desired. The term is also used for loom frame carrying the reed which parts the warp and beats up the weft and for a type of potter's wheel.

Lathrop, Julia Clifford, 1858–1932, American social worker and administrator; helped found (1899) first U.S. juvenile court.

Lathrop, Rose Hawthorne, 1851–1926, American Roman Catholic nun; daughter of Nathaniel Hawthorne. She and her husband (the author George Parsons Lathrop) were converted to Catholicism in 1891. She worked much in and near New York city for the care of the poor afflicted with incurable cancer. After her husband's death (1898), she became a nun, and as Mother (Mary) Alphonsa founded a community of Dominican nuns.

Latimer, Hugh (lă'tĭmùr), 1485?–1555, English bishop and martyr. Refused to recant Protestantism at his trial after accession of Catholic Mary I; was burned at the stake with Nicholas RIDLEY.

Latin America, Spanish-speaking, Portuguese-speaking, and French-speaking countries of North America (S of the U.S.), South America, Central America, and West Indies. The 20 republics are Argentina, Bolivia, Brazil, Chile, Colombia, Costa Rica, Cuba, Dominican Republic, Ecuador, El Salvador, Guatemala, Haiti, Honduras, Mexico, Nicaragua, Panama, Paraguay, Peru, Uruguay, and Venezuela. Term also used to include Puerto Rico, French West Indies, and other islands of West Indies where Romance languages are spoken.

Latin American Free Trade Association (LAFTA), estab. 1960, hq. Montevideo, to promote regional economic development and industrialization; organized in response to European Economic Community preferences for African markets (see EUROPEAN COMMUNITY). LAFTA aim is true Latin American common market. Members are Argentina, Brazil, Bolivia, Chile, Colombia, Ecuador, Mexico, Paraguay, Peru, Uruguay, and Venezuela. Association to be basis of Latin American Common Market, formation of which was agreed upon at conference of American presidents at Punta del Este in 1967.

Latin Empire of Constantinople: see CONSTANTINOPLE, LATIN EMPIRE OF.

Latini, Brunetto (brōōnĕt'tō lätē'nē), d. 1294?, Italian man of letters, praised by Dante in the *Divine Comedy.* Wrote first vernacular encyclopedia, in French.

Latin Kingdom of Jerusalem: see JERUSALEM, LATIN KINGDOM OF.

Latin language, Italic language of anc. Rome, standard tongue of most of the Roman Empire. It continued in Romance languages. Schoolbook Latin is that of Cicero and Caesar. The Latin of the Christian Fathers is still official language of Roman liturgy in Roman Catholic Church.

Latins, in anc. times, inhabitants of Latium. Their many small settlements united against Etruscans and Samnites, came under dominance of Rome (338 B.C.). All Latins were granted Roman citizenship after the SOCIAL WAR of 90 B.C.

Latin Way: see ROMAN ROADS.

Latium (lā'shēùm), Ital. *Lazio,* region (6,634 sq. mi.; pop. 3,922,783), central Italy, between the Apennines and the Tyrrhenian Sea; cap. Rome. It includes the CAMPAGNA DI ROMA and the former PONTINE MARSHES. The Tiber is the chief river. Region produces wine, olive oil, cereals, vegetables. Inhabited by the LATINS in ancient times, Latium later shared the history of the PAPAL STATES until its annexation by Italy (1870).

La Tour, Georges de (zhôrzh' dù lä tōōr'), 1593–1652, French painter. Used bold nocturnal light effects and simplified, solid forms, as in *Education of the Virgin* (Frick Coll., N.Y.).

La Tour, Maurice Quentin de (mōrēs' kătĕ' dù lä tōōr'), 1704–88, French portraitist in pastel. Among famous people who sat for him were Voltaire, Louis XV, and Mme de Pompadour.

La Tour d'Auvergne, Théophile Corret de (tāôfēl' kôrä' dù lä tōōr' dōvĕr'nyù), 1743–1800, French officer, celebrated for his bravery. Though a nobleman, he fought for the French Revolution and fell in battle. He refused promotion above grade of captain, was officially called "first grenadier of France."

La Trappe: see TRAPPISTS.

La Trémoille or **La Trimouille, Georges de** (zhôrzh' dù lä trämoi'yù or trēmōō'yù), c.1385–1446, French nobleman, favorite of Charles VII from 1427 to 1433. Probably in Burgundian pay, he favored negotiated peace, opposed Joan of Arc.

Latrobe, Benjamin Henry (lùtrōb'), 1764–1820, American architect, b. England. Came to U.S. in 1796, became surveyor of public buildings in 1803. Introduced Greek forms, important in classic revival; his Bank of the U.S. (now the old Philadelphia Custom House) was based on the Parthenon. Built first American cathedral, the Roman Catholic cathedral in Baltimore (1805–18). Designed Sedgely (1800), a residence near Philadelphia, an early example of Gothic revival in America. A son, **Benjamin Henry Latrobe,** 1806–78, was an eminent engineer. Another son, **John Hazlehurst Boneval Latrobe,** 1803–91, was a lawyer and philanthropist, who supported African colonization of Liberia.

Latrobe (lùtrōb'), industrial borough (pop. 11,932), SW Pa., ESE of Pittsburgh. Seat of St. Vincent Col.

Latter-Day Saints, Church of Jesus Christ of, religious sect founded (1830) in N.Y. by Joseph SMITH. Its members are called MORMONS, and hq. are in Salt Lake City. Beliefs are based on Bible, Book of Mormon, revelations to Smith (in *Doctrines and Covenants*), and *The Pearl of Great Price* (sayings ascribed to Moses and Abraham). Church is organized with Twelve Apostles. It is marked by importance of revelation, by stress on interdependence of spiritual and temporal life, and by vigorous proselytizing.

Latter Day Saints, Reorganized Church of Jesus Christ of, separatist group from Mormon Church. Estab. 1852. Hq. since 1904 at Independence, Mo.

Lattimore, Owen, 1900–, American author and educator. Author of books on Far East, and editor of *Pacific Affairs* (1934–41). Director (1938–53) of School of Internatl. Affairs at Johns Hopkins. Adviser (1941–42) to Chiang Kai-shek, and economic adviser (1945–46) Japanese Reparations Commission. Cleared 1950 of espionage charges. Twice indicted (1952, 1954) on charges of perjury before a congressional investigating committee. Indictments were dismissed (1953, 1955).

La Tuque (lä tük', town (pop. 13,023), S Que., Canada, on St. Maurice R. and NW of Quebec. Pulpmilling center with hydroelectric station.

Latvia (lăt'vēû), Lettish *Latvija,* republic (25,590 sq. mi.; 1964 pop. 2,200,000), NE Europe, bordering on Baltic Sea (W), Estonia (N), RSFSR (E), and Lithuania (S); cap. RIGA. Its incorporation in 1940 into the USSR as a constituent republic has not been recognized by U.S. (as of 1966). Latvia is a generally hilly, agr. plain (dairying, stock raising, timber). Industries produce fine and heavy machinery. Population is largely Lutheran, except in Roman Catholic Latgale region, in the NE. The regions of Kurzeme and Zemgale, S of Western Dvina R., share the history of COURLAND, of which they were part; Latgale and Vidzeme, N of the Dvina, were part of LIVONIA. With the third Polish partition (1795), all Latvia was in Russian hands, but the German "Baltic barons," settled since the times of the Livonian Knights, remained the dominating class. Devastated in First World War. Latvia was proclaimed independent in 1918 but was invaded in 1919 by Russians. Peace was restored in 1920. In 1934 the parliamentary regime was replaced by a rightist dictatorship under Karlis Ulmanis. USSR secured military bases in 1939, and in 1940 occupied Latvia and made it a constituent Soviet republic. Occupied by Germans 1941–44.

Laud, William, 1573–1645, English churchman, archbishop of Canterbury. Worked with Charles I to oust all Puritans from church positions. Parliamentarians opposed his persecution of nonconformists by tyrannical courts. By decreeing Anglican prayer book compulsory in Scotland he precipitated Bishops' Wars. Condemned by House of Commons through bill of attainder, he was executed.

laudanum: see OPIUM.

Lauderdale, James Maitland, 8th earl of (mät'lŭnd, lô'dŭrdāl), 1759–1839, Scottish statesman and author. Long an ardent Whig, he finally became a Tory. Wrote many tracts (e.g., *Inquiry into the Nature and Origin of Public Wealth,* 1804).

Lauderdale, John Maitland, duke of (lô'dŭrdāl), 1616–82, Scottish statesman. Imprisoned (1651–60) for support of Charles II. An unpopular member of the CABAL, he was powerful in Scotland.

Laudon or Loudon, Gideon Ernst, Freiherr von (both: gĕ'däôn ĕrnst' frī'hĕr fŭn lou'dôn), 1717–90, Austrian field marshal. Defeated Frederick II at Kunersdorf (1759); captured Belgrade from Turks (1789).

Laudonnière, René Goulaine de (rŭnā' gōŏlĕn' dŭ lōdônyĕr'), fl. 1562–82, French colonizer in Fla. Estab. Fort Caroline near mouth of St. Johns R. (1564). Escaped massacre of settlement by Pedro MENÉNDEZ DE AVILÉS.

Laue, Max von (mäks fŭn lou'ŭ), 1879–1960, German physicist. Won 1914 Nobel Prize in Physics for method of measuring wave lengths of X rays by using a crystal.

Lauenburg (lou'ŭnbŏŏrk), former duchy, N Germany, on lower Elbe; chief town was Lauenburg an der Elbe. Held from 1181 by a branch of Ascanian house of Saxony, upon whose extinction in 1689 it passed to Hanover. Transferred to Danish crown in 1815 (but as member of German Confederation), it was seized by Prussia in Danish War of 1864 and incorporated into Schleswig-Holstein in 1876. Bismarck was created duke of Lauenburg (1890). It ceased to be a duchy in 1918.

laughing gas, colorless gas with sweet taste and odor. It is a compound of nitrogen and oxygen, nitrous oxide. Widely used as dental anesthetic; laughing hysteria is common aftereffect.

Launcelot of the Lake, Sir: see ARTHURIAN LEGEND.

Launceston (lôn'sĕstŭn, lŏn'–), port (metropolitan pop. 57,120), N Tasmania, Australia, at junction of North Esk and South Esk; founded 1805. Second largest city of state. Exports dairy products, flour, lumber.

Laura, beloved lady of Petrarch, thought to have been Laura de Noves (1308?–1348), wife of Hugo de Sade.

Laurel. 1 Town (pop. 8,503), W central Md., NE of Washington, D.C.; patented late 17th cent. Has race track. Nearby is U.S. Fort George C. Meade. **2** City (pop. 27,889), SE Miss., SE of Jackson; founded 1881. Timber, farm products processed. Some mfg. Oil fields and refineries in area.

laurel of history and classical literature is an evergreen tree, *Laurus nobilis,* native to Mediterranean region, and called also bay and sweet bay. To the ancients it symbolized victory and merit. Its leaves, sold as

bay leaves, are used as flavoring for meats and soups. See also MOUNTAIN LAUREL.

Laurencin, Marie (märē' lōräsē'), 1885–1956, French painter. Her work usually has a young girl as the subject, done in pastel colors with a flat surface.

Laurens, Henry (lô'rŭnz), 1724–92, American Revolutionary statesman. Promoted colonial opposition to Britain. President of Second Continental Congress (1777–78). His son, **John Laurens,** 1754–82, patriot officer in American Revolution, drew up terms for surrender of Cornwallis.

Laurent, Robert (lô'rŭnt), 1890–, American sculptor. Known for sensitive interpretations of the figure.

Laurentian Mountains, range in S Que., Canada, N of St. Lawrence and Ottawa rivers. Resort area.

Laurentian Plateau (lôrĕn'shŭn, lù–), roughly shield-shaped region of rock (also called Canadian shield), the first part of the North American continent permanently elevated above sea level. It is the earth's greatest area of exposed Archaean rocks—largely of granite, gneiss, and schist. During the Pleistocene epoch ice sheets gouged out numerous lake basins, taking away much of the soil. The region is rich in natural resources, including minerals, forests, fur.

Lauria, Roger of: see ROGER OF LORIA.

Laurier, Sir Wilfrid (lô'rēā), 1841–1919, Canadian statesman, prime minister (1896–1911). Sought to develop dominion within framework of empire.

Lausanne (lōzän'), city (pop. 166,655, including Ouchy, its port on L. of Geneva), cap. of Vaud canton, SW Switzerland. Rail junction and lake port; trade and commercial center for rich agr. area; resort city and scene of many international conferences. Seat of Swiss federal tribunal. Was ruled by its bishops till 1536, when it was conquered by Bern and accepted the Reformation. School of theology, a famous center of Calvinism founded 1537, was made a university 1890. Bernese rule ended 1798, and Lausanne became (1803) cap. of liberated Vaud.

Lausanne, Conference of, 1922–23, peace conference held to write a new peace treaty with Turkey, whose new government under Kemal Pasha (see ATATURK) did not recognize the earlier Treaty of SÈVRES. The treaty, signed 1923, restored E Thrace, the Straits Zone, the Smyrna dist., and other territories to full Turkish sovereignty; abolished foreign zones of influence and capitulations; demanded no reparations. The Straits were to remain demilitarized and subject to an international convention (see DARDANELLES). A separate agreement between Turkey and Greece provided for compulsory exchange of minorities.

Lausitz and **Lausitzer Neisse:** see LUSATIA; NEISSE.

Lautero (loutä'rō), c.1533–1557, leader of Auracanian Indians in their attempts to recapture Chile from Spaniards.

Lautrec, Henri de Toulouse: see TOULOUSE-LAUTREC.

Lauzon (lōzō'), city (pop. 11,533), S Que., Canada, on St. Lawrence R. and NE of Lévis. Has large dry dock. Shipbuilding and lumbering.

Lauzun, Antonin Nompar de Caumont, duc de (ätōnē' nōpär' dù kōmō' dük dù lōzŭ'), 1633–1723, marshal of France. Despite Louis XIV's opposition, he seems to have secretly married Mlle de Montpensier (c.1681), with whom he quarreled and separated 1684. He brought James II's family to safety from England to France (1688) and in 1689–90 commanded the Irish expedition which ended in defeat at the Boyne.

lava (lä'vä), igneous rock erupted by a volcano or from a fissure on earth's surface or ocean floor. The term is applied both to liquid and hardened rock. Lavas are composed chiefly of silica and metallic oxides, varying in color and texture. Before it is exposed to the air lava is called magma. The heat and liquidity of magma, its source, and the cause of its rise in the earth are variously explained.

Lava Beds National Monument: see NATIONAL PARKS AND MONUMENTS (table).

Lavaca Bay: see MATAGORDA BAY.

SMALL CAPITALS = cross references. Pronunciation key on inside end pages. Abbreviations: p. 2.

L22

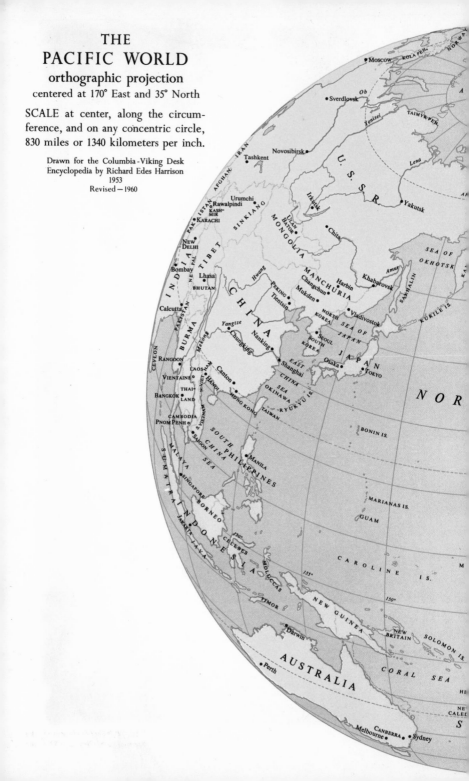

THE
PACIFIC WORLD
orthographic projection
centered at 170° East and 35° North

SCALE at center, along the circumference, and on any concentric circle,
830 miles or 1340 kilometers per inch.

Drawn for the Columbia-Viking Desk
Encyclopedia by Richard Edes Harrison
1953
Revised — 1960